Footprint South American Handbook 2007

Ben Box
83rd edition

"*Aracataca is the Macondo of [Gabriel García] Márquez's stories, the little village where South America's rickety dreams and exotic despairs are played over and over in miniature. There wasn't much there. Just another grid of pastel streets, another steel bridge, another grey river with women slapping their washing in the shallows. The bus stopped on the outskirts for a few minutes. I saw a café called April Mornings. There were the sun-baked almond trees that Márquez writes of. I heard the train whistle blow.*"

Charles Nicholl, The Fruit Palace (Picador, 1985)

South American Highlights

See colour maps at back of book

① Cartagena
Beautiful colonial city, with a dark history and sparkling beaches

② The Galápagos Islands
The greatest wildlife show on earth

③ Cotopaxi
Herds of wild horses and llamas beneath a perfect, snow-capped volcano

④ Machu Picchu and the Sacred Valley of the Incas
South America's top archaeological attraction, with the gringo capital, Cuzco, close by

⑤ Manu National Park
Home to jaguars and giant otters

⑥ Lake Titicaca
The world's highest navigable lake, home to ancient island communities

⑦ Salar de Uyuni
Blinding white salt flats, red and green lakes, flamingos and volcanoes

⑧ The Lake District
Beautiful sheets of water overlooked by forests and volcanoes for climbing and skiing

⑨ Los Llanos
Venezuela's Wild West plays host to fascinating wildlife

⑩ Canaima and the Angel Falls
Table-top mountains, 'lost worlds' and the world's highest waterfall

CARACAS

VENEZUELA

Cartagena ①

⑨

GEORGETOWN

⑩

GUYANA

⑪

BOGOTA

COLOMBIA

GALAPAGOS ISLANDS

②

QUITO

ECUADOR

③

Manaus

⑫

Amazon

Pucallpa

PERU

⑤

LIMA

④

Lake Titicaca

⑥

LA PAZ

BOLIVIA

Salar de Uyuni

⑦

PARAGUAY

CHILE

ASUNCION

Mendoza

SANTIAGO

BUENOS AIRES

MONTEVIDEO

Pacific Ocean

ARGENTINA

⑧

Chiloé

⑯

Falkland Islands

⑰

Río Gallegos

⑱

Tierra del Fuego

⑪ Iwokrama
One of the best places to see Amazonian rainforest, with a comfortable lodge and great canopy walkway

⑫ The Amazon
The world's largest river system and jungle, the combination for a once-in-a-lifetime experience

⑬ Brazil's northeastern beaches
Idyllic sands and palm trees, giant sand dunes, and all-night lambada parties

⑭ Salvador
Brazil's party city, with colonial architecture and an African soul

⑮ Iguazú Falls
Mission implausible on the Argentina-Brazil border

⑯ Península Valdés
Where Patagonia meets the Atlantic and whales and other marine mammals come to breed

⑰ Torres del Paine
Hardcore trekking at the end of the Andes

⑱ Falklands/ Malvinas
The South Atlantic's answer to the Galápagos, with amazing marine birds and mammals

Contents

Chile

Colombia

Set in stone
With their steadfast, stony gaze and red topknots, the moai of Easter Island keep their secrets secure as they watch out from Anakena Beach.

A foot in the door

If your system is jaded, South America will uplift your senses with the tropical sun rising over a palm-fringed beach, or a bracing wind blowing off the southern ice fields. Light can be blinding on the high altitude salt flats, or dense and green in the rainforest. The gentle scent of ripe guava fills the countryside, but the fire of chilli from that innocent-looking jar will electrify your taste buds.

As capybara wade through wetland shallows in the Pantanal, the spectacled bear struggles for survival in secret places in the Andes. Penguins congregate in the lee of glaciers, while tiny swifts dart through mighty waterfalls and their eternal rainbows. Volcanoes come to life and the earth trembles, yet elsewhere there are ancient, immovable tabletop plateaux. But above all is the Amazon Basin, the earth's greatest jungle, where the immensity of the trees and the smallest details of the wildlife are truly amazing.

You can explore the cities of prehispanic civilizations and the churches of colonial times, or you can immerse yourself in the present with its celebrations and its social dilemmas. Where past and present mix, there are festivals, crafts and gastronomy, from the humble potato in its umpteen varieties to the most sophisticated of wines.

If you are looking for something more active, throw yourself off a giant sand dune into a lake, or climb the highest mountain. Walk in the treetops of the rainforest, at eye level with birds and monkeys. Help homeless street kids gain a better life, or learn the martial arts of slaves. Whatever South America inspires you to do, you will find that there is no limit to the passion that it fires within you.

Contemporary South America

When the Spaniard, Francisco de Orellana, floated across the South American continent via the Amazon in 1542, he and his crew brought back tales of royal highways, grand cities and ferocious women warriors (who gave the river its name). Soon European explorers were seeking the fabulous El Dorado in what they called the 'Green Hell', but the myths gradually evaporated as scientists began to uncover the Amazon's mysteries. The indigenous cultures who survive in this vast tissue of waterways have a knowledge of the environment unmatched by science. But the threats of tree-felling, mineral exploitation and burning for unsustainable agriculture lead many to fear that, before this immense plant repository is fully understood, it will have disappeared.

Loss of the rainforest is one of many powerful symbols of rapid change in South America. Others include retreating glaciers from global warming, and the displacement of people because of civil unrest or unequal distribution of land. In parts of South America there are still a few indigenous peoples who are ignorant of technological and social

Downtown lights
Among the widest avenues in the world, the Avenida 9 de Julio in Buenos Aires is punctuated by the great obelisk of the Plaza de la República.

developments. Others shun them and lament the changes they have brought. For good or ill, South America is growing closer to the rest of the world as the demands of trade and communications create a growing interdependence between countries. At the same time, the global call to make poverty history has as much urgency in South America as elsewhere. Hunger and marginalization are seen as the root of civil strife. Recent elections have introduced a new alignment in politics and an eagerness among some politicians to work with their Latin neighbours and others to confront shared problems.

Real successors to the mythical do exist, from prehispanic Caral, in Peru, to megalopolises like São Paulo. The Incas' royal highway, Capaq Ñan, has been replaced by the Panamericana. And, yes, there are female warriors, not just guerrillas, but activists campaigning alongside their male colleagues for human, land and other rights. As a major contributor to many economies, tourism has its part to play, for travellers to this marvellous continent must take responsibility for putting something back, not plundering like the *conquistadores* of the past.

Market forces
Markets, like this one in the Peruvian Andes, are not only a place to exchange goods and produce, but also an important time for communities to come together.

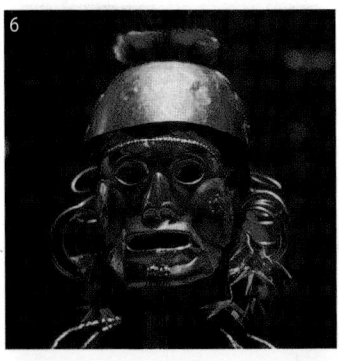

1 The trails at the feet of the jagged peaks of the Fitz Roy massif, Argentina, are one of the proverbial meccas for trekkers. ▸▸ See page 219.

2 Victoria amazonica water lilies cover the surface of an oxbow lake, like giant stepping stones. ▸▸ See page 534.

3 A lonely rhea treads the blinding white expanse of the largest salt lake in the world, the Salar de Uyuni. ▸▸ See page 284.

4 The Aragua coast of Venezuela is just one of the classic, palm-fringed places where South America meets the Caribbean. ▸▸ See page 1348.

5 During Carnaval, life becomes full colour and one of the best places to witness it is the Sambódromo in Rio de Janeiro. ▸▸ See page 372.

6 The Golden Man of Calima is just one of the thousands of fabulous examples of the ancient Colombians' art in Bogotá's renowned Gold Museum. ▸▸ See page 782.

7 The golden lion tamarin needs the utmost protection, as does its habitat, the Atlantic rainforest of Brazil. ▸▸ See page 419.

8 Dusty roads twisting and turning across the Bolivian altiplano are the lifeline between isolated towns and villages. ▸▸ See page 239.

9 Chile has some of the best rivers for rafting on the continent, with runs through temperate forest and beneath rugged mountains. ▸▸ See page 28.

10 Recent discoveries of polychrome friezes in the Huaca de Luna, near Trujillo, Peru, have uncovered an array of deities and symbols from the Moche period. ▸▸ See page 1125.

11 Lost? A llama seeks directions from a road sign in the sierras near the Chile/Bolivia border. ▸▸ See page 663.

12 Each summer, millions of holidaymakers crowd the beaches of Punta del Este, Uruguay. ▸▸ See page 1313.

The Andes

Down the length of South America runs the Andean mountain chain, which starts in the north overlooking the Caribbean and ends in the south in the fabulous towers and spires of the Chaitén Massif and the Torres del Paine National Park. Condors patrol its deep canyons and strata of rocks display colours you never knew existed in stone. Out of Lake Titicaca, the highest navigable lake in the world, strode the Inca dynasty, founding Cuzco, which has metamorphosed into the gringo capital of South America. Further south, beautiful lakes in Chile and Argentina shelter beneath snowcapped peaks. On their shores are resorts for summer watersports, fishing and winter skiing. Unlike its treeless Argentine counterpart, Chilean Patagonia is a wet and windy confusion of fjords, channels and ancient woodlands.

Forests and wetlands

In the heart of the continent, the Amazon Basin contains 20% of the world's plant and bird species, 10% of the mammals and an inestimable number of insects. In the waters live some 2,000 species of fish, plus shy giant otters, caiman and two species of freshwater dolphin. There are trees that strangle their neighbours, palms with a million thorns, plants that heal and vines that will blow your mind. Stalking in the undergrowth is the mythical jaguar, whose influence has spread through almost every religion that has come into contact with the rainforest. On its perimeter, cattle and cowboys share the land with wild birds and animals in the *llanos* of the Orinoco and the wetlands of the Brazilian/Bolivian Pantanal, while mysterious ecosystems hide on table-top mountains on the Venezuela/Brazil border and in Bolivia.

The Rio Negro reflects Brazil's Amazonian rainforest. Behind the green wall of the riverbank is a greater variety of plants, birds and animals than any other forest in the world.

A tourist boat is dwarfed by the icy-blue cliffs of the Perito Moreno Glacier, Parque Nacional de Los Glaciares, Argentina, one of the few glaciers in the world still on the move.

Islands and beaches

On the Pacific, at islands such as the Bellestas (Peru) and Isla de la Plata (Ecuador) you can see much marine life, but the destination *par excellence* is the Galápagos. On the peaks of massive volcanoes, which jut into the ocean, albatross, boobies, giant tortoises and iguanas have evolved with little instinctive fear of man, a paradise for naturalists. Meanwhile, the Atlantic coast of Brazil, all 7,408 km of it, is an endless succession of beaches, in wooded coves, dotted with islands in the south, palm tree and dune-fringed in the north.

Down through the years

When the Spanish *conquistadores* and the Portuguese colonizers arrived in South America over 500 years ago, many civilizations had risen and fallen. Most had thrived in the apparently inhospitable deserts of the Pacific coast. They left their monuments in sculptures etched into the surface of the desert, most famously at Nazca in Peru. The Incas and their contemporaries were soon overthrown and the European dominance altered every aspect of the continent. But against the odds, traditions have survived and native languages are still spoken, adapting like everything else by taking old ideas into new settings. The best way to see these processes at work is in the festivals, where Christian and indigenous religious symbols merge, brass bands blare, masqueraders represent mythical and real figures and the age-old desire to have a good time is taken to its limit.

Over the edge
Pristine forest surrounds the Kaieteur Falls, which plunge 228 m (five times higher than Niagara) over a giant step on the course of the Potaro River in Guyana.

Planning your trip

17

First-time travel guide

→ *Detailed planning information is given for each country in the relevant chapter.*

South America is a magnificently varied part of the world and tremendously hospitable. It is a tantalizing mixture of enticing images and ambiguous press reports, inspiring an air of mystery and a certain amount of trepidation. In common with many other parts of the world, South America suffers from meteorological, geological and social uncertainties. Within that context you will find some of the most dramatic landscapes on earth, biological diversity in a range of habitats, historical monuments of strength and elegance and a deep cultural resilience.

South America is a big place, so it's important not to be too ambitious on a first visit. Decide what type of holiday you want and research which countries offer what you are interested in. Then work out an itinerary in which the places you want to see and the distance between them coincides with the amount of time you have available. Over the years a Gringo Trail became firmly established, a network of places to which foreigners tended to gravitate for reasons of shared interests, lower prices, safety in numbers and so on. Some of these places have passed into legend, others are still going strong. New places are added as fashions change, or transport links are opened.

Getting around

By plane you can visit many places and airpasses, both regional and domestic, will reduce the cost of flying, but if your travel budget (or carbon-consciousness) does not stretch to air tickets, bus is the only economical alternative. Making long, or mountainous journeys by bus takes many hours, so you should build this factor into your itinerary. Trains are now few and far between and certainly cannot be relied upon as main means of transport. Car hire is expensive and tiring, but those who like driving can do well and many travellers take their own cars or motorcycles. Cycling is also popular.

When to go

It all depends on latitude: eg the far south of Argentina and Chile is busiest in the southern hemisphere summer, December-February; in winter, June-August, it is cold and snow and rain can disrupt transport. The further north you go the more the seasons fall into wet and dry. The Peruvian and Bolivian Andes are dry (and very cold at night) April-October, the rest of the year is rainy. The Sierras of Ecuador and Colombia are wet February-May and October-November. East of the Andes is wet November-April, wettest March-May in the Amazon Basin. Each chapter describes the intricacies of the weather, but changes in world climate and periodic phenomena such as El Niño can play havoc with the general rules.

Money

Take a credit or debit card, and US dollars in cash or traveller's cheques for those occasions when the ATM network isn't available (either because of remoteness or because of system failure). Euros are becoming an acceptable alternative to dollars cash in some countries.

Documents

Visa requirements vary a lot. Check before you leave. Not every country has full South American representation, nor is every country represented in South America.

Health risks → *See also Health section, page 45.*

The main health risks involve mosquitos (which transmit malaria and dengue fever); altitude sickness; tropical diseases and parasites which adequate precautions and information can help to prevent; stomach bugs; and overexposure to the sun.

Safety → *There are specific safety warnings in the relevant parts of the text.*

No entire country is a must to avoid. Most areas of **Colombia** should be treated with caution, but there are also parts which can be visited safely. Also to be treated with respect are some isolated bits of **Peru** and sensitive border areas. Big cities are more dangerous than the countryside and in busy places like bus stations and markets you need to keep your wits about you.

Cost of travelling

The cost in US$, per person per day, for two people travelling together on an economy, but not the most basic, budget is approximately:

Argentina	20-30
Bolivia	20-25
Brazil	30-40
Chile	30-40
Colombia	25
Ecuador	15-40
Paraguay	25-30
Peru	25-35
Uruguay	20-30
Venezuela	25

In the **Guianas**, allow perhaps US$25-30 per person per day for Guyana and US$25 per person per day for Suriname, but this will substantially increase if you venture into the interior. Guyane is French and expensive.

Note More than one price indicates seasonal variations in prices (eg high season in southern Argentina or Chile), differences between large cities and small towns, or including expensive areas such as jungle trips.

The cheaper countries are good places to end your journey as lower prices are better suited to dwindling travel funds. Pre-booking, including over the internet, often means you will spend more because the security of knowing you have a bed reserved for the night counts against the freedom to shop around. Usually, you do not have to book ahead (although it is comforting to have your night of arrival in the country arranged), except at major holiday times in popular resorts or for important festivals. Reserve flights in advance at all times (and reconfirm bookings) and reserve bus seats in advance when a festival is in the offing.

Sleeping → *See inside front cover for our Sleeping price codes.*
There are hotels in all price ranges. The most variety will be found in cities and main tourist centres. Youth hostels may be affiliated internationally or nationally, or not at all. Availability of campsites varies from country to country. Living with families is possible, especially if you are on a language course.

Eating → *See inside front cover for our Eating price codes.*
Local food is generally good, with lots of regional specialities, even within countries. Stick to what is local wherever you are, you'll do much better than trying to find international food. Vegetarians are best served in tourist areas, although many cities have 'healthy eating' outlets. Always drink bottled water.

Internet → *See individual town directories for cyber café listings.*
Access to the internet gets better all the time and prices in cyber cafés are often very low. Many hotels now have email for bookings.

Getting there → *See individual town Ins and outs and Transport sections.*
The easiest way to get to South America is by air (but not always by direct flight). From the USA you can get there by road, but you have to transport your vehicle around the Darién Gap between Panama and Colombia.

Best value

How much money you need to take varies from country to country. You can get by on US$20 a day in a few countries, but US$25 is the norm for good value, low (but not basic) travel. To make your money go further, ask for hotel rooms without TV (and without a bath if privacy is not an issue). Look for hostels that let you use the kitchen. Eat the *menú del día* (dish of the day, with different names in different countries), usually served at lunchtime. Investigate city bus routes, but use taxis when you have all your luggage with you or where they are the only safe option. Avoid high season or holidays, when prices rise.

⁝ Key events

Festivals play a major part in the South American calendar. Throughout the text we list important events. Here are some of the most significant dates to look out for:

31 December Reveillon, on many beaches in Brazil, especially Rio de Janeiro, a massive party to celebrate New Year. Principally at this time, but also on other dates, a number of places hold the more solemn festival of flowers, boats and candles in honour of **Yemenjá**, the Afro-Brazilian goddess of the sea.

24 January to first week in February Alacitas Fair, La Paz, Bolivia, a celebration of Ekeko, the household god of good fortune.

February/March Carnaval, celebrated almost everywhere, most famously at Oruro (including La Diablada) and Santa Cruz de la Sierra (Bolivia), Rio de Janeiro, Salvador da Bahia, São Paulo and Recife/Olinda (Brazil), Barranquilla (Colombia), Montevideo (Uruguay), Carúpano (Venezuela) and Guyane.

March Caribbean Music Festival, Cargatena, Colombia.

March/April Semana Santa, also continent-wide, but there are particularly beautiful celebrations in Ayacucho and Arequipa, Peru, while in Montevideo, Uruguay, it coincides with **Semana Criolla**, a traditional gaucho festival.

June A big month for festivals, from the Festas Juninhas, **Bumba-meu-boi** and Festa do Boi in Brazil, to **Los San Juanes** in Ecuador, **Corpus Christi**, Q'Olloriti and Inti Raymi in the Cuzco region of Peru, and **San Juan Bautista** on the Barlovento coast of Venezuela.

10 November Día de la Tradición, gaucho parades and traditional music throughout Argentina.

November Deepavali/Divali, the Hindu festival of light, is celebrated in Guyana and Suriname.

Sport and activities

Birdwatching and nature tourism

Argentina At least 980 of the 2,926 species of birds registered in South America exist in Argentina, in places with easy access. Enthusiasts head for Península Valdés, Patagonia (to see marine mammals as well as birds), the subtropical forests in the northwest, or the Iberá Marshes and Chaco savanna in the northeast. The pampas, too, have rich birdlife: flamingoes rise in a pink and white cloud, egrets gleam white against the blue sky, pink spoonbills dig in the mud and rheas stalk in the distance. Most fascinating are the oven birds, *horneros*, which build oven-shaped nests six times as big as themselves on the top of telegraph and fence posts.

Bolivia With more than 40 well-defined ecological regions and the transition zones between them, there is ample scope for enjoying wildlife. One popular tour is the four-day trip to the Salar de Uyuni (salt flats), which includes the Lagunas Colorada and Verde. Not only will you see Andean birdlife but also landscapes of unmatched, stark beauty and you will experience the bitter cold of the high altitudes. For seeing lowland birds and animals, the main options are Rurrenabaque in the lowlands of the river Beni, which is a centre for tours to the jungle and to the subtropical pampas, and the Parque Nacional Amboró, three hours west of Santa Cruz, containing ecosystems of the Amazon basin, Andean foothills and the savannahs of the Chaco plain. For table-top mountains, forests, *cerrado*, wetlands and a stunning array of wildlife, it's worth making the effort to get to the remote Parque Nacional Noel Kempff Mercado. Other opportunities include protected areas, wildlife refuges and rehabilitation centres, the sight of llamas and alpacas on any highland bus journey and even the tracks of dinosaurs.

Brazil Birdwatching can be very rewarding in Brazil. Habitats include Amazonian rainforest, the Pantanal wetlands, the subtropical forest at Iguaçu, the *cerrado* of the central plateau, the arid northeast, the Lagoa dos Patos of Rio Grande do Sul and the few remaining pockets of Mata Atlântica of the east coast. None is difficult to get to, but it would be impossible to visit every type of environment in one trip. A variety of birds can be seen, including many endemics. The system of national parks and protected areas, including those offshore (Abrolhos, Fernando de Noronha), is designed to allow access to Brazil's areas of outstanding beauty. **Pantanal Bird Club** ① *Toxx65-3624 1930, www.pantanalbirdclub.org*, is the best for serious birding. Specialists, with a good reputation, **www.birdingbraziltours.com** operate out of Manaus and cover the whole country. **Focus Tours**① *111 Malaga Rd, Santa Fe, MN 87505, T505-989 7193, www.focustours.com*, specialize in birdwatching and responsible travel. The **Focus Conservation Fund**① *www.focusconservation.org*, is a non-profit organization concerned with projects in the Pantanal, the Amazon and the Caratinga region in Minas Gerais. **Ornitholidays** ① *29 Straight Mile, Romsey, Hants, SO51 9BB, T(44) 01794-519445, www.ornitholidays.co.uk*, are the best company working in Brazil from Europe. **www.worldtwitch.com** and **www.camacdonald.com birding** are comprehensive.

Chile Birdwatching opportunities vary from the flamingoes and wildfowl of the altiplano, as found in the Parque Nacional Lauca in the far north, to the birds of the forests in the south, to the condors, geese and other species in the Torres del Paine. Mammals include those of the camel family, the llama, alpaca, vicuña and guanaco, and some rare deer, the miniature pudú and the huemul. The trees of Chile are another attraction: many deciduous varieties, the araucaria, or monkey-puzzle tree, and areas of very ancient forest, more and more of which are being protected. Also, the flowering of the desert is a sight to look out for.

Colombia Colombia claims to have more birds than any other country. There is a wide variety of habitats. Some of the more easily accessible areas are in the vicinity of Santa Marta (eg the Parque Nacional Tayrona, the marshes between Santa Marta and Barranquilla), several good spots around the capital, Parque Nacional Los Nevados, the Laguna de Sonso, near Buga, and the road from Cali to Buenaventura, around Popayán, Puracé and San Agustín, La Planada Reserve near Pasto, some of the routes into the eastern Llanos (eg Garzón to Florencia and Pasto to Mocoa) and around Leticia (eg the Parque Nacional Amacayacu). As with other remote activities, birders should ask locally if the sites they want to explore are safe.

Ecuador The Galápagos Islands are the top destination for reliably seeing wildlife close-up. They are not cheap but it is well worth paying for a good trip to the islands. A number of the species from the Galápagos may also be seen in the Parque Nacional Machalilla and on other parts of the coast; this is a less expensive option. An added bonus on the mainland coast is the opportunity to watch whales from June to September. Ecuador's other major natural attraction is its birdlife. A huge number of species in a great variety of habitats and microclimates may be seen. There are too many birdwatching spots to mention here, but they fall into five general regions: western lowlands and lower foothills, western Andes, Inter-Andean forests and *páramos*, eastern Andes and Oriente jungle. The **Jocotoco Foundation**① *www.jocotoco.com*, directed by the world's top experts on South American birds, specializes in buying up critical bird habitat in Ecuador.

Paraguay Paraguay's main asset is its wildlife, chiefly in the Chaco and national parks and reserves. It's a birdwatcher's paradise, with over 700 species, many of them endangered. For more details, contact **Fundación Moisés Bertoni** ① *www.mbertoni.org.py*, or **Guyra** ① *www.guyra.org.py*, a non-governmental organization working for the conservation of birds and their habitats. They do not officially organize visits but can be helpful and have interesting information on their website. For a list of bird species found in Paraguay and useful links see **www.bsc-eoc.org/links**. APATUR (the Paraguayan Rural Tourism Association), can arrange visits to ranches in the Chaco, or contact tour operators listed in Asunción or the Chaco sections.

Peru Nearly 20% of all the bird species in the world and 45% of all neotropical birds are found in Peru. A birding trip is possible during any month as birds breed all year round. The peak in breeding activity occurs just before the rains come in October, so it is easier to locate many birds between September and Christmas. Rainwear is recommended in the mountains, especially in the rainy season (November-April), but in the tropical lowlands it is better to take an umbrella. Besides binoculars, a telescope is useful in many areas. There are many important sites, but the key ones are the Manu Biosphere Reserve, Tambopata National Reserve, Iquitos, the Chaparrí Natural Reserve, Paracas, Lomas de Lachay, the Colca Canyon and the Huascarán Biosphere Reserve. There are too many birds to mention, but from the tiny hummingbirds to flamingoes and the Andean condor, the range is rewarding both for the beginner and the most experienced birder.

Uruguay Birdwatching is best in the east of the country, where a number of national parks have been set up in a variety of habitats. These include coastal zones, such as the sand dunes at Cabo Polonio, lakes, marshes and forest reserves on the Atlantic, Santa Teresa (which also contains important historical sites) and offshore islands. In Uruguay, though, nature tourism seldom means being in the wilderness as the majority of the land is farmed and nature reserves are small. Visit **Aves Uruguay** ⓘ *Canelones 1164, Montevideo*, T02-902 8642, *www.avesuruguay.org.uy* (in Spanish), for birding information. The Ministry of Tourism also has information on birdwatching.

Venezuela The *llanos* are a prime wildlife destination, and if you intend to go there, you should plan the timing carefully to make the most of your trip. Amazonas and the Orinoco delta also offer wildlife possibilities, but in the latter case tours can be expensive and poorly organized, so choose with caution. The Gran Sabana does not have quite the extent of wildlife that you will find in the *llanos*, but is unmatched for open landscapes. In the Andes, too, the scenery is the key, and throughout the *páramo* (open grasslands with small pockets of cloud forest above 2,500-3,000 m), the unusual *frailejón* plant (felt-leaved and with a yellow bloom) is a common sight. You may also be lucky enough to see the condor. Another significant birdwatching site is the Parque Nacional Henri Pittier in the coastal mountains between Maracay and the Caribbean. For marine birdlife, the Cuare Wildlife Sanctuary is an important nesting area. Finally, a much visited attraction is the Cueva del Guácharo, a cave near Caripe in the east.

Guyana, Suriname and Guyane Apart from Shell Beach, famous for its nesting grounds for marine turtles and colonies of scarlet ibis, the attractions of these three countries lies inland. Rivers lead to landscapes which combine savannahs and tropical forests, with excellent opportunities to see wildlife beside the waterways, on lakes and in the jungle. In Guyana, Iwokrama is one of the best places in South America for visiting Amazonian forest, with a high incidence of jaguar sightings. The Central Suriname Nature Reserve, a relatively new protected area, is just opening up to tourism.

The Falkland Islands/Islas Malvinas Although remote, the islands are a mecca for wildlife watchers. Five types of penguins are the main attraction, but albatross, giant petrels, geese, ducks and many other species can be seen close to. Marine mammals, too, are easy to see: sea lions and elephant seals on the beaches, orca and other whales and dolphins off shore.

Climbing

When planning climbs or treks in the Andes you should be aware of the effects and dangers of acute mountain sickness and cerebral and pulmonary oedema. These can be avoided by spending a few days acclimatizing to the altitude before starting your walk, and by climbing slowly. The recommended maximum altitude gain is 300 m per day. Be wary of agencies wanting to sell you trips with very fast ascents; they should ask if you are acclimatized. See the Health section, page 45, for the dangers of altitude sickness.

Argentina The Andes offer great climbing opportunities. Among the most popular peaks are Aconcagua, in Mendoza province, Pissis in Catamarca, and Lanín and Tronador, reached from the Lake District. The northern part of Los Glaciares national park, around El Chaltén, has some spectacular peaks with very difficult mountaineering. Climbing clubs (**Club Andino**) can be found in Mendoza, Bariloche, Esquel, Junín de los Andes, Ushuaia and other cities and in some places equipment can be hired.

Bolivia Some of the best mountaineering in the world can be found in Bolivia, but infrastructure is not well developed, so don't expect to be rescued if you get into trouble. With a dozen peaks at or above 6,000 m and almost a thousand over 5,000 m, most levels of skill can find something to tempt them. The season is May to September, with usually stable conditions June to August. Proper technical equipment, experience and/or a competent guide are essential to cross glaciers and climb snow and ice safely. The four ranges in which to climb are: the Cordillera Real, which has 600 5,000 m plus mountains, including six at 6,000 m or above: Illimani 6,439 m, Ancohuma 6,427 m, Illampu 6,368 m, Chearoco 6,104 m, Huayna Potosí 6,088 m (the most popular) and Chachacomani 6,000 m. A week's acclimatization at the height of La Paz or equivalent is necessary before attempting to climb above 5,000 m. Access is easy from the flat Altiplano, but public transport is not always possible. Quimza Cruz, southeast of La Paz, is hard to get to but offers some excellent possibilities. The volcanic Cordillera Occidental contains Bolivia's highest peak, Sajama (6,542 m), plus Parinacota and Pomerape. The Apolobamba range, northwest of La Paz, has many 5,000-m-plus peaks.

Brazil The most popular form of climbing (*escalada*) is rock-face climbing. In the heart of Rio, you can see, or join, climbers scaling the rocks at the base of Pão de Açúcar and on the Sugar Loaf itself. Not too far away, the Serra dos Órgãos provides plenty of challenges, not least the Dedo de Deus (God's Finger). Rio de Janeiro is the state where the sport is most fully developed, but not far behind are Paraná, Minas Gerais, São Paulo and Rio Grande do Sul.

Chile There are four different terrains: rock climbing; high mountains; ice climbing; and volcanoes. Some volcanoes and high mountains are difficult to get to and you need permission to climb. Other volcanoes, like Villarrica and Osorno are popular excursions, although access is controlled by Conaf (see page 601). The **Federación de Andinismo de Chile** and the **Escuela Nacional de Montaña** are both at Almirante Simpson 77A in Santiago.

Colombia The best possibilities for mountaineers are the national parks of Los Nevados (eg Nevado del Ruiz, Nevado de Tolima) and Sierra Nevada del Cocuy (eg Ritacuba Blanca and Ritacuba Negra check security situation and conditions before setting out). For rock and ice climbing, the Nevados and Cocuy offer some technical challenges and Suesca, north of Bogotá near Nemocón, is considered the most important centre for rock climbing in the country. The best source of information is **Mauricio Afanador**, who can be contacted at *Café y Crepes* (see Bogotá, Eating). The climbing clubs at the **Universidad Nacional** and Germán Escobar at the **Platypus Hotel** in Bogotá are also excellent sources of information. Try also **Roca Solida** ⓘ *Diagonal 127A No 28-28, Bogotá, T600 7480*, for information on climbing opportunities in and around Bogotá. Maps can be obtained at the **Instituto Geográfico Agustín Codazzi**. If you intend to climb, bring all your own equipment. It may be hard to find in Colombia. Equipment available at **Almacén Aventura** ⓘ *Cra 13, No 67-26, Bogotá, T/F313 3219* and *Cra 7, No 121-53, T213 5001*, includes rope, boots, etc; light equipment, rucksacks, tents, etc, of reasonable quality, can be bought in markets and **Exito** and **Carrefour** supermarkets.

Ecuador The country offers some exceptional high-altitude climbing, with 10 mountains over 5,000 m – most with easy access. The four most frequently climbed are Cotopaxi (technically easy with a guide and equipment), Tungurahua (an active volcano, enquire about the level of volcanic activity before climbing), Chimborazo (a long, demanding climb, with at times impassable *penitentes* – conical ice formations – near the summit) and Iliniza Norte (the only one of the 'big 10' without a glacier, but a rope is needed). The other six, Iliniza Sur, Antisana, El Altar, Sangay, Carihuairazo and Cayambe vary in degree of difficulty and/or danger. Sangay is technically easy, but extremely dangerous from the falling rocks being ejected from the volcano. Many other mountains can be climbed and the climbing clubs, guiding agencies and tour operators will give advice. Proper equipment and good guidance are essential. The dangers of inadequate acclimatization, snow blindness, climbing without a qualified guide or adequate equipment must be taken very seriously, especially on the 'easier' mountains which may lure the less experienced. Deglaciation reshapes high-altitude landscapes and alters climbing routes. Inform yourself of current conditions before undertaking an ascent. There are two climbing seasons: June to August and December to February. Allegedly, the eastern cordillera is drier December to February and the western cordillera June to August (though it is often windy in August), and Cotopaxi has more clear days than any other peak. It is best to avoid the wetter seasons from March to May and September to November. Bad weather is just predominant for the mountains on the eastern side of the eastern cordillera. Being on the equator, days and nights are 12 hours long. As a result, climbs are attempted all year round all over the country.

Mountain rescue facilities in Ecuador are rudimentary and poorly organized, so you must be as self-sufficient as possible. There's no helicopter rescue and little cooperation from the army, police or government. If you will be climbing extensively in Ecuador, it's a good idea to register with your embassy or consulate and advise them of any insurance you may have to cover the costs of rescue or repatriation by air ambulance. The first place the authorities usually contact in the event of an emergency involving a foreign climber is the embassy of their home country. Cellular phones can be used from some mountains. In an emergency contact **Safari Tours** or **Compañía de Guías de Montaña**, see under Quito, Activities and tours.

Peru The Cordillera Blanca, with Huaraz as a base, is an ice climber's paradise. Over 50 summits are between 5,000 and 6,000 m and over 20 exceed 6,000 m. There is a wide range of difficulty and no peak fees are charged (although national park entrance has to paid in the Cordillera Blanca). The **Peruvian Mountain Guide Association** (AGMP) is located in the *Casa de Guías*, Huaraz. The Cordillera Huayhuash, southeast of Huaraz, is a bit more remote, with fewer facilities, but has some of the most spectacular ice walls in Peru. In the south of the country, the Cordilleras Vilcabamba and Vilcanota are the main destinations, but Cuzco is not developed for climbing. Elsewhere in the Sierras are other peaks which are rarely climbed. Rock climbing is becoming popular in the Huaraz area, at Monterrey (for beginners) and Quebrada de Llaca. Climbing equipment can be hired in Huaraz quite easily, but the quality can be poor.

Venezuela Although there are some opportunities for climbing in the Gran Sabana, these are mostly hard to get to and are technically very challenging. The heart of Venezuelan mountaineering and trekking is the Andes, with Mérida as the base. A number of important peaks can be scaled and there are some superb hikes in the highlands. Bear in mind that high altitudes will be reached and acclimatization is essential. Similarly, suitable equipment is necessary and you may wish to consider bringing your own. For more details on climbing and mountaineering, contact **Asociación Venezolana de Instructores y Guías de Montaña**, AVIGM, T0414-311 2149, www.zonam.com.

Diving and snorkelling

Brazil The best diving in Brazil is the Atol das Rocas; only available through private charter through www.dehouche.com; very expensive but completely unspoilt, with visibility up to 40 m and with one of the highest levels of biodiversity in the tropical southern Atlantic. Fernando de Noronha has coral gardens, drop offs and wrecks which include a 50-m Brazilian navy destroyer with full armament. Visibility is up to 50 m, safe, current-free and drift diving. Amongst others, divers see at least two species of turtle, spinner dolphins, more than three species of shark, huge snapper and vast shoals of goatfish and jack. Arraial de Cabo is interesting because of the meeting of a southerly cold and northerly warm current and has the best marine life in southeast Brazil.

Colombia There are dive sites on both the Caribbean and Pacific coasts, but the former is more developed. Caribbean diving centres are Cartagena, Santa Marta and nearby Taganga, San Andrés and Providencia, the Islas de San Bernardo off the coast of Sucre, Isla Fuerte off Córdoba department and Capurganá, near the Panamanian border. On the Pacific, Bahía Solano and Gorgana Island offer excellent diving opportunities. There are dive shops in most of these places (see text). You can also contact Pedro Roa (helpful) of **Aqua Sub Diving** ① *Av Suba No 122-20 (inside the shopping centre) T613 8038, Bogotá, aquasub_dive@uole.com,* who can direct you to diving instructors belonging to the **Asociación Colombiana de Instructores de Buceo** (ACIB). A five-day PADI course costs about US$140 (2006 prices). Most of the upmarket hotels in the resorts arrange diving and snorkelling trips.

Ecuador The prime spot is the Galápagos, with more than 20 dive sites: each island has its own unique underwater environment. Off the mainland, the best place to dive is the Parque Nacional Machalilla, at Isla La Plata. Colonies of sea lions can be seen here and migrating humpback whales pass this stretch of coast between late June and September.

Venezuela Venezuela's waters are not as famous as those off neighbouring Bonaire, but they have excellent opportunities for seeing underwater flora, fauna and shipwrecks. The main areas are the national parks of Mochima and Islas Los Roques (more currents, so best for experienced divers), a number of sites to the east and west of Caracas, and in the waters off Isla de Margarita.

Fishing

Argentina The three main areas for fishing are the Northern Zone, around Junín de los Andes, extending south to Bariloche; the Central Zone around Esquel; the Southern Zone around Río Gallegos and Río Grande. The first two of these areas are in the lake district. Among the best lakes are: Lagos Traful, Gutiérrez, Mascardi, Futalaufquen (in Los Alerces National Park), Meliquina, Falkner, Villarino, Nuevo, Lacar, Lolog, Curruhué, Chico, Huechulafquen, Paimún, Epulafquen, Tromen (all in Lanín National Park), and, in the far north, Quillén. The Río Limay has good trout fishing, as do the rivers further north, the Quilquihue, Malle, Chimehuín, Collón-Curá, Hermoso, Meliquina and Caleufú. The southern fishing zone includes the Ríos Gallegos, Chico, Grande, Fuego, Ewan, San Pablo and Lago Fagnano near Ushuaia. It is famous for runs of sea trout. All rivers are 'catch and release'. The best time for fishing is at the beginning of the season, that is, in November and December (the season runs from early November to the end of March). To fish anywhere in Argentina you need a permit, which costs US$5 per day, US$15 per week, US$50 per year. In the Northern Zone forestry commission inspectors are very diligent.

Brazil There is enormous potential for angling given the number and variety of its rivers, lakes and reservoirs. Add to this the scope for sea-angling along the Atlantic coast and it is not difficult to see why the sport is gaining in popularity. Officially, the country's fish stocks are under the control of Ibama (the national parks agency) and a licence is required for fishing in any waters. The states of Mato Grosso and Mato Grosso do Sul require people fishing in their rivers to get the states' own fishing permit, which is not the same as an Ibama licence. All details on prices, duration and regulations concerning catches can be obtained from Ibama; the paperwork can be found at Ibama offices, some branches of the Banco do Brasil and some agencies which specialize in fishing. In Mato Grosso and Mato Grosso do Sul information is provided by Sema, the Special Environment Secretariat, and documents may be obtained at fishing agencies or HSBC in Mato Grosso do Sul. Freshwater fishing can be practised in so many places that the best bet is to make local enquiries on arrival. You can then find out about the rivers, lakes and reservoirs, which fish you are likely to find and what types of angling are most suited to the conditions. Favoured rivers include tributaries of the Amazon, those in the Pantanal and the Rio Araguaia, but there are many others. Agencies can arrange fishing trips and there are local magazines on the subject.

Chile The lakes and rivers of Araucanía, Los Lagos and Aisén offer great opportunities for trout and salmon fishing. The season runs from mid-November to the first Sunday in May (or from mid-September on Lago Llanquihue). A permit must be obtained, usually from the local Municipalidad, police or angling associations. The price of a permit is about US$12 for foreigners and is valid for the whole country. Some of the world's best fishing is in the Lake District, but this is a very popular region. Better still, as they are less heavily fished, are the lakes and rivers south of Puerto Montt. Some fish are catch and release only. Premiums might have to be paid to fish in private areas, or specially designated zones. Sea fishing is popular between Puerto Saavedra (Araucania) and Maullín (Los Lagos). The mountain resort of Río Blanco is where residents of Santiago and Valparaíso go to fish.

Colombia Fishing is particularly good at Girardot, Santa Marta and Barranquilla; marlin is fished off Barranquilla. There are regular competitions, especially on the Pacific coast, for instance at Golfo de Cupica. There is trout fishing, in season, in the lakes in the Bogotá area, and at Lago de Tota in Boyacá. Travel agencies in Bogotá and Medellín can arrange fishing trips.

Uruguay Fishing is a popular sport, freshwater and sea angling. The best rivers are the Uruguay and the Negro.

Venezuela Deep-sea fishing, mainly for white and blue marlin, is exceptional in the Venezuelan Caribbean, but there is also good fishing closer to shore. Here again, Los Roques is a good destination, while Macuto and Río Chico on the mainland are popular. Freshwater fishing is possible in the lakes in the Andes and in the rivers in the Llanos.

Horse riding

Argentina Many *estancias* offer horse riding, as well as fishing, canoeing, walking and birdwatching. Since *estancias* fall into four main categories, there is much variety in the type of country you can ride through. In the pampas, *estancias* tend to be cattle ranches extending for thousands of hectares; in the west they often have vineyards; northeastern *estancias* border swamps; those in Patagonia are sheep farms at the foot of the mountains or beside lakes.

Brazil Some of the best trails for horse riding are the routes that used to be taken by the mule trains that transported goods between the coast and the interior. A company like **Tropa Serrana**① *Belo Horizonte, Toxx31-3344 8986, http://tropaserrana.zip.net*, is an excellent place to start because their tours, including overnight horse treks, explore many aspects of the Minas Gerais countryside that visitors do not normally see.

Chile Treks in the mountains can be organized in Santiago, but south of Concepción and north, the Elqui and Hurtado valleys, there are more opportunities and a number of companies organize riding holidays. A popular national pastime in the centre and south is rodeo and events are held throughout the summer in stadia known as *media lunas* (half moons), culminating in the national finals in Rancagua in March. There is also horse racing throughout the country, with the Chilean Derby in February in Viña del Mar the highlight of the season.

Ecuador This is an excellent way to get to know the countryside, its people and local equestrian traditions. Horse rentals are available in many popular resort areas including Otavalo, Baños and Vilcabamba. Visits to *haciendas* throughout the country also usually offer the possibility of horse riding.

Mountain biking

Bolivia Blessed with some of the most dramatic terrain in the world and seven months of almost daily crystal-clear skies and perfect weather, Bolivia is ideal for this sport. Nevertheless, mountain biking is relatively new here. Generally speaking, many areas have yet to be explored properly and as of now there is no mountain biking guidebook. Hard-core, experienced, fit and acclimatized riders can choose from a huge range of possibilities. Either take a gamble and figure it out from a map, or find a guide and tackle the real adventure rides. Some popular rides in the La Paz region, achievable by all levels of riders, are La Cumbre to Coroico, down the so-called 'world's most dangerous road'; the Zongo Valley descent into the Yungas; Chacaltaya to La Paz, down from the world's highest ski-slope; Hasta Sorata, to the trekking paradise of Sorata. If you are plan on bringing your own mountain bike and doing some hard riding, be prepared for incredibly abusive conditions (and that's in the dry season; in the December-February wet season, the conditions are often so bad as to be unsafe). There is an almost complete absence of spare parts and very few good bike mechanics. Alternatively, there are now a number of operations offering guided mountain biking tours, but few agencies rent good quality, safe machines. The wealth of good downhill rides has encouraged a number of companies to opt for the 'quick buck' approach, using inappropriate bicycles, inexperienced guides, insufficient guide-to-client ratios, and little or no instruction during the ride. Choose a reputable company, guides who speak your language and only opt for the best, US-made bikes.

Chile This is a popular sport locally as there are lots of opportunities in the mountains and the Lake District. The Carretera Austral is also a great ride. Bikes are manufactured locally, but quality is variable.

Colombia The possibilities are, in theory, endless for this sport and Colombians are themselves keen cyclists. Because some remote parts are unsafe, it is not wise to venture off the beaten track and you should enquire locally about the security situation before setting out. An agency like **Eco-Guías** in Bogotá (see Tour operators) can give details and information may also be available at popular travellers' hotels.

Ecuador This is growing in popularity as there are boundless opportunities in the Sierra, on coastal roads and in the upper Amazon basin. What many people don't take into account is the frequently extreme conditions in which they find themselves biking. Dehydration can be a very real issue when cycling at high altitudes or in the hot tropical lowlands. You should buy bottled water wherever you can find it, but also carry a water pump or other sterilizing system. Sunscreen is essential at high altitudes even on cloudy days. Wrap around sunglasses help to restrict the amount of dust which gets into the eyes. Agencies which offer tours, rent equipment and can help plan routes are listed under Quito and other cities.

Peru This is a relatively new sport in Peru, but dedicated cyclists are beginning to open up routes which offer some magnificent possibilities. Peru has kilometre after kilometre of trails, dirt roads and single track, but very few maps to show you where to go. There is equipment for hire and tours in the Huaraz and Cuzco areas and it may be a good idea to join an organized group to get the best equipment and guiding.

Uruguay Uruguay is an ideal country for cycle touring (as opposed to mountain biking), especially along the coast, between Montevideo and Punta del Este, northeast from Punta del Este and around Colonia del Sacramento. Elsewhere, distances between services and populated areas can be great.

Parapenting/hang gliding

Brazil Hang gliding and paragliding are both covered by the **Associação Brasileira de Vôo Livre** (ABVL – Brazilian Hangliding Association) ① *R Prefeito Mendes de Moraes s/n, São Conrado, Rio de Janeiro, Toxx21-3322 0266, www.abvl.com.br*. There are state associations affiliated with ABVL and there are a number of operators offering tandem flights for those without experience. Launch sites (*rampas*) are growing in number. Among the best known is Pedra Bonita at Gávea in Rio de Janeiro, but there are others in the state. Popular *rampas* can also be found in São Paulo, Espírito Santo, Minas Gerais, Paraná, Santa Catarina, Rio Grande do Sul, Ceará, Mato Grosso do Sul and Brasília. A full list, and much else besides, can be found in the *Guia 4 Ventos Brasil*, www.guia4ventos.com.br, which also contains information on launch sites in other South American countries.

Colombia Good opportunities exist in Medellín and Cali. Contact traveller hostels there for up-to-date information.

Rafting and kayaking

Argentina There are some good whitewater rafting runs in Mendoza province, near the provincial capital and near San Rafael and Malargüe. In the Lake District there are possibilities in the Lanín, Nahuel Huapi and Los Alerces national parks.

Brazil Companies offer whitewater rafting trips in São Paulo state (eg on the Rios Juquiá, Jaguarí, do Peixe, Paraibuna), in Rio de Janeiro (also on the Paraibuna, at Três Rios in the Serra dos Órgãos), Paraná (Rio Ribeira), Santa Catarina (Rio Itajaí) and Rio Grande do Sul (Três Coroas). The Rio Novo, Jalapão, Tocantins, is an excellent, new destination. Canoeing is supervised by the **Confederação Brasileira de Canoagem** (CBCa). It covers all aspects of the sport, speed racing, slalom, downriver, surfing and ocean kayaking. For downriver canoeing, go to Visconde de Mauá (Rio de Janeiro state) where the Rio Preto is famous for the sport; also the Rio Formoso at Bonito (Mato Grosso do Sul). A recommended river for slalom is the Pranhana, Três Coroas, Rio Grande do Sul. For kayak surfing the best places are Rio, the Ilha de Santa Catarina and Ubatuba, while ocean kayaking is popular in Rio, Búzios and Santos (São Paulo).

Chile Over 20 rivers between Santiago and Tierra del Fuego are excellent for whitewater rafting. Some run through spectacular mountain scenery, such as the Río Petrohué, which flows through temperate rainforest beneath the Osorno and Calbuco volcanoes. Rafting is generally well organized and equipment is usually of a high standard. Access to headwaters of most rivers is easy. For beginners, many agencies in Santiago, Puerto Varas and Pucón offer half-day trips on Grade 3 rivers. The best Grade 4 and 5 rafting is in Futaleufú, near Chaitén. Sea kayaking is best enjoyed in the waters between Chiloé and the mainland and in the sheltered fjords off the northernmost section of the Carretera Austral. Kayaking and other watersports such as windsurfing take place in many lakes in the Lake District, notably Lagos Villarrica and Llanquihue, which holds an annual kayaking regatta.

Colombia Whitewater rafting is growing in popularity and is at present based at San Gil (Santander), Villeta and Utica (Cundinamarca) and less developed in St Agustin (Huila).

Ecuador A whitewater paradise with dozens of accessible rivers, warm waters and tropical rainforest; regional rainy seasons differ so that throughout the year there is always a river to run. The majority of Ecuador's whitewater rivers share a number of characteristics. Plunging off the Andes, the upper sections are very steep creeks offering, if they're runnable at all, serious technical Grade 5, suitable for expert kayakers only. As the creeks join on the lower slopes they form rivers navigable by both raft and kayak (ie less steep, more volume). Some of these rivers offer up to 100 km of continuous Grade 3-4 whitewater, before flattening out to rush towards the Pacific Ocean on one side of the ranges or deep into the Amazon Basin on the other. As a general rule the rivers running straight off the eastern and western slopes of the Andes are less subject to pollution than the highland rivers which drain some of the most densely populated regions of the country. Ask about water quality before signing up for a trip. Of the rivers descending to the Pacific coast, the Blanco and its tributaries are the most frequently run. They are within easy reach of Quito, as is the Quijos on the eastern side of the Sierra. In the Oriente, the main rafting and kayaking rivers are the Aguarico and its tributary the Dué, the Napo, Pastaza and Upano. See the relevant paragraphs under Quito Activities and tours, Baños and Tena.

Peru Yet more claims to some of the finest whitewater rivers in the world, Peru has some spectacular places only accessible by this type of craft: desert canyons, jungle gorges and exotic rock formations. Availability is almost year-round and all levels of difficulty can be enjoyed. Cuzco is probably the rafting capital and the Río Urubamba has some very popular trips. Further afield is the Río Apurímac, which has some of the best whitewater rafting, including a trip at the source of the Amazon. In the southeastern jungle, a trip on the Río Tambopata to the Tambopata-Candamo Reserved Zone involves four days of whitewater followed by two of drifting through virgin forest; an excellent adventure which must be booked up in advance. Around Arequipa is some first-class, technical rafting in the Cotahuasi and Colca canyons and some less-demanding trips on the Río Majes. Other destinations are the Río Santa near Huaraz and the Río Cañete, south of Lima.

Skiing

Argentina The season is from May to October, depending on the weather and the resort. Las Leñas, south of Mendoza, is of international standard. Major resorts exist on Cerro Catedral and Cerro Otto near Bariloche and Chapelco near San Martín de los Andes. Smaller resorts, with fewer facilities, can be found near Mendoza (Los Penitentes, Vallecitos and Manantiales), in the Lake District (Caviahue, Cerro Bayo; La Hoya – near Esquel) and near Ushuaia (Cerro Martial, Wallner).

Chile The season is from June to September, weather permitting. The major international ski resorts are in the Andes near Santiago, Farellones, El Colorado, La Parva, Valle Nevado, Portillo and Lagunillas. South of Santiago, skiing is mostly on the slopes of volcanoes. The larger resorts are Termas de Chillán, Villarrica/Pucón and Antillanca, but there are a great many smaller places with limited facilities which are worth the effort to get to for some adventurous fun. Details of the major resorts and some smaller ones are given in the text. Addresses of ski federations, clubs and operators are given under Santiago, Activities and tours.

Surfing

Brazil This can be enjoyed in just about every coastal state. It does not require permits; all you need is a board and the right type of wave. Best waves in the country are at Cacimba do Padre beach, Fernando de Noronha, the archipelago, 345 km out in the Atlantic. International surf championships are held here annually. Other good waves are found in the south, where long stretches of the Atlantic, often facing the swell head-on, give some excellent and varied breaks. Many Brazilian mainland surf spots are firmly on the international championship circuit, including Saquarema, in Rio de Janeiro state. Best waves in Rio de Janeiro city are at Joatinga, Prainha or Grumari beaches. One of the best states for surfing is Santa Catarina. See the website www.brazilsurftravel.com, based in Santa Catarina but with lots of info and links.

Ecuador There are a few, select surfing spots, such as Mompiche (Esmeraldas), San Mateo (Manabî), Montañita (Guayas) and Playas, near Guayaquil. Waves are generally best December to March, except at Playas where the season is June to September. In the Galápagos there is good surfing at Playa Punta Carola, outside Puerto Baquerizo Moreno on San Cristóbal.

Peru Peru is a top international surfing destination. Its main draws are the variety of wave and the year-round action. The main seasons are September to February in the north and March to December in the south, though May is often ideal south of Lima. The biggest wave is at Pico Alto (sometimes 6 m in May), south of Lima, and the largest break is 800 m at Chicama, near Trujillo. There are more than 30 top surfing beaches. For information, www.bodyboardperu.com, www.peruazul.com.pe and www.wannasurf.com, enter Peru in the search box.

Trekking

A network of paths and tracks covers much of South America and is in constant use by the local people. In countries with a large indigenous population – Ecuador, Peru and Bolivia, for instance – you can walk just about anywhere, but in the more European countries, such as Venezuela, Chile, and Argentina, you must usually limit yourself to the many excellent national parks with hiking trails. When planning treks in the Andes you should be aware of the effects and dangers of acute mountain sickness; see above under Climbing, page 22. Also be aware that the weather can deteriorate rapidly, so equip yourself accordingly. Hiking and backpacking should not be approached casually. Even if you only plan to be out a couple of hours you should have comfortable, safe footwear (which can cope with the wet) and a daypack to carry your sweater and waterproof (which must be more than showerproof). At high altitudes the difference in temperature between sun and shade is remarkable. Longer trips require basic backpacking equipment. Essential items are: backpack with frame, sleeping bag, closed cell foam mat for insulation, stove, tent or tarpaulin, dried food (not tins), water bottle, compass/GPS. Some, but not all of these things, are available locally. Hikers have little to fear from the animal kingdom apart from insects (although it's best to avoid actually stepping on a snake). You are much more of a threat to the environment than vice versa. Leave no evidence of your passing. Respect their system of reciprocity; if they give you hospitality or food, then is the time to reciprocate with presents. **South American Explorers** have good information and advice on trekking and sells books.

Argentina There is ample scope for short and long-distance trekking. The best locations are in the foothills and higher up in the Andes. Some suggestions are the valleys around Salta; San Juan and La Rioja; Mendoza and Malargüe; in the national parks of the Lake District. Around El Chaltén in Los Glaciares national park there is some of the best trekking on the continent.

Bolivia There are many opportunities for trekking in Bolivia, from gentle one-day hikes in foothills and valleys to challenging walks of several days from highlands to lowlands on Inca or gold-diggers trails. The best known are: the Choro, Takesi and Yunga Cruz hikes, all of whose starting points can be reached from La Paz; the Mapiri Trail and the Illampu Circuit, both approached from Sorata; and the Apolobamba treks in the northwest. None of these should be attempted without full planning and equipment. Various treks are outlined in the text, especially near La Paz and from Sorata. **Warning** All these trails are in remote places and robbery and violent attacks have been made on tourists and Bolivians alike. It is advisable to hike these trails in large, organized groups. The local tourist office also produces leaflets with sketch maps on walks in the vicinity of La Paz. There are also some excellent guides available through local clubs. See also Books, in Background.

Brazil This is very popular, especially in Rio de Janeiro, São Paulo, Minas Gerais, Paraná and Rio Grande do Sul. There are plenty of hiking agencies which handle tours. Trails are frequently graded according to difficulty; this is noticeably so in areas where *trilhas* ecológicas have been laid out in forests or other sites close to busy tourist areas. Many national parks and protected areas provide good opportunities for trekking (eg the Chapada Diamantina in Bahia) and local information can easily be found to get you on the right track. The latest area to come under the trekker's gaze is Jalapão in Tocantins.

Chile Trekking possibilities are endless, ranging from short, signposted trails in national parks to hikes of several days, such as the circuit of the Parque Nacional Torres del Paine. The Sendero de Chile is a project designed to link the whole country by footpath, stretching 8,500 km by 2010. Sections have been completed in all 13 regions with 1,200 km in service in 2005. The path is complete in the metropolitan region. For more information, see www.senderodechile.cl.

Colombia Trekking is popular with walks ranging from one-day excursions out of Bogotá, or at San Agustín, to three to four-day hikes. Good places for longer treks include the national parks of Los Nevados (from Ibagué, Manizales or Pereira), Sierra Nevada del Cocuy in the northeast, and Puracé (between Popayán and San Agustín). Well-trodden is the path to the Ciudad Perdida in the Sierra Nevada de Santa Marta, which has one of the country's main archaeological sites. In the departments of Boyacá and Santander there are many colonial *caminos reales*. Sources of information include tourist offices and Ministerio del Medio Ambiente (see National parks, in Colombia Essentials). See also Bogotá, Activities and tours.

Ecuador The varied landscape, diverse ecological environments and friendly villages within a compact area make travelling on foot a refreshing change from crowded buses. Hiking in the Sierra is mostly across high elevation *páramo*, through agricultural lands and past indigenous communities. There are outstanding views of glaciated peaks in the north and pre-Columbian ruins in the south. On the coast there are only a few areas developed for hiking ranging from dry forest to coastal rainforest. In the tropical rainforests of the Oriente, local guides are often required because of the difficulty in navigation and because you will be walking on land owned by local indigenous tribes. The Andean slopes are steep and often covered by virtually impenetrable cloud forests and it rains a lot. Many ancient trading routes head down the river valleys. Some of these trails are still used. Others may be overgrown and difficult to follow but offer the reward of intact ecosystems. You may be travelling across land that is either owned outright by indigenous people or jointly managed with the Ministry of the Environment. It is important to be respectful of the people and request permission to pass through or camp. Sometimes a fee may be charged by locals but it is usually minimal. The Quito Activities and tours section lists companies which rent equipment and give advice. A recommended book is *Trekking in Ecuador*, by Robert and Daisy Kunstaetter (The Mountaineers, Seattle, 2002); also www.trekkinginecuador.com.

Peru Most walking is on trails well-trodden by local people, but some of the more popular routes are becoming damaged. Little is done to maintain the trails and no guards control them; a few conservation groups are trying to remedy this. If camping, ask permission from the landowner first, and do not leave litter anywhere. There are some outstanding circuits around the peaks of the Cordilleras Blanca (eg Llanganuco to Santa Cruz, and the treks out of Caraz) and Huayhuash. The Ausangate trek near Cuzco is also good. A second type of trek is walking among, or to, ruins. The prime example is the Inca Trail to Machu Picchu, but others include those to Vilcabamba (the Incas' last home) and Choquequirao, and the treks in the Chachapoyas region. The Colca and Cotahuasi canyons also offer superb trekking.

Ways to escape

Wild landscapes

The Amazon Rainforest, covering some 6 million sq km and spilling across the borders of nine countries, is arguably the world's greatest remaining wilderness. Huge areas of the Amazon remain unexplored, but in South America, still a continent dominated by the forces of nature, there is even more, from the sweeping plains of Los Llanos in Venezuela and Colombia to the temperate rainforests of Chilean Patagonia. **Guyana** is one of the final frontiers of Latin America, with few visitors. The Iwokrama Rainforest Program is a pioneering project for research and sustainable development, one of the best places to catch a glimpse of the elusive jaguar. Alternatively there's the Rupununi Savanna for cowboy fantasies and wildlife watching. Imagine a tropical version of the American Wild West and add the chance to meet some of South America's few remaining giant otters and harpy eagles. Recently created and largely unexplored, the **Central Suriname Game Reserve** covers 10% of Suriname, deep in the country's green heart. If your ambition is to discover an unknown species or ten, this could be the place. Jewels of Brazil's endangered cerrado ecosystem, the **Chapada dos Veadeiros** and **Emas National Parks** present excellent wildlife viewing opportunities and remain strongholds of the seldom seen maned wolf and giant anteater. Emas also possesses the greatest concentration of termite mounds on the planet, which is paradise if you're an anteater! At the beginning of the rainy season (September-October) the termite larvae glow and the night time savanna lights up with it's own bioluminescent response to the Manhattan skyline. In **Noel Kempff Mercado National Park**, Bolivia's northeastern wilderness, waterfalls cascade from the cliffs of the ancient Huanchaca Plateau. This could have been another model for Conan Doyle's "Lost World" and even today reaching Noel Kempff is an adventure. Inaccessibility has preserved some of South America's rarest and most impressive flora and fauna, truly, the land that time forgot. **Esteros do Iberá**, Argentina's little known rival to the Pantanal (Brazil and Bolivia's great wetland), is a wildlife haven of marshes, forests and palm savanna providing nature's antidote to the turbulence of Buenos Aires. Experience a close encounter with the largest mammals on the planet, whale watching off Argentina's **Valdés Peninsula**. Southern Right whales breed in the Patagonian waters every year, and the almost uninhabited area is home to a host of other wildlife. You may be able to get closer still – wildlife census are carried out by willing participants using sea kayaks to collect information.

Islands and beaches
With thousands of kilometres of unspoiled coastline, South America is the ideal place to find an untouched patch of sand – a far cry from Rio's Copacabana. Good diving and beautiful beaches divided by rocky headlands, **Tayrona National Park** is little visited in troubled Colombia. This is what the Americas looked like when Columbus first gazed upon its shores – give or take the occasional hammock. On the coast of **Rio Grande do Norte and Ceará**, in Brazil, you can blast along hundreds of kilometres of undeveloped beaches in an open-topped buggy, explore the region's giant sand dunes that rise above an emerald ocean, and absorb the traditional Afro-Brazilian culture of the tiny fishing villages that dot the coastline. A far-flung Colombian Caribbean island, **Providencia** boasts gorgeous coral reefs and a distinctive English-speaking Caribbean culture. On this former hideaway of pirate Henry Morgan, who knows, you could even come upon some buried treasure! Exploring the reefs and inquisitive sea life of the **Galápagos Islands** from underwater is a truly memorable experience. Snorkelling and diving around the islands is strictly controlled for minimum impact on wildlife, although sea lions, turtles, dolphins and numerous sea bird species seem impervious to the potential threat of man. Diving in the waters of **Fernando de Noronha Islands**, Brazil, you may be accompanied by spinner dolphins, but very few tourists. Access to the islands is restricted and their waters are a protected nature reserve. Afterwards, back on the mainland, join the local party and celebrate carnival in the colonial town of Olinda.

Lost worlds and ancient cultures
South America's human history began thousands of years before Pizarro crushed the Inca Empire with horses and Spanish steel. The remains of hundreds of pre-Inca cultures litter the continent. **San Agustín**, set in flowering valleys and canyons of the upper Río Magdalena in Colombia, was once home to a great, but enigmatic civilization. Their legacy, painted burial tombs and hundreds of intricately carved statues of men and beasts, lie scattered throughout the region and can be reached on foot, horseback, or by jeep. The **Vilcabamba Mountains** of Peru were the last refuge of Manco Inca's rebellion against the Conquistadors, Vilcabamba's frozen peaks and jungled river canyons are still shrouded in mystery. The **Jesuit Missions Circuit** in Bolivia is a reminder of an idealistic past. The ornate decoration of the Mission churches stands in vivid contrast to the empty landscape that surrounds them. Millions of years before the first humans stepped onto the South American continent, the earth trembled under the weight of very different masters.

Roads to nowhere
South America is the land of the road (or river!) less travelled, a continent where opportunity beckons at every turn. Here are a couple to whet your appetite. The **Carreterra Austral** in Chile is the South's wild road, passing snow capped volcanoes, raging rivers, glacial fjords and isolated communities. Take a step off the road and there's all the windswept isolation you can handle. One of the least travelled roads into Bolivia is the route across the **Gran Chaco** in Paraguay. This peculiar area of marshland and thorn scrub has only 100,000 inhabitants in an area of 24 million ha. When it's hot, it's very hot (temperatures can reach 45°C) and when it's

wet is impassable. But the bus will get through, somehow. The bizarre scenery of the **Salar de Uyuni** can be explored on four-day jeep trips from Uyuni, Bolivia. The dazzling expanse of the world's largest salt flat and the surrounding desert are full of weird and wonderful scenery: lunar landscapes and cactus-covered islands. It's also possible by bike, but expert assistance is advised – losing your sense of direction is easy when crossing the salt.

Finding out more

Travel and safety information Local sources of information, eg tourist offices, are given in the country chapters, below. **South American Explorers** ① *126 Indian Creek Rd, Ithaca, NY, 14850, T607 277 0488, ithacaclub@saexplorers.org, www.saexplorers.org*, is a non-profit educational organization staffed by volunteers, widely recognized as the best place to go for information on South America. Highly recommended as a source for specialized information, member-written trip reports, maps, lectures, library resources. SAE publishes a 64-page quarterly journal, helps members plan trips and expeditions, stores gear, holds post, hosts book exchanges, provides expert travel advice, etc. Annual membership fee US$50 individual (US$80 couple) plus US$10 for overseas postage of its quarterly journal, The South American Explorer. The SAE membership card is good for many discounts throughout Ecuador, Peru, Argentina and, to a lesser extent, Bolivia and Uruguay. The Clubhouses in Quito, Lima, Cuzco and Buenos Aires are attractive and friendly. SAE will sell used equipment on consignment (donations of used equipment, unused medicines, etc are welcome).

See also Ron Mader's website **www.planeta.com**, which contains masses of useful information on ecotourism, conservation, travel, news, links, language schools and articles.

It is better to seek security advice before you leave from your own consulate than from travel agencies. You can contact: **British Foreign and Commonwealth Office** ① *Travel Advice Unit, T0845 850 2829*. Footprint is a partner in the Foreign and Commonwealth Office's Know before you go campaign www.fco.gov.uk/travel. US State Department's **Bureau of Consular Affairs** ① *Overseas Citizens Services, T1-888-407-4747, www.travel.state.gov*. **Australian Department of Foreign Affairs** ① *T+61-2-6261 3305, www.smartraveller.gov.au/*.

Useful websites

Website addresses for individual countries are given in the relevant chapters' Essentials sections and throughout the text. The following is a selection of sites, which may be of interest:
www.bootsnall.com/cgi-bin/gt/ samericatravelguides/index.shtml Online travel guides for South America, updated monthly.
http://gosouthamerica.about.com/ Articles and links on sights, planning, countries, culture, gay and lesbian travel.
www.lanic.utexas.edu The Latin American Network Information Center: loads of information on everything.
www.lata.org Lists tour operators, hotels, airlines, etc. Has a useful (free) guide which can also be ordered by phoning T020 8715 2913.

www.oanda.com Currency converter and for all your financial needs.
www.oas.org The Organization of American States site, with its magazine *Americas*.
www.southamericadaily.com From the World News Network, links to newspapers, plus environment, health, business and travel sites.
www.virtualtourist.com/f/4/ South America travel forum, which can take you down some interesting alleyways, lots of links, trips, etc; good exploring here.
www.putumayo.com For the lowdown on the latest Latin sounds.
www.whatsonwhen.com and **www.national-holidays.com** for worldwide information on festivals and events.

Essentials

Getting there

Before you travel

Documents → *See the Essentials section of each country for particular visa requirements.*

Passports and other important documents Latin Americans, especially officials, are very document-minded. You should always carry your passport in a safe place about your person, or if not going far, leave it in the hotel safe. If staying in a country for several weeks, it is worth while registering at your embassy or consulate. Then, if your passport is stolen, the process of replacing it is simplified and speeded up. Keep photocopies of essential documents, including your flight ticket, and some additional passport-sized photographs, or send yourself before you leave home an email message containing all important details, addresses, etc, which you can access in an emergency. It is your responsibility to ensure that your passport is stamped in and out when you cross borders. The absence of entry and exit stamps can cause serious difficulties; seek out the proper immigration offices if the stamping process is not carried out as you cross. Also, do not lose your entry card; replacing one causes a lot of trouble, and possibly expense. If planning to study in Latin America for a long period, get a student visa in advance.

Identity and membership cards Membership cards of British, European and US motoring organizations can be useful for discounts off items such as hotel charges, car rentals, maps and towing charges. Business people should carry a good supply of visiting cards, which are essential for good business relations in Latin America. Identity, membership or business cards in Spanish or Portuguese (or a translation) and an official letter of introduction in Spanish or Portuguese are also useful.

What to take

Everybody has their own preferences, but a good principle is to take half the clothes, and twice the money, that you think you will need. Listed here are those items most often mentioned. These include an inflatable travel pillow and strong shoes (footwear over 9½ English size, or 42 European size, is difficult to find in South America). Always take out a good travel insurance policy. You should also take waterproof clothing and waterproof treatment for leather footwear and wax earplugs, which are vital for those long bus trips or in noisy hotels. Also important are rubber flip flops, which can be worn in showers to avoid athlete's foot, and a sheet sleeping-bag to avoid sleeping on filthy sheets in cheap hotels. Other useful things to take with you include: a clothes line, a nailbrush, a vacuum flask, a water bottle, a universal sink plug of the flanged type that will fit any waste-pipe, string, a Swiss Army knife, an alarm clock, candles (for frequent power cuts), a torch/flashlight, pocket mirror, an adaptor, a padlock for the doors of the cheapest hotels (or for tent zip if camping), a small first-aid kit, sun hat, lip salve with sun protection, contraceptives, waterless soap and pre-moistened wipes and a small sewing kit. Always carry toilet paper, which is especially important on long bus trips. The most security-conscious may also wish to include a length of chain and padlock for securing luggage to bed or bus/train seat, and a lockable canvas cover for your rucksack. Contact lens wearers should note that lens solution can be difficult to find in Bolivia and Peru. Ask for it in a pharmacy, rather than an optician's.

Getting there

Air

Most South American countries have direct flights from **Europe**; only Paraguay does not. In many cases, though, the choice of departure point is limited to Madrid and one or two other cities (Paris or Amsterdam, for instance). Argentina, Brazil and Venezuela have the most options: UK, France, Germany, Italy, Spain, Switzerland and the UK (although neither of the last two to Venezuela). Brazil also has flights from Lisbon to a number of cities. **Air Europe** and **Air Madrid** offer no frills services from Spain to certain capitals, eg Bogotá, Quito and Lima. Where there are no direct flights connections can be made in the USA (Miami, or other gateways), Buenos Aires, Rio de Janeiro or São Paulo. **Main US gateways** are Miami, Houston, Dallas, Atlanta and New York. On the west coast, Los Angeles has flights to several South American cities. If buying airline tickets routed through the USA, check that US taxes are included in the price. Flights from **Canada** are mostly via the USA, although there are direct flights from Toronto to Buenos Aires and Santiago. Likewise, flights from **Australia** and **New Zealand** are best

JOURNEY
LATIN AMERICA

Essentials Before you travel

See the true colours of Latin America; from bustling indigenous markets to elegant colonial haciendas; from awe-inspiring ancient ruins to spectacular wildlife in pristine rainforest.
Let us show you the Latin America we know and love.

- Flights & Airpasses
- Language courses
- Small group tours
- Tailor-made travel
- Honeymoons
- Select hotels
- Family holidays

Call the UK's No 1 specialist
to Latin America.
020 8747 8315
www.journeylatinamerica.co.uk

ATOL Protected 2828 ABTA (V2522) IATA AITO

JOURNEY
LATIN
AMERICA

35

through Los Angeles, except for the **Qantas** route to Sydney which connects with **LAN** to Buenos Aires. From **Japan** there are direct flights to Brazil and from **South Africa** to Argentina and Brazil. Within **Latin America** there is plenty of choice on local carriers and some connections on US or European airlines. For airpasses, see below. To Guyana, the main routes are via the Caribbean (Port of Spain, Trinidad and Barbados) or New York, Miami and Toronto. Suriname is served by flights from Amsterdam, Miami, Port of Spain, Curaçao and Aruba, while Guyane has flights from Paris and the French-speaking Caribbean. All three have air connections with northern Brazil.

Baggage

There is no standard baggage allowance to Latin America. If you fly via the USA you are allowed two pieces of luggage up to 32 kg per case. Brazil has adopted this system, but it is not uniformly applied by all airlines. On flights from Europe there is a weight allowance of 20 or 23 kg, although some carriers out of Europe use the two-piece system, but may not apply it in both directions. The two-piece system is gaining wider acceptance, but it is always best to check in advance. Excess baggage charges can be high. The weight limits for internal flights are often lower; best to enquire beforehand.

Prices and discounts

From the UK, flights to Bogotá, Buenos Aires, Caracas, Rio and São Paulo start at between US$580-1,000 (in low season). Lima is more expensive (US$980-1,200), higher still in July and at Christmas. **From the USA**, Lima, Caracas and Bogotá are generally the cheapest destinations (around US$315-550). **From Australia**, flights to Rio de Janeiro or Buenos Aires start at about US$1,300-1,475. Most airlines offer discounted fares on scheduled flights through agencies who specialize in this type of fare. For a list of these agencies see page 37. If you buy discounted air tickets always check the reservation with the airline concerned to make sure the flight still exists. Also remember the IATA airlines' schedules change in March and October each year, so if you're going to be away a long time it's best to leave return flight coupons open. The busy seasons are 7 December-15 January and 10 July-10 September. If you intend travelling during those times, book as far ahead as possible. Between February-May and September-November special offers may be available.

Air passes

The **Mercosur Airpass** which applies to Brazil, Argentina, Chile, Uruguay and Paraguay, using several local carriers, is available to any passenger with a return ticket to a participating country. It must be bought in conjunction with an international flight; minimum stay is seven days, maximum 30; at least two countries must be visited. Maximum number of coupons is eight, the maximum number of stops per country is two. Fares are calculated on a mileage basis and range from US$237 to US$882. **TAM** also has an airpass which links Brazil with the other Mercosur countries. You must include at least two of those countries with a maximum of two stops per country (three in Brazil); minimum stay five days, maximum 30; maximum eight coupons. **Lan** has an airpass valid for travel on any of its routes in South America, on any part of its network in South America, available to anyone who has purchased a transatlantic ticket with **Lan**. It's valid for six months. The **All America Airpass**, a multi-carrier, multi-country facility put together by **Hahn Air** of Germany, is built up from individual sectors at specially negotiated rates which can be bought just as a single journey, or a multi-sector trip, as required and according to cost. There is no minimum or maximum stay. See the respective country sections for airpasses operated by national airlines.

Discount flight agents

UK and Ireland

STA Travel, T0870 163 0026, www.statravel.co.uk. 65 branches in the UK, including many university campuses. Specialists in low-cost flights and tours, good for student IDs and insurance.
Trailfinders, 194 Kensington High St, London, W8 7RG, T020-7938 3939, www.trailfinders.com. 18 branches in London and throughout the UK. Also one in Dublin and 5 travel centres in Australia.

North America

Air Brokers International, 685 Market St, Suite 400, San Francisco, CA94105, T01-800-883 3273, www.airbrokers.com. Consolidator and specialist on RTW and Circle Pacific tickets.
Discount Airfares Worldwide On-Line, www.etn.nl/discount.htm. A hub of consolidator and discount agent links.
STA Travel, 1-800-781-4040, www.statravel.com. Over 100 branches in the USA and Canada, including many university campuses.
Travel CUTS, in major Canadian cities and on university campuses, T1-866-246-9762, www.travel cuts.com. Specialist in student discount fares, IDs and other travel services. Also in California, USA.
Travelocity, www.travelocity.com. Consolidator.

Australia and New Zealand

Flight Centre, with offices throughout Australia and other countries. In Australia call T133 133 or www.flightcentre.com.au.
STA Travel, T1300-733035, www.statravel. com.au; 208 Swanston St, Melbourne, VIC 3000, T03-9639 0599, and branches throughout Australia. In NZ: 0508-782872, www.sta travel.co.nz. 130 Cuba St, PO Box 6604, Wellington, T04-385 0561, cuba@statravel.co.nz. Also in major towns and university campuses.
Travel.com.au, 80 Clarence St, Sydney, NSW 2000, T1300 130 481, www.travel.com.au.

Note Using the web for booking flights, hotels and other services directly is becoming increasingly popular and you can get some good deals this way. Be aware, though, that cutting out the travel agents is denying yourself the experience that they can give, not just in terms of the best flights to suit your itinerary, but also advice on documents, insurance, safety, routes, lodging and times of year to travel. A reputable agent will also be bonded to give you some protection if arrangements collapse while you are travelling.

Sea

Travelling as a passenger on a cargo ship to South America is not a cheap way to go, but if you have the time and want a bit of luxury, it makes a great alternative to flying. There are sailings from Europe to the Caribbean, east and west coasts of South America. Likewise, you can sail from US ports to east and west coast South America. In the main, passage is round trip only.

Useful contacts for advice and tickets
Strand Voyages (Andy Whitehouse), 1 Adam St, London WC2N 6AB, T020-7766 8220, www.strand travel.co.uk. Booking agents for all routes.
Cargo Ship Voyages Ltd, Hemley, Woodbridge, Suffolk IP12 4QF, T01473- 736265, www.cargoshipvoyages.co.uk.
The Cruise People, 88 York St, London W1H 1QT, T020-7723 2450, www.members.aol.com/ Cruiseaz/freighters.htm.

Specialist tour companies
4starSouth America, 3003 Van Ness St NW, Ste S-823, Washington DC 20008, T1-800-747 4540 (USA), T020-8002 9745 (UK), www.4starsouth america.com (tours), www.4starflights.com (flights).
Andean Trails, The Clockhouse, Bonnington Mill Business Centre, 72 Newhaven Rd, Edinburgh EH6 5QG, UK, T0131-467 7086, www.andeantrails.co.uk.
Audley Travel, 6 Willows Gate, Stratton Audley, Oxfordshire OX27 7AU, UK, T01869-276 210, www.audleytravel.com.
Austral Tours, 20 Upper Tachbrook St, London SW1V 1SH, T020-7233 5384, www.latinamerica.co.uk.

SGV Reisezentrum Weggis (Mr Urs Steiner), Seestrasse 7, CH-6353, Weggis, Switzerland, T041-390 1133, www.frachtschiffreisen.ch.
Travltips Cruise and Freighter Travel Association, PO Box 580188, Flushing, NY 11358, T800-8728584, www.travltips.com.
Internet Guide to Freighter Travel, www.geo cities.com/freighterman.geo. Don't try to get on a non-passenger carrying cargo ship to South America from a European port; it is not possible.

Chile Tours, Suite 2, Blandel Bridge House, 56 Sloane Sq, London SW1W 8AX, T020-7730 5959, www.chiletours.org. Specialist travel to Chile.
Condor Journeys & Adventures, 2 Ferry Bank, Colintrave, Argyll PA22 3AR, UK, T1700-841318, www.condorjourneys-adventures.com.
Discover Latin America, 6205 Blue Lagoon Drive, Suite 310, Miami, Florida 33126,USA, T305-266 5827, www.discoverlatinamerica.com.
Discover the World, 29 Norl Way, Banstead, Surrey, SM7 1PB, T01737 214250, www.discover-the-world.co.uk. Imaginative itineraries,

tailor-made and escorted tours, adventurous expeditions leisurely fly-drive touring.

Dragoman, Camp Green, Debenham, Suffolk IP14 6LA, UK, T01728-861133, www.dragoman.co.uk.

eXito, 108 Rutgers St, Fort Collins, CO 80525, USA, T1-800-655 4053, T970-482 3019 (worldwide), www.exito-travel.com.

Exodus Travels, Grange Mills, Weir Rd, London SW12 0NE, T0870-240 5550, www.exodus.co.uk.

ExpeditionTrips.com, 6553 California Av SW, Seattle, WA 98136, USA, T206-547 0700 , www.expeditiontrips.com.

Explore, Nelson House, 55 Victoria Rd, Farnborough, Hants GU14 7PA, UK, T0870-333 4002, www.explore.co.uk.

Exprinter Viajes, San Martin 170, 1 of 101, Buenos Aires 1004, Argentina, T0054-11 4341 6600, www.exprinterviajes.com. Tour operator with offices in Argentina, Chile, Uruguay, Peru, Paraguay, Brazil.

Galapagos Classic Cruises in conjunction with **Classic Cruises** and **World Adventures**, 6 Keyes Rd, London NW2 3XA, T020-8933 0613, www.galapagoscruises.co.uk, specialize in individual and group travel including cruises, scuba diving and land based tours to the Galapagos Islands, Peru, Chile, Costa Rica, Mexico, Honduras, Venezuela, Patagonia and Antarctica.

GAP Adventures, 19 Charlotte St, Toronto, M5V 2H5, Canada, T1-800-708 7761, www.gap.ca.

Geodyssey, 116 Tollington Park, London N4 3RB, UK, T020-7281 7788, www.geodyssey.co.uk.

Guerba Adventure & Discovery Holidays, Wessex House, 40 Station Rd, Westbury, Wilts BA13 3 JN, UK, T01373-826611, www.guerba.com.

Journey Latin America, 12 & 13 Heathfield Terrace, Chiswick, London W4 4JE, UK, T020-8747 8315, and 12 St Ann's Sq, Manchester M2 7HW, UK, T0161-832 1441, www.journeylatinamerica.co.uk.

Ladatco , 2200 S Dixie Highway, Suite 704, Coconut Grove, FL 33133, USA, T1-800- 327 6162, www.ladatco.com.

Last Frontiers, Fleet Marston Farm, Aylesbury HP18 0QT, UK, T01296-653000, www.lastfrontiers.co.uk.

Latin American Travel Association, c/o Travel PR, 133a St Margaret's Rd, Twickenham, TW1 1RG, UK, T020-8715 2913, www.lata.org.

Lost World Adventures, 337 Shadowmoor Dr, Decatur GA 30030, USA, T800-999 0558, www.lostworld.com.

MILA Tours, 100 S Greenleaf, Gurnee, IL 60031, USA, T1-800-367 7378, www.milatours.com.

Myths and Mountains, 976 Tee Court, Incline Village, NV 89451, USA, T800-670 6984, 775-832 5454, www.mythsandmountains.com.

Nature Expeditions International, 7860 Peters Rd, suite F-103, Plantation, FL 33324, USA, T1-800-869 0639, www.naturexp.com.

New Worlds, Northway House, 1379 High Rd, London, N20 9LP, T020-8445 8444, www.newworlds.co.uk. Tailor-made itineraries.

Nouveaux Mondes, Rte Suisse 7, CH-1295 Mies, Switzerland, T+41-22-950 9660, info@nouveauxmondes.com.

Oasis Overland, The Marsh, Henstridge, Somerset BA8 0TF, UK, T01963-363400, www.oasisoverland.com.

Peru For Less, US office: T1-877-269 0309; UK office: T0203 002 0571; Peru (Lima) office: T272 0542, www.peruforless.com.

Reef and Rainforest Tours Ltd, Dart Marine Park, Steamer Quay, Totnes, Devon TQ9 5AL, UK, T01803-866965, www.reefandrainforest.co.uk.

Responsible Travel.com, www.responsibletravel.com.

Select Latin America (incorporating Galapagos Adventure Tours), 79 Maltings Pl, 169 Tower Bridge Rd, London SE1 3LJ, UK, T020-7407 1478, www.selectlatinamerica.com. Tailor-made holidays and small group tours. Specialists in cruises around the Galápagos Islands, to Antarctica, Argentina and Chile.

South American Experience, 47 Causton St, London SW1P 4AT, UK, T020-7976 5511, www.southamericanexperience.co.uk.
South American Tours, Stephanstrasse 13, D-60313, Frankfurt, Germany, T+49-69-405 8970, www.southamericantours.de.
STA Travel, see Discount flight agents, above.
Steppes Latin America, 51 Castle St, Cirencester, Glos GL7 1QD, T01285 885333, www.steppeslatinamerica.co.uk.
Tambo Tours, T1-888-2-GO-PERU (246-7378), www.2GOPERU.com. Long-established adventure and tour specialist with offices in Peru and the USA. Customized trips to the Amazon and archaeological sites of Peru and Ecuador. Daily departures for groups and individuals.
Travelbag, 3-5 High St, Alton, Hants GU13 1TL, UK, T0870-814 4440, www.travelbag.co.uk.
TrekAmerica Travel Ltd, Grange Mills, Weir Rd, London SW12 0NE, UK, T0870-444 8735,
www.trekamerica.co.uk.
Tribes Travel, 12 The Business Centre, Earl Soham, Woodbridge, Suffolk, IP13 7SA, UK, T01728-685971, www.tribes.co.uk.
Trips Worldwide, 14 Frederick Pl, Clifton, Bristol BS8 1AS, UK, T0117-311 4400, www.tripsworldwide.co.uk.
Trailfinders, see Discount flight agents, above.
Tropical Nature Travel, www.tropicalnature travel.com. Ecotour company with itineraries to Ecuador, Peru and Brazil.
Tucan, 316 Uxbridge Rd, Acton, London W3 9QP, T020-8896 1600, and 217 Alison Rd, Randwick, NSW 2031, Sydney, T02-9326 6633, with affiliated travel agencies worldwide, www.tucantravel.com.
Veloso Tours, 34 Warple Way, London W3 0RG, UK, T020-8762 0616, www.veloso.com.
World Expeditions, T020-8870 2600 (UK), www.worldexpeditions.co.uk, with offices in Australia, New Zealand, USA and Canada.

Essentials Getting there

Getting around → See Getting there, above, for details of air transport including air passes.

Buses and trains

The continent has an extensive road system with frequent bus services. The buses are often comfortable; the difficulties of Andean terrain affect the quality of vehicles. In mountainous country do not expect buses to get to their destination after long journeys anywhere near on time. Do not turn up for a bus at the last minute; if it is full it may depart early. Tall travellers are advised to take aisle rather than window seats on long journeys as this allows more leg room. When the journey takes more than three or four hours, meal stops at roadside restaurants (usually with toilets), good and bad, are the rule. Usually, no announcement is made on the duration of a stop; ask the driver and follow him, if he eats, eat. See what the locals are eating – and buy likewise, or make sure you're stocked up well on food and drink at the start. For drinks, stick to bottled water or soft drinks or coffee (black). The food sold by vendors at bus stops may be all right; watch if locals are buying, though unpeeled fruit is, of course, reliable.

Where they still run, trains are slower than buses. They tend to provide finer scenery and you can normally see much more wildlife than from the road – it is less disturbed by one or two trains a day than by the more frequent road traffic.

Car

The machine A normal car will reach most places of interest, but high ground clearance is useful for badly surfaced or unsurfaced roads and for fording rivers. For greater flexibility in mountain and jungle territory 4WD vehicles are recommended. In Patagonia, main roads are gravel rather than paved: perfectly passable without 4WD, just rough and dusty. Consider fitting wire guards for headlamps, and for windscreens too. Diesel cars are much cheaper to run than petrol ones and the fuel is easily available, although in Venezuela you may have to look hard for it outside Caracas. Standard European and Japanese cars run on fuel with a higher octane rating than is commonly available in North, South or Central America, and in Brazil petrol (*gasolina*) is in fact gasohol, with a 12% admixture of alcohol.

Security Spare no ingenuity in making your car secure, inside and out (even wing mirrors, spot lamps, wheels without locking nuts can be stolen). Try never to leave the car unattended except in a locked garage or guarded parking space. Lock the clutch or accelerator to the steering wheel with a heavy, obvious chain or lock. Street children will generally protect your car fiercely in exchange for a tip.

Documents To drive your own vehicle in South America, you must have an international driver's licence. You must also have the vehicle's registration document in the name of the driver, or, in the case of a car registered in someone else's name, a notarized letter of authorization. Be very careful to keep **all** the papers you are given when you enter, to produce when you leave (see Carnet de passages, page 43).

Insurance Insurance for the vehicle against accident, damage or theft is best arranged in the country of origin. In Latin American countries it is very expensive to insure against accident and theft, especially as you should take into account the value of the car increased by duties calculated in real (ie non-devaluing) terms. If the car is stolen or written off you will be required to pay very high import duty on its value. Third-party insurance can be very difficult to find. Some countries may insist that it be bought at the border (Venezuela seems to be the only country where it is easy to obtain). If you can get the legally required minimum cover, so much the better. If not, drive with extreme caution and very defensively. Should you be involved in an accident and are uninsured, your car could be confiscated. If anyone is hurt, do not pick them up (you may become liable). Seek assistance from the nearest police station or hospital if you are able to do so.

Shipping a vehicle From Europe or the USA you can go to Panama and shop around for the best value sailing to whichever port best suits your travelling plans. There are, however, no roll-on-roll-off (RORO) services from Panama to west coast South America. You may find a RORO service from Panama to Colombia, Venezuela or Brazil, but the best bet would be to ship RORO from the USA. Otherwise find a container service if your vehicle is low enough. It is also possible to ship a vehicle from Costa Rica. Alternatively, you can ship a vehicle direct from Europe or the USA.

Driving to Heaven, by Derek Stansfield (write to: Ropley, Broad Oak, Sturminster Newton, Dorset DT10 2HG, UK, T01258-472534, £4.95 plus postage, or www.amazon.co.uk), is recommended for information on South American motoring conditions and requirements.

⁝ Carnet de passages

There are two recognized documents for taking a vehicle through customs in South America: a *carnet de passages* issued jointly by the *Fédération Internationale de l'Automobile* (FIA – Paris) and the Alliance Internationale de Tourisme (AIT-Geneva), and the *Libreta de Pasos por Aduana* issued by the *Federación Interamericana de Touring y Automóvil Club*s (FITAC). The *libreta*, a 10-page book of three-part passes for customs, should be available from any South American automobile club member of FITAC, but in practice it is only available to non-residents from the *Touring y Automóvil Club de Venezuela*. At US$400, it is not worth the effort or expense, nor is it needed to enter Venezuela. If you purchase one of these documents, get a *carnet de passages*, issued in the country where the vehicle is registered. In the UK it costs £150 for 25 pages, available from the *RAC*, www.rac.co.uk/web/know how/going_on_a_journey/driving_ abroad/carnet_de_passages. In Canada the fee is CAN$450, but in all cases you have to add on administration fees, deposits and insurance premiums, which can take the cost into the thousands, depending on the value of the car. In the USA the *AAA* does not issue the *carnet*, although the HQ in Washington DC may give advice. It is available from the *Canadian Automobile Association*, 1145 Hunt Club Road, suite 200, Ottawa K1V 0Y3, T613-247 0117, www.caa.ca, who can give full details. Also from the *AAA* of Australia, details at www.aaa.asn.au/touring/ overseas.htm. Ask the motoring organization in your home country about availability of the *carnet*.

The *carnet de passages* is recognized by all South American customs authorities and, in theory, required by all except Bolivia (in Brazil it's only necessary if you enter by ship). While entry to most countries may be possible without this document (and may not even be asked for), passage through customs will be much quicker and easier with it.

Car hire The main international car hire companies operate in all countries, but they tend to be very expensive, reflecting the high costs and accident rates. Hotels and tourist agencies will tell you where to find cheaper rates, but you will need to check that you have such basics as spare wheel, toolkit and functioning lights, etc. You'll probably have more fun if you drive yourself, although it's always possible to hire a car with driver. If you plan to do a lot of driving and will have time at the end to dispose of it, investigate the possibility of buying a second-hand car locally; since hiring is so expensive it may well work out cheaper and will probably do you just as well.

Car hire insurance Check exactly what the hirer's insurance policy covers. In many cases it will only protect you against minor bumps and scrapes, not major accidents, nor 'natural' damage (eg flooding). Ask if extra cover is available. Also find out, if using a credit card, whether the card automatically includes insurance. Beware of being billed for scratches which were on the vehicle before you hired it. This includes checking the windscreen and what procedures are involved if a new one is needed.

Car hire websites

Avis, www.avis.com. In all countries except Colombia, Guyana, Paraguay.

Budget, www.budget.com. In Argentina, Brazil, Chile, Colombia, Ecuador, Peru, Uruguay, Suriname, Venezuela.

Hertz, www.hertz.com. In all countries.

Localiza, www.localiza.com. In Argentina, Bolivia, Brazil, Chile, Ecuador, Paraguay, Peru, Uruguay.

National, www.nationalcar.com. In Argentina, Brazil, Chile, Colombia, Paraguay, Peru.

Motorcycling

The motorcycle The bike should be off-road capable. Buying a bike in the USA and driving down works out cheaper than buying one in the UK. Get to know the bike before you go, ask the dealers in your country what goes wrong with it and arrange a link whereby you can get parts flown out to you.

Security Try not to leave a fully laden bike on its own. An Abus D or chain will keep the bike secure. A cheap alarm gives you peace of mind if you leave the bike outside a hotel at night. Most hotels will allow you to bring the bike inside. Look for hotels that have a courtyard or more secure parking and never leave luggage on the bike overnight or while it is unattended. Also take a cover for the bike.

Documents A passport, international driving licence and bike registration document are necessary. Riders fare much better with a carnet de passages (see box, page 43) than without it.

Shipping Bikes may be sent from Panama to Colombia by cargo flight (eg Girag Ltda Colombia, offices at Tocumen airport – Panama, Bogotá and Barranquilla), or from Miami to Caracas. From South America to Europe, check all possibilities as it can be cheaper to fly a bike home than to ship it.

Border crossings If you do not have a carnet, do not try to cross borders on a Sunday or a holiday anywhere as a charge is levied on the usually free borders in South America. South American customs and immigration inspectors are mostly friendly, polite and efficient. If in doubt ask to see the boss and/or the rule book.

Cycling

Unless you are planning a journey almost exclusively on paved roads – when a touring bike would suffice – a mountain bike is strongly recommended. The good quality ones (and the cast-iron rule is **never** to skimp on quality) are incredibly tough and rugged, with low gear ratios for difficult terrain, wide tyres with plenty of tread for good road-holding, V brakes, sealed hubs and bottom bracket and a low centre of gravity for improved stability. A chrome-alloy frame is a desirable choice over aluminium as it can be welded if necessary. Although touring bikes, and to a lesser extent mountain bikes and spares are available in the larger Latin American cities, remember that most locally manufactured goods are shoddy and rarely last. In some countries, such as Chile and Uruguay, imported components can be found but they tend to be extremely expensive. (Shimano parts are generally the easiest to find.) Buy everything you possibly can before you leave home. *Richard's New Bicycle Book* (Pan, £12.99) makes useful reading for even the most mechanically minded (there is also *Richard's 21st century Bicycle Book*).

Remember that you can always stick your bike on a bus, canoe or plane to get yourself nearer to the heart of where you want your wheels to take you. This is especially useful when there are long stretches of major road ahead, where all that stretches before you are hours of turbulence as the constant stream of heavy trucks and long-haul buses zoom by. In almost any country it is possible to rent a bike for a few days, or join an organized tour for riding in the mountains. You should check, however, that the machine you are hiring is up to the conditions you will be encountering, or that the tour company is not a fly-by-night outfit without back-up, good bikes or maintenance

The **Expedition Advisory Centre** ① *1 Kensington Gore, London SW7 2AR, T020-7591 3008, www.rgs.org*, administered by the Royal Geographical Society, has published a useful monograph entitled *Bicycle Expeditions*, by Paul Vickers. Published in March 1990, it can be downloaded from the RGS's website. Useful websites are **Bike South America** ① *www.e-ddws.com/bsa/* and **Cyclo Accueil Cyclo** ① *chez André Coadou, 35 A, rue de Larrey, 21000 Dijon, France, www.cci.asso.fr/cac/cac.htm*, an organization of long-haul tourers who open their homes for free to passing cyclists.

Boat

Because expanding air services have captured the lucrative end of the passenger market, passenger services on the rivers are in decline. Worst hit have been the upper reaches; rivers like the Ucayali in Peru, but the trend is apparent throughout the region. The situation has been aggravated for the casual traveller by a new generation of purpose-built tugs (all engine-room and bridge), that can handle up to a dozen freight barges but have no passenger accommodation. In Peru passenger boats must now supplement incomes by carrying cargo, and this lengthens their journey cycle. In the face of long delays, travellers might consider shorter 'legs' involving more frequent changes of boat; though the more local the service, the slower and more uncomfortable it will be.

Hammocks, mosquito nets (not always good quality), plastic containers for water storage, kettles and cooking utensils can be purchased in any sizeable riverside town, as well as tinned food. Fresh bread, cake, eggs and fruit are available in most villages. Cabin bunks are provided with thin mattresses but these are often foul. Replacements can be bought locally but rolls of plastic foam that can be cut to size are also available and much cheaper. Eye-screws for securing washing lines and mosquito nets are useful, and tall passengers who are not taking a hammock and who may find insufficient headroom on some boats should consider a camp-chair.

In Venezuelan Amazonas hitching rides on boats is possible if you camp at the harbour or police post where all boats must register. Take any boat going in your direction as long as it reaches the next police post. See the special section on the Brazilian Amazon, page 536.

Maps and guidebooks

Those from the **Institutos Geográficos Militares** in the capitals are often the only good maps available in Latin America. It is therefore wise to get as many as possible in your home country before leaving, especially if travelling by land. A recommended series of general maps is that published by **International Travel Maps** (ITM) ① *530 West Broadway, Vancouver BC, V5Z 1E9, Canada, T604-879 3621, www.itmb.com*, several compiled with historical notes, by the late Kevin Healey. As well as maps of South America Southern, North East and North West (1:4M), there are maps of most of the individual countries, the Amazon Basin, Easter Island, the Galápagos, the Falklands/Malvinas and several cities. Another map series that has been mentioned is that of **New World Edition** ① *Bertelsmann, Neumarkter Strasse 18, 81673 München, Germany*, Mittelamerika, Südamerika Nord, Südamerika Sud, Brasilien (all 1:4M). London's **Stanford's** ① *12-14 Long Acre, Covent Garden, London WC2E 9LP, T020-7836 1321, www.stanfords.co.uk* (with other shops in Bristol and Manchester), also sells a wide variety of guides and maps.

Health → *Hospitals/medical facilities are listed in the Directory sections of each chapter sub-section.*

Local populations in South America are exposed to a range of health risks not encountered in the western world. Many of the diseases are major problems for the local poor and destitute. The risk to travellers is more remote but cannot be ignored. Obviously five-star travel is going to carry less risk than backpacking on a minimal budget. The health care in the region is varied. There are many excellent private and government clinics/hospitals. As with all medical care, first impressions count. If a facility is grubby, staff wear grey coats instead of white ones then be wary of the general standard of medicine and hygiene. A good tip is to contact the embassy or consulate on arrival and ask where the recommended clinics (those used by diplomats) are. Diseases you may be exposed to are caused by viruses, bacteria and parasites. Tropical South America (Bolivia, Brazil, Colombia, Ecuador, French Guiana, Guyana, Paraguay, Peru, Suriname and Venezuela) poses a greater disease risk than Temperate South America (Argentina, Chile, Falkland Islands/Islas Malvinas and Uruguay). Other health problems, such as altitude sickness, may affect you along the entire length of the Andes.

The greatest disease risk in tropical South America is caused by the greater volume of insect disease carriers in the shape of mosquitoes and sandflies. The parasitic diseases are many but the two key ones are **malaria** and South American trypanosomiasis (known as **Chagas Disease**). The key viral disease is **Dengue fever**, which is transmitted by a mosquito that bites in the day. Bacterial diseases include **tuberculosis** (TB) and some causes of traveller's **diarrhoea**. More detail will be found below.

Before you go Ideally, you should see your GP/practice nurse or travel clinic at least six weeks before your departure for general advice on travel risks, malaria and recommended vaccinations. Your local pharmacist can also be a good source of readily accessible advice. Make sure you have travel insurance, get a dental check (especially if you are going to be away for more than a month), know your own blood group and if you suffer a long-term condition such as diabetes or epilepsy make sure someone knows or that you have a Medic Alert bracelet/necklace with this information on it.

Vaccinations The following are commonly recommended for South America. The final decision, however, should be based on a consultation with your GP or travel clinic. **Polio** Recommended if nil in last 10 years. **Tetanus** Recommended if nil in last 10 years (but after five doses you have had enough for life). **Typhoid** Recommended if nil in last three years. **Yellow fever** Obligatory for most areas except Chile, Paraguay, Argentina and Uruguay. However, if you are travelling around South America it is best to get this vaccine since you will

need it for the northern areas. **Rabies** Recommended if going to jungle and/or remote areas.
Hepatitis A Recommended – the disease can be caught easily from food/water.

A-Z of health risks

Altitude sickness Acute mountain sickness can strike from about 3,000 m upwards and in general is more likely to affect those who ascend rapidly (for example by plane) and those who over-exert themselves. Acute mountain sickness takes a few hours or days to come on and presents with headache, lassitude, dizziness, loss of appetite, nausea and vomiting. Insomnia is common and often associated with a suffocating feeling when lying down in bed. You may notice that your breathing tends to wax and wane at night and your face is puffy in the mornings – this is all part of the syndrome. If the symptoms are mild, the treatment is rest and painkillers (preferably not aspirin-based) for the headaches. Should the symptoms be severe and prolonged it is best to descend to a lower altitude immediately and reascend, if necessary, slowly and in stages. The symptoms disappear very quickly – even after a few hundred metres of descent.

The best way of preventing acute mountain sickness is a relatively slow ascent. When trekking to high altitude, some time spent walking at medium altitude, getting fit and acclimatizing is beneficial. When flying to places over 3,000 m, a few hours' rest and the avoidance of alcohol, cigarettes and heavy food will help prevent acute mountain sickness.

Bites and stings This is a very rare event indeed for travellers, but if you are unlucky (or careless) enough to be bitten by a venomous snake, spider, scorpion or sea creature, try to identify the culprit, without putting yourself in further danger (do not try to catch a live snake). Snake bites in particular are very frightening, but in fact rarely poisonous – even venomous snakes can bite without injecting venom. Victims should be taken to a hospital or a doctor without delay. It is not advised for travellers to carry snake bite antivenom as it can do more harm than good in inexperienced hands. Reassure and comfort the victim frequently. Immobilize the limb with a bandage or a splint and get the patient to lie still. Do not slash the bite area and try to suck out the poison. This also does more harm than good. You should apply a tourniquet in these circumstances, but only if you know how to. Do not attempt this if you are not experienced.

Certain tropical fish inject venom into bathers' feet when trodden on, which can be exceptionally painful. Wear plastic shoes if such creatures are reported. The pain can be relieved by immersing the foot in hot water (as hot as you can bear) for as long as the pain persists.

Chagas' disease The disease occurs throughout South America, affects locals more than travellers, but travellers can be exposed by sleeping in mud-constructed huts where the bug that carries the parasite bites and defecates on an exposed part of skin. You may notice nothing at all or a local swelling, with fever, tiredness and enlargement of lymph glands, spleen and liver. The seriousness of the parasite infection is caused by the long-term effects which include gross enlargement of the heart and/or guts. Early treatment is required with toxic drugs. Prevention: always keep a light burning at night. Never scratch the bite, but swab it with disinfectant. Sleep under a permethrin-treated bed net and use insect repellents.

Dengue fever This is a viral disease spread by mosquitoes that tend to bite during the day. The symptoms are fever and often intense joint pains, also some people develop a rash. Symptoms last about a week but it can take a few weeks to recover fully. Dengue can be difficult to distinguish from malaria as both diseases tend to occur in the same countries. There are no effective vaccines or antiviral drugs though, fortunately, travellers rarely develop the more severe forms of the disease (these can prove fatal). Rest, plenty of fluids and paracetamol (not aspirin) is the recommended treatment.

Diarrhoea and intestinal upset Diarrhoea can refer either to loose stools or an increased frequency of bowel movement, both of which can be a nuisance. Symptoms should be relatively short lived but if they persist beyond two weeks specialist medical attention should be sought. Also seek medical help if there is blood in the stools and/or fever.

Adults can use an antidiarrhoeal medication such as loperamide to control the symptoms but only for up to 24 hours. In addition keep well hydrated by drinking plenty of fluids and eat bland foods. Oral rehydration sachets taken after each loose stool are a useful way to keep well hydrated. These should always be used when treating children and the elderly.

Bacterial traveller's diarrhoea is the most common form. Ciproxin (Ciprofloxacin) is a useful antibiotic and can be obtained by private prescription in the UK. You need to take one 500 mg tablet when the diarrhoea starts. If there are so signs of improvement after 24 hours the diarrhoea is likely to be viral and not bacterial. If it is due to other organisms such as those causing giardia or amoebic dysentery, different antibiotics will be required.

The standard advice to prevent problems is to be careful with water and ice for drinking. Ask yourself where the water came from. If you have any doubts then boil it or filter and treat it. There are many filter/treatment devices available. Food can also transmit disease. Be wary of salads (what were they washed in, who handled them), re-heated foods or food that has been left out in the sun having been cooked earlier in the day. There is a simple adage that says wash it, peel it, boil it or forget it. Also be wary of unpasteurised dairy products as they too can transmit diseases.

Hanta virus Some forest and riverine rodents carry hanta virus, epidemics of which have occurred in Argentina and Chile, but do occur worldwide. Symptoms are a flu-like illness which can lead to complications. Try as far as possible to avoid rodent-infested areas, especially close contact with rodent droppings. Campers and parents with small children should be especially careful.

Hepatitis Hepatitis means inflammation of the liver. Viral causes of the disease can be acquired anywhere in the world. The most obvious symptom is a yellowing of your skin or the whites of your eyes. However, prior to this all that you may notice is itching and tiredness. Pre-travel hepatitis A vaccine is the best bet. Hepatitis B (for which there is a vaccine) is spread through blood and unprotected sexual intercourse, both of which can be avoided.

Leishmaniasis A skin form of this disease occurs in all countries of South America except Chile and Uruguay. The main disease areas are in Bolivia, Brazil and Peru. If infected, you may notice a raised lump, which leads to a purplish discoloration on white skin and a possible ulcer. The parasite is transmitted by the bite of a sandfly. Sandflies do not fly very far and the greatest risk is at ground levels, so if you can sleep above ground, under a permethrin treated net, do so. In addition, use insect repellent. Seek advice for any persistent skin lesion or nasal symptom. Several weeks treatment is required under specialist supervision. The drugs themselves are toxic but if not taken in sufficient amounts recurrence of the disease is more likely.

Leptospirosis Various forms of leptospirosis occur throughout Latin America, transmitted by a bacterium which is excreted in rodent urine. Fresh water and moist soil harbour the organisms, which enter the body through cuts and scratches. If you suffer from any form of prolonged fever consult a doctor.

Malaria Malaria can cause death within 24 hours and can start as something just resembling an attack of flu. You may feel tired, lethargic, headachy, feverish; or more seriously, develop fits, followed by coma and then death. Have a low index of suspicion because it is very easy to write off vague symptoms, which may actually be malaria. If you have a temperature, visit a doctor as soon as you can and ask for a malaria test. On your return home, if you suffer any of these symptoms, have a test as soon as possible. Even if a previous test proved negative, this could save your life.

Treatment is with drugs and may be oral or into a vein depending on the seriousness of the infection. Remember ABCD: Awareness (of whether the disease is present in the area you are travelling in), Bite avoidance, Chemoprohylaxis, Diagnosis.

To prevent mosquito bites wear clothes that cover arms and legs, use effective insect repellents in areas with known risks of insect-spread disease and use a mosquito net treated with an insecticide. Repellents containing 30-50% DEET (Di-ethyltoluamide) are recommended when visiting malaria endemic areas; lemon eucalyptus (Mosiguard) is a reasonable alternative. The key advice is to guard against contracting malaria by taking the correct anti-malarials and finishing the recommended course. If you are A popular target for insect bites or develop lumps quite soon after being bitten use antihistamine tablets and apply a cream such as hydrocortisone.

Remember that it is risky to buy medicine, and in particular anti-malarials, in some developing countries. These may be sub-standard or part of a trade in counterfeit drugs.

Rabies Rabies is endemic throughout Latin America so be aware of the dangers of the bite from any animal. Rabies vaccination before travel can be considered but if bitten always seek urgent medical attention – whether or not you have been previously vaccinated – after first cleaning the wound and treating with an iodine-base disinfectant or alcohol.

Schistosomiasis (bilharzia) The mansoni form of this flat worm occurs in Suriname and Venezuela (check the CDC, WHO websites and a travel clinic specialist for up to date information for affected locations). The form that penetrates the skin after you have swum or waded through snail infested water can cause a local itch soon after, fever after a few weeks and much later diarrhoea, abdominal pain and spleen or liver enlargement. A single drug cures this disease.

Sun Take good heed of advice regarding protecting yourself against the sun. Overexposure can lead to sunburn and, in the longer term, skin cancers and premature skin aging. The best advice is simply to avoid exposure to the sun by covering exposed skin, wearing a hat and staying out of the sun if possible, particularly between late morning and early afternoon. Apply a high-factor sunscreen (greater than SPF15) and also make sure it screens against UVB. A further danger in tropical climates is heat exhaustion or more seriously heatstroke. This can be avoided by good hydration, which means drinking water past the point of simply quenching thirst. Also when first exposed to tropical heat take time to acclimatize by avoiding strenuous activity in the middle of the day. If you cannot avoid heavy exercise it is also a good idea to increase salt intake.

Ticks Ticks usually attach themselves to the lower parts of the body often when walking in areas where cattle have grazed. They take a while to attach themselves strongly, but swell up as they start to suck blood. The important thing is to remove them gently, so that they do not leave their head parts in your skin because this can cause a nasty allergic reaction some days later. Do not use petrol, vaseline, lighted cigarettes, etc to remove the tick, but, with a pair of tweezers remove the beast gently by gripping it at the attached (head) end and rock it out in very much the same way that a tooth is extracted. **Typhus**, carried by ticks, can also occur. There is usually a reaction at the site of the bite and a fever. Certain tropical flies which lay their eggs under the skin of sheep and cattle also occasionally do the same thing to humans with the unpleasant result that a maggot grows under the skin and pops up as a boil or pimple. The best way to remove these is to cover the boil with oil, vaseline or nail varnish so as to stop the maggot breathing, then to squeeze it out gently the next day.

Underwater health If you plan to dive make sure that you are fit do so. The **British Sub-Aqua Club** (BSAC), Telford's Quay, South Pier Road, Ellesmere Port, Cheshire CH65 4FL, UK, T01513-506200, F01513-506215, www.bsac.com, can put you in touch with doctors who will carry out medical examinations. Check that any dive company you use are reputable and have appropriate certification from the **Professional Association of Diving Instructors** (PADI), Unit 7, St Philips Central, Albert Rd, St Philips, Bristol, BS2 OTD, T0117-3007234, www.padi.com.

Water There are a number of ways of purifying water. Dirty water should first be strained through a filter bag and then boiled or treated. Bring water to a rolling boil for several minutes. There are sterilizing methods that can be used and products generally contain chlorine (eg Puritabs) or iodine (eg Pota Aqua) compounds. There are a number of water sterilizers now on the market available in personal and expedition size. Make sure you take the spare parts or spare chemicals with you and do not believe everything the manufacturers say.

Other diseases and risks There are a range of other insect-borne diseases that are quite rare in travellers, but worth finding out about if going to particular destinations. One example is river blindness (Onchocerciasis), carried by blackflies found in parts of Venezuela. Also remember that unprotected sex always carries a risk. You can lessen this by using condoms, a femidom or if you want to be completely safe, by avoiding sex altogether.

Websites
www.cdc.gov Centres for Disease Control and Prevention (USA).
www.dh.gov.uk/PolicyAndGuidance/Health AdviceForTravellers/fs/en Department of Health advice for travellers.
www.fitfortravel.scot.nhs.uk Fit for Travel (UK), a site from Scotland providing a quick A-Z of vaccine and travel health advice requirements for each country.
www.fco.gov.uk Foreign and Commonwealth Office (FCO), UK.

www.itg.be Prince Leopold Institute for Tropical Medicine.
www.nathnac.org National Travel Health Network and Centre (NaTHNaC).
www.who.int World Health Organisation.

Books
Dawood, R, editor, *Travellers' health*, 3rd ed, Oxford: Oxford University Press, 2002.
Warrell, David, and Sarah Anderson, editors, *Expedition Medicine*, The Royal Geographic Society, ISBN 1 86197 040-4.

Essentials A-Z

Children → *For health matters, see page 45. Visit www.babygoes2.com.*
Travel with children can bring you into closer contact with South American families and, generally, presents no special problems – in fact the path is often smoother for family groups. Officials tend to be more amenable where children are concerned and they are pleased if your child knows a little Spanish or Portuguese. Moreover, thieves and pickpockets seem to have some traditional respect for families, and may leave you alone because of it! **Note:** Buy nappies/diapers at every available opportunity, in case of short supply later on.

People contemplating overland travel in South America with children should remember that a lot of time can be spent waiting for public transport. Even then, buses can be delayed on the journey by bad weather. Travel on trains, while not as fast or at times as comfortable as buses, allows more scope for moving about. Beware of doors left open for ventilation especially if air-conditioning is not working. If hiring a car, check that it has rear seat belts.

On all long-distance buses you pay for each seat, and there are no half-fares if the children occupy a seat each. For shorter trips it is cheaper, if less comfortable, to seat small children on your knee. Often there are spare seats which children can occupy after tickets have been collected. In city and local excursion buses, small children generally do not pay a fare, but are not entitled to a seat when paying customers are standing. On sightseeing tours you should always bargain for a family rate – often children can go free. All civil airlines charge half for children under 12, but some military services don't have half-fares, or have younger age limits. Children's fares on Lloyd Aéreo Boliviano are considerably more than half, and there is only a 7 kg baggage allowance. (LAB also checks children's ages on passports.) Note that a child travelling free on a long excursion is not always covered by the operator's travel insurance; it is advisable to pay a small premium to arrange cover.

Food can be a problem if the children are not adaptable. It is easier to take food such as biscuits, drinks and bread with you on longer trips than to rely on meal stops where the food may not be to taste. Avocados are safe and nutritious; they can be fed to babies as young as six months and most older children like them. A small immersion heater and jug for making hot drinks is invaluable, but remember that electric current varies. Try and get a dual-voltage one (110v and 220v).

In all **hotels**, try to negotiate family rates. If charges are per person, always insist that two children will occupy one bed only, therefore counting as one tariff. If rates are per bed, the same applies. In either case you can almost always get a reduced rate at cheaper hotels. Occasionally when travelling with a child you will be refused a room in a hotel that is 'unsuitable'. On river boat trips, unless you have very large hammocks, it may be more comfortable and cost effective to hire a two-berth cabin for two adults and a child. (In restaurants, you can normally buy children's helpings, or divide one full-size helping between two children.)

Disabled travellers

In most of South America, facilities for the disabled are severely lacking. For those in wheelchairs, ramps and toilet access are limited to some of the more upmarket, or most recently built hotels. Pavements are often in a poor state of repair or crowded with street vendors. Most archaeological sites, even Machu Picchu, have little or no wheelchair access.

Visually or hearing-impaired travellers are also poorly catered for, but there are experienced guides in some places who can provide individual attention. There are also travel companies outside South America who specialize in holidays which are tailor-made for the individual's level of disability. Some moves are being made to improve the situation. In Chile all new public buildings are supposed to provide access for the disabled by law; PromPerú has initiated a programme to provide facilities at airports, tourist sites, etc; Quito's trolley buses are supposed to have wheelchair access, but they are often too crowded to make this practical. While disabled South Americans have to rely on others to get around, foreigners will find that people are generally very helpful. The **Global Access – Disabled Travel Network** website, www.globalaccessnews.com, is useful. Another informative site, with lots of advice on how to travel with specific disabilities, plus listings and links belongs to the **Society for Accessible Travel and Hospitality**, www.sath.org. Also see **www.access-able.com**.

Eating → *See inside front cover for our Eating price guide.*

Food in South America is enticingly varied and regionally based. Within one country you cannot guarantee that what you enjoyed on the coast will be available in the sierras. It is impossible to list here what is on offer in each country and there is a section on food and drink in each chapter's Essentials section. Here are a few tasters, though: fish from Amazonian rivers, from Chilean Pacific waters, and fresh from Andean lakes; or try *ceviche*, raw fish marinated in lemon juice and chili (best in Peru and Ecuador). If **meat** is your thing, go to an Argentine or Uruguayan *parrillada* (barbecue), or a Brazilian *churrascaría* – at the rodizio restaurants, they will bring the meat until you can eat no more. Also in Brazil, there's the traditional *feijoada* (meat and beans, with a lot more besides) and the African-style food of Bahia. An Andean speciality is *cuy*, guinea pig and don't forget that the potato is native to the Andes, with more varieties than you can imagine. Chicken is the basis of many dishes, such as *ajiaco* in Colombia. Corn (maize) and yucca are staples and in many places starchy vegetables are the main form of carbohydrate. Chinese restaurants tend to offer good value and where there are large immigrant communities you'll find excellent Japanese or Italian restaurants. Pizza is pretty ubiquitous, sometimes genuine, sometimes anything but. Then there's fruit, fruit and more fruit in all the tropical regions, eaten fresh or as ice cream, or as a juice.

In all countries except Brazil and Chile (where cold meats, cheese, eggs, fruit, etc generally figure) breakfast usually means coffee or tea with rolls and butter, and anything more is charged extra. In Colombia and Ecuador breakfast usually means eggs, a roll, fruit juice and a mug of milk with coffee; say "breakfast without eggs" if you do not want that much. **Vegetarians** should be able to list all the foods they cannot eat; saying "*soy vegetariano/a*" (I'm a vegetarian) or "*no como carne*" (I don't eat meat) is often not enough. Most restaurants serve a daily special meal, usually at lunchtime, which is cheap and good. Other than that you can expect to pay from US$7 in Peru, Ecuador or Bolivia, to US$15 in Uruguay on breakfast and dinner per day.

Gay and lesbian travellers

Much of Latin America is quite intolerant of homosexuality. Rural areas tend to be more conservative in these matters than cities. It is therefore wise to respect this and avoid provoking a reaction. In Brazil, gay men, while still enjoying more freedom than in many countries, should exercise reasonable discretion. For the gay or lesbian traveller, however, certain cities have active communities and there are local and international organizations which can provide information. The best centres are **Buenos Aires** (Argentina), **Santiago** (Chile), **Rio de Janeiro** and other cities in Brazil, **Lima** (Peru) and **Quito** (Ecuador). Helpful general websites include: www.bluway.com, www.gayscape.com, www.outandabout.com. In Argentina: **www.mun dogay.com** (in Spanish). Brazil: **www.riogayguide.com** (lots of information). In Chile: **www.gay chile.com** (very useful, in Spanish, English). In Ecuador: **www.quitogay.net** (in Spanish and English). In Peru: www.**gaylimape.tripod.com/about.htm** (good site, in English, lots of links and information), **www.deambiente.com/web** and **www.gayperu.com** (both in Spanish).

Internet

Email is common and public access to the internet is becoming widespread with cybercafés opening in both large and small towns. In large cities an hour in a cyber café will cost between US$0.50-2, with some variation between busy and quiet times. Speed varies enormously, from city to city, café to café. Away from population centres service is slower

and more expensive. Remember that for many South Americans cyber cafés provide their only access to a computer, so it can be a very busy place and providers can get overloaded. We list some cybercafés in the text, but in most cities, cybercafés are too numerous to mention. Two websites which give information on cybercafés are: **www.world66.com/netcafeguide** and **www.netcafes.com**.

Language → *See page 1534 for a full list of Spanish words and phrases.*

The official language of the majority of South American countries is Spanish. The exceptions are Brazil (Portuguese), Guyana and the Falklands/Malvinas (English), Suriname (Dutch) and Guyane (French). English is often spoken by wealthy and well-educated citizens, particularly in Colombia, but otherwise the use of English is generally restricted to those working in the tourism industry. The basic Spanish of Hispanic America is that of southwestern Spain, with soft 'c's' and 'z's' pronounced as 's', and not as 'th' as in the other parts of Spain. There are several regional variations in pronunciation, particularly in the River Plate countries, which are noted in the accompanying box. Differences in vocabulary also exist, both between peninsular Spanish and Latin American Spanish, and between the usages of the different countries.

Without some knowledge of Spanish (or Portuguese) you will become very frustrated and feel helpless in many situations. English, or any other language, is absolutely useless off the beaten track. Some initial study, to get you up to a basic vocabulary of 500 words or so, and a pocket dictionary and phrase-book, are most strongly recommended: your pleasure will be doubled if you can talk to the locals. Not all the locals speak Spanish (or Portuguese); you will find that in the more remote highland parts of Bolivia and Peru, and lowland Amazonia, some people speak only their indigenous languages, though there will usually be at least one person in each village who can speak Spanish (or Portuguese).

If you are going to Brazil, you should learn some Portuguese. Spanish is not adequate: you may be understood but you will probably not be able to understand the answers. Language classes are available at low cost in a number of centres in South America, for instance Quito. See the text for details, under Language courses.

AmeriSpan ① *117 South 17th St, Ste 1401, Philadelphia, PA 19103, T215-751 1100 (worldwide), T1-800-879 6640 (USA), T020-8123 6086 (UK), T69-2222 7597 (Germany), SKYPE: amerispan, www.amerispan.com*, offers Spanish immersion programmes, educational tours, volunteer and internship positions throughout Latin America. Language programmes are offered in Argentina, Bolivia, Brazil, Chile, Ecuador, Peru, Uruguay and Venezuela. **LanguagesAbroad.com**① *386 Ontario St, Toronto, Ontario, Canada, M5A 2V7, T416-925 2112, toll free 1-800-219 9924 (0800-404 7738 – UK), www.languages abroad.com*, offers Spanish and Portuguese programmes in every South American country except Colombia, Paraguay and Uruguay. They also have language immersion courses throughout the world. Similarly, **Cactus**① *4 Clarence House, 30-31 North St, Brighton BN1 1EB, T0845-130 4775, www.cactuslanguage.com*, and **Spanish Abroad**① *5112 N, 4th St, Suite 103, Phoenix, AZ 85018, USA, T602-778 6791, www.spanishabroad.com*. For a list of Spanish schools, see www.planeta.com/schoolist.html.

Local customs and laws

Appearance There is a natural prejudice in all countries against travellers who ignore personal hygiene and have a generally dirty and unkempt appearance. Most Latin Americans, if they can afford it, devote great care to their clothes and appearance; it is appreciated if visitors do likewise. Buying clothing locally can help you to look less like a tourist. In general, clothing requirements in Brazil are less formal than in the Hispanic countries. It is, however, advisable for men visiting upmarket restaurants to wear long trousers (women in shorts may also be refused entry). As a general rule, it is better not to wear shorts in official buildings, cinemas, inter-state buses and on flights. Also in Brazil, it is normal to stare and comment on women's appearance, and if you happen to look different or to be travelling alone, you will attract attention. Single women are very unlikely to be groped or otherwise molested (except at Carnaval), but nevertheless Brazilian men can be extraordinarily persistent, and very easily encouraged.

Courtesy Remember that politeness – even a little ceremoniousness – is much appreciated. Men should always remove any headgear and say *"con permiso"* (*"com licença"* in Brazil) when entering offices, and be prepared to shake hands (this is much more common in Latin America than in Europe or North America); always say *"Buenos días"* (until midday) or *"Buenas tardes"* (*"Bom dia"* or *"Boa tarde"* in Brazil) and wait for a reply before proceeding further. Always remember that the traveller from abroad has enjoyed greater advantages in life than most Latin American minor officials and should be friendly and courteous in consequence. Never be impatient. Do not criticize situations in public; the officials may know more English than you think and they can certainly interpret gestures and facial expressions. Be judicious about discussing politics with strangers. Politeness can be a liability, however, in some situations; most Latin Americans are disorderly queuers. In commercial transactions (such as buying a meal and goods in a shop), politeness should be accompanied by firmness, and always ask the price first (arguing about money in a foreign language can be very difficult).

Politeness should also be extended to street traders; saying *"No, gracias"* or *"Não, obrigado/a"* with a smile is better than an arrogant dismissal. Whether you give money to beggars is a personal matter, but your decision should be influenced by whether a person is begging out of need or trying to cash in on the tourist trail. In the former case, local people giving may provide an indication. Giving money to children is a separate issue, upon which most agree; don't do it. There are occasions where giving food in a restaurant may be appropriate, but first inform yourself of local practice.

Moira Chubb, from New Zealand, suggests that if you are a guest and are offered food that arouses your suspicions, the only courteous way out is to feign an allergy or a stomach ailment. If worried about the purity of ice for drinks, ask for a beer.

Colour The people of Brazil represent a unique racial mix: it is not uncommon for the children of one family to be of several different colours. However, visitors of Afro-Caribbean origin may encounter racial prejudice, or at least become the focus of some curiosity.

Money
Cash See each country's Money section in Essentials for exchange rates. The three main ways of keeping in funds while travelling are with cash, either US dollars or, in a growing number of places, euros; credit cards/current account cards; US dollars travellers' cheques (TCs – increasingly hard to exchange). Sterling and other currencies are not recommended. Though the risk of loss is greater, the chief benefit of US dollar notes is that better rates and lower commissions can usually be obtained for them. In many countries, US dollar notes are only accepted if they are in excellent, if not perfect condition (likewise, do not accept local currency notes in poor condition). Low-value US dollar bills should be carried for changing into local currency if arriving in a country when banks or *casas de cambio* (exchange shops) are closed (US$5 or US$10 bills). They are very useful for shopping: shopkeepers and *casas de cambio* tend to give better exchange rates than hotels or banks (but see below). The better hotels will normally change travellers' cheques for their guests (often at a poor rate), but if you are travelling on the cheap it is essential to keep in funds. At weekends, on public holidays and when travelling off the beaten track always have plenty of local currency, preferably in small denominations. When departing by air, do not leave yourself too little money to pay the airport departure tax which, unless included in your ticket price, is never waived.

Plastic Emergency contact numbers for credit card loss or theft are given in the relevant country. It is straightforward to obtain a cash advance against a credit card. Many banks are also linked to one, if not both of the main international **ATM** (automatic telling machine) acceptance systems, Plus and Cirrus. Coverage is not uniform throughout the continent, though, so it may be wise to take two types of cards. Frequently, the rates of exchange on ATM withdrawals are the best available. Find out before you leave what ATM coverage there is in the countries you will visit and what international 'functionality' your card has. Check if your bank or credit card company imposes handling charges. Obviously you must ensure that the account to which your debit card refers contains sufficient funds. Before travelling, it may be worth setting up two bank accounts: one with all your funds but no debit card, the other with no funds but which does have a debit card. As you travel, use the internet to transfer money from the full account to the empty account when you need it and withdraw cash from an ATM. That way, if your debit card is stolen, you won't be at risk of losing all your capital.

By using a debit card rather than a credit card you incur fewer bank charges, although a credit card is needed as well for some purchases. With a credit card, obtain a credit limit sufficient for your needs, or pay money in to put the account in credit. If travelling for a long time, consider a direct debit to clear your account regularly. Do not rely on one card, in case of loss. If you do lose a card, immediately contact the 24-hour helpline of the issuer in your home country (keep this number in a safe place).

For purchases, credit cards of the Visa and MasterCard (Eurocard, Access) groups, American Express (Amex), Carte Blanche and Diners Club can be used. Credit card transactions are normally at an officially recognized rate of exchange; but are often subject to tax. For card security, insist that imprints are made in your presence and that any imprints incorrectly completed should be torn into tiny pieces. Also destroy the carbon papers after the form is completed (signatures can be copied from them). Visa ATM locations: www.visalatam.com; MasterCard: www.mastercard.com; for American Express information: www.americanexpress.com; for Western Union agents: www.westernunion.com.

Money transfer Money can be transferred between banks. A recommended method is, before leaving, to find out which local bank is correspondent to your bank at home, then when you need funds, telex your own bank and ask them to telex the money to the local bank (confirming by fax). Give exact information to your bank of the routing number of the receiving bank. Cash in dollars, local currency depending on the country, can be received within 48 banking hours.

Traveller's cheques (TCs). These are convenient but they attract thieves (though refunds can of course be arranged) and you will find that they are more difficult to change than dollar bills. American Express, Visa or Thomas Cook US$ traveller's cheques are recommended, but less commission is often charged on Citibank traveller's cheques, if they are cashed at Latin American branches of that bank. Most banks charge a high fixed commission for changing traveller's cheques because they don't really want to be bothered. *Casas de cambio* may be better for this service. Some establishments may ask to see the customer's record of purchase before accepting.

Exchange When changing money on the street if possible, do not do so alone. If unsure of the currency of the country you are about to enter, check rates with more than one changer at the border, or ask locals or departing travellers. Whenever you leave a country, sell any local currency before leaving, because the further away you get, the less the value of a country's money.

Post → *Local post offices are listed in the Directory sections of each chapter sub-section.*
Postal services vary in efficiency from country to country and prices are quite high; pilfering is frequent. All mail, especially packages, should be registered. Check before leaving home if your embassy will hold mail, and for how long, in preference to the Poste Restante/General Delivery (Lista de Correos) department of a country's Post Office. (Cardholders can use American Express agencies.) If there seems to be no mail at the Lista under the initial letter of your surname, ask them to look under the initial of your forename or your middle name. Remember that there is no W in Spanish; look under V, or ask. For the smallest risk of misunderstanding, use title, initial and surname only. If having items sent to you by courier (such as DHL), do not use poste restante, but an address such as a hotel: a signature is required on receipt.

Radio
World Band Radio South America has more local and community radio stations than practically anywhere else in the world; a shortwave (world band) radio offers a practical means to brush up on the language, sample popular culture and absorb some of the richly varied regional music. International broadcasters such as the BBC World Service, the Voice of America, Boston- (Mass) based Monitor Radio International (operated by Christian Science Monitor) and the Quito-based Evangelical station, HCJB, keep the traveller abreast of news and events, in both English and Spanish.

Compact or miniature portables are recommended, with digital tuning and a full range of shortwave bands, as well as FM, long and medium wave. Detailed advice on radio models (£150 for a decent one) and wavelengths can be found in the annual publication, **Passport to World Band Radio** ⓘ *International Broadcasting Services Ltd, USA, £11.55.* Details of local stations is listed in **World Radio TV Handbook (WRTH)** ⓘ *Wohlfarth Gert GmbH, £12,* www.amazon.co.uk, prices. Both of these, free wavelength guides and selected radio sets are available from the **BBC World Service Bookshop** ① *Bush House Arcade, Bush House, Strand, London WC2B 4PH, UK, T020-7557 2576.*

Responsible tourism

Travel to the furthest corners of the globe is now commonplace and the mass movement of people for leisure and business is a major source of foreign exchange and economic development in many parts of South America. In some regions (eg the Galápagos Islands and Machu Picchu) it is probably the most significant economic activity.

The benefits of international travel are self-evident for both hosts and travellers: employment, increased understanding of different cultures, business and leisure opportunities. At the same time there is clearly a downside to the industry. Where visitor pressure is high and/or poorly regulated, adverse impacts to society and the natural environment may be apparent. Paradoxically, this is as true in undeveloped and pristine areas (where culture and the natural environment are less 'prepared' for even small numbers of visitors) as in major resort destinations.

The travel industry is growing rapidly and increasingly the impacts of this supposedly 'smokeless' industry are becoming apparent. These impacts can seem remote and unrelated to an individual trip or holiday (eg air travel is clearly implicated in global warming and damage to the ozone layer, resort location and construction can destroy natural habitats and restrict traditional rights and activities), but individual choice and awareness can make a difference in many instances, and collectively, travellers are having a significant effect in shaping a more responsible and sustainable industry.

Of course travel can have beneficial impacts and this is something to which every traveller can contribute. Many national parks are part funded by receipts from visitors. Similarly, travellers can promote patronage and protection of important archaeological sites and heritage through their interest and contributions via entrance and performance fees. They can also support small-scale enterprises by staying in locally run hotels and hostels, eating in local restaurants and by purchasing local goods, supplies and arts and crafts. In fact, since the early 1990s there has been a phenomenal growth in tourism that promotes and supports the conservation of natural environments and is also fair and equitable to local communities. This 'ecotourism' segment is probably the fastest-growing sector of the travel industry and provides a vast and growing range of destinations and activities in South America.

While the authenticity of some ecotourism operators' claims needs to be interpreted with care, there is clearly both a huge demand for this type of activity and also significant opportunities to support worthwhile conservation and social development initiatives. Organizations such as **Conservation International** ① *T001-202-912 1000, www.ecotour.org*, the **International Ecotourism society** ① *T001-202-347 9203, www.ecotourism.org,* **Planeta** ① *www.planeta.com*, and **Tourism Concern** ① *T44-20-7133 3330, www.tourism concern.org.uk*, have begun to develop and/or promote ecotourism projects and destinations and their websites are an excellent source of information for sites and initiatives throughout South America. Additionally, organizations such as, **Earthwatch** ① *T44-1865-318838 or in the US 978-461 0081, www.earthwatch.org/europe/,* and **Discovery Initiatives** ① *T44-1285-643333, www.discoveryinitiatives.com*, offer opportunities to participate directly in scientific research and development projects throughout the region.

South America offers unique and unforgettable experiences – often based on the natural environment, cultural heritage and local society. These are the reasons many of us choose to travel and why many more will want to do so in the future. Shouldn't we provide an opportunity for future travellers and hosts to enjoy the quality of experience and interaction that we take for granted?

Safety → *For specific local problems, see under the individual countries in the text.*

Drugs Users of drugs, even of soft ones, without medical prescription should be particularly careful, as some countries impose heavy penalties – up to 10 years' imprisonment – for even the simple possession of such substances. In this connection, the planting of drugs on travellers, by traffickers or the police, is not unknown. If offered drugs on the street, make no response at all and keep walking. Note that people who roll their own cigarettes are often suspected of carrying drugs and subjected to intensive searches.

Keeping safe Generally speaking, most places in South America are no more dangerous than any major city in Europe or North America. In provincial towns, main places of interest, on day time buses and in ordinary restaurants the visitor should be quite safe. Nevertheless, in large cities (particularly in crowded places, eg bus stations, markets), crime exists, most of which is opportunistic. If you are aware of the dangers, act confidently and use your common sense, you will lessen many of the risks. The following tips are all endorsed by travellers. Keep all documents secure; hide your main cash supply in different places or under your clothes: extra pockets sewn inside shirts and trousers, pockets closed with a zip or safety pin, moneybelts (best worn under rather than outside your clothes at the waist), neck or leg pouches, a thin chain for attaching a purse to your bag or under your clothes and elasticated support bandages for keeping money and cheques above the elbow or below the knee have been repeatedly recommended. Be extra-vigilant when withdrawing cash from an ATM: make sure you are not being watched; never give your card to anyone, however smart he may look or plausible he may sound as a 'bank employee' wishing to swipe your card to check for problems. Keep cameras in bags; take spare spectacles (eyeglasses); don't wear expensive wrist-watches or jewellery. If you wear a shoulder-bag in a market, carry it in front of you.

Ignore mustard smearers and paint or shampoo sprayers, and strangers' remarks like "what's that on your shoulder?" or "have you seen that dirt on your shoe?" Furthermore, don't bend over to pick up money or other items in the street. These are all ruses intended to distract your attention and make you easy prey for an accomplice to steal from. Take local advice about being out at night and, if walking after dark, walk in the road, not on the pavement/sidewalk.

Ruses involving 'plainclothes policemen' are infrequent, but it is worth knowing that the real police only have the right to see your passport (not your money, tickets or hotel room). Before handing anything over, ask why they need to see it and make sure you understand the reason. Insist on seeing identification and on going to the police station by main roads. On no account take them directly back to your lodgings. Be even more suspicious if he seeks confirmation of his status from a passer-by. A related scam is for a 'tourist' to gain your confidence, then accomplices create a reason to check your documents. If someone tries to bribe you, insist on a receipt. If attacked, remember your assailants may well be armed, and try not to resist.

Leave any valuables you don't need in safe-deposit in your hotel when sightseeing locally. Always keep an inventory of what you have deposited. If there is no safe, lock your bags and secure them in your room (some people take eyelet-screws for padlocking cupboards or drawers). Hostels with shared rooms should provide secure, clean lockers for guests. If you lose valuables, always report to the police and note details of the report – for insurance purposes.

When you have all your luggage with you, be careful. From airports take official taxis or special airport buses. Take a taxi between bus station/railway station and hotel. Keep your bags with you in the taxi and pay only when you and your luggage are safely out of the vehicle. Make sure the taxi has inner door handles and do not share the ride with a stranger. Avoid night buses; never arrive at night; and watch your belongings whether they are stowed inside or outside the cabin (roof top luggage racks create extra problems, which are sometimes unavoidable – make sure your bag is waterproof). Major bus lines often issue a luggage ticket when bags are stored in the hold of the bus. Finally, never accept food, drink, sweets or cigarettes from unknown fellow travellers on buses or trains. They may be drugged, and you would wake up hours later without your belongings.

Rape This can happen anywhere. If you are the victim of a sexual assault, you are advised in the first instance to contact a doctor (this can be your home doctor if you prefer). You will need tests to determine whether you have contracted any sexually-transmitted diseases; you may also need advice on post-coital contraception. You should also contact your embassy, where consular staff are very willing to help in such cases.

Police Whereas in Europe and North America we are accustomed to law enforcement on a systematic basis, in general, enforcement in Latin America is achieved by periodic campaigns. The most typical is a round-up of criminals in the cities just before Christmas. In December, therefore, you may well be asked for identification at any time, and if you cannot produce it, you will be jailed. If a visitor is jailed his or her friends should provide food every day. This is especially important for people on a diet, such as diabetics. In the event of a vehicle accident in which anyone is injured, all drivers involved are automatically detained until blame has been established, and this does not usually take less than two weeks. Never

⚡ Second languages and anomalies

Argentina English is the second most common language; French and Italian (especially in Patagonia) may be useful. In Spanish, the chief variant pronunciations are the replacement of the 'll' and 'y' sounds by a soft 'j' sound, as in 'azure' (though rarely in Mendoza or the northwest), the omission of the 'd' sound in words ending in '-ado', the omission of final 's' sounds, the pronunciation of 's' before a consonant as a Scottish or German 'ch', and the substitution in the north and west of the normal rolled 'r' sound by a hybrid 'rj'. In grammar the Spanish 'tú' is replaced by 'vos' and the second person singular conjugation of verbs has the accent on the last syllable eg vos tenés, podés, etc. In the north and northwest, the Spanish is closer to that spoken in the rest of Latin America.

Bolivia Outside the cities, especially in the highlands, Aymara and Quechua are spoken by much of the indigenous population. In the lowlands, some Tupi Guaraní is spoken.

Chile The local pronunciation of Spanish, very quick and lilting, with the 's' dropped and final syllables cut off, can present difficulties to the foreigner.

Colombia Colombia has arguably the best spoken Spanish in Latin America, clearly enunciated and not too fast. This is particularly true in the highlands.

There are several indigenous languages in the more remote parts of the country.

Ecuador Quichua is the second official language, although it is little used outside indigenous communities in the highlands and parts of Oriente.

Paraguay Guaraní is the second official language. Most people are bilingual and, outside Asunción, speak Guaraní. Many people speak a mixture of the two languages known as *jopara*.

Peru Quechua, the Andean language that predates the Incas, has been given some official status and there is much pride in its use. It is spoken by millions of people in the Sierra who have little or no knowledge of Spanish. Aymara is used in the area around Lake Titicaca. The jungle is home to a plethora of languages but Spanish is spoken in all but the remotest areas.

Suriname The native language, called Sranan Tongo, originally the speech of the Creoles, is now a lingua franca understood by all groups, and English is widely used.

Guyane Officials do not usually (or deliberately not) speak anything other than French, but Créole is more commonly spoken.

In the Guianas, the Asians, Maroons and Amerindians still speak their own languages among themselves.

offer a bribe unless you are fully conversant with the customs of the country. (In Chile, for instance, it would land you in serious trouble if you tried to bribe a *carabinero*.) Wait until the official makes the suggestion, or offer money in some form which is apparently not bribery, for example "In our country we have a system of on-the-spot fines (*multas de inmediato*). Is there a similar system here?" Do not assume that an official who accepts a bribe is prepared to do anything else that is illegal. You bribe him to persuade him to do his job, or to persuade him not to do it, or to do it more quickly, or more slowly. You do not bribe him to do something which is against the law. The mere suggestion would make him very upset. If an official suggests that a bribe must be paid before you can proceed on your way, be patient (assuming you have the time) and he may relent.

Shopping
Handicrafts, like food, enjoy regional distinctiveness, especially in items such as textiles. Each region, village even, has its own characteristic pattern or style of cloth, so the choice is enormous. Throughout the Andes, weaving has spiritual significance as well as a practical side. Reproductions of pre-Columbian designs can be found in pottery and jewellery and many crafts people throughout the continent make delightful items in gold and silver. Musical

instruments (eg from Bolivia), gaucho wear, the mate drinking gourd and silver straw (*bombilla*), soapstone carvings and all manner of ceramics, from useful pots to figurines are just some of the things you can bring home with you. Remember that handicrafts can almost invariably be bought more cheaply away from the capital, though the choice may be less wide. **Gemstones** are good in Brazil; emeralds in Colombia. Leather goods are best in the cattle countries, Argentina, Uruguay, Brazil and Colombia, while Peru is now marketing native cotton. Buy your **beachwear** in Brazil; it is matchless. **Bargaining** seems to be the general rule in most countries' street markets, but don't make a fool of yourself by bargaining over what, to you, is a small amount of money.

Sleeping → *See inside front cover for our Sleeping price codes.*

Hotels For about US$10, a cheap but not bad hotel room can be found in most countries, although in some of the Andean countries you may not have to pay that much. In some countries, it is more common for rooms to be priced per person, than per room. This is reflected in the text. For those on a really tight budget, it is a good idea to ask for a boarding house – *casa de huéspedes*, *hospedaje*, *pensión*, *casa familial* or *residencial* (according to country) – they are normally to be found in abundance near bus and railway stations and markets. Good-value hotels can also be found near truckers' stops/service stations; they are usually secure. There are often great seasonal variations in hotel prices in resorts. Remember, cheaper hotels don't always supply soap, towels and toilet paper; in colder (higher) regions they may not supply enough blankets, so take a sleeping bag. To avoid price hikes for gringos, ask if there is a cheaper room.

  Experiment in International Living Ltd① *287 Worcester Rd, Malvern, Worcestershire WR14 1AB, T0800-018 4015 or 01684-562577, and offices worldwide, www.eiluk.org,* can arrange stays with families from one to four weeks in Argentina, Chile, Ecuador and Brazil. This has been recommended as an excellent way to meet people and learn the language. They also offer gap year opportunities.

  Unless otherwise stated, it is assumed that hotels listed in the book are clean and friendly and that rooms have shower and toilet. In any class, hotel rooms facing the street may be noisy always ask for the best, quietest room. **Note:** The electric showers used in innumerable hotels should be checked for obvious flaws in the wiring; try not to touch the rose while it is producing hot water. **Cockroaches** are ubiquitous and unpleasant, but not dangerous. Take some insecticide powder if staying in cheap hotels; Baygon (Bayer) has been recommended. Stuff toilet paper in any holes in walls that you may suspect of being parts of cockroach runs.

Toilets Many hotels, restaurants and bars have inadequate water supplies. **Almost without exception used toilet paper should not be flushed down the pan, but placed in the receptacle provided**. This applies even in quite expensive hotels. Failing to observe this custom will block the pan or drain, a considerable health risk. It is quite common for people to stand on the toilet seat (facing the wall – easier to balance).

Youth hostels Organizations affiliated to the Youth Hostels movement exist in Argentina, Brazil, Colombia, Chile, Peru and Uruguay. There is an associate organization in Ecuador. More information in the country sections and from **Hostelling International** (was the International Youth Hostel Federation). Independent sites on hostelling are the **Internet Guide to Hostelling**, www.hostels.com, and **www.hostelworld.com**.

Camping Organized campsites are referred to in the text immediately below hotel lists, under each town. If there is no organized site in town, a football pitch or gravel pit might serve. Obey the following rules for 'wild' camping: (1) arrive in daylight and pitch your tent as it gets dark; (2) ask permission to camp from the parish priest, or the fire chief, or the police, or a farmer regarding his own property; (3) never ask a group of people – especially young people; (4) never camp on a beach (because of sandflies and thieves). If you can't get information from anyone, camp in a spot where you can't be seen from the nearest inhabited place, or road, and make sure no one saw you go there. In Argentina and Brazil, it is common to camp at gas/petrol stations. As Béatrice Völkle of Gampelen, Switzerland, adds, camping wild may be preferable to those organized sites which are treated as discos, with only the afternoon reserved for sleeping.

If taking a cooker, the most frequent recommendation is a multifuel stove (eg MSR International, Coleman Peak 1), which will burn unleaded petrol or, if that is not available, kerosene, benzina blanca, etc. Alcohol-burning stoves are simple, reliable, but slow and you have to carry a lot of fuel: for a methylated spirit-burning stove, the following fuels apply, *alcohol desnaturalizado*, *alcohol metílico*, *alcohol puro* (*de caña*) or *alcohol para quemar*. Ask for 95%, but 70% will suffice. In all countries fuel can usually be found in chemists/pharmacies. Gas cylinders and bottles are usually exchangeable, but if not can be recharged; specify whether you use butane or propane. Gas canisters are not always available. The Camping Clube do Brasil gives 50% discounts to holders of international campers' cards.

Student travellers

Student cards must carry a photograph if they are to be of any use in Latin America for discounts. If you are in full-time education you will be entitled to an International Student Identity Card, which is distributed by student travel offices and travel agencies in 77 countries. The ISIC gives you special prices on all forms of transport such as air, sea, rail, and access to a variety of other concessions and services. If you need to find the location of your nearest ISIC office contact: The **ISIC Association** ① *c/o IAS, Keizersgracht 174-176, 1016 DW Amsterdam, The Netherlands, T+31-20-421 2800, www.istc.org.*

Telephone → *Local dialling codes are listed at the beginning of each town entry.*

The most common method of making phone calls is with a pre-paid card. These are sold in a variety of denominations in, or just outside, phone offices. Phone offices (*centros de llamadas*, *locutorios*) are usually private, sometimes with lots of cabins, internet and other services, at other times just a table in a doorway. Public phone booths are also operated with phone cards, very rarely with coins or tokens. With privatization, more and more companies are competing on the market, so you can shop around. Net2phone is quite common and SKYPE can also be used. If you want to use a mobile phone, either take your own if your provider has an agreement with a local operator (these vary from country to country), or buy a local SIM card. Phones must be tri- or quad-band; again, this varies. Rental (not cheap) and buying a pay-as-you-go phone is possible, but you will have to check the range of the phone. The area covered is often small and rates rise dramatically once you leave it. Fax services are also available should you need them. AT&T's 'USA Direct', Sprint and MCI are all available for calls to the USA. Other countries such as the UK and Canada have similar systems; obtain details before leaving home.

Women travellers

Many women travel alone or in pairs in South America without undue difficulty. Attitudes and courtesy towards western women, especially those on their own, vary from country to country. The following hints have mainly been supplied by women, but most apply to any single traveller. First-time exposure to countries where sections of the population live in extreme poverty or squalor and may even be starving can cause odd psychological reactions in visitors. So can the exceptional curiosity extended to visitors, especially women. Simply be prepared for this and try not to over-react. When you set out, err on the side of caution until your instincts have adjusted to the customs of a new culture. If, as a single woman, you can befriend a local woman, you will learn much more about the country you are visiting. Unless actively avoiding foreigners like yourself, don't go too far from the beaten track; there is a very definite 'gringo trail' which you can join, or follow, if seeking company. This can be helpful when looking for safe accommodation, especially if arriving after dark (which is best avoided). Remember that for a single woman a taxi at night can be as dangerous as wandering around on your own. At borders dress as smartly as possible. Travelling by train is a good way to meet locals, but buses are much easier for a person alone; on major routes your seat is often reserved and your luggage can usually be locked in the hold. It is easier for men to take the friendliness of locals at face value; women may be subject to much unwanted attention. To help minimize this, do not wear suggestive clothing and do not flirt. By wearing a wedding ring, carrying a photograph of your 'husband' and 'children', and saying that your 'husband' is close at hand, you may dissuade an aspiring suitor. When asked how long you are travelling, say only for a short time because a long journey may give the impression that you are wealthy (even if you are not). If politeness fails, do not feel bad about showing offence and departing. When accepting a social invitation, make sure that someone knows the address and the time you left. Ask if you can bring a friend (even if you do not intend to do so). A good rule is always to act with confidence, as though you know where you are going, even if you do not. Someone who looks lost is more likely to attract unwanted attention. Do not disclose to strangers where you are staying.

Working/volunteering in South America

If you are seeking more than casual work in any South American country, there will be income tax implications which you should research at the relevant consulate before leaving home. **Voluntary work** falls generally into three main categories: community projects, conservation and teaching. A number of organizations can arrange a 'voluntourism' package for you, in which you will probably have to pay for your airfare and raise money before you go. You will probably be working at grass-roots level and conditions may be harsh. But at the same time you will be contributing to the local community or its environment and gaining a new perspective on travelling.

Gap year/career breaks There is some overlap between volunteering and gap year or career break tourism as many people who make this type of trip are going to do some form of work . There is an increasing amount of help for students on a gap year and, in the UK at least, a well-planned and productive gap year can be a positive advantage when it comes to university and job application. The career-break market is growing fast and there is help on-line to guide you. Some organizations guide you all the way through the planning and finding something to do; others are quite specific in the type of project or country in which they operate. Here is a list of ideas: **www.gapyear.com**, **www.gap.org.uk** and **www.yearoutgroup.org** for that year away. For a range of options, try **www.gvi.co.uk** (Global Vision International), or **www.i-to-i.com**. More specific (but not limited to South America) are **www.raleigh.org.uk** (Raleigh International), **www.rain forestconcern.org** (Rainforest Concern), with environmental projects in Bolivia, Brazil, Chile, Colombia, Ecuador and Peru, **www.handsupholidays.com**, with project vacations in Argentina, Brazil and Peru, **www.madventurer.com**, **www.questoverseas.com** (Quest Overseas, which also runs expeditions) and **www.thepodsite.co.uk** (Personal Overseas Development), with projects only in Peru, **www.outreachinternational.co.uk** (Outreach), with projects in Ecuador, **www.teaching-abroad.co.uk**, for more than teaching, in Argentina, Bolivia, Chile and Peru, and **www.vso.org.uk** (Voluntary Service Overseas), working in Guyana.

Specifically in Brazil, there are two websites with information on volunteering: **www.portaldovoluntario.org.br** and **www.voluntarios.com.br**, both in Portuguese. Catalytic Communities, **www.comcat.org**, also has projects in Brazil. In Colombia, Peace Brigades International, **www.peacebrigades.org/index.html**, which protects human rights and promotes nonviolent transformation of conflicts, employs foreign nationals who often work as human rights monitors and observers. Fluent Spanish is essential. 'Voluntourism' in Ecuador attracts many visitors. Several language schools operate volunteering schemes in conjunction with Spanish classes. Environmental conservation: **www.cecia.org** (Corporación Ornitológica del Ecuador, CECIA), works with bird conservation; **www.arcoiris.org.ec** (Fundación Arcoiris), works with a variety of nature conservation and sustainable community development projects in the far south of the country; **www.jatunsacha.org** (Fundación Jatun Sacha), has many different sites at which volunteers can work, all in exceptional natural areas; **www.fnatura.org** (Fundación Natura), a large Ecuadorean NGO, promotes environmental awareness and education. For other options in the continent, contact South American Explorers, see above.

If looking for a paying job, visit the **International Career and Employment Center**, **www.internationaljobs.org**. To teach in international Baccalaureate (IB) schools in South America, you will need to be a qualified subject teacher (primary or secondary level) with between one and two years' experience. Go to **www.ibo.org/** for a list of bilingual schools. You do not have to speak Spanish to work in a bilingual school. Most schools offer private health care packages and annual free flights home.

Another resource is **www.vacationwork.co.uk**, the site of Vacation Work, who publish a number of books, including Susan Griffith's *Work your Way around the World*, 12th edition, 2005.

Argentina

፧ Footprint features

Introduction

Argentina is a hugely varied country, from the blistering heat of the Chaco in the north to the storms of Tierra del Fuego in the south. In between these extremes, there is so much to enjoy – from nights tangoing in the chic quarters of Buenos Aires to long days riding with gauchos in the grasslands of the pampas. You can climb to the roof of the Americas, raft Andean rivers or ski with celebrities. You can visit the birthplace of revolutionary Che Guevara and the resting place of a dinosaur known to have been bigger than T Rex. In the northwest, canyons of rocks eroded into unimaginable shapes lead to sleepy villages and staging posts on the colonial trade routes. At the northern border with Brazil, 275 waterfalls cascade into a great gorge at Iguazú. Swifts dart behind the torrents of water and birds and butterflies are easy to see in the surrounding forest. This is a must on anyone's itinerary. Endangered mammals, giant storks and anacondas live side-by-side in the Iberá marshes. In the dried-up river beds of San Juan, there are exotic rockforms at Talampaya and Ischigualasto. On the Patagonian coast, at Península Valdés, Southern right whales and elephant seals come to breed in the sheltered bays, while estuaries are home to colonies of penguins and pods of dolphin. Lonely roads cross the vast, empty plateau inland, leading to the petrified remains of giant forests and a cave with 10,000 year-old paintings of hands and animals. The Andean mountain chain ends in a jagged finale at the peaks of the Chaitén Massif, with some of the best trekking on the continent. To set the taste buds tingling, the vineyards of Mendoza and the traditional Welsh tearooms of the Chubut valley hang out the welcome sign. And (vegetarians look away), don't forget the meat, barbecued on an open wood fire at the end of the day.

★ Don't miss...

1 **A tango in Buenos Aires** Tango is Buenos Aires' dance and its passion, page 88.
2 **Mendoza** Taste some of the best wines on the continent, page 120.
3 **Salta and the northwest** Romantic city and starting point for multi-coloured gorges, high plateaux and green oases, page 145.
4 **Iguazú Falls** The mightiest falls in South America, page 174.
5 **Península Valdés** *The* place to see marine life: whales, elephant seals and penguins, page 203.
6 **Los Glaciares National Park** Unforgettable landscape of jagged mountains, southern beech forest and glaciers, page 216.

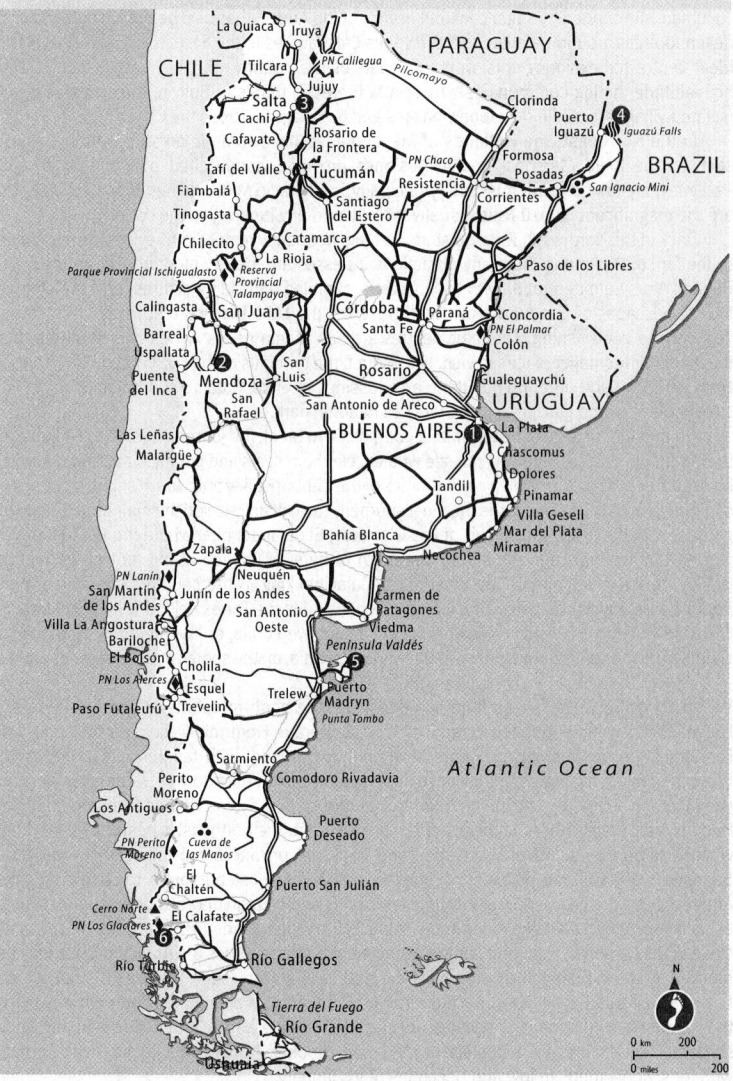

Argentina

Essentials

Planning your trip

The capital, **Buenos Aires**, has a distinctly European feel, its architecture mostly 20th-century, though earlier buildings can be found in San Telmo district. The central docklands have been reclaimed as an upmarket restaurant zone and the Palermo district, with its large parks, has become increasingly popular for eating out. Across the Río de la Plata is Uruguay; just northwest is Tigre, on the Paraná delta, a popular spot for escaping the city; to the southeast are coastal resorts which lead round to the most famous, Mar del Plata. West and south of Buenos Aires stretch the grasslands of the pampas, home of the *gaucho* (cowboy) and large *estancias*.

Through **Northwest Argentina** a string of cities gives access to the Andean foothills and the higher peaks. On the way to the mountains are Córdoba, an important industrial centre close to resorts in the Sierras de Córdoba, and Santiago del Estero, Argentina's oldest city. From Tucumán, surrounded by sugar cane but in view of the Andes, there is a beautiful route through desert foothills around Cafayate and the Valles Calchaquíes to the fine city of Salta. This is the ideal centre for exploring this wonderful part of the country with its remote valleys and high-altitude mining communities. From Salta there are routes to Bolivia, through an area of isolated villages, to Chile over lonely passes and to Paraguay across the Chaco.

In the **Northeast**, the wetlands of Mesopotamia have some interesting wildlife zones, such as the Iberá Marshes, and in Misiones province, sandwiched between Brazil and Paraguay, are ruined Jesuit missions, principally San Ignacio Miní. The highlight of this region are the magnificent Iguazú Falls, usually included on any itinerary to the country.

Back in the Northwest, **Ruta 40** starts its long, frequently remote journey beside the Andes to the far south. Among the many attractions it passes are the city of Mendoza, on the main Buenos Aires-Santiago road, with its vineyards, climbing and skiing centres, and the strange lunar landscapes of San Juan province. It traverses the **Lake District**, renowned for its lovely scenery and good fishing. The main centres are San Martín de los Andes and Bariloche, but there are many smaller places to visit, like Esquel, the terminus of the Old Patagonian Express. From Bariloche and other points, there are crossings to Chile. Ruta 40 continues south to the stunning peaks and glaciers of Los Glaciares national park.

On the Atlantic side of **Patagonia**, a good place to break the journey is Puerto Madryn and the Península Valdés. Here you can see whales, elephant seals and guanaco at close quarters. Just south of here are the Welsh communities of the Chubut Valley and, south again, three areas of petrified forest. Río Gallegos is the most southerly town of any size on the mainland. One road goes west to the most visited part of Los Glaciares, El Calafate, near where the Perito Moreno glacier tumbles into Lago Argentino. Just north of here, El Chaltén at the foot of the jagged FitzRoy massif has some of the most spectacular trekking in the country. This increasingly popular area now forms part of the circuit which includes the Torres del Paine national park in Chile. Beyond Río Gallegos is Tierra del Fuego, shared with Chile; on the Argentine side is what claims to be the southernmost town in the world, Ushuaia, on the shores of the Beagle Channel.

When to go Climate ranges from sub-tropical in the north to cold temperate in Tierra del Fuego. The densely populated central zone is temperate. From mid-December to the end of February Buenos Aires can be oppressively hot and humid, with temperatures of 27-35°C (80-95°F) and an average humidity of 70%. The city virtually shuts down in late December and early January as people escape on holiday. Autumn can be a good time to visit and spring in Buenos Aires (September-October) is often very pleasant. The Northeast is best visited in winter when it is cooler and drier. Corrientes and Misiones provinces are increasingly wet from September. The winter is also a good time to visit the Northwest, but routes to Chile across the Andes may be closed by snow at this time and spring and autumn may be better: summer rains, especially in Jujuy, can make roads impassable. In the winter (June-August) establishments may close in the far south, transport can be restricted and routes across the Andes to Chile may be blocked by snow. Spring and autumn are the best seasons for visiting the Lake District. Ideally Patagonia should be visited in December or February-April, avoiding the winter months when the weather is cold and many services are closed. There are also school holidays in July when some facilities such as youth hostels may be heavily booked. Note that Bariloche is very popular with for school groups in July and December/early January.

Finding out more The national office of the **Secretaría de Turismo** ① *Av Santa Fe 883, Buenos Aires, To800-5550016, www.turismo.gov.ar*. For free tourist information anywhere in the country To800-555 0016 (0800-2000). Addresses of other tourist offices are given in the text. For tourist information abroad, contact Argentine embassies and consulates.

National parks Administración de Parques Nacionales, Santa Fe 690, opposite Plaza San Martín, T4311 0303, Monday-Friday 1000-1700, has leaflets on national parks. Also library (**Biblioteca Perito Moreno**), open to public Tuesday-Friday 1000-1300, 1400-1700. **www.patri monionatural.com** has information on Argentina's national parks and monuments.

Tourist offices

Each province has a tourist office, Casa de Provincia, in Buenos Aires, Mon-Fri 1000-1630/1730.
Buenos Aires Province, Av Callao 237, T4371 7046, www.casaprov.gba.gov.ar. Also www.bue.gov.ar.
Catamarca, Av Córdoba 2080, T/F4374 6891, www.catamarca.gov.ar.
Chaco, Av Callao 322, T4372 5209, www.ecomchaco.com.ar.
Chubut, Sarmiento 1172, T4382 2009, www.chubut.com.ar.
Córdoba, Av Callao 332, T4373 4277, www.cba.gov.ar.
Corrientes, San Martín 333, p 4, T/F4394 2808, www.corrientes.gov.ar.
Entre Ríos, Suipacha 844, T4326 2573, www.turismo.entrerios.gov.ar.
Formosa, Hipólito Yrigoyen 1429, T4381 2037, www.casadeformosa.gov.ar.
Jujuy, Av Santa Fe 967, T 4393 6096, www.casadejujuy.gov.ar.
La Pampa, Suipacha 346, T4326 1145, www.turismolapampa.gov.ar.
La Rioja, Av Callao 745, T4815 1929, www.larioja.gov.ar/turismo.
Mar del Plata, Av Corrientes 1660, local 16, T4384 5658, www.mardelplata.gov.ar.
Mendoza, Av Callao 445, T 4374 1105, www.mendoza.gov.ar.
Misiones, Santa Fe 989, T 4322 1097, www.misiones.gov.ar/turismo.
Municipalidad de la Costa, B Mitre 737, T 4394 2330, www.lacostaturismo.com.ar.
Neuquén, Maipú 48, T4343 2324, www.neuquen.gov.ar.
Río Negro, Tucumán 1916, T4371 7078, www.rionegrotur.com.ar.
Salta, Diagonal Norte 933, T4326 2456, www.turismosalta.gov.ar.

San Juan, Sarmiento 1251, T4382 9241, www.sanjuan.gov.ar.
San Luis, Azcuénaga 1083, T5778 1621, www.sanluis.gov.ar.
Santa Cruz, 25 de Mayo 279, T4325 3102, www.epatagonia.gov.ar.
Santa Fe, Montevideo 373, p 2, T5811 4327,
Santiago del Estero, Florida 274, T4326 9418, www.mercotur.com/santiagodelestero.
Tierra del Fuego, Sarmiento 745, T4311 0233, www.tierradelfuego.org.ar.
Tucumán, Suipacha 140, T 4322 0010, www.tucumanturismo.gov.ar.
  For tourist information on **Patagonia**, see www.patagonia.com.ar and http://patagonia-argentina.com. For Patagonia and bookings for cheap accommodation and youth hostels, contact **Asatej**, see Useful addresses on page 98.

Websites

www.liveargentina.com Tourist information for the whole country. In several languages.
www.museosargentinos.org.ar/museos Argentina's museums.
http://ar.yahoo.com, www.grippo.com.ar, www.google.com.ar Argentine search engines.
www.terra.com.ar News, entertainment, weather, tourism and Spanish phone directory.
www.mercotour.com Information on travel and other matters in Argentina, Uruguay, Chile and Brazil, in Spanish, English and Portuguese.
www.meteonet.com.ar Useful web site for forecasts and weather satellite images.
www.alojar.com.ar Accommodation search engine and tourist information in Spanish.
www.tageblatt.com.ar *Argentinisches Tageblatt*, German-language weekly, very informative.
www.buenosairesherald.com Buenos Aires Herald, English language daily.

Maps Several series of road maps are available including those of the **ACA** (best and up-to-date road maps, see below), the Firestone road atlas and the **Automapa**, www.auto mapa.com.ar (regional maps, Michelin-style, high quality). Topographical maps are issued by the **Instituto Geográfico Militar** ① *Av Cabildo 381, Buenos Aires, T4576 5578 (one block from Subte Ministro Carranza, Line D, or take bus 152), open Mon-Fri, 0800-1300, www.igm.gov.ar.* 1:500,000 sheets cost US$3 each and are 'years old'; better coverage of 1:100,000 and 1:250,000, but no city plans. Take passport if intending to buy maps.

Touching down

Airport taxes US$18 for all flights, payable in pesos, dollars or euros (check with the agent selling your flight ticket if these charges have been included in the price). Montevideo and Punta del Este from Aeroparque are subject to US$8 tax. All internal taxes are payable only in pesos. When in transit from one international flight to another, you may be obliged to pass through immigration and customs, have your passport stamped and be made to pay an airport tax on departure. There is a 5% tax on the purchase of air tickets.

Business hours Banks, government offices, insurance offices and business houses are not open on Saturday; normal office hours are 0900-1200, 1400-1900. **Banks:** 1000-1500 but time varies according to the city, and sometimes according to the season. **Government offices:** 1230-1930 (winter) and 0730-1300 (summer). **Post offices:** stamps on sale during working days 0800-2000 but 0900-1300 on Saturday. **Shops:** 0900-2000, many close at 1300 on Saturday. Outside the main cities many close for the daily afternoon siesta, reopening at about 1700. 24-hour opening is allowed except on Monday.

In an emergency Police T101. If robbed or attacked, call the tourist police, **Comisaría del Turista**, Av Corrientes 436, Buenos Aires, T011-4346 5748 (24 hrs) or T0800-999 5000, English spoken, turista@policiafederal.gov.ar. **Urgent medical service** T107.

International phone code +54. Ringing: equal tones with long pauses. Engaged: equal tones with equal pauses.

Official time GMT -3.

Tipping 10% in restaurants and cafés. Porters and ushers are usually tipped.

VAT/IVA 21%; VAT is not levied on medicines, books and some foodstuffs.

Voltage 220 volts (and 110 too in some hotels), 50 cycles, AC, European Continental-type plugs in old buildings, Australian three-pin flat-type in the new. Adaptors can be purchased locally for either type (ie from new three-pin to old two-pin and vice-versa).

Weights and measures Metric.

Visas and immigration Passports are not required by citizens of neighbouring countries who hold identity cards issued by their own governments. No visa is necessary for British citizens and nationals of EU and other western European countries, citizens of Australia, Canada, Israel, Japan, New Zealand, South Africa and the US, who are given a tourist card ('tarjeta de entrada') on entry and may stay for three months, which can be renewed only once for another three months (fee US$35) at the **Dirección Nacional de Migraciones** ① *Av Antártida Argentina 1355 (Retiro), Buenos Aires, T4317 0200, open 0800- 1300*. For all others there are three forms of visa, valid for a maximum of up to one year, renewable: a tourist visa (usually valid for three months and multiple entry, providing a ticket out of Argentina and a bank proof of a minimum amount of money for expenses; fees vary depending on the country of origin; can be extended 30 days), a business visa and a student visa. If leaving Argentina on a short trip, check on re-entry that border officials look at the correct expiry date on your visa, otherwise they will give only 30 days. Carry your passport at all times; backpackers are often targets for thorough searches – just stay calm; it is illegal not to have identification to hand.

At land borders if you don't need visa, 90 days' permission to stay is usually given without proof of transportation out of Argentina. Make sure you are given a tourist card, otherwise you will have to obtain one before leaving the country. If you need a 90-day extension for your stay then leave the country (eg at Iguazú), and 90 further days will be given on return. Visa extensions may also be obtained from the address above, ask for 'Prorrogas de Permanencia'. No renewals are given after the expiry date. To authorize an exit stamp if your visa or tourist stamp has expired, go to Dirección Nacional de Migraciones and a 10-day authorization will be given for US$17, providing a proof of transportation out of the country. Alternatively, you can forego all the paperwork by paying a US$17 fine at a border immigration post.

Argentine embassies and consulates Visit www.mrecic.gov.ar for a full list of addresses.

Money The currency is the peso, divided into 100 centavos. Peso notes in circulation: 2, 5, 10, 20, 50 and 100. Coins in circulation: 1, 5, 10, 25 and 50 centavos and 1 peso. Exchange rate July 2006: US$1 = 3.18 pesos, 1 euro = 3.94 pesos. Foreigners are advised to use credit cards to withdraw cash, where possible, and for making payments. If paying in cash, do so in pesos because, away from the capital especially, dollars are often not accepted for fear of forgeries. ATMs (known as Cajeros Automáticos) can be found everywhere throughout the country except the smallest towns. They are usually Banelco or Link, accepting international cards. Changing TCs can involve lengthy bureaucracy. When crossing a land border into Argentina, make sure you have some Argentine currency as there are normally no facilities at the border.

Credit cards American Express, Diners Club, Visa and MasterCard cards are all widely accepted in the major cities and provincial capitals, though less so outside these. There is a high surcharge on credit card transactions in many establishments; many hotels offer reductions for cash. For lost or stolen cards: **MasterCard** T0800-555 0507, **Visa** T011-4379 3333 (T0810-666 3368 from outside Buenos Aires).

Cost of travelling Budget travellers should allow about US$20 a day for food, accommodation and travel. This takes into account spending time in Patagonia, which is more expensive than the centre and north, and having to stay in hotels on those occasions where there is no hostel. Hotel prices in 2006 started at about US$7-10 pp in uncategorized establishments (US$5-6 pp in a double room), with many good rooms available from US$20-40. Breakfast will cost about US$1.25-2.50, while cheap meals range from US$4-7.50 (US$2-3 for sandwich or pizza). The average cost of internet use is US$0.50-1 per hour.

Getting around

Air Internal air services are run by **Aerolíneas Argentinas** (AR) *www.aerolineas.com.ar,* **Austral** (part of AR), **LAN Argentina**, www.lan.com, and the army airline **LADE** (in Patagonia, Buenos Aires and Paraná) *www.lade.com.ar,* which provides a good extended schedule with new Fokker F-28 jets. Some airlines operate during the high season, or are air taxis on a semi-regular schedule. Children under three travel free. **LADE** also operates discount tickets: spouse (75%) and children (37.5%). Check in two hours before flight to avoid being 'bumped off' from over-booking. Meals are rarely served on internal flights.

Under the banner **Visit Argentina, Aerolíneas Argentinas** sell coupons for **AR/Austral** domestic flights at a reduced rate in conjunction with any international **AR** flight ticket, or a little less cheaply if arriving with other international carriers. These fares range from US$26 (some flights from Salta or Mendoza) to US$269 (some flights from Bariloche), plus taxes. The coupon for the first flight must be booked before the international departure and all coupons must be booked within the valid period of the international ticket. Tickets are not refundable, changes of route are not possible but changes of date are free. For children under two years the Visit Argentina fare is 10%. It is unwise to set up too tight a schedule because of delays which may be caused by bad weather. Flights between Buenos Aires and El Calafate are often fully booked two to three weeks ahead, and there may be similar difficulties on the routes to Bariloche and Iguazú. If you are 'wait-listed' they cannot ensure a seat. Reconfirmation at least 24 hours ahead of a flight is essential.

⁝ Driving in Argentina

Roads Only 29% of Argentina's roads are paved and a further 17% improved. Most main roads are rather narrow but roadside services are good. To avoid flying stones on gravel roads (called *ripio* on maps) and dirt roads, don't follow trucks too closely, overtake with plenty of room, and pull over and slow down for oncoming vehicles. Most main roads have private tolls about every 100 km, US$0.20-1.50. Unprivatized secondary roads are generally poor. Internal checkpoints prevent food, vegetable and meat products entering Patagonia, Mendoza, San Juan, Catamarca, Tucumán, Salta and Jujuy provinces.

Safety All motorists are required to carry two warning triangles, a fire-extinguisher, a tow rope or chain, and a first aid kit. The handbrake must be fully operative and seat belts must be worn if fitted. Headlights must be on in the day-time on roads in Buenos Aires province.

Documents Full car documentation must be carried (including an invoice for the most recently paid insurance premium) together with international driving licence (for non-residents).

Organizations Automóvil Club Argentino (ACA)ⓘ *Av Libertador Gen San Martín 1850, Buenos Aires, T011-4808 4000 or T0800-888 9888, www.aca.org.ar*, has a travel documents service, car service facilities, and road maps. Foreign automobile clubs with reciprocity with ACA are allowed to use ACA facilities and discounts (with a membership card). ACA accommodation comprises: Motel, Hostería, Hotel, and Unidad Turística, and they also organize campsites. All have meal facilities of some kind.

Car hire The minimum age for renting varies by company, but usually is 21-25 (private arrangements may be possible). A credit card is required; the highest prices are in Patagonia. Discounts are available for weekly rental. 4WD vehicles are offered in some agencies throughout the country. At tourist centres such as Salta, Posadas, Bariloche or Mendoza it may be more economical to hire a taxi with driver, which includes a guide, fuel, insurance and a mechanic.

Fuel Petrol/gasoline (*nafta*) costs on average US$0.70 per litre and diesel US$0.50. Octane ratings: regular gasoline (*común*) 83; *super* 93. Unleaded fuel is widely available in 93, 95 and 97 octane. You may not export fuel from Argentina, so use up spare fuel while you are in the country. Always fill up when you can in less developed areas like Chaco and Formosa and in parts of Patagonia as filling stations are infrequent.

Bus *Coche cama* or *clase ejecutiva* buses between cities are more expensive than the *comunes*, but well worth the extra money for the comfort and fewer stops. When buying tickets at a bus office, don't assume you've been automatically allotted a seat: make sure you have one. Buses have strong a/c, even more so in summer; take a sweater for night journeys. On long-distance journeys, take food and drink, even if a meal is advertised; it's usually a small snack. Note that luggage is handled by *maleteros*, who expect a tip (US$0.35 or less is acceptable) though many Argentines refuse to pay.

Taxi Licensed taxis known as *Radio Taxi* can be hired on the street, or can be called in advance and are safer. There is also a system known as *Remise*, common in smaller towns where there are no taxis, where car and driver are booked from an office and operate with a fixed fare (more than a regular taxi).

Sleeping → *See inside front cover for our hotel grade price guide.*

Hotels Bills in four- and five-star hotels are normally quoted without 21% VAT. It is often cheaper to book a room at reception, rather than over the internet; add it to get the real price. Bed and breakfast accommodation throughout Argentina can be booked via www.argentina bandb.com.ar, in English and Spanish.

Camping Camping is very popular in Argentina and there are private sites with services and free, or cheaper municipal sites in most tourist centres (except Buenos Aires). Most are very noisy and closed off-season. The average price is US$1-3 pp if you have your own tent, plus a charge for the site in some cases. Camping is allowed at the side of major highways (not recommended) and in most national parks (not at Iguazú Falls). Many ACA and YPF service stations have an area for campers (usually free) and owners are generally friendly, but ask first. Service stations usually have hot showers. A list of camping sites is available from ACA (labelled for members, but should be easily available) and from the national tourist information office in Buenos Aires. *Guía del Acampante* is published annually, on sale at kiosks, and has a full list of campsites in Argentina with good tourist information and discount vouchers.

If you are planning a long trip, renting a motorhome is a good idea. A recommended company is **Andean Roads Motorhome Rentals**, see www.andeanroads.com for contact details and rates (starting at US$110 per day for 1 week).

Estancias An *estancia* is, generally speaking, a farm, but the term covers a wide variety of establishments. In the pampas, they tend to be cattle ranches extending for thousands of hectares; in the west they often have vineyards; northeastern estancias border swamps; those in Patagonia are sheep farms at the foot of the mountains or beside lakes. Besides accommodation, many offer horse riding, fishing, canoeing, walking or birdwatching.

Youth hostels Hostelling International Argentina, or **Red Argentina de Alojamiento para Jóvenes (RAAJ)** ① *Florida 835, p 3, of 319B, Buenos Aires, T011-4511 8712, www.hostels.org.ar*. Offers 10% discount to cardholders at their 54 hostels throughout Argentina. A HI card in Argentina costs US$14, ISIC cards also sold. **Argentina Hostels Club (AHC)** ① *www.argentinahostels.com*, is a network of independent hostels throughout the country.

Eating → *See inside front cover for our Eating price guide.*

Eating out Most Argentines have lunch around 1300, though restaurants open at 1200. Out of Buenos Aires, offices close for lunch and a siesta 1200-1700. Around 1700, many people go to a *confitería* for tea, sandwiches and cakes. Dinner often begins at 2200 or 2230, but restaurants will be mostly open from 2030. The cheapest option is always to have the set lunch as a main meal of the day and then find cheap, wholesome snacks for breakfast and supper. Also good value are *tenedor libre* restaurants – eat all you want for a fixed price.

Food National dishes are based upon plentiful supplies of beef. Many dishes are distinctive and excellent; the *asado*, a roast cooked on an open fire or grill; *puchero*, a stew, very good indeed; *bife a caballo*, steak topped with a fried egg; the *carbonada* (onions, tomatoes, minced beef), particularly good in Buenos Aires; *churrasco*, a thick grilled steak; *parrillada*, a mixed grill, mainly roast meat, offal, and sausages, *chorizos* (including *morcilla*, blood sausage), though do not confuse this with *bife de chorizo*, which is a rump steak (*bife de lomo* is fillet steak). A *choripán* is a roll with a *chorizo* inside. *Empanada* is a tasty meat pie; *empanadas de humita* are filled with a thick paste of cooked corn/maize, onions, cheese and flour *Milanesa de pollo* (breaded, boneless chicken) is usually good value. Also popular is *milanesa*, a breaded veal cutlet. *Ñoquis* (gnocchi), potato dumplings normally served with meat and tomato sauce, are tasty and often the cheapest item on the menu; they are also a good vegetarian option when served with either *al tuco* or Argentine roquefort (note that a few places only serve them on the 29th of the month, when you should put a coin under your plate for luck). *Locro* is a thick stew made of maize, white beans, beef, sausages, pumpkin and herbs. Pizzas come in all sorts of exotic flavours, both savoury and sweet. **Note**: Extras such as chips, *puré* (mashed potato) are ordered and served separately, and are not cheap. Almost uniquely in Latin America, salads are quite safe. A popular sweet is *dulce de leche* (especially from Chascomús), milk and sugar evaporated to a pale, soft fudge. Other popular desserts are *almendrado* (ice cream rolled in crushed almonds), *dulce de batata* (sweet potato preserve), *dulce de membrillo* (quince preserve), *dulce de zapallo* (pumpkin in syrup); these *dulces* are often eaten with cheese. *Postre Balcarce*, a cream and meringue cake and *alfajores*, wheat-flour biscuits filled with *dulce de leche* or apricot jam, are also very popular. Note that *al natural* in reference to fruit means canned without sugar (fresh fruit is *al fresco*) Croissants (known as *media lunas*) come in two varieties: *de grasa* (dry) and *de manteca* (rich and fluffy). For local recipes (in Spanish) *Las comidas de mi pueblo*, by Margarita Palacios, is recommended.

Drink It is best not to drink the tap water; in the main cities it is often heavily chlorinated. It is usual to drink soda or mineral water at restaurants, and many Argentines mix it with their cheaper wine and with ice, as a refreshing drink in summer. Argentine wines (including champagnes, both charmat and champenoise) are sound throughout the price range. The ordinary *vinos de la casa*, or *comunes* are wholesome and relatively cheap; the reds are better than the whites. The local beers, mainly lager-type, are quite acceptable. In restaurants wines are quite expensive. Hard liquor is relatively cheap, except for imported whisky. *Clericó* is a white-wine *sangría* drunk in summer. Vineyards can be visited in Mendoza and San Juan provinces and Cafayate (in the south of Salta province).

Festivals and events

No work may be done on the national holidays (1 January, Good Friday, 1 May, 25 May, 10 June, 20 June, 9 July, 17 August, 12 October and 25 December) except where specifically established by law. There are limited bus services on 25 and 1 January. On Holy Thursday and 8 December employers decide whether their employees should work, but banks and public offices are closed. Banks are also closed on 31 December. There are gaucho parades in San Antonio de Areco (110 km from Buenos Aires), with traditional music, on the days leading up to the Día de la Tradición, 10 November. On 30 December there is a ticker-tape tradition in downtown Buenos Aires: it snows paper and the crowds stuff passing cars and buses with long streamers.

Buenos Aires and the Pampas

→ *Phone code: 011. Colour map 8, grid B5. Pop: 2.78 million (Greater Buenos Aires 12.05 million).*

With its elegant architecture and fashion-conscious inhabitants, Buenos Aires is often seen as more European than South American. Among its fine boulevards, neat plazas, parks, museums and theatres, there are chic shops and superb restaurants. However, the enormous steaks and the passionate tango are distinctly Argentine, and to really understand the country, you have to know its capital. South and west of Buenos Aires the flat, fertile lands of the pampa húmeda stretch seemingly without end, the horizon broken only by a lonely windpump or a line of poplar trees. This is home to the gaucho, whose traditions of music and fine craftsmanship remain alive.

Ins and outs

Getting there Buenos Aires has two **airports**, Ezeiza, for international flights, and Aeroparque, for domestic flights and most services to Uruguay. Ezeiza is 35 km southwest of the centre by a good dual carriageway which links with the General Paz highway which circles the city. The safest way between airport and city is by an airport bus service run by *Manuel Tienda León*, which has convenient offices and charges US$8.50 one way. Taxis charge US$13 (plus US$1.20 toll), but do not have a good reputation for security. *Remise* taxis (booked in advance) charge US$15-20 (including toll for a return journey) airport to town; *Manuel Tienda León* and *Transfer Express* remise taxis charge around US$24. Aeroparque is 4 km north of the city centre on the riverside; *Manuel Tienda León* has buses between the airports and also runs from Aeroparque to the centre for US$3. Remises charge US$6 and ordinary taxis US$4. *Transfer Express* operates on-request *remise* taxis and vans from both airports to any point in town and between them; convenient for large groups. As well as by air, travellers from Uruguay arrive by ferry (fast catamaran or slower vessels), docking in the port in the heart of the city, or by bus. All international and interprovincial buses use the Retiro **bus terminal** at Ramos Mejía y Antártida Argentina, which is next to the Retiro railway station. Both are served by city buses, taxis and Line C of the Subte (metro). Other train services, to the province of Buenos Aires and the suburbs use Constitución, Once and Federico Lacroze stations, all served by bus, taxi and Subte. ▶▶ *For more detailed information, see Transport, page 92.*

Getting around The commercial heart of the city, from Retiro station and Plaza San Martín through Plaza de Mayo to San Telmo, east of Avenida 9 de Julio, can be explored on foot, but you'll probably want to take a couple of days to explore its museums, shops and markets. Many places of interest lie outside this zone, so you will need to use public transport. City **buses** (*colectivos*) are plentiful, see below for city guides. The fare is US$0.27. The **metro**, or Subte, has five lines; a single fare is US$0.24. Yellow and black **taxis** can be hailed on the street, but for security, book a radio taxi by phone (make sure the meter is reset when you get in). *Remise* taxis, booked only through an office, cost more but are more reliable. See Transport, below, for full details. Street numbers start from the dock side rising from east to west, but north/south streets are numbered from Avenida Rivadavia, one block north of Avenida de Mayo rising in both directions. Calle Juan D Perón used to be called Cangallo, and Scalabrini Ortiz used to be Canning (old names are still referred to). Avenida Roque Sáenz Peña and Avenida Julio A Roca are commonly referred to as Diagonal Norte and Diagonal Sur respectively.

Tourist offices National office Av Santa Fe 883, T4312 2232/5550, info@turismo.gov.ar, Mon-Fri 0900-1700, maps and literature covering the whole country. There are kiosks at Aeroparque (*Aerolíneas Argentinas* section), and at **Ezeiza Airport** daily 0800-2000. There are city-run tourist kiosks at Florida 100, junction with Roque Sáenz Peña, in Recoleta (Av Quintana 596, junction with Ortiz), in Puerto Madero, Dock 4, at Aeroparque and Ezeiza airports, at Defensa 1250 (San Telmo) and at Retiro Bus Station (ground floor). **City information** T4313 0187, Mon-Fri 0730-1800, Sat-Sun 1000-1800, municipal website www.bue.gov.ar, in Spanish, English and Portuguese. Free guided tours are usually organized by the city authorities: free leaflet from city-run offices. Audio guided tours in several languages are available for 12 different itineraries by downloading MP3 files and maps from www.bue.gov.ar. **Tango information centre** Sarmiento 1551, www.tangodata.com.ar. Privately run tourist office (very helpful) on the first floor of Galerías Pacífico, on Florida. Those overcharged or cheated can go to the **Tourist Ombudsman**, Av Pedro de Mendoza 1835 (La Boca), T4302 7816, www.defensoria.org.ar, 1000-1800, or to **Defensa del Consumidor** Esmeralda 340, T5382 6200, Mon-Fri 0900-1700. **Tigre tourist office**, Estación Fluvial, Mitre 305, T4512 4497, 0900-1700, www.tigre.gov.ar. **Centro de Guías de Tigre y Delta** T4749 0543, for guided walks and launch trips.

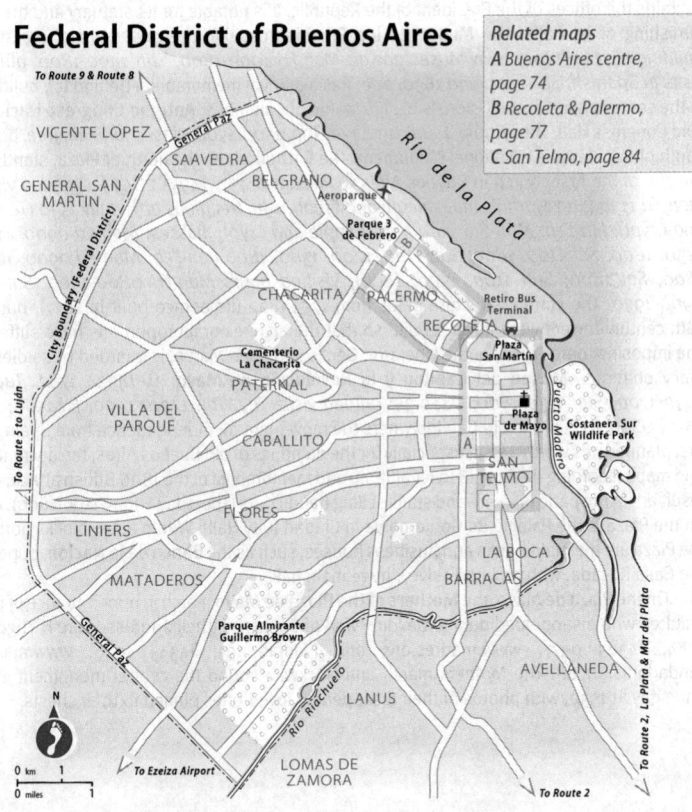

Federal District of Buenos Aires

Related maps
A Buenos Aires centre, page 74
B Recoleta & Palermo, page 77
C San Telmo, page 84

Information Good guides to bus and subway routes are **Guía T, Lumi, Peuser** and **Filcar** (usually covering the city and Greater Buenos Aires in two separate editions), US$1-9 available at news stands. Also handy is Auto Mapa's pocket-size **Plano** of the Federal Capital, or the more detailed City Map covering La Boca to Palermo, both available at news stands, US$4.30; otherwise it is easy to get free maps of the city centre from most hotels. **Buenos Aires Day & Night** is a free bi-monthly tourist magazine with useful information and a downtown map available together with similar publications at tourist kiosks and hotels. **La Nación** has a Sunday tourism section (very informative). On Friday, the youth section of **Clarín** (*Sí*) lists free entertainments. Search **Clarín**'s website (www.clarin.com) for the up-to-date page on entertainment; look at 'Sección Espectáculos'. **Página 12** has a youth supplement on Thursday called **NO**. The **Buenos Aires Herald** publishes **Get Out** on Friday, listing entertainments. Information on what's on at www.buenosairesherald.com.

Sights

The capital has been virtually rebuilt since the beginning of the 20th-century and its oldest buildings mostly date from the early 1900s, with some elegant examples from the 1920s and 30s. The centre has maintained the original lay-out since its foundation and so the streets are often narrow and mostly one-way. Its original name, 'Santa María del Buen Ayre' was a recognition of the good winds which brought sailors across the ocean.

Around Plaza de Mayo

The heart of the city is the **Plaza de Mayo**. On the east side is the **Casa de Gobierno** ① *T4344 3804, tours Mon-Fri 1600 (Spanish and English on Fri only), book at least 2 hrs earlier at Hipólito Yrigoyen 219, passport required, free.* Called the *Casa Rosada* because it is pink, it contains the offices of the President of the Republic. It is notable for its statuary and the rich furnishing of its halls. The **Museo de los Presidentes** ① *in the basement of the same building, T4344 3804, www.museo.gov.ar, Mon-Fri 1000-1800, Sun 1400-1800, guided visits in Spanish, Sun 1500 and 1630, free,* has historical memorabilia. Behind the building, in the semicircular Parque Colón, is a large statue of Columbus. **Antiguo Congreso Nacional** (Old Congress Hall, 1864-1905) ① *Balcarce 139, Thu, 1500-1700, closed Jan-Feb, free,* on the south of the Plaza, is a National Monument. The **Cathedral**, on the north of Plaza, stands on the site of the first church in Buenos Aires ① *Rivadavia 437, T4331 2845 for guided visits, Mon-Fri 1130 (San Martín's mausoleum and Crypt), 1315 (religious art), daily 1530 (Temple and Crypt); Jan-Feb: Mon-Sat 1100 both Temple and Crypt; masses: Mon-Fri 0900, 1100, 1230, 1800, Sat 1100, 1800, Sun 1100, 1200, 1300, 1800 (Jan-Feb: Mon-Fri 0900, 1230, 1800; Sat 1800; Sun 1100, 1300, 1800); visiting hours Mon-Fri 0800-1900, Sat-Sun 0900-1930.* The current structure dates from 1753-1822 (its portico built in 1827), but the 18th-century towers were never rebuilt, so that the architectural proportions have suffered. The imposing tomb (1880) of the Liberator, Gen José de San Martín, is guarded by soldiers in fancy uniforms. **Museo del Cabildo y la Revolución de Mayo** ① *T4334 1782, Tue-Fri 1030-1700, Sun 1130-1800, US$0.35; guided visits Tue, Thu 1200, 1400, Fri 1500; Sun 1630, US$0.70* is in the old Cabildo where the movement for independence from Spain was first planned. It's worth a visit, especially for the paintings of old Buenos Aires, the documents and maps recording the May 1810 revolution, and memorabilia of the 1806 British attack; also Jesuit art. In the patio is a café and stalls selling handicrafts (Thursday-Friday 1100-1800). Also on the Plaza is the Palacio de Gobierno de la Ciudad (City Hall). Within a few blocks north of the Plaza are the main banks and business houses, such as the **Banco de la Nación**, opposite the Casa Rosada, with an impressively huge main hall.

On the Plaza de Mayo, the **Mothers of the Plaza de Mayo** march in remembrance of their children who disappeared during the 'dirty war' of the 1970s (their addresses are H Yrigoyen 1584, T4383 0377, www.madres.org, and Piedras 153, T4343 1926, www.madres fundadoras.org.ar). The Mothers march anti-clockwise round the central monument every Thursday at 1530, with photos of their disappeared loved-ones pinned to their chests.

West of Plaza de Mayo

Running west from the Plaza, the Avenida de Mayo leads 1½ km to the **Palacio del Congreso** (Congress Hall), in the Plaza del Congreso ① *free guided tours from Hipólito Yrigoyen 1849, T4010 3000, www.congreso.gov.ar, passport essential, Mon, Tue, Fri 1100, 1600, 1700, tours at 1100 and 1600 are in English; also tours in Spanish, same days at 1000, 1200, 1600, 1800, from Rivadavia 1850*. This huge Greco-Roman building houses the seat of the legislature. Avenida de Mayo has several examples of fine architecture of the early 20th-century, such as the sumptuous La Prensa building (No 575, free guided visits), the traditional *Café Tortoni* (No 825), or the eclectic Palacio Barolo (No 1370), and many others of faded grandeur. Avenida de Mayo crosses the **Avenida 9 de Julio**, one of the widest avenues in the world, which consists of three major carriageways with heavy traffic, separated in some parts by wide grass borders. Five blocks north of Avenida de Mayo the great **Plaza de la República**, with a 67-m obelisk commemorating the 400th anniversary of the city's founding, is at the junction of Avenida 9 de Julio with Avenidas Roque Sáenz Peña and Corrientes. **Teatro Colón** ① *main entrance on Libertad, between Tucumán and Viamonte, T4378 7132/33, www.teatrocolon.org.ar, guided tours Mon-Sat 1100, 1200, 1300, 1430, 1500, 1600, Sun 1100, 1300, 1500 (Jan-Feb, Mon-Fri only, starting at 1100), in Spanish and English (at 1100, 1300, 1500), US$4, children or ISIC card US$0.70*, is one of the world's great opera houses. The interior is resplendent with red plush and gilt; the stage is huge, and salons, dressing rooms and banquet halls are equally sumptuous. Guided tours, including Museo del Teatro Colón, start from the entrance at Toscanini 1168 (on C Viamonte side) or from Tucumán 1171. For performance times, see page 89.

Close by is the **Museo del Teatro Nacional Cervantes** ① *Córdoba 1199, T4815 8881, Mon-Fri 1000-1800, free* displays history of the theatre in Argentina and its theatre stages performances. **Museo Judío** ① *Libertad 769, T4123 0102; for visits make an appointment with the rabbi (take identification)*, has religious objects relating to Jewish presence in Argentina in a 19th-century synagogue. Close by is **Museo del Holocausto** (Shoah Museum) ① *Montevideo 919, T4811 3588, www.fmh.org.ar, Mon-Thu 1100-1900, Fri 1100-1630, US$1 (ID required)*, a permanent exhibition of pictures, personal and religious items with texts in Spanish on the Holocaust, antisemitism in Argentina and the lives of many Argentine Jews in the pre- and post-war periods. There are also seminars, temporary art exhibitions and a library (open in the afternoon). **La Chacarita** ① *Guzmán 670, daily 0700-1800, take Subte Line B to the Federico Lacroze station*. This well known cemetery has the lovingly tended tombs of Juan Perón and Carlos Gardel, the tango singer.

North of Plaza de Mayo

The city's traditional shopping centre, Calle Florida, is reserved for pedestrians, with clothes and souvenir shops, restaurants and the elegant Galerías Pacífico. More shops are to be found on Avenida Santa Fe, which crosses Florida at Plaza San Martín. Avenida Corrientes, a street of theatres, bookshops, restaurants and cafés, and nearby Calle Lavalle (partly reserved for pedestrians), used to be the entertainment centre, but both are now regarded as faded. Recoleta, Palermo and Puerto Madero have become much more fashionable (see below). The **Basílica Nuesta Señora de La Merced** *J D Perón y Reconquista 207*, built in 1783, is a beautiful colonial church. Next door is the **Convento San Ramón**, founded in 1604, with a restaurant. **Museo y Biblioteca Mitre** ① *C San Martín 336, T4394 8240, Mon-Fri 1300-1730, US$0.70*, preserves intact the household of President Bartolomé Mitre; has a coin and map collection and historical archives. Behind Galerías Pacífico is the **Convento de Santa Catalina** ① *San Martín y Viamonte*, built in the 18th-century with a delightful patio with a restaurant (open for lunch).

The **Plaza San Martín** has a monument to San Martín in the centre and, at the north end, a memorial with an eternal flame to those who fell in the Falklands/Malvinas War of 1982. On the plaza is **Palacio San Martín** ① *Arenales 761, T4819 8092, free guided tours in Spanish and English, Thu 1100, Fri 1500, 1600, 1700*. Built 1905-1909, it is three houses linked together. This palace also hosts an excellent collection of prehispanic art. On the opposite side of the plaza is the opulent **Palacio Paz** (today Círculo Militar), ① *Av Santa Fe 750, T4311 1071, guided tours Tue and Fri 1100, 1500; Wed and Thu 1100, 1500, 1600, US$2.40 (tours in English Tue and Fri 1600, US$5)*. **Museo de Armas** ① *Av Santa Fe 702 y Maipú, T4311 1071, Mon-Fri 1300-1900, US$1*. It has all kinds of weaponry related to Argentine history, including the 1982 Falklands/Malvinas War, plus Oriental weapons.

Plaza Fuerza Aérea Argentina (formerly Plaza Británica) has the clock tower presented by British and Anglo-Argentine residents (T4311 0186, open Thu-Sun 1200-1900, free), while in

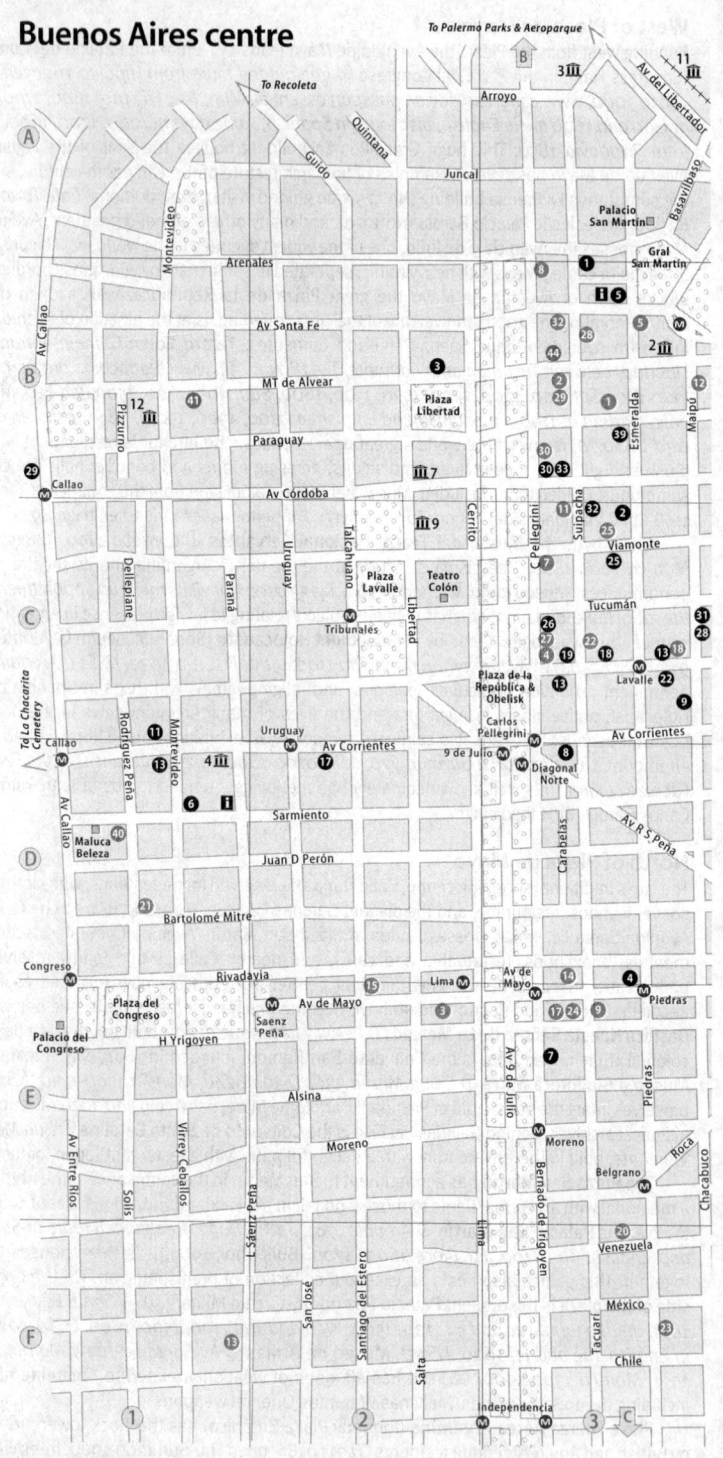

Buenos Aires centre

Argentina Buenos Aires

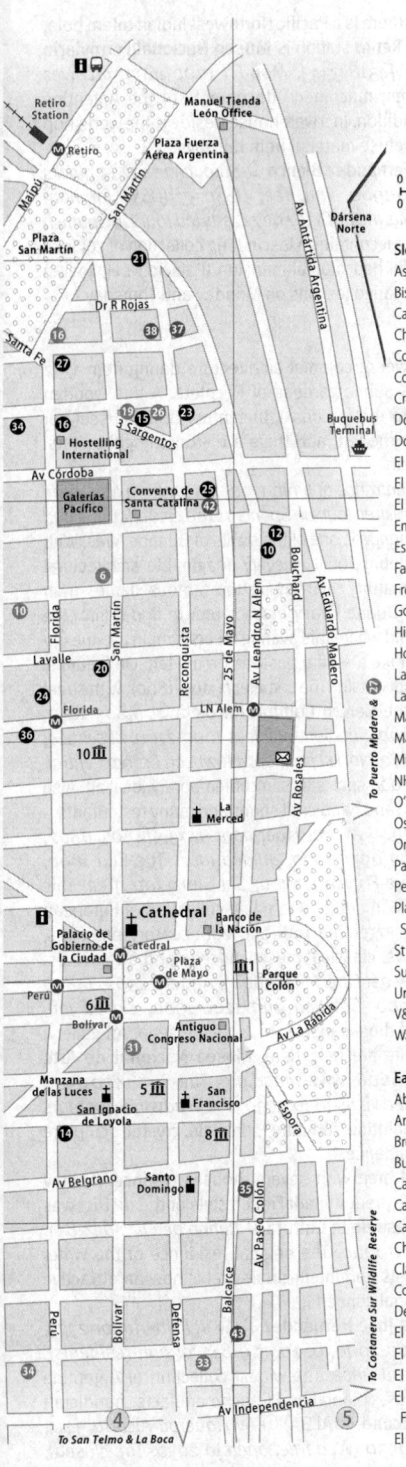

Empire Thai **15** *B4*
Exedra **30** *B3*
Florida Garden **16** *B4*
Fratello **31** *C4*
Gianni's **25** *B4/C3*
Gran Victoria **32** *C3*
Güerrín **17** *D2*
La Casona del

Sleeping 🛏
Aspen Towers **1** *B3*
Bisonte Palace **2** *B3*
Castelar **3** *E2*
Che Lagarto **20** *F3*
Colón **4** *C3*
Colonial Youth Hostel **6** *C4*
Crillon **5** *B3*
Dolmen **28** *B3*
Dorá **12** *B3*
El Cachafaz **7** *C3*
El Conquistador **29** *B3*
El Hostal de Granados **33** *F4*
Embajador **8** *B3*
España **9** *E3*
Faena Universe **27** *C5*
Frossard **10** *C4*
Goya **11** *C3*
Hilton **27** *C5*
Hostel-Inn Tango **23** *F3*
La Casa de Etty **13** *F1*
La Giralda **14** *D3*
Marbella **15** *E2*
Marriott Plaza **16** *B4*
Milhouse Hostel **17** *E3*
NH City **31** *E4*
O'Rei **18** *C3*
Ostinatto Hostel **34** *F4*
Orly **19** *B4*
Panamericano **27** *C3*
Pestana **30** *B3*
Plaza San Martín
  Suites **32** *B3*
St Nicholas **21** *D1*
Suipacha Inn **22** *C3*
Uruguay **24** *E3*
V&S **25** *C3*
Waldorf **26** *B4*

Eating 🍴
Abril **1** *B3*
Aroma **27** *B4*
Broccolino **2** *C3*
Buenos Aires Criollo **9** *C3*
Café de la Biblioteca **3** *B2*
Café Tortoni **4** *D3*
Capataz **28** *C3*
Chiquilín **6** *D1*
Clásica y Moderna **29** *B1*
Confitería Ideal **8** *D3*
Desiderio **5** *B3*
El Figón de Bonilla **10** *C5*
El Gato Negro **11** *C1*
El Navegante **12** *C5*
El Palacio de la Papa
  Frita **13** *C3/D1*
El Querandí **14** *E4*

Nonno **18** *C3*
La Chacra **33** *B3*
La Estancia **19** *C3*
La Pipeta **20** *C4*
Las Nazarenas **21** *A4*
Los Inmortales **22** *C3*
Morizono **23** *B4*
Palacio Español **7** *E3*
Richmond **24** *C4*
Saint Moritz **39** *B3*
Sorrento **36** *C4*
Tancat **34** *B4*
Tomo 1 **26** *C3*

Bars & clubs 🍸
Celta Bar **40** *D1*
Druid In **38** *B4*
El Living **41** *B1*
Kilkenny **37** *B4*
La Cigale **42** *C4*
La Trastienda **35** *E5*
Moliere **43** *F5*
Porto Pirata **38** *B4*
Temple Bar **44** *B3*

Museums 🏛
Casa de Gobierno
  (Casa Rosada) &
  Museo de los
  Presidentes **1** *D5*
Museo de Armas **2** *B3*
Museo de Arte
  Hispanoamericano
  Isaac Fernández
  Blanco **3** *A3*
Museo de Arte
  Moderno & Teatro
  General San
  Martín **4** *D1*
Museo de la
  Ciudad **5** *E4*
Museo del Cabildo
  y la Revolución
  de Mayo **6** *E4*
Museo del
  Holocausto **12** *B1*
Museo del Teatro
  Nacional Cervantes **7** *B2*
Museo Etnográfico
  JB Ambrosetti **8** *E4*
Museo Judío **9** *C2*
Museo y Biblioteca
  Mitre **10** *D4*
Museo Nacional
  Ferroviario at Retiro
  Station **11** *A3*

the **Plaza Canadá** (in front of the Retiro Station) there is a Pacific Northwest Indian totem pole, donated by the Canadian government. Behind Retiro station is **Museo Nacional Ferroviario** ① *ring the bell, free, Av del Libertador 405, T4318 3343, Mon-Fri 1000-1600, archives 1000-1400, free.* For railway fans: locomotives, machinery, documents of the Argentine system's history, the building is in very poor condition. In a warehouse beside is the workshop of the sculptor Carlos Regazzoni who recycles refuse material from railways.

Museo de Arte Hispanoamericano Isaac Fernández Blanco ① *Suipacha 1422 (3 blocks west of Retiro), T4326 3396, Tue-Sun, 1400-1900, Thu free, US$0.35 (US$1 for non-residents), for guided visits in English contact Marina at T4327 0272, guided tours in Spanish Sat, Sun 1500,* is one of the city's best museums. It contains a fascinating collection of colonial art, especially paintings and silver, in a beautiful neocolonial mansion (Palacio Noel, 1920s) with Spanish gardens; free concerts and regular tango lessons on Monday and Thursday.

Recoleta and Palermo

Nuestra Señora del Pilar, Junín 1898, is a jewel of colonial architecture dating from 1732 (renovated in later centuries), facing onto the public gardens of Recoleta. A fine wooden image of San Pedro de Alcántara, attributed to the famous 17th-century Spanish sculptor Alonso Cano, is preserved in a side chapel on the left, and there are stunning gold altars. Upstairs is an interesting museum of religious art.

Next to it, the **Cemetery of the Recoleta** ① *entrance at Junín 1790, not far from Museo de Bellas Artes (see below), T4804 7040, 0700-1800, free tours in Spanish 1100, 1500 (on Tue and Thu 1100 in English), check times as they may change* is one of the sights of Buenos Aires. With its streets and alleys separating family mausoleums built in every imaginable architectural style, La Recoleta is often compared to a miniature city. Among the famous names from Argentine history is Evita Perón who lies in the Duarte family mausoleum: to find it from the entrance go to the first tree-filled plaza; turn left and where this avenue meets a main avenue (go just beyond the Turriaca tomb), turn right; then take the third passage on the left. On Saturday and Sunday there is a good craft market in the park outside the cemetery (1100-1800), with street artists and performers. Next to the cemetery, the **Centro Cultural Recoleta** ① *T4803 1040, www.centroculturalrecoleta.org, Tue-Fri 1400-2100, Sat, Sun, holidays 1000-2100, buses 110, 102, 17, 60 (walk from corner of Las Heras y Junín, 2 blocks) from downtown, eg Correo Central, 61/62, 93, 130 to Av del Libertador y Av Pueyrredón* specializes in contemporary local art. Also the Buenos Aires Design Centre, with good design and handicraft shops and many restaurants.

Museo de Bellas Artes (National Gallery) ① *Av del Libertador 1473, T4803 0802, www.mnba.org.ar, Tue-Fri 1230-1930, Sat-Sun 0930-1930, guided tours Tue-Sun 1600, 1700, 1800, tours for children in summer Tue-Fri 1100, 1700, Sat-Sun 1700, free.* This excellent museum gives a taste of Argentine art, in addition to a fine collection of European works, particularly post-Impressionist. Superb Argentine 19th and 20th-century paintings, sculpture and wooden carvings; also film shows, classical music concerts and art courses. **Biblioteca Nacional** (The National Library) ① *Av del Libertador 1600 y Agüero 2502, T4806 6000, www.bibnal.edu.ar, Mon-Fri 0900-2000, Sat and Sun 1200-1900, closed Jan.* Housed in a modern building, only a fraction of the extensive stock can be seen. Art gallery, periodical and journal archives; cultural events are held here. **Museo Nacional de Arte Decorativo** ① *Av del Libertador 1902, T4802 6606, www.mnad.org, Tue-Sun 1400-1900 (Jan-Feb, closed Mon and Sun), US$0.70, guided visits 1630, 1730 (ask in advance for tours in English), Tue free.* It contains collections of painting, furniture, porcelain, crystal, sculpture exhibited in sumptuous halls, once a family residence.

Palermo Chico is a delightful residential area with several houses of once wealthy families, dating from the early 20th-century. The predominant French style of the district was broken in 1929 by the rationalist lines of the **Casa de la Cultura** ① *Rufino de Elizalde 2831, T4804 0553, Tue-Fri 1500-1900, Sat-Sun 1300-1900.* The original residence of the writer Victoria Ocampo was a gathering place for artists and intellectuals and is now an attractive cultural centre with art exhibitions and occasional concerts.

Museo de Motivos Populares Argentinos José Hernández ① *Av del Libertador 2373, T4802 7294, Wed-Fri 1300-1900, Sat-Sun 1000-2000, US$0.35 (US$1 for non-residents), free Sun, for guided tours in English call in advance.* The widest collection of Argentine folkloric art, with rooms dedicated to indigenous, colonial and Gaucho artefacts; handicraft shop and library. **Museo de Arte Latinoamericano (MALBA)** ① *Av Figueroa Alcorta 3415, T4808 6500, www.malba.org.ar, daily 1200-1930 (Wed free, open to 2030; Tue closed),*

Recoleta & Palermo

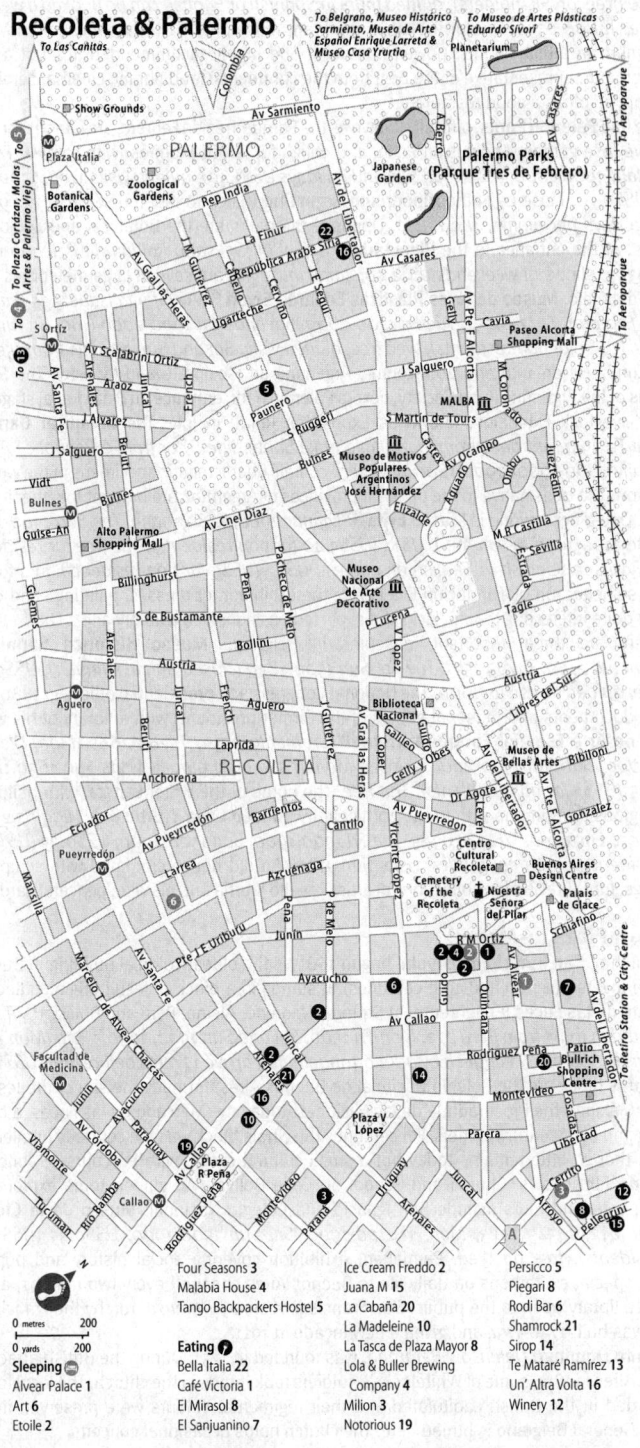

To Las Cañitas

To Belgrano, Museo Histórico
Sarmiento, Museo de Arte
Español Enrique Larreta &
Museo Casa Yrurtia

To Museo de Artes Plásticas
Eduardo Sivori

To Plaza Cortázar, Malas
Artes & Palermo Viejo

To Aeroparque

PALERMO

Show Grounds

Plaza Italia

Botanical
Gardens

Zoological
Gardens

Av Sarmiento

Colombia

Av del Libertador

A Berro

A Berro

Planetarium

Japanese
Garden

Palermo Parks
(Parque Tres de Febrero)

To Aeroparque

Rep India

La Tinur

República Árabe Siria

Av Casares

Av Casares

J M Gutiérrez

Cabello

Cerviño

E Seguí

Ugarteche

Av Gral las Heras

Getty

Cavia

Paseo Alcorta
Shopping Mall

S Ortiz

Av Scalabrini Ortiz

Arenales

Araoz

Juncal

French

J Álvarez

Beruti

J Salguero

Santa Fe

Paunero

Ruggeri

Bulnes

J Salguero

M Coronado

S Martín de Tours

MALBA

Museo de Motivos
Populares
Argentinos
José Hernández

Av Ocampo

Aguado

Castex

Ombú

Juez Pedin

Elizalde

M R Castilla

Sevilla

Estrada

Tagle

Alto Palermo
Shopping Mall

Guise-An

Bulnes

Vidt

Billinghurst

Peña

Pacheco de Melo

Av Cnel Díaz

Museo
Nacional
de Arte
Decorativo

P Lucena

V López

Austria

Güemes

Arenales

Beruti

French

S de Bustamante

Bollini

Aguero

Austria

Juncal

Aguero

Libres del Sur

Biblioteca
Nacional

Galileo

Guido

Av Gral las Heras

Av del Libertador

Museo de
Bellas Artes

Bibiloni

Aguero

Laprida

Anchorena

RECOLETA

Copér

Gelly y Obes

Dr Agote

R Leyen

Av Pte R Libertador

González

Ecuador

Barrientos

Cantilo

Av Pueyrredón

Larrea

Azcuénaga

Pueyrredón

Av Pueyrredón

Vicente López

Centro
Cultural
Recoleta

Cemetery
of the
Recoleta

Nuestra
Señora
del Pilar

Buenos Aires
Design Centre

Palais
de Glace

Schiaffino

Junín

P de Melo

Ayacucho

R M Ortiz

Av Alvear

Av del Libertador

To Retiro Station & City Centre

Marcelo T de Alvear

Av Santa Fe

Pte J E Uriburu

Paraná

Av Callao

Quintana

posadas

Rodríguez Peña

Patio
Bullrich
Shopping
Centre

Facultad de
Medicina

Charcas

Junín

Arenales

Montevideo

Parera

Junín

Ayacucho

Paraguay

Plaza V
López

Libertad

Viamonte

Av Callao

Plaza
R Peña

Montevideo

Uruguay

Arenales

Juncal

posadas

Cerrito

Tucumán

Río Bamba

Callao

Rodríguez Peña

Montevideo

Paraná

Uruguay

Arroyo

C Pellegrini

A

N

0 metres   200
0 yards   200

Sleeping
Alvear Palace 1
Art 6
Etoile 2
Four Seasons 3
Malabia House 4
Tango Backpackers Hostel 5

Eating
Bella Italia 22
Café Victoria 1
El Mirasol 8
El Sanjuanino 7
Ice Cream Freddo 2
Juana M 15
La Cabaña 20
La Madeleine 10
La Tasca de Plaza Mayor 8
Lola & Buller Brewing
  Company 4
Milion 3
Notorious 19
Persicco 5
Piegari 8
Rodi Bar 6
Shamrock 21
Sirop 14
Te Mataré Ramírez 13
Un' Altra Volta 16
Winery 12

Argentina Buenos Aires

77

US$3.40 (free for ISIC holders), guided tours in Spanish or English can be booked a week in advance, T4808 6556. One of the most important museums in the city houses renowned Latin American artists' works: powerful, moving and highly recommended. It's not a vast collection, but representative of the best from the continent. Good library, cinema, seminars and shop, also has a good restaurant.

The fine **Palermo Parks**, officially known as the Parque Tres de Febrero, are famous for their extensive rose garden, Andalusian Patio, and delightful **Jardín Japonés** (with café) ① T4804 4922, daily 1000-1800, US$1 (Sat, Sun and holidays US$1.40), guided visits 1100, 1500 and 1630, US$0.70. Close by is the **Hipódromo Argentino** (Palermo racecourse) ① T4777 9001, races 10 days per month, US$1-3.40. Opposite the parks are the Botanical and Zoological Gardens. At the entrance to the **Planetarium** ① just off Belisario Roldán, in Palermo Park, T4771 9393, shows at weekends US$1.40; small museum, are several large meteorites from Campo del Cielo. **Museo de Artes Plásticas Eduardo Sívori** ① Av Infanta Isabel 555 (Parque Tres de Febrero), T4774 9452, Tue-Fri 1200-2000, Sat and Sun 1000-2000 (1800 in winter), US$0.35 (US$1 for non-residents), Wed free, guided visits Sat and Sun anytime from 1500 to 1700. Emphasis on 19th and 20th-century Argentine art, sculpture and tapestry. The **Show Grounds** of the Argentine Rural Society, next to Palermo Park, entrance on Plaza Italia, stage the Annual Livestock Exhibition, known as Exposición Rural, in July. The **Botanical Gardens** ① Santa Fe 3951, entrance from Plaza Italia (take Subte, line D) or from C República Arabe Siria, daily 0800-1900 (0900-1800 in winter), contain characteristic specimens of the world's vegetation. The trees native to the different provinces of Argentina are brought together in one section. One block beyond is **Museo Evita** ① Lafinur 2988, T4807 9433, Tue-Sun 1300-1900 (Tue-Sun 1100-1900 in summer), US$1 (US$3.40 for non-residents), Tue free for residents; guided visits in Spanish or English on request, US$2 (US$5 for non-residents). In a former women's shelter run by Fundación Eva Perón, the exhibition of dresses, paintings and other items is quite interesting though lacks the expected passion; also a library and a café.

There are three important museums in Belgrano: **Museo Histórico Sarmiento** ① Juramento 2180, T4783 7555, Tue-Fri, Sun 1500-1830 (closed Sun in summer), US$0.35, Thu free, guided visits Sun 1600. The National Congress and presidential offices in 1880 now houses documents and personal effects of the former president, with a library of his work. **Museo de Arte Español Enrique Larreta** ① Juramento 2291, T4783 2640, Mon, Wed-Fri 1400-2000 (Sat-Sun 1500-2000), closed Mon in summer, guided visits Sun 1630,1800, US$0.35 (US$1 for non-residents), Thu free. The home of the writer Larreta, with paintings and religious art from the 14th to the 20th century. **Museo Casa Yrurtia** ① O'Higgins 2390, esq Blanco Encalada, T/F4781 0385, Tue-Fri 1300-1900, Sun 1500-1900, US$0.35 (US$1 for non-residents), Tue free, guided visits Sun 1700. An old house crammed with sculpture, paintings, furniture and the collections of artist Rogelio Yrurtia and his wife; peaceful garden.

South of Plaza de Mayo

The church of **San Ignacio de Loyola**, begun 1664, is the oldest colonial building in Buenos Aires (renovated in 18th and 19th centuries). It stands in a block of Jesuit origin, called the **Manzana de las Luces** (Enlightenment Square – Moreno, Alsina, Perú and Bolívar) ① T4342 4655, guided tours from Perú 272, Mon-Fri 1500, Sat and Sun 1500, 1630, 1800 (Mon 1300 free tour) in Spanish (in English by prior arrangement), arrive 15 mins before tour, US$1.40. Also in this block are the Colegio Nacional de Buenos Aires, formerly the site of the Jesuits' Colegio Máximo, the Procuraduría de las Misiones (today the Mercado de las Luces, a crafts market) and 18th-century tunnels. For centuries the whole block was the centre of intellectual activity, though little remains today but a small cultural centre with art courses, concerts, plays and film shows. Church and School on Calle Bolívar. All guided tours explore the tunnels; weekend tours include San Ignacio and Colegio Nacional. **Museo de la Ciudad** ① Alsina 412, T4343 2123, Mon-Fri 1100-1900, Sat-Sun 1500-1900, US$0.35 (US$1 for non-residents), free on Wed. Permanent exhibition covering social history and popular culture, special exhibitions on daily life in Buenos Aires changed every two months, and a reference library open to the public. **San Francisco** Alsina y Defensa, run by the Franciscan Order, was built 1730-1754 and given a new façade in 1911.

Santo Domingo Defensa y Belgrano, was founded in 1751. During the British attack on Buenos Aires in 1806 some of Whitelocke's soldiers took refuge in the church. The local forces bombarded it, the British capitulated and their regimental colours were preserved in the church. General Belgrano is buried here. The church holds occasional concerts.

Museo Etnográfico JB Ambrosetti ① *Moreno 350, T4345 8196, www.museo etnografico.filo.uba.ar, Wed-Sun 1500-1900 (closed Jan), US$0.70, guided visits Sat-Sun 1600*. Anthropological and ethnographic collections from the Mapuche and Argentina's northwest cultures (the latter a rich collection displayed on the first floor); also a small international room with a magnificent Japanese Buddhist altar.

San Telmo and La Boca

One of the few places which still has late colonial and Rosista buildings (mostly renovated in the 20th century) is the *barrio* of **San Telmo**, south of Plaza de Mayo. It's an atmospheric place, with lots of cafés, antique shops and little art galleries. On Sundays, it has a great atmosphere, with an antiques market at the Plaza Dorrego (see page 91), free tango shows and live music. The 29 bus connects La Boca with San Telmo.

Parque Lezama, Defensa y Brasil, originally one of the most beautiful in the city, now rather run down, has an imposing statue of Pedro de Mendoza, who (according to tradition) founded the original city in 1536 on this spot. In the park is the **Museo Histórico Nacional** ① *Defensa 1600, T4307 1182, Tue-Sun 1100-1700 (Tue-Sun 1100-1800 in summer), US$0.70; guided visits in Spanish, Sat, Sun 1500*. Argentine history, San Martín's uniforms and the original furniture and door of the house in which he died at Boulogne. In the park is the **Iglesia Ortodoxa Rusa** ① *Brasil 315; visits on Sat afternoon (women wearing trousers will be given skirts; men in shorts will be refused entry)*, with its five blue domes and a wonderful interior.

East of the Plaza de Mayo, behind the Casa Rosada, a broad avenue, Paseo Colón, runs south towards San Telmo and as Av Almirante Brown on to the old port district of **La Boca** ① *getting there: bus 152 from Av Santa Fe, or Alem, or bus 29 from Plaza de Mayo, US$0.30*, where the Riachuelo flows into the Plata. The area's distinctive brightly painted tin and wooden houses can be seen along Caminito, the little pedestrian street used as an art market. Visit the **Museo de Bellas Artes Benito Quinquela Martín** ① *Pedro de Mendoza 1835, T4301 1080, Tue-Fri 1000-1730 (in summer opens at 1100), Sat-Sun 1100-1730, US$0.35*. It has more than 1,000 works by Argentine artists, particularly Benito Quinquela Martín (1890-1977), who painted La Boca port life. Also sculptures and figureheads rescued from ships. La Boca is the poorest and roughest area within central Buenos Aires and tourists are, unfortunately, targets for crime. Don't go alone and stay within the cleaned-up, touristy part of Caminito and along the quay only as far as the museum. Avoid the area at night. The area is especially rowdy when the Boca Juniors football club is playing at home. At Boca Juniors stadium is **Museo de la Pasión Boquense** ① *Brandsen 805, T4362 1100, www.museoboquense.com, 1000-1800, US$4 for non-residents. Guided tour of the stadium in Spanish or English, 1100-1700, plus ticket to the museum, US$7 for non-residents*.

Docks and Costanera Sur

Fragata Presidente Sarmiento ① *dock 3, next to Av Alicia Moreau de Justo y Perón, Puerto Madero, T4334 9386, daily 0900-2200 (closes at 2000 in winter), US$0.70*. A sailing ship used as a naval training ship until 1961; now a museum. Nearby, in dock 4, is the **Corbeta Uruguay** ① *T4314 1090, daily 0900-2100 all year, US$0.35*, the sailing ship which rescued Otto Nordenskjold's Antarctic expedition in 1903. The **Puerto Madero** dock area has been renovated, the 19th-century warehouses becoming restaurants and bars, an attractive place for a stroll and popular nightspot. East of San Telmo on the far side of the docks, the Avenida Costanera runs as a long, spacious boulevard. A stretch of marshland reclaimed from the river forms the interesting **Costanera Sur Wildlife Reserve** ① *entrances at Av Tristán Achával Rodríguez 1550 (take Estados Unidos east from San Telmo) or next to the Buquebús ferry terminal (take Av Córdoba east), T4315 1320; for pedestrians and bikers only, Tue-Sun 0800-1800 (in summer, closes at 1900), free, bus 2 passes next to the southern entrance*, where there are more than 200 species of birds, including the curve-billed reed hunter. Free guided tours are available at weekends 1030, 1530 (daily in summer), from the administration next to the southern entrance, but much can be seen from the road before then (binoculars useful). Also free nocturnal visits every month on the Friday closest to the full moon (book Monday before, T4893 1588). It is 30 minutes walk from the entrance to the river shore, taking about three hours to walk the whole perimeter. In summer it is very hot with little shade. For details (birdwatching, in particular) contact Aves Argentinas/AOP (see page 98).

💤 Sleeping

Hotels in the upper ranges can often be booked more cheaply through Buenos Aires travel agencies. The tourist offices at Ezeiza and Jorge Newbery airports book rooms. Hotels and guest houses may display a star rating, but this does not match up to international standards. Many more expensive hotels charge different prices for *extranjeros* (non-Argentines), in US$, and there's not much you can do to get around this, since a passport is required as proof of residency. Make it clear that you'll pay in pesos in cash and you may get a reduction. Room tax (VAT) is 21% and is not always included in the price. A/c is a must in high summer. Finding hotels for Fri, Sat, Sun nights can be difficult. There are fine examples of the **Four Seasons** (www.fourseasons.com/ buenosaires), **Hilton** (www.hilton.com), **Marriott** (www.marriott.com), **Pestana** (www.pestana.com) and **N/A Town & Country Hotels** (www.newage-hotels.com) chains. Cheaper hotels in the centre may give reductions for long stays. Hotels with red-green lights or marked *Albergue Transitorio* are short-stay. All hotels will store luggage, and most have English- speaking staff.

Centre *p72, map p74*

LL Alvear Palace, Av Alvear 1891, T/F4808 2100, reservations 4804 7777, www.alvearpalace.com. The height of elegance, an impeccably preserved 1920s Recoleta palace, taking you back in time to Buenos Aires' wealthy heyday. A sumptuous marble foyer, with Louis XV-style chairs, and a charming orangery where you can take tea with superb patisseries (US$11). Antique-filled bedrooms. Unique. Recommended.

LL Faena Universe, Martha Salotti 445 (Puerto Madero), T4010 9000, www.faenahotelanduniverse.com. Set in a 100-year old silo, renovated by French designer Philippe Starck, this is not for all budgets or tastes. Eclectic decoration, staff trained to be perfect, the whole place is unique.

LL NH City Hotel, Bolívar 160, T4121 6464, www.nh-hoteles.com. Very chic indeed, with perfect minimalist design for an exclusive younger set, this is 1 of 5 in the Spanish-owned chain in central Buenos Aires (the **Crillon**, Av Santa Fe 796, T4310 2000, is now a NH hotel, due to reopen end-2006). Beautifully designed modern interiors in a 1930's building off Plaza de Mayo, and luxurious rooms. Small rooftop pool, good restaurant.

LL Panamericano, Carlos Pellegrini 551, T4348 5000, www.panamericanonews.com. Extremely smart and modern city hotel, with luxurious and tasteful rooms, a lovely covered rooftop pool, and superb restaurant, Tomo 1. Excellent service too.

L Aspen Towers, Paraguay 857, T4313 1919, www.aspentowers.com.ar. A modern minimalist foyer in this small hotel belies the traditional 1900 French-style bedrooms, all with jacuzzi baths, and all facilities, including a good breakfast and a pool.

L Bisonte Palace, MT de Alvear 910, T4328 4751, www.hotelesbisonte.com/. A rather charming place, with calm entrance foyer, which remains gracious thanks to charming courteous staff. The rooms are plain, but spacious, breakfast is ample, and this is in a good location. Very good value.

L Colón, Carlos Pellegrini 507, T4320 3500, www.colon-hotel.com.ar. With a splendid location overlooking Av 9 de Julio and Teatro Colón, in the heart of the city, extremely good value. Charming bedrooms, comfortable, pool, gym, great breakfasts, and perfect service. Highly recommended.

L Dolmen, Suipacha 1079, T4315 7117, www.hoteldolmen.com.ar. Good location, smart spacious entrance lobby, with a calm relaxing atmosphere, good professional service, modern, comfortable well-designed rooms, small pool.

L El Conquistador, Suipacha 948, T4328 3012, www.elconquistador.com.ar. A stylishly modernized '70s boutique hotel, which retains the wood and chrome foyer, but has bright modern rooms, and a lovely light restaurant on the 10th floor with great views. Well situated.

L Etoile, R Ortiz 1835 in Recoleta, T4805 2626, www.etoile.com.ar. Outstanding location, rooftop pool, rooms with balcony.

L Plaza San Martín Suites, Suipacha 1092, T4328 4740, www.plazasanmartin.com.ar. Neat modern self-contained apartments right in the city centre, comfortable and attractively decorated, with lounge and little kitchen. Sauna, gym, room service. Good value.

AL-A Art, Azcuénaga 1268, T4821 6248, www.arthotel.com.ar. Charming boutique hotel on a quiet residential street, only a few blocks from Recoleta or Av Santa Fe, simply but warmly decorated, good service, solarium, compact standard rooms.

A Castelar, Av de Mayo 1152, T4383 5000, F4383 8388, www.castelarhotel.com.ar. A wonderfully elegant 1920s hotel which retains all the original features in the grand entrance and bar. Cosy warmly-decorated bedrooms, charming staff, and excellent value. Also a spa with turkish baths and massage. Highly recommended.

A Dorá, Maipú 963, T4312 7391, www.dorahotel.com.ar. Charming and old-fashioned with

 For an explanation of the sleeping and eating price codes used in this guide, see inside the front cover. Other relevant information is found in Essentials pages 68-69.

80

comfortable rooms, good service, attractive lounge with paintings. Warmly recommended.

A Embajador, Carlos Pellegrini 1181, T4326 5302, www.embajadorhotel.com.ar. Nothing fancy, but good value for such a central location. Plain but comfortable rooms, some overlooking Av 9 de Julio, good service, small breakfast included.

A Orly, Paraguay 474, T/F4312 5344, www.orly.com.ar. Good location, and comfortable plain rooms, with helpful service.

A Waldorf, Paraguay 450, T4312 2071, www.waldorf-hotel.com.ar. Welcoming staff and a comfortable mixture of traditional and modern in this centrally-located hotel. Good value, with a buffet breakfast, English spoken. Recommended.

B Frossard, Tucumán 686, T4322 1811, www.hotelfrossard.com.ar. A lovely old 1940s building with high ceilings and the original doors, attractively modernized, and though the rooms are small (avoid No 11), the staff are welcoming, and this is good value, near C Florida.

B Goya, Suipacha 748, T4322 9269, www.goya hotel.com.ar. Welcoming and central, worth paying more for superior rooms, though all are comfortable. Good breakfast, English spoken.

C La Giralda, Tacuarí 17, T4345 3917, F4342 5561. Nicely maintained, popular with budget travellers, with discounts for long stays, no breakfast.

C Marbella, Av de Mayo 1261, T/F4383 3573, www.hotelmarbella.com.ar . Modernized, and central, though quiet, breakfast included, several languages spoken. Highly recommended.

C Suipacha Inn, Suipacha 515, T4322 0099, www.hotelsuipacha.com.ar/. Good value, neat small rooms with a/c, basic breakfast.

C Uruguay, Tacuarí 83, T4334 3456. A central and traditional old hotel, very clean and welcoming, good value but no breakfast.

D España, Tacuarí 80, T4343 5541. Delightful, old-fashioned and full of character, run by a charming eccentric old couple. Recommended.

D O'Rei, Lavalle 733, T4393 7186, cheaper without bath, central, simple but comfortable, spotless, laundry facilities, helpful staff, no breakfast.

Youth hostels

Prices are per person.

D-E Che Lagarto, Venezuela 857, T4343 4845, www.chelagarto.com. Between Monserrat and San Telmo, large light dorms and doubles with private toilet, TV and fan. Attractive tango hall, the whole ground floor is a pub and restaurant. Price includes breakfast and free internet. HI member.

E Colonial Youth Hostel, Tucumán 509 (Esq. San Martín), Microcentro, T4312-6417. Member of AHC, www.argentinahostels.com.

E El Cachafaz, Viamonte 982, T4328 1445,

www.elcachafaz.com. A renovated old house, central with dorms and **C** double rooms, breakfast and free internet access, laundry facilities.

E Garden House, Av San Juan 1271, T4304 1824, www.gardenhouseba.com.ar. Small, welcoming independent hostel for those who don't want a party atmosphere; good barbecues on the terrace guaranteed. Includes breakfast, free internet and a few **C** doubles without bath. Recommended.

E Hostal don Sancho, Constitución 4062, T4923 1422, www.hostaldonsancho.com.ar. In Boedo, a traditional tango neighbourhood (buses 15, 126, 160 and Subte E, Boedo station). Dorms and **C** double rooms with bath.

E Milhouse Hostel, Hipólito Yrigoyen 959, T4345 9604, www.milhousehostel.com. In 1890 house, lovely rooms (**C**) in double) and dorms, comfortable, free breakfast, cooking facilities, laundry, internet, tango lessons, HI discounts, very popular so reconfirm bookings at all times.

E St Nicholas, B Mitre 1691 (y Rodríguez Peña), T4373 5920/8841, www.snhostel.com. Beautifully restored old house, spotless rooms, cooking facilities, large roof terrace and a pub with daily live shows, luggage store; also **C** double rooms. Discounts for HI members.

E V&S, Viamonte 887, T4322 0994, www.hostel club.com. **C** in attractive double room with bath. A central and popular hostel, with breakfast, café, tiny kitchen, internet access, lockers, tango classes, tours arranged, warm atmosphere, welcoming. Member of AHC Argentina Hostels Club, www.argentinahostels.com. Recommended.

F-G Hostel Aguila, Espinosa 1628, T4581 6663, www.delaguilahostel.com. Good value, owned by a tango teacher (free classes), welcoming, with a large terrace. Free transfers to/from local transport terminals. Far from centre, next to the corner of Avs San Martín and Juan B Justo, where Caballito, Villa Crespo and Paternal neighbourhoods meet (buses 24, 34, 57, 109, 110).

Palermo *p76, map p77*

L Malabia House, Malabia 1555, Palermo Viejo, T4833 2410, www.malabiahouse.com.ar. Elegant but expensive B&B with individually designed bedrooms and calm sitting rooms. Recommended.

L Bo Bo, Guatemala 4882, T4774 0505, www.bobo hotel.com. On a leafy street, 7 rooms decorated in 20th-century style; some have private balconies, ideal for soaking up the atmosphere of the 'new' Palermo Viejo. Has a small good restaurant.

Youth hostels

E Casa Esmeralda, Honduras 5765, T4772 2446, www.casaesmeralda.com.ar. Laid-back, dorms and **C** doubles, neat garden with hammocks and pond. Sebastián, owner of trendy bars *La Cigale* and *Zanzibar*, offers basic comfort with great charm.

E **Tango Backpackers Hostel**, Thames 2212, T4776 6871, www.tangobp.com. Well situated for Palermo's nightlife, shared rooms and C doubles, all the usual facilities, plus restaurant, HI discount.

San Telmo p79, map p84

L-AL **Mansión Dandi Royal**, Piedras 922, T4307 7623, www.hotelmansiondandiroyal.com. A wonderfully restored 1903 residence, originally a brothel, now a small upmarket hotel with a superbly elegant tango atmosphere. Daily tango lessons and *milonga* every Wed.

B **La Casita de San Telmo**, Cochabamba 286 T/F4307 5073, www.lacasitadesantelmo.com. 7 rooms in restored 1840's house, almost all open onto a garden with a beautiful fig tree, owners are tango fans; rooms rented by day, week or month.

D **Victoria**, Chacabuco 726, T/F4361 2135. Rooms with bath, fan, kitchen and laundry facilities, no breakfast.

Youth hostels

D **Buenos Ayres**, Pasaje San Lorenzo 320, San Telmo, T4361 0694, www.buenosayreshostel.com.

On a picturesque pedestrian cobbled street, bit untidy and noisy. D doubles with bath are good.
E **El Hostal de Granados**, Chile 374, T43625600, www.hostaldegranados.com.ar. Small well-equipped rooms in an interesting building on a popular street with bars and small restaurants, lots of light, for 2 (C) to 4, with bath, breakfast included, kitchen, free internet, laundry service, reductions for longer stays.
E **Hostel-Inn Tango**, Piedras 680, T4300 5764, and **Hostel-Inn Buenos Aires**, Humberto Primo 820, T4300 7992. Both well-organized in renovated houses, popular, lively, lots of activities, and the usual facilities with use of internet, transfers, Spanish lessons and breakfasts all included. ISIC and HI discounts. Hostel-Inn is a chain of hostels in Argentina, T0800-666 4678, www.hostel-inn.com.
E **Ostinatto Hostel**, Chile 680, San Telmo. AHC member.
E **Sandanzas**, Balcarce 1351, T4300 7375, www.sandanzas.com.ar. Arty hostel run by a group of friends who've created an original and welcoming space, small but with a light airy feel, C in double, lounge and patio, free internet, DVDs, kitchen, breakfast included and free use of bikes.

Argentina B&B, www.argentina bandb.com.ar. Arranges reliable, cheap accommodation with host families in Buenos Aires and other towns. Many hosts speak English, others give you a chance to practise your Spanish.

B&T Argentina, T4821 6057, www.bytarg entina.com. Accommodation in student residences and host families; also furnished flats.

La Casa de Etty, Luis Sáenz Peña 617, T4384 6378,coret@ciudad.com.ar. Run by Esther Corcias, manager of **Organización Coret**, www.angelfire/pq/coret. For accommodation with host families, also furnished flats.

Apartments/self catering

Bahouse, T4815 7602, www.bahouse.com.ar. Very good flats, all furnished and well-located in Retiro, Recoleta, Belgrano, Palermo and the centre.

Tu Casa Argentina, Esmeralda 980, p 2B, T4312 4127, www.tucasargentina.com. Furnished flats by the day, week, month (from US$400 per month).

❼ Eating

Eating out in Buenos Aires is one of the city's great pleasures, with a huge variety of restaurants from the chic to the cheap. To try some of Argentina's excellent steak, choose from one of the many *parrillas*, where your huge slab of lean meat will be expertly cooked over a wood fire. If in doubt about where to eat, head for Puerto Madero, where there

are lots of good places serving international as well as local cuisine. In many mid- to upper- range restaurants, lunch is far cheaper than dinner. A portion at a *comidas para llevar* (take away) place costs US$2-3. Many cheaper restaurants are *tenedor libre*: eat as much as you like for a fixed price. Most cafés serve tea or coffee plus *facturas*, or pastries, for breakfast, US$0.80-1.20 (bakery shops sell 10 *facturas* for US$1).

Retiro, and the area between Plaza de Mayo and Plaza San Martín
p72, map p74

🍴 **La Chacra**, Av Córdoba 941 (just off 9 de Julio). A superb traditional *parrilla* with excellent steaks (US$16 for parrilla for 2), impeccable old-fashioned service, lively atmosphere.

🍴 **Las Nazarenas**, Reconquista 1132. Good for beef and international food.

🍴 **Morizono**, Reconquista 899. Japanese sushi and sashami, as well as other dishes.

🍴 **Sorrento** Corrientes 668 (just off Florida). Intimate, elegant atmosphere, traditional menu with good fish dishes and steak.

🍴 **Tomo 1**, Panamericano Hotel, Carlos Pellegrini 521, T4326 6695. Argentine regional dishes and international cuisine of a high standard in a sophisticated atmosphere. Very expensive.

🍴 **Broccolino**, Esmeralda 776. Good Italian food, very popular, try *pechuguitas*.

San Telmo

Sleeping		Eating ❼	Mi Tío 8
Buenos Ayres 1	La Casita de San	El Desnivel 1	
El Hostal de	Telmo 3	La Brigada 3	**Bars & clubs** ❼
Granados 7	Mansión Dandi	La Casa de Esteban	Mitos Argentinos 5
Garden House 8	Royal 4	de Luca 2	
Hostel-Inn Buenos	Sandanzas 5	La Vieja Rotisería 4	
Aires 2	Victoria 6	Lezama 6	

¶¶ Buenos Aires Criollo, Maipú 442. Serves good *parrilla*.

¶¶ Chiquilín, Sarmiento 1599. *Parrilla* and pasta, good value.

¶¶ El Establo, Paraguay y San Martín. First class parrilla, popular, "waiters all elderly characters".

¶¶ El Figón de Bonilla, Alem 673. Rustic-style atmosphere and good Spanish style cuisine.

¶¶ El Navegante, Viamonte 154. Seafood or the traditional *puchero* stew.

¶¶ El Palacio de la Papa Frita, Lavalle 735 and 954, Corrientes 1620. Great place for a filling feed, with a large menu, and quite atmospheric, despite the bright lighting.

¶¶ El Querandí, Perú 302 y Moreno. Good food in an intimate atmosphere in this place that was opened in the 1920's. Also popular café, good atmosphere, well known for its Gin Fizz, now a tango venue, too.

¶¶ Empire Thai, Tres Sargentos 427. Serves Thai food in a tasteful atmosphere.

¶¶ Exedra, Carlos Pellegrini and Córdoba. A welcoming traditional-style café right on Av 9 de Julio, set menu US$5-8, including a glass of wine.

¶¶ Fratello, Tucumán 688. Pastas and other Italian dishes in attractive Italian-style surroundings.

¶¶ La Estancia, Lavalle 941. A slightly touristy but reliable *parrilla*, popular with business people at lunchtime, good grills, US$14 for 2.

¶¶ La Pipeta, San Martín 498. Downstairs, a traditional place, established 40 years, for good food in a noisy atmosphere, closed Sun.

¶¶ Los Inmortales, Lavalle 746. Specializes in pizza, all tasty and good value to share, great salads, good service.

¶¶ Palacio Español at the Club Español, B de Irigoyen 180 (on Av 9 de Julio, near Av de Mayo). Luxurious ambience in a fine building, recommended for a quiet dinner, with very good food, basically Spanish dishes.

¶¶ Tancat, Paraguay 645. Spanish food.

¶ Abril, Suipacha y Arenales. Very good pasta; best choice of its category in the area.

¶ Capataz, Maipú 529, T4326 6086. Argentine food, *empanadas* and steak and vegetables on the *parrilla*, in a bright trendy atmosphere, good value. Delivers to home or hostel. Recommended.

¶ Gianni´s, Viamonte 834 and 25 de Mayo 757 (open 0900-1700). The set menu with the meal-of-the-day (US$5.50) makes an ideal lunch in a renovated old house. Good Risottos and salads.

¶ Gran Victoria, Suipacha 783. Good value *tenedor libre*, including parrilla, in a cheery atmosphere, also cheap set meals.

¶ Güerrín, Corrientes 1368. A Buenos Aires institution, serving incredibly cheap and filling slabs of pizza and *faina* (chick pea polenta) which you eat standing up at a zinc bar, or at tables, though you miss out on the colourful local life that way. Wonderful.

¶ La Casona del Nonno, Lavalle 827. Popular with tourists for its cheap set price menu, Italian-style food, cheap pastas and *parrilla*.

Tea rooms, café-bars and ice cream

Cafés

Aroma, Florida y M T de Alvear. A great place to relax, with a huge space upstairs, comfortable chairs for watching the world go by.

Café de la Biblioteca, M T de Alvear 1155 (Asociación Biblioteca de Mujeres). Coffee and light snacks, evening shows.

Café Tortoni, Av de Mayo 825-9. This most famous Buenos Aires café has been the elegant haunt of artists and writers for over 100 years, with marble columns, stained glass ceilings, old leather chairs, and photographs of its famous clientele on the walls. Excellent coffee and cakes, good tea, excellent tango, all rather pricey, but worth a visit.

Clásica y Moderna, Callao 892. One of the city's most welcoming cafés, with a bookshop, great atmosphere, good breakfast through to drinks at night, live music Wed-Sat. Highly recommended.

Confitería Ideal, Suipacha 384. One of the most atmospheric cafes in the city. Wonderfully old-fashioned 1930's interior, serving good coffee and excellent cakes with good service. Upstairs, tango is taught and there's tango dancing at a *milonga* here. Highly recommended.

Desiderio, Av Santa Fe y Esmeralda. Good coffee and drinks, in a nice, though noisy corner on plaza San Martín.

El Gato Negro, Av Corrientes 1669. An old pharmacy, serving a choice of coffees and teas, and good cakes.

Florida Garden, Florida y Paraguay. Another well-known café, popular for lunch, and tea.

Munchi's, Florida y MT de Alvear. New ice cream vendors in the centre where Italian tradition has been marked for decades by 'heladerías' such as **Cadore**, Av Corrientes 1695 or **El Vesuvio**, Av Corrientes 1181, the oldest of all.

Richmond, Florida 468, between Lavalle and Corrientes. Genteel, old fashioned and charming place for tea with cakes, and a basement where chess is played between 1200-2400 daily.

Saint Moritz, Esmeralda y Paraguay. Original late 1950s decor with a particularly calm atmosphere on a very busy corner.

La Recova *map p77*

Three blocks west of Plaza San Martín, under the flyover at the northern end of Av 9 de Julio, between Carlos Pellegrini and Cerrito, are several recommended restaurants.

¶¶¶ El Mirasol, Posadas 1032. Serves top quality parrilla in an elegant atmosphere.

♦♦♦ **Piegari**, Posadas 1042. Great for Italian food.
♦♦♦ **La Tasca de Plaza Mayor**, Posadas 1052.
Good Spanish food.
♦♦ **Juana M**, Carlos Pellegrini 1535 (downstairs).
Excellent choice, popular for a good range of
dishes, and very good salads.
♦♦ **Winery**, Paseo La Recova, off Libertador 500. A
chic wine bar where you can sample the best of
Argentina's fine wines, light dishes such as salads
and gourmet sandwiches. Also at Av Alem 880.

Recoleta *p76, map p77*
♦♦♦ **La Cabaña**, Rodríguez Peña 1967, T4814
0001, www.lacabanabuenosaires.com.ar. Historic
steakhouse, recreated by Orient-Express, classic
beef and other dishes and new cuisine, also offers
cookery classes. Very elegant; connected to new
Duhau-Hyatt Hotel.
♦♦♦ **Lola**, Roberto M Ortiz 1805. Well known for
superb pasta dishes, lamb and fish.
♦♦♦ **Sirop**, Pasaje del Correo, Vte Lopez 1661,
T4813 5900. Delightful chic design, delicious
French-inspired food, superb patisserie too.
Highly recommended.
♦♦ **El Sanjuanino**, Posadas 1515. Atmospheric
place offering typical dishes from the northwest:
humitas, *tamales*, and *empanadas*, as well as
unusual game dishes.
♦♦ **Rodi Bar**, Vicente López 1900. Excellent *bife*
and other dishes in this typical *bodegón*,
welcoming and unpretentious.
♦ **La Madeleine**, Av Santa Fe 1726. Great for
cheap and delicious pastas, bright and cheerful.
Recommended.

Tea rooms, café-bars and ice cream
Café Victoria, Roberto M Ortiz 1865. A
wonderful old-fashioned café, popular and
refined, great cakes.
Ice Cream Freddo, Pacheco de Melo y Callao,
Ayacucho y Quintana, Arenales y Callao, Roberto
M Ortiz y Guido and at shopping malls. Known
for the best ice cream.
Milion, Paraná 1048. Stylish bar and café in an
elegant mansion with marble stairs and a garden,
young and cool clientèle.
Un'Altra Volta, Santa Fe y Callao. Great ice
creams too. Try delicious mascarpone.

San Telmo *p79, map p84*
There are many restaurants along C Defensa, and
in the surrounding streets.
♦♦♦ **La Casa de Esteban de Luca**, Defensa 1000.
Parrilla and pastas in a lively café atmosphere,
attentive service, good.
♦♦ **La Brigada**, Estados Unidos 461, T4361 5557.
Atmospheric *parrilla*, serving excellent Argentine
cuisine and wines. Very popular, not cheap, but
recommended. Always reserve.

♦ **El Desnivel**, Defensa 855. Popular for cheap
and basic food, jam packed at weekends, good
atmosphere.
♦ **La Trastienda**, Balcarce 460. Theatre café with
lots of live events, also serving meals and drinks
from breakfast to dinner, great music, relaxed
and cool, but busy lunchtime. Recommended.
♦ **La Vieja Rotisería**, Defensa 963. Cheap
café for bargain *parrilla*, packed at weekends,
so go early.
♦ **Lezama**, Brasil 359 (on Parque Lezama). A typical
bodegón, popular with families, typical Argentine
menu, huge portions, service is rather slow.
♦ **Mi Tío**, Defensa 900. A small pizza place,
beloved by San Telmo locals.

Puerto Madero *p79*
The revamped docks area is an attractive place to
eat, and to stroll along the waterfront before
dinner. There are many good places here,
generally in stylish interiors and with good
service: along Av Alicia Moreau de Justo (from
north to south), these are recommended.
♦♦♦ **Bice**, No 192, T4315 6216. Italian-influenced
food, traditional pastas with Argentine meat and
fish.
♦♦♦ **El Mirasol del Puerto**, No 202. well known
and loved for a broad menu.
♦♦♦ **Il Gran Caruso**, Olga Cossettini 791, T4515
0707. Italian, seafood, meats and desserts.
♦♦♦ **Katrine**, No 138. Delicious fish and pasta.
♦♦♦ **Las Lilas**, No 516. Excellent parrilla, popular
with tourists.
♦♦♦ **La Parolaccia**, Nos 1052 and 1170. Pasta and
seafood, does executive lunch for US$8 Mon-Fri.
♦♦ **Siga La Vaca**, Av Alicia Moreau de Justo 1714,
T4315 6801. Huge variety of meats, tenedor libre,
price includes wine, good desserts.
♦ The cheapest places are next to the boat,
Fragata Sarmiento on Dique 3.

Palermo *p76, map p77*
This area of Buenos Aires is very popular, with
many chic restaurants and bars in Palermo Viejo
(referred to as 'Palermo Soho' for the area next to
Plaza Cortázar and 'Palermo Hollywood' for the
area beyond the railways and Av Juan B Justo) and
the Las Cañitas district (see below). It's a sprawling
district, so you could take a taxi to one of these
restaurants, and walk around before deciding
where to eat. It's also a great place to stop for
lunch, with cobbled streets and 1900s buildings,
now housing chic clothes shops.
♦♦♦ **Te Mataré Ramirez**, Paraguay 4062, T4831
9156 (also at San Isidro). A wonderful place for an
intimate dinner, Buenos Aires' only aphrodisiac
restaurant. Red velvet, cupids on the walls,
mellow live jazz, and excellent cuisine.
Highly recommended.

Katmandu, Córdoba 3547. Serves tasty Indian dishes in an exotic atmosphere.

Kayoko, Gurruchaga 1650. Serves sushi and other Japanese dishes. Cheap set menus at early 'Japo Hour' Mon-Sat 1830-2030.

Krishna, Malabia 1833. Intimate rooms or tables on the pavement for good, Indian-flavoured vegetarian dishes.

Luciana, Amenabar 1202, T4783 0975. Excellent Italian food in a trattoria atmosphere.

Sarkis, Thames 1101. Serves delicious Arabic cuisine, superb couscous and meat dishes, with belly dancers later on at weekends. Recommended.

Social Paraíso, Honduras 5182. Simple delicious dishes in a relaxed chic atmosphere. Good fish and tasty salads.

El 22, Carranza y Pasaje Voltaire and at Jufré y Godoy Cruz (Villa Crespo). Very good *parrilla* serving big portions to share. Excellent value.

La Cupertina, Cabrera y Godoy Cruz. Small and unpretentious; one of the best spots in town for *empanadas*, *locros* and different typical stews from Northwest Argentina.

Tea rooms, café-bars and ice cream

Palermo has good cafés opposite the park on Av del Libertador, including the fabulous ice creams at **Un'Altra Volta**, Av del Libertador 3060 (another branch at Echeverría 2302, Belgrano). Round the corner is **Bella Italia**, República Arabe Siria 3330, an ideal stopover for a coffee or for a light lunch. **Malas Artes**, Honduras y Borges, is one recommendable café with tables outside, of the many surrounding Plaza Cortázar, all open till the small hours. **Persicco**, Salguero y Cabello, Maure y Migueletes and Av Rivadavia 4933 (Caballito). The grandsons of **Freddo´s** founders also offer excellent ice creams.

Las Cañitas *p76, map p77*

This area of Palermo is fashionable for a wide range of interesting restaurants mostly along C Baez, and most opening at around 2000, though only open for lunch at weekends:

Baez, Baez 240. Very trendy, with lots of orange neon, serving sophisticated Italian-style food.

Novecento, across the road from De la Ostia. A lively French-style bistro, stylish but unpretentious and cosy, good fish dishes among a broad menu.

Campo Bravo, Baez y Arevalo. Stylish, minimalist, superb steaks and vegetables on the *parrilla*. Popular and recommended.

De la Ostia, Baez 212. A small, chic bistro for tapas and Spanish-style food, good atmosphere.

Eh! Santino, Baez 194. Trendy, small, Italian-style food, dark and cosy with lots of mirrors.

Morelia, Baez 260. Cooks superb pizzas on the *parrilla* or in wood ovens, and has a lovely roof terrace for summer.

El Primo, on the opposite corner from Campo Bravo. A popular *parrilla* for slightly older crowd. Cheap set menus in a relaxed atmosphere with fairy lights.

Cheap eats

For quick cheap snacks the markets are recommended. Also huge choice in basement of **Galerías Pacifico**, Florida y Viamonte. Some supermarkets have good, cheap restaurants: **Coto** supermarket, Viamonte y Paraná, upstairs. Many supermarkets have very good deli counters and other shops sell *fiambres* (smoked, cured meats) and cheeses and other prepared foods for quick, cheap eating. Good snacks all day and night at **Retiro and Constitución railway termini**. The snack bars in underground stations are also cheap. **Delicity bakeries**, several branches, have very fresh *facturas* (pastries), cakes, breads, and authentic American donuts. Another good bakery for breakfasts and salads is **Bonpler**, Florida 481, 0730-2300, with the daily papers, classical music. Other branches throughout the city.

⊙ Bars and clubs

Generally it is not worth going to clubs before 0230 at weekends. Dress is usually smart.

Bars

Boquitas Pintadas, Estados Unidos 1393 (Constitución), T4381 6064. Bar and hotel, German-run.

Buller Brewing Company, Roberto M Ortiz 1827 (Recoleta). Brew pub. Happy hour till 2100.

Irish pubs abound. St Patrick's Day, 17 Mar, has become a new reason to celebrate, especially in the pub district (corner of Reconquista and MT de Alvear). **Celta Bar**, Rodríguez Peña y Sarmiento. **Druid Inn**, Reconquista 1040. Live music weekly, English spoken, good for lunch. **The Kilkenny**, MT de Alvear 399 esq Reconquista. Open 1730-0600 (Sat opens at 2000), happy hour 1800-2000, very popular. **Porto Pirata**, next door to Druid In. **The Shamrock**, Rodríguez Peña 1220. Irish- run, popular, happy hour from 1800 till midnight. **The Temple Bar**, MT de Alvear 945.

There are good bars in San Telmo around Plaza Dorrego: **Bar Plaza Dorrego** is very atmospheric indoors, also seating on Plaza. **El Samovar de Rasputín**, Del Valle Iberlucea 1251, next to Caminito (La Boca). Good blues and rock, dinner and/or show, Fri, Sat, Sun.

In Palermo Viejo and Las Cañitas, live music usually begins 2330-2400. Good and popular are: **La Cigale**, 25 de Mayo 722, T4312 8275. **Club del Vino**, Cabrera 4737 (Palermo Soho), T4011 2582, live music, various styles including tango.

Clubs

Buenos Aires News, Paseo de la Infanta Isabel s/n, T4778 1500. Traditional spot for socialising.
El Living, M T de Alvear 1540, T4811 4730. Relaxed bar and small club.
Maluco Beleza, Sarmiento 1728. Brazilian flavour, entertaining, popular.
Mitos Argentinos, Humberto Primo 489, near Plaza Dorrego, T4362 7810. Dancing to 'rock nacional' music, on Sun tango and lunch with live music and audience participation.
Moliere, Balcarce y Chile, T4343 2623. Popular.
Niceto Club, Niceto Vega 5510, T4779 9396. Early live shows and funk or electronic music for dancing afterwards.
Pacha, Av Costanera Rafael Obligado y Pampa, T4788 4280. Electronic music.
Podestá, Armenia 1740, T4832 2776. Rock or techno in Palermo Viejo.
Opera Bay, Cecilia Grierson 225 (Puerto Madero, on dock 4), T4315 8666.

Gay clubs Most gay clubs charge US$10 entry.
Amerika, Gascón 1040, www.ameri-k.com.ar.
Glam, Cabrera 3046, www.glambsas.com.ar.
Sitges, Av Córdoba 4119. Gay and lesbian bar, near Amerika.

Jazz clubs Notorious, Av Callao 966, T4813 6888, www.notorious.com.ar. Live jazz at a music shop, daily about 2100. **La Revuelta**, Alvarez Thomas 1368, T4553 5530. Live jazz, bossa nova and tango. **Thelonious**, Salguero 1884, T4829 1562. Live jazz and tango.

Salsa clubs Escuela Integral de Arte, Defensa 1464, T4307 4384. Salsa, rumba, candombe, and capoeira classes. **La Salsera**, Yatay 961, T4864 1733. Highly regarded.

⊕ Entertainment

Details of most events are given in Espectáculos section of main newspapers, *Buenos Aires Herald* (English) on Fri and www.clarin.com (search Sección Espectáculos); also at www.tbas.com.ar.

Cinemas

The selection of films is excellent, ranging from new Hollywood releases to Argentine and world cinema; details are listed daily in all main newspapers. Films are shown uncensored and most foreign films are subtitled. Tickets best booked early afternoon to ensure good seats (average price US$3.50, with discount Wed and for first show daily; other discounts depending on cinema). Tickets obtainable, sometimes cheaper, from ticket agencies (*carteleras*), such as **Vea Más**, Paseo La Plaza, Corrientes 1660, local 2, T6320 5319 (the cheapest), **Cartelera**, Lavalle 742, T4322 1559, **Cartelera Baires**, Corrientes 1382, local 24, T4372 5058,

www.cartelera-net.com.ar, and **Entradas con Descuento**, Lavalle 835, local 27, T4322 9263. Seats can also be booked by phone with credit/debit card in shopping centres for US$0.30 each ticket. Many cinemas in shopping malls, some on Av Corrientes and on C Lavalle, also in Puerto Madero (Dock 1) and in Belgrano (Av Cabildo and environs). On Fri and Sat nights many central cinemas have *trasnoches*, late shows starting at 0100.
At **Village Recoleta** (Vicente López y Junín) there is a cinema complex with *trasnoche* programmes on Wed, Fri and Sat. Independent foreign and national films are shown during the **Festival de Cine Independiente**, held every Apr, more information on the festival at www.bafici.gov.ar.

Cultural events

Centro Cultural Borges, Galerías Pacífico, Viamonte y San Martín, p 1, T5555 5359, www.ccborges.org.ar. Varied art exhibitions, concerts, film shows and ballet; some shows with discounts for students.
Centro Cultural Konex, Av Córdoba 1235, T4813 1100, www.centroculturalkonex.org. Art and language courses, seminars and workshops, tango school, plays, music and film shows. A converted oil factory will host **Ciudad Cultural Konex**, a huge complex at Sarmiento y Jean Jaures (Abasto).
Centro Cultural Recoleta, Junín 1930, next to the Recoleta cemetery. Has many free activities (see under Sights, above).
Fundación Proa, Av Pedro de Mendoza 1929, T4303 0909, www.proa.org. Temporary exhibitions of contemporary art, photography and other cultural events in La Boca.
Luna Park stadium, Bouchard 465, near Correo Central, T4311 5100, www.lunapark.com.ar. Pop/ jazz concerts, sports events, ballet and musicals.
Museo de Arte Latinoamericano, MALBA, (address and website above), is a very active centre holding old or independent film exhibitions, seminars and conferences on arts.
Palais de Glace, Posadas 1725, T4804 1163, www.palaisdeglace.org. Temporary art and film exhibitions and other cultural events.
Teatro Gral San Martín, Corrientes 1530, T4371 0111/8 or 0800-333 5254, www.teatrosan martin.com.ar. Cultural activities, many free, including concerts, 50% ISIC discount for Thu , Fri and Sun events (only in advance at 4th floor, Mon-Fri). The theatre's **Sala Leopoldo Lugones** shows international classic films, daily, US$1.70.

Tango shows

Tango shows are mostly overpriced and tourist-oriented; they usually have touts inviting tourists in. Tango information desk at **Centro**

Cultural San Martín, Sarmiento 1551, Mon-Sat 1400-2100, www.tangodata.com.ar. Also www.tangocity.com and www.todotango.com. Every year, between end Feb-Mar the city celebrates the Festival Buenos Aires Tango, holding tango sessions, lessons, old musical films, exhibitions and a massive open-air *milonga*, open to all, in the central avenues (www.tangodata.gov.ar for details). Tango Week, leading up to National Tango Day (11 Dec), has free events all over the city, details posted around the city and at tourist offices.

Bar Sur, Estados Unidos 299, T4362 6086. 2000-0300, US$45 including all-you-can-eat pizza and empanadas, drinks extra. Good fun, public sometimes join the professional dancers.

El Querandí, Perú 302, T5199 1770. Tango show restaurant, daily show (2215) US$48 dinner including drink (2030), and show US$65.

El Viejo Almacén, Independencia y Balcarce, T4307 7388. Daily, dinner from 2000, show 2200, US$67 with all drinks, dinner and show, show only, US$47, also touristy but recommended.

Esquina Carlos Gardel, Carlos Gardel 3200 y Anchorena, T4867 6363, www.esquinacarlos gardel.com.ar. Opposite the former Mercado del Abasto, this is the only venue in Gardel's own neighbourhood; dinner at 2030 (dinner and show US$70), show at 2230 (US$47).

La Cumparsita, Chile 302, T4302 3387. Authentic, US$17 including drink and some food, 2200-0300.

La Ventana, Balcarce 431, T4331 0217. Daily dinner from 2000 (dinner and show US$70) or show with 2 drinks, 2200, US$50, very touristy but very good.

Piazzolla Tango, Florida 165 (basement), Galería Güemes, T4344 8200, www.piazzollatango.com. A beautifully restored belle epoque hall hosts a smart tango show; dinner at 2045 (dinner and show US$60), show at 2215 (US$40).

Señor Tango Vieytes 1655, Barracas, T4303 0231, www.senortango.com.ar. Spectacular show with dancers, horses etc, US$50, starts 2200 (with dinner at 2030, US$80). *Milongas* are popular events among locals, where tango and milonga are played (the latter having more cheerful music, looser steps) and take place at several locations on different days which may change; check first. Lessons are usually followed by dancing; live orchestras occasionally (US$1.70).

Centro Cultural Torquato Tasso, Defensa 1575, T4307 6506. Sun 2100 (daily lessons earlier, US$5), English spoken.

Confitería Ideal, address above, T5265 8069. Lessons 1200-1500 (Tue, Thu, Fri in English), dancing afterwards.

El Viejo Correo, Díaz Vélez 4820 (Parque Centenario), T4862 0520 or 4958 0364, daily.

La Viruta (at Centro Armenio), Armenia 1366, T4774 6357, www.lavirutatango.com. Very popular, Wed, Sun 2200, Sat 2400.

Porteño y Bailarín, Riobamba 345, T4372 6080, www.porteybailarin.com.ar. Lessons Tue, Sun at 2100, dancing at 2300.

Salón Canning, Scalabrini Ortiz 1331, T4342 4794. Daily.

Tango Discovery, Gallo 241 p 2, T4867 1888, www.tangodiscovery.com. Offers unconventional tango lessons Tue, Thu 2100.

Theatre

About 20 commercial theatres play all year round. There are many amateur theatres. You are advised to book as early as possible for a seat at a concert, ballet, or opera. Tickets for most popular shows (including rock and pop concerts) are sold also through Ticketek, T5237 7200, Entrada Plus, T4000 1010, or Ticketmaster, T4321 9700. For other ticket agencies, see Cinemas, above. TBAS, www.tbas.com.ar, publishes a complete and up-to-date list of all the performing arts events in the city online (also a free magazine). The Teatro Colón opera season runs from Apr to Nov and there are concert performances most days. Tickets sold 5 days before performance, from the C Tucumán side of the theatre, T4378 7344, Mon-Sat 0900-2000, Sun 1000-1700. The cheapest seat is US$2.70 (available even on the same day) and 'El Paraíso' tickets are available for standing room or seats in The Gods – queue for a good spot. Check for free concerts at Salón Dorado; visit www.teatrocolon.org.ar

O Shopping

Most shops close lunchtime on Sat. The main, fashionable shopping streets are Florida and Santa Fe (especially between 1,000 and 2,000 blocks). C Defensa in San Telmo is known for its antique shops. Pasaje de la Defensa, Defensa 1179, is a beautifully restored colonial house containing small shops.

Bookshops

Foreign books are hard to find and expensive. For foreign newspapers try news stands on Florida, in Recoleta district and kiosk at Corrientes y Maipú. Every Apr the Feria del Libro is held at the Rural Society grounds, on Plaza Italia; exhibitions, shows and books for sale in all languages. ABC, Maipú 870 and Rawson 2105 in Martínez suburb, www.libreriasabc.com.ar Good selection of English and German books, expensive, also sells *Footprint* books. Acme Agency, Suipacha 245, p 1. For imported English books, also Arenales 885. Asociación Dante Alighieri, Tucumán 1646. Italian books. El Ateneo, Florida 340. Has good selection of English books (basement), other branches including Av Santa Fe 1860 (in a former sumptuous cinema, lovely café) and Florida 629, www.tematika.com. **Distal**, Corrientes 913 (sells *Footprint*) with branches at Florida 528 and 738. **Joyce Proust & Co**, Tucumán 1545, p 1. Paperbacks in English, Portuguese, French, Italian; classics, language texts, good prices. **Kel Ediciones**, MT de Alvear 1369 and Conde 1990 (Belgrano), www.kelediciones.com. Good stock of English books. **Librería Rodríguez**, Sarmiento 835. Good selection of English books and magazines upstairs. **El Libro Francés**, Esmeralda 861. French bookshop. **Yenny**, at main shopping malls and airports, stocks *Footprint*, good selection of English classics.

Used and rare books Many second-hand or discount bookshops on Av Corrientes and Av de Mayo. **L'Amateur**, Esmeralda 882. For antique maps and prints. **The Antique Bookshop**, Libertad 1236, T4815 0658. Recommended. **Aquilanti**, Rincón 79, T4952 4546. For Latin American history. **British and American Benevolent Society** (*BABS Bookstore*), Av Santa Fe 512, Acassuso, T4747 3492 (take train from Retiro), Mon-Wed 0900-1800, Sat 1000-1230 (in summer, Wed mornings only). Second-hand English language books. **Entrelibros**, Av Cabildo 2280, local 80 (Belgrano). Expensive. **Galería Buenos Aires**, Florida 835 (basement). Several good used books shops here (eg *Helena de Buenos Aires*, local 32, T4311 1491, good stock of Patagonia books. **Poema 20**, Esmeralda 869, T4312 0199, dirans@uolsinectis.com.ar. Owner Diran Sirinian speaks English.

Camping equipment
Good equipment from **Buenos Aires Sports**, Panamericana y Paraná, Martínez (Shopping Unicenter, 2nd level). **Eurocamping**, Paraná 761. **Fugate** (no sign), Gascón 238 (off Rivadavia 4000 block), T4982 0203. Also repairs equipment. **Outside Mountain Equipment**, Otero 172 (Chacarita), T4856 6204, www.outside.com.ar. Camping gas available at **Britam**, B Mitre 1111, **Todo Gas**, Sarmiento 1540, and **El Pescador**, Paraguay y Libertad. **Cacique Camping**, Esteban Echeverría 3360, Munro, T4762 4475, caciquenet@ciudad.com.ar. Manufactured clothing and equipment. **Ecrin**, Mendoza 1679, T4784 4799, www.ecrin.com.ar. Imported climbing equipment. **Angel Baraldo**, Av Belgrano 270, www.baraldo.com.ar. Imported and national stock. **Montagne**, Florida 719, Paraná 834, www.montagneoutdoors.com.ar, and **Camping Center**, Esmeralda 945, www.camping-center.com.ar. Good selection of outdoor sports articles. **Costanera Uno**, at the southern end of Costanera Norte, 4312 4545,

www.costanerauno.com.ar. For nautical sports, very good. GPS repair service, **Jorge Gallo**, Liniers 1522, Tigre, T4731 0323.

Handicrafts
Alhué, Juncal 1625. Very good aboriginal- style crafts. **Arte y Esperanza**, Balcarce 234. Crafts made by aboriginal communities, sold by a Fair Trade organization. **Artesanías Argentinas**, Montevideo 1386. Aboriginal crafts and other traditional items. **Martín Fierro**, Santa Fe 992. Good handicrafts, stonework etc. Recommended. **Kelly's**, Juana Manso 1596 (Puerto Madero). A very large selection of reasonably priced Argentine handicrafts in wool, leather, wood, etc. **Plata Nativa**, Galería del Sol, Florida 860, local 41. For Latin American folk handicrafts: **Puna**, **Arte Indígena**, Galería Promenade Alvear, Av Alvear 1883, local 41, T4801 6589. Authentic hand-woven pure llama wool rugs and carpets made by Northwest Argentina aboriginal communities. Also delicate handmade silver jewellery, pottery and wooden gifts from Bolivia and Argentine Puna region.

Leather goods
Several shops are concentrated along Florida next to Plaza San Martín and also in Suipacha (900 block). **Aida**, Galería de la Flor, local 30, Florida 670. Quality, inexpensive leather goods, can make a leather jacket to measure in the same day. **All Horses**, Suipacha 1350. Quality leather clothing. **Campanera Dalla Fontana**, Reconquista 735. Leather factory, fast, efficient and reasonably priced for made-to-measure clothes. **Casa López**, MT de Alvear 640/658. The most traditional and finest leather shop, expensive. **Fortín**, Santa Fe 1245. Excellent items. **Galería del Caminante**, Florida 844. Has a variety of good shops with leather goods, arts and crafts, souvenirs, etc. **King's Game**, Maipú 984. Another good shop. **La Curtiembre**, Juncal 1173, Paraguay 670. Affordable prices for good quality articles. **Prüne**, Florida 963. Fashionable designs, many options in leather and not very expensive. **Uma**, in shopping malls and at Honduras 5225 (Palermo Viejo). The trendiest of all.

Markets
Caminito, Vuelta de Rocha (Boca), 1000-1700. Plastic arts and local crafts. **Costanera Sur**, next to the Fuente de las Nereidas. Weekends 1100-2000. Crafts, books, coins, stamps. **Feria Hippie**, in Recoleta, near cemetery. Big craft and jewellery market, Sat and Sun 1000-2200, good street atmosphere, expensive. **Feria de Mataderos**, Lisandro de la Torre y Av de los Corrales, subte E to end of line then taxi (US$3.50), or buses 36, 92, 97, 126, 141. Long way but few tourists, fair of

Argentine handicrafts and traditions, music and dance festivals, gaucho horsemanship skills, every Sun from 1000 (Sat 1800-2400 in summer); nearby *Museo de los Corrales*, Av de los Corrales 6436, T4687 1949, Sun 1200-1800 (in summer, Sat 1800-2300), US$0.35. **Mercado de las Luces**, Perú y Alsina, Mon-Fri 1000-1900, Sun 1400-1900. Handicrafts, second-hand books, plastic arts. **Parque Centenario**, Díaz Vélez y L Marechal. Weekend market, 1000-2200, local crafts, cheap handmade clothes, used items of all sorts. **Parque Lezama**, Brasil y Defensa, San Telmo. Handicraft market at weekends, 1000-2200. **Parque Rivadavia**, Av Rivadavia 4800. Second-hand books, magazines, records, tapes, CDs (daily); coins (Sun 0900-1400, under a big ombú tree). **Plaza Belgrano**, near Belgrano Barrancas station on Juramento, between Cuba y Obligado. Sat-Sun, 1000-2200 craft, jewellery, etc market. **Plaza Dorrego**, San Telmo. For souvenirs, antiques, etc, with free tango performances and live music, Sun 1000-1700, atmospheric, and interesting array of 'antiques'. **Plaza Italia**, Santa Fe y Uriarte (Palermo). Second hand textbooks and magazines (daily), handicrafts market on Sat-Sun 1000-2200.

Shopping malls

Abasto de Buenos Aires, Av Corrientes 3247, T4959 3400. In the former city's fruit and vegetable market building: cheaper clothes, good choice, cinemas. **Alto Palermo**, Col Díaz y Santa Fe, T5777 8000. Good clothes shops. **Casa Piscitelli**, San Martín 450. Has a large choice of tapes and CDs, no rock or pop. **Galerías Pacífico**, on Florida, between Córdoba and Viamonte, T5555 5110 (open 1000-2100). A beautiful mall with fine murals and architecture, many exclusive shops, cinemas and good food mall with wide choice and low prices in basement. Also good set-price restaurant on 2nd floor (lunches only). Free guided visits from the fountain on lower-ground floor (Mon-Sat 1130, 1630; Sun 1300, 1630). **Marcelo Loeb**, *galería* at Maipú 466. For antique postcards from all over the world, not cheap, same *galería* has several philatelic and numismatic shops. **Paseo Alcorta**, Salguero y Figueroa Alcorta, T5777 6500. Four levels, cinemas, supermarket, stores, many cheap restaurants (take colectivo 130 from Retiro or Correo Central, or 67 from Constitución or Recoleta). **Patio Bullrich**, Av Del Libertador 750 and Posadas 1245, T4814 7400. Chic clothes, and boutiques selling high quality leather goods.

▲ Activities and tours

Football and rugby Football fans should see Boca Juniors, matches every other Sun 1500-1900 at their stadium, cheapest entry US$5 (stadium La Bombonera, Brandsen 805, La Boca, www.boca juniors.com.ar, open for visits through the museum, T4362 1100 – see the murals; along Av Almirante Brown buses 29, 33, 53, 64, 86, 152, 168; along Av Patricios buses 10, 39, 93), or their arch-rivals, **River Plate**, www.carp.org.ar (to stadium take bus 29 from centre going north). Football season Mar-Jul, Aug-Dec, matches on Sun and sometimes on Wed, Fri or Sat. Rugby season Apr-Oct/Nov.

Horse racing Hipódromo **Argentino de Palermo**, a large, modern racecourse, popular throughout the year, and at **San Isidro**. Riding schools at both courses.

Polo The high handicap season is Sep-Dec, but it is played all year round (low season May-Aug). Argentina has the top polo players in the world. A visit to the national finals at Palermo in Nov and Dec is recommended. For information, **Asociación Argentina de Polo**, T4777 6444, www.aapolo.com.

Swimming Public baths near Aeroparque, **Punta Carrasco** (best, most expensive, also tennis courts) and **Parque Norte**, popular. **Club de Amigos**, Av Figueroa Alcorta y Av Sarmiento, T4801 1213. Only on weekdays for non-members, Dec-Mar, US$11; an indoor swimming pool is open all year round, US$7.

Tours

An excellent way of seeing Buenos Aires and its surroundings is by 3-hr tour, especially for those travelling alone, or concerned about security. Longer tours include dinner and a tango show, or a gaucho *fiesta* at a ranch (excellent food and dancing). Bookable through most travel agents. **Barbacharters**, T4824 3366, www.barbacharters.com.ar. Boat trips and fishing in the Delta and Tigre areas. **BAT, Buenos Aires Tur**, Lavalle 1444 of 10, T4371 2304, www.buenosairestur.com. City tours (US$6.50) twice daily; Tigre and Delta, daily, 6 hrs (US$15). **Buenos Aires Vision**, Esmeralda 356 p 8, T4394 4682, www.buenosaires-vision.com.ar. City tours (US$8.50), Tigre and Delta, Tango (US$60-70, cheaper without dinner) and *Fiesta Gaucha* (US$40). **Cicerones de Buenos Aires**, J J Biedma 883, T4330 0800, www.cicerones.org.ar. Non-profit organization offering volunteer "greeting"/guiding service for visitors to the city, free, safe and different. **Eternautas**, Av Roque Sáenz Peña 1124, p 4B, T4384 7874, or T15-4173 1078 (mob), www.eternautas.com. Historical, cultural and artistic tours of the city and Pampas guided in English, French or Spanish by historians and other social scientists from the University of Buenos Aires, flexible. Also cultural walks.

Horseback Riding, T4896 2188 or T15 5602 8760 (mob), www.horsebackridingbsas.com.ar. Specialises in horse rides, polo lessons, golf, fishing and tennis, all in or near Buenos Aires.
Lan&Kramer Bike Tours, T4311 5199, www.bike tours.com.ar. Daily at 0930 and 1400 next to the monument of San Martín (Plaza San Martín), 3½-4-hr cycle tours to the south or the north of the city (US$25); they also go to San Isidro and Tigre, 4½-5 hrs, US$30, bike rental at Florida 868, p 14H.
Patagonia Chopper, www.patagonia chopper.com.ar. Helicopter tours of Buenos Aires and around,15-45 mins, US$95-US$130 pp.
Smile on Sea, T15-5018 8662 (mob), www.smileonsea.com. 2-hr boat trips off Buenos Aires coast in the day and at sunset, leaving from Puerto Madero on 32-ft sailing boats (up to 5 passengers, US$165 for the whole). Also 8-hr trips to San Isidro and Delta (US$320 for 5 people) and longer holidays along the Uruguayan coast.
Urban biking, Moliere 2801 (Villa Crespo), T4568 4321 or T15-5165 9343 (mob), www.urban biking.com. 4-hr cycle tours starting next to the English clock tower in Retiro, US$24, light lunch included, also night city tours, US$18, and day tours to San Isidro and Tigre, US$33. They also rent bikes and organize cycle tours in the pampas.

Recommended travel agents
ATI, Esmeralda 567, T4329 9000, www.ati viajes.com. Mainly group travel, very efficient.
Eves Turismo, Tucumán 702, T4393 6151, www.eves.com. Helpful and efficient, recommended for flights.
Exprinter, San Martín 170 p 1, of 101, T4341 6600, Galería Güemes, www.exprinterviajes.com. 5-day, 4-night tour to Iguazú and San Ignacio Miní.
Flyer, Reconquista 617, p 8, T4313 8224, www.flyer.com.ar. English, Dutch, German spoken, repeatedly recommended, especially for *estancias*, fishing, polo, motorhome rental.
Pride Travel, Paraguay 523 p 2, T5218 6556, www.pride-travel.com. The best choice for gay and lesbian travellers; also rents apartments.

Say Hueque, Viamonte 749, p 6, of 1, T5199 2517/20, www.sayhueque.com. Good value tours by bus and plane, aimed at independent travellers, lots of options, English spoken.
Tangol, Florida 971, p 1, T4312 7276, www.tangol.com. Friendly, independent agency specializing in football and tango, plus various sports, such as polo and paragliding. Can arrange tours, plane and bus tickets, accommodation. English spoken. Discounts for students. Overland tours in Patagonia Sep-Apr.
What's Up BA, www.wubatourism.com. For a wide variety of cultural experiences around the city, including finding accommodation.

⊖ Transport

Air
Ezeiza (officially Ministro Pistarini, T5480 6111, www.aa2000.com.ar), the international airport, is 35 km southwest of the centre (also handles domestic flights to El Calafate and Ushuaia in high season). The airport has 2 terminals: 'A' for all airlines except **Aerolíneas Argentinas**, which uses 'B'. 'A' has a very modern check-in hall. There are duty free shops (expensive), exchange facilities (**Banco de la Nación; Banco Piano; Global Exchange** - rates of exchange in baggage reclaim are poorer than elsewhere) and ATMs (Visa and MasterCard), post office (open 0800-2000) and a left luggage office (US$2 per piece). No hotels nearby. There is a **Devolución IVA/Tax Free** desk (return of VAT) for purchases such as leather goods. Reports of pilfering from luggage. To discourage this have your bags sealed by Secure Bag in the check-in hall. Hotel booking service at Tourist Information desk – helpful, but prices are higher if booked in this way. A display in immigration shows choices and prices of transport into the city.

Airport buses Special buses to/from the centre are run by **Manuel Tienda León** (office in front of you as you arrive), company office and terminal at Av Madero 1299 y San Martín, behind

Sheraton Hotel in Retiro, T4315 5115, www.tiendaleon.com. To **Ezeiza**: 0400, 0500, then every 30 mins till 2100 and 2200, 2230 (be 15 mins early); from Ezeiza: 0600-2400 regular buses, then also for night arrivals, US$8.50 (US$15 return), 40-min journey, credit cards accepted. **Manuel Tienda León** will also collect passengers from addresses in centre for US$0.35 extra, book the previous day. Bus from Ezeiza to Aeroparque, 1 hr, US$8.50. Remise taxis to town or to Aeroparque, US$24. Services on request with **Transfer Express**, T0800-444 4872, reservas@ transfer-express.com.ar, airport office in front of you as you arrive, remise taxi from Ezeiza to town or to Aeroparque, US$23. **Aeroparque** (Jorge Newbery Airport), 4 km north of the centre, T5480 6111, www.aa2000.com.ar, handles all internal flights, and **AR** and **Pluna** flights to Montevideo and Punta del Este. The terminal is divided into 2 sections, 'A' for all arrivals and **AR/Austral** and **LAN** check-in desks, 'B' for **Pluna** and **LADE** check-in desks. On the 1st floor there is a **patio de comidas**, many shops and the airport tax counter. At the airport also tourist information, car rental, bus companies, bank, ATMs, exchange facilities, post office, public phones, Secure Bag (US$5 per piece) and luggage deposit (between sections A-B at the information

point), US$4 per piece a day. **Manuel Tienda León** buses to Aeroparque (see above for address), 0710-0255, every hour; from Aeroparque (departs from sector B, stops at **AR**), 0900-2000 every hour, and 2130, 20-min journey, US$3. Local buses 33 and 45 run from outside the airport to the Retiro railway station, then to **La Boca** and **Constitución** respectively. No 37 goes to **Palermo** and **Recoleta** and No 160 to **Palermo** and **Almagro**. If going to the airport, make sure it goes to Aeroparque by asking the driver, US$0.27. **Remise taxis**: are operated by **Transfer Express** and **Manuel Tienda León**, US$8 to centre, US$23-24 to Ezeiza. Taxi to centre US$4. **Manuel Tienda León** operates buses between Ezeiza and Aeroparque airports, stopping in city centre, US$8.50. **AR/Austral** offer daily flights to the main cities, for details see text under intended destination. **LADE** offers weekly flights to **Trelew** and **Bariloche** with several stops in Patagonia.

Bus

Local City buses are called *colectivos* and cover a very wide radius. They are clean, frequent, efficient and very fast. The basic fare is US$0.27, US$0.45 to the suburbs. Have coins ready for ticket machine as drivers do not sell tickets, but may give change. The bus number is not always

sufficient indication of destination, as each number may have a variety of routes, but bus stops display routes of buses stopping there and little plaques are displayed in the driver's window. No 86 (white and blue, **Empresa Duvi**, T4302 6067) runs to the centre from outside the airport terminal to the left as you leave the building, 2 hrs, US$0.45, coins only, runs all day, every 20 mins during the day. To travel to Ezeiza, catch the bus at Av de Mayo y Perú, 1 block from Plaza de Mayo (many other stops, but this is central) – make sure it has 'Aeropuerto' red sign in the window as many 86s stop short of Ezeiza.

Long distance Bus terminal at Ramos Mejía y Antártida Argentina (Subte Line C), behind Retiro station, for information T4310 0700, www.tebasa.com.ar. Information desk is at the top of long ramp to your left. All ticket offices are upstairs, even numbers to the left, foreign companies at the very end (full list at the top of the escalator). International services operate from platforms 67-75. Buenos Aires city information desk on ground floor, beside an ATM; another ATM and a bank (with exchange facilities for US$ and euros) upstairs. Locutorios with internet on ground floor. Remise taxis hiring points next to the platforms. At the basement and ground levels there are left-luggage lockers, US$0.70 for 1 day (with two 1 peso coins); **Guard pack** in the basement charges US$1-2 per day (US$2.40 for a bike); some companies store luggage for same-day departures up to 1 hr before departure, at the basement level. Fares vary according to time of year and comfort: advance booking is essential Dec-Mar, Easter, Jul and long weekends. **Coche cama** is advisable for overnight journeys: seats fully recline and food is served for just a few pesos more. Travellers have reported getting student discounts without showing evidence of status, so it's always worth asking. For further details of bus services and fares, look under proposed destinations. There are no direct buses to either of the airports.

International buses International services are run by both local and foreign companies; heavily booked Dec-Mar, especially at weekends. Do not buy Uruguayan bus tickets in Buenos Aires; wait till you get to Colonia. To **Montevideo** Bus de la Carrera, 1000, 2200 and 2300 daily, US$27, 8 hrs, with a *coche cama* at 2230 (US$29), via Zárate-Gualeguaychú-Puerto Unzué-Fray Bentos- Mercedes. CAUVI goes also to Montevideo and to **Punta del Este** (10 hrs, US$35). Direct buses to **Santiago** (Chile), 1,400 km, 20-22 hrs, US$50. To **Bolivia**: Ormeño, T4313 2259, runs 2 weekly services (Tue, Sat 1500) to **La Paz**, 55 hrs, US$74 (via Santa Cruz and Cochabamba) and **Potosí Buses** goes across the border to **Villazón**, US$56. Argentine companies

only reach the border, where you can change buses: to **La Quiaca** (US$48-53), to **Aguas Blancas** (US$53), or to **Pocitos** (US$53-57, cheaper via Tucumán). To **Asunción** (Paraguay), 1,370 km via Clorinda (toll bridge): about 15 bus companies, with executive (luxury service, 16 hrs, US$53), *diferencial* (with food, drinks, 17-18 hrs, US$33-40) and *común* (without food, but a/c, toilet, 17-18 hrs, US$27-30). Also to **Ciudad del Este** (18 hrs, US$27-33), **Encarnación** (12 hrs, US$27-33) and minor destinations in Paraguay. To **Peru** Ormeño (T4313 2259) and El Rápido Internacional (T4315 0804), direct service to **Lima** (only stops for meals, not included in the price), Mon, Wed, Sat 1800 or Tue, Fri, Sun 1800 respectively, 3 days, US$140. La Veloz del Norte, T0800-444 8356, goes to **Lima** via Paso de Jama and San Pedro de Atacama, Wed, Sun 0900, 3 days, US$150 (first meal included), if you need a visa for Chile, get one before travelling. Direct buses to **Brazil** by Pluma, T4313 3880: **São Paulo** via Paso de los Libres, 36 hrs, US$84, **Rio de Janeiro**, 42 hrs, US$91 (via **Foz do Iguaçu**, 18 hrs, US$38), **Porto Alegre**, 20 hrs, US$64, **Florianópolis**, 26 hrs, US$75, **Curitiba**, 30 hrs, US$82. To **Rio de Janeiro**, changing buses at Posadas and Foz do Iguaçu is almost half price, 50 hrs. A third route across the Río de la Plata and through Uruguay is a bit cheaper and offers a variety of transport and journey breaks.

Driving

Driving in Buenos Aires is no problem, provided you have eyes in the back of your head and good nerves. Note that traffic fines are high and police increasingly on the lookout for drivers without the correct papers. See also Essentials, page 43 for international rental agencies. **Europcar**, Maipú 965, T4311 1000, www.europcar.com.ar. **Thrifty**, Carlos Pellegrini 1576, T0810-999 8500, www.thriftyar.com.ar. There are several national rental agencies, eg **Serra Lima**, Av Córdoba 3121, T4962 8508 or T0800-777 5462, or **Dietrich**, Av Las Heras 2277, T0810-345 3438, www.dietrichrentacar.com. **Motoring Associations**: see ACA, page 68.

Ferry

To **Montevideo** and **Colonia** from Terminal Dársena Norte, Av Antártida Argentina 821 (two blocks from Av Córdoba y Alem). **Buquebus**, T4316 6500/6550, www.buquebus.com (tickets from Terminal or from offices at Av Córdoba 879): 1) Direct to **Montevideo**, 2 to 4 a day, 3 hrs, US$53 tourist class, US$63 1st class one way, vehicles US$74-84, motorcycles US$55, bus connection to Punta del Este, US$8 extra. 2) To **Colonia**, services by 2 companies: **Buquebus**: 2 ferry services a day, 3 hrs, US$18 tourist class, US$24 1st class one way, with bus connection to Montevideo (US$5 extra). Motorcycles US$20, cars US$36. **Ferrylíneas Sea Cat** operates a fast service to Colonia from same terminal, 2 to 3 daily, 1 hr, US$30 tourist class, US$36 1st class one way, vehicles US$50-55, motorcycles US$31 with bus connection to Punta del Este (US$12). See under Tigre, page 103, for services to Carmelo and Nueva Palmira.

Metro (Subte)

Five lines link the outer parts of the city to the centre. **Line 'A'** runs under Av Rivadavia, from Plaza de Mayo to Primera Junta. **Line 'B'** from central Post Office, on Av L N Alem, under Av Corrientes to Federico Lacroze railway station at Chacarita, ending at Los Incas. **Line 'C'** links Plaza Constitución with the Retiro railway station, and provides connections with all the other lines. **Line 'D'** runs from Plaza de Mayo (Catedral), under Av Roque Sáenz Peña (Diagonal Norte), Córdoba, Santa Fe and Palermo to Congreso de Tucumán (Belgrano). **Line 'E'** runs from Plaza de Mayo (Cabildo, on C Bolívar) through San Juan to Plaza de los Virreyes (connection to Premetro train service to the southwest end of the city). Note that 3 stations, 9 de Julio (Line 'D'), Diagonal Norte (Line 'C') and Carlos Pellegrini (Line 'B') are linked by pedestrian tunnels. The fare is US$0.24, the same for any direct trip or combination between lines; magnetic cards (for 1, 2, 5, 10 or 30 journeys) must be bought at the station before boarding; dollars not accepted. Trains are operated by **Metrovías**, T4555 1616, and run 0500-2230 (Sun 0800-2200). Line A, the oldest was built in 1913, the earliest in South America; it starts running Mon-Fri at 0600. Backpacks and luggage allowed. Free map (if available) from stations and tourist office.

Taxi

Taxis are painted yellow and black, and carry Taxi flags. Fares are shown in pesos. The meter starts at US$0.65 when the flag goes down; make sure it isn't running when you get in. A fixed rate of US$0.07 for every 200 m or 1-min wait is charged thereafter. A charge is sometimes made for each piece of hand baggage (ask first). About 10% tip expected. Phone a radio taxi from a phone box or locutorio, giving the address of where you are, and you'll usually be collected within 5 mins. Taxis from official rank in bus terminal are registered with police and safe. For extra security, take a remise taxi booked from a booth on the bus platform itself, more expensive but very secure (to Ezeiza US$18; to Aeroparque US$5.50). Taxis from a registered company are safer, and some 'Radio Taxis' you see on the street are false. Check that the driver's licence is displayed. Lock doors on the inside. Worst places are the two airports and

Retiro; make sure you know roughly what the fare should be before the journey: eg from Aeroparque to: Ezeiza US$13 (plus toll), Congreso US$5, Plaza de Mayo US$5, Retiro US$4, La Boca US$6. In theory fares double for journeys outside city limits (Gen Paz circular highway), but you can often negotiate. Radio Taxis (same colours and fares) are managed by several different companies (eg **Del Plata**, T4504 7776; **Pídalo**, T4956 1200; **Llámenos**, T4815 3333) and are recommended as a safer alternative; minimum fare is US$1.70.

Remise taxis operate all over the city, run from an office and have no meter. The companies are identified by signs on the pavement. Fares, which are fixed and can be cheaper than regular taxis, can be verified by phoning the office, and items left in the car can easily be reclaimed. Good companies are **Universal**, T4315 6555, www.remisesuniversal.com, and **Traslada**, T4311 5111, www.traslada.com.ar.

From centre to **Ezeiza** US$17 (plus US$1.20 toll). Fixed-price *remise taxis* for up to 4 passengers can be booked from the **Manuel Tienda León** or **Transfer Express** counter at Ezeiza, prices above. Avoid unmarked cars at Ezeiza no matter how attractive the fare may sound; drivers are adept at separating you from far more money than you can possibly owe them. Always ask to see the taxi driver's licence. If you take an ordinary taxi the Policía de Seguridad Aeroportuaria on duty notes down the car's licence and time of departure. There have been recent reports of taxi drivers taking Ezeiza airport-bound passengers to remote places, stealing all their luggage and leaving them there. If in doubt, take a *remise* or airport bus.

Tram

Old-fashioned street cars operate Mar-Nov on Sat and holidays 1600-1930 and Sun 1000-1300, 1600-1930 and Dec-Feb on Sat and holidays 1700-2030, Sun 1000-1300, 1700-2030, free, on a circular route along the streets of Caballito district, from C Emilio Mitre 500, Subte Primera Junta (Line A) or Emilio Mitre (Line E), no stops en route. Operated by **Asociación de los Amigos del Tranvía**, T4431 1073.

Train

There are 4 main terminals: 1) **Retiro** (3 lines: **Mitre, Belgrano, San Martín** in separate buildings): Mitre line (run by **TBA**, T4317 4407or T0800-333 3822, www.tbanet.com.ar). Urban and suburban services include: **Belgrano**, **Mitre** (connection to Tren de la Costa, see above), **Olivos, San Isidro**, and **Tigre** (see above); long distance services to **Rosario Norte**, 1 weekly on Fri evening, 7 hrs, US$5-6, ending at **Santa Fe**, 11 hrs, US$7-9. Belgrano line run by **Ferrovías**, T4511 8833. San Martín line for services to Pilar 2)

Constitución: Roca line (run by **Metropolitano**, www.metropolitano.com.ar). Urban and suburban services to La Plata (US$ 0.50), Ezeiza (US$0.35), Ranelagh (US$0.27) and Quilmes (US$0.20). Long distance services (run by **Ferrobaires**, T4304 0028 or T0800-222 8736, www.ferrobaires.gba.gov.ar): Carmen de Patagones, weekly, 8 hrs, US$10-12; Bahía Blanca, 5 weekly, 12½ hrs, US$5-15, food mediocre; to Mar del Plata daily, 5½-6 hrs, US$7.50-15; to Pinamar, 3 weekly, 6 hrs, US$5.50-11; to Miramar, daily, 7 hrs, US$8.50-11; to Tandil, weekly, 7½ hrs, US$5.50. 3) **Federico Lacroze** Urquiza line and Metro headquarters (run by **Metrovías**, T4555 1616, www.metrovias.com.ar). Suburban services: to General Lemos. **Trenes Especiales Argentinos**, T4551 1634, runs twice a week a train to **Posadas**, minimum 26 hrs, US$13-41, from Lacroze via the towns along Río Uruguay. 4) **Once**: Sarmiento line (run by *TBA*, see above). Urban and suburban services include **Luján** (connection at Moreno, US$0.70), **Mercedes** (US$1) and **Lobos**. A fast service runs Mon-Fri between Puerto Madero (station at Av Alicia Moreau de Justo y Perón) and Castelar. Tickets checked before boarding and on train and collected at the end of the journey; urban and suburban fares are charged according different sections of each line.

❶ Directory

Airline offices Aerolíneas Argentinas (AR) and **Austral**, Perú y Rivadavia, Av LN Alem 1134 and Av Cabildo 2900, T0810-2228 6527. **Air Canada**, Av Córdoba 656, T4327 3640. **Air France-KLM**, San Martín 344 p 23, T4317 4700. **Alitalia**, Av Santa Fe 887, T4787 7848. **American Airlines**, Av Santa Fe 881, T4318 1111, Av Pueyrredón 1997 and branches in Belgrano and Acassuso. **Avianca**, Carlos Pellegrini 1163 p 4, T4394 5990. **British Airways**, Av del Libertador 498 p 13, T0800-666 1459. **Copa**, Carlos Pellegrini 989 p 2, T0810-222 2672. **Cubana**, Sarmiento 552 p 11, T4325 0691. **Delta**, Carlos Pellegrini 1141, T0800-666 0133. **Iberia**, Carlos Pellegrini, 1163 p 1/3, T4131 1000. **LAB**, Carlos Pellegrini 141, T4323 1900. **Lan**, Cerrito y Paraguay, T0810-999 9526. **Líneas Aéreas del Estado (LADE)**, Perú 710, T5129 9000, Aeroparque T4514 1524. **Lufthansa**, M T Alvear 590, p 6, T4319 0600. **Malaysia Airlines**, Suipacha 1111 p 14, T4312 6971. **Mexicana**, Av Córdoba 1131. **Pluna**, Florida 1, T4342 7000. **TAM**, Cerrito 1030, T4819 4800 or T0810 333 3333. **United**, Av Madero 900, T0810-777 8648. **Varig**, Av Córdoba 972, p 4, T4329 9200. **Banks** ATMs are widespread for MasterCard or Visa (look for Link ATMs). The financial district lies within a small area north of Plaza de Mayo, between Rivadavia, 25 de Mayo, Av Corrientes and Florida. In non-central areas find banks/ATMs along the main avenues. Banks open Mon-Fri 1000-1500. Use credit or debit cards for withdrawing cash rather than carrying TCs. Most banks charge commission especially on TCs (as much as US$10). US dollar bills are often scanned electronically for forgeries, while TCs are sometimes very difficult to change and you may be asked for proof of purchase. Major credit cards usually accepted but check for surcharges. General MasterCard office at Perú 151, T4348 7000, www.mastercard.com/ar, open 0930-1800. Visa, Corrientes 1437 p 2, T4379 3400, www.visa.com.ar. **American Express** offices are at Arenales 707 y Maipú, by Plaza San Martín, T4310 3000 or T0810-555 2639, www.americanexpress.com.ar, where you can apply for a card, get financial services and change Amex TCs (1000-1500 only, T0810-444 2437, no commission into US$ or pesos); no commission either at **Banco de la Provincia de Buenos Aires**, several branches, or at **Banco Columbia**, Perón 350. **Citibank**, B Mitre 502, T0810-444 2484, changes only Citicorps TCs cheques, no commission; branch at Florida 199. *Casas de cambio* include **Banco Piano**, San Martín 345, T4321 9200 (has exchange facility at Ezeiza airport, 0500-2400), www.bancopiano.com.ar, changes all TCs (commission 2%). **Forex**, MT de Alvear 540, T4311 5543. **Eves**, Tucumán 702. **Banco Ciudad** at Av Córdoba 675 branch is open to tourists (providing passport) for currency exchange and TCs, Mon 1000-1800, Tue-Fri 1000-1700, Sat-Sun 1100-1800. Other South American currencies can only be exchanged in *casas de cambio*. **Western Union**, branches in Correo Argentino post offices (for transfers within Argentina) and at Av Córdoba 975 (for all transfers), T0800-800 3030. **Cultural centres** **British Council**, M T de Alvear 590, p 4, T4311 9814, F4311 7747 (Mon-Thu 0830-1700, Fri 0830-1330). **British Arts Centre** (BAC), Suipacha 1333, T4393 6941, www.britishartscentre.org.ar. English plays and films, music concerts, photography exhibitions (closed Jan). **Goethe Institut**, Corrientes 319/43, T4311 8964, German library (Mon, Tue, Thu 1230-1930, Fri 1230-1600, closed Jan) and newspapers, free German films shown, cultural programmes, German language courses. In the same building, upstairs, is the German Club, Corrientes 327. **Alliance Française**, Córdoba 946, T4322 0068, www.alianza francesa.org.ar. French library, temporary film and art exhibitions. **Instituto Cultural Argentino Norteamericano (ICANA)**, Maipú 672, T5382 1500, www.icana.org.ar. **Biblioteca Centro Lincoln**, Maipú 672, T5382 1536, www.bcl.edu.ar, Mon-Wed 1000-2000, Thu and Fri 1000-1800 (Jan and Feb Mon-Fri 1300-1900), library (borrowing for members only), English/US newspapers.

Embassies and consulates All open Mon-Fri unless stated otherwise. **Australia**, Villanueva y Zabala, T4779 3500, www.argentina.embassy.gov.au. 0830-1100, ticket queuing system; take bus 29 along Av Luis María Campos to Zabala. **Austria**, French 3671, T4802 1400, www.austria.org.ar. Mon-Thu 0900-1200. **Belgium**, Defensa 113 p 8, T4331 0066, 0800-1300, www.diplobel.org/argentina. **Bolivia**, Consulate, Alsina 1886, T4381 4171, www.embajadade bolivia.com.ar, 0830-1530, visa while you wait or a month wait (depending on the country of origin), tourist bureau. **Brazil**, Consulate, C Pellegrini 1363, p 5, T4515 6500, www.conbrasil.org.ar. 1000- 1300, tourist visa takes at least 48 hrs, US$25-110. **Canada**, Tagle 2828, T4808 1000, www.dfait-maeci.gc.ca/ argentina. Mon-Thu 0830-1230, 1330-1730, tourist visa Mon-Thu 0845-1130 **Chile**, Consulate, San Martín 439, p 9, T4394 6582, www.embajadadechile.com.ar, 0900-1330. **Denmark**, Consulate, Alem 1074, p 9, T4312 6901, www.dinamarca.org.ar. Mon-Thu 0930-1200. **Finland**, Av Santa Fe 846, p 5, T4312 0600. **France**, Santa Fe 846, p 4, T4312 2409, www.consulatfrance.int.ar, 0900-1230,

1400-1600 (by appointment). **Germany**, Villanueva 1055, T4778 2500, www.embajada-alemana.org.ar. 0830-1100. **Ireland**, Av Del Libertador 1068 p 6, T5787 0801, www.irlanda.org.ar. 0900- 1300, 1400-1530. **Israel**, Av de Mayo 701, p 10, T4338 2500, Mon-Thu 0900-1200, Fri 0900-1100. **Italy**, consulate at M T de Alvear 1125/49, T4816 6133/36, www.consitalia-bsas.org.ar, Mon, Tue, Thu, Fri 0800-1100. **Japanese Consulate**, Bouchard 547 p 17, T4318 8200, www.ar.emb-japan.go.jp, 0900-1230, 1430-1700. **Netherlands**, Olga Cossettini 831 p 3, Puerto Madero, T4338 0050, www.embajada holanda.int.ar, Mon-Thu 0900-1300, Fri 0900-1230. **New Zealand**, C Pellegrini 1427 p 5, T4328 0747, www.nzembassy.com/buenosaires. Mon-Thu 0900-1300, 1400-1730, Fri 0900-1300. **Norway**, Esmeralda 909, p 3 B, T4312 2204, www.noruega.org.ar, 0930-1400. **Paraguay**, Consulate, Viamonte 1851, T4814 4803, 0800-1330. **South Africa**, MT de Alvear 590, p 8, T4317 2900, www.embajadasudafrica.org.ar, Mon-Thu 0815-1230, 1315-1715, Fri 0815-1415. **Spain**, Consulate, Guido 1760, T4811 0070, www.mae.es/consulados/buenosaires. 0815-1430. **Sweden**, Tacuarí 147 p 6, T4329 0800, www.swedenabroad.com/buenosaires,

1000-1200. **Switzerland**, Santa Fe 846, p10, T4311 6491, www.eda.admin.ch/buenosaires_emb, open 0900-1200. **UK**, Luis Agote 2412 (near corner Pueyrredón y Guido), T4808 2200 (call T15-5114 1036 for emergencies only out of normal office hours), www.britain.org.ar. 0900-1300 (Jan-Feb 0900-1200). **Uruguay**, Consulate, Av Las Heras 1907, T4807 3045, www.embajadadel uruguay.com.ar. 0930-1730, visa takes up to 72 hrs. **US Embassy and Consulate General**, Colombia 4300, T5777 4533 (for emergencies involving US citizens, T5777 4354 or T5777 4873 after office hours), http://buenosaires. usembassy.gov/. **Internet** Prices range from US$0.50 to US$1 per hr, shop around. Most *locutorios* (phone offices) have internet access. **Language schools** All-Spanish, Talcahuano 77 p 1, T4381 3914, www.all-spanish.com.ar. One to one classes. **Argentina I.L.E.E**, Av Callao 339, p 3, T4782 7173, www.argentinailee.com. Recommended by individuals and organizations alike. **Cedic**, Reconquista 715, p 11 E, T/F4315 1156, www.cedic.com.ar. Recommended. **International Bureau of Language**, Florida 165, 3rd floor, T4331 4250, www.ibl.com.ar. Group and one-to-one lessons, all levels, recommended. **PLS**, Carabelas 241 p 1, T4394 0543, www.pls.com.ar. Recommended for travellers and executives and their families; also translation and interpreting services. **Programa Tango** adds tango lessons to Spanish. Accommodation arranged. **Universidad de Buenos Aires**, 25 de Mayo 221, T4334 7512 or T4343 1196, www.idiomas.filo.uba.ar. Offers cheap, coherent courses, including summer intensive courses. For other schools teaching Spanish, and for private tutors look in *Buenos Aires Herald* in the classified advertisements. Enquire also at *Asatej* (see Useful addresses). **Medical services** Urgent medical service: for free municipal ambulance service to an emergency hospital department (day and night) **Casualty ward, Sala de guardia**, T107 or T4923 1051/58 (SAME). Inoculations: **Hospital Rivadavia**, Av Las Heras 2670, T4809 2000, Mon-Fri, 0700-1300 (bus 10, 37, 59, 60, 62, 92, 93 or 102 from Plaza Constitución), or **Dirección de Sanidad de Fronteras y Terminales de Transporte**, Ing Huergo 690, T4343 1190, Mon 1400-1500, Tue-Wed 1100- 1200, Thu and Fri 1600-1700, bus 20 from Retiro, no appointment required (yellow fever only; take passport). If not provided, buy the vaccines in **Laboratorio Biol**, Uriburu 153, T4953 7215, or in larger chemists. Many chemists have signs indicating that they give injections. Any hospital with an infectology department will give hepatitis A. **Travel Medicine Service (Centros Médicos Stamboulian)**, 25 de Mayo 464, T4311 3000,

French 3085, T5236 7772, also in Belgrano and Flores, www.viajeros.cei.com.ar. Private health advice for travellers and inoculations centre. Public Hospitals: **Hospital Argerich**, Almte Brown esq Pi y Margall 750, T4121 0700. **Hospital Juan A Fernández**, Cerviño y Bulnes, T4808 2600/2650, good medical attention. **British Hospital**, Perdriel 74, T4309 6400, www.hospitalbritanico.org.ar. US$24 a visit. **German Hospital**, Av Pueyrredón 1640, between Beruti and Juncal, T4827 7000, www.hospitalale man.com.ar Both maintain first-aid centres (*centros asistenciales*) as do the other main hospitals. Dental treatment at Solís 2180, T4305 2530/ 2110. Excellent dental treatment centre at **Carroll Forest**, Vuelta de Obligado 1551 (Belgrano), T4781 9037, info@carroll-forest.com.ar. **Post offices** Correo Central, **Correos Argentinos**, Sarmiento y Alem, T4891 9191, www.correoargentino.com.ar, Mon-Fri, 0800-2000, Sat 1000-1300. *Poste Restante* (only to/from national destinations) on ground floor (US$0.25 per letter). Philatelic section open Mon-Fri 1000-1700, T5550 5176. **Centro Postal Internacional**, for all parcels over 2 kg for mailing abroad, at Av Comodoro Py y Antártida Argentina, near Retiro station, helpful, many languages spoken, packaging materials available, open Mon-Fri 1000-1700. Post office at Montevideo 1408 near Plaza V López, friendly staff, Spanish only. Also at Santa Fe 945 and many others. **UPS**, T0800-2222 877, www.ups.com. **DHL**, T0810-2222 345, www.dhl.com.ar. **FedEx**, T0810-3333 339, www.fedex.com.**Telephone** International and local calls, internet and fax from phone offices (*locutorios* or *telecentros*), of which there are many in the city centre.**Useful addresses Migraciones**: (Immigration), Antártida Argentina 1355, edificio 4 (visas extended mornings only), T4317 0200, www.migraciones.gov.ar, 0730-1330 (see also Visas and immigration in Essentials). **Central Police Station**: Moreno 1550, Virrey Cevallos 362, T4370 5911/5800 (emergency, T101 from any phone, free). See page 66 for **Comisaría del Turista** (tourist police). **South American Explorers**, Salguero 553, T4861 7571, baclub@ saexplorers.org, www.saexplorers.org. SAE have opened a new clubhouse in Buenos Aires, for knowledgeable advice and a comfortable meeting place for travellers, open Mon-Thu 1000-1800, Fri-Sat 1300-1700. **Aves Argentinas/AOP** (a BirdLife International partner), 25 de Mayo 749 p 2, T4312 8958, for information on birdwatching and specialist tours, good library open Wed and Fri 1500-2000 (closed Jan). Student organizations: **Asatej**: Helpful Argentine Youth and Student Travel

Organization, runs a Student Flight Centre, Florida 835, p 3, oficina 320, T4114 7600, www.asatej.com, Mon-Fri 0900-1900 (and other branches in BA: Belgrano, Monserrat, Palermo, Recoleta, Caballito), www.asatej.net. Offering booking for flights (student discounts) including cheap one-way flights (long waiting lists), hotels and travel; information for all South America; notice board for travellers, ISIC cards sold (giving extensive discounts; Argentine ISIC guide available here), English and French spoken; also runs: **Red Argentino de Alojamiento Para Jovenes** (affiliated to HI); **Asatej Travel Store**, at the same office, selling wide range of travel goods. **Oviajes**, Uruguay 385, p 6, T4371 6137, Lavalle 477 p 1, T5199 0831 and Echeverría 2498 p 1, T4785 7840/7884, www.oviajes.com.ar. Tickets and information, also issues Hostels of Americas, Nomads and Hostels of Europe, ISIC, ITIC and G0 25 cards, aimed at students, teachers and independent travellers. Cheap fares also at **TIJE**, San Martín 640 p 6, T4326 2036 or branches at Paraguay 1178, p 7, T5218 2800 and Zabala 1736, p 1, T4770 9500, www.tije.com, and at STB (STA representative), Viamonte 577 p 3, T5217 2727, www.stb.com.ar. **YMCA:** (Central), Reconquista 439, T4311 4785. **YWCA:** Tucumán 844, T4322 1550.

Around Buenos Aires

Tigre → *Population: 31,000 (Partido de Tigre -Tigre county- 301,000).*
This touristy little town, 29 km northwest of Buenos Aires, is a popular weekend destination lying on the lush jungly banks of the Río Luján, with a fun fair and an excellent fruit and handicrafts market (Puerto de Frutos) daily 1100-2000 with access from Calles Sarmiento or Perú. There are restaurants on the waterfront in Tigre across the Río Tigre from the railway line, along Lavalle and Paseo Victorica; cheaper places can be found on Italia and Cazón on the near side. North of the town is the delta of the Río Paraná: innumerable canals and rivulets, with holiday homes and restaurants on the banks and a fruit-growing centre. The fishing is excellent and the peace is only disturbed by motor-boats at weekends. Regattas are held in November. Take a trip on one of the regular launch services (*lanchas colectivas*) which run to all parts of the delta, including taxi launches – watch prices for these – from the wharf (*Estación Fluvial*). Tourist catamarans, five services daily, 1-2 hour trips, US$4-7, from Lavalle 499 on Río Tigre, T4731 0261/63, www.tigreencatamaran.com.ar, and *Río Tur* (from Puerto de Frutos, T4731 0280, www.rioturcatamaranes.com.ar). *Sturla* (Estación Fluvial, oficina 10, T4731 1300, www.sturlaviajes.com.ar) runs three 1-hour trips a day, US$4, to which can be added a barbecue at an island with a daily half-day tour (US$18); also full-day tours that include lunch and kayak excursions for US$48. Trips to the open Río de la Plata estuary are available with *Catamarán Libertad* (T4799 6030) from Puerto de Olivos on Sunday to the delta (US$4) or to Buenos Aires coasts (US$2.70), and on Saturday to the delta, US$5.
   Museo Naval ① *Paseo Victorica 602, T4749 0608, Mon-Fri 0830-1730, Sat-Sun 1030-1830, US$0.65.* Worth a visit to see the display of the origins and development of the Argentine navy. There are also relics of the 1982 Falklands/Malvinas War on display outside. **Museo de la Reconquista** ① *Av Liniers 818 (y Padre Castañeda), T4512 4496, Wed-Sun 1000-1800, free, closed Jan.* Near the location of Liniers' landing in 1806, the museum celebrates the reconquest of Buenos Aires by the Argentines from the British in 1806-1807.

Isla Martín García
This island in the Río de la Plata (Juan Díaz de Solís' landfall in 1516) used to be a military base. Now it is an ecological/historical centre and an ideal excursion from the capital, with many trails through the cane brakes, trees and rocky outcrops – interesting birds and flowers. Boat trips: four weekly from Tigre at 0900, returning 2000, three-hour journey, US$15 return (US$26 including lunch and guide; US$60 pp including weekend overnight at inn, full board). Reservations only through *Cacciola* (address under Ferries to Uruguay, above), who also handle bookings for the inn and restaurant on the island. There is also a campsite.

The Pampas

South and west of Buenos Aires the flat, fertile lands of the pampa húmeda stretch seemingly without end, the horizon broken only by a lonely windpump or a line of poplar trees. This is home to the gaucho, whose traditions of music and fine craftsmanship remain alive.

Argentina's agricultural heartland is punctuated by quiet pioneer towns, like Chascomús, and the houses of grand estancias. Argentina's former wealth lay in these splendid places, where you can stay as a guest, go horse riding, and get a great insight into the country's history and gaucho culture. The mountain range at Tandil offers great walking and marvellous views.

Luján → *Phone code: 02323. Population: 65,000.*

This is a place of pilgrimage for devout Catholics throughout Argentina. In 1630 an image of the Virgin brought by ship from Brazil was being transported to its new owner in Santiago del Estero by ox cart, when the cart got stuck, despite strenuous efforts by men and oxen to move it. This was taken as a sign that the Virgin willed she should stay there, A chapel was built for the image, and around it grew Luján. The chapel has long since been superseded by an impressive neo-Gothic basilica and the Virgin now stands on the High Altar. Each arch of the church is dedicated to an Argentine province, and the transepts to Uruguay, Paraguay and Ireland. Behind the Cabildo is the river, with river walks, cruises and restaurants (an excellent one is *L'Eau Vive* on the road to Buenos Aires at Constitución 2112, run by nuns, pleasant surroundings). Luján is a very popular spot at weekends, and there are huge pilgrimages on 5 October, 8 May and 8 December, when the town is completely packed.

Museo Histórico Colonial ① *Wed-Fri 1215-1800, Sat, Sun 1015-1800, closed Jan, US$0.30*, in the old Cabildo building, is one of the most interesting museums in the country. Exhibits illustrate its historical and political development. General Beresford, the commander of the British troops which seized Buenos Aires in 1806, was a prisoner here, as were Generals Mitre, Paz and Belgrano in later years. Next to it are museums devoted to transport and to motor vehicles and there is also a poor **Museo de Bellas Artes.**

San Antonio de Areco → *Phone code: 02326. Colour map 8, grid B5.*

San Antonio de Areco is a completely authentic, late 19th-century town, with crumbling single-storey buildings around a plaza filled with palms and plane trees, streets lined with orange trees, and an attractive *costanera* along the river bank. There are several *estancias* nearby and the town itself has historical *boliches* (combined bar and provisions store). The gaucho traditions are maintained in silver, textiles and leather handicrafts of the highest quality, as well as frequent gaucho activities, the most important of which is the **Day of Tradition** in the second week of February (book accommodation ahead), with traditional parades, gaucho games, events on horseback, music and dance. **Museo Gauchesco Ricardo Güiraldes** ① *on Camino Güiraldes, daily except Tue, 1100-1700, US$0.70*, is a replica of a typical *estancia* of the late 19th century, with impressive *gaucho* artefacts and displays on the life of Güiraldes, the writer whose best-known book, *Don Segundo Sombra*, celebrates the gaucho. Superb gaucho **silverwork** for sale at the workshop and museum of **Juan José Draghi** ① *Alvear 345, T454219*. Excellent **chocolates** at La Olla de Cobre ① *Matheu 433, T453105*, with a charming little café for drinking chocolate and the most amazing home-made *alfajores*. There is a large park spanning the river near the **tourist information centre** (address above). The **Centro Cultural y Museo Usina Vieja**, ① *Alsina 66, Tue-Fri 0800-1400, Sat, Sun, holidays 1100-1700, free*, is the city museum. There are ATMs on the plaza. The **tourist office** is at ① *Zerboni y Arellano, T453165, www.sanantoniodeareco.com.*

La Plata → *Phone code: 0221. Colour map 8, grid B5. Population: 545,000.*

La Plata, on the Río de la Plata, was founded in 1882 as capital of Buenos Aires province and is now an important administrative centre, with an excellent university. It's a well-planned city, reminiscent of Paris in places, with the French-style **legislature** and the elegant **Casa de Gobierno** on **Plaza San Martín**, central in a series of plazas along the spine of the city. On **Plaza Moreno** to the south there's an impressive Italianate palace housing the **Municipalidad**, and the **Cathedral,** a striking neo-Gothic brick construction. North of Plaza San Martín is La Plata's splendid park, the **Paseo del Bosque**, with mature trees, a boating lake and the **Museo de La Plata** ① *T425 7744, www.fcnym.unlp.edu.ar, daily 1000-1800, closed 1 Jan, 1 May, 25 Dec, US$1.50, free guided tours, weekdays 1400, 1600, Sat-Sun hourly, in Spanish and in English (phone first), highly recommended*. This museum houses an outstanding collection of stuffed animals, wonderful dinosaur skeletons and artefacts from pre-Columbian peoples throughout the Americas. 8 km northwest of the city is the **República de los Niños** ① *Col Gral Belgrano y Calle 501, daily 1000-2200, getting there: take a train from La Plata or Buenos Aires to Gonnet station, US$0.30, or bus 338, car park US$1*. This is Eva Peron's legacy, a delightful children's village with scaled-down castles, oriental palaces, a train, boat lake and restaurant. Fun for a picnic. The **Parque Ecológico** ① *Camino Centenario y San Luis, Villa Elisa, T473-2449, 0900-1930, free, getting there: take bus 273 D or E,* is another good place for families, with native forest and llamas, armadillos and ñandú roaming around.

The small municipal **tourist office** ① *Pasaje Dardo Rocha, T427 1535, Mon-Fri 1000-1700, and long weekends only,* in an Italianate palace, also houses a gallery of contemporary **Latin American art** ① *C 50 entre 6 y 7, T427 1843, www.cultura. laplata.gov.ar, 1000-1300, 1500-1800, weekends 1500-1800, free.*

Chascomus, Dolores and Tandil

To get to the heart of the pampas, stay in one of many estancias scattered over the plains. There are several accessible from the main roads to the coast, fast Ruta 2 (be prepared for tolls) and Ruta 11, near two well-preserved historic towns, Chasmomús and Dolores. At Punta Indio, 165 km from Buenos Aires, is 1920s Tudor style **Estancia Juan Gerónimo** ① *To11-493 74326, US$15pp for the day,* **L** *full board, activities included, English and French spoken.* Set on the coast in a beautiful nature reserve which protects a huge variety of fauna, the estancia offers walks and horse rides in 4,000 ha. Accommodation is simple and elegant, and the food exquisite.

Chascomús is a beautifully preserved town from the 1900's, with a rather Wild West feel to it, Chascomús is a lively place built on a huge lake, perfect for fishing and water sports. There's a great little museum **Museo Pampeano** *Muñoz y Lastra,* with gaucho artefacts. **Tourist office** ① *Libres del Sur 242,1st floor, or on the laguna. T430405, 0900-19000 daily, www.chas comus.com.ar.* Dolores is a delightful small town, like stepping back in time to the 1900's, very tranquil. **Museo Libres del Sur** ① *daily 1000-1700, US$0.30,* is an old house, full of gaucho silver, plaited leather *tablero,* branding irons, and a huge cart from 1868. The **Sierras de Tandil** are 2,000 million years old, among the world's oldest mountains, beautiful curved hills of granite and basalt, offering wonderful walking and riding. Tandil itself is an attractive, breezy town, a good base for exploring the sierras, with a couple of marvellous estancias close by. There's a park, **Parque Independencia,** with great views from the hill with its Moorish-style castle, and an amphitheatre, where there's a famous community theatre event throughout Easter week (book hotels ahead). The nearest peak, 5 km away, **Cerro El Centinela,** offers wild countryside for riding, climbing, walking, ascent by cable car, and regional delicacies at the restaurants. Very helpful **tourist information** at ① *9 de Julio 555, To2293-432073, or at the bus terminal, www.tandil.gov.ar.* Look up estancias on the Las Pampas province's website: www.vivalaspampas.com.ar and www.caminodel gaucho.com.ar, To221-425 7482.

⊕ Sleeping

Tigre *p99*
LL N/A Town & Country Hotels, Coronel Pizarro 1538, T4005 0050, www.newage-hotels.com. 19 upmarket hotels throughout Argentina.
B Cabañas del Biguá, on Arroyo Marchini, T4382 7517. Two rustic wooden cabins built on stilts, surrounded by the lush Delta vegetation, watersports. AHC member.
E Hostel Delta, Río Lujan y Abra Vieja, T4717-4648/4728-0396. For a relaxing stay on an island with sandy beaches and quite comfortable premises, including **B** doubles with bath, kayaks for rent, AHC member.

San Antonio de Areco *p100*
B Hostal Draghi, San Martín 477, T454515, draghi@arecoonline.com.ar. Charming, traditional style, very comfortable, with kitchen and bathroom.
C Los Abuelos, Zerboni y Zapiola T456390. In a renovated 1900s house, breakfast included.

C Hostal de Areco, Zapiola 25, T456118, **Posada del Ceibo,** Irigoyen y Smith, T454614.
E Res San Cayetano, Segundo Sombra 515, T456393. Basic but pleasant rooms, breakfast.
Camping Three sites in the park by the river: best is **Club River Plate,** Av del Valle y Alvear, T452744, US$3 per tent, sports club, shady sites with all facilities, pool. Also **Auto-camping La Porteña,** a beautiful spot 12 km from town on the Güiraldes *estancia.*

Estancias
Some of the province's finest *estancias* are within easy reach for day visits, offering horse riding, an *asado* lunch, and other activities. Better still, stay overnight to really appreciate the peace and beauty of these historical places. Look at estancias online: www.vivalaspampas.com.ar, www.turismo.gov.ar/eng/menu.htm (go to Active Tourism, Estancias).
L La Bamba, T456293, T011-4732 1269, www.la-bamba.com.ar. Dating from 1830,

in grand parkland, charming rooms, English-speaking owners who have lived here for generations, superb meals. Recommended.
AL El Ombú, T492080, T011-4710 2795, www.estanciaelombu.com. Fine house with magnificent terrace dating from 1890, comfortable rooms, horse riding, English-speaking owners. Recommended.
AL La Porteña, T453770, www.estancia laportenia.com.ar. House dates from 1823, where Güiraldes lived and wrote, simple spacious rooms, terrace with views of the polo pitch. Recommended.

La Plata p100

A Hotel Corregidor, C 6 No 1026, T425 6800. Upmarket, modern business hotel, well furnished, pleasant public rooms.
C Catedral, C 49 No.965, T483 0091. Modest but welcoming, modern, with fan, breakfast included.
C La Plata Hotel, Av 51 No 783, T/F422 9090. Modern, well furnished, comfortable, spacious bathrooms.

Estancias

A Casa de Campo La China, 60 km from La Plata on Ruta 11, T0221-421 2931, mceciliagargia2002@ yahoo.com.ar. A charming 1930s adobe house set in eucalyptus woods, with beautifully decorated spacious rooms off an open gallery, with open views, day visits (US$25) to ride horses, or in carriages, eat *asado*, or stay the night, guests of charming Cecilia and Marcelo, who speak perfect English. Delicious food. Highly recommended.

Chascomús p101

AL Torre Azul, Mercedes y Tandil, T422984, torre_azul@topmail.com.ar. Pool and spa, also with classy accommodation.
A La Posada, Costanera España, T423503, on the laguna, delightful, very comfortable.
D Laguna, Libres del Sur y Maipú, T426113. Best in town, good value, pleasant quiet rooms.

Estancias

Both *estancias* will collect you from Chascomús.
LL Haras La Viviana, 45 km from Chascomús, T011-4702 9633, http://haraslaviviana.com.ar. Perfect for horse riding, since fine polo ponies are bred here. Tiny cabins in gardens by a huge laguna where you can kayak or fish, very peaceful, good service, lady novelist owner is quite a character, fluent English spoken.
AL La Horqueta, 3 km from Chascomús on Ruta 20, T011-4813 1910, www.la horqueta.com. Full board, 1898 Tudor style mansion in lovely grounds with laguna for fishing, horse riding, bikes to borrow, English-speaking hosts, safe gardens especially good for children, plain food.

Dolores p101

L Dos Talas, 10 km from town, T443020, 155 13282, www.dostalas.com.ar. The most beautiful *estancia* in the pampas, and one of the oldest. An elegant house in grand parkland designed by Charles Thays, with fascinating history, visible in all the family photos, artefacts and the vast library. This is one of the few *estancias* where you are truly the owners' guests. The rooms and the service are impeccable, the food exquisite; stay for days, completely relax. Pool, riding, English spoken.

Tandil p101

A Las Acacias, Av Brasil 642, T02293-423373, www.posadalasacacias.com.ar. Attractive modern hostería in traditional-style house, good service, Italian and English spoken.
D Bed and Breakfast Belgrano 39, Belgrano 39, T02293-426989, www.cybertandil. com.ar/byb. One of the best places to stay, comfortable, in an idyllic walled garden with small pool, charming English hosts, phone in advance. Recommended.

Estancias

L Siempre Verde, T02292-498555, lasiempreverde@dilhard.com.ar. A 1900's house with traditional-style rooms, good views. The owners, descendants of one of Argentina's most important families, are very hospitable and helpful. Wonderful horse riding and walking among the sierras, fishing, *asados* on the hillside, camping. Highly recommended.
AL Ave María, 16 km from Tandil, past Cerro El Centinela, T02293-422843, www.avemaria tandil.com.ar. In beautiful gardens overlooking the rocky summits of the sierras. You're encouraged to feel at home and relax, swim in the pool or walk in the grounds, hills and woodland. Impeccable rooms, superb food and discreet staff who speak English. Highly recommended.

❼ Eating

San Antonio de Areco p100
Many *parrillas* on the bank of the Río Areco.
El Almacén, Bolivar 66. Original 1900s store and place to eat.
La Costa Reyes, Zerboni y Belgrano, on the *costanera* near the park. Delicious *parrilla*.
La Filomena, Vieytes 395. Elegant, modern, delicious food, with live music at weekends.
Ramos Generales, perfect place to try regional dishes such.
La Vuelta del Gato opposite the park. Good pizzas and salami, with traditional *patero* wine.

La Plata *p100*

Don Quijote, Plaza Paso. Delicious food in lovely surroundings, well known.

El Gran Chaparral, C 60 y C 117 (Paseo del Bosque). Good *parrilla* in the park, great steaks.

La Aguada, C 50 entre 7 y 8. Oldest restaurant in town, more for *minutas* (light meals) than big dinners, but famous for its *papas fritas* (chips – the chip soufflé is amazing).

Confitería París, C 7 y 49. The best croissants, and a lovely place for coffee.

El Modelo, C 54 y C5. Traditional *cervecería*, with good menu and great beer.

Chascomús *p101*

El Colonial, Lastra y Belgrano. Great food, and very cheap, at this traditional *parrilla*.

El Viejo Lobo, Mitre y Dolores. Very good fish.

Tandil *p101*

Plenty of *pizzerías*.

♯♯ Epoca de Quesos, San Martín y 14 de Julio, T448750. Atmospheric, delicious local produce, wines and *picadas*.

♯♯ Un Lugar, a couple of km from the centre at Av San Gabriel 2380, T155 07895 (call for directions). Recommended for excellent food in lovely surroundings, closed Mon.

♯♯ El Molino, Juncal 936. Broad menu, delicious.

♯♯ Parador del Sol in the *balneario* by Lago del Fuerte, Zarini s/n, T435697. Great pasta and salad.

♯♯ La Tranquera, Falucho y Nicaragua. Good *parrilla*, worth trying.

♯ La Amistad Pinto 736. *Tenedor libre*.

▲▲ Activities and tours

Horse riding Contact an approved guide who will take you to otherwise inaccessible privately owned land for trekking. **Eco de las Sierras**, Tandil, T442741, 156 21083, Lucrecia Ballasteros. Highly recommended guide, young, friendly and knowledgeable. **Las Patronas** stables, near Mercedes, T02324-430421, laspatronas@ yahoo.com.ar. US$35 for a complete day in the ranch with horse riding and lunch. Recommended.

Trekking and mountain biking
Horizonte Vertical, T432762, climbing and walking. **Tandil Aventuro**, T421836, trekking and mountain biking.

⊙ Transport

Tigre *p99*

Bus From central **Buenos Aires**: take No 60 from Constitución: the 60 'bajo' takes a little longer than the 60 'alto' but is more interesting for sightseeing.

Ferry To **Carmelo** (Uruguay) from Terminal Internacional, Lavalle 520, Tigre. **Cacciola**, T4749 0931, www.cacciolaviajes.com (in Buenos Aires at Florida 520, p 1, of 113, T4393 6100), 0830, 1630, 3½ hrs, US$12.50 (US$22 return). Bus connection to Montevideo, 3 hrs, US$18, US$33 return. Other bus destinations in Uruguay and overnight stays in Carmelo (from US$47 including ticket and accommodation). Connecting bus to Tigre from Carlos Pellegrini y Av Córdoba, 0635, 1445.

To **Nueva Palmira** (Uruguay) from Estación Fluvial de Tigre. **Líneas Delta Argentino**, oficina 6 at Estación Fluvial, T4731 1236, www.lineas delta.com.ar. Daily at 0745, 3 hrs, US$12 (US$21 return). Bus connection to Colonia, 5 hrs from Tigre, US$14, US$23 return. Overnight stays in Nueva Palmira and Colonia (from US$42 including ticket and accommodation). **Note**: Argentine port taxes are generally included in the fares for Argentine departures. For return tickets, port tax at Colonia is US$1.70 pp (US$16 per vehicle) and at Montevideo, US$4 pp (US$18 per vehicle).

Train From **Buenos Aires**: take train from Retiro station (FC Mitre section) to Tigre or to Bartolomé Mitre and change to the Maipú station (the stations are linked) for the **Tren de la Costa**, T4002 6000, US$2 one way, every 20 mins from Maipú Mon-Thu 0710-2300, Fri 0710-2400, Sat-Sun 0830-0010, 25 mins journey. (Buses to Tren de la Costa are 60 from Constitución, 19 or 71 from Once, 152 from centre.) Several stations on this line have shopping centres (eg San Isidro), and the terminus, Estación Delta, has the huge fun fair, El Parque de la Costa, and a casino. You can get off the train as many times as you want on the same ticket.

Luján *p100*

Bus From **Buenos Aires** (Plaza Once) Bus 52 and (Plaza Italia at Palermo) bus 57, frequent, 1 hr 50 mins with direct service, US$1.50. To **San Antonio de Areco**, 3 a day, US$1.20, Empresa Argentina, 1 hr. Train to Once station, US$0.60 (change at Moreno).

San Antonio de Areco *p100*

Bus From **Buenos Aires** (Retiro bus terminal), 2 hrs, US$3.60, every hour with Chevallier or Pullman General Belgrano. For connections to northern Argentina go to Pilar.

La Plata *p100*

Bus Terminal at Calle 4 and Diagonal 74. Information T427 3186/427 3198. To **Buenos Aires**, 1½ hrs, US$2, every 30 mins, all through the night from Retiro terminal, daytime only from Plaza Constitución. To **San Clemente del Tuyú**, US$5.

Train To/from **Buenos Aires** (Constitución), frequent, US$0.75, 1 hr 10 mins (ticket office hidden behind shops opposite platform 6).

Atlantic Coast

Among the 500 km of resorts stretching from to San Clemente de Tuyú to Monte Hermoso, the most attractive is upmarket Pinamar, with the chic Cariló next door. Villa Gesell is relaxed and friendly, while, next to it are the quiet, beautiful Mar Azul and Mar de las Pampas. Mar del Plata, Argentina's most famous resort, is a huge city with packed beaches, popular for its lively nightlife and casino; much more appealing in winter. Next to it, tranquil Miramar is great for young families, and Necochea has wild expanses of dunes to explore. Near the port of Bahía Blanca is the Sierra de la Ventana, the highest range of hills in the pampas, a great place for hiking.

Partido de la Costa

San Clemente del Tuyú is closest to the capital, the first of a string of identical small resorts known as **Partido de la Costa**, not worth a detour unless you're keen on fishing. They're old-fashioned towns, cheaper than the more popular resorts further southwest, but rather run down. There's excellent sea fishing, for shark, *pejerrey* and *brotola* from pier or boats, and fish can often be bought on the beach from local fishermen, but since the Río de la Plata flows here, the water is poor for bathing. San Clemente's main attraction is **Mundo Marino** ① *signposted from road into town, T430300, www.mundomarino.com.ar, US$5*, a sea life centre with performing seals and dolphins, fun for small children. Plenty of small hotels and campsites. At **Punta Rasa**, 9 km north, there is a lighthouse and a nature reserve, which, in summer, is home to thousands of migratory birds from the northern hemisphere. www.vidasilvestre.org.ar. There's a beautiful stretch of empty beach 15 km south of **Mar de Ajó**, the southernmost of these resorts, which belongs to one of the few *estancias* to offer horse riding on the sands, **Palantelén** ① *T02257-420983*. A peaceful place to walk and relax, delightful house, private tango lessons, charming English-speaking hosts. Highly recommended. **Tourist information** ① Mar del Tuyú, T02246-433035, www.lacostaturismo.com.ar.

Pinamar and Cariló → *Phone code: 02254.*

The two most desirable resorts on the coast, 340 km from Buenos Aires, via Ruta 11, are next to each other, with the quiet old fashioned Belgian pioneer town Ostende in between. **Pinamar** is great for young people and families, with smart *balnearios* ranging from chic, quiet places with superb restaurants, to very trendy spots with loud music, beach parties and live bands at night. There are golf courses and tennis courts, and fine hotels and smart restaurants all along the main street, Avenida Bunge, running perpendicular to the sea. It's a stylish and well-maintained resort, slightly pricey. Explore the dunes at **Reserva Dunícola**, 13 km north, by horse or 4WD. **Tourist office** ① *Av Bunge 654, T491680, www.pinamar.gov.ar, www.pinamarturismo.com.ar*, English spoken, helpful, will arrange accommodation. **Cariló**, the most exclusive resort of all, has a huge area of mature woodland, where its luxury apart-hotels and *cabañas* are all tastefully concealed. The *balnearios* are neat and exclusive – of which *Hemingway* is *the* place, full of wealthy Porteños – and there are good restaurants and shops around the tiny centre, Cerezo and Carpintero.

Villa Gesell → *Phone code: 02255. Population: 40,000.*

In contrast to the rather elite Cariló, Villa Gesell, 22 km south of Pinamar, is warm, welcoming and very laid-back. Set amid thousands of trees planted by its German founder, it has grown in recent years into a thriving tourist town, but retains its village feel. The beaches are safe and there's plenty of nightlife. In January, it's overrun by Argentine youth, far quieter in late February and March. Next to it are the two of the most tranquil and charming beach retreats: idyllic and wooded **Mar de las Pampas** and **Mar Azul** are both still underdeveloped, with fine *cabañas* to choose from. Get a map from the tourist office in Villa Gesell, or as you enter Mar de las Pampas. There's no grid system and it can be tricky finding your way around. Villa Gesell's main street is Avenida 3, pedestrianized in the evenings, full of cafés, restaurants and bars. The main **tourist office** is *at the bus terminal, T477253,* or on the right as you drive into town ① *Av de los Pioneros, 1921, T458118, open 0800-2200 daily in summer, www.villagesell.gov.ar,* very helpful, English spoken.

Mar del Plata → *Phone code: 0223. Colour map 8, grid C5. Population: 560,000.*

The oldest and most famous Argentine resort has lost much of its charm since it was built in 1874. It's now a huge city offering great nightlife in summer, but if you like some space on the beach, it's best to go elsewhere. The are hundreds of hotels, all busy (and double the price) in January-February; winter can be pleasantly warm, and much quieter. **Tourist offices** ① *Belgrano 2740, T495 1777, 0800-1500, or, more conveniently, next to ex-Hotel Provincial, 0800-2000, www.mardelplata.gov.ar.* English spoken, good leaflets on daily events with bus routes. Also lists of hotels and apartment/chalet letting agents. The province's office is ① *on the ground floor of the Hotel Provincial, Blvd Marítimo 2500 y Peralta Ramos, T495 5340, www.vivalaspampas.com.ar.* Out of season offices may be closed, or only open mornings.

The city centre is around **Playa Bristol**, with the huge casino, and **Plaza San Martín**, with pedestrian streets Rivadavia and San Martín full of shops and restaurants. 10 blocks southwest, the area of Los Troncos contains some remarkable mansions dating from Mar del Plata's heyday, from mock Tudor **Villa Blaquier** to **Villa Ortiz Basualdo** (1909), inspired by Loire chateaux, now the **Museo Municipal de Arte** ① *Av Colón 1189, daily in summer 1700-2200, US$1, including guided tour.* Rooms furnished in period style. Nearby is the splendid **Museo del Mar** ① *Av Colón 1114, T451 3553, www.museodelmar.org, from 0800-2000, 2400 on Sat, US$1.50.* It has a vast collection of 30,000 sea shells, a café and roof terrace. The **Centro Cultural Victoria Ocampo** ① *Matheu 1851, T4920569, daily in summer; ring to check current opening time, US$1.* This beautiful 1900's wooden house in lovely gardens was where the famous author entertained illustrious literary figures. Nearby is the **Villa Mitre** ① *Lamadrid 3870, Mon-Fri 0900-2000 Sat/Sun 1600-2000, in summer, US$0.70.* Owned by a descendent of Bartolomé Mitre, it has a collection of artefacts. Beaches are filled with hundreds of tiny beach huts, carpas, rented by the day for US$5-7, entitling you to use the balneario's showers, toilets, restaurants.

Beaches include fashionable **Playa Grande**, where the best hotels and shops are, as well as the famous golf course, with private *balnearios* for wealthy *porteños*, a small area open to the public; **Playa La Perla**, now packed and pretty grim, but **Playa Punta Mogotes**, further west, is by far the most appealing. The **port area**, south of Playa Grande, is interesting when the old orange fishing boats come in, and at night, for its wonderful seafood restaurants. A sea lion colony basks on rusting wrecks by the Escollera Sur (southern breakwater) and fishing is good all along the coast, where *pejerrey, corvina* and *pescadilla* abound. Lots of theatres, cinemas, and the **Casino** ① *Dec to end-Apr, 1600-0330; 1600-0400 on Sat; May-Dec, Mon-Fri 1500-0230; weekends 1500-0300; free; minimum bet US$0.50.* Lively festivals are 17 November, Day of Tradition, with gaucho-related events, the national fishing festival in late January, and the international film festival in mid-March.

Inland, 68 km west of Mar de la Plata is the town of **Balcarce** with some splendid art deco buildings and a leafy central plaza. You're most likely to visit the **Museo Juan Manuel Fangio.** Argentina's best-loved racing driver was born here, and the Municipalidad on the plaza has been turned into a great museum, housing his trophies, and many of the racing cars he drove. Recommended. There are excellent *parrillas* on the outskirts. The **Laguna Brava**, 38 km away, at the foot of the Balcarce hills, offers *pejerrey* fishing, and plentiful birdlife in lovely wooded surroundings. Visit **Estancia Laguna Brava** ① *RN 226 Km 37.5, T0223-460 8002*, for horse riding, trekking, mountain biking and water sports on the lake with fine views of Sierra Brava. **Tourist information** ① *C 17 No 671, T02266-425758.* . Frequent buses from Mar de la Plata.

Miramar → *Phone code: 02291. Colour map 8, grid C5. Population: 22,000.*

Miramar, 53 km southwest of Mar del Plata, along the coast road, is a charming small resort, known as the 'city of bicycles', and orientated towards families with small children. It has a big leafy plaza at its centre, a good stretch of beach with soft sand, and a very pleasant relaxed atmosphere; a quieter, low-key alternative to Mar del Plata. The most attractive area of the town is away from the high rise buildings on the sea front, at the **Vivero Dunícola Florentino Ameghino**, a 502 ha forest park on the beach, with lots of walks, restaurants and picnic places for *asado* among the mature trees. In town there are lots of restaurants along Calle 21, and good cafés at *balnearios* on the sea front. **Tourist office**① *on the central plaza, C 28 No 1086, T02291-420190, www.miramar-digital.com, Mon-Fri 0700-2100, Sat-Sun 0900-2100.* Helpful, accommodation lists and maps.

Necochea → *Phone code: 02262. Colour map 8, grid C5. Population: 65,000.*

Necochea is a well-established resort, famous for its long stretch of beach, and while the central area is built up and busy in the summer, further west there are beautiful empty beaches and high sand dunes. There's also a fine golf club and rafting nearby on the river Quequén. **Tourist offices**① *on the beach front at Av 79 y Av 2, T425983, www.necochea.gov.ar; also upstairs at the Municipalidad, C 56 No 2956, T422631,* English spoken, list of apartments for rent. There are banks with ATMs and *locutorios* along the pedestrianized C 83.

The **Parque Miguel Lillo** (named after the Argentine botanist) starts three blocks west of Plaza San Martín and stretches along the seafront, a wonderful dense forest of over 600 ha. There are lovely walks along paths, many campsites and picnic spots, a swan lake with paddle boats, an amphitheatre, lots of restaurants, and places to practise various sports. West of Necochea, there's a natural arch of rock at the **Cueva del Tigre**, and beyond it stretches a vast empty beach, separated from the land by sand dunes up to 100 m high, the **Médano Blanco**. This is an exhilarating area for walking or horse riding and the dunes are popular for 4WD riding. Vehicles and buses stop where the road ends at Parador Médano Blanco (a good place for lunch) where you can rent 4WDs for US$30, T155 68931.

Bahía Blanca and around → *Phone code: 0291. Colour map 8, grid C4. Pop: 300,000.*

The province's most important port and naval base, Bahía Blanca is a quiet, attractive city. It's a good starting point for exploring **Sierra de la Ventana**, 100 km north, or relaxing on beaches an hour to the east. The architecture is remarkable with many fine buildings especially around the central **Plaza Rivadavia**, notably the ornate, Italianate **Municipalidad** of 1904 and the French-style **Banco de la Nación** (1927). Three blocks north on the main shopping street, Alsina, there's the classical **Teatro Colón** (1922). Northwest of the plaza, there's the attractive **Parque de Mayo** with a fine golf course and sports centre nearby. The **Museo Histórico**① *at the side of the Teatro Municipal, Dorrego 116, 1500-2000,* has sections on the pre-Hispanic period and interesting photos of early Bahía Blanca. Not to be missed, though, is the **Museo del Puerto** ① *Torres y Carrega, 7 km away in the port area at* Ingeniero White, *weekends, 1730-2030 summer, 1500-2000 winter, getting there: bus 500A or 504 from plaza, taxi US$3.* It houses entertaining and imaginative displays on immigrant life in the early 20th century, and a quaint *confitería* on Sunday. **Tourist office** ① *in the Municipalidad on the main plaza, Alsina 65 (small door outside to the right), T459 4007, www.bahiablanca.gov.ar, Mon-Fri 0730-1900, Sat 1000-1300.* Very helpful.

At **Pehuén-Có**, 84 km east of Bahía Blanca, there's a long stretch of sandy beaches, with dunes, relatively empty and unspoilt (beware of jellyfish when wind is in the south), signposted from the main road 24 km from Bahía Blanca. It has a wild and untouristy feel, with a single hotel, several campsites well shaded, and a couple of places to eat. There's a more established resort at **Monte Hermoso**, 106 km east, with more hotels and a better organized campsite, but quiet, with a family feel, and wonderful beaches. One of the few places on the coast where the sun rises and sets over the sea.

Sierra de la Ventana → *Phone code 0291.*

The magnificent Sierra de la Ventana, the highest range of hills in the pampas, lies within easy reach of Bahía for a day or weekend visit (100 km north of Bahía Blanca). They're as old as those in Tandil, but much more accessible for long hikes, with stunning views from their craggy peaks. There are daily buses and *combis* from Bahía Blanca, but you could stop at **Tornquist**, 70 km north of Bahía Blanca by Ruta 33, a quaint place, with an attractive park in the central plaza.

The sierras are accessed within the **Parque Provincial Ernesto Tornquist**, 25 km northeast of Tornquist on Ruta 76. The entrance is signposted after the massive ornate gates from the Tornquist family home. Nearby is *Campamento Base*, T0291-491 0067, camping, basic dormitory, hot showers. At the entrance to the park itself, there's a car park and interpretation centre with *guardeparques*, who can advise on walks. From here it's a two-hour walk to the summit of **Cerro de la Ventana**, which has fantastic views from the 'window' (which gives the range its name), in the summit ridge. 5 km further along Ruta 76 is the forestry station and a visitors' centre, T0291-491 0039, with audio-visual display, from where a guided visit (only with own vehicle, 4-5 hours) is organized to natural caves (one with petroglyphs). Also from here, an hour-long trail goes to Cerro Bahía Blanca. **Villa Ventana**, 10 km further, is a pretty, wooded settlement with excellent teashop, *Casa de Heidi*, and good food at *Las Golondrinas*. Helpful **tourist office** at entrance to Village Ventana, T491 0095, *www.sierradelaventana.org.ar*.

The town of **Sierra de la Ventana**, further east, is a good centre for exploring the hills, with a greater choice of hotels than Villa Ventana, and wonderful open landscapes all around. There is a 18-hole golf course, and good trout fishing in the Río Sauce Grande. Excellent tourist office on ① *Av Roca, just before railway track, T491 5303 (same website as Villa Ventana).*

● Sleeping

Atlantic Coast *p104*

Since accommodation is plentiful all along the coast, only a small selection is listed here. Most resorts have *balnearios*, private beaches, where you pay US$3-7 per day for use of a sunshade or beach hut, showers, toilets and restaurants. Avoid January when the whole coast is packed out.

Pinamar *p104*

There are plenty of hotels in Pinamar, of a high standard, all 4-stars have a pool. Some hotels are a long way from the beach. Book ahead in Jan and Feb. All those listed are recommended.
A Del Bosque, Av Bunge 1550, T482480, elbosque@telpin.com.ar. Very attractive, though not on the beach, a smart 4 star with good service.
A Las Araucarias, Av Bunge 1411, T480812. Attractive, smaller hotel with gardens.
A Playas, Av Bunge 140, T482236, www.pina marsa.com.ar. A lovely setting with stylish rooms, and comfortable lounge, small pool, good service, a couple of blocks from the beach.
A-B Reviens, Burriquetas 79, T497010, www.hotelreviens.com. Modern, luxurious, international style, with beach access.
B Soleado Hotel, Sarmiento y Nuestras Malvinas, T490304, www.pinamarturismo.com.ar. Bright, beachfront hotel, cosy rooms.
C La Posada, Del Odiseo 324, T482267, www.pinamar.com.ar/laposada. Good value, more old-fashioned style, comfortable, close to sea and town centre.
Camping Several well equipped sites (US$5-8 per day), all near the beach at Ostende.

Villa Gesell *p104*

AL Terrazas Club, Av 2 entre 104 y 105, T462181, www.terrazasclubhotel.com.ar. The smartest in town, great service, huge breakfasts, pool and access to the *Azulmarina* Spa, T450545, www.spaazulmarina.com.ar.
B Playa, Alameda 205 y C 303, T458027. The first ever hotel, in the wooded old part of town, renovated, comfortable.

C Hostería Gran Chalet, Paseo 105 No 447 y Av 4-5, T462913. Warm welcome, comfortable rooms, good breakfast. Recommended.
E pp Hospedaje Aguas Verdes, Av 5, entre 104 y 105, T462040, clo@terra.com.ar.
Airy, with a little garden, rooms for 2-6, some English spoken.

Mar del Plata *p105*

Busy traffic makes it impossible to move along the coast in summer: choose a hotel near the beach you want.
L Costa Galana, Bv Marítimo 5725, T486 0000, reservas@hotelcostagalana.com.ar. The best by far, stylish, 5 star, at Playa Grandet.
AL Hermitage, Bv Marítimo 2657, T451 9081, www.lacapitalnet.com.ar/hermitag. Charming old-fashioned 4 star on the seafront.
A Spa República, Córdoba 1968, T492 1142, hosparep@statics.com.ar. Modern, with pool and spa, good restaurant. Recommended.
B-C Argentino, Belgrano 2225 y Entre Ríos, T493 2223, www.argentinohotel-mdp.com.ar. Modern rooms in this traditional 4 star in the city, also apartments, very good value.
C Selent, Arenales 2347, T494 0878, www.hotelselent.com.ar. Quiet with neat rooms. Recommended.
C Los Troncos, Rodríguez Peña 156, T451 8882. Small, chalet-style, handy for Güemes, garden.
D Costa Mogotes, Martínez de Hoz 2401, T484 2337. Tidy, modern, with airy confitería, near Playa Punta Mogotes.

Balcarce *p105*

C Balcarce, C 16 y 17, T422055, good.
Camping Complejo Polideportivo, Ruta 55, Km 63.5, T420251, with pools and good facilities, all kinds of sports too. Club de Pesca de Villa Laguna Brava, RN 226, Km 38.5, well organized site, with all facilities, and good fishing.

Miramar *p105*

B América, Diag Rosende Mitre 1114, T420847. One of the most attractive places in Spanish

colonial style, surrounded by trees, lots of games for children, bikes for hire, lovely gardens.
C **Brisas del Mar**, C 29 No 557, T420334. Sea front, family-run, neat rooms, cheery restaurant, attentive, good value.
Camping Lots of sites including F pp El Durazno, 2 km from town, with good facilities. Take bus 501 marked 'Playas'.

Necochea *p106*

Most hotels are in the seafront area just north of Av 2. There are at least 100 within 700 m of the beach.
B **Bahía**, Diagonal San Martín 731, T42353. Really kind owners, comfortable rooms. Recommended.
B **España**, C 89 No 215, T422896 (ACA affiliated). More modern, well suited to families, attentive staff. Recommended.
B **Presidente**, C 4 No 4040, T423800. Also 4 star and recommended for excellent service, comfortable rooms and pool.
B **San Miguel**, C 85 No 301, T/F425155 (ACA). Good service and value, comfortable, open all year.
B-C **Ñikén**, C 87 No 335, T432323, 2 blocks from the sea. Very comfortable, 4 star, pool, good facilities, good restaurant, excellent service.
C **Hostería del Bosque**, C 89 No 350, T/F420002. 5 blocks from beach, quiet, comfortable, great restaurant. Recommended.
C **Marino**, Av 79 No 253, T524140, summer only. One of the first hotels, with a wonderful staircase and patios, faded grandeur, but full of character.
Camping Camping UATRE, Av 10 y 187, T438278, the best site, a few km west of town towards Médano Blanco, great facilities, beautifully situated *cabañas*. US$1pp per day. Campsites on beach US$1 pp in season.

Bahía Blanca *p106*

AL **Austral**, Colón 159, T011-4326 0746, www.hoteles-austral.com.ar. Friendly, very good, fine views, attentive service, decent restaurant.
A **Argos**, España 149, T455 0404, www.hotel argos.com. 3 blocks from plaza, 4-star business hotel, smart rooms, good breakfast, restaurant.
B **Bahía**, Chiclana 251, T455 3050, www.bahia-hotel.com.ar. New business hotel, good value, well-equipped comfortable rooms, bright bar and *confitería*. Recommended.
C **Barne**, H Yrigoyen 270, T453 0294. Family-run, good value, welcoming.
D-E **Hospedaje Bayón**, Chiclana 487, T452 2504. Quite basic but OK, cheaper without bath, friendly.
Camping A couple of options in town, but far

better to head for Pehuen Có, see below.

Pehuén-Có *p106*

A **La Goleta**, Av Pte Perón y C 10, T481142. Modern, upmarket, lovely rooms with sea views.
C **Petit Hotel**, Av Argentina 244, T491818. Simple, modernized 1940's style, family-run, on the beach, cheap restaurant, *El Faro*, on the beach (breakfast extra). Recommended.
Camping Americano, T481149 signposted from main road 5 km before town (bus or taxi from town). Lovely shady site by beach, US$11 per group of 4 per day, hot showers, pool, restaurant, food shop, *locutorio*. Recommended. Many others, most with good facilities.

Tornquist *p106*

D **San José**, Güemes 138, T0291-494 0152. Small, quiet, modern.
Camping Parque Norte, just north on Ruta 76, T494 0661. Popular lakeside park to bathe/picnic.

Villa Ventana *p107*

Lots of accommodation in *cabañas*; municipal campsite by river with all facilities.
B **Hotel El Mirador**, before you reach the Villa, right underneath Cerro de la Ventana, T494 1338, comfortable rooms, some with tremendous views, very peaceful, good restaurant.

Sierra de la Ventana *p106*

AL **Estancia Cerro de la Cruz**, just outside Sierra town (phone for directions) T156-486957. Luxurious *estancia* with beautiful views, charming hosts. Recommended.
C **Cabañas La Caledonia** in Villa Arcadia, a couple of blocks over the railway track, T156-462003. Well equipped in pretty gardens.
C **Las Vertientes**, signposted to the left just before the turning to Sierra de la Ventana town, T491 0064, lasvertientes@ba.net. Very welcoming ranch, relaxing, horse riding, day visits, US$10pp.
D **Provincial**, Drago y Malvinas, T491 5025. Old 1940s place, quaint, fabulous views, restaurant, pool, good value.
Camping Sierra Aventura, Av San Martín y Camino a la Hoya, T452 4787, pretty site with eucalyptus trees, hot showers.

🍴 Eating

Mar del Plata *p105*

2 areas have become popular for smaller shops

● *For an explanation of the sleeping and eating price codes used in this guide, see inside the front*
● *cover. Other relevant information is found in Essentials pages 68-69.*

bars and restaurants: Around C Güemes:

♦ **El Condal**, *picadas* and drinks.
♦ **La Bodeguita**, Castelli 1252. Cuban bar with food.
♦ **Tisiano**, San Lorenzo 1332. Good pasta restaurant.

Around Alem, next to cemetery, lots of pubs and bars. Traditional favourites:

♦ **Confitería Manolo**, famous for *churros*.
♦ **Parrilla Trenelauken**, Mitre 2807.

Seafood restaurants in the Centro Comercial Puerto, many brightly lit and not atmospheric:

♦♦-♦ **Dalmacio**, Almte Brown 1958. A la carte, good quality and value.
♦ **Taberna Baska**, 12 de Octubre 3301. Seafood.
♦ **El Viejo Pop**, T480 1632. The best place, candlelit, superb paella.

Tenedor libre restaurants of all kinds along San Martín, and cheap restaurants along Rivadavia.

Necochea *p106*

There are some excellent seafood restaurants.
♦ **Cantina Venezia**, near the port at Av 59 No 259. The most famous, delicious fish.
♦ **Chimichurri**, C 83 No 345. Recommended for *parrilla*.
♦ **El Rincón de López**, Av 10 No 3288. Also worth trying for fish.
♦ **Parrilla El Loco**, Av 10 y 65. A classic, deservedly popular for superb steaks.
♦ **Río Piedra**, C 22 at the river bank, T154 64873. A superb little campsite restaurant in gorgeous surroundings.

Bahía Blanca *p106*

♦♦ **Lola Mora**, Av Alem y Sarmiento. Sophisticated, delicious Mediterranean food, in an elegant colonial-style house, US$8 for 3 courses and wine.
♦♦-♦ **Micho**, Guillermo Torres 3875, T457 0346 (but go there by taxi at night, as it's in an insalubrious area). Take bus 500 or 501. A superb chic fish restaurant at the port.
♦ **El Mundo de la Pizza**, Dorrego 53. Fabulous pizzas, lots of choice, the city's favourite.
♦ **For You**, Belgrano 69. *Tenedor libre parrilla* and Chinese food, as much as you can eat for US$3.
♦ **La Negra**, Av Alem 59. Great Italian food, excellent pastas and fish, lively atmosphere, arrive early (2100).
♦ **Santino**, Dorrego 38. Italian-influenced, quiet sophisticated atmosphere, good value and a welcoming glass of champagne. US$6 for 2 courses and wine. Recommended.
El Cofre, Dorrego 2 e Yrigoyen. Laid back, good for a coffee during the day with internet access, drink and live music at weekends with a young crowd.

La Piazza, on the corner of the plaza at O'Higgins y Chiclana. Great coffee, buzzing atmosphere, good salads, and cakes too.
Muñoz, O'Higgins y Drago. Sophisticated café.

Pehuén-Có *p106*

♦♦♦ **Marfil**, Valle Encantado 91. The smartest, delicious fish and pastas.
♦ **Pizza Jet**, Valle Encantado e Int Majluf. Hugely popular for all kinds of food, arrive before 2130.

Sierra de la Ventana *p106*

♦ **El Establo**, San Martín 121. Good value steaks.
♦ **La Angelita**, next to *Cabañas La Caledonia*, Villa Arcadia. Not to be missed, tea under the walnut trees at the old tea room, fresh scones, delicious cakes, roquefort pancakes. Highly recommended.

♦ Bars and clubs

Mar del Plata *p105*

Most nightclubs are on Av Constitución, and start at around 0200.
Chocolate, No 4471, big and chic, under 25s.
Sobremonte, No 6690, huge complex of bars and dance floors (it's fine to be over 25 here!).

Bahía Blanca *p106*

Lots of discos on **Fuerte Argentino** (along the stream leading to the park) mainly catering for under 25's: **Chocolate**, **Bonito**.
La Barraca. Best place for anyone over 25.

☉ Transport

San Clemente del Tuyú *p104*

Bus To **Mar del Plata** (and to resorts in between) are frequent, **Rápido del Sud**, **El Rápido Argentino**, US$5, 5 hrs. To **Buenos Aires**, several companies, US$4-7.

Pinamar *p104*

Bus Terminal 4 blocks north of main plaza at Av Bunge e Intermédanos, T403500. To Buenos Aires, US$12, 4-5hrs, several companies.
Trains See page 103.

Villa Gesell *p104*

Air Regular flights (in summer) from Buenos Aires to airport, 5 km away, taxi US$3, usually minibuses meet each flight. Several companies, book in advance at weekends.
Bus Direct to **Buenos Aires**, 5 hrs, US$12. To **Mar del Plata** 2 hrs, US$3.30. Also buses from Mendoza, Córdoba. Terminal at Av 3 y Paseo 140.

Argentina Atlantic Coast Listings

Mar del Plata *p105*
Air Camet airport, T478 3990, 10 km north of town. Several flights daily to **Buenos Aires**, LADE (T493 8220), AR/Austral (T496 0101). LADE also to many Patagonian towns once a week. *Remise* taxi from airport to town, mini bus US$2.
Boat Boat trips visiting **Isla de los Lobos, Playa Grande, Cabo Corrientes** and **Playa Bristol** leave from the harbour, US$2, 40 mins, summer and Sat-Sun in winter. Longer cruises on the **Anamora**, 1130, 1400, 1600, 1800, from Dársena B, Muelle de Guardacostas in the port, US$5, T489 0310.
Bus For information T451 5406. The bus terminal, in a former railway station, is central at Alberti y Las Heras, but short on services. Not a place to hang around at night. **El Rápido**, T451 0600, **Flecha bus**, T486 0512, **TAC**, T4510014, **Chevalier**, T451 8447. **La Estrella**, T486 0915. To **Buenos Aires**, 6 hrs, US$13, many companies; **Chevalier**, and **Costera Criolla**, also have *coche cama*. To **La Plata**, 6 hrs, US$12. **El Cóndor** and **Rápido Argentino**. To **San Clemente del Tuyú**, **Empresa Costamar**, frequent, 5 hrs, US$8. To **Miramar**, hourly, 45 mins, US$1.30. To **Bahía Blanca**, only **Pampa**, 6 daily, US$11, 5 ½ hrs. Change there for buses to **Bariloche** and **Puerto Madryn**.
Train To **Buenos Aires** (Constitución) from Estación Norte, Luro 4599, T475 6076, 13 blocks from the centre. Buses to/from centre 511, 512, 512B, 541. See page 103. Also services to Miramar.

Miramar *p105*
Bus 8 daily to **Buenos Aires**, many companies, US$10. To **Mar del Plata**, US$1.40, **Rápido del Sur**, from C 23 y 24, T423359. To **Necochea**, **El Rápido**, US$3.
Train See page 103. Station at C 40 y 13, T420657.

Necochea *p106*
Bus Terminal at Av 58 y Jesuita Cardiel, T422470, 3 km from the beach area; bus 513, 517 from outside the terminal to the beach. Taxi to beach area US$1. To **Buenos Aires**, US$15, **La Estrella**, **El Cóndor** and few others. To **Mar del Plata**, **El Rápido**, US$3. To **Bahía Blanca**, **El Rápido** US$10.

Bahía Blanca *p106*
Air Airport Comandante Espora, lies 11 km northeast of centre, US$3 in a taxi. Airport information T486 1456. Daily flights to **Buenos Aires** with AR/Austral (T456 0561/ 0810-2228 6527) and LADE (T452 1063). LADE has weekly flights to **Bariloche**, **Mar del Plata**, **Neuquén**, **Puerto Madryn**, **San Antonio Oeste**, **San Martín de los Andes** (may involve changes).
Bus Terminal in old railway station 18 blocks from centre, at Estados Unidos y Brown, T481

9615, connected by buses 512, 514, or taxi US$2, no hotels nearby. To **Buenos Aires** frequent, several companies, 8½ hrs, US$10-15, shop around. Most comfortable by far is **Plusmar** suite bus, US$20 (T456 0616). To **Mar del Plata**, **El Rápido**, US$10, 7 hrs. To **Córdoba**, US$18, 12 hrs. To **Neuquén**, 6 a day, 8 hrs, US$10. To **Necochea**, **El Rápido**, 5 hrs, US$8. To **Viedma Ceferino**, **Plusmar** and **Río Paraná** (to Carmen de Patagones), 4 hrs, US$5-6. To **Trelew**, **Don Otto** and others, US$28, 10½ hrs (9½ hrs to Puerto Madryn, US$23). To **Río Gallegos**, **Don Otto** US$34. To **Tornquist**, US$2, **Río Paraná** and **La Estrella/El Cóndor**, 1 hr 20 min; to **Sierra de la Ventana** (town) **La Estrella/El Cóndor** and **Expreso Cabildo**, US$. Also *combi* (shared taxi) with **Geotur** T450 1190, terminal at San Martín 455.
Train Station at Av Gral Cerri 750, T452 9196. To/from **Buenos Aires**, see page 103.

Pehuén-Có and Monte Hermoso *p106*
Bus **Combis Ariber** minibus taxi service from Bahía Blanca to either town, ring to be collected from anywhere in town, T4565523, **Combibus**, T155-700400.

Sierra de la Ventana *p106*
Bus **Geotur**, San Martín 193, T0291-491 5355, for minibus transport from Bahía (dropping you off at the entrance to the park for walking), organizing guided trekking, mountain biking and horseback excursions.

ℹ Directory

Mar del Plata *p105*
Banks *Casas de Cambio* **Jonestur**, San Martín 2574. **Amex**, at *Oti Internacional*, San Luis 1630, T494 5414. **La Moneta**, Rivadavia 2615.
Cultural centres Cultural events: reduced price tickets are often available from **Cartelera Baires**, Santa Fe 1844, local 33, or from **Galería de los Teatros**, Santa Fe 1751. **Asociación Argentina de Cultura Inglesa**, San Luis 2498, friendly, extensive library. **Internet** Broadband internet can be found everywhere.
Telephones Many *locutorios* around the town. **Useful addresses** Immigration Office: Rivadavia 3820, T492 4271, open morning.

Bahía Blanca *p106*
Banks Many ATMs on plaza for all major cards. *Casas de Cambio*: **Pullman**, San Martín 171. **Internet** Many places along Zelarrayan and Estomba near plaza. **Post offices** Moreno 34. **Telephones** Big *locutorio* at Alsina 108, also internet.

West of Buenos Aires

Rising out of the flat arid Pampa, the Sierras of Córdoba and San Luis give a dramatic setting to popular holiday towns and mountain retreats. Beyond the plains, fertile valleys stretch along the length of the Andean precordillera and climb up to the heights of Aconcagua and its neighbours. The western provinces of Mendoza, San Juan, La Rioja and Catamarca cover extreme contrasts, but Mendoza and the surrounding area to the south is popular for its excellent wines, climbing and superb ski and adventure resorts such as Malargüe.

Córdoba

→ *Phone code: 0351. Colour map 8, grid A3. Population: 1.4 million. Altitude: 440 m.*

Córdoba, the second city in the country, has some fine historic buildings and a lively university population. It is also an important route centre. Córdoba the city, capital of Córdoba Province, was founded in 1573. The site of the first university in the country, established in 1613 by the Jesuits, it now has two universities. It is an important industrial centre, the home of Argentina's motor industry, and a busy modern city with a flourishing shopping centre.

Ins and outs

Getting there Pajas Blancas airport, 13 km north of city, T475 0392, has shops, post office, a good restaurant and a *casa de cambio* (open Monday-Friday 1000-1500). The bus service (US$0.30) can be unreliable; a regular or *remise* taxi charges around US$3-5. Bus terminal at Blvd Perón 250, T434 1700. Left luggage lockers, US$0.65 per day, *remise* taxi desk, ATM, tourist office at the lower level, where the ticket offices are. Taxi US$0.65 to Plaza San Martín. Minibuses, *diferenciales*, have better services to the sierras and depart from nearby platform; tickets on bus or from offices at terminal, first floor.➤ *For further information, see Transport, page 114.*

Tourist offices Municipal tourist office in the old Cabildo, Deán Funes 15, T428 5856. Also at Centro Obispo Mercadillo (on plaza), Rosario de Santa Fe 39, T428 5600, or Patio Olmos Shopping Mall, Avenida San Juan y Vélez Sarsfield, T420 4100, as well as at the bus terminal and at the airport. All open early morning to late at night, with useful city maps and information on guided walks and cycle tours. The municipality runs good, daily city tours leaving from the Centro Obispo Mercadillo. For provincial tourist information T434 8260. See also the websites: www.cordobatrip.com and www.cordoba.net. Both in Spanish.

Sights

At the city's heart is **Plaza San Martín**, with a statue of the Liberator. On the west side is the old **Cabildo**① *Independencia 30, free, except for entry to exhibitions, 0900-2100 (Mon 1400-2100).* Built around two internal patios, the building now houses the tourist office, a small gallery, a restaurant and a bookshop. Next to it stands the **Cathedral**① *0800-1200, 1630- 2000,* the oldest in Argentina (begun 1640, consecrated 1671), with attractive stained glass windows and a richly-decorated ceiling. Look out for statues of angels resembling native Americans. Behind the cathedral is the pleasant **Plaza del Fundador**, with a statue to the city founder Jerónimo Luis de Cabrera. One of the features of this part of the city is its old churches. Near Plaza San Martín at Independencia 122 is the 16th-century **Carmelo Convent** and chapel of **Santa Teresa**, whose rooms and beautiful patio form the **Museo de Arte Religioso Juan de Tejeda** ① *Wed-Sat 0930-1230, US$0.35, guided visits also in English and French.* This houses one of the finest collections of religious art in the country. The **Manzana Jesuítica** ① *Tue-Sun 0900-1300, 1600-2000, US$1, T4332075, all guided visits (available in English) leave from Obispo Trejo 242, Tue-Sun 1000, 1100, 1700, 1800,* contained within Av Vélez Sarsfield, Caseros, Duarte Quirós and Obispo Trejo, has been declared a world heritage site by Unesco. **La Compañía** (Obispo Trejo y Caseros, built between 1640 and 1676) has a vaulted ceiling reminiscent of a ship's hull. Behind it, on Caseros, is the beautiful **Capilla Doméstica**, a private 17th century Jesuit chapel (guided visits only), next to which are two former Jesuit institutions, the main building of the **Universidad Nacional de Córdoba** and the **Colegio Nacional de Montserrat**. **La Merced** *25 de Mayo 83*, was built in the early 19th century, though its fine gilt wooden pulpit dates from the colonial period. On its exterior, overlooking Rivadavia, are fine murals in ceramic by local artist Armando Sica. Further east, at Blvd J D Perón, is the magnificent late 19th-century **Mitre railway station**, with its beautiful tiled *confitería*.

Museo Marqués de Sobremonte ① *Rosario de Santa Fe 218, 1 block east of San Martin, T4331661, Tue-Sat 1000-1600 (in summer Mon-Fri 0900-1500), US$0.35, texts in English and German*. Formerly the house of Rafael Núñez, governor of Córdoba, and now the only surviving colonial family residence in the city, the museum displays 18th and 19th provincial history. **Museo Municipal de Bellas Artes** ① *Av General Paz 33, T433 1512, Tue-Sun 0900-2100, US$0.35*. Has a permanent collection of contemporary art by celebrated Argentine artists in an early 20th-century mansion.

◉ Sleeping

Córdoba *p111, map p112*

AL NH Panorama, Alvear 251, T410 3900, www.nh-hoteles.com. Comfortable, functional, small pool, restaurant.
A Windsor, Buenos Aires 214, T422 4012, www.windsortower.com. Small, smart, warm, large breakfast.
B Cristal, Entre Ríos 58, T424 5000, www.hotel cristal.com.ar. Good, comfortable, a/c, large breakfast, excellent service.
B Heydi, Bv Illia 615, T421 8906, www.hotelheydi.com.ar. Good value, quiet, 3 star, pleasant rooms, breakfast included.
B Sussex, San Jerónimo 125, T422 9070, hotelsussex@arnet.com. A/c, with breakfast, well kept, small pool.

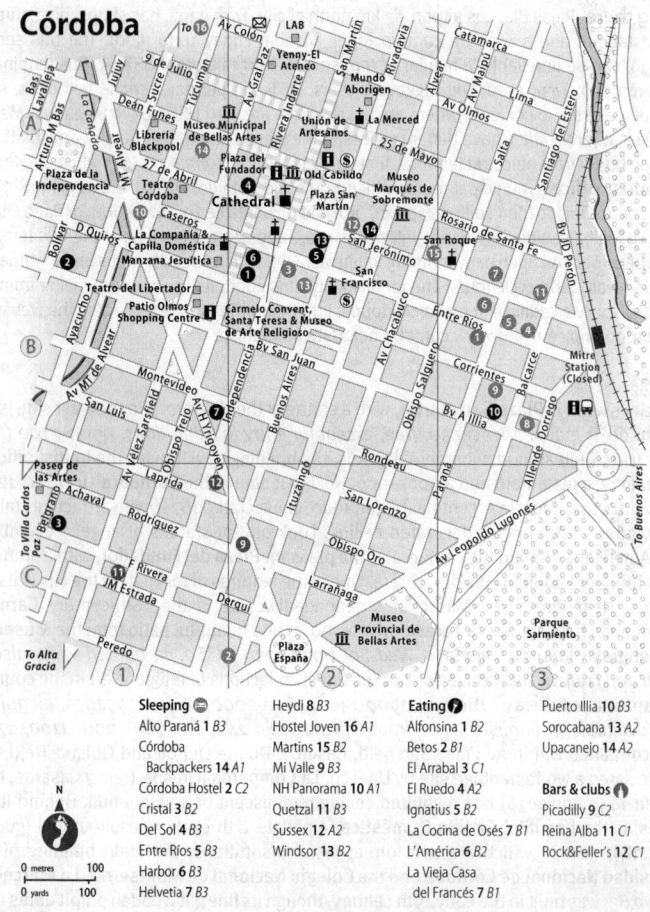

Córdoba

Sleeping ◉
Alto Paraná 1 *B3*
Córdoba
 Backpackers 14 *A1*
Córdoba Hostel 2 *C2*
Cristal 3 *B2*
Del Sol 4 *B3*
Entre Ríos 5 *B3*
Harbor 6 *B3*
Helvetia 7 *B3*

Heydi 8 *B3*
Hostel Joven 16 *A1*
Martins 15 *B2*
Mi Valle 9 *B3*
NH Panorama 10 *A1*
Quetzal 11 *B3*
Sussex 12 *A2*
Windsor 13 *B2*

Eating ❼
Alfonsina 1 *B2*
Betos 2 *B1*
El Arrabal 3 *C1*
El Ruedo 4 *A2*
Ignatius 5 *B2*
La Cocina de Osés 7 *B1*
L'América 6 *B2*
La Vieja Casa
 del Francés 7 *B1*

Puerto Illia 10 *B3*
Sorocabana 13 *A2*
Upacanejo 14 *A2*

Bars & clubs ❼
Picadilly 9 *C2*
Reina Alba 11 *C1*
Rock&Feller's 12 *C1*

N

0 metres   100
0 yards   100

C **Del Sol**, Balcarce 144, T423 3961.
Decent value, a/c and breakfast.
D **Alto Paraná**, Paraná 230, T428 1625,
hotelaltoparana@arnet.com.ar. Close to bus
terminal, hot shower, TV, breakfast, good value.
D **Córdoba Backpackers**, Deán Funes 285, T422
0593, www.cordobabackpackers.com.ar. Cheaper
with shared bath, new hostel, family atmosphere,
very helpful. Recommended.
D **Harbor**, Paraná 126, T421 7300. Cramped
rooms but very clean with welcoming staff.
D **Martins**, San Jerónimo 339, T421 2319,
martinshotel@yahoo.com.ar. Funny mix of styles,
plain rooms are OK, small bathrooms.
D **Quetzal**, San Jerónimo 579, T/F422 9106.
Refurbished, good value, breakfast extra.
E **Entre Ríos**, Entre Ríos 567, T/F423 0311. Basic,
welcoming, some rooms a/c, 1 room has wheelchair
accessbreakfast, 10% discount for ISIC members, .
E **Helvetia**, San Jerónimo 479, T421 7297.
Renovated rooms with fan, basic, nice patio.
E pp **Mi Valle**, Corrientes 586, 5 mins from the
bus terminal. Fan, small, nice, family-run.
F pp **Córdoba Hostel**, Ituzaingó 1070, T468
7359, www.cordobahostel.com.ar. In Nueva
Córdoba district, rather small but has decent
facilities for sleeping (**D** in double), cooking and
relaxing with private lockers in rooms and large
breakfasts. Small discount for HI members.
F pp **Hostel Joven**, Tablada 414. Kitchen,
internet, laundry, very good, helpful.

Estancias
Estancia Los Potreros, Casilla de correo 4, La
Cumbre, T452121, www.ride-americas.com. An
exclusive 6,000-acre working cattle farm in the
wild and scenic Cordoba hills. High standard
of accommodation, with personal attention
to detail more in keeping with a time past.
The "riders estancia"... unrivalled in its
fabulous horses.

❼ Eating

Córdoba *p111, map p112*
❦ **L'América**, Caseros 67, T4271734. Small
imaginative menu in designer restaurant, from
traditional to sushi to French, large selection of
wines, homemade bread, excellent service, also
cheap set menus.
❦ **Betos**, San Juan 450. Best *lomitos* in town,
parrilla. Recommended.
❦ **La Cocina de Osés**, Independencia 512. Nicely
decorated if rather formal, good for fish, meat
dishes and homemade pastas.
❦ **Novecento**, at the Cabildo. Smart and lively,
superb Mediterranean-style cooking, excellent
service. Lunch only, bar open 0800-2000.
❦ **Upacanejo**, San Jerónimo 171. Based on a
popular comic character (staff dressed accordingly),
parrilla serving excellent beef and chicken.
❦ **La Vieja Casa del Francés**, Independencia
508. Delicious grills, inviting atmosphere, French
owners. Recommended.
❦ **Alfonsina**, Duarte Quirós 66. Rural style in an
old house, simple meals or breakfasts with
homemade bread, also piano and guitar music
(play if you wish).

Cafés
El Ruedo, Obispo Trejo y 27 de Abril. A lively
confitería, also serving light meals.

Argentina Cordoba Listings

Ignatius, Buenos Aires y Entre Ríos. Tasty *facturas*, croissants and good music.
Puerto Illia, Bv Illia 555. By bus terminal, and open 24 hrs for breakfasts and simple meals – great if you arrive at night.
Sorocabana, Buenos Aires y San Jerónimo. Great cheap breakfasts, popular, good views on the Plaza.

❶ Bars and clubs

Cerro Las Rosas, Northwest of town, locally referred just as *Cerro*, has a lively area of bars and clubs (US$3.50 pp) along Av Rafael Núñez. **Arcimboldo**, No 4567. **Factory**, No 3964, popular club with electronic and Latin dance music. **Villa Agur**, José Roque Funes y Tristán Malbrán, is more rock and roll with food and live music.

Chateau Carreras, further northwest is another popular area. **Carreras**, on Av Ramón J Cárcano. The most popular club.

El Abasto district, on the river (about 8 blocks north of Plaza San Martín) has several good places for lower budgets: **Casa Babylon**, Bv Las Heras 48, very popular disco night Fri, rock Sat. **Dvino**, Pasaje Agustín Pérez 32 (behind Puente Alvear). Before 1900, taste wines. There are plenty of affordable options around Bv San Juan and Av Vélez Sarsfield, along La Cañada or south of Bv Illia at Nueva Córdoba district. **Reina Alba**, Obispo Trejo y F Rivera, is a redesigned old house open after dark with a chic bar. **Rita**, Independencia 1162, is a refurbished old house with a trendy clientele.

Student bars are along Rondeau between Av H Yrigoyen and Chacabuco. Less noisy are: **Rock&Feller's**, Av H Yrigoyen 320, bar and restaurant, and **Picadilly**, No 464, live jazz, blues and bossa nova after 2400. *Cuarteto* music, a Cordobés invention, is hugely popular.

❹ Entertainment

See free listings magazines *La Cova* and *Ocio en Córdoba*, local newspaper *La Voz del Interior*, and *www.cordoba.net*, for events.
Cinema Many cinemas including **Cineclub Municipal**, Bv Illia 49, **Teatro Córdoba**, 27 de Abril 275, both showing independent and foreign language films, and the new theatre in **Shopping Patio Olmos** (see below), with new releases.
Dance **Confitería Mitre**, Bv Perón 101 (in railway station), tango class before *milonga* (public place to dance) begins, US$1.30. The patio at the Cabildo on Fri has tango lessons and dance. **El Arrabal**, Belgrano y Fructuoso Rivera, restaurant with a tango show after 2400t, Fri and Sat, US$1.70 extra.
Theatre The Festival of Latinamerican Theatre is held every Oct. **Teatro del Libertador**, Av Vélez Sarsfield 367, T433 2312, is traditional and sumptuous, with a rich history.

⊙ Shopping

Bookshops Librería Blackpool, Deán Funes 395, for imported English books. **Yenny-El Ateneo**, Av Gral Paz 180. Has some English titles.
Handicrafts Mundo Aborigen, Rivadavia 155. **Paseo de las Artes**, Achával Rodríguez y La Cañada. Handicraft market, Sat-Sun 1600-2200 (in summer 1800-2300), ceramics, leather, wood and metalware. **Unión de Artesanos**, San Martín 42 (Galería San Martín, local 22).
Shopping malls Córdoba Shopping, José de Goyechea 2851 (Villa Cabrera). **Nuevocentro**, Av Duarte Quirós 1400. **Patio Olmos**, Av Vélez Sarsfield y Bv San Juan. Central.

⊖ Transport

Córdoba *p111, map p112*
Air AR/Austral run a daily shuttle service to/from **Buenos Aires**, about 1 hr. LAN also flies to Buenos Aires. Most major Argentine cities are served by AR, usually via BsAs. International flights to **Bolivia** (Santa Cruz), **Brazil** and **Chile** direct, others via BsAs.
Bus Municipal buses and electric buses (trolleys) do not accept cash. You have to buy tokens (*cospeles*) or cards from kiosks, normal US$0.30.

To **Buenos Aires**, several companies, 9-11 hrs, US$12 *común*, US$17 *coche cama*. To **Salta**, 12 hrs, US$12-14. To **Jujuy**, US$15, 12 hrs. To **Mendoza**, 10-12 hrs, frequent, US$10-12. To **La Rioja**, 6-7 hrs, US$7. To **Catamarca**, 5-7 hrs, US$7. To **San Luis**, Andesmar, Autotransportes San Juan-Mar del Plata, **TAC**, 7 hrs, US$6-8. **TAC** and **Andesmar** have connecting services to several destinations in **Patagonia**. See towns below for buses to the Sierras de Córdoba. To **Santiago** (Chile), US$20, 17-19 hrs, CATA, TAC. To **Bolivia** take Balut or Andesmar services to the border at La Quiaca (19 hrs, US$20) or Pocitos (17 hrs, US$20-23).

❶ Directory

Airline offices Aerolíneas Argentinas/ Austral, Colón 520, T410 7676. **LAB**, Colón 166, T421 6458. **LAN**, Figueroa Alcorta 206, T475 9555.
Banks Open in the morning. There are Link and Banelco ATMs at many locations. All ATMs take international credit cards. **Citibank**, Ituzaingó 238, changes Citicorp and Visa TCs (no commission). **Exprinter**, Rivadavia 47. Cash and Amex TCs (low commission). **Barujel**, Rivadavia y 25 de Mayo. Cash, Amex TCs (15% commission), Visa TCs; also Western Union branch. **Cultural centres** Asociación Argentina de Cultura Británica, Av H Yrigoyen 496, T468 1995. Good library with books, magazines, newspapers,

English teaching materials, videos and a small reading room, open Mon-Fri 0900-2000. **Consulates** Bolivia Av Rafael Núñez 3788, T481 7381. **Chile**, Crisol 280, T469 0432. **Internet** Many places charging US$0.35 per hr. **Language schools** ILEE, T4824829, www.ilee.com.ar. Spanish courses and accommodation arranged. **Medical services** Medical emergencies, T107. Hospital Córdoba, Av Patria 656, T434 9000. **Hospital Clínicas**, Santa Rosa 1564, T433 7010. **Post offices** Colón 210, parcel service on the ground floor beside the customs office. **Telephones** There are hundreds of *locutorios* throughout the city, many with a post office and internet access. **Useful addresses** Dirección Nacional de Migraciones, Caseros 676, T422 2740. **Police**, T101. **Fire department**, T100.

Around Córdoba

Sierras de Córdoba

The Sierras de Córdoba offer beautiful mountain landscapes with many rivers and streams, plus the advantage of good infrastructure and accessibility. Adventure tourism has really taken off here, so there's something for everyone in the hills and valleys. San Luis, too, has pleasant hills and is a good place to buy onyx. Popular for tourism among the upper classes in the late 19th century, the Sierras de Córdoba were opened up for mass tourism in the 1940's with the building of lots of hotels. The most visited sights lie along the valleys of **Punilla**, **Traslasierra** and **Calamuchita**, and on the east side of the **Sierra Chica**, north of Córdoba, all forming itineraries of about 70 km long each. There's a useful network of dirt roads (usually used for rally competitions!). Summer rainstorms may cause sudden floods along riversides. Beware when choosing a campsite.

Villa Carlos Paz In the Punilla Valley is this large modern town (*Phone code 03541, Population 56,000, Altitude 642 m*) on an artificial lake Lago San Roque, 36 km west of Córdoba. It is the nearest resort to Córdoba and is therefore often crowded. Trips on the lake are offered in all kinds of water-vehicles, from amphibious trucks to catamarans (stalls along Avenida San Martín, opposite bus station, US$3.30). A chair-lift runs from the Complejo Aerosilla to the summit of the Cerro de la Cruz, which offers splendid views (US$3.30). North of Villa Carlos Paz, on Ruta 38, a road branches west to Tanti from where local buses go to **Los Gigantes**, a paradise for climbers, two-day treks possible (entry US$1). Club Andino has several *refugios*; contact **Club Andino Córdoba** To351-480 5126. **Tourist information** ① *San Martín 400 and No 1000, To810-888 2729, open 0700-2100, www.sierrascordobesas.com.ar.*

Cosquín On the banks of the Río Cosquín, 26 km north of Villa Carlos Paz, Cosquín (*Phone code: 03541, Population 18,800, Altitude 708 m*) is the site of the most important **folklore festival**, in the last two weeks in January. A popular rock festival is held in early February so that accommodation is almost impossible to find between 10 January and 10 February. **Museo Camín Cosquín** ① *at Km 760, out of town, T451184, 0900-1230, 1400-1800 (closing later in summer), US$0.65.* Minerals, fossils and archaeology, recommended. Take a *remise* taxi from the town centre, US$5 (or walk two hours) to the **Pan de Azúcar** hill (1,260 m), from where there is a good view over the Punilla valley. Chairlift to top (all year round). **Tourist office** ① *Plaza Próspero Molino, T453701.*

La Falda (*Phone code: 03548, Population 15,000, Altitude 934 m*), 82 km north of Córdoba, is a good base for walking, if not an attractive town. Visit the **Trenshow** ① *Las Murallas 200, T423041, 0930-2000, US$2,* a model railway museum. **Camino de El Cuadrado** crosses the sierras eastward to Río Ceballos, passing an excellent vantage point at *Balcón de las Nubes* and the 18th-century *Estancia El Silencio*, 11 km of La Falda, where is a small museum and outdoor activities are organized. To the west, an 80-km rough winding road goes to La Higuera, across the Cumbres de Gaspar. It crosses the vast **Pampa de Olaén**, a 1,100-m high grass-covered plateau with the tiny, 18th-century chapel of **Santa Bárbara** (20 km of La Falda) and the **Cascadas de Olaén**, with three waterfalls, 2 km south of the chapel. **Tourist office** ① *Av España 50 (at the former railway station), T423007.*

North from Córdoba

Capilla del Monte About 106 km north of Córdoba and set in the heart of the Sierras, Capilla dell Monte (*Phone code 03458, Altitude 979 m*) is a good centre for trekking, paragliding and exploring this area. Excursions in the hills, particularly to Cerro Uritorco, 1,979 m, four hours via La Toma where there are medicinal waters and from where there are further walking opportunities (US$1.50). There is horse riding and tours to meditation and 'energy' centres: the location of many sightings of UFOs, the area is popular for 'mystical tourism'. **Tourist office**① *in the old railway station, open daily 0830-2030, some English spoken, T481903.*

Jesús María *(Colour map 8, grid A3. Population: 27,000. Altitude: 533 m. 51 km north of Córdoba on Ruta 9)* **Estancia de Jesús María** ① *T420126, Mon-Fri 0800-1900, Sat-Sun 1000-1200, 1400-1800 (1500-1900 in summer and spring), US$0.65, Mon free, easy 15-min walk from bus station: take Av Juan B Justo, north, turn left at Av Cleto Peña, cross bridge on river and follow a dirt road right about 300 m.* Dating from the 17th century, the estancia has the remains of its once famous winery; in the cloister is an excellent **Museo Jesuítico**, where Cuzco-style paintings, religious objects and a curious collection of plates are exhibited. **Estancia de Caroya**, ① *T426701, daily 0900-1300, 1400-1800 (1500-1900 in summer and spring), US$0.35, 20-min walk from bus station.* A rather more humble place in the southern suburbs, this estancia also dates from the 17th century; a large white building around a lovely patio, with a quaint stone chapel beside it. **Estancia de Santa Catalina** ①*T421600, Tue-Sun 1000-1800 (1100-1900 in summer), free, from the bus station, remise taxis charge US$8-10 return including 2 hrs stay.* Still in private hands, beautifully located in the countryside northwest of Jesús María, this is the largest of the *estancias* and has the most splendid buildings. Each January there is a gaucho and folklore festival, lasting 10 nights from second week; very popular. Some 4 km north of Jesús María is **Sinsacate**, a fine colonial posting inn, now a museum, with chapel attached.

At Rayo Cortado, 114 km north of Jesús María, a turning leads west to **Cerro Colorado**, 160 km north of Córdoba, the former home of the late Argentine folklore singer and composer Atahualpa Yupanqui. His house is a museum, ask in the village for the curator. There are about 35,000 rock paintings by the indigenous Comechingones in the nearby **Cerro Colorado** archaeological park ① *0800-1800, US$0.35, only with guide, 1-1½ hrs tour; there is a cheap hostería, T03522-422180, and campsite; an unpaved road, 12 km, branches off Ruta 9 at Santa Elena, 104 km north of Jesús María; getting there: Ciudad de Córdoba bus goes to/from Córdoba 3 times weekly, 4½ hrs, US$5,* and a small archaeological museum.

Southwest of Córdoba

A scenic road southwest from Villa Carlos Paz passes **Icho Cruz**, before climbing into the Sierra Grande and crossing the Pampa de Achala, a huge granite plateau at 2,000 m. At La Pampilla, 55 km from Villa Carlos Paz, is the entrance to the **Parque Nacional Quebrada del Condorito**, covering 40,000 ha of the Pampa de Achala and surrounding slopes. This is the easternmost habitat of the condor and an ideal flying school for the younger birds. Sightings are not guaranteed (Balcón Sur is a likely spot), but there's great trekking on the *pastizal de altura* (sierran grassland). Several camping places. Tours from Villa Carlos Paz. If you go with your own vehicle, park it at the NGO Fundación Cóndor (9 km before La Pampilla), beside a handicraft shop (1 km before La Pampilla) or at El Cóndor (7 km after La Pampilla). Ciudad de Córdoba and TAC buses both can stop at La Pampilla on their way to Mina Clavero (from Villa Carlos Paz: 1 hr, US$1.90). National Park administration at Sabattini 33, T433371, Villa Carlos Paz, www.carlospaz.gov.ar/pncondorito.

Mina Clavero This is a good centre, 40 km west of Córdoba, for exploring the high *sierra* and the Traslasierra Valley *(Phone code: 03544, Colour map 8, grid A3, Population: 6,800, Altitude: 915 m).* There is an intriguing museum, **Museo Rocsen**① *13 km south and about 5 km from the village of Nono, T498218, www.museorocsen.org; daily 0900 till sunset, US$1, getting there: taxi, US$1.30.* The personal collection of Sr Bouchón, it includes furniture, minerals, instruments, animals ('by far the best natural history and cultural museum, a whole day is needed to visit', Federico Kirbus). There are many hotels, *hosterías hospedajes,* campsites and restaurants around Mina Clavero; others at Cura Brochero and Nono. **Tourist office** (with ATM)① *Av San Martín y Av Mitre, T470171, mclavero.turismo@traslasierra.com, open 0900 till very late.*

South from Córdoba

Alta Gracia *(Phone code 03547, Colour map 8, grid A3, Population 42,600, Altitude 580 m).* Beside Lago Tajamar, Alta Gracia, 39 km southwest of Córdoba, has an interesting **Jesuit estancia** (a UNESCO World Heritage Site)① *T421303, Tue-Fri 0900-1300, 1500-1900, Sat, Sun 0930-1230, 1530-1830 (in summer Tue-Fri 0900-2000, Sat-Sun 0930-1230,*

1700-2000), US$0.65 (Wed free), frequent free guided visits in Spanish, also in English Tue-Sun 1000-1200, 1700-1900. The major buildings of the *estancia* are situated around the plaza. The church, completed in 1762, with a baroque façade but no tower, is open for services only. To the north of the church is the former Residence, built round a cloister and housing the **Museo del Virrey Liniers**. The **Museo Manuel de Falla**① *C Pellegrini 1100, 0900-1900, free,* is where the Spanish composer spent his last years. Beautiful views from the Gruta de la Virgen de Lourdes, 3 km west of town. Campsite at Alta Gracia; **tourist office** inside clock tower by Lago Tajamar, *T428128.*

The **Bosque Alegre and Observatory**① *21 km northwest, Fri-Sun 1000-1300, 1500-1800 (Tue-Sun, same times, in summer),* afford good views over Córdoba, Alta Gracia and the Sierra Grande. Che Guevara grew up in Alta Gracia after his parents left Rosario to live in the more refreshing environment in the foothills of the Andes. He had started to suffer from asthma, which would plague him for the rest of his life. See page 162. **Museo Casa de Ernesto Che Guevara**① *in Villa Nydia, Avellaneda 501, T428579, 0900-1850, US$0.65, from the Sierras Hotel, go north along C Vélez Sarsfield-Quintana and turn left on C Avellaneda, take bus 'Sarmiento'.* Che lived here between 1935-1937 and 1939-1943 before going to Córdoba: plenty of personal belongings from his childhood and youth, also the letter addressed to Fidel Castro where Che resigns from his position in Cuba. Texts in Spanish, but staff will translate into English, if asked.

Villa General Belgrano This completely German town (*Phone code 03546*) 85 km south of Córdoba, was founded by the surviving interned seamen from the *Graf Spee,* some of whom still live here. It is a good centre for excursions in the surrounding mountains. Genuine German cakes and smoked sausages are sold, there is an Oktoberfest, a *Fiesta de la Masa Vienesa* in Easter week, for lovers of pastries, and the *Fiesta del Chocolate Alpino* during July holidays. **Tourist office**① *Av Roca 168, T461215 (or free T125), www.elsitiodelavilla.com, 0800-2000;* climb its tower for panoramic views. Excursions can be made to **La Cumbrecita**, a charming German village 30 km west, from where Champaquí can be climbed (detailed map essential).

South of La Cumbrecita is **Villa Alpina**, a remote resort set in the forested upper valley of Río de los Reartes, 38 km west, along a poor gravel road. This is the best base for a two-day trek to the **Cerro Champaquí** (2,790 m), 19 km from the village, a rewarding hike not only for the superb mountainous scenery, but also for the chance to meet local inhabitants at the several *puestos* on the way to the summit. Expect to meet many other trekkers too in high season. Go with a local guide to avoid getting lost: information at Villa General Belgrano tourist office.

San Luis and the Sierras → *Phone code: 02652. Colour map 8, grid B2. Pop: 150,000.*

The provincial capital, founded by Martín de Loyola, the governor of Chile, in 1596, **San Luis** stands at the south end of the Punta de los Venados hills (*Altitude: 765 m. 791 km west of Buenos Aires, 412 km southwest of Córdoba*). The area is rich in minerals including onyx. Visit the **Centro Artesanal San Martín de Porras** ① *on Plaza Independencia, 0700-1300 excluding Sat and Sun.* Run by the Dominican fathers, rugs are woven here. **Tourist office** ① *Av Pres Illia y Junín, T423479, www.sanluis.gov.ar.*

Sierras de San Luis Northeast of the city are several ranges of hills, which are becoming more accessible with the building of paved roads. The western edge of the sierras can be visited by taking Ruta 9 northeast from San Luis via El Trapiche (bus from San Luis, US$4 return) to **Carolina**, where a disused goldmine can be seen. A statue of a gold miner overlooks the main plaza. Four-wheel drive vehicles can drive up Tomolasta mountain (2,000 m). From this road the Cuesta Larga descends to San Francisco del Monte de Oro, from where it is possible to follow Ruta 146 to Mina Clavero in Córdoba province.

The central part of the Sierras is best reached by Ruta 20 to **La Toma**, 70 km east of San Luís, the cheapest place to buy green onyx. North of La Toma a paved road runs as far as **Libertador General San Martín** (known as San Martín), 75 km, a good centre for exploring the rolling hills of the northern sierras.

Merlo (Phone code 02656, Altitude 700 m), almost at the San Luis-Córdoba border, is a small town on the western slopes of the Sierra de Comechingones. It enjoys a fresher climate than the pampas in summer, and the area is being promoted for its rich wildlife, particularly birds. There are many walks and excursions to *balnearios*, waterfalls and other attractions. Mountain biking, trekking, horse riding, fishing and jeep tours are all possible, run by agencies in town. **Tourist office**① *Mercau 605, T476079, www.merlo-online.com.ar.*

● Sleeping

Villa Carlos Paz *p115*
Plenty of hotels in all price categories, most with pools and parking.
B Florida, Belgrano 45, T421905, floridahotel@arnet.com.ar. Opposite bus station, 3 star, comfortable, a/c, with breakfast, pool.
C Los Sauces, Av San Martín 510, T421807, www.hotellossauces.com.ar. Another good value place next to the bus, good service, pool and restaurant, breakfast included, English spoken.
Camping ACA site, Av San Martín y Nahuel Huapi, T422132. Many others.

Cosquín *p115*
B (half board) **La Puerta del Sol**, Perón 820, T452045, lapuertadelsol@hotmail.com. Good reputation, a decent choice, pool, car hire.
D Siempreverde, Santa Fe 525 (behind Plaza Molina), T450093, siempreverdehosteria@hotmail.com. Spotless, with breakfast, welcoming and informative owner María Cristina, some rooms small, comfortable, gorgeous garden.
E Ale, Tucumán 809, T450232. Basic but clean, with bath, but no breakfast.
Camping Several campsites in the area.

La Falda *p115*
All 80 hotels are full in Dec-Feb.
C La Asturiana, Av Edén 835, T422923, hotellaasturiana@yahoo.com.ar. Simple, comfortable rooms, pool, superb breakfast.
C L'Hirondelle, Av Edén 861, T422825. Welcoming, large garden with pool, restaurant.
C Old Garden, Capital Federal 28, T422842. Central, quiet and homely, large pool, breakfast.
D El Colonial, 9 de Julio 491, T421831. Early 50s decor in the reception and dining room, large pool.
Camping Balneario 7 Cascadas, next to the dam and the seven falls (west of town), T425808. Hot showers, electricity, food shop, US$1.30 a day pp. *Remise* taxi charges US$1.70.

Capilla del Monte *p115*
C La Casona, Pueyrredón 774, T482679, silviadon48@hotmail.com. 19th century villa on a hill, surrounded by palm trees, pool, homemade meals, English spoken.
C Petit Sierras, Pueyrredón y Salta, T481667, petitsierras@capilladelmonte.com.ar. Renovated hotel with comfortable rooms. The owners run the restaurant *A Fuego Lento*, at the access of town (discounts and free transport for guests).
Camping F pp Calabalumba, 600 m north of the centre, T481903, municipal site, shady with pool, hot water, also *cabañas* for 4-6 people.

Alta Gracia *p116*
C Hispania, Vélez Sarsfield 57, T426555. Very comfortable, with breakfast, fine view of the sierras. Recommended.
Camping Los Sauces in Parque Federico Garcia Lorca, northwest of town, T420349.

Villa General Belgrano *p117*
C Alpino, Av Roca y 25 de Mayo, T461355. Decent rooms, cooking facilities, garden.
C Berna, Vélez Sarsfield 86, T/F461097, berna@tecomnet.com.ar. Next to the bus station, Swiss owners, good rooms with breakfast, large garden with pool (rates 50% higher in high season).
C La Posada de Akasha, Los Manantiales 60, T462440. Comfortable, pool, welcoming (low season rates).
F pp El Rincón, T461323, rincon@calamuchitanet.com.ar. The only hostel in town is beautifully set in dense forests and green clearings. Dormitories, double or single rooms with bath (US$4 pp) and camping (US$1.30 pp). US$1 extra for either bed linen or superb breakfasts. Meals for US$2.30 on request. 20% ISIC and HI discounts available, half price for children under 16. In high season rates are 25% higher and the hostel is usually full. 10 min-walk from terminal. Recommended.
Camping La Florida, Ruta 5, laflorida@calamuchitanet.com.ar. Open all year, US$2 pp, hot showers, pool, also *cabañas*, tours, restaurant, German owners.

La Cumbrecita
Has various hotels (**B-D**) and *hospedajes* in the **E** pp range.

San Luis *p117*
B Gran San Luis, Pres Illia 470, T425049, hotelsanluis@hotmail.com. With breakfast, restaurant (closed weekends), pool, parking.
C Aiello, PresIllia 431, T425609. With breakfast, a/c, spacious, garage, restaurant open weekdays. Recommended.
C Grand Palace, Rivadavia 657, T422059. With breakfast, parking, central, spacious, good lunches.
D Belgrano, Belgrano 1440, T435923. With breakfast, a good budget option, fan.
F pp San Luis Hostel, Falucho 646, T424188, www.sanluishostel.com.ar. The only hostel in town, dormitory accommodation, breakfast included.
Camping Rio Volcán, 4 km from town.

Sierras de San Luis *p117*

C pp **Hostería Las Verbenas**, 10 km south of Carolina, T02652-430918, www.las verbenas.com.ar. In the beautiful Pancata Valley, ideal place for exploring the area.

C **La Posta del Caminante**, Carolina, T02652-490223, www.lapostadelcaminante.com.ar. Comfortable, with breakfast, cheaper with shared bath, restaurant next door, trips to mines.

Libertador General San Martín *p117*

D **Hostería San Martín**, with bath and breakfast, meals served, good value.

Merlo *p117*

There are many hotels, *hosterías* and *residenciales* both in the town and nearby. Book in advance Jan-Feb, Easter, Jul-Aug and long weekends.

A **Villa de Merlo**, Pedernera y Av del Sol, T475335. Nice rooms, good views, quiet, relaxing, gardens with pool, sports facilities.

C **Colonial**, Av Dos Venados y P Tisera, T475388, hotelcolonial@hotmail.com. Good value, simple rooms, with breakfast, internet, quiet, central.

⊘ Eating

La Falda *p115*

† **El Cristal**, San Lorenzo 39. Very good cooking, where the locals eat.

† **Pachamama**, Av Edén 127. Health food shop with cheap organic vegetable pies, or wholemeal pizzas and *empanadas*.

Alta Gracia *p116*

†† **Hispania**, Urquiza 90. Same owners as *Hotel Hispania*, an excellent and moderately priced place serving fish and seafood.

†† **Morena**, Av Sarmiento 413. Good food in nice old house.

San Luis *p117*

†† **Rotisería La Porteña**, Junín y Gral Paz. Good food, enjoyable atmosphere.

††-† **Los Robles**, Colón 684. Parrilla with good food, wide choice, formal. Recommended.

† **Crocantes**, San Martín 630. Excellent bakery with good choice of sandwiches.

† **La Pulpería del Arriero**, 9 de Julio 753. Regional specialities with live folk music in the evening. Also has good value set menus.

▲ Activities and tours

La Falda *p115*

Mountain biking **Club Edén 201**, Av Edén 201, US$3.50 per day for hire.

Paragliding The tourist office has a list of instructors; US$23 per jump with instructor.

Tour operators

Turismo Talampaya, T470412 or 15630384, turismotalampaya@yahoo.com.ar. 4WD full-day trips to the Pampa de Olaén and Jesuit Estancia La Candelaria for US$15 pp.

VH, T424831 or 15562740, vhcabalgatas@ hotmail.com. Horse rides to nearby hills US$5/hr.

⊖ Transport

Villa Carlos Paz *p115*

Bus Villa Carlos Paz is a transport hub and there are frequent buses to **Buenos Aires** and other main destinations, as well as to the towns in the Punilla and Traslasierra valleys. To the **Calamuchita Valley** the only option is **Sarmiento** bus to Alta Gracia, 1 hr, US$0.85, several daily. To/from **Córdoba**, Ciudad de Córdoba, also Car-Cor and El Serra minibus services, 45 mins, US$0.80.

Cosquín *p115*

Bus La Calera, TAC and Ciudad de Córdoba run frequently along the Punilla valley and to Córdoba.

La Falda *p115*

Bus To **Córdoba** from La Falda US$1.70-2, **La Calera** and Ciudad de Córdoba, also minibuses. Daily buses to **Buenos Aires**.

Capilla del Monte *p115*

Bus To **Córdoba**, 3 hrs, US$3; to **Buenos Aires**, many companies daily.

Mina Clavero *p116*

Bus To **Córdoba**, US$4-6 depending on route 3-6 hrs; to **Buenos Aires**, TAC, US$17, 12 hrs; to **Mendoza**, 9 hrs, US$11.

Alta Gracia *p116*

Bus To **Córdoba**, US$0.70, every 15 mins, 1 hr.

Villa General Belgrano *p117*

Bus To/from **Córdoba**, 1½-2 hrs, US$3. To **Buenos Aires**, 11-12 hrs, US$16. To **La Cumbrecita** with Pájaro Blanco, Av San Martín 105, T461709, every 2-4 hrs, 1 hr 20 mins, US$5.50 return.

San Luis *p117*

Bus Terminal at Vía España 990 between San Martín y Rivadavia. To **Buenos Aires**, US$15-20. To **Mendoza**, US$6, 3-4 hrs.

Merlo *p117*

Bus Terminal 3 blocks from plaza. Frequent services to **San Luis**, 3 hrs, US$3; to **Buenos Aires**, TAC, Sierras Cordobesas and Chevallier, US$15-18, 10-12 hrs; to Córdoba, TAC, 5 hrs, US$6.

Mendoza and around

→ *Phone code: 0261. Colour map 8, grid B2. Population: city 148,000. Altitude: 756 m.*

At the foot of the Andes, Mendoza is a dynamic and attractive city, surrounded by vineyards and *bodegas*. The city was colonized from Chile in 1561 and it played an important role in gaining independence from Spain when the Liberator José de San Martín set out to cross the Andes from here, to help in the liberation of Chile. Mendoza was completely destroyed by fire and earthquake in 1861, so today it is essentially a modern city of low buildings and wide avenues (as a precaution against earthquakes), thickly planted with trees and gardens.

Ins and outs

Information Main **tourist office** ① *San Martín, opposite Peatonal Sarmiento, T420 1333*, very helpful, English and French spoken. At airport, *T448 0017*; at bus station, *T431 3001*. Provincial office ① *San Martín 1143, T420-2800*. All open 0900-2100. Very helpful office at the entrance to Parque San Martín ① *open Mon-Fri 0800-1300, 1600-2000, Sat 0900-1300*. All hand out maps and accommodation lists, with economical apartments for short lets, private lodgings in high season, also lists of bodegas and advice on buses. Aconcagua information and permits. Useful websites include: www.turismo.mendoza.gov.ar, www.mendoza.gov.ar.

Sights

In the centre of the city is the **Plaza Independencia**, in the middle of which is the small **Museo Municipal de Arte Moderno** and on the east side, leafy streets lined with cafés. Among the other pleasant squares nearby is the **Plaza España**, attractively tiled and with a mural illustrating the epic gaucho poem, *Martín Fierro*. **Plaza Pellegrini** (Avenida Alem y Av San Juan) is a beautiful small square where wedding photos are taken on Friday and Saturday nights, and a small antiques market.

On the west side of the city is the great **Parque San Martín** ① *0900-0200 daily, the entrance is 10 blocks west of the Plaza Independencia, reached by bus 110 'Zoo' from the centre, or the trolley from Sarmiento y 9 de Julio.* It is beautifully designed, with a famous zoo, many areas for sports and picnics, and a large lake, where regattas are held. There is also a good restaurant. The **Museo de Ciencias Naturales** ① *T428 7666, Tue-Sun 0830-1300, Tue-Fri 1400-1900, weekends 1500-1900*, has an ancient female mummy among its fossils and stuffed animals. There are views of the Andes rising in a blue-black perpendicular wall, topped off in winter with dazzling snow, into a china-blue sky. On a hill above the park is the **Cerro de la Gloria**, crowned by an astonishing monument to San Martín, with bas-reliefs depicting various episodes in the equipping of the Army of the Andes and the actual crossing. An hourly bus ('Oro Negro') runs to the top of the Cerro de la Gloria from the information office at the entrance, US$1 – it's a long walk (45 minutes).

Mendoza's interesting history can be traced through two good museums: **Museo del Pasado Cuyano** ① *Montevideo 544, T4236031, Mon-Fri 0900-1230, US$0.50*, housed in a beautiful 1873 mansion, with lots of San Martín memorabilia and an exquisite Spanish 15th-century carved altarpiece. Also recommended is **Museo del Area Fundacional** ① *Alberdi y Videla Castillo, T425 6927, Tue-Sat 0800-2000, Sun 1500-2000 US$0.50, children under 6 free, getting there: buses 10, 60, 80, 110.* It contains displays of the city pre-earthquake, with original foundations revealed, and the ruins of Jesuit church **San Francisco** opposite. The small **Acuario Municipal** (aquarium) ① *underground at Buenos Aires e Ituzaingó, daily 0900-1230, 1500-2030, US$0.50*, is fun for kids.

In the nearby suburb of Luján de Cuyo, there's a small collection of Argentine paintings in the house where Fernando Fader painted decorative murals, at the **Museo Provincial de Bellas Artes, Casa de Fader** ① *Carril San Martín 3671, Mayor Drummond, T496 0224, Tue-Fri 0900-1800, Sat-Sun 1400-1830. US$0.50, getting there: bus 200, 40 mins, in the gardens are sculptures.*

Many bodegas welcome visitors and offer tastings without pressure to buy (grape harvesting season March/April). If you've only time for one, make it **Bodega La Rural (San Felipe)** ① *at Montecaseros 2625, Coquimbito, Maipú, T497 2013, US$0.30, Tours Mon-Sat 1000-1630, Sun 1000-1300, getting there: bus 170 (subnumber 173) from La Rioja y Garibaldi.* Small, traditional with a marvellous **Museo del Vino**. (In Maipú itself, 15 km south of Mendoza, see the lovely plaza and eat good simple food at the Club Social.) Beautiful **Bodegas Escorihuela** ① *tours Mon-Fri 0930, 1030, 1130, 1230, 1430, 1530, T4242744, getting there: bus 'T' G Cruz from centre 9 de Julio, Godoy Cruz, or bus 170 subnumbers 174, 200, from Rioja, or 40 from the Plaza,* has an excellent restaurant run by renowned Francis Mallman. **Norton** ① *Ruta 15, Km 23.5, Perdriel, Luján, T488 0480, tours on the hour 0900-1200, 1400-1700, getting there: bus 380 from the terminal.* It has excellent tastings. **Pequeña Bodega** ① *Ugarte 978, La Puntilla, Luján de Cuyo, T439 2094, Mon-Fri 0900-1300, 1600-2000, getting there: take bus 10 (Ugarte) on 25 de Mayo.* The winery has a small museum. **Chandon** ① *further south on RN40, Km 29, T4909966, call for information on tour times, getting there: bus Mitre (no 380) from the terminal, platform 53 /54.* An impressive modern bodega, which makes famous wines. Finally, **Nieto Senetiner** ① *Guardia Vieja s/n, Vistalaba, T498 0315, tours Mon-Fri 1000-1600, Sat 0930-1100.* It offers wines, lunch (reserve ahead) and some accommodation. Ask agencies for tours to micro-bodegas, which usually include three wineries, such as *Domaine San Diego*, *Cabrini* and *Dolium*, with a choice of tasting, explanations and extras like local olives and walnuts.

A few other recommended trips are to the pretty village of **Cacheuta**, 29 km west, with thermal springs, to **Potrerillos**, **Puenta del Inca** and **Los Penintentes** (see Mendoza to Chile below) and to **Villavicencio**, 47 km north, good walks and a restaurant in the mountains.

Mendoza

Sleeping
Campo Base 1 *B1*
Carollo 2 *B1*
Churrasqueras del
Parque 3 *A1*
Crillon 4 *B1*
Damajuana 5 *C1*
Dam-sire 6 *B3*
Gran Hotel Balbi 8 *A1*

Gran Hotel
Mendoza 9 *B2*
Gran Hotel Ritz 10 *B1*
Hostel Internacional
Mendoza 11 *C2*
Imperial 12 *A2*
Monterrey 14 *A2*
Necochea 15 *A1*
Nutibara 16 *B1*
Palace 17 *A2*
Park Hyatt 18 *B1*
RJ Hotel del Sol 19 *A2*
San Remo 20 *B1*
Savigliano Hostel 7 *B3*

Winca's Hostel 13 *B1*

Eating
Aranjuez 1 *B2*
Boccaduro 2 *A1*
De un Rincón
de la Boca 3 *A1*
Don Otto 4 *A2*
Estancia la
Florencia 5 *B1*
Facundo 6 *B1*
La Chacra 7 *B2*
La Naturata 8 *C2*
Las Tinajas 17 *B2*

Mambrú 9 *A1*
Marchigiana 10 *A2*
Mesón Español 11 *C2*
Montecatini 12 *A1*
Mr Dog 13 *A2*
Nuevo Mundo 14 *B2*
Soppelsa 18 *A2*
Sr Cheff 15 *B2*

Bars & clubs
Vía Civit 16 *B1*

121

◑ Sleeping

Mendoza and around *p120, map p121*
Breakfast is included, unless specified otherwise. Larger hotels all have car parking.

L Park Hyatt, Chile 1124 on main plaza, T441 1234, www.mendoza.park.hyatt.com. Elegant, very comfortable, affordable (if expensive) restaurant, *Bistro M*, imaginative menu, pool, spa and casino.

A Nutibara, Mitre 867, T429 5428. Welcoming, eclectic decor if a bit outdated, pool in a leafy patio, comfortable rooms, quiet, central. Recommended.

B Gran Hotel Balbi, Las Heras 340, T423 3500, F438 0626. Splendid entrance, spacious rooms, small pool and terrace.

B Gran Hotel Mendoza, España 1210 y Espejo, T425 2000, www.hotelmendoza.com. Spacious rooms, stylish decor, central, family rooms too.

C Carollo, 25 de Mayo 1184, T423 5666. Slightly old-fashioned but hospitable, this hotel shares its pool and facilities with *Gran Princess* next door.

C Crillon, Perú 1065, T429 5161, F423 9658. Good modernized rooms, pool, warm welcome, slightly overpriced.

C Gran Hotel Ritz, Perú 1008, T423 5115, aristo@infovia.com.ar. Very comfortable, reliable, central but quiet location, excellent service. Highly recommended.

C Palace, Las Heras 70, T/F423 4200. A lovely quiet place, modern rooms, good value.

D Hostel Internacional Mendoza, España 343, T424 0018, www.hostelmendoza.net. The most comfortable hostel, HI discount, short walk south of the plaza, small rooms with bath, warm atmosphere, great food, huge range of excursions. Warmly recommended.

D Monterrey, Patricias Mendocinas 1532, T438 0901, hoteles@ciudad.com.ar. Great value, stylish, spacious, nice modern rooms.

D Necochea, Necochea 541, T425 3501. Pleasant, cheerful, very reasonable and central, free internet.

D RJ Hotel Del Sol, Las Heras 212, T438 0218. Comfortable rooms, central. Highly recommended.

D Winca's Hostel, Sarmiento 717, T425 3804, www.wincashostel.com.ar. Nice, big rooms, **F** per bed, central, garden, internet, Spanish lessons, safe, pool.

D-F Savigliano Hostel, Pedro Palacios 944, T423 7746, www.savigliano.com.ar. Rooms with bath, without (**E**) and dorms (**F**), kitchen, opposite bus station, internet, kitchen facilities, washing machine, luggage stored, helpful, tours arranged. AHC Argentina Hostels Club.

E Campo Base, Mitre 946, T429 0707, www.campo-base.com.ar. A livelier place, cramped rooms, but lots of parties and barbecues.

E Dam-sire, Viamonte 410, San José Guaymallén, T431 5142, 5 mins from terminal. Family run, spotless.

E pp Damajuana, Arístides Villanueva 282, T425 5858, www.damajuanahostel.com.ar. A great hostel, very comfortable stylish dorms also double rooms (**C**), central, pool in lovely garden.

E Imperial, Las Heras 88, T15-414 4680. Old fashioned, plain, comfortable and quiet rooms, good value.

E Lagares Hostel, Corrientes 213, T/F423 4727. Includes breakfast, free internet 24 hrs, laundry. AHC member. Recommended.

E San Remo, Godoy Cruz 477, T423 4068. Quiet, small rooms, TV, rooftop terrace, secure parking. Recommended.

Camping Camping Suizo, Av Champagnat, 9½ km from city, T444 1991, US$2 pp, modern, shady, with pool, barbecues, hot showers. Recommended. **Churrasqueras del Parque** in centre of Parque General San Martin, at Bajada del Cerro, T452 6016, 155-123124. There are 2 other sites at El Challao, 6 km west of the city centre, reached by Bus 110 (El Challao) leaving hourly from C Rioja. **Saucelandia**, at Guaymallén, 9 km east, Tirasso s/n, T451 1409. Take insect repellent.

❼ Eating

Mendoza and around *p120, map p121*
There are many open-air cafés for lunch on Peatonal Sarmiento and restaurants around Las Heras. The atmospheric indoor market on Las Heras has cheap, delicious pizza, *parrilla* and pasta. Open late.

♩♩ **Boccaduro**, Mitre 1976. *Parrilla*, popular.

♩♩ **La Chacra**, Sarmiento 55. Good set menu lunches, traditional *Mendocino* steaks.

♩♩ **Sr Cheff**, Primitivo de la Reta 1071. Long-established, good *parrilla* and fish.

♩♩ **Estancia La Florencia**, Sarmiento 698. Excellent modern *parrilla*.

♩♩ **Facundo**, Sarmiento 641. Good modern *parrilla*, good salad bar.

♩♩ **Marchigiana**, Av España 1619, T423 0751. Deservedly popular, wonderful Italian food in traditional style, charming service. Recommended.

♩♩ **Mesón Español**, Montevideo 244. Spanish food, live music at weekends. Cheap lunch menus.

♩♩ **Montecatini**, Gral Paz 370. Good Italian food and *parrilla*, more tourist oriented.

♩ **De un Rincón de la Boca**, Las Heras 485. Cheerful *pizzería* with a good range.

♩ **Don Otto**, Las Heras 242. Cheap and cheerful.

♩ **La Naturata**, Plaza Pellegrini. Delicious vegetarian food, cheap *tenedor libre*. Highly recommended.

♩ **Mambrú**, Las Heras 554 y Chile. Excellent busy *tenedor libre*.

♩ **Nuevo Mundo**, Lavalle 126. Chinese, Italian, *parrilla*, good *tenedor libre*.

¶ **Las Tinajas**, Lavalle 38, T429 1174,
www.lastinajas.net. Excellent buffet including a
wide range of salads, meats, Chinese dishes, fish,
seafood and many different desserts.

Calle Arístides Villanueva, the extension of Colón
heading west, has excellent restaurants and bars.
¶¶ **Azafrán**, Arístides Villanueva 287. Wine lover's
heaven, excellent *bodegas*, superb *picadas*.
¶¶ **Mal de Amores**, Arístides Villanueva 303.
Imaginative Mediterranean food, warm and
stylish atmosphere. Highly recommended.
¶¶ **Por Acá**, Arístides Villanueva 557. Cosy
bohemian living room for pizzas and drinks till late.
¶ **3 90 (Tres con Noventa)**, Arístides Villanueva
451. Delicious pastas, incredibly cheap, warm
cosy atmosphere. Highly recommended.
¶ **Guevar**, Arístides Villanueva y Huarpes. Eggs
with everything, a fun atmosphere.
¶ **Nativa**, Arístides Villanueva 650. Huge sandwiches.
Aranjuez, Lavalle y San Martín. Nice café, good
meeting place.
Mr Dog, popular fastfood chain, better than most.
Soppelsa, Las Heras y España. Ice cream.
Recommended.

ⓝ Bars and clubs

Mendoza and around *p120, map p121*
Blues Bar, Arístides Villanueva 687, popular,
reservations for eating T429 0240.
Soul Café, San Juan 456, T432 0828. Popular pub
with jazz, lambada, blues, theatre performances.
Vía Civit, Emilio Civit 277. Superb stylish café on
the way to Parque San Martín, exquisite pastries.

⊛ Festivals and events

Mendoza and around *p120, map p121*
The riotous wine harvesting festival, **Fiesta de la
Vendimia**, is held in the amphitheatre of the
Parque San Martín **1st weekend in Mar**. Hotels fill
up fast and prices rise; also in Jul (the ski season)
and around **21 Sep** (the spring festival).

Ⓞ Shopping

Mendoza and around *p120, map p121*
Handicrafts The main shopping area is along
San Martín and Las Heras, with good clothes,
souvenir, leather and handicraft shops. **Mercado
Artesanal**, San Martín 1133, 0830-1930 daily, for
traditional leather, baskets, weaving; also weekend
market on Plaza Independencia. Cheap shops
include: **El Turista**, Las Heras 351, and **Las Viñas**,
Las Heras 399. For higher quality head to **Raices**,
España 1092, just off Peatonal Sarmiento. Good
choice of wines at **Vinoteca**, Alem 97, T4203924.
Supermarkets Super Vea, San Martín y
Santiago del Estero, **Metro**, Colón 324.

▲▲ Activities and tours

Mendoza and around *p120, map p121*
Bike rental Piré, Las Heras 615, T425 7699,
US$4 per day. Also at **Campo Base**, see Youth
hostels above.
Climbing Information from tourist office.
Aconcagua permits from the Cuba building,
Parque San Martín (aconcagua@
mendoza.gov.ar), in summer, and directly from
the park itself at Horcones, Puente del Inca, in
winter. **Club Andinista**, F L Beltrán 357, Gillén,
T431 9870. See also page 126 for Aconcagua.
Whitewater rafting Popular on the Río
Mendoza; ask agencies for details.

Tour operators
Many agencies, especially on Paseo Sarmiento, run
trekking, riding and rafting expeditions, as well as
traditional tours to Alta Montaña and bodegas.
Asatej, San Martín 1360 (at back of shopping
arcade), T429 0029, mendoza@asatej.com.ar.
Very helpful, trips, cheap travel deals.
Biketours, T155 583413, biketour@
mendoza.com.ar. Bike tours to wine and olive-oil
producers, US$25 includes lunch.
Campo Base youth hostel (see above) runs good
expeditions, and has a helpful website in English:
www.cerroaconcagua.com. Expert guide Roger
Cangiani leads trips and gives advice on permits.
Casa Orviz, Juan B Justo 536, T425 1281,
www.orviz.com. Guides, mules, transport and hire
of mountain trekking equipment for Aconcagua.
Huentata, Las Heras 699, loc 7, T425 7444,
www.huentata.com.ar. Conventional tours, plus
Villavicencio, Cañon del Atuel, horse riding,
Aconcagua. Recommended.
Inca Expedición, Juan B Justo 343, Ciudad 5500,
T429 8494, www.aconcagua.org.ar. Climbing
expeditions, including Aconcagua.
Mendoza Viajes Peatonal Sarmiento 129, T438
0480. Comfortable coaches, professional, cheap.
Postales del Plata, Tabanera s/n, Colonia Las
Rosas, Tunayán (some 80 km south of Mendoza),
T02622-490024, www.postalesdelplata.com.
Specializes in wine tours in Mendoza and Chile,
cultural tours, fly fishing, has its own very good
lodges at Chacras de Coria and Valle de Uco.

⊖ Transport

Mendoza and around *p120, map p121*
Air El Plumerillo airport, 8 km north of centre,
T430 7837, has a bank, tourist information, shops,
restaurant and *locutorio*, but no left luggage.
Reached from the centre by bus No 60 (subnumber
68) from Alem y Salta, every hour at 35 mins past
the hour, 40 mins journey; make sure there is an
'Aeropuerto' sign on the front window.

Taxi to/from centre US$5. To **Buenos Aires**: 1 hr 50 mins, AR only. LAN to **Santiago**, daily. **Bus** Most local services have 2 numbers, a general number and a 'subnumber' in brackets which indicates the specific route. Buses within and near the city are cheaper with prepaid card which go into a machine on the bus, sold in shops, the bus terminal and **Mendobus** ticket offices everywhere. US$0.30 two trips, US$1.75 ten. There are 2 trolley bus routes, red and blue, US$0.25.

Long distance The huge bus terminal is on the east side of Av Videla, 15 mins' walk from centre (go via Av Alem, which has pedestrian tunnel), with shops, post office, *locutorio*, tourist information and supermarket (open till 2130), a good café, left luggage lockers and toilets (between platforms 38 and 39). It's not a place to linger at night. To **Buenos Aires**, 15 hrs, US$19-27, many companies including Andesmar, La Estrella, Sendas (*coche-cama* with meals and wine). To **Bariloche**, Andesmar daily, US$17, 22 hrs, book well ahead (alternatively go to Neuquén and change). To **Córdoba**, 11hrs, US$10. To **San Rafael**, many daily 3½ hrs, US$4. To/from **San Juan**, Andesmar, and others, US$5, 2 hrs. To **Tucumán**, US$12, Andesmar, Autotransportes Mendoza, TAC, all via San Juan, **La Rioja** (US$10-12), 10 hrs, and **Catamarca** 12 hrs, US$9-13. To **Salta**, Andesmar, América (via San Juan, La Rioja and Catamarca), 20 hrs, US$29-38. To **Uspallata**, 5 a day with Expreso Uspallata, US$4, 2¼ hrs. To **Potrerillos**, 1 hr, US$1.30.

Transport to Santiago, Chile Minibuses (US$10, 6 hrs) run by Chi-Ar and Nevada daily leave when they have 10 passengers. When booking, ensure that the receipt states that you will be picked up and dropped at your hotel; if not you will be dropped at the bus station. Buses to Santiago daily, 10 companies, **Chile Bus, Cata, Tur Bus** and **Tas Choapa** have been recommended, **Ahumada** has a *coche cama* at 0845. Most buses are comfortable, 6½-8 hrs, US$8, those with a/c and hostess service (includes breakfast) charge more, worth it when crossing the border as waiting time can be several hours. These companies also daily to **Viña del Mar** and **Valparaíso**, US$10. Information at Mendoza bus terminal: shop around. Book at least 1 day ahead. Passport required, tourist cards given on bus. The ride is spectacular. If you want to return, it's cheaper to buy an undated return ticket Santiago-Mendoza.

Other International buses To **La Serena**, **Covalle, Cata** and others. To **Lima**, 3-4 a week, **El Rápido**, and **Ormeño**, T431 4913, 56 hrs, US$34.

◑ Directory

Mendoza and around *p120, map p121*
Airline offices Aerolíneas Argentinas/ Austral, Peatonal Sarmiento 82, T420 4100. **Varig**, Av España 1002 y Rivadavia, T423 1000. **LAN**, Rivadavia 135, T425 7900. **Banks** Many ATMs along San Martín taking all cards. Many *casas de cambio* along San Martín, including Santiago, San Martín 1199, T420 0277, **Maguitur**, San Martín 1203, T423 3202. Most open till 2000 Mon-Fri, and some open Sat morning. **Car hire** See Essentials, page 43 for international agencies' websites. **Avis** is reliable and efficient. **Dollar** De la Reta 936, T429 9939. **Herbst** at the airport, T4482327. **Cultural centres** Alianza Francesa, Chile 1754. Instituto Dante Alighieri (Italy), Espejo 638. Instituto Cultural Argentino- Norteamericano, Chile 985. Instituto Cuyano de Cultura Hispánica (Spain), Villanueva 389. Goethe Institut, Morón 265, Mon-Fri, 0800-1200, 1600-2230, German newspapers, Spanish classes, very good.
Internet Several internet cafés in the centre and a number of *locutorios*: a huge one on San Martín y Garibaldi, with internet. **Medical facilities** Central hospital near bus terminal at Alem y Salta, T420 0600. Lagomaggiore, public general hospital (with good reputation) at Timoteo Gordillo s/n, T425 9700. Hospital Materno y Infantil Humberto Notti, Bandera de los Andes 2683, T445 0045. Medical emergencies T428 0000.
Useful addresses ACA, Avenida San Martín 985, T420 2900, and Avenida Bandera de los Andes y Gdor Videla, T431 3510. **Migraciones**, San Martín 1859, T424 3512.

South of Mendoza

San Rafael → *Phone code: 02627. Colour map 8, grid B2. Population: 107,000.*
San Rafael, 236 km south of Mendoza, is a tranquil, leafy small town in the heart of fertile land which is irrigated by snow melt from the Andes to produce fine wines and fruit. A road runs west over El Pehuenche pass to Talca (Chile). Several bodegas can be visited: the impressive champagnerie at **Bianchi** ⓘ *T422 046 informes@vbianchi.com*. Some 5 km west on Hpólito Yrigoyen, is the more intimate **Jean Rivier** ⓘ *H Yrigoyen 2385, T432675, bodega@jrivier.com*. Excellent wine. A small but interesting **natural history museum** ⓘ *Tue-Sun 0800-2000, free; Iselin bus along Av JA Balloffet*, is 6 km southeast of town at Isla Río Diamante. **Tourist office** ⓘ *Av H Yrigoyen y Balloffet, T437860, www.sanrafael.gov.ar, www.sanrafael-tour.com.*

Southwest of San Rafael is the **Cañon de Atuel**, a spectacular gorge 20 km long with strange polychrome rock formations. It is famous as a rafting centre. Daily buses, *Iselin*, go to the Valle Grande dam at the near end of the canyon, returning in the evening, US$2. Here there is plenty of accommodation, campsites, river rafting and horse riding. San Rafael tour operators run all-day tours. **Raffeish** ① *T436996, www.raffeish.com.ar*. Recommended as most professional rafting company. There is no public transport through the gorge to El Nihuel.

Las Leñas → *Altitude: 2,250 m. Season: mid-Jun to end-Oct. www.laslenas.com.*

At 182 km southwest of San Rafael, RN40 heads west into the Andes, and from it the road to the famous, chic and internationally renowned ski resort of Las Leñas. It passes **Los Molles**, at Km 30, where there is simple accommodation: Further along the Las Leñas road is the **Pozo de las Animas**, two natural pits filled with water where the wind makes a ghostly wail, hence the name (Well of the Spirits). At the end of Valle Los Molles is Las Leñas, in a spectacular setting with excellent skiing over 7 km on 41 pistes, with a maximum drop of 1,200 m. Beyond Las Leñas the road continues into Valle Hermoso, accessible December-March only.

Malargüe → *Phone code: 02627. Colour map 8, grid B2. Population: 8,600.*

Further south on Ruta 40, Malargüe is developing as a centre for hiking and horse riding in stunning open landscape nearby. Most remarkable, the **La Payunia** reserve, 208 km south, has vast grasslands and stark volcanoes where thousands of guanacos roam, best enjoyed on horseback. The **Laguna Llancanelo**, 75 km southeast, is filled with a great variety of birdlife in spring, when Chilean flamingoes come to nest. In addition, **Caverna de las Brujas** has extraordinary underground cave formations. Helpful **tourist office** on the main street (right hand side as you drive in from north), next to conference centre, *T471659 (open 0800-2300)*.

● Sleeping

San Rafael *p124*
Lots of appealing small hotels.
B Kalton, Yrigoyen 120, T430047, kalton@satlink.com. Charming, long-established, excellent service, comfortable, parking. Highly recommended.
E Tierrasoles Hostel, Alsina 245, T433449, www.tierrasoles.com.ar. HI member.
Camping Isla Río Diamante park, 15 km southeast.

Los Molles *p125*
B Hotel Termas Lahuen-Có, T499700. The best, dating from 1930's with thermal baths, meals.

Las Leñas *p125*
There are several plush hotels, **L** (phone number for all, T471100) and a disco, shop renting equipment and several restaurant. For cheaper accommodation stay in Los Molles or Malargüe.

Malargüe *p125*
Hotels issue 50% discount voucher for Las Leñas lift pass. Accommodation is generally not of a high standard, with some very poor *cabañas*.
A Río Grande, Ruta 40 Norte, T471589, hotelriogrande@slatinos.com.ar. The best, with some smart comfortable 'VIP' rooms.
C Hotel del Turismo, San Martín 224, T/F471042. Drab rooms, but good cheap

restaurant, *Puli Huén*. There's an impressive conference centre with an attractive bar.
C-E La Posta, San Martín 646, T472079. Welcoming wood-lined place with cramped rooms, also has *parrilla* at Roca 374.

▲ Activities and tours

Malargüe *p125*
The tourist office can arrange indepedent visits Llancanelo and La Payunia. Good tours with **Karen Travel**, San Martín 54, T470342, www.karentravel.com.ar. Horse riding, Cueva de las Brujas, palaeontological site Manqui Malal.

◉ Transport

San Rafael *p124*
Bus To **Mendoza**, US$4; **Neuquén**, US$10, 9 hrs.

Las Leñas *p125*
Bus From **San Rafael**, US$3.75, *colectivo* US$12.

Malargüe *p125*
Air Weekly flights **Buenos Aires** to Malargüe airport, more charter flights in the skiing season.
Bus Daily from Mendoza with TAC, minibuses with Transporte Viento Sur, both 4 hrs, U$7. Several a day from **San Rafael**. Daily buses in ski season to **Las Leñas**.

Mendoza to Chile

The route to Chile is sometimes blocked by snow in winter: if travelling by car in June-October enquire about road conditions from *ACA* in Mendoza (T431 3510). Driving without snow chains and a shovel is prohibited between Uspallata and the border, but this can be resolved in a friendly way with border police. *ACA* and Chilean Automobile Club sell, but do not rent, chains.

Potrerillos and Uspallata → *Phone code: 02624. Colour map 8, grid A1.*

Ruta 7 is the only route for motorists to the Chilean border, via **Potrerillos** and **Uspallata**. Leave the city south by Avenida J Vicente Zapata, Access Ruta 7, leading to Ruta 40. Follow signs to Potrerillos, Uspallata and Chile. From Mendoza to the Chilean border is 204 km. The construction of a dam has forced a detour around **Cacheuta**, though it's worth a side trip for its relaxing hot springs, and very comfortable hotel (see below).

Potrerillos is a pretty village for horse riding, walking and rafting. In summer you can hike from Potrerillos to Vallecitos over two days, passing from desert steppe to scenic peaks. **Vallecitos** (season July-September) is a tiny ski resort 21 km from Potrerillos (see below) along a winding *ripio* road. It has a basic ski-lodge, ski school and snack bar. www.skivallecitos.com. **Refugio San Bernado** *T154-183857*, cosy place run by mountain guides. **Los Penitentes** is a much better ski resort, 165 km west of Mendoza, on the road to Chile, named after its majestic mass of pinnacled rocks, looking like a horde of cowled monks. Good skiing on 28 pistes, very reasonably priced, with few people on slopes. For **Puente del Inca** see below.

Another recommended stopping point is the picturesque village of **Uspallata**, 52 km from Potrerillos. From here you can explore the mysterious Las Bóvedas (5 km on RN39 north) built by the Huarpe Indians under the Jesuits to melt silver, where there is a small, interesting museum. The RN39 leads north to Barreal and Calingasta (see page 129), unpaved for its first part, rough and tricky when the snow melts and floods it in summer. The tourist office in Uspallata keeps unreliable hours. There are two food shops, bakeries, a post office and a Shell station with motel, restaurant, shop and *locutorio* open 0900-2200.

Puente del Inca → *Colour map 8, grid B2. Altitude: 2,718 m.*

The road that leads from Uspallata to cross the border to Chile is one of the most dramatic in Argentina, climbing through a gorge of richly coloured rock. Surrounded by mountains of great grandeur, Puente del Inca, 72 km west of Uspallata, is a good base for trekking or exploring on horseback. The natural bridge after which the place is named is one of the wonders of South America. Bright ochre yellow, it crosses the Río Mendoza at a height of 19 m, has a span of 21 m, and is 27 m wide, and seems to have been formed by sulphur-bearing hot springs. Watch your footing on the steps; extremely slippery. There are hot thermal baths at the river just under the bridge, a bit dilapidated, but decent temperature (the guard may charge to enter). Horse treks go to Los Penitentes. Los Horcones, the Argentine customs post, is 1 km east: from here you can visit the green lake of Laguna los Horcones: follow signs to Parque Provincial Aconcagua, 2 km, where there is a Ranger station, excellent views of Aconcagua, especially morning; free camping, open climbing season only. From here a trail continues to the Plaza de Mulas base camp.

Aconcagua → *Colour map 8, grid B1. Altitude: 6,959 m.*

West of Puente del Inca on the right, there is a good view of Aconcagua, the highest peak in the Americas, sharply silhouetted against the blue sky. In 1985, a complete Inca mummy was discovered at 5,300 m on the mountain. The best time for climbing Aconcagua is from end-December to February. For camping, trekking or climbing it is first necessary to obtain a **permit**: These vary in price for high, mid or low season, and depending on the number of days. In high season (15 December to 31 January), a permit to climb Aconcagua (lasting 21 days) costs US$200, for short trekking US$20. Permits must be bought, in person only, in summer (15 November to 15 March) at **Dirección de Recursos Naturales Renovables** ① *The Cuba Building, Av Los Robles y Rotonda de Rosedal, in the Parque San Martín in Mendoza, T425 2090, Mon-Fri 0800-1800, weekends and holidays 0900-1300*. In winter permits are bought directly from the *guardería* at Laguna Horcones, at the entrance to PN Aconcagua.

There are two access routes: Río Horcones and Río Vacas, which lead to the two main base camps, Plaza de Mulas and Plaza Argentina respectively. Río Horcones starts a few kilometres from Puente del Inca, at the Horcones ranger station. About 80% of climbers use this route. From here you can go to Plaza de Mulas (4,370 m) for the North Face, or Plaza Francia (4,200 m) for the South Face. The intermediate camp for either is Confluencia (3,300 m), four hours from Horcones. Río Vacas is the access for those wishing to climb the Polish Glacier. The Plaza Argentina base camp (200 m) is three hours from Horcones and the intermediate camps are Pampa de Leñas and Casa de Piedra. From Puente del Inca, mules are available (list at the **Dirección de Recursos Naturales Renovables**① *Parque Gral San Martín, Mendoza*, about US$80-100 per day for 60 kg of gear). This only takes you to Plaza de Mulas, near which is the highest hotel in the world (see below) and an accident prevention and medical assistance service (climbing season only); crowded in summer. The same service is offered at Plaza Argentina in high season. Climbers should make use of this service to check for early symptoms of mountain sickness and oedema. Take a tent able to withstand 100 mph/160 kph winds, and clothing and sleeping gear for temperatures below -40° C. Allow at least one week for acclimatization at lower altitudes before attempting the summit (four days from Plaza de Mulas). Hotel *Plaza de Mulas*, **AL** pp full board, **C** without meals, good food, information, medical treatment, recommended, also camping area; closed in winter.

In Mendoza you can book *refugio* reservations and programmes which include trekking, or climbing to the summit, with all equipment and accommodation or camping included (see Tour operators, above). Try to agree all contract terms in advance, such as the number of members of a group, so that they aren't changed before your expedition leaves. Treks and climbs are also organized by the famous climber **Sr Fernando Grajales**① *Moreno 898, 5500 Mendoza, T493830, expediciones@grajales.net (or T421 4330 and ask for Eduardo Ibarra at Hotel Plaza de Mulas for further information)*, and by **Roger Cangiani** of Campo Base (see Mendoza Activities and tours). Near the Cementerio is **Los Puquios** T461-317603, camping, mules, guides. Further information from **Dirección de Recursos Naturales Renovables** *(see also under Mendoza, www.mendoza.gov.ar)*.

Border with Chile

The road to the Chilean border, fully paved, goes through the 3.2-km Cristo Redentor toll road tunnel to Chile (open 24 hours; US$1 for cars, cyclists are not allowed to ride through, ask the officials to help you get a lift). The last settlement before the tunnel is tiny forlorn **Las Cuevas**, 16 km from Puente del Inca, with no accommodation but a basic café and a *kiosko*. In summer you can take the old road over La Cumbre pass to the statue of El Cristo Redentor (Christ the Redeemer), an 8-m statue erected jointly by Chile and Argentina in 1904 to celebrate the settlement of their boundary dispute. Take an all day excursion from Mendoza, drive in a 4WD, after snow has melted, or walk from Las Cuevas (4½ hours up, two hours down – only to be attempted by the fit, in good weather). **Expreso Uspallata** runs buses to Mendoza.

The Chilean border is beyond Las Cuevas, but all Argentine entry and exit formalities for cars and buses are dealt with at the Argentine customs post, Ingeniero Roque Carranza at Laguna Los Horcones, near Las Cuevas. Customs are open 0730-2300. Car drivers can undertake all formalities in advance at *migraciones* in Mendoza, or Uspallata while refuelling. You can hitchhike, or possibly bargain with bus drivers for a seat, from Los Horcones to Santiago, but if you are dropped at the entrance to the tunnel, you cannot walk through. Customs officers may help to arrange a lift through to Chile.

● Sleeping

Los Penitentes *p126*
A Ayelén, in middle of village, T420299. Convenient but overpriced, poor restaurant.
B Hostería Penitentes, Villa Los Penitentes T155-090432, penitentehosteria@hotmail.com. Cheery place near slopes, good café, cheaper for several nights. Recommended.
E pp Hostel Refugio Penitentes, T0261-429 0707, www.cerroaconcagua.com. Welcoming, warm and popular. Also Aconcagua services.

Cacheuta *p126*
B Termas Cacheuta, Ruta 82, Km 38, www.termascacheuta.com. **A** at weekends, warm and inviting rustic-style rooms, lovely spa for day visits too. Recommended.

Potrerillos *p126*
B Gran Hotel Potrerillos, Ruta Nacional 7, Km 50, T02624-482010. With breakfast, faded resort hotel, nice location, pool.
Camping There is also the excellent ACA campsite, T482013, well shaded, with pool, clean.

Uspallata *p126*

A Valle Andino, Ruta 7, T420033. Modern airy place with good rooms, pool and restaurant, breakfast included.

B Hotel Uspallata, on RN 7 towards Chile, T420 066. Lovely location, spacious modernized place in big gardens away from the centre with pool, good value, comfortable rooms, cheap restaurant.

C Los Cóndores, T420002. Great value, bright rooms, restaurant, set menus. Recommended.

D Viena, Las Heras 240, T420046. Small family-run place, in need of refurbishment, breakfast.

Camping Very basic municipal site, US$2 per tent, hot water but dirty showers and toilets, poor.

Puente del Inca *p126*

B Hostería Puente del Inca, RN7, Km 175, T420266. Doubles and rooms for 4-8, huge cosy dining room, advice on Aconcagua, helpful owners, great atmosphere, warmly recommended.

E pp Hostel La Vieja Estación, 100 m off the road, next to the Puente, T0261-155 631664. Basic but cheery hostel, cheap meals provided, kitchen.

F Refugio de Montaña, small dormitories in the army barracks, helpful.

Camping Possible next to the church (but windy), also at Lago Horcones inside the park.

❶ Eating

San Rafael *p124*

❚❚ **La Fusta**, Yrigoyen 538. A good value *parrilla*.

Uspallata *p126*

❚ **Bodega del Gato**, in the centre. Good *parrilla*.

❚ **La Estancia de Elias**, Km 1146. Opposite Shell station, good food.

❚ **Pub Tibet**, at the crossroads. Bar with photos from *Seven Years in Tibet*, shot here.

▲ Activities and tours

Potrerillos *p126*

Argentina Rafting, T02624-155 691700, www.argentinarafting.com. Organizes good trips with kayaking and other adventure sports.

Desnivel Turismo Aventura, Galería Comercial local 7, T420275, desnivelturismoaventura@ yahoo.com.ar. Offers rafting, riding, mountain biking, trekking, climbing, skiing.

❂ Transport

Puente del Inca *p126*

Bus Expreso Uspallata from Mendoza for **Uspallata** and **Puente del Inca**, US$4, 3½ hrs, 2 a day in the morning, returning from Puente del Inca in the afternoon. Uspallata-Puente del Inca US$1.50. Local buses also go on from Puente del Inca to **Las Cuevas**, Expreso Uspallata, US$4 return (**Note**: take passport). You can go to **Chile** from Puente del Inca with Tur Bus at 1000 and 1400, US$10, but be sure to ask for an international ticket.

San Juan and around

→ *Phone code: 02646. Colour map 8, grid A2. Population: 122,000. Altitude: 650 m.*

San Juan, 177 km north of Mendoza, was founded in 1562 and is capital of its namesake province. Nearly destroyed by a 1944 earthquake, the modern centre is well laid-out, but lacks Mendoza's charm and sophistication. **Tourist office** ⓘ *Sarmiento Sur 24 y San Martín, T422 2431, www.ischigualasto.com, Mon-Fri, 0730-2030, Sat-Sun 0900-2000 (in theory).*

Sights

You're most likely to visit on the way to the national parks further north, but there are some *bodegas* worth visiting. One of the country's largest wine producers, *Bodegas Bragagnolo*, is on the outskirts of town at Ruta 40 y Avenida Benavídez, Chimbas (bus 20 from terminal; guided tours daily 0830-1330, 1530-1930, not Sunday). The most interesting of the museums is **Museo de Ciencias Naturales** ⓘ *Predio Ferial, Av España y Maipú, Mon-Fri 0900-1400, US$0.50.* It includes fossils from Ischigualasto Provincial Park (see below). **Museo Casa Natal de Sarmiento** ⓘ *Sarmiento Sur 21, Tue-Fri and Sun 0830-1330, 1500-2000, Mon and Sat 0830-1330, US$1, free Sun.* This is the birthplace of Domingo Sarmiento (President of the Republic, 1868-1874). **Museo Histórico Celda de San Martín** ⓘ *Laprida 57 Este, Mon-Sat 0900-1400, US$1,* includes the restored cloisters and two cells of the Convent of Santo Domingo. San Martín slept in one of these cells on his way to lead the crossing of the Andes.

The **Museo Arqueológico** of the University of San Juan ⓘ *La Laja, 20 km north, daily 0930-1700, US$2, getting there: bus 20 from San Juan, 2 a day: take the first (at 0830) to give time to return,* contains an outstanding collection of prehispanic indigenous artefacts, including several well-preserved mummies. Inexpensive thermal baths nearby. **Vallecito**, 64 km east, has a famous shrine to the **Difunta Correa**, Argentina's most loved pagan saint whose infant, according to legend, survived at her breast even after the mother's death from thirst in the desert. At roadsides everywhere you'll see mounds of plastic bottles left as offerings to ask for safe journeys, and during Holy Week 100,000 pilgrims visit the site. See the remarkable collection of personal items left in tribute in several elaborate shrines, including number plates from all over the world: photographs, stuffed animals, tea sets, hair (in plaits), plastic flowers, trophies, tennis rackets and guitars. There are cafés, toilets and souvenir stalls.

West of San Juan → *Phone code: 02648.*

Calingasta, 135 km west of San Juan, is an idyllic, secluded village in a green valley with stunning striped rocks (cider festival in April). Ruta 12 west from San Juan along the canyon of the Río San Juan has been closed by work on two dams, so to reach Calingasta you go north of San Juan to Talacasto, then take the paved Quebrada de las Burras road to Pachaco, where a bridge crosses the Río San Juan. After the bridge, police control traffic to and from Calingasta for 12 km, alternating one-way traffic on the road. Cyclists should note that there is no shade on these roads, fill up with water at every opportunity. Conslut the police before cycling from Calingasta to San Juan. **Tourist information** ⓘ *Municipalidad, Lavalle y Sarmiento, T421066.*

Barreal, 40 km south of Calingasta on the road to Uspallata, is a tranquil place between the Andes and the precordillera, with great horse riding in the mountains, trekking to Cerro Mercedaria, and wind-car racing. Tourist information, *T02648-441066.* At **El Leoncito** (2,348 m), 26 km from Barreal there are two observatories (US$3, no public transport; tours can be arranged from San Juan, or at *Hotel Barreal*) and a nature reserve with a semi-arid environment and interesting wildlife, ranger post at entrance, no facilities.

North of San Juan

Ruta 40, the principal tourist route on the east Andean slope, heads north toward Cafayate and Salta, via San José de Jachal. At Talacasto, 55 km from San Juan, Ruta 436 branches toward Las Flores (Km 180) and the Chilean border at Agua Negra pass (4,600 m; January-April, immigration, customs and ACA at Los Flores). **San José de Jachal**, 99 km north of Talacasto is a wine and olive-growing centre with many adobe buildings. From here, the undulating Ruta 40, paved but for the first 25 km to the La Rioja border, crosses dozens of dry watercourses. It continues to Villa Unión (see below), paved but for the last 15 km. The town has hotels, a campsite behind the ACA station and places to eat. Expreso Argentino bus from San Juan at 0730 arrives at 0940.

San Juan

Sleeping ◐	Capayán 4	Eating ◑	Las Leñas 3
Alkázar 1	Jardín Petit 5	Amistad 1	Listo El Pollo 4
Alkristal 2	La Toja 6	Club Sirio	Soychú 6
América 3	Nogaró 7	Libanés 'El Palito' 2	

Ischigualasto and Talampaya parks → *Phone code: 02646. Colour map 8, grid A2.*

Ruta 141 runs across the south of the province towards La Rioja province and Córdoba. Just after Marayes (133 km), paved Ruta 510 (poor in parts) goes north 135 km to **San Agustín del Valle Fértil**, the best base for exploring Ischigualasto. **Tourist information** on plaza, *T420104*.

North of San Agustín, at a police checkpoint, 56 km by paved road, a side road goes northwest for 17 km to the 62,000 ha **Parque Provincial Ischigualasto** (a UNESCO World Heritage Site), also known as **Valle de la Luna** for its bizarre sculptural desert landforms. Here the skeletons of the oldest known dinosaurs have been found (230 million years), though you'll have to visit the museum at San Juan to see their bones and fossils (US$2). **Tours and access** There is one tour route, lasting 2½ hours, visiting part of the park but encompassing the most interesting sites. You have to go with a ranger in your own vehicle and it can be crowded at holiday times. Tours from San Juan, US$20 (including breakfast, lunch and tour), 14 hours; from San Agustín US$10 for a guide (in both towns, ask at tourist office). Taxi to park US$7 from San Agustín (recommended if there are 4-5 people), more expensive out of season. You can camp opposite the ranger station, which has a small museum, but bring all food and water; expensive confitería next to ranger station. See also Activities and tours page 131.

Just beyond the police checkpoint, near Los Baldecitos, paved Ruta 150 heads east to Patquía and then to La Rioja or Chilecito. From the junction provincial Ruta 76 heads north to Villa Unión. 61 km north of Los Baldecitos a paved road goes 14 km east to the 215,000-ha **Parque Nacional Talampaya** ① *T03825-470397, 0800-1700 (summer), 0900-1700 (rest of year), US$2 for Argentines, US$4 for foreigners*, another collection of spectacular desert landforms and a UNESCO World Heritage Site. The park occupies the site of an ancient lake, where sediments have been eroded by water and wind for some 200 million years, forming a dramatic landscape of pale red hills. Numerous fossils have been found and some 600 year-old petroglyphs can be seen not far from the access to the gorge. Along the *cañón* of the Río Talapmapya, extraordinary structures have been given popular names such as 'the balconies', 'the lift', 'the crib' or 'the owl'. At one point, the gorge narrows to 80 m and rises to 143 m. A refreshing leafy spot in the centre of the gorge, 'the botanical garden', has amazing diverse plants and trees. The end of the *cañón* is marked by the imposing cliffs of 'the cathedral' and the curious 'king on a camel'. 'The chessboard' and 'the monk', 53 m high, lie not far beyond the gorge, marking the end of the so-called **Circuito El Monje**. Only accessible with 4WD vehicles, **Circuito Los Cajones** continues in the same direction up to '*los pizarrones*', an enormous wall of rock, covered with petroglyphs, and then to '*los cajones*', a narrow pass between rock walls. **Circuito Ciudad Perdida** is another possible excursion in the park, southeast of the gorge, accessible only with 4WD vehicles, leading to an area of high cliffs and a large number of breathtaking rock formations. **Tours and access** Tour operators from La Rioja and Chilecito sometimes combine a visit with nearby Ischigualasto, otherwise access is difficult (check that entrance and guide's fee are included). Independent access is possible, since buses or combis linking La Rioja and Villa Unión stop at the park entrance (a long walk to the *administración*), or better, at Pagancillo (village 30 km north), since most of the park wardens live there and will offer free transfer to the park early the following morning (contact Adolfo Páez). Excursions arranged at the *administración*: guided walks (five hours, US$5 pp); guided bike rides (2½ hours, US$4 pp, cycle and helmet provided). Vehicle guided visits (prices are for the whole group of up to eight people) for Circuito El Monje (1½ hours, US$20), Circuito Los Cajones (three hours, US$40) and Circuito Ciudad Perdida (six hours, US$50); access with own 4WD vehicle is allowed with a guide (US$5, US$10 or US$13 per vehicle for respective itineraries). Best time to visit is in the morning, for best natural light and avoiding strong afternoon winds. *Administración* has small restaurant, toilets, public telephones.

● Sleeping

San Juan *p128, map p129*
A-C hotels all include breakfast and parking.
A Alkázar, Laprida 82 Este, T421 4965, www.alkazarhotel.com.ar. Comfortable rooms, pool and gym, well run, central, good restaurant.
A América, 9 de Julio 1052 Oeste, T421 4514, www.hotel-america.com.ar. Modern, very comfortable, good service, tours arranged.

B Alkristal, Av de Circunvalacíon 1055 Sur, T425 4145, alkristal@alkazarhotel.com.ar. Very comfortable, well equipped rooms, modern, on outskirts, poor breakfast, but otherwise recommended, good value.
B Nogaró, de la Roza 132 Este, T422 7501/5, hotel@nogarosanjuan.com.ar. Big, central business hotel, pool, good restaurant.

C **Capayán**, Mitre 31 Este, T421 4222, hcapayan@
infovia.com.ar. Next to cinema on plaza,
welcoming, comfortable, good service, restaurant.
C **Jardín Petit**, 25 de Mayo 345 Este, T421 1825.
Stylish entrance and plain rooms, but warm
welcome. Recommended.
D **La Toja**, Rivadavia 494 Este, T422 2584. Simple
spartan rooms, but decent enough.
E **Triásico Hostel**, Pedro Echagüe 520 (Este),
Rawson, T4219528. AHC member.
Camping At Chimbas, 7 km north. Also **El
Paraíso**, 8 km out on C 6, US$1.85 pp, pool,
beautiful site, tennis, noisy at weekends.

Calingasta *p129*
C **La Capilla**, T421033, includes breakfast, basic
but very clean, family-run, the family also sells the
El Triunfo bus tickets, and has the only public
telephone in the village.
D **Hotel de Campo Calingasta**, T421220,
restored old colonial-style building, pool, lovely
views, very tranquil.

Barreal *p129*
B **Posada de Campo La Querencia**,
T0264-1543 64699. With breakfast, attentive
owners Adela Santarelli and Carlos Lázzaro,
relaxing, lots of adventure opportunities.
B **Posada San Eduardo**, Av San Martín s/n.
A charming colonial-style house, rooms around
a courtyard, pleasant and relaxing.
C **Hotel Turismo Barreal**, San Martín s/n,
T441090, hotelbarreal@yahoo.com.ar. Nicely
refurbished 1940s hotel, spartan rooms, and some
hostel space, good restaurant, pool, riding.
Camping Municipal site, T441241, is shady and
well maintained with pool, open all year.

San Agustín del Valle Fértil *p130*
B **Hostería Valle Fértil**, Rivadavia s/n, T420015,
www.alkazarhotel.com.ar. Good, a/c, smart, very
comfortable, with fine views, also has *cabañas*
and good restaurant.
   Hospedajes and family lodging includes:
E pp **Ischigualasto**, Mitre y Aberstein, T420146.
With bath and fan.
E pp **Los Olivos**, Santa Fe y Tucumán, T420115.
Excellent value, with restaurant.
Camping **La Majadita**, lovely campsite on
river, with hot showers and great views.
Municipal campsite by Dique San Agustin.

Parque Nacional Talampaya *p130*
F **Hotel Pagancillo**, Pagancillo,
T03825-156 66828. Shared bath,
breakfast, comfortable.
Camping Basic site next to *administración*,
US$1 pp.

❼ Eating

San Juan *p128, map p129*
❢❢ **Las Leñas**, San Martín 1670 Oeste. Huge
atmospheric and popular *parrilla*.
❢❢ **Remolacha**, Rivadavia y San Martín. Stylish,
warm atmosphere, superb Italian-inspired menu,
delicious steaks and pastas. Recommended.
❢❢ **Soychú**, de la Roza 223 Oeste. Excellent
vegetarian food. Highly recommended.
❢❢-❢ **Club Sirio Libanés 'El Palito'**, Entre Ríos 33
Sur. Pleasant decor, good tasty food, excellent
buffet. Recommended.
❢ **Amistad**, Rivadavia 47 Oeste. Chinese, good
value, lots of choice.
❢ **Listo El Pollo**, Av San Martín y Santiago del
Estero. Very good, reasonably cheap.
Also many *pizzerías, confiterías*, and cafés.

❻ Shopping

San Juan *p128, map p129*
San Juan is known for its fine bedspreads,
blankets, saddle cloths and other items made
from sheep, llama and guanaco wool, fine
leather, wooden plates and mortars and, of
course, its wines. **Mercado Artesanal**, España y
San Luis. Worth a visit. **Vinoteca San Juan**, Av
San Martín 2154 Oeste. Good selection of wines,
champagnes and olives.

▲▲ Activities and tours

San Juan *p128, map p129*
Nerja Tours, Entre Ríos 178 Sur, T421 5214,
www.nerja-tours.com.ar. Also good for local trips
and adventure tourism.
Turismo Vittorio, Sarmiento 174 Sur, T420 4000,
www.turismo-vittorio.com.ar. Conventional and
adventure tours, 4WD trips and car hire.

Barreal *p129*
Sr Ramón Luis Ossa, he can be reached at
Cabañas Doña Pipa, Mariano Moreno s/n,
T441004, ossaexpediciones@infovia.com.ar. For
mountain expeditions, he runs mule treks into
the Andes, crossing the foothills in summer, from
10 to 21 days between Nov and Apr; the
attractive *cabañas* sleep 6-8, well-equipped,
breakfast included, open all year, pool, great
views. Recommended.

❷ Transport

San Juan *p128, map p129*
Air Chacritas Airport, 14 km southeast. From
Buenos Aires with AR/Austral (Av San Martín
215 Oeste, T0810-2228 6527, or 425 0487),
also to Mendoza.

Bus Terminal at Estados Unidos y Santa Fe, 9 blocks east of centre (buses 33 and 35 go through the centre). T422 1604. To **La Rioja**, 6 hrs, US$6.50-8, 4 companies. **Catamarca**, 4 companies, US$11. **Tucumán**, 5 companies, US$12. **Córdoba**, Socasa, 20 de Julio, Autotransportes San Juan (T422 1870), 9 hrs, US$8 *coche cama*. **Buenos Aires**, 11 hrs, US$20 *semi cama*, US$30 *coche cama*). To **San Agustín** with Vallecito, 3 a day, US$5. Hourly departures to and from **Mendoza**, fares above. Also services to **Barreal** and **Calingasta** with El Triunfo, T421 4532.

Barreal *p129*
Bus From San Juan daily at 1900, **El Triunfo**, 5 hrs, US$4. Returning to San Juan at 2100. Also minibus run by José Luis Sosa, T441095, and car run by Silvio, T0264 (San Juan)-425 2370/3489.

San Agustín del Valle Fértil *p130*
Bus Empresa Mendoza from Mendoza arrives 0200, better go from San Juan, **Vallecito**, 0700, 1900, 4 hrs, a/c, US$5.

☾ Directory

San Juan *p128, map p129*
Banks Banks open 0700-1200. Many *Banelco* and *Link* ATMs accepting international credit cards in centre. **Cambio Santiago**, Gen Acha 52 Sur, T421 2332, weekdays until 2100, Sat until 1300.
Internet Several *locutorios* have internet, those at Rivadavia y Acha, on the plaza, and Mendoza 139 Sur are open on Sun. Also **Cyber Café**, Rivadavia 12 Este. **Interredes**, Laprida 362 Este. **IAC**, Acha 142 Norte. **Useful addresses** ACA, 9 de Julio y Rawson, T421 4205, helpful.

La Rioja and Catamarca

La Rioja → *Phone code: 03822. Colour map 8, grid A2. Population: 147,000.*
Founded 1591, at the edge of the plains, with views of Sierra de Velasco, La Rioja can be oppressively hot from November to March. But the town comes alive after the daily siesta and during the annual carnival, *Chaya* (in February), and the *Tinkunaco* festival (beginning on New Year's Eve and lasting four days). The city's main buildings and plazas date from the late 19th century, while the recent government of Carlos Menem, born in a little town 90 km north, has left a certain affluence. The **Church and Convent of San Francisco** ☾ *25 de Mayo y Bazán y Bustos, Tue-Sun 0900-1200, 1830- 2100, free,* contains the Niño Alcalde, a remarkable image of the infant Jesus. You can also see the cell (*celda*) in which San Francisco Solano lived and the orange tree, now dead, which he planted in 1592 (25 de Mayo 218). San Francisco helped to bring peace between the Spaniards and the indigenous people in 1593, an event celebrated at Tinkunaco. The **Convent of Santo Domingo**, Luna y Lamadrid, dates from 1623, said to be the oldest surviving church in Argentina. **Museo Arqueológico Inca Huasi** ☾ *Alberdi 650, Tue-Sat, 0900-1200, US$0.50*, owned by the Franciscan Order, contains a huge collection of fine Diaguita Indian ceramics. The **Mercado Artesanal** ☾ *Luna 790, Tue-Fri 0800-1200, 1600-2000, Sat-Sun 0900-1300,* has expensive handicrafts. The **Museo de Arte Sacro** ☾ *in the same building Tue-Sat 0800-1200,* has 18th- and 19th-century images and Cusqueña school paintings. In a beautiful and well kept house at the opposite corner, the **Museo Folklórico** ☾ *Luna 811, T428500, Tue-Sun 0900-1200, 1600-2000 (Tue-Sat 0900-1200 in summer), US$0.35, free guided visits,* gives a fascinating insight into traditional La Rioja life, with a superb collection of native deities, rustic wine-making machinery and delicate silver *mates*. Well worth a visit too for its leafy patio. There are good views of La Rioja from Cerro de la Cruz (1,648 m), 23 km west, now a centre for hang-gliding. **Tourist office** ☾ *Luna 345, T426384, www.larioja.gov.ar/turismo/.*

Chilecito → *Phone code: 03825. Colour map 8, grid A2. Population: 25,000.*
Chilecito, 129 km northwest of Patquía, is La Rioja province's second town. Founded in 1715, it has good views of Sierra de Famatina, especially from the top of El Portezuelo, an easy climb from the end of Calle El Maestro. The region is famous for its wines, olives and walnuts. **Samay Huasi** ☾ *3 km south of town, T422629, Mon-Fri 0800-1300, 1330-1930, Sat-Sun 0800-1200, 1500-1900 (closed 22 Dec-6 Jan), US$0.35.* This was the house of Joaquín V González, founder of La Plata University. He designed the gardens with native trees and strange stone monoliths expressing his love of ancient cultures; there's also a small natural history museum. It's an attractive place for a relaxing day; staying guests also welcome (**F** pp, **E** pp full board, reserve in advance). **Molino San Francisco y Museo de Chilecito** ☾ *J de Ocampo 50, Mon-Fri 0800-1200, 1600-2100, Sat-Sun 0830-1230, 1530-2000, US$0.35,* has archaeological, historical and artistic exhibits. At the **Cooperativa La Riojana** ☾ *La Plata*

646, Mon-Fri 0800, 1000, 1200; shop 0600-1400, you can watch local grapes being processed to make a wide variety of wines. Free guided visits (45 minutes) and a smart wine shop. At **Santa Florentina** (8 km northwest), there are the impressive remains of a huge early 20th century foundry, linked to Chilecito and La Mejicana mine by cable car. There are a couple of internet places. Tourist office at bus station (no phone), daily 0800- 1230, 1530-2100. For more tourist information and pictures visit www.chilecitotour.com.

Reserva Natural Laguna Brava

At Nonogasta 16 km south of Chilecito, the partly paved Ruta 40 heads west climbing through a deep narrow canyon in a series of hairpins to the Cuesta de Miranda (2,020 m). After the Cuesta is **Villa Unión**, 92 km from Nonogasta (Hotel Centro, on main plaza, has a restaurant). From here excursions can be made by four-wheel drive vehicle to the Reserva Natural Laguna Brava, 150 km north. The road goes through **Vinchina** and Jagüe (basic facilities). Further on, as you climb the Portezuelo del Peñón, the salt lake of Laguna Brava becomes visible with some of the mightiest volcanoes on earth in the background. From the left these are the perfect cone Veladero (6,436 m), Reclus (6,335 m), Los Gemelos (6,130 m), Pissis (6,882 m) the highest volcano in the world, though inactive, and Bonete (6,759 m) which is visible from Villa Unión and Talampaya. For tours in this area see under Chilecito and La Rioja. **Access**: From Jagüe 4WD and going with two vehicles are essential. Summer rainfalls and winter snow may limit the access to only a short period in the year; usually in April or early May is best. Entry US$5.

Catamarca → *Phone code: 03833. Colour map 8, grid A2. Population: 130,000. Altitude: 490 m.*

Officially San Fernando del Valle de Catamarca, the city is capital of its province, on the Río del Valle, between the Sierra de Ambato (to the west) and Ancasti (to the east), 153 km northeast of La Rioja and 240 km south of Tucumán. Now a rather run-down place, Catamarca is most famous for its textiles, and unless you're here for the poncho festival in the second fortnight in July *(feria* with high quality handicrafts, food and live music), there's little to draw you to the city. Summers are unbearably hot with temperatures up to 45°C. 37km north is the much more appealing and prettier weekend retreat of **El Rodeo** with its cooler microclimate, good walks and charming *hosterías* (tourist information T490043). In the vast open puna to the northwest, there are traces of sophisticated ancient civilizations, and the finest of the city's six museums has an outstanding collection of indigenous artefacts. **Museo Arqueológico Adán Quiroga** ① *Sarmiento 450, T437413, Mon-Fri 0700-1300, 1430-2000, Sat-Sun 1200-1900, US$0.40.* **Tourist office** ① *Av República 446, www.catamarca.com, www.catamarca.gov.ar, daily 0900-2100.* Helpful leaflets with bus times and prices. Also in Terminal Shopping by bus station on Av Güemes.

Puna west of Catamarca

The high altitude desert of the puna is spectacular, with a distinct culture and remote untouristy towns. It's most easily reached by the paved road to **Aimogasta** and on to the small settlements of Tinogasta and Fiambalá, useful staging posts if taking the Paso San Fransisco to Chile, or north to Andagalá, or to Belén, where the rough road to Antofagasta de la Sierra begins. The *Zonda*, a strong, dry mountain wind, can cause dramatic temperature increases.

Tinogasta *(Phone code 03837)* is in an oasis of vineyards, olive groves, and poplars. It is the starting point for expeditions to **Pissis** the second highest mountain in South America, 6,882 m. To get there, take Ruta 60 which crosses Tinogasta in the direction of the San Francisco pass. You have to register at the police station outside Fiambalá, take passport. Expeditions organized and horse riding with Omar Monuey, La Espiga de Oro, 25 de Mayo 436 or *Varela Viajes*, T420428. At Fiambalá, contact Jonson and Ruth Reynoso, T496214.

Fiambalá is 49 km north of Tinogasta, a peaceful place in a vine-filled valley, with **Termas de Fiambalá**, hot springs, situated 14 km east (take a taxi; make sure fare includes wait and return). 4WD vehicles may be hired for approaching the Pissis-Ojos region; ask at the Intendencia.

Border with Chile – Paso San Francisco

Fiambalá is the starting-point for the crossing to Chile via Paso San Francisco (4,726 m), 203 km northwest along a paved road. The border is open 0830-1930, T498001. On the Chilean side roads run to El Salvador and Copiapó. This route is closed by snow June-October; take enough fuel for at least 400 km as there are no service stations from Fiambalá to just before Copiapó.

Belén → *Phone code 03835. Colour map 6, grid C3. Population: 8,800. Altitude 1,000 m.*

A quiet intimate little town, Belén is famous for its ponchos, saddlebags and rugs, which you can see being woven in various workshops. The museum, **Cóndor Huasi** ① *San Martín y Belgrano, 1st floor, daily*, contains fascinating Diaguita artefacts, and you can walk up C Gral Roca to the statue of Virgin of Belén, high above the town, for good views. Important festival: Nuestra Señora de Belén, 24 December-6 January. **Tourist information** at the bus terminal a block from the plaza, *T461539, alpamicuna@cotelbelen.com.ar.*

South of Belén, Ruta 40 is paved to Chilecito via **Londres**, a quiet, pretty village. North of Belén Ruta 40 runs another 176 km, largely unpaved, to Santa María at the provincial border with Tucumán (see page 139), and on to Cafayate (page 142), or 260 km north to tiny remote **Antofagasta de la Sierra** and onwards to San Antonio de los Cobres in Salta. East of Belén, a rough and sandy road goes to **Andalgalá**, a former copper-mining town with two archaeological museums, a handicraft market, and a decent hotel **D Aquasol**. For excursions and information contact **Andalgalá Turismo**, To3835-422405, turandalgala@cotelbelen.com.ar. Very helpful.

● Sleeping

La Rioja *p132*

A/c or fan are essential for summer nights. High season is during Jul winter holidays.

A King's, Av Quiroga 1070, T422122. 4-star, buffet breakfast included, a/c gym, pool and fine rooms, also car rental.

B Plaza, San Nicolás de Bari y 9 de Julio (on Plaza 25 de Mayo), T425215, www.plazahotel-larioja.com.ar. Functional 4-star, pool on top floor, breakfast included, a/c.

C Libertador, Buenos Aires 253, T427794. Comfortable, decent rooms, a/c, with breakfast.

C Savoy, San Nicolás de Bari y Roque A Luna, T426894, hotelsavoy@infovia.com.ar. In a quiet residential area, tidy, comfortable, with breakfast and a/c, second floor best.

C Vincent Apart Hotel, Santiago del Estero y San Nicolás de Bari, T432326. Flats for up to 4, a/c, with dining room, kitchen and fridge, breakfast included, excellent value.

D Mirasol, Rivadavia 941, T420760. Quiet, comfortable, homely, though the windows look onto a corridor, breakfast extra.

D Pensión 9 de Julio, Copiapó 197 (on Plaza 9 de Julio), T426955. Attractive front patio, with breakfast, hot water, cheaper with shared bath, not very friendly.

Camping At Balneario Los Sauces, 13 km west on Ruta 75, **Camping de la Sociedad Sirio Libanesa**, hot showers, pool.

Chilecito *p132*

C Chilecito (ACA), T Gordillo y A G Ocampo, T422201, 156-66358. A/c, quite comfortable, with breakfast, safe parking, pool, restaurant has cheap set menus.

D Finca del Paimán, Mariano Moreno y Santa Rosa (San Miguel, 3 km southeast of town), T/F425102, www.fincadelpaiman.com.ar. Owner, Alejo Piehl, has opened his delightful 4½-ha farm to guests, spacious rooms, kitchen, breakfast and transport to/from Chilecito included. You can

help with fruit harvesting or jam cooking! Warmly recommended, book in advance. Also has a hostel in Chilecito, El Maestro y A Marasso, with rooms **E**, or dorms **F**, HI affiliated.

D Hostal Mary Pérez, Florencio Dávila 280, T/F423156, hostal_mp@hotmail.com. Best value, comfortable, welcoming atmosphere, good breakfast. Recommended.

E Bellia, El Maestro 188, T422181. Rooms open onto a nice garden. Breakfast included.

Camping 3 sites at Santa Florentina and Las Talas, 8 km northwest (remise taxi US$2-2.50).

Reserva Natural Laguna Brava *p133*

C Hotel Corona del Inca, Vinchina, T03825-494004, hotelcoronadelinca@ciudad.com.ar. New.

C Hotel Pircas Negras, on Ruta 76, T03825-470611.

D Hotel Noryanepat, JVGonzález 150, T03825-470372. Small rooms with a/c, good. There are several basic *hospedajes* in Vinchina.

Catamarca *p133*

Hotels are mostly unmodernized, overpriced and business-oriented.

B Casino Catamarca, Pasaje César Carman s/n (behind the ACA service station), T432928, inforcentral@hotelcasinocatamarca.com. Smart, modern and bright, well decorated rooms, discreetly hidden casino, large pool.

B Estancia Los Timones at Las Piedras Blancas, north of the city towards Las Juntas, T425230/156-93193. Recommended. Los Hermanos Vergara, run buses from Catamarca Terminal Mon-Sat, 0800, 2000.

C Arenales, Sarmiento 542, T431329, www.hotel-arenales.com.ar. Comfortable plain rooms, good bathrooms, restaurant.

C El Gran Hotel, Camilo Melet 41, T426715. Delightful, helpful owners, simple spacious rooms. Recommended.

C **Hostería El Rodeo**, in El Rodeo 37 km to the north, T490296, www.hotelguia.com/elrodeo. Daily minibus from centre.
D **El Leo III**, Sarmiento 727, T432080. Central, more comfortable than most, good value.
Camping Municipal site 5 km from centre on road to El Rodeo/Las Juntas, US$1.50, clean, friendly, hot showers.

Tinogasta *p133*
D **Hostería Novel**, Córdoba 200, T420009, near airport, friendly.
D **Viñas del Sol**, Perón 231, T420028.
E **Res Don Alberto**, A del Pino y Rivadavia, T420323.

Fiambalá *p133*
D **Hostería Municipal**, Almagro s/n, T03837-496016. Good value, also restaurant.
E pp **Complejo Turístico**, at the Termas, T496016. With cabins, also camping.

Belén *p134*
C **Belén**, Belgrano y Cubas, T461501, www.belen cat.com.ar. Comfortable, also tour operator.
D **Samai**, Urquiza 349, T461320. Old fashioned but welcoming.

● Eating

La Rioja *p132*
▐▐ **Cavadini**, Av Quiroga 1145. Good *parrilla*, informal.
▐▐ **El Corral**, Av Quiroga y Rivadavia. Traditional rustic fare and good local wines.
▐▐ **La Vieja Casona**, Rivadavia 427. Popular, smart *parrilla*.
▐▐ **Los Palotes**, H Yrigoyen 128. Varied menu, including salmon, trout, seafood and Mexican, pleasant atmosphere.
▐ **Alike**, Vélez Sarsfield e H Irigoyen. *Tenedor libre*, wide choice.
▐ **La Aldea de la Virgen de Luján**, Rivadavia 756. Lively atmosphere.

Cafés
Café del Paseo, 25 de Mayo y Luna. On main plaza in a small shopping area.
Café de la Plaza, Rivadavia e H Irigoyen. Modern, popular.
Confitería El Ciervo, C Joaquín V González opposite plaza. In the arcade of the Club Social.

Chilecito *p132*
▐ **Club Arabe**, 25 de Mayo entre Zelada y Dávila and Famatina. The usual dishes, middle eastern food on request, served under grapevines.
▐ **El Pelado**, Ocampo 15. For take away meals when all else closed.

▐ **El Rancho de Ferrito**, Luna 647. Popular *parrilla*, with local wines.
▐ **La Rosa**, Ocampo 149, T424693. Relaxing atmosphere, huge variety of pizzas, more extensive menu Fri and Sat.

Catamarca *p133*
▐▐ **La Tinaja**, Sarmiento 533. Delicious *parrilla* and excellent pastas, worth the price.
▐▐ **Salsa Criolla**, República 546 on the plaza. Traditional popular *parrilla*, sloppy service, but the beef is good. **Trattoria Montecarlo**, next door, same owner, Italian style.
▐ **Family Pizzería**, plaza. Cheap pizzas, popular.
▐ **Richmond** is the most appealing café on the plaza, stylish.
▐ **Sociedad Española**, Virgen del Valle 725. Recommended for quality and variety, paella and other Spanish specialities, friendly service; worth the 5 block walk from the plaza.

Tinogasta *p133*
In the Tinogasta/Fiambalá region the water is notoriously bad: avoid salads and ice, drink mineral water.
Restaurant Casa Grande, Constitución y Moreno. Good meals, try local wines.

Belén *p134*
Cafés
Bar El Seminario, on the plaza. Great for beer and sandwiches, fills the plaza at weekends.

● Shopping

Catamarca *p133*
Local specialities Cuesta del Portezuelo, Sarmiento 571 and **Valdez**, Sarmiento 578. You can see carpets being woven at **Mercado Artesanal**, Virgen del Valle 945, wide range of handicrafts, daily 0800-1330, 1500-2100; carpet factory Mon-Fri 0800-1200.

▲ Activities and tours

La Rioja *p132*
For excursions to Talampaya, Valle de la Luna, Laguna Brava and Corona del Inca crater (high season only), city tours and horse riding in Velasco mountains:
Aguada, T433695 or 15-675699, talampaya_aguada@ciudad.com.ar. Helpful agency with good tours.
Corona del Inca, Luna 914, T450054 or 15-663811, www.coronadelinca.com.ar.
Néstor Pantaleo, Ecuador 813, T422103. Experienced photographer, runs 4WD trips, several languages spoken.

Chilecito *p132*

This is an excellent base for amazing treks in the Famatina mountains and 1-day trips to Talampaya and Valle de la Luna.

Alejo Piehl, T/F425102, 15672612, www.fincadelpaiman.com.ar. Experienced guide (see also Sleeping, above), all inclusive 1-day tours to Talampaya and Valle de la Luna, US$30 pp, and a variety of unforgettable 1- or 2-day treks (US$35 pp) to Famatina, visiting abandoned cable car stations on the way to the summit. Occasional 4WD trips. Recommended.

Asociación Riojana de Turismo Rural, Av Perón 668, T422828. Guided visits to local farms, very cheap.

Inka Ñan, T425975, 156-71933. Leopoldo Badoul organizes excursions to the province's main attractions.

Paragliding Camel Waidatt, J V González 467, T424874, www.cuestavieja.com.

Catamarca *p133*

Mountain biking Club Mountain Bike, www.cmtbcat.com.ar.

Mountaineering Agrupación Calchaqui, Tourism block, Gral Roca, T436368. **Aníbal Vázquez**, T03835-471001, walking expeditions in Antofagasta de la Sierra.

Paragliding Eduardo Bonutto, T156-88513.

⊕ Transport

La Rioja *p132*

Air Airport T439211. To/from **Buenos Aires**, AR, T426307, flights usually stop at Catamarca or Córdoba.

Bus Terminal 7 blocks south of the Cathedral at Artigas y España (T425453). To **Buenos Aires**, Gen Urquiza and Chevallier US$18-25, 15-17 hrs. To **Mendoza** (US$10-12) and **San Juan** (US$6.50-8), 6 hrs. To **Tucumán** (US$5.50-7), several companies. To **Salta**, Andesmar, 10 hrs, US$11. Also provincial services.

Chilecito *p132*

Bus To **San Juan** and Mendoza with Vallecito, US$9-10; to **La Rioja**, several times daily, US$3. To **Córdoba**, US$8 and **Buenos Aires**, US$20, El Práctico, General Urquiza.

Catamarca *p133*

Air Airport T430080. AR/Austral (Sarmiento 589, T424450) to/from **Buenos Aires**.

Bus Terminal 5 blocks southeast of plaza at Güemes y Tucumán T437578. Taxi to/from Plaza 25 de Mayo US$0.50. To **Tucumán**, several

companies, 3½-4hrs, US$3-5. To **Buenos Aires**, 4 companies daily, 15 hrs, US$20. To **Córdoba**, 4 companies daily, 6 hrs, US$7. To **Santiago del Estero**, Mendoza, La Estrella, 4 hrs, US$5. To **Mendoza**, several companies, daily, 10 hrs, US$9-13. To **La Rioja**, several companies, US$3, 2 hrs. To **Tinogasta**, see below. To **Belén** via Londres, two companies, 5 hrs, US$5-7; **Marín** (via Aconquija).

Tinogasta *p133*

Bus To **Tucumán**, Empresa Gutiérrez, 3 weekly (daily in high season). To **Catamarca**, Empresa Gutiérrez (connection to Buenos Aires), Robledo and Rubimar, US$6; to/from **La Rioja**, El Cóndor, daily, US$4-5.

Fiambalá *p133*

Bus Empresa Gutiérrez to **Catamarca** via Tinogasta. For Belén, change at Aimogasta.

Belén *p134*

Bus From Belén to **Santa María**, **San Cayetano** (connection there with other companies to Cafayate and Salta), Mon, Wed, Fri 1400, Sat 1230, Sun 1600, 5 hrs, US$6.50. To **Tinogasta**, **Robledo**, 3 weekly, 3 hrs, US$4. To **Antofagasta de la Sierra**, El Antofagasteño, 5 weekly, 10 hrs, US$12. For more frequent services to **Catamarca** or **La Rioja**, take bus to Aimogasta, 1 hr, US$1.50.

⊕ Directory

La Rioja *p132*

Banks US$ cash changed at Banco de Galicia, Buenos Aires y San Nicolás de Bari, and at Daniel, exchange facilities at Rivadavia 525.
Internet Cool.com, Luna 684, US$0.65 per hr. Cyber Hall, Rivadavia 763. Good service with webcams, US$0.65 per hr. Cyber más, Rivadavia 909. Open 24 hrs, US$0.35 per hr. **Post offices** Perón 258. **Telephones** Several *locutorios* in the centre and at Av Quiroga e Hipólito Yrigoyen, with internet access (US$0.60 per hr) near bus terminal.

Catamarca *p133*

Banks Many ATMs for all major cards, along Rivadavia and at bus terminal, BBVA Banco Francés, Rivadavia 520. Banco de la Nación San Martín 632. **Internet** Cedecc, Esquiú 414. Taraj Net, San Martín y Ayacucho. **Post offices** San Martín 753, slow, open 0800-1300, 1600-2000. **Telephones** Most *telecentros* around Plaza 25 de Mayo, also at República 845 and Rivadavia 758, open 0700-2400, daily.

Northwest Argentina

Two of the oldest cities in Argentina, Santiago del Estero and Tucumán, are at the start of the route to the fascinating Northwest. Both have some good museums and other sites of interest, but the summer heat may urge you to press on to the mountains. You can break the journey between the two cities at the rather worn, but much-visited spa of Termas de Río Hondo. Of the two routes to the atmospheric city of Salta, the more beautiful is via Tafí del Valle, the wine-producing town of Cafayate and the dramatic canyon of the Quebrada de las Conchas or the equally enchanting Valles Calchaquíes. Pretty towns in arid landscapes, archaeological remains and the Andes in the distance make for a memorable journey.

Santiago del Estero → *Phone code: 0385. Colour map 6, grid C4. Population: 212,000.*

Founded in 1553 by conquistadores pushing south from Peru, this is the oldest Argentine city, though little of its history is visible today. It's slightly run down, but the people are relaxed and welcoming (*Altitude 200 m, 395 km north of Córdoba, 159 km southeast of Tucumán*). On the **Plaza Libertad** stand the **Municipalidad** and the **Cathedral** (the fifth on the site), with the Cabildo-like Prefectura of Police. The fine **Casa de Gobierno** is on Plaza San Martín, three blocks north. In the convent of **Santo Domingo**, Urquiza y 25 de Mayo, is one of two copies of the 'Turin Shroud', given by Philip II to his 'beloved colonies of America'. On Plaza Lugones is the church of **San Francisco**, the oldest surviving church in the city, founded in 1565, with the cell of San Francisco Solano, patron saint of Tucumán, who stayed here in 1593. Beyond it is the pleasant **Parque Francisco de Aguirre**. A highly recommended museum, **Museo de Ciencias Antropológicas** ① *Avellaneda 353, Mon-Fri 0730-1330, 1400-2000, Sat-Sun 1000-1200, free,* has a breathtaking collection of prehispanic artefacts, exquisitely painted funerary urns, flattened skulls, anthropomorphic ceramics and musical instruments. Also interesting is the **Museo Histórico Provincial** ① *Urquiza 354, Mon-Fri 0700-1300, 1400-2000, Sat-Sun 1000-1200, free.* In a 200-year old mansion, it has 18th- and 19th-century artefacts from wealthy local families. **Carnival** is celebrated in February. **Tourist office** ① *Plaza Libertad, T422 6777.*

Some 65 km north of Santiago del Estero is **Termas de Río Hondo** (phone code: 03858), Argentina's most popular spa town which has its warm mineral-laden waters piped into every hotel in the city (160 of them), making it a mecca (or Lourdes?) for older visitors with arthritic or skin conditions in July and August, when you'll need to book in advance. The hotels aside, the town is mostly run down, with a cream-coloured casino dominating the scruffy plaza and scores of *alfajores* shops. There are shops and banks all around the plaza. **Tourist office** ① *Caseros 132, T422143, or www.lastermasteriohondo.com,* helpful for accommodation advice.

● Sleeping

Santiago del Estero *p137*
B Carlos V, Independencia 110, T424 0303, hotelcarlosv@arnet.com.ar. Corner of the plaza, cheap and more luxurious, pool, good restaurant.
B Libertador, Catamarca 47, T421 9252. Smart and relaxing, spacious lounge, plain rooms, patio with pool (summer only), elegant restaurant, 5 blocks south of plaza in the better part of town.
C del Centro, 9 de Julio 131, T422 4350. Very comfortable, nice decor. Recommended.
D Savoy, Peatonal Tucumán 39, T421 2344. Good budget option, full of character and faded art nouveau grandeur, large rooms, very simple.
F Res Alaska, Santa Fe 279, T422 1360. Close to bus station, hot water, TV, fan, good value.
Camping Las Casuarinas, Parque Aguirre.

Termas de Río Hondo *p137*
B De los Pinos, Caseros y Maipú, T421043. Next best, attractive Spanish style, a little removed from the centre.
B Termal Río Hondo, T421455, www.hotel termalriohondo.com.ar. Most comfortable, modern rooms, medical services, pool, good restaurant.
Camping Two sites near river: Del Río, Av Yrigoyen y Ruta 9; La Olla, Av Yrigoyen y Lascano. Also **ACA**, on access to Dique Frontal (4 km from town), T421648; El Mirador, Ruta 9 y Urquiza. All charge about US$2 pp.

⊙ Eating

Santiago del Estero *p137*

¶¶ **Mia Mamma**, on the main plaza at 24 de Septiembre 15. A cheery place for *parrilla* and tasty pastas, with good salad starters.

¶¶ **Periko's** on the plaza, lively, popular, for *lomitos* and pizzas.

¶ **Cantina China**, Mitre and 24 de Septiembre. Very cheap Chinese *tenedor libre*.

¶ **Don Pelachi**, Urquiza y Belgrano. Good value, large choice of dishes.

Termas de Río Hondo *p137*

For dinner, try *parrilla* at **San Cayetano**, or homely **Renacimiento**, both on Sarmiento (main street), reasonably priced. Cheaper still, on Alberdi y Sarmiento is **El Chorizo Loco**, a lively pizzería.

⊖ Transport

Santiago del Estero *p137*

Air AR to **Buenos Aires**.

Bus Bus information, T421 3746. Terminal has toilets, a *locutorio*, basic café and kiosks, as well as stalls selling food. Taxi US$0.30 into town, or 8 blocks' walk. **Córdoba**, 6 hrs, US$5-7; **Jujuy**, 7 hrs, US$7; **Salta**, 6 hrs, US$11. To **Catamarca**, 1 daily at 1600, 7 hrs, US$5, otherwise go via Tucumán.

Termas de Río Hondo *p137*

Bus To **Santiago del Estero**, 1 hr, US$2 and to **Tucumán**, 2 hrs, US$2. The bus terminal is 8 blocks from the centre, but buses will stop at the plaza, opposite the casino, if asked.

Tucumán and around

→ *Phone code: 0381. Colour map 6, grid C4. Population: 700,000. Altitude: 450 m.*

San Miguel de Tucumán was founded by Spaniards coming south from Peru in 1565. Capital of a province rich in sugar, tobacco and citrus fruits, it is the biggest and busiest city in the north. It stands on a plain and is sweltering hot in summer (siesta from 1230-1630 is strictly observed), when you might prefer to retreat to the cooler mountain town of **Tafí del Valle** in the Sierra de Aconquija to the west. The **tourist office** is on the plaza① *24 de Septiembre 484, T422 2199, www.turismoentucuman.com, 0800-2200.* Also in the bus terminal and airport.

Sights

Casa Padilla (Museo de la Ciudad)① *on the west side of the main Plaza Independencia, Mon-Sat 0900-1230, 1600-1900 (in summer, mornings only),* has a small collection of art and antiques in a historical house. Also on this side is the ornate **Casa de Gobierno** and, nearby, the church of **San Francisco**, with a picturesque façade. One block north, the **Museo Arqueológico**① *25 de Mayo 265 in University building, Mon-Fri 0800-1200,* has a fine collection. On the south side of Plaza Independencia is the **Cathedral** and, two blocks south, the interesting **Casa Histórica**① *T431 0826, daily 0900-1300,1500-1900, US$1; son et lumière programme in garden nightly (not Thu, except in Jul) at 2030, adults US$2, children US$1, tickets also from tourist office on Plaza Independencia, no seats.* Here, in 1816, the country's Declaration of Independence was drawn up.

East of the centre is the **Parque de Julio**, one of the finest urban parks in Argentina. Extending over 400 ha, it contains a wide range of sub-tropical trees as well as a lake and sports facilities. The **Museo de la Industria Azucarera**① *daily 0900-1800, free,* traces the development of the local sugar industry. There are good views over the city from **Cerro San Javier**, 27 km west of the city (*Empresa Ber Bus*, US$1.50 from bus terminal).

Tafí del Valle → *Phone code: 03867. Population: 7,000. Altitude: 1,976 m.*

South of Tucumán at Acheral on RN38, Ruta 307 heads northwest out of the sugar cane fields to zigzag up through forested hills to a treeless plateau, before El Mollar and the Embalse La Angostura. Here the valley is greener and you descend gradually to Tafí del Valle, a small town and popular weekend retreat from the heat of Tucumán in the summer (106 km). It has a cool microclimate, and makes a good base for walking, with several peaks of the Sierra de Aconquija providing satisfying day-hikes. There's some excellent, if pricey, accommodation and a **cheese festival** in early February, with live music. **Tourist information** to the south of semi-circular plaza, 0800-1800 daily, no phone. Map US$1. Visit the **Capilla Jesuítica y Museo de La Banda**① *Mon-Sat 0900-1900, Sun 0900-1600 (closing early off season), US$0.50, includes a guided visit,* an 18th-century chapel and 19th-century *estancia*, with museum of archaeology and religious art. **Museo Los Tesoros de Tafí**① *at La Banda,*

T421563, is a small archaeological museum. Juan Carlos Yapura, owner, guides day walks to aboriginal sites in nearby mountains. ATM at Banco de Tucumán, Miguel Critto 311, T421033, all cards. Internet places on Av Perón and one on Av Critto.

About 5km from the main road, across the Dique La Angostura, **El Mollar** is another weekend village with campsites and *cabañas*. Boating and fishing trips are offered on the reservoir, US$3.15 half day, US$10 full day.

Amaicha, Quilmes and Santa María

From Tafí the road runs 56 km northwest over the 3,040 m Infiernillo Pass (Km 85) with spectacular views and through grand arid landscape to sunny **Amaicha del Valle** (Population 5,000; Altitude 1,997 m) with the popular **Museo Pachamama** *T421004*, highly recommended, with overview of the Calchaquí culture, geology, tapestry by Héctor Cruz for sale, US$1.20. From Amaicha the paved road continues north 15 km to the junction with Ruta 40.

Some 35 km north, the striking ruins of **Quilmes** ⓘ *0800-1830, US$0.70, includes guide and museum, café, huge gift shop, hotel*, can be found 5 km off the main road. The setting is amazing, an intricate web of walls built into the mountain side, where 5,000 members of a Diaguita tribe lived, resisting Inca, and then Spanish domination, before being marched off to Córdoba and to the Quilmes in Buenos Aires where the beer comes from. For a day's visit take 0600 Aconquija bus from Cafayate to Santa María, alight at stop 5 km from site, or take 0700 bus from Santa María; take 1130 bus back to Cafayate, US$2.

Santa María (*Population 10,000*), 22 km south of Amaicha by paved road, is a delightful, untouristy small town with an interesting archaeology museum at the **Centro Cultural Yokavil**, at the corner of the plaza ('voluntary' donation requested), pleasant hotels and a municipal campsite. Also a *locutorio* and internet places, ATM on Mitre at Banco de la Nación (only one for miles). South of Santa María, Ruta 40 goes to Belén, see page 134. Instead of going to Amaicha to get to Quilmes, you can take the Ruta 40 up the west bank of the Río Santa María: ask for the bridge over the river and turn right. The road is paved to the Catamarca/Tucumán border, thereafter *ripio*. After 15 km, you pass **Fuerte Quemado** ⓘ *free*, an archaeological site of low-walled structures amid a variety of cactus. It's 10 km further to the Quilmes turn off.

Tucumán to Salta

The speedy route to Salta is via Rosario de la Frontera and Güemes. **Rosario de la Frontera** (*Phone code 03876, Altitude 769 m*), 130 km north of Tucumán, is a convenient place for a stop, with thermal springs 8 km away. About 20 km north is the historical post house, **Posta de Yatasto**, with museum, 2 km east of the main road; campsite. About 70 km north of Rosario de la Frontera, at Lumbreras, a road branches off Ruta 9 and runs 90 km northeast to the **Parque Nacional El Rey**, one of three cloudforest parks in the northwest. Stretching from heights of over 2,300m through jungle to the flat arid Chaco in the east, it contains a variety of animal and plant life. There's free camping and marked trails, but accessible only on foot or horseback with a guide; insects are a problem. Federico Norte, **Norte Trekking** ⓘ *To387-436 11844, www.nortetrekking.com*, runs the best expeditions, US$60 pp per day, all inclusive, camping, trekking, rafting, 4WD. The park office is in Salta, at España 366, T4312683. Although drier in winter, the access road is poor, not recommended for ordinary vehicles. Park roads are impassable in the wet, November-May. There is no public transport to the park; it's best to go on an organized expedition.

● Sleeping

Tucumán *p138, map p140*
All hotels include breakfast and have fans or a/c.
A NH Grand Hotel del Tucumán, Av Soldati 380, T450 2250. Good value, luxurious, minimalist hotel, overlooking Parque 9 de Julio, outstanding food and service, pool (open to non-residents), sauna, gym. Highly recommended.
A Suites Garden Park, Av Soldati 330, T431 0700, www.gardenparkhotel.com.ar. Smart, welcoming 4-star, views over Parque 9 de Julio, pool, gym, sauna, restaurant. Also apartments.

B Carlos V, 25 de Mayo 330, T431 1666, www.redcarlosv.com.ar. Central, good service, with elegant restaurant.
B Mediterráneo, 24 de Septiembre 364, T431 0025, www.hotelmediterraneo.com.ar. Good rooms, TV, a/c. 20% discount for Footprint book owners Mon-Fri; 30% Sat-Sun.
B Premier, Crisóstomo Alvarez 510, T/F431 0381, info@redcarlosv.com.ar. Spacious comfortable rooms, modern bathrooms. Recommended.

C **Colonial**, San Martín 35, T431 1523. Near terminal on busy street, interior rooms quiet and comfortable, though dark. Minimal breakfast.

C **Dallas**, Corrientes 985, T421 8500. Very welcoming, nicely furnished rooms, good bathrooms. Recommended.

D **Argentina Norte**, Laprida 456, T430 2716, www.argentinanorte.com/hostel. Youth hostel in restored house, well-equipped kitchen, internet, English spoken, good.

D **Francia**, Crisóstomo Alvarez 467, T/F431 0781. Cheap apartments for 5, plain but comfortable high-ceilinged rooms, central, good budget option.

D **Petit**, Crisóstomo Alvarez 765, T431 1666, hotelpetit@redcarlosv.com.ar. Spacious old house with patio, quiet, cheaper without bath or fan.

D **Versailles**, Crisóstomo Alvarez 481, T422 9760, F422 9763. A touch of class, comfortable beds, and good service. Recommended.

E pp **La Estrella**, Av B Araoz 38, T421 4186. Near bus station, cheaper without bath, clean, helpful.

E **Miami**, Junín 580, T431 0265, F422 2405. Good modern hostel with discounts for HI members, pool, a/c, TV.

E **Hostería Aconquija**, Av Aconquija 2530, T425-6901, Yerba Buena. Youth hostel. AHC member.

Rosario de la Frontera *p139*

B **Termas**, Ruta 34 (6 km from bus station), T481004, hoteltermas@hotmail.com. Rambling place, good food, and thermal pool, horse riding, and golf. Baths US$2.

C **ACA hostería**, T481143. About 1 km from *Hotel Termas*, more comfortable.

Tafí del Valle *p138*

Many places, including hotels, close out of season.

A **Hostería Tafí del Valle**, Av San Martín y Gdor Campero, T421027, www.soldelvalle.com.ar. Right at the top of the town, with splendid views, good restaurant, luxurious small rooms, pool.

A **Mirador del Tafí**, T/F421219, www.mirador deltafi.com.ar. Warm attractive rooms and spacious lounge, superb restaurant, excellent views. Highly recommended.

B **Lunahuana**, Av Critto 540, T421330, www.lunahuana.com.ar. Stylish comfortable rooms, and spacious duplexes for families, also with good views.

B **La Rosada**, Belgrano 322, T421323/146, miguel_torres@sinectis.com.ar. Spacious rooms, well decorated, plenty of hot water, comfortable, excellent breakfast included, helpful staff, lots of expeditions on offer and free use of cycles.

C **Hostería Los Cuartos**, Av Juan Calchaquí s/n, T/F421444 or **Tucumán**, T0381-15587 4230, www.turismoentucuman.com/loscuartos. Old *estancia*, rooms full of character, charming hosts. Recommended. Also offer a day at the *estancia*, lunch, horse riding. Delicious *té criollo*, and farm cheese can be bought here or at cheese shop on Av Miguel Critto.

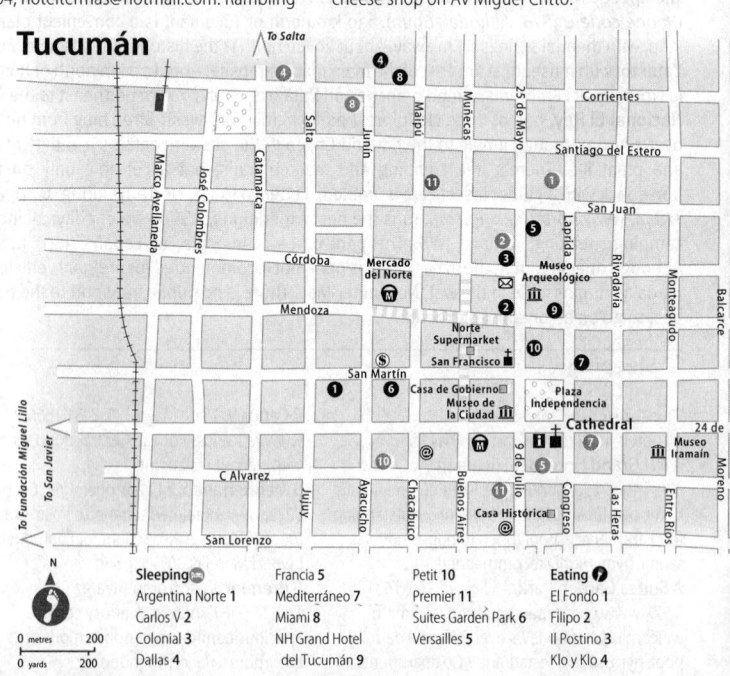

Tucumán

E Hospedaje El Valle, above the big souvenir emporium at Perón 56, T421641. Basic but clean, some rooms with bath.

E pp La Cumbre, Av Perón 120, T421768, www.lacumbretafidelvalle.com. Very welcoming, rooms for 2 to 5, bar, cooking facilities, good atmosphere. Helpful owner is a tour operator.

Camping Los Sauzales. Run down, US$2 pp plus tent. Better sites at El Mollar, among them La Mutual.

Quilmes *p139*
B Parador Ruinas de Quilmes, T03892-421075. Peaceful, very comfortable, boldly designed with weavings and ceramics, great views of Quilmes, good restaurant, free camping. Recommended.

❼ Eating

Tucumán *p138, map p140*
Many popular restaurants and cafés along 25 de Mayo, north from Plaza Independencia, and on Plaza Hipólito Yrigoyen.

♥♥ **El Fondo**, San Martín 848, T422 2161. Superb renowned steak house.

♥♥ **Klo y Klo**, Junín 663. Delightful, good range of seafood and pastas.

♥♥ **La Leñita**, 25 de Mayo 377. Recommended for excellent *parrilla*, and superb salads.

♥♥ **La Parrilla del Centro**, San Martín 391. Excellent steak, reasonable prices.

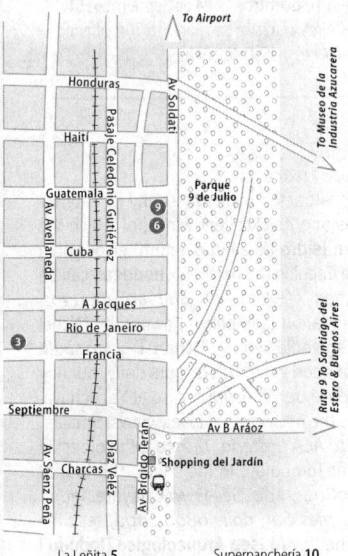

La Leñita **5**
La Mostaza **6**
La Parrilla del Centro **7**
Panadería Villecco **8**
Sir Harris **9**
Superpanchería **10**

Bars & clubs ❶
Costumbres
Argentinos **11**

♥ **Sir Harris**, Laprida y Mendoza. A Tucumán institution, good quality *tenedor libre* in cosy pub-like place. Recommended.

♥ **Il Postino**, 25 de Mayo y Córdoba. Attractive buzzing pizza place.

Cafés
Filipo, Mendoza y 25 de Mayo. Good coffee, a popular smart café, with a good atmosphere.

La Mostaza, San Martín 742. Lively and trendy café, cheap breakfasts.

Panadería Villecco, Corrientes 751. Exceptional bread, also wholemeal (*integral*).

Superpanchería, 25 de Mayo. Bright busy hot dog place with huge range of salads and toppings.

Tafí del Valle *p138*
Many places along Av Perón, including:
♥♥-♥ **El Portal de la Villa**, Av Perón 221, T03867-421834, www.elportaldelavilla.com. A big place with plenty of choice of local dishes and *parrilla*, good food, service willing but a bit amateur. Recommended.

♥♥-♥ **Parrilla Don Pepito**, Av Perón. Popular *parrilla*.

♥ **El Almacén**, Av Perón by Av Critto. A café with *menú del día*.

Cafés Panificación del Valle, Av Critto, Patio de la Empanada and Pub Aborigen.

❶ Bars and clubs

Tucumán *p138, map p140*
Costumbres Argentinos, San Juan 666 y Maipú. Good atmosphere, intimate, for late drinks.

❀ Festivals and events

Tucumán *p138, map p140*
9 Jul, Independence Day and **24 Sep**, Battle of Tucumán, are both celebrated with huge processions and partying.

❍ Shopping

Tucumán *p138, map p140*
Handicrafts Mercado Artesanal, 24 de Septiembre 565. Small, but nice selection of lace, wood and leather work. Daily 0800-1300, 1700-2200 (in summer, mornings only). **Norte** supermarket, Muñecas 137. **Regionales del Jardín**, Congreso 18. Good selection of local jams, *alfajores* etc.

▲ Activities and tours

Tafí del Valle *p138*
La Cumbre, see Sleeping, above. Energetic and helpful company, offering full day walks to

nearby peaks, waterfalls and ruins, or to Cerro Muñoz, with an *asado* at the summit, has open-sided truck.

○ Transport

Tucumán *p138, map p140*
Air Airport at Benjamín Matienzo, 10 km east of town. Bus No 120 from terminal (*cospeles*, US$0.70, required). Taxi US$4. **Cielos del Norte**, T426 5555, minibuses to/from airport to/from any place in town, US$1.50. To **Buenos Aires**, AR/ Austral (T431 1030), also to **Salta** and **Córdoba**.
Bus Bus terminal has 70 ticket offices, best to ask information kiosk opposite Disco T430 4696/422 2221. Local buses operate on *cospeles*, US$0.35, which you have to buy in advance in kiosks.

For long distance buses, the modern terminal is 6 blocks east of Plaza Independencia on Av Brigido Terán, with huge shopping complex, left luggage lockers (US$1), tourist information office (by *boletería* 1), lots of *locutorios*, toilets and banks. Bus 3 from outside terminal to San Lorenzo y 9 de Julio in centre. Taxi to centre US$0.50-1. To **Buenos Aires**, many companies, 16 hrs, US$20-25. To **Salta** direct (not via Cafayate), 4½ hrs, several companies US$7-9. To **Cafayate**, see below. To **Posadas**, La Nueva Estrella, Autotransportes Mendoza, 16 hrs, US$18-21. To **Mendoza**, 13 hrs, US$12, via Catamarca, La Rioja, and San Juan. To **Catamarca**, Aconquija and other companies, 4 hrs, US$4. To **Tinogasta**, via **Andalgalá** and **Belén**, Gutiérrez, 3 a week, daily in high season. To **Córdoba**, 8 hrs, US$7. To/from **Santiago del** Estero, 2 hrs, US$4. To **La Quiaca** (border with Bolivia), Balut, 10 hrs, US$12. To **Santiago** (Chile) via Mendoza, **Andesmar** and El Rápido Internacional, daily, 24 hrs, US$18-23.

Tafí del Valle *p138*
Bus Smart new terminal on Av Critto, with café, toilets, helpful information, T421031. To/from **Tucumán**, Aconquija, T421025, 8 daily, 2¼ hrs (4 via El Mollar, 3 hrs), US$2.80. 4 daily to **Santa María**. The 0600 and 1900 buses from Tucumán continue to **Cafayate**, 1½-2½ hrs. To **Salta**, 6 daily, 8 hrs, US$4.

○ Directory

Tucumán *p138, map p140*
Banks Most banks along San Martín especially 700 block between Junín and Maipú. **Maguitur**, San Martín 765, T431 0032, accepts TCs. **Maxicambio**, San Martín 779, T422 5399.
Car hire Avis, at airport, T426 7777, avis@ tucuman.com. **Donde Rent a Car**, Gob Gutiérrez 1384, T428 3626. **Movil Renta**, San Lorenzo 370, T431 0550, www.movilrenta.com.ar, and at airport. 20% discount for Footprint book owners.
Cultural centres Alliance Française, Laprida 456, T421 9651, free events in French.
Internet Cyber Noa, 9 de Julio y San Lorenzo and Centro Digital, Chacabuco 32. **Post offices** Córdoba y 25 de Mayo, open Mon-Fri 0800-2000. **Telephones** Lots of *locutorios* including Telecentros, at 24 de Septiembre 612, Buenos Aires y Lavalle, San Lorenzo 704, offering internet access, US$0.40 per hr.

Cafayate

→ *Phone code: 03868. Colour map 6, grid C3. Population: 8,432. Altitude: 1,660 m.*

Cafayate is a popular town for daytrippers and tourists, attracted by its dry sunny climate, its picturesque setting against the backdrop of the Andes and its excellent wines, of which the fruity white *torrontés* is unique to Argentina. **Cerro San Isidro** (five hours return) gives you a view of the Aconquija chain in the south and Nevado de Cachi in the north. Six **bodegas** can be visited, including: **Bodega La Rosa** ① *at the junction of Rutas 68 and 40, T421201, www.micheltorino.com.ar.* Hourly visits, also accommodation (see below), owned by Michel Torino, highly recommended, with superb wines and a splendid setting. **Etchart** ① *2 km south on Ruta 40, T421310.* More modest but also famous for good wine. Offers tours daily, but ring first to book. Ask to visit their boutique bodega, *San Pedro de Yacochuya.* Also at Yacochuya, **La Finca Domingo**, with handicrafts and ruins as well as the bodega, and lovely views. Smaller, but worth exploring: **Vasija Secreta**, *on outskirts, next to ACA hostería, T421503,* the oldest in the valley, English spoken. There are more vineyards at Tombolón, to the south. The **tourist office** is in a kiosk on the main plaza, *T421125, daily 0800-2200.* See www.cafayate.net.

The modest **Museo de la Vid y El Vino** ① *on Güemes Sur, daily 0800-2000,* tells the history of wine through old wine-making equipment. The tiny **Museo Arqueológico Rodolfo I Bravo** ① *Calchaquí y Colón, T421054, open on request, US$0.50,* has beautiful funerary urns, worth seeing if you haven't come across them elsewhere. ATMs at *Banco de la Nación* (but no TCs), Toscano y NS del Rosario. Also at *BanSud*, Mitre y San Martín. Internet at *Sol del Valle*, Toscana 40, on Plaza, and at Güemes Norte 105 (very popular - pick your time, open late).

Ruta 68 goes northeast from Cafayate to Salta; 6 km out of town is the rather unexpected landscape of Los Médanos (dunes), whose sand is constantly moving through thickets. The road then goes through the dramatic gorge of the Río de las Conchas (also known as the **Quebrada de Cafayate**) with fascinating rock formations of differing colours, all signposted. The road goes through wild and semi-arid landscapes. The vegetation becomes gradually denser as you near Salta, a pretty river winding by your side with tempting picnic spots.

Valles Calchaquíes

A longer alternative to Salta is to take the RN40 north of Cafayate through the stunningly varied landscape of the Valles Calchaquíes to Cachi. The mainly *ripio* road (difficult after rain) winds from the spectacular rock formations of the arid **Quebrada de las Flechas** up through Andean-foothills with lush little oases and tiny unspoilt villages at **San Carlos** (helpful tourist office on plaza), **Angastaco**, a small, modern, smart town with a *Hostería*, petrol station and bus service, and **Molinos** (all with limited bus services). The church of **San Pedro de Nolasco** in Molinos, mid-18th century, has a cactus-wood ceiling.

Cachi → *Phone code: 03868. Colour map 6, grid C3. Population: 7,200. Altitude: 2,280 m.*

Cachi is a beautiful town, in a valley made fertile by pre-Inca irrigation, set against a backdrop of arid mountains and the majestic Nevado del Cachi (6,380 m). Its rich Diaguita history, starting long before the Incas arrived in 1450, is well presented in the **Museo Arqueológico**① *Mon-Fri 0830-1930, Sat-Sun 1000-1300, US$0.30,* with painted funerary urns and intriguing petroglyphs. The simple church next door has a roof and lecterns made of cactus wood. There are panoramic views from the hill-top cemetery, 20 minutes' walk from the plaza, and satisfying walks to **La Aguada** (6 km away), or to the ruins at **Las Pailas**, 18 km west of Cachi, barely excavated. The view is breathtaking, with huge cacti set against snow-topped Andean peaks. It's a four-hour walk each way to Las Pailas (12-km track from the main road, the last part for a car is slow and rough; it leads to a farmstead from where it's 15 minutes on foot to the ruins; young man at the farm will offer to guide you). Cachi **tourist office** and Mercado de Artesanías on the plaza① *T491053, daily 0900-1300, 1500-2000.* ATM at **Banco Sud**, Güemes y Ruiz de los Llanos; internet on F Suárez on corner of passage up to Plaza, 0900-1300, 1700-2130 (connection unreliable).

From Cachi to Salta follow Ruta 40 for 11 km north to Payogasta (*Hostería*), then turn right to Ruta 33. The road climbs continuously up the Cuesta del Obispo passing a dead-straight stretch of 14 km known as La Recta del Tin-Tin through the magnificent **Los Cardones National Park**, with huge candelabra cacti, up to 6 m in height. Paving ends at the end of national park. The road reaches the summit at Piedra de Molino (3,347 m) after 43 km. Then it plunges down through the Quebrada de Escoipe, a breathtaking valley between olive green mountains, one of Argentina's great routes. The road rejoins Ruta 68 at El Carril, from where it is 37 km back to Salta.

● Sleeping

Cafayate *p142*
Accommodation is hard to find at holiday periods, but there are many places to stay. Off season, prices are much lower.
AL Bodega La Rosa, Rutas 68 y 40, T421201, www.micheltorino.com.ar. Luxurious, quiet retreat with fine food and excellent wines, set in gorgeous gardens. Highly recommended.
B Los Sauces, Calchaquí 62, T421158, directly behind the cathedral. Small tasteful rooms, breakfast included.
B-C Hostería Cafayate, T421296, www.soldel valle.com.ar. Comfortable rooms around a leafy colonial-style patio, restaurant and pool (summer only). Highly recommended.

C Emperador, Güemes 46, T03868-421268. On the Plaza, with a/c and heating, hot water, breakfast included.
C Hostal del Valle, San Martín 243, T421039, www.NorteVirtual.com. Well kept big rooms around leafy patio, charming owner. Highly recommended.
C-D Asembal, Güemes Norte y Almagro, T421065. Reasonable rooms in large building, but good value and welcoming, good restaurant, parking.
D Confort, Güemes Norte 232, T421091. Slightly kitsch but simple, hospitable staff.
D Tinkunaku, Diego de Almagro 12, 1 block from plaza, T421148. Pleasant spacious rooms, with weavings on the walls. Recommended.

E pp **Cafayate Youth Hostel**, Güemes Norte 441, on the left as you enter the town, T421440. Small, friendly, dorms and 2 doubles, shared bathrooms, English and Italian spoken, trekking organized.

E pp **El Hospedaje**, de Niño y Salta, T421680. Simple but pleasant rooms, good value.

E **Hostería Docente**, Güemes Norte 160, T421810. Light simple rooms, welcoming and central.

Campsite Municipal site **Lorohuasi** on RN40(S), T421051, US$2 pp plus tent. Hot water, pool, well maintained. Better still, **Luz y Fuerza**, T15639034, on RN40(S), quiet, good value, US$2 pp, massive pool, information on wine tours.

Valles Calchaquíes *p143*

B **Hostería Provincial de Molinos**, T03868-494002, hostaldemolinos@arnet.com.ar. Huge simple rooms arranged around big courtyards, historic building, good meals. Recommended.

Also in Molinos: **Hospedaje El Molle**, T0387-154 132488, at house called Susy Huasi, with house for 5. Next door is **Hospedaje Familiar Teasels of Molinos. Hospedaje San Agustín** at the Colegio Infantil T494015. All in E-F pp range.

E pp **Hostería Angastaco**, T03868-156 39016 or 0387-154 125636. Price includes breakfast, has bar, dining room and swimming pool (filled Jan-Mar).

Cachi *p143*

AL **El Molino de Cachi Adentro**, T491094, elmolinodecachi@salnet.com.ar. 4 km on the road to La Aguada, in restored mill, only 5 rooms, exquisite in every way.

B **El Cortijo**, opposite the ACA hotel, on Av Automóvil Club s/n, T491034, www.hostal elcortijo.com.ar. Lovely peaceful rooms, warm hospitality. Highly recommended.

B-C **Hostería Cachi**, at the top of Juan Manuel Castilla, T491904, www.soldelvalle.com.ar. Smart modern rooms, great views, pool, good restaurant, non-residents can use the pool if they eat lunch.

C **Llaqta Mawka**, Ruiz de Los Llanos s/n, up from Plaza, T491016, www.hotellllaqtamawka.todoweb salta.com.ar. Traditional frontage hides a modern block, with garden-cum-terrace, view of the Nevado de Cachi, swimming pool, discount for 3 days or more. Comfortable rooms, ample breakfast, internet, TV, good value and popular with tourists (parking on street).

D **Hospedaje Don Arturo**, Bustamante s/n, T491087. Homely, small rooms on quiet street.

E **Hospedaje El Nevado de Cachi**, Ruiz de los Llanos y F Suárez, T491912. Impeccable small

rooms around a central courtyard, hot water, *comedor* and Museo de Antigüedades Regionales.

Camping Municipal campsite at Av Travella s/n, T491053, with pool and sports complex, also *cabañas* and *albergue*.

❷ Eating

Cafayate *p142*

❚❚ **Baco**, Güemes Norte y Rivadavia, T154-028366. Parrilla, *pasta casera*, pizzas, regional dishes, *empanadas* and *picadas*. Seating inside and on street. Wine a bit pricier than elsewhere, but all local, good selection, good meat dishes.

❚❚ **La Carreta de Don Olegario**, Güemes, on Plaza. Huge and brightly lit, good set menus.

❚❚-❚ **El Rancho**, Toscano 3, T421256. On plaza, meats, regional dishes and pastas.

❚ **El Comedor Criollo**, Güemes Norte 254. A *parrilla*, also serving pasta, with *peña* at night. Recommended.

❚ **Café Bar Las Viñas**, Güemes Sur 58. Open all day, breakfasts and cheap *lomitos*.

❚ **Las Dos Marías**, San Martín 27 on Plaza. Small, serves excellent food.

❚ **El Rincón del Amigo**, San Martín 25. For great set menus and *empanadas*.

❚ **El Sol**, Güemes, on Plaza. Good for snacks and sandwiches.

Cafés

Café y Heladería Santa Bárbara, Güemes Norte 145. Ice creams and snacks.

Helados Miranda, Güemes Norte 170. Fabulous homemade ice cream, including delicious wine flavour.

Cachi *p143*

❚ **Confitería El Sol**, Ruiz de Los Llanos on the plaza. Regional food, limited menu, also offers horse riding, contact delsol_cachi@hotmail.com or T03868-156 38690.

❚ **Oliver Café**, Ruiz de Los Llanos on the plaza. For ice creams, coffee, breakfasts, fruit juices, sandwiches, pizza and fine wines.

❷ Shopping

Cafayate *p142*

Handicrafts Apart from the rather general souvenir shops, there are some fine handicrafts. Visit Calchaquí tapestry exhibition of **Miguel Nanni** on the main plaza, silver work at **Jorge Barraco**, Colón 157, T421244. Paintings by **Calixto Mamaní**, Rivadavia 452. Local pottery, woollen goods, etc are sold in the **Mercado de Artesanos Cafayetanos** on the plaza (small, pricey).

▲ Activities and tours

Cafayate *p142*
Cordillerana, de Niño 59. Tours, horses, bike hire.
MulaNegra Expedition & Adventure, San Martín 83 on Plaza, T421739. Alternative tourism, mountain bikes, excursions, riding, trekking.

⊖ Transport

Cafayate *p142*
Bus 2 bus terminals: With **El Indio** on Belgrano, ½ block from plaza, to **Santa María** (for Quilmes) 1056, arrive 1230, return at 0700. Cafayate-**San Carlos** and **Angastaco**, 1100, arrives San Carols 1200. 3 daily Cafayate-San Carlos. To Angastaco and **Cachi**, Thu only with **Marcos Rueda**. To/from **Tucumán**, Aconquija (Mitre y Rivadavia, Cafayate, open only when buses due), 3 daily, 5 hrs, US$7. **Cycle hire** Many places, consult tourist office. **Metropolitan Tours**, see Tour operators, is reliable. **Horse** Horses can be hired from **La Florida**, Bodega Etchart, 2 km south of Cafayate.

Salta → *Phone code: 0387. Colour map 6, grid C3. Population: 400,000. Altitude: 1,190 m.*

Founded in 1582, Salta, 1,600 km north of Buenos Aires, is an atmospheric city, with many fine colonial buildings, elegant plazas, stirring folkloric music and fabulous food. It lies in the broad Lerma valley, surrounded by steep and forested mountains, and is a good base for exploring the Andean regions, Cachi in the Calchaquí valleys to the south (described above) and the Quebrada de Humahuaca north of Jujuy (described in the next section).

Salta is a fascinating city to explore on foot; in a couple of hours you can get a feel for its wonderful architecture. Good maps are available from the **Provincial Tourist Office** ① *Buenos Aires 93 (1 block from main plaza), T431 0950, www.turismosalta.gov.ar. Open weekdays 0800-2100, weekends 0900-2000.* Very helpful, gives free maps, arranges accommodation in private houses in high season (July), only when hotels are fully booked. Other websites: www.turismoensalta.com of the Cámara de Turismo, Alvarado 455, p 1, T401 1002; www.iruya.com and www.redsalta.com. Local buses in the city charge US$0.25.

Sights

The heart of Salta, is **Plaza 9 de Julio**, planted with tall palms and surrounded by colonial buildings. On the plaza, the **Cabildo**, 1783, one of the few to be found intact in the country, houses the impressive **Museo Histórico del Norte** ① *Caseros 549, Tue-Sat 0930-1330, 1530-2030 (Sat 1630-2000), Sun 0930-1300, US$0.80.* The museum has displays on pre-Columbian and colonial history, independence wars, and a fine 18th-century pulpit. Opposite the Cabildo, is the 19th-century **Cathedral** (open mornings and evenings), painted pink and cream and reflected in the blue plate glass of a bank next door. It contains a huge late baroque altar and the much venerated images of the Virgin Mary and of the Cristo del Milagro, sent from Spain in 1592. The miracle was the sudden cessation of a terrifying series of earthquakes when the images were paraded through the streets on 15 September 1692. They still are, each September. Salta's newest museum, **Museo de Arqueología de Alta Montaña** (MAAM), ① *Mitre 77, T437 0499, www.maam.org.ar, Tue-Sun 0900-1300, 1600-2100, US$3.15, free Wed,* has (in theory) a superb collection of exhibits from Inca high-altitude shrines, including mummies of child sacrifices, video material in Spanish and English, also temporary exhibits. Controversy over the display of the mummies meant that, in 2005, only their photographs were on show. A block southwest of the Plaza is the **Museo de la Ciudad 'Casa de Hernández'** ① *Florida 97, T4373352, Mon-Sat 0900-1300, Mon-Fri 1530-2000, closed Sun.* This fine 18th-century mansion includes furniture and dull portraits, but a marvellous painting of Güemes. The magnificent façade of **San Francisco** church ① *on Caseros, 0730-1200, 1700-2100, free guided visits in Spanish,* rises above the skyline with its splendid tower, ornately decorated in plum red and gold. Further along Caseros, the Convent of **San Bernardo**, rebuilt in colonial style in the mid-19th century, has a beautifully carved wooden portal of 1762, but is not open to visitors.

At the end of Caseros is the **Cerro San Bernardo** (1,458 m) ① *accessible by cable car (teleférico from Parque San Martín), daily 1000-1945, US$1.35 one way, fine views, 45 mins' walk to return.* At the summit are gardens, waterfalls, a café, a silver collection and playground. Further along Avenida H Yrigoyen is an impressive **statue to General Güemes**, whose *gaucho* troops repelled seven powerful Spanish invasions from Bolivia between 1814 and 1821.

Up beyond the Güemes statue is the **Museo Antropológico**, ① *Paseo Güemes, www.antropologico.gov.ar, Mon-Fri 0800-1830, Sat 0900-1300, 1500-1800, helpful and knowledgeable staff, US$0.70.* Fascinating displays on pre-Inca cultures include painted urns, intriguing board-flattened skulls (meant to confer superiority), a mummy discovered high in the Andes and many objects from Tastil (see page 147). **Museo de Ciencias Naturales** ① *Parque San Martín, Tue-Sun 1400-1800, US$0.30,* displays a bewildering number of stuffed animals and birds; the armadillo collection is interesting.

San Antonio de los Cobres → *Phone code 0387, Population 4,000, Altitude 3,775 m.*

Sitting in the vast emptiness of the puna, San Antonio de los Cobres, 163 km by road from Salta, is a simple, remote mining town of adobe houses with a friendly Coya community. Ruta 51 leads to La Polvorilla railway viaduct (see below), 20 km, ask in town for details and beware sudden changes in the weather. Try the *quesillo de cabra* (goat's cheese) from Estancia Las Cuevas. The

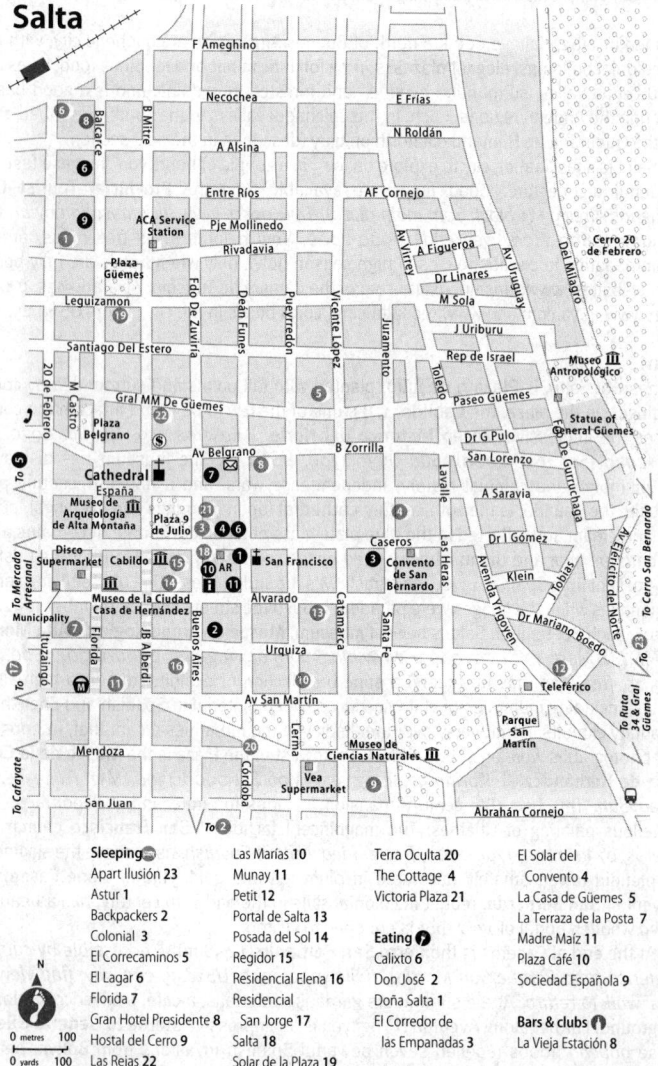

Salta

Sleeping		Terra Oculta **20**	El Solar del
Apart Ilusión **23**	Las Marías **10**	The Cottage **4**	Convento **4**
Astur **1**	Munay **11**	Victoria Plaza **21**	La Casa de Güemes **5**
Backpackers **2**	Petit **12**		La Terraza de la Posta **7**
Colonial **3**	Portal de Salta **13**	**Eating**	Madre Maíz **11**
El Correcaminos **5**	Posada del Sol **14**	Calixto **6**	Plaza Café **10**
El Lagar **6**	Regidor **15**	Don José **2**	Sociedad Española **9**
Florida **7**	Residencial Elena **16**	Doña Salta **1**	
Gran Hotel Presidente **8**	Residencial	El Corredor de	**Bars & clubs**
Hostal del Cerro **9**	San Jorge **17**	las Empanadas **3**	La Vieja Estación **8**
Las Rejas **22**	Salta **18**		
	Solar de la Plaza **19**		

N

0 metres   100
0 yards   100

⁝ Cloud line

One of the great railway journeys of South America is the Tren a las Nubes (Train to the Clouds). Engineered by Richard Maury, of Pennsylvania (who is commemorated by the station at Km 78 which bears his name) this remarkable project was built in stages between 1921 and 1948, by which time developments in road and air transport had already reduced its importance. The line includes 21 tunnels, 13 viaducts, 31 bridges, 2 loops and 2 zig-zags. From Salta the line climbs gently to Campo Quijano (Km 40, 1,520 m), where it enters the Quebrada del Toro, an impressive rock-strewn gorge. At El Alisal (Km 50) and Chorrillos (Km 66) there are zig-zags as the line climbs the side of the gorge before turning north into the valley of the Río Rosario near Puerto Tastil (Km 101, 2,675 m), missing the archaeological areas around Santa Rosa de Tastil. At Km 122 and Km 129 the line goes into 360° loops before reaching Diego de Almagro (3,304 m). At Abra Muñano (3,952 m) the road to San Antonio can be seen zig-zagging its way up the end-wall of the Quebrada del Toro below. From Muñano (3,936 m) the line drops slightly to San Antonio, Km 196. The spectacular viaduct at La Polvorilla is 21 km further at 4,190 m, just beyond the branch line to the mines at La Concordia. The highest point on the line is reached at Abra Chorrillos (4,475 m, Km 231). From here the line runs on another 335 km across a rocky barren plateau 3,500-4,300 m above sea level before reaching Socompa (3,865 m).

Note For safety reasons the Tren a las Nubes was suspended in 2005. No date for its resumption has been given (May 2006).

Huaira Huasi restaurant, used by tour groups, has a good menu. At **Santa Rosa de Tastil** there are important prehispanic ruins and a small museum (US$0.30), recommended. Basic accommodation next door to the museum, no electricity or heating, take food, water and candles. Take El Quebradeño bus (see below), a tour from Salta, or share a taxi.

The famous **Tren a las Nubes** is a 900 km, narrow gauge railway running from Salta through the town of San Antonio de los Cobres to Antofagasta, in northern Chile. San Antonio can also be reached by Ruta 51 from Salta. From **Campo Quijano**, the road runs along the floor of the Quebrada del Toro before climbing to Alto Blanco (paved section).

Ruta 51 from San Antonio de los Cobres to **San Pedro de Atacama**, Chile uses the **Sico** Pass (4,079 m). It's a spectacular route, crossing white salt lakes dotted with flamingoes and vast expanses of desert. Most of it is unpaved and the route has been replaced by that over Jama Pass (see page 154). There is a customs post at Paso Sico (you may be allowed to spend the night here), hours 0900-1900: check first in San Antonio de los Cobres if it is open. On the Chilean side continue via Mina Laco and Socaire to Toconao (road may be bad between these two points). Customs and immigration are in San Pedro de Atacama. Note that fruit, vegetables and dairy products may not be taken into Chile (search 20 km after Paso Sico). Gasoline is available in San Pedro and Calama. Obtain sufficient drinking water for the trip in San Antonio and do not underestimate the effects of altitude.

⬤ Sleeping

Salta *p145, map p146*
Book ahead in Jul holidays and around 10-16 Sep during celebrations of Cristo del Milagro. Among Salta's most desirable places to stay are its colonial-style *estancias*, known locally as *fincas*.
L El Lagar, 20 de Febrero 877, T431 9439/ 421 7943, ellagar@arnet.com.ar. An intimate boutique hotel owned by wine-making Etchart family, beautifully furnished rooms full of fine paintings, excellent restaurant, gardens (guests only). Highly recommended.
AL Finca San Antonio, Ruta 68 Km146, El Carril, T/F0387-490 2457, rcornejo@salnet.com.ar. 17th-century farm, pool, horse riding, farming activities.

AL Solar de la Plaza, Juan M Leguizamon 669, T431 5111, www.solardelaplaza.com.ar. Elegant, faultless service, sumptuous rooms, great restaurant.

AL-A Salta, Buenos Aires 1, in main plaza, T431 0740, www.hotelsalta.com. A Salta institution with neo-colonial public rooms, refurbished bedrooms, popular *confitería* and honorary membership of the Polo and Golf Club.

A pp Finca El Manantial, 25 km from Salta, T439 5506 or T156-858480, elmanantial@arnet.com.ar. Formal style, beautiful views, lovely rooms, marvellous food, swimming, farming activities.

A Finca Los Los, 40 km from Salta at the entrance to the Valles Calchaquíes, T431 7258, www.redsalta.com/loslos. Open Mar to Dec. Great hilltop views, charming rooms, beautiful gardens, pool, unforgettable horse riding to *asados* in the mountains. Handy for the airport and Cachi. Highly recommended.

A Gran Hotel Presidente, Av Belgrano 353, T/F431 2022, reservas@grhotelpresidente.com.ar. Chic and ultra-modern, very plush rooms, good restaurant with great value fixed price menu (US$7), pool, gym.

A Hostal Selva Montana, C Alfonsina Storni 2315, T492 1184, www.iruya.com/ent/selva montana. At San Lorenzo, 11 km northwest of the centre, extremely comfortable and relaxing modern hotel in traditional style, in forested hills, pool, good service. Highly recommended. Hourly bus service from Salta terminal, *Empresa Chávez*, platform 15, 30 mins, US$0.30. Last bus back about 2330.

A Portal de Salta, Alvarado 341, T431 3674, porsalta@infovia.com.ar. A/c, pleasant if faded glory, helpful, good breakfast, pool, restaurant, parking. Recommended.

A Portezuelo, Av Turística 1, T431 0104, www.portezuelohotel.com. Good views over the city, comfortable modern rooms, pool, fine restaurant, parking.

A Hostería de Chicoana, in Chicoana, 47 km south, T490 7009, martinpek@salnet.com.ar. Bohemian colonial style, English and German spoken, adventure excursions and horses for hire. Recommended.

B Colonial, Zuviría 6, T431 0805, www.hotelcolonialsalta.com. Functional, ask for the larger rooms on the plaza, with bath a/c, TV and *confitería*.

B Petit, H Yrigoyen 225, T4213012, www.todowebsalta.com.ar/petithotelsalta. Handy for the bus terminal and Cerro San Bernardo, plain pleasant rooms around a patio with pool and garden.

B Posada del Sol, Alvarado 646, T431 7300, www.hotelposadadelsol.com. With good service though dated rooms, popular with groups.

B Regidor, Buenos Aires 8, T431 1305. Smart wood panelling everywhere, small rooms, welcoming, good restaurant (no breakfast), good value.

B Victoria Plaza, Zuviría 16, T431 8500, vplaza@arnet.com.ar. Well-equipped rooms with a/c and heating, internet, *confitería*.

C Apart Ilusión (Sweet Dreams), José Luis Fuentes 743, Portezuelo Norte, T432 1081, www.aparthotel ilusion.com.ar. On the slopes of Cerro San Bernardo, beautiful views, new, well-equipped self-catering apartments, decorated with local handicrafts, English-speaking owner Sonia Alvarez, breakfast and parking available, very good value.

C Hostal del Cerro, Santa Fe 456, T431 8572, hostaldelcerro@hotmail.com. On Parque San Martín, close to bus terminal, some rooms are a bit small, but comfortable and good value, hot water, with TV, very helpful, breakfast extra, parking at nearby service station US$1.50.

D Astur, Rivadavia 752, T421 2107. Quaint little place on quiet street, good value for couples, basic rooms, handy for the train station.

D Florida, Urquiza 718, T421 2133, hotelflorida@salnet.com.ar. Stores luggage, fan, no breakfast. Recommended.

D Las Marías, Lerma 255, T422 4193, www.saltaguia.com/lasmarias. Central hostel, with breakfast, kitchen facilities, close to Parque San Martín.

D pp Las Rejas, General Güemes 569, T421 5971, www.lasrejashostel.com.ar. Very good, well-located, welcoming owners, English spoken. AHC Argentina Hostels Club.

D Munay, San Martín 656, T4224936, www.munayhotel.jujuy. Excellent budget option, new, smart rooms, warm welcome, breakfast included. Highly recommended.

D Res Elena, Buenos Aires 256, T421 1529. Quiet, 'charming', safe, a nice old doorway leads to high-ceilinged passages and rooms, courtyard with trees and plants, rooms with bath, hot water, no breakfast, free water for coffee, free medical service, run by a charming old gentleman, book in advance by phone.

D Res San Jorge, Esteco 244 y Ruiz de los Llanos 1164, T4210443, hotelsanjorge@arnet.com. Homely, with laundry and limited kitchen facilities, horse and trekking excursions (take buses 3 and 10 from bus station to San Martín y Malvinas). Recommended.

● *For an explanation of the sleeping and eating price codes used in this guide, see inside the front
● cover. Other relevant information is found in Essentials pages 68-69.*

E pp **Backpackers**, Buenos Aires 930, T4235910, www.backpackerssalta.com. 30 mins' walk from the plaza or Bus 12 from the terminal. Well-run, popular, HI affiliated, dorms, laundry, kitchen, travel information, dinners, parties and tours arranged.
E **The Cottage**, Juramento 54, T421 3668, hostalthecottage@hotmail.com. Hot water, kitchen facilities, internet, library and information, new.
E pp **El Correcaminos**, Vicente López 353, T422 0731, www.correcaminos.com.ar. 4 blocks from plaza, modern dorms, 2 doubles, shared bath, laundry, kitchen, garden.
E pp **Terra Oculta**, Córdoba 361, T421 8769, www.terraoculta.com. Party atmosphere, laid back place with small dorms, homely, kitchen, TV, email, laundry, great roof terrace bar, good annex at Av San Martín y Córdoba.

Campo Quijano *p147*
B **Hostería Punta Callejas**, T0387-490 4086. Bath, a/c, pool, tennis, riding, excursions.
Camping Municipal campsite, at entrance to Quebrada del Toro gorge, lovely spot with good facilities, hot showers, bungalows.

San Antonio de los Cobres *p146*
B **Hostería de las Nubes**, T0387-490 9059, edge of San Antonio on Salta road. Includes breakfast, comfortable, modern and spacious. Recommended.
D **Hospedaje Belgrano**, T490 9025. Welcoming, hot showers, evening meals.
E pp **Hostería Inti Huasi**, opposite the Aduana, T490 9041. Has a restaurant.

Ⓔ Eating

Salta *p145, map p146*
Salta has delicious and distinctive cuisine: try the *Locro, Humitas* and *Tamales*.
☂☂ **La Casa de Güemes**, España 730. Popular, local dishes and *parrilla*, traditionally cooked in the house where Güemes lived.
☂☂ **Don José**, Urquiza 484. Good *parrilla*.
☂☂ **Doña Salta**, Córdoba 46 (opposite San Francisco convent library). Excellent regional dishes and atmosphere, good value.
☂☂ **Sociedad Española**, Balcarce 653. Excellent, not open every day.
☂☂ **El Solar del Convento**, Caseros 444, half a block from plaza. Elegant and not expensive, champagne when you arrive, delicious steaks. Recommended.
☂☂ **La Terraza de la Posta**, España 456. Huge menu, but great for steak and *empanadas*. Cheap menus. Recommended.
☂☂-☂ **Calixto**, Deán Funes y Caseros, opposite San Francisco. Elegant but unfussy, smart service,

light jazz music, mainly meats and pastas, also serves breakfast, café and bar.
☂ **El Corredor de las Empanadas**, Caseros 117 and Zuviría 913. Delicious *empanadas* and tasty local dishes in airy surroundings.
☂ **Empanadas San Martín**, San Martín esquina Chacabuco. Large variety of *empanadas* and snacks, very popular with locals, hard to get a table on weekends.
☂ **Madre Maíz**, Alvarado 508. Very good vegetarian cooking, varied menu.
☂ **Mercado Municipal** at San Martín y Florida is unbeatable and atmospheric. Lots of good places around the Plaza 9 de Julio for *empanadas*.

Cafés
Café del Paseo at *Hotel Colonial*, Zuviría 6. Open 24 hrs, superb breakfast, good value.
Plaza Café next to *Hotel Salta* is more popular with Salteños, good for coffee or breakfast.

❶ Bars and clubs

Salta *p145, map p146*
Visit a *peña* to hear Salta's passionate folklore music live. There are many bars, called *peñas*, with excellent live bands on Balcarce towards railway station. **Balderrama**, is much touted but touristy. Head instead for: **La Casona del Molino**, Caseros 2600, T155-015934. Most authentic, in a crumbling old colonial house, good food and drink. **Gauchos de Güemes**, Uruguay 750, T492 1621, popular, delicious regional food. **La Vieja Estación**, Balcarce 885, T421 7727. Great atmosphere, good food.

❸ Festivals and events

Salta *p145, map p146*
15 Sep, Cristo del Milagro (see above); **24 Sep**, Battles of Tucumán and Salta. On **16-17 Jun**, folk music in evening and *gaucho* parade in morning around the Güemes statue. Salta celebrates **Carnival** with processions on the 4 weekends before Ash Wednesday at 2200 in Ciudad de Salta Stadium, 4 km south of town (US$0.50); also **Mardi Gras** (Shrove Tuesday) with a procession of decorated floats and dancers with intricate masks of feathers and mirrors. Water is squirted at passers-by and *bombas de agua* (small balloons to be filled with water) are sold for dropping from balconies.

❍ Shopping

Salta *p145, map p146*
Bookshops Feria del Libro, Buenos Aires 83. Huge shop, some in English. Librería Rayuela,

Alvarado 570. Foreign-language books. **Plural Libros**, Buenos Aires 220. Helpful.

Handicrafts Arts and handicrafts are often cheaper in surrounding villages. **Mercado Artesanal** on the western outskirts, at San Martín 2555, T434 2808, daily 0900-2100, take bus 2, 3, or 7 from Av San Martín in centre and get off as bus crosses the railway line. Excellent range and high quality. **Rincón del Carpincho**, Alvarado 556, makes leather boots and shoes from all kinds of leather including *carpincho*. **Siwok Crafts**, Zuviría 30. Quality wood carvings by the Wichi indigenous people, and typical *yika* woven bags.

Markets and supermarkets **Disco**, Florida y Caseros and Mitre y Leguizamon. Good supermarket. **Mercado Municipal**, San Martín y Florida, for meat, fish, vegetables, *empanadas*, *humitas* and other produce and handicrafts, closed 1300-1700 and Sun. **Norte**, 20 de Febrero y Caseros. Good supermarket. **San Francisco**, Deán Funes 596, T421 2984. 24-hr pharmacy. **Vea**, Mendoza entre Lerma y Catamarca. Good, large supermarket.

▲▲ Activities and tours

Salta *p145, map p146*
There are many tour operators, mostly on Buenos Aires, offering adventure trips and excursions; staff give out flyers on the street (likewise car hire companies). Out of season, tours often run only if there is sufficient demand; check carefully that tour will run on the day you want. All agencies charge similar prices for tours (though some charge extra for credit card payments): Salta city US$10; Quebrada del Toro US$30; Cachi US$25; Humahuaca US$30; San Antonio de las Cobres US$30; Cafayate (1 day) US$25; 2-day tour to Cafayate, Angastaco, Molinos, Cachi, US$45. The tourist office gives reports on agencies and their service.

Andino Travesías, España 202, p 2, T422 5333, www.andinosalta.com.ar. Adventurous trips combining horses, bikes and trekking.

Angelica Zaleski, T428 0861, 156-840164 (mob), angie_guide@hotmail.com. Independent guide, personalized tours by car, reasonable prices, speaks English.

Bici tours, T4394887, 156838067. Biker_s_2000@yaho.com. Specialists in cycle tours.

Hernán Uriburu, Leguizamon 446, T431 0605, www.nortetrekking.com/hru.htm. Well known and highly regarded for his horse- or mule-riding expeditions to the mountains, sleeping at locals' houses, very professional.

La Veloz Turismo, Buenos Aires 44, T401 2000, www.laveloztrismo.com.ar. English spoken.

Movitrack, Buenos Aires 28, T431 6749, www.movitrack.com.ar. Entertaining safaris in a 4WD truck, to San Antonio de los Cobres, Humahuaca, Cafayate and Iruya, also over Paso de Sico to Chile, German, English spoken, expensive. They also have an OxyBus for high-altitude journeys.

Norte Trekking, Av del Libertador 1151, Barrio Grand Bourg, T436 1844, www.nortetrekking.com. Excellent tours all over Salta and Jujuy, to Iruya, over Jama Pass to San Pedro de Atacama, hiking, horse riding, excursions to El Rey national park with experienced guide Federico Norte, knowledgeable, speaks English. Tailors tours to your interest and budget. Highly recommended.

Puna Expediciones, Agustín Usandivaras 230, T434 1875 or T154-030263, www.punaexpeditions.com.ar. Well qualified and experienced guide Luis H Aguilar organizes treks in remote areas of Salta and Jujuy. Highly recommended.

Ricardo Clark Expeditions, Caseros 121, T/F421 5390. Specialist tours for twitchers, English spoken.

Saltur, Caseros 485, T421 2012, F432 1111, saltursalta@arnet.com.ar. 4WD expeditions to national parks, Calchaquí valley, horse riding.

Turismo del Altiplano, Buenos Aires 68, T422 2394, laltiplano@hotmail.com. Conventional and adventure tourism, English spoken.

Turismo San Lorenzo, Dávalos 960, San Lorenzo. T492 1757, www.turismosanlorenzo.com. For horse riding and adventure tourism, well run. Recommended.

⊖ Transport

Salta *p145, map p146*
Air The airport is 11 km southwest, a US$1.55 shuttle bus ride to central hotels (remise taxi US$4). Bus 22 to access to airport from San Martín, US$0.35; don't be fooled by taxi touts who tell you there is no bus. LAB to **Santa Cruz** (Bolivia). AR flies to **Bs As** (2 hrs). AR, LAB to **Córdoba**.

Bus Terminal is 8 blocks east of the main plaza, T401 1143 for information. Toilets, *locutorio*, café, *panadería*, kiosks. To **Buenos Aires**, several daily, US$30 *semicama*, 20-22 hrs (TAC – T431 6600), **Panamericano**, **Balut**, **Brown**, **Chevallier** – T431 2819, **La Internacional** and others). To **Córdoba**, several daily, 12 hrs, US$12-14, *Panamericano* (T401 1118), twice daily, **Veloz del Norte**, T401 2164. To **Santiago del Estero**, 6 hrs, US$11. To **Tucumán**, 4½ hrs, several firms (*La Veloz del Norte* recommended), US$7-9. To **Mendoza** via Tucumán, several companies, eg **Andesmar**, T421 3372, daily, US$29-38 17-20 hrs. To **Jujuy**, **Balut**, **La Veloz del Norte**, **Atahualpa** and others, hourly between 0600 and 2200, 'directo', US$3, 2 hrs. To **La Rioja**, US$11, 10 hrs. To **Puerto Iguazú**,

Andesmar, US$42-52, 25 hrs, daily. To **Cafayate**, US$6, 3½ hrs, 2-4 daily, with **Marcos Rueda**, T421 4447, also to **Cachi** daily 0700, Tue and Sat 1330, Thu 1530, Sun 1700; Cachi Salta Mon-Sat 0905, Mon, Thu, Fri, Sun 1500, Sun 1615, and **Molinos**, daily except Tue and Thu, US$8.20. To **Belén**, Wed 0700 with **El Indio**, T431 9389), via Angastaco, San Carlos, Cafayate and Santa María, where you have to change bus to **Parra**, US$7.65. **El Indio** also goes daily to/from **Cafayate**, US$4.75. To **Rosario de la Frontera**, US$2.50, 2½ hrs. To **San Antonio de Los Cobres**, 5 hrs, El Quebradeño, daily, US$5.50.

International buses: To **Paraguay**: Flecha Bus (www.flechabus.com.ar) daily to Clorinda (at the border), 16 hrs, and **La Nueva Estrella**, T422 4048, 3 services weekly, US$27; buses or taxis will take you from there to Paraguay for a small fee. Alternatively travel to **Resistencia**, daily, US$19 with **La Veloz del Norte**, Flecha Bus, La Nueva Estrella, Autotransportes Mendoza or to **Formosa**, with *La Nueva Estrella*, US$25, 15 hrs, changing then, to a direct bus to Asunción. To **Chile**: Services to **Calama, San Pedro de Atacama, Antofagasta, Iquique** and **Arica** with **Géminis** and **Pullman**, T422 1366, pullmansalta@yahoo.com.ar, via Jujuy and the Jama Pass, three times a week, US$25 to **San Pedro** (Géminis, 11 hrs, US$22, stops for a meal, Pullman, 10 hrs, US$25, provides a snack) and US$25 to **Calama**, 18 hrs to Antofagasta. Géminis and Pullman offices are outside the back of the terminal, across the street, at Dionisio Puch 117. Tour operators charge US$50 to San Pedro. To **Bolivia**: To **La Quiaca**, on Bolivian border, with Balut and others, 7½ hrs, US$7-10. To **Orán**, daily, 6 hrs, US$6, and **Aguas Blancas** with Balut and La Veloz del Norte, US$8, daily for Bermejo, Bolivia; thence road connection to **Tarija**. To **Yacuiba**, via **Pocitos** (Bolivian border, see page 156), for **Santa Cruz**, US$7-12 with several companies to **Pocitos**, 6 hrs, very full, road paved; La Veloz del Norte/Leal Bus goes through to **Santa Cruz**, US$23.50.

Car hire Avis, at the airport, Ruta 51, T424 2289, salta@avis.com.ar. Efficient and very helpful, recommended. **Europe Rent A Car**, Buenos Aires 186, T422 3609. **Ruiz Moreno**, Buenos Aires 1, T431 8049, in *Hotel Salta*, helpful. **Semisa Renta Truck 4x4**, Buenos Aires 1, Local 6, T423 6295, febearzi@salnet.com.ar. **Integral**, Buenos Aires 189, T155-016451. Many others.

Train Station at 20 de February y Ameghino, 9 blocks north of Plaza 9 de Julio, taxi US$1. The **Tren a las Nubes** (Train to the Clouds, see page 147) runs between Salta and La Polvorilla

viaduct (400 km round trip). The service was closed by the provincial government in 2005. To **Socompa** (Chilean border): a cargo train with 2 passenger carriages leaves Salta Wed about 0900 (in theory), ticket office opens 0800 (queue from 0600), US$5 one way to San Antonio, US$8 one way to Socompa, 27 hrs one way via San Antonio (14 hrs). There is a dining car and a bar. Long delays are common on this route and you may do most of the journey in the dark; check locally if it is running. Take water and warm clothing. Beyond Socompa there are irregular freight trains into Chile (Augusta Victoria, Baquedano or Antofagasta): officially the Chilean railway authorities do not permit passengers to travel on this line, and it's hard to get information about departures. To travel on by train or truck may involve a wait of several days. There are only 4 buildings in Socompa: no food or accommodation, but try the Chilean customs building.

Cachi p143
Bus To **Salta**, Marcos Rueda, T491063, schedules below. To **Molinos** daily. To **Cafayate** El Indio Thu morning only, returning Thu afternoon.

❶ Directory

Salta p145, map p146
Airline offices AR, Caseros 475, T431 1331/ 0862. LAB, Caseros 529, T431 0320.
Banks Banks, open 0730-1300, all have ATMs (many on España). **Banco de la Nación**, Mitre y Belgrano. **Banco de Salta**, España 550 on main plaza. Cashes TCs. **Amex**, **Chicoana Turismo**, Zuviría 255, changes TCs. **Dinar**, Mitre 101/109; street changers opposite. **Masventas**, España 610, T431 0298, Changes dollars, euros, Chilean pesos and TCs. You can get Chilean pesos at good rates. **Cultural centres** Alliance Française, Santa Fe 20, T421 0827. **Embassies and consulates** Bolivia, Mariano Boedo 34, T421 1040, open Mon-Fri, 0900-1400 (unhelpful, better to go to Jujuy). Chile, Santiago del Estero 965, T431 1857. Belgium, Pellegrini 835, T423 4252. Spain, República de Israel 137, T431 2296, F431 0206. Italy, Santiago del Estero 497, T432 1532. France, Santa Fe 156, T431 2403. Germany, Urquiza 409, T421 6525, F431 1772, consul Juan C Kühl, helpful. **Internet** Many fast and cheap places around the centre, some 24 hrs. **Post offices** Deán Funes 160, between España and Belgrano. **Telephones** Several *locutorios* in town, some offer internet access. **Useful addresses** Immigration: Maipú 35, 0730-1230.

Jujuy → *Colour map 6, grid C4. Population: 237,000. Phone code: 0388. Altitude: 1,260 m.*

Though it lacks Salta's elegance, since there are few colonial buildings remaining, the historical city of Jujuy is the starting point for some of the country's most spectacular scenery and its distinctly Andean feel, evident in its food and music. With extremely varied landscapes, the area is rich in both contemporary and ancient culture, with prehispanic ruins at Tilcara, delightful villages and excursions. The **tourist office** on the plaza ① *Gorriti y Belgrano, Mon-Fri 0700-2100, Sat-Sun 0800-1400, 1500-2100, www.jujuy.gov.ar*, accommodation leaflet and map. Also at bus terminal 0700-2100.

Sights

San Salvador de Jujuy (pronounced Choo-Chooey, with *ch* as in Scottish loch) often referred to by locals as San Salvador, is the capital of Jujuy province and sits in a bowl of lushly wooded mountains. The city was finally established in 1593, after earlier attempts met resistance from local indigenous groups, but the city was plagued by earthquakes, sacking and the Calchaquíes Wars for the next 200 years. It struggled to prosper, then in August 1812 Gen Belgrano, commanding the republican troops, ordered the city to be evacuated and destroyed before the advancing Spanish army. This extraordinary sacrifice is marked on 23-24 August by festivities known as El Exodo Jujeño with gaucho processions and military parades.

Away from the busy shopping streets, in the eastern part of the city, is the **Plaza Belgrano**, a wide square planted with tall palms and orange trees. It's lined with impressive buildings, including the elaborate French baroque-style **Casa de Gobierno** *daily 0900-2100*, containing the famous flag Belgrano presented to the city. On the west side is the late 19th-century **Cathedral** (the original, 1598-1653, was destroyed by earthquake in 1843) containing one of Argentina's finest colonial treasures: a gold-plated wooden pulpit, carved by *indígenas* in the Jesuit missions, depicting gilded angels mounting the stairs. The modern church of **San Francisco**, Belgrano y Lavalle, contains another fine gilded colonial pulpit, with ceramic angels around it, like that at Yavi. The **Museo Histórico Franciscano** ① *daily 0900-1300, 1600-2100*, at the church, includes 17th-century paintings and other artefacts from Cuzco. There are several other museums; don't miss the **Museo Arqueológico Provincial** ① *Lavalle 434, daily 0900-1200, 1500-2100*, with beautiful ceramics from the Yavi and Humahuaca cultures, haphazardly displayed, a mummified infant, and a 2500-year old sculpture of a goddess giving birth.

There are hot springs 19 km west at **Termas de Reyes** ① *1 hr by bus Empresa 19 de Abril (línea 14) from bus terminal, hourly, US$0.50, municipal baths US$0.50 and pool US$1; also cabins with thermal water*. This resort (**Hotel Termas de Reyes** ① *T0388-492 2522, info@termasdereyes.com.ar*) is set among magnificent mountains.

● Sleeping

Jujuy *p152*

A Hostería Posta de Lozano, Ruta 9, Km 18 north, T498 0050, posta@imagine.com.ar. Good restaurant and pools with fresh mountain water.
A Jujuy Palace, Belgrano 1060, T/F423 0433, jpalace@imagine.com.ar. Conference hotel, well-equipped rooms, restaurant has good reputation.
B Panorama, Belgrano 1295, T423 2533, hotelpanorama@mail.com.ar. Business hotel, but more appealing, better value with stylish rooms.
C Fenicia, 19 de Abril 427, T/F423 1800. A welcoming place, 1980's chic, spacious rooms (ask for the ones with swish bathrooms), some with great views. Recommended.
C Internacional, Belgrano 501 (Plaza Belgrano), T423 1599, interjuy@imagine.com.ar. On north west corner of the Plaza, quiet, smart, good value. Great views over city.

D Huaico, Av Bolivia 3901, T423 5186, hotelhuaicojujuy@hotmail.com. 1½ km from the centre, near the park, useful if you're heading north, with special rates for students.
D Sumay, Otero 232, T423 5065. Rather dark, but clean, very central, helpful staff.
There are a number of cheap places near the bus terminal, of which the following are safe and comfortable, including:
E Res San Carlos, República de Siria 459, T422 2286. Shared bath, no TV, nicely maintained.
E San Antonio, Lisandro de la Torre, T422 5998, opposite terminal. Basic, looked after by 3 sisters and the whole family is kind. Recommended.
F pp Rany's, Dorrego 327 next to bus station, T423 0042. Cheaper rooms without TV, basic, but clean and the lady owner is very kind, no breakfast, but loads of cafés around.
Camping El Refugio is closest, Yala, Km 14.

🍴 Eating

Jujuy p152

🍴 **Chung King** (accommodation upstairs but not good), Alvear 627. Atmospheric for regional food. Sister restaurant next door, for '50 kinds of pizza'.

🍴 **Krysys**, Balcarce 272. Popular bistro-style *parrilla*, excellent steaks.

🍴 **La Candelaria**, Alvear 1346, some way out of town. Recommended *parrilla*, good service.

🍴 **Madre Tierra**, Belgrano 619, behind the wholemeal bakery of same name. For vegetarians (or for a break from all the meat), delicious food (open 0700-1430, 1600-2130).

🍴 **Manos Jujeños**, Sen Pérez 222. Regional specialities, the best *humitas*, charming, good for the *folclore* music at weekends.

🍴 **Ruta 9**, Lavalle 287. Another great place, slightly cheaper, for *locro* and *tamales*.

🍴 Following Lavalle across the bridge to the bus terminal (where it becomes Dorrego) there are lots of cheap *empanada* places.

Several good cafés, all on the same block of Belgrano between Lavalle and Necochea.

Color Esperanza, opposite Confitería La Royal. Bright new café serving cheap *lomitos* and burgers.

Confitería La Royal Belgrano 770. A classic café, coffee and pastries.

Pingüino is the best *heladería* in town.

Sociedad Española, opposite on the same corner. Good cheap set menus with a Spanish flavour.

Tía Bigote, Pérez y Belgrano. Café and pizzería.

🛍 Shopping

Jujuy p152

Handicrafts There are stalls near the cathedral. Centro de Arte y Artesanías, Balcarce 427. **Paseo de las Artesanías**, on the west side of the plaza.

Maps and travel guides Librería Belgrano, Belgrano 602. English language magazines and some books. **Librería Rayuela**, Belgrano 636.

Markets For food, you can't beat the Municipal market at Dorrego y Alem, near the bus terminal. Outside, women sell home-baked *empanadas* and *tamales*, and delicious goat's cheese, and all kinds of herbal cures.

Supermarkets Norte, Belgrano 825 and a bigger branch at 19 de Abril y Necochea.

🔺 Activities and tours

Jujuy p152

De Bor Turismo, Lavalle 295, T402 0241. 10% discount for ISIC members on local excursions.

Horus Turismo, Belgrano 722, T422 7247, horus@imgine.com.ar.

NASA, Senador Pérez 154, T422 3938. Guided tour to Quebrada de Humahuaca (US$30 pp, min 4

people); 4WD for rent. For information on bird watching, contact Mario Daniel Cheronaza, Peatonal 38, No 848-830, Viviendas 'El Arenal', Jujuy.

🚌 Transport

Jujuy p152

Air Airport at El Cadillal, 32 km southeast. Bus terminal at Iguazú y Dorrego, 6 blocks south of the centre, T4222134, T491 1101. Minibus to town US$2.50; taxi, US$13. Flights to **Buenos Aires**, **Córdoba**, **Tucumán** and **Salta** with AR, T423 7100.

Bus To **Buenos Aires**, 20-24 hrs, US$22 *semi cama*, several daily with **TAC**, **La Estrella**, **Panamericano**, and others. Via Tucumán to **Córdoba**, **Panamericano** and **La Veloz del Norte**, daily to **Tucumán**, 5 hrs, US$7, and **Córdoba**, 14 hrs US$15. To **Salta**, see above. To **La Quiaca**, 4-6 hrs, US$6, **Panamericano**, **Balut**, **El Quiaqueño**. Several rigorous luggage checks en route for drugs, including coca leaves. To **Humahuaca**, **Evelia** and others, US$2, 3 hrs, several daily, via Tilcara 2 hrs, US$2.50. To **Orán** and **Aguas Blancas** (border with Bolivia), daily with **Balut** and **Brown**, via San Pedro and Ledesma. To **Purmamarca**, take buses to Susques or to Humahuaca (those calling at Purmamarca village). To **Susques**, **Purmamarca** and **Andes Bus**, US$ 5, 4-6½ hrs, daily (except Mon). To **Calilegua**: various companies to Libertador Gral San Martín almost every hour, eg **Balut**, from there take a minibus, or taxi for US$1.50. All Pocitos buses pass through Libertador San Martín, eg **Panamericano**, **Estrella**, **El Rápido**.

To Chile: via the **Jama** pass (4,200 m), the route taken by most traffic, including trucks, crossing to northern Chile; hours 0900-1900. **Géminis** bus tickets sold at **Ortiz Viajes**, L N Alem 917, ortizviajes@latinmail.com.

🛈 Directory

Jujuy p152

Banks ATMs at: **Banco de Jujuy**, Balcarce y Belgrano, changes dollars. TCs can be changed at tour operators, **De Bor** and **Horus**, addresses above. **Citibank**, Güemes y Balcarce; **Bank Boston**, Alvear 802, **Banco Francés**, Alvear y Lamadrid; **Banco Salta**, San Martín 785.

Consulates Bolivia, Senador Pérez e Independencia, T424 0501, 0900-1300.

Internet Cyber Explora, Güemes 1049; Ciber Nob, Otero 317; HVA, Lavalle 390 (all US$0.50 per hour). Telecom centres at Alvear 870, Belgrano 730 and elsewhere. **Post offices** Independencia y Lamadrid. **Useful addresses** Immigration: 19 de Abril 1057, T422 2638.

Jujuy to the Chilean and Bolivian borders

Ruta 9, the Pan-American Highway, runs through the beautiful **Quebrada de Humahuaca**, a vast gorge of vividly coloured rock, with giant cacti in the higher parts, and emerald green oasis villages on the river below. (January-March ask highway police about flooding on the roads.) The whole area is very rich culturally: there are pre-Inca ruins at Tilcara (see below), and throughout the Quebrada there are fine 16th-century churches and riotous pre-Lent carnival celebrations. In Tilcara, pictures of the Passion are made of flowers and seeds at Easter and a traditional procession on Holy Thursday at night is joined by thousands of pan-pipe musicians.

For drivers heading off main roads in this area, note that service stations are far apart: at Jujuy, Tilcara, Humahuaca, Abra Pampa and La Quiaca. Spare fuel and water must be carried.

Jujuy to Chile

Beyond Tumbaya, where there's a restored 17th-century church, Ruta 52 runs 3 km west to **Purmamarca**, a quiet, picturesque village, much visited for its spectacular mountain of seven colours, striped strata from terracotta to green (best seen in the morning), a lovely church with remarkable paintings and a good handicrafts market. (Buses to Jujuy 1½ hrs, US$1.35; to Tilcara US$0.65. Salta-San Pedro de Atacama buses can be boarded here, book at Hotel Manantial del Silencio one day in advance.) It's worth staying the night in Purmamarca to appreciate the town's quiet rhythm. There's a helpful, tiny tourist office on the plaza with list of accommodation, maps and bus tickets, open 0700-1800.

From Purmamarca paved Ruta 52 leads through another *quebrada* over the 4,164 m Abra Potrerillos to the **Salinas Grandes** salt flats at about 3,400 m on the Altiplano (fantastic views especially at sunset). From here roads lead southwest past spectacular rock formations along the east side of the salt flats to San Antonio de los Cobres, and west across the salt flats via Susques to the Paso de Jama (4,400m) and Chile. The only accommodation beyond Purmamarca is at **Susques**, opposite the outstanding church (see below). There are no services or money exchange at the border. This is the route taken by most passenger and truck traffic going from Salta or Jujuy to San Pedro de Atacama.

Jujuy to Bolivia

About 7 km north of the Purmamarca turning is **La Posta de Hornillos** ① *open, in theory, Wed-Mon 0900-1800, free,* a museum in a restored colonial posting house where Belgrano stayed, also the scene of several battles. About 2 km further is **Maimará** with its brightly striped rock, known as the 'Artist's Palette', and huge cemetery, decorated with flowers at Easter.

Tilcara → *Phone code: 0388. Colour map 6, grid C3. Population: 3,500. Altitude: 2,460 m.*

Tilcara lies 22 km north of the turn-off to Purmamarca. It's the liveliest Quebrada village, the best base for exploring the area. It has an excellent handicrafts market around its pleasant plaza and plenty of places to stay and to eat. The little tourist office on Belgrano, next to *Hotel de Turismo*. Daily 0900-1200, 1500-2100 (closed Sunday afternoon). No phone. www.tilcarajujuy.com.ar. Visit the Pucará, a restored prehispanic hilltop settlement, with panoramic views of the gorge, and the superb **Museo Arqueológico** ① *daily 0900-1230, 1400-1800, US$1 for both,* with a fine collection of pre-Columbian ceramics, masks and mummies. There are four art museums in town and good walks in all directions. Recommended guide for informative trips to the puna, Iruya, Salinas Grandes, and archaeological sites, is historian **Ariel Mosca** ① *T495 5119, arielpuna@hotmail.com.* English spoken. There are fiestas at weekends in January, carnival and Holy Week. There's an ATM on the plaza, taking most international cards.

At **Uquía** is a fine church with extraordinary Cuzqueño paintings of angels in 17th-century battle dress.

Humahuaca → *Phone code: 03887. Colour map 6, grid B3. Population: 8,700. Altitude: 2,940 m.*

Although Humahuaca, 129 km north of Jujuy, dates from 1594, it was almost entirely rebuilt in the mid-19th century. Now it is visited by daily coach trips. It still has a distinctive culture of its own, though, and is a useful stopping point for travelling north up to the puna, or to Iruya. On 2 February is *La Candelaria* festival. *Jueves de Comadres, Festival de las Coplas y de la Chicha,* at the beginning of carnival is famously lively. Book accommodation ahead. ATM at *Banco de Jujuy* on main plaza, all major credit cards. On the little plaza is the church, **La Candelaria**, originally of 1631, rebuilt 1873-80, containing gaudy gold retables and 12 fine Cuzqueño paintings. Also on the plaza, tourists gather to watch a mechanical figure of San Francisco Solano blessing the town from **El Cabildo**, the neo-colonial town hall, at 1200 daily. Overlooking the town is the massive **Monumento a la Independencia Argentina**, commemorating the heaviest fighting in the country during the Wars of Independence. At **Coctaca**, 10 km northeast, there is an impressive and extensive (40 ha) series of pre-colonial agricultural terraces. To Iruya (see below).**Humahuaca**: tourist information available from the town hall, office hours.

Iruya → *Colour map 6, grid B3. Altitude: 2,600 m.*

A rough *ripio* road 25 km north of Humahuaca runs northeast from the Panamericana (RN9) 8 km to Iturbe (also called Hipólito Irigoyen), and then up over the 4,000 m Abra del Cóndor before dropping steeply, around many hairpin bends, into the Quebrada de Iruya. The road is very rough and unsuited to small hire cars, but is one of Argentina's most amazing drives. Iruya, 66 km from Humahuaca, is a beautiful hamlet wedged on a hillside, like a hide-away. Its warm, friendly inhabitants hold a colourful Rosario festival on first Sunday in October and at Easter. It is worth spending a few days here to go horse riding or walking: the hike (seven hours return) to the remote **San Isidro** is unforgettable. At Titiconte 4 km away, there are unrestored pre-Inca ruins (take guide). Iruya has no ATM or tourist information, but a public phone, and food shops.

Tres Cruces and Abra Pampa

Some 62 km north of Humahuaca on the Panamericana is Tres Cruces, where customs searches are made on vehicles from Bolivia. **Abra Pampa** (*Population 6,000*), 91 km north of Humahuaca, is a mining town. At 15 km southwest of Abra Pampa is the vicuña farm at **Miraflores**, the largest in Argentina. Information offered, photography permitted; buses go morning Monday-Saturday Abra Pampa-Miraflores.

Laguna de los Pozuelos ① *50 km northwest of Abra Pampa, Park office in Abra Pampa, T03887-491048; there are no visitor services and no bus transport, so it's best to go with a guide; the Laguna is 5 km from the road, very tough, high clearance recommended, walk last 800 m to reach the edge of the lagoon,* is a nature reserve with a lake at its centre visited by huge colonies of flamingoes. Check with the park office before going - the lake can be dry with no birds, eg in September. (Altitude 3,650 m, temperatures can drop to -25°C in winter.) *Diego Bach* leads excellent, well-informed excursions, including panning for gold as the Jesuits did. Also five-day treks on horseback to the pristine cloudforest of **Parque Nacional Baritú** ① *T03885-422797, punatours@hotmail.com,* are highly recommended.

From a point 4 km north of Abra Pampa roads branch west to Cochinoca (25 km) and southwest to **Casabindo** (62 km). On 15 August at Casabindo, the local saint's day, the last and only *corrida de toros* (running with bulls) in Argentina is held, amidst a colourful popular celebration. *El Toreo de la Vincha* takes place in front of the church, where a bull defies onlookers to take a ribbon and medal which it carries. The church itself is a magnificent building, with twin bell towers, and inside a superb series of 16th century angels in armour paintings. There is an **Albergue** *T03887-491129* (**F** per person), and buses run from Abra Pampa.

La Quiaca and Yavi → *Phone code: 03885. Altitude: 3,442 m. 5,121 km from Ushuaia. Colour map 6, grid B3.*

On the border with Bolivia, a concrete bridge links this typical border town with Villazón on the Bolivian side. Warm clothing is essential particularly in winter when temperatures can drop to -15°C, though care should be taken against sunburn during the day. On the third Sunday in October, villagers from the far reaches of the remote *altiplano* come to sell ceramic pots, sheepskins and vegetables, in the colourful three-day *Fiesta de la Olla*. Two ATMs, but no facilities for changing cash or TCs, but plenty of *cambios* in Villazón. *Farmacia Nueva*, half a block from Church, has remedies for altitude sickness. **Yavi** is 16 km east of La Quiaca. Its **church of San Francisco** (1690) ① *Tue-Sun 0900-1200 and Tue-Fri 1500-1800,* is one of Argentina's treasures, with a magnificent gold retable and pulpit and windows of onyx. Caretaker Lydia lives opposite the police station and will show you round the church. Opposite the church is the 18th-century house of the Marqués Campero y Tojo, empty, but for a small selection of handicrafts.

Border with Bolivia → *Argentine time is 1 hr later than Bolivia. Do not photograph the border area.*
The border bridge is 10 blocks from La Quiaca bus terminal, 15 minutes walk (taxi US$1).
Argentine office open 0700-2400; on Saturday, Sunday, and holidays there is a special fee of
US$1.50 which may or may not be charged. If leaving Argentina for a short stroll into Villazón,
show your passport, but do not let it be stamped by Migración, otherwise you will have to wait
24 hours before being allowed back into Argentina. Formalities on entering Argentina are
usually very brief at the border but thorough customs searches are made 100 km south at Tres
Cruces. Leaving Argentina is very straightforward, but travellers who need a visa to enter
Bolivia are advised to get it before arriving in La Quiaca.

Parque Nacional Calilegua → *Colour map 6, grid C3.*
① *Park office: San Lorenzo s/n, Calilegua, T03886-422046, pncalilegua@cooperlib.com.ar.*
*Reached by Ruta 83 from just north of Libertador, the park entrance is 10 km along the dirt
road (4WD essential when wet, hitching from Libertador possible), which climbs through the
park and beyond to Valle Grande (basic accommodation and shops), 90 km from Libertador.*
Libertador General San Martín, a sugar town 113 km northeast of Jujuy on Ruta 34 to
southeastern Bolivia, is the closest base for exploring the park, an area of peaks over 3,000 m
and deep valleys covered in cloud forest, with a huge variety of wildlife, including 260 species of
bird and 60 species of mammals (you may spot tapirs, pumas, tarucas, Andean deer and even
jaguars here) There are six marked trails of various lengths. The best trek is to the summit of
Cerro Amarillo (3,720 m), five days round trip from Aguas Negras, or three days from the village
of San Francisco (*hospedaje* and *comedores*). There is a ranger's houses at Aguas Negras, with
camping; drinking water from river nearby, and some cooking facilities and tables. Best time for
visiting is November-March. **Libertador General San Martín**: tourist office at the bus terminal.

Routes to Bolivia
From Libertador, Ruta 34 runs northeast 244 km, to the Bolivian border at Pocitos (also called
Salvador Mazza) and Yacuiba (see Eastern Bolivia, page 331). It passes through **Embarcación**
and **Tartagal** (good regional museum, director Ramón Ramos very informative). In **Pocitos**, the
border town, is F *Hotel Buen Gusto*, just tolerable. There are no *casas de cambio* here. From
Yacuiba, across the border, buses go to Santa Cruz de la Sierra. Customs at Pocitos is not to be
trusted (theft reported) and overcharging for 'excess baggage' on buses occurs. Several bus
companies including Atahualpa have services from the border to Salta and Tucumán.

An alternative route is via Aguas Blancas. At Pichanal, 85 km northeast of Libertador, Ruta
50 heads north via **Orán**, an uninteresting place (*Population 60,000*).

Aguas Blancas on the border is 53 km from Orán (restaurants, shops, but no
accommodation, nowhere to change money and Bolivianos are not accepted south of Aguas
Blancas). The passport office is open from 0700 to 1200 and 1500 to 1900. Insist on getting an exit
stamp. Buses run from Bermejo, across the river (ferry US$0.50), to Tarija. Northwest of Aguas
Blancas is the **Parque Nacional Baritú**, see above, under Abra Pampa. There are no facilities.

● Sleeping

Jujuy to Chile: Purmamarca *p154*
AL El Manantial del Silencio, Ruta 52 Km 3.5,
T0388-490 8080, www.hotelmanantial.com.ar.
Signposted from the road into Purmamarca.
Luxurious rooms, wonderful views, and charming
hosts, includes breakfast, heating , riding, pool.
C La Posta, C Santa Rosa de Lima 4 blocks up from
plaza, T4908029, www.postadepurmamarca.com.ar.
Breakfast, heating, helpful owner. Beautiful elevated
setting against the mountain, comfortable rooms.
Its restaurant, C Rivadavia at the plaza, serves
delicious local dishes (❦). Highly recommended.
D El Pequeño Inti, C Florida 10 m from plaza,
T4908089, elintidepurmamarca@hotmail.com.
Small, modern rooms around a little courtyard,
breakfast, hot water, good value. Recommended.

D El Viejo Algarrobo, C Salta behind the church,
T/F490 8038. Small but pleasant rooms, cheaper
with shared bath, good value and quality
regional dishes in its restaurant ❦).
E Hospedaje Familia García, C Lavalle ½ block
from the Plaza, T4908016, jhosep03@yahoo.com.ar.
Basic, shared bath, hot water, kitchen, family run.
E pp Hostal Las Vicuñitas, Susques,
T02887-490207, opposite the church, without
bath, hot water, breakfast available.

Jujuy to Bolivia: Maimará *p154*
C Posta del Sol, Martín Rodríguez y San Martín,
T499 7156, posta_del_sol@hotmail.com.
Comfortable, with restaurant, owner is tourist
guide and has helpful information.

Tilcara p154

Book ahead in carnival and around Easter when Tilcara is very busy.

C Posada con los Angeles, Gorriti s/n (signposted from plaza), T495 5153. Charming individually designed rooms, garden with views of mountains, relaxed atmosphere, excursions organized.

C Villar del Ala, Padilla 100, T495 5100, adriantilcara@hotmail.com. Very comfortable 1930's rooms, quiet garden with great views, pool, good food.

D Hostal La Granja, at Huacalera, Km 90, T0388-426 1766. A lovely rustic place with pool, outstanding food and service, a good base for exploring the region.

D Los Establos, Gorrito s/n (next to con los Angeles), T495 5379. Pretty, rustic rooms and well equipped *cabañas* for 2-6 people.

D Malka, San Martín s/n, 5 blocks from plaza up steep hill, T495 5197. Beautifully located *cabañas*, and an outstanding hostel, **F** pp, very comfortable rustic dorms, all with kitchen and laundry facilities, HI affiliated. Owner and guide Juan organizes a great range of trips, including several days' trek to Calilegua, horse riding and bike hire. Highly recommended.

D Quinta La Paceña, Padilla y Ambosetti, T495 5098, quintalapacena@yahoo.com.ar. Peaceful, architect-designed traditional adobe house, with stylish rooms for 2-4, gorgeous.

D Res El Antigal, Rivadavia s/n, ½ block from plaza, T495 5020. Comfortable, good beds, sunny patio, good value.

E pp **La Morada**, Debenedetti s/n, T/F495 5118. Good rooms for 2 to 5 people with cooking facilities.

E pp **Wiphala**, Jujuy 549, T495 5015. Small, warm atmosphere, kitchen.

Camping Camping El Jardín, access on Belgrano, T495 5128, US$2, hot showers, also **F** pp basic hostel accommodation.

Uquía p154

C Hostería de Uquía, next to the church, T03387-490523. Comfortable place to stay, also serves dinner.

Humahuaca p154

Accommodation is generally basic.

B Camino del Inca, on the other side of the river, T421136, tito@imagine.com.ar. Smart, well built modern place with restaurant (set menu US$4), pool, excursions. Two very simple *residenciales*.

D Hostal Azul, B Medalla Milagrosa, La Banda, T421107, www.hostalazulhumahuaca.com.ar. Across the river, smart, welcoming, new, pleasant, good restaurant and wine list, parking. Recommended.

D-E pp **Cabaña El Cardón**, T156-29072, www.elcardon.8K.com. Rural *cabaña* for 2-5 with all facilities, also regional foods, excursions and riding, charming family.

E pp **Posada El Sol**, over bridge from terminal, then 520 m, follow signs, T421466. Quiet rural area, rooms for 2-4 in a warm welcoming place, kitchen, also laundry, horse riding, owner will collect from bus station if called in advance. AHC Argentina Hostels Club.

E pp **Res El Portillo**, Tucumán 69, T421288. Dormitories are cramped, **D** rooms, nice place, shared bath, simple bar/restaurant.

Camping Across bridge by railway station, small charge for use of facilities.

Iruya p155

B Hostería de Iruya, www.hosteria deiruya.com.ar, T011-4394 9605 (Buenos Aires, www.maresur.com). A special place, extremely comfortable, with good food, and great views from the top of the village. Highly recommended.

D Hostal Federico Tercero, at *Café de Hostal*, bottom of the steep main street, T03887-156 30727. Owned by the delightful singer Jesús, with simple rooms, good food from breakfast to dinner, frequent live music.

E pp **Hosp Tacacho**, on the Plaza. Family welcome, simple rooms, great views, *comedor*.

Abra Pampa p155

E Residencial El Norte, Sarmiento 530, shared room, hot water, good food. *Res y restaurante Cesarito*, 1 block from main plaza.

Yavi p155

C Hostal de Yavi, T03887-490523, elportillo@cootepal.com.ar. Simple rooms but cosy sitting room, good food, relaxed atmosphere.

E La Casona 'Jatum Huasi', Sen Pérez y San Martín, T03885-422316, mccalizaya@ laquiaca.com.ar. Welcoming.

La Quiaca p155

C-D Hostería Munay, Belgrano 51, T423924, www.munayhotel.jujuy.com. Very pleasant, with comfortable rooms.

D Turismo, Siria y San Martín, T422243, intenmun@laquiaca.com.ar. The best place to stay: modern, comfortable rooms with TV, breakfast, pool, restaurant.

E pp **La Frontera** hotel and restaurant, Belgrano y Siria, downhill from *Atahualpa* bus stop, T422269. Good cheap food, basic but decent rooms, hospitable owner.

E Cristal, Sarmiento 539, T422255. Basic functional rooms, shared bath.

Libertador General San Martín *p117*
B Posada del Sol, Los Ceibo y Pucará, T03886-424900, posadadelsol@cooperlib.com.ar. Luxurious hotel, with pool, parking and restaurant (in different building).
D Artaza, Victoria 891, T03886-423214. With breakfast, basic hotel.
E Res Carioca, Victoria 173, T03886-421716. 3 blocks from terminal, a/c.

Orán *p156*
B Alto Verde, Pellegrini 671, T421214. Parking, pool, a/c.
C Res Crisol, López y Planes. Hot water. Recommended.

⊙ Eating

Tilcara *p154*
† **Pucará**, up the hill towards the Pucará, T495 5721. Exquisite, posh Andean food by renowned chef Garo Jurisic.
† **Pachamama**, Belgrano 590, next to *Hotel de Turismo* on the road into Tilcara. Pleasant, airy restaurant and café serving regional dishes, plus salads and pastas, reliable, popular with groups.
† **El Patio Comidas** Lavalle 352. Great range, lovely patio at the back.
† **El Rincón del Indio Chanampa**, on the Plaza. One of several cheap places, basic, serving *sandwiches de parrilla*, good snacks, live music at weekends.

Cafés
El Cafecito on the plaza. For a taste of Tilcara's culture, don't miss this place, good coffee and locally-grown herbal teas, live music at weekends from celebrated local musicians.
La Peña de Carlitos, with music from the charismatic and delightful Carlitos, also *empanadas*, and drinks.

Humahuaca *p154*
Most restaurants open only during the day, but hunt around at night for small cafés where locals eat. Popular places for lunch around the market.
† **La Cacharpaya**, Jujuy 295. Good and lively, often filled with parties at lunch time, Andean music. Recommended.
† **Humahuaca Colonial**, Tucumán 16. Good regional cooking, again, coach parties at midday.
† **El Pinocho**, Buenos Aires 452. Clean family restaurant, good value local dishes.
† **El Rancho**, Belgrano 478. Just around the corner from market, tasty local dishes and *pastas caseras*, where the locals eat.
† **Peña de Fortunato**, Jujuy y San Luis. Famous for great atmosphere and music.

158

⊙ Transport

Tilcara *p154*
El Quiaqueño combines with **Andesmar/ Brown**, passes Tilcara en route to **Jujuy** 4 times a day from 1340, and en route to **La Quiaca** 6 times a day from 1110. **Jama Bus** runs between Tilcara, Humahuaca and La Quiaca.

Humahuaca *p154*
Bus Buses to all places along the Quebrada from the terminal (toilets, *confitería*, fruit and sandwich sellers outside), to **Iruya** (see below) and to **La Quiaca**, with **Balut** and La Quiaqueña (more comfortable), several daily, 3 hrs, US$4. Rigorous police checks for drugs can cause delays on buses to La Quiaca. Keep passport with you.

Iruya *p155*
Bus Daily service from **Humahuaca** Empresa Mendoza, T03887-421016, 1030 daily, 3 hrs, US$3, returning 1515. Also excursions of several days organized by tour operators.

Yavi *p155*
Bus 4 daily from **La Quiaca**, US$0.50. Taxi available – US$9 return, including 1-hr wait.

La Quiaca *p155*
Bus Bus terminal, España y Belgrano, luggage storage. 6-8 buses a day to **Salta** (US$7-10) with **Balut** (7½ hrs), **Atahualpa** and others. Several daily to **Humahuaca** and **Jujuy**, schedules above. Take own food, as sometimes long delays. Buses are stopped for routine border police controls and searched for coca leaves. **Note**: Buses from Jujuy may arrive in the early morning when no restaurants are open and it is freezing cold outside.

Parque Nacional Calilegua *p156*
Bus From Libertador daily at 0830 going across the park to **Valle Grande** (US$4, 5 hrs), returning the same day. Also Tue, Thu, Sat to **Santa Ana** at 0600, US$4, 5 hrs, return 1430. *Remise* charges about US$2 from Libertador to Park entrance.

Aguas Blancas *p156*
Bus Between Aguas Blancas and **Orán** buses run every 45 mins, US$1, luggage checks on bus. Direct buses to **Güemes**, 8 a day, US$5; through buses to **Salta**, La Veloz del Norte, Panamericano and Atahualpa, several daily, US$8, 7-10 hrs. To **Tucumán**, *La Veloz del Norte*, *Panamericano* and La Estrella, 1 a day each company. To **Jujuy** with Balut and Brown, 3 daily. To **Embarcación**, US$2; some services from Salta and Jujuy call at **Orán** en route to **Tartagal** and **Pocitos**. Note that buses are subject to slow searches for drugs and contraband.

The Northeast

The river systems of the Paraná, Paraguay and Uruguay, with hundreds of minor tributaries, small lakes and marshlands, dominate the Northeast. Between the Paraná and Uruguay rivers is Argentine Mesopotamia containing the provinces of Entre Ríos, Corrientes and Misiones, this last named after Jesuit foundations, whose red stone ruins have been rescued from the jungle. The great attraction of this region is undoubtedly the Iguazú Falls, which tumble into a gorge on a tributary of the Alto Paraná on the border with Brazil. But the region offers other opportunities for wildlife watching, such as the national parks of the Wet Chaco and the amazing flooded plains of the Esteros del Iberá. This is also the region of mate *tea, sentimental* chamamé *music and tiny* chipá *bread.*

Up the Río Uruguay

This river forms the frontier with Uruguay and there are many crossings as you head upstream to the point where Argentina, Uruguay and Brazil meet. On the way, you'll find riverside promenades, sandy beaches and palm forests.

Gualeguaychú → *Phone code: 03446. Colour map 8, grid B5. Population: 80,000.*

On the Río Gualeguaychú, 19 km above its confluence with the Río Paraná and 220 km north of Buenos Aires, this is a pleasant town with an attractive *costanera* and a lively pre-Lenten carnival. Some 33 km southeast the Libertador Gral San Martín Bridge (5.4 km long) provides the most southerly route across the Río Uruguay, to Fray Bentos (vehicles US$4; pedestrians and cyclists may cross only on vehicles, officials may arrange lifts). The Uruguayan consulate is at Rivadavia 810, T426168. **Tourist office** ① *Plazoleta de los Artesanos, T423668, www.gualeguaychuturismo.com, 0800-2000 (closing later in summer).*

Casa de Aedo ① *San José y Rivadavia (on plaza), Wed-Sat 0900-1145, Fri-Sat also 1600-1845 (in summer afternoon times are 1700-1945).* The oldest house in the city, it served as Garibaldi's headquarters when he sacked the city in 1845. An old iron bridge crosses the river to the beautiful, 110-ha **Parque Unzué**. Nice walks can be taken along the *costanera* between the bridge and the small port, from where short boat excursions and city tours leave (also from the *balneario municipal*), T423248, high season only. **El Patio del Mate**① *G Méndez y Costanera, T424371, www.elpatiodelmate.com.ar, daily 0800-2100.* A workshop dedicated to the *mate* gourd, coming in all shapes and prices.

Concepción del Uruguay → *Phone code: 03442. Colour map 8, grid B5. Pop: 65,000.*

The first Argentine port of any size on the Río Uruguay was founded in 1783. The old town is centred on Plaza Ramírez. Overlooking the main plaza is the church of the Immaculate Conception which contains the remains of Gen Urquiza. **Palacio San José**① *32 km west of the town, www.palaciosanjose.com.ar, Mon-Fri 0830-1230, 1400-1830, Sat-Sun 0900-1745, US$1, free guided visits 1000, 1100, 1500, 1600.* Urquiza's former mansion is now a museum, with artefacts from Urquiza's life and a collection of period furniture, recommended. Take Ruta 39 west and turn right after Caseros train station. Buses to Paraná or Rosario del Tala stop at El Cruce or Caseros, 4 or 8 km away respectively, US$0.80 (take *remise* taxi from Caseros). *Remise* taxis charge about US$8 with 1½ hours wait. Tour operators run *combis* in high season US$5 including entry. The **Museo Casa de Delio Panizza** ① *Galarza y Supremo Entrerriano, 0900- 1200, 1400-1800 (1800-2100 in summer)*, in a mansion dating from 1793, contains 19th-century furnishings and artefacts. **Tourist office** ① *Galarza y Daniel Elía, T425820, www.concepcionentrerios.com.ar. Mon-Fri 0700-1300, 1400-2000, weekends 0700-2200 in high season.*

Colón → *Colour map 8, grid A5. Population: 19,200.*

Founded in 1863, Colón, 45 km north of Concepción del Uruguay, has shady streets, an attractive *costanera* and long sandy beaches, with cliffs visible from a considerable distance. Huge sand banks and densely forested islands on Río Uruguay can be visited on enjoyable boat excursions with *Ita i Cora*, www.itaicora.com. A road bridge links Colón and Paysandú, Uruguay. The most attractive part of the town is the **port district**, next to Plaza San Martín. On the plaza and the streets which go down to the riverside are fine old houses, including the former passenger terminal, now housing the **tourist office** (address above). At Avenida 12 de Abril y Paso is **La Casona** (1868), with a handicraft exhibition and shop. North of the port, Calle Alejo Peyret gives access to the *balnearios* and Calle Belgrano leads to the **Complejo Termal** ① *T424717, daily 0900-2100, US$2*, with 10 thermal pools (34°-40°).**Tourist office** ① *Av Costanera Quirós y Gouchón, T421233, www.entrerios-colon.com.ar. Monday-Friday 0630-2100, Saturday 0700-2100, Sunday 0800-2100.*

Parque Nacional El Palmar
① *51 km north of Colón. US$4 (Argentines US$2). Buses from Colón, 1 hr, US$1.50, will drop you at the entrance and it is easy to hitch the last 12 km to the park administration. Remise taxis from Colón or Ubajay offer tours, eg from Colón: US$15 for a 4-hr return trip, including tour or waiting time. There are camping facilities (electricity, hot water), with restaurant opposite, and a small shop.*
This park of 8,500 ha is on the Río Uruguay, off Ruta 14. The park contains varied scenery with a mature palm forest, sandy beaches on the Uruguay river, indigenous tombs and the remains of an 18th-century quarry and port, a good museum and many rheas and other birds. The Yatay palms grow up to 12 m and some are hundreds of years old. It is best to stay overnight as wildlife is more easily seen in the early morning or at sunset. Very popular at weekends in summer.

Refugio de Vida Silvestre La Aurora del Palmar ① *To345-490 5027, www.aurora delpalmar.com.ar, free,* is opposite the Parque Nacional El Palmar, 3 km south of Ubajay at Km 202 Ruta 14. A private reserve protecting a similar environment to that of its neighbour, La Aurora covers 1,150 ha, of which 200 are covered with a mature palm forest. There are also gallery forests along the streams and patches of *espinal* or scrub. Birds are easily seen, as are capybaras along the streams. The administration centre is only 500 m from Ruta 14 and services are well organized. There are guided excursions on horseback, on foot or canoe, two hours maximum, US$5. Camping US$2 pp a day plus US$1.50 per tent, or **D** in old railway carriages. Buses from Colón or those coming from the north will drop you at the entrance. Tell the driver you are going to La Aurora del Palmar, to avoid confusion with the national park. *Remise* taxi from Ubajay US$2. Book in advance or check availability for excursions.

Concordia → *Colour map 8, grid A5. Population: 93,800.*
Just downriver from Salto, Uruguay, Concordia, 104 km north of Colón, is a prosperous city. The Río Uruguay is impassable for large vessels beyond the rapids of Salto Chico near the city, and Salto Grande 32 km upriver, where there is a large international hydro electric dam, providing a crossing to Uruguay. Above Salto Grande the river is generally known as the Alto Uruguay. In the streets around the main **Plaza 25 de Mayo** there are some fine public buildings. The city has a range of hotels and restaurants. **Tourist office** ① *Plaza 25 de Mayo, daily 0700-2400.*

To Uruguay Take No 4 bus from the bus terminal, marked 'Puerto', for the **ferry** crossing to Salto, US$2, 15 minutes. Tickets are obtainable at a small kiosk, which shuts 15 minutes before departure, outside immigration in the building marked 'Resguardo'. Five departures Monday-Friday, four departures Saturday, two departures (0800, 1800) Sunday, 20 minutes, passengers only. The **bus** service via the Salto Grande dam is run by **Flecha Bus** and **Chadre**, two a day each, not Sunday, US$2, 1 hour, all formalities on the Argentine side, passports checked on the bus. **Bicycles** are not allowed to cross the international bridge but officials will help cyclists find a lift. The **Uruguayan consulate** is at Pellegrini 709, of 1 C, T421 0380. About 153 km upstream from Concordia is the small port of **Monte Caseros**, with the Uruguayan town of Bella Unión, on the Brazilian border, almost opposite.

Paso de los Libres → *Colour map 8, grid A5. Population: 25,000. 336 km north of Concordia.*
Linked to the larger Brazilian town of Uruguaiana by a bridge over the Alto Uruguay, Paso de los Libres was founded in 1843 by General Madariaga. It was here that he crossed the river from Brazil with his 100 men and annexed Corrientes province for Argentina. The town is not regarded as a safe border crossing.

⊜ Sleeping

Gualeguaychú *p159*

Accommodation is scarce during carnival. Prices double Dec-Mar, Easter and long weekends. The tourist office has a list of family accommodation. Many restaurants on the Costanera.

B Puerto Sol, San Lorenzo 477, T/F434017. Good rooms, a/c, next to the port, has a small resort on a nearby island (transfer included in room rate) for lazing and having a drink.

B Tykuá, Luis N Palma 150, T422625, hotel tykua@arnet.com.ar. Breakfast included, 3 blocks from the bridge (**C**) in low season).

C Amalfi, 25 de Mayo 571, T426818. Pleasant, central, old house, quite comfortable, no breakfast, helpful (**E** in low season).

C Brutti, Bolívar 591, T426048. Kind owners, decent rooms with fan and breakfast (**D** in low season).

D Lo de Juan, Alem y Bolívar, T433661. Behind the shop where Juan sells his handicrafts, good rooms with fan, no breakfast.

Camping Several sites on riverside, next to the bridge and north of it. **Costa Azul**, 200 m northeast of bridge, T423984. Shady, good location, campsite (US$4 a day), wooden cabins (**D** for 4) and small flats with cooking facilities. **El Ñandubaysal**, T423298, www.nandu baysal.com.ar. The smartest, on the Río Uruguay, 15 km southeast (US$5.50-7.50 per tent plus access fee). **Solar del Este**, east end of **C** Ituzaingó, T433303, www.solardeleste.com.ar. Resort on the Río Gualeguaychú, popular (US$3 a day).

Concepción del Uruguay *p159*

L pp Estancia San Pedro, T03442-428374/ 03445-482107, esanpedro@ciudad.com.ar. Owned by descendants of Urquiza, old rooms full of antiques, very good.

C Grand Hotel, Eva Perón 114, T422851, www.palaciotexier.com.ar. Originally a French-style mansion with adjacent theatre, superior rooms (25% pricier) have a/c and TV but not much difference from standard, both include breakfast, no restaurant.

D Centro, Moreno 130, T427429. Spotless, comfy, older front rooms and newer ones on shady patio, breakfast extra.

Colón *p159*

C Holimasú, Belgrano 28, T421305, www.hotel holimasu.com.ar. Nice patio, breakfast included, a/c extra.

C Hostería Restaurant del Puerto, Alejo Peyret 158, T422698, hosteriadelpuerto@ciudad.com.ar. Great value, lovely atmosphere in old house, breakfast included.

C Vieja Calera, Bolívar 350, T423761, viejacalera@ar.inter.net. Dark corridors lead to decent rooms, breakfast included.

D La Posada de David, Alejo Peyret 97, T423930. Pleasant family house with garden, welcoming, good rooms with breakfast, great value.

D Sophie Hostel, Laprida 128, T424836, sophiehostel@yahoo.com.ar. HI affiliated, renovated house with large garden, cooking facilities, comfortable rooms for 2, 4, 6 and 8, welcoming owner Marcela, homemade meals, great breakfast (free on your first morning), excellent information. Highly recommended.

D Sweet Rose, 25 de Mayo 10, T156 43487. Quite comfortable, small bathrooms, breakfast extra.

Camping Several sites along river bank, most US$3 per day. **Camping Municipal Playa Norte**, T422074, a few blocks north of the port district. **Piedras Coloradas**, T421451, a few hundred metres south of Av 12 de Abril.

Paso de los Libres *p160*

B Alejandro I, Col López 502, T424100. Pool, cable TV, best. Plus several in **D** range.

❼ Eating

Concepción del Uruguay *p159*

❢ **El Remanso**, Rocamora y Eva Perón. Popular, moderately priced *parrilla*.

Colón *p159*

❢ **La Cosquilla de Angel**, Alejo Peyret 180. The smartest place in town, varied moderately priced meals, including fish, adequate set menu.

❢ **El Viejo Almacén**, Gral Urquiza y Paso. Fast food.

❸ Transport

Gualeguaychú *p159*

Bus Bus terminal at Bv Artigas y Bv Jurado, T440688 (30-min walk to centre, *remise* taxi US$1.20). To **Concepción del Uruguay**, 1 hr, US$1.50. To **Fray Bentos**, 1¼ hrs, US$2.30, 2 a day (1 on Sun), arrive 30 mins before departure for immigration. To **Buenos Aires**, US$7-8, 3½ hrs, several daily.

For an explanation of the sleeping and eating price codes used in this guide, see inside the front cover. Other relevant information is found in Essentials pages 68-69.

Concepción del Uruguay *p159*

Bus Terminal at Rocamora y Los Constituyentes, T422352 (remise, US$0.40). To **Buenos Aires**, frequent, 4 hrs, US$8-9. To **Colón**, 45 mins, US$1.

Colón *p159*

Bus Terminal at Paysandú y Sourigues (10 blocks north of main plaza), T421716. Not all long distance buses enter Colón: at Ubajay (70 km north), Parador Gastiazoro, T0345- 4905026, is a busy stop for buses going north. To **Buenos Aires**, US$8-10, 5-6 hrs. To **Mercedes** (for Iberá), several companies, 6-7 hrs, US$6-8. To **Paraná**, 4-5 hrs, US$7. **To Uruguay**: via the Artigas Bridge (US$4 toll) all formalities are dealt with on the Uruguayan side. *Migraciones* officials board the bus, but non-Argentines/Uruguayans should get off bus for stamp. Bus to **Paysandú**, US$2-2.30, 45 mins.

Concordia *p160*

Bus Terminal at Justo y Yrigoyen, 13 blocks northwest of the Plaza 25 de Mayo (reached by No 2 bus). To **Buenos Aires**, US$11, 6½ hrs. To **Paraná** 5 a day.

Paso de los Libres *p160*

Bus Terminal is 1 km from town centre, near border. To **Brazil**: taxi or bus US$2.50. No bus service on Sun.

Up the Río Paraná

Several historic cities stand on the banks of the Paraná, which flows south from its confluence with the Río Paraguay. National parks protecting endangered marshes, especially at Iberá, are the highlight of the zone.

Rosario → *Phone code: 0341. Colour map 8, grid B5. Population: 1.3 million.*

The largest city in the province of Santa Fe and the third largest city in Argentina, Rosario, 295 km northwest of Buenos Aires, is a great industrial and export centre on the Río Paraná. It has a lively cultural scene with several theatres and bars where there are daily shows. It is also home of many nationally famous musicians and modern artists. The efficient **tourist office** is on the riverside park next to the Monumento a la Bandera① *Av Belgrano y Buenos Aires, T480 2230, www.rosarioturismo.com*. A free tourist card is given for discounts at several hotels, restaurants and other services. *www.viarosario.com*, for the latest events information.

The old city centre is Plaza 25 de Mayo. Around it are the **cathedral**, containing the *Virgen del Rosario*, and the **Palacio Municipal**. On the north side is the **Museo de Arte Decorativo** ① *Santa Fe 748, T480 2547, Thu-Sun 1600-2000, free*. This sumptuous former family residence houses a valuable private collection of paintings, furniture, tapestries sculptures and silverwork, brought mainly from Europe. Left of the cathedral, the *Pasaje Juramento* opens the pedestrian way to the imposing **Monumento a la Bandera**① *T/F480 2238, Mon 1400-1800, Tue-Sun 0900-1800 (in summer till 1900), US$0.35 (tower), free (Salón de las Banderas)*. This commemorates the site on which, in 1812, General Belgrano, on his way to fight the Spaniards in Jujuy, raised the Argentine flag for the first time. A tower, 70 m high, has excellent panoramic views. In the first half of November in the Parque a la Bandera (opposite the monument) *Fiesta de las Colectividades* lasts 10 nights, with stalls offering typical dishes and a stage for folk music and dances. The main show is on 11 November, Día de la Tradición. From plaza 25 de Mayo, Córdoba leads west towards plaza San Martín and beyond, the Boulevard Oroño. These 14 blocks, of which the first seven are for pedestrians only, is the largest concentration of late 19th- and early 20th-century buildings in the city in what is called the **Paseo del Siglo**. **Museo de Bellas Artes J B Castagnino**① *Av Pellegrini 2202, T480 2542, Wed-Mon 1400-2000, US$0.35*. The museum is just outside the 126-ha Parque Independencia and has an impressive collection of French impressionist, Italian baroque and Flemish works, and one of best collections of Argentine paintings and sculpture.

Che Guevara was born here in 1928. The large white house at Entre Ríos y Urquiza where he lived for the first two years of his life before his family moved to Alta Gracia, near Córdoba (see page 116), is now an insurance company. There are dozens of riverside resorts on the islands and sandbars opposite Rosario. These have restaurants, bars and all the facilities for a day out, with woods, beaches and lagoons. Some have campsites and cabins for rent. Boats depart daily in summer from *La Fluvial* or from *Costa Alta* to the resorts, each with its own transfer service. Weekend services are run the rest of the year.

⁞ True brew

Yerba mate (*ilex paraguayensis*) is made into a tea which is widely drunk in Argentina, Paraguay, Brazil and Uruguay. Traditionally associated with the gauchos, the modern mate paraphernalia is a common sight anywhere: the gourd (*un mate*) in which the tea leaves are steeped, the straw (usually silver) and a thermos of hot water to top up the gourd. It was the Jesuits who first grew *yerba mate* in plantations, inspiring one of the drink's names: *té de jesuitas*. Also used has been *té de Paraguay*, but now just *mate* or *yerba* will do. In southern Brazil it is called *ximarão*; in Paraguay *tereré*, when drunk cold with digestive herbs.

Rosario to Paraná

A new, 60-km road has been built from Rosario to **Victoria**, a pretty town overlooking the islands and canals to the west. Panoramic views from the **Mirador de la Virgen de Fátima**, west of centre (take Calle Laprida). There are many 19th- and early 20th-century buildings, several of which have wonderful ironwork on the windows. **Tourist office** is at the north access to town ① *25 de Mayo y Bv Sarmiento, T421885, 0800-1900, www.turismovictoria.com.ar*. Ask here for lodging at *estancias*.

Ruta 11 heads north to Paraná, passing the **Parque Nacional Diamante** (or **Predelta**), 2,458 ha of marshland and riverine forest of the upper delta of the Río Paraná. It protects many birds, capybaras, otters and the rare *yacaré ñato*. Access is at La Jaula, where there's a free campsite with hot showers and a 200 m footpath leading to a vantage point. Most of the park is only accessible by boat and excursions leaving from La Jaula should be arranged in advance with a tour operator in the town of Diamante. *Remises* from Diamante charge US$1.50-1.60. Entrance is free. The park administration is at Sarmiento 507 (Diamante), T0343-498 3535, predelta@apn.gov.ar. Daily 0800-2000. *Davimar*, 25 de Mayo 390, T0343-498 4104, runs boat excursions in the park for about US$10 pp. Accommodation is available at Diamante.

Paraná → *Phone code: 0343. Colour map 8, grid A5. Population: 247,600.*

About 30 km southeast of Santa Fe, the capital of Entre Ríos was, from 1854-61, capital of the Republic. The centre is on a hill offering views over the Río Paraná and beyond to Santa Fe. There are many fine buildings. In the centre is the **Plaza Primero de Mayo**, around which are the **Municipalidad**, the large **Cathedral** and the **Colegio del Huerto**, seat of the Senate of the Argentine Confederation between 1854 and 1861. The **Casa de Gobierno** at Santa Fe y Laprida has a grand façade. Take pedestrianized San Martín and half block west of the corner with 25 de Junio is the fine **Teatro 3 de Febrero** (1908). Two blocks north is the **Plaza Alvear;** on the west side of which is the **Museo de Bellas Artes** ① *Buenos Aires 355, T420 7868, Tue-Fri 0900-1200, 1600-2100, Sat-Sun 1700-2130, US$0.35*. It houses a vast collection of artists. On the north side is the **Museo de Ciencias Naturales y Antropológicas** ① *Carlos Gardel 62, T420 8894, Tue-Fri 0800-1200, 1500-1900, Sat 0830-1230, 1500-1900, Sun 0900-1200, US$0.35*. It has natural history and anthropology sections. The city's glory is **Parque Urquiza**, along the cliffs above the Río Paraná. It has a statue to Gen Urquiza, and a bas-relief showing the battle of Caseros, at which he finally defeated Rosas. **Provincial tourist office** ① *Laprida 5, on corner of Plaza Alvear, T420 7989, www.vivientrerios.com. Mon-Fri 0700-1230*.

To Santa Fe The two cities are 25 km apart, separated by several islands. The road goes under the Río Paraná by the Hernandarias tunnel, toll US$1 per car, and then crosses a number of bridges. Frequent bus service by **Etacer** and **Fluviales**, US$1, 50 minutes.

Santa Fe → *Phone code: 0342. Colour map 8, grid A4. Population: 451,600.*

Santa Fe, 184 km from Rosario, is the capital of its province and the centre of a very fertile region. It was founded by settlers from Asunción in 1573, though its present site was not occupied until 1653. The south part of the city, around the **Plaza 25 de Mayo** is the historic centre. On the Plaza itself is the majestic **Casa de Gobierno**, built in 1911-1917 in French style on the site of the historic Cabildo, in which the 1853 constitution was drafted. Opposite is the **Cathedral**, with its twin towers capped by blue cupolas. On the east side is the **Colegio de la Inmaculada**

Concepción, established by the Jesuits and including the **Iglesia de Nuestra Señora de los Milagros**, dating from 1694, more richly decorated with an ornate dome. One block south of the plaza is **the Iglesia y Convento de San Francisco** built in 1680. **Museo Histórico Provincial** ① *3 de Febrero 2553, T457 3529, all year 0830-1200, afternoon hours change frequently, closed Mon, free*. The building, dating from 1690, is one of the oldest surviving civil buildings in the country. You can swim in the river at Guadalupe beach, on the Costanera Oeste. The modern **Basílica Nuestra Señora de Guadalupe**, Javier de la Rosa 623, is the site of a popular religious pilgrimage on the third Sunday after Easter. Take bus 16 from the centre to the Costanera. **Tourist offices** at the bus terminal ① *T457 4123, 0700-1300, 1500-2100*, at Paseo del Restaurador① *Bv Pellegrini y Rivadavia, T457 1881, 0700-1900* and at Boca del Tigre① *Av Paso y Zavalía, 0700-1900*, all good, www.santafeciudad.gov.ar.

Iberá Marshes

The **Reserva Natural del Iberá** protects nearly 13,000 sq km of wetlands known as the **Esteros del Iberá**, similar to the Pantanal in Brazil. Over sixty small lakes, no more than a few metres deep, cover 20-30% of the protected area, which is rich in aquatic plants. Like islands in the *lagunas*, *embalsados* are floating vegetation, thick enough to support large animals and trees. Wildlife includes black caiman, marsh deer, capybara and about 300 species of bird, among them the *yabirú* or *Juan Grande*, the largest stork in the western hemisphere. More difficult to see are the endangered maned wolf, the 3-m long yellow anaconda, the *yacaré ñato* and the river otter. There is a visitors' centre by the bridge at the access to Carlos Pellegrini (see below), open 0730-1800. **Mercedes** (*Phone code 03773, Population 30,900*), 250 km southeast of Corrientes, gives the best access and is the only point for getting regular transport to Carlos Pellegrini. There is small **tourist office** at the bus station. The surrounding countryside is mostly grassy *pampas*, where rheas can be seen, with rocks emerging from the plains from time to time. **Carlos Pellegrini**, 120 km northeast of Mercedes (rough road), stands on beautiful *Laguna Iberá*. A one-day visit allows for a three-hour boat excursion (US$8-12 pp if not included in hotel rates), but some hotels offer more activities for longer stays, eg horse rides or guided walks.

Parque Nacional Mburucuyá

① *12 km east of the town of Mburucuyá, T03782-498022, free, 2 hotels. Buses San Antonio from Corrientes go daily to Mburucuyá, 2½ hrs, US$2.30; remises to the park, US$5.*
West of the Esteros del Iberá and 180 km southeast of Corrientes, this park covers 17,660 ha, stretching north from the marshes of the Río Santa Lucía. It includes savanna with *yatay* palms, 'islands' of wet Chaco forest, and *esteros*. The *mburucuyá* or passionflower gives the name to the park. Wildlife is easy to see. Formerly two *estancias*, Santa María and Santa Teresa, the land was donated by their owner, the Danish botanist Troels Pedersen, who identified 1,300 different plants here. Provincial route 86 (unpaved) crosses the park for 18 km leading to the information centre and free campsite (hot water and electricity).

Corrientes → *Phone code: 03783. Colour map 6, grid C6. Population: 316,500.*
Corrientes, founded in 1588 is some 30 km below the confluence of the Ríos Paraguay and Alto Paraná. The 2¾ km General Belgrano bridge across the Río Paraná (toll US$1 per car) links the city with Resistencia (25 km), from where Ruta 11 goes north to Formosa and Asunción. East of Corrientes, Ruta 12 follows the Alto Paraná to Posadas and Iguazú. The river can make the air heavy, moist and oppressive, but in winter the climate is pleasant. The city is capital of Corrientes province and the setting for Graham Greene's novel, *The Honorary Consul*. **Tourist offices**: city tourist office at ① *Plaza Cabral, daily 0700-2100*, good map. Provincial office① *25 de Mayo 1330, province and city information, Mon-Fri 0700-1300, 1500-2100, T427200, www.planetacorrientes.com.ar.*

The main **Plaza 25 de Mayo** is one of the best-preserved in Argentina. On the north side is the **Jefatura de Policía** built in 19th-century French style. On the east side is the Italianate **Casa de Gobierno** and on the south is the church of **La Merced**. Two blocks east at Mendoza 450 is the **Convent of San Francisco**, rebuilt in 1861 (the original dated from the early 17th century). Six blocks south of Plaza 25 de Mayo is the leafy Plaza de la Cruz, on which the church of **La Cruz de los Milagros** (1897) houses a cross, the Santo Madero, placed there by the founder of the city, Juan Torres de Vera – *indígenas* who tried to burn it were killed by lightning from a cloudless sky. Near the plaza, the **Museo de Ciencias Naturales 'Amadeo Bonpland'**① *San Martín 850*,

Mon-Sat 0900-1200, 1600-2000, named after the French naturalist who travelled with Alexander von Humboldt, contains botanical, zoological, archaeological and mineralogical collections. A beautiful walk eastwards, along the Avenida Costanera, beside the Paraná river leads to **Parque Mitre**, from where there are views of sunset.

⦿ Sleeping

Rosario *p162*
A Plaza del Sol, San Juan 1055, T/F421 9899, plaza@satlink.com.ar. Comfortable, spacious rooms, pool on the 11th floor with splendid views, with large breakfast.
A Riviera, San Lorenzo 1460, T/F424 2058, www.solans.com. 4-star, business hotel with good rooms, large breakfast, sauna, gym and restaurant. 3 more hotels in the same chain usually have convenient promotions:
C La Paz, Barón de Maua 36, T/F421 0905. Family-owned, central, small, though a bit run down, reasonable rooms, with breakfast.
C Rosario, Cortada Ricardone 1365 (access from Entre Ríos 900 block), T/F424 2170, hrosario@infovia.com.ar. Central, good rooms with a/c and breakfast. Larger **C** rooms in annex.
D Savoy, San Lorenzo 1022, T448 0071. Early 20th-century mansion, once Rosario's best hotel, now with faded grandeur, excellent value, attentive service, breakfast included.
Camping The nearest site is at Granadero Baigorria, 12 km north of centre, at Av Lisandro de la Torre y El Río, T471 4381. Access to beach, hot showers, sport facilities.

Victoria *p163*
B Casablanca, on Bv Moreno (by Barrio Quinto Cuartel), T424131, lopezmartin1676@ yahoo.com.ar. Breakfast included, pool in large garden, restaurant for guests only.
C Plaza, Congreso 455, T421431. Central, very pleasant, with a/c and breakfast, good value.
D Dennisse, Congreso 682, T421186. Spotless, good, breakfast (US$0.65) on the veranda.

Paraná *p163*
A-B Gran Hotel Paraná, Urquiza 976, T422 3900, www.hotelesparana.com.ar. Overlooking Plaza Primero de Mayo, 3 room categories (breakfast included), smart restaurant *La Fourchette*, gym, discounts at the Club Atlético Estudiantes.
A-B Mayorazgo, Etchevehere y Córdoba, on Costanera Alta, T423 0333, www.mayorazgo hotel.com. Upmarket, overlooking Parque Urquiza, with 4 room categories, casino, pool, gym, restaurant and fine views of the river.
B-C Paraná Plaza Jardín, 9 de Julio 60, T423 1700. In same chain as Gran Hotel Paraná, with breakfast, pleasant, roof garden.
B-C San Jorge, Belgrano 368, T/F422 1685, www.sanjorgehotel.com.ar. Renovated house,

helpful staff, older rooms are cheaper than the modern ones at the back with TV, light breakfast included, cooking facilities.
Camping La Toma, north end of C Blas Parera (10 km northeast of centre), T433 1721. US$0.35 pp plus US$1.30 per tent, hot showers, pool, shop. Bus 5 or 10 from centre.

Santa Fe *p163*
B Riogrande, San Gerónimo 2580, T450 0700, riogrande@santafe.com.ar. Santa Fe's best hotel, very good rooms, includes large breakfast.
C Castelar, 25 de Mayo y Peatonal Falucho, T/F456 0999. On a small plaza, 1930's hotel, good value, comfortable, breakfast included, restaurant.
C Hostal Santa Fe de la Veracruz, San Martín 2954, T/F455 1740, hostal_santafe@ ciudad.com.ar. Traditional favourite, also has **C** superior rooms, all good value, including large breakfast, restaurant, sauna (extra).
D Colón, San Luis 2862, T452 1586. Welcoming staff but gloomy rooms, OK, breakfast and a/c included.
D Emperatriz, Irigoyen Freyre 2440, T/F453 0061. Attractive Hispanic-style building, plain rooms, spacious, comfortable, breakfast and a/c extra.
D-E Niza, Rivadavia 2755, T/F452 2047. With fan and breakfast, adequate, a/c extra.

Esteros del Iberá *p164*
Mercedes
D Sol, San Martín 519, T420283. An old house with clean rooms and a lovely patio; with breakfast.
D World, Pujol 1162, T422508, 3 blocks from bus station. With fan and breakfast, shared bath, other meals available, Iberá information.
E pp Delicias del Iberá, Pujol 1162, T422508. Next to the *combis* to Pellegrini, excellent, shared bath, breakfast, good meals, garden.

Carlos Pellegrini
AL pp Hostería Ñandé Retá, T/F03773-499411/ 156-29109, T011-4811 2005 (in Buenos Aires), www.nandereta.com. Wooden house in a shady grove, full board, excursions included.
AL pp Posada Aguapé, T03773-499412/ 156-29759, T/F011-4742 3015 (Buenos Aires), www.iberaesteros.com.ar. On the lake with a garden and pool, comfortable rooms, attractive dining room, rates are for full board and include 2 excursions.

AL pp **Posada de la Laguna**, T03773-499413, www.posadadelalaguna.com. Run by painter Elsa Güiraldes and set on the lake, very comfortable, large neat garden and a swimming pool, full board and all excursions included.

A pp **San Juan Poriahú**, at Loreto, T03781-156 08674, T011-4791 9511 (Buenos Aires). An old estancia run by Marcos García Rams, at the northwest edge of the Esteros, full board, horse rides and boat trips to see wildlife on a property where there has been no hunting at all. Closed Jan, Feb and Jul. Access from Ruta 12.

A pp **San Lorenzo**, at Galarza, T03756-481292. Next to 2 lakes on the northeast edge of the region, splendid for wildlife watching, full board, only 3 rooms, horse rides, walks, boat trips all included. Boat excursions by night are charged separately. Access from Gobernador Virasoro (90 km), via Rutas 37 and 41. Transfer can be arranged to/from Gobernador Virasoro or Posadas for an extra charge. Closed Jan-Feb.

E pp **Posada Ypa Sapukai**, Sarmiento 212, T03773-420155, www.argentinahostels.com. Good value, nice atmosphere, excellent staff, excursion to the *laguna* is very well guided (US$8 pp), lunch or dinner US$4. AHC Argentina Hostels Club. Recommended.

F pp **Hosp Guaraní**, Calle 7 y 27, T156-29762. Basic, shared bath, owner Ana María Manzanelli arranges boat trips.

F pp **San Cayetano**, T03773-156 28763. Very basic, run by local guide Roque Pera.

Corrientes *p164*

No good value, inexpensive accommodation in the city. All those listed have a/c.

B **Corrientes Plaza**, Junín 1549, T/F466500. Business-oriented, comfortable, gym, small pool.

B **Gran Hotel Guaraní**, Mendoza 970, T433800, hguarani@gigared.com. 4-star, business-oriented with restaurant, pool and gym, parking, large breakfast included.

C **Hostal del Río**, Plácido Martínez 1098, T/F436100, hostal_del_rio@infovia.com.ar. In apartment tower overlooking the port, fine rooms, pleasantly decorated, pool, restaurant, breakfast.

C **Orly**, San Juan 867, T427248, hotelorly@arnet.com.ar. Central, pay 50% more for a better class room, with breakfast.

C **San Martín**, Santa Fe 955, T/F421061, hsanmartin@impsat1.com.ar. Central, lacks character but comfortable, with breakfast.

C **Turismo**, Entre Ríos 650, T/F433174. Riverside location, nice style but a bit outdated, smart restaurant, with breakfast, large pool, adjacent casino.

Eating

Rosario *p162*

†† **Amarra**, Av Belgrano y Buenos Aires. Good food, including fish and seafood, quite formal, cheap set menus Mon-Fri noon.

† **Bruno**, Montevideo y Av Ovidio Lagos. Homemade pastas.

† **Club Español**, Rioja 1052. Typical menu with some Iberian touches, old-fashioned.

† **Gigante**, San Martín 946. Large popular restaurant offering generous helpings of good food at incredibly low prices.

† **Pampa**, Moreno y Mendoza. A good *parrilla* with attractive 1940s decor.

† **Rich**, San Juan 1031. A classic, widely varied menu, convenient set meals including pastas, meats and salads, closed Mon. Recommended.

Cafés

Café de la Opera, Mendoza y Laprida (next to *Teatro El Círculo*). Jazz, tango, Russian folk music and food, poetry or story-telling, pretty café.

Kaffa, Córdoba 1473. Good coffee in *El Ateneo* bookshop.

La Sede, San Lorenzo y Entre Ríos. Very popular café at lunchtime.

Santa Fe *p163*

Many good eating places, with excellent meals with wine. Many places in the centre close on Sun.

† **Baviera San Martín**, San Martín 2941. Traditional, varied menu.

† **El Brigadier**, San Martín 1670. Colonial style, fish and *parrilla*.

† **Club Sirio Libanés**, 25 de Mayo 2740. Very good Middle Eastern dishes, popular Sun lunch.

† **El Quincho de Chiquito**, Av Almirante Brown y Obispo Príncipe (Costanera Oeste). Classic fish restaurant, excellent and good value.

† **Rivadavia**, Rivadavia 3299. Traditional *parrilla*.

Cafés

Las Delicias, Hipólito Yrigoyen y San Martín. Café and bakery with beautiful decor, good for coffees and pastries, fruit juices, sandwiches and alcohol.

Don Ernesto, San Martín y General López. A traditional café in the civic centre.

Tokio, on Rivadavia y Crespo (Plaza España). Another historical café.

Corrientes *p164*

† **El Solar**, San Lorenzo 830. Informal, busy at lunchtime, meals by weight.

† **Las Brasas**, Av Costanera y San Martín (near beach). Traditional mid-range *parrilla*, local fish.

† **Martha de Bianchetti**, 9 de Julio y Mendoza. Smart café and bakery.

🌣 Bars and clubs

Rosario *p162*
Good events listings in the newspaper *Rosario 12*, sold with the national edition of *Página 12*.
Albaca, Italia y Mendoza. Agreeable bar with live music in the evening.
Piluso, Catamarca y Alvear. A lively meeting place by night, also open during day.
La Traición de Rita Hayworth, Dorrego 1170. A *café concert* named after Manuel Puig's novel, live shows, usually Wed-Sun evenings, US$1-2, good food.

Santa Fe *p163*
Santa Fe has a long brewing tradition and local lagers compete with the national monopoly. Many lively bars and nightclubs along the *Costanera Este*, across the bridge on Laguna Setúbal, and the Recoleta district, north of centre.

🚍 Transport

Rosario *p162*
Air Airport at Fisherton, 15 km west of centre, T451 1226. *Remises* charge US$4-5. Transfers also arranged by the airlines. Daily flights to/from Buenos Aires with AR, 45 mins.
Bus Terminal at Santa Fe y Cafferata, about 30 blocks west of the *Monumento de la Bandera*, T437 2384. Several bus lines to centre with stops on Córdoba (eg 101, 103, 115), US$0.25; from centre, take buses on Plaza 25 de Mayo, going via C Santa Fe. *Remise* US$1.50. To **Buenos Aires**, 4 hrs, US$7. To **Córdoba**, 6 hrs, US$7. To **Santa Fe**, 2½ hrs, US$4-5.
Train Rosario Norte station, Av del Valle y Av Ovidio Lagos. To **Buenos Aires**, once a week, operated by TBA, T0800-333 3822, US$5-7.

Victoria *p163*
Bus To **Buenos Aires**, 4½-5 hrs, US$10-11. To **Paraná**, 2-3 hrs, US$2.50-3.50.

Paraná *p163*
Bus Terminal at Av Ramírez 2598 (10 blocks southeast of Plaza Primero de Mayo), T422 1282. Buses 1, 4, 5 or 9 to/from centre, US$0.35. *Remise* US$0.50. East across Entre Ríos to **Colón** on Río Uruguay, 4-5 hrs, US$7. To **Buenos Aires**, 6-7 hrs, US$11-12.

Santa Fe *p163*
Air Airport at Sauce Viejo, 17 km south. T453 4300. Daily AR to and from **Buenos Aires**.
Bus Terminal near the centre, Gen M Belgrano 2910, T457 4124. To **Córdoba**, US$8.50, 5 hrs.

Many buses to **Buenos Aires** US$11-13; to **Paraná** frequent service US$1, 50 mins; to **Rosario** very frequent, 2½ hrs, US$4-5.

Esteros del Iberá *p164*
Bus Mercedes to **Carlos Pellegrini**: Rayo Bus combis daily 1130 from Pujol 1166, T420184, T156 29598, 3 hrs, US$3.30. Combi spends an hour picking up passengers all around Mercedes after leaving the office. Returns from Pellegrini at 0400, book by 2200 the night before at the local grocery (ask for directions). Itatí II bus, T0156-29804, from bus station daily, except Sun, 1200, US$3.30 (returns 0430). Mercedes to **Buenos Aires**, 9-10 hrs, US$12-14. Mercedes to **Corrientes**, 3 hrs, US$3.30-4. To **Puerto Iguazú**, best to go via Corrientes, otherwise via any important town along Ruta 14, eg Paso de los Libres, 130 km southeast. There is a direct bus from Carlos Pellegrini to **Posadas**.

Corrientes *p164*
Air Camba Punta Airport, 10 km east of city, T458684. (Minibus picks up passengers from hotels, T450072, US$1.30.) AR (T424647) to/from Buenos Aires.
Bus To **Resistencia** US$0.70, Chaco- Corrientes, every 15 mins from Av Costanera y La Rioja at the port, 40 mins, US$0.40 return. Main terminal on Av Maipú, 5 km southeast of centre, bus No 103 (be sure toy ask the driver if goes to terminal as same line has many different routes), 20 mins, US$0.20 To **Posadas** US$6.50, 3½-4 hrs, road paved. To **Buenos Aires**, several companies, 11-12 hrs, US$13-26. To **Asunción** (Paraguay), **Crucero del Norte, El Pulqui**, 5 hrs, US$6-7.

🚹 Directory

Rosario *p162*
Airline offices Aerolíneas Argentinas, Santa Fe 1410, T424 9517. **Banks** Many banks along C Córdoba, east of plaza San Martín. Money exchange at Transatlántica, Mitre y Rioja. TCs exchanged at Banex, Mitre y Santa Fe. 2% or US$10 commission. **Internet** Several places in centre, US$0.35 per hr. **Post offices** Córdoba y Buenos Aires.

Santa Fe *p163*
Banks Banking district around San Martín y Tucumán. Exchange money and TCs at Tourfé, San Martín 2500, or at Columbia, San Martín 2275.

Corrientes *p164*
Internet Brujas, Mendoza 787, US$0.35 per hr. Many others. **Post offices** San Juan y San Martín. **Telephones** Several *telecentros* in centre.

The Chaco

The Chaco has two distinct natural zones. The Wet Chaco spreads along the Ríos Paraná and Paraguay covered mainly by marshlands with savanna and groves of caranday palms, where birdwatching is excellent. Further west, as rainfall diminishes, scrubland of algarrobo, white quebracho, palo borracho and various types of cacti characterise the Dry Chaco, where South America's highest temperatures, exceeding 45°C, have been recorded. Winters are mild, with only an occasional touch of frost in the south.

Background

This sprawling alluvial lowland rises so gently from east to west (200 m in 900 km) that the rivers which cross it are slow and meandering. It is mostly cattle country, but agriculture has developed in the central part and the southwest of Chaco province, with cotton, maize, soya, sunflower and sorghum. Much of the Chaco is inaccessible because of poor roads (many of them impassable during summer rains) and lack of public transport, but it has two attractive national parks which are reachable all year round. Resistencia and Formosa are the main cities at the eastern rim, from where almost straight Rutas 16 and 81 respectively go west across the plains to the hills in Salta province. Buses to Salta take Ruta 16, while Ruta 81 has long unpaved sections west of Las Lomitas, which make for a very hard journey after heavy rains. Presidencia Roque Sáenz Peña, 170 km northwest of Resistencia, is a reasonable place to stop over. The Chaco is one of the main centres of indigenous population in Argentina: the Toba are settled in towns by the Río Paraná and the Wichi, or Mataco, live in the western region. Less numerous are the Mocoví in Chaco and the Pilagá in central Formosa.

Resistencia → *Phone code: 03722. Colour map 6, grid C6. Population: 359,100.*

The hot and energetic capital of the Province of Chaco, Resistencia is 6½ km up the Barranqueras stream on the west bank of the Paraná and 544 km north of Santa Fe. On the Paraná itself is the little port of Barranqueras. Resistencia is known as the 'city of the statues', there being over 200 of these in the streets. Four blocks from the central Plaza 25 de Mayo is the **Fogón de los Arrieros** ① *Brown 350 (between López y Planes and French), T426418, open to non-members Mon-Sat 0900-1200, Mon-Fri 2100-2300, US$1.70.* This famous club and informal cultural centre deserves a visit. The **Museo Del Hombre Chaqueño** ① *Juan B Justo 280, Mon-Fri 0800-1200, 1600-2000, free,* is a small anthropological museum with an exhibition of handicrafts by native Wichi, Toba and Mocoví people. It has a fascinating mythology section in which small statues represent Guaraní beliefs (still found in rural areas). There are banks and *cambios* in the centre for exchange. and the **tourist office** is on Plaza 25 de Mayo, Monday-Friday 0800-2000, T458420. Provincial tourist office, Santa Fe 178, Monday-Friday 0630-2000, Saturday 0800-1200, T423547, www.chaco.gov.ar/turismo.

Isla del Cerrito, an island northeast of Resistencia at the confluence of the Ríos Paraná and Paraguay, is a provincial nature reserve of 12,000 ha, covered mainly with grassland and palm trees. At the eastern end (51 km from Resistencia) is Cerrito, a tourist complex with white sand beaches, a history museum, hotels and restaurants. Combi *Arco Iris* leaves from Juan B Justo y Avenida Alberdi at 0600, 1100, 1900 for Cerrito, one hour, stopping for 30 minutes there, US$1.20.

Parque Nacional Chaco

① *T03725-496166, 24 hrs, free, 115 km northwest of Resistencia, best visited between Apr-Oct to avoid intense summer heat and voracious mosquitoes.*
The park extends over 15,000 ha and protects one of the last remaining untouched areas of the Wet Chaco with exceptional *quebracho colorado* trees, *caranday* palms and dense riverine forests with orchids along the banks of the Río Negro. Some 340 species of bird have been sighted in the park. Mammals include *carayá* monkeys and, much harder to see, collared peccary, puma and jaguarundi. 300 m from the entrance is the visitors' centre and a free campsite with hot showers and electricity. There you can hire bicycles or horses for US$1.30 per hour. The paved Ruta 16 goes northwest from Resistencia and after about 60 km Ruta 9 branches off, leading north to Colonia Elisa and Capitán Solari, 5 km east of the park entrance, via a dirt road. If in a group, call the park in advance to be picked up at Capitán Solari. *La Estrella* run daily buses Resistencia-Capitán Solari, where *remise* taxis should not charge more than US$1 to the park. Tour operators run day-long excursions to the park from Resistencia.

Formosa → *Phone code: 03717. Colour map 6, grid C6. Population: 198,100.*

The capital of Formosa Province, 186 km above Corrientes, is the only Argentine port of any note on the Río Paraguay. Oppressively hot from November to March, the city is a good base for exploring the rivers running towards the Río Paraguay during the winter. **Tourist office** ① *José M Uriburu 820 (Plaza San Martín), 1600-2000, T420442, www.formosa.gov.ar, Mon-Fri 0700-1300.* Tourism is not well developed, but ask about guided excursions and accommodation at *estancias*.

Border with Paraguay

There are two routes into Paraguay. The easiest crossing is by road via the Puente Loyola, 4 km north of **Clorinda** (*Phone code 03718, Colour map 6, grid C6*). From Puerto Falcón, at the Paraguayan end of the bridge, the road runs 40 km northeast, crossing the Río Paraguay, before reaching Asunción. **Immigration** formalities for entering Argentina are dealt with at the Argentine end, those for leaving Argentina at the Paraguayan end. Crossing, open 24 hours. **Buses** from Puerto Falcón to Asunción run every hour, *Empresa Falcón* US$0.50, last bus to the centre of Asunción 1830.

The other route is by ferry from Puerto Pilcomayo, close to Clorinda, to Itá Enramada (Paraguay), US$0.50, five minutes, every 30 minutes. Then take bus 9 to Asunción. Argentine **immigration** is at Puerto Pilcomayo, closed at weekends for tourists. Paraguayan immigration at Itá Enramada.

Parque Nacional Río Pilcomayo

① *Access to the park is free, 24 hrs, administration centre in Laguna Blanca, Av Pueyrredón y Ruta 86, T03718-470045, Mon-Fri 0700-1430.*

Some 48,000 ha, 65 km northwest of Clorinda is this national park is recognised as a natural wetland, with lakes, marshes and low-lying parts which flood during the rainy season. The remainder is grassland with caranday palm forests and Chaco woodland. Among the protected species are aguará-guazú, giant anteaters and coatis. Caimans, black howler monkeys, rheas and a variety of birds can also be seen. The park has two entrances leading to different areas. Easiest to reach on foot is Laguna Blanca, where there is an information point and a free campsite with electricity and cold water. From there, a footpath goes to the Laguna Blanca, the biggest lake in the park. A bit further is the second entrance, leading to the area of Estero Poí, with another information point and a campsite without facilities. **Godoy** buses run from Formosa or Resistencia to the small towns of Laguna Naick-Neck, 5 km from the park (for going to Laguna Blanca) and Laguna Blanca, 8 km from the park (for going to Estero Poí). **Remise** taxis from both towns should charge no more than US$3 for these short journeys. There re police controls on the way to the park because of the proximity to the Paraguay border.

● Sleeping

Resistencia *p168*

B **Covadonga**, Güemes 200, T444444, hotel covadonga@infovia.com.ar. The city's top hotel, comfortable, a/c, breakfast, pool, sauna and gym.
C **Gran Hotel Royal**, Obligado 211, T444466, www.granhotelroyal.com.ar. Good value, comfortable, a/c, breakfast included.
D **Bariloche**, Obligado 239, T421412, jag@cpsarg.com. Best value, welcoming, good rooms with a/c, no breakfast but café at *Gran Hotel Royal*.
E **El Hotelito**, Av Alberdi 311, T459699. Ok for a night, fair rooms, shared bath, breakfast.
Camping 17 blocks northwest of plaza : Parque Dos de Febrero, Av Avalos 1000, T458366. Neat park by Río Negro, hot water and

electricity, US$0.35 pp plus US$0.65 per tent.

Formosa *p169*

A **Turismo**, San Martín 759, T431122, hoteldeturismoformosa@arnet.com.ar. Large building by the river, good views, pricey rooms with a/c and breakfast.
B **Casa Grande Apart-Hotel**, Av González Lelong 185, T431573, www.casagrande apart.com.ar. 8 blocks north of Av 25 de Mayo, by river, good 1 and 2-room apartments with kitchenette, a/c and breakfast, gym and pool.
C **Colón**, Belgrano 1068, T426547. Comfortable, a/c and breakfast.
C **Plaza**, José M Uriburu 920, T426767. On Plaza,

● *For an explanation of the sleeping and eating price codes used in this guide, see inside the front
● cover. Other relevant information is found in Essentials pages 68-69.*

good, pool, with breakfast, very helpful, some English spoken, secure parking.

E Colonial, San Martín 879, T426346. Basic, a/c, by the river.
E El Extranjero, Av Gutnisky 2660, T452276. Opposite bus terminal, OK, with a/c.
Camping Las Arianas, 10 km south (turn off Ruta 11 at El Pucu, Km 6), T427640. **Camping Banco Provincial**, 4 km south on Ruta 11, good facilities including pool, T429877.

Resistencia *p168*
♯♯ **Kebon**, Don Bosco y Güemes. Good food.
♯♯-♯ **Charly**, Güemes 213, T434019. *Parrilla* and international food, excellent, a/c, popular, open daily for lunch and dinner.
♯ **San José**, Roca y Av Alberdi. A popular café and *confitería* on Plaza 25 de Mayo with excellent pastries (try *medialunas*) and ice creams.

Formosa *p169*
♯ **El Fortín**, Mitre 602. Traditional place, good for local fish.
♯ **El Tano Marino**, Av 25 de Mayo 55. Italian, pastas are the speciality.
♯ **Yayita**, Belgrano 926. Regional dishes.

⊕ **Festivals and events**

Formosa *p169*
The world's longest **Via Crucis** pilgrimage with 14 stops along Ruta 81 (registered in the Guinness Book of Records) takes place every Easter week, starting in Formosa and ending at the border with the province of Salta, 501 km northwest. **Festival de la caña con ruda** is held on the last night of **Jul**, when Paraguayan *caña* flavoured by the *ruda* plant is drunk as a protection against the mid-winter blues. Also a good chance to try regional dishes.

⊖ **Transport**

Resistencia *p168*
Air Airport 8 km west of town (no bus), T446009. AR, T445550, to/from **Buenos Aires**.
Bus To **Corrientes**, Chaco-Corrientes buses stop opposite *Norte* supermarket on Av Alberdi e Illia, 40 mins, US$0.40 return. Modern terminal on west outskirts (bus 3 or 10 to centre, 20 mins, US$0.25; *remise* US$1.70). To **Buenos Aires** 12-13 hrs, US$13-26 several companies. To **Formosa** 2-2½ hrs, US$2.70-3.50. To **Iguazú**, 8-10½ hrs, US$11-12, some require change of bus in **Posadas**, 5½ hrs. To **Salta** (for connections to Bolivia), **FlechaBus**, La Nueva Estrella, 12½ hrs, US$17-19. To **Asunción** several companies, 5-5½ hrs, US$5-6.

Formosa *p169*
Air El Pucu airport, 5 km southwest, T452490; *remise*, US$1.70. AR (T429314) to Buenos Aires.
Bus Terminal on west outskirts, T430817 (*remise* US$0.65). To **Asunción**, 3 hrs, US$5.40. To **Resistencia**, 2½ hrs, US$2.70-3.50; to **Buenos Aires** 15-17 hrs, US$16-28.

Misiones

While Posadas is one of the main crossing points to Paraguay, most people will head northeast, through the province of the Jesuit Missions, towards Iguazú. This is a land of ruined religious establishments, gemstones and waterfalls.

Posadas → *Phone code: 03752. Population: 280,500.*
This is the main Argentine port on the south bank of the Alto Paraná, 377 km above Corrientes, and the capital of the province of Misiones. On the opposite bank of the river lies the Paraguayan town of Encarnación, reached by the San Roque bridge. The city's centre is **Plaza 9 de Julio**, on which stand the **Cathedral** and the **Gobernación**, in imitation French style. The riverside and adjacent districts are good for a stroll. Follow Rivadavia or Buenos Aires north to Avenida Andrés Guaçurarí (referred also to as Roque Pérez), a pleasant boulevard, lively at night with several bars. Immediately north of it is the small and hilly **Bajada Vieja** or old port district. There is a good **Museo Regional Aníbal Cambas**① *Alberdi 600 in the Parque República del Paraguay, 11 blocks north of Plaza 9 de Julio, T447539, Mon-Fri 0700-1900*, its permanent exhibition of Guaraní artefacts and pieces collected from the nearby Jesuit missions is worth seeing. **Tourist office**① *Colón 1985, T447540, www.conozcamisiones.com. Open daily 0800-2000.*

Border with Paraguay

Argentine immigration and customs are on the Argentine side of the bridge to Encarnación. Buses across the bridge (see Transport page 170) do not stop for formalities; you must get exit stamps. Get off the bus, keep your ticket and luggage, and catch a later bus. Pedestrians and cyclists are not allowed to cross; cyclists must ask officials for assistance. Boats cross to Encarnación, 6-8 minutes, almost every hour Monday-Friday 0800-1800, US$1. All formalities and ticket office at main building. Port access from Avenida Costanera y Avenida Andrés Guaçurarí, T425044 (*Prefectura*).

San Ignacio Miní → *Phone code: 03752. Colour map 7, grid C1.*

① *0700-1900, US$0.80, US$3.50 with guide, tip appreciated if the guards look after your luggage. Allow about 1½ hrs for a leisurely visit. Go early to avoid crowds and the best light for pictures (also late afternoon); good birdwatching. Son et lumière show at the ruins, daily after sunset, cancelled in wet weather, Spanish only, US$0.80.*

The site of the most impressive Jesuit ruins in the Misiones region, 63 km northeast of Posadas, is a good base for visiting the other Jesuit ruins and for walking. The local festival is 30-31 July. San Ignacio was founded on its present site in 1696. The 100 sq-m, grass-covered plaza is flanked north, east and west by 30 parallel blocks of stone buildings with four to 10 small, one-room dwellings in each block. The roofs have gone, but the massive metre-thick walls are still standing except where they have been torn down by the *ibapoi* trees. The public buildings, some of them still 10 m high, are on the south side of the plaza. In the centre are the ruins of a large church finished about 1724. The masonry, sandstone from the Río Paraná, was held together by a sandy mud.

Inside the entrance, 200 m from the ruins, is the **Centro de interpretación Jesuítico-Guaraní**, with representations of the lives of the Guaraníes before the arrival of the Spanish, the work of the Jesuits and the consequences of their expulsion, as well as a fine model of the mission in its heyday. **Museo Provincial** contains a small collection of artefacts from Jesuit reducciones. San Ignacio, together with the nearby missions of Santa Ana and Loreto, is a UNESCO World Heritage Site. There are heavy rains in February. Mosquitoes can be a problem.

Casa de Horacio Quiroga ① *T470124, 0800-1900, US$0.65 (includes a 40 min-guided visit; ask in advance for an English guide). Take C San Martín (opposite direction to the ruins) to its end where is Gendarmería headquarters. Turn right and on your right are two attractive wood and stone houses. After 200 m the road turns left and 300 m later, a signposted narrow road branches off.* The house of this Uruguayan writer, who lived part of his tragic life here as a farmer and carpenter between 1910 and 1916 and in the 1930s, is worth a visit. Many of his short stories were inspired by the subtropical environment and its inhabitants.

The ruins of another Jesuit mission, **Loreto** ① *0700-1830, US$0.35, getting there: no public transport to Loreto, bus drops you off on Ruta 12, otherwise take a tour from Posadas or remise from nearby towns,* can be reached by a 3 km dirt road (signposted) which turns off Ruta 12 10 km south of San Ignacio. Little remains other than a few walls, though excavations are in progress. A second ruined mission, **Santa Ana** ① *16 km south, 0700-1900, US$0.35, buses stop on Ruta 12,* was the site of the Jesuit iron foundry. Impressive high walls still stand and beautiful steps lead from the church to the wide open plaza The ruins are 700 m along a path from Ruta 12 (signposted).

San Ignacio to Puerto Iguazú

Ruta 12 continues northeast, running parallel to Río Alto Paraná, towards Puerto Iguazú. With its bright red soil and lush vegetation, this attractive route is known as the Región de las Flores. You get a good view of the local economy: plantations of *yerba mate*, manioc and citrus fruits, timber yards, manioc mills and *yerba mate* factories. The road passes through several small modern towns including Jardín America, Puerto Rico, Montecarlo and Eldorado, with accommodation, campsites, places to eat and regular bus services. Just outside Eldorado, **Estancia Las Mercedes** ① *Av San Martín Km 4, T03751-431511,* is an old *yerba mate* farm with period furnishings, open for day visits with activities like riding, boating, and for overnight stays with full board. **Wanda**, 50 km north of Eldorado, was named after a Polish princess and is famous as the site of open-cast amethyst and quartz mines which sell gems. There are guided tours to two of them, **Tierra Colorada** and **Compañía Minera Wanda** *daily 0700-1900.*

Gran Salto del Moconá

For 3 km the waters of the Río Uruguay create magnificent falls (known in Brazil as Yucuma) up to 20 m high in a remote part of Misiones. They are surrounded by dense woodland protected by the Parque Estadual do Turvo (Brazil) and the Parque Provincial Moconá, the Reserva Provincial Esmeralda and the Reserva de la Biósfera Yabotí (Argentina). Moconá has roads and footpaths, accommodation where outdoor activities can be arranged, such as excursions to the falls, trekking in the forests, kayaking, birdwatching and 4WD exploring. Alternative bases are El Soberbio (70 km southwest) or San Pedro (92 km northwest). Roads from both towns to Moconá are impassable after heavy rain. Regular bus services run from Posadas to El Soberbio or San Pedro, and from Puerto Iguazú to San Pedro, but no public transport reaches the falls.

● Sleeping

Posadas p170

A Julio César, Entre Ríos 1951, T427930. 4-star hotel with pool and gym, spacious reasonably-priced rooms, some with river views, breakfast included. Recommended.

B Continental, Bolívar 1879 (on Plaza 9 de Julio), T440990, www.hoteleramisiones.com.ar. Comfortable standard rooms and more spacious **B** VIP rooms, some have river views, restaurant on 1st floor.

B Posadas, Bolívar 1949, T440888, www.hotelposadas.com.ar. Business hotel with good standard rooms and bigger *especial* rooms, restaurant, free internet access for guests.

C City, Colón 1754, T439401, citytel@arnet.com.ar. Gloomy reception, but very good rooms, some overlooking plaza, with breakfast and a/c, restaurant on first floor, parking.

C Colonial, Barrufaldi 2419, T436149. Warm atmosphere, good value, nice rooms with a/c and breakfast, on a quiet street about 15-min walk from centre.

D Le Petit, Santiago del Estero 1630, T436031, F441101. Good value, small, a short walk from centre on a quiet street, a/c, with breakfast.

D Residencial Misiones, Félix de Azara 1960, T430133. Very hospitable, good rooms with fan, central, old house with a patio, no breakfast, cooking and laundry facilities, popular with travellers.

San Ignacio Miní p171

D El Descanso, Pellegrini 270, T470207. Comfortable small detached house, 5 blocks southwest of main Av Sarmiento.

D San Ignacio, San Martín 823, T470047. Welcoming and very informative owner Beatriz offers very good rooms with a/c and apartments for 4-5, breakfast US$1.20, evening meals.

F pp La Casa de Inés y Juan, San Martín 1291 (no sign and no phone). Laid back artist and writer's house, 2 rooms, small library and a backyard for pitching tents, where is also a small

but delightful pool and a curious bathroom. Meals on request. Recommended.

F pp El Güembé, Gendarme Medina 525, T470910. Basic, shared bath, only 100 m from the ruins, German owner Roland rents bicycles for US$3.50 a day next door at *Kiosko Alemán*.

F pp Salpeterer, Centenario y Av Sarmiento (follow main Av Sarmiento up to its end and turn right 50 m), T470362. Small, basic, tidy, cooking facilities, fan, shared bath (1 **E** room for 4 or more with own bath), no breakfast, camping facilities with electricity and hot water for US$0.65 pp per day.

Camping Two sites on the river splendidly set and very well-kept on a small sandy bay, reached after 45-min walk from town at the end of the road leading to Quiroga's house. **Club de Pesca y Deportes Náuticos**, on a hilly ground with lush vegetation. **Playa del Sol**, T470115.

Gran Salto del Moconá p172

C Hostería Puesta del Sol, C Suipacha, El Soberbio, T03755-495161 (T4300 1377 in Buenos Aires), turismocona@yahoo.com.ar. Great views, pool, restaurant, comfortable, with breakfast, a/c. For full board add US$6.50 pp. Boat excursions arranged to the falls, 7 to 8 hrs, US$20 pp (minimum 4 people). A less tiring journey to the falls is by an easy boat crossing to Brazil, then by vehicle to the Parque do Turvo, 7 hrs, meal included, US$20 pp. Otherwise, a 4WD journey on the Argentine side with more opportunities for trekking also takes 7 hrs, with a meal, US$20 pp. Also act as tour operators.

D Refugio Moconá, 3 km from access to the reserve, 8 km from the falls (or contact at Pasaje Dornelles 450, San Pedro), T03751- 470022. Rooms for 4 to 5 people with shared bath, campsite for US$4.30 a day per tent, tents for rent (US$8.50 a day), meals, boat trips and activities. Transfer with sightseeing to/from San Pedro, 2 hrs, US$85 for up to 8 people. Also act as tour operators.

● *For an explanation of the sleeping and eating price codes used in this guide, see inside the front cover. Other relevant information is found in Essentials pages 68-69.*

❼ Eating

Posadas *p170*
Most places offer *espeto corrido*, eat as much as you can *parrilla* with meats brought to the table.

❦❦❦ El Mensú, Fleming y Coronel Reguera (at Bajada Vieja district). Attractive house offering a varied menu with fish, pastas and a large selection of wines, closed Mon.

❦❦❦ Le Rendez-vous, San Martín 1786. Formal, with a French touch.

❦❦ Diletto, Bolívar 1729. For fish, such as *surubí*, and, curiously, rabbit as their speciality.

❦❦ Espeto del Rey, Ayacucho y Tucumán. *Parrilla*, good food. Try *mandioca frita* (fried manioc).

❦❦ Mentecato, San Lorenzo y La Rioja (opposite casino). Good, open when many others are closed.

❦❦ La Querencia, on Bolívar 322 (on Plaza 9 de Julio). Traditional large restaurant offering *parrilla*, *surubí* and pastas, good service.

❦❦ L'Italiano, Bolívar 1724. Proper Italian place with good pizza.

❦ Pizzería Los Pinos, Sarmiento y Rivadavia. For good food, value and service.

San Ignacio Miní *p171*
❦ La Aldea, Rivadavia y Lanusse. An attractive house serving good and cheap pizzas, *empanadas* or other simple meals.

❦ Los Hermanos, San Martín y Av Sarmiento. Kind owner, the place to go for breakfast, bread or pastries, opens 0700. Several large restaurants for tourists on the streets bordering the Jesuit site.

▲ Activities and tours

Posadas *p170*
Abra, Colón 1975, T422221, abramisiones@ arnet.com.ar. Tours to Jesuit ruins (US$30 pp), also those in Paraguay (US$23 pp) and in Brazil (US$48 pp), plus tours to waterfalls.

Guayrá, San Lorenzo 2208, T433415, www.guayra.com.ar. Tours to Iberá (US$50-65 pp if 4 people), to Saltos del Moconá (US$80 pp if 4 people), both sites in a 5-day excursion for US$240 pp (for 4), also car rental and transfer to Carlos Pellegrini (for Iberá).

⊖ Transport

Posadas *p170*
Air Gen San Martín Airport, 12 km west, T457413, reached by Bus No 8 or 28 in 40 mins, US$0.25, *remise* US$4. To **Buenos Aires**, AR (Ayacucho 1728, T432889), some flights call at Corrientes or Formosa.

Bus New terminal about 5 km out of the city at Av Santa Catalina y Av Quaranta (T456106), on the road to Corrientes. Buses No 4, 8, 15, 21, to/from centre, 20 mins, US$0.25, *remise* US$2. Travel agencies in the centre can book bus tickets in advance. To **Buenos Aires**, 12-13 hrs, US$17-25. Frequent services to **San Ignacio Miní**, 1 hr, US$1.30, and **Puerto Iguazú**, US$8, 5-6 hrs *expreso*. To **Tucumán**, La Nueva Estrella, Autotransportes Mendoza, 16-18 hrs, US$18-21. **International** To **Encarnación** (Paraguay), Servicio Internacional, 50 mins, US$0.65, leaving at least every 30 mins from platforms 11 and 12 (lower level), tickets on bus.

San Ignacio Miní *p171*
Bus Stop in front of the church, leaving almost every hour to **Posadas** (US$1.30) or to **Puerto Iguazú** (US$5-6). Do not rely on bus terminal at the end of Av Sarmiento, only a few stop there. More buses stop on Ruta 12 at the access road (Av Sarmiento).

❻ Directory

Posadas *p170*
Banks Banco de La Nación, Bolívar 1799. Round corner on Félix de Azara are Banco Río and HSBC. Citibank, San Martín y Colón. Mazza, Bolívar 1932. For money exchange, TCs accepted. **Consulates** Paraguay, San Lorenzo 179, T423858. Mon-Fri 0730-1400. All visas on the same day. **Immigration** Dirección Nacional de Migraciones, Buenos Aires 1633, T427414. **Internet** Anyway, Féliz de Azara 2067. US$0.35 per hr evenings/ weekends, otherwise US$0.50. Cyber Nick, San Luis 1847. US$0.35 before 1700, otherwise US$0.50. Mateando, on Félix de Azara, next to San Martín. US$0.35 per hr. Misiol@n, San Lorenzo 1681, open 24 hrs, US$0.35 per hr. **Post offices** Bolívar y Ayacucho.

Iguazú Falls → *Colour map 7, grid C1.*

The mighty Iguazú Falls are the most overwhelmingly magnificent in all of South America. So impressive are they that Eleanor Roosevelt remarked "poor Niagara" on witnessing them (they are four times wider). Viewed from below, the tumbling water is majestically beautiful in its setting of begonias, orchids, ferns and palms. Toucans, flocks of parrots and cacique birds and great dusky swifts dodge in and out along with myriad butterflies (there are at least 500 different species). Above the impact of the water, upon basalt rock, hovers a perpetual 30 m high cloud of mist in which the sun creates blazing rainbows.

Ins and outs Information Entry is US$10, payable in pesos, reais or dollars (guests at Hotel Sheraton should pay and get tickets stamped at the hotel to avoid paying again). Argentines pay US$4. Entry next 3 days is half price with the same ticket. Open daily 0800-1900 (1800 in winter). Visitor Centre includes information and photographs of the flora and fauna, as well as books for sale. There are places to eat, toilets, shops and a locutorio in the park. In the rainy season, when water levels are high, waterproof coats or swimming costumes are advisable for some of the lower catwalks and for boat trips. Cameras should be carried in a plastic bag. **Tourist office** ① *Aguirre 66, Puerto Iguazú, T420382, www.iguazuargentina.com. Open 0900-2200.*

The falls, on the Argentina-Brazil border, are 19 km upstream from the confluence of the Río Iguazú with the Río Alto Paraná. The Río Iguazú (*guazú* is Guaraní for big and *I* is Guaraní for water), which rises in the Brazilian hills near Curitiba, receives the waters of some 30 rivers as it crosses the plateau. Above the main falls, the river, sown with wooded islets, opens out to a width of 4 km. There are rapids for 3½ km above the 74 m precipice over which the water plunges in 275 falls over a frontage of 2,470 m, at a rate of 1,750 cu m a second (rising to 12,750 cu m in the rainy season).

Around the Iguazú Falls

Sleeping ●
Bristol Carimã 3
Das Cataratas 1

El Viejo Americano 5
Paudimar Campestre 6
San Martin 7

Sheraton Internacional
Iguazú Resort 2

Around the falls

→ In Oct-Feb (daylight saving dates change each year) Brazil is 1 hr ahead.

On both sides of the falls there are National Parks. Transport between the two parks is via the Ponte Tancredo Neves as there is no crossing at the falls themselves. The Brazilian park offers a superb panoramic view of the whole falls and is best visited in the morning when the light is better for photography. The Argentine park (which requires a day to explore properly) offers closer views of the individual falls in their forest setting with its wildlife and butterflies, though to appreciate these properly you need to go early and get well away from the visitors areas. Busiest times are holiday periods and on Sunday. Both parks have visitors' centres and tourist facilities on both sides are constantly being improved.

Parque Nacional Iguazú covers an area of 67,620 ha. The fauna includes jaguars, tapirs, brown capuchin monkeys, collared anteaters and coatimundis, but these are rarely seen around the falls. There is a huge variety of birds; among the butterflies are shiny blue morphos and red/black heliconius. From the Visitor Centre a small gas-run train (free), the **Tren de la Selva**, whisks visitors on a 25-minute trip through the jungle to the Estación del Diablo, where it's a 1-km walk along catwalks across the Río Iguazú to the park's centrepiece, the **Garanta del Diablo**. A visit here is particularly recommended in the evening when the light is best and the swifts are returning to roost on the cliffs, some behind the water (look out for full-moon tours run by the park office, US$5). Trains leave on the hour and 30 minutes past the hour. However, it's best to see the falls from a distance first, with excellent views from the two well-organized trails along the **Circuito Superior** and **Circuito Inferior**, each taking around an hour and a half. To reach these, get off the train at the **Estación Cataratas** (after 10 minutes' journey) and walk down the **Sendero Verde**. The Circuito Superior is a level path which takes you along the easternmost line of falls, Bossetti, Bernabé Mandez, Mbiguá (Guaraní for cormorant) and San Martín, allowing you to see these falls from above. This path is safe for those with walking difficulties, wheelchairs and pushchairs, though you should wear supportive non-slippery shoes. The Circuito Inferior takes you down to the water's edge via a series of steep stairs and walkways with superb views of both San Martín falls and the Gaganta del Diablo from a distance. Wheelchair users, pram pushers, and those who aren't good with steps should go down by the exit route for a smooth and easy descent. You could then return to the Estación Cataratas to take the train to Estación Garganta, 10 and 40 minutes past the hour, and see the falls close up.

At the very bottom of the Circuito Inferior, a free ferry crosses on demand to the small, hilly **Isla San Martín** where trails lead to *miradores* with good close views of the San Martín falls. The park has two further trails: **Sendero Macuco**, 7 km return, starting from near the Visitor Centre and leading to the river via a natural pool (El Pozón) fed by a slender waterfall, **Salto Arrechea** (a good place for bathing and the only permitted place in the park). **Sendero Yacaratiá** starts from the same place, but reaches the river by a different route, and ends at Puerto Macuco, where you could take the *Jungle Explorer* boat to the see the Falls themselves (see below). This trail is really for vehicles and less pleasant to walk along.

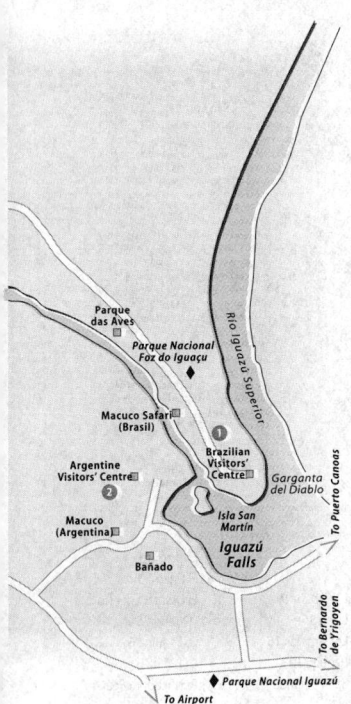

Puerto Iguazú → Phone code: 03757. Colour map 7, grid C1. Population: 19,000.

This modern town is 18 km northwest of the falls high above the river on the Argentine side near the confluence of the Ríos Iguazú and Alto Paraná. It serves mainly as a centre for visitors to the falls. The port lies to the north of the town centre at the foot of a hill: from the port you can follow the Río Iguazú downstream towards HitoTres Fronteras, a *mirador* with views over the point where the Ríos Iguazú and Alto Paraná meet and over neighbouring Brazil and Paraguay. There are souvenir shops, toilets and *La Reserva* and *La Barranca* pubs are here; bus US$0.25. **La Aripuca** ① *T423488, www.aripuca.com.ar, US$1.30, turn off Ruta 12 just after Hotel Cataratas, English and German spoken*, is a large wooden structure housing a centre for the appreciation of the native tree species and their environment. At **Güira Oga** (Casa de los Pájaros) ① *US$1, daily 0830-1800, turn off Ruta 12 at Hotel Orquídeas Palace; T423980 (mob 156-70684)*, birds that have been injured are treated and reintroduced to the wild. There is also a trail in the forest and a breeding centre for endangered species.

● Sleeping

Puerto Iguazú *p175, maps p174 and 176*
LL Sheraton Internacional Iguazú Resort, T491800, www.sheraton.com/iguazu. Fine position overlooking the falls, rooms with garden views cost less, excellent, good restaurant (buffets US$9-9.50, huge breakfast). Taxi to airport US$12. Recommended.
AL Saint George, Córdoba 148, T420633, www.hotelsaintgeorge.com. With breakfast, comfortable, attentive service, pool and

garden, good restaurant with buffet dinner, close to bus station, parking. Recommended.
B Cabañas Pirayú, Av Tres Fronteras 550, on the way to the Hito, T420393, www.pirayu.com.ar. Beautiful complex, comfortable *cabañas*, lovely river views, sports and children's games, pool, entertainment.
B-C Hostería Los Helechos, Amarante 76, T/F420338, www.argentinahostels.com. AHC

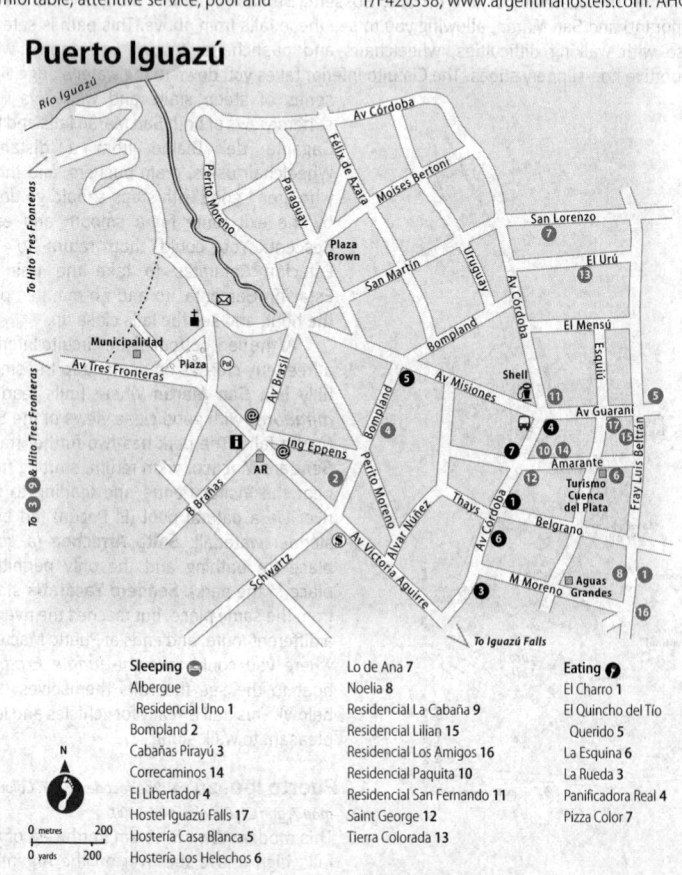

Puerto Iguazú

Sleeping ●	Lo de Ana **7**	Eating ●
Albergue	Noelia **8**	El Charro **1**
Residencial Uno **1**	Residencial La Cabaña **9**	El Quincho del Tío
Bompland **2**	Residencial Lilian **15**	Querido **5**
Cabañas Pirayú **3**	Residencial Los Amigos **16**	La Esquina **6**
Correcaminos **14**	Residencial Paquita **10**	La Rueda **3**
El Libertador **4**	Residencial San Fernando **11**	Panificadora Real **4**
Hostel Iguazú Falls **17**	Saint George **12**	Pizza Color **7**
Hostería Casa Blanca **5**	Tierra Colorada **13**	
Hostería Los Helechos **6**		

0 metres 200
0 yards 200

Argentina Hostels Club. Easy-going, popular, well maintained, with breakfast, pool, good.
C Cabañas Leñador, Ruta 12 Km 5, T421561. Family-run, pool, a/c, TV, games.
C El Libertador, Bompland 110, T/F420570. Central, helpful, large bedrooms, those at back have balconies overlooking garden and swimming pool, parking, outdated.
D Hostería Casa Blanca, Guaraní 121, 2 blocks from bus station, T421320. With breakfast, family run, large rooms, good showers, pleasant.
D Lo de Ana, San Lorenzo 70, T423415, ana10@arnet.com.ar. With breakfast, kitchen, German spoken, quiet, good.
D Res Lilian, Beltrán 183, T420968. Bright modern rooms, quiet, 2 blocks from bus terminal, with breakfast, helpful owners.
D Res Paquita, Córdoba 731, opposite terminal, T420434. Some rooms with balcony, a/c, a bit old-fashioned but nice setting.
D Res San Fernando, Córdoba y Guaraní, near terminal, T421429. With breakfast, popular, good value.
D Residencial La Cabaña, Tres Fronteras 434, T420564, iguazu@hostels.org.ar. Well run, attractive hostel, nice spaces to sit and eat, good rooms. Recommended.
D Tierra Colorada, Córdoba y El Urú 28, T420572. Quiet and comfortable, but dark rooms, good atmosphere, with breakfast.
E pp Albergue Residencial Uno, Beltrán 116, T420529, albergueuno@iguazunet.com. Institutional hostel, but OK, rooms for 2 to 8, areas to cook and wash (but no machine), tours and activities.
E pp Bompland, Av Bompland 33, T420965. More with a/c, central, family-run.
E pp Correcaminos, Amarante 48, T420967, www.correcaminos.com.ar. Hostel with shared rooms, also doubles **D**, kitchen, bar, games room.
E-F pp Hostel Iguazú Falls, Guaraní 70, T421295, www.hosteliguazufalls.com. 1 block from terminal, HI affiliated, cheaper for members, also double rooms (C-D), more expensive with breakfast and a/c, kitchen, BBQ, luggage store, laundry, internet, lovely garden, good.
E pp Noelia, Fray Luis Beltrán 119, T420729. Not far from bus terminal, neat and tidy, family-run, good value, with breakfast.
F pp Hosp José Gorgues, Fray L Beltrán 169, T420641. 5 mins from terminal, family run, quiet, garden, laundry, kitchen, good.
F pp Residencial Los Amigos, Fray L Beltrán 82, T420756. Quiet, well maintained hostel, comfy.
Camping El Viejo Americano, Ruta 12, Km 3.5, T420190, www.viejoamericano.com.ar. With 3 pools, nicely wooded gardens, also *cabañas* and a hostel, camping US$1.50 pp, food shop, electricity, games area, barbecue.

🍴 Eating

Puerto Iguazú *p175, maps p174 and 176*
♏♏ **El Quincho del Tío Querido**, Bompland 110. Recommended for *parrilla* and local fish.
♏ **El Charro**, Córdoba 106. Good food, *parrilla*, popular.
♏ **La Esquina**, Córdoba 148. Extensive buffet, beef, fish, friendly service.
♏ **La Rueda**, Córdoba 28. Good food at reasonable prices, fish, steaks and pastas. Recommended.
♏ **Pizza Color**, Córdoba y Amarante. Popular for pizza and *parrilla*.
♏ **Panificadora Real**, Córdoba y Guaraní. Good bread, open Sun evening; another branch at Victoria y Brasil in the centre.

🥾 Activities and tours

Iguazú Falls *p174, map p174*
Explorador Expediciones, offer 2 small- group tours: *Safari a la Cascada* which takes you by jeep to the Arrechea waterfall, stopping along the way to look at wildlife, with a short walk to the falls, 2 hrs, US$12. And *Safari en la Selva*, more in-depth interpretation of the wildlife all around, in open jeeps, 2 hrs, US$19. Highly recommended. T421600, T15 673318, www.hotelguia.com/turismo/explorador-expediciones, and at the *Sheraton Hotel*. The company is run by expert guide Daniel Somay. There are also night walking tours to the falls when the moon is full; on clear nights the moon casts a blue halo over the falls. The *Sheraton* rents mountain bikes for US$2.50 for a couple of hrs. Recommended guide: Miguel Castelino, Apartado Postal 22, Puerto Iguazú (3370), Misiones, T420157, focustours@aol.com.
Jungle Explorer. On *Paseo Ecológico* you float silently 3 km down the river from Estación Garganta to appreciate the wildlife on its banks, 30 mins, US$5. *Aventura Náutica* is a journey by launch to give you a soaking under the Falls, US$10. *Gran Aventura* combines the Aventura Náutica with a longer boat trip and a jeep trip along the Yacaratiá trail, 1 hr, US$24. Tickets available at all embarkation points or at *Sheraton Hotel*, T421696, www.iguazujunglexplorer.com.

Puerto Iguazú *p175, map p176*
For operators within the park, see **Jungle Explorer** and **Explorador Expediciones** above. Explorador also run recommended 2-day expeditions in 4WDs to the Salto de Moconá.
Aguas Grandes, Mariano Moreno 58, T421140, www.aguasgrandes.com. Tours to both sides of the falls and further afield, activities in the forest, abseiling down waterfalls, good fun.

Cabalgatas por la Selva, Ruta 12, just after the Rotonda for the road to the international bridge, T155-42180 (mob). For horse riding, 3-hr trips, US$12. Agencies arrange day tours to the Brazilian side (lunch in Foz), Itaipú and Ciudad del Este. Some include the new Duty Free mall on the Argentine side. Also to a gem mine at Wanda, US$10, and the Jesuit ruins at San Ignacio Miní, US$20 (better from Posadas, less driving time). **Turismo Cuenca del Plata**, Amarante 76, T421062, cuencadelplata@cuencadelplata.com. Conventional tours to the falls, and a half-day trip to a Guaraní village (touristy).

● Transport

Iguazú Falls *p174, map p174*
Bus Transportes El Práctico run every 45 mins from Puerto Iguazú bus terminal, stopping at the park entrance for the purchase of entry tickets, continuing to the Visitor Centre, US$1. First bus 0630, last 1910, journey time 30 mins. **Cars** are not allowed beyond visitor centre (car entry US$3).

Puerto Iguazú *p175, map p176*
Air Airport is 20 km southeast of Puerto Iguazú near the Falls, T422013. A bus service between airport and bus terminal connects with plane arrivals and departures, US$3. AR/Austral fly direct to **Buenos Aires**, 1 hr 40 mins.
Bus The bus terminal, at Av Córdoba y Av Misiones, has a phone office, left luggage, various tour company desks and bus offices. To **Buenos Aires**, 16-18 hrs, Tigre Iguazú, Vía Bariloche, daily, US$31 *semi cama*, US$41 *cama*. To **Posadas**, stopping at San Ignacio Miní, frequent, 5-6 hrs, US$8, *expreso*; to **San Ignacio Miní**, US$5-6. Agencia de Pasajes Noelia, local 3, T422722, can book tickets beyond Posadas for other destinations in Argentina, ISIC discounts available.
Taxi T420973/421707. Fares: to **airport** US$10, to **Argentine falls** US$10, to **Brazilian falls** US$12, to centre of **Foz** US$10, to **Ciudad del Este** US$15, to **Tierra Colorada** mine US$25 with wait.

Border with Brazil
Crossing via the Puente Tancredo Neves. When leaving Argentina, Argentine immigration is at the Brazilian end of the bridge.
Bus Leave Puerto Iguazú terminal for Foz do Iguaçu every 20 mins, US$1. The bus stops at both sides of the border for Argentine and Brazilian formalities (if you need a visa for Brazil, officially you must have one even for a day visit – immigration does not always insist).Buses also stop at the Duty Free mall. The bus does not wait for those who need stamps, just catch the next one, of whatever company. **Taxis** Between the border and Puerto Iguazú US$3.

Border with Paraguay
Crossing to Paraguay is via Puente Tancredo Neves to Brazil and then via the Puente de la Amistad to Ciudad del Este. Brazilian entry and exit stamps are not required unless you are stopping in Brazil. The Paraguayan consulate is at Bompland 355.
Bus Direct buses (non-stop in Brazil), leave Puerto Iguazú terminal every 30 mins, US$2.50, 45 mins, liable to delays especially in crossing the bridge to Ciudad del Este. Only one bus on Sun, no schedule, better to go to Foz and change buses there.

● Directory

Puerto Iguazú *p175, map p176*
Airline offices Aerolíneas Argentinas, Brasil y Aguirre, T420194/420036. **Banks** ATMs at Macro Misiones and Banco de la Nación, Av Aguirre 179. *Sheraton* has an ATM. TCs can only be changed at **Cambio Libre** in the Hito Tres Fronteras, open 0800-2200. Good exchange rates at the Brazilian border. **Embassies and consulates** Brazil, Av Córdoba 264, T421348. **Internet** Generally expensive, US$1-1.20 per hr. Intercom Iguazú, Victoria Aguirre 240, p 2, T/F423180. Telecom, Victoria Aguirre y Brasil, has internet. Other internet places around here, opposite tourist office.

Lake District

The Lake District contains a series of great lakes strung along the foot of the Andes from above 40°S to below 50°S in the Parque Nacional Los Glaciares area. This section covers the northern lakes; for convenience the southernmost lakes, including those in the Los Glaciares park area, are described under Patagonia (see page 200). The area is dramatic, beautiful and unspoilt, offering superb trekking, fishing, watersports, climbing and skiing. See the Chilean chapter, The Lake District (page 686), for map and details of the system of lakes on the far side of the Andes. These can be visited through various passes. Off season, from mid-April to June and mid-August to mid-November, many excursions, boat trips etc, run on a limited schedule, if at all. Public transport is also limited.

Neuquén and around

→ *Phone code: 0299. Colour map 8, grid C2. Population: Greater Neuquén: 290,000.*
Founded in 1904 on the west side of the confluence of the Ríos Limay and Neuquén, Neuquén is a pleasant provincial capital and a major stop en route from the east coast to the northern lakes and Bariloche. It serves both the oilfields to the west and the surrounding fruit orchards. There are also many wine *bodegas* nearby. At the Parque Centenario (be sure *not* to take the bus to Centenario industrial suburb), is a *mirador* with good views of the city and the confluence of the rivers, where they become the Negro. Visit **Museo de la Ciudad Paraje Confluencia** ① *Independencia y Córdoba*, interesting display on the Campaign of the Desert (19th-century annihilation of indigenous groups). Facing Neuquén and connected by bridge is Cipolletti, a prosperous centre of the fruit-growing region. **Tourist office** ① *Félix San Martín 182, T0299-442 4089, www.neuquentur.gov.ar. Daily 0700-2200* (don't confuse the streets Félix San Martín and General San Martín).

Villa El Chocón
The area around Villa El Chocón is rich in dinosaur fossils. Red sedimentary rocks have preserved, in relatively good condition, bones and footprints of the animals which lived in this region during the Cretaceous period about 100 million years ago. The **Museo Paleontológico Ernesto Bachmann** ① *in the civic centre, T0299-4901230, daily 0800-2100 in summer, 0900-1900 in low season, US$0.70*, displays the fossils of a giant carnivore (Giganotosaurus carolinii). Two walks beside lake to see the dinosaur footprints, guides in museum give good tours. The tourist office organizes guided tours to the 20-km long, 80-m high Cañón Escondido (or Coria) to see dinosaur footprints, three hours, US$5.

Zapala → *Phone code: 02942. Colour map 8, grid C2. Population: 35,000.*
Zapala, 185 km west of Neuquén, has an excellent geology museum, **Museo Mineralógico Professor Olsacher** ① *Etcheluz 52 (same building as bus terminal), Mon-Fri 1400-1800, free.* Among the collections of minerals, fossils, shells and rocks, is a complete crocodile jaw, believed to be 80 million years old. There is an airport, an *ACA* service station, Km 1399 Ruta 22. **Tourist office** ① *Av San Martín s/n, T02942-421132.*

● Sleeping

Neuquén *p179*
AL Del Comahue, Av Argentina 377, T443 2040, www.hahoteles.com. 4-star, extremely comfortable, spa, pool, good restaurant.
AL Express, Goya y Costa Rica, T449 0100, www.ehotelexpress.com. Handy for the airport, comfortable, business oriented, international style, nicely decorated and well-equipped, pool, golf.
A Royal, Av Argentina 143, T448 8902, www.royalhotel.com.ar. Modern, parking, breakfast included, good value.
A-B Hostal del Caminante, on Ruta 22 Km 1227, 13 km west of centre, T444 0118, www.hostaldelcaminante.com. A comfortable suburban place among fruit plantations with garden, pool and restaurant.
C Alcorta, Alcorta 84, T442 2652. Breakfast, TV in rooms, also flats for 4, good value.
D Res Inglés, Félix San Martín 534, T442 2252. Convenient, no breakfast, good value.

El Chocón *p179*
A La Posada del Dinosaurio, on the lakeshore, T0299-490 1200,

www.posadadinosaurio.com.ar. With breakfast, comfortable, modern, all rooms have lake view.

Zapala *p179*
B Hue Melén, Brown 929, T422391, hotel huemelen@zapala.com.ar. Good value, decent rooms, restaurant with best food in town.
C Coliqueo, Etcheluz 159, opposite bus terminal, T421308. Convenient and good.
C Pehuén, Elena de la Vega y Etcheluz, 1 block from bus terminal, T423135. Comfortable, recommended. There's also a municipal campsite.

● Eating

Neuquén *p179*
♯ **El Reencuentro**, Alaska 6451. Delicious *parrilla*, popular, set menu US$5.
♯ **La Birra**, Santa Fe 23. Lots of choice, welcoming, chic, modern.
♯ **Tutto al Dente**, Alberdi 49. Tasty homemade pasta and good value set meals.

⊖ Transport

Neuquén *p179*

Air Airport 7 km west of centre, T444 0244, www.anqn.com.ar. Bus **Centenario**, US$0.40, taxi US$4. AR/Austral flies to **Buenos Aires** and **Comodoro Rivadavia**; LADE flies to **Bariloche**, **Chapelco** and **Zapala**. Schedules change frequently.

Bus Terminal at Planas y Solalique, on Ruta 22, 4 km west of town. Buses US$0.35-0.70; taxi US$2.70. About a dozen companies to **Buenos Aires** daily, 12-16 hrs, US$20-35. To **Zapala** daily, 2½-3 hrs, US$5. To **San Martín de los Andes**, 6 hrs, US$12-17. To **Bariloche**, 7 companies, 5-6 hrs, US$11-16, sit on left. To **Mendoza**, Andesmar, daily, 12-13 hrs, US$23-31. To **Chile**: to **Temuco**, Igi-Llaima and El Valle, 9-10 hrs, US$24.

Zapala *p179*

Bus 3 companies to **San Martín de los Andes**, 3-3½ hrs, US$8, via Junín de los Andes. To **Bariloche**, change at San Martín. To **Temuco** (Chile) all year, various companies, 10 hrs, daily, US$20-22. Buy Chilean currency before leaving.

⊖ Directory

Neuquén *p179*

Airline offices AR/Austral, Santa Fe 52, T442 2409/0810-2228 6527. **Banks** Lots of ATMs along Av Argentina. *Casas de Cambio*: Pullman, Alcorta 144, Exterior, San Martín 23. **Internet and telephones** At lots of *locutorios* everywhere in centre. **Post offices** Rivadavia y Santa Fe.

Parque Nacional Lanín

① *US$4 to enter park. Helpful advice on walks from guardaparques at the entrance and at Puerto Canoa. Frequent buses from Junín in season, T492038 for information. Lanín National Park office, Frey 749, San Martín de los Andes, on main plaza, T429004, Mon-Fri 0800-1300, helpful but maps poor. Helpful information in Spanish is available from www.parque nacionallanin.gov.ar.*

This beautiful, large park has sparkling lakes, wooded mountain valleys and one of Argentina's most striking peaks, the snow capped Lanín Volcano. The lakes of **Huechulafquen** and **Paimún** are unspoilt, beautiful, and easily accessible for superb walking and fishing, with three *hosterías* and blissful free camping all along the lakeside. From Puerto Canoa there is a boat excursion to **Lago Epulafquen** with José Julián, T421038, US$7. Geologically, Lanín Volcano is one of the youngest of the Andes; it is extinct and one of the world's most beautiful mountains. It's a challenging and popular climb that may be completed in one long journey, starting near *Seccional de Guardaparques* (VHF 155675) at Tromen pass where you must register and all climbing equipment and experience are checked. Crampons and ice-axe are essential, as is protection against strong, cold winds. There are three *refugios*, the first of which is reached after about a 5-hour walk. Before setting off, seek advice from Lanín National Park office.

Border with Chile: the Tromen Pass

Formalities are carried out at the Argentine side of the Tromen Pass (Chileans call it Mamuil Malal). This route runs through glorious scenery to Pucón (135 km) on Lago Villarrica (Chile). It is less developed than the Huahum and Samoré (Puyehue) routes further south, and definitely not usable during heavy rain or snow (June to mid-November). Parts are narrow and steep; it is unsuitable for bicycles. (Details of the Chilean side are given under Puesco, The Lake District) There is a campsite at Puesto Tromen (though very windy), but take food as there is only one basic shop at the pass. The international bus may not pick up passengers at Tromen or on the Chilean part of the route.

Junín de los Andes → *Phone code: 02972. Colour map 8, grid B4. Population: 10,000.*

Known as the trout capital of Argentina, Junín de los Andes is a relaxed, pretty town on the broad Río Chimehuín, a less touristy option than San Martín, with many trout-filled rivers and lakes nearby, and the best base for trekking in Parque Nacional Lanín (see below). Its small museum has a collection of items from the Mapuche culture ① *on Gines Ponte, free*, and there are impressive sculptures at **Vía Christi** on the hill opposite① *US$0.65*. **Tourist office** ① *Plaza at Col Suárez y Padre Milanesio, T02972-491160, turismo@jdeandes.com.ar. Open summer 0800-2200, Mar- Nov 0800-2100.*

San Martín de los Andes → *Phone code: 02972 .Colour map 8, grid C1. Pop: 22,000.*

This picturesque and touristy little town, 40 km southwest of Junín, with its chocolate-box, chalet-style architecture, is spectacularly set at the east end of Lago Lacar. Mirador Bandurrias, 45-minute walk from the centre offers good views. There is excellent skiing on Cerro Chapelco (with varied summer activities for kids), and facilities for water skiing, windsurfing and sailing on Lago Lácar. The **tourist office** is on the main plaza① *San Martín y Rosas 790, T02972-427347, www.smandes.gov.ar. Open 0800-2100 all year, English and French spoken.* Very busy in summer, advisable to go early. Surrounded by lakes and mountains to explore, the most popular excursions are south along the **Seven Lakes Drive** (see below), north to the thermal baths at **Termas de Lahuen-Co** (also reached on foot after two days from Lagos Huechulafquen and Paimún) and to **Lagos Lolog** and **Lácar**. There's a *ripio* track along the north side of Lago Lácar with beaches and rafting at **Hua Hum**, and along the south to quieter and beautiful **Quila Quina**, where a short walk takes you to a quiet Mapuche community. Both can be reached by boat from San Martín's pier, T427380, 30 minutes one way, US$10 (plus the entry fee to the National Park) return to Quila Quina, three daily in season. Cyclists can complete a circuit around Lago Lácar, or take the cable car up to Chapelco and come back down the paths.

Border with Chile: the Hua Hum Pass

A *ripio* road along the north shore of Lago Lácar through the Lanín National Park crosses the border to Puerto Pirihueico, where a boat crosses Lago Pirihueico; bikes can be taken (the route is open all year round; for vehicle reservations T0056-631-971585, 0900-1200, www.panguipulli.cl, at least a day in advance). *Ko Ko* bus goes to the pass, two hours, and *Lafit* goes up to Panguipulli (Chile), weekly off-season, US$15, check terminal for schedule. For connections from Puerto Pirihueico to Panguipulli and beyond, see Chile chapter.

⦿ Sleeping

Junín de los Andes *p180*
AL Río Dorado Lodge & Fly shop, Pedro Illera 448, T491548, www.riodorado.com.ar. Comfortable, pricey, great for anglers, good fly shop.
A Milla Piuké, Av Los Pehuenes y JA Roca (on Ruta 234), T492378, millapiuke@ fronteradigital.net.ar. Delightful if a bit overpriced, welcoming, comfortable rooms and apartments for families. Recommended.
B Caleufu Travel Lodge, JA Roca 1323 (on Ruta 234), T492757, www.caleufutravellodge.com.ar. Excellent value, welcoming, very good rooms, neat garden, also comfortable apartments for up to 5 people. Owner Jorge speaks English. Recommended.
B Posada Pehuén, Col Suárez 560, T491569, posadapehuen@hotmail.com. A peaceful bed and breakfast with comfortable rooms, pretty garden, charming owners, good value.
C Hostería Chimehuín, Col Suárez y 25 de Mayo, T491132, www.interpatagonia.com/ hosteriachimehuin. Cosy, quaint old fishing lodge by the river, closed May. Recommended.
E pp La Casa de Marita y Aldo, 25 de Mayo 371, T491042, casademaritayaldo@hotmail.com. A cheery and popular family house with basic accommodation.
E Res Marisa, JM de Rosas 360 (on Ruta 234), T491175. A simple place with helpful owners, very good value.

Camping Mallín Beata Laura Vicuña, T491149, and La Isla, T492029, both on the river and good.

Lago Huechulafquen *p180*
AL pp Hostería Huechulafquen, T03467-450296, hosteriahuechulafquen@ yahoo.com.ar. Best, full board, comfortable cabin-like rooms, own stretch of beach, expert fishing guide.
Camping Several sites in beautiful surroundings on Lagos Huechulafquen and Paimún in Parque Nacional Lanín.

San Martín de los Andes *p181*
Single rooms are scarce. There are 2 high seasons, when rates are much higher: Jan/Feb and Jul. There are many excellent *cabañas* for families on the hill at the top of Perito Moreno. **Inmobiliaria Rohde**, San Martín 1344, T421220, www.rohde turismo.com.ar. Recommended estate agent for renting houses, cabins and apartments per day. When everywhere else is full, Tourist Office provides a list of private addresses in high season.
LL La Cheminée, Gral Roca y Mariano Moreno, T427617, www.hosterialacheminee.com.ar. Cosy cottage-like rooms, breakfast included, but no restaurant, overpriced in high season.
L Las Lengas, Col Pérez 1175, T427659, www.interpatagonia.com/laslengas. Attractive spacious rooms, warm relaxing atmosphere with pool in nice garden, peaceful part of town.

L **Alihuen Lodge**, Ruta 62, Km 5.5 (road to Lake Lolog), T426588, alihuen@smandes. com.ar. Includes breakfast, other meals available (very good), lovely location and grounds, very comfortable.

AL **Del Viejo Esquiador**, San Martín 1242, T427690, www.interpatagonia.com/ delviejoesquiador. Very comfortable, good beds, in traditional hunting lodge style, excellent service. Recommended.

A **Hostal del Esquiador**, Col Rhode 975, T427674. Well decorated rooms, lovely sitting room, good service, free internet. Great value low season.

A **Hostal del Lago**, Col Rhode 854, T427598, www.hostal-del-lago.com.ar. Relaxed homely place, basic bathrooms, good breakfast included, pretty garden.

A **La Masía**, Obeid 811, T427688, www.hosterialamasia.com.ar. Spacious, high-ceilinged chalet-style rooms, cosy bar.

B **Anay**, Capitán Drury 841, T427514, www.interpatagonia.com/anay. Excellent value, central, cosy house with welcoming owners. No credit cards; closed in Dec.

B **Casa Alta**, Obeid 659, T427456. The home of charming multilingual owners, 'beyond comparison and fantastic' (closed in low season). Book in advance.

B **Hosteria Bärenhaus**, Los Alamos 156, Barrio Chapelco (8370), T/F422775, www.baerenhaus.com. 5 km outside town, free pick-up from bus terminal and airport. Welcoming young owners, very comfortable rooms with heating, English and German spoken. Recommended.

C **Cumelén**, Elordi 931, T427304, www.inter patagonia.com/cumelen. Good choice, simple and spotless rooms, English spoken.

C **Hostería Las Lucarnas**, Col Pérez 632, T427085, hosterialaslucarnas@hotmail.com. Central, pretty, simple comfortable rooms, English spoken.

D **Rukalhue**, Juez del Valle 682 (3 blocks from terminal), T427431, www.rukalhue.com.ar. Budget choice with a rather institutional atmosphere, comfortable, well-heated, though thin-walled dorms and **C** double rooms with a poor breakfast.

E pp **Puma**, A Fosbery 535, T422443, www.pumahostel.com.ar. Discount for HI and ISIC members, small dorms with bath and **C** double room with view, laundry, kitchen facilities, bikes for hire, very well run by mountain guide owner. Recommended.

Camping ACA Camping, Av Koessler 2176, T429430, with hot water and laundry facilities, also *cabañas*. Camping Quila Quina, T426919, www.quilaquina.alojar.com.ar. Lovely site on a stream near Lago Lácar, 18 km from San Martín, with beaches, immaculate toilet blocks, restaurant and shop, access to boats and treks. Open only in summer and Easter.

Eating

Junín de los Andes *p180*

La Posta de Junín, JM de Rosas 160 (on Ruta 234). A recommended *parrilla* with good service; also trout, pizza and pastas.

Ruca Hueney, Col Suárez y Milanesio. Good steak, trout and pasta dishes.

Confitería Centro de Turismo, next to the tourist office. Café/restaurant, good for coffee and sandwiches.

San Martín de los Andes *p181*

Avataras, Tte Ramayón 765, T427104. Open only Thu-Sat from 2030, inspired, imaginative menu with cuisine from all over the world, from fondue to satay, elegant surroundings. An excellent treat. Cheaper meals at its pub.

Doña Quela, San Martín 1017. From sophisticated dishes to simple *milanesas* in a smartly renovated old hotel.

El Regional, Villegas 965. Popular for regional specialities – smoked trout, venison, wild boar, pâtés and hams, El Bolsón's homemade beer, cheerful German-style decor.

La Tasca, Mariano Moreno 866. Recommended for its venison, trout and home made pastas with a varied wine list.

Ku, San Martín 1053. Intimate atmosphere for *parrilla*, pastas and delicious mountain specialities, excellent service and wine list.

La Costa del Pueblo, Costanera opposite pier. Overlooking the lake, huge range of pastas, chicken and trout dishes, generous portions, good service. Meal of the day for US$3. Recommended.

Tío Paco, San Martín y Capitán Drury. Good lunches at this great bar/café.

La Cantina, Villegas 735. Small, family-run, daily specials, good value.

Pura Vida, Villegas 745. Small and welcoming vegetarian place serving tasty soups, also fish and chicken dishes, including a delicious chop suey with brown rice. For non-smokers and no credit cards.

Shopping

San Martín de los Andes *p181*

Abuela Goye, San Martín 807, sells delicious chocolates and runs a good café serving gorgeous cakes.

Mamusia, San Martín 601, is another recommended chocolate shop.

▲▲ Activities and tours

San Martín de los Andes p181
Cycling
Many places in the centre rent mountain and normal bikes, reasonable prices, maps provided. **HG Rodados**, San Martín 1061, T427345. Arranges excursions, rents mountain bikes, US$6 per day, also spare parts and expertise.

Fishing
In addition to licence, US$3.50 extra per day for trolling and US$1.70 for fishing in Boca del Chimehuin or Río Correntoso. Contact the tourist office for a list of fishing guides or the National Park office.
Jorge Cardillo Pesca, Villegas 1061. Fly shop, sells equipment, fishing licences and offers excursions.
Flotadas Chimehuin, at Junín de los Andes, T491313. Offers fully inclusive fishing packages with expert bilingual guides.
Orvis, Gral Villegas 835, T425892, www.sanmartinorvis.com.ar. Fly shop, sells equipment and offer fishing excursions.
Juan Carlos Aráuz, M Moreno 1193, T427376. Fishing guide.

Skiing
Chapelco has 29 km of pistes, many of them challenging, with an overall drop of 730 m. Very good slopes and snow conditions from Jul to Sep make this a popular resort with foreigners and wealthier Argentines. **Ko Ko** bus and others (from hotels) run in winter from terminal, US$4-6 one way. Details, passes, equipment hire from office at San Martín y Elordi, T427845, www.chapelco.com. At the foot of the mountain are a restaurant and a café, with 4 more restaurants and a lodge on the mountain and a small café at the top.

Tours
Prices for conventional tours are similar in most agencies: Hua Hum pass by road, US$14; Ruta de los Siete Lagos, US$18; Lago Huechulafquen, US$17.
El Claro, Col Díaz 751, T428876, www.elclaro turismo.com.ar. For conventional tours, horse riding, mountain biking and trekking.
Lanín Expediciones, San Martín 851, oficina 5, T429799, www.laninexpediciones.com. Adventure tourism for beginners or experts, from a 3-hr walk (US$9) near San Martín, winter night walks in the forest, rafting in Aluminé (US$28), trekking in Lanín area, a 3-day ascent of the volcano (US$137, discounts if booked in advance),

and a once-in-a-lifetime climb to 4,700-m Domuyo peak. Naviera Lácar & Nonthue, San Martín pier, T427380. Boat trips to Quila Quina, US$7, 30 mins one way, or guided boat excursions to Hua Hum, US$20, 5 hrs return (neither includes National Park entry fee).
Tiempo Patagónico, San Martín 950, T427113, www.tiempopatagonico.com. Excursions and adventure tourism, including rafting at Hua Hum, US$25.

⊙ Transport

Junín de los Andes p180
Transport information T492038.
Air Chapelco airport between Junín and San Martín, served by AR from Buenos Aires and LADE (office in bus terminal, San Martín de los Andes, T427672) from Buenos Aires, Esquel, Neuquén and Bariloche.
Bus Terminal at Olavarria y F San Martín, T492038. To **San Martín**, Centenario and others, 1 hr, US$2; to **Buenos Aires**, 19 hrs, US$50 *coche cama*; to **Temuco** and **Valdivia** (via Paso Tromen), 6-7 hrs, US$15 with **Empresa San Martín**. Cooperativa Litrán goes daily in summer to **Lago Paimún** (Parque Nacional Lanín), 1¼ hrs, US$4.

San Martín de los Andes p181
Air Chapelco airport, 23 km away. See under Junín de los Andes above.
Bus Terminal at Villegas 251, T427044. Café, left luggage (US$0.70), toilet facilities, *kiosko*, *locutorio*. To **Buenos Aires**, 20 hrs, US$50 *coche cama*, daily, 6 companies. To **Bariloche**, 3½-4 hrs, US$8.50 (via 7 Lagos and Villa La Angostura or via Rinconada), Vía Bariloche/Turismo Algarrobal, T422800, **Albus**, T428100, Ko Ko, T427422. La Araucana, T425065, goes to **Villa La Angostura** via Villa Traful, 5 hrs (includes a 1-hr stop in Villa Traful), US$7. **To Chile**: **Temuco** (Mon, Wed, Fri) or **Valdivia** (Tue, Thu, Sat) via Pucón with **Empresa San Martín**, T427294, US$15; **Albus**, to **Temuco** (Tue, Thu, Sat), 6 hrs, US$15.

⊙ Directory

San Martín de los Andes p181
Banks Many ATMs on San Martín. Exchange at Banco de la Nación, San Martín 687, Banco Francés, San Martín y Sarmiento and Andina, Capitán Drury 876, which also changes TCs (3% commission) Banco de la Provincia de Neuquén, Obeid y Belgrano. **Police station** Belgrano 635, T427300, or T101.

Parque Nacional Nahuel Huapi

① *US$4 payable at Nahuel Huapi National Park office, at San Martín 24, Bariloche, T02944-423111, Mon-Fri 0800-1600, Sat-Sun 0900-1500, www.parquesnacionales.gov.ar.*
Covering 709,000 ha and stretching along the Chilean border, this is the oldest National Park in Argentina. With lakes, rivers, glaciers, waterfalls, torrents, rapids, valleys, forest, bare mountains and snow-clad peaks, there are many kinds of wild animals living in the region, including the pudú, the endangered huemul (both deer) as well as river otters, cougars and guanacos. Bird life, particularly swans, geese and ducks, is abundant. The outstanding feature is the splendour of the lakes. The largest is **Lago Nahuel Huapi** (*Altitude 767 m*), 531 sq km and 460 m deep in places, particularly magnificent to explore by boat since the lake is very irregular in shape and long arms of water, or *brazos*, stretch far into the land. On a peninsula in the lake is exquisite **Parque Nacional Los Arrayanes** (see below). There are many islands: the largest is **Isla Victoria**, with its idyllic hotel. Trout and salmon have been introduced.

North of Villa La Angostura, Lagos Correntoso and Espejo both offer stunning scenery, and tranquil places to stay and walk. Navy blue Lago Traful, a short distance to the northeast, can be reached by a road which follows the Río Limay through the Valle Encantado, with its fantastic rock formations or directly from Villa La Angostura. **Villa Traful** is the perfect place to escape to, with fishing, camping, and walking. There's a tourist office at the eastern edge of town, T02944-479099, www.villatraful.info. Spectacular mountains surround the city of Bariloche, great trekking and skiing country. The most popular walks are described in Bariloche section. South of Lago Nahuel Huapi, Lagos Mascardi, Guillelmo and Gutiérrez offer horse riding, trekking and rafting along the Río Manso. See page 196 for accommodation along their shores.

The well-maintained *ripio* road known as the '**Seven Lakes Drive**', runs south from San Martín to Bariloche via Lago Hermoso and Villa La Angostura and passes beautiful unspoilt stretches of water, framed by steep, forested mountains. There are several places to stay, open summer only. An alternative route, fully paved and faster, but less scenic is via Junín de los Andes and **Confluencia** on Ruta 40 (ACA service station and a hotel, also motel *El Rancho* just before Confluencia). Round-trip excursions along the Seven Lakes route, 5 hours, are operated by several companies, but it's better in your own transport.

Villa La Angostura → *Phone code 02944. Colour map 8, grid C1. Population: 7,000.*

This pretty town, 80 km northwest of Bariloche on Lago Nahuel Huapi, is a popular holiday resort with wealthier Argentines and there are countless restaurants, hotels and *cabaña* complexes around the centre, **El Cruce** and along Ruta 231 between Correntoso and Puerto Manzano. The picturesque port, known as **La Villa**, is 3 km away at the neck of the Quetrihué Peninsula. At its end is **Parque Nacional Los Arrayanes**, with 300 year old specimens of the rare *arrayán* tree, whose flaky bark is cinnamon coloured. The park can be reached on foot or by bike (12 km each way; for a return walk start from 0900 to1400), or you could take the boat back. Boats run at least twice daily in summer from Bahía Mansa and Bahía Brava, down at La Villa, US$10 return (plus the US$4 National Park entry fee) . See also below for tours by boat from Bariloche. There is a small ski resort at **Cerro Bayo** (www.cerrobayoweb.com) with summer activities too. The **tourist office** is opposite the bus terminal ① *Av Siete Lagos 93, T02944-494124, www.villalaangostura.gov.ar. Open high season 0800-2100, low season 0800-2000.* Good maps with accommodation marked.

● Sleeping

Parque Nacional Nahuel Huapi *p184*
C **Hostería Los Siete Lagos** (27 km north of Villa La Angostura), T02944-15417152, a charming, simple place run by very knowledgeable people about the region, on the shore of Lago Correntoso, great views and the best *tortas fritas* in the region, with the breakfast. Several free campsites without facilities along the route.

Villa Traful
A **Cabañas Aiken**, T02944-479048, www.aiken.com.ar. Well-decorated wooden houses in beautiful surroundings near the lake (close to the tourist office), price is for 4-bed cabin.

B Hostería Villa Traful, T479005, www.hosteria villatraful.com. A cosy house with a tea room by the lake, also *cabañas* for 4-6 people, good value.
E pp Vulcanche Hostel, T02944-494015/028, www.vulcanche.com. Rustic log cabin, nicely located (close to the tourist office), with good dorms and **C** doubles, both including breakfast, large park for camping (US$3 pp), also cabins. Discounts to HI members.

Villa La Angostura *p184*
L Hostal Las Nieves, Av Siete Lagos 980 (1.5 km west of El Cruce), T494573, www.lasnieves.com. Small, good location with garden, very comfortable, heated swimming pool and sauna, English spoken, helpful.
L Portal de Piedra, Ruta 231 y Río Bonito (at Puerto Manzano), T494278, www.portaldepiedra.com. Small, attractive *hostería* in the woods, with heated pool and a small restaurant open in high season.
AL Hotel Angostura, Nahuel Huapi 1911, at La Villa, T494224. Built in 1938, this traditional hotel run by Familia Cilley since then has a lovely lakeside setting and a good restaurant and tea room, *Viejo Coihue*. There is a cabin for 6 (**L**) that has probably the most beautiful setting in the region. Boat excursions along the nearby shore are arranged.
A Cuyen-Co, Lago Correntoso, T494377, cuyenco@ciudad.com.ar. Family-run, big grounds, good breakfast.
A Verena's Haus, Los Taiques 268, T 494467. Adults and non-smokers only, German and English spoken, cosy, garden. Recommended.
B Río Bonito, Topa Topa 260, T494110, riobonito@ ciudad.com.ar. 2 blocks from terminal, homely, quiet, comfortable, great breakfasts. Recommended.
D Nahuel, Huiliches 41 (500 m west of El Cruce), T 494737. Good budget choice with hot water, TV, good breakfast, welcoming owners; small restaurant.
E pp Italian Hostel, Los Maquis 233 (5 blocks from terminal), T494376, www.italian hostel.com.ar. Welcoming, small, with dorms and **D** doubles, rustic, functional and nice, run by a biker who closes the place in May-Jun. Fireplace and orchard from where you can pick berries and herbs for your meals. Recommended.
E pp Hostel La Angostura, Barbagelata 157, 150 m up road behind tourist office, T494834, www.hostellaangostura.com.ar. A warm, luxurious hostel, all small dorms have bathrooms, breakfast included, good **C** doubles, young welcoming owners organize trips and rent bikes for US$6 a day too. HI discounts. Recommended.
Camping Osa Mayor, off main road, close to town, T494304, www.campingosamayor.com.ar. Well designed leafy site, all facilities, also rustic *cabañas* and dorms, helpful owner.

🍴 Eating

Parque Nacional Nahuel Huapi *p184*
Villa Traful
🍴 **Aiken**, Villa Traful. Simple meals, excellent sandwiches with home-made bread and more expensive trout dishes. Open all year round.
🍴 **Ñancu Lahuen**, Villa Traful. A chocolate shop, tea room, and restaurant serving local trout.

Villa La Angostura *p184*
🍴🍴🍴 **El Esquiador**, Las Retamas 146. If on a budget, this good, popular *parrilla* has an all-you-can-eat choice of cold starters, a main meal and a dessert for US$6.
🍴🍴🍴 **Hora Cero**, Av Arrayanes 45. Warm atmosphere and live music at weekends, popular, big range of excellent pizzas, *pizza libre* (as much as you can eat for US$2.40) on Wed and Sat is a great deal.
🍴🍴🍴 **Rincón Suizo**, Av Arrayanes 44. High season only, delicious regional specialities with a Swiss twist.
🍴🍴🍴 **Los Troncos**, Av Arrayanes 67. Great local dishes, eg trout-filled ravioli, fabulous cakes and puddings.
🍴 **Gran Nevada**, Av Arrayanes 106. Jolly place for cheap *parrilla*, and *ñoquis*.
🍴 **Los Leños**, Av Arrayanes y Cerro Belvedere, T494596. *Rotisserie* for takeaway chicken, pizzas, *empanadas* and pastas.
🍴 **Nativa Café**, Av Arrayanes 198. Relaxed and welcoming, excellent pizzas – try the smoked trout or venison topping – huge salads, good place to hang out.

🏔 Activities and tours

Villa La Angostura *p184*
Pablo Misiak, T155 12458, pablomisiak@ yahoo.com. National Park authorized guide for trekking and rafting, speaks English.

⊖ Transport

Villa La Angostura *p184*
Bus Urban buses 15 de Mayo, US$0.35, link El Cruce (main bus stop on main road, 50 m from tourist office), La Villa, Correntoso and Puerto Manzano, and go up to Lago Espejo (US$0.85) and Cerro Bayo (US$1) in high season. To/from **Bariloche**, 1¼ hrs, US$3, several companies. To **San Martín de los Andes**, 2½ hrs, US$6.50-8.50 (several companies via 7 Lagos or via Rinconada). For **La Araucana** to **San Martín**, see above. **Via Bariloche/El Valle** goes to **Osorno**, 3½ hrs, and **Puerto Montt** (Chile), 5½ hrs, US$16; Andesmar and Tas Choapa go to **Valdivia**, US$15.

Argentina Parque Nacional Nahuel Huapi *Listings*

Bariloche and around → *Phone code: 02944. Colour map 8, grid C1. Population: 89,000.*

Beautifully situated on the south shore of Lago Nahuel Huapi, at the foot of Cerro Otto, San Carlos de Bariloche is an attractive tourist town and the best centre for exploring the National Park. There are many good hotels, restaurants and chocolate shops among its chalet-style stone and wooden buildings. Others along the lake shore have splendid views. Heaving with visitors in summer months, it's less busy in March-April when the forests are in their glory.

Ins and outs

Getting there The airport is 13 km east of town, the bus and train stations 3 km east.
▶▶ *For more detailed information see Transport, page 192.*

Getting around At peak holiday times (July and December-January), Bariloche is very busy with holidaymakers and students. The best times to visit are in the spring (September-November) and autumn (March-April), or February for camping and walking and August for skiing.

Tourist information Oficina Municipal de Turismo, San Martín 662, p 6, T422484, www.barilochepatagonia.info. Daily 0800-2100. Has full list of city buses, and details of hikes and campsites in the area and is helpful in finding accommodation. Very useful for information on hiking is *Club Andino Bariloche* (*CAB*), 20 de Febrero 30, T422266, www.clubandino.org. 0900-1300, plus 1600-2100 high season. Good *Infotrekking* maps (1:50,000, US$4.50), *Guía de Sendas y Picadas* maps (1:100,000, US$3.50 and 1:50,000, US$1.70) and a guidebook of paths, US$5, for sale. When Club Andino is closed, obtain more general information at the Nahuel Huapi National Park office (see address under Parque Nacional Nahuel Huapi, above). The *Traveller's Guru* is a free paper available at many points throughout Patagonia, written in English by travellers with valuable information for backpackers.

Sights

At the heart of the city is the **Centro Cívico**, built in 'Bariloche Alpine style' and separated from the lake by Avenida Rosas. It includes the **Museo de La Patagonia** which, apart the region's fauna (stuffed), has indigenous artefacts and material from the lives of the first white settlers.

Bariloche

Sleeping
Aire Sur 1 *A1*
Albergue El Gaucho 2 *B1*
Cristal 6 *A2*
Edelweiss 4 *A1*
El Nire 7 *A3*
Familia Arko 19 *B1*
Güemes 9 *B1*
Hostel 41 Below 22 *A1*
La Bolsa 11 *B2*
La Pastorella 12 *B1*
La Sureña 13 *A1*
Marco Polo Inn 10 *A1*
Nevada 14 *A2*
Patagonia Andina 15 *B1*
Periko's 16 *B1*
Piuké 17 *A3*
Premier 18 *A2*
Ruca Hueney 20 *B2*
Tres Reyes 21 *A2*

Eating
Antigua Café 15 *A2*
El Boliche de Alberto 1 *B2*
El Boliche de Alberto
 Pastas 2 *B2*
Familia Weiss 3 *A2*
Friends 4 *A2*
Jauja 5 *B2*
Kandahar 6 *B1*
La Jirafa 7 *A2*
La Marmite 8 *A2*
Map Room 14 *A2*
Pilgrim 9 *A2*
Rock Chicken 10 *A2*
Simoca 11 *A2*
Tarquino 13 *B1*
Vegetariano 12 *B1*

Walks around Bariloche

There's a network of paths in the mountains, and several refugios allowing for treks over several days. Refugios are leased by Club Andino Bariloche. On treks to refugios remember to add costs of ski lifts, buses, food at refugios and lodging (in Club Andino refugios: US$3-7 per night, plus US$1-1.70 for cooking, or US$2-4 for breakfast, US$4-7 for dinner). Take a good sleeping bag. Horseflies (*tábanos*) infest the lake shores and lower areas in summer. Among the many great treks possible here, these are recommended: From **Llao Llao** ① *getting there: bus 20 to Llao Llao*, delightful easy circuit in Valdivian (temperate) rainforest (two hours), also climb the small hill for wonderful views. Up to **Refugio López** (2,076 m) ① *getting there: bus 10 to Colonia Suiza and López (check return times)*, five hours return, from southeastern tip of Lago Moreno up Arroyo López, for fabulous views. From Refugio López, extend this to 3-4 day trek via Refugio Italia, on Laguna Negra, to **Laguna Jacob** and **Refugio San** Martín (poorly signposted, need experience). From Cerro Catedral to **Refugio Frey** (1,700 m), beautiful setting on small lake, via Arroyo Piedritas (four hours each way), or via cable car to *Refugio Lynch* and via Punta Nevada (only experienced walkers). To beautiful **Lago Gutiérrez**, 2 km downhill from Cerro Catedral, along lake shore to the road from El Bolsón and walk back to Bariloche (four hours), or Bus 50. From **Pampa Linda**, idyllic (*hostería*, campsite – see Sleeping), walk up to Refugio Otto Meiling (5 hours each way), to tranquil Laguna Ilon (5½ hrs each way), or across Paso de las Nubes to **Puerto Frías**, boat back to Bariloche (two days, check if open: closed when boggy). Bus to Pampa Linda from outside Club Andino Bariloche in summer, **Expreso Meiling**, T529875, US$14 return or from **Transitando lo Natural** ① *20 de Febrero 25, T527926, 2¼ hours, US$14 return*. Contact *CAB* for maps, guidebooks and to check walks are open (see under Tourist information).

① *Tue-Fri 1000-1230, 1400-1900, Sat 1000-1700, US$1.* Next to it is **Biblioteca Sarmiento** ① *Mon-Fri, 0900-1900 (closed 1-15 Jan)*, a library and cultural centre. The **cathedral**, built in 1946, lies six blocks east of here, with the main commercial area on Mitre in between. Opposite the main entrance to the cathedral there is a huge rock left in this spot by a glacier during the last glacial period. On the lakeshore is the **Museo Paleontológico** ① *12 de Octubre y Sarmiento, Mon-Sat 1600-1900, US$0.70*, which displays fossils mainly from Patagonia, including an ichthyosaur and replicas of a giant spider and shark's jaws.

Around Bariloche

One of South America's most important ski centres is just a few kilometres southwest from Bariloche, at **Cerro Catedral** (see Activities and tours, page 191). You can take a boat trip from Puerto Pañuelo (Km 25.5, bus 20 or transfer arranged with tour operator, US$5.50) across Lago Nahuel Huapi to **Isla Victoria** and **Bosque de Arrayanes**, on the Quetrihué Peninsula; full or a half-day excursion (fewer options in low season), US$15 plus National Park entry (with **Turisur**, see address below, on the 1937 boat *Modesta Victoria*) or US$17 plus Park entry (with **Espacio**, T431372, on modern *Cau Cau*), take picnic lunch if you don't want to pay on board. The all-day boat trip to **Puerto Blest**, in native Valdivian rainforest, is highly recommended. From Puerto Pañuelo, sail down to Puerto Blest (hotel, restaurant), continuing by short bus ride to Puerto Alegre and again by launch to Puerto Frías. From Puerto Blest, walk through forest to the Cascada and Laguna de los Cántaros (1½ hrs). Transfer to Puerto Pañuelo can be arranged from the agency; **Catedral Turismo** (see address below), US$16 plus Park entry and US$5 extra if going to Puerto Frías.

An old train (1912) leaves three times a week in summer from Bariloche railway station for an eight-hour excursion with two stops at Ñirihuau and Los Juncos (for birdwatching) and a walk up to **Cerro Elefante**, US$16-23 (lunch optional), T423858. Some tour operators offer an excursion to El Maitén, from where the Old Patagonian Express (La Trochita) runs a tourist service a few days a week (see more information under El Bolsón and Esquel).

Avenida Bustillo runs parallel to the lakeshore west of Bariloche, with access to the mountains above. At Km 5, a cable car (teleférico) goes up to **Cerro Otto** (1,405 m) with its revolving restaurant and splendid views. Transport and other details under Activities and tours (page 191). At Km 17.7 a chairlift goes up to **Cerro Campanario** (1,049 m)① *daily 0900-1800, US$5*, with fine views of Isla Victoria and Puerto Pañuelo. At Km 18.3 **Circuito Chico** begins – a 60-km circular route around Lago Moreno Oeste, past Punto Panorámico and through Puerto Pañuelo to **Llao Llao**, Argentina's most famous hotel (details on this and others on Avenida Bustillo in Sleeping, below.) Take bus No 20, 45 mins, US$0.85, a half-day drive or tour with agency, or full day's cycle. You could also extend this circuit, returning via **Colonia Suiza** and **Cerro Catedral** (2,388 m) one of South America's most important ski centres. Whole-day trip to **Lagos Gutiérrez** and **Mascardi** and beautiful **Pampa Linda** at the base of mighty **Cerro Tronador** (3,478 m), visiting the strange **Ventisquero Negro** (black glacier), highly recommended. Several companies run 12-hour minibus excursions to San Martín de los Andes along the famous **Seven Lakes Drive**, returning via Paso Córdoba and the Valle Encantado, but these involve few stops.

Border with Chile

The Samoré (formerly Puyehue) Pass A spectacular six-hour drive. A good broad paved road, RN 40 then RN 231, goes around the east end of Lago Nahuel Huapi, then follows the north side of the lake through Villa La Angostura. It passes the junction with 'Ruta de Los Siete Lagos' for San Martín at Km 90, Argentine customs (T494996) at El Rincón, Km 105, and the pass at Km 122 at an elevation of about 1,314 m. Chilean customs (Too566-4236284) is at Pajarito, Km 145, in the middle of a forest. The border is open from the second Saturday of October to 1 May, 0800-2100, winter 0900-2000 but liable to be closed after snowfalls. Chilean currency can be bought at Samoré pass customs at a reasonable rate.

Four bus companies (**El Valle, Bus Norte, Andesmar, Tas Choapa**) run daily services from Bariloche via Samoré pass to Osorno (4-6 hours, US$16) and Puerto Montt (6-7½ hours, same fare); **Andesmar** goes to Valdivia via Osorno (see Bariloche Transport below and take passport when booking). Sit on left side for best views. You can buy a ticket to the Chilean border, then another to Puerto Montt, or pay in stages in Chile, but there is little advantage in doing this.

Via Lake Todos Los Santos The route is Bariloche to Puerto Pañuelo by road, Puerto Pañuelo to Puerto Blest by boat (1¼ hours), Puerto Blest to Puerto Alegre on Lago Frías by bus, cross the lake to Puerto Frías by boat (20 minutes), then 2 hours by road to Peulla. Leave for Petrohué in the afternoon by boat (1 hour 40 minutes), cross Lago Todos Los Santos, passing the Osorno volcano, then by bus to Puerto Montt (2 hours). This route is beautiful, but the weather is often wet. In summer a one-day journey option (*rápida*) is added to the regular two-day crossing (*normal*) that runs all-year round. **Cruce de Lagos** has the monopoly on the famous Three Lakes Crossing to Puerto Montt in Chile, US$160, and their representatives in Argentina are **Catedral Turismo** (see address below) and in Chile, **Andina del Sud**; credit cards accepted. Book in advance during the high season, and beware the hard sell. For a two-day crossing, there is an overnight stop not included in the price, in Puerto Blest (**B** accommodation, half board) or in Peulla (**L** accommodation with breakfast). Details of accommodation under Peulla, Chile. Full price is charged even if only taking sections of the crossing. The only cheaper option, recommended to cyclists, is to pay US$60 for the boat trips. Summer crossing Monday-Saturday; rest of the year Monday-Friday.

The Argentine and Chilean border posts are open every day. There is an absolute ban in Chile on importing any fresh food – meat, cheese, fruit – from Argentina. Further information on border crossings in the Lake District will be found in the Chile chapter. You are strongly advised to get rid of all your Argentine pesos before leaving Argentina; it is useful to have some Chilean pesos before you cross into Chile from Bariloche.

🌐 Sleeping

Bariloche *p186, map p186*

Prices rise in 2 peak seasons: Jul-Aug for skiing, and mid-Dec to Mar for summer holidays. If you arrive in the high season without a reservation, consult the listing published by the tourist office (address above). This selection gives lake-view, high-season prices where applicable. In low season you pay half of these prices in most cases.

LL Edelweiss, San Martín 202, T445500, www.edelweiss.com.ar. 5-star with real attention to detail, excellent service, spacious comfortable rooms, indoor pool and beauty salon. *La Tavola* restaurant is excellent. Highly recommended.

LL Llao-Llao, Av Bustillo Km 25, T448530 (in BsAs, Maipú 1300, T011-57767450), www.llaollao.com. Deservedly famous, superb location, complete luxury, golf course, pool, spa, water sports, restaurant.

LL Pire-Hue, Cerro Catedral, T011-4807 8200, www.pire-hue.com.ar. Exclusive 5-star hotel in ski resort with beautiful rooms and all facilities.

LL-L Cabañas Villa Huinid, Av Bustillo, Km 2.6, T523523, www.villahuinid.com.ar. Luxurious *cabañas* with everything you need. Recommended.

L Nevada, Rolando 250, T522778, www.nevada.com.ar. Warm and welcoming, nicely furnished rooms with minibar (spacious superior rooms), good restaurant, with traditional dishes.

L Tres Reyes, 12 de Octubre 135, T426121, reservas@hoteltresreyes.com. Traditional lakeside hotel with spacious rooms, splendid views, cheaper to reserve on the spot than by email.

L Tunquelén, Av Bustillo, Km 24.5, T448400, www.maresur.com. 4-star, quiet comfortable, splendid views, feels more secluded than *Llao-Llao*, restaurant, attentive service. Highly recommended.

AL Cristal Mitre 355, T422002, hotelcristalres@ciudad.com.ar. Central, charming, 60s style, comfortable, with TV and minibar (the superior rooms are best).

A Hostería Santa Rita, Av Bustillo, Km 7.2, T/F461028, www.santarita.com.ar. Bus 10, 20, 21, to Km 7.5. Close to the centre, peaceful lakeside views, comfortable, lovely terrace, poor breakfast.

A La Caleta, Av Bustillo, Km 1.9, T443444. *Cabañas* sleep 4, open fire, excellent value.

A La Pastorella, Belgrano 127, T424656, www.lapastorella.com.ar. Quaint little hostería, whose hospitable owners speak English, good value, safe. Recommended.

A La Sureña, San Martín 432, T422013, hosteria@infovia.com.ar. Central, cosy, small wood-panelled rooms, old-fashioned feel, with TV.

B El Ñire, O'Connor y O'Connor, T423041, www.elnire.com.ar. Small, warm and pleasant place, English spoken.

B Piuké, Beschtedt 136, T423044. Delightful, simple, nicely decorated, breakfast included, excellent value, owner Martin Walter speaks German, Hungarian and Italian, closed from Easter to 1 Jul.

C Premier, Rolando 263, T426168, www.hotelpremier.com. Good central choice (very good value in low season), small rooms with TV and larger and renovated superior rooms, English spoken. Recommended.

D Familia Arko, Güemes 691, T423109. English and German spoken, cooking facilities (no breakfast), helpful, good trekking information, beautiful garden, camping. Repeatedly recommended.

D Güemes, Güemes 715, T424785. Lovely, quiet, lots of space, very pleasant, big breakfast included, owner is a fishing expert and very knowledgeable about the lake district.

D pp Katy, Av Bustillo, Km 24.3, T448023, gringospatagonia@yahoo.de. Delightful, peaceful, garden full of flowers, charming Slovenian family Kastelic, breakfast included (also half-board). Also offers adventure tourism www.gringospatagonia.com.

D pp Mariana Pirker, 24 de Septiembre 230, T424873. Flats sleeping 2-3, German and English spoken.

D Res No Me Olvides, Av Los Pioneros Km 1, T429140, 30 mins' walk or Bus 50/51 to corner of C Videla then follow signs. Beautiful house in quiet surroundings, use of kitchen. Recommended.

E pp Aire Sur, Salta 456, T522135, airesurhostel@arnet.com.ar. Light, airy and peaceful, with views, dorms, doubles (**D**), breakfast extra, internet, laundry, cycle hire, knowledgeable owner also runs mountain bike excursions and kayaking. Recommended.

E pp Alaska, Lilinquen 328 (buses 10, 20, 21, get off at La Florida, Av Bustillo Km 7.5), T/F461564, www.alaska-hostel.com. Well run, cosy with shared rustic rooms for 4, all with bath, also double without bath (**D**), nice garden, kitchen facilities, washing machine, free internet, organizes horse riding and rafting, rents mountain bikes. machine, free internet, organizes horse riding and rafting, rents mountain bikes. Recommended. Also cabañas for 6. HI discounts. Owners run **Overland Patagonia** (see below) for trips along Ruta 40. Recommended.

E pp Hostel 41 below, Pasaje Juramento 94, T436433, www.hostel41below.com. Central, quiet, relaxing atmosphere, good light rooms for 4 and **C** doubles, some with lake views. Recommended.

E pp **La Morada**, Cerro Otto Km 5 (free transfer), T441711, www.lamoradahostel.com. Ideal place to chill out from the slopes of Cerro Otto, amazing views, very good doubles with bath (**D**), dorms, kitchen, laundry, English spoken. Highly recommended.

E pp **Marco Polo Inn**, Salta 422, T400105, www.marcopoloinn.com.ar. Central location, breakfast included, B in doubles with bath, free internet, bar and restaurant. Recommended.

E pp **Patagonia Andina**, Morales 564, T421861, www.elpatagoniaandina.com.ar. Comfortable dorms, and twin rooms (**D**) with shared bath, small kitchen, TV area, sheets included, breakfast extra, internet, advice on trekking, double-check bookings.

E pp **Periko's**, Morales 555, T522326, www.perikos.com. Welcoming, quiet and nice atmosphere, same owners as Alaska Hostel, dorms and **C** doubles with no breakfast but towels and sheets included, kitchen, washing machine, *asado* every Fri. Discounts on tours, contact with **Overland Patagonia**. Recommended.

E pp **Ruca Hueney**, Elflein 396, T433986, www.argentinahostels.com. Lovely, calm, comfortable beds with duvets, fabulous double room (**C**) with extra bunk beds, bathroom and great view, spotless kitchen, very kind owners, Spanish school. Recommended. AHC Argentina Hostels Club.

F pp **Albergue El Gaucho**, Belgrano 209, T522464, www.hostelelgaucho.com.ar. In quiet part of town, some doubles with own bath (**D**), breakfast extra, English and German spoken. Recommended.

F pp **Casa Nelly**, Beschtedt 658, T422295. Helpful, hot showers and use of kitchen, also camping.

F pp **La Bolsa**, Palacios 405 y Elflein, T423529. Relaxed atmosphere, rustic rooms with duvets on the beds - one double with bath **D** – some rooms with views, deck to sit out on, free internet. Recommended.

Camping List of sites from tourist office. These are recommended among the many along Bustillo. They charge US$2.50-3.50 pp. **Petunia**, Km 13.5, T461969, petunia@bariloche.com.ar. A lovely shady site going down to lakeside with all facilities. Shops and restaurants on most sites; these are closed outside Jan-Mar. **Selva Negra**, Km 2.95, T441013, campingselvanegra@infovia.com.ar. Very good, discounts for long stay. **El Yeti**, Km 5.7, T442073, gerezjc@ bariloche.com.ar. All facilities, also *cabañas*.

Eating

Bariloche *p186, map p186*
There are many good delicatessens for picnics.

Chez Philippe, Primera Junta 1080, T427291. Delicious local delicacies, fine French-influenced cuisine.

El Boliche de Alberto, Villegas 347, T431433. Very good steak, huge portions, popular with young travellers after 2000.

Familia Weiss, Palacios y VA O'Connor. Excellent local specialities, live music. Wild boar particularly recommended.

Friends, Mitre 302. A varied menu, including pizzas in a lively atmosphere, open 24 hrs.

Jauja, Quaglia 366. Recommended for local dishes, good value (also take-away round the corner at Elflein128, T429986).

Kandahar, 20 de Febrero 698, T424702. Atmospheric, warm and intimate, with exquisite food, run by ski champion Marta Peirono de Barber, superb wines and fabulous pisco sour. Reserve in high season. Highly recommended.

La Marmite, Mitre 329. Cosy, good service, huge range of fondues, good wild boar, delicious cakes for tea too. Recommended.

Pilgrim, Palacios 167. Irish pub, serves a good range of beers, reasonable meals too.

Tarquino, 24 de Septiembre y Saavedra. Good food and service and a fine wine selection.

The Map Room, Urquiza 248. Maps from all over the world cover the walls of this relaxing café and Irish pub, restaurant in the basement has a very varied menu.

El Boliche de Alberto Pastas Elflein 49. Good for pasta.

La Jirafa, Palacios 288. Cheery family-run place for good food, good value.

Rock Chicken, Rolando 245. Small, busy, good value fast food (also take-away).

Simoca, Palacios 264. Recommended for delicious and cheap Tucumán specialities, huge empanadas.

Vegetariano, 20 de Febrero 730, T421820. Also fish, excellent food, beautifully served, warm atmosphere, also take-away. Highly recommended.

Cafés

Antigua Café, Quaglia 320. The perfect stopover for an excellent coffee at the bar.

Panadería Trevisan, Moreno y Quaglia. For excellent bread and cakes.

Jauja on same block as Panadería Trevisan. Legendary ice creams.

For an explanation of the sleeping and eating price codes used in this guide, see inside the front cover. Other relevant information is found in Essentials pages 68-69.

Around Bariloche p187

¶¶¶ **El Patacón**, Av Bustillo Km 7, T442898. Good *parrilla* and game, pricey.

¶¶ **Cervecería Blest**, Av Bustillo Km 11.6, T461026. Wonderful brewery with delicious beers, serving imaginative local and German dishes and steak and kidney pie. Recommended.

¶¶ **Il Gabbiano**, Av Bustillo Km 24.3, T448346. Delicious Italian lunches and dinners.

¶¶ **La Raclette**, Cerro Catedral ski resort. Highly recommended, family place, open in winter.

¶¶ **Tasca Brava**, Av Bustillo Km 7, T462599. On lakeside, intimate atmosphere, Patagonian and superb Spanish cooking.

Refugio Lynch has restaurant and *confitería* up the slopes of Cerro Catedral. In **Cerro Otto** there's a revolving *confitería*, craft shop, great views. Also **Club Andino confitería**, at Refugio Berghof, 20 mins' walk from main *confitería* on summit.

Tea rooms
Meli Hue, Av Bustillo Km 24.7 (Colonia Suiza), T448029. Also recommended; has bed and breakfast, in a lavender garden and selling sweet-smelling produce.

○ Shopping

Bariloche p186, map p186
The main commercial centre is on Mitre between the Centro Cívico and Beschtedt , plus a few more shops along San Martín.
Chocolate The local stuff is excellent: several shops on Mitre. Local wines, from the Alto Río Negro, are also good. **Abuela Goye**, Mitre 258 and Quaglia 221. First rate chocolatier. **Fenoglio**, Mitre 301 y Rolando. Very good chocolate and superb chocolate ice cream. **Mamushka**, opposite *El Turista*. Better chocolate here, excellent. **El Turista**, Mitre 231/39. Aptly-named, you can watch chocolates being made here.
Outdoor Arbol, Mitre 263. Sells good quality outdoor gear, lovely clothes and gifts. **Feria Artesanal Municipal**, Moreno y Villegas.
Supermarkets Todo, Mitre 281, good selection, cheap. **Uno**, Moreno 350. **La Anónima**, Quaglia 331 and a huge **Norte** at Moreno y Onelli.

▲▲ Activities and tours

Bariloche p186, map p186
Climbing
Note that at higher levels, winter snow storms can begin as early as Apr, making climbing dangerous.
Club Andino Bariloche, see Tourist information and Walks, above. The club can contact mountain guides and provide information.

Cycling
Bikes can be hired at many places in high season. **Dirty Bikes**, V O'Connor 681, T425616, www.dirtybikes.com.ar. Very helpful for repairs too, US$7 per day. See also *Aire Sur* under Youth hostels, US$7 per day. Mountain bike excursions, **Diego Rodríguez**, T156 10287, www.adventure-tours-south.com.

Fishing
Martín Pescador, Rolando 257, also in Cerro Catedral in winter, at Shopping Mall Las Terrazas, T422275, for fishing, camping and skiing equipment.

Horse riding
Tom Wesley, in country ranch by the lake at Km 15.5, office at Mitre 385, T448193, www.tomwesley.com. Tuition and full day's riding offered.

Paragliding
Ernesto Gutiérrez, T462234, 154 13037, parapente@bariloche.com.ar. At Cerro Otto, US$45 (transfer included).

Skiing
Cerro Catedral, T423776, www.catedralaltapatagonia.com, mid-Jun to end-Aug, busiest from mid-Jul to mid-Aug for school holidays, ski lifts: 0900-1700, ski lift pass: adults US$40 per day, ski school, US$30 per hr pp. It has 100 km of slopes of all grades, allowing a total drop of 1,010 m, and 52 km of cross country skiing routes. There are also snowboarding areas and a well-equipped base with hotels, restaurants and equipment hire, ski schools and nursery care for children. Bus are run by **3 de Mayo**, 'Catedral', leaves Moreno 480 every 30 minutes in winter approximately (via Av Pioneros or via Av Bustillo), T425648, US$1.10. Cable car for Catedral T423776.
Cerro Otto, cable car passengers can take free bus leaving from huts opposite National Park office or at Mitre y Villegas, hourly 1000-1730 in summer, returning hourly 1115-1915. Ticket for both costs US$8.50 pp, T441031. Ski gear can be rented by the day from **Cebron**, Mitre 171. See also **Martín Pescador**, above.

Trekking
See Walks, on page 187. **Andescross**, T467502, 156 33581, www.andescross.com. Expert guides, all included. Trekking to Chile across the Andes, via Pampa Linda, Lago Frías, Peulla.

Tours
Check what your tour includes; cable cars and chair lifts are usually charged as extras. Tours get very booked up in season. Most travel agencies

will pick you up from your hotel, and all charge roughly the same prices: Circuito Chico US$7-9, Isla Victoria and Bosque de Arrayanes US$15-17, Tronador, Ventisquero Negro and Pampa Linda , US$15 (US$26 plus National Park entry via Lago Mascardi by boat), Puerto Blest boat trip US$18, plus National Park entry, plus US$5 for Lago Frías, Cerro Catedral US$7, El Bolsón US$15.

Aguas Blancas, Morales 564, T432799, www.aguasblancas.com.ar. Rafting on the Río Manso, all grades, with expert guides, and all equipment provided (US$37-50), also bikes and horse riding, traditional lunches included.

Catedral Turismo, Palacios 263, T425444, cattur@bariloche.com.ar. Representatives for the Lakes Crossing to Chile, boat excursions to Puerto Blest and conventional tours.

Corredor Patagónico, John O'Connor 108 p 3, T525488 or 155 84873. Representatives for **Chaltén Travel**, www.chaltentravel.com. For 2-day trips along Ruta 40 to El Chaltén, US$105, and El Calafate, US$115 (Oct-Apr) with one stopover at the town of Perito Moreno, prices for transport only, leaves Bariloche on odd days.

Del Lago Turismo, Villegas 222, T430056, info@dellagoturismo.com.ar. Very helpful, staff speak fluent English, all conventional tours, plus horse riding, rafting. Also recommended, a combined trip by boat along Lago Mascardi to Tronador.

Extremo Sur, Morales 765, T427301, www.extremosur.com. Rafting and kayaking, all levels, full day all inclusive packages.

Hans Schulz, Casilla 1017, T155 08775. Speaks German and English, arranges tours and guides.

Infinito Sur, T156 39624, www.infinito-sur.com. For climbing, trekking, mountain skiing, rafting, expeditions on the *estepa* in Argentine and Chilean Patagonia, highly experienced from Peru, Bolivia and all points south.

Overland Patagonia, Morales 555, T437654, www.overlandpatagonia.com. For a 4-day trip along Ruta 40 to El Calafate, with English-speaking guides and stops en route at Río Mayo, Estancia Los Toldos (for Cueva de las Manos) and Estancia Menelik (for Parque Nacional Perito Moreno), US$270, meals not included. Also other trips across Patagonia.

Parque Cerro Leones, Villegas 246, p 1, T529909, www.cerroleones.com. Organize a 3-hr excursion to a 130 m-long natural cave, 16 km east of Bariloche, US$8 (transfer not included; book a day in advance).

Pucara, Mitre 22, p 1, T430989. Huge range of local trips and further afield to La Trochita and Esquel as well as the Estepa.

Tronador Turismo, Quaglia 283, T421104, www.tronadorturismo.com.ar. Conventional tours, trekking and rafting. Also to Refugio Neumeyer, and to Chilean border. Great adventurous wintersports options.

Turisur, Mitre 219, T426109, www.bariloche.com/turisur. Boat trips to Bosque de Arrayanes, Isla Victoria on a 1937 ship and to Tronador via Lago Mascardi. Always reserve 1 day ahead.

Guides

Martín Angaut, T156 19829, fishing_bariloche@hotmail.com. Professional fly-fishing guide, English spoken; contact at **Martín Pescador** (see above).

Daniel Feinstein, T442259, 155 05387, defeinstein@bariloche.com.ar. For trekking, biking, kayaking, natural history expeditions. Speaks English. Experienced in Argentina and Chile.

Angel Fernández, T524609, 156 09799, angel_e_fernandez@hotmail.com. For trekking, biking, kayaking, natural history expeditions. Extremely knowledgeable and charming, speaks English. Recommended.

Transport

Bariloche *p186, map p186*

Air Airport is 13 km east of town, with access from Ruta 40, 7 km east of centre; urban bus 72 from airport to town centre, Moreno y Palacios, hourly in the afternoon, US$0.50, taxi to airport US$6. If staying on the road to Llao Llao, west of town, expect to pay more for transport to your hotel; a taxi charges US$11 from town to Llao Llao. Car rental agencies, internet, exchange, ATM, café at the airport. Many flights a day to **Buenos Aires**, with AR/Austral. *AR* also flies to **Esquel, Trelew, El Calafate** and **Ushuaia**. LADE to **Buenos Aires, Esquel** and several other destinations in Patagonia. LAN Chile flies to **Puerto Montt** and **Santiago**.

Bus Bus and train stations both 3 km east of centre; urban buses 70 and 71, to/from centre, Moreno y Rolando; also bus 10, 20, 21, 72, US$0.35. Taxi US$2. Bus information at terminal T432860. Toilets, small *confitería, kiosko, locutorio* with internet, tourist information desk. Left luggage US$2 per day. Bus company offices in town (tickets can be purchased there or at terminal): **Vía Bariloche/El Valle/Don Otto/Transportadora Patagónica**, Mitre 321, T429012; **Andesmar**, Mitre 385, T430211; **Chevallier**, Moreno 105, T423090; **TAC**, Moreno 138, T426663; **Mar y Valle**, T432269. **3 de Mayo**, for local services and Viedma, Moreno 480, T426225. Prices rise in summer. To **Buenos Aires**, 5 companies daily, 19-22 hrs, US$50 *coche cama* (recommended with **Vía Bariloche**). To **Bahía Blanca**, El Valle and El Crucero del Norte, 14 hrs, US$30. To **Mendoza**, US$35, *TAC*, 19 hrs, via Piedra del Aguila, Neuquén, Cipolletti and San

Rafael. To **Esquel**, via **El Bolsón**, fares and schedules given below. To **Puerto Madryn**, 13-14 hrs, US$25-38, with **Mar y Valle** and **Don Otto**. To **Viedma** (along Ruta 23), **3 de Mayo**, 14 hrs, US$21. To **San Martín de los Andes** (via 7 Lagos and Villa La Angostura, 1¼ hrs, US$3, or via Rinconada), **Ko Ko, Albus, Via Bariloche/Turismo Algarrobal**, US$8.50, 3½-4 hrs. To **Villa Traful** (via Confluencia), **Via Bariloche/Turismo Algarrobal** and **Albus**, 1½-2 hrs, US$3.50-4. To Chilean destinations, see under Border with Chile, above. To **Río Gallegos** (for connections to El Calafate or Ushuaia), **Don Otto/ Transportadora Patagónica** runs a direct service daily (2 hrs stop at Comodoro Rivadavia), 28 hrs, US$38, *semi cama*; change same day to **Taqsa** bus to El Calafate or following day to **Tecni Austral** bus to Ushuaia. To **El Calafate**, take bus to Río Gallegos and change there; or contact **Overland Patagonia** or **Corredor Patagónico** (see addresses under Activities and tours) for a trip along Ruta 40.

Car hire Localiza, Frey y VA O'Connor, T435374 or 156 17474, offers often low promotional rates (papers for Chile, extra US$35). Hertz (Quaglia 352, and airport, T423457), helpful, English spoken. Open, Mitre 171 local 15, T/F426325, www.opencar.com.ar, is cheaper. Likewise Lagos, Mitre 83, T428880, www.lagosrentacar.com.ar. To enter Chile, a permit is necessary; it's generally included in the price. State when booking car, allow 24 hrs. For international car rental agencies, see Essentials, page 43.

Taxi Autojet, España 11, T422408, Remises Moreno, Moreno 389, T435555.

Train To Viedma, Fri in Jan-Feb, Tren Patagónico, leaving in the afternoon, 17-hrs journey mostly at night, dusty, nice views only in the first few hours, US$10-40 (sleeper section), also carries cars. More services to **Jacobacci**, 4½ hrs, US$3.50-6.50. In Carmen de Patagones (across the river from Viedma), train to Buenos Aires, but check first. Booking office at station (T423172) closed Mon, Fri afternoon and Sun morning.

❻ Directory

Bariloche *p186, map p186*
Airline offices Aerolíneas Argentinas/ Austral, Mitre 185, T422425. LADE, Mitre 531, p 1, T423562. LAN, Moreno 234, p 1, T431043 or 0800-2222424. **Banks** Banks and exchange shops buy and sell virtually all European and South American currencies, besides US dollars. Best rates from Sudamérica, Mitre 63, T434555; all TCs (3% commission). ATMs on Mitre at 158, 427, Moreno y Quaglia, San Martin 336. **Consulates** Chile, JM de Rosas 180, T527468, helpful. **Internet** Several cybercafés and at *locutorios* in the centre, all with similar rates. **Medical facilities** Emergencies: Dial 107. Clinic: Hospital Zonal, Moreno 601, T426117. **Post offices** Moreno 175, closed Sat afternoon and Sun. **Telephones** Many *locutorios* in the centre. **Useful addresses** Customs: 24 de Septiembre 12, T425216. Immigration office: Libertad 175. **Policía Federal** (for tourist orientation), Tiscornia y Morales, open 24 hrs, T423789/423430, English spoken.

South of Bariloche

More wild and beautiful scenery can be explored along the Andes, with a few tourist centres like El Bolsón and Esquel giving access to lakes and national parks. There is trekking, rafting, skiing and fishing on offer, a train ride on the famous La Trochita and the magnificent Los Alerces national park to explore.

Bariloche to El Bolsón

The paved road from Bariloche to El Bolsón, 126 km south, passes the beautiful lakes Gutiérrez, Mascardi and Guillelmo. From the southern end of Lago Mascardi, 35 km south of Bariloche, a *ripio* road (note one-way system) runs west towards Cerro Tronador and **Pampa Linda**, the starting point for excellent trekking including the two-day walk over Paso de los Nubes to Laguna Frías (see Walks page 187 and Sleeping page 196). **Río Villegas**, about 70 km south of Bariloche, is very beautiful, and there's world class rafting to be done on the **Río Manso**.

El Bolsón and around → *Population: 40,000. Phone code: 02944. Colour map 8, grid C1.*

El Bolsón is an attractive town in a broad fertile valley, surrounded by the mountains of the cordillera and dominated by the dramatic peak of Cerro Piltriquitrón 2,284 m (hence its name: the big bag). It's a magical setting which attracted thousands of hippies to create an ideological community here in the 1970's; they now produce the handicrafts, beers, fruit and jams, sold at

The Old Patagonian Express

Esquel is the terminus of a 402-km branch-line from Ingeniero Jacobacci, a junction on the old Buenos Aires-Bariloche mainline, 194 km east of Bariloche. This narrow-gauge line (0.75 m wide) took 23 years to build, being finally opened in 1945. It was made famous outside Argentina by Paul Theroux who described it in his book *The Old Patagonian Express*. The 1922 Henschel and Baldwin steam locomotives (from Germany and USA respectively) are powered by fuel oil and use 100 litres of water every km. Water has to be taken on at least every 40 km along the route. Most of the coaches are Belgian and also date from 1922. If you want to see the engines, go to El Maitén where the workshops are.

Until the Argentine government handed responsibility for railways over to the provincial governments in 1994, regular services ran the length of the line. Since then, services have been maintained between Esquel and El Maitén by the provincial government of Chubut.

the market on Tuesday, Thursday, Saturday, 1000-1700. There are many mountain walks and waterfalls nearby, and good fishing at Lagos Puelo (see below) and Epuyén (shops and petrol available) – both within easy access. **Tourist office**① *Av San Martín y Roca. 0900-2100 all year, until 2300 in high summer. Extremely helpful with maps, treks to refugios and accommodation, English spoken. T492604, www.bolsonturistico.com.ar.*

There are waterfalls at **Cascada Escondida**, 10 km northwest of town (2-hour dusty walk, ask for short-cut through woods), a good place for a picnic. There are fine views from **Cerro Piltriquitrón** – drive or taxi 10 km, then walk one hour through the sculptures of the **Bosque Tallado** (or 6-7 hour round trip walk), food and shelter at *refugio* (1,400 m; US$3.50). Views of the valley from **Cabeza del Indio**, a good 6 km drive or bike ride from the centre, and a pleasant one hour walk up to **Cerro Amigo**: follow Gral Roca east until it becomes Islas Malvinas and continue up the hill. There is wonderful trekking in the mountains and valleys west of town on an excellent network of trails with well equipped and staffed *refugios* in superb locations; at least 8 shelters were operating in 2005-2006, most open October-March. Most shelters offer simple accommodation (US$5 pp, sleeping bag required), some meals (US$4), basic supplies including home-baked bread and home-brewed beer, camping (US$1.50 pp), and hot showers (US$1). They have radio communication with each other and with town. Additional information and compulsory registration at the Club Andino or tourist office in El Bolsón. In high season there are minibuses to the trailheads, at other times hitch or take a remise taxi for US$5.

Cholila and around → *Phone code: 02945. Population: 1,300.*

A peaceful sprawling village, 76 km south of El Bolsón, with superb views at Lago Cholila (17 km west), crowned by the Matterhorn-like mountains of Cerros Dos and Tres Picos (campsite and expensive *Hostería El Pedregoso*). Excellent fishing, canoeing and kayaking on rivers nearby. Along Valle de Cholila (Ruta 71) are several lovely old brick and wooden houses and barns. Among them are the atmospheric **wooden cabins**, where Butch Cassidy, the Sundance Kid and Etta Place lived between 1901 and 1907. They are 13 km north, east of the road, opposite a police station. One km west of the road is the *Casa de Piedra* teahouse serving *té galés* and offering basic accommodation. **Villa Lago Rivadavia**, 15 km south of Cholila lies next to the northern gates of Parque Nacional Los Alerces, with an increasing number of *cabañas*. Tourist information hut open in summer only, opposite petrol station at El Rincón; also basic information at Municipalidad in Cholila, T498040.

At **Lago Puelo** in the **Parque Nacional Lago Puelo** there are gentle walks on marked paths, boat trips across the lake on a 1931 boat, and canoes for rent. Wardens at the park entrance (free) can advise on these and a 3-day trek through magnificent scenery to Chilean border. Gorgeous homemade *alfajores* in fairy tale setting at *El Bolsonero* on the old road to Lago Puelo. Regular buses, US$0.85, from Avenida San Martín y Dorrego in El Bolsón go to the lake via Villa Lago Puelo. Boats: *Juana de Arco* ① *T493415, www.interpatagonia.com/juanadearco. Information in summer from hut in Avenida San Martín y Pellegrini*, 30-minute trip, US$5; to the Chilean border, 3 hours, US$15.

Esquel → *Phone code: 02945. Colour map 9, grid A1. Population: 30,000.*

Esquel, 293 km south of Bariloche, was originally an offshoot of the Welsh colony at Chubut, 650 km to the east, and still has a pioneer feel. A breezy open town in a fertile valley, with a backdrop of mountains, Esquel is the base for visiting the Parque Nacional Los Alerces and for skiing at **La Hoya** in winter (15 km, good 6½-hour trek in summer). Good walks from the town to Laguna La Zeta, 5 km, and to Cerro La Cruz, two hours (one way). It's also the departure point for the famous narrow gauge railway, **La Trochita** (see box, page 194). **Tourist office** ① *Av Alvear y Sarmiento, T451927, www.esquel.gov.ar. Daily 0800-2100, summer 0700-2300.*

Trevelin → *Colour map 9, grid A1. Population: 5,000.*

An offshoot of the Welsh Chubut colony (see box in Patagonia section), where Welsh is still spoken, the pretty village of Trevelin, 24 km southwest of Esquel, has a Welsh chapel (built 1910, closed) and tea rooms. The **Museo Regional** *US$0.70, 1100-1800*, in the old mill (1918) includes artefacts from the Welsh colony. The **Hogar de Mi Abuelo** *US$1.70*, is a private park and museum (*El Malacara*, named after Evans' horse), dedicated to John Evans, one of the first settlers, whose granddaughter acts as a guide. **Nant-y-fall Falls** ① *17 km southwest on the road to the border, US$1 pp including guide to 3 falls (1½-hr walk)*, are a series of impressive cascades in lovely forest. Helpful tourist office in the central plaza, *T480120, www.trevelin.org*. Has maps, accommodation booking service and English is spoken.

Parque Nacional Los Alerces → *Colour map 9, grid A1.*

① *33 km west of Esquel, US$4, December-Easter*. One of the most appealing and untouched expanses of the Andes region, this national park has several lakes including **Lago Futalaufquen**, with some of the best fishing in the area, **Lago Menéndez** which can be crossed by boat to visit rare and impressive *alerce* trees over 2000 years old, and the green waters of **Lago Verde**. Relatively undeveloped, access is possible only to the east side of the park, via a *ripio* road (which is an alternative way from Esquel to El Bolsón) with many camping spots and *hosterías*. Helpful *guardaparques* give out maps and advice on walks at the visitor centre (T471020 ext 23) in Villa Futalaufquen (southern end of Lago Futalaufquen); also a service station, two food shops, and a restaurant *El Abuelo Monje*. Fishing licences from food shops, the *kiosko* or *Hosterías Cume Hué* and *Futalaufquen*, or petrol stations in Esquel.

Trekking and tours The west half of the park is inaccessible, but there are splendid walks along footpaths on the southern shore of Lago Futalaufquen, with several waterfalls, and near Lago Verde further north. Treks at Los Alerces range from an hour to two or three days. All long treks require previous registration with the *guardaparques*; some paths are closed in autumn and winter. For longer options or when trails here are closed, try the El Bolsón area, Parque Nacional Nahuel Huapi or Parque Nacional Lanín. At Lago Futalaufquen's northern end, walk across the bridge over Río Arrayanes to Lago Verde. A longer more difficult trek is to **Cerro El Dedal**, either returning the way you came from Villa Futalaufquen or making an 8 to 10 hour loop through Puerto Limonao. Start before 1000 and carry plenty of water. Also a two-day hike through *coihue* forest to the tip of beautiful, secluded **Lago Krügger**, where you can take a boat back to Puerto Limonao. On Lago Futalaufquen is a free campsite at Playa Blanca and on Krügger is an expensive *refugio* for anglers, open January/February, and a campsite, US$5 pp. **Cerros Alto El Petiso** and **La Torta** can be climbed and there is a trekkers' shelter at the base of **Cerro Cocinero**. **Boat trips**: to El Alerzal, from Puerto Limonao, across Lago Futalaufquen along the pea-green Río Arrayanes, lined with the extraordinary cinnamon-barked trees, to Puerto Mermoud on Lago Verde. A short walk leads to Puerto Chucao, on Lago Menéndez, where another boat makes the unforgettable trip to see the majestic 2600-year old alerce trees, walking to silent Lago Cisne, past the white waters of Río Cisne. A cheaper alternative is to get to Puerto Chucao on your own and take the boat there (US$20). Boats run frequently in high season. Book through **Patagonia Verde** ① *Esquel*, or **Safari Lacustre** ① *www.brazosur.com*.

Border with Chile: Paso Futaleufú → *Colour map 9, grid A1.*

There is a campsite (**Camping Puerto Ciprés**) on the Argentine side of river. Cross the border river by the bridge after passing Argentine customs; Chilean customs is 1 km on the other side of river (one hour for all formalities). The Chilean town of Futaleufú is 10 km from the border. See p 200 for buses to the border.

South of Esquel, Ruta 40 is paved through the towns of **Tecka** and **Gobernador Costa** in Chubut province. At 38 km south of Gobernador Costa, gravelled Ruta 40 forks southwest through the town of Alto Río Senguer, while provincial Ruta 20 heads almost directly south for 141 km, before turning east towards Sarmiento and Comodoro Rivadavia. At La Puerta del Diablo, in the valley of the lower Río Senguer, Ruta 20 intersects provincial Ruta 22, which joins with Ruta 40 at the town of Río Mayo (see page 214). This latter route is completely paved and preferable to Ruta 40 for long-distance motorists; good informal campsites on the west side of the bridge across the Río Senguer.

● Sleeping

Bariloche to El Bolsón *p193*
LL Peuma Hue, access from Ruta 40 (ex-Ruta 258 Km 25, T02944-15501030, www.peuma-hue.com. Best comfort in a homely environment, on the southern shores of Lago Gutiérrez, below Cerro Catedral Sur. Charming owner Evelyn Hoter and dedicated staff make it all work perfectly, tasty home-made food, horse riding, candlelit concerts. All inclusive, varied accommodation. Highly recommended.
L Hotel Tronador, T441062, hoteltronador@bariloche.com.ar. 37 km from Bariloche, on the narrow road from Villa Mascardi to Pampa Linda (there are restricted times for going in each direction: check with tourist office), open Nov-Apr, full board, lakeside paradise, lovely rooms, beautiful gardens, charming owner, also riding, fishing and lake excursions. Also camping *La Querencia*.
L-AL El Retorno, Villa Los Coihues, on the shore of Lago Gutiérrez, T467333, www.hosteriael retorno.com. Stunning lakeside position, comfortable hunting lodge style, with a beach, tennis, very comfortable rooms (Bus 50, follow signs from the road to El Bolsón).
AL-A Hostería Pampa Linda, T490517 (in Bariloche, Villegas 246, p 1, T529909), www.tronador.com. A wonderfully comfortable, peaceful base for climbing Tronador and many other treks (plus horse riding, trekking and climbing courses), simple rooms, all with stunning views, restaurant, full board optional, packed lunch. Highly recommended. Nearby is **Refugio Pampa Linda F** pp) and **Camping Río Manso**.
AL-A Mascardi, T490518, www.mascardi.com. Luxurious hotel with a delightful setting along Lago Mascardi.
D Hostería Río Villegas, Río Manso, pleasant, restaurant, outside gates of the park, by the river.
F pp Refugio Neumeyer, 18 km south of Bariloche, office at 20 de Junio 728, T428995, www.eco-family.com. Comfortable hostel, great family centre for trekking, climbing, mountain biking in summer; cross country skiing in winter. Highly recommended.
Camping Camping Las Carpitas, 33 km from Bariloche, T490527, www.lascarpitas.com.ar. Summer only, great location, all facilities, also *cabañas*. Camping Pampa Linda, T424531.

Idyllic spacious lakeside site with trees. Camping Los Rápidos, after crossing the Río Manso to Pampa Linda, T461861, tascha@bariloche.com.ar. All facilities, attractive shaded site going down to lake, *confitería*, open all year.

El Bolsón *p193*
Difficult to find accommodation in the high season: book ahead.
B Amancay, Av San Martín 3207, T492222, www.hotelamancaybolson.com.ar. Good, comfortable and light rooms.
B Cordillera, San Martín 3210, T492235, cordillerahotel@elbolson.com. With breakfast, modern, comfortable, cheaper without TV.
B La Posada de Hamelin, Int Granollers 2179, T492030, gcapece@elbolson.com. Charming rooms, welcoming atmosphere, huge breakfasts, German spoken. Highly recommended.
B Refugio del Lago, at Lago Epuyén, T02945-499025, sophie@elbolson.com. Relaxed place with breakfast, also good meals, trekking, riding, canoes for hiring, also camping and dorms (US$3.50 pp). Recommended. Owners are mountain guides. Book in advance.
C Hostería Steiner, San Martín 670, T492224. Another peaceful place surrounded by a lovely park, wood fire, restaurant, breakfast US$1.70, German spoken.
D pp La Casona de Odile, Barrio Luján, T492753, www.interpatagonia.com/odile. Idyllic lavender farm by stream, delicious cooking, reserve ahead, English, French and German spoken, closed May-Sep. Recommended.
D Luz de Luna, Dorrego 150, T491908. Breakfast US$1, nice garden, good value, clean hotel with a variety of rooms.
D Valle Nuevo, 25 de Mayo y Belgrano, T492087, albahube@hotmail.com. Small rooms, quiet place, cooking facilities, breakfast not included, but good value. Also runs nice **Albergue Sol del Valle** next door (**E** double,**F** pp in dorm), cooking facilities. Also rents a few good value apartments with cooking facilities.
E pp El Pueblito, 4 km north in Barrio Luján, 1 km off Ruta 258 (now Ruta 40; take northbound bus along Av San Martín, US$0.50), T493560, elpueblito@elbolson.com. Cosy wooden

building in open country, cooking and laundry facilities, shop, open fire. HI discounts.
E Piltri, Saavedra 2729, T455305, lucas_breide 17@hotmail.com. Basic little place, welcoming owner, shared bath, breakfast US$1.70; also a small apartment with kitchen.
E pp Refugio Patagónico, Islas Malvinas y Pastorino, T156 35463, www.refugio patagonico.com.ar. High quality, small dorms with bath, breakfast US$1.40, in a spacious house in open fields, great views of Piltriquitrón, also camping. Recommended.
Camping Arco Iris, T155 58330. Blissful wooded setting near Río Azul, helpful owners. La Chacra, Av Belgrano 1128, T492111, campinglachacra@yahoo.com.ar, 15 mins walk from town, well shaded, good facilities, lively atmosphere in season. Quem Quem, on river bank Río Quemquemtreu, T493550. Lovely site, hot showers, good walks, free pickup from town. There are many *cabañas* in picturesque settings with lovely views in the Villa Turismo or try Las Bandurrias, Ruta 40 (ex-258), 1.5 km north of town, T492819, US$35 for a cabin for 4.

Cholila and around *p194*
AL La Rinconada, Villa Lago Rivadavia, T498091. Offers tours, horse riding, kayaking, American-owned.
B El Trébol, T/F498055, eltrebol@ar.inter.net. With breakfast, comfortable rooms with stoves, meals and half board also available, family-run, large garden, popular with fishing expeditions, reservations advised, bus stops in Cholila 4 km away.
D Cumelen Huenti, in Cholila village, T496031. With bath, heating, restaurant with good home cooking, helpful.
D pp La Pasarela, 2 km from town, T499061, www.lpuelo.com.ar. Dorms, camping, shops, fuel. Cabañas Cerro La Momia, Villa Lago Rivadavia, T011-4522 0617, www.cabanas cerrolamomia.com.ar. Very good *cabañas* for up to 6, picturesque setting among fruit orchards and wooded slopes. Restaurant, excursions arranged.
Camping F Autocamping Carlos Pellegrini, next to El Trébol, T498030. Free municipal camping in El Morro park, next to Cholila.
Camping El Abuelo, 13 km south, at Villa Lago Rivadavia, T491013.

Esquel *p195*
Hotels are often full in Jan-Feb. Ask at tourist office for lodgings in private houses.
L Cumbres Blancas, Av Ameghino 1683, T/F455100, www.cumbresblancas.com.ar. Attractive modern building, a little out of centre, very comfortable, spacious rooms, sauna, gym, airy restaurant.

AL Canela, Los Notros y Los Radales, Villa Ayelén, on road to Trevelin, T/F453890, www.canelaesquel.com. Bed and breakfast in a lovely, quiet residential area, English spoken, owner knowledgeable about Patagonia.
A La Chacra, Km 5 on Ruta 259 towards Trevelin, T452802, rinilachacra@ciudad.com.ar. Relaxing, spacious rooms, huge breakfast, Welsh and English spoken.
A Tehuelche, 9 de Julio 831, T452420, tehuelche@commlab.com.ar. Large, central, a bit overpriced, but comfortable, good restaurant.
B Angelina, Av Alvear 758, T452763. Good value, welcoming, big breakfast, English and Italian spoken.
B La Tour D'Argent, San Martín 1063, T454612, www.cpatagonia.com/esq/latour. With breakfast, bright, comfortable, overpriced, restaurant.
C Hostería Los Tulipanes, Av Fontana 365, T452748. Ample breakfast, comfortable, homely, smokers welcome. Recommended.
C La Posada, Chacabuco 905, T454095, laposada@art.inter.net. Tasteful B&B in quiet part of town, lovely lounge, very comfortable, breakfast included, excellent value.
D El Arrayán, Antártida Argentina 767, T451051. Comfortable carpeted rooms, with heating, reliable hot water, good value.
D Las Mutisias, Av Alvear 1021, T452083, lasmutisias@ciudad.com.ar. Spotless place run by Emma Cleri, helpful and very hospitable, no breakfast.
D Res El Cisne, Chacabuco 778, T452256. Basic small rooms, hot water, quiet, well kept, good value, breakfast extra.
E Lago Verde, Volta 1081, T452251, patagoniaverde@ciudad.com.ar. Breakfast extra, modern, comfortable, run by tour guides, same owners as Patagonia Verde, rooms for 2 and 3 with bath, near bus terminal, 2 blocks from La Trochita. Recommended.
F pp Casa del Pueblo, San Martín 661, T450581, www.epaadventure.com.ar. Smallish rooms but good atmosphere (D double with bath), kitchen, laundry. HI discounts.
F pp Hospedaje Rowlands, behind Rivadavia 330, T452578. Warm family welcome, Welsh spoken, breakfast extra, basic rooms with shared bath and a double with bath (E), good value.
Camping El Hogar del Mochilero, Roca 1028 (statue of backpacker at entrance), T452166. Summer only, laundry facilities, 24-hr hot water, friendly owner, free firewood for cooking. Also a basic large dorm (US$3 pp). Millalen, Av Ameghino 2063 (5 blocks from bus terminal), T456164, good services and a dorm. La Rural, 1 km on road to Trevelin, T155 07306. Well organized and shady site with facilities.

Trevelin *p195*
B Familia Pezzi, Sarmiento 353, T480146, hpezzi@intramed.com.ar. Charming family house with a beautiful garden, open Jan-Mar, English spoken. Recommended.

E-F pp Casa Verde Hostal, Los Alerces s/n, T480091, www.casaverdehostel.com.ar. 'The best hostel in Argentina', by many reckonings. Charming owners Bibiana and Charly, spacious log cabin with panoramic views of wooded mountains, comfortable dorms and **C-D** doubles, both with own bath, kitchen facilities, laundry, HI member, breakfast extra. Also a lovely rustic cabin for up to 7. English and Welsh spoken, excursions into Los Alerces, bikes for hire US$10 per day. Recommended.

Camping There are a couple of campsites in town, charging US$2-3 pp and many *cabañas*; ask for full list at Tourist office.

Parque Nacional Los Alerces *p195*
East side of Lago Futalaufquen
AL Bahía Rosales, T471044. Comfortable *cabaña* for 6 with kitchenette and bath, **B-C** in small basic cabin without bath, **F** pp for camping in open ground, restaurant, all recommended.

AL Cabañas Tejas Negras, next to Pucón Pai, T471046. Comfortable *cabañas* for 4.

AL Hostería Quimé Quipan, T471021. Comfortable rooms with lake views, dinner included. Recommended.

A pp Cume Hué, T450503, www.cumehue. com.ar. Overpriced lodge with basic rooms, full board, but great for fishing.

C Pucón Pai, T471010. Slightly spartan rooms, but good restaurant, recommended for fishing; campsite with hot showers, US$2 pp.

West side of Lago Futalaufquen
LL Hostería Futalaufquen just north of Puerto Limonao, T471008, www.brazosur.com. Idyllic lakeside setting and splendid architecture, half board, but lacking a warm welcome. Very expensive for tea.

Camping Los Maitenes, Villa Futalaufquen, excellent, US$1.50 pp. Several campsites at Lagos Rivadavia, Verde and Río Arrayanes, from free to US$3 depending on facilities.

Gobernador Costa *p196*
E Hotels Jair, good value, and *Vega*.
Camping Municipal site, all services, US$1.

🍴 Eating

El Bolsón *p193*
⫘ Arcimbaldo, Av San Martin 2790, Good value *tenedor libre*, smoked fish and draft beer, open for breakfast.

⫘ Amancay, San Martín 3217. Good *parrilla* and homemade pastas.

⫘ Cerro Lindo, Av San Martín 2524. Elegant, delicious pastas, vegetarian dishes and regional specialities.

⫘ Jauja, Av San Martín 2867. Great meeting place, delicious fish and pasta, outstanding ice cream, English spoken. Recommended.

⫙ Il Rizzo, Av San Martin y Juez Fernández, Good value pizzas, empanadas, pastas and draught beer in a lively relaxed café.

⫙ La Calabaza, Av San Martín y Hube. Good inexpensive food including vegetarian dishes, relaxed atmosphere.

⫙ Morena, Av San Martín y Hube. Small and unpretentious café/restaurant; for pizzas, pastas and some very good vegetarian meals.

⫙ Parrilla Las Brasas, Sarmiento y Belgrano. Good parrilla, also trout and pastas.

Cafés
La Saltentia, Av Belgrano 515. For a great selection of *empanadas*.

La Tosca, Perito Moreno y Roca (behind Tourist office). A very agreeable café, good sandwiches.

Esquel *p195*
⫘ Dionisio, Av Fontana 656. Good value crêpes with the most varied fillings, *picadas* with beer or wine and meat dishes in a nice house. Also a café open in the late afternoon.

⫘ Don Chiquino, behind Av Ameghino 1649. Delicious pastas in a fun atmosphere with plenty of games brought to the tables by magician owner Tito. Recommended.

⫘ Tío Vicente, Av Ameghino y Av Fontana. Very good food; parrilla and pastas with varied sauces.

⫘ Vascongada, 9 de Julio y Mitre. Traditional style, trout and other local specialities.

⫙ Casa Grande, Roca 441. Popular for its varied menu (such as lamb and trout), reasonable prices.

⫙ Los Nietos, 9 de Julio 910, T454500. Good cheap pizzas to take away.

⫙ Pizzería Don Pipo, Av Fontana 649. Good pizzas and *empanadas*.

⫙ Tío Canuto, Av Alvear 949. Restaurant/bar with live music, tango shows and lessons, open Tue-Sun 1900-0300.

Cafés
María Castaña, Rivadavia y 25 de Mayo. Popular, good coffee.

Melys, Miguens 346, off Ameghino 2000. Plentiful Welsh teas and a good breakfast.

Trevelin *p195*
⫘ Patagonia Celta, 25 de Mayo s/n. Delicious local specialities, trout and vegetarian dishes, best in town. Recommended.

♦ **Parrilla Oregon**, Av San Martín y Laprida. Large meals, set menus based on parrilla and pastas.
♦ **Parrilla del Club**, Av San Martín y Libertad. Simple, cheap, good meals.
♦ **Nain Maggie**, Perito Moreno 179. Tea room, offering *té galés* and *torta negra*, expensive.

O Shopping

Esquel *p195*
Casa de Esquel (Robert Müller), 25 de Mayo 415. Wide range of new and secondhand books on Patagonia, also local crafts.
La Anónima, 9 de Julio y Belgrano. Big supermarket.
Los Vascos, 25 de Mayo y 9 de Julio. Traditional store founded in 1926, worth seeing.

▲ Activities and tours

El Bolsón *p193*
Grado 42, Av. Belgrano 406, T493124, www.grado42.com. Tours to El Maitén to take La Trochita, 7 hrs, US$20; also short excursions in the surroundings (US$9) and day trips to Parque Nacional Los Alerces (US$29). Agency for bus tickets Lago Pulelo-Esquel via Cholila and Los Alerces, daily in summer, 6 hrs, US$6 plus US$1 transfer El Bolsón-Lago Puelo.
Maputur, Perito Moreno 2331, T491139, www.maputur.com.ar. Horse rides, paragliding and mountain bikes for hire (US$7 per day).
Patagonia Adventures, Hube 418, T493280, www.argentinachileflyfishing.com. Rafting, paragliding, fishing, boat trip on Lago Puelo to remote forest lodge, horse riding to Chile.

Esquel *p195*
Fishing
Tourist office has a list of guides.

Skiing
One of Argentina's cheapest, with laid back family atmosphere, **La Hoya**, 15 km north, has 22 km of pistes, 8 ski-lifts. For skiing information ask at **Club Andino Esquel**, Pellegrini 787, T453248; travel agencies run minibuses to La Hoya from Esquel; US$5 return, ski pass US$15. Equipment hire US$4-8 a day.

Tours
Esquel Expediciones, T451763, moranjack@ciudad.com.ar. Bespoke adventure trips, trekking and canoeing in the national park, to the gold mine, up Rio Futaleufú to Chile, walking in Valdivian rainforest, with experienced mountain guide Jack Moran.
Gales al Sur, at bus terminal and at the airport,

T455757. Adventure tours with mountain bikes, horses, canoes or a good pair of boots. Also bikes for rent (US$10 per day) and transfer to/from airport for all flights.
Patagonia Verde, 9 de Julio 926, T454396, www.patagonia-verde.com.ar. Boat trips to El Alerzal on Lago Menéndez, rafting on Río Corcovado, tickets for 'La Trochita' and for Ruta 40 to El Calafate. Also short local excursions and ski passes. English spoken.

● Transport

El Bolsón *p193*
Bus No terminal. Vía Bariloche/Don Otto/Transportadora Patagónica, Roca y Sarmiento (one block from Tourist office), T455554, and Av Belgrano y Perito Moreno (both bus stops and ticket sales) to **Bariloche**, 2 hrs, US$5; to **Esquel**, 2½ hrs, US$5; to **Río Gallegos**, 26 hrs, US$34. **Mar y Valle**, Perito Moreno 2331, T491440, to **Bariloche, Esquel** and **Puerto Madryn** (US$20-34). **Andesmar/Chevallier**, Av Belgrano y Perito Moreno, T492178, to **Bariloche, Esquel** and **Mendoza**; also tickets to **El Chaltén** and **El Calafate** (US$112) with **Corredor Patagónico/ Chaltén Travel**, along Ruta 40. To **Lago Puelo, El Hoyo** and other nearby towns, **La Golondrina** and **Nehuén**, stops along Av San Martín. **La Golondrina** runs a service in high summer from Lago Pulelo to Lago Verde in Los Alerces.

Esquel *p195*
Air Airport, 20 km east of Esquel, by paved road, US$7 by taxi, US$2.50 by **Gales al Sur** minibus (see Activities and tours, above). To **Buenos Aires** and **Trelew** with AR (Av Fontana 408, T453614). LADE (Av Alvear 1085, T452124) to **Bariloche, Comodoro Rivadavia, El Bolsón, El Calafate, El Maitén, Mar del Plata, Puerto Madryn** and several other destinations in Patagonia.
Bus Smart terminal at Av Alvear 1871, T451584, US$1 by taxi from centre, it has toilets, *kiosko*, *locutorio* with internet, café, tourist information desk, left luggage (US$0.70 per day). To Buenos Aires change in Bariloche, with **Andesmar**, T450143, or **Via Bariloche**, T453528, (US$55 *coche cama*). To **Bariloche**, (via El Bolsón, 2½ hrs, US$5), 4-5hrs, US$ 8-12, **Don Otto** (T453012), **Andesmar, Mar y Valle** (T453712), **Vía Bariloche**. To **Puerto Madryn**, Don Otto and Mar y Valle, 9 hrs, US$17-27. Mar y Valle to **Trelew** US$20, 8 hrs nightly or 0800 Tue and Sat. To **Río Gallegos** (for connections to El Calafate or Ushuaia), Don Otto/Transportadora Patagónica runs a direct service daily (2 hrs stop at Comodoro Rivadavia), 22 hrs, US$32, *semi cama*. To **Trevelin**, Vía Trevelin (T455222) and Jacobsen (T453528), Mon-Fri, hourly 0600-2300, every 2 hrs weekends, 30 mins, US$0.85. To **Coyhaique** (Chile), via Paso

Coyhaique or via Paso Huemules, ETAP, T454756, 14 hrs, US$29.

Train La Trochita – the Old Patagonian Express: tourist services: Esquel to **Nahuel Pan** (19 km), 4 weekly in summer, 3 to 1 weekly in low season, 2½-3 hrs, US$8.50; El Maitén to **Desvío Thomae**, 3 weekly in summer, 1 weekly in low season, 3 hrs, US$8.50. El Maitén to **Leleque**, only in summer, 6½ hrs, US$14. Special service Esquel-El Maitén return for the *Fiesta del Tren a Vapor*, 7½ hrs one way, US$27 return, book in advance. Information in El Maitén, T02945-495190, in Esquel T451403. Tickets from tour operators, or from Esquel station office, Urquiza y Roggero.

Parque Nacional Los Alerces p195
Bus From Esquel (Transportes Esquel, T453529) runs daily in Jan-Feb and 2-3 weekly off season at 0800 from Esquel to Lago Pulelo, 6 hrs, US$6, along the east side of Lago Futalaufquen, passing **Villa Futalaufquen** 0915, **Lago Verde** 1030, **Lago Rivadavia** 1045 and Cholila (sit on left). On the return it passes Lago Rivadavia at 1830, Lago Verde 1845 and Villa Futalaufquen 1945, back in Esquel 2100. Extra frequencies in high summer from Esquel up to Lago Verde and from Lago Pulelo up to Lago Verde (**Bus La Golondrina**), US$3.50 and throughout the year from Esquel up to Villa Futalaufquen.

Border with Chile: Paso Futaleufú p195
Buses from Esquel to **Paso Futaleufú** (La Balsa), Mon and Fri (also Wed in summer) 0800, 1730, Jacobsen, T453528, 1¼ hr, US$3. Connecting with bus to Futaleufú (US$3) and from there to Chaitén, **Trans Cordillera**, T258633 and Ebenezer, between them 4 times a week, and daily Jan-Feb. Very little traffic for hitching. From Esquel to **Carrenleufú** at the Palena border crossing (via Corcovado), 3½ hrs, US$5, Jacobsen, Sun, Mon 1600 and Wed, Fri 1000 , return Mon, Tue 0600, Wed, Fri 1600.

⊙ Directory

Esquel p195
Banks Banco de la Nación, Av Alvear y Roca, open 0800-1300; changes US$ and euros. ATM accepts all cards. ATMs also at Banco del Chubut, Av Alvear 1147, Banco Patagonia, 25 de Mayo 739, Bansud, 25 de Mayo 752. Exchange also at Finan City, Av Fontana 673. **Internet** Cyber Club, Av Alvear 961. Cyberplanet, San Martín 976. **Post offices** Av Alvear 1192. **Telephones** Many *locutorios* in centre, including **Cordillera**, 25 de Mayo 526. El Alerce, 9 de Julio y 25 de Mayo.

Patagonia

Patagonia is the vast, windy, mostly treeless plateau covering all of southern Argentina south of the Río Colorado. The Atlantic coast is rich in marine life; penguins, whales and seals can all be seen around Puerto Madryn. The far south offers spectacular scenery in the Parque Nacional Los Glaciares, with the mighty Moreno and Upsala glaciers, as well as challenging trekking around Mount Fitz Roy. The contrasts are extreme: thousands of handprints can be found in the Cueva de las Manos, but in most of Patagonia there's less than one person to each sq km; far from the densely wooded Andes, there are petrified forests in the deserts; and the legacy of brave early pioneers is the over-abundance of tea and cakes served up by Argentina's Welsh community in the Chubut valley.

Patagonia's appeal lies in its emptiness. Vegetation is sparse, since a relentless dry wind blows continually from the west, raising a haze of dust in summer, which can turn to mud in winter. Rainfall is high only in the foothills of the Andes, where dense virgin beech forests run from Neuquén to Tierra del Fuego. During a brief period in spring, after the snow melt, there is grass on the plateau, but in the desert-like expanses of eastern Patagonia, water can be pumped only in the deep crevices which intersect the land from west to east. This is where the great sheep estancias lie, sheltered from the wind. There is little agriculture except in the north, in the valleys of the Colorado and Negro rivers, where alfalfa is grown and cattle are raised. Centres of population are tiny and most of the towns are small ports on the Atlantic coast. Only Comodoro Rivadavia has a population over 100,000, thanks to its oil industry. Patagonia has attracted many generations of people getting away from it all, from Welsh religious pioneers to Butch Cassidy and the Sundance Kid, and tourism is an increasingly important source of income.

Ins and outs

Getting there

Air There are flights to many towns throughout Patagonia; most are to or from Buenos Aires. Main air services are given in the text below. Bear in mind that it's usually cheaper to buy internal flights in Argentina. Prepare for delays in bad weather. Many Air Force **LADE** flights in the region south of Bariloche must be booked in advance from the flight's departure point. The baggage allowance is 15 kg. Flights are often heavily booked, but check again on the day of the flight even if it is sold out. **LADE** ① *T011-5129-9000, or 0810-810 5233, www.lade.com.ar*, tickets are much cheaper for a long flight with stops than buying separate segments.

Road The principal roads in Patagonia are the Ruta 3, which runs down the Atlantic coast, and the Ruta 40 on the west. One of Argentina's main arteries, Ruta 3 runs from Buenos Aires to Ushuaia, interrupted by the car ferry crossing through Chilean territory across the Magellan Strait to Tierra del Fuego. It is mostly paved, except between Río Gallegos and San Sebastián (80 km north of Río Grande) and for 65 km south of Tolhuin. Regular buses run along the whole stretch, more frequently between October and April, and there are towns with services and accommodation every few hundred km. However, Ruta 40 is a wide unpaved *ripio* track which zigzags across the moors from Zapala to Lago Argentino, near El Calafate, ending at Cabo Vírgenes. It's by far the more interesting road, lonely and bleak, with little traffic even in the tourist summer season, offering fine views of the Andes and plenty of wildlife as well as giving access to many National Parks. The east-west road across Patagonia, from south of Esquel in the Lake District to Comodoro Rivadavia, is paved, and there's a good paved highway running from Bariloche through Neuquén to San Antonio Oeste.

Many of the roads in southern Argentina are *ripio* – gravelled – limiting maximum speeds to 60 km per hour, or less where surfaces are poor, very hard on low-clearance vehicles. Strong winds can also be a hazard. Windscreen and headlight protection is a good idea (expensive to buy, but can be improvised with wire mesh for windscreen, strips cut from plastic bottles for lights). There are cattle grids (*guardaganados*), even on main highways, usually signposted; cross them very slowly. Always carry plenty of fuel, as service stations may be as much as 300 km apart and as a precaution in case of a breakdown, carry warm clothing and make sure your car has anti-freeze. Petrol prices in Chubut, Santa Cruz and Tierra del Fuego provinces are 40% cheaper than in the rest of the country (10-15% for diesel).

There are good hotels at Perito Moreno and El Calafate, and basic accommodation at Gobernador Gregores and Río Mayo. In summer hotel prices are very high, especially in El Calafate and El Chaltén. In some places there may not be enough hotel beds to meet demand. Camping is increasingly popular and *estancias* may be hospitable to travellers who are stuck for a bed. Many *estancias*, especially in Santa Cruz province, offer transport, excursions and food as well as accommodation: see www.estanciasdesantacruz.com. **ACA** establishments, which charge roughly the same prices all over Argentina, are good value in Patagonia. As very few hotels and restaurants have a/c or even fans, it can get uncomfortably hot in January.

Viedma, Carmen de Patagones and around

These two pleasant towns (Phone code 02920, Colour map 8, grid C4) lie on opposite banks of the Río Negro, about 27 km from its mouth and 270 km south of Bahía Blanca. Patagones is older and charming, but most services are in Viedma (*Population*: 50,000), capital of Río Negro Province. A quiet place, its main attraction is the perfect bathing area along the shaded south bank of the river. **El Cóndor** is a beautiful beach 30 km south of Viedma, three buses a day from Viedma in summer, with hotels open January-February, restaurants and shops, free camping on beach 2 km south. And 30 km further southwest is the sealion colony, **Lobería Punta Bermeja**, daily bus in summer from Viedma; hitching easy in summer.

Carmen de Patagones (*Population 16,000*) was founded in 1779 and many early pioneer buildings remain in the pretty streets winding down to the river. There's a fascinating museum, **Museo Histórico** ① *JJ Biedma 64, T462729, daily 0930-1230, 1900-2100, Sun afternoon only.* Helpful **tourist office** at ① *Bynon 186, T462054.* The two towns are linked by two bridges and a four-minute frequent ferry crossing.

Bahía San Blas is an attractive small resort and renowned shark fishing area, 100 km from Patagones (tourist information at www.bahiasanblas.com). Almost due west and 180 km along the coast, on the Gulf of San Matías, is **San Antonio Oeste** (*Phone code*: 02934. *Population*: 14,000), and 17 km south, the popular beach resort, **Las Grutas**. The caves themselves are not really worth visiting; but the water is famously warm. Las Grutas is closed in the winter, but very crowded in the summer; accessible by bus from San Antonio hourly US$1. San Antonio is on the bus routes north to Bahía Blanca and south as far as Río Gallegos and Punta Arenas.

⬤ Sleeping

Viedma *p201*

B Austral, 25 de Mayo y Villarino, T422615, viedma@hoteles-austral.com.ar. Modern.

B Nijar, Mitre 490, T422833. Most comfortable, smart, modern, good service.

C-D Spa Inside, 25 de Mayo 174, T430459. Good value, lovely and quiet, with steam baths.

D Peumayen, Buenos Aires 334, T425222. Old-fashioned friendly place on the plaza.

Camping Good municipal site near the river, US$2 per person, all facilities including hot showers.

Estancias AL La Luisa and San Juan, both 40 km away in wilder country, T02920-463725, eleri@ viedma.com.ar. Traditional Patagonia *estancias* with English speaking owners, riding, cattle mustering, good hospitality, open Dec-Mar. Highly recommended.

Bahía San Blas *p202*

Lots of accommodation, Including **Resort Tiburón**, T02920-499202, www.tiburonresort.com.ar.

❼ Eating

Viedma *p201*

ⴲ-ⴲ **La Ochava**, Alsina y 25 de Mayo. New, good food and atmosphere.

ⴲ **La Balsa**, on the river at Colón y Villarino. The best restaurant, cheap but delicious seafood.

⬤ Transport

Viedma *p201*

Air LADE (Saavedra 403, T/F424420) fly to **Buenos Aires**, **Mar del Plata**, **Bahía Blanca**, **Neuquén**, **San Martín de Los Andes**, **San Antonio Oeste**, **Puerto Madryn**, **Trelew** and **Comodoro Rivadavia**.

Bus Terminal in Viedma at Av Pte Perón y Guido, 15 blocks from plaza; taxi US$1. To **Buenos Aires** 14 hrs, 3 daily, US$20, Don Otto/La Estrella/ Cóndor. To **San Antonio Oeste**, 2½ hrs, several daily, US$4, Don Otto. To **Bahía Blanca**, 4 hrs, 4 daily, US$5.

Train Tren Patagónico every Sun in Jan-Feb to **Bariloche**, US$10-40 (sleeper), www.patagonia. com.ar/rionegro/bariloche/tren_patagonico.php

---

Puerto Madryn and around

→ *Phone code: 02965. Colour map 9, grid A3. Population: 58,000.*

Puerto Madryn is a pleasant, breezy seaside town 250 km south of San Antonio Oeste. It stands on the wide bay of Golfo Nuevo, the perfect base for the Península Valdés and its extraordinary array of wildlife, just 70 km east. It was the site of the first Welsh landing in 1865 and is named after the Welsh home of the colonist, Jones Parry. Popular for skin diving and the nature reserves, the town's main industries are a huge aluminium plant and fish processing plants. You can often spot whales directly from the coast at the long beach of **Playa El Doradillo**, 16 km northeast (October-December). **EcoCentro** ⓘ *Julio Verne 3784, T457470, www.eco centro.org.ar, daily 1000-1800, US$5, reductions for students.* An inspired interactive sea life information centre, art gallery and café, it is perched on a cliff at the south end of town. **Museo de Ciencias Naturales y Oceanográfico**ⓘ *Domecq García y J Menéndez, Mon-Fri 0900-1200, 1430-1900, Sat 1430-1900, US$1.* This informative museum is worth a visit. The **tourist office** is at ⓘ *Av Roca 223, T/F453504, www.madryn.gov.ar, Mon-Fri 0700-2100, Sat-Sun 0830-1330, 1530-2030,* helpful. On 7 March the Battle of Patagones (1827) is celebrated in a week-long colourful fiesta of horse displays and fine food.

Around Puerto Madryn

With **elephant seal** and **sea lion** colonies at the base of chalky cliffs, breeding grounds for **Southern right whales** in the sheltered Golfo Nuevo and the Golfo San José, and **guanacos**, **rheas**, **patagonian hares** and **armadillos** everywhere on land, the area around Puerto Madryn, especially the Península Valdés, is a spectacular region for wildlife. Whales can be seen from June to mid December, particularly interesting with their young September-October.

Keeping up with the Joneses

On 28 July 1865, 153 Welsh immigrants landed at Puerto Madryn, then a deserted beach deep in *indígena* country. After three weeks they pushed, on foot, across the parched pampa and into the Chubut river valley, where there is flat cultivable land along the riverside for a distance of 80 km upstream. Here, maintained in part by the Argentine Government, they settled, but it was three years before they realized the land was barren unless watered. They drew water from the river, which is higher than the surrounding flats, and built a fine system of irrigation canals. The colony, reinforced later by immigrants from Wales and from the US, prospered,

but in 1899 a great flood drowned the valley and some of the immigrants left for Canada. The last Welsh contingent arrived in 1911. The object of the colony had been to create a 'Little Wales beyond Wales', and for four generations they kept the Welsh language alive. The language is, however, dying out in the fifth generation. There is an offshoot of the colony of Chubut at Trevelin, at the foot of the Andes nearly 650 km to the west, settled in 1888 (see page 195). It is interesting that this distant land gave to the Welsh language one of its most endearing classics: *Dringo'r Andes* (Climbing the Andes), written by one of the early women settlers.

The sea lion breeding season runs from late December to late January, but visiting is good up to late April. Bull elephant seals begin to claim their territory in the first half of August and the breeding season is late September/early October. Orcas can be seen attacking seals at Punta Norte in February/March. Conservation officials can be found at the main viewpoints, informative but only Spanish spoken. The *EcoCentro* in Puerto Madryn, studies the marine ecosystems. **Punta Loma** ⓘ *0800-1200, 1430-1930; US$3.30 (free with Península Valdés ticket), information and video, many companies offer tours, taxi US$15 (8.30 one way - walk back).* This is a sea lion reserve 15 km southeast of Puerto Madryn; sea lions can even be seen in Puerto Madryn harbour. See also Puerto Deseado, page 210 and Punta Tombo, page 208.

Península Valdés

The Península Valdés, near Puerto Madryn, in the Chubut province, has an amazing array of wildlife: marine mammals including Southern Right Whales, penguins and guanacos. There are other penguin colonies on the coast, a fine palaeontological museum in Trelew and villages where Welsh settlers set up home. Several estancias offer excellent hospitality for those who wish to get to know the vastness of this land. The best way to see the wildlife is by car. See Puerto Madryn for car hire; fuel will cost about US$10 for the return trip. A taxi costs US$70 per vehicle for the day. Take your time, roads are all unpaved except the road from Puerto Madryn to Puerto Pirámide. In summer there are several shops, but take sun protection and drinking water.

The Golfos Nuevo and San José are separated by the Istmo Carlos Ameghino, which leads to **Península Valdés** *US$12*, a bleak, but beautiful treeless splay of land. In depressions in the heart of the peninsula are large salt flats; Salina Grande is 42 m below sea level. At the entrance to the peninsula, on the isthmus, there is an interesting Visitors' Centre with wonderful whale skeleton. Near the entrance, Isla de los Pájaros can be seen in Golfo San José, though its seabirds can only be viewed through fixed telescopes (at 400 m distance); best time is September to April. The main tourist centre of the Peninsula is **Puerto Pirámide** (*Population 400*), 90 km east of Puerto Madryn, where boat trips leave to see the whales in season (sailings controlled by Prefectura, according to weather). There's plentiful accommodation and eating places here (tourist information, T495084, aldeaturistica@infovia.com).

Punta Norte (176 km) at the north end of the Valdés Peninsula, isn't usually included in tours, but has elephant seals and penguins (September-March) below its high, white cliffs, best seen at low tide. There's a reasonably priced restaurant. At **Caleta Valdés**, 45 km south of Punta Norte, you can see elephant seals at close quarters, and there are three marked walks. At **Punta Delgada** (at the south of the peninsula) elephant seals and other wildlife can be seen. The beach on the entire coast is out of bounds; this is strictly enforced.

☺ Sleeping

Puerto Madryn *p202, map p204*
Book ahead in summer, and whale season. Note that non-Argentines will often be charged more in the pricier hotels.

AL Bahía Nueva, Av Roca 67, T451677, www.bahianueva.com.ar. One of the best sea front hotels, quite small but comfortable rooms, professional staff, cheaper in low season.

AL Península Valdés, Av Roca 155, T471292, www.hotelpeninsula.com.ar. Luxurious minimalist sea front hotel with great views, spa, sauna and gym (bookings from outside Argentina 30% extra).

AL Tolosa, Roque Sáenz Peña 253, T471850, tolosa@hoteltolosa.com.ar. Extremely comfortable, modern, great breakfasts. Disabled access. Recommended.

A-B Villa Pirén, Av Roca 439, T/F456272, www.piren.com.ar. Excellent modern rooms and apartments in smart seafront place.

B Hostería Torremolinos, Marcos A Zar 64, T453215. Nice, modern, well decorated rooms.

B Marina, Av Roca 7, T/F454915, teokou@infovia.com.ar. Great value little seafront apartments for up to 5 people, book ahead.

B Playa, Av Roca 187, T451446, www.playahotel.com.ar. Good sea front location, the slightly pricier more modern rooms are worth it.

B Santa Rita, Gob Maiz 370, T471050. Welcoming, comfy, wash basins in rooms, good value with dinner included, also kitchen facilities. Often recommended.

B-C Res Verona, 25 de Mayo 874, T451509, hotel_verona@hotmail.com. New, with breakfast, also has 3 apartments, excellent value.

C Muelle Viejo, H Yrigoyen 38, T471284. Ask for the comfortable modernized rooms in this funny old place. Rooms for 4 are excellent value, kitchen facilities.

Puerto Madryn

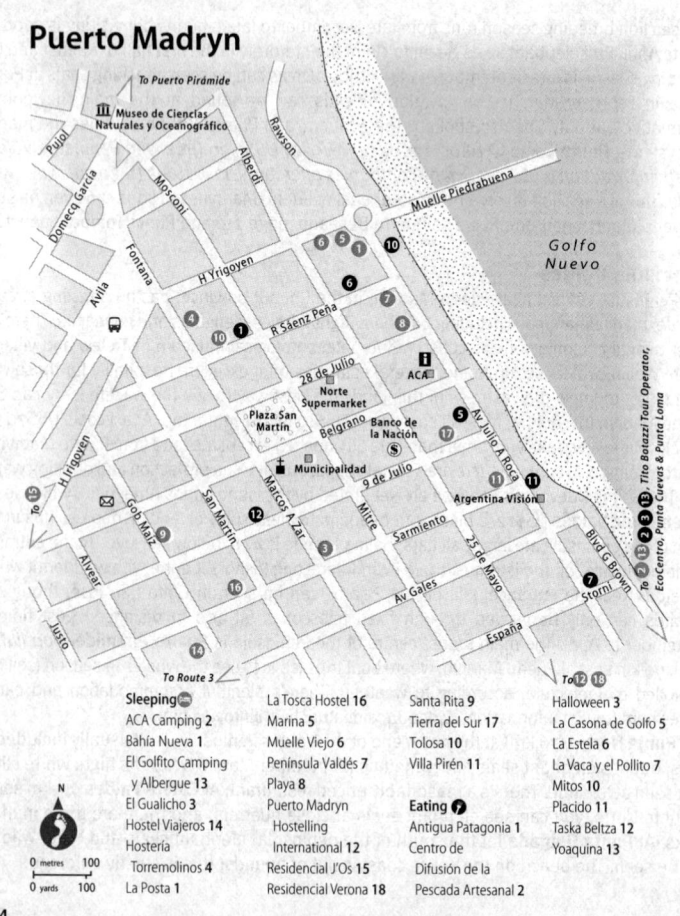

Sleeping ☺
ACA Camping **2**
Bahía Nueva **1**
El Golfito Camping
  y Albergue **13**
El Gualicho **3**
Hostel Viajeros **14**
Hostería
  Torremolinos **4**
La Posta **1**

La Tosca Hostel **16**
Marina **5**
Muelle Viejo **6**
Península Valdés **7**
Playa **8**
Puerto Madryn
  Hostelling
  International **12**
Residencial J'Os **15**
Residencial Verona **18**

Santa Rita **9**
Tierra del Sur **17**
Tolosa **10**
Villa Pirén **11**

Eating ❼
Antigua Patagonia **1**
Centro de
  Difusión de la
  Pescada Artesanal **2**

Halloween **3**
La Casona de Golfo **5**
La Estela **6**
La Vaca y el Pollito **7**
Mitos **10**
Placido **11**
Taska Beltza **12**
Yoaquina **13**

D La Posta, Roca 33, T472422, residencial laposta@infovia.com.ar. Small rooms, welcoming, with breakfast, on the sea front, also apartments, popular in high season.

D Residencial J'Os, Bolívar 75, T471433, residencialjos@infovia.com.ar. Nice little place, breakfast included.

D Tierra del Sur, 9 de Julio 57, T471379, tierradelsuralojamiento@yahoo.com.ar. New, good breakfast, kitchen very helpful.

E El Gualicho, Marcos A Zar 480, T454163. Best budget option, new hostel, nicely designed, enthusiastic owner, free pick up from bus terminal, *parrilla*, garden, some double rooms, bikes for hire. Highly recommended.

E pp Hostel Viajeros, Gob Maíz 545, T456457, www.hostelviajeros.com. With basic breakfast, small rooms with 4 beds or doubles (**C**), big kitchen/dining room, lawn, TV, helpful.

E pp La Tosca Hostel, Sarmiento 437, Chubut, T456133, www.argentinahostels.com. Also has doubles (**C**), AHC member.

E Puerto Madryn Hostelling International, 25 de Mayo 1136, T/F474426, madryn@hostels.org.ar. 10 blocks from the centre of town, modern house, garden, laundry, kitchen facilities, bike rental, doubles too, English and French spoken.

Camping All closed out of season. ACA, Blvd Brown, 3.5 km south of town at Punta Cuevas, T452952. Open Sep-Apr, hot showers, café, shop, no kitchen facilities, shady trees, close to the sea.

Many people camp on the beach, though there is a municipal site **El Golfito**, Camping y Albergue, at Ribera Sur, 1 km before *ACA* site on same road along beach (gives student discount) T454544. All facilities, very crowded, US$2 pp and US$2 per tent for 1st day. Also room with bunkbeds, **F** pp. Bus from town stops 100 m before entrance.

Península Valdés *p203*
Puerto Pirámide
A-C ACA Motel, T495004, www.piramides.net. Poor restaurant, camping. There is also an **ACA** service station (daily) with good café and shop.

B Estancia El Sol, T495007, with restaurant.

B Paradise Pub, T495030. Helpful, good value food and beer, good atmosphere.

B Cabañas en el Mar, T495049, www.piramides.net. Recommended.

D Español, T495031. Basic but pleasant.

Camping Municipal campsite by the black sand beach, T495000, US$2.50 pp (free out of season), hot showers US$0.50, good, get there early to secure a place. Do not camp on the beach: people have been swept away by the incoming tide.

Punta Delgada
Staying at estancias on the peninsula is a great way to appreciate the wildlife.

LL-L Faro Punta Delgada, T458444, or 15 406304, www.puntadelgada.com. In a lighthouse, amazing setting, half and full board, excellent food, very helpful. Recommended; book in advance.

Punta Cantor
La Elvira, T15 406183 (office in Puerto Madryn T474248), www.laelvira.com. Traditional Patagonian dishes and comfortable accommodation (B&B, half and full board available).

🍴 Eating

Puerto Madryn *p202, map p204*
Excellent fish restaurants, but pricier than in the rest of Argentina. You should try at least one plate of *arroz con mariscos* (rice with a whole selection of squid, prawns, mussels and clams).

▼▼▼ Placido, Av Roca 508. On the beach, stylish, intimate, excellent service, seafood and vegetarian.

▼▼▼ Taska Beltza, 9 de Julio 345, T15 668085, Without doubt, the best in town, chef 'El Negro' cooks superb paella – book ahead, closed Mon.

▼▼ Antigua Patagonia, Mitre y RS Pena. Large *parilla* and seafood restaurant, warm atmosphere, good value set menu.

▼▼ Centro de Difusión de la Pescada Artesanal, Brown, 7th roundabout, T15 538085. Authentic cantina, where the fishermen's families cook meals with their catch, go early.

▼▼ La Estela, Sáenz Peña 27. Highly recommended for meat dishes.

▼▼ La Vaca y el Pollito, Av Roca y A Storni. Built into the wooden hull of a boat, cosy, *parrilla*, seafood and pastas.

▼▼ Yoaquina, Blvd Brown between 1st and 2nd roundabouts, T456058. Relaxed. Beachfront, eat outside in summer, good seafood, open from breakfast to after dinner, cheap lunch menu.

▼ La Casona de Golfo, Av Roca 349. Good value *tenedor libre parrilla*, seafood, and 'helados libre'.

▼ Halloween, Av Roca 1355. Pizza and *empanadas*.

▼ Náutico, Av Julio Roca y Albarracín. Good food and service, mainly fish, always full of locals.

▼ Norte, 28 de Julio 136, Takeaway food at this supermarket: *empanadas*, vegetable tortillas.

Cafés
Mitos, 28 de Julio 64. Stylish café with good atmosphere. Recommended.

París 43, RS Peña y 25 de Mayo, T458166. Good place for coffees.

🌙 Bars and clubs

Puerto Madryn *p202, map p204*
Havanna, Av Roca y 28 de Julio. Smart, buzzing.

Margarita, next to *Ambigu*, RS Peña y Av Roca. Late night drinks and live music.

▲ Activities and tours

Puerto Madryn *p202, map p204*
Diving
Puerto Madryn is a diving centre, with several shipwrecked boats in the Golfo Nuevo. A 1st dive ('bautismo') for beginners costs about US$30 dive.
Safari Submarino, Blvd Brown 1070, T474110.
Ocean Divers, Blvd Brown (between 1st and 2nd roundabout), T472569; advanced courses (PADI) and courses on video, photography and underwater communication.
Lobo Larsen, Av H Yrigiyen 144, T15 516314, www.lobolarsen.com. Good equipment and boat, guide speaks English, professional, US$48 for 2 open-water dives.

Mountain bike hire
US$5 for 3 hrs, US$8.50 all day.
Future Bike, Juan B Justo 683, T15 665108.
Na Praia, on the beach at Blvd Brown and Perlotti, T473715.
XT Mountain Bike, Av Roca 742, T472427.

Tours
Many agencies do similar 12-hr tours to the Península Valdés, about US$38, plus US$12 entrance to the Peninsula. They include the interpretation centre, Puerto Pirámides (the whales boat trip is US$12 extra), Punta Delgada and Caleta Valdés. Take water and lunch, and shop around to find out how long you'll spend at each place, how big the group is, and if your guide speaks English. Tours to see the penguins at Punta Tombo and Welsh villages are better from Trelew. Recommended for Península Valdés:
Argentina Visión, Av Roca 536, T451427, www.argentinavision.com. Also 4WD adventure trips and *estancia* accommodation at Punta Delgada, English and French spoken.
Ryan's Travel, Yrigoyen 257, loc 4, www.ryanstravel.com.ar. Very helpful (also have offices in El Calafate and Ushuaia).
Tito Botazzi, Blvd Brown 1070, T474110. Small groups and good bilingual guides.

Península Valdés *p203*
Full-day tours take in Puerto Pirámide (with whale-watching in season), plus some, but not necessarily all, of the other wildlife viewing points. Prices are US$ 14 pp, in some cases including the entry to the national park; boat trip to see whales US$12 if not included in tour price. On all excursions take drink, food if you don't want to eat in the expensive restaurants, and binoculars. Most tour companies stay about 1 hr on location.
Tito Bottazzi, T495050. Recommended.

Hydrosport, near the ACA, T495065, hysport@infovia.com.ar. Rents scuba equipment and boats, and organizes land and sea wildlife tours to see whales and dolphins. Tours do not run after heavy rain in the low season.

⊖ Transport

Puerto Madryn *p202, map p204*
Air Airport 10 km west; LADE to **Buenos Aires**, **Bahía Blanca**, **Viedma**, **Trelew**, **Comodoro Rivadavia** and other Patagonian airports. More flights to **Bariloche**, Buenos Aires, and El Calafate from Trelew. Buses to Trelew stop at entrance to airport if asked. Taxi US$20. Direct bus to Trelew airport, **Puma**, US$3.50, leaves 1½ hrs before flight and takes arriving passengers to Puerto Madryn.
Bus Terminal at Irigoyen y San Martín (behind old railway station), T451789. To **Buenos Aires**, 18 hrs, several companies, **Andesmar** recommended. To **Bahía Blanca**, 9 ½ hrs with **Don Otto**, 2000, US$23. To **Río Gallegos**, 18 hrs; US$18, **El Pingüino** (connecting to El Calafate, Punta Arenas, Puerto Natales), **Andesmar, TAC, Don Otto**. To **Trelew**, 1 hr, every hr, US$2 with **28 de Julio, Mar y Valle**. To **Bariloche**, 15 hrs, US$25-38, daily, except Weds, **Mar y Valle** and Andesmar (has better *semi cama*).
Car hire Expensive, and note large excess for turning car over. Drive slowly on unpaved *ripio* roads; best to hire 4WD! **Puerto Madryn Turismo**, Roca 624, T452355. **Localiza** has an office (see Car Hire in Essentials). **Sigma**, T15-699465, www.sigmarentacar.com. Will deliver car to your hotel.
Taxi There are taxis outside the bus terminal, T452966/474177, and on the main plaza.

Península Valdés *p203*
28 de Julio **bus** company from Puerto Madryn to Puerto Pirámide, daily at 1000, returns 1800, US$2 each way, 1 hr.

❶ Directory

Puerto Madryn *p202, map p204*
Airline offices Aerolíneas Argentinas, Roca 303, T421257. **LADE**, Roca 117, T451256.
Banks Lots of ATMs at the following: Banco Nación, 9 de Julio 117. Banco del Chubut, 25 de Mayo 154 and Río, Mitre 102. **Internet** Internet Centro Madryn, 25 de Mayo y Belgrano. US$0.60 per hr. Re Creo, Roque Sáenz Peña 101.
Medical services For emergencies call 107 or 451240. **Post offices** Belgrano y Maiz, 0900-1200, 1500-1900. **Telephones** Many *locutorios* in the centre.

Trelew and the Chubut Valley

→ *Phone code: 02965. Colour map 9, grid A3. Population: 88,000.*

Pronounced 'Trel-ay-Oo', Trelew is a busy town, with an excellent museum and a shady plaza, which hosts a small handicraft market at weekends. Evidence of Welsh settlement remains only in a few brick buildings: the 1889 **Capilla Tabernacl**, on Belgrano, between San Martín and 25 de Mayo, and the **Salón San David**, a 1913 Welsh meeting hall. On the road to Rawson, 3 km south, is one of the oldest standing Welsh chapels, **Capilla Moriah**, from 1880, with a simple interior and graves of many original settlers in the cemetery. **Museo Paleontológico Egidio Feruglio**① *Fontana 140, T432100, www.mef.org.ar, Mon-Fri 1000-2000 spring and summer, 1000-1800 rest of year, Sat-Sun 1000-2000, US$5.* This is an excellent museum, which presents the origins of life and dynamically poised dinosaur skeletons. It has free tours in English, German and Italian; also a café and shop. Also has information about **Parque Paleontológico Bryn-Gwyn**, 8 km from Gaiman (see below). **Museo Regional Pueblo de Luis** ① *Fontana y 9 de Julio, Mon-Fri 0800-2000, Sat closed, Sun 1700-2000, US$0.65.* In the old 1889 railway station, it has displays on indigenous societies, failed Spanish attempts at settlement and on Welsh colonization. **Tourist office** on the plaza① *Mitre 387, T420139, Mon-Fri 0800-1400, 1500-2100, Sat-Sun 0900-1300, 1500-2000. www.trelew.gov.ar.*

Gaiman and around → *Colour map 9, grid A3. Population: 4,400.*

A small pretty place with old brick houses retaining the Welsh pioneer feel, Gaiman hosts the annual Eisteddfod (Welsh festival of arts) in October. It's renowned for delicious, and excessive 'traditional' Welsh teas and its fascinating, tiny museum, **Museo Histórico Regional Galés** ① *Sarmiento y 28 de Julio, US$0.50, Tue-Sun 1500-1900,* revealing the spartan lives of the idealistic Welsh pioneers. Curator Mrs Roberts is very knowledgeable. **Geoparque Bryn Gwyn** ① *8 km south of town, T432100, www.mef.org.ar, end Sep-end Mar, daily 1000-1900, US$2.50, getting there: taxi from Gaiman US$1.70.* Fossil beds 40 million years old are shown, there is a visitor centre. **El Desafío**① *2 blocks west of plaza, US$2.50, tickets valid 2 months,* is a quaint private theme-park comprising pergolas and dinosaurs made of rubbish.

Dolavon, founded in 1919, is a quiet settlement, with a few buildings reminiscent of the Welsh past. The main street, Avenida Roca, runs parallel to the irrigation canal built by the

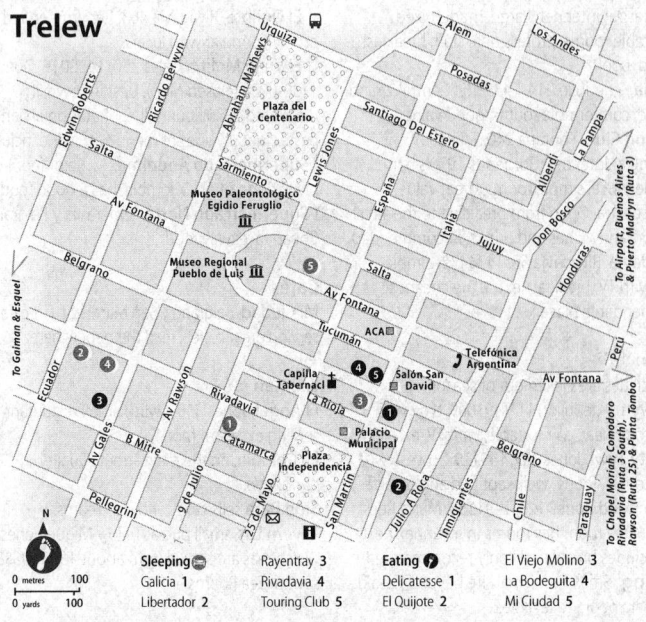

Trelew

Sleeping ⬤
Galicia 1
Libertador 2
Rayentray 3
Rivadavia 4
Touring Club 5

Eating ⬤
Delicatesse 1
El Quijote 2
El Viejo Molino 3
La Bodeguita 4
Mi Ciudad 5

settlers, where willow trees now trail into the water, and there's a Welsh chapel, **Capilla Carmel** at one end. The old flour mill at Maipú y Roca dates from 1927 and can be visited – the key is kept in the Municipalidad, Roca 188 (next to *Banco Provincial del Chubut*). There's *Autoservicio Belgrano* at the far end of San Martin, for food supplies, but no tea rooms, and nowhere to stay. The **municipal campsite**, two blocks north of the river, is free, with good facilities.

In the irrigated valley between Dolavon and Gaiman, you'll see more Welsh chapels tucked away among fringes of tall *alamo* (poplar) trees and silver birches (best if you're in your own transport). The **San David chapel** (1917) is a beautifully preserved brick construction, with an elegant bell tower, and sturdy oak-studded door, in a quiet spot surrounded by birches.

Paved Ruta 25 runs from Dolavon west to the upper Chubut Valley, passing near the **Florentino Ameghino** dam, a good leafy spot for a picnic. From Ameghino to Tecka on Ruta 40 (south of Trevelin) is one of the most beautiful routes across Patagonia from the coast to the Andes, lots of wildlife to be seen. It goes through Las Plumas (mind the bridge if driving), Los Altares, which has an ACA motel, camping, fuel and some shops, and Paso Los Indios.

South of Trelew

Punta Tombo ① *Park entrance US$4. Tours from Trelew and Puerto Madryn, US$17; 45 mins at the site, café and toilets. Access from Ruta 1, a ripio road between Trelew and Camarones. Closed after Mar.* This nature reserve is 107 km south of Trelew, open from September, when huge numbers of Magellanic penguins come here to breed. Chicks can be seen from mid-November; they take to the water January to February. It's fascinating to see these creatures up close, but noisy colonies of tourists dominate in the morning; it's quieter in the afternoon. You'll see guanacos, hares and rheas on the way. Another large **penguin colony** ① *all year, US$5* – with lots of other marine life – is at Cabo Dos Bahías, easily reached from the town of **Camarones** 275 km north of Comodoro Rivadavia. The Guarda Fauna is 25 km from town.

● Sleeping

Trelew *p207, map p207*

A **Libertador**, Rivadavia 31, T/F420220. Modern, highly recommended for service and comfortable rooms, breakfast included.

A **Rayentray**, San Martín y Belgrano, T434702, rcvcentral@ar.inter.net. Large, modernized, comfortable rooms, professional staff, breakfast included, pool.

C **Galicia**, 9 de Julio 214, T433802. Central, grand entrance, comfortable rooms, good value.

C **Touring Club**, Fontana 240, T/F433997, htouring@ar.inter.net. Gorgeous 1920's bar, faded elegance, simple rooms, great value, breakfast extra. Open from breakfast to the small hours for sandwiches and drinks. Recommended.

D **Rivadavia**, Rivadavia 55, T434472. Simple rooms with TV, breakfast extra, the cheapest recommendable place.

Gaiman *p207*

Most facilities are closed out of season.

B **Ty Gwyn**, 9 de Julio 111, T491009, tygwyn@cpsarg.com. Neat, comfortable, with TV, excellent.

C **Gwesty Tywi**, Jones 342, T491292, gwestywi@infovia.com.ar. Pretty, well-kept bed and breakfast.

C **Plas y Coed**, Jones 123, T491133. Marta Rees' delightful tea room has rooms in an annex next door, includes breakfast. Highly recommended.

Camping Small municipal site beyond Casa de Té Gaiman, poor, no facilities.

● Eating

Trelew *p207, map p207*

† **La Bodeguita**, Belgrano 374. Delicious pastas and pizzas, with interesting art on the walls.

† **Delicatesse**, Belgrano y San Martin. Best pizzas in town, cheery place, popular with families.

† **El Quijote**, Rivadavia 463. Recommended *parrilla*, popular with locals.

† **El Viejo Molino** Gales 250, T428019. Open 1130-0030 (closed Mon), best in town, in renovated 1886 flour mill, for Patagonian lamb, pastas, good value set menu with wine included.

† **Supermercado Anónima**, Av Belgrano, 1 block north of Av Colombia, has a good food hall.

† **Supermercado Norte**, Soberanía y Belgrano. Cheap takeaway food.

Cafés

Mi Ciudad, Belgrano y San Martin. Smart café serving great coffee; read the papers here.

Gaiman *p207*

El Angel, Jones 850. Stylish small restaurant serving excellent food.

La Colonia, on the main street. Quality *panadería*.

Siop Bara sells cakes and ice creams.

Tavern Las, small pub at Tello y Miguel Jones. Welsh teas are served from about 1500 (US$5) by several Tea Rooms.

Plas Y Coed (see Sleeping, above). The best, and oldest; Marta Rees is a wonderful raconteur and fabulous cook.

Ty Gwyn, 9 de Julio 111. Larger, more modern and welcoming; generous teas.

Ty Nain, Yrigoyen 283. The prettiest house and full of history, owned by Mirna Jones.

▲ Activities and tours

Trelew *p207, map p207*
Agencies run tours to Punta Tombo, US$18, Chubut Valley (half-day), US$10, both as full day US$22. Tours to Península Valdés are best done from Puerto Madryn.

Nievemar, Italia 98, T434114, www.nievemartours.com.ar. Punta Tombo and Valdés, bilingual guides (reserve ahead), organized and efficient.

Patagonia Grandes Espacios, Belgrano 338, T435161. Good excursions to Punta Tombo and Gaiman, but also palaeontological trips, staying in chacras, whale watching. Recommended.

⊖ Transport

Trelew *p207, map p207*
Air AR have flights to/from **Buenos Aires**, **El Calafate** and **Ushuaia**. LADE flies to Patagonian airports from **Viedma** to **Comodoro Rivadavia**, as well as **Bariloche**. Airport 5 km north of centre; taxis about US$6-8. Local buses to/from Puerto Madryn stop at the airport entrance if asked, turning is 10 mins walk, US$3.50; AR runs special bus service to connect with its flights.
Bus Terminal on Plaza del Centenario, T420121. **Mar y Valle** and **28 de Julio** both go frequently to

Gaiman, 30 mins; US$1, and **Dolavon** 1 hr, US$1.50, to **Puerto Madryn**, 1 hr, US$2, to **Puerto Pirámide**, 2½ hrs; US$5.

To **Buenos Aires**, 20 hrs; US$20, several companies go daily, including TAC, El Pingüino, Que Bus, Don Otto, Andesmar, El Cóndor. To **Comodoro Rivadavia**, 5 hrs, US$8, many companies, to **Río Gallegos**, 17 hrs; US$20, many companies. To **Esquel**, 10hrs, US$11.

Companies Andesmar, T433535; El Pingüino, T427400; Don Otto, T429496; TAC, T431452; El Cóndor, T431675; 28 de Julio/ Mar y Valle, T432429; Que Bus, T422760.
Car hire Expensive. Airport desks are staffed only at flight arrival times and cars are snapped up quickly. All have offices in town. See Essentials at front of book for international agencies.

Camarones *208*
Bus Mon, Wed, Fri 0800 from **Trelew** to Camarones, El Nañdú, T427499, US$6.50, 3 hrs, returns same day 1600.
Taxi From Camarones to Cabo Dos Bahías, US$10.

❶ Directory

Trelew *p207, map p207*
Airline offices Aerolineas Argentinas, 25 de Mayo 33, T420170. LADE, Terminal de Omnibus, offices 12 /13, T435740. **Banks** Open Mon-Fri 0830-1300. Banco de la Nación, 25 de Mayo y Fontana. Banco del Sud, 9 de Julio 320, cash advance on Visa. **Internet** 25 de Mayo y Rivadavia. **Post offices** 25 de Mayo and Mitre. **Telephones** Telefónica, Roca y Pje Tucumán, and several *locutorios* in centre.

Comodoro Rivadavia and inland

→ *Phone code: 0297. Colour map 9, grid A2. Population: 145,000.*
The largest city in the province of Chubut, 375 km south of Trelew, oil was discovered here in 1907. It looks rather unkempt, reflecting changing fortunes in the oil industry, the history of which is described at the **Museo del Petroleo** ① *3 km north, San Lorenzo 250, T455 9558, Tue-Fri 0900-1800, Sat-Sun 1500-1800, getting there: taxi US$4.* There's a beach at Rada Tilly, 8 km south (buses every 30 minutes); walk along beach at low tide to see sea lions. **Tourist office** ① *Rivadavia y Pellegrini, T446 2376, www.comodoro.gov.ar, Mon-Fri 0900-1400,* English spoken. Also in bus terminal.

Sarmiento → *Colour map 9, grid A2. Population: 10,000. Phone code 0297.*
If you're keen to explore the petrified forests south of Sarmiento and the Cueva de las Manos near Perito Moreno, take the road to Chile running west from Comodoro Rivadavia. It's 156 km to Colonia Sarmiento (known as Sarmiento), a quiet relaxed place, sitting just south of two large lakes, Musters and Colhué Huapi. This is the best base for seeing the 70 million-year old **petrified forests** of fallen araucaria trees. Most accessible is the **Bosque Petrificado José Ormachea** ① *32 km south of Sarmiento on a ripio road, warden T4898047, US$3.30.* Less easy to reach is the bleaker **Víctor Szlapelis** petrified forest, some 40 km further southwest

along the same road (follow signposts, road from Sarmiento in good condition). From December to March a *combi* service runs twice daily: contact Sarmiento tourist office. Taxi Sarmiento to forests, US$20 (three passengers), including 1 hour wait. Contact Sr Juan José Valero, the park ranger, for guided tours, Uruguay 43, T0297-489 8407 (see also the Monumento Natural Bosques Petrificados). **Tourist office** ① *Pietrobelli 388, T489 8220, www.coloniasarmiento.gov.ar,* is helpful, has map of town, arranges taxi to forests.

Comodoro Rivadavia to Río Gallegos

Caleta Olivia (*Population 13,000*) lies on the Bahía San Jorge, 74 km south of Comodoro Rivadávia, with hotels (one opposite bus station, good) and a municipal campsite near beach. A convenient place to break long bus journeys; see the sound sculptures, **Ciudad Sonora** ① *at* **Pico Truncado** *(a few simple hotels, campsite, tourist information T499 2202), daily bus service,* 58 km southwest, where the wind sings through marble and metal structures.

In a bizarre lunar landscape surrounding the Laguna Grande, **Monumento Natural Bosques Petrificados** is the largest examples of petrified trees, araucarias 140 million years old, lie in a desert which was once, astonishingly, a forest. There is a museum and a 1-km nature walk. No charge but donations accepted; please do not remove 'souvenirs'. Tours from Puerto Deseado with Los Vikingos *(address on page 211). Access by Ruta 49 which branches off 91 km south of Fitz Roy. No facilities. Nearest* campsite at Estancia La Paloma, on Ruta 49, 24 km before the entrance, T0297-443503.

Puerto Deseado (*Phone code 0297, Colour map 9, grid B3, Population 10,000*) is a pleasant fishing port on the estuary of the Río Deseado, which drains, strangely, into the Lago Buenos Aires in the west. It's a stunning stretch of coastline and the estuary is a wonderful nature reserve, with Magellanic penguins, cormorants, and breeding grounds of Commerson's dolphin - one of the most beautiful in the world. **Cabo Blanco**, 72 km north, is the site of the largest fur seal colony in Patagonia, breeding season December-January. The **tourist office** is in the *vagón histórico*, San Martín 1525, T487 0220, turismo@pdeseado.com.ar.

The quiet **Puerto San Julián** (*Phone code 02962, Colour map 9, grid B2, Population 6,100*) is the best place for breaking the 780 km run from Comodoro Rivadavia to Río Gallegos. It has a fascinating history, little of which is visible today. The first mass in Argentina was held here in 1520 after Magellan had executed a member of his mutinous crew. Francis Drake also put in here in 1578, to behead Thomas Doughty, after amiably dining with him. There is much wildlife in the area: red and grey foxes, guanacos, wildcats in the mountains, rheas and an impressive array of marine life in the coastal Reserva San Julián. Recommended zodiac boat trip run by **Excursiones Pinocho** ① *T454333,* to see Magellanic penguins (September-March), cormorants and Commerson's dolphins. Ceramics are made at the **Escuela de Cerámica**; good handicraft centre at Moreno y San Martín. There is a regional museum at the end of San Martín on the waterfront. **Tourist office** ① *San Martín 1126, T454396, centur@uvc.com.ar.*

Piedrabuena (*Population 4,200*) on Ruta 3 is 125 km south of San Julián on the Río Santa Cruz. On Isla Pavón, south of town on Ruta 3 at the bridge over Río Santa Cruz, is a tourist complex, with popular wooded campsite and wildlife park, T497498, liable to get crowded in good weather; the river is popular for water sports. **Hostería Municipal Isla Pavón** T02966-156 38380, is a new four-star catering for fishers of steelhead trout. National trout festival in March. 33 km further south, a dirt road branches 22 km to **Parque Nacional Monte León**, land formerly owned by Douglas Tompkins (see Parque Pumalin in Chaitén, Chile) which includes the Isla Monte León, an important breeding area for cormorants and terns, where there is also a penguin colony and sea lions. There are impressive rock formations and wide isolated beaches at low tide. Campsite with basic facilities.

● Sleeping

Comodoro Rivadavia *p209*
A Lucania Palazzo, Moreno 676, T449 9338, www.lucania-palazzo.com. Most luxurious, superb rooms, sea views, good value, huge American breakfast, sauna and gym included. Recommended.
B Comodoro, 9 de Julio 770, T447 2300, info@comodorohotel.com.ar. Buffet breakfast included, pay extra for larger rooms.

D Azul, Sarmiento 724, T447 4628, Breakfast extra, quiet old place with lovely bright rooms, kind, great views from the *confitería*.
D Rua Marina, Belgrano 738, T447 6877. With TV and breakfast, good budget choice.
E Hospedaje Cari Hué, Belgrano 563, T447 2946. Best budget choice, breakfast extra, shared bath, nice owners who like backpackers!

Sarmiento *p209*

B Chacra Labrador, 10 km from Sarmiento, T0297-489 3329, agna@coopsar.com.ar. Excellent small *estancia*, breakfast included, other meals extra and available for non-residents, English and Dutch spoken, runs tours to petrified forests at good prices, will collect guests from Sarmiento (same price as taxi).

D Colón, Perito Moreno 650, T489 4212. One of the better cheap places in town.

D Ismar, Patagonía 248, T489 3293.

D Hostería Los Lagos, Roca y Alberdi, T493046. Good, heating, restaurant.

Camping Club Deportivo Sarmiento, 25 de Mayo y Ruta 20, T4893103.

Puerto Deseado *p210*

L Estancia La Madrugada, T011-5371 5555, lwalker@caminosturismo.com.ar, or ats@ caminosturismo.com.ar. Accommodation and meals, excursions to sea lion colony and cormorant nesting area, English spoken. Highly recommended.

A Isla Chaffer, San Martín y Mariano Moreno, T4872246. Modern, central.

B Los Acantilados, Pueyrredón y España, T4872167, acantur@puertodeseado.com.ar. Beautifully located, good breakfast.

Puerto San Julián *p210*

A Bahía, San Martín 1075, T454028, nico@ sanjulian.com.ar. Modern, comfortable, good value. Recommended.

A Estancia La María, 150 km northwest of Puerto San Julián, offers transport, accommodation and meals and visits to fascinating caves with paintings of human hands, guanacos etc 4,000-12,000 years old, less visited than the Cueva de las Manos. Contact Fernando Behm in San Julián, Saavedra 1163, T452328.

B Municipal, 25 de Mayo 917, T452300. Very nice, well run, good value, no restaurant.

B Res Sada, San Martín 1112, T452013. Fine, hot water, but on busy main road, poor breakfast.

Camping Good municipal campsite Magallanes 650 y M Moreno, T452806. US$1 pp plus US$0.50 for the use of shower (US$1.70 per vehicle), repeatedly recommended, all facilities.

Eating

Comodoro Rivadavia *p209*

⊘⊘ La Barra, San Martín 686. For breakfast, coffee or lunch.

⊘⊘ Cayo Coco, Rivadavia 102. Excellent pizzas, good service.

⊘⊘ Dionisius, 9 de Julio y Rivadavia. Elegant *parrilla*, set menu US$5.

⊘⊘ La Nueva Rosada, Belgrano 861. Good for beef or chicken.

⊘⊘ Peperoni, Rivadavia 348. Cheerful, modern, pastas.

⊘ La Barca, Belgrano 935. Good *tenedor libre*.

⊘ Superquick in *La Anónima* supermarket, San Martín y Güemes. Cheap food.

Café El Sol, Av Rivadavia y 25 de Mayo. Good café to hang out in.

Puerto Deseado *p210*

⊘ La Casa de Don Ernesto, San Martín 1245. Seafood and *parrilla*.

⊘ El Pingüino, Piedrabuena 958. *Parrilla*.

⊘ El Viejo Marino, Pueyrredón 224. Considered best by locals.

Puerto San Julián *p210*

⊘ Rural, Ameghino y Vieytes. Good, but not before 2100. A number of others. Also bars and tearooms.

⊘ Sportsman, Mitre y 25 de Mayo. Excellent value.

⛰ Activities and tours

Puerto Deseado *p210*

Darwin Expediciones, España 2601, T156 247554.

Los Vikingos, Estrada 1275, T156 245141/ 487 0020, vikingo@puertodeseado.com.ar. Both offer excursions by boat to Ría Deseado reserve and Reserva Provincial Isla Pingüino.

⊘ Transport

Comodoro Rivadavia *p209*

Air Airport, 13 km north. Bus No 6 to airport from bus terminal, hourly (45 mins), US$0.25. Taxi to airport, US$4.50. To **Buenos Aires**, AR/Austral. LADE flies to all Patagonian destinations once or twice a week, plus **Bariloche**, **El Bolsón** and **Esquel**.

Bus Terminal in centre at Pellegrini 730, T446 7305; has luggage store, good *confitería* upstairs, toilets, excellent tourist information office 0800-2100, some kiosks. Services to **Buenos Aires** 2 daily, 28 hrs, US$45. To **Bariloche**, 14½ hrs, US$19, Don Otto, T447 0450. To **Esquel** (paved road) 8 hrs direct with ETAP, T447 4841, and *Don Otto*, US$13. In summer buses usually arrive full; book ahead. To **Río Gallegos**, daily, 10-12 hrs, US$17-21 (see below for companies). To **Puerto Madryn**, US$10-12, and **Trelew**, US$8, several companies. To/from **Sarmiento** and **Caleta Olivia**, see below. To **Coyhaique** (Chile), US$15, 12 hrs, twice a week.

Sarmiento *p209*
Bus Frequent service to/from **Comodoro
Rivadavia**, US$5, 2½ hrs.
To **Chile** via **Río Mayo**, 0200, twice weekly; seats
are scarce in Río Mayo. From Sarmiento you can
reach **Esquel** (448 km north along Rutas 20 and
40); overnight buses on Sun stop at Río Mayo,
take food for journey.

Caleta Olivia *p210*
Bus To **Río Gallegos**, Andesmar, Sportman
(overnight) and El Pingüino (by day), US$13-16,
9½ hrs. Many buses to/from **Comodoro
Rivadavia**, 1 hr, US$2.50-3 (**La Unión** and
Sportman at terminal, T0297-485 1134), and
several daily to **Puerto Deseado**, La Unión and
Sportman, 2½-3 hrs, US$7.50. To **Perito Moreno**
and **Los Antiguos**, 5-6 hrs, several daily.

Puerto San Julián *p210*
Air LADE (Berutti 985, T452137) flies weekly to
Comodoro Rivadavia, **Gobernador Gregores**,
Puerto Deseado and **Río Gallegos**.
Bus To/from **Río Gallegos**, El Pingüino,
6 hrs, US$8.

🌐 Directory

Comodoro Rivadavia *p209*
Airline offices Aerolineas Argentinas,
9 de Julio 870, T444 0050. LADE, Rivadavia
360, T447 0585. **Banks** Many ATMs and
major banks along San Martín. Change money
at **Thaler**, San Martín 270, Mon-Sat 1000-1300,
or at weekends ETAP in bus terminal. **Post
offices** San Martín y Moreno.

Río Gallegos and around

→ *Phone code: 02966. Colour map 9, grid C2. Population: 79,000.*

The capital of Santa Cruz Province, 232 km south of Piedrabuena, on the estuary of the Río
Gallegos, this pleasant open town was founded in 1885 as a centre for the trade in wool and
sheepskins, and boasts a few smart shops and some excellent restaurants. The delightful
Plaza San Martín, 2 blocks south of the main street, Avenida Roca, has an interesting
collection of trees, many planted by the early pioneers, and a tiny corrugated iron cathedral,
with a wood-panelled ceiling in the chancel and stained glass windows. The small **Museo de
los Pioneros** ① *Elcano y Alberdi, daily 1000-2000, free,* is worth a visit. Interesting tour
given by the English-speaking owner, a descendent of the Scottish pioneers; great photos of
the first sheep-farming settlers. **Museo de Arte Eduardo Minichelli** ① *Maipú 13, Mon-Fri
0800-1900, Sat-Sun and holidays 1500-1900 (closed Jan/Feb),* has work by local artists.
Museo Regional Provincial Manuel José Molina ① *in the Complejo Cultural Santa Cruz, Av
San Martín y Ramón y Cajal 51, Mon-Fri 1000-1800 1100-1900,* has rather dull rocks and
fossils and a couple of dusty dinosaur skeletons. **Museo Malvinas Argentinas** ① *Pasteur 74,
Mon and Thu 0800-1300, Tue, Wed, Fri 1300-1800, 3rd Sun on month 1530-1830.* More
stimulating, it aims to inform visitors, with historical and geographical reasons, why the
Malvinas are Argentine. The provincial **tourist office** is at ① *Roca 863, T437447,
www.riogallegos.gov.ar, Mon-Fri 0900-2100, Sat 1000-2000, Sun 1000-1500,
1600-2000.* Helpful, English spoken, has list of *estancias*, and will phone round hotels for
you. Also at airport, limited opening hours. Small desk at bus terminal, T442159.

Cabo Vírgenes ① *134 km south of Río Gallegos, US$2.30,* is where a nature reserve
protects the second largest colony of Magellanic penguins in Patagonia. There's an
informative self-guided walk to see nests among the *calafate* and *mata verde* bushes. Good
to visit from November, when chicks are born, with nests under every bush, to January. Great
views from the Cabo Vírgenes lighthouse. *Confitería* close by with snacks and souvenirs
Access from *ripio* Ruta 1 for 3½ hours. About 13 km north of Cabo Vírgenes is **Estancia Monte
Dinero** ① *T428922, www.montedinero.com.ar*, where the English-speaking Fenton family
offers accommodation (**A**), food and excursions; excellent. Tours to both with tour operators
listed below, US$30 including lunch at Estancia Monte Dinero.

🛏 Sleeping

Río Gallegos *p212, map p213*
A Santa Cruz, Roca 701, T420601. Good value,
spacious rooms with good beds, full buffet
breakfast US$3.50 extra . Recommended.

A-B Comercio, Roca 1302, T422458,
hotelcomercio@informacionrgl.com.ar. Good
value, including breakfast, nice design,
comfortable, cheap *confitería*.

B **Apart Hotel Austral**, Roca 1505, T435855.
Modern, good value, particularly the duplexes,
basic kitchen facilities, breakfast US$1.70 extra.
B **Croacia**, Urquiza 431, T421218. Comfortable,
huge breakfasts, helpful owners, a good choice.
Recommended.
B **Sehuen**, Rawson 160, T425683,
hotelsehuen@hotmail.com. Good, cosy, helpful,
with breakfast.
C **París**, Roca 1040, T420111. Simple rooms, good
value, with breakfast.
C-D **Covadonga**, Roca 1244, T420190. Small
rooms with TV, breakfast extra.
D **Nevada**, Zapiola 480, T435790. Good
budget option, nice simple rooms, cable TV,
no breakfast.
D **Oviedo**, Libertad 746, T420118. A cheaper
budget option, breakfast extra, laundry, café,
parking.
Camping Camping ATSA, Ruta 3, en route
to bus terminal, T420301, US$1.70 pp plus
US$1.70 for tent. Club Pescazaike, Paraje
Guer Aike, Ruta 3, pescazaike@ciudad.com.ar,
US$1 pp per day plus US$5 per tent, also
quincho and restaurant, and Chacra Daniel,
Paraje Río Chico, 3.5 km from town, T423970,
US$1.70 pp per day plus US$2.40 per tent,
parrilla and facilities.

🍴 Eating

Río Gallegos *p212, map p213*
🍴🍸 **Club Británico**, Roca 935, T427320. Good
value, excellent steaks, "magic".
🍸 **Buena Vista**, Sarmiento y Gob Lista, T444114,
near the river, looking across Plaza de la República.
Most chic, not expensive, imaginative menu.
🍸 **Confitería Díaz**, Roca 1157. For pizzas
and pastas.
🍸 **El Dragón**, 9 de Julio 29. Cheap, varied *tenedor
libre*.
🍸 **El Horreo**, Roca 863, next door to Puesto
Molino. Serves delicious lamb dishes and good
salads.
🍸 **Puesto Molino**, Roca 862, Opposite the tourist
office. Inspired by *estancia* life, excellent pizzas
(US$5 for two) and *parrilla* (US$10 for 2).
🍸 **La Vieja Esquina**, Sarsfield 90.

🛍 Shopping

Río Gallegos *p212, map p213*
Souvenirs and crafts Artesanías Keóken,
San Martín 336. Good leather and weavings.
Curtumbre Monte Aymond, Roca 870. Also
fine traditional leather goods. **Prepap**, Ramón
y Cajal 51.

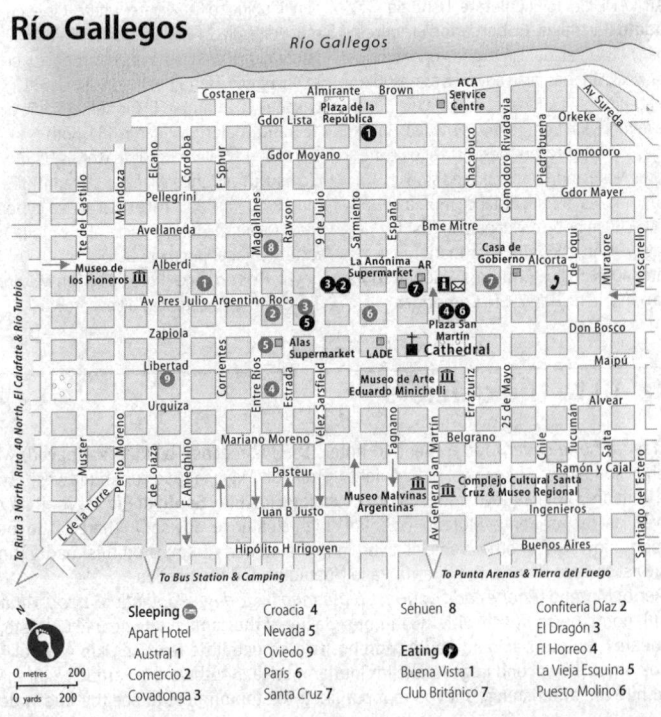

Río Gallegos

Supermarkets Alas, Zapiola y Estrada. La Anónima, Roca y España, larger branch on Lisandro de la Torre, near bus terminal.

▲ Activities and tours

Río Gallegos *p212, map p213*
For tours contact **Transporte Terrestre Guanacóndor**: Juan José Nauta (Estancia Telken), T432079, and **Transporte Lago Posadas**, T432431. All day tour with option of collecting from Bajo Caracoles or *Estancia Los Toldos*, US$20-27 for a 10-hour tour to Cueva de las Manos. Both these operators also do the spectacular **Circuito Grande Comarca Noroeste**, one of the highlights of Santa Cruz, taking in some of the province's most dramatic scenery. From Perito Moreno to Bajo Caracoles, Cueva de las Manos, Lago Posadas, Paso Roballos, Monte Zeballos, Los Antiguos. The tourist office can also advise, T02963-432222.

⊙ Transport

Río Gallegos *p212, map p213*
Air Airport 10 km from centre. Taxi (*remise*) to/from town US$2.50. Now that the airport has opened at El Calafate, most flights go directly there. There are still regular flights to/from **Buenos Aires**, **Ushuaia** and **Río Grande** direct, with AR. LADE flies to **El Calafate**, **Ushuaia**, **Comodoro Rivadavia**, **Gobernador Gregores** and many other Patagonian airports once or twice a week. Book as far in advance as possible.
Bus Terminal, T442159, at corner of Ruta 3 and Av Eva Perón, 3 km from centre (crowded, no left luggage, *confitería*, toilets, kiosks); taxi to centre US$1, bus Nos 1 and 12 from posted stops around town. For all long distance trips, turn up with ticket 30 mins before departure. To **El Calafate**, 4-5 hrs, US$7-10, **Sportman**, **Taqsa** and **Interlagos**. To **Los Antiguos**, Quebek Tours (Taqsa) daily 15 hrs, US$25. To **Comodoro**

Rivadavia, **Andesmar**, **El Pingüino** (T442169), **Don Otto** (only daytime service) and **TAC**, 10-12 hrs, US$17-21. For **Bariloche**, Don Otto/Transportadora Patagónica, daily, 28 hrs, US$38, *semi cama*.

To **Buenos Aires**, 36 hrs, several daily El Pingüino, Don Otto, Andesmar, US$60-70. To **Río Grande** and **Ushuaia** Tecni Austral, Mon-Sat, at 1000, US$29, 11½ hrs.

To Chile: **Puerto Natales**, El Pingüino, Bus Sur, Ghisoni, 3 weekly, 4-5 hrs, US$9-14. To **Punta Arenas**, El Pingüino and others, 4-5 hrs, US$9-12 daily. **By car** make sure your car papers are in order (go first to tourist office for necessary documents, then to the customs office at the port, at the end of San Martín, very uncomplicated). For road details, see Tierra del Fuego sections in Argentina and Chile.
Car hire Localiza, Sarmiento 237, T424417. Cristina, Libertad 123, T425709. Essential to book rental in advance in season.
Taxi Taxi ranks plentiful, rates controlled, *remise* slightly cheaper.

⊙ Directory

Río Gallegos *p212, map p213*
Airline offices Aerolineas Argentinas, San Martín 545, T422020/0810-222-86527. LADE, Fagnano 53, T422326. **Banks** Change Tcs here if going to El Calafate, where it is even more difficult. 24-hr ATMs for all major international credit and debit cards all over town. **Banco Tierra del Fuego**, Roca 831, changes TCs. **Cambio El Pingüino**, Zapiola 469, and **Thaler**, San Martín 484. Both will change Chilean pesos as well as US$. **Consulates** Chile, Mariano Moreno 136, Mon-Fri, 0900-1300. **Internet** J@va cybercafe (next to British Club on Roca); also various *locutorios* offer internet services, US$0.60 per hr. **Post office** Roca 893 y San Martín. **Telephone** *Locutorios* all over town.

Ruta 40 to the glaciers

Río Mayo (*Phone code 02903*; fuel and hotels **D-E**) is reached by Ruta 22 (paved) which branches southwest 74 km west of Sarmiento. From Río Mayo, a road continues west 140 km to the Chilean border at Coyhaique Alto for Coyhaique in Chile. **South of Río Mayo** Ruta 40 is unpaved as far as Perito Moreno (124 km, high-clearance advised). There is no public transport and very few other vehicles even in mid-summer. At Km 31 on this road a turning leads west to Lago Blanco, to Chile via Paso Huemules and Balmaceda.

Perito Moreno (*Phone code 02963. Colour map 9, grid B2. Population: 1,700. Altitude: 400 m*), not to be confused with the famous glacier of the same name near El Calafate, nor with nearby Parque Nacional Perito Moreno, is a spruce little town, 25 km west of Lago Buenos Aires, the second largest lake in South America. Southwest is Parque Laguna, with varied bird life and fishing. But you're most likely to stop off here to see the **Cueva de las**

Manos (see below). Two ATMs, but nowhere to change travellers cheques. **Tourist office** ① *San Martín 1222, open 0700-2300, T432222/020*, can advise on tours. Also has information on Patagonian *estancias*, in English.

Ruta 40 is unpaved and rough south of Perito Moreno; 124 km south, a marked road runs 46 km northeast to the famous **Cueva de las Manos** ① *US$1.70, under 12 free, a ranger at the site gives information*. In a beautiful volcanic canyon is an intriguing series of galleries with 10,000-year-old paintings of human hands and animals in red, orange, black, white and green. Worth the trip for the setting, especially early morning or evening.

After hours of spectacular emptiness, even tiny **Bajo Caracoles** (*Population 31*) is a relief: a few houses with an expensive grocery store and very expensive fuel. From here Ruta 41 goes 99 km northwest to **Paso Roballos**, continuing to Cochrane in Chile.

Parque Nacional Perito Moreno

① *Free. Park office in Gobernador Gregores, Av San Martín 409, T02962-491477. Accessible only by own transport, Nov-Mar.*

South of Bajo Caracoles, 101 km, is a crossroads. Ruta 40 heads southeast while the turning northwest goes to remote Parque Nacional Perito Moreno (free), at the end of a 90-km *ripio* track. There is trekking and abundant wildlife among the large, interconnected system of lakes below glaciated peaks, though much of the park is dedicated to scientific study only. Lago Belgrano, the biggest lake, is a vivid turquoise, its surrounding mountains streaked with a mass of differing colours. Ammonite fossils can be found. . The Park ranger, 10 km beyond the park entrance, has maps and information on wildlife, none in English. Camping is free: no facilities, no fires. There is no public transport into the park but it may be possible to arrange a lift with estancia *workers from Hotel Las Horquetas. www.parquesnacionales.com, has information.*

From the Parque Moreno junction to Tres Lagos, Ruta 40 improves considerably. East of the junction (7 km) is *Hotel Las Horquetas* (closed) and 15 km beyond is Tamel Aike village (police station, water). After another 34 km Ruta 40 turns sharply southwest, but if you need fuel before Tres Lagos, you must make a 72 km detour to Gobernador Gregores (always carry spare). At **Tres Lagos** a track turns off northwest to Lago San Martín. From Tres Lagos Ruta 40 deteriorates again and remains very rugged until the turnoff to the Fitz Roy sector of Parque Nacional Los Glaciares. 21 km beyond is the bridge over Río La Leona, with delightful *Hotel La Leona* whose café serves good cakes. Near here are petrified tree trunks 30 m long, protected in a natural reserve.

Border with Chile: Los Antiguos: from Perito Moreno Ruta 43 (paved) runs south of Lago Buenos Aires to **Los Antiguos**, 60 km west, 2 km from the Chilean border (*Phone code 02963*). **Tourist office** ① *Av 11 de Julio 446, T491261, open 0800-2200 in summer, morning only other times. www.losantiguos.gov.ar.*

● Sleeping

Río Mayo *p214*
L Estancia Don José, San Martín 313, T420015 or 0297-156 249155, www.guenguel.com.ar. Excellent *estancia* accommodation, with superb food, rooms and cabins. The family business involves sustainable production of guanaco fibre.

Perito Moreno *p214*
C Austral, San Martín 1327, T432538. With breakfast, has a decent restaurant, slightly better than Belgrano.
D Belgrano, San Martín 1001, T432019. Unhelpful staff, usually booked by Ruta 40 long-distance bus companies.
Camping Two campsites: Municipal site

2 km at Laguna de los Cisnes, T432072.
Estancias Two estancias on RN40: 28 km south:
A Telken, sheep station of the Nauta family, T02963-432079, telkenpatagonia@ argentina.com or jarinauta@yahoo.com.ar. Comfortable accommodation Oct-Apr, camping US$5, all meals available, breakfast US$3-6, Lunch US$10, dinner US$15, tea US$5-7, English and Dutch spoken, horse treks and excursions (Cueva de las Manos US$80, and others). Highly recommended.
B Hostería Cueva de Las Manos, 20 km from the cave at Estancia Las Toldos, 60 km south, 7 km off the road to Bajo Caracoles, T02963-432856/839 (Buenos Aires 4901 0436, F4903 7161). Open 1 Nov-5 Apr, closed

● *For an explanation of the sleeping and eating price codes used in this guide, see inside the front*
● *cover. Other relevant information is found in Essentials pages 68-69.*

Christmas and New Year, runs tours to the caves, horse riding.

E Estancia Turística Casa de Piedra, 75 km south of Perito Moreno on Ruta 40, in Perito Moreno ask for Sr Sabella, Av Perón 941, T02963-432199. Price is for rooms, camping **G**, hot showers, homemade bread, use of kitchen, excursions to Cueva de las Manos and volcanoes by car or horse.

Bajo Caracoles *p215*
D Hotel Bajo Caracoles, hospitable, meals.

Parque Nacional Perito Moreno *p215*
Nearest accommodation is **B** full board **Estancia La Oriental**, T02962-452196, elada@uvc.com.ar. Open Nov-Mar, with horse riding, trekking. See www.cielospatagonicos.com or www.estanciasdesantacruz.com, for other *estancias* in Santa Cruz: *Menelik* near PN Perito Moreno, and *El Cóndor*, on the southern shore of Lago San Martín, 135 km from Tres Lagos.

Tres Lagos *p215*
E Restaurant Ahoniken, Av San Martín. Has accommodation.
Camping At Estancia La Lucia, US$2.50, water, barbecue, 'a little, green paradise'; supermarket, fuel.

Los Antiguos *p215*
A Antigua Patagonia, on Ruta 43, T491055, www.antiguapatagonia.com.ar. Luxurious rooms with beautiful views, excellent restaurant. Also arranges small tours to the Cueva de las Manos and nearby Monte Cevallos.
A Hostería La Serena, at Km 29, further details from Geraldine des Cressonières, T02963-432340. Offers very comfortable accommodation, excellent home-grown food, organizes fishing and trips in Chilean and Argentine Lake Districts, open Oct-Jun.
C Argentino, Av 11 de Julio 850, T491132, comfortable, restaurant.
E pp **Albergue Padilla**, San Martín 44 (just off main street) T491140. Cheapest, comfortable shared rooms, *quincho* and garden.

Also camping. Sells El Chaltén travel tickets and receives passengers off the bus from El Chaltén.
Camping An outstanding **Camping Municipal**, 2 km from centre on Ruta Provincial 43, T491265, with hot showers, **F** pp.

🍴 Eating

Perito Moreno *p214*
Good food at **Pipach**, next to *Hotel Austral*, *Parador Bajo Caracoles*, or pizzas at **Nono's**, 9 de Julio y Saavedra.

🚌 Transport

Río Mayo *p214*
Air LADE flights to Esquel and Comodoro Rivadavia once a week, T420060.
Bus For **Sarmiento** and **Coyhaique** go from bus office in the centre. Mon-Fri at 0300 Giobbi buses take Ruta 40 north from Río Mayo direct to Esquel.

Perito Moreno *p214*
Bus Terminal on edge of town next to petrol station, T432072. If crossing from Chile at Los Antiguos, 2 buses daily in summer, 1 hr, US$2, **La Unión** T432133. To **El Chaltén** and **El Calafate**, Chaltén Travel, see next paragraph, at 1000. To **Comodoro Rivadavia**, with **La Unión** and Sportman, 6 hrs, US$9-10.

Los Antiguos *p215*
It is nearly impossible to hitchhike between Perito Moreno and El Calafate. Hardly any traffic and few services.
Bus To **Comodoro Rivadavia**, US$9-12, **La Unión** © Perito Moreno, T491093) and **Sportman** (11 de Julio 445, T491333), daily, 7½ hrs, via **Perito Moreno** and **Caleta Olivia**. *Albergue Padilla* sells tickets. To **El Chaltén** and **El Calafate**, via Perito Moreno, **Chaltén Travel**, www.chaltentravel.com, mid-Nov-Apr, every other (odd) day at 0900, US$66. It's an unforgettable 13-hr, 660-km journey over the emptiness of Patagonia. To **Chile**, La Unión to **Chile Chico**, 8 km west, US$1, 45 mins (for routes from Chile Chico to Coyhaique, see Chile chapter).

Parque Nacional Los Glaciares

This park, the second largest in Argentina, extends over 724,000 ha. 40% of it is covered by ice fields (*hielos continentales*) from which 13 major glaciers descend into two great lakes, Lago Argentino and, further north, Lago Viedma, linked by the Río La Leona, flowing south from Lago Viedma. The only accessible areas of the park are the southern area around Lago Argentino, accessible from El Calafate, and the northern area around Cerro El Chaltén (Fitz Roy). Access to the central area is difficult and there are no tourist facilities.

Ins and outs

Access to the southern part of the park is from El Calafate, US$10. Office in El Calafate, Av del Libertador 1302, T491005, losglaciares@apn.gov.ar, helpful, English spoken. **National Park Office** In El Calafate : Av del Libertador 1302, T491005, www.losglaciares.com; in El Chaltén: across the bridge at the entrance to the town, T493004, Jan-Feb 0700-2200, low season: 0900-1600. An informative talk about the National Park and its paths is given to all incoming bus passengers. Both hand out helpful trekking maps of the area, with paths and campsites marked, distances and walking times. Note that the hotel, restaurant and transport situation in this region changes greatly from year to year.

El Calafate and around → *Phone code: 02902. Colour map 9, grid B1. Population: 8,000.*

This town sits on the south shore of **Lago Argentino** and exists almost entirely as a tourist centre for the **Parque Nacional los Glaciares**, 50 km away. An ever- growing number of hotels, hostels and *cabañas* can't quite accommodate the hordes at times in January and February, but the town is empty and quiet all winter. It's neither cheap nor attractive, but the Lago Argentino is beautiful, and the shallow part at Bahía Redonda is good for birdwatching in the evenings. **Tourist office** ① *in the bus terminal, T491090, www.elcalafate.gov.ar. Helpful staff speak several languages. Summer: Oct-Apr daily 0800-2300; low season: daily 0800-2200. See also www.calafate.com.*

For the main excursions to the glaciers, see below. At **Punta Gualicho** (or Walichu) on the shores of Lago Argentino 7 km east of town, there are cave paintings (badly deteriorated). A recommended 15-minute walk is from the Intendencia del Parque, following Calle Bustillo up the road towards the lake through a quiet residential area to **Laguna Nímez** ① *US$0.70, guides at the entrance in summer (likely to be closed in low season, though still a nice area away from busy centre)*, a bird reserve (fenced in), with flamingos, ducks,

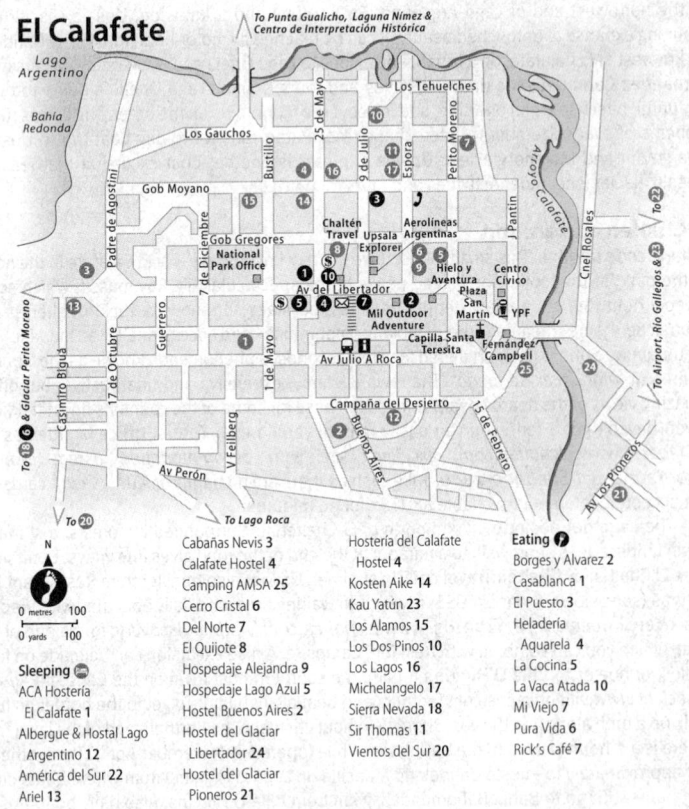

El Calafate

Sleeping
ACA Hostería
  El Calafate **1**
Albergue & Hostal Lago
  Argentino **12**
América del Sur **22**
Ariel **13**

Cabañas Nevis **3**
Calafate Hostel **4**
Camping AMSA **25**
Cerro Cristal **6**
Del Norte **7**
El Quijote **8**
Hospedaje Alejandra **9**
Hospedaje Lago Azul **5**
Hostel Buenos Aires **2**
Hostel del Glaciar
  Libertador **24**
Hostel del Glaciar
  Pioneros **21**

Hostería del Calafate
  Hostel **4**
Kosten Aike **14**
Kau Yatún **23**
Los Alamos **15**
Los Dos Pinos **10**
Los Lagos **16**
Michelangelo **17**
Sierra Nevada **18**
Sir Thomas **11**
Vientos del Sur **20**

Eating
Borges y Alvarez **2**
Casablanca **1**
El Puesto **3**
Heladería
  Aquarela **4**
La Cocina **5**
La Vaca Atada **10**
Mi Viejo **7**
Pura Vida **6**
Rick's Café **7**

and abundant birdlife. **Centro de Interpretación Histórica** ⓘ *Av Brown y Bonarelli, US$2.70*, has a very informative anthropological and historical exhibition about the region, with pictures and bilingual texts, also a very relaxing café/library. There are several *estancias* within reach, offering a day on a working farm, *asado al palo,* horse riding and accommodation. **Estancia Alice 'El Galpón del Glaciar'** ⓘ *T492509, Buenos Aires T011-4311 8614, www.estanciaalice.com.ar.* **Estancia Nibepo Aike** ⓘ *on Brazo Sur of Lago Argentino in the National Park, 55 km southwest (book at Av Libertador 1215 p 1, T02966-436010),* beautiful setting in a more remote area, traditional 'estancia' style with original furniture, delightful meals served and an optional boat trip on Brazo Sur. **'Cerro Frías'** ⓘ *25 km west, T492808, www.cerrofrias.com,* excursion includes one meal and an ascent of Cerro Frías (1,030 m) for great views; options are by horse, on 4WD vehicles or on foot. See also **Helsingfors,** in Sleeping below, or visit www.estanciasdesantacruz.com.

Glaciar Perito Moreno

At the western end of Lago Argentino (80 km from El Calafate) the major attraction is the Glaciar Perito Moreno, one of the few glaciers in the world that is moving. It descends to the surface of the water over a 5-km frontage and a height of about 60 m. Several times in the past, it advanced across the lake, cutting the Brazo Rico off from the Canal de los Témpanos; then the pressure of water in the Brazo Rico broke through the ice and reopened the channel. This spectacular rupture last occurred in March 2006. The glacier can be seen close up from a series of wooden walkways descending from the car park. Weather may be rough. The vivid blue hues of the ice floes, with the dull roar as pieces break off and float away as icebergs from the snout, are spectacular, especially at sunset. ➤➤ *See Transport, page 224, for further details.*

Glaciar Upsala

At the northwest end of Lago Argentino, 60 km long and 4 km wide, Upsala Glacier is a stunning expanse of untouched beauty. It can be reached by motor-boat from Punta Bandera, 50 km west of El Calafate, on a trip that also goes to Lago Onelli and Spegazzini glaciers (with **Fernández Campbell**, see under Activities and tours) . Small Lago Onelli is quiet and very beautiful, beech trees on one side, and ice-covered mountains on the other. The lake is full of icebergs of every size and sculpted shape. **Mar Patag** runs a two-day boat trip to Upsala, Spegazzini and Moreno glaciers. **Upsala Explorer** is another boat excursion that reaches Upsala glacier (see under Activities and tours for both).

El Chaltén and around

(Phone code 02962) This small tourist town lies 217 km northwest of El Calafate in the north of the park, at the foot of the jagged peaks of the spectacular Fitz Roy massif, which soars steeply from the Patagonian steppe, its sides too steep for snow to stick. Chaltén is the Tehuelche name meaning the 'smoking mountain', and occasionally at sunrise the mountains are briefly lit up bright red for a few seconds, a phenomenon known as the 'sunrise of fire', or *'amanecer de fuego'*. The town is windy, expensive and unattractive, but offers amazing views of the nearby peaks and it's the base for some of the country's finest trekking. If you haven't got a tent, you can easily rent all you'll need. **Tourist office** ⓘ *Güemes 21, T493011, www.elchalten.com, excellent site with accommodation listed, Mon-Fri 0900-2000, Sat-Sun 1300-2000.* Take cash as there are no banks or ATMs. Credit cards are not accepted. Internet is available at US$2 for 30 minutes.

The **Lago del Desierto,** 37 km north of El Chaltén, is surrounded by forests, a stunning virgin landscape. A short walk to a mirador at the end of the road gives fine views. Excursions from El Chaltén by **Chaltén Travel** daily in summer, US$12; also transfer from **Restaurant Las Lengas** (see below), T493023, US$10, with 2-hr waiting time, and daily boat trips with **Viedma Discovery** i *Güemes s/n, T493103, www.elchalten.com/viedmadiscovery,* to the end of the lake, which you can combine with trekking. Campsite. A nice excursion can be made on foot, cycles, or horses to **Villa O'Higgins** (Chile), the southernmost town on the Carretera Austral (check at www.villaohiggins.com for tours and boat availability). To get to the border on foot, walk up a path alongside the east shores 4½ hours to reach the northern end of the lake, from where is a 2-hour walk up to the border with Chile (open only November-April). Then, other 15 km approximately to Puesto Candelario Mancilla on Lago O'Higgins, from where boats cross in 3 hours, US$30 to Bahía Bahamóndez, 7 km from Villa O'Higgins. Also daily boat trips on

> **❝❞** Chaltén is the Tehuelche name meaning the 'smoking mountain', and occasionally at sunrise the mountains are briefly lit up bright red for a few seconds, a phenomenon known as the 'sunrise of fire'...

Lago Viedma to pass Glaciar Viedma, with ice trekking optional in the day-long tour (with **Viedma Discovery**). The *estancia Hostería El Pilar* (see Sleeping) is a base for trekking up Río Blanco or Río Eléctrico, or try the multi activity adventure circuit. Highly recommended.

Trekking and climbing

Trekking The two most popular walks are to **1) Laguna Torre** (three hours each way). After 1-1½ hours you'll come to Mirador Laguna Torre with great view of Cerro Torre and Fitz Roy, and 1¼ hours more to busy Camping De Agostini near the lake, where you have fantastic views. **2) Laguna de Los Tres** (four hours each way). Walk 1¼ hours up to Camping Capri, great views of Fitz Roy, then another hour to Camping Poincenot. Just beyond it is Camping Río Blanco (only for climbers, registration at the National Park office required). From Río Blanco you can walk another hour, very steep, to Laguna de los Tres where you'll get a spectacular view (not a good walk if it's cloudy). You can connect the two paths by taking one that takes about two hours and branches off south, northwest of Laguna Capri, passes by Lagunas Madre e Hija and reaches the path to Laguna Torre, west of the Mirador. This may be too long for a day. From El Chaltén to Laguna Torre along this route takes about seven hours. **3) Loma del Pliegue Tumbado** (four hours each way). To a viewpoint where you can see both cordons and Lago Viedma: marked path from Park Ranger's office, a good day walk, best in clear weather. **4) Laguna Toro** (seven hours each way). For more experienced trekkers, to wild glacial lake. **5) Up Río Blanco to Piedra del Fraile** (seven hours each way, two hours each way from the road to Lago del Desierto). A beautiful walk out of the National Park to campsite with facilities, and Refugio Piedra del Fraile, neither is free. Recommended. The best day walks are Laguna Capri, Mirador Laguna Torre, both of which have great views after an hour or so. Most paths are very clear and well worn, but a map is essential, even on short walks: the park information centre gives helpful maps of treks. If you wish to buy maps, the best are by *Zagier and Urruty*, www.patagoniashop.net, 1:50,000 (US$5-10); 1:100,000 (US$7.50), updated quite regularly and available in shops in El Calafate and El Chaltén. For trekking on horseback with guides: **Rodolfo Guerra** *T493020* (also hires animals to carry equipment, but poor organization); **El Relincho** *T493007*. In summer **Restaurant Las Lengas** (see below) runs a regular minibus to Lago del Desierto passing by some starting points for treks and by Hostería El Pilar.

Climbing Base camp for Fitz Roy (3,405 m) is Campamento Río Blanco (see above). Other peaks include Cerro Torre (3,102 m), Torre Egger (2,900 m), Cerro Solo (2,121 m), Poincenot (3,002 m), Guillaumet (2,579 m), Saint-Exupery (2,558 m), Aguja Bífida (2,394 m) and Cordón Adela (2,938 m): most of these are for very experienced climbers. Generally the best time is mid February to end March; November-December is very windy; January is fair; winter is extremely cold, but weather is unpredictable and it all depends on the specific route being climbed. Permits for climbing are available at the national park information office. Guides are available in El Chaltén. **Fitz Roy Expediciones** ① *L Terray 212, T493107, www.fitzroyexpediciones.com.ar*. Owned by experienced guide Alberto del Castillo, organizes trekking and adventure excursions including on the *Campo de Hielo Continental*, ice climbing schools, and fabulous longer trips. Must be fit, but no technical experience required; equipment provided. Email with lots of notice to reserve. Highly recommended. **Casa De Guías** ① *Av Costanera Sur, T493118, www.casade guias.com.ar*, are experienced climbers who lead groups to nearby peaks, to the Campo de Hielo Continental and on easier treks. **Mermoz** ① *San Martín 493, T493098, mermoz@ infovia.com.ar*, for trips across Lago del Desierto, including bus transfer, helpful.

El Calafate to Chile

If travelling from El Calafate to Torres del Paine by car or bike, you'll cross this bleak area of steppe. About 40 km before reaching the border there are small lagoons and salt flats with flamingoes (between El Calafate to Punta Arenas it is also possible to see guanacos and condors). From Calafate you can take the paved combination of Ruta 11, RN 40 and RN 5 to La Esperanza (165 km), where there's fuel, a campsite and a large but expensive *confitería* (**D** with bath). From La Esperanza, Ruta 7 heads west (not completely paved) along the valley of the Río Coyle. A shorter route (closed in winter) missing Esperanza, goes via El Cerrito and joins Ruta 7 at *Estancia Tapi Aike*. Ruta 7 continues to the border crossing at Cancha Carrera and then at Cerro Castillo meets the good *ripio* road between Torres del Paine (20 km north) and Puerto Natales (60 km south). For bus services along this route see under El Calafate.

Río Turbio → *Phone code 02902. Colour map 9, grid C2. Population: 6,600.*

A charmless place, 267 km west of Río Gallegos, 30 km from Puerto Natales (Chile), you're most likely to visit en route to or from Torres del Paine in Chile. The site of Argentina's largest coalfield hasn't recovered from the depression hitting the industry. It has a cargo railway, connecting it with Punta Loyola; Mina 1 is where the first mine was opened. There is a ski centre: **Valdelén** has six pistes and is ideal for beginners, also scope for cross-country skiing between early June and late September. **Tourist information** in the municipality ① *Juan José Paso 237, T421679, www.rioturbio.gov.ar.*

Border with Chile

1) Paso Mina Uno/Dorotea is 5 km south of Río Turbio. Open all year, 0900-0100. On the Chilean side this runs south to join the main Puerto Natales-Punta Arenas road. **2) Paso Casas Viejas** is 33 km south of Río Turbio via 28 de Noviembre. Open all year, 090-0100. On the Chilean side this runs west to join the main Puerto Natales-Punta Arenas road. **3) Paso Río Don Guillermo (or Cancha Carrera)** is 48 km north of Río Turbio, this is the most convenient crossing for Parque Nacional Torres del Paine. Open all year, 0900-2300. Argentine customs are fast and friendly. On the Chilean side the road continues 7 km to the Chilean border post at Cerro Castillo, where it joins the road from Puerto Natales to Torres del Paine.

● Sleeping

Parque Nacional los Glaciares *p216*

LL Estancia Helsingfors, 73 km northwest of La Leona, on Lago Viedma, T/F02966-420719 (in Bs As: T011-4315 1222), www.helsingfors.com.ar. Fabulous place in splendid position on Lago Viedma, stylish rooms, welcoming lounge, delicious food (full board), and excursions directly to glaciers and to Laguna Azul, by horse or trekking, plus boat trips. Open Oct-Apr.

LL Los Notros, 70 km west of Calafate on the road to the Moreno glacier, T/F499510 (in Bs As: T011-4814 3934), www.losnotros.com. Exclusive retreat with wonderful views of the glacier, spacious rooms, all-inclusive packages.

Camping AMSA, Olavarría 65 (50 m off the main road, turning south at the fire station), T492247. Hot water, open in summer, US$3.50 pp. **El Huala**, 42 km from El Calafate, on the road to Lago Roca. Free with basic facilities, open all year round. **Lago Roca**, 50 km from El Calafate, T499500, beautifully situated, US$3 pp, bike hire, fishing licences, restaurant/confitería, open Oct-Apr. (Ferretería Chuar, 1 block from bus terminal, sells gas for camping.)

El Calafate *p217, map p217*

Prepare to pay far more for accommodation here than elsewhere in Argentina. El Calafate is very popular in Jan-Feb, so book all transport and accommodation in advance. Best months to visit are Oct, Nov and Mar, Apr when it is less crowded and less overpriced. Many hotels open only from Sep/Oct to Apr/May.

LL El Quijote, Gob Gregores 1155 , T491017, elquijote@cotecal.com.ar. A very good hotel, spacious, well-designed with traditional touches, tasteful rooms with TV, restaurant *Sancho* (from US$10 for 3 courses), English spoken.

LL Kau Yatún, Estancia 25 de Mayo (10 blocks from centre, east of arroyo Calafate), T491059, www.kauyatun.com. Renovated main house of a former estancia, very comfortable, offering only half board or all inclusive packages that include excursions in the National Park.

LL Kosten Aike, Gob Moyano 1243, T492424, www.kostenaike.com.ar. Relaxed yet stylish, elegant spacious rooms, jacuzzi, gym, excellent restaurant, *Ariskaiken* (open to non residents), cosy bar, garden, English spoken. Recommended.

LL Los Alamos, Gob Moyano y Bustillo, T491144, www.posadalosalamos.com. Extremely comfortable, charming rooms, good service, lovely gardens and without doubt the best restaurant in town, *La Posta*.

L Sierra Nevada, Av del Libertador 1888, T493129, sierranevada@cotecal.com.ar. Breakfast included, well- equipped, TV, all rooms with lake views, 'smart-rustic' style.

AL Cabañas Nevis, Av del Libertador 1696, T493180, www.cabanasnevis.com.ar. Owner Mr Patterson offers very nice cabins for 5 and 8 (price quoted is for 5), some with lake view, great value. Recommended.

AL Hostería del Calafate Hostel, 25 de Mayo y Gob Moyano, T491256. Same owners as Calafate Hostel round the corner, small, extremely functional, plainly decorated, with TV, PC with internet and minibar in every room.

AL Michelangelo, Espora y Gob Moyano, T491045, michelangelohotel@cotecal.com.ar. Lovely, quiet, welcoming, TV, breakfast included, superb restaurant. Recommended.

AL-A Vientos del Sur, up the hill at Río Santa Cruz 2317, T493563, www.vientosdelsur.com. Very hospitable, calm, comfortable, TV, good views, kind family attention.

AL-D Hosp Alejandra, Espora 60, T491328. Overpriced doubles with bath, good value **D** doubles with shared bath, no breakfast but you can make your own. Also one flat for 5 with TV. Recommended.

A ACA Hostería El Calafate, Valentín Feilberg 51, T491004, F491027. In need of some renovation, yet good with simple, rather small rooms, restaurant.

A Ariel, Av Libertador 1693, T493131, www.hotelariel.com.ar. Modern, functional, well maintained, TV, with breakfast.

A-C Cerro Cristal, Gob Gregores 989, T491088, www.cerrocristalhotel.com.ar. Comfortable, quiet, free internet and TV, breakfast included, very good value in low season.

B Los Lagos, 25 de Mayo 220, T491170, loslagos@cotecal.com.ar. Very comfortable, cheerful, breakfast included, TV; good value.

B Sir Thomas, Espora 257, T492220, hospedajesirthomas@cotecal.com.ar. Modern, comfortable wood-lined rooms, breakfast extra.

B-F pp Albergue y Hostal Lago Argentino, Campaña del Desierto 1050-61 (near bus terminal), T491423, hostellagoargentino@ cotecal.com.ar. **F** pp shared dorms with kitchen facilities, too few showers when full, nice atmosphere, good flats and **B** doubles with breakfast on a neat garden.

C del Norte, Los Gauchos 813, T491117, delnorte@cotecal.com.ar. Open all year, kitchen facilities, quite comfortable rooms with or without bath, breakfast extra, owner organizes tours (*Cal-Tur* agency).

C Posada Nakel Yenú, Pto. San Julian 244, T493711. Price includes breakfast, also has apartments (**A**), AHC member, www.argentinahostels.com.

E pp América del Sur, up the hill on C Puerto Deseado, access from Col Rosales east of Arroyo Calafate, T493525, www.americahostel.com.ar. Panoramic views from this comfortable, relaxed hostel, welcoming, well-heated rooms, with breakfast (**E** pp dorms for 4, **B** doubles with views, one room adapted for wheelchair users), chill-out area, fireplace, internet access, kitchen facilities. Warmly recommended.

E pp Calafate Hostel, Gob Moyano 1226, 400 m from bus terminal, T492450, www.calafate hostels.com. A huge log cabin with good rooms: **E** pp dorms with or without bath, breakfast extra, **B** doubles with bath and breakfast. Kitchen facilities, internet access, lively sitting area. Book a month ahead for Jan-Feb and call ahead for free shuttle from airport, HI discounts, helpful travel agency, Chaltén Travel (see below).

E pp Hosp Lago Azul, Perito Moreno 83, T491419. Charming Sra Echeverría and her husband Horacio, a Calafate pioneer, offer traditional Patagonian hospitality, 2 rooms for 3, shared bath. Highly recommended.

E Hostel Buenos Aires, Buenos Aires 296, 200 m from terminal, T491147. Homely, quiet, kind owner, comfortable **B** doubles with bath and breakfast, **C** doubles without bath, **E** pp dorms for up to 8, no breakfast, kitchen facilities, helpful, good hot showers, luggage store.

E pp Hostel del Glaciar 'Libertador', Av del Libertador 587 (next to the bridge), T491792, www.glaciar.com. HI discounts, open year round. Smaller and pricier than 'Pioneros', rooms are good and well-heated, all with own bath (**E** pp dorms for 4 and **AL** doubles), breakfast extra, cooking facilities, internet access. Free transfer from bus terminal. Owners run **Patagonia Backpackers** (see below under Activities and tours).

E pp Hostel del Glaciar 'Pioneros', Los Pioneros 251, T/F491243, www.glaciar.com. Discount for HI members, open mid Sep to mid Apr. Accommodation for all budgets: standard **B** doubles (also for 3 and 4) with bath, superior **A** doubles with bath, shared dorms up to 4 beds, **E** pp. Many languages spoken, lots of bathrooms, internet access, kitchen facilities, no breakfast, free shuttle from bus terminal. Very popular, so book well in advance and double-check. *Punto de Encuentro* restaurant with some vegetarian options. Owners run **Patagonia Backpackers** (see below under Activities and tours).

E Los Dos Pinos, 9 de Julio 358, T491271, losdospinos@cotecal.com.ar. Popular place ranging from basic dorms (**F** pp), rather cramped and no heating, to good *cabañas* for 6 or 7(**AL**), tiny little studio flats, very good value, for 2 (**A**) and a campsite (**F** pp), all sharing the friendly TV room where you can cook, tours to glacier.

El Chaltén *p218*
In high season places are likely to be full: book ahead. Most places close in low season.
L El Pilar (see above), T/F493002, www.hosterielpilar.com.ar. Country house in a spectacular setting at the meeting of Ríos Blanco and de las Vueltas, with clear views of Fitz Roy. A chance to sample the simple life with access to less-visited northern part of the park. Simple comfortable rooms, great food, very special. Owner Marcelo Pagani is an experienced mountain guide.
L Hostería El Puma, Lionel Terray 212, T493095, www.elchalten.com/elpuma. A little apart, splendid views, lounge with log fire, tasteful stylish furnishings, comfortable, transfers and big American breakfast included. Can also arrange tours through their excellent agency Fitz Roy Expeditions, see Climbing, above. Recommended.
L Hostería Posada Lunajuim, Trevisán s/n, T/F493047, www.elchalten.com/lunajuim. Stylish yet relaxed, comfortable (duvets on the beds!), lounge with wood fire, with full American breakfast. Recommended.
AL Fitz Roy Inn, Av San Martín, T493062, caltur@cotecal.com.ar. Overpriced place with pleasant rooms, often filled with package tour clients, breakfast included. Also restaurant and travel agency Cal Tur.
B Hospedaje La Base, Lago del Desierto s/n, T493031. Good rooms for 2, 3 and 4, all with bath, tiny kitchen, self service breakfast included, great video lounge. Recommended.
B-C Nothofagus, Hensen s/n, T493087, www.elchalten.com/nothofagus. Cosy bed and breakfast, simple rooms with and without bath, good value. Recommended. AHC Argentina Hostels Club, www.argentinahostels.com.
E pp **Albergue Patagonia**, T/F493019, www.elchalten.com/patagonia. HI-affiliated, small, rooms for 4, 5, or 6, kitchen, video room, bike hire, laundry. Information on Chaltén, also run excursions to Lago del Desierto.
E pp **Albergue Rancho Grande**, San Martín s/n, T493005, rancho@cotecal.com.ar. HI-affiliated, in a great position at the end of town with good open views and attractive restaurant and lounge, accommodates huge numbers of trekkers in rooms for 4, with shared bath, breakfast extra. Also **B** doubles, breakfast extra. Helpful, English

spoken. Recommended. Reservations in Calafate Hostel/Chaltén Travel, Calafate.
E pp **Cóndor de los Andes**, Av Río de las Vueltas y Halvorsen, T493101, www.condordelosandes.com. Nice little rooms for up to 6 with bath, sheets included, breakfast US$2, laundry service, library, kitchen, quiet.
Camping Camping Madsen, northern end of town, free, no facilities, and **El Refugio**, off San Martín just before Rancho Grande (US$3 pp plus US$2 for hot shower). A gas/alcohol stove is essential for camping as open fires are prohibited in campsites in of the National Park. Take plenty of warm clothes and a good sleeping bag. It is possible to rent equipment in El Chaltén, ask at park office or Rancho Grande.
In the National Park Confluencia, Poincenot, Capri, Laguna Toro, De Agostini. None has services, all river water is drinkable. Pack up all rubbish and take it back to town, do not wash within 70 m of rivers. Camping Piedra del Fraile on Río Eléctrico is behind park boundary, privately owned, has facilities.

Río Turbio *p220*
C Hostería Capipe, Dufour, 9 km from town, T482935, www.hosteriacapipe.com.ar.
C De La Frontera, 4 km from Rio Turbio, Paraje Mina 1, T421979. The most recommendable.
C Nazó, Gob Moyano 464, T421800, nazo@oyikil.com.ar. In town.

🍴 Eating

El Calafate *p217, map p217*
🍴🍴 **El Puesto**, Gob Moyano y 9 de Julio, T491620. Tasty thin-crust pizzas in a cosy old house. Pricier regional meals and takeaway. Recommended.
🍴🍴 **La Cocina**, Av del Libertador 1245. Good pizza and pasta, including a large variety of pancakes.
🍴🍴 **La Vaca Atada**, Av del Libertador 1176. Good homemade pastas and more elaborate and expensive dishes based on trout and king crab.
🍴🍴 **Mi Viejo**, Av del Libertador 1111. Popular *parrilla*, US$5.50 for grilled lamb.
🍴🍴 **Pura Vida**, Av Libertador 2000 block, near C 17. Comfortable sofas, homemade Argentine food, vegetarian options, lovely atmosphere, lake view. Recommended.
🍴🍴 **Rick's Café**, Av del Libertador 1091. Lively *parrilla* with good atmosphere.
🍴 **Universo**, Av del Libertador y 9 de Julio. Unpretentious and modest as El Calafate used to be. Good basic meals.

🍴 *For an explanation of the sleeping and eating price codes used in this guide, see inside the front cover. Other relevant information is found in Essentials pages 68-69.*

Cafés

Borges y Alvarez, Av del Libertador 1015 (Galería de los Gnomos). A lively café/bookshop, open till 0100, good place to hang out.
Casablanca, 25 de Mayo y Av del Libertador. Jolly place for omelettes, hamburgers, vegetarian, US$7 for steak and chips.
Heladería Aquarela, Av del Libertador 1177. The best ice cream - try the *calafate*.

El Chaltén *p218*
There's nowhere really cheap to eat.
♯ **Estepa**, Cerro Solo y Antonio Rojo. Small, intimate place with good, varied meals.
♯ **Pangea**, Lago del Desierto y San Martín. Open for lunch and dinner, drinks and coffee, calm, good music, varied menu. Recommended.
♯ **Patagonicus**, Güemes y Madsen. Lovely warm place with salads, *pastas caseras* and fabulous pizzas for 2, US$3-8, open midday to midnight. Recommended.
♯ **Ruca Mahuida**, Lionel Terray s/n. Widely regarded as the best restaurant with imaginative and well prepared food.
♯ **Zaffarancho** (behind Rancho Grande), bar-restaurant, good range and reasonably priced.
♮ **Fuegia**, San Martín s/n. Pastas, trout, meat and vegetarian dishes. Dinner only, recommended.
♮ **Josh Aike**. Excellent *confitería*, homemade food, beautiful building. Recommended.
♮ **Las Lengas**, Viedma y Güemes, opposite tourist office, cheaper than most. Plentiful meals, basic pastas and meat dishes. US$3 for meal of the day. Owner runs a minibus to Lago del Desierto.
♮ **Domo Blanco**, Costanera y De Agostini, and Güemes y Río de las Vueltas. Delicious ice cream.

Río Turbio *p220*
♮ **Restaurant El Ringo**, near bus terminal, will shelter you from the wind.

⊙ Bars and clubs

El Chaltén *p218*
Cervecería Bodegón El Chaltén, San Martín s/n. Brews its own excellent beer, also pizzas, *empanadas*, coffee and cakes.

○ Shopping

El Calafate *p217, map p217*
La Anónima. Supermarket Av del Libertador y Perito Moreno.

El Chaltén *p218*
El Gringuito, Av Antonio Rojo, has the best choice. **Stella Maris**, small supermarket on San Martín y Lago del Desierto. Fuel is available next to the bridge.

▲ Activities and tours

El Calafate *p217, map p217*
Most agencies charge the same rates for excursions.
Chaltén Travel, Av del Libertador 1174, T492212 (in Bs As T011-4326 7282), www.chalten travel.com. Most helpful, huge range of tours: glaciers, *estancias*, trekking, and bus to El Chaltén. Also sell tickets along the Ruta 40 to Perito Moreno and Los Antiguos, departures mid-Nov-Apr on even days, US$66 transport only, English spoken.
Fernández Campbell, Av del Libertador 867, T491155, www.solopatagonia.com.ar. Memorable day-boat excursions to Upsala glacier and Lago Onelli (and Spegazzini glacier in summer); lunch extra in summer at restaurant on Bahía Onelli, US$60 plus transfer to Punta Bandera departure point. Recommended. Also 45-min boat trip to the front of Moreno glacier from a pier 1 km away from walkways, US$8.50 plus transfer from El Calafate.
Hielo y Aventura, Av del Libertador 935, T492205, www.hieloyaventura.com. Minitrekking includes walk through forests and 2-hr trek on Moreno glacier (crampons included), US$110. Also half-day boat excursion to Brazo Sur for a view of spectacular glaciers, including Moreno, US$40. Recommended.
Lago San Martín, Av del Libertador 1215, p 1, T492858, lagosanmartin@cotecal.com.ar. Operates with Estancias Turísticas de Santa Cruz, helpful.
Mar Patag, T011-5031 0756, www.cruceros marpatag.com. Exclusive 2-day boat excursion to Upsala, Spegazzini and Moreno glaciers, US$165.
Mil Outdoor Adventure, Av del Libertador 1029, T491437, www.miloutdoor.com. Excursions in 4WD to panoramic views, 3-6 hrs, US$35-65.
Mundo Austral, Av del Libertador 1114, T492365, F492116. For all bus travel and glaciers, helpful bilingual guides.
Patagonia Backpackers, at Hostels del Glaciar, T491243, www.glaciar.com. Alternative Glacier tour, entertaining, informative, includes walking, US$26. Recommended constantly. Also Supertrekking en Chaltén, Oct-Apr, 2-day hiking trip, featuring the best treks in the Fitz Roy massif, including camping and ice trekking, US$135. Highly recommended. Also sells tickets for **Navimag** ferries (Puerto Natales-Puerto Montt).
Upsala Explorer, 9 de Julio 69, T491133, www.upsalaexplorer.com.ar. Spectacular full-day experience visiting Upsala glacier by boat, superb lunch at remote Estancia Cristina (vegetarians catered for on request), and excursions to Mirador del Upsala, weather permitting, US$110.

Argentina Parque Nacional Los Glaciares *Listings*

⊙ Transport

El Calafate *p217, map p217*
Air Airport, T491230, 22 km east of town, **Transpatagonia Expeditions**, T493766, runs service from town to meet flights, US$7 open return. Taxi (T491655/492655), US$9.50.
AR/Austral flies daily to/from **Buenos Aires**. Many more flights in summer to **Bariloche**, **Ushuaia** and **Trelew** (office at 9 de Julio 57, T492815). **LADE** flies to **Ushuaia**, **Comodoro Rivadavia**, **Río Gallegos** and **Esquel** (office at Julio A Roca 1004, Loc 4, T491262). To **Puerto Natales Aerovías** Dap Nov-Mar only, representatives at **Aventura Andina**, Av del Libertador 761, T491726. Airport tax US$6.
Bus Terminal on Roca 1004, 1 block up stairs from Av del Libertador. To **Perito Moreno** glacier daily with **Taqsa** (T491843) or **Cal-Tur** (T491842), US$10. To **El Chaltén** daily with **Taqsa**, **Chaltén Travel** (T492212, at 0800), **Los Glaciares**, **Cal-Tur**, 4-5 hrs, US$32 return. To **Río Gallegos** daily with **Sportman** (T02966-15 464841), **Taqsa**, **Interlagos/Pingüino** (T491179), 4 hrs, US$7-10. To **Ushuaia** and **Bariloche** take bus to Río Gallegos for connections: **Taqsa** runs a 0300 service for the best connections; check first. Taxi (*remise*) to **Río Gallegos**, with Remises Perito Moreno, T491745, 4 hrs, US$135 irrespective of number of passengers, up to 4 people.
Direct bus services to Chile (Take passport when booking bus tickets to Chile.) To **Puerto Natales**, daily in summer with **Cootra** (T491444), via Río Turbio, 7 hrs, or with **Turismo Zaahj** (T491631), Wed, Fri, Sun, US$17 (advance booking recommended, tedious border crossing). **Note**: Argentine pesos cannot be exchanged in Torres del Paine.
Car hire Average price about US$45 per day. **Cristina**, Av del Libertador 1711, T491674, crisrenta@rnet.com.ar. **Localiza**, Av del Libertador 687, T491398, localizacalafate@hotmail.com. **ON Rent a Car**, Av del Libertador 1831, T493788 or T02966-15629985, onrentacar@cotecal.com.ar. All their vehicles have a permit for crossing to Chile, included in the fee. Bikes for hire, US$17 per day.

Glaciar Perito Moreno *p218*
Boat A 45-min boat trip departs from a pier 1 km away from walkways and gets closer to the glacier's front, US$8.50; can be arranged independently through **Fernández Campbell** (see above) or is offered with the regular excursions. Another boat trip and a minitrekking on the glacier are organised by **Hielo y Aventura** (see Activities and tours for both). In all cases go early.
Bus From El Calafate with **Taqsa**, **Cal-Tur**, US$16 return; also guided excursions. Many agencies in El Calafate also run minibus tours (park entry not included). Out of season trips to the glacier may be difficult to arrange. Taxis US$80 for 4 passengers round trip including wait at the glacier.

El Chaltén *p218*
Bus In summer, buses fill quickly: book ahead. Fewer services off season. Daily buses to **El Calafate**, 4-5 hrs, US$27 return, companies given above, El Chaltén phone numbers: **Chaltén Travel** T493005, **Cal Tur** T493062. **Overland Patagonia** does trips to **Bariloche** in 4 days, staying at *estancias* and visiting **Cueva de las Manos**, www.overlandpatagonia.com. **Chaltén Travel**, at Albergue Rancho Grande or office on Av Güemes y Lago del Desierto, www.chaltentravel.com, also runs a Nov-Apr service along Ruta 40 to Los Antiguos via Perito Moreno, odd days at 0900.

Río Turbio *p220*
Bus To **Puerto Natales**, 2 hrs, US$2, several daily with **Cootra** (Tte del Castillo 01, T421448, cootra@oyikil.com.ar), **Bus Sur**, **Lagoper** (Av de Los Mineros 262, T411831). To **El Calafate**, **Cootra**, 4 hrs, US$10. **Río Gallegos**, 5 hrs, US$10 (**Taqsa**).

⊙ Directory

El Calafate *p217, map p217*
Banks Best to take cash as high commission is charged on exchange, but there are ATMs at airport, **Banco de la Provincia de Santa Cruz**, Av del Libertador 1285, and at **Banco de Tierra del Fuego**, 25 de Mayo 34. **Thaler**, Av del Libertador 1242 changes money and TCs. **Post office** Av del Libertador 1133. **Telephone** Open Calafate, Av del Libertador 996, huge locutorio for phone and also 20 fast internet places, central but expensive. More convenient, also big and with a café is **Centro Integral de Comunicaciones**, Av del Libertador 1486.

Tierra del Fuego → Colour map 9, grid C3.

The island at the extreme south of South America is divided between Argentina and Chile, with the tail end of the Andes cordillera providing dramatic mountain scenery along the southern fringe of both countries. There are lakes and forests, mostly still wild and undeveloped, offering good trekking in summer and downhill or cross-country skiing in winter. Until a century ago, the island was inhabited by four ethnic groups, Selknam (Onas), Alcaluf, Haush and Yamana. They were removed by settlers who occupied their land to introduce sheep and many died from disease. Their descendants (except for the extinct Haush) are very few in number and live on the islands. Many of the sheep farming estancias which replaced the indigenous people can be visited. Ushuaia, the island's main city, is an attractive base for exploring the southwest's small national park, and for boat trips along the Beagle channel to Harberton, a fascinating pioneer estancia. There's good trout and salmon fishing, and a tremendous variety of bird life in summer. Autumn colours are spectacular in March and April.

Ins and outs

Getting there There are no road/ferry crossings between the Argentine mainland and Argentine Tierra del Fuego. You have to go through Chilean territory. (Accommodation is sparse and planes and buses fill up quickly from Nov to Mar. Essential to book ahead.) From Río Gallegos, Ruta 3 reaches the Chilean border at Monte Aymond (67 km; open 24 hours summer, 0900-2300 April-October), passing Laguna Azul. For bus passengers the border crossing is easy; hire cars need a document for permission to cross. 30 km into Chile is **Punta Delgada**, with a dock 23 km beyond for the 20-minute Magellan Strait ferry-crossing over the Primera Angostura (First Narrows) to **Bahía Azul** (cosy tea room). Boats run every 90 minutes, 0830-2215, in low season, more frequently in summer, US$20 per vehicle, www.tabsa.cl. Some 140 km southeast is Chilean San Sebastián, and then 14 km east, across the border (24 hours), is Argentine San Sebastián, with a basic ACA motel (**D**), T02964-425542; service station open 0700-2300. From here the road is paved to Río Grande (see below). The other ferry crossing is **Punta Arenas-Porvenir**. RN255 from Punta Delgada goes west 113 km to the intersection with the Punta Arenas-Puerto Natales road. 5 km north of Punta Arenas centre, at Tres Puentes, there is a ferry crossing to Porvenir (Tuesday-Sunday, 2 hours 20 minutes, US$45 per vehicle, www.tabsa.cl), from where a 234 km road runs east to Río Grande (six hours) via San Sebastián. The main road from San Sebastián (Argentina) to Ushuaia is paved, apart from the 65km from **Tolhuin** to Rancho Hambre. All other roads are *ripio* (unsurfaced). **Note** Fruit and meat may not be taken onto the island, nor between Argentina and Chile. ▶▶ *For further details, see Transport, page 232. For details of transport and hotels on Chilean territory, see the Chile chapter.*

Río Grande → *Population: 53,000. Phone code: 02964. Colour map 9, grid C2.*

Río Grande is a sprawling modern town in windy, dust-laden sheep-grazing and oil-bearing plains. (The oil is refined at San Sebastián in the smallest and most southerly refinery in the world.) The *frigorífico* (frozen meat) plant and sheep-shearing shed are among the largest in South America. Government tax incentives to companies in the 1970s led to a rapid growth in population; the subsequent withdrawal of incentives has produced increasing unemployment and emigration. The city was founded by Fagnano's Salesian mission in 1893; you can visit the original building **La Candelaria** ① *11 km north, T430667, Mon-Sat 1000-1200, 1500-1900, Sun 1500-1900, US$0.70, afternoon teas, US$3, getting there: taxi US$6 with wait*. The museum has displays of indigenous artefacts and natural history. Río Grande's **Museo de la Ciudad** ① *Alberdi 555, T430414, Mon-Fri 0900-1700, Sat 1500-1900* is also recommended for its history of the pioneers, missions and oil. **Local festivals**: Sheep shearing in January. Rural exhibition and handicrafts 2nd week February. Shepherd's day, with impressive sheepdog display first week March. **Tourist office**, Instituto Fueguino de Turismo office ① *Espora 533, T424326, www.tierradelfuego.org.ar, Mon-Fri 0900-2100, Sat 1000-2000, till 1700 in winter.*

● Sleeping

Río Grande *p225*

Book ahead, as there are few decent choices.
Several estancias offer full board and some,
mainly on the northern rivers, have expensive
fishing lodges: see www.tierradelfuego.org.ar.
LL Estancia Viamonte, 40 km southeast on the
coast, T430861, www.estanciaviamonte.com.
For an authentic experience of Tierra del Fuego,
built in 1902 by pioneer Lucas Bridges, writer of
Uttermost Part of the Earth, to protect the
indigenous Ona peoples, this working *estancia*
has simple and beautifully furnished rooms in a
spacious cottage. Reserve a week ahead, riding
and trekking also arranged. Delicious meals.
AL-A Posada de los Sauces, Elcano 839, T430868,
posadadelossauces@speedy.com.ar. Best by far,
with breakfast, beautifully decorated, comfortable,
good restaurant, cosy bar.
B Atlántida, Belgrano 582, T431915, atlantida@
netcombbs.com.ar. Modern, uninspiring but
good value, with breakfast, cable TV.
B Isla del Mar, Güemes 963, T422883,
www.hotelguia.com/hoteles/isladelmar. On sea
shore, bleak and a bit run down, but breakfast
included and staff are friendly.
E pp Argentino, San Martín 64, T422546,
hotelargentino@yahoo.com. Cheap place
with thin walls, also has doubles (**C**) and
rooms with or without bath, poor breakfast,
kitchen facilities.

● Eating

Río Grande *p225*

♥♥♥ **La Nueva Colonial**, Av Belgrano y Lasserre.
Delicious pasta, warm family atmosphere.
♥♥♥ **La Rueda**, Islas Malvinas 998. Excellent *parrilla*.
♥ **La Nueva Piamontesa**, restaurant and 24-hr
grocery store at Av Belgrano y Mackinlay,
T426332, take away.
♥ **Leymi**, 25 de Mayo 1335. Cheap fixed menu.
♥ **Pope Pizzas**, Av Belgrano 383.

● Bars and clubs

Río Grande *p225*

Epa!, Rosales 445 just off the plaza. Trendy bar.

● Transport

Río Grande *p225*

Air Airport 4 km west of town, T420600. Taxi US$2.
To **Buenos Aires**, AR daily, 3½ hrs direct. **LADE** flies
to **Río Gallegos** and **Comodoro Rivadavia**.
Bus To **Punta Arenas**, Chile, via Punta Delgada,
7-9 hrs, **Pacheco** (T425611) and **Tecni Austral**
(Moyano 516, T430610), US$20. To **Río Gallegos**,
Tecni Austral, Mon-Sat, 8 hrs, US$20. To **Ushuaia**,
3½-4 hrs, **Tecni Austral**, Mon-Sat 1800, US$8.50,
Pacheco, **Montiel** (25 de Mayo 712, T420997) and
Líder (Perito Moreno 635, T420003), US$10.
Car hire Europcar, Av Belgrano 423, T430365.
Localiza, San Martín 642, T430191.

● Directory

Río Grande *p225*

Airline offices Aerolineas Argentinas, San
Martín 607,T424467. LADE, Lasserre 447, T422968.
Banks ATMs: 4 banks on San Martín between
100 and 300. Exchange is difficult: if coming from
Chile, buy Argentine pesos there. **Post
offices** Rivadavia 968. **Supermarkets** La
Nueva Piamontesa, see Eating, above. Norte, San
Martín y Piedrabuena, good selection; also **La
Anónima** on San Martín.

Ushuaia and around → *Phone code: 02901. Colour map 9, grid C2. Population: 45,000.*

Situated 212 km southwest of Río Grande on new road via Paso Garibaldi, the most southerly
town in Argentina and growing fast, Ushuaia is beautifully positioned on the northern shore of
the Beagle Channel, which is named after the ship in which Darwin sailed here in 1832. Its
streets climb steeply towards snow-covered Cerro Martial and there are fine views over the
Beagle Channel to the jagged peaks of Isla Navarino (Chile). **Tourist offices** ① *San Martín 674,
esq Fadul, T/F432000, www.e-ushuaia.com. Mon-Fri 0800-2000, Sat, Sun and holidays
0900-2000.* 'Best in Argentina', very helpful English speaking staff, who will find you
accommodation in summer. Information available in English, French, German and Portuguese.
There is also a tourist office at the port and a desk at the airport. **Oficina Antártica**, at Muelle
Turístico, T421423 (ext 33), daily in summer 0800-1900; Monday-Friday 0900-1700 in low
season, provides general information on Antarctica with a small library with navigational charts.

Sights

First settled by missionary Thomas Bridges, whose son Lucas became a great defender of the
indigenous peoples here, Ushuaia's fascinating history is still visible in its old buildings and

at **Estancia Harberton**, 85 km west (see below). A penal colony for many years, the old prison, **Presidio** ⓘ *Yaganes y Gob Paz, at the back of the Naval Base, Mon-Sun 0900-2000, US$5 for foreigners*, houses the small **Museo Marítimo**, with models and artefacts from seafaring days, and, in the cells of most of the huge five wings, the **Museo Penitenciario**, which details the history of the prison (be prisoner for an hour, Monday-Friday evenings in high season, to book T436321, US$8.50, not for under 15s). There is also an art gallery and an Antarctic hall. During the excellent guided visits (in Spanish only) a replica of the lighthouse that inspired Jules Verne's novel is seen from inside. Highly recommended. **Museo del Fin del Mundo** ⓘ *Maipú y Rivadavia, T421863, www.tierradelfuego.org.ar/museo, daily 0900-2000 (Oct-Feb, Jul), 1200-1900 (Mar-Jun, Ago-Sep), US$3.50, students US$1.70*. In the 1912 bank building, it has small displays on indigenous peoples, missionaries and first settlers, as well as nearly all the birds of Tierra del Fuego (stuffed). Recommended. The building also contains an excellent library with helpful staff. **Museo Yámana** ⓘ *Rivadavia 56, T422874, www.tierradelfuego.org.ar/mundoyamana, daily 1000-2000 high season, 1200-1900 low season, US$1.70*. Scale models depicting the geological evolution of the island and the everyday life of Yamana people, texts in English, also recommended. Centro Beagle ⓘ *Luis Pedro Fique 121, T432090, www.centrobeagle.com, Oct-Mar 1200-2400, closed Mon*, is a representation of Fitzroy's ship, with a model Yámana village where meals are served. Its main attraction is a dramatisation of Darwin's visit to Tierra del Fuego, *La Aventura del Beagle*, one-hour show, full of humour, in English and Spanish. Local events: winter solstice, the longest night with a torch-light procession and fireworks, 20-21 June.

Tren del Fin del Mundo ⓘ *T431600, www.trendelfindelmundo.com.ar, 3 departures daily in summer, 1 in winter, US$17 tourist, US$32 1st class return, plus US$7 park entrance and US$2.50 for taxi to the station, tickets at station, travel agencies, or from Tranex kiosk in the port, sit on left outbound for the best views*, is the world's southernmost steam train, running new locomotives and carriages on track first laid by prisoners to carry wood to Ushuaia. A totally touristy experience with relentless commentary in English and Spanish, 50-minute ride from the Fin del Mundo station, 8 km west of Ushuaia, into Tierra del Fuego National Park (one way of starting a hike).

Cerro Martial, about 7 km behind the town, offers fine views down the Beagle Channel and to the north. Take a chairlift (*aerosilla*), daily 1000-1800, US$3.50. To reach the chairlift, follow Magallanes out of town, allow 1½ hours. *Gonzalo* and *Kaupen* run minibus services from the corner of Maipú and Roca, several departures daily in summer, US$3-4 return. Taxis charge US$3 to the base, from where you can walk down all the way back. From the top you can walk 90 minutes to **Glaciar Martial**. Splendid tea shop and *cabañas* at the base, *refugio* up at the Cerro. Excursions can also be made to **Lagos Fagnano** and **Escondido**.

The **Estancia Harberton** ⓘ *T422742, ngoodall@tierradelfuego.org.ar, US$5, daily 15 Nov- 15 Apr, except 25 Dec, 1 Jan and Easter, museum: US$1.70*, the oldest on the island and run by descendants of British missionary, Thomas Bridges, whose family protected the indigenous peoples here, is 85 km from Ushuaia on Ruta J. It's a beautiful place, offering guided walks through protected forest and delicious teas or lunch (reserve ahead), in the *Mánakatush casa de té* overlooking the bay. The impressive **Museo Acatushún** ⓘ *www.acatushun.org*, has skeletons of South American sea mammals and birds, the result of 23 years' scientific investigation in Tierra del Fuego, with excellent tours in English. You can camp free, with permission from the owners, or stay in cottages. Access is from a good unpaved road which branches off Ruta 3, 40 km east of Ushuaia and runs 25 km through forest before the open country around Harberton; marvellous views, about two hours (no petrol outside of Ushuaia and Tolhuin). Boat trips to Harberton, twice weekly in summer, allow 1-2 hours on the estancia. Regular daily minibus service with **Ebenezer** from Maipú y 25 de Mayo, US$20 return.

Short boat excursions from Ushuaia are highly recommended, though the Beagle Channel can be very rough. These can be booked through most agencies, and leave from the *Muelle Turístico*, where all operators have ticket booths. Trip to the sea lion colony at Isla de los Lobos, Isla de los Pájaros and Les Eclaireurs lighthouse: 2½-3 hours on catamaran, US$20-27; 4½ hours on the *Patagonian Adventure*, US$30 including 1 hour trekking on Bridges island and hot drink; or on a sailing boat *Patagonia Explorer* in summer, 4½ hours, US$40. To Isla de los Lobos, Isla de los Pájaros, Les Eclaireurs lighthouse, and the Isla Martillo penguin colony (Oct-Mar only): 4½-6½ hours, US$44. To Isla de los Lobos, Isla de los Pájaros, Isla Martillo penguin colony, Les Eclaireurs lighthouse and Estancia Harberton: 9 hours round trip on catamaran, US$49, summer only. To the National Park, 5-5½ hrs, US$35-60, includes lunch.

Sea trips: Cruceros Australis ① *www.australis.com*, operates two luxury cruise ships (one weekly each) from Ushuaia to Punta Arenas, via Puerto Williams and around Cabo de Hornos, 4-5 days, from US$1,244 pp in summer (book through agencies); frequently recommended. Ushuaia is also the starting point, or the last stop en route to Antarctica for several cruises from October to March that usually sail for 10-20 days along the western shores of the Antarctic peninsula and the South Shetland Islands. Other trips include stops at Falkland/Malvinas archipelago and at South Georgia. Cheapest fare to Antarctica with ship *Ushuaia* ① *www.antarpply.com, every 10 days Nov-Feb, around US$2,900 pp in advance in a twin cabin (US$2,500 pp for last minute reduction, if available and booked a few days before departure). Book through travel agencies.* **Ushuaia Boating** ① *Gob Paz 213 (or at the Muelle Turístico),* T436193 or 154-59949, operates all year round a channel crossing to Puerto Navarino, 30 minutes, and then to Puerto Williams, 90 minutes, US$100 one way. From Puerto Williams there are frequent ferries to Punta Arenas. At **Muelle AFASYN**, near the old airport, T435805, ask about possible crossings with a club member to Puerto Williams, about 4 hours, from US$80, or if any foreign sailing boat is going to Cabo de Hornos or Antarctica.

Parque Nacional Tierra del Fuego

① *US$7, getting there: in summer buses and minibuses, US$5 return to Lago Roca and to Lapataia, US$7, run by several companies, leaving from the tourist pier at Maipú y Roca and from Maipú y 25 de Mayo. Tierra del Fuego National Park Office, San Martín 1395, T421315, Mon-Fri 0900-1600, has a basic map. Tourist office and National Park office have details and a basic map of park, with walks. See below for Camping.*

Covering 63,000 ha of mountains, lakes, rivers and deep valleys, this small but beautiful park stretches west to the Chilean border and north to Lago Fagnano, though large areas are closed to tourists. Public access is allowed from the park entrance 12 km west of Ushuaia, where you'll be given a basic map with marked walks. **1) Senda Costera**, 6.5 km, three hours each way. Along the shore from Ensenada (where boat trips start). From Lago Roca, continue along to Bahía Lapataia, crossing the broad green river, where there are more short paths to follow. **2) Senda Hito XXIV**, along Lago Roca, 4 km, 90 minutes one way, lots of birdlife. **3) Cerro Guanaco** (1,106 m), 4 km, four hours one way. Challenging hike up through forest to splendid views. Campsite in a good spot at Lago Roca, with *confitería*, it's best to go early morning or afternoon to avoid the tour buses. You'll see geese, the torrent duck, Magellanic woodpeckers and austral parakeets. There are no

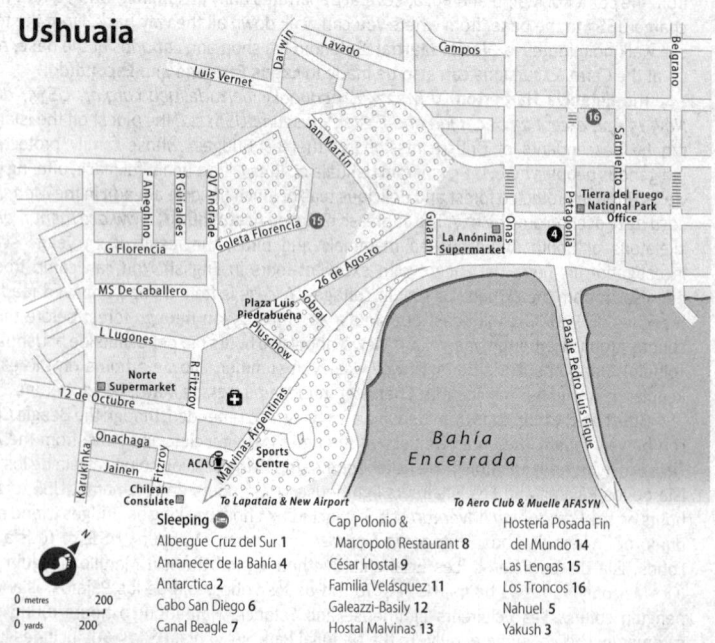

Ushuaia

Sleeping	Cap Polonio &	Hostería Posada Fin
Albergue Cruz del Sur **1**	Marcopolo Restaurant **8**	del Mundo **14**
Amanecer de la Bahía **4**	César Hostal **9**	Las Lengas **15**
Antarctica **2**	Familia Velásquez **11**	Los Troncos **16**
Cabo San Diego **6**	Galeazzi-Basily **12**	Nahuel **5**
Canal Beagle **7**	Hostal Malvinas **13**	Yakush **3**

legal crossing points to Chile. Helpful *guardaparque* (ranger) at Lago Roca. Remember that the weather can be cold, damp and unpredictable, even in summer; winter days are short.

🛏 Sleeping

Ushuaia *p226, map p228*

The tourist office has a comprehensive list of all officially registered accommodation and will help with rooms in private homes, campsites etc. An excellent choice is to stay with Ushuaia families on a b&b basis.

LL Las Hayas, Camino Glaciar Martial, Km 3, T430710, www.lashayashotel.com.ar. Ushuaia's only 5 star, spectacular setting high up on the mountain, breakfast included, pool, sauna, gym, sports, shuttle from town and transfer from airport. Recommended.

L-AL Canal Beagle, Maipú y 25 de Mayo, T432303, www.hotelcanalbeagle.com.ar. Good value ACA hotel (discounts for members), with a small pool, gym, sauna and clear views over the channel from some rooms, expensive restaurant.

AL Cap Polonio, San Martín 746, T422140, www.hotelcappolonio.com.ar. Smart, central, modern, comfortable, TV, free internet, restaurant/café *Marcopolo*, a bit overpriced.

AL-A Las Lengas, Goleta Florencia 1722, T423366, www.maresur.com. A nice setting for a hotel that has seen better days; some rooms with channel views.

A Cabo San Diego, 25 de Mayo 368, T435600, www.cabosandiego.com.ar. Apart-hotel with spacious apartments, equipped for cooking, comfortable, with breakfast. Excellent value.

A César Hostal, San Martín 753, T421460, www.hotelcesarhostal.com.ar. Central, often booked by groups, reasonable value, good rooms, breakfast included, *Restaurant del Angel*.

A Hostería Posada Fin del Mundo, Gob Valdez 281, T437345, www.posadafindelmundo.com.ar. Family atmosphere, comfortable rooms, good value.

B Hostal Malvinas, Gob Deloqui 615, T/F422626, hostalmalvinas@speedy.com.ar. Comfortable but small rooms, small breakfast, free tea and coffee.

B Nahuel, 25 de Mayo 440, T423068, byb_nahuel@yahoo.com.ar. Charming and talkative Sra Navarrete has a comfortable place with channel views from the upper rooms and the terrace.

C Galeazzi-Basily, Gdor Valdez 323, T423213, www.avesdelsur.com.ar. Easily the best, beautiful family home run by Frances, Alejandro and their sons, incredible welcome, in pleasant area 5 blocks from centre, breakfast included, free internet. Also excellent value *cabañas* in the backyard. Recommended.

C Los Troncos, Gob Paz 1344, T/F421895. Comfortable house owned by Clarisa Ulloa, breakfast, cable TV and free internet.

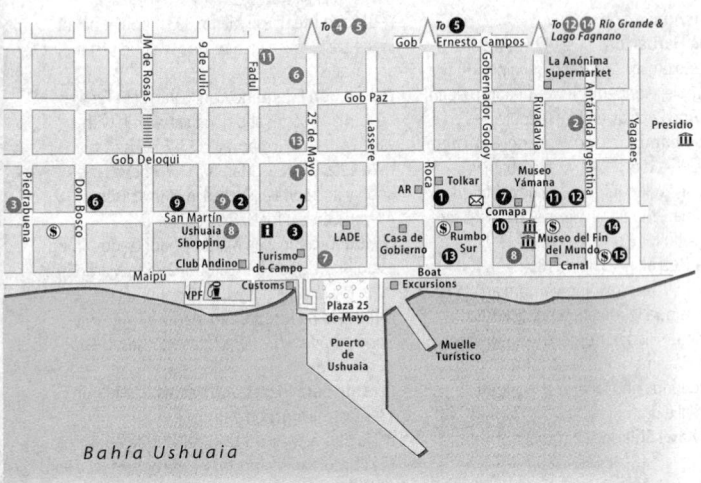

Eating 🍴
Barcito Ideal 1
Bodegón Fueguino 9
Café Tante Sara 2
El Nuevo Galeón 3
El Turco 4

Kaupé 5
La Baguette 6
La Estancia 7
Martinica 14
Moustacchio 10
Parrilla La Rueda 11

Tante Sara
 Pizzas & Pastas 12
Tía Elvira 13
Volver 15

Bars & clubs 🍸
Lennon Pub 8

D pp **Familia Velásquez**, Juana Fadul 361, T421719, almayo@arnet.com.ar. Cosy, welcoming house of a pioneer, with breakfast, cooking and laundry facilities, good.

E pp **Amanecer de la Bahía**, Magallanes 594, T424405, www.ushuaiahostel.com.ar. Light, spacious, shared rooms for 4, but cramped for 6, also good double and triples **C** with shared bath, kitchen facilities, breakfast, luggage store and own parking, AHC Argentina Hostel Club, www.argentinahostels.com.

E pp **Yakush**, Piedrabuena 118 y San Martín, T435807, www.hostelyakush.com.ar. Very-well run, central with spacious dorms, with breakfast, free internet, light kitchen and dining room and a steep garden with views. Recommended.

F pp **Albergue Cruz del Sur**, Deloqui 636, T434099, www.xdelsur.com.ar. Welcoming Italian owner Luca, a nice, relaxed and small house with library, kitchen facilities and free tea, coffee and mate, book in advance, good for smokers.

F pp **Antarctica**, Antártida Argentina 270, T435774, www.antarcticahostel.com. Central, welcoming, spacious chill-out room, excellent 24-hr bar, dorms for 6 and large **C** doubles, breakfast and internet included, bike rental (US$8.50 per day) and the omnipresence of Tino, the dog. Recommended.

Camping On the western edge of town at **Ushuaia Rugby Club** (Km 4) US$2.50 pp, friendly owners, all facilities.

Around Ushuaia p226

LL Estancia Harberton, T422742, ngoodall@ tierradelfuego.org.ar. 2 restored buildings on the channel, simple, wonderful views, heating. Open 15 Nov-15 Apr. Price given for 6 people.

A **Cabañas Khami**, on Lago Fagnano, 8 km from Tolhuin, T02964-156 11243, www.cabanias khami.com.ar. Well-equipped, rustic cabins, good value with linen. Mountain bikes and horses for hire. Price given for 6 people.

A **Hostería Petrel**, RN 3, Km 3186, T02901-433569, hpetrel@infovia.com.ar. Secluded position in forest on the fjord-like Lago Escondido, 50 km from Ushuaia towards Río Grande. Decent rooms with bath, good restaurant overlooking lake, and tiny basic *cabañas*. Idyllic but pricey.

C **Parador Kawi Shiken**, 4 km south of Tolhuin on RN3, Km 2945, T02964-424380, www.hotelguia.com/hoteles/kawi-shiken/. Rustic, 3 rooms, shared bath, *salón de té* and restaurant, horse riding.

D pp **Refugio Solar del Bosque**, 19 km from Ushuaia, RN3, Km 3020, T156 06176, www.solar-del-bosque.com.ar. A basic hostel for walkers, arranges excursions.

Camping On Ruta 3 heading for Río Grande is **Camping del Solar del Bosque** (Km 19), T156 06176, US$2.50 pp, hot showers. **Camping Haruwen**, in the Haruwen Winter Sports complex (Km 36), T/F156 04893, US$2.50 per tent, electricity, shop, bar, restaurant , winter and summer activities.

Camping inside the Parque Nacional Tierra del Fuego Camping Lago Roca, T433313, 21 km from Ushuaia, by forested shore of Lago Roca, a beautiful site with good facilities, reached by bus Jan-Feb, expensive small shop, cafetería. There are also various sites with no facilities, eg **Bahía Ensenada** 14 km from Ushuaia; **Río Pipo** 16 km; **Las Bandurrias, Cauquenes** and **Laguna Verde**, 20 km from Ushuaia.

❷ Eating

Ushuaia *p226, map p228*
Lots of restaurants along San Martín and Maipú. Ask around for currently available seafood, especially *centolla* (king crab; US$14 on average) and *cholga* (giant mussels). Much cheaper if prepare your own meal; **Pesquera del Beagle**, Maipú 227, sells *centollón* (US$3 per kg; US$11 per kg ready to eat) and *centolla* (US$9 per kg; US$18 per kg ready to eat, just add lemon).

♈♈♈ **Kaupé**, Roca 470 y Magallanes. Best restaurant in town, dishes, eg king crab, meat.

♈♈♈ **Volver**, Maipú 37. Delicious seafood in atmospheric 1898 house, with ancient newspaper all over the walls.

♈♈ **Barcito Ideal**, San Martín 393. Popular haunt in the past; now a picturesque seafood restaurant and a café.

♈♈ **Bodegón Fueguino**, San Martín 859. Tapas, homemade pastas and good roast lamb with varied sauces in a renovated 1896 house.

♈♈ **La Estancia**, San Martín 253. A cheery and good value *parrilla*. Packed in high season. All-you-can-eat for US$7.

♈♈ **Moustacchio**, San Martín y Gdor Godoy. Long established, good for seafood. On San Martín 272, there is a cheaper all-you-can-eat branch.

♈♈ **Parrilla La Rueda**, San Martín y Rivadavia. Good *tenedor libre* (US$7) for beef, lamb and great salads.

♈♈ **Tante Sara Pizzas and Pastas**, San Martín 137. Tasty filling food. Also takeaway.

♈♈ **Tía Elvira**, Maipú 349. Excellent seafood.

♈ **El Turco**, San Martín 1410. One of the few good cheap places, serving generous milanesas, pastas, pizzas and beef. Very popular with locals.

♈ **Martinica**, San Martín entre Antártida Argentina y Yaganes. Cheap, small, busy, sit at the bar facing the *parrilla* and point to your favourite beef cut. Also take-away (T432134) and good meals of the day.

Cafés

Café Tante Sara, San Martin y Fadul. Opposite the tourist office, is the best, smart, good coffee, tasty sandwiches.

El Nuevo Galeón, San Martín y 25 de Mayo. Good toasted sandwiches and coffee.

La Baguette, Don Bosco y San Martín. Best fresh takeaway sandwiches, also delicious *empanadas* and *facturas* (pastries).

♬ Bars and clubs

Ushuaia *p226, map p228*

Küar, Av Perito Moreno 2232, east of town. Wonderful setting by the Beagle channel; restaurant/bar/brewery open from 1500.

Lennon Pub, Maipú y Gob Godoy. Good place for a late night drink, with live music.

○ Shopping

Ushuaia *p226, map p228*

Ushuaia's tax free status doesn't produce as many bargains as you might hope. Lots of souvenir shops on San Martín and several offering good quality leather and silver ware.

Atlántico Sur, San Martín 627, is the (not especially cheap) duty free shop.

Boutique del Libro, 25 de Mayo 62. A good range of books on Patagonia and Antarctica.

La Anónima, Gob Paz y Rivadavia and San Martín y Onas. Large supermarket.

Norte, 12 de Octubre y Karukinka. Supermarket, takeaway, fresh food, and fast-food diner.

Popper, San Martín 740. Sells outdoor clothes, camping and fishing gear.

Vraie, San Martín y 25 de Mayo. Lots of clothes.

World's End, San Martín y Lasserre. Books on the area, as well as T shirts and key rings.

▲ Activities and tours

Ushuaia *p226, map p228*

Sports Centre on Malvinas Argentinas on west side of town (close to seafront). Swimming pool.

Fishing

Trout season is Nov-mid Apr, licences US$7 (an extra fee is charged for some rivers and lakes).

Asociación de Caza y Pesca at Maipú 822, Mon-Fri 1800-2100, sells licences.

Hiking and, climbing

Club Andino, Fadul 50, T422335, www.club andinoushuaia.com.ar. For advice, Mon-Fri 1000-1230, 1400-2130; Sat 1000-1400. Sells maps and trekking guidebooks; free guided walks once in a month in summer. The winter sports resorts along

Ruta 3 (see below) are an excellent base for summer trekking and many arrange excursions.

Nunatak, 19.5 km from Ushuaia, nunatak@ tierradelfuego.org.ar, is a small centre run by Gustavo Giró, who organizes eg day-treks to Glaciar Ojo de Albino past Laguna Perdida, US$40.

Skiing

Ushuaia is becoming popular as a winter resort with several centres for skiing, snowboarding and husky sledging. By far the best is **Cerro Castor complex**, 27 km from town, T499302, www.cerrocastor.com. 20 km of pistes, a vertical drop of 772 m and powder snow. Attractive centre with complete equipment rental for snowboarding and snowshoeing. Ski pass US$29 per day. Excellent cross country skiing, with various new centres along Ruta 3 at 18-36 km east of Ushuaia, of which **Tierra Mayor**, 21 km from town, T155 13463, is the largest and recommended. In a beautiful wide valley between steep-sided mountains, offering half and full day excursions on sledges with huskies for hire, as well as cross country skiing and snowshoeing. Equipment hire and restaurant.

Tours

Lots of companies now offer imaginative adventure tourism expeditions. All agencies charge the same fees for excursions; ask tourist office for a complete list: Tierra del Fuego National Park, 4 hrs, US$15 (entry fee US$7 extra); Lagos Escondido and Fagnano, 7 hrs, US$32 with lunch. With 3 or 4 people it might be worth hiring a *remise* taxi.

All Patagonia, Juana Fadul 48, T430725, www.allpatagonia.com. Trekking, ice climbing, and tours; trips to Cabo de Hornos and Antarctica.

Canal, Rivadavia 82, T437395, www.canal fun.com. Huge range of activities, trekking, canoeing, riding, 4WD excursions. Recommended.

Comapa, San Martín 245, T430727, www.comapa.com. Conventional tours and adventure tourism, bus tickets to Punta Arenas and Puerto Natales, trips to Antarctica, Cabo de Hornos and Navimag ferries for Puerto Natales-Puerto Montt (10% ISIC discount for Navimag tickets).

Compañía de Guías de Patagonia, www.companiadeguias.com.ar. The best agency for walking guides, expeditions for all levels, rock and ice climbing (training provided), US$55 pp for a day-trek and climb on ice, including all equipment, transport. Recommended.

Rumbo Sur, San Martín 350, T421139, www.rumbosur.com.ar. Flights, buses, conventional tours, plus Antarctic expeditions, mid-Nov to mid-Mar, English spoken.

Tolkar, Roca 157, T431412, www.tolkarturismo.com.ar. Flights, bus tickets to

Argentina and Chile, trips to Cabo de Hornos and to Antarctica, conventional and adventure tourism, mountain biking to Lago Fagnano. **Travel Lab**, San Martín y 9 de Julio, T436555, travellabush@speedy.com.ar. Tren del Fin del Mundo, unconventional tours, mountain biking, trekking etc, trips to Cabo de Hornos and Antarctica, Navimag ferries, English and French spoken, helpful. **Turismo de Campo**, 25 de Mayo 64, T/F437351, www.turismodecampo.com. Adventure tourism, English/French speaking guides, boat and trekking trips in the National Park, bird watching, sailing and trips to Antarctica.

● Transport

Ushuaia *p226, map p228*

Air Book ahead in summer; flights fill up fast. In winter flights often delayed. Taxi to airport US$2.50 (no bus). Schedules tend to change from season to season. Airport tourist information only at flight times, T423970. To **Buenos Aires** (Aeroparque or Ezeiza), 3½ hrs, **El Calafate**, 1 hr, and **Río Gallegos** with AR/Austral and LADE (longer flights). AR/Austral also flies to **Trelew**, LADE to **Comodoro Rivadavia**. In summer Aerovías DAP and LAN fly to **Punta Arenas**.

Bus Urban buses from west to east across town, most stops along Maipú, US$0.45. Tourist office provides a list of minibus companies that run daily from town (stops along Maipú) to nearby attractions, eg Harberton, Lago Fagnano, National Park. Passport needed when booking international bus tickets. Buses always booked up Dec-Mar; buy your ticket to leave as soon as you arrive. To **Río Grande**, 3½-4 hrs, bus **Tecni Austral**, Mon-Sat 0530, US$8.50, leaves from Roca y Deloqui, book through **Tolkar** (address above), and combis **Líder** (Gob Paz 921, T436421), and **Montiel** (San Martín 1547, T421366), both US$10.

To **Río Gallegos**, Tecni Austral, 11½ hrs, US$29 (through Tolkar). To **Punta Arenas**, Tecni Austral, Mon, Wed, Fri 0530, 11½ hrs, US$29 (through Tolkar); also Oct-Apr, **Pacheco**, Barría and Sur, 12-13 hrs, US$35 (book through Comapa, address above). To **Puerto Natales**, Oct-Apr, **Bus Sur**, 15 hrs, US$40.

Car hire Localiza, San Martín 1222, T430739. Europcar, Maipú 857, T430786.

Taxi Cheaper than remises, T422007, T440225. Remises Carlitos, T422222; Bahía Hermosa, T422233.

● Directory

Ushuaia *p226, map p228*

Airline offices Aerolíneas Argentinas, Roca 116, T421091. **Aerovías DAP**, Deloqui 555, p 4, T431110. **LADE**, San Martín 542, shop 5, T/F421123. **Banks** Banks open 1000-1500. ATMs are plentiful all along San Martín, using credit cards is easiest (but Sat, Sun and holidays machines can be empty), changing TCs is difficult and expensive. Banco de Tierra del Fuego, San Martín 396 (also open on summer weekends 1000-1300 for exchange only), Agencia de Cambio Thaler, San Martín 877, also open weekends, 1000-1300, 1700-2030. **Consulates** Chile, Jainen 50, T421279. Germany, Rosas 516. **Internet** Many broadband cyber cafés and *locutorios* along San Martín. **Post offices** San Martín y Godoy, Mon-Fri 0900-1900, Sat 0900-1300. **Telephones** *Locutorios* all along San Martín. **Useful addresses** Dirección Nacional de Migraciones, Beauvoir 1536, T422334. Biblioteca Popular Sarmiento, San Martín 1589, www.bpsarmiento.com.ar. Mon-Fri 1000- 1800, library with a good range of books about the region.

Bolivia

Introduction

On Bolivia's Altiplano you are so far up it will make your head spin. Every day, the highest capital in the world transforms itself from a melée of indigenous markets and modern business into a canyon of glittering stars as the lights come on at nightfall.

Bolivia has some of the most bio-diverse conservation areas in South America: Madidi, Amboró and Noel Kempff Mercado all have an incredible range of habitats and variety of flora and fauna and you should visit at least one on your journey. If you fancy a trek, there are adventurous trails within a day of the capital, while anyone nostalgic for the revolutionary days of the 60s can retrace the final steps of Che Guevara. For a fun bike ride, try one of the most dangerous roads in the world, from the mountain heights to the lush Yungas valleys, through waterfalls and round hairpins – but do go with an expert.

In Bolivia you learn to expect the unexpected. On the largest salt flat on earth, a vast blinding-white expanse, you lose track of what is land and what is sky. At La Diablada festival in Oruro, dancers wear masks of the scariest monsters you could ever dream of. To visit the mines at Potosí, once the silver lode for the Spanish Empire, you buy dynamite and coca leaves as presents for the labourers. Flamingoes feed from red and green lakes rimmed by volcanoes. Dalí-esque rock structures dot the Altiplano. Turn the corner and you can swim with pink river dolphins in jungle waters, or fish for piranhas in the pampas. Before you go home, you can fill your bags with everything from the beautiful autumnal colours of the textiles, to packs of dried llama foetuses, which protect homes from evil spirits.

★ Don't miss...

1 **Isla del Sol** Take a boat trip on Lake Titicaca to the fabled birthplace of the Incas, the Island of the Sun, and spend a few days walking through tiny villages that seem to belong to another age, page 265.

2 **Coroico** It's only a short run from the breathless altitudes of La Paz to the subtropical, flower and fruit-filled Yungas, but what a run. It's a hair-raising, tortuous 70-km ride to the town of Coroico, and the best way to go is on a mountain bike, page 274.

3 **La Diablada** At Oruro, in the southern Altiplano, a major mining town becomes the scene of one of Latin America's greatest carnivals. Fearsome devils with gruesome masks dance through the streets, page 279.

4 **Salar de Uyuni** The mining town of Uyuni is the gateway to the world's highest, largest salt flats. Beyond are the bright red Laguna Colorada and the jade green Laguna Verde, soda lakes where flamingos feed, page 284.

5 **Madidi** This national park is one of the most bio-diverse regions on earth, stretching from savannahs to cloud forest and providing habitats for some 1,000 bird species, monkeys, jaguar and other cats, page 314.

6 **Chiquitano Missions** Six exceptional Jesuit missions, among Bolivia's finest examples of colonial art and craftsmanship, page 331.

Essentials

Planning your trip

Where to go **La Paz** is the best place to start, as many international flights land here and it is closest to the well-travelled overland routes from Peru and Chile. The capital is easy to explore, but you do need to adjust to the altitude, which will leave you temporarily breathless. La Paz is, after all, the highest capital city in the world. There are some good museums and churches, and an indigenous market area. Daytrips include the pre-Inca city of **Tiahuanaco**, which is close to the beautiful **Lake Titicaca**. To appreciate the lake, a night or more on its shores is recommended. Northeast of La Paz, over the cordillera, are the **Yungas**, deep subtropical valleys, rich in vegetation, where a town like **Coroico** can provide welcome relief from the rigours of the Altiplano. Equally pleasant and lower than La Paz is **Sorata**, a good base for trekking and climbing.

South of La Paz is the mining city of **Oruro**, which hosts one of the most famous Latin American carnival celebrations, including the **Diablada** dance, usually held in mid- to late February. Southeast are the colonial cities of **Potosí**, where Spain garnered much of its imperial wealth from abundant silver deposits and present-day miners scour the mountain for meagre pickings, and **Sucre**, Bolivia's official capital, with an array of fine buildings. **Uyuni** and **Tupiza**, further south again, are the jumping-off places for trips to high-altitude puna with stunning salt flats, coloured lakes, flamingoes and horizons of volcanoes. **Tarija**, southeast of Potosí, is best known for its fruits and wine, dinosaur remains and Mediterranean climate (and thus its nickname 'the Andalucía of Bolivia'). Continuing beyond here you come to the Argentine border.

East of La Paz is **Cochabamba**, Bolivia's third largest city and centre of one of the country's main agricultural zones. The **Parque Nacional Toro Toro**, with its dinosaur tracks, rock paintings, canyons and waterfalls, is a tough but stunning excursion. Further east is **Santa Cruz**, now the country's most economically important (and largest) city, from where you can visit **Amboró**, **Noel Kempff Mercado** and other national parks, as well as follow in the footsteps of Che Guevara, take in **Samaipata**, the country's second most important archaeological site, see the beautiful **Jesuit missions** of the Chiquitanía, or take the train to Corumbá in Brazil. Like its eastern neighbour, Bolivia has a **Pantanal** wetland, just now opening up to tourism, with opportunities to see a magnificent range of wildlife.

From La Paz you can fly into the Beni region, in the heart of the Bolivian Amazon. **Rurrenabaque** is the chief destination and starting point for the fantastic Chalalán Ecolodge in the **Parque Nacional Madidi**, which claims a greater bio-diversity than anywhere else on earth. Outside of Rurrenabaque, the further north you go the fewer tourists you will meet. April to October are the months to visit, although insects are year-round tenants.

When to go The most popular season for visitors is June to August, while some of the best festivals, eg Carnival and Holy Week, fall during the wet season, which is considered to be from December to March. The country has four climatic zones: (1) The Puna and Altiplano; average temperature, 10° C, but above 4000 m may drop as low as -25°C at night from June to August. By day, the tropical sun raises temperatures to above 20°C. Rainfall on the northern Altiplano is 400-700 mm, much less further south. Little rain falls upon the western plateau between May and November, but the rest of the year can be wet. (2) The Yungas north of La Paz and Cochabamba, among the spurs of the Cordillera; altitude, 750-1500 m; average temperature 24°C. (3) The Valles, or high valleys and basins gouged out by the rivers of the Puna; average temperature 19° C. Rainfall in the Yungas valleys is 700-800 mm a year, with high humidity. (4) The tropical lowlands; altitude 150m to 750 m; rainfall is high but seasonal (heaviest November to March, but can fall at any season); large areas suffer from alternate flooding and drought. The climate is hot, ranging from 23° to 25°C in the south and to 30°C in the north. Occasional cold, dust-laden winds from the south, the *surazos*, lower the temperature considerably.

Finding out more Tourism is under the control of the **Viceministerio de Turismo** ① *Av Mariscal Santa Cruz (El Prado) y Loayza, Edificio Cámara de Comercio, p 11, T02-237 5129, www.turismobolivia.bo, Mon-Fri 0830-1630*. They have Centros de Información Turística, **InfoTur**, at international arrivals in El Alto airport (T02-285 2543) and Viru Viru (Santa Cruz, T03-336 9595) ① *0600-2200, English spoken*. They are planning other information centres. See under each city for addresses of tourist offices.

National parks For information: **Servicio Nacional de Áreas Protegidas** ① *Sernap, Loayza 178, Edif La Papelera, La Paz, T231 7742, www.sernap.gov.bo.*Also **Fundación para el Desarrollo del Sistema Nacional de Áreas Protegidas** ① *Fundesnap, Pasaje Villegas 1140, La Paz, T211 3364, www.fundesnap.org.*

Websites

Tourism, culture and general information
www.bolivia.com (Spanish) News, tourism, entertainment and information on regions.
www.boliviacontact.com (English and Spanish) A comprehensive tourist guide to the country.
www.bolivia.gov.bo Government portal.
www.boliviahostels.com (English, French, German and Spanish) An independent network offering budget accommodation in Bolivia.
www.bolivian.com (Spanish and English) A comprehensive tourist guide to the country.
www.lanic.utexas.edu Search 'Bolivia', is an excellent database on various topics indigenous to Bolivia, maintained by the University of Texas, USA.
www.megalink.com Links to other Bolivian sites.
www.noticiasbolivianas.com Here you'll find all the Bolivian news in one place.

www.andes-mesili.com The site of climbing guide and author Alain Mesili, with lots of interesting links to more than just adventure.

Wildlife and nature
www.fobomade.org.bo (Spanish) website of the Foro Boliviano Sobre Medio Ambiente y Desarrollo. For environmental issues.
www.redesma.org site of the Red de Desarrollo Sostenible y Medio Ambiente (Spanish and English) has lots of links to sustainable development topics and organizations.
http://wcs.org/sw-around_the_globe/latina merica/centralandes/ World Conservation Society site with information on the Gran Chaco and on Northwestern Bolivia.

Maps Instituto Geográfico Militar ① *see under La Paz, Shopping, for address.* IGM map prices for topographical sheets start at US$5 original, US$3.75 photocopy. IGM maps were prepared some 20 years ago and do not show trails or passes for trekking. *Mapa Turístico* (good general road map of the country) US$4.40. **Liam P O'Brien** has a 1:135,000, full colour, shaded relief topographic map of the Cordillera Real, US$10 per copy, also a 1:2,200,000 full colour travel map of Bolivia highlighting the National Parks from map distributors (**Bradt, Stanfords**, etc). **Walter Guzmán Córdova** colour maps, 1:150,000, of Choro-Takesi-Yunga Cruz, Mururata-Illimani, Huayna Potosí Oruro-Potosi-Salar de Uyuni, Illampu-Ancohuma, Titicaca-Tiwanaku-Yungas, Nigruni-Condoriri, La Paz department, Santa Cruz department, Sajama and Mapa Físico-Político-Vial (1:2,250,000, road map), available from bookshops in La Paz (see Shopping), US$6.70-7.50. The **German Alpine Club** (**Deutscher Alpenverein**) produces two maps of Sorata-Ancohuma-Illampu and Illimani, but are not available in La Paz.

Visas and immigration A passport only, valid for one year beyond date of visit, is needed for citizens of almost all Western European countries (except Malta), Japan, North and South American countries, Australia and New Zealand. Irish citizens are advised to check with a

⁝ Touching down

Airport taxes A departure tax of US$25, payable in dollars or bolivianos, cash only, is levied on leaving by air. On internal flights an airport tax of US$2.25 must be paid. Tax on airline tickets 14.9%.

Business hours 0900-1200 (sometimes 1230 in La Paz), and 1400-1800 (sometimes 1900 in La Paz). Sat is a half day. Opening and closing in the afternoon are several hours later in the provinces. **Banks**: 0900-1600 (*BCP* 0900-1800) some open 0900-1200, or 1300 on Saturday.

In an emergency Robberies should be reported to the *Policía Turística*, they will issue a report for insurance purposes but stolen goods are rarely recovered. In La Paz: Calle Hugo Estrada 1354, Plaza Tejada Sorzano frente al estadio, Miraflores, next to Love City Chinese restaurant, T222 5016. In cities which do not have a Policía Turística report robberies to the *Policía Técnica Judicial* (PTJ), Departamento de Robos. Police T110.

International phone code +591. Equal tones with long pauses: ringing. Equal tones with equal pauses: engaged. **IDD prefix** 0010 (Entel), 0011 (AES Communications Bolivia), 0012 (Teledata), 0013 (Bolivaitel).

Official time GMT -4.

Tipping Up to 10% in restaurants is generous, Bolivians seldom leave more than a few coins; otherwise give a tip for a service provided, eg, to a taxi driver who has been helpful (an extra Bs 0.50-1), to someone who has looked after a car or carried bags (usual tip Bs 0.50-1).

VAT/IVA 13%.

Voltage Varies considerably. Generally 110 volts, 50 cycles AC in La Paz, but newer districts and buildings have 220 volts; 220 volts 50 cycles AC elsewhere, but check before using any appliance. (You may even find 110 and 220 in the same room.) Sockets usually accept both continental European (round) and US-type (flat) 2-pin plugs.

Weights and measures Metric.

Bolivian embassy before leaving home as there has been confusion over requirements for them in recent years. Many are granted 90 days on entry, others are entitled to only 30. Extensions can be arranged at immigration. Nationals of all other countries require a visa. Some nationalities must gain authorization from the Bolivian Ministry of Foreign Affairs, which can take six weeks. Other countries which require a visa do not need authorisation (visas in this case take one to two working days). You must check with a Bolivian consulate in advance. Visa extensions and costs vary depending on your nationality. If your country is entitled to 90 days but you were given less on entry then visa extensions up to 90 days are free. If your nationality is only entitled to 30 days, extensions cost US$21 for 30 additional days. Extensions are granted in immigration offices in La Paz, Cochabamba and Santa Cruz. There should be a statutory 72 hours period outside Bolivia before renewing a visa but 24 hours is usually acceptable. On arrival ensure that visas and passports are stamped with the same, correct date of entry or this can lead to 'fines' later. If you outstay your visa the current fine is US$1.25 per day. Business visitors (unless passing through as tourists) are required to obtain a visa from a Bolivian consulate. This costs £61.50 (or equivalent); applicants should check all requirements and regulations on length of stay and extensions in advance. A student visa costs £31, or equivalent.

Bolivian embassies and consulates For a full list, see www.rree.gov.bo/inimin.htm

Money The currency is the boliviano (Bs), divided into 100 centavos. There are notes for 200, 100, 50, 20 and 10 bolivianos, and 5, 2 and 1 boliviano coins, as well as 50, 20 and 10 centavos. Bolivianos are often referred to as pesos; expensive items, including hotel rooms, are often quoted in dollars. **Exchange rate** in March 2006: US$1 = Bs 7.97; 1 euro = Bs 10.14.

Many *casas de cambio* and street changers accept euros as well as dollars. When changing money, try to get notes in small denominations. Bs 100 notes are very difficult to change in La Paz and impossible elsewhere. Change is often given in forms other than money:

! Driving in Bolivia

Road A small percentage of Bolivian roads are paved and under 25% are gravel-surfaced. All roads, whatever their surface, may be closed in the rainy season (November- March). Road tolls vary from US$0.50 to US$2.50 for journeys up to 100 km.

Safety Take great care on the roads, especially at night. Too many truck drivers are drunk, almost never dip their headlights, and many private vehicles drive with faulty headlights.

Documents To bring a private vehicle into Bolivia temporary admission must be sought, but is not easily obtainable; a *carnet de passages* is recommended. You must also have an International Driving Permit. Always carry your passport, driving licence and registration documents. Bureaucracy regulations are tight and police checks frequent. If you are asked for a 'contribution' to the police force (*colaboración*), always ask for a receipt (*factura*).

Organizations Automóvil Club Boliviano, Av 6 de Agosto y Arce, La Paz, T243 2231. Check here for any special documents or permits that may be required.

Car hire The minimum age for hiring a car is 25. Rates tend to be very expensive. The rental company may only require a national licence, but a policeman may ask to see an international licence.

Fuel 85 and 92 octane; both contain lead. *Especial* (85) US$0.47, *premium* (92) US$0.60. Diesel costs US$0.46 per litre. Costs are higher in the Amazon lowlands.

eg, cigarettes, sweets, or razor blades. Some larger *casas de cambio* will give US$ cash in exchange for travellers' cheques, usually with a commission (3-5%). *Banco Unión* (at the main branch in cities where they have more than one) gives US$ cash for TCs at 1% commission, minimum US$5, efficient service. If arriving on Fri night, bring bolivianos or US dollars cash as it is difficult to change travellers' cheques at the weekend (in La Paz, try *El Lobo* restaurant, usually changes TCs at any time, good rates, or *Hotel Gloria*, good rates for most western currencies). American Express cards are not as useful as Visa, or, to a lesser extent, MasterCard. In all cities and large towns there are plenty of 24-hour cash machines (ATMs). Those displaying the *Enlace* sign are the best, accepting pretty much every foreign card. See Ins and outs, La Paz, **Safety**, on ATM scams; these are worst in La Paz, but may occur elsewhere.

Cost of travelling Bolivia is cheaper to visit than most neighbouring countries. Food, accommodation and transport are all cheap. Budget travellers can get by on US$20-25 per person per day for two travelling together. A basic hotel costs as little as US$3-5 per person, breakfast US$1-2, and a set lunch (*almuerzo*) costs around US$1.50-2.50. The average cost of using the internet is US$0.40 per hour.

Getting around

Air Internal air services are run by **Lloyd Aéreo Boliviano (LAB)** *www.labairlines.com* (in financial difficulties in 2006, with reduced services and an uncertain future), **Aero Sur** *www.aerosur.com*, **Amazonas** *www.amazonas.com*, and – occasionally – the military air service, **TAM**. Always reconfirm TAM flights as it is phasing out its civilian transport business. LAB offers a 45-day domestic airpass for US$155-250 for four flights between the main cities. Many flights radiate from La Paz, Santa Cruz or Cochabamba. Note that a 'through' flight may require a change of plane, or be delayed waiting for a connecting flight coming from elsewhere. Only on international flights is overnight lodging provided during delays. Insure your bags heavily as they tend to get left around and LAB is reluctant to give compensation. If your internal flight is delayed keep your baggage with you and do not check it in until the flight is definitely announced. There have been reports of theft.

Bus Buses ply most of the roads (inter-urban buses are called *flotas*, urban ones *micros*, also minibuses and *trufis* – shared taxis). You should always try to reserve, and pay for, a seat as far as possible in advance and arrive in good time, but substantial savings can be made by buying tickets just before departure, as there is fierce competition to fill seats. In many cases, buses do not leave at the scheduled time as they try to fill seats and depart up to an hour late. A small charge is made for use of major bus terminals; payment is before departure. In the wet season, bus travel is subject to long delays and detours, at extra cost, and cancellations are not uncommon. Conversely, in the dry season journeys can be very dusty. On all journeys, take food and toilet wipes. It is best to travel by day, not just so you can see the scenery and avoid arriving at your destination at night, but also because drivers work long hours and there is less chance of them falling asleep in daylight. Bus companies are responsible for any luggage packed on the roof. Trucks congregate at all town markets, with destinations chalked on the sides. They can be cheaper than buses but this depends on the amount of competition. Think before hitching a ride as fatal accidents occur, especially in the Altiplano and Yungas regions, where mountainous terrain presents a hazard. **Note**: On election day no public transport runs whatsoever; only cars with a special permit may be on the road. Civil disturbance is not uncommon in Bolivia, taking the form of strikes, demonstrations in major cities and frequent road blocks throughout the country, some lasting a few hours, others weeks. Try to be flexible in your travel plans if you encounter such disruptions and make the most of the attractions where you are staying if overland transport is not running.

Train There are passenger trains to the Argentine border at Villazón from Oruro, via Uyuni and Tupiza. Another line runs from Uyuni to Calama in Chile. The only other public railways of significance run from Santa Cruz to the Brazil border and southward. The new Santa Cruz terminal is amazingly efficient, and has connections with bus lines as well. Always check departure times in advance.

Sleeping → *See inside front cover for our hotel grade price guide.*
Hotels and hostales Hotels must display prices by law (prices listed in this book include 20% tax and service charge). The number of stars awarded each hotel is regulated by law as well and is a fairly accurate assessment of an establishment's relative status.

Camping Camping is safe almost anywhere except near settlements (unless unavoidable). Warm sleeping gear essential, even in the lowlands in the winter. Sleeping bags are also useful for keeping warm on buses in the Andes.

Youth hostels Youth hostels are not necessarily cheaper: many middle range *residenciales* are affiliated to the HI. For information: **Hostelling International Bolivia** ① *C Guillermo Loayza 119, Sucre, T04-644 4071, www.HostellingBolivia.org*. In La Paz ① *Socabaya 457, p1, Hotel Torino, T240 9569*. In Santa Cruz ① *T370 1294*. At affiliated establishments, members usually receive a 10% discount. They also sell the HI card, US$40 and the ISIC card, US$20. Another website listing hostels is http://boliviahostels.com, but they are not necessarily affiliated.

Eating → *See inside front cover for our Eating price guide.*
Eating out In the *pensiones* and cheaper restaurants a basic lunch (*almuerzo* – usually finished by 1300) and dinner (*cena*) are normally available. The *comida del día* is the best value in any class of restaurant. Lunch can also be obtained in many of the modern market buildings in the main towns; eat only what is cooked in front of you. Dishes cooked in the street are not safe. Llama meat contains parasites similar to those in pork, so make sure it has been cooked for a long time and is hot when you eat it. Be very careful of salads, which may carry a multitude of amoebic life as well vile bacteria.

Food Bolivian highland cooking is usually very tasty and often *picante*. Local specialities which you should try include *empanadas* (cheese pasties) and *humitas* (maize pies); *pukacapas* are *picante* cheese pies. Recommended main dishes include *sajta de pollo*, hot spicy chicken with onion, fresh potatoes and *chuño* (dehydrated potatoes), *parrillada* (a Bolivian kind of mixed grill), *fricase* (juicy pork dish served with *chuño*), *silpancho* (fried breaded meat with eggs, rice and bananas), *saice*, a dish of minced meat with picante sauce, served with rice, potatoes, onions and tomatoes, *pique macho*, roast meat with chips, onion and pepper, and *ají de lengua*, ox-tongue with chilis, potatoes and *chuño* or *tunta* (another kind of dehydrated potato). The soups are also good, especially a *chairo* soup made of meat, vegetables, *chuño* and *ají* (hot pepper) to which the locals like to add *llajua* or *halpahuayca* (hot sauces always set on restaurant tables) to make it even more *picante*. *Salteñas* are meat or chicken pasties (originating from Salta, Argentina), eaten regularly by Bolivians, mostly in the morning. Some are *muy picante* (very hot) with red chili peppers, but *medio picante* and *poco picante* ones can normally be obtained.

In the lowland Oriente region, the food usually comes with cooked banana and yucca. The bread in this region is often sweet with cheese on top, and the rice bread is also unusual. In the north lowlands, many types of wild meat are served in tourist restaurants and on jungle tours. Bear in mind the turtles whose eggs are eaten are endangered and that other species not endangered soon will be if they stay on the tourist menu.

Standard international cuisine is found at most good hotels and restaurants. Big cities and popular tourist destinations have an increasing number of cafés and restaurants which offer decent international cuisine at reasonable prices aimed at the traveller market. The best cheap option is always the *comida del día*, served in any class of restaurant for about US$1 and up. Markets are often the only choice for breakfast where restaurants do not open early, but check hygiene conditions. Dishes cooked on the street are not safe.

Drink The several makes of local, lager-type **beer** are recommendable; *Paceña* and *Ducal* are the best-selling brands. *El Inca* is a dark beer, sweet, like a stout, while *singani*, the national spirit, is distilled from grapes, and is cheap and strong. *Chuflay* is *singani* and a fizzy mixer, usually 7 Up. Good **wines** are produced by La Concepción vineyard, near Tarija. *Chicha* is a fermented maize drink, popular in Cochabamba; it is not always alcoholic. In the countryside, look for the white flag outside the houses selling *chicha*. The hot maize drink, *api* (with cloves, cinnamon, lemon and sugar), is good on cold mornings. Bottled **water** is easily available but make sure the seal is unbroken (rain water is sometimes offered as an alternative). The local tap water should not be drunk without first being sterilized. Local water purifier is 'Lugol Fuerte Solución', an iodine-based product, US$1.75 per small bottle; also *iodo* from *farmacias*, US$0.50. For milk, try sachets of *Leche Pil* (plain, chocolate or strawberry-flavoured), at US$0.45 each.

Festivals and events

In Andean regions, **Carnaval Campesino** begins on **Ash Wednesday** and lasts for five days, ending with **Domingo de Tentación** in many small towns. Two weeks before Carnaval is **Jueves de Compadres** and one week before Jueves de Compadres, **Shrove Tuesday** is celebrated as **Martes de Challa**, when house owners make offerings to Pachamama and give drinks to passers-by. Carnaval is celebrated in many cities and towns usually with a *corso* parade with floats and folkloric dances, parties and water throwing. **2 February**: **Virgen de la Candelaria**, in rural communities, Copacabana, Santa Cruz. **Palm Sunday** (Domingo de Ramos) is the occasion for parades to the church throughout Bolivia; the devout carry woven palm fronds, then hang them outside their houses. **Corpus Christi** is also a colourful festival. **3 May**: **Fiesta de la Invención de la Santa Cruz**, various parts. **2 June**: **Santísima Trinidad** in Beni Department. **24 June**: **San Juan**, all Bolivia. **29 June**: **San Pedro y San Pablo**, at Tiquina and Tihuanaco. **25 July**: **Fiesta de Santiago** (St James), Altiplano and lake region. **16 August**: **San Roque**, patron saint of dogs; the animals are adorned with ribbons and other decorations. **1 and 2 November**: **All Saints and All Souls**, any local cemetery. **18 November**: **Beni's Departmental anniversary**, especially in Trinidad. For other festivals on the Altiplano enquire at hotels or tourist office in La Paz. Remember cities are very quiet on national holidays, but colourful celebrations will be going on in the villages. Beware of water-filled balloons thrown during carnival in even the coldest weather. Hotels are often full at the most popular places, for instance Copacabana on Good Friday; worth booking in advance.

Public holidays 1 January, New Year's Day; Carnival Week, Monday, Shrove Tuesday, Ash Wednesday; Holy Week: Thursday, Friday and Saturday; 1 May, Labour Day; Corpus Christi (movable); 16 July, La Paz Municipal Holiday; 5-7 August, Independence; 2 November, Day of the Dead; Christmas Day.

La Paz and around → *Phone code: 02. Colour map 6, grid A2. Population: 1.2 million.*

The minute you arrive in La Paz, the highest capital city in the world, you realize this is no ordinary place. La Paz's airport is at a staggering 4,000 m above sea level. The sight of the city, lying 500 m below, at the bottom of a steep canyon and ringed by snow-peaked mountains, takes your breath away – literally. For at this altitude breathing can be a problem.

The Spaniards chose this odd place for a city on 20 October 1548, to avoid the chill winds of the plateau, and because they had found gold in the Río Choqueyapu, which runs through the canyon. The centre of the city, Plaza Murillo, is at 3,636 m, about 400 m below the level of the Altiplano and the new city of El Alto, perched dramatically on the rim of the canyon.

Ins and outs

Getting there La Paz has the highest commercial **airport** in the world, at El Alto, high above the city at 4,058 m; T281 0122/3. A taxi from the airport to the centre takes about 30 minutes, US$5. There are 3 main **bus terminals**; the bus station at Plaza Antofagasta, the cemetery district for Sorata, Copacabana and Tiahuanaco, and Villa Fátima for Coroico and the Yungas.
▸▸ *For more detailed information see Transport, page 257.*

Getting around There are two types of city bus: *micros* (small, old buses), which charge US$0.15 in the centre, US$0.20 from outside centre; and the faster minibuses (small vans), US$0.20 in the centre, US$0.30 outside. *Trufis* are fixed route collective taxis, with a sign with their route on the windscreen, US$0.30 in the centre, US$0.40 pp outside. Prices vary with demand, they are slightly higher at rush hour. Taxis are often, but not always, white. There are three types: regular honest taxis which may take several passengers at once, fake taxis which have been involved in robberies (see below), and radio taxis which take only one group of passengers at a time. Since it is impossible to distinguish between the first two, it is best to pay a bit more for a radio taxi which has a sign and number on the roof and can be ordered by phone; note the number when getting in. Radio taxis charge US$1 in the centre, US$2 outside.

Orientation The city's main street runs from **Plaza San Francisco** as Avenida Mcal Santa Cruz, then changes to Avenida 16 de Julio (more commonly known as the Prado) and ends at **Plaza del Estudiante**. The business quarter, government offices, central university (UMSA) and many of the main hotels and restaurants are in this area. From the Plaza del Estudiante, Avenida Villazón splits into Avenida Arce, which runs southeast towards the wealthier residential districts of **Zona Sur** and Avenida 6 de Agosto which runs through **Sopocachi**, an area full of restaurants, bars and clubs. In the valley, 15 minutes south of the centre, is Zona Sur, home to the resident foreign community. It has international shopping centres, supermarkets with imported items and some of the best restaurants and bars in La Paz (see page 252). Zona Sur begins after the bridge at La Florida beside the attractive Plaza Humboldt. The main road, Avenida Ballivián, begins at C 8 and continues up the hill to San Miguel on C 21 (about a 20-minute walk). Sprawled around the rim of the canyon is **El Alto**, now a city in its own right and reputedly the fastest growing in South America. Its population of 1 million is mostly indigenous immigrants from the countryside. El Alto is connected to La Paz by motorway (toll US$0.25, motorbikes and cycles free) and by a new road to Obrajes and the Zona Sur. Buses from Plaza Eguino and Pérez Velasco leave regularly for Plaza 16 de Julio, El Alto. Buses to and from La Paz always stop at El Alto in an area called *terminal*, off Av 6 de Marzo, where transport companies have small offices. If not staying in La Paz, you can change buses here and save a couple of hours. There is ample accommodation in the area.

Best time to visit Because of the altitude, nights are cold the year round. In the day, the sun is strong, but the moment you go into the shade or enter a building, the temperature falls. From Dec-Mar, the summer, it rains most afternoons, making it feel colder than it actually is. The two most important festivals, when the city gets particularly busy, are **Alasitas** (last week of Jan and first week of Feb) and **Festividad del Señor del Gran Poder** (end May/early Jun). See Festivals, page 252.

Tourist offices The **Alcaldía Municipal de La Paz** has information centres at: ① *Plaza del Estudiante at the lower end of El Prado between 16 de Julio and México, T237 1044, Mon-Fri 0900-1900, Sat-Sun 0930-1300*, very helpful, English and French spoken; ① *Plaza Alonso de Mendoza, Mon-Fri 0900-1200, 1500-1800* and ① *the Terminal, T228 5858, Mon-Fri 0700-2300, Sat 0700-1500, Sun 1500-2300*. See www.lapaz.bo/paginas/turismo. A private office is at Linares 932, which has a good selection of guide books for reference, purchase or exchange.

Safety Fake police, fake narcotics police and fake immigration officers (usually plain-clothed but carrying a forged ID) have been known to take people to their 'office' and ask to see all their documents and money, they then rob them. Legitimate police do not ask people for documents in the street unless they are involved in an accident, fight, etc. If approached, try to walk away and seek assistance from as many bystanders as possible. Never get in a vehicle with the 'officer' nor follow them to their 'office'. Many of the robberies are very slick, involving taxis and various accomplices. Take only radio taxis, identified by their dome lights and phone numbers. Lock the doors and never allow other passengers to share your cab, the extra security is well worth the extra cost. If someone else gets in, get out at once. The scams often include a fake tourist who first shares the taxi; when the fake police officer arrives he shows his money and has it returned, all to reassure the real tourist who is then robbed. Also if smeared or spat-on, walk away, don't let the good Samaritan clean you up, they will clean you out instead. The worst areas for all the above are the Cemetery neighbourhood where all the local buses arrive, and around Plaza Murillo. Other areas, eg Sopocachi, are generally safer.

Warning for ATM users: scams to get card numbers and PINs have flourished, especially in La Paz. Make sure that nobody is watching or filming you from a distance. You have no obligation to show cards to anyone. The tourist police post warnings in hotels.

See **Touching down**, page 238 for what to do in an emergency.

Sights

There are few colonial buildings left in La Paz; probably the best examples are in **Calle Jaén** (see below). Late 19th-, early 20th-century architecture, often displaying European influence, can be found in the streets around Plaza Murillo, but much of La Paz is modern. The **Plaza del Estudiante** (Plaza Franz Tamayo), or a bit above it, marks a contrast between old and new styles, between the commercial and the more elegant. The **Prado** itself is lined with high-rise blocks dating from the 1960s and 1970s.

Around Plaza Murillo
Plaza Murillo, three blocks north of the Prado, is the traditional centre. Facing its formal gardens are the huge, graceful **Cathedral**, the **Palacio Presidencial** in Italian renaissance style, usually known as the **Palacio Quemado** (burnt palace) twice gutted by fire in its stormy 130-year history, and, on the east side, the **Congreso Nacional**. In front of the Palacio Quemado is a statue of former President Gualberto Villarroel who was dragged into the plaza by an angry mob and hanged in 1946. Across from the Cathedral on Calle Socabaya is the **Palacio de los Condes de Arana** (built 1775), with beautiful exterior and patio. It houses the **Museo Nacional de Arte** ① *T240 8600, www.mna.org.bo, Tue-Sun 0900-1230, 1500-1900, US$1.25*. It has a fine collection of colonial paintings including many works by Melchor Pérez Holguín, considered one of the masters of Andean colonial art, and which also exhibits the works of contemporary local artists. Calle Comercio, running east-west across the Plaza, has most of the stores and shops. West of Plaza Murillo is the **Museo Nacional de Etnografía y Folklore** ① *in the palace of the Marqueses de Villaverde, Ingavi 916, T240 8640, Tue-Sat 0900-1230, 1500-1900, Sun 0900-1230, free until renovations are completed*. Undergoing renovation since 2005, new sections are gradually being opened to show, eventually, the cultural richness of Bolivia by geographic region.

Northwest of Plaza Murillo is **Calle Jaén**, a picturesque colonial street with a restaurant/peña, a café, craft shops, good views and four museums housed in colonial buildings ① *known as Museos Municipales, Tue-Fri 0930-1230, 1500-1900, Sat-Sun 0900-1230, US$0.50 good for all 4*. **Museo Costumbrista** ① *on Plaza Riosinio, at the top of Jaén, T228 0758*, has miniature displays depicting incidents in the history of La Paz and well-known Paceños, as well as miniature replicas of reed rafts used by the Norwegian Thor Heyerdahl, and the Spaniard Kitin

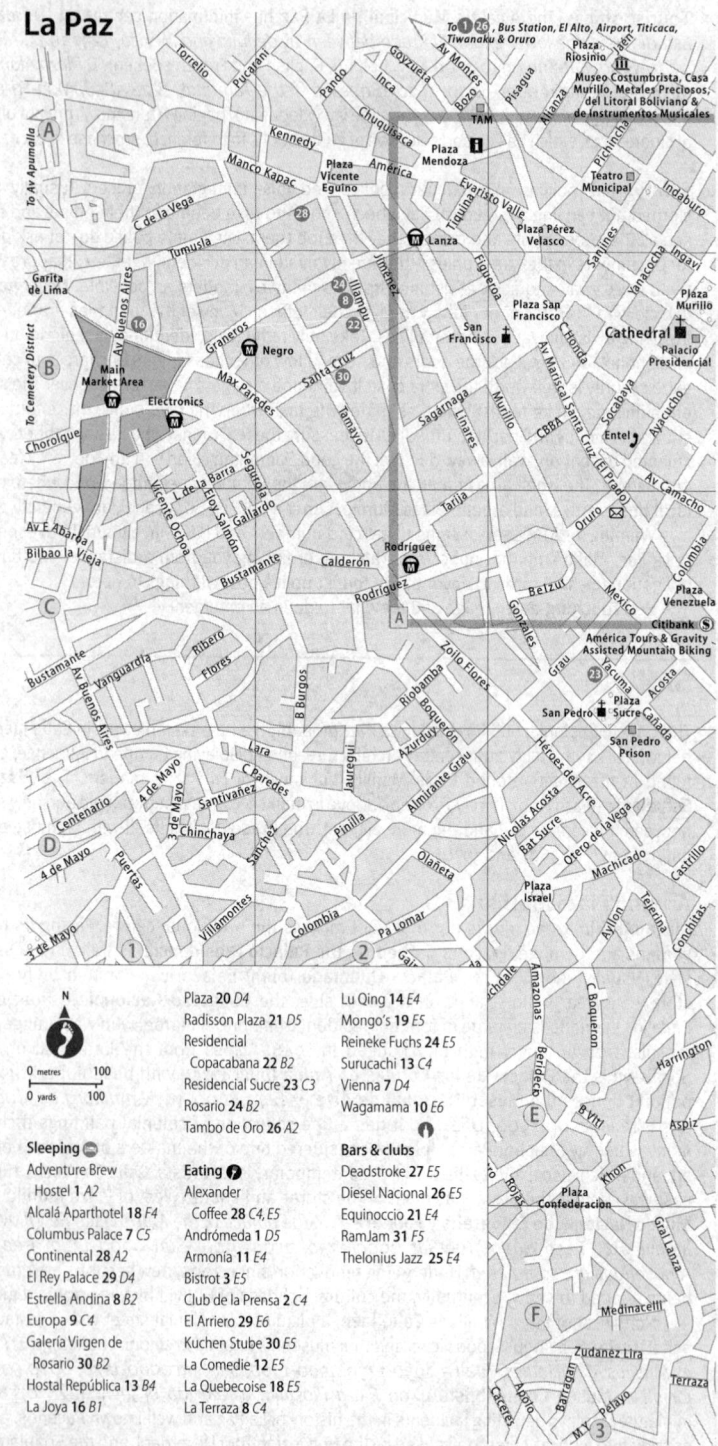

La Paz

To ①, Bus Station, El Alto, Airport, Titicaca, Tiwanaku & Oruro

Plaza Riosinio

Museo Costumbrista, Casa Murillo, Metales Preciosos, del Litoral Boliviano & de Instrumentos Musicales

Plaza Mendoza

Teatro Municipal

Plaza Vicente Eguino

Plaza Pérez Velasco

Lanza

Plaza San Francisco

Plaza Murillo

San Francisco

Cathedral

Negro

Palacio Presidencial

Main Market Area

Electronics

Entel

Garita de Lima

To Cemetery District

Rodríguez

Plaza Venezuela

Citibank

América Tours & Gravity Assisted Mountain Biking

Calderón

Rodríguez

San Pedro

Plaza Sucre

San Pedro Prison

Plaza Israel

Plaza Confederación

Plaza Medinacelli

Bolivia La Paz Sights

N

| 0 metres | 100 |
| 0 yards | 100 |

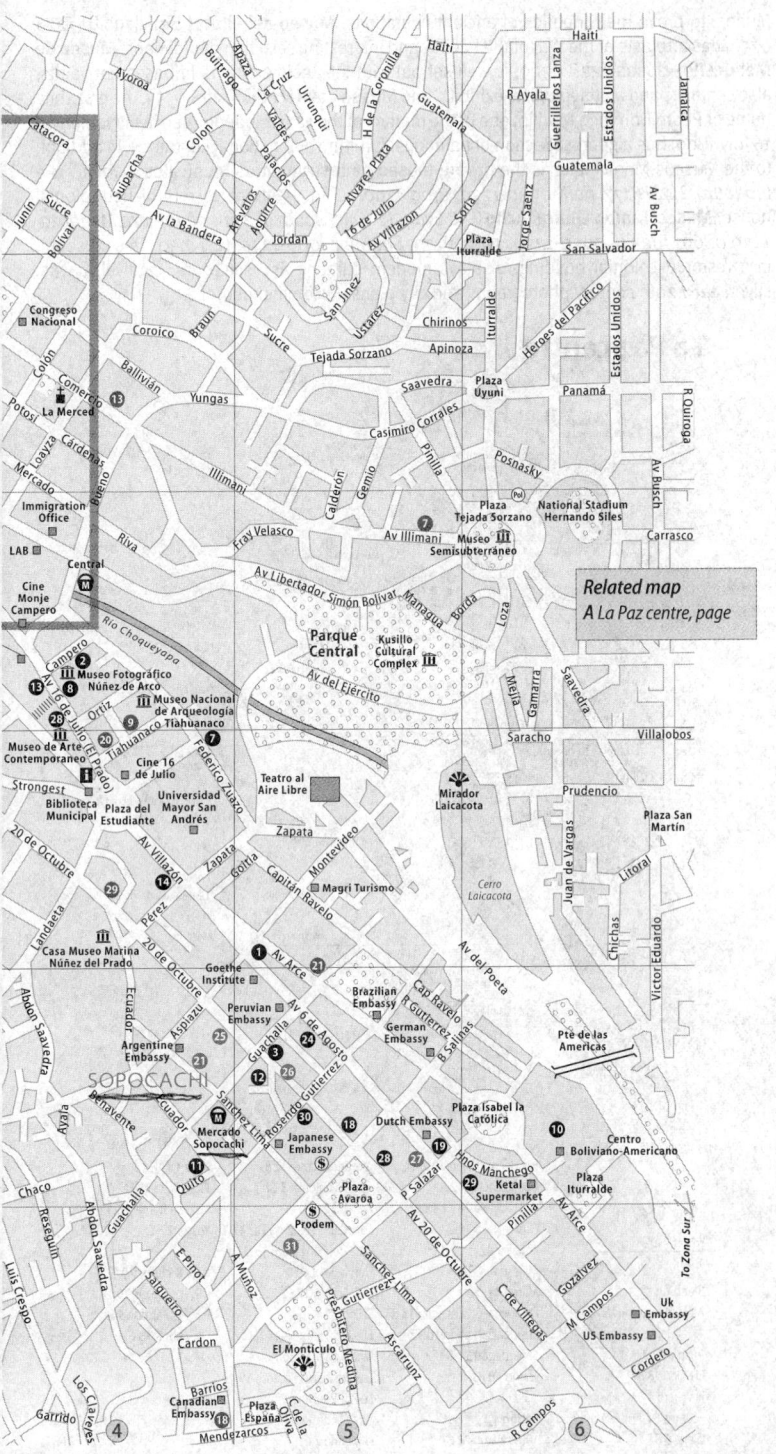

Related map
A La Paz centre, page

SOPOCACHI

245

Muñoz, to prove their theories of ancient migrations. **Museo del Litoral Boliviano** ① *T228 0758*, has artefacts of the War of the Pacific, and interesting selection of old maps. **Museo de Metales Preciosos** *T228 0329*, is well set out with Inca gold artefacts in basement vaults, also ceramics and archaeological exhibits, and **Museo Casa Murillo** *T228 0553*, the erstwhile home of Pedro Domingo Murillo, one of the martyrs of the La Paz independence movement of 16 July 1809, has a good collection of paintings, furniture and national costumes. In addition to the Museos Municipales is the private **Museo de Instrumentos Musicales** ① *Jaén 711 e Indaburo, T240 8177, daily 0930-1230, 1400-1700, US$0.65*, in a nicely refurbished colonial house. **Museo Tambo Quirquincho** ① *C Evaristo Valle, south of Jaén, near Plaza Mendoza, T239 0869, Tue-Fri, 0930-1230, 1500-1900, Sat-Sun, 1000-1230, US$0.50*. This museum, in a restored colonial building, displays modern painting and sculpture, carnival masks, silver, early 20th century photography and city plans. Recommended.

La Paz centre

Sleeping 🛏		
Alojamiento París 8 A3	Majestic 11 B1	
Arcabucero 1 C1	Milton 17 D1	
Austria 2 B2	Président & La Kantuta 13 B2	
El Solario 3 B1	Residencial Latino 10 A3	
El Viajero 4 C1	Sagárnaga 15 C1	
Fuentes 6 C1	Torino 16 B3	
Gloria 5 B2		
Hospedaje Milenio 19 A3		
Hostal Cactus 12 B1		
Hostal Maya 18 C1		
Hostal Naira 7 C2		
Ingavi 9 A2		

Eating 🍴
- 100% Natural 1 C1
- Alexander Coffee 2 B3
- Angelo Colonial 3 C1
- Banais 12 B2
- Café Confitería de la Paz 4 C2
- Casa del Corregidor 16 D2
- Dumbos 18 D3
- El Calicanto 17 B2
- El Lobo 5 B1
- Eli's Pizza Express 18 D3
- Jackie Chan 6 C2
- La Casa de Los Paceños 19 A3
- Le Pot-Pourri des Gourmets 7 C1
- O Mundo 7 C1
- Pepe's 14 C1
- Pizzería Italia 9 C1
- Pizzería Romana 21 B1
- Yussef 22 C1

Bars & clubs 🍸
- Oliver's Travels 20 C2
- Peña El Parnaso 15 C2
- Sol y Luna 23 C2

Tiny treats

One of the most intriguing items for sale in Andean markets is *Ekeko*, the god of good fortune and plenty and one of the most endearing of the Aymara folk legends. He is a cheery, avuncular little chap, with a happy face, a pot belly and short legs. His image, usually in plaster of Paris, is laden with various household items, as well as sweets, confetti and streamers, food, and with a cigarette dangling cheekily from his lower lip. Believers say that these statues only bring luck if they are received as gifts. The *Ekeko* occupies a central role in the festival of Alacitas, the Feast of Plenty, which takes place in La Paz at the end of January. Everything under the sun can be bought in miniature: houses, trucks, buses, suitcases, university diplomas; you name it, you'll find it here. The idea is to have your mini-purchase blessed by a *Yatiri*, an Aymara priest, and the real thing will be yours within the year.

Plaza San Francisco up to the cemetery district

At the upper end of Avenida Mcal Santa Cruz is the **Plaza San Francisco** with the **church and monastery of San Francisco** ① *local weddings can be seen on Sat 1000-1200, the church opens for Mass at 0700, 0900, 1100 and 1900, Mon-Sat, and also at 0800, 1000 and 1200 on Sun.* Dating from 1549, this is one of the finest examples of colonial religious architecture in South America and well worth seeing. The **Cultural Museo San Francisco** ① *Plaza San Francisco 503, 0900-1800 daily (0900-2100 Jun-Aug), US$2.50, allow 1½-2 hrs for visit, guides available free but tip appreciated, some speak English and French*, offers access to various areas of the church and convent which were previously off limits, including the choir, crypt (open 1400-1730), roof, various chapels and gardens. Fine art includes religious paintings from the 17th, 18th and 19th centuries, plus visiting exhibits and a hall devoted to the works of Tito Yupanqui, the indigenous sculptor of the Virgen de Copacabana. There is a pricey but good café at entrance. Behind the San Francisco church a network of narrow cobbled streets rise steeply up the canyon walls. Much of this area is a permanent street market. Handicraft shops, travel agencies, hotels and restaurants line the lower part of **Calle Sagárnaga** (here you find the highest concentration of tourists and pick-pockets). The amazing **Mercado de Hechicería**, 'witchcraft market', on Calles Melchor Jiménez and Linares, which cross Santa Cruz above San Francisco, sells fascinating charms, herbs and more gruesome items like llama foetuses. **Museo de la Coca** ① *Linares 906, daily 1000-1900, US$1, shop with coca sweets for sale.* Devoted to the coca plant, its history, cultural significance, medical values, political implications, this excellent museum has texts in Spanish and English. In the same building as the Museo de la Coca is the **Museo de Arte Texil Andino Boliviano** ① *Mon-Sat 1000-1930, Sun 100-1700, US$1*, a small collection of old traditional weavings (not to be confused with the larger Museo de Textiles Andinos Bolivianos in Miraflores).

Further up, from Illampu to Rodríguez and in neighbouring streets, is the produce-based **Rodríguez market** ① *daily, but best on Sun morning.* Turning right on Max Paredes, heading north, is **Avenida Buenos Aires**, one of the liveliest streets in the Indian quarter, where small workshops turn out the costumes and masks for the Gran Poder festival, and with great views of Illimani, especially at sunset. Continuing west along Max Paredes towards the **cemetery district**, the streets are crammed with stalls selling every imaginable item. Transport converges on the cemetery district (for more information see page 257). See also Safety, above, page 243.

The Prado, Sopocachi, Miraflores and Zona Sur

Museo de Arte Contemporáneo Plaza ① *Av 16 de Julio 1698, T233 5905, www.museo plaza.com, daily 0900-2100, US$1.25.* In a 19th-century house which has been declared a national monument, there is an excellent selection of contemporary art from national and international artists. Rotating exhibits, some work for sale. The new **Museo Fotográfico Nuñez de Arco** ① *16 de Julio 1615, Mon-Fri 1000-1300, 1500-2000, Sat 10-1300, US$1.90* has an interesting photo collection of the early excavations of Tiawanaku and old photos of La Paz and surroundings. Just off the Prado (go down the flight of stairs by the Hotel Plaza) is **Museo**

Nacional de Arqueología or **Tiahuanaco** (Tiwanaku) ① *Tiwanacu 93 entre Bravo y F Zuazo, T231 1621, www.bolivian.com/arqueologia, Tue-Fri 0900-1230, 1500-1900, Sat 1000-1230, 1500-1830, Sun 1000-1300, US$1.25*. It contains good collections of the arts and crafts of ancient Tiwanaku and items from the eastern jungles. It also has a two room exhibition of gold statuettes and objects found in Lake Titicaca. In Sopocachi district, above Avenida 6 de Agosto, is **Casa Museo Marina Núñez del Prado** ① *Ecuador 2034, T242 4175, www.bolivian.com/cmnp, daily 0930-1300, Tue-Fri 1500-1900 (may be closed afternoons and weekends), US$0.75, students US$0.30.* It houses an excellent collection of Marina Núñez's sculptures in the family mansion. By Plaza España, is **El Montículo**, a lovely park with great views of the city. On Avenida Libertador Simón Bolívar, from where there are great views of Mt Illimani, is the indigenous produce **Central Market** (called **Mercado Camacho**). Further east is the residential district of Miraflores where you'll find **Museo de Textiles Andinos Bolivianos** ① *Plaza Benito Juárez 488, Miraflores, T224 3601, Mon-Sat 0930-1200, 1500-1800, Sun 1030-1230, US$1.90*, with good displays of textiles from around the country, detailed explanations and a knowledgeable owner. Outside the Hernan Siles national football stadium is the **Museo Semisubterráneo** ① *Plaza Tejada Sorzano*, a sunken garden full of restored statues and other artefacts from Tiahuanaco, some of them badly eroded from traffic pollution. The **Kusillo Cultural Complex** ① *Av del Ejército, T222 6371, www.quipus bolivia.org and www.kusillo.org, museum hours Tue-Fri 0900-1300, 1500-1900, US$0.75*, features interactive exhibits on Bolivian culture, shops selling native crafts, a Museum of Science and Play and the highest funicular railway in the world (great views).

⦿ Sleeping

Around Plaza Murillo *p243, maps p244 and p246*

L Presidente, Potosí y Sanjines 920, T240 6666, www.hotelpresidente-bo.com. 'The highest 5-star in the world'. Includes breakfast, gym and sauna, pool, all open to non-residents, internet, bar, disco, excellent service, comfortable, good food.

A Gloria, Potosí 909, T240 7070, www.hotel gloria.com.bo. Modern, central, cable TV, price includes buffet breakfast, 2 restaurants, one is vegetarian, excellent food and service, run **Gloria Tours** (www.gloriatours.com.bo). Recommended.

C Hostal República, Comercio 1455, T220 2742, marynela@ceibo.entelnet.bo. **D** with shared bath, old house of former president, hot water, luggage stored, helpful, laundry service, good café, free internet, reserve in advance.

D The Adventure Brew Hostel, Av Montes 533, T246 1614, www.theadventurebrewhostel.com. With solar-heated showers, **E** pp in dorm, on-site microbrewery, includes pancake breakfast, rooftop terrace with great views of the city and Illimani, nightly BBQs, use of kitchen, convenient to the bus station, scheduled to open in mid-2006.

E Alojamiento París, Av Sucre 949, T228 5029. Electric shower, **E-F** shared bath, good value.

E Ingavi, Ingavi 727, T232 3645. Nice rooms with infrequent hot water, good value, poor service.

E Residencial Latino, Junín 857 y Sucre, T228 5463. With hot water, cheaper without bath, in a refurbished colonial house with patios, a pleasant simple hostel, good value.

E Tambo de Oro, Armentia 367, T228 1565, F228 2181. Near bus station, hot showers, TV, good value, safe for luggage.

E Torino, Socabaya 457, T240 6003. Ask for better rooms in new section, with or without bath, run-down rooms in old section, HI member, popular with backpackers, prices go up in high season, free book exchange, good service, internet café (pricey) and good restaurant next door for breakfast and good value lunch (weekdays 1200-1500).

E-F Austria, Yanacocha 531, T240 8540, hotelaustria@acelerate.com. Without bath, **G** pp in shared room, basic, hot water but only three showers, safe deposit, laundry, TV lounge, use of kitchen, book in advance, bus to Copacabana leaves here 0800-0830.

E-F Hospedaje Milenio, Yanacocha 860, T228 1263. Electric shower, basic, good value, family house, homely, helpful owner, quiet, kitchen.

Plaza San Francisco up to the cemetery district *p247, maps p244 and p246*

B Hostal Naira, Sagárnaga 161, T235 5645, www.hostalnaira.com. Hot water, comfortable but pricey, rooms around courtyard, some are dark, price includes buffet breakfast in Café Banais, safety deposit boxes.

B Rosario, Illampu 704, T245 1658, www.hotel rosario.com. 3-star, excellent buffet breakfast, cable TV, modem connection, sauna, laundry, internet café *Jiwhaki* (free for guests, great view), good restaurant, stores luggage, very helpful staff. Highly

---

⬤ *For an explanation of the sleeping and eating price codes used in this guide, see inside the front*
● *cover. Other relevant information is found in Essentials pages 240-241.*

recommended. *Turisbus* travel agency downstairs (see Tour operators, page 257), Cultural Interpretation Centre explains items for sale in nearby 'witches' market'.

C Continental, Illampu 626, T/F245 1176, hotelcontinental626@hotmail.com. **E** without bath, nice rooms, stores luggage, member of Hostelling International Bolivia.

C Galería Virgen de Rosario, C Santa Cruz 583, p 4, T246 1015, hgaleria@ceibo.entelnet.bo. Great rooms, lots of daylight, includes breakfast, cable TV, safety boxes, nice staff, helpful, good value.

C La Joya, Max Paredes 541, T245 3841, www.hotelajoya.com. **D** without bath or breakfast, TV, modern and comfy, lift, laundry, popular area with free pickup from town centre, close to bus and train station.

C Sagárnaga, Sagárnaga 326, T235 0252, www.hotel-sagarnaga.com. **D** in plain rooms without TV, includes breakfast, solar-powered hot water, laundry, English spoken, *peña*, ATM.

D Arcabucero, C Viluyo 307, Linares (close to Museo de Coca), T/F231 3473. Pleasant new rooms in converted colonial house, excellent value but check the beds, breakfast extra.

D Estrella Andina, Illampu 716, T245 6421, juapame_2000@hotmail.com. Price includes breakfast, all rooms have a safe, English spoken, family run, comfortable, tidy, helpful, internet access, roof terrace, very nice.

D Fuentes, Linares 888, T231 3966, www.hotelf uentesbolivia.com. Cheaper without bath, includes breakfast, nice colonial style hotel with comfortable rooms, good value, new in 2006.

D Hostal Maya, Sagárnaga 339, T231 1970, mayahost_in@hotmail.com. **D-E** with shared bath, some rooms spacious, with balconies, others windowless and small, internet, money exchange, laundry, safe deposit, massage, luggage store, cable TV in living room.

D Majestic, Santa Cruz 359, T245 1628. Simple rooms, comfortable, laundry, safe, breakfast.

D Milton, Illampu y Calderón 1124, T236 8003, F236 5849. **E** without bath, hot water, includes breakfast, restaurant, expensive laundry, safe parking around corner, popular, will store luggage, excellent views from roof of this concrete block.

D Res Copacabana, Illampu 734, T245 1626, www.hostalcopacabana.com. Hot water, good showers, **E** without bath, soft beds, includes breakfast, changes TCs, simple, OK.

D Res Sucre, Colombia 340, on Plaza Sucre, T249 2038, F248 6723. **E** without bath, quiet area, hot water, big rooms, no double beds, luggage stored, helpful.

E El Viajero, Illampu 807, T245 3465, www.viajero.LoboPages.com. **E-F** without bath, **G** pp in dorm, a reasonable hostel, decorated with plants, dorm has lockers.

E-F El Solario, Murillo 776, T236 7963, elsolariohotel@yahoo.com. Central, good shared bathrooms, luggage store, use of kitchen, internet, international phone calls, laundry and medical services, taxi service, travel agency, good value.

E-F Hostal Cactus, Jiménez 818 y Santa Cruz, T245 1421. Shared showers (electric), helpful, kitchen facilities, luggage store, basic but peaceful, in a great location.

The Prado, Sopocachi, Miraflores and Zona Sur *p247, map p244*

LL Europa, Tiahuanacu 64, T231 5656, next to the Museo Nacional de Arqueología, www.hotel europa.com.bo. Excellent facilities and plenty of frills, internet in rooms, health club, several restaurants including a good café. Recommended.

LL Radisson Plaza, Av Arce 2177, T244 1111, www.radisson.com/lapazbo. 5-star hotel with all facilities, excellent buffet in restaurant (see Eating below), still referred to as the Sheraton.

L Casa Grande, Av Ballivian 1000 y C 17, Calacoto, T279 5511, www.casa-grande.com.bo. Beautiful, top quality apartments, includes buffet breakfast, wireless internet, airport pickup, restaurant, very good service, discounts or longer stays.

L **Plaza**, Av 16 de Julio 1789, T237 8311, www.plazabolivia.com.bo. Excellent hotel with good value restaurant (see below), peña show on Fri, includes breakfast, internet, pool.

AL **El Rey Palace**, Av 20 de Octubre 1947, T241 8541, www.hotel-rey-palace-bolivia.com. Includes breakfast, large suites with bath tub, internet, excellent restaurant, stylish, modern.

A **Alcalá Aparthotel**, Sanjinés 2662 at Plaza España, Sopocachi, T241 2336, alcapt@zuper.net. Nice, comfortable, spacious, furnished apartments, includes breakfast, 20% discount per month.

B **Columbus Palace**, Illimani 1990 by Plaza Tejada Sorzano, Miraflores, T224 2444, www.hotel-columbus.com. Includes buffet breakfast, internet, comfortable modern rooms, restaurant with buffet lunch.

B **EHT Sopocachi**, Macario Pinilla 580 at the base of El Montículo, T241 0312, ehtsopo@ccaoba.entelnet.bo. Spacious furnished apartments with kitchenette, good location and views, US$750 per month.

⊙ Eating

Around Plaza Murillo *p243, maps p244 and p246*

♦♦ **La Casa de los Paceños**, Sucre 856, T228 0955, also at Los Pinos 200 in Calacoto. Tourist restaurant, excellent Bolivian food, à la carte only.

♦ **El Calicanto**, Sanjines 467, T240 8008. Good food including regional specialities, renovated colonial house, live music at weekends.

♦ **Club de la Prensa**, C Campero 52. With a pleasant garden, limited menu is typical Bolivian – meat and fish only, in copious quantities – lively company.

♦ **Hotel Gloria**, Potosí 909. Vegetarian, popular for *almuerzo*, US$3, buffet lunch or dinner US$2.15; international restaurant, daily 1200-1500, 1800-2230.

♦ **La Kantuta**, in *Hotel Presidente*, Potosí 920. Excellent food, good service.

Cafés

Alexander Coffee, Potosí 1091. Part of a chain, sandwiches, salads, coffee, pastries.

Café Berlín, Mercado 1377 y Loayza and at Av Montenegro 5, Calacoto. Coffee, sweets, omelettes, breakfast, popular with locals, smokey, 0800-2300.

Café Confitería de la Paz, Camacho 1202, on the corner where Ayacucho joins Av Mcal Santa Cruz. Good if expensive tea room, traditional, meeting place for businessmen and politicians, great coffee and cakes.

Plaza San Francisco up to the cemetery district *p247, maps p244 and p246*

♦♦ **Casa del Corregidor**, Murillo 1040, T236 3633. Centrally heated, Spanish colonial restaurant with

mainly Bolivian dishes, excellent food, bar, Mon-Sat 1730-2300, peña from 2100.

♦♦ **Tambo Colonial**, in *Hotel Rosario* (see above). Excellent local and international cuisine, good salad bar, huge buffet breakfast, peña at weekend. Recommended.

♦♦♦ **Pizzería Romana**, Santa Cruz 260. Good pizzas and pastas, good value.

♦ **100% Natural**, Sagárnaga 345. Range of healthy, tasty fast foods ranging from salads to burgers and llama meat, good breakfasts, closed Sun.

♦ **Angelo Colonial**, Linares 922. Excellent food, vegetarian options, and ambience, candlelight, antiques, good music, internet access, open early for breakfast, can get very busy. Has a hostal at Av Santa Cruz 1058, with hot water, safe, convenient.

♦ **El Lobo**, Santa Cruz 441. Huge portions, Israeli dishes, good meeting place, noticeboard, popular.

♦ **Jackie Chan**, Cochabamba 100 (just south of Av Mcal Santa Cruz). Good Chinese, excellent value, popular with locals.

♦ **Le Pot-Pourri des Gourmets**, Linares 906, close to Sagárnaga. Bolivian and a variety of main courses including vegetarian, *almuerzo* US$2.20, pastries, snacks, hot and cold drinks, quiet, homely, music, exceptional value, great atmosphere but slow service.

♦ **Pizzería Italia**, Illampu 840 and 809, 2nd floor, T712 1234. Thin-crust pizza, pasta and international food.

♦ **Yussef**, Sagárnaga 380, second floor (poorly signed). Lebanese, great mezze, good for vegetarians, good value and relaxed atmosphere.

Cafés

Banais, Sagárnaga 161, same entrance as *Hostal Naira*. Coffee, sandwiches and juices, buffet breakfast, laid-back music and computer room downstairs.

O Mundo, Linares 906. Open only until 1500, below *Le Pot Pourri des Gourmets*, from which you can order food, good range of drinks.

Pepe's, Pasaje Jiménez 894, off Linares. Welcoming little café with good all-day breakfasts, sandwiches, omelettes, tables outside, cards and dominoes, magazines and guidebooks.

The Prado, Sopocachi, Miraflores and Zona Sur *p247, map p244*

♦♦♦ **Chalet la Suisse**, C 23, on the main avenue between Cs 24 and 25, Zona Sur, T279 3160. Serves excellent fondue, steaks, booking essential on Fri evening.

♦♦ **El Arriero**, Av 6 de Agosto 2535 (Casa Argentina), Sopocachi, also on C 17, Zona Sur. The best barbecue in the city with large portions.

♦♦ **Bistrot**, Fernando Guachalla 399, Sopocachi, in Alliance Française. Swish new restaurant with French menu, vegetarian options, sandwiches.

High Lander's, Final Sánchez Lima 2667, Sopocachi, T243 0023. Very good Tex-Mex fare, nice atmosphere, good views from the end of the street, Mon-Fri 1200-1500, 1700-2300, Sat 1800-2330.

La Comedie, Pasaje Medinacelli 2234, Sopocachi, T242 3561. 'Art café restaurant', contemporary, with a mainly French menu, good salads and cocktails.

La Tranquera, Capitán Ravelo 2123 next to Hotel Camino Real, T244 1103. Good international food, grill and salad bar, daily 1200-1600, 1900-2300.

Radisson Plaza Hotel, Av Arce 2177, T244 1111. Excellent buffet in 5-star setting, daily 1200-1500, delicious, friendly to backpackers.

Reineke Fuchs, Jáuregui 2241, Sopocachi. Many European beers and food in a German-style bar (closed for renovation in mid-2006).

The Lounge, Presbitero Medina 2527, T241 0585. American/Bolivian run, chilled atmosphere, western and Latin food, art exhibitions, excellent toilets, popular.

Utama, in *Plaza* hotel, Av 16 de Julio 1789). 2 restaurants: **Utama** on the top floor, with the views, 1700-2300, à la carte, and **Uma**, on the ground floor, for breakfast and lunch, buffet lunch US$6.15. Recommended.

Vienna, Federico Zuazo 1905, T244 1660, www.restaurantvienna.com. German, Austrian and local food, excellent food, atmosphere and service, live piano music, popular, open Mon-Fri 1200-1400, 1830-2200, Sun 1200-1430. Frequently recommended.

Wagamama, just behind *Jalapeños*, Pasaje Pinilla 2557, T243 4911. Open Tue-Sat 1200-1430, 1900-2000 (closed Sun and Mon) serving huge plates of sushi, complimentary tea, excellent service, popular with ex-pats.

Andrómeda, Av Arce 2116, T244 0726. Renowned for superb-value lunches, closing at time of going to press and reopening after as French bistro.

Armonía, Ecuador 2286 y Quito. Nice vegetarian buffet lunch, Mon-Sat 1200-1430.

Eli's Pizza Express, Av 16 de Julio 1400 block. English spoken, open daily including holidays (also at Comercio 914), very popular, maybe not the best pizza in La Paz, but certainly the largest omelettes.

La Quebecoise, 20 de Octubre 2387, Sopocachi, T212 1682, Mon-Fri 1200-1500, 1900-2300, Sat 1900-2300. French Canadian, good value for buffet, grill and take-away, pleasant atmosphere.

Lu Qing, 20 de Octubre 2090 y Aspiazu, T242 4188. Chinese food, large choice of dishes, set meals on weekdays, Mon-Sat 1130-1500, 1830-2300, Sun 1100-1530.

Mongo's, Hnos Manchego 2444, near Plaza Isabela la Católica, T244 0714. Open 1900-0300, live music Mon and Tue, Mexican and Bolivian dishes, burgers, snacks, open fires, bar, club after midnight, popular with gringos and locals.

The Olive Tree, Campos 334 y 6 de Agosto, Edificio Iturri. Closed Sat evening and Sun, good salads, soups and sandwiches.

Surucachi, 16 de Julio 1598 (El Prado), T231 2135. Bolivian specialties, good value set lunches on weekdays, plus à la carte.

Cafés

Alexander Coffee (Café Alex), Av 16 de Julio 1832, T231 2790, also at 20 de Octubre 2463 Plaza Avaroa, Av Montenegro 1336, Calacoto, and the airport. Excellent coffee, smoothies, muffins, cakes and good, salads and sandwiches, open 0730-0000. Recommended.

Dumbos, Av 16 de Julio, near *Eli's* and Cinema. For meat and chicken *salteñas*, ice creams, look for the dancing furry animals outside.

Fridolin, Av 6 de Agosto 2415, T215 3188, and Comercial La Chiwiña, San Miguel, Calacoto. *Empanadas, tamales*, savoury and sweet (Austrian) pastries, coffee, breakfast.

Kuchen Stube, Rosendo Gutiérrez 461, Sopocachi. Excellent cakes, coffee and German specialities, Mon -Fri 0930-1230, 1500-1900.

La Terraza, 16 de Julio 1615, T231 0701, 0630-0000; 20 de Octubre 2171 y Gutierrez,

0730-0000; Av Montenegro y C 8, Calacoto, 0730-0000. Excellent sandwiches and coffee, pancakes, breakfasts, make your own salads, in modern, US-style cafés.

🍸 Bars and clubs

The epicentre for nightlife in La Paz is currently Plaza Avaroa in Sopocachi. Clubs are clustered around here and crowds gather Fri and Sat nights.

San Francisco up to the cemetery district
p247, maps p244 and p246
Oliver's Travels, Murillo 1014. Fake English pub serving breakfasts, PG Tips, curries, fish and chips, pasta, sports channels, music, travel agency, very good book exchange, popular meeting place.
Sol y Luna, Murillo 999 y Cochabamba. Opens 1800. Dutch run, good breakfasts, snacks and cocktails, nice atmosphere, guide books for sale. Recommended.

The Prado, Sopocachi, Miraflores and Zona Sur *p247, map p244*
The Britannia, Av Ballivián on the left between C 15 y 16, Calacoto, Zona Sur, T279 3070. Open daily from 1700, closed Sun, cosy, popular with expats, bar snacks, designed as English pub, now with an Asian restaurant too.
Deadstroke, Av 6 de Agosto 2460, Sopocachi. US-style pub, café and billiards bar, food, drinks (good value for beer), billiards, pool and other games, opens 1700.
Diesel Nacional, Av 20 de Octubre entre Gutiérrez y Guachalla, Sopocachi. A hip, modern club with an industrial theme.
Equinoccio, Sánchez Lima 2191, Sopocachi. Top venue for live music and bar, Thu-Sat.
Fak'n Tacos, Belisario Salinas opposite Presbitero Medina. Bizarre upstairs bar with a boxing ring for patrons' use, potent drinks, including the `fishbowl`.
Ja Ron, 20 de Octubre esq Pasaje Medinacelli, Sopacachi. Bright bar with a bohemian feel, tree trunks for tables, potent cocktails, happy hour 1800-2100, stays open till 0200.
RamJam, C Presbitero Medina 2421, Sopacachi, T242 2295. Above Plaza Avaroa, open 1900-0300 or later, an energetic place aimed at gringos and upmarket locals, with coffee, curry, Sun evening roasts, micro-brewery beer and cable TV, dancing, packed Fri and Sat nights.
Ozone, an oxygen bar, is due to open on the premises in 2006.
Theolonius Jazz Bar, 20 de Octubre 2172, Sopacachi, T233 7806. Tue-Sat from 1700. Renowned for jazz (what else?), but it is expensive, with an extra charge to see the jazz.

🎭 Entertainment

For up-to-the-minute information on cinemas and shows, check *La Prensa* or *La Razón* on Fri, or visit www.la-razon.com. Best entertainment for visitors are the folk shows (*peñas*), which present the wide variety of local musical instruments.

Around Plaza Murillo *p243, maps p244 and p246*
Bocaisapo, Indaburo 654 y Jaén. Live music in a bar; no cover charge.
El Calicanto. See Eating, above.
Marka Tambo, Junín 710, T228 0041. Wed-Sat 2000-0100, US$7 all inclusive, repeatedly recommended (also sells woven goods and serves lunch Mon-Sat 1200-1500).

Above Plaza San Francisco *p247, maps p244 and p246*
Casa del Corregidor, see under Eating above. Good dinner show Mon-Thu, no cover charge, Fri and Sat *peña* US$4, both 2100, good, colonial atmosphere, traditional music and dance.
El Parnaso, Sagárnaga 189, T231 6827. Daily starting at 2030, meals available, purely for tourists but a good way to see local costumes and dancing.
Cinemas Films mainly in English with Spanish subtitles. Expect to pay around US$3.15.
Theatre Teatro Municipal Alberto Saavedra Pérez has a regular schedule of plays, opera, ballet and classical concerts, at Sanjines y Indaburo, T240 6183. The National Symphony Orchestra is very good and gives inexpensive concerts. Next door is the **Teatro Municipal de Cámara**, a small studio-theatre which shows dance, drama, music and poetry. **Casa Municipal de la Cultura 'Franz Tamayo'**, almost opposite Plaza San Francisco, hosts a variety of exhibitions, paintings, sculpture, photography, videos, etc, most of which are free. It publishes a monthly guide to cultural events, free from the information desk at the entrance. The **Palacio Chico**, Ayacucho y Potosí, in old Correo, operated by the Secretaría Nacional de Cultura, also has exhibitions (good for modern art), concerts and ballet, Mon-Fri 0900-1230, 1500-1900, closed at weekends, free. It is also in charge of many regional museums. Listings available in Palacio Chico.

🎉 Festivals and events

La Paz *p242, maps p244 and p246*
Jan/Feb: the **Alacitas Fair**, from 24 Jan to first week of Feb, in Parque Central up from Av del Ejército, also in Plaza Sucre/San Pedro (see box).
End May/early Jun Festividad del Señor de Gran Poder, the most important festival of the year, with a huge procession of costumed and

masked dancers on the 3rd Sat after Trinity. **Jul** Fiestas de Julio, a month of concerts and performances at the Teatro Municipal, with a variety of music, including the University Folkloric Festival. **8 Dec**, festival around Plaza España, not very large, but colourful and noisy. On **New Year's Eve** there are spectacular fireworks displays; view from higher up. See page 241 for national holidays and festivals outside La Paz.

O Shopping

La Paz *p242, maps p244 and p246*

Bookshops Los Amigos del Libro, Mercado 1315, T220 4321, also Av Montenegro y C 18 (San Miguel) and El Alto airport. They sell a few tourist guide books and will also ship books. Gisbert, Comercio 1270, libgis@entelnet.bo. Books, stationery, will ship overseas. Yachaywasi, just below Plaza del Estudiante, opposite *Hotel Eldorado*. Large selection, popular with students.

Camping equipment Kerosene for pressure stoves is available from a pump in Plaza Alexander, Pando e Inca. Caza y Pesca, Edif Handal Center, no 9, Av Mcal Santa Cruz y Socabaya, T240 9209. English spoken. The Base Adventure Store, Av 16 de Julio 1490, Edif Avenida, basement. Camping gear and clothing, head lamps, no rentals.

Handicrafts Above Plaza San Francisco (see page 247), up Sagárnaga, by the side of San Francisco church (behind which are many handicraft stalls in the Mercado Artesanal), are booths and small stores with interesting local items of all sorts, best value on Sun morning when prices are reduced. The lower end of Sagárnaga is best for antiques. At Sagárnaga 177 is an entire gallery of handicraft shops. On Linares, between Sagárnaga and Santa Cruz, high quality alpaca goods are priced in US$. Also in this area are many places making fleece jackets, gloves and hats, but shop around for value and service. Artesanía Sorata, Linares 862, and

Sagárnaga 311. Mon-Sat 0930-1900 (and Sun 1000-1800 high season), specializes in dolls, sweaters and weavings. Ayni, Illampu 704, www.hotelrosario.com/ayni. Fair trade shop in Hotel Rosario, featuring Aymara work. Comart Tukuypai, Linares 958, T/F231 2686, www.terranova.nu/comart. High-quality textiles from an artisan community association. Comercio Doryan, Sagárnaga y Murillo, eg Wari, unit 12, Comercio Doryan, closed Sun. High quality alpaca goods, will make to measure very quickly, English spoken, prices reasonable. Kunturi, Nicolás Acosta 783, T249 4350. You will find wonderful handicrafts produced by the Institute for the Handicapped, including embroidered cards. LAM shops on Sagárnaga. Good quality alpaca goods. Millma, Sagárnaga 225, and Claudio Aliaga 1202, San Miguel, Zona Sur, closed Sat afternoon and Sun. Alpaca sweaters (made in their own factory) and antique and rare textiles. Mother Earth, Linares 870. High-quality alpaca sweaters with natural dyes. Toshy on Sagárnaga. Top quality knitwear (closed Sat afternoon).

Jewellery There are good jewellery stores throughout the city: for example Joyería King's, Loayza 261, www.bolivia.com/empresas/kings/index.html, Torre Ketal, C 15, Calacoto, T277 2542. Gold and silver jewellery and souvenirs using native, Andean designs.

Maps IGM: head office at Estado Mayor General, Av Saavedra 2303, Miraflores (far from the centre), T214 9484, Mon-Thu 0830-1630, Fri 0830-1200, take passport to buy maps. IGM's Oficina 5, Juan XXIII 100 (mud track between Rodríguez y Linares), Mon-Thu 0800-1200 and 1430-1800, Fri 0800-1400, will order maps from HQ. Librería IMAS, Av Mcal Santa Cruz entre Loayza y Colón, T235 8234. Ask for the map collection and check what is in stock. Maps are also sold in the Post Office on the stalls opposite the Poste Restante counter.

Markets In addition to those mentioned in the Sights section (page 247), the 5-km sq **El Alto** market is on Thu and Sun (the latter is bigger). Take a Ceja bus from along the Prado to Desvío. At the toll plaza on the autopista, change buses for one marked 16 de Julio; most other passengers will be doing the same, follow them. Arrive around 1000 and stay to 1600. Goods are cheap. Don't take anything of value, just a bin liner to carry your purchases. **Mercado Sopocachi**, Guachala y Ecuador, a well-stocked covered market selling foodstuffs, kitchen supplies, etc.

Musical instruments Many shops on Sagárnaga/Linares, for example **El Guitarrón**, Sagárnaga 303 esq Linares, and **Marka 'Wi**, Sagárnaga 851. **Pasaje Linares**, the stairs off C Linares, has a number of shops selling just instruments.

Shopping malls and supermarkets
Hipermaxi, Cuba y Brazil, Miraflores. An out-of-centre mall. **Shopping Norte**, Potosí y Socabaya. Modern mall with restaurants and expensive merchandise. **Supermercado Ketal**, C 21, San Miguel, and Av Arce y Pinillo, near Plaza Isabel la Católica. Regular supermarket. **Supermercado Zatt**, Av Sánchez Lima 2362 near Plaza Avaroa. Has the best selection of dried foods etc for trekking.

▲ Activities and tours

La Paz *p242, maps p244 and p246*
City tours
Sightseeing, T279 1440, city tours on a double-decker bus, 2 circuits, downtown and Zona Sur with Valle de la Luna (1 morning and 1 afternoon departure to each), departs from Plaza Isabel la Católica and can hop on at Plaza San Francisco, tour recorded in 7 languages, US$6 for both circuits, daily except first Mon of each month.

Climbing, hiking and trekking
Guides must be hired through a tour company. For Maps, see Essentials, page 237 and Shopping, above. For books on trekking and climbing, see page 1520.
Ricardo Albert at *Inca Travel*, Av Arce 2116, Edif Santa Teresa.
Alberth Bolivia Tours, Illampu 773, T245 8018, alberthbolivia@hotmail.com. Good for climbing and trekking, good value, helpful, Juan speaks English, equipment rental.
Altiplano-Extreme, Av Pablo Sánchez 6532, T272 1994, www.altiplano-extreme.com.
Andean Summits, Aranzaes 2974, Sopocachi, T242 2106, www.andeansummits.com. For mountaineering and other adventure trips off the beaten track.

Azimut Explorer, Sagárnaga 213, Galería Chuquiago, of 11, T233 3809. Guide Juan Villarroel is one of the best.
Iván Blanco Alba, *Asociación de Guías de Montaña y Trekking*, Chaco 1063.
Bolivian Mountains, Murillo 947, T231 3197, www.bolivianmountains.com. A high-quality mountaineering outfit, with experienced guides and good equipment, not cheap.
Club Andino Boliviano, C México 1638, T231 0863, can provide a list of guides and works with the Bolivian association of mountain guides.
Club de Excursionismo, Andinismo y Camping, Riobamba 502, www.clubceac.com. Helps people find the cheapest way to go climbing, trekking, etc; foreigners may join local groups. Each week there is a meeting and slide show.
Trek Bolivia, C Sagárnaga 392, T/F231 7106. Organizes expeditions in the Cordillera.

Football
Popular and played on Wed and Sun at the **Siles Stadium** in Miraflores (Micro A), which is shared by both La Paz's main teams, Bolívar and The Strongest. There are reserved seats.

Golf
Mallasilla, the world's highest course, 3,318 m. Non-members can play at Mallasilla on weekdays, when the course is empty, no need to book. Club hire, green fee, balls and a caddy (compulsory) also costs US$37. The course is in good condition and beautiful (take water).

Snooker/pool/other
Picco's, Edif 16 de Julio, Av 16 de Julio 1566. Good tables and friendly atmosphere.
San Luis, Edif México, 2do Sótano, C México 1411. Friendly atmosphere.
YMCA sportsground and gymnasium: opposite the University of San Andrés, Av Villazón, and clubhouse open to the public, Av 20 de Octubre 1839 (table tennis, billiards, etc).

Tour operators
Adventure Planet, C Vicenti 850, Sopocachi, T242 3855, www.planetaventura.com. Adventure travel, including mountaineering, trekking and climbing, plus 4WD tours.
Akhamani Trek, Illampu 707, T237 5680, tourtrek@ceibo.entelnet.bo. Trekking in Sorata and Coroico, also day trips, English spoken, safe, good porters, well-organized.
America Tours SRL, Av 16 de Julio 1490 (El Prado), Edificio Avenida PB, No 9, T237 4204, www.america-ecotours.com. Cultural and ecotourism trips to many parts of the country (including the renowned Chalalán Lodge near Rurrenabaque, the Che Guevara Trail and

Parque Nacional Noel Kempff Mercado), rafting, trekking and horse-riding, English spoken. Highly professional and recommended. Basic book exchange.

Bolivian Journeys, Sagárnaga 363, p 1, T/F235 7848. Camping, mountain bike tours, equipment rental (with large shoe sizes), maps, English and French spoken, very helpful.

Carmoar Tours, C Bueno 159, headed by Günther Ruttger T231 7202, carmoar@zuper.net. Has information for the Inca Trail to Coroico, rents trekking gear.

Crillon Tours, Av Camacho 1223, T233 7533, www.titicaca.com. With 24-hr ATM for cash on credit cards. In USA, 1450 South Bayshore Dr, suite 815, Miami, FL 33131, T305-358 5353, darius@titicaca.com. A very experienced company. Joint scheduled tours with Lima arranged. Fixed departures to Salar de Uyuni and much more. Full details of their Lake Titicaca services can be found on page 271.

Detour, Av Mariscal Santa Cruz, Edif Camara Nacional de Comercio, T236 1626. Good for flight tickets, very professional, English spoken.

Eco Adventures, Sagárnaga 368, T231 0272, www.ecoadventurebolivia.com. Another biking specialist (US$39 to Cocoico), with good levels of customer care and equipment (Trek bikes).

Explore Bolivia, Sagárnaga 339, Galería Sagárnaga of 1, T/F239 1810, explobol@ceibo.entelnet.bo. Adventure sports, good bikes (Trek).

Et-n-ic, Illampu 863, T7064 3566, www.visitabolivia.com. Overland tours throughout Bolivia, Swiss staff, good reports.

Fremen, Edif Handal, Av Mariscal Santa Cruz y Socabaya, pb, of 13, T240 8200, www.andes-amazonia.com. They also have offices in Cochabamba, Santa Cruz, Uyuni, Trinidad and Atlanta (GA). They run the *Flotel Reina de Enín* on the Río Mamoré (US$423pp double occupancy for 5 day trip), *El Puente* Hotel in Villa Tunari (C) and are involved with *Proyecto Tayka*, Red de Hoteles de los Andes, a chain of hotels in the Salar de Uyuni-Reserva Avaroa area (see page 287).

Gloria tours/Hotel Gloria, Potosi 909, T240 7070, www.hotelgloria.com.bo See Sleeping.

Gravity Assisted Mountain Biking, Av 16 de Julio 1490, Edificio Avenida, PB, of 10 (across the hall from, and part of, América Tours), T231 3849, www.gravitybolivia.com. A wide variety of mountain biking tours throughout Bolivia, including the world- famous downhill ride to Coroico (US$50). Also offers rides more challenging than the Coroico ride, including technical single-track and high-speed abandoned dirt roads, complete with coaching and all the safety equipment needed. Highly professional and recommended. Quality book exchange, sells new and used guidebooks, and gives a free T-shirt with every ride. Often full so worth booking on their web site in advance.

Madidi Travel, Jiménez 806 esq Santa Cruz, T245 0069, www.madidi-travel.com. Responsible tourism in the Madidi area, including to the private Serere Sanctuary, also to other parts of Bolivia, all proceeds directly support conservation in Madidi, tours from 3-day, 2-nights to over 10, all tailored to travellers' needs and local conditions.

Magri Turismo, Capitán Ravelo 2101, PO Box 4469, T244 2727, www.bolivianet.com/magri. Amex representative, gives TCs against American Express card but doesn't change TCs, offers Amex emergency services and clients' mail. Recommended for tours in Bolivia, travel services.

Nuevo Continente, at *Hotel Alem*, Sagárnaga 344, T237 3423, quiquisimo@mixmail.com. Recommended for trip to Zongo, Clemente is a good driver, cheap service to airport, very helpful.

Pachamama Tours, Sagárnaga 189 y Murillo Shopping Doryan p2, of 35, T/F211 3179, www.magicbolivia.com. Cheap air fares within South America, very knowledgeable and professional for local tours, English spoken, also arranges cultural tours to indigenous groups.

Tauro Tours, Mercado 1362, Galería Paladium

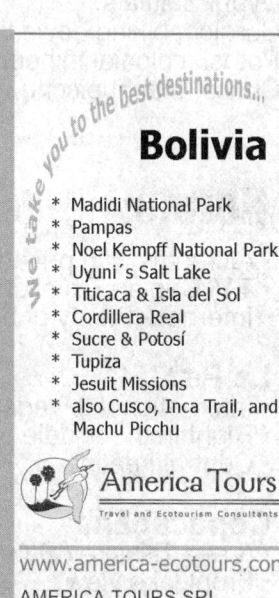

Mezz, local 'M', T220 1846, F220 1881. Top end adventure tours, jeep trips everywhere, run by the highly experienced and trained Carlos Aguilar.

Toñito Tours, Sagárnaga 189, Comercio Doryan, of 9, T233 6250, www.bolivian expeditions.com. Tours of the **Salar de Uyuni**, also book bus and train tickets, very helpful, hire out sleeping bags.

Transturin, C Alfredo Ascarrunz 2518, Sopocachi, PO Box 5311, T242 2222, www.travelbolivia.com. Full travel services with this long-standing company, with tours ranging from La Paz to the whole country. Details of their Lake Titicaca services will be found on page 268.

Tupiza Tours, Av Tejada Sorzano 855, Edif Dica, entre Puerto Rico y Costa Rica, Zona Miraflores, T224 4282 (248 9107 out of office hours), 7260 0026 mob, Hmitru@entelnet.bo. For La Paz tours and tours to the southwest from Uyuni or Tupiza.

Turisbus, Illampu 704, T245 1341, www.turisbus.com. Helpful, trekking equipment rented, agent for PeruRail, tickets to Puno and Cuzco, also local and Bolivian tours. Recommended.

Turismo Balsa, Capitán Rvelo 2104, T244 0817, www.turismobalsa.com. City and tours throughout Bolivia (recommended), see also under Puerto Pérez, page 268. Also international flight deals.

⊖ Transport

La Paz *p242, maps p244 and p246*
Air
Cotranstur minibuses, white with 'Cotranstur' and 'Aeropuerto' written on the side and back, go from Plaza Isabel La Católica, anywhere on the Prado and Av Mcal Santa Cruz to the airport between 0800-0830 to 1900-2000, US$0.50 (allow about 1 hr), best to have little luggage, departures from the airport every 5 mins or so. Colectivos from Plaza Isabel La Católica charge US$3 pp, carrying 4 passengers. Radio-taxi is US$5 to airport, US$6.50 from Zona Sur. There is an *Enlace* ATM for Cirrus, Plus, Visa and MasterCard credit/debit cards in the international departures hall for taking out local cash and a bank which changes cash, OK rates. To change money when bank is closed, ask at the departure tax window near information. The international departures hall is the main concourse, with all check-in desks, and is the hall for all domestic arrivals and departures. Tourist office at Arrivals. Bar/restaurant and café (cheaper) upstairs. For details of services, see under destinations. Note that **TAM** uses the nearby military airport.

Bus
For information, TT228 6061. Buses to: **Oruro**, **Potosí**, **Sucre**, **Cochabamba**, **Santa Cruz**, **Tarija** and **Villazón**, leave from the main terminal at Plaza Antofagasta (micros 2, M, CH or 130), see under each destination for details. Taxi to central hotels, US$1. The terminal (open 0700-2300) has a tourist booth by the main entrance, internet, a post office, **Entel**, restaurant, luggage store, near the main entrance and several private kiosks at the rear, US$0.30 per bag (0530-2200) and agencies, such as **Turisbus**, **Diana**, **Vicuña** (cheaper than their offices in town). Touts find passengers the most convenient bus and are paid commission by the bus company. Buses to **Chokilla** and **Yanachi** leave from a street just off Plaza 24 de Septiembre at 0800 and 1500, 3-4 hrs, US$2.75.

To **Copacabana**, several bus companies (tourist service) pick-up travellers in their hotels (in the centre) and also stop at the main terminal, tickets from booths at the terminal (cheaper) or agencies in town. They all leave about 0800, 3½ hrs, US$2.50, return from Copacabana about 1100. When there are not enough passengers for each company, they pool them. **Diana Tours** T228 2809, **Milton Tours** T228 6349, **Nuevo Continente** T228 5191, **Turisbus** T245 1341 (more expensive). You can also book this service all the way to Puno, US$6.25.

Public buses to **Sorata**, **Copacabana** and **Tiahuanaco** leave from the Cemetery district. Companies include **Flota Copacabana**, **Manco Kapac**, **2 de Febrero**, **Ingavi**, **Trans Perla Andina**. To get to the Cemetery district, take any bus or minibus marked 'Cementerio' going up C Santa Cruz (US$0.17). On Plaza Reyes Ortiz are **Manco Kapac**, recommended, and **2 de Febrero** for **Copacabana** and **Tiquina**. From the Plaza go up Av Kollasuyo and at the 2nd street on the right (Manuel Bustillos) is the terminal for minibuses to **Achacachi**, **Huatajata** and **Huarina**, and buses for **Sorata**. Several micros (20, J, 10) and minibuses (223, 252, 270, 7) go up Kollasuyo; look for 'Kollasuyo' on the windscreen in most, but not all cases. Taxi US$1. Buses to **Coroico and the Yungas** leave from Villa Fátima (25 mins by micros B, V, X, K, 131, 135, or 136, or *trufis* 2 or 9, which pass Pérez Velasco coming down from Plaza Mendoza, and get off at the service station, C Yanacachi 1434). See Safety, above (page 243).

International buses From Plaza Antofagasta terminal: to **Buenos Aires**, US$85, Mon and Fri with **Ormeño**, 54 hrs. Alternatively, go to Villazón and change buses in Argentina. To **Arica** via the frontier at Tambo Quemado and Chungará **Pullmanbus** at 0630, **Cuevas** at 0700, **Zuleeta** at 0600, 1200 and 1300, **Nuevo Continente** at 0815, US$11.25-12.50. Connecting service for Iquique and Santiago. To **Cuzco**: colectivos and agencies to **Puno** daily with different companies, most easily booked through travel agencies, US$15, 10 hrs. **Note**: Of the various La Paz-Puno services, only **Transturin** does not make you change to a Peruvian bus once over the border. For luxury and other services to Peru see under Lake Titicaca below. To **Lima**, **Ormeño** daily at 1630, **Nuevo Continente** at 0800, US$70, 26 hrs.

Car hire

Imbex, Av Montes 522, T245 5432, www.imbex.com. Well-maintained Suzuki jeeps from US$50 per day, including 120 km free for 4-person 4WD. Highly recommended. **Kolla Motors**, Av Sánchez Lima 2321, T241 9141. Well-maintained 6-seater 4WD Toyota jeeps, insurance and gasoline extra. **Petita Rent-a-car**, Valentín Abecia 2031, Sopocachi Alto, T242 0329, www.rentacarpetita.com. Swiss owners Ernesto Hug and Aldo Rezzonico. Recommended for well-maintained 4WD jeeps, etc, also offer adventure tours, German, French, English spoken. Recommended. Also arranges fishing trips. Ernesto also has garage for VW and other makes, Av Jaimes Freyre 2326, T241 5264. Highly recommended. Car Park on corner of Ingavi and Sanjines, US$1.35 for 24 hrs, safe and central. See page 43 in Essentials for multinational car hire websites.

Taxi

Standard taxis charge US$0.75 pp for short trips within city limits. A *trufi* US$0.20 in the centre, US$0.40 pp beyond the centre. Taxi drivers are not tipped. At night, for safety, only take **radio taxis** (radio móvil), which are named as such, have a unique number and radio communication (e.g. **Alfa** T232 2427, **La Rápida** 239 2323). They charge US$1 in centre and US$2 to suburbs. Also good value for tours for 3 people, negotiate price. **Eduardo Figueroa**, T278 6281, taxi driver and travel agent. Recommended. **Adolfo Monje Palacios**, in front of *Hotel El Dorado* or T235 4384. Highly recommended for short or long trips. **Oscar Vera**, Simón Aguirre 2158, Villa Copacabana, La Paz, T223 0453, specializes in trips to the Salar de Uyuni and the Western Cordillera, speaks English. Recommended.

❶ Directory

La Paz *p242, maps p244 and p246*
Airline offices Aerolíneas Argentinas, Edif Petrolero, El Prado, Mezanine, of 13, T235 1711, F239 1059. **Aero Sur**, Av 16 de Julio 1616, p 11, T231 2244. **Amaszonas**, Av Saavedra 1649, T211 1104. **American Airlines**, Av 16 de Julio 1440, Edif Herman, T239 2127, www.aa.com. **British Airways** and **Iberia**, Ayacucho 378, Edif Credinform p 5, T220 3885, F220 3950. **LanChile**, Av 16 de Julio 1566, p 1, T235 8377, www.lanchile.com. **Lloyd Aéreo Boliviano (LAB)**, Camacho 1460, T800-103001. **KLM**, Montenegro 778 (altos Librería Lectura), T277

4212. **Lufthansa**, Av 6 de Agosto 2512 y P Salazar, T243 1717, F243 1267. **TACA**, El Prado 1479, Of 401, T231 3111, toll free T800-108222. **TAM** (Mercosur), Heriberto Gutiérrez 2323, T244 3442. **Transportes Aéreo Militar (TAM)**, Av Montes 738 esq Serrano, T237 9286, Mon-Fri 0830-1200 and 1430- 1830. **Varig**, Av Mcal Santa Cruz 1392, Edif Cámara de Comercio, T231 4040, F239 1131. **Banks** *Enlace* ATMs at many sites in the city. **Bisa**, Av Gral Camacho 1333, open 0830-1200, 1430-1800, Sat 1000-1300, good service, changes US$ cash. Cash advance (in bolivianos) on Visa at **Banco Santa Cruz**, also known as *BSCH* (branch in Shopping Norte is open Sat afternoon), **Banco Mercantil**, Mercado 1190 (good, quick service), and **Banco Nacional**. BCP, Comercio y Yancocha, long hours Mon-Fri 0830-1800, Sat 0900-1200, US$ cash only. **Prodem**, Av Camacho esq Colón 1277, T215 0297, Illampu 784 y Santa Cruz, T214 7723, Sánchez Lima y Salinas and other branches, changes US$ cash. **Amex**, see *Magri Turismo* under Tour operators. **Visa**, Av Camacho 1448, p 11 y 12, T231 8585 (24 hrs), F211 6525, for cancelling lost or stolen credit cards. **Exchange houses**: Sudamer, Colón 256 y Camacho, open Mon-Fri till 1800, Sat till 1200. Good rates for currencies other than US$ including euros, 2% commission on US$ or euro TCs into dollars, and US$ TCs into bolivianos, frequently recommended. **Unitours**, Mercado y Loayza. Good rates for US$ cash. Very few deal in Argentine and Chilean pesos. Street changers on corners around Plaza del Estudiante, Camacho, Colón and Prado, OK rates. **Cultural centres** Alliance Française, Guachalla 399 esq Av 20 de Octubre T244 2075, www.afbolivia.org, French-Spanish library, videos, newspapers, and cultural gatherings information. Call for opening hours. **Centro Boliviano Americano (CBA)**, Parque Zenón Iturralde 121, T243 0107 (10 mins walk from Plaza Estudiante down Av Arce), www.cba.edu.bo. Has public library and recent US papers. **Goethe-Institut**, Av 6 de Agosto 2118, T244 2453, www.goethe.de. Excellent library, recent papers in German, CDs, cassettes and videos free on loan, German books for sale. **Cycle spares** See Gravity Assisted Mountain Biking under *América Tours* in Tour operators, above, very knowledgeable, www.gravity bolivia.com. In Calacoto: **Nosiglia Sport**, Av Costanera 28, T274 9904, nossport@ ceibo.entelnet.bo. **Embassies and consulates** Argentina, Aspiazú 497, Sopocachi, T241 7737, embarbol@ caoba.entelnet.bo. 24 hrs for visa, 0900-1330. Brazil, Av Arce, Edif Multicentro, T244 0202, embajadabrasil@acelerate.com. 0830-1700, Mon-Fri (visas take 2 days). **Canadian Consulate**,

Edif Barcelona p 2, Victor Sanjinez 2678, Plaza España, T241 4453, 0900-1200. **Danish Consulate**, Av Arce 2799 and Cordero, Edif Fortaleza, p 9, T243 2070, lpbamb@um.dk. Mon-Fri, 0800-1600. **French Consulate**, Av Hernando Siles 5390, esq C 08 Obrajes, T214 9900, amfrabo@ ceibo.entelnet.bo. Take microbus N, A or L down Av 16 de Julio, Mon-Thu 0800-1300, 1430-1730, Fri 0800-1230. **German**, Av Arce 2395, T244 0066, info@embajada-alemana-bolivia.org. Mon-Fri 0900-1200. **Italy**, Av 6 de Agosto 2575, PO Box 626, T243 4955, ambitlap@ceibo.entelnet.bo. Mon-Fri 0830-1300. **Japan**, Rosendo Gutiérrez 497, esq Sánchez Lima, PO Box 2725, T241 9110, embjapon@ceibo.entelnet.bo. Mon-Fri 1030-1230, 1400-1800. **Netherlands Consulate**, Av 6 de Agosto 2455, Edif Hilda, p 7, T244 4040, nllap@caoba. entelnet.bo. 0900-1200. **Paraguayan Consulate**, Edif Illimani, p 1, Av 6 de Agosto y P Salazar, good visa service, T243 3176, embapar@acelerate.com. Mon-Fri 0830-1100. **Peru**, F Guachalla 300, Sopocachi, T244 1250, embbol@caoba.entelnet.bo. Mon-Fri 0900-1600, visa US$10 in US$, issued same day if you go early. **Spanish Consulate**, Av 6 de Agosto 2827 and Cordero, T243 0118, embespa@ ceibo.entelnet.bo. Mon-Fri 0830-1500. **Swedish Consulate**, Av 14 de Septiembre 5080 y C5 Obrajes, T/F243 4943, open 0900-1200. **Switzerland**, Av 13 esq Av 14 de Septiembre, T275 1001, vertretung@paz.rep.admin.ch. Mon-Fri 0900-1200. **UK**, Av Arce 2732, T243 3424, ppa@megalink.com. Mon-Thu 0830-1330, Fri 0830-1200, visa section open 0900-1200 has a list of travel hints for Bolivia, doctors, etc. **USA**, Av Arce 2780 y Cordero, T216 8000, http://bolivia.usembassy.gov, Mon-Fri 0800-1730. **Internet** There are many internet cafés in the centre of La Paz, opening and shutting all the time. Cost US$0.40 per hr, fast connections, long hours, but many closed Sun. **Language schools** Alliance Française (see

also above). **Centro Boliviano Americano** (address under Cultural centres above), US$140 for 2 months, 1½ hrs tuition each afternoon. **Instituto de La Lengua Española**, María TeresaTejada, C Aviador esq final 14, No 180, Achumani, T279 6074, T715-56735 (mob), sicbol@caoba. entelnet.bo. One-to-one lessons US$7 per hr. Recommended. **Speak Easy Institute**, Av Arce 2047, between Goitia and Montevideo, just down from Plaza del Estudiante, T/F244 1779, speakeasy institute@yahoo.com. US$6 for one-to-one private lessons, cheaper for groups and couples, Spanish and English taught, very good. **Private Spanish lessons** from: Cecilia Corrales, José María Camacho 1664, San Pedro, T248 7458, besteaching75@hotmail.com. **Isabel Daza Vivado**, Murillo 1046, p 3, T231 1471, T706-28016 (mob), maria_daza@hotmail.com. US$3 per hr. **Enrique Eduardo Patzy**, Mendez Arcos 1060, Sopocachi, T241 5501 or 776-22210, epatzy@hotmail.com. US$6 an hr one-to-one tuition, speaks English and Japanese. Recommended. **Medical services** For hospitals, doctors and dentists, contact your consulate or the tourist office for recommendations. **Ambulance service**: T222 4452. **Health and hygiene**: Unidad Sanitaria La Paz, on Ravelo behind *Hotel Radisson Plaza*, yellow fever shot and certificate for US$12. **Ministerio de Desarollo Humano, Secretaría Nacional de Salud**, Av Arce, near *Radisson Plaza*, yellow fever shot and certificate, rabies and cholera shots, malaria pills, bring own syringe (US$0.20 from any pharmacy). **Centro Piloto de Salva**, Av Montes y Basces, T236 9141, 10 mins walk from Plaza San Francisco, for malaria pills, helpful. **Laboratorios Illanani**, Edif Alborada p 3, of 304, Loayza y Juan de la Riva, T231 7290, open 0900-1230, 1430-1700, fast, efficient, hygienic, blood test US$4.75, stool test US$9.50. Tampons may be bought at most *farmacias* and supermarkets. The daily papers list chemists/pharmacies on duty (*de turno*). For

contact lenses, **Optaluis**, Comercio 1089, well-stocked. **Post offices** Correo Central, Av Mcal Santa Cruz y Oruro, Mon-Fri 0800-2000, Sat 0830-1800, Sun 0900-1200. Another on Linares next to Museo de Coca, 0830-2000. Stamps are sold only at the post offices. Good philately section/museum on 1st floor of Correo Central. There are a number of shops selling good postcards. *Poste Restante* keeps letters for 2 months, no charge. Check the letters filed under all parts of your name. For the procedure for sending parcels and for mailing prices, see page 244. Don't forget moth balls (difficult to buy – try C Sagárnaga) for textile items. To collect parcels costs US$0.15. Express postal service (top floor) is expensive. DHL, Av Mcal Santa Cruz 1297,

T0800-4020, expensive and slow. FedEx, Rosendo Gutiérrez 113 esq Capitán Ravelo, T244 3537. UPS, Av 16 de Julio 1479, p 10. **Telephones** There are *cabinas* for competing phone companies everywhere. **Useful addresses** Immigration: to renew a visa go to **Migración Bolivia**, Av Camacho 1433, T220 2981. Mon-Fri 0830-1600, go early. Drop passport and tourist card at the booth on the right as you walk into the office in the morning and collect stamped passport in the afternoon. **Tourist Police:** C Hugo Estrada 1354, Plaza Tejada Sorzano frente al estadio, Miraflores, next to *Love City* Chinese restaurant, T222 5016. Open 24 hrs, for insurance claims after theft, helpful.

Around La Paz

South of La Paz

To the south of the city are dry hills of many colours, topped by the **Muela del Diablo**, a striking outcrop. Here is the **Valle de la Luna**, or 'Moon Valley', which has a nice terraced cactus garden worth walking through; the climate in this valley is always much warmer than in the city. About 3 km from the bridge at Calacoto the road forks. Get out of the minibus (see Transport, page 262) at the turning and walk a few minutes east to the Valle entrance, or get out at the football field which is by the entrance. Take good shoes and water. Just past the Valle de la Luna is **Mallasa** where there are several small roadside restaurants and cafés and the **Hotel Oberland** (see page 248). The **zoo** ① *on the road to Río Abajo, entrance just past Mallasa after Valle de la Luna, daily 0900-1700, US$0.50 adults, US$0.25 children*. In a beautiful, wide open park-like setting, conditions for the animals and birds are relatively good, but the public is allowed to feed the animals. Quad biking is available behind the zoo.

Tiahuanaco

① *The site is open 0900-1700, US$10 for foreigners, including entry to museum. Allow 4 hrs to see the ruins and village. See also Transport, page 263.*
This remarkable archaeological site, 72 km west of La Paz, near the southern end of Lake Titicaca, takes its name from one of the most important pre-Columbian civilizations in South America. It is now the most popular excursion from La Paz. Many archaeologists believe that Tiahuanaco existed as early as 1600 BC, while the complex visible today probably dates from the eighth to the 10th centuries AD. The site may have been a ceremonial complex at the centre of an empire which covered almost half Bolivia, south Peru, north Chile and northwest Argentina. It was also a hub of trans-Andean trade. The demise of the Tiahuanaco civilization, according to studies by Alan Kolata of the University of Illinois, could have been precipitated by the flooding of the area's extensive system of raised fields (*Sukakollu*), which were capable of sustaining a population of 20,000. The Pumapunka section, 1 km south of the main complex may have been a port, as the waters of the lake used to be much higher than they are today. The raised field system is being reutilized in the Titicaca area.

One of the main structures is the **Kalasasaya**, meaning 'standing stones', referring to the statues found in that part: two of them, the Ponce monolith (centre of inner patio) and the Fraile monolith (southwest corner), have been re-erected. In the northwest corner is the Puerta del Sol, originally at Pumapunku. Its carvings, interrupted by being out of context, are thought to be either a depiction of the creator God, or a calendar. The motifs are exactly the same as those around the Ponce monolith. The **Templo Semisubterráneo** is a sunken temple whose walls are lined with faces, all different, according to some theories depicting states of health, the temple being a house of healing; another theory is that the faces display all the ethnicities of the world. The **Akapana**, originally a pyramid (said to have been the second largest in the world, covering over 28,000 sq m), still has some ruins on it and, since August 2004, is being excavated. At **Pumapunku**, some of whose blocks weigh between 100 and 150 tonnes, a natural disaster may have put a sudden end to the construction before it was finished. Most of the best statues are in the **Museo Tiahuanaco** or the **Museo Semisubterráneo** in La Paz (see page 247). There is a small museum at the ticket office, the **Museo Regional Arqueológico de Tiahuanaco**, containing a well-illustrated explanation of the raised field system of agriculture. Next to the site museum is La Cabaña del Puma restaurant where lunch costs about US$2.

Guidebooks in English *Tiwanaku*, by Mariano Baptista, Plata Publishing Ltd, Chur, Switzerland, or Discovering Tiwanaku by Hugo Boero Rojo. *Guía Especial de Arqueología Tiwanaku*, by Edgar Hernández Leonardini, a guide on the site, recommended. Written guide material is difficult to come by; hiring a good guide costs US$10. A map of the site with a historical explanation in English (published by Quipus) is sold at the ticket office, US$2.50. Locals sell copies of Tiahuanaco figures; cheaper here than La Paz.

The nearby **Tiahuanaco village** still has remnants from the time of independence and the 16th-century church used pre-Columbian masonry. In fact, Tiahuanaco for a long while was the 'quarry' for the altiplano. For the festival on 21 June, before sunrise, there are colourful dances and llama sacrifices. On the 8th day of carnival (Sunday), there is a colourful carnival. Souvenirs for sale, bargain hard, do not take photographs.

By road to Chile

The main route to Chile is via Tambo Quemado (see page 279), but an alternative route, on which there are no trucks, is to go by good road direct from La Paz via Viacha to Santiago de Machaco (130 km, petrol); then 120 km to the border at Charaña (**F Alojamiento Aranda**; immigration behind railway station), very bad road. In Visviri (Chile) there is no fuel, accommodation, electricity, ask for restaurant and bargain price. From Visviri a regular road runs to Putre, see Chile chapter.

Trekking and climbing near La Paz

Four so-called 'Inca Trails' link the Altiplano with the Yungas, taking you from the high Andes to the sub-tropics, with dramatic changes in weather, temperature and vegetation. Each has excellent sections of stonework and they vary in difficulty from relatively straightforward to quite hard-going. In the rainy season going can be particularly tough.

Takesi Trail Start at **Ventilla** (see Transport, page 263), walk up the valley for about three hours passing the village of Choquekota until the track crosses the river and to the right of the road, there is a falling-down brick wall with a map painted on it. The Takesi and Alto Takesi trails start here, following the path to the right of the wall. The road continues to Mina San Francisco. In the first hour's climb from the wall is excellent stone paving which is Inca or pre-Inca, depending on who you believe, either side of the pass at 4,630 m. There are camping possibilities at *Estancia Takesi* and in the village of Kakapi you can sleep at the **G Kakapi Tourist Lodge**, 10 beds with good mattresses, solar shower and toilet. It is run by the local community and sponsored by Fundación Pueblo. It is also possible to camp. You also have to pass the unpleasant mining settlement of Chojlla, between which and Yanakachi is a gate where it is necessary to register and often pay a small 'fee'. Yanakachi has a number of good places to stay, several good hikes and an orphanage you can help at. The Fundación Pueblo office on the plaza has information. Buy a minibus ticket on arrival in Yanakachi or walk 45 minutes down to the La Paz-Chulumani road for transport. The trek can be done in one long day, especially if you organize a jeep to the start of the trail, but is more relaxing in two or three. If you take it slowly, though, you'll have to carry camping kit. Hire mules in Choquekhota for US$8 per day plus up to US$8 for the muleteer. A 2-3 day alternative is from Mina San Francisco to El Castillo and the village of Chaco on the La Paz-Chulumani road. This trek is called La Reconquistada and has the distinction of including a 200 m disued mining tunnel.

Choro Trail (La Cumbre to Coroico) Immediately before the road drops down from La Cumbre to start the descent to Las Yungas, there is a good dirt road leads up to the *apacheta* (narrow pass) where the trail starts properly. Cloud and bad weather are normal at La Cumbre (4,660 m): you have to sign in at the Guardaparque post on the way to the pass. The trail passes Samaña Pampa (small shop, sign in again, camping US$0.60), Chucura (pay US$1.20 fee, another shop, camping), Challapampa (camping possible, US$0.60, small shop), the Choro bridge and the Río Jacun-Manini (fill up with water at both river crossings). In 2005 new bridges across the rivers were in place. At Sandillani it is possible to stay at the lodge or camp in the carefully-tended garden of a Japanese man, Tamiji Hanamura, who keeps a book with the names of every passing traveller. He likes to see postcards and pictures from other countries. There is good paving down to Villa Esmeralda, after which is Chairo (lodging and camping), then to Yolosa. It takes three days to trek from La Cumbre to Chairo, from where you can take a truck to Yolosa (it runs when there are enough people: US$2.25 each, but preferable to a long, dreary walk past construction sites for the new La Paz-Coroico road). From Yolosa it is 8 km uphill to Coroico with regular transport for US$1.20 per person. The Choro Trail has a reputation for unfriendliness and occasional robbery, take care.

Yunga Cruz (Chuñavi to Chulumani) The best, but hardest of the four 'Inca' trails: from Chuñavi follow the path left (east) and contour gently up. Camping possible after two hours. Continue along the path staying on left hand side of the ridge to reach Cerro Khala Ciudad (literally, Stone City Mountain, you'll see why). Good paving brings you round the hill to join a path coming from Quircoma (on your right); continue, heading north, to Cerro Cuchillatuca and then Cerro Yunga Cruz, where there is water and camping is possible. After this point water and camping are difficult and normally impossible until you get down to Sikilini. The last water and camping possibilities are all within the next hour, take advantage of them. Each person should have at least two litres of water in bottles. For water purification, only use iodine-based preparations (iodine tincture, *iodo* in *farmacias* costs US$0.50: use five drops per litre.) There are some clearances on the way down but no water. Colectivos run from Sikilini to Chulumani. Starting in Chuñavi the trek takes three days. The Yunga Cruz trail is badly littered - clean up after yourself.

Huayna Potosí Huayna Potosí is normally climbed in two days, with one night camped on a glacier at 5,600 m. There is a refugio *Huayna Potosí*, which costs US$10 per night, plus food. Contact at Illampu 626, T/F02-245 6717, bolclimb@mail.megalink.com or La Paz agencies for further information. Average cost is US$140 for two-day tour including all equipment except sleeping bag. The starting point for the normal route is at Zongo, whose valley used to have a famous ice cave (now destroyed by global warming). See Climbing, page , and Activities and tours below for details of guides.

● Sleeping

South of La Paz *p260*
A-B Gloria Urmiri, Urmiri, T237 0010, www.hotelgloria.com.bo. At hot springs 2 hrs from La Paz, price for weekend (wide range of choices depending on the type of tub), cheaper weekdays; B full board shared bath, cheaper Mon-Fri. Transport US$5.60 pp return. Entry to pools: US$2.50 pp small pool, US$3.15 large pool, includes use of sauna. Massage available, camping US$1.50, reservations required.
B Allkamari, in Valle de las Animas, 30 mins from town on the road to Palca, T279 1742, allkamari@ casalunaspa.com. Reservations required, cabins in a lovely valley between the Palca and La Animas canyons, a retreat with nice views of Illimani and Huayna Potosí, a place to relax and star-gaze, **AL** cabin for up to 8, **D** pp in dorm, includes breakfast, solar heating, jacuzzi included, meals on request, use of kitchen, horse and bike rentals, massage, shamanic rituals, taxi from Calacoto US$4.50, bus No 42 from the cemetery to Uni (7 daily weekdays, hourly weekends), get off at Iglesia de las Animas and walk 1 km.

B Oberland, Calle 2 y 3, Mallasa, PO Box 9392, 12 km from centre, T274 5040, www.h-oberland.com. A Swiss-owned, chalet-style restaurant (excellent, not cheap) and hotel (also good) with older resort facilities, gardens, cabañas, sauna, pool (open to public – US$2 - very hot water), beach volley, tennis. Permits camping with vehicle.

Tiahuanaco village *p261*
There are a few places to sleep and eat, including: **E Tiahuanco**, rooms with bath, also restaurant. Market day in Tiahuanaco is Sun; do not take photos then.

● Transport

Valle de la Luna *p260*
Minibus A can be caught on the Prado. If you do not want to walk in the valley, stay on the bus to the end of the line and take a return bus, 2 hrs in all. Alternatively take Micro 11 ('Aranjuez' large, not small bus) from C Sagárnaga, near Plaza San Francisco, US$0.65, and ask driver where to get off. Most of the

local travel agents organize tours to the Valle de la Luna. These are very brief, 5 mins stop for photos in a US$15 tour of La Paz and surroundings; taxis cost US$6.

Tiahuanaco p260

To get to Tiahuanaco, **Cooperativa Turismo** has tourist service with pick up from central hotels, or the terminal, at 0830, return at 1400, US$7.50. Otherwise take any **Micro** marked 'Cementerio' in La Paz, get out at Plaza Félix Reyes Ortiz, on Mariano Bautista (north side of cemetery), go north up Aliaga, 1 block east of Asín to find Tiahuanaco micros, US$1, 1½ hrs, every 30 mins, 0600 to 1700. Tickets can be bought in advance. **Taxi** for 2 costs about US$20-25 (can be shared), return, with unlimited time at site (US$30-40 including El Valle de la Luna). Some **buses** go on from Tiahuanaco to Desaguadero; virtually all Desaguadero buses stop at Tiahuanaco. Return buses (last back 1730-1800) leave from south side of the Plaza in village. Most tours from La Paz start at US$6.50 pp (not including site entrance or lunch, US$2.10) stopping at Laja and the highest point on the road before Tiahuanaco. Some tours include El Valle de la Luna. Minibuses (vans) to **Desaguadero**, from José María Asín y P Eyzaguirre (Cemetery district) US$1.25, 2 hrs, most movement on Tue and Fri when there is a market at the border.

Takesi Trail p261

Take a Palca/Ventilla **bus** from outside *comedor popular* in C Max Paredes above junction with C Rodríguez, daily at 0530, US$1; or take any bus going to Bolsa Negra, Tres Ríos or Pariguaya (see Yunga Cruz below). Alternatively, take any **micro** or minibus to Chasquipampa or Ovejuyo and try hitching a lift with anything heading out

of La Paz. If there isn't any transport, haggle with drivers of empty minibuses in Ovejuyo; you should be able to get one to go to Ventilla for about US$4. To **Mina San Francisco**: hire a **jeep** from La Paz; US$70, takes about 2 hrs. **Veloz del Norte** (T02-221 8279) leaves from Ocabaya and Av Las Américas in Villa Fátima, 0900 and 1400; 3½ hrs, continuing to Chojlla. Buses to La Paz (US$2.85) leave from Yanakachi at 0545 and 1245-1300 or 1400 daily.

Choro Trail p261

To the *apacheta* pass beyond **La Cumbre**, take a radio **taxi** from central La Paz for US$10, stopping to register at the Guardaparque hut. Or take a taxi to Villa Fátima in La Paz (US$1) then a bus to La Cumbre (US$1), 30 mins; make sure the drive knows you want to get off at La Cumbre.

Yunga Cruz Trail p262

Take the **bus** to **Pariguaya** between 0730-0830 Mon-Sat, from C Gral Luis Lara esq Venacio Burgoa near Plaza Líbano, San Pedro, US$2, 6 hrs to Chuñavi, US$2.25; 6½ hrs to Lambate (3 km further on). Buses to **Tres Ríos** and **Barro Negro/Tabacaya** depart at same time but stop well before Chuñavi. It's not possible to buy tickets in advance, be there at 0700.

Huayna Potosí p262

The mountain can be reached by transport arranged through tourist agencies (US$70) or the refugio. **Camión** from Plaza Ballivián in El Alto early morning or midday Mon, Wed, Fri (return next day), **taxi** (US$30), or **minibus** in the high season. If camping in the Zongo Pass area, stay at the site maintained by Miguel and family near the white house above the cross.

Lake Titicaca

Lake Titicaca is two lakes joined by the Straits of Tiquina: the larger, northern lake (Lago Mayor, or Chucuito) contains the Islas del Sol and de la Luna; the smaller lake (Lago Menor, or Huiñamarca) has several small islands. The waters are a beautiful blue, reflecting the hills and the distant cordillera in the shallows of Huiñamarca, mirroring the sky in the rarified air and changing colour when it is cloudy or raining. A boat trip on the lake is a must.

Ins and outs
Getting there A paved road runs from La Paz to the Straits of Tiquina (114 km El Alto-San Pablo). ▸▸ *See Transport page 272 for more details.*

La Paz to Copacabana
Puerto Pérez The closest point to the capital on Lake Titicaca, Puerto Pérez, 72 km from La Paz, was the original harbour for La Paz. It was founded in the 19th century by British navigators as a harbour for the first steam boat on the lake (the vessel was assembled piece by piece in Puno). Colourful fiestas are held on New Year's Day, Carnival, 3 May and 16 July (days may change each year). There are superb views of the lake and mountains.

Huatajata Further north along the east shore of the lake is Huatajata, with *Yacht Club Boliviano* (restaurant open to non-members, Saturday, Sunday lunch only, sailing for members only) and *Crillon Tours' International Hydroharbour* and *Inca Utama Hotel* (see below).
   Beyond here is **Chúa**, where there is fishing, sailing and *Transturin's* catamaran dock (see below). The public telephone office, *Cotel*, is on the plaza just off the main road.

Islands of Lake Huiñamarca
On **Suriqui** (1½ hours from Huatajata) in Lake Huiñamarca, a southeasterly extension of Lake Titicaca, you can visit the museum/craft shops of the Limachi brothers (now living at the *Inca Utama* cultural complex). The late Thor Heyerdahl's *Ra II*, which sailed from Morocco to Barbados in 1970, his *Tigris* reed boat, and the balloon gondola for the Nasca (Peru) flight experiment (see page 1171), were also constructed by the craftsmen of Suriqui. Reed boats are still made on Suriqui, probably the last place where the art survives. On **Kalahuta** there are *chullpas* (burial towers), old buildings and the uninhabited town of Kewaya. On **Pariti** there is Inca terracing and very good examples of weaving.
   From Chúa the main road reaches the east side of the Straits at **San Pablo** (clean restaurant in blue building, with good toilets). On the west side is San Pedro, the main Bolivian naval base, from where a paved road goes to Copacabana. Vehicles are transported across on barges, US$4. Passengers cross separately, US$0.35 (not included in bus fares) and passports are checked. Expect delays during rough weather, when it can get very cold.

Copacabana → *Phone code: 02. Colour map 6, grid A2.*
A little town on Lake Titicaca 158 km from La Paz by paved road, Copacabana has a heavily restored, Moorish-style **cathedral**. ① *Mon-Fri 1100-1200, 1400-1800, Sat-Sun, 0800-1200, 1400-1800, only groups of 8 or more, US$0.20.* It contains a famous 16th century miracle-working Dark Virgin of the Lake, also known as the Virgin of Candelaria, one of the patron saints of Bolivia. If going during Carnival or on a religious holiday, arrive early and be prepared to hold onto your place, as things tend to get very crowded. The cathedral itself is notable for its spacious atrium with four small chapels; the main chapel has one of the finest gilt altars in Bolivia. The basilica is clean, white, with coloured tiles decorating the exterior arches, cupolas and chapels. Vehicles are blessed in front of the church daily, especially on Sunday. There are 17th and 18th century paintings and statues in the sanctuary. Entrance at side of Basilica opposite *Entel*. **Tourist office** ① *kiosk on Plaza 2 de Febrero*, is helpful when open.
   On the headland which overlooks the town and port, Cerro Calvario, are the Stations of the Cross (a steep climb – leave plenty of time if going to see the sunset). On the hill behind the town (Cerro Sancollani) overlooking the lake, roughly southeast of the Basilica, is the **Horca del Inca**, two pillars of rock with another laid across them (probably a sun clock, now covered in graffiti), US$3. There is a path marked by arrows. Boys will offer to guide you: fix

Bolivia Lake Titicaca

66 99 The basilica is clean, white, with coloured tiles decorating the exterior arches, cupolas and chapels. Vehicles are blessed in front of the church daily...

price in advance if you want their help. There's a lovely walk along the lakeside north to Yampupata, 17 km (allow 6 hours), through unspoilt countryside. At the village, or at Sicuani ask for a rowing boat to Isla del Sol, or trip on the lake (US$3.50). Motor boats cost more but are quicker. There are *alojamientos* and places to eat in Sicuani and Yumpapata.

Isla del Sol
The site of the main Inca creation myth (there are other versions) is a short distance by boat from Copacabana. Legend has it that Viracocha, the creator god, had his children, Manco Kapac and Mama Ocllo, spring from the waters of the lake to found Cuzco and the Inca dynasty. A sacred rock at the island's northwest end is worshipped as their birthplace. On the east shore near the jetty for *Crillon Tours*' hydrofoils and other craft is the Fuente del Inca, a pure spring, and Inca steps leading up from the water. A 2 km walk from the landing stage takes one to the main ruins of Pilcocaina, a two storey building with false domes and superb views. The community-run **Museo Comunitario de Etnografía** (or Mueso Templo del Sol) ① *daily 0900-1200, 1300-1800, multi-site ticket US$0.60,* celebrates costumes used in sacred dances. Southeast of the Isla del Sol is the Isla de la Luna (or Coati), which also may be visited – the best ruins are an Inca temple and nunnery, both sadly neglected.

Border with Peru
The west side of Lake Titicaca The road goes from La Paz 91 km west to **Guaqui,** formerly the port for the Titicaca passenger boats. The road crosses the border at **Desaguadero** 22 km further west and runs along the shore of the lake to Puno. (There are three La Paz-Puno routes, see also page 1194.) Bolivian immigration is just before the bridge, open 0830-1230 and 1400-

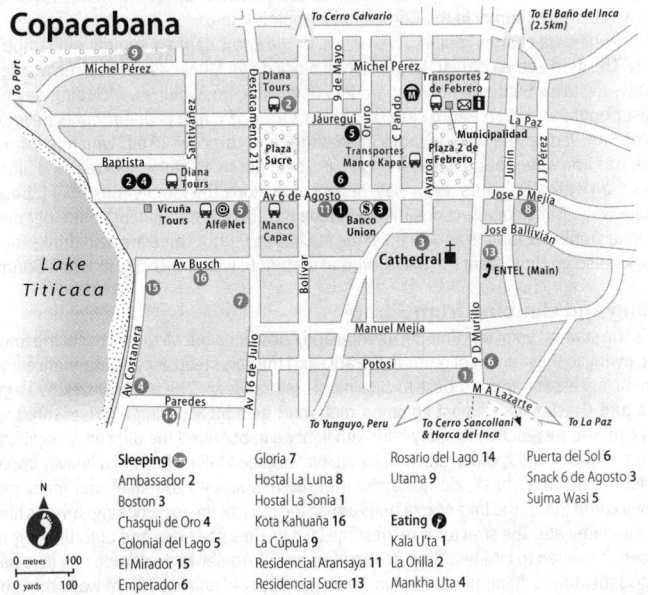

2030. Get exit stamp, walk a few hundred metres across the bridge then get entrance stamp on the other side. Get Peruvian visas in La Paz. There are a few basic hotels and restaurants on both sides of the bridge. Money changers on Peruvian side give reasonable rates.

Via Copacabana From Copacabana a new, paved 'panoramic' highway leads south to the Bolivian frontier at Kasani, then to Yunguyo. Do not photograph the border area. For La Paz tourist agency services on this route see under International Buses (page 257) and under Activities and tours page 271. The border is open 0830-1930 (Bolivian time). Buses/colectivos stop here and at the Peruvian side; or you can walk, 500 m, between the two posts. If crossing into Bolivia with a motorcycle, do not be fooled into paying any unnecessary charges to police or immigration. Going to Peru, money can be changed in Yunguyo but better rates are to be found in Puno. Coming into Bolivia, the best rates are at Copacabana.

East side of Lake Titicaca

From Huarina, a road heads northwest to Achacachi (market Sunday; fiesta 14 September). Here, one road goes north across a tremendous marsh to **Warisata**, then crosses the altiplano to Sorata (see below). Paving of this road commenced in 2005.

At Achacachi, another road runs roughly parallel to the shore of Lake Titicaca, through **Ancoraimes** (Sunday market), **Carabuco** (with colonial church), **Escoma**, which has an Aymara market every Sunday morning, to **Puerto Acosta**, 10 km from the Peruvian border. It is a pleasant, friendly town with a large plaza and several simple places to stay and eat. The area around Puerto Acosta is good walking country. From La Paz to Puerto Acosta the road is paved as far as Escoma, then good until Puerto Acosta (best in the dry season, approximately May to October). North of Puerto Acosta towards Peru the road deteriorates and should not be attempted except in the dry season. An obelisk marks the international frontier at Cerro Janko Janko, on a promontory high above the lake with magnificent views. Here are hundreds of small stone storerooms, deserted except during the busy Wednesday and Saturday smugglers' market, the only days when transport is plentiful. You should get an exit stamp in La Paz before heading to this border (only preliminary entrance stamps are given here). There is a Peruvian customs post 2 km from the border and 2 km before Tilali, but Peruvian immigration is in Puno.

Sorata → *Phone code: 02. Colour map 6, grid A2. Population: 8,000. Altitude: 2,578 m.*

Sorata, 163 km from La Paz, is a beautiful colonial town nestled at the foot of Mount Illampu; around it are views over lush, alpine-like valleys. The climate is delightful. Nearby are some challenging long-distance hikes and, closer to the Peruvian border is more adventurous hiking and climbing country in the Cordillera de Apolobamba.

The town has a charming plaza, with views of the snow-capped summit of Illampu on a clear day. The market area is near the plaza, half block down Muñecas on the right. Market day is Sunday; fiesta 14 September. There are lots of walking possibilities, including day hikes. The most popular is to **San Pedro cave** ① *0800-1700, US$1, toilets at entrance*, beyond the village of San Pedro. The walk is more interesting than the cave itself, which is formed in gypsum, has an underground 'lake' and is lit. It's best not to go alone. It is reached either by road, a 12 km walk (2½ hours) each way, or by a path along the Río San Cristóbal (about 3½ hours one way). Get clear directions before setting out. Take water, at least 1 litre per person, or else take sterilizing tablets and fill up at the tap in San Pedro. There are also drinks for sale. Taxi trucks also go there from the plaza, with a 30-minute wait, for US$5, most on Sunday.

Trekking and climbing from Sorata

Sorata is the starting point for climbing **Illampu** and Ancohuma but all routes out of the town are difficult, owing to the number of paths in the area and the very steep ascent. Experience and full equipment necessary and it's best to hire mules (see below). The 2-4 day trek to **Lagunas Chillata and Glaciar** is the most common route and gets busy during high season. Laguna Chillata can also be reached in a day-hike with light gear, but mind the difficult navigation and take warm clothing, food, water, sun protection, etc. Laguna Chillata has been heavily impacted by tourism (remove all trash, do not throw it in the pits around the lake) and many groups frequently camp there. The Inka Marka ruins are on the back of the rock looking towards Illampu from Laguna Chillata. The structures nearest the lake are in a sad state and unfortunately many have been converted to latrines. The **Circuito Illampu**, a 8-10 day high-altitude trek (five passes over 4,500 m) around Illampu, is excellent. It can get very cold and it is a hard walk, though very beautiful with nice campsites on the way. Some food can be bought in Cocoyo on the third day. You must be acclimatized before setting out. A new option is the **Trans-Cordillera Trek**, 12 days from Sorata to Huayna Potosí, or 20 days all the way to Illimani at the opposite (south) end of the Cordillera Real. **Note**: Laguna San Francisco, along the Illampu Circuit, has for many years been the scene of repeated armed holdups. In late 2005 this was the only place in the Sorata area not considered safe and guided trekking parties were passing though in the small hours of the night to avoid contact with the local population.

Cordillera Apolobamba

The Area Protegida Apolobamba forms part of the Cordillera Apolobamba, the north extension of the Cordillera Real. The range itself has many 5,000 m-plus peaks, while the conservation area of 483,744 ha protects herds of vicuña, huge flocks of flamingoes and many condors. The area adjoins the Parque Nacional Madidi (see page 314). This is great trekking country and the five-day **Charazani to Pelechuco** mountain trek is one of the best in the country (see *Footprint Bolivia* for details). It passes traditional villages and the peaks of the southern Cordillera Apolobamba. **Charazani**, the main starting point, is the biggest village in the region (3,200 m). Its three-day fiesta is around 16 July. There are some **G** *alojamientos*, restaurants and shops. **Pelechuco** (3,600 m) is a basic village, also with **G** *alojamientos*, cafés and shops. The road to Pelechuco goes through the Area Protegida, passing La Cabaña, 5 km outside of which are the reserve's HQ. Visitors are welcome to see the vicuñas and there is accommodation and food.

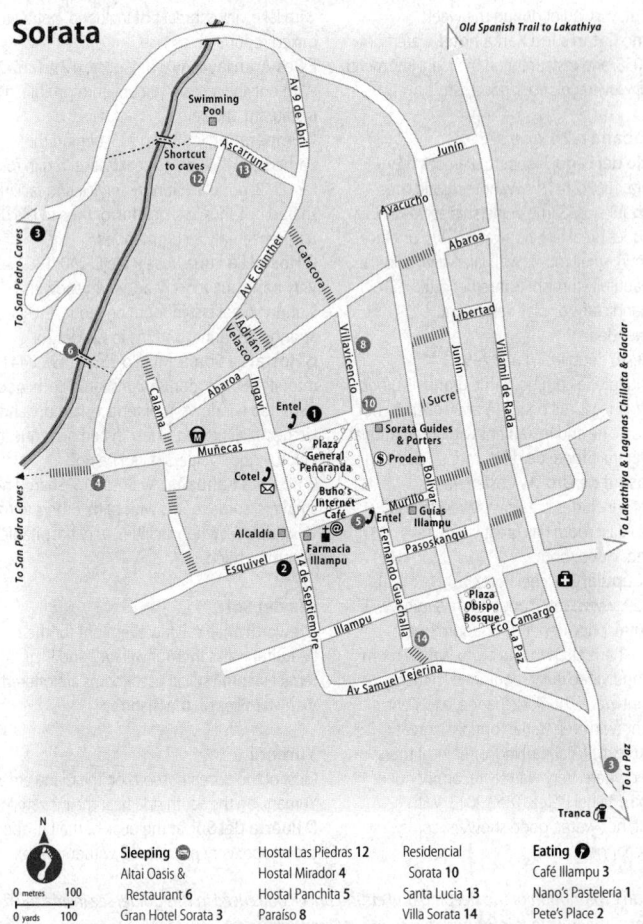

Sorata

Old Spanish Trail to Lakathiya

Sleeping
Altai Oasis & Restaurant **6**
Gran Hotel Sorata **3**
Hostal Las Piedras **12**
Hostal Mirador **4**
Hostal Panchita **5**
Paraíso **8**

Residencial Sorata **10**
Santa Lucia **13**
Villa Sorata **14**

Eating
Café Illampu **3**
Nano's Pastelería **1**
Pete's Place **2**

⊜ Sleeping

La Paz to Copacabana *p264*
Puerto Pérez
L Hotel Las Balsas, owned and operated by *Turismo Balsa* (see La Paz Tour Operators, page 254, or T/F02-281 3226). In a beautiful lakeside setting, with views of the cordillera, all rooms have balcony over the lake, willing to negotiate out of season, fitness facilities including pool, jacuzzi, sauna. Excellent restaurant with fixed price lunch or dinner good value at US$12.

C Hostería Las Islas, nearby on the Plaza. Shared bath, hot water, heated rooms, comfortable but can get crowded, *Blue Note* jazz bar next door.

Huatajata
B Hotel Titicaca, between Huatajata and Huarina, Km 80 from La Paz, T02-237 4877, F239 1225 (address in La Paz, Potosí y Ayacucho 1220, p 2). Beautiful views, sauna, pool, good restaurant, very quiet during the week.

F Máximo Catari's Inti Karka hotel, waterfront, T0811 5058, and restaurant on the road. Full menu, open daily, average prices, good fish.

Copacabana *p264, map p265*
B Rosario del Lago, Rigoberto Paredes y Av Costanera, T862 2141, www.hotelrosario.com/lago. **A** in Jul-Aug. Same ownership as *Rosario*, La Paz, includes breakfast, hot water, *Turisbus* office (see below), small rooms with lake view, colonial style, beautifully furnished, internet café US$0.75 per hr, handicrafts display, restaurant. Recommended.

B Gloria, 16 de Julio, T/F862 2094, www.hotelgloria.com.bo. Same group as *Gloria* in La Paz, price is full board (**A** at weekends) hot water, bar, café and restaurant with international and vegetarian food, gardens, money exchange.

B-C Chasqui de Oro, Av Costanera 55, T862 2343. Includes breakfast, lakeside hotel, café/breakfast room has great views, trips organized, video room.

B-D La Cúpula, C Michel Pérez 1-3, T862 2029, www.hotelcupula.com. 5 mins' walk from centre, price depends on room (most expensive have kitchen and bath), sitting room with TV and video, fully- equipped kitchen, library, hot water, book exchange, excellent restaurant (with vegetarian options), great breakfast (extra), car parking, offer local tours, German owners. Very warmly recommended.

D Utama, Michel Pérez, T862 2013. With breakfast, hot water, good showers, comfy, book exchange.

E Boston, Conde de Lemos, near Basilica, T862 2231. **F** without bath, good, quiet.

E Colonial del Lago, Av 6 de Agosto y Av 16 de Julio, T862 2270, www.titicacabolivia.com. Bright rooms, some with lake view, **F** without bath, breakfast included, garden, good restaurant and *peña*.

E Res Sucre, Murillo 228, T862 2080. Hot water, parking, quiet, good cheap breakfast, laundry US$1.20, offers tours of lake.

E-F Ambassador, Bolívar y Jáuregui, T/F862 2216. Comfortable, rooms downstairs around courtyard, dorms upstairs, heater US$2 per day, hot water, rooftop restaurant, reduction for more than 1 night or with IH card, 10% with student card, luggage store, parking. Recommended.

F El Mirador, Av Costanera y Busch, T862 2289, elmiradorhotel@hotmail.com. In a pink building with lake views, breakfast included, hot water, mixed reports on service.

F Res Aransaya, Av 6 de Agosto 121, T862 2229. With hot shower, simple but comfortable, good restaurant and café.

G Emperador, C Murillo 235, behind the Cathedral, T862 2083. Breakfast served in room for US$2, popular, laundry service and facilities, shared hot showers, helpful for trips to Isla del Sol. Repeatedly recommended.

G Hostal La Luna, José P Mejía 260, T862 2051. Very basic but very cheap, warm showers, laundry, breakfast in room on request (US$1), can arrange discounts on trips to Isla del Sol.

G Hostal La Sonia, Murillo 253, T7196 8441 (mobile). Some rooms with shared bath, good beds, big windows, roof terrace, laundry and kitchen facilities, breakfast in bed on request, very helpful, good value but can be noisy.

G pp Kota Kahuaña, Av Busch 15. Shared hot showers, some rooms with bath, others with lake view, quiet, kitchen facilities, very hospitable. Recommended.

Isla del Sol *p265*
It is worthwhile staying overnight for the many beautiful walks through villages and Inca terraces, some still in use. Rooms are offered by many families on the island.

Yumani
Most of the dozen *posadas* on the island are at Yumani, on the south side near the Inca steps.
D Puerta del Sol, at the peak of the hill above the village. Very popular. (**G** without bath).

⊜ *For an explanation of the sleeping and eating price codes used in this guide, see inside the front*
⚫ *cover. Other relevant information is found in Essentials pages 240-241.*

Nearby is the owner's father's hostel, **G Templo del Sol**, with clean rooms, comfy beds, electric showers and a good restaurant.

F El Imperio del Sol, peach-coloured house. Comfortable, no running water.

F Inti Kala, opposite *Templo del Sol*. Shared electric showers, fantastic views, great value, serves good meals.

G There are several others, all basic but clean, few have hot water (although the island has electricity), meals provided US$1.50-2.

Pilcocaina

G Albergue Inca Sama, next to Pilcocaina ruins. Sleep on mattresses on floor, good food, also camping in typical tents (contact via *Hotel Playa Azul*, Copacabana, T862 2228, or La Paz T235 6566), Sr Pusari, offers boat service from Copacabana and trips to the north of island.

Challa

G Posada del Inca, at Challa, on the northeast coast, right on the beach. 8 double rooms, very basic outside toilets, no showers, contact Juan Mamani Ramos through *Entel* office, food is provided and beer or *refrescos* are for sale.

G pp Qhumphuri, mid-island on the east coast, 1 hr from the Inca Steps, 1 hr from the Inca ruins in the north. Simple but comfortable rooms with bath, local furniture, great views, restaurant serves all meals (extra cost), tasty food, cooking facilities, owner Juan Ramos Ticona interested in sustainable development.

Challapampa

Several places to stay around the Plaza in Challapampa, at the north end of the island.

G Posada Manco Kapac, one of 2 basic hostales owned by Lucio Arias and his father, Francisco (Lucio can also arrange boat tickets). Price depends on whether you have a shower or a bucket. Room for 35 people and a garden for camping, hot showers and views of Illampu. The second hostel has the same name but is further up the beach.

La Posada del Inca, a restored colonial hacienda, owned by *Crillon Tours* and only available as part of a tour with *Crillon*, see below. *Magri Turismo* also owns a hotel on the island. See La Paz, Tour operators on page 254. See also *Transturin's* overnight options on page 271.

Sorata *p266*

D-E Altai Oasis, T7151 9856 (mobile), resaltai@hotmail.com. At the bottom of the valley in a beautiful setting, with cabins (**C**), rooms with bath and camping (US$1.25 pp), transport to town US$3 for 5 people, quiet, well-designed,

with good restaurant, owners Johnny and Roxana Resnikowski. Recommended.

D-E Gran Hotel Sorata (Ex-*Prefectural*), on the outskirts immediately above the police checkpoint, T281 7378, call from Plaza for free pick-up. Spacious although bathrooms (electric showers) a bit tired, breakfast included, free filtered water, large garden with great views, swimming pool (open to non-residents for US$0.50), games room, good restaurant, internet café, accepts credit cards. Not always open.

F Hostal El Mirador, Muñecas 400, T289 5008. With showers and toilets, kitchen, laundry facilities, sun terrace.

F Hostal Las Piedras, just off Ascarrunz, T7191 6341 (mobile). New, well-designed and mellow, European run, cheaper with shared bath, very helpful, good breakfasts. Recommended.

F Hostal Panchita, on plaza, T813 5038. Shared bath, large rooms, hot water, basic but good value, sunny courtyard and good restaurant.

F pp Paraíso, Villavicencio 117, T213 6671. Pleasant, fairly modern, American breakfast US$1.80, hot water, restaurant.

F Res Sorata, just off plaza, T213 6672, resorata@entelnet.bo. Administrator Louis Demers, from Quebec, and the proprietor are helpful. The garden is lovely, older rooms (with

shared bath) are basic, newer ones (with private bath) are adequate and good value. Restaurant with good lunch/dinner US$2.75, breakfast US$2, washing machine US$1.50, DVDs to watch, slow internet access US$3.60 per hr.

F Santa Lucía, Ascarrunz, T213 6686, santa_lucia@yahoo.com. Modern, carpeted rooms, comfortable, cheaper with shared bath, patio, helpful.

F Villa Sorata, F Guachalla, T213 5241. Large, well-furnished rooms, electric shower, terrace with lovely views, nice small courtyard, good value but the owner lives abroad and staff are often absent.

---

❼ Eating

Huatajata *p264*
Inti Raymi. With fresh fish and boat trips (US$22 per boat). There are other restaurants of varying standard, most lively at weekends and in the high season.

Copacabana *p264, map p265*
♛♛ La Orilla, Av 6 de Agosto, close to lake. Open daily 1000-2200, usually, warm, atmospheric, tasty food with local and international choices. Recommended.
♛ Kala U'ta, Av 6 de Agosto. Nice atmosphere, good vegetarian food, coffee and chocolate.
♛ Mankha Uta, lake end of Av 6 de Agosto. Warm, good service, cheap but uninspiring set meals, movies, Play Station and big sound system.
♛ Puerta del Sol, Av 6 de Agosto. Similar to others on this avenue, excellent trout, eat in or takeaway.
♛ Snack 6 de Agosto, Av 6 de Agosto. 2 branches, good trout, big portions, some vegetarian dishes, serves breakfast. Also has good rooms for rent, **D** with bath, **E** without, breakfast extra, laundry.

♛ Sujma Wasi, Jáuregui 127. Open 0730-2300, excellent food and atmosphere, good breakfasts, vegetarian lunch, wide range of books on Bolivia.
Good breakfasts and other meals, especially fish, in the market on C Abaroa.

Sorata *p266*
There are several Italian restaurants on the plaza, all quite similar (♛♛-♛), none is outstanding.
♛♛-♛ Altai Oasis (see Sleeping, above). Good breakfasts and other meals, home-gown vegetables, local honey, regarded as best in town.
♛♛-♛ Café Illampu, on the way to San Pedro cave. Swiss-run, excellent sandwiches, bread and cakes, camping US$1 (an extra US$0.50 to hire tent), mountain bikes for hire, closed Tue and Feb-Mar.
♛♛-♛ Pete's Place, Esquivel y 14 de Septiembre, 2nd floor. Vegetarian dishes and set menus, also meat, very good, British owner Pete is a good source of information, open Tue-Sat 0830-2200.
♛ Nano's Pastelería, Muñecas on the plaza. Thu-Sat 1700-2200, Sun 0930-1200, good sweets and snacks.
♛ Royal House, off Muñecas by the market. For set meals.

❀ Festivals and events

Copacabana *p264, map p265*
Note: At these times hotel prices quadruple.
1-3 Feb Virgen de la Candelaria, massive procession, dancing, fireworks, bullfights. **Easter**, with candlelight procession on Good Friday. **23 Jun**, San Juan, also on Isla del Sol. **4-6 Aug**, La Virgen de Copacabana.

Sorata *p266*
Fiesta San Pedro, **7 days after Easter**. Feria Agro-Eco-Turística in **Jun**. Fiesta Patronal del Señor de la Columna, **14 Sep**, is the main festival.

▲ Activities and tours

Lake Titicaca *p264*

Crillon Tours (address under La Paz, Tour operators, page 254) run a hydrofoil service on Lake Titicaca with excellent bilingual guides. Tours stop at their Andean Roots cultural complex at *Inca Utama*: the Bolivian History Museum includes a recorded commentary; a 15-min video precedes the evening visit to the Kallawaya (Native Medicine) museum. The **Inca Utama Hotel** (**AL**) has a health spa based on natural remedies; the rooms are comfortable, with heating, electric blankets, good service, bar, good food in restaurant, reservations through *Crillon Tours* in La Paz. *Crillon* is Bolivia's oldest travel agency and is consistently highly recommended. Also at *Inca Utama* is an observatory (*Alajpacha*) with two telescopes and retractable thatched roof for viewing the night sky, a floating restaurant and bar on the lake (*La Choza Náutica*), a 252-sq m floating island, a colonial-style tower with 15 deluxe suites, panoramic elevator and 2 conference rooms. Health, astronomical, mystic and ecological programmes are offered. The hydrofoil trips include visits to Andean Roots complex, Copacabana, Islas del Sol and de la Luna, Straits of Tiquina and past reed fishing boats. See Isla del Sol, Sleeping, for *La Posada del Inca*. Crillon has a sustainable tourism project with Urus-Iriuitos people on floating islands by the Isla Quewaya. Trips can be arranged to/from Puno (bus and hydrofoil excursion to Isla del Sol) and from Copacabana via Isla del Sol to Cuzco and Machu Picchu. Other combinations of hydrofoil and land-based excursions can be arranged (also jungle and adventure tours). All facilities and modes of transport connected by radio. In Puno, *Crillon*'s office is at *Arcobaleno Tours*, Lambayeque 175, T351052, arcobaleno@ titicacalake.com, where all documentation for crossing the border can be done.

Transturin (see also La Paz, Tour operators, page 254) run catamarans on Lake Titicaca, either for sightseeing or on the La Paz-Puno route. The catamarans are more leisurely than the hydrofoils of *Crillon* so there is more room and time for on-board entertainment, with bar, video and sun deck. From their dock at Chúa, catamarans run day and day/night cruises starting either in La Paz or Copacabana. Puno may also be the starting point for trips. Overnight cruises involve staying in a cabin on the catamaran, moored at the Isla del Sol, with lots of activities. On the island, Transturin has the *Inti Wata* cultural complex which has restored

Inca terraces, an Aymara house and the underground *Ekako* museum. There is also a 50-passenger totora reed boat for trips to the Polkokaina Inca palace. All island-based activities are for catamaran clients only. Transturin runs through services to Puno without a change of bus, and without many of the formalities at the border. **Transturin** offers last minute, half-price deals for drop-in travellers (24-48 hrs in advance, take passport): sold in Copacabana only, half-day tour on the lake, continuing to Puno by bus, or La Paz; overnight Copacabana-Isla del Sol-Copacabana with possible extension to La Paz. Sold in La Paz only: La Paz-Isla del Sol-La Paz, or with overnight stay (extension to Puno possible on request).

Turisbus (see La Paz, Tour operators page 254 and *Hoteles Rosario*, La Paz, and *Rosario del Lago*, Copacabana) offer guided tours in the fast launches *Titicaca Explorer I* (28 passengers) and *II* (8 passengers) to the Isla del Sol, returning to Copacabana via the Bahía de Sicuani for trips on traditional reed boats. Also La Paz-Puno, with boat excursion to Isla del Sol, boxed lunch and road transport, or with additional overnight at *Hotel Rosario del Lago*.

Sorata *p266*
Mountain biking
Hoodoo Bike Tours, Plaza Gral Peñeranda, T7127 6685 (in La Paz, *Oliver's Travels*, Murillo y Tarija), www.hoodoobiketours.com. Plenty of good routes, including multi-day trips (eg to Rurrenabaque) with emphasis on fairly extreme.

Trekking guides
It is much cheaper to go to Sorata and ask about trekking there than to book up a trek with an agency in La Paz. Conversely, buy all your trekking food in La Paz as Sorata shops are poorly supplied. Asociación de Guías y Porteadores, T213 6698. Another guiding association is **Asociación de Guías Illampu**, Murillo entre Guachalla y Bolívar. Both offer similar services, quality and prices. Louis at *Residencial Sorata* can arrange guides and mules. Daily prices: guide prices start at US$12, porters and mules extra, remember you have to feed your guide/porter. When trekking avoid sedimented glacier melt water for drinking and treat with iodine all other water.

⊖ Transport

La Paz to Copacabana *p264*
Puerto Pérez
Bus Regular minibus service from **La Paz** Cementerio district: across from the cemetery, above the flower market, ask for buses to Batallas, price US$0.75.

Huatajata
Bus **La Paz**-Huatajata/Tiquina, US$0.85, Transportes Titikaka, Av Kollasuyo 16, daily from 0400, returning between 0700 and 1800.

Islands in Lago Huiñamarca *p264*
Ferry Máximo Catari (see Huatajata, Sleeping, above) arranges boats to the islands in Lago Huiñamarca, Pariti, Kalahuta and Suriqui: prices from US$25-US$40, 1 hr boat trip US$7.50, sailing boat for 3 US$16-20 for a day (boat trips recommended). Boats can also be hired in Tiquina for trips to Suriqui, US$3 per person in a group.

Copacabana *p264, map p265*
If arriving in Bolivia at Copacabana and going to La Paz, see Safety on page 243, for scams in the Cemetery district, where public transport arrives.
Bus Agency buses: several agencies go from La Paz to **Puno**, stopping at Copacabana for lunch, or with an open ticket for continuing to Puno later. They charge US$12-15 and depart La Paz 0800; La Paz- Copacabana takes 4½ hrs. They continue to the Peruvian border at Kasani and on to Puno, stopping for immigration formalities and changing money (better rates in Copacabana or Puno). 3½ hrs to Puno, US$2.50-4 depending on season, depart Copacabana around 1200-1400. It's also possible to catch a tour bus to **Cuzco**, usually depart around 1400, tickets US$17-20, change bus in Puno, tour company arranges connection. Tour buses Copacabana-La Paz charge US$3. To/from **La Paz**, US$2 plus US$0.35 for Tiquina crossing, 3½ hrs, several departures daily between 0700-1800 with **Manco Capac**, T862 2234, or 245 3035, La Paz or **2 de Febrero**, T862 2233, or 237 7181, La Paz. Both have offices on Copacabana's main plaza and in La Paz at Plaza Reyes Ortiz, opposite entrance to cemetery. Buses also from main terminal, US$3. Buy bus tickets as soon as possible as all buses are usually full by day of travel, especially Sun. 1-day trips from La Paz are not recommended as they allow only 1½-2 hrs in Copacabana. (See also Frontier via Copacabana page 266.) Bus to **Huatajata**, US$2 and to **Huarina**, US$2.50.
Car From **La Paz** to Copacabana (direct), 4 hrs, take exit to 'Río Seco' in El Alto.

Isla del Sol *p265*
Ferry Inca Tours and Titicaca Tours run motor boats to the island; both have offices on Av 6 de Agosto in Copacabana, as do other companies. Boats leave Copacabana at 0800, 1100 and 1300, US$1.20 pp. To hire a private boat for 12 costs US$70. Boats go to the north and south end: check on the day for return times. If you go to the north end, you have enough time to walk the length of the island (take food and water, allow 3 hrs). With

the same ticket you can stay on the island and return another day. Other options are: half-day tours and tours which include north and south of Isla del Sol and Isla de La Luna in one day (not recommended, too short). Full-day tour US$4-5 pp (more if you stay overnight). Expensive express boats may also be taken to Isla del Sol from Yampupata (see page 265), but none returns to Yampupata.

Border with Peru p265
Via Guaqui and Desaguadero
Bus Road paved all the way to Peru. Buses from La Paz to Guaqui and Desaguadero depart from same location as micros for Tiahuanaco (see above) every 30 mins, US$1.55, 1½-2 hrs. From Desaguadero to **La Paz** last bus departs 1700, buses may leave later if enough passengers, but charge a lot more.

Via Copacabana
Bus In Peru, bus starts at **Yunguyo**. *Colectivo* Copacabana-Kasani US$0.50 pp, Kasani- Yunguyo US$0.60 pp. Make sure, if arranging a through ticket La Paz-Puno, that you get all the necessary stamps en route, and find out if your journey involves a change of bus. Note the common complaint that through services La Paz-Puno (or vice versa) deteriorate once the border has been crossed, eg smaller buses are used, extra passengers taken on, passengers left stranded if the onward bus is already full, drivers won't drop you where the company says they will.

East side of Lake Titicaca p266
Bus **La Paz** (Reyes Cardona 772, Cancha Tejar, Cementerio district, T238 2239)-Puerto Acosta, 5 hrs, US$3.75, daily 0600, more on Sun. Transport past Puerto Acosta only operates on market days, Wed and Sat, and is mostly cargo trucks. Bus Puerto Acosta-La Paz at about 1400. There are frequent minivans to La Paz from **Escoma**, 25 km from Puerto Acosta; trucks from the border may take you this far.

Sorata p266
Bus From **La Paz** with **Trans Unificada Sorata** (from C Manuel Bustillos 683, 2 blocks up from Cementerio in La Paz), 0500-1600, 4½ hrs, US$1.65; from Sorata every hour daily 0400-1400 (till 1700 Fri and Sun). To **Rurrenabaque**: jeeps run between Sorata and **Santa Rosa**, down the valley past Consata. From Santa Rosa transport can be arranged to Mapiri and all the way to

Rurrenabaque (a very long rough ride with interesting vegetation and views). To, or from **Peru**, change buses at Huarina for Copacabana.

Cordillera Apolobamba p267
Charazani
Bus From Calle Reyes Cardona, Cemetery district, La Paz, daily, 10 hrs, US$4.40, very crowded.

Pelechuco
Bus From **La Paz** (same street as for Charazani) leave on Wed and Thu, 1100, US$6, 18-24 hrs, returning Fri 2000 and Sat 1600. Jeeps charge US$250 to Charazani and US$300 to Pelechuco.

● Directory

Copacabana *p264, map p265*
Banks Banco Unión, 6 de Agosto opposite Oruro, reasonable rates of exchange, TCs at US$2 commission, cash advance on Visa and MasterCard 3% commission. **Prodem**, Av 6 de Agosto entre Oruro y Pando, for cash advances on Visa or MasterCard, 5% commission, changes US$ cash. No ATM in town. Several *artesanías* on Av 6 de Agosto buy and sell US$ and Peruvian soles. **Internet** Alcadi, next to post office, opposite cathedral, US$2.40 per hr. **Alf@Net**, Av 6 de Agosto, next to *Hostal Colonial*, 0830-2200, US$2, has book exchange. In Municipal building, Plaza 2 de Febrero, US$2.95 per hr. **Ifa-Internet**, Av 16 de Julio y Jáuregui, Plaza Sucre. US$3.50 per hr. **Post offices** Plaza 2 de Febrero, open Tue-Sat 0900- 1200, 1430-1830, Sun 0900-1500, *poste restante*. **Telephones** Entel, open 0800-1230, 1330-2000, international phone and fax, accept US$.

Sorata *p266*
Banks Prodem, on main plaza, variable hours Tue-Sun, changes US$ cash at fair rates, 5% commission on Visa/MasterCard cash advances. Nowhere in town to change TCs. **Internet** Buho's Internet Café, on the plaza, 0900-1800. US$3 per hr, very slow connection but a cosy place. **Medical services** Hospital: Villamil de Rada e Illampu. Has oxygen and X-ray. There is an adequately equipped pharmacy. **Post offices** On the plaza, 0830-1230, 1500-1800, but La Paz Correo is more reliable. **Telephones** Several around the plaza, rates vary considerably from place to place, so shop around.

The Yungas

Only a few hours from La Paz are the subtropical valleys known as The Yungas. These steep, forested slopes, squeezed in between the Cordillera and the Amazon Lowlands, provide a welcome escape from the chill of the capital. The warm climate of The Yungas is also ideal for growing citrus fruit, bananas, coffee and coca leaves for the capital.

La Paz to the Yungas

The most commonly-used route to the Yungas is via **La Cumbre**, northeast of La Paz. The road out of La Paz circles cloudwards over La Cumbre pass at 4,660 m; the highest point is reached in half an hour; all around are towering snowcapped peaks. Soon after **Unduavi** the paving ends, the road becomes 'all-weather' and drops over 3,400 m to the green subtropical forest in 80 km. The roads to Chulumani and Coroico divide just after Unduavi, where there is a *garita* (check point), the only petrol station, and lots of roadside stalls. From Unduavi leading to Yolosa, the junction 8 km from Coroico, is steep, twisting, clinging to the side of sheer cliffs, and it is slippery in the wet. It is a breathtaking descent (best not to look over the edge if you don't like heights) and its reputation for danger is more than matched by the beauty of the scenery. A new road from La Paz, including a 2½-km tunnel, is being built to Coroico via Chuspipata and Yolosa. It is due for completion in 2006, but opened, incomplete, in late 2005 (buses still used the old road). For the La Cumbre-Coroico hike (Choro), see page 261. **Gravity Assisted Mountain Biking** (address under La Paz, Tour operators) run La Cumbre-Coroico down the so-called "World's Most Dangerous Road" with top quality bikes (with hydraulic disc brakes), English speaking guides, helmet, gloves, vehicle support throughout the day, four hours La Cumbre-Yolosa, then transport to Coroico and/or back to La Paz. Free next day transport back to La Paz. Recommended. Other companies do this trip too, but quality varies, and going with a reputable company is a sensible option. Cheaper operators often have to cut corners. Many bike companies take riders back to La Paz the same day, but Coroico is worth much more of your time than that. Note that the road is especially dangerous mid-December to mid-February and many companies will not run downhill bike tours at this time.

Coroico → *Phone code: 02. Colour map 6, grid A3.*

The little town of Coroico is perched on a hill at 1,760 m amid beautiful scenery. The hillside is covered with orange and banana groves; coffee is also grown and condors circle overhead. Coroico is a first-class place to relax with several good walks. A colourful four-day festival is held 19-22 October. On 2 November, All Souls' Day, the cemetery is festooned with black ribbons. A good walk is up to the waterfalls, starting from **El Calvario**. Follow the stations of the cross by the cemetery, off Calle Julio Zuazo Cuenca, which leads steeply uphill from the plaza. Facing the chapel at El Calvario, with your back to the town, look for the path on your left. This leads to the falls which are the town's water supply (Toma de Agua) and, beyond, to two more falls. **Cerro Uchumachi**, the mountain behind El Calvario, can be climbed following the same stations of the cross, but then look for the faded red and white antenna behind the chapel. From there it's about 1½ hours' steep walk to the top (take water). A third walk goes to the pools in the **Río Vagante**, 7 km off the road to Coripata; it takes about three hours. The **Cámara Hotelera** on the plaza functions as a **tourist information centre**. There have been several incidents of young women being raped or attacked in this area; do not hike alone in this area.

Caravi → *Phone code: 02. Colour map 6, grid A2. Altitude: 600 m.*

From the road junction at Yolosa the lower fork follows the river northeast 75 km to Caranavi, an uninspiring town 156 km from La Paz. From here the road continues towards the settled area of the Alto Beni, at times following a picturesque gorge. Market days are Friday and Saturday. There is a range of hotels and *alojamientos* and buses from La Paz (Villa Fátima) to Rurrenabaque pass through. Beyond Caranavi, 70 km, is **Guanay** at the junction of the Tipuani and Mapiri rivers (basic lodging). From here there is river transport to Rurrenabaque.

Chulumani and around → *Phone code: 02. Colour map 6, grid A2. Altitude: 1,640 m.*

The capital of Sud Yungas, 124 km from La Paz, is a charming, relaxed little town with beautiful views and many hikes. There's a **fiesta** on 24 August (lasts 10 days) and a lively market every weekend. The road from Unduavi goes through **Puente Villa**, where a road branches north to Coroico through Coripata. The **tourist office** ① *main plaza, Mon-Fri 0900-1330, 1500-2200, Sat, Sun 0700-2200, but frequently shut,* sells locally grown coffee, teas, jams and honey. **Apa Apa Ecological Park** ① *10 km away, US$25 for up to 5 people park fee including transport and hiking guide (no reduction for fewer people),* is the last area of original Yungas forest with lots of interesting wildlife. The road to **Irupana,** a colonial village 1½ hours from Chulumani, passes the turn-off to the park. Ask to get off and walk 15 minutes up to the *hacienda* of Ramiro Portugal and his wife, Tildi (both speak English), who manage the park; you can use their pool after trek (3 rooms, full-board accommodation and campsite with bathrooms, US$10 per tent). Or T213 6106 to arrange transport from town, taxi US$3 one way; or T279 0381 (La Paz), or write to Casilla 10109, Miraflores, La Paz.

● Sleeping

Coroico *p274*
Hotel rooms can be difficult to find at holiday weekends and prices are higher.
B El Viejo Molino, T/F213 6004, valmar@ waranet.com. 2 km on road to Caranavi, 5-star, pool, jacuzzi, games room etc.
B Gloria, C Kennedy 1, T/F213 6020, www.hotel gloria.com.bo. Full board with bath (**A-B** at weekend), cheaper Mon-Fri. Spacious, large pool and a kiddies' pool, breakfast extra, restaurant, internet, free transport from plaza.
B-D Esmeralda, reservations: Casilla PO Box 92 25, La Paz, T221 36017, www.hotelesmeralda.com, www.coroico-info.com. 10 mins uphill from plaza. Renovated suites with great views, de luxe rooms, **E** pp without private bath, dormitories **F** pp, hot showers, satellite TV and DVD, free pick-up (ring from **Totaí Tours**), German owned, English spoken, hikes arranged, and tours by open-sided truck to coca fields and waterfalls, TCs (no commission), credit cards accepted, phones, book exchange, cinema room, breakfast US$2, buffet restaurant, Finnish sauna, garden, good pool, laundry, high-speed internet access US$1 per hr, wi-fi zone, welding facilities for overland drivers, express van to La Paz, book ahead.
D Bella Vista, C Héroes del Chaco (2 blocks from main plaza), T7156 9237 (mob). Beautiful rooms and views, **E** without bath, 2 racquetball courts, terrace, bike hire, restaurant, pool.
D Don Quijote, 500 m out of town, on road to Coripata, T213 6007, quijote@mpoint.com.bo. With bath, pool, quiet, English spoken.
D Hostal Kory, at top of steps leading down from the plaza, T243 1311. Pool, terrace, **E** without bath, hot showers, kitchen, restaurant, snacks, laundry.
D-F pp Sol y Luna, 15-20 mins beyond *Hotel Esmeralda,* T7156 1626 (or Maison de la Bolivie, 6 de Agosto 2464, Ed Jardines, La Paz, T244 0588, lamaisontour@acelerate.com), www.solyluna-bolivia.com. 7 *cabañas* with bath and kitchen, splendid views, 2 apartments for 4 people, 2 rooms with bath, 7 rooms with shared bath for 1-4 people, meals available, vegetarian specialities and Indonesian banquet, camping US$2.50 pp (not suitable for cars), garden, pool, laundry service, and shiatsu massage (US$12), very good value, Sigrid, the owner, speaks English, French, German and Spanish. Recommended.
F pp El Cafetal, Miranda, 10-min walk from town, T719-33979 (mob). French-run, very nice, restaurant with excellent French/Indian/vegetarian cuisine, good value. Highly recommended.
G La Residencial Coroico, F Reyes Ortiz. Without bath, basic, hot shower extra.

G **Residencial de la Torre**, Julio Zuazo Cuenca. Welcoming place with a flowery courtyard, sparse rooms, no alcoholic drinks allowed.

Chulumani *p274*
D **Huayrani**, just off Junín, T213 6351. Lovely views, garden, more expensive in winter.
E **Country House**, 400 m out of town. Bed and breakfast, pool, good value but rock hard beds, restaurant with home cooking.
E **Hostal Familiar Dion**, Alianza, just off the plaza, T213 6070. Modern, roof terrace, includes breakfast, laundry and use of kitchen, F without bathroom and breakfast, very good.
E **Panorama**, top of hill on Murillo, T213 6109. Some rooms with view, garden, breakfast, pool.
G **Alojamiento Danielito**, Bolívar. Hot water extra, laundry facilities, good view.
G **El Mirador**, on Plaza Libertad, T213 6117. Cheaper without bath, good beds, restaurant, noisy at weekends from disco.

Puente Villa *p275*
C **Hotel Tamapaya**, T02-270 6099, just outside town, beautiful setting, shower, good rooms, pool.

● Eating

Coroico *p274*
🍴 **Bamboo**, Iturralde. Good Mexican food and pleasant atmosphere, live music some nights with cover charge. Happy hour 1800-1900.
🍴 **Back-stube**, opposite *Hostal Kory*. German owned, set lunch (including vegetarian), wiener schnitzels, breakfasts, nice atmosphere.
🍴 **Pizzería Italia**, on the plaza. Possibly the best Italian in town.

Cafés
Café de la Senda Verde, Plazuela Julio Zuazo Cuenca. Open daily 0630-1900. Home roasted Yungas coffee, healthy breakfasts, toasted sandwiches and more, very nice.
Snack Hawaii, Plaza M V García Lanza. Basic snack bar on the plaza, open all-day, breakfast, burgers, sandwiches, juices, also has money exchange.

Chulumani *p274*
🍴 **Chulumani**, on Plaza. Pleasant. *Almuerzo*.
🍴 **La Hostería** on Junín close to the *tranca*. Pizzas and hamburgers.
🍴 **El Mesón**, on Plaza. Open 1200-1330 only, good cheap lunches.

▲ Activities and tours

Coroico *p274*
Cycling
CXC, Pacheco 79. Good bikes, US$20 for 6 hrs

including packed lunch, a bit disorganized but good fun and helpful.

Horse riding
El Relincho, Don Reynaldo, T719-13675/23814 (mob), 100 m past *Hotel Esmeralda* (enquire here, ask for Fernando), US$25 for 4 hrs with lunch.

Tour operators
Eco Adventuras and **Inca Land Tours**, both on the main plaza. **Bala Tours**, T03-892 2527, balatours@yahoo.com, and **Enin Tours**, T03-892 2487, enintours@yahoo.com, off Rurrenabaque, run tours to Guanay by 4WD then boat to Rurrenabaque, with 2 camps along the way, all inclusive, guide and cook, US$140 for 4-6 people.

● Transport

Coroico *p274*
Bus From La Paz all companies are on C Yanacachi, beside YPFB station in Villa Fátima: Turbus Totaí (T221 8385), US$2.25, 3 hrs, several daily from 0730-1630 each way, as does **Flota Yungueña** (T221 3513; on the plaza in Coroico); worth booking in advance. Best views on left hand side on the descent to Yungas. Extra services run on Sun. It can be difficult to book journeys to La Paz on holidays and on Sun evenings/Mon mornings (though these are good times for hitching). Trucks and pick-ups from La Paz may drop you at Yolosa, 7 km from Coroico; there is usually transport Yolosa-Coroico, US$1, or you can walk, uphill all the way, 2 hrs. To **Caranavi**, direct bus at 1300, continues to Rurrenabaque arriving at 0700 next day, US$8. Buses, trucks and pick-ups run from Yolosa to **Rurrenabaque** via Caranavi, daily at 1500 with **Yungueña**, except Sun at 1730, with **Turbus Totaí**, US$8.75, 13-15 hrs, they will take you down to Yolosa to catch the bus from La Paz. In Coroico trucks leave from the market.

Chulumani *p274*
Bus From **La Paz**: **Trans San Bartolomé**, Virgen del Carmen 1750, Villa Fátima, T221 1674, daily at 0800-1600 or when full, 4 hrs, US$2.50. **Trans Arenas**, daily at 0730-1800, US$2.25. **Trans 24 de Agosto micros**, 15 de Abril 408 y San Borja, T221 0607, 0600-1600, when full. Buses return to La Paz from the plaza, micros from the *tranca*.

● Directory

Coroico *p274*
Banks Banco Mercantil, on Central Plaza. Mon-Fri 0830-1230, 1430-1830, Sat 0900- 1230, cash advances (no commission) on MasterCard and Visa. **Prodem**, J Suazo Cuenca, on main plaza, changes US$ cash, cash advance on Visa or

MasterCard, 5% commission. **Internet** Carlos, who lives on C Caja de Agua, T/F213 6041, has an internet café, will exchange Spanish for English lessons. **Language classes** Siria León Domínguez, Julio Zuazo Cuenca 062, T7195 5431, siria_leon@yahoo.com.es. US$3.60 per hr, also has rooms for rent and makes silver jewellery, excellent English. **Medical** services **Hospital:** T213 6002, the best in the Yungas, good malaria advice. **Police** East side of main plaza. **Post offices** on plaza.

Telephones Entel, on Sagárnaga next to *Flota Yungueña*, for international and local calls. Cotel, next to church, phones, public TV.

Chulumani *p274*
Banks On Plaza Libertad, **Banco Unión**, changes US$100 or more only in cash and TCs (5% commission), Mon-Fri 0830-1200, 1430- 1800. Cooperativa San Bartolomé, changes cash Mon-Fri 0800-1200, 1400-1700, Sat-Sun 0700-1200. **Internet** In tourist office, US$1.05 per hr.

Southwest Bolivia

The mining town of Oruro, with one of South America's greatest folkloric traditions, shimmering salt flats, coloured lakes and surrealistic rock formations combine to make this one of the most fascinating regions of Bolivia. Add some of the country's most celebrated festivals and the last hide-out of Butch Cassidy and the Sundance Kid and you have the elements for some great and varied adventures. The journey across the altiplano from Uyuni to San Pedro de Atacama is now a popular route to Chile and there are other routes south to Argentina.

Oruro

→ *Phone code: 02. 30 km southeast of La Paz. Colour map 6, grid A2. Population: 236,110. Altitude: 3,706 m.*

The mining town of Oruro is the gateway to the altiplano of southwest Bolivia. It's a functional place which explodes into life once a year with its famous carnival, symbolised by La Diablada. Not far to the west is the national park encompassing Bolivia's highest peak, Sajama. The **tourist office**, ① *Montes 6072, Plaza 10 de Febrero, T/F525 0144. Mon-Fri 0800-1200, 1400-1800* is very helpful and informative. Another kiosk is outside *Entel* on C Bolívar (same hours). Colour map and guide (Spanish only), US$1.

Although Oruro became famous as a mining town, there are no longer any working mines of importance. It is, however, a major railway junction and the commercial centre for the mining communities of the altiplano, as well as hosting the country's best-known carnival (see page 279). Several fine buildings in the centre hint at the city's former importance, notably the baroque concert hall (now a cinema) on Plaza 10 de Febrero and the **Casa de la Cultura** (Museo Simón I Patiño) ① *Soria Galvarro 5755, Mon-Fri 0900-1200, 1400-1830, US$0.30*. Built as a mansion by the tin baron Simón Patiño, it is now run by the Universidad Técnica de Oruro, and contains European furniture and a carriage imported from France, also houses temporary exhibitions. There is a good view from the Cerro Corazón de Jesús, near the church of the Virgen del Socavón, five blocks west of Plaza 10 de Febrero at the end of Calle Mier.

The **Museo Etnográfico Minero** ① *inside the Church of the Virgen del Socavón, entry via the church 0900-1200, 1500-1800, US$0.50*, contains mining equipment and other artefacts from the beginning of the century as well as a representation of *El Tío* (in Catholic terminology the devil.) **Museo Antropológico** ① *south of centre on Av España, Mon-Fri 0900-1200, 1400-1800, Sat-Sun 1000-2000, 1500-1800, US$0.50, good guides, getting there: take micro A heading south or any trufi going south*. It has a unique collection of stone llama heads as well as impressive carnival masks. The **Museo Mineralógico** ① *part of the University, Mon-Fri 0800-1200, 1430-1700, US$0.60, getting there: take micro A south to the Ciudad Universitaria*, has over 5,500 mineral specimens. **Casa Arte Taller Cardozo Velásquez,** ① *Junín 738 y Arica, east of the centre, T527 5245, www.catcarve.org, Mon-Sat 0930-1200, US$0.45*. Contemporary Bolivian painting and sculpture is displayed in the Cardozo Velásquez home, a family of seven artists.

Parque Nacional Sajama

A one-day drive to the west of Oruro is the **Parque Nacional Sajama** ① *park headquarters in Sajama village, T02-513 5526, www.sajamabolivia.com, US$2.50*, established in 1942 and covering 81,000 ha. The park contains the world's highest forest, consisting mainly of the rare queñual tree (Polylepis tarapacana) which grows up to an altitude of 5,200 m. The scenery is wonderful and includes views of three volcanoes (Sajama – Bolivia's highest peak at 6,542 m – Parinacota and Pomerape). The road is paved and leads across the border into the Parque Nacional Lauca in Chile. You can trek in the park, with or without porters and mules, but once you move away from the Río Sajama or its major tributaries, lack of water is a problem.

Sajama village → *Population: 500. Altitude: 4,200 m.*

In Sajama village, visitors are billeted with family-run *alojamientos* (**G**) on a rotatating basis. All are basic to very basic, especially the sanitary facilities; no showers or electricity, solar power for lighting only. There are many small comedores but food supplies are limited. It can be very windy and cold at night; a good sleeping bag, gloves and hat are essential. Crampons, ice axe and rope are needed for climbing the volcanoes and can be hired in the village. Local guides charge US$50 per day. Horses can be hired, US$8 per day including guide. Good bathing in hot springs 7 km northwest of village; jeeps can be rented to visit, US$5-6. Many villagers sell alpaca woolen items.

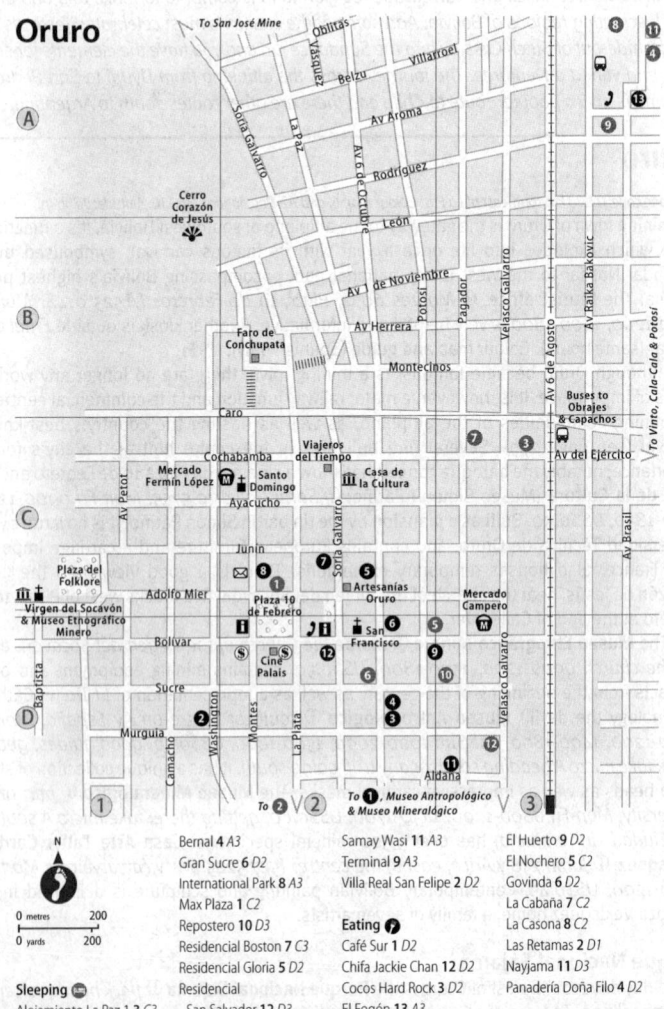

Oruro

N

0 metres 200
0 yards 200

Sleeping 🛏
Alojamiento La Paz 1 *3 C3*

Bernal 4 *A3*
Gran Sucre 6 *D2*
International Park 8 *A3*
Max Plaza 1 *C2*
Repostero 10 *D3*
Residencial Boston 7 *C3*
Residencial Gloria 5 *D2*
Residencial
San Salvador 12 *D3*

Samay Wasi 11 *A3*
Terminal 9 *A3*
Villa Real San Felipe 2 *D2*

Eating 🍴
Café Sur 1 *D2*
Chifa Jackie Chan 12 *D2*
Cocos Hard Rock 3 *D2*
El Fogón 13 *A3*

El Huerto 9 *D2*
El Nochero 5 *C2*
Govinda 6 *D2*
La Cabaña 7 *C2*
La Casona 8 *C2*
Las Retamas 2 *D1*
Nayjama 11 *D3*
Panadería Doña Filo 4 *D2*

La Diablada festival

On the **Saturday before Ash Wednesday**, Los Carnavales de Oruro include the famous **Diablada** ceremony in homage to the miraculous Virgen del Socavón, patroness of miners, and in gratitude to Pachamama, the Earth Mother. The entire procession starts its 5 km route through the town at 0700, reaching the Sanctuary of the Virgen del Socavón at 0400 on Sunday. There the dancers invoke her blessing and ask for pardon. The company then proceeds to the Av Cívica amphitheatre, where the dancers perform two masques. Afterwards, the dancers all enter the sanctuary, chant a hymn in Quechua and pray for pardon. The **Diablada** was traditionally performed by indigenous miners, but several other guilds have taken up the custom. The Carnival is especially notable for its fantastically imaginative costumes. The working-class Oruro district known as La Ranchería is particularly famous for the excellence of its costumes.

The **Gran Corso del Carnaval** takes place on the Sunday, a very spectacular display. Monday is **El Día del Diablo y del Moreno** in which the Diablos and Morenos, with their bands, compete against each other on Avenida Cívica in demonstrations of dancing. Every group seems to join in, in 'total marvellous chaos'. The action usually parades out of the amphitheatre, ending up at the Plaza de Armas. At dusk dancers and musicians go their separate ways, serenading until the early hours. By Tuesday the main touristic events have ended. **Carnaval del Sur** takes place, with ch'alla rituals to invoke ancestors, unite with Pachamama and bless personal possessions. This is also the día del agua on which everyone throws water and sprays foam at everyone else (though this goes on throughout carnival; plastic tunics are sold for US$0.20 by street vendors).

The Friday before carnival, traditional miners' ceremonies are held at mines, including the sacrifice of a llama. Visitors may only attend with a guide and permission from Comibol, via the tourist office. The Sunday before carnival the groups practise and make their final pledges. In honour of its syncretism of Andean, pre-Columbian tradition and Catholic faith, the Oruro Carnaval has been included on UNESCO's Heritage of Humanity list.

Seating Around the Plaza de Armas, along Avenida 6 de Agosto and on Avenida Cívica, seats cost US$5-10 a day, bought from the Alcaldía in the plaza, or whichever business has erected stands outside its building. Seats on Avenida Bolívar, etc, cost US$5 a day from the shops which built stands. You can wander freely among the dancers and take photographs.

Sleeping For the hotel of your choice it's best to book in advance for carnival; prices range from US$10 per person without bath, to US$20 per person with, to US$100 per person per day in the better places. The tourist office has list of all householders willing to let rooms; host and guest arrange the price, at least US$10 per person. Most hotels sell only three-night packages.

Transport Prices from La Paz triple. Organized day trips from La Paz cost US$30-45, including transport departing 0430, food and a seat in the main plaza, returning at 1600-1700 (missing the last eight to nine hours).

By road to Chile
The shortest and most widely used route from La Paz to Chile is the road to **Arica** via the border at Tambo Quemado (Bolivia) and **Chungará** (Chile). From La Paz take the highway south towards Oruro. Immediately before Patacamaya, turn right at green road sign to Puerto Japonés on the Río Desaguadero, then on to Tambo Quemado. Take extra petrol (none available after Chilean border until Arica), food and water. The journey is worthwhile for the breathtaking views.

Bolivian **customs and immigration** are at Tambo Quemado, where there are a couple of very basic places to stay and eat. Border control is open daily 0800-2000. Shops change bolivianos, pesos chilenos and dollars. From Tambo Quemado there is a stretch of about 7 km of 'no-man's land' before you reach the Chilean frontier at Chungará. Here the border crossing, which is set against the most spectacular scenic backdrop of Lago Chungará and Volcán Parinacota, is thorough but efficient; open 0800-2100. Expect a long wait behind lines of lorries. Drivers must fill in 'Relaciones de Pasajeros', US$0.25 from kiosk at border, giving details of driver, vehicle and passengers. Do not take any livestock, plants, fruit, vegetables, or dairy products into Chile.

An alternative crossing from Oruro: several bus companies travel southwest to Iquique, via the border posts of **Pisiga** (Bolivia) and **Colchane** (Chile). The road is paved 40 km to Toledo and in 2005 work was in progress for paving other sections along this road. There is also service from Oruro to Arica via Patacamaya and Tambo Quemado.

South of Oruro

Machacamarca, about 30 minutes south of Oruro, has a good railway museum. Further south, the road runs between the flat plain of Lago Poopó and the Cordillera Azanaque, a very scenic ride. There are thermal baths at **Pazña**, about 1 hour from Oruro.

About 65 km south is the **Santuario de Aves Lago Poopó** (a Ramsar site since 2003), an excellent bird reserve on the lake of the same name. The lake dries up completely in winter. The closest place to Oruro to see flamingos and other birds is **Lago Uru Uru** (the northern section of the Poopó lake system), go to Villa Challacollo on the road to Pisiga (minibuses 102, 10, 5 or blue micros) and walk from there. Birds start arriving with the first rains in October or November. Further along, at Km 10 is Chusakeri, where chullpas can be seen on the hillside.

Access to the lake is a little closer from **Huari**, 15 minutes south of Challapata along a paved road. Huari (124 km south of Oruro) is a pleasant little town with a large brewery; there is a small museum and Mirador Tatacuchunita, a lookout on nearby Cerro Sullka. Sunsets over the lake are superb. There are a couple of basic *alojamientos*, eg **G** 25 de Mayo, 2 blocks from the plaza towards Challapata, shared bath, cold water in morning only. It is about 8 km walk from Huari to the lake, depending on the water level. Near the lake is the Uru-Muratos community of **Llapallapani** with circular adobe homes, those with straw roofs are known as *chillas* and those with conical adobe roofs are *putukus*. A community tourism programme, with *putuku* cabins, remains to be completed (2005). Boats can be hired when the water level is high, at other times Poopó is an unattainable mirage. There is good walking in the Cordillera Azanaque behind Huari; take food, water, warm clothing and all gear. **Challapata** (*fiesta* 15-17 July) has several places to stay, eg *Res Virgen del Carmen*, by main plaza, and a gas station.

Atlantis in the Andes Jim Allen's theory of Atlantis is well known around Oruro and a video about it is on display at the bus station (see www.geocities.com/webatlantis). **Pampa Aullagas**, the alleged Atlantis site, is 196 km from Oruro, southwest of Lago Poopó. Access is from the town of **Quillacas** along a road which branches west from the road to Uyuni just south of Huari. It can also be reached from the west through Toledo and Andamarca. A visit here can be combined with visits to the Salar de Coipasa.

Southwest of Lago Poopó, off the Oruro-Pisiga-Iquique road (turn off at **Sabaya**), is the **Salar de Coipasa**, 225 km from Oruro. It is smaller and less visited than the Salar de Uyuni, and has a turquoise lake in the middle of the salt pan surrounded by mountains with gorgeous views and large cacti. At the edge of the Salar is **Coquesa** (lodging available), which has a mirador and tombs with mummies ① *US$1.25 entry to each site*. Coipasa is northwest of the Salar de Uyuni and travel from one to the other is possible with a private vehicle along the impressive **Ruta Intersalar**. Along the way are tombs, terracing and ancient irrigation canals at the archaeological site of **Alcaya** ① *US$1.25*, gradually being developed by the local community (near **Salinas de Garci Mendoza**, locally known as Salinas). Nearby are the towering volcanic cones of Cora Cora and Tunupa. Access to the north end of the Salar de Uyuni is at **Jirira**.

Note: Getting stranded out on the altiplano or, worse yet on the salar itself, is dangerous because of extreme temperatures and total lack of drinking water. It is best to visit this area with a tour operator that can take you, for example, from Oruro through the salares to Uyuni. Travellers with their own vehicles should only attempt this route following extensive local inquiry or after taking on a guide to avoid becoming lost or bogged. The edges of the salares are soft and only established entry points or ramps should be used to cross onto or off the salt.

😴 Sleeping

Oruro *p277, map 278*

B Max Plaza, Adoplfo Mier at Plaza 10 de Febrero, T525 2561. Includes breakfast, comfortable carpeted rooms, good central location.

B Villa Real San Felipe, San Felipe 678 y La Plata, south of the centre, T525 4993, www.villarealsanfelipe.com. Quaint small hotel with nicely furnished but small rooms, heating, includes buffet breakfast, sauna and whirlpool, restaurant, tour operator, best hotel in town.

C Gran Sucre, Sucre 510 esq 6 de Octubre, T527 6800, www.hotebol.com. Nicely refurbished old building, includes buffet breakfast, cheaper rooms on the ground floor, heaters on request. Recommended.

C Samay Huasi, Av Brasil 232 opposite the terminal, T527 6737. Modern, includes breakfast, bright rooms, hot water, internet, 30% discount for IYHF members. Recommended.

D Repostero, Sucre 370 y Pagador, T525 8001. Hot water, includes breakfast, renovated carpeted rooms are pricier but better value than the old rooms, secure parking.

E Bernal, Brasil 701, opposite bus terminal, T527 9468. Modern, good value, excellent hot showers, cheaper with shared bath, heaters on request, restaurant, tours arranged. Recommended.

E Res Gran Boston, Pagador 1159 y Cochabamba, T527 4708. Nicely refurbished house, internal rooms around a covered patio, electric shower, cheaper with shared bath, good value, new in 2005.

E Res San Salvador, V Galvarro 6325 near train station, T527 6771. Hot water, **F** with shared bath, electric shower, best in this area.

E Terminal, 21 de Enero y Bakovic opposite the terminal, T527 3431. Modern, hot water, cheaper with shared bath.

F Res Gloria, Potosí 6059, T527 6250. 19th century building, private toilet, shared electric shower, cheaper with shared toilet, basic but clean.

F-G Alojamiento La Paz I, Cochabamba 180, T527 4882. Shared bath, basic, clean, hot shower extra.

Sajama *p278*

AL Tomarapi Ecolodge, north of Sajama in Tomarapi community, near Caripe, T02-241 4753, ecotomarapi@hotmail.com. Including full board (good food) and guiding service with climbing shelter at 4,900 m, helpful staff, simple but comfortable, with bath, hot water, heating.

South of Oruro *p280*

E-F Posada Doña Lupe, Jirira, T527 2094-Oruro. Hot water, cheaper without bath, use of kitchen but bring your own food, no meals available, caters to tour groups, pleasant, comfortable.

F Alojamiento Paraíso, Sabaya. Take sleeping bag, shared bath, cold water, meals on request or take own food, sells petrol.

G Doña Wadi, Salinas de Garci Mendoza, 1½ blocks from main plaza. Shared bath, hot water, basic but clean, meals available

🍴 Eating

Oruro *p277, map 278*

🍴 La Cabaña, Junín 609. Comfortable, smart, good international food, bar, Sun and Mon 1200-1530 only.

🍴 Nayjama, Aldana esq Pagador. Best in town, huge portions.

🍴-🍴 Chifa Jackie Chan, Bolívar 615 esq S Galvarro. Good Chinese food, open 1100-2300.

🍴-🍴 El Fogón, Brasil y 21 de Enero. Best of a poor lot by the bus terminal. The many greasy chicken places by the terminal are best avoided.

🍴-🍴 Las Retamas, Murguía 930 esq Washington. Excellent set lunches (🍴), Bolivian and international dishes à la carte, very good pastries, pleasant atmosphere, out of the way but worth the trip. Recommended.

🍴 Cocos Hard Rock, 6 de Octubre y Sucre. Set meals, local and international dishes.

🍴 La Casona, Pres Montes 5970, opposite Post Office. A good *pizzería*.

🍴 Govinda, 6 de Octubre 6071. Excellent vegetarian, Mon-Sat 0900-2130.

🍴 El Huerto, Bolívar 359. Good, vegetarian options, open Sun.

Cafés

Café Arte, 6 de Octubre y León. Cafetería, bar, books to browse.

Café Sur, Arce 163, near train station. Live entertainment, seminars, films, Tue-Sat, good place to meet local students.

El Nochero, Av 6 de Octubre 1454, open 1700-2400, good coffee.

Notre Dame, Murguía y Pagador. Café-bar, books to browse.

Panadería Doña Filo, 6 de Octubre esq Sucre. Excellent savoury snacks and sweets, closed Sun, takeaway only.

🎵 Bars and clubs

Oruro *p277, map 278*

Bravos, Montesinos y Pagador. Varied music.

Imagine, 6 de Octubre y Junín. Latin and other music.

O Shopping

Oruro *p277, map 278*

Crafts On Av La Paz the 4 blocks between León and Belzu, 48-51, are largely given over to workshops producing masks and costumes for Carnival. **Artesanías Oruro**, A Mier 599, esq S Galvarro. Lovely selection of regional handicrafts produced by 6 rural community cooperatives; nice sweaters, carpets, wall-hangings.

Markets **Mercado Campero**, V Galvarro esq Bolívar. Sells everything, also *brujería* section for magical concoctions. **Mercado Fermín López**, C Ayacucho y Montes. Food and hardware. C Bolívar is the main shopping street. **Irupana**, S Galvarra y A Mier. Good selection of natural foods and snacks.

▲ Activities and tours

Oruro *p277, map 278*

Charlie Tours, Brasil 232 at *Hotel Samay Huasi*, T527 6737, charlietours@yahoo.com. Regional tours including Salares de Coipasa and Uyuni, transport service.

Freddy Barrón, T527 6776, lufba@hotmail.com. Tours and transport, speaks German.

Viajeros del Tiempo, Soria Galvarro 1232, T527 1166. Offers trips to the nearby mines, hot pools and other attractions, open Mon-Fri 0900-1230, 1500-1930, Sat 0900-1200, phone in advance.

⊖ Transport

Oruro *p277, map 278*

Bus Bus terminal 10 blocks north of centre at Bakovic and Aroma, T525 3535, US$0.20 terminal tax to get on bus. Micro No 2 to centre, or any saying 'Plaza 10 de Febrero'. To **Challapata** and **Huari**: several companies go from the Oruro terminal to Challapata, about every hour, US$1, 1¾ hrs, and Huari, US$1.25, 2 hrs, last bus back leaves Huari about 1630. You can also take a bus to Challapata and a shared taxi from there to Huari, US$0.30. Daily services to: **La Paz** at least every hour 0400-2200, US$1.25-1.90, 3½ hrs;. **Cochabamba**, US$2.50, 4 hrs, 9 daily with Copacabana, more with other companies. **Potosí**, US$2.50 day bus, US$3.75 at night, 5 hrs, several daily, Copacabana *bus cama* at 2345 US$10. **Sucre** Bustillo 1100 and 2000, US$5, Copacabana at 2230, *semi-cama* US$10, *bus cama* US$15, 10 hrs. **Tarija**, Belgrano at 2030, US$7.50-10, 16 hrs. **Uyuni**, several companies, all depart 1900-2100, US$2.50, US$3.75 on Wed, 7 hrs. **Todo Turismo**, Aroma 232 opposite the bus station, T511 1889, www.touringbolivia.com, offers a tourist bus departing from La Paz, stopping in Oruro, night departures only, US$20. To **Tupiza**, via Potosí, Boquerón at 1230, **Illimani** at 1630, US$9.75,

11-12 hrs, continuing to Villazón, US$10, 13-14 hrs. **Santa Cruz**, Bolívar at 2000, US$7.50, *bus cama* at 2130, US$11.25, 11 hrs. **Pisiga** (Chilean border), Trans Pisiga, Av Dehene y España, T526 2241, at 2000 and 2030, or with Iquique bound buses, US$3.75, 4-5 hrs. **International buses** (US$2 to cross border): to **Iquique** via Pisiga, several companies at 0100, Interbus at 0500 and 1200, Bernal at 1230, US$11.25, *bus cama* US$13.75, 10 hrs. **Arica** via Patacamaya and **Tambo Quemado** (US$3.75, 4 hrs), several companies between 1200 and 1300, US$11.25, 10 hrs.

Radio-taxis Sajama, T528 0801, provide transport to regional attractions.

Train Two companies run services from Oruro to **Uyuni** and on to **Villazón** via Tupiza. Each has an executive and two other classes of seat: Expreso del Sur, Tue and Fri at 1530, arriving in Uyuni at 2220 ; Wara Wara del Sur Sun and Wed at 1900, arriving in Uyuni at 0220. Fares: Expreso del Sur to Uyuni: *Ejecutivo* US$10, *Salón* US$5.50, *Popular* US$3.75; Tupiza: US$20.75, US$10.25 and US$ 6.70 respectively: Villazón: US$23.30, US$11.60 and US$8.20. Wara Wara del Sur to Uyuni: *Ejecutivo* US$8.40, *Salón* US$4.25, *Popular* US$3.55; Tupiza: US$15.15, US$7.30 and US$ 6.10 respectively: Villazón: US$18.30, US$9.15 and US$7.30. For details of trains from Uyuni to **Villazón** and for trains from Uyuni to Oruro, see Uyuni. For return times from Villazón, see page 291. Passengers with tickets Villazón-La Paz are transferred to a bus at Oruro. To check train times, T527 4605 (or La Paz 02-241 6545). In Nov-Jan and Jul you must have a lot of patience to get a ticket; demand is very high.

Sajama *p278*

To get to the park, take a La Paz-Oruro bus and change at Patacamaya. Mini-vans from Patacamaya (in front of **Restaurant Capitol**) to Sajama Sun-Fri 1300, 3 hrs, US$2. Sajama to **Patacamaya** Mon-Fri 0600-0700, some days via **Tambo Quemado**, confirm details and weekend schedule locally. From Tambo Quemado to Sajama about 1530 daily, 1 hr, US$0.65. Or take a La Paz-Arica bus, ask for Sajama, try to pay half the fare, but you may be charged full fare.

South of Oruro *p280*

Public transport to **Coipasa** is very scarce. Trans Pisiga, address above, goes every second Tue to Copaisa, US$3, 6 hrs. You can also ride with one of the buses to Iquique and get off at the turnoff, but it is difficult to hire a private vehicle for onward transportation in this sparsely populated area. There is transport going around the southern end of Poopó. Oruro to **Salinas**, 5 per week (different schedule every day), from Avs Caro y Ejército, US$2.60, 7 hrs.

❶ Directory

Oruro *p277, map 278*
Banks Banco Bisa, Bolívar at Plaza 10 de Febrero, fair rates for US$ cash, US$6 flat rate for TCs (max US$500), cash advances on Visa and Mastercard, Mon-Fri 0900-1600, Sat 0900-1300. BCP, Bolívar esq Montes at Plaza 10 de Febrero, fair rates for US$ cash, Visa and Mastercard ATM, Mon-Fri 0900-1800, Sat 0900-1300. **Casa de Cambio** at the Terminal Terrestre, US$, euros, pesos chilenos and argentinos, soles, cash only, fair rates, daily 0800-2000. **Internet** Many in town, rates US$0.30-0.35. **Post offices** Presidente Montes 1456, half block from plaza. **Telephones** Many *cabinas* in town. **Useful addresses** Immigration, S Galvarro entre Ayacucho y Cochabamba.

Uyuni → *Phone code: 02. Colour map 6, grid B3. Population: 11,320. Altitude: 3,665 m.*

Uyuni lies near the eastern edge of the Salar de Uyuni and is one of the jumping-off points for trips to the salt flats, volcanoes and multi-coloured lakes of southwest Bolivia. Still a commercial and communication centre, Uyuni was, for much of this century, important as a major railway junction. A statue of an armed railway worker, erected after the 1952 Revolution, dominates Avenida Ferroviaria. Most services are near the station. **Museo Arqueológico and Antropológico de los Andes Meridionales** ① *Arce y Potosí, Mon-Fri 1000-1200, 1400-1800, Sat-Sun 0900-1300, US$0.35*. A small museum with local artifacts. Market on Avenida Potosí between the clock and Avaroa sells everything almost every day. Fiesta 11 July. There is a Railway Cemetery outside town with engines from 1907-1950s, now rusting hulks.

Pulacayo, 30 minutes ride from Uyuni, is a town at the site of a 19th-century silver mine. Here you can see the first locomotive in Bolivia and the train robbed by Butch Cassidy and the Sundance Kid. Information and tours from the Uyuni clock tower, Arce at Avenida Potosí.

Tourist office ① *Av Potosí 13, Mon-Fri 0830-1200, 1400-1830, Sat-Sun 0830-1200, T693 2060 and ask for the tourist office*. **Ranking Bolívia** ① *Potosí 9 y Arce, T693 2102, rankingbolivia@hotmail.com, daily 0830-2000*. Good source of local and regional information, database of tour operators based on traveller's reports, café, crafts, books and other products, video room, a place to hang out while waiting for transport, English spoken. Part of an internationally funded project which ended in 2005 and is attempting to continue independently.

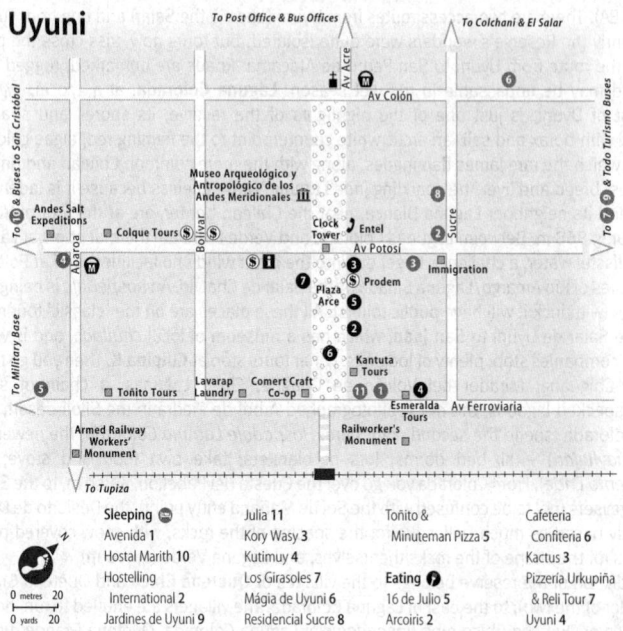

Uyuni

Sleeping	Julia 11	Toñito &	Cafetería
Avenida 1	Kory Wasy 3	Minuteman Pizza 5	Confitería 6
Hostal Marith 10	Kutimuy 4		Kactus 3
Hostelling	Los Girasoles 7	**Eating**	Pizzería Urkupiña
International 2	Mágia de Uyuni 6	16 de Julio 5	& Reli Tour 7
Jardines de Uyuni 9	Residencial Sucre 8	Arcoíris 2	Uyuni 4

0 metres **20**
0 yards **20**

Salar de Uyuni

Crossing the Salar de Uyuni, the largest and highest salt lake in the world, is one of the great Bolivian trips. Driving across it is a fantastic experience, especially during June and July when the bright blue skies contrast with the blinding white salt crust. Farther south, and included on tours of the region, are the towering volcanoes, multi-coloured lakes (including Colorada and Verde) with abundant birdlife, weird rock formations, thermal activity and endless puna that make up some of most fabulous landscapes in South America.

Trips to the Salar de Uyuni enter via the *terraplén* (ramp) at Colchani and include stops to see traditional salt mining techniques and the Ojos del Agua, where salt water bubbles to the surface of the slat flat, perhaps a call at a salt hotel (see Sleeping, below) and a visit to the **Isla del Pescado** ① *entry US$1*, so-called because of its shape (also known as Incahuasi – Inca House). This is a coral island, raised up from the ocean bed, covered in tall cactii. There is a walking trail with superb views, a *Mongo's* café, basic lodging and toilets. If on an extended tour (see below), you may leave the Salar by another *terraplén*, eg Puerto Chupica in the southwest.

San Cristóbal

The original village of **San Cristóbal**, southwest of Uyuni, was relocated in 2002 to make way for a Canadian-owned open-pit mine, said to be one of the largest silver deposits in South America. The original church (1650) had been declared a national monument and was therefore rebuilt in its entirety. Ask at the Fundación San Cristóbal Office for the church to be opened as the interior artwork, restored by Italian techniques, is worth seeing. The fiesta is 27-28 July. San Cristóbal and other towns in the area, eg Alota (see below) and Culpina K, were offered tourism projects by the company in exchange for permission to allow the mine to proceed. Dubbed *pueblos auténticos* (authentic towns), they have yet to escape the look of the new money spent on them. The road San Cristóbal-Uyuni is paved to start with, then becomes good gravel (watch out for stones flung up by speeding trucks).

Reserva Nacional de Fauna Andina Eduardo Avaroa

① *Office at Avaroa entre Potosí y Colón, Uyuni, T693 2225/693 2400, www.bolivia-rea.com, excellent map for sale, US$3.75 (not included in tour price; pay in bolivianos). Park ranger/entry points are near Laguna Colorada, Lagunas Verde and Blanca, close to the Chilean border, and at Sol de Mañana, near Quetena Chico.*

In the far southwest of Bolivia, in the Lípez region, is the 714,000-ha **Reserva Nacional Eduardo Avaroa** (REA). There are two access routes from Uyuni (one via the Salar) and one from Tupiza. Until recently the Reserve's wonders were quite isolated, but tours now criss-cross the puna, many on the route from Uyuni to San Pedro de Atacama. Roads are unmarked, rugged truck tracks and may be impassable in the wet season. **Laguna Colorada**, at 4,270 m, 346 km southwest of Uyuni, is just one of the highlights of the reserve, its shores and shallows encrusted with borax and salt, an arctic white counterpoint to the flaming red, algae-coloured waters in which the rare James flamingoes, along with the more common Chilean and Andean flamingoes, breed and live. The sparkling jade **Laguna Verde** (lifeless because it is laden with arsenic) and its neighbour Laguna Blanca, near the Chilean border, are at the foot of Volcán Licancábur, 5,868 m. Between Lagunas Colorada and Verde there are thermal pools at Laguna Blanca (blissful water, a challenge to get out into the bitter wind - no facilities) and at Polques, on the shores of Río Amargo/Laguna Salada by the Salar de Chalviri. An *hospedaje* is being built at Polques (with luck it will have public toilets). All these places are on the `classic' tour route, across the Salar de Uyuni to **San Juan**, which has a museum of local *chullpas*, and is where most tour companies stop: plenty of lodgings. Other tours stop at **Culpina K**. Then you go to the Salar de Chiguana, Mirador del Volcán de Ollagüe, Cinco Lagunas, a chain of small, flamingo-specked lagoons, the much-photographed Arbol de Piedra in the Siloli desert, then Laguna Colorada (spend the second night here: *Hospedaje Laguna Colorada*, the newer and better *Huayllajara* – six-bed dorms, lots of blankets, take own food and stove, and *Campamento Ende*). From Colorada you go over the Cuesta del Pabellón, 4,850 m, to the Sol de Mañana geysers (not to be confused with the Sol de Mañana entry point), the Desierto de Dalí, a pure sandy desert as much Daliesque for the spacing of the rocks, with snow-covered peaks behind, as for the shape of the rocks themselves, and Laguna Verde (4,400 m).

Jurisdiction of the reserve belongs to the villages of **Quetena Chico** and Quetena Grande (the smaller of the two), to the east of Laguna Colorada. The villagers are entitled to run lodging in the reserve: Quetena Chico runs *hospedajes* at Laguna Colorada. Quetena Grande runs *La*

Cabaña at Hito Cajónes (see below). In Quetena Chico is the reserve's visitors information centre, **Centro Ecológico Ch'aska** ① *daily 0730-1800, will charge entry fee (amount not determined end-Oct 2005)*, informative displays about the region's geology, vulcanology, fauna, flora, natural and human history; a worthwhile stop. The village has three *hospedajes* (eg *Piedra Preciosa* and *Hostal Quetena*, both **G**, hot water extra), and places to eat.

From Tupiza Tour operators in Tupiza run trips to the REA and Salar de Uyuni and go to places not included on tours from Uyuni. These include the beautiful Lagunas Celeste and Negra below Cerro Uturunco, which is near Quetena Chico; the **Valle de las Rocas**, 4,260 m, between the villages of **Alota** and Villa Mar (a vast extension of rocks eroded into fantastic configurations, with polylepis trees in sheltered corners); and isolated communities in the puna. The high altitude scenery is out of this world. *Alojamientos* in the villages on the tour routes cannot be booked. You turn up and search for a room. All provide kitchen space for the tour's cook or independent traveller to prepare meals, take your own stove, though. See also Tayka/Fremen in Uyuni, Activities and tours, below. There is public transport from Uyuni into the region, but rarely more than one bus a week, with several hours rough travelling. If travelling independently, note that there are countless tracks and no signposts.

Crossing into Chile
There is a REA ranger station near Lagunas Blanca and Verde: if coming from Bolivia, have your park entry receipt at hand, if crossing from Chile pay the entry fee. Alongside is a *refugio*, La Cabaña, operated by Quetena Grande, US$5 pp in comfortable but very cold dorms, solar-powered lighting, hot water seldom works, cooking facilities but you must bring your own food (in high season book in advance – tour agencies can do this by radio). There is good climbing and hiking in the area with outstanding views. You must register at the ranger station before heading out and they may insist that you take a guide (eg to climb Licancábur, US$30 for guide plus US$40 for transport). Mind the altitude, intense solar radiation and lack of drinking water.

From the ranger station it is 5 km to the border at Hito Cajónes (on the Chilean side referred to as Hito Cajón), 4,500 m. Bolivian immigration, open about 0800-2100, charges US$2 in any currency (no other border crossing makes this charge). Other than immigration, there are no services or facilities of any kind at the border. A further 6 km along a good dirt road into Chile is the intersection with the fully paved road from San Pedro de Atacama to Paso de Jama, the border between Chile and Argentina. From this intersection, it is 40 km and 2,000 m downhill to San Pedro. Chilean customs and immigration are just outside San Pedro and can take 45 minutes at busy times. See Transport, page 287, for further details.

● Sleeping

Uyuni *p283, map p283*
Water is frequently cut off and may only be available between 0600 and 1200.
A Los Girasoles, Santa Cruz 155, 3½ blocks from clock tower, T693 3323, www.girasoleshotel.com. Buffet breakfast, bright and warm (especially 2nd floor), comfortable, nicely decorated, heaters available, best in town. Recommended.
B Jardines de Uyuni, Potosí 133, T693 2989. Includes breakfast, rustic style but comfortable, hot water, heaters available, open fire in lounge, parking.
C Kory Wasy, Av Potosí, entre Arce y Sucre, T693 2670, kory_wasy@hotmail.com. **D** low season, overpriced but breakfast is included, good fun, sunny lobby but many dark rooms, restaurant, tour agency.
C Mágia de Uyuni, Av Colón 432, T693 2541, Magia_Uyuni@yahoo.es. All rooms have bath, Includes breakfast. Recommended. **C Toñito**, Av Ferroviaria 60, T693 3186, www.bolivian

expeditions.com. Spacious rooms with good beds, good breakfast included, TV, **E** with shared bath and no breakfast, very helpful, laundry, internet, tours.
D-E Hostelling International, Potosí y Sucre, T693 2228. Hot water, cheaper without bath, kitchen facilities, modern and popular, discount for IYHF members.
D-E Julia, Ferroviaria 314 y Arce, T693 2134. Spacious comfortable rooms, unreliable hot water.
E Avenida, Av Ferroviaria 11, opposite train station, T693 2078. **F** with shared bath, basic, limited water and shower facilities, basic, quite old, frequently used by travellers, parking.
E Kutimuy, Avaroa esq Av Potosí, near market, T693 2391 (owned by Colque Tours, so often full of groups). Includes continental breakfast, warm rooms, electric showers, **F** without bath.
F Residencial Sucre, Sucre 132, T693 2047, residencial.sucre.uyuni@gmail.com. Hot water,

cheaper without bath, basic but adequate, very welcoming and warm though the 3 stars on the sign is optimistic!

G pp Hostal Marith, Av Potosí 61, T693 2174. Good budget option (better value without private bath), hot showers from 0830, simple, sunny patio with laundry sinks.

Salar de Uyuni *p284*

These *hoteles de sal* are generally visited on tours, seldom independently.

L Palacio de Sal, on the edge of the salar, near the ramp outside Colchani (book through **Jardines de Uyuni**, see above, operated by **Hidalgo Tours**, Junín esq Bolívar, T622 5186, Potosí, uyusalht@ceibo.entelnet.bo). Price is half-board. Spacious, comfortable luxury salt hotel, decorated with large salt sculptures, heating, hot water, sauna, lookout on second storey with views of the salar. It was relocated from its original location on the salar.

AL Luna Salada, north of Colchani near entrance to the salar, T2693 22423 (mob), rodri_lara@yahoo.com. Half-board, private bath, hot water. **A** (high season).

C Playa Blanca, on the Salar de Uyuni, about 10 km from the Colchani access and 70 km from Isla del Pescado, T693 2115 (Uyuni). **D** in low season, half-board, all furnishings made of salt blocks, shared bath, no showers, single beds only, all solid and liquid waste is removed in barrels. This is the only hotel left on the salar and it is not clear if it will remain here, hotels were asked to leave for environmental reasons. A stop for most tours, day visitors must consume something in order to take photographs, use of toilet US$0.60. Playa Blanca has a second salt hotel in Colchani, same price, half-board, private bath, no shower. See also **Tayka/Fremen** in Activites and tours, below.

San Cristóbal *p284*

B Hotel San Cristóbal, purpose-built, owned by the community, in centre. The bar is inside a huge oil drum, all metal furnishings. The rest is comfortable if simple, very hot water, good breakfast included, evening meal extra.

G pp Alojamiento behind the internet office. Basic rooms with several beds, separate bath, hot water extra. Owners keep ñandúes.

G pp Alojamiento Ali, a bit more expensive, but not much difference, rooms with 3 beds, hot water extra.

🍴 Eating

Uyuni *p283, map p283*

Plenty of small places serving *menú del día* (one traveller advises "follow the police or army officers"). Avoid eating in market. This is not a good place to get ill.

🍴-🍴 16 de Julio, Arce entre Avs Ferroviaria y Potosí. Opens 0700, good value set lunch, à la carte in the evening, veggie options, meeting place.

🍴-🍴 Kactus, Arce y Potosí, p2. International food, homemade pasta, good pancakes, slow service.

🍴 Arco Iris, Plaza Arce. Good Italian food, pizza, and atmosphere, occasional live music.

🍴 La Loco, Av Potosí. Gringo food, with music and drinks till late, open fire, popular.

🍴 Minuteman, pizza restaurant attached to *Toñito Hotel* (see above), good pizzas and soups.

▲▲ Activities and tours

Uyuni *p283, map p283*

Organization of tours from Uyuni to the Salar is much improved, but even good companies, their guides or vehicles have their off days. Travel is in 4WD Landcruisers, cramped for those on the back seat, but the staggering scenery makes up for any discomfort. Always check the itinerary, the vehicle, the menu (vegetarians should be prepared for an egg-based diet), what is included in the price and what is not (accommodation is normally not included – add US$3-4.50 pp per night). Trip prices are based on a 6-person group – it is easy to find other people in Uyuni, especially in high season, Apr-Sep. If there are fewer than 6 you each pay more. Trips are the standard 3 to 4-day trip (Salar de Uyuni, Lagunas Colorada and Verde, back to Uyuni), the Uyuni-San Pedro de Atacama trip, including the Salar and lakes, and Uyuni to Tupiza via all the sights. Prices range from US$65-220 pp depending on agency, departure point and season. Agencies in Potosí and La Paz also organize tours, but in some cases this may involve putting you on a bus to Uyuni where you meet up with one of the Uyuni agencies and get the same quality tour for a higher price. If the tour seriously fails to match the contract and the operator refuses any redress, complaints can be taken to the tourism office in Uyuni (see above) and then to the **Director Regional de Turismo**, La Prefectura del Departamento de Potosí, C La Paz, Potosí (T02-622 7477). For the latest recommendations, speak to travellers who have just returned from a tour and try the following:

🔴 *For an explanation of the sleeping and eating price codes used in this guide, see inside the front*
⚫ *cover. Other relevant information is found in Essentials pages 240-241.*

Tour operators

Andes Salt Expeditions, 55 Arce Main Square, T693 2116, www.andes-salt-uyuni.com.bo. Recommended especially for their tours of the salt flat salar and colour lagoons.

Andes Travel Office, Ayacucho 222, T693 2227. Good reports, run by Belgian Isabelle and Iver.

Colque Tours, Av Potosí 54, T/F693 2199, www.colquetours.com. Well-known but consistently mixed reports, has its own hostals on the edge of the Salar and by Laguna Verde and a branch in San Pedro de Atacama.

Esmeralda, Av Ferroviaria esq Arce, T693 2130, esmeraldaivan@hotmail.com. Good tours – cheaper end of market.

Kantuta, Av Arce y Av Potosí, T693 3084, kantutatours@hotmail.com. Run by 3 eager brothers, also volcano-climbing tours, good food.

Reli Tours, Av Arce 42, T693 3209, www.reli tours.com. Reliable, good vehicles and food.

Tayka/Fremen, Sucre entre Uruguay y México, T693 2987, www.andes-amazonia.com. Proyecto Tayka, Red de Hoteles de los Andes, a chain of hotels in the Salar de Uyuni-Reserva Avaroa area, is a joint venture between Fremen, Fundación Prodem and 4 local communities. Hotels have 14 rooms with private bath, hot water, heating, restaurant, price in **AL** range: **Hotel de Sal** at Tahua, just north of the Salar de Uyuni, west of Salinas de Garcimendoza, and **Hotel de Piedra** at San Pedro de Quemez south of the Salar. To open in 2006, **Hotel del Desierto** at Ojo de Perdiz, Comunidad Soniquera, north of Laguna Colorada, and **Hotel de los Volcanes** at San Pablo de Lípez.

Toñito Tours, Av Ferroviaria 152, T693 3186, www.bolivianexpeditions.com. Offers a variety of tours (also in La Paz, see page 254), with their own hotel at Bella Vista on the edge of the Salar.

San Cristóbal *p284*

Llama Mama, www.llamamama.com. 60 km of exclusive bicycle trails descending 2-3 or 4 hrs, depending on skill, 3 grades, US$200, all inclusive, taken up by car, with guide and communication.

Suri 4x4, www.suri4x4.com. US$250 for up to 5 for whole-day tours to the Salar de Uyuni.

⊙ Transport

Uyuni *p283, map p283*

Bus Offices are on Av Arce, north of Colón. To **La Paz**, **16 de Julio** daily at 2000 (La Paz-Uyuni, daily 1530), **Panasur** Wed and Sun at 1800 (La Paz-Uyuni Tue and Fri 1730), US$6.25, 12 hrs, or transfer in Oruro. Tourist buses with **Todo Turismo**, C Santa Cruz next to *Hotel Los Girasoles*, www.touringbolivia.com, Tue and Sun at 2000, Fri at 2330, US$25, 11 hrs, 1 additional departure in high season (La Paz office, Plaza Antofagasta 504, Edif Paula, p1, opposite the bus terminal, T211 9418, depart Mon, Wed and Sat, 2100) **Oruro**, several companies 2000-2130, US$2.50-3.75; **Todo Turismo** (see above), US$20. To **Potosí** several companies 0930-1000 and 1900-2000, US$3.10, 6 hrs, spectacular scenery. To **Sucre 6 de Octubre** at 1900, or transfer in Potosí, US$5, 9 hrs. To **Tupiza** with **11 de Julio**, Wed, Fri and Sun 0900, US$4.40, 8 hrs, ramshackle buses. 6-8 passenger jeeps with **12 de Octubre** or **11 de Julio**, daily 0600, US$6.25, 5 hrs. For **Tarija** change in Potosí or Tupiza.

Regional services To **San Cristóbal**, from Av Potosí y Ayacucho, next to *Hostal Marith*, daily 1400, US$1.90, returns 0600. To **Vila Vila, San Cristóbal, Culpina K, Serena, Alota, Villa Mar, Soniquera, Quetena**, Trans Nor Lípez, Sun 1000, US$5 to Quetena, 10 hrs, return Wed 0300.

To **Alota** and **Colcha K**, 11 de Julio, Fri 1100, US$2.50, return Wed 1100. To **Soniquera** (between Villa Mar and Quetena), Sun 1100, US$3.15, 5 hrs, return Wed 0700.

Road and train A road and railway line run south from Oruro, through Río Mulato, to Uyuni (323 km). The road is sandy and, after rain, very bad, especially south of Río Mulato. The train journey is quicker and more scenic. Check services on arrival, T693 2153. **Expreso del Sur** leaves for **Oruro** on Thu and Sun at 0005, arriving 0700. Wara Wara del Sur service leaves on Tue and Fri at 0145, arriving 0910 (prices for both under Oruro). To **Atocha, Tupiza** and **Villazón** Expreso del Sur leaves Uyuni on Tue and Fri at 2240, arriving, respectively, at 0045, 0400 and 0705. **Wara Wara** leaves on Sun and Wed at 0250, arriving 0500, 0835 and 1205. The ticket office opens at 0830 and 1430 each day and one hour before the trains leave. It closes once tickets are sold – get there early or buy through a tour agent.

Travelling to Chile Chile is 1 hr ahead of Bolivia from mid-Oct to Mar. Do not attempt to take coca leaves across the border; it is an arrestable offence. Also Chile does not allow dairy produce, tea bags (of any description), fruit or vegetables to be brought in.

The easiest way is to go to San Pedro de Atacama as part of your jeep trip to the Salar and *lagunas* (see above). **Colque Tours**, address above, as well as running Salar and Lagunas tours that take you to **San Pedro de Atacama**, has a direct jeep leaving their office every day at 1900, US$25 pp, 16 hrs. They also run 2 mini-buses daily from their camp near the ranger station at Hito Cajones to San Pedro de Atacama, departing 1000 and 1700, US$5, 1 hr including stop at immigration. There is another vehicle from Hito Cajones to San Pedro de Atacama (*tránsito público*), most days at about 1000, same price. At other times onward transport to San Pedro must be arranged by your agency, this can cost up to US$60 if it is not included in your tour. The ranger station may be able to assist in an emergency. The *tránsito público* leaves San Pedro for Hito Cajones at 0800 or 0830. It is usually booked through an agency in town. Occasionally it runs in the afternoon.

There is a train service to **Calama** leaving 0330 Mon, US$13.20. Tickets are sold Fri-Sun. It should take 16 hrs but involves a 1-hr change of trains at Avaroa (arrives at Avaroa at 0800), then it's 40 mins to Ollagüe, where Chilean customs take 2-4 hrs. All passports are collected and stamped in the rear carriage and should be ready for collection after 1-2 hrs; queue for your passport,

no names are called out. After that it is an uncomfortable 8 hrs to Calama. Train Avaroa-Uyuni Thu 1200, arrives 1630. **Predilecto** has a bus to Calama which leaves from the terminal (T694 2330) Wed and Sun 0300, US$11, 15 hrs (depending on border crossing).

If driving your own vehicle, from **Colchani** it is about 60 km across to the southern shore of the **Salar**. The tracks made by other vehicles can be seen in the dry season: follow them. The salt is soft and wet for about 2 km around the edges so only use established ramps. It is 20 km from the southern shore to Colcha K, a military checkpoint. From there, a poor gravel road leads 28 km to San Juan then the road enters the Salar de Chiguana, a mix of salt and mud which is often wet and soft with deep tracks which are easy to follow. 35 km away is Chiguana, another military post, then 45 km to the end of this Salar, a few kilometres before border at Ollagüe. This latter part is the most dangerous; very slippery with little traffic. Alternatively, take the route that tours use to Laguna Colorada and continue to Hito Cajones. **Toñito Tours** of Uyuni will let you follow one of their groups and even promise help in the event of a break-down. There is no gasoline between Uyuni and Calama (Chile) if going via Ollagüe, or San Pedro de Atacama. Keep to the road at all times, and never venture from the shoulder at night. It is a hard trip and the road is impassable after rain. There are still a few unmarked sections along the border that are mined, although both sides downplay this unfortunate situation.

🌐 Directory

Uyuni *p283, map p283*
Banks Banco de Crédito, Av Potosí, entre Bolívar y Arce, changes cash occasionally. **Prodem**, Arce near Av Potosí, US$ cash at fair rates, Visa and Mastercard cash advances 5% comission, Mon-Fri 0830-1230 and 1430-1800, Sat 0830-1130. Several **casas de cambio** along Av Potosí, rates vary greatly, shop around, poor rates for TCs. **Internet** Many places in town, US$0.55 per hr. **Post offices** Av Arce esq C Cabrera. **Telephones** Several offices in town. **Useful addresses** Immigration: Av Sucre 94, corner of Av Potosí, T693 2062, open daily 0830-1200, 1400-1900 for visa extensions.

San Cristóbal *p284*
Bank For exchange at weekends only.
Internet By satellite, US$1.20 per hr.
Telephones Public phone in entrance to Hotel San Cristóbal.

Tupiza → *Phone code: 02. Colour map 6, grid B3. Population: 20,000. Altitude: 2,990 m.*

Set in a landscape of colourful, eroded mountains and stands of huge cactii, Tupiza, 200 km south of Uyuni, is a pleasant town with a lower altitude and warmer climate than Uyuni, making it a good alternative for visits to the Reserva Nacional Eduardo Avaroa and the Salar. There are also many things to do in the area and is best known as the place from which to take **Butch Cassidy and the Sundance Kid tours**. You can take bike rides, horse and jeep tours in the surroundings, eg the Quebrada Palala with the nearby 'Stone Forest', the Valle de los Machos and the Quebrada Seca. The Cañón del Inca is another site well worth visiting and there is a difficult and beautiful full-day trek: Tupiza-Cañón del Inca-Palala-Tupiza (guides or detailed route description available from Tupiza Tours). Another local option is *turismo rural*, staying in nearby rural communities, arranged by local agencies usually in conjunction with horse riding tours. The statue in the main plaza is to **Avelino Aramayo** (1802-1882), of the Aramayo mining dynasty, pre-eminent in the late 19th, early 20th centuries. **Chajra Huasi**, a palazzo-style, abandoned home of the Aramayo family across the Río Tupiza, may be visited. Beautiful sunsets over the fertile Tupiza valley can be seen from the foot of a statue of Christ on a hill behind the plaza. Market days are Monday, Thursday and Saturday, with local produce sold in the northern part of town; there is also a daily market at the north end of Avenida Chichas.

   IGM office ① *ground floor of Sub-Prefectura, next to the church, Mon-Fri 0800-1200 and 1500-1800*, topographic maps of southern Departamento de Potosí (including Salar de Uyuni and Lípez regions).

San Vicente → *Population: 400. Altitude: 4,500 m.*
Tupiza is the centre of Butch Cassidy and the Sundance Kid country and there are tours following their last few days. On 4 November 1908, they held up an Aramayo company payroll north of Salo. (**Aramayo hacienda** in Salo, one hour north of Tupiza, still stands. One-day tours from Tupiza go to the site of the hold-up, Huaca Huañusca.) Two days later they were killed by a four-man military police patrol in San Vicente, a silver and antimony mining camp. (Shoot out site off main street – ask locals.) Butch and Sundance are buried in the cemetery, but the grave has yet to be identified (ask around for the keyholder). An investigation of the supposed grave by the Nova project in 1991 proved negative, but see *Digging Up Butch and Sundance*, by Anne Meadows (Bison Books, 1996). There is no lodging, but ask at the mine office, who may find you a room. To get to San Vicente there are tours from hotels and agencies in Tupiza (see Listings, below); there is public transport once or twice a week from Tupiza or Atocha.

South to Argentine border → *Bolivian time is 1 hr behind Argentina.*
Villazón (81 km south of Tupiza) The Argentine border is here at Villazón (Phone code: 02; Cotevi phone company prefix 596, Entel 597, Population: 13,000, Altitude: 3,443 m). There is not much to see (good indoor market). The border area must not be photographed.

Border with Argentina Bolivian immigration office is on Avenida República de Argentina just before bridge; open daily 0600-2000. They issue entry and exit stamps. Officials are efficient. For Argentine immigration see page 156. Once in Bolivia, boys offer to wheel your bags uphill to the bus stations, US$0.65, but they will ask for more. Change all your bolivianos into dollars or pesos, because there are no exchange facilities in La Quiaca and bolivianos are not accepted in Argentina. The Argentine consulate is at Plaza 6 de Agosto 117, upstairs; open Monday-Thursday 1000-1300.

● Sleeping

Tupiza *p289*
D Mitru, Av Chichas 187, T/F694 3001, www.tupiza tours.com. In new rooms with bath, **E** in older rooms with bath, **E** with shared bath (only 4 rooms left), **A** for suite with sitting room. All include breakfast. Very good, hot water, pool, games room, cable TV, parking, use of kitchen, luggage store,

safes, book exchange, laundry (discount for hotel guests) and clothes-washing facilities, surcharge on credit card payments and TCs.
E Mitru Anexo, Abaroa 20, T694 3002. **F** with shared bath, includes breakfast, nicely renovated in 2005, restaurant, use of kitchen, use of pool and games room at **Hotel Mitru**.

D-E **La Torre**, Av Chichas 220, T694 2633,
latorrehotel@yahoo.es. **F** with shared bath and
no TV, includes breakfast, lovely refurbished
house, comfortable rooms, good value, great
service, use of kitchen. Recommended.
E **Hostal Pedro Arraya**, Av P Arraya 494,
T694 2734, hostalarraya@hotmail.com.
Convenient to bus and train stations, **F** with
shared bath, hot water, includes breakfast,
modern comfortable rooms, use of kitchen,
laundry, terrace, good value.
E **Hostal Valle Hermoso**, Av Pedro Arraya 478,
T694 2592, www.bolivia.freehosting.net. Good hot
showers, breakfast included (**F** with shared bath
and no breakfast), pleasant TV/breakfast room,
breakfast extra, book exchange, tourist advice,
Butch Cassidy video, firm beds, motorbikes can be
parked in restaurant, accepts credit cards and TCs
(5% extra). Second location, **Valle Hermoso 2**, Av
Pedro Arraya 585, T694 3441, near the bus station,
refurbished house, 3 simple rooms with bath,
several dorms for 6 or 8 with bunk beds, same
prices as No 1, new in 2005, 10% discount for IYHF
members in both locations.
F **Renacer Chicheño**, Barrio Ferroviario, Casa 18,
T694 2718, hostalrenacer-ch@hotmail.com.
Cheaper with shared bath, includes basic
breakfast, family home, use of kitchen.
F **Res Centro**, Av Santa Cruz 287, 2 blocks from
station, T694 2705. Nice patio, motorbike and car
parking, couple rooms with bath, most shared,
basic but clean, hot water on request, parking,
helpful owner, good value.

South to Argentine border: Villazón *p289*
D-E **Res El Cortijo**, 20 de Mayo 338, behind post
office, T596 2093. Breakfast included, some rooms
with bath, intermittent hot water, restaurant.
E **Grand Palace**, 25 de Mayo 52, 1 block
southwest of bus terminal, T596 5333. Safe, hot
water, **F** without bath, TV, no breakfast.
Recommended (but up for sale in late 2005).
E **Hostal Plaza**, Plaza 6 de Agosto 138, T597 3535.
Modern, smart, **F** without bath, TV, comfortable,
good restaurant, *La Perla*, underneath hotel.
F **Hostal Buena Vista**, Av Antofagasta 508, T596
3055. Good rooms, shared bath, hot showers
US$1.05, close to the train and bus stations,
above reasonable restaurant.
G **Res Martínez**, 25 de Mayo 13, 1 block
southwest of bus station. Well signed, shared
bath, hot water.
G **Res Panamericano**, C 20 de Mayo 384, T596
2612. Shared bath, risky electric showers, sagging
beds, laundry facilities, parking.

🍽 Eating

Tupiza *p289*

Tupiza is famous for its *tamales*, a delicious scrap
of spicy dried llama meat encased in a ball of
corn mash and cooked in the leaves of the plant.
🍴-🍴 Two places outside town serve speciality
meals in rural surrounds on weekends only. La
Estancia, 2 km north in Villa Remedios, best on
Sun, *picante de cabrito* (spicy goat). La Campiña,
in Tambillo Alto, 45 mins' walk north along the
river, *cordero a la cruz* (lamb on the spit) and
lechón (suckling pig).
🍴 **California**, Cochabamba on main plaza,
0800-2300 daily. Breakfast, pizza, vegetarian and
regional dishes, popular with gringos.
🍴 **El Escorial**, Chichas esq Abaroa. Good value set
meal at midday, à la carte in the evening.
🍴 **Il Bambino**, Florida y Santa Cruz. Recommended,
especially for *salteñas*, closed Sat and Sun evenings.
🍴 **La Casa de Irma**, in supermarket *Frial Castro*,
Florida. Only prepares meals for groups with
several hours advance notice, lasagnes, chicken,
meat and vegetarian dishes.
🍴 **Los Helechos**, next door to *Mitru Anexo* on
Abaroa. Burgers and main courses, vegetarian
options, good salad bar, closed alternate Suns.

South to Argentine border: Villazón *p289*
Better to cross the border to La Quiaca to eat.
🍴 **Snack Pizzería Don Vicco**, J M Deheza, round
corner from *Hotel Grand Palace*.
🍴 **Chifa Jardín**, on the Plaza. Chinese, looks tatty
but huge helpings.
🍴 **El Repostero**, opposite market. Serves good
breakfasts and lunches.
🍴 **Snack El Turista**, Edificio de Turismo. Open at
0900 for breakfast.

⛰ Activities and tours

Tupiza *p289*

One-day jeep tours US$11-12; horse riding
US$2-2.50; 2-day San Vicente plus colonial town
of Portugalete US$55; Salar de Uyuni and Reserva
Avaroa, 4 days with Spanish speaking guide,
US$85-100 low season, US$90-120 high season
(tours out of Tupiza are more expensive than those
out of Uyuni because of the additional 400 km
travelled). Prices per person based on groups of 6,
add US$10 per day for English speaking guide.
Some agencies include in their price entrance fees
to Reserva Avaroa and Isla del Pescado.
Tupiza Tours, in *Hotel Mitru* (address above), are
the most experienced and are at the higher end of
the market. They have additional tours: 'triathlon' of

🔴 *For an explanation of the sleeping and eating price codes used in this guide, see inside the front*
⚫ *cover. Other relevant information is found in Essentials pages 240-241.*

riding, biking and jeep in the surroundings, US$22 pp (frequently recommended), and extensions to the Uyuni tour.

Valle Hermoso Tours, inside *Hostal Valle Hermoso 1*, T/F694 2592. Also recommended, offers similar tours, as do several new agencies. Most hotels listed have an agency.

Transport

Tupiza *p289*
Bus There is small, well-organized, bus terminal at the south end of Av Pedro Arraya. To **Villazón** 0400, 1430, US$1.50, 2½ hrs. To **Potosí**, 1000, 2000, US$5.25, 7 hrs (change here for **Sucre**). Road from Potosí which goes on south to Villazón is 2-way, dirt, with a bridge over the Río Suipacha. To **Tarija**, 1930, 2000, US$5, 8 hrs (change here for **Santa Cruz**). To **Uyuni**, 11 de Julio, Mon, Thu, Sat at 1000, US$4.40, 8 hrs, poor vehicles; also 6-8 passenger jeeps daily at 0600 and 1030 (**12 de Octubre**) US$6.25, 5 hrs. To **Oruro**, 1200, 2030, US$6.25, 13 hrs (change here for **Cochabamba**). Expreso Tupiza has a direct bus to **La Paz** at 1000 (La Paz-Tupiza at 1930, 15 hrs), otherwise via Potosí, 17 hrs, US$7.50.
Train Train station ticket office open Mon-Sat 0800-1100, 1530-1730, and in the early morning half an hour before trains arrive. To **Villazón**: Expreso del Sur Wed and Sat 0410, arriving 0705; Wara Wara Mon and Thu at 0905, arriving 1205. To **Atocha**, **Uyuni** and **Oruro**, *Expreso del Sur* Wed and Sat at 1825; *Wara Wara* Mon and Thu at 1905. Fares are given under Oruro.

South to Argentine border: Villazón *p289*
Bus Bus terminal is near plaza, 5 blocks from the border. There are lots of company offices jumbled together. Taxi to border, US$0.35 or hire porter, US$0.65, and walk across. From **La Paz**, several companies, 18 hrs, US$8.75 (even though buses are called 'direct', you may have to change in Potosí, perhaps to another company), depart La Paz 1630, depart **Villazón** 0800-0830. To **Potosí** several between 0800-0830 and 1800-1900, 10 hrs by day, 12 hrs at night, US$6 (terrible in the wet,

can take 24 hrs; freezing at night). To **Tupiza**, several daily, US$1.50. To **Tarija**, beautiful journey but most buses overnight only, daily at 2000-2030, US$3, 6½ hrs, very cold on arrival but passengers can sleep on bus until daybreak.
Road An unpaved road goes to Tarija, improved for the last 16 km. The road linking Potosí with Villazón via Camargo is in poor condition and about 100 km longer than the better road via Tupiza.
Train Station about 1 km north of border on main road, taxi US$2.35. To **Tupiza**, **Atocha**, **Uyuni** and **Oruro**: Expreso del Sur Wed, Sat, 1530, **Wara Wara del Sur** Mon, Thu 1530. Ticket office opens 0800; take a number and wait till you are called.

Directory

Tupiza *p289*
Banks Banco de Crédito, on main plaza, Mon-Fri 0830-1230, 1430-1700, fair rates for cash, US$5 commission for Visa/MasterCard cash advances. **Prodem**, Cochabamba on main plaza, Mon-Fri 0830-1230, 1430-1800, Sat 0900-1200, fair rates for cash, 5% commission for Visa/MasterCard cash advances. **Cooperativa El Chorlque**, Av Santa Cruz 300 y Abaroa, Mon-Fri 0900-1600, Sat 0900-1100, cash only. **Cambios Latin America**, Abaroa y Santa Cruz, open daily or knock on door (long hours), bargain for best cash rate, 6% commission for Tcs. **Tupiza Tours** gives cash against Visa, Mastercard (no ATM) and TCs. **Internet** Many internet places, US$0.70 per hr. **Post offices** On Abaroa, northwest of plaza, Mon-Fri 0830-1800, Sat 0900-1700, Sun 0900-1200. **Telephones** Several Entel offices, including one on the plaza and another across the street from the bus station.

South to Argentine border: Villazón *p289*
Banks Banco de Crédito, Oruro 111, changes cash only; try the *casas de cambio* on Av República de Argentina, uphill from the border. **Internet** Several internet places, US$1.50 per hour. **Post offices** Av Independencia, opposite side to bus station. **Telephones** Several Entel office the corner of Plaza 6 de Agosto and Gilberto Cortez.

Central and Southern Highlands

This region boasts two World Cultural Heritage sites, the mining city of Potosí, the source of great wealth for colonial Spain and of indescribable hardship for many Bolivians, and Sucre, the white city and Bolivia's official capital. In the south, Tarija is known for its fruit and wines and its traditions which set it apart from the rest of the country.

Potosí → *Phone code: 02. Colour map 6, grid B3. Population: 112,000. Altitude: 4,070 m.*

Potosí is the highest city of its size in the world. It was founded by the Spaniards on 10 April 1545, after they had discovered indigenous mine workings at Cerro Rico, which dominates the city. Immense amounts of silver were once extracted. In Spain 'es un Potosí' (it's a Potosí) is still used for anything superlatively rich. By the early 17th century Potosí was the largest city in the Americas, but over the next two centuries, as its lodes began to deteriorate and silver was found elsewhere, Potosí became little more than a ghost town. It was the demand for tin – a metal the Spaniards ignored – that saved the city from absolute poverty in the early 20th century, until the price slumped because of over-supply. Mining continues in Cerro Rico – mainly tin, zinc, lead, antimony and wolfram.

Ins and outs

Getting there The airport is 5 km out of town on the Sucre road. The bus terminal is 20 minutes downhill walk or a short taxi or micro ride from the centre of town on Avenida Universitaria below rail station, T624 3361. **Entel**, post office, police, US$0.10 terminal tax.
▶ *For more detailed information see Transport, page 296.*

Tourist office On Plaza 6 de Agosto, T622 7405, gobmupoi@cedro.pts.entelnet.bo. Town maps US$0.40 (English, French, German and Spanish), better than glossy US$0.60 map (Spanish only), helpful. Open Monday-Friday 0800-1200, 1400-1800 (allegedly). The police station by the Alcaldía has a photo album showing common scams. Beware fake "plainclothes policemen", usually preceded by someone asking you for the time. The official police wear green uniforms and work in pairs. ▶ *See La Paz, page 243 for Safety hints.*

Sights

Large parts of Potosí are colonial, with twisting streets and an occasional great mansion with its coat of arms over the doorway. UNESCO has declared the city to be 'Patrimonio de la Humanidad' (World Cultural Heritage site). Some of the best buildings are grouped round the Plaza 10 de Noviembre. The old Cabildo and the Royal Treasury – Las Cajas Reales – are both here, converted to other uses. The **Cathedral** ① *faces Plaza 10 de Noviembre, Mon-Fri 0930-1000, 1500-1730, Sat 0930-1000, guided tour only, US$1.*

The **Casa Nacional de Moneda**, or Mint, is nearby ① *on C Ayacucho, T622 2777, Tue-Sat 0900-1200, 1400-1830, Sun 0900-1200, US$3, US$3 to take photos, US$3 for video, entry by regular, 2-hr guided tour only (in English at 0900, usually for 10 or more people).* Founded in 1572, rebuilt 1759-1773, it is one of the chief monuments of civil building in Hispanic America. Thirty of its 160 rooms are a museum with sections on mineralogy, and an art gallery in a splendid salon on the first floor. One section is dedicated to the works of the acclaimed 17th-18th century religious painter Melchor Pérez de Holguín. Elsewhere are coin dies and huge wooden presses which made the silver strips from which coins were cut. The smelting houses have carved altar pieces from Potosí's ruined churches. You cannot fail to notice the huge, grinning mask of Bacchus over an archway between two principal courtyards. Erected in 1865, its smile is said to be ironic and aimed at the departing Spanish. Wear warm clothes, as it is cold inside.

Convento y Museo de Santa Teresa ① *Chicas y Ayacucho, T622 3847, 0900-1100, 1500-1700, only by guided tour in Spanish or English, US$3.15, US$1.50 to take photos, US$25(!) for video.* A guide is obligatory to this interesting collection of colonial and religious art. Among Potosí's baroque churches, typical of 18th-century Andean or 'mestizo' architecture, are the Jesuit **Compañía** church ① *on Ayacucho, 0800-1200, 1400-1800*, with an impressive bell-gable. **San Francisco** ⓘ *Tarija y Nogales, T622 2539, Mon-Fri 0900-1200, 1430-1700, Sat 0900-1200, US$1.50, US$1.50 to take photos, US$3 for video*, with a fine organ, worthwhile for the views from the tower and roof, museum of ecclesiastical art, underground tunnel system. Also **San Lorenzo** (1728-1744) *on Héroes del Chaco*, with a rich portal and fine views from the tower. **San Martín** *on Hoyos*, with an uninviting exterior, is beautiful inside, but is normally closed for fear of theft. Ask the German Redemptorist Fathers to show you around; their office is just to the left of their church. Other churches to visit include **Jerusalén** ⓘ *Plaza del Estudiante, Mon-Sat 1430-1830, US$0.75*, with **Museo Sacro** displaying gold work and painting. On the opposite side of Plaza del Estudiante is **San Bernardo** ⓘ *Mon-Fri 0800-1200, 1400-1800*, which houses the Escuela Taller Potosí where you can see a display of restoration work. **San Agustín** *Bolívar y Quijarro,* with crypts and catacombs (the whole city was interconnected by tunnels in colonial times) is open only by prior arrangement with the tourist office. Tour starts at 1700, US$0.10.

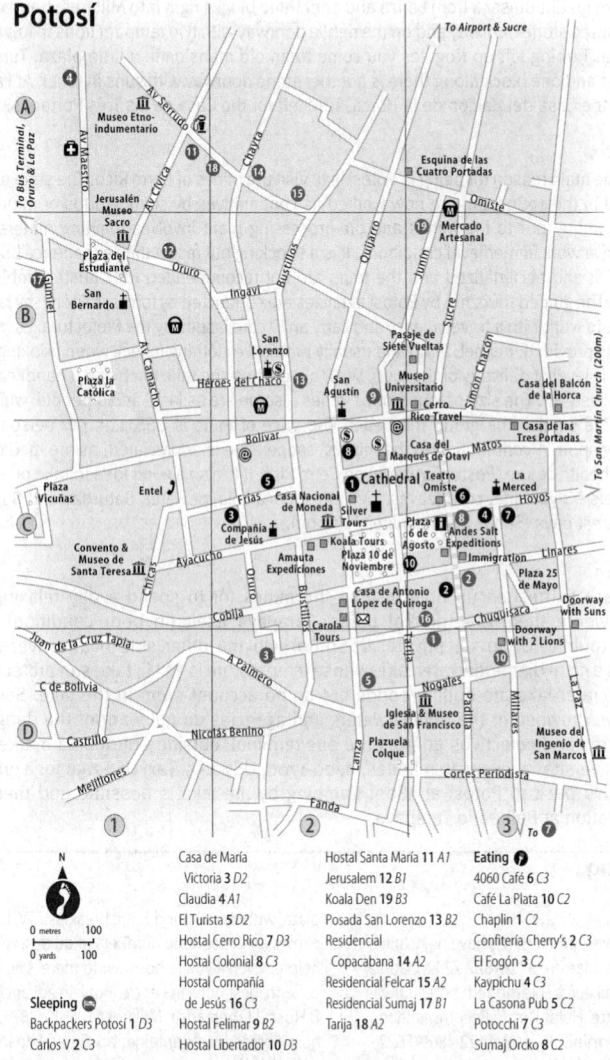

Potosí

N

0 metres 100
0 yards 100

Sleeping 🛏
Backpackers Potosí 1 *D3*
Carlos V 2 *C3*
Casa de María
   Victoria 3 *D2*
Claudia 4 *A1*
El Turista 5 *D2*
Hostal Cerro Rico 7 *D3*
Hostal Colonial 8 *C3*
Hostal Compañia
   de Jesús 16 *C3*
Hostal Felimar 9 *B2*
Hostal Libertador 10 *D3*

Hostal Santa María 11 *A1*
Jerusalem 12 *B1*
Koala Den 19 *B3*
Posada San Lorenzo 13 *B2*
Residencial
   Copacabana 14 *A2*
Residencial Felcar 15 *A2*
Residencial Sumaj 17 *B1*
Tarija 18 *A2*

Eating 🍴
4060 Café 6 *C3*
Café La Plata 10 *C2*
Chaplin 1 *C2*
Confitería Cherry's 2 *C3*
El Fogón 3 *C2*
Kaypichu 4 *C3*
La Casona Pub 5 *C2*
Potocchi 7 *C3*
Sumaj Orcko 8 *C2*

293

Teatro Omiste (1753) *on Plaza 6 de Agosto,* has a fine façade. The **Museo Universitario** ① *C Bolívar 698, Mon-Fri, 0800-1200, 1400-1800, US$0.75,* displays archaeology and some good modern Bolivian painting. **Museo del Ingenio de San Marcos** ① *Betanzos y La Paz, T622 2781, 1000-2300; restaurant 1200-2300, information office 1130-1230, 1430-1530, exhibition Mon-Sat 1300-2000.* This is a well-preserved example of the city's industrial past, with machinery used in grinding down the silver ore. It also has a restaurant, cultural activities and an exhibition of Calcha textiles. **Museo Etno-indumentario** (also known as **Fletes**) ① *Av Serrudo 152, T622 3258, Mon-Fri 0900-1200, 1400-1800, Sat 0900-1200, US$1.10, includes tour in Spanish and German.* This very interesting museum has a thorough display of the different dress and customs and their histories of Potosí department's 16 provinces.

In Potosí, 2,000 colonial buildings have been catalogued. At Quijarro and Omiste is the Esquina de las Cuatro Portadas (two houses with double doors), or Balcón de Llamacancha. Off Junín, see the Pasaje de Siete Vueltas (the passage of the seven turns). There is a fine stone doorway (house of the Marqués de Otavi, now a bank) in Junín between Matos and Bolívar. At Lanza 8 was the house of José de Quiroz and of Antonio López de Quiroga (now a school). Turn up Chuquisaca from Lanza and after three blocks right into Millares; here on the left is a sculpted stone doorway and on the right a doorway with two rampant lions in low relief on the lintel. Turning left up Nogales you come to an old mansion in a little plaza. Turn left along La Paz and one block along there is another stone doorway with suns in relief. At La Paz y Bolívar is the Casa del Balcón de la Horca. Turn left for the Casa de las Tres Portadas.

Mine tours

For many, the main reason for being in Potosí is to visit the mines of Cerro Rico. The state mines were closed in the 1980s and are now worked as cooperatives by small groups of miners. A 4½-hour morning tour to the mines and ore-processing plant involves meeting miners and seeing them at work in medieval conditions. It is a shocking but fascinating experience but you need to be fit and acclimatized and the tours are not recommended for claustrophobics or asthmatics. The guided tours run by Potosí agencies are conducted by former miners; by law all guides have to work with a travel agency and carry an ID card issued by the Prefectura. Essential equipment is provided: helmet, lamp and usually protective clothing (check when booking and ask about the level of difficulty of the tour). Wear old clothes and take torch and a handkerchief to filter the dusty air. The size of tour groups varies – some are as large as 20 people, which is excessive. The smaller the group the better. The price of tours is US$11.25 per person and includes transport. A contribution to the miners' cooperative is appreciated, as are medicines for the new health centre (*Posta Sanitaria*) on Cerro Rico. It is also a good idea to take presents for the miners – dynamite, coca leaves, cigarettes, Coca-cola, or water. Saturday and Sunday are the quietest days (Sunday is the miners' day off).

Tarapaya

A good place to freshen up after visiting the mines (or to spend a day relaxing) is Tarapaya, where there are thermal baths, Tarapaya itself (in poor condition) and Miraflores (public, US$0.30, private, US$0.60). On the other side of the river from Tarapaya is a 50 m diameter crater lake, whose temperature is 30° C; take sun protection. Below the crater lake are boiling ponds but on no account swim in the lake. Several people have drowned in the boiling waters and agencies do not warn of the dangers. Buses, micros and colectivos go from the bus terminal, outside Chuquimia market on Avenida Universitaria, every 30 minutes, 0700-1700, US$0.55. Taxi US$7.50 for a group. Last colectivo back to Potosí at 1800. Camping by the lake is possible and there is accommodation at Balneario Tarapaya.

● Sleeping

Potosí *p292, map p293*
Unless otherwise stated hotels have no heating.
B Claudia, Av Maestro 322, T622 2242, claudia_hotel@hotmail.com. This modern hotel is away from the centre. Helpful staff. Recommended.
B Hostal Colonial, Hoyos 8, T622 4809, F622 7146. A pretty colonial house near the main

plaza, with heating and basic breakfast, TV, has names and telephone numbers of guides, very helpful, even if you're not staying there, safe parking, best hotel in centre. Book in advance.
B Hostal Libertador, Millares 58, T622 7877, hostalib@cedro.pts.entelnet.bo. Central heating, quiet, helpful, comfortable, parking.

C Hostal Cerro Rico, Ramos 123 entre La Paz y Millares, T/F622 3539. Very good rooms upstairs, heating, hot water, **D** without bath, cable TV, internet, helpful, parking.

C Jerusalem, Oruro 143, T/F622 2600, hoteljer@cedro.pts.entelnet.bo. Pleasant, with breakfast, **F** without bath, helpful, *comedor*, parking, laundry, good value.

D Hostal Compañía de Jesús, Chuquisaca 445, T622 3173. Central, attractive, good value, includes breakfast.

D Hostal Felimar, Junín 14, T622 4357. Hot water, includes breakfast, very good, 2 roof-top suites, basement rooms have no exterior windows but warm, quiet.

E Carlos V, Linares 42 on Plaza 6 de Agosto, T622 5121. With breakfast, **F** without bath, occasional hot water 0700-1200, luggage store, 2400 curfew.

E Hostal Santa María, Av Serrudo 244, T622 3255. Hot water, cold rooms, cafeteria, popular.

E El Turista, Lanza 19, T622 2492, F622 2517. Also *LAB* office, helpful, hot showers, breakfast (US$1), great view from top rooms, good value. Recommended but poor beds.

E Koala Den, Junín 56, T622 6467, see *Koala Tours*, below, but book separately. Refurbished, with heated dormitory (**F**) and shared showers, private rooms with bath and breakfast, TV and video and use of kitchen.

F Casa de María Victoria, Chuquisaca 148, T622 2132. All rooms open onto colonial courtyard, **G** without bath, lukewarm water, stores luggage, popular as budget choice, arranges mine tours, owner speaks English, good breakfast, leave nothing unattended, poor beds.

F Res Felcar, Serrudo 345 y Bustillos, T622 4966. Shared bath, hot water 0800-1600, popular, nice patio garden.

F Tarija, Av Serrudo 252, T622 2711. Poorly signed but the more expensive rooms are good, **G** without bath, helpful, large courtyard for parking.

G pp Backpackers Potosí, Chuquisaca 460 y Padilla, T04-644 0889, potosi@boliviahostels.com. Recent addition to the network of budget hostels.

G Posada San Lorenzo, C Bustillos 967, opposite market. Colonial building, courtyard, no showers.

G Res Copacabana, Av Serrudo 319, T622 2712. Single or shared rooms, restaurant, separate hot showers, will change $ cash, safe car park.

G Res Sumaj, Gumiel 12, T622 3336. Small dark rooms with shared bath, kitchen, laundry, TV lounge, helpful, popular with travellers.

● Eating

Potosí *p292, map p293*
Good value food in Mercado Central, between Oruro, Bustillos, Héroes del Chaco and Bolívar, breakfast from 0700, fresh bread from 0600.

†¶-¶ La Casona Pub, Frías 34, T622 2954. Good food (meat fondue and trout recommended) and beer, nice atmosphere and service, open Mon-Sat 1000-1230, 1815-2400.

†¶-¶ El Fogón, Oruro y Frías, T622 4969. Upmarket pub-restaurant, good food and atmosphere, open 1200-1500, 1800-2400.

†¶-¶ Potocchi, Millares 24, T622 2467. Great traditional food, opens 0800, *peña* most nights.

¶ Chaplin, Quijarro y Matos 10. Pleasant, good breakfasts and fast food, vegetarian options, best *tucumanos*, closed 1200-1500 and Sun.

¶ Kaypichu, Millares 24. Vegetarian, stylish, good breakfasts, open 0700-1300 and 1600-2100, closed Mon.

¶ Sumaj Orcko, Quijarro 46. Large portions, cheap set lunch, reasonably priced, very popular with travellers, heating.

Cafés
4060 Café, Hoyos entre Padilla y Millares. 'Hip' place serving interesting food, more upmarket surroundings and pricier than others.

Café La Plata, Plaza 10 de Noviembre at Linares. For breakfast and then 1500-2200, closed Sun, good for coffee, cookies and cakes, wine and beer. English and French spoken. **Confitería Cherry's**, Padilla 8. Good cakes, popular, good breakfast, cheap, slow service, open 0800.

● Festivals and events

Potosí *p292, map p293*
8-10 Mar is San Juan de Dios, with music, dancing, parades etc. In **May** there is a market on C Gumiel every Sun, with lotteries and lots of fun things for sale. Fiesta de Manquiri: on 3 consecutive Sat at the **end of May/beginning of Jun** llama sacrifices are made at the cooperative mines in honour of *Pachamama*; the same occurs on **1 Aug**, the Ritual del Espíritu. Carnaval Minero, 2 weeks before carnival in Oruro, includes Tata Ckascho, when miners dance down Cerro Rico and El Tío (the *Dios Minero*) is paraded. San Bartolomé, or the Fiesta de Chutillos, is held from the middle of **Aug**, with the main event being processions of dancers on the weekend closest to the **24th-26th**; Sat features Potosino, and Sun national, groups. Costumes can be hired in *artesanía* market on C Sucre. Hotel and transport prices go up by 30% for the whole of that weekend. In **Oct**, Festival Internacional de la Cultura, in Potosí and Sucre. **10 Nov**, Fiesta Aniversario de Potosí. Potosí is sometimes called the 'Ciudad de las Costumbres', especially at Corpus Cristi, Todos Santos and Carnaval, when special cakes are baked, families go visiting friends, etc.

✪ Shopping

Potosí p292, map p293
Germán Laime, Sucre 38. Tailor, will make items (jackets, bags, etc) to customers' wishes.
Mercado Artesanal, at Sucre y Omiste, sells handwoven cloth and regional handicrafts. Some Fridays the merchants organize music, food and drink (ponche), not to be missed.
Mercado Central (see address above), sells mainly food and produce but silver is sold near the C Oruro entrance.

▲ Activities and tours

Potosí p292, map p293
Trips to the Salar de Uyuni, Laguna Colorada and Laguna Verde are expensive here. See page 284 for advice on booking a trip.

The following have been recommended:
Amauta Expediciones, Ayacucho 17, T622 5515. For trips to Uyuni, the lagoons and the mines. Gerónimo Fuentes has been recommended and speaks English. 15% of income goes to the miners.
Andes Salt Expediciones, Plaza Alonso de Ibáñez 3, T622 5175, www.bolivia-travel.com.bo. Recommended guides. Run by Braulio Mamani, who speaks English. Daily city tours, bus and flight tickets, also have n office inj Uyuni.
Carola Tours, Lanza y Chuquisaca. Guide and owner Santos Mamani is recommended.
Cerro Rico Travel, Bolívar 853, T622 7044, T718-35083 (mob), jacky_gc@yahoo.com. Jaqueline knows the mines well and speaks good English. Also English and French guides for trips to village artesanía markets north of the city and to colonial haciendas, horse and mountain bike hire, treks, trips to Toro Toro including cave visits.
Hidalgo Tours, Junín y Bolívar 19, T622 5186, uyusalht@ceibo.entelnet.bo. Upmarket and specialized services within the city and to Salar de Uyuni. Efraín Huanca has been recommended for mine tours.
Koala Tours, Ayacucho 5, T/F622 2092, www.koalatoursbolivia.com. Run by Eduardo Garnica Fajardo who speaks English and French. Excellent mine tours by former miners, Juan Mamani Choque and Pedro Montes Caria have been recommended. The company donates 15% of its fees to support on-site health-care facilities. Frequently recommended. They also have a hostal, The Koala Den, see Sleeping, and an internet café, see below.
Silver Tours, Quijarro 12, Edif Minero, T622 3600, www.silvertours.8m.com. One of the cheaper firms, guide Fredi recommended.

⊕ Transport

Potosí p292, map p293
Air Aero Sur (C Cobija 25, T622 2898), to **La Paz** 0800 Mon-Sat; **TAM** to/from **La Paz**, Mon. Flights frequently cancelled. Beware theft in the terminal.
Bus When you buy your ticket you check your luggage into the operator's office and it is then loaded directly onto your bus. Daily services: to **La Paz** 1830-1930, US$5, 10 hrs by paved road, bus cama with **Flota Copacabana** US$7.50 (all departures from La Paz 1830-2030). To travel by day, go to **Oruro**, 0700 and 1900, US$2.50, 5 hrs. To **Cochabamba** 1830 and 1900, US$4.50, 12 hrs. To **Sucre** 4 daily 0700-1800, US$3, 3 hrs. Cars run to Sucre, taking 5 passengers, 2½ hrs, US$3.75 pp, drop-off at your hotel. To **Santa Cruz** 1900 (change in Sucre or Cochabamba), US$12, 18 hrs. To **Villazón** 0800, 1900, US$6, 10-12 hrs. To **Tarija** 1800, US$6.70-7.45, 12 hrs, spectacular journey but crowded bus. Buses to **Uyuni** leave from either side of the railway line (uphill the road is called Av Antofagasta or 9 de Abril, downhill it is Av Universitaria), 5 daily 1030 to 1930, US$3.10, 6 hrs, superb scenery; book in advance.
A **taxi** in town costs US$1.

⊕ Directory

Potosí p292, map p293
Banks There are ATMs around the centre. **Banco Nacional**, Junín 4-6. Exchange for US$ TCs and cash. **Banco Mercantil**, Sucre y Ayacucho. 1% commision on US$ TCs, no commission on Visa cash withdrawals. Almost opposite is **Casa Fernández** for cash exchange. **Banco de Crédito**, Bolívar y Sucre. Cash withdrawals on Visa. **Prodem**, Bolívar y Junín. Cash advances on Visa and MasterCard, 5% commission, also changes US$ cash. Many shops on Plaza Alonso de Ibáñez and on Bolívar, Sucre and Padilla display 'compro dólares' signs. **Internet** All US$0.75 per hr. **Café Candelaria**, Ayacucho 5, T622 8050, also crafts, postcards, book exchange (see Koala Tours, above). **Tuko's Café**, Junín 9, p 3, T622 5489, tuco25@hotmail.com. Open 0800-2300, 'the highest net café in the world'; lots of information, English spoken, popular music, videos, good food. Another opposite bus terminal. **Post offices** Lanza 3, Mon-Fri 0800-2000, Sat 0800-1800, Sun 0900-1200. **Telephones** Entel, on Plaza Arce at end of Av Camacho, T624 3496. Also at Av Universitaria near bus terminal, and on Padilla, opposite Confitería Cherys. **Useful** addresses Migración: Linares esq Padilla, T622 5989. Mon-Fri 0830-1630, closed lunchtime, beware unnecessary charges for extensions. **Police station:** on Plaza 10 de Noviembre.

Sucre → *Phone code: 04. Colour map 6, grid B3. Population: 131,769. Altitude: 2,790 m.*

Sucre has grown rapidly since the mid-1980s following severe drought which drove campesinos from the countryside and the collapse of tin mining in 1985. Founded in 1538 as La Plata, it became capital of the audiencia of Charcas in 1559. Its name was later changed to Chuquisaca before the present name was adopted in 1825 in honour of the first president of the new republic. Sucre is sometimes referred to as La Ciudad Blanca, owing to the tradition that all buildings in the centre are painted in their original colonial white. This works to beautiful effect and in 1992 UNESCO declared the city a 'Patrimonio Histórico y Cultural de la Humanidad' (World Cultural Heritage site). There are two universities, the older dating from 1624.

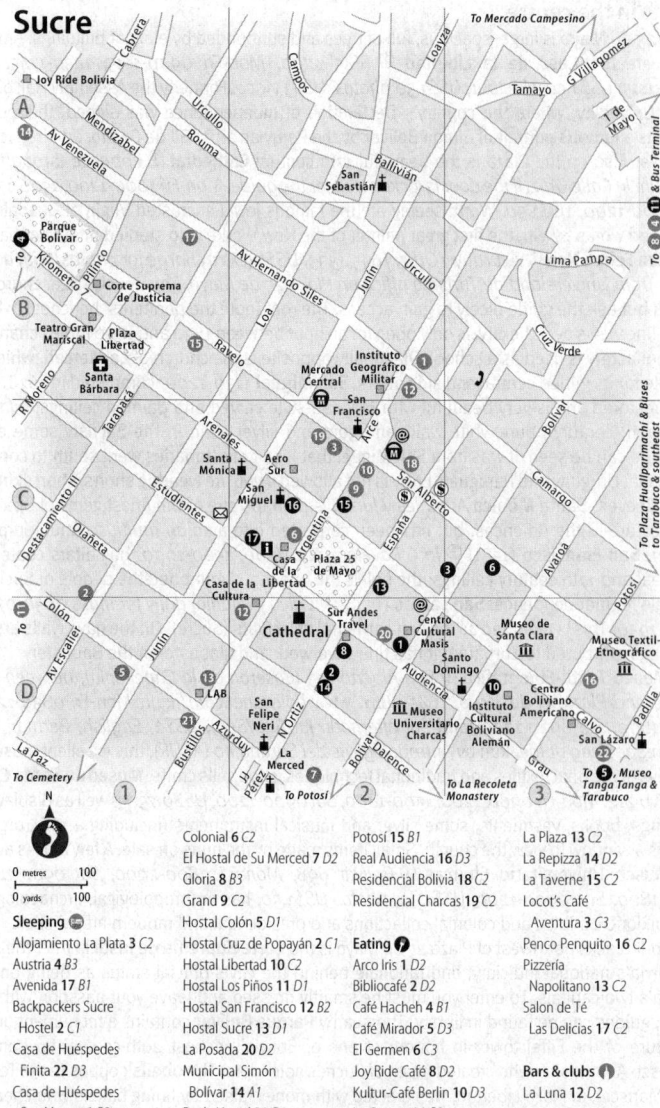

Colonial **6** *C2*
El Hostal de Su Merced **7** *D2*
Gloria **8** *B3*
Grand **9** *C2*
Hostal Colón **5** *D1*
Hostal Cruz de Popayán **2** *C1*
Hostal Libertad **10** *C2*
Hostal Los Piños **11** *D1*
Hostal San Francisco **12** *B2*
Hostal Sucre **13** *D1*
La Posada **20** *D2*
Municipal Simón
Bolívar **14** *A1*
Paola Hostal **21** *D1*

Potosí **15** *B1*
Real Audiencia **16** *D3*
Residencial Bolivia **18** *C2*
Residencial Charcas **19** *C2*

Eating 🍴
Arco Iris **1** *D2*
Bibliocafé **2** *D2*
Café Hacheh **4** *B1*
Café Mirador **5** *D3*
El Germen **6** *C3*
Joy Ride Café **8** *D2*
Kultur-Café Berlin **10** *D3*
La Casona **11** *B3*

La Plaza **13** *C2*
La Repizza **14** *D2*
La Taverne **15** *C2*
Locot's Café
Aventura **3** *C3*
Penco Penquito **16** *C2*
Pizzería
Napolitano **13** *C2*
Salon de Té
Las Delicias **17** *C2*

Bars & clubs 🍷
La Luna **12** *D2*

0 metres 100
0 yards 100

Sleeping 🛏
Alojamiento La Plata **3** *C2*
Austria **4** *B3*
Avenida **17** *B1*
Backpackers Sucre
Hostel **2** *C1*
Casa de Huéspedes
Finita **22** *D3*
Casa de Huéspedes
San Marcos **1** *B2*

Ins and outs

Getting there Juana Azurduy de Padilla airport is 5 km northwest of town (T645 4445). **Bus terminal** is on north outskirts of town, 2 km from centre on Ostria Gutiérrez, T645 2029; taxi US$0.75; Micro A or *trufi* No 8. Taxis cost US$0.45 per person within city limits. ►► *For more detailed information see Transport, page 302.*

Information Tourist office, Estudiantes 25, T644 7644, open Mon-Fri 0900-1200, 1500-1830, very helpful, English and French spoken, sells copies of town map, US$0.15; also at the bus station, allegedly open Monday-Friday 1000-1230, 1500-1730, Saturday 0800-1200; and at the airport, to coincide with incoming flights. For country maps try **Instituto Geográfico Militar**, Arce 172, 1st floor, T645 5514. Open Monday-Friday 0830-1200, 1430-1800. As in Potosí and La Paz, beware fake police and immigration officials and gangs of youths by the market.

Sights in the centre

Plaza 25 de Mayo is large, spacious, full of trees and surrounded by elegant buildings. Among these are the **Casa de la Libertad** ① *T645 4200, Mon-Fri 0900-1115, 1430-1745, Sat 0930-1115, US$1.50 with tour; US$1.50 photos, US$3 video.* Formerly the Assembly Hall of the Jesuit University, where the country's Declaration of Independence was signed, this house contains a famous portrait of Simón Bolívar by the Peruvian artist Gil de Castro, admired for its likeness. Also on the Plaza is the beautiful 17th century **Cathedral** ① *entrance through the museum in Calle Ortiz, if the door is locked wait for the guide, Mon-Fri 1000-1200, 1500-1700, Sat 1000-1200, US$1.50.* Worth seeing are the famous jewel-encrusted Virgin of Guadalupe, 1601, and works by Viti, the first great painter of the New World, who studied under Raphael.

San Felipe Neri ① *Azurduy y Ortiz, T645 4333, US$1 (extra charge for photos) with a free guide from Universidad de Turismo office on Plaza 25 de Mayo.* The neoclassical church is closed but ask the guide nicely to gain access. The roof (note the penitents' benches), which offers fine views over the city, is only open for an hour between 1630 and 1800 (times change). The monastery is used as a school. Diagonally opposite is the church of **La Merced**, which is notable for its gilded central and side altars. **San Miguel** *1130-1200,* completed in 1628, has been restored and is very beautiful with Moorish-style carved and painted ceilings, *alfarjes* (early 17th century), pure-white walls and gold and silver altar. In the Sacristy some early sculpture can be seen. It was from San Miguel that Jesuit missionaries went south to convert Argentina, Uruguay and Paraguay. Entry is not allowed if you are wearing shorts, short skirts or short sleeves. **Santa Mónica** *Arenales y Junín,* is perhaps one of the finest gems of Spanish architecture in the Americas, but has been converted into a *salón multiuso* (multipurpose space). **San Francisco** (1581) ① *in C Ravelo, 0700-1200, 1500-1900,* has altars coated in gold leaf and 17th century ceilings; the bell is the one that summoned the people of Sucre to struggle for independence. **San Lázaro** (1538) ① *Calvo y Padilla, daily for mass 0630-0730, 1830-1930.* This is regarded as the first cathedral of La Plata (Sucre). On the nave walls are six paintings attributed to Zurbarán; it has fine silverwork and alabaster in the Baptistery.

Museo Textil-Etnográfico ① *San Alberto 413 (Caserón de la Capellanía), between San Lázaro and Plaza 25 de Mayo, T645 3841, www.bolivianet.com/asur, Mon-Fri 0830-1200, 1430-1800, Sat 0930-1200 (and Sat afternoon Jul/Aug/Sep), US$2, English, German and French-speaking guide.* Run by *Antropológicas del Surandino* (*ASUR*), this excellent museum displays of regional textiles and traditional techniques, shop sells crafts. **Museo de Santa Clara** ① *Calvo 212, Mon-Fri 0900-1200, 1500-1800, Sat 0900-1200, US$0.75.* As well as displays of paintings, books, vestments, some silver and musical instruments (including a 1664 organ), there is a window to view the church. Small items made by the nuns on sale. A few blocks away, the **Museo Universitario Charcas** ① *Bolívar 698, Mon-Fri 0800-2000, Sat 0900-1200, 1500-1800, Sun 0900-1200, US$1.50, photos US$1.50,* has anthropological, archaeological and folkloric exhibits, and colonial collections and presidential and modern-art galleries.

Four blocks northwest of Plaza 25 de Mayo is the **Corte Suprema de Justicia** *free,* the seat of Bolivia's national judiciary, and rationale behind the city's official status as being one of Bolivia's two capitals. To enter you must be smartly dressed and leave your passport with the guard; guides can be found in library. The nearby **Parque Bolívar** contains a monument and a miniature of the Eiffel tower in honour of one of Bolivia's richest 20th-century tin barons, Francisco Argandoña, who created much of Sucre's splendour. The **obelisk** opposite the Teatro Gran Mariscal, in Plaza Libertad, was erected with money raised by fining bakers who cheated on the size and weight of their bread. Also on this plaza is the Hospital Santa Bárbara (1574).

Sights outside the centre

Southeast of the city, at the top of Dalence, lies the Franciscan monastery of **La Recoleta** with good views over the city and the **Museo de la Recoleta** ① *C Pedro de Anzúrez, Mon-Fri 0900-1130, 1430-1630, US$1.20 for entrance to all collections, guided tours only*. It is notable for the beauty of its cloisters and gardens; the carved wooden choir stalls above the nave of the church are especially fine (see the martyrs transfixed by lances). In the grounds is the Cedro Milenario, a 1,400-year-old cedar. **Tanga Tanga** ① *Iturricha 297, La Recoleta, T644 0299, Tue-Sun 0900-1200, 1430-1800*, is an interactive children's museum with art, music, theatre, dance and books (the excellent *Café Mirador* is in the garden). Behind Recoleta monastery a road flanked by Stations of the Cross ascends an attractive hill, **Cerro Churuquella**, with large eucalyptus trees on its flank, to a statue of Christ at the top. In the cemetery are mausoleums of presidents and other famous people, boys give guided tours; take Calle Junín south to its end, 7 to 8 blocks from main plaza.

About 5 km south on the Potosí road is the **Castillo de la Glorieta** ① *daily 0830-1200, 1400-1800, US$1*. The former mansion of the Argandoña family, built in a mixture of contrasting European styles with painted ceilings, is in the military compound. Ask to see the paintings of the visit of the pope, in a locked room. Take any bus marked 'Liceo Militar' from the Plaza, or bus or trufi 4 or E. Some 7 km north of Sucre is **Cal Orcko** ① *T645 1863, guided tours at 1000 and 1230, tours in English are available for US$2*. At this extensive area of dinosaur footprints, found in the Fancesa cement works, tracks from three types of dinosaur have been identified. Recommended, but don't expect any high-tech explanations or tourist facilities. Tour agencies charge US$10 per person as do taxi drivers who have trained as guides (untrained drivers charge US$7); ask tourist office for approved drivers. **Dino Truck** leaves daily 0930, 1200, 1430 from main plaza, US$4, minimum five people, good explanations in English.

Tarabuco → *Colour map 6, grid B4. Altitude: 3,295 m.*

Tarabuco, 64 km southeast of Sucre, is best known for its colourful ndigenous market on Sunday, with local people in traditional dress. It starts around 0930-1000 and is very popular with tourists, but still an enjoyable experience. Those in search of a bargain should have an idea about the quality on offer. The *Phujllay* independence celebration in mid-March is very colourful and lively. No one sleeps during this fiesta. There is budget accommodation. Try the Plaza or food stalls in market offering tasty local dishes. A good guide is *Alberto* from Sucre tourist office, US$45 for a full day in a car for four people. The market is not held at Carnival (when all Tarabuco is dancing in Sucre), Easter Sunday or on the holiday weekend in November.

Sucre to Paraguay

A road runs southeast from Sucre, through Tarabuco, to **Monteagudo** where there are several hotels including **E Fortín** ① *Plaza 20 de Agosto 1-2, T647 2135*, with bath, TV, includes breakfast, **F Alojamiento los Naranjos**, on road to bus terminal, hot showers, and a few restaurants. There are daily buses from Monteagudo to **Santa Cruz** (book early), US$8, 14 hours. The road then joins the road south from Santa Cruz to **Camiri** and **Boyuibe** (see page 328), from where a road heads east to the border with Paraguay at **Hito Villazón** (not to be confused with Villazón on the border with Argentina, see page 289). Most public transport goes south through Villamontes and a new road east to Paraguay, or continues south to **Yacuiba** on the border with Argentina (see page 329). The journey is beautiful through mountains. The easiest way to reach **Paraguay** from Sucre is to take a bus to Santa Cruz, then an international bus to **Asunción**. Alternatively, take the bus to Camiri (*Emperador* at 1730 or *Andes Bus*, 1800, on alternate days, 18 hours, US$4.30). From Camiri take a colectivo to **Villamontes** (three hours, US$5), but stop in Boyuibe to get an exit stamp. In Villamontes, catch the Santa-Cruz-Asunción bus around 0600. Bargain hard not to pay the full Santa Cruz-Asunción fare. (See also page 328.)

● Sleeping

Sucre *p297, map p297*
A Real Audiencia, Potosí 142, T/F646 0823, realaudiencia2000@hotmail.com. Modern, large rooms, excellent restaurant, heated pool. Recommended.

B El Hostal de Su Merced, Azurday 16, T644 2706, sumerced@mara.scr.entelnet.bo. Beautifully-restored colonial building, more character than any other hotel in the city, owner speaks fluent French and English (as do staff), good breakfast buffet, internet, sun terrace, restaurant. Recommended.

B Paola Hostal, C Colón 138, T645 4978, www.scr.cnb.net/~molincom. Comfortable, helpful hotel, with bath and jacuzzi, laundry, cafeteria for snacks, internet facilities, airport transfer.

B La Posada, Audiencia 92, T646 0101, www.laposadahostal.com. Smart, colonial- style, comfortable, good courtyard restaurant.

B Refugio Andino Bramadero, 30 km from the city, details from Raul y Mabel Cagigao, Avaroa 472, T645 5592, bramader@yahoo.com. Cabins or rooms, well-furnished, full board, drinks and transport included, excellent value, owner Raul is an astronomer and advises on hikes, book in advance. Recommended.

C Colonial, Plaza 25 de Mayo 3, T645 4079, hoscol@mara.scr.entelnet.bo. Some rooms noisy, but generally recommended, good breakfast included.

C Hostal Cruz de Popayán, Loa 881 y Colón, T644 0889, popayan@boliviahostels.com. **E** without bath, also has dorms (**F** pp), breakfast included, free internet, in a colonial building, rooms around 3 courtyards, use of kitchen, coffee shop, laundry service, book exchange, can arrange transport and language classes, many good reports.

C Hostal Libertad, Arce y San Alberto, p 1, T645 3101, F646 0128. Spacious comfortable rooms, hot water and heating, TV, some rooms with good views.

C Hostal Sucre, Bustillos 113, T645 1411, hostalsucre@hotmail.com. Comfortable if plain rooms around 2 patios, TV, room service, breakfast included.

C Kantu Nucchu, 21 km southwest of Sucre, details from Augusto Marion, San Alberto 237, T438 0312, tursucre@mara.scr.entelnet.bo. With bath, kitchen, full board, **G** pp without meals, peaceful, colonial hacienda, hiking, swimming. Recommended.

C-D Municipal Simón Bolívar, Av Venezuela 1052, T645 5508, F645 1216. Including breakfast in patio, helpful and comfortable, restaurant.

D Austria, Av Ostria Gutiérrez 506, near bus station, T645 4202. Hot showers, redecorated, great beds and carpeted rooms, some cable TV, cafeteria, parking, **F** rooms available and, next door, **G** in the *Alojamiento* (parking extra).

D Grand, Arce 61, T645 1704, F645 2461. Comfortable (ask for room 18), ground floor at the back is noisy, hot showers, includes poor

breakfast in room, good value lunch in *Arcos* restaurant, laundry, safe, motorcycle parking. Recommended.

D Hostal los Piños, Colón 502, T645 4403, H-Pinos@mara.scr.entelnet.bo. Comfortable, hot showers, nice garden, quiet, peaceful, includes breakfast, laundry, kitchen, parking.

D Res Charcas, Ravelo 62, T645 3972, hostalcharcas@latinmail.com. **E** without bath, good value, huge breakfast extra, hot showers, runs bus to Tarabuco on Sun.

E Casa de huéspedes Finita, Padilla 233, T645 3220, delfi_eguez@hotmail.com. 2 rooms with bath, others without, breakfast included, hot water, heaters, **D** with full board for long stay, works with students studying Spanish.

E Hostal Colón, Colón 220, T645 5823, colon220@bolivia.com. Clean, laundry, helpful owner speaks English and German and has tourist information, breakfast included, coffee room, very nice.

E Hostal San Francisco, Av Arce 191 y Camargo, T645 2117, hostalsf@cotes.net.bo. Breakfast and other meals available, quiet, patio, laundry, excellent value.

E Res Bolivia, San Alberto 42, T645 4346, F645 3239. **F** without bath, spacious rooms, electric showers, fair beds, includes breakfast, clothes washing not allowed, safe and helpful.

F Avenida, Av H Siles 942, T645 2387. Hot showers, breakfast US$1, laundry, helpful, use of kitchen.

F pp Backpackers Sucre Hostel, Loa 891 esq Colón, T644 0889, backpackers-sucre@ boliviahostels.com. A good bet for travellers, includes breakfast, safe, internet, laundry, luggage store, travel information. Recommended.

F Casa de Huéspedes San Marcos, Arce 223, T646 2087. **G** without bath, flower-filled patio, use of kitchen, quiet. Recommended.

G Alojamiento La Plata, Ravelo 32, T645 2102. Without bath, limited shower facilities, basic, noisy, good beds, popular with backpackers (lock rooms at all times).

G Gloria, Av Ostria Gutiérrez 438, T645 2847, opposite bus station. Great value.

G Potosí, Ravelo 262, T/F645 1975, castro@sucre.bo.net. Basic rooms around courtyard, popular, helpful, internet, good value, better rooms at the front.

● *For an explanation of the sleeping and eating price codes used in this guide, see inside the front cover. Other relevant information is found in Essentials pages 240-241.*

🍴 Eating

Sucre *p297, map p297*

Many fruit juice and snack stalls in the central market; clean stalls also sell cheap meals (US$0.75-1.40). The local sausages and chocolate are recommended.

🍴 **Arco Iris**, Bolívar 567. Swiss restaurant, good service and food, *peña* on Sat, excellent *rösti*, live music some nights.

🍴 **El Huerto**, Ladislao Cabrera 86, T645 1538. International food with salad bar, good *almuerzo*, in a beautiful garden. Take a taxi there at night.

🍴 **La Casona**, Ostria Guitiérrez 401, near bus terminal. Stylish, *platos típicos*, good value.

🍴 **El Germen**, San Alberto 231. Vegetarian, set lunches (US1.80), excellent breakfast, US$1.05-2.10, open Mon-Sat 0800-2200, book exchange, German magazines. Recommended.

🍴 **Pizzería Napolitano**, Plaza 25 de Mayo 30. Pizzas and pasta, home-made ice cream, good lunch options till 1700.

🍴 **La Plaza**, Plaza 25 de Mayo 33. Good food, popular with locals, set lunch US$2.10, open 1200-2400.

🍴 **La Repizza**, N Ortiz 78. Good value lunches, good pizzas in evening.

🍴 **La Taverne** of the *Alliance Française*, Aniceto Arce 35, ½ block from plaza. Closed Sun evening, *peñas* Fri-Sat in Jul and Aug, good French food, also regular cultural events.

Cafés

Amanecer, Junín 855, German *pastelería*, run by social project supporting disabled children, opens 1530.

Bibliocafé, N Ortiz 50, near plaza. Good pasta and light meals, *almuerzo* US$3 1100-1600, closes 2000 (opens 1800 on Sun), music and drinks.

Café Hacheh, Pastor Sainz 233. Great coffee bar with art gallery, tasty lunch and fresh juices, open 1100-2400 (at 1700 on Sun), '70s style. Highly recommended.

Café Mirador, Iturricha 297 in Tanga Tanga museum garden, La Recoleta. Not cheap, but great coffee, fine views, good snacks and music.

Joy Ride Café, N Ortiz 14, same Dutch owner as *Joy Ride Bolivia* (see Tour operators). Great food and drink, good salads, open 0730 till late (0900 at weekends), very popular, upstairs lounge shows films Sun-Thu. Recommended.

Kultur-Café Berlin, Avaroa 326, open 0800-2400 (except Sun). Good breakfasts, German newspapers, *peña* every other Fri (in same building as *Instituto Cultural Boliviano Alemán – ICBA*), popular meeting place.

Locot's Café Aventura, Bolívar 465, T691 5958, www.locotsbolivia.com. Open 0800 till late, fun, bright café serving international, Mexican and Bolivian food, live music and theatre, European/Bolivian owned, also has agency offering 'adrenaline activities', mountain biking, hiking, riding, paragliding.

Penco Penquito, Arenales 108. Excellent coffee and cakes.

Salon de Té Las Delicias, Estudiantes 50. Great cakes and snacks, open 1600-1900.

Tertulias, Plaza 25 de Mayo 59. Italian and other dishes, breakfasts, poor service.

La Vieja Bodega, N Ortiz 38. Good value, cheapish wine.

🍸 Bars and clubs

Sucre *p297, map p297*

La Luna, Argentina 65, back of Casa de la Cultura. Video pub with occasional live music, popular.

Mitsubanía, Av del Maestro y Av Venezuela. Club popular with local, younger, fashionable crowd, mixture of music with lots of *cumbia*, US$3 for men, women do not pay.

Rock Bar Chatarra, Junín esq Colón. Popular bar, open late, well-decorated.

🎉 Festivals and events

Sucre *p297, map p297*

24-26 May: Independence celebrations, most services, museums and restaurants closed on 25. **8 Sep**: Virgen de Guadalupe, 2-day fiesta. **Sep**: Festival Internacional de la Cultura, 2nd week, shared with Potosí. **21 Sep**: Día del Estudiante, music around main plaza.

🛍 Shopping

Sucre *p297, map p297*

Handicrafts Antropológicos del Surandino, *ASUR*, San Alberto 413, T642 3841 (in the *Museo Textil-Etnográfico*). Weavings from around Tarabuco and from the Jalq'a. Weavings are more expensive, but of higher quality than elsewhere. **Artesanías Calcha**, Arce 103, opposite San Francisco church. Recommended, knowledgeable proprietor. **Chocolates para Tí**, San Alberto, just off Plaza, T 645 4260, www.chocolates-para-ti.com. One of the best chocolate shops in Sucre. Others can be found on Arce and Arenales. **Fundación Aprecia**, Raul F de Córdova 49, just off Colón, T642 4718. A workshop for blind weavers making beautiful rugs (they can make to order with advance notice).

Markets The central market is clean and colourful with many stalls selling *artesanía*, but beware theft. A bus from the central market will take you to the **Mercado Campesino** near football stadium.

▲ Activities and tours

Sucre *p297, map p297*

Candelaria Tours, Audiencia No 1, C 322, T646 1661, F646 0289. Organizes excursions and also organizes Bolivian textile fashion shows, English spoken.

Joy Ride Bolivia, N Ortiz 14, T642 5544, www.joyridebol.com. Top quality quad and dirt bike trips, European standards of safety and bike-to-bike radio, insurance, take motorcycle licence for dirt bikes, car licence for quads, also hiking trips. Sign up and get information at Joy Ride Café (see above).

Locot's Adventure, see Locot's Café Aventura under Eating, above. For many types of adventure sport.

Seatur, Plaza 25 de Mayo 24, T/F646 2425, seatur@latinmail.com. Local tours, English, German, French spoken.

Sur Andes, N Ortiz 6, T645 3212, F645 2632. Organizes trekking from half a day to 5 days, eg to pre-Columbian sites such as **Pumamachay** and the **Camino Prehispánico** (take sleeping bag and good shoes, all else provided, but no porters).

❷ Transport

Sucre *p297, map p297*

Air Aero Sur flies to **La Paz** and **Santa Cruz**, LAB flies to **Cochabamba** and **Santa Cruz**. Few flights are daily. **Aero Sur**, Arenales 31, T646 2141. **LAB**, Bustillos 121, T645 2666 (Toll free 0800 3001). Airport minibus goes from entrance and will drop you off on Siles y Junín, and returns from here, 1½ hrs before flight (not always), US$0.70, 20-30 mins. Taxi US$4-5. *Trufis* No 1 and F go from entrance to H Siles y Loa, 1 block from main plaza, US$0.55, 25 mins.

Bus Daily to/from **La Paz** at 1830-2000, 13 hrs, US$7.50-10 (Flota Copacabana and Trans Copacabana have *bus-cama*). To **Cochabamba**: several companies daily at 1830, arriving 0630, US$4.50-5.25 (Trans Copacabana *bus-cama*, US$7.50). To **Potosí**: 3 hrs on a paved road, frequent departures between 0630 and 1800, US$3. Silito Lindo taxis take 4 people to Potosí for US$3.75; T644 1014. To **Tarija**: several companies, 16hrs, US$5.25-6. To **Uyuni**: 0700 (Emperador), 0800 (Trans Capital), 9 hrs, US$5. Or catch a bus to Potosí and change; try to book the connecting bus in advance – see *Trans Real Audencia*. To **Oruro**: 1700 with **Emperador** via Potosí, arrives 0300, US$5 (*bus-cama*, US$15). To **Santa Cruz**: many companies go between 1600 and 1730, 15 hrs, US$6-7.50. To **Villazón**: at 1300 (Transtin Dilrey, direct) and 1400 (Villa Imperial, via Potosí) both 15 hrs, US$8.20. Trans Real Audencia, Arce 99 y

San Alberto (same entrance as Hostal Libertad), T644 3119, for hassle-free bus tickets reservations to: **Potosí** (US$3), **Uyuni** (US$6.70), **Villazón** and **Tupiza** (US$7.45), **Tarabuco** (Sun 0700 from outside office, US$3 return).

To Tarabuco Buses (US$1.25) and trucks (very crowded) leave 0630 or when full from Plaza Huallparimachi, Av Manco Capac, or across the railway (take micro B or C from opposite Mercado), 2½ hrs (or taxi, US$45). On Sunday only, at least one bus will wait on Ravelo by the market for travellers, charging US$3 return to Tarabuco. Shared trufi taxis can be arranged by hotels, with pick-up service, starting at 0700, US$3.25 return. First bus back 1300; you must return on the bus you went on. *Andes Bus* run tourist services, departing 0800 (or when full), returning 1430, US$3, book at office, take food and drink. Transport more difficult on weekdays; take an early bus and return by truck.

Car hire Imbex, Serrano 165, T646 1222, www.imbex.com. Recommended.

Road 164 km from **Potosí** (fully paved) 366 km to **Cochabamba** (for 1st hr from Sucre road is OK, terrible to **Epizana**, then paved).

❸ Directory

Sucre *p297, map p297*

Banks There are many *Enlace* 24hr ATMs around town. **Banco Nacional**, España esq San Alberto. Cash given on Visa and MasterCard US$3 commission, good rates for dollars, TCs changed, 5% commission. Diagonally opposite is **Banco Santa Cruz**. Good rates for cash, advances on Visa, MasterCard and Amex, US$10 fee. Travel agencies' rates are good and at **España**, España 134, T646 0189, changes for TCs, 3% commission into US$, free into bolivianos, 9% commission on euro TCs. **Casa de Cambio Ambar**, San Alberto 7, T645 1339. Good rates for TCs. Cambios of Camargo and Arce buy and sell cash $ as well as Argentine, Chilean and Brazilian currency, but not as good rates as *cambios*. Many shops and street changers on Hernando Siles/Camargo buy and sell $ cash. **Cultural centres** The Instituto Cultural Boliviano-Alemán (Goethe Institute), Avaroa 326, T645 2091, www.icba-sucre.edu.bo. Shows films, has German newspapers and books to lend (0930-1230 and 1500-2100), runs Spanish, German, Portuguese and Quechua courses and has the *Kulturcafé Berlín* (see above). Spanish lessons cost from US$6 for 45 mins for 1 person, with reductions the more students there are in the class. The *ICBA* also runs a folk music *peña* on Fri. **Centro Cultural Masis**, Bolívar 561, T645 3403. Promotes the Yampara culture through textiles, ceramics, figurines and music. Instruction in Quechua, traditional Bolivian music

(3 hrs a week for US$15 a month, recommended) and handicrafts; stages musical events and exhibitions; items for sale. Open Mon-Sat 1430-2000 (knock if door closed); contact the director, Roberto Sahonero Gutierres at the centre Mon, Wed and Fri. **Alianza Francesa**, Aniceto Arce 35, T645 3599, www.afbolivia.org/_es/sucre.php. Offers Spanish classes. **Centro Boliviano Americano**, Calvo 301, T644 1608, http://lapaz.usembassy.gov/cbasucre/cba.htm. Library open Mon-Fri 0900-1200, 1500-2000 (good for reference works). Recommended for language courses. The **Centro Cultural Hacheh** (see address for *Café Hacheh* above), run by Felix Arciénega, Bolivian artist who organizes folk and jazz concerts, conferences, exhibitions and discussions, and is the editor of an art and poetry journal 'Hacheh'. **Casa de la Cultura**, Argentina 65, presents art exhibitions, concerts, folk dancing etc. **Embassies and consulates** Germany, Eva Kasewitz de Vilar, Rosendo Villa 54, T645 1369, ekvilar@mara.scr.entelnet.bo. Italy, Vice Consul, Martín Cruz 51, T645 5858. **Paraguay**, Plaza 25 de Mayo 28, T642 2999. **Perú**, Avaroa 472, T645 5592. **Internet** Many around town, generally slow connections, average

US$0.60 per hr. **Language schools** Academia Latinoamericana de Español, Dalence 109, T646 0537, www.latinoschools.com. Professional, good extracurricular activities, US$90 for 5 full days (US$120 for private teacher – higher prices if you book by phone or email). **Bolivian Language School**, C Kilómetro 7 250, T644 3841, www.bolivianspanishchool.com. Near Parque Bolívar, pleasant school, good value, excellent teachers. **Margot Macias Machicado**, Olañeta 345, T642 3567, www.spanish-classes.8m.net. US$5 per hr. Recommended. **Sofia Sauma**, Loa 779, T645 1687, sadra@mara.scr.entelnet.bo. US$5 per hr. Private teachers advertise in bars etc. **Medical services** For hospitals, doctors and dentists, contact your consulate or the tourist office for recommendations. **Post offices** Ayacucho 100 y Junín, open till 2000 (1600 Sat, 1200 Sun), good service. *Poste Restante* is organized separately for men and women. **Telephones** Entel, España 252. 0730-2300. **Useful addresses** Immigration: Pastor Sáenz 117, T645 3647, Mon-Fri 0830-1630. Police radio patrol: T110 if in doubt about police or security matters.

Tarija → *Phone code: 04. Colour map 6, grid B4. Population: 109,000. Altitude: 1,840 m.*

Tarija, a pleasant, small city, with a delightful climate and streets and plazas planted with flowering trees, is often called the 'Andalucía of Bolivia' for its resemblance to that region of Spain. It is known for its fruit and wines and its traditions which set it apart from the rest of the country. The best time to visit is from January onwards, when the fruit is in season. The *indígena* strain is less evident here than elsewhere in Bolivia, but Tarija has a strong cultural heritage. Founded 4 July 1574 in the rich valley of the Río Guadalquivir, the city declared itself independent of Spain in 1807, and for a short time existed as an independent republic before joining Bolivia. In Plaza Luis de Fuentes there is a statue to the city's founder, Capitán Luis de Fuentes Vargas. The **tourist office** ① *on the main plaza in the Prefectura, T663 1000, Mon-Fri 0800-1200, 1430-1830*, is helpful, city map and guide for US$0.20 each. Also at Sucre y Bolívar.

Sights The oldest and most interesting church in the city is the **Basílica de San Francisco** ① *corner of La Madrid y Daniel Campos, 0700-1000, 1800-2000, Sun 0630-1200, 1800-2000*. It is beautifully painted inside, with praying angels depicted on the ceiling and the four evangelists at the four corners below the dome. The library is divided into old and new sections, the old containing some 15,000 volumes, the new a further 5,000. The oldest book is a 1501 *Iliad* incorporating other works. There are also old manuscripts and 19th century photograph albums. To see the library, go to the door at Ingavi 0137. Tarija's **university museum** ① *Trigo y Lema, Mon-Fri 0800-1200, 1500-1800 (Sat opens at 0900), free, small donation appreciated,* contains a palaeontological collection (dinosaur bones, fossils, remains of an Andean elephant), as well as smaller mineralogical, ethnographic and anthropological collections. **Casa Dorada** ① *Trigo y Ingavi (entrance on Ingavi), Mon-Fri 0900-1200, 1500-1800, Sat 0900-1200, guided tours only; donation (minimum US$0.30).* Also known as Maison d'Or, it is now the Casa de Cultura, begun in 1886. It belonged to importer/exporter Moisés Narvajas and his wife Esperanza Morales and has been beautifully restored inside and out; the photography room contains pictures of Tarijan history and the restoration of the house. Near Parque Bolívar (shady, pleasant) is another of Narvajas' houses, the **Castillo de Beatriz** Bolívar between *Junín and O'Connor*; much of house is off-limits, but ask the owner if it is possible to visit. If no answer, enquire at the museum.

Outside the centre The outskirts of the city can be a good place to look for **fossils**: take a micro or taxi in the direction of the airport. 5 km out of town, before the police control (*garita*), you see lovely structures of sand looking like a small canyon (*barrancos*). Here have been found bones, teeth, parts of saurian spines, etc; things come to the surface each year after the rains. You may have to go a long way from the city. About 15 km from the centre is the charming village of **San Lorenzo**. Just off the plaza is the **Museo Méndez** ① *0900-1230, 1500-1830, minimum US$0.30 entry,* the house of the independence hero Eustaquio Méndez, 'El Moto'. The small museum exhibits his weapons, his bed, his 'testimonio'. At lunchtime on Sunday, many courtyards serve cheap meals. Take a trufi from Barrio del Carmen, at the roundabout just north of San Juan Church. They return from San Lorenzo plaza; 45 mins, US$0.45.The road to San Lorenzo passes **Tomatitas** (5 km) a popular picnic and river bathing area.

Bodegas **Aranjuez** bodega is a short walk across the river at Avenida Los Sauces 1976 (shop at 15 de Abril O-0241): ask Sr Milton Castellanos at the Agrochemical shop at Trigo 789 (Monday-Friday 1000-1200, 1500-1730, Saturday 0900-1200); he can also arrange visits to *Campos de Solana* (shop 15 de Abril E-0259). Farther afield is the **Rugero Singani** bodega at **El Valle de Concepción**, 36 km south of Tarija. An appointment must be made with Ing Sergio Prudencio Navarro, Bodegas y Viñedos de la Concepción at La Madrid y Suipacha s/n, T664 3763. Ing Prudencio will show visitors round the vineyards and the bodega. *Trufis* go from Parada del Chaco every 20-30 minutes, US$0.75, return from plaza. Note that all *bodegas* are closed Saturday afternoon and Sunday. See also Activities and tours page 305.

To Argentina → *Bolivia is 1 hr behind Argentina.*
The road to Villazón, 189 km, is the shortest route to Argentina, but a tiring six hours in all (only the first 15 km is paved). The alternative route via Bermejo is the most easily reached from Tarija, 210 km, the views are spectacular (sit on right); not recommended in the rainy season or a month or so after. The first 50 km out of Tarija, and the last 20 km to Bermejo are paved. Many buses daily, usually at night, some early morning, 4-5 hours, US$7.75, truck US$4.50. At **Bermejo** (Population 13,000, Altitude: 415 m) there a few hotels and two *casas de cambio* on main street. Note there are thorough customs searches here and it's very hot. (Expect to spend up to 4 hrs to pass at customs and immigration. Electronic goods must be entered in your passport for later checks.) Cross river by ferry to Aguas Blancas, in Argentina. From Tarija to Yacuiba/Pocitos border is 290 km (see page 156). Daily buses to Yacuiba 0700-1800, 12 hours, US$5-8, mostly old buses, *Expresos Tarija* and *Narváez* are best.

● Sleeping

Tarija *p303*
Blocks west of C Colón have a small O before number (oeste), and all blocks east have an E (este); blocks are numbered from Colón outwards. All streets north of Av Las Américas are preceded by N.
L Los Parrales Resort, Urb Carmen de Aranjuez Km 3.5, T664 8444 (ask for Lic Miguel Piaggio), parrales@mail.com. Only 5-star accommodation in southern Bolivia and worth it, European style amenities, can arrange city and vineyard tours and to Argentina, phone in advance for off-season discounts.
A Los Ceibos, Av Víctor Paz Estenssoro y La Madrid, T663 4430, ceibhot@cosett.com.bo. Including excellent buffet breakfast, large rooms, mini-bar, good restaurant, pool and cocktail bar.
A Gran Hotel Tarija, Sucre N-0770, T664 4777. Modernized, comfortable, parking, central.
A Victoria Plaza, on Plaza Luis de Fuentes, T664 2600, F664 2700. 4-star, includes buffet breakfast in *Café-Bar La Bella Epoca*, laundry service.

B Hostal Loma de San Juan, Bolívar s/n (opposite Capela Loma de San Juan), T664 4206. Comfortable, pool, sumptuous buffet breakfast included.
B La Pasarela, 10 km north of Tarija near the village of Coimata, T666 1333, www.lapasarel hotel.com. Belgian-owned hotel/restaurant/bar, includes breakfast, country views, tranquil, family atmosphere, living room, jacuzzi, swimming pool, internet, mountain bikes, laundry and camping.
C Gran Hostal Baldiviezo, La Madrid O-0443, T/F663 7711, administracion@ghb.htmlplanet.com. New hotel, central, good beds and facilities.
D Hostal Carmen, Ingavi O-0784 y R Rojas, T664 3372, vtb@olivo.tja.entelnet.bo. Shower, good value, **E** without cable TV, some ground floor rooms without exterior windows, good breakfast, transfer stand at airport, tour agency, book in advance.
E Amancayas (formerly **Res Rosario**), Ingavi 0-0777, residen_rosario@latinmail.com.

F without bath, showers, cable TV, quiet, good value. Recommended but for the laundry.
E Hostería España, Alejandro Corrado O-0546, T664 1790. Hot showers, **F** without bath, pleasant.
E Zeballos, Sucre 0966, T664 2068. Nice atmosphere, **F** without bath, with breakfast, cable TV, quiet, safe, laundry, 5 mins from plaza.
G Alojamiento Familiar, Rana S 0231 y Navajas, T664 0832. Shared hot shower, no breakfast, modern, helpful, close to bus terminal, traffic noise.

🍴 Eating

Tarija *p303*
Many restaurants (and much else in town) close between 1400 and 1600.
🍴🍴 **La Taberna Gattopardo**, on main plaza. Pizza, *parrillada* with Argentine beef, local wines, snacks, excellent salads, good value, opens 0700-0200 daily.
🍴 **Cabaña Don Pedro**, Padilla y Av Las Américas. Good typical, moderately- priced food.
🍴 **Cabaña Don Pepe**, D Campos N-0138, near Av Las Américas. Excellent steaks at moderate prices, *peña* at weekends with local folk music.
🍴 **Chifa New Hong Kong**, Sucre O-0235. Smart, Chinese, good service.
🍴 **Chingo's**, on Plaza Sucre, is popular and serves cheap local food.
🍴 **Club Social Tarija**, east side of the plaza. Pleasant, old-fashioned, haunt of Tarija's business community, excellent *almuerzo* for US$1.80. Recommended.
🍴 **El Solar**, Campero y V Lema. Vegetarian, set lunch, Mon-Sat 0800-1400 only.
🍴 **Gringo Limón**, Trigo N-0345. Pay by weight, nothing special.
🍴 **Mateo's**, Trigo N-0610. Excellent *almuerzo* US$3 (includes salad bar), good value evening meals with a wide selection of local and international dishes, pasta a speciality, closed 1530-1900 and Sun.
🍴 **Pizzería Europa**, main plaza west side. Internet (US$0.90 per hr), good *salteñas*.

Cafés
Bagdad Café, on Plaza Sucre. Also has live music at night.
La Fontana, La Madrid y Campos, is good for ice cream, snacks and coffee. For a cheap breakfast try the market. Try the local wines, eg Aranjuez, La Concepción, Santa Ana de Casa Real or Kohlberg, the singani (a clear brandy, San Pedro de Oro and Rugero are recommended labels), also local beer, Astra.

✹ Festivals and events

Tarija *p303*
The city is famous for its colourful niño (child) processions on **15 Mar**, Día de Tarija. In **late Apr**, Exposur is held, approximately 20 km northwest of city; admission free; local and regional crafts, cuisine, and dances; much commercial activity as well. In the 3-day San Roque festival from the **1st Sun in Sep** the richly-dressed saint's statue is paraded through the streets; wearing lively colours, cloth turbans and cloth veils, the people dance before it and women throw flowers from the balconies. Dogs are decorated with ribbons for the day.
On **2nd Sun in Oct** the flower festival commemorates the **Virgen del Rosario** (celebrations in the surrounding towns are recommended, eg San Lorenzo and Padcaya). Another flower festival takes place in San Lorenzo in **Easter** week. Also in **Oct**, on 2 weekends mid-month, there is a **beer festival** on Av de las Américas. **La Virgen de Chaguaya**, **15 Aug**, people walk from Tarija to Santuario Chaguaya, south of El Valle, 60 km south of the city. For less devoted souls, Línea P *trufi* from Plaza Sucre, Tarija, to Padcaya, US$1; bus to Chaguaya and Padcaya from terminal daily, 0700, returns 1700, US$1.35.

▲ Activities and tours

Tarija *p303*
Internacional Tarija, Sucre 721, T664 4446, F664 5017. Flights and tours, helpful.
Mara Tours, Gral Trigo N-739, T664 3490, marvin@olivo.tja.entelnet.bo. Helpful.
VTB, at *Hostal Carmen* (see Sleeping above). All tours include a free city tour; 4-6 hr trips including singani bodegas, US$19 pp; comprehensive 10 hr "Tarija and surroundings in 1 Day", US$27; can also try your hand at an excavation with their palaeontology specialist!
Viva Tours, Sucre 0615, T663 8325, vivatour@cosett.com.bo. Vineyard tours US$30 with lunch.

☉ Transport

Tarija *p303*
Air LAB flies to **Santa Cruz** and **Cochabamba**; Aero Sur flies to **La Paz** and **Santa Cruz**. Schedules change frequently; also flights are frequently cancelled and/or delayed. **LAB** office: Trigo N-0319, T644 2473. **TAM** office: La Madrid O-0470, T664 5899. **Aero Sur** office: 15 de Abril entre Daniel Campos y Colón, T663 0894. Taxi to

● *For an explanation of the sleeping and eating price codes used in this guide, see inside the front*
● *cover. Other relevant information is found in Essentials pages 240-241.*

Bolivia Tarija Listings

airport, US$3.75, or *micro* A from Mercado Central which drops you 1 block away. Some hotels have free transport to town, you may have to call them. On arrival at Tarija, reconfirm your return flight immediately. Airport information T664 3135.

Bus The bus station is in the outskirts on Av de Las Américas (30 min walk from centre, 7-8 mins from airport), T663 6508. Daily on the 935 km route **Potosí-Oruro-La Paz**, depart 0700 and 1700 (20 hrs, US$11.25; check which company operates the best buses, eg **San Lorenzo** has heating). To **Potosí** (386 km), daily at 1630, 12 hrs, US$6.70-7.45 with **AndesBus, San Lorenzo, San Jorge** and **Emperador**. To **Sucre**, direct with Andesbus (recommended), **Emperador** and **Villa Imperial**, depart 1600-1630, 17-18 hrs, US$5.25-6, check if you have to change buses in Potosí. To **Villazón**, several companies daily, depart morning and afternoon, 7 hrs, US$4.50, unpaved road. To **Santa Cruz**, several companies, US$10.45-12, 24 hrs over rough roads, last 140 km from Abapó is paved; via Entre Ríos, Villamontes, Boyuibe and Camiri, between Entre Ríos and Villamontes is spectacular. Trucks to all destinations depart from Barrio La Loma, 10 blocks west of market.

● Directory

Tarija *p303*
Banks Many ATMs accept foreign cards. **Banco Mercantil**, Sucre y 15 de Abril. Exchanges cash and gives cash against Visa and MasterCard (US$5 authorization charge). **Banco de Crédito**, Trigo N-0784, **Banco Nacional**, Av Trigo, all change TCs. Dollars and Argentine pesos can be changed at a number of casas de cambio on Bolívar between Campos and Sucre. **Embassies and consulates** Argentina, Ballivián N-0699 y Bolívar, T664 4273, Mon-Fri, 0830-1230. **Germany**, Campero 321, T664 2062, methfess@olivo.tja.entelnet.bo, helpful. **Internet** Café Internet Tarija On-Line, Campos N-0488, US$0.75 per hr. **Pizzería Europa** (see above), US$0.90 per hr. 2 on Plaza Sucre. **Language classes** Julia Gutiérrez Márquez, T663 2857, gringo108@hotmail.com. Recommended for language classes and information. **Post offices** V Lema y Sucre. Also at bus terminal. **Telephone** Entel, on main plaza, at V Lema y D Campos and at terminal.

Cochabamba and around

→ *Phone code: 04. Colour map 6, grid A3. Population: 594,790. Altitude: 2,570 m.*

Set in a bowl of rolling hills at a comfortable altitude, Cochabamba's unofficial title is 'City of Eternal Spring'. Its inhabitants enjoy a wonderfully warm, dry and sunny climate. Its parks and plazas are a riot of colour, from the striking purple of the bougainvillaea to the subtler tones of jasmin, magnolia and jacaranda. Bolivia's fourth largest city was founded in 1571. Today it is an important commercial and communications centre, while retaining a small-town, rural feel.

The fertile foothills surrounding the city provide much of the country's grain, fruit and coca. Markets, colonial towns and archaeological sites are all close by too. Further afield, the dinosaur tracks and great scenery at Torotoro National Park are worth an exhausting trip. The lowland route to Santa Cruz de la Sierra, now preferred to the old road over the mountains, has great birdwatching and the animal refuge in Villa Tunari deserves your support.

Ins and outs
Getting there and around The city is 394 km from La Paz by road, now completely paved. Neither airport, nor bus station are far from the centre. Buses and taxis serve both. The city is divided into four quadrants based on the intersection of Avenida Las Heroínas running west to east, and Avenida Ayacucho running north to south. In all longitudinal streets north of Heroínas the letter N precedes the four numbers. South of Heroínas the numbers are preceded by S. In all transversal streets west of Ayacucho the letter O (Oeste) precedes the numbers and all streets running east are preceded by E (Este). The first two numbers refer to the block, 01 being closest to Ayacucho or Heroínas; the last two refer to the building's number. ►► *For more detailed information see Transport, page 312.*

Information The central **tourist office** is at Colombia E-0340, between 25 de Mayo y España, T422 1793, helpful, excellent city map and free guide; Monday-Friday 0830-1630. The tourist police are here for complaints, also at Jorge Wilstermann airport. **Note:** You need to guard against theft around the markets and Plaza San Antonio and you should not climb San Sebastián and La Coronilla hills because of robbery.

Cochabamba

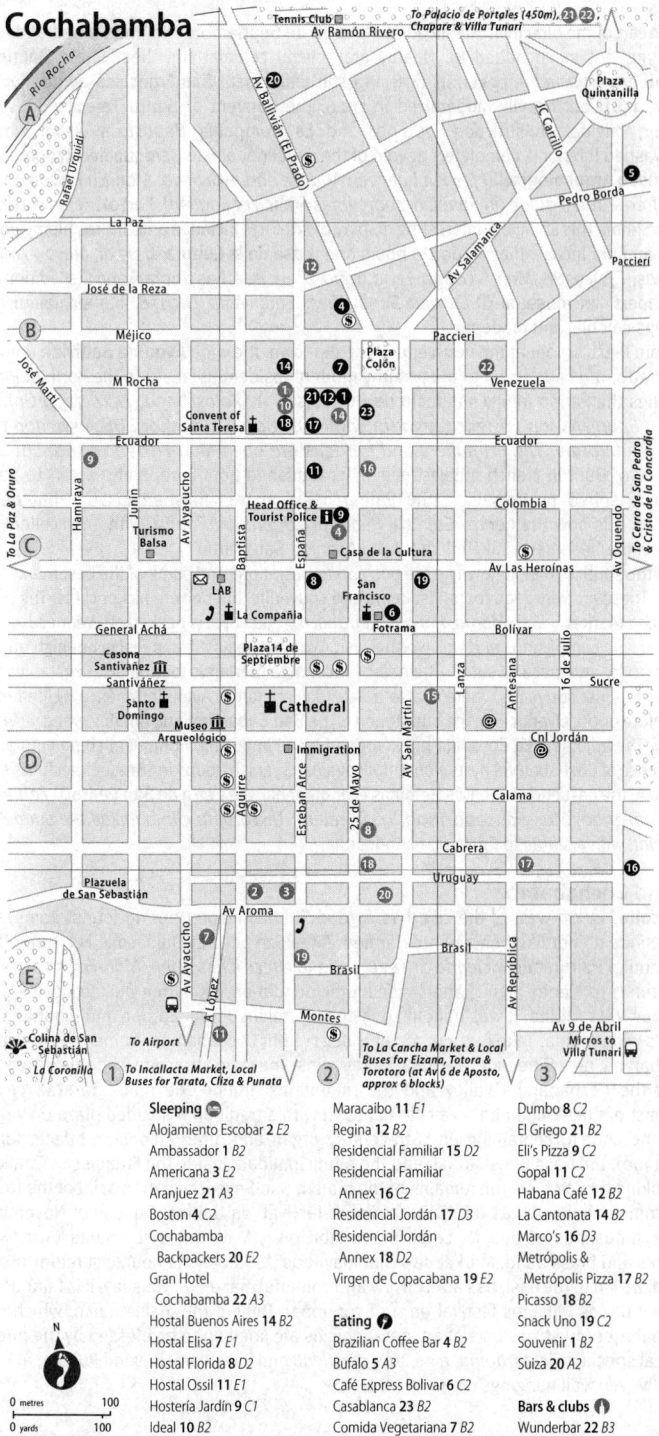

Sleeping 🛏
Alojamiento Escobar **2** *E2*
Ambassador **1** *B2*
Americana **3** *E2*
Aranjuez **21** *A3*
Boston **4** *C2*
Cochabamba
  Backpackers **20** *E2*
Gran Hotel
  Cochabamba **22** *A3*
Hostal Buenos Aires **14** *B2*
Hostal Elisa **7** *E1*
Hostal Florida **8** *D2*
Hostal Ossil **11** *E1*
Hostería Jardín **9** *C1*
Ideal **10** *B2*

Maracaibo **11** *E1*
Regina **12** *B2*
Residencial Familiar **15** *D2*
Residencial Familiar
  Annex **16** *C2*
Residencial Jordán **17** *D3*
Residencial Jordán
  Annex **18** *D2*
Virgen de Copacabana **19** *E2*

Eating 🍴
Brazilian Coffee Bar **4** *B2*
Bufalo **5** *A3*
Café Express Bolivar **6** *C2*
Casablanca **23** *B2*
Comida Vegetariana **7** *B2*

Dumbo **8** *C2*
El Griego **21** *B2*
Eli's Pizza **9** *C2*
Gopal **11** *C2*
Habana Café **12** *B2*
La Cantonata **14** *B2*
Marco's **16** *D3*
Metrópolis &
  Metrópolis Pizza **17** *B2*
Picasso **18** *B2*
Snack Uno **19** *C2*
Souvenir **1** *B2*
Suiza **20** *A2*

Bars & clubs 🍸
Wunderbar **22** *B3*

Sights

At the heart of the old city is the arcaded **Plaza 14 de Septiembre** with the **Cathedral** dating from 1571, but much added to. Nearby are several colonial churches: **Santo Domingo** *Santiváñez y Ayacucho*, begun in 1778 and still unfinished; **San Francisco** *25 de Mayo y Bolívar*, 1581, but heavily modernized in 1926; the **Convent of Santa Teresa** *Baptista y Ecuador*, original construction 1760-90; and **La Compañía** *Baptista y Achá*, whose whitewashed interior is completely devoid of the usual riot of late Baroque decoration.

Museo Arqueológico ① *Jordán between Aguirre and Ayacucho, Mon-Sun 0800-1700, US$2, free student guide (in Spanish, sometimes French or English)*. Part of the Universidad de San Simón, this small but interesting display of artefacts includes amerindian hieroglyphic scripts and pre-Inca textiles, good 1½ hours tour. **Casa de la Cultura** ① *25 de Mayo y Av Las Heroínas, T425 9788, Mon-Fri 0800-1200, 1430-1830, free*, has a library and first editions of newspapers. Its **museum** ① *Casona Santiváñez, Santiváñez O-0156*, has exhibitions of paintings colonial and modern.

From Plaza Colón, at the north end of the old town, the wide **Avenida Ballivián** (known as **El Prado**) runs northwest to the wealthy modern residential areas. To the north of Plaza Colón lies the Patiño family's **Palacio de Portales** ① *Av Potosí 1450, T424 3137, Guided tours in Spanish Mon-Fri 1700, 1730 (in English), 1800, Sat at 1100, US$1.50, don't be late, useful library. The art gallery and gardens are open Mon-Fri 1700-1800, Sat-Sun 1000-1200*. Built in French renaissance style, furnished from Europe and set in 10 ha of gardens inspired by Versailles, the Patiño mansion was finished in 1927 but never occupied. It is now the *Centro Cultural Pedagócico Simón J Patiño*, with an excellent art gallery in the basement. Take micro G from Avenida San Martín.

To the south of the old town lie the bus and train stations and some of the best markets in Bolivia. These are very good for tourist items and souvenirs, but beware pickpockets. The huge **La Cancha market** ① *San Martín, Punata, República y Pulacayo*, is packed on Wednesday and Saturday with campesinos and well worth a visit. Woollen items are expensive but high quality (US$35-50 for an alpaca sweater). The nearby **Incallacta market** is for fruit and vegetables but also sells tourist souvenirs. There is also a Saturday market at Avenida América y Libertador, best before 0900. Overlooking the bus station is the **San Sebastián hill**, offering grand views of the city. The adjoining **La Coronilla hill** is topped by an imposing monument commemorating the defence of Cochabamba by its womenfolk against Spanish troops in 1812 (neither hill is safe to visit). At the east end of Avenida Heroínas is another hill, the **Cerro de San Pedro** ① *cable car Sun 0900-1900, Mon-Sat 1000-1800, US$1 return; US$0.15 to climb inside the statue for viewpoint*, with a statue to Cristo de la Concordia.

Around Cochabamba

Quillacollo, 13 km west of the city, has a good Sunday market but no tourist items; the *campesinos* do not like being photographed. A few km beyond Quillacollo is a turn-off to the beautiful **Pairumani** *hacienda* ① *T426 0083 to check if it is open, Mon-Fri 1500-1600, Sat 0900-1130*. Centre of the Patiño agricultural foundation, 8 km from Quillacollo, It is also known as **Villa Albina**. It was built in 1925-1932, furnished from Europe and inhabited by Patiño's wife, Albina. Take bus 7 or 38, or trufi 211 from Cochabamba. Some 27 km west of Cochabamba, near Sipe-Sipe, are **Inka-Rakay** ruins. The main attraction is the view from the site of the Cochabamba valley and the mountains around the ruins. **Tarata**, 33 km southeast of Cochambamba, is a colonial town with a traditional arcaded plaza on which stand the church, containing an 18th-century organ and other colonial artefacts (daily 0800-1300), the Casa Consistorial, and the Municipalidad. Inside the **Franciscan Convent** overlooking the town are the remains of the martyr, San Severino, patron saint of the town, more commonly known as the 'Saint of Rain'; festival, on the last Sunday of November, attracts thousands of people. Large procession on 3 May, day of La Santa Cruz, with fireworks and brass band. Market day Thursday (bus US$0.65, one hour, last return 1800). **Punata**, 48 km to the east, has a very lively and colourful market on Tuesday. It is famous for its Señor de los Milagros festival on 24 September. Behind the main church, which has many baroque/mestizo works of art, new vehicles are lined up to be blessed by the priest. The local speciality is *garapiña*, a mixture of *chicha* and ice-cream. Beyond Punata, at Villa Rivera, woven wall hangings are produced.

Parque Nacional Torotoro

ⓘ *US$3, local guide US$5 per day, plus his food for trips of over a day; tourist information is available at the national park office, open daily, ask here about all tours, guides, etc.* In the province of Potosí, but best reached from Cochabamba (135 km), is **Torotoro**, a small village, set amid beautiful rocky landscape (*Tinku* festival 25 June; *Santiago* 24-27 July). The village is in the centre of the Parque Nacional Torotoro, covering an area of 16,570 ha and declared a National Park in 1989. Attractions include caves, a canyon, waterfalls, pictographs, ruins, fossilized dinosaur tracks and rock paintings, some of which can be seen by the Río Toro Toro just outside the village (ask directions, or take a young guide). This trip is highly recommended and tour operators now offer packages there. You should be able to speak Spanish.

Umajalanta cave, which has many stalactites and a lake with blind fish, is about 1½ hrs' walk northwest of Torotoro, with an hour's caving; a guide is necessary from the park office, US$5 per person in a group of 2-5 (take a head torch if possible). **El Vergel** waterfall can be reached without a guide, but you need good directions. The falls are fantastic, and the walk along the river bed is great fun if you like rock-hopping and skipping over pools. Fossils can be seen at Siete Vueltas, an afternoon's walk, but you need a guide. Mario Jaldín (Spanish speaking only) is knowledgeable. He lives two doors to the right of *Alojamiento Charcas*. He also leads a four-day trek to see canyons, condors, orchids, many birds and, if lucky, the Andean Bear and pumas; $80-100 per person, depending on the size of the group, includes camping gear and food, bring your own sleeping bag.

Cochabamba to Santa Cruz

The road via Chapare descends to the lowlands, with superb birdwatching on the way. The roads are manned by army and police and foreigners are subject to scrutiny. In the coca-growing territory around Villa Tunari the police advise not to stray from the main road.

The lowland road from Cochabamba to Santa Cruz runs through Villa Tunari, Sinahota and Chimoré (a centre for DEA operations; three hotels). The road is paved Villa Tunari-Santa Cruz. **Villa Tunari** is a relaxing place and holds an annual Fish Fair 5 and 6 August, music and dancing, delicious meals. **Parque Ecoturístico Machía** ⓘ *just outside town, free, but donations welcome*, offers good trails through semi-tropical forest. Beside the park is **Inti Wara Yassi** ⓘ *Villa Tunari, T04-413 6572, or www.intiwarayassi.org for full information, donations welcome, to take photos US$2.25 and videos US$3.75*. This project rehabilitates animals back into the wild. Volunteering involves building rehabilitation facilities, and feeding and carrying out basic animal husbandry on a variety of monkeys, birds, wild cats and small land mammals. Living accommodation is basic, work is challenging but if you're lucky affords fascinating up-close encounters with native wildlife. A new park, Parque Ambue Ari, between Santa Cruz and Trinidad, is around 600 ha of jungle teeming with wildlife, rehabilitating pumas, monkeys, birds and bears. There is much to do and few volunteers, so lots of flexibility and opportunities, and a freer routine to allow for yoga or a morning nap after the animals' breakfast! Delicious food is provided. For transport from Cochabamba see page 312.

The mountain road The 500 km road via the mountains and Epizana to Santa Cruz is not paved and the new lowland route is preferred by most transport. Before the Siberia pass, 5 km beyond Montepunco (Km 119), the 23 km road to Pocona and Inkallajta turns off. The Inca ruins of **Inkallajta** (1463-1472, rebuilt 1525), on a flat spur of land at the mouth of a steep valley, are extensive and the main building of the fortress is said to have been the largest roofed Inca building. There are several good camping sites. The Cochabamba Archaeological Museum has some huts where visitors can stay, free, but take sleeping bag and food. Water available at nearby waterfall. **Totora**, on the Sucre road, is a beautiful, unspoiled colonial village. **Aiquile**, south of Totora and 217 km from Cochabamba, is famous for its wooden *charangos* and there's a festival in late October/early November, ask tourist office. Sunday market, for which the town fills up on Saturday. The town was devastated by an earthquake in 1998, so much of it remains in a partially re-built state.

🔵 Sleeping

Cochabamba *p306, map p307*
There are many cheap and basic places to stay near the bus station, most are short-stay and the

area is unsafe.
AL Aranjuez, Av Buenos Aires E-0563, T428 0076, www.aranjuezhotel.com. 4-star, small, colonial

style, good restaurant, jazz in the bar Fri-Sat night, small pool open to public (US$1). Recommended.

A Ambassador, España N-0349, T425 9001, ambass@comteco.entelnet.bo. Modern, central and reasonable, includes breakfast, good restaurant.

A Gran Hotel Cochabamba, Plaza Ubaldo Anze, T428 2551, cbbhotel@bo.net. Beautifully set in the north part of the city (2 blocks from Los Portales at La Recoleta), with garden, swimming pool (US$3 for non-guests) and tennis courts, popular with tour groups. Recommended.

B Americana, Esteban Arce S-788, T425 0554, americana@mail.infornetcbba.com.bo. Fan, helpful, lift, laundry, parking, *Rodizio* grill next door, good service.

C Boston, C 25 de Mayo 0167, T422 8530, hboston@supernet.com.bo. Restaurant, luggage deposit, quiet rooms at back, safe parking. Recommended but cheaper rooms not so good.

C Ideal, España N-0329, T423 5175, F425 9430. Includes breakfast, TV, restaurant, comfortable, good value but can be noisy at weekends from bar below.

C Regina, Reza 0359, T425 7382, hregina@ supernet.com.bo. Spacious, efficient, breakfast extra, restaurant.

E Alojamiento Escobar, Aguirre S-0749, T422 5812. Recently upgraded, good value (not to be confused with *Residencial* at Uruguay E-0213).

E Hostal Buenos Aires, 25 de Mayo N-0329, T425 4005. **F** without bath, pleasant, clean communal baths, breakfast US$1.35.

E Hostal Elisa, Agustín López S-0834, T425 4404, F423 5102. **F** without bath, good showers, hot water, good breakfast US$2.25, modern, garden, 2 blocks from bus station, laundry service, very popular with travellers, helpful owner, but small single rooms and area is a bit dodgy at night.

E Hostal Florida, 25 de Mayo S-0583, T425 7911, floridah@elsito.com. **F** without bath or cable TV, hot water, noisy, popular, laundry service, safe deposit box, internet, breakfast.

E Hostería Jardín, Hamiraya N-0248, T424 7844, jaguirre@latinmail.com. **F** without bath, garden, safe car and motorcycle parking, good breakfast included, basic but good value, in a nice area.

E Res Jordán, C Antesana S-0671, T422 9294. Youth hostel, *ABAJ* affiliate, modern, basic, with cable TV and small pool. Annex (**E**) at 25 de Mayo S-0651, T422 5010.

F Hostal Ossil, Agustín López S-0915, close to bus terminal, T425 4476. New, good rooms, cooking facilities, helpful, good value.

F Maracaibo, Agustín López S-0925, T422 7110. Close to bus terminal, popular, safe.

F Res Familiar, Sucre E-0554, T422 7988. Pleasant, secure, good showers. Its annex at 25 de Mayo N-0234 (entre Colombia y Ecuador),

T422 7986, is also pleasant, with a big court-yard, shared bath, hot water, comfortable.

G pp Cochabamba Backpackers, Av Aroma E-437 entre 25 de Mayo y San Martín, T425 7131, backpackers-cochabamba@boliviahostels.com. Close to bus station, a member of this network of Bolivian hostels.

G Virgen de Copacabana, Av Arce S-0875 y Brasil, T422 7929, near bus station. Electric showers, shared bath, good breakfast US$0.75, motorcycle parking, stores luggage, noisy TV, otherwise recommended.

Parque Nacional Torotoro *p309*

Several hostales have opened recently in Torotoro and there is electricity in some.

G Alojamiento Charcas, near bus terminal, with very good restaurant serving hot, filling meals, US$1 pp (order dinner in the morning).

G De Los Hermanos, very basic rooms, supposedly running water, delightful owner with friendly pets.

Cochabamba to Santa Cruz *p309*
Villa Tunari

B Los Araras, across bridge on main road to Santa Cruz, T413 4116, hisc_marco@yahoo.com. **C** midweek, large rooms, nice gardens, good breakfast, HI affiliated.

B-C Las Palmas, T411 4103, 1 km out of town. With breakfast, pool and good restaurant, changes US$ cash, a bit run down.

C Bibosi, Plaza Principal, T428 0814. Pleasant, with gardens and pool.

C El Puente, Av de la Integración, 3 km from town, T425 9322 (book in advance at offices of *Fremen* Travel Agency). With breakfast and bath, cabins from 2 people to family-size, pool, tours to Carrasco national park, the hotel has a stream and natural pools.

F Las Palmas 2, corner of plaza. With bath, breakfast, fan, swimming pool (not very clean).

G La Querencia, Beni 700, T413 6548. Pleasant terrace on river front, avoid noisy rooms at front, good cheap food, clothes-washing facilities.

G San Mateo, opposite *Baviera* restaurant, by the river. Shared bath, choice of beds (hard or soft), helpful.

Several other hotels; also 2 internet cafés, *Entel* office and post office.

Totora

G Residencial Colonial, behind the church. Hot water in mornings, restaurant also.

Aiquile *p309*

F Hostal San Pablo, 1 block from plaza. No sign but the best option, clean, family run and comfortable.

⁞ Fiesta de la Virgen de Urkupiña, Quillacollo

The festival lasts four days with much dancing and religious ceremony; its date varies each year between June and August. Plenty of transport from Cochabamba, hotels all full. Be there before 0900 to be sure of a seat, as you are not allowed to stand in the street. The first day is the most colourful with all the groups in costumes and masks, parading and dancing in the streets till late at night. Many groups have left by the second day and dancing stops earlier. The third day is dedicated to the pilgrimage. (Many buses, micros and *trufis* from Heroínas y Ayacucho, 20 minutes, US$0.30.)

● Eating

Cochabamba *p306, map p307*

The bars and restaurants centre around España, Ecuador and Colombia, Plaza Colón and Av Ballivián and north of Río Rocha near Av Santa Cruz. A few km north of the city, in the village of Tiquipaya, are many comida criolla restaurants, eg El Diente, recommended.

ŤŤŤ La Cantonata, España N-0409, T425 9222. Among the best Italian restaurants in Bolivia. Highly recommended.

ŤŤŤ Suiza, Av Ballivián 820, T425 7103. Popular, recommended for international cuisine, good value.

ŤŤ Bufalo, Torres Sofer, p 2, Av Oquendo N-0654. Brazilian *rodizio* grill, all-you-can-eat buffet for US$7.50, great service. Highly recommended.

ŤŤ Comida Vegetariana, M Rocha E-0375. Good filling food, buffet lunch and breakfast, mostly soy-protein based dishes, but also serves chicken, closed Sun.

ŤŤ El Griego, España N-0386. Good kebabs and lots of pasta dishes, colourful walls and modern art.

ŤŤ Habana Café, M Rocha E-0348. Genuine Cuban food and drinks, can get lively at night, open 1200-last person leaves.

ŤŤ Marco's, Av Oquenda entre Cabrera y Uruguay. Good Peruvian ceviche, Sat-Sun 1200-1500.

ŤŤ Metrópolis, España N-0299. Good pasta dishes, huge portions, good vegetarian options, noisy. **Metrópolis Pizza** next door is good value.

ŤŤ Picasso, España 327, entre Ecuador y Mayor Rocha. Good value Italian and Mexican.

Ť Eli's Pizza, 25 de Mayo N-0254 y Colombia. Son of the famous La Paz branch, great pizzas and serves Mexican fast food.

Ť Gopal, C España 250, Galería Olimpia. Hare-krishna, US$1.50 for vegetarian lunch 1200-1500 only, closed Sun, English spoken, very good.

Ť Incallacta market (see page 308) has excellent food for under US$1.

Ť Snack Uno, Av Heroínas E-0562. Good lunches and dinners including vegetarian.

Brazilian Coffee Bar, Av Ballivián just off Plaza Colón. Upmarket, tables on pavement.

Café Express Bolívar, Bolívar entre San Martín y 25 de Mayo. Great coffee in a delightful old-fashioned café.

Café Otoño, 25 de Mayo y Mayor Rocha, T452 3903. Nicely decorated, simple but tasty dishes, good service.

Casablanca, 25 de Mayo entre Venezuela y Ecuador. Next to Google internet café, attractive, buzzing, good food and a wide selection of coffee, popular for wine and cocktails in the evening.

Dumbo, Av Heroínas 0440. Good ice-cream parlour, popular eating and meeting spot, also does cheap meals.

Souvenir, 25 de Mayo N-0391. *Salteñas*, crêpes and *confitería*, popular in the early evening.

Unicornio, Heroínas y Baptista. Large, attractive, popular gringo hangout, pricey.

Parque Nacional Torotoro *p309*

Ť Salón de Té, Torotoro, run by Lydia García, provides good meals with prior notice, good breakfasts, bakes bread and cakes, welcoming.

Cochabamba to Santa Cruz: Villa Tunari *p309*

ŤŤ El Bosque, west end of town, 1 km past toll booth. German, run by botanists, with orchid garden, one of the best in town.

ŤŤ Surubi, also known as Cuqui, 1 km west of town. A good restaurant with fish specialities, also has tents for camping.

ŤŤ-Ť Baviera, near the bridge on main road. Good steak and fish, good value, tourist information, also has rooms to let with hot water.

ŤŤ-Ť El Jazmín, opposite *Las Palmas*. Gringo hangout serving good pizza.

● Bars and clubs

Cochabamba *p306, map p307*

Chilimania, M Rocha E-0333. Good for drinking and dancing.

D'Mons, Tarija y América. Mix of Latin, contemporary and classic American music, open 2300, US$4 including first drink.
Lujos, Beni E-0330. Nice atmosphere. Mix of Latin, contemporary and classic American music, open 2300, US$4 including first drink.
Panchos, M Rocha E-0311, just off España. A lively dancing and drinking place.
Wunderbar, Venezuela E-0635. Cable TV sports on Mon, music, darts upstairs, ribs, wings, subs, opens 1930.

🎭 Entertainment

Cochabamba *p306, map p307*
Peñas Totos, M Rocha y Ayacucho, T452 2460. Fri night 2000-0300; may open on Sat. Free entry.
Theatre Teatro Achá, España y Las Heroínas, T422 1166. Concerts and plays. **Tra La La**, Plazuela 4 de Noviembre, T428 5030. Popular productions, comedy, music and dance.

🎉 Festivals and events

Cochabamba *p306, map p307*
Carnival is celebrated 15 days before Lent. Rival groups (*comparsas*) compete in music, dancing, and fancy dress, culminating in El Corso on the last Sat of the Carnival. **Mascaritas** balls also take place in the carnival season, when the young women wear long hooded satin masks. **14 Sep: Day of Cochabamba**.

🛍 Shopping

Cochabamba *p306, map p307*
Alpaca Fotrama, factory at Av Circunvalación 0413, T422 5468, outlet at Bolívar 0439. Cooperative for alpaca sweaters, rugs, alpaca wool (pricey).
Bookshops Los Amigos del Libro, Ayacucho S-0156, T450 4150, in *Hotel Portales*, Av Pando 1271, and *Gran Hotel Cochabamba*, in the Torres Sofer shopping centre and at Jorge Wilsterman airport. Good, stocks US and English magazines as well as *South American Handbook*. City map and guide in colour for US$2.50.

🥾 Activities and tours

Cochabamba *p306, map p307*
Vicuñita Tours, Av Ayacucho 350, T452 0194. Specializes in local and regional travel, also overseas reservations (T03-334 0591 for Santa Cruz office).

🚌 Transport

Cochabamba *p306, map p307*
Air Jorge Wilstermann airport, T459 1820. Airport bus is Micro B from Plaza 14 de Septiembre,
312

US$0.40; taxis from airport to centre US$3.10. Reconfirm all flights (and obtain reconfirmation number), and arrive early for international flights. Several flights daily to/from **La Paz** (35 mins) and **Santa Cruz** (45 mins) with LAB and **Aero Sur** (book early for morning flights). *LAB* also to **Sucre**, **Trinidad** and **Tarija**. International flights to **Asunción**, **Buenos Aires**, Lima and São Paulo. LAB, Salamanca 675, open 0800, T0800-30011. **Aero Sur**, Av Villarroel 105, esq Av Oblitos (Pando), T440 0909/459 0077 (airport).
Bus *Micros* and *colectivos*, US$0.20; *trufis*, US$0.30. Anything marked 'San Antonio' goes to the market. *Trufis* C and 10 go from bus terminal to the city centre. The main bus terminal is on Av Ayacucho on opposite side from Montes and Punata (T155). To **Santa Cruz**, 10 hrs, 0530-2200, US$3-4.50 (*buscama* US$7.50); only minibuses take the old mountain road via Epizana, from Av 9 de Abril y Av Oquendo, all day. See page 309. To/from **La Paz** many companies, shop around for best times, services and prices (about US$2.50, *buscama* US$4.50-6), by night or day, 7 hrs on paved road. Bus to **Oruro**, US$2.50, 4 hrs, buses hourly. To **Potosí**, US$4.50- 5.25 via Oruro, several companies 1830-2000. Daily to **Sucre**, US$4.50- 5.25, 10 hrs, several companies between 1930 and 2030 (**Flota Copacabana** and **Trans Copacabana** recommended; latter *buscama* US$8.90). To **Sucre** by day; take a bus to Aiquile (see below), then a bus at 2400-0100 passing en route to Sucre (if you want to take a truck in daylight, wait till next day). Local buses leave from Av Barrientos y Av 6 de Agosto, near La Coronilla for **Tarata**, **Punata** and **Cliza**. Av República y Av 6 de Agosto to **Epizana** and **Totora**. Av Oquendo y 9 de Abril (be careful in this area), to **Villa Tunari**, US$2.70, 4-5 hrs, several daily; **Chimoré**, US$5.75; **Eterazama**, US$5.75; **Puerto Villarroel**, US$4, 6-8 hrs (from 0800 when full, daily); **Puerto San Francisco**, US$6.50.
Taxi About US$0.50 from anywhere to the Plaza, more expensive to cross the river; double after dark.

Parque Nacional Torotoro *p309*
Air Travel to Torotoro is sometimes impossible overland in the wet season (end Nov-Mar), as flooded rivers wash out roads, but it is possible to fly quite cheaply as a group. Swiss pilot **Eugenio Arbinsona** charges US$120 for up to 5 passengers in his Cessna. It takes only 25 mins, but he may be persuaded to lengthen the journey by flying you through a canyon or two on the way. T424 6289 or (T0717-23779 (mob).
Bus Check schedules with Gonzalo Milán, Comercial El Dorado, Honduras 646, Cochabamba, T422 0207, also very helpful on accommodation and activities. Transport to Torotoro goes in convoy from Av República y 6

de Agosto at 0600 Sun and Thu, be there at 0530, US$4 in a bus or the cab of a truck, US$3 in the back, 8 hrs on an improved dirt road via Aiquile, with stops at Cliza market and for lunch. Transport returns to **Cochabamba** every Mon and Fri, 0600. Groups can arrange with Gonzalo Milán to be picked up at a hotel. Alternatively, pay in advance and arrange to be picked up in Cliza where buses/trucks stop at 0800.

Cochabamba to Santa Cruz *p309*
Inkallajta
Best to go Thu or Sat when **micros** leave when full from 0700 from 6 de Agosto y República, Cochabamba, passing the sign to the ruins, from where it's a 12 km walk. Otherwise take a micro to the checkpoint 10 km from Cochabamba, then a truck to Km 119 sign, walk towards Pocona or take a truck for 15 km, to where a large yellow sign indicates the trail. After 10 km the trail divides, take the downhill path and the ruins are a further 2 km.

Totora
Bus Daily buses from **Cochabamba**, 6 de Agosto y República at 1600, also at 1430 on Sat; return 0500 Mon-Sat, 1100 Sun.

Aiquile
Bus Daily buses except Sun from Cochabamba with **Flotas Aiquile** (Av Barrientos S-2365) and **Trans Campero** (Av Barrientos S-2291, 100 m past Av 6 de Agosto junction, *trufis* 1, 10, 14, 16, 20 pass in front), 5 hrs; 1300, return at 1700. All nightly buses from Sucre to Cochabamba and Santa Cruz pass Aiquile between 2300 and 0130 (buses from Santa Cruz to Sucre pass 0400-0500); few sell tickets only to Aiquile. *Unificado* has an office on the main road in Aiquile beneath the shabby **Alojamiento Turista** with buses leaving every day for **Sucre** (0100), **Cochabamba** (1100) and **Santa Cruz** (2130). Daily bus from Totora at 1600.

❶ Directory

Cochabamba *p306, map p307*
Banks Visa and MasterCard at *Enlace* ATMs all over the town (especially on Av Ballivián) and next to the bus terminal. Cash on Visa or MasterCard from many banks; no commission on bolivianos. **Bisa**, Aguirre y Calama. Best rates for cash and Amex TCs, changes euro TCs at 5% commission. **Ef€c**, Plaza 14 de Septiembre S-0262, changes TCs into dollars at 2% commission. Money changers congregate at most major intersections, especially outside *Entel*, and on Plaza Colón, poor rates. **Cultural centres** Centro Boliviano Americano, 25 de Mayo N-0365, T422 1288, www.cbacoch.org.

Library of English-language books, open 0900-1200 and 1430-1900; also offers language classes. **Alianza Francesa**, Santiváñez O-0187, T422 1009, afcbba@ afbolivia.org. **Instituto Cultural Boliviano- Alemán**, Lanza 727, T412 323, icbacbba@ supernet.com.bo. Spanish classes. **Embassies and** consulates **Argentina**, F Blanco E-0929, T425 5859, consuladoar@ entelnet.bo. Visa applications 0830-1300. **Brazil**, Edif Los Tiempos Dos, Av Oquendo, p 9, T425 5860, cchbrvc14@ supernet.com.bo. Open 0830-1130, 1430-1730. **Germany**, España esq Av Heroínas, Edif La Promotora, p 6, of 602, T425 4024, coricba@ pino.cbb.entelnet.bo. **Italy**, Av Humboldt 932, T424 5809. **Netherlands**, Av Oquendo 654, Torres Sofer p 7, T423 0888. 0830-1200, 1400-1630 Mon-Fri. **Paraguay**, Av Gral Achá O-0107, Edif América p 6, T458 1801. 0830-1230, 1430-1830 Mon-Fri. **Peru**, Pedro Blanco y Santa Cruz, edif Continental of 3H, T448 6157, conbba@ aceletrate.com. 0800-1200, 1400- 1800 Mon-Fri. **Spain**, Colombia O-655, T458 2281, Mon-Fri 0900-1200, 1430-1730. **Sweden**, Barquisimeto, Villa La Glorieta, T/F424 5358, arvidsson@ comteco.entelnet.bo, Mon- Fri 0930-1200. **USA**, Av Oquendo, Torres Sofer p 6, T425 6714. 0900- 1200 (will also attend to Britons and Canadians). **Internet** Many cybercafés all over town, charging US$0.60 per hr. **Language classes** Sra Blanca De La Rosa Villareal, Av Libertador Simón Bolívar 1108, esq Oblitas (T424 4298). US$5 per hr. Runawasi, J Hinojosa, Barrio Juan XXIII s/n, T/F424 8923, www.runawasi.org. Spanish and Quechua, also has accommodation. **Sra Alicia Ferrufino**, JQ Mendoza N-0349, T428 1006. US$10 per hr, **Elizabeth Siles Salas**, T423 2278, silessalas@latinmail.com. **Reginaldo Rojo**, T424 2322, frojo@supernet.com.bo. US$5 per hr. **María Pardo**, Pasaje El Rosal 20, Zona Queru Queru behind Burger King on Av América, T428 4615. US$5 per hr, also teaches Quechua. **Carmen Galinda Benavides**, Parque Lincoln N-0272, T424 7072. **Maricruz Almanzal**, Av San Martín 456, T422 7923, maricruz_almanza@ hotmail.com. US$5 for 50 mins, special offers. See also Cultural centres, above. **Medical facilities** For hospitals, doctors and dentists, contact your consulate or the tourist office for advice. **Post offices** Av Heroínas y Ayacucho, next to *LAB* office (entrance on Ayacucho), Mon-Fri 0800- 2000, Sat 0800-1800, Sun 0800-1200. **Telephones** Entel, Gral Achá y Ayacucho, international phone, fax (not possible to make AT&T credit card calls), open till 2300. **Useful addresses** Immigration Office:, Jordán y Arce, p 2, T422 5553, Mon-Fri 0830-1630.

Northern Lowlands

Bolivia's Northern lowlands account for about 70% of national territory. From scrubby east lowlands to dense tropical jungle in the north, this is pioneer country; home to missionaries, rubber tappers and cocaine refiners. Improved roads to Rurrenabaque and Trinidad are opening up the area and wildlife expeditions are becoming increasingly popular. Beni department has 53% of the country's birds and 50% of its mammals, but destruction of forest and habitat is proceeding at an alarming rate.

Madidi and Rurrenabaque

Caranavi to San Borja

From Caranavi, a road runs north to Sapecho. Beyond Sapecho, the road passes through Palos Blancos 7 km from the bridge (Saturday market day, several cheap lodgings). The road between Sapecho and Yucumo is now a very good all-weather gravel surface, three hours from Sapecho *tránsito*. There are *hospedajes* (**F**) and restaurants in **Yucumo** where a road branches northwest, fording rivers 13 times on its way to Rurrenabaque. From Yucumo it is 50 km (1-2 hours, truck at 0730) to **San Borja**, a small, wealthy-looking cattle-raising centre with hotels (**D-F**) and restaurants clustered near the plaza. From San Borja the road goes east to Trinidad via **San Ignacio de Moxos**. There are 5-6 river crossings and, in the wetlands, flamingoes, blue heron and waterfowl. The road passes through part of the Pilón Lajas Reserve (see below).

Parque Nacional Madidi

ⓘ *Contact the director, Ivan Arnold, C Libertad s/n junto a orillas del río Beni, San Buenaventura, T03-892-2540, www.sernap.gov.bo/madidi/. Visit also www.ecobolivia.org for information on Madidi. Insect repellent and sun protection are essential.*

Parque Nacional Madidi is quite possibly the most bio-diverse of all protected areas on the planet. It is the variety of habitats, from the freezing Andean peaks of the Cordillera Apolobamba in the southwest (reaching nearly 6,000 m), through cloud, elfin and dry forest to steaming tropical jungle and pampas (neo-tropical savannah) in the north and east, that account for the array of flora and fauna within the park's boundaries. In an area roughly the size of Wales or El Salvador are an estimated 1,000 bird species, 10 species of primates, five species of cat (with healthy populations of jaguar and puma), giant anteaters and many reptiles. Madidi is at the centre of a bi-national system of parks. The Heath river on the park's north-western border forms the Bolivia/Peru frontier and links with the Tambopata National Reserve in Peru. To the southwest the Area Protegida Apolobamba protects extensive mountain ecosystems.

Pilón Lajas Biosphere Reserve and Indigenous Territory

ⓘ *Official park headquarters are at the park's northernmost point, less than 1 km south of Rurrenabaque, US$6 pp. Contact Sernap's representative, Juan Carlos Miranda, C Campero esq C Busch, Rurrenabaque, T03-892 2245, www.sernap.gov.bo.*

Beyond the Beni River in the southeast runs the Pilón Lajas Biosphere Reserve and Indigenous Territory, home to several native groups. Together with Madidi, it constitutes approximately 60,000 sq km, one of the largest systems of protected land in the neotropics. Unfortunately, much of this land is under pressure from logging interests, and the government has allocated precious little resources to combat encroachment. The Pilón Lajas Biosphere Reserve and Indigenous Territory in the Beni, under the auspices of UNESCO, has been set up. The reserve has one of the continent's most intact Amazonian rainforest ecosystems, as well as an incredible array of tropical forest animal life. NGOs have been working with the people of La Unión, Playa Ancha, Nuevos Horizontes and El Cebó to develop sustainable forestry, fish farming, beekeeping, cattle ranching, *artesanía* and even fruit wines; tours are run by **Donato Tours** (see Activities and tours, below), US$22 including lunch and transport.

Rurrenabaque → *Phone code: 03. Population: 10,000.*

The charming, picturesque jungle town of Rurre (as the locals call it), on the Río Beni, is the main jumping off point for tours in the Bolivian Amazon. Across the river is San

Buenaventura. Despite its growth as a trading, transport and ecotourism centre, Rurre is nice to walk around, although the climate is usually humid.

An hour upstream from Rurre is **San Miguel del Bala**, in a beautiful setting on the edge of Madidi. Opened in 2004, it gives a good taste of the jungle, offers day trips and has en suite cabins where you can stay, bars and a plunge pool.

● Sleeping

Madidi *p314*

AL Chalalán Ecolodge, at San José de Uchupiamonas, in Madidi, 5 hrs up-river from Rurrenabaque. Addresses: C Sagarnaga 189 esq Murillo, Edif Michel Shoping Doryan 2do Nivel, of 35, T/F02-231 1451, or in Rurrenabaque 892 2419, reservas@chalalan.com, oficinalapaz@chalalan.com or oficinarurrenabaque@chalalan.com. This is Bolivia's top ecotourism project. It was founded by the local community, Conservation International (www.ecotour.org/destinations/chalalan.htm) and the Interamerican Development Bank. Accommodation is in thatched cabins, and activities include fantastic wildlife-spotting and birdwatching, guided and self-guided trails, river and lake activities, and relaxing in pristine jungle surroundings. A 5-day trip includes travel time from La Paz: tours cost about US$100 per person per night, depending on group size and length of stay. Air fares are an extra US$110.

AL Wizard's Mountain Jungle Lodge (Cerro del Brujo), near Madidi and the Tacana community, T02-279 1742, www.boliviamistica.com. Ecolodge offering jungle and pampas tours, wide range of therapies, shamanic rituals, and a canopy walkway, price is for 2 days, 1 night pp, many other options available, including community tourism at **Villa Alcira** in the Tacana community.

Pilón Lajas *p314*

A pp Mapajo, Mapajo Ecoturismo Indígena, C Comercio, Rurrenabaque, T03-892 2317, www.mapajo.com. A community-run ecolodge 2 hrs by boat from Rurrenebaque has 4 *cabañas* without electricity (take a torch and batteries), cold showers and a dining room serving traditional meals. Minimum stay is 3 days. You can visit the local community, walk in the forest, go birdwatching, etc. Take insect repellent, wear long trousers and strong footwear. Recommended.

Rurrenabaque *p314*

In high season hotels fill up very quickly.

B Hotel Safari, Comercio on the outskirts by the river (a hot walk), T892 2410. Beautiful garden and comfortable rooms, pool, terrace and a good restaurant. Recommended.

D Beni, Comercio, by ferry, T892 2408. Best rooms have a/c and TV, hot showers extra,

cheaper without bath or a/c (but with fan). Spacious, pleasant, good service.

E Asaí, C Vaca Díez, T892 2439. Electric showers, quiet, laundry area, courtyard and hammocks, luggage store, breakfast extra.

E Oriental, on plaza, T892 2401. Electric showers, cheaper without bath, small breakfast included, quiet, hammocks in garden. Recommended.

E Rurrenabaque, Vaca Díez y Bolívar, T892 2481. Safe, hot water, cooking and laundry facilities, good.

F Hostal Eden, southern end of C Bolívar, T892 2452. **G** without bath, hot water, breakfast available, has hammocks and kitchen, laundry, family run, helpful and good value.

F El Porteño, Comercio y Vaca Díez, T892 2558. Some big rooms with TV, bath, fan, comfortable beds, courtyard with hammocks, quite good.

F Jazmín, Comercio entre Aniceto Arce y Av Santa Cruz, T892 2337. Variety of rooms, some with bath, good value, fan, cold showers, hammock space. Recommended.

F pp Toucan, Aniceto Arce entre Avaroa y Bolívar. Rooms with electric fan and shower (hot water for 10 mins pp), includes breakfast, clean, pleasant.

G pp Jislene, C Comercio, T892 2526. Erlan Caldera and family very hospitable, hot water, fan, basic, good breakfast if booked in advance, information, helpful.

G Santa Ana, 1 block north of plaza on Avaroa, T892 2399. Cheaper without bath in hammock area, basic but clean, electric showers, poor water pressure, thin mattresses, laundry, luggage store, pretty courtyard, car park.

G Tuichi, C Avaroa y Santa Cruz, T7198 3582. Cheaper without bath (but shared bathrooms are dirty), cold showers, luggage storage, kitchen and laundry facilities, fan, good value, accepts TCs, good meeting place.

● Eating

Rurrenabaque *p314*

♥♥ Juliano, C Comercio. 'French-Italian' cuisine, good pasta and fish dishes, friendly atmosphere and bar outside.

♥♥ La Perla de Rurre, Bolívar y Díez. Smartest place in town, for meat and fish under a shady tree.

♥ Camila's, Santa Cruz. Good Mexican and Italian food, fast food.

♥ La Chocita, just south of ferry, by the river. Simple fish restaurant, popular, especially for the

315

almuerzo. **La Cabaña**, another riverside restaurant, is next door.

¶ Club Social Rurrenabaque, on Comercio 1 block north of Santa Cruz. Vegetarian dishes on request, good juices, fishburgers.

¶ El Tacuara, opposite *Camila's*. Good range of dishes, also for breakfast. Good *almuerzos* and fruit juices in the market.

¶ Pizzería Italia, Comercio, T892 2611, next to Moskkito. A tasty variety of pizzas, young crowd.

Cafés

Café Bar Madidi, C Comercio. Coffees, juices, some vegetarian dishes.

Moskkito Bar, just downriver from *El Porteño*. Good for ½-price cocktails 1900-2100.

Pachamama, Avaroa sud, at south end of town. English/Bolivian café/bar, snacks, river view, films, playstation, internet and a book exchange.

▲ Activities and tours

Rurrenabaque *p314*

Jungle tours normally last 4 days and 3 nights (US$15-25 per day). The jungle is very hot and humid in the rainy season with many more biting insects and far fewer animals to be seen. You see a lot of wildlife on a 4-day Pampas tour (US$25-30 per day), which involves a 4-hr jeep ride to the Río Yacuma, then a series of boat trips. You see howler, squirrel and capuchin monkeys, caiman, capybara, pink dolphins, possibly anacondas and a huge variety of birds. The weather and general conditions are more pleasant than in the jungle; season Jul to Oct. For pampas and jungle tours, 1-day trips are reportedly a waste of time as it takes 3 hrs to reach the jungle. It is recommended to go with an established company as competition is forcing down prices and, consequently, quality and standards of guiding. Some agencies offer ecologically unsound practices such as fishing, feeding monkeys, catching caiman; before signing up for a tour ask if the operator respects the environment. Pampas tours may involve wading through knee-deep water; wear appropriate shoes. The tourist office can advise on the quality of tours. Bear in mind that it is cheaper to book tours in Rurrenabaque than La Paz and mosquito nets are much cheaper than in La Paz.

Tour operators

Agencia Fluvial, at *Hotel Tuichi*, T892 2372, runs jungle tours on the Río Tuichi, normally 4 days, but shorter by arrangement, US$25 pp per day (payable in dollars) including food, transport and mosquito nets (write to Tico Tudela, *Agencia Fluvial*, Rurrenabaque). Take swimming costume and insect repellent. Also 3-day 'Pampas Tours' on a boat to Río Yacuma, US$30 pp per day. Tico

Tudela has opened *Hotel de la Pampa* near Lago Bravo, 2½ hrs from Rurrenabaque, as a base for visiting Lago Rogagua (birds) and Río Yacuma. Fully inclusive tours (including meals and accommodation) US$40 pp per day.

Aguila Tours, Av Avaroa, T892 2478, jungle and pampas tours (can be booked through *Eco Jungle Tours*, C Sagárnaga, La Paz).

Bala Tours, Av Santa Cruz, T892 2527, www.bala tours.com. Arranges 'Pampas' and 'Jungle' tours, good base camp in the Pampas. Recommended.

Donato Tours, C A Arce, T7179 5722 (mob). For regular tours and A Day for the Community.

Indígena Tours, Abaroa s/n, T892 2091. Good value tours, food and accommodation, helpful.

Turismo Ecológico Social (TES), Av Santa Cruz, next to tourist information office, T7128 9664, turismoecologicosocial@ hotmail.com. Day tours to 4 local communities and the Pilón Lajas buffer zone, US$25 pp including lunch, water and guides.

❷ Transport

Caranavi to San Borja *p314*

Bus Flota Yungueña daily except Thu at 1300 from San Borja to **La Paz**, 19 hrs via Caranavi. **Yucumo** is on the La Paz-Caranavi-

Rurrenabaque and San Borja bus routes. Rurrenabaque-La Paz bus passes through about 1800. If travelling to Rurrenabaque by bus or truck take extra food in case there is a delay for river levels to fall. The road surface Caranavi-San Borja is good; San Borja-San Ignacio poor, long stretches are rutted and pot-holed; San Ignacio-Trinidad is good. Also San Borja to **Rurrenabaque** (Buses 1 de Mayo, T03-895 3467, US$4.40), **Santa Rosa**, **Riberalta**, **Guayaramerín** Thu, Sat, Sun. Minibuses and *camionetas* run daily between San Borja and **Trinidad** throughout the year, US$15, about 7 hrs including 20 mins crossing of Río Mamoré on ferry barge (up to 14 hrs in wet season); **1 de Mayo** to **San Ignacio** (US$8), **Trinidad** and **Santa Cruz**. Gasoline available at Yolosa, Caranavi, Yucumo, San Borja and San Ignacio.

Rurrenabaque *p314*
Air New airport due for completion in 2007. Flights with **Amazonas** (C Santa Cruz, T892 2472), daily from **La Paz**, US$52 in 12-seater plane. **Aero Sur** © Santa Cruz 450, T892 2396) flies 3 times a week. **TAM** © Santa Cruz, T892 2398), 4 a week, US$58 one way from **La Paz**. Book all flights as early as possible and buy return to La Paz on arrival. Check flight times in advance; they change frequently. Expect delays and cancellations in wet season. Airport tax US$2. Motorcycle taxi from town, US$1.

Bus To/from **La Paz** via Caranavi daily at 1100 with **Flota Yungueña** and **Totaí**; 18-20 hrs, US$8.20. Returns at 1100. **Flota Unificada** leaves La Paz (also from Villa Fátima) on Tue, Thu, Fri, Sat at 1030, same price. Continues to **Riberalta** and **Guayaramerín**; return departure time depends on road conditions. **Flota Yungueña** also has a 1030 bus which leaves Villa Fátima and continues to Riberalta and Guayaramerín.
Rurrenebaque-**Riberalta** should take 14-16 hrs, but can take 6 days or more in the wet. Take lots of food, torch and be prepared to work. To **Trinidad**, Tue, Thu, Sat, Sun at 2230 with **Trans Guaya** via **Yucumo** and **San Borja**, US$18.

⊙ Directory

Rurrenabaque *p314*
Banks Prodem, Av Comercio 21 entre Vaca Díez y Santa Cruz, T892 2616. Changes US$ cash at fair rates, cash advance on Visa or MasterCard, 5% commission. **Bala Tours** will give cash advance against credit cards at 7.5% commission. Try hotels or agencies for small amounts. TCs can be used as payment for tours, but are difficult to cash. Try **Agencia Fluvial**, 5% commission. Most agencies accept credit cards for tours. **Internet** *Camila's*, next to restaurant of same name on Santa Cruz, US$3 per hr. **Post offices** On C Bolívar. Open Sat. **Telephones** Entel, on C Comercio, 2 blocks north of plaza; also at Santa Cruz y Bolívar.

Riberalta to Brazil

Riberalta → *Phone code: 03. Colour map 3, grid B6. Population: 60,000. Altitude: 175 m.*
This town, at the confluence of the Madre de Dios and Beni rivers, is off the beaten track and a centre for brazil nut production. Change cash in shops and on street. Recent reports indicate an increase in theft and rape – worth knowing when the bus drops you in the middle of the night and everything is closed. Some 25 km away is Tumi-Chucua situated on a lovely lake. Nearby are the **Nature Gardens**. Here you can fish in the lake, good for birdwatching. They also have lots of information on the rainforest, the rubber boom and brazil nut production. Contact **Dr Willy Noack**, T/F352 2497 for further information.

Guayaramerín and border with Brazil → *Phone code: 03. Colour map 4, grid C1.*
Guayaramerín is a cheerful, prosperous little town on the bank of the Río Mamoré, opposite the Brazilian town of Guajará-Mirim. It has an important *Zona Libre*. Passage between the two towns is unrestricted; boat trip US$1.65 (more at night).

Bolivian immigration Avenida Costanera near port; open 0800-1100, 1400-1800. Passports must be stamped here when leaving, or entering Bolivia. On entering Bolivia, passports must also be stamped at the Bolivian consulate in Guajará-Mirim. For Brazilian immigration, see page 562. The Brazilian consulate is on 24 de Septiembre, Guayaramerín, T855 3766, open 0900-1300, 1400-1700; visas for entering Brazil are given here. To enter Brazil you must have a yellow fever certificate, or be inoculated at the health ministry (free). Exchange money on the Bolivian side (but not travellers' cheques) as there is only an ATM at the Banco do Brasil in Guajará-Mirim; no facilities for cash.

Cobija → *Phone code: 03. Colour map 3, grid B5. Population: 15,000.*

The capital of the lowland Department of Pando lies on the Río Acre which forms the frontier with Brazil. A new, single-tower suspension bridge is being built across the river to Brasiléia. As a duty-free zone, shops in centre have a huge selection of imported consumer goods at bargain prices. Brazilians and Peruvians flock here to stock up. As this is a this border area, watch out for scams and cons.

● Sleeping

Riberalta *p317*
Ask for a fan and check the water supply.

D Colonial, Plácido Méndez 1. Charming colonial casona, large, well-furnished rooms, no singles, nice gardens and courtyard, comfortable, good beds, helpful owners. Recommended.

D Comercial Lazo, NG Salvatierra, T852 8326. **F** without a/c, comfortable, laundry facilities, good value.

F Res Los Reyes, near airport, T852 8018. With fan, safe, pleasant but noisy disco nearby on Sat and Sun.

G Res El Pauro, Salvatierra 157. Basic, shared baths, good café.

Guayaramerín *p317*
B Esperanza out of town in nearby Cachuela Esperanza, reserve through **America Tours** in La Paz, T02-237 4204, www.america-ecoturs.com. Eco-friendly.

C San Carlos, 6 de Agosto, 4 blocks from port, T855 2152/3. With a/c (**D** without), hot showers, changes dollars cash, TCs and reais, swimming pool, reasonable restaurant.

There are also **F-G** places, eg **Santa Ana**, close to the airport.

Cobija *p318*
E Prefectural Pando, Av 9 de Febrero, T842 2230. Includes breakfast, *comedor* does good lunch, manager Sr Angel Gil, helpful.

F Res Cocodrilo, Av Molina, T842 2215. Comfortable, good atmosphere, rooms with fan.

G Res Frontera, 9 de Febrero, T842 2740. Good location, basic but clean, fan.

❼ Eating

Riberalta *p317*
❢ **Club Social Progreso**, on plaza. Good value *almuerzo*, excellent fish.

❢ **Club Social Riberalta**, on Maldonado. Good *almuerzo* US$3.50, smart dress only.

❢ **Tucunare**, M Chávez/Martínez. Recommended.

❢ Good lunch at *comedor popular* in market, US$1.50.

Guayaramerín *p317*
The following places are all on the plaza:

❢ **Gipsy**, good *almuerzo*.

❢ **Heladería Tutti-Frutti**, on road to airport. For ice cream, excellent.

❢ **Los Bibosis**, popular with visiting Brazilians.

❢ **Made in Brazil**, good coffee.

❢ **Only**, 25 de Mayo/Beni, good *almuerzo* for US$2.50, plus Chinese.

Cobija *p318*
❢❢-❢ **La Esquina de la Abuela**, opposite *Res Cocodrilo*, good food, not cheap.

❢ Good cheap meals in *comedor popular* in central market.

❸ Transport

Riberalta *p317*
Air Expect delays in the wet season.

Amazonas (Chuquisaca y Sucre, T852 3933) flies from La Paz. **TAM** flies to **Cochabamba**, **Santa Cruz** and **La Paz**, Fri (US$100 to La Paz); office Av Suárez y Chuquisaca, T852 3924. **LAB** office at M Chávez 77, T852 2239 (0800-3001). Check all flight details in advance.

Bus Several companies (including **Yungueña**) to **La Paz**, via **Rurrenabaque** and **Caranavi** Tue-Sat at 1100, also Tue, Thu, Sat at 1000; US$22.40 (same price to Rurrenebaque, 18 hrs). To **Trinidad** with **8 de Diciembre** Mon, Wed, Thu, Sat, Sun at 0830, also **Trans Guaya** daily at 0930, via Rurrenabaque; to **Guayaramerín** several daily, US$3, 3 hrs. To **Cobija** several companies, none with daily service.

Ferry Cargo boats carry passengers along the **Río Madre de Dios**, but they are infrequent. There are not many boats to Rurrenabaque.

Guayaramerín *p317*
Air **Amaszonas** (F Román y Mamoré, T855 3731) flies from La Paz. **TAM** flies to **Cochabamba**, **Santa Cruz** and **La Paz**; office at 16 de Julio (road to airport). **LAB** office at 25 de Mayo 652, T855 3540 (0800-3001).

● *For an explanation of the sleeping and eating price codes used in this guide, see inside the front*
● *cover. Other relevant information is found in Essentials pages 240-241.*

Bus Terminal is 2½ km from centre. To/from **La Paz**, Flota Yungueña, daily 0830 (1030 from La Paz), 36 hrs, US$22.40. Also **Flota Unificada**, leaving La Paz Tue, Thu, Fri, Sat 1030, US$26.90. To **Riberalta** 3 hrs, US$3, daily 0700-1730. To **Trinidad** Fri, 30 hrs, US$23. To **Rurrenabaque**, US$16. To **Cobija** 4 a week. To **Santa Cruz** via Trinidad, 1-2 a week, 2½ days. Buses depart from Gral Federico Román. Roads are very difficult in wet season.

Ferry Check the notice of boats leaving port on the Port Captain's board, prominently displayed near the immigration post on the riverbank. Boats up the Mamoré to **Trinidad** are fairly frequent – a 3-day wait at the most.

Cobija *p318*

Air Aero Sur, Coronel Cornejo 123, T842 3132, flies 3 days a week to **La Paz**. Also Amaszonas, Cornejo 121, T842 3844, 4 times a week. LAB office at F Molina 139, T842 2170. TAM office on 2 de Febrero, T842 2267.

Bus Flota Yungueña to **La Paz** via Riberalta and Rurrenabaque Sat at 0700 (check times first, T842 2318). To **Riberalta** with several bus companies and trucks, depart from 2 de Febrero,

most on Wed, Fri, Sun at 0600; good all-weather surface; 5 river crossings on pontoon rafts, takes 10-11 hrs.

Taxi These are very expensive, charging according to time and distance, eg US$10 to the outskirts, US$12 over the international bridge to Brasiléia. Besides taxis there are motorbike taxis (much cheaper). **Brasiléia** can also be reached by **canoe**, US$0.35. The bridge can be crossed on foot as well, although one should be dressed neatly in any case when approaching Brazilian customs. Entry/exit stamps (free) are necessary and yellow fever vaccination certificate also (in theory), when crossing into Brazil.

⊙ Directory

Cobija *p318*

Banks Lots of money changers along Av 2 de Febrero. Most shops will accept dollars or reais, or exchange money.
Internet Internet place near the university, 100 m from the plaza. **Post offices** on plaza.
Telephones Entel, on C Sucre, for telephone calls internal and abroad and fax, much cheaper than from Brazil.

Cochabamba to Trinidad

Villa Tunari to the Lowlands

Another route into Beni Department is via the lowland road between Cochabamba and Santa Cruz. At Ivirgazama, east of Villa Tunari, the road passes the turn-off to **Puerto Villarroel**, 27 km further north, from where cargo boats ply irregularly to Trinidad in about four to 10 days. You can get information from the Capitanía del Puerto notice board, or ask at docks. **E-G Amazonas Eco-hotel** *T/F04-423 5105*, with restaurant, boat trips arranged. There are very few stores in Villarroel. Sr Arturo Linares at the Cede office organizes boat trips to the jungle – not cheap.

Trinidad → *Phone code: 03. Colour map 6, grid A3. Population: 86,000. Altitude: 237 m.*

The hot and humid capital of the lowland Beni Department, founded 1686, is a dusty city in the dry season, with many streets unpaved. There are two ports, Almacén and Varador, check which one your boat is docking at. Puerto Varador is 13 km from town on the Río Mamoré on the road between Trinidad and San Borja; cross the river by the main bridge by the market, walk down to the service station by the police checkpoint and take a truck, US$1.70. Almacén is 8 km from the city. The main mode of transport in Trinidad is the motorbike (even for taxis, US$0.40 in city); rental on plaza from US$2 per hour, US$8 per half day. The **tourist office** i *in the Prefectura building at Joaquín de Sierra y La Paz, ground floor, T462 1305, ext 116*, is very helpful, sells guide and city map, US$2. Transport can be arranged from the airport.

Hire a motorbike or jeep to go to the river; good swimming on the opposite bank; boat hire US$5. 8 km from town is the Laguna Suárez, with plenty of wildlife; the water is very warm, the bathing safe where the locals swim, near the café with the jetty (elsewhere there are stingrays and alligators). See under Eating, below. Motorbike taxi from Trinidad, US$1.30.

About 17 km north is **Chuchini** with the **Madriguera del Tigre** ⊙ *contact Efrem Hinojoso at Av 18 de Noviembre 543, T462 1811*, an ecological and archaeological centre, accessible by road in dry season and by canoe in wet season. Three days and two nights US$210 per person, including accommodation and meals; also including Museo Arqueológico del Beni, containing human remains, ceramics and stone objects from pre-Columbian Beni culture, said to be over 5,000 years old.

San Ignacio de Moxos → *Electricity is supplied in town from 1200- 2400.*

San Ignacio de Moxos, 90 km west of Trinidad, is known as the folklore capital of the Beni Department. The traditions of the Jesuit missions are still maintained with big *fiestas*, especially during Holy Week; 31 July is the town's patron saint's day, one of the country's most famous celebrations. *Macheteros*, who speak their own language, comprise 60% of the population.

Magdalena and Bella Vista

Magdalena, northeast of Trinidad, stands on the banks of the Río Itonama. There is an abundance of wildlife and birds in the surrounding area. The city's main festival, Santa María Magdalena, is on 22 July attracting many visitors from all over. Drinking water is available and electricity runs from 1800-2400. There is a bank (changes travellers' cheques), an *Entel* office and Post Office on the plaza.

East of Magdalena, **Bella Vista** on the Río Blanco is considered by many to be one of the prettiest spots in northeast Bolivia. Lovely white sandbanks line the Río San Martín, 10 minutes' paddling by canoe from the boat moorings below town (boatmen will take you, returning later by arrangement; also accessible by motorcycle). Check that the sand is not covered by water after heavy rain. Other activities are swimming in the Río San Martín, canoeing, hunting, good country for cycling. Three well-stocked shops on plaza, but none sells mosquito repellent or spray/coils (bring your own, especially at the beginning of the wet season). No banks.

Ⓢ Sleeping

Trinidad *p319*

A Gran Moxos, Av 6 de Agosto y Santa Cruz, T462 3305, F462 2240. Includes breakfast, a/c, fridge bar, cable TV, phone, good restaurant, accepts Visa and MasterCard.

C-D Hostal Aguahi, Bolívar y Santa Cruz, opposite *TAM*, T462 5570, F462 5569. A/c, fridge, comfortable, swimming pool in pleasant garden.

C-D Monte Verde, 6 de Agosto 76, T462 2750. With or without a/c, fridge bar, includes breakfast, owner speaks English. Recommended.

D Copacabana, Matías Carrasco 627, 3 blocks from plaza, T462 2811, copabeni@yahoo.com. Good value, **F** pp without bath.

D-E Hostal Jarajorechi, Av 6 de Agosto y 27 de Mayo, T462 1716. With bath and breakfast, comfortable, ecotourism centre offering jungle expeditions, equipment and transport hire.

D-E Res Castedo, Céspedes 42, T462 0937, 200 m from bus terminal. A/c or fan, cheaper without bath, breakfast.

F Paulista, Av 6 de Agosto 36, T462 0018. Cheaper without bath, comfortable, good restaurant.

F Res Oriental, 18 de Noviembre near Vaca Díez, T462 2534. Good value, shared bath, helpful, good food, but not very clean.

G Res 18 de Noviembre, Av 6 de Agosto 135, T462 1272. Laundry facilities, OK but noisy.

San Ignacio de Moxos *p320*

There are a few cheapish *residencias* (**E-F**) on the main plaza, several other basic *alojamientos* on and around plaza.

Magdalena *p320*

There are some basic hotels and restaurants.
B Internacional, T03-886 2210, info@hwzinc.com. With breakfast, pools, beautiful setting.

Bella Vista *p320*

F Hotel Pescador, owner Guillermo Esero Gómez very helpful and knowledgeable about the area, shared bath, provides meals for guests, offers excursions.

ⓔ Eating

Trinidad *p319*

Cheap meals, includes breakfast, served at the fruit and vegetable market. Try delicious sugar cane juice with lemon.

♥♥ Balneario Topacare is a restaurant and bathing resort with swimming pool 10 mins out of town on Laguna Suárez, delicious local specialities, lunch or dinner, beautiful location, excellent bird watching, favourite spot for locals at weekends.

♥♥ Pescadería El Moro, Bolívar 707 y Natusch. Excellent fish. Also several good fish restaurants in Barrio Pompeya, south of plaza across river.

♥ Carlitos, on Plaza Ballivián. Recommended.

♥ La Casona, Plaza Ballivián. For good pizzas and set lunch, closed Tue.

♥ Club Social 18 de Noviembre, N Suárez y Vaca Díez on plaza. Good lunch for US$1.35.

♥ La Estancia, Barrio Pompeya, on Ibare entre Muibe y Velarde. Excellent steaks.

Cafés
Heladería Oriental, on plaza. Good coffee, ice-cream, cakes, popular with locals.
Kivón cafeteria on main plaza. Burgers, ice cream and snacks.

San Ignacio de Moxos *p320*
Restaurants do not stay open late.
♯♯ **Casa Suiza**, good European food.
♯ **Donchanta**, recommended for meat dishes.
♯ **Isireri**, on plaza, good and cheap set lunches and delicious fruit juices.

▲▲ Activities and tours

Trinidad *p319*
Most agents offer excursions to local *estancias* and jungle tours down river to **Amazonia**. Most *estancias* can also be reached independently in 1 hr by hiring a motorbike.
Amazonia Holiday, 6 de Agosto 680, T462 5732, F462 2806. Good service.
Fremen, Cipriano Berace 332, T462 2276, fremensl@sauce.ben.entelnet.bo. Run speed boat trips along the **Mamoré** and **Iboré** rivers and to **Parque Nacional Isiboro**, US$80 per day; their *Flotel Reina de Enin* offers tours of more than 1 day, US$80 pp per day, good food.
Moxos, 6 de Agosto 114, T462 1141, turmoxos@sauce.ben.entelnet.bo. Recommended.
Paraíso Travel, 6 de Agosto 138, T/F462 0692, paraiso@sauce.ben.entelnet.bo. Does 'Conozca Trinidad' packages.
Tarope Tours, 6 de Agosto 57, T/F462 1468. For flights.

◉ Transport

Villa Tunari to the Lowlands:
Puerto Villarroel *p319*
From Cochabamba you can get a bus to **Puerto Villarroel** (see Cochabamba Transport, Bus), **Puerto San Francisco**, or **Todos Santos** on the Río Chapare.

Trinidad *p319*
Air AeroSur, 6 de Agosto 76, T462 3402, to **Santa Cruz**. Flights also with **Amaszonas** (18 de Noviembre 267, T346 2426) to **La Paz, Riberalta, Guayaramerín, Cobija** and **Santa Cruz**, and LAB (Santa Cruz 322, T462 1277) to **Cochabamba**. TAM, Bolívar s/n entre 18 de Noviembre y Santa Cruz, T462 2363, at airport, T462 0355, to **Bella Vista, Magdalena, Riberalta, Guayaramerín, Santa Cruz** and **La Paz** (do not leave any valuables in baggage that you check in). Airport,

T462 0678. Taxi to airport US$1.20.
Bus Bus station is on Rómulo Mendoza, between Beni and Pinto, 9 blocks east of main plaza. Motorbike taxis will take people with backpacks from bus station to centre for US$0.45. Several *flotas* daily to/from **La Paz** via San Borja and Caranavi, 20-21 hrs, depart 1730, US$17.50 (see also under San Borja, Transport). To **Santa Cruz** (12 hrs in dry season, US$5.80) and **Cochabamba** (US$11.60), with Copacabana, Mopar and Bolívar at 1700, 1730 and 1800; irregular morning service (generally 0900). Trinidad to Casarabe is paved and Santa Cruz to El Puente; otherwise gravel surface on all sections of unpaved road. To **Rurrenabaque** (US$18), **Riberalta** (US$21.15) and **Guayaramerín** (US$23), connecting with bus to **Cobija**; Guaya Tours Sun, Mon, Thu, Fri at 1030; road often impassable in wet season, at least 24 hrs to **Rurrenabaque**.
Ferry Cargo boats down the Río Mamoré to **Guayaramerín** take passengers, 3-4 days, assuming no breakdowns, best organized from Puerto Varador (speak to the Port Captain). **Argos** is recommended as friendly, US$22 pp, take water, fresh fruit and toilet paper. Ear-plugs are also recommended as hammocks are strung over the engine on small boats; only for the hardy traveller.

San Ignacio de Moxos *p320*
Bus The Trinidad to San Borja bus stops at the *Donchanta* restaurant for lunch, otherwise difficult to find transport to San Borja. Minibus to Trinidad daily at 0730 from plaza, also *camionetas*, check times before.

Magdalena *p320*
Road An unpaved road goes to Trinidad via San Ramón (pick-up US$10.50), passable only in the dry season. San Ramón to Magdalena takes 6 hrs on motorbike taxi, US$16.

Bella Vista *p320*
Air There are TAM flights; ask at the office on the road nearest the river, 2-3 blocks east of plaza.

◉ Directory

Trinidad *p319*
Banks Banco Mercantil, J de Sierra, near plaza. Changes cash and TCs, cash on Visa. Banco Ganadero, Plaza Ballivián. Visa agent. Street changers on 6 de Agosto (US dollars only). **Post offices and telephones** (Open daily till 1930) in same building at Av Barace, just off plaza.

Santa Cruz and Eastern Lowlands

In contrast to the highlands of the Andes and the gorges of the Yungas, eastern Bolivia is made up of vast plains stretching to the Chaco of Paraguay and the Pantanal wetlands of Brazil. Agriculture is well-developed and other natural resources are fully exploited, bringing prosperity to the region. There are a number of national parks with great biodiversity, such as Amboró and Noel Kempff Mercado. Historical interest lies in the pre-Inca ceremonial site at Samaipata, the beautiful Chiquitano Jesuit missions and, of much more recent date, the trails and villages where Che Guevara made his final attempt to bring revolution to Bolivia.

Santa Cruz → *Phone code: 03. Colour map 6, grid A4. Population: 1,284,000. Altitude: 416 m.*

As little as 50 years ago, what is now Bolivia's largest city was a remote backwater, but rail and road links ended its isolation and the exploitation of oil and gas in the Department of Santa Cruz helped fuel the city's rapid development. Santa Cruz is far removed from most travellers' perceptions of Bolivia. Formerly a haven for narcotraficantes, it is now less opulent, although agribusiness is an important economic concern. The city centre still retains much of its colonial air and during the lunchtime hiatus when the locals (who like to call themselves cambas) take refuge from the overwhelming heat, it can almost seem like its original self. Here, too, you can witness the incongruous sight of immigrant Mennonite farmers and their families, who fled persecution in the USA and Canada, going about their business in the presence of Bolivia's most open and laid-back population.

Ins and outs
Getting there The international **airport** is at **Viru-Viru**, about 13 km north of the city. Airport bus every 20 minutes from the bus terminal, 25 minutes (US$0.70), also *colectivos*. Taxi, US$8.50. From airport take bus to bus terminal then taxi to centre. Long distance and local **buses** leave from the new combined bus/train terminal, **Terminal Bimodal**, Avenida Montes on the southeastern edge of the city between Avenida Brasil and Tres Pasos, between the second and third *anillos*. T348 8382. No 12 bus to/from the centre, taxi US$1.50. The city has ten ring roads, Anillos 1, 2, 3, 4 and so on. Equipetrol suburb, where many hotels and bars are situated, is northwest of the heart of the city between Anillos 2 and 3.

Tourist office Prefectura del Departamento (Direcciones), on the north side of the main plaza, T333 2770 ext 144. New and impressive; videos; guided tours. Information kiosk at the airport. Also **Organización y Gestión del Destino Turístico Santa Cruz** (OGD-SCZ), Av Las Américas 7, Torres Cainco p 5, T339 2925, www.destinosantacruz.com/es/home/welcome.asp. Local guide books: *Guía Turística Metropolitana de Santa Cruz* (Spanish/English) and *Handbook of Santa Cruz* (English), both published by Editora Exclusiva (T336 8655, www.scbbs.net/ exclusiva), US$4, and *Santa Cruz Turístico* (Spanish), published by APAC (T332 2287), US$5.

Sights
The Plaza 24 de Septiembre is the city's main square with the huge **Cathedral** ① *museum Tue, Thu, Sun 1000-1200, 1600-1800, US$0.75*, the Casa de Cultura and the Palacio Prefectural set around it. **Casa de la Cultura** has occasional exhibitions, a museum, giftshop and also an archaeological display; also plays, recitals, concerts and folk dancing. The heart of the city, with its arcaded streets and buildings with low, red-tiled roofs and overhanging eaves, retains a colonial feel, despite the profusion of modern, air-conditioned shops and restaurants. Five blocks north of the Plaza is **Parque El Arenal** in which is a mural by the celebrated painter, Lorgio Vaca, depicting the city's history. Nearby is the **Museo Etno-Folklórico** ① *Beni y Caballero, T335 2078, Mon-Fri 0830-1200, 1430-1830, US$0.75*, which houses a collection of artefacts from lowland cultures. **Museo de Historia Natural, Noel Kempff Mercado** ① *Av Irala 565 entre Velasco e Independencia, T/F337 1216, www.museonoelkempff.org, Mon-Fri 0800-1200, also Mon-Tue 1500-1830, US$0.15*. It has a video library. Contact this museum for trips and information to Parque Nacional Noel Kempff Mercado (see page 333). Some 12 km on the road to Cotoca are the **Botanical Gardens** (micro o colectivo from C Suárez Arana, 15 minutes).

⊜ Sleeping

Santa Cruz *p322, map p323*

LL Las Buganvillas, Av Roca y Coronado 901, T355 1212, www.buganvillas.com.bo. 5-star in all respects, all amenities, located between the Río Piraí and Feria Exposición complex.

LL Los Tajibos, Av San Martín 455 in Barrio Equipetrol, 5-star, T342 1000, www.lostajiboshotel.com. A/c, *El Papagayo* restaurant good (*ceviche* recommended), business centre, *Viva Club Spa* has sauna, swimming pool for residents only.

L House Inn, Colón 643, T336 2323, www.houseinn.com.bo. 5-star suites with computer in each room, unlimited internet use, price includes taxes and breakfast, 2 pools, sauna, restaurant, a/c, parking, modern.

A Las Américas, 21 de Mayo esq Seoane, T336 8778, americas@cotas.com.bo. A/c, discount for longer stay, parking, arranges tours and car rental, restaurant, bar, 5-star service.

B Asturias, Moldes 154, T333 9611, www.hotel asturias.net. A/c, quiet, nice pool and gardens,

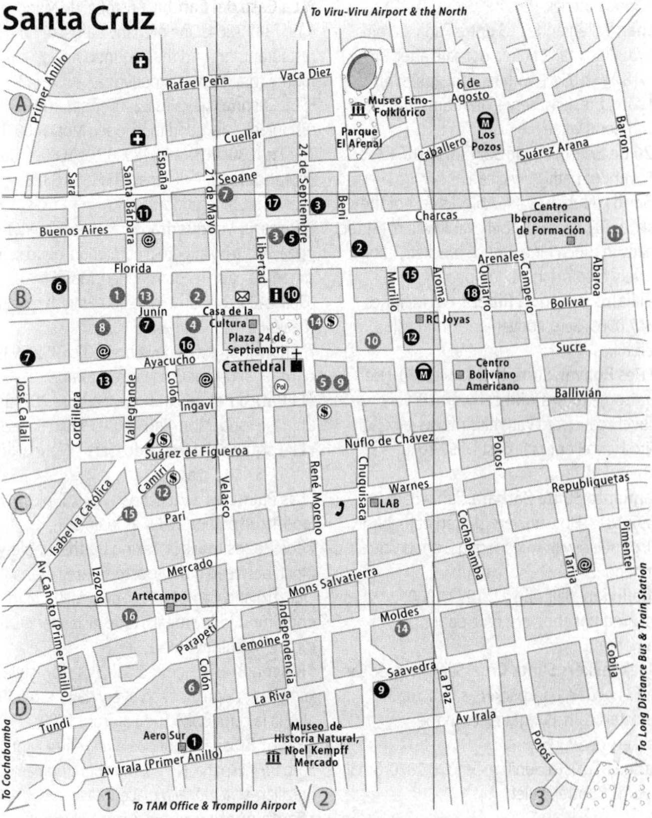

Santa Cruz

To Viru-Viru Airport & the North

Museo Etno-Folklórico

Parque El Arenal

6 de Agosto

Los Pozos

Centro Iberoamericano de Formación

Casa de la Cultura

Plaza 24 de Septiembre

Cathedral

RC Joyas

Centro Boliviano Americano

Museo de Historia Natural, Noel Kempff Mercado

To Cochabamba

To Long Distance Bus & Train Station

To TAM Office & Trompillo Airport

N

0 metres 200
0 yards 200

Sleeping ⊜
Alojamiento Santa
  Bárbara 1 *B1*
Asturias 14 *D2*
Backpackers
  Santa Cruz 16 *D1*

Bibosi 2 *B1*
Colonial 3 *B2*
Copacabana 4 *B1*
Crismar 15 *C1*
Excelsior 5 *B2*
House Inn 6 *D1*
Las Américas 7 *B2*
Posada El Turista 8 *B1*
Residencial 26
  de Enero 12 *C1*
Residencial
  Ballivián 9 *B2*
Residencial Bolívar 10 *B2*

Residencial Sands 11 *B3*
Viru-Viru 13 *B1*

Eating 🍴
Capri 1 *D1*
El Boliche 2 *B2*
El Patito Pekín 3 *B2*
Il Gatto 5 *B2*
Kivón 16 *B1*
La Casona 15 *B2*
La Esquina
  del Pescado 6 *B1*
Las Palmeras 7 *B1*

Michelangelo 9 *D2*
Pizzería Marguerita 10 *B2*
Rincón Brasil 17 *B2*
Sabor Brasil 11 *B1*
Su Salud 18 *B3*
Tía Lía 12 *B2*
Vegetariano 13 *B1*

Bars & clubs 🍸
Irlandés 14 *B2*

Bolivia Santa Cruz Listings

323

internet, bar and restaurant, a good choice.

B Colonial, Buenos Aires 57, T333 3156, F333 9223. A/c, breakfast, restaurant, comfortable.

B Viru-Viru Junín 338, T/F336 7500. Includes breakfast, a/c, cheaper with fan, pleasant, central.

C Bibosi, Junín 218, T334 8548, bibosi@scbbs-bo.com. **D** with shared bath, breakfast included, internet. Recommended.

C Copacabana, Junín 217, T332 1843, F333 0757. **B** with a/c, **E** without bath, TV, laundry service, includes breakfast, restaurant, very good.

C Excelsior, René Moreno 70, T332 5924, excelsior@cotas.net. Includes breakfast, good rooms, good lunches.

D Crismar, Vallegrande 285 entre Pari y Camiri, by the '7 Calles' market (area not safe after 2100), T337 1918. With a/c, **E** with fan, cheaper with shared bath, breakfast served in rooms, basic but clean and good value.

E Res 26 de Enero, Camiri 32, T332 1818, F333 7518. **F** without bath, very clean.

E Res Sands, Arenales 749, 7 blocks east of the main plaza, T337 7776. Unbelievable value, better than many in much higher price brackets, cable TV, fan, very comfortable beds, pool.

E pp **Williams y Patricia Ribera**, Los Melones 622, T347 0909. Safe, convenient, good value, very helpful.

E-F pp **Res Bolívar**, Sucre 131, T334 2500. Hot showers, some rooms with bath, others very small, lovely courtyard with hammocks, alcohol prohibited, excellent breakfast US$2.10. Recommended.

F Alojamiento Santa Bárbara, Santa Bárbara 151, T332 1817. Hot showers, shared bath, basic, helpful, popular, will store luggage, good value. Recommended.

F Res Ballivián, Ballivián 71, T332 1960. Basic, shared hot showers, nice patio. Recommended.

G pp **Backpackers Santa Cruz**, Salvatierra 555 y Izozog, T312 0033, backpackers-santacruz@ boliviahostels.com. Budget place in the Backpackers network.

G Posada El Turista, Junín 455, T336 2870. Small basic rooms, central, quiet.

⊙ Eating

Santa Cruz *p322, map p323*
Barrio Equipetrol is the area for the poshest restaurants and nightlife. Most restaurants close Mon. The bakeries on Junín, Los Manzanos and España sell the local specialities.

₸₸₸ El Boliche, Arenales 135. Open 1930 onwards, serves good crêpes, fondues and salads.

₸₸₸ Il Gatto, 24 de Septiembre 285. Bright and clean, good pizzas, US$2.25 buffet 1200-1500.

₸₸₸ Michelangelo, Chuquisaca 502. Excellent Italian. Mon-Fri 1200-1400, 1900-2330, Sat evenings only.

₸₸₸ Yorimichi, Av Busch 548, T334 7717. Japanese, one of the city's best restaurants, could easily put some Tokyo restaurants to shame, closed 1430-1900 and all day Sun.

₸₸ La Buena Mesa, Av Cristóbal de Mendoza 1401, T342 1248. Excellent for barbecued steak.

₸₸ Capri, Irala 634, "The best pizzas in town".

₸₸ Churrasquería El Palenque, Av El Trompillo y Santos Dumont, T352 6022. Open 1200-1400,1830-2330, closed Tue, excellent for barbecued steak.

₸₸ La Casa del Camba, Cristóbal de Mendoza 539, T342 7864. One of many barbecue restaurants around the Segundo Anillo, "a must for the total camba experience."

₸₸ La Casona, Arenales 222. German-run restaurant, very good food, open Mon 1600-2000, Tue-Fri 1030-1430, 1600-2000, Sat 1000-1400.

₸₸ Mandarin 2, Av Potosí 793, T334 8388. Excellent Chinese food.

₸₸ Pizzería Marguerita, northwest corner of the plaza. A/c, truly superb filet mignon, good service, coffee, bar, also recommended, Mon-Fri 0900-2400, Sat-Sun 1600-2400. Finnish owner, speaks English, German.

₸₸ Shanghai, Av 26 de Febrero 27, T352 3939. Another excellent Chinese restaurant.

₸ El Patito Pekín, 24 de Septiembre 307. Basic Chinese food, Mon-Sun 1100-1400, 1800-2000.

₸ La Esquina del Pescado, Sara y Florida. For fish, US$1.60 a plate.

₸ Las Palmeras, Ayacucho y Callali. Typical *camba* food, large portions. Also at Junín 381.

₸ Los Pozos market, taking up the whole block between 6 de Agosto, Suárez Arana, Quijarro and Campero, is open daily, clean, good for midday meals, food aisles serve local and Chinese food.

₸ Rincón Brasil, Libertad 358. Brazilian-style *por kilo* place, popular, open every day 1130-1500, also (à la carte only) Tue-Sat from 1800.

₸ Sabor Brasil, off Buenos Aires, entre Santa Bárbara y España, No 20. Another popular Brazilian-style *por kilo* place.

₸ Santa Ana, Ingavi 164. Good value buffet lunch in a shady patio.

₸ Su Salud, Quijarro 115. Tasty vegetarian food, filling lunches, huge portions. Recommended.

₸ Tía Lía, Murillo 40. US$1.50 (US$2.25 weekends) for all the beef, chorizos, pork and chicken you want from a *parrillada*, huge selection of salads, pasta and bean dishes, Mon-Fri 1100-1500, Sat-Sun 1100-1600.

₸ Vegetariano, Ayacucho 444. Breakfast, lunch and dinner, good.

Cafés

There are lots of very pleasant a/c cafés and ice cream parlours, where you can get coffee, ice cream, drinks, snacks and reasonably-priced meals.
Alexander Coffee at Av Monseñor Rivero 400 in Zona El Cristo, T337 8653. For good coffee.
Fridolin, Pari 254 and Av Cañoto y Florida. Two good places for coffee and pastries.
Kivón, Ayacucho 267. Highly recommended for ice cream; also at Quijarro 409 in Mercado Los Pozos.

🎵 Bars and clubs

Santa Cruz *p322, map p323*
Bar Irlandés Irish Pub, 3o Anillo Interno 1216 (between Av Cristo Redentor and Zoológico), T343 0671. Irish-themed pub, food available, English-speaking owner. Also *Café Irlandés*, Plaza 24 de Septiembre, Edificio Shopping Bolívar No 157 overlooking main plaza, T333 8118, live music Wed and Sat evening. Recommended.
MAD, Av San Martín 155, T336 0333. One of the best known and most popular clubs.
Moosehead, next to Bar Iralndés on 3o Anillo. Canadian bar/restaurant.

❀ Festivals and events

Santa Cruz *p322, map p323*
Cruceños are famous as fun-lovers and their music, the *carnavalitos*, can be heard all over South America. Of the various festivals, the brightest is **Carnival**, renowned for riotous behaviour, celebrated for the **15 days before Lent**: music in the streets, dancing, fancy dress and the coronation of a queen. Beware the following day when youths run wild with buckets and balloons filled with water – no one is exempt. The *mascaritas* balls also take place during the pre-Lent season at *Caballo Blanco* when girls have the right to demand that men dance with them, and wear satin masks covering their heads completely, thus ensuring anonymity. **24 Sep** is a holiday. **Misiones de Chiquitos** is an international music festival held every even year, concerts in Santa Cruz, San Javier, Concepción, among other places, including Renaissance and Baroque recitals.
International film festival held every odd year in same locales. Contact *APAC* for info: T333 2287.

⦿ Shopping

Santa Cruz *p322, map p323*
Bookshops El Ateno, Cañoto y 21 de Mayo, T333 3338. Books in English, access to internet.
Los Amigos del Libro, Igavi 14, T332 7937, sells foreign language books and magazines. International magazines and newspapers often on sale in kiosks on main Plaza, eg *Miami Herald*, after arrival of daily Miami flight.
Handicrafts Artecampo, Salvatierra 407 esq Vallegrande, T334 1843. Run by a local NGO, sells handicrafts made in rural communities in the department, high quality, excellent value. **Manos Indígenas**, Cuéllar 16, T337 2042. For fabrics and weavings from a number of indigenous groups.
Museo de Historia in the Casa de Cultura. Best local crafts; hours are sporadic, call ahead, T355 0611. All proceeds go to *La Mancomunidad*, a local outfit that supports indigenous craftsmen and their families. **Vicuñita Handicrafts**, Ingavi e Independencia, T333 4711. By far the best and biggest selection from altiplano and lowlands. Very honest, will ship. Artesanía shops on Libertad and on Plaza 24 de Septiembre y Bolívar
Jewellery Gemas de Bolivia, Casco Viejo, p 2 (esq 21 de Mayo y Junín), T357 3623, rbirt@scbbs.com. Outstanding selection of local and Brazilian stones. Honest, very reasonable prices, English spoken. Repeatedly recommended. **RC Joyas**, Bolívar 262, T333 2725. Jewellery and Bolivian gems, the manager produces and sells good maps of Santa Cruz City and department.
Markets Bazar Siete Calles, mainly for clothing, but food and fruit is sold outside, main entrance is in 100 block of Isabel La Católica, also on Camiri and Vallegrande, past Ingavi. **Los Pozos**, see under Eating. Open daily; in summer it's full of exotic fruits. Beware of bag-snatching. There is a fruit and vegetable market at Sucre y Cochabamba, and a large indigenous market on Sun near the bus terminal.

🔺 Activities and tours

Santa Cruz *p322, map p323*
Jean Paul Ayala,
jpdakidd@roble.scz.entelnet.bo. Recommended for birdwatching trips, speaks English.
Mario Berndt, T342 0340, tauk@em.daitec-bo.com. Does large-scale tailored tours off the beaten track, mostly to the Altiplano, requires approx 3 months notice, speaks English, German and Spanish and is very knowledgeable about the area.
Cambatur, Sucre 8, T334 9999, cambatur@cotas.com.bo. Best in city by far for local, regional, international. Ask for Cynthia Otalora; speaks English, French and Portuguese. She is a member of the *Asociación Cruceña – Guías de Turismo* and can arrange private city tours, T345 1741 or 773 44471 (mob).
Fremen, Beni 79, T333 8535, F336 0265. Local tours, also jungle river cruises.
Magri Turismo, Warnes esq Potosí, T334 5663, www.magri-amexpress.com.bo. American Express agent. Recommended.

⊖ Transport

Santa Cruz *p322, map p323*
Air Airport information T181; the terminal has
Emigration/Immigration office, **Entel** office,
luggage lockers, duty free shop, restaurant
(expensive), bank open 0830-1830, changes cash
and TCs, withdrawal on Visa and MasterCard (when
closed try **AASANA** desk, where you pay airport
tax). LAB flies at least twice daily to **La Paz** and
Cochabamba, and to **Sucre** and **Tarija**. Aero Sur
flies to **La Paz** (several daily), **Cochabamba**,
Sucre, **Tarija** and **Puerto Suárez**. Flights also with
Amazonas to **Trinidad**. International
destinations include most South American
capitals, as well as **Salta** and **Córdoba**, **Rio de
Janeiro**, **São Paulo** and **Manaus**, plus some US
gateways and cities in Mexico and Central America.
Bus Daily buses to **Cochabamba** (US$3-4.50,
10 hrs), many *flotas* leave between 0600-0900 and
1630-2100. Direct to **Sucre** daily between 1700-
1800, 14 hrs, US$6-7.50. **Oruro** and **La Paz** 17 hrs,
US$10-12.50, between 1700-2200 (some are
buscama); change in Cochabamba for daytime
travel. To **Camiri** (US$3.75), **Yacuiba** and **Tarija**,
daily, several companies; 26-32 hrs to Tarija. To
Trinidad, several daily, 12 hrs, US$4.50, all depart
1700 or 1900. **International**: Empresa Yacyretá,
Mon, Tue, Thu, Sat, 2030 **Santa Cruz- Asunción**,
US$45, minimum 24 hrs via Villamontes and
the Chaco, for information T362 5557. **Stel
Turismo**, T349 7762, runs the same route 2000
daily. See page 328 for the route to Paraguay
across the Chaco.
Taxi About US$1.15 inside 1st Anillo (US$1.50 at
night), US$1.30 inside 3rd Anillo, fix fare in advance.
Train Ferroviaria Oriental, T7164 8421. To
Quijarro (for Brazil), see page 333, and **Yacuiba**
(for Argentina), see page 329.

⊖ Directory

Santa Cruz *p322, map p323*
Airline offices Aerolíneas Argentinas, Edif
Banco de la Nación Argentina, on main Plaza,
T333 9776. **Aero Sur**, Irala 616, T336 7400.
Amazonas, Aeropuerto El Trompillo, of 10, T357
8988. **American Airlines**, Beni 167, T334 1314.
LAB, Warnes y Chuquisaca, T334 4596, or
800-103001. **TAM**, 21 de Mayo, T337 1999.
Banks Enlace ATMs in airport departure lounge
and throughout downtown; also in Equipetrol.
Banco Mercantil, René Moreno y Suárez de
Figueroa. Cash advance on Visa, changes cash and
TCs. Medicambio on Plaza 24 de Septiembre will
change TCs into dollars at 3% commission,
excellent reputation. **Menno Credit Union**, 10 de
Agosto 15, T332 8800, small office in Mennonite
area of town, open 0900-1600, changes TCs, 1%

commission, English, German and Dutch spoken.
Street money changers on Plaza 24 de Septiembre
and around bus terminal; they exchange
guaraníes. **Car hire** Aby's, 3rd Anillo 1038, esq
Pasaje Muralto 1038 (opposite zoo), T345 1560.
Across, 4th Anillo, esq Radial 27 (400 m from Av
Banzer Oeste), T344 1717. US$70 per day for basic
Suzuki 4x4 (200 km per day) with insurance.
Barron's, Av Alemana 50 y Tajibos, T342 0160,
www.rentacarbolivia.com. **Cultural centres**
Centro Boliviano Americano, Cochabamba 66,
T334 2299, www.cba.com.bo. Library with US
papers and magazines, English classes, some
cultural events. Centro Cultural Franco Alemán,
Av Velarde 200, T332 9906, www.ccfranco
aleman.org. Joint cultural institute with language
courses, cultural events, library (internet access),
both open Mon-Fri 0900-1200, 1530-2000.
Centro de Formación de la Cooperación
Española, Arenales 583, T335 1322,
www.aeci.org.bo (concerts, films, art exhibitions,
lectures, etc), very good. **Embassies and
consulates** Argentina, in Edif Banco de la
Nación Argentina, Plaza 24 de Septiembre, Junín
22, T334 7133, Mon-Fri 0800-1300. **Belgium**,
Parque Industrial Mz14, edif Dismac, T348 7216.
Brazil, Av Busch 330, near Plaza Estudiantes, T334
4400, Mon-Fri 0900-1500. It takes 24 hrs to process
visa applications, reported as unhelpful. **Denmark**,
Landívar 401, T352 5200, Mon-Fri, 0900-1200,
1500-1800. **France**, Alemania y Mutualista, off the
3rd ring, T343 3434, Mon-Fri 1630-1800. **Germany**,
Libertad esq Strongest, Edif Plaza Libertad, of 201,
T345 3914, Mon-Fri 0800-1200. **Israel**, Av Banzer
171, T342 4777, hobsch@infonet.bo. **Italy**, C
Chaco, Edif Honnen p 1, T353 1796, Mon-Fri
0830-1230. **Netherlands**, Av Roque Aguilera 300,
3rd ring, between Grigotá and Paraí, T335 4498,
ludo@alke.net, Mon-Fri 0900-1230. **Paraguay**,
Manuel Ignacio Salvatierra 99, Edif Victoria, of 1A,
T336 6113. Colour photo required for visa, Mon-Fri
0730-1400. **Spain**, Monseñor Santiesteban 237,
T332 8921, Mon-Fri 0900-1200. **UK**, Av Las
Américas y Gral Saavedra, Torre Cainco, T331 3330,
cwollgar@cdcgroup.com. **USA**, Güemes Este 6,
Equipetrol, T333 0725, Mon-Fri 0900-1130.
Internet cybercafés everywhere, US$0.40-0.80
per hr. **Medical services** For hospitals,
doctors and dentists, contact your consulate or
the tourist office for advice. **Post office** C Junín
146. **Telephone** Entel, Warnes 36 (entre
Moreno y Chuquisaca), T332 5526, local and
international calls and fax, open Mon-Fri
0730-2330, Sat, Sun and holidays 0730-2200. Also
small *Entel* office at Quijarro 267. **Useful
addresses** Immigration: 3er Anillo Interno esq
Av Cronenbold, opposite the zoo, T333
6442/2136, Mon-Fri 0830-1200, 1430-1800,
service can be very slow.

Southeastern Bolivia

The highlights of this area are southwest of Santa Cruz: the pre-Inca ruins of Samaipata, the nearby Parque Nacional Amboró and the newly-developed Che Guevara Trail, on which you can follow in the final, fatal footsteps of the revolutionary. Heading further south takes you to Argentina and Paraguay.

Samaipata → *Phone code: 03. Colour map M6, grid A4. Altitude: 1,650 m.*

From Santa Cruz the spectacular old mountain road to Cochabamba runs along the Piray gorge and up into the highlands. Some 120 km from Santa Cruz is Samaipata, a great place to relax mid-week, with good lodging, restaurants, hikes and riding, and a helpful ex-pat community. Local *artesanías* include ceramics. At weekends the town bursts into life as crowds of Cruceños come to escape the city heat and to party.

The **Centro de Investigaciones Arqueológicas y Antropológicas Samaipata** has a collection of pots and vases with anthropomorphic designs, dating from 200 BC to 200 AD and, most importantly, provides information on the nearby pre-Inca ceremonial site commonly called **El Fuerte** ① *daily 0900-1700, Centro 0930-1230, 1430-1830; US$4 for El Fuerte and Centro de Investigaciones, US$0.75 for Centro only, ticket valid 4 days. Guides available at El Fuerte, US$5.* This sacred structure (1,970 m) consists of a complex system of channels, basins, high-relief sculptures, etc, carved out of one vast slab of rock. Latest research on dates is conflicting. Some suggests that Amazonian people created it around 1500 BC, but it could be later. There is evidence of subsequent occupations and that it was the eastern outpost of the Incas' Kollasuyo (their Bolivian Empire). It is no longer permitted to walk on the rock, so visit the museum first to see the excellent model. El Fuerte is 9 km from the town; 3 km along the highway, then 6 km up a rough, signposted road (taxi US$4.50); two hours' walk one way, or drive to the entrance. Pleasant bathing is possible in a river on the way to El Fuerte.

Vallegrande and La Higuera

Some 115 km south of the Santa Cruz-Cochabamba road is La Higuera, where Che Guevara was killed. On 8 October each year, people gather there to celebrate his memory. La Higuera is reached through the colonial town of **Vallegrande** where, at **Hospital Nuestro Señor de Malta** ① *no fee, but voluntary donation to the health station*, you can see the old laundry building where Che's body was shown to the international press on 9 October 1967. Near Vallegrande's air strip you can see the results of excavations carried out in 1997 which finally unearthed his physical remains (now in Cuba), ask an airport attendant to see the site. Vallegrande has a small archaeological museum, above which is the **Che Guevara Room** *US$0.30*.

The schoolhouse in La Higuera where Che was executed is being turned into a museum. Another **museum** *T03-942 2003*, owned by René Villegas, is open when he is in town. Guides, including Pedro Calzadillo, headmaster of the school, will show visitors to the ravine of El Churo, where Che was captured on 8 October 1967. In 2004 the **Ruta del Che** (Che Guevara Trail) was opened, following the route of Che and his band as they feld the Bolivian army. It takes three to six days, depending on how much you do and how you travel. The trail is run by the Bolivian government, CARE International and local communities. Tour operators offer packages.

Parque Nacional Amboró

This vast (442,500 ha) protected area lies only three hours west of Santa Cruz. Amboró encompasses three distinct major ecosystems and 11 life zones and is home to thousands of animal, plant and insect species (it is reputed to contain more butterflies than anywhere else on earth). The park is home to 712 species of birds, including the blue-horned curassow, the very rare quetzal and cock-of-the-rock, red and chestnut-fronted macaws, hoatzin and cuvier toucans, and most mammals native to Amazonia, such as capybaras, peccaries, tapirs, several species of monkey, and jungle cats like the jaguar, ocelot and margay, and the increasingly rare spectacled bear. There are also numerous waterfalls and cool, green swimming pools, moss-ridden caves and large tracts of virgin rainforest. The park itself is largely inaccessible and much wading is required to get around, but there is good trekking in the surrounding buffer zone which is where most tours operate. There are two places to base yourself: Samaipata (see also page 327) and Buena Vista. Most entrances to the park involve crossing the Río Surutú, which is usually in flood in the wet season. The park is administered by **SERNAP** ① *Santa Cruz office at Calle 9 Oeste 138, Barrio Equipetrol, T339 4310, Mon-Fri 0800-1200, 1400-1800*, officious with no maps and little practical information. Topographic maps of the area can be obtained at the IGM in Santa Cruz ① *Av Tres Pasos al Frente near the Tercer Anillo, Barrio Petrolero Sur, T346 3040, 0830-1230, 1500-1800.* Note that there are many biting insets so take repellent.

Access from Buena Vista Northwest of Santa Cruz by paved road is the sleepy town of Buena Vista. The most popular entrance to the park is Las Cruces, 35 km away, reached by a daily morning bus whose route runs alongside the Río Surutú for several km. From Las Cruces, the trail leads directly to the settlement of Villa Amboró, in the park's buffer zone. Also in the buffer zone is Macañucú which has the best services in the park, with horse riding, hiking trails, guides, camping, kitchens and showers (US$20 pp per day), radio contact with the park office. There is a national park office just over a block from the plaza in Buena Vista, T932 2032 (permit free). Office is closed Sunday and siesta time. They can help with guides and suggestions.

Access from Samaipata Many agencies in Samaipata offer excursions. If going on your own, access is via **Mairana**, 17 km by minibus from Samaipata over a bad, but beautiful road (several basic hotels and roadside eateries), the meal stop for long distance buses between Santa Cruz and Sucre; you can catch these if there are seats available. Shared taxis from Santa Cruz to Mairana with **Cotrama** ① *Humberto Vásquez y Primer Anillo*, leave when full throughout the day, 3 hours, US$3.50. Local trucks and shared taxis from Mairana to La Yunga, US$1.50 per person, more for an *expreso*. At **La Yunga** (US$2 entry fee), there are community-run cabins, **E**, with shared bath, no shower, lovely views, meals available with advance notice. Guides from La Yunga charge US$15 per day to explore the buffer zone; take all your own trekking gear and provisions. Taxi Samaipata-La Yunga, 30 km, US$12 one way. The village of **Quirusillas** is 1½-2 hours by minibus from Mairana . As the area is close to the mountains, there is more rain than further east, with plenty of greenery and cloud forest. Quirusillas has two basic places to stay and a cemetery set on a hill overlooking a small valley. Lago Quirusillas is about 6 km away via a steep dirt road.

There is a minibus service from Mairana to Vallegrande (see above) and overnight buses to Cochabamba along the old road with **Expreso Surumi** on Tuesday, Friday and Sunday, 1530, 12 hours, US$4.50 (passengers sleep in the locked bus in a Cochabamba market area until dawn).

To Paraguay
South of Santa Cruz the road passes through Abapó and Camiri. A paved road heads south from Camiri, through Boyuibe, Villamontes and Yacuiba to Argentina (see below). At Boyuibe another road heads east to Paraguay, used less now than a new road from Villamontes (see below) to Mariscal Estigarribia in the Paraguayan Chaco. It is possible, albeit foolish, to drive from Boyuibe into Paraguay direct on the old road in a truck or 4WD, high clearance vehicle, carry insect repellent, food and water for a week. No help can be relied on in case of a breakdown; a winch is advisable, especially after rain. There are some rivers to ford and although they are dry in the dry season they can be impassable if there is rain in the area. The new route, once you leave the paved road at Villamontes, should be treated with the same respect. At Boyuibe (*Alojamiento Boyuibe*, has hot showers, restaurant, and two others, all **G**) all buses stop at Parador-Restaurante Yacyretá, on main road, owners are helpful, sell bus tickets to Asunción and have rooms to rent; change cash here (poor rates). Fuel and water are available.

Villamontes → *Phone code: 04. Colour map 6, grid B4.*
South of Boyuibe is Villamontes (280 km east of Tarija) renowned for fishing and infamous for its heat. It holds a Fiesta del Pescado in August. It is a friendly town on the edge of the Gran Chaco and is on the road and rail route from Santa Cruz to the Argentine border at Yacuiba. You can change buses here to/from Paraguay on the Santa Cruz-Yacuiba bus route, or to/from Tarija, or if coming from Sucre. There are two banks (no ATM, exchange limited), *TAM* office (T672 2135) and internet café (next to *El Arriero* restaurant) on Plaza 15 de Abril. *Entel* is one block northeast of this plaza.

The road to Paraguay runs east to **Ibibobo**. The first 80 km is an all-weather gravel surface. Bolivian exit stamps are given at Ibibobo. If travelling by bus, passports are collected by driver and returned on arrival at Mcal Estigarribia, Paraguay, with Bolivian exit stamp. Paraguayan immigration and thorough drugs searches take place in Mcal Estigarribia. See under Santa Cruz, page 326, for international bus services, and see the Chaco section of the Paraguay chapter for road conditions, etc. From Ibibobo to the frontier at Picada Sucre is 75 km, then it's 15 km to the border and another 8 km to the Paraguayan frontier post at **Fortín Infante Rivarola**. There are no police or immigration officials at the border.

To Argentina (Yacuiba) → *Colour map 6, grid B4. Population: 11,000.*

From Santa Cruz the route goes Boyuibe, Villamontes and Yacuiba, a prosperous city at the crossing to Pocitos in Argentina. From Villamontes to Yacuiba road is paved, but no bridges; river crossings tricky in wet season. In Yacuiba, there are **Entel** and Correos. Argentine consul at Comercio y Sucre. The border crossing is straightforward. Passengers leaving Bolivia must disembark at Yacuiba, take a taxi to Pocitos on the border (US$0.40, beware unscrupulous drivers) and walk across to Argentina.

● Sleeping

Samaipata *p327*

Rooms may be hard to find at weekends in high season. Most cabins listed have kitchen, bathroom, barbecue and hammocks.

C Cabañas de Traudi, across the road from *La Vispera*, T944 6094, traudiar@cotas.com.bo. Cabins for 2-8, also **E** lovely rooms (**F** with shared bathroom), heated pool US$1.50 for non residents, sitting area with open fire, TV and music system, ceramics shop, great place.

B Campeche, T944 6046, campeche@scbbs-bo.com. For 2-6 people, all self-catering, quiet, hot water, **D** midweek, **E** without kitchen.

C Landhaus, most central of all the *cabañas*, T944 6033. Beautiful place with a small pool, sun loungers, garden, hammocks, parking, internet and sauna (US$20 for up to 8 people), also rooms only with shared bathroom **E** pp; excellent restaurant and café.

C La Víspera, 1.2 km south of town, T944 6082, www.lavispera.org. Dutch-owned organic farm with accommodation in 4 cosy cabins, camping US$3 (US$4 to hire tent), delicious local produce for breakfast, US$3 pp. Very peaceful; Margarita and Pieter know pretty much everything about the local area and can arrange all excursions through *Bolviajes*. Highly recommended.

Several other *cabañas* west of town, but all very expensive.

E Andoriña, 2 blocks from plaza, T944 6333, www.andorina-samaipata.blogspot.com. To open mid-2006, enthusiastic owners Andrés and Doriña, very helpful and knowledgeable, Dutch and English spoken, serve breakfast and juices. Also offer nature photography courses and a wide variety of other activities in the area.

E Hostería Mi Casa, Bolívar, T944 6292. Pretty flower patio, snack bar, **F** with shared bath, 1 *cabaña* (**D**); being renovated in 2006.

F Aranjuez, on the main road at the entrance to town, T944 6223. Upstairs terrace, clothes washing area, food available, includes breakfast, good value.

F Don Jorge, Bolívar, T944 6086. Cheaper with shared bath, hot showers, good beds, large shaded patio, good set lunch.

F Residencial Kim, near the plaza, T944 6161. Use of kitchen, **G** with shared bath, family-run, spotless, good value. Recommended.

G Alojamiento Vargas, around corner from museum. Clothes-washing facilities, use of kitchen, breakfast, owner Teresa is helpful. Recommended.

G Paola, western corner of plaza. Family-run, breakfast extra, good beds, warm showers, use of kitchen, good restaurant, can arrange guides to Amboró and El Fuerte and book microbus to Santa Cruz, rents mountain bikes US$1.25 per hr.

Vallegrande and La Higuera *p327*

F La Sede de los Ganaderos, 1 block from plaz, T942 2176. Includes breakfast, hot water, large rooms, comfortable, parking.

G pp Alojamiento Teresita, Escalante y Mendoza. Has good rooms. In La Higuera you can camp in the school, but ask permission, US$0.30.

Parque Nacional Amboró *p327*

L Flora y Fauna, known as '*Doble F*', Buena Vista, T03-333 8118, Santa Cruz. Hilltop cabins, viewing platforms for birdwatchers, well-planned trails (same owner as *Café Irlandés* in Santa Cruz).

B Pozoazul, on the bypass, Buena Vista, T03-932 2091. A/c, kitchen, pool, good restaurant, helpful, also camping US$14 including showers and pool.

D Sumuqué, Av 6 de Agosto 250, Buena Vista, T932 2080. Cabins in pleasant gardens, trails.

F Nadia, Buena Vista, T03-932 2049. Central, small, family run.

CARE has funded cabins on the far bank of the Río Surutú just past Villa Aguiles on the road from Buena Vista to the river. Good trails, well located in the multiple-use area with lots of flora and fauna.

Villamontes *p328*

C Gran Hotel Avenida, 3 blocks east of Plaza 15 de Abril, T672 2297, F672 2412. A/c, includes breakfast, helpful owner, parking.

C pp El Rancho, 3 km from centre opposite station (taxi US$0.45) T672 2059, F672 2985. Lovely rooms, a/c, TV, excellent restaurant, also annexe **F** pp. Recommended.
E Res Miraflores, 500 block of main Av.
F without bath, basic, not very clean, owner Rolando Rueda arranges fishing trips.
F Res Raldes, 1 block from Plaza 15 de Abril, T672 2088. **G** pp without bath, neat rooms, poor showers.

To Argentina: Yacuiba p329
C Hotel París, Comercio y Campero, T682 2182. The best.
C Monumental, Comercio 1270, T682 2088. Includes breakfast.
D Valentín, Avenida San Martín 1462, opposite rail station, T682 2645, F682 2317. **E** without bath, excellent value

❶ Eating

Samaipata p327
♥♥♥ El Descanso en Los Alturas. Wide choice including excellent steaks and pizzas.
♥♥ Café Hamburg, Bolívar. Laid back, bar, food (including vegetarian), well stocked book exchange, internet US$2.25 per hr (only after 1900), see *Roadrunners* tour agency below.
♥ There are several restaurants on and around the plaza, most of which are cheap. Good *almuerzo* (US$1.05) at Media **Vuelta**.

Cafés
Café Baden, 1 km towards Santa Cruz, good for ice cream and tortes as well as steak and *schweizer würstsalat*.
Chakana bar/restaurant/café open every day 0900-late, Dutch-owned, relaxing, *almuerzos* for US$2.25, good snacks and salads, seats outside, a book exchange, cakes and ice cream.
Panadería Gerlinde, near the Santa Cruz-Cochabamba main road. For superb biscuits, bread, homemade pastas, herbs, cheese, yoghurts and cold meats, Swiss-run, open daily 0700-2200. Also has a weekend stall in the market.

Vallegrande and La Higuera p327
♥ Café Santa Clara, on the plaza. Decent food and beer, Che-inspired work, the young waiter is very helpful.
♥ Hong Kong. Chicken, cheap, good service.
♥ El Mirador. Huge portions of meat, good.

Villamontes p328
♥ Churrasquería Argentina, ½ block from Plaza 15 de Abril. For pizzas and grilled meat.
♥ Parillada El Arriero, Plaza 15 de Abril. Good, cheap meals.

Bar Cherenta, Plaza 15 de Abril. Favoured by locals.
Heladería Noelia, halfway from the plaza to bus station. Good for ice cream, popular.

▲▲ Activities and tours

Samaipata p327
All those in this list are recommended and offer trips to similar destinations. Expect to pay US$15-20 pp in a group of 4.
Gilberto Aguilera, T944 6050, considered the most knowledgeable local guide, good value tours.
Amboró Tours, T/F944 6293, erickamboro@ cotas.com.bo. Run by Erick Prado who speaks only Spanish.
Michael Blendinger, T944 6227, mblendinger@ cotas.com.bo. German guide raised in Argentina who speaks English, runs fully- equipped 4WD tours, short and long treks, horse rides, specialist in nature and archaeology. Accommodation in cabins available, also inclusive packages.
Roadrunners, Olaf and Frank, T944 6193. Speak English, enthusiastic, lots of information and advice, recommended tour of El Fuerte. See La Víspera, above, Margarita and Pieter, Bolviajes. All lead trips to Amboró and other interesting places.

Parque Nacional Amboró p327
Amboró Adventures, on the plaza in Buena Vista, T03-932 2090. Excursions include guide and transportation, but not food.
Amboró Tours, near the park office in Buena Vista, T03-932 2093, 716 33990 (mob), rodosoto@ hotmail.com. Tours with very basic accommodation, simple food and include transport and guides, about US$50 pp per day, expensive for what's offered. Independent guides cost US$10 per day in Buena Vista.

❸ Transport

Samaipata p327
Bus From **Santa Cruz** to Samaipata, only Sucre-bound buses leave from the new bus station. Shared taxis and mini-buses leave from the vicinity of the old bus station, eg **Expreso Samaipata**, Av Omar Chávez Ortiz 1147 y Solís de Olguín, 2½ hrs, US$3.50. *Colectivos* in Samaipata will pick you up from your hotel, or else take you from the petrol station. Buses and *micros* leaving Santa Cruz for **Sucre** pass through **Samaipata** between 1800 and 2000; tickets can be booked with 2 days' notice through **Roadrunners**. Early morning transport from Samaipata to Santa Cruz: **Montenegro** from *Heladería Dany* on the plaza (buy tickets here the day before), Mon-Sat 0430, Sun 1500, 3 hrs, US$2; mini-bus from Mairana passes through Samaipata daily at 0445 near *Residencial Kim*, ask for details in

advance; **Picaflor** from Samaipata plaza at 0600 daily. You can get to **Samaipata** by bus from Sucre; these leave at night and arrive soon after dawn, stopping in Mairana or Mataral for breakfast, about ½ hr before Samaipata.

Vallegrande and La Higuera *p327*
Bus Trans Vallegrande and others from Av Grigota, 3o Anillo, daily buses at 0900, 1400, 1930 from Santa Cruz to **Vallegrande** via **Samaipata**, 5 hrs, US$4.30. Best to book in advance. From Vallegrande market, a daily bus departs 0800 to **Pucara** (45 km), from where there is transport (12 km) to **La Higuera**. Taxi Vallegrande-La Higuera US$25-30.

Parque Nacional Amboró *p327*
Bus Leave regularly from beside Santa Cruz terminal hourly from 0500-1500 (also minibuses from Montero, US$1, and buses from Villa Tunari, US$5) to **Buena Vista**. See p 328 for how to get to **Mairana** and **La Yunga**.

Villamontes *p328*
Air TAM flies to **La Paz**, **Sucre** and **Tarija** on Sun and **Santa Cruz** on Sat.
Bus To **Tarija** via Entre Ríos (unpaved road, 10 hrs) daily 1800, US$7.50. To **Santa Cruz** at 1030, 12 hrs, US$4.50, **Sucre** at 1930, US$7.50, and **La Paz** at

2000, US$9. Also to **Camiri**, **Tupiza**, **Villazón**.
Train The **Santa Cruz-Yacuiba** trains stop here: Tren Mixto on Tue, Thu, Sat at 0400, returning to **Santa Cruz** on Tue, Thu and Sat at 1930, and the Ferrobus on Mon and Fri.

To Argentina: Yacuiba *p329*
Bus Good connections in all directions. To **Santa Cruz**, about 20 companies run daily services, mostly at night, 14 hrs, US$13. To **Tarija**, daily morning and evening. To **Potosí-Oruro-La Paz**, with Trans Yacuiba and Expreso Tarija. Daily to **Sucre** with Flota Copacabana.
Train Santa Cruz-Yacuiba trains: Ferrobus Sur on Thu, Sun 1800, 11 hrs, *cama* US$16.10, *semi-cama* US$14.30; return to Santa Cruz Mon, Fri 1800. Tren Mixto Mon, Wed, Fri 1700, 15½ hrs, returning from Yacuiba Tue, Thu, Sat, 1700, Pullman US$12, 1st class US$5.55, 2nd class US$4.40.

❶ Directory

Samaipata *p327*
Banks No ATMs. The Cooperativa near plaza changes US$ cash at fair rates. **Internet** At Entel on the plaza and Andoriña (see Sleeping), both slow and expensive, US$1.50-2 per hr.
Telephone Several cabinas around the plaza.

Eastern Bolivia

The vast and rapidly-developing plains to the east of the Eastern Cordillera are Bolivia's richest area in natural resources. For the visitor, the beautiful churches of former Jesuit Chiquitano missions east of Santa Cruz are worth a visit and further east is Bolivia's portion of the Pantanal. The Noel Kempff Mercado national park, meanwhile, is one of the natural wonders of South America.

Chiquitano Jesuit Missions

Six Jesuit churches survive east of Santa Cruz: San Javier, Concepción, Santa Ana, San Rafael, San Miguel and San José de Chiquitos. All are UNESCO World Heritage Sites. The first four were built by the Swiss Jesuit, Padre Martin Schmidt, the other two (plus the one at San Ignacio de Velasco, demolished in 1948, see below) were built by other priests. Besides organizing *reducciones* and constructing churches, for each of which he built an organ, Padre Schmidt wrote music (some is still played today on traditional instruments) and he published a Spanish-Idioma Chiquitano dictionary based on his knowledge of all the dialects of the region. He worked in this part of the then-Viceroyalty of Peru until the expulsion of the Jesuits in 1767 by order of Charles III of Spain.

Access to the mission area is by bus or train from **Santa Cruz**: a paved highway runs north to San Ramón (139 km) and on north, to San Javier (45 km), turning east here to Concepción (68 km) and San Ignacio (unpaved). One road continues east to San Matías and the Brazilian border (good gravel); others head south either through San Miguel, or Santa Ana to meet at San Rafael for the continuation south to San José de Chiquitos. By rail, leave the Santa Cruz-Quijarro train at San José and from there travel north. The most comfortable way to visit is by jeep, in four days. The route is straightforward and fuel is available. For jeep hire, see page 330. For information on the Chiquitano area, visit www.fcbcinfo.org, the site (in Spanish and English) of the **Fundación para la Conservación del Bosque Chiquitano** ① *C Fortín Platanillos 190, Santa Cruz, T/F03-334 1017*. See also **www.chiquitania.com** for historical and practical information.

San Javier The first Jesuit mission in Chiquitos (1691), its church built by Padre Schmidt between 1749 and 1752. The original wooden structure has survived more or less intact and restoration was undertaken between 1987 and 1993 by the Swiss Hans Roth. Subtle designs and floral patterns cover the ceiling, walls and carved columns. One of the bas-relief paintings on the high altar depicts Martin Schmidt playing the piano for his indigenous choir. The modern town prospers from extensive cattle ranching. Many fine walks in the surrounding countryside; also good for cycling with an all-terrain bike. Local *fiesta*, 3 December.

Concepción The village is dominated by its magnificent cathedral, completed by Padre Schmidt in 1756 and totally restored by the late Hans Roth 1975-1982. The interior of this beautiful church has an altar of laminated silver. In front of the church is a bell-cum-clock tower housing the original bells and behind it are well-restored cloisters. On the beautiful plaza is the **Museo Misional**① *Mon-Sat 0830-1200, 1400-1730, Sun 1000-1200, US$0.50*, and there is a new **Hans Roth Museum**, dedicated to the restoration process. There is a tourist office, which can arrange trips to nearby ranches and communities. Various restaurants in town.

San Ignacio de Velasco A lack of funds for restoration led to the demolition of San Ignacio's Jesuit church in 1948. A modern replacement contains the elaborate high altar, pulpit and paintings and statues of saints. A museum in the Casa de la Cultura on the plaza has a few musical instruments from the old church. Laguna Guapomó on the outskirts of town is good for swimming, boating and fishing. *Entel* two blocks from plaza.

Santa Ana, San Rafael and San Miguel The church in **Santa Ana** (founded 1755, constructed after the expulsion of the Jesuits), is a lovely wooden building, currently being restored. Sr Luis Rocha will show you inside; ask for his house at the shop on the plaza where the bus stops. Two *alojamientos* in town and meals at Sra Silva's *Pensión El Tacú*, next to church. **San Rafael**'s church was completed by Padre Schmidt in 1748. It is the most authentic (still retaining its original thatched roof), and one of the most beautifully restored (Concepción's also vying for this title), with frescoes in beige paint over the exterior (*Hotel Paradita*, **F**, and two restaurants on plaza). The frescoes on the façade of the church (1766) at **San Miguel** depict St Peter and St Paul; designs in brown and yellow cover all the interior and the exterior side walls. The mission runs three schools and workshop; the sisters are very welcoming and will gladly show tourists around. Some 4 km away is the **Santuario de Cotoca**, beside a lake where you can swim; ask at *La Pascana* for transport. (*Alojamiento y Restaurant La Pascana*, on plaza, basic, cheap meals; just up the hill are two other *alojamientos* and *Entel*.) Most traffic from San Ignacio goes via San Miguel, not Santa Ana, to San Rafael. If visiting these places from San Ignacio, it's probably better to go to San Rafael first, then go back via San Miguel. A day trip by taxi from San Ignacio to these villages costs US$35-40 (negotiate).

San José de Chiquitos → *Phone code: 03. Colour map 6, grid B5.*

One complete side of the plaza of this dusty little town is occupied by the superb frontage of the Jesuit mission, begun in the mid-1740s. The stone buildings, in Baroque style, are connected by a wall. They are the restored chapel (1750); the church, unfinished at the expulsion of the Jesuits, with a triangular façade and side walls standing (restoration work in progress); the four-storey bell-tower (1748); the mortuary (*la bóveda* – 1754), with one central window but no entrance in its severe frontage. Behind is a long colonnaded hall. There is an *Entel* office and a hospital. On Monday, Mennonites bring their produce to sell to shops and to buy provisions. The colonies are 50 km west and the Mennonites, who speak English, German, plattdeutsch and Spanish, are happy to talk about their way of life.

About 2 km south from San José is the **Parque Nacional Histórico Santa Cruz la Vieja** ① *daily US$2, pool US$0.75*. This includes a monument to the original site of Santa Cruz (about 1540), a *mirador* giving views over the jungle and, 5 km into the park, a religious shrine. The park's heavily-forested hills contain much animal and bird life; various trails with grand views; guides available from the small village in the park (take insect repellent). It gets very hot so start early and take plenty of water. About 2 km past the entrance, at the end of the road at the foot of high hills, is a large swimming pool fed by a mountain stream, often dirty and short of water. The park and pool are best visited by car or taxi because it is a very hot, dusty walk there (allow over one hour on foot).

Parque Nacional Noel Kempff Mercado

In the far northeast corner of Santa Cruz Department, **Parque Nacional Noel Kempff Mercado** (named after a pioneer of conservation in Bolivia) *US$8*, is one of the world's most diverse natural habitats. It covers 1,583,809 ha (roughly the same size as Massachusetts) and encompasses seven ecosystems, within which are at least 130 species of mammals (including black jaguars), 620 species of birds (including nine types of macaw), 70 species of reptiles and 110 species of orchid. Highlights include the **Huanchaca** or **Caparú Plateau**, which with its 200-500 m sheer cliffs and tumbling waterfalls is another candidate for Sir Arthur Conan Doyle's *Lost World* (Colonel Percy Fawcett, who discovered the plateau in 1910, was a friend of the writer). The three best-known waterfalls are Arco Iris, Federico Ahlfeld on the Río Paucerna and the 150-m high Catarata del Encanto. The **Reserva Biológica Laguna Bahía**, in the southwest quadrant, has some tremendous hiking across the high plateau, through breathtaking scenery. For information on the park, contact the **Fundación de Amigos de la Naturaleza** ① *FAN, Km 7 Carretera Antigua a Cochabamba, Santa Cruz, T03-355 6800, ask for Richard Vaca, www.fan-bo.org*, which manages the park. Also visit www.noelkempff.com (Proyecto de Acción Climática).

To Brazil

There are three routes from Santa Cruz: by air to Puerto Suárez, by rail to Quijarro, or by road via San Matías. Puerto Suárez is near Quijarro and these two routes lead to Corumbá on the Brazilian side, from where there is access to the southern Pantanal. The San Matías road links to Cáceres, Cuiabá and the northern Pantanal in Brazil.

Puerto Suárez → *Phone code: 03. Colour map 6, grid B6. Population: 21,000.*

On the shore of Laguna Cáceres, this is a friendly, quiet, small town, with a shady main plaza. There is a nice view of the lake from the park at the north end of Avenida Bolívar. The area around the train station is known as *Paradero*. Do not venture into the market area unless you are looking to contract any one of innumerable intestinal illnesses, and/or have your pockets picked. Fishing and photo tours to the ecologically-astonishing Pantanal can be arranged more cheaply than on the Brazilian side. You can also arrange river tours and day trips to Brazil; these are generally most easily done through a hotel, although they will add a 10-15% service charge (see below). For information on the province, see www.gbusch.info.

Quijarro → *Phone code: 03. Colour map 6, grid B6. Population: 15,000.*

The eastern terminus of the Bolivian railway, and the gateway to Brazil, is Quijarro, a growing town with a new railway station (in 2005). It is quite safe by day, but caution is recommended at night. The water supply is often unreliable, try the tap before checking in to a hotel. Prices are much lower than in neighbouring Brazil and there are some decent places to stay.

Border with Brazil

The municipality by the border is known as Arroyo Concepción. You need not have your passport stamped if you visit Corumbá for the day. Otherwise get your exit stamp at Bolivian immigration (see below), formalities are straightforward. There are no formalities on the Brazilian side, you must get your entry stamp in the Corumbá bus station/*rodoviária* (see page 588). Yellow Fever vaccination is compulsory to enter Bolivia and Brazil, have your certificate at hand when you go for your entry stamp, otherwise you may be sent to get revaccinated. Bolivian immigration is at the border at Arroyo Concepción, on right just before bridge (open 0800-1200, 1400-1730 daily), or at Puerto Suárez airport, where Bolivian exit/entry stamps are issued. Money changers right at the border offer the worst rates. Ask around in the small shops past the bridge and check the rate with several of them before changing. The Brazilian consulate is in Santa Cruz, or in Puerto Suárez. See Transport, below, for taxis from the border.

Via San Matías to Cáceres

The road route from Santa Cruz is via San Ignacio de Velasco to San Matías, a busy little town with hotels and restaurants then on to Cáceres and Cuiabá. From Santa Cruz it is a three-day trip, roads permitting. See under San Ignacio, page , for bus information. Get your passport stamped in San Ignacio as there is no passport control in San Matías, but plenty of military checks en route. Once in Brazil go to immigration in Cáceres or, on Sun, to Polícia Federal in Cuiabá.

● Sleeping

Chiquitano Jesuit Missions *p332*
San Javier
Also several hotels in **F-G** range in town.
C Momoqui, Av Santa Cruz before plaza, T963 5095, hotelmomoqui@hotmail.com. Cabins in nice garden, with pool, pleasant, no restaurant.
C Gran Hotel El Reposo del Guerrero, T963 5022. Cheaper Mon-Fri and with shared bath, includes breakfast, comfortable, restaurant, bar.
E-F Alojamiento Ame-Tauna, on plaza opposite church, T963 5018. Cheaper with shared bath, hot showers, clean.

Concepción
B Gran Hotel Concepción, on plaza, T964 3031, granhotelconcepcion@ hotmail.com. Excellent service, including buffet breakfast, pool, gardens, bar, very comfortable. Highly recommended.
B pp Estancia La Pailita, 7 km north of Concepción (15 mins by taxi), karin_meyer 1960@yahoo.de. Full board, Swiss-owned, German, French and English spoken, 2 guest rooms with solar power, Swiss, local and vegetarian food, activities include riding, swimming, nature treks, working on the farm.
C Apart Hotel Los Misiones, 1 block from church, T964 3021. Pleasant rooms around a courtyard, small pool, also has an apartment, good value.
D-F Colonial, ½ block from plaza, T964 3050. Good value, with hot shower, garden, hammocks on veranda, breakfast extra.
F Residencial Westfalia, 2 blocks from plaza, T964 3040. Cheaper without bath, German-owned, nice patio, good value.

San Ignacio de Velasco
AL La Misión, Plaza 31 de Julio, T962 2333, hotel-lamision@unete.com. Luxurious, colonial style with a/c, cable TV and pool, rooms of various standards and prices, includes buffet breakfast, tours arranged.
E Casa Suiza, at the end of C Sucre, 5 blocks west of plaza (taxi US$0.75). Small guesthouse run by Horst and Cristina, German and French spoken, full board, excellent food, very comfortable, family atmosphere, hires horses. Highly recommended.
E Palace, on the plaza. With hot shower, includes breakfast, comfortable, good value. Other hotels (**C-F**) and places to eat near plaza.

San José de Chiquitos *p332*
D Alojamiento San Miguel, Velasco entre Géricke y 25 de Mayo. With fan, not the friendliest place.
D Turubó, on the plaza, T972 2037. With a/c, **E** with fan, cheaper with shared bath, variety of different rooms, good location, laundry service.

E Hotel Denisse, Mons Géricke, 4 blocks east of plaza, T972 2230. With bath, a/c, cheaper with fan, nice patio, clean and comfortable, good value.

Parque Nacional Noel Kempff Mercado *p333*
There are 2 lodges in the park: 15 beds at a renovated ranch at Flor de Oro, with access to hikes in the pampas and forests, and river excursions to the Arco Iris and Federico Ahlfeld falls and to bays. At Los Fierros there are 30 beds at a more rustic facility, **B** pp including 3 meals. From here you can visit many different habitats and El Encanto falls. There are other lodging possibilities in small towns bordering the park and some camping is available. In all cases, contact *FAN* (Fundación Amigos de la Naturaleza – see above).

Puerto Suárez *p333*
AL pp Centro Ecológico El Tumbador, T03- 762 8699, T7106 7712 (mob), eltumbador@yahoo.com. A non-profit- making organization working for sustainable development in the Bolivian Lowlands runs ½-day to 4-day river, trekking and 4WD tours from its research station and lodge on the lake; prices from US$82 per person all-inclusive.
C Bamby, Santa Cruz 31 y 6 de Agosto, T976 2015. A/c, **D** with fan, cheaper with shared bath, comfortable.
C-D Sucre, Bolívar 63 on main plaza, T976 2069. A/c, with bath, pleasant, good restaurant.
D Beby, Av Bolívar 111, T976 2270. A/c, **E** with shared bath and fan.
D Ejecutivo, at south end of Bolívar, T976 2267. A/c, parking, cheaper with fan.
D Roboré, 6 de Agosto 78, T976 2170. Fan, **E** with shared bath, basic, restaurant next door.

Quijarro *p333*
B-C Bibosi, Luis Salazar s/n, main street 3 blocks east of train station, T978 2044, htlbibosi@ hotmail.com. With a/c, **D** with fan, breakfast, pool, patio, restaurant, comfortable rooms with fridge, upscale for where it is.
D Oasis, Av Argentina 20, T978 2159. A/c, fridge, cheaper with shared bath and a/c, **E** with fan, OK.
D San Silvestre, Av Naval s/n, side street 3 blocks east of train station, T978 2088. With a/c, **E** with fan, simple breakfast, rooms are hot but away from noise and dust of the main street.
D Yoni, Av Brazil opposite the station, T978 2109. A/c, fridge, **E** with shared bath and fan, OK, mosquito netting on windows.

Border with Brazil *p333*
L El Pantanal Resort, Arroyo Concepción, T978 2020, www.elpantanalhotel.com. With all mod

cons (poor internet connection), gateway to the Pantanal. They arrange cruises, tours and transport, expensive but worth it, discounts in dry season (very busy in Jan-Feb).

🍴 Eating

Chiquitano Jesuit Missions *p332*
🍴 **Ganadero**, San Javier, in Asociación de Ganaderos on plaza. Best restaurant in town with excellent steaks. Others on plaza.

San José de Chiquitos *p332*
🍴 **Caseta de las Vivanderas**, just outside train station. Open 2100-2400 (after train arrives), serves all typical favourites. Recommended.
🍴 **El Raffa**, between *la tranca* and petrol station on outskirts of town is highly recommended for *churrasco típico*.
🍴 **El Solar**, on plaza. Hamburgers, milanesa, and salchipapa.
🍴 **Plaza America**, by main plaza. Set meals and à la carte, lunch only.
🍴 **Romanazzi Pizzería**, Géricke. Run by elderly Italian-Bolivian who makes her own pizzas entirely from scratch. Visit at least 2 hrs before wishing to dine and describe what you'd like, very much worth the wait.

Puerto Suárez *p333*
🍴 **Al Paso**, Bolívar 43, near Plaza, opposite *Parillada Jenecherú*. Very good value set meals and à la carte, popular.
🍴 Several small inexpensive restaurants on Bolívar 100 block, eg **El Taxista**.

Quijarro *p333*
🍴 Restaurant at **Hotel Bibosi** is the only better option, otherwise check the basic eateries along the main street but keep an eye on cleanliness. Avoid the food stalls in the street and market.

⛰ Activities and tours

Puerto Suárez *p333*
R B Travel, Bolívar 65 by Plaza, T976 2014, for airline tickets, helpful.

🚌 Transport

Chiquitano Jesuit Missions *p332*
San Javier
Línea 31 del Este micros from Santa Cruz, 4 hrs, US$3.50, several between 0800 and 1730; a few **buses** from the Terminal Bimodal, or from S Arana y Barron. To **Concepción** at 1130, 1830, 1½ hrs, US$1.50.

Concepción
Bus Many buses between Santa Cruz and San Ignacio pass through about midnight, but drop you at the gas station on the main road, several blocks from plaza; ask around for transport to centre. **Misiones del Oriente**, on the plaza to Santa Cruz and San Ignacio, **31 del Este micros**, 1 block from plaza, to **Santa Cruz** (US$4.50), and **Flota Jenecheru**, 2 blocks from plaza, buses to **Santa Cruz** and **San Ignacio** (3½ hrs, US$2.80).

San Ignacio de Velasco
Bus Bus companies are based around the market. From **Santa Cruz**, Flota Chiquitana, from new terminal 1900 daily, 10 hrs, US$6.70; also **Expreso Misiones del Oriente** daily at 1930, T337 8782. From **San Ignacio**: Flota Chiquitano and **Trans Velasco** at 1900; **Trans Joá** at 2030 (office on plaza). These companies and several others go to **San Matías** for Brazil (see below), 7 hrs, US$7.50. Some continue to **Cáceres**, 1 hr from San Matías on a paved road. To **San José de Chiquitos**, Transical B, Mon, Wed, Fri, Sat 1430, **Trans Bolivia**, Tue, Thu, Sun at 0700, US$4.25, 4½ hrs. Micros to **Santa Ana**, **San Rafael** and **San Miguel** from market area; also Transical B bus, 5 a day to **San Miguel**, 1 hr, US$1.40, and **Trans Bolivia** to **San Rafael** 0700, 1430, 1½-2 hrs, US$1.40.

San José de Chiquitos *p332*
Bus To **San Ignacio**, Transical B and Trans Bolivia, as above, each goes every day. Both go via **San Rafael** and **San Miguel**. Leave at 0700 and 1200; US$3. Overnight bus to **Santa Cruz**, dry season only (May-Oct), US$6 one way. Don't try to drive the unpaved road on this route to Brazil without 4WD, the sandy surface is hell for small cars.
Train Schedule from **Santa Cruz** as for Quijarro (see below), 8 hrs to San José, standard: Pullman US$6, 1st class US$3.15; luxury: *cama* US$24.80, *semi-cama* US$20. To **Quijarro** daily except Sun at 2130; Pullman US$13.15, 1st class US$4.20. **Ferrobus** Sun, Tue, Thu at 2340; *cama* US$21.35, *semi-cama* US$18.20. It is possible to reserve seats on either service at the train station up to a week in advance. Trains to San José are usually delayed by an hour or 2. Always reconfirm.

Parque Nacional Noel Kempff Mercado *p333*
Air A paved road runs north from San Ignacio de Velasco to La Florida on the park's southwest edge; a bus runs this route. Access by plane from Santa Cruz is to **Flor de Oro**, in the north/central sector, or to **Los Fierros**, the park's official headquarters, in the south. Flights also go to smaller places, but are irregular. All flights should be arranged through **FAN**. The road journey is long and arduous, eg 13-18 hrs by 4WD to Los

Fierros from Santa Cruz, via Concepción and La Florida (40 km west of Los Fierros).

Bus 2 weekly buses run from San Ignacio de Velasco to **Piso Firme** on the park's western edge (24 hrs, US$9), from where boats can be chartered to Flor de Oro, 5-9 hrs, US$250. Journey times depend on the season, state of the roads and river conditions. Tours can be arranged with operators in La Paz, Santa Cruz and San Ignacio de Velasco. Prices for a 7-day/6-night tour range from US$915-1170, not including flights (**América Tours**, La Paz). Shorter tours are available.

Puerto Suárez *p333*

Air The simplest way to Brazil is to fly to **Puerto Suárez**, then share a taxi to the border. The airport is 6 km north of town, T976 2347; airport tax US$2. Flights on Mon and Fri to/from Santa Cruz with **Aero Sur**. Don't buy tickets for flights originating in Puerto Suárez in Corumbá, these cost more.
Taxi To **Paradero** US$1.65; to airport US$2; to **Quijarro** or the border, US$5 (day), US$6 (night) or US$0.80 pp in a colectivo.
Train The station for Puerto Suárez is about 3 km from town. It is the 1st station west of Quijarro.

Quijarro *p333*

Taxi To the border (**Arroyo Concepción**) US$0.40 pp; to **Puerto Suárez** US$0.65 pp, more at night.

If arriving from Brazil, you will be approached by Bolivian taxi drivers who offer to hold your luggage while you clear immigration. These are the most expensive cabs (US$5 to Quijarro, US$15 to Puerto Suárez) and best avoided. Instead, keep your gear with you while your passport is stamped, then walk 200 m past the bridge to a commercial area where other taxis wait (US$0.40 to Quijarro, US$0.65 to Puerto Suárez).
Train There is no direct service between Santa Cruz and Brazil. All trains from Santa Cruz go via San José de Chiquitos to Quijarro, from where travellers must go by *colectivo* to the border post (beware overcharging, fare should be US$0.40 pp), then by bus to Corumbá. **Tren del Este**, 20 hrs stopping at all intermediate stations, Mon-Sat 1315 (returns at 1145), *Super Pullman* US$14.50, *Primera* US$6.50. **Expreso Oriental** 15 hrs stopping at San José de Chiquitos, Roboré, and Puerto Suárez on Mon, Wed, Fri 1700, returning Tue, Thu, Sun 1630, same fares as Tren del Este. A **Ferrobus** runs Tue, Thu, Sun at 1900, returning Mon, Wed, Fri 1900, same stops as Expreso Oriental, 12½ hrs, US$25 *semi-cama*, US$30 *cama* (not as luxurious as it claims). Take food, drinking water, insect repellent and a torch, whichever class you are travelling. From Mar-Aug take a sleeping bag for the cold; be prepared for delays. There is a

computerized reservation system and tickets may be purchased several days in advance. Ticket office on ground floor of Quijarro station is open Mon-Sat 0730-1200, 1430-1800, Sun 0730-1100. There may be queues of 1-2 hrs; purchase tickets directly at the train station and avoid all touts, middlemen and agencies. Passport or some form of ID required to buy tickets but entry/exit stamps are not checked. At Quijarro station, **Willy Solís Cruz**, Roboré 22, T978 2204, wiland_54@ hotmail.com, runs a left-luggage room, speaks English, very helpful, assists with ticket purchases, has laundry and cooking facilities (has been known to let people sleep in the luggage room). Note that times of departure from Quijarro are approximate as they depend on when trains arrive. 500 m from station is a modern, duty-free a/c shopping complex with banks, restaurants and pool.

Small **bus** terminal 3 blocks from the train station. To **Santa Cruz** Mon-Sat 1400, 1700, Sun 1200, minimum 24 hrs, US$10. This is an arduous journey and can take several days in the rainy season; the road is poor, buses run-down, and breakdowns frequent.

⬤ Directory

Chiquitano Jesuit Missions *p332*
San Ignacio de Velasco **Banks** Prodem, Velasco esq Sucre, T962 2099. Cash advances on Visa and MasterCard, 5% commission, also changes US$ cash.

San José de Chiquitos *p332*
Banks No ATMs, nowhere to change TCs. Banco Unión on main plaza, US$ cash only, fair rates. **Telephone and internet** Several *cabinas* around the plaza. No internet.

Puerto Suárez *p333*
Airline offices Aero Sur, Bolívar 43, T976 2110. TAM, C del Chaco s/n, T976 2205. **Banks** Supermercado Tocale changes Bolivianos, reais and US$, cash only. **Embassies and consulates** Brazilian Consulate, Av Raúl Otero Reich y C Suárez Abego, T976 2040, vcbrasil@entelnet.bo.

Quijarro *p333*
Banks Bolivianos, reais and US$ cash traded along Av Brazil opposite the station by changers with large purses sitting in lawn chairs; beware of tricks. No ATMs; nowhere to change TCs.
Telephone and internet Several phone and internet places along the main street opposite the train station..

Brazil

✷ Footprint features

Introduction

Described as the sexiest nation on earth, Brazilians know how to flirt, flaunt and have fun. The Rio Carnival, with its intoxicating atmosphere and costumes to die for, is the most exuberant of a whole calendar of festivals. In this, the world's fifth largest country, football, looking good and dancing are the national passions. Everyone seems to be seduced by the sounds of samba... and by the beach.

The coast of Brazil, all 7,408 km of it, has provided a suitable stretch of sand for every volleyball champion, surfer, dune-buggy driver and party animal. Just off shore there are many islands to sail to, from the huge Marajó with its water buffalo, to highly developed Santa Catarina, to the marine paradise of Abrolhos National Park.

But Brazilians also have a spiritual side to match their hedonistic streak. Many religions flourish, most obviously the African-based candomblé, which lives happily alongside Catholicism. In the 16th to 18th centuries, when Brazil was rich in gold and diamonds, the Portuguese colonists expressed their faith in some of the most beautiful baroque buildings created anywhere at that time.

For a change from cosmopolitan life, trek through the hills of the Chapada Diamantina, take the long road into the Pantanal wetlands and watch for hyacinth macaws and capybara, sling a hammock on a river boat up the mighty Amazon, or take a walk with the wildlife in the rainforest.

★ Don't miss...

1 **Rio de Janeiro** One of the quintessential images of South America is Rio's setting of beaches, mountains and islands in the bay. Another is its carnival. And don't forget the football, or the nightlife...where do you stop? Page 348.

2 **Ouro Preto** In the heart of Minas Gerais is the capital of Brazilian baroque, built on the wealth of precious metals, and birthplace of the rebellion against colonial rule, page 417.

3 **Bahia** The city of Salvador is Africa in Brazil, with a culture that has survived the slave trade in religion, music and cuisine. There's also a fine colonial heritage and some great beaches, page 462.

4 **Northeastern beaches** The states of Ceará and Rio Grande do Norte have beaches to die for: clear waters, golden sands and brightly-coloured cliffs. There are dunes made for buggies, party towns and quiet hideaways, page 491.

5 **The Amazon** Over half of Brazilian national territory is the Amazon Basin (which spreads beyond the country's borders). Travel between the few centres of population is by riverboat and the jungle provides fabulous wildlife viewing opportunities, page 534.

6 **Pantanal** This vast wetland is one the world's greatest wildlife preserves. Rivers criss-cross the plains where giant storks, giant guinea-pigs (*capybara*), giant fish and much else of a more regular size live alongside great herds of cattle, page 579.

Brazil

Essentials

Planning your trip

Where to go **Rio de Janeiro** was for a long time *the* image of Brazil, with its beautiful setting – the Sugar Loaf and Corcovado overlooking the bay and beaches, its world renowned carnival, the nightlife and its *favelas* (slums – which are now being incorporated into tourism). It is still a must on many itineraries, but Rio de Janeiro state has plenty of other beaches, national parks and colonial towns (especially **Paraty**) and the imperial city of Petrópolis. **São Paulo** is the country's industrial and financial powerhouse; with some fine museums and its cultural life and restaurants are very good. All the São Paulo coast is worth visiting and inland there are hill resorts and colonial towns. The **state of Minas Gerais** contains some of the best colonial architecture in South America in cities such as Ouro Preto, Mariana, São João del Rei and Diamantina. All are within easy reach of the state capital, Belo Horizonte. Other options in Minas include national parks with good hill scenery and bird-watching and hydrothermal resorts.

The atmosphere of the South is dominated by its German and Italian immigrants. The three states, Paraná, Santa Catarina and Rio Grande do Sul have their coastal resorts, especially near Florianópolis, capital of Santa Catarina. **Rio Grande do Sul** is the land of Brazil's *gaúchos* (cowboys) and of its vineyards, but the main focus of the region is the magnificent **Iguaçu Falls** in the far west of Paraná, on the borders of Argentina and Paraguay.

The Northeast is famous for beaches and colonial history. Combining both these elements, with the addition of Brazil's liveliest African culture, is **Salvador de Bahia**, one of the country's most famous cities and a premier tourist destination. Huge sums of money have been lavished on the restoration of its colonial centre and its carnival is something special. Inland, Bahia is mostly arid sertão, in which a popular town is **Lençóis**, a historical monument with a nearby national park. The highlight of the southern coast of Bahia is the beach and party zone around **Porto Seguro**, while in the north the beaches stretch up to the states of Sergipe and Alagoas and on into Pernambuco. **Recife**, capital of Pernambuco, and its neighbour, the colonial capital **Olinda**; also mix the sea, history and culture, while inland is the major handicraft centre of Caruaru. Travelling around to the north-facing coast, there are hundreds of beaches to choose from, some highly developed, others less so. You can swim, surf or ride the dunes in buggies. Last stop before the mouth of the Amazon is **São Luís**, in whose centre most of the old houses are covered in colonial tiles.

Through the North flows the **Amazon**, along which river boats ply between the cities of Belém, Santarém and Manaus. From **Manaus** particularly there are opportunities for exploring the jungle on adventurous expeditions or staying in lodges. North of Manaus is the overland route through Boa Vista to Venezuela. The forest stretches south to the central tableland which falls to the Pantanal in the far west. This seasonal wetland, the highlight of the Centre West, is one of the prime areas for seeing bird and animal life in the continent. At the eastern end of the Centre West is **Brasília**, built in the 1960s and now a World Heritage Site in recognition of its superb examples of modern architecture. Also in this region is one of the largest river islands in the world (Bananal – a mecca for fishing) and the delightful hill and river landscapes of **Bonito** in Mato Grosso do Sul.

When to go   Brazil is a tropical country, but the further south you go the more temperate the winters become and there are places in the coastal mountains which have gained a reputation for their cool climate and low humidity. The heaviest rains fall at different times in different regions: November to March in the southeast, December to March in the centre west and April to August on the northeast coast around Pernambuco (irregular rainfall causes severe draughts). The rainy season in the north and Amazônia can begin in December and is heaviest March to May, but it is getting steadily shorter, possibly as a result of deforestation. It is only in rare cases that the rainfall can be described as either excessive or deficient. Few places get more than 2,000 mm: the coast north of Belém, some of the Amazon Basin, and a small area of the Serra do Mar between Santos and São Paulo, where the downpour has been harnessed to generate electricity.

May to September is usually referred to as winter, but this is not to suggest that this is a bad time to visit. On the contrary, April to June and August to October are recommended times to go to most parts of the country. One major consideration is that carnival falls within the hottest, wettest time of year (in February), so if you are incorporating carnival into a longer

Touching down

Airport tax The amount of tax depends on the class of airport. All airports charge US$36 for international departure tax. In some circumstances, this tax is collected when you buy your flight tickets (eg in the UK), but you must check if this is the case. If it has not been collected you will have to pay on leaving Brazil. First class airports charge R$9.50 domestic tax; second class airports R$7; domestic rates are lower still in third and fourth class airports. Tax must be paid on checking in, in reais or US dollars. Tax is waived if you stay in Brazil less than 24 hours.

Business hours 0900-1800 Monday-Friday for most businesses, which close for lunch some time between 1130 and 1400. **Shops**: open on Saturday till 1230 or 1300. **Government offices**: 1100-1800 Monday-Friday. **Banks**: 1000-1600, but closed on Saturday.

In an emergency Ambulance T192. Directory enquiries T102. Police T190.

International phone code +55 Ringing: equal tones with long pauses. Engaged: equal tones, equal pauses.

Official time Brazilian standard time is GMT -3; of the major cities, only the Amazon time zone, Manaus, Cuiabá, Campo Grande and Corumbá are different (GMT -5). The state of Acre is GMT -4. Clocks go forward one hour in summer for approximately five months (usually between October and February or March). (This does not apply to Acre.)

Tipping Tipping is usual, but less costly than in most other countries, except for porters. Restaurants, 10% of bill if no service charge but small tip if there is; taxi drivers, none; cloakroom attendants, small tip; cinema usherettes, none; hairdressers, 10-15%; porters, fixed charges but tips as well; airport porters, about US$0.65 per item.

VAT Rate varies from 7 to 25% at state and federal level; average 17-20%.

Voltage Varies, see individual town directories. Sockets also vary, often combination sockets for twin flat and twin round pin.

Weights and measures Metric.

holiday, it may be wet wherever you go. Also bear in mind that mid-December to February is the national holiday season, which means that hotels, planes and buses may be full and many establishments away from the holiday areas may be shut.

The average annual temperature increases steadily from south to north, but even on the Equator, in the Amazon Basin, the average temperature is not more than 27°C. The highest recorded was 42°C, in the dry northeastern states. From the latitude of Recife south to Rio, the mean temperature is from 23° to 27°C along the coast, and from 18° to 21°C in the Highlands. From a few degrees south of Rio to the boundary with Uruguay the mean temperature is from 17° to 19°C. Humidity is relatively high in Brazil, particularly along the coast.

Finding out more Tourism is in the hands of the **Ministério do Turismo** ① *Esplanada dos Ministérios, Bloco U, 2nd and 3rd floors, Brasília, www.turismo.gov.br (in many languages)*. For information abroad, contact Brazil's representation overseas: France, T+33-1-5353 6962; Germany, T+49-69-9750 3251; Italy, T+39-2-8633 7791; Japan, T+81-8-5565 7591; Portugal, T+351-21-340 4668; Spain, T+34-91-503 0687, UK, T+44-207-7396 5551, USA, T+1-646-756 2590. Tourist information bureaux are not usually helpful with information on cheap hotels and it is difficult to get information on neighbouring states. The expensive hotels provide tourist information magazines for their guests. Telephone directories (not Rio) contain good street maps.

National parks are run by **Ibama**, the **Instituto Brasileiro do Meio Ambiente e dos Recursos Naturais Renováveis** (Brazilian Institute of Environmental Protection): ① *SCEN Trecho 2, Av L-4 Norte, Edif Sede de Ibama, CEP 70818-900, Brasília, DF, Toxx61-3226 5094, www.ibama.gov.br*. The Institute is underfunded, understaffed and visitors may find it difficult to get information. National parks are open to visitors, usually with a permit from Ibama. See also the Ministério do Meio Ambiente website, www.mma.gov.br. For further details, see individual parks.

Useful websites

See also the Tourist office sites under individual cities in the text.

www.ipanema.com Insider's guide to Rio In English.

www.copacabana.com On Copacabana in Portuguese.

www.maria-brazil.org A fun site with info, tips, recommendations, mostly about Rio, but other regions, too.

The following embassy sites have lots of information: **www.brasilemb.org** (USA); **www.brazil.org.uk** (UK).

www.atbrazil.com Hotels and resorts guide, currency converter and general info.

www.brazilmax.com Bill Hinchberger's "Hip Gringo's Guide" to Brazil with loads of news, cultural articles and travel information and a strong ecological angle.

www.brazilianmusic.com Introductions to musical styles and musicians, and more.

www.vivabrazil.com A 'virtual trip', with news, history, chat.

www.wwf.org.br The World Wide Fund for nature in Brazil.

www.cartacapital.com.br Independent news magazine (Portuguese).

Maps and guides Editora Abril publishes *Quatro Rodas*, a motoring magazine, as well as excellent maps and guides in Portuguese and English from US$15. Its *Guia Brasil* is a type of Michelin Guide to hotels, restaurants (not the cheapest), sights, facilities and general information on hundreds of cities and towns in the country, including good street maps (we acknowledge here our debt to this publication). It also publishes an excellent guide to São Paulo, Sampa (in Portuguese), a guide to cheap travel, *Viajar Bem e Barato* and a *Guia das Praias*, with descriptions of all Brazil's beaches. All are available at news stands and bookshops all over the country. For information about the *Quatro Rodas* guides, see www.abril.com.br.

Visas and immigration Consular visas are not required for stays of up to 90 days by tourists from Austria, Belgium, Denmark, France, Germany, Ireland, Israel, Italy, Netherlands, New Zealand, Norway, South Africa, Spain, Sweden, Switzerland and the UK. For them, only the following documents are required at the port of disembarkation: a passport valid for at least six months; and a return or onward ticket, or adequate proof that you can purchase your return fare, subject to no remuneration being received in Brazil and no legally binding or contractual documents being signed. Visas are required by US and Canadian citizens, Japanese, Australians and people of other nationalities, and those who cannot meet the requirements above, must get a visa before arrival, which may, if you ask, be granted for multiple entry. Visas are valid form date of issue. Visa fees vary from country to country, so apply to the Brazilian consulate, in the country of residence of the applicant. The consular fees range from US$30 to US$52 (for Australians), to US$100 for US citizens. Do not lose the emigration permit given to you when you enter Brazil. If you leave the country without it, you may have to pay a fine.

Foreign tourists may stay a maximum of 180 days in any one year. 90-day renewals are easily obtainable, but only at least 15 days before the expiry of your 90-day permit, from the Polícia Federal. You will have to fill out three copies of the tax form at the Polícia Federal, take them to a branch of Banco do Brasil, pay US$15 and bring two copies back. You will then be given the extension form to fill in and be asked for your passport to stamp in the extension. Regulations state that you should be able to show a return ticket, cash, cheques or a credit card, a personal reference and proof of an address of a person living in the same city as the office (in practice you simply write this in the space on the form). Some offices will only give you an extension within 10 days of the expiry of your permit. Some points of entry, such as the Colombian border, refuse entry for longer than 30 days, renewals are then for the same period, insist if you want 90 days. For longer stays you must leave the country and return (not the same day) to get a new 90-day permit. If your visa has expired, getting a new visa can be costly (US$35 for a consultation, US$30 for the visa) and may take up to 45 days. If you overstay your visa you will be fined US$7 per day, with no upper limit. After paying the fine to Polícia Federal, you will be issued with an exit visa and must leave within eight days. **Note**: Officially, if you leave Brazil within the 90-day permission to stay and then re-enter the country, you should only be allowed to stay until the 90-day permit expires. If, however, you are given another 90-day permit, this may lead to charges of overstaying if you apply for an extension. For UK citizens a joint agreement allows visits for business or tourism of up to six months a year from the date of first entry.

Identification You must always carry identification when in Brazil; it is a good idea to take a photocopy of the personal details in your passport, plus that with your Brazilian immigration stamp, and leave your passport in the hotel safe deposit. Always keep an independent record of your passport details. It is a good idea to register with your consulate to expedite document replacement if yours gets lost or stolen.

Brazilian embassies and consulates Visit www.mre.gov.br/portugues/enderecos/embaixadas.asp for a full list of addresses.

Money The unit of currency is the real, R = $ (plural reais). It floats freely against the dollar. Any amount of foreign currency and 'a reasonable sum' in reais can be taken in; residents may only take out the equivalent of US$4,000. Notes in circulation are: 100, 50, 10, 5 and 1 real; coins 1 real, 50, 25, 10 and 5 centavos. Real **exchange rate** with US$: 2.20; with euro: 2.81 (May 2006). Banks open 1000-1600 (1630 Mon-Fri).

Credit cards By far the best way to travel in Brazil is with a credit or debit card, preferably Visa, withdrawing money from ATMs. For Visa the best are **Banco 24 Horas** (maximum withdrawal per day R$1,000) and **Bradesco** (maximum withdrawal per day R$600). Take another credit card stowed away for emergencies in case of robbery. For MasterCard, HSBC has the best ATM network (maximum withdrawal per day R$600). Charges are around US$3 per withdrawal. Emergency phone numbers: MasterCard T0800-891 3294; Visa T1-410-581 9994, call collect.

Banks In major cities banks will change cash and travellers' cheques. If you keep the exchange slips, you may convert back into foreign currency up to 50% of the amount you exchanged.

Take US dollars in cash, or euros, and perhaps a few travellers' cheques as a back-up. The commission on travellers' cheques can be as much as US$20 **per cheque**.

Cost of travelling Accommodation in every price range is good value. Owing to the strengthening of the real against other currencies in 2006, Brazil has become expensive for the traveller. It is hard to find a room costing less than US$15 per person, although dormitories are cheaper (US$10-15); in the cities and holiday centres hotels cost more, about US$25. Eating is relatively cheaper and *comida a kilo* (pay by weight) restaurants are good value. Bus prices are reasonable, but because of long distances, costs can mount up. Internal air prices, though, are high. Prices are highest in Rio and São Paulo.

Safety Although Brazil's big cities suffer high rates of violent crime, this is mostly confined to the *favelas* (slums), which should be avoided unless accompanied by a tour leader, or NGO. If the worst does happen and you are threatened, try not to panic, but hand over your valuables. Do not resist, but report the crime to the local tourist police, who should be your first port of call in case of difficulty. The situation is much more secure in smaller towns and in the country. Also steer well clear of areas of drug cultivation and red light districts. In the latter drinks are often spiked with a drug called 'Goodnight Cinderella'. See the Safety section in Essentials at the beginning of the book for general advice.

Police There are several types of police: **Polícia Federal**, civilian dressed, who handle all federal law duties, including immigration. A subdivision is the **Polícia Federal Rodoviária**, uniformed, who are the traffic police. **Polícia Militar** are the uniformed, street police force, under the control of the state governor, handling all state laws. They are not the same as the Armed Forces' internal police. **Polícia Civil**, also state-controlled, handle local laws; usually in civilian dress, unless in the traffic division. In cities, the Prefeitura controls the **Guarda Municipal**, who handle security. **Tourist police** operate in places with a strong tourist presence.

Getting around

Air Because of the great distances, flying is often the most practical option. Internal air services are highly developed and the larger cities are linked several times a day. All national airlines offer excellent service on their internal flights. The largest airlines are **TAM** ① T0800-123100, www.tam.com.br, and **Varig** ① T0800-997000, www.varig.com.br. **Penta** have a wide and cheap network in the Amazon region and **Pantanal** T0800-125833, operate flights mainly between São Paulo and Mato Grosso do Sul.

The no-frills, ticketless airline **Gol** ① *To800-280 0465, English-speaking operators or www.voegol.com.br (website in Portuguese)*, provides a good service. Book Gol flights at a travel agent and pay by credit card. Similar, newer airlines are **Bra** ① *offices throughout Brazil, www.voebra.com.br*, **Ocean Air**, www.oceanair.com.br, and **Trip** ① *To300 789 8747, www.voetrip.com.br*. Internal flights often have many stops and are therefore quite slow. Most airports have left-luggage lockers (US$2 for 24 hours). Seats are often unallocated on internal flights: board in good time.

Varig and TAM offer 21-day air passes, but since deregulation these are not as good value as they used to be. The Varig and TAM **airpasses** cover all Brazil and each costs US$411 for four coupons. Additional coupons, up to a maximum of nine, cost US$100 each. All sectors must be booked before the start of the journey. Two flights forming one connection count as one coupon. The same sector may not be flown more than once in the same direction. Date or route changes are charged at US$30. There is no child discount, but infants pay 10%. For the TAM airpass, passengers may arrive in Brazil on any carrier. Varig passengers must arrive on a Star Alliance carrier. Routes must be specified before arrival.

All airpasses must be purchased outside Brazil, no journey may be repeated and none may be used on the Rio-São Paulo shuttle. Remember domestic airport tax has to be paid at each departure. Hotels in the Tropical and Othon chains, and others, offer discounts of 10% to Varig airpass travellers. Promotions on certain destinations offer a free flight, hotel room, etc; enquire when buying the airpass. Converting the voucher can take some hours, do not plan an onward flight immediately, check at terminals that the airpass is still registered, faulty cancellations have been reported. Cost and restrictions on the airpass are subject to change.

Small scheduled domestic airlines operate Brazilian-built Bandeirante 16-seater prop-jets into virtually every city and town with any semblance of an airstrip.

Bus There are three standards of **bus**: *comum* or *convencional*, which are quite slow, not very comfortable and fill up quickly; *executivo* (executive), which are a few reais more expensive, comfortable (many have reclining seats), but don't stop to pick up passengers en route and are therefore safer; *semi-leito* and *leito* (literally, bed), which run at night between the main centres, offering reclining seats with foot and leg rests, toilets, and sometimes refreshments, at double the normal fare. For journeys over 100 km, most buses have chemical toilets. A/c can make leito buses cold at night, so take a blanket or sweater (and plenty of toilet paper); on some services blankets are supplied. Some companies have hostess service. Ask for window seats (*janela*), or odd numbers if you want the view.

Buses stop frequently (every two to four hours) for snacks. The cleanliness of these *postos* is generally good, but standards of comfort on buses and in *postos* vary, which can be important on long journeys.

Bus stations for interstate services and other long-distance routes are called *rodoviárias*. They are normally outside the city centres and offer snack bars, lavatories, left-luggage stores ('*guarda volume*'), local bus services and information centres. Reliable bus information is hard to come by, other than from companies themselves (most take credit cards). Buses usually arrive and depart in very good time.

Taxi Taxi meters measure distance/cost in reais. At the outset, make sure the meter is cleared and shows tariff '1', except 2300-0600, Sun, and in Dec when '2' is permitted. Check the meter works, if not, fix price in advance. Radio taxi service costs about 50% more but cheating is less likely. Taxi services offered by smartly-dressed individuals outside larger hotels usually cost twice as much as ordinary taxis. If you are seriously cheated, note the taxi number and insist on a signed bill, threatening to go to the police; it can work. **Note**: Be wary of Moto Taxis. Many are unlicensed and a number of robberies have been reported.

Hitchhiking Hitchhiking (*carona* in Portuguese) is not a safe option and is difficult everywhere; drivers are reluctant to give lifts because passengers are their responsibility. Try at the highway-police check points on the main roads (but make sure your documents are in order) or at the service stations (*postos*).

Boat The main areas where boat travel is practical (and often necessary) are the Amazon region, along the São Francisco River and along the Atlantic coast. There are also some limited transport services through the Pantanal.

⁞ Driving in Brazil

Road Around 10% of roads are paved and several thousand more all-weather. The best highways are heavily concentrated in the southeast; those serving the interior are being improved to all-weather status and many are paved. Some main roads are narrow and therefore dangerous. Many are in poor condition.

Safety Try to never leave your car unattended except in a locked garage or guarded parking area.

Documents To drive in Brazil you need an international licence. A national driving licence is acceptable as long as your home country is a signatory to the Vienna and Geneva conventions. (See Motoring, Essentials.) There are agreements between Brazil and all South American countries (but check in the case of Bolivia) whereby a car can be taken into Brazil (or a Brazilian car out of Brazil) for a period of 90 days without any special documents. For cars registered in other countries, you need proof of ownership and/or registration in the home country and valid driving licence (as above). A 90-day permit is given by customs and procedure is very straightforward. Make sure you keep *all* the papers you are given when you enter, to produce when you leave.

Car hire Renting a car in Brazil is expensive: the cheapest rate for unlimited mileage for a small car is about US$65 per day. Minimum age for renting a car is 21 and it is essential to have a credit card. Companies operate under the terms *aluguel de automóveis* or *autolocadores*.

Fuel Fuel prices vary from week to week and region to region. *Gasolina comun* costs about US$1.35 per litre with *gasolina maxi* and *maxigold* a little more. *Alcool comun*; *alcool maxi* and diesel cost a little less. There is no unleaded fuel. Fuel is only 85 octane. It is virtually impossible to buy premium grades of petrol anywhere. With alcohol fuel you need about 50% more alcohol than regular gasoline. Larger cars have a small extra tank for 'gasolina' to get the engine started; remember to keep this topped up. Diesel fuel is cheap.

Train There are 30,379 km of railway track which are not combined into a unified system and most passenger services have been withdrawn. Brazil has two gauges and there is little transfer between them. Two more gauges exist for the isolated Amapá Railway and the tourist-only São João del Rei line. There are passenger services in the state of São Paulo. There are plans to reopen the line from São Paulo state through Mato Gross to Sul to Corumbá on the Bolivian border. Initial prospects are for tourist services in Mato Grosso do Sul (2006-07).

Sleeping → *See inside front cover for our hotel grade price guide.*

Hotels Usually hotel prices include breakfast; there is no reduction if you don't eat it. In the better hotels (category **A** and upwards) the breakfast is well worth eating: rolls, ham, eggs, cheese, cakes, fruit. Normally the apartamento is a room with bath; a quarto is a room without bath. *Pousadas* are the equivalent of bed-and-breakfast, often small and family run, although some are very sophisticated and correspondingly priced. The type known as *hotel familiar*, to be found in the interior – large meals, communal washing, hammocks for children – is much cheaper, but only for the enterprising. The service stations (*postos*) and hostels (*dormitórios*) along the main roads provide excellent value in room and food, akin to truck-driver type accommodation in Europe, for those on a tight budget. The star rating system for hotels (five-star hotels are not price-controlled) is not the standard used in North America or Europe. Business visitors are strongly recommended to book in advance, and this can be easily done for Rio or São Paulo hotels with representation abroad. If staying more than three nights in a place in low season, ask for a discount. Motels are specifically intended for very short-stay couples: there is no stigma attached and they usually offer good value (the rate for a full night is called the pernoite), though the decor can be a little unsettling.

Roteiros de Charme This is a private association of hotels and *pousadas* in the southeast and northeast, which aims to give a high standard of accommodation in establishments typical of the town they are in. If you are travelling in the appropriate budget range (our **AL** price range upwards), you can plan an itinerary which takes in these hotels, with a reputation for comfort and good food. Roteiros de Charme hotels are listed in the text and any one of them can provide information on the group, or visit www.roteirosdecharme.com.br.

Youth hostels For information about youth hostels contact **Federação Brasileira de Albergues da Juventude**① *R dos Andrades 1137, conj 214, Porto Alegre, Rio Grande do Sul, CEP 90020-007, Toxx51-3226 5380, www.albergues.com.br*. Its annual book and website provide a full list of good value accommodation. Another site for the Federação is www.hostel.org.br (Rio de Janeiro based, Toxx21-2286 0303). Also see the *Internet Guide to Hostelling*, which has list of Brazilian youth hostels: www.hostels.com/br.html. Low-budget travellers with student cards (photograph needed) can use the **Casa dos Estudantes** network.

Camping Members of the Camping Clube do Brasil or those with an international campers' card pay only half the rate of a non-member, which is US$10-15 per person. The Club has 43 sites in 13 states. For enquiries, **Camping Clube do Brasil** ① *R Senador Dantas 75, 29 andar, 20037-900 – Centro, Rio de Janeiro, T021-2210 3298, www.campingclube.com.br. In São Paulo, R Minerva 156, 05007-030 – Perdizes, T011-3864 7133, F3871 9749. In Curitiba, Al Dr Muricy 650, conj 161, CEP 80020-902, T/F041-224 7869. In Belo Horizonte, Av Amazonas 115, sala 1301, CEP 30180-000, T/F031-3201-6989. In Salvador, R Portugal 3, grupo 404/410, CEP 40015-000, T071-3243 0029, F242 1954.* It may be difficult to get into some Clube campsites during the high season (January to February). Private campsites charge about US$8 per person. For those on a very low budget and in isolated areas where there is no camp site, service stations can be used as camping sites (Shell stations recommended); they have shower facilities, watchmen and food; some have dormitories; truck drivers are a mine of information. There are also various municipal sites; both types are mentioned in the text. Campsites often tend to be some distance from public transport routes and are better suited to those with their own transport. Never camp at the side of a road; wild camping is generally not possible. Good camping equipment may be purchased in Brazil and there are several rental companies. Camping gas cartridges are easy to buy in sizeable towns in the south, eg in HM shops. Quatro Rodas' Guia Brasil lists main campsites, see page 341. Most sizeable towns have laundromats with self service. Lavanderias do the washing for you but are expensive.

Eating → *See inside front cover for Eating price guide.*

The main meal is usually taken in the middle of the day; cheap restaurants tend not to be open in the evening. The most common dish is *bife* (*ou frango*) *com arroz e feijão*, steak (or chicken) with rice and the excellent Brazilian black beans. The most famous dish with beans is the *feijoada completa*: several meat ingredients (jerked beef, smoked sausage, smoked tongue, salt pork, along with spices, herbs and vegetables) are cooked with the beans. Manioc flour is sprinkled over it, and it is eaten with kale (*couve*) and slices of orange, and accompanied by glasses of aguardente (unmatured rum), usually known as *cachaça* (booze), though *pinga* (drop) is a more polite term. Almost all restaurants serve the *feijoada completa* for Saturday lunch (that means up to about 1630).

Throughout Brazil, a mixed grill, including steak, served with roasted manioc flour (*farofa*; raw manioc flour is known as *farinha* goes under the name of *churrasco* (originally from the cattlemen of Rio Grande do Sul), served in specialized restaurants known as churrascarias or *rodízios*; good places for large appetites Bahia has some excellent fish dishes (see note on page 490); some restaurants in most of the big cities specialize in them. *Vatapá* is a good dish in the north; it contains shrimp or fish sauce with palm oil, or coconut milk. *Empadinhas de camarão* are worth trying; they are shrimp patties, with olives and heart of palm.

Minas Gerais has two splendid special dishes involving pork, black beans, farofa and kale; they are *tutu á mineira* and *feijão tropeiro*. A white hard cheese (*queijo prata*) or a slightly softer one (*queijo Minas*) is often served for dessert with bananas, or guava or quince paste. *Comida mineira* is quite distinctive and very wholesome and you can often find restaurants serving this type of food in other parts of Brazil.

Meals are extremely large by European standards; portions are usually for two and come with two plates. Likewise beer is brought with two glasses. If you are on your own and in a position to do so tactfully, you may choose to offer what you can't eat to a person with no food. Alternatively you could ask for an *embalagem* (doggy bag) or get a take away called *a marmita* or *quentinha*, most restaurants have this service but it is not always on the menu. Many restaurants now serve *comida por kilo* where you serve yourself and pay for the weight of food on your plate. Unless you specify to the contrary many restaurants will lay a *coberto opcional*, olives, carrots, etc, costing US$0.65-1. **Warning** Avoid mussels, marsh crabs and other shellfish caught near large cities: they are likely to have lived in a highly polluted environment. In a restaurant, always ask the price of a dish before ordering.

For **vegetarians**, there is a growing network of restaurants in the main cities. In smaller places where food may be monotonous try vegetarian for greater variety. Most also serve fish. Alternatives in smaller towns are the Arab and Chinese restaurants.

If travelling on a tight **budget**, remember to ask in restaurants for the *prato feito* or *sortido*, a money-saving, excellent value table-d'hôte meal. The *prato comercial* is similar but rather better and a bit more expensive. *Lanchonetes* are cheap eating places where you generally pay before eating. *Salgados* (savoury pastries), *coxinha* (a pyramid of manioc filled with meat or fish and deep fried), *esfiha* (spicey hamburger inside an onion-bread envelope), *empadão* (a filling – eg chicken – in sauce in a pastry case), *empadas* and *empadinhas* (smaller fritters of the same type), are the usual fare. In Minas Gerais, *pão de queijo* is a hot roll made with cheese. A *bauru* is a toasted sandwich which, in Porto Alegre, is filled with steak, while further north it has tomato, ham and cheese filling. *Cocada* is a coconut and sugar biscuit.

Imported **drinks** are expensive, but there are some fair local wines. Chilean and Portuguese wines are sometimes available at little more than the cost of local wines. The Brahma, Cerpa and Antárctica beers are really excellent, of the lager type, and are cheaper by the bottle than on draught. Buying bottled drinks in supermarkets, you may be asked for empties in return. The local firewater, aguardente (known as cachaça or pinga), made from sugar-cane, is cheap and wholesome, but visitors should seek local advice on the best brands; São Francisco, Praianinha, Maria Fulô, '51' and Pitu are recommended makes. Mixed with fruit juices of various sorts, sugar and crushed ice, cachaça becomes the principal element in a *batida*, a delicious and powerful drink; the commonest is a lime batida or *batida de limão*; a variant of this is the *caipirinha*, a cachaça with several slices of lime in it, a *caipiroska* is made with vodka. Cachaça with Coca-Cola is a *cuba*, while rum with Coca-Cola is a *cuba libre*. Some genuine Scotch whisky brands are bottled in Brazil; they are very popular because of the high price of Scotch imported in bottle; Teacher's is the most highly regarded brand. Locally made gin, vermouth and campari are very good.

There are plenty of local soft drinks. Guaraná is a very popular carbonated fruit drink. There is an excellent range of non-alcoholic fruit juices, known as sucos: *caju* (cashew), *pitanga*, *goiaba* (guava), *genipapo*, *graviola* (chirimoya), *maracujá* (passion fruit), *sapoti* and *tamarindo* are recommended. Vitaminas are thick fruit or vegetable drinks with milk. *Caldo de cana* is sugar-cane juice, sometimes mixed with ice. Remember that água mineral, available in many varieties at bars and restaurants, is a cheap, safe thirst-quencher (cheaper still in supermarkets). Apart from the ubiquitous coffee, good tea is grown and sold. **Note:** If you don't want sugar in your coffee or suco, you must ask when you order it. *Água de côco* or *côco verde* (coconut water from fresh green coconut) cannot be missed in the Northeast.

Festivals and events → See also Carnival section page 372.

National holidays are 1 January (New Year); three days up to and including Ash Wednesday (Carnival); 21 April (Tiradentes); 1 May (Labour Day); Corpus Christi (June); 7 September (Independence Day); 12 October, Nossa Senhora Aparecida; 2 November (All Souls' Day); 15 November (Day of the Republic); and 25 December (Christmas). The local holidays in the main cities are given in the text. Four religious or traditional holidays (Good Friday must be one; other usual days: 1 November, All Saints Day; 24 December, Christmas Eve) must be fixed by the municipalities. Other holidays are usually celebrated on the Monday prior to the date.

Telephones

Important telephone changes: All ordinary phone numbers in Brazil are changing from seven to eight figure numbers. The process was still under way as this guide went to press. Where confirmed, eight-digit numbers have been included in the text. Where numbers have changed an electronic message should redirect callers. If a seven-digit number included in the text doesn't work, try putting 3 as the first digit.

Rio de Janeiro → *Phone code: 0xx21. Colour map 4, grid C3.*

Brazilians say: God made the world in six days; the seventh he devoted to Rio. (Pronounced 'Heeoo' by locals). Rio has a glorious theatrical backdrop of tumbling wooded mountains, stark expanses of bare rock and a deep blue sea studded with rocky islands. From the statue of Christ on the hunchbacked peak of Corcovado, or from the conical Pão de Açúcar (Sugar Loaf), you can experience the beauty of a bird's-eye view over the city which sweeps 220 km along a narrow alluvial strip on the southwestern shore of the Baía de Guanabara. Although best known for the curving Copacabana beach, for Ipanema – home to the Girl and beautiful sunsets, and for its swirling, reverberating, joyous Carnival, Rio also has a fine artistic, architectural and cultural heritage from its time as capital of both imperial and republican Brazil. But this is first and foremost a city dedicated to leisure: sport and music rule and a day spent hang gliding or surfing is easily followed by an evening of jazz or samba.

Ins and outs

Getting there **Aeroporto Internacional** Antônio Carlos Jobim (Galeão) is on the Ilha do Governador. Left luggage only in Terminal 1. The air bridge from São Paulo ends at Santos Dumont airport in the town centre. Taxis from here are much cheaper than from the international airport. There are also frequent buses. International and buses from other parts of Brazil arrive at the **Rodoviária Novo Rio** (main bus station) near the docks. ▶▶ *See also Transport, page 375.*

Getting around Because the city is a series of separate districts connected by urban highways and tunnels, you will need to take public transport. An underground railway, the **Metrô**, runs under some of the centre and the south and is being extended. Buses run to all parts, but should be treated with caution at night when taxis are a better bet.

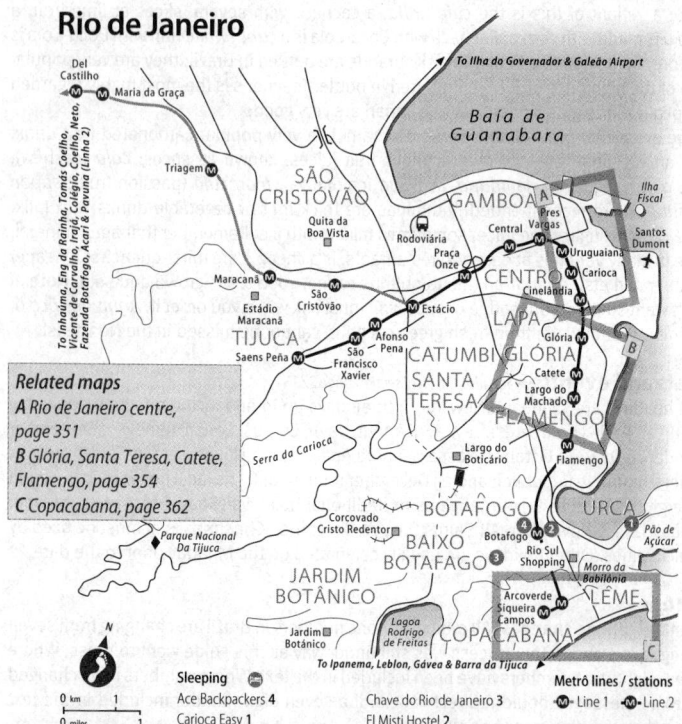

Rio de Janeiro

Related maps
A Rio de Janeiro centre, page 351
B Glória, Santa Teresa, Catete, Flamengo, page 354
C Copacabana, page 362

Sleeping
Ace Backpackers **4**
Carioca Easy **1**
Chave do Rio de Janeiro **3**
El Misti Hostel **2**

Metrô lines / stations
🚇 Line 1   🚇 Line 2

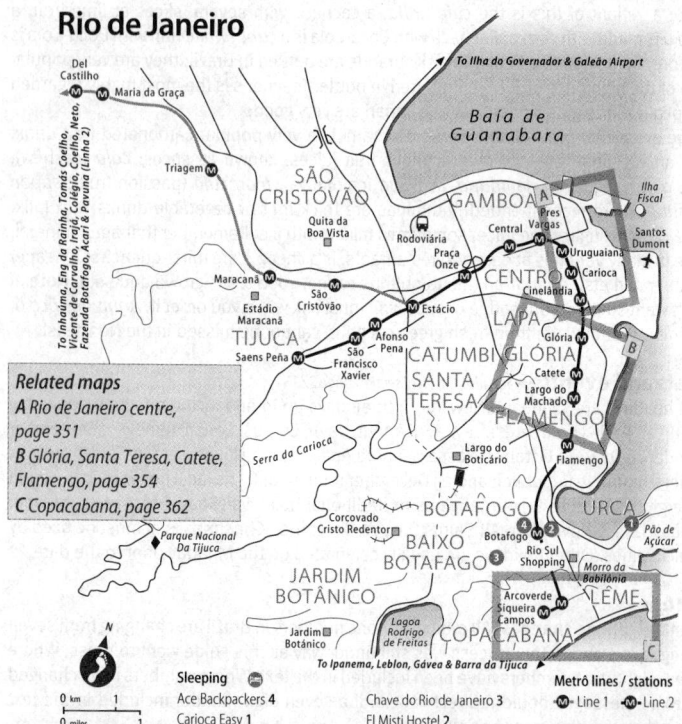

Climate Rio has one of the healthiest climates in the tropics. Trade winds cool the air. June, July and August are the coolest months with temperatures ranging from 22°C (18° in a cold spell) to 32°C on a sunny day at noon. December to March is hotter, from 32°C to 42°C. Humidity is high. It is important, especially for children, to guard against dehydration in summer by drinking as much liquid as possible. October to March is the rainy season. Annual rainfall is about 1,120 mm.

Tourist offices Riotur, R da Assembléia 10, 9th floor, T2217 7575, www.riodejaneiro-turismo.com.br/pt (also in English). Main information office: Av Princesa Isabel 183, Copacabana, T2541 7522, Monday-Friday 0900-1800, helpful with English and German spoken by some staff, has good city maps and a very useful free brochure RIO, in Portuguese and English. More information stands can be found at the international airport (0600-2400) and at Rodoviária Novo Rio (0800-2000), both very friendly and helpful in finding accommodation. **Alô Rio** is an information service in English and Portuguese, T2542 8080/0800-707 1808, daily from 0900-1800. **TurisRio**, R da Ajuda 5, 12th floor, T2215 0011, www.turisrio.rj.gov.br. Information on the state of Rio de Janeiro, Monday-Friday 0900-1700, with stands at the bus station and Jobim airport. A good A-Z-type street guide to Rio is *Guia Quatro Rodas do Rio* (the *Guia Quatro Rodas do Brasil*, published annually in November, has a good Rio section). *Trilhas do Rio*, by Pedro da Cunha e Meneses (Editora Salamandra, 2nd edition), US$22.50, describes walking trips around Rio. The guide *Restaurantes do Rio*, by Danusia Bárbara, published annually by Senac at around US$10 (in Portuguese only), is worth looking at for the latest ideas on where to eat in both the city and state of Rio. Many hotels provide guests with the weekly *Rio This Month*. There is an online Favela news agency with news, comment and links, aimed at helping people understand better this aspect of the city: www.anf.org.br. ▶ *See also Tour operators, page 374.*

Safety The majority of visitors enjoy Rio's glamour and the rich variety of experience it has to offer without any problems. It is worth remembering that, despite its beach culture, carefree atmosphere and friendly people, Rio is one of the world's most densely populated cities. If you live in London, Paris, New York or Los Angeles and behave with the same caution in Rio that you do at home, you will be unlucky to encounter any crime. The **Tourist Police** ① *Av Afrânio de Melo Franco 159, Leblon (in front of the Casa Grande theatre), T3399 7170, 24 hrs*, publish a sensible advice leaflet (available from hotels and consulates: consulates also issue safety guidelines). Tourist police officers are helpful, efficient and multilingual. All the main tourist areas are patrolled. If you have any problems, contact the tourist police first.

Extra vigilance is needed on the beaches at night. Don't walk on the sand. Likewise in the backstreets between the Copacabana Palace and Rua Figueiredo de Magalhães. Santa Teresa is now far safer and better policed than before, but caution is needed walking between Santa Teresa and Lapa at night and around the small streets near the Largo das Neves.

Background

The Portuguese navigator, Gonçalo Coelho, arrived at what is now Rio de Janeiro on 1 January 1502. Thinking that the Baía de Guanabara (the name the local *indígenas* used) was the mouth of a great river, they called the place the January River. Although the bay was almost as large and as safe a harbour as the Baía de Todos Os Santos to the north, the Portuguese did not take of advantage of it. In fact, it was first settled by the French, who, under the Huguenot Admiral Nicholas Durand de Villegagnon, occupied Lage Island on 10 November 1555, but later transferred to Seregipe Island (now Villegagnon), where they built the fort of Coligny.

In early 1559-1560, Mem de Sá, third governor of Brazil, mounted an expedition from Salvador to attack the French. The Portuguese finally took control in 1567. Though constantly attacked by *indígenas*, the new city grew rapidly and when King Sebastião divided Brazil into two provinces, Rio was chosen capital of the southern captaincies. Salvador became sole capital again in 1576, but Rio again became the southern capital in 1608 and the seat of a bishopric.

Rio de Janeiro was by the 18th century becoming the leading city in Brazil. Not only was it the port out of which gold was shipped, but it was also the focus of the export/import trade of the surrounding agricultural lands. On 27 January 1763, it became the seat of the Viceroy. After independence, in 1834, it was declared capital of the Empire and remained so for 125 years.

Orientation

The city is usually divided into north and south zones, Zona Norte and Zona Sul, with the historical and business centre, O Centro, in between. The parts that most interest visitors are the centre itself and the Zona Sul, which has the famous districts of Flamengo, Botafogo, Urca, Copacabana, Ipanema, Leblon and then out to the newer suburb of Barra de Tijuca.

The city's main artery is the Avenida Presidente Vargas, 4½ km long and over 90 m wide. It starts at the waterfront, divides to embrace the famous Candelária church, then crosses the Avenida Rio Branco in a magnificent straight stretch past the Central do Brasil railway station, with its imposing clock tower, until finally it incorporates a palm-lined, canal-divided avenue. The second principal street in the centre is the Avenida Rio Branco, nearly 2 km long, on which only a few ornate buildings remain, by Cinelândia and the Biblioteca Nacional. Some of the finest modern architecture is to be found along the Avenida República do Chile, such as the Petrobrás, the Banco Nacional de Desenvolvimento Econômico and the former Banco Nacional de Habitação buildings and the new Cathedral.

City centre and Lapa

Around Praça 15 de Novembro

Praça 15 de Novembro (often called Praça XV) has always been one of the focal points in Rio. Today it has one of the greatest concentrations of historic buildings in the city. The last vestiges of the original harbour, at the seaward end of the Praça, have been restored. The steps no longer lead to the water, but a new open space leads from the Praça to the seafront, beneath the Avenida Pres Kubitschek flyover. This space now gives easy access to the ferry dock for Niterói. At weekends an antiques, crafts, stamp and coin fair is held from 0900-1900.

On Rua 1 de Março, across from Praça 15 de Novembro, there are three buildings related to the Carmelite order. The convent of the **Ordem Terceira do Monte do Carmo**, started in 1611, is now used as the Faculdade Cândido Mendes. The order's present church, the **Igreja da Ordem Terceira do Carmo** ① *also in R Primeiro de Março, Mon-Fri 0800-1400, Sat 0800-1200, is the other side of the old cathedral (see below) from the convent.* It was built in 1754, consecrated in 1770 and rebuilt between 1797 and 1826. It has strikingly beautiful portals by Mestre Valentim, the son of a Portuguese nobleman and a slave girl. He also created the main altar of fine moulded silver, the throne and its chair and much else.

Between the former convent and the Igreja da Ordem Terceira do Carmo is the old cathedral, the **Igreja de Nossa Senhora do Carmo da Antiga Sé**, separated from the Carmo Church by a passageway. It was the chapel of the Convento do Carmo from 1590 until 1754. A new church was built in 1761, which became the city's cathedral. In the crypt are the alleged remains of Pedro Alvares Cabral, the Portuguese explorer (though Santarém, Portugal, also claims to be his last resting place).

The **Paço Imperial** (former Royal Palace) ① *T2533 4407, Tue-Sun 1100-1830*, is on the southeast corner of the Praça 15 de Novembro. This beautiful colonial building was built in 1743 as the residence of the governor of the Capitania. It later became the Paço Real when the Portuguese court moved to Brazil. After Independence it became the Imperial Palace. It has an exhibition space and the Bistro and Atrium restaurants. Recommended.

Igreja de São José ① *R São José e Av Pres Antônio Carlos, Mon-Fri 0900-1200, 1400-1700, Sun 0900-1100*, is considerably altered since its 17th-century construction. The current building dates from 1824.

On the northwest side of the Praça 15 de Novembro, you go through the Arco do Teles and the Travessa do Comércio to Rua do Ouvidor. The **Igreja Nossa Senhora da Lapa dos Mercadores** ① *R do Ouvidor 35, Mon-Fri 0800-1400*, was consecrated in 1750, remodelled 1869-72 and has been fully restored. Across the street, with its entrance at R 1 de Março 36, is the church of **Santa Cruz dos Militares**, built 1780-1811. It is large, stately and beautiful and has been well renovated in a 'light' baroque style.

The Church of **Nossa Senhora da Candelária** (1775-1810) ① *on Praça Pio X (Dez), at the city end of Av Pres Vargas where it meets R 1 de Março, Mon-Fri 0730-1200, 1300-1630, Sat 0800-1200, Sun 0900-1300*, has beautiful ceiling decorations and romantic paintings.

The **Centro Cultural Banco do Brasil (CCBB)** ① *entrances on Av Pres Vargas and R 1 de Março 66, T3808 2000, Tue-Sun 1230-1900*, is highly recommended for good exhibitions. It has a library, multimedia facilities, a cinema, concerts (US$6 at lunchtime) and a restaurant.

Opposite is the **Espaço Cultural dos Correios** ① *R Visconde de Itaboraí 20, T2503 8770, Tue-Sun 1300-1900*, which holds temporary exhibitions and a postage stamp fair on Saturdays. **Casa França-Brasil** ① *R Visconé de Itaboraí 253 and Av Pres Vargas, T2253 5366, Tue-Sun 1200-2000*, dates from the first French Artistic Mission to Brazil and it was the first neoclassical building in Rio. **Espaço Cultural da Marinha** ① *Av Alfredo Agache at Av Pres Kubitschek, US$3.65 for museum and 1-hr boat trip*, this former naval establishment now contains museums of underwater archaeology and navigation and the Galeota, the boat used by the Portuguese royal family for sailing around the Baía de Guanabara. Moored outside is the warship, Bauru and boats give access to the beautiful **Ilha Fiscal** ① *T3870 6879, Tue-Sun 1200-1700, boats to Ilha Fiscal, Fri, Sat, Sun, 1300, 1430, 1600*.

Just north of Candelária, on a promontory overlooking the bay, is the **Mosteiro** (monastery) **de São Bento** ① *daily 0800-1230, 1400-1730, shorts not allowed*. Every Sun at 1000, mass is

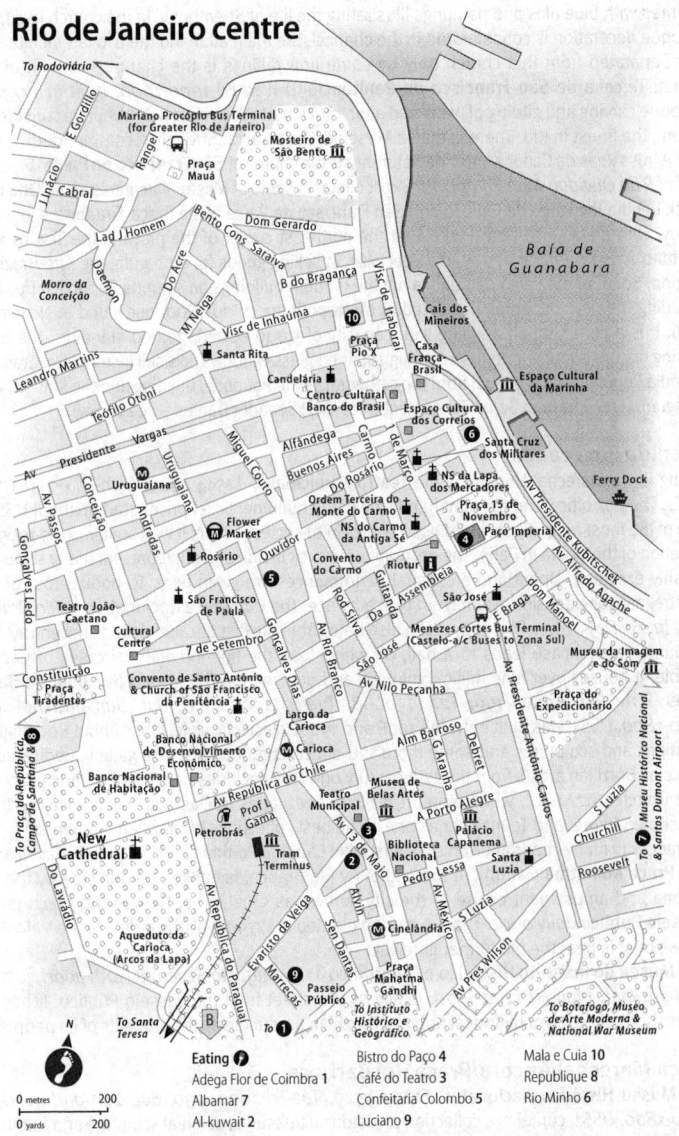

Rio de Janeiro centre

Eating 🍴
Adega Flor de Coimbra 1
Albamar 7
Al-kuwait 2

Bistro do Paço 4
Café do Teatro 3
Confeitaria Colombo 5
Luciano 9

Mala e Cuia 10
Republique 8
Rio Minho 6

sung with Gregorian chant and music, which is free, but arrive an hour early to get a seat. On other days, mass is at 0715. It contains much of what is best in the 17th and 18th century art of Brazil. São Bento is reached either by a narrow road from R Dom Gerardo 68, or by a lift whose entrance is at R Dom Gerardo 40 (taxi from centre US$5). The main body of the church is adorned in gold and red. The carving and gilding is remarkable, much of it by Frei Domingos da Conceição. The paintings, too, should be seen. The Chapels of the Immaculate Conception (Nossa Senhora da Conceição) and of the Most Holy Sacrament (Santíssimo Sacramento) are masterpieces of colonial art. The organ, dating from the end of the 18th century, is very interesting.

Around Largo da Carioca

The second oldest convent in the city is the **Convento de Santo Antônio**, on a hill off the Largo da Carioca, built 1608-1615. Santo Antônio is a particular object of devotion for women looking for a husband and you will see them in the precincts. The church has a marvellous sacristy adorned with blue tiles and paintings illustrating the life of St Anthony. In the church itself, the baroque decoration is concentrated in the chancel, the main altar and the two lateral altars.

Separated from this church only by some iron railings is the charming church of the Ordem Terceira de **São Francisco da Penitência** ① *Wed-Fri 1000-1600, built in 1773*. Its Baroque carving and gilding of walls and altar, much more than in its neighbour, is considered among the finest in Rio. There is also a Museu de Arte Sacra. Strongly recommended.

Across Ruas da Carioca and 7 de Setembro is the church of **São Francisco de Paula** ① *upper end of R do Ouvidor, Mon-Fri 0900-1300*. It contains some of Mestre Valentim's work. One long block behind the Largo da Carioca and São Francisco de Paula is the **Praça Tiradentes**, old and shady, with a statue to Dom Pedro I. At the northeast corner of the praça is the **Teatro João Caetano** T2221 0305. Shops nearby specialize in selling goods for umbanda, the Afro-Brazilian religion. South of the Largo da Carioca are the modern buildings on Avenida República do Chile including the new cathedral, the **Catedral Metropolitana** *0800-1800*, dedicated in November 1976. It is a cone-shaped building with capacity of 5,000 seated, 20,000 standing. The most striking feature is four enormous 60 m-high stained-glass windows. It is still incomplete. Crossing Avendia República do Paraguai from the cathedral, is the Petrobrás building and the station, with museum, for the tram to Santa Teresa (entrance on R Senador Dantas – see below).

Avenida Rio Branco

Facing Praça Marechal Floriano is the **Teatro Municipal** ① *T2544 2900, Mon-Fri 0900-1700, US$2*. The box office is at the right hand side of the building; ticket prices start at about US$15. One of the most magnificent buildings in Brazil in the eclectic style, it was built in 1905-1909, in imitation of the Opéra in Paris. The decorative features inside and out represent many styles, all lavishly executed. Opera and orchestral performances are given here. To book a tour of the theatre, ask for extension – ramal – 935 in advance. The **Biblioteca Nacional** ① *Av Rio Branco 219, T2262 8255, Mon-Fri 0900, US$1*, also dates from the first decade of the 20th century. The monumental staircase leads to a hall, off which lead the fine internal staircases of Carrara marble. It houses over nine million volumes and documents. The **Museu Nacional de Belas Artes** ① *Av Rio Branco 199, T2240 0068, Tue-Fri 1000-1800, Sat, Sun and holidays 1400-1800, US$1*, was built between 1906 and 1908, in eclectic style. It has about 800 original paintings and sculptures and some thousand direct reproductions. One gallery, dedicated to works by Brazilian artists from the 17th century onwards, includes paintings by Frans Janszoon Post (Dutch 1612-1680), who painted Brazilian landscapes in classical Dutch style, and the Frenchmen Debret and Taunay. It has one of the best collections of Brazilian modernism in the country, with many important works by artists like Cândido Portinári and Emiliano Di Cavalcánti.

Praça Mahatma Gandhi, at the end of Av Rio Branco, is flanked on one side by the old cinema and amusement centre of the city, known as Cinelândia. Next to the praça is the **Passeio Público** *daily 0900-1700*, a garden planted in 1779-83 by the artist Mestre Valentim, whose bust is near the old former gateway.

Museu do Instituto Histórico e Geográfico ① *Av Augusto Severo 8 (10th floor), just off Av Beira Mar, Mon-Fri 1200-1700*, is across the street from the Passeio Público. It has an interesting collection of historical objects, Brazilian products and the artefacts of its peoples.

Praça Marechal Âncora/Praça Rui Barbosa

The **Museu Histórico Nacional** ① *T2240 9529, Tue-Fri 1000-1730, Sat, Sun and holidays 1400-1800, US$1*, contains a collection of historical treasures, colonial sculpture and furniture, coins, maps, paintings, arms and armour, silver and porcelain. Newly renovated it has a collection of beautiful colonial coaches, including one used by the emperor. **Museu da Imagem e do Som** ① *also on Praça Rui Barbosa, Mon-Fri 1300-1800*, has many photographs of Brazil and modern Brazilian paintings; also collections and recordings of Brazilian classical and popular music and a non-commercial cinema Friday-Sunday.

Zona Norte

West of the centre

Palácio do Itamaraty (Museu Histórico e Diplomático) ① *Av Marechal Floriano 196, guided tours Mon, Wed, Fri hourly 1315-1615*, became the president's residence between 1889 and 1897 and then the Ministry of Foreign Affairs until the opening of Brasília. Recommended.

About 3 km west of the public gardens of the Praça da República (beyond the Sambódromo – see box, Carnival, page 372) is the **Quinta da Boa Vista** *daily 0700-1800*, formerly the Emperor's private park, from 1809 to 1889. If you are comfortable in crowds, perhaps the best time to visit is Saturday or Sunday afternoon. It is full of locals looking for fun and relaxation and therefore more police are on hand. **Note** Quinta da Boa Vista has had the problem of thieves operating by the park entrance and in the park itself.

Museu Nacional ① *in the Quinta da Boa Vista, 1000-1600, closed Mon, US$2. The safest way to reach the museum is by taking a taxi to the main door. Having said that, it can be reached by Metrô to São Cristóvão, then cross the railway line and walk a few metres to the park. This is safer than taking a bus.* In the entrance hall is the famous Bendegó meteorite, found in the State of Bahia in 1888; its original weight, before some of it was chipped, was 5,360 kg. The museum also has important collections which are poorly displayed. The building was the principal palace of the Emperors of Brazil, but only the unfurnished Throne Room and ambassadorial reception room on the second floor reflect past glories. The Museum contains collections of Brazilian indigenous weapons, dresses, utensils etc, of minerals and of historical documents. There are also collections of birds, beasts, fishes and butterflies. Despite the need for conservation work, the museum is still worth visiting. **Museu de Fauna** ① *also in the Quinta da Boa Vista, Tue-Sun 1200-1700*, contains a most interesting collection of Brazilian fauna.

Maracanã Stadium ① *T2568 9962, 0900-1700 (0800-1100 on match days), a guided tour of the stadium (in Portuguese) from Gate 16 costs US$6 and of the museum, US$0.50. The stadium was being renovated in 2006.* Highly recommended for football fans. This is one of the largest sports centres in the world, with a capacity of 200,000. Matches are worth going to if only for the spectators' samba bands. There are three types of ticket, but prices vary according to the game (expect to pay US$7.50-10). Agencies charge much more for tickets than at the gate. It is cheaper to buy tickets from club sites on the day before the match. Seats in the white section have good views. Maracanã is now used only for major games; Rio teams play most matches at their home grounds (still a memorable experience, about US$2 per ticket). Maracanã can be visited most safely during a game with www.bealocal.com, T9643 0366: all is organized including transport from hotel/hostel, tickets and a safe area from which to watch the game.

Santa Teresa → *see map, page 354*

Known as the coolest part of Rio, and a haven for artists and intellectuals, this hilly inner suburb southwest of the centre, boasts many colonial and 19th century buildings, set in narrow, curving, tree-lined streets. Today the old houses are lived in by artists, intellectuals and makers of handicrafts. As Rio's up and coming place to stay, it has hostels, hotels and homestays (including the upper floor of the former home of Ronnie Biggs, the British, 1960s great train robber). Most visitors in the daytime will arrive by tram. If you stay to the end of the line, Largo das Neves, you will be able to appreciate the small-town feel of the place. There are several bars here, including Goiabeira, simple and charming with a nice view of the praça. The essential stop is the Largo do Guimarães, which has some not to be missed eating places (see Eating.)

Chácara do Céu ① *R Murtinho Nobre 93, T2285 0891, www.visualnet.com.br/cmaya, Tue-Sun 1200-1700, US$1, take the Santa Teresa tram to Curvelo station, walk along R Dias de Barros, following the signposts to Parque das Ruínas*. Also called Fundação Raymundo Ottoni de Castro Maia, it has a wide range of art objects and modern painters, including Brazilian;

exhibitions change through the year. The **Chalé Murtinho**① *R Murtinho 41, daily 1000-1700*, was in ruins until it was partially restored and turned into a cultural centre called **Parque das Ruínas** in 1998. There are exhibitions, a snack bar and superb views.

Santa Teresa is best visited on the traditional open-sided **tram** *US$0.40 one way*, the bondinho. Take the Metrô to Cinelândia, go to R Senador Dantas then walk along to R Profesor Lélio Gama (look for Banco do Brasil on the corner). The station is up this street. Take the Paula Mattos line (a second line is Dois Irmãos) and enjoy the trip as it passes over the **Arcos da Lapa** aqueduct, winding its way up to the district's historic streets. At Largo das Neves, the tram turns round for the journey back to R Prof L Gama. Normally a policeman rides each bondinho, but you are advised not to take valuables (see Safety, in Ins and outs above). Buses Nos 206 and 214 run from Avenida Rio Branco in the centre to Santa Teresa. At night, only take a taxi.

Glória, Santa Teresa, Catete, Flamengo

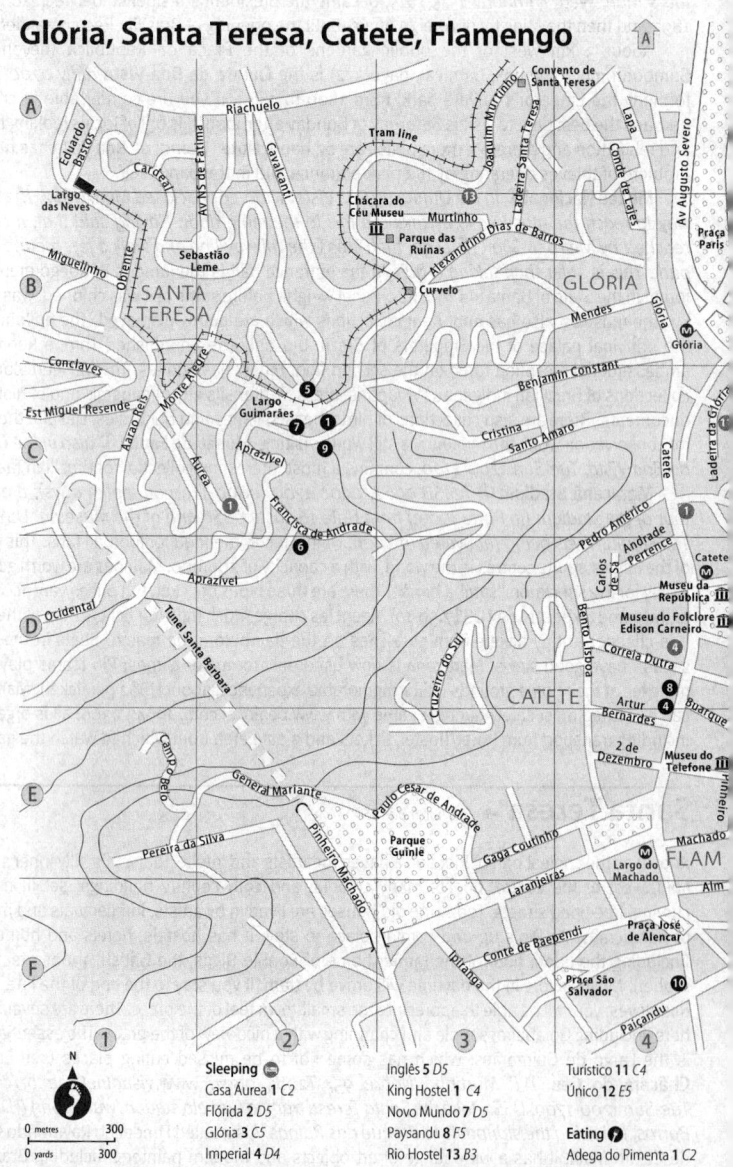

Sleeping
Casa Áurea **1** *C2*
Flórida **2** *D5*
Glória **3** *C5*
Imperial **4** *D4*

Inglês **5** *D5*
King Hostel **1** *C4*
Novo Mundo **7** *D5*
Paysandu **8** *F5*
Rio Hostel **13** *B3*

Turístico **11** *C4*
Único **12** *E5*

Eating
Adega do Pimenta **1** *C2*

Zona Sul → *see map, page 354*

The commercial district ends where Avenida Rio Branco meets the Avenida Beira Mar. This avenue, with its royal palms and handsome buildings, coasting the Botafogo and Flamengo beaches, makes a splendid drive, Avenida Infante Dom Henrique, along the beach over re-claimed land (the Aterro), leading to Botafogo and through two tunnels to Copacabana.

Glória, Catete and Flamengo

On the Glória and Flamengo waterfront, with a view of the Pão de Açúcar and Corcovado, is the **Parque do Flamengo**, designed by Burle Marx, opened in 1965 during the 400th anniversary of the city's founding and landscaped on 100 ha reclaimed from the bay. Security in the park is in the hands of vigilante policemen and it is a popular recreation area. (**Note**: Beware armed robbery in Parque do Flamengo.) **Museu de Arte Moderna** ① *Av Infante Dom Henrique 85, city end of Parque Flamengo, T2240 4944, www.mamrio.com.br, Tue-Sun 1200-1700 (last entry 1630), US$2.* This spectacular building near the National War Memorial, suffered a disastrous fire in 1978. The collection is being rebuilt and several countries have donated works.

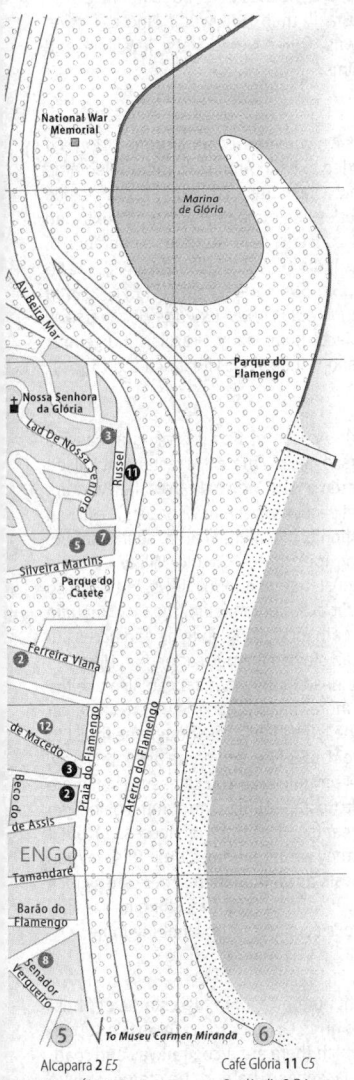

The **Monumento aos Mortos da Segunda Guerra Mundial/National War Memorial** ① *Av Infante Dom Henrique 75, opposite Praça Paris, crypt and museum open Tue-Sun 1000-1700, but beach clothes and rubber-thonged sandals are not permitted*, to Brazil's dead in the Second World War. The Memorial takes the form of two slender columns supporting a slightly curved slab, representing two palms uplifted to heaven. In the crypt are the remains of Brazilian soldiers killed in Italy in 1944-1945. The beautiful little church on the Glória Hill, overlooking the Parque do Flamengo, is **Nossa Senhora da Glória do Outeiro** ① *church, 0800-1200 (only Sat-Sun) and 1300-1700 weekdays, is reached by bus 119 from the centre and 571 from Copacabana.* It was the favourite church of the imperial family; Dom Pedro II was baptized here. The building is polygonal, with a single tower. It contains some excellent examples of blue-faced Brazilian tiling. Its main altar, of wood, was carved by Mestre Valentim. The adjacent museum of religious art keeps the same hours, but is closed on Monday.

Parque do Catete is a charming small park with birds and monkeys between Praia do Flamengo and the Palácio do Catete, which contains the **Museu da República** ① *R do Catete 153, T2557 3150, Tue-Sun 1200-1700, US$2.50. Signs in Portuguese only. Take bus 571 from Copacabana, or the*

Alcaparra **2** *E5*
Alho e Óleo **3** *E5*
Amazônia **4** *D4*
Aprazível **6** *D2*
Bar do Arnaudo **5** *C2*

Café Glória **11** *C5*
Catelândia **8** *D4*
Espírito Santa **9** *C2*
Lamas **10** *F4*
Sobrenatural **7** *C2*

Metrô to Catete station. The palace was built in 1858-1866. In 1887 it was converted into the presidential seat, until the move to Brasília. The first floor is devoted to the history of the Brazilian republic. The museum is highly recommended.

Museu do Folclore Edison Carneiro ① *R do Catete 181, T2285 0441, Tue-Fri 1100-1800, Sat-Sun 1500-1800, free, signs in Portuguese, no flash photography, take bus 571 from Copacabana, or the Metrô to Catete station*. This museum's collection should not to be missed. There is an exhibit of small ceramic figures representing everyday life in Brazil, some very funny, some scenes animated by electric motors. There are fine Candomblé and Umbanda costumes, religious objects, ex-votos and sections on many of Brazil's festivals. It has a small, but excellent library, with helpful, friendly staff for finding books on Brazilian culture, history and anthropology.

The **Museu Carmen Miranda** ① *Rui Barbosa 560, Parque do Flamengo (in front of the Morro da Viúva) T 5512 5970. Mon-Fri 1100-1700, US$0.30*, houses over 3,000 items related to the famous Portuguese singer who emigrated to Brazil, then Hollywood, and is forever associated with Rio. These include her famous gowns, fruit-covered hats, jewellery and reviews, recordings and occasional showings of her films.

Botafogo

Museu Villa-Lobos ① *R Sorocaba 200, T2266 3845, www.museuvillalobos.org.br, Mon- Fri 1000-1700, free*. Such was the fame and respect afforded to Latin America's most celebrated composer that Rio de Janeiro founded this museum only a year after his death in 1960. Inside the fine 19th-century building is the collection includes instruments, scores, books and recordings. The museum has occasional shows and concerts, and supports a number of classical music projects throughout Brazil. **Museu do Índio** ① *R das Palmeiras 55, T2286 8899, www.museudoindio.org.br, Tue-Fri 1000-1730, Sat-Sun 1300-1700, US$1.75, 10-min walk from Botafogo Metrô; from Catete, bus 571 (Glória-Leblon) passes Ruas Bento Lisboa and São Clemente*. The museum houses 12,000 objects from many Brazilian indigenous groups. There is also a small, well-displayed handicraft shop (shop closes for lunch 1200-1400).

Pão de Açúcar (Sugar Loaf mountain)

① *Getting there: see Transport, page 376.* The Pão de Açúcar, or Sugar Loaf, is a massive granite cone at the entrance to Guanabara Bay that soars to 396 m. There is a restaurant (mixed reports on food, closes 1900) and a playground for children on the **Morro da Urca**, half way up, where there are also shows at night (consult the cultural sections in the newspapers). You can get refreshments at the top. The sea level cable car station is in a military area, so it is safe to visit. At Praia Vermelha, the beach to the south of the rock, is the Círculo Militar da Praia Vermelha restaurant, which is open to the public (no sign). It has wonderful views, but is not so good for food or service; stop there for a drink anyway. From Praia Vermelha, the Pista Cláudio Coutinho runs around the foot of the rock. It is a paved path for walking, jogging and access to various climbing places. It is open until 1800, but you can stay on the path after that. Here you have mountain, forest and sea side-by-side, right in the heart of the city. You can also use the Pista Coutinho as a way of getting up the Pão de Açúcar more cheaply than the US$16 cable-car ride. About 350 m from the path entrance is a track to the left which leads though the forest to Morro de Urca, from where the cable car can be taken for US$8 (you can come down this way, too, but if you take the cable car from sea level you must pay full fare). You can save even more money, but use more energy, by climbing the Caminho da Costa, a path to the summit of the Pão de Açúcar. Only one stretch, of 10 m, requires climbing gear (some say it is not necessary), but if you wait at the bottom of the path for a group going up, they will let you tag along. This way you can descend to Morro de Urca by cable car for free and walk down from there. There are 35 rock routes up the mountain, with various degrees of difficulty. The best months for climbing are April to August. See Sport, page 371, for climbing clubs; there is also a book on climbing routes.

Corcovado

Corcovado is a hunch-backed peak, 710 m high, surmounted by a 38 m high statue of Christ the Redeemer, O Cristo Redentor, which was completed on 12 October 1931. There is a superb view from the top (sometimes obscured by mist), to which there are a cog railway and road; taxis, cooperative minivans and train put down their passengers behind the statue. Private cars are only allowed as far as Paineiras, from where you can catch train or cabs. The 3.8 km railway itself offers fine views. Average speed is 15 kph on the way up and 12 kph on the way down. There is a new exhibition of the history of the railway. From the upper terminus there is a system of escalators, one with a panoramic view, to the top, near which there is a café (alternatively you can climb 220 steps up). To see the city by day and night ascend at 1500 or 1600 and descend on the last train, approximately 1815. Mass is held on Sunday in a small chapel in the statue pedestal. To reach the vast statue of Cristo Redentor at the summit of Corcovado, you have to go through Laranjeiras and Cosme Velho. The road through these districts heads west out of Catete. See Transport, page 377.

The **Museu Internacional de Arte Naif do Brasil** (MIAN) ① *R Cosme Velho 561, T2205 8612, www.museunaif.com.br, Tue-Fri 1000-1800, Sat, Sun and holidays 1200-1800; closed Mon, US$3.20; discounts for groups, students and senior citizens.* This is one of the most comprehensive museums of Naive and folk paintings in the world. It is only 30 m uphill, on the same street as the station for Corcovado. There is a permanent collection of some 8,000 works by Naive artists from about 130 countries. MIAN has a good shop at Avenida Atlântica 1998.

Those who want to see what Rio was like early in the 19th century should go to the **Largo do Boticário** *R Cosme Velho 822,* a charming small square in neo-colonial style. Much of the material used in creating the effect of the square came from old buildings demolished in the city centre. The square is close to the terminus for the Corcovado cog railway.

Copacabana → *Tourist police patrol Copacabana beach until 1700.*

Built on a narrow strip of land (only a little over 4 sq km) between mountain and sea, Copacabana has one of the highest population densities in the world: 62,000 per sq km, or 250,000 in all. Copacabana began to develop when the Túnel Velho (Old Tunnel) was built in 1891 and an electric tram service reached it. Weekend villas and bungalows sprang up; all have now gone. In the 1930s the Copacabana Palace Hotel was the only tall building; it is now one of the lowest on the beach. The opening of the Túnel Novo (New Tunnel) in the 1940s led to an explosion of population which shows no sign of having spent its force. Unspoilt art deco blocks towards the Leme (city) end of Copacabana are now under preservation order.

There is almost everything in this 'city within a city'. The shops, mostly in Avenida Nossa Senhora de Copacabana and the Rua Barata Ribeiro, are excellent. Even more stylish shops are to be found in Ipanema, Leblon and in the various large shopping centres in the city. The city's glamorous nightlife is beginning to move elsewhere and, after dark, Copacabana, has lost some of its former allure. A fort at the far end of the beach, Forte de Copacabana, was an important part of Rio's defences and prevents a seashore connection with the Ipanema and Leblon beaches. Parts of the military area are now being handed over to civilian use, the first being the Parque Garota de Ipanema at Arpoador, the fashionable Copacabana end of the Ipanema beach.

The world-famous beach is divided into numbered postos, where the lifeguards are based. Different sections attract different types of people, eg young people, artists and gays. The safest places are in front of the major hotels which have their own security, eg the Meridien on Copacabana beach or the Caesar Park on Ipanema. The Caesar Park also has 24-hour video surveillance during the summer season, which makes it probably the safest patch of sand in Rio. See Transport page 377.

Ipanema and Leblon → *see map, page 364*

Beyond Copacabana are the seaside suburbs of Ipanema and Leblon. The two districts are divided by a canal from the Lagoa Rodrigo de Freitas to the sea, beside which is the Jardim de Alá. Ipanema and Leblon are a little less built-up than Copacabana and their beaches tend to be cleaner. Praia de Arpoadar at the Copacabana end of Ipanema is a peaceful spot to watch surfers, with the beautiful backdrop of Morro Dois Irmãos; excellent for photography, walk on the rocks. There is now night-time illumination on these beaches. The seaward lane of the road running beside the beach is closed to traffic until 1800 on Sundays and holidays; this makes it popular for rollerskating and cycling (bicycles can be hired).

Gávea, Lagoa and Jardim Botânico

Backing Ipanema and Leblon is the middle-class residential area of **Lagoa Rodrigo de Freitas**, by a saltwater lagoon on which Rio's rowing and small-boat sailing clubs are active. The lake is too polluted for bathing, but the road which runs around its shores has pleasant views. Avenida Epitácio Pessoa, on the eastern shore, leads to the Túnel Rebouças which runs beneath Corcovado and Cosme Velho.

Well worth a visit are the **Jardim Botânico** (Botanical Gardens) ① *T2294-9349, www.jbrj.gov.br, 0800-1700, US$2, getting there: 8 km from the centre, see Transport,* *below.* These were founded in 1808. The most striking features are the transverse avenues of 30 m high royal palms. Among the more than 7,000 varieties of plants from around the world are examples of the pau-brasil tree, now endangered, and many other threatened species. There is a herbarium, an aquarium and a library (some labels are unclear). A new pavilion contains sculptures by Mestre Valentim transferred from the centre. Many improvements were carried out before the 1992 Earth Summit, including a new Orquidário and an enlarged bookshop.

The **Planetário** ① *Padre Leonel Franco 240, Gávea, T2274 0096, www.rio.rj.gov.br/planetario, tours at 1400, observations on Fri at 2000, Sat-Sun at 1630, 1800 and 1930, getting there: buses 176 and 178 from the centre and Flamengo; 591 and 592 from Copacabana.* Inaugurated in 1979, the planetarium has a sculpture of the Earth and Moon by Mario Agostinelli. There are occasional chorinho concerts on Thursday or Friday.

Southern suburbs

Leblon to Barra da Tijuca

The Pedra Dois Irmãos overlooks Leblon. On the slopes is Vidigal favela. From Leblon, two inland roads take traffic west to the outer seaside suburb of Barra da Tijuca: the Auto Estrada Lagoa-Barra, which tunnels under Dois Irmãos, and the Estrada da Gávea, which goes through Gávea.

Parque da Cidade ① *daily 0700- 1700, free, getting there: buses, Nos 593, 592, 174, 170, 546, leave you just short of the entrance, but it should be OK to walk the last part if in a group, similarly, do not walk the trails in the park alone.* A pleasant park a short walk beyond the Gávea bus terminus, it has a great many trees and lawns, the Museu Histórico da Cidade, with views over the ocean. The proximity of the Rocinha favela (see below) means the park is not very safe. Carry a copy of your passport here because of frequent police checks. Beyond Leblon the coast is rocky. A third route to Barra da Tijuca is the Avenida Niemeyer, which skirts the cliffs on the journey past Vidigal, a small beach where the Sheraton is situated. Avenida Niemeyer carries on round the coast to São Conrado. On the slopes of the Pedra da Gávea, through which the Avenida Niemeyer has two tunnels, is the Rocinha favela.

The flat-topped **Pedra da Gávea** can be climbed or scrambled up for magnificent views, but beware of snakes. Behind the Pedra da Gávea is the Pedra Bonita. A road, the Estrada das Canoas, climbs up past these two rocks on its way to the Parque Nacional Tijuca. There is a spot on this road which is one of the chief hang-glider launch sites in the area (see page 371). See also Transport page 377.

Barra da Tijuca

This rapidly developing residential area is also one of the principal recreation areas of Rio, with its 20-km sandy beach and good waves for surfing. At the westernmost end is the small beach of Recreio dos Bandeirantes, where the ocean can be very rough. The channels behind the Barra are popular with jetskiers. It gets very busy on Sundays. There are innumerable bars and restaurants, clustered at both ends, campsites (see page 364), motels and hotels: budget accommodation tends to be self-catering. Although buses do run as far as Barra, getting to and around here is best by car. A cycle way links Barra da Tijuca with the centre of the city. A bit further out is the **Museu Casa do Pontal** ① *Estrada do Pontal 3295, Recreio dos Bandeirantes, Sat and Sun only, 1400-1800, a collection of Brazilian folk art. Recommended.*

Parque Nacional Tijuca

① *National park information, T2208 4194. See also transport page 377.*
The Pico da Tijuca (1,022 m) gives a good idea of the tropical vegetation of the interior and a fine view of the bay and its shipping. A two to three hr walk leads to the summit: on entering the park at Alto da Boa Vista (0600-2100), follow the signposts (maps are displayed) to Bom Retiro, a good picnic place (1½ hours' walk). At Bom Retiro the road ends and there is another hour's walk up a fair footpath to the summit (take the path from the right of the Bom Retiro drinking fountain; not the more obvious steps from the left). The last part consists of steps carved out of the solid rock; look after children at the summit as there are several sheer drops, invisible because of bushes. The route is shady for almost its entire length. The main path to Bom Retiro passes the Cascatinha Taunay (a 30 m waterfall) and the Mayrink Chapel (built 1860). Beyond the Chapel is the restaurant A Floresta. Other places of interest not passed on the walk to the peak are the Paulo e Virginia Grotto, the Vista do Almirante

and the Mesa do Imperador (viewpoints). Allow at least five to six hours for the excursion. Maps of the park are available. If hiking in the national park other than on the main paths, a guide may be useful if you do not want to get lost: Sindicato de Guías, T2267 4582.

Parque Estadual da Pedra Branca ① *Núcleo Camorim, Camorim, Jacarepaguá, T3417 3642, www.ief.rj.gov.br*. The largest urban forest in the world is also in Rio, though few Cariocas are aware of it. Pedra Branca is the city's best kept natural secret, protecting an astounding 12,500 ha of pristine rainforest, lakes and mountains, which are home to over 500 animal species. A number are threatened or critically endangered. There are many trails in the park, including one leading to the highest peak in Rio de Janeiro, the Pedra Branca (1,024 m).

Ilha de Paquetá

The island, the second largest in Guanabara Bay, is noted for its gigantic pebble shaped rocks, butterflies and orchids. At the southwest tip is the interesting Parque Darke de Mattos, with beautiful trees, lots of birds and a lookout on the Morro da Cruz. The island has several beaches, but ask about the state of the water before bathing. The only means of transport are bicycles and horse-drawn carriages (US$20 per hr, many have harnesses which cut into the horse's flesh). Neither is allowed into the Parque Darke de Mattos. A tour by trenzinho, a tractor pulling trailers, costs US$1.65, or just wander around on foot, quieter and free. Bicycles can be hired. The island is very crowded at weekends and on public holidays, but is usually quiet during the week. The prices of food and drink are reasonable. See Transport page 377.

● Sleeping

All hotels **AL-A** and above in the following list are a/c. A 10% service charge is usually added to the bill and tax of 5% or 10% may be added (if not already included). Note that not all higher-class hotels include breakfast in their room rates. The best and safest places to stay in Rio are Ipanema and southern Copacabana and there are a number of decent, new budget hostels in these areas. With a few notable exceptions, Rio's other hotels in the higher and mid-range are a mix of anonymous business chain towers and fading leftovers from the 1970s, complete with period decor. Economy hotels are found mainly in the 3 districts of Rio: Flamengo/Botafogo (best), Lapa/Fátima and Saúde/Maúa: choose with care in those districts. The city is noisy. An inside room is cheaper and much quieter. Always ask for the actual room price: it usually differs from that quoted, frequently much lower. Prices rise considerably pricier over New Year and Carnaval. Reserve well in advance, especially budget accommodation.

Santa Teresa *p353, map p354*
Santa Teresa is hilly and offers views out over Rio but is inconvenient for transport.
B-C Casa Áurea, R Áurea 80, Santa Teresa, T2242 5830, www.casaaurea.com.br. Small hotel in a converted colonial house. Rooms are bright and

airy and service attentive. Breakfast is served in a little garden visited by marmosets in the mornings.

Glória, Catete and Flamengo *p355, map p354*
Glória, Catete and Flamengo are primarily residential areas between the centre and Copacabana. Catete, and Glória to the north and Flamengo to the south, lie next to a park landscaped by Burle Marx and a beautiful beach lapped by a filthy sea. They have good bus and Metrô connections, but are not as safe as Ipanema.
   Many great deals and charming options for B&Bs to be found on www.camaecafe.com.br (R Progresso 67, next to Largo das Neves, Santa Teresa, T2224 5689). They include Ronnie Biggs's former home and Mestre Valentim's castle-folly on their books.
LL-L Glória, R do Russel 632, Glória, T2555 7572, www.hotelgloriario.com.br. Rio's other stylish and elegant 1920s hotel. Not as grand as the Copacabana Palace but with far more charm than any others in Copacabana or Ipanema. Rooms have mock Edwardian decoration. Two pools, spa and in-house theatre. Highly recommended.
LL-L Novo Mundo, Praia Flamengo 20, Catete, T2557 4355, www.hotelnovomundo-rio.com.br. Standard 4-star rooms, suites with balcony views of the Sugar Loaf. Recommended but noisy.

● *For an explanation of the sleeping and eating price codes used in this guide, see inside the front*
● *cover. Other relevant information is found in Essentials pages 345-347.*

L Flórida, Ferreira Viana, 71/81, Catete, T2556 5242, www.windsorhoteis.com. Business-orientated hotel, bars (for private hire), restaurant, and modestly decorated modern rooms.

A Inglês, R Silveira Martins 20, Glória, T2558 3052, www.hotelingles.com.br. Popular cheapie next to the metro and in front of the Museu da República. The better rooms have been refurbished and have a/c.

A Paysandu, Paysandu, R Paissandu 23, Flamengo T2558 7270, www.paysanduhotel.com.br. Wonderful art deco tower next to the Palácio de República and Flamengo gardens, with spartan rooms but helpful staff, good location, organized tours available.

B Imperial, R do Catete 186, T2556 5212, Catete, www.imperialhotel.com.br. One of the city's very first grand hotels (late 19th- century). Rooms either in the grander, older main building, or the modern annexe (modern, US motel-style), better equipped but overlooking the parking lot.

B Turístico, Ladeira da Glória 30, Glória, T2557 7698, F2558 5815. With breakfast, a/c, tourist information provided, mixed reports, some highly favourable.

C Único, Ferreira Viana 54, Catete, T2205 9932, F2205 8149. Plain rooms with TV, a/c and fridge. Recommended.

D Rio Hostel, R Joaquim Murtinho 361, T3852 0827, Santa Teresa, www.riohostel.com. Dormitories (**B** in double room), with breakfast, kitchen, bar, pool, internet, laundry service, hot water, airport pick-up US$17, relaxed, English spoken, events and trips organized. Owner loves English and Australians and has an inexplicable fixation with Jamie Oliver.

D-E King Hostel, R Barão de Guaratiba 20, Catete, www.kingalbergue.hpg.ig.com.br. Cheap and cheerful hostel with dorms and doubles, a stroll from Catete metro.

Botafogo *p356*
Another quiet, middle class neighbourhood with a great beach lapped by dirty water. Convenient for public transport and Mall shopping but care should be taken at night.

AL O Veleiro, T2554 8980, PO Box 62602, Praia de Botafogo, RJ 22252-970, www.oveleiro.com. Address given only with reservation. B&B with a great breakfast, Canadian/ Carioca owned, pick-up

and drop-off from airport or bus station, tours, guiding, very helpful staff. Recommended, but neighbourhood noisy at times.

D Chave do Rio de Janeiro, R general Dionísio 63, Botafogo, T2286 0303, www.riohostel.com.br. IYHA, cheaper for members, laundry and cooking facilities, superb breakfast, noisy. Recommended.

D-E pp Ace Backpackers, R São Clemente 23, 1st floor, Botafogo, T2527 7452, www.ace hostels.com.br. Popular, lively, small but spotless dorms and rooms, kitchen, internet, tours, laundry. Other branches in Paraty and São Paulo.

D-E El Misti Hostel, R Praia de Botafogo 462, casa 9, T2226 0991, www.elmistihostel.com. Converted colonial house with 6 dorms, shared bath, doubles. **B**, kitchen, internet, capoeira classes, tour service. Convenient for public transport.

Pão de Açúcar: Urca *p356*

A-D Carioca Easy, R Marechal Cantuária 168, Urca, T2295 7805, www.cariocahostel.com.br. Bright little hostel in a colonial house in one of the safest and most spectacular neighbourhoods in Rio; at the base of Sugar Loaf. Pool, kitchen, bike rental, boat trips, dorms and doubles.

Copacabana *p357, map p362*

LL Copacabana Palace, Av Atlântica 1702, T2548 7070, www.copacabana palace.com.br. Justifiably world famous hotel with distinguished guest list, dripping in 1920's elegance. Go for cocktails and dinner if you can't afford to stay. Cipriani (♥♥♥), is the best restaurant for formal evening dining in Rio with a chef from the Hotel Cipriani in Venice. Very good seafood and modern Italian fare.

LL Le Méridien, Av Atlântica 1020, T0800-111554, www.meridien- br.com. Air France hotel with pool, quite small rooms, breakfasts with a wonderful view, also good for business travellers.

LL Marriott, Av Atlantica 2600, T2545 6500, www.marriott.com. Rio's newest top end business hotel, specifically designed with a gamut of services for the business visitor.

LL Pestana Río Atlântica, Av Atlântica 2964, T2548 6332, www.pestana.com. Part of the Portuguese Pestana group, an excellent choice, spacious bright rooms and a rooftop pool and terrace with sweeping views, very high standards. Recommended.

AL Grandarell Ouro Verde, Av Atlântica 1456, T2542 1887, www.grandarrell.com.br. The best small hotel in Copacabana with spacious, well-decorated rooms and a decent restaurant. Good for families – the hotel has a Kid's club.

Brazil Rio de Janeiro Listings

AL-A Hotel Santa Clara, Rua Décio Vilares, 316, T2256 2652, T/F2547 4042, www.hotel santaclara.com.br. Quiet, central location, a/c, TV, telephone, en suite bath, attentive service, breakfast included, tours arranged.

A Debret, Av Atlântica 3564, T2522 0132, www.de bret.com. Bright, spacious seafront rooms, others are a little dark, modern. Good, helpful staff.

A Rio Copa, Av Princesa Isabel 370, T2275 6644, www.riocopa.com. Best Western, simple, well-maintained rooms 2 blocks back from beach. English-spoken. Recommended.

A-B Atlantis Copacabana, Av Bulhões de Carvalho 61, T2521 1142, atlantishotel@ uol.com.br. Fading Arpoador hotel in a quiet, safe street very close to the beach. Small rooftop pool, sauna, very good value.

A-B Copacabana Sol, R Santa Clara 141, T2549 4577, www.copacabanasolhotel.com.br. Safe, helpful, quiet, with good breakfast, simple rooms.

D Che Lagarto Copacabana, R Anita Garibaldi 87, T2256 2778, www.chelagarto.com. HI members. Includes breakfast and welcome drink. Rooms with toilet and a/c. Also **Che Lagarto Budget**, T2257-3133, 304 Santa Clara, from US$14.

D pp Copacabana Praia, R Tte Marones de Gusmão 85, Bairro Peixoto, T2235 3817. Dorms and doubles in a large place in a quiet residential area 600m from beach, no breakfast.

D Shenkin Hostel, R Santa Clara 304, T2257 3133. Party hostel with its own bar 5 mins' from the beach, dorms, singles, doubles, good value.

D-E Mario's Hostel, R Leopoldo Miguez 10, T 3185 6604, www.marioshostel.com. Dorms, singles and doubles 2 mins from the beach, airport pickup, kitchen, internet and a shared sitting room.

D-E Mellow Yellow, R General Barbosa Lima 51, T2547 1993, www.mellowyellow.com.br. Nothing mellow about this enormous party hostel. But it is always packed, has its own bar, live music, tour services, internet facilities and free airport pick-up.

D-E Rio Backpackers, Travessa Santa Leocádia 38, T2236 3803, www.riobackpackers.com.br. Another popular hostel, bright, with small dorms, singles and doubles (**A-B**), very helpful, English spoken, kitchen, internet, good fun.

Ipanema, Leblon and further west
p357, map p364
Note: Rio Universe, a new Fasano 'boutique'

Copacabana

hotel is due to open in Ipanema in 2006-07: www.riouniverse.com.br.

LL La Maison, R Sergio Porto 58, Gávea, T7812 5836, www.lamaisonario.com. A boutique hidden away in a converted colonial townhouse on a quiet back street. Resolutely OTT decor, but the bedrooms are more understated and the views of the forest and Corcovado from the breakfast area are magnificent.

LL La Suite, R Jackson de Figueiredo, 501, Joá, 00 55 21 2484 1962, fxdussol@hotmail.com. Versace meets Louis XIV in a riot of colour that Elton John would swoon over in this 7-room boutique between Leblon and Barra da Tijuca. Fabulous location - the pool sits eyrie-like over the exclusive beach at Joá with sweeping views out towards São Conrado. Every room has a terrace, view and a marble bathroom.

LL Best Western Sol Ipanema, Av Vieira Souto 320, T2525 2020, www.bestwestern.com. Huge breakfast, good member of the US chain, popular.

LL Marina Palace and Marina All Suites, Av Delfim Moreira 630 and 696, T2294 1794, www.hotelmarina.com.br. Two 1980s towers almost next door to each other. The former has smart, modern but standard rooms and a rooftop pool, the latter is a luxury boutique with 'designer' suites, with the excellent Bar D'Hotel (▼▼▼), light but very well-flavoured fish dishes served in cool surroundings. Also very good breakfasts and cocktails.

L Arpoador Inn, Francisco Otaviano 177, T2523 0060, F2511 5094. Well-maintained, if undistinguished rooms, seafront restaurant, off-season special offers are a good deal.

L Mar Ipanema, R Visconde de Pirajá 539, T3875 9190, www.maripanema.com. One block from the beach, simple, smart, modern rooms.

AL-A San Marco, R Visconde de Pirajá 524, T2540 5032, www.sanmarcohotel.net. Renovated 2-star 2 blocks from beach, with simple rooms and a free caipirinha for every internet booking, very helpful, internet US$2.70 per hr. Price includes breakfast. Recommended.

A Ipanema Inn, Maria Quitéria 27, behind Caesar Park, T2523 3092, F2511 5094. Good value and location.

A-D The Lighthouse, R Barão da Torre 175, casa 20, T2522 1353, www.thelighthouse.com.br. One private room for up to 4, and a dorm for 8, use of kitchen, internet, very helpful, New Zealand/Brazilian owners.

C-D Che Lagarto Ipanema, R Paul Redfern 48, T2512 8076, www.chelagarto.com. Bright red party hostel with young staff and a terrace with views of Corcovado, dorms and doubles (**B**), cheaper with HI card. See also Copacabana, above.

C-D Casa 6, R Barão da Torre 175, casa 6, T2247 1384, www.casa6ipanema.com. Charming, colourful but simple French-owned B&B in a townhouse 3 blocks from the beach. Also has doubles (**A**), good long stay rates.

C-D Crab Hostel, R Prudente de Morais 903, T2267 7353, www.crabhostel.com.br. A block from the beach with a pool, sauna, cable TV and dorms with en suites, poor service reported.

C-D Harmonia, R Barão da Torre 175, casa 18, T2523 4905, www.hostelharmonia.com. 3 blocks from beach, doubles or dormitories, cheaper without breakfast, kitchen facilities, English, Spanish, German and Swedish spoken, good internet. At casa 14 in the same building is **Hostel Ipanema**, T2247 7269.

C-E Ipanema Beach House, R Barão da Torre 485, T3202 2693, www.ipanemahouse.com. Dorms and doubles all with shared baths. Great little hostel with rooms arranged around a garden and small pool. Small bar, kitchen, internet and tours, good service.

Casarão **6**
Cervantes **3**
Churrascaria Palace **5**
La Trattoria **7**
Marakesh **9**
Siri Mole & Cia **11**

Taberna do Leme **10**
Traiteurs de France **12**

Camping

Camping Clube do Brasil, Av Sen Dantas 75, 29th floor, Centro, CEP 20037-900, T2210 3171, www.camping-club.com.br. Has 2 beach sites at Barra da Tijuca: Av Sernambetiba 3200, T2493 0628 (bus 233 from centre, 702 or 703 from the airport via Zona Sul, US$5 – a long way from the centre), sauna, pool, bar, café, US$12 (half price for members), during Jan and Feb this site is often full and sometimes restricted to members of the Camping Clube do Brasil; a simpler site at Estrada do Pontal 5900, T2437 8400, lighting, café, good surfing, US$6. Both have trailer plots.

If travelling by trailer, you can park at the **Marina Glória** car park, where there are showers and toilets, a small shop and snack bar. Pay the guards to look after your vehicle.

Self-catering apartments

A popular form of accommodation in Rio, available at all price levels: eg furnished apartments for short-term let, accommodating up to 6, cost US$300 per month in Maracanã, about US$400 in Saúde, Cinelândia, Flamengo. Copacabana, Ipanema and Leblon prices range from about US$25 a day for a simple studio, starting at US$500-600 a month up to US$2,000 a month for a luxurious residence sleeping 4-6. Heading south past Barra da Tijuca, virtually all the accommodation available is self-catering. Renting a small flat, or sharing a larger one, can be much better value than a hotel room. Blocks consisting entirely of short-let apartments can

attract thieves, so check the (usually excellent) security arrangements; residential buildings are called prédio familial. Higher floors (alto andar) are considered quieter.

Apart-Hotels are listed in the Guia 4 Rodas and Riotur's booklet. Agents and private owners advertise in Balcão (like the UK's Exchange and Mart), twice weekly, O Globo or Jornal do Brasil (daily); under 'Apartamentos – Temporada'; advertisements are classified by district and size of apartment: 'vagas e quartos' means shared accommodation; 'conjugado' (or 'conj') is a studio with limited cooking facilities; '3 Quartos' is a 3-bedroom flat. There should always be a written agreement when renting.

The following rent apartments in residential blocks:

Apartments Rio de Janeiro, www.rentinrio.com, with contact numbers in the USA and UK.

Copacabana Holiday, R Barata Ribeiro 90A, Copacabana, T2542 1525, www.copacabana holiday.com.br. Recommended, well-equipped small apartments from US$500 per month, minimum 30 days let.

Fantastic Rio, Av Atlântica 974, Suite 501, Copacabana, BR-22020-000, T/F2543 2667, hpcorr@hotmail.com. All types of furnished accommodation, owned by Peter Corr.

Rio Flat Rental, R Leopoldo Miguez, l 61, Copacabana, T9956 5147, www.rioflatrental.com. Fully furnished flats, 24-hr security. Free pick-up from the airport.

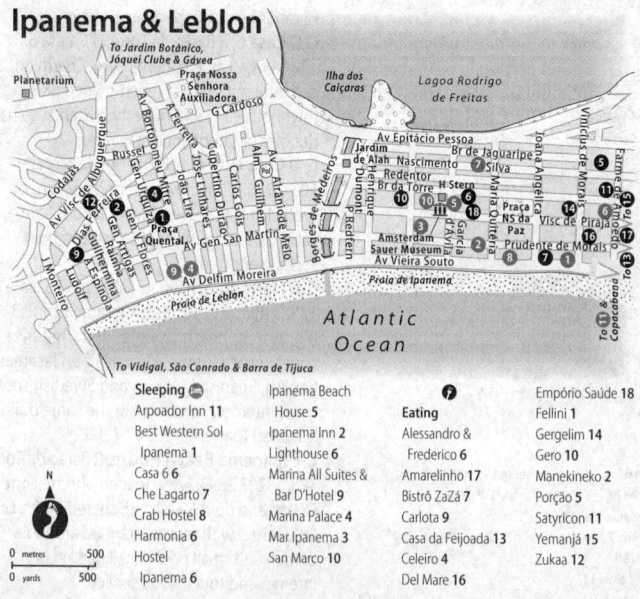

Ipanema & Leblon

Sleeping		
Arpoador Inn 11	Ipanema Beach	
Best Western Sol	House 5	**Eating**
Ipanema 1	Ipanema Inn 2	Alessandro &
Casa 6 6	Lighthouse 6	Frederico 6
Che Lagarto 7	Marina All Suites &	Amarelinho 17
Crab Hostel 8	Bar D'Hotel 9	Bistrô ZaZá 7
Harmonia 6	Marina Palace 4	Carlota 9
Hostel	Mar Ipanema 3	Casa da Feijoada 13
Ipanema 6	San Marco 5	Celeiro 4
		Del Mare 16

Empório Saúde 18	
Fellini 1	
Gergelim 14	
Gero 10	
Manekineko 2	
Porção 5	
Satyricon 11	
Yemanjá 15	
Zukaa 12	

Youth hostel associations and B&Bs
ALBERJ (for Rio), R da Assembléia 10, l 61,
T2531 2234, F2531 1943.
Federação Brasileira (Brazil), at Chave do
Rio de Janeiro hostel. For web bookings see
www.hostelworld.com.

🍴 Eating

The best of Rio's many restaurants are in
Copacabana, Ipanema or Leblon. Expect to pay
US$30+ per person in the better restaurants. You
can eat well for an average US$5 per person, less if
you choose the prato feito at lunchtime (US$2-
7.50), or eat in a place that serves food by weight
(starting at about US$0.65 per g). Avoid mussels!
Most restaurants are closed on 24 and 25 Dec.

Grill or barbecue houses (*churrascarias*) are
relatively cheap, especially by European standards.
There are many at São Conrado and Joá, on the
road out to Barra da Tijuca. Look for the
'Churrascaria Rodízio', where you are served as
much as you can eat. Galetos are lunch counters
specializing in chicken and grilled meat, very
reasonable. In the shopping centres there is
usually a variety of restaurants and snack bars
grouped around a central plaza where you can
shop around for a good meal. Most less-expensive
restaurants in Rio have basically the same type of
food (based on steak, fried potatoes and rice) and
serve large portions. La Mole, at 11 locations,
serves good, cheap Italian food, very popular. Rio
lacks that almost ubiquitous Brazilian institution,
the corner bakery, and a decent breakfast can be
hard to find. But there are plenty of stand-up juice
bars serving fruit juices made from as many as 25
different fruits, all of which are wonderful.

City centre and Lapa *p350, map p351*
Many restaurants in the business district are open
only for weekday lunch. Many lanchonetes in this
area offer good, cheap meals. R Miguel Couto
(opposite Santa Rita church) is called the **Beco
das Sardinhas** because on Wed and Fri in
particular is full of people eating sardines and
drinking beer. There are several Arab restaurants
on Av Senhor dos Passos, which are also open Sat
and Sun. In addition to those listed there are
plenty of cafes, including a few new chic options
on R Lavradio in Lapa; where the lively Sat
antiques market is held.

♛♛♛ Republique, Praça da República 63 (2nd floor),
T2532 9000. Refurbished and designed by the
architect Chicô Gouveia. Chef Paulo Carvalho cooks
a mix of Portuguese, Italian and French dishes.
♛♛ Adega Flor de Coimbra, R Teotônio Regadas
34, Lapa. Founded 1938, Portuguese food and
wines, speciality *bacalhau* (dried cod). Very good.
♛♛ Café do Teatro, Rio Branco, Teatro Municipal.
Traditional Portuguese and Brazilian cuisine for a
mostly business clientele. No shorts or sandals.
Weekday lunch only.
♛♛ Café Glória, R do Russel 734, Lapa, T2205 9647.
Open daily for lunch and dinner. Beautiful Art
Nouveau building, helpful staff, excellent food.
♛♛ Confeitaria Colombo, R Gonçalves Dias 32,
near Carioca Metrô station. Recommended for
atmosphere and the only one of its kind in Rio.
Over 100 years old, it has the original belle époque
decor, open 0900-1800, no service charge so tip
the excellent waiters. More modern but similar
establishments in some of the main hotels.
♛ Albamar, Praça Marechal Âncora 184-6, T2240
8428. Good, reasonably priced fish and seafood,
with lovely views of the bay. Open 1130-1600
Mon, 1130-2200 Tue-Sat.
♛ Al-kuwait, Av Treze de Maio, T2240 1114.
Charming Middle Eastern fan-cooled restaurant
with wood panelling in unprepossessing alley off
Treze de Maio. No English menu but helpful staff.
Try a traditional kofta or the daily special. Open
1100-2300, closed Sat and Sun.

¶ **Bistro do Paço**, Praça 15 de Novembro 48 (Paço Imperial), T2262 3613. Excellent, good value food in attractive surroundings, Swiss-run. Recommended. Open 1130-2000 Mon-Fri, 1200-1830 Sat and Sun.

¶ **Fiorino**, Av Heitor Beltrão 126, Tijuca, T2567 4476. Delicious, home-cooked Italian food with indulgent deserts. Recommended.

¶ **Luciano**, R das Marrecas 44. One of several functional, fairly cheerless all-you-can-eat buffets on this street, very cheap.

¶ **Mala e Cuia**, R Candelária 92, T2253 4032. For comida mineira. Recommended – also in Ipanema and Copacabana.

¶ **Rio Minho**, R do Ouvidor 10, T2509 2338. Excellent seafood in an historic building.

Santa Teresa p353, map p354

¶¶¶ **Aprazível**, R Aprazível 62, Santa Teresa, T3852 4935. Decent but unspectacular Brazilian dishes and seafood with tables outdoors in a tropical garden overlooking Guanabara Bay. This is a good Sun lunch spot when they have Choro and Samba performed by Rio's equivalent of the Buena Vista Social Club.

¶¶ **Adega do Pimenta**, R Almte Alexandrino 296, Santa Teresa. Daily 1130-2200, Sun 1100-1800, closed Sat, Tue. A very small German restaurant in the Largo do Guimarães with excellent sausages, sauerkraut and cold beer.

¶¶ **Bar do Arnaudo**, Largo do Guimarães, R Almte Alexandrino 316, Santa Teresa, T2252 7246. A modest-looking restaurant decorated with handicrafts but serving generous portions of wonderful Northeast Brazilian cooking. Try the *carne do sol* (sun-dried beef, or jerky) with *feijão de corda* (brown beans and herbs), or the *queijo coalho* (a country cheese, grilled).

Glória, Catete and Flamengo p355, map p354

There are many cheap and mid-range eating places on R do Catete; all much of a muchness.

¶¶ **Alcaparra**, Praia do Flamengo 144, Flamengo, T2557 7236. Elegant traditional Italian popular with politicians and business people. Overlooking the sea.

¶¶ **Alho E Óleo**, R Buarque de Macedo 13, Flamengo, T2557 8541. Fashionable Italian with a strong emphasis on pasta. Recommended.

¶¶ **Espírito Santa**, R Almirante Alexandrino 264, T2508 7095, www.espiritosanta.com.br. Great little arty restaurant with a wonderful sweeping view of the city and a cool club in the basement. Imaginative menu based on Amazon cooking, including *tacacá*, which literally tingles in the mouth as you eat it.

¶¶ **Lamas**, Marquês de Abrantes 18A, Flamengo. Steak, seafood and general Brazilian fare have been served here for over 130 years. Excellent value, great atmosphere, opens late, popular with Brazilian arts/media people. Recommended.

¶¶ **Sobrenatural**, R Almirante Alexandrino 432, T2224 1003. Closed Mon, open lunchtime and evening. A charming rustic restaurant serving fish caught daily on owner's boat. For a light lunch, order a mix of excellent appetisers. Recommended.

¶ **Amazônia**, R do Catete 234B, Catete. Downstairs for fixed-price counter service, upstairs for good, reasonably priced evening meals. Recommended.

¶ **Catelândia**, R do Catete 204, Catete. Excellent and cheap, pay by weight.

Botafogo p356

In Baixo Botafogo, those on a budget will find a number of enticing bars and restaurants on R Visconde de Caravelas.

¶¶ **Carême Bistrô**, R Visconde de Caravelas 113, Botafogo, T 2537 5431. An elegant and intimate little restaurant serving the best French food in Rio. Recommended.

¶¶ **Raajmahal**, R Gen Polidoro 29. One of the few restaurants offering authentic Indian food.

¶ **Aurora**, R Visconde de Caravelas corner of R Capitão Salomão 43. Varied menu and good value simple fare.

¶ **Botequim**, R Visconde de Caravelas No 184. Also has a varied menu and is good value.

¶ **Cobal Humaitá** is a daytime fruit market with many popular restaurants (Mexican tacos, pizzeria)

¶ **Chez Michou** and the ubiquitous chain restaurant **Habib's**, both in Rio Sul Shopping. Serve, respectively, crêpes and Arabic fast-food.

Copacabana, Ipanema and Leblon p357, maps p362 and p364

¶¶¶ **Alessandro & Frederico**, R Garcia D'Ávila, 134 loja D, Ipanema, T2521 0828. Upmarket café with decent café latte and breakfasts. Great juice bar next door.

¶¶¶ **Bistrô ZaZá**, R Joana Angélica 40, Ipanema. Hippy-chic, pseudo Moroccan/ French restaurant, good fish dishes and cocktails and good fun. Evenings are best for intimate dining when the tables are lit by candles.

¶¶¶ **Carlota**, R Dias Ferreira 64, Leblon, T2540 6821. The best of many on a street lined with restaurants and bars. Great unpretentious Mediterranean food in an elegant dining room.

¶¶¶ **Gero**, R Aníbal de Mendonça 157, Ipanema, T2239 8158. Light Italian fare and excellent fish in a beautiful, minimalist space.

¶¶¶ **Manekineko**, R Dias Ferreira, 410, Leblon, T2540 7641, www.manekineko.com.br. Exquisite Japanese and Japanese fusion cooking served in an intimately designed modern dining room.

TTT Porcão, Barão de Torre 218, Ipanema, T2522 0999 (also on Av NS de Copacabana). One of the city's best churrascarias, serving all manner of meat in unlimited quantities for a set price.

TTT Satyricon, R Barão da Torre 192, Ipanema, T2521 0627. The best seafood in Rio; especially the squid. Lively crowd in a large dining room. Avoid Sat when there is a seafood buffet.

TTT Zukaa, R Dias Ferreira 233, Leblon, T3205 7154. One of the most fashionable restaurants in Rio with an exciting and eclectic fusion of everything – French and Japanese, American fast food and Italian.

TT Casa da Feijoada, Prudente de Morais 10, Ipanema, T2523 4994. Serves an excellent feijoada all week. Generous portions.

TT Churrascaria Palace, R Rodolfo Dantas 16B, Copacabana. 20 different kinds of barbecued meat served on a spit at your table with buffet salads to accompany. Good value.

TT Fellini, R General Urquiza 104, Leblon, T2511 3600, www.fellini.com.br. The best per kilo in the city with a range of delicious buffet options and plenty for vegetarians.

TT Gergelim, R Vinícius de Moraes, 121, Ipanema T2523 7026. Vegetarian whole food in an a/c café atmosphere. Good puddings.

TT Mala e Cuia, R Barata Ribeiro 638, Copacabana, T2545 7566. Comida mineira at one of the restaurants in this recommended chain (also in the centre).

TT Rodizio Carretão, R Visconde de Pirajá 112, Ipanema, www.carretaochurrascaria.com.br. Good atmosphere, good food, reasonably priced (rises to TTT at weekends).

TT Siri Mole & Cia, R Francisco Otaviano 90, T2233 0107. Excellent Bahian seafood and Italian coffee in elegant a/c. At the upper end of this price bracket.

TT Yemenjá, R Visconde de Pirajá 128, Ipanema, T2247 7004. Bahian cooking such as moqueca, vatapa cooked in dende palm or coconut oil.

T A Marisquera, Barata Ribeiro 232, Copacabana, T2547 3920. Reasonable seafood dishes and Brazilian standards – eg meat, rice, beans, chips.

T Aipo and Aipim, Av Nossa Senhora de Copacabana 391b, 599 and 920, Copacabana, and R Visconde de Pirajá 145, Ipanema, T2267 8313. Plentiful tasty food sold by weight at this popular chain.

T Amarelinho, R Farme de Amoedo 62, Ipanema. Great corner lanchonete with tables outside, fresh food, good value, friendly, open until 0300. Recommended.

T Casarão, Souza Lima 37A, Copacabana. Cheap but decent café food and breakfasts.

T Celeiro, R Dias Ferreira 199, Leblon. Some of the best salads in the city, and light food by weight.

T Cervantes, Barata Ribeiro 07-B e Prado Júnior 335B, Copacabana. Stand-up bar or sit-down, a/c restaurant, open all night, queues after 2200. Said to serve the best sandwiches in town, a local institution.

T Del Mare, on the corner of Prudente de Morais and Vinícius de Morais. Recommended.

T Empório Saúde, R Visconde de Pirajá, 414, Ipanema, T2522 1494. Closed Sun and evenings. A large variety of vegetarian cooking from quiches to stews.

T La Trattoria, Av Atlântica, opposite Hotel Excelsior. Italian, good food and service, very reasonable. Recommended.

T Marakesh, Av NS de Copacabana 599. Good value pay by weight food.

T Taberna do Leme, corner of Princesa Isabel and Av NS Copacabana. A simple, friendly bar/restaurant with helpful waiters with tables on pavement. Comprehensive menu all in English includes delicious crab pancakes. Warmly recommended for eating as well as drinking.

T Traiteurs de France, Av NS de Copacabana 386, Copacabana. Delicious tarts and pastries, not expensive.

There are stand-up bars selling snacks all around Copacabana and Ipanema.

Gávea, Jardim Botânico and Lagoa *p357*

Gávea is the grungy heartland of trendy 20-something Rio, while Jardim Botânico and Lagoa appear, at first sight, to offer no end of exciting upmarket dining opportunities. They're mostly all show and poor value. Here are a few exceptions:

TTT Olympe, R Custódio Serrão 62, Lagoa, T2537 8582. Elegant French restaurant named after its chef who cooks a mixture of traditional cuisine and Franco-Brazilian fusions. Recommended.

TT Árabe da Gávea, Gávea shopping mall, R Marquês de São Vicente 52, T2294 2439. By far the best Arabic restaurant in Rio.

TT Dom João, R Pacheco Leão, Jardim Botânico, T3874 2819. Elegant colonial building with a mixed menu of respectable dishes. Good if you are in the area.

TT Guimas, R José Roberto Macedo Soares, Baixo Gávea, T2259 7996. One of the places where the under 30s come to be seen, especially after 2200 towards the end of the week and on Mon, before moving down the street to the two tatty bars on the corner of the street and Praça Santos Dumont. The restaurant serves simple, traditional Portuguese food, at only a handful of tables.

T Les Artistes, R Marquês de São Vicente 75, T2239 4242, Baixo Gávea. Another bar/ restaurant most notable for who goes not what is served; but only after 2200 on Fri when there is drum 'n bass.

♦ Bars and clubs

Rio nightlife is young and vivacious. The current hotspots are **Lapa** at weekends: once a down-at-heel area and still not entirely safe, but undergoing a great renaissance, with a string of clubs along Mem de Sá and Lavradio with dance steps from samba and forró to techno and hip hop. **Santa Teresa** is increasingly lively and is often used as a drinking spot before moving onto Lapa, or a night spot in its own. There is a cluster of bars around the Largo das Neves. Similarly busy, even on Sun and Mon is **Baixa Gávea**, where beautiful 20-somethings gather around Praça Santos Dumont. In **Ipanema/ Leblon**, there is always activity on and around Av General San Martin and Rua Dias Ferreira. **Copacabana** nightlife is mostly seedy and tawdry. Discos like Help are sad places full of visiting males panting after the lowest common denominator. Exceptions to this rule are the clubs like Bunker, the only one to play European club music in Rio. The guidebook O Guia dos Botequins do Rio de Janeiro, describes Rio's best, most traditional bars and their history, US$20. You can find it in the Livraria da Travessa (see Shopping), together with similar books; some in English.

Bars Wherever you are, there's one near you. Beer costs around US$1.50 for a large bottle, but up to US$5 in the plusher bars; where you are often given an entrance card which includes 2 drinks and a token entrance fee. A cover charge of US$3-7 may be made for live music, or there might be a minimum consumption charge of around US$3, sometimes both. Snack food is always available. Copacabana, Ipanema and Leblon have many beach barracas, several open all night. The seafront bars on Av Atlântica are great for people-watching; though avoid those towards Leme as they tend to offer more than beer. The big hotels have good cocktail bars.

Clubs Clubs in Rio are either fake Europe (eg Melt and Bunker) and US (eg Nuth and 00), or samba halls undergoing a renaissance (eg Scenarium and Carioca da Gema).

Centre, Lapa and Santa Teresa
p350, map p351
Lapa is without doubt the centre of Rio nightlife and should not be missed if you are in Rio over a weekend. Ideally come early on Sat for the afternoon market and live street tango, eat and stay for a bar and club crawl. Always be wary of pickpockets around Lapa. See also Samba schools.
Bar do Mineiro, on the Largo dos Guimarães, R Pascoal Carlos Magno 99, T2221 9227. A very popular Santa Teresa bar.
Carioca da Gema, Av Mem de Sá 79, Centro, T2221 0043. Great samba club café, second only to Rio Scenarium, good food too.

Club 6, R das Marrecas 38, Lapa. Huge pounding European/NYC dance club with everything from hip hop to ambient house.
Dama da Noite, R Gomes Freire 773, Lapa. Samba, Chorinho and crepes in the pátio.
Espírito Santa, see Santa Teresa, Eating. The basement club has great Rio funk from DJ Zod on Sat from 2200, Very popular.
Mercado, R do Mercado 32, Centro. A little bar with live Chorinho every Thu from 2030.
Rio Scenarium, R do Lavradio 20, Lapa, T3852 5516, www.rioscenarium.com.br. Three-storey Samba club in a colonial house used as a movie prop warehouse. Overflowing with Brazilian exuberance and joie de vivre, with people dancing furiously, to the bizarre backdrop of a 19th-century apothecary's shop or a line of mannequins wearing 1920s outfits. This is Rio at its Bohemian best. Buzzes with beautiful people of all ages on Fri. Arrive after 2300.
Sacrilégio, Av Mem de Sá 81, next to Carioca da Gema, Lapa, T2507 3898. Samba, Chorinho, Pagode and occasional theatre. Close to many other bars.
Semente, R Joaquim Silva 138, T2242 5165. Popular for Samba, Choro and Salsa from 2200 Mon-Sat, US$2.50 cover; minimum consumption US$2. Book a table at weekends. Great atmosphere both inside and in the streets outside. Recommended.

Glória, Flamengo and Botafogo
p355, map p354
Look out for the frequent free live music performances at the Marina da Glória and along Flamengo beach during the summer.
Casa de Matriz, R Enrique de Novais 107, Botafogo. Great little grungey club with a bar, Atari room, small cinema and 2 dance floors. Full of Rio students.
Porão, under the Anglican church hall, R Real Grandeza 99, Botafogo. British ex-pats meet here on Fri night.

Copacabana and Ipanema
p357, maps p362 and p364
There is frequent live music on the beaches of Copacabana and Ipanema, and along the Av Atlântica throughout the summer; especially around New Year.
Acádemia da Cachaça, R Conde de Bernadotte 26-G, Leblon; with another branch at Av Armando Lombardi 800, Barra da Tijuca. The best cachaças, great caipirinhas and traditional Brazilian dishes. Good on Fri.
Barril 1800, Av Vieira Souto 110, Ipanema. Nice place to watch the sunset. Highly recommended.
Bip Bip, R Almirante Gonçalves 50, Copacabana. Botequim bar which attracts a crowd of jamming musicians every Tue, also Sun for great atmosphere.

Bom Bar, R General San Martin 1011, Leblon. A downstairs bar and an upstairs club, packed after 2300, especially Sat.

Bunker, R Raul Pompeira 94, Copacabana. European-style dance club where the likes of DJs Marky and Patife play. Busy from Wed-Sat, kicks off at about 0200. The queues have become a party in themselves – at the bar next door.

Caroline Café, R JJ Seabra 10, Jardim Botânico, T2540 0705, www.carolinecafe.com. Popular bar with Rio's young and good-looking middle classes. Kicks off after 2130. Food too.

Devassa, Av General San Martin 1241, Leblon. A two-floor pub/restaurant/bar which is always heaving. Brews its own beer.

Empório, R Maria Quitéria 37, Ipanema. Street bar which attracts hordes. Mon is busiest.

A Garota de Ipanema, R Vinícius de Morais 49, Ipanema. Where the song 'Girl from Ipanema' was written. Now packed with foreigners on the package Rio circuit listening to Bossa. For the real thing head up the street to Toca do Vinícius on Sun afternoon (see below).

Melt, R Rita Ludolf 47, T2249 9309. Downstairs bar and upstairs sweaty club. Occasional performances by the cream of Rio's new samba funk scene, usually on Sun. Always heaving on Thu.

Shenanigans, R Visconde de Pirajá 112, Ipanema. Obligatory mock-Irish bar with Guinness and Newcastle Brown. Not a place to meet the locals.

Sindicato do Chopp, Av Atlântica 3806, Copacabana, and R Farme de Amoedo 85, Ipanema. Good value for meals as well as the obvious.

Vinícius, R Vinícius de Morais 39, Ipanema, 2nd floor. Mirror image of the Garota de Ipanema with slightly better acts and food.

Gávea, Jardim Botânico and Lagoa *p357*
00 (Zero Zero), Av Padre Leonel Franca 240, Gávea. Mock LA bar/restaurant/club with a small outdoor area. Currently the trendiest club in Rio for Brazil's equivalent of Sloanes or Valley Girls. Gay night on Sun.

Bar Lagoa, Av Epitácio Pessoa 1674, Lagoa. Attracts a slightly older, arty crowd on weekday evenings.

Clan Café, R Cosme Velho 564 (in front of the Corcovado train station). Great little gem of a sit down Choro and Samba club with live music every night and decent bar food.

Cozumel, Av Lineu de Paula Machado 696, Jardim Botânico. The Rio equivalent of a foam disco, with free margaritas, tacky music and a crowd most of whom are looking not to go home alone.

Mistura Fina, Av Borges de Medeiros 3207, T2537 2844. Downstairs restaurant, upstairs jazz

nd bossa nova club. One of the few places not oriented solely to the young.

Sítio Lounge, R Marques de Sao Vicente 10, Gávea. The nearest thing Rio has to a lounge bar, good for a chilled out Sat night.

El Turf (aka Jockey Club), opposite the Jardim Botânico, Praça Santos Dumont 31. Opens at 2200, gets going at 2300, you may have to wait to get in at the weekend if you arrive after midnight, no T-shirts allowed, very much a Rio rich kid singles and birthday party place; another branch in Rio Sul Shopping Centre.

Barra da Tijuca *p358*
Nuth, R Armando Lombardi 999, Barra da Tijuca, www.nuth.com.br. Barra's slickest club; very mock Miami with snacks. Mix of tacky Brazilian and Eurotrash music and some samba funk live acts. Expensive.

Pepe, at Posto 2, Barra da Tijuca beach. Very popular with young people.

◉ Entertainment

Rio de Janeiro *p348, maps p348 and p351*
Cinemas
There are cinemas serving subtitled Hollywood films and major Brazilian releases on the top floor of almost all the malls. The normal seat price is US$3, discounts on Wed and Thu (students pay half price any day of the week).
Centro Cultural do Banco do Brasil, see Sights, T2808 2020. One of Rio's better arts centres with the best art films and exhibitions from fine art to photography (Metro: Uruguaiana).
Cinemateca do MAM, Infante Dom Henrique 85, Aterro do Flamengo, T2210 2188. Cinema classics, art films and roving art exhibitions and a good café with live music. Views of Guanabara Bay from the balconies.
Estaçao Ipanema, R Visconde de Pirajá 605, Ipanema. European art cinema, less mainstream US and Brazilian releases.

Live music
Many young Cariocas congregate in Botafogo for live music. There are free concerts throughout the summer, along the Copacabana and Ipanema beaches, in Botafogo and at the parks: mostly samba, reggae, rock and MPB (Brazilian pop): there is no advance schedule, information is given in the local press (see below). Rio's famous jazz, in all its forms, is performed in lots of enjoyable venues, see the press. See www.samba-choro.com.br, for more information. Also see Clan Café, Melt, Nuth and Mistura Fina in Bars and clubs, above.
Canecão, R Venceslau Brás 215, Botafogo, T2295 3044. This big, inexpensive venue has live

concerts most nights, see press for listings. For a taste of some purely local entertainment, make your way down here on Mon nights.

Centro Cultural Carioca, R do Teatro 37, T2242 9642 for advance information, www.centroculturalcarioca.com. An exciting venue that combines music (mostly samba) and dance, 1830-early morning. This restored old house with wrap-around balconies and exposed brick walls is a dance school and music venue that attracts a lovely mix of people. Professional dancers perform with musicians; after a few tunes the audience joins in. Thu is impossibly crowded; Sat is calmer. Bar food available. US$3 cover charge. Highly recommended.

Praia do Vermelha at Urca. Residents bring musical instruments and chairs onto beach for an informal night of samba from 2100-midnight, free. Bus No 511 from Copacabana.

Rhapsody, Av Epitácio Pessoa 1104, Lagoa, T2247 2104. Piano bar restaurant with mixture of Brazilian and Diana Krall-style crooning.

Toca do Vinícius, Vinícius de Moraes 129, Ipanema. Rio's leading Bossa Nova and Choro record shop with live concerts from some of the finest past performers every Sun lunchtime and 2000 Sun in summer.

⊕ Festivals and events

Rio de Janeiro *p348, maps p348 and p351*
Less hectic than Carnival, but very atmospheric, is the festival of **Iemanjá** on the night of **31 Dec**, when devotees of the orixá of the sea dress in white and gather on Copacabana, Ipanema and Leblon beaches, singing and dancing around open fires and making offerings. The elected Queen of the Sea is rowed along the seashore. At midnight small boats are launched as offerings to Iemanjá. The religious event is dwarfed, however, by a massive New Year's Eve party, called **Reveillon** at Copacabana. The beach is packed as thousands of revellers enjoy free outdoor concerts by big-name pop stars, topped with a lavish midnight firework display. It is most crowded in front of Copacabana Palace Hotel. Another good place to see fireworks is in front of Le Meridien, famous for its fireworks waterfall at about 10 mins past midnight. **Note**: Many followers of Iemanjá are now making their offerings on 29 or 30 Dec and at Barra da Tijuca or Recreio dos Bandeirantes to avoid the crowds and noise of Reveillon. The festival of **São Sebastião**, patron saint of Rio, is celebrated by an evening procession on **20 Jan**, leaving Capuchinhos Church, Tijuca, and arriving at the cathedral of São Sebastião. On the same evening, an **umbanda festival** is celebrated at the Caboclo Monument in Santa Teresa. **Carnival 5-8**

Feb 2005, **26 Feb-1 Mar** 2006 (see page 372). **Festas Juninas: Santo Antônio** on **13 Jun**, whose main event is a mass, followed by celebrations at the Convento do Santo Antônio and the Largo da Carioca. Throughout the state of Rio, the festival of **São João** is a major event, marked by huge bonfires on the night of **23-24 Jun**. It is traditional to dance the quadrilha and drink quentão, cachaça and sugar, spiced with ginger and cinnamon, served hot. The Festas Juninas close with the festival of **São Pedro** on **29 Jun**. Being the patron saint of fishermen, his feast is normally accompanied by processions of boats. **Oct** is the month of the feast of **Nossa Senhora da Penha**.

⊙ Shopping

Rio de Janeiro *p348, maps p348 and p351*
Bookshops Argumento, R Dias Ferreira 417, Leblon. Sells imported English books.
FNAC has a megastore at Barra Shopping, with French, English and other imported titles, CDs.
Livraria da Travessa, Travessa do Ouvidor 11-A, superb new branch at Av Rio Branco 44 and R Visconde de Pirajá 572, Ipanema. Excellent. Broad selection of novels, general books, magazines and guidebooks in English. Great café upstairs at the Ipanema branch for a coffee while you read.
Saraiva has a megastore at R do Ouvidor 98, T507 9500, also with a music and video shop and a café; other branches in Shopping Iguatemi and Shopping Tijuca. **Siciliano**, Av Rio Branco 156, loja 26. European books, also at Nossa Senhora de Copacabana 830 and branches; French books at No 298. **Da Vinci**, Av Rio Branco 185 lojas 2, 3 and 9. All types of foreign books.

Fashion Fashion is one of the best buys in Brazil; with a wealth of Brazilian designers selling clothes of the same quality as European or US famous names at a fraction of the price. Rio is the best place in the world for buying high fashion bikinis. The best shops in Rio are on Garcia D'Ávila and R Nascimento Silva, which runs off it, in Ipanema. This is where some of the best Brazilian designers like Andrea Saletto and Rosana Bernardes, together with international big name stalwarts like Louis Vuitton and Cartier. Most of the international names, together with all the big names Brazilian names like Lenny (Brazil's best bikinis), Alberta, Salinas, Club Chocolate and so on are housed in the **Fashion Mall** in São Conrado.

Saara is a multitude of little shops along R Alfândega and R Senhor dos Passos (between city centre and Campo Santana), where clothing bargains can be found (especially jeans, kanga beach wraps and bikinis); it is known popularly as 'Shopping a Céu Aberto'. Little shops on Aires Saldanha, Copacabana (1 block back from beach), are good for bikinis and cheaper than in shopping centres.

Jewellery Amsterdam Sauer, R Garcia D'Ávila 105, with10 shops in Rio and others through- out Brazil. They offer free taxi rides to their main shop. Antônio Bernardo, R Garcia d'Ávila 121, Ipanema, T2512 7204, and in the Fashion Mall. Brazil's foremost jeweller who has been making beautifully understated jewellery with contemporary designs for nearly 30 years. Internationally well known, but available only in Brazil. H Stern, next door to Amsterdam Sauer at R Visconde de Pirajá 490/R Garcia Dávila 113, Ipanema, has 10 outlets, plus branches in major hotels.

There are several good jewellery shops at the Leme end of Av NS de Copacabana. Mineraux, Av NS de Copacabana 195. For mineral specimens as against cut stones, Belgian owner.

Markets Northeastern market at Campo de São Cristóvão, with music and magic, on Sun 0800-2200 (bus 472 or 474 from Copacabana or centre). A recommended shop for northeastern handicrafts is Pé de Boi, R Ipiranga 55, Laranjeiras, www.pedeboi.com.br. Sat antiques market on the waterfront near Praça 15 de Novembro, 1000-1700. Also in Praça 15 de Novembro is Feirarte II, Thu-Fri 0800-1800. Feirarte I is a Sun open-air handicrafts market (everyone calls it the Feira Hippy) at Praça Gen Osório, Ipanema, 0800-1800, items from all over Brazil. A stamp, coin and postcard market is held in the Passeio Público on Sun, 0800-1300. Markets on Wed 0700-1300 on R Domingos Ferreira and on Thu, same hrs, on Praça do Lido, both Copacabana (Praça do Lido also has a Feirarte on Sat-Sun 0800-1800). Sunday market on R da Glória, colourful, cheap fruit, vegetables and flowers; early-morning food market, 0600-1100, R Min Viveiros de Castro, Ipanema. There is a cheap market for just about anything, especially electronic goods, outside Metro stop Uruguaiana. Excellent food and household-goods markets at various places in the city and suburbs (see newspapers for times and places).

Music Modern Sound Música Equipamentos, R Barata Ribeiro 502D, Copacabana. For a large selection of Brazilian music, jazz and classical.
Toca do Vinícius, see Live music, above.

Shopping malls Rio Sul, at the Botafogo end of Túnel Novo, has almost everything the visitor may need. Some of the services in Rio Sul are: Telemar (phone office) for international calls at A10-A, Mon-Sat 1000-2200; next door is Belle Tours Câmbio, A10. There is a post office at G2. A good branch of Livraria Sodiler is at A03. For Eating and Entertainment, see above; live music at the Terraço; the Ibeas Top Club gym; and a cinema. A US$5 bus service runs as far as the

Sheraton passing the main hotels, every 2 hrs between 1000 and 1800, then 2130.

Other shopping centres, which include a wide variety of services, include Cassino (Copacabana), Norte Shopping (Todos os Santos), Plaza Shopping (Niterói), Barra in Barra da Tijuca (see page 358) and The Fashion Mall in São Conrado, see above.

▲ Activities and tours

Rio de Janeiro *p348, maps p348 and p351*
There are hundreds of gyms and sports clubs; most will not grant temporary (less than 1 month) membership. Big hotels may allow use of their facilities for a small deposit.

Cycling Rio Bikers, R Domingos Ferreira 81, room 201, T2274 5872. Tours and bike hire.
Stop Bike, T2275 7345, Copacabana. Bike rental.
Diving Squalo, Av Armando Lombardi 949-D, Barra de Tijuca, T/F2493 3022, squalo1@hotmail.com. Offers courses at all levels, NAUI and PDIC training facilities, also snorkelling and equipment rental.
Football See under Maracanã stadium, page 353.
Hang-gliding HiltonFlyRio Hang Gliding Center, T2278 3779/9964 2607 (mob), www.hiltonflyrio.com. DeHilton Carvalho is an ABVL certified instructor, very experienced.
Just Fly, T/F2268 0565, T9985 7540 (mob), www.justfly.com.br. US$80 for tandem flights with Paulo Celani (licensed by Brazilian Hang Gliding Association), pick-up and drop-off at hotel included, in-flight pictures US$15 extra, flights all year, best time of day 1000-1500 (5% discount for South American and Brazil Handbook readers on presentation of book at time of reservation). Super-fly, T3322 2286, www.riosuperfly.com.br. Regarded as the best hang-gliding operator from the Pedra Bonita. Tandem Flight and Rio by Jeep, T9693 8800, www.deltaflight.com.br. Tandem flight tours above Rio from Pedra Bonita Mountain with instructors licensed by the Brazilian Hang- Gliding Association. Contact Ricardo Hamond. Ultra Força Ltda, Av Sernambetiba 8100, Barra da Tijuca, T3399 3114; 15 mins.
Helicopter rides Helisight, R Visconde de Pirajá 580, loja 107, Térreo, Ipanema, T2259 6995, www.helisight.com.br. Prices from US$100 pp for flights from Lagoa or Pão de Açucar over Sugar Loaf and Corcovado.
Horse racing and riding Jockey Club Racecourse, by Jardím Botânico and Gávea, meetings on Mon and Thu evenings and Sat and Sun 1400, entrance US$1-2, long trousers required. Take any bus marked 'via Jóquei'. Sociedade Hípico Brasileiro, Av Borges de Medeiros 2448, T527 8090, Jardim Botânico. For riding.

Carnival

Carnival in Rio is spectacular. On the Friday before Shrove Tuesday, the mayor of Rio hands the keys of the city to Rei Momo, the Lord of Misrule, signifying the start of a five-day party. Imagination runs riot, social barriers are broken and the main avenues, full of people and children wearing fancy dress, are colourfully lit. Areas throughout the city such as the Terreirão de Samba in Praça Onze are used for shows, music and dancing. *Bandas* and *blocos* (organized carnival groups) seem to be everywhere, dancing, drumming and singing.

There are numerous samba schools in Rio divided into two leagues, both of which parade in the Sambódromo. The Carnival parades are the culmination of months of intense activity by community groups, mostly in the city's poorest districts. Every school presents 2,500-6,000 participants divided into *alas* (wings) each with a different costume and 5-9 *carros alegóricos*, beautifully designed floats. Each school chooses an *enredo* (theme) and composes a samba (song) that is a poetic, rhythmic and catchy expression of the theme. The *enredo* is further developed through the design of the floats and costumes. A *bateria* (percussion wing) maintains a reverberating beat that must keep the entire school, and the audience, dancing throughout the parade. Each procession follows a set order with the first to appear being the *comissão de frente*, a choreographed group that presents the school and the theme to the public. Next comes the *abre alas*, a magnificent float usually bearing the name or symbol of the school. Schools are given between 65 and 80 minutes and lose points for failing to keep within this time. Judges award points to each school for components of their procession, such as costume, music and design, and make deductions for lack of energy, enthusiasm or discipline.

The **Sambódromo** is a permanent site at R Marquês de Sapucai, Cidade Nova, is 600 m long with seating for 4 3,000 people. Designed by Oscar Niemeyer and built in 1983-1984, it handles sporting events, conferences and concerts during the rest of the year.

Rio's ***bailes*** (fancy-dress balls) range from the sophisticated to the wild. The majority of clubs and hotels host at least one. The Copacabana Palace hotel's is elegant and expensive whilst the Scala club has licentious parties. It is not necessary to wear fancy dress; just join in, although you will feel more comfortable if you wear a minimum of clothing to the clubs. The most famous are the Red & Black Ball (Friday) and the Gay Ball (Tuesday) which are both televized.

Bandas and ***blocos*** can be found in all neighbourhoods and some of the most popular and entertaining are Cordão do Bola Preta (meets at 0900 on Saturday in Rua 13 de Maio 13, Centro), Simpatia é Quase Amor (meets at 1600 Sunday in Praça General Osório, Ipanema) and the transvestite Banda da Ipanema (meets at 1600 on Saturday and Tuesday in Praça General Osorio, Ipanema). It is necessary to join a bloco in advance to receive their distinctive T-shirts, but anyone can join in with the bandas.

The expensive hotels offer special Carnival breakfasts from 0530. Caesar Park is highly recommended for a wonderful meal and a top-floor view of the sunrise over the beach.

Tickets The Sambódromo parades start at 1900 and last about 12 hours. Gates (which are not clearly marked) open at 1800. There are *cadeiras* (seats) at ground level, *arquibancadas* (terraces) and *camarotes* (boxes). The best boxes are reserved for tourists and VIPs and are very expensive or by invitation only.

Parapenting Barra Jumping, Aeroporto de Jacarepaguá, Av Ayrton Senna 2541, T3326 2304, www.barrajumping.com.br. Tandem jumping (Vôo duplo). Several other people offer tandem jumping; check that they are accredited with the Associação Brasileira de Vôo Livre. Ask for the **Parapente Rio Clube** at São Conrado launch site, tandem flight US$75-80.

Seats are closest to the parade, but you may have to fight your way to the front. Seats and boxes reserved for tourists have the best view, sectors 3, 5, 7, 9 and 11 all have good views (4, 7 and 11 house the judging points). 6 and 13 are at the end when dancers might be tired, but have more space. The terraces, while uncomfortable, house the most fervent fans, tightly packed; this is where to soak up the atmosphere but not take pictures (too crowded). Ticket are sold at banks and travel agencies as well as the Maracanã Stadium box office; expect to pay in the hundreds of dollars. Tickets are usually sold out before Carnaval weekend but touts outside can generally sell you tickets at inflated prices. Samba schools have an allocation of tickets which members sometimes sell, if you are offered one of these check its date. Tickets for the champions' parade on the Saturday following Carnival are much cheaper. Taxis to the Sambódromo are negotiable and will find your gate, the nearest metrô is Praça Onze and this can be an enjoyable ride in the company of costumed samba school members. You can follow the participants to the *concentração*, the assembly and formation on Avenida Presidente Vargas, and mingle with them while they queue to enter the Sambódromo.

Sleeping and security Reserve accommodation well in advance. Virtually all hotels raise their prices during Carnival, although it is usually possible to find a room. Your property should be safe inside the Sambódromo, but the crowds outside can attract pickpockets; as ever, don't brandish your camera, and only take the money you need for fares and food.

Taking part Most samba schools accept a number of foreigners and you will be charged upwards of US$125 (+

tax) for your costume (the money helps fund poorer members of the school). You should be in Rio for at least two weeks before carnival. Attend fittings and rehearsals on time and show respect for your section leaders – enter into the competitive spirit of the event.

Rehearsals *Ensaios* are held at the schools' *quadras* from October on and are well worth seeing. (Go by taxi, as most schools are based in poorer districts.) Tour agents sell tickets for glitzy samba shows, which are nothing like the real thing.

Samba Schools Acadêmicos de Salgueiro, R Silva Teles 104, Andaraí, T2288 3065, www.salgueiro.com.br. **Beija Flor de Nilópolis**, Pracinha Wallace Paes Leme 1025, Nilópolis, T2791 2866, www.beija-flor.com.br. **Imperatriz Leopoldinense**, R Prof. Lacê 235, Ramos, T2560 8037, www.imperatriz leopoldinense.com.br. **Mocidade Independente de Padre Miguel**, R Coronel Tamarindo 38, Padre Miguel, T3332 5823, www.mocidad eindependente.com.br. **Portela**, R Clara Nunes 81, Madureira, T2489 6440, www.gresportela.com.br. **Primeira Estação de Mangueira**, R Visconde de Niterói 1072, Mangueira, T3872 6786, www.mangueira.com.br. **Unidos da Viradouro**, Av do Contorno 16, Niterói, T2628 7840, www.unidosdoviradouro.com.br.

Useful information Freephone T0800-701 1250 (24 hrs, English, Spanish, Portuguese). **Riotur**'s guide booklet gives information on official and unofficial events (in English). The entertainment sections of newspapers and magazines such as *O Globo*, *Jornal do Brasil*, *Manchete* and *Veja Rio* are worth checking. *Liga Independente das Escolas de Samba do Rio de Janeiro*, T3213 5151, http://liesa.globo.com, for schools' addresses and rehearsal times and lots more information.

Rock climbing and hill walking Clube Excursionista Carioca, R Hilário Gouveia 71, room 206, T2255 1348. Recommended for enthusiasts, meets Wed and Fri. **ECA**, Av Erasmo Braga 217, room 305, T2242 6857. Personal guide US$100/

day. **Paulo Miranda**, R Campos Sales 64/801, RJ20270-210, T/F2264 4501. **Rio Hiking**, T 2507 4417, 9721 0594 (mob), www.rio hiking.com.br. Hiking tours to the top of Rio's mountains.

Tours

Most hotels offer tours, usually on a commission basis to a separate operator. Shop around if you have the time and want more choice. Organized trips to Samba shows cost US$50 including dinner, good, but it's cheaper to go independently.
Atlantic Forest Jeep Tour, T2495 9827, T9974 0218 (mob). Jeep tours to the Parque Nacional Tijuca (see above), and trips to coffee fazendas in the Paraíba Valley, trips to Angra dos Reis and offshore islands and the Serra dos Órgãos.
Brazil Expedition, R Visconde Piraja 550 lj 201, Ipanema, T2513 4091, www.brazilexpedition.com. Backpacker bus trips south to Paraty and Ilha Grande with stops along the Costa Verde. Day trips and Rio 'starter packs', accommodation advice. Recommended.
Dantur, Largo do Machado 29 (Galeria Condor) loja 47, T2557 7144. Helena speaks English and is friendly and helpful.
Favela Tour, Estr das Canoas 722, Bl 2, apt 125, Sao Conrado, T3322 2727, T9989 0074/9772 1133 (mob), www.favelatour.com.br. Guided tours of Rio's favelas, safe, different and interesting, US$20, 3 hrs. Also ask Marcelo Armstrong, the owner, about eco tours, river rafting and other excursions. He speaks English, French, Spanish, Italian and can provide guides in German and Swedish. For the best attention and price call Marcelo direct rather than through a hotel desk. Recommended.
Fenician Tours, Av NS de Copacabana 335, T2235 3843. Offers a cheaper tour than some at US$30 including transport from/to hotel.
Jeep Tours, T3890 9336, T9977 9610 (mob), www.jeeptour.com.br. Among their tours are escorted groups to favelas.
Marlin Tours, Av NS de Copacabana office 1204, T2548 4433, bbm.info@openlink.com.br. Recommended for hotel, flights and tours. Robin and Audrey speak English.
Metropol, R São José 46, T2533 5010, www.metropolturismo.com.br. Eco, adventure and culture tours to all parts of Brazil.
Rejane Reis Exotic Tours, T2422 2031, www.exotictours.com.br. Focuses on a tourism workshop in Rocinha favela. They also offer hang gliding, ultralights, paragliding, sailing, diving, voodoo, and daytime tours.
Rio G, R Teixeira de Melo, 25-A, Ipanema, T3813-0003, www.riogtravel.com. Very helpful, English spoken, specialists in the GLBT market.
Saveiros Tour, R Conde de Lages 44, Glória, T2225 6064, www.saveiros.com.br. Offers tours in sailing schooners around the bay and down the coast, also 'Baía da Guanabara Histórica' historical tours.
Travel Café, R Cosme Velho 513, T2285 8302. City tours, rafting, sky diving, horse riding, night tours and packages along the Costa Verde, English spoken.

Turismo Clássico, Av NS de Copacabana 1059/805, T2523 3390, classico@infolink.com.br. Warmly recommended.
Turismo Vida Sol e Mar LTD, Praia do Rosa Imbituba, Santa Catarina, CEP8878000, T3355 6111, www.vidasolemar.com.br. 9 years of experience. Right whale watching, dolphin watching, horse riding and surf school.
www.bealocal.com. As well as guided tours to football matches, see under Maracanã stadium, page 353, also offer recommended visits to favelas.

Guides

Cultural Rio, R Santa Clara 110/904, Copacabana, T3322 4872, T9911 3829 (mob), www.culturalrio.com.br. Tours escorted personally by Professor Carlos Roquette, English and French spoken, almost 200 options available, entirely flexible to your interests.
Fábio Sombra, T2295 9220, T9729 5455 (mob), fabiosombra@hotmail.com. Offers private and tailor-made guided tours focusing on the cultural aspects of Rio and Brazil.
Itaporã Ecoturismo, T2245 4080/9387 4501 (mob), www.itaporaecotur.com.br. Run by Geiza Monteiro, small group or individual tours and walks around Rio.
Rio Life, R Visc de Pirajá 550, office 215, Ipanema, T2259 5532, T9637 2522 (mob), www.travelrio.com. Good company offering personalised tours run by Luiz Felipe Amaral who speaks good English.

⊕ Transport

Rio de Janeiro *p348, maps p348 and p351*

Air

Rio has 2 airports: **Antônio Carlos Jobim International Airport** (T3398 3773), previously called Galeão, and the **Santos Dumont** airport on Guanabara Bay (T3814 7070), for domestic flights. **Jobim international airport** is situated on Governador Island some 16 km from the centre of Rio. It is in 2 sections: international and domestic. There is a **Pousada Galeão (AL)**, comfortable, good value if you need an early start, follow signs in airport.

There are a/c taxis; Cootramo and Transcopass have fixed rates (US$25 Copacabana). Buy a ticket at the counter near the arrivals gate before getting into the car. Fixed rate taxi fares from Terminal 2 are US$10 to Centro, US$17 to Copacabana/Ipanema, US$20 to Barra da Tijuca. Credit cards accepted by some companies. The hire is for the taxi, irrespective of the number of passengers. Make sure you keep the ticket, which carries the number to phone in case of difficulty. Ordinary taxis also operate with the normal meter reading (about US$16, but some may offer cheaper rates from Copacabana to the airport, US$9-10). Do not negotiate with a driver on arrival, unless you are a frequent visitor. Beware pirate taxis which are unlicensed. It is better to pay extra for an official vehicle than run the risk of robbery.

The a/c 'Real' bus runs frequently from the 1st floor of the airport to Recreio dos Bandeirantes via the municipal rodoviária and city centre, Santos Dumont Airport, Flamengo, Copacabana, Ipanema and Leblon. Fares are collected during the journey, to anywhere in Rio US$4.50. The driver will stop at requested points (the bus runs along the seafront from Leme to Leblon), so it's worth checking a map so that you can specify your required junction. The bus returns by the same route. Town buses M94 and M95, Bancários/ Castelo, take a circular route passing through the centre and the interstate bus station. They leave from the 2nd floor of the airport.

There are câmbios in the airport departure hall. There is also a câmbio on the 1st floor of the international arrivals area, but it gives worse rates than the Banco do Brasil, 24-hr bank, 3rd floor, which has Visa ATMs and will give cash advances against Visa. Duty-free shops are well-stocked, but not especially cheap. Duty free is open to arrivals as well as departures. Only US dollars or credit cards are accepted on the air-side of the departure lounge. There is a wider choice of restaurants outside passport control.

The **Santos Dumont** airport on Guanabara Bay, right in the city, is used for Rio-São Paulo shuttle flights, other domestic routes, air taxis and private planes. The shuttle services operate every 30 mins from 0630 to 2230. Sit on the right-hand side for views to São Paulo, the other side coming back, book in advance for particular flights. The main airport, on Governador Island, some 16 km from the centre of Rio, is in 2 sections, international and domestic (including the jet shuttle from Rio to São Paulo).

Bus

Local There are good services, but buses are very crowded and not for the aged or infirm during rush hours; buses have turnstiles which are awkward if you are carrying luggage. Hang on tight, drivers live out Grand Prix fantasies. At busy times allow about 45 mins to get from Copacabana to the centre by bus. The fare on standard buses is US$0.55 and suburban bus fares are US$1. Bus stops are often not marked. The route is written on the side of the bus, which is hard to see until the bus has actually pulled up at the stop. Private companies operate air-conditioned frescão buses which can be flagged down practically anywhere: **Real, Pegaso, Anatur**. They run from all points in Rio Sul to the city centre, Rodoviária and the airports. Fares are US$2 (US$2.40 to the international

airport). City Rio is an a/c tourist bus service with security guards which runs between all the major parts of the city. Good maps show what sites of interest are close to each bus stop, marked by grey poles and found where there are concentrations of hotels. T0800 258060.

Long distance Rodoviária Novo Rio, Av Rodrigues Alves, corner with Av Francisco Bicalho, just past the docks, T2291 5151. Some travel agents sell interstate tickets, or will direct you to a bus ticket office in the centre. Agencies include: **Dantur Passagens e Turismo**, Av Rio Branco 156, subsolo loja 134, T2262 3424/3624; **Itapemirim Turismo**, R Uruguaiana 10, loja 24, T2509 8543, both in the centre; **Guanatur**, R Dias da Rocha 16A, Copacabana, T2235 3275; and an agency at R Visconde de Pirajá 303, loja 114, Ipanema. They charge about US$1 for bookings. Buses run from Rio to all parts of the country. It is advisable to book tickets in advance. The rodoviária has a **Riotur** information centre, which is very helpful, T2263 4857. Left luggage costs US$4. There are câmbios for cash only. The local bus terminal is just outside the rodoviária: turn right as you leave and run the gauntlet of taxi drivers – best ignored. The air conditioned Real bus (opposite the exit) goes along the beach to São Conrado and will secure luggage, US$1.30 to Copacabana. If you need a taxi collect a ticket, which ensures against overcharging, from the office inside the entrance (to Flamengo US$10). On no account give the ticket to the taxi driver. The main bus station is reached by buses M94 and M95, Bancários/Castelo, from the centre and the airport; 136, 172, Rodoviária/Glória/ Flamengo/Botafogo; 127, 128, 136, Rodoviária/Copacabana; 170, Rodoviária/ Gávea/São Conrado; 128, 172, Rodoviária/ Ipanema/Leblon.

Distances in km to some major cities with approximate journey time in brackets: Juiz de Fora, 184 (2¾ hrs); Belo Horizonte, 434 (7 hrs), São Paulo, 429 (6 hrs); Vitória, 521 (8 hrs); Curitiba, 852 (12 hrs); Brasília, 1,148 (20 hrs); Florianópolis, 1,144 (20 hrs); Foz do Iguaçu, 1,500 (21 hrs); Porto Alegre, 1,553 (26 hrs); Salvador, 1,649 (28 hrs); Recife, 2,338 (38 hrs); Fortaleza, 2,805 (48 hrs); São Luís, 3,015 (50 hrs); Belém, 3,250 (52 hrs).

International bus Asunción, 1,511 km via Foz do Iguaçu, 30 hrs (**Pluma**), US$70; **Buenos Aires** (Pluma), via Porto Alegre and Santa Fe, 48 hrs, US$91 (book 2 days in advance); **Santiago de Chile**, with Pluma US$135, or **Gen Urquiza**, about 70 hrs.

Car

Service stations are closed in many places Sat and Sun. Road signs are notoriously misleading in Rio and you can easily end up in a favela. Take care if driving along the Estr da Gávea to São Conrado as it is possible to enter unwittingly Rocinha, Rio's biggest slum.

Metro

The Metrô provides good service, clean, a/c and fast. Line 1: between the inner suburb of Tijuca (station Saens Peña) and Siqueira Campos (Copacabana – being extended to Ipanema), via the railway station (Central), Glória and Botafogo. Line 2: from Pavuna, passing Engenho da Rainha and the Maracanã stadium, to Estácio. It operates 0500-2400 Mon-Sat, 0700-2300 Sun and holidays. The fare is US$0.65 single; multi-tickets and integrated bus/Metrô tickets are available. Changes in bus operations are taking place because of the extended Metrô system; buses connecting with the Metrô have a blue-and-white symbol in the windscreen.

Taxi

The fare between Copacabana and the centre is US$9.50. Between 2300 and 0600 and on Sun and holidays, 'tariff 2' is used. Taxis have red number plates with white digits (yellow for private cars, with black digits) and have meters. Smaller ones (mostly Volkswagen) are marked TAXI on the windscreen or roof. Make sure meters are cleared and on tariff 1, except at those times mentioned above. Only use taxis with an official identification sticker on the windscreen. Don't hesitate to argue if the route is too long or the fare too much. Radio Taxis are safer but more expensive, eg **Cootramo**, T3976 9944 , **Coopertramo**, T2560 2022, **Centro de Táxi**, T2593 2598, **Transcoopass**, T2590 6891. Luxury cabs are allowed to charge higher rates. Inácio de Oliveira, T2225 4110, is a reliable taxi driver for excursions, he only speaks Portuguese. Recommended. **Grimalde**, T2267 9812, has been recommended for talkative daytime and evening tours, English and Italian spoken, negotiate a price. Also **Eduardo**, T3361 1315 or 9708 8542, a/c taxi.

Pão de Açúcar *p356*

Bus Bus 107 (from the centre, Catete or Flamengo) and 511 from Copacabana (512 to return) take you to the cable-car station, Av Pasteur 520, at the foot.

Cable car Praia Vermelha to Morro de Urca: first car goes up at 0800, then every 30 mins (or when full), until the last comes down at 2200 (quietest before 1000). From Urca to Sugar Loaf, the first connecting cable car goes up at 0815 then every 30 mins (or when full), until the last leaves the summit at 2200; the return trip costs US$16 (US$8 to Morro de Urca, half-way up, or from Morro de Urca to the top). Termini are ample and efficient and the present Italian cable cars carry 75 passengers. Even on the most crowded days there is little queuing.

Corcovado *p356*

Take a **Cosme Velho bus** to the cog railway station at Rua Cosme Velho 513: from the centre or Glória/Flamengo No 180; from Copacabana take No 583, from Botafogo or Ipanema/Leblon No 583 or 584; from Santa Teresa Microônibus Santa Teresa. The **train** runs every 20-30 mins between 0800 and 1830, journey time 10 mins (cost: US$16 return; single tickets available). **Trem do Corcovado**, R Cosme Velho 513, T2558 1329, www.corcovado.com.br. **Taxis** and minivans from Paineiras charge US$6.50 pp. Also, a 206 bus does the very attractive run from Praça Tiradentes (or a 407 from Largo do Machado) to Silvestre (the railway has no stop here now). An active walk of 9 km will take you to the top. For safety reasons go in company, or at weekends when more people are about. If going by **car** to Corcovado, the entrance fee is US$5 for the vehicle, plus US$5 pp. Coach trips tend to be rather brief and special taxis, which wait in front of the station, offer tours of Corcovado and Mirante Dona Marta for US$13.

Copacabana *p357, map p362*

Bus To and from the city centre are plentiful and cost US$0.55. The buses to take are Nos 119, 154, 413, 415, 455, 474 from Av Nossa Senhora de Copacabana. If you are going to the centre from Copacabana, look for 'Castelo', 'Praça 15', 'E Ferro' or 'Praça Mauá' on the sign by the front door. 'Aterro' means the expressway between Botafogo and downtown Rio (not open on Sun). From the centre to Copacabana is easier as all buses in that direction are marked. The 'Aterro' bus does the journey in 15 mins.

Jardim Botânico *p357*

Bus Take bus No 170 from the centre, or any bus to Leblon, Gávea or São Conrado marked 'via Jóquei'; from Glória, Flamengo or Botafogo take No 571, or 172 from Flamengo; from Copacabana, Ipanema or Leblon take No 572 (584 back to Copacabana).

Ipanema and Leblon *p357, map p364*

Bus Run from Botafogo Metrô terminal to Ipanema: some take integrated Metrô-Bus tickets; look for the blue signs on the windscreen. Many buses from Copacabana run to Ipanema and Leblon.

Barra da Tijuca *p358*

Bus From the city centre to Barra, 1 hr, are Nos 175, 176; from Botafogo, Glória or Flamengo take No 179; Nos 591 or 592 from Leme; and from Copacabana via Leblon No 523 (45 mins-1 hr). A taxi to Zona Sul costs US$20 (US$30 after 2400). A comfortable bus, Pegasus, goes along the coast from the Castelo bus terminal to Barra da Tijuca

and continues to Campo Grande or Santa Cruz, or take the free 'Barra Shopping' bus. Bus 700 from Praça São Conrado (terminal of bus 553 from Copacabana) goes the full length of the beach to Recreio dos Bandeirantes.

Parque Nacional Tijuca *p358*

Bus Take bus No 221 from Praça 15 de Novembro, No 233 (which continues to Barra da Tijuca) or 234 from the rodoviária or from Praça Sáens Pena, Tijuca (the city suburb, not Barra – reached by Metrô), for the park entrance. Jeep tours are run by Atlantic Forest Jeep Tour, daily; T2495 9827, T9974 0218 (mob), or contact through travel agencies.

Ilha de Paquetá *p359*

Ferry Services that leave more or less every 2 hrs from Praça 15 de Novembro, where there is a general boat terminal; there are boats from 0515 (0710 on Sun and holidays) to 2300, T2533 7524, or hydrofoils between 1000 and 1600, Sat and Sun 0800-1630 hourly, T2533 4343 or Paquetá 3397 0656 (fare US$1 by boat, 1 hr, US$5 by hydrofoil, 20 mins' journey, which more than doubles its price Sat, Sun and holidays). Buses to Praça 15 de Novembro: No 119 from Glória, Flamengo or Botafogo; Nos 154, 413, 455, 474 from Copacabana, or No 415 passing from Leblon via Ipanema. Other boat trips: Several agencies offer trips to Paquetá. Some also offer a day cruise, including lunch, to Jaguanum Island (see under Itacuruçá) and a sundown cruise around Guanabara Bay.

---

❶ Directory

Rio de Janeiro *p348, maps p348 and p351*
Airline offices **Aerolíneas Argentinas**, R São José 70, 8th floor, Centro, T2292 4131, airport T3398 3520. **Air France**, Av Pres Antônio Carlos 58, 9th floor, T2532 3642, airport T3398 3488. **Alitalia**, Av Pres Antônio Carlos 58, 9th floor, T2292 4424. **American**, Av Pres Wilson 165, 5th floor, T2210 3126, airport T3398 4053. **Avianca**, Av Pres Wilson 165, offices 801-08, T2240 4413. **Bra**, Central Rio, T3213 3233, Copacabana T3208 4009, www.voebra.com.br. Offices in both airports. **British Airways**, T0300-789 6140. **Continental**, R da Assembléia 10, sala 3711, T0800-554777. **Gol**, T0800 2800465, www.voegol.com.br. **Iberia**, Av Pres Antônio Carlos 51, 9th floor, T2282 1336, airport T3398 3168. **Lan Chile**, R da Assembléia 92, office 1301, T2220 9722. **LAB**, Av Calógeras 30A, T2220 9548. **Lufthansa**, Av Rio Branco 156D, T3687 5000. **Ocean Air**, T4004 4040, www.oceanair.com.br. Offices in both airports. **RioSul/Nordeste**, Av Rio Branco 85, 11th floor, T2507 4488 (has an advance check-in desk in Rio

Sul Shopping). **TAM**, Praça Floriana 19, 28th floor, T2524 1717, airport T3398 2133. **TAP**, Av Princesa Isabel 7, T 3873 7787, airport, T3398 3455. **United**, Av Atlântica 2600, T0800-162323. **Varig**, Av Rio Branco 277G, T2220 3821, information, T0800-997000 bookings; airport T3398 3522.

Banks Citibank, R Assembléia 100, T2291 1232, changes large US$ TCs into smaller ones, no commission, advances cash on Eurocard/MasterCard. ATM at branch on Av NS de Copacabana at Siqueira Campos. **Banco do Brasil**, there are only 2 branches in Rio which will change US$ TCs, Praia de Botafogo, 384A, 3rd floor (minimum US$200) and the central branch at R Sen Dantas 105, 4th floor (minimum US$500 – good rates). **Banco do Brasil** at the International Airport is open 0800-2200. The international airport is probably the only place to change TCs at weekends. **Banco 24 horas** ATMs around town and in airports. Good for Visa card withdrawal. Visa cash withdrawals also at **Banco do Brasil** (many ATMs at the R Sen Dantas branch, no queues) and **Bradesco** (personal service or machines). MasterCard and Cirrus cash machines at most **HSBC** branches in Centro, Copacabana, Ipanema and other locations. Some **BBV** branches have Visa and MasterCard ATMs. Also at Santos Dumont airport. **Money changers: American Express**, Av Atlântica 1702, loja 1, T2548 2148 Mon-Fri 0900-1730, Av Pres Wilson 231, 18th floor, Centro, and at Jobim/Galeão airport, T3398 4251 (VIP room 1st floor), good rates (daily 0630-2230); credit card line 0800 785050. Most large hotels and reputable travel agencies will change currency and TCs. Copacabana (where rates are generally worse than in the centre) abounds with câmbios and there are many also on Av Rio Branco. **Câmbio Belle Tours**, Rio Sul Shopping, ground floor, loja 101, parte A-10, Mon-Fri 1000-1800, Sat 1000-1700, changes cash. In the gallery at Largo do Machado 29 are **Câmbio Nick** at loja 22 and, next door but one, **Casa Franca**. **Car hire** For international car rental websites, see Car hire, Essentials, page 43. **Interlocadora**, international airport T3398 3181, domestic airport T2240 0754; **Telecar**, R Figueiredo Magalhães 701, Copacabana, T2235 6778, www.telecar.com.br. Many agencies on Av Princesa Isabel, Copacabana. A credit card is essential for hiring a car. Recent reports suggest it is cheaper to hire outside Brazil. You may also obtain fuller insurance this way. **Cultural centres** Alliance Francaise, R Duvivier 43/103, Copacabana and Rua Garcia d'Avila 72, Ipanema, T2259 4489, www.rioaliancafrancesa.com.br. **British Council**, R Jardim Botânico, 518R, T2105 7500, www.britishcouncil.org.br. **German Cultur-InstTut** (Goethe), R do Passeio 62, 2nd

floor, T2533 4862, www.goethe.de/br/rio. Tue-Wed 1000-1200, Thu 1530-2000, Fri 1530-1800, Sat 0900-1300. See also **Casa-França-Brasil**, p 351. **Embassies and consulates** Argentina, Praia de Botafogo 228,T2553 1646, consar.rio@openlink.com.br. Very helpful over visas, 1130-1600. **Australia**, Av Presidente Wilson 231, no 23, T3824 4624, honconau@terra.com.br. Mon-Fri 9000-1300, 1430-1800. **Austria**, Av Atlântica 3804, T2102 0020, rio-de-janeiro-gk@bmaa.gv.at. **Canada**, Av Atlântica, 1130, 5th floor, T2543 3004, rio@international.gc.ca. **Denmark**, Av Rio Branco 50, 15th floor, T2233 0303, riodejaneirodk@terra.com.br. **France**, Av Pres Antônio Carlos 58, T3974 6699, consulatrio@rionet.com.br. **Germany**, R Pres Carlos de Campos 417, T2554 0004, gkrioalemao@terra.com.br (also serves Minas Gerais). **Ireland**, R 24 de Maio 347, Riachuelo, T2501 8455, rioconsulate@ireland.com. **Japan**, Praia do Flemengo 200, 10th floor, T3461 9595. **Netherlands**, Praia de Botafogo 242, 10th floor, T2157 5400, rio@minbuza.nl. **Paraguay**, Praia de Botafogo 242, 2nd floor, T2553 2294, cg@consulado paraguayrj.com.br. **Sweden, Finland** and **Norway**, R Lauro Müller 116/2206, Rio Sul Shopping Center, Botafogo, T2541 7732, cg.riodejaneiro@mfa.no. **Switzerland**, R Cândido Mendes 157, 11th floor, T2221 1867, vertretung@rio.rep.admin.ch. **UK**, Praia do Flemengo 284, 2nd floor. T2555 9600, consular.rio@fco.gov.uk (consular section is open Mon-Fri 0900-1230, the consulate's hrs are 0830-1700), Metrô Flamengo, or bus 170, issues a useful 'Guidance for Tourists' pamphlet. **Uruguay**, Praia de Botafogo 242, 6th floor,T2553 6030. **USA**, Av Pres Wilson 147, T3823 2000. Mon-Fri 0830-1100. **Internet** Throughout the city. @point, Barra Shopping, Av das Americas 4666, Barra da Tijuca. Several places in Rio Sul Shopping, Botafogo. Many on Av NS de Copacabana and others on R Visconde de Pirajá, Ipanema. Locutório at R Francisco Sá 26, T2522 6343. Internet, phone, fax, open 0800-2000 daily. **Phone Serv**, Av NS de Copacabana 454 loja B. Internet and phone. **Tudo é Fácil**, 3 branches in Copacabana: R Xavier da Silveira, 19; Av Prado Júnior 78 and R Barata Ribeiro 396. Well-organized, with identification cards so once registered you can bypass the front desk, telephone booths and scanners, US$2 per hr, discounts for extended use. A cheap place is at R Barata Ribeiro 370C. **Language courses** Instituto Brasil- Estados Unidos, Av Copacabana 690, 5th floor, 8-week course, 3 classes a week, US$200, 5-week intensive course US$260. Good English library at same address. **IVM Português Prático**, R do Catete 310, sala 302, US$18 per hr

for individual lessons, cheaper for groups. Helpful staff. Recommended. **Cursos da UNE** (União Nacional de Estudantes), R Catete 243, include cultural studies and Portuguese classes for foreigners. Private lessons with **Camila Queiraz**, T8828 3196/3339 3485, reasonable prices.
Medical services Vaccinations at **Saúde de Portos**, Praça Mcal Âncora, T2240 8628/ 8678, Mon-Fri 1000-1100, 1500-1800 (international vaccination book and ID required). **Policlínica**, Av Nilo Peçanha 38. Recommended for diagnosis and investigation. A good public hospital for minor injuries and ailments is **Hospital Municipal Rocha Maia**, R Gen Severiano 91, Botafogo, T2295 2295/2121, near Rio Sul Shopping Centre. Free, but there may be queues. **Hospital Miguel Couto**, Mário Ribeiro 117, Gávea, T2274 6050. Has a free casualty ward. **Health:** Dentist: English- speaking, **Amílcar Werneck de Carvalho Vianna**, Av Pres Wilson 165, suite 811. **Dr Mauro Suartz**, R Visconde de Pirajá 414, room 509, T2287 6745. Speaks English and Hebrew, helpful. **Post offices** The central Post Office is on R 1 de Março 64, at the corner of R do Rosário. Av NS de Copacabana 540 and many other locations. All handle international post. There is a post office at

Galeão airport. Poste Restante: Correios, Av NS de Copacabana 540 and all large post offices (letters held for a month, recommended, US$0.10 per letter). **Federal Express**, Av Calógeras 23 (near Santa Luzia church) T2262 8565, is reliable.
Telephones International calls can be made at Telemar offices: Av NS de Copacabana 540, 2nd floor; Jobim international airport (24 hrs); Novo Rio rodoviária; R Dias da Cruz 192, Méier-4, 24 hrs, 7 days a week; Praça Tiradentes 41, a few mins' walk from Metrô Carioca; R Visconde de Pirajá 111, Ipanema; R do Ouvidor 60, Centro. International telephone booths are blue. Larger Embratel offices have fax, as do many larger Correios. **Useful addresses** Immigration: Federal Police, Praça Mauá (passport section), entrance at Av Venezuela 2, T2291 2142. To renew a 90-day visa, US$12.50. **Ibama**, Praça 15 de Novembro 42, 8th floor, T2506 1734, edson.azeredo@ ibama.gov.br. **Student Travel Bureau**, Av Nilo Peçanha 50, sala 3103, Centro, T3526 7700, and R Visconde de Pirajá 550, lj 201, Ipanema, T2512 8577, www.stb.com.br (offices throughout the country) has details of travel, discounts and cultural exchanges for ISIC holders.

East of Rio

It is not only the state capital that is blessed with beautiful beaches, forests and mountains. There are chic resorts, surfing centres and emerald green coves, national parks in rainforest-clad hills and strange rocky mountains, and fine historical towns dating from both the colonial and imperial epochs. Within easy reach of Rio are the popular coastal resorts of Cabo Frio and Búzios and the imperial city of Petrópolis.

Niterói → *Phone code: 0xx21. Colour map 7, grid B5. Population: 459,451.*
This city is reached across Guanabara Bay by ferries which carry some 200,000 commuters a day. Founded in 1573, Niterói has various churches and forts, plus buildings associated with the city's period as state capital (until 1960). Many of these are grouped around the Praça da República. The **Capela da Boa Viagem** (1663) stands on a fortified island, attached by a causeway to the mainland. The most important historical monument is the **Fortaleza Santa Cruz** ① *T2710 7840, daily 0900-1600, US$1.50, go with guide.* Dating from the 16th century and still a military establishment, it stands on a promontory which commands a fine view of the entrance to the bay. It is about 13 km from the centre of Niterói, on the Estrada Gen Eurico Gaspar Dutra, by Adão e Eva beach.

The **Museu de Arqueologia de Itaipu** ① *20 km from the city, T2709 4079, Wed-Sun 1300-1800*, is in the ruins of the 18th century Santa Teresa Convent and also covers the archaeological site of Duna Grande on Itaipu beach. **Museu de Arte Contemporânea-Niterói** ① *Mirante da Praia da Boa Viagem, T2620 2400, www.macniterio.com, Tue-Sun 1000-1800, US$1, Sat 1300-1900, free*, is an Oscar Niemeyer project and worth visiting. It is best seen at night, especially when the pond beneath the spaceship design is full of water. **Tourist office: Neltur** ① *Estrada Leopoldo Fróes 773, São Francisco, T2710 2727, 5 km from ferry dock, www.niteroiturismo.com.br.*

Local beaches Take bus no 33 from the boat dock, passing Icaraí and São Francisco, both with polluted water but good nightlife, to the fishing village of Jurujuba. About 2 km further along a narrow road are the attractive twin beaches of Adão and Eva beneath the Fortaleza da Santa Cruz (see above). To get to the ocean beaches, take a 38 or 52 bus from Praça Gen Gomes

Carneiro to Piratininga, Camboinhas, Itaipu (see the archaeology museum, above) and Itacoatiara. These are fabulous stretches of sand and the best in the area, about 40 minutes' ride through picturesque countryside.

Lagos Fluminenses

To the east of Niterói lie a series of salt-water lagoons, the Lagos Fluminenses. The first major lakes, Maricá and Saquarema are muddy, but the waters are relatively unpolluted and wildlife abounds in the surrounding scrub and bush. An unmade road goes along the coast between Itacoatiara and Cabo Frio, giving access to the long, open beaches of Brazil's **Costa do Sol**.

In the holiday village of **Saquarema**, the little white church of Nossa Senhora de Nazaré (1675) is on a green promontory jutting into the ocean. Saquarema is a fishing town and one of the top spots for quality consistent pumping surf in Brazil.

The largest lake is **Araruama** (220 sq km), famous for its medicinal mud. The salinity is extremely high, the waters calm, and almost the entire lake is surrounded by sandy beaches, making it popular with families looking for safe, unpolluted bathing. The almost constant breeze makes the lake perfect for windsurfing and sailing. There are many hotels, youth hostels and campsites in the towns by the lakes and by the beaches. All around are saltpans and the wind pumps used to carry water into the pans. At the eastern end of the lake is **São Pedro de Aldeia**, which, despite intensive development, still retains some of its colonial charm.

Cabo Frio → *Phone code: 0xx22. Colour map 7, grid B5. Population: 140,000.*

Cabo Frio, 156 km from Rio, is a popular holiday and weekend haunt of Cariocas because of its cooler weather, white sand beaches, sailing and good underwater swimming. **Forte São Mateus**, 1616, is now a ruin at the mouth of the Canal de Itajurú, which connects the Lagoa Araruama and the ocean. A small headland at its mouth protects the nearest beach to the town, Praia do Forte, which stretches south for about 7½ km to Arraial do Cabo. The canal front, Av dos Pescadores, is pretty, lined with palm trees, restaurants and schooners tied up at the dock. It leads around to the bridge, which crosses to the Gamboa district. **Convento Nossa Senhora dos Anjos** (1696), Largo de Santo Antônio in the town centre, houses the **Museu de Arte Religiosa e Tradicional** ① *Wed-Fri 1400- 2000, Sat-Sun 1600-2000*. Above the Largo de Santo Antônio is the **Morro da Guia**, which has a look-out and an 18th-century chapel (access on foot only). The beaches of **Peró** and **Conchas** ① *'São Cristovão' (with 'Peró' on its notice board) or 'Peró' bus, US$0.65, 15-20 mins, has lots of condos, but not many places to stay,* are lovely (a headland, Ponta do Vigia, separates the two and you can walk from one to the other). Peró. **Tourist office** ① *Av Américo Vespúcio s/n, Praia do Forte, at the junction of Av do Contorno and Av João Pessoa, T2647 6227/1689.* Kiosks in the centre sell maps.

Búzios → *Phone code: 0xx24. Colour map 7, grid B5. Population: 18,208. www.buzioschannel.com.br.*

Known as a lost paradise in the tropics, this village, 192 km from Rio, found fame in the 1964 when Brigite Bardot was photographed sauntering barefoot along the beach. The world's press descended on the sophisticated, yet informal resort, following the publicity. Originally a small fishing community, founded in 1740, Búzios remained virtually unknown until the 1950s when its natural beauty started to attract the Brazilian jet-set who turned the village into a fashionable summer resort. The city gets crowded at all main holidays, the price of food, accommodation and other services rises substantially and the traffic jams are long and stressful.

During the daytime, the best option is to head for one of the 25 beaches. The most visited are Geribá (many bars and restaurants; popular with surfers), Ferradura (blue sea and calm waters), Ossos (the most famous and close to the centre), Tartaruga and João Fernandes. Schooner trips of two to three hours pass many of the beaches: US$14-20. Escuna Queen Lory, T2623 1179. **Tourist office:** at Manguinhos, T0800-249999 (24 hours), on the western edge of the peninsula, and at Praça Santo Dumont, T2623 2099. See www.buziosonline.com.br.

Petrópolis → *Phone code: 0xx24. Post code: 25600. Colour map 7, grid B5. Population: 286,537.*

A steep scenic mountain road from Rio leads to this summer resort, 68 km north of Rio, known for its floral beauty and hill scenery, coupled with adventure sports. Until 1962 Petrópolis was the 'summer capital' of Brazil. Now it combines manufacturing industry (particularly textiles) and tourism. There are possibilities for whitewater rafting, hiking, climbing, riding and cycling in the vicinity. Petrópolis celebrates its foundation on 16 March. Patron saint's day, São Pedro de Alcântara, 29 June. **Tourist office:** Petrotur ① *Praça Liberdade, T2246 9377,* *www.petropolis.rj.gov.br/fctp*, Mon-Tue 0900-1830, Wed-Sat 0900-2000, Sun 0900-1600. Very helpful, good English. There are kiosks in the main sites of interest.

The **Museu Imperial** (Imperial Palace) ① *R da Imperatriz 220, T2237 8000, Tue-Sun 1100-1700, US$3.65*, is Brazil's most visited museum. It is an elegant building, neoclassical in style, fully furnished and equipped. It is so well-kept you might think the imperial family had left the day before, rather than in 1889. It's worth a visit just to see the Crown Jewels of both Pedro I and Pedro II. In the palace gardens is a pretty French-style tearoom, the Petit Palais. The Gothic-style **Catedral de São Pedro de Alcântara** ① *Tue-Sat 0800-1200, 1400-1800*, completed in 1925, contains the tombs of the Emperor and Empress. The Imperial Chapel is to the right of the entrance. The summer home of air pioneer **Alberto Santos Dumont** ① *R do Encanto 22, Tue-Sun 0930-1700, US$1*, is known as 'A Encantada' and is worth a visit. The interior of the **Casa de Petrópolis** ① *R Ipiranga 716, T2237 2133, Tue-Sun 1100-1900, Sat 1100-1300, US$2*, is completely original and over-the-top, but has been lovingly restored. It holds art exhibitions and classical concerts. A charming restaurant in the old stables is worth a stop for coffee, if not for lunch. **Orquidário Binot** ① *R Fernandes Vieira 390, T2248 5665, Mon-Fri 0800-1100, 1300-1600, Sat 0700-1100, take bus to Vila Isabel*, has a huge collection of orchids from all over Brazil (plants may be purchased).

Serra dos Órgãos

① *Tue-Sun 0800-1700, best months for trekking Apr-Sep, US$1, with an extra charge for the path to the top. For information from Ibama, Av Rotariana s/n, Alto Teresópolis, T2642 2374, www.ibama.gov.br.*

The Serra dos Órgãos, so called because their strange shapes are said to recall organ-pipes, is an 11,000-ha national park (created in 1939, the second oldest in the country). The main attraction is the precipitous Dedo de Deus ('God's Finger') Peak (1,692 m). The highest point is the 2,263 m Pedra do Sino ('Bell Rock'), up which winds a 14-km path, a climb of three to four hours. The west face of this mountain is one of the hardest climbing pitches in Brazil. Another well-known peak is the Pedra do Açu (2,245 m) and many others have names evocative of their shape. Near the Sub-Sede (off BR-116, just outside the park) is the **Von Martius natural history museum** *0800-1700*. By the headquarters (Sede) entrance is the Mirante do Soberbo, with views to the Baía de Guanabara. To climb the Pedra do Sino, you must sign a register (under 18 must be accompanied by an adult and have authorization from the park authorities).

Further information on the area from the **Teresópolis** tourism office ① *Mirante Soberba, BR 116, T2642 1737, www.teresopolison.com, Mon-Fri 0900-1800, Sat 0900-1700, Sun 0900-1300*. On the outskirts of town on the main road to Rio de Janeiro and opposite the Mirante; very helpful with lots of maps and pamphlets.

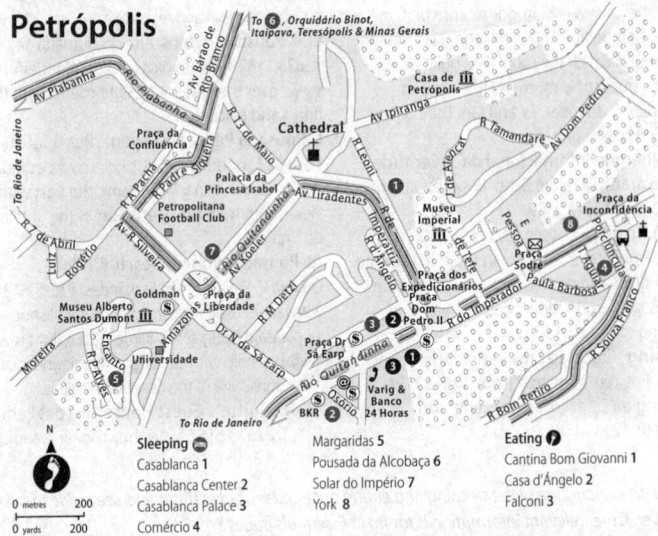

Petrópolis

Sleeping
Casablanca 1
Casablanca Center 2
Casablanca Palace 3
Comércio 4

Margaridas 5
Pousada da Alcobaça 6
Solar do Império 7
York 8

Eating
Cantina Bom Giovanni 1
Casa d'Ángelo 2
Falconi 3

😴 Sleeping

Cabo Frio *p380*

A Othon Sítio do Portinho, R Cnel Ferreira 281, Portinho, T2644 9264, www.pousadasitiodo portinho.hpg.com.br. Cheaper in low season. Very nice rooms set in gardens in a residential suburb, a/c and all usual facilities, pool and bar.

B Pousada Água Marinha, R Rui Barbosa 996b, Centro, T2643 8447, p.aguamarinha@uol.com.br. **C** in low season, white rooms with comfortable beds, a/c, fan, TV, frigobar, breakfast, pool and parking. About 4 blocks from Praia do Forte.

B Pousada Suzy, Av Júlia Kubitschek 48, T2643 1742. 100 m from rodoviária, **C** in low season, with a/c, cheaper with fan. Shared rooms for 8, **D**. Plain rooms but not spartan, pool, sauna, garage.

C Pousada Velas ao Vento, Av Júlia Kubitschek 5, T2644 1235. Between rodoviária and centre. Cheaper in low season, comfortable, set back from the main road but still a bit of traffic noise. Hot water, a/c, helpful owner and staff.

D Marina dos Anjos, R Bernado Lens 145, Arraial do Cabo, T2622 4060, www.marinadosanjos.com.br. Superior HI hostel with spruce dorms and doubles, facilities including a games room, sun terrace and links to tour companies and dive shops.

Peró

AL La Plage, R das Badejos 40, T2647 1746, www.redebela.com.br. **B** in low season; fully-equipped suites, those upstairs have sea view, excellent for families. Right on the beach, services include pool and bar, à la carte restaurant, hydromassage, sauna, 24 hr cyber café, garage.

B Pousada Espírito do Mar, R Anequim s/n, T2644 3077, www.espiritodomar.com.br. **C** in low season. Orange building with central swimming pool around which the rooms are built. Good, spacious but simple rooms, with extra bed available. A/c, frigobar, TV and fan. The bus to Cabo Frio passes outside.

E pp **Albergue Internacional da Juventude de Muxarabi**, R Leonor Santa Rosa, 13, Jardim Flamboyant, T2643 0369.

D Peró Hostel, R Coutrin 13, T2647 7605, www.perohostel.com.br. Smart modern HI hostel with doubles and dorms, many with their own terraces, some with fridge, good services including tours and Tai Chi.

Camping Clube do Brasil, Estrada dos Passageiros 700, 2 km from town, T2643 3124. Camping da Estação, on the same road, at No 370, T2643 1786.

Búzios *p380*

Prior reservations are needed in summer, at holidays such as Carnival and the New Year's Eve, and weekends. For cheaper options and better availability, try Cabo Frio.

The best rooms on the peninsula are not on the beaches, but on the Morro do Humaitá, superb views, 10 mins' walk from the town centre. Hire a beach buggy. Several private houses rent rooms, especially in summer and holidays. Look for the signs: 'Alugo Quartos'.

LL Boca do Ceu, Mirante de João Fernandes, Rua Hum s/n, T2623 4713, www.bocadoceu.com. Super luxurious, and very expensive, private home/mini pousada (owned by a famous Uruguayan interior designer) with the best views on the peninsula out across a carefully designed swimming pool and garden. All the fittings are by famous names.

LL Hotel Pérola Búzios, Av José Bento Ribeiro Dantas 222, Armação dos Búzios - Centro, 28950-000, T2620 8507, www.perolabuzios.com. Full facilities, accommodates up to 450 people. The only hotel in Búzios that can cater for such large numbers for meetings etc.

LL-L Casas Brancas, Alto do Humaitá 8, T2623 1458, www.casasbrancas.com.br. Far and away the best hotel in Búzios; a series of rooms perched on the hill in mock-Mykonos buildings with separate terraces for the pool and spa areas, wonderfully romantic at night when all is lit by candlelight. If you can't afford to stay go for dinner.

LL-L El Cazar, Alto do Humaitá 6, T2623 1620. Next door to Casas Brancas and almost as luxurious; though a little darker inside. Beautiful artwork, tasteful and relaxing.

LL-L Pousada Byblos, Alto do Humaitá 14, T2623 1162, www.byblos.com.br. Wonderful views over the bay, bright, light rooms with tiled floors and balconies.

L Pousada Pedra Da Laguna, Rua 6, lote 6, Praia da Ferradura, T2623 1965, www.pedrada laguna.com.br. Spacious rooms, the best with a view 150m from the beach. Part of the Roteiros do Charme.

AL Pousada Hibiscus Beach, R 1 No 22, Quadra C, Praia de João Fernandes, T2623 6221, www.hibiscusbeach.com.br. A peaceful spot, 15 pleasant bungalows, garden, pool, light meals available, help with car/buggy rentals and local excursions. One of the best beach hotels.

AL-A Brigitta's Guest House, Rua das Pedras 131, T/F2623 6157, www.buziosonline.com.

🍷 *For an explanation of the sleeping and eating price codes used in this guide, see inside the front* ● *cover. Other relevant information is found in Essentials pages 345-347.*

brigitta. Beautifully decorated little pousada where Bardot once stayed, just 4 rooms on the main street, delightful restaurant, bar and tea house overlooking the water are worth a visit.

A Casa da Ruth, R dos Gravatás, Geribá, T2623 2242, www.buziosturismo.com/casadaruth. Simple mock-Greek rooms in lilac overlooking the beach and pool.

C-E Praia dos Amores, Av José Bento Ribeiro Dantas 92, T2623 2422. IYHA, not far from the bus station, next to Praia da Tartaruga and just under 1 km from the centre. The best value in Búzios. Recommended.

C-E Ville Blanche, R Turibe de Farias 222, T2623 1840. New simple pousada, central, dorms for up to 10, and bright, tiled floor doubles with balconies.

E Country Camping Park, R Maria Joaquina Justiniano 895 (off Praça da Rasa), Praia Rasa, Km 12, T2629 1155, www.buzioscamping.com.br. Chalets and a well-run, shady campsite 1 km from the beach (directions on web site).

Petrópolis *p380, map p381*

LL Pousada da Alcobaça, R Agostinho Goulão 298, Correas, T2221 1240, www.pousadada alcobaca.com.br. Delightful, family-run country house in flower-filled gardens, pool and sauna. Worth stopping by for tea on the terrace, or dinner at the restaurant. Recommended.

LL Solar do Império, Av Koeler 276, T2103 3000, www.solardoimperio.com.br. Converted neo-classical colonial mansion set in gardens on Petrópolis's grandest street. Fittings evoke the imperial era but modern facilities include a pool, sauna and ofuro hot tub.

A Casablanca, R da Imperatriz 286, T2242 6662, F2242 5946. Most atmospheric of the 3 in this chain, cheaper rooms in modern extension, good restaurant, pool. Also **B Casablanca Center**, Gen Osório 28, T2242 2612, F2242 6298; and **B Casablanca Palace**, R 16 de Março 123, T2242 0162, F2242 5946.

A Margaridas, R Bispo Pereira Alves 235, T2242 4686, near Trono de Fátima. Chalet-style in lovely gardens with a swimming pool, charming proprietors.

B York, R do Imperador 78, T2243 2662, F2242 8220. A short walk from the Rodoviária, convenient, helpful, the fruit and milk at breakfast come from the owners' own farm. Recommended.

C Comércio, R Dr Porciúncula 55, T2242 3500, opposite the Rodoviária. Shared bath, very basic.

Brazil East of Rio Listings

Serra dos Órgãos/Teresópolis *p381*
Ibama has some hostels, US$5 full board, or US$3 first night, US$2 thereafter, a bit rough. There is also the Refugio do Parque, 2 km from park entrance of Teresópolis side, T9687 4539 (mob), refugiodoparque@bol.com.br. Rooms with bath and dormitories with shower, breakfast and soup-and-bread supper included.
L-AL Regua, c/o Nicholas Locke, Cachoeiras de Macacu, T2745 3998, www.regua.co.uk. Private rainforest reserve with very comfortable accommodation in a spacious wooden house and guided walks through pristine forest. Families of South America's largest and rarest primate, the woolly spider monkey live here, excellent birding.
L-AL Serra dos Tucanos, Cachoeiras do Macacu, T2649 1557, www.serradostucanos.com.br. British-run lodge in the Parque Estadual Três Picos near Teresópolis, with some of the very best bird-watching, guiding and facilities in the Atlantic coast forest. Cabins around a spring-water swimming pool. Airport transfers from Rio.
C-E Recanto do Lord, R Luiza Pereira Soares 109, Teresópolis, T2742 5586, www.teresopolis hostel.com.br. Big, ugly but well-equipped, dorms and doubles, wonderful mountain views and organized tours and 'adventure' trips in the Serra dos Órgãos.

❷ Eating

Cabo Frio *p380*
There's a neat row of restaurants on Av dos Pescadores, most offering fish, local meats, or pastas. They have seating on the pavement under awnings, French-style. Upstairs are a number of bars and nightclubs.
ᵀᵀᵀ-ᵀᵀ Picolino, R Mcal F Peixoto 319, T2643 2436. In a nice old building, very smart, mixed menu but mostly local fish and seafood, but also some international dishes.
ᵀᵀ Hippocampo, R Mcal F Peixoto 283, T2645 5757. Mostly seafood.
ᵀᵀ "In" Sônia, Av dos Pescadores 140 loja 04. Good service and tasty fish, many dishes for 2.
ᵀᵀ Populeti, Av dos Pescadores e Trav Maçonica, T2645 3876. Homemade pastas, a/c, entrance in Shopping Crystal Palace. **Galeto do Zé** (below it) for snacks. Also **Do Zé** on Av dos Pescadores, T2643 4277, serving Brazilian specialities.
ᵀᵀ Tonto, Av dos Pescadores next to "In" Sônia. Serves pizza and local dishes (T2645 1886 for delivery), has a bar too.
ᵀᵀ ᵀ Kilo-Kura, Av Teixeira e Souza 121-A. Good self-service lunches, very popular.
ᵀ Bacalhauzinho, Praça Porto Rocha. Portuguese.
ᵀ Branca, Praça Porto Rocha. Lunches à kilo 1100-1700, also fast food, pizza after 1800, coffee, pastries and cakes, good, a big, popular place.

ᵀ Chico's, Av Teixeira e Souza 30, upstairs in Centro Comercial Víctor Nunes da Rocha, T2645 7454. Smart, does breakfast, self-service.

Búzios *p380*
There are many restaurants on and around R das Pedras and one of the charms of Buzios is browsing. The cheaper options tend to be off the main drag. There are plenty of beachside barracas all over the peninsula (closed out of season). A few places on Praça Santos Dumont off Rua das Pedras offer sandwiches and self-service food, including the homely La Prima on Av Manuel Turibo de Farias, which doubles as a bakery. There's a small supermarket a couple of doors away.
ᵀᵀᵀ Acquerello, R das Pedras 130, T2623 6576. Smart a/c seafood and Italian restaurant with a reasonable wine list. The best on the street.
ᵀᵀᵀ Satyricon, Av José Bento Ribeiro Dantas 500, Praia da Armação (in front of Morro da Humaitá), T2623 1595. Buzios's most illustrious restaurant specialising in Italian seafood. Decent wine list.
ᵀᵀᵀ Moqueca Capixaba, R Manoel de Carvalho 116, Centro, T2623 1155. Bahian seafood with dishes cooked in coconut or dende oil.
ᵀ Banana Land, R Manoel Turíbio de Farias 50, T2623 0855. Cheap and cheerful per kilo buffet.
ᵀ Chez Michou, R das Pedras, 90, Centro, T2623 2169. An open-air bar with videos, music and dozens of choices of pancakes accompanied by ice cold beer. Always crowded.
ᵀ Fashion Cafe, R das Pedras 151, T2623 2697. Fast food and pizzas with a young crowd and a live band.

Petrópolis *p380, map p381*
ᵀᵀᵀ Falconi, R do Imperador 757. Traditional Italian. Recommended.
ᵀ Cantina Bom Giovanni, R do Imperador 729 upstairs. Popular, Italian, lunch and dinner.
ᵀ Casa d'Ángelo, R do Imperador 700, by Praça Dom Pedro II. Traditional tea house with self service food that doubles as a bar at night.

❶ Bars and clubs

Búzios *p380*
In season Búzios nightlife is young, beautiful and buzzing. Out of season it is non-existent. The bulk of the bars and the handful of clubs are on R das Pedras. These include **GuapoLoco**, a bizarrely shaped Mexican theme bar and restaurant with dancing. There are plenty of others including more upscale wine bar style options like **Café Concerto**. **Privelege**, Av José Bento Ribeiro Dantas 550, R Orla Bardot. One of Brazil's best European-style dance clubs with pumping techno, house and

hip hop and 5 rooms including a cavernous dance floor, sushi bar and lounge.

Ta-ka-ta ka-ta, R das Pedras 256. Strewn with motorbike parts and covered with graffiti.

⊖ Transport

Niterói *p379*

Road The toll on the Rio-Niterói bridge for cars is US$0.90. Bus 996 Gávea-Jurujuba, 998 Galeão-Charitas, 740-D and 741 Copacabana-Charitas, 730-D Castelo Jurujba, US$0.80-1.

Ferry From the 'barcas' at Praça 15 de Novembro (ferry museum at the terminal), ferry boats and launches cross every 10 mins to Niterói (15-20 mins, US$0.65). There are also catamarans ('aerobarcas') every 10 mins (about 3 mins, US$3.25). Of the frequent ferry and catamaran services from Praça 15 de Novembro, Rio, the slow, cheaper ferry gives the best views.

Lagos Fluminenses: Saquarema *p380*

Bus Mil e Um (1001) **Rio**-Saquarema, every 2 hrs 0730-1800, 2 hrs, US$4.50.

Cabo Frio *p380*

Air A new airport has opened linking the area with **Belo Horizonte, Brasília, Rio de Janeiro** and **São Paulo**.

Bus **Urban**: Salineira and Montes Brancos run local services. US$1 to **Búzios, São Pedro da Aldeia, Saquarema, Araruama** and **Arraial do Cabo**. US$0.65 for closer destinations. The urban bus terminal is near Largo de Santo Antônio, opposite the BR petrol station.

Long distance: The rodoviária is well within the city, but a fair walk from centre and beaches. City buses stop nearby. To **Belo Horizonte** US$28-32 (a/c). To **Petrópolis** US$14.50. 1001 to **Rio de Janeiro**, Niterói US$5.40, to **São Paulo** US$30 at 2100.

Búzios *p380*

Bus Mil e Um from Novo Rio, T0xx21-2516 1001,US$10.50, 2½ hrs (be at the bus terminal 20 mins before departure). Departures every 2 hrs from 0700 to 1900 daily. You can also take any bus to **Cabo Frio** (many more during the day), from where it's 30 mins to Búzios. Buy the ticket in advance on major holidays. Búzios' rodoviária is a few blocks' walk from the centre. Some pousadas are within 10 mins on foot, eg La Coloniale,

Brigitta's, while others need a local bus (US$0.65) or taxi. Buses from Cabo Frio run the length of the peninsula and pass several pousadas.

Car Via BR-106 takes about 2½ hrs from Rio.

Petrópolis *p380, map p381*

Bus From **Rio** every 15 mins throughout the day (US$4) with **Única Fácil**, Sun every hr, 1½ hrs, sit on the left hand side for best views. Return tickets are not available, so buy tickets for the return on arrival in Petrópolis. The ordinary buses leave from the rodoviária in Rio; a/c buses, hourly from 1100, from Av Nilo Peçanha, US$5. To **Teresópolis** for the Serra dos Órgãos, **Viação Teresópolis**, 8 a day, US$4. **Salutário** to **São Paulo**, daily at 2330.

Serra dos Órgãos

Bus **Rio-Teresópolis**: buses leave every 30 mins from the Novo Rio rodoviária. Book the return journey as soon as you arrive at Teresópolis; rodoviária at R 1 de Maio 100. Fare US$4.80.

Car The park has 2 dependencies, both accessible from the BR-116: the Sede (HQ, Av Rotariano, Alto Teresópolis, T/F0xx21-2642 1070) is closer to Teresópolis, the highest city in the state of Rio de Janeiro, while the Sub-Sede is just outside the park proper, off the BR-116.

❶ Directory

Cabo Frio *p380*

Internet Cyber Mar, CC V Nunes da Rocha, Av Teixeira e Souza 30. A/c, open 0800-2000 daily. Cyber Tel, Praça Porta Rocha 56, in gallery next to Banco do Brasil, T2649 7575. Only 3 machines, but good and fast.

Búzios *p380*

Internet buzios@internet, Av J B Ribeiro Dantas, 97, close to Shopping One.

Petrópolis *p380, map p381*

Banks Banco do Brasil, R Paulo Barbosa 81. A Banco 24 Horas ATM is by the Varig office at R Marechal Deodoro 98. Travel agencies with exchange: BKR, R Gen Osório 12, **Goldman**, R Barão de Amazonas 46, and **Vert Tur**, R 16 de Março 244, from 1000-1630. **Internet** Compuland, R do Imperador opposite Praça Dr Sá Earp. **Post offices** R do Imperador 350. **Telephones** Telerj, R Marechal Deodoro, just above Praça Dr Sá Earp.

West of Rio

One of the main attractions near the inland highway to São Paulo is the Itatiaia National Park, a good area for climbing, trekking and birdwatching. If you want a really beautiful route, though, take the Rio de Janeiro-Santos section of the BR101, which hugs the forested and hilly Costa Verde southwest of Rio.

Dutra Highway

The Dutra Highway, BR-116, heads west from Rio towards the border with São Paulo. It passes the steel town of **Volta Redonda** and some 30 km further west, the town of **Resende**. In this region, 175 km from Rio, is **Penedo** (five buses a day from Resende) which in the 1930s attracted Finnish settlers who brought the first saunas to Brazil. There is a Finnish museum, a cultural centre and Finnish dancing on Saturday. This popular weekend resort also provides horse riding, and swimming in the Portinho River. There are plenty of mid-range and cheap hotels in town. For tourist information, Toxx24-3351 1876.

Parque Nacional Itatiaia

① *Entry per day is $10 per car. Information can be obtained from Ibama, Toxx24-3352 1461, for the local headquarters, or Toxx21-3224 6463 for the Rio de Janeiro state department. Avoid weekends and holidays if you want to see wildlife.*

This park, being so close to Rio and São Paulo, is a must for those with limited time who wish to see some of world's rarest birds and mammals in a whole range of different ecosystems. Trails from one hour to two days go through deep valleys shrouded in pristine rainforest, hiding icy waterfalls and clear-water rivers. The 30,000 ha mountainous park is Brazil's oldest, founded in 1937 to protect Atlantic Coast Rainforest in the Serra de Mantiqueira. Important species include jaguar, puma, brown capuchin and black-face titi monkeys. The park is particularly good for birds with a list of 350+, with scores of spectacular tanagers, humming, cotingas and manakins. The best trails head for Pedra de Taruga and Pedra de Maçã and the Poranga and Véu de Noiva waterfalls. The Pico das Agulhas Negras and the Serra das Prateleiras (up to 2,540 m) offer decent rock climbing. There is a **Museu de História Natural** ① *1000-1600, closed Mon*, near the headquarters, with a depressing display of stuffed animals from the 1940s.

Information and maps can be obtained at the park office. The **Administração do Parque Nacional de Itatiaia** operates a refuge in the park, which acts as a starting point for climbs and treks. Although buses do run through the park calling at the hotels, hiring a car to visit Itatiaia is the best option.

Costa Verde (Emerald Coast)

The Rio de Janeiro-Santos section of the BR101 is one of the world's most beautiful highways, running along the aptly called Emerald Coast, which is littered with islands, beaches, colonial settlements and mountain fazendas. It is complete through to Bertioga (see page 407), which has good links with Santos and São Paulo. Buses run from Rio to Angra dos Reis, Paraty, Ubatuba, Caraguatatuba and São Sebastião, where it may be necessary to change for Santos or São Paulo.

Itacuruçá, 91 km from Rio, is a delightful place to visit. Separated from the town by a channel is the Ilha de Itacuruçá, the largest of a string of islands stretching into the bay. Further offshore is Ilha de Jaguanum, around which there are lovely walks. Saveiros (schooners) sail around the bay and to the islands from Itacuruça: Passamar, T9979 2429. Ilha de Itacuruçá can also be reached from **Muriqui**, a popular beach resort 9 km from Itacuruçá. There are hotels on the island. **Mangaratiba**, 22 km down the coast, is half-way from Rio to Angra dos Reis. Its beaches are muddy, but the surroundings are pleasant and better beaches can be found outside town.

Angra dos Reis → *Phone code: 0xx24. Post code: 23900. Colour map 7, grid B4. Pop: 119,247.*

Said to have been founded on 6 January 1502 (O Dia dos Reis – The Day of Kings), this is a small port, 151 km southwest of Rio, with an important fishing and shipbuilding industry. It has several small coves with good bathing within easy reach and is situated on an enormous bay full of islands. Of particular note are the church and convent of **Nossa Senhora do Carmo**, built in 1593 (Praça Gen Osório), the **Igreja Matriz de Nossa Senhora da Conceição** (1626) in the centre of town, and the church and convent of **São Bernardino de Sena** (1758-1763) on the Morro do Santo Antônio. On the Largo da Lapa is the church of **Nossa Senhora da Lapa da Boa Morte** (1752), with a sacred art museum. On the Península de Angra, just west of the town, is the **Praia do Bonfim**, a popular beach, and a little way offshore the island of the same name, on which is the hermitage of Senhor do Bonfim (1780). **Tourist information** is opposite the bus station on the Largo da Lapa, very good, T3336 51175, ext 2186.

Ilha Grande → *Phone code: 0xx21.*

Ilha Grande is a mountain ridge covered in tropical forest sticking out of an emerald sea and fringed by some of the world's most beautiful beaches. As there are no cars and no roads either, just trails through the forest, the island is still relatively undeveloped. Much of it forms part of a State Park and **Biological Reserve**, and cannot even be visited. The island was a notorious pirate lair, then a landing port for slaves. By the 20th century it had become the site of an infamous prison for the country's most notorious criminals (closed in 1994 and now overgrown rubble). The weather is best from March to June and, like everywhere along the coast, the island is over-run during the Christmas, New Year and Carnaval period. **Convention and Visitors Bureau**, at the ferry port on arrival ⓘ *T021-2220 4323, Mon-Sat 0800-1800, Sun 0900-1300.* All information on website www.ilhagrande.com.br.

The beach at **Vila do Abraão** may look beautiful to first arrivals but those further afield are far more spectacular. The two most famous are **Lopes Mendes**, two hours walk from Abraão, and **Aventureiro**, six hours, but it can be reached via the Maria Isabel or Mestre Ernani boats (T3361 9895 or T9269 5877), which leave from the quay in front of the BR petrol station in Angra dos Reis. Good beaches closer to Abraão include the half moon bay at **Abraãozinho** (15 minutes walk) and **Grande das Palmas** which has a delightful tiny whitewashed chapel (one hour 20 minutes walk), both east of town. Lagoa Azul, Freguesia de Santana and Saco do Céu are all boat trips. Good treks include over the mountains to Dois Rios, where the old jail was situated (13 km one way, about three hours), Pico do Papagaio (980 m) through forest, a stiff, three-hour climb (guide is essential) and Pico da Pedra d'Água (1,031 m).

Paraty → *Phone code: 0xx24. Post code: 23970. Colour map 7, grid B4. Population: 29,544.*

Paraty, 98 km from Angra dos Reis, is one of Brazil's prettiest colonial towns, whose centre has been declared a national historic monument in its entirety. It was the chief port for the export of gold in the 17th century and a coffee-exporting port in the 19th century. At the weekend Paraty buzzes with tourists who browse in the little boutiques and art galleries, or buy souvenirs from the indigenous Guaraní who sell their wares on the cobbles. Many of the numerous little bars and restaurants, like the pousadas, are owned by expat Europeans, who are determined to preserve Paraty's charm. During the week, especially off season, the town is quiet and intimate. Much of the accommodation available is in colonial buildings, some sumptuously decorated, with flourishing gardens or courtyards. The town centre is out of bounds for motor vehicles; heavy chains are strung across the entrance to the streets. In spring the roads are flooded, while the houses are above the water level. **Centro de Informações Turísticas** ⓘ *Av Roberto Silveira, near the entrance to the historical centre, T3371 1266, daily 0900-1600.* More information is available at www.paraty.com.br (Portuguese, English, Spanish) and www.paraty.tur.br (Portuguese, English, French).

There are four churches: **Santa Rita** (1722), built by the 'freed coloured men' in elegant Brazilian baroque, faces the bay and the port. It houses an interesting **Museum of Sacred Art** ⓘ *Wed-Sun 0900-1200, 1300-1800, US$1.* **Nossa Senhora do Rosário e São Benedito** (1725, rebuilt 1757) ⓘ *R do Comércio, Tue 0900-1200,* built by black slaves, is small and simple. **Nossa Senhora dos Remédios** (1787-1873) ⓘ *Mon, Wed, Fri, Sat 0900-1200, Sun 0900-1500,* is the town's parish church, the biggest in Paraty. **Capela de Nossa Senhora das Dores** (1800) is a small chapel facing the sea that was used mainly by the wealthy whites in the 19th century (Ms Grassa will open it for visitors if requested in advance). There is a great deal of distinguished Portuguese colonial architecture in delightful settings. **R do Comércio** is the main street in the historical centre. The **Casa da Cadeia**, close to Santa Rita church, is the former jail and is being converted into a historical museum. On the northern headland is a small fort, **Forte do Defensor Perpétuo**, built in 1822.

The town's environs are as beautiful as Paraty itself. Just a few kilometres away lie the forests of the Ponta do Juatinga peninsula, fringed by wonderful beaches, washed by little waterfalls and still home to traditional fishing communities. At **Fazenda Murycana**, an old sugar estate and 17th century cachaça distillery, you can taste and buy the different types of cachaça. It has an excellent restaurant. Mosquitoes can be a problem, take repellent and don't wear shorts. If short of time, the one must is to take a boat trip round the bay; some of its islands are home to rare animals. Boats also go to wonderful beaches like **Praia da Conçeicao**, **Praia Vermelha** and **Praia da Lula**, all of which have simple restaurants and are backed by forest and washed by gentle waves. Further south are **Saco da Velha**, protected by an island, and **Paraty Mirim** (17 km, also reached by bus, four a day, three on Sunday). The **Gold Trail**, hiking on a road dating from the 1800s, can be done on foot or horseback. Many other adventure sports are available (see Activities and tours below).

Trindade

Trindade, 30 km south of Paraty, may not be as beautiful in its own right but its setting, sandwiched between rainforested slopes and emerald sea, is spectacular. It has a long, broad beach and has long been a favourite with surf hippies from São Paulo and Rio who come in droves over Christmas and New Year. It is gradually finding its place on the international backpacker circuit as the campsites, pousadas and restaurants are cheap and cheerful. It's also the last stop on the South American Experience backpacker bus tour.

Note If travelling along the coast into São Paulo state as far as Guarujá, do not drive or go out alone after dark.

🛏 Sleeping

Parque Nacional de Itatiaia *p386*
Basic accommodation in cabins and dormitories is available in Itatiaia village, strung along the road leading to the park.

LL Simon, Km 13 on the road in the park, T3352 1122, www.hotelsimon.com.br. Price is for 3 days, full board. A 1970s concrete block at the top of the park, which marks the trailhead for the higher walks to Agulhas Negras and Três Picos. Wonderful views from fading rooms.

L-AL Hotel Donati, T3352 1110, www.hoteldonati.com.br. Delightful, mock Swiss chalets and rooms, set in tropical gardens visited by animals every night and early morning. A series of trails lead off from the main building and the hotel can organize professional birding guides. Decent restaurant and 2 pools. Highly recommended. Map on web site.

B Hotel Cabanas de Itatiaia, T3352 1252. Magical views from these comfortable but ridiculously Swiss chalets on a hillside. Pool and good restaurant too.

C pp Cabanas da Itatiaia, T3352 1152. Simple chalets in secondary forest in the lower reaches of the park. The sister hotel (Aldeia dos Pássaros) opposite has a pool. Both share facilities and are very helpful. Great breakfasts, good off season rates and a riverside sauna.

C Hotel Alsene, at 2,100 m, 2 km from the side entrance to the park, take a bus to São Lourenço and Caxambu, get off at Registro, walk or hitch from there (12 km). Very popular with climbing and trekking clubs, dormitory or camping, chalets available, hot showers, fireplace, evening meal after everyone returns, drinks but no snacks.

Ipê Amarelo, R João Maurício Macedo Costa 352, Campo Alegre, T/F3352 1232. IYHA.
Camping Camping Clube do Brasil site is entered at Km 148 on the Via Dutra.

Costa Verde: Itacuruçá *p386*
A-B Resort Atlântico, Praia do Axixá, T/F2680 7168, www.divingbrasil.com. Dutch/Brazilian-owned pousada, helpful, good breakfast, English spoken, meals available, diving courses (PADI).

Angra dos Reis *p386*
B Caribe, R de Conceição 255, T3365 0033, F3365 3450. Central. Recommended.

C-E Angra Hostel, Praça da Matriz 152 (at the corner of Rua do Comércio), T3364 4759. Simple hostel (HI) with reasonable breakfast and internet. A block from the quays (just on the other side of the road from the post office) and convenient if you miss a boat.

Ilha Grande *p387*
There are many pousadas in Abraão and reservations are only necessary in peak season or on holiday weekends. Ignore dockside hotel touts who lie about hotel closures and flash pictures of their lodgings to unsuspecting tourists. Numerous eating places serve the usual fish/chicken, beans and rice options.

Abraão
B Ancoradouro, R da Praia 121, T3361 5153, www.ancoradouro.ilhagrande.com. Simple rooms with en suites in a beach front building, 10 mins' walk east of the jetty.

B-C Farol dos Borbas, Praia do Abraão, T3361 5260, www.ilhagrandetour.com.br. A minute from the jetty. Simple, well-maintained rooms with tiled floors, fan, breakfast tables and chairs. The best rooms have balconies, the worst have no windows. Boat trips organized.

C Porto Girassol, T3361 527, R do Praia 65, portogirasol@ilhagrande.com. Simple rooms in a mock-colonial beachhouse 5 mins east of the jetty.

C-D Pousada Cachoeira, Rua do Bicão, T3361 9521, www.cachoeira.com. Lovely little pousada with a dining room palapa and living area, cabins and a terrace of rooms nestled in a forest garden next to a fast-flowing stream. Good breakfasts and boat tours. English and German spoken. Cheaper prices per person.

C-E Aquário Hostel, Praia Abraão, T3361 3405, www.aquario.ilhagrande.com. Beautifully located on a spit next to the beach and with scruffy rooms and dorms, spacious, airy public areas including a bar, huge sea-water swimming pool and wonderful ocean views.

C-E Che Lagarto Ilha Grande, Praia Abraão, left side of the beach on the way to Praia da Julia, T7814-4455, www.chelagarto.com. HI member. Includes breakfast and welcome drink. Open 2006; basic dorms and doubles, some with private toilet, a/c and sea view, a loud bar, barbecue area and numerous tours and activities on offer.

D Estalagem Costa Verde, R. Amâncio Felicio de Souza 239a, T3104 7490, www.estalagem costaverde.com.br. In the town ½ a block behind the church. Bright hostel with light, well-decorated rooms, great value.

F pp Albergue Holdandés, R Assembléia de Deus, T3361 5034, www.holandeshostel.com.br. Four little chalets and rooms lost in the forest, great atmosphere, be sure to reserve, HI affiliated.

Outside of town

LL Sítio do Lobo, T2227 4138, www.sitiodolobo.com.br. Access is only by boat. An architect commissioned house converted into a small boutique hotel, sitting on an isolated peninsula. The views are marvellous; the best room are the suites; others overlook the pool. The best food on the island.

LL-L Sankay, T3365 1090, Enseada do Bananal (1 hr by boat from Angra or Abraão), www.pousadasankay.com.br. Another beautiful little pousada perched on a peninsula with wonderful views. 5 rooms from 4 to 6 people, sauna and bar. Price includes boat transfers, breakfast, dinner and a boat trip.

Paraty *p387*

Over 300 hotels and pousadas; in mid-week look around and find a place that suits you best. Browse through www.paraty.com.br/frame.htm for yet more options.

LL Pousada Pardieiro, R do Comércio 74, T3371 1370, www.pousadapardieiro.com.br. Quiet, with a calm, sophisticated atmosphere, a colonial building with lovely gardens, delightful rooms facing internal patios and a little swimming pool. Always full at weekends, no children under 15.

LL Pousada Picinguaba, T12-3836 9105, www.picinguaba.com. Stylish French-owned hotel in a converted convent some 30 km from Paraty; with superior service, an excellent restaurant and simple, elegant (fan-cooled) rooms. Marvellous views out over a bay of islands. Booking ahead essential.

L Bromelias Pousada & Spa, Rodovia Rio-Santos, Km 562, Graúna, T/F3371 2791, www.pousadabromelias.com.br. Asian-inspired with its own aromatherapy products and massage treatments, tastefully decorated chalets in the Atlantic coastal forest. Pool, sauna and restaurant.

L Pousada do Ouro, R Dr Pereira (or da Praia) 145, T/F371 2221, www.pousadaauro.com.br. Near Paraty's eastern waterfront, once a private home built from a gold fortune, suites in the main building, plainer rooms in an annexe, open-air poolside pavilion in a tropical garden. Has had many famous guests.

L Pousada do Sandi, Largo do Rosário 1, T3371 2100, www.pousadadosandi.com.br. 18th-century building with a grand lobby, comfortable, adjoining restaurant and pool.

L-AL Pousada Mercado do Pouso, Largo de Santa Rita 43, T/F3371 1114, www.mercadode pouso.com.br. Historic building close to water-front, good sea views, family atmosphere, no pool.

AL Le Gite d'Indaitiba, Rodovia Rio-Santos (BR-101) Km 562, Graúna, T3371 7174, www.legitedindaiatiba.com.br. French owned, stylish chalets set in gardens on a hillside. Sweeping views of the bay, and French food to match the location.

AL Morro do Forte, R Orlando Carpinelli, T/F371 1211, www.pousadamorrodoforte.com.br. Out of the centre, lovely garden, good breakfast, pool, German owner Peter Kallert offers trips on his yacht. Recommended.

AL-A Hotel Coxixo, R do Comércio 362, T3371 1460, www.hotelcoxixo.com.br. Converted colonial building in the heart of the town, owned by movie-star Maria Della Costa. The best rooms in the hotel and in Paraty are the upper floor colonial suites.

AL-B Pousada Arte Colonial, R da Matriz 292, T3371 7231, www.paraty.com.br/ artecolonial. One of the best deals in Paraty: colonial building in the centre decorated with style and a genuine personal touch by its French owner. Helpful, breakfast included. Highly recommended.

A Pousada do Corsário, Beco do Lapeiro 26, T3371 1866, www.pousadadocorsario.com.br. New building with a pool and its own gardens; next to the river and 2 blocks from the centre, simple but stylish rooms, most with hammocks outside. Highly recommended.

B Solar dos Gerânios, Praça da Matriz, T/F33711550, www.paraty.com.br/geranio. Beautiful colonial family house on main square in traditional rustic style, excellent value, English spoken. Warmly recommended.

C Marendaz, R Patitiba 9, T3371 1369. Family-run, simple, charming, a block from the historical centre.

C Pousada Miramar, Abel de Oliveira 19, T3371 2132. One room has its own kitchen, good value. Recommended.

D Pousada do Careca, Praça Macedo Soares, T3371 1291. Very simple rooms in the historic centre, those without street windows are musty.

D-E Che Lagarto Paraty, R Dr Derly Ellena 9, T3371 1369, www.chelagarto.com. HI member, rates include breakfast and welcome drink. Rooms with private toilet and a/c.

Casa do Rio, R Antônio Vidal 120, T3371 2223, www.paraty.com.br/casadorio. Peaceful little hostel with riverside courtyard and hammock, kitchen, breakfast included. Offers jeep and horse riding trips. Recommended.

Camping Camping Beira-Rio, just across the bridge, before the road to the fort. Camping Club do Brasil, Av Orlando Carpinelli, Praia do Pontal, T3371 1877. Small, good, very crowded in Jan and Feb, US$8 pp. Also at Praia Jabaquara, T3371 2180.

Trindade p388

B Garni Cruzeiro do Sul, Rua Principal (first on the right as you enter the village), T3371 5102, www.hotelgarnicruzeirodosul.com.br. Smart little beachside pousada with duplex rooms, most of which have sea views.

D-F Ponta da Trindade Pousada & Camping, T3371 5113. Simple rooms with fan, sand-floored campsite with cold water showers and no power.

D Chalé e Pousada Magia do Mar, T3371 5130. Thatched roofed hut with space for four. Views out over beach.

D Pousada Marimbá, R. Principal, T3371 5147. Simple colourful rooms and a little breakfast area.

🍴 Eating

Paraty *p387*
The best restaurants in Paraty are in the historic part of town and are almost as good as any you will find in Rio or São Paulo. Watch out for surreptitious cover charges for live music. The less expensive restaurants, those offering *comida a quilo* (pay by weight) and the fast food outlets are outside the historical centre, mainly on Av Roberto Silveira. Paraty has some plates unique to the region, like peixe à Parati – local fish cooked with herbs, green bananas and served with pirão, a mixture of manioc flour and the sauce that the fish was cooked in.

₸₸₸ Bartolomeu, R Samuel Costa 176, T3371 3052. Argentinian steaks, delicious salads from a chef trained in Rio´s Gourmet restaurant. Good atmosphere and cocktails.

₸₸₸ Copa de Ouro, R Dr Pereira 145, T3371 1311. Very good seafood and Brazilian dishes. Recommended.

₸₸₸ do Hiltinho, R Mcal Deodoro 233, T3371 1432. Decent seafood, including local dishes.

₸₸₸ Merlin O Mago, R do Comércio 376, T3371 2157, www.paraty.com.br/merlin.htm. Franco-Brazilian cooking in an intimate dining room/bar, by a German Cordon Bleu-trained chef and illustrious photojournalist. The best in town.

₸₸ Café Paraty, R da Lapa and Comércio. Sandwiches, appetizers, light meals, also bar with live music nightly (cover charge), a local landmark. Open 0900-2400.

₸₸ Dona Ondina, R do Comércio 2, by the river. Family restaurant with well-prepared simple food (closed on Mon, Mar and Nov), good value.

₸₸ Punto Di Vino, R Mcal Deodoro 129, T3371 1348. Wood-fired pizza and calzoni served with live music and a good selection of wine.

₸₸ Thai Brasil, R Dona Geralda 345, 3371 0127, www.thaibrasil.com.br. Beautiful restaurant ornamented with handicrafts and hand-painted furniture, the cooking loosely resembles Thai, without spices.

₸ Sabor da Terra, Av Roberto Silveira, next to Banco do Brasil. Reliable, if not bargain-priced, self service food, closes 2200.

🍸 Bars and clubs

Paraty *p387*
Bar Coupé, Praça Matriz. A popular hang-out with outside seating, good bar snacks and breakfast.
Bar Dinho, Praça da Matriz at R da Matriz. Good bar with live music at weekends, sometimes mid-week.
Grupo Contadores, The Puppet Show, R Dona Geralda 327, T3371 1575, ecparaty@ax.apc.org. Wed, Sat 2100, US\$12: a silent puppet theatre for adults only which has toured throughout the USA and Europe. Not to be missed.
Umoya, R Comendador José Luiz. Video bar and café, live music at weekends.

🎉 Festivals and events

Paraty *p387*
Feb/Mar: Carnival, hundreds of people cover their bodies in black mud and run through the streets yelling like prehistoric creatures (anyone can join in). **Mar/Apr**: Semana Santa, with religious processions and folk songs. **Mid-Jul**: Semana de Santa Rita, traditional foods, shows, exhibitions and dances. **Aug**: Festival da Pinga, the cachaça fair at which local distilleries display their products and there are plenty of opportunities to over-indulge. **Sep** (around the 8th): Semana da Nossa Senhora dos Remédios, processions and religious events. **Sep/Oct**: Spring Festival of Music, concerts in front of Santa Rita church. The city is decorated with lights for Christmas. **31 Dec**: New Year's, a huge party with open-air concerts and fireworks (reserve accommodation in advance). As well as the Dança dos Velhos (see Music and dance, page 1510), another common dance in these parts is the ciranda, in which everyone, young and old, dances in a circle to songs accompanied by guitars.

The **Festa Literária Internacional de Parati** (FLIP, www.flip.org.br), which is organized by Bloomsbury publishing house, occurs every northern summer and is one of the most important literary events in Latin America. It is always attended by big name writers.

🥾 Activities and tours

Parque Nacional de Itatiaia *p386*
Information on treks can be obtained from **Clube Excursionista Brasileira**, Av Almirante Barroso 2, 8th floor, Rio de Janeiro, T0xx21-2220 3695.
Wildlife guides Edson Endrigo, T3742 8374, www.avesfoto.com.br. Birding trips in Itatiaia and throughout Brazil. English spoken. **Ralph Salgueiro**, T3351 1823, www.ecoralph.com.

Angra dos Reis *p386*
Boat trips Trips around the bay are available, some with a stop for lunch on the island of Gipóia (5 hrs). Several boats run tours from the Cais de Santa Luzia and there are agencies for saveiros in town, boats depart between 1030-1130 daily, US\$10-12 (during Jan and Feb best to reserve in advance).
Diving Aquamaster, Praia da Enseada, T3365 2416. US\$60 for 2 dives with drinks and food, take a 'Retiro' bus from the port in Angra.

Ilha Grande *p387*

Boat trips US$13 without food or drinks, but include fruit. Ask about trips to good scuba diving sites around the coast.

Cycling Bikes can be hired and tours arranged; ask at pousadas.

Paraty *p387*

Antígona, Praça da Bandeira 2, Centro Histórico, T/F3371 1165. Daily schooner tours, 5 hrs, bar and lunch on board. Recommended.

Fausto Goyos, T9914 5506. Offers off-road tours in an ex-US military jeep to rainforest, waterfalls, historical sites, also photo safaris. He also has highly professional horse riding tours and offers lodging in youth-hostel style rooms, with or without meals.

Paraty Tours, Av Roberto Silveira 11, T/F371 1327. English and Spanish spoken.

Soberana da Costa, R Dona Geraldo 43, in Pousada Mercado do Pouso, T/F3371 1114. Also offers schooner trips in the bay. Recommended.

Transport

Parque Nacional de Itatiaia *p386*

Bus Itatiaia lies just off the main Sao Paulo-Rio motorway. There are connections to Itatiaia town or nearby Resende from both **Rio** and **São Paulo**. There is only 1 way into the park from Itatiaia town and 1 main road within it – which forks off to the various hotels, all of which are signposted. Four times a day (variable hours), a bus marked '504 Circular' leaves Itatiaia town for to the Park, calling at the hotels and stopping at the Simon. Coming from Resende this may be caught at the crossroads before Itatiaia. Through tickets to São Paulo are sold at a booth in the large bar in the middle of Itatiaia main street.

Costa Verde: Mangaratiba *p386*

Bus From Rio Rodoviária with **Costa Verde**, several daily, US$5.65.

Angra dos Reis *p386*

Bus To **Angra** at least hourly from Rio's rodoviária with **Costa Verde**, several direct, T516 2437, accepts credit cards, comfortable buses take the 'via litoral', sit on the left, US$8, 2½ hrs. From Angra to **São Paulo**, 5 buses daily (3 on Sat), US$16. To **Paraty**, many buses leave from bus station or just flag the bus down at bus stops on the highway, US$4.

Ilha Grande *p387*

Ferry Barcas SA, T21-4004 3113/2533 7524: **Angra**-Abraão Mon-Fri 1530, Sat-Sun 1330. Abraão-Angra: daily 1000. **Magaratiba**-Abraão

daily 0800 and Fri 2200; Abraão-Mangaratiba daily 1730. US$2 during the week, US$6 at weekends. 2 hrs to both destinations. Direct service to Rio with Eterno Beira Mar, T9955 9174/3361 9533, eternobeiramar@ zipmail.com.br, or ask for Alexandra (T8196 9895 mob) at the ferry dock on Ilha Grande at 0930. Eterno Beira Mar sails at 1000 to Mangaratiba, where a minivan or taxi will take you to Rio (hotel, bus station, airport, wherever); also does the journey in reverse, US$20. During the Brazilian summer, fishing boats (*escunas*) usually leave Mon-Fri at 1320, 1430 and 1630 from the Cais da Lapa quay in Angra. They return from Abraão at 0730, 0830 and 1630 and go to Mangaratiba at 1000. There are also frequent impromptu fishing boat trips on demand between Angra and Abraão, usually before lunchtime only and most frequently in summer months. Around US$6.50.

Paraty *p387*

Bus To **Fazenda Murycana** take a Penha/ Ponte Branca bus from the rodoviária, 4 a day; alight where it crosses a small white bridge and then walk 10 mins along a signed, unpaved road.

Rodoviária at the corner of R Jango Padua and R da Floresta. 9 buses a day go to **Rio** (241 km), 4½ hrs, US$13, **Costa Verde** – see under Angra dos Reis for details; to **Angra dos Reis** (98 km, 1½ hrs, every 1 hr 40 mins, US$5, also **Colitur**). 3 a day to **Ubatuba** (75 km, just over 1 hr, Colitur, US$5). To **São Paulo**, 4 a day (304 km via São José dos Campos, 5½ hrs, US$10.50, **Reunidas**, booked up quickly, very busy at weekends). To **São Sebastião**, 2 a day with **Normandy** (who also go to Rio twice a day). On holidays and in high season, the frequency of bus services usually increases.

Directory

Ilha Grande *p387*

No **banks** or money changing on the island. **Internet** Several places in Abraão.

Paraty *p387*

Banks Banco do Brasil, Av Roberto Silveira, not too far from the bus station, exchange 1000-1500, long queues and commission. 2 ATMs in town for Visa and MasterCard, 0600-2200. **Internet** Many places but connection is not cheap. **Post offices** R Mcal Deodoro e Domingos Gonçalves de Abreu, 0800-1700, Sun 0800-1200. **Telephones** Telerj for international calls, Praça Macedo Soares, opposite the tourist office. Local and long distance calls can be made from public phones.

São Paulo → *Phone code: 0xx11. Colour map 7, grid B4.*

The city of São Paulo is vast and can feel intimidating at first. But this is a city of separate neighbourhoods, only a few of which are interesting for visitors and, once you have your base, it is easy to negotiate. Those who don't flinch from the city's size and who are prepared to spend money and time here, and who get to know Paulistanos, are seldom disappointed. (The inhabitants of the city are called Paulistanos, to differentiate them from the inhabitants of the state, who are called Paulistas.) Nowhere in Brazil is better for concerts, clubs, theatre, ballet, classical music, all round nightlife, restaurants and beautifully designed hotels.

Ins and outs

Getting there There are air services from all parts of Brazil, Europe, North and South America to the international **airport** at Guarulhos, also known as Cumbica, Avenida Monteiro Lobato 1985, T6445 2945 (30 km from the city). Varig has its own terminal for international flights, adjoining the old terminal which all other airlines use. The local airport of Congonhas, 14 km from the city centre on Avenida Washington Luiz, is used for the Rio-São Paulo shuttle, some flights to Belo Horizonte and Vitória and private flights only, T5090 9000. The **main rodoviária** is Tietê (T3235 0322), which is very convenient and has its own Metrô station. There are three other bus stations for inter-state bus services. ►► *For more detailed information, see Transport, page 410.*

Getting around and orientation Much of the centre is pedestrianized, so walking is the only option if you wish to explore it. The best and cheapest way to get around São Paulo is on the Metrô system, which is clean, safe, cheap and efficient, though rather limited. Bus routes can be confusing and slow due to frequent traffic jams, but buses are safe, clean and only crowded at peak hours. All the rodoviárias (bus stations) are on the Metrô, but if travelling with luggage, take a taxi. The **Old Centre** (Praça da República, Sé, Santa Cecília) is a place to visit but not to stay. The central commercial district, containing banks, offices and shops, is known as the Triângulo, bounded by Ruas Direita, 15 (Quinze) de Novembro, São Bento and Praça Antônio Prado, but it is rapidly spreading towards the Praça da República. **Jardins**, the city's most affluent inner neighbourhood, is a good place to stay and to visit, especially if you want to shop and eat well. Elegant little streets hide hundreds of wonderful restaurants and accommodation ranges from the luxurious to the top end of the budget range. You are safe here at night. The northeastern section of Jardins, known as **Cerqueira César**, abuts one of São Paulo's grandest modern avenues, **Paulista**, lined with skyscrapers, shops and a few churches and museums including MASP (Museu de Arte de São Paulo). There are metro connections from here and a number of good hotels. **Ibirapuera Park and around**: the inner city's largest green space is home to a handful of museums, running tracks, a lake and frequent free live concerts on Sun. The adjoining neighbourhoods of Moema and Vila Mariana have a few hotels, but **Moema**, **Itaim** and **Vila Olimpia** are among the nightlife centres of São Paulo with a wealth of streetside bars, designer restaurants and European-style dance clubs. Hotels tend to be expensive as they are near the new business centre on Avenidas Brigadeiro Faria Lima and Luis Carlos Berrini. **Pinheiros and Vila Madalena** are less chic, but equally lively at night and with the funkiest shops.

Beware of assaults and pickpocketing in São Paulo. Thieves often use the mustard-on-the-back trick to distract you while someone else robs you. The areas around Luz station, Praça da República and Centro are not safe at night, and do not enter favelas.

Tourist offices There are tourist information booths with English speaking staff in domestic and international arrivals (ground floor) at Guarulhos airport (Cumbica); and tourist booths in the Tietê bus station and in the following locations throughout the city: **Praça da República** ① *T3231 2922, daily 0900-1800*, very helpful; **Praça Dom José Gaspar** ① *corner of Av São Luís, T3214 0209, Mon-Fri 0900-1800*; **Avenida Paulista at Parque Trianon** ① *T251 0970, daily except Sat 0900-1800*; and on **Avenida Brig Faria Lima** ① *opposite the Iguatemi Shopping Center, T3031 1277, Mon-Fri 0900-1800*. An excellent map is available free at all these offices, as well as free maps and pamphlets in English. Editora Abril also publish maps and an excellent guide, *Sampa* (Portuguese). Also visit www.cidadedesaopaulo.com (Portuguese, English and Spanish), www.guiasp.com.br and www.gringoes.com.br.

National parks Ibama, Alameda Tietê 637, Jardim Cerqueira César, T3066 2662, F3066 2675.

Climate São Paulo sits on a plateau at around 800 m and the weather is temperamental. Rainfall is ample and temperatures fluctuate greatly: summer 20-30° C (occasionally peaking into the high 30s or 40s), winter 15-25° C (occasionally dropping to below 10° C). The winter months (April-October) are also the driest, with minimal precipitation in June/July. Christmas and New Year are wet. When there are thermal inversions, air pollution can be troublesome.

Background

Until the 1870s São Paulo was a sleepy, shabby little town known as 'a cidade de barro' (the mud city), as most of its buildings were made of clay and packed mud. The city was transformed at the end of the 19th century when wealthy landowners and the merchants of Santos began to invest. Between 1885 and the end of the century the boom in coffee and the arrival of large numbers of Europeans transformed the state out of all recognition. By the end of the 1930s São Paulo state had one million Italians, 500,000 each of Portuguese and immigrants from the rest of Brazil, nearly 400,000 Spaniards and nearly 200,000 Japanese. It is the world's largest Japanese community outside Japan. In the early 20th century, numbers of Syrian-Lebanese came to São Paulo. Nowadays, it covers more than 1,500 sq km – three times the size of Paris.

São Paulo

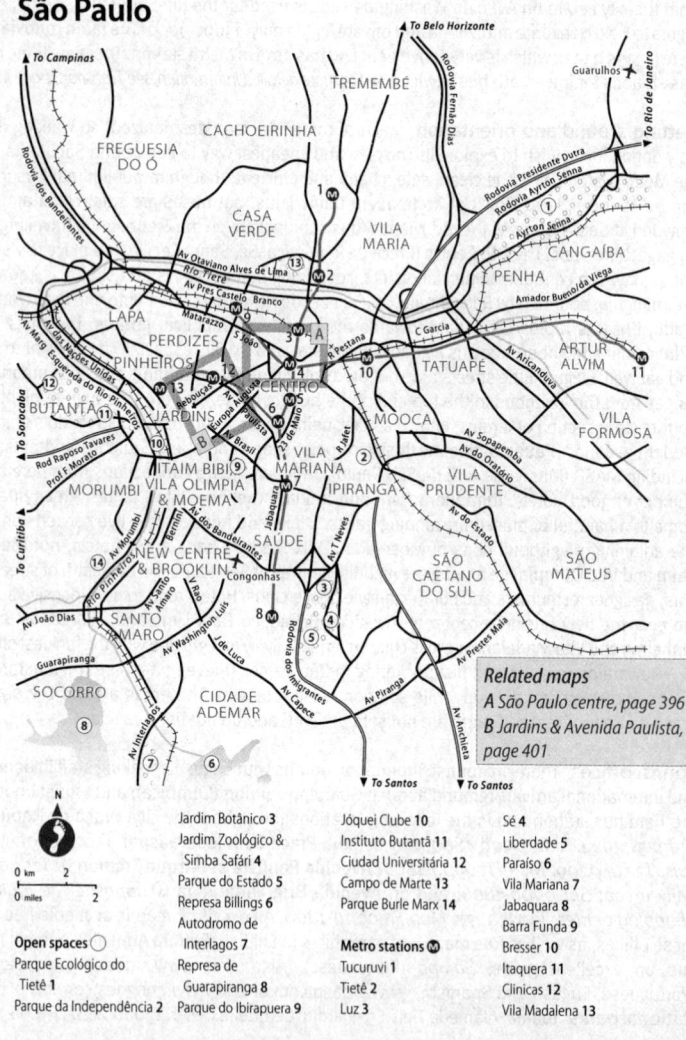

Related maps
A São Paulo centre, page 396
B Jardins & Avenida Paulista, page 401

N

0 km   2
0 miles   2

Open spaces ○
Parque Ecológico do
Tietê 1
Parque da Independência 2

Jardim Botânico 3
Jardim Zoológico &
Simba Safári 4
Parque do Estado 5
Represa Billings 6
Autodromo de
Interlagos 7
Represa de
Guarapiranga 8
Parque do Ibirapuera 9

Jóquei Clube 10
Instituto Butantã 11
Ciudad Universitária 12
Campo de Marte 13
Parque Burle Marx 14

Metro stations Ⓜ
Tucuruvi 1
Tietê 2
Luz 3

Sé 4
Liberdade 5
Paraíso 6
Vila Mariana 7
Jabaquara 8
Barra Funda 9
Bresser 10
Itaquera 11
Clinicas 12
Vila Madalena 13

Old Centre

A focal point of the centre is the **Parque Anhangabaú**, an open space between the Triângulo and the streets which lead to Praça da República (Metrô Anhangabaú is at its southern end). Beneath Anhangabaú, north-south traffic is carried by a tunnel. Crossing it are two viaducts: **Viaduto do Chá**, which is open to traffic and links R Direita and R Barão de Itapetininga. Along its length sellers of potions, cures, fortunes and trinkets set up their booths. The **Viaduto Santa Ifigênia**, an iron bridge for pedestrians only, connects Largo de São Bento with Largo de Santa Ifigênia.

On **Largo de São Bento** is the **Igreja e Mosteiro de São Bento**, an early 20th century building (1910-22) on the site of a 1598 chapel. Due south of São Bento is the **Martinelli building** ① *on R Líbero Badaró at Av São João, Mon-Sat 0900-1530, entry to 26th floor, free*, the city's first skyscraper. On Praça Antônio Prado stands the **Antigo Prédio do Banco do São Paulo** ① *Mon-Fri 0900-1800, the ground floor used for fairs and exhibitions*. The **Pátio do Colégio (Museu de Anchieta)** ① *Praça Pátio do Colégio, T3105 6899, Metrô Sé, Tue-Sun 0900-1700, US$3*. The newly renovated building is an exact replica of the original Jesuit church and college but dates from 1950s. Most of the buildings are occupied by the Museu de Anchieta, named after the Jesuit captain who led the first mission. This houses, amongst other items a 17th-century font used to baptize indigenous people and a collection of Guaraní art and artefacts from the colonial era and a modernist painting of the priest, by Italian Albino Menghini.

A short distance southeast of the Pátio do Colégio is the **Solar da Marquesa de Santos**, an 18th-century residential building, which now contains the **Museu da Cidade** ① *R Roberto Simonsen 136, Tue-Sun, 0900-1700*. The **Praça da Sé** is a huge open area south of the Pátio do Colégio, dominated by the **Catedral Metropolitana**, a massive, peaceful space. The cathedral's foundations were laid over 40 years before its inauguration during the 1954 festivities commemorating the fourth centenary of the city. It was fully completed in 1970. This enormous building in neo-Gothic style has a capacity for 8,000 worshippers in its five naves. The interior is mostly unadorned, except for the two gilt mosaic pictures in the transepts: on the north side is the Virgin Mary and on the south Saint Paul.

West of the Praça da Sé, along R Benjamin Constant, is the Largo de São Francisco. Here is the **Igreja da Ordem Terceira de São Francisco**. The convent was inaugurated in 1647 and reformed in 1744. To the right is the Igreja das Chagas do Seráphico Pai São Francisco (1787), painted like its neighbour in blue and gold. Across the Viaduto do Chá is the **Teatro Municipal** *T3223 3022*, one of the few distinguished early 20th-century survivors that São Paulo can boast. Viewing the interior may only be possible during a performance; as well as the full evening performances, look out for midday, string quartet and 'vesperais líricas' concerts.

Praça da República

In Praça da República the trees are tall and shady. There are also lots of police. Near the Praça is the city's tallest building, the **Edifício Itália** on the corner of Avenida Ipiranga and Avenida São Luís. There is a restaurant on top and a sightseeing balcony. If you walk up Avenida São Luís, which has many airline offices and travel agencies (especially in the Galeria Metrópole), you come to Praça Dom José Gaspar, in which is the **Biblioteca Municipal Mário de Andrade**, surrounded by a pleasant shady garden.

North of the centre

About 10 minutes' walk from the centre is the old **Mercado Municipal** ① *R Cantareira 306, Mon-Sat 0400-1600*, covering 27,000 sq m. **Parque da Luz** on Avenida Tiradentes, (110,000 sq m) was formerly a botanical garden. It is next to the Luz railway station. There are two museums near the park: the **Museu de Arte Sacra** ① *Av Tiradentes 676, T3326 3336, Tue-Sun 1300-1800*, is modern and tasteful, housed in the serene **Igreja e Convento Nossa Senhora da Luz** (1774), still partially occupied. It has a priceless, beautifully presented collection including works by Aleijadinho, Benedito Calixto, Mestre Athayde and Francisco Xavier de Brito. The convent is one of the few colonial buildings left in São Paulo; the chapel dates from 1579. The **Pinacoteca do Estado** (State Art Collection) ① *Av Tiradentes 141, T229 9844, Tue-Sun 1000-1800, free* and its neighbouring sister gallery, the **Estação Pinacoteca** ① *Largo General Osório 66, T3337 0185, daily 1000-1730, US$2*, preserve the best collection of modernist Brazilian art outside the Belas Artes in Rio, together with important works by Europeans like Picasso and Chagall. Both have good cafés, the Pinacoteca has a very good art bookshop.

Liberdade

Directly south of the Praça da Sé, and one stop on the Metrô, is Liberdade, the central Japanese district, now also home to large numbers of Koreans and Chinese. The Metrô station is in Praça da Liberdade, in which there is an oriental market every Sunday (see Shopping). The Praça is one of the best places in the city for Japanese food. **Museu da Imigração Japonesa** ① *R São Joaquim 381, 3rd floor, T3209 5465, www.nihonsite.com.br/muse, Tue-Sun 1330-1730, US$3*, is excellent, with a roof garden; ask at the desk for an English translation of exhibits.

West of the Old Centre

Jardins and Avenida Paulista

Either Metrô station Vergueiro or Paraíso is convenient for the southeastern end of Avenida Paulista, the highlight of which is **MASP**. This is the common name for The **Museu de Arte de São Paulo** ① *Av Paulista 1578 (above the 9 de Julho tunnel); T3251 5644, www.masp.art.br, the nearest Metrô is Trianon-MASP; bus 805A from Praça da República goes by MASP, Tue-Sun 1100-1800 (Thu 1100-2000, free), US$8.* The museum has the finest collection of European masters in the southern hemisphere with works by artists like Raphael, Bellini, Bosch, Rembrandt, Turner, Constable, Monet, Manet and Renoir. Also some interesting work by Brazilian artists, including Portinari. Temporary exhibitions are also held and when a popular show is on, it can take up to an hour to get in. There is a very good art shop.

São Paulo centre

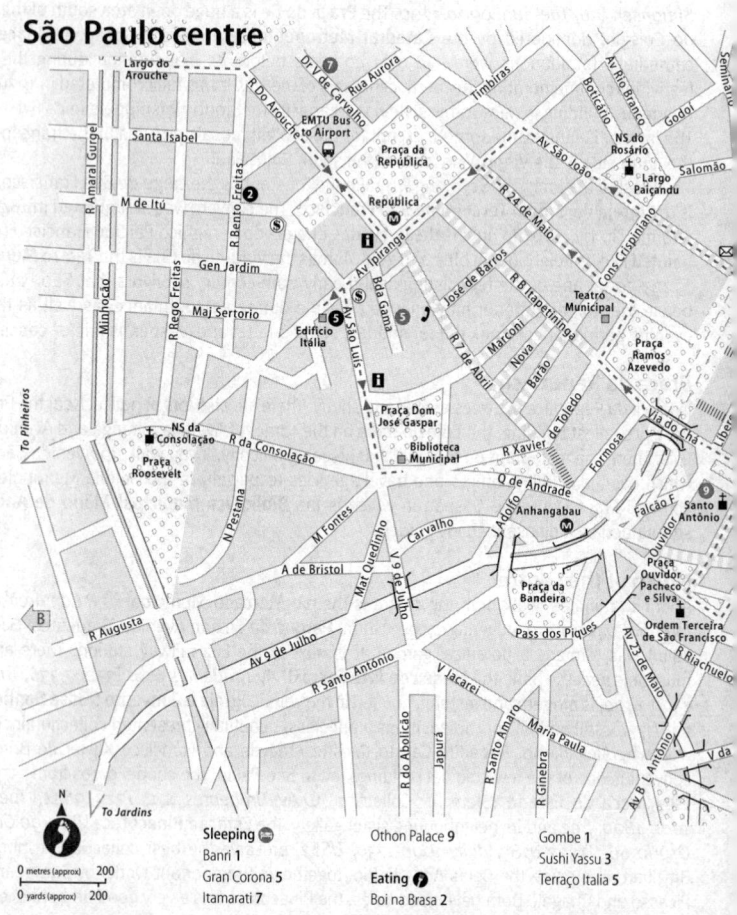

Sleeping
Banri 1
Gran Corona 5
Itamarati 7

Othon Palace 9

Eating
Boi na Brasa 2

Gombe 1
Sushi Yassu 3
Terraço Italia 5

Opposite MASP is **Parque Tenente Siqueira Campos** *daily 0700-1830*, which covers two blocks on either side of Alameda Santos; a bridge links the two parts of the park. It is a welcome green area in the busiest part of the city. The **Museu da Imagem e do Som** (MIS) ① *Av Europa 158, T3085 1498, Tue-Fri 1400- 1800*, has photographic exhibitions, archives of Brazilian cinema and music, and a nice café. Next to MIS is the **Museu Brasiliero da Escultura** (MuBE); free to temporary exhibitions and recitals in the afternoons. Av Europa continues to Av Brigadeiro Faria Lima, on which is the **Casa Brasileira** ① *Av Faria Lima 2705, T3032 3727, Tue-Sun 1300-1800*, a museum of Brazilian furniture. It also holds temporary exhibitions.

Cidade Universitária and Morumbi

The Cidade Universitária is on the west bank of the Rio Pinheiros, opposite the district of Pinheiros. The campus also contains the famous **Instituto Butantã** (Butantã Snake Farm and Museum) ① *Av Dr Vital Brasil 1500, T3726 7222, www.butantan.gov.br, Tue-Sun 0900-1700, US$1, getting there: from Praça da República take bus marked 'Butantã' or 'Cidade Universitária' (Nos 701U or 792U) along Av Paulista, and ask to be let out at Instituto Butantã.* The snakes are milked for their poison six times a day. It also deals with spider and scorpion venom, has a small hospital and is a biomedical research institute. Visitors see the museum of poisonous animals and public health, with explanations in Portuguese and English. The **Museu de Arte Contemporâneo** (MAC) ① *T3091 3039, www.mac.usp.br, Tue-Sat 1200-1800, Sun 1000-1800, free*, with an important collection of Brazilian and European modern art, is in the Prédio Novo da Reitoria. Also the **Museu de Arqueologia e Etnologia** (MAE) ① *R Reitoria 1466,*

To Luz, Pinacoteca Museum & Tietê

To Liberdade & ❶❷❸
Historic buildings walk – ◄ – ◄ –

T3091 4905, with Amazonian and ancient Mediterranean collections. Not far from the Butantã Institute, just inside Cidade Universitária, is the **Casa do Bandeirante** ① *Praça Monteiro Lobato, T3031 0920*, the reconstructed home of a 17th-century pioneer.

On the west bank of the Rio Pinheiros, just southeast of the Cidade Universitária, is the palatial **Jóquei Clube/Jockey Club** ① *Av Lineu de Paula Machado 1263, T3816 4011*, racecourse in the Cidade Jardim area. Take Butantã bus from República. Race meetings are held Monday and Thursday at 1930 and weekends at 1430. It has a **Museu do Turfe** ① *Tue-Sun, closed Sat-Sun mornings.*

Morumbi is a smart residential district due south of the Cidade Universitária. In the area are the state government building, **Palácio dos Bandeirantes** *Av Morumbi 4500*, the small, simple **Capela de Morumbi** *Av Morumbi 5387*, and the Morumbi stadium of São Paulo Football Club, which holds 100,000 people. Motor racing fans might like to visit the Morumbi cemetery, last resting place of Ayrton Senna; take 6291 bus to R Profesor Benedito Montenegro.

Museu da Fundação Maria Luisa e Oscar Americano ① *Av Morumbi 3700, Morumbi, T3742 0077, Tue-Fri 1100-1830, Sat-Sun 1000-1830*, is a private collection of Brazilian and Portuguese art and furniture. The garden has fascinating paths, patios and plants. It is close to the Palácio dos Bandeirantes.

Burle Marx Park ① *Av Dona Helena Pereira de Moraes 200, Morumbi, daily 0700-1900*. Designed by famous landscape designer Burle Marx, it has trails leading through the Mata Atlântica (Atlantic rainforest).

South of the Old Centre

Ibirapuera

The **Parque do Ibirapuera** ① *entrance on Av Pedro Álvares Cabral, daily 0600-1730*, was designed by Oscar Niemeyer and landscape artist Roberto Burle Marx for the city's fourth centenary in 1954. Within its 1.6 million sq m is the **Assembléia Legislativa** and a **planetarium** ① *T5549 9688, shows Sat, Sun at 1530 and 1730, US$5*. After many years of refurbishment it now has state-of-the-art fittings. Buy tickets 30 minutes before the show. Also in the park is the **Museu de Arte Moderna** (MAM) ① *T5549 9688, www.mam.org.br, Tue, Wed, Fri 1200-1800, Thu 1200-2200, Sat-Sun 1000-1800, US$2, students half price, free all Tue and Fri after 1700*, with art exhibitions and sculpture garden (see Nuno Ramos' Craca – Barnacle). It has a great café restaurant and art shop. **Museu Afro-Brasileiro** ① *T5579 0593, Wed-Sun 1000-1800, free*: temporary exhibitions, theatre, dance and cinema spaces, photographs and panels devoted to exploring African Brazil. **Pavilhão Japonês** ① *T3573 6543, Sat, Sun 1000-1700*, exhibition space showing works from Japanese and Japanese-Brazilian artists, designed by Japanese and built exclusively with materials from Japan. It is set in Japanese gardens and has a traditional tea house upstairs. Bicycles can be hired from local character Maizena beside the city hall, Prodam, US$1.25 for a bike without gears, US$2 with gears, leave document as security. Buses to Ibirapuera, 574R from Paraíso Metrô station; 6364 from Praça da Bandeira; to Cidade Universitária 702U or 7181 from Praça da República. Every even-numbered year the **Bienal Internacional de São Paulo** (São Paulo Biennial) at Ibirapuera has the most important show of modern art in Latin America, usually in September (next in 2006).

Parque da Independência

In the suburb of Ipiranga, 5½ km southeast of the city centre, the Parque da Independência contains the **Monumento à Independência;** ① *Mon-Fri 0900-2100, Sat 0900-1700*. Beneath the monument is the Imperial Chapel, with the tomb of the first emperor, Dom Pedro I, and Empress Leopoldina **Casa do Grito** *Tue-Sun 0930-1700*, the little house in which Dom Pedro I spent the night before his famous cry of Ipiranga – 'Independence or Death' – is preserved in the park. The **Museu Paulista** ① *T6165 8000, Tue-Sun 0900-1645, US$1*, contains old maps, traditional furniture, collections of old coins and of religious art and rare documents, and a department of *indígena* ethnology. Behind the Museum is the **Horto Botânico/Ipiranga Botanical Garden** and the **Jardim Francês** ① *Tue-Sun 0900-1700, getting there: take bus 478-P (Ipiranga-Pompéia for return) from Ana Rosa, or take bus 4612 from Praça da República.*

Parque do Estado (Jardim Botânico)

This large park, a long way south of the centre, at **Água Funda** ① *Av Miguel Estefano 3031-3687, T5573 6300, Wed-Sun 0900-1700, getting there: take Metrô to São Judas on the Jabaquara line, then take a bus, contains the Jardim Botânico*, with lakes and trees and places for picnics, and a very fine orchid farm worth seeing during November-December (orchid exhibitions in April and November).

Excursions

In Tremembé, a little beyond Cantareira, 30 minutes north of downtown, is the **Horto Florestal** ① *R do Horto 931, in Parque Estadual Alberto Löfgren, T6231 8555, daily 0600-1800*, which contains examples of nearly every species of Brazilian woodland flora, 15 km of natural trails, a museum, a view of São Paulo from Pedra Grande on the right of the entrance to the park. **Embu** (M'Boy – Big Snake), 28 km from São Paulo, is a colonial town which has become a centre for artists and craftsmen. The town itself, on a hill, is surrounded by industry and modern developments and the colonial centre is quite small. Many of the old houses are painted in bright colours and most contain arts, furniture, souvenir or antiques shops. On Sunday afternoons there is a large and popular arts and crafts fair (0900-1800). On Monday almost everything is closed. In the Largo dos Jesuítas is the church of **Nossa Senhora do Rosário** (1690) and the **Museu de Arte Sacra** ① *Tue-Fri 1300-1700, Sat-Sun 1000-1700*.

● Sleeping

For both business and leisure, São Paulo has by far the best hotels in Brazil. The best area to stay is northeastern Jardins (also known as Cerqueria César), which is safe and well-connected to the Metrô via Av Paulista. There are cheapies in the centre, but this is an undesirable area at night.

Old Centre p395, map p396

L Othon Palace, R Líbero Badaró 190, T3291 5000, www.othon.com.br. The only business hotel of quality in the Triângulo; in a 1950s heritage building.
AL Gran Corona, Basílio da Gama 101, T3214 0043, www.grancorona.com.br. In a small street. Comfortable, good services, good restaurant. Warmly recommended.
B Itamarati, Av Dr Vieira de Carvalho 150, T222 4133, www.hotelitamarati.com.br. Good location, safe. Highly recommended and very popular.

Liberdade p396

B Banri, R Galvão Bueno 209, T3207 8877. Good, Chinese owners, near the Metrô station. Recommended.

Jardins, Avenida Paulista and around
p396, map p401

LL Emiliano, R Oscar Freire 384, T3069 4369, www.emiliano.com.br. Bright and beautifully designed, with attention to every detail and the best suites in the city. No pool but a relaxing small spa. Excellent Italian restaurant, location and service.
LL Fasano, R Vittorio Fasano 88, T3896 4077 www.fasano.com.br. One of the world's great hotels with decor like a modernist gentleman's club designed by Armani, a fabulous pool and the best formal haute cuisine restaurant in Brazil. Excellently positioned in Jardins.
LL Renaissance, Al Santos 2233 (at Haddock Lobo), T3069 2233, http://marriott.com/property/propertyPage/Sãobr. The best business hotel off Av Paulista with standard business rooms, a good spa, gym, pool and 2 squash courts.
LL Unique, Av Brigadeiro Luis Antônio 4700, Jardim Paulista, T3055 4700, www.hotel unique.com. The most ostentatious hotel in the country, an enormous half moon on concrete uprights with curving floors, circular windows and beautiful use of space and light. The bar on the top floor is São Paulo's answer to the LA Sky Bar and is always filled with the rich and famous after 2130.
LL-AL George V, R José Maria Lisboa 1000, T3088 9822, www.george-v.com.br. Apartments with living rooms, fully equipped kitchens, huge bathrooms and comprehensive business services. Shared facilities include sauna, indoor pool and gym. Special deals through the web site.

LL-AL Golden Tulip Park Plaza, Al Lorena 360, T3058 4055, www.parkplaza.com.br. Modern tower with apartments, spa and well- equipped modern gym. Good value.
L-A The Landmark Residence, Al Jaú 1607, T3082 8677, www.landmarkresidence.com.br. Spacious apartments, shared gym, gardens and modest business centre. Good location.
AL Transamérica Ópera, Al Lorena 1748, T3062 2666, www.transamericaflats.com.br. Prices go up to **LL**. Conservatively decorated but elegant and well-maintained modern flats between the heart of Jardins and Av Paulista.
A Dona Ziláh, Av França 1621, Jardim Paulista, T3062 1444, www.zilah.com. Little pousada in a renovated colonial house, well-maintained, decorated with a personal touch. Excellent location, bike rental and generous breakfast included.
A-B Ibis São Paulo Paulista, Av Paulista 2355, T3523 3000, www.accorhotels.com.br. Great value, modern business standard rooms with a/c, right on Paulista, cheaper at weekends.
B Formule 1, R Vergueiro 1571, T5085 5699, www.accorhotels.com.br. Another great value business-style hotel, apartments big enough for 3 make this an **E** option for those in a group. Right next to Paraíso Metro in a safe area, a/c.
B Paulista Garden, Al Lorena 21, T/F3885 8498, www.paulistagardenhotel.com.br. Small, simple rooms with a/c, cable TV and fridge, close to Ibirapuera Park.
B-C Pousada dos Franceses, R dos Franceses 100, Bela Vista, T3262 4026, www.pousadados franceses.com.br. Plain little pousada 10 mins' walk from Brigadeiro Metrô, with dorms, doubles and singles, free internet, TV room, breakfast included.

South of the Old Centre p398
Avenida Brig Faria Lima and
Avenida Luis Carlos Berrini

The area known as the New Centre has no sights of interest for the tourist, however it has the plushest, most expensive hotels.
LL Hyatt São Paulo, Av das Nações Unidas 13301, T6838 1234, http://Sãopaulo.hyatt.com. A superb business hotel, with spa, pool, state of the art business centre and marvellous views from the upper floor suites.
LL-AL Blue Tree Towers, Av Brigadeiro Faria Lima 3989, Vila Olímpia, T3896 7544, www.bluetree.com.br. Modern business hotel with excellent service, ideally positioned for Faria Lima, Vila Olímpia and Itaim, pool, massage, gym, sauna and business centre.
C ACE Hostel, R Gastão da Cunha 253, Congonhas Airport, T5034 2472, www.bed andbreakfast.com.br. Pocket-sized hostel in a

brightly painted house near Congonhas. Services include TV, DVD and movies, broadband, kitchen, laundry, book exchange and pick-up. Tours of São Paulo available.

D Praça da Árvore, R Pageú 266, Saúde, T5071 5148, www.spalbergue.com.br. Well-kept pousada in a quiet street, cheaper for HI members, helpful, 2 mins from Praça do Árvore metro, kitchen, laundry and internet service (overpriced).

D Primavera, R Mariz e Barros 346, Vila Santa Eulália (bus 4491 from Parque Dom Pedro in the centre), T215 3144. Cooking and laundry facilities, friendly staff.

Associação Paulista de Albergues da Juventude, R 7 de Abril 386, Conj 22, T/F3258 0388, www.alberguesp.com.br.

🍴 Eating

Old Centre *p395, map p396*
Restaurants in the old centre tend to be lunchtime only; there are many per kg options and padarias.

₸₸₸ **Terraço Italia**, Av Ipiranga 344, T3257 6566. Average and overpriced Italian food with the best restaurant views in the city – out over an infinity of skyscrapers. Come for a coffee.

₸₸-₸ **Boi na Brasa**, R Bento Freitas by Praça da República. Very good meat dishes and feijoada at a reasonable price.

₸ **Café da Pinacoteca**, Pinacoteca Museum, Praça da Luz 2, T3326 0350. Portuguese style café with marble floors and mahogany balconies. Great coffee, sandwiches and cakes.

Liberdade *p396*
₸₸ **Gombe**, R Tomás Gonzaga 22, T3209 8499. Renowned for grilled tuna and noodle dishes.

₸₸ **Sushi Yassu**, R Tomás Gonzaga 98, T3209 6622. The best of Liberedade's traditional Japanese restaurants. Excellent sushi/sashimi combinations.

Jardins *p396, map p401*
Those on a budget can eat to their stomach's content in per kg places or, if looking for cheaper still, in bakeries (*padarias*). There is one of these on almost every corner. They all serve sandwiches like Misto Quentes, Beirutes and Americanos – delicious Brazilian burgers made from decent meat and served with ham, egg, cheese or salad. They always have good coffee, juices, cakes and set lunches (almoços) for a very economical price. Most have a designated sitting area – either at the padaria bar or in an adjacent room. Juices are made from mineral or filtered water.

₸₸₸ **Café Antique**, R Haddock Lobo 1416, T3062 0882. French cooking by Erick Jacquin, a Maître Cuisinier de France, in an informal but traditional dining room atmosphere.

₸₸₸ **Charlô Bistro**, R Barão de Capanema 440 (next to DOM), T3088 6790 (with another branch at the Jockey Club, Av Lineu de Paula Machado 1263, Cidade Jardim, T3034 3682). One of the premier VIP and old family haunts in the city run by a scion of one of the city's establishment families. Decked out in tribute to a Paris brasserie and with food to match.

₸₸₸ **DOM**, R Barão de Capanema 549, T3088 0761. São Paulo's evening restaurant of the moment – Alex Attala has won the coveted Veja best chef of the year award twice. Contemporary food, fusing Brazilian ingredients with French and Italian styles and served in a large modernist dining room.

₸₸₸ **Fasano**, in Hotel Fasano (see Sleeping), T3896 4077. Long regarded as the best restaurant for gourmets in São Paulo. A huge choice of modern Italian and French cooking from chef Salvatore Loi. Diners have their own lowly-lit booths in a magnificent dining room, exemplary wine list, formal dress.

₸₸₸ **Gero**, R Haddock Lobo 1629, T3064 0005. Fasano's version of a French Bistrô a Côte, but serving pasta and light Italian. Ever so casual design; be prepared for a long wait at the bar alongside people who are there principally to be seen. Reservations are not accepted.

₸₸₸ **Jun Sakamoto**, R Lisboa 55, T3088 6019. Japanese with a touch of French; superb fresh ingredients (some of it flown in especially from Asia and the USA).

₸₸₸ **La Tambouille**, Av 9 de Julho 5925, Jardim Europa, T3079 6276. The favourite 'old money' Franco-Italian restaurant. Excellent wine list.

₸₸₸ **Laurent**, Al Lorena 1899, Cerqueira César, T3062 1452. The best French cooking in the country, French style, Brazilian ingredients.

₸₸₸ **Massimo**, Al Santos 1826, Cerqueira César, T3284 0311. One of São Paulo's longest established Italian restaurants serving Northern Italian food. Credit cards are not accepted, despite the costly price.

₸₸₸ **Rubaiyat Figuera**, R Haddock Lobo 1738, T3063 3888. The most interesting of the Rubaiyat restaurant group, with Argentinian steaks prepared by Argentinian chef Francis Mallman. Very lively for Sun lunch, light and airy and under a huge tropical fig tree. The best meat is served at another restaurant in the chain, Baby Beef Rubaiyat, Av Brig Faria Lima 2954, T3078 9488.

🔴 *For an explanation of the sleeping and eating price codes used in this guide, see inside the front*
🔴 *cover. Other relevant information is found in Essentials pages 345-347.*

¶ **A Mineira**, Al Joaquim Eugénio de Lima 697, T3283 2349. Self-service Minas food by the kilo. Lots of choice. Cachaça and pudding included.

¶ **Baalbeck**, Al Lorena 1330, T3088 4820. Lebanese cooking vastly superior to its luncheonette setting. Great falafel.

¶ **Camelo**, R Pamplona 1873, T3887 8764. More than 40 superior pizzas with a choice of dough as well as topping.

¶ **Fran's Café**, Av Paulista 358, and throughout the city. Open 24 hrs, the Brazilian equivalent of Starbuck's but with proper coffee and light meals.

¶ **Kayomix**, R da Consolação 3215, T3082 2769. Brazilian Oriental fusions like salmon taratare with shimeji and shitake.

¶ **Namesa**, R da Consolação 2967, T3088 7498. Great little gourmet snacky dishes, created by the chef from DOM.

¶ **Restaurante do MASP**, Av Paulista 1578, T3253 2829. In the basement of the museum, reasonably priced standards like lasagna and stroganoff often with a garnish of live music.

¶ **Sattva**, R da Consolação 2904, T3083 6237. Light vegetarian curries, stir fries, salads and pastas.

¶ **Sujinho**, R da Consolação 2068, Consolação, T3256 8026. South American beef in large portions, other carnivorous options also available.

¶ **Cheiro Verde**, R Peixoto Gomide 1413, T289 6853 (lunch only). Hearty veggie food, like

Jardins & Avenida Paulista

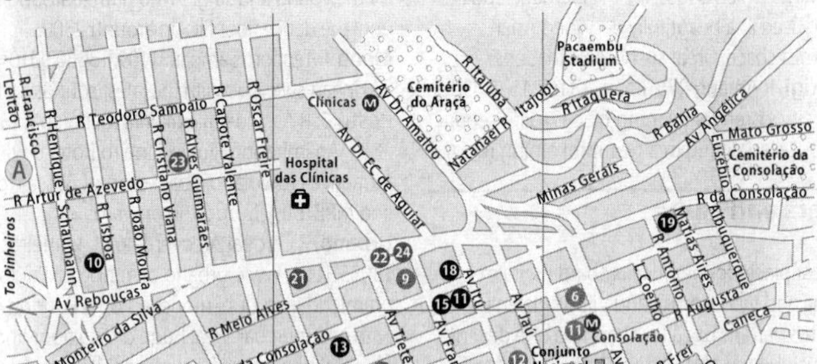

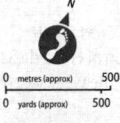

0 metres (approx) 500
0 yards (approx) 500

Sleeping 🛏
Dona Zilah **9** *A2*
Emiliano **1** *B2*
Fasano **2** *B2*
Formule 1 **3** *C3*
George V **4** *B2*

Golden Tulip Park
Plaza **5** *C3*
Ibis São Paulo Paulista **6** *A3*
Landmark Residence **12** *B2*
Paulista Garden **8** *C2*
Pousada dos
Franceses **10** *C3*
Renaissance **11** *B3*
Transamérica Ópera **13** *B2*
Unique **14** *C2*

Eating 🍴
A Mineira **1** *C3*

Baalbeck **2** *B2*
Café Antique **3** *B2*
Camelo **4** *C2*
Charlô Bistro **6** *B2*
Cheiro Verde **5** *B2*
DOM **7** *B2*
Fran's Café **8** *B2,C3*
Gero **9** *B2*
Jun Sakamoto **10** *A1*
Kayomix **11** *A2*
La Tambouille **12** *C1*
Laurent **13** *B2*
MASP **16** *B3*

Massimo **14** *B3*
Namesa **15** *A2*
Rubaiyat
Figuera **17** *B1*
Sattva **18** *A2*
Sujinho **19** *A3*
Tâmara Café **20** *B3*

Bars & clubs 🍸
Apollinari **21** *A2*
Balcão **22** *A2*
Da Dida **24** *A2*
Finnegan's Pub **23** *A1*

401

vegetable crumble in gorgonzola sauce and pasta with buffalo mozarella and sun dried tomato.

¶ Tâmara Cafe, Al Santos 1518, T288 1248 (lunchtimes only). Arabic cooking with good kibe, kofta and falafel.

South of the Old Centre *p398*
Vila Olímpia and Itaim
Restaurants here are ultra, ultra trendy; full of the beautiful posing in beautiful surroundings. We include only a handful of the best.

¶¶¶ Boo, R Viradouro 132, T3078 7477. Opposite Kosushi, with a carbon copy crowd, Luso-Asian cooking and a beautiful garden setting.

¶¶¶ Kosushi, R Viradouro 139, Itaim Bibi, T3167 7272. The first of São Paulo's chic Japanese restaurants which began life in Liberdade and is now housed in a beautifully designed Asian modernist space. Great sushi combinations.

¶¶¶ Parigi, R Amauri 275, Itaim, T3167 1575. One of the city's premier evening places to be seen; Franco-Italian dining in a beautiful dining room.

⊙ Bars and clubs

The best places for nightlife are Jardins, Itaim, Moema and Vila Olímpia, and Vila Madalena/ Pinheiros. Jardins has a few bars and one decent live music venue. Vila Olímpia, Itaim and Moema have a series of funky, smart bars overflowing onto the street, filled with an eclectic mix of after-workers, clubbers, singles and couples; all united by being under 40 and having money. These sit alongside imitation US and European club/lounge bars playing techno, hip hop and the like. The busiest streets for a bar wander are Rua Atílio Inocenti near the junction of Av Juscelino Kubitschek and Av Brigadeiro Faria Lima, Av Hélio Pellegrino and Rua Araguari, which runs behind it. Vila Madalena is younger still, more hippy-chic, but is the best part of town to hear live, Brazilian music and uniquely Brazilian close dances like Forró, as opposed to international club sounds. The liveliest streets are Aspicuelta and Girasol.

Jardins *p396, map p401*
Apollinari, R Oscar Freire 1206, T3061 9965. Smart restaurant/bar frequented by the city's glitterati.
Bar Balcão, R Dr Melo Alves 150, T3063 6091. After work meeting place, very popular with young professionals and media types who gather on either side of the long low wooden bar which winds its way around the room like a giant snake.
Bar da Dida, R Dr Melo Alves 98, T3088 7177. Funky little street bar with pavement tables attracting a Bohemian, studenty clientele. A few doors up from *Balcão*.
Finnegan's Pub, R Cristiano Viana 358, Pinheiros.

One of São Paulo's various Irish bars, this one actually run by an Irishman, popular with ex-pats.

West of the Old Centre *p393*
Vila Madalena/Pinheiros
AMP Galaxy, R Fradique Coutinho 352, T3085 7867, www.ampgalaxy.com.br. A fusion of retro 50s bar and café, clothing boutique and, after 2300, packed dance floor with alternate live music and DJs. The crowd is 20-something and bohemian.
Grazie a Dio, R Girassol, 67, T3031 6568, www.grazieadio.com.br. The best bar in Vila Madalena for live music, different band every night, samba on Sun. Great for dancing, always packed.
A Marcenaria, R Fradique Coutinho 1378, T3032 9006, www.amarcenaria.com.br. The bar of choice for the young and single who gather around 2130, until the dance floor fills up around 2300.
Mood, R Teodoro Sampaio 1109, T3060 9010. European-style club with the latest sounds and DJs.
Posto 6, R Aspicuelta 644, Vila Madalena, T3812 7831. An imitation Rio de Janeiro Boteco with an attractive crowd and a backdrop of Bossa Nova and MPB. Busy from 2100 onwards.
Urbano, R Cardeal Arcoverde 614, Pinheiros, T3085 1001, www.urbano.com.br. Sao Paulo's premier dance club, modelled on a London club with a lounge bar area, huge dance floor and a combination of live bands and DJs. Popular with musicians and creative industry people.

South of the Old Centre *p398*
Itaim, Moema and Vila Olímpia
Liquid Lounge, Av Hélio Pellegrino 801, Vila Olímpia, T3849 5014, www.liquidlounge. com.br. Pulsing European-style dance club with a smart bar area. Always busy.
Lov.E Club & Lounge, R Pequetita 189, Vila Olímpia, T 3044 1613. Trance, house, drum 'n' bass; famous name DJs.
Na Mata Café, R da Mata 70, Itaim, T3079 0300, www.namata.com.br. Popular flirting and pick-up spot with a dark dance room, varied Brazilian and European dance tunes and select live bands.

✪ Entertainment

São Paulo *p393, maps p396 and p401*
See the Guia da Folha section of Folha de São Paulo and Veja São Paulo of the weekly news magazine Veja for listings.
Cinema Entrance is usually half price on Wed; normal seat price is US$5 in the centre, US$7-8 in R Augusta, Av Paulista and Jardins. Cine clubs: **Cine SESC**, R Augusta 2075, and cinemas at: **Museu da Imagem e do Som**, **Centro Cultural Itaú** and **Centro Cultural São Paulo**.

Theatre The Teatro Municipal (see Sights) is used by visiting theatrical and operatic groups, as well as the City Ballet Company and the Municipal Symphony Orchestra who give regular performances. There are several other 1st-class theatres: **Aliança Francesa**, R Gen Jardim 182, Vila Buarque, T3017 5699, www.aliancafrancesa.com.br. **Paiol**, R Amaral Gurgel 164, Vila Buarque, T221 2462; among others. Free concerts at **Teatro Popular do Sesi**, Av Paulista 1313, T3284 9787, at midday, under MASP (Mon-Sat); see also Museums.

⊛ Festivals and events

São Paulo *p393, maps p396 and p401*
Foundation of the City 25 Jan. Carnival in **Feb** (most attractions are closed).This includes the parades of the escolas de samba in the Anhembi sambódromo – the São Paulo special group parades on the Fri and Sat and the Rio group on the Sun and Mon to maximise TV coverage. World's biggest **Gay Pride** march takes places in the Brazilian winter - usually **May** - on Av Paulista. In Jun there are the **Festas Juninas** and the **Festa de São Vito**, the patron saint of the Italian immigrants. **Festa da Primavera** in **Sep**. In Dec there are various Christmas and New Year festivities. Throughout the year, there are countless anniversaries, religious feasts, international fairs and exhibitions, look in the press or the monthly tourist magazines to see what is on while you are in town. See Sights for the São Paulo Biennial.

○ Shopping

São Paulo *p393, maps p396 and p401*
Bookshops Duas Cidades, R Bento Freitas 158, near República. Good selection of Brazilian and Spanish American literature. **La Selva**, in various shopping malls, also at airports. Sells books in English. **Letraviva**, Av Rebouças 1986. Mon-Fri 0900-1830, Sat 0900-1400, specializes in books and music in Spanish. **Librairie Française**, R Barão de Itapetininga 275, ground floor. Wide selection, also at R Professor Atilio Innocenti 920, Jardins. **Livraria Cultura**, Av Paulista 2073, loja 153, also at Shopping Villa-Lobos, Avdas Nações Unidas 4777, Jardim Universale. New books in English, including guidebooks. **Livraria Freebook**, R da Consolação 1924, ring bell for entry. Wide collection of art books and imported books in English. **Livraria Kosmos**, Av São Luís 258, loja 6. International stock. **Livrarias Saraíva**, in various shopping malls. Sells books in English. **Livraria Triângulo**, R Barão de Itapetininga 255, loja 23, Centro, sells books in English. **Sodiler**, Shopping Market Place, Av Nações Unidas 13947, Brooklin, loja 121A, floor T.

Handicrafts Casa dos Amazonas, Al Jurupis 460. For souvenirs. **Ceará Meu Amor**, R Pamplona 1551, loja 7. Good quality lace from the northeast. **Galeria Arte Brasileira**, Al Lorena 2163, galeria@dialdata.com.br. Good value. **Sutaco**, handicrafts shop at República Metrô station. This promotes items from the State of São Paulo, Tue-Fri 1000-1900, Sat 1000-1500; there is a showroom at R Augusta 435, 6th floor.
Jewellery There are many other shops selling Brazilian stones, including branches of **H Stern** and **Amsterdam Sauer**.
Maps Quatro Rodas, Mapograf, Cartoplam, and the map given out by the tourist kiosks; RGN Public Ltda produces a map which is given out free in various places and which is adapted to show its sponsors' locations. A variety of maps and timetables are sold in news stands. **Editorial Abril**, Av das Nações Unidas 7221, T3037 2087, www.abril.com.br. Map, magazine and guide book publisher. **Geo Mapas**, R Gen Jardim 645, 3rd floor, Consolação. Private map publisher (40% discount for volume purchases), excellent 1988 1:5,000,000 map of Brazil, town maps. **Mapolândia**, 7 de Abril 125, 1st floor.
Open-air markets Antiques market, below the Museu de Arte de São Paulo. Sun, 1000-1700. **Arts and handicrafts**, are also sold in Parque Tenente Siqueira Campos/Trianon on Sun from 0900-1700. **Flea markets**, in the main square of the Bixiga district (Praça Don Orione) and in Praça Benedito Calixto in Pinheiros. On Sun. **Ceasa flower market**, Av Doutor Gastão Vidigal 1946, Jaguaré. Tue and Fri 0700-1200, should not be missed. **'Hippy' market**, on Praça da República. Sun, reopened after temporary closure, but with stricter licensing than in the old days. **'Oriental' fair**, Praça da Liberdade. Sun 1000-1900, good for Japanese snacks, plants and some handicrafts, very picturesque, with remedies on sale, tightrope walking, gypsy fortune tellers, etc.
Shopping centres Typical of modern development are the huge Iguatemi, Ibirapuera and Morumbi shopping centres. They include luxurious cinemas, snack bars and most of the best shops in São Paulo. Other malls include Paulista and Butantã. On a humbler level are the big supermarkets of El Dorado (Av Pamplona 1704) and Pão de Açúcar (Praça Roosevelt, near the Hilton); the latter is open 24 hrs a day (except Sun). São Paulo is relatively cheap for film and clothes (especially shoes).

⊖ Transport

São Paulo *p393, maps p396 and p401*
Air From the international airport Guarulhos (also known as Cumbica), T6445 2945, there are airport taxis which charge US$45-52 on a ticket system

(the taxi offices are outside Customs, 300 m down on the left; go to get your ticket then take your bags right back to the end of the taxi queue). Fares from the city to the airport are US$45-52 and vary from cab to cab. **Emtu bus service** every 30 mins from Guarulhos to Praça da República 343 (northwest side, corner of R Arouche), US$8.50, 30-45 mins, very comfortable (in the airport buy ticket at the booth in Domestic Arrivals); the same company runs services from Guarulhos to the main bus terminal, Tietê (hourly), US$8, and to Congonhas airport, T5090 9000. Buses run to Bresser bus station from Guarulhos and there are other buses to Jabaquara bus terminal, without luggage space, usually crowded. Also **Airport Bus Service**, T0800-999701, www.airportbusservice.com.br. US$8 to centre. Inter-airport bus US$16. From Congonhas airport, there are about 400 flights a week to Rio.

Airport information Money exchanges, in the arrivals hall, Guarulhos, 0800-2200 daily. Post office on the 3rd floor of Asa A. The Infraero Sala VIP has been recommended for coffee, cable TV for US$5. Mon-Fri 0800 to 1800. See Ins and outs above for the tourist office.

Bus Maps of the local bus and metro system are available at depots, for example Anhangabaú. Some city bus routes are run by trolley buses. Take an SP-Pinheiros bus from Clínicas, which takes the main highway to Embu; 40 mins, US$1. Get out at Largo 21 de Abril in Embu. To return to São Paulo, walk up R da Matriz from Largo 21 de Abril, turn left down Av Júnior, then left again on R Solano Trindade to a junction where the buses stop.

The main rodoviária for long distance buses is Tietê, which handles buses to the interior of São Paulo state, all state capitals (but see also under Barra Funda and Bresser below) and international buses. The **left luggage** charges US$1 per day per item. You can sleep in the bus station after 2200 when the guards have gone; tepid showers cost US$2.65.

Buses from Tietê: To **Rio**, 6 hrs, every 30 mins, US$16.50 (leito, 25), special section for this route in the rodoviária, ask how to take the coastal route via Santos ('via litoral') unless you wish to go the direct route. To **Florianópolis**, 11 hrs (US$31, leito 48). To **Porto Alegre**, 18 hrs, US$40 (leito, 68). **Curitiba**, 6 hrs, US$13.50-16.50. **Salvador**, 30 hrs, US$68 (executive, 85). **Recife**, 40 hrs, US$80. **Cuiabá**, 24 hrs, US$56. **Porto Velho**, 60 hrs (or more), US$100. **Brasília**, 16 hrs, US$40 (leito, 80). **Foz do Iguaçu**, 16 hrs, US$29. **São Sebastião**, 4 hrs US$10.50 (say 'via Bertioga' if you want to go by the coast road, beautiful journey but few buses take this route).

International buses from Tietê: to **Montevideo**, via Porto Alegre, with TTL, departs Mon, Thu, Sat 2200, 31 hrs, US$100, cold a/c at night, plenty of meal stops, bus stops for border formalities, passengers disembark only to collect passport and tourist card on the Uruguayan side (also EGA, same price, US$67 to **Chuy**, Tue, Fri, Sun). To **Buenos Aires**, Pluma, 36 hrs, US$145. To **Santiago**, Pluma or Chilebus, 56 hrs, US$130, Chilebus, poor meals, but otherwise good, beware overbooking. To **Asunción** (1,044 km), 18 hrs with Pluma (US$57, leito 112), **Brújula** or RYSA, all stop at Ciudad del Este. **Cometa del Amambay** runs to **Pedro Juan Caballero** and **Concepción**.

There are 3 other bus stations: Barra Funda, T3666 4682, with Metrô station, for buses from cities in southern São Paulo state, **Campo Grande**, 14 hrs, US$44, and many places in Paraná. Bresser, T6692 5191, on the Metrô, is for destinations in Minas Gerais. Buses from Santos arrive at **Jabaquara**, T5012 2256, at the southern end of the Metrô. To **Santos**, US$4.65, and destinations on the southern coast of São Paulo state, use Jabaquara station. Buses from here for Santos leave every 15 mins, taking about 50 mins, last bus at 0100, US$4.80. Buses at Bresser, **Cometa** (6967 7255) or **Transul** (T6693 8061) go to Minas Gerais: **Belo Horizonte**, 10 hrs, US$20, 11 a day (leito 40); 9 a day with Gontijo. **Translavras** and **Útil** also operate out of this station. Prices are given under destinations.

Car The rodízio, which curbs traffic pollution by restricting car use according to number plate, may be extended beyond the winter months. Check.

Metrô Two lines intersect at Praça de Sé: north-south from Tucuruvi to Jabaquara; east-west from Corinthians Itaquera to Barra Funda (the interchange with Fepasa and RFFSA railways and site of the São Paulo and Paraná rodoviária); an extension east to Guaianases is under construction. A 3rd line runs from Vila Madalena in the west, along Av Paulista, to Ana Rosa in the south, joining the Jabaquara line at Paraíso and Ana Rosa. A 4th line is being built from Vila Sônia to Luz. The system is clean, safe, cheap and efficient; the 2 main lines operate from 0500-2400, Ana Madalena to Ana Rosa 0600-2030. Fare US$1, US$8 for a book of 10 tickets; backpacks are allowed. Combined bus and Metrô ticket are available, US$1.30, for example to Congonhas airport. Information T286 0111.

Taxi Taxis display cards of actual tariffs in the window (starting price US$4). There are ordinary taxis, which are hailed on the street, or at taxi stations such as Praça da República, radio taxis and deluxe taxis. For **Radio Taxis**, which are more expensive but involve fewer hassles, **Central Radio Táxi**, T6914 6630; **São Paulo Rádio Táxi**, T5583 2000; **Fácil**, T6258 5947; **Aero Táxi**, T6461 4090; or look in the phone book; calls are not accepted from public phones.

Train São Paulo has 4 stations: 1) **Estação da Luz** for commuter trains between the northwest and southeast of São Paulo state. There is also a Metrô stop here. A train runs from Luz 8 times a day to connect with the **tourist train** from Paranapiaçaba to Rio Grande da Serra, US$0.65. 2) **Barra Funda**, services go to São José do Rio Preto (overnight), Barretos, Londrina, Maringá, Sorocaba and Ponta Grossa. There is a Metrô station and a rodoviária at Barra Funda; 3) **Júlio Prestes station**, for commuter services to the west; T0800 550121 for these three. 4) **Roosevelt**, T6942 1199, for commuter trains to the east.

---

❶ Directory

São Paulo *p393, maps p396 and p401*
Airline offices Aerolíneas Argentinas, Araújo 216, 6th floor, T259 0319 (Guarulhos airport 6445 3806). Alitalia, Av São Luís 50, cj 291, T3257 1922 (6445 3791). American Airlines, Araújo 216, 9th floor, T0800 703 4000 or 3214 4000 (6445 3808). Bra, T6445 4310, sales offices all over the city, in shopping centres and at both airports, see www.voebra.com.br. British Airways, Av São Luís 50, 32nd floor, T3145 9700 (6445 2021). Gol, T0800-280 0465, www.voegol.com.br. Iberia, Araújo 216, 3rd floor, T2507 6711 (6445 2060). JAL, Av Paulista 542, 2nd floor, T251 5222 (6445 2040). Lufthansa, R Gomes de Carvalho 1356, 2nd floor, T3048 5868 (6445 2220). OceanAir, Av Washington Luis 7059, Av: Washington Luis 7059, Santo Amaro, T2176 1000, or 4004 4040. Rio-Sul, R Bráulio Gomes 151, T5561 2161. TAM, R da Consolação 247, 3rd floor, T0300-123 1000 (24 hrs), or 3155 6700 (6445 3474). TAP, Av São Luís 187, T255 5366 (6445 2400). United, Av Paulista 777, 9-10th floor, T3145 4200/ 0800-162323 (6445 3283). Varig, R da Consolação 362/372, Av Paulista 1765, T5091 7000 (Guarulhos 6445 2825, Congonhas 535 0216).
Banks There are many national and international banks; most can be found either in the Triângulo, downtown, or on Av Paulista, or Av Brigadeiro Faria Lima. Hours 1000-1600; but some vary. All have different times for foreign exchange transactions (check at individual branches). Many Banco 24 Horas ATMs in the city. Banco do Brasil will change cash and TCs and will advance cash against Visa. All transactions are done in the foreign exchange department of any main branch (eg Av São João 32, Centro), but queues are long. Citibank, Av Ipiranga 855, or Av Paulista 1111 (1100-1500), cash on MasterCard. Banespa, for example at R Duque de Caxias 200, Centro, or Praça da República 295, accepts Visa, TCs and cash. MasterCard, cash against card, R Campo Verde 61, 4th floor, Jardim Paulistano. MasterCard ATMs at branches of HSBC Bank. American Express, Al

Santos 1437 (Hotel Mofarrej Sheraton) T251 3383, Av Maria Coelho Aguiar 215, Bloco F, 8th floor, T3741 8478 and Guarulhos international airport, terminal 1, 1st floor of Asa A, T6412 3515. Western Union at Banco Itamarati, T0800-119837. Money changers: there are many câmbios on or near Praça da República. There are none near the rodoviária or Tietê hotels. Interpax, Praça da República 177, loja 13, changes cash (many currencies) and TCs, 0930-1800, Sat 0930-1300. Amoretur, Praça da República 203, will change TCs. Coraltur, Praça da República 95. Most travel agents on Av São Luís change TCs and cash at good rates, but very few are open on Sat. Avencatur, Av Nações Unidas 1394, Morumbi, changes TCs, Deutschmarks, good rates.
Car hire See Car hire, Essentials for international car rental agencies, page 43. Interlocadora, several branches, São Luís T255 5604, Guarulhos T6445 3838, Congonhas T240 9287. **Cultural centres** Centro Brasileiro Britânico, R Ferriera de Araújo 741, Pinheiros, T3039 0567. American Library, União Cultural Brasil-Estados Unidos, R Col Oscar Porto 208. Goethe-Instituto, R Lisboa 974, T3088 4288 (Mon-Thu 1400-2030). Centro Cultural Fiesp, Av Paulista 1313, T3146 7405, 0900-1900 Tue-Sun, has foreign newspapers and magazines. See under Entertainment for Alliance Française Theatre. **Consulates** Argentina, Av Paulista 1106, T284 1355 (0900-1300, very easy to get a visa here). Australia, R Tenente Negrão 140, T3849 6281. Bolivia, R Oscar Freire 379, T3081 1618, www.embolivia.cjb.net. 0900-1700. Canada, Av Nações Unidas 12901, T5509 4343, spalo-immigration@dfait-maeci.gc.ca. 0800-1100, 1500-1600, Fri 0800-0930, 1200-1300. Denmark, R Oscar Freire 379, T3061 3625, 0900-1700, Fri until 1400 only. France, Av Paulista 1842, 14th floor, T3371 5400, www.ambafrance.org.br. 0830-1200. Germany, Av Brigadeiro Faria Lima 2092, T3814 6644, info.saopaulo@alemanha.org.br. 0800-1130 (also serves Paraná). Italy, Av Higienópolis 436, T3826 9022, notarile@italconsul.org.br. Israel, Av Brig Faria Lima 1713, T3815 7788. Japan, Av Paulista 854, T287 0100, cgjsp@nethall.com.br. Netherlands, Av Brigadeiro Faria Lima 1779, T3813 0522, 0900-1200. New Zealand, Av Campinas 579, T3148 0613, www.tradenz.govt.nz. Norway and Sweden, R Oscar Freire 379, 3rd floor, T883 3322 (Norway), 3061 1700 (Sweden) (Caixa Postal 51626), 0900-1300. Paraguay, R Bandeira Paulista 600, 15th floor, T3849 0455, 0830-1600. Peru, R Votuverava 350, T3819 1793, viceconsulperu@ originet.com.br. 0900-1300. UK, R Ferreira Araújo 741, 2nd floor, Pinheiros, T3094 2700, saopaulo@ gra-bretanha.org.br. US, R Henri Dunant 500, Chácara Santo Antônio, T5186 7000, www.consuladoamericanosp.org.br. 0800-1700. **Internet** at Av Paulista 1499, conj 1001 (Mêtro

Trianon), 1100-2200, English spoken, secondhand books; **Saraíva Megastore**, Shopping El Dorado, US$3; **Kiosknet**, Shopping Light, 4th floor, R Cel Xavier de Toledo 23, opposite Teatro Municipal, T3151 3645, US$2.50 per hr; **Monkey Paulista**, Al Santos 1217 (Jardins, off Av Paulista behind Citibank). Superfast connection, US$0.70-1.15 per hr, more expensive at weekends. O Porão, R Tamandaré 1066, near Verqueiro metro station. **Language courses** Universidade de São Paulo (USP) in the Cidade Universitária has courses available to foreigners, including a popular Portuguese course, registry is through the **Comissão de Cooperação Internacional**, R do Anfiteatro 181, Bloco das Colméias 05508, Cidade Universitária. **Medical services** Hospital Samaritano, R Conselheiro Brotero 1486, Higienópolis, T824 0022. Recommended. Emergency and ambulance T192, no charge. Fire: T193. **Post offices** Correio Central, Praça

do Correio, corner Av São João and Prestes Máia. Booth adjoining tourist office on Praça da República, weekdays only 1000-1200, 1300-1600, for letters and small packages only. UPS, Brasinco, Alameda Jaú 1, 1725, 01420 São Paulo. **Federal Express**, Av São Luís 187, Galeria Metropole, loja 45, is reliable, also at Av das Nações Unidas 17891; DHL, Av Vereador José Diniz 2421. **Telephone** Telefônica, R 7 de Abril 295, near Praça da República; many other offices. **Embratel**, Av São Luís 50, and Av Ipiranga 344. For the international operator dial 000111; for international collect calls dial 000107. Red phone boxes are for national calls, blue ones for international phone calls. **Useful addresses** Police: Deatur, special tourist police, Av São Luís 91, T3120 3984; Guarulhos airport T6445 2686; Congonhas airport T5090 9032. **Radio Patrol**, T190. **Federal Police**, Av Prestes Maia 700, 1000-1600 for visa extensions.

São Paulo coast

On the coast there are fine beaches, although pollution is sometimes a problem. The further northeast or southwest you go from the port of Santos, the more unspoilt the beaches become, with some areas of special natural interest.

Santos → *Phone code: 0xx13. Post code: 11000. Colour map 7, grid C4. Population: 417,983.*

Santos, on an island about 5 km from the open sea, is the most important Brazilian port. Over 40% by value of all Brazilian imports and about half the total exports pass through it. Santos is also a holiday resort with magnificent beaches and views. The scenery on the routes crossing the Serra do Mar is superb. The roadway includes many bridges and tunnels. From Rio the direct highway, the Linha Verde (see pages 386 and 407) is also wonderful for scenery. The port is approached by the winding Santos Channel; at its mouth is an old fort (1709). The centre of the city, on the north side of the island, is being renovated. Due south, on the Baía de Santos, is **Gonzaga**, where hotels and bars line the beachfront. Between these two areas, the eastern end of the island curves round within the Santos Channel. **Tourist offices**: at the rodoviária, T3219 2194, Ponta da Praia, T3236 9996, and Orquidário Municipal (limited opening). Information by phone T0800-173887.

Sights The best way get around the centre of Santos is by the newly restored Victorian trams which leave on guided tours from in front of the Prefeitura Municipal on Praça Visconde de Mauá. The tram passes in front of most of the interesting sights, including the *azulejo*-covered houses on Rua do Comércio. The streets around **Praça Mauá** are very busy in the daytime. **Museu do Café** ① *R 15 de Novembro 95, T3219 5585, www.museudocafe.com.br, Tue-Sat 0900-1700, Sun 1000-1700*. The old Bolsa Oficial de Café was closed to all but rich men up until the mid-20th century, but is now a delightful museum, with large wall paintings by Benedito Calixto and a very impressive art deco stained-glass ceiling. Upstairs is a small but very well-presented collection of displays. The lobby café serves some of the best coffee in Brazil. Two churches in the centre are **Santo Antônio do Valongo** (17th century, but restored), which is by the railway station on Largo Monte Alegre, and the **Capela da Ordem Terceira de Nossa Senhora do Carmo** (1760, also later restored), Praça Barão do Rio Branco. **Fundação Pinacoteca** ① *Av Bartolomeu de Gusmão 15, T3288 2260, www.pinacoteca.unisanta.br, Tue-Sun 1400-1900, free.* A large collection of ecclesiastical paintings and landscapes by one of Brazil's most distinguished early 19th-century artists and housed in one of Santos's few remaining coffee mansions.

At **Santos Football Stadium and Museum** ① *Princesa Isabel 77, Vila Belmiro, T3257 4000, www.santosfc.com.br*, the ground floor houses a collection of trophies and photographs chronicling the history of Pele's club, including several cabinets devoted to him and containing his shirts, boots and other memorabilia. **Monte Serrat**, just south of the city centre, has at its summit a semaphore station and look-out post which reports the arrival of all ships in Santos harbour. There is also a church, dedicated to Nossa Senhora da Monte Serrat. The top can be reached on foot or by **funicular** ① *every 30 mins, US$8*. **Museu do Mar** *R República do Equador 81*, is in the eastern part of the city; with a collection that includes several thousand shells. In the western district of José Menino is the **Orquidário Municipal**, municipal orchid gardens, in the **Praça Washington** ① *daily 0800-1745, bird enclosure 0800-1100, 1400- 1700, US$1*. The flowers bloom October to February, orchid show in November.

The **Ilha Porchat**, a small island reached by a bridge at the far end of Santos/São Vicente bay, has beautiful views of the high seas on one side and of the city and bay on the other. The lookout was designed by Oscar Niemeyer and, in summer, there is lively nightlife here.

Itatinga, 30 km from Santos in the Serra do Mar, has remnants of Atlantic forest, mangrove and sandbanks. The area is full of wildlife. There are trails graded according to difficulty. Visitors go with one of the travel agencies officially permitted to lead groups: contact the tourism office (see above). Access is either via the village of Itatinga by boat, three hours, then by street car. Or take the BR-101 (Santos-Rio) road, a three-minute crossing by boat and then 7.5 km by street car.

São Sebastião → Phone code: 0xx12. Post code: 11600. Colour map 7, grid B4. Population: 58,038.

East of Santos, a vehicle ferry (free for pedestrians) crosses from Ponta da Praia to **Guarujá**, from where a road (SP-061) runs to **Bertioga**. The coastal road beyond Bertioga is paved, and the Rio-Santos highway, 1-2 km inland, provides a good link to São Sebastião. Beyond Praia Boracéia are a number of beaches, including **Camburi**, surrounded by the Mata Atlântica, into which you can walk on the Estrada do Piavu (bathing in the streams is permitted, but use of shampoo is forbidden). There are several good hotels and restaurants in Camburi and at Praia de Boracéia. The road carries on from Camburi, past clean beach **Maresias**, a fashionable place for surfers.

From Maresias it is 21 km to São Sebastião. In all there are 21 good beaches and an adequate, but not overdeveloped tourist infrastructure. The natural attractions of the area include many small islands offshore and a large portion of the **Parque Estadual da Serra do Mar** on the mainland, with other areas under protection for their different ecosystems. Trails can be walked through the forests. There are also old sugar plantations. In the colonial centre is a **Museu de Arte Sacra**, R Sebastião Neves 90, in the 17th century chapel of São Gonçalo. The town's parish church on Praça Major João Fernandes was built in the early 17th century and rebuilt in 1819. There is a **Museu do Naufrágio** near the church (free) exhibiting shipwrecks and natural history of the local area. **Tourist office** ① *Av Dr Altino Arantes 174, T4522 1808*.

The beaches within 2-3 km of São Sebastião harbour are polluted; others to the south and north are clean and inviting. Ilhabela tends to be expensive in season, when it is cheaper to stay in São Sebastião.

Ilhabela → Phone code: 0xx12. Pop: 20,836; rising to 100,000 in high season.

The island of São Sebastião, known popularly as Ilhabela, is of volcanic origin, roughly 390 sq km in area. The four highest peaks are Morro de São Sebastião, 1,379 m, Morro do Papagaio, 1,309 m, Ramalho, 1,28 m, and Pico Baepi, 1,025 m. All are often obscured by mist. Rainfall on the island is heavy, about 3,000 mm a year. The slopes are densely wooded and 80% of the forest is protected by the Parque Estadual de Ilhabela. The only settled district lies on the coastal strip facing the mainland, the Atlantic side being practically uninhabited except by a few fisherfolk. The island abounds with tropical plants, flowers, and wild fruits, whose juice mixed with *cachaça* and sugar makes a delicious cocktail. The terraced **Cachoeira da Toca** ① *US$4, includes insect repellent*, waterfalls amid dense jungle close to the foot of the Baepi peak give cool freshwater bathing; lots of butterflies. You can walk on a signed path, or go by car; it's a few kilometres from the ferry dock. The locals claim there are over 300 waterfalls on the island, but only a few of them can be reached on foot. In all shady places, especially away from the sea, there thrives a species of midge known locally as *borrachudo*. A locally sold repellent (Autan) keeps them off for some time, but those allergic to insect bites should remain on the inhabited coastal strip. There is a small hospital (helpful) by the church in town. **Secretaria Municipal de Turismo** ① *R Bartolomeu de Gusmão 140, Pequeá, T3896 2440, www.ilhabela.com.br.*

No alterations are allowed to the frontage of the main township, **Ilhabela**. It is very popular during summer weekends, when it is difficult to find space for a car on the ferry. It is, however, a nice place to relax on the beach, with good food and some good value accommodation.

Visit the old **Feiticeira** plantation, with underground dungeons. The road is along the coast, sometimes high above the sea, towards the south of the island (11 km from the town). You can go by bus, taxi, or horse and buggy. A trail leads down from the fazenda to the beautiful beach of the same name. Another old fazenda is **Engenho d'Água**, which is nearer to the town, which gives its name to one of the busiest beaches (the fazenda is not open to the public).

Beaches and watersports On the mainland side the beaches 3-4 km either side of the town are polluted: look out for oil, sandflies and jellyfish on the sand and in the water. There are some three dozen beaches around Ilhabela, only about 12 of them away from the coast facing the mainland. **Praia dos Castelhanos**, reached by the rough road over the island to the Atlantic side (no buses), is recommended. Several of the ocean beaches can only be reached by boat. The island is considered the **Capital da Vela** (of sailing) because its 150 km of coastline offers all types of conditions. There is also plenty of adventure for divers.

Ubatuba → *Phone code: 0xx12. Post code: 11680. Colour map 7, grid B4. Population: 66,861.*

This is one of the most beautiful stretches of the São Paulo coast with a whole range of watersports on offer. In all, there are 72 beaches, some large, some small, some in coves, some on islands. They are spread out over a wide area, so if you are staying in Ubatuba town, you need to use the buses which go to most of them. The commercial centre of Ubatuba is at the northern end of the bay. Here are shops, banks, services, lots of restaurants (most serving pizza and fish), but few hotels. These are on the beaches north and south and can be reached from the Costamar bus terminal. **Comtur** tourist office is on ① *Av Iperoig opposite R Profesor Thomaz Galhardo, To800-771 7400; www.ubatuba.com.br,* very helpful.

Saco da Ribeira, 13 km south, is a natural harbour which has been made into a yacht marina. Schooners leave from here for excursions to **Ilha Anchieta** (or dos Porcos), a popular four-hour trip. On the island are beaches, trails and a prison, which was in commission from 1908-1952. Agencies run schooner trips to Ilha Anchieta and elsewhere. Trips leave Saco da Ribeira at 1000, returning 1500, four-hour journey, US$26 per person. A six-hour trip can be made from Praia Itaguá, but in winter there is a cold wind off the sea in the afternoon, same price. The Costamar bus from Ubatuba to Saco da Ribeira (every 20 minutes, 30 minutes, US$1) drops you at the turn-off by the Restaurante Pizzaria Malibu.

Straddling the border of São Paulo and Rio de Janeiro states is the **Parque Nacional Serra da Bocaina** ① *permission to visit must be obtained in advance from Ibama, Toxx12-3117 2183/88 in São José do Barreiro, the nearest town*. It rises from the coast to its highest point at Pico do Tira (or Chapéu) at 2,200 m, encompassing three strata of vegetation.

Southwest from Santos

Itanhaém (*Phone code: 0xx13*), 61 km from Santos, has a pretty colonial church of Sant'Ana (1761), Praça Narciso de Andrade, and the Convento da Nossa Senhora da Conceição (1699-1713, originally founded 1554), on a small hill. There are several good seafood restaurants along the beach, hotels and camping. There are more beaches 31 km south of Itanhaém at **Peruíbe**, where the climate is said to be unusually healthy owing to a high concentration of ozone in the air. Local rivers have water and black mud which has been proven to contain medicinal properties. There are plenty of places to stay and to eat in Peruíbe (none close to the bus station, some close out-of-season). Peruíbe marks the northernmost point of the **Estação Ecológico Juréia-Itatins** ① *contact the Instituto Florestal, R do Horto 931, CEP 02377-000, São Paulo, Toxx11-6997 5000, for permission to visit the ecological station*. The station was founded in 1986 and protects 820 sq km of Mata Atlântica, "as it was when the Portuguese arrived in Brazil". The four main ecosystems are restinga, mangrove, Mata Atlântica and the vegetation at 900 m on the Juréia mountain range.

Iguape → *Phone code: 0xx13. Colour map 7, grid C3. Population: 27,427.*

At the southern end of Juréia-Itatins is the town of Iguape founded in 1538. Typical of Portuguese architecture, the small **Museu Histórico e Arqueológico** ① *R das Neves 45, Tue-Sun 0900-1730*, is housed in the 17th-century Casa da Oficina Real de Fundição. There is also a **Museu de Arte Sacra** ① *Sat-Sun 0900-1200, 1330-1700*, in the former Igreja do Rosário, Praça Rotary. The **tourist office** is at 9 de Julho 63, T6841 3358.

Opposite Iguape is the northern end of the **Ilha Comprida** with 86 km of beaches (some dirty and disappointing). This **Área de Proteção Ambiental** ① *the Ibama office of the Area de Proteção Ambiental Cananéia-Iguape-Peruíbe is at R da Saúde s/n, Canto do Morro, Iguape, T6841 2692/2388*, is not much higher than sea level and is divided from the mainland by the Canal do Mar Pequeno. The northern end is the busiest and on the island there are good restaurants, hotels, supermarkets – fresh fish is excellent. There is also accommodation.

Cananéia and Ilha do Cardoso → *Colour map 7, grid C3. Population: 12,298.*

At the southern end of Ilha Comprida, across the channel, is Cananéia, 270 km from São Paulo. The colonial centre, around Praça Martim Afonso de Souza and neighbouring streets, contains the 17th-century church of **São João Batista** and the **Museu Municipal**. To the south are a number of good beaches and the waterways are popular with fisherfolk. For guides, contact Manoel Barroso, Avenida Independencia 65, T013-3851 1273, Portuguese only. Recommended. Cananéia has several hotels, starting in price range **B**.

To reach the densely wooded Ilha do Cardoso, a Reserva Florestal e Biológica, take a ferry from the dock at Cananéia, four hours, three daily (T3851 1268). Alternatively, drive 70 km along an unpaved road, impassable when wet, to **Ariri**, from where the island is 10 mins by boat. The tiny village of Marujá, which has no electricity, has some rustic pousadas and restaurants. There are designated camping areas and lots of idyllic beaches; best for surfing is Moretinho.

● Sleeping

Santos *p406*
Many beachfront hotels on Av Pres Wilson, cheap hotels are near the Orquidário Municipal (Praça Washington), 1-2 blocks from the beach.
AL Atlântico, No 1, T3289 4500, www.atlantico-hotel.com.br. Good, a/c, sauna, restaurant, bar.
B Hotel Natal, Av Marechal Floriano Peixoto 104, T3284 2732, www.hotelnatal.com.br. Safe, Comfortable, with cable TV, fridge, full breakfast.

Ilhabela *p407*
Several in the **L-AL** price range and some in the **A-B** range, mostly on the road to the left of the ferry.
AL Ilhabela, Av Pedro Paulo de Morais 151, T3896 1083, www.hotelilhabela.com.br. Family-oriented, gym, pool, good breakfast. Recommended.
A Pousada dos Hibiscos, Av Pedro Paulo de Morais 714, T3896 1375, www.pousadados hibiscos.com.br. Good atmosphere, swimming pool. Recommended.
A Vila das Pedras, R Antenor Custódio da Silva 46, Cocaia, T3896 2433, www.viladas pedras.com.br. 11 chalets in a forest garden, tastefully decorated, nice pool.
C Estância das Bromélias Pousada, Av Col José Vicente Faria Lima 1243, Perequê, T3896 3353, www.estanciadasbromelias.com.br. Welcoming, chalets for 5, great breakfast, garden, pool, horse riding and jeep excursions, very good.
Camping Pedras do Sino, at Perequê, near ferry dock, and at Praia Grande, 11 km south.

Ubatuba *p408*
At all holiday times it is expensive, with no hotel less than US$30. On many of the beaches there are hotels and pousadas, ranging from luxury resorts to more humble establishments.

AL Saveiros, R Lucian Strass 65, Praia do Lázaro, 14 km from town, T3842 0172, www.hotel saveiros.com.br. Pretty *pousada* with pool, restaurant, English spoken.
A São Charbel, Praça Nóbrega 280, T3832 1090, www.saocharbel.com.br. Helpful, comfortable, a/c, TV, restaurant, bar, swimming pool, etc.
A São Nicolau, R Conceição 213, T/F3832 5007. Good, TV, fridge, good breakfast.
A Xaréu, R Jordão Homem da Costa 413, T/F3832 1525. Pleasant, quiet. Recommended.
D Pousada Taiwan, R Felix Guisard Filho 60, T3832 6448. Fan or a/c, with breakfast, TV, fridge.
J S Brandão, R Nestor Fonseca 173, Jardim Sumaré, CEP 11880-000, T3832 2337. 0700-2300, near the Tropic of Capricorn sign south of town.
Cora Coralina, Rodovia Oswaldo Cruz, Km 89, T011-258 0388. 0800-2300, near Horto Florestal.
Camping There are about 10 sites in the vicinity, including 2 **Camping Clube do Brasil** sites at Lagoinha (25 km from town) and Praia Perequê-Açu, 2 km north.

Iguape *p408*
B-C Silvi, R Ana Cândida Sandoval Trigo 515, T6841 1421, silvihotel@virtualway.com.br. With bath and breakfast, simple but good.
Camping At Praia da Barra da Ribeira, 20 km north. Wild camping is possible at Praia de Juréia, the gateway to the ecological station.

▲▲ Activities and tours

Ubatuba *p408*
Companies offer trekking tours graded according to difficulty lasting from 2 hrs to 2 days. More details from the guide association, T9141 3692.

Rodeo Romeos

Some 422 km northwest of São Paulo and 115 km northwest of the city of Ribeirão Preto, is **Barretos**, where, in the third week in August, the **Festa do Peão Boiadeiro** is held. This is the biggest annual rodeo in the world. The town is taken over as up to 600,000 fans come to watch the horsemanship, enjoy the concerts, eat, drink and shop in what has become the epitome of Brazilian cowboy culture. Tours from the UK are run by Last Frontiers, see page 38.

⊜ Transport

Santos *p406*

Bus In Santos US$0.80; to **São Vicente**, US$1.20. To **São Paulo** (50 mins, US$4.80) every 15 mins, from the rodoviária near the city centre, José Menino or Ponta da Praia (opposite the ferry to Guarujá). (The 2 highways between São Paulo and Santos are sometimes seriously crowded, especially at rush hours and weekends.) To **Guarulhos/ Cumbica airport**, Expresso Brasileiro 3-4 daily, US$6.50, allow plenty of time as the bus goes through Guarulhos, 3 hrs. TransLitoral from Santos to **Congonhas airport** then to **Guarulhos/Cumbica**, 4 daily, US$9.50, 2 hrs. To **Rio** (Normandy company), several daily, 7½ hrs, US$29; to Rio along the coast road is via São Sebastião (US$9.25, change buses if necessary), Caraguatatuba and Ubatuba.
Taxi All taxis have meters. The fare from Gonzaga to the bus station is about US$6.50.

São Sebastião *p407*

Bus 2 buses a day from **Rio** with Normandy, 0830 and 2300 (plus 1630 on Fri and Sun), to Rio 0600 and 2330, heavily booked in advance, US$16.60 (US$6.50 from Paraty); 4 a day from **Santos**, 4 hrs, US$9.25; 4 Litorânea buses a day also from **São Paulo**, US$11, which run inland via São José dos Campos, unless you ask for the service via Bertioga, only 2 a day (bus to Bertioga US$4.50). Daily buses from São Paulo to **Camburi**, 160 km, en route to São Sebastião/Ilhabela, US$4.80.

Ilhabela *p407*

Bus A bus runs along the coast. **Litorânea** from **São Paulo** connects with a service right through to Ilhabela; office in Ilhabela at R Dr Carvalho 136.
Ferry At weekends and holidays the 15-20 min ferry between São Sebastião and Perequê runs non-stop day and night. During the week it does not sail 0130-0430. Free for foot passengers; cars US$9.25 weekdays, US$13 at weekends.

Ubatuba *p408*

Bus There are 3 bus terminals: 1) Rodoviária Costamar, R Hans Staden e R Conceição, serves all local destinations; 2) Rodoviária at R Profesor Thomaz Galhardo 513 for São José buses to Paraty, US$3, Normandy services (to Rio, US$12) and some Itapemirim buses; 3) Rodoviária Litorânea, the main bus station: go up Conceição for 8 blocks from Praça 13 de Maio, turn right on R Rio Grande do Sul, then left into R Dra Maria V Jean. Buses from here go to **São Paulo**, 3½ hrs, US$10.25.
Taxi In town are a rip-off, for example US$8 from the centre to the main bus terminal.

Iguape *p408*

Bus To Iguape: from **São Paulo, Santos**, or **Curitiba**, changing at Registro.
Ferry A continuous ferry service runs from Iguape to **Ilha Comprida** (free but small charge for cars); buses run until 1900 from the ferry stop to the beaches. From Iguape it is possible to take a boat trip down the coast to **Cananéia** and **Ariri**. Tickets and information from Dpto Hidroviário do Estado, R Major Moutinho 198, Iguape, T841 1122. It is a beautiful trip, passing between the island and the mainland.

⊙ Directory

Santos *p406*

Embassies and consulates Britain, R Tuiuti 58, 2nd floor, Caixa Postal 204, T3219 6622, daw@wilson.com.br. Denmark, R Frei Gaspar 22, 10th floor, 106, CP 726, T3219 6455, 1000-1100, 1500-1700. **Internet** Viva Shop, in Shopping Parque Balneario, Av Ana Costa, US$3 per hr. **Post offices** Main post office at R Cidale de Toledo 41, Centro, also at R Tolentino Filgueiras 70, Gonzaga.
Telephones International calls: can be made at R Galeão Carvalhal 45, Gonzaga.
Voltage 220 AC, 60 cycles.

Ubatuba *p408*

Internet Chat and Bar, upper floor of Ubatuba Shopping, US$3 per hr. **Post offices** One on R Dona Maria Alves between Hans Staden and R Col Dominicano. **Telephones** Telesp, is on Galhardo, close to Sérgio restaurant.

Minas Gerais and Espírito Santo

Minas Gerais was once described as having a heart of gold and a breast of iron. Half the mineral production of Brazil comes from the state, including most of the iron ore. Minas Gerais also produces 95% of all Brazil's gemstones. All this mineral wealth has left the state a legacy of sumptuous colonial cities built on gold and diamond mining. Streets of whitewashed 18th-century houses with deep blue or yellow window frames line steep and winding streets leading to lavishly decorated churches with rich gilt interiors. The colonial gold mining towns of Minas Gerais are the highlights of any visit. There are also other attractions: rugged national parks, which are great for trekking, lots of festivals and a famous cuisine, the comida mineira. The state of Minas Gerais, larger than France, is mountainous in the south, rising to the 2,787 m peak of Agulhas Negras in the Mantiqueira range, and in the east, where there is the Parque Nacional Caparaó containing the Pico da Bandeira (2,890 m). The capital, Belo Horizonte is culturally very active. From Belo Horizonte north are undulating grazing lands, the richest of which are in the extreme west: a broad wedge of country between Goiás in the north and São Paulo in the south, known as the Triângulo Mineiro. The coastal state of Espírito Santo is where mineiros head to for their seaside holidays. The most popular beaches are south of Vitória, the state capital, while north of the city are several turtle-nesting beaches. Inland are immigrant towns.

Brazil Minas Gerais & Espírito Santo

Belo Horizonte & Pampulha

Related map
A Belo Horizonte centre, page 413

Sleeping		Eating	
Ouro Minas Palace 1	Chalé Mineiro 3	Aurora 1	Xapuri 2
Pousadinha Mineira 2			

Belo Horizonte → *Phone code: 0xx31. Post code: 30000. Colour map 7, grid B5.*

Belo Horizonte (Population 4.8 million, Altitude 800 m) is surrounded by mountains and enjoys an excellent climate (16°-30°C) except for the rainy season (December-March). It was founded on 12 December 1897 and is one of Brazil's fastest growing cities, now suffering from atmospheric pollution. The third largest city in Brazil is a hilly city with streets that rise and fall and trees lining many of the central avenues. The large **Parque Municipal** is an oasis of green in the heart of downtown; closed at night and on Monday, except for a small section in the southwest corner (the Parque Municipal is not too safe, so it's best not to go alone). The main commercial district is around Av Afonso Pena; at night the movimento shifts to Savassi, southwest of the centre, where all the good eating places are.

Ins and outs
Tourist offices The municipal information is **Belotur** ① *R Pernambuco 284, Funciários, T3277 9797, www.pbh.gov.br/belotur*. Very helpful, with lots of useful information and maps. The monthly *Guia Turístico* for events, opening times etc, is freely available. Belotur has offices also at the southwest corner of Parque Municipal, at Confins and Pampulha airports, and at the rodoviária (particularly polyglot). **Setur** ① *Praça Rio Branco 56, T3272 8567, www.turismo. mg.gov.br*. The tourism authority for the state of Minas Gerais is very helpful. **Ibama** ① *Av do Contorno 8121, Cidade Jardim, CEP 30110-120, Belo Horizonte, T3337 2624, F3335 9955*.

Sights
The principal building in the Parque Municipal is the **Palácio das Artes** ① *Afonso Pena 1537, T3237 7234, 1000-2200, Sun 1400-2200*, which contains the **Centro de Artesanato Mineiro** (with craft shop), an exhibition of painting in Minas Gerais, a cinema, three theatres and temporary exhibitions. On the stretch of Avenida Afonso Pena outside the Parque Municipal an open-air market operates each Sunday morning (0800-1430). The avenue is transformed by thousands of coloured awnings covering stalls selling every conceivable type of local handicraft. Six blocks up Avenida João Pinheiro from Avenida Afonso Pena is the **Praça da Liberdade**, which is surrounded by fine public buildings, some in eclectic, fin-de-siècle-style, others more recent. At the end of the Praça is the **Palácio da Liberdade** *Sun 0900-1800 only*. The Praça itself is very attractive, with trees, flowers, fountains which are lit at night and joggers and walkers making the most of the paths. The **railway station**, with a museum on the 2nd floor showing a model railway, is part of a complex which includes a number of buildings dating from the 1920s around the **Praça da Estação** (also called Praça Rui Barbosa).

    Museu Mineiro ① *Av João Pinheiro 342, T3269 1168, Tue-Fri 1230-1830, Sat-Sun 1000-1600*, houses religious and other art. **Museu Histórico Abílio Barreto** ① *Av Prudente de Morais 202, Cidade Jardim, T3296 3896, bus 2902 from Av Afonso Pena*, in an old fazenda, is the last reminder of Belo Horizonte's predecessor, the village of **Arraial do Curral d'el Rey**. It has historical exhibits. **Jardim Botânico e Museu de História Natural** ① *Instituto Agronómico, R Gustavo da Silveira 1035, Cidade Nova, T3461 5805, Tue-Fri 0800-1130, 1330-1700, Sat-Sun 0900-1600 (take bus 8001)*, has geological, palaeontological and archaeological displays.

    About 8 km northwest from the centre is the picturesque suburb of **Pampulha**, famous for its modern buildings and the artificial lake, created in the 1930s by Brasilia architect Oscar Niemeyer and landscaped by Roberto Burle Marx. The **Igreja São Francisco de Assis** ① *Av Otacílio Negrão de Lima Km 12, T3441 9325*, was inaugurated in 1943. The painter Cândido Portinari installed beautiful blue and white tiles depicting Saint Francis' life on the exterior. On the wall behind the altar is a powerful composition also by Portinari. On the opposite shore is the glass and marble **Museu de Arte de Pampulha** (MAP) ① *Av Octacílio Negrão de Lima 16585, T3443 4533, Tue-Sun 0900-1900, free*. It has a fine collection of modern art from Minas Gerais. The **Casa do Baile** ① *Av Octacílio Negrão de Lima 751, T3277 7433, 0900-1900 daily except Mon, free*, is a perfect example of Niemeyer's fascination with the curved line. Just south of the lake is the **Mineirão** football stadium, about 750 m away. This is the second largest stadium in Brazil after the Maracanã stadium in Rio. Seats cost between US$4 and US$9.

    In the southern zone of the city, just 3 km from the central area, the **Parque de Mangabeiras** ① *Thu-Sun 0800-1800, is on the Serra do Curral at between 1,000 m and 1,400 m above sea level*. There are good views of the city, especially from the Mirante da Mata. Three forest trails have been laid out.

😴 Sleeping

Belo Horizonte *p412, maps p411 and p413*
You may spend the night in the rodoviária only if you have an onward ticket (police check at 2400). There are cheaper options near the rodoviária and in R Curitiba, but many of these hotels are not used for sleeping in. You will have a more comfortable stay in one of the youth hostels.
LL Ouro Minas Palace, Av Cristiano Machado 4001, T3429 4001 (toll free 0800-314000), www.ourominas.com.br. The most luxurious hotel in the city with palatial suites, including several for women only on the top floors, excellent service, pool, sauna, gym, excellent business facilities, not central but within easy reach of the centre and airports.

L Grandarrell Minas, R Espírito Santo 901, T3248 0000, www.grandarrell.com.br. One of the best business hotels in the centre, full business facilities including fax and email modems in rooms, rooftop pool, not much English spoken.
L Le Flamboyant, R Rio Grande do Norte 1007, Savassi, T3261 7370, www.clan.com.br. Well-maintained flats with separate sitting room with TV, kitchen with cooker, pool. Some flats have two bedrooms.
L Liberty Palace, R Paraíba 1465, Savassi, T2121 0900, www.libertypalace.com.br. Business hotel in the Savassi restaurant district, standard rooms with spacious bathrooms, 24-hr room service, IDSL in all rooms and a well-appointed business centre.

Belo Horizonte centre

Sleeping 😴	Othon Palace **8**	Chico Mineiro **1**	Taste Vin **6**
Chalé Mineiro **1**	São Salvador **10**	Dona Derna **2**	Vecchio Sogno **7**
Continental **2**	Villa Emma **9**	Dona Lucinha **3**	
Esplanada **3**		Flor de Líbano **4**	**Bars & clubs** 🍸
Grandarrell Minas **4**	**Eating** 🍴	Kauhana **10**	de James **14**
Le Flamboyant **5**	A Cafeteria **8**	La Traviata **11**	de João **15**
Liberty Palace **6**	Café da Travessa **9**	Sushi Beer **12**	Koyote **16**
O Sorriso do Lagarto **7**	Café Tina **13**	Sushi Naka **5**	

N

0 metres   300
0 yards   300

413

L Othon Palace, Av Afonso Pena 1050, T3247 0000, www.hoteis-othon.com.br. 1980s hotel, glass-fronted, excellent, safe, good restaurant, pool, helpful staff, lower floors can be noisy.

AL Villa Emma, R Arturo Toscanini 41, Savassi, T32823388, www.clan.com.br. The cheapest option in Savassi, spacious flats in need of a lick of paint, with 2 bedrooms, separate living area and kitchen. Internet access in some rooms.

B Esplanada, Av Santos Dumont 304, T3273 5311. An upmarket cheapie with bright rooms with en-suites, soap and towels, generous breakfasts and triples available for little more than doubles. Prices are negotiable.

D Continental, Av Paraná 241, T3201 7944. Central, quieter interior rooms. Recommended.

D São Salvador, R Espírito Santo 227, T3222 7731. Small, the best rooms are the triples with en suites, reasonable breakfast. One of many similar cheapies in the area.

E pp Chalé Mineiro, R Santa Luzia 288, Santa Efigênia, T3467 1576, www.chalemineiro hostel.com.br. Attractive, HI affiliated, with a small pool, dorms, a shared kitchen, TV lounge and telephones. Towels and bed linen are extra.

E pp O Sorriso do Lagarto, R Padre Severino 285, Savassi, T3283 9325, www.osorrisodolagarto.com.br. Simple, small hostel in a converted town house with kitchen, internet, breakfast, lockers, washing machines and a living area with DVD player.

Pousadinha Mineira, R Araxá 514, Floresta, 15 mins from the rodoviária, T3423 4105. HI, cheaper for members, being renovated in 2006.

● Eating

Belo Horizonte *p412, maps p411 and p413*
Mineiros love their food and drink and Belo Horizonte has a lively café dining and bar scene. Savassi overflows with street cafés, bars and restaurants and is the best place in the city for a food browse. There is a lively, cheap food market on R Tomé de Souza, between Pernambuco and Alagoas, in Savassi every night between 1900 and 2300. Pampulha has the best of the fine dining restaurants; which are well worth the taxi ride. And there are plenty of cheap per kilo restaurants and *padarias* near the budget hotels in the city centre.

††† Aurora, R Expedicionário Mário Alves de Oliveira 421, Sao Luís, T3498 7567. One of the best restaurants in town, garden setting next to Lago da Pampulha. Imaginative menu fusing Mineira and Italian techniques and making use of unusual Brazilian fruits. Closed Mon-Tue.

††† Taste Vin, R Curitiba 2105, Lourdes, T3292 5423. Excellent French, soufflés and provençale seafood. The wine list includes decent Brazilian options. Recommended.

††† Vecchio Sogno, R Martim de Carvalho 75 and R Dias Adorno, Santo Agostinho, under the Assembléia Legislativo, T3292 5251. The best Italian in the city with an inventive menu fusing Italian and French cuisine with Brazilian ingredients, excellent fish. Lunch only on Sun.

†††-†† Xapuri, R Mandacaru 260, Pampulha, T3496 6198. Great atmosphere, live music, very good food, a bit out of the way but recommended. Closed Mon.

†† Chico Mineiro, R Alagoas 626, corner of Av Brasil, T3261 3237. Good local chicken specialities, lunchtime only except till 0100 at weekends.

†† Dona Derna, R Tomé de Souza 1380, Savassi, T3223 6954. A range of restaurants in one. Upstairs is Italian fine dining with excellent dishes and a respectable wine list. Downstairs on weekdays is traditional Italian home cooking and by night a chic pizzeria called Memmo.

†† Sushi Naka, R Gonçalves Dias 92, Funcionários, T3287 2714. Japanese, excellent sushi, sashimi and soups. Close to the centre.

††-† La Traviata, Av Cristovão Colombo 282, Savassi, T3261 6392. A little moody Italian with terrace, strong on meat and fish, reasonable pasta and pizzas, good value house wine.

††-† Sushi Beer, R Tomé de Souza, Savassi, T3221 1116. A large open air dining area overlooked by a long bar, superior per kilo Minas and Japanese food, plus meats and pizzas.

† Dona Lucinha, R Sergipe 811, Savassi, T3261 5930 and R Padre Odorico 38 (São Pedro), T3227 0562. Self service, decent meat dishes, generous portions. Lunch only on Sun. Recommended.

† Flor de Líbano, R Espírito Santo 234. Very cheap and good.

† Kauhana, R Tomé de Souza, Savassi, T3284 8714. Tasty wood-fire cooked pizzas both savoury and sweet, pleasant open-air dining area.

† Mala e Cuia, a chain of restaurants serving good comida mineira at R Gonçalves Dias 874, Savassi, T3261 3059, Av Antônio Carlos 8305, Pampulha, T3441 2993, Av Raja Gabaglia 1617, São Bento.

Cafés

A Cafeteria, Av Cristovão Colombo 152, Savassi, T3223 9901. Salads, great sandwiches in pitta bread and a range of mock-Italian standards served to a lively young crowd and accompanied by live music most nights. One of several such café bars on the corner of Colombo and Albuquerque.

● *For an explanation of the sleeping and eating price codes used in this guide, see inside the front*
● *cover. Other relevant information is found in Essentials pages 345-347.*

Café da Travessa, Getúlio Vargas 1405 at Praça Savassi, T3223 8092. Great little café cum book and CD shop. Dishes range from rosti to Brazilian tapas, pasta and wraps, pizzas upstairs, great coffee. From breakfast until late.

Café Tina, Av Cristovão Colombo 336, Savassi, T3261 5068. Bohemian café serving soups, risottos and delicious puddings to an arty crowd. Closed Mon.

❶ Bars and clubs

Belo Horizonte *p412, maps p411 and p413*
Rua Tomé de Souza in Savassi has umpteen lively bars, particularly between Paraíba and Sergipe. The beer and caipirinhas are cheap and plentiful. Try **Bar de João**, **Bar de James**, or **Bar Koyote**.
Alambique, Av Raja Gabáglia 3200, Chalé 1D, Estoril, T3296 7188. Specializes in cachaça, with mineira appetizers, designed like a country house.

❀ Festivals and events

Belo Horizonte *p412, maps p411 and p413*
The city celebrates **Maundy Thursday**; Corpus Christi; **15 Aug**, **Assunção** (Assumption); **8 Dec**, **Conceição** (Immaculate Conception).

⊙ Shopping

Belo Horizonte *p412, maps p411 and p413*
Gemstones **Manoel Bernardes**, Av Contorno 5417, Savassi. Very reasonable.
Markets See above for the Sun **handicraft fair** on Av Afonso Pena. **Mercado Central**, Av Augusto de Lima 744. Large and clean, open every day.

▲ Activities and tours

Belo Horizonte *p412, maps p411 and p413*
For information on the cultural and adventure tourism possibilities on the **Estrada Real**, the colonial gold and diamond roads from Minas Gerais to Paraty and Rio de Janeiro, go to the head office at R Álvares Maciel 59, 11th floor, Santa Efigênia, T3241 7166.
Ametur, R Alvarengo Peixoto 295, loja 102, Lourdes, T/F3292 2139. Open 0900-1200, 1400-1900, has information on fazendas which welcome visitors and overnight guests.
Amo-Te, Associação Mineira dos Organizadores do Turismo Ecológico, R Monte Verde 125, Alípio de Melo, T3477 5430, oversees ecotourism in Minas Gerais. For companies which arrange trekking, riding, cycling, rafting, jeep tours, canyoning, visiting national parks, or fazendas, speak to Amo-Te in the first instance.
Master Turismo (Amex representative), R da

Bahia 2140, T3330 3655, www.master turismo.com.br. At Sala VIP, Aeroporto de Confins, and Av Afonso Pena 1967, T3330 3603 (very helpful). Runs 10-day/9-night tours on the Estrada Real (see above).
Oasis Turismo, A de Lima 479/815, Centro, T3274 6422. Very helpful, manager Jacqueline.
Ouro Preto Turismo, Av Afonso Pena 4133, T3287 0505, www.ouropretotour.com.
Reveture, R Espírito Santo 1892, 1st floor, Lourdes, T3337 2500, www.revetour.com.br.
Tropa Serrana, Tullio Marques Lopes Filho, T3344 8986, http://tropaserrana.zip.net. For recommended horse riding tours.

❷ Transport

Belo Horizonte *p412, maps p411 and p413*
Air The international airport is near Lagoa Santa, at Confins, 39 km from Belo Horizonte, T3689 2700. Taxi to centre, US$54, cooperative taxis have fixed rates to different parts of the city. Airport bus, either *executivo* from the exit, US$14, or comfortable normal bus (Unir) from the far end of the car park hourly, US$2.65, both go to/from the rodoviária.

Closer to the city is the national airport at Pampulha, which has shuttle services from several cities, including Rio and São Paulo, T3490 2001. Urban transportation to/from this airport is cheaper than from Confins. From Pampulha airport to town, take blue bus 1202, 25 mins, US$0.65, passing the rodoviária and the cheaper hotel district.
Bus The city has a good public transport system: red buses run on express routes and charge US$1; yellow buses have circular routes around the Contorno, US$0.65; blue buses run on diagonal routes charging US$0.85. There are also buses which integrate with the regional, overground Metrô.

The rodoviária is by Praça Rio Branco at the northwest end of Av Afonso Pena, T3271 3000/8933. The bus station has toilets, post office, phones, left-luggage lockers (attended service 0700-2200), shops and is clean and well-organized. Buses leave from the rather gloomy platforms beneath the ticket hall. Do not leave belongings unattended.

To **Rio** with **Cometa** (T3201 5611) and **Útil** (T3201 7744), 6½ hrs, US$16.75 (ordinary), leito, US$34. To **Vitória** with **São Geraldo** (T3271 1911), US$23 and semi-leito US$32. To **Brasília** with **Itapemirim** (T3291 9991) and **Penha** (T3271 1027), 10 hrs, 6 a day including 2 leitos, only one leaves in daylight (0800), US$25.25, leito US$51. To **São Paulo** with **Cometa** and **Gontijo** (T3201 6130), 10 hrs, US$20. To **Foz do Iguaçu**, US$55, 22 hrs. To **Salvador** with Gontijo, US$53, 24 hrs,

at 1900 daily, and São Geraldo at 1800. São Geraldo also goes to **Porto Seguro**, 17 hrs, direct, via Nanuque and Eunápolis, US$44. To **Campo Grande** with Gontijo (at 1930) and Motta (3 a day), US$41-46, a good route to Bolivia, avoiding São Paulo. All major destinations served. For buses within Minas Gerais, see under destination.
Train To **Vitória**, see below.

◑ Directory

Belo Horizonte *p412, maps p411 and p413*
Airline offices American, Av Bernardo Monteiro 1539, Funcionários, T3274 3166. Bra, T3263 0000, www.voebra.com.br. Office in the airports and bookable through most high street travel agencies. Gol, www.voegol.com.br. Office in the airports and bookable through most high street travel agencies. TAM, R Marília de Dirceu 162, Lourdes, T0300-231000/3349 5500. United, Av Olegário Maciel 2251, Lourdes, T3339 6060. Varig/Rio Sul/Nordeste, Av Getúlio Vargas 840, T0300-7887000, Confins airport T3689 2244.
Banks Banco do Brasil, R Rio de Janeiro 750, Av Amazonas 303; cash is given against credit cards at Banco Itaú, Av João Pinheiro 195. Citibank, R Espírito Santo 871. Visa ATM at Bradesco, R da Bahia 947. **Master Turismo**, see Tour operators, above. American Express representative. Changing TCs is difficult, but hotels will change them for guests at a poor rate. **Embassies and consulates** Austria, R José Américo Cançado Bahia 199, T3333 5363, F3333 1046. **Denmark**, R Paraíba 1122, 5th floor, T3269 8626, F3269 8785. **France**, Av do Contorno 5417/2, Cruzeiro, T4501 3737, Manoel@mbernardes.com.br. Italy, Av Afonso Pena 3130, 12th floor, T3281 4211. Netherlands, R Sergipe 1167, loja 5, T3227 5275. Spain, Av Raja Gabáglia 1001, sl 910, T/F32754480. UK, R dos Inconfidentes 1075, sala 1302, Savassi, T3261 2072, britcon.bhe@terra.com.br. **Internet** Many places throughout the city. **Language classes** Carlos Robles, T3281 1274, gatirobles@vol.com.br. Has a network of schools in Brazil, speaks good English. **Medical services** Mater Dei, R Gonçalves Dias 2700, T3339 9000. Recommended. **Post offices** Av Afonso Pena 1270, with fax, philatelic department and small museum, closes 1800; poste restante is behind the main office at R de Goiás 77. The branch office on R da Bahia is less busy. **Telephones** Telemig, Av Afonso Pena 1180, by the Correios, daily 0700-2200; also at the rodoviária, Confins airport, and others in the centre. **Voltage** 120-220 AC, 60 cycles.

East and south of Belo Horizonte

Most of the colonial cities lie southeast and south of Belo Horizonte and many people choose to visit them on the way to or from Rio as they make for the most charming and restful of stopping places. Ouro Preto is the most famous and a much more pleasant place to stay than the state capital. Mariana is a good day trip from Ouro Preto. Further south are Congonhas, with its remarkable statuary, São João del Rei, with some beautiful colonial architecture, and Tiradentes, the most heavily visited of the Minas colonial towns after Ouro Preto. In the far south of the state, closer to the road to São Paulo, is one of Brazil's main New Age sites, São Tomé das Letras.

Sabará → *Colour map 7, grid B5. Population: 115,352.*
East of the state capital by 23 km is the colonial gold-mining (and steel-making) town of Sabará, strung along the narrow steep valleys of the Rio das Velhas and Rio Sabará. **Secretaria de Turismo** ① *R Pedro II 223, T3672 7690, www.sabara.mg.gov.br.*

Rua Dom Pedro II is lined with beautiful 18th-century buildings. Among them is the **Solar do Padre Correa** (1773) at No 200, now the **Prefeitura**; the **Casa Azul** (also 1773), No 215; and the **Teatro Municipal**, former Opera House (1770 – the second oldest in Brazil). At the top of R Dom Pedro II is the Praça Melo Viana, in the middle of which is **Nossa Senhora do Rosário dos Pretos** ① *church and museum Tue-Sun 0800-1100, 1300-1700.* The church was left unfinished at the time of the slaves' emancipation. There is a museum of religious art in the church. To the right of the church as you face it is the **Chafariz do Rosário** (the Rosário fountain). In R da Intendência is the museum of 18th century gold mining in the **Museu do Ouro**. ① *Tue-Sun 1200-1730, US$1.30.* It contains exhibits on gold extraction, plus religious items and colonial furniture. Another fine example is the **Casa Borba Gato** *R Borba Gato 71*; the building currently belongs to the Museu do Ouro.

The church of **Nossa Senhora do Carmo** (1763-1774) ① *US$1.30 (includes a leaflet about the town)*, with doorway, pulpits and choirloft by Aleijadinho (see Box) and paintings by Athayde, is on R do Carmo. **Nossa Senhora da Conceição** ① *Praça Getúlio Vargas, free*, built 1701-1720, has much visible woodwork and a beautiful floor. The carvings have much gilding,

O Aleijadinho

Antônio Francisco Lisboa (1738-1814), the son of a Portuguese architect and a black slave woman, was known as O Aleijadinho (the little cripple) because in later life he developed a maiming disease (possibly leprosy) which compelled him to work in a kneeling (and ultimately a recumbent) position with his hammer and chisel strapped to his wrists. His finest work, which shows a strength not usually associated with the plastic arts in the 18th century, is probably the set of statues in the gardens and sanctuary of the great Bom Jesus church in Congonhas do Campo, but the main body of his work is in Ouro Preto, with some important pieces in Sabará, São João del Rei and Mariana.

there are painted panels and paintings by 23 Chinese artists brought from Macau. The clearest Chinese work is on the two red doors to the right and left of the chancel. **Nossa Senhora do Ó**, built in 1717 and showing Chinese influence, is 2 km from the centre of the town at the Largo Nossa Senhora do Ó (take local bus marked 'Esplanada' or 'Boca Grande').

If you walk up the Morra da Cruz hill from the Hotel do Ouro to a small chapel, the Capela da Cruz or Senhor Bom Jesus, you can get a wonderful view of the whole area.

Caeté → *Colour map 7, grid B5. Population: 36,299.*

A further 25 km is Caeté, which has several historical buildings and churches. On the Praça João Pinheiro are the **Prefeitura** and **Pelourinho** (both 1722), the **Igreja Matriz Nossa Senhora do Bom Sucesso** (1756 rebuilt 1790) *daily 1300-1800*, and the **Chafariz da Matriz**. Also on the Praça is the tourist information office in the Casa da Cultura (T6511855). Other churches are **Nossa Senhora do Rosário** (1750-1768), with a ceiling attributed to Mestre Athayde, and **São Francisco de Assis**. The **Museu Regional** ① *R Israel Pinheiro 176, Tue-Sun 1200-1700*, in the house of the Barão de Catas Altas, or Casa Setecentista, contains 18th and 19th century religious art and furniture.

Parque Natural de Caraça

The **Parque Natural de Caraça** ① *0700-2100; if staying overnight you cannot leave after 2100, US$6.50 per vehicle*, is a remarkable reserve about 120 km east of Belo Horizonte. It has been preserved so well because the land belongs to a seminary, part of which has been converted into a hotel. The rarest mammal in the park is the maned wolf; the monks feed them on the seminary steps in the evening. Also endangered is the southern masked titi monkey. Other primates include the common marmoset and the brown capuchin monkey. Some of the bird species at Caraça are endemic, others rare and endangered. The trails for viewing the different landscapes and the wildlife are marked at their beginning and are quite easy to follow.

Ouro Preto → *Phone code: 0xx31. Post code: 35400. Colour map 7, grid B5. Population: 66,277.*

Founded in 1711, this famous former state capital has cobbled streets that wind up and down steep hills, crowned with 13 churches. Mansions, fountains, terraced gardens, ruins, towers shining with coloured tiles, all blend together to maintain a delightful 18th-century atmosphere. October-February is the wettest time, but the warmest month of the year is February (average 30ºC). The coldest months are June-August, with the lowest temperatures in July (10ºC).

Tourist office ① *Praça Tiradentes 41, opens 0800, T3551 2655*, Portuguese only spoken, very helpful. The **Secretaria de Turismo** ① *Casa de Gonzaga, R Cláudio Manoel 61, T3559 3200*, has lists of hotels, restaurants and local sites and a map. A local guide for a day, **Associação de Guias de Turismo (AGTOP)**, can be obtained through the tourist office, T3559 3269 at the tourist office, or 3221 2655 (guide Cássio Antunes is recommended). The **Guiding Association** (T3551 2504) offers group tours of US$40 for 1 to 10 people. If taking a guide, check their accreditation. The tourist office and most historic buildings have several books for sale, including Lucia Machado de Almeida's *Passeio a Ouro Preto*, US$8 (in Portuguese, English and French). See also www.ouropreto.com.br (in Portuguese).

Most churches charge a conservation tax of US$1.50-5; bags and cameras are taken at the entrance and guarded in lockers (visitors keep the key). Churches are all closed Monday.

Sights In the central **Praça Tiradentes** is a statue of the leader of the **Inconfidentes**, Joaquim José da Silva Xavier. Another Inconfidente, the poet Tomás Antônio Gonzaga lived at R Cláudio Manoel 61, close to São Francisco de Assis church. On the north side of the praça (at No 20) is a famous **Escola de Minas** (School of Mining), founded in 1876, in the fortress-like **Palácio dos Governadores** (1741-1748); it has the interesting **Museu de Mineralogia e das Pedras** ① *Tue-Fri 1200-1700, Sat-Sun 0900-1300, US$2*, with 23,000 stones from around the world. On the south side of the Praça, No 139, is the **Museu da Inconfidência** ① *T3551 1121, Mon-Fri 0800-1800, US$2*, a fine historical and art museum in the former **Casa de Câmara e Cadeia**, which has some drawings by Aleijadinho and the Sala Manoel da Costa Athayde, in an annex. In the Casa Capitular of NS do Carmo is **Museu do Oratório** ① *T3551 5369, 0930-1200, 1330-1730 daily*, a collection of beautiful 18th and 19th-century prayer icons and oratories including many made of egg and sea shell. **Casa dos Contos** ① *R São José 12, T3551 1444, 1230-1730 Tue-Sat, 0900-1500 Sun and holidays, US$0.65*. Built between 1782-1784, it is the Centro de Estudos do Ciclo de Ouro (Centre for Gold Cycle Studies) and a museum of money and finance. The **Casa Guignard** ① *R Conde de Bobadela 110, T3551 5155, 1200-1800 Tue-Fri, 0900-1500 Sat, Sun and holidays, free*, displays the paintings of Alberto da Veiga Guignard. The **Teatro Municipal** ① *in R Brigadeiro Musqueiro, daily 1230-1800*, is the oldest functioning theatre in Latin America. It was built in 1769.

São Francisco de Assis (1766-1796) ① *Largo de Coimbra, 0830-1145, 1330-1640, US$2.65*; the ticket also permits entry to NS da Conceição (keep your ticket for admission to the museum). This church is considered to be one of the masterpieces of Brazilian baroque. Aleijadinho worked on the general design and the sculpture of the façade, the pulpits and many other features. Mestre Athayde (1732-1827) was responsible for the painted ceiling. **Nossa Senhora da Conceição** (1722) ① *0830-1130, 1330-1700, Sun 1200-1700*, is heavily gilded and contains Aleijadinho's tomb. It has a museum devoted to him. **Nossa Senhora das Mercês e Perdões** (1740-1772) ① *R das Mercês, 1000-1400*, was rebuilt in the 19th century. Some sculpture by Aleijadinho can be seen in the main chapel. **Santa Efigênia** (1720-1785) ① *Ladeira Santa Efigênia e Padre Faria, 0800-1200*; Manuel Francisco Lisboa (Aleijadinho's father) oversaw the construction and much of the carving is by Francisco Xavier de Brito (Aleijadinho's mentor). It has wonderful panoramic views of the city. **Nossa Senhora do Carmo** (1766-1772) ① *R Brigadeiro Mosqueira, 1330-1700*, has a museum of sacred art with Aleijadinho sculptures. **Nossa Senhora do Pilar** (1733) ① *Praça Mons Castilho Barbosa, 1200-1700*, also contains a religious art museum. Entry is shared with São Francisco de Paula, Ladeira de São José (1804). **Nossa Senhora do Rosário** *Largo do Rosário*, dated from 1785, has a curved façade. The interior is much simpler than the exterior, but there are interesting side altars.

The **Mina do Chico Rei** ① *R Dom Silvério, 0800-1700, US$2*, is not as impressive as some other mines in the area, but is fun to crawl about in; restaurant attached. Near the Padre Faria Church (NS do Rosário dos Brancos) is another small mine, **Mina Bem Querer** *US$1.30*, with a swimming pool with crystal clear water that runs through the mine. Between Ouro Preto and Mariana is the **Minas de Passagem** ① *US$10, 0900-1730, last admissions at 1645*, gold mine, dating from 1719. A guided tour visits the old mine workings and underground lake (take bathing suit).

Mariana → *Phone code: 0xx31. Post code: 35420. Colour map 7, grid B5. Population: 46,710.*
Streets are lined with beautiful, two-storey 18th century houses in this old mining city, which is much less hilly than Ouro Preto. Mariana's historical centre slopes gently uphill from the river and the Praça Tancredo Neves, where buses from Ouro Preto stop. **Tourist office: Secretaria de Cultura e Turismo de Mariana** ① *Praça Tancredo Neves, T3557 9044*. The tourist office will help with guides and tours and offer a map and a free monthly booklet, *Mariana Agenda Cultural*, packed with local information including accommodation and eating.

Sights The first street parallel with the Praça Tancredo Neves is R Direita, and is home to the 300-year-old houses. At No 54 is the **Casa do Barão de Pontal** ① *Tue 1400-1700*, whose balconies are carved from soapstone, unique in Minas Gerais. The ground floor of the building is a museum of furniture. At No 35 is the **Museu-Casa Afonso Guimarães** (or Alphonsus de Guimaraens) *free*, the former home of a symbolist poet: photographs and letters. No 7 is the **Casa Setecentista**, which now belongs to the Patrimônio Histórico e Artístico Nacional.

R Direita leads to the Praça da Sé, on which stands the **Cathedral** ① *Basílica de Nossa Senhora da Assunção, organ concerts are given on Fri at 1100 and Sun at 1200, US$10*. The portal and the lavabo in the sacristy are by Aleijadinho. The painting in the beautiful interior and side altars is by Manoel Rabello de Sousa. Also in the cathedral is a wooden German organ (1701), a gift to the first diocese of the Capitania de Minas do Ouro in 1747. The **Museu Arquidiocesano** ① *on R Frei Durão, 0900-1200, 1300-1700, closed Mon, US$2*, has fine church furniture, a gold and silver collection, Aleijadinho statues and an ivory cross. Opposite is the **Casa da Intendência/Casa de Cultura** ① *No 84, 0800-1130, 1330-1700*, which holds exhibitions and has a museum of music. On the south side of Praça Gomes Freire is the **Palácio Arquiepiscopal**, while on the north side is the **Casa do Conde de Assumar**, who was governor of the Capitania from 1717 to 1720.

From Praça Gomes Freire, Travessa São Francisco leads to Praça Minas Gerais and one of the finest groups of colonial buildings in Brazil. In the middle of the Praça is the **Pelourinho**, the stone monument to Justice, at which slaves used to be beaten. On one side of the square is the fine **São Francisco church** (1762-1794) *daily 0800-1700*, with pulpits designed by Aleijadinho, paintings by Mestre Athayde, who is buried in tomb No 94, a fine sacristy and one side-altar by Aleijadinho. At right angles to São Francisco is **Nossa Senhora do Carmo** (1784) *daily 1400-1700*, with steatite carvings, Athayde paintings, and chinoiserie panelling. Across R Dom Silvério is the **Casa da Câmara e Cadéia** (1768), at one time the Prefeitura Municipal. On Largo de São Pedro is **São Pedro dos Clérigos** (begun in 1753), one of the few elliptical churches in Minas Gerais. Restoration is under way.

Capela de Santo Antônio *on R Rosário Velho*, wonderfully simple and the oldest in town. It is some distance from the centre. Overlooking the city from the north, with a good viewpoint, is the church of **Nossa Senhora do Rosário**, R do Rosário (1752), with work by Athayde and showing Moorish influence.

Parque Nacional Caparaó
① *Contact R Vale Verde s/n, Alto do Caparaó, CEO 36836-000, Toxx32-3266 9090.*
This is one of the most popular parks in Minas (on the Espírito Santo border), with good walking through stands of Atlantic rainforest, páramo and to the summits of three of Brazil's highest peaks: Pico da Bandeira (2,890 m), Pico do Cruzeiro (2,861 m) and Pico do Cristal (2,798 m). The park, surrounded by coffee farms, features rare Atlantic rainforest in its lower altitudes and Brazilian alpine on top. Loss of forest and floral biodiversity has adversely affected wildlife, but there are nonetheless a number of Atlantic coast primates, like the brown capuchins, together with a recovering bird population. From the park entrance (where a small fee has to be paid) it is 6 km on a good unpaved road to the car park at the base of the waterfall. From the hotel (see below) jeeps (US$25 per jeep) run to the car park at 1,970 m (2½ hours' walk), then it's a three to four hour walk to the summit of the Pico da Bandeira, marked by yellow arrows; plenty of camping possibilities, the highest being at Terreirão (2,370 m). This is good walking country. It is best to visit during the dry season (April-October). It can be quite crowded in July and during Carnival. See Transport, below, for how to get there.

Congonhas → *Phone code: 0xx31. Post code: 36404. Colour map 7, grid B5. Population: 41,256.*
This hill town is connected by a paved 3½ km road with the Rio-Belo Horizonte highway. Most visitors spend little time in the town, but go straight to **O Santuário de Bom Jesus de Matosinhos** ① *Tue-Sun 0700-1900, there are public toilets on the Alameda das Palmeiras, the information desk at the bus station will guard luggage and you can visit the sanctuary between bus changes*, which dominates Congonhas. The great pilgrimage church was finished in 1771; below it are six linked chapels, or pasos (1802-1818), showing scenes with life-size Passion figures carved by Aleijadinho and his pupils in cedar wood. These lead up to a terrace and courtyard. On this terrace (designed in 1777) stand 12 prophets, sculpted by Aleijadinho between 1800 and 1805. Carved in soapstone with dramatic sense of movement, they constitute one of the finest works of art of their period in the world. Inside the church, there are paintings by Athayde and the heads of four sainted popes (Gregory, Jerome, Ambrose and Augustine) sculpted by Aleijadinho for the reliquaries on the high altar. To the left of the church, as you face it, the third door in the building alongside the church is the Room of Miracles, which contains photographs and thanks for miracles performed.

On the hill are souvenir shops, the Colonial Hotel and Cova do Daniel restaurant (both are good, hotel **E**). From the hotel the Alameda das Palmeiras sweeps round to the **Romarias**, which contains the Espaço Cultural, the headquarters of the local tourist office, workshops, the museums of mineralogy and religious art and the Memória da Cidade. To get there take bus marked 'Basílica' which runs every 30 minutes from the centre of the rodoviária to Bom Jesus, 5 km, US$0.45. A taxi from the rodoviária costs US$5, US$10 return including the wait while you visit the sanctuary. In town, the bus stops in Praça JK. You can walk up from Praça JK via Praça Dr Mário Rodrigues Pereira, cross the little bridge, then go up Ruas Bom Jesus and Aleijadinho to the Praça da Basílica. **Tourist office**: Fumcult, in the Romarias T3731 1300 ext 114.

São João del Rei → *Phone code: 0xx32. Post code: 36300. Colour map 7, grid B5. Pop: 78,616.*

This colonial city is at the foot of the Serra do Lenheiro. A good view of the town and surroundings is from Alto da Boa Vista, where there is a Statue of Christ (Senhor dos Montes). São João del Rei is very lively at weekends, but feels far less of a tourist museum piece than nearby Tiradentes (see below). Through the centre of town runs the Corrego do Lenheiro (sadly a winding stream no more); across it are two fine stone bridges, A Ponte da Cadeia (1798) and A Ponte do Rosário (1800). **Tourist office: Secretaria de Turismo**, in the house of Bárbara Heliodora ① *Praça Frei Orlando 90, T3337 1783, 0900-1700*. Free map.

There are five 18th century churches in the town, three of which are splendid examples of Brazilian colonial building. **São Francisco de Assis** (1774) ① *Praça Frei Orlando, 0830-1700, closed Mon, US$1.30*. The façade, with circular towers, the doorway intricately carved and the greenish stone framing the white paint to beautiful effect was designed by Francisco de Lima Cerqueira and his disciple Aniceto de Souza Lopez. Inside are two sculptures by the same artists, about whom nothing is known beyond their names in the church's records and that they carried out the work in 1774. The six side altars are in wood; restoration has removed the plaster from the altars, revealing fine carving in sucupira wood.

Basílica de Nossa Senhora do Pilar (the Cathedral) ① *R Getúlio Vargas (formerly R Direita), open afternoons*, built 1721, has a 19th century façade which replaced the 18th century original. It has rich altars and a brightly painted ceiling. In the sacristy are portraits of the Evangelists. **Nossa Senhora do Carmo** ① *Praça Dr Augusto Viegas (Largo do Carmo), open afternoons*, very well restored, is all in white and gold. Construction commenced in 1733. Almost opposite São Francisco is the house of **Bárbara Heliodora** which contains the **Museu Municipal Tomé Portes del Rei**, with historical objects and curios, and, downstairs, the tourist office (see above). The **Museu Ferroviário** (railway museum) ① *Av Hermílio Alves 366, T3371 8485, Tue-Sun 0900-1130, 1300-1700, US$0.65 (see below for the train to Tiradentes)*, is well worth exploring. The museum traces the history of railways in general and in Brazil in brief. You can walk along the tracks to the round house, in which are several working engines in superb condition, an engine shed and a steam-operated machine shop, still working. It is here that the engines get up steam before going to couple with the coaches for the run to Tiradentes. On days when the trains are running, you can get a good, close-up view of operations even if not taking the trip; highly recommended.

Tiradentes → *Phone code: 0xx32. Post code: 36325. Population: 5,759.*

This charming little town, 15 km from São João, with its nine streets and eight carefully restored, baroque churches, is at the foot of the green Serra São José. Neat whitewashed cottages trimmed in yellow and blue hide art galleries, restaurants, souvenir shops and pousadas, all busy with tourists even during the week. It is especially busy during Holy Week, when there are numerous religious processions. It was founded as São José del Rei on 14 January 1718. After the ousting of the emperor in 1889 the town was renamed in honour of the martyr of the Inconfidência. **Tourist office** is in the Prefeitura, R Resende Costa 71.

Sights The **Igreja Matriz de Santo Antônio** (1710-1736) ① *daily 0900-1700, US$1.30, no photography*, contains some of the finest gilded wood carvings in the country. The church has a small but fine organ brought from Porto in the 1790s. The upper part of the reconstructed façade is said to follow a design by Aleijadinho. In front of the church are also a cross and a sundial by him. **Santuário da Santíssima Trindade**, on the road which leads up behind the Igreja Matriz de Santo Antônio, is 18th century, while the room of miracles associated with the annual Trinity Sunday pilgrimage is modern.

The charming **Nossa Senhora do Rosário** church (1727) ① *on a small square on R Direita, Wed-Mon 1200-1600, US$0.65*, has fine statuary and ornate gilded altars. **São João Evangelista** ① *Largo do Sol, Wed-Mon 0900-1700*, is in a lovely open space. It is a simple church, built by the Irmandade dos Homens Pardos (mulattos). Beside Igreja São

66 99 One of the five highest places in Brazil, São Tomé has attracted many new age visitors and its hotels are graded in UFOs instead of stars...

João Evangelista is the **Museu Padre Toledo**, the house of one of the leaders of the Inconfidência Mineira. It exhibits some handsome colonial furniture and a painted roof depicting the Five Senses. At the junction of R da Câmara and R Direita is the **Sobrado Ramalho**, said to be the oldest building in Tiradentes. It has been beautifully restored as a cultural centre. **Nossa Senhora das Mercês** (18th century) ① *Largo das Mercês, Sun 0900-1700*, has an interesting painted ceiling and a notable statue of the Virgin. The magnificent **Chafariz de São José** (public fountain, 1749) is still used for drinking, clothes washing and watering animals. You can follow the watercourse into the forest of the Serra de São José (monkeys and birds can be seen).

The **steam train** ① *runs on Fri, Sat, Sun and holidays, 1000 and 1415 from São João del Rei, returning from Tiradentes at 1300 and 1700, US$10.50*, on the line between São João del Rei and Tiradentes (13 km) has been in continuous operation since 1881, using the same locomotives and rolling stock, running on 76 cm gauge track, all lovingly cared for. The maximum speed is 20 km per hour.

São Tomé das Letras and around → *Phone code: 0xx35. Colour map 7, grid B4. Population: 6,204.*

A beautiful hilltop town in **southern Minas**, one of the five highest places in Brazil, São Tomé has attracted many new age visitors and its hotels are graded in UFOs instead of stars. It is said to be a good vantage point for seeing UFOs, which draw crowds at weekends. Nearby are caves with inscriptions, which some say are extraterrestrial in origin. It is believed that there are many places with special energies. Behind the town are rocky outcrops on which are the Pyramid House, the Cruzeiro (Cross, 1,430 m, with good 360° views), the Pedra da Bruxa and paths for walking or, in some parts, scrambling. A quarry town since the beginning of the 20th century, there is evidence of the industry everywhere you look. **Tourist office** ① *R José Cristiano Alves 4.*

On the main Praça is the frescoed 18th-century **Igreja Matriz** beside the fenced cave in which are the faded red rock paintings ('letras') of the town's name. A second church, the **Igreja das Pedras** (Nossa Senhora do Rosário – 18th century) is on a Praça to the left as you enter town (R Ernestina Maria de Jesus Peixoto). It is constructed in the same style as many of the charming old-style buildings, with slabs of the local stone laid on top of each other without mortar. The post office and Bemge Bank are in the group of buildings at the top right of the Praça, facing the Gruta São Tomé.

In the surrounding hills are many caves, waterfalls and rapids. Some of these places make a good hike from the town, but you can also visit several in a day on an organized tour. T3237 1283 or enquire at Néctar shop on R José Cristiano Alves. Tours run on weekends and holidays from the Praça at 1000 and 1400 to waterfalls, caves, etc, T3237 1353 and ask for Jaime or Iraci. The Carimbado cave is especially rich in myths and legends. Shangri-lá, which is a beautiful spot, is also called the Vale do Maytréia.

● Sleeping

Sabará *p416*

A Pousada Solar das Sepúlvedas, R da Intendência 371, behind the Museu do Ouro, T3671 2705. Grand, rooms with TV, pool.

C Hotel do Ouro, R Santa Cruz 237, Morro da Cruz, T3671 5622. With bath, hot water, with breakfast, marvellous view, best value.

Parque Natural de Caraça *p417*

AL Hospedaria do Caraça, the seminary hotel, for reservations write to Santuário do Caraça, Caixa Postal 12, 35960-000 – Santa Bárbara, MG, T0xx31-3837 2698. It has pleasant rooms; room rates vary, price is full board. There is a restaurant serving good food which comes from farms within the seminary's lands. Lunch is served 1200-1330.

Ouro Preto *p417*

Prices indicated here are for high season; many hotels offer, or will negotiate, lower prices outside holiday times or when things are quiet.

Ask at the tourist office for accommodation in *casas de família*, reasonably priced. Avoid touts who greet you off buses and charge higher prices than those advertised in hotels; it is difficult to get hotel rooms at weekends and holiday periods.

AL Pousada do Mondego, Largo de Coimbra 38, T3551 2040, www.mondego.com.br. Beautifully kept colonial house in a fine location by São Francisco church, room rates vary according to view, small restaurant, Scotch bar, popular with groups. Recommended (a Roteiro de Charme hotel, see page 346), the hotel runs a jardineira bus tour of the city, 2 hrs, minimum 10 passengers, US$10 for non-guests.

AL Pousada Solar de NS do Rosário, Av Getúlio Vargas 270, T3551 5200, www.hotelsolar dorosario.com.br. Fully restored historic building with a highly recommended restaurant, bar, sauna, pool; all facilities in rooms.

AL-A Pousada Mirante do Café, Fazenda Alto das Rubiáceas, Santo Antônio do Leite, 25 km west of Ouro Preto, T3335 8478, www.mirante docafe.com.br. Coffee farm with full board available, visits allowed during coffee harvest, pool, trails, horse riding and other leisure activities.

A Luxor Pousada, R Dr Alfredo Baeta 16, Praça Antônio Dias, T3551 2244, www.luxor hoteis.com.br. Converted colonial mansion, no twin beds, comfortable but spartan, good views, restaurant good but service slow.

B Pousada Casa Grande, R Conselheiro Quintiliano, 96, T/F3551 4314, www.hotel pousadacasagrande.com.br. Including breakfast, safe, good views. Recommended.

C Colonial, Trav Padre Camilo Veloso 26, close to Praça Tiradentes, T3551 3133, www.hotelc olonial.com.br. With new rooms and refurbished older rooms, pleasant.

C Hospedária Antiga, R Xavier da Veiga 1, T3551 2203. Spacious rooms in a restored colonial house. Recommended.

C Pousada Itacolomi, R Antônio Pereira 167, T3551 2891. Next door to the Museu da Inconfidência, small but well kept with good rates for the 3-room apartments.

C Pousada Nello Nuno, R Camilo de Brito 59, T3551 3375. Cheaper rooms have no bath, friendly owner Annamélia speaks some French. Highly recommended.

C Pousada Tiradentes, Praça Tiradentes 70, T3551 2619. Spartan rooms, but well-kept and moderately comfortable, TV, fridge, conveniently located.

C Pouso Chico Rey, R Brig Musqueira 90, T3551 1274. Fascinating old house with Portuguese

colonial furnishings, very small and utterly delightful (but plumbing unreliable), book in advance.

C Solar das Lajes, R Conselheiro Quintiliano 604, T/F3551 3388, www.solardaslajes.com.br. A little way from centre but with an excellent view and a pool, well run.

D Pousada dos Bandeirantes, R das Mercês 167, T3551 1996. Behind the São Francisco de Assis church and offering beautiful views.

D Pousada São Francisco de Paula, Padre JM Pen 202, next to the São Francisco de Paula church, T3551 3456, 100 m from rodoviária. One of the best views of any in the city, from the rooms or from a hammock in the garden. Rooms with and without bath or breakfast, dormitory, use of a kitchen, multilingual staff, excursions. Snacks are available. Recommended (book in after 1200).

E Brumas, R. Pe José Marcos Pena 68, 150 m downhill from rodoviária, just below São Francisco de Paula church, T3551 2944, www.brumasonline.cjb.net. Hostel with dormitory, kitchen and laundry and superb views. Don't walk down from bus station after dark.

Camping Camping Clube do Brasil, Rodovia dos Inconfidentes Km 91, 2 km north, T3551 1799. Expensive but good.

Students may be able to stay, during holidays and weekends, at the self-governing student hostels, known as *repúblicas* (very welcoming, 'best if you like heavy metal music' and 'are prepared to enter into the spirit of the places'). The Prefeitura has a list of over 50 repúblicas with phone numbers, available at the Secretaria de Turismo. Many are closed between Christmas and Carnival.

Mariana *p418*

B Pousada Solar dos Corrêa, R Josefá Macedo 70 and R Direita, T/F3557 2080. Central, restored 18th-century town house with spacious a/c rooms, with breakfast, TV, fridge in room, parking.

B Pousada do Chafariz, R Cônego Rego 149, T3557 1492. Converted colonial building, TV, fridge, parking, breakfast included.

C Providência, R Dom Silvério 233, T3557 1444. Along the road that leads up to the Basílica; has use of the neighbouring school's pool when classes finish at noon, small rooms, quiet.

C-D Central, R Frei Durão 8, T/F3557 1630. A charming but run-down colonial building on the attractive Praça Gomes Freire. Recommended but avoid downstairs rooms.

Parque Nacional Caparaó *p419*

A Caparaó Parque, T3747 2559, 2 km from the park entrance, 15 mins' walk from the town of Alto Caparaó, nice. Ask where camping is permitted.

C São Luiz, in **Manhumirim** (Population: 20,025), good value, but **Cids Bar**, next door, Travessa 16 do Março, has better food.

São João del Rei p420
AL **Beco do Bispo**, Beco do Bispo 93, 2 mins west of São Francisco de Assis, T/3371 8844, www.becodobispo.com.br. The best in town, bright a/c rooms with firm mattresses, hot showers, cable TV, pool, convenient, very helpful English speaking staff. Organizes tours. Highly recommended.
AL **Lenheiros Palace**, Av Pres Tancredo Neves 257, T/F3371 8155. A modern hotel with good facilities, parking, Lenheiros Casa de Chá tea house, breakfast, no restaurant.
A **Ponte Real**, Av Eduardo Magalhães 254, T/F3371 7000. Also modern, comfortable, sizeable rooms, good restaurant.
C **Aparecida**, Praça Dr Antônio Viegas 13, T3371 2540. Central, by the bus and taxi stop, has a restaurant and lanchonete.
C **Pousada Casarão**, opposite São Francisco church, in a converted mansion, Ribeiro Bastos 94, T3371 7447. In a delightful converted mansion house, firm beds, TV, fridge, swimming pool, games room.
D **Brasil**, Av Presidente Tancredo Neves 395, T3371 2804. In an old house full of character and staircases, on the opposite side of the river from the railway station, cheap. Recommended but basic, no breakfast.
D **Sinha Batista**, R Manock Anselmo 22, T3371 5550. The best of the cheaper options, quite large rooms in a colonial building conveniently located by the central canal.

Tiradentes p420
L **Solar da Ponte**, Praça das Mercês (proprietors John and Anna Maria Parsons), T3355 1255, www.solardaponte.com.br. Has the atmosphere of a country house, the price includes breakfast and afternoon tea, only 12 rooms, fresh flowers in rooms, bar, sauna, lovely gardens, swimming pool, light meals for residents only, for larger meals, the hotel recommends 5 local restaurants (it is in the Roteiros de Charme group, see page 346). For horse-riding treks, contact John Parsons here. Recommended.
A **Pousada Mãe D'Água**, Largas das Forras 50, T3355 1206. Including breakfast but not tax, very nice, outdoor pool in garden.
A **Pousada Três Portas**, R Direita 280A, T3355 1444. Charming, central, in restored town house, has sauna, thermal pool, hydromassage, heating.
A **Pouso das Gerais**, R dos Inconfidentes 109, T3355 1234, www.pousodasgerais. com.br. Fresh fan-cooled rooms, TV, marble basins, central, quiet, pool, breakfast included. Recommended.

B-C **Pousada do Arco Iris**, R Frederico Ozanan 340, T3355 1167. The best of a string of pousadas in houses on this stretch of road just out of town. Swimming pool, popular, family-run, 5 rooms only. Price includes breakfast. Book ahead.
C **Pousada do Alferes**, R dos Inconfidentes 479, T3355 1303. Simple but central on the main shopping street close to main square.
C **Pousada do Laurito**, R Direita 187, T3355 1268. Central, good value, very popular with international backpackers.

São Tomé das Letras p421
Streets are hard to follow because their names seem to change almost from one block to the next; numbering is also chaotic. There are lots of pousadas and rooms to let all over town, also many restaurants and bars.
B **Pousada Arco-Iris**, R João Batista Neves 19, T/F3237 1212. Rooms and chalets, sauna, swimming pool.
C **dos Sonhos II** (do Gê), Trav Nhá Chica 8, T3237 1235. Very nice, restaurant, swimming pool, sauna. Recommended.
D pp **Fundação Harmonia**, Estrada para Sobradinho s/n, Bairro do Canta Galo, T3237 1280. 4 km from town, but shop on the main Praça. The community emphasizes several disciplines for a healthy lifestyle, for mind and body, 'new age', workshops, massage, excursions, vegetarian food, clean accommodation.
D-E pp **Pousada Souza Reis**, Praça do Rosário 540, T3237 1264. Next to Igreja de Pedra, with bath and breakfast, TV, good value, helpful.

● Eating

Ouro Preto p417
Try the local liquor de jaboticaba.
♙ **Adega**, R Teixeira Amaral 24, T3551 4171. Vegetarian smorgasbord, all you can eat, 1130-1530. Highly recommended.
♙ **Casa Grande** and **Forno de Barro**, both on Praça Tiradentes (Nos 84 and 54 respectively). Decent Mineira cooking.
♙ **Ouro Grill**, R Sen Rocha Lagoa 61. Self-service at lunchtime, US$5, good value after 1600.
♙ **Taverna do Chafariz**, R São José 167, T3551 2828. Good local food. Recommended.
♙ **Beijinho Doce**, R Direita 134A. Delicious pastries and cakes, try the truffles.
♙ **Café & Cia**, R São José 187, T3551 0711. Closes 2300, very popular, comida por kilo at lunchtime, good salads, juices.
♙ **Deguste**, R São José next to Banco Itaú. Good value.
♙ **Pasteleria Lampião**, Praça Tiradentes. Good views at the back (best at lunchtime).

¶ Vide Gula, R Sen Rocha Lagoa 79ª, T3551 4493.
Food by weight, good, friendly atmosphere.
Recommended.

Mariana *p418*
¶¶ Engenho Nôvo, Praça da Sé 26. Bar at night,
English spoken by the owners and clients.
Recommended.
¶¶ Mangiare della Mamma, D Viçoso 27. Italian.
Recommended.
¶¶ Tambaú, R João Pinheiro 26. Regional food.
¶ Panela de Pedra in the Terminal Turístico
serves food by weight at lunchtime.

São João del Rei *p420*
¶¶¶ Churrascaria Ramón, Praça Severiano
de Resende 52. One of the town's better
churrascarias with generous portions and plenty
of side dishes.
¶¶ Quinto do Ouro, Praça Severiano de Rezende
04, T3371 7577. Tasty and well- prepared regional
food. Said to be the best Mineira cooking in town.
¶¶ Portal del Rey, Praça Severiano de Rezende 134.
Comida à kilo, Minas and Arabic food; good value.
¶ Restaurant 611, R Getúlio Vargas 145, T3371
8793. Very cheap but excellent Mineira cooking –
eat as much as you like for less than US$2. Plenty
of choice, very popular.

Tiradentes *p420*
There are many restaurants, snack bars and
lanchonetes in town and it is a small enough place
to wander around and see what takes your fancy.
¶¶¶ Estalagem, R Ministro G Passos 280. Excellent
and generous traditional Mineira meat dishes.
¶¶¶ Quartier Latin, R São Francisco de Paula 46,
Praça da Rodoviária, T3355 1552. French, cordon
bleu chef, excellent.
¶¶¶ Quinto de Ouro, R Direita 159. Mineira and
international dishes. Recommended.
¶¶¶ Theatro da Vila, R Padre Toledo 157, T3355
1275. Inventive and delicious Franco-Brazilian
fusion cooking served in intimate rustic-chic
dining room. Views out towards the Serra across
the restaurant garden which has a little theatre
with performances in summer.
¶¶¶ Virados do Largo, Largo do Ó. Good Mineira
food and service.
¶ Maria Luisa Casa de Chá, Largo do Ó 1,
diagonally opposite Aluarte, T3355 1502. Tea,
cakes and sandwiches in an arty Bohemian
atmosphere. Great for breakfast.

☻ Bars and clubs

Tiradentes *p420*
Aluarte, Largo do Ó 1, is a bar with live music in
the evening, nice atmosphere, US$4 cover
charge, garden, sells handicrafts.

☻ Festivals and events

Ouro Preto *p417*
Ouro Preto is famous for its **Holy Week**
processions, which in fact begin on the Thu
before Palm Sunday and continue (but not
every day) until Easter Sunday. The most famous
is that commemorating Christ's removal from
the Cross, late on Good Friday. Many shops
close during this holiday, and on winter
weekends. Attracting many Brazilians, **Carnival**
here is also memorable. In **Jun**, **Corpus Christi**
and the **Festas Juninas** are celebrated. Every
Jul the city holds the **Festival do Inverno da
Universidade Federal de Minas Gerais**
(UFMG), the Winter Festival, about 3 weeks of
arts, courses, shows, concerts and exhibitions.
Also in **Jul**, on the 8th, is the **anniversary of the
city**. **15 Aug**: Nossa Senhora do Pilar, patron
saint of Ouro Preto. **12-18 Nov**: Semana de
Aleijadinho, a week-long arts festival.

Congonhas *p419*
Congonhas is famous for its **Holy Week**
processions, which have as their focus the Bom
Jesus church. The most celebrated ceremonies are
the **meeting of Christ and the Virgin Mary** on the
Tue, and the dramatized **Deposition from the
Cross** late on **Good Friday**. The pilgrimage
season, first half of **Sep**, draws thousands. **8 Dec**,
Nossa Senhora da Conceição.

São João del Rei *p420*
Apr, Semana Santa; **15-21 Apr**, Semana da
Inconfidência. **May or Jun**, Corpus Christi. **First
2 weeks of Aug**, Nossa Senhora da Boa Morte,
with baroque music (novena barroca). Similarly, **12
Oct**, Nossa Senhora do Pilar, patron saint of the
city. **8 Dec**, founding of the city. FUNREI, the
university (R Padre José Maria Xavier), holds
Inverno Cultural in **Jul**.

☻ Shopping

Ouro Preto *p417*
Gems are not much cheaper from freelance
sellers in Praça Tiradentes than from the shops,
and in the shops, the same quality of stone is
offered at the same price. If buying on the
street, ask for the seller's credentials. Buy
soapstone carvings at roadside stalls and bus
stops rather than in cities; they are much
cheaper. Many artisans sell carvings, jewellery
and semi-precious stones in Largo de Coimbra
in front of São Francisco de Assis church.
Recommended are: **Gemas de Minas**, Conde
de Bobadela 63; and   **Manoel Bernardis**, Conde
de Bobadela 48.

⊖ Transport

Sabará *p416*
Bus Viação Cisne No 1059 from R Catete, **Belo Horizonte**, US$1, 30 mins, circular route.

Parque Natural de Caraça *p417*
Turn off the BR-262 (towards Vitória) at Km 73 and go via Barão de Cocais to Caraça (120 km). There is no public transport to the seminary. **Buses** go as far as **Barão de Cocais**, from where you have to take a taxi, US$15 one way. You must book the **taxi** to return for you, or else **hitch** (which may not be easy). The park entrance is 10 km before the seminary. The alternatives are either to hire a **car**, or take a guide from Belo Horizonte, which will cost about US$100 (including guiding, transport and meals). It is possible to stay in **Santa Bárbara** (D Hotel Karaibe. D Santa Inés), 25 km away on the road to Mariana and hitchhike to Caraça. 11 buses a day from Belo Horizonte – Santa Bárbara (fewer on Sat and Sun).

Ouro Preto *p417*
Bus Note: Don't walk from the rodoviária to town at night; robberies have occurred. The rodoviária is at R Padre Rolim 661, near São Francisco de Paula church, T3551 1081. A 'Circular' bus runs from the rodoviária to Praça Tiradentes, US$0.55. Taxi US$3. 11 buses a day from Belo Horizonte (2 hrs, Pássaro Verde), US$4.70, taxi US$40. Day trips are run. Book your return journey to **Belo Horizonte** early if returning in the evening; buses get crowded. Bus to/from **Rio**, Útil, 3 a day, US$20, 12 hrs (book in advance). There are also Útil buses to **Congonhas** on the new Caminho de Ouro highway and services to **Conselheiro Lafaiete**, 3-4 a day via Itabirito and Ouro Branco (see below), US$5, 2¾ hrs. Other Útil services to Rio go via Belo Horizonte. Direct buses to **São Paulo**, 3 a day with Cristo Rei, 11 hrs, US$25. **Gontijo** go to Salvador via Belo Horizonte.

Mariana *p418*
Bus Mariana is only 12 km from Ouro Preto and can easily be visited as a side trip. Buses run between the Escola de Minas near Praça Tiradentes in Ouro Preto and the Secretaria de Cultura e Turismo de Mariana, Praça Tancredo Neves, every 30 mins.

Parque Nacional Caparaó *p419*
Bus The park is 49 km by paved road from Manhuaçu (about 190 km south of Governador

Valadares) on the Belo Horizonte-Vitória road (BR-262). There are buses from **Belo Horizonte** (twice daily with **Pássaro Verde**), Ouro Preto or Vitória to **Manhumirim**, 15 km south of Manhuaçu. From Manhumirim, take a bus direct to Alto Caparaó, 8 a day, US$1.30. By **car** from the BR-262, go through Manhumirim, Alto Jaquitibá and Alto Caparaó village, then 1 km further to the Hotel Caparaó Parque.

Congonhas *p419*
Bus The Rodoviária is 1½ km outside town; bus to town centre US$0.55; for 'Basílica', see above. To/from **Belo Horizonte**, 1½ hrs, US$4, 8 times a day. To **São João del Rei**, 2 hrs, US$4.80, tickets are not sold until the bus comes in. Bus to **Ouro Preto**: direct on the new Caminho de Ouro highway, or go via Belo Horizonte or Conselheiro Lafaiete.

São João del Rei *p420*
Bus Rodoviária is 2 km west of the centre. Buses to **Rio**, 5 daily with **Paraibuna** (3 on Sat and Sun), 5 hrs, US$13-16. Cristo Rei to **São Paulo**, 8 hrs, 5 a day, and **Translavras**, 4 a day, US$16.50. **Belo Horizonte**, 3½ hrs, US$8.50. To **Tiradentes** with Meier, 8 a day, 7 on Sat, Sun and holidays, US$0.90.

Tiradentes *p420*
Bus Last bus back to **São João del Rei** is 1815, 2230 on Sun; fares are given above. **Taxi** To **São João del Rei** costs US$13. Around town there are pony-drawn taxis; ponies can be hired for US$6.50.

São Tomé das Letras *p421*
Bus There are 3 daily buses (2 on Sun) to São Tomé from **Tres Corações**, the birthplace of Pelé, the legendary football star (to whom there is a statue in Praça Col José Martins), US$2.15, 1½ hrs (paved road). Tres Corações has hotels and regular buses to **Belo Horizonte**, US$13, 5½ hrs, and **São Paulo**, US$10.25.

⊕ Directory

Ouro Preto *p417*
Banks Banco do Brasil, R São José 189, high commission, changes TCs. Bradesco, corner of Senador Rocha Lagoa and Padre Rolim, opposite the Escola de Minas. Banco 24 Horas, Praça Alves de Brito, next to Correios. **Internet** Point Language School, Xavier da Veiga 501. **Post offices** Praça Alves de Brito. **Voltage** 110 volts AC.

Espírito Santo

The coastal state of Espírito Santo is where mineiros head to for their seaside holidays. The most popular beaches are south of Vitória, the state capital, while north of the city are several turtle-nesting beaches. Inland are immigrant towns.

Vitória and around → *Phone code: 0xx27. Post code: 29000. Colour map 7, grid B6.*

Five bridges connect the island on which Vitória stands with the mainland. The state capital is beautifully set, its entrance second only to Rio's, its beaches quite as attractive, but smaller, and the climate is less humid. Port installations at Vitória and nearby Ponta do Tubarão have led to some beach and air pollution at places nearby. It is largely a modern city: The upper, older part of town, reached by steep streets and steps, is less hectic than the lower harbour area, but both are full of cars. The car-parking boys have their work cut out to find spaces. **Tourist offices**: Only in the rodoviária and at the airport. The airport office is helpful and friendly, with map and leaflets. The rodoviária stand is staffed by students and has little information to give away. For the Secretaria de Turismo, T3322 8282, or 3382 6357/9927 4152. Disque turismo T1677, www.vitoria.es.gov.br. **Ibama**, Avenida Marechal Mascarenhas de Moraes 2487, Caixa Postal 762, Vitória ES, CEP 29000, T3227 5067.

On Av República is the large **Parque Moscoso**, an oasis of quiet, with a lake and playground. Colonial buildings still to be seen in the upper city are the **Capela de Santa Luzia** (1551)① *R José Marcelino, Mon-Fri 0800-1800*. It has a painted altar, otherwise a small open space; the church of **São Gonçalo** (1766)① *R Francisco Araújo, closed to the public*, and the ruins of the **Convento São Francisco** (1591). In the **Palácio Anchieta**, or **do Governo**① *Praça João Climaco (upper city-packed with parked cars)*, is the tomb of Padre Anchieta, one of the founders of São Paulo. Praça João Climaco has some restored buildings around it, including the green Casa do Cidadão. The **Teatro Carlos Gomes** *on Praça Costa Pereira*, often presents plays, also jazz and folk festivals.

Urban beaches such as **Camburi** can be affected by pollution (about 10% according to official sources), but it is pleasant, with a fair surf. Several buses run from the centre to Camburi, but look for one with Av Beira Mar on the destination board, eg No 212. Buses pass Praia do Canto, a smart district with good restaurants and shops, then cross A Ponte de Camburi.

Vila Velha, reached by A Terceira Ponte (the Third Bridge) across the bay, is a separate municipality from Vitória. The Third Bridge, a toll road, is a sweeping structure and one of the symbols of the city. It has an excellent series of beaches: Praia da Costa is the main one, with others, including Itaparica, heading south. The second main symbol of Vila Velha is the monastery of **Nossa Senhora da Penha** (1558) *daily 0530-1645*, on a high hill with superb views of the bay, bridge and both cities. The Dutch attacked it in 1625 and 1640. Minibuses take the infirm and not-so-devout up the hill for US$0.55 return, 0630-1715 (you have to use the phone in the upper car park if you want a ride down). A museum in the convent costs US$0.35. From here you will see that Vila Velha is neither old, nor a small town. It's a built up beachfront city, noisy at times, but the sea suffers less from pollution than Camburi. Vila Velha is the place of origin of Garoto chocolates, whose factory can be visited on weekdays (T3320 1709 for times). **Tourist information**: T3139 9015, www.vilavelha.es.gov.br.

Some 14 km south of Vila Velha is **Barra do Jucu**, which has bigger waves, and the **Reserva de Jacarenema**, which preserves coastal ecosystems.

Inland from Vitória

Santa Leopoldina or **Domingos Martins**, both around 45 km from Vitória, are less than an hour by bus (Pretti to Santa Leopoldina five a day, four on Sunday, Aguia Branca to Domingos Martins; Friday 1700 only). Both villages preserve the architecture and customs of the first German and Swiss settlers who arrived in the 1840s. Domingos Martins (also known as Campinho) has a Casa de Cultura with some items of German settlement. Santa Leopoldina has an interesting **museum**① *Tue-Sun 0900-1100, 1300-1800*, which covers the settlers' first years in the area.

Along the BR-262 west towards Minas Gerais, most of the hills are intensely worked, with very few patches of Mata Atlântica remaining. A significant landmark is the **Pedra Azul**, a huge granite outcrop, with a sheer face (a bit like a massive tombstone). From the side you can see a spur which looks like a finger pointing to the summit. It's a Parque Etadual, whose entrance is on the BR-262. The Pedra Azul bus stop is at the turn-off to the town of Alonso Cláudio ('region of waterfalls'). There are many pousadas around Pedra Azul and the corridor between it and the next town, **Venda Nova do Imigrante**, some 10 km, is obviously in full development. This is a pretty place to stop, with well-tended flower beds along the main street, plenty of eating places, handicrafts and local Italian produce and at least one hotel (Alpes).

Santa Teresa is a charming hill town two hours, 78 km by bus from Vitória. A brochure from the Prefeitura lists local sites of interest including waterfalls, valley views and some history. It also lists where to stay and eat. Fazendas also offer accommodation, days out and rural pursuits. See Santa Teresa's website, www.santateresa-es.com.br for more. In the Galeria de Arte, just past the rodoviária, shops sell handicrafts and lots of sweet things, honey, jams, liqueurs, sweet wines and biscuits. Stalls on the side of the main road also sell local products. There is a museum, botanical garden and small zoo for study of Mata Atlântica wildlife at the **Museu Mello Leitão** ① *Av José Ruschi 4, T3259 1182, 0800-1200, 1300-1700 (closed Mon morning, US$1.* Its library includes the works of the hummingbird and orchid scientist, Augusto Ruschi. Hummingbird feeders are hung outside the administration building.

Guarapari and beaches south of Vitória → *Colour map 7, grid B6. Pop: 88,400.*

South of Vitória (54 km) is Guarapari, whose beaches are the closest to Minas Gerais, so they get very crowded at holiday times. The beaches also attract many people seeking cures for rheumatism, neuritis and other complaints, from the radioactive monazitic sands. Information about the sands can be found at **Setuc** ① *in the Casa de Cultura, Praça Jerônimo Monteiro, T3261 3058,* and at the Antiga Matriz church on the hill in the town centre, built in 1585.

A little further south (20 km) is the fishing village of **Ubu**, then, 8 km down the coast, **Anchieta**. Near here are Praia de Castelhanos (5 km east, on a peninsula) and **Iriri**, a small village with two beaches, Santa Helena and Inhaúma. There is accommodation in these places. The next spot down the coast, 5 km, is **Piúma**, a calm, little-visited place, renowned for its craftwork in shells. About 3 km north of the village is Pau Grande beach, where you can surf. The resort town of **Marataízes**, with good beaches, hotels and camping, is 30 km south of Piúma. It is just north of the Rio state border. Planeta buses go to Mataraízes and Piúma from Vitória.

Turtle beaches

The **Reserva Biológica Comboios** ① *for information, contact Projeto Tamar, Av Paulino Müller 1111, Vitória, T3222 1417, www.projetotamar.org.br, or Toxx27-3274 1209,* 104 km north of Vitória via Santa Cruz, is designed to protect the marine turtles which frequent this coast. **Regência**, at the mouth of the Rio Doce, 65 km north of Santa Cruz, is part of the reserve and has a regional base for Tamar, the national marine turtle protection project.

Linhares, 143 km north of Vitória on the Rio Doce, has good hotels (**E** Modenezi, opposite bus terminal, with bath) and restaurants. It is a convenient starting place for the turtle beaches. Besides those at the mouth of the Rio Doce, there is another Tamar site at **Ipiranga** ① *for information, also contact Tamar, Toxx27-3274 2097,* 40 km east of Linhares by an unmade road.

Itaúnas and around → *Colour map 7, grid B6.*

The most attractive beaches in the state are around **Conceição da Barra** (Population: 26,494; pleasant beach hotels). Corpus Christi (early June) is celebrated with an evening procession for which the road is decorated with coloured wood chips.

Itaúnas ① *getting there: bus from the bakery in Conceição da Barra at 0700, returns 1700,* 27 km north by road, or 14 km up the coast, has been swamped by sand dunes, 30 m high. From time to time, winds shift the sand dunes enough to reveal the buried church tower. Itaúnas has been moved to the opposite river bank. The coast here, too, is a protected turtle breeding ground (Tamar, Caixa Postal 53, Conceição da Barra, Toxx27-762 5196). There are a few pousadas and a small campsite at Itaúnas and other hotels 3 km further north at Guaxindiba.

● Sleeping

Vitória *p426*

A Alice Vitória, R Cnel Vicente Peixoto 95, Praça Getúlio Vargas, T3322 1144, and round the corner, **B São José**, Av Princesa Isabel 300, T3223 7222, www.gruponeffa.com.br. In the busy lower city, good rooms with a/c, TV, comfy beds, typical business hotels, special offers. Both share ₮₮-₮ Pizza Gourmet restaurant, which serves pizza, quick dishes and local specialities, open till 2300, modern cafeteria style, clean, clinical but OK.

C Avenida, Av Florentino Avidos 347, T3071 1031. With breakfast, cheaper without fridge, with TV, simple, thin mattresses, noisy avenue outside. Recommended.

C Vitória, R Cais de São Francisco 85, T3223 0222. Near Parque Moscoso. Comfortable rooms, some with round beds, a/c, TV, rambling building, good restaurant Mar e Sol. Quieter than Avenida.

D Cidade Alta, R Dionisio Rosendo 213, T3322 7188. Cheaper rooms without TV, with breakfast, hot water. Strange place on Cathedral praça, cavernous, basic, full of character.

D Imperial, 7 de Setembro, corner Praça Costa Pereira, T3233 5017. Noisy but cheap, cheaper without TV or bath, good value but tatty, hot water, fan, has its own à kilo restaurant (nearby are lots of other cheap eating places – see below).

Adequate hotels can be found opposite the rodoviária. eg **Minas, Lírio, Spala, JS** and **Príncipe** nearby, which looks posher.

Camburi

A Aruan, Av Dante Michelini 1497, T3334 0777, www.grupohp.com.br. Good beachfront hotel with rooms with views, comfortable, free sauna, pool and internet, massage at R$15, restaurant serving wide variety of dishes, safes in rooms, helpful. In same group (same phones and www): **Porto do Sol**, Av Dante Michelini 3957, and **A Vitória Palace**, R José Teixeira 323, Praia do Canto, T3325 0999.

B Alvetur, Av Dante Michelini 877, T3225 3911, alvetur@matrix.com.br. All the usual facilities of a beachfront hotel, outside a bit faded and plain lobby, but rooms are well-furnished if unfussy, big TV! In same group are **Mata da Praia**, Av Adalberto Simão Nader 133, T3227 9422, matadapraia@matrix.com.br, and **Aeroporto**, R Ary Ferreira Chagas 35, T3325 7888, haeroporto@ ebr.com.br (large rooms, well-furnished, good breakfast), both on way to airport from Camburi beach, and **C Camburi**, Av Dante Michelini 1007, T3334 0303 (rather tatty outside and in lobby).

Vila Velha

B Itaparica Praia, R Itapemirim 30, Coqueirão de Itaparica, Vila Velha, T3329 7385, www.hotelita

parica.com.br. More expensive in high season, rooms with sea view cost a bit more. Huge rooms with fridge and TV, pool, garage, quiet, safe and good. Next door is a good café serving breads cakes, Pão e Companhia (which has other branches).

C Forte Príncipe, R Aracruz 169, Coqueiral de Itaparica, in Vila Velha, 8 km from Vitória, T3339 1605, ask for Marcelo, www.forteprincipe.com.br. Cheaper without a/c and for HI members, all rooms with 2 floors, **F** pp in dorm, kitchen, TV, OK, no meals, garage. Convenient for Carone supermarket, beach and buses.

Jardim da Penha, R Hugo Viola 135, Vitória, T3324 0738, F3325 6010, take 'Universitário' bus, get off at first University stop.

Inland from Vitória: Santa Teresa *p426*

A Pierazzo, Av Getúlio Vargas 115, T3259 1233, pierazzohotel@uol.com.br. Central, nice rooms with frigobar, a/c, comfortable, helpful, small pool, sauna. Recommended.

Itaúnas and around:
Conceição da Barra *p427*

B Pousada Mirante, Av Atlântica 566, T3762 1633. With a/c, completely renovated, spotless, English spoken.

B Pousada Porto Márlin, Praia Guaxindiba, T3762 1800, www.redemarlin.com.br. With a/c, TV, fridge, seaview, waterpark, restaurant and bar.

For other places see www.portonet.com.br/ cb/pousadas.asp).

Camping Camping Clube do Brasil, full facilities, Rodovia Adolfo Serra, Km 16, T3762 1346.

● Eating

Vitória *p426*

A local speciality is *Moqueca capixaba*, a seafood dish served in an earthenware pot. It is a variant of the moqueca which is typical of Bahia. Note that it's big enough for 2 people, but you can get half portions. It is served with rice and siri desfiado, crab and shrimp in a thick sauce, very tasty. Several places on R Joaquim Lírio, Praia do Canto, from breads to pastas to seafood. Lots of lanches etc on R G Neves at Praça Costa Pereira, in the city centre, and pizzas and others on R 7 de Setembro.

₮₮₮ Pirão, R Joaquim Lírio 753, Praia do Canto. Specializes in moqueca, also fish, seafood and a couple of meat dishes. Well-established and rightly highly regarded. Ask for a bib to keep your front clean. Closed in the evening.

₮ Restaurante Expresso, G Neves 22, T3223 1091. A better class of self-service for lunch, good choice and puddings, a/c, clean, popular.

Cafés/padarias

Cheiro Verde, R Prof Baltazar, next to Pão Gostoso. Churrascaria and comida caseira, self-service.

Expressa, as above, next door and open later in afternoon, on G Neves. For good breads, cakes, savouries and cold stuffs.

Pão Gostoso, R Prof Baltazar. Also selling breads, cakes, savouries and cold stuffs.

Inland from Vitória: Santa Teresa *p426*
Zitu's, Av Getúlio Vargas 79. Self-service, good local food. There are many other eating places in the town.

◑ Bars and clubs

Vitória *p426*
The junction of Joaquim Lírio and João da Cruz in Praia do Canto is known as O Triângulo (or Bermuda Triangle). 2 bars at the junction, **Bilac** and **Búfalo Branco** are very popular Fri and Sat with young crowd. Another bar is **Apertura**, J Lírio 811, quieter. All serve food. Many other places in the area, including The Point Plaza. From centre take any bus going to Camburi and get out opposite São José supermarket just before Ponte de Camburi.

◒ Transport

Vitória *p426*
Air Eurico Salles airport is at Goiaberas, 11 km from the city. Several buses go there eg Nos 162, 163, 122, 212. Taxi from centre US$9.50.
Bus City buses are mostly green, US$0.50. No 212 is a good route, from rodoviária to airport, marked Aeroporto; make sure it says Via Av Beira Mar: it goes right along the waterfront, past the docks (ask to be let off for Av Princesa Isabel in centre), Shopping Vitória opposite the State Legislative Assembly, by the Third Bridge, MacDonald's near InJoy internet (look for inverted V arch on right side and immediately ring bell to get off – McDonald's is across the avenue), São José supermarket just before Ponte de Camburi, all along Camburi beach, then turns left to airport.
To Vila Velha: from Vitória take a yellow 500 bus marked 'Vilha Velha' from Praça Getúlio Vargas, or a 514 from Av Mal Mascarenhas de Moraes. No 508 connects Camburi and Vila Velha. Buses back to Vitória leave from the rodoviária, or a stop on Champagnat, almost opposite Carone supermarket, fare US$0.60. In Vila Velha, to get to Coqueiral de Itaparica (see Sleeping), go to the rodoviária and change to a blue bus, Linhas Alimentadores, No 605 or 606, marked T Ibes (ask where to get off) – you shouldn't have to pay for

this connection. For NS da Penha, ask to be let off the yellow bus into Vila Velha on Av Henrique Moscoso at or near R Antônio Ataíde, which you go down (right from direction of bus) to R Vasco Coutinho then turn right.

The rodoviária is a 15-min walk west of the centre; many buses go there and there is a city bus stop just outside. It has good lanches, sweet shops and toilets (R$0.70). **Rio**, 8 hrs, US$22 (leito 44). **Belo Horizonte**, see above. **Ouro Preto**, São Geraldo US$18, 6 hrs, poor road, also **Itapemirim**, which goes to other Minas Gerais destinations. **Rio Doce** to **Juiz da Fora** and **southern Minas Gerais**. **São Paulo**, US$38, 16 hrs (leito 69). **Salvador**, 18 hrs, US$69, **Aguia Branca** at 1700; **Porto Seguro** direct 11 hrs with lots of stops **Aguia Branca**, 2 a day, US$35; alternatively, take a bus to Eunápolis, then change to buses which run every hour. **Alvorada** bus from Vitória to **Guarapari**, 1½ hours, several daily, US$3.
Train Daily passenger service to **Belo Horizonte**, departs 0700, arrives Belo Horizonte at 1940, returns 0730, arrives 2100; US$17 executivo (very comfortable), US$11 econômico. T0800 992233, CAP Centro de atendimento de pasageiros. The station is called Pedro Nolasco, Km 1 BR-262: take a yellow bus saying 'Ferroviária', best is No 515 going to Campo Grande; to the city (cross the main road outside the station), Praia do Canto and Camburi, take a 'T Laranjeiras via Beira Mar' bus.

Inland from Vitória: Santa Teresa *p426*
Bus Several buses daily from **Vitória** rodoviária with **Lirio dos Vales**, US$4.25, most go via Fundão on the BR-101 going north, all paved. Fewer buses via Santa Leopoldina, not all paved, a beautiful journey.

◐ Directory

Vitória *p426*
Airline offices TAM, R Eugênio Neto 111, T3325 1222. **Varig, RioSul, Nordeste**, R Eugênio Neto 68, T3227 1588, Mon-Fri 0900-1730, Sat 0900-1200. For both, take Praia do Canto bus 101 and ask for Praia Shopping – they are opposite each other. **Banks** Banco do Brasil, Praça Pio XII, câmbio 1000-1600. ATM for Visa. Other banks close by. HSBC, Av Princesa Isabel 43, changes TCs, but very slow and 6% commission. **Car rental** Agencies at airport. **Internet** In Joy, Av Saturnino de Brito 169, Praia do Canto, T3225 2114, close behind McDonalds. Loads of machines, fast, US$0.55 per hr. Mon-Fri 1000- 2200, Sat-Sun 1200-2200. **Telephones** Rios phone office (Telemar) on Praça Costa Pereira.

North of Belo Horizonte

Diamantina, the most remote of the colonial cities to the north of the State capital is reached from Belo Horizonte by taking the paved road to Brasília (BR-040). Turn northeast to **Curvelo**, beyond which the road passes through the impressive rocky country of the Serra do Espinhaço. Equally remote is the town of Serro, while in the Serra do Espinhaço itself is the Cipó national park, protecting high mountain grassland and rare species.

Diamantina → *Phone code: 0xx38. Post code: 39100. Colour map 7, grid A5. Population: 44,259.*
This centre of a once active diamond industry Diamantina has excellent colonial buildings. Its churches (difficult to get into, except for the modern cathedral) are not as grand as those of Ouro Preto, but it is the least spoiled of all the colonial mining cities, with carved overhanging roofs and brackets. This very friendly, beautiful town is in the deep interior, amid barren mountains. It is lively at weekends. President Juscelino Kubitschek, the founder of Brasília, was born here. His **house** ① *R São Francisco 241, Tue-Thu 0900-1700, Fri-Sat 0900-1800, Sun 0900-1400*, is now a museum. Festivals include Carnival, 12 September is O Dia das Serestas, the Day of the Serenades, for which the town is famous; this is also the anniversary of Kubitschek's birth. **Departamento de Turismo** ① *Casa de Cultura, Praça Antônio Eulálio 53, 3rd floor, T3531 1636*; pamphlets, reliable map, friendly and helpful, free tour of churches with guide (tip guide).

Sights The oldest church in Diamantina is **Nossa Senhora do Rosário** *Largo Dom Joaquim, Tue-Sat 0800-1200, 1400-1800, Sun 0800-1200*, built by slaves in 1728. **Nossa Senhora do Carmo** *R do Carmo, Tue-Sat 0800-1200, 1400-1800, Sun 0800-1200*, dates from 1760-1765 and was built for the Carmelite Third Order. It is the richest church in the town, with fine decorations and paintings and a pipe organ, covered in gold leaf, made locally.

São Francisco de Assis ① *R São Francisco, just off Praça JK, Sat 0800-1200, 1400-1800, Sun 0900-1200*, was built between 1766 and the turn of the 19th century. It is notable for its paintings and has been renovated (2006)S. Other colonial churches are the **Capela Imperial do Amparo** (1758-1776), **Nossa Senhora das Mercês** (1778-1784) and **Nossa Senhora da Luz** (early 19th century). The **Catedral Metropolitana de Santo Antônio** *on Praça Correia Rabelo*, was built in the 1930s in neo-colonial style to replace the original cathedral.

After repeated thefts, the diamonds of the **Museu do Diamante** ① *R Direita 14, Tue-Sat 1200-1730, Sun 0900-1200, US$1*, are now kept in the Banco do Brasil. The museum houses an important collection of materials used in the diamond industry, plus oratories and iron collars used to shackle slaves. **Casa de Chica da Silva** ① *Praça Lobo Mesquita 266, Tue-Sat 1200-1730, Sun 0900-1200, free*. Chica da Silva was a slave in the house of the father of Padre Rolim (one of the Inconfidentes). She became the mistress of João Fernandes de Oliveira, a diamond contractor. Chica, who died 15 February 1796, has become a folk-heroine among Brazilian blacks.

Behind the 18th century building which now houses the **Prefeitura Municipal** (originally the diamonds administration building, Praça Conselheiro Matta 11) is the **Mercado Municipal** or **dos Tropeiros** (muleteers) *Praça Barão de Guaicuí*. The **Casa da Glória** *R da Glória 297, Tue-Sun 1300-1700*, is two houses on either side of the street connected by an enclosed bridge. It contains the Instituto Eschwege de Geologia.

Walk along the **Caminho dos Escravos**, the old paved road built by slaves between the mining area on Rio Jequitinhonha and Diamantina. A guide is essential (ask at the Casa de Cultura), and beware of snakes and thunderstorms. Along the river bank it is 12 km on a dirt road to **Biribiri**, a pretty village with a well-preserved church and an abandoned textile factory. It also has a few bars and at weekends it is a popular, noisy place. About half-way, there are swimming pools in the river; opposite them, on a cliff face, are animal paintings in red. The age and origin are unknown. The plant life along the river is interesting and there are beautiful mountain views.

At **São Gonçalo do Rio das Pedras** and **Milo Verde** (35 and 42 km south of Diamantina on an unsealed road), there are trails for hiking and riding, waterfalls and some colonial buildings in the towns. Simple lodging is available.

The sleepy little town of **São Gonçalo do Rio Preto**, which sits next to a beautiful mountain river, is famous for its traditional festivals. It lies some 60 km from Diamantina on the edge of the **Parque Estadual de São Gonçalo do Rio Preto**, an area of pristine *cerrado* filled with flowering trees and particularly rich in birdlife. There are *pousadas* in São Gonçalo and cabins in the park (reachable by taxi). Guides are also available.

Serro → *Phone code: 0xx38. Post code: 39150. Colour map 7, grid B5. Population: 21,012.*
From Diamantina, 92 km by paved road and reached by bus from there or from Belo Horizonte, is this unspoiled colonial town on the Rio Jequitinhonha. It has six fine baroque churches, a museum and many beautiful squares. It makes queijo serrano, one of Brazil's best cheeses, being in the centre of a prosperous cattle region. The most conspicuous church is **Santa Rita** on a hill in the centre of town, reached by a long line of steps. On the main Praça João Pinheiro, by the bottom of the steps, is **Nossa Senhora do Carmo**, arcaded, with original paintings on the ceiling and in the choir. The town has two large mansions: those of the **Barão de Diamantina** *Praça Presidente Vargas*, now in ruins, and of the **Barão do Serro** ① *across the river on R da Fundição, Tue-Sat 1200-1700, Sun 0900-1200*, beautifully restored and used as the town hall and Casa de Cultura. The **Museu Regional Casa dos Ottoni**, *Praça Cristiano Ottoni 72*, is an 18th-century house with furniture and objects from the region. There are hotels in town.

Parque Nacional da Serra do Cipó

① *Toxx31 3718 7228, www.guiaserradocipo.com.br/parquenacional.*
About 105 km northeast of Belo Horizonte, **Parque Nacional da Serra do Cipó**, 33,400 sq km of the Serra do Espinhaço, covers important cerrado and gallery forest habitats, which provide a home for rare bird species like the Cipó Canastero and Grey-backed Tachuri, as well as endangered mammals such as maned wolf and monkeys such as the masked titi and brown capuchin. There are a number of carnivorous plants. The predominant habitat is high mountain grassland, with rocky outcroppings. Take a guide because the trails are unmarked; ask locally.

● Sleeping

Diamantina *p430*
All are within 10 mins walking distance of the centre unless otherwise stated.
AL Pousada do Garimpo, Av da Saudade 265, T3531 1044, www.pousadadogarimpo.com.br. Plain, well-kept rooms in a smart hotel on the outskirts, pool, sauna, restaurant serving some of the city's best Minas cooking.
A Relíquias do Tempo, R Macau de Baixo 104, T3531 1627, www.diamantinanet.com.br/pousadareliquiasdotempo. Cosy rooms in a pretty 19th-century house just off Praça JK, decorated like a colonial family home, generous breakfasts.
B Tijuco, R Macau de Melo 211, T3531 1022, www.hoteltijuco.com.br. A deliciously dated Niemeyer building with tastefully renovated plush wood interior and rooms which retain their 60s feel, great views.
B-C Montanhas de Minas, R da Roman 264, T3531 3240, www.montanhasdeminas.com.br. Spacious rooms with stone floors, some with balconies, decent breakfasts.
C Pousada da Seresta, R Jogo da Bola 415, T3531 2368. Rambling colonial house, quiet, good views.
C-D Pousada Ouro de Minas, R do Amparo 90A, T3531 2306. Simple well-kept rooms with tiny bathrooms in a converted colonial house.
C-D Santiago, Largo Dom João 133, T3431 3407, hotelsantiago@jk.net. Plain, small but spruce rooms, reasonable breakfast.
C-D Pousada dos Cristais, R Joga da Bola 53, T3531 3923, www.diamantinanet.com.br/pousadadoscristais. A range of simple, large rooms in white on the edge of town, with views across the mountains.

C-E Pousada Dona Daizinha, R Direita 131, T3531 1351. Simple wood-floor rooms in a colonial house; some with space for up to 5. Very good breakfast and friendly service.

Parque Nacional da Serra do Cipó *p431*
LL Toucan Cipó, exclusively through www.dehouche.com as part of a tour. Luxury *fazenda* in prisitine *cerrado* forest cut by clear-water streams. Very rich in bird and mammal life.
AL-A Cipó Veraneio, Rodovia MG-10, Km 95, Jaboticatubas, www.cipoveraneiohotel.com.br. Comfortable a/c rooms with cable TV, fridge, in terraces of stone cabins, pool, sauna, very good tour operator and a *cachaça* distillery just up the road which produces some of Minas's finest.

❷ Eating

Diamantina *p430*
♈♈♈ Cantina do Marinho, R Direita 113, T3531 1686. Formal, decorated with bottles of wine, black-tie waiters is celebrated for its *Salmão Provençale* and *Bacalhau*. Set lunch ♈.
♈♈ Caipirão, R Campos Carvalho 15, T3531 1526. Minas cooking with buffet lunch cooked over a traditional wood-fired clay oven, evening à la carte.
♈♈ Grupiara, R Campos Carvalho 12, T3531 3887. Decent regional cooking, convivial atmosphere, good value per kilo options at lunch.
♈♈ Recanto do Antônio, Beco da Tecla 39, T3531 1147. Minas food and decent steaks, chic rustic dining room in a colonial house.
♈ Sisisi, Beco da Mota 89, T3531 3071. Pasta, Minas cooking and good value *prato feito* at lunchtime.

① Bars and clubs

Diamantina *p430*
Apocalipse Point, Praça Barão de Guaicuí 78, T3531 9296. Sertaneja and Axe music. Lively.
Café a Baiuca, Rua da Quitanda. Coffee bar by day, funky bar by night with music DVDs and a crowd spilling out into the street.
Espaço B, R Beco da Tecla. A bookshop café serving crêpes and draught beer until late.

⊛ Festivals and events

Diamantina *p430*
Vesperatas, musicians and singers serenade from balconies along the colonial streets and drum troupes and bands parade every other Sat.

▲ Activities and tours

Diamantina *p430*
Diamantina Tour, Praça dos Garimpeiros 616, T8801 1802. City tours, adventure activities

(rappel and trekking) and trips to nearby natural attractions and Biri Biri. From US$8 pp per day.
Real Receptivo, R Campos Carvalho 19 loja 12, T3531 1636, www.realreceptivo.com.br. City tours and trips to nearby natural attractions.

⊜ Transport

Diamantina *p430*
Bus To **São Gonçalo do Rio Preto**, one bus per day. 6 buses a day to **Belo Horizonte**, via Curvelo, with **Pássaro Verde**: 2½ hrs to **Curvelo**, US$3, to **Belo Horizonte**, US$20, 5 hrs. To **Bahia**, 2 buses to **Araçuaí** per day (4 hrs); from here combis and buses run to **Itaubim** from where there are connections to Porto Seguro and other destinations in Bahia. For **Brasília**: 1 bus a day to **Montes Claros** for connections, also to Parque Nacional Grande Sertão Veredas; or connect in **Curvelo**, take any Belo Horizonte bus.

Parque Nacional da Serra do Cipó *p431*
Bus Take bus to Serro (2 daily) for Santa Ana do Riacho and the Serra do Cipó.

Southern Brazil → *Population: 9.5 million.*

Southern Brazil comprises three states: Paraná, Santa Catarina and Rio Grande do Sul. Paraná has one of the premier tourist sites in South America, the Iguaçu Falls, described in its own section (see page 457). The Paraná coastline, albeit short, has a large area of coastal rainforest and little beach-fringed islands, like Ilha do Mel. Its main port, Paranaguá, is connected with the capital, Curitiba, by one of the most impressive railways in South America. It is the coast, however, from which Santa Catarina gains most of its reputation, with highly regarded surfing beaches and a growing interest in whale watching. Inland, the state has a distinctive European feel, including frosty and snowy winters in the highest parts. The culture of the region has been heavily influenced by large immigrant communities from Japan, Germany, Poland, Italy, Syria and the Ukraine. In Rio Grande do Sul this can be seen (and tasted) in the Italian communities, well-known for their wines. The southernmost state, as well as having yet more beaches, has some beautiful national parks, the remnants of Jesuit missions and the south's largest industrial centre, Porto Alegre. But above all, this is the land of the gaúcho, the Brazilian cowboy.

Curitiba and around → *Phone code: 0xx41. Post code: 80000. Colour map 7, grid C2.*

Situated in the Serra do Mar, Curitiba is regarded as one of Brazil's model cities for quality of life. It has something of a European feel, with leafy squares and a street that is open 24 hours. It makes a pleasant base for exploring the coast and the surrounding mountains, and is the start of one of the world's most spectacular railway journeys.

Ins and outs

Tourist offices Paranatur ① *R Deputado Mário de Barros 1290, Centro Cívico, T3313 3500, www.pr.gov.br/turismo*. **Disque Turismo** ① *T3254 1516 (state), T3352 8000 (city)*; also booths at the airport and Rodoferroviária (T3320 3121, 0700-1300). **Kiosk** ① *R 24 Horas, T3324 7036, 0800-2400, 2200 at weekends*. Annual *Guía Turística de Curitiba e Paraná*, US$4, on sale at kiosks; free weekly leaflet, *Bom Programa*, available in shops, cinemas, paper stands.

Sights

One of the cleanest cities in Latin America, the capital of Paraná state has extensive open spaces and some exceptionally attractive modern architecture. The commercial centre is the busy R 15 de Novembro, part of which is a pedestrian area called **Rua das Flores**. The **Boca Maldita** is a particularly lively part where local artists exhibit. On Praça Tiradentes is the **Cathedral** ① *R Barão do Serro Azul 31, T3324 5136*, built in neo-gothic style and inaugurated in 1893 (restored in 1993). Behind the cathedral, near Largo da Ordem, is a pedestrian area with a flower clock and old buildings, very beautiful in the evening when the old lamps are lit – nightlife is concentrated here. The oldest church in Curitiba is the **Igreja de Ordem Terceira da São Francisco das Chagas**, built in 1737 in Largo da Ordem. Its most recent renovation was in 1978-1980. In its annex is the **Museu de Arte Sacra** *T3321 3265*. The **Igreja de Nossa Senhora do Rosário de São Benedito** was built in the Praça Garibáldi in 1737 by slaves and was the Igreja dos Pretos de São Benedito. It was demolished in 1931 and a new church was inaugurated in 1946. A mass for tourists, Missa do Turista, is held on Sunday at 0800. An art market is held in **Praça Garibáldi** on Sunday mornings. **Museu Paranaense** ① *in the Palácio São Francisco, R Kellers 289, T3304 3300, www.pr.gov.br/museupr/, Tue-Fri 0930-1730, Sat-Sun 1100-1500,* holds permanent and temporary exhibitions, including documents, manuscripts, ethnological and historical material, stamps, works of art, photographs and archaeological pieces.

Museu de Arte Contemporânea ① *R Desembargador Westphalen 16, Praça Zacarias, T3222 5172, Tue-Fri 1000- 1900, Sat-Sun 1000-1600,* displays Brazilian contemporary art in its many forms, with an emphasis on artists from Paraná. All that remains of the old **Palácio Avenida** ① *Travessa Oliveira Belo 11, T3321 6249,* is the façade, which was retained during remodelling works in 1991. Nowadays it has offices, an auditorium for 250 people and cultural activities. A fine example of the use of steel and glass is **Rua 24 Horas**, where the whole street is protected by an arched roof. The street's shops, bars and restaurants never close. On Saturday mornings there is a small fish fair at **Praça Generosa Marques**.

North of the centre, the **Solar do Barão** ① *R Presidente Carlos Cavalcanti 53, T3321 3240,* built in 1880-1883, is used for concerts in the auditorium and exhibitions. The **Passeio Público**, in the heart of the city (closed Monday), inaugurated in 1886. It has three lakes, each with an island, and playground. The **Centro Cívico** is at the end of Av Dr Cândido de Abreu, 2 km from the centre: a monumental group of buildings dominated by the **Palácio Iguaçu**, headquarters of the state and municipal governments. In a patio behind it is a relief map to scale of Paraná. The **Bosque de João Paulo II** behind the Civic Centre on R Mateus Leme, was created in December 1980 after the Pope's visit to Curitiba. It also contains the **Memorial da Imigração Polonesa no Paraná** (Polish immigrants memorial). The **Museu Oscar Niemeyer** ① *R Mal Hermes 999, T3350 4400, Tue-Sun 1000-1800, US$2,* which opened in 2003 was designed by, and is devoted to the famous Brazilian modernist architect who designed Brasília and was a disciple of Le Corbusier, together with other Paranense artists. The stunning principal building is shaped like a giant eye. An underground passage, lined with exhibits and photographs, links it to a sculpture garden.

About 4 km east of the rodoferroviário, the **Jardim Botânico Fanchette Rischbieter** has a fine glass house, inspired by Crystal Palace in London. The gardens are in the French style and there is also a **Museu Botânico** ① *R Ostoja Roguski (Primeira Perimetral dos Bairros), T3362 1800 (museum), 0600-2000.* Take the orange Expreso buses from Praça Rui Barbosa.

Parque Nacional Vila Velha → *Colour map 7, grid C2.*

① *The park office (phone, toilets, lanchonete, tourist information) is 300 m from the highway and the park a further 1½ km (entrance – also to Furnas, keep the ticket – US$2.50 – opens 0800). Allow all day if visiting all 3 sites (unless you hitch, or can time the buses well, it's a lot of walking).*

West of Curitiba on the road to Ponta Grossa is the **Museu Histórico do Mate** ① *T3304 3300, free, BR 277 at Km 17 (closed for restoration in 2006),* an old water-driven mill where mate was prepared. On the same road is Vila Velha, 91 km from Curitiba: the sandstone rocks have been weathered into most fantastic shapes. About 4 km away are the **Furnas** *US$0.25,* three water holes, the deepest of which has a lift (US$1.30 – not always working) which descends almost to water level. Also in the park is the Lagoa Dourada (surrounded by forest) whose water level is the same as that in the Furnas.

● **Sleeping** → *See Telephone, page 347, for important phone changes.*

Curitiba *p432, map p434*

There are some good value hotels in the
A and **B** categories. Some of the cheaper central
hotels are seedy and charge by the hour. There
are good hotels southeast of the centre in the
vicinity of the Rodoferroviária, but the cheaper
ones are close to the wholesale market, which
operates noisily throughout the night.

L Bourbon & Tower, R Cândido Lopes 102, T3221
4600, www.bourbon.com.br. Good modern hotel
in the centre with a mock old-fashioned charm,
rooms have jacuzzis, business centre.

L Grand Hotel Rayon, R Visconde de Nácar
1424, T2108 1100, www.rayon.com.br. Central,
much the best option for business travellers with
all the expected services, pool, saunas, well-
equipped gym and travel agency.

AL Del Rey, R Ermelino de Leão 18, T2106 0099,
www.hoteldelrey.com.br. Central, upmarket yet
relaxed, large rooms, good restaurant, gym, good
value. Recommended.

AL Slaviero Braz, Av Luis Xavier 67, T3017 1000,
www.hotelslaviero.com.br. Refurbished hotel in a

1940s building preserved as 'Patrimonio
Historico', business facilities.

A Deville Express, R Amintas de Barros 73,
T3883 4777, www.deville.com.br. New
central hotel with a bar, small modest
restaurant, a/c, with fridge.

A-B King's, Av Silva Jardim 264, T3322 8315,
king@kinghotel.com.br. Good apartment hotel,
secure. Highly recommended.

B Bourbon Express, Av Visconde de Guarapuava
4889, T3342 7990, www.bourbon.com.br. A/c,
modern and comfortable, good breakfast,
wireless internet in rooms US$3/day, attentive
service, good value.

B Lumini, R Gen Carneiro, T/F3264 5244,
www.hotellumini.com.br. Good apartment hotel
in a quiet street, all rooms a/c.

B Nova Lisboa, Av 7 de Setembro 1948, T3264
1944. With breakfast, bargain for cheaper rates
without breakfast. Recommended.

B O'Hara, R 15 de Novembro 770, T3232 6044,
hotelohara@ig.com.br. Good location, fan, excellent
breakfast, parking.

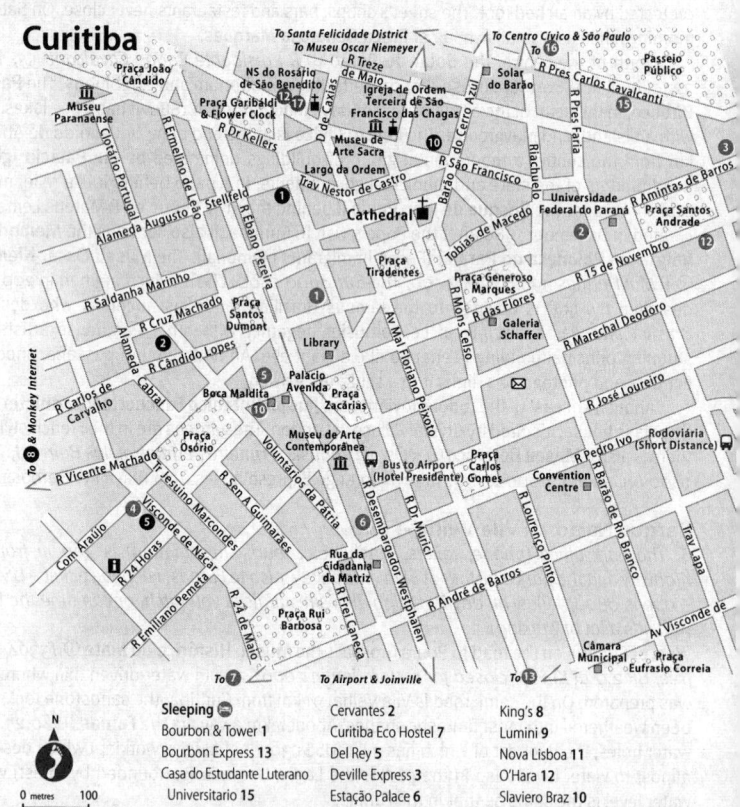

Sleeping ●

Bourbon & Tower 1	Cervantes 2
Bourbon Express 13	Curitiba Eco Hostel 7
Casa do Estudante Luterano	Del Rey 5
Universitario 15	Deville Express 3
Casa dos Estudantes 16	Estação Palace 6
	Grand Hotel Rayon 4

King's 8
Lumini 9
Nova Lisboa 11
O'Hara 12
Slaviero Braz 10

C Cervantes, R Alfredo Bufrem 66, T3222 9593, cervantes@brturbo.com.br. Central, small but cosy.
C Estação Palace, R Des Westphalen, 126, T3322 9840, www.hotel-curitiba.com.br/estacao. Excellent for price, 24-hr room service and internet, rather stark but immaculate. Recommended.
E Casa do Estudante Luterano Universitario, R Pr Cavalcanti, T3324 3313. For those with ISIC student cards, good.
E Casa dos Estudantes, Parque Passeio Público, north side. Also for those with ISIC student cards, 4 nights or more.
E pp Curitiba Eco Hostel, R Luiz Tramontin 1693, Campo Comprido, T3274 7979, www.curitibaeco hostel.com.br. Cheaper for HI members, **C** in double room, youth hostel association for Paraná is located in this suburb outside the centre – catch a bus from the Rodoviária to Praça Rui Barbosa, marked Expreso Centenário, then change to a Tramontina bus to the door.
Camping Camping Clube do Brasil, BR-116, Km 84, 16 km towards São Paulo, T358 6634.

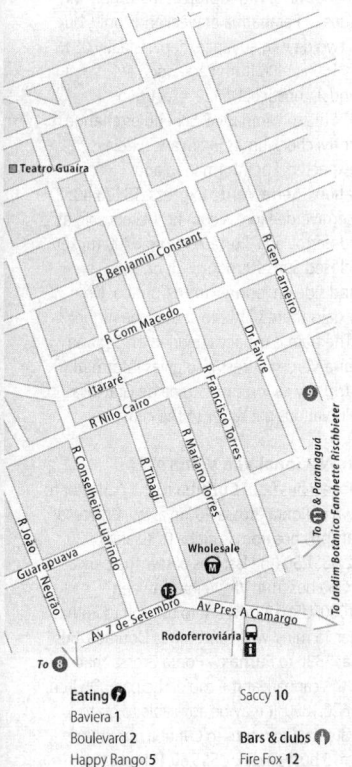

🍴 Eating

Curitiba *p432, map p434*
Cheap food also near the old railway station and good meals in the bus station. Close to the Rodoferroviária is the market, where there are a couple of lanchonetes. Hot sweet wine sold on the streets in winter helps keep out the cold.
🍴🍴🍴 Boulevard, R Vol da Patria 539 (centre). The city's most celebrated restaurant serving a mix of French, Italian and Brazilian cooking. Closed Sun.
🍴🍴 Baviera, Al Augusto Stellfield, at Av Dr Murici (centre). A Curitiba institution, established over 30 years and serving pizza in an intimate beer cellar setting. Also deliver. Open 1830-0100.
🍴🍴 Saccy, R São Franscisco 350. Pizza, tapas and a popular bar with very good live music.
🍴🍴 Salmão, R Emiliano Perneta 924. In historic house, delicious fish and pizza, special promotions, live music every night, open until 0100. Short taxi ride from centre.
🍴 Kisco, 7 de Setembro near Tibagi. Good, huge prato do dia, friendly.
🍴 Happy Rango, Av Visconde de Nacar, 1350, near R 24 horas. Brightly lit, basic corner joint selling fast food and pizzas, open 24 hrs.
🍴 Mister Sheik, Av Vicente Machado, 534. Arabic fast food in pitta with salad, popular for deliveries. Recommended.

🍸 Bars and clubs

Curitiba *p432, map p434*
A cluster of bars at the Largo da Ordem have tables and chairs on the pavement, music, and bar food: **Fire Fox**, Av Jaime Reis 46, flanked by **Tuba's** and **The Farm**.

🎬 Entertainment

Curitiba *p432, map p434*
Cinema There are cinemas in several shopping centres, and other places showing international films. Tickets are usually US$4-5 Mon-Thu, and US$6-8 at weekends. Best to look in the newspaper for music and what's on in the bars, clubs and theatres; *Gazeta do Povo* has a what's on section called *Caderno G*.
Theatres Theatre festival in Mar. **Teatro Guaíra**, R 15 de Novembro, T3304 7999, www.pr.gov.br/ teatroguaira. For plays and revues (also has free events – get tickets early in the day).

🛍 Shopping

Curitiba *p432, map p434*
Handicrafts Feira de Arte e Artesanato, Praça Garibáldi, Sun 0900-1400.

Lojas de Artesanato, Casa de Artesanato Centro, R Mateus Leme 22, T352 4021.
Lojas de Artesanato 'Feito Aqui', Dr Muricy 950, International Airport and Shopping Mueller.
Lojas Leve Curitiba, at several locations, R 24 Horas, Afonso Pena airport, Ópera de Arame, Jardim Botánico, Memorial de Curitiba.

▲▲ Activities and tours

Curitiba *p432, map p434*
BMP Turismo, R Brigadeiro Franco, 1845, T3322 8566. American Express representative, emergency cash available with Amex.
Rostel, R 13 de Maio 894, Alto São Francisco, T3322 2610, www.rostelturismo.com.br. Very helpful.
Scubasul, in same building as Rostel, T3232 0198, www.scubasul.com.br. Advice on diving, courses arranged, reasonable prices.

⊖ Transport

Curitiba *p432, map p434*
Air Afonso Pena (21 km away) for international and national flights, T3381 1515; good services: ATMs, left luggage, hotel booking desk, and cafés. Daily flights from Rio, São Paulo, Buenos Aires, Asunción, and cities in the interior of Paraná state. Two types of bus run from the Rodoferroviária to the airport, making several stops along the way: **Aeroporto Executivo**, 0500-2330 daily, 20 mins, US$3; regular city bus, 40 mins, US$1.

Bus There are several route types on the integrated transport system and you are advised to pick up a map with details. **Express** are red and connect the transfer terminals to the city centre, pre-paid access, they use the silver 'tubo' bus stops; **Feeder** orange conventional buses connect the terminals to the surrounding neighbourhoods; **Interdistrict** green buses run on circular routes connecting transfer terminals and city districts without passing through the centre; **Direct or speedy** silver grey buses use the 'tubo' stations to link the main districts and connect the surrounding municipalities with Curitiba; **Conventional** yellow buses operate on the normal road network between the surrounding municipalities, the Integration Terminals and the city centre; **City circular** white mini buses, **Linha Turismo**, circle the major transport terminals and points of interest in the traditional city centre area. US$4.50 (multi-ticket booklets available), every 30 mins from 0900-1700, except on Mon. First leaves from R das Flores, narrow street in front of McDonalds. Three stops allowed.

Short-distance bus services within the metropolitan region (up to 40 km) begin at Terminal Guadalupe at R João Negrão s/n. The

Terminal Rodoviário/Estação Rodoferroviária is on Av Afonso Camargo s/n, T3320 3000, for other cities in Paraná and other states. Restaurants, banks, bookshops, shops, phones, post office, pharmacy, tourist agency, tourist office and public services are all here. Frequent buses to **São Paulo** (6 hrs, US$13-16.50) and **Rio** (12 hrs, US$33, leito US$56). To **Foz do Iguaçu**, 10 a day, 10 hrs, US$20. **Porto Alegre**, 10 hrs, US$23.
Florianópolis, US$16, 4½ hrs; **Blumenau** 4 hrs, US$8.50, 3 daily with **Penha/ Catarinense**. Good service to most destinations in Brazil. **Pluma** bus to **Buenos Aires** (change buses at Foz de Iguaçu) and to **Asunción**. TTL runs to **Montevideo**, 26 hrs, 0340 departure (semi-cama).

Train Rodoferroviária, Av Afonso Camargo s/n. There are two trains running on the line from Curitiba to **Morretes** and **Paranaguá**: the **Litorina**, a modern a/c railcar with on-board service with bilingual staff, which stops at Morretes, with a halt at Marumbi Park station; hand luggage only; tickets can be bought two days in advance; departs Sat, Sun and holidays 0915, returns 1500, US$51 one way, 3 hrs. Also the **Trem Classe Convencional**, which runs daily to Morretes, with a stop at Marumbi, and continues to Paranaguá at weekends only, buy tickets two days in advance, departs daily 0815, returns 1500 (1400 from Paranaguá at weekends), turístico, US$22, executivo US$34, 4 hrs to Paranaguá. Schedules change frequently; check times in advance; delays to be expected. For information and reservations, **Serra Verde Express**, T3323 4007, www.serraverdeexpress.com.br. Tickets sold at the Rodoferroviária, Portão 8, from 0700 (ticket office closed Sun afternoon). Sit on the left-hand side on journey from Curitiba. On cloudy days there's little to see on the higher parts. The train is usually crowded on Sat and Sun. Serra Verde Express also gives information about trips by car on the Estrada de Graciosa and sells various packages to the coast.

Parque Nacional Vila Velha *p433*
Bus Take a bus from **Curitiba** to the park, not to the town of Ponta Grossa 26 km away. **Princesa dos Campos** bus from Curitiba 0730 and 0930, 1½ hrs, US$7.50 (the last bus passes the park at 1600). One bus from Vila Velha between 1530-1600, US$0.85, 4½ km to turn-off to Furnas (another 15 mins' walk) and Lagoa Dourada. Bus Mon-Sat 1330 to **Furnas** – Ponta Grossa that passes the car park at the top of the park. On Sun, 1200,1620,1800. It may be advisable to go to Ponta Grossa and return to Curitiba from there (114 km, 6 buses a day, US$5.60, **Princesa dos Campos**, also with buses to **Foz do Iguaçu**, 9 hrs), www.princesadoscampos.com.br.

☉ Directory

Curitiba *p432, map p434*
Airline offices BRA, T3323 1073, airport T3381 1383. **TAM**, R Ermelino Leão 511, T3219 1200. **Trip**, at airport, T3381 1710. **Varig**, at airport, T3381 1644. **Banks** Bradesco, R 15 de Novembro 155, Visa ATM. Plus or Cirrus associated credit cards can cash money at Citibank, R Marechal Deodoro 711 or at Buenos Aires 305 near Shopping Curitiba. Cotação, R Marechal Deodoro 500, 2nd floor, Centro. Also Galeria Suissa, R Marechal Deodoro 280, open Sat when many others are closed. Diplomata, R Presidente Faria 145 in the arcade. **Cultural centres** British Council, R Pres Faria 51, T3232 2912, curitiba@britishcouncil.org.br. Instituto Goethe, R Reinaldino S de Quadros 33, T3262 8422, www.goethe.de/ins/br/cur/deindex.htm. **Embassies and consulates** Austria, R Cândido Hartmann 570, Ed Champagnat, 28th floor, T3336 1166, Mon-Fri 1000-1300. **Denmark**, R Prof Francisco Ribeiro 683, T3641 1112, saio@novozymes.com. **France**, R Conselheiro Laurindo 490, 10th floor, T3320 5805, consuldefrance@softcall.com.br. **Germany**, R Emiliano Perneta 297, 2nd floor, T3222 6920, Mon-Fri 0800-1200. **Netherlands**, Av Candido de Abreu 469, conj 1606, T353 2630,

holland@telecorp.com.br, open 1400-1700, except emergencies. **UK**, R Pres Faria 51, 2nd floor, T3322 1202, consulado.britanico@mais.sul.com.br. Mon-Fri 0830-1200, 1400-1730. **Uruguay**, Av Carlos Cavalho 417, 32 floor, T3225 5550, conurucur@terra.com.br . **Internet** at Livraria Saraiva in Shopping Crystal, Livraria Curitiba, R das Flores (US$2 per hr), and Estação Plaza Shopping (four blocks from Rodoferroviária) after 1100. Also in R 24 Horas at **Digitando o Futuro** and **Internet 24 Horas**, in the bookshop, open 24 hrs, US$3 per hr. **Get On**, R Visc de Nacar 1388. **Monkey**, Av Vicente Machado 534, corner with R Brigadeiro. Cool, modern with lots of computers and internet games, open daily till 2400. **Medical services** Emergency: T190 for Police and T193 for ambulance or fire. The Cajuru Hospital is at Av São José 738, T3362 1121, and the Evangélico is at Al Augusto Stellfeld 1908, T3322 4141, both of which deal with emergencies. **Post offices** main post office is at Mal Deodoro 298; post offices also at R 15 de Novembro and R Pres Faria. **Telephones** Tele Centro-Sul, information, T102. **Embratel**, Galeria Minerva, R 15 de Novembro. **Useful addresses** Visa extensions: Federal police, Dr Muricy 814, 1000-1600. **Voltage** 110 V, 60 cycles.

Paranaguá and the coast

The railway to the coast winds its way around the slopes of the Marumbi mountain range, across rushing rivers and through the forest to the sea. There are pretty colonial towns en route. The coast itself only has a few beaches, but in compensation has some of the richest biodiversity in Brazil.

Curitiba to Paranaguá

Two roads and a railway run from Curitiba to Paranaguá. The railway journey is the most spectacular in Brazil. There are numerous tunnels with sudden views of deep gorges and high peaks and waterfalls as the train rumbles over dizzy bridges and viaducts. Near Banhado station (Km 66) is the waterfall of Véu da Noiva; from the station at Km 59, the mountain range of **Marumbi** can be reached. See page 436 for schedules and fares. Of the roads, the older, cobbled Estrada da Graçiosa, with numerous viewpoints and tourist kiosks along the way, is much more scenic than the paved BR277.

Parque Nacional Marumbi

Marumbi Park is a large area of preserved Atlantic rainforest and is a UNESCO World Heritage site and Biosphere Reserve. The forest in the 2,343 ha park is covered in banana trees, palmito and orchids. There are rivers and waterfalls and among the fauna are monkeys, snakes and toucans. A climbing trail reaches 625 m to Rochedinho (two hours). Hands need to be free to grasp trees, especially during the rainy season (December to March), when trails are muddy. The last five minutes of the trail is a dangerous walk along a narrow rock trail. At the park entrance, notify administration of your arrival and departure. There is a small museum, video, left luggage and the base for a search and rescue unit at weekends. Volunteer guides are available at weekends. Wooden houses can be rented for US$55 a night; take torch. Camping is free. To get there take the Paranaguá train from Curitiba at 0815, arriving Marumbi at 1020. Return at 1540 to Curitiba. If continuing the next day to Paranaguá your Curitiba-Marumbi ticket is valid for the onward journey.

Morretes → *Colour map 7, grid C3. www.morretes.com.br.*

Morretes, founded in 1721, is one of the prettiest colonial towns in southern Brazil. Whitewashed colonial buildings with painted window frames straddle the pebbly river and church spires stick up from a sea of red tiled roofs against the backdrop of forested hills. The Estrada da Graciosa road passes through Morretes and the train stops here too. Most of the numerous restaurants serve the local speciality, Barreado, a meat stew cooked in a clay pot – originally a day in advance of Carnaval in order to allow women to escape from their domestic chores and enjoy the party. There are a handful of pousadas too and a series of walks into the mountains. **Antonina**, 14 km from Morretes is as picturesque, less touristy, and sits on the Baía do Paranaguá. It can be reached by local bus from Morretes.

Paranaguá → *Phone code: 0xx41. Colour map 7, grid C3. Population: 128,000.*

The centre of Paranaguá is a pleasant place to stroll, especially around the waterfront. Colonial buildings decay in the heat and humidity; some are just façades encrusted with bromeliads. There is an interesting city **museum** ①*R General Carneiro 66, T3423 2511, www.proec.ufpr.br, Tue-Fri 0930-1200, 1300-1800, Sat-Sun 1200-1800, US$1,* housed in a formidable 18th-century Jesuit convent. Other attractions are a 17th-century fountain, the church of **São Benedito**, and the shrine of **Nossa Senhora do Rocio**, 2 km from town. **Tourist information**: R General Carneiro 258, Setor Histórico, T3425 4542. Boat schedules, toilet, and left-luggage available, www.paranagua.pr.gov.br.

The Paranaguá region was an important centre of indigenous life. Colossal shell middens, called **Sambaquis**, some as high as a two-storey building, protecting regally-adorned corpses, have been found on the surrounding estuaries. They date from between 7,000 and 2,000 years ago, built by the ancestors of the Tupinguin and Carijo people who encountered the first Europeans to arrive here. The Spanish and Portuguese disputed the bay and islands when gold was found in the late 16th century. More important is the area's claim to be one of Latin America's biodiversity hotspots and the best place on the Brazilian coast to see rare rainforest flora and fauna. Mangrove and lowland subtropical forests, islands, rivers and rivulets here form the largest stretch of Atlantic coast rainforest in the country and protect critically endangered species (see below). Most of the bay is protected by a series of national and state parks, but it is possible to visit on an organized tour from Paranaguá. The **Barcopar** cooperative, access from Praça 29 de Julho (Palco Tutóia), T3422 8159, www.barcopar.com.br, offers a range of excellent trips in large and small vessels ranging from two hours to two days, US$6-60 per person.

Ilha do Mel

Ilha do Mel sits in the mouth of the Baía de Paranaguá and was of strategic use in the 18th century. On this popular weekend escape and holiday island there are no roads, no vehicles and limited electricity. Outside of Carnaval and New Year's it is a laid back little place. Bars pump out Bob Marley and Maranhão reggae; surfers lounge around in hammocks and barefooted couples dance forró on the wooden floors of simple beachside shacks. Much of the island is forested, its coastline is fringed with broad beaches, broken in the south by rocky headlands.

The rugged eastern half, where most of the facilities are to be found is fringed with curving beaches and capped with a lighthouse, Farol das Conchas, built in 1872 to guide shipping into the bay. The flat, scrub forest-covered western half is predominantly an ecological protection area, its northern side watched over by the Fortaleza Nossa Senhora dos Prazeres, built in 1767 on the orders of King José I of Portugal, to defend what was one of the principal ports in the country. The best surf beaches are Praia Grande and Praia de Fora. Both are about 20 minutes' walk from the Nova Brasilia jetty. Fortaleza and Ponta do Bicho on the north shore are more tranquil and are safe for swimming. They are about 45 minutes' walk from the jetty or five minutes by boat. Farol and Encantadas are the liveliest and have the bulk of the accommodation, restaurants and nightlife. A series of well-signposted trails, from 20 minutes to three hours, cover the island and its coast. It is also possible to take a long day walking around the entire island, but the stretch along the southern shore between Encantadas and Nova Brasilia has to be done by boat. **Information**: www.ilhadomelonline.com, www.pousadasilhadomel.com.br.

Superagui National Park

The island of Superagui and its neighbour, Peças, the focus for the Guaraqueçaba Environmental Protection Area which is part of the Nature Conservancy's parks in peril programme (http://parks inperil.org). They also form a national park and UNESCO World Heritage Site. Access to the park and accommodation can be arranged through the village on Superagui beach, just north of Ilha do Mel. Many endangered endemic plants and animals live in the park, including hundreds of endemic orchids, Atlantic rainforest specific animals like brown howler monkeys and large colonies of Red-tailed Amazons (a parrot on the red list of critically endangered species and which can be seen nowhere else). There are also jaguarundi, puma and jaguar. The *indígena* village is one of several Guarani villages in the area; other inhabitants are mostly of European descent, living off fishing. There is superb swimming from deserted beaches, but watch out for stinging jelly fish. Contact Ibama on the island, 2 km out of the village, for information.

● Sleeping → *See Telephone, page 347, for important phone changes.*

Morretes *p438*

A Pousada Graciosa, Estrada da Graciosa Km 8 (Porto da Cima village), T3462 1807, www.morretes.com.br/pousadagraciosa. Much the best in the area; some 10 km north of Morretes with simple but comfortable wooden chalets set in rainforest. No children under 12.
B Pousada Cidreira, R Romulo Pereira 61, T3462 1604, loizetycidreira@uol.com.br. Central, plain tiled rooms, TV, most with balconyand. Breakfast.
C Hotel Nhundiaquara, R General Carneiro 13, T3462 1228, F3462 1267. Smart, beautifully set on the river, but service, public areas and rooms do not match up to the exterior, with breakfast.

Paranaguá *p438*

AL Camboa, R João Estevão (Ponta do Caju), T3423 2121, www.hotelcamboa.com.br. Full- or half-board available. Family resort, tennis courts, large pool, saunas, trampolines, a restaurant and a/c rooms, out of town near the port. Book ahead.
AL San Rafael, R Julia Costa 185, T3423 2123, www.sanrafaelhotel.com.br. Business hotel with plain rooms, restaurants, pool and jacuzzis.
D Ponderosa, R Pricilenco Corea 68 at 15 Novembro, T3423 2464. A block east and north of the boat dock, some rooms with a view.
D Pousada Itiberê, R Princesa Isabel 24, T3423 2485. Very smart spartan rooms, some with sea views, helpful service from the elderly Portuguese owner, shared bath, 3 blocks east of the boat dock.
Camping Arco Iris, Praia de Leste, on the beach, 29 km south of Paranaguá, T458 2001.

Ilha do Mel *p438*

All rooms are fan cooled unless otherwise stated.
A-B Long Beach, Praia Grande, T9944 9204, www.lbeach.cjb.net. Best on the beach, chalets for up to 6, very popular with surfers. Book ahead.
B Caraguatá, Encantadas, T3426 9097, pousada caraguata@uol.com.br. A/c, fridge, close to jetty.
B Pôr do Sol, Nova Brasilia, T3426 8009, www.pousadapordosol.com.br. Simple, elegant rooms around a shady garden, large deck with cabins and hammocks by the beach. Breakfast.
C Enseada, Farol, T9978-1200, pousadaenseada@ uol.com.br. 4 rooms with en suites, TVs and fridges, charmingly decorated. Lots of rescued cats.

C Dona Quinota, Fortaleza, T3426 8171/9978 3495, http://donaquinota.zeta.8x.com.br. Little blue and cream cottages right on the beach, 3 km from Nova Brasilia. Includes breakfast and supper. **Dona Clara** next door is very similar.
C Recanto do Frances, Encantadas, T3426 9105, www.recantodofrances.com.br. Full of character, with each chalet built in a different style to represent a different French city. 5 mins from Prainha or Encantadas. Good crêpe restaurant.
D pp Aconchego, Nova Brasilia, T3426 8030, www.cwb.matrix.com.br/daconchego. Very clean, beachside deck with hammocks, TV and breakfast area, charming. Includes breakfast.
D D'Lua, Farol, T3426 8031, daluapousada_ ilhadomel@hotmail.com. Basic and hippy with a friendly new-age owner, Jô (closed low season).
D Farol da Ilha, Farol, T3426 8017/ 9136 2138. Dorms and double rooms in a garden, surf boards for rent. Price includes generous breakfast.
D Girassol, Farol, T3426 8006, heliodasilva@ onda.com.br. Wooden rooms in a little fruit tree and bougainvillea garden, close to jetty. Breakfast.
D Plâncton, Farol at Fora, T3426 8061. A range of wooden buildings in a hummingbird-filled garden, fresh atmosphere, Italian food in high season.
D Recanto da Fortaleza, Ponta do Bicho, T3426 8000, www.ilhadomelpousada.com.br. The best of the 2 next to the Fort, basic cabins, free pick-up by boat from Nova Brasilia (ring ahead), bike rental. Price includes breakfast and dinner.
D pp Recanto Tropical, Farol, opposite D'Lua, T3426 8054. Open out of season, good breakfast.
    You can rent a fisherman's house on Encantadas, ask for **Valentim's Bar**, or for Luchiano. Behind the bar is **Cabanas Dona Maria**, shared showers, cold water; food available if you ask in advance. Many pousadas and houses with rooms to rent (shared kitchen and living room). Shop around, prices from US$10 double, low season, mid-week.
Camping There are mini campsites with facilities at Encantadas, Farol and Brasília. Camping is possible on the more deserted beaches (good for surfing). If camping, watch out for the tide, watch possessions and beware of the bicho de pé which burrows into feet (remove with a needle and alcohol) and the borrachudos (discourage with Autan repellent).

🍴 Eating

Morretes *p438*
🍴🍴🍴 **Armazém Romanus** R Visc Do Rio Branco 141. Family-run restaurant with the best menu and wine list in the region, dishes from home- grown ingredients, including barreado and desserts.
🍴🍴🍴 **Terra Nossa** R 15 de Novembro 109. Barreado, pasta, pizzas and fish, generous portions.
🍴 **Madalozo** R Alm Frederico de Oliveira 16, overlooking the river. Good barreado and generous salads.

Paranaguá *p438*
🍴🍴🍴 **Casa do Barreado** R José Antônio da Cruz. Barreado buffet from a well established eatery.
🍴🍴🍴 **Danúbio Azul** R 15 de Novembro 95. The best in town, fish and chicken dishes, pastas and pizzas; all in enormous quantities. 1 block back from the sea at the east end of town.
🍴 **Divina Gula** R 15 de Novembro 165. Until 1400 only, sea food buffet and feijoada at weekends. 3 blocks east of the Ilha do Mel dock.
🍴 **Rosa** R Praia 16. Decent seafood including good risotto. A block west of the Ilha do Mel boat dock.

Ilha do Mel *p438*
Many pousadas serve food, some only in season (Christmas-Carnaval). Many have live music or dancing (especially in high season) after 2200.
🍴🍴 **Fim da trilha**, Prainha (Fora de Encantadas), T3426 9017. Spanish seafood restaurant, one of the best on the island. Also has a *pousada*.
🍴 **Colmeia**, Farol. Snacks, crepes and good cakes and puddings.

🍴 **Mar e Sol**, Farol. Huge portions of fish, chicken with chips and rice and a small selection of more adventurous dishes like bass in shrimp sauce.
🍴 **Toca do Abutre**, Farol. Live music and the usual huge portions of fish or chicken with rice, beans and chips.
🍴 **Zorro**, Encantadas. One of several cheap seafront restaurants, forró dancing in the evenings.

🚍 Transport

Ilha do Mel *p438*
Ferry By ferry from Paranaguá to Encantadas and Nova Brasilia, at 0930 and 1500, 1 hr 40 mins, US$5, boats leave from R Gen Carneiro (R da Praia) in front of the Tourist Information kiosk; by ferry from **Pontal do Paraná** (Pontal do Sul), daily from 0800 to 1800 (last boat from island to mainland) every hr at weekends, less frequently in the week. From **Paranaguá**, take the **bus** to Pontal do Sul (many daily, 1½ hrs, US$0.80), then wait for the ferry, US$3.20. There are handicraft stalls at the ferry point. The last bus back to Paranaguá leaves at 2200. Alternatively, go to the small harbour in Paranaguá and ask for a boat to Ilha do Mel, US$20 one-way (no shade). Make sure the ferry goes to your chosen destination (Nova Brasília or Encantadas are the most developed areas).

Superagui National Park *p438*
Ferry From Paranaguá Sat 1000 arriving 1400, return Sun 1530 (two stops en route), US$8 one way. Private boats from Praia da Fortaleza on Ilha do Mel run if the weather is good. Commercially organized tours are available through Ibama T252 0180, or Barcopar, T422 8159.

Santa Catarina

Famous for its beaches and popular with Argentine and Paraguayan holidaymakers in high summer, this is one of the best stretches of Brazilian coast for surfing, attracting 1½ million visitors to the 170 beaches just in the summer months of January and February. For the rest of the year they are pleasant and uncrowded. Immigrant communities, such as the German, give a unique personality to many towns and districts with the familiar European pattern of mixed farming. Rural tourism is important and the highlands, 100 km from the coast, are among the coldest in Brazil, giving winter landscapes reminiscent of Europe, or Brazil's southern neighbours.

Florianópolis ➔ *Phone code: 0xx48. Colour map 5, grid B5. Population: 342,315.*
Half way along the coast of Santa Catarina is the state capital and port of Florianópolis, founded in 1726 on the Ilha de Santa Catarina. The island is joined to the mainland by two bridges, one of which is Ponte Hercílio Luz, the longest steel suspension bridge in Brazil (closed for repairs). The newer Colombo Machado Salles bridge has a pedestrian and cycle way beneath the roadway. The natural beauty of the island, beaches and bays make Florianópolis a magnet for holidaymakers in summer. The southern beaches are usually good for swimming, the east for surfing, but be careful of the undertow. **Tourist office: Setur**, head office at ① *Portal Turístico de Florianópolis, mainland end of the bridge, Av Eng Max de Souza 236, Coqueiros, T3952 7000, open 0800-2000 (Sat-Sun 1800).* Office

in the Largo da Alfândega, *T222 4906, Mon-Fri 0800-1830, Sat-Sun 0800-1800*. At Rodoviária, Avenida Paulo Fontes, *T212 3127*, free maps; www.guiafloripa.com.br, www.pmf.sc.gov.br turismo and for the state www.sc.gov.br.

In the 1960s Florianópolis port was closed and the aspect of the city's southern shoreline was fundamentally changed, with land reclaimed from the bay. The two main remnants of the old port area are the late 19th-century **Alfândega** and **Mercado Público**, both on Rua Conselheiro Mafra, fully restored and painted ochre. In the Alfândega is a **handicraft market** *① Mon-Fri 0900-1900, Sat 0900-1200*. The market is divided into boxes, some are bars and restaurants, others **shops** *① T3224 0189, Mon-Fri 0600-1830, Sat 0600-1300*, a few fish stalls open on Sun. The **Cathedral** *on Praça 15 de Novembro*, was completed in 1773. **Forte Santana** (1763), beneath the Ponte Hercílio Luz, houses a **Museu de Armas Major Lara Ribas**

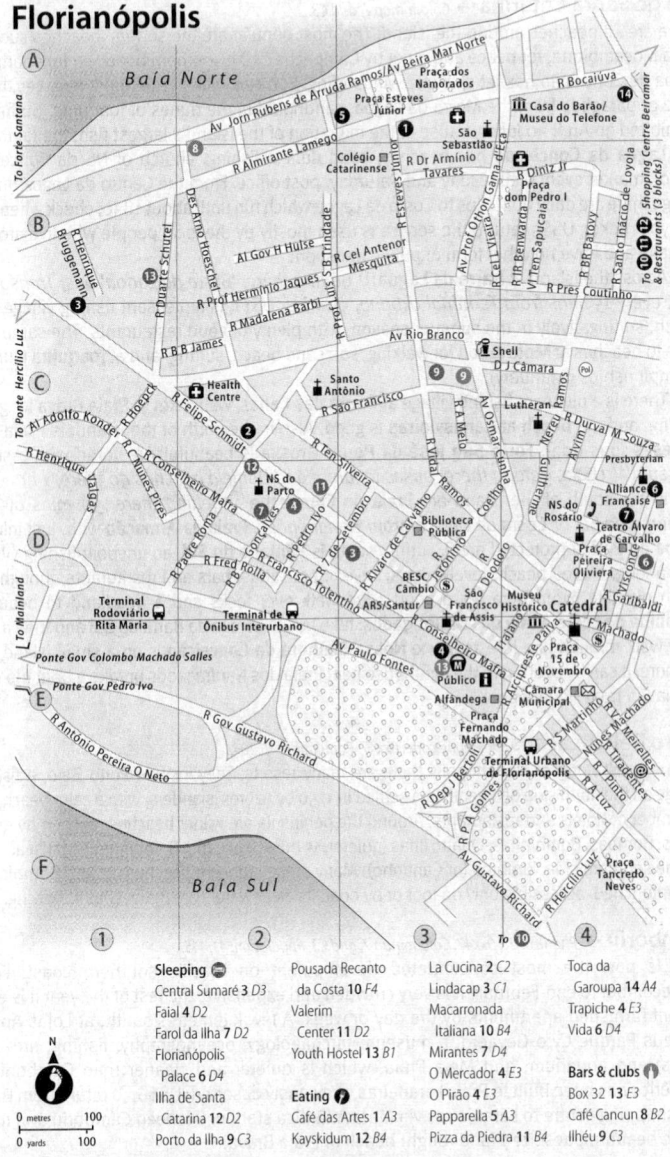

Florianópolis

ⓘ *Tue-Sun 0830-1200, 1400-1800 (Mon 1400-1800), free*, with a collection of guns and other items, mostly post Second World War. **Museu Histórico** ⓘ *in the 18th-century Palácio Cruz e Souza, Praça 15 de Novembre, Tue-Fri 0800-1900, Sat 1300-1900, Sun 1530-1900*, contains furniture, documents and objects belonging to governors of the state. **Museu de Antropologia** ⓘ *Trindade University Campus, Mon-Fri 0900-1200, 1300-1700*, has a collection of stone and other archaeological remains from the cultures of the coastal *indígenas*. **Museu do Homem Sambaqui** ⓘ *at the Colégio Catarinense, R Esteves Júnior 711, Mon-Fri 1330-1630*, exhibits pieces from the sambaqui culture and fossils. There is a look-out point at **Morro da Cruz** ⓘ *getting there: take Empresa Trindadense bus, US$0.80, waits 15 mins, or walk*. **Boat trips** *from US$12.75*, can be made in the bay with **Scuna Sul** ⓘ *T225 1806 or 9971 1806, www.scunasul.com.br.*

Ilha de Santa Catarina → *Colour map 7, grid C3.*

There are 42 beaches around the island. The most popular are the surfers' beaches such as Praia Moçambique; for peace and quiet try Campeche or the southern beaches; for sport, the Lagoa de Conceição has jet skis and windsurfing. You can walk in the forest reserves, hang glide or paraglide from the Morro da Lagoa, sandboard in the dunes of Joaquina. Surfing is prohibited 30 April-30 July because of the migration of the island's largest fish, the tainha.

Lagoa da Conceição has beaches, sand dunes, fishing, church of NS da Conceição (1730), market every Wednesday and Saturday, post office. From the Centro da Lagoa on the bridge there are daily boat trips to Costa da Lagoa which run until about 1830, check when you buy your ticket, US$5 return, the service is used mostly by the local people who live around the lake and have no other form of public transport.

Across the island at **Barra da Lagoa** ⓘ *getting there: 'Barra da Lagoa' bus, Transol No 403, every 15 mins from Terminal Urbano, 55 mins, US$1*, is a pleasant fishing village and beach, surfing, lively in the summer season, with plenty of good restaurants. The same bus goes to beaches at **Mole** (good for walking, soft sand beach, surfing) and at **Joaquina** (surfing championships in January).

There is a pleasant fishing village at **Ponta das Canas**, walk 1 km to Praia Brava for good surfing, and the beach at **Canasvieiras** is good. Also in the north of the island, is **Praia dos Ingleses** (bus 602). **Forte São José da Ponta Grossa** is beautifully restored with a small museum ⓘ *US$2, getting there: buses to Jurerê and Daniela beaches go there, 1 hr.*

In the south of the island are **Praia do Campeche** ⓘ *getting there: 30 mins by bus (Pantano do Sul or Costa de Dentro) from Florianópolis*, **Praia da Armação** with, just inland, **Lagoa do Peri** (a protected area). Further south is **Pântano do Sul**, an unspoilt fishing village with a long, curved beach, lovely views, several pousadas, bars and restaurants, though not much nightlife. From here it's a good 4-km walk over rocks and a headland to beautiful **Lagoinha do Leste**. **Praia dos Naufragados**: take bus to Caieira da Barra do Sul and then a one hour walk through fine forests. **Forte Nossa Senhora da Conceição** is on a small island just offshore. It can be seen from the lighthouse near Praia dos Naufragados or take a boat trip with Scuna Sul from Florianópolis.

Porto Belo Beaches → *Phone code: 0xx47. Population: 10,704.*

On the coast north of Florianópolis there are many resorts. They include Porto Belo, a fishing village on the north side of a peninsula settled in 1750 by Azores islanders, with a calm beach and a number of hotels and restaurants. Around the peninsula are wilder beaches reached by rough roads: Bombas, Bombinhas, Quatro Ilhas (quieter, 15 mins' walk from Bombinhas), Mariscal, and, on the southern side, Zimbros (or Cantinho). Many of the stunning beaches around **Bombinhas** are untouched, accessible only on foot or by boat. Its clear waters are marvellous for diving.

Camboriú → *Phone code: 0xx47. Colour map 7, grid C3. Population: 41,445.*

This is now the most concentrated development on Brazil's southern coast. From 15 December to end-February it is very crowded and expensive; the rest of the year it is easy to rent furnished apartments by the day or week. A few kilometres south, at Lojas Apple, there is Parque Cyro Gevaerd, a museum (archaeology, oceanography, fishing, arts and crafts) and aquarium; and Meia Praia, which is quieter and cleaner than Camboriú. A teleférico has been built to Praia Laraneiras, previously deserted; US$6.50 return from Barra Sul shopping centre to Laranjeiras via Mata Atlântica station. Between Camboriú and Itajaí is the beautiful, deserted (and rough) beach of Praia Brava.

Blumenau → *Phone code: 0xx47. Post code: 89100. Colour map 7, C3. Pop: 261,808. Voltage: 220 AC.*

Some 47 km up the Rio Itajaí-Açu (61 km by paved road from Itajaí) is this prosperous city, where high-tech and electronics industries are replacing textiles as the economic mainstay. The surrounding district was settled mostly by Germans. It is clean and orderly with almost caricatured Germanic architecture. See the **Museu da Família Colonial** ① *Av Duque de Caxias 78, Mon-Fri 0800-1130, 1330-1730, Sat morning only, US$0.20,* German immigrant museum. Also worth a visit is the **German Evangelical Church**, and the houses, now **museums** *0800-1800,* of **Dr Bruno Otto Blumenau** and of **Fritz Müller** (a collaborator of Darwin), who bought the Blumenau estate in 1897 and founded the town. **Tourist office:** T3326 6797, www.blumenau.sc.gov.br.

Oktoberfest, the second largest street party in Brazil, after Carnival is usually held in the first half of October. During the day the narrow streets are packed around the Molemann Centre, which contains a mixture of bars, live music and of course, Chopp beer. At 1900 the doors of the Oktoberfest pavilion open for different events, including drinking competitions, the 'sausage Olympics', traditional dress and cake making competitions. There is also a fun fair and folk dancing shows. Visitors report it is worth attending on weekday evenings but weekends are too crowded. It is repeated, but called a 'summer festival', in the three weeks preceding Carnival.

At **Pomerode**, 33 km west of Blumenau, the north German dialect of Plattdeutsch is still spoken and there are several folkloric groups keeping alive the music and dance of their ancestors. The **Museu Pomerano** ① *Rodovia SC 418, Km 3,* tells the story of the colonial family. **Museu Ervin Kurt Theichmann** ① *R 15 de Novembro 791,* has sculptures. The **Confeitaria Torten Paradies** *R 15 de Novembro 211,* serves excellent German cakes. Festa do Pomerania in January. www.pomerode.sc.gov.br.

São Francisco do Sul

→ *Phone code: 0xx47. Colour map 7, grid C3. Population: 32300. www.saofranciscodosul.com.br.*

Some 80 km up the coast at the mouth of the Baia de Babitonga, São Francisco do Sul is the port for the town of Joinville, 45 km inland at the head of the Rio Cachoeira. There is an interesting **Museu Nacional do Mar** reflecting Brazil's seafaring history. The centre has over 150 historical sites and has been protected since 1987. The **cathedral** was built between 1699 and 1719 and still has its original walls made with sand, shells and whale oil. There are some excellent **beaches** nearby.

Joinville itself (*Phone code 0xx47*) is the state's largest city. It lies 2 km from the main coastal highway, BR-101, by which Curitiba and Florianópolis are less than two hours away. The industry does not spoil the considerable charm of the city. The **Alameda Brustlein**, better known as the **R das Palmeiras**, is an impressive avenue of palm trees leading to the **Palácio dos Príncipes**. The trees have been protected since 1982. The **Cathedral** ① *on Av Juscelino Kubitscheck with R do Príncipe,* is futuristic with spectacular windows recounting the story of man. The **Casa da Cultura** (Galeria Municipal de Artes 'Victor Kursansew') ① *R Dona Fransisca 800, Mon-Fri 0900-1800, Sat 0900-1300,* also contains the School of Art 'Fritz Alt', the School of Music 'Vila Lobos' and the School of Ballet. A number of museums and exhibition centres reflect the history of, and immigration to the area and the city's artistic achievements. In July, Joinville hosts the largest dance festival in the world, which attracts around 4,000 dancers who stay for 12 days and put on shows and displays ranging from jazz, folklore, classical ballet and other styles. There is also an annual beer festival, Fenachopp, in October. There are many good restaurants and good air and road links to other parts of Brazil. **Tourist office** at the corner of Praça Nereu Ramos with R do Príncipe. **Promotur**, R 15 de Novembro 4543, Glória, T3453 2663, www.promotur.com.br. Also www.joinville.sc.gov.br.

Southern Santa Catarina

At **Praia do Rosa**, 101 km south of Florianópolis, is the headquarters of the Right Whale Institute (**Instituto Baleia Franca** *www.institutobaleiafranca.com*) ① *Ibama: Area de Proteção Ambiental da Baleia Franca, Av Mauro Ramos 1113, CCP660, 88020-301 Florianópolis, T212 3300,* and one of Brazil's prime **whale-watching** sites. The right whales come to the bay to calve from May to November and trips can be arranged to see them. The institute's base is the **Pousada Vida, Sol e Mar** ① *T3254 4199, www.vidasolemar.com.br,* which has cabins, pool, restaurant and surf school. There are other lodgings at Praia do Rosa (eg **AL A Morada dos Bougainvilles**, T3355 6100, www.pousadabougainville.com.br, and **Pousada Caminho do Rei**, T3355 6062, www.caminhodorei.com.br) and other fine beaches in the area. The nearest major town is Imbituba.

Laguna → *Phone code: 0xx48. Colour map 7, grid C3. Population: 47,568.*

Some 15 km from Tubarão is the small fishing port of Laguna. The town, founded in 1676, was the capital of the Juliana Republic in 1839, a short-lived separatist movement led by Italian idealist Guiseppe Garibáldi. At Laguna is the **Anita Garibáldi Museum**, containing documents, furniture, and personal effects of Garibáldi's devoted lover.

About 16 km away (by ferry and road) are beaches and dunes at **Cavo de Santa Marta**. Also from Laguna, take a Lagunatur or Auto Viação São José bus to **Farol** ① *getting there: 4 buses a day Mon-Fri, 1 on Sat, US$2, beautiful ride*. You have to cross the mouth of the Lagoa Santo Antônio by ferry (10 minutes) to get to Farol; look out for fishermen aided by dolphins (botos). Here is a fishing village with a **lighthouse** (Farol de Santa Marta) ① *guided tours available, getting there: taxi, US$10, not including ferry toll*, built by the French in 1890 of stone, sand and whale oil. It is the largest lighthouse in South America and has the third largest view in the world. It may be possible to bargain with fishermen for a bed, or there are campsites at Santa Marta Pequena by the lighthouse, popular with surfers.

São Joaquim → *Colour map 7, grid C2. Population: 22,836. Altitude: 1,360 m.*

Buses from the coalfield town of Tubarão (27 km from Laguna) go inland to Lauro Müller, then over the Serra do Rio do Rastro (beautiful views of the coast in clear weather) to **Bom Jardim da Serra** which has an apple festival every April. The road continues to **São Joaquim**. The highest town in southern Brazil, it regularly has snowfalls in winter; a very pleasant town with an excellent climate. 11 km outside the town on the way to Bom Jardim da Serra is the **Parque Ecológico Vale da Neve** (Snow Valley). It is an easy hike and very beautiful, the entrance is on the main road, US$3, and there is a restaurant. The owner is American and an English speaking guide will take you for a 1½-hour walk through the forest. The **Parque Nacional de São Joaquim** in the Serra Geral (33,500 ha, on paper only, much of the land is still private) has canyons containing sub-tropical vegetation, and araucaria forest at higher levels. There is no bus (local Ibama office, To48-278 4002, Secretaria de Turismo de São Joaquim, To49-233 2790, www.serracatarinense.com).

● Sleeping → *See Telephone, page 347, for important phone changes.*

Florianópolis *p440, map 441*
AL-A Valerim Plaza, R Felipe Schmidt 705, T0800-702 3000, www.hotelvalerim.com.br. Three-star, more modern than Valerim Center, buffet restaurant open till 2300.
AL-A Porto da Ilha, R Dom Jaime Câmara 43, T3322 0007, hotel@portodailha.com.br. Central, comfortable, **A-B** at weekends. Recommended.
A Faial, R Felipe Schmidt 603, T3225 2766, www.hotelfaial.com.br. Comfortable and traditional hotel with good restaurant. Also owns the **Farol da Ilha**, R Bento Gonçalves 163, T3225 3030, www.hotelfaroldailha.com.br, which is good too, convenient for the bus station.
A Florianópolis Palace, R Artista Bittencourt 14, T3224 9633, www.floph.com.br. Large a/c rooms, pool, sauna, 1970s hotel.
B Valerim Center, R Felipe Schmidt 554, T0800-702 3000. Large rooms, hot water, hard beds.
C Pousada Recanto da Costa, R 13 de Maio 41. With breakfast, hot water, laundry facilities, parking, 15 mins' walk from centre.
D Central Sumaré, R Felipe Schmidt 423, T222 5359. Breakfast, good value, rooms vary from **C** with bath, to **E**.
E pp Ilha de Santa Catarina, R Duarte Schutel 227, T225 3781, alberguesfloripa@uol.com.br. HI, breakfast included, cooking facilities, clean, some

traffic noise, very friendly, will store luggage. Prices rise in Dec-Feb; more expensive for non-members. Recommended.
Camping Camping Clube do Brasil, São João do Rio Vermelho, north of Lagoa da Conceição, 21 km out of town; also at Lagoa da Conceição, Praia da Armação, Praia dos Ingleses, Praia Canasvieiras. 'Wild' camping allowed at Ponta de Sambaqui and Praias Brava, Aranhas, Galheta, Mole, Campeche, Campanhas and Naufragados; 4 km south of Florianópolis, camping site with bar at Praia do Sonho on the mainland, beautiful, deserted beach with an island fort nearby. 'Camping Gaz' cartridges from **Riachuelo Supermercado**, on R Alvim and R São Jorge.

Ilha de Santa Catarina *p442*
Barra da Lagoa
C Pousada Floripaz, Servidão da Prainha 20 (across hanging bridge at bus station, take bus 403 from terminal municipal), T3232 3193, www.qlitoral.com.br/floripaz. Book in advance, safe, family run, helpful owners, will organize tours by boat and car on island. Highly recommended.
Apartments José Irineu e Terezinha, T0xx48-9981 6060, juliane.s.s@zipmail.com.br.

Apartments to rent 200 m from beach, fully-equipped, about US$110 a month.
Camping Marina da Barra, T3232 3199. Beautiful clean site, helpful owner.

Joaquina

A Joaquina Beach, R A Garibaldi Santiago, T232 5059, reservas@joaquinabeachhotel.com.br. Pleasant hotel with a/c. safes, sea views more expensive, buffet breakfast.
D Pousada Dona Zilma, R Geral da Praia da Joaquina 279, T3232 5161. Quiet, safe. Recommended.

Ponta das Canas

A Moçambique, T/F3266 1172, www.mocambique.com.br. In centre of village, noisy at weekends. Also has beach hotel, Moçambique Praia.

Praia dos Ingleses

C Companhia Inglesa, R Dom João Becker 276, T3269 1350, www.hotelciainglesa.com.br. Little beach hotel with pool and helpful staff. Recommended for families.
C Marcos Barroso, T9983 4472. Good value apartments.

Praia do Campeche

L-AL Pousada Natur Campeche, Servidão Família Nunes 59, T3237 4011, www.natur campeche.com.br. Also has a hotel at Av Pequeno Príncipe 2196, a little cheaper, both with gardens, quiet, pousada has a pool and is closer to the beach.
L-A Pousada Vila Tamarindo, Av Campeche 1836, T3237 3464, www.tamarindo.com.br. Tranquil setting with lovely views, gardens, helpful staff, good buffet breakfast.
AL Hotel São Sebastião da Praia, Av Campeche 1373, T/F3338 2020, www.hotelsaosebastiao.com.br. Resort hotel on splendid beach, offers special monthly rate Apr to Oct, excellent value.

Near Pântano do Sul

B Pousada Sítio dos Tucanos, Estrada Geral da Costa de Dentro 2776, T3237 5084, www.pousadasitiodostucanos.com. **AL** in high season. English, French, Spanish spoken, spacious bungalows in garden setting, excellent organic food. Very highly recommended. Take bus to Pântano do Sul, walk 6 km or telephone and arrange to be picked up by German owner.
D Albergue do Pirata, R Rosalia P Ferreira 4973, Pântano do Sul, T9960 1344. Hostelling International. With breakfast, natural surroundings, lots of trails.

Blumenau *p443*

Reservations are essential during Oktoberfest.
A-B Glória, R 7 de Setembro 954, T3326 1988, hotelgloria@hotelgloria.com.br. German-run, excellent coffee shop, best deal is 'meal of soups', US$2.30 for salad bar, 4 soups, dessert and wine.
C Herrmann, Floriano Peixoto 213, T3322 4370. One of the oldest houses in Blumenau, rooms with or without bath, excellent big breakfast, German spoken. Many cheap hotels do not include breakfast.
Grün Garten Pousada, R São Paulo 2457, T3323 4332. Youth hostel, 15 mins' walk from rodoviária.
Camping Municipal campsite, 3 km out on R Pastor Osvaldo Hesse; Paraíso dos Poneis, 9 km out on the Itajaí road, also Motel; Refúgio Gaspar Alto, 12 km out on R da Glória.

São Francisco do Sul *p443*

A Zibamba, R Fernandes Dias 27, T/F444 2077. Central, good restaurant.

Joinville *p443*

AL Anthurium Parque, São José 226, T/F433 6299, anthurium@anthurium.com.br. Colonial building, once home to a bishop, good value, English spoken, pool, sauna.
AL Tannenhof, Visconde de Taunay 340, T/F3433 8011, www.tannenhof.com.br. 4-star, pool, gym, traffic noise, excellent breakfast, restaurant.
C Mattes, 15 de Novembro 801, T422 3582, www.hotelmattes.com.br. Good facilities, big breakfast, German spoken. Recommended.
D Novo Horizonte, R Paraíba 766, T422 7269, at bus station. Basic, clean.

Laguna *p444*

B Turismar, Av Beira Mar 207, T647 0024, F647 0279. 2-star, view over Mar Grosso beach, TV.
C Beiramar, T644 0260, 100 m from Recanto, opposite Angeloni Supermarket. No breakfast, TV, rooms with view over lagoon.
C Recanto, Av Colombo 17, close to bus terminal. With breakfast, modern but basic.

São Joaquim *p444*

C Maristela, R Manoel Joaquim Pinto 220, T233 0007. No heating so can be cold, helpful, good breakfast; 5 mins' walk from rodoviária.
C Nevada, R Manoel Joaquim Pinto 190 (also 5 mins' walk from rodoviária), T/F233 0259. Expensive meals.

Bom Jardim da Serra

D Moretti, Rua Antão de Paula Velho, T232 0106. Family atmosphere, owner very helpful.
Camping Clube do Brasil site.

🍴 Eating

Florianópolis *p440, map 441*
Take a walk along Rua Bocaiúva, east of
R Almte Lamego, to find the whole street
filled with Italian restaurants, barbecue
places and an exclusive fish restaurant,
Toca da Garoupa (turn on to R Alves de Brito
178). **Don Pepé Forno a Lenha** is a great place
to go for a quiet romantic meal with a
serenador (cover charge added to bill for
singer). Shrimp dishes are good everywhere. A
popular place to start a night out (after 2100) is
the **Nouvelle Vague**, more commonly known
as A Creperia, buzzing every weekend, wide
selection of sweet and savoury pancakes.
Lindacap, R Felipe Schmidt 1132 (closed
Mon). Recommended, good views.
Macarronada Italiana, Av Beira Mar Norte
2458. Good Italian food.
O Mercador, Box 33/4 in the Mercado Público.
Self-service specializing in fish and seafood.
O Pirão overlooks the market square in the
Mercado Público. Elegant, self-service, open
1100-1430.
Papparella, Almte Lamego 1416. Excellent
giant pizzas.
Pizza da Piedra, next door to Macarronada
Italiana. Another good place for pizza.
Trapiche, Box 31 in the Mercado Público. Also
self-service fish and seafood (see also Bars, below).
La Cucina, R Padre Roma 291. Vegetarian buffet
lunch, Mon-Sat, pay by weight, good, vegetarian
choices. Recommended.
Kayskidum, Av Beira Mar Norte 2566.
Lanchonete and crêperie, very popular.
Mirantes, R Alvaro de Carvalho 246, Centro.
Self-service buffet, good value.
Vida, R Visc de Ouro Preto 298, next to Alliance
Française. Good vegetarian.
Café das Artes, R Esteves Junior 734 at north
end. Nice café with excellent cakes.
Cía Lanches, Ten Silveira e R Trajano, downstairs.
For a wide selection of juices and snacks.
Laranja Madura, **Sabor e Sucos** and
Lanchonete Dias Velho all in Edif Dias Velho at
R Felipe Schmidt 303. All have a good choice of
juices and snacks.

Ilha de Santa Catarina *p442*
Lagoa da Conceição
Bodeguita, Av das Rendeiras 1878.
Very good value and atmosphere.
Oliveira, R Henrique Veras.
Excellent seafood.

Barra da Lagoa
Meu Cantinha, R Orlando Shaplin 89.
Excellent seafood.
Ponta das Caranhas, R Jornalista M de
Menezes 2377, T232 3076. Excellent seafood,
lovely location on the lake.

Blumenau *p443*
Cavalinho Branco, Av Rio Branco 165. Good
German food and huge meals.
Deutsches Eck, R 7 de Septembro 432.
Recommended, especially carne pizzaiola.
Frohsinn, Morro Aipim (panoramic view).
Good German food.
Gruta Azul, Rodolfo Freygang 8. Good, popular.
Amigo, Peixoto 213. Huge cheap meals.
Internacional, Nereu Ramos 61. Chinese, very
good, moderate prices.
Patisseria Bavaria, Av 7 Septembro y
Zimmerman. Very good cakes and fruit juices,
friendly and caring staff.

🍸 Bars and clubs

Florianópolis *p440, map 441*
Free open air concert every Sat morning at the
market place near the bus terminal.
    To find out about events and theme nights check
the Beiramar centre for notices in shop windows,
ask in surf shops or take a trip to the University of
Santa Catarina in Trindade and check out the
noticeboards. The news-paper *Diário Catarinense*
gives details of the bigger events, eg Oktoberfest. The
Mercado Público in the centre, which is alive with
fish sellers and stalls during the day, has a different
atmosphere at night; the stall, **Box 32**, is good for
seafood and becomes a bar specializing in cachaça
for hard working locals to unwind.
Café Cancun, Av Beira Mar Norte, T225 1029.
Wed-Sat from 2000, bars, restaurant, dancing,
sophisticated.
Empórium, Bocaiúva 79. A shop by day and
popular bar at night.
Ilhéu, Av Prof Gama d'Eça e R Jaime Câmara. Bar
and club open until early hrs, tables spill outside,
very popular with locals, fills up quickly, music a
mixture of 1980s and 1990s hits but dance floor
shamefully small.

Ilha de Santa Catarina *p442*
Throughout the summer the beaches open their
bars day and night. The beach huts of Praia Mole
invite people to party all night (bring a blanket).
Any bars are worth visiting in the Lagoa area
(around the Boulevard and Barra da Lagoa); the

🍷 *For an explanation of the sleeping and eating price codes used in this guide, see inside the front*
⚫ *cover. Other relevant information is found in Essentials pages 345-347.*

Confraria das Artes here is reckoned to be one of the coolest places in Brazil.

☻ Festivals and events

Florianópolis *p440, map 441*
In **Dec** and **Jan** the whole island dances to the sound of the Boi-de-Mamão, a dance which incorporates the puppets of Bernunça, Maricota (the Goddess of Love, a puppet with long arms to embrace everyone) and Tião, the monkey. The Portuguese brought the tradition of the bull, which has great significance in Brazilian celebrations. Around **Easter** is the Festival of the Bull, **Farra de Boi**. It is only in the south that, controversially nowadays, the bull is killed on Easter Sunday. The festival arouses fierce local pride and there is much celebration.

⊖ Transport

Florianópolis *p440, map 441*
Air International and domestic flights arrive at Hercílio Luz airport, Av Deomício Freitas, 12 km from town, T331 4000. Take Ribeiroense bus 'Corredor Sudoeste' from Terminal Urbano.
Bus There are 3 bus stations for routes on the island, or close by on the mainland: Terminal de Ônibus Interurbano between Av Paulo Fontes and R Francisco Tolentino, west of the Mercado Público; Terminal Urbano between Av Paulo Fontes and R Antônio Luz, east of Praça Fernando Machado; a terminal at R Silva Jardim and R José da Costa. Yellow micro buses (Transporte Ejecutivo), starting from the south end of Praça 15 de Novembro and other stops, charge US$1-US$2 depending on destination. Similarly, normal bus fares vary according to destination, from US$0.85.

International and buses from other Brazilian cities arrive at the rodoviária Rita Maia on the island, at the east (island) end of the Ponte Colombo Machado Salles.

Daily buses to **Porto Alegre** (US$21, 7 hrs), **São Paulo**, 9 hrs (US$31, leito US$48), **Rio**, 20 hrs (US$41 convencional, US$56 executive, US$72 leito); to **Foz do Iguaçu** (US$37, continuing to Asunción US$40), to **Curitiba** US$16. To **Blumenau** US$9, 3 hrs. To **São Joaquim** at 1145, 1945 with Reunidos, 1815 with Nevatur, 5-6 hrs, US$12; to **Laguna** US$7.
International buses Montevideo, US$69, daily, by TTL. **Buenos Aires**, US$75, Pluma, buses very full in summer, book 1 week in advance.

Porto Belo Beaches *p442*
Bus Florianópolis to Porto Belo, several daily with Rainha, fewer at weekends, more frequent buses to **Tijuca**, **Itapema** and **Itajaí**, all on the

BR-101 with connections. Buses from Porto Belo to the beaches on the peninsula.

Camboriú *p442*
Bus From **Florianópolis**, **Joinville** and **Blumenau**. TTL buses Montevideo-São Paulo stop here at about 1800, a good place to break the journey.

Blumenau *p443*
Bus Rodoviária is 7 km from town (get off at the bridge over the river and walk 1 km to centre). Bus to the rodoviária from Av Presidente Castelo-Branco (Beira Rio). There are connections in all directions from Blumenau. To **Curitiba**, US$9.50, 4 hrs, 3 daily (Penha and Catarinense). To **Pomerode** Coletivos Volkmann (T387 1321) Blumenau-Pomerode daily US$1, 1 hr; check schedule at tourist offices.

São Francisco do Sul *p443*
Bus Terminal is 1½ km from centre. Direct bus (Penha) daily to **Curitiba** at 0730, US$8, 3½ hrs.

Laguna *p444*
Bus To/from **Porto Alegre**, 5½ hrs, with Santo Anjo Da Guarda; same company goes to **Florianópolis**, 2 hrs, US$7, 6 daily.

São Joaquim *p444*
Bus To **Florianópolis** 0700 and 1700 via Bom Retiro (Reunidos) and 0800 via Tubarão (Nevatur), 5½ hrs, US$12. Florianópolis-Bom Jardim da Serra, US$13.

☻ Directory

Florianópolis *p440, map 441*
Airline offices TAM, T0800 570 5700. Varig, at airport, T3331 4154. **Banks** Banco do Brasil, Praça 15 de Novembro, exchange upstairs, 1000-1 500, huge commission on cash or TCs. ATMs downstairs, some say Visa/Plus. Banco Estado de Santa Catarina (BESC), câmbio, R Felipe Schmidt e Jerônimo Coelho, also Praça 15 de Novembro 341, 1000-1600, no commission on TCs. Money changers on R Felipe Schmidt outside BESC. **Car hire** Auto Locadora Veleiros, R Silva Jardim 1050, T3225 8207, hotel_veleiros@ uol.com.br. Locarauto, Silva Jardim 816, T3225 9000. **Internet** Moncho, Tiradentes 181. Internet café on R Felipe Schmidt 705. And others. **Post offices** Praça 15 de Novembro 5. **Telephones** Praça Pereira Oliveira 20. **Voltage** 220 volts AC.

Blumenau *p443*
Banks Câmbios/travel agencies: Vale do Itajaí Turismo e Cambio, Av Beira Rio 167, very helpful, German spoken.

Rio Grande do Sul → *Population: 10.2 million.*

Rio Grande do Sul is gaúcho country; it is also Brazil's chief wine producer. The capital, Porto Alegre, is the most industrialized city in the south, but in the surroundings are good beaches, interesting coastal national parks and the fine scenery of the Serra Gaúcha. On the border with Santa Catarina is the remarkable Aparados da Serra National Park. In the far west are the remains of Jesuit missions. Look out for local specialities such as comida campeira, te colonial and quentão. In southern Rio Grande do Sul there are great grasslands stretching as far as Uruguay to the south and Argentina to the west. In this distinctive land of the gaúcho, or cowboy (pronounced ga-oo-shoo in Brazil), people feel closer to Uruguay and Argentina than Brazil (except where football is concerned). The gaúcho culture has developed a sense of distance from the African-influenced society of further north. This separationist strain was most marked in the 1820s and 1830s when the Farroupilha movement, led by Bento Gonçalves, proclaimed the República Riograndense in 1835.

Porto Alegre → *Phone code: 0xx51. Colour map 7, inset. Population: 1,360,590.*

The capital of Rio Grande do Sul is where cowboy culture meets the bright lights. It lies at the confluence of five rivers (called Rio Guaíba, although it is not a river in its own right) and thence into the great freshwater lagoon, the Lagoa dos Patos, which runs into the sea. The freshwater port is one of the most up-to-date in the country and Porto Alegre is the biggest commercial centre south of São Paulo. It is also one of the richest and best educated parts of Brazil and held the first three World Social Forums (2001-2003), putting the city in a global spotlight. Standing on a series of hills and valleys on the banks of the Guaíba, it has a temperate climate through most of the year, though the temperature at the height of summer can often exceed 40°C and drop below 10°C in winter.

Ins and outs
Tourist offices To800-517686, www2.portoalegre.rs.gov.br/turismo. **Porto Alegre Turismo** ① *Travessa do Carmo 84, Cidade Baixa, T3212 3464, daily 0830-1800; also at airport; Usina do Gasômetro, Tue-Sun 0900-2100; Mercado Público, Mon-Fri 0900-1900, Sat 0900-1800; Mercado do Bom Fim, Loja 12, T3333 1873, daily 0900-2000, and various shopping centres.* The market area in Praça 15 de Novembro and the bus terminal are dangerous at night. Thefts have been reported in Voluntários da Pátria and Praça Parcão.

Sights
The older residential part of the town is on a promontory, dominated previously by the **Palácio Piratini** (Governor's Palace) and the imposing 1920s **cathedral** on the **Praça Marechal Deodoro** (or da Matriz). Also on, or near this square, are the neoclassical **Theatro São Pedro** (1858), the **Solar dos Câmara** (1818, now a historical and cultural centre), the **Biblioteca Pública** – all dwarfed by the skyscraper of the **Assembléia Legislativa** – and the **Museu Júlio de Castilhos** ① *Duque de Caxias 1231, T3221 3959, Tue-Fri 1300-1800, Sat 1400-1800,* which has an interesting historical collection about the state of Rio Grande do Sul. Down Rua General Câmara from Praça Marechal Deodoro is the **Praça da Alfândega**, with the old customs house and the Museu de Arte de Rio Grande do Sul (see below). A short walk east of this group, up Rua 7 de Setembro, is Praça 15 de Novembro, on which is the neoclassical **Mercado Público**, selling everything from religious artefacts to spice and meat. For art from the state, visit the **Museu de Arte do Rio Grande do Sul** ① *Praça Senador Florêncio (Praça da Alfândega), T3227 2311, www.margs.org.br, Tue-Sun 1000-1900, free.* **Museu de Comunicação Social** ① *R dos Andradas 959, T3224 4252, Mon-Fri 0900-1800, Sat 0900-1200,* in the former A Federação newspaper building, deals with the development of the press in Brazil since the 1920s.

A large part of **Rua dos Andradas** (Rua da Praia) is permanently closed to traffic and by around 1600 it is jammed full of people. Going west along Rua dos Andradas, you pass the wide stairway that leads up to the two high white towers of the church of **Nossa Senhora das Dores**. At the end of the promontory, the **Usina do Gasômetro** has been converted from a thermoelectric station into a cultural centre. Its enormous chimney has become a symbol for the city. There is a café in the bottom of it. The sunset from the centre's balcony is stunning. In the **Cidade Baixa** quarter are the colonial **Travessa dos Venezianos** (between Ruas Lopo Gonçalves and Joaquim Nabuco) and the **house of Lopo Gonçalves**, which houses the **Museu de Porto Alegre Joaquim José Felizardo** ① *R João Alfredo 582, T3226 7570, Tue-Sun 0900-1200, 1330-1800, free*, a collection on the history of the city.

The central **Parque Farroupilha** (called Parque Redenção) which has many attractions and on Sundays there is a feira of antiques, handicrafts and all sorts at the José Bonifácio end. The **Jardim Botânico** (Bairro Jardim Botânico, bus 40 from Praça 15 de Novembro), is on Rua Salvador França 1427, Zona Leste.

The 5-km wide **Rio Guaíba** lends itself to every form of boating and there are several sailing clubs (see Activities and tours, below). You can see a good view of the city, with glorious sunsets, from the **Morro de Santa Teresa** (take bus 95 from the top end of Rua Salgado Filho, marked 'Morro de Santa Teresa TV' or just 'TV'). Another good sunset-viewing spot is the Usina do Gasômetro.

Porto Alegre beach resorts

The main beach resorts of the area are to the east and north of the city. Heading east along the BR-290, 112 km from Porto Alegre is **Osório**, a pleasant lakeside town with a few hotels. From here it is 18 km southeast to the rather polluted and crowded beach resort of **Tramandaí** ① *getting there: 5 buses daily from Porto Alegre, US$3.50.* The beaches here are very popular, with lots of hotels, bars, restaurants, and other standard seaside amenities. Extensive dunes and lakes in the region provide an interesting variety of wildlife and sporting opportunities. The beach resorts become less polluted the further north you travel, and the water is clean by the time you reach Torres (see below). Among the resorts between the two towns is **Capão da Canoa**, with surfing at Atlântida beach. The Lagoa dos Quadros, inland, is used for windsurfing, sailing, water-skiing and jet-skiing.

Torres → *Phone code: 0xx51. Colour map 7, inset. Population: 30,880.*
Torres is a well developed resort, with a number of beaches, several high class, expensive hotels, a wide range of restaurants, professional surfing competitions and entertainment. Torres holds a ballooning festival in April. There is an annual independence day celebration, when a cavalcade of horses arrives in town on 16 September from Uruguay. Torres gets its name from the three huge rocks, or towers, on the town beach, Praia Grande. Fishing boats can be hired for a trip to **Ilha dos Lobos**, a rocky island 2 km out to sea, where sea lions spend the winter months. Dolphins visit Praia dos Molhes, north of the town, the year round and whales can occasionally be seen in July. The tourist office is at R Rio Branco 315, T664 1219/626 1937.

There is a paved road running south from Tramandaí along the coast to **Quintão**, giving access to many beaches. Of note is **Cidreira**, with Hotel Farol on the main street (**D** with bath). Bus from Porto Alegre US$3.40.

● **Sleeping** → *See Telephone, page 347, for important phone changes.*

Porto Alegre *p448, map p450*
Hotels in the area around R Garibáldi and Voluntários da Patria between Av Farrapos and rodoviária are overpriced and used for short stays.
AL-A Continental, Lg Vespasiano Júlio Veppo 77, T3027 1900, www.hoteiscontinental.com.br. High standards, cheaper at weekends, pool, gym. Recommended.
A Ritter, Lg Vespasiano Júlio Veppo 55, opposite rodoviária, T3228 4044, www.ritterhoteis.com.br. Four-star and 3-star wings, English, French, German spoken, bar, small pool, sauna. Fine restaurant, good service. Recommended.
A Conceição Center, Av Sen Salgado Filho 201, T3227 6088, www.hoteisconceicao.com.br. Respectable city hotel with well-kept rooms, a/c. Has a cheaper sister hotel.
B Lancaster, Trav Acelino de Carvalho 67, T3224

4737, www.hotel-lancaster-poa.com.br. Central, quiet, a/c, restaurant.
C Erechim, Av Júlio de Castilhos 341, near Rodoviária, T3228 7044, www.hotel erechim.com.br. Youth hostel member, with or without bath, noisy and some rooms smelly.
C-D América, Av Farrapos 119, T/F3226 0062, www.hotelamerica.com.br. Bright, large rooms with sofas, garage, also affiliated to youth hostel association. Recommended.
C-D Elevado, Av Farrapos 65, T/F3224 5250, www.hotelelevado.com.br. Youth hostel association member, big rooms, microwave and coffee, good value.
C-D Palácio, Av Vigário José Inácio 644, T3225 3467. Central, hot water, safe.
Camping Praia do Guarujá, 16 km out on Av Guaíba.

🅕 Eating

Porto Alegre *p448, map p450*

The Central Market along the Praça is lined with lancherias. Vegetarians might try some of the campeiro soups and casseroles.

🍴🍴🍴 Al Dente, R Mata Bacelar 210, Auxiliadora, T3342 8534. Expensive northern Italian cuisine. Closed Sun.

🍴🍴🍴 Chopp Stübel, R Quintino Bocaiúva 940, Moinhos de Vento, T3332 8895. Open 1800-0030, closed Sun, German food. Recommended.

🍴🍴🍴 Wunderbar, R Marquês do Herval 598, Moinhos de Vento, T3222 4967. German cooking, very busy 1830 till last diner leaves. Recommended, welcoming.

🍴🍴🍴-🍴🍴 514 Lobby Bar and Restaurant, Av Alberto Bins 514 (in Plaza São Rafael Hotel), T3220 7000. Daily lunch 1200-1430, dinner 1900-2300 (not Sun). Steaks, pasta and fish, good soups.

🍴🍴 Atelier de Massas, R Riachuelo 1482, T3225 1125. Lunch and dinner, Italian, closed Sun, fantastic pastas and steaks, excellent value.

🍴🍴 Coqueiros, R João Alfredo 208, T3227 1833. 1130-1430, 1930-2400, closed Sun and Mon evening. Cheap and cheerful churrasco.

🍴🍴 Gambrinus, Central Market ground level, Praça 15 de Novembro. T3226 6914. Lunch and dinner, regional cooking, closed Sun.

🍴🍴 Komka, Av Bahia 1275, San Geraldo, T3222 1881. 1130-1430, 1900-2300, closed Sun, also do churrasco. Recommended.

🍴 Chalé da Praça 15, Praça 15 de Novembro. Average gaúcho food but recommended for early evening drinks and snacks.

🍴 Ilha Natural, R Gen Câmara 60, T3224 4738. Self-service vegetarian, lunch only Mon-Fri.

🍴 Lancheria Primavera, Av Farrapos 187. Good breakfasts (toasties and juice) if staying nearby. 0630-1930 closed Sun. Staff also run red metal shack round corner on R Dr Barros Cassal serving tasty German hotdogs and burgers.

🍴 Nova Vida, R Demétrio Ribeiro 1182, T3226 8876. 1100-1500, closed Sun, vegetarian, good lasagne.

🍴 Spaguetti Express, Centro Comercial Nova Olária, Lima e Silva 776. Good Italian.

Porto Alegre

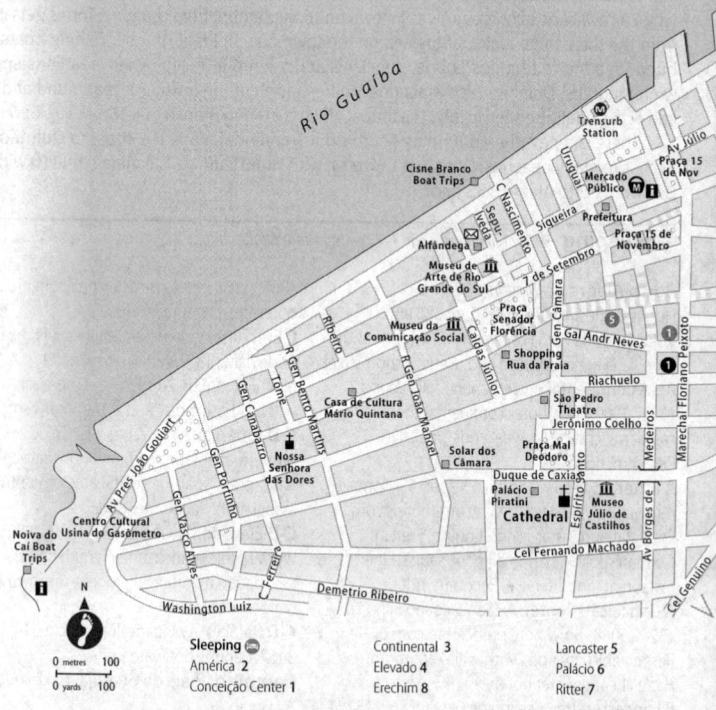

Sleeping 🛏️
América **2**
Conceição Center **1**
Continental **3**
Elevado **4**
Erechim **8**
Lancaster **5**
Palácio **6**
Ritter **7**

Cafés

Café Dos Cataventos, in Casa de Cultura Mário Quintana, R dos Andrades 736, in courtyard. Also **Restaurant Majestic** on roof, T3226 0153. Both serve good drinks, snacks and meals. Fantastic rooftop sunsets. 1200-2300.

The café in **Usina do Gasômetro** is very good for sandwiches and speciality coffee. Cheap.

🍷 Bars and clubs

Porto Alegre *p448, map p450*
Bars
On weekend nights, thousands spill out of the huge beer bars and clubs along Av Goethe between R Vasco de Gama and R Dona Laura in Rio Branco (a US$2.65 taxi ride from the centre).
Bar do Goethe, R 24 de Outubro 112, Moinhos de Vento, T3222 2043. Reunion each Tue, 2030, for foreign language speakers.
Bar do Nito, Av Cel Lucas de Oliveira 105, Moinhos de Vento. T3333 6221. Popular music bar.
Cía Sandwiches, Getúlio Vargas 1430, T3233 7414. 1800-0200, beer, sandwiches and music.

Sargeant Peppers, Dona Laura 329, T3331 3258. Live music Thu-Sat, closed Mon.

Clubs

Dr Jekyll, Travessa do Carmo 76, Cidade Baixa. T32269404. Open from 2200. Closed Sun.
Ossip, Av República 677 e João Afredo, T3224 2422. Pleasant wine bar.
Wanda Bar, R Comendador Coruja 169, Floresta. T3224 4755. Gay nightclub, open from 2030.

🎭 Entertainment

Porto Alegre *p448, map p450*
Art galleries Casa de Cultura Mário Quintana, R dos Andradas 736, T3221 7147. A lively centre for the arts, with exhibitions, theatre, pleasant bar etc, open 0900-2100, 1200-2100 Sat-Sun.
Theatre São Pedro, Praça Mal Deodoro, T3227 5100. Free noon and late afternoon concerts Sat, Sun, art gallery, café.

🎉 Festivals and events

Porto Alegre *p448, map p450*
The main event is on **2 Feb** (a local holiday), with the festival of **Nossa Senhora dos Navegantes** (Iemanjá), whose image is taken by boat from the central quay in the port to the industrial district of Navegantes. **Semana Farroupilha** celebrates gaúcho traditions with parades in traditional style, its main day being on **20 Sep**. The Carnival parade takes place in Av A do Carvalho, renamed Av Carlos Alberto Barcelos (or Roxo) for these 3 days only, after a famous carnival designer. **Feira do Livro** in Praça da Alfândega, **Oct-Nov**.

🛍 Shopping

Porto Alegre *p448, map p450*
Bookshops Livraria Londres, Av Osvaldo Aranha 1182. Used books in English, French and Spanish and old Life magazines.
Markets There is a street market (leather goods, basketware etc) in the streets around the central Post Office. Good leather goods are sold on the streets. Sun morning handicraft and bric-a-brac market (plus sideshows) Av José Bonifácio (next to Parque Farroupilha). There is a very good food market.
Shopping centres The Praia de Belas shopping centre, among the largest in Latin America, is a US$2 taxi ride from town.

🚶 Activities and tours

Porto Alegre *p448, map p450*
Two **boats trips** around islands in estuary:
Cisne Branco, from Cais do Porto, near Museu de

To Guaíba Bridge
To Guaíba Bridge
Garibáldi
Conceição
Carlos Chagas
Carlos Vicente
Av Maua
de Castilhos
Chaves Barcelos
Comendador Pereira
Pátria
To Airport
Farrapos
Voluntários da Pátria
Senhor dos Passos
Pinto Bandeira
Av Alberto Bins
Otávio Rocha
Vig José Inácio
Dr Flores
R dos Andradas
Av Independência
Gal Vitorino
Prof Annes Dias
Sen Salgado Filho
Sarmento Leite
Moinhos de Vento district, restaurants & Av Goethe
Av João Pessoa
Av dos Andra da Rocha
Osvaldo Aranha
Paulo Gama
University
Av Loureira da Silva
Sarmento Leite
Luis Englert
Setembrina
Parque Farroupilha
To Museu de Porto Alegre Joaquim José Felizardo

Eating 🍴
514 **2**
Atelier de Massas **1**
Chopp Stübel **3**
Wunderbar **4**

Arte de Rio Grande do Sul, T3224 5222. Several sailings on Sun, fewer mid-week, 1 hr, US$5. **Noiva do Caí**, from the Usina do Gasômetro, T3211 7662. Several on Sun, fewer mid- week, one hr, US$2 (check winter schedules).

⊜ Transport

Porto Alegre *p448, map p450*
Air The international airport is on Av dos Estados, 8 km from the city, T3358 2000.
Bus 1st-class local minibuses (*Lotação*), painted in a distinctive orange, blue and white pattern, stop on request, fares about US$0.80. Safer and more pleasant than normal buses (US$0.45). There are regular buses to the rodoviária. **Torres**, 9 a day, US$8.

International and interstate buses arrive at the rodoviária at Largo Vespasiano Júlio Veppo, on Av Mauá with Garibáldi, T3210 0101, www.rodoviaria-poa.com.br. Facilities include a post office and long-distance telephone service until 2100. There are 2 sections to the terminal; the ticket offices for interstate and international destinations are together in 1 block, beside the municipal tourist office (very helpful). The intermunicipal (state) ticket offices are in another block; for travel information within the state, ask at the very helpful booth on the station concourse.

To **Rio**, US$80, 24 hrs with **Itapemirim**; **São Paulo**, US$40 (leito US$68), 18 hrs; **Florianópolis**, US$21, 7 hrs with **Santo Anjo** (take an executivo rather than a convencional, which is a much slower service); **Curitiba**, from US$23 convencional to US$40 leito, coastal and Serra routes, 11 hrs; **Rio Grande**, US$13, every 2 hrs from 0600, 4 hrs. **Foz do Iguaçu**, US$35-40, 13 hrs. To **Jaguarão** on Uruguayan border at 2400, 6 hrs, US$13. **Uruguaiana**, US$23, 8 hrs. Many other destinations.
International buses Note: Take your passport and tourist card when purchasing international bus tickets. To **Montevideo**, with TTL executivo daily 2030 US$58 (leito Fri only at 2100), or take an ordinary bus to border town of Chuí, 7 hrs, US$32, then bus to Montevideo (US$12). To **Asunción** with Unesul at 1900, Tue, Fri, 18 hrs via **Foz do Iguaçu**. There are bus services to **Buenos Aires**, US$64, 19 hrs with **Pluma**, 1805 daily, route is Uruguaiana, Paso de los Libres, Entre Ríos and Zárate. For **Misiones** (Argentina), take 2100 bus (not Sat) to Porto Xavier on the Río Uruguay, 11 hrs, US$20, get exit stamp at police station, take a boat to San Javier, US$2.50, go to Argentine immigration at the port, then take a bus to Posadas (may have to change in Leandro N Além).
Metrô Trensurb, to the Mercado Público, via the rodoviária, US$0.50.

Road Good roads radiate from Porto Alegre, and Highway BR-116 is paved to Curitiba (746 km). To the south it is paved (mostly in good condition), to Chuí on the Uruguayan border, 512 km. In summer visibility can be very poor at night owing to mist, unfenced cows are a further hazard. The paved coastal road to Curitiba via Itajaí (BR-101), of which the first 100 km is the 4-lane Estrada General Osório highway, is much better than the BR-116 via Caxias and Lajes. The road to Uruguaiana is entirely paved but bumpy.

⊕ Directory

Porto Alegre *p448, map p450*
Banks Banco do Brasil, Av dos Estados 1515, T371 1955 (also has Visa/Plus ATM), and Av Assis Brasil 2487, T341 2466. 1000-1500, good rates for TCs. Branch at Uruguai 185 has Visa/Plus ATM. Many branches of **Bradesco** have Visa ATMs, also **Banco 24 Horas** for Visa ATMs. **Citibank**, R7 de Setembro 722, T3220 8619. MasterCard ATMs at any **HSBC** branch. **MasterCard**, cash against card, R 7 de Setembro 722, 8th floor, Centro. **Exprinter**, R Hilário Ribeiro 292 (best for cash). For other addresses consult tourist bureau brochure.
Cultural centres Instituto Goethe, 24 de Outubro 122, T3222 7832, www.goethe.de/br/poa/demail.htm. Mon-Fri, 0930-1230, 1430-2100, occasional concerts, bar recommended for German Apfelkuchen. **Embassies and consulates** Argentina, R Coronel Bordini 1033, Moinhos de Vento, T/F3321 1360, caleg@zaz.com.br. 1000-1600. **France**, R Ramiro Barcelos 1172, cj 217, T3222 6467, chfpoa@terra.com.br. **Germany**, R Prof Annes Dias 112, 11th floor, Centro, T3224 9592. 0830-1130. **Italy**, R José de Alencar 313, T3230 8200, urp.poa@embitalia.org.br. 0900-1200. **Japan**, Av João Obino 467, Alto Petrópolis, T3334 1299, cjpoa@terra.com.br. 0900-1130, 1400-1700. **Spain**, R Ildefonso Simões Lopes 85, Três Figueiras, T3338 1300, consuladoesp@terra.com.br. 0900-1430. **UK**, R Antenor Lemos 57 cj. 303, Menino Deus, T3232 1414, britcon@terra.com.br. 0830-1230, 1330-1630. **Uruguay**, Av Cristóvão Colombo 2999, Higienópolis, T3325 6200, conurugran@terra.com.br, 0900-1500. **Internet** Places in the centre, as well as Livraria Saraiva Megastore, Shopping Praia de Belas, Mon-Sat 1000-2200. PC2, Duque de Caxias 1464, T3227 6853. Portonet, R Mal Floriano 185, T3227 4696, 0900-2100.
Language courses Portuguese and Spanish, **Matilde Dias**, R Pedro Chaves Barcelos 37, Apdo 104, T3331 8235, malilde@estadao.com.br. **Post offices** R Siqueira Campos 1100, Centro, Mon-Fri 0900-1800, Sat 0900-1230. **Telephones** R Borges de Medeiros 475, and upstairs at rodoviária.

Rio Grande do Sul state

Mountains, vineyards, cowboys, waterfowl and ruined Jesuit missions are all part of the mix that makes up Brazil's southernmost state.

Serra Gaúcha → *Population: Canela, 33,625; Gramado, 29,593.*

The Serra Gaúcha boasts stunningly beautiful scenery, some of the best being around the towns of Gramado and Canela, about 130 km north of Porto Alegre. There is a distinctly Swiss/Bavarian flavour to many of the buildings in both towns. It is difficult to get rooms in the summer/Christmas. In spring and summer the flowers are a delight, and in winter there are frequently snow showers. This is excellent walking and climbing country among hills, woods, lakes and waterfalls. For canoeists, the Rio Paranhana at Três Coroas is renowned, especially for slalom. Local crafts include knitted woollens, leather, wickerwork, and chocolate.

Gramado, at 850 m on the edge of a plateau with views, provides a summer escape from the 40° C heat of the plains. It lives almost entirely by tourism and the main street, Avenida Borges de Medeiros, is full of kitsch artisan shops and fashion boutiques. In the summer, thousands of hydrangeas (hortênsias) bloom. About 1.5 km along Avenida das Hortênsias towards Canela is the **Prawer Chocolate Factory** ① *Av das Hortênsias 4100. T3286 1580, www.prawer.com.br, free tours of the truffle-making process and free tasting. 0830-1130, 1330-1700, closed weekends.* Opposite is the incongruous but good **Hollywood Dream Car Automobile Museum** ① *Av das Hortênsias 4151, T3286 4515, 0900-1900, US$2.10,* with a collection of dating back to a 1929 Ford Model A and Harley Davidson motorbikes from 1926. For a good walk/bike ride into the valley, take the dirt road Turismo Rural 28, Um Mergulho no Vale (A Dive into the Valley), which starts at Avenida das Hortênsias immediately before Prawer. Each August, Gramado holds a festival of Latin American cinema. **Tourist office** ① *Av das Hortênsias 2029, T3286 0200, www.gramadosite.com.br.* Internet at **Cyber** ① *Av Borges de Medeiros 2016, 1300-2300, US$2.80 per hr.*

A few kilometres along the plateau rim, **Canela** is less tourism and shopping-oriented than its neighbour ① *frequent bus service from Gramado, 10 mins.* **Tourist office** ① *R Dona Carlinda 455, T3282 2200, www.canelaturismo.com.br.* Voltage is 220 V AC.

About 7 km away is the **Parque Estadual do Caracol** ① *T278 3035, 0830-1800, US$1.75,* with a spectacular 130-m high waterfall where the Rio Caracol tumbles out of thick forest. A 927-step metal staircase ("equivalent to a 45-storey building") leads to the plunge pool. There is an 18-km circular bike route continuing on to **Parque Ferradura**, where there is a good view into the canyon of the Rio Cai. From the Ferradura junction, take the right to continue to the **Floresta Nacional** ① *T282 2608, 0800-1700, free,* run by Ibama From here, the dirt road continues round to Canela. Another good hike or bike option is the 4-km track southeast of Canela past Parque das Sequóias to **Morro Pelado**. At over 600 m, there are spectacular views from the rim edge.

Parque Nacional de Aparados da Serra → *Colour map 7, inset.*

① *Wed-Sat 0900-1700, US$2.10 plus US$1.75 for car, T251 1262. Further information from Porto Alegre tourist office or Ibama, R Miguel Teixeira 126, Cidade Baixa, Porto Alegre, CEP 90050-250, T3228 7290.*

The major attraction at the Parque Nacional de Aparados da Serra is a canyon, 7.8 km long and 720 m deep, known locally as the Itaimbezinho. Here, two waterfalls cascade 350 m into a stone circle at the bottom. For experienced hikers (and with a guide) there is a difficult path to the bottom of Itaimbezinho. One can then hike 20 km to Praia Grande in Santa Catarina state. As well as the canyon, the park, its neighbour, the **Parque Nacional da Serra Geral**, and the surrounding region have several bird specialities. The park is 80 km from São Francisco de Paula (18 km east of Canela, 117 km north of Porto Alegre).

Tourist excursions, mostly at weekends, from **São Francisco de Paula** (a few hotels and *pousadas*; tourist information at southern entrance to town, www.saofranciscodepaula.tur.br). At other times, take a bus to Cambará do Sul (0945, 1700, 1¼ hours, US$2.65): several pousadas and **D Pousada dos Pinheiros** ① *Estrada Morro Agudo, T3282 2503, pousadadospinheiros@via-rs.net, 12 km from Cambará, off road to Aparados da Serra and Praia Grande turn right (signposted) for 2 km,* rustic cabins, breakfast and dinner at isolated farm amid stunning scenery. Recommended.

Caxias do Sul and around

→ *Phone code: 0xx54. Post code: 95000. Colour map 7, inset. Population: 360,419.*

This city's population is principally of Italian descent and it is an expanding and modern city, the centre of the Brazilian wine industry. Vines were first brought to the region in 1840 but not until the end of the century and Italian immigration did the industry develop. The church of **São Pelegrino** has paintings by Aldo Locatelli and 5 m-high bronze doors sculptured by Augusto Murer. There is a good **Museu Municipal** ① *R Visconde de Pelotas 586, T3221 2423, Tue-Sat 0830-1130, 1330-1700, Sun 1400-1700*, with displays of artefacts of the Italian immigration. Italian roots are again on display in the **Parque de Exposições Centenário**, 5 km out on R Ludovico Cavinato. January-February is the best time to visit. There is a tourist information kiosk in Praça Rui Barbosa. The **rodoviária** ① *R Ernesto Alves 1341, T228 3000*, is a 15-minute walk from the main praça, but many buses pass through the centre. **Tourist office** ① *R Ludovico Cavinatto, 1431, T3222 1875, www.caxias.tur.br*.

Caxias do Sul's festival of grapes is held February to March. Many adegas accept visitors (but do not always give free tasting). Good tour and tasting (six wines) at Adega Granja União, R Os 18 de Forte 2346. Visit also the neighbouring towns and sample their wines: **Farroupilha** 20 km from Caxias do Sul. **Nova Milano**, 6 km away (bus to Farroupilha, then change – day trip). **Bento Gonçalves**, 40 km from Caxias do Sul. **Garibáldi**, which has a dry ski slope and toboggan slope – equipment hire, US$5 per hr. A restored steam train leaves Bento Gonçalves for a 1½-hour trip to **Carlos Barbosa**; called 'a rota do vinho' (the wine run), it goes through vineyards in the hills. US$30 round trip, including wines, with live band; reserve in advance through **Giordani Turismo** ① *R Erny Hugo Dreher 227 sala 01, Bento Gonçalves, T3452 6042*. Another worthwhile trip is to **Antônio Prado**, 1½ hours by Caxiense Bus. The town is now a World Heritage Site because of the large number of original buildings built by immigrants in the Italian style.

Jesuit Missions → *Colour map 7, grid C1. Colour map 8, grid A6.*

West of **Passo Fundo**, 'the most gaúcho city in Rio Grande do Sul', are the **Sete Povos das Missões Orientais**. The only considerable Jesuit remains in Brazilian territory (very dramatic) are at **São Miguel das Missões**, some 50 km from **Santo Ângelo**. At São Miguel, now a World Heritage Site, there is a church, 1735-1745, and small **museum** *0900-1800*. A son et lumière show in Portuguese is held daily, in winter at 2000, and later in summer, although all times rather depend on how many people there are. The show ends too late to return to Santo Ângelo. Gaúcho festivals are held on some Sunday afternoons, in a field near the Mission.

Border with Argentina → *Colour map 8, grid A6.*

In the extreme west are **Uruguaiana**, a cattle centre 772 km from Porto Alegre, and its twin Argentine town of Paso de los Libres, also with a casino. A 1,400 m bridge over the Rio Uruguai links the cities. Brazilian immigration and customs are at the end of the bridge, five blocks from the main praça; exchange and information in the same building. Since 2003 this border crossing has not been recommended as Paso de los Libres was not safe. Should you cross here, there are hotels in each town. **Note:** Exchange rates are better in the town than at the border.

South of Porto Alegre → *Colour map 7, inset.*

South of Quintão a track runs to the charming town of **Mostardas** (www.mostardas.rs.gov.br; **D Hotel Mostardense** ① *R Bento Conçalves 203, T3673 1368*, good), thence along the peninsula on the seaward side of the Lagoa dos Patos to São José do Norte, opposite Rio Grande (see below). Mostardas is a good base for visiting the national park **Lagoa do Peixe** ① *information: Praça Luís Martins 30, Mostardas, T3673 1464, free*, park has no infrastructure. This is one of South America's top spots for migrating birds: flamingos and albatross are among the visitors. The main lake (which has highest bird concentration) is about 20 km from Mostardas and the town of **Tavares**. The park is, however, under threat from invasive planting of trees.

São Lourenço do Sul About 40 km to the south (towards Rio Grande) begins the Costa Doce of the Lagoa dos Patos. São Lourenço (*Phone code oxx53, Population 43,691, www.saolourenco.net*) is a good place to enjoy the lake, the beaches, fish restaurants and watersports. The town hosts a popular four-day festival in March. On the BR-116, **Pelotas** is the second largest city in the State of Rio Grande do Sul, 271 km south of Porto Alegre, on the

Rio São Gonçalo which connects the shallow Lagoa dos Patos with the Lagoa Mirim. There are many good hotels and transport links to all of the state and the Uruguay border at Chuí.

South of Pelotas on the BR-471, is the **Taim** water reserve on the Lagoa Mirim. Many protected species, including black swans and the quero-quero (the Brazilian lapwing). Information T262 1500, or from Ibama in Porto Alegre.

Rio Grande Some 59 km south of Pelotas, at the entrance to the Lagoa dos Patos, is the city Rio Grande (*Phone code: 0xx53, Population: 186,544*). It is the distribution centre for the southern part of Rio Grande do Sul, with significant cattle and meat industries. During the latter half of the 19th century Rio Grande was an important centre, but today it is a rather poor town, notable for the charm of its old buildings. The **Catedral de São Pedro** dates from 1755-1775. **Museu Oceanográfico** ① *2 km from centre on Av Perimetral, T3232 9107, daily 0900-1100, 1400-1700, bus 59 or walk along waterfront*, has an interesting collection of 125,000 molluscs. The tourist kiosk is at junction of R Duque de Caxias and R Gen Becaleron.

Excursions To **Cassino**, a popular seaside town on the ocean, 24 km, over a good road. Travelling south, beaches are Querência (5 km), Stela Maris (9 km), Netuno (10 km), all with surf. The breakwater (the Barra), 5 km south of Cassino, no bus connection, through which all vessels entering and leaving Rio Grande must pass, is a tourist attraction. Barra-Rio Grande buses, from the east side of Praça Ferreira pass the Superporto. Across the inlet from Rio Grande is the little-visited settlement of **São José do Norte**, founded in 1725. There are ferries every half hour, 30 minutes, São José to Rio Grande; there are also three car ferries daily, T232 1500. Tourist information from R Gen Osório 127. Buses run north to Tavares and Mostardas.

Border with Uruguay: coastal route → *Colour map 7, inset. Population: 5,167.*

The Brazilian border town is **Chuí**. The BR-471 from Porto Alegre and Pelotas skirts the town and carries straight through to Uruguay, where it becomes Ruta 9. The main street crossing west to east, Avenida Internacional (Avenida Uruguaí on the Brazilian side, Avenida Brasil in Uruguay) is lined with clothes and household shops in Brazil, duty free shops and a casino in Uruguay. São Miguel fort, built by the Portuguese in 1737, now reconstructed with period artefacts, is worth a visit. A lighthouse 10 km west marks the Barro do Chuí inlet, which has uncrowded beaches and is visited by sea lions. Brazilian immigration is about 2½ km from the border, on BR-471, road to Pelotas. Buses stop at customs on both sides of the border, except those from Pelotas, on which you must ask the bus to stop for exit formalities. International buses make the crossing straightforward: the company holds passports; hand over your visitor's card on leaving Brazil and get a Uruguayan one on entry. Have luggage available for inspection. Make sure you get your stamp, or you will have trouble leaving Brazil.

Entering Brazil From Uruguay, on the Uruguayan side, the bus will stop if asked, and wait while you get your exit stamp (with bus conductor's help); on the Brazilian side, the appropriate form is completed by the rodoviária staff when you purchase your ticket into Brazil. The bus stops at Polícia Federal (BR-471) and the conductor completes formalities while you sit on the bus.

Border with Uruguay: inland routes → *Colour map 8, grid A6.*

At **Aceguá**, 60 km south of Bagé, there is a crossing to the Uruguayan town of Melo, and further east, **Jaguarão** with the Uruguayan town of **Rio Branco**, linked by the 1½ km long Mauá bridge across the Rio Jaguarão.

Entering Uruguay Before crossing into Uruguay, you must visit Brazilian Polícia Federal to get an exit stamp; if not, the Uruguayan authorities will send you back. The crossing furthest west is **Barra do Quaraí** to Bella Unión, via the Barra del Cuaraim bridge. This is near the confluence of the Rios Uruguai and Quaraí. Thirty kilometres east is another crossing from **Quaraí** to **Artigas** in a cattle raising and agricultural area.

The southern interior of the state is the region of the real gaúcho. Principal towns of this area include **Santana do Livramento**. Its twin Uruguayan city is Rivera. All one need do is cross the main street to Rivera, but by public transport this is not a straightforward border. The town has hotels and a youth hostel.

● Sleeping → *See Telephone, page 347, for important phone changes.*

Serra Gaúcha *p453*
Gramado

Plenty of hotels and places to eat (mostly expensive).

A Chalets do Vale, R Arthur Reinheimer 161 (off Av das Hortênsias at about 4700), T3286 4151, chaletsdovale@via-rs.net. 3 homely chalets in lovely setting, kitchen, TV, good deal for groups of 4/ families.

D Albergue Internacional de Gramado, Av das Hortênsias 3880, T295 1020, www.gramado hostel.com.br. Cosy and new, dormitory accommodation, **B** in double room, cheaper for HI members.

Canela

AL-A Serra Verde, Av Osvaldo Aranha 610, T282 6511, www.serraverdehotel.com.br. With thermal pools, sauna, massage, TV and internet, parking, very good.

A Bela Vista, R Oswaldo Aranha 160, T/F282 1327, near rodoviária. Good breakfasts.

C Pousada Schermer, Travessa Romeu 30, T282 1746. Very good indeed.

C Turis Café, R Oswaldo Aranha 223, T282 2774. Breakfast, English speaking staff.

D pp Pousada do Viajante, R Ernesto Urbani 132, T282 2017. Kitchen facilities, dormitories and double rooms.

Camping Camping Clube do Brasil, 1 km from waterfall in Parque do Caracol, 1 km off main road, signposted (8 km from Canela), T282 4321. Sell excellent honey and chocolate. **Sesi**, camping or cabins, R Francisco Bertolucci 504, 2½ km outside Canela, T/F282 1311. Clean, restaurant.

Caxias do Sul *p454*

Hotels fill up early in the afternoon.

C Grande, R Independência 1064, Farroupilha, T/F261 1025, 2 blocks from the church where the buses from Caxias do Sul stop, no breakfast, clean.

C Pérola, Marquês de Herval 237, T223 6080. Good value.

C Somensi, R Siba Paes 367, Bento Gonçalves, T453 1254, near the Pipa Pórtico and Cristo Rei church in the upper town. And others.

D Pousada Casa Mia, Trav Niterói 71, Bento Gonçalves, T451 1215. HI youth hostel.

Camping Palermo, 5 km out on BR-116 at Km 118, T222 7255. **Recanto dos Pinhais**, on BR-453 towards Lajeado Grande at Km 23. At Garibáldi, Camping Clube do Brasil, estrada Gen Buarque de Macedo 4 km.

Jesuit Missions *p454*
São Miguel

In the evening it is difficult to find a good place to eat, try one of the 2 snack bars for hamburgers.

B Hotel Barichello, Av Borges do Canto 1567, T3381 1272. Nice and quiet, restaurant with churrasco for lunch.

D Pousada das Missões, youth hostel, next to the ruins, T3381 1030, pousada.missoes@ terra.com.br. Very good.

Santo Ângelo

AL-B Maerkli, Av Brasil 1000, T/F3313 2127. Recommended.

D Comércio, Av Brasil 1178, T3312 2542. Good for the price, a bit run down.

D Hotel Nova Esperança, Trav Centenário 463, T3312 1173. Behind bus station, without breakfast.

South of Porto Alegre: Rio Grande *p455*

A Atlântico Rio Grande, R Duque de Caxias 55, T3231 3833. Recommended, good value.

C Paris, R Mal F Peixoto 112, T3231 3866. Old, charming and recommended.

Border with Uruguay: coastal route *p455*
Chuí

B Bertelli Chuí, BR-471, Km 648, 2 km from town, T3265 1266, www.bertellichuihotel.com.br. Comfortable, with pool.

D Rivero, Colômbia 163-A, T3265 1271. With bath, without breakfast.

D San Francisco, Av Colombia e R Chile. Shower, restaurant.

● Eating

Serra Gaúcha: Canela *p453*

♥♥ Bifão e Cia, Av Osvaldo Aranha 301, T282-9156. For meat, good local food and ambience.

South of Porto Alegre: Rio Grande *p455*

♥♥ Blue Café, R Luis Loréa 314. Expresso machine and good cake. 0830-1930 (2300 Fri when jazz/blues music).

♥♥ Parrillada Don Lauro, R Luís Loréa 369. Uruguayan steak in nice restaurant, fairly cheap.

♥ Rio's, R Val Porto 393. Vast but good churrascaria.

♥ Tia Laura, 29 km from town on BR-392 north to Pelotas. Excellent, specializes in home cooking and café colonial.

● *For an explanation of the sleeping and eating price codes used in this guide, see inside the front*
● *cover. Other relevant information is found in Essentials pages 345-347.*

⊙ Transport

Border with Argentina *p454*
Uruguaiana/ Paso de los Libres
Taxi or **bus** across the bridge about US$4.50.
Buses connect the bus stations and centres of
each city every 30 mins; if you have to disembark
for visa formalities, a following bus will pick you
up without extra charge. There are buses to
Porto Alegre. Planalto buses run from
Uruguaiana via Barra do Quaraí/Bella Unión to
Salto and **Paysandú** in Uruguay.

South of Porto Alegre *p454*
Lagoa do Peixe
For local transport José Carlos Martins Cassola
T673 1186, Itamar Velho Sessin T673 1431. From
Mostardas you can hop off the 1045 **bus** which
passes through the northern end of the park on its
way to the beach (basic hotels and restaurants).
Three buses a week between Mostardas/Tavares
and São José do Norte (130 km), via Bojuru.

São Lourenço do Sul
Bus From **Porto Alegre** US$8.50, 6 a day.

Rio Grande
Bus Frequent daily to and from **Pelotas**
(56 km), 1 hr, US$2.25, **Bagé** (280 km), **Santa
Vitória** (220 km), and **Porto Alegre** (5 a day,
US$13, 4 hrs). All buses to these destinations
go through Pelotas. Road to Uruguayan
border at **Chuí** is paved, but the surface is
poor (5 hrs by bus, at 0700 and 1430). Bus
tickets to Punta del Este or Montevideo at
2330 from rodoviária.

Border with Uruguay: coastal route *p455*
Chuí
Bus Rodoviária on R Venezuela. Buses run from
Chuí to **Pelotas** (6-7 daily, US$10, 4 hrs), **Rio
Grande** (0700, 1400, 5 hrs, US$8) and **Porto
Alegre** (1200, 2400, 7¾ hrs, US$32).

Border with Uruguay: inland route *p455*
Santana do Livramento
Bus Rodoviária is at Gen Salgado Filho e Gen
Vasco Alves. Bus to **Porto Alegre**, 2 daily, 7 hrs,
US$26.50; 3 daily to **Uragaiana**, 4 hrs, US$13;
services also to São Paulo and other
destinations.

Foz do Iguaçu

*The Iguaçu Falls are the most stunning waterfalls in South America. Their magnitude, and
the volume of water that thunders over the edge, has to be seen to be believed. They are
32 km from the city of Foz do Iguaçu. For a description of the falls, maps and an account of
road links between Argentina, Brazil and Paraguay, see the Argentina chapter, page 174.*

Ins and outs

Tourist offices Foz do Iguaçu: Secretaria Municipal de Turismo, Praça Getúlio Vargas
69, T3521 1461, 0700-2300, www.fozdoiguacu.pr.gov.br. Very helpful, English spoken.
There is a 24-hour tourist help line number, T0800-451516. Very helpful. Airport tourist
information is also good, open for all arriving flights, gives map and bus information,
English spoken. Helpful office, free map, at the rodoviária, English spoken.

Parque Nacional Foz do Iguaçu → *Colour map 7, grid C1.*

ⓘ *US$9, payable in reais only, includes transport within the park. The park is open daily,
0900-1700 in winter, and to 1800 in summer (check if the park is closed until 1300 on
Mon); www.cataratasdoiguacu.com.br.*
The Brazilian national park was founded in 1939 and the area was designated a World Heritage
Site by UNESCO in 1986. Fauna most frequently encountered are little and red brocket deer,
South American coati, white-eared opossum, and a sub-species of the brown capuchin
monkey. The endangered tegu lizard is common. Over 100 species of butterflies have been
identified, among them the electric blue Morpho, the poisonous red and black heliconius and
species of Papilionidae and Pieridae. The bird life is especially rewarding for birdwatchers. Five
members of the toucan family can be seen.

Take a bus or taxi to the park's entrance, 17 km from Foz. There's a smart modern **visitors
centre** here, with toilets, ATM, a small café, a large souvenir shop and a Banco do Brasil
câmbio (0800-1900). An **Exposição Ecolôgica** has information about the natural history of
the falls and surrounding park (included in entry fee). Nature lovers are advised to visit first
thing in the morning, preferably in low season, as crowds can significantly detract from the

experience of the falls and surrounding park (at peak times like Semana Santa up to 10,000 visitors a day arrive). From the entrance, shuttle buses leave every 10-15 minutes for the 8-km journey to the falls, stopping first at the start of the **Macuco Safari** (see below). From there it's another 10 minutes' drive to the Hotel Tropical das Cataratas and the start of a 1.2 km paved walk to the falls. This is an easy walk, taking you high above the Rio Iguaçu, giving splendid views of all the falls on the Argentine side from a series of galleries. At the end of the path, you can walk down to a viewing point right almost under the powerful Floriano Falls, a dramatic view, since you're in the middle of the river, though you will get completely soaked. A catwalk at the foot of the Floriano Falls goes almost to the middle of the river to give a good view of the Garganta del Diablo. From here, there are 150 steps up to the **Porto Canoas** complex (there is a lift for those who find stairs difficult); you can also return the way you came, and walk a little further along the road. The Porto Canoas complex consists of a big souvenir shop, toilets, a café, a fast food place (mixed reports) and smart **restaurant** ① *buffet lunch US$15, 1200-1600, good value*, all with good view of the river above the falls. Return to the visitor centre and entrance either by the free shuttle bus, by walking back along the forest path as far as Hotel das Cataratas (good lunch with a view of the falls) and take the bus from there. The whole visit will take around two hours, plus time for lunch. Never feed wild animals and keep your distance when taking photos; coatis have been known to attack visitors with food.

Foz do Iguaçu and around → *Phone code 0xx45. Population 301,400.*

A small, modern city, 28 km from the falls, with a wide range of accommodation and good communications by air and road with the main cities of southern Brazil and Asunción in Paraguay. The **Parque das Aves bird zoo** ① *Rodovia das Cataratas Km 16, 100 m before the*

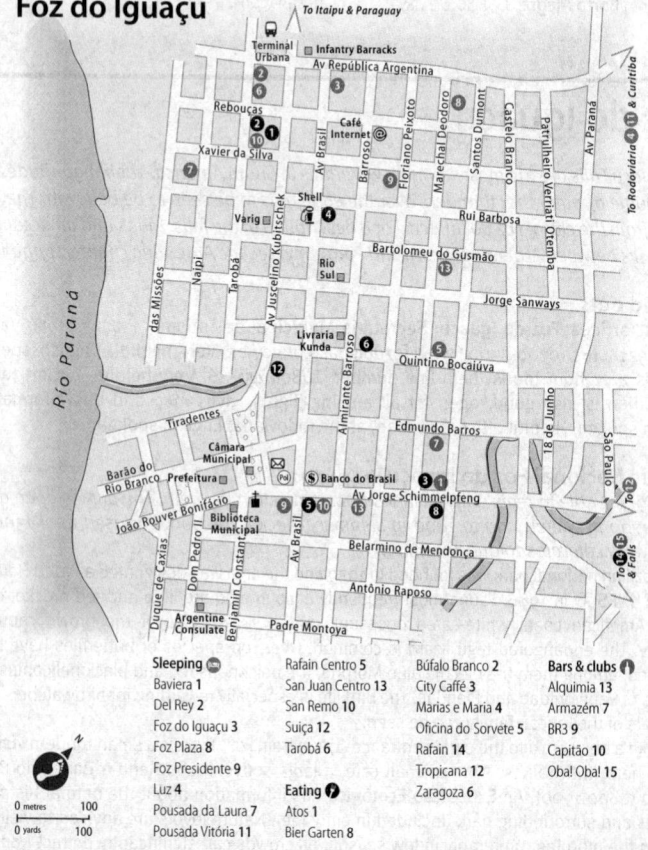

Foz do Iguaçu

Sleeping
Baviera 1
Del Rey 2
Foz do Iguaçu 3
Foz Plaza 8
Foz Presidente 9
Luz 4
Pousada da Laura 7
Pousada Vitória 11
Rafain Centro 5
San Juan Centro 13
San Remo 10
Suiça 12
Tarobá 6

Eating
Atos 1
Bier Garten 8
Búfalo Branco 2
City Caffé 3
Marias e Maria 4
Oficina do Sorvete 5
Rafain 14
Tropicana 12
Zaragoza 6

Bars & clubs
Alquimia 13
Armazém 7
BR3 9
Capitão 10
Oba! Oba! 15

entrance to the park, *T/F529 8282, www.parquedasaves.com.br, 0830-1700, US$10*, has received frequent good reports. It contains Brazilian and foreign birds, many species of parrot and beautiful toucans, in huge aviaries through which you can walk, with the birds flying and hopping around you. There are other birds in cages and a butterfly and hummingbird house.

The **Itaipu dam** ① *on the Río Paraná 12 km north, a short film is shown at the visitor centre 10 mins before each guided visit, all free, at 0800, 0900, 1000, 1400, 1500, 1530, Mon-Sat, check times with tourist office, and take passport, T3520 6999, www.itaipu.gov.br*, is the site of the largest single power station in the world built jointly by Brazil and Paraguay. Construction of this massive scheme began in 1975 and it became operational in 1984. The main dam is 8 km long, creating a lake which covers 1,400 sq km. The 18 turbines have an installed capacity of 12,600,000 Kw and produce about 75 bn Kwh a year, providing 80% of Paraguay's electricity and 25% of Brazil's. The Paraguayan side may be visited from Ciudad del Este. There is also the **Ecomuseu de Itaipu** ① *Av Tancredo Neves, Km 11, Mon 1400-1700, Tue-Sat 0900-1100, 1400-1700*, and **Iguaçu Environmental Education Centre** *free with guide*, are geared to educate about the preservation of the local culture and environment, or that part which isn't underwater. Recommended.

Border with Argentina

If entering Argentina only for the day, there is no need to obtain a Brazilan exit stamp but you must get Argentine stamps for any visit. The city bus between Foz do Iguaçu and Puerto Iguazú therefore only stops and waits at the Argentine border post, not the Brazilian one. If you are crossing from one country to the other for an extended period and need stamps from both, then you can ask the bus driver for a transfer, get off at the Brazilian border post and get on the next bus through without paying again. If entering Brazil only for the day, in principle a stamp is required, especially if you need a visa. In practice it is seldom asked for and adds considerably to travel time because the bus will not wait for you at the Brazilian border post.

Between October-February Brazil is 1 hr ahead of Argentina. It takes about two hours to get from Foz to the Argentine falls, very tiring when the weather is hot.

Border with Paraguay → *Brazil is 1 hr ahead of Paraguay.*

The Ponte de Amizade/Puente de Amistad (Friendship Bridge) over the Río Paraná, 6 km north of Foz, leads straight into the heart of Ciudad del Este. Paraguayan and Brazilian immigration formalities are dealt with at opposite ends of the bridge. Ask for relevant stamps if you need them. A large new customs complex is being built at the Brazilian end of the bridge (2006).

● Sleeping

Foz do Iguaçu *p457, map p458*
Note: Av Juscelino Kubitschek and the streets south of it, towards the river, are unsafe at night. Many prostitutes around R Rebouças and Almirante Barroso. Taxis are only good value for short distances when you are carrying all your luggage.
AL Rafain Centro, Mal Deodoro 984, T/F3521 3500, www.rafaincentro.com.br. Smart, comfortable, attractive pool area, good restaurant, WiFi internet connection.
AL Suiça, Av Felipe Wandscheer 3580, T3525 3232, www.hotelsuica.com.br. Some way out of the city, but charming, comfortable, Swiss manager, helpful with tourist information, attractive pool.
A Foz do Iguaçu, Av Brasil 97, T3521 4455, www.hotelfozdoiguacu.com.br. Smart, attractive pool and terrace, well-designed rooms, good value.
A Foz Plazza Hotel, R Marechal Deodoro 1819, T/F3523 1448, fozplazza@uol.com.br. Serene and very nice.

A-B Foz Presidente, R Xavier da Silva 1000, T/F3572 4450, www.fozpresidentehoteis.com.br. Good value, decent rooms, restaurant, pool, with breakfast, convenient for buses.
B 15 de Julho, Almte Barroso 1794, T3574 2664, F3572 8849. A/c, cheaper with fan, TV, hot water, pool, German and some English spoken, overpriced.
B Baviera, Av Jorge Schimmelpfeng 697, T3523 5995, www.hotelbavieraiguassu.com.br. Chalet-style exterior, on main road, central for bars and restaurants, comfortable, if rather gloomy rooms.
B San Juan Centro, R Marechal Deodoro 1349, T3523 1512, or 0800415505, www.sanjuan hoteis.com.br. A/c, comfortable, excellent buffet breakfast, popular, good value. Recommended.
B Tarobá, R Tarobá 1048, T3025 2199, www.hoteltaroba.com.br. Bright and welcoming, small pool, nice rooms, helpful, a/c, good breakfast, free internet. Recommended.
C Luz, Av Costa e Silva Km 5, near Rodoviária, T3522 3535, www.luzhotel.com.br. A/c, TV, pool. Recommended.

C Del Rey, R Tarobá 1020 e República Argentina, T3523 2027. Nothing fancy, but perennially popular, little pool, great breakfasts. Recommended.

C Pousada Evelina Navarrete, R Irlan Kalichewski 171, Vila Yolanda, T/F3574 3817, pousada.evelina@foznet.com.br. Lots of tourist information, English, French, Italian, Polish and Spanish spoken, lots of information, good breakfast and location, near Chemin Supermarket, near Av Cataratas on the way to the falls. Recommended.

C San Remo, Xavier da Silva 563 at Tarobá, T3523 1619, roberto_171@hotmail.com. Scrupulously clean though small rooms with TV, all you can eat breakfast, English, Spanish and Hebrew spoken. In-house travel agency.

D Pousada da Laura, R Naipi 671, T/F3572 3374. Secure and run by the enthusiastic Laura who speaks some Spanish, English, Italian and French. The hostel has a kitchen, laundry facilities and en suites and is a good place to meet other travellers. Good breakfasts too.

D pp Pousada Vitória, R Nereu Ramos 285, Parque Presidente, near bus station, T573 4664/9967 6183 (mob). Hot shower, helpful, Spanish and English spoken.

D pp (in high season IYHA members only): **Paudimar Campestre**, Av das Cataratas Km 12.5, Remanso Grande, near airport, T/F3529 6061, www.paudimar.com.br. From airport or town take Parque Nacional bus (0525-0040) and get out at Remanso Grande bus stop, by Hotel San Juan, then take the free shuttle (0700-1900) to the hostel, or 1.2 km walk from main road. Camping as well, pool, soccer pitch, quiet, kitchen and communal meals, breakfast. Highly recommended. For assistance, ask for owner, Gladis. The hostel has telephone, fax and internet for guests' use. Tours run to either side of the falls (good value). Paudimar desk at rodoviária.

Camping Camping E Pousada Internacional, R Manêncio Martins 21, 1½ km from town, T3529 8883, www.campinginternacional.com.br. For vehicles and tents, US$10 pp (half with International Camping Card), also basic cabins (**E**), helpful staff, English, German and Spanish spoken, pool, restaurant. **Note**: Camping is not permitted by the Hotel das Cataratas and falls.

Outside Foz do Iguaçu *p458*
LL Hotel das Cataratas (Tropical), directly overlooking the Falls, 28 km from Foz, T2102 7000, www.tropicalhotel.com.br. Some discount may be offered in slack periods for holders of the Brazil Air Pass. Generally recommended but caters for lots of groups, attractive colonial-style building with pleasant gardens (where a lot of wildlife can be seen at night and early morning) and pool. Non-residents can eat here, midday

and evening buffets; also à-la-carte dishes and dinner with show.
On the road to the falls (Rodovia das Cataratas) are:
L San Martin, Km 17, T3521 8088, www.hotelsanmartin.com.br. Attractive 4-star, a/c, TV, pool, sports, nightclub, several eating options, luxury, comfortable. Recommended.
AL Bristol Carimã, Km 10, T3521 3000, www.carima.com.br. 4-star, popular with groups, well laid out, lots of facilities, good restaurant, pool, bars, good value.

Foz do Iguaçu *p458, map p458*
¶¶¶ Búfalo Branco, R Rebouças 530, T3523 9744. Superb all you can eat churrasco, includes filet mignon, bull's testicles, salad bar and desert. Sophisticated surroundings and attentive service. Highly recommended.
¶¶¶ Cabeça de Boi, Av Felipe Wandscheer, Km 6, T3525 3358 . Live music, buffet, churrasco, but coffee and pastries also.
¶¶¶ Rafain, Av das Cataratas, Km 6.5, T3523 1177, closed Sun. Out of town, take a taxi or arrange with travel agency. Set price for excellent buffet with folkloric music and dancing (2100-2300) from throughout South America, touristy but very entertaining. Recommended.
¶¶¶ Zaragoza, R Quintino Bocaiúva 882, T3574 3084. Large and upmarket, for Spanish dishes and seafood. Recommended.
¶¶ Atos, Av Juscelino Kubitschek 865, T3572 2785. Per kilo buffet with various meats, salads, sushi and puddings. Lunch only.
¶¶ Bier Garten, Av Jorge Schimmelpfeng 550, T3523 3700. Pizzeria and choparia, beer garden in name only but some trees.
¶¶ Tropicana, Av Juscelino Kubitschek 228, T3574 1701. All-you-can-eat pizza or churrascaria with salad bar, good value.

Cafés
City Caffé, Av Jorge Schimmelpfeng 898. Stylish café open daily 0800-2330 for sandwiches, Arabic snacks and pastries.
Marias e Maria, Av Brasil 505. Good confeitaria.
Oficina do Sorvete, Av Jorge Schimmelpfeng 244, open daily 1100-0100. Excellent ice- creams, a popular local hang-out.

Bars and clubs

Foz do Iguaçu *p458, map p458*
Bars, all doubling as restaurants, concentrated on Av Jorge Schimmelpfeng for 2 blocks from Av Brasil to R Mal Floriano Peixoto. Wed to Sun are best nights; crowd tends to be young.
Alquimia, Av Jorge Schimmelpfeng 334, T3572 3154. Popular, nightclub, Dancing, attached, open 2400-0500.

Armazém, R Edmundo de Barros 446, T3572
7422. Intimate and sophisticated, attracts
discerning locals, good atmosphere, mellow live
music, US$1 cover. Recommended.
BR3, Av Jorge Schimmelpfeng corner with Av
Brasil. Modern, open till 2400.
Capitão Bar, Av Jorge Schimmelpfeng 288 and
Almte Barroso, T3572 1512. Large, loud and
popular, nightclub attached.
Oba! Oba!, Av das Cataratas 3700,
T529 6596 (Antigo Castelinho). Live samba
show Mon-Sat 2315-0015, very popular,
US$12 for show and drink.

▲ Activities and tours

Parque Nacional Foz do Iguaçu *p457*
Tours
Macuco Safari Tour, T3529 6262,
www.macuco safari.com.br, 1 hr 40 mins,
US$45, involves a ride down a 3-km path
through the forest in open electric jeeps. Then
a fast motor boat whisks you close to the falls
themselves (similar to Jungle Explorer on the
Argentine side, but more expensive and the
guides aren't as good). Portuguese, English and
Spanish spoken, take insect repellent. Helicopter
tours over the falls leave from near the entrance,
US$30 pp, 8 mins. Apart from disturbing visitors,
they disturb bird life and so the altitude has
been increased, making the flight less attractive.
Lots of companies on both sides organize
conventional tours to the falls, useful more for
convenience rather than information, since they
collect you from your hotel. Half day, US$13,
plus park entrance price.

Foz do Iguaçu *p458, map p458*
Tours
There are many travel agents on Av Brasil. Beware
of overcharging by touts at the bus terminal.
Caribe Tur at the airport, Hotel das Cataratas and
other branches, T3529 7505, runs tours from the
airport to the Argentine side and Hotel das
Cataratas (book hotel direct, not at the airport).
STTC Turismo, Ruth Campo Silva
(recommended guide), Hotel Bourbon, Rodovia
das Cataratas, T/F3529 8580, (American Express).
Several branches.

● Transport

Parque Nacional Foz do Iguaçu *p457*
Bus Leave from the Terminal Urbana in Foz, Av
Juscelino Kubitschek and República Argentina,
every 40 mins from 0730-1800, and are clearly
marked '400, Parque Nacional'. You can get on
or off at any point on the route past the airport
and Hotel das Cataratas, 40 mins, US$1 one way,

payable in reais or pesos (the driver waits
at the Park entrance while passengers
purchase entry tickets, which are checked by a
park guard on the bus). Taxi US$9.50, US$40
return including waiting (negotiate in advance).

Foz do Iguaçu *p458, map p458*
Air Iguaçu international airport, 18 km south of
town near the falls. In Arrivals is **Banco do Brasil**
and **Caribe Tours e Câmbio**, car rental offices,
tourist office and an official taxi stand, US$10.50 to
town centre (US$15 from town to airport). All
buses marked Parque Nacional pass the airport in
each direction, US$0.65, 0525-0040, does not
permit large amounts of luggage but backpacks
OK. Many hotels run minibus services for a small
charge. Daily flights to **Rio, São Paulo, Curitiba**
and other Brazilian cities.
Bus For transport to the falls see above under
Parque Nacional Foz do Iguaçu. Long distance
terminal (Rodoviária), Av Costa e Silva, 4 km from
centre on road to Curitiba; bus to centre, any bus
that says 'Rodoviária', US$0.90. Taxi US$5.25.
Book departures as soon as possible. As well as
the tourist office (see above), there is a Cetreme
desk for tourists who have lost their documents,
Guarda Municipal (police) and luggage store. To
Curitiba, Pluma, Sulamericana, 9-10 hrs, paved
road, US$20. To **Guaíra** via Cascavel only, 5 hrs,
US$13. To **Florianópolis**, Catarinense and
Reunidas, US$37, 14 hrs. Reunidas to **Porto
Alegre**, US$35-40. To **São Paulo**, 16 hrs, Pluma
US$40, executivo 6 a day, plus one leito.
To **Rio** 22 hrs, several daily, US$50. To **Campo
Grande**, US$37.

Foz do Iguaçu and around:
Itaipu dam *p459*
Bus Runs from outside the Terminal Urbano to
the visitor centre, US$0.65, marked `Usina Itaipu'.
The Noelia company in Puerto Iguazú includes
Itaipu in its tours of the Brazilian side of the falls,
US$15, T422722.

Border with Argentina:
Foz do Iguaçu/ Puerto Iguazú *p459*
Bus Marked 'Puerto Iguazú' run every
20 mins from the Terminal Urbana, crossing
the border bridge; 30 mins' journey,
3 companies, US$2. See above for procedures
regarding entry stamps. **Note**: Be sure you
know when the last bus departs from Puerto
Iguazú for Foz (usually 1900); last bus from
Foz 1950. Combined tickets to Puerto Iguazú
and the falls cost more than paying separately.
For buses to **Buenos Aires**, see Puerto Iguazú,
Transport for the options. There is a Pluma bus
direct from Foz and you can also go to Posadas
via Paraguay.

Border with Paraguay:
Foz do Iguaçu/ Ciudad del Este *p459*
Bus (Marked Cidade-Ponte) leave from the Terminal Urbana, Av Juscelino Kubitschek, for the Ponte de Amizade (Friendship Bridge), US$0.55. To **Asunción**, **Pluma** (0700), RYSA (direct at 1430, 1830), from Rodoviária, US$15 (cheaper if bought in Ciudad del Este).

Car If crossing by private vehicle and only intending to visit the national parks, this presents no problems. Another crossing to Paraguay is at **Guaíra**, at the northern end of the Itaipu lake. It is 5 hrs north of Iguaçu by road and can be reached by bus from Campo Grande and São Paulo. Ferries cross to Saltos del Guaira on the Paraguayan side (see page 1049).

❻ Directory

Foz do Iguaçu *p458, map p458*
Airline offices Gol, Rodovia das Cataratas, Km 16.5, T3521 4296. **TAM**, R Rio Branco 640, T3523 8500 (offers free transport to Ciudad del Este for its flights, all cross-border documentation dealt with). **Varig**, Av Juscelino Kubitscheck 463 , T3523 2111.

Banks It is difficult to exchange on Sun but quite possible in Paraguay where US dollars can be obtained on credit cards. There are plenty of banks and travel agents on Av Brasil. **Banco do Brasil**, Av Brasil 1377. Has ATM, high commission for TCs. **Bradesco**, Av Brasil 1202. Cash advance on Visa. HSBC, Av Brasil 1151, for MasterCard ATM. **Banco 24 Horas** at Oklahoma petrol station. Câmbio at **Vento Sul**, Av Brasil 1162, no TCs, good rates for cash. Also **Corimeira**, Av Brasil 148. **Embassies and consulates** Argentina, Travessa Eduardo Bianchi 26, T3574 2969. Open Mon-Fri 1000-1500. **France**, R Francisco Fogaça do Nascimento 800, T3529 6850, royal.service@fnn.net, 0800-1200, 1430-1700. **Paraguay**, Edmundo de Barros s/n, T3523 2898. **Internet** Several including **Cafe Internet**, R Rebouças 950, 0900-2200, Sun 1600-2200, US$1.50 per hr. **Zipfoz.com**, R Barão do Rio Branco 412, corner with Av Juscelino Kubitschek. Smart, a/c, US$1.50 per hr. **Medical services** Free 24-hr clinic, Av Paraná 1525, opposite Lions Club, T573 1134. Few buses: take taxi or walk (about 25 mins). **Post offices** Praça Getúlio Vargas 72. **Telephones** Several call centres. **Voltage** 110 volts a/c.

Salvador de Bahia

➔ *Phone code: 0xx71. Post code: 40000. Colour map 5, grid C5. Population: 3.02 million.*

Salvador, the third largest city in Brazil, is capital of the state of Bahia, dubbed 'Africa in exile' for its mixture of African and European which finds its most powerful expression in Carnival. Often referred to as Bahia, rather than Salvador, the city is home to a heady mix of colonial buildings, beautiful beaches, African culture and pulsating musical rhythms. It stands on the magnificent Bahia de Todos os Santos, a sparkling bay dotted with 38 islands. The bay is the largest on the Brazilian coast covering an area of 1,100 sq km. Rising above the bay on its eastern side is a cliff which dominates the landscape and, perched on top, 71 m above sea level, are the older districts with buildings dating back to the 17th and 18th centuries. Beyond the state capital are many fine beaches, particularly in the south around Porto Seguro, while inland is the harsh sertão, traversed by the Rio São Francisco.

Ins and outs
Getting there Luis Eduardo Magalhães airport is 32 km from city centre. The **Rodoviária** is 5 km from the city with regular bus services to the centre and Campo Grande; the journey can take up to one hour especially at peak periods. ➔➔ *For further information, see Transport, page 490.*

Getting around The broad peninsula on which the city of Salvador is built is at the mouth of the Bahia de Todos Os Santos. On the opposite side of the bay's entrance is the Ilha de Itaparica. The commercial district of the city and its port are on the sheltered, western side of the peninsula; residential districts and beaches are on the open Atlantic side. The point of the peninsula is called Barra, which is itself an important area. The centre of the city is divided into two levels, the Upper City (or Cidade Alta) where the Historical Centre lies, and the Lower City (Cidade Baixa) which is the commercial and docks district. The two levels are connected by a series of steep hills called *ladeiras*. The easiest way to go from one level to the other is by the 74-m high **Lacerda** lift which connects Praça Cairu in the lower city with Praça Municipal in the upper (renovated 2003). There is also the Plano Inclinado Gonçalves, a funicular railway which leaves from behind the Cathedral going down to Comércio, the commercial district (closes 1300 on Saturday and all Sunday). Most visitors limit themselves to the Pelourinho and historical centre, Barra, the Atlantic suburbs and the Itapagipe peninsula, which is north of the centre. The roads and avenues between these areas are straightforward to follow and are well-served by public transport. Other parts of the city are not as easy to get around, but have less of a tourist interest. If going to these areas a taxi may be advisable until you know your way around. ▸▸ *For more detailed information, see Transport, page 490.*

Climate Temperatures range from 25°C to 32°C, never falling below 19°C in winter. Humidity can be high, which may make the heat oppressive. It rains somewhat all the year but the main rainy season is between May and September. Nevertheless, the sun is never far away.

Tourist offices Bahiatursa, R das Laranjeiras 12, Historical Centre, T3117 3000, www.bahiatursa.ba.gov.br, open daily 0830-2200, English and German spoken. Rodoviária, T3450 3871, good, English spoken; airport, T3204 1244, open daily 0800-2245, friendly; in the Mercado Modelo, T3241 0242, Monday-Saturday 0900-1800; Sac Shopping Centre, Avenida Centenario 2992, T3264 4566. Useful information (often only available in Portuguese) includes Bahia Cultural, the month's programme of events with maps of themed points of interest. **Bahiatursa** has lists of hotels and accommodation in private homes. Map, US$1.20, not all streets marked; also a free map, clear map of the historic centre. Offices have noticeboards for messages. The offices also have details of travel throughout the State of Bahia. See also www.bahia.com.br. T131-06000030 for tourist information in English, www.sct.ba.gov.br is the Secretaria de Cultura e Turismo's website. **Maps:** from **Departamento de Geografia e Estadística**, Avenida Estados Unidos (opposite Banco do Brasil, Lower City): also from news stands including the airport bookshop, US$1.50.

Security The authorities have made efforts to police the old part of the city and Barra, which are now well-lit at night. The civil police are reported to be very sympathetic and helpful. Police are little in evidence after 2300, however, and at night you should leave valuables securely in your hotel. Also at night, the areas around and in the lifts and buses are unsafe. Do not walk down any of the links between the old and new city, especially the Ladeira de Misericôrdia, which links the Belvedere, near the Lacerda Lifts, with the lower city. As in all large cities, use your common sense and be very careful of your possessions at all times and in all districts. There have been reports of armed muggings on the sand dunes surrounding Lagoa do Abaeté. Do not visit them alone. Should a local join you at your table for a chat, leave at once if drugs are mentioned.

Background

On 1 November 1501, All Saints' Day, the navigator Amérigo Vespucci sailed into the bay. As the first European to see it, he named it after the day of his arrival. The first Governor General, Tomé de Sousa, arrived on 23 March 1549 to build a fortified city to protect Portugal's interest from constant threats of Dutch and French invasion. Salvador was formally founded on 1 November 1549 and remained the capital of Brazil until 1763. By the 18th century, it was the most important city in the Portuguese Empire after Lisbon, ideally situated in a safe, sheltered harbour along the trade routes of the 'New World'.

The city's first wealth came from the cultivation of sugar cane and tobacco, the plantations' workforce coming from the West coast of Africa. For three centuries Salvador was the site of a thriving slave trade. Even today, Salvador is described as the most African city in the Western Hemisphere and the University of Bahia boasts the only chair in the Yoruba language in the Americas. The influence permeates the city: food sold on the street is the same as in Senegal and Nigeria, Bahian music is fused with pulsating African polyrhythms, men and women nonchalantly carry enormous loads on their heads, fishermen paddle dug-out canoes in the bay, the pace of life is a little slower than elsewhere. The pulse of the city is candomblé, an Afro-Brazilian religion in which the African deities of Nature, the Goddess of the sea and the God of creation are worshipped. These deities (or orixás) are worshipped in temples (terreiros) which can be elaborate, decorated halls, or simply someone's front room with tiny altars to the orixá. Candomblé ceremonies may be seen by tourists – but not photographed – on Sunday and religious holidays. Contact the tourist office, Bahiatursa, or see their twice monthly calendar of events. Salvador today is a city of 15 forts, 166 Catholic churches, 1,000 candomblé temples and a fascinating mixture of old and modern, rich and poor, African and European, religious and profane. It is still a major port exporting tropical fruit, cocoa, sisal, soya beans and petrochemical products. Its most important industry, though, is tourism. Local government has done much to improve the fortunes of this once rundown, poor and dirty city and most visitors feel that the richness of its culture is compensation enough for any problems they may encounter. The Bahianas – black women who dress in traditional 18th century costumes – are street vendors who sit behind their trays of delicacies, savoury and seasoned, made from the great variety of local fish, vegetables and fruits. Their street food is one of the musts for visitors.

Sights

Centro Histórico

There is much more of interest in the Upper than in the Lower City. From Praça Municipal to the Carmo area 2 km north along the cliff is the Centro Histórico (Historical Centre), now a national monument and also protected by UNESCO. It was in this area that the Portuguese built their fortified city and where today stand some of the most important examples of colonial architecture in the Americas. This area is undergoing a massive restoration programme funded by the Bahian state government and UNESCO. Colonial houses have been painted in pastel colours. Many of the bars have live music which spills out onto the street on every corner. Patios have been created in the open areas behind the houses with open air cafés and bars. Artist ateliers, antique and handicraft stores have brought new artistic blood to what was once the bohemian part of the city. Many popular traditional restaurants and bars from other parts of Salvador have opened new branches here. Its transformation has also attracted many tourist shops and the area can get crowded.

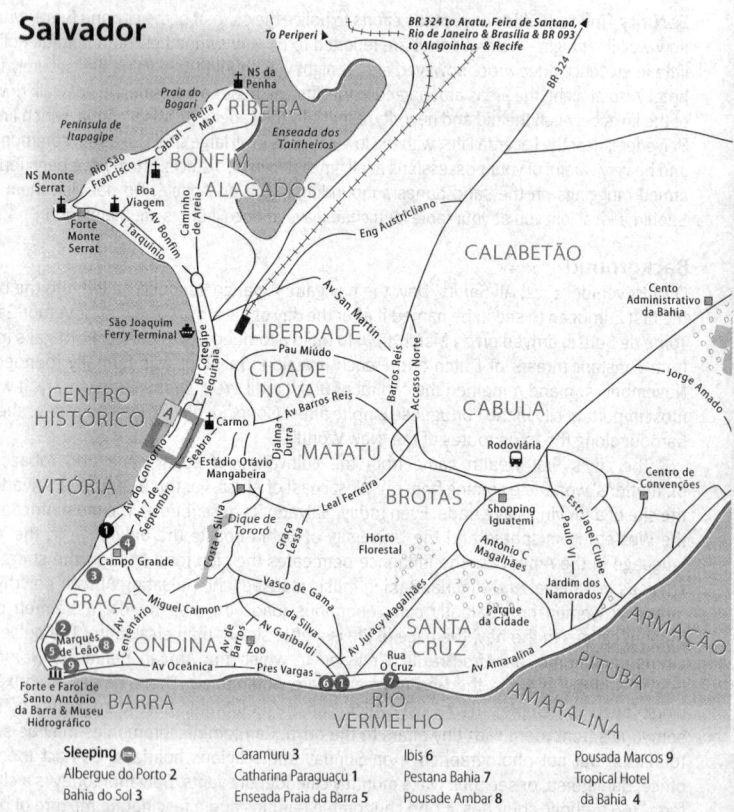

Salvador

Praça Municipal, Praça de Sé and Terreiro de Jesus

Dominating the Praça Municipal is the old Casa de Câmara e Cadeia or **Paço Municipal** (Council Chamber – 1660), while alongside is the **Palácio Rio Branco** (1918), once the Governor's Palace now the headquarters of Bahiatursa, the state tourist board (no office open to the public). Leaving it with its panoramic view of the bay, R Misericôrdia goes north passing the **Santa Casa Misericôrdia** ① *0800-1000, 1400-1700, T3322 7666* (1695 – see the high altar and painted tiles), to Praça da Sé. This praça with its mimosa and flamboyant trees leads into Terreiro de Jesus, a picturesque praça named after the church which dominates it. Built in 1692, the **church of the Jesuits** became the property of the Holy See in 1759 when the Jesuits were expelled from all Portuguese territories. The façade is one of the earliest examples of baroque in Brazil, an architectural style which was to dominate the churches built in the 17th and 18th centuries. Inside, the vast vaulted ceiling and 12 side altars in baroque and rococo frame the main altar completely leafed in gold. The tiles in blue, white and yellow in a tapestry pattern are also from Portugal. It houses the tomb of Mem de Sá. The church is now the city Cathedral (**Catedral Basílica**) *0900-1100, 1400-1700*; parts are currently being renovated. On the eastern side of the square is the church of **São Pedro dos Clérigos** *Sun 0800-0930*, which is beautifully renovated, while close by, on the south-side, is the church of the **Ordem Terceira de São Domingos** (Dominican Third Order) ① *Mon-Fri 0800-1200, 1400-1700, US$0.30*, which has a beautiful painted wooden ceiling and fine tiles. Nearby is **Museu Afro-Brasileiro** ① *in the former Faculty of Medicine building, Terreiro de Jesus, Mon-Fri 0900-1800, Sat-Sun 1000-1700, US$1.65, students US$0.85*, compares African and Bahian Orixás (deities) celebrations, beautiful murals and carvings, all in Portuguese. **Museu Arqueológico e Etnográfico** ① *in the basement of the same building, Mon-Fri 0900-1700, US$0.55*, houses archaeological discoveries from Bahia (stone tools, clay urns etc), an exhibition on indígenas from the Alto Rio Xingu area (artefacts, tools, photos), recommended. There is a museum of medicine located in the same complex.

Facing Terreiro de Jesus is Praça Anchieta and the church of **São Francisco**. ① *0830-1700, entry to cloisters US$0.25, church free*. Its simple façade belies the treasure inside. The entrance leads to a sanctuary with a spectacular painting on the wooden ceiling, by local artist José Joaquim da Rocha (1777). The main body of the church is the most exuberant example of baroque in the country. The cedar wood carving and later gold leaf was completed after 28 years in 1748. The cloisters of the monastery are surrounded by a series of blue and white tiles from Portugal. Next door is the church of the **Ordem Terceira de São Francisco** (Franciscan Third Order – 1703) ① *daily 0800-1200, 1300-1700, US$1.30, students US$0.65*. It has a façade intricately carved in sandstone. Inside is a quite remarkable Chapter House with striking images of the Order's most celebrated saints.

Largo do Pelourinho

Leading off the Terreiro de Jesus is R Portas do Carmo (formerly Alfredo Brito), a charming, narrow cobbled street lined with fine colonial houses painted in different pastel shades. This street leads into the Largo do Pelourinho (Praça José Alencar), which was completely renovated in 1993.

Represa do Ipitanga

BA 337

Av Luiz Viana Filho

To Lagoa de Abaeté, Airport & Estrada do Coco
to Arembepe & Praia do Forte

R Prof Pinto de Aguiar

R Dorival Caymmi

To Lagoa de Abaeté

Av Otávio Mangabeira

ITAPOÃ
PLACAFOR
PIATÃ
JAGUARIBE
CORSARIO

Parque Pituaçu

BOCA DO RIO

To Lagoa de Abaeté

Related map
A *Salvador Centro Histórico*,
page 466

N

0 km   1
0 miles   1

Villa Romana 8

Eating
Chez Bernard 1
Solar Do Unhão 1

Considered the finest complex of colonial architecture in Latin America, it was once the site of a pillory where unscrupulous tradesmen were publicly punished and ridiculed. After the cleaning of the area, new galleries, boutiques and restaurants are opening, and at night the Largo is lively, especially on Tuesday (see Nightlife below). **Nosso Senhor Do Rosário Dos Pretos church** *small entry fee*, the so-called Slave Church, dominates the square. It was built by former slaves over a period of 100 years. The side altars honour black saints. The painted ceiling is very impressive, the overall effect being one of tranquillity in contrast to the complexity of the Cathedral and São Francisco.

At the corner of Portas do Carmo and Largo do Pelourinho is a small museum to the work of Jorge Amado, who died in 2002, **Casa da Cultura Jorge Amado** ① *Mon-Sat 0900-1900, free*. Information is in Portuguese only, but the café walls are covered with colourful copies of his book jackets. The Carmo Hill is at the top of the street leading out of Largo do Pelourinho. **Museu Abelardo Rodrigues** ① *Solar Ferrão, Pelourinho, R Gregório de Mattos 45, 1300-*

Salvador Centro Histórico

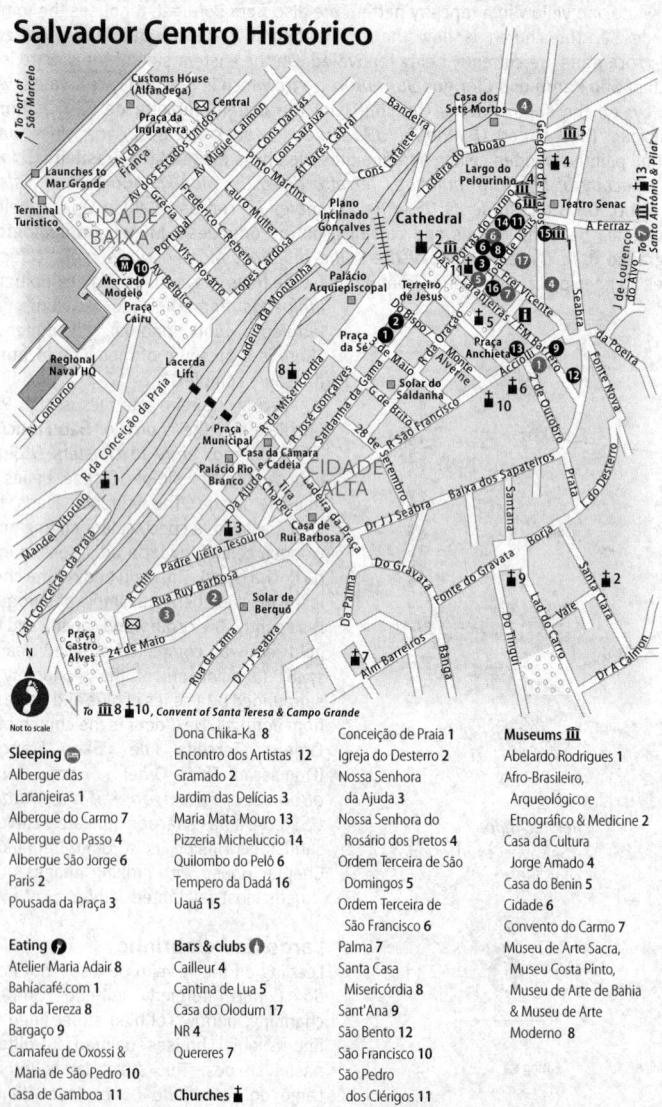

Not to scale

Sleeping 🛏
Albergue das
   Laranjeiras **1**
Albergue do Carmo **7**
Albergue do Passo **4**
Albergue São Jorge **6**
Paris **2**
Pousada da Praça **3**

Eating 🍴
Atelier Maria Adair **8**
Bahíacafé.com **1**
Bar da Tereza **8**
Bargaço **9**
Camafeu de Oxossi &
   Maria de São Pedro **10**
Casa de Gamboa **11**
Coffee Shop **1**

Dona Chika-Ka **8**
Encontro dos Artistas **12**
Gramado **2**
Jardim das Delícias **3**
Maria Mata Mouro **13**
Pizzeria Micheluccio **14**
Quilombo do Pelô **6**
Tempero da Dadá **16**
Uauá **15**

Bars & clubs 🍸
Cailleur **4**
Cantina de Lua **5**
Casa do Olodum **17**
NR **4**
Quereres **7**

Churches ✝
Carmo **13**

Conceição de Praia **1**
Igreja do Desterro **2**
Nossa Senhora
   da Ajuda **3**
Nossa Senhora do
   Rosário dos Pretos **4**
Ordem Terceira de São
   Domingos **5**
Ordem Terceira de
   São Francisco **6**
Palma **7**
Santa Casa
   Misericórdia **8**
Sant'Ana **9**
São Bento **12**
São Francisco **10**
São Pedro
   dos Clérigos **11**

Museums 🏛
Abelardo Rodrigues **1**
Afro-Brasileiro,
   Arqueológico e
   Etnográfico & Medicine **2**
Casa da Cultura
   Jorge Amado **4**
Casa do Benin **5**
Cidade **6**
Convento do Carmo **7**
Museu de Arte Sacra,
   Museu Costa Pinto,
   Museu de Arte de Bahia
   & Museu de Arte
   Moderno **8**

Funicular Railway ┼┼┼┼

To 🏛8 ✝10, *Convent of Santa Teresa & Campo Grande*

1900 except Mon, US$0.55, is a religious art museum, with objects from the 17th, 18th and 19th centuries, mainly from Bahia, Pernambuco and Maranhão. **Museu da Cidade** ① *Largo do Pelourinho, weekdays except Tue 0930-1800, Sat 1300-1700, Sun 0930-1300, free*, has exhibitions of arts and crafts and old photographs. From the higher floors of the museum you can get a good view of the Pelourinho. **Casa do Benin** ① *Mon-Fri 1000-1800, below NS do Rosario dos Pretos*, shows African crafts, photos, a video show on Benin and Angola.

The **Carmo church** (Carmelite Third Order, 1709) ① *Mon-Sat 0800-1130 and 1400-1730, Sun 1000-1200, US$0.40*, houses one of the sacred art treasures of the city, a sculpture of Christ made in 1730 by a slave who had no formal training, Francisco Xavier das Chagas, known as O Cabra. One of the features of the piece is the blood made from whale oil, ox blood, banana resin and 2,000 rubies to represent the drops of blood. **Museu do Carmo** ① *in the Convento do Carmo, Mon-Sat 0800-1200, 1400-1800, Sun 0800-1200, US$0.15*, has a collection of icons and colonial furniture.

South of the Praça Municipal
Rua Chile leads to **Praça Castro Alves**, with its monument to Castro Alves, who started the campaign which finally led to the Abolition of Slavery in 1888. Two streets lead out of this square, Avenida 7 de Setembro, busy with shops and street vendors selling everything imaginable, and, parallel to it, R Carlos Gomes. **Museu de Arte Sacra** ① *R do Sodré 276 (off R Carlos Gomes), Mon-Fri 1130-1730, US$2*, is in the 17th century convent and church of Santa Teresa, at the bottom of the steep Ladeira de Santa Teresa. Many of the 400 carvings are from Europe, but some are local. Among the reliquaries of silver and gold is one of gilded wood by Aleijadinho (see page 417). **São Bento church** ① *Av 7 de Setembro, Mon-Sat 0630-1230, 1600- 1900, Sun 0700-1130, 1700-1900*, was rebuilt after 1624, but it has fine 17th century furniture.

Both streets eventually come to **Campo Grande** (also known as Praça Dois de Julho). In the centre of the praça is the monument to Bahian Independence, 2 July 1823. Avenida 7 de Setembro continues out of the square towards the Vitória area. There are some fine 19th century homes along this stretch, known as Corredor da Vitória. The **Museu de Arte Moderna** ① *off Av Contornom, T3329 0660, Tue-Fri 1300-2100, Sat 1500-2100 and Sun 1400-1900*, converted from an old sugar estate house and outbuildings, is only open for special exhibitions. The restaurant (Solar do Unhão) is still there and the buildings are worth seeing for themselves (take a taxi there as access is dangerous). **Museu Costa Pinto** ① *Av 7 de Setembro 2490, weekdays 1430-1900, but closed Tue, Sat-Sun 1500-1800, US$2.50*, is a modern house with collections of crystal, porcelain, silver, furniture etc. It also has the only collection of balangandãs (slave charms and jewellery), highly recommended. **Museu de Arte da Bahia** ① *Av 7 de Setembro 2340, Vitória, Tue-Fri 1400-1900, Sat-Sun 1430-1900, US$1.60*, has interesting paintings of Brazilian artists from the 18th to the early 20th century.

Barra
From Praça Vitória, the avenue continues down Ladeira da Barra (Barra Hill) to Porto da Barra. The best city beaches are in this area. Also in this district are the best bars, restaurants and nightlife. The Barra section of town has received a facelift with a new lighting system. The pavements fill with people day and night and many sidewalk restaurants and bars are open along the strip from Porto da Barra as far as the Cristo at the end of the Farol da Barra beach. Great attention to security is given. A little further along is the **Forte de Santo Antônio da Barra** and **lighthouse**, 1580, built on the spot where Amérigo Vespucci landed in 1501. It is right at the mouth of the bay where Bahia de Todos Os Santos and the South Atlantic Ocean meet and is the site of the first lighthouse built in the Americas. The interesting **Museu Hidrográfico** ① *Tue-Sat 1300-1800, US$1.30*. It has a good café for watching the sunset, is housed in the upper section of the Forte de Santo Antônio, fine views of the bay and coast, recommended.

Atlantic beach suburbs
The promenade leading away from the fort and its famous lighthouse is called Avenida Oceânica, which follows the coast to the beach suburbs of **Ondina**, Amaralina and Pituba. The road is also called Avenida Presidente Vargas, but the numbering is different. Beyond Pituba are the **best ocean beaches** at Jaguaripe, **Piatã** and Itapoã. En route the bus passes small fishing colonies at Amaralina and Pituba where jangadas can be seen. A jangada is a small raft peculiar to the northeastern region of Brazil used extensively as well as dug-out canoes.

Near Itapoã is the **Lagoa do Abaeté**, surrounded by brilliant, white sands. This is a deep, freshwater lake where local women traditionally come to wash their clothes and then lay them out to dry in the sun. The road leading up from the lake offers a panoramic view of the city in the distance, the coast, and the contrast of the white sands and fresh water less than 1 km from the sea and its golden beaches. **Note:** See Security page 463. Near the lighthouse at **Itapoã** there are two campsites on the beach. A little beyond the campsites are the magnificent ocean beaches of Stella Maris and Flamengo, both quiet during the week but very busy at the weekends. Beware of strong undertow at these beaches. Apart from Porto da Barra, all the beaches before Itapoã are polluted with sewage (a new system is under construction). The Sunday paper, A Tarde, publishes the condition of the beaches.

Bonfim and Itapagipe

See also the famous church of **Nosso Senhor do Bonfim** on the Itapagipe peninsula in the suburbs north of the centre, whose construction began in 1745. It draws endless supplicants (particularly on Friday and Sunday) offering favours to the image of the Crucified Lord set over the high altar; the number and variety of ex-voto offerings is extraordinary. The processions over the water to the church on the third Sunday in January are particularly interesting. Also on the Itapagipe peninsula is a colonial fort on **Monte Serrat** point, and at Ribeira the church of **Nossa Senhora da Penha** (1743). The beach here has many restaurants, but the sea is polluted (bus from Praça da Sé or Avenida França).

Itaparica

Across the bay from Salvador lies the island of Itaparica, 29 km long and 12 km wide. The town of Itaparica is very picturesque, with a fair beach in the town, and well worth a visit. Take a bus or kombi by the coast road (Beira Mar) which passes through the villages of Manguinhos, Amoureiras and Ponta de Areia. The beach at Ponta de Areia is one of the best on the island and is very popular. There are many barracas on the beach, the best and busiest is Barraca Pai Xango, always very lively.

In Itaparica there are many fine residential buildings from the 19th century, plus the church of **São Lourenço**, one of the oldest in Brazil, and there are delightful walks through the old town. During the summer months the streets are ablaze with the blossoms of the beautiful flamboyant trees. The beaches at **Mar Grande** are fair but can be dirty at times. There are many pousadas in Mar Grande and at the nearby beaches of Ilhota and Gamboa (both to the left as you disembark from the ferry).

From Bom Despacho there are many buses, kombis and taxis to all parts of the island, including beaches at Ponta de Areia, Mar Grande, Berlinque, **Aratuba** and **Cacha Pregos**. Kombi and taxis can be rented for trips but be prepared to bargain. There are also buses to other towns such as Nazaré das Farinhas, Valença (see below) and also **Jaguaribe**, a small, picturesque colonial port. Both of these towns are on the mainland connected by a bridge on the southwest side of the island, turn off between Mar Grande and Cacha Pregos (bus company, **Viazul**). There are good beaches across the bay on the mainland, but a boat is needed to reach these (US$16).

🛏 Sleeping → *See Telephone, page 347, for important phone changes.*

The Centro Histórico is the ideal place to stay; the Pelourinho if you're on a tight budget and Santo Antônio if you are looking for reasonably priced hotels with real charm and character. Barra also has some cheap options but is increasingly seedy. Business visitors will find the best hotels in Rio Vermelho, overlooking the ocean and a 10-min taxi ride from the centre. Self-contained a/c apartments with kitchens and hotel services can be rented by the day. Standards are generally high.

Centro Histórico *p464, map p466*
B-C Pousada da Praça, Rui Barbosa, 5, T3321 0642, www.pousadadapracahotel.com.br.

Simple, pretty, old colonial house, quiet, secure, big breakfast, rooms with and without bath, **E** pp in shared room. Insist on a receipt; the streets around can be noisy.
C Arthemis, Praça da Sé 398, Edif Themis, 7th floor, T322 0724, arthemis@arthemis com.br. Fan, wonderful views over bay and old city. Recommended restaurant with French chef.
C Paris, R Rui Barbosa 13, T321 3922. Cheaper without a/c, shared showers, breakfast, restaurant in same building. Recommended.
D pp **Albergue do Carmo**, R do Carmo 06, 3 mins' walk north of Pelourinho, T3326 3750, www.alberguedocarmo.com.br. Smart

dormitories, **B** double room, sea view, cheaper with church view and for members, kitchen, lockers, English spoken, internet. Recommended.
D Albergue das Laranjeiras, R Inácio Acciolli 13, Pelourinho, T/F3321 1366, www.laranjeiras hostel.com.br. In a beautiful colonial building in the heart of the historical district, can be noisy, café downstairs, English spoken. **A** double, **B** with shared bath, cheaper for HI members. Good for meeting other travellers. Warmly recommended.
D Albergue do Passo, R Ladeira do Passo 3, T3326 1951, passoyouthhostel@yahoo.com. Safe, with breakfast, group rates available, English, French and Spanish spoken. Recommended.
E pp **Albergue São Jorge**, R das Portas do Carmo 25, Pelourinho, T3266 7092, www.saojorgehostel.com. Dorms, shared rooms and doubles (**B-C**), under new ownership, refurbished, with breakfast, kitchen and laundry facilities, lockers, internet access available.

Santo Antônio
L Pousada Redfish, Ladeira do Boqueirão 1, T/F3243 8473, www.hotelredfish.com. Incredibly stylish, modern design in a rebuilt historic building. English-owned, 2 suites with terraces, spacious rooms, a/c, art gallery.
AL Pousada do Boqueirão, R Direita do Santo Antônio 48, T3241 2262, www.pousada boqueirao.com.br. Family-run, beautiful house overlooking bay, remodelled, relaxed atmosphere, most European languages spoken, great food, first class in all respects.
AL Pousada das Flores, R Direita de Santo Antônio 442, near Santo Antônio fort, T/F3243 1836, www.pflores.com.br. Brazilian/French owners, excellent breakfast, beautiful old house.
A Pousada Villa Carmo, R do Carmo 58, T/F3241 3924, contato@pousadavillacarmo.com.br. Italian/Brazilian owned, many European languages spoken, very comfortable, rooms with fan or a/c.
A-B Pousada Baluarte, R Baluarte, 13, T3327 0367, www.pousadabaluarte.com. Bohemian household, lovely owners, 5 rooms, cheaper without bath, the home made breakfasts are excellent.
B-C Pousada Hilmar, R Direita de Santo Antônio 136, T3243 4959, www.pousadahilmar.com.br. Several types of room with and without a/c and TV, with breakfast, a good option in a quiet street.
C Pensão Von Sandt Platz, R Direita de Santo Antônio 351, T/F3316 6551, manaschu@ cpunet.com.br. Relaxing family house of Nazaré Schubeler, sumptuous breakfasts, legendary caipirinhas, free email facilities, laundry, "prepare to be mothered".
D pp **Nalvas**, R Direita de Santo Antônio 22. 4-bed rooms, fan, no towel, use of kitchen, related travel agency at No 22, good value.

Campo Grande/Vitória
Upmarket residential area, between Barra and city centre, convenient for museums.
L Tropical Hotel da Bahia, Av 7 de Setembro 1537, Campo Grande, T2105 2000, www.tropicalhotel.com.br. Well-run, convenient for city centre, very much a business hotel.
AL Bahia do Sol, Av 7 de Setembro 2009, T3338 8800, www.bahiadosol.com.br. Comfortable, safe and frigobar in room, family run, good breakfast and restaurant, bureau de change. Highly recommended (no pool).
C Caramuru, Av 7 de Setembro 2125, Vitória, T3336 9951. Cosy, with lounge and terrace, safe parking. Recommended.

Barra *p467*
AL Villa Romana, R Lemos Brito 14, T3264 6522, www.villaromana.com.br. 1960s hotel with basic a/c rooms and a pool, good location. Recommended.
A-B Mansion Villa Verde, R da Palmeira 190, T3264 3597, www.pousadavillaverde.com. **A-C** in low season, reduced rates for longer stay, a/c studios with kitchen and double room with fan, garden, terrace, hammocks, safe, very good. Recommended.
B-C Enseada Praia da Barra, R Barão de Itapoã 60, Porto da Barra, T3235 9213. Breakfast, safe, money exchanged, credit cards, laundry bills high, otherwise good value, near beach.
B-C Pousada Ambar, R Afonso Celso 485, T3264 6956, www.ambarpousada.com.br. Good service, breakfast, convenient, run by Paulo and Christine (French, also speaks English).
B-D Barra, R Dr Arturo Neiva 4, T3245 2600, www.alberguebarravento.com.br. HI, 30 m from beach, cheaper for members and in low season, suites and dorms, with breakfast, cyber café, kitchen and laundry.
C-D Pousada Santa Maria, Av 7 de Setembro 3835, T3264 4076, pousadasmaria@hotmail.com. Excellent breakfast, English and German spoken, TV, laundry service, internet, restaurant/bar, exchange, car rental.
D Albergue do Porto, R Barão de Sergy 197, T3264 6600, www.alberguedoporto.com.br. One block from beach, short bus ride or 20 mins on foot from historical centre. IYHA hostel in

● *For an explanation of the sleeping and eating price codes used in this guide, see inside the front*
● *cover. Other relevant information is found in Essentials pages 345-347.*

beautiful turn-of-the-century house, breakfast, convenient, English spoken, double rooms with a/c and bath available (**AL-C**, depending on season), kitchen, laundry facilities, safe, TV lounge, games room, internet, courtyard. Highly recommended.

D-E Pousada Marcos, Av Oceânica 281, T3264 5117, www.pousadamarcos.com.br. Youth hostel-style, great location near the lighthouse, very busy, notices in Hebrew for potential travelling companions, efficient.

Private apartments Rooms to let in private apartments: **Carmen Simões**, R 8 de Dezembro 326. Safe, helpful. **Gorete**, R 8 de Dezembro 522, Apt 002, Edif Ricardo das Neves, Graça, T264 3016, gorete@cpunet.com.br. Convenient, use of kitchen, patio, internet, safe.

Atlantic beach suburbs p467

LL Pestana Bahia, R Fonte de Boi 216, Rio Vermelho, T/F2103 8000, www.pestana.com. One of the best in Salvador, all comfort and facilties including for the disabled.

AL Catharina Paraguaçu, R João Gomes 128, Rio Vermelho, T3334 0089, www.hotel catharinaparaguacu.com.br. Charming, small, colonial-style, tastefully decorated.

AL Sol Bahia Atlântico, R Manoel Antônio Galvão 1075, Patamares, 17 km from the city (next to one of the best beaches in Salvador), T3206 0500, www.solbahia.com.br. Modern family hotel set high on the hill with great views of the coastline with a pool, restaurant and sauna, private tram connects the higher and lower parts of the resort and there is free transport to the beach (around ½ km away).

A Ibis, R Fonte do Boi 215, T3330 8300, www.accorhotels.com.br. Large hotel in this budget business chain, safe, a/c and with sea views from the upper floors. Great value.

Itapoã

LL Sofitel, R Passargada s/n, T2106 8500, www.sofitel.com. Another superb hotel, in a park with 9-hole golf course, 5 mins from airport, shuttle bus to centre, all facilities.

L Catussaba, R Alameida da Praia, 25 km from the city, T3374 8000, www.catussaba.com.br. Elegant resort hotel with a mock colonial interior and beautiful gardens which lead out to the beach. Beware of ocean currents when swimming. Convenient for the airport. Recommended.

AL Villa Farol, Praia do Pedra do Sal, T3374 2107. Small Swiss-run pousada, pool, homely, great restaurant *Le Jardin*, 1 block from beach. First class.

C-D Casa Grande, R Minas Gerais 122, Pituba, T3248 0527. HI hostel some 15 km from the centre, laundry and cooking facilities.

D Pousada Glória, R do Retiro 46, T/F3375 1503. A basic pousada near the beach, no breakfast.

Camping Note that sea bathing is dangerous off shore near the campsites. **Camping Clube do Brasil**, R Visconde do Rosário 409, Rosário, T3242 0482. **Ecológica**, R Alameida da Praia, near the lighthouse at Itapoã, take bus from Praça da Sé direct to Itapoã, or to Campo Grande or Barra, change there for Itapoã, about 1 hr, then 30 mins walk, T3374 3506. Bar, restaurant, hot showers. Highly recommended.

Pensionatos These are places to stay in shared rooms (up to 4 per room); part or full board available. **Pierre Marbacher**, R Carlos Coqueijo 68A, Itapoã, T3249 5754 (Caixa Postal 7458, 41600 Salvador). He is Swiss, owns a beach bar at Rua K, speaks English and rents houses or rooms.

At Carnival it's a good idea to rent a flat; the tourist office has a list of estate agents. They can also arrange rooms in private houses; however, caution is advised as not all householders are honest.

Itaparica p468

AL Pousada Arco Iris, Estrada da Gamboa 102, Mar Grande, T3633 1316. Magnificent building and setting in mango orchard, expensive, good if slow restaurant, Manga Rosa. They have camping facilities next door, shady, not always clean.

A Quinta Pitanga, R da Alegria 10, in Itaparica town, T3631 1834. Beautifully decorated by the owner Jim Valkus, 3 suites and 2 singles, beachfront property, a retreat, excellent restaurant. Expensive but highly recommended, accepts day visitors and offers artists' residencies (www.sacatar.org).

C Pousada Casarão da Ilha, near the church in the main praça, Mar Grande, T3633 1083. Spacious rooms with a great view of Salvador across the bay, swimming pool, a/c.

C Pousada Sonho do Verão, R São Bento 2, opposite Pousada Arco Iris, Mar Grande, T3633 1316. Chalets and apartments, cooking facilities, French and English spoken. Like other pousadas they rent bicycles (US$3 per hr); they also rent horses (US$5 per hr).

C-D Pousada Icaraí, Praça da Piedade, Itaparica town, T3631 1110, hicarai@hotmail.com. Charming, good location.

C-D Pousada Zimbo Tropical, Estrada de Cacha Pregos, Km 3, Rua Yemanjá, Aratuba, T/F3638 1148. French/Brazilian-run, good breakfast, evening meals available. Recommended.

● Eating

Local specialities

The main dish is *moqueca*, seafood cooked in a sauce made from coconut milk, tomatoes, red and green peppers, fresh coriander and *dendê* (palm oil). It is traditionally cooked in a wok-like earthenware dish and served piping hot at the table. Served with moqueca is *farofa* (manioc flour) and a hot pepper sauce which you add at your discretion, it's usually extremely hot so try a few drops before venturing further. The dendê is somewhat heavy and those with delicate stomachs are advised to try the *ensopado*, a sauce with the same ingredients as the moqueca, but without the palm oil.

Nearly every street corner has a Bahiana selling a wide variety of local snacks, the most famous of which is the *acarajé*, a kidney bean dumpling fried in palm oil which has its origins in West Africa. To this the Bahiana adds *vatapá*, a dried shrimp and coconut milk pâté (also delicious on its own), fresh salad and hot sauce (pimenta). For those who prefer not to eat the palm oil, the *abará* is a good substitute. Abará is steamed, wrapped in banana leaves. Seek local advice on which are most hygienic stalls to eat from. Two good Bahianas are Chica, at Ondina beach (on the street at the left side of Mar A Vista Hotel) and Dinha at Largo da Santana (very lively in the late afternoon), who serves acarajé until midnight, extremely popular. Bahians usually eat acarajé or abará with a chilled beer on the way home from work or on the beach at sunset. Another popular dish with African origins is *Xin-Xin de Galinha*, chicken on the bone cooked in dendê, with dried shrimp, garlic and squash.

Centro Histórico *p464, map p466*

Casa do Benin, Praça José Alencar 29, Pelourinho. Afro-Bahian, great surroundings, try the shrimp in the cashew nut sauce, closed Mon and 1600-1900.

Maria Mata Mouro, R Inácio Accioly 8, Pelourinho. International menu, excellent service, relaxing atmosphere, closed Sun night.

Pizzeria Micheluccio, R Portas do Carmo 31, Pelourinho. Best pizzas in Pelourinho. Daily 1200 till late.

Uauá, R Gregório de Matos 36, Pelourinho, T3321 3089. Elegant, colonial restaurant and bar, typical Bahian cuisine.

Atelier Maria Adair, R J Castro Rabelo 2. Specializing in coffees and cocktails, owner Maria is a well known artist whose highly original work is on display.

Casa da Gamboa, R João de Deus 32, 1st floor. 1200-1500 and 1900-2400, closed Mon. Also at R Newton Prado 51 (Gamboa de Cima), beautifully located in old colonial house overlooking the bay, good reputation. Mon-Sat 1200-1500, 1900-2300, not cheap.

Casa da Roça, R Luis Viana 27. Near the Carmo church, pizzas, caipirinhas and live music at weekend.

Jardim das Delícias, R João de Deus 12, Pelourinho, T321 1449. Elegant restaurant and antiques shop with tropical garden, very reasonable for its setting, classical or live music.

Senac, Praça José Alencar 19, Largo do Pelourinho, T3324 4552. State-run catering school, a selection of 40 local dishes, buffet, lunch 1130-1530, dinner 1830-2130, all you can eat for US$16, inconsistent quality but very popular, folkloric show Thu-Sat 2030, US$5.

Quilombo do Pelô, R Portas do Carmo 13, Pelourinho, T3322 4371. Rustic Jamaican restaurant, open daily from 1100, good food with relaxed, if erratic service, vegetarian options.

Tempero da Dadá, R Frei Vicente 5. Open daily 1130 till late, closed Tue, Bahian cuisine, owners Dadá and Paulo are genial hosts, extremely popular.

Bar da Tereza, R J Castro Rabelo 16. Open 0900-2300, good wholemeal snacks and juices.

Carvalho, R Conselheiro Cunha Lopez 33, Centro. Comida a kilo, tasty, excellent fish, clean.

Dona Chika-Ka, R J Castro Rabelo 10. 1100-1500 and 1900-0200. Good local dishes. Open gates beside Dona Chika-Ka lead to an open square, Largo de Quincas Berro d'Água (known locally as Quadra 2M) with many bars and restaurants.

Encontro dos Artistas, R das Laranjeiras 15, T321 1721, Ribeiro dos Santos 10, Passo – Pelourinho. Cheap.

Gramado, Praça da Sé. One of few food-by-weight restaurants in area, basic, lunch only.

Bahiacafé.com, Praça da Sé 20. Funky, Belgian-run internet café, good breakfasts, excellent food, English spoken.

Coffee Shop, Praça da Sé. Cuban-style café serving sandwiches; main attraction is excellent coffee, and tea served in china cups, doubles as cigar shop.

Between Historical Centre and Barra

Baby Beef, Av AC Magalhães 3363, Iguatemi, T3270 3000. Among the best churrascarias in Salvador, top class restaurant, excellent service, extremely popular, open daily 1200-1500 and 1900-2300.

Chez Bernard, R Gamboa de Cima 11, T3329 5403. French cuisine, open daily except Sun.

Solar Do Unhão, on Av Contorno, in a beautiful 18th-century sugar estate on the edge of the bay, T3321 5559. Lunch and dinner (fair Bahian cuisine) with the best folklore show in town, expensive; also good for sunset drinks. A good jam session takes place every Sat night (Aug-Mar) in the grounds. Guest musicians are welcome. It is best to go by taxi as bus connections are difficult.

¶¶ **Beni-Gan**, Praça A Fernandes 29, Garcia. An excellent Japanese restaurant, intimate atmosphere, Tue-Sun 1900 till midnight.
¶¶ **Recanto das Coroas**, underneath the Hotel Arthemis. Looks uninviting but the food is excellent.
¶¶ **Ristorante d'Italia**, Av 7 de Setembro, 1238, Campo Grande. Has won awards. Very reasonable, with large portions, closed Sun night, music some evenings.
¶ **Kentefrio**, Av 7 de Setembro 379. The best of several good snack bars on this avenue, clean, counter service only, closed Sun.

In and near Mercado Modelo

¶¶-¶ **Camafeu De Oxossi** and **Maria De São Pedro**, at the bottom of the Lacerda Lift, at Praça Cairu, in the famous **Mercado Modelo**. On the upper floor of the market are 2 very good restaurants, both specializing in Bahian dishes, great atmosphere, good view of the port, daily 1130-2000, Sat lunchtime is particularly busy. Opposite the Mercado Modelo, the Paes Mendonça supermarket self-service counter (¶) is good value, 1100-1500, 1st floor.

Barra *p467*

¶¶¶ **Frutos Do Mar**, R Marquês de Leão 415. The best Bahian restaurant in the area.
¶¶ **Ban Zai**, Av 7 de Setembro 3244, Ladeira da Barra, by the yacht club. Sushi bar, always busy, open daily except Mon.
¶¶ **Caranguejo do Farol**, Av Oceânica 231, above the road. Specializing in crab, extremely busy.
¶¶ **Mon Filet**, R Afonso Celso 152. Good steaks, pastas, open 1830-2400.
¶¶ **Yan Ping**, on R Airosa Galvão. Good Chinese, open daily 1100 until midnight, reasonably priced, generous portions.
¶ **Mediterrânio**, R Marques de Leão 262. Pay by weight, open daily for lunch only.
¶ **A Porteira**, R Afonso Celso 287. Open for lunch only, pay by weight northeastern Brazilian food.

Near the lighthouse at the mouth of the bay (Farol Da Barra) there are a number of good fast food places: **Micheluccio**, Av Oceânica 10, good pizza, always busy. Next door is **Baitakão**, good hamburgers and sandwiches.

Atlantic beach suburbs *p467*

There is an interesting fish market at Largo da Mariquita, Ondina, with a number of stalls serving food from noon until the small hours, clean, good atmosphere, popular with locals.
¶¶¶ **Bargaço**, Rua P, Qd 43, Lotes 18/19, Jardim Armação, T3231 5141. Traditional seafood restaurant, Bahian cuisine. Daily 1200 to midnight.

¶¶ **Cantina Famiglia-Salvatore**, Largo da Mariquita 45, Ondina. Delicious, authentic Italian pasta, 2 other branches.
¶¶ **Extudo**, Largo Mesquita 4, Ondina. Good varied menu, lively bar at night, attracts interesting clientèle, open 1200-0200, closed Mon, not expensive.
¶¶ **Margarida**, R Feira de Santana 2, Parque Cruz Aguiar, Ondina, T3335 0225. Open daily for lunch 1130-1500, original dishes, pasta, seafood, meat, imaginative salads, pay by weight, great desserts, very friendly owners, attracts interesting clientèle.
¶ **Brisa**, R Sargento Astrolábio 150, Pituba. Mon-Sat, 1100-1500, excellent wholefood restaurant, small, simple, cheap, owner Nadia is very friendly, organizes a small organic market Thu 0700-1000.
¶ **Manjericão**, R Fonte do Boi (the street leading to Pestana), Ondina. Excellent wholefood menu, Mon-Sat 1100-1600.
¶ **Rodeio**, Jardim dos Namorados, Pituba, T240 1762. Always busy, good value 'all you can eat' churrascaria, open daily from 1130-midnight.

Itapoã

¶¶¶ **Mistura Fina**, R Professor Souza Brito 41, T3375 2623. Seafood, pasta dishes, open daily 1000-midnight.
¶¶ **O Lagostão**, R Agnaldo Cruz 12, T3375 3646. Bahian cuisine, open daily 1100 till midnight.

The beaches from Patamares to Itapoã are lined by *barracas*, thatched huts serving chilled drinks and freshly cooked seafood dishes, ideal for lunch and usually very cheap.

Itparica *p468*

Philippe's Bar and Restaurant, Largo de São Bento, Mar Grande. French and local cuisine, information in English and French.
Restaurant Rafael in the main praça, Mar Grande. For pizzas and snacks.

There are many Bahianas selling *acarajé* in the late afternoon and early evening in the main praça by the pier at Mar Grande.

☉ Bars and clubs

Nightlife is concentrated on and around the Pelourinho where there is always a free live street band on Tue and at weekends. The Pelourinho area is also good for a bar browse; though be wary after 2300. There are many bars on the Largo de Quincas Berro d'Água, especially along R Portas do Carmo. R João de Deus and its environs are dotted with simple pavement bars with plastic tables. Aside from the big *axê* carnaval stars like Daniela Mercury and Ivete Sangalo, the most famous Salvador musicians are the *maracatú* drum orchestras like **Olodum**, **Ilê Aiyê** and Carlinhos

Brown's **Timabalada** (see below). There is live music all year round but the best time to hear the most frenetic performers, particularly the *axê* stars, is during Carnaval.

Pelourinho *p465*

Bahia Café, Quartel dos Aflitos (at the far end of the square). An expansive and very popular bar with good bay views. Very popular.

Bar do Reggae and **Praça do Reggae**, Ladeiro do Pelourinho, by Nossa Senhora dos Rosarios dos Pretos. Live reggae bands every Tue and more frequently closer to carnival.

Cailleur, R Gregório de Matos 17. Good café and great chocolate, open daily 0930-2100, bar service continues till 0100.

Cantina da Lua, Terreiro de Jesus. Daily, popular, good place to meet, flower boxes and more security ensure less hassle for open-air diners.

Casa do Olodum, R das Laranjeiras, T3321 5010, http://olodum.uol.com.br. Olodum's headquarters where they perform live every Tue and Sun at 1930 to packed crowds.

Ilê Aiyê, R do Curuzu 197, Liberdade, Barra, T3256 1013, www.ileaiye.com.br. Ilê Aiyê's headquarters. Details of live performances throughout Salvador are published here.

NR, almost directly opposite Casa do Olodum at R Gregório de Matos 15. A great after-hours bar with live music (which is not always so great). There's a US$0.50 charge if you sit down.

Quereres, R Frei Vicente 7. Lively little club in a colonial house playing Brazilian samba funk, hip hop and *axê*.

Barra *p467*

Most Barra nightlife happens at the Farol da Barra (lighthouse). R Marquês de Leão is very busy, with lots of bars with tables on the pavement. Like the Pelourinho, the whole area is good for a browse, but be wary of pickpockets.

Habeas Copos, R Marquês de Leão 172. Famous and traditional street side bar, very popular.

Mordomia Drinks, Ladeira Da Barra. Enter through a narrow entrance to an open air bar with a spectacular view of the bay, very popular.

Atlantic suburbs *p467*

Once the bohemian section of town the nightlife in Rio Vermelho rivals Pelourinho. There are a number of lively bars around the Largo de Santana, a block west of the Hotel Catharina Paraguaçu.

Café Calypso, Trav Prudente Moraes 59, Rio Vermelho. Live Brazilian rock on Tue and Fri.

Havana Music Bar, R Cardeal da Silva, Rio Vermelho. Live bands Wed-Sat, best after 2230.

Pimentinha, Boca do Rio. One of the few clubs to be lively on Mon.

Teatro Sesi Rio Vermelho, R Borges dos Reis 9, Rio Vermelho, T334 0668. The best place in the city to see contemporary Salvador bands live.

🎭 Entertainment

Salvador de Bahia *p462, maps p464 and p466*
The Fundação Cultural do Estado da Bahia edits *Bahia Cultural*, a monthly brochure listing monthly cultural events. These can be found in most hotels and Bahiatursa information centres. Local newspapers *A Tarde* and *Correio da Bahia* have good cultural sections listing all events in the city.

Cinema The main shopping malls at Barra, Iguatemi, Itaigara and Brotas, and **Cineart** in Politeama (Centro), run more mainstream movies. The impressive Casa do Comércio building near Iguatemi houses the **Teatro do SESC** with a mixed programme of theatre, cinema and music Wed-Sun.

Music

During the winter (Jul-Sep) ring the blocos to confirm that free rehearsals will take place.

Ara Ketu, T3264 8800 www.araketu.com, hails from the sprawling Periperi suburb in the Lower City. Once a purely percussion band Ara Ketu has travelled widely and borrowed on various musical forms (samba, candomblé, soukous etc) to become a major carnival attraction and one of the most successful bands in Bahia. Rehearsals take place on Wed nights on Av Contorno. As these get very full, buy tickets in advance from Av Oceânica 683, Barra Centro Comercial, Sal 06, T3247 6784.

Banda Olodum (address above) drumming troupe made famous by their innovative powerhouse percussion and involvement with Paul Simon, Michael Jackson and Branford Marsalis, their weekly rehearsals take place in front of packed crowds.

Didá Neguinho do Samba was the musical director of Olodum until he founded Didá, an all-woman drumming group based along similar lines to Olodum. They rehearse on Fri nights in the Praça Teresa Batista, Pelourinho. Starts 2000, US$10.

Filhos de Gandhi, the original African drumming group and the largest, was formed by striking stevedores during the 1949 carnival. The hypnotic shuffling cadence of Filhos de Gandhi's afoxé rhythm is one of the most emotive of Bahia's carnival.

Ilê Aiyê, address above. Established in Liberdade, the largest suburb of the city, Ilê Aiyê is a thriving cultural group dedicated to preserving African traditions which under the guidance of its president Vovô is deeply committed to the fight against racism. Rehearsals take place mid week at

Boca do Rio and on Sat nights in front of their headquarters at Ladeira do Curuzu in Liberdade. **Timbalada**, T3355 0680, www.timbalada.com. Carlinhos Brown is a local hero. He has become one of the most influential musical composers in Brazil today, mixing great lyrics, innovative rhythms and a powerful stage presence. He played percussion with many Bahian musicians, until he formed his own percussion group, Timbalada. He has invested heavily in his native Candeal neighbourhood: the Candy All Square, a centre for popular culture, is where the Timbalada rehearsals take place every Sun night. 1830, US$20 from Sep to Mar. Not to be missed.

Artists and bands using electronic instruments and who tend to play in the *trios eléctricos* draw heavily on the rich rhythms of the drumming groups creating a new musical genre known as **Axé**. The most popular of such acts are **Chiclete com Banana**, www.chicletecombanana.com.br, and **Ivete Sangalo**. Also look out for the internationally famous **Daniela Mercury**. **Gerónimo** was one of the first singer/songwriters to use the wealth of rhythms of the Candomblé in his music and his song *E d'Oxum* is something of an anthem for the city.

All the above have albums released and you can find their records easily in most record stores. See Shopping in the Pelourinho. Also try Billbox in Shopping Barra on the 3rd floor.

Theatre
Castro Alves, at Campo Grande (Largo 2 de Julho), T3339 8000, www.tca.ba.gov.br, seats 1400 and is considered one of the best in Latin America. It also has its own repertory theatre, the **Sala de Coro**, for more experimental productions. The theatre's Concha Acústica is an open-air venue used frequently in the summer, attracting the big names in Brazilian music. **Theatro XVIII**, R Frei Vicente, T 3332 0018, www.theatroxviii.com.br, an experimental theatre in the Pelourinho. **Teatro Gregório de Matos** in Praça Castro Alves offers space to new productions and writers. **Vila Velha**, Passéio Público, Gamboa da Cima, T3336 1384. A historically important venue where many of the *tropicalistas* first played. Nowadays it has an eclectic programme of modern dance, theatre and live music. **Grupo Teatro Olodum** often works here.

⊛ Festivals and events

Salvador de Bahia *p464, maps p464 and p466*
6 Jan (Epiphany); Ash Wednesday and **Maundy Thursday**, half-days; **2 Jul** (Independence of Bahia); **30 Oct**; Christmas Eve, half-day. An

important local holiday is **Festa do Nosso Senhor do Bonfim**; it takes place on the 2nd Sun after Epiphany, but the washing or *lavagem* of the Bonfim church, with its colourful parade, takes place on the preceding Thu (usually mid-Jan). The **Festa da Ribeirav** is on the following Mon. Another colourful festival is that of the fishermen of Rio Vermelho on **2 Feb**; gifts for Yemanjá, Goddess of the Sea, are taken to sea in a procession of sailing boats to an accompaniment of candomblé instruments. The Holy Week processions among the old churches of the upper city are also interesting.
For Carnival, see box.

⊙ Shopping

Pelourinho *p465*
Bookshops Graúna, Av 7 de Setembro 1448, and R Barão de Itapoã 175, Porto da Barra, many English titles. **Livraria Brandão**, R Ruy Barbosa 104, Centre. Secondhand English, French, Spanish and German books. **Livraria Planeta**, Carlos Gomes 42, loja 1, sells used English books. **Handicrafts** The major carnival afro blocos have boutiques selling T-shirts etc. **Boutique Olodum**, on Praça José Alencar, **Ilê Aiyê**, on R Francisco Muniz Barreto 16 and **Muzenza** next door. On the same street is **Modaxé**, a retail outlet for clothes manufactured by street children under the auspices of the Projeto Axé, expensive. **Artesanato Santa Bárbara**, R Portas do Carmo 7. Excellent hand-made lace products. **Atelier Portal da Cor**, Ladeira do Carmo 31. Run by a co-operative of local artists, Totonho, Calixto, Raimundo Santos, Jô, good prices. Recommended. **Casa do Índio**, Ladeira do Carmo 27. Indigenous artefacts and art, restaurant and bar open here till late, good surroundings. **Instituto Mauá**, R Gregório de Matos 27. Open Tue-Sat 0900-1800, Sun 1000-1600, good quality Bahian handicrafts at fair prices, better value and better quality for traditional crafts than the Mercado Modelo. **Loja de Artesanato do SESC**, Largo Pelourinho. Mon-Fri 0900-1800 (closed for lunch), Sat 0900-1300, similar store to Instituto Mauá. **Rosa do Prado**, R Inacio Aciolly, 5. Cigar shop packed with every kind of Brazilian 'charuto' imaginable. **Jewellery** In the Pelourinho are: **Casa Moreira**, Ladeira da Praça, just south of Praça da Sé. Exquisite jewellery and antiques, most very expensive, but some affordable charms. **Scala**, Praça da Sé. Handmade jewellery using locally mined gems (eg. acquamarine, amethyst and emerald), workshop at back. **Markets** Mercado Modelo, at Praça Cairu, lower city, offers many tourist items such as wood carvings, silver-plated fruit, leather goods, local musical instruments. Lace items for sale are

often not handmade (despite labels), are heavily marked up, and are much better bought at their place of origin (for example Ilha de Maré, Pontal da Barra and Marechal Deodoro). **Cosme e Damião**, musical instrument sellers on 1st floor, has been recommended, especially if you want to play the instruments. Bands and dancing, especially Sat (but very much for money from tourists taking photographs), closed at 1200 Sun. The largest and most authentic market is the **Feira de São Joaquim**, 5 km from Mercado Modelo along the sea front: barkers, trucks, burros, horses, boats, people, mud, all very smelly, every day (Sun till 1200 only), busiest on Sat morning; interesting African-style pottery and basketwork; very cheap. (The car ferry terminal for Itaparica is nearby.) Every Wed from 1700-2100 there is a **handicrafts fair** in the 17th century fort of Santa Maria at the opposite end of Porto da Barra beach.

Music in the Pelourinho Brazilian Sound, R Francisco Muniz Barreto 18, for the latest in Brazilian and Bahia CDs. **Oficina de Investigação Musical**, Portas do Carmo 24. Hand-made traditional percussion instruments (and percussion lessons, US$15 per hr), Mon-Fri 0800-1200 and 1300-1600.

Shopping centres Barra and Iguatemi are the largest and best stocked. They are the most comfortable places to shop - havens of a/c cool in the heat of summer.

▲ Activities and tours

Salvador de Bahia *p464, maps p464 and p466*
Boat and bus tours Available from several companies. All-day boat trip on Bahia de Todos Os Santos last from 0800-1700 including a visit to Ilha dos Frades, lunch on Itaparica (US$13 extra), US$20 pp. City tours also cost US$20 pp

Capoeira A sport developed from the traditional foot-fighting technique introduced from Angola by African slaves. The music is by drum, tambourine and berimbau; there are several different kinds of the sport. If you want to attempt Capoeira, the best school is **Mestre Bimba**, R das Laranjeiras, T3322 0639, open 0900-1200, 1500-2100, basic course in Capoeira regional, US$32 for 20 hours. Another Capoeira regional school is **Filhos de Bimba**, R Durval Fraga, 6, Nordeste, T3345 7329. There are schools in Forte de Santo Antônio behind Pelourinho which teach Capoeira Angola, but check addresses at the tourist office. Exhibitions take place in the Largo do Pelourinho every Friday evening around 2000, very authentic, in the upper city. You can also see capoeiristas in public spaces like the Pelourinho, outside the Mercado Modelo and at Campo Grande. They may be picturesque but are not always genuine experts; they often expect a contribution, too; but real Capoeira should be free. Negotiate a price before taking pictures. At the Casa da Cultura at Forte de Santo Antônio there is also free live music on Saturday night.

Tour operators and guides
Dieter Herzberg, T3334 1200. A recommended guide who speaks German,
Tatur Turismo, Av Tancredo Neves 274, Centro Empresarial Iguatemi, Sala 228, Bloco B, T3450 7216, www.tatur.com.br. Run by Irishman, Conor O'Sullivan. English spoken. Specializes in Bahia, arranges private guided tours and can make any necessary travel, hotel and accommodation arrangements. Highly recommended.

⊖ Transport

Salvador de Bahia *p464, maps p464 and p466*
Air An a/c bus service every 30-40 mins between the new Luis Eduardo Magalhães Airport and the centre, a distance of 32 km, costs US$1.60. It takes the coast road to the city, stopping at hotels en route. Service starts from the airport at 0500 (last bus 2200, 0600-2200 at weekends) and from Praça da Sé at 0630 (last bus 2100). Also ordinary buses, US$0.65. 'Special' taxis to both Barra and centre (buy ticket at the airport desk next to tourist information booth), US$60; normal taxis (from outside airport), US$25, bus-taxi service, US$13. Allow plenty of time for travel to the airport and for check-in. ATMs are in a special area to the extreme right as you arrive, a good place to get money. **Banco do Brasil** is to the extreme left, open Mon-Fri 0900-1500. **Jacarandá** exchange house is in front of international arrivals, open 24 hrs a day, but poor rates and only good for changing a small amount (count your money carefully). Tourist information booth open 24 hrs, English spoken, has list of hotels and useful map.

Daily flights to all the main cities.

Bus Local buses US$0.90, executivos, a/c, US$1.80, US$2 or US$4 depending on the route. On buses and at the ticket-sellers' booths, watch your change and beware pickpockets (one scam used by thieves is to descend from the bus while you are climbing aboard). To get from the old city to the ocean beaches, take a 'Barra' bus from Praça da Sé to the Barra point and walk to the nearer ones; the Aeroporto executivo leaves Praça da Sé, passing Barra, Ondina, Rio Vermelho, Amaralina, Pituba, Costa Azul, Armação, Boca do Rio, Jaguaripe, Patamares, Piatã and Itapoã, before turning inland to the airport. The glass-sided Jardineira bus goes to Flamengo beach (30 km from the city) following the coastal route; it passes all the best beaches; sit on the right hand side for best views. It leaves from the

Praça da Sé daily 0730-1930, every 40 mins, US$2. For beaches beyond Itapoã, take the executivo to Stella Maris and Flamengo beaches. These follow the same route as the Jardineira. During Carnival, when most streets are closed, buses leave from Vale do Canela (O Vale), near Campo Grande.

Long distance bus from the Rodoviária (T450 4500); bus RI or RII, 'Centro- Rodoviária-Circular'; in the centre, get on in the Lower City at the foot of the Lacerda lift; buses also go to Campo Grande (US$0.90). A quicker executive bus from Praça da Sé or Praça da Inglaterra (in front of McDonalds), Comércio, run to Iguatemi Shopping Centre, US$2, weekdays only, from where there is a walkway to the rodoviária (take care in the dark, or a taxi, US$13). To **Belém** US$64 comercial with **Itapemirim**. To **Recife**, US$24-32, 13 hrs, 2 a day and 1 leito, **Itapemerim**, T358 0037. To **Rio** (28 hrs, US$60, leito US$120, Itapemirim, good stops, clean toilets, recommended). To **São Paulo** (30 hrs), US$68, leito US$95 (0815 with **Viação Nacional**, 2 in afternoon with São Geraldo). To **Fortaleza**, 19 hrs, US$76 at 0900 with Itapemerim. **Ilhéus**, 7 hrs, **Aguia Branca**, comercial US$19, leito US$39, several. To **Lençóis** 3 a day, 8 hrs, US$23 with **Real Expresso**. **Belo Horizonte**, Gontijo, T358 7448, at 1700, US$50 comercial, US$65 executivo, São Geraldo at 1800. There are daily bus services to **Brasília** along the fully paved BR-242, via Barreiras, 3 daily, 23 hrs, **Paraíso**, US$50. Frequent services to the majority of destinations; a large panel in the main hall lists destinations and the relevant ticket office.
Taxi Taxi meters start at US$0.65 for the 'flagdown' and US$0.13 per 100 m. They charge US$20 per hr within city limits, and 'agreed' rates outside. Taxi Barra-Centro US$4 daytime; US$5 at night. Watch the meter, especially at night; the night-time charge should be 30 higher than daytime charges.

Itaparica *p468*
Ferry The main passenger ferry leaves for Bom Despacho from São Joaquim (buses for Calçada, Ribeira stop across the road from the ferry terminal; the 'Sabino Silva – Ribeira' bus passes in front of the Shopping Barra). First ferry from Salvador at 0540 and, depending on demand, at intervals of 45 mins thereafter; last ferry from Salvador at 2230. Returning to Salvador the 1st ferry is at 0515 and the last at 2300. In summer ferries are much more frequent. Information from **COMAB/Ferry Fácil**, open 0700-2300 at terminal. A one way ticket for foot passengers Mon-Fri is US$1.30, Sat-Sun US$1.60. Catamarans depart for Bom Despacho twice daily, US$2 (US$2.65 at weekends). **Mar Grande** can be reached by a smaller ferry (**Lancha**) from the Terminal

Marítimo in front of the Mercado Modelo in Salvador. The ferries leave every 45 mins and the crossing takes 50 mins, US$2.40 return.

● Directory

Salvador de Bahia *p464, maps p464 and p466*
Airline offices BRA, at airport, T3204 1027, www.voebra.com.br. Gol, T3204 1608. Ocean Air, T3204 1502. TAM, Praça Gago Coutinho, T0800-570 5700. TAP, AvTancredo Neves 1632, salas 1206/7, T0800-707 7787. Varig Galeria Hotel Grande Rio, R Padre Fraga s/n, T3862 2500. At airport T3204 1050. **Banks** Banks are open 1000-1600. Selected branches of major banks have ATMs for Visa, eg Bradesco, also Banco 24 Horas. Don't change money on the street especially in the Upper City where higher rates are usually offered. Changing at banks can be bureaucratic and time-consuming. Citibank, R Miguel Calmon 555, Comércio, centre, changes TCs. Branch at R Almte Marquês de Leão 71, Barra, has ATM. MasterCard ATMs at branches of HSBC. Also at Credicard, 1st floor, Citibank building, R Miguel Calmon 555, Comércio. Figueiredo, opposite Grande Hotel da Barra on Ladeira da Barra will exchange cash at good rates. Shopping Tour in Barra Shopping centre changes dollars, as will other tour agencies. If stuck, all the big hotels will exchange, but at poor rates. **Car hire** If renting a car check whether credit card or cash is cheapest. See page 43, for multinational car rental agencies.
Embassies and consulates France, Trav Francisco Gonçalves 1, sala 401, Comércio, T3241 0168, Mon, Tue, Thu morning only. Germany, R Jogo do Carneiro 49, Saúde, T3242 2670, Mon-Fri 0900-1200. Italy, Av 7 de Setembro 1238, Centro, T3329 5338, viconitbahia@svn.com.br, Mon, Wed, Fri 1500-1800. Netherlands, R Largo do Carmo 04, Sl 101, Santo Antônio, T3241 3001, Mon-Fri 0900-1100. Switzerland, Av Tancredo Neves 3343, 5th floor, sala 506b, T3341 5827. UK, R Caetano Moura 35, T3247 8216, lhanson@uol.com.br. USA, Av Tancredo Neves 1632, Sala 1401, Salvador Trade Center - Torre Sul, Caminho das Árvores, T3113 2090, amcon@svn.com.br. Mon-Fri, 1400-1600. **Internet** There are numerous internet cafés throughout the touristy parts of the city. **Language classes** Casa do Brasil, R Milton de Oliveira 231, Barra, www.casadobrazil.com.br. Diálogo, R Dr João Pondé 240, Barra, T3264 0007, www.dialogo-brazilstudy.com. With optional dance, *capoeira* and cookery classes, accommodation with host families. **Medical services** Clinic: Barão de Loreto 21, Graça. Medical: yellow fever vaccinations free at Delegação Federal de Saúde, R Padre Feijó, Canela. **Post offices** Main post office and

poste restante is in Praça Inglaterra, in the Lower City, open Mon-Fri 0800-1700, Sat 0800-1200. Several other offices, including R Portas do Carmo 43, rodoviária, airport, Barra and Iguatemi Shopping Malls. **Useful addresses Immigration**: (for extensions of entry permits), Policia Federal, Av O Pontes 339, Aterro de Água de Meninos, Lower City, T3319 6082, open 1000-1600. Show an outward ticket or sufficient funds for your stay, visa extension US$17.50. **Tourist Police**: R Gregório de Matos 16, T3321 1092. **Delegacia de Proteção ao Turista**, Praça José de Anchieta 14, T3322 7155.

Inland from Salvador

There are strong historical associations inland from Salvador, seen in the colonial exploitation of sugar and diamonds. Lençóis, famous for the latter, also has some beautiful countryside, which is ideal for trekking. On the coast south of Salvador, there is a whole string of popular resorts. It was on this part of what is now Brazil that the Portuguese first made landfall. Bahia's north coast runs from the Coconut Highway onto the Green Line, just to give of an idea of how the shore looks – and don't forget the beaches there, too.

The Recôncavo

The area around Salvador, known as the Recôncavo Baiano, was one of the chief centres of sugar and tobacco cultivation in the 16th century. Some 73 km from Salvador is **Santo Amaro da Purificação**, an old sugar centre sadly decaying, noted for its churches (often closed because of robberies), municipal palace (1769), fine main praça, birthplace of the singers Caetano Veloso and his sister Maria Bethania and ruined mansions including Araújo Pinto, former residence of the Barão de Cotegipe. Other attractions include the splendid beaches of the bay, the falls of Vitória and the grotto of Bom Jesus dos Pobres. The festivals of **Santo Amaro**, 24 January-2 February, and **Nossa Senhora da Purificação** on 2 February itself are interesting. There is also the **Bembé do Mercado** festival on 13 May. Craftwork is sold on the town's main bridge. There are no good hotels or restaurants.

Cachoeira and São Félix

At 116 km from Salvador and only 4 km from the BR-101 coastal road are the towns of Cachoeira (Bahia's 'Ouro Preto', *Population: 30,416*) and São Félix (*Population 13,699*), on either side of the Rio Paraguaçu below the Cachoeira dam. Cachoeira was twice capital of Bahia: once in 1624-1625 during the Dutch invasion, and once in 1822-1823 while Salvador was still held by the Portuguese. There are beautiful views from above São Félix.

Cachoeira's main buildings are the **Casa da Câmara e Cadeia** (1698-1712), the **Santa Casa de Misericórdia** (1734 – the hospital, someone may let you see the church), the 16th-century **Ajuda** chapel (now containing a fine collection of vestments), and the Convent of the **Ordem Terceira do Carmo**, whose church has a heavily gilded interior. Other churches are the **Matriz** with 5 m-high azulejos, and **Nossa Senhora da Conceição do Monte**. There are beautiful lace cloths on the church altars. All churches are either restored or in the process of restoration. The **Museu Hansen Bahia**, R Ana Néri, houses fine engravings by the German artist who made the Recôncavo his home in the 1950s. There is a great wood-carving tradition in Cachoeira. The artists can be seen at work in their studios. Best are Louco Filho, Fory, both in R Ana Néri, Doidão, in front of the Igreja Matriz and J Gonçalves on the main praça. A 300 m railway bridge built by the British in the 19th century spans the Rio Paraguaçu to São Felix where the Danneman cigar factory can be visited to see hand-rolling. Tourist office: Casa de Ana Néri, Cachoeira.

Lençóis → *Phone code: 0xx75. Colour map 5, grid C4. Population: 8,910.*

This historical monument and colonial gem was founded in 1844 to exploit the diamonds in the region. While there are still some *garimpeiros* (gold prospectors), it is not precious metals that draw most visitors, but the climate, which is cooler than the coast, the relaxed atmosphere and the wonderful trekking and horse riding in the hills of the Chapada Diamantina. A few of the options are given below under Excursions, and pousadas and tour operators offer guiding services to point you in the right direction. This is also a good place for buying handicrafts. **Tourist office**, Avenida Sete de Setembro 10, T3334 1271.

Parque Nacional da Chapada Diamantina → *Colour map 5, grid C4.*

Palmeiras, 50 km from Lençóis, is the headquarters of the Parque Nacional da Chapada Diamantina (founded 1985), which contains 1,500 sq km of mountainous country. There is an abundance of endemic plants, waterfalls, large caves (take care, and a strong torch, there are no signs and caves can be difficult to find without a guide), rivers with natural swimming pools and good walking tours. **Parque Nacional da Chapada Diamantina** Information, **Ibama**, R Barão do Rio Branco 25, Palmeiras, Toxx75-332 2420, parnadiamantina@hotmail.com.

Excursions near Lençóis and in the Chapada Diamantina ① *local guides can often arrange transport to the more remote excursions, certainly this is possible when groups are involved.* Near the town, visit the **Serrano** with its wonderful natural pools in the river bed, which give a great hydro massage. A little further away is the **Salão de Areia**, where the coloured sands for the bottle paintings come from. **Ribeirão do Meio** is a 45-minute walk from town; here locals slide down a long natural water chute into a big pool (it is best to be shown the way it is done and to something to slide in). **Gruta do Lapão**, three hours from Lençóis, guide essential, is in quartz rock and therefore has no stalagmites. Some light rock climbing is required. **Cachoeira da Primavera**, two very pretty waterfalls close to town, recommended. **Cachoeira Sossego**, two hours from town, a 'picture postcard' waterfall, swimming pool, recommended. **Morro de Pai Inácio**, 30 km from Lençóis, has the best view of the Chapada, recommended at sunset (bus from Lençóis at 0815, 30 minutes, US$1). In the park is the **Cachoeira da Fumaça** (Smoke Waterfall, also called **Glass**), 384 m, the second highest in Brazil. To see it, go by car to the village of **Capão** and walk 2½ hours. The view is astonishing; the updraft of the air currents often makes the water flow back up creating the 'smoke' effect. Olivia Taylor at the Pousada dos Duendes offers a three-day trek, the village of Capão and Capivara and Palmital falls from US$45.

🔵 **Sleeping** → *See Telephone, page 347, for important phone changes.*

Cachoeira *p477*
B Pousada do Convento de Cachoeira, Praça da Aclamação, T3425 1716. In a restored 16th-century convent, good restaurant.
C Pousada Labarca, R Inocêncio Boaventura 37, T3425 1070, cecilia.thomas@bol.com.br. Nice *pousada* with art gallery, paintings by Argentine owner, organizes local trips and to candomblé ceremonies.
C Santo Antônio, Praça Maciel,01, near the rodoviária, T3425 1402. Basic, safe, laundry facilities. Recommended.

Lençóis *p477*
L Portal de Lençóis, R Chacara Grota, at the top of the town, T3334 1233, www.portalhoteis.tur.br. 15 smart chalets in a mini-resort on the edge of the park, with pool, sauna, restaurant, bar and play area for kids. Activities and walks organized.
L-AL Hotel de Lençóis, R Altinha Alves 747, T3369 5000, www.hoteldelencois.com.br. Rooms organized in terraces set in a grassy garden on the edge of the park. Good breakfast, pool and restaurant.
L-AL Canto das Águas, Av Senhor dos Passos, T/F3334 1154, www.lencois.com.br. Riverside hotel with a/c or fan, pool, efficient, best rooms are in the new wing.
B Águas Claras, R P Benjamin 27, T3334 1471 (100 m from the rodoviária). Simple, well-looked-after rooms; some with a fridge.

B O Casarão, Av 7 de Setembro 85, T3334 1198. Modest *pousada* with a/c or fan, fridge. Recommended.
B-C Estalagem de Alcino, R Tomba Surrão 139, T3334 1171. An enchanting, beautifully-restored period house furnished with 19th-century antiques. Most have shared bathrooms. Superb breakfast served in hummingbird-filled garden. Highly recommended.
B-C Pousalegre, R Boa Vista 95, T3334 1916. Dormitories only with hot shared showers, tasty breakfast and good vegetarian restaurant.
C Casa da Geleia, R Gen Viveiros 187, T3334 1151, casadageleia@hotmail.com. 6 smart chalets set in a huge garden at the entrance to the town, English spoken, good breakfast (Ze Carlos is a keen birdwatcher and an authority on the region, Lia makes excellent jams).
C Casa de Hélia, R da Muritiba 3, T3334 1143, www.casadehelia.com.br. Attractive little guest-house, English and some Hebrew spoken, good facilities, legendary breakfast. Recommended.
C Tradição, R José Florêncio, T334 1137. Plain rooms with TV, breakfast, fridge, mosquito nets.
D Pousada dos Duendes, R do Pires, T/F3334 1229. English-run *pousada*, shared hot showers, breakfast (vegetarians and vegans catered for), welcoming, comfortable. Their tour agency, (**Saturno** on R Miguel Calmon) arranges tours and treks from 1 to 11 days and more, Olivia Taylor is very helpful.

Camping **Alquimia**, 2 km before Lençóis, T3334 1213, and **Camping Lumiar**, near Rosário church in centre, T3334 1241, with popular restaurant. Recommended.

House rental
Mostly very simple houses to rent: **Juanita** on R do Rosário rents rooms and offers washing and cooking facilities. **Claudia and Isabel**, R da Baderna 95, T3334 1229, rent houses all over town.

🍴 Eating

Cachoeira and São Félix *p477*
🍴🍴 **Do Nair**, R 13 de Maio. Delicious food and sometimes Seresta music.
🍴 **Cabana do Pai Thomaz**, 25 de Junho 12, excellent Bahian food, good value, also an hotel, **B** with private bath and breakfast.
🍴 **Xang-hai**, São Félix. Good, cheap food. Warmly recommended. Try the local dish, *maniçoba* (meat, manioc and peppers).

Lençóis *p477*
🍴🍴 **Artistas da Massa**, R Miguel Calmon. Italian dishes, mainly pasta and pizza.
🍴🍴 **Picanha na Praça**, opposite the bandstand on the square above the main praça. Good steaks.
🍴 **Goody**, R da Rodaviária s/n. Good simple cooking.

🍸 Bars and clubs

Lençóis *p477*
Bar Lençóis, on main praça. For drinks, good *cachaça* and *caipirinhas*.
Doce Bárbaros, R das Pedras 21. Lively bar almost any night of the week.

✳ Festivals and events

Cachoeira *p477*
São João (**24 Jun**), 'Carnival of the Interior' celebrations include dangerous games with fireworks. **Nossa Sehora da Boa Morte** (**early Aug**) is also a major festival. A famous candomblé ceremony at the Fonte de Santa Bárbara is held on **4 Dec**.

⦿ Shopping

Lençóis *p477*
The Mon morning market is recommended. There is a local craft market just off the main praça every night.
Artesanato Areias Coloridas, R das Pedras, owned by Taurino, is the best place for local sand paintings made in bottles. These are inexpensive. They will make one as you wait.

Jota, the most original for ceramic work, whose workshop can be visited. Take the steps to the left of the school near the Pousada Lençóis.

▲ Activities and tours

Lençóis *p477*
Cirtur, R da Bandeira 41, T3334 1133, cirtur@neth.com.br.
Lentur, Av 7 de Setembro 16, T/F3334 1271. Speak to Paulo, who organizes day trips to nearby caves and to see the sunset at Morro do Pai Inácio.
Pé de Trilha Turismo Aventura, Praça 7 de Setembro, T3334 1124. Guiding, trekking, rent camping equipment, etc, can make reservations for most of the *pousadas* in the Chapada Diamantina. Represented in Salvador by **Tatur Turismo**.
Venturas e Aventuras, Praça Horácio de Matos 20, T3334 1304. Excellent trekking expeditions, up to 6 days.

Guides
Each pousada generally has a guide attached to it to take residents on tours, about US$20-30. The following are recommended:
Edmilson (known locally as Mil), R Domingos B Souza 70, T3334 1319. Knows the region extremely well, knowledgeable and reliable.
Ereas, R José Florêncio 60, T3334 1155. The only specialist birding guide in the town.
Roy Funch, T/F3334 1305, royfunch@gd.com.br. The ex-director of the Chapada Diamantina National Park is an excellent guide and has written a visitors' guide to the park, which is available in English. (It is recommended as the best for information on the geography and trails of the Chapada.) Highly recommended. He can be booked through www.elabrasil.com from the USA or UK.
Índio, contact at **Pousada Diangela**, R dos Minheiros 60, Centro Histórico. Reliable, goes off the beaten track.
Luiz Krug, contact via Pousada de Lençóis, T3334 1102. An independent guide specializing in geology and caving. He speaks English.
Trajano, contact via **Casa da Hélia**, T3334 1143, Speaks English and some Hebrew and is a good-humoured guide for treks to the bottom of the Cachoeira da Fumaça.

⊖ Transport

Cachoeira *p477*
Bus From **Salvador** (Camurjipe) every hr or so from 0530; **Feira Santana**, 2 hrs, US$4.

Air Airport, Km 209, BR-242, 20 km from town T3625 8100.
Bus Real Expresso from **Salvador** 3 a day, US$23, *comercial*. Book in advance, especially at weekends and holidays. Buses also from **Recife**, **Ibotirama**, **Barreiras** or **Brasília**, 16 hrs, US$44 (take irregular bus to Seabra, then 2 a day to Brasília).

 Directory

Lençóis *p477*
Banks There are several banks with cashpoints and money changing facilities in town, including a Banco do Brasil and a Bradesco. **Post offices** main square, 0900-1700, Mon-Fri.

South of Salvador

On the coast south of Salvador, there is a whole string of popular resorts. It was on this part of what is now Brazil that the Portuguese first made landfall. Bahia's north coast runs from the Coconut Highway onto the Green Line, just to give of an idea of how the shore looks – and don't forget the beaches there, too.

Valença → *Phone code: 0xx71. Colour map 7, grid A6. Population: 77,509.*

In this small, attractive town, 271 km south of Salvador via a paved road, two old churches stand on rising ground; the views from Nossa Senhora do Amparo are recommended. It is at the mouth of the Rio Una, which enters an enormous region of mangrove swamps. The main attraction is the beaches on the mainland (Guabim, 14 km north) and on the island of Tinharé. **Secretaria de Turismo**, T3641 8610. Avoid touts at the rodoviária.

Tinharé and Morro de São Paulo → *Phone code: 0xx75.*

Tinharé is a large island (1½ hours south of Valença by boat) separated from the mainland by the estuary of the Rio Una and mangrove swamps, so that it is hard to tell which is land and which is water. The most popular beaches and pousadas are at Morro de São Paulo. Immediately south is the island of **Boipeba**, separated from Tinharé by the Rio do Inferno. Accommodation is split between the little town where the riverboat ferry arrives, the adjacent beach, Boca da Barra, which is more idyllic and the fishing village of Moreré half an hour's boat ride to the south, US$20 (high tide only).

  Morro de São Paulo is on the headland at the northernmost tip of Tinharé, lush with ferns, palms and birds of paradise. The village is dominated by the lighthouse and the ruins of a colonial fort (1630), built as a defence against European raiders. It has a landing place on the sheltered landward side, dominated by the old gateway of the fortress. From the lighthouse a path leads to a ruined look out with cannon, which has panoramic views. The fort is a good point to watch the sunset from. Dolphins can be seen in August. Fonte de Ceu waterfall is reached by walking along the beach to **Gamboa** then inland. Watch the tide; it's best to take a guide, or take a boat back to Morro (US$0.50-1). No motor vehicles are allowed on the island. On 7 September there's a big festival with live music on the beach. For more information visit www.morrodesaopaulo.com.br. **Note:** There is a port tax of US$1 payable at the prefeitura on leaving the island.

Itacaré → *Phone code: 0xx73.*

This picturesque fishing village sits in the midst of remnant Atlantic Coast rainforest at the mouth of the Rio de Contas. Some of Bahia's best beaches stretch north and south. A few are calm and crystal clear, the majority are great for surfing. There are plenty of beaches within walking distance of town. Itacaré is rapidly becoming a sophisticated resort town for the São Paulo middle classes and is very busy with Brazilian tourists in high season. Much of the accommodation here is tasteful, blending in with the natural landscape and there are many excellent restaurants and lively if still low key nightlife. Pousadas are concentrated on and around Praia da Concha, the first beach south of the town centre. North of Itacaré is the **Peninsula de Maraú**, fringed with beautiful beaches to its tip at **Barra Grande** and fast becoming the focus of Europeans seeking a slice of paradise. Already, luxury resorts are being built. To explore the area fully you will need a car. **Secretaria de Turismo de Itacaré** ① *T3251 2134, www.itacare.com.br.*

Brazil Inland from Salvador Listings

Ilhéus → *Phone code: 0xx73. Post code: 45650. Colour map 7, grid A6. Population: 222,127.*

At the mouth of the Rio Cachoeira, 462 km south of Salvador, the port serves a district which produces 65% of all Brazilian cocoa. A bridge links the north bank of the river with Pontal, where the airport is located. Ilhéus is the birthplace of Jorge Amado (1912-2002) and the setting of one of his most famous novels, *Gabriela, cravo e canela* (Gabriela, Clove and Cinnamon). The church of **São Jorge** (1556), the city's oldest, is on the Praça Rui Barbosa; it has a small museum. In Alto da Vitória is the 17th century **Nossa Senhora da Vitória**, built to celebrate a victory over the Dutch. The **Secretaria de Turismo** is at ① *R Santos Dumont s/n, anexo da Prefeitura, 5th floor, T2101-5500.*

North of Ilhéus, two good beaches are Marciano, with reefs offshore and good surfing, and Barra, 1 km further north at the mouth of the Rio Almada. South of the river, Pontal beaches can be reached by 'Barreira' bus; alight just after Hotel Jardim Atlântico. Between Ilhéus and **Olivença** are more fine beaches.

Porto Seguro and around

→ *Phone code: 0xx73. Post code: 45810. Colour map 7, grid A6. Population: 95,721.*

About 400 km south of Ilhéus on the coast is the old town of Porto Seguro. In 1500, Pedro Álvares Cabral sighted land at Monte Pascoal south of Porto Seguro. As the sea here was too open, he sailed north in search of a secure protected harbour, entering the mouth of the Rio Burnahém to find the harbour he later called Porto Seguro (safe port). Where the first mass was celebrated, a cross marks the spot on the road between Porto Seguro and Santa Cruz Cabrália. A rather uncoordinated tourist village, **Coroa Vermelha**, has sprouted at the site of Cabral's first landfall, 20 minutes by bus to the north of Porto Seguro.

Porto Seguro itself is Bahia's second most popular tourist destination, with charter flights from Rio and São Paulo and plenty of hustle and bustle. Contact the **Secretaria de Turismo de Porto Seguro**, Praça dos Pataxós, T3288 3708, turismo@portonet.com.br. Information desk at Praça Manoel Ribeiro Coelho 10. A website for the entire coast is www.portonet.com.br.

To its historical quarter, **Cidade Histórica**, take a wide, steep, unmarked path uphill from the roundabout at the entrance to town. Three churches (Nossa Senhora da Misericórdia-1530, Nossa Senhora do Rosário-1534, and Nossa Senhora da Pena-1718), the former jail and the monument marking the landfall of Gonçalo Coelho comprise a small, peaceful place with lovely gardens and panoramic views.

Only 10 mins north of Coroa Vermelha, **Santa Cruz Cabrália** is a delightful small town at the mouth of the Rio João de Tiba, with a splendid beach, river port, and a 450-year-old church with a fine view. A good trip from here is to Coroa Alta, a reef 50 minutes away by boat, passing along the tranquil river to the reef and its crystal waters and good snorkelling. Daily departure at 1000. A recommended boatman is Zezé on the square by the river's edge, helpful, knowledgeable. The trip costs around US$15 without lunch. A 15-minute river crossing by ferry to a new road on the opposite bank gives easy access to the deserted beaches of **Santo André** and **Santo Antônio**. Hourly buses from Santa Cruz to Porto Seguro (23 km).

Arraial da Ajuda → *Colour map 7, grid A6.*

Across the Rio Buranhém south from Porto Seguro is the village of Arraial da Ajuda, the gateway to the idyllic beaches of the south coast. Set high on a cliff, there are great views of the coastline from behind the church of Nossa Senhora da Ajuda in the main praça. Each August there is a pilgrimage to the shrine of Nossa Senhora da Ajuda. Ajuda has become very popular with younger tourists (especially Israelis) and there are many pousadas, from the very simple to the very sophisticated, restaurants, bars and small shops. The town has grown out of its former 'hippie' image, becoming more rave oriented. Parties are held almost every night, on the beach or in the main street, called the Broadway. At Brazilian holiday times (especially New Year and Carnival) it is very crowded.

The **beaches**, several protected by a coral reef, are splendid. The nearest is 15 minutes' walk away. During daylight hours those closest to town (take 'R da Praia' out of town to the south) are extremely busy; excellent barracas sell good seafood, drinks, and play music. The best beaches are Mucugê, Pitinga ('bronzeamento irrestrito' or nude sunbathing) and Taipé.

Trancoso → *Phone code 0xx73.*

Some 15 km from Ajuda, 25 km south of Porto Seguro by paved road, is Trancoso. This pretty, peaceful town, with its beautiful beaches (Praia dos Nativos is the most famous), has become very chic, with the rich and famous from home and abroad buying properties and shopping in the little boutiques. In summer it can get packed. Trancoso has an historic church, São João Batista (1656). From the end of Praça São João there is a fine coastal panorama. It is possible to walk along the beach to Ajuda via the village of Rio da Barra; allow three hours.

Caraíva → *Phone code 0xx73. www.caraiva.com.br.*

This atmospheric, peaceful fishing village on the banks of the Rio Caraíva, 65 km south of Porto Seguro, and near the Pataxó Indian Reserve has no wheeled vehicles, no electricity nor hot water, but has marvellous beaches and is a real escape from the more developed Trancoso and Porto Seguro. Despite the difficulty of getting there, it is becoming increasingly popular. Good walks are north to Praia do Satu (Sr Satu provides an endless supply of coconut milk), or 6 km south to a rather sad Pataxó Indian village (watch the tides). Horses can be hired from Pousada Lagoa or Pizzaria Barra Velha. Boats can be hired for US$40 per day from Zé Pará to Caruípe beach, snorkelling at Pedra de Tatuaçu reef and Corombau (take your own mask and fins) or for diving (best December to February). Prainha river beach, about 30 minutes away, and mangrove swamps can also be visited by canoe or launch. The high season is December-February and July; the wettest months are April-June and November. Use flip-flops for walking the sand streets and take a torch. There are no medical facilities and only rudimentary policing.

Parque Nacional de Monte Pascoal → *Colour map 7, grid A6.*

South of Porto Seguro, reached by a 14 km paved access road at Km 796 of the BR-101, the Parque Nacional de Monte Pascoal set up in 1961 to preserve the flora, fauna and birdlife of the coastal area in which Europeans made landfall in Brazil (Caixa Postal 24, CEP 45836-000 Itamaraju, Toxx73-3294 1110). The Pataxó Indian reservation is located at Corombau village, on the ocean shore of the park. Corombau can be reached by schooner from Porto Seguro.

Caravelas and around → *Colour map 7, grid A6. Population: 20,103.*

Further south still, 107 km from Itamaruju (93 km south of Eunápolis), is this charming town, rapidly developing for tourism, but a major trading town in 17th and 18th centuries. Caravelas is in the mangroves; the beaches are about 10 km away at Barra de Caravelas (hourly buses), a fishing village. There are food shops, restaurants and bars.

The **Parque Nacional Marinho dos Abrolhos** is 70 km east of Caravelas. Abrolhos is an abbreviation of Abre os olhos: 'Open your eyes' from Amérigo Vespucci's exclamation when he first sighted the reef in 1503. Established in 1983, the park consists of five small islands (Redonda, Siriba, Guarita, Sueste, Santa Bárbara), which are volcanic in origin, and several coral reefs. The warm current and shallow waters (8-15 m deep) make for a rich undersea life (about 160 species of fish) and good snorkelling. The park is best visited in October-March. Humpback whales breed and give birth from July to December. Diving is best December to February. The archipelago is administered by Ibama and a navy detachment mans a lighthouse on Santa Bárbara, which is the only island that may be visited. Permission from **Parque Nacional Marinho dos Abrolhos** ① *Praia do Kitomgo s/n, Caravelas, Bahia 45900, Toxx73-3297 1111, or Ibama, Av Juracy Magalhães Junior 608, CEP 41940-060, Salvador, T/Foxx71-3240 7913.* Visitors are not allowed to spend the night on the islands, but may stay overnight on schooners.

● Sleeping → *See Telephone, page 347, for important phone changes.*

Valença *p480*
AL Portal Rio Una, R Maestro Barrinha, T/F3741 5050, www.portalhoteis.tur.br. Resort hotel by the riverside with a pool, tennis courts and organized activities.
A do Porto, Av Maçônica 50, T3641 5226, hdoporto@vca.mma.com.br. Helpful, safe, good breakfast, good restaurant.
C Guabim, Praça da Independência 74, T3641 4114, guaibimhotel@ig.com.br. Modest with bath and buffet breakast, good Akaurius restaurant.

C Valença, R Dr H Guedes Melo 15, T3641 2383. Comfortable, good breakfast. Recommended.

Tinharé and Morro de São Paulo *p480*
Expensive Dec-Mar, cheaper and more tranquil during the rest of the year. Very crowded during public holidays.

Morro de São Paulo
There are many cheap pousadas and rooms to rent near the fountain (Fonte Grande) but this part of town is very hot at night.

B Pousada Colibri, R do Porto de Cima 5, T3652 1056, pousadacolibri@svn.com.br. Up some steep steps to the left of the street. Cool, always a breeze blowing, excellent views, only 6 apartments, Helmut, the owner, speaks English and German.

C Pousada Gaúcho, R da Prainha 79, T3652 1243. On same street as the steps to Pousada Colibri. Huge breakfast, shared bath.

There are a number of beach hotels on Morro de São Paulo are at the bottom of the main street where one turns right on to the first beach (Primeira Praia).

L-AL Pousada Farol do Morro, T3652 1036, www.faroldomorro.com.br. Little huts running up the hill all with a sea view and served by a private funicular railway, pool.

AL Pousada Vista Bela, R da Biquinha 15, T3652 1001, petruscamello@terra.com.br. Owner Petruska is extremely welcoming, good rooms, those to the front have good views and are cooler, all have fans, hammocks.

C Pousada Ilha do Sol, T3652 1576. Modest but scrupulously clean, good views.

On 3rd beach (Terceira Praia)

AL Pousada Fazenda Caeira, T3652 1042, www.fazendacaeira.com.br. Spacious, airy chalets in a coconut grove overlooking the sea, good breakfasts, library, games room.

AL-B Fazenda Vila Guaiamú, T3652 1035, www.vilaguaiamu.com.br. 7 tastefully decorated chalets set in tropical gardens visited by marmosets, tanagers and rare cotingas, excellent food. The hotel has a spa and the Italian photographer-owner runs an ecotourism project protecting a rare species of crab which lives in the fazenda's river. Guided walks available. Highly recommended.

C Pousada Aradhia, T3652 1239. Balconies with ocean view, very good facilities.

Boipeba

A Pousada Tassimirim, ½-hr walk south of town, T3653 6030, or 9981 2378 (R Com Madureira 40, 45400-000 Valença), www.ilhaboipeba.org.br/ pousadas.html. Bungalows, bar, restaurant, including breakfast and dinner.

A-C Santa Clara, Boca da Barra, T3653 6085, www.santaclaraboipeba.com. Californian-owned, with the island's best restaurant, large, tasteful cabins and a good-value room for 4 at **D** pp. Therapeutic massages available. Highly recommended.

B-C Horizonte Azul, Boca da Barra, T3653 6080, www.ilhaboipeba.org.br/pousadas.html. Next to Santa Clara, a range of chalets in a hillside garden visited by hundreds of rare birds. Owners speak English and French. Lunch available. Highly recommended.

C Pousada Moreré, Moreré town, T9981 1303. Simple rooms with fan. Good restaurant and bar. The owner is the island's *prefeito*.

Itacaré *p480*

LL Txai Resort, Praia de Itacarezinho, T2101 5000, www.txai.com.br. The most self-consciously exclusive resort in Bahia; on a deserted beach with very tasteful bungalows overlooking a deep blue pool shaded by its own stand of palms. Excellent spa and a full range of activities including diving and horse riding.

LL-L Villa de Ocaporan, between the town and Praia da Concha, T3251 2470, www.villadeo caporan.com.br. Brightly coloured, spacious chalets around a charming little pool, good Bahian restaurant.

A-B Art Jungle, T9996 2167, artjungle@ itacare.com. 6 tree houses in a modern sculpture garden in the middle of forest, great views. A favourite with celebrities, but relatively unpretentious nonetheless.

A-B Pousada da Lua, Praia da Concha, T3251 2209, www.pousadadalua.com. A handful of little chalets in forest filled with marmosets and parakeets. Great breakfast.

B Pousada Litoral, R de Souza 81, 1 block from where buses stop, T3251 3046. The owner João Cravo speaks English and can organize tours to remote beaches and hire fishing boats. Recommended.

Ilhéus *p481*

Plenty of cheap hotels near the municipal rodoviária in centre and *pousadas* along the coast to Olivença.

A Ilhéus Praia, Praça Dom Eduardo (on beach), T3634 2533, www.ilheuspraia.com.br. Pool, helpful. Recommended.

Porto Seguro *p481*

Prices rise steeply Dec-Feb and Jul. Off-season rates can drop by 50%, for stays of more than 3 nights: negotiate. Outside Dec-Feb rooms with bath and hot water can be rented for US$150 per month.

AL Alegrete Porto, Av Navegantes 567, T3288 1738, www.portonet.com.br/alegrete. All facilities, very helpful. Recommended.

AL Estalagem Porto Seguro, R Marechal Deodoro 66, T3288 2095, hotelestalagem@ hotelestalagem.com.br. In an old colonial house, relaxing atmosphere, a/c, TV, pool, good breakfast. Highly recommended.

AL Pousada Casa Azul, 15 de Novembro 11, T/F3288 2180, p.casazul@uol.com.br. TV, a/c, good pool and garden, quiet part of town.

AL Vela Branca, R Dr Antonio Ricaldi (Cidade Alta), T3288 2318, www.velabranca.com.br.

Luxury resort with a wonderful view out over the water. Beautiful pool, tennis courts, sauna and spacious a/c rooms.

B Pousada Jandaias, R das Jandaias 112, T3288 2611, www.jandaias.com.br. Fan, great breakfast.

B Pousada dos Navegantes, Av 22 de Abril 212, T3288 2390, www.portonet.com.br/navegantes. A/c, TV, pool, conveniently located. Recommended.

B-C Pousada Da Orla, Av Portugal 404, T/F3288 1131. Fan, good breakfast, great location. Highly recommended.

C-D Pousada Aquárius, R Pedro Álvares Cabral 174, T/F3288 2738. No breakfast, family run, central.

Camping Camping Mundaí Praia, US$10 per night, T3679 2287. **Tabapiri Country**, BR-367, Km 61.5, next to the rodoviária on the road leading to the Cidade Histórica, T3288 2269.

Around Porto Seguro:
Santa Cruz Cabrália p481
B Victor Hugo, Villa de Santo Antônio, Km 3, T3671 4064, www.portonet.com.br/victorhugo. Smart, tasteful, right on the beach.

E pp Maracaia, Coroa Vermelha on road to Porto Seguro, Km 77.5, T3672 1155, www.maracaia hostel.com.br. Low season price, HI affiliated.

Arraial da Ajuda p481
At busy times, don't expect to find anything under US$15 pp in a shared room for a minimum stay of 5-7 days. Camping is best at these times.

L Pousada Pitinga, Praia Pitinga, T3575 1067, www.pousadapitinga.com.br. Bold architecture amid Atlantic forest, a hideaway, great food and pool, a Roteiros de Charme hotel.

AL Pousada Canto d'Alvorada, Esterada d' Ajuda 1993, T3575 1218. **B** out of season, Swiss run, 7 cabins, restaurant, laundry facilities.

A Pousada Erva Doce, Estrada do Mucugê 200, T3575 1113, www.ervadoce.com.br. Good restaurant, well appointed chalets (**AL** in high season).

A Pousada do Roballo, T3575 1053, www.pousadadoroballo.com.br. Good grounds, welcoming, good pool.

B Pousada Flamboyant, Estrada do Mucugê 89, T3575 1025, www.flamboyant.tur.br. Pleasant courtyard, pool, good breakfast.

B Pousada Tubarão, R Bela Vista 74, beyond the church on the right, T3575 1086, tubarao@arraial.com.br. Good view of the coastline, cool, good restaurant.

C O Cantinho, Praça São Bras, T3575 1131, pousadacantinho@arraialnet.com.br. Terraces of smart rooms, a/c or fan, nice courtyard, excellent breakfast, discounts off season.

C-E pp Arraial d'Ajuda Hostel, R do Campo 94, T3575 1192, www.arraialdajudahostel.com.br. Backpacker hostel with HI discounts, with breakfast, snack bar, pool, good location.

C-D Pousada Alto Mar, Rua Bela Vista 114, historical centre, behind the main church on the square, T3575 1935, www.jungleimmersion.pro.br. With breakfast, hot water, safe, good views of the port, use of kitchen, free internet, ask for special packages.

Camping Generally, Arraial da Ajuda is better for camping than Porto Seguro. **Chão do Arraial**, 5 mins from Mucugê beach, shady, good snack bar, also hire tents. Recommended. **Praia**, T3575 1020, on Mucugê Beach, good position and facilities.

Trancoso p481
There are many houses to rent, very good ones are rented by Clea who can be contacted at **Restaurant Abacaxi**. Also **Condominio dos Nativos**, condominiodosnativos@bol.com.br. Owned by Gustavo and Ana, excellent double-bedroom villas with kitchen and patio, 3 mins from beach, organize horse-riding, day trips, very welcoming.

LL-AL Mata N'ativa, Estrada Velha do Arraial (next to the river on the way to the beach), T3668 1830, www.matanativapousada.com.br. The best in town, a series of elegant cabins in a lovingly maintained garden by the riverside, cheaper in low season. Owners Daniel and Daniela are very hospitable. Good English, Spanish and Italian. Recommended.

AL Caipim Santo, T3668 1122, to the left of the main praça, capimsanto@capimsanto.com.br . With breakfast, the best restaurant in Trancoso. Recommended.

There are other, cheaper *pousadas*. About 500 m inland away from main praça (known as the 'quadrado') lies the newer part of Trancoso (known as the 'invasão') with some good value *pousadas*.

Caraíva p482
A Pousada da Barra, T9985 4302, www.caraiva.com. **AL** in Dec-Jan. Rooms and bungalows between the river and sea, bar and restaurant in high season, boat trips. Horse riding and other excursions arranged.

A Pousada Lagoa, T3225 5845, or 9985 6862, www.lagoacaraiva.com.br. Chalets and

---

● *For an explanation of the sleeping and eating price codes used in this guide, see inside the front*
● *cover. Other relevant information is found in Essentials pages 345-347.*

bungalows under cashew trees, good restaurant, popular bar, own generator, internet. The owner, Hermínia, speaks English and is very helpful and can arrange local trips and excursions.
A-C Pousada da Terra, far end of village near Indian reserve, T9985 4417, www.caraiva.com.br/terra. With breakfast, bar, safe, also houses for rent. Recommended.

Caravelas p482
B Pousada Caravelense, Praça Teófilo Otoni 2, T3297 1182. TV, fridge, good breakfast, excellent restaurant. Recommended.
D Beco Shangri-lá, Sete de Setembro 219, T3297 1059. Simple rooms with bath, breakfast.
D Pousada Juquita, Praia do Grauçá, Barra de Caravelas, T3674 1038. Use of kitchen, big breakfast, bath, airy rooms, the owner is Secka who speaks English.

● Eating

Tinharé and Morro de São Paulo p480
There are plenty of restaurants in Morro de São Paulo town and on the 2nd and 3rd beaches. Most of them are OK though somewhat overpriced. For cheap eats stay in a *pousada* which includes breakfast, stock up at the supermarket and buy seafood snacks at the *barracas* on the 2nd beach.
Belladonna on the main street. Good Italian restaurant with great music, a good meeting point, owner Guido speaks Italian, English and French, open evenings only.
Bianco e Nero, Morro town. Reasonably good pizza, pasta and grilled food.
Chez Max, 3rd beach. Simple but decent seafood in a pretty restaurant overlooking the sea.
Comida Natural, on the main street. Good breakfasts, comida a kilo, good juices.

Itacaré p480
There are plenty of restaurants in Itacaré, most of them on Rua Lodônio Almeida. Menus here are increasingly chic and often include a respectable wine list.
Casa Sapucaia, Rua Lodônio Almeida, T251 3091. Sophisticated Bahian food with an international twist.
Dedo de Moça, Rua Plínio Soares (next to the São Miguel Church), T251 3391. One of Bahia's best restaurants, with dishes which combine Brazilian ingredients with French and Oriental techniques.
Boca de Forno, Rua Lodônio Almeida 134, T251 2174. The busiest restaurant in Itacaré, serving good wood-fired pizzas in tastefully decorated surroundings.

O Restaurante, Rua Pedro Longo 150, T251 2012. One of the few restaurants with a *prato feto*, and a mixed seafood menu.

Ilhéus p481
Try the local drink, *coquinho*, coconut filled with cachaça. Also try *suco de cacau* at juice stands.
Vesúvio, Praça Dom Eduardo, next to the cathedral, made famous by Amado's novel (see above). Good but pricey.
Os Velhos Marinheiros, Av 2 de Julho. A recommended eating place on the waterfront.
Nogar, Av Bahia 377, near sea. Pizzas and pasta.

Porto Seguro p481
Cruz de Malta, R Getúlio Vargas 358. Good seafood.
Anti-Caro, R Assis Chateaubriand 26. Good. Recommended. Also antique shop, good atmosphere.
Les Agapornis, Av dos Navegantes 180. Wide selection of crêpes and pizzas.
Tres Vintens, Av Portugal 246. Good imaginative seafood dishes. Recommended.
Vida Verde, R Dois de Julho 92, T2882766. Vegetarian food, open 1100-2100 except Sun.
da Japonêsa, Praça Pataxós 38. Excellent value with varied menu, open 0800-2300. Recommended.
Pau Brasil, Praça dos Pataxós. Good breakfast.
Ponto do Encontro, Praça Pataxós 106. Good simple food, owners rent rooms, open 0800-2400.
Preto Velho, on Praça da Bandeira. Good value à la carte or self-service.

Arraial da Ajuda p481
Don Fabrizio, Estrada do Mucugê 402, T575 1123. The best Italian in town, in an upmarket open air restaurant with live music and reasonable wine.
Manguti, Estrada do Mucugê, T575 2270, www.manguti.com.br. Reputed by some to be the best in town, meat, pasta, fish alongside other Brazilian dishes. Very popular and informal.
Mineirissima, Estrada do Mucugê, T575 3790. Good value pay by weight with very filling Minas Gerais food and moquecas. Opens until late but menu service only after 1800.
Nipo, Estrada do Mucugê 250, T575 3033. Reasonably priced but decent Japanese with hotel delivery.
Pizzaria do Arraial, Praça São Bras s/n. Basic pizzeria and pay by weight restaurant.
Paulinho Pescador, Estrada do Mucugê. Open 1200-2200, excellent seafood, also chicken and meat, one price (US$5), English spoken, good service, popular, there are often queues for tables.

Carnival in Bahia

Carnival officially starts on Thursday night at 2000 when the keys of the city are given to the Carnival King 'Rei Momo'. The unofficial opening though is on Wednesday with the Lavagem do Porto da Barra, when throngs of people dance on the beach. Later on in the evening is the Baile dos Atrizes, starting at around 2300 and going on until dawn, very bohemian, good fun. Check with *Bahiatursa* for details on venue, time etc (see under Rio for carnival dates).

Carnival in Bahia is the largest in the world and it encourages active participation. It is said that there are 1½ million people dancing on the streets at any one time.

There are two distinct musical formats. The **Afro Blocos** are large drum-based troupes (some with up to 200 drummers) who play on the streets accompanied by singers atop mobile sound trucks. The first of these groups was the Filhos de Gandhi (founded in 1949), whose participation is one of the highlights of Carnival. Their 6,000 members dance through the streets on the Sunday and Tuesday of Carnival dressed in their traditional costumes, a river of white and blue in an ocean of multicoloured carnival revellers. The best known of the recent **Afro Blocos** are Ilê Aiye, Olodum, Muzenza and Malê Debalê. They all operate throughout the year in cultural, social and political areas. Not all of them are receptive to foreigners among their numbers for Carnival. The basis of the rhythm is the enormous surdo (deaf) drum with its bumbum bumbum bum anchorbeat, while the smaller repique, played with light twigs, provides a crack-like overlay. Ilê Aiye take to the streets around 2100 on Saturday night and their departure from their headquarters at Ladeira do Curuzu in the Liberdade district is not to be missed. The best way to get there is to take a taxi to Curuzu via Largo do Tanque thereby avoiding traffic jams. The ride is a little longer in distance but much quicker in time. A good landmark is the Paes Mendonça supermarket on

Recommended barracas are **Tem Q Dá** and **Agito** on Mucugê beach and **Barraca de Pitinga** and **Barraca do Genésio** on Pitinga.

Trancoso *p481*
Food in Trancoso is expensive. Those on a tight budget should shop at the supermarket between the main square and the new part of town. There are numerous fish restaurants in the *barracas* on the beach. None is cheap.
₸₸₸ **Cacao**, on the main square, T668 1266. One of the best in town with a varied international and Brazilian menu. Pleasant surrounds.
₸₸ **Laila**, in the new shopping area just before the main square. Elegant little restaurant serving good Moroccan and Lebanese food.
₸₸ **Silvana e Cia**, in the historical centre. Respectable Bahian food at a fair price.
₸ **Portinha**, on the main square. The only place serving food at a reasonable price. Excellent pay by weight options and good if overpriced juices.

Caraíva *p482*
There is forró dancing 0100-0600 at **Pelé** and **Ouriços** on alternate nights in season.

₸₸₸ **Bar do Pará**, by the river. Serves the best fish in the village, US$7-8 (try sashimi or moqueca). Also has simple lodging, **Pousada da Canoa**.

⊕ Bars and clubs

Morro de São Paulo *p480*
There is always plenty going on in Morro. The liveliest bars are **87** and **Jamaica**, both on the 2nd beach. These tend to get going after 2300 when the restaurants in town empty.

Itacaré *p480*
There is frequent extemporaneous forró and other live music all over the city and most restaurants and bars have some kind of music between Oct and Apr.

Porto Seguro *p481*
Porto Seguro is famous for the lambada. There are lots of bars and street cafés on Av Portugal. **Pronto Socorro do Choppe**, **Doce Letal 50** and **Studio Video Bar** are all lively places.
Porto Prego on R Pedro Álvares Cabral. A good bar for live music, small cover charge.
Sotton Bar, Praça de Bandeira. Lively.

the corner of the street from where the bloco leaves. From there it's a short walk to the departure point.

The enormous **trios eléctricos** 12 m sound trucks, with powerful sound systems that defy most decibel counters, are the second format. These trucks, each with its own band of up to 10 musicians, play songs influenced by the **afro blocos** and move at a snail's pace through the streets, drawing huge crowds. Each **Afro Bloco** and **bloco de trio** has its own costume and its own security personnel who cordon off the area around the sound truck. The **bloco** members can thus dance in comfort and safety.

There are three official Carnival routes. The oldest, Osmar, is from Campo Grande to Praça Castro Alves near the old town. The **blocos** go along Avenue 7 de Setembro and return to Campo Grande via the parallel R Carlos Gomes. The best night at Praça Castro Alves is Tuesday (the last night of Carnival) when the famous 'Encontro dos trios' (Meeting of the Trios) takes place.

Trios jostle for position in the square and play in rotation until dawn (or later!) on Ash Wednesday. It is not uncommon for major stars from the Bahian (and Brazilian) music world to make surprise appearances.

The second route is Dodô, from Farol da Barra to Ondina. The **blocos alternativos** ply this route. These are always **trios eléctricos** connected with the more traditional blocos who have expanded to this now popular district. The third and newest route is Batatinha, in the historic centre and the streets of Pelourinho. No trios eléctricos take part on this route, but marching bands, folkloric groups and fancy-dress parades.

Day tickets for these are available the week leading up to Carnival. Check with *Bahiatursa* for information on where the tickets are sold for the stands. There is little or no shade from the sun so bring a hat and lots of water. Best days are Sunday to Tuesday. For those wishing to go it alone, just find a barraca in the shade and watch the blocos go by.

Arraial da Ajuda *p481*
The lambada is danced at the **Jatobar** bar (summer only), by the church on the main square (opens 2300 - pensão at the back is cheap, clean and friendly). **Limelight** has raves all year round. Many top Brazilian bands play at the beach clubs at Praia do Parracho during the summer, entry is about US$20. Entry to other beach parties is about US$10. There is also a capoeira institute; ask for directions.

⊛ Festivals and events

Ilhéus *p481*
Festa de São Sebastião (**17-20 Jan**), Carnival, Festa de São Jorge (**23 Apr**), Foundation day, **28 Jun**, and Festa do Cacau throughout **Oct**.

▲ Activities and tours

Porto Seguro *p481*
Diving Portomar Ltda, R Dois de Julho 178, T3288 2606. Arranges diving and snorkelling trips to the coral reefs offshore, professional instructors, equipment hire.

Tour operators
Several agencies at the airport.
Brazil travel, Av 22 de Abril 200, T/F3288 1824, braziltravel@braziltravel.tur.br. Dutch- run travel agency, all types of trips organized, English, German, Dutch, French and Spanish spoken.
Companhia do Mar, Praça dos Pataxós 15, T3288 2107. Daily trips by schooner to coral reefs. The most popular is to Recife de Fora, with good snorkelling; it leaves daily at 1000, returns 1630, pay extra for snorkelling gear.

⊖ Transport

Valença *p480*
Bus Long-distance buses from new rodoviária, Av Abel de Aguiar Queirós, Aguazinha, T3641 4805. Local buses from the old rodoviaria. Many buses a day to/from **Salvador**, 5 hrs, US$9, several companies including Águia Branca.
Ferry For the shortest route to Valença, take the ferry from São Joaquim to Bom Despacho on Itaparica island, from where it is 130 km to Valença via Nazaré das Farinhas. To/from **Bom Despacho** on Itaparica, **Camarujipe** and **Águia Branca**, 16 a day, 1 hr 45 mins, US$4.80.

Tinharé and Morro de São Paulo *p480*

Air Air taxi from Salvador airport US$50 1-way, 20 mins, **Addey** T3377 1993, www.addey.com.br.

Ferry From Salvador, several companies operate a catamaran (1 hr 30 mins) service from the Terminal Marítimo in front of the Mercado Modelo to Morro de São Paulo. Times vary according to the weather and season. **Catamara Gamboa do Morro**, T9975 6395. Part of the trip is on the open sea, which can be rough. Boats leave every day from **Valença** for Gamboa (1½ hrs) and Morro de São Paulo (1½ hrs) from the main bridge in Valença 5 times a day (signalled by a loud whistle). The fare is US$3.40. A *lancha rápida* taking 25 mins travels the route between Valença and Morro, US$8. Only buses between 0530-1100 from Salvador to Valença connect with ferries. If not stopping in Valença, get out of the bus by the main bridge in town, don't wait till you get to the rodoviária, which is a long way from the ferry. Private boat hire can be arranged if you miss the ferry schedule. A responsible local boatman is **Jario**. He also offers excursions to other islands, especially **Boipeba**. There is a regular boat from Valença to Boipeba on weekdays 1000-1230 depending on tide, return 1500-1700, 3-4 hrs.

Itacaré *p480*

Bus The rodoviária is a few mins' walk from town. Porters are on hand with barrows to help with luggage. Frequent buses 0700-1900 to **Ilhéus** (the nearest town with an airport), 1 hr 40 mins, US$2.65 along the newly paved road. To **Salvador**, change at **Ubaitaba** (3 hrs, US$4), Ubaitaba-Salvador, 6 hrs, US$16, several daily.

Ilhéus *p481*

Bus Rodoviária is 4 km from the centre on Itabuna road. Several daily to **Salvador**, 7 hrs, US$19 (leito US$37, **Expresso São Jorge**); 0620 bus goes via Itaparica, leaving passengers at Bom Despacho ferry station on the island – thence 50-mins ferry to Salvador. To **Eunápolis**, 5 hrs, US$7.20, this bus also leaves from the central bus terminal. Other destinations served; local buses leave from Praça Cairu. Insist that taxi drivers have meters and price charts.

Porto Seguro *p481*

Air Airport T3288 1880. Regular flights from **Rio**, **São Paulo**, **Salvador** and **Belo Horizonte**. Taxi airport-Porto Seguro, US$9.50. Also buses.

Bus From Porto Seguro: **Salvador** (Águia Branca), daily, 12 hrs, US$30. **Vitória**, daily, 11 hrs, US$35. **Ilhéus**, daily 0730, 5½ hrs, US$14. **Eunápolis**, 1 hr, US$2.65. For **Rio** direct buses (**São Geraldo**), leaving at 1745, US$47 (leito 92), 18 hrs, from Rio direct at 1600 (very cold a/c, take

warm clothes), or take 1800 for Ilhéus and change at Eunápolis. To **Belo Horizonte** daily, direct, US$44 (São Geraldo). Other services via Eunápolis (those going north avoid Salvador) or Itabuna (5 hrs, US$12).

The rodoviária has reliable luggage store and lounge on the 3rd floor, on the road to Eunápolis, 2 km from the centre, regular bus service (30 mins) through the city to the old rodoviária near the port. Local buses US$0.30. Taxis charge US$5 from the rodoviária to the town or ferry (negotiate at quiet times).

Arraial da Ajuda *p481*

Ferry Across the Rio Buranhém from Porto Seguro take 15 mins to the south bank, US$0.80 for foot passengers, US$4.20 for cars, every 30 mins day and night. It is then a further 5 km to Arraial da Ajuda, US$0.65 by bus; kombis charge US$1 pp; taxis US$6.50.

Trancoso *p481*

Bus Buses run regularly on the newly paved road between Porto Seguro, Ajuda and Trancoso, at least every hour in high season: US$2.65 Porto Seguro-Trancoso, US$1.60 Ajuda-Trancoso. Arriving from the south, change buses at Eunápolis from where the newly paved Linha Verde road runs.

Caraíva *p482*

Caraíva can only be reached by **canoe** across the river. Access roads are poor and almost impossible after heavy rain. There are services several times a day from Trancoso, which is the easiest point of access. **Aguia Azul** bus company takes this route from Porto Seguro at 1500. If arriving by bus from the south, change to **Aguia Azul** bus in Itabela, departs at 1500, or take a taxi, about 50 km. Heading south take the bus to Eunápolis at 0600, 3 hrs.

Parque Nacional de Monte Pascoal *p482*

From Caraíva there is a river crossing by **boats** which are always on hand. **Buses** run from **Itamaraju** 16 km to the south, at 0600 on Fri-Mon.

Caravelas *p482*

Bus To **Teixeira de Freitas** (4 a day), **Salvador**, **Nanuque** and **Prado**. **Flights** from **Belo Horizonte**, **São Paulo** and **Salvador** to Caravelas; otherwise fly to Porto Seguro.

Parque Nacional Marinho dos Abrolhos

The journey to the islands takes 1-6 hrs depending on the boat. Tours are available from Caravelas (about US$225 for a slow 2½ day tour by saveiro). 1-day tours can be made in a faster boat (US$130) from Abrolhos or the Marina Porto Abrolhos.

ⓘ Directory

Porto Seguro *p481*
Banks Banco do Brasil, Av Beira Mar, open 1000-1500, changes TCs and US$ cash, also Visa ATM. Also at airport. **Bradesco**, Av Getúlio Vargas, Visa ATM. **Bicycle hire** Oficina de Bicicleta, Av Getúlio Vargas e R São Pedro, about US$13 for 24 hrs. Also at Praça de Bandeira and at 2 de Julho

242. **Car hire** Several companies at the airport.
Post offices In the mini-shopping centre on the corner of R das Jandaias and Av dos Navegantes.

Arraial da Ajuda *p481*
Banks Mobile Banco do Brazil in the main square during high season. **Internet** Various places in town.

North from Salvador

The paved BA-099 coast road from near Salvador airport is known as the Estrada do Coco (Coconut Highway, because of the many plantations) and for 50 km passes some beautiful beaches. The best known from south to north are Ipitanga (with its reefs), Buraquinho, **Jauá** (with reefs, surfing, pools at low tide, clean water), Arembepe (with a Tamar turtle protection project, famous hippy village in 1960s), Guarajuba, Itacimirim, Castelo Garcia D'Ávila (with its 16th century fort) and Forte. Regular buses serve most of these destinations.

Praia do Forte

The former fishing village, 80 km north of Salvador, takes its name from the castle built by a Portuguese settler, Garcia D'Ávila, in 1556 to warn the city to the south of enemy invasion. Praia do Forte is now a pleasant resort town with all but one of the streets of sand and lovely beaches. Inland from the coast is a restinga forest, which grows on sandy soil with a very delicate ecosystem. Near the village is a small *pantanal* (marshy area), which is host to a large number of birds, caymans and other animals. Birdwatching trips on the pantanal are rewarding. The **Tamar Project** ⓘ *Caixa Postal 2219, CEP 40223-970, Rio Vermelho, Salvador, Bahia, T0xx71-3676 1020, F3676 1067,* preserves the sea turtles which lay their eggs in the area. Praia do Forte is now the headquarters of the national turtle preservation programme and is funded by the Worldwide Fund for Nature.

The coast road north

The Linha Verde (the extension of the Estrada do Coco) runs for 142 km to the border of Sergipe, the next state north; the road is more scenic than the BR-101, especially near Conde. There are very few hotels or pousadas in the more remote villages. The most picturesque are **Imbassaí, Subaúma, Baixio** (very beautiful, where the Rio Inhambupe meets the sea) and **Conde**. Sítio do Conde on the coast, 6 km from Conde, has many pousadas, but the beaches are not very good. Sítio do Conde is an ideal base to explore other beaches at Barra do Itariri, 12 km south, at the mouth of a river (fine sunsets). The last stop on the Linha Verde is **Mangue Seco**. A steep hill rising behind the village to tall white sand dunes offers superb view of the coastline. There are plenty of small cheap places to stay along the seafront from the jetty, none with addresses or phone numbers (the village is tiny). There are simple restaurants around the main square next to the church. The beach has a handful of *barracas* serving cheap fish. Access from Sergipe is by boat on the Rio Real from Pontal (10-minute crossing). Buses run between Pontal and Estância twice a day. The ferry across the river usually leaves before 1000 in the morning. A private launch will cost US$10, but it usually possible to find someone to share the ride.

🛏 Sleeping → *See Telephone, page 347, for important phone changes.*

North from Salvdor: Jauá *p489*
B Lagoa e Mar, Praia de Jauá, T/F3672 1573, www.hotellagoaemar.com.br. Very good breakfast, spacious bungalows, swimming pool, 350 m to beach, restaurant, helpful, transport to airport, 10% discount to Footprint owners.

Praia do Forte *p489*
Prices rise steeply in the summer season. It may be difficult to find cheap places to stay.
LL-L Praia do Forte EcoResort, Av do Farol, T3676 4000, www.praiadoforte.com. Large scale family resort set in tropical gardens on the beach and with programmes to visit the nearby protected

areas. Room are spacious, well appointed and comfortable. Service, which includes a spa and entertainment, is excellent. Beautiful pool.

AL Pousada Solar da Lagoa, R do Forte, T3676 1271, www.solardalagoa.com.br. Smart chalets with room enough for 4, a decent pool and excellent service. Price is for full board.

AL-A Ogum Marinho, Av Alameda do Sol, T3676 1165, www.ogummarinho.com.br. A/c, cheaper with fan, nice little courtyard garden, good restaurant and service.

A Pousada Casa de Praia, Praça dos Artistas 08-09, T3676 1362, www.casadepraia.tur.br. Good value and location rooms, with and without a/c, popular.

A Sobrado da Vila, Av do Sol, T/F3676 1088, www.sobradodavila.com.br. Best in the village itself with a range of individually decorated rooms with balconies and a good-value restaurant, convenient for restaurants.

A-B Pousada João Sol, R da Corvina, T3676 1054, www.pousadajoaosol.com.br. 6 well-appointed and newly refurbished chalets. The owner speaks English, Spanish and German. Great breakfast.

B Pousada Tatuapara, Praça dos Artistas, T3676 1015, manfredweftrich@uol.com.br. Spacious and well-maintained, fan, fridge, good breakfast.

C Tia Helena, just east of the Praça dos Artistas, T3676 1198. Helena, the motherly proprietor provides an excellent meal and enormous breakfast, simple rooms, well-kept, reductions for 3-day stays.

D Albergue da Juventude, Praia do Forte, R da Aurora 3, T3676 1094, www.albergue.com.br. Smart youth hostel with decent shared rooms and rooms with en suites (**C**), a large breakfast, fan, kitchen and shop, cheaper for HI members.

🍴 Eating

Praia do Forte *p489*

🍴🍴 **Bar Da Souza**, Av do Sol, on the right as you enter the village. Best seafood in town, open daily, live music at weekends. Recommended.

🍴🍴 **O Europeu**, Alameda do Sol, T3676 0232. English owned, with the most adventurous menu in town. The owner, William, is knowledgeable about the area. Good little arts and crafts shop upstairs.

🍴 **Cafe Tango**, Praça das Artistas. Pleasant open-air tea and coffee bar with great pastries and cakes.

🍴 **La Crêperie**, Alameda do Sol. Excellent crêpes, Tue to Sun, good music, popular, owner Klever very friendly.

🍴 **Pizzaria Le Gaston**, Alameda do Sol. Good pizza and pasta, also good home-made ice-creams, daily.

🔺 Activities and tours

Praia do Forte *p489*

Praia do Forte is ideal for windsurfing and sailing owing to constant fresh Atlantic breezes.

Odara Turismo, in the EcoResort Hotel, T3676 1080. Imaginative tours to surrounding areas and outlying villages and beaches using 4WD vehicles. They are very friendly and informative. Recommended. The owners, Norbert and Papy, speak English and German.

⊖ Transport

Praia do Forte *p489*

Bus From **Salvador** (US$2.65): Santa Maria/Catuense leave 5 times daily from rodoviária, 1½ hrs.

Recife and the northeast coast

The eight states north of Bahia are historically and culturally rich, but generally poor economically. Steeped in history are, for instance, Recife, Olinda, or São Luís and cultural heritage abounds (eg 'Forró' and other musical styles, many good museums, lacework, ceramics). There is a multitude of beaches: if established resorts aren't your thing, you don't have to travel far for somewhere more peaceful, while off the beaten track are some which have hardly been discovered.

Pernambuco was the seat of Dutch Brazil in the 17th century. Its capital, Recife, and close neighbour, Olinda, have the most creative music scene in the northeast and their famous wild carnival draws thousands of visitors.

Recife → *Phone code: 0xx81. Post code: 50000. Colour map 5, grid B6. Population: 1.42 million.*

The capital of Pernambuco State, 285 km north of Maceió and 839 km north of Salvador, was founded on reclaimed land by the Dutch prince Maurice of Nassau in 1637 after his troops had burnt Olinda, the original capital. The city centre consists of three portions, always very busy by day; the crowds and the narrow streets, especially in the Santo Antônio district, can make it a confusing city to walk around. Recife has the main dock area, with commercial buildings associated with it. South of the centre is the residential and beach district of Boa Viagem, reached by bridge across the Bacia do Pina. Olinda, the old capital, is only 7 km to the north (see page 500).

Ins and outs
Tourist offices Empetur (for the State of Pernambuco), main office, Complexo Viário Vice-Governador Barreto Guimarães s/n, Salgadinho, T3427 8000, between Recife and Olinda, www.empetur.pe.gov.br. Branches at airport – 24 hours, T3224 2361 (helpful but few leaflets, English spoken), and Praça of Boa Viagem, T3463 3621 (English spoken, helpful). Maps are available, or can be bought at newspaper stands in city; also sketch maps in monthly guides Itinerário Pernambuco and Guia do Turista. For the **Secretaria de Turismo da Prefeitura do Recife**, T3224 7198. **Secretaria de Desenvolvimento Econômico, Turismo e Esportes**, Rua Montevidéu, 220, Boa Vista, T3216 1500, www.turismo.pe.gov.br. Hours of opening of museums, art galleries, churches etc are published in the Diário de Pernambuco and Jornal do Comércio. The former's website has lots of tourist information, www.dpnet.com.br/ turismo/ or via www.pernambuco.com.

Opportunistic theft is unfortunately common in the streets of Recife and Olinda (especially on the streets up to Alto da Sé, Olinda). Prostitution is reportedly common in Boa Viagem – choose nightclubs with care.

Sights
The best sights are the churches of **Santo Antônio do Convento de São Francisco** (1606) *in the R do Imperador*, which has beautiful Portuguese tiles, and adjoining it the finest sight of all, the **Capela Dourada** (Golden Chapel, 1697) ① *Mon-Fri 0800-1130, 1400-1700, Sat morning only, US$1, no flash photography*; it is through the Museu Franciscano de Arte Sacra. **São Pedro dos Clérigos** (1782) ① *in São José district, daily 0800-1130, 1400-1600*, should be seen for its façade, its fine wood sculpture and a splendid trompe-l'oeil ceiling. **Nossa Senhora da Conceição dos Militares** (1771) ① *R Nova 309, Mon-Fri 0800-1700*, has a grand ceiling and a large 18th century primitive mural of the battle of Guararapes (museum next door). Other important churches are **Santo Antônio** (1753-91) ① *Praça da Independência, Mon-Fri 0800-1200, 1400-1800, Sun 1700-1900*, rebuilt in 1864. **Nossa Senhora do Carmo** (1663) ① *Praça do Carmo, Mon-Fri 0800-1200, 1400-1900, Sat-Sun 0700-1200*. **Madre de Deus** (1715) ① *in R Madre de Deus in the district of Recife, Tue-Fri 0800-1200, 1400-1600*, with a splendid high altar, and sacristy. The **Divino Espírito Santo** (1689) ① *Praça 17 in Santo Antônio district, Mon-Fri 0800-1630, Sat 0800-1400, Sun 1000-1200*, the original church of the Jesuits. There are many others.

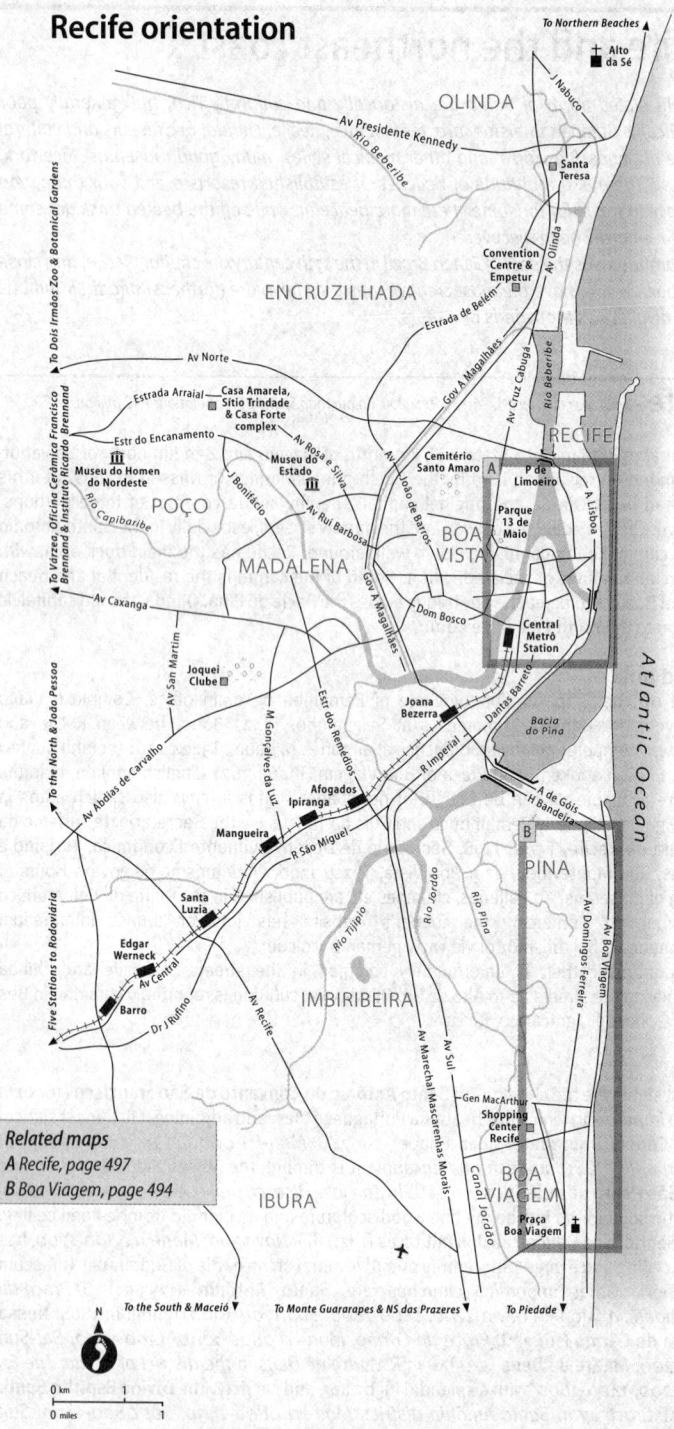

Recife orientation

To Northern Beaches

Alto da Sé

J Nabuco

OLINDA

Av Presidente Kennedy

Rio Beberibe

Santa Teresa

Av Olinda

Convention Centre & Empetur

ENCRUZILHADA

Estrada de Belém

Av Cruz Cabugá

Rio Beberibe

RECIFE

Av Norte

Av A Magalhães

Estrada Arraial

Casa Amarela, Sítio Trindade & Casa Forte complex

Estr do Encanamento

Av Rosa e Silva

Museu do Estado

Cemitério Santo Amaro

A

P de Limoeiro

A Lisboa

Museu do Homen do Nordeste

J Bonifácio

POÇO

Rio Capibaribe

Av do Sol

Av Rui Barbosa

Av João de Barros

Parque 13 de Maio

BOA VISTA

MADALENA

Av A Magalhães

Dom Bosco

Central Metrô Station

Av Caxanga

Joaquei Clube

Av San Martim

M Gonçalves da Luz

Estr dos Remédios

Joana Bezerra

Dantas Bareto

R Imperial

Bacia do Pina

B

Av Abdias de Carvalho

Afogados Ipiranga

Mangueira

R São Miguel

Rio Tijipió

Rio Jiquiá

Rio Pina

PINA

A de Góis H Bandeira

Av Boa Viagem

Av Domingos Ferreira

Santa Luzia

Edgar Werneck

Av Central

Dr J Rufino

Barro

Av Recife

IMBIRIBEIRA

Av Sul

Av Marechal Mascarenhas Morais

Gen MacArthur

Shopping Center Recife

BOA VIAGEM

Canal Jordão

Five Stations to Rodoviária

To the North & João Pessoa

IBURA

Praça Boa Viagem

Related maps
A *Recife*, page 497
B *Boa Viagem*, page 494

Atlantic Ocean

N

0 km   1
0 miles   1

To Dois Irmãos Zoo & Botanical Gardens

To Várzea, Oficina Cerâmica Francisco Brennand & Instituto Ricardo Brennand

To the South & Maceió

To Monte Guararapes & NS das Prazeres

To Piedade

Forte do Brum ① *Tue-Fri 0900-1600, Sat-Sun 1400-1600* (built by the Dutch in 1629) is an army museum. **Forte das Cinco Pontas** (with **Museu da Cidade do Recife**) ① *Mon-Fri 0900-1800, Sat-Sun 1300-1700, US$0.50 donation advised*, with a cartographic history of the settlement of Recife, was built by the Dutch in 1630 and altered by the Portuguese in 1677. The two forts jointly controlled access to the port at the northern and southern entrances respectively. The first Brazilian printing press was installed in 1706 and Recife claims to publish the oldest daily newspaper in South America, Diário de Pernambuco, founded 1825 (but now accessible on www.dpnet.com.br/). The distinctive lilac building is on the Praça da Independência.

The artists' and intellectuals' quarter is based on the **Pátio de São Pedro**, the square round São Pedro dos Clérigos. Sporadic folk music and poetry shows are given in the square Wednesday to Sunday evenings (T3426 2728) and there are atmospheric bars and restaurants.

The square is an excellent shopping centre for typical northeastern craftware (clay figurines are cheapest in Recife). Not far away, off Avenida Guararapes, two blocks from central post office, is the **Praça do Sebo**, where the city's second-hand booksellers concentrate; this Mercado de Livros Usados is off the R da Roda, behind the Edifício Santo Albino, near the corner of Avenida Guararapes and R Dantas Barreto. You can also visit the city markets in the São José and Santa Rita sections.

The former municipal prison has now been made into the **Casa da Cultura** ① *T3284 2850 to check what's on in advance, Mon-Sat 0900-1900, Sun 0900-1400*. Many of the cells have been converted into art or souvenir shops and with areas for exhibitions and shows (also public conveniences). Local dances such as the ciranda, forró and bumba-meu-boi are held as tourist attractions. Among other cultural centres are Recife's three traditional **theatres, Santa Isabel** ① *Praça da República, open to visitors Mon-Fri 1300-1700*, built in 1850. **Parque** ① *R do Hospício 81, Boa Vista, 0800-1200, 1400-1800*, restored and beautiful. **Apolo** ① *R do Apolo 121, 0800-1200, 1400-1700*. The **Museu do Estado** ① *Av Rui Barbosa 960, Graças, Tue-Fri 0900-1700, Sat-Sun 1400-1700*, has excellent paintings by the 19th-century landscape painter, Teles Júnior. **Museu do Trem** ① *Praça Visconde de Mauá, Tue-Fri 0800-1200, 1400-1700, Sat 0900-1200, Sun 1400-1700*, small but interesting, especially the Henschel locomotive.

West of the centre is the **Museu do Homem do Nordeste** ① *Av 17 de Agosto 2223, Casa Forte, Tue-Fri 1100-1700, Sat-Sun 1300-1700, US$1*. It comprises the **Museu de Arte Popular**, containing ceramic figurines (including some by Mestre Alino and Zé Caboclo); the **Museu do Açúcar**, on the history and technology of sugar production, with models of colonial mills, collections of antique sugar bowls and much else; the **Museu de Antropologia**, the **Nabuco Museum** (No 1865) and the modern museum of popular remedies, **Farmacopéia Popular**. Either take the 'Dois Irmãos' bus (check that it's the correct one, with 'Rui Barbosa' posted in window, as there are two) from in front of the Banorte building near the post office on Guararapes, or, more easily, go by taxi.

Oficina Cerâmica Francisco Brennand ① *Av Caxangá, Várzea, T3271 2466, www.brennand.com.br*. A museum and 19th-century ceramics factory set in mock-Moorish gardens and filled with Brennand's extraordinary Gaudiesque ceramic sculptures and paintings. The artist, who is one of Brazil's most illustrious, can sometimes be seen walking here, cane in hand looking like an old Sigmund Freud. **Instituto Ricardo Brennand**, ① *Alameda Antônio Brennand s/n, Várzea, T2121 0370, www.institutoricardobrennand.org.br*. Another scion of the Brennand family has built this fantasy castle on the outskirts of the city to house his art collection. This is one of the most important in the country and includes the largest assemblage of New World Dutch paintings in the world (with many Franz Posts), Brazilian modern art, armoury and medieval maps.

Boa Viagem

Boa Viagem, the main residential and hotel quarter, is currently being developed at its northern end. The 8-km promenade commands a striking view of the Atlantic, but the beach is backed by a busy road, is crowded at weekends and not very clean. During the January breeding season, sharks come close to the shore. You can go fishing on jangadas at Boa Viagem with a fisherman at low tide. The main praça has a good market at weekends. Take any bus marked 'Boa Viagem'; from Nossa Senhora do Carmo, take buses marked 'Piedade', 'Candeias' or 'Aeroporto' – they go on Av Domingos Ferreira, two blocks parallel to the beach, all the way to Praça Boa Viagem (at Avenida Boa Viagem 500). Back to the centre take buses marked 'CDU' or 'Setubal' from

Boa Viagem

To Recife Centre

Boa Viagem detail

Atlantic Ocean

N

| 0 metres | 200 |
| 0 yards | 200 |

Sleeping
Aconchego 1
Coqueiral 2
Hostel Boa Viagem 9
Maracatus do Recife 3
Pousada da Julieta 5
Pousada da Praia 6
Recife Monte 7
Uzi Praia 8

Eating
Bargaço 1
Chica Pitanga 2
Churrascaria Porcão 3
Ilha da Kosta 5
La Capannina 6
La Maison 7
Parraxaxa 8
Peng 9
Realeza 10
Romana 11
Sushimi 4
Tempero Verde 12
Tio Dadá 13

Bars & clubs
Baltazar 14

Avenida Domingos Ferreira. About 14 km south of the city, a little beyond Boa Viagem and the airport, on Guararapes hill, is the historic church of **Nossa Senhora dos Prazeres** ① *Tue-Fri 0800-1200, 1400-1700, Sat 0800-1200, closed to tourists on Sun*. It was here, in 1648-1649, that two Brazilian victories led to the end of the 30-year Dutch occupation of the northeast in 1654. The church was built by the Brazilian commander in 1656 to fulfil a vow. Boa Viagem's own fine church dates from 1707.

Beaches south of Recife

About 30 km south of Recife, beyond Cabo, is the beautiful and quiet **Gaibu** beach, with scenic Cabo de Santo Agostinho on the point 5 km east of town. It has a ruined fort. To get there, take bus 'Centro do Cabo' from the airport, then frequent buses – 20 minutes – from Cabo. **Itapuama** beach is even more empty, both reached by bus from **Cabo** (Population 140,765), Pernambuco's main industrial city, which has interesting churches and forts and a **Museu da Abolição**. At nearby **Suape** are many 17th-century buildings and a biological reserve.

    Porto de Galinhas, further south still, is a beautiful beach. It has cool, clean water, and waves. Because of a reef close to the shore, swimming is only possible at high tide (take heed of local warnings), but jangadas make trips to natural swimming pools. A rash of recently built upmarket resorts is changing its rustic atmosphere. To find a more peaceful spot, walk 3 km south to Pontal Maracaipe, or take a buggy to Praia Carneiros. Porto de Galinhas information centre, T3552 1728, 0900-1900, www2.uol.com.br/portodegalinhas/.

🛏 Sleeping

Boa Viagem is the main tourist district and the best area to stay. All hotels listed in this area are within a block or two of the beach. There is not much reason to be in the city centre and accommodation here is of a pretty low standard.

Recife *p491, map p497*
A Recife Plaza, R da Aurora 225, T3231 1200, www.recifeplazahotel.com.br, Boa Vista, overlooking the Rio Capibaribe. Comfortable old fashioned business hotel with a reasonable restaurant which is very popular at lunchtime.
A Pousada Villa Boa Vista, R Miguel Couto 81, Boa Vista, T3223 0666, www.pousadavilla boavista.com.br. The only modern hotel in town, with plain, comfortable a/c rooms (all with powerful showers), around a courtyard. Quiet, safe, a 5 minute cab ride from the centre.
D América, Praça Maciel Pinheiro 48, Boa Vista, T3221 1300. Frayed, very simple rooms with low foamy beds, the best of which are on the upper floors and offer a good view out over the city.
D Central, Av Manoel Borba 209, Boa Vista, T3222 4001. A splendid 1920s building with original French-style open-lifts and plain, but freshly painted rooms, enormous old iron bathtubs, upper floors have wonderful views.

Boa Viagem *p493, map 494*
A Recife Monte, R Petrolina e R dos Navegantes 363, T3465 7422, F3465 8406. Very smart and good value for category, caters to business travellers.
B Aconchego, Félix de Brito 382, T3326 2989, aconchego@novaera.com.br. Motel style rooms

around pleasant pool area, a/c, sitting room, English-speaking owner, will collect from the airport.
C Coqueiral, R Petrolina, 43, T3326 5881. Dutch-owned (Dutch, English, French spoken), a/c, small and homely with pretty breakfast room. Recommended.
C Uzi Praia, Av Conselheiro Aguiar 942, T/F3466 9662. A/c, cosy, sister hotel across the road.
D Pousada da Julieta, R Prof Jose Brandão 135, T3326 7860, hjulieta@elogica.com.br. 1 block from beach, very good value. Recommended.
D Pousada da Praia, Alcides Carneiro Leal 66, T3326 7085. A/c, TV, safe, a/c, rooms vary (some tiny), very helpful, popular with Israelis. Roof-top breakfast room.

Beaches south of Recife: Gaibu *p495*
C Pousada Aguas Marinhas, Av Beira Mar 56, Gaibu, T3522 6346. A/c, comfortable, fridge, **E** without bath, with breakfast, French spoken, very nice.
C-E Hostel Boa Viagem, R Aviador Severiano Lins 455, T3326 9572, www.hostelboaviagem.com.br. From doubles and singles with a/c to dormitories, well-located hostel, excellent value, good bathrooms, pool, owners speak French and are from Caruaru so can arrange trips. Call ahead to arrange transport from airport or bus station.
E Maracatus do Recife, R Maria Carolina 185, T3326 1221, alberguemaracatus@yahoo.com. Hostel with good breakfast, no hot water, simple, cooking facilities, pool, safe, mosquitoes can be a problem.

Camping There is no camping within the city. For information on camping throughout Pernambuco state, call **Paraíso Camping Clube**, Av Dantas Barreto 512, loja 503, T3224 3094.

Private accommodation During Carnival and for longer stays at other times, private individuals rent rooms and houses in Recife and Olinda; listings can be found in the classified ads in *Diário de Pernambuco*, or ask around the streets of Olinda. This accommodation is generally cheaper, safer and quieter than hotels.

❼ Eating

Recife centre *p491, map p497*
TTT Leite (lunches only), Praça Joaquim Nabuco 147/53 near Casa de Cultura. Old and famous, good service, smart (another branch in Boa Viagem, at Prof José Brandão 409).

TTT Lisboa á Noite, R Geraldo Pires 503. Good, reasonable, open Sun evenings.

TT Casa de Tia, Gamboa do Carmo 136. Lunch only, must arrive by 1215, try cosido, a meat and vegetable stew, enough for 2.

TT Galo D'Ouro, Gamboa do Carmo 83. Well-established, international food.

TT O Vegetal, R Cleto Campelo e Av Guararapes (2nd floor) behind Central Post Office, lunch only, closed Sat-Sun.

TT Tivoli, R Matias de Albuquerque, Santo Antônio. Lunches downstairs, a/c restaurant upstairs, good value.

T Buraquinho, Pátio de Sao Pedro. Lunch only, all dishes good, generous servings of caipirinha, friendly.

T Casa dos Frios, da Palma 57, loja 5. Delicatessen/sandwich bar, salads, pastries.

T Gellattos, Av Dantas Barreto, 230. Great sucos (try the delicious guarana do amazonas with nuts), hamburgers and sandwiches.

T Savoy Bar, Av Guararapes. The haunt of Pernambucan intellectuals since 1944, with poetry all over the walls and the legend that Sartre and De Beauvoir once ate there, buffet Mon-Sat 1100-1500, US$2, also lunch by weight. Lanchonetes abound in the city, catering to office workers, but tend to close in evening.

Boa Viagem *p493, map p494*
Restaurants on the main beach road of Av Boa Viagem are pricey; venture a block or two inland for cheaper deals. Be careful of eating the local small crabs, known as guaiamum; they live in the mangrove swamps which take the drainage from Recife's mocambos (shanty towns).

TTT Bargaço, Av Boa Viagem 670. Typical northeastern menu specialising in seafood, sophisticated with small bar.

TTT La Maison, Av Boa Viagem, 618, T3325 1158. Fondue restaurant in low-lit basement, with rosé wine and peach melba on menu.

TT La Capannina, Av Cons Aguiar 538, T3465 9420. Italian, pizzas, salad, pasta and sweet and savoury crêpes, delivery service.

TT Chica Pitanga, R Petrolina, 19, T3465 2224. Upmarket, excellent food by weight.

TT Churrascaria Porção, Av Eng Domingos Ferreira 4215. Good for meat and salad eaters alike, very popular.

TT Ilha da Kosta, R Pe Bernardino Pessoa, 50, T3466 2222. Self-service seafood, sushi, pizza and Brazilian cuisine, open 1100 to last client and all afternoon.

TT Parraxaxa, R Baltazar Pereira, 32, T9108 0242. Rustic-style, award-winning, northeastern buffet, including breakfast. Recommended.

TT Sushimi, T3463 6500. Classic, Japanese fast-food in suitably sterile surroundings. One of a range of options in Shopping Center Recife (open 1000-2200, T3464 6000) in Boa Viagem.

T Peng, Av Domingos Ferreira, 1957. Self-service, some Chinese dishes, bargain, rather than gourmet food, in area with few other restaurants.

T Realeza, Av Boa Viagem, on corner with Av Atlântico. Beachfront location, hamburgers, snacks and pizza.

T Romana, R Setubal 225. Deli/bakery with a few tables and chairs, pastries, coffee, yoghurt for breakfast or snack.

T Tempero Verde, R S H Cardim, opposite Chica Pitanga. Where the locals go for a bargain meal of beans, meat and salad, US$1.50, simple, self-service, pavement tables.

T TioDadá, R Baltazar Pereira 100. Loud, TV screens, good value portions of beef.

❽ Bars and clubs

Recife centre *p491*
Most bars (often called 'pubs', but nothing like the English version) stay open until dawn. The historic centre of Recife Antigo has been restored and is now an excellent spot for nightlife. Bars around R do Bom Jesus such as **London Pub**, No 207, are the result of a scheme to renovate the dock area. The Graças district, west of Boa Vista, on the Rio Capibaribe, is popular for bars and evening entertainment. Discos tend to be expensive and sophisticated. Best times are around 2400 on Fri or Sat, take a taxi. The Pina zone, north of the beginning of Boa Viagem, is one of the city's major hang-out areas with lively bars, music and dancing. Try to visit a northeastern Forró where couples dance to typical music, very lively especially Fri and Sat, several good ones at Candeias.

Calypso Club, R do Bom Jesus. US$5, has live

local bands playing anything from traditional music to rock.

The 2 most popular nightclubs (both enormous, 2300 to dawn) are **Downtown Pub**, R Vigário Tenório, disco, live music, US$5, and **Fashion Club**, Av Fernando Simões Barbosa 266, Boa Viagem in front of Shopping Centre Recife, T3327 4040, US$8. Techno and rock bands.

Boa Viagem *p493, map p494*
Baltazar, R Baltazar Pereira 130, T3327 0475. Live music nightly, bar snacks, large and popular. Open 1600 to early hours.
Papillon Bar, Av Beira Mar 20, Piedade, T3341 7298. Forró Wed-Sat.

Recife

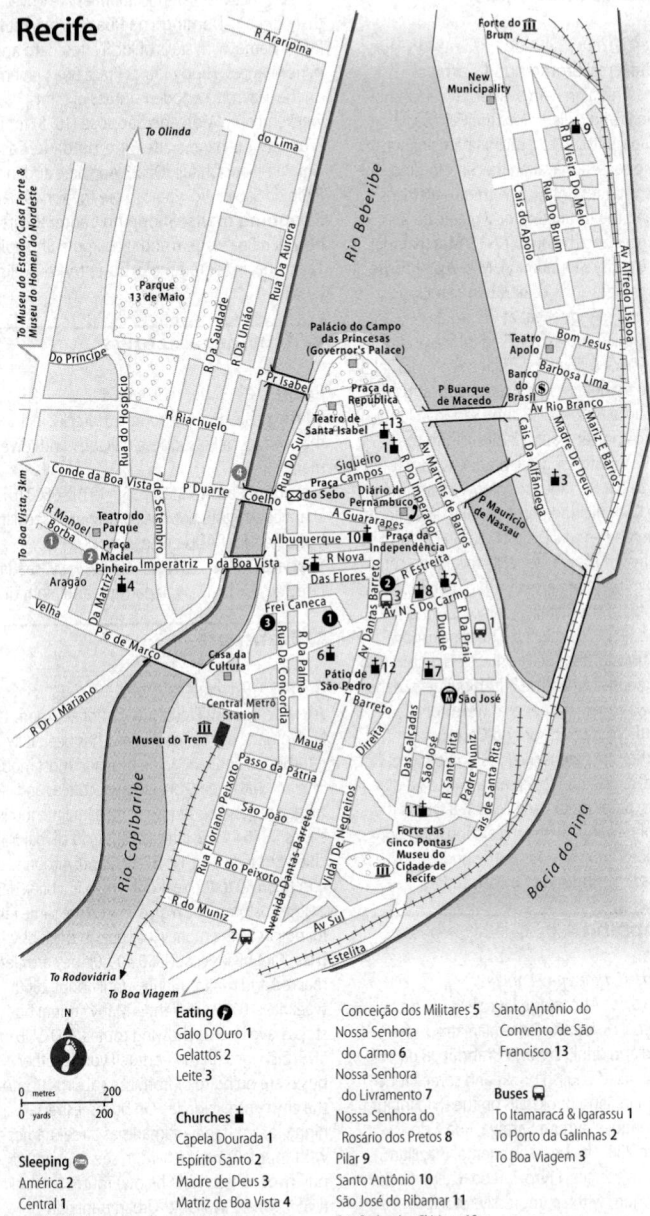

N

| 0 | metres | 200 |
| 0 | yards | 200 |

Sleeping 💤
América **2**
Central **1**
Recife Plaza **4**

Eating 🍴
Galo D'Ouro **1**
Gelattos **2**
Leite **3**

Churches ⛪
Capela Dourada **1**
Espírito Santo **2**
Madre de Deus **3**
Matriz de Boa Vista **4**
Nossa Senhora da
Conceição dos Militares **5**
Nossa Senhora
do Carmo **6**
Nossa Senhora
do Livramento **7**
Nossa Senhora do
Rosário dos Pretos **8**
Pilar **9**
Santo Antônio **10**
São José do Ribamar **11**
São Pedro dos Clérigos **12**

Santo Antônio do
Convento de São
Francisco **13**

Buses 🚌
To Itamaracá & Igarassu **1**
To Porto da Galinhas **2**
To Boa Viagem **3**

🎭 Entertainment

Recife *p491, map p497*

Theatre Agenda Cultural details the cultural events for the month, free booklet from tourist offices. Shows in the **Recife/Olinda Convention Center**, US$10, traditional dances in full costume.

🎉 Festivals and events

Recife *p491, maps p494 and 497*

1 Jan, Universal Brotherhood. **Carnival** in Recife features a pre-carnavalesca week of shows, processions and balls, before the Galo da Madrugada, with up to a million participants officially opens Carnaval on the Sat morning. The festival continues until Tue with trios elétricos, samba and the distinctive local maracatu and frevo dances and rhythms. **12-15 Mar**, parades to mark the city's foundation. **Mid-Apr**, Pro-Rock Festival, a week-long celebration of rock, hip-hop and manguebeat at Centro de Convenções, Complexo de Salgadinho and other venues. Check Diário de Pernambuco or Jornal do Comércio for details. **Jun**, Festejos Juninos. The days of Santo Antônio (13 Jun), São João (24 Jun), São Pedro and São Paulo (29 Jun), form the nuclei of a month-long celebration whose roots go back to the Portuguese colony. Intermingled with the Catholic tradition are Indian and African elements. The annual cycle begins in fact on **São José's day**, **19 Mar**, historically the 1st day of planting maize; the harvest in Jun then forms a central part of the festejos juninos. During the festivals the forró is danced. This dance, now popular throughout the Northeast, is believed to have originated when the British builders of the local railways held parties that were 'for all'. **11-16 Jul**, Nossa Senhora do Carmo, patron saint of the city. **Aug** is the Mes do Folclore. **Oct**, Recifolia, a repetition of carnival over a whole weekend; dates differ each year. **1-8 Dec** is the festival of Iemanjá, with typical foods and drinks, celebrations and offerings to the goddess; also **8 Dec**, Nossa Senhora da Conceição.

🛍 Shopping

Recife *p491, maps p494 and 497*

Bookshops Almanque Livros, Largo do Varadouro 418, loja 58. Bohemian atmosphere, sells food and drink. **Livraria Brandão**, R da Matriz 22 (used English books and some French and German), and bookstalls on the R do Infante Dom Henrique. **Livraria Saraiva**, Rua 7 de Setembro 280. The best selection of Brazilian literature in the city. **Livro 7**, R do Riachuelo 267. An emporium with an impressive stock. **Melquísidec Pastor de Nascimento**, a local

character, has a second-hand stall at Praça do Sebo. **Sodiler** at Guararapes airport has books in English, newspapers, magazines; also in the Shopping Center Recife.

Markets Afogados market. For herbal remedies and spices. **Cais de alfandega**, Recife Barrio, market of local work, 1st weekend of every month. **Casa da Cultura**; the permanent craft market. Prices for ceramic figurines are lower than Caruaru. **Domingo na Rua**, Sun market in Recife Barrio, with stalls of local artesanato and performances. **Hippy fair** at Praça Boa Viagem, on the sea front, wooden statues of saints, weekend only. **Mercado São José** (1875) for local products and handicrafts. **Sítio Trindade**, Casa Amarela. Sat craft fair. On 23 Apr, here and in the Pátio de São Pedro, you can see the *xangô* dance.

Shopping malls Shopping Center Recife between Boa Viagem and the airport. **Shopping Tacaruna**, in Santo Amaro, buses to/from Olinda pass it.

⛰ Activities and tours

Recife *p491, maps p494 and 497*

Diving Offshore are some 20 wrecks, including the remains of Portuguese galleons, with diverse marine life.

Mergulhe Coma, T3552 2355, T9102 6809 (mob), atlanticdivingasr@hotmail.com. English speaking instructors for PADI courses.

Seagate, T3426 1657/9972 9662, www.seaga terecife.com.br. Daily departures and night dives.

🚌 Transport

Recife *p491, maps p494 and 497*

Air The Gilberto Freyre international airport, 12 km from the city in Boa Viagem, has been fully refurbished and is now the best and most modern in Brazil; with plenty of places for coffees and magazines and boutiques of elegant little tourist shops. T3464 4188. Internal flights to all major cities. Bus to airport, No 52, US$0.50. Airport taxis cost US$6.50 to the seafront. There is a bank desk before customs which gives much the same rate for dollars as the moneychangers in the lobby.

Bus City buses cost US$0.40-80; they are clearly marked and run frequently until about 2300 weekdays, 0100 weekends. Many central bus stops have boards showing routes. CID/SUB or SUB/CID signs on the front tell you whether buses are going to or from the suburbs from/to the city centre (cidade). On buses, especially at night, look out for landmarks as street names are written small and are hard to see. Integrated bus-**metrô** (see Train below) routes and tickets (US$1.30) are available. Urban transport information, T158. See below for buses to Olinda and other destinations outside the city. Taxis are plentiful; fares double on Sun, after 2100 and on holidays; number shown on meter is the fare; don't take the taxi if a driver tells you it is km. **Porto de Galinhas** can be reached by bus from the southern end of Av Dantas Barreto, 8 a day, 7 on Sun, 0700-1700, US$1.65. Buses leave for **Igarassu** from Av Martins de Barros, in front of Grande Hotel, Recife, 45 mins, US$1.30.

The rodoviária, mainly for long-distance buses, is 12 km outside the city at São Lourenço da Mata (it is called Terminal Integrado dos Passageiros, or TIP, pronounced 'chippy'). T3452 1999. There is a 30-min metrô connection to the central railway station, entrance through Museu do Trem, opposite the Casa da Cultura, 2 lines leave the city, take train marked 'Rodoviária'. From Boa Viagem a taxi all the way costs US$26, or go to Central Metrô station and change there. Bus US$1.30, 1 hr, from the centre or from Boa Viagem. The train to the centre is much quicker than the bus. Bus tickets are sold at Cais de Santa Rita (opposite EMTU) and **Fruir Tur**, at Praça do Carmo, Olinda.

To **Salvador**, daily 1930, 12 hrs, US$24-32. To **Rio**, daily 2100, 44 hrs, US$77-100. To **São Paulo**, 1630 daily, 50 hrs, US$80-96. To **Foz do Iguaçu**, Fri and Sun 1030, 55 hrs, US$120. To **Brasília**, daily 2130, 39 hrs, US$65-90. To **Belo Horizonte**, daily 2115, 34 hrs, US$60. To **João Pessoa**, every 20-30 mins, 2 hrs, US$3.40. To **Caruaru**, see below. Buses to Olinda, see below; those to the beaches beyond Olinda from Av Dantas behind the post office. To **Cabo** (every 20 mins) and beaches south of Recife from Cais de Santa Rita.

Train Commuter services, known as the **Metrô** (but not underground), leave from the central station; they serve the rodoviária (frequent trains, 0500-2300, US$0.50 single). To reach the airport, get off the Metrô at Central station (not Joana Bezerra, which is unsafe) and take a bus or taxi (US$10.50) to Boa Viagem.

⊙ Directory

Recife *p491, maps p494 and 497*
Airline offices BRA, T3327 9911, or airport T3464 4655. **Gol**, T3464 4793. **TAM**, airport T3462 6799/ 0800-123100. **TAP**, Praça Min Salgado Filho, Imbiribeira, T3465 0300. **Trip**, at airport, T3464 4610. **Varig**, R Conselheiro Aguiar 456, T3464 4440. **Banks** Banks open 1000-1600, hours for exchange vary 1000-1400, sometimes later. **Banco do Brasil**, Shopping Centre Boa Viagem (Visa), helpful. **MasterCard**, cash against card, Av Conselheiro Aguiar 3924, Boa Viagem. **Citibank**, Av Marques de Olinda 126 and Av Cons Aguiar 2024, MasterCard with ATM. Also at branches of **HSBC**, eg Av Conde de Boa Vista 454

and Av Cons Aguiar 4452, Boa Viagem, and at **Banco 24 Horas. Bradesco**, at: Av Cons Aguiar 3236, Boa Viagem; Av Conde de Boa Vista; Rua da Concórdia 148; Getúlio Vargas 729; all have credit card facility, 24-hr ATMs but no exchange. **Exchange: Anacor**, Shopping Center Recife, loja 52, also at Shopping Tacaruna, loja 173. **Norte Câmbio Turismo**, Av Boa Viagem 5000, and at Shopping Guararapes, Av Barreto de Menezes.
Cultural centres British Council, Domingos Ferreira 4150, Boa Viagem, T2101 7500, recife@britishcouncil.org.br. 0800-1500, reading room with current English newspapers, very helpful. **Alliance Française**, R Amaro Bezerra 466, Derby, T3222 0918, www.af.rec.br. **Embassies and consulates Denmark**, Av M de Olinda 85, Ed Alberto Fonseca 2°, T3224 0311, F3224 0997. Open 0800-1200, 1400-1800. **France**, Av Conselheiro Aguiar 2333, 6th floor, T3465 3290, consulfr@hotlink.com.br. **Germany**, R Antônio Lumack do Monte 128, 16th floor, Boa Viagem, T3463 5350, info.recife@ alemanha.org.br, Mon-Fri 0900-1200, serving the Northeast. **Japan**, R Padre Carapuceiro 733, 14th floor, Boa Viagem, T3327 7264. **Netherlands**, Av Conselheiro Aguiar 1313/3, Boa Viagem, T3465 6764. **Sweden**, R Ernesto de Paula Santos, Boa Viagem, T3465 2940. **Switzerland**, Av Conselheiro Aguiar 4880, loja 32, Boa Viagem, T3326 3144. **UK**, Av Cons Aguiar 2941, 3rd floor, Boa Viagem, T3465 0230, recife@british consulate.org.br. 0800-1130. **US**, Gonçalves Maia 163, Boa Vista, T3421 2441, F3231 1906.
Internet Internet access in bookshop (signposted) in Shopping Centre Recife in Boa Viagem. Also, **Lidernet**, Shopping Boa Vista, city centre. **popul@r.net**, R Barão de Souza Leão, near junction with Av Boa Viagem. Open daily 0900-2100. **Medical services** Unimed, Av Bernardo Vieira de Melo 1496, Guararapes, T3462 1955/3461 1530, general medical treatment. **Unicordis**, Av Conselheiro Aguiar 1980, Boa Viagem, T3326 5237, equipped for cardiac emergencies; also at Av Conselheiro Roas e Silva 258, Aflitos, T421 1000. **Note**: Dengue fever has been resurgent in Recife. **Post offices** Including poste restante, Central Correios, 50001, Av Guararapes 250. In Boa Viagem, Av Cons Aguiar e R Col Sérgio Cardim.
Telephones Embratel, Av Agamenon Magalhães, 1114, Parque Amorim district; also Praça da Independência. **International telephones: Telemar**, Av Conselheiro Aguiar, Av Herculano Bandeira 231, and Av Conde da Boa Vista, all open 0800-1800. **Useful addresses Ibama**, Av 17 de Agosto 1057, Casa Forte, T3441 6338, F3441 5033. **Tourist Police**, T3326 9603/3464 4088.

Brazil Recife Listings

499

Around Recife

"Around Recife" is a bit of literary license because this section deals with not only fine colonial towns not far from the state capital, but also the Fernando de Noronha archipelago, way out in the Atlantic. Of the former, Olinda is one of the best examples in Brazil and only minutes from Recife. In the drier interior is Caruaru, a fascinating market town. Fernando de Noronha, best reached from Recife (hence its inclusion here), has a wonderful marine environment and is ideal for those who are seeking a remote destination.

Olinda → *Phone code: 0xx81. Post code: 53000. Colour map 5, grid B6. Population: 367,902.*

The old capital of Brazil founded in 1537 and named a World Heritage Site by UNESCO in 1982 is about 7 km north of Recife. A programme of restoration, partly financed by the Netherlands government, was initiated in order to comply with the recently conferred title of National Monument, but many of the buildings are still in desperate need of repair. The compact network of cobbled streets is steeped in history and invites wandering. This is a charming spot to spend a few relaxing days and a much more appealing base than Recife.

Many of the historic buildings have irregular opening hours, but can be viewed from the outside. The Tourist Office (Praça do Carmo, T3429 9279, open daily 0900-2100) provides a complete list of all historic sites with a useful map, Sítio Histórico. Guides with identification cards wait in Praça do Carmo. They are former street children and half the fee for a full tour of the city (about US$15) goes to a home for street children. If you take a guide you will be safe from mugging which, unfortunately, occurs.

The **Basílica e Mosterio de São Bento** ① *R São Bento, Mon-Fri 0830-1130, 1430-1700, mass Sat 0630 and 1800; Sun 1000*, with Gregorian chant. Monastery closed except with written permission. Founded 1582 by the Benedictine monks, burnt by the Dutch in 1631 and restored in 1761, this is the site of Brazil's first law school and the first abolition of slavery. The magnificent gold altar was on loan to New York's Guggenheim Museum at the time of writing. Despite its weathered exterior, the **Convento de São Francisco** (1585) ① *Ladeira de São Francisco, Tue-Fri 0700-1130, 1400-1700, Sat 0700-1200, US$0.40, mass Tue 1900, Sat 1700 and Sun 0800*, has splendid woodcarving and paintings, superb gilded stucco, and azulejos in the Capela de São Roque within the church of **Nossa Senhora das Neves** in the same building. Make the short, but very steep, climb up to the **Alto da Sé** for memorable views of the city and the coastline stretching all the way to Recife. Here, the simple **Igreja da Sé** (1537) ① *Mon-Fri 0800-1200, 1400-1700*, a cathedral since 1677, was the first church to be built in the city. Nearby, the **Igreja da Misericórdia** (1540) ① *R Bispo Coutinho, daily 1145-1230, 1800-1830*, has fine tiling and gold work. On a small hill overlooking Praça do Carmo, the **Igreja do Carmo** church (1581) has been closed for several years, with restoration planned.

There are some houses of the 17th century with latticed balconies, heavy doors and brightly-painted stucco walls, including a house in Moorish style at **Praça João Alfredo 7**, housing the Mourisco restaurant and a handicrafts shop, Sobrado 7. The local colony of artists means excellent examples of regional art, mainly woodcarving and terracotta figurines, may be bought in the Alto da Sé, or in the handicraft shops at the **Mercado da Ribeira** *R Bernardo Vieira de Melo* (Vieira de Melo gave the first recorded call for independence from Portugal, in Olinda in 1710). Handicrafts are also sold at good prices in the Mercado Eufrásio Barbosa, by the junction of Av Segismundo Gonçalves and Santos Dumont, Varadouro. There is a **Museo de Arte Sacra** ① *R Bispo Coutínho, Tue-Fri 0900-1300*, in the former Palacio Episcopal (1696). At R 13 de Maio 157, in the 18th century jail of the Inquisition, is the **Museu de Arte Contemporânea** *same hours as Museu Regional*. The **Museu Regional** ① *R do Amparo 128, Tue-Fri, 0900-1700, Sat and Sun 1400-1700*, is excellent. **Museu do Mamulengo** ① *Amparo 59, 0900-1800, Sat-Sun 1100-1800*, has Pernambucan folk puppetry.

The **beaches** close to Olinda are reported to be seriously polluted. Those further north from Olinda, beyond Casa Caiada, are beautiful, usually deserted, palm-fringed; at **Janga**, and **Pau Amarelo**, the latter can be dirty at low tide (take either a 'Janga' or 'Pau Amarela' bus, Varodouro bus to return). At many simple cafés you can eat sururu (clam stew in coconut sauce), agulha frita (fried needle-fish), miúdo de galinha (chicken giblets in gravy) and casquinha de caranguejo (seasoned crabmeat and farinha de dendê served in crabshells). Visit the Dutch fort on Pau Amarelo beach; small craft fair here on Saturday nights.

Igarassu → *Colour map 5, grid B6, Population 82,277.*

Igarassu, 39 km north of Recife on the road to João Pessoa, has the first church ever built in Brazil (SS Cosme e Damião, built in 1535), the Livramento church nearby, and the convent of Santo Antônio with a small museum next door. The church of Sagrado Coração is said to have housed Brazil's first orphanage. Much of the town (founded in 1535) is a National Monument.

Caruaru → *Colour map 5, grid C6. Population: 253,634. Altitude: 554 m.*

The paved road from Recife passes through rolling hills, with sugar cane and large cattle fazendas, before climbing an escarpment. As the road gets higher, the countryside becomes drier, browner and rockier. Caruaru, 134 km west of Recife, is a busy, modern town, one of the most prosperous in the agreste in Pernambuco. It is also culturally very lively, with excellent local and theatre and folklore groups.

Caruaru is most famous for its markets. The Feira da Sulanca is basically a clothes market supplied mostly by local manufacture, but also on sale are jewellery, souvenirs, food, flowers and anything else that can go for a good price. The most important day is Monday. There is also the Feira Livre or do Troca-Troca (free, or barter market). On the same site, Parque 18 de Maio, is the Feira do Artesanato, leather goods, ceramics, hammocks and basketware, all the popular crafts of the region. It is tourist-oriented but it is on a grand scale and is open daily 0800-1800.

The little clay figures (figurinhas or bonecas de barro) originated by Mestre Vitalino (1909-1963), and very typical of the Nordeste, are the local speciality; most of the local potters live at **Alto da Moura** ① *getting there: bus, 30 mins, bumpy, US$0.65*, 6 km away, where a house once owned by Vitalino is open (the **Casa Museu Mestre Vitalino**), with personal objects and photographs, but no examples of his work.

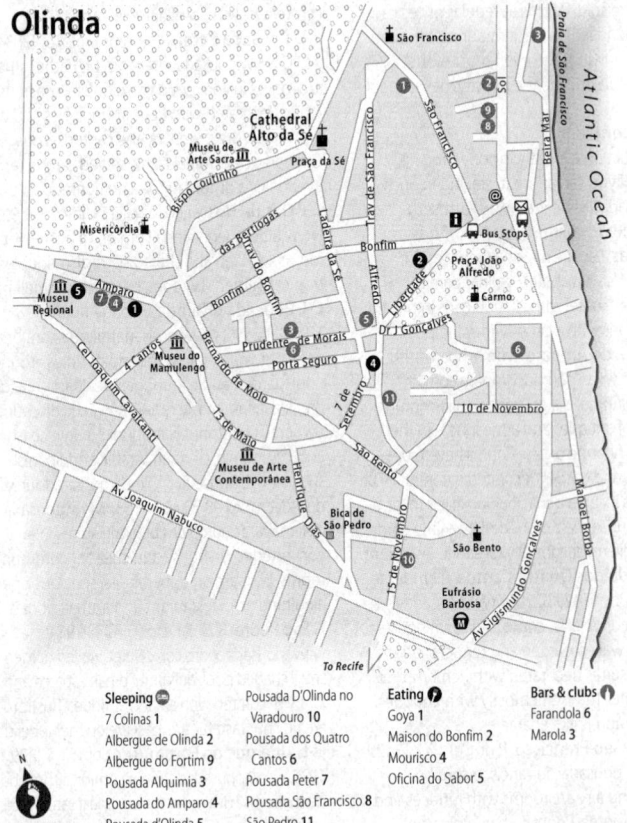

Olinda

N

Not to scale

Fernando de Noronha → *1 hr behind Brazilian Standard Time.*

This small archipelago 345 km off the northeast coast was declared a Marine National Park in 1988. There are many unspoilt beaches and interesting wildlife and excellent scuba-diving and snorkelling. Only one island is inhabited and is dominated by a 321 m peak. It is part of the state of Pernambuco administered from Recife. The islands were discovered in 1503 by Amérigo Vespucci and were for a time a pirate lair. In 1738 the Portuguese built the Forte dos Remédios (begun by the Dutch), later used as a prison in this century, and a church to strengthen their claim to the islands. Remains of the early fortifications still exist.

Vila dos Remédios, near the north coast, is where most people live and socialize. At Baía dos Golfinhos is a lookout point for watching the spinner dolphins in the bay. On the south side there are fewer beaches, higher cliffs and the coastline and islands are part of the marine park.

All development is rigorously controlled by Ibama, to prevent damage to the nature reserve. Many locals are dependent on tourism and most food is brought from the mainland; prices are about double. Entry to the island is limited to two plane-loads per day. There is a daily tax of US$15 for the first week of your stay. In the second week the tax increases each day. Take sufficient reais as dollars are heavily discounted. For information, contact the national park office, Al do Boldró s/n Fernando de Noronho, Toxx81-3619 1171. The rains are from February- July; the island turns green and the sea water becomes lovely and clear. The dry season is August-March, but the sun shines all year round. No repellent available for the many mosquitoes.

◉ Sleeping

Olinda *p500, map p501*
Prices at least triple during Carnival when 5-night packages are sold. Rooms at regular prices can often be found in Boa Viagem during this time. All of the following, and even most of the cheaper hotels outside the old city, have a pool.

Historic centre
Accommodation is mostly in converted mansions. If you can afford it, staying in one of these pousadas is the ideal way to absorb Olinda's colonial charm.

AL 7 Colinas, Ladeira de Sao Francisco 307, T/F3439 6055, www.hotel7 colinas.com.br. Spacious, new hotel with all mod cons in private gated grounds with a large swimming pool.

AL Pousada do Amparo, R do Amparo 199, T3439 1749, www.pousadoamparo.com.br. Olinda's best hotel is a gorgeous, 18th-century house, full of antiques and atmosphere in the Roteiros do Charme group. Rooms have four poster beds and each is decorated differently. The public areas include a spacious, art-filled foyer, a pool and sauna area surrounded by a little garden and an excellent, delightfully romantic restaurant.

B-C Pousada dos Quatro Cantos, R Prudente de Morais 441, T3429 0220, www.pousada4 cantos.com.br. A large converted town house with a little walled garden and terraces, bright rooms and suites decorated with Pernambuco arts and crafts, furnished mostly with antiques, welcoming and full of character.

C Pousada São Francisco, R do Sol 127, T3429 2109, www.pousadasaofrancisco.com.br. Well-kept and airy a/c rooms with terraces and pokey bathrooms. Pool and bar in pleasant gardens visited by hummingbirds in the early morning, restaurant, parking. Outside the historic centre but within walking distance.

C-D Pousada Peter, R do Amparo 215, T/F3439 2171, www.pousadapeter.com.br. Rather small a/c rooms in converted town house, spacious lobby decorated with Pernambuco arts and crafts and colourful art work by the cantankerous German owner. Breakfast is served on the terrace overlooking distant Recife and the modest pool.

C-E Olinda Hostel, R do Sol 233, T3429 1592, www.alberguedeolinda.com.br. HI hostel, 8-bed rooms with fan and shared bath, also doubles, tropical garden, TV room, hammocks, small pool.

C-E Pousada d'Olinda, P João Alfredo 178, T/F3494 2559, www.pousadadolinda.com.br. Basic but well-kept dorms and doubles around a pool, garden and communal breakfast area, good breakfast, lunchtime restaurant, 10% discount for owners of Footprint Handbooks in low season, English, French, German, Arabic and Spanish spoken. C-E Pousada D'Olinda no Varadouro, R 15 de Novembro 98, T3439 1163, www.pousada dolindavaradouro.com.br. Little suites in a converted town house and cheaper communal rooms, best are on upper floors, spacious open air dining area/restaurant and a small pool.

D São Pedro, R 27 Janeiro 95, T3439 9546, www.pousadapedro.com. Quiet, walled garden, small shaded pool, delightful breakfast area and lobby decorated with art and antiques. Rustic rooms are tiny but tasteful, a/c, best are on the upper floor.

D-E Albergue do Fortim, R do Sol 151, T3429 1939, www.pousadadofortim.com.br. Simple but clean rooms with a/c at the cheapest rates in Olinda. Some are big enough for 4. Breakfast US$2 extra.

Outside the historic centre

Hotels on R do Sol and in Bairro Novo are below the old city and on the roads heading north.

B Oh! Linda Pousada, Av Ministro Marcos Freire 349, Bairro Novo, T3439 2116. Recommended.

C Cinco Sóis, Av Ministro Marcos Freire 633, Bairro Novo, T/F3429 1347. A/c, fridge, hot water, parking.

D Pousada Alquimia, R Prudente de Morais 292, T3429 1457. Simple, lovely house, good breakfast, caring owners whose son is a painter with a workshop at the front.

D Cheiro do Mar, Av Ministro Marcos Freire 95, T3429 0101. Very good small hostel with some doubles (room No 1 is noisy), cooking facilities, ask driver of 'Rio Doce/Piedade' or 'Bairra de Jangada/ Casa Caiada' bus (see below) to drop you at Albergue de Juventude on the sea front.

Camping Olinda Camping, R Bom Sucesso 262, Amparo, T3429 1365. US$5 pp, space for 30 tents, 5 trailers, small huts for rent, quiet, well-shaded, on bus route, recommended.

Caruaru *p501*

Cheap hospedarias are around the central Praça Getúlio Vargas. Lots of cheap lunch restaurants.

A Grande Hotel São Vicente de Paulo, Av Rio Branco 365, T3721 5011, F3721 5290. Good, a/c, central, laundry, garage, bar, restaurant, pool, TV.

C Centenário, 7 de Setembro 84, T3722 4011, F3721 1033. Also suites, good breakfast, pool, central, can be noisy, otherwise recommended.

C Central, R Vigário Freire 71, T3721 5880. Suites or rooms, all with a/c, TV, good breakfast, in the centre. Recommended.

Fernando de Noronha *p502*

LL Pousada Maravilha, T3619 1290. One of the finest beach hotels in South America. Luxurious bungalows (and smaller annex rooms on a hill overlooking the Bahia do Sueste. Understated good taste in the public areas which overlook an infinity pool and the Atlantic. Excellent restaurant, gym, sauna, massage and help with tours and services on the island. Transfer from Rio, São Paulo or Recife can be arranged.

LL Zé Maria, R Eunice Cordeiro 1, T3619 1258, www.pousadazemaria.com.br. Spacious bungalows with generous beds, verandahs with hammocks and views to the Morro do Pico, small deep-blue half-moon pool.

L Solar dos Ventos, T3619 1347, www.pousadasolardosventos.com.br. Next to the Maravilha, shares the same spectacular view, but not in the sameleague, well-appointed bungalows, no pool.

AL Pousada do Vale, T3619 1293, www.pousadadovale.com. Well-run pousada, comfortable rooms, best are the duplex wooden bungalows. 300 m from Vila dos Remedios town centre.

AL Pousada dos Corais, Residencial Floresta Nova, Quadra "D" Casa 07, T3619 1147, www.pousadacorais.com.br. 8 small, plain a/c rooms around a little pool. Good breakfast.

C Verde Livre, Vila Remédios, T3619 1312. With a/c, TV, fridge and breakfast, simple but good.

⑦ Eating

Olinda *p500, map p501*

Several lanchonetes and fast-food options along the seafront. The traditional Olinda drinks, **Pau do Índio** (contains 32 herbs) and **Retetel**, are both made on the R do Amparo. Also try tapioca, a local dish made of manioc with coconut or cheese.

♥♥♥ Goya, R do Amparo, 157. Regional food, particularly seafood, beautifully presented.

♥♥♥ Oficina do Sabor, R do Amparo, 355. Consistently wins awards, pleasant terrace overlooking city, food served in hollowed-out pumpkins and lots of vegetarian options.

♥♥ Maison do Bomfim, R do Bonfim, 115. Serene, fan-cooled, rustic-style restaurant, French cuisine, as well as Brazilian and Italian.

♥♥ Samburá, Av Min Marcos Freire 1551. With terrace, try caldeirada and pitu (crayfish), lobster in coconut sauce or daily fish dishes, very good.

♥ Mourisco, Praça João Alfredo 7. Excellent, good value food by weight in lovely, part-covered, garden, delicious deserts. Warmly recommended.

Fernando de Noronha *p502*

♥♥♥ Ecologiku's, Estr Velha do Sueste, T3619 1807. Opened sided restaurant with a little garden, great Bahian food, delicious *moqueca*. Good *caipirinhas*.

♥♥♥ Porto Marlin, Porto de Santo Antônio, T3619 1452. Good Japanese food à la carte with an all you can eat buffet on Thu and Sat from 1800.

♥ Jacaré, Praça Pres Eurico Dutra (next to the Banco Real), T3619 1947. Best value on the island with lunchtime seafood and general Brazilian buffet.

♥ Açai e Raizes, BR363, Floresta Velha, T3619 0058. Roadside sandwich bar with good snacks, puddings and delicious cream of *cupuaçu* and *açai*.

Cia da Lua, Bosque dos Flamboyantes, T3619 1631. Decent coffee, snacks, sandwiches, internet access and car and buggy rental.

⑧ Bars and clubs

Olinda *p500, map p501*

Every Fri night bands of wandering musicians walk the streets serenading passers-by. Each Sun from 1 Jan to Carnival there is a mini Carnival in the streets.

Beginning at dusk, but best after 2100, the Alto da Sé becomes the scene of a street fair, with arts, crafts, makeshift bars and barbecue stands, and impromptu traditional music; even more animated at Carnival. Plenty of funky bars on R do Sol.

Cantinho da Sé, Ladeira da Sé 305. Lively, good view of Recife, food served.
Farandola, R Dom Pedro Roeser 190, behind Carmo church. Mellow bar with festival theme and 'big-top' style roof. Warmly recommended.
Marola, Trav. Dantas Barreto 66. Funky wooden barraca on rocky shoreline specializing in seafood, great caiprifrutas (frozen fruit drink with vodka – try the cashew), can get crowded. Recommended.
Pernambucanamente, Av Min Marcos Freire 734, Bairro Novo. Live, local music every night.

Fernando de Noronha *p502*
Vila dos Remédios town has several bars; including a pizzeria with lively weekend forró from 2200 on weekends, and a bar with live reggae nightly in high season.

⊛ Festivals and events

Olinda *p500, map p501*
At Olinda's **carnival** thousands of people dance through the narrow streets of the old city to the sound of the frevo, the brash energetic music which normally accompanies a lively dance performed with umbrellas. The local people decorate them with streamers and straw dolls, and form themselves into costumed groups to parade down the R do Amparo; **Pitombeira** and **Elefantes** are the best known of these groups. **Foundation Day** is celebrated with 3 days of music and dancing, **12-15 Mar**, night time only.

Caruaru *p501*
17 Dec-2 Jan, Festas Natalinas; Semana Santa, Holy Week, with lots of folklore and handicraft events; **18-22 May**, city's anniversary. **13 Jun** Santo Antônio and **24 Jun** São João, the latter a particularly huge forró festival, are part of Caruaru's Festas Juninas. **Sep**, Micaru, a street carnival; also in **Sep**, Vaquejada (a Brazilian cross between rodeo and bull fighting), biggest in the northeast.

▲ Activities and tours

Olinda *p500, map p501*
Viagens Sob O Sol, Prudente de Moraes 424, T3429 3303, transport offered to all parts, any type of trip arranged, also car hire.
Victor Turismo, Av Santos Domont 20, Loja 06, T3494 1467. Day and night trips to Recife.

Fernando de Noronha *p502*
Boat trips and jeep tours are available; it is also possible to hire a beach buggy. **Locadora Ilha do Sol**, T3619 1132, or 9985 4051, www.pousadadovale.com, for buggy rental and guided tours of the island. You can hitch everywhere as everyone stops. There are good hiking, horse riding and mountain biking possibilities, but you must either go with a guide or ranger in many parts.
Diving Diving is organized by **Atlantis Divers**, T0xx81-3619 1371, **Águas Claras**, T3619 1225, in the hotel grounds, and **Noronha Divers**, T3619 1112. Diving costs between US$65-100 and equipment rental from US$65. This is the diving mecca for Brazilian divers with a great variety of sites to explore and fish to see.
Surfing Iaponã, T3619 1947, or 9635 7176, iapadosurf@hotmail.com. Classes from one of the island's best; US$25 per class including equipment.

⊖ Transport

Olinda *p500, map p501*
Bus From **Recife**: take any bus marked 'Rio Doce', No 981 which has a circular route around the city and beaches, or No 33 from Av Nossa Senhora do Carmo, US$0.80 or 'Jardim Atlântico' from the central post office at Siqueira Campos; from Boa Viagem, take bus marked 'Piedade/Rio Doce' or 'Bairra de Jangada/Casa Caiada' (US$0.80, 30 mins). Change to either of these buses from the airport to Olinda: take 'Aeroporto' bus to Av Domingos Ferreira, Boa Viagem, and ask to be let off; and from the Recife Rodoviária: take the metrô to Central station and then change. In all cases, alight in Praça do Carmo. Taxi drivers between Olinda and Recife try to put meters onto rate 2 at the Convention Centre (between the 2 cities), but should change it back to 1 when queried (taxi to Recife US$10.50, US$16 to Boa Viagem at night).

Caruaru *p501*
Bus The rodoviária is 4 km from the town; buses from Recife stop in the centre. Bus from centre, at the same place as Recife bus stop, to rodoviária, US$0.50. Many buses from TIP in **Recife**, 2 hrs, US$4.

Fernando de Noronha *p502*
Air Daily flights from **Recife** with Trip and Varig, 2 hrs, US$400. From Natal package tours are available via Recife.

ⓘ Directory

Olinda *p500, map p501*
Banks There are no facilities to change TCs, or ATMs in the old city. **Banco do Brasil**, R Getúlio Vargas 1470. **Bradesco**, R Getúlio Vargas 729, Visa ATM. **Bandepe** on the same Av has MasterCard ATM. **Internet** Study Web, Praça do Carmo, US$1.20, 30 mins, a/c. Olind@.com, Av Beira Mar 15, US$1.50, 30 mins. **Post offices** Praça do Carmo, open 0900-1700. **Telephones** International calls can be made at **Telemar** office on Praça do Carmo, Mon-Sat 0900-1800.

South of Recife

Two small states, Alagoas and Sergipe, are wedged between Pernambuco and Bahia. For no good reason, most people pass through, but there are some good examples of colonial architecture and, like the entire northeast coast, some fine beaches.

Important telephone changes All ordinary phone numbers in Brazil are changing from seven to eight figure numbers, a process still under way as this guide went to press. Where confirmed, eight-digit numbers have been included in the text, but if a seven-digit number doesn't work, try putting 3 as the first digit.

South to Alagoas
There are many interesting stopping points along the coast between Recife and Maceió. The main highway, BR-101, heads a little inland from the coast, crossing the state border near Palmares. It then continues to Maceió. On the coast the Pernambuco-Alagoas border is by São José da Coroa Grande, after which a coastal road, unpaved in parts, runs to Barra do Camaragibe. Just after the mouth of the Rio Camaragibe is Praia do Morro, Pedra do Cebola and Carro Quebrado, where beach buggies can be hired for trips up the coast. Further south is **Barra de Santo Antônio**, a busy fishing village, with a palm fringed beach on a narrow peninsula, a canoe-ride away. The beaches nearby are beautiful: to the south, near the village of Santa Luzia, are Tabuba and Sonho Verde. Two unspoilt fishing villages, which have good places to stay and are pretty much close to paradise are **Japaratinga** ① *Pousada Doze Cabanas, Toxx82-3297 1338, www.dozecabanas.com.br* (has been recommended) and **Maragogi** *www.maragogionline.com.br*; try **Pousada Mariluz** *Toxx82-3296 1511, www.pousada mariluz.com.br*, or **Portal do Maragogi** *www.portaldomaragogi.cjb.net*. The natural pools at the reef of As Galés are beautiful; trips can be arranged at the Frutos do Mar restaurant.

Maceió and around → *Phone code: 0xx82. Post code: 57000. Colour map 5, grid C6.*
The capital of Alagoas state (*Population 797,759, Voltage 220 volts AC, 60 cycles*) is mainly a sugar port, but for tourism it's friendly, safe and good value. Two of its old buildings, the **Palácio do Governo**, which also houses the **Fundação Pierre Chalita** (Alagoan painting and religious art) and the church of **Bom Jesus dos Mártires** (1870, covered in tiles), are particularly interesting. Both are on the Praça dos Martírios (or Floriano Peixoto). The **cathedral**, Nossa Senhora dos Prazeres (1840), is on Praça Dom Pedro II. The helpful **tourist office** is at Setur ① *R Boa Vista 453, Centro, T3315 5700* (also at airport and rodoviária). The municipal tourist authority is **Seturma** ① *R Sá e Albuquerque 310, T3336 4409*; information post on Pajuçara beach, by Hotel Solara. Also visit www.turismomaceio.com.br and www.maceioumbarato.com.br.

Lagoa do Mundaú, a lagoon whose entrance is 2 km south at **Pontal da Barra**, limits the city to the south and west: excellent shrimp and fish are sold at its small restaurants and handicraft stalls; a nice place for a drink at sundown. Boats make excursions in the lagoon's channels. Beyond the city's main dock the beachfront districts begin; within the city, the beaches are smarter the further from the centre you go. The first, going north, is **Pajuçara** where there is a nightly craft market. At weekends there are wandering musicians and entertainers. Further out, **Jatiúca, Cruz das Almas** and **Jacarecica** (9 km from centre) are all good for surfing. The beaches, some of the finest and most popular in Brazil, have a protecting coral reef a kilometre or so out. Bathing is much better three days before and after full or new moon, because tides are higher and the water is more spectacular. Jangadas take passengers to a natural swimming pool 2 km off Pajuçara beach (**Piscina Natural de Pajuçara**), at low tide you can stand on the sand and rock reef (beware of sunburn). You must check the tides, there is no point going at high tide. Jangadas cost US$5 per person per day (or about US$20 to have a jangada to yourself). On Sunday or local holidays in the high season it is overcrowded (at weekends lots of jangadas anchor at the reef selling food and drink).

By bus (22 km south), past Praia do Francês, the attractive colonial town and former capital of Alagoas, **Marechal Deodoro**, overlooks the Lagoa Manguaba. The 17th-century **Convento de São Francisco**, Praça João XXIII, has a fine church (Santa Maria Magdalena) with a superb baroque wooden altarpiece, badly damaged by termites. You can climb the church's tower for views. Adjoining it is the **Museu de Arte Sacra** ① *Mon-Fri 0900-1300, US$0.40, guided tours available, payment at your discretion*. Also open to visitors is the

505

Igreja Matriz de Nossa Senhora da Conceição (1783). The town is the birthplace of Marechal Deodoro da Fonseca, founder of the Republic; the modest **house** ① *Mon-Sat 0800-1700, Sun 0800-1200, free,* where he was born is on the R Marechal Deodoro, close to the waterfront. On a day's excursion, it is easy to visit the town, then spend some time at beautiful **Praia do Francês**. The northern half of the beach is protected by a reef, the southern half is open to the surf. Along the beach there are many barracas and bars selling drinks and seafood; also several pousadas.

Penedo → *Phone code: 0xx82. Post code: 57200. Colour map 5, grid C6. Population: 56,993.*

This charming town, some 35 km from the mouth of the Rio São Francisco, with a nice waterfront park, Praça 12 de Abril, was originally the site of the Dutch Fort Maurits (built 1637, razed to the ground by the Portuguese). The colonial town stands on a promontory above the river. Among the colonial architecture, modern buildings on Av Floriano Peixoto do not sit easily. On the Praça Barão de Penedo is the neoclassical **Igreja Matriz** (closed to visitors) and the 18th century **Casa da Aposentadoria** (1782). East and a little below this square is the Praça Rui Barbosa, on which are the **Convento de São Francisco** (1783 and later) and the church of **Santa Maria dos Anjos** (1660). As you enter, the altar on the right depicts God's eyes on the world, surrounded by the three races, one Indian, two negroes and the whites at the bottom. The church has fine trompe-l'oeil ceilings (1784). The convent is still in use. Guided tours are free. The church of **Rosário dos Pretos** (1775-1816), on Praça Marechal Deodoro, is open to visitors. **Nossa Senhora da Corrente** (1764), on Praça 12 de Abril, and **São Gonçalo Garcia** (1758-1770) ① *Av Floriano Peixoto, Mon-Fri 0800-1200, 1400-1700.* Also on Avenida Floriano Peixoto is the pink **Teatro 7 de Setembro** (No 81) of 1884. The **Casa de Penedo** ① *R João Pessoa 126 (signs point the way up the hill from F Peixoto), Tue-Sun 0800-1800,* displays photographs and books on, or by, local figures. **Tourist information:** in the Casa da Aposentadoria.

An interesting crossing into Sergipe can be made by frequent ferry (car and foot passengers) from Penedo to **Neópolis**.

Aracaju → *Phone code: 0xx79. Post code: 49000. Colour map 5, grid C5. Population: 461,534.*

Capital of Sergipe founded 1855, it stands on the south bank of the Rio Sergipe, about 10 km from its mouth, 327 km north of Salvador. In the centre is a group of linked, beautiful parks: **Praça Olímpio Campos**, in which stands the cathedral, **Praça Almirante Barroso**, with the Palácio do Governo, and **Praças Fausto Cardoso** and **Camerino**. Across Av Rio Branco from these two is the river. There is a handicraft centre, the **Centro do Turismo** ① *in the restored Escola Normal, on Praça Olímpio Campos, Rua 24 Horas, 0900-1300, 1400-1900;* the stalls are arranged by type (wood, leather, etc). The city's beaches are at **Atalaia**, 16-km by road, and the 30-km long **Nova Atalaia**, on Ilha de Santa Luzia across the river. It is easily reached by boat from the Hidroviária (ferry station), which is across Avenida Rio Branco from Praça Gen Valadão. For tourist information, try **Turismo Sergipe**, Travessa Baltazar Góes 86, Edifício Estado, T3179 1937, www.setur.se.gov.br.

São Cristóvão is the old state capital, 17 km southwest of Aracaju on the road to Salvador. It was founded in 1590 by Cristóvão de Barros. It is the fourth oldest town in Brazil. Built on top of a hill, its colonial centre is unspoiled: the **Museu de Arte Sacra e Histórico de Sergipe** contains religious and other objects from the 17th to the 19th centuries; it is in the **Convento de São Francisco** ① *Tue-Fri 1000-1700, Sat-Sun 1300-1700.* Also worth visiting (and keeping the same hours) is the **Museu de Sergipe** in the former **Palácio do Governo** *both are on Praça de São Francisco.* Also on this square are the churches of **Misericórdia** (1627) and the **Orfanato Imaculada Conceição** (1646, permission to visit required from the Sisters), and the **Convento de São Francisco**. On Praça Senhor dos Passos are the churches **Senhor dos Passos** and **Terceira Ordem do Carmo** (both 1739), while on the Praça Getúlio Vargas (formerly Praça Matriz) is the 17th century **Igreja Matriz Nossa Senhora da Vitória** ① *Tue-Fri 1000-1700, Sat-Sun 1500-1700.*

Estância → *Colour map 5, grid C5*

On the BR-101, almost midway between Aracaju and the Sergipe-Bahia border, and 247 km north of Salvador, is Estância, one of the oldest towns in Brazil. Its colonial buildings are decorated with Portuguese tiles. The month-long festival of **São João** in June is a major event. There are pleasant hotels, but most buses stop at the Rodoviária, which is on the main road (four hours from Salvador).

Sleeping → See Telephone, page 347, for important phone changes.

Maceió *p505*

It can be hard to find a room during the Dec-Mar holiday season, when prices go up. There are many hotels on Praia Pajuçara, mostly along Av Dr Antônio Gouveia and R Jangadeiros Alagoanos.

L Enseada, Av A Gouveia 171, T231 4726, www.hotelenseada.com.br. 1980s business hotel on the waterfront with a pool and restaurant. Recommended.

L-AL Sete Coqueiros, Av A Gouveia 1335, T3231 8583, www.setecoqueiros.com.br. 3-star, a/c, TV, phone, good restaurant, pool.

A Velamar, Av A Gouveia 1359, T3327 5488, atendimento@hotelvelamar.com.br. A/c, TV, fridge, safes in rooms.

B Buongiorno, R Jangadeiros Alagoanos 1437, T3327 4447, vapini@ig.com.br. A/c, fridge, English-speaking owner, helpful.

B Casa Grande da Praia, R Jangadeiros Alagoanos 1528, T3231 3332, hcgpraia@matrix.com.br. A/c and TV, cheaper without. Recommended.

B Costa Verde, R Jangadeiros Alagoanos 429, T3231 4745. Bath, fan, good family atmosphere, English, German spoken.

B Pousada Cavalo Marinho, R da Praia 55, Riacho Doce (15 km from the centre), facing the sea, T/F355 1247, pcavalomarinho@ uol.com.br. Use of bicycle, canoes and body boards including, hot showers, German and English spoken, tropical breakfasts, Swiss owner. Further from the centre, but very highly recommended (nearby is **Lua Cheia**, good food and live music at night).

B Sol de Verão, R Eng Mário do Gusmão 153, Ponta Verde beach, T/F3231 6657. Small rooms without baths and some larger and more expensive a/c options with en suites.

Alagamar, R Prefeito Abdon Arroxelas 327, T3231 2246, alag@superig.com.br. Excellent hostel, good location and value. IH affiliated, requires reservations Dec-Feb, Jul and Aug.

Camping Camping **Clube do Brasil** site on Jacarecica beach, T235 3600, a 15-min taxi drive from the town centre. **Camping Pajuçara**, at Largo da Vitória 211, T231 7561, clean, safe, food for sale.

Penedo *p386*

A São Francisco, Av Floriano Peixoto 237, T3551 2273, www.hotelsaofrancisco.tur.br. Standard rooms have no a/c, TV, fridge. Recommended except for poor restaurant.

B Pousada Colonial, Praça 12 de Abril 21, T3551 2355, F3551 3737. Luxo and suite have phone, TV and fridge, suites have a/c, spacious, good cheap restaurant, front rooms with view of Rio São Francisco.

C Pousada Estilo, Praça Jacome Calheiros 79, T551 2465. Cheaper without TV, quiet, river views, very nice.

C Turista, R Siqueira Campos 143, T3551 2237. With bath, fan, hot water. Recommended.

Aracaju *p506*

A range of hotels in the centre, including:

A Grande, R Itabaianinha 371, T3211 1383, F3211 1388. A/c, TV, fridge, central, **Quartier Latin** restaurant.

B Brasília, R Laranjeiras 580, T3214 2964, F3214 1023. Good value, good breakfasts. Recommended.

Eating

Maceió *p505*

Local specialities include oysters, *pitu*, a crayfish (now becoming scarce), and *sururu*, a kind of cockle. Local ice cream, Shups, recommended. Many good bars and restaurants in Pajuçara, eg on Av Antônio Gouveia. The beaches for 5 km from the beginning of Pajuçara to Cruz das Almas in the north are lined with barracas (thatched bars), providing music, snacks and meals until 2400 (later at weekends). Vendors on the beach sell beer and food during the day: clean and safe. There are many other bars and barracas at Ponto da Barra, on the lagoon side of the city. Most hotels offer free transport to restaurants; ask at reception.

TTT Spettus, Av Silvio Carlos Viana 1911, Ponta Verde. Excellent churrascaria, fine service and worth the expense.

TT Divina Gula, R Eng Paulo Brandão Nogueira 85, Jatiúca, T235 1016. Minas specialities, very good, huge helpings, also *cachaçaria*.

TT New Hakata, R Eng Paulo Brandão Nogueira 95, Jatiúca, T325 6160. Good Japanese with *rodizios* on Tue.

T Nativa, Osvaldo Sarmento 56. Vegetarian, good views.

T O Natural, R Libertadora Alagoana (R da Praia) 112. Vegetarian.

Aracaju *p506*

T Gonzaga, Rua Santo Amaro 181, T224 7278. Lunch only, good value, popular, excellent traditional dishes.

Festivals and events

Maceió *p505*

27 Aug: Nossa Senhora dos Prazeres; **16 Sep:** Freedom of Alagoas; **8 Dec:** Nossa Senhora da Conceição; **15 Dec:** Maceiofest, 'a great street party with trios elêctricos'; Christmas Eve; New Year's Eve, half-day.

⊙ Transport

Maceió *p505*

Air 20 km from centre, taxi about US$30. Buses to airport from near Hotel Beiriz, R João Pessoa 290 or in front of the Ferroviária, signed 'Rio Largo'; alight at Tabuleiro dos Martins, then 7-8 mins walk to the airport, bus fare US$1.

Bus Frequent local buses, confusingly marked, serve all parts of the city. Bus stops are not marked: it is best to ask where people look as if they are waiting. The 'Ponte Verde/ Jacintinho' bus runs via Pajuçara from the centre to the rodoviária, also take 'Circular' bus (25 mins Pajuçara to rodoviária); Taxis from town run to all the northern beaches, but buses run as far as Ipioca (23 km). The Jangadeiras bus marked 'Jacarecica-Center, via Praias' runs past all the beaches as far as Jacarecica. From there you can change to 'Riacho Doce-Trapiche', 'Ipioca' or 'Mirante' buses for Riacho Doce and Ipioca. To return take any of these options, or take a bus marked 'Shopping Center' and change there for 'Jardim Vaticana' bus, which goes through Pajuçara. Buses and kombis to Marechal Deodoro, Praia do Francês and Barra de São Miguel leave from R Zacarias Azevedo, near the ferroviária: bus US$1, kombi US$1.30 to Marechal Deodoro, 30 mins, calling at Praia do Francês in each direction. Last bus back from Praia do Francês to Maceió at 1800.

The rodoviária is 5 km from centre, on a hill with good views and cool breezes. Taxi, US$9.50 to Pajuçara. Bus to **Recife**, 10 a day, 3½ hrs express (more scenic coastal route, 5 hrs) US$12. **Maceió-Aracaju**, 5 hrs, US$12 with Bonfim. To **Salvador**, 10 hrs, 4 a day, US$27 (rápido costs more).

Penedo *p386*

Bus 451 km from **Salvador** (US$15-19, 6 hrs, daily bus 0600, book in advance), at same time for **Aracaju** (US$8). Buses south are more frequent from **Neópolis**, 6 a day (0630-1800) to Aracaju, 2 hrs, US$4.80. 115 km from **Maceió**, 5 buses a day in either direction, US$7.20-8.80, 3-4 hrs. **Rodoviária**: Av Duque de Caxias, behind Bompreço supermarket.

Aracaju *p506*

Bus Interstate rodoviária is 4 km from centre, linked by local buses from adjacent terminal (buy a ticket before going on the platform). To **Salvador**, 6-7 hrs, 11 a day with **Bonfim**, US$14.50-19.

João Pessoa → *Phone code: 0xx83. Post code: 58000. Colour map 5, grid B6. Pop: 597,934.*

It is a bus ride of two hours through sugar plantations over a good road from Recife (126 km) to João Pessoa, capital of the State of Paraíba on the Rio Paraíba. It's a pleasant, historical town with a rich cultural heritage. The beaches, beside the turquoise waters of the Atlantic, are wonderful. At Ponta do Seixas is the most easterly point in Brazil; near here the Transamazônica highway begins its immense, if not controversial, route west into the heart of the country. The **Centro de Turismo** is at Tambaú ① *To800-281 9229, www.pbtur.pb.gov.br, with branches at rodoviária and the airport; all open 0800-1900.*

Sights

João Pessoa is a capital that retains a small town atmosphere. In the **Centro Histórico** is the São Francisco Cultural Centre (Praça São Francisco 221), one of the most important baroque structures in Brazil, with the beautiful church of **São Francisco** which houses the **Museu Sacro e de Arte Popular** ① *Tue-Sat 0800-1100, Tue-Sun 1400-1700.* Other tourist points include the **Casa da Pólvora**, now the **Museu Fotográfico Walfredo Rodríguez** (Ladeira de São Francisco) ① *Mon-Fri 0800-1200, 1330-1700.* Also the **Teatro Santa Roza** (1886) ① *Praça Pedro Américo, Varadouro, Mon-Fri 1400-1800.* João Pessoa's parks include the 17-ha **Parque Arruda Câmara**, north of the centre, and **Parque Solon de Lucena** or **Lagoa**, a lake surrounded by impressive palms in the centre of town, the city's main avenues and bus lines go around it.

The beachfront stretches for some 30 km from Ponta do Seixas (south) to the port of **Cabedelo** (north), on a peninsula between the Rio Paraíba and the Atlantic Ocean. This is Km 0 of the Transamazônica highway. The ocean is turquoise green and there is a backdrop of lush coastal vegetation. About 7 km from the city centre, following Av Presidente Epitáceo Pessoa is the beach of **Tambaú** ① *getting there: bus No 510 'Tambaú' from outside the rodoviária or the city centre, alight at Hotel Tropical Tambaú,* which has many hotels and restaurants. Regional crafts, including lace-work, embroidery and ceramics are available at Mercado de Artesanato, Centro de Turismo, Almte Tamandaré 100. The town's main attractions are its beaches, where most tourists stay. About 14 km south of the centre is the

Cabo Branco lighthouse at Ponta do Seixas, the most easterly point of continental Brazil and South America; there is a panoramic view from the cliff top. **Cabo Branco** is much better for swimming than **Tambaú**. Take bus 507 'Cabo Branco' from outside the rodoviária to the end of the line; hike up to the lighthouse.

The best known beach of the state is **Tambaba**, the only official nudist beach of the Northeast, 49 km south of João Pessoa in a lovely setting. Two coves make up this famous beach: in the first bathing-suits are optional, while the second one is only for nudists. Strict rules of conduct are enforced. Between Jacumã (many hotels, restaurants) and Tambaba are several nice beaches such as **Tabatinga** which has summer homes on the cliffs and **Coqueirinho**, surrounded by coconut palms, good for bathing, surfing and exploring caves.

☁ Sleeping → *See Telephone, page 347, for important phone changes.*

João Pessoa *p508*

All those listed are at Tambaú, unless indicated otherwise:

L Caiçara, Av Olinda 235, T/F2106 1000, www.hot caicara.com.br. A slick, business orientated place with a pleasant restaurant attached.

L Tropical Tambaú, Av Alm Tamandaré 229, T2107 1900, www.tropicalhotel.com.br. An enormous round building on the seafront which looks like a military bunker and has motel-style rooms around its perimeter. Comfortable and with good service. Recommended.

L Xênius, Av Cabo Branco 1262, T3015 3519, www.xeniushotel.com.br. Popular standard 4 star with a pool, good restaurant and well kept but standard a/c rooms (low-season reductions).

AL-A Royal Praia, Coração de Jesus, T2106 3000, www.royalhotel.com.br. Comfortable a/c rooms with fridges around a pool.

B-C Tambía Praia, R Carlos Alverga 36, T247 4101, www.tambiahotel.hpg.com.br. Centrally located and 1 block from the beach. Intimate, with balconies and sea view. Recommended.

B-C Villa Mare Apartment Hotel, Av Négo 707, T226 2142, www.pbnet.com.br/ openline/george. Comfortable apartments for 2 or 3 people with full amenities per night or from US$400-500 per month. Helpful staff. Recommended.

C Solar Filipéia, Av Incognito Coração de Jesus 153, T3247 3744, www.solarfilipeia.com.br. Brand new, very smart hotel with large, bright rooms with bathrooms in tile and black marble and excellent service. A real bargain.

D Pousada Mar Azul, Av João Maurício 315, T226 2660. Very clean large rooms, the best are on the upper level, right on the oceanfront road. Some have a/c and private bathrooms, others have fans. Well kept, safe and a real bargain.

D-E Hostel Manaíra, R Major Ciraulo 380, Manaíra, T247 1962, www.manairahostel.br2.net. Friendly, brand new hostel close to the beach, with a pool, internet, barbecue, cable TV and breakfast. A real bargain.

☯ Eating

João Pessoa *p508*

There are few options in the centre, other than the stalls in Parque Solon de Lucena next to the lake, beside which are some simple restaurants. Every evening on the beachfront, stalls are set up selling all kinds of snacks and barbecued meats. At Cabo Branco there are many straw huts on the beach serving cheap eats and seafood.

♥♥♥ Adega do Alfredo, Coração de Jesus. Very popular traditional Portuguese restaurant in the heart of the club and bar area.

♥♥♥ Gulliver, Av Olinda 590, Tambaú. Fashionable French/Brazilian restaurant frequented by João Pessoa's upper middle classes.

♥♥ Mangaí, Av General Édson Ramalho 696, Manaíra. This is one of the best restaurants in the northeast to sample the region's cooking. There are almost 100 different hot dishes to choose from, sitting in copper tureens over a traditional wood-fired stove some 20 m long.

♥♥ Cheiro Verde, R Carlos Alverga 43. Self service, well established, regional food.

♥♥ Sapore d'Italia, Av Cabo Branco 1584, Standard Italian fare including pizza.

☯ Bars and clubs

João Pessoa *p508*

There are many open bars on and across from the beach in Tambaú and Cabo Branco. The area known as Feirinha de Tambaú, on Av Tamandaré by the *Tambaú Hotel* and nearby streets, sees much movement even on weekend nights, with R Coração do Jesus being the centre. There are numerous little bars and *forró* places here.

☯ Festivals and events

João Pessoa *p508*

Pre-carnival celebrations are renowned: the bloco Acorde Miramar opens the celebrations the Tue before Carnival and on Wed, known as **Quarta Feira de Fogo**, thousands join the

Muriçocas de Miramar. Celebrations for the patroness of the city, **Nossa Senhora das Neves**, take place for 10 days around **5 Aug**.

▲ Activities and tours

João Pessoa *p508*
Half-day city tours (US$6), day trips to Tambaba (US$8) and Recife/Olinda (US$15) organized by **Vida Mansa**.
Navegar, Artur Monteiro de Paiva 97, Bessa. Buggy tours (US$32 to Jacumã).
Preocupação Zero Turismo, Av Cabo Branco 2566, T226 4859, F226 4599. Local and regional tours, floating bars.
Roger Turismo, Av Tamandaré 229, www.rogerturismo.com.br. A range of tours, some English-speaking guides.

⊖ Transport

João Pessoa *p508*
Air Aeroporto Presidente Castro Pinto, Bayeux, 11 km from centre, 232 1200; national flights. Taxi to centre costs US$10.50, to Tambaú US$16.
Bus Most city buses stop at the rodoviária and go by the Lagoa (Parque Solon de Lucena). Take No 510 for Tambaú, No 507 for Cabo Branco.

Rodoviária is at R Francisco Londres, Varadouro, 10 mins from the centre, T221 9611; luggage store; PBTUR information booth is helpful. Taxi to the centre US$2, to Tambaú US$6.50. To **Recife** with Boa Vista or Bonfim, every 30 mins, US$3.20, 2 hrs. To **Natal** with Nordeste, every 2 hrs, US$9

convencional, US$10.50 executivo, 3 hrs. To **Fortaleza** with Nordeste, 2 daily, 10 hrs, US$35. To **Salvador** with Progresso, 4 weekly, US$40, 14 hrs. To **Belém** with Guanabara, daily at 1000, US$60, 36-39 hrs.

⊙ Directory

João Pessoa *p508*
Airline offices BRA, T2106 9595, at airport T232 2520. **TAM**, Av Senador Rui Carneiro 512, T247 2400 (airport T232 2747). **Varig**, Av Getúlio Vargas 183, Centro, T3232 1274 (airport), 0800-997000.
Banks Banco do Brasil, Praça 1817, 3rd floor, Centro, helpful, or Isidro Gomes 14, Tambaú, behind Centro de Turismo, poor rates. MasterCard Cirrus and Amex cashpoints at Banco 24 Horas, kiosk in front of Centro de Turismo, Tambaú, and HSBC, R Peregrino de Carvalho 162, Centro. PB Câmbio Turismo, Visconde de Pelotas 54C, Centro, open Mon-Fri 1030-1630, cash and TCs. **Internet** Many cybercafés in Tambaú: at telephone office in Centro de Turismo, Almte Tamandaré 100. **Post offices** Main office is at Praça Pedro Américo, Varadouro; central office is at Parque Solon de Lucena 375; also by the beach at Av Rui Carneiro, behind the Centro de Turismo.
Telephones Calling stations at: Centro de Turismo, Tambaú; Av Epitácio Pessoa 1487, Bairro dos Estados; rodoviária and airport.
Useful numbers Polícia Federal, T0800 218 3033.

Natal → *Phone code: 084. Colour map 2, grid B6. Population: 713,000.*

Natal, capital of Rio Grande do Norte, located on a peninsula between the Rio Potengi and the Atlantic Ocean, is one of the most attractive cities of Brazil's northeast coast, as well as a popular destination for those seeking sun and good beaches. The air is said by NASA to be the second purest in the world, after Antarctica. The inventors of the beach-buggy must have had Rio Grande do Norte in mind as the dunes and strand that surround the city are ideal for daredevil stunts and whizzing along the open sands.

Ins and outs
Tourist offices Secretaria de Turismo do Estado (SETUR), R Mossoró 359, Petrópolis, T232 2496, www.setur.rn.gov.br. Information booths at Centro de Turismo, T211 6149 (see Shopping, below), Avenida Pres Café Filho s/n, Praia dos Artistas (0800-2100 daily), Central do Cidadão, Praia Shopping, T232 7234 (see Shopping, below, there is also a Polícia Federal office here), Cajueiro de Pirangi, Parnamirim, T238 2347 (see Around Natal, below), rodoviária, T232 7310 and airport, T643 1043. For information T205 2428 (Disque Passagem), or, for the Polícia Federal T204 5500, and for the Tourist Police T232 7404 (Delegacia do Turista).

Sights
The oldest part is the **Ribeira** along the riverfront where a process of renovation has been started. The **Cidade Alta**, or Centro, is the main commercial centre and Avenida Rio Branco its principal artery. The main square is made up by the adjoining **praças: João Maria, André de**

Albuquerque, **João Tibúrcio** and **7 de Setembro**. At Praça André de Albuquerque is the old cathedral (inaugurated 1599, restored 1996). The small church of **Santo Antônio** ① *R Santo Antônio 683, Cidade Alta, 0800-1700 Tue-Fri, 0800-1400 Sat*, dates from 1766. It has a blue and white façade, a fine, carved wooden altar and a sacred art museum.

On a hill overlooking Ribeira is the **Centro do Turismo** ① *R Aderbal de Figueiredo 980, off R Gen Gustavo C Farias*, Petrópolis (see Bars and nightclubs, and Shopping, below). A converted prison with a wide variety of handicraft shops, art gallery, antique shop and tourist information booth, it offers good view of the Rio Potengi and the sea. At Praia do Forte, the tip of Natal's peninsula, is the **Forte dos Reis Magos** ① *T221 0342, 0800-1630 daily except Christmas Day, New Year and Carnaval, US$1*. The star-shaped fort was begun in 1598 and is now the city's main historical monument. Its blinding white walls contrast with the blue of sea and sky. You can wander round the interior rooms, mostly empty although the former military prison now houses a lanchonete, and there are guides. The easiest way to get there is by taxi or on a tour; no buses go to the entrance, from where you have to walk along a causeway to the fort. Between it and the city is a military installation.

The **Museu Câmara Cascudo** ① *Av Hermes de Fonseca 1440, Tirol, T211 8404, Tue-Fri 0800-1700, US$1*, has exhibits on archaeological digs, Umbanda rituals and the sugar, leather and petroleum industries. **Museu do Mar** ① *Av Dinarte Mariz (Via Costeira), Praia de Mãe Luiza, T215 4433, Mon-Fri 0800-1130, 1400-1700, free*. It has aquariums with regional sea life and exhibits with preserved specimens. At Mãe Luiza is a lighthouse with beautiful views of Natal and surrounding beaches (take a city bus marked 'Mãe Luiza'). It is only open on Sunday, until 1700; at other times T221 2631.

A large ecological zone, the **Parque das Dunas**, separates the commercial centre from Ponta Negra, 12.5 km away, the beach and nightlife spot where most visitors stay.

Beaches

Natal has excellent beaches, some of which are also the scene of the city's nightlife. East of the centre, from north to south are: **Praia do Forte**, **do Meio**, **dos Artistas**, **de Areia Preta** and **Mãe Luzia**. The first two have reefs offshore, therefore little surf, and are appropriate for windsurfing. The others are urban beaches and local enquiries regarding pollution are recommended before bathing. Mãe Luzia marks the start of the **Via Costeira**, which runs south along the ocean beneath the towering sand dunes of **Parque das Dunas** (access restricted to protect the 9 km of dunes), joining the city to the neighbourhood and popular beach of Ponta Negra. A cycle path parallels this road and provides great views of the coastline. Lining Mãe Luzia and Barreira d'Água (the beach across from Parque das Dunas) are the city's four and five-star hotels.

Furthest south is vibrant and pretty **Ponta Negra**, justifiably the most popular beach. The seafront, Avenida Erivan França, is a car-free promenade for much of its length; the remainder is the busiest part of town. It has many hotels, from albergues up to three and four-star, restaurants and bars (see below). The northern end of the beach is good for surfing, while the

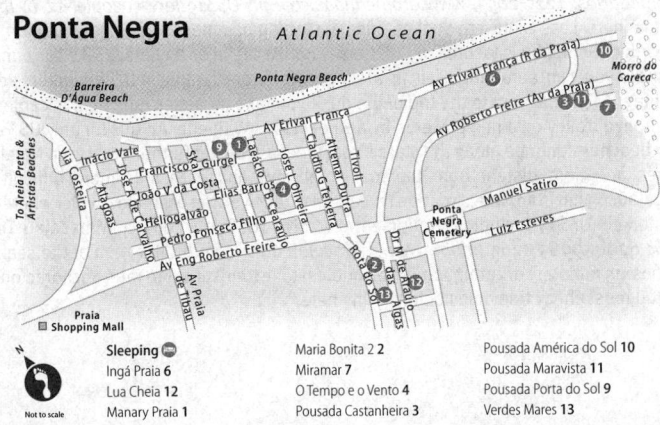

Sleeping	Maria Bonita 2 2	Pousada América do Sol 10
Ingá Praia 6	Miramar 7	Pousada Maravista 11
Lua Cheia 12	O Tempo e o Vento 4	Pousada Porta do Sol 9
Manary Praia 1	Pousada Castanheira 3	Verdes Mares 13

Brazil Natal

southern end is calmer and suitable for swimming. At the south end of the beach is **Morro do Careca**, a 120-m high dune with a sand-skiing slope surrounded by vegetation. Although no longer used for sand-skiing, it remains one of the 'postcards' of the city.

Around Natal

The coast south of the city is referred to as **Litoral Sul**, to the north as **Litoral Norte**. Dune buggies are the only way to travel here. Tours are available through travel agencies (see below).

Pirangi do Norte, 25 km from Natal, has calm waters, is popular for watersports and offshore bathing (500 m out) when natural pools form between the reefs. In the town is the world's largest cashew-nut tree (cajueiro maior do mundo, entry US$0.75); branches springing from a single trunk cover an area of some 8,400 sq m, a whole city block. A guide on site offers a brief explanation and there is a look-out for seeing the tree from above. Outside are handicraft stalls, tourist information and musicians.

Beyond Barreta is the long, pristine beach of **Malembar**, access on foot or by a five-minute boat ride across the mouth of the **Lagoa Guaraíra** from Tibau do Sul at the south end. The ferries to/from Tibau do Sul costs US$7 return; buggy drivers should not add this fee to a day tour. Crossings are determined by the state of the tide (times are critical and you should follow the buggy driver's instructions regarding departure times). Around **Tibau do Sul** the lovely beaches circled by high cliffs, the lagoons, Atlantic forest and the dolphins are some of the attractions that make this one of the most visited stretches of the southern coast (it can get crowded during holiday periods and weekends). South of town there are fine, wide, white-sand beaches, separated by rocky headlands, set against high cliffs and coconut groves.

At Praia do Madeiro and neighbouring **Baía dos Golfinhos**, the ocean is calm and clear and dolphins can often be seen (ask locally for the best time). Between Praia do Madeiro and Pipa, on a 70-m high dune, is the **Santuário Ecológico de Pipa** ① *0800-1600, US$4*. This 60-ha park was created in 1986 to conserve the mata atlântica forest; there are 17 trails and lookouts over the cliffs which afford an excellent view of the ocean and dolphins.

Praia da Pipa, 3 km further south (85 km from Natal), is popular with Brazilians and foreigners alike, for its beautiful beaches and charming restaurants. The town is expanding rapidly and its nightlife is the talk of the area.

The coast **north of Natal** is known for its many impressive, light-coloured sand dunes, some reaching a staggering 50 m in height. A 25-minute ferry crossing on the Rio Potengi takes you from Natal to **Redinha**, an urban beach, with ocean and river bathing, and buggies to hire.

The best-known beach in the state, **Genipabu** is 30 km north of the city. Its major attractions are very scenic dunes and the Lagoa de Genipabu, a lake surrounded by cashew trees and dunes where tables are set up on a shoal in the water and drinks served. There are also many bars and restaurants on the sea shore. The dunes are a protected **Parque Ecológico** *T9974 8265*, and only authorized buggy drivers are allowed to enter. All buggy tours go through the dunes and make the most of the vehicles' manoeuvrability on the fantastic slopes and hollows: prepare yourself for "emoção". At the top of a dune overlooking the lake and coast are lots of colourful umbrellas and handicraft stalls. **Camel rides** ① *dromedários, T225 2053, www.dromedunas.com.br, US$19 for 2 people, 12-14 mins*, start from here. Less exotic are **donkey rides** ① *starting at a mere US$0.65 per person*.

North of Genipabu is **Jacumã**, 49 km from Natal. At Lagoa de Jacumã, a lake surrounded by dunes, you can aerobunda, sit in a sling and fly on a cable into the water. Really refreshing. To get back up to the top of the dune you take the fusca funicular, a 'cable car' made from a trolley on a rail, powered by a wheel-less VW Beetle. All this for only US$1.75. Lovely beaches continue along the state's coastline; as you get further away from Natal the beaches are more distant from the main highways and access is more difficult. At **Maracajaú**, 63 km from Natal, low tide reveals an extensive area of shallow water where you can snorkel (US$15 including equipment), or dive (US$30); contact **Maracajaú Diver** ① *T261 6200, 9983 4264 (mob), www.maracajau diver.com.br*. It's 7 km out to sea and launches (15 minutes) or catamarans (30 minutes) take tourists out to rafts anchored on the reef. You must check tide times before going here.

Natal *p510*

The **Via Costeira** is a strip of enormous, upmarket beachfront hotels, which are very isolated, with no restaurants or shops within easy walking distance. **Ponta Negra** is the ideal place to stay, with its attractive beach and concentration of restaurants. Economical hotels are easier to find in the city proper but there is otherwise not much reason to stay there (no nightlife and a long way from the action). Prices of beach hotels below are for the high season (Dec-Feb and Jul), unless otherwise stated.

In the centre

LL Maine, Av Salgado Filho 1791, Lagoa Nova, T4005 5774, www.hotelmaine.com.br. On the principal avenue leading from the centre to Ponta Negra. Full service in this 4-star hotel, including free internet service, restaurant with panoramic views.

B Natal Center, R Santo Antônio 665, T221 2355. Business hotel in the city centre, rooms with a/c, fridge and TV, restaurant and pool.

C Casa Grande, R Princesa Isabel 529, T211 0555. 'Big house' built around family home, popular with business visitors. A/c, cheaper without bath (also low season discounts), good breakfast, pleasant, excellent value. Recommended.

D Natal, Av Rio Branco 740, Centro, T3222 2792, www.hotelnatal.com. On a busy part of the main street, well-established, a/c, cheaper with fan, popular with local guests.

Near rodoviária

There are several in the area, but the only reason to stay here is if arriving very late or departing very early.

B Pousada Esperança, Av Capt Mor Gouveia 418, T205 1955. With bath, a/c, cheaper with fan or without bath.

Beaches *p511*
Praia do Meio, Praia dos Artistas and Praia de Areia Preta

The distinction between these 1st 2 beaches is often blurred. Most hotels here are on the beachfront Av Pres Café Filho, the numbering of which is illogical. Many pousadas open for just 1 season, then close for good.

AL Praia do Sol, Av Pres Café Filho 750, Praia dos Artistas, T202 4848. Opposite beach, quiet, a/c, TV, frigobar, swimming pools, bar and restaurant. Recommended.

A Bruma, Av Pres Café Filho 1176, Praia dos Artistas, T/F202 4303, www.hotelbruma.com.br. Slick, intimate, beachfront balconies, also has more expensive suites, pool, terrace. Recommended.

C Beira Mar, Av Pres Café Filho 886, Praia do Meio, T202 1470. Motel-style, on the beach front, with breakfast, a/c, small pool, good value (**E** for more than 2 nights), popular. Recommended.

D Pousada do Paxá, Av Pres Café Filho 11, T202 2848. Clean, beachfront, breakfast extra, real bargain, but also has more expensive rooms. Recommended.

Ponta Negra *p511, map p511*

Here, too, the street numbering is pretty chaotic.

LL-L Manary Praia, R Francisco Gurgel 9067, T/F3204 2900, www.manary.com.br. Price depends on view from room; phone in advance as prices vary greatly according to month. This is a very stylish hotel on a quiet corner, some rooms overlook the pool/ terrace and beach, all are very comfortable, 'neocolonial' design using local materials, member of the Roteiro de Charme group, see page 346. Recommended.

AL Hotel e Pousada O Tempo e o Vento, R Elias Barros 66, T/F3219 2526, www.otempoeovento.com.br. **C** in low season, a/c, fridge, safe in room, pool and wet bar, clean, luxo rooms are very comfortable, good breakfast. Recommended.

A Ingá Praia, Av Erivan França 17, T3219 3436, www.ingapraiahotel.com.br. **B** without sea view, **C** in low season (service tax not included). Very comfortable, clean and cosy, rooms have all the expected facilities. Recommended.

A Miramar, Av da Praia 3398, T219 2131. Price reduced by half in low season. Quite high up with good views, family-run, very clean, internet for guests 0800-1800, restaurant, 2 pools, games room, English spoken.

A-B Pousada Castanheira, Rua da Praia 221, T3236 2918, www.pousadacastanheira.com.br. **C** in low season, English/Brazilian owners, comfortable spacious rooms with TV, fridge and safe, small pool, breakfast room with sea view, room service, parking, very helpful staff. Recommended.

B Maria Bonita 2, Estrela do Mar 2143, T236 2941, F219 2726. With a/c, **C** with fan, not as close to the beach as most, but near the Broadway and its nightlife.

C Pousada Maravista, Rua da Praia 223, T236 4677, marilymar@hotmail.com. One of the cheaper options, next to Pousada Castanheira, high-ceilinged rooms, hot showers, TV, fan, good breakfast, simple, English spoken, Marilyn is very welcoming. Recommended.

C Pousada Porta do Sol, R Francisco Gurgel 9057, T236 2555, pousadaportadosol@digizap.com.br. Clean and tidy, good seafront location, TV, fridge, a/c except in rooms with sea breeze, some fans, good mattresses, excellent breakfast, pool, good value, English and French spoken (ask for Patrick or Suerda). Recommended.

D pp Lua Cheia, R Dr Manoel Augusto Bezerra de Araújo 500, Ponta Negra, T3236 3696, www.luacheia.com.br. HI hostel in 'castle' with 'medieval' **Taverna Pub** in basement (see Bars and nightclubs below). Includes breakfast. Highly recommended.

D Pousada América do Sol, Rua Erivan França 35, T3219 2245, www.pousadaamericado sol.com.br. Price per person in albergue-style rooms with bath, hot water, lockers, cheaper without a/c, popular, simple, use of kitchen, breakfast included. Also has pousada rooms at **B** (half-price in low season), a/c, TV, frigobar, includes breakfast, parking.

D Verdes Mares, R das Algas 2166, Conj Algamar, Ponta Negra, T236 2872, F236 2872. HI hostel, includes breakfast, discount in low season, quiet, comfortable. Also recommended.

Around Natal: Praia da Pipa *p512*

In Pipa more than 30 pousadas and many private homes offer accommodation. See www.pipa.com.br for some listings.

AL Ponta do Madeiro, Rota do Sol, Km 3, Tibaú do Sul, T3246 4220, www.pontado madeiro.com.br. Beautifully set in Mata atlântica with access to Madeiro beach, between Pipa and Tibaú, 3 types of chalet in gardens, pool, restaurant, trips on land and sea.

AL Sombra e Água Fresca, Praia do Amor, Km 1, T3246 2258, www.sombraeaguafresca.com.br. **A** in low season. A/c, fridge, pools, restaurant with beautiful view especially at sunset.

AL Toca da Coruja, Av Baía dos Golfinhos, T3246 2226, www.tocadacoruja.com.br. Comfortable chalets and rooms (cheaper in low season), with all facilities including safe in room, in gardens with lots of trees, quiet, member of the Roteiros de Charme group, see page 346.

A Pousada da Bárbara, 1st right after church in centre, T246 2351, pousadadabarbara@ yahoo.com.br. **B** in low season, 20 m from town beach, rooms with a/c TV, hot shower and veranda, swimming pool, very good.

A Pousada Bicho Preguiça, R Praia do Amor 15, T246 2370, www.pipabicho preguica.com.br. A variety of rooms with cable TV, a/c, frigobar, internet for guests, 24-hr restaurant and bars.

B-C Pousada Pomar da Pipa, R da Mata, T3246 2256, www.pomardapipa.com. 150 m from praça, quiet, beautiful garden, very helpful, good value.

C-D Vera-My house, T9988 5154, veramyhouse @uol.com.br. With bath, **E** pp in dormitory, use of kitchen, no breakfast. Good value, friendly. Recommended.

● Eating

Natal *p510*

Prawns feature heavily on menus here as Natal is the largest exporter in Brazil.

♥♥♥ Raro Sabor, R Seridó 722, Petrópolis. Exclusive bistro serving international dishes, emphasis on French cuisine. Closed Mon.

♥♥ Bella Napoli, Av Hermes da Fonseca 960, Tirol. Good Italian food.

♥♥ Camarões Express, Av Sen Salgado Filho 2234, Natal Shopping. Express prawns in 15 styles. Open for lunch only at weekends.

♥♥ Mangaí, Av Amintos Barros 3300, Lagoa Nova. Very good regional food (carne do sol, tapioca and many other sertaneja dishes) in rustic atmosphere, open 0600-2200, closed Mon. Recommended.

♥♥ Marenosso, in the Centro do Turismo (see below). Specializes in seafood and local dishes like carne do sol, sweets, expresso coffee.

♥♥ Thin-San, Av Hermes da Fonseca 890, Tirol. Good Chinese food, popular.

♥ China Palace, Av Afonso Pena 554, Petrópolis. For cheap lunches, a mixture of Chinese and Brazilian dishes, self-service.

♥ Habib's, also in Natal Shopping. A branch of the cheap Middle Eastern food chain.

♥ A Macrobiótica, Princesa Isabel 524, vegetarian, shop, lunch only. Next door is **Neide**, at No 530, for coffee and sweets.

Beaches: Ponta Negra *p511*

♥♥♥ Sobre Ondas, Av Erivan França 14. Seafood and international dishes, average food, underwater theme, has internet.

♥♥♥ Tereré, Rota do Sol 2316. All-you-can-eat barbecue, including Argentinian beef, ribs, as well as fish and salad.

♥♥ Barraca do Caranguejo, Av Erivan França 1180. Live music nightly from 2100. 12 different types of prawn dish for US$6.75, rodízio style.

♥♥ Beterraba, Av Erivan França 108, Santa Fe Mall. Upstairs, overlooking street and sea, specializes in grills and salads, fruit salads and juices.

♥♥ Camarões, Av Eng Roberto Freire 2610. Also at Natal Shopping Centre. Touristy, but very good seafood.

♥♥ Cipó Brasil, Av Erivan França 3 and Rua Aristides Porpinho Filho 3111 (behind Lua Cheia youth hostel). Jungle theme, 4 levels, sand floors, lantern-lit, dishes and rinks well-presented. Serves pizzas and crêpes (house speciality), good for cocktails, live music nightly after 2100. In the same group is **Casa de Taipa**, Rua Dr Manoel E B de Araújo 130A, next to Taverna Pub (see below), serving tapioca, salads, juices and coffee.

♥♥ Ponta Negra Grill, Av Erivan França 22. Large, several terraces, popular for steaks, seafood and cocktails, lively.

♥ Grande Muralha, Av Erivan França 12, Casa Branca Center. Upstairs, Chinese, Japanese and Brazilian food with executive meals at good prices.

Cafés

Dulce France, Av Afonso Pena 628, Vila Colonial Shopping, corner of R Mossoró. Café selling crêpes, salads and coffee.

The malls in Ponta Negra have a variety of cafés and bars:

Ponta Negra Mall, Av Erivan França 24. Smart stalls sell sandwiches and snacks, also shops and Fellini restaurant. It can be accessed from Av Roberto Freire.

Santa Fe Mall, Av Erivan França 108. With Beach Café, Blackout Beer (popular in early evening), Beterraba restaurant (see above) and Bistro de Suisse for pizzas, pastas, meats and drinks.

🍸 Bars and clubs

Natal *p510*
Ponta Negra beach is lively at night and the venue for a full-moon party, when there is live music all night.

Aquamarina Praia, Av Roberto Freire 22a, Ponta Negra. Pavement beachfront bar, attached to restaurant/hotel, large TV screen, open 24 hrs. Also has internet.

Blackout B52, Rua Chile 25. 1940s theme, best night is 'Black Monday'.

Centro de Turismo (see Shopping below) has Forró com Turista, a chance for visitors to learn this fun dance, Thu at 2200; many other enjoyable venues where visitors are encouraged to join in.

Downtown Pub, Rua Chile 11. 4 bars, dancefloor, games area, cybercafé, live bands, open Thu-Sat. Both popular bar/nightclubs are in the Ribeira district, in restored historic buildings.

Taverna Pub, R Dr Maneol, A B de Araújo, 500, Ponta Negra. Medieval-style pub in youth hostel basement. Eclectic (rock, Brazilian pop, jazz, etc.) live music Tue-Sun from 2200, best night Wed. Recommended. This street and the one that joins it by Taverna/Lua Cheia is known as 'Broadway', with lots of bars and cafés.

Zás-Trás, Rua Apodi 500, Tirol. Daily shows, except Sun, with a variety of local dances and presentations and a comedy act. Also has handicraft shops and a restaurant.

🎉 Festivals and events

Natal *p510*
In **Jan** is the Festa de Nossa Senhora dos Navegantes when numerous vessels go to sea

from Praia da Redinha, north of town. **Mid-Dec** sees Carnatal, the Salvador-style out of season carnival, a lively 4-day music festival with dancing in the streets.

🛍 Shopping

Natal *p510*
Handicrafts Centro Municipal de Artesanato, Av Pres Café Filho, Praia do Meio. Daily 1000-2200. Sand-in- bottle pictures are very common in Natal. **Centro de Turismo**, R Aderbal de Figueiredo, 980, off R Gen Gustavo C Farias, Petrópolis. A converted prison with a wide variety of handicraft shops, art gallery, antique shop, café, restaurant and tourist information booth, offers good view of the Rio Potengi and the sea, open daily 0900-1900, Thu at 2200 is Forró com Turista (see above).

Shopping centres Natal Shopping, Av Senador Salgado Filho 2234, Candelária, between Ponta Negra and the centre. Large mall with restaurants, ATMs, cinemas and 140 shops. Free shuttle bus service to major hotels.

Praia Shopping, Av Eng Roberto Freire 8790, Ponta Negra. Smart shops, including **AS Livros** book and coffee shop (lojas 505-506); food hall with lots of options and a **Habib's**. There are more restaurants outside, mostly fast food, on Rua Praia de Genipabu. It also has internet, exchange (see Directory, below) and the **Central do Cidadão**. This facility has a tourist office (see above), post office, federal police office and Banco do Brasil with ATM; open Tue-Fri 1000-2200, Sat 1000-1800.

🚴 Activities and tours

Natal *p510*
Boat tours To natural swimming pools at Pirangi do Norte, 25 km south of Natal, and to the nearby beaches of the Litoral Sul are available from **Marina Badauê**, Pirangi do Norte, T238 2066. A 2-hr tour includes hotel pick-up, a snack (or breakfast if you take an early tour), and allows time for a swim, US$11.15 per person. The company has a restaurant and bar at the seashore. Boat trips to Barra do Cunhaú, 86 km south of Natal, go through mangroves, visit an island and a salt mine with **Passeio Ecológico Cunhaú**, T211 1123; see beaches above.

Diving Miami Dive, T202 4727, natalnautica @natal.digi.com.br. For groups of up to 10, beginners' courses, dives up to 20 m. Associated with Império do Sol chalets in Pipa, T3246 2381, www.imperiodosol.com.br. See also Maracajaú in The Northern Coast, above.

Tour operators

A city tour costs US$20; if it includes the northern beaches US$25-30, including southern beaches US$40-45. Buggy tours are by far the most popular, US$100 for a full day in high season, US$85 in low season (shorter options are available). If you book direct with the buggy owner, rather than through a hotel or agency, there will be a discount. The price should include all commissions and ferry crossings. Buggy drivers (bugueiros) have an association (APCBA, R Projetada 405, Praia de Genipabu, Extremoz, T225 2061, www.angelfire.com/nt2/apcbarn/) and all members must be approved by Setur and Detran. Look for the sign 'Autorizado Setur' plus a number on the buggy.
Cariri Ecotours, T3086 3601/3234 4068, www.caririecotours.com.br. Mainly 4WD tours throughout Ceará, the Sertão, Paraíba and Pernambuco, to natural monuments and archaeological sites, with a strong ecological emphasis. Also works with **Aventura** (www.aventuraturismo.com.br) for coastal Land Rover trips. Trustworthy, excellent guides.
Cascadura Turismo e Viagens Ecológicas, R Praia de Bessa 2089, sl 101, Ponta Negra, www.cascadura.net. Land Rover tours to beaches and the interior, to historical and cultural sites, also packages to Fernando de Noronha.

⊙ Transport

Natal *p510*
Air Aeroporto Augusto Severo, Parnamirim, T644 1000. The airport has a tourist office, VIP Câmbio, ATMs, car hire, restaurants and shops.
Bus Rodoviária, Av Capitão Mor Gouveia 1237, Cidade da Esperança, T232 7310. Regional tickets are sold on street level, interstate on the 2nd floor. To **Recife**, 5 daily, US$13 convencional, US$21 executivo, 4 hrs. With **Nordeste** to **Mossoró**, US$13 convencional, US$21 executivo, 4 hrs. To **Aracati**, US$16, 5½ hrs. To **Fortaleza**, US$23 semi-leito, US$33 executivo, US$53 leito, 7½ hrs. To **João Pessoa**, see above. With **São Geraldo** to **Maceió**, buses both direct and via Recife, US$29 convencional, US$43 executivo, 10 hrs. To **Salvador**, US$67 executivo, 20 hrs. With **Boa Esperança** to **Teresina**, US$53 convencional, US$67 executivo, 17-20 hrs. To **Belém**, US$95, 32 hrs.
Taxi Taxis are expensive compared to other cities; US$10 for 10-min journey.

Around Natal *p512*
Pirangi do Norte
Bus From Natal, new rodoviária, Viação Campos, T205 4787, many daily, US$0.90 to Pirangi, 1 hr.

Tibau do Sul and Pipa
Bus From Natal **Transul**, T205 2711, 6 a day to Tibau do Sul and on to Pipa, and **Oceano** buses, T3203 2440, www.expresso-oceano.com.br, from the new rodoviária, several daily, US$3.30. **Oceano** and VW combis go to **Goianinha** from where buses run south to João Pessoa.
Buggy tours Rivatur, Tibau do Sul, T246 4244 or 9982 8331 (mob), ask for Rivaldo, rivatur@uol.com.br. Tours south and north of Natal and to the interior and Paraíba; US$100 for 5 hrs, US$175 for 8 hrs, US$24 to Natal, with sightseeing. Also arranges boat (US$13) and horse rides (US$15).

Redinha
Bus Regular **Oceano** buses, T3203 2440, www.expresso-oceano.com.br, from the old rodoviária to Redinha.
Ferry Frequent ferry service for Redinha from **Cais Tavares de Lira**, Ribeira (Natal), weekdays 0530-1900, weekend and holidays 0800-1830, US$0.65 per person, US$4 for car. If on a buggy tour, the fare is included in the cost.

Genipabu
Bus Guanabara from the old rodoviária every 30 mins from 0530, till 2030, T205 3300.

Jacumã
Bus Riograndense, T205 4388, from **Natal**, 1100 and 1800 to **Jacumã** (0730 and 1800, Sun).

❶ Directory

Natal *p510*
Airline offices BRA, Av Prudente de Morais 507, Petrópolis, T3221 1155, at airport, T3643 2132. **TAM**, Av Afonso Pena 844, Tirol, T201 2020, at airport, T643 1260, freephone 0800-570 5700. **Trip**, Av Prudente de Morais 4283, sala2, T3643 1450. **Varig**, R Mossoró 598, Petrópolis, at airport T3644 1050. **Banks** Banco 24 horas, Natal Shopping, Cirrus, Visa, MasterCard and Plus. Banco do Brasil, Seafront ATM, Ponta Negra for Cirrus, Visa, MasterCard and Plus. Also, Av Rio Branco 510, Cidade Alta, US$ cash and TCs at poor rates, cash advances against Visa, Mon-Fri 1000-1600. Dunas Câmbio, Av Roberto Freire 1776, Loja B-11, Capim Macio (east of Parque das Dunas), T2193840, cash and TCs, 0900-1700. Natal Câmbio, in Natal Shopping, open Mon-Sat 1000-2200. Ponta Negra Câmbio, Av Erivan França 91, cash and TCs, Mon-Fri 0900-2200, Sat 1000-2100, Sun 0900-2000. Praia Câmbio in Praia Shopping, open Mon-Sat 0900-2200, Sun 0900-1700. Sunset Câmbio, Av Hermes da Fonseca 628, Tirol, cash and TCs, 0900-1700. **Car hire**

BR Rede Brasil, Av Eng Roberto Freire 9100, Ponta Negra, T3236 3344, www.redebrasil natal.com.br. Dudu Locadora, Av Rio Branco 420, Centro, T211 7000. There are many other rental agencies on Av Eng Roberto Freire for cars and buggies. Buggy rental about US$45 a day, price depends on make. **Embassies and consulates** Italy, R Auta de Souza 275, Centro, T222 6674. Spain, R Amintas Barros 4200, Lagoa Nova, T206 5610. **Internet** Café Arte and LM in Galeria Princesa Isabel, Av Princesa Isabel, Centro, Mon-Fri 0800-190, Sat 0900-1400. Both US$2.80 per hr, former serves coffee and lunches. InterJato in Praia Shopping, US$0.55 for 10 mins, then charges 10 centavos per min. International Center Call, Av Erivan França 91, Ponta Negra, internet, scanner, international, cellular and card phones, open 0900-2200, Sun 1000-2000. Sobre Ondas, Ponta Negra (also bar and restaurant, see above), open 0900-2400, 15 centavos 1 min. **Post offices** R Princesa Isabel 711, Centro; Av Rio Branco 538, Centro, Av Engenheiro Hildegrando de Góis 22, Ribeira, Av Praia de Ponta Negra 8920, Ponta Negra. **Telephone** R Princesa Isabel 687 and R João Pessoa, Centro; Av Roberto Freire 3100, Ponta Negra, Shopping Cidade Jardim, Av Roberto Freire, Ponta Negra; and rodoviária.

Fortaleza and the north coast

→ *Phone code: 0xx88 outside metropolitan Fortaleza, but prefix numbers beginning with 3 with 0xx85.*

The state of Ceará has been dubbed A Terra da Luz, Land of Light. It has some of the finest beaches in Brazil, scenic dunes and almost constant sunshine. The sophisticated capital, Fortaleza, is still home to jangadas (traditional fishing boats), while its nightlife is famous throughout the country. As well as the mysterious Parque Nacional de Sete Cidades, Piauí shares with Maranhão the remarkable Parnaíba delta, which is beginning to be recognized as a major ecological site with great tourist potential. The Parque Nacional Lençóis Maranhenses, across the delta, is a landscape of fabulous sand dunes and crystal lakes. Maranhão's capital, São Luis is one of Brazil's UNESCO sites of worldwide cultural importance, because of its colonial centre.

Fortaleza → *Phone code: 0xx85. Post code: 60000. Colour map 5, grid B5. Population: 2.1 million.*

Fortaleza, the fifth largest city in Brazil, is a busy metropolis with many highrise buildings, an important clothes manufacturing industry, many hotels and restaurants and a lively nightlife. Fishermen's *jangadas* still dot the turquoise ocean across from the beach and transatlantic cruise ships call in for refuelling. The mid-day sun is oppressive, tempered somewhat by a constant breeze; evening temperatures can be more pleasant, especially by the sea. The wettest months are March to July, known locally as "winter".

Ins and outs
Tourist offices Setur, state tourism agency; Centro Administrativo Virgílio Távora, Cambeba, T3101 4639, www.setur.ce.gov.br. Information booths at Centro de Turismo, has maps, information about beach tours (0700-1800, Sunday 0700-1200); rodoviária (0600-1800 daily), airport (24 hours) and Farol de Mucuripe (0700-1730). Disque Turismo 24-hour 0800-991516. Posta Telefônica Beira Mar, on Beira Mar almost opposite Praiano Palace, information, sells Redenção tickets to Jericoacoara, good range of postcards and clothes, papers and magazines. Tourist police, R Silva Paulet 505, Aldeota, T433 8171.

Safety In Fortaleza avoid the Serviluz favela between the old lighthouse (Av Vicente de Castro), the favela behind the railway station, the Passeio Público at night, Av Abolição at its eastern (Nossa Senhora da Saúde church) and western ends. Also be careful at Mucuripe and Praia do Futuro. Generally, though, the city is safe for visitors.

Sights
Praça do Ferreira, from which pedestrian walkways radiate, is the heart of the commercial centre. The whole area is dotted with shady squares. **Fortaleza Nossa Senhora da Assunção**

① *Av Alberto Nepomuceno, T255 1600 in advance for permission to visit, daily 0800-1100,* *1400-1700*, originally built in 1649 by the Dutch, gave the city its name. Near the fort, on R Dr João Moreira, is the 19th century **Passeio Público** or Praça dos Mártires, a park with old trees and statues of Greek deities. West of here, a neoclassical former prison (1866) houses the **Centro de Turismo do Estado** (Emcetur) ① *Av Senador Pompeu 350, near the waterfront,* *T0800-991516, closed Sun*, with museums, theatre and high-quality craft shops (bargaining expected). It houses the **Museu de Arte e Cultura Populares** and the **Museu de Minerais** *T212 3566*. Further west along R Dr João Moreira, at **Praça Castro Carreira** (commonly known as Praça da Estação), is the nicely refurbished train station **Estação João Felipe** (1880).

The **Teatro José de Alencar** ① *on the praça of the same name, T229 1989, Mon-Fri* *0800-1700, hourly tours, some English speaking guides, US$1, Wed free*, was inaugurated in 1910. This magnificent iron structure was imported from Scotland and is decorated in neo-classical and art nouveau styles. It also houses a library and art gallery. The new **cathedral**, completed in 1978, in gothic style but built in concrete, stands beside the new, semi-circular **Mercado Central** with beautiful stained glass windows. Both are on Praça da Sé, at Av Alberto Nepomuceno. The **Museu do Maracatu** ① *Rufino de Alencar 231, at Teatro São* *José*, houses costumes of this ritual dance of African origin.

The new and exciting **Centro Dragão do Mar de Arte e Cultura** at R Dragão do Mar 81, Praia de Iracema hosts music concerts, dance, and art and photography exhibitions. It has various entrances, from Ruas Almirante Barroso, Boris and from junction of Monsenhor Tabosa, Dom Manuel and Castelo Branco. This last one leads directly to three museums: on street level, the **Memorial da Cultura Cearense**, with changing exhibitions; on the next floor down is an art and cultural exhibit; in the basement is an excellent audio-visual museum of **El Vaqueiro**. Also at street level is the Livraria Livro Técnico. There is a planetarium with a whispering gallery underneath. The centre also houses a contemporary art museum (**Museu**

Fortaleza

de Arte Contemporânea do Ceará) ① *T3488 8617, www.dragaodomar.org.br, Tue-Thu 1000-1730, Fri-Sun 1400-2130, US$0.75 for entry to each museum/gallery, free on Sun.* This area is very lively at night (see Entertainment below).

Fortaleza has 25 km of beaches, many of which are the scene of the city's nightlife; those between Barra do Ceará (west) and Ponta do Mucuripe (east) are polluted. **Praia de Iracema** is one of the older beach suburbs with some original turn-of-the-century houses. East of Iracema, the **Avenida Beira Mar** (Avenida Presidente Kennedy) connects **Praia do Meireles** with Volta da Jurema and **Praia do Mucuripe**, 5 km from the centre. Fortaleza's main fishing centre, jangadas, bring in the catch here. **Praia do Futuro**, 8 km southeast of the centre, is the most popular bathing beach, 8 km long, unpolluted, with strong waves, sand dunes and fresh-water showers, but no natural shade; there are many vendors and barracas serving local dishes. Thursday night, Saturday and Sunday are very busy. A city bus marked 'P Futuro' from Praça Castro Carreira, 'Praia Circular', does a circular route to Praia do Futuro; a bus marked 'Caça e Pesca' passes all southeast beaches on its route. Praia do Futuro has few hotels or buildings because the salt-spray corrosion is among the strongest in the world. About 29 km southeast of the centre is **Praia Porto das Dunas**, popular for watersports including surfing; the main attraction is **Beach Park** *US$25*, a water park.

Northwest of the centre is **Praia Barra do Ceará**, 8 km, where the Rio Ceará flows into the sea. Here are the ruins of the 1603 Forte de Nossa Senhora dos Prazeres, the first Portuguese settlement in the area. The beaches west of the Rio Ceará are cleaner, lined with palms and have strong waves. A new bridge across this river gives better access to this area, for example, **Praia de Icaraí**, 22 km, and **Tabuba**, 5 km further north. Beyond Tabuba, 37 km from Fortaleza, is **Cumbuco**, a lively beach, dirty in high season, chaotic bars, horse riding, dunes which you can sandboard down into a rainwater lake, palm trees.

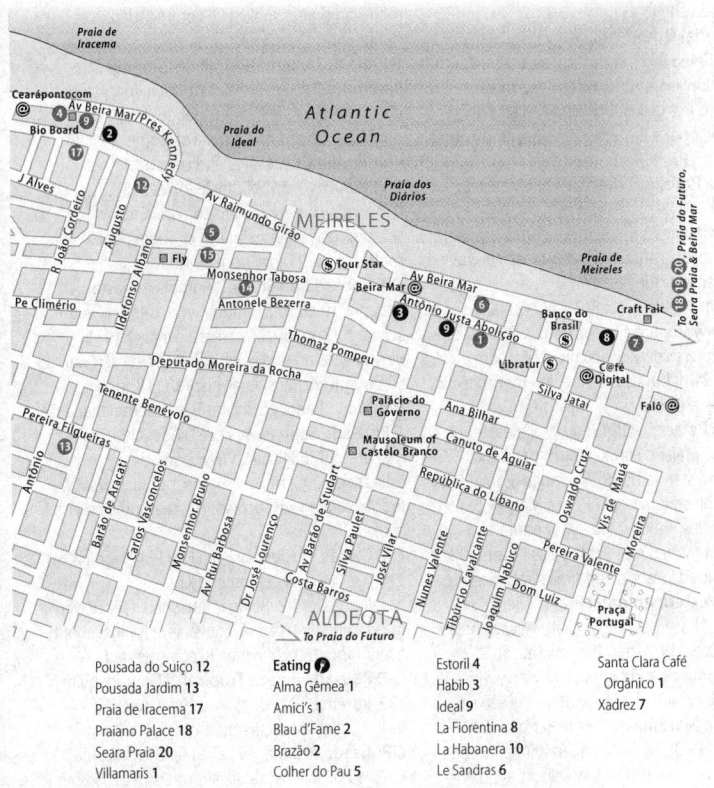

Pousada do Suíço 12	**Eating** ❼	Estoril 4	Santa Clara Café
Pousada Jardim 13	Alma Gêmea 1	Habib 3	Orgânico 1
Praia de Iracema 17	Amici's 1	Ideal 9	Xadrez 7
Praiano Palace 18	Blau d'Fame 2	La Fiorentina 8	
Seara Praia 20	Brazão 2	La Habanera 10	
Villamaris 1	Colher do Pau 5	Le Sandras 6	

Brazil Fortaleza

Fortaleza *p517, map p518*

Almost all hotels offer reduced prices in the low season. There are many pousadas in the Iracema/ Meireles area, but they change frequently.

In the centre

C Caxambu, Gen Bezerril 22, T226 6656. Reduction in low season. a/c, TV, fridge, room service, with breakfast, probably best bet in centre (opposite Cathedral), good value.

D Passeio, R Dr João Moreira 221, Centro, T226 9640, F253 6165. Opposite Passeio Público (which is not so enticing when the prostitutes are about) and near Centro Turismo, homely, rooms with high ceilings, a/c or fan, gloomy passages, good value.

E pp Backpackers, R Dom Manuel 89, T3091 8997. Central, basic, shared bathrooms, no breakfast, helpful owner.

E Big, Gen Sampaio 485, on Praça da Estação in centre, T212 2066. All rooms with fan, cheaper without TV, even cheaper without bath, simple breakfast, OK, but caution needed at night, right in thick of the central scrum.

By the beach

LL-L Imperial Othon Palace, Av Beira Mar 2500, Meireles, T3466 5500, www.othon.com.br. Beach front location, large hotel with all facilities common to this group, business and tourists catered for, pool, sauna, massage (recommended feijoada on Sat).

LL-L Seara Praia, Av Beira Mar 3080, Meireles, T4011 2200, www.hotel seara.com.br. 30% cheaper in low season, smart, comfortable luxury hotel with pool, gym, cyber café, French cuisine.
    In the same group are:
L Beira Mar, Av Beira Mar 3130, T3242 5000, Meireles, www.hotelbeiramar.com.br. Some rooms seafront, others side view, comfortable rooms, safe, pool, 24-hr business centre (internet), parking, good value, especially in low season.

L Praiano Palace, Av BM 2800, Meireles, T4008 2200, www.praiano.com.br. Much the same services and standards, but not quite as luxurious, opposite the craft fair. And **Ponta Mar**, Av BM 2200, Meireles, T4006 2200, www.ponta mar.com.br. Aimed more at the business market, but still a good location and similar facilities.

AL Best Western Colonial Praia, R Barão de Aracati 145, Iracema, T4005 4644, www.colonial praiahotel.com.br. 4-star, **B** in low season, pleasant grounds and big pool, low-rise, which is unusual, popular with families, laundry service.

AL-A Agua Marinha, Av Almte Barroso 701, Iracema, T219 0303, www.aguamarinha hotel.com.br. Less 10% in low season, a/c, TV, room safe, fridge and generally comfortable, pool, internet.

A-C Alfa Residence, Av Mons Tabosa 1320, Meireles, T248 2020. Associated with Coimbra Residence Flat, Prime Plus car hire, all in same block. Apartments with a/c, TV, fridge, unfussy but welcoming, can use pool and sauna at Coimbra.

A Ibis, Atualpa Barbosa de Lima 660, Iracema, T3219 2121, www.accorhotels.com.br. Breakfast extra, in Accor style, with usual facilities, pool.

B Abrolhos Praia, Av Abolição 2030, Meireles, T/F248 1217. Pleasant, TV, fridge, hot shower, a/c, rooms a bit spare but no different from others in this category, soft beds, discount in low season, 1 block from beach, internet.

B Pousada Icaraí, Praia Icaraí, just before town on curve in road, T0xx85-318 2000. English/Brazilian owners, ask for Fiona. A good out-of-town base with beautiful gardens, lots of budgerigars flying free, pools, restaurant, near beach and bus to Fortaleza.

B Pousada Jardim, Idelfonso Albano 950, Aldeota, T226 9711, www.hoteljardim.com.br. No sign outside, nice garden, excursions arranged, many languages spoken. Recommended, 20% discount for Handbook users.

B Praia de Iracema, Raimundo Girão 430, Iracema, T219 2299. 20% discount in low season, a/c, TV, fridge, safe in room, coffee shop, pool, brightly coloured bed covers, on corner so traffic outside, but OK for value and comfort.

B Villamaris, Av Abolição 2026, Meireles, T248 0112, www.hotelvillamaris.com.br. **C** in low season, cosy, security guard, TV, fridge, small rooftop pool, 1 block from beach.

B-C Pousada do Suiço, R Antônia Augusto 141, Iracema, T9992 9481 (mob), www.pension-vom-schweizer.com.br/. Must reserve mid-Oct-Feb. Very private, no sign, quiet street, variety of rooms, some with kitchens, small pool, a/c, TV, fridge, Swiss run, changes cash and TCs. Recommended.

C Pousada Salinas, Av Zezé Diogo 3300, Praia do Futuro, T3234 3626, www.pousada salinas.com.br. **D** in low season, popular, a/c, TV, fridge, parking, just across from sea, some English spoken.

C-D Ondas Verdes, Av Beira Mar 934, Iracema, T219 0871, www.centernet.psi.br/ hotelondasverdes. Being refurbished, fan, TV, very good value for location, convenient for just about everything, French owner. Recommended.

C-D Pousada Beleza Tropical, R Dom Joaquim 132, Iracema, T219 0515. a/c, hot water, TV, fridge, breakfast by the pool, good.

C Pousada Atalaia, Av Beira Mar 814, Iracema, T/F3219 0755, www.atalaiahostel.com.br. Hostel,

E in dormitory, a/c, fan, TV, good breakfast, prices fall in low season.

D Albergue Praia de Iracema, Av Almte Barroso 998, T3219 3267, www.aldeota.com/albergue. Basic hostel but busy, helpful staff.

Camping Barra Encantada, Praia do Barro Preto, Iguape, 42 km southeast (reservations in Fortaleza, T370 1173), US$9 pp, Camping Club members US$4 pp, see Eastern Coast below.

Fazenda Lagoa das Dunas, Uruaú (115 km southeast), T244 2929, US$4 pp Camping Club members, US$9 pp others; also rents rooms.

Fortaleza Camping Club, R Pedro Paulo Moreira 505, Parque Manibura, Água Fria, 12 km, T273 2544, many trees for shade, US$7 pp.

🍴 Eating

Fortaleza p517, map p518
Centre
There are several options around and in the railway station.

♥♥♥ Xadrez, Emcetur restaurant, in the old prison. Good atmosphere, overpriced, open to 2400, reported safe to 2100.

♥ Alivita, Barão do Rio Branco 1486. Good for fish and vegetarian, lunch only, Mon-Fri.

♥ Fonte de Saúde, R Pedro 339. Excellent vegetarian food, sold by weight, and a wide range of fruit juices.

Iracema and Dragão do Mar
Two good areas for places to eat, with plenty of variety. There are many eating places of various styles at the junction of Tabajaras and Tremembés, mostly smart.

♥♥ Alma Gêmea, R Dragão do Mar 30. Bar and restaurant with good atmosphere by the cultural centre.

♥♥ Amici's, R Dragão do Mar 80. Pasta, pizza and lively atmosphere in music-filled street, evenings only. Some say it's the best at the cultural centre.

♥♥ Colher do Pau, R Tabajaras 412, Iracema. Opens daily at 1830, sertaneja food, seafood, indoor and outdoor seating, live music. Recommended.

♥♥ Estoril, R dos Tabajaras 397, Iracema. Varied food in this landmark restaurant, which is also a restaurant school.

♥ Blau d'Fame, R João Cordeiro 41, Iracema. Good self-service, serving lunch much later than others, especially on Sat.

♥ Brazão, R João Cordeiro corner of Av R Girão, Iracema, next to Blau d'Fame. The only place open 24 hrs, but the food is not that special.

Urban beaches
Several good fish restaurants at Praia de Mucuripe, where the boats come ashore

between 1300 and 1500. Rua J Ibiapina, at the Mucuripe end of Meireles, 1 block behind beach, has pizzerias, fast food restaurants and sushi bars.

♥♥♥-♥♥ La Fiorentina, Osvaldo Cruz 8, corner of Av Beira Mar, Meireles. Some seafood expensive, but fish, meats, pasta, unpretentious, attentive waiters, good food, frequented by tourists and locals alike.

♥♥♥-♥♥ Le Sandras, Av Santos Dumont 938, Aldeota. Successor to Sandras of Praia do Futuro. Brightly painted old building, cool yellow inside, tasteful, elegant with outdoor, indoor and a/c seating, garden, French-trained owner, novo cearanse and Mediterranean cooking, lobster still a speciality, good food.

♥ Churrascaria Picanha de Veras, R Carlos Vasconcelos 660, Aldeota. Good for chicken.

♥ Dom Pastel, R Carlos Vasconcelos 996, Aldeota. Pay-by-weight.

♥ Habib, Av Abolição, corner with Av Barão de Studart, Meireles (and other branches). Modern middle-eastern fast-food restaurant, excellent service, set menus are a bargain, good deserts. Recommended.

♥ Ideal, Av Abolição e José Vilar, Meireles. Open 0530-2030, bakery serving lunches, small supermarket and deli, good, handy.

Out of town
♥♥♥ Carneiro de Ordones, R Azevedo Bolão 571, Parquelândia, near North Shopping. Crowded with locals at weekends for every kind of lamb dish.

Lá na Roça, opposite the church, in the district of Eusébio. Excellent *sertaneja* restaurant, very popular on Sun, pay by weight, go early to be sure of a table – all local dishes and sweets. Eusébio is reached from the CE 040, the road to Iguape and Aquiraz. On this road out of the city is the best place for tapioca shacks. As well as the rough traditional shacks, there is a whole complex for tapioca sellers at the Estrada do Fio.

Fazenda do Joe, T0xx85-260 1610. One of several country restaurants. German, open for lunch weekends and holidays only, also sells German breads and sausages. Has a pousada too.

Casa de Farinha, CE 040 Km 13. Mon-Fri 1100-1500 à la carte only, Sat, Sun and holidays 1100-1800 self-service *sertaneja* food, very good. It is also a working cassava/manioc mill and museum so you can see the whole process of making tapioca. A good place to take kids, plenty of games for them.

Delicias de Cana, Km 18. A working sugar mill, selling rapa dura flavoured with fruits and nuts (cashew – of course, sesame).

La Habanera, Praça da Igreja in Iracema, Av Beira Mar e Ararius. Café, wicker chairs, marble tables, old photos of Fidel, Che, et al, coffee and cigars.

Santa Clara Café Orgânico, R Dragão do Mar 81, at end of red girder walkway (or upstairs depending which way you go), www.santa clara.com.br. Café, delicious organic coffees, juices, cold drinks, plus sandwiches and desserts.

☾ Bars and clubs

Fortaleza *p517, map p518*
Fortaleza is renowned for its nightlife and prides itself with having the liveliest Mon night in the country. *Forró* is the most popular dance and there is a tradition to visit certain establishments on specific nights. **Mon** Forró is danced at the **Pirata Bar**, Iracema, US$5, open-air theme bar, from 2300, and other establishments along R dos Tabajaras and its surroundings. **Tue** Live golden oldies at **Boate Oásis**, Av Santos Dumont 6061, Aldeota.
Wed Regional music and samba-reggae at **Clube do Vaqueiro**, city bypass, Km 14, by BR-116 south and E-020, at 2230. **Thu** Live music, shows and crab specialities at the beach shacks in Praia do Futuro, **Chico do Caranguejo**, lively bar with some sex tourism. Also recommended for crab is **Atlântico**. For music, Rebu (traditional) and Vila Galé (for tourists). **Fri** Singers and bands play regional music at **Parque do Vaqueiro**, BR-020, Km 10, past city bypass. **Sat** Forró at **Parque Valeu Boi**, R Trezópolis, Cajueiro Torto, **Forró Três Amores**, Estrado Tapuio, Eusébio and **Cantinho do Céu**, CE-04, Km 8. **Sun** Forró and música sertaneja at **Cajueiro Drinks**, BR-116, Km 20, Eusébio.

Some of the best areas for entertainment, with many bars and restaurants are: the Av Beira Mar, Praia de Iracema, the hill above Praia de Mucuripe and Av Dom Luís. The streets around Centro Cultural Dragão do Mar on R Dragão do Mar are lively every night of the week. Brightly painted, historic buildings house restaurants where musicians play to customers and the pavements are dotted with cocktail carts.
Caros Amigos, R Dragão do Mar, 22. Live music at 2030: Tue, Brazilian instrumental; Wed, jazz; Thu, samba; Sun, Beatles covers, $US1 (also shows music on the big screen).
Restaurant e Crêperie Café Crème, R Dragão do Mar 92, live music on Tue.

❀ Festivals and events

Fortaleza *p517, map p518*
6 Jan, Epiphany; Ash Wednesday. 19 Mar, São José; Christmas Eve; New Year's Eve, half-day. The **Festas Juninas** in Ceará are much livelier than carnival. A festival, the **Regata Dragão do Mar**, takes place at Praia de Mucuripe on the last Sun in **Jul**, during which the traditional jangada (raft) races take place. Also during the last week of Jul, the out-of-season Salvador-style carnival, **Fortal**, takes place along Avs Almte Barroso, Raimundo Giro and Beira Mar. On **15 Aug**, the

local Umbanda terreiros (churches) celebrate the **Festival of Iemanjá** on Praia do Futuro, taking over the entire beach from noon till dusk, when offerings are cast into the surf. Well worth attending (members of the public may 'pegar um passo' – enter into an inspired religious trance – at the hands of a pai-de-santo). For 4 days in **mid-Oct** Ceará Music, a festival of Brazilian music, rock and pop, is held Marina Park.

◯ Shopping

Fortaleza *p517, map p518*
Bookshops Livraria Livro Técnico, see Dragão do Mar, above, has several branches, on Dom Luís, Praça Ferreira, Shopping Norte and at UFC university. **Livraria Nobel** bookstore and coffee shop in Del Paseo shopping centre in Aldeota. **Siciliano**, bookstore and coffee shop in new part of Iguatemi shopping mall, with just a bookstore in the old part.
Handicrafts Fortaleza has an excellent selection of locally manufactured textiles, which are among the cheapest in Brazil, and a wide selection of regional handicrafts. The local craft specialities are lace and embroidered textile goods; also hammocks (US$15 to over US$100), fine alto-relievo wood carvings of northeast scenes, basket ware, leatherwork and clay figures (*bonecas de barro*). Bargaining is OK at the **Mercado Central**, Av Alberto Nepomuceno (closed Sun), and the **Emcetur Centro de Turismo** in the old prison (see above). Crafts also available in shops near the market, while shops on R Dr João Moreira 400 block sell clothes. Every night (1800-2300) there are stalls along the beach at Praia Meireiles. Crafts also available in the commercial area along Av Monsenhor Tabosa.
Shopping centres The biggest is **Iguatemi**, south of Meireles on way to Centro de Convenções; it also has modern cinemas. Others are **Aldeota** and **Del Paseo** in Aldeota, near Praça Portugal.

▲ Activities and tours

Fortaleza *p517, map p518*
Diving Projeto Netuno/Manta Diving Center, R Oswaldo Cruz 2453, Dionísio Torres, T3264 4114, www.pnetuno.com.br.
Surfing Surfing is popular on a number of Ceará beaches. Kite surfing also catching on.
Trekking The Fortaleza chapter of the Trekking Club do Brasil has walks once a month to different natural areas; visitors welcome, US$20 for transport and T-shirt, T212 2456.
Windsurfing A number of Ceará beaches are excellent for windsurfing. Equipment can be rented in some of the popular beaches such as Porto das Dunas and in the city. **Bio Board**, Av

Beira Mar 914, T3242 1642, www.bio
board.com.br. Looks after equipment for you,
windsurf school, Açaizeiro Café with açaí, juices,
sandwiches upstairs (opens 1000 till 2000, 1900
Sat, 1800 Sun), also travel agency. **Windclub**, Av
Beira Mar 2120, Praia dos Diários, T9982 5449.
Equipment rental, lessons also available.

Tour operators
Many operators offer city and beach tours. Others
offer adventure trips further afield, most common
being off-road trips along the beaches from Natal
in the east to the Lençois Maranhenses in the west.
Ceará Saveiro, Av Beira Mar 4293, T263 1085.
Saveiro and yacht trips, daily 1000-1200 and
1600-1800 from Praia de Mucuripe.
Dunnas Expedições, R Silva Paulet 1100, Aldeota,
T3264 2514, www.dunnas.com.br. Off-road tours
with a fleet of white Land Rover Defenders,
experienced, environmentally and culturally aware,
very helpful and professional staff. Recommended.
Martur, Av Beira Mar 4260, T263 1203. Sailing
boat and schooner trips, from Mucuripe, same
schedule as Ceará Saveiro.
Sunny Tour, Av Prof A Nunes Freire 4097,
Dionísio Torres, T0xx85-9986 5689, also has a
bus-cum-stand on Av Beira Mar near the craft fair.
Offers beach tours (eg 3 in 1 day, 6 in 4 days, trips
to Jericoacoara).

⊖ Transport

Fortaleza *p517, map p518*
Air Aeroporto Pinto Martins, Praça Eduardo
Gomes, 6 km south of centre, T3477 1200. Airport
has a tourist office, T477 1667, car hire, food hall
upstairs, small internet facility at US$3 per hr,
Laselva bookstore and Banco do Brasil (changes
cash, US$20 commission on TCs, open 1100-1500).
Direct flights to major cities. Bus 404 from airport
to Praça José de Alencar in the centre, US$0.80,
also 066 Papicu to Parangaba and 027 Papicu to
Siqueira, or luxury Guanabara service from Beira
Mar via Iracema, a/c, US$1; taxis US$12 to centre,
Av Beira Mar or Praia do Futuro, more at night
depending on destination. Use Cooperativa Taxi
Comum or Taxi Especial Credenciado.
Bus Rodoviária at Av Borges de Melo 1630,
Fátima, 6 km south from centre, T256 2100, info
T256 4080 or 24-hr Disque Turismo. Many city
buses (US$0.80) including 'Aguanambi' 1 or 2
which go from Av Gen Sampaio, 'Barra de
Fátima-Rodoviária' from Praça Coração de Jesus,
'Circular' for Av Beira Mar and the beaches, and
'Siqueira Mucuripe' from Av Abolição. Taxi to
Praia de Iracema, or Av Abolição US$7.50. There is
a luggage store. Opposite the rodoviária is Hotel
Amuarama, which has a bar and restaurant;
there's also a lanchonete.

Nordeste: To **Mossoró**, 10 a day, US$10.50,
Natal, 8 daily, US$23, semi-leito, US$33
executivo, US$53 leito, 7½ hrs. **João Pessoa**, 2
daily, US$35 semi-leito, US$48 leito, 10 hrs. **Boa
Esperança**, stops at Fortaleza on its Belém-Natal
route only. **Itapemirim** to **Salvador**, US$77,
1900, 23 hrs. **Guanabara**, T256 0214, to **Recife**, 5
daily, US$39 executivo, US$52 leito, 12 hrs, book
early for weekend travel. **Guanabara** to
Teresina, several daily, US$27, leito US$47, 10
hrs; to **Parnaíba** US$24; to **Belém**, 2 daily, US$65
executivo, 23 hrs. **Piripiri**, for **Parque Nacional
de Sete Cidades**, US$20, 9 hrs, a good stop en
route to Belém, also Guanabara, who go to **São
Luís**, 3 daily, US$44, 18 hrs.
   In Ceará: Guanabara to **Sobral** US$7, **Ubajara**
0800, 1800, return 0800, 1600, 6 hrs, US$11. Also
Ipu Brasília to **Sobral** US$12.25, and to
Camocim 1120, 1530. To **Majorlândia**, US$5.

⊙ Directory

Fortaleza *p517, map p518*
Airline offices BRA, T3261 1919, at airport
T3477 1423. **TAM**, Av Santos Dumont 2849,
Aldeota, T261 0916, T0800-570 5700. **Trip**, at
airport T3477 1747 **Varig**, at airport, T3477 1720.
Banks Banco do Nordeste, R Major Facundo
372, a/c, helpful, open 0900-1630.
Recommended. TCs exchanged and cash with
Visa at **Banco do Brasil**, R Barão do Rio Branco
1500, also on Av Abolição (high commission on
TCs). **Banco Mercantil do Brasil**, Rua Major
Facundo 484, Centro, Praca do Ferreira: cash
against MasterCard. Cirrus/MasterCard ATM at
international airport; others at **HSBC** and **Banco
24 Horas** throughout the city. ATM for Cirrus/
MasterCard and Visa outside cinema at Centro
Cultural Dragão do Mar. Also at Av Antonio Sales
and Iguatemi Shopping. Exchange at **Tropical
Viagens**, R Barão do Rio Branco 1233, **Libratur**,
Av Abolição 2194, open 0900-1800 Mon-Fri,
0800-1200 Sat; also has kiosk outside Othon hotel
on Av Beira Mar which is open every day till 2300.
Recommended. More câmbios on Av Mons
Tabosa: eg **TourStar**, No 1587, **Sdoc**, No 1073.
Car hire Many car hire places on Av
Monsenhor Taboso, eg **Shop**, No 1181, T219
7788, **Reta**, No 1171, T219 5555, **Amazônia**, No
1055, T219 0800/9983 2796, and many more at
the junction with Ildefonso Albano. **Brasil Rent a
Car**, Av Abolição 2300, T0xx85-3242 0868. There
are also many buggy rental shops. **Note**: When
driving outside the city, have a good map and be
prepared to ask directions frequently as road
signs are non-existent, or placed after junctions.
Embassies and consulates Belgium,
R Eduardo Garcia 909, Aldeota, T3091 5185,
consulbelce@ig.com.br. **France**, R João Cordeiro

831, Iracema, T3226 3470. **Germany**, R Dr Lourenço 2244, Meireles, T3246 2833, DghonkonsulBRD@aol.com. **Italy**, Rua M Dibe 80, Parque Wáshington Soares, T273 2606. **Netherlands**, R Dom Luis 880, T461 2331, consuladoholanda@tradetec.com.br. **Sweden** and **Norway**, R Leonardo Mota 501, Aldeota, T242 0888, marcos@emitrade.com.br. **Switzerland**, R Dona Leopoldina 697, Centro, T226 9444. **UK**, R Leonardo Mota, 501, Meireles, T3242 0888, annette@edsonqueiroz.com.br. **US**, Av Santos Dumont 2828, sala 708, T3486 1306. **Internet** Many internet cafés around the city. **Beira Mar Internet Café**, Av Beira Mar 2120A, Meireles, open 0800-0200, US$2.60 per hr (discounts with receipt from Habib's), also international phones, coffee. Outside Avenida Shopping, Av Dom Luís 300, US$2.50 per hr. **Abrolhos Praia**, Av Abolição 2030, Meireles, part of hotel of same name, US$1.25 per hr, open daily0800-2000, closes 1400 Sat and all day Sun. **Cyber Net**, Av Beira Mar 3120 in small mall, smart, US$2.20 per hr. **Ligue.com**, Osvaldo Cruz in Beiramar Trade Center. **Cearápontocom**, Av Beira Mar e R dos Ararius, across from La Habanera. US$3 per hr, popular, cafés around it. **Internet Express**, R Barão de Aracati opposite Colonial Praia, opens 0800. Via Veneto Flat, Av Abolição 2324, has **C@fé Digital**, open to the public, US$2.25 per hr, open Sun evening. 2 doors from Pousada Casa Nossa is **Falô**, Av Abolição 2600 block, 0800-2000 daily, US$1.50 per hr, also phones. Others in Pôlo Comercial at Av Mons Tabosa e Ildefonso Albano. **Medical services** Instituto Dr José Frota (IJF), R Barão do Rio Branco 1618, T255 5000. Recommended public hospital. **Post offices** Main branch at R Senador Alencar 38, Centro; Av Monsenhor Tabosa 1109 and 1581, Iracema; at train station; opposite rodoviária. Parcels must be taken to Receita Federal office at Barão de Aracati 909, Aldeota (take 'Dom Luiz' bus). **Telephones** International calls from **Emcetur** hut on Iracema beach and from offices of **Telemar**; at rodoviária and airport.

Coast east of Fortaleza

Aquiraz, 31 km east of Fortaleza, first capital of Ceará which conserves several colonial buildings and has a religious art museum, is the access point for the following beaches: **Prainha**, 6 km east, a fishing village and 10 km long beach with dunes, clean and largely empty. You can see jangadas coming in daily in the late afternoon. The village is known for its lacework: you can see the women using the bilro and labirinto techniques at the **Centro de Rendeiras**. 18 km southeast of Aquiraz is **Praia Iguape**, another fishing and lacework village, 3 km south of which is **Praia Barro Preto**, wide, tranquil, with sand dunes, palms and lagoons. All these beaches have accommodation.

Cascavel (*Colour map 5, grid B5*), 62 km southeast of Fortaleza (Saturday crafts fair), is the access point for the beaches of **Caponga** and **Águas Belas**, where traditional fishing villages coexist with fancy weekend homes and hotels.

Some 4 km from **Beberibe**, 78 km from Fortaleza, is **Morro Branco**, with a spectacular beach, coloured craggy cliffs and beautiful views. Jangadas leave the beach at 0500, returning at 1400-1500, lobster is the main catch in this area. The coloured sands of the dunes are bottled into beautiful designs and sold along with other crafts such as lacework, embroidery and straw goods. Jangadas may be hired for sailing (one hr for up to six people US$30). Beach buggies (full day US$100) and taxis are also for hire. The beach can get very crowded at holiday times. There re pousadas, or you can rent fishermen's houses. Meals can also be arranged at beach-front bars. South of Morro Branco and 6 km from Beberibe is **Praia das Fontes**, which also has coloured cliffs with sweet-water springs; there is a fishing village and a lagoon. South of Praia das Fontes are several less developed beaches including **Praia Uruaú** or **Marambaia**. The beach is at the base of coloured dunes, there is a fishing village with some accommodation. Just inland is Lagoa do Uruaú, the largest in the state and a popular place for watersports. Buggy from Morro Branco US$45 for four.

Canoa Quebrada → *Colour map 5, grid B5. Visit www.canoa-quebrada.com.*

On the shores of the Rio Jaguaribe, **Aracati** is the access point to the southeastern-most beaches of Ceará; it is along the main BR-304. The city is best known for its Carnival and for its colonial architecture.

About 10 km from Aracati is Canoa Quebrada on a sand dune, famous for its labirinto lacework and coloured sand sculpture, for sand-skiing on the dunes, for the sunsets, and for the beaches. There are many bars, restaurants and forró establishments. Canoa Quebrada is beginning to suffer from unplanned development. To avoid biting insects (bicho do pé), wear shoes. There is nowhere to change money except Banco do Brasil in Aracati. In the second half of July the Canoarte Festival takes place, it includes a jangada regatta and music festival. South of Canoa Quebrada and 13 km from Aracati is **Majorlândia**, an attractive village, with many-coloured sand dunes and a wide beach with strong waves, good for surfing; the arrival of the fishing fleet in the evening is an important daily event; lobster is the main catch. It is a popular weekend destination with beach homes for rent and Carnaval here is lively.

Community tourism Some 120 km east of Fortaleza, in the district of Beberibe, is **Prainha do Canto Verde**, a small fishing village on the vast beach, which has an award-winning community tourism project. There are guesthouses (eg **E Dona Mirtes**, with breakfast, will negotiate other meals), houses for rent (**D Casa Cangulo**, or **Vila Marésia**), restaurants (good food at Sol e Mar), a handicraft cooperative, jangada and catamaran cruises, fishing and walking trails. Each November there is a Regata Ecológica, with jangadas from up and down the coast competing. (For the regatta, Christmas and Semana Santa, add 30% to prices.) This is a simple place, which lives by artesanal fishing (ie no big boats or industrial techniques) and has built up its tourism infrastructure without any help from outside investors (they have been fighting the speculators since 1979). It's a very friendly place and foreigners are welcome to get to know how the fisher folk live; knowledge of Portuguese is essential. For information on Prainha do Canto Verde, contact **René Schärer** ① *Toxx88-413 1426, fishnet@ uol.com.br*, Swiss, also speaks English, or **Lagomar** *Toxx85 9608 8222*. The tourism coordinator is **Antônio Aires** *www.fortalnet.com.br/~fishnet*. To get to Prainha do Canto Verde, take a São Benedito bus to Aracati or Canoa Quebrada, buy a ticket to Quatro Bocas and ask to be let off at Lagoa da Poeira, two hours from Fortaleza. If you haven't booked a transfer in advance, Márcio at the Pantanal restaurant at the bus stop will take you, US$3.65.

    Ponta Grossa is near Icapuí, the last municipality before Rio Grande do Norte (access from Mossoró), from where you then head to Redonda. Ponta Grossa is down a sand road just before Redonda. Both Ponta Grossa and Redonda are very pretty places, nestled at the foot of the cliffs, but Ponta Grossa has its own community tourism development. One of the main attractions of Ponta Grossa is that, offshore, is one of the few places where manatees (peixe boi marinho) visit. You can try to spot them from the cliffs. Beach trips go from Canoa Quebrada to Ponta Grossa for lunch, but if you want to stay here, you need to speak Portuguese. Cabins for rent are under construction and there are restaurants/bars. The tourism coordinator is **Eliabe** ① *Toxx88-432 5001, or 9964 5846*.

    For further information on community tourism and the preservation of traditional ways of life in Ceará, contact **Instituto Terramar** ① *R Pinho Pessoa 86, Joaquim Távora, Fortaleza, Toxx85-3226 4154, www.terramar.org.br*.

⬤ **Sleeping** → *See Telephone, page 347, for important phone changes.*

Canoa Quebrada *p524*
There are several pousadas in town. Villagers will let you sling your hammock or put you up cheaply (Verónica recommended, European books exchanged; Sr Miguel rents good clean houses for US$10 a day).
B Pousada Sete Mares, R Quatro Ventos 400, T3368 2247, www.pousada7mares hpg.com.br. A recommended pousada with a/c chalets, pool.
C Pousada California, R Nascer do Sol 136, T3421 7039, www.californiacanoa.com. Prices vary according to room and season, a/c, **E** pp in dorm, TV, pool, bar, internet, buggy tours, horse riding, kite surfing, book exchange, several languages spoken, use of kitchen.
C Pousada Lua Morena, R Principal, T3421 7030, www.canoaquebrada.com. A variety of chalets with direct access to beach, with a/c,

fridge, TV, hot water, pool, good value, English, Dutch and German spoken.
C Pousada Quebramar, on the beach front, T416 1044. With breakfast, safe, hot water.
D-E Pousada Alternativa, R Francisco Caraço, T3421 7276, www.geocities.com/ pousadaalternativa. Rooms with a/c and bath, cheaper with fan and without fridge, central, safe.

⬤ **Transport**

Coast east of Fortaleza *p524*
Bus Daily bus service from Fortaleza rodoviária to **Prainha**, 11 daily, US$1.30; **Iguape**, hourly between 0600 and 1900, US$1.50. To **Caponga**: direct bus from Fortaleza rodoviária (4 a day, US$1.70) or take a bus from Fortaleza to Cascavel (80 mins) then a bus from Cascavel (20

mins). For bus information in Fortaleza, São Benedito, T272 2544, at rodoviária: to **Beberibe**, 10 a day, US$2.65; **Cascavel**, US$1.50; **Morro Branco**, 0745, 1000, 1515, 1750, US$3; **Canoa Quebrada**, 0830, 1100, 1340, 1540 (plus 1730 Sun), US$5.65; **Aracati**, 0630, 0830, 1100, 1340, 1540, 1900, last back at 1800, US$5.20.

Natal-Aracati bus via Mossoró, 6 hrs, US$10; from Mossoró (90 km) US$3.20, 2 hrs; **Fortaleza**-Aracati (142 km), besides São Benedito, Guanabara or Nordeste many daily, US$5, 2 hrs; Aracati-**Canoa Quebrada** from Gen Pompeu e João Paulo, US$0.90; taxi US$4.20.

Coast west of Fortaleza

Paracuru, a fishing port which has the most important Carnaval on the northwest coast, is two hours by bus from Fortaleza. West of Paracuru, about 120 km from Fortaleza and 12 km from the town of Paraipaba, is **Lagoinha**, a very scenic beach, with cliffs, dunes and palms by the shore; a fishing village is on one of the hills.

Some seven hours by bus and 230 km from Fortaleza is the sleepy fishing village of **Almofala**, home of the Tremembés Indians who live off the sea and some agriculture. There is electricity, but no hotels or restaurants, although locals rent hammock space and cook meals. Bathing is better elsewhere, but the area is surrounded by dunes and is excellent for hiking along the coast to explore beaches and lobster-fishing communities. In Almofala, the church with much of the town was covered by shifting sands and remained covered for 50 years, reappearing in the 1940s; it has since been restored. There is also a highly praised turtle project.

Jijoca de Jericoacoara (Gijoca) is near the south shore of scenic Lagoa Paraíso (or Lagoa Jijoca), the second largest in the state. There are pousadas on its shore. It is excellent for windsurfing as it has a "comfortable" wind, very good for beginners and those gaining experience (Jericoacoara is for 'professionals'). There is also good for kite surfing. **Note**: The low season, August to November, is the windy season.

Jijoca is one of the access points for **Jericoacoara**, or 'Jeri' (*Phone code*: oxx88). One of the most famous beaches of Ceará and all Brazil (if not the world), it has towering sand dunes, deserted beaches with little shade, cactus-covered cliffs rising from the sea and interesting rock formations. The most famous is the **Pedra Furada**, a rock arch by the sea. Its atmosphere has made it popular with Brazilian and international travellers, with crowds at weekends mid-December to mid-February, in July and during Brazilian holidays. Many places full in low season, too. Jericoacoara is part of an environmental protection area which includes a large coconut grove, lakes, dunes and hills covered in caatinga vegetation. The village east of Jeri, **Preá**, is much quieter, with simple fish restaurants (see Transport, below).

Parnaíba → *Phone code: 0xx86. Post code: 64200. Colour map 5, grid A4. Population: 132,282.*
Parnaíba is a relaxed, friendly place, with a regular connection here to Tutóia, for boats across the Parnaíba delta (see page 526). A tour in the delta costs US$25 per person. Porto das Barcas, a pleasant shopping and entertainment complex, has several good restaurants and a large open-air bar on the riverside. The tourist office, **Piemtur**, is at R Dr Oscar Clark 575 and at Porto das Barcas, T321 1532.

Parque Nacional Lençóis Maranhenses → *Colour map 5, grid A3.*
Crossing the Parnaíba delta, which separates Piauí from Maranhão, is possible by boat arriving in Tutóia: an interesting trip through swamps sheltering many birds. This truly amazing park has 155,000 ha of beaches, lakes and dunes, with very little vegetation and largely unstudied wildlife. It is a strange landscape of shifting white dunes, stretching about 140 km along the coast between **Tutóia** and Primeira Cruz, west of **Barreirinhas**. The best time to visit is during the rainy season (June-September), when the dune valleys fill with water. Reflections of the sky make the water appear vivid blue, a spectacular contrast against brilliant white sand. **Parque Nacional Lençóis Maranhenses** ① *national park office: Av Joaquim Soeiro de Carvalho 746, CEP 65590-000, Barreirinhas, Toxx98-349 1155.* Ribamar at **Ibama**, Avenida Jaime Tavares 25, São Luís, T231 3010, is helpful on walks and horse rides.

São Luís → *Phone code: 0xx98. Post code: 65000. Colour map 5, grid A3. Population: 870,028.*

The capital of Maranhão state, 1,070 km west of Fortaleza, founded in 1612 by the French and named after St Louis of France, is in a region of heavy tropical rains, but the surrounding deep forest has been cut down to be replaced by babaçu palms. It stands upon São Luís island between the bays of São Marcos and São José. The urban area extends to São Francisco island, connected with São Luís by three bridges. An old slaving port, the city has a large black population, and has retained much African culture. **São Luís**, Avenida Jaime Tavares 26B, Praia Grande, T3231 2000, R Dr Cesário Combra 129, Centro, Avenida Ana Jansen s/n. Ponta d'Areia, T3227 8484 and at the airport and rodoviária, www.turismo.ma.gov.br/pt/. Also www.guiasaoluis.com.br.

The old part, on very hilly ground with many steep streets, is still almost pure colonial. The historical centre is being restored with UNESCO support and the splendid results (eg the part known as Reviver) rival the Pelourinho of Salvador. The damp climate stimulated the use of ceramic tiles for exterior walls, and São Luís shows a greater variety of such tiles than anywhere else in Brazil, in Portuguese, French and Dutch styles. The commercial quarter (R Portugal, also called R Trapiche) is still much as it was in the 17th century. The best shopping area is R de Santana near Praça João Lisboa. There is a Funai shop at R do Sol 371 and a Centro do Artesanato in the main street of the São Francisco suburb, over the bridge from the city.

The **Palácio dos Leões** (Governor's Palace) ① *Av Dom Pedro II, free guided visits Mon, Wed and Fri 1400-1700*, has beautiful floors of dark wood (jacarandá) and light (cerejeira), French furniture and china and great views from terrace. The restored **Fortaleza de Santo Antônio**, built originally by the French in 1614, is on the bank of the Rio Anil at Ponta d'Areia. The **Fábrica Canhamo** (CEPRAMA) ① *R São Pantaleão 1232, Madre de Deus, near Praia Grande, T3232 2187, Mon-Fri 0900-1900*, a restored factory, houses an arts and crafts centre. The **Centro da Creatividade Odylo Costa Filho** ① *R da Alfândego 200, Praia Grande, T231 4058, Mon-Fri 0800-2200*, is an arts centre with theatre, cinema, exhibitions, music, a bar and café; a good meeting place.

São Luís historic centre

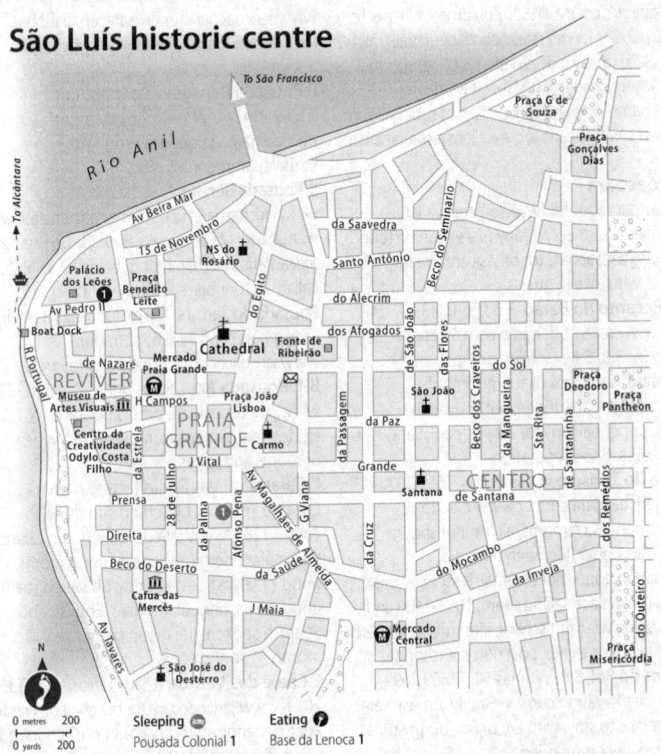

Sleeping 🛏	Eating 🍴
Pousada Colonial 1	Base da Lenoca 1

The best colonial churches are the **Cathedral** (1629) *on Praça Dom Pedro II*, and the churches of **Carmo** (1627) *Praça João Lisboa*, **São João Batista** (1665) *Largo São João*, **Nossa Senhora do Rosário** (1717) *on R do Egito*, and the 18th century **Santana** *R de Santana*. On Largo do Desterro is the church of **São José do Desterro**, finished in 1863, but with some much older parts.

The **Cafua das Mercês** ① *R Jacinto Maia 43, Mon-Fri 1330-1700*, is a museum housed in the old slave market, worth the effort to find: a building opposite the Quartel Militar. Also visit the Casa dos Negros, next door. **Museu de Artes Visuais** ① *Av Portugal 289, Mon-Fri 0800-1300, 1600-1800*, shows ceramics and post war art.

Alcântara → *Colour map 5, grid A3. Population: 21,291.*

Some 22 km away by boat is Alcântara the former state capital, on the mainland bay of São Marcos. Construction of the city began at the beginning of the 17th century and it is now a historical monument. There are many old churches, such as the ruined **Matriz de São Matias** – 1648, and colonial mansions (see the **Casa**, and **Segunda Casa, do Imperador**, also the old cotton barons' mansions with their blue, Portuguese tiled façades). In the Praça Gomes de Castro is the pillory, the **Pelourinho** (1648), also a small museum (0900-1300, US$0.25) and the **Forte de São Sebastião** (1663) now in ruins. See also the **Fonte de Mirititiua** (1747). Canoe trips go to **Ilha do Livramento**, good beaches, good walking around the coast (can be muddy after rain), mosquitoes after dark. A rocket-launching site has been built nearby.

● **Sleeping** → *See Telephone, page 347, for important phone changes.*

Coast west of Fortaleza *p526*

Jijoca de Jericoacoara

A-B Pousada do Paulo, Córrego do Urubu s/n, T0xx88-3669 1181, www.jericoacoara.tur.br/pousadadopaulo. Has a windsurf school, US$18.50 for beginner's course, US$20 equipment hire per hr, US$50 per day, longer rates negotiable. It's also a good place to stay (prices depends on season and cabin, lovely location with lake views, garden, beach, hammocks and various sizes of cabin, all very nice, some with TV and a/c; excellent restaurant, bar.

Jericoacoara

4-5-day packages for Reveillon are available, but prices rise steeply. Many places can be found on www.jericoacoara.tur.br. Ask around for families who take in guests.

LL-L Recanto do Barão, R do Forró 433, T3242 0685, www.recantodobarao.com. 21 rooms mostly for 3 to 5 (ie families, groups), nicely decorated with hibiscus theme, lots of hammocks, a/c, TV, fridge, hot shower, big rooms, upper balcony for sunset, pool, Land Rover tours. Good reputation.

A Casa do Turismo, R das Dunas, T669 2000, www.jericoacoara.com or www.casado turismo.com. Nice rooms, all a/c, hot shower, TV, some with upper floor with mattress. Information, tours, horse rental, Redenção bus tickets (only place selling them, 1030-1400 and 1730-2200), windsurf school, kite surf, sandboard rental, telephone calls, post office, exchange.

A-C Por do Sol, R das Dunas 50, T3669 2099, pordosoljeri@yahoo.com.br. Family atmosphere, lovely place to stay, with a/c or fan, buggy trips arranged. Recommended.

B Casa Nostra, R das Dunas, T3669 2035, www.jericoacoara.tur.br/casanostra/index.html. Nice rooms, good breakfast, money exchange, Italian spoken. Recommended.

B Isalana Praia, R Principal, T3660 1334, www.jericoacoara.tur.br/isalanapraiahotel/index.html. A/c, minibar, TV, very helpful, ask for Will Louzada.

B Pousada Papagaio, Beco do Forró, T3669 2142, www.jericoacoara.tur.br/pousadapapagaio/index.html. With bath, recommended, tours.

B Pousada Renata, T3669 2061, www.jericoacoara.tur.br/pousadadarenata. Owned by the sister of Fernanda at Pousada do Paulo at Jijoca. Patio with hammocks, breakfast, English, Italian and German spoken. Renata also has **Pousada do Serrote**, 100 m from Praia da Malhada, same phone, and 9961 5522 (mob), www.jericoacoara.tur. Br/pousadadoserrote.

B-C Pousada Azul, R das Dunas, T3669 2182, www.jericoacoara.tur.br/azulpousada. Under new ownership, redecorated, variety of rooms and suites.

C Calanda, R das Dunas (across from Casa do Turismo, by setting sun dune), T3669 2285, www.jericoacoara.tur.br/calanda. With solar energy, Swiss run, good rooms, good breakfast, restaurant with varied menu, good views, helpful, German, English and Spanish spoken, full moon party every month. Warmly recommended.

C Chalé dos Ventos, R São Francisco 50, T3669 2023, www.jericoacoara.tur.br/ chaledosventos. Price depends on room, chalet on 2 floors, good views, great breakfast, nice atmosphere.

C Pousada do Véio, T3669 2015, www.jericoacoara.tur.br/pousadadoveio. All rooms with a/c, bath, hot water and fan, some have a/c and fridge.

D Pousada Tirol, R São Francisco 202, T669 2006. HI-affiliated, non-members pay more, also has double rooms at **B** (**C** in low season), with breakfast, hot water, safe, helpful, great fun. Recommended. Also has very busy cyber café, US$3 per hr – 10 mins free use for all guests.

Parnaíba *p526*

LL Cívico, Av Gov Chagas Rodrigues, T322 2470, www.hotelcivico.com.br. With a/c, good breakfast. Recommended.

AL Pousada dos Ventos, Av São Sebastião 2586, Universidade, T/F323 2555, www.pousada dosventos.com.br. Pool. Recommended.

C Pousada Chalé Suiço, Av Padre R J Vieira 448, Fátima, T321 3026, www.chalesuico.com.br. Cheaper without a/c or breakfast, bar, laundry, pool, tours arranged, wind- surfing, sandboarding, buggies and bikes.

D Pousada Rio Mar, Av São Sebastião 5013. Pleasant, quiet, TV, pool, good breakfast, helpful, many languages spoken. Other basic hotels in the centre.

Parque Nacional Lençóis Maranhenses *p526*
Tutóia

C Pousada Em-Bar-Cação, R Magalhães de Almeida 1064, T479 1219. On the beach, breakfast US$3. Recommended for good food and tiquira, a drink made of manioc.

Barreirinhas

C Pousada do Baiano, T0xx98-349 1130. Pousadas at Praia Cabure, 5 hrs by boat from Barreirinhas (or truck from Tutóia), friendly, fresh seafood daily.

C Pousada Igarape, R Coronel Godinho 320, Centro, T0xx98-3349 0641, igarape@backpacker. com.br. Clean, good.

C Pousada Lins, Av Joaquim Soeiro de Carvalho 550, T0xx98-3349 1494. Shared bath, good but shop around before taking their tours.

São Luís *p527, map p527*

Many cheap hotels can be found in R da Palma, very central (eg **G Pousada Ilha Bela**, safe), and R Formosa.

A Pousada Colonial, R Afonso Pena 112, T3232 2834, www.clickcolonial.com.br. In a beautiful restored, tiled house, a/c, comfortable. Recommended.

B São Marcos, Saúde 178, T3221 6263. Restored colonial house, a/c, family-run. Recommended.

B-C Lord, R Nazaré 258, T/F3221 4655, facing Praça Benedito Leite, lord@elo.com.br. Comfortable, good breakfast. Recommended.

C Pousada Solar dos Nobres, R 13 de Maio 82, Centro, T232 5705. Bright, welcoming, superb breakfast, very good.

D Hotel Casa Grande, Rua Isaac Martins 94, Centro, T232 2432. Basic, single, double, triple rooms, no a/c, big windows facing the bay. Recommended.

E Solar das Pedras, R da Palma 127, T/F232 6694, aj.solardaspedras.ma@ bol.com.br. Good breakfast, helpful, no a/c, lots of mosquitoes, but nice location.

Alcântara *p528*

Ask for hammock space or rooms in private houses, friendly but no great comfort; provide your own mineral water.

B Pousada do Mordomo Régio, R Grande 134, T337 1575. TV, refrigerator, good restaurant.

C Pousada do Pelourinho, Praça de Matriz 55, T337 1257. Breakfast, good restaurant, shared bath. Recommended.

🍴 Eating

Coast west of Fortaleza: Jericoacoara *p526*

There are several restaurants serving vegetarian and fish dishes.

♥♥ Carcará, R do Forró. Restaurant and bar, northeastern specialities, seafood and pastas, said to be "o mais fino" in town.

♥♥ Espaço Aberto, R Principal. Meat dishes, delicious seafood, salads, pleasant atmosphere. Recommended.

♥♥ Naturalmente On the beach. Nice atmosphere, wonderful crêpes. Recommended.

♥♥ Pizzaria Banana, R Principal 26. Many choices of pizza, salads, sandwiches, good.

♥♥ Pizzaria Dellacasa, R Principal, next to the phone office. Good variety of pizzas, pastas, salads, art gallery.

♥♥ Pizzaria Reggae, R Principal. Another pizza place, with a Caribbean theme.

♥♥ Taverna, R Principal. Cantina and restaurant, lovely pasta and pizza, crêpes, expresso coffee. Drinks.

♥♥ Tudo na Brasa, R Principal. Recommended for the churrascaria.

♥ A Casa da Tia Angelita, for tortas, tapiocas and other local fare.

● *For an explanation of the sleeping and eating price codes used in this guide, see inside the front*
● *cover. Other relevant information is found in Essentials pages 345-347.*

⍥ Tempero da Terra, R São Francisco. Restaurant and lanchonete, comida caseira, meat and fish dishes, nothing fancy, but well cooked and tasty.

São Luís *p527, map p527*
R da Estrela has many eating places with good food and outdoor terraces. R dos Afogados has many places for lunch. There is further choice in the São Francisco district, just across bridge.
⍤⍤⍤ La Bohème, R Isaac Martins 48. Very good food, live music, expensive, popular.
⍤⍤ Base de Edilson, R Alencar Campos 31. Shrimp only, excellent.
⍤⍤ Base da Lenoca, R Don Pedro II 181. Good view, seafood, big portions.
⍤⍤ Tia Maria, Av Nina Rodrigues 1 (Ponta d'Areia). Seafood. Recommended.
⍥ Cia Paulista, R Portugal e R da Estrela. Good, simple food, cheap.
⍥ Naturalista Alimentos, R do Sol 517. Very good, natural foods shop and restaurant, open till 1900.

Alcântara *p528*
⍤⍤-⍥ Bar do Lobato, on the praça. Pleasant, with good, simple food, fried shrimps highly recommended.

⍤ Bars and clubs

Coast west of Fortaleza: Jericoacoara *p526*
Forró nightly in high season at R do Forró, Wed and Sat in low season, 2200. Action moves to bars when forró has stopped about 0200. There are also frequent parties to which visitors are welcome. Once a week in high season there is a folk dance show which includes capoeira. After forró, **Padaria Santo Antônio** opens, selling special breads, coconut, banana, cheese, 0230-0700.

⍤ Festivals and events

São Luís *p527, map p527*
On **24 Jun** (São João) is the **Bumba-Meu-Boi**. For several days before the festival street bands parade, particularly in front of the São João and São Benedito churches. There are dances somewhere in the city almost every night in Jun. In **Aug**, São Benedito, at the Rosário church.

Alcântara *p528*
Principal festivals: **Festa do Divino**, at **Pentecost** (Whitsun); **29 Jun**, São Pedro; **early Aug**, São Benedito.

⍤⍤ Activities and tours

Coast west of Fortaleza:
Jericoacoara *p526*
Clube dos Ventos, R das Dunas, T3669 2288, www.clubedosventos.com. Same owner as Casa de Turismo, equipment hire US$18 per hr, US$44 per day for experienced, US$13 and US$31 for beginners, US$270 deposit (R$700). Basic course US$55.55, 3 hrs and up. Kite surfing at Preá and Lagoa Jijoca.
Jeri Off Road, T0xx88-3669 2022, 9961 4167 (Mob). João Gaúcho runs adventure trips in the area. Recommended, but popular. They also have a travel agency run by Paula Salles.
Buggy tours Cost US$44.45 for a buggy to all the sites. Associação de Bugueiros, ABJ, R Principal, barraca near Ibama. If seeking a bugueiro who speaks English, Spanish, Italian and French, ask for Alvaro, the school teacher, who is Uruguayan.

⍤ Transport

Coast west of Fortaleza *p526*
Lagoinha
Bus from **Fortaleza**, 6 daily with Brasileiro, 3 hrs, US$3.50.

Almofala
Bus From **Fortaleza Redenção** to Almofala 0700, 1730, US$9.

Jijoca and Jericoacoara
Bus Redenção buses from Fortaleza to **Jijoca** and **Jericoacoara** from the rodoviária 1030, 1700 and the Av Beira Mar at the Posta Telefônica opposite Praiano Palace Hotel 30 mins later. The day bus goes via Jijoca and the night bus via Preá. The journey takes 6 hrs and costs US$13 one way. Always check times of the Redençao buses from Fortaleza as they change with the season. The night bus requires an overnight stop in Preá: make your own way to Jeri next day. A jardineira (open-sided 4WD truck) meets the Redenção bus from Fortaleza, at Jijoca (included in the Redenção price). Buses return from Jeri at 0730, 1400 (via Preá) and 2230 (via Jijoca); the jardineira leaves from Casa do Turismo (see above for ticket sale times). Hotels and tour operators run 2 or 3-day tours to Jeri from Fortaleza. If not on Redenção or a tour, 'guides' will besiege new arrivals in Jijoca with offers of buggies, or guiding cars through the tracks and dunes to Jeri for US$7.25. If you don't want to do this, ask if a pick-up is going: US$2-5 pp up front, 22 km, 30 mins. In a buggy it's US$21 per buggy.

If coming from Belém or other points north and west, go via Sobral (from Belém US$38, 20 hrs), where you change for Cruz, 40 km east of Jijoca, a small pleasant town with basic hotels (there is only one bus a day Sobral-Cruz, US$10, 3-4 hrs, but Redenção runs to **Cruz** from Fortaleza 0900, 1030, 1630, 1830, US$9.50. Either continue to Jijoca the next day (Cruz-Jijoca, daily about 1400, US$1.65, meets jardineira for Jeri, Cruz-Jericoacoara, US$3) or take an horário pick-up Cruz-Jijoca.

An alternative from the west, especially if going through Parnaíba, is by buggy or jardineira from **Camocim** (a pleasant town at the mouth of the Rio Coreaú, facing the dunes on the eastern shore), which is 1½ hrs by road from Parnaíba. It has several hotels and eating places. You take a ferry across the river then the vehicle; they leave between 0900-1030. You can break the journey from Camocim to Jericoacoara at villages such as **Nova Tatajuba** (on the west margin of the outflow of Lagoa Grande; the beach is wide, dunes follow the shore, the ocean is clear and calm and there is a fishing village with a few basic pousadas), or **Guriú** where hammock space can be found. There is good bird watching here. Walk 4 hrs, or take a boat across the bay to Jericoacoara. The journey along the beach has beautiful scenery. In Jericoacoara ask around for buggy or jardineira rides to Camocim, about US$15-20 pp.

Parque Nacional Lençóis Maranhenses *p526*
Bus Parnaíba-Tutóia: bus, 4 hrs, US$9; river boat up the Parnaíba delta, 3 a week (ask at the port as departures depend on the tide), 8 hrs, US$9. Recommended. Private boat hire is also possible. **São Luís- Barreirinhas**: bus, 4 hrs on a new road, US$16. Ask at **Solar das Pedras** youth hostel about minivan trips, same price as bus. Private tour buses, US$23, organized bus tours cost US$95. 4WD trips into the park from Barreirinhas cost US$13. Plane (single propeller), 40 mins, US$48 pp. Recommended. A fabulous experience giving panoramic views of the dunes, pilots **Amirton**, T225 2882, or **Fénix** in Barreirinhas. Agencies charge about US$270 for a tour with flight.
Ferry Excursions from/to **Barreirinhas**: regular boat service between Barreirinhas and

Atins (7 hrs return, US$6.65): boat along Rio Preguiça, 4 hrs then 1 hr walk to the dunes, US$16. The only forms of transport that can get across the dunes right into the park are a **jeep** or a **horse**, both about US$20. It is a 2-3 hr walk from Barreirinhas to the park; you will need at least another 2 hrs in the dunes. At Mandacuru, a popular stop on tours of the area, the lighthouse gives a very impressive view.

Alcântara *p528*
Ferry
Ferries cross the bay daily, leaving São Luís dock or from São Francisco district at about 0700 and 0930, returning from Alcântara about 0830 and 1600: check time and buy the ticket at the hidroviária (west end of R Portugal, T3232 0692) the day before as departure depends on the tides. The journey takes 90 mins, return US$20, worth paying extra for 'panorámica' seat. The sea can be very rough between Sep and Dec. There are sometimes catamaran tours bookable through tour operators in São Luís, meals not included.

São Luís *p527, map p527*
Air Internal flights only, 15 km from centre, T3217 6133; buses ('São Cristovão') to city until midnight, US$1.
Bus Rodoviária is 12 km from the centre on the airport road, 'Rodoviária via Alemanha' bus to centre (Praça João Lisboa), US$0.65. Bus to **Fortaleza**, US$44, 4 a day, 18 hrs. To **Belém**, 13 hrs, US$26, **Transbrasiliana**. Also to **Recife**, US$60, 25 hrs, all other major cities and local towns.

❶ Directory

São Luís *p527, map p527*
Banks TCs at Banco do Brasil, Praça Deodoro. HSBC, off Praça João Lisboa. Accepts Master Card/Maestro. **Agetur**, R do Sol 33-A, T231 2377.
Language courses Portuguese lessons: Sra Amin Castro, T227 1527. Recommended.
Medical services Clínica São Marcelo, R do Passeio 546, English speaking doctor.
Telephones Embratel, Av Dom Pedro II 190.

West of Fortaleza

Western Ceará

At 340 km from Fortaleza and at 840 m is **Ubajara** ① *T634 1300 ext 231 for tourist information*, with an interesting Sunday morning market selling produce of the sertão. About 3 km from town is **Parque Nacional Ubajara**① *the Ibama office is at the park entrance, 5 km from the caves, Toxx85-634 1388, www.ibama.gov.br, there is bar by the entrance serving juices, snacks, refrigerantes, etc*, with 563 ha of native highland and caatinga brush. The park's main attraction is the Ubajara cave on the side of an escarpment. Fifteen chambers totalling 1,120 m have been mapped, of which 360 are open to visitors. Access is along a 6-km footpath and steps (2-3 hours, take water) or with a **cablecar**① *T634 1219, 0900-1430, last up at 1500, US$2, locals US$0.20 – they use it as a means of transport*, which descends the cliff to the cave entrance. Lighting has been installed in nine caverns of the complex. An Ibama guide leads visitors in the cave, which is completely dry and home to 14 types of bat. At one point the lights are turned out to appreciate total blackness. Several rock formations look like animals: horse's head, jacaré, snake. The views of the sertão from the upper cablecar platform are superb. In the national park there is a new easy walkway through the woods with stunning views at the end. Start either to the left of the Park entrance, or opposite the snack bar near the cable car platform. The locals' route, and another good trail through caatinga, is from Araticum, 8 km, which is 7 km by bus from Ubajara.

Teresina → *Phone code: 0xx86. Post code: 64000. Colour map 5, grid B3. Population: 715,360.*

About 435 km up the Rio Parnaíba is the state capital. The city is reputed to be the hottest after Manaus (temperatures rise to 42°C). The **Palácio de Karnak** (the old governor's palace)①① *just west of Praça Frei Serafim, Mon-Fri 1530-1730*, contains lithographs of the Middle East in 1839 by David Roberts RA. Also see the **Museu do Piauí**① *Praça Marechal Deodoro, Tue-Fri 0800-1730, Sat-Sun 0800-1200, US$0.80*. There is an interesting **open market** by the Praça Marechal Deodoro and the river is picturesque, with washing laid out to dry along its banks. The market is a good place to buy hammocks, but bargain hard. Every morning along the river bank there is the **troca-troca** where people buy, sell and swap. An undercover complex (**Mercado Central do Artesanato**) *Mon-Fri 0800-2200*, has been built at R Paissandu 1276 (Praça Dom Pedro II). Most of the year the river is low, leaving sandbanks known as coroas (crowns). There is a good, clean supermarket on Praça Marechal Deodoro 937 with fresh food. Local handicrafts include leather and clothes. **Teresina**: Piemtur, R Acre s/n, Centro de Convenções, Cabral, T3221 7100, www.piemtur.pi.gov.br. Information office at R Magalhães Filho s/n (next to 55 N, English spoken); kiosks at rodoviária and airport. **Singtur** (Sindicato dos Guías de Turismo de Piauí), R Paissandu 1276, T215 7894, singtur-pi@bol.com.br, has information booths at the Centro de Artesanato (helpful), the Encontro das Águas, Poty Velho and on the shores of the Rio Poty.

Parque Nacional de Sete Cidades → *Colour map 5, grid B4.*

① *0800-1700, US$1.35 plus US$4.55 for compulsory guide.*

Unusual eroded rock formations decorated with mysterious inscriptions are to be found in the Parque Nacional de Sete Cidades, 12 km from Piracuruca, 190 km northeast of Teresina. The rock structures are just off the Fortaleza-Teresina road. From the ground it looks like a medley of weird monuments. The inscriptions on some of the rocks have never been deciphered; one theory suggests links with the Phoenicians, and the Argentine Professor Jacques de Mahieu considers them to be Nordic runes left by the Vikings. There is plenty of birdlife, and iguanas, descending from their trees in the afternoon. Ibama hostel in the park, **C**, T3223 3366, pleasant, good restaurant, natural pool nearby, camping (US$6.50). Local food is limited and monotonous: bring a few delicacies, and especially fruit. Piripiri is a cheap place to break the Belém-Fortaleza journey; several good hotels. **Parque Nacional de Sete Cidades**: For park information, contact **Ibama**, Rod Min Vicente Fialho, Piripiri, CEP 64260-000, T3343 1342. Colourful brochures with good map.

● Sleeping → *See Telephone, page 347, for important phone changes.*

Western Ceará: Ubajara *p532*

A Pousada da Neblina, Estrada do Teleférico, 2 km from town, near the park, T/F3634 1270. In beautiful cloud forest, swimming pool, with breakfast and private shower (**C** without breakfast) restaurant open 1100-2000. Meals recommended. Campground (US$15 per tent).

C Marina Camping, on Ibiapina road 4 km south from Ubajara town, T3634 1364. Restaurant, pool, sauna, good value.

D Paraíso, in the centre of Ubajara town, T3634 1728. Reckoned to be the best in town.

D Hotel Churrascaria Ubajara, R Juvêncio Luís Pereira 370, Ubajara town, T3634 1261. Small restaurant.

D Sítio do Alemão, take Estrada do Teleférico 2 km from town, after the Pousada da Neblina turn right, signposted, 1 km to Sítio Santana, in the coffee plantation of Herbert Klein, T0xx88-9961 4645, www.sitio-do-alemao.20fr.com. Here, down a path, there are 3 small chalets, with full facilities, and 2 older ones with shared bath, **E**, view from breakfast/hammock area to Sertão, excursions, bicycle hire offered, if chalets are full Mr Klein may accommodate visitors at the house (Caixa Postal 33, Ubajara, CE, CEP 62350-000). No meals other than breakfast but Casa das Delícias in Ubajara will send lasagne if necessary. Warmly recommended. **Note**: camping is not allowed in the national park.

Teresina *p532*

Many cheap hotels and dormitórios around Praça Saraiva. Many other cheap ones in R São Pedro and in R Alvaro Mendes.

LL Rio Poty, Av Marechal Castelo Branco 555, Ilhota, T4009 4009, www.riopoty.com.br. 5-star. Recommended.

A-B Sambaíba, R Gabriel Ferreira 230-N, T3222 6712, hotelsambaiba@bol.com.br. 2-star, central, good.

C-D Fortaleza, Felix Pacheco 1101, Praça Saraiva, T3221 2984. Fan, basic. Recommended.

C-D Grande, R Alvaro Mendes 906, T3221 2713. Very friendly and clean.

C-D Teresinha, Av Getúlio Vargas 2885, opposite rodoviária, T3221 0919. With a/c, cheaper with fan.

● Eating

Teresina *p532*

Many eating places for all pockets in Praça Dom Pedro II.

♥♥ Camarão do Elias, Av Pedro Almeida 457, T232 5025. Good seafood.

♥♥ Pesqueirinho, R Domingos Jorge Velho 6889, in Poty Velho district. For fish dishes.

♥ Sabores Rotisserie, R Simplício Mendes 78, Centro. By kg, good quality and variety.

● Festivals and events

Teresina *p532*

Teresina is proud of its **Carnival**, which is then followed by **Micarina**, a local carnival in **Mar**. There is much music and dancing in **Jul** and **Aug**, when there is a **Bumba-meu-Boi**, the Teresina dance festival, **Festidanças**, and a convention of itinerant guitarists.

● Transport

Western Ceará: Ubajara *p532*

Guanabara **bus** from **Fortaleza**, 0800, 1800, return 0800, 1600, 6 hrs, US$10.75.

Teresina *p532*

Air Flights to **Fortaleza, Brasília, Rio, São Paulo, São Luís, Belém, Manaus**. Buses from outside the airport run straight into town and to the rodoviária.

Bus Rodoviária, T3218 1514. The bus trip from **Fortaleza** is scenic and takes 9 hrs (US$27). There are direct buses to **Belém** (13 hrs, US$31), **Recife** (16 hrs, US$36) and to **São Luís** (7 hrs, US$16).

Parque Nacional de Sete Cidades and Piripiri *p532*

Bus Free **Ibama** bus service leaves the Praça da Bandeira in Piripiri (26 km away, rodoviária T3276 2333), at 0700, passing *Hotel Fazenda Sete Cidades* at 0800 (**B**, at Km 63 on BR-222, T0xx86- 3232 3030, camping US$4.50; also has a free pick-up to the park), reaching the park 10 mins later. Return at 1630, or hitchhike (to walk takes all day, very hot, start early). Taxi from Piripiri, US$20, or from Piracuruca, US$28. Bus Teresina-Piripiri and return, throughout the day 2½ hrs, US$5. Bus São Luís-Piripiri, 3 a day, 10 hrs, US$20. Several daily buses Piripiri-**Fortaleza**, 9 hrs, US$20. Bus Piripiri-**Ubajara**, marked 'São Benedito', or 'Crateús', 2½ hrs; US$5, first at 0700 (a beautiful trip).

● Directory

Teresina *p532*

Banks There are ATMs for both Visa and MasterCard, eg Banco 24 Horas – TecBan, Av João XXIII 2220.

The Amazon

The area is drained by the mighty Amazon, which in size, volume of water – 12 times that of the Mississippi – and number of tributaries has no equal in the world. At the base of the Andes, far to the west, the Amazonian plain is 1,300 km wide, but east of the confluences of the Madeira and Negro rivers with the Amazon, the highlands close in upon it until there is no more than 80 km of floodplain between them. Towards the river's mouth – about 320 km wide – the plain widens once more and extends along the coast southeastwards into the state of Maranhão and northwards into the Guianas.

Brazilian Amazônia, much of it still covered with tropical forest, is 56% of the national area. Its jungle is the world's largest and densest rain forest, with more diverse plants and animals than any other jungle in the world. It has only 8% of Brazil's population, and most of this is concentrated around Belém (in Pará), and in Manaus, 1,600 km up the river. The population is sparse because other areas are easier to develop.

Northern Brazil consists of the states of Pará, Amazonas, Amapá and Roraima. The states of Rondônia and Acre are dealt with under Southern Amazônia, see page 561.

Ins and outs

Climate The rainfall is heavy, but varies throughout the region; close to the Andes, up to 4,000 mm annually, under 2,000 at Manaus. Rains occur throughout the year but the wettest season is between December and May, the driest month is October. The humidity can be extremely high and the temperature averages 26°C. There can be cold snaps in December in the western reaches of the Amazon basin. The soil, as in all tropical forest, is poor.

Travel up the Amazon River

Rivers are the arteries of Amazônia for the transport of both passengers and merchandise. The two great ports of the region are Belém, at the mouth of the Amazon, and Manaus at the confluence of the Rio Negro and Rio Solimões. Manaus is the hub of river transport, with regular shipping services east to Santarém and Belém along the lower Amazon, south to Porto Velho along the Rio Madeira, west to Tabatinga (the border with Colombia and Peru) along the Rio Solimões and northwest to São Gabriel da Cachoeira along the Rio Negro. There is also a regular service connecting Belém and Macapá, on the northern shore of the Amazon Delta, and Santarém and Macapá. The size and quality of vessels varies greatly, with the largest and most comfortable ships generally operating on the Manaus-Belém route. Hygiene, food and service are reasonable on most vessels but **overcrowding** is a common problem. Many of the larger ships offer air-conditioned berths with bunkbeds and, for a higher price, 'suites', with a private bathroom (in some cases, this may also mean a double bed instead of the standard bunkbed). The cheapest way to travel is 'hammock class'; on some routes first class (upper deck) and second class (lower deck) hammock space is available, but on many routes this distinction does not apply. Some new boats have air-conditioned hammock space. Although the idea of swinging in a hammock may sound romantic, the reality is you will probably be squeezed in with other passengers, possibly next to the toilets, and have difficulty sleeping because of **noise** and an aching back. Most boats have some sort of rooftop bar serving expensive drinks and snacks.

Riverboat travel is no substitute for visiting the jungle. Except for a few birds and the occasional dolphin, little wildlife is seen. However, it does offer an insight into the vastness of Amazônia and a chance to meet some of its people. Extensive local inquiry and some flexibility in one's schedule are indispensable for river travel. **Agencies** on shore can inform you of the arrival and departure dates for several different ships, as well as the official (highest) prices for each, and they are sometimes amenable to bargaining. Whenever possible, **see the vessel** yourself (it may mean a journey out of town) and have a chat with the captain or business manager to confirm departure time, length of voyage, ports of call, price, etc. Inspect cleanliness

⬤ *The Amazon system is 6,577 km long, of which 3,165 km are in Brazilian territory. Ships of up to*
⬤ *4-5,000 tonnes regularly negotiate the Amazon for a distance of about 3,646 km up to Iquitos, Peru.*

Paradise lost?

Successive modern Brazilian governments have made strenuous efforts to develop Amazônia. Roads have been built parallel to the Amazon to the south (the Transamazônica), from Cuiabá (Mato Grosso) northwards to Santarém (Pará), and northeast from Porto Velho through Humaitá to the river bank opposite Manaus. Unsuccessful attempts were made to establish agricultural settlements along these roads; major energy and mining projects for bauxite and iron ore are bringing rapid change. More environmental damage has been caused to the region by gold prospectors (garimpeiros), especially by their indiscriminate use of mercury, than by organized mining carried out by large state and private companies using modern extraction methods. The most important cause of destruction, however, has been large scale deforestation to make way for cattle ranching, with logging for hardwoods for the Asian markets coming a close second.

There is a gradually growing awareness among many Brazilians that their northern hinterland is a unique treasure and requires some form of protection and recently some encouraging moves have been made. On the other hand, government is still intent upon some form of development in the region, as its seven-year Avança Brasil programme demonstrated. Scientists argued in 2001 that if the plan went ahead, its road improvement and other elements would lead to a loss of between 28% and 42% of Amazon rainforest by 2020, with only about 5% of the region untouched. This report led to a reassessment of the plan.

in the kitchen, toilets and showers. All boats are cleaned up when in port, but if a vessel is reasonably clean upon arrival then chances are that it has been kept that way throughout the voyage. You can generally arrange to sleep on board a day or two before departure and after arrival, but be sure to secure carefully your belongings when in port. If you take a berth, lock it and keep the key even if you will not be moving in right away. If you are travelling hammock class, board ship at least 6-8 hours before sailing in order to secure a good spot (away from the toilets and the engine and check for leaks in the deck above you). Be firm but considerate of your neighbours as they will be your intimate companions for the duration of the voyage. Always keep your gear locked. Take some light warm clothing, it can get very chilly at night.

Compare fares for different ships and remember that prices may fluctuate with supply and demand. Most ships sail in the evening and the first night's supper is not provided. Empty cabins are sometimes offered to foreigners at reduced rates once boats have embarked. **Payment** is usually in advance. Insist on a signed ticket indicating date, vessel, class of passage, and berth number if applicable.

All ships carry cargo as well as passengers and the amount of cargo will affect the length of the voyage because of weight (especially when travelling upstream) and loading/unloading at intermediate ports. All but the smallest boats will transport vehicles, but these are often damaged by rough handling. Insist on the use of proper ramps and check for adequate clearance. Vehicles can also be transported aboard cargo barges. These are usually cheaper and passengers may be allowed to accompany their car, but check about food, sanitation, where you will sleep (usually in a hammock slung beneath a truck), and adequate shade.

The following are the **major shipping routes** in Amazônia, indicating main intermediate ports, average trip durations, and basic fares. Facilities in the main ports are described in the appropriate city sections below. There are many other routes and vessels providing extensive local service. All **fares shown are one-way only** and include all meals unless otherwise stated.

Boat services
Belém-Manaus via Santarém, Óbidos and Parintins on the lower Amazon. 5-6 days upriver, four days downriver, including 18-hour stop in Santarém, US$130 upriver, US$120 down; suites and double berths also available. Vehicles are also carried. The Belém-Manaus route is very busy. Try to get a cabin.

Belém-Santarém, 2½ days upriver, 1½ days downriver, US$52. All vessels sailing Belém-Manaus will call in Santarém.

Santarém-Manaus, same intermediate stops as above. Two days upriver, 1½ days downriver, US$52. All vessels sailing Belém-Manaus will call in Santarém and there are many others operating only the Santarém-Manaus. Speedboats (lanchas) are sometimes available on this route, 16 hours sitting, US$65.

Belém-Macapá (Porto Santana) non-stop, 24 hours on large ships, double berth US$130, hammock space US$36 pp, meals not included but can be purchased onboard (expensive), vehicle US$105, driver not included. Same voyage via Breves, 36-48 hours on smaller riverboats, hammock space US$30 pp including meals. See page 542.

Macapá (Porto Santana)-Santarém via Boca do Jari, Prainha, and Monte Alegre on the lower Amazon, two days upriver, 1½ days downriver, berth US$155, hammock US$48.

Manaus-Porto Velho via Humaitá on the Rio Madeira (from where there are buses to Porto Velho, saving about 24 hrs). Tuesday and Friday, five days upriver, 3½ days downriver (up to seven days when the river is low), US$93.

Manaus-Tefé 36 hours, US$52. Boats every 2 days to Tabatinga (flights Manaus-Tefé- Tabatinga).

Manaus-Tabatinga via Fonte Boa (three days), Tonantins (four days), São Paulo de Olivença (five days) and Benjamin Constant along the Rio Solimões. Six days upriver (depending on cargo), three days downriver, US$120 upriver, cheaper down (the Voyager fleet is recommended).

Manaus-São Gabriel da Cachoeira. Leaving from Porto Raimundo in Manaus not the main boat port, six days along the Rio Negro, US$120.

What to take

A hammock is essential on all but the most expensive boats; it is often too hot to lie down in a cabin during day. Light cotton hammocks seem to be the best solution. Buy a wide one on which you can lie diagonally; lying straight along it leaves you hump-backed. A climbing carabiner clip is useful for fastening hammocks to runner bars of boats. It is also useful for securing baggage, making it harder to steal.

Health → *See also Health, Essentials, page 45.*

There is a danger of malaria in Amazônia. Mosquito nets are not required when in motion as boats travel away from the banks and too fast for mosquitoes to settle, though repellent is a boon for night stops. From April to October, when the river is high, the mosquitoes can be repelled by Super Repelex spray or K13. A yellow-fever inoculation is strongly advised; it is compulsory in some areas and may be administered on the spot with a pressurized needle gun. The larger ships must have an infirmary and carry a health officer. Drinking water is generally taken on in port (ie city tap water), but taking your own mineral water is a good idea.

Food

Ample but monotonous, better food is sometimes available to cabin passengers. Meal times can be chaotic. Fresh fruit is a welcome addition; also take plain biscuits, tea bags, seasonings, sauces and jam. Fresh coffee is available; most boats have a bar of sorts. Plates and cutlery may not be provided. Bring your own plastic mug as drinks are served in plastic beakers which are jettisoned into the river. A strong fishing line and a variety of hooks can be an asset for supplementing one's diet; with some meat for bait, piranhas are the easiest fish to catch. Negotiate with the cook over cooking your fish. The sight of you fishing will bring a small crowd of new friends, assistants, and lots of advice – some of it useful.

   In Amazônia Inevitably fish dishes are very common, including many fish with indengous names, eg matrinchã, jaraqui, pacu, tucunaré, and tambaqui, which are worth trying. Pirarucu is another delicacy of Amazonian cuisine, but because of overfishing it is in danger of becoming extinct. Also shrimp and crab dishes (more expensive). Specialities of Pará include duck, often served in a yellow soup made from the juice of the root of the manioc (tucupi) with a green vegetable (jambu); this dish is the famous pato no tucupi, highly recommended. Also tacaca (shrimps served in tucupi), vatapá (shrimps served in a thick sauce, highly filling, simpler than the variety found in Salvador), maniçoba (made with the poisonous leaves of the bitter cassava, simmered for eight days to render it safe – tasty). Caldeirada, a fish and vegetable soup, served with pirão (manioc puree) is a speciality of Amazonas. There is also an enormous variety of tropical and jungle fruits, many unique to the region. Try them fresh, or in ice creams or juices. Avoid food from street vendors.

Belém and around

From Belém, the great city near the mouth of the Amazon, to Parintins, site of a renowned annual festival, on the border with Amazonas state, it is 60 hours by boat. This section deals with the first few stops on the river, plus the route through Amapá state to the frontier with French Guiane.

Belém → *Phone code: 0xx91. Post code: 66000. Colour map 5, grid A1. Population: 1.3 million.*

Belém (do Pará) is the great port of the Amazon. It is hot (mean temperature, 26°C), but frequent showers freshen the streets. There are some fine squares and restored historic buildings set along broad avenues. Belém used to be called the 'City of Mango Trees' and there are many such trees remaining.

Tourist offices Belém Belemtur ① *Av José Malcher 592, T3242 0900, belemtur@ cinbesa.com.br.* Also at airport, T3211 6151. **Paratur** ① *Praça Mestro Waldemar Henrique s/n, T3212 0575, www.paratur.pa.gov.br.* Helpful, many languages spoken; good map of Belém in many languages (but some references are incorrect). Town guidebook, US$3. **Ibama** ① *Av Conselheiro Furtado 1303, Batista Campos, CEP 66035-350, T3241 2621, F3223 1299.*

Belém has its share of crime and is prone to gang violence. Take sensible precautions especially at night. Police for reporting crimes, R Santo Antônio e Trav Frei Gil de Vila Nova.

Sights The largest square is the **Praça da República** where there are free afternoon concerts; the main business and shopping area is along the wide Av Presidente Vargas leading to the river and the narrow streets which parallel it. The neoclassical **Teatro da Paz** (1868-1874) ① *Tue-Fri 0900-1800, tours US$2,* is one of the largest theatres in the country. It stages performances by national and international stars and also gives free concert and theatre shows; worth visiting, recently restored. Visit the **Cathedral** (1748) ① *Mon 1500-1800, Tue-Fri 0800-1100, 1530-1800,* another neoclassical building which contains several remarkable paintings. It stands on Praça Frei Caetano Brandão, opposite the 18th-century **Santo Aleixandre** church, which is noted for its wood carving. The 17th-century **Mercês** church (1640), near the market, is the oldest church in Belém; it forms part of an architectural group known as the Mercedário, the rest of which was heavily damaged by fire in 1978 and is being restored.

Belém

Sleeping
Amazônia 2
Fortaleza 1
Grão Pará 11
Itaoca 4
Le Massilia 4
Machado's Plaza 10

Novo Avenida 5
Palácio 6
Palácio das Musas 6
Regente 7
Sete Sete 8
Unidos 9
Vila Rica 12

Eating
Açaí at Hilton Hotel 11
Boteco das Onze 5
Cantina Italiana 1
Churrascaria Rodeio 3
Churrascaria Tucuruvi 4

Doces
Bárbaros 8
Govinda 10
Lá em Casa 6
Mãe Natureza 9
Miako 7
Sabor Paraense 2

The **Basílica of Nossa Senhora de Nazaré** (1909) ① *Praça Julho Chermont on Av Magalhães Barata, Mon-Sat 0500-1130, 1400-2000, Sun 0545-1130, 1430-2000*, built from rubber wealth in romanesque style, is an absolute must for its stained glass windows and beautiful marble. A museum at the basilica describes the Círio de Nazaré religious festival. The **Palácio Lauro Sodré** or **Museu do Estado do Pará** ① *Praça Dom Pedro II, T3225 3853, Mon-Fri 0900-1800, Sat-Sun 1900-1200*, a gracious 18th-century Italianate building, contains Brazil's largest framed painting, 'The Conquest of Amazônia', by Domenico de Angelis. The **Palácio Antônio Lemos**, **Museu da Cidade** ① *Tue-Fri 0900-1200, 1400-1800, Sat-Sun 0900-1300*, which houses the **Museu de Arte de Belém** and is now the **Prefeitura**, was originally built as the Palácio Municipal between 1868 and 1883. In the downstairs rooms there are old views of Belém; upstairs the historic rooms, beautifully renovated, contain furniture, paintings etc, all well explained.

The Belém market, known as '**Ver-o-Peso**' was the Portuguese Posto Fiscal, where goods were weighed to gauge taxes due (hence the name: 'see the weight'). It now has lots of gift shops selling charms for the local African-derived religion, umbanda; the medicinal herb and natural perfume stalls are also interesting. It is one of the most varied and colourful markets in South America; you can see giant river fish being unloaded around 0530, with frenzied wholesale buying for the next hour; a new dock for the fishing boats was built just upriver from the market in 1997. The area around the market swarms with people, including many armed thieves and pickpockets.

In the old town, too, is the **Forte do Castelo** ① *Praça Frei Caetano Brandão 117, T3223 0041, daily 0800-2300*. The fort overlooks the confluence of the Rio Guamá and the Baía do Guajara and was where the Portuguese first set up their defences. It was rebuilt in 1878. The site also contains the Círculo Militar restaurant (entry US$1.30; drinks and salgadinhos served on the ramparts from 1800 to watch the sunset; the restaurant serves Belém's best Brazilian food). At the square on the waterfront below the fort the açaí berries are landed nightly at 2300, after picking in the jungle (açaí berries ground up with sugar and mixed with manioc are a staple food in the region).

At the **Estação das Docas**, the abandoned warehouses of the port have been restored into a complex with an air-conditioned interior and restaurants outside. The Terminal Marítimo has an office of Valverde Tours, which offers sunset and nighttime boat trips. The Boulevard das Artes contains the Cervejaria Amazon brewery, with good beer and simple meals, an archaeological museum and arts and crafts shops. The Boulevard de Gastronomia has smart restaurants and the 5-star Cairu ice cream parlour (try açaí or the Pavê de Capuaçu). Also in the complex are ATMs, internet café, phones and good toilets.

The **Bosque Rodrigues Alves** ① *Av Almte Barroso 2305, T3226 2308, 0900-1700, closed Mon*, is a 16-ha public garden (really a preserved area of original flora), with a small animal collection; yellow bus marked 'Souza' or 'Cidade Nova' – any number – 30 minutes from 'Ver-o-Peso' market, also bus from Cathedral. The **Museu Emílio Goeldi** ① *Av Magalhães Barata 376, Tue-Thu 0900-1200, 1400-1700, Fri 0900-1200, Sat-Sun 0900-1700, US$1.30, additional charges for specialist area*, takes up a city block and consists of the museum proper (with a fine collection of Marajó Indian pottery, an excellent exhibition of Mebengokre Indian lifestyle) and botanical exhibits including Victoria Régia lilies. Take a bus from the Cathedral.

A return trip on the ferry from Ver-o-Peso to **Icaoraci** provides a good view of the river. Several restaurants here serve excellent seafood; you can eat shrimp and drink coconut water and appreciate the breeze coming off the river. Icaoraci is 20 km east of the city and is well-known as a centre of ceramic production. The pottery is in Marajoara and Tapajonica style. Take the bus from Av Presidente Vargas to Icaoraci (one hr). Open all week but best on Tuesday to Friday. Artisans are friendly and helpful, will accept commissions and send purchases overseas.

The nearest beach is at **Outeiro** (35 km) on an island near Icaoraci, about an hour by bus and ferry (the bus may be caught near the Maloca, an *indígena*-style hut near the docks which serves as a nightclub). A bus from Icaoraci to Outeiro takes 30 minutes. Further north is the island of **Mosqueiro** (86 km) ① *buses Belém-Mosqueiro every hr from rodoviária, US$2, 80 mins*, accessible by an excellent highway. It has many beautiful sandy beaches and jungle inland. It is popular at weekends when traffic can be heavy (also July) and the beaches can get crowded and polluted. Many hotels and weekend villas are at the villages of Mosqueiro and Vila; recommended (may be full weekends and July). Camping is easy and there are plenty of good places to eat.

Ilha do Marajó → *Colour map 5, grid A1.*

At almost 50,000 sq km, the world's largest island formed by fluvial processes is flooded in rainy December to June and provides a suitable habitat for water buffalo, introduced from India in the late 19th century. They are now farmed in large numbers (try the cheese and milk). It is also home to many birds, crocodiles and other wildlife, and has several good beaches. It is crowded at weekends and in the July holiday season. The island was the site of the pre-Columbian Marajoaras culture.

Ponta de Pedras

Boats leave Belém (near Porto do Sal, seat US$4.35, cabin US$47 for two, five hours) most days for Ponta de Pedras (**D Hotel Ponta de Pedras**, good meals, buses for Soure or Salvaterra meet the boat). Bicycles for hire (US$1 per hour) to explore beaches and the interior of the island. Fishing boats make the eight-hour trip to Cachoeira do Arari (one pousada, **D**) where there is a Marajó museum. A 10-hour boat trip from Ponta de Pedras goes to the Arari lake where there are two villages, Jenipapo built on stilts, forró dancing at weekends, and Santa Cruz which is less primitive, but less interesting (a hammock and a mosquito net are essential). There is a direct boat service to Belém twice a week.

Soure → *Colour map 5, grid A1. Population: 20,000.*

The 'capital' of the island has fine beaches: Araruna (2 km – take supplies and supplement with coconuts and crabs, beautiful walks along the shore), do Pesqueiro (bus from Praça da Matriz, 1030, returns 1600, eat at Maloca, good, cheap, big, deserted beach, 13 km away) and Caju-Una (15 km). Small craft await passengers from the Enasa boats, for Salvaterra village (good beaches and bars: seafood), 10 minutes, or trips are bookable in Belém from Mururé, T3241 0891. There are also 17th-century Jesuit ruins at Joanes as well as a virgin beach. Changing money is only possible at very poor rates. Take plenty of insect repellent.

Macapá → *Phone code: 0xx96. Post code: 68900. Colour map 2, grid C6. Population: 283,308.*

The capital of Amapá State is situated on the northern channel of the Amazon Delta and is linked to Belém by boat and daily flights. Along with Porto Santana it was declared a Zona Franca in 1993 and visitors flock to buy cheap imported electrical and other goods. Each brick of the **Fortaleza de São José do Macapá**, built between 1764 and 1782, was brought from Portugal as ballast; 50 iron cannons remain. Today it is used for concerts, exhibits, and colourful festivities on the anniversary of the city's founding, 4 February. In the handicraft complex (**Casa do Artesão**) ① *Av Azárias Neto, Mon-Sat 0800-1900*, craftsmen produce their wares onsite. A feature is pottery decorated with local manganese ore, also woodcarvings, leatherwork and indigenous crafts. **São José Cathedral**, inaugurated by the Jesuits in 1761, is the city's oldest landmark.

The riverfront is a very pleasant place for an evening stroll. The **Complexo Beira-Rio** has food and drink kiosks, and a nice lively atmosphere. The pier (trapiche) has been rebuilt and is a lovely spot for savouring the cool of the evening breeze, or watching sunrise over the Amazon. There is a monument to the equator, **Marco Zero** (take Fazendinha bus). The equator also divides the nearby enormous football stadium in half, aptly named O Zerão. South of here, at Km 12 on Rodovia Juscelinho Kubitschek, are the **botanical gardens**. **Fazendinha** (16 km from the centre) is a popular local beach, very busy on Sunday. **Curiarú**, 8 km from Macapá, was founded by escaped slaves, and is popular at weekends for dancing and swimming.

Tourist offices: Detur, Avenida Raimundo Álvares da Costa 18, Centro, T223 0627. Branch at airport. State website: www.amapa.net. Ibama, R Hamilton Silva 1570, Santa Rita, CEP 68.906-440, Macapá, T/F214 1119.

Border with Guyane → *Colour map 2, grid B6.*

The main road crosses the Rio Caciporé and continues to the border with Guyane at **Oiapoque** (*Population: 13,000*), on the river of the same name. It is 90 km inland from the Parque Nacional Cabo Orange, Brazil's northernmost point on the Atlantic coast. About 7 km to the west is Clevelândia do Norte, a military outpost and the end of the road in Brazil. Oiapoque is remote, with its share of contraband, illegal migration, and drug trafficking. It is also the gateway to gold fields in the interior of both Brazil and Guyane. Visitors should take care late at night; the town is popular with French Guiana weekenders, most of them single men in search of the town's numerous women of ill repute. Prices here are high, but lower than in neighbouring Guyane. The

Cachoeira Grande Roche rapids can be visited, upstream along the Oiapoque River, where it is possible to swim, US$30 per motor boat. The road north to the Guyane border (BR-156) is unpaved from Tatarugalzinho and is difficult in parts, especially during the wet season (but open throughout the year). It is advisable to carry extra fuel, food and water from Macapá onwards. Immigration officers will stamp you out the day before if you want to make an early start to Guyane. A bridge linking Guyane and Amapá is under construction and the road is asphalted all the way to Cayenne. As combis to Cayenne leave before lunch it is best to get to St-Georges before 1000. There is already much deforestation along the Brazilian side of the road and many Brazilian *garimpeiros* and hunters are causing havoc in Guyane.

⊜ Sleeping → *See Telephone, page 347, for important phone changes.*

Belém *p537, map p537*

There are now a few decent mid-range hotels in the city and a few clean, well-kept bargains in the upper budget category. The cheapest rooms are still very scruffy in Belém: consider an upgrade, this is a place where US$3-4 can make an enormous difference.

L Machado's Plaza, R Henrique Gurjão 200, T4008 9800, www.machadosplazahotel.com.br. Bright, brand new hotel with smart and tastefully decorated a/c rooms, a small business centre, plunge pool and a pleasant a/c breakfast area. Good value.

AL Itaoca, Av Pres Vargas 132, T4009 2400, itaoca@canal13.com.br. Well kept, bright a/c rooms, the best are on the upper floors away from the street noise, and with river views. Decent breakfast.

AL Regente, Av Gov José Malcher 485, T3181 5000, www.hotelregente.com.br. Small, refurbished a/c rooms with standard 3 star fittings above a noisy street. Popular with US tour groups.

AL Vila Rica, Av Júlio César 1777, T3257 1522, www.hotelvilarica.com.br/hotel_belem.htm. 5 mins from airport, helpful with transfers, very good.

A Le Massilia, R Henrique Gurjão 236, T3224 2834, www.massilia.com.br. Intimate, French owned boutique hotel with chic little duplexes and more ordinary doubles. Excellent French restaurant (ŢŢŢ) and a tasty French breakfast.

B-C Grão Pará, Av Pres Vargas 718, T3224 9600. A/c rooms with contemporary fittings, smart, hot water, the best have superb river views, excellent breakfast, great value.

B-C Novo Avenida, Av Pres.Vargas 404, T3223 8893, www.hotelnovoavenida.com.br. Slightly frayed but spruce rooms with decent breakfast. Groups of can sleep in large rooms for **E** pp. Very good value.

C Sete Sete, Trav 1 de Março 673, T3222 7730. Refurbished, clean but still gloomy little rooms, good breakfast, convenient location, but be careful after dark.

C Unidos, Ó de Almeida 545, T3229 0600. Simple, spacious a/c rooms with cable TV and clean en suites.

D Palácio das Musas, Trav Frutuoso Guimarães 275, T3212 8422. Big rooms, shared bath.

D-E Fortaleza, Trav Frutuoso Guimarães 276, T3212 1055. Unkempt hotel with a range of basic wood-floor rooms and dorms around a communal sitting area. Popular with backpackers. Careful in this area after dark.

D-E Palácio, Trav Frutuoso Guimarães, T3212 8422. Opposite and almost identical to the *Fortaleza*, though with scruffier communal areas and slightly cleaner rooms, and a restaurant/snack bar.

D pp Amazônia, Av Gov José Malcher 592, Nazaré (between Quintino Bocaiúva and Rui Barbosa), T4008 4800, www.amazonia hostel.com.br. Good hostel.

Ilha do Marajó *p539*
Soure

B Ilha do Marajó, 2a Travessa 10, 15 mins' walk from centre, T/F3741 1315, himarajo@ interconect.com.br. A/c, bath, pool, popular with package tours.

B Marajó, Praça Inhangaíba 351, Centro, T3741 1396. A/c, bath, clean, helpful owner, renovated 2005.

D Pousada Asa Branca, Rua 4, T3741 1414. A/c, **E** with fan, breakfast, dirty, poor food.

Salvaterra

A Pousada das Guarás, Av Beira Mar, Salvaterra, T/F4005 5656, www.pousadadosguaras.com.br. Well-equipped, tour programme, on beach.

Joanes

B Pousada Ventania do Rio-Mar, take bus, US$1.20 from Foz do Cámara, T3646 2067, 9992 5716 (mob), www.pousadaventania.com. Near the beach, with bath and breakfast, fan, hammocks, laundry service, arranges tours on horseback or canoe, Belgian and Brazilian owners. Ask about their social integration projects with locals.

Macapá *p539*

AL Ceta Ecotel, R do Matodouro 640, Fazendinha, T227 3396, www.ecotel.com.br. 20 mins from town centre by taxi. All furniture made on site, a/c,

sports facilities, gardens with sloths and monkeys, ecological trails. Highly recommended.
AL-A Atalanta, Av Coracy Nunes 1148, T223 1612. 10 mins walk from the river. The best business-style hotel in town with a rooftop pool and comfortable, modern a/c rooms, includes generous breakfast.
A Pousada Ekinox, R Jovino Dinoá 1693, T223 0086, www.ekinox.com.br. Nice atmosphere, a/c, book and video library, excellent meals and service, riverboat tours available. Recommended.
C Glória, Leopoldo Machado 2085, T222 0984. A/c, minibar, TV.
D Mercúrio, R Cândido Mendes 1300, 2nd floor, T224 2766. 2 blocks from river. With breakfast, basic, large musty rooms with a/c.
D Vista Amazônica, Av Beira Rio 1298, T222 6851. Right opposite the Amazon, simple but well maintained rooms and good restaurant.
D-E Santo Antônio, Av Coriolano Jucá 485, T222 0226, 1 block south and half a block east of Praça da Bandeira. Best rooms are on upper floors, cheaper with fan, good breakfast extra; **E** in dormitory.

Border with Guyane: Oiapoque *p539*
Plenty of cheap, poorly-maintained hotels along the waterfront.
C Amapá, R Lélio Silva 298, near the Praça (1 block from the bus stop), T521 1768. A/c, bath, no breakfast. Recommended.
D Kayama, Av Joaquim Caetano da Silva 760, T521 1256. A/c and bath, **E** with fan, poor showers, lots of people hanging about, basic, international calls.
D Pousada Central, Av Coracy Nunes 209, one block from the river, T521 1466. A/c, bath, **E** with fan and shared bath.
E Mini Hotel, Av Coaracy Nunes, near bus stop, T521 1241. Fan, bath.

❶ Eating

Belém *p537, map p537*
All the major hotels have good restaurants.
₮₮₮ Açaí Hilton Hotel, Av Pres Vargas 882, T3242 6500. Recommended for regional dishes and others, Sun brunch or daily lunch and dinner.
₮₮₮ Boteco das Onze, Praça F C Brandão s/n, T3224 8599. About the best regional cooking in Belem with live music every night and a view over the river.
₮₮₮ Churrascaria Rodeio, Trav Pres Eutíquio 1308 and Rodovia Augusto Montenegro Km 4,

T3248 2004. A choice of 20 cuts of meat and 30 buffet dishes for a set price. Well worth the short taxi ride to eat all you can.
₮₮₮ Churrascaria Tucuruvi, Trav Benjamin Constant 1843, Nazaré, T3235 0341. Good value.
₮₮₮ Lá em Casa, Av Governador José Malcher 247 (also in Estação das Docas). Try menu paraense, good cooking, fashionable.
₮₮ Cantina Italiana, Trav Benjamin Constant 1401. Very good Italian, also delivers.
₮₮ Mãe Natureza, Manoel Barata 889, T3212 8032. Vegetarian and wholefood dishes in a bright clean dining room. Lunch only.
₮₮ Miako, Trav 1 de Março 766, behind Praça de República. Very good Japanese, oriental and international food.
₮₮ Sabor Paraense, R Sen Manoel Barata 897, T3241 4391. A variety of fish and meat dishes served in a bright, light dining room.
₮ Doces Bárbaros, Benjamin Constant 1658, T3224 0576. Cakes, snacks, sandwiches and decent coffee. Lunch only.
₮ Govinda, Ó de Almeida 198. Basic but tasty vegetarian food. Lunch only. **₮** Good snack bars serving *vatapá* (the Bahian dish), tapioca rolls etc, are concentrated on Assis de Vasconcelos on the eastern side of the Praça da Republica.

Macapá *p539*
₮₮₮ Chalé, Av Pres Vargas 499. Nice atmosphere and good food.
₮₮ Cantinho Baiano, Av Beira-Rio 1, Santa Inês, T223 4153. Good seafood. 10 mins walk south of the fort. Many other restaurants along this stretch about 1½ km beyond the Cantino Baiano including the **Vista Amazônica**, see Sleeping, above.
₮₮ Martinho's Peixaria, Av Beira-Rio 810. Another good fish restaurant.
₮ Bom Paladar Kilo's, Av Pres Vargas 456. Good pay-by-weight buffet.
₮ Sorveteria Macapá, R São José 1676, close to centre. Excellent ice cream made from local fruit.

❶ Bars and clubs

Belém *p537, map p537*
Many venues around Av Doca de Souza Franco, often just called 'Doca', especially popular Thu. The Reduto district is also very popular at night.
African Bar, Praça Waldemar Henrique 2. Rock or Samba, weekends only.
Baixo Reduto, R Quintino Bocaiúva, Reduto. Blues on Wed; Brazilian pop, Thu; rock, Fri and jazz, Sat.

● *For an explanation of the sleeping and eating price codes used in this guide, see inside the front*
● *cover. Other relevant information is found in Essentials pages 345-347.*

Bar Teatro Bora Bora, R Bernal do Couto 38, restaurant, bar and nightclub. MPB and Pagode open from 2100 until late Thu-Sun.

Cachaçaria Água Doce, R Diogo Móia 283 esq Wandenkolk. Specializes in fine cachaças, good appetizers, live music, informal atmosphere.

Colarinho Branco Chopperia, Av Visconde de Souza Franco 80, near the river. Open Tue-Sun 1800 to last customer, nightly performers of Brazilian popular music.

Escapóle, Rodovia Augusto Montenegro 400. Huge dance hall with various types of music, live and recorded, frequented by all age groups, open Wed-Sat from 2200 (take a radio taxi for safety), no a/c, dress informally.

Olê Olá, Av Tavares Bastos 1234. Disco, live music and dance floor. Thu-Sun, 2230 to last customer.

❀ Festivals and events

Belém p537, map p537

Círio, the Festival of Candles in **Oct**, is based on the legend of the Nossa Senhora de Nazaré, whose image was found on the site of her Basílica around 1700. On the 2nd Sun in Oct, a procession carries a copy of the Virgin's image from the Basílica to the cathedral. On the Mon, 2 weeks later, the image is returned to its usual place. There is a Círio museum in the crypt of the Basílica, enter at the right side of the church; free. (All hotels are fully booked during Círio.)

Macapá p539

Marabaixo is the traditional music and dance of the state of Amapá; a festival held 40 days after Easter. The sambódromo, near Marco Zero, is used by Escolas de Samba during Carnaval and by Quadrilhas during the São João festivities.

O Shopping

Belém p537, map p537
Belém is a good place to buy hammocks, look in the street parallel to the river, 1 block inland from Ver-o-Peso.

Arts and crafts market, Praça da República every weekend. Seed and bead jewellery, whicker, hammocks and raw cotton weave work, toys and other nic-nacs. Mostly predictable but the odd gem.

Complexo São Brás, Praça Lauro Sodré. Has a handicraft market and folkloric shows in a building dating from 1911.

Parfumaria Orion, Trav Frutuoso Guimarães 268. Sells a variety of perfumes from Amazonian plants, much cheaper than tourist shops.

▲ Activities and tours

Belém p537, map p537
Most of the larger hotels organize city and one-day boat tours.

Amazon Star, R Henrique Gurjão 236, T/F3241 8624, amazonstar@amazonstar. com.br. City and river tours, Ilha de Marajó hotel bookings and tours, very professional, good guides, jungle tours, books flight tickets. Repeatedly recommended.

Amazônia Sport & Ação, Av 25 de Setembro, 2345, T3226 8442. Extreme sports, diving, rock-climbing.

Macapá p539

Awara, Av Presidente Vargas 2396-B, T/F222 0970. Recommended for city and r iver tours, English and French spoken.

Marco Zero, R São José 2048, T223 1922, F222 3086. Recommended for flights.

⊖ Transport

Belém p537, map p537
Air Bus 'Perpétuo Socorro-Telégrafo' or 'Icoaraci', every 15 mins from the Prefeitura, Praça Felipe Patroni, to the airport, 40 mins, US$0.65. Taxi to airport, US$13 (ordinary taxis are cheaper than Co-op taxis, buy ticket in advance in Departures side of airport). ATMs for credit cards in the terminal. Airport T3210 6272.

Daily flights south to **Brasília** and other Brazilian cities, and west to **Santarém** and **Manaus**. To **Paramaribo** and **Cayenne**, 2 a week with Surinam Airways. Travellers entering Brazil from Guyane may need a 60-day visa (takes 2 days) before airlines will confirm their tickets. Internal flights also offered by Varig, Nordeste and TAM.

Bus The rodoviária is at the end of Av Governador José Malcher 5 km from the centre (T3246 8178). Take Aeroclube, Cidade Novo, No 20 bus, or Arsenal or Canudos buses, US$0.65, or taxi US$6.50 (day), US$9.25 (night) (at rodoviária you are given a ticket with the taxi's number on it, threaten to go to the authorities if the driver tries to overcharge). It has a good snack bar and showers (US$0.15) and 2 agencies with information and tickets for riverboats. Regular bus services to all major cities. To **Santarém**, via Marabá (on the Transamazônica) once a week (US$60, more expensive than by boat and can take longer, goes only in dry season). **Transbrasiliana** go direct to Marabá, 16 hrs, US$27. To **São Luís**, 2 a day, US$26, 13 hrs, interesting journey through marshlands. To **Fortaleza**, US$46-53 (24 hrs), several companies. To **Recife**, US$69, 34 hrs.

Ferry To **Santarém, Manaus**, and intermediate ports (see River Transport, Amazônia, page 535). All larger ships berth at

Portobrás/Docas do Pará (the main commercial port) at Armazém (warehouse) No 10 (entrance on Av Marechal Hermes, corner of Av Visconde de Souza Franco). The guards will sometimes ask to see your ticket before letting you into the port area, but tell them you are going to speak with a ship's captain. Ignore the touts who approach you. Macamazónia, R Castilho Franca, sells tickets for most boats, open Sun. There are 2 desks selling tickets for private boats in the rodoviária; some hotels recommend agents for tickets. Purchase tickets from offices 2 days in advance. Smaller vessels (sometimes cheaper, usually not as clean, comfortable or safe) sail from small docks along Estrada Nova (not a safe part of town). Take a Cremação bus from Ver-o-Peso.

To **Macapá (Porto Santana)**, the quickest (12 hrs) are the catamaran Atlântico I or the launches Lívia Marília and Atlântico II (slightly slower), all leaving at 0700 on alternate days. Other boats take 24 hrs: **Silja e Souza** (Wed) of Souzamar, Trav Dom Romualdo Seixas corner R Jerônimo Pimentel, T3222 0719, and **Almirante Solon** (Sat) of Sanave (Serviço Amapaense de Navegação, Castilho Franca 234, opposite Ver-o-Peso, T3222 7810), slightly cheaper, crowded, not as nice. Via Breves, ENAL, T3224 5210 (see River Transport in Amazônia, page 535). Smaller boats to Macapá also sail from Estrada Nova.

Ilha do Marajó p539
Ferry From Belém docks the Enasa ferry sails to Soure on Fri at 2000 (4 hrs, US$6.50). There are daily boats to Foz do Cámara at 0630, 0700 and 1300 (1½-3 hrs US$5). Then take a bus to Salvaterra and a ferry to Soure. Boats return from Foz do Cámara at 0800 and 1100. There is a 'taxi-plane' service to Soure leaving Belém at 0630 returning 1600, US$40.

Macapá p539
Air Varig (Av Hildemar Maia s/n, Santa Rita, T3223 4686), and **TAM** (T223 2688), fly to Belém and other Brazilian cities. **Gol** fly to Belém (at night), Brasília and São Paulo.
Bus New rodoviária on BR-156, north of Macapá. To **Amapá**, **Calçoene** and **Oiapoque** (15-17 hrs, US$20), at least 2 daily. The road is from Amapá to the border is due to be paved; before then you may have to get out and walk up hills, bus has no a/c.
Ferry Ships dock at Porto Santana, 30 km from Macapá (frequent buses US$1.70, or share a taxi US$20). To **Belém**, **Silja e Souza** of Souzamar, Cláudio Lúcio Monteiro 1375, Santana T281 1946, and **Almirante Solon** of Sanave, Av Mendonça Furtado 1766, T223 0244. See under Belém, River Services, for other boats. Purchase tickets from offices 2 days in advance. Also smaller and

cheaper boats. The faster (12 hr) catamaran Atlântico I or launches leave for Belém most days. **São Francisco de Paula I** sails to **Santarém** and **Manaus**, not going via Belém.

Border with Guyane: Oiapoque p539
Air Flights to **Macapá** Mon-Fri with Penta, office on the waterfront, T/F521 1117. While waiting for flights to Cayenne from St-Georges, it is much cheaper to stay on the Brazilian side.
Bus At least 2 a day for **Macapá**, 12-15 hrs (dry season), 14-24 hrs (wet season), US$20. Also shared jeeps, US$15 in the back, or US$37 in the cabin. You may be asked to show your Polícia Federal entry stamp and Yellow Fever vaccination certificate either when buying a ticket from the offices on the waterfront or at the bus station when boarding for Macapá.
Ferry Crossing to Guyane: motorized canoes cross to St-Georges de L'Oyapock, 10 mins downstream, US$5 pp, bargain for return fare. A vehicle ferry will operate until the bridge is completed.

❶ Directory

Belém p537, map p537
Airline offices BRA, T3073 8800, at airport T3210 6227. **Penta**, Av Sen Lemos 4700, T3244 7777. **Surinam Airways**, R Gaspar Viana 488, T3212 7144, airport 211 6038, English spoken, helpful with information and documentation. **Varig**, Av Pres Vargas 768, T3224 3344, airport T3257 0481. **Banks** Banco do Brasil, Av Pres Vargas (near Hotel Central), good rates, Visa ATMs, and other Brazilian banks (open 0900-1630, but foreign exchange only until 1300). **HSBC**, Av Pres Vargas near Praça da República has MasterCard Cirrus and Amex ATMs. **Banco de Amazônia** (Basa), on Pres Vargas, gives good rates for TCs (Amex or Citicorp only), but does not change cash. Itaú, R Boaventura 580, good TCs and cash rates. Since 2002 all **Casas de câmbio** have been closed, so money can only be changed at banks during the week. At weekends hotels will only exchange for their guests, while restaurants may change money, but at poor rates. Exchange rates are generally the best in the north of the country. **Embassies and consulates** Denmark (Consul Arne Hvidbo), R Senador Barata 704, sala 1503, T3241 1588 (PO Box 826). **Finland and Sweden**, Av Senador Lemos 529, Umarizal, T3222 0148. **Germany**, R Tiradentes 67, sala 204, T3212 8366, hsteffen.bel@orm.com.br. **UK**, Edif Palladium Centre, room 410, Av Gov José Malcher 815, T3222 5074, britbel@veloxmail.com.br. **USA**, Edifício Síntese 21, Av Conselheiro Furtado 2865, T3259 4566. **Venezuela**, opposite French

Consulate, Av Pres Pernambuco 270, T3222 6396 (Venezuelan visa for those entering overland takes 3 hrs, costs US$30 for most nationalities, but we are told that it is better to get a visa at Manaus, Boa Vista or before you leave home. **Internet** Amazon, 2nd floor of Estação das Docas. In Shopping Iguatemi, US$1.90 per hr. **Medical services** Health: a yellow fever certificate or inoculation is mandatory. It is best to get a yellow fever vaccination at home (always have your certificate handy) and avoid the risk of recycled needles. Medications for malaria prophylaxis are not sold in Belém pharmacies. Bring an adequate supply from home. **Clínica de Medicina Preventativa**, Av Bras de Aguiar 410 (T3222 1434), will give injections, English spoken, open 0730-1200, 1430-1900 (Sat 0800-1100). **Hospital Ordem Terceira**, Trav Frei Gil de Vila Nova 2, doctors speak some English, free consultation but it's a bit primitive. Surgery open Mon 1300-1900, Tue-Thu 0700-1100, 24 hrs for emergencies. The British consul has a list of English-speaking doctors. **Post offices** Av Pres Vargas 498, but international parcels are only accepted at the Post Office on the praça at the corner of Trav Frutuoso Guimarães e R 15 de Novembro, next door to NS das Mercês (hard to find). **Telephones** For phone calls: Telemar, Av Presidente Vargas. Fax at the Post Office, Av Pres Vargas. **Voltage** 110 AC, 60 cycles.

Macapá *p539*
Banks Banco do Brasil, R Independência 250, cash, Visa, ATM and TCs. Visa ATM also at Bradesco, Cândido Mendes 1316. MasterCard and Amex ATM at HSBC, Av Pres Vargas. Casa Francesa, Independência 232, changes euros (euros can be bought in Macapá and Belém). **Embassies and consulates** For the French honorary consul, ask at Pousada Ekinox, visas for Guyane have to be obtained from Brasília which can take a while. **Post offices** Av Coriolano Jucá. International calls can be made at São José 2050, 0730-1000.

Border with Guyane: Oiapoque *p539*
Banks Exchange: It is possible to exchange US$ and reais to euros, but dollar rates are low and TCs are not accepted anywhere. Banco do Brasil, Av Barão do Rio Branco, open 1000-1500, and Bradesco, have Visa facilities to withdraw reais which can be changed into euros. Casa Francesa, on the riverfront, and one câmbio in the market sell reais for US$ or euros. Rates are worse in St-Georges. Best to buy euros in Belém, or abroad. **Post offices** Av Barão do Rio Branco, open 0900-1200, 1400-1700. **Useful addresses** Immigration: Polícia Federal, for Brazilian exit and entry stamps, is on the road behind the church about 500 m from the river.

Belém to Manaus

A few hours up the broad river from Belém, the region of the thousand islands is entered. The passage through this maze of islets is known as 'The Narrows' and is perhaps the nicest part of the journey. The ship winds through 150 km of lanes of yellow flood with equatorial forest within 20 m or 30 m on both sides. On one of the curious flat-topped hills after the Narrows stands the little stucco town of **Monte Alegre**, an oasis in mid-forest (airport; some simple hotels, **D-E**). There are lagoon cruises to see lilies, birds, pink dolphins; also village visits (US$25-40 per day).

Santarém → *Phone code: 0xx93. Post code: 68000. Colour map 4, grid A5. Population: 262,538.*
The third largest city on the Brazilian Amazon is small enough to walk around. It was founded in 1661 as the Jesuit mission of Tapajós; the name was changed to Santarém in 1758. There was once a fort here and attractive colonial squares overlooking the waterfront remain. Standing at the confluence of the Rio Tapajós with the Amazon, on the southern bank, Santarém is half-way (two or three days by boat) between Belém and Manaus. Most visitors breeze in and out on a stopover by boat or air. **Tourist office: SANTUR**, Tv Inácio Corrêa 22, T/F3523 2434, good information available in English.

The yellow Amazon water swirls alongside the green-blue Tapajós; the **meeting of the waters**, in front of the market square, is nearly as impressive as that of the Negro and Solimões near Manaus. A small **Museu dos Tapajós** in the old city hall on the waterfront, now the **Centro Cultural João Fora** *closed Sat*, downriver from where the boats dock, has a collection of ancient Tapajós ceramics, as well as various 19th century artefacts. The unloading of the fish catch between 0500 and 0700 on the waterfront is interesting. There are good beaches nearby on the Rio Tapajós.

Alter do Chão

Some 34 km west of Santarém is this friendly village on the Rio Tapajós, at the outlet of Lago Verde. Of particular interest is the **Centro do Preservação de Arte Indígena** ① *R Dom Macedo Costa, T527 1110, 0800-1200, 1300-1700*, which has a substantial collection of artefacts from tribes of Amazônia and Mato Grosso. Good swimming in the Tapajós from the beautiful, clean beach.

Óbidos and around → *Phone code: 0xx93. Population: 46,500.*

At 110 km up-river from Santarém (five hours by boat), Óbidos is located at the narrowest and deepest point on the river. It is a picturesque and clean city with many beautiful, tiled buildings and some nice parks. Worth seeing are the **Prefeitura Municipal** *T547 1194*, the cuartel and the **Museu Integrado de Ôbidus** ① *R Justo Chermont 607, Mon-Fri 0700-1100, 1330-1730*. There is also a **Museu Contextual**, a system of plaques with detailed explanations of historical buildings throughout town. The airport has flights to Manaus, Santarém and Parintins.

Just across the Pará-Amazonas border, between Santarém and Manaus, is **Parintins** (*Phone code: 0xx92. Post code: 69150-000*), 15 hours by boat upriver from Óbidos. Here, on the last three days of June each year, the **Festa do Boi** draws over 50,000 visitors. Since the town has only two small hotels, everyone sleeps in hammocks on the boats that bring them to the festival from Manaus and Santarém. The festival consists of lots of folkloric dancing, but its main element is the competition between two rival groups, the Caprichoso and the Garantido, in the bumbódromo, built in 1988 to hold 35,000 spectators.

● Sleeping → *See Telephone, page 347, for important phone changes.*

Santarém *p544*

AL Amazon Park I, Av Mendonça Furtado 4120, T3523 2800, amazon@netsan.com.br. Swimming pool, 4 km from centre, taxi US$4.

A-B Mirante, Trav Francisco Correa, 115, T3522 0275, www.mirantehotel.com. Homely, a/c, fridge, TV, some rooms with balcony, individual safes, internet, good value. Recommended.

B-C Brasil Grande Hotel, Trav 15 de Agosto 213, T3522 5660. Family-run, with restaurant.

B-C New City, Trav Francisco Correia 200, T3523 2351. A/c, frigobar, good, will collect from airport.

B-C Santarém Palace, Rui Barbosa 726, T3523 2820. A/c, TV, fridge, comfortable.

C Brasil, Trav dos Mártires 30, T3523 6665. Nice, family-run, includes good breakfast, communal bath, good food, good service.

C Horizonte, Trav Senador Lemos 737, T522 5437, horizontehotel@bol.com.br. With a/c, **F** with fan, modern.

C-D Rios, R Floriano Peixoto 720, T522 5701. Large rooms, comfortable, a/c, fridge and TV.

Alter do Chão *p545*

A Pousada Tupaiulândia, Pedro Teixeira 300, T0xx93-3527 1157. A/c, unimpressive but OK, very helpful, good breakfast for US$5, next to telephone office opposite bus stop.

D Pousada Villa Praia, first on the right as you enter the village, T3527 1130. Large rooms, a/c, very helpful staff, good value.

Óbidos *p545*

Several in our **C** price range.

C Braz Bello, R Corrêia Pinto, on top of the hill. Shared bath, full board available.

C Pousada Brasil, R Correia Pinto. Basic, with bath, cheaper without.

● Eating

Santarém *p544*

¶¶ **Mascote**, Praça do Pescador 10. Open 1000-2330, restaurant, bar and ice-cream parlour.

¶¶ **Mascotinho**, Praça Manoel de Jesus Moraes, on riverfront. Bar/pizzeria, popular, outside seating, good view.

¶¶ **Santa Antônio**, Av Tapajós 2061. Churrasco and fish.

¶ **Lucy**, Praça do Pescador. Good juices and pastries. Recommended.

Alter do Chão *p545*

Lago Verde, Praça 7 de Setembro. Good fresh fish, try caldeirada de tucunaré, huge portions.

● *For an explanation of the sleeping and eating price codes used in this guide, see inside the front*
● *cover. Other relevant information is found in Essentials pages 345-347.*

⊛ Festivals and events

Santarém *p544*
29 Jun, São Pedro, with processions of boats on the river and boi-bumbá dance dramas.

Alter do Chão *p545*
2nd week in Sep, Festa do Çairé, religious processions and folkloric events.

▲ Activities and tours

Santarém *p544*
Amazon Jungle Tours, R Galdino Veloso 200, T3529 0146, 9903 7320 (mob), radarfinder@hotmail.com. Tours from 1 to 7 days by boat, English, French and Spanish spoken.
Amazon Tours, Trav Turiano Meira 1084, amazonriver@netsan.com.br, www.amazonriver.com. The owner Steve Alexander is a very friendly, helpful man who can give you lots of hints on what to do. He also organizes excursions for groups to remote areas which are quite expensive. Recommended.
Coruá-Una Turismo, R Dr Hugo Mendonça 600, T518 1014. Offers various tours, Pierre d'Arcy speaks French. Recommended.
Santarém Tur, in Amazon Park, and at R Adriano Pimental 44, T3522 4847, www.santaremtur.com.br. Owned by Perpétua and Jean-Pierre Schwarz (speaks French), friendly, helpful, also group tours (group of 5, US$65 per day pp). Recommended.
Gil Serique, Av Bartolomeu de Gusmão 883, T522 5174, www.youramazon.org. English-speaking guide. Recommended.
Tapam Turismo, Trav 15 de Agosto, 127 A, T523 2422. Recommended.

⊖ Transport

Santarém *p544*
Air 15 km from town, T523 1021. Internal flights only. Buses run to the centre or waterfront. From the centre the bus leaves in front of the cinema in Rui Barbosa every 80 mins from 0550 to 1910, or taxis (US$10.50 to waterfront). The hotels Amazon Park and New City have free buses for guests; you may be able to take these.
Bus Rodoviária is on the outskirts (T522 3392), take 'Rodagem' bus from the waterfront near the market, US$0.25. Santarém to **Marabá** on the Rio Tocantins with Transbrasiliana. From Marabá there are buses east and west on the Transamazônica. Enquire at the rodoviária for other destinations. Road travel during rainy season is always difficult, often impossible.
Ferry To **Manaus**, **Belém**, **Macapá**, **Itaituba**, and intermediate ports (see River transport, page 535). Boats to Belém and Manaus dock at the Cais do Porto, 1 km west, take 'Floresta-Prainha', 'Circular' or 'Circular Externo' bus; taxi US$5. Boats to other destinations, including Macapá, dock by the waterfront by the centre of town. Local service to **Óbidos**, US$13, 4 hrs, Oriximiná US$16.50, Alenquer, and **Monte Alegre** (US$13, 5-8 hrs).

Alter do Chão *p545*
Bus Tickets and information from the bus company kiosk opposite Pousada Tupaiulândia. From Santarém: bus stop on Av São Sebastião, in front of Colégio Santa Clara, US$1.30, about 1 hr.

Óbidos and around: Parintins *p545*
Ferry Apart from boats that call on the **Belém-Manaus** route, there are irregular sailings from **Óbidos** (ask at the port). Journey times are about 12-15 hrs from **Manaus** and 20 from **Santarém**. There is also a small airport with **flights** to Manaus, **Óbidos** and **Santarém**.

⊙ Directory

Santarém *p544*
Airline offices Penta, Trav 15 de Novembro 183, T523 2532. **Varig**, Av Rui Barbosa, 790, T523 2488. **Banks** Cash withdrawals on Visa at Banco do Brasil, Av Rui Barbosa 794. It is very difficult to change dollars (impossible to change TCs anywhere), try travel agencies. **Internet** Tapajós On Line, Mendonça Furtado 2454, US$3.50 per hr. **Post office** Praça da Bandeira 81. **Telephones** Posto Trin, R Siquiera Campos 511. 0700-1900 Mon-Sat, 0700-2100 Sun.

Manaus → *Phone code: 0xx92. Post code: 69000. Colour map 4, grid A3. Population 1.4 million*

The next city upriver is Manaus, capital of Amazonas State – the largest in Brazil. Once an isolated urban island in the jungle, it now sprawls over a series of eroded and gently sloping hills divided by numerous creeks (igarapés). The city is growing fast and 20-storey modern buildings are rising above the traditional flat, red-tiled roofs, but an impressive initiative in 2001 saw the start of a significant restoration programme in which historic buildings have been given a new lease of life and theatres, cultural spaces and libraries created. Manaus is an excellent port of entry for visiting the Amazon. Less than a day away are river islands and tranquil waterways. The opportunities for canoeing, trekking in the forest and meeting local people should not be missed and, once you are out of reach of the urban influence, there are plenty of animals to see. There is superb swimming in the natural pools and under falls of clear water in the little streams which rush through the woods, but take locals' advice on swimming in the river (electric eels and various other kinds of unpleasant fish, apart from the notorious piranhas, abound and industrial pollution of the river is growing).

Ins and outs → *Manaus is 1 hr behind Brazilian standard time (2 hrs Oct-Feb, Brazil's summer time).*
Getting there Boats dock at different locations depending on where they have come from. The **docks** are quite central. The **airport** is 18 km from the centre, the **bus terminal** 9 km. Both are served by local buses and taxis.

Getting around All city bus routes start below the cathedral in front of the port entrance; just ask someone for the destination you want. The city centre is easily explored on foot (although bear in mind an average temp of 27ºC). ▶▶ *See Transport, page 554, for further details.*

Tourist office AmazonasTur (state tourism office), R Saldanha Marinho 321, T2123 3800, www.amazonastur.am.gov.br. Open 0800-1700. Offices at Avenida Eduardo Ribeiro 666, near Teatro Amazonas, T3231 1998. Open Monday-Friday 0800-1700, Saturday 0800-1200. Limited English and information. At the airport, open daily 0700-2300, T3652 1120. Also in Amazonas Shopping Center, T3648 1396, in the new cruise ship terminal at the docks (open when a ship is in town) and in a trailer at the Rodoviária. **ManausTur**, Avenida 7 de Setembro 157, T3622 4948, manaus@pmm.am.gov.br. Town map from Amazon Explorers, or news kiosks. Weekend editions of A Crítica, newspaper, list local entertainments and events. See also www.manausonline.com.

Security Manaus is a friendly, if busy city and a good deal safer than the big cities of southern Brazil. As in any city, the usual precautions against opportunist crime should be taken, especially when arriving at night (see River transport in Amazônia on staying on boats in port). Bars along R Joaquim Nabuco are reported particularly unsafe. This street, R dos Andrades, R 10 de Julho and the port area are not places to hang around after dark. A tourist police force, **Politur**, assists visitors. See below for advice on choosing a jungle tour.

Sights
Dominating the centre is a **Cathedral** built in simple Jesuit style on a hillock; very plain inside or out. Nearby is the main shopping and business area, the tree-lined Avenida Eduardo Ribeiro; crossing it is Av 7 de Setembro, bordered by ficus trees. **Teatro Amazonas** ① *Praça São Sebastião, T3622 1880 for information on programmes, Mon-Sat 0900-1600, 20-min tour US$7. Recommended.* About same price for a concert. This opulent theatre was completed in 1896 during the great rubber boom following 15 years of construction. It has been restored four times and should not be missed. There are ballet, theatre and opera performances several times a week and free popular Brazilian music on Monday nights, June-December. **Igreja São Sebastião** (1888), on the same praça, has an unusual altar of two giant ivory hands holding a water lily of Brazil wood.

On the waterfront, the **Mercado Adolfo Lisboa** *R dos Barés 46*, was built in 1902 as a miniature copy of the now demolished Parisian Les Halles. The wrought ironwork which forms much of the structure was imported from Europe and is said to have been designed by Eiffel. The remarkable **harbour installations**, completed in 1902, were designed and built by a Scottish engineer to cope with the up to 14 m annual rise and fall of the Rio Negro. The large passenger ship floating dock is connected to street level by a 150 m-long floating ramp, at the end of which, on the harbour wall, can be seen the high water mark for each year since it was built. When the water is high, the roadway floats on a series of large iron tanks measuring 2½m in diameter. The large beige **Alfândega** (Customs House) ① *R Marquês de Santa Cruz, Mon-Fri 0800-1200, 1400-1600*, stands at the entrance to the city when arriving by boat. It was entirely prefabricated in England, and the tower once acted as lighthouse.

The **Biblioteca Pública Estadual** (Public Library) ① *R Barroso 57, T234 0588, Mon-Fri 0730-1730*, inaugurated in 1871, features an ornate European cast iron staircase. It is well stocked with 19th century newspapers, rare books and old photographs, and worth a visit. The **Centro Cultural Pálacio Rio Negro** ① *Av 7 de Setembro, T3232 4450, Tue-Fri 1000-1700*,

Sat-Sun 1600-2100, was the residence of a German rubber merchant until 1917 and later the state government palace. It now holds various cultural events, including exhibitions, houses the Museu-Biblioteca da Imagem e do Som, shows and films; there is also a café.

There is a curious little church, **Igreja do Pobre Diabo** ① *corner of Av Borba and Av Ipixuna in the suburb of Cachoeirinha*; it is only 4 m wide by 5 m long, and was built by a tradesman, the 'poor devil' of the name. Take Circular 7 Cachoeirinha bus from the cathedral to Hospital Militar.

On Praça da Polícia is the very small **Museu Tiradentes** ① *closed 2006*, run by the military police and holds selected historical items and old photographs. A short distance away is **Museu do Homem do Norte** ① *Av 7 de Setembro 1385 (near Av J Nabuco), T3232 5373, Mon-Fri 0900-1200, 1300-1700, US$1*, which reviews the way of life of the Amazonian population; social, cultural and economic aspects are displayed with photographs, models and other pieces. **Instituto Geográfico e Histórico do Amazonas** ① *R Frei José dos Inocentes 117 (near Prefeitura), T3232 7077, Mon-Fri 0900-1200, 1300-1600, US$0.50*, located in a fascinating older district of central Manaus, houses a museum and library of over 10,000 books which thoroughly document Amazonian life through the ages, **Museu do Índio** ① *R Duque de Caxias 296, T3635 1922, Mon-Fri 0800-1130, 1400-1630, Sat 0830-1130, US$3*, kept by the Salesian missionaries: this interesting, if rather run down, museum's collection includes handicrafts, ceramics, clothing, utensils and ritual objects from the various indiegenous tribes of the upper Rio Negro; excellent craft shop.

Manaus

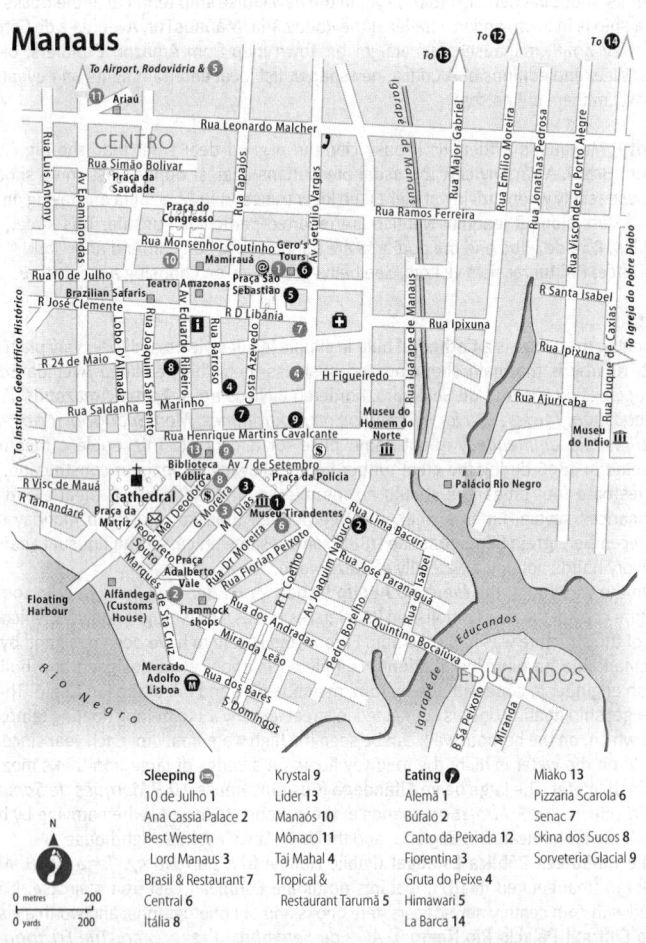

Sleeping		Krystal 9	Eating	Miako 13
10 de Julho 1		Lider 13	Alemã 1	Pizzaria Scarola 6
Ana Cassia Palace 2		Manaós 10	Búfalo 2	Senac 7
Best Western		Mônaco 11	Canto da Peixada 12	Skina dos Sucos 8
Lord Manaus 3		Taj Mahal 4	Fiorentina 3	Sorveteria Glacial 9
Brasil & Restaurant 7		Tropical &	Gruta do Peixe 4	
Central 6		Restaurant Tarumã 5	Himawari 5	
Itália 8			La Barca 14	

N

0 metres   200
0 yards   200

Botanic Gardens, **Instituto Nacional de Pesquisas Amazonas** (INPA) ① *Estrada do Aleixo, at Km 3, not far from the Museu de Ciências Naturais da Amazônia, T643 3377, Mon-Fri 0900-1100, 1400-1630, Sat-Sun 0900-1600, US$2, take any bus to Aleixo*. At the centre for scientific research in the Amazon, labs (not open to the public) investigate farming, medicines and tropical diseases in the area. There is a small museum and restaurant, lots of birds, named trees and manatees (best seen Wednesday and Friday mornings when the water is changed), caimans and giant otters; worth a visit. **Museu de Ciências Naturais da Amazônia** ① *Al Cosme Ferreira, Colonia Cachoeira Grande, 15 km from the city, T3644 2799, Mon-Sat 0900-1700, US$4, difficult to get to, take 'São José-Acoariquarape/ Tropolis' bus 519 to Conjunto Petro, then 2 km walk*. Best to combine with a visit to INPA, and take a taxi from there. The museum has a pavilion with insects and fish of the region. **Jardim Botânico 'Chico Mendes'** (Horto Municipal) ① *Av André Araujo s/n, daily 0800-1200, 1400-1700, buses 'Aleixo', 'Coroado*. 'The botanical gardens contain a collection of plants from the Amazon region. The **zoo** ① *Estrada Ponta Negra 750 (look for the life-size model jaguar), T3625 2044, Tue-Sun 0900-1630, US$0.65, plus US$1 for trail, getting there: take bus 120 or 207, 'Ponta Negra', from R Tamandaré, US$1*. It is run by CIGS, the army jungle-survival unit. It has been expanded and improved and has a 800-m trail which leads into the zoo itself.

About 15 km from Manaus is the confluence of the yellow-brown Solimões (Amazon) and the blue-black Rio Negro, which is itself some 8 km wide. The two rivers run side by side for about 18 km (says one traveller) without their waters mingling. Tourist agencies run boat trips to this spot (US$60-160). The simplest route is to take a taxi or No 713 'Vila Buriti' bus to the Careiro ferry dock, and take the car ferry across. The ferry (very basic, with no shelter on deck and no cabins) goes at 0700 returning 1000, and 1500 returning 1800 (approximately). Small private launches cross, 40 minutes' journey, US$10-15 per seat, ask for the engine to be shut off at the confluence, you should see dolphins especially in the early morning. Alternatively, hire a motorized canoe from near the market (US$15 approximately; allow 3-4 hours to experience the meeting properly). A 2-km walk along the Porto Velho road from the Careiro ferry terminal will lead to a point from which Victoria Regia water lilies can be seen in April/May-September in ponds, some way from the road. Agencies can arrange tours.

Arquipélago de Anavilhanas, the largest archipelago in a river in the world, is in the Rio Negro, some 100 km upstream from Manaus, near the town of Novo Airão. There are hundreds of islands, covered in thick vegetation. When the river is low, white sand beaches are revealed, as well as the roots and trunks of the trees. Tour companies arrange visits to the archipelago (see below).

Mamirauá ① *4-day, 3-night package US$360 all inclusive ("worth every penny"). Reservations through Toxx97-3343 4672, www.mamiraua.org.br. Can also be booked through Iguana Tours (see Tour operators), or contact through their web site or through their shop next to Teatro Amazonas on R 10 de julho 495 (see Shopping). Book well in advance*. All profits go to local projects and research. Daily flights Manaus-Tefé, then 1½ hours by boat to lodge. This sustainable development reserve, at the confluence of the Rios Solimões, Japurá and Auti-Paraná, is one of the best places to see the Amazon. It protects flooded forest (várzea) and is listed under the Ramsar Convention as an internationally important wetland. In the reserve Uakari is a floating lodge with 10 suites. Lots of mammals and birds to see, including cayman, dolphin and harpy eagles, also the endangered pirarucu fish. Visitors are accompanied by guides the whole time.

Tours from Manaus

There are two types of tours: those based at **jungle lodges** and **river boat trips**. Most tours, whether luxury or budget, combine river outings on motorised canoes with piranha fishing, caiman spotting, visiting local families and short treks in the jungle. Specialist tours include fishing trips and those aimed specifically at seeing how the people in the jungle, caboclos, live. Booking in advance on the internet is likely to secure you a good guide (who usually works for several companies and may get booked up). Be sure to ascertain in advance the exact itinerary of the tour, that the price includes everything (even drink and tips), that guides are knowledgeable and will accompany you themselves and that there will be no killing of anything rare. Ensure that others in your party share your expectations and are going for the same length of time. Choose a guide who speaks a language you can understand. A shorter tour may be better than a long, poor one. Packaged tours, booked overseas, are usually of the same price and quality as those negotiated locally.

Note: There are many hustlers at the airport and on the street (particularly around the hotels and bars on Joaquim Nabuco and Miranda Leão), and even at the hotels. It is not wise to go on a tour with the first friendly face you meet; all go-betweens earn a commission so recommendations cannot be taken at face value. Employing freelance guides not attached to a company is potentially dangerous. Make enquiries and check for official and ABAV (Brazilian Association of Travel Agents) credentials personally. Secretaria de Estado da Cultura e Turismo is not allowed by law to recommend guides, but can provide you with a list of legally registered companies. Unfortunately, disreputable operations are rarely dealt with in any satisfactory manner and most continue to operate. When you are satisfied that you have found a reputable company, book direct with the company itself and ask for a detailed, written contract if you have any doubts.

Flights over the jungle give a spectacular impression of the extent of the forest. Bill Potter, resident in Manaus, writes: "opposite Manaus, near the junction of the Rio Negro and the Rio Solimões, lies the **Lago de Janauri**, a small nature reserve. This is where all the day or half-day trippers are taken, usually combined with a visit to the 'meeting of the waters'. Although many people express disappointment with this area because so little is seen and/or there are so many 'tourist-trash' shops, for those with only a short time it is worth a visit. You will see some birds and with luck dolphins. In the shops and bars there are often captive parrots and snakes. The area is set up to receive large numbers of tourists, which ecologists agree relieves pressure on other parts of the river. Boats for day trippers leave the harbour constantly throughout the day, but are best booked at one of the larger operators. Remember that in the dry season, one-day tours may not offer much to see if the river is low."

Those with more time can take the longer cruises and will see various ecological environments. To see virgin rainforest, a five-day trip by boat is needed. Most tour operators operate on both the Rio Solimões and the Rio Negro. The Rio Negro is considered easier to navigate, generally calmer and with fewer biting insects, but as it is a black water river with forest growing on poor soil and the tannin-filled waters are acidic, there are fewer frutiferous trees and fish and therefore fewer animals. The tributaries of the Solimões have higher concentrations of wildlife; including biting insects. Currently most Solimões tours go to the Rio Mamori area via the Port Velho highway and the Mamori river. There is plenty of deforestation along the initial stages of this river. The best lodges for wildlife are the furthest from Manaus but don't expect to see lots of animals. This is difficult anywhere in the Amazon, but you should see caiman, macaws, boa constrictors and river dolphins. It is the immensity of the forest and rivers and the seemingly limitless horizons, as well as a glimpse of the extraordinary way of life of the Amazon people, which make these tours exciting. For the best wildlife options in the Brazilian Amazon head for Alta Floresta, the Mamirauá reserve near Tefé (see above), or the little visited forests of northern Roraima.

Generally, between April and September excursions are only by boat; in the period October-March the Victoria Regia lilies virtually disappear. If using a camera, do remember to bring a fast film as light is dim.

Prices vary, but usually include lodging, guide, transport, meals and activities. The recommended companies charge within the following ranges (per person): one day, US$50-100; three days, eg to Anavilhanas Archipelago, US$195-285. Longer, specialized, or more luxurious excursions will cost significantly more. Most river trips incorporate the meeting of the waters on the first day, so there is no need to make a separate excursion. For Lodges, see under Sleeping, below.

What to take Leave luggage with your tour operator or hotel in Manaus and only take what is necessary for your trip. Long sleeves, long trousers, shoes and insect repellent are advisable for treks where insects are voracious. Take a mosquito net (and a hammock mosquito net if going on a cheaper tour) for trips in February-June. A hat offers protection from the sun on boat trips. Bottled water and other drinks are expensive in the jungle, so you may want to take your own supplies.

Manaus p546, map p548

10% tax and service must be added to bills. Hotel booking service at airport (see Transport, below, on taxi drivers' ruses). The best option is the area around the Teatro Amazonas, where the Italianate colonial houses and cobbled squares have been refurbished. A less good alternative is the Zona Franca, which is convenient for shops, banks, restaurants and the port area, but is not very safe at night. Av Joaquim Nabuco and R dos Andradas have many cheap hotels (**E**), most of which charge by the hour and all of which are in an area which is undesirable after dark.

LL Taj Mahal Continental, Av Getúlio Vargas 741, T3627 3737, www.grupotajmahal.com.br. Large, impressive, one of best hotels in city, popular, tour agency, revolving restaurant, massage and high level of service. Recommended.

LL Tropical, Av Coronel Teixeira 1320, Ponta Negra, T2123 5000, www.tropicalhotel.com.br. A lavish, 5-star Varig hotel 20 km outside the city (taxi to centre, US$25). Wave pools, beach with new dock, departure point for river cruises and agency which arranges them, tennis courts, churrascaria, pool, 24-hr coffee shop, open to well-dressed non-residents. Take minibus from R José Paranaguá in front of Petrobras building at the corner of Dr Moreira, US$6.50 return, 0830, 0930, 1130 to hotel, 1200, 1400, 1500, 1800 to town, or take Ponta Negra bus, US$1, then walk. It is rarely full, except in Jan-Feb.

L Best Western Lord Manaus, R Marcílio Dias 217, T3622 2844, bwmanaus@internext.com.br. Pleasant, spacious a/c lobby and standard, though well-presented rooms.

AL-A Krystal, Rua Barroso 54, T3233 7535. A range of small though business-like, well-maintained modern a/c rooms.

AL-A Mônaco, R Silva Ramos 20, T2121 0004, monaco@internext.com.br. The furniture and fittings may be a bit old-fashioned and plastic, but wonderful views from the top floor rooms, restaurant and little pool.

A Ana Cassia Palace, R dos Andradas 14, T3622 3637, www.hotelanacassia.com.br. Gloriously faded, large rooms, some with great views of port, restaurant, pool.

A Brasil, Av Getúlio Vargas 657, T3233 7271, www.hotelbrasil.tur.br. Mid-market option close to centre, faded rooms and tiny bathrooms and balconies, small pool.

A Lider, Av 7 de Setembro 827, T3633 1326, liderhotel@internext.com.br. Small, modern a/c rooms with little breakfast tables. The best are at the front on the upper floors. Very well-kept.

A Manaós, Av Eduardo Ribeiro 881, T3633 5744, www.hotelmanaos.brasilcomercial.com. Recently renovated; smart a/c rooms with marble floors, decent breakfast, next to Teatro Amazonas.

A-B Central, R Dr Moreira 202, T3622 2600, www.hotelcentralmanaus.com.br. A business hotel in the Zona Franca, check rooms thoroughly as many are very scruffy, but a few are good, excellent breakfast.

B-C 10 de Julho, R Dez de Julio 679, T3232 6280, www.hoteldezdejulho.com. Near opera house, a/c, much the best cheap option, very clean though simple rooms (some with a/c and hot water), efficient, laundry, tour operator and English speaking staff.

C Itália, Rua Guilherme Moreira 325, T234 7934. Very simple but well kept rooms in the heart of the Zona Franca, the best are on the upper floors. Generous breakfast.

Camping There are no campsites near Manaus; it is difficult to find a good, safe place to camp wild.

Lodges near Manaus

There are several lodges within a few hrs boat or car journey from Manaus. Most emphasize comfort (although electricity and hot water is limited) rather than a real jungle experience and you are more likely to enjoy a nice buffet in pleasant company than come face to face with rare fauna. Nevertheless, the lodges are good if your time is limited and you want to have a brief taste of the Amazon rainforest. Agencies for reservations are also listed. Most of the lodges around Manaus apply the term 'ecotourism' very loosely. Very few of the lodges are locally owned and only a small percentage of labour is drawn from local communities. Only a handful of people have benefited from a boom which has seen the total number of beds rise from just 6 in 1979 to over 1000 today. See www.viverde.com.br for general information on lodges.

LL Acajatuba Jungle Lodge, office at Conj Vila Municipal, Rua 07, no 87, Adrianópolis, T3642 0358, www.acajatuba.com.br. A 40-apartment lodge in a beautiful area on lake Acajatuba just below the Anavilhanas islands, 70 km from Manaus. Good piranha fishing, plenty of caiman and lots of várzea forest. It's close to Ariaú. Service can be patchy.

● For an explanation of the sleeping and eating price codes used in this guide, see inside the front
● cover. Other relevant information is found in Essentials pages 345-347.

LL Ariaú Amazon Towers, Rio Ariaú, 2 km from Archipélago de Anavilhanas, Manaus office at R Leonardo Malcher 699, T2121 5000, www.ariau towers.com.br. 60 km and 2 hrs by boat from Manaus on a side channel of the Rio Negro. Complex of towers connected by walkways, beach (Sep-Mar), trips to the Anavilhanas islands in groups of 10-20. Rates pp: US$280 for 2-days/1-night, US$400, 3 nights/4 days. Highly recommended.

LL Amazon Ecopark Lodge, Igarapé do Tarumã, 20 km from Manaus, 15 mins by boat, jungle trails; 60 apartments with shower, bar, restaurant, T9146 0594, www.amazonecopark.com.br. Comfortable lodge with 60 apartments and a decent restaurant only 15 mins from Hotel Tropical and used by them for many of their day trips. Pleasant guided walks but poor for wildlife.

LL Amazon Lodge, contact T656 3357. A floating lodge on Lago do Juma, 80 km from Manaus, 30 mins by Careiro ferry, then 1½ hrs by bus, then 2 hrs by boat, 12 basic apartments with cold shower, restaurant, good excursions. Highly recommended as an excellent choice for wildlife.

LL Amazon Village, Lago do Puraquequara, 60 km, contact T3633 1444, avillage@internext.com.br. 2 hrs by boat from Manaus, a comfortable lodge on dry land, with nice cabins, 32 apartments with cold shower, restaurant. Recommended.

LL Juma Lodge, T3232 2707, www.jumahotel.com.br. Small lodge on the Rio Juma, idyllic location near the Rio Mamori, 2½ hrs south of Manaus by road and boat, all-inclusive packages. One of the best options for wildlife.

LL Pousada dos Guanavenas on Ilha de Silves, T656 1500, www.guanavenas.com.br. 300 km from Manaus on the road to Itacoatiara then by boat along the Rio Urubu, views of Lago Canacari. Comfortable rooms with a/c and hot water and a good restaurant on a black water lake some 4-5 hrs from Manaus, but in an area with abundant wildlife.

L Wild Cabanas, book through Brazilian Safaris (see Tour operators), www.wildcabana.com. Comfortable rooms and hammock space in a large maloca-like building on a caiman-filled lake close to the Rio Mamori. One of the best options for backpackers.

L-AL Rainforest Lodge, contact MS Empreendimentos, T3233 9182, rflodge@n3.com.br. On the banks of Lago Januacá, 4 hrs from Manaus, 14 bungalows with fans, pool, restaurant, snack bar.

AL Boa Vida Jungle Resort, contact T3633 2501, F3232 2482. 53 km from Manaus by route AM-10, direction Itacoatiara, 7 apartments and 6 chalets, shower, fridge, bar, restaurant, fishing, boating. A good area for wildlife and little visited.

AL Aldeia dos Lagos Lodge, Silves Project, T/F 5282124. Simple floating lodge on a lake, run in conjunction with the local community and WWF. Good for birds and caiman.

Amazon Youth Hostel, near the town of Maués, southeast of Manaus. Contact Doña Nailê or Joe Maldonado, T9127 7941. US$75 per week in dormitory, US$150 per week in cabin, no electricity, take your own food and hammock, kitchen, lounge, hiking, canoeing. **Rico Airlines**, address below, fly Manaus-Maués US$75, 1 hr, or boat at 1600, arrive 1100 next day, US$25 (take own hammock). In Maués go to Casa Quixada store and take a water taxi to the hostel, US$30 per group.

🍴 Eating

Manaus p546, map p548
Many restaurants close on Sun nights and Mon. City authorities grade restaurants for cleanliness: look for A and B.

ᵀᵀᵀ La Barca, R Recife 684, T642 3040. Wide variety of fish dishes, very swanky, popular, often has live music.

ᵀᵀᵀ Himawari, R 10 de Julho 618. Swish, sushi and Japanese food, attentive service, opposite Teatro Amazonas, open Sun night, when many restaurants close. Recommended.

ᵀᵀᵀ Miako, R São Luís 230. Japanese.

Restaurant Tarumã in Tropical Hotel (see above). Dinner only.

ᵀᵀ Búfalo, churrascaria, Av Joaquim Nabuco 628. Best in town, US$7, all you can eat Brazilian barbecue.

ᵀᵀ Canto da Peixada, R Emílio Moreira 1677 (Praça 14 de Janeiro). Superb fish dishes, lively atmosphere, unpretentious, close to centre, take a taxi.

ᵀᵀ Fiorentina, R José Paranaguá 44, Praça da Polícia. Fan-cooled, traditional Italian, including vegetarian dishes, average food but one of best options in centre, watch out for the mugs of wine! Great feijoada on Sat, half-price on Sun.

ᵀᵀ Peixaria Moronguetá, floating boat restaurant, with view of Meeting of the Waters, regional food, also caters for big groups. Transfer daily from R Jaith Chaves 30, CEASA, T615 3362.

ᵀᵀ Pizzaria Scarola, R 10 de Julho 739, corner with Av Getúlio Vargas. Standard Brazilian menu, pizza delivery, popular.

ᵀ Alemã, R José Paranaguá, Praça da Polícia. Food by weight, great pastries, hamburgers, juices, sandwiches.

ᵀ Brasil, Av Getúlio Vargas next to hotel of same name, see above. Food by weight, juice and sandwich kiosk outside hotel.

ᵀ Gruta do Peixe, R Saldanha Marinho 609. Self-service and pratos in attractive basement, lunch only. Recommended.

¶ **O Naturalista**, R 7 de Setembro 752, 2nd floor. Vegetarian, lunch only.

¶ **Senac**, R Saldanha Marinho, 644. Cookery school, self-service, open daily, lunch only. Highly recommended.

¶ **Skina dos Sucos**, Eduardo Ribeiro e 24 de Maio. Regional fruit juices and snacks.

¶ **Sorveteria Glacial**, Av Getúlio Vargas 161 and other locations. Recommended for ice-cream.

Bars and clubs

Manaus *p546, map p548*
The city has very lively nightlife - especially live forró and pagodé. **Mon** Coração Blue, Estrada Ponta Negra, live forró and general dance in a large club, US$2 entrance. **Tue** Hollywood Rock, Estrada Ponta Negra, live pagodé, US$2 entrance. **Wed** Antares, Estrada Dom Pedro, Kisia, live brega (a frenetic northern Brazilian form of forró), US$2. **Thu** Clube do Forró, Estrada do Aleixo, live forró, US$2. **Fri** Simbola, Estrada Ponta Negra, big club with 3 floors playing a mix of club music, forró and pagodé, US$3.50. **Sat** numerous clubs especially Simbola and Taliãsm Forró club in Cachoeirinha. **Sun** Hollywoodand Simbola.
Bar do Armando, 10 de Julho e Tapajós, behind the Teatro. Bohemian atmosphere, good place for drinking outside.
DJ (Djalma) Oliveira, T9112 3942, specialises in taking people out to sample Manaus club life, is cheaper than taxis and speaks a little English. He can be booked through Gero's Tours.
O Laranjinha, Ponta Negra, is lively any week night and has a live Boi Bumba dance show on Wed. Be wary of 'piranhas' of the female, human kind after midnight.
Tucano nightclub in the Tropical Hotel attracts Manaus's wealthy citizens on Thu-Sat, as does its bingo club. Nearby Ponta Negra beach becomes extremely lively late on weekend nights and during holidays, with outdoor concerts and samba in the summer season.

Entertainment

Manaus *p546, map p548*
Performing arts For Teatro Amazonas and Centro Cultural Pálacio Rio Negro, see above.
Teatro da Instalação, R Frei José dos Inocentes, T/F234 4096. Performance space in recently restored historic buildings with free music and dance (everything from ballet to jazz), Mon-Fri May-Dec at 1800. Charge for performances Sat and Sun. Recommended.
Funfair In Praça da Saudade, R Ramos Ferreira, there is a Sun funfair from 1700; try prawns and calaloo dipped in tacaca sauce.

Festivals and events

Manaus *p546, map p548*
6 Jan: Epiphany; Ash Wednesday, half-day; Maundy Thursday; **24 Jun**: São João; **14 Jul**; **5 Sep**; **30 Oct**; **1 Nov**, All Saints Day, half-day; Christmas Eve; New Year's Eve, half-day.
Feb: Carnival dates vary – 5 days of Carnival, culminating in the parade of the Samba Schools. 3rd week in **Apr**: Week of the Indians, indigenous handicraft. In **Jun**: Festival do Amazonas; a celebration of all the cultural aspects of Amazonas life, indigenous, Portuguese and from the northeast, especially dancing; **29 Jun**: São Pedro, boat processions on the Rio Negro. In **Sep**: Festival da Bondade, last week, stalls from neighbouring states and countries offering food, handicrafts, music and dancing, SESI, Estrada do Aleixo Km 5. **Oct**: Festival Universitário de Música – FUM, the most traditional festival of music in Amazonas, organized by the university students, on the University Campus. **8 Dec**: Procissão de Nossa Senhora da Conceicão, from the Igreja Matriz through the city centre and returning to Igreja Matriz for a solemn mass.

Shopping

Manaus *p546, map p548*
Since Manaus is a free port, the whole area a few blocks off the river front is full of electronics shops. All shops close at 1400 on Sat and all day Sun.
Bookshops Livraria Nacional, R 24 de Maio 415. Stocks some French books. **Paper Comunicação**, Av J Nabuco 2074-2. For maps. Usados CDs e Livros, Av Getúlio Vargas 766. Selection of used books, English, German, French and Spanish. Valer, R Ramos Ferreira 1195. A few English classics stocked, best bookshop in city.
Handicrafts There are many handicrafts shops in the area around the Teatro Amazonas, including **Ecoshop**, R 10 de Julho 509a, www.eco shop.com.br, which also has a good little a/c café and the **Mamirauá Shop**, R 10 de Julho 495, with a range of indigenous crafts and books and information on the Mamirauá Reserve. In the Praça do Congresso, Av E Ribeiro, there is a very good Sun craftmarket. The souvenir shop at the INPA has some interesting Amazonian products on sale. For hammocks go to R dos Andradas, many shops. **Central Artesanato**, R Recife s/n, near Detran. For local craft work. **Selva Amazônica**, Mercado Municipal. For wood carvings and bark fabric.
Markets and supermarkets Go to the Mercado Adolfo Lisboa (see above) early in the

morning when it is full of good quality regional produce, food and handicrafts, look out for guaraná powder or sticks, scales of pirarucu fish (used for manicure), and its tongue used for rasping guaraná (open Mon- Sat 0500-1800, Sun and holidays 0155-1200). There is a good supermarket at the corner of Av Joaquin Nabuco and Av Sete de Setembro. **Shopping Amazonas**, outside the city, is a mall with cinema, supermarket, fast food.

▲▲ Activities and tours

Manaus *p546, map p548*
Check agencies' licences from tourist office and ABAV. If in the least doubt, use only a registered company.

Swimming For swimming, go to Ponta Negra beach by Soltur bus, US$1, though the beach virtually disappears beneath the water in Apr-Aug; popular by day and at night with outdoor concerts and samba in the summer season. Every Sun, boats leave from the port in front of the market to beaches along Rio Negro, US$2.65, leaving when full and returning at end of the day. This is a real locals' day out, with loud music and food stalls on the sand. Good swimming at waterfalls on the Rio Tarumã, where lunch is available, shade, crowded at weekends. Take Tarumã bus from R Tamandaré or R Frei J dos Inocentes, 30 mins, US$1.10 (very few on weekdays), getting off at the police checkpoint on the road to Itacoatiara.

Tour operators

Amazon Clipper Cruises, R Sucupira 249, Conj Kissia, Planalto, T656 1246. Informed guides, well-planned activities, comfortable cabins and good food.
Amazon Jungle Tours, R Dr Moreira 163, 1st floor, T3231 1067, www.arquipelagotours.com.br. A range of boat and trekking trips throughout the Rio Negro. Their Anavilhanas trips are very good.
Amazonatours, T3232 8271/9624 2419 or in Spain 34-61-521 9070, www.amazonatours.com. Spanish/Brazilian run agency offering trips further afield and to their small lodge in the Tupana Natural Reserve. Recommended.
Brazilian Safaris, R 10 de Julho 632, T8112 7154, www.braziliansafaris.com. Ground operator for many of the smaller agencies with their own lodge off the Rio Mamori and a range of good budget trips.
Gero's Tours, R 10 de Julho 679, T9983 6273, www.amazongerotours.com. Backpacker-oriented tours south of the Solimões, and bookings made for lodges everywhere. Gero, the owner is very friendly and dedicated.
The Global Heritage Expeditions, R Floriano Peixoto 182, www.amazonpda.hpg.com.br.

Sandro Gama speaks English, small group tours in the Amazon basin.
Heliconia, R Col Salgado 63, Aparecida, T3234 5915, www.heliconia-amazon.com. Run by French researcher Thérèse Aubreton.
Iguana Tour, R 10 de Julho 679, T3633 6507, www.amazonbrasil.com.br. Short and long tours, plenty of activities, many languages spoken.
Jaguar Adventure Tours R Marciano Armond, Vila Operária 23A, Cachoeirinha, T3663 2998, www.objetivonet.com.br/jaguartours. Carlos Jorge Damasceno, multilingual, deep jungle exploration with an ecological slant and visits to remote historical and indigenous settlements.
Swallows and Amazons, R Quintino Bocaiúva 189, Suite 13, T/F3622 1246, www.swallows andamazonstours.com. Mark and Tania Aitchison offer a wide range of riverboat tours and accommodation (up to 15 days), prices start at US$65-120 per day; they have their own houseboat Dona Tania, covered motorized canoe and 8-room private jungle lodge, The Over Look Lodge, just before the Anavilhanas islands. Very comprehensive service, with full assistance for travellers (reservations, email, transfers, medical, etc), English, French and Spanish speaking guides.

Guides

Guides are licensed to work only through tour agencies, so it is safest to book guides through approved agencies. Advance notice and a minimum of 3 people for all trips offered by these guides:
Samuel Basilio, T9616 3124, samuelbasilio@ hotmail.com. A guide from the upper Rio Negro specialising in long expeditions; has worked on many BBC documentaries as a location finder.
Moreno Ortelli, T9605 0519, morenojivaro@ hotmail.com. One of the few guides in Manaus who knows his birds. Excellent knowledge of indigenous culture and fascinating trips to explore this. Many languages.
Matthias Raymond, T8115 5716, raymathias@ hotmail.com. A Waipixana indigenous guide offering trips to further reaches of the forest including the Pico da Neblina (with notice). Many languages.

⊖ Transport

Manaus *p546, map p548*
Air Airport T3652 1210. **International flights**: LAB to **Miami** and **Santa Cruz** (Bolivia), twice a week. **Varig** flies 4 times a week to **Caracas**. To the **Guyanas, Meta** (no office in town) flies from the small Eduardinho airport (by main airport) twice

a week to **Georgetown** and **Paramaribo**, via Boa Vista. **Internal flights**: there are frequent internal flights with **Varig, Penta, TAM** and **Tavaj. Rico Airlines** fly to Tefé, Tabatinga and other Amazon destinations. Domestic airport tax US$7. The taxi fare to or from the airport is US$16-19, with meter (check the driver uses it). Many taxi drivers are paid commission by hotels and will assure you that the hotel of your choice is either closed or doubles up as a brothel. Ignore them. They also tell arrivals that no bus to town is available: not true: bus 306 marked 'Aeroporto Internacional' (or from R Tamandaré near the cathedral), US$1.30. No buses 2300-0700. It is sometimes possible to use the more regular, faster service run by the Tropical Hotel; many tour agencies offer free transfers without obligation. Check all connections on arrival. Local flights leave from airport terminal 2: make sure in advance of your terminal. **Note**: Check in time is 2 hrs in advance. Allow plenty of time at Manaus airport, formalities are very slow especially if you have purchased duty-free goods. The restaurant serves good à la carte and buffet food through the day. Many flights depart in the middle of the night and while there are many snack bars there is nowhere to rest.

Bus Manaus rodoviária is 9 km out of town at the intersection of Av Constantino Nery and R Recife. Take a local bus from centre, US$0.65, marked 'Aeroporto Internacional' or 'Cidade Nova' (or taxi, US$6.50). Local buses to Praça 14 or the airport leave from Praça Adalberto Vale (take airport bus and alight just after Antárctica factory) or take local bus to Ajuricaba.

Ferry To **Santarém**, Belém, Porto Velho, Tefé, Tabatinga (for Colombia and Peru), São Gabriel da Cachoeira, and intermediate ports (see River Transport, page 535). Almost all vessels now berth at the first (downstream) of the floating docks which is open to the public 24 hrs a day. Tickets are sold at booths at the boat terminal in front of the docks. A tourist

office in a purpose- built shopping complex on the dockside will help travellers buy tickets (avoiding touts) and will translate for you as you look over the boats. The names and itineraries of departing vessels are displayed here as well as on the docked boats themselves. The port is relatively clean, well organized, and has a pleasant atmosphere.

ENASA (the state shipping company) sells tickets for private boats at its office in town (prices tend to be high here), T633 3280. Local boats and some cargo barges still berth by the concrete retaining wall between the market and Montecristi. Boats for São Gabriel da Cachoeira and Novo Airão go from São Raimundo, up river from the main port. Take bus 101 'São Raimundo', or 112 'Santo Antônio', 40 mins; there are 2 docking areas separated by a hill, the São Raimundo balsa, where the ferry to Novo Airão, on the Rio Negro, leaves every afternoon (US$13); and the Porto Beira Mar de São Raimundo, where the São Gabriel da Cachoeira boats dock (most departures Fri). **Note**: Departures to the less important destinations are not always known at the **Capitânia do Porto**, Av Santa Cruz 265, Manaus. Be careful of people who wander around boats after they've arrived at a port: they are almost certainly looking for something to steal.

Immigration For those arriving by boat who have not already had their passports stamped (eg from Leticia), the immigration office is on the first of the floating docks. Take the dock entrance opposite the cathedral, bear right, after 50 m left, pass through a warehouse to a group of buildings on a T section.

Road The Catire Highway (BR 319) from Manaus to Porto Velho (868 km), has been officially closed since 1990. Enquire locally if the road is passable for light vehicles; some bridges are flimsy. The alternative for drivers is to ship a car down river on a barge, others have to travel by boat (see below).

❶ Directory

Manaus *p546, map p548*

Airline offices BRA, Av Santos Dumont s/n, Tarumã, T3631-0007. **LAB**, Av 7 de Setembro 993, T3633 4200. **Meta**, Av Santos Dumont 1350, T3652 1105. **Rico Airlines**, R 24 de Maio 60-D, T4009 8333, www.voerico.com.br. **TAM**, Av Joaquim Nabuco 1846 Sl-2, T3233 7744. **Trip**, Av Boulevard Álvaro Maia 2166, Adrianópolis, T3652 1243. **Varig**, Marcílio Dias 284, T3622 3090, English spoken, helpful. **Banks** Banco do Brasil, Guia Moreira, and airport changes US$ cash, 8% commission, both with ATMs for Visa/Plus, Cirrus/ MasterCard. Most offices shut at 1500; foreign exchange operations 0900-1200 only, or even as early as 1100. **Bradesco**, Av 7 de Setembro 895/293, for Visa ATM. **HSBC**, R Dr Moreira,226. ATM for Visa, Cirrus, MasterCard and Plus. **Credicard**, Av Getúlio Vargas 222 for Diner's cash advances. Cash at main hotels; **Câmbio Cortez**, 7 de Setembro 1199, converts TCs into US$ cash, good rates, no commission. Do not change money on the streets. **Embassies and consulates** Austria, Rua 5, 4 Qde Jardim Primavera T3642 1939. **Belgium**, 13 qd D conj Murici, T3236 1452. **Colombia**, R 24 de Maio 220, Rio Negro Center, T3622 6078, double check whether a Colombian tourist card can be obtained at the border. **Denmark**, R Timbiras 306, T3646 5330, also handles Norway. **Finland**, R Marcílio Dias 131, T3622 6276. **France**, Av Visc de Sepetiba 17, Flores, T3648 5959. **Germany**, Av 24 Maio 220, Ed Rio Negro Centre, sala 812, T3622 8800, 1000-1200. **Italy**, R Rio Madeira 68, lj 8, N Sra das Graças, T3234 7391. **Japan**, R Fortaleza 416, T3232 2000. **Netherlands**, R M Leão 41, T3622 1366. **Peru**, Rua H, 12, Morada do Sol, Aleixo, T3642 3012. **Portugal**, R Ferreira Pena 37, T3633 1235. **Spain**, Al Cosme Ferreira 1225, Aleixo, T3644 3800. **Sweden**, R Rio Quixito 86, T3616 9043. **UK**, R Poraquê 240, Distrito Industrial, T3237 7869, F3237 6437, vincent@internext.com.br. **US**, R Franco de Sá 310, Ed Atrium, São Francisco, T3611 333; will supply letters of introduction for US citizens. **Venezuela**, R Rio Jataí 839, T3233 6006, 0800-1200. Everyone entering Venezuela overland needs a visa. The requirements are: 1 passport photo, an onward ticket and a yellow fever certificate, US$30 (check with a Venezuelan consulate in advance for changes to these regulations). **Internet** Many around the Teatro including **Loginet**, R 10 de Julho 625. **Amazon Cyber Cafe**, Av Getúlio Vargas 626, corner with R 10 de Julho, US$1.50 per hr. Another at No 188, 0800-2300, US$2 per hr. **Discover Internet**, R Marcílio Dias 304, next to Praça da Polícia, cabins in back of shop with Internet phones and scanners, US$1.50 per hr. **Internext**, R 24 de Maio 220, US$3 per hr. **Medical services** Clínica São Lucas, R Alexandre Amorin 470, T3622 3678, reasonably priced, some English spoken, good service, take a taxi. **Hospital Tropical**, Av Pedro Teixeira (D Pedro I) 25, T3238 1711. Centre for tropical medicine, not for general complaints, treatment free, some doctors speak a little English. Take buses 201 or 214 from Av Sete de Setembro in the city centre. **Pronto Soccoro 28 de Agosto**, R Recife 1581, T3642 4272, free for emergencies. **Post offices** Main office including poste restante on Marechal Deodoro. On the 1st floor is the philatelic counter where stamps are sold, avoiding the long queues downstairs. Staff don't speak English but are used to dealing with tourists. For airfreight and shipping, Alfândega, Av Marquês Santa Cruz (corner of Marechal Deodoro), Sala 106. For airfreight and seamail, Correio Internacional, R Monsenhor Coutinho e Av Eduardo Ribeiro (bring your own packaging). **Telephone** International calls can be made from local call boxes with an international card. Also **Telemar**, Av Getúlio Vargas 950 e R Leo Malcher. **Useful addresses** Police: to extend or replace a Brazilian visa, take bus from Praça Adalberto Vale to Kissia Dom Pedro for Polícia Federal post, people in shorts not admitted, T3655 1517. **Ibama**: R Ministro João Gonçalves de Souza s/n, BR-319, Km 01, Distrito Industrial, Caixa Postal 185, CEP 69900-000, T3613 3277.

Amazon frontiers

To get to the border with Colombia and Peru, a river boat is the only alternative to flying and this, of course, is the true way to experience the Amazon. On the route to Venezuela, buses and trucks have almost entirely replaced river traffic to Boa Vista, from where roads go to Santa Elena de Uairén and Lethem in Guyana.

Rondônia and Acre, lands which mark not just the political boundaries between Brazil and Peru and Bolivia, but also developmental frontiers between the forest and colonization. Much of Rondônia has been deforested. Acre is still frontier country with great expanses of forest in danger of destruction.

Manaus to Colombia, Peru, Venezuela and Guyana

Benjamin Constant and around → *Phone code: 0xx97. Colour map 3, grid A5.*
Benjamin Constant is on the border with Peru, with Colombian territory on the opposite bank of the river. The **Ticuna Indian Museum** *Av Castelo Branco 396*, display photographs, costumes, traditional art and music. **Tabatinga** (*Phone code 0xx97*) is 4 km from Leticia (Colombia). The Port Captain in Tabatinga is reported as very helpful and speaks good English. **Note**: The port area of Tabatinga is called Marco. A good hammock will cost US$20 in Tabatinga (try Esplanada Teocides) or Benjamin Constant. A mosquito net for a hammock is essential if sailing upstream from Tabatinga; much less so downstream. **Note**: In this area, carry your passport at all times.

Border with Colombia and Peru
Check all requirements and procedures before arriving at this multiple border. Enquire carefully about embarkation/disembarkation points and where to go through immigration formalities. If waiting for transport, Tabatinga has convenient hotels for early morning departures, but Leticia has the best money changing facilities and more internet facilities (try the bookshop next to the church). **Note**: When crossing these borders, check if there is a time difference (for example, Brazilian summer time, usually mid-October to mid-February). **Consulates Brazilian** ① *Cra 9, No 13-84, Leticia, T08-592 7530, brvcleticia@yahoo.com.br, 1000-1600, Mon-Fri, onward ticket and 2 black-and-white photos needed for visa (photographer nearby); allow 36 hrs, efficient, helpful.* **Peruvian**① *Cra 11, No 5-32, Leticia, T08-592 7204, coplet@telecom.com.co, 0900-1300; no entry or exit permits are given here.*

Brazilian immigration Entry and exit stamps are given at the Polícia Federal, 2 km from the Tabatinga docks, best to take a taxi, 24 hours. Proof of US$500 or an onward ticket may be asked for. There are no facilities in Benjamin Constant. One-week transit in Tabatinga is permitted. The Colombian consulate is near the border on the road from Tabatinga to Leticia, opposite Restaurant El Canto de las Peixadas. Open 0800-1400. Tourist cards are issued on presentation of two passport photos. **Note**: If coming from Peru, you must have a Peruvian exit stamp and a yellow fever certificate.

Colombian immigration DAS ① *C9, No 9-62, T59-24878, secamaadm@das.gov.co, Leticia, and at the airport.* Exit stamps to leave Colombia by air or overland are given by DAS no more than 1 day before you leave. If flying into Leticia prior to leaving for Brazil or Peru, get an exit stamp while at the airport. Check both offices for entry stamps before flying into Colombia. To enter Colombia you must have a tourist card to obtain an entry stamp, even if you are passing through Leticia en route between Brazil and Peru (the Colombian consul in Manaus may tell you otherwise; try to get a tourist card elsewhere). The Colombian Consular Office in Tabatinga issues tourist cards; 24-hr transit stamps can be obtained at the DAS office. If visiting Leticia without intending to go anywhere else in Colombia, you may be allowed to enter without immigration or customs formalities (but travellers' cheques cannot be changed without an entry stamp). ① *Travel between Colombia and Brazil and Peru is given below. Travel from/into Colombia is given under Leticia.* **Note**: There are no customs formalities for everyday travel between Leticia and Tabatinga.

Peruvian immigration Entry/exit formalities take place at Santa Rosa. Every boat leaving and entering Peru stops here. There is also an immigration office in Iquitos (Mcal Cáceres 18th block, T235371), where procedures for leaving can be checked. There is no Brazilian consulate in Iquitos No exchange facilities in Santa Rosa; reais and dollars are accepted, but soles are not accepted in Leticia and only occasionally in Tabatinga.

Manaus to Venezuela and Guyana

The road which connects Manaus and Boa Vista (BR-174 to Novo Paraíso, then the Perimetral, BR-210, rejoining the BR174 after crossing the Rio Branco at Caracaraí) can get badly potholed. There are service stations with toilets, camping, etc, every 150-180 km, but all petrol is low octane. Drivers should take a tow cable and spares, and bus passengers should prepare for delays in the rainy season. At Km 100 is Presidente Figueiredo, with many waterfalls and a famous cave with bats, shops and a restaurant. About 100 km further on is a service station at the entrance to the **Uaimiri Atroari Indian Reserve**, which straddles the road for about 120 km. Private cars and trucks are not allowed to enter the Indian Reserve between sunset and sunrise, but buses are exempt from this regulation. Nobody is allowed to stop within the reserve at any time. At the northern entrance to the reserve there are toilets and a spot to hang your hammock (usually crowded with truckers overnight). At Km 327 is the village of Vila Colina with Restaurante Paulista, good food, clean, you can use the shower and hang your hammock. At Km 359 there is a monument to mark the equator. At Km 434 is the clean and pleasant Restaurant Goaio. Just south of Km 500 is Bar Restaurante D'Jonas, a clean, pleasant place to eat, you can also camp or sling a hammock. Beyond here, large tracts of forest have been destroyed for settlement, but already many homes have been abandoned.

At **Caracaraí**, a busy port with modern installations on the Rio Branco, a bridge crosses the river for traffic on the Manaus-Boa Vista road. It has hotels in our **D-E** range. Boa Vista has road connections with the Venezuelan frontier at Santa Elena de Uairén (237 km, paved, the only gasoline 110 km south of Santa Elena) and Bonfim for the Guyanese border at Lethem. Both roads are open all year.

Boa Vista → *Phone code: 0xx95. Post code: 69300. Colour map 2, grid B2. Population: 200,568.*

The capital of the extreme northern State of Roraima, 785 km north of Manaus, is a pleasant, clean, laid-back little town on the Rio Branco. Tourism is beginning here and there are a number interesting new destinations opening up, many offering a chance to explore far wilder and fauna-rich country than that around Manaus. The landscape is more diverse, too, with a mix of tropical forest, savannah and highlands dotted with waterfalls. The area immediately around the city has been heavily deforested. It has an interesting modern cathedral; also a museum of local indigenous culture (poorly kept). There is swimming in the Rio Branco, 15 minutes from the town centre (too polluted in Boa Vista), reachable by bus only when the river is low. **Tourist office:** Detur ① *Av Capitão Julio Bezerra 193, T3623 2365, www.rr.gov.br.* Information is available at the rodoviária, T3623 1238; also in the Prefeitura's tourist office, R Floriano Peixoto, Centro, beside the Orla Tuamanan, open Tuesday-Sunday 1600-2200.

Border with Venezuela

Border searches are thorough and frequent at this border crossing. If entering Brazil, ensure in advance that you have the right papers, including yellow fever certificate, before arriving at this border. Officials may give only two months' stay and car drivers may be asked to purchase an unnecessary permit. Ask to see the legal documentation. Everyone who crosses this border must have a visa for Venezuela. Check requirements beforehand. See the Directory, below, for the Venezuelan consulate. There is another Venezuelan consulate in Manaus (see above). On the Brazilian side there is a basic hotel, Pacaraima Palace, a guest house, camping and a bank.

Border with Guyana → *Colour map 2, grid B3. Population: 9,326.*

The main border crossing between Brazil and Guyana is from **Bonfim**, 125 km (all paved) northeast of Boa Vista, to Lethem. The towns are separated by the Rio Tacutu, which is crossed by small boats for foot passengers, 5 minutes, US$2; vehicles cross by ferry on demand. The river crossing is 2.5 km from Bonfim, 1.6 km north of Lethem. A bridge is under construction. Formalities are strict on both sides of the border: it is essential to have a yellow fever vaccination both to leave Brazil and to enter Guyana The bus passes through Brazilian Immigration where you receive your exit stamp before stopping at the river. After the crossing, there are taxis to the Guyana Immigration office (US$3). You are given a visa for the exact amount of time you stipulate staying. The border is open 24 hours, but officials tend to leave immigration after 1800.

There is no Guayanese consul in Boa Vista, so if you need a visa for Guyana, you must get it in São Paulo or Brasília (see Guyana Documents in Essentials). Reais can be changed into Guyanese dollars in Boa Vista. There are no exchange facilities in Lethem, but reais are accepted in town.

● Sleeping → *See Telephone, page 347, for important phone changes.*

Benjamin Constant and around *p557*
There are a number of very cheap, simple *pousadas* in town.
B Benjamin Constant, R Getulio Vargas 36, beside ferry, T415 5638. A/c, some rooms with hot water and TV, good restaurant, arranges tours, postal address Apto Aéreo 219, Leticia, Colombia. Recommended.

Tabatinga
There are decent places to stay near the boat companies for Peru.
C Pousada do Sol, general Sampaio, T412 3355. With sauna and pool, simple rooms, helpful.
D-E Travellers Jungle Home, R Marechal Rondón 86. Small hostel and tour operator with Brazilian and French owners.

Boa Vista *p558*
Accommodation is generally expensive. Economic hardship has caused an increase in crime, sometimes violent.
AL Aipana Plaza, Joaquim Nabuco 53, T3224 4116, aipana@technet.com.br. Best in town with plain rooms decorated with photos of Roraima, hot water, a/c, cable TV, attractive pool area with a shady little bar.
A Uiramutam Palace, Av Capt Ene Garcez 427, T3224 9757, uiramutam@technet.com.br. Business hotel with modest rooms, a/c, cable TV and large bathrooms. Decent pool.
B Barrudada, R Araújo Filho 228, T3623 1378. Simple a/c rooms in a modern tower block very close to the centre. The best on the upper floors have views out to the river. Breakfast and lunch included.
C Eusêbio's, R Cecília Brasil 1107, T3623 0300, F3623 9131. Spruce, modest rooms with a/c and en suites with c/w showers. The best are airy and on the upper floors. Pleasant pool and a laundry service. Has a good a/c restaurant (♥♥) serving fish, *feijoada* and meat dishes and a generous breakfast.
D Terraço, Av Cecília Brasil 1141. Without bath, noisy, friendly. **D-E Ideal**, R Araújo Filho 481, T3224 6342. Simple but well kept rooms, some have a/c, generous breakfast and convenient for the centre.

Camping Rio Caaumé, 3 km north of town (unofficial site, small bar, clean river, pleasant).

Border with Guyana: Bonfim *p558*
D Bonfim, owned by Mr Myers, who speaks English and is very helpful, fan, shower.

---

❷ Eating

Benjamin Constant and around *p557*
Eat at **Pensão Cecília**, or **Bar-21 de Abril**, which is cheaper.

Tabatinga
Canto do Peixado, on main street. Excellent food. Highly recommended.
Lanchonete e Sorveteria Mallet, fresh juices, ice creams, burgers, popular.

Boa Vista *p558*
There are several restaurants serving snacks and juices on the riverside along R Floriano Peixoto.
♥♥ Peixada Tropical, R Pedro Rodrigues at Ajuricaba, T224 6040. A range of river fish dishes in various styles from Bahian sauces to Milanesa.
♥ 1000 Sabores, R Araújo Filho e Benjamin Constant. Pizzas, snacks and juices. Open early and closing late.
♥ Café com Leite Suiço, at Santa Cecilia, 15 mins by car on road to Bom Fim. Open 0630-1300 for regional food, US$4, good.
♥ Catequeiro, Araújo Filho e Benjamin Constant. Recommended *prato feito*.
♥ Frangão, R Homen de Melo e Cecília Brasil. Barbecued chicken, fish accompanied by salads, rice, beans etc.
♥ La Góndola, Benjamin Constant e Av Amazonas. Good.

Border with Guyana: Bonfim *p558*
There is a café at the rodoviária, opposite the church, whose owner speaks English and gives information. **Restaurante Internacional**, opposite the rodoviária, on other side from church; another restaurant a bit further from the rodoviária serves good food. Local speciality, fried cashew nuts.

🍷 Bars and clubs

Boa Vista *p558*

R Floriano Peixoto is lively after dark at weekends when there is live music in and around the **Orla** Taumanan; a complex of little bars and restaurants. **Toca**, Orla Taumanan, T9971 5454. River cruises and parties with live music and dancing.

⛰ Activities and tours

Benjamin Constant around around: Tabatinga *p557*

Travellers Jungle Home, R Marechal Rondon, 86. English and French owners, budget prices.

Boa Vista *p558*

Acqua, R Floriano Peixoto 505, T224 6576. Tours and boat trips on Rio Branco and surrounding waterways (jungle, beaches, Indian reservations). Guide Elieser Rufino is recommended.
Roraima Adventures, R Sebastião Diniz 787, T3624 9611, 9115 4171 (mob), www.roraima-brasil.com.br. A range of interesting trips to little known and little visited parts of Roraima including the spectacular Tepequem and Serra Grande mountains and the Rio Uraricoera, which is replete with wildlife. Pre-formed groups get the best prices, which are competitive with Manaus. Helpful with visas for Venezuela.

⊖ Transport

Border with Colombia and Peru *p557*
Brazil to Colombia
Air Varig to Manaus 3 times a week. Also smaller local airlines. From the airport at Tabatinga to town by minibus, US$1. See also under Leticia (Colombia) page 878. Regular minibus from airport to Leticia, US$0.90.
Ferry From Manaus to Benjamin Constant boats normally go on to Tabatinga, and start from there when going to Manaus. Boat services from Manaus to Benjamin Constant, 7 days, or more; to Manaus, 4 days, or more. They usually wait 1-2 days in both Tabatinga and Benjamin Constant before returning to Manaus; you can stay on board. It's quicker to get off the river boat in Benjamin Constant and take a fast ferry, US$2, 2 hrs, to Tabatinga, than stay on the river boat for the crossing from Benjamin Constant. Boats arrive in Benjamin Constant at 0600, so you can take the 0700 ferry and have a enough time in Tabatinga to get exit stamps and book the launch to Iquitos for the next day. For information on boats to/from Manaus, see Manaus Shipping and River Transport in Amazônia.
Taxi Travel between Tabatinga and Leticia is very informal; taxis between the 2 towns charge US$5

560

(more if you want to stop at immigration offices, exchange houses, etc; beware of taxi drivers who want to rush you expensively over the border before it 'closes'), or US$1 in a colectivo (more after 1800).

Brazil to Peru
Ferry Santa Rosa-Tabatinga or Leticia, US$2.50 (in reais, soles or pesos). Between Tabatinga and Iquitos in Peru there are 3 companies with 20-seater speedboats, US$60 one way, buy ticket 1 day in advance. They take 11-12 hrs. Departure from Tabatinga is 0530 (be there 0500). There are also cheaper, slower lanchas, which 2 days (US$15-17.50 hammock, US$25-30 cabin). Boat services are given under **Iquitos** in the Peru chapter. Passengers leaving and entering Peru must visit immigration at Santa Rosa when the boat stops there. For entry into Brazil, formalities are done in Tabatinga; for Colombia, in Leticia.

Boa Vista *p558*
Air Flights to **Manaus** US$80 with **Meta**, **Varig** or **Rico** and to **Georgetown**. Also flights to São Paulo, Rio de Janeiro, Belém etc. Book through **Aguia**, R Benjamin Constant 1683B, T3624 1516. The owner speaks some English. No left luggage, information or exchange facilities at the airport, which is 4 km from the centre. Bus 'Aeroporto' from the centre is US$0.50. Taxi to rodoviária, US$6.50, to centre US$9, 45 mins walk.
Bus (See also Border Crossings below.) Rodoviária is on the town outskirts, 3 km at the end of Av Ville Roy; taxi to centre, US$6.50, bus US$0.60, 10 mins (marked '13 de Setembro' or 'Joquey Clube' to centre). The local bus terminal is on Av Amazonas, by R Cecília Brasil, near the central praça. It is difficult to get a taxi or bus to the rodoviária in time for early morning departures; as it's a 25-min walk, book a taxi the previous evening. To **Manaus**, US$37, several companies including **Eucatur** (T224 0505), 12 hrs, at least 6 daily, executivo service at 1800/1900 with meal stop. Advisable to book. Buses between Boa Vista and **Caracaraí** take 8 hrs.

Border with Venezuela *p558*
Bus One bus a day goes from Boa Vista rodoviária to **Santa Elena de Uairén**, stopping at all checkpoints, US$20, 4 hrs, take water. It is possible to share a taxi, US$10 pp. There are through buses to **Ciudad Guayana, Ciudad Bolívar** (eg Caribe), US$40.

Border with Guyana: Bonfim *p558*
Bus Boa Vista-Bonfim 6 a day US$8, 2½ hrs; colectivos charge US$18. **Ferry**: to cross the river, take a canoe (see above), US$2.65 (no boats at night).

● Directory

Benjamin Constant around around:
Tabatinga *p557*
Banks Banco do Brasil, Av da Amizade. Has a Visa cash point and changes TCs at poor rate. Best to change money in Leticia. Dollars are accepted everywhere; Colombian pesos are accepted in Tabatinga, Peruvian soles rarely accepted.
Internet Infocenter, Av da Amizade 1581.

Boa Vista *p558*
Airline offices Gol, Praça Santos Dumont 100, T3224 5824. **Meta**, Praça Santos Dumont 100, T3224 7490. **Varig**, R Araújo Filho 91, T3224 2425.
Banks US$ and Guyanese notes can be changed in Boa Vista. TCs and cash in Banco do

Brasil, Av Glaycon de Paiva 56, 1000-1300 (minimum US$200), has Visa/Plus ATM. There is no official exchange agency and the local rates for bolívares are low: the Banco do Brasil will not change bolívares. HSBC, Av Ville Roy 392, MasterCard ATM. **Bradesco**, Av Jaime Brasil 441, Visa ATM. Best rate for dollars, **Casa Pedro José**, R Araújo Filho 287, also changes TCs and bolívares; **Timbo's** (gold and jewellery shop), Av B Constant 170, will change money.
Embassies and consulates Guyana, R Benjamin Constant 1171, T9112 7017, open mornings only. **Venezuela**, Av Benjamin Constant 968, T623 9285, Mon-Fri 0830-1300. Visas available, relaxed service, allow 24-48 hrs.
Medical services Yellow fever inoculations are free at a clinic near the hospital.

Southern Amazônia

Porto Velho → *Phone code: 0xx69. Post code: 78900. Colour map 4, grid B1. Population: 450,000.*
This city stands on a high bluff overlooking a curve of the Rio Madeira. It prospered during the local gold and timber rush and although these activities have slowed, the city continues to grow. At the top of the hill, on Praça João Nicoletti, is the **Cathedral**, built in 1930, with beautiful stained glass windows; the **Prefeitura** is across the street. The principal commercial street is Avenida 7 de Setembro, which runs from the railway station and market hall to the upper level of the city, near the rodoviária. The centre is hot and noisy, but not without its charm, and the port and old railway installations are interesting. In the old railway yards known as Praça Madeira-Mamoré are the **Museus Ferroviário** and **Geológico** *both 0800-1800*, the **Casa do Artesão** (see Shopping) and a promenade with bars by the river, a wonderful place to watch the sunset. A neoclassical **Casa do Governo** faces Praça Getúlio Vargas, while Praça Marechal Rondon is spacious and modern. There are several viewpoints overlooking the river and railway yards: **Mirante I** (with restaurant) is at the end of R Carlos Gomes; **Mirante II** (with a bar and ice cream parlour), at the end of R Dom Pedro II. There is a clean fruit and vegetable market at the corner of R Henrique Dias and Avenida Farquhar and a dry goods market three blocks to the south, near the port. **Tourist office:** Setur/Ro, Av Pdte Dutra 3004, Caiari, CEP 78900-550, T223 3496, www.setur.ro.gov.br. See also www.guiarondonia.com.br and www.ronet.com.br/marrocos.

About 5 km northeast of the city is the **Parque Nacional Municipal**, a small collection of flora in a preserved area of jungle and one of very few parks in the city. The **Cachoeira de Santo Antônio**, rapids on the Rio Madeira, 7 km upriver from Porto Velho, is a popular destination for a swim during the dry season; in the rainy season the rapids may be underwater and swimming is dangerous. Access is by boat, taking a tour from Porto Cai N'Água, one hour; or by city bus No 102, Triângulo, which runs every 50 minutes from the city bus terminus or from the bus stop on R Rogério Weber, across from Praça Marechal Rondon. Gold dredges may be seen working near Porto Velho, ask around. Malaria is common and the drinking water is contaminated with mercury (from gold panning).

The BR-364 → *Colour map 4, grid C2.*
The Marechal Rondon Highway, BR-364, is fully paved to Cuiabá, 1,550 km. A result of the paving of BR-364 is the development of farms and towns along it; least population density is in the south between Pimenta Bueno and Vilhena. From Porto Velho south, the towns include **Ariquemes** (202 km from Porto Velho). (*Phone code 0xx69, post code: 78930, buses hourly from 0600, 3-4 hrs, hotels, bank*); **Ji Paraná** (*376 km, post code 78960, phone code: 0xx69*), on the shores of the Rio Machado, a pleasant town with a small riverside promenade, which has several bars, lively at night; several hotels. **Note:** At the Mato Grosso state border, proof of yellow-fever inoculation is required: if no proof is presented, a new shot is given.

Parque Nacional Pacaás Novos → *765,800 ha.*

The Parque Nacional Pacaás Novos, lies west of the BR-364; it is a transitional zone between open plain and Amazonian forest. The majority of its surface is covered with cerrado vegetation and the fauna includes jaguar, brocket deer, puma, tapir and peccary. The average annual temperature is 23°C, but this can fall as low as 5°C when the cold front known as the friagem blows up from the South Pole. Details from **Ibama** ① *Av Tancredo Neves s/n, Campo Novo, T3239 2992, or Av Jorge Teixeira 3559, CEP 78.904-320, Toxx69-223 3598, Porto Velho.*

The Madeira-Mamoré Railway → *See www.efmm.net.*

Porto Velho was the terminus of the Madeira-Mamoré railway. It was supposed to go as far as Riberalta, on the Rio Beni, above that river's rapids, but stopped short at Guajará Mirim. Over 6,000 workers died during its construction (1872-1913). The BR-364 took over many of the railway bridges, leaving what remained of the track to enthusiasts to salvage what they could. The line no longer works, but the roundhouse, recently restored, has two antique locomotives, a collection of skulls and other items on display. Mr Johnson at the station speaks English.

Guajará Mirim → *Phone code: 0xx69. Colour map 4, grid B1. Population: 38,045.*

From Porto Velho, the paved BR-364 continues 220 km southwest to Abunã (hotels **E**), where the BR-425 branches south to Guajará Mirim. The BR-425 is a fair road, partly paved, which uses the former rail bridges (in poor condition). It is sometimes closed March-May. Across the Mamoré from Guajará Mirim is the Bolivian town of Guayaramerín, which is connected by road to Riberalta, from where there are air services to other Bolivian cities. Guajará Mirim is a charming town. The **Museu Municipal** ① *T541 3362, 0500-1200, 1400-1800,* is at the old Guajará Mirim railway station beside the ferry landing; interesting and diverse. Highly recommended. Banco do Brasil only changes money in the morning.

Border with Bolivia

Get Brazilian exit and entry stamps from **Polícia Federal** *Av Presidente Dutra 70, corner of Av Quintino Bocaiúva, T541 4021.* The Bolivian consulate is at Avenida Beira Rio 505, T541 5876, Guajará Mirim; visas are given here.

Rio Branco → *Post code: 69900. Phone code: 0xx68. Colour map 3, grid B6. Population: 253,059.*

The BR-364 runs west from Porto Velho to Abunã (239 km), then in excellent condition, 315 km to Rio Branco the capital of the State of Acre. This intriguing state, rich in natural beauty, history and the seringueiro culture, is still very much off the beaten track. During the rubber boom of the late 19th century, many Nordestinos migrated to the western frontier in search of fortune. As a result, the unpopulated Bolivian territory of Acre was gradually taken over by Brazil and formally annexed in the first decade of the 20th century. In compensation, Bolivia received the Madeira-Mamoré railroad, as described above. In 1913, Rio Branco became capital of the new Território Federal do Acre, which attained statehood in 1962. The chief industries remain rubber and castanho-de-pará (Brazil nut) extraction, but timber and ranching are becoming increasingly important and improved road access is putting the state's tropical forests at considerable risk. Despite improved air and road links, Rio Branco remains at the 'end of the line', a frontier outpost whose depressed economy, high unemployment and prevalent drug-running make the city unsafe at night.

The Rio Acre is navigable upstream as far as the Peru and Bolivia borders. It divides the city into two districts called Primeiro (west) and Segundo (east), on either side of the river. In the central, Primeiro district are **Praça Plácido de Castro**, the shady main square; the **Cathedral**, Nossa Senhora de Nazaré, along Av Brasil; the neo-classical **Palácio Rio Branco** on R Benjamin Constant, across from Praça Eurico Gaspar Dutra. There is a market off R Epaminondas Jácome. Two bridges link the districts. In the Segundo district is the **Calçadão da Gameleira**, a pleasant promenade along the shore, with plaques and an old tree marking the location of the original settlement. There are several large parks in the city; the **Horto Forestal**, popular with joggers, in Vila Ivonete (1° distrito), 3 km north of the centre ('Conjunto Procon' or 'Vila Ivonete' city-buses), has native Amazonian trees, a small lake, paths and picnic areas.

Museu da Borracha (Rubber Museum) ① *Av Ceará 1177, Mon-Sat 0730-1900,* in a lovely old house with a tiled façade, has information about the rubber boom, archaeological artefacts, a section about Acreano Indians, documents and memorabilia from the annexation and a display about the Santo Daime doctrine (see excursions below). Recommended. **Casa**

do Seringueiro ① *Av Brasil 216, corner of Av Getúlio Vargas*, has a good exhibit on rubber tappers and on **Chico Mendes** in particular; the Sala Hélio Melo has a display of Melo's paintings, mainly on the theme of the forest. **Tourist office: SEICT/AC**, R Mal Deodoro 219 fourth floor, Centro, T223 1390, seict@ac.gov.br.

Note Rio Branco time is one hour behind Porto Velho and Manaus time; this means two hours behind Brazilian Standard Time.

Border with Bolivia and Peru

The BR-317 from Rio Branco heads south and later southwest, parallel to the Rio Acre; it is paved as far as **Xapuri** (the location of the Fundação Chico Mendes); one very basic lodging and two restaurants. The road continues to **Brasiléia** (four buses daily to/from Rio Branco, five hours in the wet, faster in the dry, US$6.50; three hotels, two basic lodgings, several restaurants – La Felicitá is good, Polícia Federal give entry/exit stamps), opposite the Bolivian town of Cobija on the Rio Acre. A striking, single-tower suspension bridge crosses the river. It is possible to stay in Epitaciolândia (**C Hotel Kanda**, five minutes' walk from the police post) and cross into Bolivia early in the morning. Ask the bus driver to let you off near Polícia Federal, open 0700-2200, to get passport stamped. Cobija is opposite. If going to Peru, a taxi from Polícia Federal to the Rodoviária costs US$1.30.

The road ends at Assis Brasil (120 km) where the Peruvian, Bolivian and Brazilian frontiers meet. Across the Rio Acre are Iñapari (Peru), border crossing difficult, even out of the wet season, and Bolpebra, Bolivia. A bus service operates only in the dry season beyond Brasiléia to Assis Brasil, 0700 and 1230, 2½ hours; access in the wet season is by 4WD vehicles. In **Assis Brasil**, there are three hotels, two restaurants (including a good churrascaria on the main street), some shops, a bank which does not change US dollars (the hotel owner may be persuaded to oblige). Cross to Iñapari from Assis Brasil (another distinctive suspension bridge is being built here), then take a shared taxi to Iberia or Puerto Maldonado. Immigration is open 0800-1830. **Note:** There is no Polícia Federal in the village, get entry/exit stamps in Brasiléia. Take small denomination dollar bills or Peruvian soles as there is nowhere to change money on the Peruvian side.

⬤ **Sleeping** → *See Telephone, page 347, for important phone changes.*

Porto Velho *p561*

The city is less safe than it used to be; do not walk around alone after dark nor during the day near the railway station and port. From the rodoviária, take bus No 301 'Presidente Roosevelt' (outside Hotel Pontes), which goes to railway station at riverside, then along Av 7 de Setembro as far as Av Marechal Deodoro. It passes several hotels.

AL Rondon Palace, Av Gov Jorge Teixeira 491, corner Jacy Paraná, away from the centre, T223 3420. A/c, fridge, restaurant, pool, travel agency.

AL Vila Rica, Av Carlos Gomes 1616, T3224 3433, www.hotelvilarica.com.br. Tower block with restaurant, pool and sauna, member of a Brazilian chain.

A Central, Tenreiro Aranha 2472, T2181 2500, www.enter-net.com.br/hcentral. A/c, TV, fridge, reliable and remodelled. Recommended.

B Pousada da Sete, Av 7 de Setembro 894, T221 8344. On No 301 bus route (see above). A/c, cheaper with fan, **D** with shared bath.

D Líder, Av Carlos Gomes, near rodoviária. Honest, welcoming, reasonably clean, fan, coffee. Recommended.

D Missionero, Av 7 de Setembro 1180, T221 4080. On No 301 bus route (see above). Good, a/c, cheaper with fan, **E** with shared bath, fan. Recommended.

D Tía Carmen, Av Campos Sales 2995, T221 7910. Very good, honest, good cakes in lanche in front of hotel. Recommended.

E Yara, Av 7 do Septembre y R Gonçalves Dias. On No 301 bus route (see above). Shared room with breakfast, safe, helpful staff.

Guajará Mirim *p562*

AL Pakaas Palafitas Lodge, Estrada do Palheta Km 18, T/F3541 3058, www.pakaas.com.br. 28 bungalows in a beautiful natural setting, price is per person per day.

B Jamaica, Av Leopoldo de Mato 755, T/F3541 3721. A/c, fridge, parking.

⬤ *For an explanation of the sleeping and eating price codes used in this guide, see inside the front cover. Other relevant information is found in Essentials pages 345-347.*

B Lima Palace, Av 15 de Novembro 1613, T3541 3421. A/c, fridge, parking.
C Chile, Av Q Bocaiúva. Good value, includes breakfast. Recommended.
C Fénix Palace, Av 15 de Novembro 459, T3541 2326. Highly recommended.
C Mamoré, R M Moraes, T3541 3753. Clean, friendly.
Centro Deportivo Afonso Rodrigues, Av 15 de Novembro, T541 3732. There's a basic dorm, **E**, opposite the rodoviária.

Rio Branco *p562*
Few economical hotels in the centre, but a reasonable selection of these by the rodoviária.
AL Pinheiro Palace, Rui Barbosa 91, T3223 7191, pinheiro@mdnet.com.br. In 1° distrito (west bank), a/c, pool. Recommended.
A Rio Branco, R Rui Barbosa 193, T3224 1785, by Praça Plácido de Castro in 1° distrito. A/c, fridge, TV, nice but simple.
B Albemar, R Franco Ribeiro 99, T3224 1396. In 1° distrito (west bank), a/c, fridge, TV, good breakfast, good value. Recommended.
B Rodoviária, R Palmeiral 468, T3221 4434. In 2° distrito (east bank), in Cidade Nova by the rodoviária. A/c, fridge TV, **D** with shared bath, fan, good value.
B Triângulo, R Floriano Peixoto 893, T3224 9265. In 1° distrito (west bank), a/c, TV, fridge, restaurant.
D Xapuri, Nações Unidas 187, T3222 7268. In 1° distrito (west bank), shared bath, fan, basic, 15 mins' walk from the centre.

🍴 Eating

Porto Velho *p561*
There are plenty of snack bars and *padarias* throughout the city. **Note**: Avoid eating much fish because of mercury contamination.
🍴🍴🍴 **Caravela do Madeira**, R José Camacho 104. The city's business lunch venue, a/c, international menu.
🍴🍴🍴-🍴🍴 **Barcaça Gourmet**, Av Pinheiro Machado 3258, Centro, T3223 3334. Excellent menu with a variety of prices, a/c, singer most evenings.
🍴🍴 **Almanara**, R José de Alencar 3064. Good authentic Lebanese food, popular, not cheap. Recommended.
🍴🍴 **Bella Italia**, Joaquim Nabuco 2205. Italian, pizza and comida caseira.
🍴🍴 **Emporium**, Av P Machado e Av Dutra. Mid-range, nice atmosphere, good meats and salads, expensive drinks, open 1800-2400.
🍴 **Churrascaria Natal**, Av Carlos Gomes 2783. Good meat and chicken.
🍴 **Churrascaria Ponto Certo**, Av Rio Madeira 45. Excellent meats, good view of the river, closed Mon.

Guajará Mirim *p562*
Oasis, Av 15 de Novembro 460. The best place to eat. Recommended (closed Mon).

Rio Branco *p562*
Local specialities *Tacacá*; a soup served piping hot in a gourd (cuia) combines manioc starch (goma), cooked jambu leaves which numb the mouth and tongue, shrimp, spices and hot pepper sauce; recommendation from Sra Diamor, Boulevar Augusto Monteiro 1046, Bairro 15 in the 2° distrito (bus Norte-Sul from the centre), other kiosks in town, ask around.
🍴🍴 **Anexos**, R Franco Ribeiro 99, next to Albemar Hotel. Popular for meals and drinks.
🍴🍴 **Churrascaria Triângulo**, R Floriano Peixoto 727. As much charcoal-grilled meat as you can eat. Recommended.
🍴🍴 **Kaxinawa**, Av Brasil at Praça Plácido de Castro. Best in town for Acreano regional food.
🍴🍴 **Pizzaria Tutti Frutti**, Av Ceará 1132, across from the Museu da Borracha. Pizzas, ice cream, not cheap.
🍴🍴-🍴 **Remanso do Tucunaré**, R José de Melo 481, Bairro Bosque. Fish specialties.
🍴 **Casarão**, Av Brasil 310, next to the telephone office. Good food and drink.

Cafés
Sorveteria Arte Sabor, Travessa Santa Inés 28, corner Aviarsio, 1° distrito, 15 mins' walk from the centre. Excellent home made ice cream, many jungle fruit flavours. Recommended.

🛍 Shopping

Porto Velho *p561*
Bookshops Livraria da Rose, Av Rogério Weber 1967, opposite Praça Marechal Rondon, exchanges English paperbacks; Rose, the proprietor, speaks English, friendly. Other bookshops nearby.
Indian handicrafts Casa do Índio, R Rui Barbosa 1407 and Casa do Artesão, Praça Madeira-Mamoré, behind the railway station, Thu-Sun 0800-1800.
Supermarkets Supermercado Maru, 7 de Setembro e Joaquim Nabuco.

🚌 Transport

Porto Velho *p561*
Air Airport 8 km west of town, T225 1339. Take bus marked 'Aeroporto' (last one between 2400-0100). Daily flights to many Brazilian cities.
Bus Rodoviária is on Jorge Teixeira between Carlos Gomes and Dom Pedro II, T225 2891. From town take 'President Roosevelt' bus No 301 (if on Av 7 de Setembro, the bus turns at Av Marechal

Deodoro); 'Aeroporto' and 'Hospital Base' (No 400) also go to rodoviária. Health and other controls at the Rondônia- Mato Grosso border are strict. To break up a long trip is much more expensive than doing it all in one stretch.

Bus to/from **Humaitá**, 4 a day, US$6.50, 3 hrs (last from Humaitá at 1600, after that taxis charge US$10.50 pp). To **São Paulo**, 60-plus hrs, US$100. To **Cuiabá**, 23 hrs, US$60, expensive food and drink is available en route. To **Guajará-Mirim**, see below. To **Rio Branco**, Viação Rondônia, 6 daily, 8 hrs, US$9.25. Daily bus with **Eucatur** from Cascavel (Paraná, connections for Foz do Iguaçu) via Maringá, Campo Grande and Cuiabá to Porto Velho (Porto Velho-Campo Grande 36 hrs, US$80). To **Cáceres** for the Pantanal, 18 hrs, US$40.

Ferry See River Transport, page 535. Passenger service from **Porto Cai N'Água** (which means 'fall in the water', watch out or you might!), for best prices buy directly at the boat, avoid touts on the shore. Boat tickets for Manaus are also sold in the rodoviária. The Rio Madeira is fairly narrow so the banks can be seen and there are several 'meetings of waters'. Shipping a car: São Matheus Ltda, Av Terminal dos Milagros 400, Balsa, takes vehicles on pontoons, meals, showers, toilets, cooking and sleeping in your car is permitted.

Road Road journeys are best done in the dry season, the 2nd half of the year.

The BR-364: Ji Paraná p561
Bus To **Porto Velho**, US$21, 16 hrs; to **Cuiabá**, 15 hrs, US$37.

Guajará Mirim p562
Bus From **Porto Velho** to Guajará Mirim, 5½ hrs or more depending on season, 8 a day with **Viação Rondônia**, US$24. Taxi from Porto Velho rodoviária, US$32 pp for 4-5, 3 hrs, leaves when full.

Guajará Mirim/Guayaramerín p562
Speedboat across the Rio Mamoré (border with Bolivia), US$2.10, 5-min crossing, operates all day, tickets at the waterside; **ferry** crossing for vehicles, T3541 3811, Mon-Sat 0800-1200, Mon-Fri 1400-1600, 20-min crossing.

Rio Branco p562
Air The airport is on AC-40, Km 1.2, in the 2° distrito. Taxi from the airport to the centre US$25 flat rate, but going to the airport the meter is used, which usually comes to less. By bus, take 'Norte-Sul' or 'Vila Acre'. Flights with Varig daily to **Porto Velho**, Manaus, Brasília and São Paulo.

Bus Rodoviária on Av Uirapuru, Cidade Nova, 2° distrito (east bank); city bus 'Norte-Sul' to the centre. To **Porto Velho**, Viação Rondônia, 6 daily, 8 hrs, US$9.25. To **Guajará Mirim**, daily with **Rondônia** at 1130 and 2200, 5-6 hrs, US$13; or take Inácio's Tur shopping trip, 3 per week. From Rio Branco the BR-364 continues west (in principle) to Cruzeiro do Sul and Japim, with a view to reaching the Peruvian frontier further west when completed.

Car Prices for car rentals with the nationwide agencies are higher in Acre than in other states.

---

❶ Directory

Porto Velho p561
Airline offices TAM, RJ Castilho 530, T221 6666, or T0800-570 5700. **Trip**, T3222 0879. **Banks** Banks are open in the morning only; **Banco do Brasil**, Dom Pedro II 607 e Av José de Alencar, cash and TCs with 2% commission, minimum commission US$15, minimum amount exchanged US$200. **Marco Aurélio Câmbio**, R José de Alencar 3353, T9984 0025 (mob), efficient, good rates, Mon-Fri 0900-1500. **Parmetal** (gold merchants), R Joaquim Nabuco 2265, cash only, good rates, open Mon-Fri 0730-1800, Sat 0730-1300. Exchange is difficult elsewhere in Rondônia. **Car hire** Silva Car, R Almte Barroso 1528, Porto Velho, T221 1423/6040. **Internet** Games and Videos, Av 7 de Setembro 1925. US$1.70 per hr. **Medical services** Hospital Central, R Júlio de Castilho 149, T/F224 4389, 24 hr emergencies. Dentist: at Carlos Gomes 2577; 24-hr clinic opposite. **Post offices** Av Presidente Dutra 2701, corner of Av 7 de Setembro. **Telephones** Tele Centro Sul, Av Presidente Dutra 3023 e Dom Pedro II, 0600-2300 daily. **Voltage** 110 volts AC, Guajará-Mirim also, elsewhere in Rondônia 220 volts.

Rio Branco p562
Airline offices BRA, T3223 1400. Varig, R Marechal Deodoro 115, T3224 2226. **Post offices** On the corner of R Epaminondas Jácome and Av Getúlio Vargas. **Telephones** On Av Brasil between Marechal Deodoro and Av Getúlio Vargas, long delays for international calls.

Brasília and Goiás

The Centre West is the frontier where the Amazon meets the central plateau. It is also Brazil's frontier with its Spanish American neighbours. Lastly, it contains the border between the expansion of agriculture and the untouched forests and savannahs. On this region's eastern edge is Brasília, the symbol of the nation's commitment to its empty centre. Although not generally viewed as a tourist attraction, Brasília is interesting as a city of pure invention along the lines of Australia's Canberra and Washington in the United States. Its central position makes it a natural crossroads for visiting the north and interior of Brazil and, when passing through, it is well worth undertaking a city tour to view its innovative modern design.

Goiás is quite a mixture: colonial mining towns, a modern, planned state capital and centres which owe their existence to rapidly expanding agriculture. There are two fine national parks, Emas and Chapada dos Veadeiros. An interesting festival, with processions on horseback, is held in Pirenópolis during May/June. In Tocantins, Brazil's newest state, Jalapão is a fantastic landscape, fast-becoming a desirable destination.

Brasília → *Phone code: 0xx61. Post code: 7000. Colour map 7, grid A3. Population: 2.1 million (2000).*

Ins and outs

Orientation The Eixo Monumental divides the city into Asa Sul and Asa Norte (north and south wings) and the Eixo Rodoviário divides it east and west. Buildings are numbered according to their relation to them. For example, 116 Sul and 116 Norte are at the extreme opposite ends of the city. The 100s and 300s lie west of the Eixo and the 200s and 400s to the east; Quadras 302, 102, 202 and 402 are nearest the centre and 316, 116, 216 and 416 mark the end of the Plano Piloto. Residential areas made up of large six-storey apartment blocks, called the 'Super-Quadras'. All Quadras are separated by feeder roads, along which are the local shops. There are also a number of schools, parks and cinemas in the spaces between the Quadras (especially in Asa Sul), though not as systematically as was originally envisaged.

Brasília: Plano Piloto

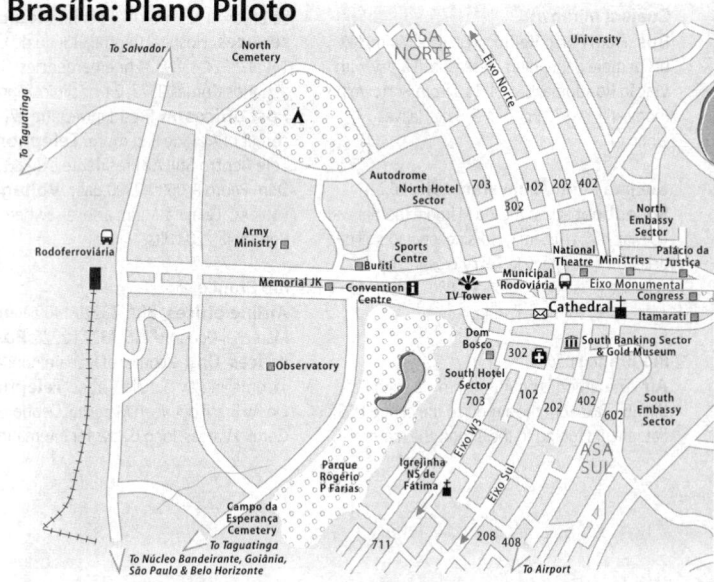

The main shopping areas, with more cinemas, restaurants and so on, are situated on either side of the city bus station (rodoviária). There are now several green areas. The private residential areas are west of the Super-Quadras, and on the other side of the lake. At right angles to these residential areas is the 'arrow', the 8-km long, 250 m wide **Eixo Monumental**. The main north-south road (Eixo Rodoviário), in which fast-moving traffic is segregated, follows the curve of the bow; the radial road is along the line of the arrow – intersections are avoided by means of underpasses and cloverleaves. Motor and pedestrian traffic is segregated in residential areas. A limited Metrô has been built to the southwestern suburbs. It is worth telephoning addresses away from the centre to ask how to get there. ▸▸ *See Transport page 577 for more details.*

Climate The climate is mild and the humidity refreshingly low, but overpowering in dry weather. The noonday sun beats hard, but summer brings heavy rains and the air is usually cool by night. Altitude: 1,171 m.

Tourist offices Setur (Secretaria de Turismo), SCN Q04 bloco B, T3429 7600, www.setur.df. gov.br (Portuguese). The **Brasília e Região Convention & Visitors Bureau**, SNC Q 1 bloco C, Edifício Brasília Trade Center, Sala 2004, T3328 6878, www.brasiliaconvention.com.br (Portuguese and English), also has lots of information. There is a small stand at rodoviária (daily 0800-2000), friendly but not very knowledgeable. Airport tourist office, open daily 0800-2000, will book hotels, limited English and information, no maps of the city. The **Ministério do Turismo** is at Esplanada dos Ministérios, Bloco U, 2nd and 3rd floors, www.turismo.gov.br (in many languages). The information office in the centre of Praça dos Tres Poderes has a colourful map and lots of useful text information. The staff are friendly and have interesting information about Brasília and other places in Goiás – only Portuguese spoken. **Maps** Infomaps publish a comprehensive map of the city showing attractions and principal hotels. It is available from Arte Capital shops in the Airport, Patio Brasil Shopping, the lobby of the Blue Tree Park hotel and Matriz in the Asa Norte as well as the larger newsagents.

Background

The purpose-built federal capital of Brazil succeeded Rio de Janeiro (as required by the Constitution) on 21 April 1960. The creation of an inland capital had been urged since the

Lago Do Paranoá

Palácio da Alvorada
Palácio do Jaburu
Palácio do Planalto
Praça dos Três Poderes
Avenida das Nações

N

0 metres 200
0 yards 200

beginning of the 19th century, but it was finally brought into being after President Kubitschek came to power in 1956, when a competition for the best general plan was won by Professor Lúcio Costa, who laid out the city in the shape of a bent bow and arrow. (It is also described as a bird, or aeroplane in flight.) Only light industry is allowed in the city and its population was limited to 500,000; this has been exceeded and more people live in a number of shanty towns, with minimal services, located well away from the main city, which is now a UNESCO World Heritage Site. Brasília is on undulating ground in the unpopulated uplands of Goiás, in the heart of the undeveloped Sertão. The official name for central Brasília is the Plano Piloto.

Sights

At the tip of the arrow is the **Praça dos Três Poderes**, with the Congress buildings, the Palácio do Planalto (the President's office), the Supremo Tribunal Federal opposite it and the Ministério da Justiça and Palácio Itamaraty respectively below them. Nineteen tall Ministry buildings line the Esplanada dos

Ministérios, west of the Praça, culminating in two towers linked by a walkway to form the letter H, representing Humanity. They are 28 storeys high: no taller buildings are allowed in B7rasília. Where the bow and arrow intersect is the city bus terminal (rodoviária), with the cultural and recreational centres and commercial and financial areas on either side. There is a sequence of zones westward along the shaft of the arrow; a hotel centre, a radio city, an area for fairs and circuses, a centre for sports, the **Praça Municipal** (with the municipal offices in the Palácio do Buriti) and, lastly (where the nock of the arrow would be), the combined bus and railway station (rodoferroviária) with the industrial area nearby. Other than the Santuário Dom Bosco and the JK bridge, the most impressive buildings are all by Oscar Niemeyer, Brazil's leading architect.

The **Palácio da Alvorada**, the President's official residence (not open to visitors), is on the lakeshore. The 80-km drive along the road round the lake to the dam is attractive. There are spectacular falls below the dam in the rainy season. Between the Praça dos Três Poderes and the lake are sites for various recreations, including golf, fishing and yacht clubs, and an acoustic shell for shows in the open air. The airport is at the eastern end of the lake. Some 395 ha between the lake and the northern residential area (Asa Norte) are reserved for the Universidade de Brasília, founded in 1961. South of the university area, the Av das Nações runs from the Palácio da Alvorada along the lake to join the road from the airport to the centre. Along it are found all the principal embassies. Also in this area is the attractive vice- presidential residence, the **Palácio do Jaburu** (not open to visitors). This area is very scenic.

A fine initial view of the city may be had from the **television tower** ① *West Eixo Monumental, Mon 1400-2000, Tue-Sun 0800-2000*, which has a free observation platform at 75 m up; also bar and souvenir shop. If the TV tower is closed, the nearby Alvorada hotel has a panoramic terrace on the 12th floor (lift to 11th only): ask at reception. A good and cheap way of seeing Brasília is by taking bus rides from the municipal rodoviária at the centre: the destinations are clearly marked. The circular bus routes 106, 108 and 131 go round the city's perimeter. If you go around the lake by bus, you must change at the Paranoá dam; to or from Paranoá Norte take bus 101, 'Rodoviária', and to and from Sul, bus 100, bypassing the airport. Tours from 1300-1700, start from the downtown hotel area and municipal rodoviária (US$12-20). Many hotels arrange city tours (see also Tour operators). Some buildings are open 1000-1400 Saturday-Sunday, with guided tours in English, well worth going.

Praça dos Três Poderes: **Congress** ① *Mon-Fri 0930-1200, 1430-1630 (take your passport), guides free of charge (in English 1400-1700)*. Visitors may attend debates when Congress is in session (Friday morning). Excellent city views from the 10th floor in Annex 3. The **Palácio do Planalto** ① *Sun 0930-1330, 30-min tours*, may also be visited. The guard is changed ceremonially at the Palácio do Planalto on Friday at 1730. The President attends if he is available. Opposite the Planalto is the Supreme Court building, **Supremo Tribunal Federal**. **Espaço Lúcio Costa** ① *0900-1800 Tue-Sun, free*, contains a model of Plano Piloto, sketches and autographs of the designer's concepts and gives the ideological background to the planning of Brasília. (Town clothes (not shorts or minis) should be worn when visiting all these buildings.) The **Museu Histórico de Brasília** ① *Tue- Sun and holidays 0900-1800*, is really a hollow monument, with tablets, photos and videos telling the story of the city. The sculpture 'Os Candangos' in front of the Planalto is a symbol of the city. By Bruno Giorgi, it pays homage to the candangos, or pioneer workers who built Brasília on empty ground. The marvellous building of the Ministry of Foreign Affairs, the **Itamarati** ① *guided visits Mon, Wed, Fri 1500-1700, free*, has modern paintings and furniture and beautiful water gardens. Opposite the Itamarati is the **Palácio da Justiça** ① *Mon-Fri, 0900-1200, 1500-1700*, with artificial cascades between its concrete columns. The **Panteão Tancredo Neves** is a 'temple of freedom and democracy', built 1985-1986 by Niemeyer. It includes an impressive homage to Tiradentes, the precursor of Brazilian independence.

Niemeyer is well into his nineties but still working. His **Procuradaria Geral da República**, comprising two glass cylinders, one suspended from a concrete cog, opened in 2002. The **Museu Nacional de Brasília**, on the Conjunto Cultural da República (next to the cathedral), and the adjacent **Biblioteca Nacional** will open in early 2007. They are the last grand projects Niemeyer designed for the capital. The former is particularly impressive, a huge dome of white concrete, blank but for a door half way up, sitting in a shallow pool of water which reflects it like a mirror. This door is reached by a long sinuous ramp. Inside there will be a 700-seat auditorium and state-of-the-art galleries.

¶¶**Vercelli**, SCLS 410, bloco D, loja 34. Lunch only. Pizzas, pastas and a great deal more on a huge menu.

¶**Cedro do Líbano**, SCS, quadra 06, bloco A, loja 218, Edif Carioca. Self-service, some Arabic dishes, friendly, closes 2200.

¶**Centro Venâncio 2000** at the beginning of Av W3 Sul, has several budget options, including Salada Mista, lunch only.

¶ **Naturama**, SCLS 102, bloco B, loja 9. Vegetarian and wholefood dishes, lunchtime.

Places serving prato feito or comercial (cheap set meals) can be found all over the city, especially on Av W3 and in the Setor Comercial Sul. Other good bets are the Conjunto Nacional and the Conjunto Venâncio, 2 shopping/office complexes on either side of the municipal rodoviária. Tropical fruit flavour ice-cream can be found in various parlours, eg Av W3 Norte 302. Freshly made fruit juices in all bars.

⭕ Bars and clubs

Brasília *p566*
Arena Café, CA 7, bloco F1, loja 33. Popular gay bar with DJs from Thu to Sat.

Bar Brasília, SHC/S CR, quadra 506, bloco A, loja 15, parte A. Little boteco with '50s decor, draught beer and wooden tables. Lively after 1900, especially Fri.

Bier Fass, SHIS Q 5, bloco E, loja 52/53, T3248 3400. Cavernous bar/restaurant with live music Tue-Sun and 20/30s crowd. Happy hour from 1800.

Café Cancun, Shopping Liberty Mall, SCN, cuadra 3, bloco D, loja 52. Tacky Mexican restaurant by day and teen and 20-something beautiful people club alter dark.

Clube de Choro, SDC, quadra 3, bloco G. Wed-Sat, one of the best clubs in the country devoted to the music which gave rise to samba. Top names from all over Brazil as well as the city itself. Great atmosphere. Tickets sold 9 days in advance.

Frei Caneca, Brasília Shopping, SCN, quadra 5, bloco A, lojas 82s/94s. Similar to Café Cancun. Dreadful 'flashback' night on Thu, most interesting at weekends.

Gates Pub, Av W3 Sul 403, T3225 4576, www.gatespub.com.br. Great for forró dancing and live music with a young, middle class crowd.

UK Brasil Pub, SCLS 411, bloco B, loja 28. Some of the best live bands in the city play here. Guinness, sandwiches, all ages.

❻ Entertainment

Brasília *p566*
Information about entertainment etc is available in 2 daily papers, *Jornal de Brasília* and *Correio Brasiliense*. Any student card (provided it has a photograph) will get you into the cinema/theatre/concert hall for half price.

Cinema Pier 21, SCSS, Trecho 2, Cj 32/33, is an enormous complex with 13 cinema screens, nightclubs, restaurants, video bars and children's theme park.

Theatre There are 3 auditoria of the **Teatro Nacional**, Setor Cultural Norte, Via N 2, next to the bus station, T3325 6239, foyer open 0900- 2000, box office open at 1400; the building is in the shape of an Aztec pyramid. The Federal District authorities have 2 theatres, the **Galpão** and **Galpãozinho**, between Quadra 308 Sul and Av W3 Sul. There are several other concert halls.

⭕ Shopping

Brasília *p566*
Bookshops Livraria Sodiler in Conjunto Nacional and at the airport. English books (good selection).

Handicrafts Artíndia, SRTVS, Qd 702, also in the rodoviária and at the airport. For Amerindian handicrafts. **Feira hippy** at the base of the TV tower Sat, Sun and holidays. Leather goods, wood carvings, jewellery, bronzes. **Galeria dos Estados**, which runs underneath the eixo from Setor Comercial Sul to Setor Bancário Sul, 10 mins' walk from municipal rodoviária, south along Eixo Rodoviário Sul. For handicrafts from all the Brazilian states.

Shopping malls The best shopping centres are Shopping Brasília below the southern hotel zone and Patio Brasília below the northern. Both have a wide range of boutiques and fast food restaurants. There are many others.

⛰ Activities and tours

Brasília *p566*
Many tour operators have their offices in the shopping arcade of the Hotel Nacional.

3-4 hr city tours with English commentary can also be booked at the airport by arriving air passengers – a convenient way of getting to your hotel if you have heavy baggage. Some tours have been criticized as too short, others that the guides speak poor English, and for night-time tours, the flood lighting is inadequate on many buildings.

Presmic Turismo, SIA trecho 03, lotes 625/695, Shopping SIA, sala 208C, T3225 0155. Full, half-day and night-time city tours (0845, 1400 and 1930 respectively).

Toscana SCLS 413, Bloco D, loja 22/24, T242 9233. Recommended as cheap and good.

⊖ Transport

Brasília *p566*

Air Airport, 12 km from centre, T3364 9224. Frequent daily flights to **Rio** and **São Paulo** (1½ hrs in both cases) and to main cities. Bus 102 or 118 to airport, regular, US$1, 30 mins. Taxi is US$13 (meter rate 2 used to airport), worth it. Left luggage facilities at airport (tokens for lockers, US$0.65).

Bus The bus terminal (rodoviária, T3363 2281) beside the railway station, from which long-distance buses leave, has post office (0800-1700, Sat 0800-1200) and telephone facilities. Bus 131 between rodoviária, the municipal terminal, and rodoferroviária, US$1.65; taxi rodoferroviária to Setor Hoteleiro Norte, US$12. There are showers (US$0.65). Both bus stations have large luggage lockers. To **Rio:** 17 hrs, 6 comuns (US$43) and 3 leitos (about US$85) daily. To **São Paulo:** 16 hrs, 7 comuns (about US$40) and 2 leitos (about US$90) daily (**Rápido Federal** recommended). To **Belo Horizonte:** 12 hrs, 9 comuns (US$27) and 2 leitos (US$53) daily. To **Belém:** 36 hrs, 4 daily (US$74, **Trans Brasília** T233 7589). To **Salvador:** 24 hrs, 3 daily (US$53). To **Cuiabá:** 17½ hrs (US$40) daily at 1200 with **São Luis**. For **Mato Grosso:** generally Goiânia seems to be the better place for buses. **Barra do Garças:** 0830 and 2000, takes 9 hrs with **Araguarina**, T233 7598, US$18 return. All major destinations served. Bus tickets for major companies sold at the rodoviária.

❶ Directory

Brasília *p566*

Airline offices BRA, at airport, T2105 0909. GOL, airport, T364 9370, premium rate number, T0300-789 2121. TAM, SHN Hotel Nacional, Gallery Store, 36/37, T325 1300; airport, T365 1000, or 4002 5700. Varig, Camara os Deputados/Anexo 4, Praça dos Três Poderes, T3326 9930; airport, T3364 9583, or 4003 7000.

Banks Foreign currency (but not always Amex cheques) can be exchanged at branches of: Banco Regional de Brasília, SBS Q 1, Bl E, and Banco do Brasil, Setor Bancário Sul, latter also at airport (ATM, bank open weekends and holidays), charges US$20 commission for TCs. MasterCard office, SCRN 502, Bl B, loja 31-32, T225 5550, for cash against card; ATMs at Citibank, SCS Quadra 06, bloco A, loja 186, T215 8000, HSBC, SCRS 502, bloco A, lojas 7/12, and Banco 24 Horas at airport, and all over the city, including the Rodoferroviária. Good exchange rates at Hotel Nacional and hotels with 'exchange-turismo' sign. **Car hire** All large companies are represented at the airport and the Car Rental Sector. Multinational agencies and

Interlocadora, airport, T0800-138000.Unidas, T2365 2266 at airport, Mon-Fri 0800-1800.

Cultural centres British Council, Ed Centro Empresarial Varig, SCN Q 04 bloco B, Torre Oeste Conjunto 202, T2106 7500, brasilia@british council.org.br. Cultura Inglesa, SHCGN 703 Área Especial 170370-700, T327 5400, gerente.asa.norte2@culturainglesa.net. American Library, Casa Thomas Jefferson, SEPS 706/906, Conj B, T3443 6588, www.thomas.org.br. Aliança Francesa, SEPS EQ 708/ 907 Lote A, T3242-7500, www.afbrasilia.org.br. Instituto Cultural Goethe, Av W5 Sul, SEPS-EQS 707/907, bloco F, salas 103-137, T3244 6776, www.goethe.de/brasilia.

Embassies and consulates Australia, SES Av das Nações, Qd 801, conjunto K, lote 7, T3226 3111, www.brazil.embassy.gov.au. Austria: SES, Av das Nações 40, T3443 3111, emb.austria@ terra.com.br. Canada: SES, Av das Nações Q 803 lote 16, T3424 5400, www.dfait-maeci.gc.ca/ brazil. Denmark: Av das Nações Q 807, lote 26, T3445 3443, www.ambbrasilia.um.dk. Finland: SES, Av das Nações Q 807, lote 27, T3443 7151, brasilia@finlandia.org.br. France: SES, Av das Nações Q801, L04, T3312 9100, www.amba france.org.br. Germany: SES, Av das Nações Q807, L25, T3442 7000, www.brasilia.diplo.de/ pt/Startseite.htm. Guyana: SHIS QI 05, conj 19, casa 24, Lago Sul, T248 0874, embguyana@ apis.com.br. Israel, SES, Av das Nações, Q 809, lote 38, T2105 0500, info@brasilia.mfa.gov.il. Netherlands: SES, Av das Nações Q 801, lote 5, T3961 3200, www.embaixada-holanda.org.br/. New Zealand, SHIS QI 09, conj 16, casa 01, Lgo Sul, T248 9900, zelandia@terra.com.br. South Africa: SES, Av das Nações Q 801, lote 06, T3312 9500, www.africadosul.org.br. Sweden: Av das Nações Q 807, lote 29, T443 1444, swebra@opengate.com.br. Switzerland: SES, Av das Nações Q 811, lote 41, T3443 5500, www.eda.admin.ch/brasilia. UK: SES, Quadra 801, Conjunto K lote 8 (with British Commonwealth Chamber of Commerce), Av das Nações, T3329 2300, contato@reinounido.org.br. US: SES, Av das Nações Q801, L03, T3312 7000, www.embaixada-americana.org.br. Venezuela: SES, Av das Nações Q803, lote 13, T2101 1011, embven2@ rudah.com.br. **Internet** Café.Com.Tato, CLS 505, bloco C, loja 17, Asa Sul, open daily. Liverpool Coffee Shop, CLS 108, R da Igreijinha. **Post offices** Poste restante, Central Correio, 70001; SBN-Cj 03, BL-A, Ed Sede da ECT, the central office is in the Setor Hoteleiro Sul, between Hotels Nacional and St Paul. Another post office is in Ed Brasília Rádio, Av 3 Norte.

Goiás

Goiânia → *Phone code: 062. Colour map 4, grid A1. Population: 1.1 million.*
The state capital is famous for its street cafés and is a good place to stop between Brasília and the rest of the Cent West. It is a spacious city, founded in 1933, with well-lit main avenues radiating out from the central **Praça Cívica**, on which stand the Government Palace and main Post office. Goiânia has more parks and gardens than any other of Brazil's large cities and many are filled with interesting forest and cerrado plants, as well as marmosets and remarkably large numbers of birds. **Tourist office**: Sictur, Centro Administrativo, Praça Cívica, 7th floor, CEP 74319-000, T3565 4292. **Dirtur**, R 30 corner of R 4, Centro de Convenções, CEP 74025-020, T217 1121, F217 2256. Extensive information, maps and bus routes in Novo Guia Turístico de Goiás, readily available at news stands, US$2.25. Visit www.portalgoiania.com.

The **Museu Zoroastro Artiaga** ① *Praça Cívica 13, T201 4676*, has a small but interesting collection of indigenous and historical objects, fossils and religious items as well as cases depicting indigenous and early settler life in Goiás. **Museu Antropológico do UFG** ① *Praça Universitária, 1 km east of Praça Cívica, 0900-1700 Mon-Fri*, houses wide-ranging ethnographic displays on the *indígenas* of the Centre West. The **Museu de Arte de Goiânia** ① *R 1 605, T524 1190, 0800-1700 Mon-Fri, 0800-1300 Sat, free*, in the Bosque dos Buritis gardens has a room showcasing the work of a number of local artists including Siron Franco, who is nationally renowned. The **Casa do Indio** is a centre for indigenous arts and craft production and an important meeting place for indigenous peoples like the Xavantes. The shop there sells a variety of handicrafts. The **Memorial do Cerrado Museum** ① *Av Bela Vista Km 2, Jd Olímpico, T562 4141, 0800-2200 Mon-Sat, 0800-1800 Sun, US$2.65*, just outside the city, provides an interesting introduction to Cerrado life, with reconstructions of indigenous villages, quilombos and colonial streets as well as planted cerrado vegetation.

Cidade de Goiás (Goiás Velho) → *Phone code: 062. Colour map 1, grid C5.*
This delightful town (*Population 30,000*) nestled amid cerrado-covered ridges is one of Central Brazil's hidden gems. Its cobbled streets lined with Portuguese whitewash and brilliant yellow and blue façades and elegantly simple baroque churches have been awarded UNESCO World heritage status. The town was founded in 1727 as Vila Boa and like its Minas counterparts became rich on gold, before becoming the capital of Goiás state, which it remained until just before the Second World War. The **tourist office** is housed in the Quintal do Vinte, a beautiful 18th-century, former barracks on Praça Brasil Caiado (daily 0900-1700). No English is spoken. The Museu Casa de Cora Coralina is a better source of information. Churches are usually open in the mornings and closed on Monday.

The most interesting streets in the colonial part of town spread out from the two principal plazas, Praça Brasil Caiado and, immediately below it towards the river, Praça do Coreto. The former is dominated by a lavish baroque fountain which once supplied all the town's water. The oldest church, **São Francisco de Paula** (1763) *Praça Zacheu Alves de Castro*, sits on a platform overlooking the market and the Rio Vermelho. It has a beautiful 19th Century painted ceiling by André Antônio da Conceição, depicting the life of St Francis. **Nossa Senhora da Abadiá** *R Abadia s/n*, has a similarly understated but impressive painted ceiling, whilst the other 18th-century churches like **Nossa Senhora do Carmo** *R do Carmo – on the riverside*, and **Santa Bárbara** *R Passo da Pátria*, are even simpler. The latter sits on a hill a kilometre or so east of the town affords wonderful sunset views. The **Museu das Bandeiras** ① *Praça Brasil Caiado/Largo do Chafariz, T3371 1087, Tue-Fri 0900-1700, Sat 1200-1700, Sun 0900-1300, US$1.30*, was once the centre of local government. Its rooms, furnished with period pieces, sit over a small but forbidding dungeon. The old governor's palace, the **Palacio Conde dos Arcos** ① *Praça do Coreto, T3371 1200, Tue-Sat 0800-1700, Sun 0900-1300, US$1.30*, has a display of 19th-century furniture and plaques describing the town's life in colonial times. The **Museu de Artes Sacras** ① *Praça do Coreto, T3371 1200, Tue-Sat 0800-1700, Sun 0900-1300, US$1.30*, houses some 18th-century church silverware and a series of painted wooden statues by one of Brazil's most important religious sculptors, José Joaquim da Veiga Valle. A stroll from the Praça do Coreto, downhill and across the river will bring you to the **Museu Casa de Cora Coralina** ① *R do Cândido 20, T3371 1990, Tue-Sun 0900-1700, US$1.30*, the former home of Goiás's most respected writer, with a collection of her belongings and a restful walled riverside garden at the back. The staff here are extremely helpful and knowledgeable about the city, though they speak no English. The 18th-century **Mercado Municipal**, next to the old rodoviária, 500 m west of the central Praça do Coreto, is a wonderful spot for cheap lunches, breakfasts and photography. Little artisan shops are springing up all over the town.

Pirenópolis → *Colour map 1, grid C5. Phone Code: 062. Population: 23,000. Altitude: 770 m.*
This lovely colonial silver mining town, 165 km due west of Brasília, has a well-preserved centre. It's almost as pretty as Cidade de Goiás and is National Heritage Site. The city is the nation's unofficial silver capital and is a good place to stock up on presents. It's also a favourite weekend haunt for the capital's middle classes who congregate in the lively restaurants and bars which line the northern end of Rua do Rosário. One of Brazil's most unusual and vibrant festivals takes place here every May/June (see below) and at weekends the Praça Central fills with country folk in stetsons and spurs, blasting out Sertanejo music from their souped-up cars. **Tourist office: Centro de Atendimento ao Turista**, R do Bonfim 14, Centro Histórico, T3331 2633, www.pirenopolis.tur.br. Poor English.

The **Igreja Matriz Nossa Senhora do Rosário**, which has been restored after being gutted by a fire in 2002, is the oldest church in the state (1728). It is open to the public, but its lavish interior is sadly no more. **Nosso Senhor de Bonfim** (1750-1754) houses an impressive lifesize crucifix from Bahia and was transported here on the backs of 260 slaves. **Nossa Senhora do Carmo** *daily 1300-1700*, serves as a museum of religious art. **Museu Família Pompeu** ⓘ *R Nova 33, 1300-1700 Tue-Fri, 1300-1500 Sat, 0900-1200 Sun*, displays the best collection of pictures and documents devoted to the history of the city (in Portuguese only). The tiny, private **Museu das Cavalhadas** ⓘ *R Direita 37, officially 0800-1700, Fri-Sat but sporadic, US$1.30*, has a collection of masks and costumes from the Festa do Divino. **Fazenda Babilônia** ⓘ *25 km southwest by paved road, 0800-1700 Sat-Sun only, US$2.65*, is a fine example of an 18th-century sugar fazenda, now a small museum, original mill, no public transport.

Chapada dos Veadeiros

These table top mountains, drained by countless fast-flowing rivers which rush through deep gorges and plummet over spectacular waterfalls are less famous, but much bigger than Diamantina or Guimarães. And unlike both those areas its forests have never been felled (it was designated a World Heritage Site by UNESCO in 2001). The Chapada is covered in cerrado forest – a habitat of such floral diversity that it has recently been declared a biological hotspot by Conservation International. Rare mammals including jaguar, maned wolf, puma, tapir, ocelot and giant anteater are abundant and although no one has yet compiled a serious bird list spectaculars and rarities include red shouldered macaw, coal crested finch, helmeted manakin and various key indicator species like rusty margined guan and bare face currasow. King vultures are abundant. At present trips within the park itself are limited to day visits only; but there are plans to change this as walks of as long as nine days can be easily organized at a good price. Entry to the park without a guide is not permitted and visits to the surrounding countryside without one not recommended – it is easy to get lost and guides are not expensive. The park is reached by paved state highway 118 to **Alto Paraiso de Goiás**, then a newly paved road around 40 km west to **São Jorge** (1 km from park entrance). Alto Paraiso is best for visits to the eastern sections of the Chapada, São Jorge for the park itself.

Parque Nacional Emas

ⓘ *Permission to visit from Ibama R 229 No 95, Setor Universitário, 74605-090 Goiânia, Toxx62-3901 1900. Day trips are not recommended, but 4-day, 3-night visits to the Park can be arranged through agencies (eg Focus Tours).*
In the far southwest of the state, covering the watershed of the Araguaia, Taquari and Formoso rivers, is the small **Parque Nacional Emas**, 98 km south of Mineiros just off the main BR-364 route between Brasília and Cuiabá (112 km beyond Jataí). Almost 132,868 ha of undulating grasslands and cerrado contain the **world's largest concentration of termite mounds**. Pampas deer, giant anteater, greater rhea, or 'ema' in Portuguese, and maned wolf are frequently seen roaming the grasses. The park holds the greatest concentration of blue-and-yellow macaws outside Amazônia, and blue-winged, red-shouldered and red-bellied macaws can also be seen. (There are many other animals and birds.) Along with the grasslands, the park supports a vast marsh on one side and rich gallery forests on the other. As many of the interesting mammals are nocturnal, a spotlight is a must.

Goiânia *p573*

The best hotels are 1 km from the centre in the Setor Oeste which has many restaurants and bars. Most hotels in the centre are frayed 1970s blocks.

L Castro's Park, Av República do Líbano 1520, Setor Oeste, T3096 2000, www.castros park.com.br. 5-star tower a few blocks from the centre, gym, pool, best for business. Plenty of restaurants and bars nearby.

L Papillon, Av Republica do Libano 1824, T3219 1500, www.papillonhotel.com.br. Modern rooms and suites, pool, gym, sauna, business facilities, very popular, book ahead.

AL Address, Av República do Líbano 2526, T3257 1000, www.addresshotel.com.br. Well-equipped business hotel, the best, in the city, modern rooms with separate living areas, broadband access, gym, pool, restaurant, bar, good views from the upper floors.

A-B Rio Vermelho, R 4 No26, T3213 2555, www.hotelriovermelho.com.br. Simple, in a quiet street with lots of cheap restaurants, cheapest with fan, close to the centre.

B Oeste Plaza, 389 Rua 2, Setor Oeste, T3224 5012. Well-maintained, modern, small a/c rooms, those on higher floors have good views, small pool and gym.

C Karajás, Av Goiás and R 3 No 860, T3224 9666. Good value in a once luxury hotel now fallen somewhat from grace, convenient.

C Goiânia Palace, Av Anhangüera 5195, T3224 4874, Goiâniapalace@terra.com.br. Art deco building with a range of rooms from simple doubles with fan to suites, good breakfast, well located.

D Antoninho's, R 68 No 41, T3223 1815. Very basic but well looked after, only a few rooms have windows, safe, good breakfast.

D Paissandú, Av Goiás 1290 at R 55, T3224 4925. Very simple, fan or a/c, 8 blocks north of the centre.

Camping Itanhangá municipal site, Av Princesa Carolina, 13 km, T292 1145. Attractive wooded location, reasonable facilities.

Cidade de Goiás *p573*

AL-A Vila Boa, Av Dr Deusdete Ferreira de Moura, 1 km southeast of the centre on the Morro do Chapéu do Padre, T3371 1000. The best in town, though inconvenient for the centre, pool, bar, restaurant and good views.

A Casa da Ponte, R Moretti Foggia s/n, T3371 4467. An art deco building next to the bridge across the Rio Vermelho, a/c rooms, the best overlook the river.

B-C Pousada do Ipê, R Cel Guedes de Amorim 22, T3371 2065. Rooms around a courtyard

dominated by a huge mango tree. The annexe has a pool and bar.

B-C Pousada do Vovô Jura, R Sta Barbara 38, T3371 1746. Colonial house set in a little garden with views out over the river and Serra.

C-D Pousada do Sol, R Americano do Brasil, T3371 1717. Well maintained, fans, friendly and central.

D Pousada Reis, R 15 Novembro 41, T3371 1565. A simple cheapie next to the Sonho offering similar rooms but shoddier service.

D Pousada dos Sonhos, R 15 Novembro 22, T3372 1224. Simple and convenient, plain rooms with shared bath, good breakfast.

Camping Cachoeira Grande campground, 7 km along the BR-070 to Jussara (near the tiny airport). Attractive, well-run, with bathing place and snack bar. More basic site (**Chafariz da Carioca**) in town by the river.

Pirenópolis *p574*

At Festa do Divino (see below) it's essential to book ahead or visit from Brasília.

A Casa Grande, R Aurora 41, T3331 1758, www.casagrandepousada.com.br. Chalets in a tropical garden with a pool gathered around a large colonial house on the edge of town.

A Casarão, R Direita 79, T3331 2662, www.ocasarao.pirenopolis.tur.br. A converted colonial town house decorated with antiques, garden and small pool, a/c rooms with 4 poster beds, mosquito nets.

C Pouso do Sô Vigario, R Nova 25, T3331 1206, www.pousadaspirenopolis.com.br. Small rooms but pleasant public areas, good location, decent breakfast in a little garden next to the pool.

C Rex, Praça da Matriz, T331 1121. Five rooms, all with fridge and TV, arranged around a courtyard. Good breakfast and location.

C-D Arvoredo, R Direita s/n, T3331 3479, www.arvoredo.tur.br. Peaceful, small pool, views over the town. Simple rooms with large beds and excellent special rates during the week.

E-F Arco Iris, R dos Pirenus s/n, T3331 1686. Very simple but well-kept, fan, shared bath, no breakfast.

Camping Roots, R dos Pirenus 96, camproots@yahoo.com. In easy reach of the centre with power, hot water and some English speaking staff.

Chapada dos Veadeiros *p574*
Alto Paraíso

AL-A Camelot, on the main road just north of town, T3446 1449, www.pousadacamelot. com.br. Delightfully kitsch mock-Arthurian castle with proper hot showers and comfortable a/c rooms with satellite TV.

AL-A Portal da Chapada, 9km along the road to São Jorge, T3446 1820, www.portalda chapada.com.br. The best choice for birdwatchers, with cabins in the cerrado. Comfortable with a/c.

A Casa Rosa, R Gumersindo 233, T3446 1319, www.pousadacasarosa.com.br. Good a/c rooms, the best in chalets near the pool.

C-D Pousada do Sol, R Gumersindo 2911, T3446 1201. Small and simple, with a range of rooms, the best with balconies and fridges.

São Jorge
Prices often go up 30% at weekends.

AL Casa das Flores, T9976 0603, www.pousada casadasflores.com.br. Elegant, tastefully decorated rooms (candle-lit), sauna, pool and great breakfast.

AL-A Áquas de Março, T3347 2082, www.chapadadosveadeiros.com.br. A range of simple rooms decorated by local artists' work, pleasant garden, saunas, good breakfast.

AL-A Trilha Violeta, T3455 1088, www.trilha violeta.com.br. Fan, rooms around a bougainvillea filled garden. Reasonable restaurant.

D Casa Grande, T9623 5515/446 1388, www.pousadacasagrande.com.br. Simple but well looked after, good breakfast.

Camping Tatoo, at the top of town, tattoo@ travessia.tur.br, or tattoosj@yahoo.com.br. Powered sites from only US$3. Pizzas from wood oven, small bar, English spoken, very helpful.

Parque Nacional Emas p574
Mineiros
A Pilões Palace, Praça Alves de Assis, T661 1547. Restaurant, comfortable.

B Boi na Brasa, R Onze 11, T661 1532. No a/c, good churrasco restaurant attached.

C Mineiros Hotel, next to Boi na Brasa. With bath and huge breakfast, good lunch. Recommended.

Dorm accommodation at the park headquarters; kitchen and cook available but bring own food.

🍴 Eating

Goiânia p573
Gioanian cooking is like that of neighbouring Minas – meat heavy, with huge portions of accompanying vegetable dishes and of course beans and rice. The city has a good range of restaurants and bars, especially around Praça Tamandaré and Av Rep de Líbano in the Setor Oeste. Other mid-range options exist on and around Av Anhaguera between Tocantins and Goiás. Street stands (pamonharías) sell pamonha

snacks, tasty pastries made with green corn, sweet, savoury, or picante/spicy; all are served hot and have cheese in the middle, some include sausage.

₸₸₸ Bella Luna, R 10 704 (Praça Tamandaré). Excellent pizza, pasta and northern Italian dishes.

₸₸₸ Celson & Cia, R 15 539 at C 22. Very popular Goiás and Mineira meat restaurant with a good cold buffet. Evenings only except at weekends.

₸₸₸ Chão Nativo, Av Rep Líbano 1809. The city's most famous Goiânian restaurant also serving local and Mineira food. Lively after 2000 and lunchtime on weekends.

₸₸ China, R 7 623 (Praça Tamandaré). Chinese and Japanese food in a/c surroundings.

₸₸ Floresta, R 2 at R 9. Lively corner bar with grilled steaks, Brazilian standards and snacks ($). Open until late.

₸₸ Tribo do Açai, R 36 590. Buzzing little fruit juice bar with excellent buffet salads and health food.

₸₸ Walmor, R 3 1062 at R 25-B. Large portions of some of Brazil's best steaks, attractive open-air dining area, best after 2000.

₸ Buffalo's Grill, Praça Tamandaré. Pizzas, grilled meat, sandwiches and crêpes. Open 24 hrs.

₸ Giraffa, Av Rep Líbano 1592. Fast food with some more sumptuous set plates.

₸ Mineiro, R 4 No 53. Good Mineira per kilo buffet with lots of choice and some veggie options. One of several on this block.

₸ Primo Patio, Av Rep Líbano (opposite Castro's Plaza). Pizza, pasta and grilled steak and chicken.

Cidade de Goiás p573
₸₸ Dali, R 13 de Maio 26, T3372 1640. Riverside restaurant offering a broad range of international and local dishes.

₸₸ Flor do Ipê, Praça da Boa Vista 32 (end of the road leading from the centre across the bridge, T3372 1133. The best Goiânian food, enormous variety, lovely garden setting. Highly recommended.

₸ Degus't Fun Pizzaria, R Quinta Bocaiuva (next to Praça do Coreto), T3371 2800. Pizza, casseroles, soups and very friendly service from a mother and daughter team.

Pirenópolis p574
There are plenty of options along R do Rosário, serving a surprising range of international food including some vegetarian and Asian options. Many have live music at night (and an undisclosed cover charge – be sure to ask). There are cheaper options near the Igreja Bonfim in the upper part of town.

₸₸ Caffe e Tarsia, R do Rosário 34, T3331 1274, www.caffetarsia.com.br. One of the best in town with rich Goiás cooking, a decent wine list and live music at the weekends.

₸ Chiquinha, R do Rosário 19. Serves local cuisine (heavy on meat).

⋔ Bars and clubs

Goiânia p573

Goiânia is surprisingly lively, with some of the best nightlife in central Brazil. This is especially true around the various festivals and carnival. There is an active gay scene and plenty of choices of clubs and bars. Most locals tend to drink in the restaurants; many of which double up as bars (see above) before heading to a club at around 2300.

⊛ Festivals and events

Cidade de Goiás p573

Many festivals here and a very lively arts scene. The streets blaze with torches during the solemn Fogaréu processions of Holy Week, when hooded figures re-enact Christ's descent from the cross and burial. Carnaval is a good deal more joyous and still little known to outsiders. Plans are to make carnival a series of traditional masked balls, as it was at the turn of the 20th century.

Pirenópolis p574

Festa do Divino Espírito Santo, held 45 days after Easter (Pentecost- May/Jun), is one of Brazil's most famous and extraordinary folkloric/religious celebrations. It lasts three days, with medieval costumes, tournaments, dances and mock battles between Moors and Christians, a tradition held annually since 1819. The city throbs with life over this period.

⊙ Shopping

Pirenópolis p574

There are many jewellery and arts and crafts shops. Two of the best jewellers are **Cristiano**, who has travelled extensively in South America as is reflected in his designs, and **Rodrigo Edson Santos**, R do Rosário 3, T3331 3804.

⚠ Activities and tours

Goiânia p573

Travel agents in town can arrange day tours. **Turisplan Turismo**, R 8 No 388, T224 1941. Also sells regular bus tickets.

Cidade de Goiás p573

Frans and Susana Leeuweenberg (through Serra Dourada). Birding and wildlife trips in the surrounding area (or anywhere in Goiás – with advanced notice) from a husband and wife team of biologists who have been working hard to protect the cerrado for many years. English, French and Dutch spoken.
Serra Dourada Aventura, no fixed office, reachable on T3371 4277 or 9238 5195, through

www.vilaboadegoias.com.br or orlei@vilaboadegoias.com.br. Hiking in the Serra Dourada and bespoke trips to the wilds of the Rio Araguaia (with notice). Very good value.

Pirenópolis p574

There are plenty of walks and adventure activities in the cerrado and hills, birding is good and there is a reasonably healthy population of maned wolf and the various South American cats, including jaguar. The landscape is rugged, with many waterfalls and canyons. Guides are essential as many of the attractions are well off the beaten track.
Drena, R do Carmo 11 (across the bridge and up the hill, on the left), T3331 3336. A range of walks and adventure activities, good value, well-run, very good English spoken. They organize trips to **Santuário de Vida Silvestre Vagafogo**, T3335 8490, the private reserve of Evandro Engel Ayer: good birding (species list and library) and many interesting animals. Evandro is very knowledgeable and helpful, speaks good English and serves one of the best light lunches in Goiás. **Mosterio Buddhisto**, a simple Zen monastery near a series of beautiful cascades in the heart of pristine cerrado forest. Day visits with light walks or longer term retreats. Particularly magical at sunset.

Chapada dos Veadeiros p574

By far the easiest way to visit is with one of the tour operators in Alto Paraíso. Prices vary according to season and group number.
Alternativas, T3446 1000, www.alternativas.tur.br. Light adventure activities and treks, run by locals, excellent and really go out of the way to help. Sasa speaks good English. Recommended.
Chapada Ecotours, T3446 1345, www.transchapada.com.br. Light adventure and visits to the major sights.
EcoRotas, R dos Nascentes 129, T3446 1820, www.altoparaiso.com. Van-based tours to the principal sights. Suitable for all ages.
Travessia, T3446 1595, www.travessia.tur.br. Treks of several days to over a week and rappelling and canyoning from one of the country's most respected instructors, Ion David. Little English.

⊖ Transport

Goiânia p573

Air Santa Genoveva, 6 km northeast off Rua 57, T3265 1500. Flights to **Brasília**, **São Paulo** and other cities. Taxi from centre US$8.
Bus Rodoviária on Rua 44 No 399 in the Norte Ferroviário sector, about a 40-min walk to downtown (T3229 0070). Buses 'Rodoviária-Centro' (No 404) and 'Vila União-Centro' (No 163) leave from stop on city side of terminal, US$1; No 163 goes on to the Praça Tamandaré.

To **Brasília**, 207 km, at least 15 departures a day, 2½ hrs, US$6.50, and **São Paulo**, 900 km via Barretos, US$33, 14½ hrs, leito services at night. To **Cidade de Goiás**, 136 km, hourly from 0500, 2½ hrs, US$6.50. **Pirenópolis** 0700 and 1700, 2 hrs, US$6.50. **Campo Grande**, 935 km, 4 services daily, 18 hrs, US$40. To **Cuiabá** (Mato Grosso), 916 km on BR-158/070 via Barra do Garças, or 928 km on BR-060/364 via Jataí (both routes paved, most buses use the latter route), 4 buses a day, US$33, 15-16 hrs, continuing to Porto Velho (Rondônia) and Rio Branco (Acre) – a very trying journey indeed.

Cidade de Goiás p573

Bus The rodoviária is 2 km out of town. Regular services to Goiânia (2½ hrs), Aruanã, Barra do Garças and Jussara. All buses stop at the old bus station (rodoviária velha) next to the Mercado Municipal. Ask to get out here.

Pirenópolis p574

Bus 2 a day to **Brasília** (2-4 hrs) and 2 per day to **Goiânia** (3 hrs).

Chapada dos Veadeiros p574

Bus At least 2 per day Brasília-Alto Paraíso (3-4 hrs) and on to São Jorge. One a day to **Palmas** in Tocantins.

Parque Nacional Emas p574

Car 6 hrs' drive from Campo Grande, 20 hrs from Goiânia, paved road poor. The road to the park is unpaved; twice weekly **bus** from Mineiros.

Tocantins

To the north of Goiás, and extracted from that state in 1988, is Tocantins, dominated by vast rivers, cerrado forests and, increasingly soya plantations. The state was formed largely at the whim of one powerful landowner, José Wilson Siqueira Campos; who for the first decade of its existence ran the state like a personal fiefdom. Although new to tourism Tocantins has some stunning scenery and is the only state in the country to have Amazonian forest, Pantanal, cerrado forest and sertão. The greatest draw is **Jalapão**, a region of sweeping yellow sand-dunes, vast plains cut by fast-flowing clear-water rivers and dotted with table top mountains eroded into bizarre shapes. The air is so clear that it is possible to see for hundreds of kilometres to every horizon; and the landscape so empty that cars can be heard from miles away. There is plentiful wildlife too - including maned wolf, puma and some of the world's rarest birds including Brazilian merganser and Spix's macaw.

The capital of Tocantins is **Palmas** (Phone code oxx63. Colour map 5, grid C1, www.palmas.to.gov.br), a modern planned city laid out in an incomprehensible mathematical plan and on the edge of the dammed and flooded Tocantins river. Brazil's newest city is an interesting detour on the highway between Belém (1,282 km away) and Brasília (973 km). There are waterfalls in the surrounding mountains and beaches on the River Tocantins, which make for a relaxing stop on an otherwise long drive. The BR-153 is close to the city and provides a good road connection, both north to Maranhão, Pará, and south to Goiás.

⊜ Sleeping → *See Telephone, page 347, for important phone changes.*

Tocantins p578
There are numerous hotels in Palmas.
A Pousada dos Girassóis, 103-C. cj 3, lt 44, T3219 4500, www.pousadadosgirassois.com.br. The best in town with standard 3 star rooms with fitted furniture and a/c and the best restaurant in town. Jalapão tours leave from here.

▲ Activities and tours

Tocantins p578
Korubo Expedicoes, T011-3667 5053, www.korubo.com.br. Excellent tours to Jalapão staying in their luxurious purpose-built safari camp, modelled on those in Botswana and with white-water rafting, trekking, jeep trips and wildlife tours included in the price.

⊙ Transport

Tocantins p578
Air Airport, Av NS 5, 2 km from centre, T216 1237. Flights to Belém, Brasília, Goiânia and São Paulo.
Bus City buses are plentiful and cheap. Rodoviária, Acsuso 40, T216 1603.

The Pantanal

This vast wetland, which covers a staggering 21,000 sq km (the size of Belgium, Portugal, Switzerland and Holland combined), between Cuiabá, Campo Grande and the Bolivian frontier, is one of the world's great wildlife preserves. Parts spill over into Bolivia, Paraguay and Argentina to form an area totalling some 100,000 sq km. Partly flooded in the rainy season (see page 579), the Pantanal is a mecca for wildlife tourism or fishing. Whether land or river-based, seasonal variations make a great difference to the practicalities of getting there and what you will experience. A road runs across Mato Grosso do Sul via Campo Grande to Porto Esperança and Corumbá, both on the Rio Paraguai; much of the road is across the wetland, offering many sights of birds and other wildlife.

Ins and outs

Wildlife → www.geocities.com/RainForest/1820/ (Portuguese and English).

The Pantanal plain slopes some 1 cm in every kilometre north to south and west to east to the basin of the Rio Paraguai and is rimmed by low mountains. One hundred and seventy five rivers flow from these into the Pantanal and after the heavy summer rains they burst their banks, as does the Paraguai itself; to create vast shallow lakes broken by patches of high ground and stands of *cerrado* forest. Plankton then swarm to form a biological soup that contains as many as 500 million microalgae per litre. Millions of amphibians and fish spawn or migrate to consume them. And these in turn are preyed upon by waterbirds and reptiles. Herbivorous mammals graze on the stands of water hyacinth, sedge and savanna grass and at the top of the food chain lie South America's great predators - the jaguar, ocelot, maned wolf and yellow anaconda. In June at the end of the wet when the sheets of water have reduced to small lakes or canals wildlife concentrates and then there is nowhere on earth where you will see such vast quantities of birds or such enormous numbers of crocodilians. Only the plains of Africa can compete for mammals and your chances of seeing a jaguar or one of Brazil's seven other species of wild cat are greater here than anywhere else on the continent. There are over 700 resident and migratory bird species in the Pantanal and birding along the Transpantaneira road in the north or in one of the fazendas in the south can yield as many as 100 species a day; especially between late June and early October. Many species overlap with the Amazon region, the Cerrado and Chaco and the area is particularly rich in waterbirds. Although the Pantanal is often described as an ecosystem in its own right, it is in reality made up of many distinct habitats which in turn have their own, often distinct biological communities. Botanically it is a mosaic, a mixture of elements from the Amazon region including *várzea* and gallery forests and tropical savanna, the *cerrado* of central Brazil and the dry *chaco* of Paraguay.

Only one area is officially a national park, the **Parque Nacional do Pantanal Matogrossense** in the municipality of Poconé, 135,000 ha of land and water, only accessible by air or river. Permission to visit the park needs to be obtained at **Ibama** ① *R Rubens de Mendonça, Cuiabá, CEP 78008, T6441511/1581*. Hunting in any form is strictly forbidden throughout the Pantanal and is punishable by four years imprisonment. Fishing is allowed with a licence (enquire at travel agents for latest details); it is not permitted in the spawning season or piracema (1 October-1 February in Mato Grosso do Sul, 1 November-1 March in Mato Grosso). Like other wilderness areas, the Pantanal faces important threats to its integrity. Agro-chemicals and garimpo mercury washed down from the neighbouring planalto are a hazard to wildlife. Visitors must share the responsibility of protecting the Pantanal and you can make an important contribution by acting responsibly and choosing your guides accordingly: take out your rubbish, don't fish out of season, don't let guides kill or disturb fauna, don't buy products made from endangered species and report any violation of these norms to the authorities.

When to go

The Pantanal is good for seeing wildlife year-round. However, the dry season between July and October is the ideal time as animals and birds congregate at the few remaining areas of water.

During these months you are very likely to see jaguars. This is the nesting and breeding season, when birds form vast nesting areas, with thousands crowding the trees, creating an almost insupportable cacophony of sounds. The white sand river beaches are exposed, caiman bask in the sun, and capybaras frolic amid the grass. July sees lots of Brazilian visitors who tend to be noisy, decreasing the chances of sightings. From the end of November to the end of March (wettest in February), most of the area, which is crossed by many rivers, floods. At this time mosquitoes abound and cattle crowd on to the few islands remaining above water. In the southern part, many wild animals leave the area, but in the north, which is slightly higher, the animals do not leave.

What to take

Most tours arrange for you to leave your baggage in town, so you need only bring what is necessary for the duration of the tour with you. In winter (June-August), temperatures fall to 10° C, warm clothing and covers or sleeping bag are needed at night. It's very hot and humid during summer and a hat and sun protection, factor 30 or above, is vital. Wear long sleeves and long trousers and spray clothes as well as skin with insect repellent. Insects are less of a problem July-August. Take insect repellent from home as mosquitoes, especially in the North Pantanal, are becoming immune to local brands. Drinks are not included in the price of packages and tend to be over-priced, so if you are on a tight budget bring your own. Most importantly, make sure you take a pair of binoculars.

Getting there

There are three options for visiting the Pantanal: by tour, through a working ranch (*fazenda*) or by self-drive. Entry into the northern Pantanal comes either via the Transpantaneira road in the north, reached from the city of Cuiabá, which cuts through the wetland and is lined with fazendas, or the town of Barão do Melgaço which is surrounded by large lakes and rivers and is not as good for wildlife. In the south the access points are Campo Grande, Corumbá and Miranda, which offers access to many of the *fazendas*. *Fazendas* in the northern or southern Pantanal can also be booked directly; most now have websites and a tour of them can be taken with a hire car.

Types of tour

Tourist facilities in the Pantanal currently cater to four main categories of visitors. **Sport fishermen** usually stay at one of the numerous speciality lodges scattered throughout the region, which provide guides, boats, bait, ice and other related amenities. Bookings can be made locally or in any of Brazil's major cities. **All-inclusive tours** combining air and ground transportation, accommodation at the most elaborate fazendas, meals, guided river and land

tours, can be arranged from abroad or through Brazilian travel agencies. This is the most expensive option. **Moderately priced tours** using private guides, camping or staying at more modest fazendas can be arranged locally in Cuiabá (where guides await arrivals at the airport) or through the more reputable agencies in Corumbá. **The lowest priced tours** are offered by independent guides in Corumbá, some of whom are unreliable and travellers have reported at times serious problems here (see below). For those with the minimum of funds, a glimpse of the Pantanal and its wildlife can be had on the bus ride from Campo Grande to Corumbá, by lodging or camping near the ferry crossing over the Rio Paraguai (Porto Esperança), and by staying in Poconé and day-walking or hitching south along the Transpantaneira. **Note**: Whatever your budget, take binoculars!

Choosing a tour

Most tours combine 'safari' jeep trips, river-boat trips, piranha fishing and horse riding with accommodation in lodges. Excursions often take place at sunset and sunrise as these are the best times for spotting bird and wildlife. A two-day trip, with a full day taken up with travel each way, allows you to experience most of what is on offer. Longer tours tend to have the same activities spread out over a longer period of time. The best way to enjoy a tour is not to have fixed expectations about what you will see, but to take in the whole experience that is the Pantanal.

Many budget travellers en route to or from Bolivia make Corumbá their base for visiting the Pantanal. Such tourists are often approached, in the streets and at the cheaper hotels, by salesmen who speak foreign languages and promise complete tours for low prices. They then hand their clients over to agencies and/or guides, who often speak only Portuguese, and may deliver something quite different. Some travellers have reported very unpleasant experiences and it is important to select a guide with great care anywhere. By far the best way is to speak with other travellers who have just returned from a Pantanal tour. Most guides also have a book containing comments from their former clients. Do not rush to sign up when first approached, always compare several available alternatives. Discuss the planned itinerary carefully and try to get it in writing (although this is seldom possible – threaten to go to someone else if necessary). Try to deal directly with agencies or guides, not salesmen (it can be difficult to tell who is who). Always get an itemized receipt. Bear in mind that a well-organized three-day tour can be more rewarding than four days with an ill-prepared guide. There is fierce competition between guides who provide similar services, but with very different styles. Although we list a few of the most reputable guides below, there are other good ones and most economy travellers enjoy a pleasant if spartan experience. Remember that travellers must shoulder part of the responsibility for the current chaotic guiding situation in Corumbá. Act responsibly and don't expect to get something for nothing.

It appears to be the case that once a guide is recommended by a guidebook, he ceases to guide and sets up his own business working in promoting and public relations, using other guides to work under his name. Guides at the airport give the impression that they will lead the tour, but they won't. Always ask who will lead the party and how big it will be. Less than four is not economically viable and he will make cuts in boats or guides.

Campo Grande and around

Campo Grande → *Phone code: 0xx67. Post code: 79000. Colour map 7, grid B1. Pop: 663,621.*
Capital of the State of Mato Grosso do Sul. It was founded in 1899. It is a pleasant, modern city. Because of the terra roxa (red earth), it is called the 'Cidade Morena'. In the centre is a shady park, the **Praça República**, commonly called the Praça do Rádio after the Rádio Clube on one of its corners. Three blocks west is **Praça Ari Coelho**. Linking the two squares, and running through the city east to west, is Av Afonso Pena; much of its central reservation is planted with yellow ypé trees. Their blossom covers the avenue, and much of the city besides, in spring. The municipal **Centro de Informação Turística e Cultural** ① *Av Noroeste 5140 corner Afonso Pena, T/F324 5830, Tue-Sat 0800-1900, Sun 0900-1200*, sells maps and books. Housed in Pensão Pimentel, a beautiful mansion built in 1913, it also has a database about services in the city and cultural information.

Some distance from the centre is the large **Parque dos Poderes**, which contains the Palácio do Governo and other secretariats, paths and lovely trees. Even larger is the 119-ha

Parque das Nações Indígenas. Despite its name this is almost completely covered with recreational grassy areas and ornamental trees. But it's a very pleasant place for a stroll or quiet read and has good birdlife and a couple of museums: **Museu de Arte Contemporânea** ① *R Antônio Maria Coelho 6000, Tue-Sun 1200-1800, US$2*. This preserves the largest collection of modern art in the state and one of the largest in the Centre West; permanent and temporary exhibitions. **Museu Dom Bosco (Indian Museum)** ① *Av Afonso Pena, Parque das Nações Indígenas, T312 6491, Tue-Fri 0800-1800, Sat 1300-1800, Sun 0800-1200, 1400-1700, US$1.50*, contains relics from the various tribes who were the recipients of the Salesians aggressive missionary tactics in the early and mid-20th century. The largest collections are from the Tukano and Bororo people from the Upper Rio Negro and Mato Grosso respectively, both of whose cultures the Salesians were responsible for almost completely wiping out. There is also a rather depressing display of stuffed endangered species (mostly from the Pantanal, though some are from other areas of Brazil or other countries), two-headed calves and seashells from around the world.

Bonito → *Phone code: 0xx67. Post code: 79290. Colour map 6, grid B6. Population: 17,000.*

The municipality of Bonito, 248 km from Campo Grande, is in the Serra do Bodoquena. It is surrounded by beautiful *cerrado* forest cut by clear-water rivers rich with fish and dotted with plunging waterfalls and deep caves. It has become Brazil's foremost ecotourism destination; which in Brazilian terms means that families come here to romp around in Nature: from light adventure activities like caving to gentle rafting and snorkelling, all with proper safety measures and great even for small children. Despite the heavy influx of visitors plenty of wildlife appears around the trails when it's quiet. The wet season is January to February; December to February is hottest, July to August coolest. **Tourist office** Comtur ① *Praça Rachid Jauli (no English spoken), www.bonito-ms.com.br or www.guiabonito pantanal.com.br*. Bonito is prohibitively expensive for those on a budget. All the attractions in the area can only be visited with prior booking through a travel agent. As taxis are exorbitant, it is best to book with one of the few agencies who offers tours and transport. Owners also enforce limits on the number of daily visitors so, at busy times, pre-booking is essential. Bonito is very popular, especially during December to January, Carnival, Easter, and July (at these times advance booking is essential).

Some 26 km from Bonito is **Lagoa Azul**. The cave is named after a lake 50 m long and 110 m wide, 75 m below ground level. The water, 20°C, is a jewel-like blue as light from the opening is refracted through limestone and magnesium. Prehistoric animal bones have been

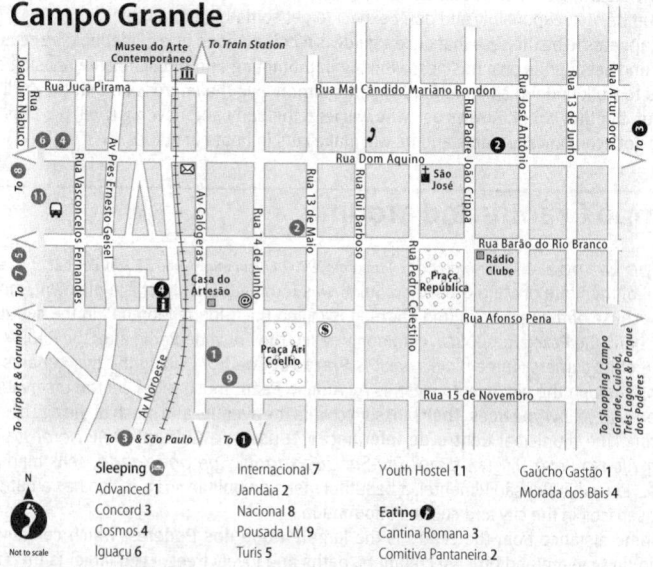

Campo Grande

Sleeping
Advanced 1
Concord 3
Cosmos 4
Iguaçu 6

Internacional 7
Jandaia 2
Nacional 8
Pousada LM 9
Turis 5

Youth Hostel 11

Eating
Cantina Romana 3
Comitiva Pantaneira 2

Gaúcho Gastão 1
Morada dos Bais 4

found in the lake. The light is at its best January-February, 0700-0900, but is fine at other times. A 25-ha park surrounds the cave. You must pay a municipal tax, US$10; if not using your own transport, a car for four costs US$20. Also open is **Nossa Senhora Aparecida cave**, which has superb stalactites and stalagmites; no tourism infrastructure.

The **Balneário Municipal** ① *7 km on road to Jardim, US$4*, on the Rio Formoso, with changing rooms, toilets, camping, swimming in clear water, plenty of fish to see (strenuous efforts are made to keep the water and shore clean). **Hormínio waterfalls** ① *13 km, US$1*, eight falls on the Rio Formoso, suitable for swimming; bar and camping. **Rafting** on the Rio Formoso: 2½ hours, minimum four people, US$15 per person, a mixture of floating peacefully downriver, swimming and shooting four waterfalls, lifejackets available; arranged by many agencies. The **Aquário Natural** *US$25*, is one of the springs of the Rio Formoso. To visit you must have authorization from the owners; you can swim and snorkel with five types of fish. Do not swim with suntan oil on. Other tours are: from the **springs of the Rio Sucuri** to its meeting with the Formoso (permission required to visit), about 2 km of crystal-clear water, with swimming or snorkelling, birdwatching, very peaceful; **Aquidaban**, a series of limestone/marble waterfalls in dense forest; **Rio da Prata** *US$24*, a spring with underground snorkelling for 2 km, stalactites, bats, very beautiful, also parrots and other animals can be seen on the trip, The **fishing** season is from 1 March-31 October. In late October, early November is the piracema (fish run), when the fish return to their spawning grounds. Hundreds can be seen jumping the falls. **Note:** Bonito's attractions are nearly all on private land and must by visited with a guide. Owners also enforce limits on the number of daily visitors so, at busy times, pre-booking is essential.

Ponta Porã → *Post code: 79900. Phone code: 0xx67. Population: 67,000*

There is a paved road from Campo Grande to the Paraguayan border to Ponta Porã, separated from Pedro Juan Caballero in Paraguay only by a broad avenue. With paved streets, good public transport and smart shops, Ponta Porã is more prosperous than its neighbour, although Brazilians cross the border to play the casino and visit the cheaper shops. In addition to the free movement of people and goods, the blending of cultures here is impressive. There are many *Brasiguayos* with one parent of each nationality and *Portoñol* is the common tongue. There are many banks on Av Brasil (one block back from the border) with ATMs but no exchange facilities; many cambios on the Paraguayan side.

Border with Paraguay → *Colour map 7, grid B2.*

There are no border posts between the two towns. The **Brazilian Polícia Federal** ① *Av Pres Vargas 70, ½ block back from the border street, T3431 1428, Mon-Fri 0730-1130, 1330- 1730*, is closed weekends but officers on duty might provide an entry stamp if you are on a bus that is passing through. The Paraguayan consulate in Ponta Porã (Av Pres Vargas 130, T3431 6312) does not issue visas, the nearest ones that do are in São Paulo, Curitiba and Foz do Iguaçu. **Check requirements carefully**, and ensure your documents are in order: without the proper stamps you will inevitably be sent back somewhere later on in your travels. Taking a taxi between offices can speed things up if pressed for time; drivers know border crossing requirements; US$10.

Campo Grande to Corumbá

BR-262 is paved from Campo Grande to Corumbá and the Bolivian border. The scenery is marvellous. Some 200 km west of Campo Grande is **Miranda**, where a road heads south to Bodoquena and Bonito. As a gateway to the Pantanal and Bonito, it is far closer to both than either Corumbá or Campo Grande. Many of the best of the southern Pantanal fazendas lie here, too. Every October Miranda throws the spectacular **Festa do Homen Pantaneiro**, four days of rodeos, lassoing and general revelry (dates vary each year). There is a tourist booth just outside the bus station, opposite the **Zero Hora** bakery and supermarket. **Rail services** to Corumbá, onwards to Bolivia and eventually to Campo Grande are due to recommence in 2006/2007. Internet at **Star Informática**, R Francisco Rebúa 149. The town has both a **Bradesco** and a **Banco do Brasil**.

To the southern Pantanal

Many tours out of Campo Grande and Miranda take a dirt road running off the BR 262 Campo Grande-Corumbá highway called the **Estrada Parque**. It begins half way between Miranda and Corumbá at a turn off called **Buraco da Piranha** (the Piranha hole), heads north into the

Pantanal and then, after 51 km, turns west to Corumbá at a point called the **Curva do Leque**. This is the overland access point to **Nhecolândia**, a region particularly rich in wildlife. Although there are excellent fazendas off the Estrada Parque road there are an increasing number opening up to tourism around Miranda.

💤 Sleeping → *See Telephone, page 347, for important phone changes.*

Campo Grande *p581, map p582*

The better hotels are in the centre. There is a wide variety of cheaper hotels in the streets around the rodoviária so it is easy to leave bags in the *guarda volumes* and shop around. This area is not safe at night.

L Jandaia, R Barão do Rio Branco 1271, T3316 7700, www.jandaia.com.br. The city's best hotel, aimed at a business market. Modern well-appointed rooms (with IDSL) in a tower, pool, gym and some English spoken.

A Advanced, Av Calógeras 1909, T3321 5000, www.hoteladvanced.com.br. Spacious if spartan rooms with hot showers, in an 80s block, very small pool, cheaper with fan.

A Internacional, Allan Kardec 223, T384 4677. Quiet street near rodoviária. Modern, comfortable with a/c or fan and some renovated suites, small pool, restaurant.

B Concord, Av Calógeras 1624, T384 3081. A standard town hotel with a small pool and recently renovated a/c rooms with modern fittings.

B Iguaçu, R Dom Aquino 761, T3322 4621, www.hoteliguacu.com.br. **D** with fan. Very popular well-kept hotel next to the rodoviária with smart, simple a/c rooms with cable TV. Good breakfast.

C-D Pousada LM, R 15 de Novembro 201, T321 5207, www.lmhotel.com.br. Tiny, basic en suites around a courtyard, all with a TV, fridge and some with terraces. Cheaper with fan.

D Cosmos, R Dom Aquino 771, near the rodoviária, T384 4270. Simple but bright and well-kept 1980s rooms with decent mattresses and en suites.

D Nacional, R Dom Aquino, 610, T383 2461, hotelnacional@ig.com.br. Simple, quiet rooms with fans, some rooms with bath, proper mattresses in a well-kept hotel with a TV room and internet, good value.

D Turis, R Alan Kardec 200, T382 7688. Airy, a/c or with fans, all on bright terrace, all with bath.

D R Joaquim Nabuco 185, opposite rodoviária, T321 0505, ajcampogrande@hotmail.com. Simple, musty little rooms with saggy foam mattresses and frayed bathrooms. Laundry, kitchen, internet; reception open 24 hrs. Ecological expeditions offer Pantanal trips from their office next door. Their other branch at R

Barão Rio Branco 343, T325 6874, has marginally better rooms for 10% more; but the mattresses are still hot and foamy.

Bonito *p582*

AL Pira Miuna, R Luis da Costa Leite 1792, T3255 1058, www.piramiunahotel.com.br. Ugly building with the most comfortable a/c rooms in the centre and a large pool area with jacuzzis and a bar.

AL Pousada Olho d'Água, Rod Três Morros, Km 1, T3255 1430, olhodagua@vip2000.net. Comfortable cabins with fan, set in a garden next to a small lake. Horse riding, bike rental, solar-powered hot water and great food from the vegetable garden. Recommended.

A Tapera, Estrada Ilha do Padre, Km 10, on hill above Shell station on road to Jardim, T3255 1700. Fine views, cool breezes, peaceful, a/c, very comfortable, own transport an advantage.

C Canaã, R Col Pilad Rebuá 1376, T3255 1282. A scruffy lobby leads to gloomy though well-maintained motel-style rooms with a/c and bath.

C-E Albergue do Bonito, R Lúcio Borralho 716, T/F255 1462, www.ajbonito.com.br. Price pp in dorm, HI affiliated hostel, English spoken, pool, laundry facilities, use of kitchen, hot showers, secure parking, rents bicycles.

C-E Pousada São Jorge, Av Col Pilad Rebuá 1605, T255 1956, www.pousadasaojorge.com.br. Clean dorms with bunks and en suites (the best with 2 bathrooms) and a pleasant public dining area with snack bar. Price per person for dorms.

D pp Pousada Muito Bonito, Pilad Rebuá 1448, T/F3255 1645. With bath, or rooms with bunkbeds, nice patio, excellent, helpful owners, including breakfast, also with tour company (Mario Doblack speaks English, French and Spanish). Warmly recommended.

D pp Pousada Rio do Peixe, R 29 de Maio 820, T3255 2212, pousadariodopeixe@viabonito.com.br. More expensive with TV, Italian-owned, very helpful, excellent breakfast, tours arranged.

Camping At Ilha do Padre, 12 km north of Bonito, T/F255 1430. On island with natural pools, very pleasant, no regular transport. 4 rustic cabins with 4 bunk beds, or 2 bunks and a double, US$10 pp. Youth hostel with dorms, US$6 pp, same price for camping. Toilets,

---

For an explanation of the sleeping and eating price codes used in this guide, see inside the front cover. Other relevant information is found in Essentials pages 345-347.

showers, clothes washing, meals, bar, electricity, lots of trees. You can swim anywhere, to enter the island for a day US$3. Camping also at **Poliana** on Rio Formosa, 100 m past Ilha do Padre, T255 1267. Very pleasant.

Ponta Porã *p583*

AL-A Barcelona, R Guia Lopes 45, T3431 3061, www.hotelbarcelonapp.com.br. Maze-like building, a/c, restaurant, indoor pool, parking.
A Pousada do Bosque, Av Pres Vargas 1151, T3431 1181, www.hotelpousadado bosque.com.br. 'Fazenda style' with lovely grounds and pool, sports fields, restaurant, parking, comfortable rooms with a/c and fridge.
A-B Interpark, Av Brasil 3684, T3431 1577, www.grupointerhoteis.com.br. Comfortable modern rooms with a/c and fridge, small pool, restaurant.
D Guarujá, R Guia Lopes 63, T3431 1619. With a/c and fridge, cheaper with fan, parking, faded but functional.
D Vila Velha, Av Marechal Floreano 2916, T3431 2760. Private bath, electric shower, fan, basic.

Campo Grande to Corumbá: Miranda *p583*

A-D Águas do Pantanal, Av Afonso Pena 367, T3242 1242, www.aguasdopantanal.com.br. Much the best in town, comfortable a/c rooms and cheaper backpacker accommodation, attractive pool surrounded by tropical flowers, helpful travel agency. Usually have a rep waiting at the rodoviária.
C Pantanal, Av Barão do Rio Branco 609, T3242 1068. Well-maintained a/c rooms with en suites along a gloomy corridor, pool.
D-E Diogo, Av Barão do Rio Branco s/n, T242 1468. Very simple but well-kept doubles, triples and quadruples, some with a/c.

To the southern Pantanal *p583*

LL Refúgio Ecológico Caiman, 36 km from Miranda, T011-3706 1800 (São Paulo), www.caiman.com.br. The most comfortable, stylish accommodation in the Pantanal. Tours and guiding are excellent. A member of the Roteiros de Charme group (see p 346).
LL-L Fazenda Xaraés, Estrada Parque, www.xaraes.com.br. One of the most luxurious fazendas, with a pool, tennis court, sauna, air strip and surprisingly plain but well-appointed a/c rooms. The immediate environs have been extensively cleared, but there are some wild areas of savanna and *cerrado* nearby and there are giant otter in the neighbouring Rio Abodrai.
L-AL Fazenda Bela Vista, Estrada Parque, www.pousadabelavista.com.br. On the banks of the Rio Papagaio in the foothills of the Serra do Urucum hills in a transition zone between Pantanal and higher ground. Bird and primate life is very rich. Guiding is good, but express your interest in wildlife beforehand.
L-AL Fazenda Rio Negro, Estrada Parque, T3326 0002, www.fazendarionegro.com.br. A Conservation International project based at a 13,000-ha farm on the shores of the Rio Negro. One of the oldest fazendas in the Pantanal (1920s). Guiding is good, but express your interest in wildlife beforehand.
AL Cacimba de Pedra, Estr Agachi, T9982 4655, www.cacimbadepedra.com.br. A Jacaré caiman farm and pousada in beautiful dry deciduous forest with abundant wildlife. A/c rooms sit in front of an inviting pool.
AL Fazenda San Francisco, turn off BR 262 30km west of Miranda, T3242 3333, www.fazendasanfrancisco.tur.br. One of the best places in the Pantanal for wild cats, preserved through Roberto Coelho's pioneering Gadonça project (www.procarnivoros.org.br), a great success here. Birdwatching is also excellent. Accommodation simple in rustic a/c cabins around a pool in a garden filled with rheas. Food and guides are excellent.
AL Fazenda Santa Inés, Estr . La Lima Km 19, www.fazendasantaines.com.br. A very comfortable family-oriented fazenda overlooking an artificial lake. Tours are aimed firmly at the Campo Grande weekend market and although there is little wildlife here, food is excellent and there is a range of light adventure activities for kids.
AL Pousada Rio Vermelho, off Estrada Parque, T3321 4737, www.pousadariovermelho.com.br. A rustic fazenda in a wild area on the banks of a river famous for its population of jaguars. Simple, well-kept a/c rooms. Coordinate with other visitors through the fazenda in advance as the fazenda lies well off the Estrada Parque.
AL-A Fazenda Meia Lua, BR-262 Km 551, 10 mins from Miranda, T9988 2284, www.fazendameialua.com.br. Charming newly-opened fazenda with a pool, lovely garden filled with hummingbirds and accommodation in a/c cabins or simple a/c rooms, attentive owners.
AL-A Fazenda Baia Grande, Estr La Lima Km 19, T3382 4223, www.fazendabaiagrande.com.br. Very comfortable a/c rooms around a pool in a garden. The fazenda is surrounded by savanna and stands of cerrado. The owner, Alex is very eager to please and enthusiastic.
A Fazenda 23 de Março, T3321 4737, www.fazenda23demarco.com.br. Simple, rustic fazenda with 4 rooms and programmes oriented to budget travellers. Visitors can learn to lasso, ride a bronco and turn their hand to other Pantanal cowboy activities.

🍴 Eating

Campo Grande *p581, map p582*

Local specialities *Caldo de piranha* (soup), *chipa* (Paraguayan cheese bread), sold on streets, delicious when hot, and local liqueur, *pequi com caju*, which contains *cachaça*. There are many cheap restaurants around the rodoviária and many other in a/c surrounds in the Shopping Campo Grande mall (R Afonso Pena 4909).

🍴🍴🍴 **Gaúcho Gastão**, R 14 de Julho 775, T3384 4326. The best churrascaria in a town, famous for its beef, comfortable, a/c, lunch only.

🍴🍴🍴 **Comitiva Pantaneira**, R Dom Aquino 2221, T3383 8799. Hearty, tasty and very meaty regional dishes served by waiters in cowboy gear, or as a buffet, lunchtime only.

🍴🍴 **Cantina Romana**, R da Paz, 237, T3324 9777. Over 20 years serving Italian dishes, salads and a lunchtime buffet, good atmosphere.

🍴🍴-🍴 **Sabor en Quilo**, R Barão do Rio Branco 1118 and R Dom Aquino 1786, T3383 3911/3325 5102. Self-service per kilo restaurants with plenty of choice including sushi on Sat, lunchtime only.

🍴 **Morada dos Bais**, Av Noroeste, 5140, corner with Afonso Pena, behind tourist office. Brazilian and Italian dishes, snacks and coffee served in a pretty courtyard, lunchtime only.

Bonito *p582*

🍴🍴-🍴🍴 **Santa Esmeralda**, R Cel Pilad Rebuá 1831. Respectable Italian food in one of the few a/c dining rooms.

🍴🍴 **Cantinho do Peixe**, R 31 de Março 1918, T3255 3381. A la carte Pantanal fish dishes including good *pintado na telha* (grilled surubim).

🍴🍴 **Tapera**, R Cel Pilad Rebuá 480, T3255 1110. Good, home-grown vegetables, breakfast, lunch, pizzas, meat and fish dishes, opens 1900 for evening meal.

🍴 **Da Vovó**, R Sen F Muller 570, T3255 2723. A great per kilo serving Minas and local food all cooked in a traditional wood-burning aga. Plenty of vegetables and salads.

🍴 **Mercado da Praça**, R 15 Novembro 376, T3255 2317. The cheapest in town, a snack bar in the local supermarket offering sandwiches, juices, etc, open 0600-0000.

Campo Grande to Corumbá: Miranda *p583*

🍴🍴 **Cantina Dell'Amore**, Av Barão do Rio Branco 515, T3242 2826. The best in town with fish, passable pasta and jacaré steak.

🍴 **Zero Jora**, Av Barão do Rio Branco at the rodoviária, T3242 1330. 24 hour snack bar, provision shop and out the back, with its own private waterfall, a passable, good value per kilo restaurant.

🛍 Shopping

Campo Grande *p581, map p582*

Arts and crafts There is a market (Feira Livre) on Wed and Sat. Local native crafts, including ceramics, tapestry and jewellery, are good quality. A local speciality is Os Bugres da Conceição, squat wooden statues covered in moulded wax. **Arte do Pantanal**, Av Afonso Pena 1743. **Barroarte**, Av Afonso Pena 4329. Very good selections. **Casa do Artesão**, Av Calógeras 2050, on corner with Av Afonso Pena. Housed in an historic building, Mon-Fri 0800-2000, Sat 0800-1200.

Shopping centre Shopping Campo Grande, Av Afonso Pena 4909, www.shoppingcampo grande.com.br, is the largest shopping mall in the city.

🏞 Activities and tours

Campo Grande *p581, map p582*

City Tour, T3321 0800 or through larger hotels. Half day tours of the city's sights including the Museu Dom Bosco and the Parque das Nações Indígenas.
Ecological Expeditions, R Joaquim Nabuco 185, T321 0505, www.pantanaltrekking.com and in Corumbá. Attached to the youth hostel at the bus station. Budget camping trips and lodge-based trips in Nhecolândia (sleeping bag needed) for 3, 4 or 5 days ending in Corumbá.
Impacto, R Padre João Crippa 686, T384 8175, www.impactotour.com.br. Very helpful, Pantanal and Bonito tours. Prices vary according to standard of accommodation; a wide range is offered. 2-day packages for 2 people from US$190-600. English spoken.
Open Door, R Allan Kardec 87, Galeria Maria Auxiliadora, Sala 4, T3321 8303/3388 1189, www.opendoortur.com.br. Specialists in the Southern Pantanal and Amazon and booking agents for flights and buses.

Bonito *p582*

There is very little to choose between agencies in Bonito, who offer the same packages for the same price, so shop around to see which you like the feel of best. English speakers are hard to come by. We list only those who also offer transport or a specialist service such as cave diving.
Impacto, R Cel Pilad Rebuá 1515, T3255.1414, see above under Campo Grande. English speaking staff and the possibility of organized transport. These can be pre-booked through their efficient head office in Campo Grande or through Águas do Pantanal tours in Miranda.
Ygarapé, R Cel Pilad Rebuá 1956, T3255 1733, www.ygarape.com.br. One of the few to speak even basic English and to offer transport to the sights. Also PDSE accredited cave diving.

Campo Grande to Corumbá: Miranda *p583*
Both of the operators below can organize lodging during the Festa do Homen Pantaneiro.
Águas do Pantanal Tours, Águas do Pantanal hotel, Av Afonso Pena 367, T3242 1242, www.aguasdopantanal.com.br. Well-organized tours to the fazendas around Miranda, to those on the Estrada Parque, to the sights around Bonito. They also run exclusive 1 or 2-day trips on the Rio Salobrinha to the Sanctuario Baía Negra, a little-visited river which is great for snorkelling and teeming with wildlife.
Marcello Yndio, lives in Bonito, contact him via T9638-3520 (mob), yndian@hotmail.com, marcelloyndio@gmail.com or marcelloyndio@yahoo.com.br. Kadiweu indigenous guide with many years experience. Very good English, French, Spanish and Italian and decent Hebrew. Great for small groups who want to get off the beaten track. Prices are competitive with budget operators in Campo Grande and Corumbá.

● Transport

Campo Grande *p581, map p582*
Air Daily flights to most major cities. Airport T3368 6000. City bus No 158, 'Popular' stops outside airport. Taxi to airport, US$8. Banco do Brasil at airport exchanges dollars; Bradesco just outside has a Visa ATM. Airport also has tourist information booths, car rental and airline offices. It is safe to spend the night at the airport.
Bus Rodoviária is in the block bounded by Ruas Barão do Rio Branco, Vasconcelos Fernandes, Dom Aquino and Joaquim Nabuco, T3321 8797, all offices on 2nd floor. At V Fernandes end are town buses, at the J Nabuco end state and interstate buses. In between are shops and lanchonetes, 1 km walk from Praça República. Taxi to rodoviária, US$4.80.
  São Paulo, US$40, 14 hrs, 9 buses daily, 1st at 0800, last at 2400, leito US$45. **Cuiabá**, US$28, 10 hrs, 12 buses daily, leito at 2100 and 2200 US$65. To **Brasília**, US$43, 23 hrs at 1000 and 2000. To **Goiânia**, São Luís 1100, 2000, 15 hrs on 1900 service, US$45, others 24 hrs. **Corumbá**, with Andorinha, 8 daily from 0600, 6 hrs, US$22. Campo Grande-Corumbá buses connect with those from Rio and São Paulo, similarly those from Corumbá through to Rio and São Paulo. Twice daily direct service to **Foz do Iguaçu** (17 hrs) with Integração, US$37. To **Ponta Porã** for Paraguay, see below.

Bonito *p582*
Bus Rodoviária is on the edge of town. From **Campo Grande**, US$15, 5½-6 hrs, 1500, returns at 0530. Bus uses MS-345, with a stop at Autoposto Santa Cruz, Km 60, all types of fuel, food and drinks available.

Ponta Porã *p583*
Bus The rodoviária is 3 km out on the Dourados road (Brazilian city buses from the *ponto* in the centre to Rodoviaria, São Domingos or Sanga Puitã, 20 mins, US$1; taxi US$6. To/from **Campo Grande**, Expresso Queiroz, 11 daily, 5 hrs, US$21; From Ponta Porã to **Bonito** or **Corumbá**, change at **Jardim** (a friendly little town with a good services, offering access to various natural attractions similar to those of Bonito at more modest prices): Ponta Porã-Jardim, **Cruzeiro do Sul** (www.cruzeirodosulms.com.br) at 0600 and 1530 Mon-Sat, 4 hrs, US$14; connect the following day at 0500 from Jardim to Corumbá (Corumbá to Jardim at 1400) via Bonito, 7 hrs, US$26. Also Jardim to Miranda, 1430 daily, 4 hrs, US$13. To **São Paulo**, Motta at 3 a day, 14 hrs, US$61, US$80 *leito*.

Campo Grande to Corumbá: Miranda *p583*
Bus Campo Grande-Miranda, 12 a day, 2-3 hrs, US$12.To **Corumbá**; 10 daily, 3-4 hrs, US$12. To **Bonito**, 1 daily, 2-3 hrs, US$8 at 1630.

● Directory

Campo Grande *p581, map p582*
Airline offices BRA, T382 1535. Trip, T3368 6137. TAM, office at airport, T0800-570 5700. Varig, R Barão do Rio Branco 1356, Centro, T325 4070, or 4003 7000. **Banks** ATMs at Banco do Brasil, 13 de Maio e Av Afonso Pena, open 1000-1500, commission US$10 for cash, US$20 for TCs, regardless of amount exchanged. Visa ATM at Bradesco, 13 de Maio e Av Afonso Pena. HSBC, R 13 de Maio 2837, ATM. Banco 24 horas, R Maracaju, on corner with 13 de Junho. Also at R Dom Aquino e Joaquim Nabuco. Overcash Câmbio, R Rui Barbosa 2750, open Mon-Fri 1000-1600. **Car hire** Agencies on Av Afonso Pena and at airport. **Embassies and consulates** Bolivia, R João Pedro de Souza 798, T382 2190. Paraguay, R 26 Agosto 384, T721 4430. **Internet** Cyber Café Iris, Av Alfonso Pena 1975. Also in the youth hostel (see above) and at Cyber Café, R Alan Kardec 374, T3384 5963, near the Hotel Turis. **Medical services** Yellow and Dengue fevers are both present in Mato Grosso do Sul. Get your immunizations at home. **Post offices** On corner of R Dom Aquino e Calógeras 2309 and Barão do Rio Branco corner Ernesto Geisel. **Telephones** Telems, R 13 de Maio e R 15 de Novembro, daily 0600-2200.

Bonito *p582*
Banks Banco do Brasil, R Luiz da Costa Leite 2279, for Visa. Hoteliers and taxi drivers may change money. **Post offices** R Col Pilad Rebuá. **Telephones** Santana do Paraíso.

Corumbá→ *Phone code: 0xx67. Post code: 79300. Pop: 95,701.*

Situated on the south bank by a broad bend in the Rio Paraguai, 15 minutes from the Bolivian border, Corumbá offers beautiful views of the river, especially at sunset. It is hot and humid (70%); cooler in June to July, very hot from September to January. It has millions of mosquitoes in December to February. The municipal tourist office, **Sematur**① *R América 969, T231 6996*, provides general information and city maps.

There is a spacious shady **Praça da Independência** and the port area is worth a visit. Av Gen Rondon between Frei Mariano and 7 de September has a pleasant palm lined promenade which comes to life in the evenings. The **Forte Junqueira**, the city's most historic building, which may be visited only through a travel agency, was built in 1772. In the Serra do Urucum to the south is the world's greatest reserve of manganese, now being worked. Corumbá has long been considered the best starting point for the southern part of the Pantanal and although many operators have shifted base to Campo Grande or Miranda, the town still offers various boat and jeep trips and access to the major hotel and farm accommodation. Almost all of the Campo Grande agencies have offices here and there are still a number of upmarket cruise companies along the water front.

Border with Bolivia

Over the border from Corumbá are Arroyo Concepción, Puerto Quijarro and Puerto Suárez. From Puerto Quijaro a 650-km railway runs to Santa Cruz de la Sierra. There is a road of sorts. There are flights into Bolivia from Puerto Suárez.

Brazilian immigration Formalities are constantly changing so check procedures in advance. In 2006 Brazilian Polícia Federal only stamped passports only at their office in the rodoviária ① *Mon-Fri 0800-1100, 1400-1600, Sat-Sun 1400-1700*, long queues for entry stamps but much quicker for exit. If leaving Brazil merely to obtain a new visa, remember that exit and entry must not be on the same day. Money changers at the border and in Quijarro offer the same rates as in Corumbá. The **Bolivian consulate** is at ① *R Antônio Maria Coelho 881, Corumbá, T231 5605. Mon-Fri, 0800-1600, Sat and Sun closed. A fee is charged to citizens of those countries which require a visa. A yellow fever vaccination certificate is required; go to R 7 de Setembro, Corumbá, for an inoculation (preferably get one at home).*

⏺ Sleeping → *See Telephone, page 347, for important phone changes.*

Corumbá *p588*
Although there are hostels around the bus station, this is a 10-min walk to the centre of town on the river bank where most of the hotels, restaurants and tour operators lie.
A-B Águas do Pantanal, R Dom Aquino Corrêa 1457, T3231 6582, www.aguasdopantanal hotel.com.br. The smartest in town together with the Nacional Palace, a/c rooms in a 1980s tower, pool and sauna.
A-B Nacional Palace, R América 936, T3234 6000, www.hnacional.com.br. Smart, modern a/c rooms, a decent pool and parking.
C-D Angola, R Antônio Maria 124, T3231 7727. Huge, scruffy, a/c and with fan. Internet via shared terminals. Safe as it is in front of the Polícia Federal.
C-E Salette, R Delamaré 893, T3231 6246. Cheap and cheerful with a range of rooms, the cheapest with fans and shared bathrooms. Recommended.
D Premier, R Antônio Maria Coelho 389, T3231 4937. Basic, small a/c rooms without windows. Prices are negotiable.

D Santa Rita, R Dom Aquino 860, T3231 5453. Modern, well-kept, a/c, all rooms TV and bath.
D-E Corumbá IYHA, R Colombo 1419, T3231 1005, www.corumbahostel.com.br. New, well-equipped modern hostel with helpful staff and a pool. Fan or a/c rooms and dorms.

⏺ Eating

Corumbá *p588*
Local specialities These include *peixadas corumbaenses*, a variety of fish dishes prepared with the catch of the day; as well as ice cream, liquor and sweets made of *bocaiúva*, a small yellow palm fruit, in season Sep-Feb. There are several good restaurants in R Frei Mariano. Lots of open-air bars on the river front.
♦♦♦-♦♦ Avalom, R Frei Mariano 499, T3231 4430. Chic little restaurant bar with streetside tables and decent pasta, pizza and fish. Especially busy after 2100 on Fri.

¶¶ Laço de Ouro, R Frei Mariano 556, T3231 7371. Very popular fish restaurant with a lively atmosphere and tables spilling out onto the street.
¶¶ Almanara, R América 961. Arabic and Turkish food.
¶¶-¶ Peixeria de Lulú, R Dom Aquino 700, T3232 2142. A local institution selling good river fishes for many years.
¶ Panela Velha, R 15 de Novembro 156, T3232 5650. Popular lunchtime restaurant with a decent, cheap all you can eat buffet.
¶ Verde Frutti, R Delamare 1164, T3231 3032. A snack bar with a wide variety of juices and great, ice-cold *acai na tigela*.

⊕ Festivals and events

Corumbá *p588*
2 Feb, Festa de Nossa Senhora da Candelária, Corumbá's patron saint, all offices and shops are closed. **24 Jun**, Festa do Arraial do Banho de São João, fireworks, parades, traditional food stands, processions and the main event, the bathing of the image of the saint in the Rio Paraguai. **21 Sep**, Corumbá's anniversary, includes a Pantanal fishing festival held on the eve. **Early-mid Oct**, Festival Pantanal das Águas, with street parades featuring giant puppets, dancing in the street and occasional water fights.

◉ Shopping

Corumbá *p588*
Shops tend to open early and close by 1700.
Casa do Artesão, R Dom Aquino Correia 405. Open Mon-Fri 0800-1200, 1400-1800, Sat 0800-1200, good selection of handicrafts, small bookshop, friendly staff but high prices.
CorumbArte, Av Gen Rondon 1011. For good silk-screen T-shirts with Pantanal motifs.
Livraria Corumbaense, R Delamaré 1080. For state maps.
Supermarkets Frutal, R 13 de Junho 538, open 0800-2000. Ohara, Dom Aquino 621.

▲ Activities and tours

Corumbá *p588*
Ecological Expeditions, R Antônio Maria 78 (see under Campo Grande, above, for more details).
Green Track, R Antônio João, Corumbá, T3231 2258, with representatives in Campo Grande at their bus station office. One of the longest established budget tour operators offering camping and lodge based trips to Nhecolândia starting in Campo Grande or Corumbá, where they have a budget hostel. Basic, but good value tours.

Mutum Turismo, R Frei Mariano 17, T3231 1818, www.mutumturismo.com.br. Cruises and upmarket tours (mostly aimed at the Brazilian market) and help with airline, train and bus reservations.
Pantur, R América 969, T3231 2000, www.pantur.com.br. Packages to Bonito and the fazendas on the Estrada Parque, including some of the less visited like Bela Vista and Xaraes. Flights and bus tickets can be booked here too.

Fishing and river cruises
These all leave from Corumbá.
Pérola do Pantanal, in the Hotel Nacional (see above), T3231 1470, www.perolado pantanal.com.br. Fishing and 'eco' tours on their large river boat the *Kalypso* with options on additional jeep trips on the Estrada Parque.
O Pantaneiro, R Manoel Cavassa 225, quays, T3231 3372, www.opantaneirotur.com.br. Cruises on by far the most comfortable modern boat sailing out of Corumbá, with day excursions in small launches.

⊖ Transport

Corumbá *p588*
Air Airport, R Santos Dumont, 3 km, T231 3322. Daily flights to **Campo Grande**, **Cuiabá** and **São Paulo**. No public transport from airport to town, you have to take a taxi. Car hire at the airport.
Bus The rodoviária is on R Porto Carreiro at the south end of R Tiradentes, next to the railway station. City bus to rodoviária from Praça da República, US$1; taxis are extortionate but mototaxis charge US$0.85. Andorinha services to all points east. To **Campo Grande**, 7 hrs, US$22, 13 buses daily, between 0630 and midnight, interesting journey ('an excursion in itself') – take an early bus to see plentiful wildlife, connections from Campo Grande to all parts of Brazil.

Border with Bolivia: Corumbá/Arroyo Concepción *p588*
Bus Leaving Brazil, take Canarinho city bus marked Fronteira from the port end of R Antônio Maria Coelho to the Bolivian border (15 mins, US$0.60), walk over the bridge to Bolivian immigration, then take a colectivo to Quijarro or Puerto Suárez. Taxi from Corumbá rodoviaria to Bolivian border US$11, negotiable. Ask to be taken directly to Bolivian immigration, not to a Bolivian cab who will hold your luggage while your passport is stamped. Overcharging and sharp practices are common. Touts at the Corumbá rodoviária offer hotels, Pantanal tours and railway tickets

to Santa Cruz. The latter cost double the actual fare and are not recommended.

When travelling from Quijarro, take a taxi or walk to the Bolivian border to go through formalities. Just past the bridge, on a small side street to the right, is the bus stop for Corumbá, take a bus to the rodoviária for Polícia Federal, US$0.60, don't believe taxi drivers who say there is no bus.

Train The schedules of trains from Puerto Quijarro to Santa Cruz are given on page 336. Timetables change frequently, so check on arrival in Corumbá. It may be best to stay in Quijarro to get a good place in the queue for tickets.

● Directory

Corumbá p588

Banks Banco do Brasil, R 13 de Junho 914, ATM. HSBC, R Delamare 1068, ATM. **Car hire** Unidas, R Frei Mariano 633, T/F231 3124. **Internet** Caffe.com, R Frei Mariano 635, T231 7730. PantanalNET, Rua América 403,Centro, US$2.50 per hr. **Post offices** main at R Delamaré 708; branch at R 15 de Novembro 229. **Telephones** R Dom Aquino 951, near Praça da Independência, open 0700-2200 daily. To phone Quijarro/Puerto Suárez, Bolivia, it costs slightly more than a local call, dial 214 + the Bolivian number.

Cuiabá and around

Cuiabá

→ *Phone code: 0xx65. Post code: 78000. Colour map 7, grid A1. Pop: 483,346. Altitude: 176 m.*

The capital of Mato Grosso state on the Rio Cuiabá, an upper tributary of the Rio Paraguai, is in fact two cities: Cuiabá on the east bank of the river and Várzea Grande, where the airport is, on the west. It is very hot; coolest months for a visit are June, July and August, in the dry season.

Cuiabá has an imposing government palace and other fine buildings round the green **Praça da República**. On the square is the **Cathedral**, with a plain, imposing exterior, two clock-towers and, inside, coloured-glass mosaic windows and doors. Behind the altar is a huge mosaic of Christ in majesty, with smaller mosaics in side chapels. Beside the Cathedral is the leafy **Praça Alencastro**. On **Praça Ipiranga**, at the junction of Avs Isaac Póvoas and Tenente Col Duarte, a few blocks west of the central squares, there are market stalls and an iron bandstand from Huddersfield, UK. On a hill beyond the praça is the church of **Bom Despacho**, built in the style of Notre Dame de Paris (in poor condition, closed to visitors). In front of the Assembléia Legislativa, Praça Moreira Cabral, is a point marking the **Geogedesic Centre of South America** (see also under Chapada dos Guimarães). **Museus de Antropologia, História Natural e Cultura Popular** ① *in the Fundação Cultural de Mato Grosso, Praça da República 151, Mon-Fri 0800-1730, US$0.50 (closed late 2005)*, has historical photos, a contemporary art gallery, stuffed Pantanal fauna, indigenous, archaeological finds and pottery. At the entrance to Universidade de Mato Grosso, 10 minutes by bus from the centre (by swimming pool), is the small **Museu do Índio/Museu Rondon** ① *T3615 8489, www.ufmt.br/icms/museurondon/museurondon, Tue-Sun 0800-1100, 1330-1700, US$1*, with artefacts from tribes mostly from the state of Mato Grosso. Particularly beautiful are the Bororo and Rikbaktsa headdresses made from macaw and currasow feathers and the Kadiwéu pottery (from Mato Grosso do Sul). **Tourist information** at **Secretaria de Desenvolvimento do Turismo**, Sedtur, in the Centro Político Administrativo ① *T/F613 9300, www.sedtur.mt.gov.br, Mon-Fri, 0700-1800*. Good maps, helpful, contact them if you have any problems with travel agencies; also book hotels and car hire, some English and Spanish spoken. Also at the airport, T682 2213, ext 2252. **Ramis Bucair**, R Pedro Celestino 280, is good for detailed maps of the region. City maps also from **Hotel Best Western**.

Cuiabá to Pantanal → *Colour map 6, grid A6.*

A paved road turns south off the main Cuiabá-Cáceres road to **Poconé** (102 km from Cuiabá, hotels, 24-hour gas station – closed Sunday). From here, the Transpantaneira runs 146 km south to Porto Jofre (just a petrol station, petrol and diesel, but no alcohol available). The road is of earth, in poor condition, with ruts, holes and many bridges that need care in crossing. Easiest access is in the dry season (July-September), which is also the best time for seeing birds and, in September, the trees are in bloom. In the wet, especially January-February, there is no guarantee that the Transpantaneira will be passable. The wet season, however, is a good time to see many of the shyer animals because more fruit, new growth and other high calorie foods are available, and there are fewer people.

Campos de Jofre, about 20 km north of Porto Jofre, is said to be magnificent between August and October. In Poconé one can hitch to Porto Jofre, or hire a vehicle in Cuiabá. You will get more out of this part of the Pantanal by going with a guide; a lot can be seen from the Transpantaneira in a hired car, but guides can take you into fazendas some 7 km from the Transpantaneira and will point out wildlife. Recommended guides in Cuiabá are under Tour operators. Although there are gas stations in **Pixaim** (a bridge across the Rio Pixaim, two hotels and a tyre repair shop) and Porto Jofre, they are not always well stocked, best to carry extra fuel.

Barão de Melgaço → *Colour map 7, grid A1.*

On Rio Cuiabá, 130 km from Cuiabá (TUT bus at 0730 and 1500, US$8.50), Barão de Melgaço is reached by two roads: the shorter, via Santo Antônio de Leverger, unpaved from Santo Antônio to Barão (closed in the wet season), or via São Vicente, longer, but more pavement. The way to see the Pantanal from here is by boat down the Rio Cuiabá. Boat hire, for example from Restaurant Peixe Vivo on waterfront, up to US$100 for a full day; or enquire with travel agencies in Cuiabá. The best time of day would be sunset, but this may mean returning after dark. Initially the river banks are farms and small habitations, but they become more forested, with lovely combinations of flowering trees (best seen September-October). After a while, a small river to the left leads to Chacororé and Sia Mariana lakes, which join each other via an artificial canal which has led the larger of the two lakes to drain into the smaller and begin to dry out. Boats can continue beyond the lakes to the Rio Mutum, but a guide is essential because there are many dead ends. The area is rich in birdlife and the waterscapes are beautiful.

Cuiabá

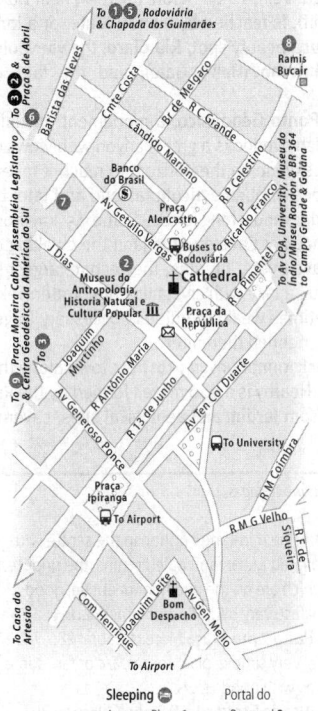

Sleeping
Amazon Plaza 6
Best Western Mato
  Grosso Pálace 2
Ipanema 5
Mato Grosso 7
Nacional 1
Panorama 9

Portal do
Pantanal 3
Pousada
Ecoverde 8

Eating
Choppão 2
Getúlio 3

Cáceres → *Phone code: 065. Post code: 78200. Colour map 6, grid A6. Population: 85,857.*

On the banks of the Rio Paraguai, 200 km west of Cuiabá, Cáceres is very hot but clean and hospitable. It has a number of well preserved 19th century buildings, painted in pastel colours.

The **Museu Histórico de Cáceres** ① *R Antônio Maria by Praça Major João Carlos*, is a small local history museum. The main square, Praça Barão de Rio Branco, has one of the original border markers from the Treaty of Tordesillas, which divided South America between Spain and Portugal; it is pleasant and shady during the day. In the evenings, between November and March, the trees are packed with thousands of chirping swallows (andorinhas). The praça is surrounded by bars, restaurants and ice cream parlours and comes to life at night. The city is known for its many bicycles as most people seem to get around on two wheels. Until 1960, Cáceres had regular boat traffic, today it is limited to a few tour boats and pleasure craft. The town is at the edge of the Pantanal. Vitória Regia lilies can be seen north of town, just across the bridge over the Rio Paraguai along the BR-174. Local festivals are the Piranha Festival, mid-March; International Fishing Festival in mid-September; annual cattle fair.

Border with Bolivia

An unpaved road runs from Cáceres to the Bolivian border at San Matías. Brazilian immigration is at Polícia Federal, Av Getúlio Vargas. Ask here for Fiscales Federales, which is the customs point for those entering or leaving by private vehicle. Leaving Bolivia, get your passport stamped at Bolivian immigration (1000-1200, 1500-1700), then get your passport stamped at Cáceres, nowhere in between, but there are luggage checks for drugs.

Chapada dos Guimarães
→ *Phone code: 065. Post code: 78195. Population 15,755. Colour map 7, grid A1.*

Some 68 km northeast of Cuiabá lies one of the oldest plateaux on earth. It is one of the most scenic areas of Brazil and visitors describe it as an energizing place. The pleasant town of Chapada dos Guimarães, the main centre, is a base for many beautiful excursions in this area; it has the oldest church in the Mato Grosso, **Nossa Senhora de Santana** (1779), a bizarre blending of Portuguese and French baroque styles, and a huge spring-water public swimming pool (on R Dr Pem Gomes, behind the town). Formerly the centre of an important diamond prospecting region, today Chapada is a very popular destination for Cuiabanos to escape the heat of the city at weekends and on holidays. It is a full day excursion from Cuiabá through lovely scenery with many birds, butterflies and flora. There is a post office at R Fernando Corrêa 848. The Festival de Inverno is held in last week of July, and Carnival is very busy. Accommodation is scarce and expensive at these times. The **Secretaria de Turismo e Meio Ambiente** office, R Quinco Caldas 100, near the praça, provides a useful map of the region and organizes tours. Weekdays 0800-1100, 1300-1800.

The Chapada is an immense geological formation rising to 700 m, with rich forests, curiously-eroded rocks and many lovely grottoes, peaks and waterfalls. A **national park** has been established in the area just west of the town, where the **Salgadeira** tourist centre offers bathing, camping and a restaurant close to the Salgadeira waterfall.

The beautiful 85 m **Véu da Noiva** waterfall (Bridal Veil), 12 km before the town near Buriti (well-signposted, ask bus from Cuiabá to let you off), is reached by a short route, or a long route through forest. Other sights include the **Mutuca** beauty spot, **Rio Claro**, the viewpoint over the breathtaking 80 m-deep **Portão do Inferno** (Hell's Gate), and the falls of **Cachoeirinha** (small restaurant) and **Andorinhas**.

About 8 km east of town is the **Mirante do Ponto Geodésico**, a monument officially marking the Geodesic Centre of South America, which overlooks a great canyon with views of the surrounding plains, the Pantanal and Cuiabá's skyline on the horizon; to reach it take R Fernando Corrêa east. Continuing east, the road goes through agricultural land and later by interesting rock formations including a stone bridge and stone cross. Some 45 km from Chapada you reach the access for **Caverna do Francês** or Caverna Aroe Jari ('the dwelling of the souls' in the Bororo language), a sandstone cave over 1 km long, the second largest in Brazil; it is a 1-km walk to the cave, in it is Lagoa Azul, a lake with crystalline blue water. Take your own torch/flashlight (guides' lamps are sometimes weak). A guide is necessary to get through fazenda property to the cave, but not really needed thereafter.

Other excursions are to the **Cidade de Pedra** rock formations, 25 km from town along the road to the diamond prospecting town of Água Fria. Nearby is a 300 m wall formed by the Rio Claro and 60 km from town are the **Pingador** and **Bom Jardim** archaeological sites, caverns with petroglyphs dating back some 4,000 years.

● **Sleeping** → *See Telephone, page 347, for important phone changes.*

Cuiabá *p590, map p591*

L Amazon Plaza, Av Getúlio Vargas 600, T2121 2000, www.hotelamazon.com.br. By far the best in the centre with very smart modern rooms, good views over the city, shady pool area, excellent service includes broadband in all rooms.

AL Best Western Mato Grosso Pálace, Joaquim Murtinho 170, T3624 7747, www.hotelmatogrosso.com.br. Conveniently located behind the Praça República, standard 3 star rooms with cable TV, fridge, hot showers.

B-C Mato Grosso, R Comandante Costa 252, T3614 7777, www.hotelmatogrosso.com.br. The

best value mid-range option in the centre with renovated a/c or fan-cooled rooms, the brightest of which are on the 2nd floor or above, good breakfast, very helpful. Recommended.

B-C Panorama, Praça Moreira Cabral 286, T3322 0072. Very simple, plain rooms, a/c or fan, some rooms with good views.

C Pousada Ecoverde, R Pedro Celestino 391, T3624 1986, joelsouza@terra.com.br. The best value, if idiosyncratic option, rooms with spacious bathrooms in a converted town house. Facilities include excellent tour agency, laundry service, internet and free airport/bus station pick-up (with 12 hrs notice).

By the rodoviária

B Nacional, Jules Rimet 22, T3621 3277. Right opposite the front of the bus station and convenient for those who don't need to go into town. Plain a/c rooms with renovated en suites..

C Ipanema, Jules Rimet 12, T3621 3069. Opposite the front of the bus station and with very well kept rooms, a/c or fan, cable TV, internet access, huge lobby TV for films or football. Many other options between here and the **Nacional**.

D pp Portal do Pantanal, Av Isaac Povoas 655, T/F3624 8999, www.portaldopantanal.com.br. HI hostel, with breakfast, cheaper with fan, internet access US$3 per hr, laundry, use of kitchen.

Cuiabá to Pantanal *p590*

Fazendas are listed according to distance in kms from Poconé

L Pouso Alegre, km 36 , T626 1545, www.pousalegre.com.br. Rustic pousada, simple accommodation, a/c or fan. One of the largest fazendas and overflowing with wildlife and particularly good for birds (especially on the morning horseback trail). Many species not yet seen elsewhere in the northern Pantanal have been catalogued here. Their remote oxbow lake is particularly good for water birds. Birding guides provided with advance notice. Best at weekends when the very knowledgeable owner Luís Vicente is there.

L Pousada Rio Claro, Km 42, book through Natureco. Comfortable fazenda with a pool and simple a/c rooms on the banks of the Rio Claro which has a resident colony of giant otters.

L Pousada Rio Clarinho, Km 42, book through Fauna Tour. Charming budget option on the Rio Clarinho which makes up in wildlife what it lacks in infrastructure. The river has rare water birds, as well as river and giant otters and occasionally tapir.

L Fazenda Santa Teresa, Km 75. A working fazenda, rustic, a/c or fan, pool, hearty food. There are giant otters in the river adjacent to the farm which are fed daily for show; making sightings almost guaranteed.

A Araras Lodge, Km 32, T682 2800, www.araraslodge.com.br. Book direct or through Fauna Tour or Natureco. One of the most comfortable with 14 a/c rooms; pool, excellent tours and food, homemade *cachaça* and a walkway over a private patch of wetland filled with capybara and cayman. Very popular with small tour groups from Europe. Book ahead.

A Fazenda Piuval, Km 10, T3345 1338, www.pousadapiuval.com.br.The first fazenda on the Transpantaneira and one of the most touristy, with scores of day visitors at weekends. Rustic farmhouse accommodation, pool, excellent horse and walking trails and boat trips on their vast lake.

Barão de Melgaço

L Pousada Passárgada, Sia Mariana, Barão de Melgaço, T3713 1128, in Barão de Melgaço on riverside, through **Nature Safaris**, Av Marechal Rondon, Barão de Melgaço, or agencies in Cuiabá. Much cheaper if booked direct with the owner, Maré Sigaud, Mato Grosso, CEP 786807, Pousada Passárgada, Barão de Melgaço. Programmes from 3 days up, full board, boat, Land Rover and trekking expeditions, transport from Barão de Melgaço either by boat or 4WD can be arranged with the owner who speaks English, French and German. Closed Dec-Feb.

C Barão Tour Hotel, in Barão de Melgaço town. Apartments with a/c, restaurant, boat trips and excursions (Cuiabá T322 1568). There are a handful of cheaper options near the waterfront.

Cáceres *p591*

A Caiçaras, R dos Operários 745, corner R Gen Osório, T3223 3187, F3223 2692. Modern, with a/c rooms and cheaper options without a fridge.

A-B Ipanema, R Gen Osório 540, T3223 1177, www.ipanemahotelmt.com.br. Simple town hotel with a/c rooms, a pool and a restaurant.

B-D Rio, Praça Major João Carlos 61, T3223 3387, F3223 3084. A range of rooms - the cheapest with no a/c and shared bathrooms.

C-D Charm, Col José Dulce 405, T/F3223 4949. A/c and fan-cooled rooms, with or without a shared bath.

D-E União, R 7 de Setembro 340. Near the rodoviária. Fan, cheaper with shared bath, basic but good value.

Chapada dos Guimarães *p592*

AL-A Solar do Inglês, R Cipriano Curvo 142, T3301 1389, www.chapadadosguimaraes.com.br. In an old converted house near town centre with 7 rooms each with bath, TV and frigobar. Garden, swimming pool and sauna. Breakfast and afternoon tea included.

A Estância San Francisco, at the entrance to town from Cuiabá (MT 251, Km 61), T3791 1102, F3791 1537. On a 42-ha farm with 2 lakes, said to have the best breakfast in town fresh from the farm. Good for birds.

B Turismo, R Fernando Corrêa 1065, a block from rodoviária, T3791 1176, F3791 1383. A/c rooms with a fridge, cheaper with fan, restaurant, breakfast and lunch excellent, very popular, German-run; Ralf Goebel, the owner, is very helpful in arranging excursions.

B-C Rio's Hotel, R Tiradentes 333, T3791 1126. A/c rooms with a fridge, cheaper with fan, cheaper with shared bath, good breakfast.

C Pousada Bom Jardim, Praça Bispo Dom Wunibaldo s/n, T3791 1244. Fan, comfortable, parking, good breakfast. Recommended.

D São José, R Vereador José de Souza 50, T3791 1152. Fan, cheaper with shared bath and no fan, hot showers, basic, no breakfast, good, owner Mário sometimes runs excursions.

Camping Aldeia Velha, in the Aldeia Velha neighbourhood at the entrance to town from Cuiabá, T322 7178 (Cuiabá). Fenced area with bath, hot shower, some shade, guard.

🍴 Eating

Cuiabá *p590, map p591*
City centre restaurants only open for lunch. On Av CPA are many restaurants and small snack bars. There are several cheap restaurants and lanchonetes on R Jules Rimet across from the rodoviária.

🍴🍴🍴 **Getúlio**, Av Getúlio Vargas 1147, T3264 9992. An a/c haven from the heat with black tie waiters, excellent food, with meat specialities, pizza, good buffet lunch on Sun. Live music upstairs on Fri and Sat from significant cult Brazilian acts.

🍴🍴🍴-🍴🍴 **Choppão**, Praça 8 de Abril, T3623 9101. A local institution, buzzing at any time of the day or night. Go for huge portions of delicious food or just for *chopp* served by fatherly waiters. The house dish of chicken soup promises to give diners drinking strength in the early hours and is a meal in itself. Warmly recommended.

🍴🍴 **Panela de Barro**, R Cmdte Costa 543. Self-service, a/c lunchtime restaurant with a choice of tasty regional dishes.

🍴🍴-🍴 **Miranda's**, R Cmdte Costa 716. Decent self-service per kilo lunchtime restaurant with good value specials.

🍴 **Lanchonete da Marilda**, R Cmdte Costa 675. Simple snack bar with generous *prato feito*.

Cáceres *p591*
🍴🍴🍴 **Corimbá**, R 15 de Novembro s/n, on riverfront. Fish specialities, and general Brazilian food.

🍴 **Gulla's**, R Cel José Dulce 250. Buffet by kilo, good quality and variety. Recommended.

🍴 **Panela de Barro**, R Frei Ambrósio 34, near rodoviária. *Comida caseira* with the usual gamut of meat dishes with squash, rice, black beans and salads.

Chapada dos Guimarães *p592*
Pequi is a regional palm fruit with a spikey inside, used to season many foods; *arroz com pequi* is a rice and chicken dish.

🍴🍴🍴 **Nivios**, Praça Dom Wunibaldo 631. The best place for good regional food.

🍴🍴🍴 **O Mestrinho**, R Quinco Caldas 119. Meat, regional dishes, *rodízio* at weekends.

🍴🍴🍴 **Trapiche**, R Cipriano Curvo 580. Pizza, drinks, regional dishes.

🍴 **Choppada** (O Chopp da Chapada), R Cipriano Curvo near Praça. Drinks and meals, regional dishes, live music at weekends.

🍴 **Fogão da Roça**, Praça Dom Wunibaldo 488. Good *comida mineira* in generous portions. Recommended.

🍷 Bars and clubs

Cuiabá *p590, map p591*
Cuiabá is quite lively at night, bars with live music and dance on Av CPA. Av Mato Grosso also has many bars and restaurants. 4 cinemas in town.

Café Cancun, R Candido Mariano at São Sebastião. One of a chain of popular Brazilian club bars attracting a mid-20s to 40s crowd.

Rush, Isaac Povoas at Presidente Marquês. Teen and twenty something techno cub bar. **Tucano**, bar/restaurant, Av CPA. Beautiful view, specializes in pizza, open daily 1800-2300. Recommended.

🛍 Shopping

Cuiabá *p590, map p591*
Handicrafts in wood, straw, netting, leather, skins, Pequi liquor, crystallized caju fruit, compressed guaraná fruit (for making the drink), indigenous objects on sale at the airport, rodoviária, craft shops in centre, and daily market, Praça da República, interesting. Fish and vegetable market, picturesque, at the riverside.

Casa de Artesão, Praça do Expedicionário 315, T321 0603. Sells all types of local crafts in a restored building. Recommended.

Chapada dos Guimarães *p592*
Crafts, indigenous artefacts, sweets and locally made honey from **Casa de Artes e Artesanato Mato Grossense**, Praça Dom Wunibaldo. Regional sweets from **Doceria Olho de Sogra**, Praça Dom Wunibaldo 21. **João Eloy de Souza Neves** is a local artist, his paintings, music and history about Chapada (*Chapada dos Guimarães da descoberta aos dias atuais*) are on sale at **Pousada Bom Jardim**.

⛰ Activities and tours

Cuiabá *p590, map p591*
You should expect to pay US$60-90 per person per day for tours in the Pantanal. All these agencies arrange trips to the Pantanal. Budget trips are marginally more expensive than those in

---

● *For an explanation of the sleeping and eating price codes used in this guide, see inside the front cover. Other relevant information is found in Essentials pages 345-347.*

Brazil Cuiabá & around Listings

the Southern Pantanal (around $10 per day), but accommodation based in fazendas is more comfortable. For longer or special programmes, book in advance.

Fauna Tour/Eco do Pantanal - Pousada Eco do Pantanal, R Campo Grande 487, T3624 1996, T998 37475 (mob; 24 hrs), pousadaecodopantanal@ gmail.com. One of several budget operators in town, but much the best option. 2 to 5-day tours to the Pantanal, Chapada and Rio Xingu with excellent wildlife guides; ask for Alex Gomes Ramos (T9204 5827). Camping trips available between Jun and Oct with advance notice.

Natureco, R Benedito Leite 570, T3321 1001, www.pantanaltour.net. Fazenda-based Pantanal tours, trips to the Chapada dos Guimarães and to Nobres - the Bonito of Mato Grosso. Specialist birding and wildlife guides available with advance notice. Some English spoken

Wildlife guides for the Pantanal and Mato Grosso

Recommended birding and wildlife guides for the northern Pantanal and Mato Grosso are listed below. All guides work freelance for other companies as well as employing other guides for trips when busy. Most guides await incoming flights at the airport; compare prices and services in town if you don't wish to commit yourself at the airport. The tourist office recommends guides; this is not normal practice and their advice is not necessarily impartial.

Giuliano Bernardon, T8115 6189, giubernardon@gmail.com. Young birding guide from the Chapada dos Guimarães, with a good depth of knowledge and experience in the Chapada, Pantanal, Mato Grosso Amazon and Atlantic coastal forest.

Paulo Boute, Boute Expeditions, R Getúlio Vargas 64, Várzea Grande, near airport, T3686 2231, pauloboute@uol.com.br. One of the most experienced birding guides in the Pantanal; works from home and speaks good English and French.

Fabricio Dorileo, fabriciodorileo18@yahoo.com.br or through Eduardo Falcão, rejaguar@bol.com.br. Excellent birding guide with good equipment, good English and many years experience in the Pantanal and Chapada dos Guimarães.

Pantanal Bird Club, T3624 1930, 9981 1236 (mob), www.pantanalbirdclub.org. Good for even the most exacting clients, PBC are the most illustrious birders in Brazil with many years experience, owner Braulio Carlos. Tours throughout the area and to various parts of Brazil.

Joel Souza, owner of Pousada Ecoverde, see above. Can be contacted at Av Getúlio Vargas 155A, next to Hotel Presidente, T641 1386, T9282 3201 (mob), joelsouza@terra.com.br. Speaks English, German and Italian, knowledgeable and

very helpful, checklists for flora and fauna provided, will arrange all transport, accommodation and activities, tends to employ guides rather than guiding himself.

Chapada dos Guimarães *p592*

4-hr tours are about US$26 pp, minimum 5 persons; 7-8 hr tours, US$32 pp, minimum 5; horseback day tour, US$32 pp, minimum 2; an 8-10 km hike with a guide, US$26 pp, minimum 2; bicycle tour with guide, US$26 pp, minimum 2. Tours from Cuiabá cost US$45-52 pp, but a one-day tour is insufficient for a full appreciation of what the area has to offer.

Guides   Jorge Belfort Mattos from **Ecoturismo Cultural**, Praça Dom Wunibaldo 464, T/F3791 1393. Recommended tours, he speaks English and knows the area well; several 4-6 hr itineraries from US$20-50 pp (minimum 4 people or prices increase).

Cássio Martins of AC Tour, R Tiradentes 28, T3791 1122, often waits at the rodoviária.

José Paulino dos Santos is a guide working with the **Secretaria de Turismo e Meio Ambiente**, T3791 1245.

⊖ Transport

Cuiabá *p590, map p591*

Air   Airport in Várzea Grande, T682 2213. By air to most major cities. ATMs outside include **Banco do Brasil** and **Bradesco** for Visa, MasterCard/ Cirrus; there is a post office and a **Sedtur** office (not always open). Taxi to centre US$15, 'Aeroporto' bus from Praça Ipiranga US$0.50. There is a direct Airport-Rodoviária bus; bus stop is by the farmacia outside airport.

Bus   Many bus routes have stops in the vicinity of Praça Ipiranga. Rodoviária is on R Jules Rimet, Bairro Alvorada, north of the centre; town buses stop at the entrance. Bus No 202 from R Joaquim Murtinho behind the cathedral, 20 mins. Comfortable buses (toilets) to **Campo Grande**, 10 hrs, US$28, 12 buses daily, leito at 2000 and 2100, US$65. **Goiânia**, 14 hrs, US$32; direct to **Brasília**, 24 hrs, US$30, leito US$60. To **Porto Velho**, 6 **Eucatur** buses a day (T621 2551), US$60, 21 hrs. **Andorinha** (T621 3416) 1700 bus São Paulo-Cuiabá connects with Porto Velho service. Several to **São Paulo**, eg **Motta** (T621 1159), US$56. Connections to all major cities.

Cáceres *p591*

Bus   Rodoviária, Terminal da Japonesa, T224 1261. **Colibri/União Cascavel** buses Cuiabá-Cáceres, US$12, many daily between 0630-2400 (book in advance), 3½ hrs. Cáceres-Porto Velho, US$43.

Ferry For information on sailings, ask at the Capitânia dos Portos, on the corner of the main square at waterfront. At the waterfront you can hire a boat, US$6.50 per hr pp, minimum 3.

Border with Bolivia:
Cáceres/San Matías *p591*
Bus The bus fare Cáceres-San Matías is US$12 with Transical-Velásquez, Mon-Sat at 0630 and 1500, Sun 1500 only (return at same times), 3 hrs.

Chapada dos Guimarães *p592*
Bus 7 departures daily to and from Cuiabá (Rubi 0700-1900, last back to Cuiabá 1800), 1½ hrs, US$3.65.
Car Hiring a car in Cuiabá is the most convenient way to see many of the scattered attractions, although access to several of them is via rough dirt roads which may deteriorate in the rainy season; drive carefully as the area is prone to dense fog.

❶ Directory

Cuiabá *p590, map p591*
Airline offices TAM, T0800-570 5700. Trip, T3682 2555. Varig, R 15 de Novembro 230, Bairro Porto, and at airport T4003 7000. **Banks** Banco do Brasil, Av Getúlio Vargas e R Barão de Melgaço,

commission US$10 for cash, US$20 per transaction for TCs, very slow for TCs, but best rates, also has ATM; Incomep Câmbio, R Gen Neves 155, good rates. It is difficult to get cash advances on credit cards especially MasterCard, for Visa try Banco do Brasil. **Car hire** Agencies have offices at the airport. **Embassies and consulates** Bolivia: Rua Paramaribo 174, Qd 08 Lote 06, Jardim das Américas , T627 7087, open Mon-Fri 0900-1700. **Internet** Copy Grafic, Praça Alencastro 32, fax and email, English spoken, friendly. Netnave, in Três Américas shopping centre, Av Brasília 200, 2nd floor. Not central but fast access, multimedia machines, US$2.50 per hr. Oxis, Pres Marques e Cândido Marino, fast connection, US$1 per hr. Also available in Library, free. **Post offices** Main branch at Praça da República, fax service. **Telephones** R Barão de Melgaço 3209, 0700-2200, also at rodoviária, 0600-2130, international service. **Voltage** 110 volts AC, 60 cycles.

Cáceres *p591*
Banks Banco do Brasil, R Cel José Dulce 234. HSBC, R Cel José Dulce 145. Casa de Câmbio Mattos, Comandante Bauduino 180, next to main praça, changes cash and TCs at good rates. **Internet** Available at US$1.50 per hr. **Telephones** Praça Barão de Rio Branco s/n.

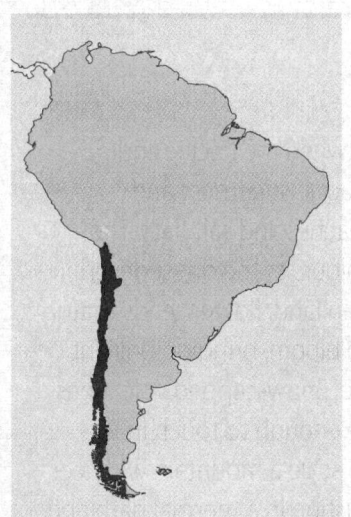

Chile

Footprint features

Introduction

Chile is a ribbon of land squashed between the Pacific and the Andes. Its landscape embraces glacial wilderness and moonscapes, lakes and volcanoes, beaches and salt flats. The north is characterized by the burnt colours of the driest desert in the world. Should rain fall in this barren land, flower seeds that have lain in wait seize the moment to bloom, bringing brilliant colours where no life seemed possible. Snow-capped volcanoes in the Lauca National Park seem close enough to touch in the rarefied air. In one day it is possible to scale a mountain with ice axe and crampons, soak off the exhaustion in a thermal bath and rest beneath the stars of the Southern Cross. Real stargazers will want to visit the astronomical observatories near La Serena, while lovers of mystery will head south for the folklore of Chiloé, Land of Seagulls. The Chilean Lake District is the homeland of the Mapuche, the people who resisted the Spaniards and who proudly maintain their culture and traditions. The lakes themselves are beautiful, set in farm land, overlooked by yet more snow-capped volcanoes. Before the road peters out, blocked by fjords and icefields, the Carretera Austral reveals ancient woodlands, hot springs beside the sea, mountains like castles and raging, emerald rivers – a paradise for fishing and cycling. To reach the ultimate goal of trekkers and birdwatchers, the fabulous granite towers and spires of the Torres del Paine National Park, you have to take a boat, or fly, or make the long haul through Argentina. There are seaports of every size, with their fishing boats, pelicans and sea lions. The most romantic is Valparaíso, described by one observer as 'a Venice waiting to be discovered', with its warren of streets and brightly painted houses, its singular lifts up to the clifftops and its old bars.

Chile

★ Don't miss...

1 **Valparaíso** One of the great ports of the entire Pacific seaboard. Its hills are UNESCO World Heritage sites, up and down the coast are beach resorts and the seafood is out of this world, page 627.

2 **Lauca National Park** In the thin air of the altiplano, snow-capped volcanoes seem to be just arm's length away, waterfowl wade at the margins of lakes and shy vicuña graze the windswept grasses, page 668.

3 **Lake District** A string of lakes of all different shapes and sizes stretches along the western foothills of the Andes. In many are mirrored the perfect cones of volcanoes. Some buzz with holidaymakers, others are ideal for a spot of solitude, page 684.

4 **Chiloé** The fabled island of seagulls, full of legends, wooden churches and forests. Take a ferry from the mainland; watch out for dolphins in the surrounding waters; ride a horse along the beaches, page 717.

5 **Carretera Austral** Over 1,000 km of largely unpaved road runs through a spectacular landscape of ancient forests, tree-lined fjords, glaciers and dramatic volcanoes. This is one of the best places for mountain biking, with many lakes, hot springs and townships to explore, page 725.

6 **Torres del Paine** The Mecca for all long-distance hikers is one of the world's most stunning national parks: massive granite towers overlook white and turquoise lakes, wild-flower meadows and forests, page 750.

Chile

Essentials

Planning your trip

Where to go A great many of Chile's attractions are outdoors, in the national parks, adventure sports, etc, but the capital, **Santiago**, has a rich cultural life (museums, handicrafts shopping) and is a good base for visiting nearby areas. These include the vineyards of the Maipo Valley, the Andean foothills in the Cajón del Maipo and the ski resorts. The port of Valparaíso and the beach resorts to north and south, principally Viña del Mar, are only a couple of hours away.

North of Santiago is La Serena, a popular seaside resort, from which can be reached the Elqui Valley, where Chilean pisco is made, and three major astronomical observatories. Heading north, the land becomes more barren, but every few years after rain, usually September to October, the flowers that have lain dormant in the desert burst into bloom; if you are in the area, a sight not to be missed. Inland from Antofagasta, the next main city, a road goes to Calama, the huge copper mine at Chuquicamata and the isolated Andean town and popular tourist resort of San Pedro de Atacama. Its attractions are lunar landscapes, hot geysers, salt flats and the way of life at high altitude. Alternatively, from Antofagasta you can take the spectacular coast road to the **Far North** and the ports of Iquique, near which are several archaeological sites, thermal springs and abandoned nitrate mines, and Arica, the last main town before Peru. The road route into Bolivia from Arica passes through the magnificent Parque Nacional Lauca, with its wealth of Andean bird and animal life, high lakes and remote volcanoes.

South of Santiago, the longitudinal highway runs south through the Central Valley passing through or near a number of cities, such as Rancagua, Talca, Chillán and Concepción (the country's second city). There are national parks which deserve a visit in both the Andean foothills and the coastal range of mountains. You can visit vineyards, thermal springs, unspoilt beaches or simply enjoy real Chilean rural life.

The **Lake District** is home to the popular lakes of Villarrica and Llanquihue, but many others are far less developed. Protected areas of great beauty and first-class opportunities for adventure sports and fishing abound. Temuco, at the northern end of this region, is the centre of Mapuche culture and has a huge produce market. Wooded Valdivia, near the coast, is worth a detour for the trip to the rivermouth to see the ruined Spanish forts that protected this outpost of the empire. The southern gateway to the Lake District is Puerto Montt, the starting point for the long haul south. The city's fishing harbour, Angelmó, with its market and food stalls, is not to be missed. From Puerto Montt you can cross to Argentina by road and ferries on Lago Todos los Santos and neighbouring Lagos Frías and Nahuel Huapi on the way to Bariloche.

The island of **Chiloé**, a short bus and ferry ride from Puerto Montt, has a distinctive culture and a green landscape which is the result of its Pacific coastal climate. On the mainland, running south from Puerto Montt, the Carretera Austral has opened up an area of forests, lakes and rivers, linking small communities of settlers. The biggest town is Coyhaique and there are regular excursions by sea and air to the stunning glacier at the Laguna San Rafael. A four-day sea voyage from Puerto Montt takes you to Puerto Natales in **Chilean Patagonia**, near Chile's most dramatic national park, the Torres del Paine. Hiking around the vertical mountains with their forested slopes, past lakes and glaciers, in the presence of a multitude of southern Andean wildlife is an unforgettable experience (but do allow for the unpredictability of the weather). If you prefer not to venture this far south by ship, there are regular flights to the main city of Chilean Patagonia, Punta Arenas, and there is no problem crossing from Argentina by road or by ferry from **Tierra del Fuego**. The contrast between this southernmost part of the country with the dry, desert north could not be greater.

When to go The best times to visit vary according to geographical location. For the heartland, any time between October and April is good, but the most pleasant seasons are spring (September to November) and autumn (March-April). In Santiago itself, summers (December to February) are roasting hot and winters (June-August) polluted. The heat of the north is less intense from June to September. In the south December to March, summer, is the best time. Along the Carretera Austral this is the only realistic time to travel because at other times ferry schedules are restricted and in mid-winter many transport services do not run at all. Further south, there is more leeway. The Torrres del Paine park is open year round, though snow, fewer hours of daylight and reduced accommodation mean that only day hikes are feasible in winter.

🔡 Touching down

Airport taxes Airport tax is US$26 for international flights; US$8 for domestic flights. There is a surcharge on Transandean flights of US$10.
Business hours Banks: 0900-1400, closed on Saturday. **Government offices**: 1000-1230 (the public is admitted for a few hours only). **Other offices**: 0830-1230, 1400-1800 (Monday-Friday). **Shops (Santiago)**: 1030-1930, 0930-1330 Saturday.
In an emergency Emergency (Carabineros) T133. **Police** (Investigaciones) T134. **Policia Internacional**, head office Gral Borgoña 1052, Santiago, T02-737 2443/1292, handle immigration, lost tourist cards.
International phone code +56.

Ringing: a double ring repeated regularly. Engaged: equal tones with equal pauses.
Official time GMT -4; -3 in summer. Clocks change from mid-September or October to early March.
Tipping In restaurants, if service is not included in the bill, tip 10%; tip a few pesos in bars and soda fountains. Porters: US$1 or US$0.15 a piece of luggage. Taxi-drivers are not tipped.
VAT/IVA 19%
Voltage 220 volts AC, 50 cycles. Sockets are 3 round pins in a line, which will accept 2-pin plugs.
Weights and measures The metric system is obligatory but the quintal of 46 (101.4 lbs) is used.

Chile Essentials

Also bear in mind that January to February in the Lake District and further south are the busiest months, with raised prices, hotels and buses full, lots of backpackers on the road and advance booking often essential. In this holiday season business visitors may find making appointments difficult, but otherwise any time of year is good for working in Santiago.

Finding out more The national secretariat of tourism, **Sernatur** *www.sernatur.cl*, has offices throughout the country (addresses given in the text). City offices provide town maps and other information. A recommended book is Turistel, published annually in four parts, Norte, Centro, Sur and a camping guide with road map, with information and a wealth of maps covering the whole country and neighbouring tourist centres in Argentina (eg Mendoza, San Martín de los Andes, Bariloche), in Spanish only. Each volume costs between US$10-13, depending where you buy it, but buying the whole set is better value; they can be found in bookshops and news stands in most city centres. See www.turistel.cl (in Spanish). **Conaf** (the Corporacíon Nacional Forestal) ① *Presidente Bulnes 285, Santiago, T390 0125, www.conaf.cl*, publishes a number of leaflets and has documents and maps about the national park system. **CODEFF** (Comité Nacional Pro-Defensa de la Fauna y Flora) ① *Luis Uribe 2620, Ñuñoa, Santiago, T274 7461, www.codeff.cl*, can also provide information on environmental questions.

Websites

www.chile.cl (Spanish and English), and **www.visit-chile.org** (English, Spanish, French), both have information on Chile.
www.prochile.cl (Spanish) and **www.chile info.com** (English), focus on business.
www.senderodechile.cl Information on the project to build a trekking/mountain biking path running the whole length of Chile.
www.gobiernodechile.cl Government site.
www.terra.cl Chilean version of Terra, covers much of Latin America in Spanish.
www.chip.cl Chile Information Project, Av Santa María 227, of 12, Recoleta, Santiago, gives access to *The Santiago Times* English-language daily, travel

information, hotels, history, wine and LOM books.
www.gaychile.com Gay events in Chile.
www.chileaustral.com or **www.inter patagonia.com** Information on Patagonia.
www.valparaisochile.cl Valparaíso info.
www.ancientforests.org/chile.htm Site of Ancient Forest International, Box 1850, Redway, CA 95560, T/F707-923 4475, USA. Information regarding Chilean forests.
www.greenpeace.cl Eco-issues (Spanish).
www1.elmostrador.cl Online newspaper.
www.newsreview.cl Site of *The News Review*, Santiago English paper.
www.condor.cl *Cóndor*, German magazine.

Maps The **Instituto Geográfico Militar** ① *Dieciocho 369, Santiago, T410 9363, www.igm.cl*, publishes a *Guía Caminera*, with roads and city plans (available only at IGM offices, not 100% accurate). It also has detailed geophysical and topographical maps of the whole of Chile, useful for climbing; expensive (US$11) but the Biblioteca Nacional, Alameda 651 (T360 5200) will allow you to photocopy parts of each map. **Matassi maps** (JLM Mapas) ① *F02-236 4808, jmatassi@ interactiva.cl, US$5.50-6.50*, usually with a red cover, are good value but often contain errors. The *Turistel Guides* (see above) are very useful for roads and towns, but not all distances are exact and that the description 'ripio' (gravel) usually requires high clearance; 'buen ripio' should be OK for ordinary cars. Good road maps are also published by Tur-Bus and Copec.

Visas and immigration Passport (valid for at least six months) and tourist card only are required for entry by all foreigners except citizens of Guyana, Dominica, Kuwait, Egypt, Saudi Arabia and UAE, most African countries, Cuba and some former Eastern bloc countries, who require visas. It is imperative to check tourist card and visa requirements before travel. National identity cards are sufficient for entry by citizens of Argentina, Brazil, Colombia, Paraguay, and Uruguay. Tourist cards are valid for 90 days. For nationals of Greece, Indonesia and Peru validity is 60 days; Belize, Costa Rica, Malaysia and Singapore 30 days. Tourist cards can be obtained from immigration offices at major land borders and Chilean airports; you must surrender your tourist card on departure. If you wish to stay longer than 90 days (as a tourist), you must buy a 90-day extension from the Departamento de Extranjería (address under Santiago Useful addresses, page 624), or any local *gobernación* office. It costs US$100. To avoid this, make a day-trip to Argentina, Bolivia or Peru and return with a new tourist card (the authorities don't like it if you do this more than 3-4 times). An onward ticket is required. Tourist card holders may change their status to enable them to stay on in employment if they have a contract; they need to contact the Extranjería in whichever province they will be working. On arrival you will be asked where you are staying in Chile. **Note**: On arrival by air, US citizens will be charged an administration fee of US$100, Canadians US$55, Australians US$34 and Mexicans US$15 (this is a reciprocal tax payable because Chileans have to pay the equivalent amount when applying for visas to enter these countries). This tax is not charged at land borders. The permission is valid for multiple entry and for the life of the passport. The tax should be paid in cash, but cheques are accepted. For some nationalities a visa will be granted within 24 hours upon production of an onward ticket, for others (eg Guyana), authorization must be obtained from Chile. For other nationalities who need a visa, a charge is made. To travel overland to or from Tierra del Fuego a multiple entry visa is essential since the Argentine- Chilean border is crossed more than once (it is advisable to get a multiple entry visa before arriving, rather than trying to change a single entry visa once in Chile). A student card is useful for getting discounts on buses, etc. They can be obtained from Hernando de Aguirre 201, of 602, Providencia, T411 2000, and cost US$15, photo and proof of status required; www.isic.cl.

Chilean embassies and consulates Visit www.minrel.gov.cl for a complete list.

Money The unit of currency is the peso, its sign is $. Notes are for 1,000, 2,000, 5,000, 10,000 and 20,000 pesos and coins for 1, 5, 10, 50, 100 and 500 pesos. Small businesses and bus drivers do not look kindly upon being presented with high denomination notes, especially in the morning. Peso **exchange rate** with US$: 525, and with euro: 669 (May 2006). MasterCard emergency T1230-020-2012; Visa emergency T020-631 7003, or call collect +44-20-7937 8091, F+44-17-3350 3670; Amex emergency T0800-201022.

Plastic/TCs/banks (ATMs) The easiest way to obtain cash is by using ATMs which operate under the sign Redbanc (www.redbanc.cl, for a full list); they take Cirrus (MasterCard), Maestro and Plus (Visa) and permit transactions up to US$400 per day. Instructions are available in English. Visa and MasterCard are common in Chile. American Express and Diner's Club are less useful. Travellers' cheques are most easily exchanged in Santiago, but you get better value for cash US dollars or euros. Even slightly damaged foreign notes may be rejected for exchange. Exchange shops (casas de cambio) are open longer hours and often give slightly better rates than banks. It is always worth shopping around. Rates get worse as you go north from Santiago. Official rates are quoted in daily newspapers. Occasionally, prices may be quoted in US dollars; check if something seems cheap. Remember that in some hotels foreigners who pay with US dollars cash or travellers' cheques are not liable for VAT.

Cost of travelling The average cost for a traveller on an economical budget is about US$30-40 per day for food, accommodation and land transportation (more for flights, tours, car hire etc). Cheap accommodation costs US$8-15. Breakfast in hotels, if not included in the price, is about US$2.50 (instant coffee, roll with ham or cheese, and jam). Alojamiento in private houses and hostels (bed, breakfast and often use of kitchen) costs US$8-13 per person (bargaining may be possible). Internet costs US$0.60-1 per hour. Southern Chile is much more expensive between 15 December and 15 March. Santiago tends to be more expensive for food and accommodation than other parts of Chile.

Safety Chile is one of the safest countries in South America for the visitor. Law enforcement officers are *carabineros* (green military uniforms), who handle all tasks except immigration. *Investigaciones*, in civilian dress, are detective police who deal with everything except traffic.

Getting around

Air Most flights of **LAN** www.lan.com, and its subsidiary, **Lan Express**, between Santiago and major towns and cities, are given in the text. It has a very efficient electronic ticketing system. **Sky** www.skyairline.cl, whose network is not as extensive as LAN, and **Aerolíneas del Sur**, T02-210 9000, with a smaller network still, are newer airlines. Try to sit on the left flying south, on the right flying north to get the best views of the Andes. LAN's 'South America Air Pass' can be used just in Chile. It must be purchased abroad in conjunction with an international ticket and reservations made well ahead since many flights are fully booked in advance. If arriving in Chile on LAN or Iberia, a six-coupon Pass costs US$520, if on another carrier US$725. The minimum number of coupons is three. Date changes are allowed for US$15. Maximum stay is six months. Easter Island may be included on the Pass. **Note**: Book well in advance (several months) for flights to Easter Island in Jan-Feb. If arriving in Chile on LAN, ask about discounts on individual sector, domestic flights. Check with the airlines for student and other discounts. It is best to confirm domestic flights at least 24 hours before departure.

Bus Buses are frequent and on the whole good. Apart from holiday times, there is little problem getting a seat on a long-distance bus. Salón-cama services run between main cities on overnight services; **Tur-Bus** www.turbus.com, and **Pullman** www.pullman.cl, have the most extensive networks. Standards on routes vary but Tur-Bus is better than Pullman, especially on long journeys. Tur-bus itineraries can be checked and tickets bought online. Prémium buses have six fully reclining seats. Salón-cama means 25 seats, semi-cama means 34 and Classico means 44. Stops are infrequent. Since there is lots of competition between bus companies, fares may be bargained lower, particularly just before departure. Prices are highest between December-March and during festivals such as Easter and the Independence celebrations in September. Students may get discounts, amount varies, but not usually in high season. Most bus companies will carry bicycles, but may ask for payment.

Hitchhiking Hitchhiking is generally easy and safe throughout Chile, although you may find that in some regions traffic is sparse, so you are less likely to catch a lift.

Taxis Taxis have meters, but agree beforehand on fares for long journeys out of city centres or special excursions. In some places a surcharge is applied late at night. Taxi drivers may not know the location of streets away from the centre. There is no need to tip unless some extra service, like the carrying of luggage, is given. Black colectivos (collective taxis) operate on fixed routes identified by numbers and destinations. They have fixed charges, often little more expensive than buses, which increase at night and which are usually advertised in the front windscreen. They are flagged down on the street corner (in some cities such as Puerto Montt there are signs). Take small change as the driver takes money and offers change while driving. Yellow colectivos also operate on some inter-urban routes, leaving from a set point when full.

Train There are 6,560 km of line, of which most are state owned. Passenger services in the south go from Santiago to Puerto Montt. Passenger services north of the Valparaíso area have ceased, though there are regional train lines in the Valparaíso and Concepción areas. Trains in Chile are moderately priced, and not as slow as in other Andean countries. See Santiago, Transport, page 622, rail company offices.

Sleeping → *See inside front cover for our hotel grade price guide.*

On hotel bills IVA (VAT) is charged at 19%. Check on arrival whether hotel rates include IVA. (In expensive hotels, if you pay in US$ cash or TCs, you may not have to pay IVA, but unless the establishment has an agreement with the government, hotels are not allowed to exclude IVA for dollar payments.) When booking make certain whether meals are included in the price and don't rely on the list in the bedroom for prices. In popular tourist destinations, especially in the south in high season, many families offer accommodation: these are advertised by a sign in the window. People often meet buses to offer rooms, which vary greatly in quality and cleanliness; have a look before committing. See *www.backpackerschile.com* or *www.backpackersbest.cl*, in English, German and Spanish, for suggestions on good accommodation at reasonable prices. In summer especially, single rooms can be hard to find.

Camping Camping is easy but not always cheap at official sites. A common practice is to charge US$10 for up to five people, with no reductions for any less. Copec run a network of 33 'Rutacentros' along Ruta 5 which have showers, cafeterias and offer free camping. Free camping is also available at many filling stations. If camping, trekking, cycling or skiing, consider taking all your own equipment because, although it may be available in Chile, it will be expensive. Also note that in the Lake District and Chiloé, between mid-December and mid-January, huge horseflies *távanos*) can be a real problem when camping, hiking and fishing: do not wear dark clothing.

Youth hostels There are youth hostels throughout Chile; average cost about US$5-15 pp. Although some hostels are open only from January to the end of February, many operate all year round. The IH card is usually readily accepted, but YHA affiliated hostels are not necessarily the best. In summer many are usually crowded and noisy, with only floor space available. Chilean YHA card costs US$5. A Hostelling International card costs US$15. These can be obtained from **Asociación Chilena de Albergues Turísticos Juveniles** ① *Hernando de Aguirre 201, of 602, Providencia, Santiago, T411 2050, www.hostelling.cl*, together with a useful guidebook of all hostels in Chile, *Guía Turística de los Albergues Juveniles*. In summer there are makeshift hostels in many Chilean towns, usually in the main schools; they charge US$3-4 per person.

Eating → *See inside front cover for our Eating price guide.*

Eating out Breakfast is poor: instant coffee or tea with bread and jam are common, although some hostels serve better fare. Lunch is about 1400 and dinner not before 2030. *Onces* (Elevenses) is tea taken at 1700, often accompanied by a snack. Good, cheap meals can be found in *Casinos de Bomberos*, or around the market. Most restaurants offer a cheaper set meal at lunchtime; it is called *colación* or *el menú* and may not be included on the *menu la carta*.

Food A very typical Chilean dish is *cazuela de ave*, a nutritious stew containing large pieces of chicken, pumpkin potatoes, rice, and maybe onions, and green peppers. *Valdiviano* is another stew, common in the south, consisting of beef, onion, sliced potatoes and eggs. *Empanadas de pino* are turnovers filled with meat, onions, raisins, olives and egg chopped up together. *Pastel de choclo* is a casserole of meat and onions with olives, topped with a maize-meal mash, baked in an earthenware bowl. *Humitas* are mashed sweetcorn mixed with butter and spices and baked in sweetcorn leaves. *Prieta* is a blood sausage stuffed with cabbage leaves. A normal *parrillada* or *asado* is a giant mixed grill served from a charcoal brazier. *Bife a lo pobre* (a poor man's steak) can be just the opposite: it is a steak topped by two fried eggs, chips and fried onions. The Valparaíso speciality is the *chorrillana*, chips topped with fried sliced steak, fried onions and scrambled eggs, while in Chiloé you can enjoy a *curanto*, a meat, shellfish and potato stew traditionally cooked in a hole in the ground.

What gives Chilean food its personality is the **seafood**. The delicious congrio fish is a national dish, and *caldillo de congrio* (a soup served with a massive piece of kingclip, onions and potatoes) is excellent. A *paila* can take many forms (the paila is simply a kind of dish), but the commonest are made of eggs or seafood. *Paila Chonchi* is a kind of bouillabaisse, but has more flavour, more body, more ingredients. *Parrillada de mariscos* is a dish of grilled mixed seafood, brought to the table piping hot on a charcoal brazier. Other excellent local fish are the *cojinoa*, the *albacora* (swordfish) and the *corvina* (bass). A range of mussels (*choritos/cholgas*) is available, as are abalone (*locos*), clams (*almejas*) and razor clams (*machas*). Some bivalve shellfish may be periodically banned because they carry the disease **marea roja** (which is fatal in humans). *Cochayuyo* is seaweed, bound into bundles, described as 'hard, leathery

⁞ Driving in Chile

Road Most roads are in good condition and many are paved. The main road is the Panamericana (Ruta 5) from La Serena to Puerto Montt. A paved coastal route running much of the length of Chile is due to open 2007. Motorways tolls are very expensive, but the charge includes towing to the next city and free ambulance in case of accident.

Safety In the south (particularly on the Carretera Austral), and in the desert north, always top up your fuel tank and carry spare fuel (you may have to buy a can if renting a car). *Carabineros* (national police) are strict about speed limits (100-120 kph on motorways): Turistel maps mark police posts. Car drivers should have all their papers in order and to hand as there are occasional checks.

Documents For drivers of private vehicles entering Chile, customs type out a *título de importación temporal de vehículos* (temporary admission), valid for the length of stay granted by immigration. Your immigration entry/exit card is stamped 'entrada con vehículo' so you must leave the country with your vehicle (so you cannot make an excursion to Bariloche, for example, without your car). Insurance is obligatory and can be bought at borders. A *carnet de passages* is not officially required for foreign-owned motorcycles: a temporary import paper is given at the border.

Organizations Automóvil Club de Chile, Av Andrés Bello 1863, Providencia, Santiago, T600-464 4040, www.automovil club.cl. Seven route maps of Chile, US$6 each or US$3 each if affiliated to motor organization. It has a car hire agency (with discounts for members or affiliates).

Car hire Shop around as there is a lot of competition. Reputable Chilean companies offer much better value than the well-known international ones, although rates may not always include insurance or 19% VAT. In northern Chile, where mountain roads are bad, check rental vehicles very carefully before setting out. Hire companies charge a large premium to collect the car from another city, so unless making a round-trip it makes economic sense to travel by public transport, then rent a car locally. If intending to leave the country in a hired car, you must obtain authorization from the hire company.

Fuel Gasoline costs US$0.80-0.90 a litre; it becomes more expensive the further north and further south you go. Unleaded fuel, 93, 95 and 97 octane, is available in all main cities. Diesel is widely available. Larger service stations usually accept credit cards, but check before filling up.

thongs'. The *erizo*, or sea-urchin, is also commonly eaten as are *picorocos* (sea barnacles) and the strong flavoured *piure*. *Luche* is dried seaweed, sold as a black cake, like 'flakey bread pudding' to be added to soups and stews. **Avocado** pears (*paltas*) are excellent, and play an important role in recipes. Make sure that vegetables are included in the price for the main dish; menus often don't make this clear. Local **fast food** is excellent. *Completos* are hot dogs with a huge variety of fillings. A *barros jarpa* is a grilled cheese and ham sandwich and a *barras luco* is a grilled cheese and beef sandwich. *Sopaipillas* are cakes made of a mixture including pumpkin, served in syrup. Ice cream is very good; try *lúcuma* and *chirimoya* flavours.

Drink Tap **water** is safe to drink in main cities but bottled water is safer for the north. The local **wines** are very good; the best are from the central areas. The bottled wines cost from US$1.80 upwards. The *Guía de vinos de Chile*, published every year in January (English edition available) has ratings and tasting notes for all Chilean wines on the market. **Beer** is quite good and cheap (about US$0.80 for a litre bottle, plus US$0.30 deposit in shops). Draught lager is known as Schop. Chilean brewed beers include Cristal and Royal Guard (light), Escudo (Amber), Austral (good in the far south) and Heineken. In Valdivia, Kunstmann brews three types of beer, good. Malta, a brown ale, is recommended for those wanting a British-type beer. There are good local breweries in Valparaíso and Llanquihue near Puerto Varas.

Pisco, made from grapes, is the most famous spirit. It is best drunk as a 'Pisco Sour' with lime or lemon juice and sugar. **Manzanilla** is a local liqueur, made from *licor de oro* (like Galliano); *crema de cacao*, especially **Mitjans**, has been recommended. Two popular drinks are **vaina**, a mixture of brandy, egg and sugar and **cola de mono**, a mixture of aguardiente, coffee, milk and vanilla served very cold at Christmas. **Chicha** is any form of alcoholic drink made from fruit, usually grapes. **Cider** (*chicha de manzana*) is popular in the south. **Mote con huesillo**, made from wheat hominy and dried peaches, is a soft drink, refreshing in summer.

Coffee is generally instant except in expresso bars such as **Café Haiti, Café Brasil** and **Tío Pepe**. Elsewhere specify *café-café*, *expresso* or *cortado*. Tea is widely available. If you order *café*, or *té*, *con leche*, it will come with lots of milk; if you want just a little milk, you must specify that. After a meal, try an *agüita* (infusion) – hot water in which herbs such as mint or aromatics suh as lemon peel, have been steeped. There is a wide variety, very refreshing.

Festivals and events

1 January, New Year's Day; Holy Week (Friday and Saturday); 1 May, Labour Day; 21 May, Navy Day; Corpus Christi; 27 June, St Peter and Paul; 15 August, Assumption; 18, 19 September, Independence Days; 12 October, Columbus' arrival in America; 1 November, All Saints Day; 8 December, Immaculate Conception; 25 December.

Santiago and around

→ *Phone code: 02. Colour map 8, grid B1. Population: nearly 6 million. Altitude: 600 m.*

Santiago, the political, economic and financial capital of Chile, is one of the most beautifully set of any South American city, standing in a wide plain with the magnificent chain of the Andes in full view – rain and pollution permitting. Nearly 40% of Chileans live in and around Santiago, which is now the fifth largest city in South America. It's a modern industrial capital, full of skyscrapers, bustle, noise and traffic, and smog is a problem especially between April and September. Santiago bursts with possibilities, with its parks, museums, shops and hectic nightlife, and is also within easy reach of vineyards, beaches and Andean ski resorts.

Ins and outs

Getting there The airport is 26 km northwest of the centre. **Turbus**, US$2.50, and **Centropuerto**, US$2, run from airport to city centre. There are also shuttle services to/from hotels and private addresses (US$8-10) and taxis (US$14-20). The railway station, Estacíon Alameda, which only serves the south of the country, is on the Alameda, as are the four main bus terminals. All can be reached by buses, taxi or the Metro. The bus terminals are Alameda, for Pullman Bus and Tur-Bus services; next door is Terminal Santiago, for the south of the country, and some international destinations (metro Universidad de Santiago); San Borja, for regional and national destinations (metro Estación Central); Los Héroes (nearest the centre, metro Los Héroes) for some southern, northern and international routes; new terminal at Metro Pajaritos, for Valparaíso, Viña del Mar, the coast (airport buses stop here). ▶▶ *See also Transport on page 620.*

Getting around The Metro (underground railway) has four lines at present, Line 1 east-west, Lines 2, 4 and 5 north-south. Fares range from US$0.70 to US$0.88 depending on time of day. The east-west line follows the main axis, linking the bus and train stations, the centre, Providencia and beyond. Metrobus services connect the subway with outlying districts. City buses: the old system of yellow *micros* is being replaced by *Transantiago* (2005-2010); details under Transport, below. You pay by *multivía* ticket. Taxis are abundant and not expensive. Colectivos (collective taxis) run on fixed routes to the suburbs.

Tourist offices Servicio Nacional de Turismo Sernatur ① *Av Providencia 1550, metro Manuel Montt, next to Providencia Municipal Library, T731 8336, info@sernatur.cl, Mon-Fri 0845-1830, Sat 0900-1400*, maps, brochures and posters. Good notice board. **Information office** also at the airport daily 0900-2100. **Municipal Tourist Board** ① *Casa Colorada, Merced 860, metro Plaza de Armas, T336700*, good free booklet: *Historical Heritage of Santiago: A Guide for visitors in English and Spanish*, on historic buildings, and walking tours on Wed, 1500. Almost all museums are closed on Monday and on 1 November.

Orientation The centre of the old city lies between the Mapocho and the Avenida O'Higgins, which is usually known as the Alameda. From the Plaza Baquedano (usually called Plaza Italia), in the east of the city's central area, the Mapocho flows to the northwest and the Alameda runs to the southwest. From Plaza Italia the C Merced runs due west to the Plaza de Armas, the heart of the city, five blocks south of the Mapocho. A new urban motorway runs the length of Santiago from east to west under the course of the Río Mapocho.

Best time to visit There is rain during the winter, but the summers are dry. The rain increases to the south. On the coast at Viña del Mar it is 483 mm a year, but is less inland. Temperatures, on the other hand, are higher inland than on the coast. There is frost now and then, but very little snow falls. Temperatures can reach 33° C in January, but fall to 13° C (3° C at night) in July. Days are usually hot, the nights cool.

Security Like all large cities, Santiago has problems of theft. Pickpockets and bag-snatchers, who are often well-dressed, operate especially on the Metro and around the Plaza de Armas.

Sights
Around the Plaza de Armas On the eastern and southern sides of the Plaza de Armas there are arcades with shops; on the northern side is the post office and the Municipalidad; and on the western side the Cathedral and the archbishop's palace. The **Cathedral**, much rebuilt, contains a recumbent statue in wood of San Francisco Javier, and the chandelier which lit the first meetings of Congress after independence; it also houses an interesting museum of religious art and historical pieces (0930-1230, 1530-1830, free). In the Palacio de la Real Audiencia on the Plaza de Armas is the **Museo Histórico Nacional** ① *No 951, T411 7000, www.dibam.cl/historico_nacional, Tue- Sun 1000-1730, US$0.80, free on Sun, signs in Spanish*, covering the period from the Conquest until 1925.

Just west of the Plaza is the **Museo Chileno de Arte Precolombino** ① *in the former Real Aduana, Bandera 361, www.precolombino.cl, Tue-Sun 1000-1800, US$3, displays in English*. Its representative exhibition of objects from the pre-Columbian cultures of Central America and the Andean region is highly recommended for the quality of the objects and their presentation. The former Congress building, a block west of the Cathedral, is now occupied by the Ministry of Foreign Affairs (it can be visited for free; the new Congress building is in Valparaíso). At Calle Merced 864, close to the Plaza de Armas, is the **Casa Colorada** (1769), home of the Governor in colonial days and then of Mateo de Toro, first president of Chile. It is now the **Museo de Santiago** ① *www.munistgo.cl/colorada, Tue-Sat 1000-1800, Sun and holidays, 1100-1400, US$2, students free*. It covers the history of Santiago from the Conquest to modern times, with excellent displays and models, some signs in English, guided tours. From the Plaza de Armas Paseo Ahumada, a pedestrianized street lined with cafés runs south to the Alameda four blocks away, crossing Huérfanos.

Four blocks north of the Plaza de Armas is the interesting **Mercado Central** *21 de Mayo y San Pablo*. The building faces the Parque Venezuela, on which is the Cal y Canto metro station and, at its western end, the former **Mapocho Railway Station**, now a cultural centre. If you head east from Mapocho station, along the river, you pass through the Parque Forestal (see below), before coming back to Plaza Italia.

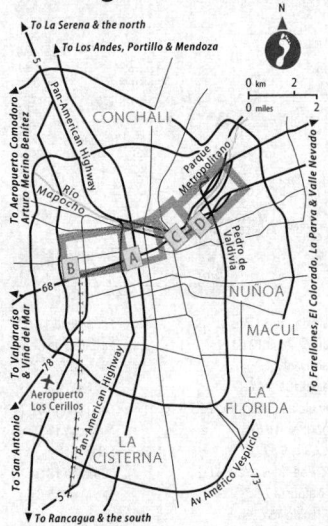

Santiago orientation

To La Serena & the north
To Los Andes, Portillo & Mendoza

To Aeropuerto Comodoro Arturo Merino Benítez

Pan-American Highway

Río Mapocho

CONCHALÍ

Parque Metropolitano

A C D
B

Pedro de Valdivia

To Valparaíso & Viña del Mar

68

NUÑOA

MACUL

Aeropuerto Los Cerrillos

To San Antonio

Pan-American Highway

LA FLORIDA

LA CISTERNA

To Farellones, El Colorado, La Parva & Valle Nevado

To Rancagua & the south

Av Américo Vespucio

0 km   2
0 miles   2

N

Related maps
A Santiago centre, page 608
B West of centre, page 616
C Bellavista & Lastarria, page 614
D Providencia, page 610

Along the Alameda The Alameda runs through the heart of the city for over 3 km. It is 100 m wide, and ornamented with gardens and statuary: the most notable are the equestrian statues of Generals O'Higgins and San Martín; the statue of the Chilean historian Benjamín Vicuña MacKenna who, as mayor of Santiago, beautified Cerro Santa Lucía (see below); and the great monument in honour of the battle of Concepción in 1879.

From the Plaza Italia, where there is a statue of Gen Baquedano and the Tomb of the Unknown Soldier, the Alameda skirts, on the right, Cerro Santa Lucía, and on the left, the Catholic University. Beyond the hill the Alameda goes past the neoclassical **Biblioteca Nacional** on the right, Moneda 650 (good concerts, temporary exhibitions). Beyond, on the left, between calles San Francisco and Londres, is the oldest church in Santiago: the red-walled church and monastery of **San Francisco**. Inside is the small statue of the Virgin which Valdivia carried on his saddlebow when he rode from Peru to Chile. The **Museo Colonial San Francisco** ① *beside Iglesia San Francisco, Londres 4, T639 8737, www.museo sanfrancisco.cl, Tue-Sun 1000-1300, 1500-1800, US$1.50,* houses religious art, including one room with 54 paintings of the life of St Francis; in the cloisters is a room containing Gabriela Mistral's Nobel medal. South of San Francisco is the Barrio París-Londres, built 1923-1929, now restored. Two blocks north of the Alameda is **Teatro Municipal** ① *C Agustinas, tours Tue 1300-1500, Sun 1100-1400, US$3.*

Santiago centre

Sleeping	Eating ⓕ	
Libertador 5 *D3*	Café Caribe 3 *C2*	Fra Diavolo 17 *D3*
Majestic 6 *B1*	Café Colonia 12 *C3*	La Caleta de Don
París 9 *D3*	Café Haití 2 *C3*	Beno 8 *D2*
Residencial	Café Ikabaru 4 *C3*	Las Tejas 9 *D2*
Londres 10 *D3*	Círculo de Periodistas 16 *D1*	Lung Fung 10 *C3*
Santa Lucía 11 *C3*	Congreso 14 *B1*	Masticón 11 *D2*
	Da Carla 5 *B3*	Salón de Té
Sleeping	El 27 de Nueva York 6 *D2*	Cousiño 18 *C2*
Fundador 12 *D2*	El Naturista 7 *D3*	San Marco 5 *B3*
Galerías 3 *D3*	El Rápido 15 *C2*	
	Bar Central 13 *A2*	
	Bar Nacional No 2 15 *C2*	

A little further west along the Alameda, is the Universidad de Chile; the Club de la Unión is almost opposite. Nearby, on Calle Nueva York is the **Bolsa de Comercio**; the public may view the trading, bur passport required. One block further west is the Plaza de la Libertad. To the north of this Plaza, hemmed in by the skyscrapers of the Centro Cívico, is the **Palacio de la Moneda** (1805), the Presidential Palace containing historic relics, paintings and sculpture, and the elaborate 'Salón Rojo' used for official receptions. Although the Moneda was damaged by air attacks during the military coup of 11 September 1973 it has been fully restored. (Ceremonial changing of the guard every other day, 1000, never on Sunday; Sunday ceremony is performed Monday. The courtyards, with sculptures and carabineros in dress uniform, are open to all – entry from the north.) There is a large new Centrol Cultural here ① *T355 6500, www.ccplm.cl, Tue-Sun 1000-2100, US$1.15. Films US$2.30*. It has exhibition halls, a cinema and a handicrafts centre.

West of the centre Barrio Brasil, with Plaza Brasil at its heart and the Basílica del Salvador two blocks from the plaza, is one of the earliest parts of the city. It has some fine old buildings, especially around C Concha y Toro, but now it's a more bohemian, studenty neighbourhood with modern amenities and plenty of places to stay and eat (Metro República). Five blocks south of the Alameda at this point is the **Palacio Cousiño** ① *C Dieciocho 438, www.palaciocousino.cl, Metro Toesca, Tue-Fri 0930-1330, 1430-1700, Sat, Sun and holidays 0930-1330, US$2.40, guided tours only, in Spanish or English, visitors have to wear cloth bootees to protect the floors*. This large mansion in French rococo style has a superb Italian marble staircase and other opulent items. Recommended.

   Parque O'Higgins ① *about 10 blocks south of Alameda; take Metro Line 2 to Parque O'Higgins station, getting there: bus from Parque Baquedano via Avs MacKenna and Matta*. It has a small lake, playing fields, tennis courts, swimming pool (open from 5 December), an open-air stage, a club, the racecourse of the Club Hípico and an amusement park, **Fantasilandia** ① *daily in summer, at weekends until 2000 only in winter, US$7-9, unlimited rides*. There are kite-flying contests on Sunday, good 'typical' restaurants, craft shops, an aquarium, an insect, reptile and shellfish museum and the **Museo del Huaso** ① *Mon-Fri 1000-1700, Sun and holidays 1000-1400, free, a collection of criollo clothing and tools*. On 19 September there is a huge military parade in the park.

   The Alameda continues westwards to the **Planetarium** ① *Alameda 3349, US$4.50*. Opposite it on the southern side, the railway station (Estación Central or Alameda). On Avenida Matucana, running north from here, is the very popular Parque Quinta Normal (at Avenida D Portales). It was founded as a botanical garden in 1830. Near the park is **Museo Artequín** ① *Av Portales 3530, Tue-Fri 0900- 1700, Sat, Sun and holidays 1100-1800, US$1*. Housed in the Chilean pavilion built for the 1889 Paris International Exhibition, it contains prints of famous paintings and activities and explanations of the techniques of the great masters. Recommended. The new Quinta Normal metro station has an underground cultural centre with theatres and a free art cinema (part of the Metro Arte project), which shows independent films. The government is building an enormous public library 200 m from the station, in front of which is **Centro Cultural Matucana**, with several exhibition halls and a theatre. (**Museo de la Solidaridad Salvador Allende** formerly by the park, is closed – May 2006 – for possible relocation; T682 4954, www.mssa.cl, for information.)

East of the centre Cerro Santa Lucía *closes at 2100*, bounded by Calle Merced to the north, Alameda to the south, Calles Santa Lucía and Subercaseaux, is a cone of rock rising steeply to a height of 70 m (reached by a series of stairs and a lift from the Alameda). It can be climbed from the Caupolicán esplanade, on which, high on a rock, stands a statue of that Mapuche leader, but the ascent from the northern side of the hill, where there is an equestrian statue of Diego de Almagro, is easier. A plaque to Darwin, who climbed the hill, has a quotation giving his impressions. There are striking views of the city from the top (reached by a series of stairs), where there is a fortress, the Batería Hidalgo (closed to the public). It is best to descend the eastern side, to see the small Plaza Pedro Valdivia with its waterfalls and statue of Valdivia.

   Parque Forestal lies due north of Santa Lucía hill and immediately south of the Mapocho. **Museo Nacional de Bellas Artes** ① *www.dibam.cl/bellas_artes, Tue-Sun 1000-1845, US$0.80, quiet café*, is in an extraordinary example of neoclassical architecture. It has a large display of Chilean and foreign painting and sculpture; contemporary art exhibitions are held several times a year. In the west wing is the **Museo de Arte Contemporáneo** ① *www.mac*.

uchile.cl. **Parque Balmaceda** (Parque Gran Bretaña), east of Plaza Italia, is perhaps the most beautiful in Santiago (the Museo de los Tajamares, which holds monthly exhibitions, is here).

Between the Parque Forestal, Plaza Italia and the Alameda is the **Lastarria** neighbourhood (Universidad Católica Metro). For those interested in antique furniture, objets d'art and old books, the area is worth a visit, especially the **Plaza Mulato Gil de Castro** *C José V Lastarria 305*. Occasional shows are put on in the square, which has a mural by Roberto Matta and a new visual arts museum. The **Museo Arqueológico de Santiago** ① *in Plaza Mulato Gil de Castro, Lastarria 307, Mon-Fri 1000-1400, 1530- 1830, Sat 1000-1400, free*, exhibits Chilean archaeology, anthropology and pre-Columbian art. Nearby, on Lastarria, is the Jardín Lastarria, a cul-de-sac of craft and antique shops.

The **Bellavista district**, on the north bank of the Mapocho from Plaza Italia at the foot of Cerro San Cristóbal (see below), is the main focus of nightlife in the old city. Around Calle Pío Nono are restaurants and cafés, theatres, entertainments, art galleries and craft shops (especially those selling lapis lazuli). **La Chascona** ① *F Márquez de la Plata 0192, Bellavista, T777 8741, www.neruda.uchile.cl/chascona.html, daily except Mon, 1000-1300, 1500-1800, US$2 guided visits only*. This was the house of the poet Pablo Neruda and is now headquarters of the Fundación Pablo Neruda (see page 635).

Providencia East of Plaza Italia, the main east-west axis of the city becomes **Avenida Providencia** which heads out towards the residential areas, such as **Las Condes**, at the eastern and upper levels of the city. It passes through the neighbourhood of Providencia, a modern area of shops, offices, bars and restaurants around Pedro de Valdivia and Los Leones metro stations (particularly Calle Suecia), which also contains the offices of Sernatur, the national tourist board. At Metro Tobalaba it becomes Avenida Apoquindo. Here, in **El Bosque Norte**, there are lots more good, mid-range and expensive restaurants.

Museo Ralli ① *Sotomayor 4110, Vitacura (further east still), Tue-Sun 1000-1600, closed in summer, free*, has an excellent collection of works by modern European and Latin American artists, including Dali, Chagall, Bacon and Miró.

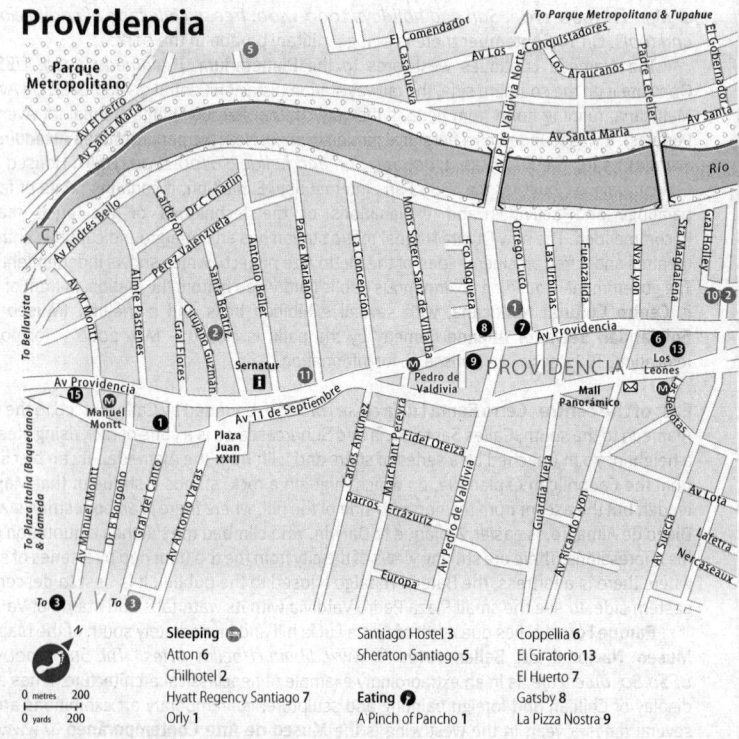

Providencia

Sleeping 🛏
Atton **6**
Chilhotel **2**
Hyatt Regency Santiago **7**
Orly **1**
Santiago Hostel **3**
Sheraton Santiago **5**

Eating 🍴
A Pinch of Pancho **1**
Coppellia **6**
El Giratorio **13**
El Huerto **7**
Gatsby **8**
La Pizza Nostra **9**

0 metres   200
0 yards   200

The sharp, conical hill of **San Cristóbal**, to the northeast of the city, forms the **Parque Metropolitano** ① *there are 2 entrances: from Pío Nono in Bellavista and further east from Pedro de Valdivia Norte. Getting there: by funicular: every few minutes from Plaza Caupolicán at the northern end of C Pío Nono (it stops on its way at the Jardín Zoológico near the Bellavista entrance), US$2.30 return, 1000-2000 daily. By teleférico from Estación Oasis, Av Pedro de Valdivia Norte via Tupahue to San Cristóbal, the funicular's upper station, summer only, Mon 1430-1830, Tue-Fri 1030-1830, Sat-Sun 1030-1900, US$3 combined funicular/teleférico ticket. An open bus operated by the teleférico company runs to San Cristóbal and Tupahue from the Bellavista entrance with the same schedule as the teleférico itself. To get to Tupahue at other times you must take the funicular or a taxi (or walk to/from Pedro de Valdivia Metro station, about 1 km). By taxi either from the Bellavista entrance (much cheaper from inside the park as taxis entering the park have to pay entrance fee), or from Metro Pedro de Valdivia.* It is the largest and most interesting of the city's parks. On the summit (300 m) stands a colossal statue of the Virgin, which is floodlit at night; beside it is the astronomical observatory of the Catholic University which can be visited on application to the observatory's director. Further east in the Tupahue sector there are terraces, gardens, and paths; in one building there is a good, expensive restaurant Camino Real, T232 1758) with a splendid view from the terrace, and an Enoteca (exhibition of Chilean wines: you can taste one of the three 'wines of the day', US$1.50 per glass, and buy if you like, though prices are higher than in shops). Nearby is the Casa de la Cultura which has art exhibitions and free concerts at midday on Sunday. There are two good swimming pools (see Sports below). East of Tupahue are the Botanical Gardens, with a collection of Chilean native plants, guided tours available.

Cementerio General ① *take any Recoleta bus from C Miraflores to get there.* In the barrio of Recoleta, just north of the city centre, this cemetery contains the mausoleums of most of the great figures in Chilean history and the arts, including Violeta Para, Víctor Jara and Salvador Allende. There is also an impressive monument to the victims, known as "*desaparecidos*" (disappeared) of the 1973-1990 military government.

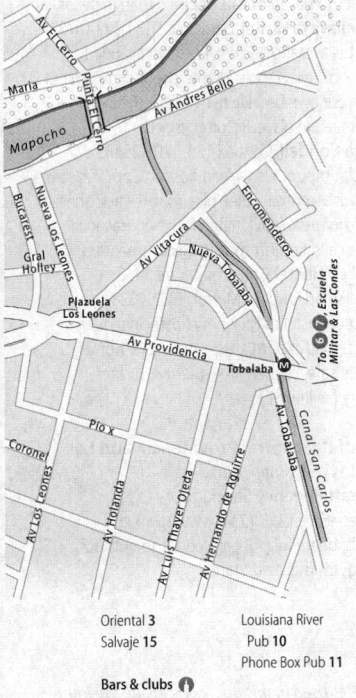

Oriental **3**
Salvaje **15**

Louisiana River
Pub **10**
Phone Box Pub **11**

Bars & clubs ●
Brannigan Pub **2**

● Sleeping

Santiago centre *p607, map p608*
Note: Check if breakfast and 19% tax are included in the price quoted.
LL Fundador, Paseo Serrano 34, T387 1200, www.hotelfundador.cl. Helpful, charming, good service and location, pool, spa, bar, restaurant, internet.
LL Galerías, San Antonio 65, T470 7400, www.hotelgalerias.cl. Excellent, large rooms, good location, welcoming.
AL Majestic, Santo Domingo 1526, T695 8366, hotelmajestic@hotelmajestic.cl. With breakfast, good Indian restaurant open to non- residents, pool, English spoken, internet.
A Libertador, O'Higgins 853, T639 3137, www.hotellibertador.cl. Helpful, stores luggage, good restaurant, rooftop pool, but noisy location.
B Santa Lucía, Huérfanos 779, p 4, T639 8201, santalucia@terra.cl. Garage 2 blocks away, comfortable, quiet restaurant.
B-C París, París 813, T664 0921. Great location, good meeting place, luggage store, breakfast and internet extra. Recommended, but can be noisy. Book in advance in summer.
C Res Londres, Londres 54, T/F638 2215. Old mansion with original features in lovely area, perfect location, without breakfast, cheaper without bath, pleasant common rooms, good,

safe, laundry service, often full, often refuses to take advance bookings. Recommended.

C-E Che Lagarto Santiago, Tucapel Jiménez 24, T699 1493, www.chelagarto.com. Metro Los Héroes. HI hostel, part of South American chain. Free breakfast and internet. Rooms with private toilet and fan, **D** pp in dorms. Comfortable common areas, kitchen facilities, internet.

D pp **Hostelling Internacional Santiago**, Cienfuegos 151, T671 8532, www.hisantiago.cl (5 mins from Metro Los Héroes). Modern, satellite TV, no cooking facilities, sterile, cafeteria, parking. Information from YHA, Hernando de Aguirre 201, of 602, Providencia, T233 3220, www.hostelling.cl. Supplies student cards (2 photos required and proof of student status, though tourist card accepted), US$14-16.

West of the centre *p609, map p616*
A Happy House Hostel, Catedral 2207, T688 4849, www.happyhousehostel.cl. Also dormitories **D** pp. Luxury hostel in restored mansion with all mod-cons, spacious kitchen and common areas, internet, pool table, bar, sauna, jacuzzi, roof terrace, full breakfast, free tea and real coffee all day, book exchange, English and French spoken, lots of info. Highly recommended.

B Hostal Río Amazonas, Barrio Brasil, Rosas 2234, between C Maturana and Av Ricardo Cumming, T671 9013, www.hostalrio amazonas.cl. Convenient, central, good, charming hosts, internet access, helpful.

B La Casa Roja, Agustinas 2113, Barrio Brasil, T696 4241, www.lacasaroja.cl. Doubles with and without bath (**C**), **E** pp in dormitory, huge converted historic house, great location, kitchen facilities, meals extra, internet, convenient for metro and lots of amenities, fun, but not if you want a quiet time.

C Hostal Internacional Letelier, Cumming 77, 3 blocks from Alameda, T965 6861. Very helpful, no meals, internet, Spanish lessons arranged.

Near bus terminals and Estación Central *map p616*
A Tur Hotel Express, O'Higgins 3750, p 3, in the Turbus Terminal, T685 0100. Comfortable business standard with breakfast, cable TV, a/c, free internet. Particularly useful if you need to take an early flight as buses leave for the airport from here.

C Res Mery, Pasaje República 36, off 0-100 block of República, T696 8883, m.mardones@ entelchile.net. Big green building down an alley, without bath, quiet. Recommended.

D SCS Habitat, Scott's Place, San Vicente 1798, T683 3732, scshabitat@yahoo.com. **E-F** in dorms, kitchen, laundry facilities, lots of interesting information, huge breakfast, popular (some mixed reports), English spoken, maps and camping equipment sold/rented, cycles for hire, safe bike parking. To get there take taxi from bus station.

E pp **Federico Scoto 130**, T779 9364. Attentive hosts, good food, kitchen facilities, often full.

East of the centre: Bellavista *p610, map p614*
A Monte Carlo, Subercaseaux 209, T639 1569, montecarlo@manquehue.cl. At foot of Santa Lucía, modern, restaurant, heating, stores luggage, good.

B Hostal Casa Grande, Vicuña MacKenna 90, T222 7347, Baquedano metro, www.hostal casagrande.cl. **C** without bath, quiet, good value.

B Hostal Forestal, Cnel Santiago Bueras 120, T638 1347, www.hostalforestal.cl. Doubles (some with bath) and dorms (**D-E** pp), with breakfast, on a quiet side street near the Plaza Italia. Comfy lounge with internet and big screen TV, barbeque area, kitchen facilities, good information, English spoken. Recommended.

B Hostal Río Amazonas Plaza Italia, Vicuña Mackenna 47, T635 1631, www.hostalrio amazonas.cl. In a restored mansion, with breakfast, internet, good value, helpful, much cheaper to pay in dollars or euros than in pesos.

B-C Bellavista Hostel, Dardignac 0184, T732 8737, www.bellavistahostel.com. Breakfast included, European- style, **D** pp in dorms, sheets provided but make your own bed, kitchen facilities, free internet, good meeting place. Recommended.

C Casa Condell, Condell 114, T209 2343, Salvador metro. Also 4-bed dorms, **E** pp. Pleasant old house, central, quiet, nice roof-terrace, shared baths, no breakfast, kitchen facilities, free local phone calls, English spoken. Recommended.

D pp **Eco Hostel Chile**, Gral Jofré 349B (Universidad Católica Metro), T222 6833, www.ecohostel.cl. Nice new hostel in a quiet district, shady courtyards, hammocks, hot shower, safe, kitchen, free internet, lockers, laundry facilities.

East of the centre: Providencia and Las Condes *p610, map p610*
LL Hyatt Regency Santiago, Av Las Condes 4601, T218 1234, www.hyatt.cl. Superb, beautifully decorated, large outdoor pool, gym, Thai restaurant.

● *For an explanation of the sleeping and eating price codes used in this guide, see inside the front*
● *cover. Other relevant information is found in Essentials pages 604-605.*

LL **Sheraton Santiago**, Santa María 1742, T233 5000, www.sheraton.cl. One of the best, good restaurant, good buffet lunch, and all facilities.
AL **Atton**, Alonso de Córdova 5199, Las Condes, T422 7979, www.atton.cl. Good value, very helpful, internet in rooms, full disabled access. Recommended.
AL **Orly**, Pedro de Valdivia 027, Metro Pedro de Valdivia, T231 8947, www.orly hotel.com. Small, comfortable, convenient, Cafetto café attached with good value meals.
A **Chilhotel**, Cirujano Guzmán 103, T235 0713, metro Manuel Montt, www.chilhotel.cl. Small, comfortable, family-run, includes breakfast, luggage store, airport transfer US$19. Recommended.
A **El Patio Suizo**, Condell 847, T494 1214, www.patiosuizo.com. Metro Parque Bustamante. Comfortable Swiss-run B&B in a quiet residential part of Providencia, TV, patio, internet, English, German spoken. Recommended.
A **Marilú's Bed and Breakfast**, Rafael Cañas 246 C, T235 5302, www.bedandbreakfast.cl. Comfortable, **B** with shared bath, no Tcs, good beds, English and French spoken, secure. Highly recommended.
D pp **Santiago Hostel**, Dr Barros Borgoño 199, T226 49894, hostelsantiago@yahoo.com. Dorms only, European style youth hostel, with breakfast, kitchen facilities, garden, internet, excellent skiing information.

Near airport
B pp **Hacienda del Sol y La Luna**, 4 Hijuela 9978, Pudahuel, T/F601 9254. English, German and French spoken.

Accommodation with families

C pp **Antonio y Ana Saldivia**, Guillermo Tell 5809, La Reina (near Las Condes), T226 6267. Breakfast, dinner extra, quiet, bus 244 from Alameda.

D Cecilia Parada, Llico 968, T226 6267. 1 block from Metro Departamental, washing machine, gardens, quiet.

D pp **Rodrigo Sauvageot**, Gorbea 1992, dept 113, T672 2119. Includes breakfast, phone first.

E pp **Sra Fidela Monge**, San Isidro 261, Apt H, T222 1246. Shared bathroom, breakfast. Recommended.

E pp **Sra Lucía**, Catedral 1029, p 10, dept 1001, T696 3832. Central, safe, cooking facilities, wonderful views.

E pp **Sra Irma Jiménez**, Santo Domingo 3673B, near Quinta Normal, T357 5397. Double room, shared bath, use of kitchen, family atmosphere, laundry service, very good.

Longer stay accommodation

See the classified ads in *El Mercurio*; flats, homes and family pensiones are listed by district, or in *El Rastro* (weekly), or try the notice board at the tourist office. Estate agents handle apartments, but often charge ½ of the first month's rent as commission, while a month's rent in advance and 1 month's deposit are required. Recommended apartments are **Santa Magdalena**, Helvecia 244, Las Condes, T374 6875, www.santamagdalena.cl.

⑦ Eating

Some of the best seafood restaurants are to be found in the Mercado Central (by Cal y Canto Metro, lunches only), at the Vega Central market on the opposite bank of the Mapocho and on Av Cumming and C Reyes in Barrio Brasil. Visit *El Mercurio* online, www.emol.com, and go to "tiempo libre", to search for types of restaurants and areas of the city. It is

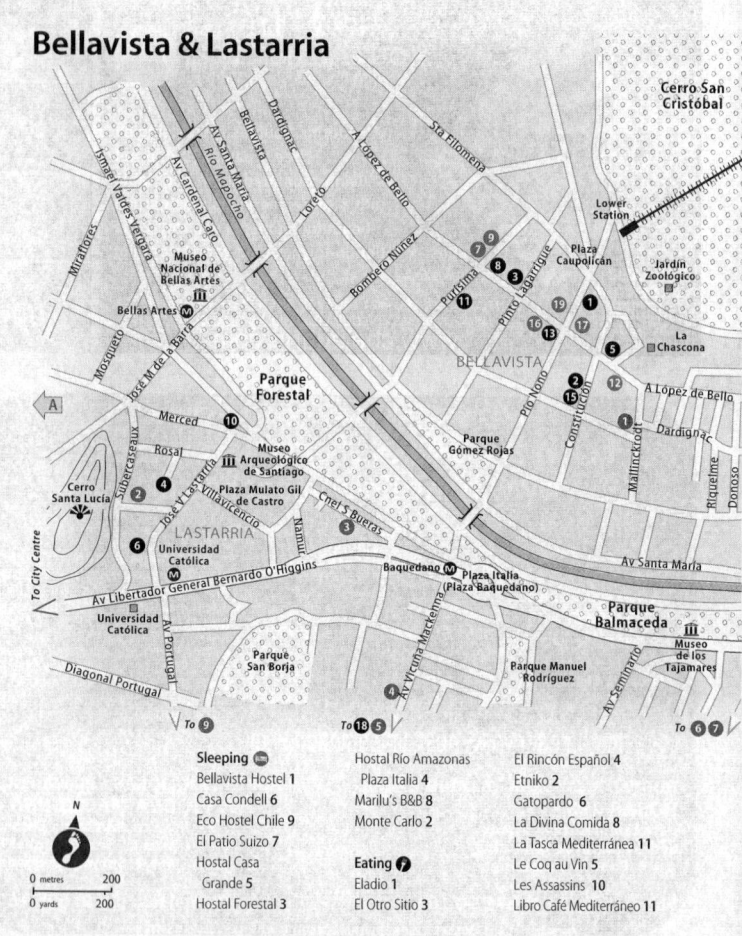

Bellavista & Lastarria

Sleeping 💤
Bellavista Hostel 1
Casa Condell 6
Eco Hostel Chile 9
El Patio Suizo 7
Hostal Casa
  Grande 5
Hostal Forestal 3

Hostal Río Amazonas
  Plaza Italia 4
Marilu's B&B 8
Monte Carlo 2

Eating ⑦
Eladio 1
El Otro Sitio 3

Hostal Río Amazonas
Plaza Italia 4
El Rincón Español 4
Etniko 2
Gatopardo 6
La Divina Comida 8
La Tasca Mediterránea 11
Le Coq au Vin 5
Les Assassins 10
Libro Café Mediterráneo 11

difficult to eat cheaply in the evening apart from fast food, so if you're on a tight budget, make the *almuerzo* your main meal.

Santiago centre *p607, map p608*

♦♦♦-♦♦ Da Carla, MacIver 577. Traditional Italian food, good.

♦♦♦-♦♦ San Marco, 2 doors from Da Carla. Even better than its neighbour, also Italian.

♦♦ Congreso, Catedral 1221. Good meat and wines, popular at lunchtime.

♦♦ El 27 de Nueva York, Nueva York 27. Central, good international menu, live music.

♦♦ Faisán d'Or, Plaza de Armas. Good pastel de choclo, pleasant place to have a drink and watch the world go by.

♦♦ Fra Diavolo, París 836. Lunches only, excellent food and service, popular.

♦♦ Lung Fung, Agustinas 715. Delicious oriental food, large cage in the centre with noisy parrots.

Tercera Compañía de Bomberos **18**	HBH **7**
Tragaluz **15**	La Casa en el Aire **12**
Venezia **13**	La Otra Puerta **19**
	Restaurant/Pub Evelyn **9**

Bars & clubs ♦
Bogart **16**
Disco Salsa **17**

♦ Bar Central, San Pablo 1063. Cheap, typical food. Recommended.

♦ Bar Nacional No 2, Bandera 317. Popular, local specialities, good for quantity.

♦ Círculo de Periodistas, Amunátegui 31, p 2. Unwelcoming entrance, good value lunches. Recommended.

♦ El Naturista, Moneda 846. Excellent vegetarian, "healthy portions", closes 2100.

♦ El Rápido, next to Bar Nacional No 2. Specializes in empanadas, good food, good fun, "happening locals' joint".

♦ La Caleta de Don Beno, San Diego 397. Excellent *parrilladas*, also seafood, popular. Recommended.

♦ Las Tejas, San Diego 234, south of the Alameda. For typical dishes and drinks, rowdy.

♦ Masticón, San Diego 152, south of the Alameda. Good service, excellent value.

♦ Torres, Alameda 1570. Traditional bar/restaurant, good ambience, live music at weekends.

Cafés

Café Caribe and **Café Haití**, both on Paseo Ahumada and elsewhere in centre and Providencia. Good coffee, institutions for the Santiago business community.

Café Colonia, MacIver 133. Splendid variety of cakes, pastries and pies, fashionable and pricey.

Café Ikabaru, Huérfanos 709. Good coffee, popular and intimate.

Café Manila, Ahumada 357. Central, quiet, very pleasant place for a snack or more.

Salón de Té Cousiño, Cousiño 107. Good coffee, snacks and *onces*, very popular, but not cheap.

West of centre *p609, map p616*

♦♦ Las Vacas Gordas, Cienfuegos 280, Barrio Brasil. Good value grilled steaks, nice wine selection, very popular so book in advance.

♦♦ Los Chinos Ricos, Brasil 373, on the Plaza. Good Chinese.

♦♦ Mansión de la Novia, Agustinas 2859. Chilean food, elegant.

♦♦ Ostras Azócar, Gral Bulnes 37. Reasonable prices for oysters. Several other seafood restaurants in same street.

East of the centre: Bellavista and Lastarria *p610, map p610*

♦♦♦ El Otro Sitio, López de Bello 53. Peruvian, excellent food, elegant, good service.

♦♦ Eladio, Pío Nono 251. Good steaks, Argentine cuisine, excellent value.

♦♦♦ La Divina Comida, Purísima 93. Italian with 3 rooms: Heaven, Hell and Purgatory, good seafood.

♦♦♦ Le Coq au Vin, López de Bello 0110. French, excellent, good value. Highly recommended.

Etniko, Constitución 172. Tasty, inventive Japanese food, including sushi.

El Rincón Español, just off C Rosal, Lastarria. Spanish, good paella, reasonably priced.

Gatopardo, next door to El Rincón Español. Good value, Mediterranean cuisine. Highly recommended.

La Tasca Mediterránea, Purísima 165. Good food, extensive menu including seafood. Recommended.

Les Assassins, Merced 297. Good French cuisine.

Tragaluz, Constitución 124. Good Chilean food, not cheap.

Venezia, Pío Nono, corner of López de Bello. Huge servings, good value.

Libro Café Mediterráneo, Purísima, next door to La Tasca Mediterránea. Popular with students, lively, cheap.

Tercera Compañía de Bomberos, Vicuña Mackenna 097. Good food, very cheap. Recommended.

East of the centre: Providencia *p610, map p610*

El Giratorio, 11 de Septiembre 2250, p16. French revolving restaurant, good food.

El Huerto, Orrego Luco 054, Providencia, T233 2690. Vegetarian. Open daily, live music Fri and Sat evenings, varied menu, very good, popular. Recommended.

La Pizza Nostra, Av Providencia 1975. Pizzas and good Italian food, real coffee, also at Av Las Condes 6757 and Luis Thayer Ojeda 019.

Oriental, Manuel Montt 584. Excellent Chinese. Highly recommended.

Salvaje, Av Providencia 1177. Good international menu, open-air seating, good value. Warmly recommended.

A Pinch of Pancho, Gral del Canto 45. Very good fish and seafood.

Gatsby, Av Providencia 1984. American food, as-much-as-you- can-eat buffet and lunch/dinner, snack bar open till 2400, tables

Santiago west of centre

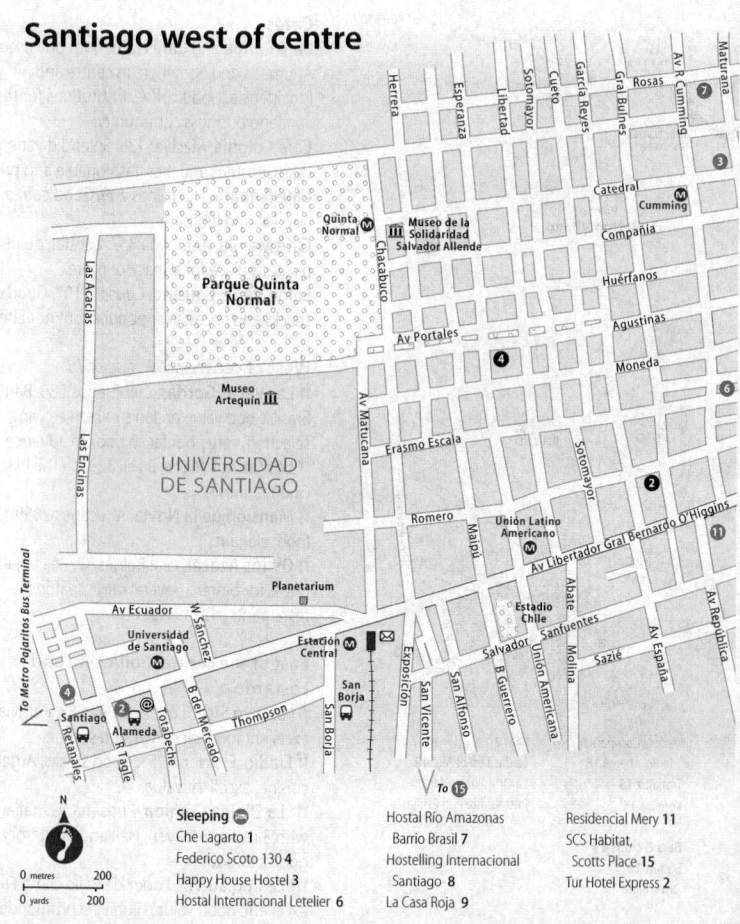

Sleeping
Che Lagarto **1**
Federico Scoto 130 **4**
Happy House Hostel **3**
Hostal Internacional Letelier **6**

Hostal Río Amazonas
Barrio Brasil **7**
Hostelling Internacional
Santiago **8**
La Casa Roja **9**

Residencial Mery **11**
SCS Habitat,
Scotts Place **15**
Tur Hotel Express **2**

outside in warm weather, good (also has a good branch at the airport).

Cafés
For snacks and ice cream there are several good places on Av Providencia including **Coppellia**, No 2211, **Bravissimo**, No 1406, and **El Toldo Azul**, No 1936. Also **Salón de Té Tavelli**, drugstore precinct, Av Providencia 2124.

East of the centre: Las Condes *p610*
TTTT **Cuerovaca**, El Mañío 1659, Vitacura, T246 8936. Serves fantastic steaks, Argentine and Chilean cuts.
TTTT **El Madroñal**, Vitacura 2911, T233 6312. Spanish, excellent, booking essential.
TTTT **Sakura**, Vitacura 4111. Japanese, sushi, very good.
TTTT-TT **Diego Pizza**, El Bosque Norte y Don Carlos. Nice atmosphere, good cocktails, popular.

Eating **⦿**
Las Vacas Gordas **1**
Los Chinos Ricos **3**
Mansión de la Novia **4**
Ostras Azócar **2**

TTT-TT **Mare Nostrum**, La Concepción 281. Good for seafood.
TT **Le Fournil**, Vitacura 3841, opposite Cuerovaca. Excellent French bakery and restaurant, popular a lunchtime.

⦿ Bars and clubs

For all entertainments, nightclubs, cinemas, theatres, restaurants, concerts, *El Mercurio* Online website has all listings and a good search feature, www.emol.com. Listings in weekend newspapers, particularly *El Mercurio* and *La Tercera*. Also *Santiago What's On*. Lively areas to head for are: **Bellavista**, good selection of varied restaurants, bars, clubs and salsotheques. Reasonable prices (Metro Baquedano). Avs Suecia and Gral Holley in **Providencia**, much of it pedestrianized. Lots of bars and some restaurants, clubs and salsotheques (Metro Los Leones). **El Bosque Norte**, chic bars and expensive restaurants for the Chilean jetset (Metro Tobalaba). **Barrio Brasil**, a number of bars and restaurants dotted around the Plaza Brasil and on Avs Brasil and Cumming. Popular with Chilean students (Metro República). **Plaza Ñuñoa**, a number of good bars dotted around the Plaza in the middle-class suburb of Ñuñoa.

East of the centre: Bellavista *p610*, map *p614*
Bogart, Av López de Bello 34. Disco-rock bar.
Disco Salsa, Pío Nono 223. Good atmosphere, salsa and dance classes.
HBH Bars, Pío Nono 129 and Purísima y López de Bello, also at Irarrázaval 3176, near Plaza Ñuñoa, and Gral Holley 124, Providencia. Bavarian-style beer brewed to traditional recipes in Temuco.
La Casa en el Aire, López de Bello 125. Pleasant atmosphere, live music. Recommended.
La Otra Puerta, Pío Nono 348. Lively salsoteca with live music.
Peña Nano Parra, San Isidro 57. Good folk club, cheap.
Restaurant/Pub Evelyn, Purísima 282. Austrian beers on tap, good atmosphere, not cheap.

East of the centre: Providencia
p610, map *p610*
Brannigan Pub, Av Suecia 35. Good beer, live jazz, one of many good bars on this avenue.
Flannery's Irish Geo Pub, Encomenderos 83. Beer, food, live music Wed and Fri, internet.
Golden Bell Inn, Hernando Aguirre 27. Popular with ex-pats.
Louísiana River Pub, Suecia y Gral Holly. Live music.
Phone Box Pub, Av Providencia 1652. Serves imported British beers, popular with locals.

East of the centre: Las Condes *p610*
Country Village, Av Las Condes y Estoril.
Mon-Sat from 2000, Sun lunchtime onwards, live
music Fri and Sat.
Heaven, Recoleta 345. US$12 pp, Thu-Sat
2330-0500.
Ilé Habana, Bucaré, just off Suecia. Bar with salsa,
often live, and a good dance floor.
Morena, Av Las Condes 10120. Good dance floor
and sound system, techno, open till 0200, live
music weekends.

Further east on Av Las Condes at Paseo San
Damián are several popular bar-restaurants
including **T'quila** (annex of Santa Fe, No 10690, a
colourful, popular Mexican restaurant).

Ñuñoa
Club de Jazz de Santiago, José Pedro
Alessandri 85, T274 2997, www.clubdejazz.cl.
Regular live jazz in candle-lit bar, pleasant.

⊕ Entertainment

Santiago *p606, maps p608, p610, p615, p616*
There's a good guide to daily cinema in the free
newspapers, *La Hora* and *tmg*, given out at
metro stations on weekday mornings.
Cinemas 'Ciné Arte' (quality foreign films) is
popular. Cinemas specializing in this type of film
include: **El Biógrafo**, Lastarria 181, T633 4435.
Casa de Extensión UC, Alameda 390, T635 1994.
Normandie, Tarapacá 1181, T697 2979.
Tobalaba, Av Providencia 2563, T231 6630.
Try also Goethe-Institut (address below). Many
multiplex cinemas across the city show
mainstream releases, nearly always in the original
English with subtitles. Seats cost US$4-6 with
reductions on Wed (elsewhere in the country
the day varies).
Classical concerts Free concerts are
sometimes given in San Francisco church in
summer. Arrive early for a seat.
Theatres **Teatro Municipal**, Agustinas y San
Antonio. Stages international opera, concerts by
the Orquesta Filarmónica de Santiago, and the
Ballet de Santiago, throughout the year. On Tue
at 2100 there are free operatic concerts in the
Salón Claudio Arrau; tickets range from US$7 for a
very large choral group with a symphony
orchestra, and US$8 for the cheapest seats at the
ballet, to US$70 for the most expensive opera
seats. Some cheap seats are often sold on the day
of concerts. **Teatro Universidad de Chile**, Plaza
Italia, is the home of the Orquesta y Coro
Sinfónica de Chile and the Ballet Nacional de
Chile. There are a great number of theatres which
stage plays in Spanish, either in the original
language or translations.

⊕ Festivals and events

Santiago *p606, maps p608, p610, p615, p616*
During **Nov** there is a **free fair** in the Parque
Forestal on the banks of the Río Mapocho, lasting a
fortnight. In **Oct** or **Nov** there are a sumptuous
flower show and an annual agricultural and
industrial show (known as **Fisa**) in Parque Cerrillos.
Religious festivals and ceremonies continue
throughout **Holy Week**, when a priest washes the
feet of 12 men. The image of the Virgen del
Carmen (patron of the Armed Forces) is carried
through the streets by cadets on **16 Jul**.

⊕ Shopping

Santiago *p606, maps p608, p610, p615, p616*
Antique stores in Plaza Mulato Gil de Castro and
elsewhere on Lastarria (Merced end).
Bookshops Book prices are high compared
with neighbouring countries and Europe.
Apostrophes, Merced 324. Specializes in French
books, book exchange, internet service. **Books**,
Av Providencia 1652, Metro Pedro de Valdivia,
T235 1205. Second-hand English books,
exchange for best deal. **Chile Ilustrado**, next to
Books at Av Providencia 1652, T235 8145,
chileil@tnet.cl. Specializes in books relating to
Chile, flora, fauna, history and anthropology
(mostly in Spanish). **Feria Chilena del Libro**,
Huérfanos 623, and in Drugstore precinct,
Providencia 2124. Largest bookshop in Santiago,
a few travel books and maps. **LOM Ediciones**,
Estación Mapocho, Mon-Fri 1000-2000, Sat
1000-1400. Very good, large stock from its own
publishing house (literature, history, sociology,
art, politics), also bar and reading room with
recent Chilean papers and magazines. **Librería
Albers**, Vitacura 5648, Las Condes, T218 5371,
F218 1458. Spanish, English and German, good
selection, cheaper than most, helpful, also
German and Swiss newspapers. **Librairie
Française**, Estado 337. Books and newspapers.
Librería Inglesa, Huérfanos 669, local 11, Pedro
de Valdivia 47, Providencia 2653, Vitacura 5950,
www.libreriainglesa.cl. Good selection of English
books. **Librería Universitaria**, Alameda 1050,
T695 1529, in unmistakable yellow building next
to Universidad de Chile metro. Good selection of
books in Spanish. **South American Way**,
Apoquindo 6856, Las Condes, T211 8078. Sells
books in English. **The English Reader**, Los
Leones 116, T334 7388, www.englishreader.cl.
Specializes in books in English.

For cheap English books, try the second-hand
book kiosks on San Diego between Eleuterio
Ramírez and Cóndor, 4 blocks south of Plaza
Bulnes.

Camping equipment Camping gas cartridges (Italian substitute for Camping Gaz) can be bought at **Fabri Gas**, Bandera y Santo Domingo. Imported camping goods from **Club Andino** and **Federación de Andinismo** (see below). **Casa Italiana**, Tarapacá 1120. Repair of camping stoves. **La Cumbre**, Apoquindo 5258, Las Condes, T220 9907, la_cumbre@email.com. Dutch-owned, very helpful. Industria Yarur, Rosas 1289 y Teatinos, T672 3696 (metro Cal y Canto). Sells wide range of Doite products (Chilean, good value). **Mountain Service**, PO Box 233 Correo 35, Providencia, www.mountainservice.cl. English spoken, tents, stoves, clothing, equipment rental, recommended. **Outdoors & Travel**, Encomenderos 206, Las Condes, T/F335 7104. German/Chilean owned, clothing, equipment, maps. For second-hand equipment look for adverts in cheaper hotels or try **Luz Emperatriz Sanhuela Quiroz**, Portal Lyon, Loc 14, Providencia 2198 (Metro Los Leones), expensive for new equipment, as is **Patagonia**, Centro Comercial Alto Las Condes, where there are three other similar stores.

Handicrafts Chile Vivo, Dardignac 15, Bellavista, T735 0227, chilevivo@latinmail.com. Typical handicrafts, jewellery making, art gallery, internet café, owner Doris Berdichevsky is very helpful. **Cooperativa Almacén Campesino**, Purísima 303, Bellavista, T737 2127. A cooperative association in an attractive colonial building, selling handicrafts from all over Chile, including attractive Mapuche weavings, wood carvings, pottery and beautiful wrought copper and bronze. Highly recommended for variety, quality and value. Prices are similar to those in similar shops in Temuco. Ask about shipping. **Los Graneros del Alba**, or **El Pueblo de Artesanos**, beside and behind the Iglesia de los Dominicos, on Av Apoquindo 9085. Open 1030-2100 in summer, 1000-1900 in winter. All types of ware on sale, classes given in some shops, interesting. To get there, take a No 326 or 327 bus from Av Providencia, marked 'Camino del Alba'; get out at the junction of Apoquindo y Camino del Alba and walk up to the church. **Plaza Artesanos de Manquehue**, Av Manquehue Sur, block 300-600, just off Apoquindo. Good range of modern Chilean crafts, from ceramics to textiles, at the biggest craft market in Chile. Take any bus east from Providencia or Escuela Militar which goes via Apoquindo. **Prisma de los Andes**, Santo Domingo 1690 T673 0540, Metro Santa Ana. Textiles, crafts, tapestries, rucksacks, bags, kids clothes etc.

Jewellery The gemstone lapis lazuli can be found in shops on C Bellavista between Pío Nono and Yáñez, but is cheaper in the arcades on south side of the Plaza de Armas and in the **Centro** Artesanal Santa Lucía (Santa Lucía Metro, south exit) which also has a wide variety of woollen goods, jewellery, some folk music and other miscellanea. **Amitié**, Ricardo León y Av Providencia (Metro Los Leones) and **Dauvin Artesanía Fina**, Providencia 2169, Local 69 (Metro Los Leones) have also been recommended.

Maps See Essentials, page 602, and Driving in Chile Box. **Librería Australis**, Av Providencia 1670, local 5. All sorts of local, regional and trekking maps.

Markets For food: Mercado Central, between Puente y 21 de Mayo by the Río Mapocho (Cal y Canto Metro) is excellent but quite expensive. There is a cheaper market, the **Vega Central**, on the opposite bank of the river. There are craft markets in an alleyway, 1 block south of the Alameda between A Prat and San Diego, on the 600 to 800 blocks of Santo Domingo (including pieces from neighbouring countries) and at Pío Nono y Santa María, Bellavista. The **Bío Bío** flea market on C Bío Bío, Metro Franklin (follow crowds) on Sat and Sun morning is huge; everything under the sun, lots of it having fallen off the back of a lorry.

Music Feria de Disco, Paseo Ahumada and in numerous malls. The biggest chain, often sell tickets for rock concerts. **Musimundo**, Huérfanos 930 (with listening stations) and Providencia 2266, megastores.

Shopping malls Numerous; generally open daily 1000-2100. **Alto Las Condes**, Av Kennedy 9001; **Apumanque**, Manquehue y Apoquindo; **Mall del Centro**, Rosas 900 block, just north of the Plaza de Armas. The most central. **Parque Arauco**, Av Kennedy 5413, north of Metro Escuela Militar; **Plaza Vespucio** at terminus of Línea 5, Bellavista de La Florida.

Wine El Mundo del Vino, Isidora Goyenechea 2931, T244 8888. For all types of Chilean wines, good selection across the price range. **Vinopolis**, El Bosque Norte 038 and Pedro de Valdivia 036. Mon-Fri 0900-2300, Sat 1000-2300, Sun 1000-2200. Also at airport. Sells all types of Chilean wines, good selection across the price range. **The Wine House**, Vitacura 2904, Mall Parque Arauco, loc 333.

▲▲ Activities and tours

Santiago *p606, maps p608, p610, p615, p616*
Cricket Sat in summer at Club Príncipe de Gales, Las Arañas 1901 (bus from Tobalaba Metro), see www.cricketchile.cl for more information.
Cycling For new models, parts and repairs at best prices go to San Diego, 800 and 900 blocks, south of the Alameda.

Football Main teams including Colo Colo who play at the **Estadio Monumental**, T688 3244 (reached by any bus to Puente Alto; tickets from Cienfuegos 41), **Universidad de Chile**, Campo de Deportes, Ñuñoa, T239 2793 (Estadio Nacional, Grecia 2001, T238 8102) and **Universidad Católica** who play at San Carlos de Apoquindo, reached by bus from Metro Escuela Militar, tickets from Andrés Bello 2782, Providencia, T231 2777.

Horse racing Club Hípico, Blanco Encalada 2540, highly recommended, entry to main stand US$5, every Sun and every other Wed. Hipódromo Chile every Sat.

Skiing and climbing Club Alemán Andino, El Arrayán 2735, T242 5453. Open Tue and Fri, 1800-2000, May-Jun. **Club Andino de Chile**, Enrique Foster 29, ski club (open 1900-2100 on Mon and Fri). **Federación de Andinismo de Chile**, Almte Simpson 77A (T222 0888, www.feach.cl). Open daily (frequently closed Jan/Feb), has a small museum, library (weekdays except Wed 1930-2100), shop selling guides and equipment. Escuela Nacional de Montaña (ENAM), at same address, T222 0799, holds seminars and courses and has the addresses of all the mountaineering clubs in the country. It has a mountaineering school. **Skitotal**, Apoquindo 4900, of 40-42, T246 0156, for 1-day excursions and good value ski hire. Equipment hire is much cheaper in Santiago than in ski resorts. Sunglasses are essential. For ski resorts in the Santiago area see below, page .

Swimming Antilen, Cerro San Cristóbal. Open daily in summer except Mon 1000-1500 (check if they are open in winter, one usually is). In Parque O'Higgins, 1330-1830 summer only, US$3. Olympic pool in Parque Araucano (near Parque Arauco Shopping Centre, Metro Escuela Militar), open Nov-Mar Tue-Sat 0900-1900. Tupahue, Cerro San Cristóbal. Large pool with cafés, entry US$10 but worth it.

Tennis Municipal courts in Parque O'Higgins. Estadio Nacional, Av Grecia y Av Marathon, has a tennis club which offers classes.

Tours A number of agencies offer day trips from Santiago. Typical excursions are to the Wine Valleys, Isla Negra (Pablo Neruda's seaside villa), visits to nearby haciendas and adventure tours such as whitewater rafting, rock climbing or trekking in the Cajón del Maipo, southeast of the city. Many agencies advertise in the Sernatur tourist office (see above).

Asatej Student Flight Centre, H de Aguirre 201, Oficina 401, T335 0395, chile@asatej.com. For cheap flights and youth travel. Recommended.
Tajamar, Orrego Luco 023, Providencia, T336 8000, www.tajamar.cl. Good for flights.
Turismo Cocha, El Bosque Norte 0430, PO Box 191035, Providencia, Metro Tobalaba, T600-464 1000, www.cocha.com.

Adventure tours and trekking
Altue Expediciones, Encomenderos 83, p 2, Las Condes (above Geo Pub), T232 1103, altue@entelchile.net. For wilderness trips including tour of Patagonia. Recommended.
Antarctic Expeditions, Av Vitacura 2771, of 904, Las Condes, T236 5179, www.antarctic.cl. Expeditions to Patagonia and Antarctica from Punta Arenas on board their 'Antarctic Dream'.
Azimut 360, General Salvo 159, Providencia, T235 1519, www.azimut.cl. Adventure and ecotourism including mountaineering all over Chile, low prices. Highly recommended.
Catamaranes del Sur, Pedro de Valdivia Norte 0210, Providencia, T231 1902, offers tours of Chilean Patagonia. In Puerto Chacabuco: José Miguel Carrera 50, T351112, www.catamaranesdelsur.cl.
Patagonia Connection SA, Fidel Oteíza 1921, of 1006, Providencia (Metro Pedro de Valdivia), T225 6489, www.patagonia-connection.com. For excursion by boat Puerto Montt-Coyhaique/Puerto Chacabuco-Laguna San Rafael.
Racies, Plaza Corregidor Zañartu 761, T/F638 2904. Cultural tours, including Robinson Crusoe Island and Antarctica.
Santiago Adventures, Coyancura 2270, of 801, Providencia, T415 0667, www.santiagoadventures.com. US-run, offering adventure day tours, wine tours, city tours, skiing and Patagonia.
Sportstours, Moneda 970, p 18, T549 5200, www.sportstour.cl. German-run, 5-day trips to Antarctica (offices also at Hotels Carrera, and San Cristóbal), only for tours organized from abroad.
Turismo Cabo de Hornos, Av Vitacura 2898, Las Condes, T374 0161, hornos@entelchile.net. For DAP flights and Tierra del Fuego/Antarctica tours.
Valle Nevado, Av Vitacura 5250, No 304, Vitacura, T477 7000, www.vallenevado.com. Skiing, trekking and mountain biking.

⊖ Transport

Santiago p606, maps p608, p610, p615, p616
Air
International and domestic flights leave from **Arturo Merino Benítez Airport** at Pudahuel, 26 km northwest of Santiago, off Ruta 68, the motorway to Viña del Mar and Valparaíso. The terminal has most facilities, including Afex cambio, ATMs, Sernatur office which will book accommodation and a fast-food plaza. Left luggage US$7.50 per bag per day. Airport information T601 8758/690 1900.

Airport taxi, about US$14-20 but bargain hard and agree fare beforehand: more expensive with meter. Taxi to airport is much cheaper, US$10-12, if flagged down in the street rather than booked by

Chile Santiago & around Listings

620

phone. Frequent bus services to/from city centre by 2 companies: **Tur Bus**, from Terminal Alameda, US$2.50, every 30 mins; and **Centropuerto** (T601 9883, from Metro Los Héroes), US$2, first from centre 0600, last from airport 2230, every 10 mins. Buses leave from outside airport terminal and, in Santiago, call at Estación Central, Terminal Santiago, Metro Pajaritos and most other regular bus stops. (Beware the yellow bus marked Aeropuerto which stops 2 km short of the Airport). **Delfos** (T601 1111), **Navett** (T695 6868), **Transfer** (T777 7707), **TransVip** (T677 3000) and others run minibus services between the airport and hotels or other addresses: US$7-8 to/from city centre; US$10 to Las Condes. To go to the airport, book the previous day.

Bus

Local Yellow buses called *micros* are being replaced by Transantiago (www.transantiago.cl), new buses designed to reduce congestion and pollution. Bus lines will be main, for long journeys, and local and will integrate with the metro system. Payment will be by prepaid *multivía* card. *Micros* will be withdrawn by 2010. City buses display a number, the route and the fare (in 2006 US$0.65 - always retain your ticket until you get off, in case an inspector boards). There are also *colectivos* (collective taxis) on fixed routes to the suburbs. Routes are displayed with route numbers. Taxis (black with yellow roofs) are abundant, and not expensive, with a minimum charge of US$0.30, plus US$0.10 per 200 m. Taxi drivers are permitted to charge more at night, but in the daytime check that the meter is set to day rates. At bus terminals, drivers will charge more – best to walk a block and flag down a cruising taxi. Avoid taxis with more than one person in them especially at night. For journeys outside the city arrange the charge beforehand. Various radio taxi services operate, but rates are above those of city taxis.

Long distance There are frequent, and good, interurban buses to all parts of Chile. Take a look at the buses before buying the tickets (there are big differences in quality among bus companies); ask about the on-board services, many companies offer drinks for sale, or free, and luxury buses have meals, videos, headphones. Reclining seats are standard and there are also *salón cama* sleeper buses. Fares from/to the capital are given in the text. On Fri evening, when night departures are getting ready to go, the terminals can be chaotic. There are 5 bus terminals: 1) **Terminal de Buses Alameda**, which has a modern extension called Mall Parque Estación with left luggage (US$3.40 per day), ATMs and internet, O'Higgins 3712, Metro Universidad de Santiago, T270 1500. All **Pullman-Bus** and

Tur-Bus services go from here, they serve almost every destination in Chile, good quality but prices a little higher than others. 2) **Terminal de Buses Santiago**, O'Higgins 3878, 1 block west of Terminal Alameda, T376 1755, Metro Universidad de Santiago. Services to all parts of southern Chile, including Punta Arenas. Also international departures. Has left luggage from 0700. 3) **Terminal San Borja**, O'Higgins y San Borja, 1 block west of Estación Central, 3 blocks east of Terminal Alameda, Metro Estación Central (entrance is, inconveniently, via a busy shopping centre), T776 0645. Mainly departures to the Central Valley area, but also to northern Chile. Booking offices and departures organized according to destination. 4) **Terminal Los Héroes on Tucapel Jiménez**, just north of the Alameda, Metro Los Héroes, T420 0099. Left luggage 0630-2330. Booking offices of 8 companies, to the north, the south and Lake District and some international services (Lima, Asunción, Montevideo, Buenos Aires, Bariloche, Mendoza). 5) **Metro Pajaritos**, to Valaparaíso, Viña del Mar and places on the central coast; efficient new terminal with café, toilets, public phones. Some long-distance buses call at Las Torres de Tajamar, Providencia 1108, which is more convenient if you are planning to stay in Providencia.

Note: See the note under Taxis about not taking expensive taxis parked outside bus terminals, but note that official Tur-Bus taxis are good and reliable. Also check if student rates are available (even for non-students), or reductions for travelling same day as purchase of ticket; it is worth bargaining over prices, especially shortly before departure and out of summer season.

International buses Most services leave from Terminal Santiago, though there are also departures from Terminal Los Héroes. There are frequent services from Terminal Santiago through the Cristo Redentor tunnel to **Mendoza** in Argentina, 6-7 hrs, US$12, many companies, departures around 0800, 1200 and 2200, touts approach you in Terminal Santiago. Many of these services continue to **Buenos Aires**, 24 hrs, US$35, and many companies in Terminal Santiago have connections to other Argentine cities (eg **Bahía Blanca**, **Córdoba**, **San Juan**, **Bariloche** and **Neuquén**). There are also minibuses from the Terminal Santiago, US$15, 6 hrs, shorter waiting time at customs. To **Lima**, **Ormeño** (Terminal Santiago), Tue and Fri 0900, 51 hrs, US$60, it is cheaper to take a bus to Arica, a colectivo to Tacna, then bus to Lima.

Car

Car hire Prices vary a lot so shop around first. Tax of 19% is charged, usually included in price quoted. If possible book a car in advance.

Information boards full of flyers from companies at airport and tourist office. A credit card is usually asked for when renting a vehicle. Many companies will not hire a car to holders of drivers licences in left hand drive countries unless they have an international licence. Remember that in the capital driving is restricted according to licence plate numbers; look for notices in the street and newspapers. Main international agencies and others are available at the airport (see Essentials, page 43 for agency web addresses). **Automóvil Club de Chile** car rental from head office (see Maps), discount for members and members of associated motoring organizations. **Rosselot**, Av Vicuña Mackenna 1911, T585 4260, www.rosselot.cl. Also at airport, T690 1374. Reputable Chilean firm with national coverage. **Seelmann**, Las Encinas 3057, Ñuñoa, T09-331 0591. English and German spoken. **Verschae**, Manquehue Sur 660, T202 7266, www.verschae.com. Good value, branches throughout country.

Ferry operators
Navimag, Av El Bosque Norte 0440, p 11, Las Condes, T442 3120, www.navimag.com. For services from **Puerto Montt** to **Puerto Chacabuco, Puerto Natales** and **Laguna San Rafael**. M/n Skorpios: Augusto Leguía Norte 118, Las Condes, T477 1900, www.skorpios.cl. For luxury cruise out of Puerto Montt to **Laguna San Rafael** and adventure strips from Puerto Natales to Puerto Edén and the Campo Hielo del Sur. **Note**: Check schedules with ferry companies rather than Sernatur.

Metro
See www.metrosantiago.cl. Line 1 runs west-east between **San Pablo** and **Escuela Militar**, under the Alameda; Line 2 runs north-south from **Einstein** to **La Cisterna** (with further extension north in progress); Line 4 runs from **Tobalaba** on Line 1 south to **Plaza de Puente Alto**; Line 5, from **Quinta Normal** via **Baquedano** south to **Vicente Valdés** on Line 4. Line 4A from La Cisterna (Line 2) to Vicuña Mackenna (Line 4) is under construction. The trains are fast, quiet, and very full. The first train is at 0630 (Mon-Sat), 0800 (Sun and holidays), the last about 2245. Fares vary according to time of journey; there are 2 charging periods: high 0715-0900, 1800-1930, US$0.88; economic, at all other times, US$0.70. The simplest solution is to buy a *tarjeta multivía*, US$2.85 (US$0.95 for subsequent top-ups), a charge card from which the appropriate fare is deducted. Blue metrobus services connect with the metro at various stations for outlying districts, fare US$0.40.

Train
All trains leave from **Estación Central (Alameda)** at O'Higgins 3170. The line runs south to **Rancagua**, **Talca**, **Chillán**, **Concepción**, **Temuco** and **Puerto Montt**. The train leaves at 2200, arriving in Temuco at 0800. Fares: US$26.50, *salón* class, or US$36 *preferente*. To continue to Puerto Montt change in Temuco to the Victoria-Puerto Montt line, twice a day. There is a connecting bus service from Temuco to Valdivia, Villarrica and Pucón. Meals are good but not cheap. There are also frequent local Metrotren services to Rancagua and San Fernando. For reservations: T585 5000, open till 2230, www.efe.cl. **Booking offices**: Alameda O'Higgins 3170, T585 5990, Mon-Sat 0700-2245, Sun 0800-2245; Universidad de Chile metro, loc 10, T688 3297, Mon-Fri 0900-2000, Sat 0900-1400; Morandé 115, Plaza Constitución, T585 5016, Mon-Fri 0800-1900. Left luggage office at Estación Alameda. **Note**: Schedules change with the seasons, so check timetables in advance. Summer services are booked up a week in advance.

⊕ Directory

Santiago *p606, maps p608, p610, p615, p616*
Airline offices Aerolíneas Argentinas, Roger de Flor 2921, Las Condes, T210 9300. **American Airlines**, Huérfanos 1199, T679 0000. **Avianca**, Isidora Goyenechea 3365, Las Condes, T270 6612. **Continental**, Fidel Oteiza 1921, Suite 703, T200 2100. **Delta**, Av Vitacura 2700. Las Condes. **Iberia**, Bandera 206, p 8, T870 1010. **KLM**, Américo Vespucio Sur 100, of 202, T290 9696. **LAB**, Augusto Leguia Norte 100, p 7, Las Condes, T481 3523. **LAN**, Américo Vespucio 901, T526 2000, sales offices: Huérfanos 926, and Av Providencia y Av Pedro de Valdivia, Mon-Fri 0900-1900, Sat 0900-1230 (to avoid queues, buy tickets at the office in the airport). **Lufthansa**, Av El Bosque Norte 500, p 16, Las Condes, T630 1655. **Sky Airline**, Fuenzalida 55, Providencia, and Huérfanos 815, T600-600 2828. **Varig**, El Bosque Norte 0177, p 9, T707 8007. **Banks** (Banks, open 0900-1400, closed on Sat. Exchange rates are published in El Mercurio.) For Cirrus/MasterCard and Visa ATMs go to any bank or Copec petrol station with Redbanc sign. Visa at **Corp Banca**, Huérfanos y Bandera, but beware hidden costs in 'conversion rate', and **Banco Santander**, Av Providencia y Pedro de Valdivia, no commission. **Banco de Chile**, Ahumada 251 and other branches, minimum of formalities. **Citibank**, Av Providencia 2653. **American Express**, Andrés Bello 2711, p 9, T350 6700, Tobalaba metro, also at Blanco Viajes, Gen Holley 148, T636 9100, blancoviajes@blancoviajes.cl. Some Amex services at branches of **Viajes Falabella**

throughout the city. **Casas de Cambio** (exchange houses) in the centre are mainly situated on Paseo Ahumada and Huérfanos (metro Universidad de Chile or Plaza de Armas). Use them, not banks, for changing TCs. **Exprinter**, Bombero Ossa 1053, good rates, low commission. **Afex**, Moneda 1140, good rates for TCs. In Providencia several on Av Pedro de Valdivia. Some casas de cambio in the centre open Sat morning (but check first). Dollars can only be bought for Chilean pesos in casas de cambio. Most cambios charge 3% commission to change US$ TCs into US$ cash; check beforehand. Only residents can buy dollars against credit cards. Always avoid street money changers (particularly common on Ahumada and Agustinas): they pull any number of tricks, or will usually ask you to accompany them to somewhere obscure. The passing of forged notes and muggings are reported. **Cultural centres** Centro Cultural Matucana, Av Matucana 100 y Moneda, T682 4502, www.m100.cl. Art exhibitions, cheap films, sculpture workshop, café. Instituto Chileno Británico de Cultura, Santa Lucía 124, T413 2000, www.britanico.cl. 0930-1900, except 1330-1900 Mon, and 0930-1600 Fri, has British papers and library (also in Providencia, Darío Urzúa 1933, and Las Condes, Av Américo Vespucio Sur 631), runs language courses. British Council, Eliodoro Yáñez 832, near Providencia, T410 6900, www.britishcouncil.org/chile.htm. Instituto Chileno Francés de Cultura, Merced 298 (Francisco Noguera 176, Providencia, while being remodelled), T470 8060, www.icf.cl. In a beautiful house. Instituto Chileno Alemán de Cultura, Goethe-Institut, Esmeralda 650, T462 1800, www.goethe.de/ins/cl/sao/deindex.htm. Instituto Chileno Norteamericano de Cultura, Moneda 1467, T0800-200863, www.norte americano.cl. Good for US periodicals, cheap films on Fri. Also runs language courses and free Spanish/English language exchange hours (known as Happy Hours) which are a good way of meeting people. **Embassies and consulates** Argentina, Miraflores 285, T582 2500, www.embargentina.cl/. Consulate Vicuña MacKenna 41, T582 2606. Australians need letter from their embassy to get visa here, open 0900-1400 (visa US$25, free for US citizens), if you need a visa for Argentina, get it here or in the consulates in Concepción, Puerto Montt or Punta Arenas, there are no facilities at the borders. Australia, Isidora Goyenechea 3261, T550 3500, www.chile.embassy.gov.au, 0900-1200. Austria, Barros Errázuriz 1968, p 3, T223 4774. Belgium, Av Providencia 2653, depto 1103, T232 1071. Bolivia, Santa María 2796, T232 8180 (Metro Los Leones). 0930-1400. Canada, Nueva Tajamar 481, p 12, T362 9660, www.dfait-maeci.gc.ca/

latin-america/chile/embassy/embassy-en.asp (prints a good information book). Denmark, Jaques Cazotte 5531, T218 5949. France, Condell 65, T470 8000, www.france.cl. Germany, Las Hualtatas 5677, T463 2500. Israel, San Sebastián 2812, p 5, T750 0500. Italy, Clemente Fabres 1050, T470 8400. Japan, Av Ricardo Lyon 520, p 1, T232 1807. Netherlands, Av Apoquindo 3500, p 13, Las Condes, T756 9200. New Zealand, Av El Golf 99, of 703, Las Condes, T290 9800, embajada@ nzembassy.cl. Norway, San Sebastián 2839, T234 2888, www.noruega.cl/info/embassy.htm. Peru, Andrés Bello 1751, T235 6451 (Metro Pedro de Valdivia). South Africa, Av 11 de Septiembre 2353, p 17, T231 2862, www.embajada- sudafrica.cl. Spain (Consul General), Av. 11 de Septiembre 2353, p 9, T233 4070, cogsantiagodechile@mae.es. Sweden, 11 de Septiembre 2353, Torre San Ramón, p 4, Providencia, T940 1700, www.embajadasuecia.cl. Switzerland, Av Americo Vespucio Sur 100, p 14, T263 4211, F263 4094, metro Escuela Militar. Open 1000-1200. United Kingdom, El Bosque Norte 0125 (Metro Tobalaba), Casilla 72-D, T370 4100, www.britemb.cl. Will hold letters, consular section (F370 4170) open 0930- 1230. United States, Andrés Bello 2800, T232 2600, www.embajadaeeuu.cl. **Hospitals** Emergency hospital at Marcoleta 377 costs US$60. For yellow fever vaccination and others (but not cholera). Hospital San Salvador, J M Infante 551, T225 6441, Mon-Thu 0800-1300, 1330-1645, Fri 0800-1300, 1330-1545. Also Vaccinatoria Internacional, Hospital Luis Calvo, MacKenna, Antonio Varas 360. Clínica Central, San Isidro 231, T222 1953, open 24 hrs. Note: If you need to get to a hospital, it is better to take a taxi than wait for an ambulance. **Internet** Internet cafés are everywhere; usual price US$0.60-1 per hr. **Language schools** Bellavista, Calle del Arzobispado 0609, Providencia, T732 3443, www.escuelabellavista.cl. Group and individual classes, lodging with families, free activities. Escuela de Idiomas Violeta Parra, Ernesto Pinto Lagarrigue 362, Recoleta-Barrio Bellavista, T735 8240, www.tandemsantiago.cl. Courses aimed at budget travellers, information programme on social issues, arranges accommodation and visits to local organizations and national parks. Instituto Chileno-Suizo de Idiomas y Cultura, José Victorino Lastarria 93, p 2 (Metro Universidad Católica), T638 5414, www.chilenosuizo.cl. Coordinates stays in Chile for foreign-language students, courses in several languages, cyber café, meeting place, study area and art gallery. Natalis Language Centre, Vicuña Mackenna 6, p 7, T222 8721, www.natalislang.com. Many private teachers, including Lucía Araya Arévalo, T749 0706 (home), 731 8325 (office), 09-480 3727 (mob), lusara5@hotmail.com. Speaks German and English. **Carolina Carvajal**, Av El Bosque Sur 151, dpto Q, Las Condes, T734 7646, ccarvajal@ interactiva.cl. Exchange library, internet access. Highly recommended. **Patricio Ríos**, Tobalaba 7505, La Reina, T226 6926. Speaks English. Recommended. **Patricia Vargas Vives**, JM Infante 100, of 308, T/F244 2283, www.escueladeespanol.cl. Qualified and experienced (US$12.50 per hr). Recommended.

Post offices Plaza de Armas and Moneda between Morandé and Bandera. Also sub offices in Providencia at Av 11 de Septiembre 2092, Manuel Montt 1517, Pedro de Valdivia 1781, Providencia 1466, and in Estación Central shopping mall. These open Mon-Fri 0900-1800, Sat 0900-1230. Poste restante well organized (though only kept for 30 days), passport essential, list of letters and parcels received in the hall of central Post Office (one list for men, another for women, indicate Sr or Sra/Srta on envelope); Plaza de Armas office also has philatelic section,

0900-1630, and small stamp museum (ask to see it). If sending a parcel, the contents must first be checked at the Post Office. Paper, tape etc on sale. **Telephones** The cheapest call centres are on Calles Bandera, Catedral and Santo Domingo, all near the Plaza de Armas. International calls from here are half the price of main offices, eg **Entel**, Huérfanos 1133, Mon-Fri 0830-2200, Sat 0900-2030, Sun 0900-1400, calls cheaper 1400-2200. **Useful addresses** Immigration For extension of tourist visa, or any enquiries regarding legal status, go to **Departamento de Extranjería**, Agustinas 1235, p 2 (opposite Palacio de la Moneda), T550 2400. Mon-Fri 0900-1200. Take a numbered ticket from the machine and wait your turn. There are 3 options: Informaciones, Residencias/Visas, Estampados; if unsure which to choose, take tickets for all three while waiting for Informaciones. **Policia Internacional**: For lost tourist cards, etc, see Touching down Box, p 601.

Around Santiago

Pomaire

In this little town 65 km west of Santiago, pottery can be bought and the artists can sometimes be seen at work. The area is rich in clay and the town is famous for its cider in the apple season, for its *chicha de uva* and for its Chilean dishes, recommended.

Vineyards

Several vineyards in the Santiago area can be visited. **Cousiño-Macul** ① *Av Quilin 7100, Peñalolén, on east outskirts of the city, offers tours Mon-Fri at 1100, 1500, Sat at 1100, phone first T351 4175, vtaparticular@cousinomacul.cl, US$9.50, getting there: take bus 390 from Alameda, or 391 from Merced, both marked Peñalolén.* **Concha y Toro** ① *at Pirque, near Puente Alto, 40 km south of Santiago, T476 5269, www.conchaytoro.cl/visit/f_tours.html, short tour (3 a day in Spanish, 3 in English), Mon-Sat, US$11, includes free wine glass and 2 tastings; book 4 days in advance, getting there: take Metro to Bellavista de La Florida (end of Línea 5), then blue Metrobus to Pirque.* The **Undurraga vineyard** ① *Santa Ana, southwest of Santiago, T372 2850, www.undurraga.cl, 4 tours in English and Spanish Mon-Fri, 3 on Sat, Sun (reserve 2 days in advance), US$9.50, getting there: take a Melipilla bus (but not Rutabus 78) to the entrance.* **Viña Santa Rita** ① *Padre Hurtado 0695, Alto Jahuel, Buín, 45 km south, T362 2520 (362 2590 weekends), rrivas@santarita.cl, good tour in English and Spanish, US$4 (free if you dine in the restaurant), reserve 2 days in advance, daily except Sun at specific times, getting there: take a bus from Terminal San Borja to Alto Jahuel.* Santiago tour operators (eg TourisTur) offer full-day tours to vineyards, US$40 for two.

Upper Maipo Valley

Southeast of Santiago is the rugged, green valley of the **Cajón del Maipo**. A road runs through the villages of San José de Maipo, Melocotón and San Alfonso, near which is the **Cascada de Animas** waterfall. At **El Volcán** (1,400 m), 21 km beyond San Alfonso, there are astounding views, but little else (the village was wiped away in a landslide). From El Volcán the road (very poor condition) runs east to the warm natural baths at **Baños Morales** ① *from Oct, US$3.80, brown water*; no mains electricity in the village. About 12 km further east up the mountain are **Baños Colina**, hot thermal springs. This area is popular at weekends and holiday times, but is otherwise deserted. There are horses for hire. If visiting this area or continuing further up the mountain, be prepared for military checks.

Ski resorts

There are six main ski resorts near Santiago, four of them around the mountain village of **Farellones**. Farellones, on the slopes of Cerro Colorado at 2,470 m, only 32 km from the capital and reached by road in under 90 minutes, was the first ski resort built in Chile. Now it is more of a service centre for the three other resorts, but it provides accommodation, has a good beginners area with fairly basic equipment for hire and is connected by lift to El Colorado. Popular at weekends, it has several large restaurants. It offers beautiful views for 30 km across 10 Andean peaks and incredible sunsets. Daily ski-lift ticket, US$22; a combined ticket for all four resorts is also available, US$40-50 depending on season. One-day return shuttles are available from Santiago, US$5; enquire **Ski Club Chile** ① *Goyenechea Candelaria 4750, Vitacura (north of Los Leones Golf Club), T211 7341.*

El Colorado *www.elcolorado.cl*, is 8 km further up Cerro Colorado and has a large ski lodge at the base, offering all facilities, and a restaurant higher up. There are nine lifts giving access to a large intermediate ski area with some steeper slopes. Lift ticket US$26. **La Parva**, nearby at 2,816 m, is the upper class Santiago weekend resort with 13 lifts, 0900-1730. Accommodation is in a chalet village and there are some good bars in high season. Good intermediate to advanced skiing, not suitable for beginners. Lift ticket, US$26; equipment rental, US$10-15 depending on quality.

Valle Nevado ① *T02-477 7000, www.vallenevado.com*, is 16 km from Farellones and owned by Spie Batignolles of France. It offers the most modern ski facilities in Chile. There are 34 runs accessed by nine lifts. The runs are well prepared and are suitable for intermediate level and beginners. There is a ski school and heli-skiing. Lift ticket US$30 weekdays, US$42 weekends. In summer, this is a good walking area, but altitude sickness can be a problem.

Portillo *www.skiportillo.cl*, 2,855 m, is 145 km north of Santiago and 62 east of Los Andes near the customs post on the route to Argentina. One of Chile's best-known resorts, Portillo is on the Laguna del Inca, 5½ km long and 1½ km wide; this lake, at an altitude of 2,835 m, has no outlet, is frozen over in winter, and its depth is not known. It is surrounded on three sides by accessible mountain slopes. The runs are varied and well prepared, connected by 12 lifts, two of which open up the off-piste areas. This is an excellent family resort, with a highly regarded ski school. Cheap packages can be arranged at the beginning of and out of season. Lift ticket US$20, equipment hire US$21. There are boats for fishing in the lake (afternoon winds can make the homeward pull much longer than the outward pull). Out of season this is another good area for walking, but get detailed maps before setting out.

Lagunillas is 67 km southeast of Santiago in the Cajón del Maipo. Accommodation is in the lodges of the **Club Andino de Chile** (see Skiing page 620). Lift ticket US$17; long T-bar and poma lifts, US$15; easy field. Being lower than the other resorts, its season is shorter, but it is also cheaper.

Santiago to Argentina

The route across the Andes via the Redentor tunnel is one of the major crossings to Argentina. Before travelling check on weather and road conditions beyond Los Andes. See International Buses, page 621. Some 77 km north of Santiago is the farming town of **Los Andes**. There is a monument to the Clark brothers, who built the Transandine Railway to Mendoza (now disused), and several workshops where hand-painted ceramics are made (the largest is Cala, Rancagua y Gen Freire). The town has several hotels and a tourist office on the main plaza, opposite the post office. The road to Argentina follows the Aconcagua valley for 34 km until it reaches the village of **Río Blanco** (1,370 m). East of Río Blanco the road climbs until Juncal where it zig-zags steeply through a series of 29 hairpin bends at the top of which is Portillo.

Border with Argentina Los Libertadores The old pass, with the statue of Christ the Redeemer (**Cristo Redentor**), is above the tunnel on the Argentine side. On the far side of the Andes the road descends 203 km to Mendoza. The 4 km long tunnel is open 24 hours September-May, 0700-2300 Chilean time June-August, toll US$3. The Chilean border post of Los Libertadores is at Portillo, 2 km from the tunnel. Bus and car passengers are dealt with separately. Bicycles must be taken through on a pick-up. There may be long delays during searches for fruit, meat and vegetables, which may not be imported into Chile. For Argentine formalities, see page 127. A Casa de Cambio is in the customs building in Portillo. Note that, entering Argentina, Chilean emigration, Argentine immigration and all customs formalities are done at the Argentine check point, while entering Chile you do everything on the Chilean side.

● Sleeping

Upper Maipo Valley *p624*
A-B pp **Refugio Alemán Lo Valdés**, 14 km east of El Volcán, just after Baños Morales, T245 4424 or 09-824 2123. Stone-built chalets in a splendid region, full board, generator, good food, good for mountain excursions, open all year.
E **Pensión Díaz**, Río Maipo s/n, T861 1496. Basic, good food.
E pp **Res Los Chicos Malos**, T288 5380. Comfortable, with breakfast, fresh bread, good meals, dirty bathrooms; free campsite.
D pp **Res El Tambo**, Baños Colina, full board, restaurant, also camping. No shops so take food.

Ski resorts *p625*
LL **Hotel Portillo**, Portillio, reservations: Renato Sánchez 4270, Las Condes, T02-263 0606, www.skiportillo.cl. Lakefront suites, family apartments and bunk rooms without or with bath (from B up), on the shore of Laguna del Inca. Cinema, nightclub, swimming pool, sauna and medical service, parking charges even if you go for a meal, self-service lunch, open all year.
L **Condominio Nueva Parva**, La Parva, reservations in Santiago at Av El Bosque Norte 0177, p 2, T02-339 8482 , www.laparva.cl. Good hotel and restaurant.
L **Posada Farellones**, Fareloones, T02-201 3704, www.skifarellones.com. Cosy and warm, Swiss-style, decent restaurant, transport to slopes.
B pp **Refugio Club Alemán Andino** see page 620. Hospitable, good food.

Hotel and apartment accommodation for weekly rental in El Colorado. Also several hotels (in our LL bracket) and restaurants in Valle Nevado.

Santiago to Argentina *p625*
L **Baños El Corazón**, at San Esteban, 2 km north of Los Andes, T034-482852. With full board, use of swimming pool but thermal baths extra, take bus San Esteban/El Cariño (US$0.50).

● Transport

Pomaire *p624*
Bus From Santiago take the Melipilla bus from outside the San Borja terminal, every few mins, US$1 each way, Rutabus 78 goes on the motorway, 1 hr, other buses via Talagante take 1 hr 25 mins (alight at side road to Pomaire, 2-3 km from town, colectivos every 10-15 mins – these buses are easier to take than the infrequent, direct buses).

Upper Maipo Valley *p624*
Bus From Bellavista La Florida on Metro Line 5 (follow signs to Transporte Intermodal) to San José de Maipo every 30 mins, about every 2 hrs to El Volcán, 2½ hrs; to **Baños Morales**, 0830 daily, returns 1830, US$3.80, 3 hrs; buy return on arrival to ensure seat back. Otherwise hitch.

Ski resorts *p625*
Bus From Santiago leave from Av Apoquindo 4900 (Escuela Militar Metro), daily from 0730 in season, essential to book in advance, **Ski Total**, T246 0156, US$15 return. **Centro de Esqui El Colorado**, T02-246 3344, leaves from same place daily at 0800 in season to Farellones and El Colorado. Also **Manzur Expediciones**, T777 4284. Wed, Sat and Sun 0830 from Baquedano metro in season to Farellones, Valle Nevado, El Colorado, Lagunillas and Portillo. It is easy to hitch from the junction of Av Las Condes/El Camino Farellones (petrol station in the middle), reached by a Barnechea bus. Portillo is easily reached by any bus from Santiago or Los Andes to **Mendoza**; you may have to hitch back. Public transport goes up to San José de Maipo, 17 km west of the resort. Bus from Metro Parque O' Higgins, Av Norte-Sur, or west side of Plaza Ercilla, every 15 mins, US$1, 2 hrs.

Santiago to Argentina *p625*
Bus Terminal is 1 block from the plaza. To **Santiago** US$2.50. To **Mendoza** (Argentina); Mendoza buses drop at **Portillo** ski resort, US$6.

Valparaíso and around

Sprawling over a crescent of forty-two hills (cerros) that rear up from the sea, Valparaíso, the capital of V Región, is unlike any other Chilean city. The main residential areas obey little order in their layout and the cerros have a bohemian, slightly anarchic atmosphere. Here you will find mansions mingling with some of Chile's worst slums and many legends of ghosts and spirits. It is an important naval base and, with the new Congress building, it is also the seat of the Chilean parliament. Pacific beaches close to the capital include the international resort of Viña del Mar, Reñaca, Concón and several others. On the same stretch of coast is the port of San Antonio. This coastline enjoys a Mediterranean climate; the cold sea currents and coastal winds produce much more moderate temperatures than in Santiago and the central valley. Rainfall is moderate in winter and the summers are dry and sunny.

Valparaíso → *Phone code: 032. Colour map 8, grid B1. Population: 290,000.*

First settled in 1542 (but not officially 'founded' until the end of the 20th century), Valparaíso became a small port used for trade with Peru. It was raided by pirates, including Sir Francis Drake, at least seven times in the colonial period. The city prospered from independence more than any other Chilean town. It was used in the 19th century by commercial agents from Europe and the US as their trading base in the southern Pacific and became a major international banking centre as well as the key port for US shipping between the East Coast and California (especially during the gold rush) and European ships that had rounded Cape Horn. Its decline was the result of the development of steam ships which stopped instead at the coal mines around Concepción and the opening of the trans-continental railway in the United States and then the Panama Canal in 1914. It then declined further owing to the development of a container port in San Antonio, the shift of banks to Santiago and the move of the middle-classes to nearby Viña del Mar, but Valparaíso is now reviving. It is officially the Cultural Capital of Chile and much work is being done to renovate the historical centre and museums and to build new galleries. The **tourist office** is in the Municipalidad building ① *Condell 1490, Oficina 102, Mon-Fri 0830-1400, 1530-1730 (closed March 2006)*. Also by Muelle Prat, the pier off Plaza Sotomayor. **Note:** There are two private kiosks at the bus terminal which give details on, and transport to, selected hotels. If you want impartial advice, go to one of the municipal offices.

Sights

Little of the city's colonial past survived the pirates, tempests, fires and earthquakes of the period. Most of the principal buildings date from after the devastating earthquake of 1906 (further serious earthquakes occurred in July 1971 and in March 1985) though some impression of its 19th century glory can be gained from the banking area of the lower town which is known as **El Plan**. This is the business centre, with once fine office buildings on narrow streets strung along the edge of the bay. Above, covering the hills ('cerros'), is a fantastic, multicoloured agglomeration of fine mansions, tattered houses and shacks, scrambled in oriental confusion along the narrow back streets. Superb views over the bay are offered from most of the 'cerros'. The lower and upper cities are connected by steep winding roads, flights of steps and 15 ascensores or funicular railways dating from the period 1883-1914. The most unusual of these is **Ascensor Polanco** (entrance from Calle Simpson, off Avenida Argentina, a few blocks from the bus station), which is in two parts, the first of which is a 160 m horizontal tunnel through the rock, the second a vertical lift to the summit on which there is a *mirador*. Bag-snatching is not uncommon in El Puerto (the old port). One of the best ways to see the lower city is on the historic **trolley bus**, which takes a circular route from the Congress to the port (US$0.30). Some of the cars, imported from Switzerland and the US, date from the 1930s. Another good viewpoint is from top of Ascensor Barón, near the bus terminal. **Note:** Between Plazas Echaurren and Aduana is the 'barrio chino' or red light district, pretty seedy at night.

The old heart of the city is the **Plaza Sotomayor**, dominated by the former Intendencia (Government House), now used as the seat of the admiralty. Opposite is a fine monument to the 'Heroes of Iquique' (see page 661). Bronze plaques on the Plaza illustrate the movement of the shoreline over the centuries and an opening, protected by a glass panel, shows parts of the original quay, uncovered when a car park was being excavated. The modern passenger quay is one block away (with poor, expensive handicraft shops) and nearby is the railway station for trains to Viña del Mar and Limache. The streets of El Puerto run on either side from Plaza Sotomayor. Serrano runs northwest for two blocks to the Plaza Echaurren, the oldest plaza in Valparaíso, once the height of elegance, today the home of sleeping drunks. Nearby stands the stucco church of **La Matriz**, built in 1842 on the site of the first church in the city. Remnants of the old colonial city can be found in the hollow known as El Puerto, grouped round La Matriz. **Museo del Mar Almirante Cochrane** ① *Merlet 195, Tue-Sun 1000-1800, free*, has temporary exhibitions and has good views over the port. Take Ascensor Cordillera from C Serrano, off Plaza Sotomayor, to Cerro Cordillera; at the top, on Plazuela Eleuterio Ramírez, take C Merlet to the left.

Further northwest, along Bustamante lies the Plaza Aduana from where Ascensor Artillería rises to the bold hill of **Cerro Artillería**, crowned by a park, the huge Naval Academy and the **Museo Naval** ① *Tue-Sun 1000-1800, US$0.85*, with naval history 1810-1880 and exhibitions on Chile's two naval heroes: Lord Cochrane and Arturo Prat. Avenida Altamirano runs along the coast at the foot of Cerro Playa Ancha to **Las Torpederas**, a popular, picturesque bathing beach. The **Faro de Punta Angeles**, on a promontory just beyond Las Torpederas, was the first lighthouse on the West Coast.

Both **Cerro Concepción** and **Cerro Alegre** have fine architecture and scenic beauty. Artists and students have long lived there, lending them a slightly bohemian feel, and the cerros are becoming deservedly very popular with visitors. A signed, 2-km walk starts at the top of Ascensor Turri (Cerro Concepción), leading to Paseo Mirador Gervasoni and Calle Pupudo through a labyrinth of narrow streets and stairs (the municipal tourist office has a good map). Two museums on these hills are: **Museo Municipal de Bellas Artes** ① *Paseo Yugoslavo, Cerro Alegre; take Ascensor El Peral from Plaza de la Justicia, off Plaza Sotomayor*. To reopen after refurbishment in 2006. Housed in the impressive Palacio Baburizza, it displays Chilean landscapes and seascapes and some modern paintings by Chilean and contemporary artists. **Casa de Lukas** ① *Paseo Mirador Gervasoni 448, Cerro Concepción, US$0.80, Tue-Sun, summer 1100-2200, winter 1030-1400, 1530-1830*. This beautiful villa is dedicated to the work of Chile's most famous caricaturists and is recommended.

Southeast of Plaza Sotomayor Calles Prat, Cochrane and Esmeralda run through the old banking and commercial centre to Plaza Aníbal Pinto, around which are several of the city's oldest bars and cafés. On Esmeralda, just past the Turri Clock Tower and Ascensor is the building of **El Mercurio de Valparaíso**, the world's oldest Spanish-language newspaper still in publication, first published in 1827. Further east is the Plaza Victoria with the Cathedral. Near Plaza Victoria is the **Museo de Historia Natural** and **Galería Municipal de Arte** ① *both in 19th century Palacio Lyon, Condell 1546, Tue-Fri 1000-1300, 1400-1800, Sat 1000-1800, Sun 1000-1400; former closed for renovation 2006*. Above Plaza Victoria on Cerro Bellavista is the **Museo al Cielo Abierto**, a collection of 20 street murals on the exteriors of buildings, designed by 17 of Chile's most distinguished contemporary artists. It is reached by the Ascensor Espíritu

Valparaíso

Sleeping	Residencial Eliana **8**	Sra Silva **10**
Casa Patricia **5**	Residencial El	Villa Kunterbunt **4**
Grand House **2**	Rincón Universal **7**	
Hostal Kolping **1**	Robinson Crusoe **3**	Eating
María Pizarro **6**	Sra Mónica Venegas **9**	Bambú **1**

0 metres 200
0 yards 200

Santo at the end of Calle Huito, or by walking downhill from Casa "La Sebastiana", former house of **Pablo Neruda** ① *Ferrari 692, Av Alemania, Altura 6900 on Cerro Florida, T256606, Tue-Fri 1030-1410, 1530-1800. Sat, Sun, holidays, 1030-1800; in summer, Tue-Sun 1030-1850, US$3.50, Tue-Fri students half-price; getting there: bus O from Av Argentina, US$0.40, or colectivo from Plazuela Ecuador, US$0.60*. This has interesting displays, guides in English, wonderful views and is worth a visit (see also his house at Isla Negra, below). It has an art gallery and a small café. East of Plaza Victoria, reached by following Calle Pedro Montt is Plaza O'Higgins (antiques market on Sunday mornings – see Shopping), which is dominated by the huge square arch of the imposing new Congreso Nacional. Small boats make 30-minute tours of the harbour from near Plaza Sotomayor (Spanish only). US$1.90 pp, wait for boat to fill up or pay US$15 to hire a whole boat, recommended if sunny.

● Sleeping

Valparaíso *p627, maps p628 and p630*
El Plan
AL-A Puerta de Alcalá, Pirámide 524, T227478, www.hotelpuertadealcala.cl. Good standard of facilities, reasonable restaurant.
C Condell, Pasaje Pirámide, T212788. Central, comfortable, somewhat noisy, breakfast extra.
C Hostal Kolping, Valdés Vergara 622, T216306, kolpingvalparaiso@yahoo.es. Without bath, pleasant, quiet, good value.

Cerros Alegre and Concepción
The best option is to stay on one of the Cerros, eg Alegre or Concepción. The bus terminal area is quite rough and dirty El Plan is noisy and not too safe at night. After dark C Chacabuco is frequented by rent boys and transvestites.
A Brighton, Paseo Atkinson 151, Co Concepción, T223513, brighton-valpo@ entelchile.net. New building in traditional style, good views, small rooms beautifully furnished, live tango and

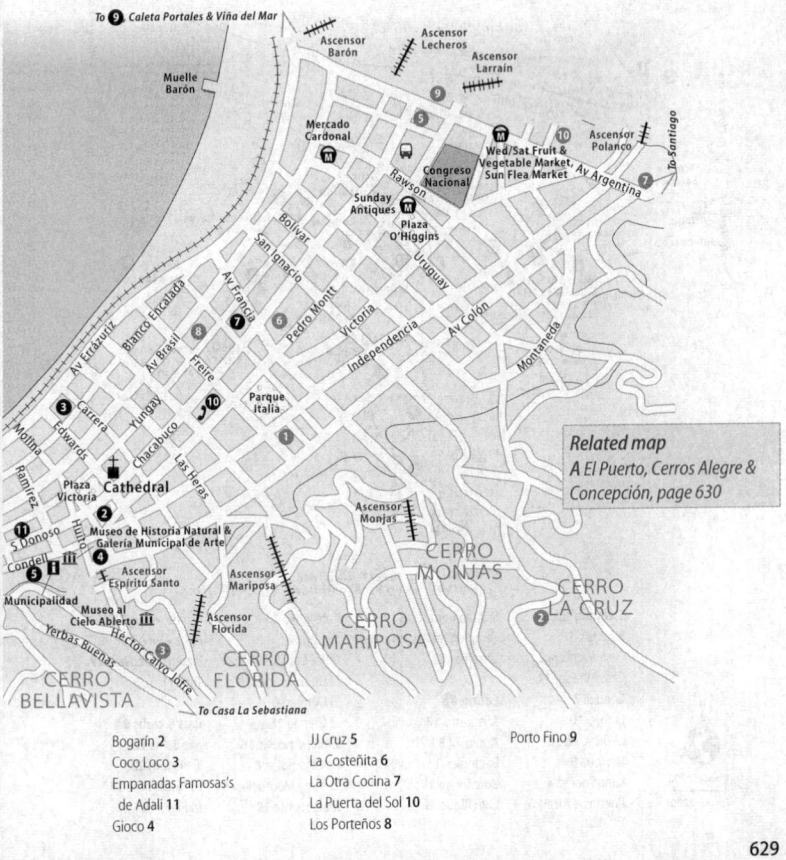

Bogarín **2**
Coco Loco **3**
Empanadas Famosas's de Adali **11**
Gioco **4**

JJ Cruz **5**
La Costeñita **6**
La Otra Cocina **7**
La Puerta del Sol **10**
Los Porteños **8**

Porto Fino **9**

bolero music in the bar at weekends, good restaurant (not cheap).

A-B Café Vinilo, Almte Montt 448, T230665, www.cafevinilo.cl. New loft and rooms at this popular café.

A-B Templeman Apartments, Pierre Loti 65B, Co Concepción, T257067, chantalder ementeria@hotmail.com. Stylish self-contained apartments, stylish, peaceful. Recommended.

B-C Luna Sonrisa, Templeman 833, Co Alegre, T734117, www.lunasonrisa.cl. Some rooms with private bath, **E** pp in first-class dorms, newly restored, bright, comfortable, large kitchen, patio, tours arranged, English, French spoken, good breakfast (fresh fruit/juice, wholemeal bread, real coffee etc), helpful and informative, already popular and highly recommended. Also very comfortable self-contained apartment on top floor, all mod cons, **A**, sleeps 2 or 3. Owner is author of *Footprint Chile*.

C Casa Aventura, Pasaje Gálvez 11, off C Urriola, Cerro Concepción, T755963, www.casaventura.cl.

Dorms **E** pp. Popular backpacker hostel in restored traditional house. No single rooms, shared bath, good breakfast, German and English spoken, Spanish classes offered, good value tours, informative, kitchen facilities. Generally recommended, but check beds before choosing.

C Casa Mirador, Abtao 457, T257098, hostalcasamirador@yahoo.es. Shared bath, with breakfast, good views.

C La Bicyclette, Almte Montt 213, Cerro Alegre, T222415. Basic, bright rooms, shared bath, book exchange, lovely patio, French run, rents bicycles.

C La Nona, Galos 660, Cerro Alegre, T495706. Comfortable, welcoming, plenty of information, English spoken.

C Sr Juan Carrasco, Abtao 668, Co Concepción, T210737. Dorms **E** pp. Dingy but great views from terrace, good meeting place.

Other Cerros

L-AL Robinson Crusoe, Héctor Calvo Jofre 389, Co Bellavista. T495499, www.hotels.tk/robinson.

El Puerto, Cerros Alegre & Concepción

Sleeping
Brighton 1
Casa Aventura 2
Casa Mirador 11
Condell 7
El Yoyo 10
La Bicyclette 8
La Nona 9
Luna Sonrisa 4
Puerta de Alcalá 5

Sr Juan Carrasco 3
Templeman Apartments 6
Ultramar 12

Eating
Allegretto 17
Apolo 77 8
Bar Inglés 1
Bote Salvavidas 2
Café Riquet 3

Café Vinilo 13
Cinzano 4
Color Café 5
El Desayunador 18
El Dominó 6
El Gremio 15
Gloria Vuscovic 16
La Colombina 8
Le Filou Montpellier 9
Mastodonte 19

Pan de Magia 21
Pasta e Vino 20
Pizzería Napolitana 7
Turri 11

Bars & clubs
Axe Bahía 12
El Irlandés 22
La Piedra Feliz 14
La Playa 10

0 metres 200
0 yards 200

Beautiful rooms and spectacular views, peaceful, many rooms have shared bath.

L-B Ultramar, Pérez 173, Cerro Cárcel, T210000, www.hotelultramar.cl. Boutique hotel in a converted Italiante building (1907), modern design, buffet breakfast, free internet, café.

A The Grand House, Federico Varela 25, Cerro La Cruz, T212376, www.thegrandhouse.cl. Rooms cheaper with shared bath, excellent breakfast, charming house, almost Victorian decor, "a true gem".

B-C Villa Kunterbunt, Av Quebrada Verde 192, Co Playa Ancha,T288873. Shared rooms **D**. Lovely building, fine views from top floor (ask for La Torre), with first-class breakfast, garden, English and German spoken, very helpful. Highly recommended. Bus 1, 2, 5, 6, 17, 111, N, colectivo 150, 151, 3b all pass by.

D El Yoyo, Subida Ecuador 355, Co Yungay, T591087, elyoyo355@latinmail.com. **E** pp in dorms, refurbished in 2005-06, with breakfast, kitchen facilities, new bar area, friendly, English spoken.

Near the terminal
C Casa Patricia,12 de Febrero 315, T220290, T09-6347239 (mob). Shared hot showers, family accommodation, use of kitchen, good local knowledge.

C Res El Rincón Universal, Argentina 825, T/F235184, www.elrinconuniversal.cl. With breakfast, laundry, study, cable TV, internet, good, the area can be intimidating at night.

E pp María Pizarro, Chacabuco 2340, Casa No 2, T230791. Lovely rooms, central, quiet, kitchen.

E pp Res Eliana, Av Brasil 2164, T755872. Large old house, without breakfast, slightly rough area.

E pp Sra Mónica Venegas, Av Argentina 322, Casa B, T215673, 2 blocks from bus terminal.

E pp Sra Silvia, Pje La Quinta 70, Av Argentina, 3 blocks from Congress, T216592. Quiet, kitchen facilities. Not safe at night.

⊘ Eating

Valparaíso *p627, maps p628 and p630*
El Plan
¶¶¶ Bote Salvavidas, by Muelle Prat. Elegant fish restaurant overlooking the port.

¶¶¶ Coco Loco, Blanco 1781 pisos 21 y 22, T227614. Plush revolving restaurant 70 m above the bay, extensive menu.

¶¶ Bar Inglés, Cochrane 851 (entrance also on Blanco Encalada). Historic bar dating from the early 1900s, a chart shows the ships due in port. Good food and drink. Recommended.

¶¶ La Costeñita, Blanco 86. Good seafood.

¶¶ La Otra Cocina, Yungay 2250, near Francia. Good seafood, cosy, good service.

¶¶ Los Porteños, Valdivia 169 and Cochrane 102. Perennial favourite for fish and shellfish, terse service but good food.

¶¶ At Caleta Membrillo, 2 km northwest of Plaza Sotomayor (take any Playa Ancha bus), there are several good fish restaurants including **Club Social de Pescadores**, Altamirano 1480, good, and **El Membrillo**.

¶¶-¶ Cinzano, Plaza Aníbal Pinto 1182. The oldest bar in Valparaíso, also serving food. Flamboyant live music at weekends, noted for tango (no dancing by guests allowed). Service can be awful.

¶ Bambú, Pudeto 450, Mon-Sat 1000-1800. Vegetarian lunches only.

¶ Calaguala, 2nd floor of the market (off Plaza Echaurren). There are many cheap restaurants here, all cheap with large portions, but this is a cut above the rest (closed in the evenings).

¶ El Dominó, Cumming 67. Traditional, serves empanadas, chorillanas etc.

¶ Empanadas Famosas's de Adali, S Donoso 1379-81. Some of the best empanadas in Valparaíso.

¶ Gioco, Molina 586-B (in yoga centre, no sign). Vegetarian set lunches with fruit juices.

¶ JJ Cruz, Condell 1466. Valparaíso's most traditional restaurant/museum, famous for its chorillana, open all night, very popular.

¶ La Puerta del Sol, Montt 2033. Traditional Chilean dishes, great chips served outside.

¶ Mastodonte, Esmeralda 1139. No nonsense, very good value, traditional food in incredibly kitsch surroundings. Excellent service and cheap beer.

¶ There are many super-cheap restaurants on Pedro Montt and behind the bus station.

Bogarín, Plaza Victoria. Great juices and snacks.

Café do Brasil, Condell 1342. Excellent coffee, juices, sandwiches.

Café Riquet, Plaza Aníbal Pinto. Comfortable, expensive, good coffee and breakfast.

Cioccolata, Condell 1235. Good coffee and cakes.

Hespería, Victoria 2250. Classic old-time coffee emporium, the internet annex makes a strange contrast.

La Pérgola Café, Almte Montt 51, near Plaza Aníbal Pinto. Small expensive place serving great salads and quiches, cakes, pastries, also wine and beer, local artwork and jewellery for sale.

Cerros Alegre and Concepción
¶¶¶ Apolo 77, Paseo Yugoeslavo 15, Cerro Alegre, below La Colombina in the same building. Wee prepared dishes using local ingredients but international influences. Recommended.

¶¶¶ La Colombina, Paseo Yugoeslavo 15, Cerro Alegre, T236254. Fish and seafood, good food and wines, fine views.

ΨΨΨ **Pasta e Vino**, Templeman 352, Cerro Concepción, T496187. Wonderfully inventive, tasty pasta dishes. Advance booking essential.
ΨΨΨ **Turri**, Templeman 147, Cerro Concepción, T259198. Reasonable food, slightly snooty service, wonderful views, something of a tourist trap.
ΨΨ **Allegretto**, Pilcomayo 529, Cerro Concepción, T968839. Top notch pizzas, also ice-cream. Delivery service.
ΨΨ **Pizzería Napoletana**, Lautaro Rosas y Templeman. Pizza and pasta, good (wine and service less good).
ΨΨ **Poble Nou**, Urriola 476, Cerro Alegre. Catalan tapas bar.
ΨΨ-Ψ **Café Vinilo**, Almte Montt 448. Good mix of traditional food and innovation, lunchtime only, lively, with international feel, house beers, art displays, good place to meet people.
Ψ **El Gremio**, Pasaje Gálvez 173. Trendy, ultra-modern bar serving inventive lunches. Vegetarian available.
Ψ **Gloria Vuscovic**, Monte Alegre 280. Offers good set lunches in a delightful old house.
Ψ **Le Filou Montpellier**, Almte Montt 382. French-run, Sat menu deservedly popular.
Color Café, Papudo 526, Co Concepción. Cosy arty café serving tea and real coffee, fresh juice, good cakes, snacks and all-day breakfasts, regular live music, art exhibits, local art and craft for sale.
El Desayunador, Almte Montt y Dimalow. Breakfast bar open early. Wide range of teas, cakes etc, also serves vegetarian lunches.
Lavanda Café, Almte Montt 454. Enjoy an expresso while having your clothes washed!
Pan de Magia, Almte Montt 738 y Templemann, Co Alegre. Artesanal bakery selling cakes, cookies, and by far the best wholemeal bread in town.

Other Cerros

ΨΨΨ **Porto Fino**, Bellamar 301, Co Esperanza, T629939. Great views, classiest restaurant.
ΨΨΨ-ΨΨ **Gato Tuerto**, in Fundación Valparaíso building, Calvo 205, Co Bellavista. Thai and oriental food. Great views.
Gori, Av Alemania 6985 (on the way to La Sebastiana). Excellent value for *empanadas*.

Bars and clubs

Valparaíso *p627, maps p628 and p630*

El Plan

As a general rule there are 3 main sectors for nightlife in El Plan: **Errázuriz** is for live music/dancing, mixed crowd, slightly more classy than the rest; between Plaza Sotomayor and Plaza Echauren are young/studenty pubs, some with live music; and **Subida Ecuador** is loud and full of boozed-up young lads (single women beware!). Calle Ecuador has dozens of bars, of varying quality; some can be very rough, eg El Muro.
Axe Bahía, Errázuriz 1084. Salsa and Cuban music.
El Irlandés, on Blanco. Decent Irish-run Irish bar with bitter on tap and a good selection of beer, live music at weekends.
La Piedra Feliz, Errázuriz 1054. Every type of music depending on the evening, large pub, live music area, and dance floor, entrance US$5.
La Playa, Serrano 567, near Plaza Sotomayor. Old English-style bar, live music, student crowd.

Cerros Alegre and Concepción

Brighton (see Sleeping). Great views at night.

Festivals and events

New Year is celebrated by a spectacular firework display launched from the harbour and naval ships, which is best seen from the Cerros. The display is televised nationally and about a million visitors come to the city at this time. Book well in advance; accommodation doubles or trebles in price for the night, but it's well worth it: dinner with a view US$50-170).

Shopping

Valparaíso *p627, maps p628 and p630*
Bookshops Crises, on Pedro Montt by the bus terminal. Excellent new and second-hand bookshop, small selection in English. **Cummings 1**, just off Plaza Aníbal Pinto. Wide selection of new and used books in English and other languages. **Librería Ivens**, on Plaza Aníbal Pinto. Good general bookshop, the oldest in Valparaíso.
Department stores Ripleyand Falabella, both on Plaza Victoria.
Markets Large antiques market on Plaza O'Higgins every Sun. Very good selection, especially old shipping items. Along Av Argentina there is a huge, colourful fruit and vegetable market on Wed and Sat and a crowded flea market on Sun. Good locally made handicrafts on Cerros Alegre and Concepción.

Activities and tours

Turismo Nuevo Mundo, Blanco 951, p 3, T253817, www.turismonuevomundo.cl. Local tours, English spoken, has offices in Argentina and US.

For an explanation of the sleeping and eating price codes used in this guide, see inside the front cover. Other relevant information is found in Essentials pages 604-605.

⊖ Transport

Valparaíso *p627, maps p628 and p630*
Ascensores US$0.15-0.20, slightly more expensive going up than down.
Bus US$0.35 within El Plan, US$0.45 to Cerros, US$0.60 to Viña del Mar from C Errázuriz. Green bus 'Verde Mar' (O) from Av Argentina near the bus terminal to Plaza Aduana gives fine panoramic views of the city and bay.

Long distance terminal is on Pedro Montt 2800 block, corner of Rawson, 1 block from Av Argentina; plenty of buses between terminal and Plaza Sotomayor. To **Santiago**, 1 hr 20 mins, US$5.70, with **Tur-Bus**, **Cóndor** and **Pullman** from Pajaritos in Santiago, frequent (book on Sat to return to the capital on Sun, or buy a return ticket, US$8.40). From the **airport**, take a bus to Pajaritos, US$2.30, cross the platform and take a bus to Valparaíso. To return to the airport, catch any Santiago bus and ask to be let off at the 'parada de taxis' before the Cruce de Pudahuel. Taxis wait here to go to the airport for US$6.65 (about 7 mins' ride, compared with an hour if you go into Santiago). Taxis run 0700-2000 (2300 in summer). Only take a taxi with an official Airport Taxi sticker (pirates overcharge).

To **Concepción**, 8 hrs, US$10. To **Puerto Montt**, 14 hrs, US$18; to **Pucón** about 12 hrs, US$15 (Tur-Bus). To **La Serena**, 7 hrs, US$18. To **Calama**, 24 hrs, US$25. To **Arica**, 29 hrs, US$25, also salón cama services. To Argentina: to **Mendoza** 4 companies, 7 hrs, US$10-20.
Taxi More expensive than Santiago: a short run under 1 km costs US$1. Taxi colectivos, slightly more expensive than buses, carry sign on roof indicating route, very convenient.
Train Regular service on Merval, the Valparaíso metropolitan line between Valparaíso, **Viña del Mar** (US$0.40), **Quilpué** and **Limache** (US$0.75); services every 30 mins. Trains are 70 years old, made by FIAT, but are being replaced by a new fleet. Work on a new tunnel through Viña means slight delays (until sometime in 2006).

❶ Directory

Valparaíso *p627, maps p628 and p630*
Airline offices LAN, Esmeralda 1048, T251441.
Banks Banks open 0900 to 1400, but closed on Sat. Many Redbanc ATMs on Blanco and Prat, and also one in the bus terminal. Casas de Cambio: Many on Esmeralda; also **Exprinter**, Prat 887 (the building with the clocktower at junction with Cochrane). Good rates, no commission on TCs, open Mon-Fri 0930-1400, 1600-1830. New York, Prat 659. Best rates for US$ and euro cash on 3rd floor of stock exchange, Urriola y Prat. **Cultural centres** Parque Cultural ex-Cárcel de Valparaíso, C Castro s/n, Cerro Cárcel, T219179, www.culturart.cl, or see www.redcultural.cl for programmes. The converted former prison has guided tours, exhibitions, shows, lecturers, etc. Opposite is the Disidentes cemetery, worth a visit, good views. **Instituto Chileno- Norteamericano**, Esmeralda 1069. Library, free internet for members, regular cinema nights. **Embassies and consulates** Argentina, Blanco 890, of 204, T213691. Germany, Blanco 1215, of 1102, T256749. Peru, Errázuriz 1178, of 71, T253403. Spain, Brasil 1589, p 2, T214466. Sweden, Errázuriz 940, T250305. UK, Blanco 1190, p 5, T/F213063. **Internet** Average price US$0.80 per hr. Many places in El Plan. On Cerro Alegre, at Templeman y Urriola. **Post offices** Pedro Montt entre San Ignacio y Bolívar. Also on C Prat. **Telephones** Lots of cheap call centres in El Plan, shop around.

Viña del Mar and around

→ *Phone code: 032. Colour map 8, grid B1. Population: 304,203.*
Northeast of Valparaíso via Avenida España which runs along a narrow belt between the shore and precipitous cliffs is one of South America's leading seaside resorts, Viña del Mar. A mixture of fashionable seaside destinations and fishing communities lines the coast to the north, while south of Valparaíso are more popular resorts at the mouth of the Río Maipo. Pablo Neruda's famous seaside home at Isla Negra is also found here. For a change from the sea visit La Campana national park with its native woodlands, panoramic views and Darwinian associations. For **tourist information** in Viña del Mar try Sernatur ① *Valparaíso 507, of 305, T683355, infovalparaiso@sernatur.cl*. Municipal office on Plaza Vergara.

The older part of Viña del Mar is situated on the banks of a dried-up estuary, the Marga Marga, which is crossed by bridges. Around Plaza Vergara and the smaller Plaza Sucre to its south are the **Teatro Municipal** (1930) and the exclusive **Club de Viña**, built in 1910. The municipally owned Quinta Vergara, formerly the residence of the shipping entrepreneur Francisco Alvarez, lies two blocks south. The **Palacio Vergara**, in the gardens, houses the **Museo de Bellas Artes** and the **Academia de Bellas Artes** ① *T680618, museum hours Tue-Sun 1000-1400, 1500-1800, US$0.50*. Part of the grounds is a playground, and there

633

is a modern outdoor auditorium where concerts are performed in the summer, and in February an international song festival, one of the premier music events is held. Tickets from the Municipal theatre, or Ticketmaster.

On a headland overlooking the sea is **Cerro Castillo**, the summer palace of the President of the Republic. Just north, on the other side of the lagoon is the Casino, built in the 1930s and set in beautiful gardens, US$5 to enter (open all year). It now includes a five-star hotel, see Sleeping, below.

The main beaches, Acapulco and Mirasol are located to the north, but south of Cerro Castillo is Caleta Abarca, also popular. The coastal route north to Reñaca provides lovely views over the sea. East of the centre is the **Valparaíso Sporting Club** with a racecourse (meetings every Friday) and playing fields. North of here in the hills are the **Granadilla Golf Club** and a large artificial lake, the **Laguna Sausalito**, adjacent to which is the **Estadio Sausalito** ① *US$2.50, children under 11, US$1.75, getting there: take colectivo No 19 from C Viana (home to Everton soccer team, among many other sporting facilities).* It has an excellent tourist complex with swimming pools, boating, tennis courts, sandy beaches, water skiing, restaurants, etc.

Museo de la Cultura del Mar ① *in the Castillo Wolff, on the coast near Cerro Castillo, T625427, Tue-Sat 1000-1300, 1430-1800, Sun 1000-1400*, contains a collection on the life and work of the novelist and maritime historian, Salvador Reyes. **Palacio Rioja** ① *Quillota 214, Tue-Sun, visitors 1000-1330, 1500-1730, US$1*, was built in 1906 by a prominent local family and now used for official municipal receptions, ground floor preserved in its original state. Recommended. **Museo Sociedad Fonk** ① *C 4 Norte 784, Tue-Fri 1000-1800, Sat-Sun 1000-1400, US$1.50, children US$0.30*, is an archaeological and natural history museum, with objects from Easter Island and the Chilean mainland, including Mapuche silver. Recommended.

Jardín Botánico Nacional ① *8 km southeast of the city, US$1, getting there: take bus 20 from Plaza Vergara or the Merval train to Laboral.* Formerly the estate of the nitrate baron Pascual Baburizza, this is now administered by Conaf. Covering 405 ha, it contains over 3,000 species from all over the world and a collection of Chilean cacti, but the species are not labelled. It's a good place for a picnic.

Viña del Mar

Sleeping 🛏
Andalué 2
Cap Ducal 3
Del Mar 4
Gala 5
Genrosz 7
Girasoles de
   Agua Santa 11
Offenbacher Hof 6
Residencial Blanchait 8
Residencial Capric 9
Residencial Victoria 8
Residencial Villarica 10

Eating 🍴
Africa 1
Alster 2
Café Big Ben 6
Café Journal 3
Club Giacomo 8
Fellini 9
La Flor de Chile 7
Las Delicias del Mar 4
Mangiarbene 9
Pizzería Mama Mía 4
Samoiedo 5
Shawarma Kabab 10

Resorts north of Viña del Mar

North of Viña del Mar the coast road runs through **Las Salinas**, a popular beach between two towering crags, **Reñaca** (long beach, upmarket, good restaurants) and **Cochoa**, where there is a sealion colony 100 m offshore, to **Concón** (18 km). Beware if cycling from Valparaíso, the road is very bad with lots of traffic. There is a much faster inland road, between Viña del Mar and Concón, on the southern shore of a bay at the mouth of the Río Aconcagua. It has six beaches and is famous for its seafood restaurants. Horses can be hired here. **Quintero** (*Population 16,000*) 23 km north of Concón, is a slightly dilapidated fishing town on a rocky peninsula with lots of small beaches (hotels and residenciales).

Horcón (also known locally as Horcones) is set back in a cove surrounded by cliffs, a pleasant small village, mainly of wooden houses. On the beach young travellers sell cheap and unusual jewellery and trinkets, while horses drag the small fishing boats out of the sea. Vegetation is tropical with many cacti on the cliff tops. Packed out in January-February, the rest of the year it is a charming place, populated by fishermen and artists. A new condominium by Caucau beach has off-set some of the charm of the village. Further north is well-to-do **Maitencillo** (*Population 1,200*), with a wonderful long beach, heaving in high summer but a ghost town off season. Some 14 km beyond is **Zapallar** (*Population 2,200*) a fashionable resort. A hint of its former glory is given by a number of fine mansions along Avenida Zapallar. At **Cachagua**, 3 km south, a colony of penguins may be viewed from the northern end of the beach. **Papudo** (*Phone code 033, Population 2,500*), 10 km further north, was the site of a naval battle in November 1865 in which the Chilean vessel Esmeralda captured the Spanish ship Covadonga. Following the arrival of the railway Papudo rivalled Viña del Mar as a fashionable resort in the 1920s but it has long since declined. With its lovely beach and fishing port, it is an idyllic spot.

Resorts south near the mouth of the Río Maipo

San Antonio is a commercial centre for this part of the coast. It is a container and fishing port and is the terminal for the export of copper brought by rail from El Teniente mine, near Rancagua. To the south are the resorts of Llolleo and Rocas de Santo Domingo. **Cartagena**, 8 km north of San Antonio, is the most popular resort on this part of the coast. The centre is around the hilltop Plaza de Armas. To the south is the picturesque Playa Chica, overlooked by many of the older hotels and restaurants; to the north is the Playa Larga. Between the two a promenade runs below the cliffs; high above hang old houses, some in disrepair but offering spectacular views. Cartagena is packed sas n in summer, but out of season it is a good centre for visiting nearby resorts of Las Cruces, El Tabo and El Quisco. There are many hotels and bus connections are good. For more information on Cartagena, look at www.cartagena-chile.cl

North of Cartagena in the village of **Isla Negra** is the beautifully-restored **Museo-Casa Pablo Neruda** ① T035-461284, *to book English guide, open 1000-1800 at weekends, phone to check (see also his house, La Chascona, under Santiago Sights, and La Sebastiana, under Valparaíso Sights), US$5. It is open for guided tours in Spanish, or English, Tue-Sun 1000-2000 in summer, rest of year Tue-Fri 1000-1400, 1500-1800.* Bought by Neruda in 1939, and constantly added to over time, this house, overlooking the sea, was his writing retreat in his later years. It contains artefacts gathered by Neruda from all over the world. Neruda and his last wife, Mathilde, are buried here; the touching gravestone is beside the house. The house has a good café specializing in Neruda's own recipes.

Parque Nacional La Campana

This 8,000-ha park *US$2*, includes Cerro La Campana (1,828 m) which Darwin climbed in 1836 and Cerro El Roble (2,200 m). Some of the best views in Chile can be seen from the top. Near Ocoa there are areas of Chilean palms (*kankán* – which give edible, walnut-sized coconuts in March-April), now found in its natural state in only two locations in Chile. There are three entrances: at Granizos (from which the hill is climbed), reached by paved road from Limache, 4 km west, via Olmué; at Cajón Grande (with natural bathing pools), reached by unpaved road which turns off the Olmué-Granizos road; at Palmar de Ocoa to the north reached by unpaved road (10 km) leading off the Pan-American Highway at Km 100 between Hijuelas and Llaillay.

● Sleeping

Viña del Mar *p633, map p634*
There are lots of small hotels in the Norte-Poniente quadrant, mostly **B**; discounts often possible in low season. There are also lots of cheaper places around Von Schroeders y Valparaíso, but this can be a rough area at night. Out of season agencies rent furnished apartments. In season it's cheaper to stay in Valparaíso.

LL Hotel del Mar, Perú y Los Héroes, T500600, www.hoteldelmar.cl. Very expensive, luxurious hotel on the upper floors of the casino, panoramic views, suites, pool, spa, tours, several restaurants.

LL-L Gala, Arlegui 273, loc 10, T321500, www.galahotel.cl. All mod-cons in excellent suites.

AL Cap Ducal, Marina 51, T626655, www.capducal.cl. Old mansion charm, with an elegant restaurant, good seafood.

A-B Offenbacher Hof, Balmaceda 102, T621483, www.offenbacher-hof.cl. A good place to stay, peaceful, clean and helpful. Recommended.

B Andalué, 6 Poniente 124, T684147, F684148. With breakfast, central. Recommended.

B Genross, Paseo Monterrey 18, T661711, genrosshotel@hotmail.com. Beautiful mansion, airy rooms, garden patio and sitting room, informative, English spoken.

B Girasoles de Agua Santa, Pasaje Monterey 78, off Agua Santa, T482339, www.hostalgirasoles.cl. Slightly upscale B&B in a quiet sidestreet, **D** pp with HI card, shared bath, pleasant, but not so convenient for the beaches (25 mins walk). Also has a branch in Cerro Alegre, Valparaíso.

C Res Blanchait, Valparaíso 82A, T974949, www.blanchait.cl. With breakfast, hot water, good service.

C-D Res Capric, von Schroeders 39, T978295. Dark rooms, with breakfast, TV (special rates for HI card holders).

D Res Victoria, Valparaíso 40, T977370. With bath and breakfast, central.

D Res Villarica, Arlegui 172, T881484, F942807. Shared bath, good.

Resorts north of Viña del Mar *p635*
Concón
Several *cabañas* and motels.

Horcón
Lots of cabañas in Horcón, generally **B-C** for 4 people, shop around.

C Arancibia, T796169. D without bath, pleasant gardens, good food.

C-D Juan Esteban, Pasaje Miramar, Casa 2, T796056, www.juanesteban.cl. English, Portuguese, Italian spoken, nice terrace with view, rooms and fully equipped cabañas, E pp for 4-6 people. Recommended.

Papudo
Many more on Chorrillos.

B Carande, Chorrillos 89, T791105. Best in town, quiet.

B De Peppino, Concha 609, T791108. Cabins for 4-6 people.

Resorts south near the mouth of the Río Maipo *p635*
A Rocas de Santo Domingo, La Ronda 130, San Antonio, T444356, F444494. Generally good, including breakfast, but staff unfriendly, restaurant, 20 minutes to sea.

D Violeta, Condell 140, Cartagena, T450372. Swimming pool, good views.

E pp Hostal Casa Azul, Av Santa Luisa s/n, Isla Negra, T035-461154. Shared bath, hot showers, garden, kitchen and laundry facilities, breakfast included, helpful. Highly recommended.

E pp Res Carmona, Playa Chica, Cartagena, T450485. Small rooms, basic, good value.

E pp Res Paty's, Alcalde Cartagena 295, Cartagena, T450469. Nice spot, good value.

● Eating

Viña del Mar *p633, map p634*
Many good bars and restaurants on and around San Martín between 2 and 8 Norte. Cheap bars and restaurants around Calle Valparaíso and Von Schroeders. Not too safe at night.

♥♥♥ Fellini, 3 Norte 88. Fresh pasta, good.

♥♥♥ Mangiarbene, 6 Poniente 121, T686358. Good pastas, fish and seafood, good service, desserts and wine selection.

♥♥♥-♥♥ Las Delicias del Mar, San Martín 459. Award-winning seafood restaurant, "brilliant food, wine and service".

♥♥ Pizzería Mama Mía, San Martín 435. Good pizzas and good value.

♥ Africa, Valparaíso 324. Extraordinarily kitsch façade, pasta and fast food.

♥ Café Journal, Alvarez near Von Schroeders. Great set lunch, good beer, student favourite at night. Recommended.

● *For an explanation of the sleeping and eating price codes used in this guide, see inside the front*
● *cover. Other relevant information is found in Essentials pages 604-605.*

¶ Club Giacomo, Villanelo 131. A Viña institution, traditional set lunches with a pool hall annex.
¶ La Flor de Chile, 8 Norte 607 y 1 Poniente. Good, typical Chilean food.
¶ Shawarma kabab, Ecuador 255. Cheap, authentic middle-eastern fare.

Cafés
Alster, Valparaíso 225. Elegant but pricey.
Café Big Ben, Valparaíso 469 in Galería Cristal. Good coffee, good food.
Samoiedo, Valparaíso 637. Confitería, old-time café.

Resorts north of Viña del Mar *p635*
Concón
Good seafood empanadas at bars. Excellent seafood restaurants at Caleta Higuerilla, Av Borgoño (**Aquí Jaime** being the most expensive but also the best), and at La Boca (eg **El Loro**, **Ementerio**); cheaper picadas in Alto Higuerillas.

Horcón
Many places serve lunch from the catch of the day.
¶¶ El Ancla, cabañas and restaurant. Recommended.
¶ El Roti Schop. Famous for its *empanadas*.

Papudo
¶¶ La Maison des Fous, Blanco 151, restaurant/piano bar, unusual, good food.

① Bars and clubs

Viña del Mar *p633*, map *p634*
Barlovento, 2 Norte y 5 Poniente. The designer bar in Viña, on 3 floors with a lovely roof terrace, serves great pizzas.

▲ Activities and tours

Resorts north of Viña del Mar *p635*
Ritoque Expediciones, just north of Concón, T032-816344/0-82099734. Horse riding, 1 or half-day trips to lakes, sand dunes, scrubland, beaches, you can help herd cows or just gallop, also full moon rides, can collect from Valparaíso or Viña, English spoken. Highly recommended.

⊖ Transport

Viña del Mar *p633*, map *p634*
Bus Terminal at Av Valparaíso y Quilpué (rebuilt in 2005). To **Santiago**, US$5.50, 1½ hrs, frequent, same companies as for Valparaíso from Pajaritos in Santiago, heavily booked in advance for travel on Sun afternoons. Long distance services: prices and itineraries similar to Valparaíso. **Note**: Beware pickpockets around shops in the terminal.
Train Services on the Valparaíso Metropolitan line (Merval) stop at Viña (details under Valparaíso).

Resorts north of Viña del Mar *p635*
Bus From Valparaíso and Viña del Mar: to **Concón** several, eg bus 1, 111 or 10, US$0.60; to **Quintero** and **Horcón**, **Sol del Pacífico**, every 30 mins, US$1.20, 2 hrs; to **Zapallar** and **Papudo**, **Sol del Pacífico**, 4 a day (2 before 0800, 2 after 1600), US$3. All of these from Av Libertad in Viña, or Errázuriz in Valparaíso.

Resorts south near the mouth of the Río Maipo *p635*
Bus From San Antonio: buses to **Valparaíso**, Pullman Bus, every 30 mins until 2000, US$3; to **Santiago**, Pullman Bus, every 20 mins in summer, US$3. Regular bus services to **Isla Negra** from Santiago (**Pullman Bus**) and Valparaíso (**Pullman Lago Peñuelas**), 1½ hrs, US$3.

Parque Nacional La Campana *p635*
Euro Express micros from C Errázuriz in Valparaíso and 1 Norte in Viña del Mar go to within 1 km of Granizos and Cajón Grande, US$1, 1½ hrs, or take the train to Limache (1 hr), and a micro or any colectivo marked "Olmue" to Granizos. No public transport to Ocoa. Get a bus to La Calera and bargain with a taxi or colectivo driver. Expect to pay US$12-15.

① Directory

Viña del Mar *p633*, map *p634*
Banks Many Redbanc ATMs on Libertad near 7 y 8 Norte; also on C Valparaíso (but this is not a safe area at night). Many casas de cambio on Arlegui.
Cultural centres Centro Cultural, Libertad 250 in the Palacio Carrasco, holds regular exhibitions.
Internet Several the length of Calle Valparaíso, prices range from US$0.60-0.80 per hr.
Telephones Several on C Valparaíso.

North of Santiago

Along the coast is a mixture of fishing villages, deserted beaches and popular resorts, while inland the scenery is wonderfully dramatic but little visited. The land becomes less fertile as you go further north. Ovalle is a good centre for trips to see petroglyphs and the coastal forests at the Parque Nacional Fray Jorge. The largest resort is La Serena, from where access can be made to the Elqui Valley, one of Chile's major pisco-producing regions and one of the world's major astronomical centres.

From the Río Aconcagua to the Río Elqui is a transitional zone between the fertile heartland and the northern deserts. The first stretch of the Pan-American Highway from Santiago is inland through green valleys with rich blue clover and wild artichokes. North of La Ligua, the Highway mainly follows the coastline, passing many beautiful coves, alternately rocky and sandy, with good surf, though the water is very cold. The valleys of the main rivers, the Choapa, Limarí and Elqui, are intensively farmed using irrigation to produce fruit and vegetables. There is a striking contrast between these lush valley floors and the arid mountains with their dry scrub and cactus. In some areas, condensation off the sea provides sufficient moisture for woods to grow. Rainfall is rare and occurs only in winter. On the coast the average temperature is 15° C in winter, 23° in summer; the interior is dry, with temperatures reaching 33° in summer, but it is cooler in winter and very cold at night.

Ovalle to La Serena

Ovalle and around → *Phone code: 053. Colour map 8, grid A1. Population: 53,000.*

This town lies inland, 412 km north of Santiago, in the valley of the Río Limarí, a fruit-growing and mining district. Market days are Monday, Wednesday, Friday and Saturday, till 1600; the market feria modelo) is off Benavente (east of the centre). The town is famous for its talabarterías (saddleries), products made of locally mined lapis lazuli, goats cheese and dried fruits. Wine is produced in the Limarí Valley and tours to *bodegas* such as Tamaya and Tabila are arranged under the Ruta del Vino heading. **Museo del Limarí** ⓘ *in the old railway station, Covarrubias y Antofagasta, Tue-Fri 0900-1300, 1500-1900, Sat-Sun 1000-1300, US$1, free on Sun*, has displays of petroglyphs and a good collection of Diaguita ceramics and other artefacts. Unofficial tourist information kiosk on the Plaza de Armas.

Monumento Nacional Valle del Encanto ⓘ *about 22 km southwest of Ovalle, 0800-1800, US$0.50, getting there: no local bus service; you must take a southbound long distance bus and ask to be dropped off – 5 km walk to the valley; flag down a bus to return; alternatively, use a tour operator like Tres Valles, Libertad 496, T629650*. This is a most important archaeological site. Artefacts from hunting peoples from over 2,000 years ago have been found but the most visible remains date from the Molle culture (AD 700). There are over 30 petroglyphs as well as great boulders, distributed in six sites. There are camping facilities.

Termas de Socos ⓘ *35 km southwest of Ovalle on the Pan- American Highway, bus US$2*, has a swimming pool and individual tubs fed by thermal springs, as well as sauna, jacuzzi and water massage (entrance US$5, very popular). It also boasts a reasonable hotel (**AL**, T02-681692, Casilla 323, full board) and a campsite (**F** per tent, but bargain) nearby.

Monumento Nacional Pichasca ⓘ *47 km northeast of Ovalle, 0800-1800, US$2.20, getting there: daily buses from Ovalle to San Pedro pass the turn off about 42 km from the city, from here it is 3 km to the park and about 2 km more to sites of interest*. An unpaved and largely winding road leads to the park, which contains petrified tree trunks, archaeological remains, including a vast cave with vestiges of ancient roof paintings, and views of rock formations on the surrounding mountains.

Parque Nacional Fray Jorge ⓘ *90 km west of Ovalle and 110 km south of La Serena at the mouth of the Río Limarí, Sat, Sun and public holidays only, 0900-1600, last departure 1800, US$2.50*. Visits closely controlled owing to risk of fire. The Park is reached by a dirt road leading off the Pan-American Highway. It contains original forests which contrast with the otherwise barren surroundings. Receiving no more than 113 mm of rain a year, the forests survive because of the almost constant covering of fog. Waterproof clothing is essential when you visit.

The good inland road between Ovalle and La Serena makes an interesting contrast to Ruta 5 (Panamericana), with a fine pass and occasional views of the Andes across cacti-covered plains and semi-desert mountain ranges. North of Ovalle 61 km a side road runs 44 km southeast (last 20 km very bad) to **Andacollo** (*Population 10,216, Altitude 1,050 m*). This old town, in an area of alluvial gold washing and manganese and copper mining, is one of the great pilgrimage sites in Chile. In the enormous **Basilica** (1893), 45 m high and with a capacity of 10,000, is the Virgen del Rosario de Andacollo. The **Fiesta Grande** from 23-27 December attracts 150,000 pilgrims. The ritual dances date from a pre-Spanish past. Colectivos run to the festival from Benavente, near Colocolo, in La Serena, but 'purists' walk (torch and good walking shoes essential). There is also a smaller festival, the Fiesta Chica on the first Sunday of October. The tourist office on the Plaza arranges tours to the Basilica and to mining operations.

Coquimbo → *Phone code: 051. Colour map 8, grid A1. Population: 106,000.*
On the same bay as La Serena, 84 km north of Ovalle, is this important port, with one of the best harbours on the coast and major fish-processing plants. The city is strung along the north shore of a peninsula. On the south shore lies the suburb of Guayacán, with an iron-ore loading port, a steel church designed by Eiffel, an English cemetery and a 83-m high cross to mark the Millennium (US$1.50 to climb it). In 1981 heavy rain uncovered 39 ancient burials of humans and llamas which had been sacrificed; they are exhibited in a small museum in the Plaza Gabriela Mistral. Tours of nearby islands with sealions go from beside the fish market, can be cold and rough but boats have blankets and life vests (US$2). Nearby is **La Herradura**, 2½ km from Coquimbo, slightly more upmarket and with the best beaches. Resorts further south, **Totoralillo** (12 km), **Guanaqueros** (37 km) and **Tongoy** (50 km), have good beaches and can be reached by rural buses or colectivos. A tourist kiosk in Plaza de Armas is open in the summer only.

La Serena → *Phone code: 051. Colour map 8, grid A1. Population: 120,000.*
La Serena, built on a hillside 2 km inland from Bahía de Coquimbo, is an attractive city and tourist centre, 11 km north of Coquimbo (473 km north of Santiago) and is the capital of IV Región (Coquimbo). The city was founded by Juan de Bohón, aide to Pedro de Valdivia, in 1544, destroyed by Diaguita Indians in 1546 and rebuilt by Francisco de Aguirre in 1549. The city was sacked by the English pirate Sharpe in 1680. In the colonial period the city was the main staging-post on the route north to Peru. In the 19th century the city grew prosperous from copper-mining. While retaining colonial architecture and churches, the present-day layout and style have their origins in the 'Plan Serena' drawn up in 1948 on the orders of Gabriel González Videla, a native of the city. Main **Sernatur** ① *Matta 461, of 108, in Edificio de Servicios Públicos (next to the post office on the Plaza de Armas), T225199, infocoquimbo@ sernatur.cl, Mon-Fri 0845-1830 (2030 in summer), Sat- Sun 1000-1400 (1000-1400, 1600-2000 in summer). Kiosks at bus terminal (summer only) and Balmaceda y Prat, helpful, open Mon-Sat 1100-1400, 1600-1900 (allegedly). Also private kiosk at the bus terminal; do not confuse with Sernatur.*

Around the attractive Plaza de Armas are most of the official buildings, including the Post Office, the **Cathedral** (built in 1844 and featuring a carillon which plays every hour) and the **Museo Histórico Casa González Videla** ① *Tue-Sat 0900-1300, 1600-1900, Sun 1000-1300, US$0.80,* which includes several rooms on the man's life. Ticket are also valid for **Museo Arqueológico** ① *Cordovez y Cienfuegos, Tue-Sat 0900-1300, 1600-1900, Sun 1000-1300, US$0.80.* It has an outstanding collection of Diaguita and Molle Indian exhibits, especially of attractively decorated pottery, also Easter Island exhibits. There are 29 other churches, several of which have unusual towers. La Recova, the craft market, at Cienfuegos y Cantournet, includes a large display of handicrafts and, upstairs, several good restaurants. One block west of the Plaza de Armas is the **Parque Pedro de Valdivia** ① *daily 1000-2000, US$1.25.* One block south is the delightful **Parque Japonés**, "El Jardín del Corazón".

Avenida Francisco de Aguirre, a pleasant boulevard lined with statues and known as the Alameda, runs from the centre to the coast, terminating at the **Faro Monumental** *US$0.45,* a small, neo-colonial mock-castle and lighthouse, now a pub. A series of beaches stretch from here to Peñuelas, 6 km south, linked by the Av del Mar. Many apartment blocks, hotels, cabañas and restaurants have been built along this part of the bay. Most activity is around the middle of the beach, where swimming is safest. If you don't like crowds, head for the northern or southern extremes.

Elqui Valley

The valley of the Río Elqui is one of the most attractive oases in this part of northern Chile. There are orchards, orange groves, vineyards and mines set against the imposing, arid mountains. The Elqui Valley is the centre of pisco production with nine distilleries, the largest being Capel in Vicuña. Huancara. Elqui is also well-known as a centre of mystical energy and is one of the main astronomical centres of the world, with three important observatories. Tour operators in La Serena and Coquimbo (including Ingservtur and GiraTour), receive tickets from the observatories and arrange tours to Tololo and La Silla (to Tololo US$22 per person). Book tours up to 3-4 months ahead in holiday times.

At 2,200 m, 89 km southeast of La Serena in the Elqui Valley, 51 km south of Vicuña, **El Tololo** ① *www.ctio.noao.edu, visitors by permit only every Sat 0900-1200, 1300-1600; for permits (free) write to Casilla 603, La Serena, T051-205200, then pick your permit up before 1200 on the day before (the office is at Colina Los Pinos, on a hill behind the new University – personal applications can be made here for all three observatories), they will insist that you have private transport; you can hire a taxi, US$35 for the whole day, but you will require the registration number when you book* belongs to Aura, an association of US and Chilean universities. It possesses one of the largest telescopes in the southern hemisphere (4-m diameter), seven others and a radio telescope. At 2,240 m, 150 km northeast of La Serena **La Silla** ① *www.ls.eso.org, registration in advance in Santiago essential (Alonso de Córdoba 3107, Santiago, T02-463 3000) or write to Casilla 567, La Serena, T224527, every Sat, 1430-1730, except Jul-Aug* belongs to ESO (European Southern Observatory), and comprises 14 telescopes. From La Serena it is 114 km north along Route 5 to the turn-off, then another 36 km. At 2,510 m, 156 km northeast of La Serena, 30 km north of La Silla **Las Campanas** ① *T207301, or write to Casilla 601, La Serena, www.lco.cl, open with permission every Sat 1430-1730* belongs to the Carnegie Institute, has four telescopes and is a smaller facility than the other two. To get there, follow Route 5 to the same junction as for La Silla, take the turning for La Silla and then turn north after 14 km. La Silla and Las Campanas can be reached without private transport by taking any bus towards Vallenar two hours, US$3.25, getting out at the junction (*desvío*) and hitch from there.

The road up the valley is paved as far as Pisco Elqui, 37 km beyond **Vicuña**, the valley's capital. This small, friendly town, 66 km east of La Serena, was founded in 1821. On the west side of the plaza are the municipal chambers, built in 1826 and topped in 1905 by a medieval-German-style tower, the Torre Bauer, imported by the German-born mayor of the time. The tourist office is on Plaza de Armas. There is an ATM. There are good views from Cerro La Virgen, north of town. The **Capel Pisco distillery** ① *1½ km east of Vicuña, to the right of the main road, guided tours (in Spanish) are offered Dec-Feb, daily 1000-1800, free, no booking required.* **Museo Gabriela Mistral** ① *Gabriela Mistral 759, Mon-Sat 1000-1900, Sun 1000-1800, US$1,* contains manuscripts, books, awards and many other details of the poet's life. Next door is the house where the poet was born. **Observatorio Astronómico Comunal de Vicuña** ① *Gabriela Mistral 260, Vicuña, T411352, www.mamalluca.org, on Cerro Mamalluca, 6 km north of Vicuña, 1500 m above sea level, offers tours to the public at 2030, 2230, 0030, 0230 in summer, 1830, 2030, 2230 in winter, price is US$6.65 for tour, including talk and viewing through telescope, plus US$2.85 for transport, guides in Spanish and English for groups of 5 or more, book in advance.*

From Vicuña a 46-km road runs south through the Andes to the village of **Río Hurtado**, a secluded, picturesque place in a spectacular valley. Beyond the village the old trading route from Argentina, known as the Inka Trail, leads to Vado Morrillas, 3 km west of Hurtado. Along the trail are rock paintings, old indigenous campsites and aqueducts.

From Vicuña the road runs through Paihuano (camping) to **Monte Grande**, where the schoolhouse where Gabriela Mistral lived and was educated by her sister is now a **museum** US$0.50. The poet's tomb is at the edge of town, opposite the Artesanos de Cochiguaz pisco distillery, which is open to the public. (Buses from the plaza in Vicuña.) Here the road forks, one branch leading to the Cochiguaz valley. There is no public transport. Along this road are several new age settlements; it is said that the valley is an important energy centre. There are several campsites. At night, there is no better place on earth to star gaze. When the moon is new, or below the horizon, the stars seem to be hanging in the air; spectacular shooting stars can be seen every couple of seconds, as can satellites crossing the night sky. The other branch leads to **Pisco Elqui**, an attractive village with the newly restored church of Nuestra Señora del Rosario on a shady plaza. It's also famous for its night skies and beautiful scenery.

Here there is the Tres Erres pisco plant (open for visits). There is a juice bar and pancake restaurant on the plaza and a well-stocked supermarket one block from the plaza. Horses can be hired, with or without guide, US$4 per hour with guide, recommended – ask at the Hotel Elqui. Pisco Elqui is also a new age centre, where all sorts of alternative therapies and massages are available.

Border Paso Agua Negra Paso Agua Negra (4,775 m) is reached by unpaved road from Rivadavia. Chilean immigration and customs at Juntas, 84 km west of the border, 88 km east of Vicuña. Border open 0800-1700; January-April only, check rest of year. No public transport beyond Rivadavia. Tell officials if you intend to camp between border posts.

● Sleeping

Ovalle and around *p638*
A Turismo, Victoria 295, T623258, F623536. Pleasant, comfortable, parking, modern but could be better maintained.
B-C Gran Hotel, Vicuña Mackenna 210 (entrance through Galería Yagnam), T621084, yagnam@terra.cl. Decent rooms, negotiate for a good price and a quiet room.
D Roxy, Libertad 155, T620080. Constant hot water, big rooms, patio, slightly rundown. Recommended.
F pp Res Socos, Socos 22, T629856. Breakfast extra, lots of other extras, family run.
F pp Venecia, Libertad 261, T620968. Safe and welcoming. Recommended.

Parque Nacional Fray Jorge
Two campsites, one in the desert and one at the admin area, both with hot showers; also rooms available at an old hacienda, **F** pp, and a cabaña, **B**.
Camping US$16 pp including park entry.

Coquimbo *p639*
Generally accommodation is much cheaper than in La Serena. Several hotels in La Herradura.
C Iberia, Lastra 400, T312141. Cheaper without bath, pleasant and recommended.
C Prat, Bilbao y Aldunate, T311845. Comfortable, also pleasant, with breakfast.
D Vegamar, Las Heras 403, T311773. With bath, basic.
Camping F Camping La Herradura, T263867. For up to 5 people.

La Serena *p639, map p642*
Route 5 from La Serena to Coquimbo is lined with cheap accommodation. There are no buses along Av del Mar, but it is only ½ km off Route 5. The tourist office in the bus terminal has accommodation information, helpful. Do not be pressurised at the bus station into choosing rooms. There is much more choice than touts would have you believe. Similarly, do not be pressurized in hotels to buy tours: established agencies may give better service and deals.

AL Francisco de Aguirre, Córdovez 210, T222991. 4-star, with breakfast, good rooms, reasonable restaurant.
A Mediterráneo, Cienfuegos 509, Casilla 212, T/F225837. Includes good breakfast. Recommended.
A Pucará, Balmaceda 319, T211966, F211933. With breakfast, modern, helpful, quiet.
B Berlín, Córdovez 535, T222927, F223575. Safe, efficient, good value.
B-C El Punto, Andrés Bello 979, T228474, www.punto.de. **E** pp without bath, with breakfast, tastefully decorated, comfortable, café, laundry, parking, English and German spoken, arranges tours to Elqui Valley. Recommended.
C Hostal Villanueva de La Serena, Colón 290, T550260, www.hostalvillanueva.cl. Large rooms, clean with hot water, TV and breakfast.
C Res Suiza, Cienfuegos 250, T216092, residencial.suiza@terra.cl. With breakfast, good beds, excellent value. Highly recommended.
C-D Hostal Croata, Cienfuegos 248, T/F224997, hostalcroata@entelchile.net. **E** without bath, with breakfast, laundry facilities, cable TV, patio, hospitable. Recommended.
D Casa de María Pizarro, Las Rojas 18, T229282. Very welcoming, laundry facilities, camping, helpful. Book in advance.
D Gregoria Fernández, Andrés Bello 1067, T224400, gregoria_fernandez@hotmail.com. Very helpful, good beds, with and without bath, close to terminal, excellent breakfast, garden, good local information; if full she will divert you to her mother's house, also good but less convenient for the bus station. Highly recommended.
D Rosa Canto, Cantournet 976, T213954. Kitchen, comfortable, family run, good value.
E pp Amunátegui 315. Kitchen facilities, patio, good beds. Recommended.
E pp Backpacker Lodging, El Santo 1058, T227580. Kitchen facilities, central, camping.
E pp Casa de Huéspedes, El Santo 1410, T213557. Convenient for bus terminal, including breakfast, hot water, cable TV. Recommended.
E pp Celia Rivera, Las Rojas 21, T215838. Near terminal, use of kitchen, nice place.

E Edith González, Los Carrera 889, T221941/224978. F without bath, cooking and laundry facilities, meets passengers at bus terminal. Recommended.

E Hostal El Hibisco, Juan de Dios Peni 636, T211407. Delightful hosts, welcome drink, good breakfast included.

E pp Hostal Gladys, Pasaje Alberto Coddou 1360 (by Plaza de Armas), T551267, or 09-540 3636 (mob). Breakfast available US$2.85, TV, hot water, free internet, kitchen and laundry facilities, bicycles for rent, helpful, Gladys works at tourist information in bus terminal (15 mins away).

E pp Hostal Jofre, Rgto Coquimbo 964 (entre Peni y Amunátegui), T222335, hostaljofre@hotmail.com. With breakfast, good beds, garden, kitchen, free internet, discount for teachers, students and retired people, cheaper Apr-Oct, near bus terminal.

E pp Res Carvajal, Av El Santo 1056, T/F224059. Family home, kitchen facilities, central camping.

E pp Res El Loa, O'Higgins 362, T210304. Without bath, with breakfast, good inexpensive home cooking, good value.

E pp Res Lorena, Cantournet 950, T223330, hostal_lorena@msn.com. Quiet, pleasant.

E pp Res Petit, de la Barra 586, T212536. Hot water.

Lodging for visitors, Mauricio Betrios y Mary Rosas, San Juan de Dios Peni 636, T211407. Hot shower, includes breakfast, student place, helpful, kitchen facilities, laundry.

Camping Hipocampo, 4 km south on Av del Mar (take bus for Coquimbo and get off at Colegio Adventista, US$7.50 site by Playa El Pescador), T214316. **Maki Payi**, 153 Vegas Norte, about 5 km north of La Serena, near sea, T213628. Self-contained cabins available.

Elqui Valley *p640*
Vicuña
A Halley, Gabriela Mistral 542, T412070, www.valledeelqui.cl/hotelhalley.htm. Rooms

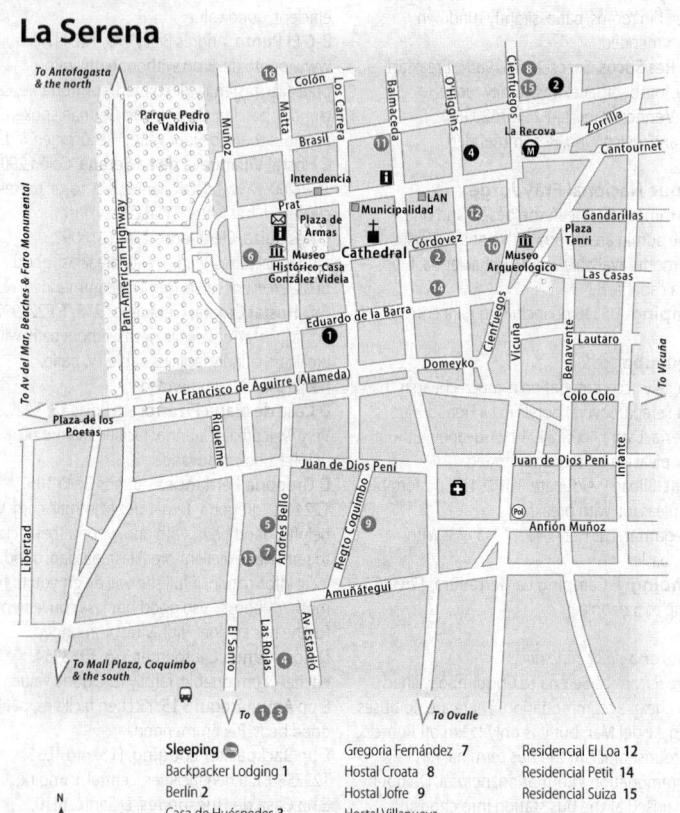

La Serena

Chile Ovalle to La Serena Listings

To Antofagasta & the north

Parque Pedro de Valdivia

To Av del Mar, Beaches & Faro Monumental

Pan-American Highway

Colón
Los Carrera
Matta
Balmaceda
O'Higgins
Cienfuegos
Zorrilla

Brasil

Muñoz

Intendencia

Prat
Plaza de Armas
Municipalidad
LAN

Museo Histórico Casa González Videla
Cathedral
Córdovez

Eduardo de la Barra

Av Francisco de Aguirre (Alameda)

Plaza de los Poetas

Riquelme
Libertad

Juan de Dios Peni

Andrés Bello
Rgto Coquimbo

Amunátegui

El Santo
Las Rojas
Av Estadio

To Mall Plaza, Coquimbo & the south

To Ovalle

La Recova
Cantournet
Gandarillas
Plaza Tenri
Las Casas
Museo Arqueológico
Vicuña
Benavente
Lautaro
Colo Colo
To Vicuña
Domeyko
Juan de Dios Peni
Infante
Anfión Muñoz

N

0 metres 200
0 yards 200

Sleeping
Backpacker Lodging 1
Berlín 2
Casa de Huéspedes 3
Casa de María Pizarro 4
Celia Rivera 4
El Punto 5
Francisco de Aguirre 6
Gregoria Fernández 7
Hostal Croata 8
Hostal Jofre 9
Hostal Villanueva de la Serena 16
Mediterráneo 10
Pucará 11
Residencial Carvajal 13
Residencial El Loa 12
Residencial Petit 14
Residencial Suiza 15

Eating
Bavaria 1
Donde El Guatón 2
La Mía Pizza 4

around a courtyard, Victorian-style, very good, with breakfast.

A-B Hostería Vicuña, Sgto Aldea 101, T411301, www.hosteriavicuna.cl. Swimming pool, tennis court, restaurant.

B Sol del Valle, Gabriela Mistral 743, T411078. Including breakfast, swimming pool, vineyard, restaurant.

C La Elquina, O' Higgins 65, T411317. Includes breakfast, D without bath, relaxed, quiet, lovely garden, laundry and kitchen facilities. Recommended.

C Valle Hermoso, Gabriela Mistral 706, T411206. Comfortable, parking.

Camping Camping y Piscina Las Tinajas, east end of Chacabuco. Swimming pool, restaurant.

Río Hurtado

B Hacienda Los Andes, Vado Morrillos, T691822, www.haciendalosandes.com. German-Austrian management at this highly regarded colonial-style hacienda, all meals of local produce with organic fruit and vegetables, horse riding, trekking, biking and many other outdoor activities, from 1 to 8 days, English spoken. Camping available, **F** pp. Access from Vicuña or Ovalle via Monumento Nacional Pichasca.

Pisco Elqui

Prices are much lower outside Jan-Feb.

AL Misterios de Elqui, C Prat, T1982544, www.misteriosdeelqui.cl. Plush cabañas, sleep 2 or 4, swimming pool, good expensive restaurant.

A-B Los Dátiles, Prat s/n, T1982540, elqui_datil@yahoo.com. Cabañas sleep 5, swimming pool, good restaurant.

A-B El Tesoro del Elqui, T051-451069, www.tesoro-elqui.cl. Cabañas for up to 4, dormitory for up to 4 with shared bath (**D**), café, pool, German spoken.

C Elqui, O'Higgins s/n by the plaza. T1982523.

Hot shower, central, swimming pool, good restaurant. Recommended.

F Hospedaje, Prat 17. Cheapest option, friendly, watch out for fleas.

Camping F Camping El Olivo, restaurant, pool, excellent facilities, closed in winter.

⊘ Eating

Ovalle *p638*

¶ Club Social Arabe, Arauco 255. Spacious glass-domed premises, limited selection of Arab dishes.

¶ La Bocca, Benavente 110. Specializes in shellfish.

¶ Casino La Bomba, Aguirre 364. Run by fire brigade, good value almuerzos.

¶ Club Comercial, Aguirre 244 (on plaza), open Sun for general Chilean fare.

¶ El Quijote, Arauco 294. Good seafood, intimate atmosphere.

¶ Yum Yum, V MacKenna 21. Good, cheap, lively.

Coquimbo *p639*

The seafood restaurants tend to be better than La Serena.

¶¶-¶ Sal y Pimienta del Capitán Denny, Aldunate 769. Mainly fish in Chilean style, one of the best in town, pleasant, old fashioned.

¶¶ Mai Lai Fan, Av Ossandón 1. Good Chinese.

¶¶ La Picada, Costanera near statue of O'Higgins. Excellent, try the pebre.

¶ La Bahía, Pinto 1465. Good food and value.

¶ La Barca, Ríos y Varela. Modest, good food.

La Serena *p639, map p642*

Most restaurants close off season on Sun. For good fish lunches (middle range/cheap) try the restaurants on the top floor of the Recova market.

¶¶ Bavaria, E de la Barra 489. International menu, good service, chain restaurant.

¶¶ Ciro's, Av de Aguirre 431, T213482. Old-fashioned, good lunch. Recommended.

Chile Ovalle to La Serena Listings

Donde El Guatón, Brasil 750. Parrillada, paradise for meat eaters, also good seafood.

La Mía Pizza, O'Higgins 360, T215063. Italian, good value (branch on Av del Mar 2100 in summer).

Pastissima Limitado, O'Higgins 663. Wide variety of pizzas, delicious pancakes, live music and dancing at weekends.

Mai Lai Fan, Cordóvez 740. Good Chinese, good value almuerzo.

Plaza Royal, Prat 465. Light meals and snacks, pleasant. Recommended.

Qahlûa, Balmaceda 655. Good fish, seafood, popular.

Taiwan, Cantournet 844. Good Cantonese.

Bocaccio, Prat y Balmaceda. Modern, popular, good cakes.

Bravissimo, Balmaceda 545. For the best ice cream.

Café do Brasil, Balmaceda 461. Good coffee.

Colonial, Balmaceda 475 (next to Brasil). Real coffee, sandwiches, salads, good.

Tahiti, Córdovez 540, local 113. Real coffee, pastries.

Elqui Valley: Vicuña *p640*

Club Social de Elqui, Gabriela Mistral 435. Attractive patio, good value *almuerzo*, not so good in the evening.

Halley, Gabriela Mistral 404. Good meat, also *chopería*, swimming pool (US$5 pp).

Michel, Gabriela Mistral 180. Popular, good value almuerzo.

Yo Y Soledad, Gabriela Mistral 364. Inexpensive, good value.

🌓 Bars and clubs

La Serena *p639, map p642*
Bar Real, Los Carrera y Cordovez, on the plaza. Nice bar with colonial-style interior.
Café del Patio, Prat 470. Café with bar, Tijuana Blues from 2100 with live music to the early hours. On Sat offers The Beatles Club from 2300.

🎡 Festivals and events

Coquimbo *p639*
Coquimbo hosts **La Pampilla**, by far the biggest independence day celebrations in Chile. Between 200-300,000 people come from all over the country for the fiesta, which lasts for a week from **14-21 Sep**. It costs a nominal US$1.50 to enter the main dancing area peñas cost extra); plenty of typical Chilean food and drink.

⊙ Shopping

La Serena *p639, map p642*
Bicycle repairs Mike's Bikes, Av F de Aguirre 004, T224454. Good parts, rental, information on cycle routes.
Handicrafts Cema-Chile, Los Carrera 562, and La Recova handicraft market, see Sights.
Supermarkets Las Brisas, Cienfuegos y Cordóvez. Mall Plaza, shopping centre on the Panamericana next to the bus terminal.

🚠 Activities and tours

La Serena *p639, map p642*
Approximate tour prices: Valle del Elqui US$24, Parque Nacional Fray Jorge US$38, Tongoy US$30, Isla Damas US$40, observatory US$20, city tour US$10.
Elqui Valley Tours, Balmaceda 551B. Good for local tours, enthusiastic guides.
Elquitour, Matta 522, T214846. Good travel agency.
Ingservtur, Matta 611, T/F220165, www.ingservtur.cl. Guided tours to Valle del Encanto, Fray Jorge, Andacollo, Isla Chañaral, Valle del Elqui and to observatories. Expensive.
Lancuyén, O'Higgins 336, T214744, www.turismolancuyen.cl. Tours of the region, including Limarí Valley Ruta del Vino tours.
More Tour, Av F de Aguirre 343, T09-885 1045, moretour20@hotmail.com. Knowledgeable guides, attentive, good tours.
Talinay Adventure Expeditions and **Inca Travel**, both at Café del Patio, Prat 470 (Talinay T218658 or 09-623 5481, www.talinay chile.4mg.com). Both offer a range of local tours including Valle del Elqui, Mamalluca, Reserva Nacional Pingüino de Humboldt, also trekking and climbing.

⊖ Transport

Ovalle and around *p638*
Bus Ovalle has 2 long-distance bus terminals, Terrapuerta Limarí, next to Feria Modelo, near Benavente 500 block, which all major companies use, and Terminal Media Luna, by the Rodeo on Aritzía Oriente. Local buses leave from the terminal next to Terrapuerto Limarí. Buses to **Santiago**, several, 6½ hrs, US$7; to **Valparaíso**, 6 hrs, US$8; to **La Serena**, 20 a day, 1½ hrs, US$2.50; to **Antofagasta**, 14 hrs, US$16; to **Arica**, 24 hrs, US$21.

Parque Nacional Fray Jorge
Round trip in **taxi** from Ovalle, US$30, Abel Olivares Rivera, T Ovalle 620352.

Andacollo
Colectivo from Ovalle, US$2; **bus**, US$1.40.

Coquimbo *p639*
Bus Terminal at Varela y Garriga. To
La Serena, US$0.45.

La Serena *p639, map p642*
Air Aeropuerto Gabriela Mistral, 5 km east of the
city. To Santiago, **LAN/Lan Express**; also to
destinations in northern Chile.
Bus City buses US$0.25. Bus terminal, El Santo y
Amunátegui (about 8 blocks south of the centre).
Tur-Bus office, Balmaceda entre Prat y Cordovez.
Buses daily to **Santiago**, several companies, 7-8
hrs, US$8 (classic), US$10 semi-cama)-13
salón-cama). To **Valparaíso**, 7 hrs, US$18. To
Caldera, 6 hrs, US$7. To **Calama**, US$28.30, 16 hrs.
To **Antofagasta**, 12-13 hrs, several companies,
US$18, and to **Iquique**, 17 hrs, and **Arica**, 20 hrs.
To **Vicuña** and **Pisco Elqui**, see below. To
Coquimbo, bus No 8 from Av Aguirre y
Cienfuegos, US$0.45, every few minutes.
Car hire Daire, Balmaceda 3812, T226933,
recommended, good service; **Flota Verschae**, Av
Balmaceda 3856, T241685, good value,
recommended; La Florida at airport, T271947.
Taxi US$0.75 + US$0.20 per every 200 m.
Colectivos with fixed rates, destination on roof;
also to Coquimbo from Aguirre y Balmaceda, and
Ovalle and Vicuña from Domeyko y Balmaceda.

Elqui Valley: Vicuña *p640*
Bus To **La Serena**, about 10 a day (more in
summer), most by **Vía Elqui/Megal Bus**, first
0800, last 1930, 1 hr, US$1.75, colectivo from
Plaza de Armas US$2.50. To **Pisco Elqui**, 10 a
day, Vía Elqui, 1 hr, US$2. Buses from Pisco Elqui
to La Serena go via Vicuña, US$2.50.

⊕ Directory

La Serena *p639, map p642*
Airline offices LAN, Prat y Balmaceda,
T225981, also an office in the Mall Plaza.
Banks ATMs at most banks and outside Las
Brisas supermarket. Corp Banca, O'Higgins 529,
Visa. Casas de cambio: Cambio Caracol,
Balmaceda 460, in the basement, building closed
1400-1600. Cambio Intercam, De la Barra 435B.
La Portada, Prat 515, open all day Sat. If heading
north note that La Serena is the last place to
change TCs before Antofagasta. **Cultural
centres** Instituto Chileno Francés de Cultura,
Cienfuegos 632, T224993. Library, films, etc.
Centro Latino-Americano de Arte y Cultura,
Balmaceda 824, T229344. Dance workshops, art
gallery, artesanía. **Internet** Cybercafé at
Ingservtur, Matta 611. Cyber-Bazaar 2000, Av F
de Aguirre 343-A. Net Café, Cordovez 285,
T212187, also bar. Shalom, Av F de Aguirre 343.
Telephones Telefónica, Cordovez 446 and La
Recova market. Entel, Prat 571.

North of La Serena

North of the Río Elqui, the transitional zone continues to the mining and agro-industrial centre
of Copiapó. Thereafter begins the desert, which is of little interest, except after rain. Then it is
covered with a succession of flowers, insects and frogs, in one of the world's most spectacular
wildlife events. Rain, however, is rare: there is none in summer; in winter it is light and lasts
only a short time. Annual precipitation at Copiapó is about 115 mm. Drivers must beware of
high winds and blowing sand north of Copiapó.

The Huasco valley is an oasis of olive groves and vineyards. It is rugged and
spectacular, dividing at Alto del Carmen, 30 km east of Vallenar, into the Carmen and
Tránsito valleys. There are pisco distilleries at Alto del Carmen and San Félix. A sweet wine
known as Pajarete is also produced.

Reserva Nacional Pingüino de Humboldt

Some 72 km north of La Serena, a road branches west off the Panamericana to **Punta de
Choros**. This is the departure point for the Humboldt Penguin Natural Reserve, on Islas
Chañaral, Choros and Damas. Besides penguins, there are seals, sea lions, a great variety of
seabirds and, offshore, a colony of grey dolphin. Isla Damas has interesting flora, too. No
public transport to Punta de Choros (42 km from Panamericana). Tours run from La Serena,
0830-1800. Permission to land on Isla Damas (US$2.50) from Conaf in Punta de Choros,
T051-272798. There's a tourist information kiosk on the Pan-American Highway at the south
end of Chañaral (closed winter). If it is closed, go to the Municipalidad.

Vallenar → *Phone code: 051. Colour map 8, grid A1. Population: 47,000. Altitude: 380 m.*
This is the chief town of the Huasco valley, 194 km north of La Serena. It has a pleasant Plaza de
Armas, with marble benches. About seven blocks southeast is the **Museo del Huasco** ⓘ *Sgto*

Aldea 742, Tue-Fri 1500-1800, US$0.70. It contains historic photos and artefacts from the valley. At the mouth of the river, 56 km west, is the pleasant port of Huasco (cheap seafood restaurants near the harbour). The staff at the Municipalidad on Plaza de Armas are helpful.

Copiapó → *Phone code: 052. Colour map 6, grid C2. Population: 127,000. Altitude: 400 m.*

The valley of the Río Copiapó, generally regarded as the southern limit of the Atacama desert, is an oasis of farms, vineyards and orchards about 150 km long. Copiapó is an important mining centre. Founded in 1744, Copiapó became a prosperous town after the discovery in 1832 of the third largest silver deposits in South America at Chañarcillo (the mine was closed in 1875). The discoverer, Juan Godoy, a mule-driver, is commemorated at Matta y O'Higgins. Fiesta de la Candelaria, first Sunday in February. **Museo Mineralógico** ① *Colipí y Rodríguez, 1 block east from Plaza Prat, Mon-Fri 1000-1300, 1530-1900, Sat 1000-1300, US$0.80.* This is the best of its type in Chile. Many ores shown are found only in the Atacama desert. The museum at the railway station opens irregularly, but the Norris Brothers steam locomotive and carriages used in the inaugural journey between Copiapó and Caldera in 1851 (the first railway in South America) can be seen at the Universidad de Atacama about 2 km north of the centre on Avenida R Freire. Helpful **tourist office** ① *Los Carrera 691, north side of Plaza Prat, T212838, infoatacama@sernatur.cl.*

Border with Argentina: Paso San Francisco

Paso San Francisco is reached either by poor unpaved road northeast from Copiapó, via the Salar de Maricunga and Laguna Verde or by an unpaved road southeast from El Salvador: the two roads join near the Salar de Maricunga, 96 km west of Paso San Francisco. On the Argentine side a paved road continues to Tinogasta. Chilean immigration and customs are near the Salar de Maricunga, 100 km west of the border, open 0900-1900; US$2 per vehicle charge for crossing Saturday, Sunday and holidays. This crossing is liable to closure in winter: T052-238032 for road reports. Always take spare fuel.

Caldera and around → *Phone code: 052. Colour map 6, grid C2. Population: 12,000.*

This is a port and terminal for the loading of iron ore, 73 km west of Copiapó. **Iglesia de San Vicente** (1862) on the Plaza de Armas was built by English carpenters working for the railway company. **Bahía Inglesa**, 6 km south of Caldera, 6 km west of the Highway, is popular for its beautiful white sandy beaches and unpolluted sea (very expensive and can get crowded January-February and at weekends). It was originally known as Puerto del Inglés after the visit in 1687 of the English 'corsario', Edward Davis.

Chañaral → *Phone code: 052. Colour map 6, grid C2. Population: 12,000.*

The valley of the Río Salado, 130 km in length, less fertile or prosperous than the Copiapó or Huasco valleys, is the last oasis south of Antofagasta. Chañaral, a town with old wooden houses perched on the hillside at the mouth of the Salado, is 93 km north of Caldera. In its heyday it was the processing centre for ore from the nearby copper mines of El Salado and Las Animas. Now it is a base for visits to beaches and the Parque Nacional Pan de Azúcar.

Parque Nacional Pan de Azúcar

① *US$4. Conaf office in Caleta Pan de Azúcar, 0830-1800 daily, maps available. There are heavy fines for driving in 'restricted areas' of the park.*

The park, north of Chañaral, consists of the Isla Pan de Azúcar on which Humboldt penguins and other sea-birds live, and some 43,754 ha of coastal hills rising to 800 m. There are fine beaches (popular at weekends in summer). Fishermen near the Conaf office offer boat trips round Isla Pan de Azúcar to see the penguins, US$5 per person. Vegetation is mainly cacti, of which there are 26 species, nourished by frequent sea mists camanchaca). The park is home to 103 species of birds as well as guanaco and foxes. Pollution from nearby copper mining is a threat. There are two entrances: north by good secondary road from Chañaral, 28 km to Caleta Pan de Azúcar; from the Pan-American Highway 45 km north of Chañaral, along a side road 20 km (road in parts deep sand and very rough, 4WD essential).

Taltal → *Phone code: 055. Colour map 6, grid C2. Population: 9,000.*

This is the only town between Chañaral and Antofagasta, a distance of 420 km. Along Avenida Prat are several wooden buildings dating from the late 19th century, when Taltal prospered as a mineral port of 20,000 people. It is now a fishing port with a mineral processing plant. North 72 km is the Quebrada El Médano, a gorge with ancient rock-paintings along the upper valley walls.

⊜ Sleeping

Reserva Nacional Pingüino de Humboldt: Punta de Choros p645
C Cabañas Los Delfines, Pilpilen s/n, sitio 33, T09-639 6678 (mob). Cabins for up to 6. There are other sleeping and eating options in the area.

Vallenar p645
Listed hotels and restaurants all recommended.
A Hostería Vallenar, Ercilla 848, T614379, hotval@ctc.cl. Excellent, pool, restaurant with good breakfast.
B Cecil, Prat 1059, T614071. A good modern hotel with hot water and a swimming pool.
C Hostal Camino del Rey, Merced 943, T/F613184. Cheaper without bath, good value.
D Vall, Aconcagua 455, T613380. With breakfast, parking, good value.
E Viña del Mar, Serrano 611, T611478. Nice rooms, *comedor*, a good choice.

Copiapó p646
AL Diego de Almeida, O'Higgins 656, Plaza Prat, T/F212075, dalmeida@tnet.cl. TV, fridge, good restaurant, bar and pool.
A Hostería Las Pircas, Av Copayapu 095, T213220, hosteria.laspirca@chilnet.cl. Bungalows with nice rooms, pool, good breakfast, restaurant.
B San Francisco de la Selva, Los Carrera 525, T217013, hosanco@entelchile.net. Pleasant modern hotel, central, with TV, café-bar, garage.
B-C Montecatini, Infante 766, T211363, hotelmontecatini@123click.cl. Large rooms around a beautiful courtyard, helpful, excellent value, pool.
C Palace, Atacama 741, T212852. Comfortable, central, good breakfast, patio.
D Res Rocío, Yerbas Buenas 581, T215360. **F** without bath, good value, attractive patio.
E Res Nuevo Chañarcillo, Rodríguez 540, T212368. Without bath (more with), comfortable, nice lounge. Recommended.
F Res Chacabuco, O'Higgins 921, T213428. Cheaper with shared bath, quiet, near bus terminal.
F Res Torres, Atacama 230, T240727. Shared bath, hot water, quiet, good value.

Caldera p646
It's cheaper to stay in Caldera than Bahía Inglesa in summer.
A-B Hostería Puerta del Sol, Wheelwright 750, T315205. Includes tax, cabins with kitchen and all mod cons, swimming pool, view over bay.

A-B Portal del Inca, Carvallo 945, T315252. Cabins with kitchen, English spoken, restaurant not bad, order breakfast on previous night.
B Costanera, Wheelwright 543, T316007. Takes credit cards, simple rooms.
E pp Res Millaray, Cousiño 331, Plaza de Armas. Good value, basic.

Bahía Inglesa
A Cabañas Paraíso, Av Costanera 6000, T09-218 0050. Cabins up to 6, with kitchen solar-powered, on beach. Recommended.
A Los Jardines de Bahía Inglesa, Av Copiapó, cabañas, T315359. Open all year, good beds, comfortable.
B Camping Bahía Inglesa, Playa Las Machas, T315424. Fully equipped cabañas for up to 5 persons, **C** tent site.
B El Coral, Av El Morro, T315331. Restaurant overlooking sea, has some cabins, good seafood, groups welcome, open all year.

Chañaral p646
B Hostería Chañaral, Müller 268, T480055. Spacious rooms, attentive service, except in the restaurant, although the food is good.
C Jiménez, Merino Jarpa 551, T480328. Without bath, modern, patio with lots of birds, restaurant good value. Recommended.
C Nuria, Costanera 302, T480903. Good, if a little basic, with breakfast, parking.
D La Marina, Merino Jarpa 562. Basic, without bath, patio, beware overcharging.
D Sergio Molina, Pinto 583, T09-972 0077 (see Pan de Azúcar Activities and tours). Shared bath, kitchen and laundry facilities, nice family.

Parque Nacional Pan de Azúcar p646
Camping E per site, no showers, take all food and drinking water; also 2 cabañas, T213404.

Taltal p646
C Hostal de Mar, Carrera 250, T611612. Comfortable, modern.
C Hostería Taltal, Esmeralda 671, T611173, btay@entelchile.net. Sea view, excellent restaurant, good value *almuerzo*.
D San Martín, Martínez 279, T611088. Without bath, good *almuerzo*.

🍴 Eating

Vallenar *p645*

Cheap eating places along south end of Av Brasil.
🍴 **Bavaria**, Serrano 802. Chain restaurant, good.
🍴 **Pizza Il Boccato**, Plaza O'Higgins y Prat.
Good coffee, good food, popular.
🍴 **La Pica**, Brasil y Faez. Good for cheap
meals, seafood, cocktails.

Copiapó *p646*

🍴 **Bavaria**, Chacabuco 487 (Plaza Prat) and
round corner on Los Carrera. Good variety on
offer, restaurant upstairs, cafetería downstairs.
🍴 **El Corsario**, Atacama 245. Good food, value
and atmosphere.
🍴 **Benbow**, Rodríguez 543. Good value almuerzo,
extensive menu.
🍴 **Chifa Hao Hwa**, Colipi 340 and Yerbas Buenas
334. Good Chinese, one of several in town.
🍴 **Don Elias**, Los Carrera e Yerbas Buenas.
Excellent seafood, popular.
🍴 **La Pizza de Tito**, Infante y Chacabuco. Pizzas
with good fillings, sandwiches and almuerzos.

Caldera *p646*

🍴 **El Pirón de Oro**, Cousiño 218. Good but pricey.
🍴 **Miramar**, Gana 090. At pier, good seafood.

Chañaral *p646*

🍴 **Rincón Porteño**, Merino Jarpa 567. Good
and inexpensive.

Taltal *p646*

🍴 **Club Social Taltal**, Torreblanca 162. The old
British club (see the ballroom and poker room),
excellent, good value.
🍴 **Caverna**, Martínez 247. Good seafood.

🥾 Activities and tours

Vallenar *p645*

If it rains (usually Sep-Oct) a guided tour of the
desert in flower can be done with **Roberto
Alegría**, T613865.
Agencia de Viajes Irazu, Prat 1121A,
T/F619807. They do not organize excursions,
but will organize flights.

Parque Nacional Pan de Azúcar *p646*

Subsole Atacama Adventure (Sergio Molina -
see Sleeping above), Merino Jarpa s/n, Chañaral,
T09-972 0077, kekomoli@123mail.cl. Specializes
on tours in the park, US$28, enthusiastic
and knowledgeable.

🚌 Transport

Vallenar *p645*

Bus Each bus company has its own terminal:
Tur-Bus, Merced 561; **Pullman**, opposite (the
most frequent buses going north); **Tas Choapa**,
next door. To **La Serena**, 2 hrs, US$4. To **Copiapó**,
2 hrs, US$4. To **Valparaíso**, 10 hrs, US$13.15.

Copiapó *p646*

Air Airport 12 km north of town. **LAN/Lan
Express**, Colipi 484, T213512, daily to/from
Santiago, also to northern destinations.
Bus Terminal 3 blocks from centre on Freire
y Chacabuco. To **Santiago** US$15, 12 hrs.
To **La Serena** US$7.50, 5 hrs. To **Caldera**,
US$1-2, 1 hr.

Caldera *p646*

Bus Buses on the Panamericana do not go into
Caldera, but stop at Cruce Caldera, outside town
(Restaurante Hospedaje Mastique, Km 880, is a
good place to eat and stay, **D**). Buses to **Copiapó**
and **Santiago**, several daily. To **Antofagasta**,
US$11, 7 hrs. To travel north, it may be better to
take a bus to **Chañaral** (Inca-bus US$2), then
change. Between Bahía Inglesa and Caldera
colectivos charge US$1 all year; frequent bus
service Jan-Feb US$0.30.

Chañaral *p646*

Bus Terminal Merino Jarpa 854. Frequent
services to **Antofagasta** US$10, 5 hrs, and
Santiago, US$18.

Parque Nacional Pan de Azúcar *p646*

A **taxi** costs US$25 from Chañaral, or hitch a lift
from fishermen at sunrise.

Taltal *p646*

Bus To **Santiago**: 3 a day; to **Antofagasta**,
Tur-Bus, US$5. Many buses bypass Taltal: to
reach the Panamericana take a taxi, US$8.

ⓘ Directory

Copiapó *p646*

Banks Redbanc ATMs at central banks and in
Plaza Real shopping mall. **Bicycle repairs**
Biman, Los Carrera 998A, T/F217391, excellent.
Cultural centres Casa de la Cultura,
O'Higgins 610, Plaza Prat. Wide range of arts,
workshops, artesanía shops, good café El
Bramador. **Internet** Zona Virtual, Rodríguez y
Colipi, T240308. Terra, Chacabuco 380, US$1
per hr. **Post offices** Los Carrera y Colipi, Plaza
Prat. **Telephones** Telefónica, O'Higgins 531;
Entel, Colipi 484.

Far north

Antofagasta, capital of the Second Region, is a major port for the export of copper from La Escondida and Chuquicamata. It is also a major commercial centre and home of two universities. The coast north of Antofagasta is much more picturesque than the aridity surrounding much of the Panamerican Highway. Two possible stops are the fishing port of Mejillones and Tocopilla, beneath towering cliffs. Despite this being the driest region, the climate is delightful. Temperature varies from 16° C in June/July to 24° C January/February, never falling below 10° C at night.

From the mining service centre of Calama, the route heads up to the altiplano with its saltflats and lunar landscapes. In an oasis on the Río San Pedro is the historic town of San Pedro de Atacama. This has become a popular destination for visitors seeking high altitudes, clear skies, steaming geysers and volcanic horizons. It is also, increasingly, a staging post on the route between Bolivia's Salar de Uyuni and the Pacific Ocean. The Atacama Desert extends over most of the Far North to the Peruvian border. The main cities are Iquique and Arica; between them are old mineral workings and geoglyphs. Large areas of the Andean highland have been set aside as national parks; the most visited is Lauca with its volcanoes and lakes.

Antofagasta and around

→ *Phone code: 055. Colour map 6, grid C2. Population: 225,316.*

The largest city in Northern Chile, Antofagasta, 1,367 km north of Santiago, is not especially attractive in itself, but its setting beside the ocean and in view of tall mountains is dramatic. The **tourist office** ① *Prat 384, p 1, T451818, infoantofagasta@sernatur.cl, Mon-Fri 0930-1200, 1400-1700,* is very helpful. There is also a kiosk on Balmaceda ① *Mon-Fri 0930-1300, 1530-1930, Sat-Sun 0930-1300;* kiosk at airport (open summer only). **Conaf,** Argentina 2510, Antofagasta, T383332, antofaga@conaf.cl.

In the main square, Plaza Colón, is a clock tower donated by the British community in 1910 to commemorate 100 years of Chilean independence. It is a replica of Big Ben in London. Calle A Prat, which runs southeast from Plaza Colón, is the main shopping street. Two blocks north of Plaza Colón, at the old port, is the former Aduana, built as the Bolivian customs house in Mejillones and moved to its current site after the War of the Pacific. It houses the **Museo Histórico Regional** ① *Tue-Sat 1000-1300, 1530-1830, Sun 1100-1400, US$1, children half-price; museoanto@terra.cl,* which has fascinating visual displays (explanations in Spanish only) on life on land and in the oceans, development of civilization in South America, minerals, human artefacts, recommended. Opposite are the former Capitanía del Puerto (now the administrative offices and library of the Museo Regional) and the former Resguardo Marítimo (now housing Digader, the regional coordinating centre for sport and recreation).

East of the port are the buildings of the Antofagasta and Bolivia Railway Company (FCAB) dating from the 1890s and beautifully restored, but still in use. **Museo del Ferrocarril a Bolivia** ① *Bolívar 255, T206311, www.fcab.cl, make reservation 48 hrs in advance,* has an interesting museum of the history of the Antofagasta-Bolivia railway, with photographs, maps, instruments and furniture. **Museo Geológico** ① *Av Angamos 0610, inside the university campus. Gchong@socompa.ucn, Mon-Fri, 0900-1200, 1500-1800, free, colectivo 3 or 33 from town centre,* is the mineral museum of the Universidad Católica del Norte. Tours of the port by boat leave from **La Cabaña de Mario** ① *C Aníbal Pinto s/n between the Museo Regional and the Terminal de Pescadores, 30 mins, US$3.50.*

The fantastic cliff formations and symbol of the **Second Region at La Portada** are 16 km north, reached by any bus for Mejillones from the Terminal Centro (or ask at a travel agency). Taxis charge US$11 (for a small extra fee, taxis from the airport will drive past La Portada). Hitching is easy. From the main road it is 2 km to the beach which, though beautiful, is too dangerous for swimming; there is an excellent seafood restaurant La Portada) and café (open lunch-time only). A number of bathing beaches are also within easy reach.

Juan López, 38 km north of Antofagasta, is a windsurfers' paradise. The sea is alive with birds, especially opposite Isla Santa María. For those with their own transport, follow the road

out of Juan López to the beautiful cove at Conchilla. Keep on the track to the end at Bolsico.
Mejillones (*Population 5,500*), a little fishing port 60 km north of Antofagasta, stands on a good natural harbour protected from westerly gales by high hills. Until 1948 it was a major terminal for the export of tin and other metals from Bolivia: remnants of that past include a number of fine wooden buildings: the Intendencia Municipal, the Casa Cultural (built in 1866) and the church (1906), as well as the Capitanía del Puerto.

Sleeping

Antofagasta and around *p649, map p650*
AL Antofagasta, Balmaceda 2575, T/F228811. Garage, pool, lovely view of port and city, good but expensive restaurant (bar serves cheaper snacks), with breakfast, beach, but rooms facing the city are noisy due to all night copper trains.
A Plaza, Baquedano 461, T269046, hplaza@chilesat.net. TV, salon de té, pool and sports, parking. Recommended, also has apartments.

B Colón, San Martín 2434, T261851, F260872. With breakfast, comfortable, hot water, quiet, cash only.
B Marsal, Prat 867, T268063, marsalhotel@ terra.cl. Modern, very comfortable, Catalan owner. Recommended.
B Nadine, Baquedano 519, T227008, F265222. TV in rooms, parking, bar, cafetería serving real coffee, pastries and ice cream.
B Parina, Maipú 446, T223354, F266396. Modern, comfortable, restaurant, conference centre, good value.

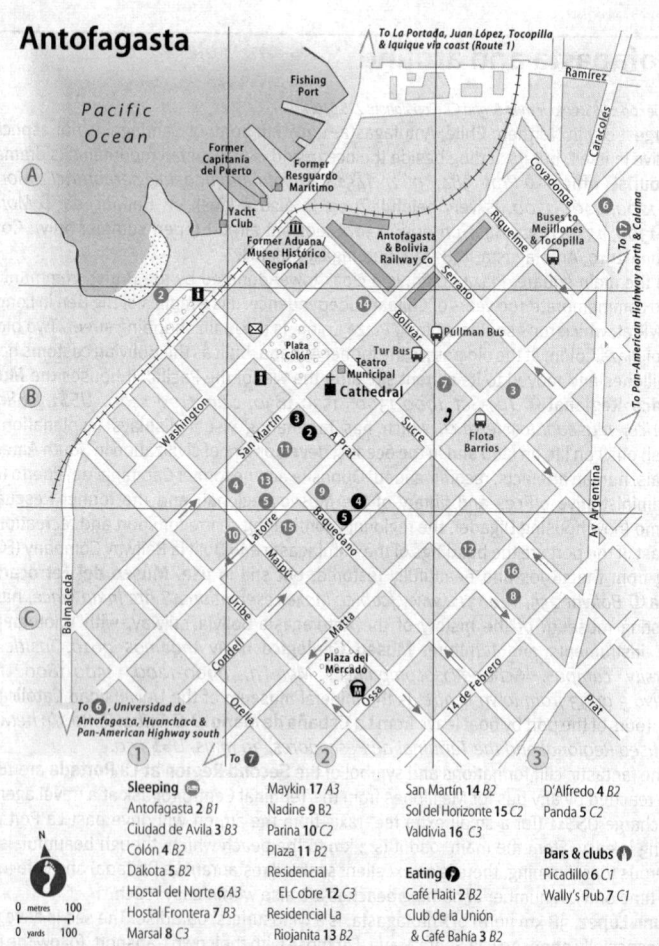

Antofagasta

Sleeping			
Antofagasta 2 *B1*	Maykin 17 *A3*	San Martín 14 *B2*	D'Alfredo 4 *B2*
Ciudad de Avila 3 *B3*	Nadine 9 *B2*	Sol del Horizonte 15 *C2*	Panda 5 *C2*
Colón 4 *B2*	Parina 10 *C2*	Valdivia 16 *C3*	
Dakota 5 *B2*	Plaza 11 *B2*		**Bars & clubs**
Hostal del Norte 6 *A3*	Residencial	**Eating**	Picadillo 6 *C1*
Hostal Frontera 7 *B3*	El Cobre 12 *C3*	Café Haiti 2 *B2*	Wally's Pub 7 *C1*
Marsal 8 *C3*	Residencial La	Club de la Unión	
	Riojanita 13 *B2*	& Café Bahía 3 *B2*	

0 metres 100
0 yards 100

The slow train to Uyuni

The line between Calama and Oruro in Bolivia is the only section of the old Antofagasta and Bolivia Railway still open to passenger trains. It is a long, slow journey but well worthwhile for the scenery. The journey is very cold, both during the day and at night (-15°C, no heating on board). From Calama the line climbs to reach its highest point at Ascotán (3,960 m); it then descends to 3,735 m at Cebollar, skirting the Salar de Ascotán. Chilean customs are at Ollagüe and the train is searched at Bolivian customs at Avaroa, eight hours. From the border the line runs northeast to Uyuni, 204 km (eight hours), crossing the Salar de Chiguana and running at an almost uniform height of 3,660 m. Uyuni is the junction with the line south to the Argentine frontier at Villazón. Río Mulato is the junction for Potosí, but it is much quicker to travel by bus from Uyuni.

B San Martín, San Martín 2781, T263503, F268159. TV, parking, safe, convenient for Tur-Bus and Pullman, but very tatty.
B Sol del Horizonte, Latorre 2450, T/F221886, hotelsoldelhorizonte@123click.cl. Cable TV, bar, pleasant, good value.
C Dakota, Latorre 2425, T251749. With breakfast and cable TV, popular, good value. Recommended.
D Ciudad de Avila, Condell 2840, T/F221040. TV, restaurant, good value. Recommended.
D Hostal del Norte, Latorre 3162, T251265, F267161. Without bath, comfortable, quiet.
D Hostal Frontera, Bolívar 558, T281219. Good hot shower, good beds, TV, convenient for Tur-Bus and Pullman.
D Maykin, Condell 3130, T/F259400. Modern, helpful, good value. Recommended, but takes in short-stay guests.
D Valdivia, Ossa 2642, T265911. Recommended.
E pp Res El Cobre, Prat 749, T225162. Without bath, clean, but unattractive.
E pp Res La Riojanita, Baquedano 464, T226313. Basic, very helpful, noisy but recommended.
Camping To the south on the road to Coloso are: **Las Garumas**, Km 6, T247763 ext 42, **E** per site (bargain for lower price out of season), **C** for cabins, cold showers and beach (reservations Av Angamos 601, casilla 606). **Rucamóvil**, Km 11, T223929 and 7 cabañas. Both open year-round, expensive.

Juan López
A Hotel La Rinconada, 10 km from Juan López, T261139. A cabaña and camping complex, prices for up to 5 people.
C Hostería Sandokan, Juan López, T223022. Standard facilities.

🍴 Eating

Antofagasta *p649, map p650*
🍴🍴🍴 **Club de la Unión**, Prat 474, p 2. Open to non-members, excellent almuerzo and service.
🍴🍴 **D'Alfredo**, Condell 2539. Pizzas, good.
🍴🍴 **El Arriero**, Condell 2644. Good service, cheaper set lunch, popular, live music.
🍴🍴 **Chifa Pekín**, Ossa 2135. Chinese, smart.
🍴🍴 **Panda**, Condell y Baguedano. Self-service, eat all you can for US$8.
🍴🍴 **Pizzante**, Carrera 1857. Good pasta, seafood.
🍴🍴 **Tío Jacinto**, Uribe 922. Good seafood.
🍴 **Casa Vecchia**, O'Higgins 1456. Good value.
🍴 **Chicken's House Center**, Latorre 2660. Chicken, beef and daily specials, open till 2400.
🍴 **Oliver Café Plaza**, Plaza Colón. Self-service, modern. Recommended.

Above the market are several good places selling cheap seafood *almuerzos* and super-cheap set lunches. Good fish restaurants in Terminal Pesquero Centro and at Caleta Coloso, 8 km south. Many restaurants and bars are closed on Sun.

Cafés
It is hard to find coffee or breakfast before 0900.
Café Bahía, Prat 474. For real coffee.
Café Haiti, in Galería at Prat 482. Real coffee.

Panaderías
Chez Niko's, Ossa 1951. **La Palmera**, Ossa 2297. **Panadería El Sol**, Baquedano 785. **Heladería Latorre**, Baquedano y Latorre. Have ice-cream.

🍸 Bars and clubs

Antofagasta *p649, map p650*
The most popular clubs are south of the town in Balneario El Huascar.
Bar Picadillo, Av Grecia 1000. Lively atmosphere, also good food.

Chile Antofagasta & around Listings

651

Castillo Pub, Pasaje Carrera 884.
Live music, good food with good
value almuerzo, fun.
Wally's Pub, Toro 982. British expat-style with
darts and beer, closed Sun.

● Entertainment

Antofagasta *p649, map p650*
Teatro Municipal, Sucre y San Martín, T264919.
Modern, state-of-the art theatre.
Teatro Pedro de la Barra, Condell 2495. Theatre
run by University of Antofagasta, regular
programme of plays, reviews, concerts etc, high
standard, details in press.

● Festivals and events

Antofagasta *p649, map p650*
29 Jun, San Pedro, patron saint of the
fishermen: the saint's image is taken out
by launch to the breakwater to bless the first
catch of the day. On the last weekend of **Oct**,
the foreign communities put on a joint festival
on the seafront, with national foods, dancing
and music.

○ Shopping

Antofagasta *p649, map p650*
Bookshops Librería Andrés Bello, Condell
2421. Good selection. **Librería Universitaria**,
Latorre 2515. Owner Germana Fernández
knowledgeable on local history. **Multilibro**,
opposite Librería Universitaria. Very good selection
of Chilean and English-language authors.
Markets Feria Modelo O'Higgins (next to
fish market on Av Pinto). Excellent fruit and veg,
also restaurants. The municipal market is at
Matta y Uribe.
Supermarkets Las Brisas, Baquedano 750.
Korlaert, on Ossa 2400-2500 block. **Líder** on road
to La Portada.

▲ Activities and tours

Antofagasta *p649, map p650*
Many tour companies offer packages to the
Atacama, but it is generally better to book tours
in San Pedro de Atacama.
Intitour, Baquedano 460, T266185,
intitour@dtl.net. English speaking guides.
Maerz (Joseph Valenzuela Thompson), PO Box
55, T243322, maerz@entelchile.net. For tours in
German.
Tatio Travel, Washington 2513, T/F263532.
English spoken, tours arranged for groups or
individuals. Highly recommended.

● Transport

Antofagasta and around *p649, map p650*
Air Cerro Moreno Airport, 22 km north. Taxi to
airport US$10, but cheaper if ordered from hotel.
Bus US$4 or less, Aerobus (T221047), Tur Bus and
others. **LAN/Lan Express** and **Sky** fly daily to
Santiago, **Arica**, **Iquique** and **Calama**; LAN/Lan
Express also to **Copiapó** and **La Serena**.
Bus No main terminal; each company has its
own office in town (some quite a distance from
the centre). Buses for **Mejillones** and **Tocopilla**
depart from the Terminal Centro at Riquelme
513. Minibuses to Mejillones leave from Latorre
2730. Bus company offices: **Flota Barrios**, Condell
2682, T268559; **Géminis**, Latorre 3055, T263968;
Pullman Bus, Latorre 2805, T262591; **Tur-Bus**,
Latorre 2751, T264487. To **Santiago**, many
companies: 18 hrs, US$20 semi cama, US$30
cama; book 2 days in advance. If all seats to the
capital are booked, catch a bus to **La Serena** (12
hrs, US$15, or US$20 cama service), or **Ovalle**, 14
hrs, US$15, and re-book. To **Valparaíso**, US$20.
To **Copiapó**, 7 hrs, US$12. Frequent buses to
Iquique, US$10, 6 hrs. To **Arica**, US$11, 11 hrs.
To **Chuquicamata**, US$5, frequent, 3 hrs. To
Calama, several companies, US$4.50, 3 hrs; to
San Pedro de Atacama, Tur-Bus 3 daily, 5 hrs,
US$5.50, or via Calama.
  To **Salta, Argentina** Géminis, Wed, Sun 0700,
via Calama, San Pedro de Atacama, Paso de Jama
and Jujuy, US$34, 18 hrs. **Tur-Bus**, Wed and Sun
0615, US$42. Also check with **Pullman Bus**, who
run services via San Pedro de Atacama and Jujuy.

Juan López
Bus At weekends in summer only, also
minibuses daily in summer from Latorre y Sucre,
Antofagasta.

● Directory

Antofagasta *p649, map p650*
Airline offices LAN, Paseo Prat, T265151. Sky,
Velásquez 890, T459090. **Banks** It's impossible
to change TCs south of Antofagasta until you
reach La Serena. **Corp Banca**, Plaza Colón for
Visa. ATMs at major banks around Plaza Colón,
Hotel Antofagasta, and Las Brisas and Tricot
supermarkets. **Casas de Cambio** are mainly on
Baquedano, such as Ancla, No 524, Mon-Fri
0900-1400, 1600-1900 (at weekends try ice
cream shop next door) and shopping centre at
No 482-98. Car hire: **First**, Bolívar 623, T225777.
Iqsa, Latorre 3033, T264675.
Consulates Argentina, Blanco Encalada 1933,
T220440. **Bolivia**, Washington 2675, p 13,
T225010. **France and Belgium**, Baquedano 299,

T268669. **Germany**, Pérez Zujovic 4940, T251691. **Italy**, Matta 1945, of 808, T227791. **Netherlands**, Washington 2679, of 902, T266252. **Spain**, Rendic 4946, T269596. **Cultural centres** Instituto Chileno Norteamericano, Carrera 1445, T263520. **Instituto Chileno Alemán**, Bolívar 769, T225946. **Centro Cultural Nueva Acrópolis**, Condell 2679, T222144, lots of

activities, talks, discussions. **Internet** Intitour, see Activities and tours above, US$0.60 per hr. Cybercafé, Maipú y Latorre, US$1.30 per hr. Sucre 671, US$0.80 per hr. **Post offices** on Plaza Colón. 0830-1900, Sat 0900-1300. Also at Washington 2613. **Telephones** Telefónica, Condell 2529 and 2750 (open Sun). **Entel Chile**, Condell 2451.

North of Antofagasta

Tocopilla → *Phone code: 055 Colour map 6, grid B2. Population: 24,600.*
Tocopilla is 187 km north of Antofagasta via the coastal road and 365 km via the Pan-American Highway. It has one of the most dramatic settings of any Chilean town, sheltering at the foot of 500-m high mountains that loom inland. There are some interesting early 20th century buildings with wooden balustrades and façades, there is a good range of eating places and the town is very friendly. The port facilities are used to unload coal and to export nitrates and iodine from María Elena and Pedro de Valdivia. There are two good beaches: Punta Blanca (12 km south) and Balneario Covadonga, with a swimming pool.

East of Tocopilla a good paved road runs up the narrow valley 72 km to the Pan-American Highway. From here the paved road continues east to Chuquicamata. North of the crossroads 81 km is **Quillagua**, officially the driest place in the world (customs post, all vehicles and buses are searched) and 111 km further is the first of three sections of the Reserva Nacional del Tamarugal. In this part are the **Geoglyphs of Cerro Pintados**, some 400 figures (humans, animals, geometric shapes) on the hillside (3 km west of the highway). The second part of Tamarugal is near La Tirana (see page 663), the third 60 km north of Pozo Almonte.

The coastal road from Tocopilla north to Iquique is now a very good paved road, 244 km, offering fantastic views of the rugged coastline and tiny fishing communities. The customs post at **Chipana-Río Loa** (90 km north) searches all southbound vehicles for duty-free goods; 30 minutes delay. Basic accommodation is available at **San Marcos**, a fishing village, 131 km north. At **Chanaballita**, 184 km north there is a hotel, cabañas, camping, restaurant, shops. There are also campsites at **Guanillos**, Km 126, **Playa Peruana**, Km 129 and **Playa El Aguila**, Km 160.

Calama → *Phone code: 055. Colour map 6, grid B2. Population: 106,970. Altitude: 2,265 m.*
Calama lies in the oasis of the Río Loa, 202 km north of Antofagasta. Initially a staging post on the silver route between Potosí and Cobija, it is now an expensive, unprepossessing modern city, serving the nearby mines of Chuquicamata and Radomiro Tomic. Calama can be reached from the north by Route 24 via Chuquicamata, or, from the south, by a paved road leaving the Pan-American Highway 98 km north of Antofagasta at Carmen Alto (petrol and food). This road passes many abandoned nitrate mines *oficinas*. **Tourist office** ① *Latorre 1689, T345345, calamainfotour@entelchile.net, Mon-Fri 0900-1300, 1430-1900*. Map, city tours, helpful but information not always accurate.

Two kilometres from the centre on Avenida B O'Higgins is the **Parque El Loa** *daily 1000-1800*, which contains a reconstruction of a typical colonial village built around a reduced-scale reproduction of Chiu Chiu church. Nearby in the park is the **Museo Arqueológico y Etnológico** ① *Tue-Sun 1000-1300, 1540-1930*, with an exhibition of prehispanic cultural history. Also the **Museo de Historia Natural** ① *Wed-Sun, 1000-1300, 1430-2000, US$0.65*, with an interesting collection on the oficinas and on the region's ecology and palaeontology.

Chuquicamata → *Phone code: 055. Colour map 6, grid B2. Altitude: 2,800 m.*
North of Calama 16 km is the site of the world's largest open-cast copper mine, employing 8,000 workers and operated by Codelco (the state copper corporation). Everything about Chuquicamata is huge: the pit from which the ore is extracted is four km long, two km wide and 730 m deep; the giant trucks, with wheels over 3½ m high, carry 310 ton loads and work 24 hours a day; in other parts of the plant 60,000 tons of ore are processed a day. Guided tours, by bus, in Spanish (also in English if enough people) leave from the office of **Chuqui**

Ayuda (a local children's charity) ① *near the entrance at the top end of the plaza, Mon-Sat 1400, 1500 (less frequent in low season, tourist office in Calama has details), 1 hr, US$2 requested as a donation to the charity; register at the office 1 hr in advance; passport number essential, filming permitted in certain areas.* In order to get on the tour, the tourist office in Calama recommends that you catch a colectivo from Calama at 0800, US$1 (ask them where it leaves from). From Calama: yellow colectivo taxis (marked 'Chuqui') from Abaroa entre Vargas y Ramírez, corner of the main plaza, US$1.75 to town centre, US$2 at night and to mine gates, 15 minutes.

From Calama it is 273 km north to Ollagüe, on the Bolivian border. (There is no petrol between Calama and Uyuni in Bolivia. If really short try buying from the carabineros at Ollagüe or Ascotán, the military at Conchi or the mining camp at Buenaventura, 5 km from Ollagüe.) The road follows the Río Loa, passing Chiu Chiu (33 km), one of the earliest Spanish settlements in the area. Just beyond this oasis, a small turning branches off the main road to the hamlet of **Lasana**, 8 km north of Chiu Chiu. Petroglyphs are clearly visible on the right-hand side of the road. There are striking ruins of a pre-Inca pukará, a national monument; drinks are on sale. If arranged in advance, Línea 80 colectivos will continue to Lasana for an extra charge Pre-book the return trip, or walk back to Chiu Chiu. At **Conchi**, 25 km north of Lasana, the road crosses the Río Loa via a bridge dating from 1890 (it's a military zone, so no photographs of the view are allowed). Beyond Chiu Chiu the road deteriorates, with deep potholes, and, north of Ascotán carabinero checkpoint at 3,900 m), it becomes even worse (ask about the conditions on the Salares at Ascotán or Ollagüe before setting out, especially in December/January or August). The desert to the eastern side of the road by minefields. There are many llama flocks along this road and flamingoes on the salares.

Ollagüe → *Colour map 6, grid B2. Altitude: 3,690 m.*

This village, on the dry floor of the Salar de Ollagüe, is surrounded by a dozen volcanic peaks of over 5,000 m. The border with Bolivia is open 0800-2100; US$2 per vehicle charge for crossings 1300-1500, 1850-2100. A bad unmade road from Ollagüe runs into Bolivia and it is on the new Ruta Altiplanica, or "Inca Road" which runs from San Pedro de Atacama via El Tatio, Ascotán and Colchane to Visviri, with a planned continuation to Cuzco. There is a municipal hostel and the Andean Project ① *T+44-20-8571 0737, John Barker, treasurer,* plans to build a hostel here. Food and drink is available in town. At this altitude the days are warm and sunny, nights cold (minimum -20° C). There are only 50 mm of rain a year, and water is very scarce. Ollagüe can be reached by taking the Calama-Uyuni train, but if you stop off, hitching is the only way out.

Between Chiu Chiu and El Tatio (see below), **Caspana** (*Population 400, Altitude 3,305 m*) is beautifully set among hills with a tiny church dating from 1641 and a museum with interesting displays on Atacameño culture. Basic accommodation is available (the nearest to El Tatio; see Lican Huasi, page). A poor road runs north and east through valleys of pampas grass with llama herds to **Toconce**, which has extensive prehispanic terraces set among interesting rock formations. There are archaeological sites nearby and the area is ideal for hiking. Further information from the tourist office in Calama, who may also help with arranging transport, or T321828, toconce@mixmail.com.

🛏 Sleeping

Tocopilla *p653*
C Vucina, 21 de Mayo 2069, T/F813088. A busy, modern hotel, good rooms and a good restaurant.
E pp **Casablanca**, 21 de Mayo 2054, T813222. Helpful, good restaurant, good value.
F pp **Res Royal**, 21 de Mayo 1988, T/F811488. Helpful, basic, without breakfast or bath.

Calama *p653*
L Park, Camino Aeropuerto 1392, T319900, F319901 (Santiago T233-8509). First class, pool, bar and restaurant. Recommended.
AL El Mirador, Sotomayor 2064, T310294, www.hotelmirador.cl. Price includes bath,

internet, parking, TV and breakfast, good atmosphere and services, pleasant rooms, helpful.
AL Hostería Calama, Latorre 1521, T341511, www.hotelcalama.co.cl. Comfortable, good food and service. Also owns **A Alfa**, Sotomayor 2016, T342496, hotelalfa@hotelalfa.cl. Central, comfortable, cable TV, but overpriced, breakfast included (neither juice nor fruit is fresh). Helpful staff, good cafeteria, airport transfer from both hotels.
A Lican Antai, Ramírez 1937, T341621, hotellicanantai@terra.cl. With breakfast, central, good service and good restaurant, TV.

B Res Alecris, Félix Hoyos 2153, T341616.
C without bath, single, double and triple rooms,
well-maintained, very clean, family atmosphere,
popular with miners, police, safe (CCTV, near
police station), no breakfast, modern, sunny
courtyard. Chatty owner Alejandro.
C Cavour, Sotomayor 1841, T314718. Hot water,
TV, no breakfast, rooms off an open-air corridor,
simple, hospitable.
C San Sebastián, Pinto 1902, T343810. Meals
available, family run, rooms with bath and TV in
annex across the street.
C-D Hostal Splendid, Ramirez 1960, T341841.
Good central place to stay, hot water, often full.
E pp **Claris Loa**, Granaderos 1631, T311939.
Quiet, good value, central.
E pp **Génesis**, Granaderos 2148, T342841.
Cheaper without bath, near Géminis bus
terminal. Recommended.

❶ Eating

Calama *p653*
On pedestrian part of C Eleuterio Ramírez,
several cafés, juice bars, heladerías and fast
food places.
†† Bavaria, Sotomayor 2095. Good restaurant
with cafetería downstairs, real coffee, open
0800, very popular, also cheaper café at
Latorre 1935, upstairs.
†† Los Braseros de Hanstur, Sotomayor 2030.
Good ambience, good food.
†† Mariscal JP, Félix Hoyos 2127. Best seafood in
town, worth that bit extra (has another branch in
the Mercado Central at Latorre 1974).
†† Mexicano, Latorre 1986A. Genuine Mexican
cuisine, live music at weekends.
††-† Club Croata, on Abaroa, Plaza 23 de Marzo.
Excellent value 4-course almuerzo, good service.
††-† Nueva Chong Hua, Abaroa 2006.
Best Chinese in Calama.

Cafés
Bon Apetit, Sotomayor 2131, open 0800-1530,
1900-2400. Set lunches, salón de té and café.
Panadería y Pastelería Alemana, Latorre 1998.
Good, with OK *empanadas*.
Pastelería Delicius, Sotomayor 1950. *Panadería,
pastelería*, also selling chocolates.
Tilomonte, Ramírez 1929. For breads and cakes.

❷ Shopping

Calama *p653*
Craft stalls On Latorre 1600 block.
Market On Antofagasta between Latorre and
Vivar, selling fruit juices and crafts.
Supermarkets El Cobre, Vargas 2148.
Económico, Grecia 2314.

▲ Activities and tours

Calama *p653*
Several agencies run 1-day and longer tours to
the Atacama region, including San Pedro; these
are usually more expensive than tours from San
Pedro and require a minimum number for the
tour to go ahead. Operators with positive
recommendations include: **Turismo
Buenaventura**, T/F341882, buenventur@
entelchile.net. Recommended tours of the
Atacama region.

⊖ Transport

Tocopilla *p653*
Bus Bus company offices are on 21 de Mayo.
Buses to **Antofagasta** many daily, US$3, 2½ hrs.
To **Iquique**, along coastal road, 3 hrs, US$4,
frequent. To **Chuquicamata** and **Calama**, 2 a
day, 3 hrs, US$5.

Calama *p653*
Air Airport is modern and efficient with Redbanc
ATM, restaurant upstairs, shop with internet. **Lan
Express** (Latorre 1726, T600-526 2000), daily, to
Santiago, via Antofagasta; **Sky** (Latorre 1497,
T310190) 6 days a week. **Lan Express** also flies to
Iquique and **Arica** twice a week. Taxi to town
US$7.50 (courtesy vans from Hotels Calama, Alfa
and Lican Antai - phone in advance). Also buses
into town. Recommended service with **Alberto
Molina**, T324834; he'll pick you up at your hotel.
Bus No main terminal, buses leave from
company offices: **Flota Barrios**, Ramírez 2298;
Frontera, Antofagasta 2041, T318543; **Géminis**,
Antofagasta 2239, T341993; **Kenny Bus**, Vivar
1954; **Pullman**, Balmaceda y Sotomayor,
T311410; **Tur-Bus**, Balmaceda 1852, T316699.
To **Santiago** 23 hrs, US$37.75). To **La Serena**,
usually with delay in Antofagasta, 15 hrs,
US$28.30. To **Antofagasta**, 3 hrs, several
companies, US$4.50. To **Iquique**, 6 hrs, via
Chuquicamata and Tocopilla, US$9.50, most
overnight, but Tur-Bus have one early morning
and one mid-afternoon service. To **Arica**,
usually overnight, US$10, 11 hrs, or change
in Antofagasta. To **Chuquicamata** (see above).
To **San Pedro de Atacama**, Tur-Bus several
daily, **Atacama**, Abaroa 2106, T364295, 3 a
day, US$2.30, **Frontera**, Antofagasta 2041,
T318543, several a day, US$1.90, 1½ hrs.
Transfer Licancábur direct from Calama
airport to San Pedro, US$7, reserve in advance,
T09-942 5978, F055-334194, and Toconao, see
below. **Buses Manchego**, Alonso de Ercilla
2142, T316612, and **Atacama** (Wed, Sun
2400) go to **Ollagüe**, US$5.70. **To Argentina**
Géminis on Wed and Sun, 1130, 11 hrs;

Tur-Bus, Wed, Sun 0915, US$38. **Note** Thieves operate at the bus stations.

Local transport Public transport runs on a *colectivo* system, black cabs with a number on the roof. Just ask which number goes where you want to and flag it down. US$0.65 by day, US$0.75 after 2100. **Taxis**, basic fare US$3.80.

Car hire A hired car shared between several people is an economic alternative for visiting the Atacama region. A 4WD jeep (necessary for the desert) costs US$80 a day, a car US$63. All offices close Sat 1300 till Mon morning. Airport offices only open when flights arrive. IQSA, O'Higgins 877, T310281. If intending to drive in the border area, visit the police in San Pedro to get maps of which areas may have landmines. See Essentials, page 43 for agency web addresses.

Train Station on Av Balmaceda opposite Sotomayor, T348900. To **Uyuni** (Bolivia), weekly service, Wed 2300, though often doesn't leave till early next morning. If on time the train arrives in **Ollagüe** at 0700. The Chilean engine returns to Calama and you have to wait up to 7 hrs for the Bolivian engine. You have to disembark at the border for customs and immigration. Interpol is in a modern building 400 m east of the station. Through fare to Uyuni is US$13.20. Book seats (passport essential) on Mon, Tue or Wed from the **Ferrocarril** office at the station (closed

1300-1500 for lunch), or a local travel agency. Catch the train as early as possible: although seats are assigned, the designated carriages may not arrive; passengers try to occupy several seats to sleep on, but will move if you show your ticket. Sleeping bag and/or blanket essential. Restaurant car operates to the border, cheap. Money can be changed on the train once in Bolivia, but beware forged notes.

● Directory

Calama *p653*

Banks Exchange rates are generally poor especially for TCs. Many Redbanc ATMs on Latorre and Sotomayor. Several **cambios**, eg **Marbumor**, 2 branches on Sotomayor (at Latorre and Av Balmaceda), changes US$, TCs, Argentine pesos and bolivianos, **Moon Valley**, Vivar 1818, and **Parina**, Sotomayor 1984, US$ only. **Consulates** Bolivia, Latorre 1395, T341976, apply for visas before 1500, helpful. **Internet** Many places in the centre, usually under US$1 per hr. **Post offices** Granaderos y V Mackenna. 0830-1300, 1530-1830, Sat 0900-1230, will not send parcels over 1 kg. **Telephones** Lots of phone offices. Entel, Sotomayor opposite Hotel Alfa, is good for phone, fax and internet.

San Pedro de Atacama → *Phone code: 055. Colour map 6, grid B2. Population: 2,824.*

San Pedro de Atacama (*Altitude 2,436 m*), 103 km southeast of Calama (paved, no fuel, food or water along the way) is a small town, more Spanish-Indian looking than is usual in Chile. Long before the arrival of the Spanish, the area was the centre of the Atacameño culture. There is a definite sense of history in the shady streets and the crumbling ancient walls, which drift away from the town into the fields, and then into the dust. Owing to the clear atmosphere and isolation, there are wonderful views of the night sky. Lunar landscapes, blistering geysers and salt flats are all close by. Now famous among visitors as the centre for excursions in this part of the Atacama, San Pedro can be overrun with visitors in summer. The **tourist office** on the plaza ⓘ *Toconao y Gustavo Le Paige, T851420, sanpedrodeatacama@sernatur.cl, open Mon-Fri 1000-1330, 1500-1930, Sat 1000-1400.* Helpful, has a useful suggestions book. See also www.sanpedroatacama.com. **Note:** The main tourist season October-end February is accompanied by high prices and pressure on resources.

The **Iglesia de San Pedro**, dating from the 17th century, has been heavily restored (the tower was added in 1964). The roof is made of cactus. Nearby, on the Plaza, is the **Casa Incaica**, the oldest building in San Pedro. **Museo Arqueológico** ⓘ *museospa@entelchile.net, Mon-Fri, 0900-1300, 1500- 1900; Sat-Sun, 1000-1200, 1500-1800, US$1.50.* The collection of Padre Gustave Paige, a Belgian missionary who lived in San Pedro between 1955 and 1980, is now under the care of the Universidad Católica del Norte. It is a fascinating repository of artefacts, well organized to trace the development of prehispanic Atacameño society. Labels on displays (in Spanish) are good, and there is a comprehensive booklet in Spanish and English.

Around San Pedro de Atacama

The Valle de la Luna with fantastic landscapes caused by the erosion of salt mountains, is a nature reserve 12 km west of San Pedro. It is crossed by the old San Pedro-Calama road. Although buses on the new Calama-San Pedro road will stop to let you off where the old road branches off 13 km northwest of San Pedro (signposted to Peine), it is far better to travel from San Pedro on the old road, either on foot (allow three hours there, three hours back; no lifts), by bicycle (only for the fit and difficult after sunset) or by car (a 20-km round trip is possible). The Valle is best seen at sunset (if the sky is clear), although this is also the most crowded time. Do not leave any rubbish behind on desert excursions – the dry climate preserves it perfectly. Take water, hat, camera and torch. Camping is forbidden.

North of San Pedro along the river is the **Pukará de Quitor**, a pre-Inca fortress restored in 1981. The fortress, which stands on the west bank of the river, was stormed by the Spanish under Pedro de Valdivia. A further 4 km up the river there are Inca ruins at Catarpe. At **Tulor**, 12 km southwest of San Pedro, there is an archaeological site where parts of a stone-age village (dated 800 BC-500 AD) have been excavated; can be visited on foot, or take a tour, US$5 pp. Nearby are the ruins of a 17th century village, abandoned in the 18th century because of lack of water.

El Tatio (*Altitude 4,500 m*), the site of geysers, is a popular attraction. From San Pedro it is reached by a maintained road which runs northeast past the thermal pools at **Puritama** (28 km, worth a visit). The geysers are at their best 0630-0830, though the spectacle varies: locals say the performance is best when weather conditions are stable. Warning: People have been killed or seriously injured by falling into the geysers, or through the thin crust of the mud. Do not stand too close as the geysers can erupt unexpectedly. A swimming pool has been built nearby (take costume and towel). There is no public transport and hitching is impossible. If going in a hired car, make sure the engine is suitable for very high altitudes and is protected with antifreeze. If driving in the dark it is almost impossible to find your way: the sign for El Tatio is north of the turn off (follow a tour bus). Tours arranged by agencies in San Pedro and Calama; nearest *hospedaje* in Caspana (see above).

Toconao (*Population 500*), 37 km south of San Pedro de Atacama, is on the eastern shore of the Salar de Atacama. All houses are built of bricks of white volcanic stone, which gives the village a very characteristic appearance totally different from San Pedro. The 18th-century church and bell tower are also built of volcanic stone. East of the village is a

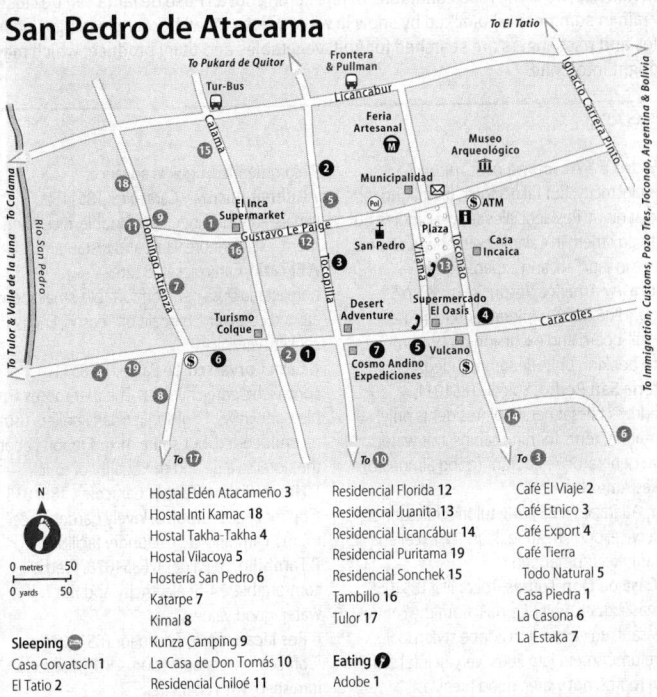

San Pedro de Atacama

N
0 metres 50
0 yards 50

Sleeping 🛏
Casa Corvatsch 1
El Tatio 2

Hostal Edén Atacameño 3
Hostal Inti Kamac 18
Hostal Takha-Takha 4
Hostal Vilacoya 5
Hostería San Pedro 6
Katarpe 7
Kimal 8
Kunza Camping 9
La Casa de Don Tomás 10
Residencial Chiloé 11

Residencial Florida 12
Residencial Juanita 13
Residencial Licancábur 14
Residencial Puritama 19
Residencial Sonchek 15
Tambillo 16
Tulor 17

Eating 🍴
Adobe 1

Café El Viaje 2
Café Étnico 3
Café Export 4
Café Tierra
Todo Natural 5
Casa Piedra 1
La Casona 6
La Estaka 7

beautifully green gorge called the Quebrada de Jérez, filled with fruit trees and grazing cattle (entry US$1). Worth visiting are the vineyards which produce a unique sweet wine. The quarry where the stone sillar) is worked can be visited, about 1½ km east (the stones sound like bells when struck).

South of Toconao is one of the main entrances to the **Salar de Atacama** ① *entry is controlled by Conaf in Toconao, US$3.50*. This vast 300,000-ha salt lake (the third largest expanse of salt flats in the world) is home to the pink flamingo and other birds (though most of the flamingos have moved to lakes higher in the Andes and numbers depend on breeding times). The air is so dry that you can usually see right across the Salar. A huge lake half a metre below the surface contributes to a slight haze in the air. The area is also rich in minerals. Three areas of the Salar form part of the **Reserva Nacional de los Flamencos**, which is in seven sectors totalling 73,986 ha and administered by Conaf in San Pedro.

From Toconao the road heads south through scenic villages to the mine at Laco (one poor stretch below the mine), before proceeding to Laguna Sico (4,079 m), and Paso Sico to Argentina.

Border with Bolivia and Argentina
→ *Between Oct and Mar, Chilean time is 1 hr later than Bolivian.*

Hito Cajón for the border with Bolivia is reached by road 47 km east of San Pedro. The first 35 km are the paved road to Paso de Jama (see below), then it's unpaved to Hito Cajón. From the border it is 7 km north to Laguna Verde. Chilean immigration and customs are in San Pedro, open 0900-1200, 1400-1600. For the Bolivian consulate, see under Calama. Bolivian immigration only gives 1 month entry here.

The ride from San Pedro de Atacama to Salta on a fully paved road through the 4,400-m **Paso de Jama** is spectacular. It stays high on the puna, going by snow-capped peaks, lakes and salt pans, before reaching the Argentine border post, 160 km from San Pedro. There are no money changing facilities nor any other services here. Be prepared for cold. The road continues paved on the Argentine side to Susques and Jujuy. This is much more popular than the **Paso Sico** route, which is hardly used by any public or heavy traffic (paved to Socaire on the Chilean side, about 40% paved in Argentina to San Antonio de los Cobres, slow going on the unpaved parts). **Chilean immigration** and customs are in San Pedro. When crossing by private vehicle, check the road conditions before setting out as Paso de Jama can be closed by heavy rain in summer and blocked by snow in winter. **Note** At all border crossings, incoming vehicles and passengers are searched for fruit, vegetables and dairy produce, which may not be brought into Chile.

● Sleeping

San Pedro de Atacama *p656, map p657*
There is electricity, but take a torch (flashlight) for walking at night. Residenciales supply candles, but better to buy them in Calama beforehand. Rooms are scarce in Jan/Feb, and expensive.
L Explora, Av Américo Vespucio Sur 80, p 5, Santiago, T206 6060, explora@entelchile.net. Luxury full-board and excursion programme, advance booking only. Recommended.
L Hostería San Pedro, Solcor, T851011, hsanpedro@chilesat.net. Pool (residents only), petrol station, tents for hire, cabins, hot water, has own generator, restaurant (good almuerzo), bar, takes Amex but no Tcs.
L Tulor, Atienza, T/F851248, tulor@chilesat.net. Good service, pool, heating, laundry, excellent restaurant. Recommended.
AL La Casa de Don Tomás, Tocopilla, T851055, dontomas@rdc.cl. A bit of a walk from the centre, but pleasant, quiet, modern adobe style, pool under refurbishment late 2005, very helpful staff, no TV in rooms, hot water, good breakfast.

Recommended, book in advance.
AL Kimal, Atienza y Caracoles, T851159, kimal@entelchile.net. Comfortable, nice living room, excellent breakfast and restaurant.
A El Tatio, Caracoles, T851263, hoteleltatio@usa.net. Comfortable, small rooms, around courtyard, bargain off season, English spoken, very nice.
B Casa Corvatsch, Le Paige, T/F851101, corvatsch@entelchile.net. Cheaper rooms **F** pp, pleasant views, English/German spoken, usually recommended, but some mixed reports about the hotel's value and the quality of tours.
B Hostal Takha-Takha, Caracoles, T851038. **F** pp for cheaper rooms, lovely garden, nice rooms, camping **G** pp, laundry facilities.
B Tambillo, Le Paige, T/F851078. Pretty, comfortable, 24-hr electricity and hot water, good value.
B Res Licancábur, Toconao, T851007, **C** off-season, cheaper rooms **E-F** pp, nicely furnished, with character.

B-D Mama Tierra, Pachamama 615,
T851418. With and without bath, kitchen,
hot showers, hammocks in garden, mini mart
next door, helpful, some English spoken.
Recommended.
B-E Res Puritama, Caracoles 113, T851540.
Simple but comfortable, large patio, kitchen
facilities, good showers, camping possible,
nice big dogs.
C Hostal Inti Kamac, Atienza, T851200. Pleasant
veranda, hot water, easy-going, basic but clean,
stores luggage, good value.
C Katarpe, Atienza, T851033,
katarpe@galeon.com. Comfortable, warm, quiet,
nice patio, good value. Recommended.
C Res Chiloé, Atienza, T851017. Hot water,
sunny veranda, good beds and bathrooms,
rooms with bath **A,** good meals, laundry
facilities, luggage store.
C Res Juanita, on the plaza, T851039,
09-491 7663 (mob), newgeston@ hotmail.com.
E without bath, hot water, run-down,
restaurant on site.
D Hostal Vilacoya, Tocopilla. Set around
courtyard, comfortable beds, hot water,
helpful, well-equipped kitchen, luggage store,
free internet access.
D La Quinta Adela, Toconao, T851272,
qtadela@cvmail.cl. Hot water, no breakfast.
D pp Res Sonchek, Calama 370, T851112.
Pleasant but strict, shared bath, also dormitory,
no towels, laundry facilities, use of kitchen,
garden, restaurant, French and English spoken,
mixed reports.
E pp Casa de Nora, Tocopilla, T851114.
Family accommodation, simple rooms, lovely
patio. Recommended.
E pp Hostal Edén Atacameño, Toconao,
T851154. Renovated, rooms with and without
bath, hot water, laundry, parking, also camping
with laundry and cooking facilities, **F.**
E pp Res Florida, Tocopilla, T851021. Without
bath, basic, noisy, patio, hot water evenings only
in dirty shared showers, laundry facilities,
no singles available.
E pp Sumaj-Jallpa, Volcán El Tatio 703, on edge
of town, T851416. Prices vary, some rooms more
expensive, Swiss-Chilean owned, spacious,
kitchen, pool table, new.
Camping F pp Kunza, Antofagasta
y Atienza, T851183, but nightclub next door
at weekends. See also Swimming pools,
in Activities and tours, below.
Rural tourism Red de Turismo Rural Lican
Huasi, Caracoles 349, T851593,
likanhuasi@gmail.com. A network of *casas de
huéspedes* in San Pedro and villages in the ll
Region, such as Solor, Socaire, Ollagüe, Caspana
and Chiu-Chiu, with good facilities.

Around San Pedro de Atacama:
Toconao *p657*
There are basic residenciales.
F pp, Residencial Valle deToconao, on Láscar.
Nice and quiet. And others.

🍴 Eating

San Pedro de Atacama *p656, map p657*
Few places are open before 1000. Most places
offer an evening special for under US$10.
🍴 **Adobe**, Caracoles. Open fire, internet, good
atmosphere and meeting place, loud music.
🍴 **Café Etnico**, Tocopilla 423, cafeetnico@
hotmail.com. Good food, cosy, book exchange,
internet (free for diners), also has a wine club.
🍴 **Café Export**, Toconao y Caracoles.
Nice decor, enormous *empanadas* (big enough
to share), vegetarian options, real coffee, English
spoken, loud music.
🍴 **Casa Piedra**, Caracoles. Open fire, also has a
cheap menu, many of the waiters are musicians,
good food and cocktails. Recommended.
🍴 **La Casona**, Caracoles. Good food, vegetarian
options, cheap almuerzo, large portions. Popular
and recommended.
🍴 **La Estaka**, Caracoles 259, T851201. Wood fire,
cane roof, jazz music, pizzería and other dishes,
good food but quite slow service, bar and book
exchange, lively after 2300.
🍴 **Café Kebab**, Toconao 544. Good for breakfast
and coffee, good value.
🍴 **Café Tierra Todo Natural**, Caracoles. Excellent
fruit juices, "the best bread in the Atacama", real
coffee, yoghurt, best for breakfast, opens earliest.
🍴 **Café El Viaje**, Tocopilla in the Casa de la
Arte. Nice patio, vegetarian food, travel
information, internet access.

🛍 Shopping

San Pedro de Atacama *p656, map p657*
Handicrafts Agrupación de Artesanos,
beside the Biblioteca (opposite the school), is the
place to go for local handicrafts. The *feria* which
runs off the Plaza is mostly foreign goods, eg
from Peru and Ecuador.
Supermarkets El Inca, Calama y Le Paige. For
fruit and vegetables. El Oasis, Caracoles y Vilama.

🚠 Activities and tours

San Pedro de Atacama *p656, map p657*
Mountain biking Bicycles for hire all over
town, by the hour or full day: US$7.60 for
'professional' model, cheaper for 'amateur'.
Tracks in the desert can be really rough, so
check the bike's condition and carry a torch if
riding after dark.

Horse hire US$9.50. **Campamento Base**, Toconao 544, T851451, basecamp@mail.com. A bit more expensive than others (US$80-100 a day), but offers full insurance, for all levels of ability, good breakfast, good guides, English and German spoken (Stephan will give 5% discount to Footprint owners). Also offers rock climbing and has a good vegetarian café. Highly recommended. **Pangea**, Tocopilla, T851111. English spoken, US$2 per hr, US$15 per day. Recommended. Mountaineering: Some climbs go to very high altitude – be acclimatized.

Sand boarding Desert Sports, Toconao 447A/B, T851373, cabanasports@hotmail.com. Good value, tuition, pizzería, also rents mountain bikes. Recommended.

Swimming pools Piscina Oasis, at Pozo Tres, only 3 km southeast but walking there is tough and not recommended. Open all year daily (except Mon) 0500-1730, US$1.50 to swim, sometimes empty. Camping US$3, good showers and picnic facilities, very popular at weekends.

Tour operators

Usual tour rates (may rise in high season): to Valle de la Luna, US$9.50. To the Salar de Atacama, Toconao and Altiplano lakes, 0700-1800, US$40. To El Tatio (begin at 0400) with trekking, US$26 (take swimming costume and warm clothing). El Tatio and villages, US$40. Beware of tours to Valle de la Luna leaving too late to catch sunset – leave before 1600. Before taking a tour, check that the agency has dependable vehicles, suitable equipment (eg oxygen for El Tatio), a guide who speaks English if so advertised, and that the company is well-established. Report any complaints to the municipality or Sernatur.

Andean Summits, Bolivian company, www.andeansummits.com. Has a local office here for cross-border expeditions.

Atacama Connection, Caracoles y Toconao, T851421, www.atacamaconnection.com. For local tours, trekking, private tours.

Cactus Tours, Atienza 419. Good tours to local sites.

Cordillera Traveller, Toconao 447B, T851111, ctraveler@123mail.cl. Good value.

Cosmo Andino Expediciones, Caracoles s/n, T/F851069, cosmoandina@entelchile.net. Very professional and experienced, several languages spoken, owner Martin Beeris (Martín El Holandés). Recommended.

Desert Adventure, Caracoles s/n, T/F851067, www.desertadventure.cl. Good guides and range of trips, English spoken. Recommended.

Labra, Caracoles s/n, T851137. Expert guide Mario Banchón, English and German spoken. Recommended.

Rancho Cactus, Toconao, T851506, F851052. Offers horse riding with good guides to Valle de la Luna and other sites (Farolo and Valerie – speaks French and English), not for experienced riders.

Southern Cross Adventure, Toconao 544 (see under Santiago, Tour operators).

Space, Caracoles 166, T851935/09-817 8354 (mob), www.spaceobs.com. Run by Alain, who speaks 3 languages and gives tours 2000-2330 to study the night sky, hot drink included but wear all your warmest clothes.

Turismo Colque, Caracoles, T851109, www.colquetours.com. Runs tours to Laguna Verde, Laguna Colorado, Uyuni and other sites in Bolivia. 3 days, changing vehicles at the border as the Bolivian authorities refuse permits for Chilean tour vehicles, basic accommodation, take food and especially water (1-day tour to Laguna Verde possible), entrance to Eduardo Avaroa Reserve in Bolivia is included. Passports are stamped en route (check if you need a visa for Bolivia in advance – consulate is in Calama).

Vulcano, Caracoles s/n, T851023. Mountain climbs, adventure tours to infrequently-visited areas, mountain bike hire. Recommended.

Transport

San Pedro de Atacama *p656, map p657*
Bus To **Calama**: US$2.30 (**Atacama**) - US$1.90 (**Frontera**, many daily), 1½ hrs, Tur-Bus, Licancábur 294, T851549, open 0700-2045, several including 1800 (continues to Antofagasta). Frequencies vary with more departures in Jan-Feb and some weekends. Book in advance to return from San Pedro on Sun afternoon. Tur-Bus to **Arica**, 2030, US$15. Tur-Bus to **Santiago**, 4 a day, 3 on Sun, US$39.20. Frontera to **Socaire**, Mon, Thu, Fri 1930, Sun 1230, 2200, US$3.25; to **Toconao**, 4 a day (3 on Sun), US$0.95. **To Argentina**: Géminis, on Toconao (changes bolivianos), Wed and Sun 1130, to **Salta**, US$40, 9 hrs, reserve in advance and book Salta hotel as bus arrives 0100-0200 (schedules change often). **Pullman** (in the Frontera office), Wed, Sun 1045, US$40.

Border with Bolivia

Tránsito público leaves San Pedro for **Hito Cajón** at 0800 or 0830 and costs US$5.70, return about 1000 Chilean time. It is usually booked through an agency in town. Occasionally it runs in the afternoon. Tránsito público from the border to San Pedro takes passengers to their hotels after passing through immigration.

Directory

San Pedro de Atacama *p656, map p657*
Banks Redbanc ATM for Mastercard, Maestro

and Cirrus on Le Paige, opposite the Museum. Also at Caracoles y Domingo Atienza. The cambio on Toconao, casi Caracoles, changes TCs, 1030-1800 daily. Some places change euros; ask around. **Internet** Several places in town. **Post offices** in the Casa Parroquial on the Plaza,

open 0900-1230, 1430-1800. **Telephones** Telefónica in Galería Peral at Caracoles 317, local 4, also has internet. Also at Caracoles y Vilama. **Entel** is on the corner of Plaza at Vilama, in the arcade.

Iquique and around

The Cordillera de la Costa slowly loses height north of Iquique, terminating at the Morro at Arica (see page 666): from Iquique north it drops directly to the sea and as a result there are few beaches along this coast. Inland the central depression (pampa) 1,000-1,200 m is arid and punctuated by salt-flats south of Iquique. Between Iquique and Arica it is crossed from east to west by four gorges. East of this depression lies the sierra, the western branch of the Andes, beyond which is a high plateau, the altiplano (3,500-4,500 m) from which rise volcanic peaks. In the altiplano there are a number of lakes, the largest of which, Lago Chungará (see page 668), is one of the highest in the world. The coastal strip and the pampa are rainless; on the coast temperatures are moderated by the Pacific, but in the pampa variations of temperature between day and night are extreme, ranging from 30°C to 0°C. The altiplano is much colder.

Iquique → *Phone code: 057. Colour map 6, grid B2. Population: 145,139.*

Iquique is an attractive port and city with well-preserved historical buildings. Around it the desert pampa stretches north, south and to the mountains. Several oases also have strong historical associations, either in the form of geoglyphs, the last evidence of peoples long vanished, or the ghost towns of nitrate operations. Mamiña and Pica are thermal resorts within easy reach of Iquique; both are beautiful, tranquil places.

The name of the capital of I Región (Tarapacá) and one of the main northern ports, is derived from the Aymara word *ique-ique*, meaning place of 'rest and tranquillity'. The city, 492 km north of Antofagasta and 47 km west of the Pan-American Highway, is situated on a rocky peninsula at the foot of the high Atacama pampa, sheltered by the headlands of Punta Gruesa and Cavancha. The city, which was partly destroyed by earthquake in 1877, became the centre of the nitrate trade after its transfer from Peru to Chile at the end of the War of the Pacific. A short distance north of town along Amunátegui is the **Free Zone (Zofri)** ① *Mon-Sat 0800-2100, limit on tax free purchases US$650 for foreigners, US$500 for Chileans, getting there: colectivo from the centre US$0.50*. It is worth visiting this giant shopping centre, which sells all manner of imported items, including electronic goods. It is much better value than Punta Arenas. **Tourist office** ① *Serrano 145, of 303, T312238, infoiquique@sernatur.cl, Mon-Fri, 0830-1630*. Masses of information, helpful.

In the centre of the old town is the **Plaza Prat**. On the northeast corner of the Plaza is the Centro Español, built in Moorish style by the local Spanish community in 1904; the ground floor is a restaurant, on the upper floors are paintings of scenes from Don Quijote and from Spanish history. Three blocks north of the Plaza is the old Aduana (customs house) built in 1871; in 1891 it was the scene of an important battle in the Civil War between supporters of President Balmaceda and congressional forces. Part of it is now the Museo Naval, focusing on the Battle of Iquique, 1879. Along Calle Baquedano, which runs south from Plaza Prat, are the attractive former mansions of the 'nitrate barons', dating from between 1880 and 1903. The finest of these is the **Palacio Astoreca** ① *Baquedano y O'Higgins, Tue-Fri 1000-1400, 1500-1900, Sat-Sun 1000-1300, US$1*. Built in 1903, it was subsequently the Intendencia and now a museum of fine late 19th century furniture and shells. **Museo Regional** ① *Baquedano 951, Mon-Fri 0800-1300, 1500-1850, Sat 1030-1300, Sun (in summer) 1000-1300, 1600-2000*, contains an archaeological section tracing the development of prehispanic civilizations in the region; an ethnographical collection of the Isluga culture of the Altiplano (AD 400), and of contemporary Aymara culture; also a section devoted to the nitrate era which includes a model of a nitrate office and the collection of the nitrate entrepreneur, Santiago Humberstone. Sea lions and pelicans can be seen from the harbour. There are **cruises** ① *US$2.50, 45 mins, minimum 10-15 people*, from the passenger pier.

The **beaches** at Cavancha just south of the town centre are good; those at Huaiquique are reasonable, November-March. There are restaurants at Cavancha. Piscina Godoy is a fresh water swimming pool on Av Costanera at Aníbal Pinto and Riquelme, open in the afternoon, US$1 There are several hills where you can paraglide, good for beginners.

Around Iquique

Humberstone, a large nitrate town, is now abandoned. It is at the junction of the Pan-American Highway and the road to Iquique. Entry by 'donation', US$1.50, guided tours Saturday-Sunday, leaflets available. Colectivo from Iquique US$2; phone near site for booking return. Though closed since 1961, you can see the church, theatre, pulpería (company stores) and the swimming pool (built of metal plating from ships' hulls). Nearby are the ruins of other mining towns including Santa Laura. Local tour companies run trips to the area, including Humberstone, Santa Laura, Pisagua and **Pozo Almonte**, 52 km east (*Population c. 5,400*). This town was the chief service provider of the nitrate companies until their closure in 1960. The **Museo Histórico Salitrero** ① *on the tree-shaded plaza, Mon-Fri 0830-1300 and 1600-1900*, displays artefacts and photographs of the nitrate era.

To Cerro Pintados (see page 653) take any bus south, US$2.50, and walk from the Pan-American Highway then hitch back or flag down a bus. From Pozo Almonte 74 km (paved), **Mamiña** (*Population c. 600, Altitude 2,750 m*) has abundant thermal springs and

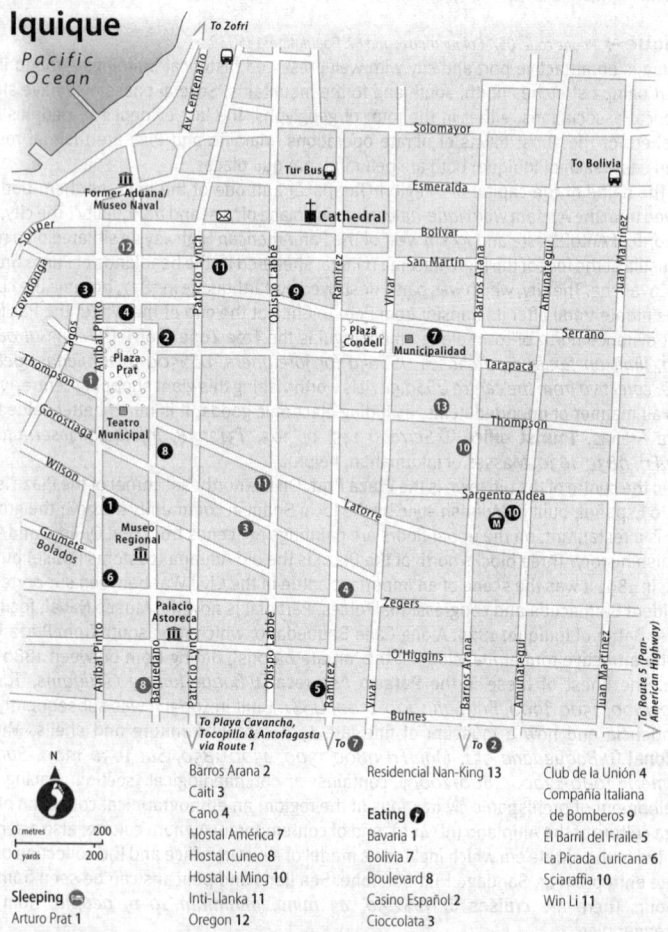

a mud spring (**Baño Los Chinos** *0930-1300*). The therapeutic properties of the waters and mud are Mamiña's main claim to fame. Mineral water from the spring is sold throughout northern Chile. There are ruins of a prehispanic pukará (fortress) and a church, built in 1632, the only colonial Andean church in Chile with two towers. An Aymara cultural centre, Kaspi-kala, has an artesanía workshop and outlet.

La Tirana (*Population 550, Altitude 995 m*) is famous for a religious festival to the Virgen del Carmen, held from 10 to 16 July, which attracts some 80,000 pilgrims. Over 100 groups dance night and day, starting on 12 July. All the dances take place in the main plaza in front of the church; no alcohol is served. Accommodation is impossible to find, other than in organized camp sites (take tent) which have basic toilets and showers. It is 10 km east of the Pan-American Highway (70 km east of Iquique), turn-off 9 km south of Pozo Almonte. **Pica** (*Population 1,767, Altitude 1,325 m*), 42 km from La Tirana, was the most important centre of early Spanish settlement in the area. Most older buildings date from the nitrate period when it became a popular resort. The town is famous for its pleasant climate, citrus groves and two natural springs, the best of which is **Cocha Resbaladero** ① *0700-2000 all year, US$2, snack bar, changing rooms, beautiful pool, tourist office opposite.*

Many other sites around Iquique, including the Giant of the Atacama (see below), are difficult to visit without a car.

From Iquique to the Bolivian Border

At **Huara** (*Population 450*), 33 km north of Pozo Almonte, a road turns off the Pan-American Highway to **Colchane**. At 13 km east of Huara are the huge geoglyphs of Cerro Unitas, with the giant humanoid figure of the Gigante del Atacama and a sun with 24 rays, on the sides of two hills (best seen from a distance). This road is in a terrible state, with long-term roadworks and a diversion heavily damaged by lorries. Some buses from Iquique to La Paz and Oruro pass through, or La Paloma at 2300 from Esmeralda y Juan Martínez. 173 km northeast is the Bolivian border at Pisiga (open daily 0800-1300, 1500-1800).

Northwest of Colchane, the **Parque Nacional Volcán Isluga** ① *Park Administration at Enquelga, 10 km north of the entrance, but guardaparques are seldom there, Arica T58-250570 for details of hospedaje at the guardería,* covers 174,744 ha at altitudes above 2,100 m and is some of the best volcanic scenery in northern Chile. (**D** pp). The village of **Isluga**, near the park entrance, 6 km northwest of Colchane, has an 18th century Andean walled church and bell tower. Wildlife varies according to altitude but includes guanacos, vicuñas, llamas, alpacas, vizcachas, condors and flamingoes.

The Pan-American Highway runs across the Atacama desert at an altitude of around 1,000 m, with several steep hills which are best tackled in daylight (at night, sea mist, camanchaca, can reduce visibility). At **Zapiga**, 80 km north of Pozo Almonte, there is a crossroads: east through Camiña (*Population 500, Altitude: 2,400 m*), a picturesque village in an oasis, 67 km east of Zapiga along a poor road. Thence mountain roads lead across the Parque Nacional Volcán Isluga to Colchane. The westerly branch runs 41 km to **Pisagua** (*Population 200*), formerly an important nitrate port, now a fishing village. Several old wooden buildings are National Monuments. The fish restaurants make a pleasant stop for a meal. Mass graves dating from just after the 1973 military coup were discovered near here in 1990. At Km 57 north of Huara there is a British cemetery at Tiliviche dating from 1825. The Geoglyphs of Tiliviche representing a group of llamas (signposted, to left, and easily accessible), Km 127, can be seen from the highway.

🛏 Sleeping

Iquique *p661, map p662*
Accommodation is scarce in the weeks before Christmas as many Chileans visit Iquique to shop in the Zofri. All hotels in the list are recommended.
AL-A Arturo Prat, Aníbal Pinto 695, Plaza Prat, T427000, www.hotelarturoprat.cl. 4-star, pool, health suite, expensive restaurant, tours arranged.
A Atenas, Los Rieles 738, T431100, atenashotel2000@yahoo.es. Pleasant, personal, good value, good service and food.

A Barros Arana, Barros Arana 1302, T412840, hotelba@entelchile.net. Modern, pool, good value.
A Cano, Ramírez 996, T315580, www.iqq.cl/hotelcano. Big rooms, nice atmosphere, good value.
B Inti-Llanka, Obispo Labbé 825, T311104, www.inti-llanka.cl. Nice rooms, helpful, good value.

C Caiti, Gorostiaga 483, T/F423038. Pleasant, with breakfast and all mod cons, rooms fairly basic and staff not very helpful.

C-D Hostal América, Rodríguez 550, near beach, T427524, transjaws81@hotmail.com. Shared bath, no breakfast, motorcycle parking, good value.

C-D Hostal Cuneo, Baquedano 1175, T428654, hostalcuneo@hotmail.com. Modern, nice rooms, shared bath, helpful, pleasant, good value.

C-D Hostal Li Ming, Barros Arana 705, T421912, www.hostal.cl. Simple, good value, small rooms.

C-D Res Nan-King, Thompson 752, T330961. Small but nice rooms, well-kept.

D pp Oregon (also called Durana), San Martín 294, T410959. Central, hot water, breakfast included.

Around Iquique *p662*
Mamiña

There are several hotels and residenciales offering rooms with bath fed by the springs and full board.

AL pp Refugio del Salitre, T751203, tmami@chilesat.net. Secluded, nice rooms and lovely views, helpful, pool.

A pp Los Cardenales, T438182, T09-545 1091 (mob). Beautifully designed, comfortable, superb food, English and German spoken, pool.

B pp Llama Inn, T419893, pierangelam@hotmail.com. Room only, good meals extra (including vegetarian on request), comfortable, pool.

B pp Termal La Coruña, T09-543 0360. Good, Spanish cuisine, horse riding, nice views, very helpful.

Pica

A Santa Rosa, Sector Comiño, Lote B, T741670, www.resortsantarosa.cl. Large rooms and stylish cabins (**AL**) with kitchen and patio, lovely gardens, quiet, good restaurant, excellent value.

C-D Los Emilios, Cochrane 201, T741126. With breakfast, interesting old building with nice lounge and patio, pool. Recommended.

C-D O'Higgins, Balmaceda 6, T721524. Modern, well furnished.

D San Andrés, Balmaceda 197, T741319. With breakfast, basic, good restaurant.

● Eating

Iquique *p661, map p662*

The restaurants on the wharf on the opposite side of Av Costanera from the bus terminal are poor value. Many chifas including **Win Li**, San Martin 439, and 6 cheaper ones on Tarapacá 800/900 blocks. There are several good, cheap seafood restaurants on the 2nd floor of the central market, Barros Arana y Latorre, eg **Toyita**.

♦♦♦ Otelo, Valenzuela 775. Italian specialities, seafood.

♦♦ Bavaria, Pinto 926. Expensive restaurant, reasonably priced café serving real coffee, snacks and almuerzo.

♦♦ Boulevard, Baquedano 790. Good, French, English and French spoken.

♦♦ Casino Español, Plaza Prat. Good meals well served in beautiful building.

♦♦ Club de la Unión, Plaza Prat. Roof terrace with panoramic views, open lunchtimes only, good food.

♦♦ Colonial, Plaza Prat. Fish and seafood, popular, good value.

♦♦ El Barril del Fraile, Ramírez 1181. Good seafood, nice atmosphere.

♦♦ Sciaraffia, Sgto Aldea 803 (Mercado Centenario). Open 24 hrs, good value, large choice.

♦ Bolivia, Serrano 751. *Humitas* and *salteñas*. Recommended.

♦ Compañía Italiana de Bomberos, Serrano 520. Authentic Italian cuisine, excellent value almuerzo, otherwise more expensive.

♦ La Picada Curicana, Pinto y Zegers. Good local cuisine, good value menu de la casa.

Cioccolata, Pinto 487 (another branch in the Zofri). Very good coffee and cakes.

Jugos Tarapacá, Tarapacá 380. Good fruit juices.

Salon de Té Ricotta, Vivar y Latorre. Very popular for onces, quite expensive.

Splendid, Vivar 795. Good onces, inexpensive.

Tropical, Baquedano y Thompson. Recommended for juices and snacks.

Via Pontony, Baquedano y Zegers. Fruit juices and empanadas, good.

Around Iquique: Pica *p663*

Try the local alfajores, delicious cakes filled with cream and mango honey.

♦♦ El Edén, Riquelme 12. 1st class local food in delightful surroundings.

♦ La Mía Pappa, Balmaceda, near plaza. Good selection of meat and juices, attractive.

♦ La Palmera, Balmaceda 115. Excellent almuerzo, popular, near plaza.

♦ La Viña, Ibáñez 70. Good cheap *almuerzo*.

● *For an explanation of the sleeping and eating price codes used in this guide, see inside the front*
● *cover. Other relevant information is found in Essentials pages 604-605.*

🍷 Bars and clubs

Iquique *p661, map p662*
Santa Fé, Mall Las Américas, locales
10-11-193. Mexican, live music, great
atmosphere, very popular.
Taberna Barracuda, Gorostiaga 601. For late
night food, drink, video entertainment, dancing,
nice decor, nice atmosphere.

⛰ Activities and tours

Iquique *p661, map p662*
The tourist office maintains a full list of operators.
Parapenting Contact the Zone Norte branch
of the Chilean Hanggliding Association,
www.achvl.cl.
Altazor Skysports, Vía 6 manzana A, sitio 3, Bajo
Molle, T380110, www.altazorsky sports.com.
Avitours, Baquedano 997, T527692,
www.avitours.cl. Tour to Pintados, La Tirana,
Humberstone, Pica, etc, some bilingual guides,
day tours start at US$20.
Paraventura, T329041/09-874 1334,
www.paraventura.cl. Frank Valenzuela, qualified
tandem pilot, professional and helpful, great
40-min flights. Highly recommended.

🚌 Transport

Iquique *p661, map p662*
Air Diego Aracena international airport,
35 km south at Chucumata. Taxi US$9.50; airport
transfer, T310800, US$3.20 for 3 or more
passengers, unreliable. LAN and Sky fly to **Arica,
Antofagasta** and **Santiago**. LAN/Lan Express
also fly to **Calama, Copiapó** and **La Serena**. See
Getting there, Essentials, for international flights.
Bus Terminal at north end of Patricio Lynch (not
all buses leave from here); bus company offices
are near the market on Sgto Aldea and B Arana.
Tur-Bus, Esmeralda 594, T472987 (420634 at
terminal), with Redbanc ATM and luggage store.
Pullman, in terminal T426522. Southbound
buses are searched for duty-free goods, at
Quillagua on the Pan-American Highway and at
Chipana on the coastal Route 1. To **Arica**, buses
and colectivos, US$5, 4½ hrs. To **Antofagasta**,
US$10, 8 hrs. To **Calama**, 6 hrs, US$9.50. To
Tocopilla along the coastal road, buses and
minibuses, several companies, 4 hrs, US$4. To **La
Serena**, 18 hrs, US$18. To **Santiago**, 28 hrs,
several companies, US$21 (US$32 salón cama).

International buses To **Bolivia** Litoral,
T423670, daily to **Oruro**, US$8, and **La Paz**,
US$12. **Salvador** and others from Esmeralda near
Juan Martínez around 2100-2300, US$8-13 (may
have a cold wait for customs to open at 0800).
Car hire Iqsa, Labbé 1089, T/F417068. **Procar**,
Serrano 796, T/F413470.

Around Iquique *p662*
Mamiña
Bus Transportes Tamarugal, Barros Arana 897,
Iquique, daily 0800, 1600, return 1800, 0800, 2½
hrs, US$4, good service. Also **Mamiña**, Latorre
779, daily.

Pica
Bus Minibus **Iquique**-Pica: San Andrés, Sgto
Aldea y B Arana, Iquique, daily 0930, return
1800; **Pullman Chacón**, Barros Arana y Latorre,
many daily; **Santa Rosa**, Barros Arana 777, daily
0830, 0930, return 1700, 1800. US$2.50
one-way, 2 hrs.

🛈 Directory

Iquique *p661, map p662*
Airline offices LAB, Serrano 442, T418396.
LanChile, Tarapacá 465, T427600, and in Mall
Las Américas. Sky, Ramírez 411, T415013.
Banks Numerous Redbanc ATMs in the centre
and the Zofri. Cambios: **Afex**, Serrano 396, for
TCs. Money Exchange, Lynch 548, loc 1-2. Best
rates for TCs and cash at casas de cambio in the
Zofri, eg Wall Street (sells and cashes Amex
TCs). **Consulates** Bolivia, Gorostiaga 215,
Departamento E, T421777. Mon-Fri 0930-1200.
Italy, Serrano 447, T421588. Netherlands,
Tarapacá 123, T390900. Peru, Zegers 570,
T411466. Spain, Manzana 2, Sitio 5 y 9, Zofri,
T422330. **Internet** Fassher Internet, Vivar
1497, p 2. US$0.80 per hr. Same price is
PC@NET Computación, Vivar 1373. More
central is Obispo Labbé y Serrano, US$1.50 per
hr. **Language schools** Academia de
Idiomas del Norte, Ramírez 1345, T411827,
idiomas@chilesat.net. Swiss run, Spanish classes
and accommodation for students. **Post
offices** Correo Central, Bolívar 485.
Telephones Telefónica, Serrano 620. Entel,
Tarapacá 476. **Note** Correos and phone
companies all have offices in the Plaza de
Servicios in the Zofri.

Arica and Lauca

The Lauca national park, the most northerly in Chile, has some of the country's most stunning scenery: high lakes, snow-capped volcanoes, lava fields and varied bird life. Small Andean villages near the park retain their Aymara culture. Lauca is easily reached from Arica, Chile's northernmost city, which is the main outlet for Bolivian trade and is even closer to Peru. It's a busy place, dominated by the rocky headland of El Morro.

Arica → *Phone code: 058. Colour map 6, grid A1. Population: 174,064.*

Arica, 20 km south of the Peruvian border, is built at the foot of the Morro headland and is fringed by sand dunes. The Andes can be clearly seen from the anchorage. Arica used to be the principal route for travellers going overland to Bolivia, via the Parque Nacional Lauca. Now there is competition from the San Pedro de Atacama-Uyuni route, so new routes are being considered to link this part of the coast with San Pedro, via the high altitude national parks. This is an important port and route-centre. The road route to La Paz via Tambo Colorado is now paved and Arica is a popular seaside destination for landlocked Bolivians, as well as Chileans. A 63-km railway runs north to Tacna in Peru. Regrettably, Arica is also becoming a key link in the international drugs trade. The Sernatur tourist office ① *San Marcos 101, T252054, in a kiosk next to the Casa de la Cultura, Mon-Fri 0830-1330, 1500-1900,* is very helpful, English spoken, good map, list of tour companies. Head office is at ① *Prat 305, p 2, T232101, infoarica@sernatur.cl.* Municipal kiosk also on San Marcos, opposite Sernatur, opens at 0830.

The **Morro**, with a good view from the park on top (10 minutes' walk by footpath from the southern end of Colón), was the scene of a great victory by Chile over Peru in the War of the Pacific on 7 June 1880. **Museo Histórico y de Armas** ① *summit of the Morro, daily 0830-2000 (2200 Jan-Feb), US$0.60,* contains weapons and uniforms from the War of the Pacific.

At the foot of the Morro is the **Plaza Colón** with the cathedral of San Marcos, built in iron by Eiffel. Though small it is beautifully proportioned and attractively painted. It was brought to Arica from Ilo (Peru) in the 19th century, before Peru lost Arica to Chile, as an emergency measure after a tidal wave swept over Arica and destroyed all its churches. Eiffel also designed the nearby Aduana (customs house) which is now the **Casa de la Cultura** *Mon-Fri 0830-2100.* Just north of the Aduana is the La Paz railway station; outside is an old steam locomotive (made in Germany in 1924) once used on this line. In the station is a memorial to John Roberts Jones, builder of the Arica portion of the railway. The Casa Bolognesi, Colón y Yungay, is a fine old building painted blue and white. It holds temporary exhibitions.

Worthwhile sights outside Arica include the **Museo Arqueológico de San Miguel** ① *at Km 13 on the road east to the Azapa valley, T224248, www.uta.cl/masma/, daily Jan-Feb 0900-2000, Mar-Dec 1000-1800, US$2, getting there: take a yellow colectivo from P Lynch y Chacabuco and 600 block of P Lynch, US$1.* Built around an olive press, it contains a fine collection of pre-Columbian weaving, pottery, wood carving and basketwork from the coast and valleys, and also seven mummified humans from the Chinchorro culture (8000-1000 BC), the most ancient mummies yet discovered. Explanations in several languages are loaned free at the entrance. In the forecourt of the museum are several boulders with pre-Columbian petroglyphs. In San Miguel itself is an old cemetery and several typical restaurants. On the road between Arica and San Miguel there are several groups of geoglyphs of humans and llamas ('stone mosaics') south of the road (signed to Cerro Sagrado, Cerro Sombrero – an Azapa Archaeological Circuit is advertised). North of Arica along Route 11, between Km 14 and Km 16, is the **Lluta valley** where you can see along the hillsides four groups of geoglyphs, representing llamas, and eagle and human giants. The road continues through the Parque Nacional Lauca and on to Bolivia. Take a bus from Mackenna y Chacabuco.

By road to Bolivia

1) Via **Chungará** (Chile) and **Tambo Quemado** (Bolivia). This, the most widely used route, begins by heading north from Arica on the Pan-American Highway (Route 5) for 12 km before turning right (east towards the cordillera) on Route 11 towards Chungará via Putre and Parque Nacional Lauca. The road passes **Termas de Juasi** ① *just after Km 130, look for sign, US$2,* rustic thermal baths, with mud baths and a small swimming pool. This road is now paved to La Paz, estimated driving time six hours. 2) Via **Visviri** (Chile) and **Charaña** (Bolivia), following the La Paz-Arica railway line. This route should not be attempted in wet weather.

Arica

Arica centre

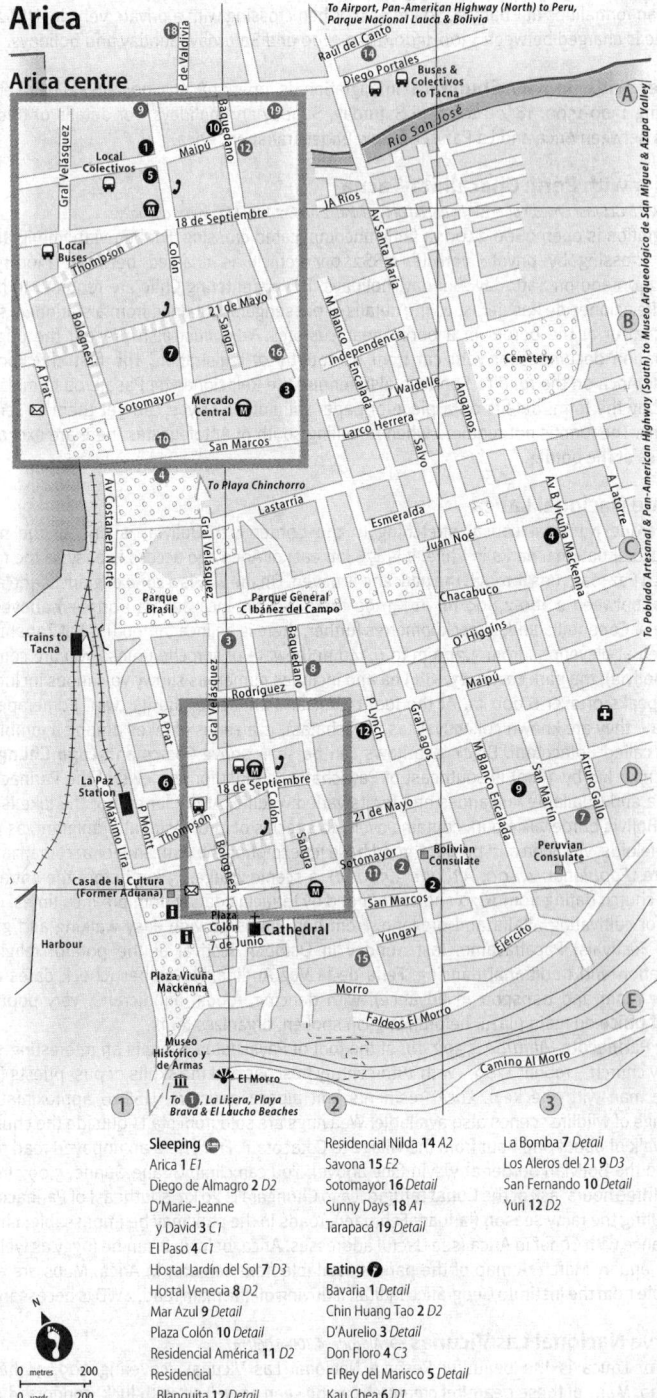

To Airport, Pan-American Highway (North) to Peru,
Parque Nacional Lauca & Bolivia

Río San José

Raúl del Canto

Diego Portales

Buses &
Colectivos
to Tacna

Local
Colectivos

Local
Buses

Mercado
Central

To Playa Chinchorro

Lastarria

Esmeralda

Juan Noé

Chacabuco

O'Higgins

Parque
Brasil

Parque General
C Ibáñez del Campo

Maipú

Trains to
Tacna

Rodríguez

Baquedano

La Paz
Station

18 de Septiembre

21 de Mayo

Bolivian
Consulate

Peruvian
Consulate

Sotomayor

Casa de la Cultura
(Former Aduana)

San Marcos

Plaza
Colón

Cathedral

7 de Junio

Yungay

Harbour

Ejército

Plaza Vicuña
Mackenna

Morro

Faldeos El Morro

Museo
Histórico y
de Armas

El Morro

Camino Al Morro

To La Lisera, Playa
Brava & El Laucho Beaches

0 metres 200
0 yards 200

Chile Arica & Lauca

Sleeping
Arica **1** *E1*
Diego de Almagro **2** *D2*
D'Marie-Jeanne
  y David **3** *C1*
El Paso **4** *C1*
Hostal Jardín del Sol **7** *D3*
Hostal Venecia **8** *D2*
Mar Azul **9** *Detail*
Plaza Colón **10** *Detail*
Residencial América **11** *D2*
Residencial
  Blanquita **12** *Detail*

Residencial Nilda **14** *A2*
Savona **15** *E2*
Sotomayor **16** *Detail*
Sunny Days **18** *A1*
Tarapacá **19** *Detail*

Eating
Bavaria **1** *Detail*
Chin Huang Tao **2** *D2*
D'Aurelio **3** *Detail*
Don Floro **4** *C3*
El Rey del Marisco **5** *Detail*
Kau Chea **6** *D1*

La Bomba **7** *Detail*
Los Aleros del 21 **9** *D3*
San Fernando **10** *Detail*
Yuri **12** *D2*

667

Border with Bolivia: Visviri Immigration is open 0800-2400. Chilean formalities at Visviri, Bolivian formalities at Charaña, 10 km east. When crossing with a private vehicle, US$2 per vehicle is charged between 1300-1500, 1850-2100 and Saturday, Sunday and holidays.

Border with Bolivia: Chungará Immigration is open 0800-2100; US$2 per vehicle crossing 1300-1500, 1850-2100 and Saturday, Sunday and holidays. For details of through buses between Arica and La Paz see below under Transport, Arica.

Border with Peru: Chacalluta-Tacna
→ *Between Oct-Mar Chilean time is 1 hr ahead of Peruvian, 2 hrs Oct-Feb/ Mar, varies annually.*
Immigration is open 0800-2400; a fairly uncomplicated crossing. For Peruvian immigration. When crossing by private vehicle, US$2 per vehicle is charged between 1300-1500, 1850-2400 and on Saturday, Sunday, holidays. Drivers entering Chile are required to file a form, Relaciones de Pasajeros, giving details of passengers, obtained from a stationery store in Tacna, or at the border in a booth near Customs. You must also present the original registration document for your car from its country of registration. The first checkpoints outside Arica on the road to Santiago also require the Relaciones de Pasajeros form. If you can't buy the form, details on a piece of paper will suffice or you can get them at service stations. The form is not required when travelling south of Antofagasta. There are exchange facilities at the border.

Parque Nacional Lauca
The Parque Nacional Lauca, stretching to the border with Bolivia, is one of the most spectacular national parks in Chile. It is 176 km east of Arica and access is easy as the main Arica-La Paz road runs through the park and is paved. On the way is a zone of giant candelabra cactus, between 2,300-2,800 m. At Km 90 there is a pre-Inca pukará (fortress) above the village of Copaquilla and, a few kilometres further, there is an Inca tambo (inn) at Zapahuira. Situated at elevations from 3,200 m to 6,340 m (beware of soroche unless you are coming from Bolivia), the park covers 137,883 ha and includes numerous snowy volcanoes including three peaks of over 6,000 m. At the foot of Volcán Parinacota and its twin, Pomerape (in Bolivia – they are known collectively as Payachatas), is a series of lakes among a jumble of rocks, called Cotacotani. Black lava flows can be seen above Cotacotani. **Lago Chungará** (4,517 m, 7 km by 3 km) is southeast of Payachatas, a must for its views of the Parinacota, Sajama and Guallatire volcanoes and for its varied wildlife. At the far end of the lake is the Chile/Bolivia border. The park contains over 140 species of bird, resident or migrant, as well as cameloids, vizcacha and puma. A good base for exploring the park and for acclimatization is **Putre** (*Population 4,400, Altitude 3,500 m*), a scenic village, 15 km before the entrance with a church dating from 1670 and surrounded by terracing dating from pre-Inca times, now used for cultivating alfalfa and oregano. From here paths provide easy walking and great views. Festivals: Pacahayame, last Sunday in October, festival of the potato: religious celebration and traditional dancing. Feria de la Voz Andina, November (check dates and reserve room and transport in advance), with dancing, foods, handicrafts, very popular. **Tourist office** on main plaza, helpful, English spoken, organizes tours.

At **Parinacota** (*Altitude 4,392 m*), at the foot of Payachatas, there is an interesting 17th century church – rebuilt 1789 – with 18th-century frescoes and the skulls of past priests (ask for the man with the key). Local residents knit alpaca sweaters, US$26 approximately; weavings of wildlife scenes also available. Weavings are sold from stalls outside the church. It's a walk of about one hour from the village to Cotacotani. From here an unpaved road runs north to the Bolivian border at Visviri (see above). You can climb Guane Guane, 5,097 m, in two to three hours, ask at the **Conaf refugio**. Lago Chungará is 20 km southeast of Parinacota.

During the rainy season (January-February), roads in the park may be impassable; check in advance with Conaf in Arica (see Useful addresses, Arica, below). It can be foggy as well as wet in January-March. A map of the park is available from Sernatur in Arica. Maps are also available from the Instituto Geográfico Militar. If driving off the main road, 4WD is necessary.

Reserva Nacional Las Vicuñas → *Altitude: 4,300-6,060 m*
South of Lauca is the beautiful Reserva Nacional Las Vicuñas, covering 209,131 ha of altiplano. Many of these beautiful creatures can be seen as well as, with luck, condors, rheas and other birds. Administration is at Guallatiri, reached by turning off the Arica-La Paz road

onto the A147 2 km after Las Cuevas, where there is also a Conaf office. The same road leads into the Monumento Natural Salar de Surire, for which the same weather and road conditions apply. The Salar, also at 4,300 m, is a drying salt lake of 17,500 ha. It has a year-round population of 12,000-15,000 flamingos (Chilean, Andean and James). Administration is in **Surire**, 45 km south of Guallatiri and 129 km south of Putre. A normal car can reach Surire in the dry season, but a high clearance vehicle is essential for all other roads and, in the summer wet season (January to March, also August), 4WD vehicle: take extra fuel. In the wet, roads may be impassable. There is no public transport to these wildlife reserves, but tours can be arranged in Putre or Arica. Ask tour operators such as Latinorizons about routes through these parks from Arica to San Pedro de Atacama. Also check with Conaf in Arica about road conditions and whether the parks are closed at any time.

● Sleeping

Arica *p666, map p667*
In Jan-Feb the municipality supplies cheap basic accommodation, ask at the tourist office. Cheap residenciales on Prat 500 block, Velázquez 700 block and P Lynch 600 block. Others opposite the bus terminal.
AL Arica, San Martín 599, about 2 km along shore (frequent micros and colectivos), T254540, www.panamericanahoteles.cl. Best, price depends on season, good value, good and reasonable restaurant, tennis court, pool, lava beach (not safe for swimming), American breakfast.
AL-A El Paso, Gen Velásquez 1109, T254507, www.hotelelpaso.cl. Bungalow style, pleasant gardens, swimming pool, with breakfast, good restaurant Araksaya.
AL-A Savona, Yungay 380, T231000, reservas@hotelsavona.cl. Comfortable, 3-star, quiet. Highly recommended.
B Diego de Almagro, Sotomayor 490, T224444, F221240. Helpful, comfortable, parking, stores luggage. Recommended.
B Plaza Colón, San Marcos 261, T/F254424, www.hotelplazacolon.cl. With breakfast, comfortable, convenient.
B Sotomayor, Sotomayor 367, T232970, www.hotelsotomayor.cl. Comfortable, helpful, restaurant, parking, cheaper if paying in dollars.
C Hotel D'Marie- Jeanne y David, Velásquez 792, T/F258231, hotelmariejeanneydavid@hotmail.com. With breakfast, TV, laundry, parking, snacks in café, French spoken.
D Hostal Jardín del Sol, Sotomayor 848, T232795, F231462. With breakfast, safe, kitchen facilities, large patio, laundry, very helpful staff. Often recommended.
D Hostal Venecia, Baquedano 741, T252877, hostalvenecia@gmail.com. Spotless, small rooms. Recommended.
D Res América, Sotomayor 430, T254148, viosa_40@hotmail.comrnet.cl. Hot water, hospitable, good value.
D Res Nilda, Raúl del Canto 947, T222743. Very nice casa de familia, kitchen facilities, laundry, near bus terminal and Playa Chinchorro.

D Res Tres Soles, Población Juan de Noé 921, Pasaje 15, T227207, tressolesarica@hotmail.com. E without bath, opposite bus terminal, quiet, meals available, English spoken, convenient, helpful.
D Tarapacá, Maipú 455, T252680, hoteltarapaca@hotmail.com. With breakfast, helpful, laundry.
E pp Mar Azul, Colón 665, T256272, www.hotelmarazul.cl. Small rooms and family rooms, fan, TV, restaurant, small pool, sauna.
E pp Res Blanquita, Maipú 472, T232064, residencialblanquita@hotmail.com. Breakfast extra, pleasant, good value, laundry and kitchen facilities.
E pp Sunny Days, Tomás Aravena 161 (a little over half way along P de Valdivia, 800 m from bus terminal), T241038, sunnydaysarica@ hotmail.com. All-you-can- eat breakfast, hot water, kitchen, laundry facilities, videos, book exchange, bikes and body boards for rent, nice atmosphere, lots of information. Recommended.

Parque Nacional Lauca *p668*
There are 2 Conaf refuges in the park (but check in advance with Conaf in Arica that they are open): at **Lago Chungará**, and **Las Cuevas** (emergencies only, no tourist facilities). Chungará has cooking facilities, hot showers, **E** pp, sleeping bag essential, take your own food, candles and matches. Advance booking recommended.

Putre
If arriving from Bolivia, remember that no fresh produce may be brought across the border into Chile, so plan accordingly if using a Conaf refugio.
AL Hostería Las Vicuñas, T/F228564. Bungalow-style, helpful, heating, restaurant, does not accept TCs or credit cards.
A Casa Barbarita, belonging to Alto Andino Nature Tours (see below), T300013, casa@birdingaltoandino.com. 2 bedroom house, heating, cooking facilities, naturalist library, information in English.
C Res La Paloma, O'Higgins 353, T09-1979319, lapalomahugopaco@hotmail.com. **D** with shared

bath, hot showers after 0800 unless requested, no heating but lots of blankets, good food in large, warm restaurant, indoor parking; supermarket opposite.
D Hostal Cali, Baquedano. **E** with shared bath, pleasant, no heating, hot water, good restaurant, supermarket.
E Hostal Chez Charlie, contact through *Latinorizons* (see Activities and tours, below). Comfortable, shared bath, hot water, good value, French and English spoken.
E Res Rosamel, Latorre y Carrera, on plaza, T300051. Hot water, pleasant, good restaurant.
Camping Sra Clementina Cáceres, blue door on C Lynch, allows camping in her garden.

Parinacota
Accommodation is available with various families, ask at the food and artesanía stands. You can camp behind the Conaf office for free, great site.

Reserva Nacional Las Vicuñas: Salar de Surire *p669*
At Surire there is a Conaf refugio, 4 beds, very clean, prior application to Conaf in Arica essential. There is also a campsite at Polloquere, 16 km south of Surire, no facilities.

● Eating

Arica *p666, map p667*
Many good places on 21 de Mayo and offering meals, drinks, real coffee, juices and outdoor seating.
♥♥ Los Aleros del 21, 21 de Mayo 736. Recommended for seafood and service.
♥♥ D'Aurelio, Baquedano 369. Italian specialities, good pasta, seafood.
♥♥ Bavaria, Colón 613, upstairs. Good restaurant, coffee and cakes.
♥♥ Don Floro, V MacKenna 847. Good seafood and steaks, good service. Highly recommended.
♥♥ Chin Huang Tao, Lynch 224. Excellent Chinese.
♥♥ Maracuyá, San Martín 0321. Seafood, splendid location on the coast.
♥♥ El Rey del Marisco, Colón 565, upstairs. Excellent seafood, not always welcoming.
♥ Acuario, Muelle Turístico. Good food in fishy environment, good value *menu de casa*.
♥ La Bomba, Colón 357, at fire station. Good value almuerzo, friendly service.
♥ Kau Chea, 18 de Septiembre y Prat. Chinese, good value.
♥ San Fernando, Baquedano y Maipú. Simple breakfast, good value almuerzo. There are many other cheap restaurants on Baquedano 600/700 blocks.
♥ Yuri, Maipú y Lynch. Good service, cheap lunches. Recommended.

Parque Nacional Lauca: Putre *p668*
♥ Bar Kuchamarka, Baquedano between La Paloma supermarket and Hostal Cali. Popular, good, food available.

☺ Entertainment

Arica *p666, map p667*
Teatro Municipal de Arica, Baquedano 234. Wide variety of theatrical and musical events, exhibitions. Recommended.

☻ Festivals and events

Arica *p666, map p667*
24-26 Jan, folk music and dance carnival. **Late Feb**, Ginga Carnaval, annual group dance competition, 3 nights. **29 Jun**, San Pedro, religious service at fishing wharf and boat parades. First weekend of **Oct**, Virgen de las Peñas, pilgrimage to the site of the Virgin, 4-5 hrs inland.

○ Shopping

Arica *p666, map p667*
Many shopping galerías in the centre, also pharmacies, electrical appliances and clothes shops Ferias for clothes on Velázquez.
Bookshop Andrés Bello, Sotomayor 363, wide selection.
Crafts Poblado Artesanal, Plaza Las Gredas, Hualles 2825 (take bus 2, 3 or 7). Expensive but especially good for musical instruments, open Tue-Sun 0930-1300, 1530-1930, peña Fri and Sat 2130.
Markets Feria Turística Dominical, Sun market, along Chacabuco between Valásquez and Mackenna. Good prices for llama sweaters. Mercado Central, Sotomayor y Sangra, between Colón and Baquedano. Mostly fruit and vegetables. Smaller fruit and veg market, with food stalls, on Colón between 18 de Septiembre and Maipú.

Parque Nacional Lauca: Putre *p668*
Putre has several stores, 2 bakeries and several private houses selling fresh produce. Petrol is more expensive than in Arica but available in cans from the Cali and Paloma supermarkets and from ECA, a government subsidized market on the plaza (cheapest). Other than a small shop with limited supplies in Parinacota, no food is available outside Putre. Take drinking water with you as water in the park is not safe.

▲ Activities and tours

Arica *p666, map p667*
Surfing Strong currents at Playa Las Machas which is popular with surfers. Good

surfing on **La Isleta** near Club de Yates
and on **Playa Chinchorro**.

Swimming Olympic pool in **Parque
Centenario**, Tue-Sun, US$0.50. Take No 5A bus
from 18 de Septiembre. The best beach for
swimming is **Playa Chinchorro**, north of town.
Buses 7 and 8 run to beaches south of town – the
first 2 beaches, La Lisera and El Laucho, are both
small and mainly for sunbathing. Playa Brava is
popular for sunbathing but not swimming
(dangerous currents).

Tours operators

All charge similar prices for tours: Valle de
Azapa US$12; city tour US$10; Parque Nacional
Lauca, see page 668.
Globo Tour, 21 de Mayo 260, T/F231085. Very
helpful for international flights.
Latinorizons, Bolognesi 449, T/F250007,
www.latinorizons.com. Specializes in tours
to Parque Nacional Lauca and the Altiplano,
small groups in four-wheel drive Landcruiser;
also tourist train rides from Arica, bike rental.
Recommended.
Raices Andinas, Sotomayor 195, T233305,
www.raicesandinas.com. Specializes in Altiplano
trips. Recommended.

Parque Nacional Lauca *p668*
One-day tours are offered by most tour operators
and some hotels in Arica, daily in season,
according to demand at other times, US$17-20
pp with breakfast and light lunch; but some find
the minibuses cramped and dusty. You spend all
day in the bus (0730-2030) and you will almost
certainly suffer from soroche. You can leave the
tour and continue on another day as long as you
ensure that the company will collect you when
you want (tour companies try to charge double
for this). Much better are 1½-day tours,
1400-1800 next day (eg Latinorizons), which
include overnight in Putre and a stop on the
ascent at the Aymara village of Socorama, US$56.
For 5 or more, the most economical proposition
is to hire a vehicle. Full-day tours of the National
Park starting at 0830, arranged in Putre, cost
US$45, covering all aspects of Lauca.
Alto Andino Nature Tours, Baquedano 299,
Putre (Correo Putre) T09-282 6195 ,
www.birdingaltoandino.com. Allow a week for
reply to email. Run general tours and upscale,
specialist bird-watching tours to remote areas of
the park, to the Salar de Surire and Parque
Nacional Isluga and to low-level parts of
Atacama; English spoken, owner is an
Alaskan biologist.
Freddy Torrejón and Eva Mamami,
T058-253361. Run tours to local sites and offer
accommodation and meals.

Tour Andino, C Baquedano, Putre, T09-011
0702, www.tourandino.com. Comfortable 4WD
tours from 1 to 4 days with Justino (owner) to
Lauca and other areas, excellent, knowledgeable,
flexible, about US$25 pp. Recommended.
Turismo Taki, is located in Copaquila, about 45
km west of Putre, 100 km east of Arica.
Restaurant, camping site and excursions to
nearby pucarás, Inca tambo and cemetery, good
local food, English and Italian spoken.

☉ Transport

Arica *p666, map p667*
Air Airport 18 km north of city at Chacalluta,
T211116. Taxi to town US$6, colectivo US$3.50
per person. Flights to **La Paz**, LAB and LAN; to
Santiago, LAN, Lan Express and Sky via Iquique
and, less frequently, **Antofagasta**. LanChile/Lan
Express also to **Calama, Copiapó** and **La
Serena**. To **Lima**, from Tacna (Peru), enquire at
travel agencies in Arica.
Bus Local buses run from 18 de Septiembre at
Bolognesi, US$0.25. Long distance bus terminal
at Av Portales y Santa María, T241390, many
buses and colectivos (eg No 8) pass (US$0.25, or
US$0.50); terminal tax US$0.15. All luggage is
carefully searched for fruit 30 mins prior to
boarding and at two stops heading south. Bus
company offices at bus terminal: **Pullman**,
T223837; **Tur-Bus**, T241059. Local services: **Flota
Paco** (La Paloma), Germán Riesco 2071 (bus U
from centre).

To **Iquique**, frequent, US$5, 4½ hrs, also
collective taxis, several companies, all in the
terminal. To **Antofagasta**, US$11, 11 hrs. To
Calama and **Chuquicamata**, 11 hrs, US$10,
several companies, all between 2000 and 2200.
To **San Pedro de Atacama**, 2200, 11½ hrs,
US$15. To **La Serena**, 20 hrs, US$24. To
Santiago, 28 hrs, a number of companies, eg
**Carmelita, Pullman, Ramos Cholele, Tur-Bus,
Fénix** and **Flota Barrios** US$22-26, also salón
cama services, US$34 (most serve meals of a kind,
somewhat better on the more expensive services;
student discounts available). To **Viña del Mar**
and **Valparaíso**, US$25, also salón cama services.
International buses See below for transport
to Bolivia and Peru. **Géminis**, T241647, to **Jujuy**
and **Salta**, Argentina, Tue and Sat, and **Tramaca**,
T222586, Tue 2300.
Car hire **American**, Gen Lagos 559, T252234,
servturi@entelchile.net. **Automóvil Club de
Chile**: Chacabuco 460, T252878, F232780.
Cactus, Baquedano 635, T257430,
cactusrent@latinmail.com. **Ghama**, Diego
Portales 840, of 161, T225158. **Hertz**, Av Andrés
Bello 1469 and at airport, has been
recommended for good service. Several others

and at Chacalluta airport. Rates start at US$26 per day, up to US$50-60 for 4WD. Antifreeze is essential for Parque Nacional Lauca, 4WD if going off paved roads.

Taxi Colectivos on fixed routes within city limit line up on Maipú entre Velásquez y Colón (all are numbered), US$0.50 pp (more after 2000). Taxis are black and yellow and are scarce; hire a colectivo instead, US$1.20-1.50.

Border with Bolivia *p668*

Bus To **La Paz**, Bolivia, at least 4 companies from terminal, US$11-15, most via Putre and Chungará (some daily). Buses from Arica to Visviri, **Humire**, T220198/260164, Tue and Fri, 1030, US$7, also Sun 0830 en route to La Paz; **Martínez**, Tue and Fri 2230 en route to La Paz, both from terminal. Colectivos from Arica US$10. In Visviri take a jeep across the border to Charaña. Buses from Charaña to La Paz, leave before 1000, US$11, 7 hrs. Trucks leave in the afternoon.

Border with Peru *p668*

Colectivos Run from the international bus terminal on Diego Portales to **Tacna**, US$3 pp, 1½ hrs. There are many companies and you will be besieged by drivers. For quickest service take a Peruvian colectivo heading back to Peru. Give your passport to the colectivo office where your papers will be filled. After that, drivers take care of all the paperwork. Chile Lintur,T225038; **San Andrés**, T260167; **San Remo**, T260509; **El Morro**, T262477; **Perú Express**, T249970. Colectivos will pick you up from hotel. Also buses from the same terminal, US$1.50, 2½ hrs. For Arequipa it is best to go to Tacna and catch an onward bus there.

Parque Nacional Lauca *p668*

Bus La Paloma buses leave Germán Riesco 2071, Arica for **Putre** daily at 0630, 4 hrs, US$2.50, returning from La Paloma supermarket 1300 (book in advance); **Jurasi** collective taxi leaves Arica daily at 0700, picks up at hotels, T222813, US$6.50. If you take an Arica-La Paz bus for Putre, it is about 4 km from the crossroads to the town at some 4,000 m, tough if you've come straight up from sea level.

Martínez and **Humire** buses run to **Parinacota** Tue and Fri. Hostal Cali runs buses to Bolivia. Bus to La Paz from Putre crossroads or Lago

Chungará can be arranged in Arica (same fare as from Arica).

Hitchhiking Hitching back to Arica is not difficult; you may be able to bargain on one of the tour buses. Trucks from Arica to La Paz sometimes give lifts, a good place to try is at the Poconchile control point, 37 km from Arica.

⊙ Directory

Arica *p666, map p667*

Airline offices LAB, C Prat, Edif Empresarial, T258259. **LanChile**, 21 de Mayo 345, T251641 (closes 1330 on Sat). **Sky**, Chacabuco 314, loc 52, T251816. **Banks** Many Redbanc ATMs on 21 de Mayo and by Plaza Colón. Money changers on 21 de Mayo and its junction with Colón, some accept TCs. **Cambio**, in Cosmo Center, Colón 600, cash and TCs, reasonable rates. **Consulates** Bolivia, P Lynch 298, T231030. Peru, San Martín 235, T231020. **Cultural centres** Instituto Chileno-Británico de Cultura (library open Mon-Fri 0900-1200, 1600-2100), Baquedano 351, T232399, Casilla 653. **Internet** Plenty of locutorios with internet and cyber cafés in the centre, eg on 21 de Mayo or Bolognesi, average price US$0.75-1 per hr. **Post offices** Prat 375, down pedestrian walkway. Mon-Fri 0830-1330, 1500-1900, Sat 0900-1230. To send parcels abroad, contents must be shown to Aduana (1st floor of post office) on Mon-Fri 0800-1200. Your parcel will be wrapped, but take your own carton. DHL, Colón 351. **Telephones** Entel, 21 de Mayo 345. Open 0900-2200. Telefónica, Colón 430 and at 21 de Mayo 211.Many other phone offices. **Useful addresses** Conaf, Av Vicuña MacKenna 820, T201200, tarapaca@conaf.cl. Mon-Fri 0830-1300, 1430-1630 (take Colectivo 1). Aug-Nov is best season for mountain climbing; permits needed for summits near borders. Write, email or visit **Dirección Nacional de Fronteras y Límites del Estado** (DIFROL) Bandera 52, p 5, Santiago, F56-2-697 1909.

Parque Nacional Lauca: Putre *p668*

Banks Bank in Putre changes dollars but commission on TCs is very high.

Central Valley

One of the world's most fecund and beautiful landscapes, with snowclad peaks of the Andes to the east and the Cordillera de la Costa to the west, the Central Valley contains most of Chile's population. A region of small towns, farms and vineyards, it has several protected areas of natural beauty. Five major rivers cross the Central Valley, cutting through the Coastal Range to the Pacific: from north to south these are the Rapel, Mataquito, Maule, Itata and Biobío. Some of the river valleys provide ideal conditions for growing grapes and making wine and you can wander between vineyards. This is also Chilean cowboy country and at rural shows you can see displays of horsemanship.

Rancagua to Chillán

Rancagua → *Phone code: 072. Colour map 8, grid B1. Population: 167,000.*
The capital of VI Región (Libertador Gen Bernardo O'Higgins) lies on the Río Cachapoal, 82 km south of Santiago. Founded in 1743, it is a service and market centre. At the heart of the city is an attractive tree-lined plaza, the Plaza de los Héroes, and several streets of single-storey colonial-style houses. In the centre of the plaza is an equestrian statue of O'Higgins. The main commercial area lies along Avenida Independencia, which runs west from the plaza towards the bus and rail terminals. The National Rodeo Championships are held at the end of March, with plenty of opportunities for purchasing cowboy items. **Tourist office** ① *Germán Riesco 277, T230413, inforancagua@sernatur.cl.*

For information on the Cachapoal wine producing zone, with details on tours and vineyard visits, see the **Ruta del Vino** ① *Comercio 435, Rancagua, T553684, www.cachapoal wineroute.cl.* Around Santa Cruz and **San Fernando** (51 km south of Rancagua) is the Colchagua Valley, another wine-producing zone. For the Ruta del Vino here ① *Plaza de Armas 298, Santa Cruz, T072-823199, www.colchaguavalley.cl.*

Curicó → *Phone code: 075. Colour map 8, grid B1. Population: 103,919. Altitude: 200 m.*
Between the Ríos Lontué and Teno, 192 km from Santiago, Curicó is the only town of any size in the Mataquito Valley. It was founded in 1744. In mid-March is the Fiesta de la Vendimia with displays on traditional wine-making. In the Plaza de Armas there are fountains and a monument to the Mapuche warrior, Lautaro, carved from the trunk of an ancient beech tree. There is a steel bandstand, built in New Orleans in 1904, which is a national monument. The church of San Francisco (1732), also a national monument, partly ruined, contains the 17th century Virgen de Velilla, brought from Spain. Overlooking the city, the surrounding countryside and with views to the distant Andean peaks is Cerro Condell (100 m); it is an easy climb to the summit from where there are a number of walks. **Torres wine bodega** ① *5 km south of the city, T310455, 0900-1230, 1500-1730, no organized tour, Spanish only, worthwhile, getting there: take a bus for Molina from the local terminal or outside the railway station and get off at Km 195 on the Pan-American Highway.* For information on the vineyards of Curicó, see the **Ruta del Vino de Curicó** ① *Merced 341, p 2, Curicó, T328972, www.rvvc.cl.* The **tourist office** is at Gobernación Provincial ① *Plaza de Armas, Mon-Fri 0900-1330, 1600-1800,* helpful.

Area de Protección Radal Siete Tazas
① *Oct-Mar, administration is in Parque Inglés, entry US$5.70, US$1.90 for students.*
The park is in two parts, one at Radal, 65 km east of Curicó, the other at Parque Inglés, 11 km further on. At Radal, the Río Claro flows through a series of seven rock bowls (*siete tazas*) each with a pool emptying into the next by a waterfall. The river goes through a canyon, 15 m deep but only 1½ m wide, ending abruptly in a cliff and a beautiful waterfall. There is excellent trekking in the park, through beautiful woods and scenery, similar to what can be found further south, but with a better climate.

Talca → *Phone code: 071. Colour map 8, grid B1. Population: 175,000.*
At 56 km south of Curicó (258 km from Santiago via dual carriageway) this is the most important city between Santiago and Concepción. It is a major manufacturing centre and the capital of VII Región (Maule). Founded in 1692, Talca was destroyed by earthquakes in 1742 and 1928. **Museo O'Higginiano** ① *just off the Plaza de Armas at 1 Norte y 2 Oriente, Tue-Fri 1030-1300, 1430-1845, Sat-Sun 1000-1300.* This museum is in a colonial mansion in which Bernardo O'Higgins lived as a child. The house was later the headquarters of O'Higgins' Patriot Government in 1813-14 (before his defeat at Rancagua). In 1818 O'Higgins signed the declaration of Chilean independence here: the room (Sala Independencia) is decorated and furnished in period style. The museum also has a collection of regional art. The **Maule valley** ① *information from the Villa Cultural Huilquilemu, 7 km southeast of Talca, T071-246460, www.valledelmaule.cl,* is another wine producing region, with vineyards that can be visited. The **tourist office** is at ① *4 Oriente y 1 Sur, infomaule@sernatur.cl, Mon-Fri 0830-1930 (1730 winter).*

Constitución and the coast
At the mouth of the Río Maule, 89 km from San Javier on the Pan-American Highway (south of Talca), **Constitución** is an important port and seaside resort. The coast, especially to the north, is beautiful, while south a paved road runs through thick forest to the small towns of Chanco, **Pelluhue** and Curanipe. There are black sand beaches and dunes in this little visited part of Chile.

Vilches
① *US$1.50, 2-2½ hrs, getting there: 4 buses a day, 5 on Sun, US$2.30, 2 hrs.*
This is the starting point for the climb to the volcanoes **Quizapu** (3,050 m) and **Descabezado** (3,850 m). For walks on Descabezado Grande and Cerro Azul (ice axe and crampons needed) contact recommended guide Carlos Verdugo Bravo, Probación Brilla El Sol, Pasaje El Nickel 257, Talca (Spanish only). The Reserva Nacional Altos del Lircay 2 km from Vilches, covers 12,163 ha and includes three peaks, several small lakes and the Piedras Tacitas, a stone construction supposedly made by the aboriginal inhabitants of the region. There are good hikes: Laguna del Alto, eight hours, and El Enladrillado, 12 hours; you can also hike between Radal and Vilches in three days. A visitors' centre and administration are near the entrance and the Talca municipal tourist office has maps.

To the border with Argentina: Paso Pehuenche
A road south of Talca, paved for the first 65 km, runs southeast from the Panamericana along **Lago Colbún** and up the broad valley of the Río Maule to reach the Argentine border at Paso Pehuenche. At the western end of the lake is the town of Colbún, from where a road goes to Linares on the Panamericana. Thermal springs 5 km south of Colbún at Panimávida, and 12 km, Quinamávida. Campsites on south shore. Paso Pehuenche (2,553 m) is reached by poor unpaved road southeast from Lago Colbún. Chilean customs is at La Mina, 106 km from Talca, 60 km from the border (Camping La Querencia, 4 km west of La Mina). On the Argentine side the road continues to Malargüe and San Rafael. The border is open December-March 0800-2100, April-November 0800-1900.

Chillán → *Phone code: 042. Colour map 8, grid B1. Population: 146,000. Altitude: 118 m.*
Chillán, 150 km south of Talca, is capital of Ñuble province and a service centre for this agricultural area. Following an earthquake in 1833, the site was moved slightly to the northwest, though the older site, Chillán Viejo, is still occupied. Further earthquakes in 1939 and 1960 ensured that few old buildings have survived. Chillán was the birthplace of Bernardo O'Higgins (Arturo Prat, Chile's naval hero, was born 50 km away at Ninhue). The Fiesta de la Vendimia is an annual wine festival held in the third week in March. **Tourist office** ① *18 de Septiembre 455, at the side of Gobernación, T042-223272, infochillan@sernatur.cl.* Street map of city, leaflets on skiing, Termas de Chillán, etc.

The centre of the city is **Plaza O'Higgins**, on which stands the modern **Cathedral** designed to resist earthquakes. Northwest of the Plaza O'Higgins, on the Plaza Héroes de Iquique, is the **Escuela México** ① *daily 1000-1300, 1500-1830.* It was donated to the city after the 1939 earthquake. In its library are murals by the great Mexican artists David Alvaro Siqueiros and Xavier Guerrero which present allegories of Chilean and Mexican history. The **Mercado y Feria Municipal** (covered and open markets at Riquelme y Maipón) sell regional arts and crafts and have many cheap, good restaurants, serving regional dishes; open daily, Sunday until 1300. Three blocks further south is the **Museo Naval El Chinchorro** ① *Collin y I Riquelme, Tue-Fri 0930-1200, 1500-1730*, containing naval artefacts and models of Chilean vessels. In Chillán Viejo (southwest of the centre) there is a monument and park at **O'Higgins' birthplace** *park 0830-2000*. It has a 60 m long mural depicting his life (an impressive, but sadly faded, mosaic of various native stones), and a Centro Histórico y Cultural, with a gallery of contemporary paintings by regional artists.

Quinchamalí is 27 km southwest of Chillán, a little village famous for the originality of its craftsmen in textiles, basketwork, black ceramics, guitars and primitive paintings (all on sale in Chillán market). Handicraft fair, second week of February.

Termas de Chillán

East of Chillán 82 km by good road (paved for the first 50 km), 1,850 m up in the Cordillera, are thermal baths and, above, the largest ski resort in southern Chile. There are two open-air thermal pools (officially for hotel guests only) and a health spa with jacuzzis, sauna, mud baths

Chillán

Sleeping	Libertador 6	Club Comercial 2
Claris 2	Quinchamalí 7	Jai Yang 5
Cordillera 3		La Casa Nostra 6
Floresta 4	**Eating**	La Masc'a 7
Gran Hotel Isabel Riquelme 1	Arcoiris 1	
Hospedaje Sonia Segui 5	Café París 3	

etc. Suitable for families and beginners and cheaper than centres nearer Santiago, the ski resort has 28 runs, nine lifts, snowboarding and other activities. It also has two hotels (the five-star Gran Hotel, and the 3-star Pirigallo) and condominium apartments. Season: middle December to the end of March. Information and reservations from **Chillán Ski Centre** ① *Panamericana Norte 3651, T042-434200, www.termaschillan.cl, lift pass US$30 per day, US$20 per half-day, equipment hire about US$25 pp.*

● Sleeping

Rancagua *p673*
AL Camino del Rey, Estado 275, T232314, hotelcaminodelrey@terra.cl. 4-star, suites with full facilities, best in town.
A Rancagua, San Martín 85, T232663, www.hotelrancagua.galeon.com. Quiet, good accommodations, secure parking. Recommended.
B-C España, San Martín 367, T230141, noraberriosf@latinmail.com. Cheaper without bath, central, pleasant, laundry service.

San Fernando
L Viña Casa Silva, Angostura, San Fernando (Casilla 97), T072-716519, www.casasilva.cl. Turn off the Panamericana at Km 133. Elegant hacienda with homemade furniture and 7 luxury rooms, shared country-style living rooms, hot water, cable TV, delicious food and wine from their own vineyard. Recommended.

Curicó *p673*
A Comercio, Yungay 730, T310014, info@hotelcomercio.cl. Cheaper without bath, 3-star, clean. Recommended.
C Prat, Peña 427, T311069. Pleasant patio vines and figs, cheaper without bath, breakfast, hot water, laundry facilities.
D Res Colonial, Rodríguez 461, T314103, resicolonial@terra.cl. Good, basic, cable TV, cheaper without bath, helpful, use of kitchen, patio.

Area de Protección Radal Siete Tazas *p673*
Campsite at Radal village, next to river and minimarket, US$2.50 pp. Several *hosterías* and campsites at Parque Inglés.

Talca *p674*
AL Cabañas Entre Ríos, Panamericana Sur Km 250, 8 km north, T223336. Very good value, excellent breakfast, pool, very helpful owner. Highly recommended.
A-D Casa Chueca, Camino Las Rastras, 4 km from Talca by the Río Lircay, Casilla 143, T197 0096, T09-837 1440 (mob), casachueca@ hotmail.com (also www.trekkingchile.com). Phone hostal from bus terminal for directions on how to get there. With breakfast, very good vegetarian food (US$6), cheaper rooms with

shared bath, Austrian and German owners, many languages spoken, lovely setting, swimming pool, mountain bikes, good tours (including climbing) arranged. Also Spanish classes, see www.spanish-for-travellers.com. Enthusiastically recommended.
A-B Cordillera, 2 Sur 1360, T221817, www.cordillerahotel.cl. Decent standard, serves a good breakfast.
B Hostal del Puente, 1 Sur 407, T220930, hostaldelpuente@adsl.tie.cl. Large breakfast extra, family-owned, parking in central courtyard. Recommended for atmosphere, price and surroundings.
C Hostal del Río, 1 Sur 411, T225448, hostaldelrio@hotmail.com. New rival to Del Puente next door, a little cheaper, also good.
D pp Hosp Santa Margarita, at Pelarco, 18 km northwest, T/F09-335 9051. Swiss run, with breakfast, other meals available, reservations advised (Casilla 1104, Talca). Dec-Mar only.

Constitución and the coast: Pelluhue *p674*
D pp Res Hostería Las Palmeras, Condell 837, T09-579 2431. In an old, tatty house, great atmosphere, meals extra.

To the border with Argentina: Lago Colbún *p674*
C pp Ecological Reserve Posada Campesina, at Rabones on the road Linares/ Panimávida, T09-752 0510, full board, estancia offering forest trails, trekking and horseback expeditions, English spoken, highly recommended.

Chillán *p674, map p675*
Lots of cheap hospedajes on Constitución 1-300.
AL Quinchamalí, El Roble 634, T223381, hotelquinchamali@entelchile.net. Central, quiet, hot water and heated lounge.
A Gran Hotel Isabel Riquelme, Constitución 576, T213663, hotelir@termaschillan.cl. Decent option for the price, with cable TV, restaurant, laundry, parking.
B Cordillera, Arauco 619, on Plaza de Armas, T215211, hotelcordillera@entelchile.net. 3-star, small, all rooms with heating, good.
C Claris, 18 de Septiembre 357, T221980. Welcoming, hot water, **E** pp without bath.

C **Floresta**, 18 de Septiembre 278, T222253.
Quiet, old fashioned and welcoming.
D **Libertador**, Libertad 85, T223255. Large
rooms, without breakfast, parking, good, a few
mins' walk from the railway station.
E pp **Hosp Sonia Segui**, Itata 288, T214879.
Good, especially breakfast and the beds, huge
almuerzo, helpful, but noisy and bathrooms dirty.

Termas de Chillán *p675*

At Las Trancas on the road to the Termas, Km
70-76 from Chillán are:
LL **Robledal**, T432030, www.hotelrobledal.cl.
Pleasant rooms, bar, restaurant, sauna and
jacuzzi, tours offered.
L **Parador Jamón, Pan y Vino**, Casilla 618,
Chillán, T222682, www.nevadosdechillan.cl.
Arranges horse riding expeditions. There are
many other cabañas in the village and Galería de
Arte de Luis Guzmán Molina, a painter from
Chillán, Entrada por Los Pretiles Km 68.5.
Camping available 2 km from the slopes.

🍴 Eating

Rancagua *p673*

There eating places west of Plaza de los Héroes,
eg on Independencia and Astorga.

Curicó *p673*

♦♦♦-♦♦ **Club de la Unión**, Plaza de Armas.
Good, elegant.
♦♦ **American Bar**, Yungay 647. Real coffee, small
pizzas, good sandwiches, pleasant atmosphere,
open early morning to late afternoon including
weekends. Recommended.
♦♦ **El Fogón Chileno**, M Montt 399. Good
for meat and wines.
♦ **Café-Bar Maxim**, Prat 617. Light meals,
beer and wine.
♦ **Centro Italiano Club Social**, Estado 531.
Good, cheap meals.

Chillán *p674, map p675*

The Chillán area is well-known for its *pipeño* (very
young) wine and *longanizas* (sausages).
♦♦ **Arcoiris**, El Roble 525. Vegetarian.
♦♦ **Café París**, Arauco 666. Fine restaurant
upstairs, good bar.
♦♦ **Los Adobes**, in Chillán Viejo, on Parque
O'Higgins. Good food and service.
♦ **Club Comercial**, Arauco 745. Popular at
lunchtime, good value almuerzo, popular
bar at night.
♦ **Jai Yang**, Libertad 250. Good Chinese.
♦ **La Copucha**, 18 de Septiembre y Constitución.
Inexpensive meals and sandwiches.
♦ **La Masc'a**, 5 de Abril 544. Excellent meals,
empanadas de queso, drinks.

⛰ Activities and tours

Constitución and the coast *p674*

For information, tours and lodging in this area,
contact Alejandro of **Ruta Verde**, T744 8224,
tours@rutaverde.cl. Speaks English, good
fun. Recommended.

🚌 Transport

Rancagua *p673*

Bus The terminal for regional buses is at Doctor
Salinas 1165, just north of the market. Frequent
services to **Santiago** from terminal at O'Carroll
1039, US$1.75, 1¼ hrs. Tur-Bus has its terminal
at O'Carroll 1175, T241117.
Train Train station on Av La Marina, T230361.
Main line services between Santiago and
Concepción and Chillán stop here. Also regular
services to/from **Santiago** on Metrotren, 1¼ hrs,
10-13 a day, US$2.65.

Curicó *p673*

Bus Long distance terminal at Prat y Maipú. Local
buses, including to coastal towns, as well as some
long distance services, from Terminal Plaza, Prat y
Maipú. **Pullman del Sur** terminal, Henríquez y
Carmen. Many southbound buses bypass Curicó,
but can be caught by waiting outside town. To
Santiago US$4.75, 2½ hrs, several companies,
frequent. To **Talca** every 15 mins, US$2.30, 1 hr.
To **Temuco**, Alsa and Tur-Bus, US$7.
Train Station is at the end of Prat, 4 blocks west
of Plaza de Armas, T310028. To/from **Santiago**, 6
a day, 2 hrs, US$6. To/from **Chillán**, 6 a day, 2¼
hrs, US$6.

Talca *p674*

Bus Terminal at 12 Oriente y 2 Sur. To **Chillán**,
frequent, US$2. To **Temuco**, US$7, 5½ hrs. To
Puerto Montt, US$11, 10 hrs. Train: station at
2 Sur y 11 Oriente, T226254. To **Santiago**, 5 a
day, US$5.

Chillán *p674, map p675*

Bus Two long-distance terminals: Central, Brasil y
Constitución (Tur-Bus, Línea Azul, Tas Choapa,
Alsa-LIT); Northern, Ecuador y O'Higgins for other
companies. Local buses leave from Maipón y Sgto
Aldea. To **Santiago**, 5½ hrs, US$7-11. To
Concepción, every 30 mins, 1¼ hrs, US$3. To
Curicó 2 a day, US$5. To **Temuco**, 4½ hrs, US$5.
Train Station, 5 blocks west of Plaza de Armas
on Brasil, T222424. To **Santiago**, 6 daily,
4½ hrs, salón US$10.

Area de Protección Radal Siete Tazas *p673*

Take a **minibus** from Terminal Plaza, Curicó, to
Molina, 26 km south, US$0.75; from Molina bus at

1700 weekdays, 0800 Sun, to **Radal** village in
summer, return 0730 (1800 Sun), 3 hrs, US$2. It's
a further 6.5 km to Siete Tazas and 11 km to
Parque Inglés. Access by car is best as the road
through the park is paved.

Termas de Chillán *p675*
Ski **buses** run from **Libertador** 1042 at 0800
and from Chillán Ski Centre, subject to demand,
US$30 (includes lift pass). Summer bus service
(Jan-mid-Mar), from **Anja**, 5 de Abril 594, Thu,
Sat, Sun only, 0730, US$5 return, book in
advance. **Taxi** US$30 one way, 1½ hrs. At busy
periods hitching may be possible from Chillán
Ski Centre.

🄳 **Directory**

Talca *p674*
Banks Edificio Caracol, Oficina 15, 1 Sur 898, for
US$ cash. **Internet** 1 Poniente 1282 and 2 Sur
1661 (free, reserve in advance). **Post offices** 1
Oriente s/n. **Telephones** Telefónica,
1 Sur 1156 and 1 Sur 835.

Chillán *p674, map p675*
Banks Better rates than banks at Casa de
Cambio, Constitución 550, or Café de París (ask for
Enrique Schuler). **Internet** Gateway, Libertad
360. **Planet**, Arauco 683, p 2. **Post offices** In
Gobernación on Plaza de Armas.
Telephones Entel, 18 de Septiembre 746.
Telefónica, Arauco 625.

Concepción and around

→ *Phone code: 041. Colour map 8, grid B1. Population: almost 250,000.*
The third biggest city in Chile (516 km from Santiago) and the most important city in southern
Chile, is also a major industrial centre. Capital of VIII Región (Biobío), Concepción is 15 km up
the Biobío River. Founded in 1550, Concepción became a frontier stronghold in the war
against the Mapuche after 1600. Destroyed by an earthquake in 1751, it was moved to its
present site in 1764. The climate is very agreeable in summer, but from April to September the
rains are heavy; the annual average rainfall, nearly all of which falls in those six months, is
from 1,250 mm to 1,500 mm. The **tourist office** ① *Caupolicán 85*, T041-741415,
infobiobio@sernatur.cl, provides regional information. Also at Aníbal Pinto 460, T741337.

Sights
In the attractive **Plaza de Armas** at the centre are the **Intendencia** and the **Cathedral**. It was
here that Bernardo O'Higgins proclaimed the independence of Chile on 1 January 1818. **Cerro
Caracol** can easily be reached on foot starting from the statue of Don Juan Martínez de Rozas in
the Parque Ecuador, arriving at the Mirador Chileno after 15 minutes. From here it is another 20
minutes' climb to **Cerro Alemán**. The **Biobío** and its valley running down to the sea lie below. On
the far side of the river you see lagoons, the largest of which, **San Pedro**, is a watersport centre.
    The **Galería de la Historia** ① *Lincoyán y V Lamas by Parque Ecuador, Mon 1500-1830,
Tue-Fri 1000-1330, 1500-1830, Sat-Sun 1000-1400, 1500-1930, free*, is a depiction of the
history of Concepción and the region; upstairs is a collection of Chilean painting. The **Casa del
Arte** ① *Roosevelt y Larenas, Tue-Fri 1000- 1800, Sat 1000-1600, Sun 1000-1300, free*,
contains the University art collection; the entrance hall is dominated by La Presencia de
América Latina, by the Mexican Jorge González Camerena (1965), a mural depicting Latin
American history. Free explanations are given by University Art students.
    The **Museo y Parque Hualpen** ① *Tue-Sun 1000-1300, 1400-1900, free*, is a house built
around 1885 (a national monument) and its gardens. It contains beautiful pieces from all over
the world, two hour visit, recommended. The park also contains Playa Rocoto, at the mouth of
the Río Biobío. Take a city bus to Hualpencillo from Freire, ask the driver to let you out then
walk 40 minutes, or hitch. Go along Avenida Las Golondrinas to the Enap oil refinery, turn left,
then right (it is signed).

Talcahuano → *Population: 244,000.*
At the neck of a peninsula, Talcahuano has the best harbour in Chile. It is Chile's main naval
station and an important commercial and fishing port. Two good roads run from Concepción.
The **Huáscar** ① *Tue-Sun 0900-1230, 1330-1730, US$1.50 (surrender passport at main gate)*,
a relic of the War of the Pacific, is in the naval base and can be visited. On Península Tumbes is
Parque Tumbes, owned by Codeff: paths lead along the coast, no services, no admission charge
(details from Codeff office in Concepción).

Costa del Carbón

South of the Biobío is the Costa del Carbón, the main coal producing area of Chile, linked with Concepción by road and two bridges over the Biobío. **Lota** (Population 52,000, 42 km south of Concepción) was, until its closure in 1997, the site of the most important **coalmine** in Chile ① *T870682, guided tours by former miners, 1000-1700, US$5*. In the church on the main plaza you can see a virgin made of coal. The **Parque de Lota** ① *daily 1000-1800, till 2000 in summer, US$2.50, no picnicking*, covers 14 ha on a promontory to the west of the town. It was

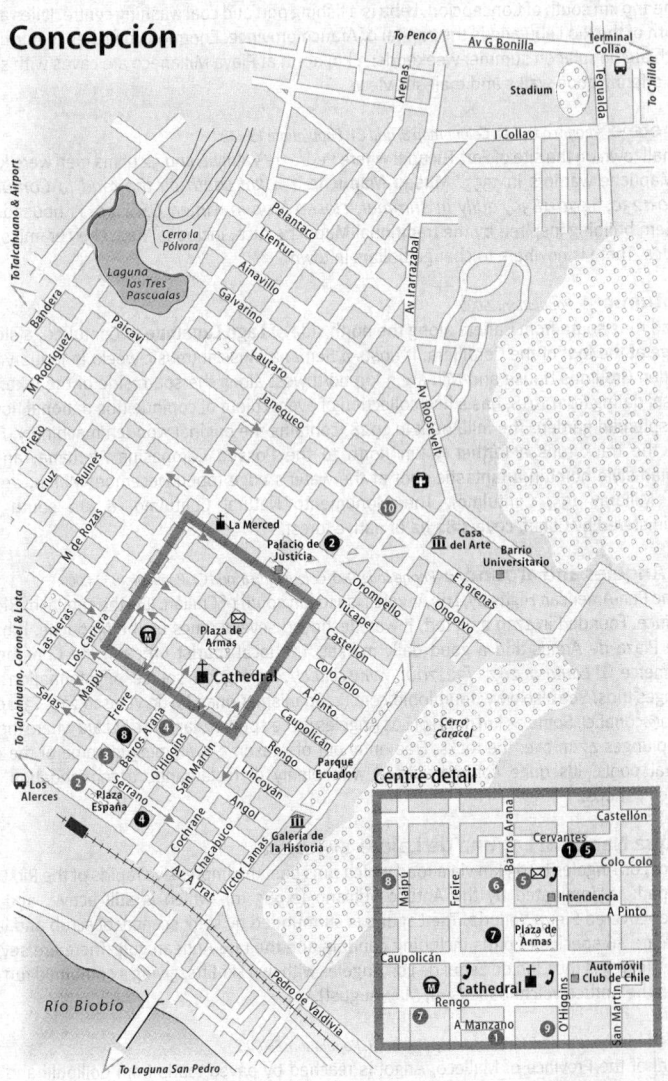

Concepción

Sleeping 😴
Alborada 1
Cecil 2
Concepción 3
El Dorado 4
Maquehue 5
Residencial Antuco 6
Residencial Central 7

Residencial Colo Colo 8
Residencial O'Higgins 9
Residencial San Sebastián 6
Silvia Uslar 10

Eating 🍴
Big Joe Saloon 1
Casino de Bomberos 2

El Rancho de Julio 4
Le Château 5
Piazza 7
Yiet-Xiu 8

N

0 metres 300
0 yards 300

the life's work of Isadora Cousiño, whose family owned the mine. Laid out by English landscape architects in the last century, it contains plants from all over the world, ornaments imported from Europe, romantic paths and shady nooks offering views over the sea, and peafowl and pheasants roaming freely. South of Lota the road runs past the seaside resort of **Laraquete** where there are miles of golden sands.

Lebu → *Phone code: 041. Population: 20,000.*

Some 149 km south of Concepción, Lebu is a fishing port and coal washing centre. It lies at the mouth of the Río Lebu and is the capital of Arauco province. Enormous beaches to north and south are popular on summer weekends: 3 km north at Playa Millaneco are caves with steep hills offering good walks and majestic views.

Cañete → *Phone code: 041. Colour map 8, grid C1. Population: 15,642.*

A small town on the site of Fort Tucapel where Pedro de Valdivia and 52 of his men were killed by Mapuche warriors in 1553. **Museo Mapuche** ① *1 km south on the road to Contulmo, 0930-1230, 1400-1830, daily in summer, closed Mon in winter, US$1.50*, is housed in a modern building inspired by the traditional Mapuche ruca; includes Mapuche ceramics and textiles. There is nowhere to change dollars in town.

Contulmo → *Population: 2,000.*

A road runs south from Cañete along the north side of **Lago Lanalhue** to Contulmo, a sleepy village at the foot of the Cordillera. It hosts a Semana Musical (music week) in January. The wooden Grollmus House and Mill are 3 km northwest along the south side of the lake. The house, dating from 1918, has a fine collection of every colour of copihue (the national flower) in a splendid garden. The mill, built in 1928, contains the original wooden machinery. From here the track runs a further 9 km north to the Posada Campesina Alemana, an old German-style hotel in a fantastic spot at the water's edge (open December-March, details from Millaray 135, Contulmo). The Monumento Natural Contulmo, 8 km south and administered by Conaf, covers 82 ha of native forest.

Los Angeles and around → *Phone code: 043. Colour map 8, grid C1. Population: 114,000.*

On the Pan-American Highway, Los Angeles is 110 km south of Chillán. It is the capital of Biobío province. Founded in 1739 as a fort, it was destroyed several times by the Mapuche. It has a large Plaza de Armas and a good daily market. The local **tourist office** in the Chamber of Commerce ① *Lautaro 267, T321700, www.ccla.cl/*, is a good source of information and arranges trips. See also www.tourbiobio.com (in Spanish). **Conaf**, JM de Velasco 275, T321086, hsoto@conaf.cl. Some 25 km north of Los Angeles is the spectacular **Salto El Laja** where the Río Laja plunges 47 m over the rocks. Free entry out of season – swimming in some of the cool natural pools. It's quite commercialized with plenty of restaurants, accommodation and souvenir shops.

Parque Nacional Laguna de Laja → *Entry US$1.30.*

East of Los Angeles by 93 km via a road which runs past the impressive rapids of the Río Laja, this park is dominated by the Antuco volcano (2,985 m), which is still active, and the glacier-covered Sierra Velluda. The Laguna is surrounded by stark scenery of scrub and lava. There are 46 species of birds including condors and the rare Andean gull. There are several trails. Nearby is the Club de Esquí de Los Angeles with two ski-lifts, giving a combined run of 4 km on the Antuco volcano (season, May-August).

Angol → *Phone code: 045. Colour map 8, grid C1. Population: 39,000.*

Capital of the Province of Malleco, Angol is reached by paved roads from Collipulli and Los Angeles. Founded by Valdivia in 1552, it was seven times destroyed by the *indígenas* and rebuilt. The church and convent of San Beneventura, northwest of the attractive Plaza de Armas, built in 1863, became the centre for missionary work among the Mapuche. El Vergel, founded in 1880 as an experimental fruit-growing nursery, now includes an attractive park and the **Museo Dillman Bullock** ① *Mon-Fri 0900-1900, Sat-Sun 1000-1900, US$1. 5 km from town, colectivo No 2*, with pre-Columbian indigenous artefacts. **Angol**: There is an excellent **tourist office** on O'Higgins s/n, T045-711255, across bridge from bus terminal. **Conaf**, Prat 191, p 2, T711870.

Parque Nacional Nahuelbuta

ⓘ *All year (snow Jun-Sep), US$4.50.*
Situated in the coastal mountain range at an altitude of 800-1,550 m, this beautiful park covers 6,832 ha of forest and offers views over both the sea and the Andes. Although the forest includes many species of trees, the monkey puzzle araucaria) is most striking; some are over 2,000 years old, 50 m high and 3 min diameter. There are also 16 species of orchids as well as pudu deer, Chiloé foxes, pumas, black woodpeckers and parrots. There is a **Visitors' Centre** ⓘ *at Pehuenco, 5 km from the entrance, summer only 0800-1300, 1400-2000, rough maps are available at the park entrance for US$0.25, camping is near the Visitors' Centre, US$9 – there are many free campsites along the road from El Cruce to the entrance.*

● Sleeping

Concepción *p678, map p679*
Good budget accommodation is hard to find.
AL Alborada, Barros Arana 457, T911121, www.hotelalborada.cl. Good 4-star with all mod cons, disabled friendly, tours offered.
AL El Dorado, Barros Arana 348, T229400, www.hoteleldorado.co.cl. Comfortable, central, cafeteria, parking.
A Concepción, Serrano 512, T620851, hotelconcepcion@entelchile.net.
Central, comfortable, heating, English spoken. Recommended.
C Cecil, Barros Arana 9, T230677, near railway station. With breakfast, quiet. Highly recommended.
C Maquehue, Barros Arana 786, p 8, T210261, hotelmaquehue@hotmail.com. Good services, with restaurant and laundry service. Highly recommended.
C Res Antuco, Barros Arana 741, flats 31-33, T235485. Entry in Galería Martínez. Recommended.
C Res San Sebastián, Barros Arana 741, flat 35, T910240. Reductions for HI, also entered via the Galería Martínez. Recommended.
D pp **Res Central**, Rengo 673, T227309. With breakfast, large rooms, a bit run down.
D Res Colo Colo, Colo Colo 743, T227118. With breakfast, some single rooms have bath.
D-E Res O'Higgins, O'Higgins 457, T221086. Without breakfast, comfortable.
E pp **Silvia Uslar**, Edmundo Larenas 202, T227449 (not signed). Excellent, good breakfast, quiet, comfortable.

Costa del Carbón: Lota *p679*
E Res Rome, Galvarino 233, T041-876257. Near main plaza in Lata Bajo, good rooms, with breakfast, patio, welcoming.

Lebu *p680*
A Hostería Millaneco, at Playa Millaneco, T/F511540. Cabañas sleep 7, good restaurant.
D pp **Central**, Pérez 183, T/F511904. **E** without bath, parking. Recommended.

D Gran, Pérez 309, T511939. **E** without bath, old fashioned, comedor.
E Res Alcázar, Alcázar 144. With breakfast, cold water.

Cañete *p680*
B Nahuelbuta, Villagrán 644, T611073, hotelnahuelbuta@lanalhueturismo.cl. Cheaper without bath, pleasant, parking.
D pp **Derby**, Mariñán y Condell, T611960. Without bath, basic, restaurant.
D pp **Gajardo**, 7° de la Línea 817 (1 block from plaza). Without bath, old fashioned, pleasant.

Contulmo *p680*
B Contulmo, Millaray 116, T894903. **E** pp without bath, hospitable. Recommended.
D Central, Millaray 131, T618089, hotelcentral@lanalhueturismo.cl. Without bath, no sign, very hospitable.

Lago Lanalhue
B pp **Hostal Licahue**, 4 km north of Contulmo towards Cañete (Casilla 644, Correo Contulmo) T09-870 2822 (mob). With breakfast, also full board, attractively set overlooking lake, pool. Highly recommended.
Camping Camping Huilquehue, 15 km south of Cañete on lakeside. **Elicura**, Playa Blanca, 10 km north of Contulmo. Clean, US$6. Recommended. **Playa Blanca**, Playa Blanca, 10 km north of Contulmo. Clean.

Los Angeles *p680*
AL Gran Hotel Müso, Valdivia 230 (Plaza de Armas), T313183, www.hotelmuso.cl. Good restaurant open to non-residents.
B Res Santa María, Plaza de Armas, T328214. Hot shower, TV, hospitable but rundown and overpriced.
D Private house at Caupolicán 651. Large breakfast, good value. Opposite, also No 651, basic, cheaper.
D pp **Res Angelina**, Colo Colo 335. Basic, good hot shower.

Outside town

A Hostería Salto del Laja (Casilla 562, Los Angeles, Salto El Laja, T321706, www.saltodellaja.cl). Good rooms, restaurant, 2 swimming pools (dirty), on an island overlooking the falls.

B Complejo Turístico Los Manantiales, Salto El Laja, T/F314275, with camping.

B-C pp El Rincón, Panamericana Sur Km 494 (20 km north of Los Angeles), exit El Olivo (Cruce La Mona) 2 km east, T09-441 5019, elrincon@cvmail.cl. Beautiful property beside a small river, restful, South American and European cuisine, includes vegetarian, Spanish classes, tours arranged, English, French, German and Spanish spoken. Recommended.

Parque Nacional Laguna de Laja *p680*

B Refugio Chacay, 21 km from the lake, T043-222651. It offers food, drink and bed, closed in summer.

E pp Hostería del Bosque, in Abanico. Restaurant, also good campsite.

E 2 other refugíos: Digeder, 11 km from the park entrance, and **Universidad de Concepción**, both on slopes of Volcán Antuco, for both T041-229054, office O'Higgins 740.

E pp house with orange gates at park bus stop takes guests, food extra. Only wild camping possible.

Angol *p680*

D pp La Posada, at El Vergel, T712103. Full board, nice hotel.

D Millaray, Prat, 2 blocks west of Plaza. Shared bath, good.

E pp Puren 539. Basic *hospedaje* with shared hot shower.

⦿ Eating

Concepción *p678, map p679*

♈♈♈ Le Château Colo Colo 340. French, seafood and meat, closed Sun.

♈♈ Big Joe Saloon, O'Higgins 808, just off plaza. Popular at lunchtime, open Sun evening, good breakfasts, vegetarian meals, snacks and pizzas.

♈♈ Piazza, 631, p 2r. Good pizzas.

♈♈ El Rancho de Julio, O'Higgins 36. Argentine *parrillada*.

♈ Casino de Bomberos, O'Higgins y Orompello. Good value lunches.

♈ Yiet-Xiu, Angol 515. Good, cheap Oriental cuisine.

Cafés

Café El Dom, Caupolicán 415. One of several cafés near the Plaza de Armas, good, open Sun morning.

Café Haiti, Caupolicán 515. Open Sun morning, good coffee.

Fuente Alemana, Caupolicán 654. A recommended *fuente de soda* near the Plaza.

La Capilla, Vicuña MacKenna 769. Good ponches, popular.

Nuria, Barros Arana 736. Very good breakfasts and lunches, good value.

QuickBiss, O'Higgins between Tuscapel and Castellón. Salads, real coffee, good service, good lunches.

Saaya 1, Barros Arana 899. Excellent panadería/pastelería/rotisería.

Treinta y Tantos, Prat 356. Nice bar, good music, wide selection of empanadas, good breakfasts and lunches. Recommended.

Talcahuano *p678*

♈♈ Benotecas, on the seafront, has a row of 4 restaurants sharing one window facing the harbour, superb fish and seafood in each one, reasonable prices, recommended.

♈♈ Domingo Lara, Aníbal Pinto 450, seafood specialities, excellent.

♈ Fine seafood at low prices can also be found in the market.

Cañete *p680*

♈ Café Nahuel, just off the plaza. For real coffee.

♈ Don Juanito, Riquelme 151. A very good eating place recommended by the locals.

Los Angeles *p680*

♈♈♈ El Arriero, Colo Colo 235. Good parrillas and international dishes.

♈♈ D'Leone, Av Alemania 686. Good lasagne and other Italian dishes.

♈♈♈ Rancho de Julio, Colón 720. Excellent parrilla.

♈ Julio's Pizzas, Colón 542. Good pizzería.

⦿ Shopping

Concepción *p678, map p679*

The main shopping area is north of the Plaza de Armas.

Handicrafts Feria Artesanal, Freire 757.

Malls and supermarkets Las Brisas, Freire y Lincoyán. Supermarket. Galería Internacional, Caupolicán y Barros Arana is worth a visit. Plaza del Trébol mall with multi-screen cinemas north

● For an explanation of the sleeping and eating price codes used in this guide, see inside the front
● cover. Other relevant information is found in Essentials pages 604-605.

of the city off the road to Talcahuano (near the airport). Take any bus for Talcahuano. **Supermercado Unimarc**, Chacabuco 70.

▲ Activities and tours

Concepción *p678, map p679*
Alta Luz, San Martín 586, p 2, T217727. Tours to national parks.
Chile Indomito Adventure, Serrano 551, of 3, T221618, Trekking in Reserva Nacional Ralco.
South Expeditions, O'Higgins 680, p 2, of 218D, T/F232290. Rafting, horseriding, fishing and trekking expeditions, 1 and 2-day programmes.

Los Angeles *p680*
Interbruna Turismo, Caupolicán 350, T313812, interbruna@hotmail.com. For local excursions, car rental or air tickets.

⊖ Transport

Concepción *p678, map p679*
Air Airport north of the city, off the main road to Talcahuano. Taxi US$6. Flights daily to and from **Santiago** (Lan Express and Sky); Lan Express less frequently to **Valdivia, Osorno** and **Puerto Montt**; both fly to **Temuco**.
Bus Main long distance terminal, known as Terminal Collao, is 2 km east, on Av Gen Bonilla, next to athletics stadium. (To the city centre take a bus marked 'Hualpencillo' from outside the terminal and get off in Freire, US$0.40, taxi US$3.) **Tur-Bus, Línea Azul** and **Buses Bío Bío** services leave from Terminal Camilo Henríquez 2 km northeast of main terminal on J M García, reached by buses from Av Maipú in centre, via Terminal Collao. To **Santiago**, 6½ hrs, US$8. To **Valparaíso**, 8 hrs, US$10 (most via Santiago). To **Los Angeles**, US$3. To **Loncoche**, 5½ hrs, US$7. To **Pucón**, 8 hrs, US$8. To **Valdivia**, 7 hrs, US$8. To **Puerto Montt** several companies, US$10, about 9 hrs bus cama US$20). Best direct bus to **Chillán** is Línea Azul, 2 hrs, US$2. For a longer and more scenic route, take the Costa Azul bus which follows the old railway line, through Tomé, Coelemu and Ñipas on to Chillán (part dirt-track, takes 5½ hrs). Services to **Lota, Lebu, Cañete** and **Contulmo** are run by J Ewert (terminal at Carrera y Tucapel) and **Los Alerces** (terminal at Prat y Maipú). To **Talcahuano** frequent service from Plaza de Armas (bus marked 'Base Naval'), US$0.30, 1 hr, express US$0.50, 30 mins.
Train Station at Prat y Barros Arana, T226925. Regular nightly train to/from **Santiago**, 9 hrs; clase preferente US$15, turista US$10. Also suburban services from Talcahuano to Chiguayante. Booking offices at the station and at Galería Plaza, local 13, T225286.

Costa del Carbón: Lota *p679*
Bus Concepción-Lota, 1½ hrs, US$0.50. Many buses by-pass the centre: catch them from the main road.

Cañete *p680*
Bus Leave from 2 different terminals: J Ewert, Inter Sur and **Thiele** from Riquelme y 7° de la Línea, Jeldres, Erbuc and other companies from the Terminal Municipal, Serrano y Villagrán. To **Santiago**, Inter Sur, daily, 12 hrs. To **Concepción**, 3 hrs US$3.50. To **Lebu** US$1.50. To **Angol** US$3.50.

Contulmo *p680*
Bus To **Concepción**, Thiele, US$4.50, 4 hrs; to **Temuco**, Thiele and Erbuc, US$4; to **Cañete**, frequent, US$1.

Los Angeles *p680*
Bus Long distance bus terminal on northeast outskirts of town, local terminal at Villagrán y Rengo in centre, by market. To **Salto de Laja**, every 30 mins with JB, US$2 return. To **Santiago**, 6½ hrs, US$8, cama US$20. To **Viña del Mar** and **Valparaíso**, 8 hrs, US$11. Every 30 mins to **Concepción**, US$2.50, 2 hrs. To **Temuco**, US$6, hourly. To **Curacautín**, daily at 0945, 1600, 3 hrs, US$6 (otherwise change in Victoria).

Parque Nacional Laguna de Laja *p680*
Bus ERS Bus from Los Angeles (Villagrán 507, by market) to **Abanico**, 20 km past Antuco (6 a day, US$1.50), then 2 hrs walk to park entrance (hitching possible). Or bus to **Antuco**, 2 hrs, weekdays 5 daily, 2 on Sun and festivals, last return 1730, US$1.35, then hitch last 24 km. Details from Conaf in Los Angeles (see above).

Angol *p680*
Bus To **Santiago** US$6.50, **Los Angeles**, US$1.35. To **Temuco**, Trans Bío-Bío, frequent, US$2.50.

Parque Nacional Nahuelbuta *p681*
Bus In Dec-Feb there is a direct bus from **Angol**, Sun 0800, return 1700. Bus to **Vegas Blancas** (27 km from Angol) 0700 and 1600 daily, return 0900 and 1600, 1½ hrs, US$1.20, get off at El Cruce, from where it is a pleasant 7 km walk to park entrance.

⊕ Directory

Concepción *p678, map p679*
Airline offices LanChile, Barros Arana 560, T248824. Sky, T218941 **Banks** ATMs at banks, most of which are on O'Higgins. Several cambios in Galería Internacional, entrances at Barros Arana

565 and Caupolicán 521. **Consulates** Argentina, San Martín 472, of 52, T230257. **Cultural centres** Alliance Française, Colo Colo y Lamas. Library, concerts, films, cultural events. **Chilean- British Cultural Institute**, San Martín 531. British newspapers, library. **Chilean-North American Institute**, Caupolicán 301 y San Martín. Library. **Internet** In the centre. **Post offices** O'Higgins y Colo Colo. **Telephones** Telefónica, Colo Colo 487, Angol 483. **Entel**, Barros Arana 541, Caupolicán 567, p 2.

Useful addresses Automóvil Club de Chile, O'Higgins 630, Of 303, T245884, for information and car hire (T222070). **Codeff** (Comité Nacional pro Defensa de la Fauna y Flora), Caupolicán 346, oficina E, p 4, T226649.

Los Angeles *p680*
Banks ATMs at banks and at supermarket at Av Alemania 686. **Agencia Interbruna**, Caupolicán 350, T313812, F325925, best rates.

Lake District

The Lake District, stretching southwards from Temuco to Puerto Montt, is one of Chile's most beautiful regions. There are some 12 great lakes of varying sizes, as well as imposing waterfalls and snowcapped volcanoes. There are a number of good bases for exploring. Out of season many facilities are closed, in season (from mid-December to mid-March), prices are higher and it is best to book well in advance, particularly for transport. About 20,000 Mapuches live in the area, particularly around Temuco. Although Mapudungun is becoming less prevalent, there are possibly 100,000 more of mixed descent who speak the native tongue, nearly all of them bilingual.

Temuco and around

→ *Phone code: 045. Colour map 8, grid C1. Population: 227,000. Altitude: 107 m.*

Although at first sight rather grey and imposing, Temuco is a lively university city and one of the fastest growing commercial centres in the south. Founded in 1881 after the final treaty with the Mapuches and the arrival of the railway, this city is the capital of IX Región (Araucanía), 677 km south of Santiago. Temuco is proud of its Mapuche heritage and it is this that gives it its distinctive character, especially around the outdoor market. The **Sernatur office** is at ① *Bulnes 586, on main plaza, T211969, infoaraucania@sernatur.cl. Daily in summer 0830-2030, Mon-Fri 0900-1200, 1500-1700 in winter.* It has good leaflets in English. Also in the municipal market. **Conaf** is at Bilbao 931, T298114, temuco@conaf.cl. Sernap for fishing permits, Miraflores 965. North and east of the city are five national parks and reserves, notably Conguillío with its araucaria forests, and flora and fauna found nowhere else. It is great for hiking, or touring by car or even mountain bike. There are also various skiing opportunities.

Sights

The centre is the Plaza Aníbal Pinto, around which are the main public buildings including the cathedral and the Municipalidad. Very little of the old city remains; practically every wooden building burned down following the 1960 earthquake. Temuco is the Mapuches' market town and you may see some, particularly women, in their typical costumes in the huge produce market, the **Feria** *Lautaro y Pinto*, one of the most fascinating markets in Chile. Mapuche textiles, pottery, woodcarving, jewellery etc are also sold inside and around the municipal market, Aldunate y Diego Portales (it also sells fish, meat and dairy produce), but these are increasingly touristy and poor quality. There is a handicraft fair every February in the main plaza. The **Casa de la Mujer Mapuche** ① *in the Gymnasium, between Corvalín and Almte Barroso, Padre las Casas suburb, T09-169 4682, Mon-Fri 0900-1300, 1500-1900, getting there: take bus 8a or 10, colectivo 13a,* sells many crafts, including textiles made by a Mapuche weavers' co-operative, all with traditional designs. **Museo de la Araucanía** ① *Alemania 84, Mon-Fri 0900-1700, Sat 1100-1645, Sun 1100-1300, US$1 (free Sun), getting there: take bus 1 from the centre.* It is devoted to the history and traditions of the Mapuche nation, with a section on German settlement. For information on visits to Mapuche settlements, eg Chol Chol, go to the

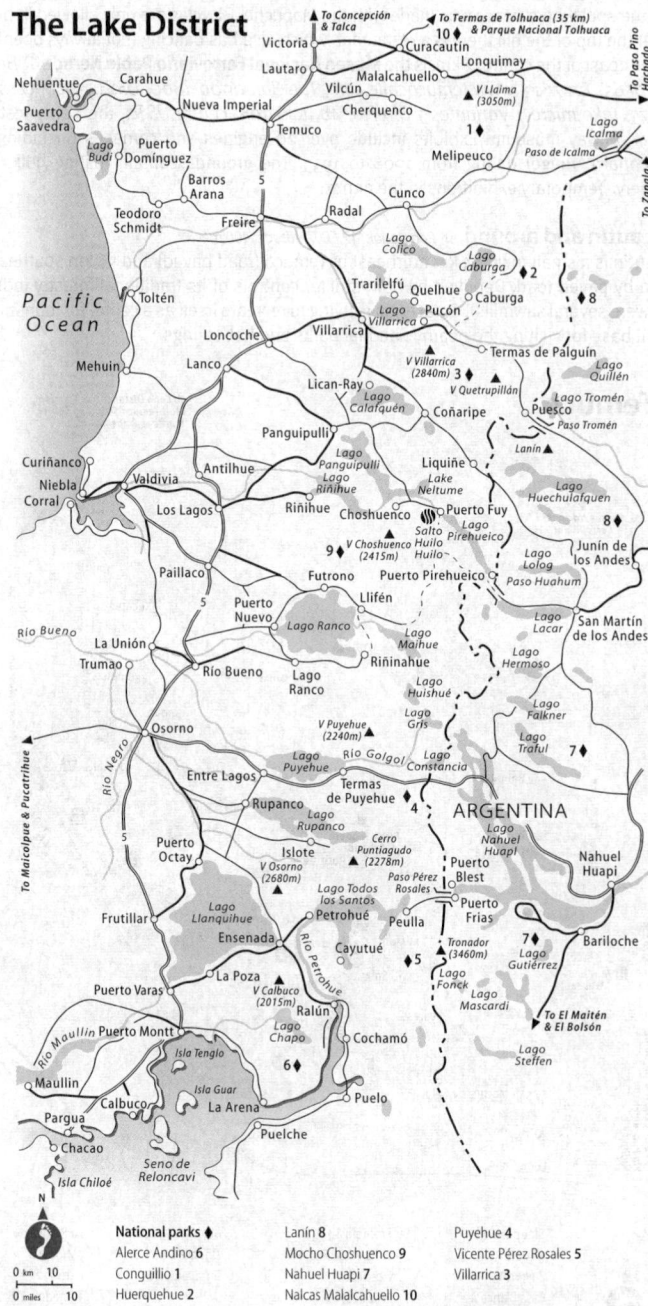

The Lake District

Pacific Ocean

ARGENTINA

National parks ♦
Alerce Andino **6**
Conguillio **1**
Huerquehue **2**

Lanín **8**
Mocho Choshuenco **9**
Nahuel Huapi **7**
Nalcas Malalcahuello **10**

Puyehue **4**
Vicente Pérez Rosales **5**
Villarrica **3**

0 km   10
0 miles   10

Sernatur office in the Plaza. There are views of **Temuco from Cerro Ñielol** ① *US$1, 0830-2030*. This park has a fine collection of native plants in the natural state, including the national flower, the copihue rojo. This is a good site for a picnic and it has an excellent visitors' centre. A tree marks the spot where peace was made with the Mapuche. Bicycles are only allowed in before 1100. At the top of the hill there is a restaurant, which also has dancing (not always open).

Northeast of the centre, 2 km, is the **Museo Nacional Ferroviario Pablo Neruda** ① *Barros Arana 0565, T227613, www.temucochile.com, Tue-Sun 0900-1800, US$1.75, concessions US$0.75, take micro 1 Variante, 9 Directo, 4b, taxi from centre US$2,* the newly restored national railway museum. Exhibits include over 20 engines and carriages (including the presidential carriage) dating from 1908 to 1953. The grounds contain rusting hulks and machinery. Temporary exhibitions in the annex.

Curacautín and around → *Population: 12,500. Altitude: 400 m.*

Curacautín is a small town 84 km northeast of Temuco (road paved) and 56 km southeast of Victoria by paved road. Deprived by new, stricter controls of its traditional forestry industry (there were several sawmills), Curacautín is trying to recreate itself as a centre for tourism. It is a useful base for visiting the nearby national parks and hot springs.

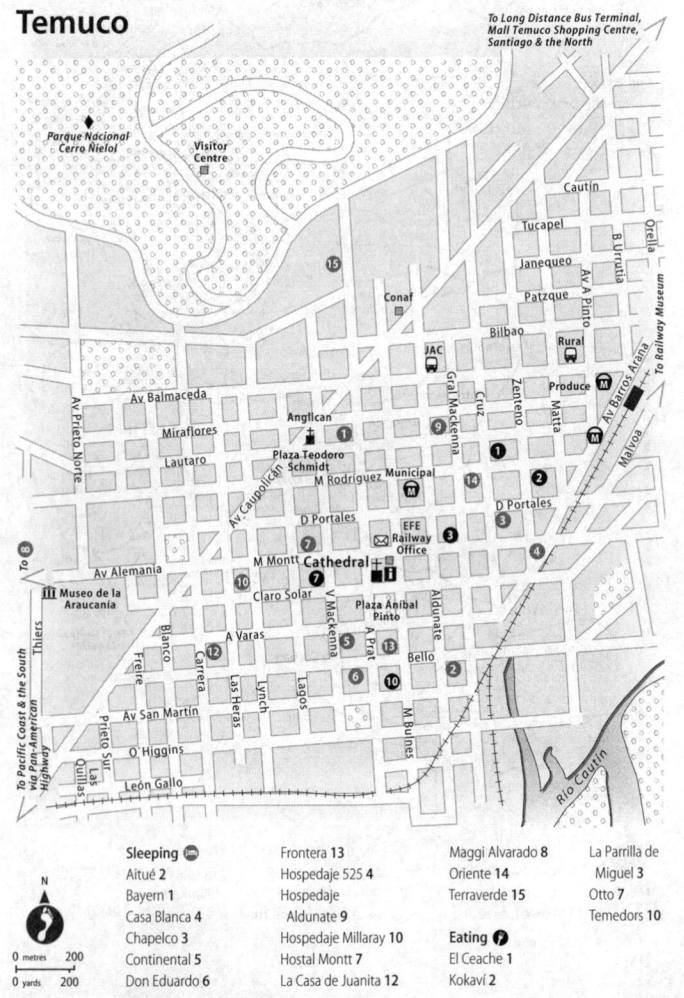

Temuco

Sleeping
Aitué 2
Bayern 1
Casa Blanca 4
Chapelco 3
Continental 5
Don Eduardo 6

Frontera 13
Hospedaje 525 4
Hospedaje
Aldunate 9
Hospedaje Millaray 10
Hostal Montt 7
La Casa de Juanita 12

Maggi Alvarado 8
Oriente 14
Terraverde 15

Eating ❼
El Ceache 1
Kokaví 2

La Parrilla de
Miguel 3
Otto 7
Temedors 10

Termas de Manzanar, are indoor hot springs, 17 km east of Curacautín (US$5, open all year, run down, overpriced) are reached by bus from Temuco and Victoria. The road passes the Salto del Indio (Km 71 from Victoria; cabañas US$1), and Salto de la Princesa, 3 km beyond Manzanar hostería, camping).

The beautiful pine-surrounded **Termas de Tolhuaca** ① *all year, US$2.50-5, getting there: taxi from Curacautín US$21*, are 35 km to the northeast of Curacautín by unpaved road, or 82 km by rough, unpaved road from just north of Victoria (high clearance four-wheel drive vehicle essential). And 2 km north of the Termas is the **Parque Nacional Tolhuaca** ① *Dec-Apr, taxi from Curacautín US$17*, including waterfalls, two lakes, superb scenery and good views of volcanoes from Cerro Amarillo. Park administration is near Laguna Malleco, with a campsite nearby. Much of the park, together with the neighbouring Reserva Nacional Malleco, was severely damaged by forest fires in early 2002. It will take several decades fully to recover, but some half-day trails are open.

Reserva Nacional Nalcas Malalcahuello
Northeast of Curacautín, this 31,305 ha park is on the slopes of the **Lonquimay** volcano. It is much less crowded than nearby Parque Nacional Conguillio. The volcano began erupting on Christmas Day 1988; the new crater is called Navidad. To see it, access is made from Malalcahuello, 15 km south and half-way between Curacautín and Lonquimay town. In the park, which is one of the best areas for seeing unspoilt araucaria forest, Conaf has opened several marked trails, from one hour to two days in length. There is a municipal refugio at the foot of the volcano. The teacher at Malalcahuello school, José Córdoba, organizes tours and horse riding for groups. Sra Naomi Saavedra at Res Los Sauces arranges transport. From Malalcahuello it is a one-day hike to the Sierra Nevada mountain, or a two-day hike to Conguillio national park (with equipment and experience, otherwise use a guide). **Conaf** office on main road in Malalcahuello gives information, as does **La Suizandina**, which gives good access to treks and the ascent of the volcano, see Sleeping, below.

Los Arenales ski resort ① *season Jun-Sep, taxi from Curacautín US$17, in winter access from Lonquimay town side only*, is at Las Raices Pass on the road from Malalcahuello to Lonquimay town. Four lifts go up to 2,500 m with great views, ski pass US$17. It is a good, small resort with a nice restaurant. Also in winter, the main route from Malalcahuello to Lonquimay town, goes through the ex-railway tunnel of **Las Raices** *toll US$1.50*. At 4.8 km it was, until recently, the longest tunnel in South America. Now it's in poor condition, unlit and has constant filtration. There is talk of repair, but it's unwise to go through by bicycle.

Parque Nacional Conguillio
East of Temuco by 80 km, this is one of the most popular parks in Chile ① *Dec-Mar, US$4*, but is deserted outside January/February and weekends. In the centre is the 3,125 m **Llaima volcano**, which is active. There are two large lakes, **Laguna Verde** and **Laguna Conguillio**, and two smaller ones, **Laguna Arco Iris** and **Laguna Captrén**. North of Laguna Conguillio rises the snow covered **Sierra Nevada**, the highest peak of which reaches 2,554 m. This is the best place in Chile to see araucaria forest, which used to cover an extensive area in this part of the country. Other trees include cypresses, lenga and winter's bark. Birdlife includes the condor and the black woodpecker and there are foxes and pumas.

Crampons and ice-axe are essential for climbing Llaima, as well as experience or a guide. Climb south from Guardería Captrén. Allow five hours to ascend, two hours to descend. Information on the climb is available from **Guardería Captrén**. There is a range of walking trails, from 1 km to 22 km in length. Details are available from park administration or **Conaf** in Temuco. Llaima ski resort, one of the prettiest in Chile, is reached by poor road from Cherquenco, 30 km west (high clearance vehicle essential).

There are three entrances: From Curacautín, north of the park: see Transport below; from Melipeuco, 13 km south of the southern entrance at Truful-Truful (open all year); and from Cherquenco to the west entrance near the Llaima ski resort. It is then a two or three day hike around Volcán Llaima to Laguna Conguillio, which is dusty, but with beautiful views of Laguna Quepe, then on to the Laguna Captrén guardería. Information on all three roads into the park and administration by Lago Conguillio. There is a Visitors' Centre at Laguna Captrén.

Border with Argentina

Paso Pino Hachado (1,884 m) can be reached either by paved road, 77 km southeast from Lonquimay, or by unpaved road 103 east from Melipeuco. On the Argentine side this road continues to Zapala. Chilean immigration and customs are in Liucura, 22 km west of the border, open December-March 0800-2000, April-November 0800-1800. Very thorough searches and 2-3 hour delays reported. Buses from Temuco to Zapala and Neuquén use this crossing: see under Temuco. **Paso de Icalma** (1,298 m) is reached by unpaved road, 53 km from Melipeuco, a good crossing for those with their own transport. On the Argentine side this road continues to Zapala. Chilean immigration is open December-March 0800-2100, April-November 0800-1900.

● Sleeping

Temuco *p684, map p686*

Accommodation in private houses, category **E** minimum, can be arranged by tourist office.

L Terraverde, Prat 0220, T239999, www.pan americanahoteles.cl. Best 5-star hotel in town.

AL Frontera, Bulnes 726, T200400, www.hotelfrontera.cl. With breakfast, good business standard, large conference room.

A Aitué, A Varas 1048, T212512, www.hotelaitue.cl. Business standard, central, bar, English spoken, comfortable.

A Continental, Varas 708, T238973, www.turismochile.cl/continental. Popular with business travellers, old fashioned building, charming, large rooms with antique furniture, heating, with breakfast, good restaurant, popular bar, cheaper rooms without bath, parking. Neruda stayed here once. Recommended.

A Don Eduardo, Bello 755, T214133, www.hoteldoneduardo.cl. Parking, suites with kitchen. Recommended.

A Holiday Inn Express, Av R Ortega 01800, T223300, www.holidayinnexpress.cl. A member of the Chileanized version of this chain, good value, with breakfast, a/c, heating, free internet, pool, out of town but worth considering if driving.

A-B Bayern, Prat 146, T276000, www.inter patagonia.com/hotelbayern. Standard 3-star. Small rooms, clean, helpful, buffet breakfast, parking, cheaper in dollars than pesos.

A-B Hostal Montt, M Montt 637, T910400, www.hostalmontt.cl. Comfortable if overpriced, some rooms with bath, parking, TV, breakfast included, gym.

B Chapelco, Cruz 401, T749393, www.hotelchapelco.cl. Airy, slightly run-down, cable TV, laundry, internet in lobby, comfortable, good service. Recommended.

B-C La Casa de Juanita, Carrera 735, T213203. Cheaper without bath, breakfast, hot water, laundry, heating, parking. Many others in this range on Bello, west of plaza.

B-D Casa Blanca, Montt 1306 y Zenteno, T272667, www.hostalcasablanca.cl. **E** single with shared bath, slightly run down, but cheap alternative for room without private bath, includes breakfast.

C Blanco Encalada 1078, T234447. Use of kitchen, good breakfast.

C Oriente, M Rodríguez 1146, T/F233232, h-oriente@123mail.cl. Old but clean, good value rooms, cheaper without bath, heating, TV, parking, laundry, breakfast extra, some rooms with no windows. Recommended.

C Hosp Aldunate, Aldunate 187, T270057. **D-E** singles, cooking facilities, some rooms with TV and bath.

C-D Hospedaje 525, Zenteno 525, T233982. Without breakfast, new section has small rooms with bath, good value, older part has poor beds but also good value.

C-D Maggi Alvarado, Recreo 209, T263215. Small rooms (**E** singles), helpful, student place, nice atmosphere.

D Hosp Millaray, Claro Solar 471, T645720. Simple, basic, but unfriendly. Other private houses on this street, **E** pp.

F pp Hospedaje, unnamed but signed, at Aldunate 12. With hot shower and cable TV.

Curacautín and around *p686*

B Plaza, Yungay 157 (main plaza), T881256. Restaurant good but pricey, accommodation overpriced.

C Hostal Las Espigas, Miraflores 315, T881138, rivaseugenia@hotmail.com. Good rooms (**E** singles), kitchen, breakfast, dinner available on request.

E pp Turismo, Tarapacá 140, T881116. Good food, hot shower, comfortable, good value if old-fashioned.

Termas de Manzanar

L-A Termas de Manzanar, T/F045-881200, termasmanzanar@indecom.cl. Overpriced, but also simple rooms with bath.

A-B Anden Rose, 5 km west of Manzanar, Casilla 123, Curacautín, T056-9-869 1700, www.andenrose.com. **E** pp in dorms, with breakfast, camping **F**, restaurant, bike, horse, kayak rental, tours arranged, German run.

D Hostería Abarzúa, Km 18, T045-870011. Simple, full board available, also campsite.

Termas de Tolhuaca

AL pp **Termas de Tolhuaca**, T045-881164, www.termasdetolhuaca.cl. With full board, including use of baths and horse riding, very good.

E pp **Res Roja**, food, camping near the river.
Campsite 10 km past the Termas, US$3.80 pp (US$15 with car), pleasant, cold water.

Lonquimay

A La Suizandina, Km 83 Carretera Internacional a Argentina, T045-1973725 or 09-884 9541, www.suizandina.com. Hostel 3 km before Malalcahuello Erbuc bus from Temuco 2½ hrs), with a range of rooms from private room with heating and large Swiss breakfast, to shared rooms **D-E** pp, camping US$5, laundry, book exchange, bike and ski rental, horse riding, travel and trekking information, German and English spoken, good meals available. "Like being in Switzerland". Recommended.
C pp **Centro de Ski Lonquimay**, 10 km from the bus stop. With breakfast, full board also available, open only in season.
C-D Res Los Sauces, in Malalcahuello, T09-883 7880. Singles **E** pp, some rooms with bath, use of kitchen extra, hot water, good value, breakfast US$1.90, dinner US$4.75, full board available.

Parque Nacional Conguillio *p687*

AL-A La Baita, in the park, 3 km south of Laguna Verde, T416410, on-line bookings at www.labaitaconguillio.cl/labaita. Cabins with electricity, hot water, kitchen and wood stoves, charming, lots of information, Italian/Chilean owned.
A cabañas Laguna Conguillio, summer only, sleep 6, no sheets or blankets, gas stove, and café/shop. Also campsite (US$15 per tent, hot water, showers, firewood), and a cheaper campsite *camping de mochileros* at Ñires, US$5.70 pp, with hot shower, US$2 for firewood).
B-E Adela y Helmut, Faja 16000, Km 5 Norte, Cunco (on the way to Melipeuco, 16 km from Cunco, website has directions, phone for pick-up from bus stop; pick-up from Temuco US$28.50), T09-724 4479, www.adelayhelmut.com. Guesthouse and restaurant on a Mapuche/German owned farm, room for families and for backpackers in 6-bed dorm, kitchens, hot showers, solar heating, mountain bike rental, 4WD tours, good reports. Ask about horse riding and rafting (www.esmeraldaraft.de) at neighbouring properties.
C-D Hospedaje Icalma, Aguirre 729, Melipeuco, T581108. More spacious, with shower and breakfast, new facilities. Recommended.
D Germania, Aguirre 399, Melipeuco. Basic, good food.

Camping Camping Los Pioneros, 2 km out of town on road to the park, hot water.

🍴 Eating

Temuco *p684, map p686*
Many good restaurants around Av Alemania and Mall Mirage, about 10 blocks west of centre. Make for the produce market or the rural bus terminal, where there are countless restaurants serving very cheap set meals at lunch.
🍴🍴 **La Parrilla de Miguel**, Montt 1095. Good for meat and wine.
🍴🍴 **Otto**, V MacKenna 530. German food, cakes.
🍴 **El Ceache**, Cruz 231. Typical Chilean food, good value set lunch.
🍴 **Kokavi**, Rodríguez y Zenteno. Mapuche restaurant, popular at lunchtime.
🍴 **Temedors**, San Martín 827. Good value lunch.
Marriet, Prat 451, loc 21. Excellent coffee.

Termas de Manzanar

🍴🍴 **La Rotonda del Cautín**, T1971478. Good food, friendly.

Parque Nacional Conguillio *p687*

Buy supplies in Temuco, Curacautín or Melipeuco: much cheaper than the shop in the park. **Restaurant Los Troncos**, Aguirre 352. Recommended. Also **Ruminot**, on same street.

🛍 Shopping

Temuco *p684, map p686*
Camping equipment Eltit supermarket, O'Higgins y Fresia. **Outdoors & Travel**, Lincoyán 361, clothing, equipment, maps.
Crafts Best choice in the indoor municipal market at Aldunate y Portales. **Fundación Chol-Chol**, Sector Rengalil, Camino Temuco-Nueva Imperial Km 16, T614007, www.chol chol.org. Contact Johanna Pérez (speaks English), or Esteban Bastias. A non-profit organization which sells traditional Mapuche textiles, naturally dyed and hand woven by local women.
Supermarket Las Brisas, Caupolicán y Montt, and Rodríguez 1100 block. There is a modern shopping mall north of city; buses 2 or 7. **Frutería Las Vegas**, Matta 274, dried fruit (useful for climbing/trekking).

⛰ Activities and tours

Temuco *p684, map p686*
Tours to Parque Nacional Conguillio cost generally US$40; to Villarrica volcano US$70.

⊖ Transport

Temuco *p684, map p686*

Air Manquehue Airport 6 km southwest of the city. There is an airport transfer service to the city and to hotels in Villarrica and Pucón, US$12 (may not run out of season). Taxis charge US$6. There is no public bus. LanChile, Lan Express to **Santiago, Concepción, Pucón, Osorno, Valdivia, Puerto Montt, Balmaceda** and **Punta Arenas**. Sky to **Santiago, Concepción, Pucón** and **Puerto Montt**.

Bus New long-distance bus terminal north of city at Pérez Rosales y Caupolicán, city bus 2, 7 or 10; colectivo 11P; taxi US$2.50. JAC has its own efficient terminal at Balmaceda y Aldunate, 7 blocks north of the Plaza. NarBus and Igi-Llaima are opposite. Buses to **Santiago**, overnight, 9 hrs, US$8 salón-cama US$22). To **Concepción**, Bío Bío (Lautaro entre Prat y Bulnes), US$5, 4½ hrs. To **Chillán**, 4 hrs, US$5. Cruz del Sur, 3 a day to **Castro**, 10 a day to **Puerto Montt** (US$6, 5½ hrs). To **Valdivia**, JAC, several daily, US$4.50, 2½ hrs. To **Osorno** US$4, 4 hrs. To **Villarrica** and **Pucón**, JAC, many between 0705 and 2045, 1½ hrs, and 2 hrs, US$3-3.50. Buses to neighbouring towns leave from Terminal Rural, Pinto y Balmaceda. To **Coñaripe**, 3 hrs, and **Lican Ray**, 2 hrs. To **Panguipulli**, Power and Pangui Sur 3 hrs, US$3. Pangui Sur to **Loncoche**, US$1.50, **Los Lagos**, US$2.50, **Mehuin** in summer only.

To **Curacautín** via Lautaro, Erbuc, US$2, 4 daily, 2 hrs. To **Lonquimay**, Erbuc, 4 daily, 3½ hrs, US$3. To **Contulmo**, US$4, 2 hrs, **Cañete**, US$4 and **Lebu**, Erbuc and Thiele.

Buses to Argentina: Igi Llaima and Narbus to **Junín de los Andes**, early morning but not daily, US$20, advance sales only. **Ruta Sur** (Miraflores 1151) to **Zapala**, 10-12 hrs (US$25), 3 a week. To **Neuquén**, 7 companies, 16 hrs (US$20), via Paso Pino Hachado. To **Bariloche** you have to change bus in Osorno, US$18.

Car hire Automóvil Club de Chile, Varas 687, T248903 for car hire and at airport. **Christopher Car**, Varas 522, T215988, recommended. **Euro**, MacKenna 426, T210311, helpful, good value. **Full Famas**, at airport and in centre T215420, highly recommended.

Train Station at Barros Arana y Lautaro Navarro, T233416, www.efe.cl. There is another ticket office at Bulnes 582, T233522, open Mon-Fri 0900-1300, 1430-1800, Sun 0900-1300. To

Santiago: at 2200, 9 hrs: fares *salón* US$26.50, *preferente* US$36, restaurant car mid-price (or take your own food). To **Puerto Montt** at 0800 and 1540, US$8.60.

Curacautín *p686*

Bus Terminal on the main road, by the plaza. Buses to/from **Temuco, Los Angeles** and **Santiago**. **Taxi** from Temuco airport US$40.

Lonquimay

Bus Bus Erbuc from **Temuco** via Lautaro, US$2 to **Malalcahuello**, 4 a day, 2½ hrs, 3½ to Lonquimay town, US$3. **Taxi** Curacautín-Malalcahuello US$12.

Parque Nacional Conguillio *p687*

For touring, hire a 4WD vehicle in Temuco.

To the northern entrance: **taxi** from Curacautín to Laguna Captrén, US$25 one way. To **Melipeuco** (stops at Hospedaje Icalme), Narbus from rural bus terminal, Temuco, 2½ hrs, US$2.85. Transport can be arranged from Melipeuco into the park (ask in grocery stores and hospedajes, US$25 one way). To the western entrance: Daily **buses** from Temuco to Cherquenco, from where there is no public transport to the park. Private transport is the best way to see the area.

⊕ Directory

Temuco *p684, map p686*

Airline offices LanChile, Bulnes 699, T272138. Sky, T747300, or 600-600 2828 for information. **Banks** Many ATMs at banks on Plaza Aníbal Pinto. Also at the JAC bus terminal (Visa). Many cambios around the plaza, all deal in dollars and Argentine pesos. Good rates at Germaniotour, M Montt 942, after 1100. **Bicycle repairs** on Balmaceda, **Don Cheyo**, No 1266, another at No 1294, **Monsalves**, No 1448, opposite rural bus terminal. Several others on Portales eg **Oxford, Bianchi**. **Consulates** Netherlands, España 494, Honorary Consul, Germán Nicklas, is friendly and helpful. **Internet** Many on Prat and Mackenna, south of the Plaza, US$0.50-0.65 per hr. **Hospitals** Manuel Montt 115. **Motor mechanic** ServiTren, Edgardo Schneider Reinike and Peter Fischer (peocito@yahoo.de), Matta 0545 y Ruta 5, T/F212775, for cars and motorcycles, German spoken. **Post offices** Portales 839.

Lagos Villarrica, Calafquén and Panguipulli

Wooded Lago Villarrica, 21 km long and about 7 km wide, is one of the most beautiful in the region, with the active, snow-capped Villarrica volcano (2,840 m) to the southeast. Villarrica and Pucón, resorts at the lake's southwest and southeast corners, are among the more expensive in the region, but are definitely worth a visit. South of Lago Villarrica, a necklace of six lakes with snowy peaks behind, form picture-postcard views. Calafquén and Panguipulli are the most visited, but there are also hot springs, national parks and interesting routes to Argentina.

Villarrica → *Phone code: 045. Colour map 8, grid C1. Population: 27,000. Altitude: 227 m.*

The quiet town of Villarrica, pleasantly set at the extreme southwest corner of the lake, can be reached by a 63-km paved road southeast from Freire (24 km south of Temuco on the Pan-American Highway), or from Loncoche, 54 km south of Freire, also paved. Founded in 1552, the town was besieged by the Mapuche in the uprising of 1599: after three years the surviving Spanish settlers, 11 men and 13 women, surrendered. The town was refounded in 1882. The **Muestra Cultural Mapuche** ① *Pedro de Valdivia y Zegers, open all summer*, features a Mapuche ruca and handicraft stalls. There is a livestock market every Monday about 1400; riding equipment for sale. In January and February Villarrica has a summer programme with many cultural and sporting events (including the Semana de Chilenidad) and on 18-19 September the Gran Fiesta Campestre de Villarrica is held in the indoor riding arena of the Parque Natural Dos Ríos, with typical foods, music, dancing, competitions and shows. **Dos Ríos** is 13 km west of Villarrica between the Ríos Voipir and Toltén, a private nature park with bed-and-breakfast accommodation (**A, B** without breakfast), cafetería, lots of sports, especially riding, fishing, boating, birdwatching: T09-419 8064, www.dosrios.de. **Chamber of tourism office** ① *on Gral Urrutia, Plaza de Armas, open daily in summer*. Offers accommodation.

Pucón → *Phone code: 045. Colour map 8, grid C1. Population: 13,000. Altitude: 227 m.*

Pucón, on the southeastern shore of Lago Villarrica, 26 km east of Villarrica, is the major tourist centre on the lake. The black sand beach is very popular for swimming and watersports. Between New Year to end-February it is very crowded and expensive; off season it is very pleasant. Apart from the lake, other attractions nearby include whitewater rafting, winter sports (see Skiing below) and several **canopy** (see Ziplining under Activities and tours) sites. **Tourist office** in the municipal building ① *O'Higgins 483, T441125/443238*, sells fishing licences (US$1 per month). Do not confuse with the Chamber of Tourism at the entrance to Pucón from Villarrica. It is not recommended to visit the lake on your won (robbery reported, 2005).

There is a pleasant *paseo*, the **Otto Gudenschwager**, which starts at the lake end of Ansorena (beside Gran Hotel Pucón, Holzapfel 190, T441001) and goes along the shore. Launch excursions from the landing stage at La Poza at the end of O'Higgins, US$7 for two hours.

Walk 2 km north along the beach to the mouth of the Río Trancura (also called Río Pucón), with views of the volcanoes Villarrica, Quetrupillán and Lanín. To cross the Río Pucón: head east out of Pucón along the main road, then turn north on an unmade road leading to a new bridge; from here there are pleasant walks along the north shore of the lake to Quelhue and Trarilelfú, or northeast towards Caburga, or up into the hills through farms and agricultural land, with views of three volcanoes and, higher up, of the lake. The journey to Caburga (see below) is a perfect mountain bike day trip.

Parque Nacional Villarrica

The park has three sectors: **Volcán Villarrica** *US$6*, **Volcán Quetrupillán** and the **Puesco sector** which includes the slopes of the Volcán Lanín on the Argentine border. Each sector has its own entrance and ranger station. A campsite with drinking water and toilets is below the refuge, 4 km inside the park. The Villarrica volcano, 2,840 m, 8 km south of Pucón, can be climbed up and down in eight to nine hours, good boots, ice axe and crampons, sunglasses, plenty of water, chocolate and sun block essential. Beware of sulphur fumes at the top – occasionally agencies provide gas masks, otherwise take a cloth mask moistened with lemon juice – but on good days you can see into the crater with lava bubbling at 1,250°.

Entry to Volcán Villarrica is permitted only to groups with a guide and to individuals who can show proof of membership of a mountaineering club in their own country. Several agencies take excursions, US$50, including park entry, guide, transport to park entrance and hire of equipment (no reduction for those with their own equipment); at the park entrance equipment is checked. Entry is refused if the weather is poor. Reputable travel agencies will not start out if the weather is bad: establish in advance what terms apply in the event of cancellation and be prepared to wait a few days. Many guides, all with equipment; ask for recommendations at the tourist office. For US$4 you can take the ski lift for the first part of the ascent; this is recommended as it saves 400 m climbing on scree.

Skiing ⓘ *Lift pass US$18-30 full day, to restaurant only US$7; ski season is Jul-Sep, occasionally longer. Equipment rental US$18 per day, US$100 per week. Information on snow and ski-lifts (and, perhaps, transport) from tourist office or Gran Hotel Pucón.* The Pucón resort, owned by the Gran Hotel Pucón, is on the eastern slopes of the volcano, reached by a track, 35 minutes. The centre offers equipment rental, ski instruction, first aid, restaurant and bar as well as wonderful views from the terrace. The centre is good for beginners; more advanced skiers can try the steeper areas. (Skiing trips to the summit are very tough going and only for the fit.)

Lagos Caburga and Colico
Lago Caburga (spelt locally Caburgua), a very pretty lake in a wild setting 25 km northeast of Pucón, is unusual for its beautiful white sand beach (it also has a black sand beach – other beaches in the area are of black volcanic sand). The west and much of the shores of the lake are inaccessible to vehicles. The north shore can be reached by a road from Cunco via the north shore of Lago Colico, a more remote lake north of Lago Villarrica. The village of Caburga, at the southern end is reached by a turning off the main road 8 km east of Pucón. The southern end of the lake and around Caburga is lined with campsites. There is a supermarket in Caburga. Rowing boats may be hired US$2 per hour. Just off the road from Pucón, Km 15, are the Ojos de Caburga, beautiful pools fed from underground, particularly attractive after rain (entry US$0.50; ask bus driver to let you off). Alternatively, take a mountain bike from Pucón via the Puente Quelhue.

Parque Nacional Huerquehue
ⓘ *The park is open officially only Dec-Mar, but you can get in at other times, US$7.50 (students and teachers half-price), the warden is very helpful.*
East of Lago Caburga, the park includes steep hills and at least 20 lakes, some of them very small. Entrance and administration are near Lago Tinguilco, the largest lake, on the western edge of the park. The park entrance is 7 km (3 km uphill, 3 km down, one along Lago Tinquilco) from Paillaco, which is reached by an all-weather road which turns off 3 km before Caburga. From the entrance there is a well-signed track north to three beautiful lakes, Lagos Verde, Chico and Toro (private car park, US$1.50, 1½ km along the track). The track zig-zags up (sign says 5 km, but worth it) to Lago Chico, then splits left to Verde, right to Toro. From Toro you can continue to Lago Huerquehue and Laguna los Patos (camping). People in the park rent horses and boats. Take your own food.

South of the Huerquehue Park on a turning from the Pucón-Caburga road there are **Termas de Quimey-Co**, about 29 km from Pucón, campsite, two cabins and hotel **Termas de Quimey- Co** *T045-441903*, new, less ostentatious or expensive than **Termas de Huife Hostería** ⓘ *T441222, www.termashuife.cl, Pucón, Km 33*, US$12 high season (US$9 low), including use of pool, modern, pleasant (hotel offers daily shuttle from/to Pucón, or taxi from Pucón, US$23 return with taxi waiting, US$16 one way). Beyond Huife are the hot springs of **Los Pozones**, Km 35, set in natural rock pools, US$5, US$7 at night (a good time to go). The road there is rough.

Cañi Forest Sanctuary, south of Parque Nacional Huerquehue and covering 500 ha, was the first private forest reserve established in Chile. It contains 17 small lakes and is covered by ancient native forests of coihue, lenga and some of the oldest araucaria trees in the country. From its highest peak, **El Mirador**, five volcanoes can be seen. There is a self-guided trail, US$8 plus transport; for tours with English-speaking guide, contact **the Cañi Guides Program** ⓘ *Hostería ¡école! in Pucón (see Sleeping), or see www.ecole.cl.*

Route to Argentina
From Pucón a road runs southeast via Curarrehue to the Argentine border. At Km 18 there is a turning south to the **Termas de Palguín**. There are many beautiful waterfalls within hiking distance: for example, Salto China (entry US$0.60, restaurant, camping); Salto del Puma

(US$0.60) and Salto del León (US$1.25), both 800 m from the Termas. From Pucón take Bus Regional Villarrica from Palguín y O'Higgins at 1100 to the junction (10 km from Termas); last bus from junction to the Termas at 1500, so you may have to hitch back. Taxi from Pucón, US$20.

Near Palguín is the entrance to the Quetrupillán section of the Parque Nacional Villarrica (high clearance vehicle necessary, horses best), free camping, wonderful views over Villarrica Volcano and six other peaks. Ask rangers for the route to the other entrance.

The road from Pucón to Argentina passes turnings north at Km 23 to **Termas de San Luis** and Km 35 to **Termas de Pangui** (15 km from main road), both with hotels, the latter with teepees (To45-411388 and o45-442039 respectively). It continues to Curarrehue, from where it turns south to Puesco and climbs via **Lago Quellelhue**, a tiny gem set between mountains at 1,196 m to reach the border at the **Mamuil Malal** or **Tromén Pass**. To the south of the pass rises the graceful cone of Lanín volcano. On the Argentine side the road runs south to Junín de los Andes, San Martín de los Andes and Bariloche.

Chilean immigration and customs at Puesco, open Dec-Mar 0800-2100, Apr-Nov 0800-1900, US$2 per vehicle at other times. There are free Conaf campsites with no facilities at Puesco and 5 km from the border near Lago Tromén. Daily bus from Pucón, 1800, two hours, US$2. It's a hard road for cyclists, but not impossible.

Lago Calafquén → *Colour map 8, grid C1. Population: 1,700. Altitude: 207 m.*

Dotted with small islands, Lago Calafquén is a popular tourist destination. **Lican-Ray** 25 km south of Villarrica on a peninsula on the north shore, is the major resort on the lake. There are two fine beaches each side of the rocky peninsula. Boats can be hired (US$2 per hour) and there are catamaran trips (US$3; trips to islands US$11 per hour). Although very crowded in season, most facilities close by the end of March and, out of season, Lican-Ray feels like a ghost town. 6 km to the east is the river of lava formed when the Villarrica volcano erupted in 1971. The **tourist office**, on the plaza, is open daily in summer, Monday-Friday off season.

Coñaripe (*Population 1,253*), 21 km southeast of Lican-Ray at the eastern end of Lago Calafquén, is another popular tourist spot. Its setting, with a 3-km black sand beach surrounded by mountains, is very beautiful. From here a road (mostly ripio) around the lake's southern shore leads to Lago Panguipulli (see below) and offers superb views over Villarrica volcano, which can be climbed from here. Most services are on the Calle Principal. **Tourist office**, on the plaza, open 15 November-15 April daily, otherwise weekends only.

Termas Vergara are 14 km northeast of Coñaripe by a steep ripio road which continues to Palguín. There are nice pools, a campsite and minimarket. **Termas Geometricas** ⓘ *3 km beyond Termas Vergara, www.termasgeometricas.cl, US$16.* These good new pools are geometrically-shaped and are linked by wooden walkways.

From Coñaripe a road runs southeast over the steep **Cuesta Los Añiques** offering views of tiny Lago Pellaifa. The **Termas de Coñaripe** are at Km 16. Further south at Km 32 are the **Termas de Liquiñe** ⓘ *8 different thermal centres, from US$4 to US$7 pp.* Opposite Liquiñe are the new Termas Río de Liquiñe, good heated cabañas, good food, personal spa bath, large outdoor thermal pool. From there you can walk up to the thermal source, US$0.25 to cross river by boat, one hour excursion. There is a road north to Pucón through Villarrica National Park, high-clearance and 4WD vehicle essential.

The border with Argentina, **Paso Carirriñe**, is reached by unpaved road from Termas de Liquiñe. It is open 15 October-31 August. On the Argentine side the road continues to San Martín de los Andes.

Lago Panguipulli and around

→ *Phone code: 063. Colour map 8, grid C1. Population: 8,000. Altitude: 136 m.*

The lake is reached by paved road from Lanco on the Pan-American Highway or unpaved roads from Lago Calafquén. A road leads along the beautiful north shore, wooded with sandy beaches and cliffs. Most of the south shore is inaccessible by road. **Panguipulli**, at the northwest corner of the lake in a beautiful setting, is the largest town in the area. The streets are planted with roses: it is claimed that there are over 14,000. The Iglesia San Sebastián is in Swiss style, with twin towers; its belltower contains three bells from Germany. Fishing excursions on the lake are recommended. Boat hire US$3. There are also good rafting opportunities on rivers in the area. In the last week of January is Semana de Rosas, with dancing and sports competitions. **Tourist office**, by the plaza, is open daily December-February, otherwise weekdays only.

Choshuenco (*Population 622*) lies 23 km east of Panguipulli at the eastern tip of the lake. To the south is the Reserva Nacional Mocho Choshuenco (7,536 ha) which includes two volcanoes: Choshuenco (2,415 m) and Mocho (2,422 m). On the slopes of Choshuenco the Club Andino de Valdivia has ski-slopes and three refugios. This can be reached by a turning from the road which goes south from Choshuenco to Enco at the east end of Lago Riñihue (the lake southwest of Lago Panguipulli). East of Choshuenco a road leads to Lago Pirehueico, via the impressive waterfalls of Huilo Huilo, where the river channels its way through volcanic rock before thundering down into a natural basin. The falls are three hours' walk from Choshuenco, or take the Puerto Fuy bus and get off at Alojamiento Huilo Huilo (see Sleeping, below), from where it is a five-minute walk to the falls.

East of Choshuenco is **Lago Pirehueico**, a long, narrow and deep lake, surrounded by virgin lingue forest. It is totally unspoilt except for some logging activity. There are no roads along the shores of the lake, but two ports. **Puerto Fuy** (*Population: 300*) is at the north end 21 km from Choshuenco, 7 km from Neltume. **Puerto Pirehueico** is at the south end. A ferry runs between the two ports, then a road to the Argentine border crossing at Paso Huahum.

The border with Argentina, **Paso Huahum** (659 m), is a four-hour walk from Puerto Pirehueico (very hard for cyclists with steep climbs, no public transport to border). On the Argentine side the road, with buses, leads to San Martín de los Andes and Junín de los Andes. Chilean immigration is open summer 0800-2100, winter 0800-2000.

● Sleeping

Villarrica *p691*

Lodging in private homes in our **C-D** range can be found on blocks Muñoz 300 and 400, Koerner 300 and O'Higgins 700 and 800. More upmarket accommodation is on the lakefront.

LL Villarrica Park Lake, Km 13 on the road to Pucón, T450000, www.villarricaparklakehotel.cl. 5-star, all rooms overlook the lake, spa with pools, sauna and solarium, fishing trips.

L-AL El Ciervo, Koerner 241, T411245, www.hotelelciervo.cl. German spoken, beautiful location, pool. Recommended.

AL Hotel Yachting Kiel, Koerner 153, T411631, www.chile-hotels.com/kielhost.htm. **A** off season, lakeside, good.

AL-A Hotel y Cabañas El Parque, 3 km east on Pucón road, T411120, reservas@ hotelelparque.cl. Lakeside with beach, tennis courts, with breakfast, good restaurant set meals. Recommended.

AL-B Hostería de la Colina, Las Colinas 115, overlooking town, T411503, www.hosteria delacolina.com. With breakfast, variety of rooms and cabins, large gardens, good service, internet, good restaurant, English spoken. Recommended.

A-B Bungalowlandia, Prat 749, T/F411635, www.bungalowlandia.cl. Cabañas for 2, dining room, good facilities, pool.

A-B Hostería Bilbao, Henríquez 43, T411186, bilbao@7lagos.com. Small rooms, pretty patio, good restaurant.

B Kolping, Riquelme 399, T/F411388. Good breakfast. Recommended.

C Hostería Rayhuen, Pedro Montt 668, T411571, guido-castillo@entelchile.net. Lovely garden. Recommended.

C La Torre Suiza, Bilbao 969, T/F411213, www.torresuiza.com. Some rooms with bath (**B**), **E** pp in dorms, kitchen facilities, camping, cycle rental, book exchange, lots of info, good breakfast included, reserve in advance. "Very Swiss". Recommended.

C-D Chilepeppers, Vicente Reyes 546, T414694, www.chilepeppers.cl. **E** pp in dorms, new, basic, cramped dorms, kitchen, internet, barbeque area, a fun place.

C-D Hospedaje Nicolás, Anfion Muñoz 477, T410232. **E** pp singles. Simple rooms with bath. Breakfast included.

D Vicente Reyes 854, T414457. Good breakfast, good bathrooms but only one for 4-5 rooms, use of kitchen, camping in garden. Also **D** Vicente Reyes 773. Family of Elena Martínez, pleasant, cheaper without bath.

E Hosp y Restaurante Rayen, Zegers 950, T412056. Cosy, with TV, breakfast, good food including typical and vegetarian dishes.

E pp **Maravillas del Sur**, Bilbao 821, T411444. With bath and breakfast, good value, parking.

E pp **Res San Francisco**, Julio Zegers 646. Youth hostel, shared rooms.

Camping Many sites east of town on Pucón road, open in season only: nearest is **E** Los Castaños, T412330, up to 6 people.

Pucón *p691*

In summer (Dec-Feb) rooms may be hard to find. Plenty of alternatives (usually cheaper) in Villarrica. Prices below are Jan-Feb. Off-season rates are 20-40% lower and it is often possible to negotiate. Many families offer rooms, look for the signs or ask in bars/restaurants. Touts offer rooms to new arrivals; check that they are not way out of town.

LL Antumalal, 2 km west, T441011, www.antumalal.com. Luxury class, very small, picturesque chalet-type, magnificent views of the lake (breakfast and lunch on terrace), gardens, with meals, open year round, pool.

L Interlaken, Colombia y Caupolicán, T441276, F441242. Chalets, open Nov-Apr, water skiing, pool, TCs changed, no restaurant.

AL Hostería El Principito, Urrutia 291, T441200. Good breakfast.

AL-A Los Maitenes, Fresia 354, T441820, www.hotelmaitenes.cl. Light and airy, comfortable, homely, breakfast, TV.

A Gudenschwager, Pedro de Valdivia 12, T442326, hotelgudenschwager@yahoo.com. Classic Bavarian type, views over lake, volcano and mountains, attentive staff, comfortable, excellent restaurant (open in summer only).

A Munich, Alderete 275, T/F442293. Modern, spacious, German and English spoken.

A La Posada, Valdivia 191, T441088, laposada@unete.com. Cheaper without bath, full board available, also spacious cabins (**C** low season), small breakfast.

B Cabañas Ruca Malal, O'Higgins 770, T442297, www.rucamalal.cl. Lovely cabins in a pretty garden, spacious, well-equipped and decorated, various sizes, pool.

B Hostería Gerónimo, Alderete 665, T/F443762, www.geronimo.cl. Quiet, smart, bar, restaurant, open all year.

B Hostería Millarrahue, O'Higgins 460, T411610. Good, inexpensive restaurant.

B Kernayel, 1 km east at Camino Internacional 1395, T442164, www.kernayel.cl. Cabins and comfortable rooms, heating, hot water, good breakfast, pool.

B-C La Tetera, Urrutia 580, T/F441462, www.tetera.cl. 6 rooms, some with bath, with breakfast, German and English spoken, book swap, information centre, good Spanish classes, agency for Navimag ferries, book in advance. Recommended.

C Casa de Campo Kila-Leufu, about 20 km east on road to Curarrehue, T09-711 8064, www.kilaleufu.cl. **E** pp in small dorms. Rooms on the Martínez family farm, contact Margot or Peter in advance, English spoken, price includes breakfast, home-grown food served, horse riding, boat tours, treks, camping facilities. Recommended.

C Hosp Víctor, Palguín 705, T443525, www.pucon.com/victor. **E** pp without bath, new, comfortable, kitchen use, TV, laundry, internet, information, good.

C Hostería ¡école!, Urrutia 592, T441675, www.ecole.cl. Private rooms, singles, shared rooms and dormitory, good vegetarian and fish restaurant, ecological shop, ancient forest treks,

information, language classes, massage, hostelling discount, best to reserve in advance.
C Res Lincoyán, Av Lincoyán 323, T441144, www.lincoyan.cl. Cheaper without bath, comfortable.

C-D Donde Germán, Brasil 640, T442444, www.dondegerman.cl. **E** pp in dorms. Fun, organizes tours, internet, book in advance.

C-D Hostal Backpackers, Palguín 695, T441373, www.backpackerspucon.tk. With or without bath, quiet, next to JAC buses, kitchen, internet, 10% discount on Politur activities, Navimag reservations, tourist information, new.

Camping There are many camping and cabin establishments. Those close to Pucón include: **F** pp **La Poza**, Costanera Geis 769, T441435, hot showers, good kitchen. Recommended. West along Lago Villarrica: **A-B Huimpalay-Tray**, Km 12, T450079 (Santiago 231 4248). Gorgeous location on lake, well-equipped. Recommended all round. **Saint John**, Km 7, T441165/92, Casilla 154, open Dec-Mar, also hostería. Several sites en route to volcano, including: **C** per site **L'Etoile**, Km 2, T442188, in attractive forest. **Mahuida**, Km 6. Cheaper sites en route to Caburga.

Private houses
E pp **Hosp Graciela**, Pasaje Rolando Matus 521 (off Av Brasil). Comfortable, good food.
E pp **Hosp Irma Torres**, Lincoyán 545. Cooking facilities.
E pp **Hosp Lucía**, Lincoyán 565, T441721, luciahostal@hotmail.com. Safe, quiet, cooking facilities.
E pp **Hosp Sonia**, Lincoyán 485, T441269, www.pucon.com/sonia. Use of kitchen, meals.
E pp **Tr@vel Pucón**, Blanco Encalada 190, T444093. Garden, tours, kitchen, Spanish classes, near Tur-Bus terminal.
E-F pp **Adriana Molina**, Lincoyán 312. With breakfast, helpful.
E-F pp **Familia Acuña**, Palguín 223 (ask at *peluquería* next door). Without breakfast, kitchen and laundry facilities.
F pp **Roberto y Alicia Abreque**, Perú 170. Basic, noisy, popular, kitchen and laundry facilities, information on excursions.

Lago Caburga *p692*
B Landhaus San Sebastián, east of Lago Caburga, F045-1972360, www.landhaus-chile.com. With bath and breakfast, good meals, laundry facilities, English and German spoken, Spanish classes.
D Hostería Los Robles, near the lake shore, T236989. Views, restaurant, campsite, closed out of season.

Parque Nacional Huerquehue *p692*
B-D Refugio Tinquilco, 3½ km from park entrance, where forest trail leads to lakes Verde and Toro, T02-777 7673, T09-822 7153 (mob), patriciolanfranco@entelchile.net. Most expensive rooms with bath, cheapest for bed and no sheets, meals extra, heating, hot water, 24-hr electricity, sauna, cooking facilities, very good. Recommended.
C Hospedaje Carlos Alfredo Richard, southwest shore of the lake, 2 km from park entrance, parque_huerquehue@hotmail.com. Large rooms with bath, hot water, breakfast included, restaurant, rowing boats for hire (also at Arauco 171 in Pucón, shared rooms, use of kitchen, internet access).
E pp 2 German speaking families, the Braatz and Soldans, offer accommodation, no electricity, food and camping (US$6); they also rent rowing boats on the lake. **E** pp Nidia Carrasco Godoy runs a hospedaje in the park, T09-443 2725 (mob). With breakfast, hot water, camping.
Camping only at the park entrance, 2 sites, US$8. 1½ km before the park entrance.

Route to Argentina: Termas de Palguín *p692*
C Rancho de Caballos (Casilla 142, Pucón), T441575. Restaurant with vegetarian dishes, laundry and kitchen facilities; also, cabañas and camping, horse riding, self-guided trails, English and German spoken.

Lago Calafquén *P693*
Lican-Ray
C Hostería Inaltulafquen, on Playa Grande, Casilla 681, T431115, F410028. With breakfast, English spoken, comfortable.
C Hosp Los Nietos, Manquel 125, Playa Chica, T431078. Without breakfast.
D Res Temuco, G Mistral 515, Playa Chica, T431130. Without bath, with breakfast, good.
Camping Floresta, T211954, **B** for 6 people, ½ km east of town. 6 sites to west and many along north shore towards Coñaripe.

Coñaripe
E pp **Hospedaje Chumay**, on Plaza, T317287, turismochumay@hotmail.com. With restaurant, internet, tours, some English spoken, good.
Camping Sites on beach charge US$20, but if you walk ½-¾ km from town you can camp on the beach free. Cold municipal showers on beach, US$0.35.

Termas de Coñaripe
L-AL pp **Termas de Coñaripe**, T411407. Excellent hotel with four pools, good restaurant, cycles and horses for hire. Full board available.

Termas de Liquiñe

A pp **Termas de Liquiñe**, T063-317377. Full board, cabins, restaurant, hot pool, small native forest **E** for accommodation in private houses.
E-F pp **Hosp La Casona**, Camino Internacional, T045-412085. Hot shower, good food, comfortable; tours from Lican-Ray in summer, US$17, 0830-1830 with lunch.

Panguipulli *p693*

B Hostería Quetropillán, Etchegaray 381, T311348. Comfortable.
D Central, Valdivia 115, T311331. Good breakfast. Recommended.
D Olga Berrocal, JM Carrera 834. Small rooms.
D Eva Halabi, Los Ulmos 62, T311483. Good breakfast.
E-F pp **Hostal Orillas del Lago**, M de Rosas 265, T311710 (or 312499 if no reply, friends have key). From plaza walk towards lake, last house on left, 8 blocks from terminal. Good views, kitchen, backpacker place.
Camping El Bosque, P Sigifredo 241, T311489, US$7.50 per site. Small, good, but not suitable for vehicle camping, hot water. Also 3 sites at Chauquén, 6 km southeast on lakeside.

Choshuenco

D Hostería Rayen Trai, María Alvarado y O'Higgins. Former yacht club with accommodation and good food, open all year.
E pp **Alojamiento Huilo Huilo**, Km 9 east from Choshuenco (1 km before Neltume). Basic but comfortable and well situated for walks, good food.
E-F pp **Hostería Rucapillán**, San Martín 85, T318220, rucapi@telsur.cl. Restaurant which lets out rooms, English spoken, tours.

Lago Pirehueico

E Hostal Kaykaen, Puerto Fuy. Meals, use of kitchen, bike rental. One of several private houses offering accommodation.
F pp **Restaurant Puerto Fuy**, Puerto Fuy. Hot water, good food.
F pp **Restaurant San Giovani**, Puerto Fuy. Family atmosphere, good rooms, breakfast and other meals. There is also accommodation in private houses.
Camping On the beach (take own food).

O Eating

Villarrica *p691*

♔♔♔ **El Tabor**, S Epulef 1187. Excellent but pricey.
♔♔♔ **La Cava de Roble**, Valentín Letelier 658, p 2, T416446. Excellent grill, specialises in exotic meat and game, extensive wine list
♔♔ **Rapa Nui**, V Reyes 678. Good, closed Sun.

♔♔ **El Rey de Mariscos**, Letelier 1030. Good seafood.
♔♔ **The Travellers**, Letelier 753. Varied menu including vegetarian, Asian food, good bar, English spoken.
♔ **Alternativa**, V Reyes 739. Good almuerzo.
♔ **Café 2001**, Henríquez 379. Coffee and ice cream, good.
♔ **Casa Vieja**, Letelier y Muñoz. Good value set lunch, family run.
♔ **Pastelería Sweet**, Prat 709. Excellent homemade cakes and pies, smoothies, nice deck overlooking lake.

Pucón *p691*

See Sleeping for other recommendations.
♔♔♔ **Ana María**, O'Higgins 865. Classic Chilean.
♔♔♔ **La Maga**, Fresia 125. Uruguayan grill, good, if pricey.
♔♔♔ **Puerto Pucón**, Fresia 251. Spanish, stylish.
♔♔ **La Buonatesta**, Fresia 243. Good pizzería.
♔♔ **El Fogón**, O'Higgins 480. Very good.
♔♔ **El Palet**, Fresia 295. Genuine local food, good value. Recommended.
♔♔ **El Refugio**, Lincoyán 348. Some vegetarian dishes, expensive wine.
♔♔ **Nafis Pucón**, Fresia 477. Middle eastern cuisine, good value, helpful.

Cafés and bars

Several bars on O´Higgins.
Fresia Strasse, Fresia 161. Good coffee and cake.
Holzapfel Backerei, Holzapfel 524. German café. Recommended.
Vagabundo, Fresia 135. Good value meals.

Lago Calafquén: Lican-Ray *p693*

♔♔-♔ **Café Ñaños**, Urrutia 105. Very good, reasonable prices, helpful owner.
♔♔-♔ **Restaurant-Bar Guido's**, Urrutia 405. Good value.

Panguipulli *p693*

♔♔-♔ **Café Central**, M de Rosas 750. Fixed menu.
♔♔-♔ **El Chapulín**, M de Rosas 639. Good food and value. Several cheap restaurants in O'Higgins 700 block.

O Shopping

Pucón *p691*

Camping equipment Eltit supermarket, O'Higgins y Fresia. **Outdoors & Travel**, Lincoyán 361, clothing, equipment, maps.

▲ Activities and tours

Villarrica *p691*

Fundo Huifquenco, just south of town (0.5 km) along Av Matta, T415040, www.fundohuif

quenco.cl. A large working farm, trails, horseriding, carriage tours, bicycle hire, meals (book in advance). Prices from US$8.

Vuelatour, Camilo Henríquez 430, loc 1, T415766. General tour agency, trips to thermal springs etc, Navimag, LAN agent, airport transfer, car hire.

Pucón *p691*

Pucón and Villarrica are celebrated as centres for fishing on Lake Villarrica and in the beautiful Lincura, Trancura and Toltén rivers. In high season, sports shops open, especially for biking and watersports.

Fishing Local tourist office will supply details on licences and open seasons etc.

Horse riding Enquire at La Tetera for Hans Bacher (Austrian), or Rancho de Caballos (German run, see Termas de Palguín, above). Day excursions US$55, also half-day US$35. **Centro de Turismo Ecuestre Huepil Malal**, T09-643 2673, www.huepil-malal.cl. Rodolfo Coombs and Carolina Pumpin, PO Box 16, Pucón, 40 mins from town. Highly recommended.

Hydrospeeding Fabrice Pini, Colo Colo 830, US$55 for 30 mins.

Mountain biking Bike hire from US$1.50 per hr to US$10 per day from several travel agencies on O'Higgins.

Thermal springs There are dozens of thermal springs in the area, ranging from the upmarket to the natural. Transport is provided by tour operators.

Watersports Water-skiing, sailing, windsurfing at Playa Grande beach by Gran Hotel and La Poza beach end of O'Higgins (more expensive than Playa Grande, not recommended). Playa Grande: waterskiing US$10 for 15 mins, Laser sailing US$11 per hr, sailboards US$10 per hr, rowing boats US$4 per hr.

Whitewater rafting Very popular on the Río Trancura. Many agencies offer trips (see below), Trancura Bajo (grade 3), US$15; Trancura Alto (grade 4), US$30.

Ziplining Called **Canopy** (sliding from platform to platform along a metal cord). 6 agencies can arrange this, US$15-20 including transport.

Tour operators

Tour operators arrange trips to thermal baths, trekking to volcanoes, whitewater rafting, etc. For falls, lakes and termas it's cheaper, if in a group, to flag down a taxi and bargain. Many agencies, so shop around: prices vary at times, quality of guides and equipment variable. In high season, when lots of groups go together, individual attention may be lacking. Prices for climbing Villarrica are given below. Tours to Termas de

Huife, US$20 including entry.

Aguaventura, Palguín 336, T444246, www.aguaventura.com. French-run, in summer kayaking and rafting specialities, in winter "snowshop" for ski and snowboard rental, volcano climbing, trekking.

Anden Sport, O'Higgins 535, T441048, anden-sport-tours@tie.cl. Agency specializing in skiing, rafting, trips to springs, hiking tours.

Politur, O'Higgins 635, T/F441373, www.politur.com. Well-established and responsible.

Roncotrack, O'Higgins y Arauco. Quadbike excursions and "ethnotourism".

Sol y Nieve, O'Higgins esq Lincoyán, T/F444098. Well established, trekking, rafting. Recommended.

Trancura, several offices on O'Higgins, T441189, www.trancura.com. The biggest and cheapest of the agencies. Recommended for trips to thermal springs (they have their own **termas**), but questionable safety standards for rafting and climbing.

Several other reputable agencies including **Kayak Pucón, Aventur, Turismo Lafquén, Sur Expediciones.**

Lago Calafquén: Coñaripe *p693*

Hiking to Villarrica Volcano is organized by Leo Barrios at Hospedaje Chumay, who also runs trips to various thermal springs, as does the tourist office in summer.

● Transport

Villarrica *p691*

Bus Terminal at Pedro de Valdivia y Muñoz. JAC at Bilbao 610, T411447, and opposite for Pucón and Lican-Ray. Terminal Rural for other local services at Matta y Vicente Reyes. To **Santiago**, 10 hrs, US$20, several companies. To **Pucón**, with **Vipu-Ray** (main terminal) and JAC, in summer every 15 mins, 40 mins' journey, US$0.50; same companies to **Lican-Ray**, US$1. To **Valdivia**, JAC, US$3.50, 3 a day, 2½ hrs. To **Coñaripe** (US$1.60) and **Liquiñe** at 1600 Mon-Sat, 1000 Sun. To **Temuco**, JAC, US$3. To **Loncoche** (Ruta 5 junction for hitching), US$1.50. To **Panguipulli**, go via Lican-Ray, occasional direct buses. Buses to Argentina: buses from Temuco to **Junín de los Andes** pass through Villarrica, fares are the same as from Temuco, T412733, book in advance. Note that if the Tromén pass is blocked by snow buses go via Panguipulli instead of Villarrica and Pucón.

Pucón *p691*

Air Airport 2 km on Caburga road. **Lan Express** and **Sky** fly to **Santiago** via Temuco in summer, 2-3 times a week each.

Bus No municipal terminal: each company has its own terminal: **JAC**, Uruguay y Palguín;

Tur-Bus, O'Higgins, 1180, east of town; Igi Llaima and Cóndor, Colo Colo y O'Higgins. JAC to **Villarrica** (US$0.50), **Temuco** (frequent, US$3, 2 hrs, rápido US$3.50, 1¾ hr) and **Valdivia** (US$5, 3 hrs). Tur-Bus direct to **Valdivia, Osorno** and **Puerto Montt**, 6 hrs, US$6, daily. To **Santiago**, 10 hrs, US$12, many companies, early morning and late evening; semi cama service by Tur-Bus and JAC, US$40. Colectivos to **Villarrica** from O'Higgins y Palguín. Buses to Argentina: Buses from Temuco to **Junín** pass through Pucón, fares are the same as from Temuco.

Car hire Prices start at US$25 for a car. Christopher Car, O'Higgins 335, T/F449013. Pucón Rent A Car, Camino Internacional 1395, T441922, kernayel@cepri.cl. **Sierra Nevada**, Palguín y O'Higgins.

Taxi Co-operative, T441009.

Lago Caburga *p692*
Taxi day trips from Pucón, US$30 return. JAC bus departs regularly for Caburga (US$1 single), and there are colectivos from Ansorena y Uruguay or you can try hitching. If walking or cycling, turn left 3 km east of Pucón (sign to Puente Quelhue) and follow the track (very rough) for 18 km through beautiful scenery. Recommended.

Parque Nacional Huerquehue *p692*
Bus Direct to park, take JAC from Pucón, 3 a day in summer, US$2.85, 1 hr. JAC from Pucón to Paillaco, 1½ hrs, US$1, Mon-Fri 0700, 1230, 1700, Sat-Sun 0700, 1600, returns immediately – last at 1800.

Lago Calafquén and around *p693*
Lican-Ray
Bus Leave from offices around plaza. To **Villarrica**, 1 hr, US$1, JAC frequent in summer. In summer, there are direct buses from **Santiago** (Tur-Bus US$12, 10 hrs, salón-cama US$30) and **Temuco** (US$3). To **Panguipulli**, Mon-Sat 0730.

Coñaripe
Bus To **Panguipulli**, 7 a day (4 off season), US$1.80 and 16 daily to **Villarrica**, US$1. Nightly bus direct to **Santiago**, Tur-Bus and JAC.

Panguipulli *p693*
Bus Terminal at Gabriela Mistral y Portales. To **Santiago** daily, US$20. To **Valdivia**, frequent (Sun only 4), several lines, 2 hrs, US$3. To **Temuco** frequent, Power and Pangui Sur, US$2, 3 hrs. To **Puerto Montt**, US$7. To **Choshuenco**, Neltume and Puerto Fuy, 3 daily, 3 hrs. To **Coñaripe** (with connections for Lican-Ray and Villarrica), 7 daily Mon-Fri, 4 Sat, 1½ hrs, US$2.

Lago Pirehueico
Bus Daily Puerto Fuy to **Panguipulli**, 2 daily, 2 hrs, US$3.
Ferry The **Mariela** sails from Puerto Fuy to Puerto Pirehueico, 2-3 hrs, US$1.50, cars US$16, bikes $3. A beautiful crossing (to take vehicles reserve in advance at the Hotel Quetropillán in Panguipulli). Schedule: twice daily each way. In summer there is a daily bus service to **Argentina**.

🅞 Directory

Villarrica *p691*
Banks ATMs at banks on Pedro de Valdivia between Montt and Alderete. **Carlos Huerta**, A Muñoz 417, **Central de Repuestos**, A Muñoz 415 (good rates), **Turcamb**, Henríquez 576, and **Cristopher Exchange**, Valdivia 1061, all change TCs and cash. **Bicycle shops** Mora Bicicletas, G Korner 760, helpful. **Internet** At the Central de Llamadas, Henríquez 567, 2nd floor. Cybercafé Salmon, Letelier y Henríquez. **Post offices** A Muñoz 315. Open 0900-1300, 1430-1800 (Mon-Fri), 0900-1300 (Sat). **Telephones** Entel, Henríquez 440 and 575. Telefónica, Henríquez 544.

Pucón *p691*
Airline offices LanChile, Urrutia y Costanera, daily 1000-1400, 1800-2200. **Banks** ATMs in Banco Santander, O'Higgins y Fresia, Eltit, supermarket, O'Higgins, Banco BCI, Fresia y Alderete, and in casino. Several casas de cambio on O'Higgins. Eltit, also changes TCs, but rates for TCs in Pucón are poor. **Internet** Several sites on O'Higgins, US$2 per hr. Also at Palguín y O'Higgins. **Post offices** Fresia 183. **Telephones** Telefónica, Gen Urrutia 472. Entel, Ansorena 299.

Valdivia and Osorno

Valdivia is a very pleasant city at the confluence of the Ríos Calle Calle and Cruces, which form the Río Valdivia. It is set in rich agricultural land receiving some 2,300 mm of rain a year. To the north of the city is a large island, Isla Teja, where the Universidad Austral de Chile is situated. The student population adds zest to the nightlife. At the mouth of the Rio Valdivia are a group of historic forts which make a good day's outing from the city. Osorno, further south, is not such a tourist city, but it is a base for visiting the attractive southern lakes.

Valdivia → *Phone code: 063. Colour map 8, grid C1. Population: 127,000. 839 km south of Santiago.*

Valdivia was one of the most important centres of Spanish colonial control over Chile. Founded in 1552 by Pedro de Valdivia, it was abandoned as a result of the Mapuche insurrection of 1599 and the area was briefly occupied by Dutch pirates. In 1645 it was refounded as a walled city, the only Spanish mainland settlement south of the Río Biobío. The coastal fortifications at the mouth of the river also date from the 17th century. They were greatly strengthened after 1760 owing to fears that Valdivia might be seized by the British, but were of little avail during the Wars of Independence: overnight on 2 February 1820 the Chilean naval squadron under Lord Cochrane seized San Carlos, Amargos and Corral and turned their guns on Niebla and Mancera, which surrendered the following morning. From independence until the 1880s Valdivia was an outpost of Chilean rule, reached only by sea or by a coastal route through Mapuche territory. From 1849 to 1875 Valdivia was a centre for German colonization of the Lake District. **Tourist offices** ① *Av Prat 555, by the dock, T342300, infovaldivia@sernatur.cl.* Good map of region and local rivers, list of hotel prices and examples of local crafts with artisans' addresses. Open daily in summer, weekdays only off season. **Conaf,** Ismael Váldez 431, T245200. **Automóvil Club de Chile,** García Reyes 49075, T250376, also for car hire.

Sights The city centre is the tree-lined, shady **Plaza de la República**. A pleasant walk is along **Avenida Prat** (or **Costanera**), which follows the bend in the river, from the bus station to the bridge to **Isla Teja,** the **Muelle Fluvial** (boat dock) and the riverside market. Boats can be hired at the bend for US$2.50 per hour. Sealions lounge around the dock. On Isla Teja, near the library in the University, are a **botanic garden** and **arboretum** with trees from all over the world (open during daylight hours). On boat trips round the island you can see lots of waterfowl. The 30-ha **Parque Saval** on the island has areas of native forest as well as the Lago de los Lotos (beautiful blooms in spring), entry US$0.50. Also on Isla Teja is the **Museo Histórico y Antropológico** ① *daily, 1000-1300, 1400-1800, off season closed Mon, US$2.* Run by the University, it contains archaeology, ethnography and history of German settlement. Next door is the **Museo de Arte Moderno** ① *open Jan-Feb, Tue-Fri 1000-1300, 1400-1800, Sat-Sun 1000-1300, 1500-1900, US$0.60.* Off season it is only open for occasional exhibitions.

The surrounding district has lovely countryside of woods, beaches, lakes and rivers. The various rivers are navigable and there are pleasant journeys by rented motor boat on the **Ríos Futa** and **Tornagaleanes** around the **Isla del Rey**. Boat tours go to the **Santuario de la Naturaleza Río Cruces** ① *Boat Isla del Río, daily 1415, 6 hrs, US$15 pp.* The Refuge is an area which flooded as result of the 1960 earthquake; lots of bird species are visible. In summer there is a regular steam train service to **Antilhue** (20 km) ① *Ecuador 2000, T214978, every Sun Jan-Feb, other weekends and holidays throughout the year, phone to check. US$5, 1½-hr trip, return 2 hrs later,* where the train is met by locals selling all sorts of local culinary specialities. This is the only steam train in Chile (the engine dates from 1913), good; book in advance.

Parque Oncol ① *27km northwest of Valdivia, park entry US$1.50, www.parqueoncol.cl, buses Sat-Sun 1005, return 1700, T278100,* 754 ha of Valdivian native forest, with several trails and lookouts, zipline (*canopy*) site, picnic area and campsite.

Coastal resorts near Valdivia

At the mouth of the Río Valdivia there are attractive villages which can be visited by land or river boat. The two main centres are Niebla on the north bank and Corral opposite on the south bank. **Niebla,** 18 km from Valdivia, is a spread-out resort with seafood restaurants and accommodation (also plenty of cabañas and campsites on the road from Valdivia). To the west of the resort is the **Fuerte de la Pura y Limpia Concepción de Monfort de Lemus** ① *daily in summer 1000-1900, closed Mon in winter, US$1.15, Wed free, tourist information and telephone office nearby,* on a promontory. Partially restored in 1992, it has an interesting museum on Chilean naval history.

Corral, a fishing port with several good restaurants is 62 km from Valdivia by road (unsuitable for cars without four-wheel drive or high clearance). The Castillo de San Sebastián, with 3 m wide walls was defended by a battery of 21 guns. It has a museum and offers a view upriver. In summer there are re-enactments of the 1820 storming of the Spanish fort by the Chileans (daily, 1200 and 1800). *Entry US$2.* North along the coast are the remains of Castillo San Luis de Alba de Amargos (3 km) Castillo de San Carlos, with pleasant beaches (4 km). The coastal walks west and south of Corral are splendid.

In midstream, between Niebla and Corral is **Isla Mancera** a small island, fortified by the Castillo de San Pedro de Alcántara, which has the most standing buildings. The island is a pleasant place to stop, but it can get crowded when an excursion boat arrives.

Osorno and around → *Phone code: 064. Colour map 8, grid C1. Population: 132,000.*

Founded in 1553, abandoned in 1604 and refounded in 1796, Osorno later became one of the centres of German immigration. On the large Plaza de Armas stands the modern cathedral, while to the east of the plaza along MacKenna are a number of late 19th-century mansions built by German immigrants, now National Monuments. **Museo Histórico Municipal** ① *Matta 809, entrance in Casa de Cultura, Mon-Sun 1100-1900 in summer; winter Mon-Fri 0930-1730, Sat 1500-1800, US$1,* includes displays on natural history, Mapuche culture, refounding of the city and German colonization. The **Museo Interactivo de Osorno** (MIO) ① *in the former train station, 3 blocks southwest of the plaza, www.municipalidadosorno.cl/mio/proyecto mio.htm, Mon-Sat 0845-1245, 1445-1815, Fri closes 1715, Sat pm only,* is an interactive science museum designed for both children and adults. **Tourist offices**: Sernatur in provincial government office ① *Plaza de Armas, O'Higgins 667, p 1, T237575, infosorno@ sernatur.cl.* Municipal office in the bus terminal and kiosk on the Plaza de Armas. Both open December-February. Contact **Club Andino**, O'Higgins 1073, for advice on skiing.

About 47 km east of Osorno, **Lago Puyehue** (*Colour map 8, grid C1, Altitude 207 m*) is surrounded by relatively flat countryside. At the western end is **Entre Lagos** (*Population 4,000*) and the **Termas de Puyehue** ① *US$15 pp, 0900-2000,* is at the eastern end.

The **Parque Nacional Puyehue**, east of Lago Puyehue, stretches to the Argentine border. On the east side are several lakes and two volcanic peaks: **Volcán Puyehue** (2,240 m) in the north (access via private road US$2.50) and **Volcán Casablanca** (also called Antillanca, 1,900 m). Park administration is at Aguas Calientes, 4 km south of the Termas de Puyehue. There is a ranger station at Anticura. Leaflets on attractions are available.

At **Aguas Calientes** there is an **open-air pool** ① *0830-1900, US$2, free for campers,* with very hot thermal water beside the Río Chanleufú, and a very hot **indoor pool** ① *Mon-Fri in season only, 0830-1230, 1400-1800, Sat, Sun and holidays year-round 0830-2030, US$6, children US$3.*

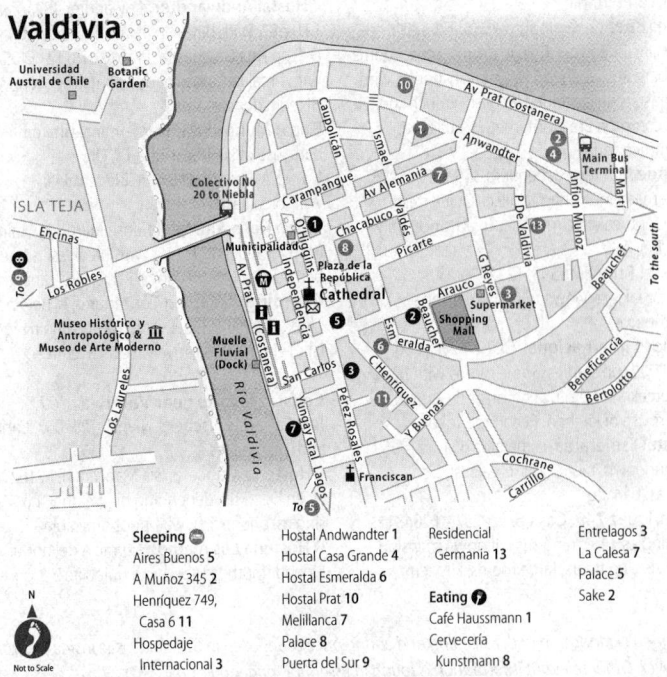

Valdivia

Sleeping 🛏
Aires Buenos **5**
A Muñoz 345 **2**
Henríquez 749,
Casa 6 **11**
Hospedaje
Internacional **3**

Hostal Andwandter **1**
Hostal Casa Grande **4**
Hostal Esmeralda **6**
Hostal Prat **10**
Melillanca **7**
Palace **8**
Puerta del Sur **9**

Residencial
Germania **13**

Eating 🍴
Café Haussmann **1**
Cervecería
Kunstmann **8**

Entrelagos **3**
La Calesa **7**
Palace **5**
Sake **2**

From Aguas Calientes the road continues 18 km southeast to Antillanca on the slopes of **Volcán Casablanca**, past three small lakes and through forests. This is particularly beautiful, especially at sunrise, with the snow-clad cones of Osorno, Puntiagudo and Puyehue forming a semicircle. The tree-line on Casablanca is one of the few in the world made up of deciduous trees (southern beech). From Antillanca it is possible to climb Casablanca for even better views of the surrounding volcanoes and lakes, no path, seven hours return journey, information from Club Andino in Osorno. Attached to the Hotel Antillanca is one of the smallest ski resorts in Chile; there are three lifts, ski instruction and first aid available. Skiing quality depends on the weather: though rain is common it often does not turn to snow. See under Osorno for buses. No public transport from Aguas Calientes to Antillanca; try hitching – always difficult, but it is not a hard walk.

Border with Argentina: Paso Puyehue

Chilean immigration Oopen the second Saturday in October to 1 May 0800-2100, otherwise 0800-1900. The Chilean border post is at Pajaritos, 4 km east of **Anticura**, which is 22 km west of the border. For vehicles entering Chile, formalities are quick (about 15 minutes), but includes the spraying of tyres, and shoes have to be wiped on a mat. This route is liable to closure after snow. Cyclists should know that there are no supplies between Entre Lagos and La Angostura (Argentina).

● Sleeping

Valdivia *p699, map p701*
Prices are often cheaper in low season.
L-AL Puerta del Sur, Los Lingües 950, Isla Teja T224500, www.hotelpuertadelsur.com. 5 star, all facilities, the best.
AL Melillanca, Alemania 675, T212509, www.melillanca.cl. 4-star. Recommended.
A Palace, Chacabuco y Henríquez, T213319, hotelpalace@surnet.cl. Good, comfortable.
B Aires Buenos, Gral Lagos 1036, T206304, www.airesbuenos.cl. **E** pp in dorms. Some rooms with bath, refurbished 19th-century house, with breakfast, tours arranged, English, French spoken, good common areas, internet, HI affiliated. Recommended.
B Donde Marcelo, Janequero 355, T/F205295, dondemarcelo@valdiviachile.cl. Quiet, fresh bread for breakfast, must pay in advance, thin walls, helpful.
B Hostal Prat, Prat 595, T222020. TV, good breakfast, views to industrial zone over the river.
B-C Hosp Internacional, García Reyes 660, T212015. **D** pp singles. Some rooms with bath, with breakfast, helpful, English and German spoken, use of kitchen. Recommended.
C Hostal Esmeralda, Esmeralda 651, T215659. A bit rundown, big rooms, breakfast, also cabañas, parking.
D Henríquez 749, Casa 6, T222574, F204313. **E** pp singles. Charming tumbledown mansion, wildly sloping floors, large rooms, kitchen,

laundry, internet, some English spoken. Highly recommended.
E pp **Riquelme 15**, T218909. With breakfast, good value.

Around the bus terminal

B-C Hostal Casa Grande, Anwandter 880, T202035. With bath, TV, attractive old house, great views, laundry facilities. Highly recommended.
C Hostal Andwandter, Anwandter 482, T218587. With bath, breakfast, TV, hot water.
D-E pp **Res Germania**, Picarte 873, T212405. With breakfast, poor beds, German spoken, HI reductions.
E pp **A Muñoz 580**, near terminal. Shared bath, use of kitchen, cable TV, OK.
E-F pp **A Muñoz 345**, outside terminal. With breakfast.
E-F pp **Hosp Ana María**, José Martí 11, 3 mins from terminal, T222468. With breakfast, shared bath, use of kitchen, good value, also cabañas.
Camping Camping Centenario, in Rowing Club on España. **E** per tent, overlooking river. Isla Teja, T213584, lovely views over river.

Coastal resorts near Valdivia *p700*

B-C Cabañas Fischers, Niebla, T282007. Cabins and 2 campsites.
C Hostería Mancera, Isla Mancera, T/F216296. Open Dec-Mar, depending on weather, no singles, phone first, water not drinkable.
D Hostería Los Alamos, Corral. A delightful hideout for those seeking a quiet life.

● *For an explanation of the sleeping and eating price codes used in this guide, see inside the front* ● *cover. Other relevant information is found in Essentials pages 604-605.*

D pp **Villa Santa Clara**, Niebla, T282018 (Casilla 52, Valdivia). With breakfast, kitchen and laundry, also cabañas.
E pp **Residencial Mariel**, Tarapacá 36, Corral, T471290. Modern, good value.

Osorno *p701*
AL **Waeger**, Cochrane 816, T233721, hotelwaeger@telsur.cl. 4-star, restaurant, comfortable. Recommended.
B **Eduviges**, Eduviges 856, T/F235023, www.hoteleduviges.cl. Spacious, quiet, attractive, gardens, also cabañas. Recommended.
B-C **Res Riga**, Amthauer 1058, T232945, resiriga@telsur.cl. Pleasant. Highly recommended but heavily booked in season.
C **Res Hein**, Cochrane 843, T234116. **D** without bath, old-fashioned, spacious, family atmosphere.

Near bus terminal
E pp **Amunátegui 520**. Good.
E pp **Res Sánchez**, Los Carrera 1595, T232560, crisxi@telsur.cl. Family-owned, with breakfast, shared bath, use of kitchen, basic, like stepping back 50 years.
Camping Municipal site off Ruta 5 near south entrance to city, open Jan-Feb only, good facilities, US$5 per site, swimming pool.

Around Osorno *p701*
Lago Puyehue
L pp **Hotel Termas de Puyehue**, at the Termas de Puyehue, T232157/371272. Cheaper May-mid-Dec. 2 thermal swimming pools (one indoors, very clean), well maintained, meals expensive, in beautiful scenery, heavily booked Jan-Feb (postal address Casilla 27-0, Puyehue, or T Santiago 231 3417, F283 1010).
B **Hostería Isla Fresia**, on own island, T236951, Casilla 49, Entre Lagos, transport provided.
E pp **Hosp Millarey**, Ramírez 333, Entre Lagos, T371251. With breakfast, excellent.
Camping Camping No Me Olvides, Km 56, on south shore of Lake Puyehue. US$10, also cabañas. Playa Los Copihues, Km 56.5, on south shore of Lake Puyehue. Hot showers, good.

Aguas Calientes and Antillanca
L **Chanleufú**, Aguas Calientes, T236988. Good cabañas (cheaper in off season), also camping, US$4 pp with hot water, also has a poorly-stocked shop – better to take your own food, and an expensive café.
A **Hotel Antillanca**, T235114, www.skiantillanca.cl. More expensive with full board. Includes free mountain biking and parapenting, at foot of Volcán Casablanca, restaurant/café, with pool, sauna, friendly club-like atmosphere.

Camping At Aguas Calientes, US$15 for one, US$19 for 2 or more, only one toilet block with hot water. Conaf refugio on Volcán Puyehue, but check with Conaf in Anticura whether it is open. Los Derrumbes, 1 km from Aguas Calientes, no electricity, US$20 per site.

🍴 Eating

Valdivia *p699, map p701*
Several fish restaurants on the Costanera facing the boat dock serve good food and have nice atmosphere. There are others upstairs in the municipal market.
🍴🍴 **La Calesa**, Yungay 735. Peruvian and international, music, art gallery, pier. Highly recommended.
🍴🍴 **La Cava del Buho**, Av Alemania 660. Very good food, service and interesting decor.
🍴🍴 **Cervecería Kunstmann**, Ruta T350, No 950, T292969, www.cerveza-kunstmann.cl. On road to Niebla. Restaurant serving German/Chilean food, brewery with 5 types of beer, beautiful interior, museum. Recommended.
🍴🍴 **Palace**, Arauco y P Rosales. Popular, good atmosphere.
🍴🍴 **Ritual**, Prat 233. Trendy new bar/ restaurant on the waterfront, varied menu, good food.
🍴🍴 **Sake**, Beauchef 629. Claims to be Japanese but really serves generic "oriental" food. Take-away service available.
🍴🍴 **Selecta**, Picarte 1093. Pleasant, excellent fish and meat.
🍴🍴-🍴 Good seafood in the market.
🍴 **Chester's**, Henríquez 314. Good, popular.

Cafés
La Baguette, Libertad y Yungay. Panadería with French-style cakes, brown bread. Repeatedly recommended.
Café Express, Picarte 764. Real coffee.
Café Haussmann, O'Higgins 394. A Valdivia institution. Good tea, cakes and *crudos*.
Café Moro, Independencia y Libertad. Airy café with a mezzanine art gallery. Popular bar at night.
Entrelagos, Pérez Rosales 622. Ice cream and chocolates.

Coastal resorts near Valdivia *p700*
Las Delicias, Niebla, T213566. With restaurant with 'a view that would be worth the money even if the food wasn't good'. Also cabañas and camping.

Osorno *p701*
Good cheap restaurants in the municipal market.
🍴🍴🍴 **Atelier**, Freire 468. Fresh pasta, good.
🍴🍴 **Dino's**, Ramírez 898, on the plaza. Restaurant upstairs, bar/cafeteria downstairs, good.

¶¶ **Peter's Kneipe**, M Rodríguez 1039. Excellent German restaurant.

¶¶-¶ **Club de Artesanos**, MacKenna 634. Decent Chilean fare.

¶ **Café Central**, on Plaza. Good food and coffee.

¶ **Panadería**, at Ramírez 977. Bakery with good wholemeal bread.

¶ **Travels**, in bus terminal for cheap snacks.

¶ **Waldis**, on Plaza de Armas. Real coffee.

Around Osorno: Lago Puyehue *p701*

¶¶ **Chalet Suisse**, Ruta 215, Km 55, on the south lakeshore (Casilla 910, Osorno, T Puyehue 647208, Osorno 064-234073). Hostería, restaurant with excellent food.

¶¶ **Pub del Campo**, Entre Lagos. Reasonable prices. Highly recommended.

¶¶ **Restaurant Jardín del Turista**, Entre Lagos. Very good.

⊛ Festivals and events

Valdivia *p699, map p701*
Semana Valdiviana, in **mid-Feb**, culminates in Noche Valdiviana on the Sat with a procession of elaborately decorated boats which sail past the Muelle Fluvial. Accommodation is scarce during festival.

O Shopping

Valdivia *p699, map p701*
Bookshop/cultural centre Librería/Centro Cultural 787, Pérez Rosales 787. Old mansion, with café and art exhibitions.
Supermarket Hiper-Unico, Arauco 697 (4-screen cinema at Plaza Dos Ríos next door). There's a colourful riverside market with livestock, fish etc.

▲ Activities and tours

Valdivia *p699, map p701*
To Corral and Niebla and other boat trips along the river, many the kiosks along the Muelle Fluvial. Boats will only leave with a minimum of 10 passengers, so off-season organize in advance. Full list of operators in the tourist information office. Prices: city US$3.50pp; Isla Teja US$6pp; Corral-Mancera US$13-25. Several other options.

Sea kayaking.
Mi Pueblito Expediciones, San Carlos 190, T245055, www.pueblitoexpediciones.cl. Offer classes and trips in sea kayaks in the waters around Valdivia, US$15-25 for 4-5 hrs.

⊖ Transport

Valdivia *p699, map p701*
Air LanChile/Lan Express to/from **Santiago** every day via Temuco, or Concepción.
Bus Terminal at Muñoz y Prat, by the river. To **Santiago**: several companies, 10 hrs, most services overnight, US$12, salón cama US$30. Half-hourly buses to/from **Osorno**, 2 hrs, several companies, US$4. To **Panguipulli**, US$3, Empresa Pirehueico, about every 30 mins, US$3. Many daily to **Puerto Montt**, US$5, 3 hrs. To **Puerto Varas**, 2¾ hrs, US$4. To **Frutillar**, 2½ hrs. To **Villarrica**, by JAC, 6 a day, 2½ hrs, US$3.50, continuing to **Pucón**, US$4.50, 3 hrs. Frequent daily service to Riñihue via Paillaco and Los Lagos. To Argentina: to **Bariloche** via Osorno, 7 hrs, Bus Norte, US$14; to **Junín de los Andes**, Igi-Llaima, 4 times a week, San Martín, 3, US$18.

Coastal resorts near Valdivia *p700*
Ferry The tourist boats to **Isla Mancera** and **Corral** offer a guided half-day tour (US$13-25, some with meals) from the Muelle Fluvial, Valdivia (behind the tourist office on Av Prat 555). The river trip is beautiful, but you can also take a **bus** (orange No 20) to Niebla from outside bus station or along Calles Andwanter and Carampangue in Valdivia, regular service between 0730 and 2100, 30 mins, US$0.65 (bus continues to Los Molinos), then cross to Corral by boat, every 20 mins, US$1.20. There are occasional buses from Valdivia to Corral.

Osorno *p701*
Air Lan Express, Matta 862, T314900, daily flights Osorno-**Santiago**, via Concepción and/or Temuco.
Bus Main terminal 4 blocks from Plaza de Armas at Errázuriz 1400. Left luggage open 0730-2030. Bus from centre, US$0.30. To **Santiago**, frequent, US$13, salón cama US$30, 11½ hrs. To **Concepción**, US$10. To **Temuco**, US$4. To **Pucón** and **Villarrica**, Tur-Bus, frequent, US$6. To **Frutillar**, US$1.50, **Llanquihue**, **Puerto Varas** and **Puerto Montt** (US$2.30) services every 30 mins. To **Puerto Octay**, US$1.50, hourly. To **Bariloche**, 5 hrs, US$14. Local buses to **Entre Lagos**, **Puyehue** and **Aguas Calientes** leave from the Mercado Municipal terminal, 1 block west of the main terminal.

Around Osorno: Lago Puyehue *p701*
Bus To **Entre Lagos** from Osorno, frequent services in summer, Expreso Lago Puyehue and Buses Barria, 1 hr, US$1.20, reduced service off-season. Some buses by both companies continue to **Aguas Calientes** (off-season according to demand) 2 hrs, US$2. Buses that continue to Aguas Calientes do not stop at the

lake (unless you want to get off at Hotel Termas de Puyehue and clamber down).

Border with Argentinian: Anticura *p702*
Bus To Anticura, 2-3 buses daily from **Osorno**, 3 hrs, US$4.50. Several bus companies run daily services from **Puerto Montt** via Osorno to Bariloche along this route (see under Puerto Montt for details). Although less scenic than the ferry journey across Lake Todos Los Santos and Laguna Verde (see page 706) this crossing is far cheaper, more reliable and still a beautiful trip (best views from the right hand side of the bus).

❶ Directory

Valdivia *p699, map p701*
Airline offices LanChile, Maipú 271, T218841/258840. **Banks** Redbanc ATM at Supermercado Hiper-Unico (see above). Good rates for cash at **Banco Santander**, P Rosales 585, **Corp Banca** (Visa), Picarte 370, will change cash and TCs. **Banco Santiago**, Arauco e Independencia, MasterCard. Casa de Cambio at Carampangue 325, T213305. **Turismo Austral**, Arauco y Henríquez, Galería Arauco, accepts TCs. **Internet** Café Phonet, Libertad 127. **Centro Internet Libertad**, Libertad 7. **Post offices** O'Higgins y Maipú.

Osorno *p701*
Banks ATMs at Bancos BCI, MacKenna 801, and **Santiago**, MacKenna 787 (Visa). For good rates try **Cambio Tur**, MacKenna 1010, T234846. **Turismo Frontera**, Ramírez 949, local 11 (Galería Catedral). **Internet** 3 internet places in the mall at Freire 542. **Chat-Mail-MP3**, P Lynch 1334, near Colón.

Southern lakes

This is one of the most beautiful areas in a part of Chile which already has plenty to boast about. Lago Llanquihue, with its views to volcanoes and German-influenced towns, adjoins the Parque Nacional Vicente Pérez Rosales. The oldest national park in the country, this contains another beautiful lake, Todos los Santos, three major volcanoes, waterfalls and a memorable lakes route to Argentina. The region ends at the Seno de Reloncaví, a peaceful glacial inlet, often shrouded in soft rain.

Lago Llanquihue

The lake, covering 56,000 ha, is the second largest in Chile. Across the great blue sheet of water can be seen two snowcapped volcanoes: the perfect cone of Osorno (2,680 m) and the shattered cone of Calbuco (2,015 m), and, when the air is clear, the distant Tronador (3,460 m). The largest towns, Puerto Varas, Llanquihue and Frutillar are on the western shore, linked by the Pan-American Highway. There are roads around the rest of the lake: that from Puerto Octay east to Ensenada is very beautiful, but is narrow with lots of blind corners, necessitating speeds of 20-30 kph at best in places (see below).

Puerto Octay → *Phone code: 064. Colour map 8, grid C1. Population: 2,500.*

A peaceful, picturesque small town at the north tip of the lake with a backdrop of rolling hills, Puerto Octay was founded by German settlers in 1851. The town enjoyed a boom in the late 19th century when it was the northern port for steamships on the lake. The church and the enormous German-style former convent survive from that period. **Museo el Colono** ⓘ *Independencia 591, Tue-Sun 1500-1900, Dec-Feb only,* has displays on German colonization. Another part of the museum, housing agricultural implements and machinery for making chicha, is just outside town on the road to Centinela. 3 km south along an unpaved road is the Peninsula of Centinela, a beautiful spot with a launch dock and watersports. From the headland are fine views of the volcanoes and the Cordillera of the Andes; a very popular spot in good weather, good for picnics (taxi US$2.50 one way). Rowing boats and pedalos can be hired.

Frutillar Bajo → *Phone code: 065. Colour map 8, grid C1. Population: 9,000. Altitude: 70 m.*

About half-way along the west side of the lake, Frutillar is divided into Frutillar Alto, just off the main highway, and Frutillar Bajo beautifully situated on the lake, 4 km away. (Colectivos run between the two towns, five minutes, US$0.50.) Frutillar Bajo is possibly the most attractive – and expensive – town on the lake. At the north end of the town is the Reserva Forestal Edmundo Winckler, run by the Universidad de Chile, 33 ha, with a guided trail through native woods. **Museo Colonial Alemán** ⓘ *daily 0930-1900 summer, Tue-Sun*

0930-1400, 1530-1800 winter, US$2, includes a watermill, replicas of two German colonial houses with furnishings and utensils of the period, a blacksmith's shop (personal engravings for US$5), a campanario (circular barn with agricultural machinery and carriages inside), gardens and handicraft shop. In late January to early February there is a highly regarded classical music festival and a new, state-of-the-art concert hall is being built for this on the lakefront (accommodation must be booked well in advance). Tourist office on lakeside opposite Club Alemán, helpful.

Puerto Varas and around → *Phone code: 065. Colour map 8, grid C1. Population: 22,000.*
This beauty spot was the southern port for shipping on the lake in the 19th century. It is a more popular centre for visiting the southern lakes than Puerto Montt, 20 km to the south. The Catholic church, built by German Jesuits in 1918, is a copy of the church in Marieenkirche in the Black Forest. North and east of the **Gran Hotel Puerto Varas** (1934) are German style mansions dating from the early 20th century. **Parque Philippi**, on top of the hill, is pleasant; walk up to Hotel Cabañas del Lago on Klenner, cross the railway and the gate is on the right. Puerto Varas is a good base for trips around the lake. On the south shore two of the best beaches are **Playa Hermosa** (Km 7) and **Playa Niklitschek** (entry fee charged). **La Poza**, at Km 16, is a little lake to the south of Lago Llanquihue reached through narrow channels overhung with vegetation. **Isla Loreley**, an island on La Poza, is very beautiful (frequent boat trips); a concealed channel leads to yet another lake, the Laguna Encantada. The **tourist office** is at ① *San Francisco 441, T232402, F233315, 0900-2100 in summer*, helpful, finds cheap accommodation, also has an art gallery. Beware of places offering "tourist information", eg on pier. They may be only giving information about their paying members' services. Many places close in the off-season.

Ensenada
East of Puerto Varas by 47 km, Ensenada is at the southeast corner of Lake Llanquihue, which is the town's main attraction. Minibuses run from Puerto Varas, frequent in summer (see below).

Volcán Osorno
North of Ensenada, Osorno volcano can be reached from Ensenada, or from a road branching off the Puerto Octay-Ensenada road at Puerto Klocker, 20 km southeast of Puerto Octay. Weather permitting, Aqua Motion (see Puerto Varas, Activities and tours) organize climbing expeditions with local guide, transport from Puerto Montt or Puerto Varas, food and equipment, US$150 pp payment in advance (minimum group of two, maximum of six with three guides) all year, setting out from the refugio at La Burbuja. They check weather conditions the day before and offer 50% refund if climb is abandoned because of bad weather. From La Burbuja it is six hours to the summit. Conaf do not allow climbing without a guide and insist on one guide to every two climbers. Only experienced climbers should attempt to climb right to the top, ice climbing equipment essential.

Parque Nacional Vicente Pérez Rosales
① *Free entry. The park is infested by horseflies in Dec and Jan: cover up as much as possible with light- coloured clothes which may help a bit.*
Lago Todos los Santos The most beautiful of all the lakes in southern Chile, this long, irregularly shaped sheet of emerald-green water has deeply wooded shores and several small islands rising from its surface. In the waters are reflected the slopes of Volcán Osorno. Beyond the hilly shores to the east are several graceful snow-capped mountains, with the mighty Tronador in the distance. To the north is the sharp point of Cerro Puntiagudo, and at the northeastern end Cerro Techado rises cliff-like out of the water. The ports of **Petrohué** at its western and **Peulla** at its eastern ends are connected by boat. Trout and salmon fishing are excellent in several parts including Petrohué. Conaf has an office in Petrohué with a visitors' centre, small museum and 3D model of the park. There is a guardaparque office in Puella. Park offices have details of walks. There are no roads round the lake and the only scheduled vessel is the Andina del Sud service with connections to Bariloche (Argentina), but private launches can be hired for trips (tickets for two-hour lake tours are sold on the Petrohué-Puella ferry). Isla Margarita, the largest island on the lake, with a lagoon in the middle, can be visited (in summer only) from Petrohué, boats by Andina del Sud leave 1500, US$40. Walking to Laguna Margarita is difficult because of fallen trees.

Petrohué, 16 km northwest of Ensenada, is a good base for walking. The **Salto de Petrohué** *US$2.25*, is 6 km from Petrohué (unpaved, dusty, lots of traffic; bus US$1), 10 km (paved) from Ensenada. Near the falls is a snackbar; there are also two short trails, the Senderos de los Enamorados and Carileufú. **Peulla**, is a good starting point for hikes in the mountains. The Cascadas Los Novios, signposted above the Hotel Peulla, are stunning.

For crossing the border with Argentina, **Paso Pérez Rosales**. Chilean immigration is in Peulla, 30 km west of the border, open summer 0800-2100, winter 0800-2000.

Seno de Reloncaví

The Reloncaví estuary, the northernmost of Chile's glacial inlets, is recommended for its local colour, its sealions, dolphins and its peace. **Ralún**, a small village at the northern end of the estuary, is 31 km southeast from Ensenada by a poorly paved road along the wooded lower Petrohué valley. Roads continue, unpaved, along the east side of the estuary to Cochamó and Puelo and on the west side to Canutillar. In Ralún there is a village shop and post office. Just outside the village there are thermal springs, reached by boat, US$2.50 pp.

Cochamó, 17 km south of Ralún on the east shore of the estuary, is a pretty village, with a fine wooden church similar to those on Chiloé, in a striking setting, with the estuary and volcano behind. **Puelo**, further south, on the south bank of the Río Puelo, is a most peaceful place. From here the road (very rough) continues to Puelche on the Carretera Austral.

● Sleeping

Puerto Octay *p705*
C Hosp Raquel Mardorf, Germán Wulf 712. **E** for single room. Comfortable, large breakfast. Owners have ▌ Restaurante La Cabaña at No 713.
B-C Zapato Amarillo, 35 mins' walk north of town, T/F391575, www.zapatoamarillo.8k.com. **D-E** in dorm. Excellent, book in advance in high season, use of spotless kitchen, great breakfasts with homemade bread, German and English spoken, mountain bikes, canoes, tours (house has a grass roof). Highly recommended.
E-F pp Hosp La Naranja, Independencia 361. Without bath, with breakfast, restaurant.
Camping El Molino, beside lake, US$5 pp. Recommended.

Centinela
L-AL Hotel Centinela, T 391326, www.hotelcentinela.cl. Newly restored, superb views, also has cabañas, excellent restaurant, bar, open all year.
C-D Hostería La Baja, Casilla 116, T391269. **E** singles. Beautifully situated at the neck of the peninsula, with breakfast and bath.
Camping Municipal site on lakeside, US$10 per site. Cabañas on the peninsula.

East of Puerto Octay
D pp Hostería Irma, 2 km south of Las Cascadas. Very pleasant, good food; also farmhouse accommodation and camping.

Frutillar *p705*
Frutillar Bajo
AL Ayacara, Av Philippi 1215, T421550. Beautiful rooms with lake view, welcoming, have a pisco sour in the library in the evening.

A Casona del 32, Caupolicán 28, T421369. With breakfast, comfortable old house, central heating, English and German spoken, excellent.
A Hosp El Arroyo, Av Philippi 989, T421560. With breakfast. Highly recommended.
A Residenz/Café am See, Av Philippi 539, T421539. Good breakfast.
A Winkler, Av Philippi 1155, T421388. Cabins. Recommended.
B Hosp Costa Azul, Av Philippi 1175, T421388. Mainly families, good breakfasts.
B Hosp Trayén, Av Philippi 963, T421346. With bath, nice rooms, good breakfast.
B Hosp Vivaldi, Av Philippi 851, T421382, Sra Edith Klesse. Quiet, comfortable, excellent breakfast and lodging, also family accommodation. Recommended.
C Av Philippi 451, T421204. Good breakfast.
C Pérez Rosales 590. Excellent breakfast.

North of Frutillar Bajo
AL Salzburg, T421589 or Santiago 206 1419. Excellent, restaurant, sauna, mountain bikes, arranges tours and fishing.

Frutillar Alto
Several places to stay along Carlos Richter (main street). Cheap accommodation in the school, sleeping bag required.
D Faralito, Winkler 245. Cooking facilities (owner can be contacted at shop at Winkler 167, T421440).
Camping Los Ciruelillos, 2 km south, T339123. Most services. Playa Maqui, 7 km north of Frutillar, T339139. Fancy, expensive.

Puerto Varas *p706*

LL Colonos del Sur, Del Salvador 24, T233369, www.colonosdelsur.cl. Good views, good restaurant, tea room. Also at Estación 505.

L Bellavista, Pérez Rosales 60, T232011, www.hotelbellavista.cl. Cheerful, restaurant, overlooking lake. Recommended.

L Licarayén, San José 114, T232305, info@hotelicarayen.cl. Overlooking lake, comfortable, book in season. Recommended.

L-AL Los Alerces, Pérez Rosales 1281, T232060, reservalosalerces@hotmail.com. 4-star hotel, with breakfast, cabin complex (price depends on season when rest of hotel is closed), attractive, helpful.

AL Cabañas del Lago, Klenner 195, T232291, calago@entelchile.net. On Phiippi hill overlooking lake, good breakfast, restaurant. Also self-catering cabins sleeping 5 (good value for groups), heating, sauna.

AL Gran Reserva, Mirador 106, T346876, www.granreserva.cl. Behind the Casino, good hotel with great views from breakfast room.

A Amancay, Walker Martínez 564, T232201, cabamancay@chile.com. Cabañasfor 4, also has rooms, **D** with bath, **E** without, includes breakfast, good, German spoken. Recommended.

A Loreley, Maipo 911, T232226. Homely, quiet. Recommended.

B-C Hostería Outsider, San Bernardo 318, T/F232910, www.turout.com. With bath, some rooms with internet, real coffee, meals, horse riding, rafting, sea kayaking, climbing.

B-D Casa Azul, Manzanal 66 y Rosario, T232904, www.casa azul.net. **D** pp in dorms. Lovely building, some rooms with bath, good buffet breakfast (US$4), kitchen facilities, limited heating, garden, German and English spoken. Reserve in advance in high season.

C Casa Margouya, Santa Rosa 318, T511648. **D-E** in shared rooms, with breakfast. Bright, colourful, kitchen, slightly cramped, information, French run, English spoken.

C Compas del Sur, Klenner 467, T232044, www.compassdelsur.cl. **E** pp in shared rooms, Chilean-Swedish run, kitchen facilities, internet, small breakfast included (US$1 for extras), helpful, German, English, Swedish spoken. Highly recommended, but reserve in advance in high season (may be closed in low season).

C Hosp Ellenhaus, Martínez 239, T233577, www.ellenhaus.cl. More expensive with bath, **E** pp in dorms, laundry facilities, lounge, hospitable.

C Las Dalias, Santa Rosa 707, T233277. Quiet, cheaper with shared bath, central, good breakfast, parking, German spoken.

C-D Res Alemana, San Bernardo 416, T232419. With breakfast, without bath.

D Hospedaje Amac, San Bernardo 313, T234216. Apartment-style, comfortable if a bit rundown, heating in lounge, TV, use of kitchen, hot water.

E pp Hosp Don Raúl, Salvador 928, T234174, hospedajedonraul@hotmail.com. Laundry and cooking facilities, camping **F** pp.

E pp Patiperros, Mirador 135, T235050, www.jardinsa.cl. New hostel, comfortable, with breakfast.

Camping Wild camping and use of barbecues is not allowed on the lake shore. Sites on south shore of Lago Llanquihue east of Puerto Varas: **Campo Aventura**, San Bernardo 318, Puerto Varas, T/F232910, www.campo-aventura.com. 2 lodges with camping facilities, excellent horse riding, fishing, birdwatching, Spanish classes and vegetarian food.

Also: **Conaf**, Km 49, site at Puerto Oscuro, beneath road to volcano, very good. **Playa Hermosa**, Km 7, T252223, fancy, take own supplies, recommended. **Playa Niklitschek**, Km 8, T338352. Full facilities. **Playa Venado**, Camping Municipal, Km 20. **Trauco**, Imperial 433.

Ensenada *p706*

AL-B Cabañas Brisas del Lago, T212012, www.brisasdellago.cl. Chalets for 6 on beach, good restaurant nearby, supermarket next door. Highly recommended for self-catering.

AL-B Hotel Ensenada, Km 45, T212028, www.hotelensenada.cl. Olde-worlde, good food (closed in winter), good view of lake and Osorno Volcano, runs tours, hires mountain bikes (guests only). Also hostal in the grounds, cooking facilities, cheaper.

C Hosp Ensenada, T338278. Excellent breakfast.

C Ruedas Viejas, T/F212050, for room, also cabins, about 1 km west from Ensenada. Basic, damp, restaurant.

Camping **Montaña**, central Ensenada. **E** per site. Fully equipped, nice beach sites. Also at Playa Larga, 1 km further east, US$10 and at Puerto Oscuro, 2 km north, US$8. **Trauco**, 4 km west, T212033. Large site with shops, fully equipped, US$4-9 pp.

Volcán Osorno *p706*

The Club Andino Osorno (address under Osorno) has 3 refugios: north of the summit at

For an explanation of the sleeping and eating price codes used in this guide, see inside the front cover. Other relevant information is found in Essentials pages 604-605.

708

La Picada (20 km east of Puerto Klocker) at 950 m; south of the summit: **La Burbuja**, 14 km north of Ensenada at 1,250 m; and, 15 km from Ensenada at 1,200 m **Refugio Teski Club**, **D** pp, bunk accommodation, restaurant and bar, sleeping bag useful, bleak site just below snow line; a good base for walking.

Parque Nacional Vicente Pérez Rosales *p706*
There is a small shop in Andino del Sud building but best to take your own food.

At Petrohué

L Fundo El Salto, near Salto de Petrohué, www.fly-fish-chile.com/index.htm. Run by New Zealanders, mainly a fishing lodge, good home cooking, fishing trips arranged.
L Hotel Petrohué, T065-212025, www.petrohue.com. Excellent views, recently reopened, **LL** for half-board, also has cabins, pool, cosy, restaurant.
D pp **Familia Küschel** on other side of river (boat across). With breakfast, meals available, electricity only 3 hrs in afternoon, OK, camping US$5. Albergue in the school in summer. Conaf office can help find cheaper family accommodation.

Peulla

L Hotel Peulla, T02-196 4183, hpeullareservas@terra.cl. Including dinner and breakfast, cheaper out of season. Beautiful setting by the lake and mountains, restaurant and bar, expensive meals (lunch poor), cold in winter, often full of tour groups (tiny shop at back of hotel).
C pp **Res Palomita**, 50 m west of Hotel Peulla. Half board, family-run, simple, comfortable but not spacious, shared rooms, separate shower, book ahead in season, lunches, expensive tours available.
Camping Camping and picnicking in the national park is forbidden. At Petrohué on far side beside the lake, US$5 per site, no services, cold showers, locals around the site sell fresh bread (local fishermen will ferry you across, US$0.50). At Peulla, opposite Conaf office, US$1.50. Good campsite 1½ hrs' walk east of Peulla, take food. A small shop in Peulla sells basic goods, including fruit and veg.

Seno de Reloncaví

Ralún *p707*
Lodging (**E** pp) is available at restaurants El Refugio and Navarrito and **E** pp Posada El Encuentro and **F** pp Posada Campesino.

Cochamó *p707*

B Campo Aventura (San Bernadino 318, Puerto Varas) T/F065-232910, www.campo-aventura.com. Offers accommodation 4 km south of Cochamó in Valle Río Cochamó, full board available, local food, camping **E** Kitchen, sauna. Also at their other base in the valley of La Junta. They specialize in horseback and trekking between the Reloncaví Estuary and the Argentine border, 2-10 days.

E Cochamó, T216212. Basic but clean, often full with salmon farm workers, good meals.

E pp **Edicar**, on seafront by the dock/ramp. With breakfast, hot shower, very good value.

E Hosp Maura, JJ Molina 12. Beautiful location overlooking the estuary, excellent food, good for kids, highly recommended.

Also a large number of pensiones, cabañas, a campsite and a few eating places.

Puelo *p707*

Basic lodging is available at the restaurant or with families – try Roberto and Olivia Telles, no bath/shower, meals on request, or Ema Hernández Maldona; 2 restaurants.

❶ Eating

Puerto Octay *p705*

❢**Restaurante Baviera**, Germán Wulf 582. Cheap and good.

Frutillar Bajo *p705*

❢❢**Club Alemán**, Av Philippi 747. Good but not cheap.

❢❢-❢**Guten Apetit**, Philippi 1285. Lunch/café, mid-range to cheap.

❢**Casino de Bomberos**, Philippi 1060. Upstairs bar/restaurant, memorable painting caricaturing the firemen in action.

Cafés

Many German-style cafés and tea-rooms on C Philippi (the lakefront) eg **Salón de Te**, Frutillar, No 775.

Der Volkladen, O'Higgins y Philippi. Natural products, chocolates and cakes, natural cosmetics.

Puerto Varas *p706*

❢❢❢**Merlín**, Imperial 0605, on road out of town. Most rate it highly.

❢❢**Di Carusso**, San Bernardo 318. Italian trattoria. Recommended.

❢❢**Ibis**, Pérez Rosales No 1117, at the Puerto Chico end. Recommended.

❢❢**La Olla**, V Pérez Rosales 1971, on lakefront, 1 km east of town. Good, popular for seafood, fish and meat.

❢❢❢**Mediterráneo**, Santa Rosa 068. Good international and local food, interesting varied menu.

❢**El Amigo**, San Bernardo 240. Large portions, good value.

Cafés

Café Danés, Del Salvador 441. Coffee and cakes.

Giorgio Café, San Bernardo 318. Danish-run, good food. Recommended.

Punto Café, Del Salvador 348. Cybercafé, bar and art gallery.

Terranova, Santa Rosa 580. Pleasant, helpful café on main plaza.

Ensenada *p706*

Most eating places close off season. There are a few pricey shops. Take your own provisions.

❢**Ruedas Viejas** is the cheapest eating place.

❢**Canta Rana** is recommended for bread and kuchen.

❍ Shopping

Puerto Varas *p706*

Supermarkets Las Brisas, Salvador 495. Vyhmeister, Gramado 565. Good selection.

▲▲ Activities and tours

Puerto Varas *p706*

Cycling Thomas Held Expeditions, Martínez 239, T/F311889. Cycle hire US$20 per day. Turismo Biker, in Terranova Café, www.turismobiker.com. Touring and downhill as well as standard tours.

Fishing Licence US$2.50 a year, obtainable from Municipalidad. Expeditions organized by many operators.

Horse riding Cabañas Puerto Decher, Fundo Molino Viejo, 2 km north, T338033, guided tours, minimum 2 people, mixed reports. **Quinta del Lago**, Km 25 on road to Ensenada, T338275, www.quintadellago.com. All levels catered for, US$7 per hr, also trips in ox cart and cabañas. See also Campo Aventura, above.

Ziplining (*canopy*), offered by several operators.

Tours

Most tours operate in season only (1 Sep-15 Apr). **Al Sur**, Del Salvador 100, T232334, F232300, www.alsurexpeditions.com. Rafting on Río Petrohué, good camping equipment, tours, trekking maps, English spoken, official tour operators to Parque Pumalín.

Andina del Sud, Del Salvador 72, T232511. Operate 'lakes' trip to Bariloche, Argentina via

Lago Todos los Santos, Peulla, Cerro Tronador (see under Puerto Montt, To Argentina), plus other excursions.

Aqua Motion, C San Francisco, T/F232747, www.aquamotion.cl. For trekking, rafting and climbing, German and English spoken, good equipment, several other activities.

Kokayak, Ruta 225, Km 40 (lodge at Km 37), T09 310 5272, www.paddlechile.com. Kayaking and rafting trips, good equipment and after-trip lunch.

Tranco Expeditions, San Pedro 422, T311311. Trekking on volcano, rafting, fishing and more. Recommended.

Travel Art, Imperial 0661, T232198, www.travelart.cl. Biking and hiking tours.

Seno de Reloncaví: Cochamó *p707*
Sebastián Contreras C Morales, T216220, is a recommended independent guide who offers tours on horseback and hires out horses.

❷ Transport

Puerto Octay *p705*
Bus To **Osorno** hourly, US$2; to **Frutillar** (1 hr, US$0.90), **Puerto Varas** (2 hrs) and **Puerto Montt** (3 hrs, US$2) Thaebus, 5 a day. Around the east shore: to **Las Cascadas** (34 km), 2-3 daily.

Frutillar Bajo *p705*
Bus Most leave from opposite the Copec station in Alto Frutillar. To **Puerto Varas** (US$0.75) and **Puerto Montt** (US$1.50), frequent, Full Express. To **Osorno**, Turismosur 1½ hrs, US$1.50. To **Puerto Octay**, Thaebus, 6 a day, US$0.90.

Puerto Varas *p706*
Bus To **Santiago**, normal US$24, semi cama US$36, cama US$48, Tur-Bus, 12 hrs. To **Puerto Montt**, 30 mins, Thaebus and Full Express every 10 mins, US$1.30. Same frequency to **Frutillar** (US$0.75, 30 mins) and **Osorno** (US$2, 1½ hrs). To **Valdivia** US$4. To **Bariloche**, Andina del Sud, by lakes route, see above. Buses, eg Cruz del Sur, Tas Choapa, daily, 7 hrs, US$12. Minibuses to **Ensenada** and leave from San Bernardo y Martínez, hourly. Taxi from Puerto Montt airport, US$16.

Parque Nacional Vicente Pérez Rosales *p706*
Minibuses Every 30 mins to Petrohué from Puerto Montt and Puerto Varas in summer (US$3.80, 1¼ hrs from Puerto Varas), much less frequent off season. Last bus to Ensenada at 1800.

Ferry The boat between Petrohué and Peulla costs US$41 return or one way (book in advance). It leaves Petrohué at 1100, Peulla at 1630 (not Sun, 1 hr 40 mins – most seating indoors, no cars carried, cycles free), commentaries in Spanish, English and German. This connects with the Andina del Sud tour bus between Puerto Montt and Bariloche (see under Puerto Montt). Local fishermen make the trip across the lake, charging less than the public service and their boats have no shelter if it rains.

Seno de Reloncaví *p707*
Bus From Puerto Montt to **Ralún** via Ensenada, 7 a day, **Bohle** and **Fierro**, between 1000 and 1930, 6 on Sat, return 0700-1830, US$2. **Fierro** buses also go to Cantillar via Ensenada and Ralún. To **Cochamó**, Bus Fierro from Puerto Montt via Puerto Varas, Ensenada and Ralún, 4 daily, US$3.40, 2½ hrs. To **Puelo**: Buses Bohle from Puerto Montt, Sun 0900 and 1500 (from Puerto Varas 30 minutes later). Daily buses from Cochamó Mon-Sat 0745 and 1645, Sun 1100 and 1500. Boats: In summer boats sail up the Estuary from Angelmó. Tours from Puerto Montt US$30. Off season the Carmencita sails once a week, leaving Puelo Sun 1000 and Angelmó Wed 0900 (take warm clothes, food and seasickness pills if it's windy).

❶ Directory

Frutillar Bajo *p705*
Useful services Toilet, showers and changing cabins for beach on O'Higgins. Banco Santander, on the lakeside, has Redbanc ATM.

Puerto Varas *p706*
Banks Redbanc ATMs at several banks. Turismo Los Lagos, Del Salvador 257 (Galería Real, local 11). Daily 0830-1330, 1500-2100, Sun 0930-1330, accepts TCs, good rates. **Internet** Ciber Service, Salvador 264, loc 6-A. George's, San Ignacio 574. Av Gramado 560, p 2. San José 380, p 2. **Post offices** San José y San Pedro. **Telephones** 4 agencies in town.

Puerto Montt and Chiloé

→ Phone code: 065. Colour map 8, grid C1. Population: 160,000.

Just 20 minutes south of Puerto Varas, and 1,016 km south of Santiago, Puerto Montt is the gateway to the shipping lanes to the south, namely the island of Chiloé and the wilds of Patagonia. It's a rapidly growing, disordered modern city, developing in line with a boom in salmon fishing. Angelmó, a fishing port 2 km west, is most popular with visitors for its seafood restaurants and handicraft shops, but is not worth a visit of more than a day or two.

Puerto Montt

Ins and outs

Tourist offices Puerto Montt: Sernatur has two offices: in the Gobernación Provincial building on the Plaza de Armas. Daily in summer 0900-1300, 1500-1900, Monday to Friday in winter 0830-1300, 1400-1800. Also in the Intendencia Regional, Avenida Décima Región 480 (p 2), T256999, infoloslagos@sernatur.cl, 0830-1300, 1330-1730 Monday to Friday. See www.puerto monttchile.cl for information on the web. For more information and town maps, go to the kiosk just southeast of the Plaza de Armas run by the municipality. Open till 1800 on Saturday. Telefónica del Sur and Sernatur operate a phone information service (INTTUR), dial 142 (cost is the same as a local call). Dial 149 for pharmacy information, 148 for the weather, 143 for the news. The service operates throughout the Tenth Region. **Conaf** is at Ochogavia 458, but cannot supply information on national parks. **Automóvil Club de Chile**, Esmeralda 70, T252968.

Sights

The capital of X Región (Los Lagos) was founded in 1853 as part of the German colonization of the area. Good views over the city and bay are offered from outside the Intendencia Regional on Avenida X Region. The port is used by fishing boats and coastal vessels, and is the departure

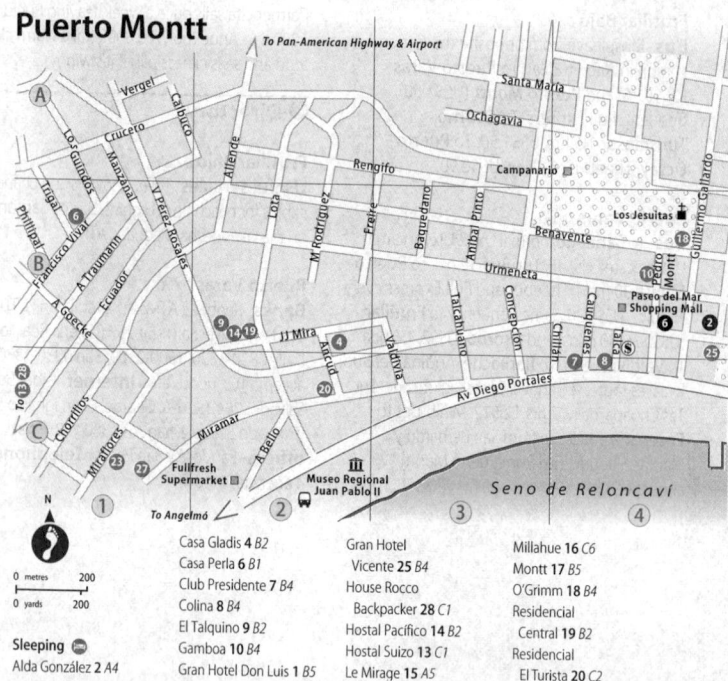

Puerto Montt

To Pan-American Highway & Airport

Seno de Reloncaví

Sleeping
Alda González **2** A4

Casa Gladis **4** B2
Casa Perla **6** B1
Club Presidente **7** B4
Colina **8** B4
El Talquino **9** B2
Gamboa **10** B4
Gran Hotel Don Luis **1** B5

Gran Hotel
  Vicente **25** B4
House Rocco
  Backpacker **28** C1
Hostal Pacífico **14** B2
Hostal Suizo **13** C1
Le Mirage **15** A5

Millahue **16** C6
Montt **17** B5
O'Grimm **18** B4
Residencial
  Central **19** B2
Residencial
  El Turista **20** C2

Chile Puerto Montt & Chiloé

point for vessels to Puerto Chacabuco, Laguna San Rafael and for the long haul south to Puerto Natales. A paved road runs 55 km southwest to Pargua, where there is a ferry service to Chiloé.

The **Iglesia de los Jesuitas on Gallardo**, dating from 1872, has a fine blue-domed ceiling; behind it on a hill is the campanario (clock tower). **Museo Regional Juan Pablo II** ① *Portales 997 near the bus terminal, daily 1030-1800, US$1*, documents local history and has a fine collection of historic photos of the city; also memorabilia of the last Pope's visit. The fishing port of **Angelmó**, 2 km west, has become a tourist centre with seafood restaurants and handicraft shops (reached by Costanera bus along Portales and by collective taxi Nos 2, 3, 20 from the centre, US$0.30).

The wooded **Isla Tenglo**, reached by launch from Angelmó (US$0.50 each way), is a favourite place for picnics. Magnificent view from the summit. The island is famous for its curantos, served by restaurants in summer. Boat trips round the island from Angelmó last 30 minutes, US$8. **Parque Provincial Lahuen Nadi** contains some ancient trees in swampland, more accessible than some of the remoter forests. Take the main road to the airport, which leads off Ruta 5. After 5 km, turn right (north) and follow the signs. West of Puerto Montt the Río Maullin, which drains Lago Llanquihue, has some attractive waterfalls and good fishing (salmon). At the mouth of the river is the little fishing village of **Maullin**, founded in 1602.

To Argentina via Lago Todos Los Santos

This popular but ever more expensive route to Bariloche, involving ferries across Lago Todos Los Santos, Lago Frías and Lago Nahuel Huapi is outstandingly beautiful whatever the season, though the mountains are often obscured by rain and heavy cloud. The route is via Puerto Varas, Ensenada and Petrohué falls (20 minutes stop) to Petrohué, where it connects with catamaran service across Lago Todos Los Santos to Peulla. Lunch stop in Peulla two hours (lunch not included in fare: Hotel Peulla is expensive, see page 709 for alternatives). Chilean customs in Peulla, followed by a 1½-hour bus ride through the Paso Pérez Rosales to Argentine customs in Puerto Frías, 20 minute boat trip across Lago Frías to Puerto Alegre and bus from Puerto Alegre to Puerto Blest. From Puerto Blest it is a beautiful ½ hour catamaran trip along Lago Nahuel Huapi to Puerto Pañuelo (Llao Llao), from where there is a 45-minute bus journey to Bariloche (bus drops passengers at hotels, camping sites or in town centre). From 1 May to 30 August this trip is done over two days with overnight stay in Peulla, add about US$90 to single fare for accommodation in Hotel Peulla. (Baggage is taken to Hotel Peulla automatically but for alternative accommodation see under Peulla.)

Sea routes south of Puerto Montt

To Puerto Natales The dramatic 1,460 km journey first goes through Seno Reloncaví and Canal Moraleda. From Bahía Anna Pink along the coast and then across the Golfo de Penas to Bahía Tarn it is a 12-17 hours sea crossing, usually rough. The journey continues through Canal Messier, Angostura Inglesa, Paso del Indio and Canal Kirke (one of the narrowest routes for large shipping). Navimag's vessel Magallanes makes the journey. It calls at Puerto Chacabuco en route south and north, and stops off Puerto Edén on Isla Wellington (one hour south of Angostura Inglesa). This is a fishing village with one hospedaje (20 beds), three shops, scant provisions, one off-licence, one café, but no camping, or running water. Population is 180, plus five carabineros and the few remaining Alacaluf Indians. It is the drop-off point for exploring Isla Wellington, which is largely untouched, with stunning mountains. If stopping, take food; maps (not very accurate) available in

Residencial Emita 23 *C1*
Vista Hermosa 27 *C1*

Eating 🍴
Café Central 2 *B4*
Café Haussman 1 *B5*
Café Real 2 *B4*

Centro Español 3 *B5*
Club Alemán 4 *B5*
Club de Yates 5 *C5*
Dino 6 *B4*
Milton Plaza 7 *B5*

Santiago. Passengers on the Magallanes may disembark for an hour on Wednesday morning to walk around the village (on Saturday sailing north - hot wine is served after the visit). Between November and March, the Magallanes also visits the Pío XI, or Bruggen Glacier, the largest in South America, for an hour on the southward journey. Going north it stops at the Amalia or Brujo Glacier (depending on weather conditions) on Friday evening.

● Sleeping

Puerto Montt *p712, map p712*
Accommodation is expensive in season, much cheaper off season. Check with the Tourist Office.
LL-L Gran Hotel Vicente, Varas 447, T432900, www.granhoteldonvicente.cl. With breakfast, excellent restaurant, seafood. Recommended.
L Club Presidente, Portales 664, T251666, www.presidente.cl. 4-star, with breakfast, very comfortable, also suites. Recommended.
L-AL Gran Hotel Don Luis, Quillota 146, T259001, www.hoteldonluis.cl. New 4-star, gym, sauna, business centre etc.
AL-A O'Grimm, Gallardo 211, T252845, www.ogrimm.com. With breakfast, cosy, central, restaurant with occasional live music.
A Montt, Varas y Quillota, T253651. **B** without bath, decent restaurant.
B Hostal Pacífico, J J Mira 1088, T256229. With breakfast, cable TV, parking, comfortable. Discounts for foreign visitors. Recommended.
B Le Mirage, Rancagua 350, T255125, F256302. With breakfast, small rooms.
B-C Hostal Suizo, Independencia 231, T/F252640, rossyoelckers@yahoo.es. **E** pp in shared rooms, some rooms with bath. With small breakfast, painting and Spanish classes, German and Italian spoken, Spanish classes. The house is as quirky as the owner. Convenient for Navimag.
B-C Millahue, Copiapó 64, T253829, www.hotelmillahue.cl. With breakfast, modern, good restaurant.
C Colina, Talca 81, T253502, hotcolina@hotmail.com. Spacious, good restaurant, bar, car hire. Good value. Recommended.
C Gamboa, Pedro Montt 157, T252741. Some rooms with bath, with breakfast, TV, comfortable, warm.
C Res Emita, Miraflores 1281, T250725, hospedaje_emita@hotmail.com. **E** singles, some rooms with bath, includes breakfast with homemade bread, safe.
C-D Casa Perla, Trigal 312, T262104, www.casaperla.com. **E** pp in shared rooms. With breakfast, French, English spoken, helpful, meals, Spanish classes offered off season. Recommended.

C-D House Rocco Backpacker, Pudeto 233, T/F272897, hospedajerocco@hotmail.com. **E** in dorms. Renovated, with breakfast, real coffee, English spoken, laundry, quiet residential area, convenient for Navimag. Recommended.
C-D Res El Turista, Ancud 91, T263838. **E** singles. With and without bath, with breakfast, comfortable, small rooms, heating. Recommended.
D El Talquino, Pérez Rosales 114 esq JJ Mira, T253331, eltalquino@hotmail.com. **F** singles. Includes breakfast, hot water, family-run, cosy. Recommended, but noisy bars nearby.
D Vista Hermosa, Miramar 1486, T319600. **E-F** singles, with breakfast, very good, without bath, ask for front room (10 mins' walk from terminal).
E pp **Alda González**, Gallardo 552, T253334. With or without bath, with breakfast, cooking facilities, popular. Recommended.
E pp **Hosp Vista al Mar**, Vivar 1337, T255625, www.hospedajevistaalmar.unlugar.com. Helpful, welcoming, good breakfast, phone for a lift from bus station.
E-F pp **Hosp El Valle**, Chorrillos 1358, T258464. Hot showers, internet.
E pp **Mercedes Fuentes**, Aníbal Pinto 315, T273463. Bed and breakfast with shared bath, spacious rooms, helpful family, father is tour guide.
E pp **Res Central**, Lota 111, T257516. Use of kitchen, basic, popular with Chileans. Several lodgings in **E-F** pp range on C Huasco, east of the Plaza de Armas.
F pp **Casa Gladis**, Ancud 112 y Mira. Some double rooms, or dormitory style, kitchen and laundry facilities, crowded.
Camping Camping Anderson, 11 km west, American-run, hot showers, private beach, home-grown fruit, vegetables and milk products.
Camping Metri, 30 km southeast on Carretera Austral, T251235, Fierro bus, US$2 per tent.
Camping Municipal at Chinquihue, 10 km west (bus service), open Oct-Apr, fully equipped with tables, seats, barbecue, toilets and showers. Small shop, no kerosene.

● *For an explanation of the sleeping and eating price codes used in this guide, see inside the front*
● *cover. Other relevant information is found in Essentials pages 604-605.*

● Eating

Puerto Montt *p712, map p712*
Local specialities include *picoroco al vapor*, a
giant barnacle whose flesh looks and tastes
like crab, and curanto.

In Angelmó, there are several dozen small,
seafood restaurants in the old fishing port, past
the fish market, very popular, ask for *té blanco*
(white wine – they are not legally
allowed to serve wine).

Other seafood restaurants in Chinquihue, west
of Angelmó. In Pelluco (4 km east), many seafood
restaurants, including **Pazos**, T252552. Best
curanto in Puerto Montt. **Azurro**, good Italian
restaurant and, around the corner, a great
pub called **Taitao**, façade like a galleon.

TTT Centro Español, O'Higgins 233. Very good.

TTT Club Alemán, Varas 264. Old fashioned,
good food and wine.

TTT Club de Yates, Costanera east of centre.
Excellent seafood.

TT Café Haussman, San Martín y Urmeneta.
German cakes, beer and *crudos*. Recommended.

TT New Harbour Café, San Martín 185 y
Urmeneta. Good coffee and atmosphere
(closed Sin lunchtime).

TT Puerto Café, Angelmó 2456 (above Travellers).
Vegetarian dishes, real coffee, English spoken.
Recommended.

T Café Central, Rancagua 117. Spartan, generous
portions (sandwiches and pichangas). Giant TV
screen for football enthusiasts.

T Café Real, Rancagua 137. For empanadas,
pichangas, congrío frito, and lunches.

T Dino, Varas 550. Restaurant upstairs,
snacks downstairs (try the lemon juice).

T La Nave, A Varas 1006. Good value seafood,
also *residencial*.

T Milton Plaza, Urmeneta y O´Higgins.
Good seafood and snacks, doubles as a pool
hall. Recommended.

Cafés

Asturias, Angelmó 2448. Often recommended.

Café Plaza, Urmeneta 326. Good location, pool
table, nice atmosphere.

● Shopping

Puerto Montt *p712, map p712*
Woollen goods and Mapuche-designed rugs can be
bought at roadside stalls in Angelmó and on
Portales opposite the bus terminal. Prices are much
the same as on Chiloé, but quality is often lower.

Bookshop Libros, Portales 580. Small
selection of English novels.

Supermarkets Fullfresh, opposite bus
terminal, open 0900-2200 daily. Also in the Paseo
del Mar shopping mall, Talca y A Varas, and in the
old railway station. Santa Isabel, Varas y Chillán.

▲ Activities and tours

Puerto Montt *p712, map p712*
Rafting Alsur, Varas 445, T/F287628.

Sailing 2 Yacht Clubs in Chinquihue:
Club de Deportes Náuticas, founded by British
and Americans in 1940s, more oriented towards
small boat sailing, windsurfing, watersports.
Marina del Sur (MDS), T/F251958. Modern, bar
and restaurant, sailing courses, notice board for
crew tripulante) notices, MDS Charters office (also
Santiago T/F231 8238) specializes in cruising the
Patagonian channels. Charters US$2,200-8,500
per week depending on size of boat.

Tour operators

There are many tour operators. Some companies
offer 2-day excursions along the Carretera Austral
to Hornopirén, US$100 including food and
accommodation. Most offer 1-day excursions to
Chiloé (US$20) and to Puerto Varas, Isla Loreley,
Laguna Verde, and the Petrohué falls: both these
tours are much cheaper from bus company
kiosks inside the bus terminal, eg Bohle, US$15
to Chiloé, US$11 to the lakes. We have received
good reports about:

Andina del Sud, very close to central tourist
kiosk, Varas 437-445, T257797/257686. Sells a
daily tour at 0830 (not Sun) to Puerto Varas,
Parque Nacional V Pérez Rosales, Petrohué, Lago
Todos los Santos, Peulla and back, and to other
local sights, as well as skiing trips to the Osorno
volcano (see below for trip to Bariloche).

Petrel Tours, San Martín 167, of 403, T/F251780,
petrel@telsur.net.

Travellers, Casilla 854, General Bulnes 1009, 22 de
Mayo, T262099, www.travellers.cl. Close to 2nd
port entrance and Navimag office, open Mon-Fri
0900-1330, 1500-1830, Sat 0900-1400 for booking
for Navimag ferry Puerto Edén to Puerto Natales,
bespoke incoming tours, car hire, also runs
computerized tourist information service, map
display, TV, real coffee, English-run.

● Transport

Puerto Montt *p712, map p712*
Air El Tepual Airport is 13 km northwest of
town. ETM bus from terminal 1½ hrs before
departure, US$2; also meets incoming flights.
ETM minibus service to/from hotels, US$4 pp,
T294294. Taxi US$12. **Lan Express** flies to
**Santiago, Concepción, Temuco, Valdivia,
Balmaceda** and **Punta Arenas**, most daily. Sky
also flies to Santiago, Temuco, Balmaceda and
Punta Arenas daily. In Jan, Feb and Mar you may

well be told that flights are booked up, but cancellations may be available from the airport. To **Chaitén**, Aerotaxi del Sur daily, US$72.

Bus Terminal (very crowded, well- organized, but beware hotel touts) on sea front at Portales y Lota, has Telephone, restaurants, casa de cambio (left luggage, US$1.50 per item for 24 hrs). To **Puerto Varas** (US$1.35), **Llanquihue**, **Frutillar** (US$1.50), **Puerto Octay** (US$2) and **Osorno** (US$2.30) minibuses every few mins, **Expreso** Puerto Varas, Thaebus and Full Express. To **Ensenada** and **Petrohué**, Buses JM several daily. To **Pucón**, US$6. To **Temuco** US$6, to **Valdivia**, US$5, 3½ hrs. **Concepción**, US$10. To **Santiago**, *clásico* 12 hrs, US$18, *cama* US$36-40, several companies including **Tur-Bus**, very good, and **Tas Choapa Royal Class**. To **Punta Arenas**, **Austral** and **Ghisoni**, between 1 and 3 times a week, US$53-70 depending on company (bus goes through Argentina via Bariloche), 32-38 hrs. Take plenty of food for this "nightmare" trip. Book well in advance in Jan-Feb and check if you need a multiple-entry Chilean visa. Also book any return journey before setting out. For services to Chiloé, see page 717.

To Argentina via Lago Todos Los Santos The route is operated only by **Andina del Sud** see under Tour operators. Bus from company offices daily at 0800; the fare is a hefty US$160 one way. Note that the trip may be cancelled if the weather is poor; difficulty in obtaining a refunds or assistance have been reported. Try both Puerto Montt and Puerto Varas offices if you want to take the trip in sections. If you take the boat from Petrohué to Peulla, you can cross to Argentina and take public transport on to Bariloche (bus and boat). In high season you must book ahead.

Buses to Argentina via Osorno and the Puyehue pass Daily services to Bariloche on this route via Osorno, US$15, 7 hrs, are run by **Cruz del Sur, Río de la Plata, Tas Choapa** and **Bus Norte**. Out of season, services are reduced. Buy tickets for international buses from the bus terminal, not through an agency. Book well in advance in Jan and Feb; ask for a seat on the right hand side for the best views.

Car hire Automotric Angelmó, Talca 79. Cheap and helpful. **Automóvil Club de Chile**, Ensenada 70, T254776, and at airport (US$235 per week). **Autovald**, Portales 1330, T256355. Cheap rates. **Full Famas**, Portales 506, T258060 and at airport. Helpful, good value, has vehicles that can be taken to Argentina. See Essentials, page 43 for international agencies.

Ferry To **Puerto Natales**: The **Magallanes** sails to Puerto Natales throughout the year on Mon at 1600, taking 4 days and 3 nights, arriving in Puerto Natales Thu between 0800 and 1200. It returns on Fri 0600, arriving Puerto Montt Mon morning.

Check-in in Puerto Montt must be done between 0900 and 1200 on day of departure. In Puerto Natales check-in is on Thu 1600-2000; passengers embark 2100, but dinner is not included. Confirm times and booking 48 hrs in advance. The fare, including meals, ranges from US$355 pp in C berth (sheets are extra, take your own or a sleeping bag), to US$1,750 double in cabin with a view (high season prices, Nov-Mar; US$275 and US$1,260 respectively May-Sep). First class is recommended. 10% discount on international student cards in cabin class only. Cars are carried for US$368, motorcycles for US$60. Payment by credit card or foreign currency is accepted in all Navimag offices. The vessel is a mixed cargo/passenger ferry which includes live animals in the cargo. On board is a book exchange, video films are shown, there are guided talks and information sessions and you can play bingo. Food is good and plentiful and includes vegetarian options at lunch and dinner. Passengers tend to take their own food and alcohol. Standards of service and comfort vary, depending on the number of passengers and weather conditions. Take seasickness tablets, or buy them on board (you'll be advised when to take them!). **Booking** Tickets can be booked through many travel agencies, Navimag offices throughout the country, or direct from www.navimag.cl. Book well in advance for departures between mid-Dec and mid-Mar especially for the voyage south (Puerto Natales to Puerto Montt is less heavily booked). It is well worth going to the port on the day of departure if you have no ticket. Departures are frequently delayed by weather conditions – or even advanced. For details and next season's fares see Navimag's website. **Note** It is cheaper to fly and quicker to go by bus via Argentina. The route does not pass Laguna San Rafael.

To **Puerto Chacabuco**: Navimag's ferry Puerto Edén sails every Wed and Sat to Puerto Chacabuco (80 km west of Coyhaique), returning Tue and Fri. The cruise to Puerto Chacabuco lasts about 24 hrs. The fares are from US$58 for bunks, cars US$157, motorcycles US$40, bicycles US$25. There is a small canteen; long queues if the boat is full. Food is expensive so take your own. This same vessel goes to Laguna San Rafael from Puerto Montt, on specific dates depending on the time of year. It is a 5-day, 4-night trip, with activities, all meals and a boat trip to the glacier. Accommodation ranges from US$400 to US$838. You can also do the return trip from Puerto Chacabuco, or Puerto Montt-Laguna San Rafael-Puerto Chacabuco (www.navimag.cl, for fares and dates).

To **Chaitén**: Naviera Austral operates the *Pincoya*, twice a week, and the *Alexandrina*, also twice a week, 10½ hrs, US$31, cars US$131, US$13 for a bicycle.

To **Laguna San Rafael**: The m/n Skorpios 1 and 2 of **Skorpios Cruises** leave Puerto Montt (vessel 2) or Puerto Chacabuco (1) for a luxury cruises with various itineraries. The fare varies according to season, type of cabin and number of occupants: double cabin from US$1,100 Skorpios 2. Generally service is excellent, the food superb, and at the glacier, you can chip ice off the face for your whisky. After the visit to San Rafael the ships visit Quitralco Fjord where there are thermal pools and boat trips on the fjord. From Puerto Montt it's a 6-day cruise. Skorpios' latest vessel 3 sails from Puerto Natales to Glaciar Pío XI in the Campo de Hielo Sur, 6 days/5 nights, fares from US$1,780. **Compañía Naviera Puerto Montt** offers 6-day, 6-night trips to the glacier for US$900 on board the *Quellón*. **Patagonia Connection SA**, Fidel Oteíza 1921, of 1006, Providencia, Santiago, T225 6489, www.patagonia-connection.com. Operates Patagonia Express, a catamaran which runs from Puerto Chacabuco to Laguna San Rafael via Termas de Puyuhuapi, see page 729. Tours lasting 4 to 6 days start from Puerto Montt and include the catamaran service, the hotel at Termas de Puyuhuapi and the day excursion to Laguna San Rafael. High season 20 Dec-20 Mar, low season 11 Sep-19 Dec and 21 Mar-21 Apr. High season fares for a 6-day tour from US1430-2100, all inclusive, highly recommended.

Other routes: See under Castro and Chaitén for details of sailings between Chiloé and the mainland.

Shipping offices in Puerto Montt: Cruce de Lagos, www.lakecrossing.cl, includes departures to **Puerto Varas** and **Bariloche**. **Naviera Austral**, Angelmó 2187, T270400, www.navieraustral.cl. **Navimag** (Naviera Magallanes SA), Terminal Transbordadores,

Angelmó 2187, T432300, www.navimag.cl. Skorpios Cruises, Angelmó 1660 y Miraflores, T252619, www.skorpios.cl. **Transmarchilay Ltda**, Angelmó 2187, T270430, www.tmc.cl. **Train** Twice a day to **Temuco**, US$8.60, 6 hrs 20 mins.

❶ Directory

Puerto Montt *p712, map p712*
Airline offices LAN, O'Higgins y Urmeneta, T253141. **Sky**, T437555, or 600-600 2828 for information. **Banks** Many ATMS in the city. Commission charges vary widely. **Afex**, Portales 516. **Inter**, Talca 84. For cash, TCs, no commission on Amex. **Turismo Los Lagos**, Varas 595, local 13. La Moneda de Oro at the bus terminal exchanges some Latin American currencies (Mon-Sat 0930-1230, 1530-1800). Obtain Argentine pesos before leaving Chile. **Note**: This is the last city on the mainland with Visa ATM before Coyhaique. **Consulates** Argentina, Cauquenes 94, p 2, T253996, quick visa service. Germany, Varas y Gallardo, p 3, of 306. Tue-Wed 0930-1200. **Netherlands**, Chorillos 1582, T253003. **Spain**, Rancagua 113, T252557. **Cycle repairs** Kiefer, Pedro Montt 129, T253079. 3 shops on Urmeneta, none very well stocked. **Internet** Latin Star, Av Angelmó 1684, T310036. Internet café, cheap phone rates, stamps, fax, book exchange, English spoken, helpful. Others on Av Angelmó near Navimag. 3 internet cafés on San Martín (eg No 232). **Motorcycle repairs** Miguel Schmuch, Urmeneta 985, T/F258877. **Post offices** Rancagua 126. Open 0830-1830 (Mon-Fri), 0830-1300 (Sat). **Telephones** Pedro Montt 114 and Chillán 98. Entel, Urmeneta y Pedro Montt. Telefónica del Sur, A Varas entre Talca y Pedro Montt.

Chiloé → *Colour map 9, grid A1.*

The island of Chiloé is 250 km long, 50 km wide and covers 9,613 sq km. Thick forests cover most of its western side. The hillsides in summer are a patchwork quilt of wheat fields and dark green plots of potatoes. The population is 116,000 and most live on the sheltered eastern side. The west coast, exposed to strong Pacific winds, is wet for most of the year. The east coast and the offshore islands are drier, though frequently cloudy. The culture of Chiloé has been strongly influenced by isolation from Spanish colonial currents, the mixture of early Spanish settlers and Mapuche indians and a dependence on the sea. Religious and secular architecture, customs and crafts, combined with delightful landscapes, all contribute to Chiloé's uniqueness.

Ins and outs
Getting there Regular ferries cross the straits of Pargua between Pargua, 55 km southwest of Puerto Montt on the mainland, and Chacao on Chiloé. Dolphins, seals and birds can be seen. **Buses:** Puerto Montt to Pargua, frequent, US$2, one hour, though most buses go through to Ancud (3½-4 hours) and Castro. Transport to the island is dominated by **Cruz del**

Sur, who also own Trans Chiloé and have their own ferries. Cruz del Sur run frequent services from Puerto Montt to Ancud and Castro, six a day to Chonchi and Quellón; their fares are highest but they are faster (their buses have priority over cars on Cruz del Sur ferries). **Fares from Puerto Montt**: to Ancud, Cruz del Sur US$4.50, Trans Chiloé US$4.50, **Quellén Bus** (independent company), US$4; to Castro, Cruz del Sur US$7.50, Trans Chiloé US$6 and Quellén Bus; to Chonchi, US$7, Quellón, US$9. There are direct bus services from Santiago, Osorno, Valdivia, Temuco and Los Angeles to Chiloé. Buses drive on to the ferry (passengers may leave the bus). **Ferries** About 24 crossings daily, 30-minute crossing, operated by several companies including Transmarchilay and Cruz del Sur; all ferries carry buses, private vehicles (cars US$10 one way, motorcycles US$6, bicycles US$3) and foot passengers (US$1).
➤ *For further information, see Transport, page 723.*

Background

The original inhabitants of Chiloé were the Chonos, who were pushed south by the Mapuches invading from the north. The first Spanish sighting was by Francisco de Ulloa in 1553 and in 1567 Martín Ruiz de Gamboa took possession of the islands on behalf of Spain. The small Spanish settler population divided the indigenous population and their lands between them. The rising of the Mapuche after 1598 which drove the Spanish out of the mainland south of the Río Biobío left the Spanish community on Chiloé (some 200 settlers in 1600) isolated. During the 17th century, for instance, it was served by a single annual ship from Lima.

The islanders were the last supporters of the Spanish Crown in South America. When Chile rebelled the last of the Spanish Governors fled to the island and, in despair, offered it to Britain. Canning, the British Foreign Secretary, turned the offer down. The island finally surrendered in 1826.

The availability of wood and the lack of metals have left their mark on the island. Some of the earliest churches were built entirely of wood, using wooden pegs instead of nails. These early churches often displayed some German influence as a result of the missionary work of Bavarian Jesuits. Two features of local architecture often thought to be traditional are in fact late 19th century in origin. The replacement of thatch with thin tiles (*tejuelas*) made from alerce wood, which are nailed to the frame and roof in several distinctive patterns, and *palafitos* or wooden houses built on stilts over the water.

The island is also famous for its traditional handicrafts, notably woollens and basketware, which can be bought in the main towns and on some of the off-shore islands, as well as in Puerto Montt.

Although the traditional mainstays of the economy, fishing and agriculture, are still important, salmon farming has become a major source of employment. Seaweed is harvested for export to Japan. Tourism provides a seasonal income for a growing number of people. Nevertheless, the relatively high birth rate and the shortage of employment in Chiloé have led to regular emigration.

Ancud and around → *Phone code: 065. Colour map 9, grid A1. Population: 30,000.*

Ancud lies on the north coast of Chiloé 30 km west of the Straits of Chacao at the mouth of a great bay, the Golfo de Quetalmahue. Founded in 1767 to guard the shipping route around Cape Horn, it was defended by two fortresses, the Fuerte San Antonio and Fuerte Ahui on the opposite side of the bay. The port is dominated by the **Fuerte San Antonio**, built in 1770, the site of the Spanish surrender of Chiloé to Chilean troops in 1826. Close to it are the ruins of the **Polvorín del Fuerte** (a couple of cannon and a few walls). A lovely 1 km walk north of the fort leads to the secluded beach, **Arena Gruesa**. 2 km east is a **mirador** offering good views of the island and across to the mainland, even to the Andes on a clear day. Near the Plaza de Armas is the **Museo Regional** ① *summer daily 1100-1900, winter Tue-Fri 0900-1300, 1430-1830, Sat 1000-1330, 1430-1800, US$1, reductions for students*. As well as an interesting collection on the early history of Chiloé, it has good shops and café. **Tourist office**: Sernatur ① *Libertad 665, T622800, infochiloe@sernatur.cl. Mon-Fri 0830-2000, Sat-Sun (summer only) 0900-1800*. Ask here about the Agro Turismo programme, staying with farming families.

To **Faro Corona**, the lighthouse on Punta Corona, 34 km west, along the beach, offers good views with birdlife and dolphins (2-3 buses daily). The duty officer may give a tour, recommended. To **Pumillahue** ① *27 km southwest, 2-3 buses daily*, where nearby there is a penguin colony (the birds are seen early morning or late afternoon): hire a fishing boat to see it, US$5.50 per person. No bus is suitable for seeing the birds.

Chepu, population 230, on the coast southwest of Ancud (38 km) is famed for its sea-fishing and the drowned forest (Valley of Dead Trees, devastated by a tsunami in 1960) and environment of its river (a wide range of birds here). The **Mirador de Chepu** information centre, run by Fernando and Amory Uslar, gives views of the wetlands, information about the flora, fauna and tourist options, has a café and rents kayaks (US$3 per hour). Chepu is also the northern entry for the Parque Nacional Chiloé, see page 720.

Ancud to Castro

There are two routes: direct along Route 5, the Pan-American Highway, crossing rolling hills, forest and agricultural land, or via the east coast along unpaved roads passing through small farming and fishing communities. The two main towns along the coastal route, **Quemchi** (*Population 1,700, basic accommodation*) and Dalcahue, can also be reached by roads branching off Route 5.

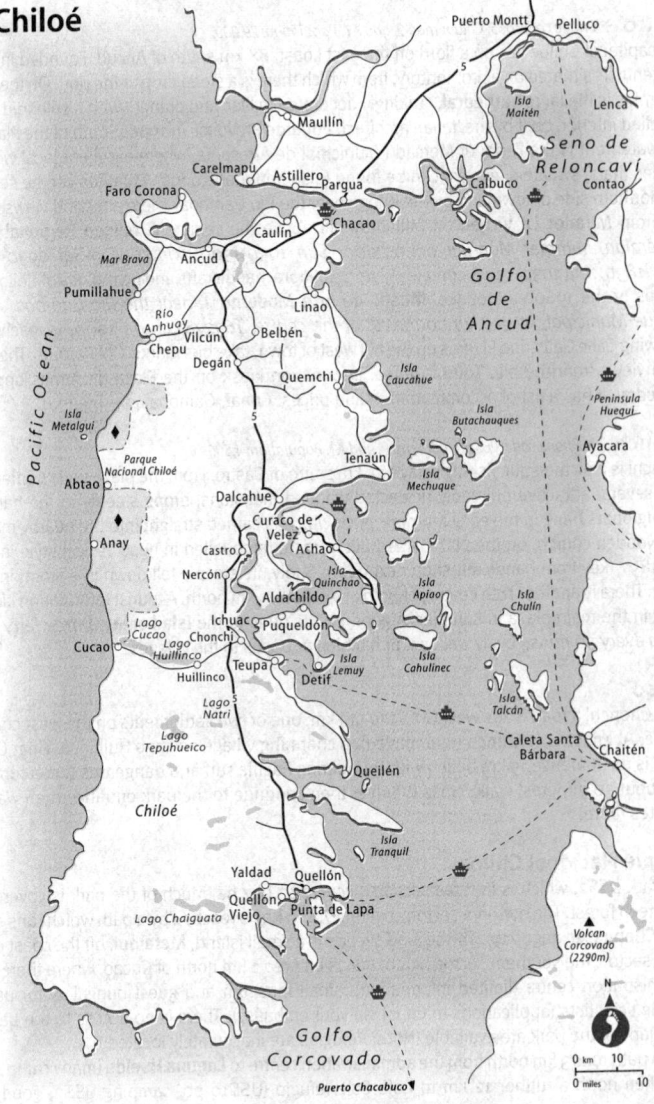

Chiloé

Dalcahue (*Population 5,000*), 74 km south of Ancud, is more easily reached from Castro, 30 km further south. It is one of the main ports for boats to the offshore islands, including Quinchao and Mechuque. The wooden church on the main plaza dates from the 19th century. The market is on Sunday, from 0700 to 1300; good quality. Tourist kiosk in season. There are various basic hotels (**D-F** pp) and a restaurant. Buses to Castro, hourly, 40 minutes, US$1. Also collective taxis.

Quinchao Island

The main settlement on this island is **Achao**, a quiet, pretty fishing village with a market. Its wooden church, built in 1730 and saved by a change of wind from a fire which destroyed much of the town in 1784, is a fine example of Chilote Jesuit architecture. The original construction was without use of nails. The tourist office at Serrano y Progreso is open between December and March only. There are various hotels (**D-F** pp) and restaurants, and don't miss the oysters sold on the beach.

Castro → *Phone code: 065. Colour map 9, grid A1. Population: 29,000.*

The capital of Chiloé lies on a fjord on the east coast, 88 km south of Ancud. Founded in 1567, the centre is situated on a promontory, from which there is a steep drop to the port. On the Plaza de Armas is the large **Cathedral**, strikingly decorated in lilac and orange, with a splendid wood panelled interior, built by the Italian architect, Eduardo Provosoli in 1906. South of the Plaza on the waterfront is the **Feria**, or Mercado Municipal de Artesanía, where excellent local woollen articles (hats, sweaters, gloves) can be found (also imported goods). Palafitos can be seen on the northern side of town and by the bridge over the Río Gamboa. There are good views of the city from **Mirador La Virgen** on Millantuy hill above the cemetery. **Museo Regional** ① *on Esmeralda, summer Mon-Sat 0930-2000, Sun 1030-1300; winter Mon-Sat 0930-1300, 1500-1830, Sun 1030-1300*, contains history, folklore, handicrafts and mythology of Chiloé and photos of the 1960 earthquake. **Museo de Arte Moderno** ① *near the Río Gamboa, in the Parque Municipal, over 3 km northwest of the centre, T632787, 1000-1900*, is reached by following Calle Galvarino Riveros up the hill west of town, take bus marked 'Al Parque'. There are good views from the hill. **Tourist office**: Information kiosk on the Plaza de Armas opposite Cathedral. It has a list of accommodation and prices. **Conaf**, Gamboa 424, T532501.

Chonchi → *Phone code: 065. Colour map 9, grid A1. Population: 4,500.*

Chonchi is a picturesque fishing village 25 km south of Castro. From the plaza Calle Centenario, with several attractive but sadly neglected wooden mansions, drops steeply to the harbour. Fishing boats bring in the early morning catch which is carried straight into the nearby market. The wooden church, on the plaza, was built in 1754, remodelled in neoclassical style in 1859 and 1897 (key from handicraft shop next door). Sadly, its steeple fell down in a storm in early 2002. There is another 18th century church at Vilopulli, 5 km north. A tourist information kiosk is open in the main plaza in summer. A good excursion is to the **Isla Lemuy** ① *free ferry 4 km south every 30 mins*; lovely walking, or hitching or buses to the villages.

Cucao

From Chonchi a road leads west to Cucao, 40 km, one of two settlements on the west coast of Chiloé. At Km 12 is **Huillinco** (road paved), a charming village on Lago Huillinco. Near Cucao there is an immense 15 km beach with thundering Pacific surf and dangerous undercurrents. It's about 30 minutes' walk: cross the river then continue to the park entrance then walk 10 minutes more.

Parque Nacional Chiloé

The Park *US$2*, which is in three sections, covers 43,057 ha. Much of the park is covered by evergreen forest. The northern sector, covering 7,800 ha, is reached by a path which runs south from **Chepu** (see page 719). The second section is a small island, **Metalqui**, off the coast of the north sector. The southern sector, 35,207 ha, is entered 1 km north of Cucao, where there is an administration centre (limited information), small museum and guest bungalow for use by visiting scientists (applications to Conaf via your embassy). There is no access to the park by car. Maps of the park are available (**Note:** Refugios are inaccurately located.)

A path runs 3 km north from the administration centre to **Laguna Huelde** (many camp sites) and then north a further 12 km to Cole Cole refugio (US$10 pp, camping US$2, good site) offering great views, best done on horseback (return journey to/from Cucao nine hours by horse, five hours one way on foot). The next refugio is at **Anay** (US$10 pp), 5 km further north on the Río Anay. There are several other walks but signposting is limited. Many houses in Cucao rent horses at US$3 per hour, US$22 per day (check horses and equipment carefully). **Miguelangelo Allende** has been recommended. If you hire a guide you pay for his horse too. Horseflies are bad in summer (wear light coloured clothing).

Quellón → *Phone code: 065. Colour map 9, grid A1. Population: 13,500. 92 km south of Castro.*

There are pleasant beaches nearby at Quellón Viejo (with an old wooden church), Punta de Lapa and Yaldad. The launch Puerto Bonito sails three times daily in summer from the pier, US$12.50 to tour the bay passing Punta de Lapa, Isla Laitec and Quellón Viejo. A trip can also be made to Chaiguao, 11 km east, where there is a small Sunday morning market. Horses can be hired US$2.50 per hour. Also kayaks with a guide, US$2.50 per hour. Camping US$3.50. **Museo de Nuestros Pasados** ① *Ladrilleros 255*, includes reconstructions of a traditional Chilote house and mill. **Tourist office**: kiosk on the Plaza de Armas open mid-December to mid-March. Ask about hospedajes not listed in their information leaflet. Amazing views of the mainland on a clear day.

● Sleeping

Ancud *p718*

L-AL Hostería Ancud, San Antonio 30, T622340, resancud@sumet.cl. Nice views of the bay, attractive, very comfortable, helpful, restaurant.
A-B Hostería Ahui, Costanera 906, T622415, hosteriaahui@terra.com. With breakfast, full of charm, good views.
A-B Montserrat, Baquedano 417, T/F622957, hotelmontserrat@hotmail.com. With breakfast, good views, attractive.
B-C Hostal Vista al Mar, Costanera 918, T622617, www.vistaalmar.cl. **E** pp in dorms, also self catering apartments **B**. Views over the bay, heating, internet, laundry, dinner served in barn in summer.
B-C Mundo Nuevo, Costanera 748, T628383, www.newworld.cl. **E** pp in dorms. With breakfast, comfortable, great views over the bay, lots of info, heating, good showers, kitchen facilities, car hire, one room has a boat-bed, English and German spoken. Highly recommended.
C Hosp San José, Las Américas 661, T629944, hostalsanjose6@hotmail.com. **E** singles. With breakfast, good family atmosphere, nice views from lounge, hot water, some rooms with bath, use of kitchen, internet, tours offered, bicycle hire. Recommended.
C Hostal Lluhay, Cochrane 458, T622656. Meals served. Attentive, nice lounge. Recommended.
C Lacuy, Pudeto 219 near Plaza de Armas, T/F623019, hotellacuy@yahoo.es. With breakfast, restaurant. Recommended.
C-D Hosp Alto Bellavista, Bellavista 449, T622384. Very helpful, good breakfast, some rooms with bath, **E-F** pp shared rooms.
C-D Hosp Sra Martha, Lautaro 988, T623748, martaalvarado@latinmail.com. **E** singles. With breakfast, TV, kitchen facilities, good beds.
D Hosp Alinar, Ramírez 348. Hospitable, a good choice in this range.

D Hosp Santander, Sgto Aldea 69. **E-F** pp without bath. Recommended.
E pp **Elena Bergmann**, Aníbal Pinto 382. Use of kitchen, parking.
E pp **Hosp Austral**, A Pinto 1318, T624847, hospedajeaustral@hotmail.com. Cosy wooden house, near bus station, with breakfast, shared bath, family of Mirta Ruiz, very welcoming, dinner extra. Recommended.
E-F pp **Familia Vallejos**, Aníbal Pinto 738, T622243. Very friendly, basic. Recommended.
E-F pp **Hosp Su Casa**, Los Alerces 841, T623382. Excellent breakfast, hot shower, TV room.
E-F pp **Pudeto 331**, T622535. Without bath, old fashioned, very nice.
E-F pp **San Bernardo**, Errázuriz 395, T622657. Good dormitory accommodation.
F pp **Hosp Don Luis**, Av Almte Latorre 1225, T620325. With basic breakfast, private and shared rooms, good shared hot showers, friendly family, lots of information, use of kitchen.
In summer the school on Calle Chacabuco is used as an albergue.
Camping Arena Gruesa, Av Costanera Norte 290, T623428, arenagruesa@yahoo.com. **Playa Gaviotas**, 5 km north, T09-653 8096 (mob). **Playa Larga Huicha**, 9 km north, **E** per site, bath, hot water, electricity.

Castro *p720*

Hotels on San Martín are convenient for the bus terminals. Several lodgings on Los Carrera 500-700 blocks, in our **E** pp range.
AL Alerce Nativo, O'Higgins 808, T632267. Heating, helpful, breakfast, also has cabañas and restaurant 4 km south of Castro.
AL Hostería Castro, Chacabuco 202, T632301, www.hosteriadecastro.cl. Attractive building, wonderful views. Recommended.

AL Unicornio Azul, Pedro Montt 228, T632359, www.chiloeweb.com/pweb/unicornioazul. Good views over bay, comfortable, restaurant.
AL Cabañas Trayen, 5 km south of Castro, T633633, www.trayenchiloe.cl. **A** off season, lovely views, cabins for 4 to 6.
B Casita Española, Los Carrera 359, T635186. Heating, TV, parking. Recommended.
B Chilhue, Blanco Encalada 278, T632956. Good.
B-C Hostal Quelcún, San Martín 581, T632396. Cheaper without bath, some rooms small, heating, helpful.
D Hosp Sotomayor, Sotomayor 452, T632464. With breakfast, TV, quiet, small beds.
E pp **Eyzaguirre 469**. Comfortable. Recommended.
E pp **Freire 758**. Breakfast, good value.
E pp **Hosp Chiloé**, San Martín 739. Breakfast. Recommended.
E pp **Hosp El Molo**, O'Higgins 486, T635026. Comfortable, safe, welcoming, internet.
E pp **Hosp Victoria**, Barros Arana 745. Warm water. Recommended.
E pp **Lidia Low**, San Martín 890. With good breakfast, warm showers, use of kitchen, family home.
E pp **Lodging El Mirador**, Barros Arana 127, T633795. With breakfast, **C** with bath, cosy, relaxing, kitchen, broadband internet US$1.15. Recommended.
E pp **María Zuñiga**, Barros Arana 140, T635026. Includes breakfast, comfortable, cooking facilities, secure. Recommended.
E pp **Pensión Victoria**, San Martín 747. Small rooms, pretty.
E pp **Res Capullito**, San Martín 709. Quiet.
F pp Basic accommodation Dec-Feb in the **Gimnasio Fisical**, Freire 610, T632766. With breakfast.
Camping Camping Pudú, Ruta 5, 10 km north of Castro, T635109, cabins, showers with hot water, sites with light, water, children's games. Several sites on road to Chonchi.

Chonchi *p720*
A Posada El Antiguo Chalet, Gabriela Mistral, T671221. **B** in winter, charming, beautiful location, very good.
B-C Cabañas Amankay, Centenario 421, T671367. Homely, kitchen facilities.
C-D Esmeralda By The Sea, on waterfront 100 m east of market, T/F671328, esmeraldachonchi@hotmail.com. **E** pp in dorms. With breakfast, being remodelled in 2006, shared bath, dinner available, attractive, welcoming, English spoken, use of internet US$0.60, bunkhouse for 8, cooking facilities, book exchange, rents bicycles, boat trips offered, Landcruiser tours. Recommended.
D Hosp Mirador, Alvarez 198. With breakfast, **E-F** singles. Recommended.
D Huildin, Centenario 102, T671388. Without bath, old fashioned, good beds, also cabañas A, garden with superb views, parking.
D Res Turismo, Andrade 299, T671257. Without bath, with breakfast.
F pp **Sra Fedima**, Aguirre Cerda 176. Own sleeping bag required, use of kitchen, good.
Camping Los Manzanos, Aguirre Cerda y Juan Guillermo, T671263. **E** per site.

Cucao *p720*
E pp **Chela**, close to beach and within walking distance of park. Helpful, use of kitchen, good breakfast extra.
E pp **Hosp El Arrayan**, T633040, ask for Erice or Ojede. Friendly, good food and restaurant.
E pp **Hosp Paraíso**, T633040 (Sra Luz Vera), ask for Sra Edvina for horse-hire.
E pp **Posada Cucao**, T633040. With breakfast, meals.
E pp **Provisiones Pacífico**, with full board or demi-pension, friendly, good, candles provided, no hot water.
E pp **Parador Darwin**, after the bridge, Cucao sector, T633040. Breakfast, vegetarian and other meals, real coffee, fresh bread for sale. Recommended.
Camping Several campsites.

Huillinco
E pp **Residencia**, good food, or stay at the post office

Quellón *p721*
B Melimoyu, P Montt 375, T681250. Good beds, parking.
E pp **La Paz 303**, unnamed. With shared hot water.
F pp **Albergue**, Ladrilleros, near Carrera Pinto. Dormitory accommodation.
F pp **Las Brisas**, P Montt 555, T681413. Without bath, basic.
F pp **Club Deportes Turino**, La Paz 024. Floor space and camping, cold water, kitchen facilities, basic, open Dec-Feb only.

Eating

Ancud *p718*
Excellent cheap seafood restaurants in the market area.
ΨΨ **El Cangrejo**, Dieciocho 155. Seafood. Highly recommended.
ΨΨ **Hamburguería**, Av Prat. Much better than name suggests, good seafood.
ΨΨ **La Pincoya**, Prat 61, on waterfront. Good food, service and views.

¶¶ Mar Pacífico, Pudeto 346. Typical Chilote fare.
¶¶ Sacho, in the market. Renowned for its *curantos*.
¶ Pingüino, in an alley behind the market. Very cheap, decent lunches.

Cafés
La Candela, Pudeto y Libertad. Cosy, nice range of snacks, drinks and light meals.

Castro *p720*
Breakfast before 0900 is difficult to find. By the market many places offer set lunch, usually fish dishes. In the market, try *milcaos*, fried potato cakes with meat stuffing. Also *lic or de oro*, like Galliano.
¶¶ Donde Eladio, Lillo 97. Meat and seafood specialities.
¶¶ Octavio's, Pedro Montt 261. Good food and nice views over bay, specializes in seafood.
¶ Don Camilo, Ramírez 566. Average food, also has pleasant accommodation.
¶ Palafito restaurants near the Feria Artesanía on the waterfront offer good food and good value, including **Rapa Nui**, **Mariela** and **La Amistad**.
¶ Playa, Lillo 93. Good seafood.
¶ Sacho, Thompson 213. Good sea views, clean.

Cafés
Años Luz, San Martín on corner of Plaza. Good café/bar/restaurant, live music at weekends, great cocktails.
La Brújula del Cuerpo, Plaza de Armas. Fast food, good coffee, snacks.
Stop Inn Café, Martín Ruiz shopping centre, Gamboa. Good coffee.

Chonchi *p720*
¶¶ La Parada, Centenario 133. Good selection of wines, erratic opening hours. Recommended.
¶ El Alerce, Aguirre Cerda 106. Good seafood, excellent value.
¶ El Trébol, Irrazával 187. Good food and good views.

Quellón *p721*
¶¶ Fogón Las Quilas, La Paz 053, T206. Famous for lobster. Recommended.
¶¶ Los Suizos, Ladrilleros 399. Swiss cuisine, good, slow service, internet.
¶ El Coral, 22 de Mayo. Good, reasonably priced, superb views.
¶ Rucantú on P Montt. Good food and value.

O Shopping

Castro *p720*
Bookshops Anay, Serrano 357, **El Tren**, Thompson 229 and **Libros Chiloé**, Blanco

Encalada 204. All for books on Chiloé. Cassettes of typical Chilote music are widely available.
Handicrafts Cema-Chile outlet on Esmeralda.
Market The municipal market is on Yumbel, off Ulloa, uphill northwest of town: fish and vegetables.
Supermarket Beckna, O'Higgins y Aldea. Bakes good bread.

Chonchi *p720*
Handicrafts From **Opdech** (Oficina Promotora del Desarrollo Chilote), on the waterfront, and from the parroquia, next to the church (open Oct-Mar only).

▲ Activities and tours

Ancud *p718*
Austral Adventures, Cochrane 432, T/F625977, www.austral-adventures.com. Bespoke tours on land and sea. Good English speaking guides, lots of interesting choices. Ask director Britt Lewis about the return of blue whales to Chiloé's waters.
Paralelo 42, Latorre 558, T622458. Tours to Río Chepu area, including 2-day kayak trips, guide Carlos Oyarzun.
Patagón Chiloé, Bellavista 491, T622128, patagonchiloe@hotmail.com. Tours to the penguin colony and Chepu.

Castro *p720*
Tours to Parque Nacional Chiloé US$33, to Isla Mechuque (east of Dalcahue) US$45.
Pehuén Expediciones, Blanco Encalada 299, T632361, pehuentr@entelchile.net. LanChile agency, horse riding, trips to national park and islands.
Sergio Márquez, local guide, Felipe Moniel 565, T632617, very knowledgeable, has transport.
Turismo Isla Grande, Thompson 241, Navimag agents.
Turismo Queilén, Gamboa 502, T632776. Good tours to Chonchi and Chiloé National Park. Recommended.

⊖ Transport

Ancud *p718*
Bus Terminal on the east outskirts at Aníbal Pinto y Marcos Vera, reached by bus, or Pudeto colectivos. To **Castro**, US$2.50, frequent (see below), 1½ hrs. To **Puerto Montt**, frequent services by Cruz del Sur, Trans Chiloé and Queilén Bus, US$4.50. To **Quemchi** via the coast, 2 hrs, US$1.50.

Quinchao *p720*
Ferry From **Dalcahue**, frequent, free for pedestrians and cyclists. Arriagada **buses**

from **Ancud**, 5 a day. Frequent to **Castro**, US$1.50, **Achao Express**.

Castro *p720*
Bus Frequent services to **Chonchi**, choose between buses **Cruz del Sur**, **Queilén Bus** and others), minibuses and colectivos (from Esmeralda y Chacabuco). **Arroyo** and **Ocean Bus** both run to **Cucao**, 6 a day in season, first 0930, last back 1600 1½ hrs, US$2.65 (1200 and 1600 off season, avoid Fri when school children are going home – much slower, lots of stops). To **Dalcahue** frequent services by **Gallardo** and **Arriagada**, also colectivos from San Martín 815. To **Achao** via Dalcahue and Curaco de Vélez, Arriagada, several daily, last return from Achao 1730, US$2.65. To **Puqueldón** on the island of Lemuy, Gallardo, Mon-Fri 1315, US$2. To **Quemchi**, 2 a day, 1½ hrs, US$2.50. To **Quellón**, Regional Sur and Trans Chiloé, frequent. To **Queilén**, Queilén Bus, 6 a day, US$2.50.

Long distance buses leave from 2 terminals: Cruz del Sur, T632389, **Trans Chiloé** and Arriagada from Cruz del Sur terminal on San Martín 500 block behind the cathedral. Other services leave from the Municipal Terminal, San Martín, 600 block (2 blocks further north). Frequent services to **Ancud** and **Puerto Montt** by Cruz del Sur, Trans Chiloé and Queilén Bus. Cruz del Sur also run to **Osorno**, **Valdivia**, **Temuco**, **Concepción** and **Santiago**. Bus Norte to Ancud, Puerto Montt, Osorno and Santiago daily. To **Punta Arenas**, Queilén Bus, Mon, 36 hrs, US$60.
Ferry Naviera Austral's *Pincoya* sails Castro-**Chaitén** on Wed, Sat, Sun, US$30, US$23 without a seat.

Chonchi *p720*
Buses and **taxis** to **Castro**, frequent, US$1.15, from main plaza. Services to **Quellón** (US$1.90) and **Queilén** from Castro and Puerto Montt also call here.

Cucao *p720*
Bus From Castro see above; in season as many as 4 buses a day, last departure 1600, reduced service off-season; hitching is very difficult. Taxi from Chonchi US$4.50.

Quellón *p721*
Bus To **Castro**, 2 hrs, frequent, Cruz del Sur, US$3; also to **Ancud** and **Puerto Montt**.
Ferry Naviera Austral's *Pincoya* sails Quellón-Chaitén on Fri and Alexandrina on Wed, 7 hrs, US$28, US$20 without seat. Off season services are irregular, perhaps one ferry per week.

⊕ Directory

Ancud *p718*
Banks ATMs at BCI, off plaza. **Post offices** On corner of Plaza de Armas at Pudeto y Blanco Encalada. **Telephones** Plaza de Armas. Mon-Sat 0700-2200.

Castro *p720*
Banks Many of the banks in the centre have ATMs for credit and bank cards (pesos only). Banco de Chile with ATM at Plaza de Armas, accepts TCs (at a poor rate). BCI, Plaza de Armas, MasterCard and Visa ATM. Better rates from **Julio Barrientos**, Chacabuco 286, cash and TCs. **Bicycle hire** San Martín 581. **Post offices** On west side of Plaza de Armas. **Telephones** Latorre 289. Entel: O'Higgins entre Gamboa y Sotomayor.

Quellón *p721*
Banks Banco del Estado, commission charged on TCs, no credit cards, no commission on US$ cash. **Shipping offices** Naviera Austral, (www.navieraustral.cl) and Navimag (www.navimag.cl), Pedro Montt 457, Quellón, T682207.

Carretera Austral

A third of Chile lies to the south of Puerto Montt, but until recently its inaccessible land and rainy climate meant that it was only sparsely populated and unvisited by tourism. The Carretera Austral, or Southern Highway, has now been extended south from Puerto Montt to Villa O'Higgins, giving access to the spectacular virgin landscapes of this wet and wild region, with its mountains, fjords and islands, hitherto isolated communities, and picturesque ports. Ships were the only means of access and remain important for exporting the timber grown here, and for bringing visitors; see page 713. There is great hiking at Ventisquero Colgante, whitewater rafting at Futaleufú, and thermal springs at Chaitén and Puyuhuapi, as well as the unspoilt national parks of Hornopirén, Queulat and Parque Pumalin.

Puyuhuapi is the perfect place to break the journey, but the main town is Coyhaique, and from nearby Chacabuco, boats leave for the magnificent glacier of Parque Nacional Laguna San Rafael. Coyhaique is the only settlement of any size on the Carretera Austral. It's a good starting point for exploring the Carretera and for trekking (eg at Cerro Castillo), and fishing expeditions, for instance on the Río Baker, an angler's paradise further south. Coyhaique is also a good place for booking San Rafael Glacier trips. The Carretera extends to Villa O'Higgins, beyond which the southern icefields and their glaciers bring the roadway to a halt.

The southernmost section of the Carretera Austral, 443 km, ends at Villa O'Higgins and is the wildest and most dramatic, with beautiful unspoilt landscapes around Lago General Carrera. The fairy tale peaks of Cerro Castillo offer challenging trekking, and there's world class fishing in the turquoise waters of Río Baker. A road runs off to Puerto Ibañez for lake crossings to Chile Chico, a convenient border crossing to Argentina.

Ins and outs

Getting there and around This road can be divided into three major sections: **Puerto Montt-Chaitén**, **Chaitén-Coyhaique**, and **Coyhaique-Villa O'Higgins**. The road is paved only for about 150 km north and south of Coyhaique, from Puerto Chacabuco to Villa Cerro Castillo. Currently, it's 'ripio' (loose stones) and many sections are extremely rough and difficult after rain. Cyclists can't expect to make fast progress and motorists need to carry sufficient fuel and spares, especially if intending to detour from the highway itself, and protect windscreens and headlamps from stones. Unleaded fuel is available all the way to Villa O'Higgins. There is now a road between Puerto El Vagabundo and Caleta Tortel, and the Carretera Austral is connected by a free ferry between Puerto Yungay and Río Bravo, where it continues to Villa O'Higgins. So far, there is little infrastructure for transport or accommodation among the tiny rural hamlets, so allow plenty of time for bus connections, and bring cash, as there are few banking facilities along the whole route. Having your own transport here is definitely preferable. Camping will give you more freedom for accommodation, and there are many beautiful sites, though note that food supplies are limited and tend to be expensive. ▸▸ *For further information, see Transport, page 739.*

Best time to visit The landscape throughout the region is lushly green because there is no real dry season. On the offshore islands and the western side of the Andes annual rainfall is over 2,000 mm, though inland on the steppe the climate is drier and colder. Westerly winds are strong, especially in summer, but there's plenty of sunshine too, especially around Lago General Carrera (described in the Southern Section), which has a warm microclimate. January and February are probably the best months for a trip to this region.

Information Portal for the Aisén region (in Spanish): www.patagoniachile.cl.

Puerto Montt to Chaitén

This section of the Carretera Austral, 242 km, includes two, sometimes three ferry crossings. Before setting out, it is imperative to check when the ferries are running and, if driving, make a reservation: do this in Puerto Montt (not Santiago), at the Naviera Austral office, Angelmó 2187, T065-270430. The alternative to this section is by ferry from Puerto Montt or Quellón to Chaitén.

The road (Ruta 7) heads east out of Puerto Montt, through Pelluco and after an initial rough stretch follows the shore of the beautiful Seno Reloncaví. It passes the southern entrance of the **Parque Nacional Alerce Andino** ① *US$5, no camping within park boundaries*, which contains one of the best surviving areas of alerce trees, some over 1,000 years old (the oldest is estimated at 4,200 years old). Wildlife includes pudú, pumas, vizcachas, condors and black woodpeckers. There are two entrances: 2½ km from Correntoso (35 km east of Puerto Montt) at the northern end of the park (with ranger station and campsite) and 7 km east of Lenca (40 km south of Puerto Montt) at the southern end. There are three other ranger posts, at Río Chaicas, Lago Chapo and Sargazo. Ranger posts have little information; map is available from Conaf in Puerto Montt.

At 46 km from Puerto Montt (allow one hour), is the first ferry at **La Arena**, across the Reloncaví Estuary to **Puelche**. See Transport, page 739, for Ferry details. **Río Negro** is now called **Hornopirén** after the volcano above it. From here you catch the second ferry, to Caleta Gonzalo, one of the centres for the Parque Pumalin (see below). At the mouth of the fjord is Isla Llancahué, good for hiking in the forests amid beautiful scenery.

Parque Pumalin

Caleta Gonzalo is the entry point for Parque Pumalin for visitors from the north. On the quay is a smart café serving excellent (and pricey) organic food, a visitor centre selling tasteful handicrafts, and cabañas for rent, tiny and perfectly designed, with lake views. The park, created by the US billionaire Douglas Tompkins, is a private reserve of 320,000 ha which has been given Nature Sanctuary status. Covering large areas of the western Andes, with virgin temperate rainforest, the park is spectacularly beautiful, and is seen by many as one of the most important conservation projects in the world. You can visit the model farm, a native tree nursery and an apiculture project, producing delicious honey, sold in the visitor centre. There are several self guided trails, showing examples of ancient alerce trees, rainforest and waterfalls (check which paths shown on maps are actually open). **Information centres** ① *Buin 356, Puerto Montt, T065-250079; Fiordo Reñihué, Caleta Gonzalo, T1712-196-4151 (not always open); O'Higgins 62, Chaitén, T065-731341. In USA T415- 229-9339, www.parquepumalin.cl.*

South of Caleta Gonzalo the Carretera Austral winds through the park's beautiful unspoilt scenery, and there is a steep climb on the ripio road to Laguna Blanca, with panoramic views. At Caleta Santa Bárbara, 12 km from Chaitén, there's a wonderful sweeping black sand beach fringed with woodland and with views of the mighty Morro Vilcum, good for swimming and wild camping.

Chaitén → *Phone code: 065. Colour map 9, grid A1. Population: 3,258.*

The capital of Palena province, Chaitén is rather a bland town and a port for ferries to Puerto Montt and Quellón. Its charms lie in the splendour of its setting, against thickly forested vertical mountains, the dramatic peak of volcano Michimahuida, and the broad open bay of Corcovada. There's great hiking nearby and it's a base for exploring Parque Pumalin. The rustic, open-air thermal pools, **Termas El Amarillo** ① *dawn to 2100, US$3pp, highly recommended, several cabañas nearby*, in the middle of the beautiful forest, are 25 km away. It is becoming a popular centre for adventure tourism. Most facilities are along the coast road, Av Corcovado, with good views of the bay. There is excellent fishing nearby, especially to the south in the Ríos Yelcho and Futaleufú and in Lagos Espolón and Yelcho (see below). Fishing licences are sold at the Municipalidad on the plaza. Visits are possible to the offshore sealion colony at Isla Puduguapi. **Tourist office** ① *Av B O'Higgins 284, Plaza de Armas, T731082, infopalena@sernatur.cl.* Better information at Chaitur, see Activities and tours, page 727.

🍽 Sleeping

Puerto Montt to Chaitén *p725*
Hornopirén
Electricity 1900-0100.
A Hotel Termas de Llancahué, Isla Llancahué. To get there, make arrangements by phoning T09-642 4857. The hotel will send an open boat for you; the 1-hr crossing affords views of dolphins

and fur seals. Price is for full board (excellent food), hot spring at the hotel.
C-D Hornopirén, Carrera Pinto 388, T217256. Cabañas and restaurant at the water's edge. Recommended.
D Holiday Country, O'Higgins 666, T217220. Hot shower, restaurant.

D pp **Hostería Catalina**, Ingenieros Militares s/n, T217359, www.hosteriacatalina.cl. With bath, a good place to stay.

Parque Pumalin *p726*
Camping Sites, of which there are several, are exemplary, run on strict conservation lines, with well-designed picnic shelters and good washing facilities (but no hot water): US$8 per tent. Cabañas (**AL**), sleep up to 4; meals extra.

Chaitén *p726*
A **Brisas del Mar**, Av Corcovada 278, T731284, cababrisas@telsur.cl. Pleasant cabañas for 4 to 6 facing sea, but no view, best restaurant in town.
A-B **Schilling**, Corcovado 230, T731295. With breakfast, heating, restaurant.
B **Mi Casa**, Av Norte 206, up on hill at end of Diego Portales, T731285, hmicasa@telsur.cl. Small pleasant rooms, and fine views from the restaurant which serves good fish. Recommended.
C **Cabañas Tranqueras del Monte**, Av Norte s/n (head for Mi Casa and turn left), T731379, tranquer@telsur.cl. Splendid views over bay, well-equipped, comfortable cabañas, also **B** rooms, superb breakfasts, charming hosts Doria and Francisco, very knowledgeable, speak perfect English. Also offer a good package to explore the Carretera Austral. Highly recommended.
D pp **Corcovado**, Av Corcovado 408, T731221. Rather superior place, also facing sea, wood panelled rooms with comfortable beds, most with bath, restaurant (US$5 for 2 courses). Cabañas for 4 too.
D pp **Llanos**, Av Corcovdo 378, T731332. Small place facing the sea with kind owners and lovely rooms, dinner in restaurant (US$5 for 2 courses). Good mechanic next door.
E pp **Hosp Rita**, Almte Riveros y A Prat, T731502. Warm, Rita runs a great place with comfy beds in whitewashed rooms, good atmosphere, use of kitchen. Recommended.
Camping Los Arrayanes, fabulous setting, right on the sea with great views of Volcán Corcovado, hot showers, and fire places.

🍴 Eating

Chaitén *p726*
🍴 **El Flamengo**, Corcovado 218. Family run, plain but good fish dishes, also serves meat.
🍴 **El Quijote**, O'Higgins 42. More modest, also recommended.

⛰ Activities and tours

Chaitén *p726*
Chaitur, O'Higgins 67, T731429, nchaitur@hotmail.com. This should be your first port of call in Chaitén. Run by Nicholas, a charming and helpful North American with information and booking for all buses and boats, and internet access. Excellent, personalized excursions to places far and near: Parque Pumalin, hiking at Ventisqueo Yelcho (astounding white glacier), Santa Bárbara beach, boat excursions, fishing, horses, trekking, mountain biking, very reasonable prices.

🚍 Transport

Puerto Montt to Chaitén *p725*
Parque Nacional Alerce Andino
Bus To the north entrance: take a **Fierro** or **Río Pato** bus to **Correntoso** (or **Lago Chapo** bus which passes through Correntoso), several daily except Sun, then walk. To the south entrance: take any **Fierro** bus to **Chaicas, La Arena, Contau** and **Hornopirén**, US$1.50, getting off at Lenca sawmill, then walk (signposted).

La Arena to Puelche
Ferry Across the Reloncaví Estuary, 30 mins, every 1½ hrs, US$10 for a car, US$6 for motorcycle, US$3 for bicycle, US$1 for foot passengers, 0715-2045 daily. Arrive at least 30 mins early to guarantee a place; buses have priority. Roll-on roll-off type operating all year.

Hornopirén
Bus Fierro (T253022) and Jordán (T254938) run Mon-Sat 0800 and 1330 (Sun 1500, 1730) from **Puerto Montt**, US$5.35; return 0530, 1330 Mon-Sat, 1245, 1500 Sun.
Ferry Hornopirén to **Caleta Gonzalo**, Naviera Austral, daily 1600, 5 hrs (may be much longer if the ferry cannot dock in rough weather). Going north the ferry leaves Caleta Gonzalo at 0900, daily. Fare for cars US$111 (capacity 21), motorbikes US$22, passengers US$18 (capacity 80), bicycles, US$11.50. Ferry operates Jan-Feb only and can be very busy; there can be a 2-day wait for vehicles to get on the ferry.

Chaitén *p726*
Air Flights to **Puerto Montt** with Aerotaxi del Sur, daily, 35 mins, US$72.
Bus Several companies operate minibuses along the Carretera Austral to Coyhaique from next to Chaitur, O'Higgins 67: in Jan-Feb up to 6 a week, in

● For an explanation of the sleeping and eating price codes used in this guide, see inside the front
● cover. Other relevant information is found in Essentials pages 604-605.

winter 2 a week with overnight stop in La Junta or Puyuhuapi. Even in summer, prepare to wait extra days. All details from **Chaitur**, T731429. To **La Junta** US$9, 4 hrs; to **Puyuhuapi** US$13, 5 hrs; to **Coyhaique** US$25, 11 hrs. Buses travel full, so are unable to pick up passengers en route. To **Futaleufú**, US$9, 5 hrs, **Chaitur**, daily 1530 except Sun, US$8, daily, 0900, US$9. To **Caleta Gonzalo**, daily Jan-Feb 0700 to connect with boats. Hitching the whole route is slow, even in summer.

Ferry Port about 1 km north of town. To **Puerto Montt**, Naviera Austral, *Pincoya* Sun and Mon, *Alexandrina* Wed and Fri to **Puerto Montt**, and Thu (*Pincoya*) and Sat (*Alexandrina*) to **Quellón** and Wed, Fri, Sun to Castro (Chiloé). **Navimag** office, Carrera Pinto 188, T731570. **Naviera Austral**, Av Corcovado 266, T731272. **Note**: All boat services vary season to season: check with the local office. Reduced service in winter.

❶ Directory

Chaitén
Banks There is 1 ATM on the plaza, for Maestro, Mastercard and Cirrus, not Visa. There is no other ATM between here and Coyhaique. Banco del Estado, O'Higgins y Libertad, on plaza, changes dollars and TCs in working hours.

Chaitén to Coyhaique

This section of the Carretera Austral, runs 422 km though breathtaking and varied scenery, passing tiny villages, most notably the idyllic Puyuhuapi, where there are thermal pools, and good trekking in Parque Nacional Queulat. A road branches off east to the Argentine border, the picturesque Futaleufú, with excellent rafting, and west to Puerto Cisnes.

Puerto Cárdenas, 46 km south of Chaitén, is on the northern tip of **Lago Yelcho**, a beautiful lake on Río Futaleufú surrounded by hills, much loved by anglers for its salmon and trout. Further south at Km 60, a path leads to **Ventisquero Yelcho** (two hours' walk there), a dramatic glacier with high waterfalls.

At **Villa Santa Lucía**, an uninspiring modern settlement 87 km south of Chaitén, with basic food and accommodation, a road branches east to the Argentine border. There are two crossings: Futaleufú and Palena, both reached from **Puerto Ramírez** past the southern end of Lago Yelcho, 24 km east of Santa Lucia. Here the road divides: the north branch runs along the valley of the Río Futaleufú to Futaleufú and the southern one to Palena. The scenery is spectacular, but the road is hard going: single track ripio, climbing steeply in places (tough for bikes; allow plenty of time). Don't leave litter, take out all rubbish.

Futaleufú → *Phone code: 065.*
This once tranquil border town, 8 km west of the border, is growing into a hugely popular tourist centre. The rickety houses, neatly slatted with alerce wood, and spruce vegetable gardens, nestle in a bowl amid steep mountains on the Río Espolón. There is good hiking and some of the most challenging white water rafting in the world on the Río Futaleufú. **Lago Espolón**, west of Futaleufú, reached by a turning 41 km northeast of Villa Santa Lucía, is a beautiful lake in an area enjoying a warm microclimate: 30° C in the day in summer, 5° C at night, with excellent fishing at the lake's mouth. Several cabañas and campsites. Banco del Estado on the plaza has no ATM, but may change cash. **Tourist office** ❶ *O'Higgins and Prat, T721370/721241*, for accommodation and maps of walks.

Border with Argentina
Chilean immigration is in Futaleufú. Straightforward crossing. The border is just west of the bridge over the Río Grande. For Argentinian immigration, see page 195. Change money in Futaleufú; nowhere to change at the border but you can pay the bus fare to Esquel (Argentina) in US dollars. Alternatively, cross into Argentina further south near **Palena**, which is 8 km west of the border and has a Chilean immigration office. Note that if entering from Argentina, no fresh produce may be brought into Chile.

La Junta is a village 151 km south of Chaitén. It has a service station, where there's a minimarket (selling stove alcohol) and phone. From the village you can visit **Lago Rosselot**, surrounded by forest in the **Reserva Nacional Lago Rosselot**, 9 km east of La Junta. The same road continues east, 74 km, to Lago Verde and the Argentine border. Another excursion, by road and boat, is to the fishing village of Raúl Marín.

Puyuhuapi → *Phone code: 067. Population: 500.*

With the most idyllic setting along the whole Carretera Austral, Puyuhuapi lies in a tranquil bay at the northern end of the Puyuhuapi fjord, 45 km south of La Junta. The blissful thermal pools at Termas de Puyuhuapi are nearby. The village was founded by four German-speaking Sudeten families in 1935, and handwoven carpets are still made here by the Hopperditzel brothers, now world renowned. **Alfombras de Puyuhuapi** ① *T325131, www.puyuhuapi.com, daily in summer 0830-1930, closed lunch, English spoken*. This is the best stopping point between Chaitén and Coyhaique with phone, fuel, shops, but no banking facilities: hotel owners will change dollars.

South of Puyuguapi, 24 km, is the 154-ha **Parque Nacional Queulat** ① *Conaf, La Junta, epinto@patagoniachile.cl, daily Dec-Mar 0830-2100, rest of year 0830-1830, US$3, camping US$11 per spot, Conaf campsite with cold showers*. Luis Lepio, T325139, runs bus service to park daily if there's demand, Mon to Fri, 1030, also guide for fly fishing. It is most visited for the spectacular hanging glacier, **Ventisquero Colgante**. 2.5 km off the road passing the guardeparques' house, you'll find parking and camping areas. Three walks begin from here: a short stroll through the woodland to a viewpoint of the Ventisquero, or cross the river where the path begins to Laguna Tempanos, where boats cross the lake in summer. The third, 3.25 km, takes 2½ hours to climb to a panoramic viewpoint of the Ventisquero, where you can watch the ice fall into huge waterfalls like sifted sugar.

Puerto Cisnes

At 59 km south of Puyuhuapi, a winding road branches west and follows the Río Cisnes 35 km to Puerto Cisnes (*Population 1,784*), a quiet fishing village at the mouth of the river on Puyuhuapi fjord, set amongst steep mountains. The Río Cisnes, 160 km in length, is recommended for rafting or canoeing, with grand scenery and modest rapids except for the horrendous drop at Piedra del Gato. Good camping in the forest, and fuel is available in the village.

At 89 km south of Puyuhuapi is **Villa Amengual** and, at Km 92, a road branches east, 104 km to La Tapera and to the Argentine border. Chilean immigration is 12 km west of the border, open daylight hours only. On the Argentine side the road continues to meet up with Ruta 40, a section with few services for fuel or food.

Coyhaique → *Phone code: 067. Colour map 9, grid A1. Population: 43,297.*

A growing centre for tourism, Coyhaique, 420 km south of Chaitén, is a busy small town perched on a hill between the Ríos Simpson and Coyhaique. It's a good idea to get cash here as there are no banks along the Carretera Austral. The **Museo Regional de la Patagonia Central** ① *Baquedano 310, Tue-Sun winter 0830-1730, summer 0900-2000, US$1 is in the Casa de Cultura*. It traces local history through photos of the first pioneers. From the bridge over the Río Simpson look for the **Piedra del Indio**, a rock outcrop which looks like a face in profile. **Tourist offices**: In the bright green cabin in the plaza, helpful, with details on buses and accommodation. **Sernatur** office (less helpful) ① *Bulnes 35, T231752, infoaisen@sernatur.cl. Mon-Fri 0830-2100, Sat-Sun 1100-2000*. **Conaf**, Av Ogana 1060, T212109, aysen@conaf.cl.

Just outside the town, the **Reserva Forestal Coihaique** ① *information from Conaf*, has some trails for walking or biking, with several picnic grounds and a campsite on the river bank. A satisfying walk is up to Cerro Cinchao, and great views from Sendero Los Leñeros to Laguna Verde. Walk to laguna Verde and Laguna Venus particularly recommended. Follow Baquedano to the end, over bridge, and past the guardeparque's hut where all the trails begin. There are well-marked walks of between 20 minutes and five hours. Ski centre **El Fraile**, 29 km from Coyhaique, is 1599 m above sea level, with five pistes, powder snow, in the middle of nire and pine forests (1,000 people capacity).

Border with Argentina: Coyhaique Alto

A 43-km road runs east to this crossing. On the Argentine side the road leads through Río Mayo and Sarmiento to Comodoro Rivadavia. **Chilean immigration** is at Coyhaique Alto, 6 km west of the border, open May-August 0800-2100, September- April 0700-2300.

Puerto Aisén and Puerto Chacabuco

→ *Phone code: 067. Colour map 9, grid A1. Population: 13,050.*

The paved road between Coyhaique and Puerto Aisén passes through **Reserva Nacional Río Simpson**, with beautiful waterfalls, lovely views of the river and excellent fly-fishing. Administration is at the entrance; campsite opposite turning to Santuario San Sebastián, US$5.

Puerto Aisén is 65 km west of Coyhaique at the meeting of the rivers Aisén and Palos. Formerly the region's major port, it has been replaced by Puerto Chacabuco, 15 km to the west, and though it remains an important centre for services, there's little of interest for the visitor. It's also very wet. In summer, the *Apulcheu* sails regularly down the Aisén Fjord to Termas de Chiconal, a spectacular two hour trip by boat, US$30 – book in the tourist office or **Turismo Rucaray**, on the plaza, rucaray@entelchile.net. **Tourist office** in the Municipalidad, Prat y Sgto Aldea, Dec-Feb only. www.portchacabuco.cl, gives information on shipping movements.

The longest suspension bridge in Chile and a paved road lead to **Puerto Chacabuco** 15km away; a regular bus service runs between the two. The harbour, rather a charmless place, is a short way from the town.

Balmaceda

From Coyhaique, the Carretera Austral heads south past huge bluffs, through deforested pasture and farmsteads edged with alamo trees, before entering flatter plains and rolling hills. At around Km 41, a paved road runs east to Balmaceda on the Argentine border at Paso Huemules (no accommodation). **Chilean immigration** is open May-July 0800-2000, September-April 0730-2200.

Puerto Ibáñez

The Carretera Austral starts to climb again, past the entrance to the Reserva Nacional Cerro Castillo (see below). It winds up through the attractive narrow gorge of Río Horqueta, to a pass between Cerro Castillo and its neighbours, before dropping down a 6-km slalom into the breathtaking valley of Río Ibáñez. (This is currently the most southerly paved section and the road is safe and wide here). Here the road forks east to Puerto Ibáñez, a further 31 km away, for the ferry crossing of vast Lago General Carrera.

Coyhaique

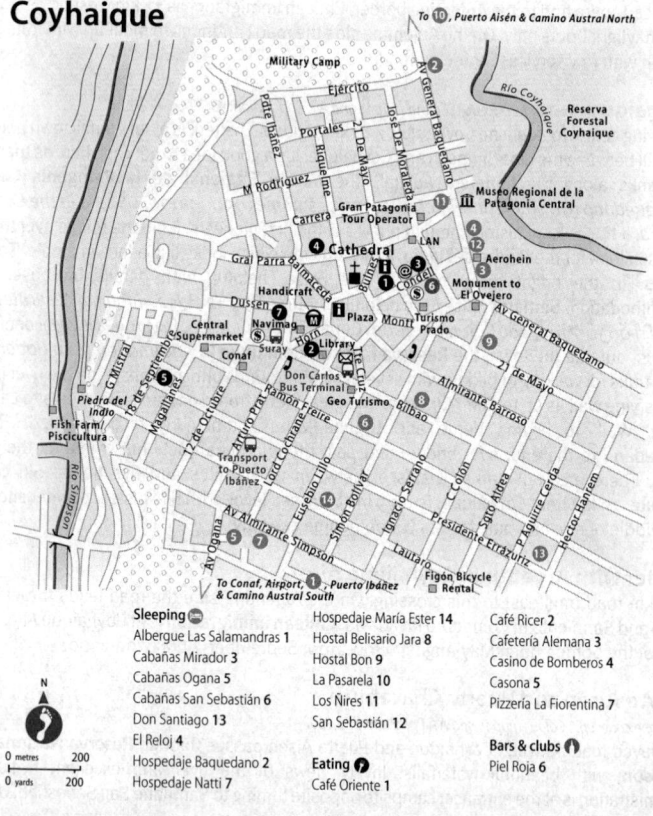

Sleeping		
Albergue Las Salamandras 1	Hospedaje María Ester 14	Café Ricer 2
Cabañas Mirador 3	Hostal Belisario Jara 8	Cafetería Alemana 3
Cabañas Ogana 5	Hostal Bon 9	Casino de Bomberos 4
Cabañas San Sebastián 6	La Pasarela 10	Casona 5
Don Santiago 13	Los Ñires 11	Pizzería La Fiorentina 7
El Reloj 4	San Sebastián 12	
Hospedaje Baquedano 2		Bars & clubs
Hospedaje Natti 7	Eating	Piel Roja 6
	Café Oriente 1	

Puerto Ibáñez (*Population 828*) is the principal port on the Chilean section of the lake, and as such you'll probably just pass through to reach the ferry. It is, however, a centre for distinctive pottery, leather production and vegetable growing (you can visit potters and buy salad from greenhouses). Local archaeology includes rock art and the largest Tehuelche cemetery in Patagonia. There are various hotels, but no other services. Fuel (sold in 5-litre containers) is available at Luis A Bolados 461 (house with five laburnum trees outside). Most shops and restaurants are closed Sunday. There are some fine waterfalls, the Salto Río Ibáñez, 6 km north.

Villa Cerro Castillo

From the turning to Puerto Ibáñez the Carretera Austral goes through Villa Cerro Castillo (Km 8), a quiet village in a spectacular setting beneath the striking, jagged peaks of **Cerro Castillo**, overlooking the broad valley below. There's a petrol station, public phone, several food shops and a tiny tourist information kiosk by the road side (January-February only), with details of guides offering trekking to the Cerro, among them Jorge Aguilar and Francisco Calderón.

The village is a good place to stop for a few days with two appealing attractions. There's a truly spectacular four-day trek around the fairytale castle peaks of Cerro Castillo, in the **Reserva Nacional Cerro Castillo**, whose entrance is 64 km south of Coyhaique. The walk starts at Las Horquetas Grandes, a bend in the river Río Ibáñez, 8 km south of the park entrance, where any bus driver will let you off. It follows Río La Lima to the gorgeous Laguna Cerro Castillo, then animal trails around the peak itself, returning to the village (accommodation or bus back to Coyhaique). This is a challenging walk: attempt it only if fit, and ideally, take a guide, as trails are poorly marked (IGM map essential, purchase in advance in Coyhaique). The guardería is on the Senda Ibáñez, 50 m to the left of the main road (as you head south), opposite Laguna Chinguay to the right, with access to walks and campsite (camping US$5, November-March, take equipment – there are no refugios). The picnic ground is open summer 0830-2100, winter to 1830.

A few kilometres south of the village, **La Cueva de las Manos** ⓘ *US$1 charged Dec-Apr.* In a shallow cave, a few handprints have been made on the side of vertical rocks high above the Río Ibáñez. There's no clue to their significance, but they're in a beautiful place with panoramic views. This makes a delightful two hours' walk. The site is accessible all year, signposted clearly from the road.

⦿ Sleeping

Chaitén to Coyhaique *p728*
Lago Yelcho
L-A **Cabañas Yelcho en la Patagonia**, T731337, www.yelcho.cl. A smart fishing lodge on banks of the lake with comfortable rooms and cabañas, tastefully decorated with views straight to the lake (booked solid Jan-Feb); also attractive campsite, all facilities. Recommended.

Villa Santa Lucía
D pp Several places on main street: ask at Nachito, the café where the bus stops, which serves good breakfasts.
San Antonio and El Trébol, are basic, but the most recommendable. Another, opposite Nachito, is a last resort only. None has hot water.

Puerto Ramírez
Hostería Río Malito has rooms, camping and fishing. Also **Hospedaje Las Casas**. Far better to stay in Futaleufú, if plans allow.

Futaleufú *p728*
L El Barranco, O'Higgins 172, T721314, www.elbarrancochile.cl. Elegant rustic rooms,

luxurious, pool, good restaurant, and expert fishing guides, horses and bikes for hire, half and full board available.
L **Río Grande**, O'Higgins y Aldea, T721320, www.exchile.com. Also upmarket but not such good value, spacious attractive rooms, international restaurant, popular with rafting groups.
B pp **Antigua Casona**, Rodríguez y Cerda, T721311, pcoronadop@yahoo.es. Very attractive old house, owners speak English and have a delightful country house Posada Anchileufú, T721311.
B Cosy cabañas in secluded riverside setting at Río Espolón, T721216, follow Cerda to the end, also recommended parrilla.
D pp **Hospedaje Adolfo**, O'Higgins 302, T721256, hospedajeadolfo@hotmail.com. Best value in this range, very comfortable rooms in family home.
E pp **Continental**, Balmaceda 595, T721222. Oldest in town, no breakfast, basic, welcoming.
Camping There are lots of campsites, many beautifully situated on river bank.

Border with Argentina: La Junta *p729*

AL **Espacio y Tiempo**, T314141, www.espacioytiempo.cl. Spacious rooms, warm and cosy atmosphere, restaurant, attractive gardens, fishing expeditions. Recommended.
D **Café Res Patagonia**, Lynch 331, T314120. Good meals, small rooms, poor bathrooms.
D **Hostería Valderas**, Varas s/n, T314105. Includes breakfast, good value.
D **Res Copihue**, Varas 611, T314184. Without bath, includes breakfast, meals.

Puyuhuapi *p729*

LL **Hotel Termas de Puyuhuapi**. Reservations: Patagonia Connection, Santiago, T225 6489, F274 8111 or directly at the Hotel Termas de Puyuhuapi, T/F325103, www.patagonia-connection.com. Splendidly isolated on a nook in the sea fjord, the hotel owns the thermal baths: outdoors by the fjord so that you can dive in for a refreshing swim afterwards, or in the lovely indoor spa complex where there are jacuzzis of sea water, good for sufferers of arthritic and skin conditions, expert massage facilities. Good packages for de-stressing with all activities from riding, trekking, mountain biking, yoga and the thermals included. Room price includes use of baths, boat transfer to hotel, full board US$40 extra, excellent restaurant. Guests met at Balmaceda airport, or arrive by boat from Puerto Chacabuco, taking in the San Rafael lake and glaciers (US$1000 for 2 for 4 nights, all included). Highly recommended. Boats leave frequently from a 2 hrs' walk from town, US$3 each way, 10 mins' crossing.
AL **Cabañas Aonikenk**, Hamburgo 16, T325208. Small cosy cabañas for 2-6, by waterfront, friendly owner also runs good little café.
AL **El Pangue**, 18 km north, T325128, cpangue@entelchile.net. Luxurious cabañas in splendid rural setting, horseriding, restaurant, trekking, pool, great views, restful. Recommended.
A **Hostería Alemana**, Otto Uebel 450, T325118. A large traditional wooden house on the water, very comfortable, lovely lake views and garden. Recommended.
A-B **Casa Ludwig**, Otto Uebel s/n, T/F325220, www.casaludwig.cl. **B** with shared bath. Open Nov-Mar; enquire in advance at other times (**B**). In a beautiful 4-storey house built by first German settlers, with wonderful views of bay, charming owner Luisa offers a range of rooms, including the snug attic with shared bath, good breakfast included, very comfortable; Luisa is knowledgeable about the area, speaks German and English. Highly recommended.
D pp **Res Elizabeth**, Llantureo y Henríquez, T325106. Includes breakfast, homely place.

Puerto Cisnes *p729*

A-C **Cabañas Río Cisnes**, Costanera 101, T346404. Cabins sleep 4 to 8. Owner, Juan Suazo, offers fishing trips in his boat.
D **Res El Gaucho**, Holmberg 140, T346514. With bath and breakfast, dinner available.
  Also various cabañas: **Brisas del Sur**, T346587, **Portal del Mar**, T346439, and **Cerro Gilberto**, T346440, all fine.

Villa Amengual

E pp **Res El Encanto**, Fca Castro 33-A, T188-2-1964517. With restaurant and café, one of several cheap options in town.

Coyhaique *p729, map p730*

Plentiful accommodation is of a higher standard, and more expensive than elsewhere in southern Chile. The tourist office has a list.
L **Hostal Belisario Jara**, Bilbao 662, T/F234150, www.belisariojara.itgo.com. Most distinctive and delightful, an elegant and welcoming small place, with TV and excellent breakfast. Recommended.
L-AL **El Reloj**, Baquedano 828, T231108, htlelreloj@patagoniachile.cl. Tasteful, quiet place with a good restaurant, charming, comfortable wood panelled rooms.
AL **Los Ñires**, Baquedano 315, T232261, www.doncarlos.cl. Bland but pleasant place with comfortable rooms, good restaurant.
A **San Sebastián**, Baquedano 496, T/F233427. Modern, spacious rooms with great views over the Reserva, with breakfast, good value. Recommended. Also **Cabañas San Sebastián**, Freire 554, T231762, cabsebastian@hotmail.com. Central, very good.
B **Cabañas Mirador**, Baquedano 848, T233191. Attractive, well-equipped cabañas, also **C** rooms in lovely gardens with panoramic views of the Reserva Forestal, and Río Coyhaique below, great value. Recommended.
B-G **Cabañas Ogana**, Av Ogana Pasaje 8, 185, T232353. Cooking facilities, with breakfast, helpful, also camping and cabañas.
C **Hostal Bon**, Serrano 91, T231189. Simple but very welcoming place, with multilingual owner. They also have cabañas near Reserva Forestal 1km away.
D **Albergue Las Salamandras**, Sector Los Pinos, 2 km south in attractive forest, T/F211865, www.salamandras.cl. Double rooms, dorms (**E** pp) and camping, kitchen facilities, winter sports and trekking (Jun-Oct). Recommended.
E **Don Santiago**, Errázuriz 1040, T231116. With parking and kitchen, good value.
E pp **Hospedaje Baquedano**, Baquedano 20, T232520, Patricio y Gedra Guzmán. Welcoming, well-maintained, lovely place, simple cabañas, with splendid views over the Reserva Forestal, very

helpful hosts who speak English, space for camping, access to river, great value. Recommended.

E pp Hospedaje María Ester, Lautaro 544, T233023. With breakfast, also has cabañas (**C**) with bath, hot water and kitchenette.

E Hosp Natti, Av Simpson 417, T231047. Basic little rooms, laundry next door.

Many more hospedajes and private houses with rooms; ask tourist office for a list.

Cabañas

AL Los Pinos, Camino Teniente Vidal, Parcela 5, T234898. Fishing area, near river and beach and natural park.

A La Pasarela, T240700, Km 1.5 Carretera a Aisén. Good atmosphere, comedor.

A Río Simpson, T/F232183, riosimpsoncab@ hotmail.com, Km 3 road to Pto Aisén. Very reasonable for 6, fully equipped, horse hire, fishing.

B Don Joaquin Cabañas, Km 2 Camino Aerodromo, T214553, www.coyhaique.com. Attractively built of wood, on banks of Río Simpson, well-equipped, for 4 to 8 people, with TV and full service.

Camping Tourist office on plaza or Sernatur in Coyhaique have a full list of all sites in XI Región. There are many camping sites in Coyhaique and on the road between Coyhaique and Puerto Aisén, eg at Km 1, 2 (**Camping Alborada**, US$8.50 per site, T238868, hot shower), 24, 25, 35, 37, 41, 42 (**Camping Río Correntoso**, T232005, US$15 per site, showers, fishing, Automobile Club discount) and 43. Camping in Reserva Forestal, Km 1, towards Puerto Aisen. See above for access details.

Puerto Aisén and Puerto Chacabuco *p729*

Accommodation is hard to find, most is taken up by fishing companies in both ports. There are several places to eat along Tte Merino and Aldea in Puerto Aisén.

AL Hotel Loberías del Sur, José Miguel Carrera 50, Puerto Chacabuco, T351115. Comparatively luxurious, the restaurant serves the best food in the area. Owned by Catamaranes del Sur (see Shipping, below), which also has a nearby nature reserve, Parque Aiken del Sur.

AL-A Patagonia Green, 400m from bridge (on Pto Chacabuco side), T336796, www.patagoniagreen.cl. Nice cabins for up to 5, kitchen, heating, TV, gardens, arranges tours to Laguna San Rafael, fishing, mountain biking, riding, trekking etc, English spoken.

B Caicahues, Michimalonco 660, Puerto Aisén, T336326. The most recommended in this port.

C Hosp San Jorge, Ramírez y Serrano Montaner, Puerto Aisén, T333587. A pleasant place to stay.

D pp Hosp La Estrella, José Miguel Carrera 412, Puerto Chacabuco, T351127. Pleasant, good value.

D Hosp Luisa, Av Municipal 546, Puerto Aisén, T332719. Good, welcoming.

D Res Serrano Montaner, Montaner 471, Puerto Aisén, T332574. Very pleasant and helpful. Recommended.

E pp Hosp Marclara, Caupolicán 970, Puerto Aisén, T333030. Good value.

Puerto Ibáñez *p730*

Various hotels in our **C-E** range, also a campsite.

B Hostería Shehen Aike, Luis Risopatrón 55, T423284, info@shehenaike.cl. Swiss owned, large cabins, lots of ideas for trips, bike rental, organizes tours, fine food, welcoming.

E Hospedaje Don Francisco, San Salvador y Lautaro. Very hospitable, good food. **E Vientos del Sur**, Bertrán Dixon 282, T423208. Good, nice family, dormitories, check the bill, cheap meals but not as good as the lodging.

Villa Cerro Castillo *p731*

There are several lodgings, all **E** pp.

E pp La Querencia, Higgins 460, T411610. Comfortable rooms with shared bath, meals.

E pp Res Villarrica, O'Higgins 59, next to Supermercado Villarrica, T419200. Welcoming, hot showers, and meals too, kind owners can arrange trekking guides and horse riding.

❼ Eating

Futaleufú *p728*

❈ El Encuentro, O'Higgins 653. Reasonable prices, cheerful, fish.

❈ Futaleufú, Cerda 407. Serves meat dishes and local foods.

❈ Martín Pescador, Balmaceda y Rodríguez, T721279. For the best fish meals, rustic.

❈ El Copihue, Cerda y Prat. Cheap pizza and pasta.

Cafés

La Antigua Casona is the best café and bar, cosy and stylish, serving delicious food and wines.

Puyuhuapi *p729*

❈ Café Rossbach. Run by the descendants of the original German settlers, an attractive place by the water for delicious salmon.

❈ Lluvia Marina, next to Casa Ludwig, veronet@entelchile.net. The best café, also selling handicrafts. Superb food in relaxed atmosphere, a great place to just hang out, owner Veronica is very helpful.

Coyhaique *p729*, map *p730*

❈ Café Ricer, Horn 48. Central, warm and cosy, handy meeting place, serving breakfast to dinner, with good vegetarian options.

♥♥ **Casona**, Obispo Vielmo 77, T238894. Justly reputed as best in town, charming family restaurant serves excellent fish, congrio especially, but best known for grilled lamb.
♥ **Casino de Bomberos** next to the fire station, Gral Parra 365, T231437. For great atmosphere and a filling lunch. Recommended.
♥ **Pizzería La Fiorentina**, Prat 230. Tasty pizzas, good service. Recommended.

Cafés
Cafe Oriente, Condell 201. Coyhaique's oldest, was moved on rollers several blocks to its present position. Serves a good lunch and tasty cakes.

❶ Bars and clubs

Coyhaique *p729, map p730*
Piel Roja, Moraleda y Condell. Good music, drinking and dancing, popular with Europeans, open Wed, Fri, Sat 1000-0500 for dancing, pub other nights. Recommended.

❍ Shopping

Coyhaique *p729, map p730*
Handicrafts Artesanía Manos Azules, Riquelme 435. Sells fine handicrafts. **Feria de Artesanía** on the plaza.
Supermarkets Brautigam, Horn 47. Stocks fishing and camping gear. **Central**, Magallanes y Bilbao, open daily till 2230 and at Lautaro y Cochrane. **Multimas**, Lautaro 339, y Prat.

▲▲ Activities and tours

Futaleufú *p728*
Austral Excursiones, Hnos Carrera 500, T721239. Offers rafting, riding, mountain biking and canoeing or kayaking trips.
Centro Aventura Futaleufú (at Río Grande hotel), O'Higgins 397, T721320, www.exchile.com. Also for rafting, riding, mountain biking and canoeing or kayaking.
Rancho Las Ruedas, Pilota Carmona s/n, T721294. The best horseriding in the area.

Coyhaique *p729, map p730*
Tours only operate Dec to Mar.
Geo Turismo, E Lillo 315, T256100, www.geoturismopatagonia.cl. Impressive range of conventional tours and more specialized tours for photographers, fishing, kayaking, all equipment and expert guides included, horse riding and trekking, English spoken. San Rafael Glacier combined with other destinations, also goes to Caleta Tortel, taking boat from there to Steffens glacier, La Isla de los Muertos and Jorge Montt glacier. Fly drive holidays from Chaitén or

Coyhaique, allowing you to leave the car at the other end, car hire US$75 per day, plus 18% IVA .
Gran Patagonia, Parra 97, T214770, www.granpatagonia.cl. English spoken, can organize Laguna San Rafael by boat and 45 min flights, which leave daily in summer. Also trips along the Carretera Austral.
Patagonia Adventure Expeditions, Riquelme 372, T/F219894, www.adventurepatagonia.com. Jonathan and Ian, both English speakers, organize professional adventure tourism, from half day trips to 22 day, multi-environment expeditions. Area of speciality is the Northern Patagonian ice cap, all extended adventures happen there. Also fishing.
Turismo Prado, 21 de Mayo 417, T231271, www.turismoprado.cl. Good travel agent for flights and excursions, changes money and TCs without commission. Trips to Laguna San Rafael by charter flight, US$200pp, unforgettable 4-hr round trip.

❍ Transport

Futaleufú *p728*
Bus To/from **Chaitén**: see above. Bus to Puerto Montt, Tue and Fri, US$33.

Border with Argentina *p728*
Bus From west side of plaza in Futaleufú, a Jacobsen bus runs to the border, 3 times a week, and daily Jan-Feb, US$3, 30 mins, connecting with services to Trevelin and Esquel. From **Chaitén** to Palena, **Expreso Yelcho** bus twice weekly in summer, US$12, 5½ hrs.

La Junta
Bus To **Coyhaique**, daily except Sat with Becker, 7 hrs, US$13. To **Chaitén**, 4 hrs, US$11. To **Puerto Cisnes**, Empresa Entre Verde (T314275), US$7.

Puyuhuapi *p729*
Bus To **Coyhaique** 6 times a week in summer, also private minibuses: ask at food shops.

Puerto Cisnes *p729*
Bus To **Coyhaique**, Transportes Terra Austral, T346757, **Bus Alegría**, T346434, run a daily (not Sun) service, US$11.

Coyhaique *p729, map p730*
Air Most flights from Balmaceda (see page 730), although Coyhaique has its own airport, Tte Vidal, about 5 km southwest of town. **Don Carlos** (www.doncarlos.cl), to **Chile Chico** (Mon-Sat, US$44), **Cochrane** (Mon, Thu, US$74) and **Villa O'Higgins** (Mon, Thu, US$111, recommended only for those who like flying, with strong stomachs, or in a hurry).

Bus Don Carlos, Subteniente Cruz 63, T232981, www.doncarlos.cl; **Suray**, A Prat 265, T238387; **Inter Lagos**, at bus terminal, T240840, www.turismointerlagos.cl. Full list of buses from tourist information. Terminal at Lautaro and Magallanes, but few buses use this. Most leave from their own bus company offices.

To **Puerto Aisén**, minibuses run every 45 mins, 1 hr **Suray** and **Inter Lagos**, US$2. Suray continues to **Puerto Chacabuco**, 20 mins, US$0.75. To **Puerto Ibáñez** on Lago Gen Carrera, several minibus companies (connect with ferry to Chile Chico) pick up 0530-0600 from your hotel, 3 hrs, book the day before (eg **Dario Figueroa Castro**, T08-977 9737, **Miguel Acuña**, T251579, **Don Tito Segovia**, T250280), US$6.

Buses on the **Carretera Austral** vary according to demand, and they are always full so book early. Bikes can be taken by arrangement. North to **Chaitén**, Becker (T232167), M&C Tours (Parra 329, T242626) and **Daniela** (at terminal, T09-512 3500), between them 6 days a week, US$25; in winter these stop overnight in La Junta, only northbound buses stop at Pto Aisén. To **Puerto Cisnes**, Terra Austral (T254335), **Alegría** (T231350), Mon-Sat, US$10. South to **Cochrane** daily in summer with either **Don Carlos**, or **Inter Lagos**, US$15. All buses stop at **Cerro Castillo**. (US$5), **Bahía Murta** (US$10), **Puerto Tranquilo** (US$11) and **Puerto Bertrand** (US$15).
To Argentina: Giobbi, T232067, at Terminal Municipal, run buses **Comodoro Rivadavia**, US$30, via Sarmiento. Daily buses from Com Rivadavia to Bariloche. Other options are given under Balmaceda and Chile Chico.
Car hire If renting a car, a high 4WD vehicle is recommended for Carretera Austral. Buy fuel in Coyhaique, several stations. There are several rental agencies in town.
Ferry Navimag, Paseo Horn 47, T233306, F233386.
Taxi US$5 to airport (US$1.65 if sharing). Fares in town US$2, 50% extra after 2100. Taxi colectivos (shared taxis) congregate at Prat y Bilbao, average fare US$0.50.

Puerto Aisén and Puerto Chacabuco *p729*
Bus See under **Coyhaique**.
Ferry Navimag's Puerto Edén sails each Fri from Puerto Chacabuco to Puerto Montt, taking about 24 hrs (fares given under Sea routes south of Puerto Montt, page 713). It diverts from its schedule in summer to run a 5-day trip from Puerto Montt to Laguna San Rafael, calling at Puerto Chacabuco. Catamaranes del Sur also have sailings to Laguna San Rafael, US$299 for a 1-day trip, US$550 for 3 days. Shipping Offices: **Agemar**, Tte Merino 909, T332716, Puerto Aisén.

Catamaranes del Sur, J M Carrera 50, T351115, www.catamaranesdelsur.cl. **Navimag**, Terminal de Transbordadores, Puerto Chacabuco, T351111, F351192. It is best to make reservations in these companies' offices in Puerto Montt, Coyhaique or Santiago. For trips to Laguna San Rafael, see below (page 717).

Balmaceda *p730*
Air Balmaceda airport is used by LAN/Lan Express and Sky for flights from **Santiago** via **Puerto Montt** for Coyhaique. Don Carlos flies to **Chile Chico** US$41. Airlines run connecting bus services to/from Coyhaique, US$2 (leave town 2 hrs before flight). Minibuses to/from hotels, US$4.50, several companies. Taxi from airport to Coyhaique, 1 hr, US$6.
Bus Daily to **Coyhaique**, 0800, US$1.70.

Puerto Ibáñez *p730*
Bus Minibus to **Coyhaique**, 2½ hrs, US$6. There is a road to **Perito Moreno**, Argentina, but no public transport.
Ferry The car ferry, **Chelenco** sails from Puerto Ibañez to **Chile Chico**, daily in summer, less often otherwise, US$3 per adult, US$1.50 for bikes, cars US$45, uncomfortable 2½ hr crossing, take food and warm clothing, as the ferries are completely open. Passports required, reservations possible in Coyhaique: **Mar del Sur**, Baquedano 146A, T231255; in Chile Chico T411864. At the quay, Café El Refugio has toilets and sells sandwiches and snacks. Minibuses meet the ferry in Puerto Ibáñez for Coyhaique, and buses meet the ferry in Chile Chico for Los Antigos, see page 739.

Villa Cerro Castillo *p731*
Bus 6 a week in summer to both **Coyhaique** and **Cochrane**, Don Carlos, Inter Lagos (T258203) and **Amin Ali** (T09-313 1402).

❶ Directory

Coyhaique *p729, map p730*
Airline offices Aerohein, Baquedano 500, T232772, aerohein@entelchile.net. Don Carlos, address under Bus, above. LAN, Parra 402 , T600-526 2000. Sky, Prat 203, T240827.
Banks Several Redbanc ATMs in centre. Casas de cambio: Turismo Prado, see Tour operators. Emperador, Bilbao 222, T233727. **Bicycle rental** Figón, Simpson y Colón, T234616, check condition first, also sells spares. **Bicycle repairs** Tomás Madrid Urrea, Pasaje Foitzich y Libertad, F252132. Recommended.
Internet Cyber Patagonia, 21 de Mayo 525. Cheap, good. Another branch at Prat 360, p 2. Others in centre. **Language schools**

Baquedano International Language School, Baquedano 20, at Hospedaje de Sr Guzmán (see Sleeping), T232520, www.patagoniachile.cl/com/bils. US$300 per week course including lodging and all meals, 4 hrs a day one-to-one tuition, other activities organized at discount rates. **Post offices** Cochrane 202. **Telephones** Entel, Prat 340, also has internet access, US$1.35 per hr.

Puerto Aisén *p729*
Banks Banco de Crédito, Prat, for Visa. Banco de Chile, Plaza de Armas, changes cash, not TCs. Redbanc ATM in Puerto Chacabuco. **Post offices** on south side of bridge. **Telephones** On south side of Plaza de Armas, next to Café Rucaray, which posts boat information and has internet. Entel, Aldea 1202. Internet access.

Lago General Carrera and around

Southwest of Villa Cerro Castillo, the Carretera continues to afford stunning views, for instance minty-green Lago Verde and the meandering Río Manso, with swampy vegetation punctuated by the silver stumps of thousands of burnt trees, huge mountains behind. Lago General Carrera (Lago Buenos Aires in Argentina) straddles the border and, at 2,240 sq km, is the second largest lake in South America. It's an area of outstanding beauty. Sheltered from the icy west winds by the Campo de Hielo Norte, the region also has the best climate in Southern Chile, with little rain and some 300 days of sunshine. The lake crossing is by ferry between Chile Chico and Puerto Ibáñez (see above), but if you're not in a hurry, it's worth taking time to follow the Carretera Austral around the lake's western shores.

Bahía Murta (*Km 198, Population 586*), 5 km off the Camino, lies at the northern tip of the central 'arm' of the lake. There is a tiny tourist information hut, which opens summer 1000-1430, 1500-1930. Petrol is available from a house with a sign just before Puerto Murta. There's a public phone in the village.

Back on the Carretera Austral, **Puerto Río Tranquilo**, Km 223, is a slightly larger hamlet where the buses stop for lunch: fuel is available, with accommodation and meals in the house next door (see Sleeping, below). Capilla del Marmol, in fact a limestone cliff vaguely resembling sculpted caves, is reached by a wonderful boat ride (ask at petrol station, pay no more than US$30 per boat).

El Maitén, Km 273 south of Coihaique, an idyllic spot at the southwest tip of Lago Gen Carrera, is where a road branches off east along the south shore of the lake towards Chile Chico, while the Carretera Austral continues south to Puerto Bertand. There are two excellent places to stay, La Pasarela and Cabañas Mallín Colorado (see Sleeping, below). All Cochrane buses pass by the entrances to these establishments and will drop off/pick up passengers.

South of El Maitén the Carretera Austral becomes steeper and more winding (in winter this stretch, all the way to Cochrane, is icy and dangerous). At Km 284, is the hamlet of **Puerto Bertrand**, lying by the dazzling turquoise waters of Río Baker. As this river is world renowned for fly fishing, good accommodation in Puerto Bertrand is either in one of the luxury cabañas that cater for wealthy anglers, or is a simple room above the village shop and phone box Hostería Puerto Bertrand, see Sleeping, below).

At **Puerto Guadal**, 10 km east of El Maitén, there are shops, a post office, petrol and a lovely stretch of lakeside beach. Minibus to Chile Chico three to four a week in summer, fewer in winter. Further east are the villages of Mallín Grande (Km 40) and Fachinal (locals will let you stay for free if you have a sleeping bag). Parts of this road were built into the rock face, giving superb views, but also dangerous, unprotected precipices.

Chile Chico → *Population: 3,757.*

This is a quiet town in a fruit-growing region, 122 km east of El Maitén. It has an annual fruit festival at end-January. There are fine views from Cerro de las Banderas. It's 9 km to Los Antiguos, Argentina, where food and accommodation are preferable. **Laguna Jeinimeni**, 52 km from Chile Chico, is a beautiful place with excellent fishing, where you can also see flamingos and black necked swans. The **tourist office** (usually closed) is in the Casa de la Cultura on O'Higgins. An unofficial purple tourist kiosk on the quay where the ferry arrives, sells bus tickets for Ruta 40 (Argentina), but has some accommodation information. Municipal website: www.chilechico.cl.

Border with Argentina

Chilean immigration 2 km east of Chile Chico. Open 0800-2000. Argentine side closes for lunch 1300-1400. Remember that you can't take fresh food across in either direction, and you'll need ownership papers if crossing with a car.

Cochrane → *Population: 2,996.*

From Puerto Bertand heading south, the road climbs up to high moorland, passing the confluence of the Ríos Neff and Baker (there is a mirador – lookout – here), before winding into Cochrane, 343 km south of Coyhaique. The scenery is splendid all the way; the road is generally rough but not treacherous. Watch out for cattle on the road and take blind corners slowly. Sitting in a hollow on the Río Cochrane, Cochrane is a simple place, sunny in summer, good for walking and fishing. The **Reserva Nacional Lago Cochrane**, 12 km east, surrounds Lago Cochrane. Campsite at Playa Vidal. Boat hire on the lake costs US$12. Northeast of Cochrane is the beautiful **Reserva Nacional Tamango** ① *ask in the Conaf office about visiting because some access is through private land and tourist facilities are rudimentary, US$3*. It has lenga forest, a few surviving huemul deer as well as guanaco, foxes and lots of birds including woodpeckers and hummingbirds. Access 9 km northeast of Cochrane, along Río Cochrane. There are marked paths for walks between 45 minutes and five hours, up to Cerro Tamango (1,722 m) and Cerro Temanguito (1,485 m). Take water and food, and windproof clothing if climbing the Cerros. The views from the reserve are superb, over the town, the nearby lakes and to the Campo de Hielo Norte to the west. It is inaccessible in the four winter months. **Tourist office** ① *Esmerelda y Dr Steffens, T522115.*

Caleta Tortel → *Population: 448.*

The Carretera Austral runs south of Cochrane and, after 105km, at the rather bleak looking Puerto Vagabundo, the road branches west to Caleta Tortel. This quiet village at the mouth of the river, was until very recently accessible only by water and has no streets, only walkways of cypress wood (slippery when wet). Surrounded by mountainous land with abundant vegetation, it has a cool, rainy climate, and its main trade is logging, though this is declining as the town looks towards tourism. Located between the Northern and Southern Ice Fields, Tortel is within reach of two glaciers: **Glaciar Steffens** is to the north, a three-hour boat journey and 2½-hour walk, crossing a glacial river in a rowing boat. A speedboat for nine people costs US$100 and a lancha US$120 for 12. **Glaciar Jorge Montt** is to the south, five hours by lancha through landscapes of pure ice and water, US$220 for 12 people, two hours by speedboat, US$170 for nine. Another boat trip is to the Isla de los Muertos, which has an interesting history. There is a post office, open Monday-Friday 0830-1330. For all information and boat charters, contact the Municipality, T/F067-211876. The phone office number is T234815.

Villa O'Higgins

The Carretera Austral runs to Puerto Yungay (122 km from Cochrane), then another 110 km to **Villa O'Higgins**. There is one free ferry crossing between Yungay (military base) and Río Bravo (1000, 1200, 1500 from Yungay, return 1100, 1300, 1600, 4-5 cars). The road beyond Río Bravo is very beautiful, but often closed by bad weather (take food – no shops on the entire route, few people and few vehicles for hitching). Tourist information is available from the Municipalidad, Lago Christie 121, T/F067-211849, www.villaohiggins.cl. **Conaf**, Av Lago Cisnes s/n, T211849.

It is possible to go from Villa O'Higgins to El Chaltén, Argentina. The road continues 7 km south to Bahía Bahamóndez on Lago O'Higgins (bus US$3), from where a boat leaves three times a week in summer, 3 hours, US$35, to Chilean immigration at Candelario Mancila ① *open Nov-Apr 0800-2200*. Then you have to trek or ride 14 km to the Argentine border (US$20 on horseback) and a further 5 km to Argentine immigration on Lago del Desierto. Then you take a boat across the lake, US$20, and finally a bus to El Chaltén, US$12. With this combination of bus, boat and horse this can be done in a day (depart Villa O'Higgins 0800, arrive El Chaltén 2130; full details on www.villaohiggins.cl). You can pay for each portion of the route separately. The route closes in late April. (Boats on Lago O'Higgins also make excursions to the O'Higgins and Chico glaciers.) With the opening of this route it is possible to do the Carretera Austral and go on to Argentina's Parque Nacional Los Glaciares and Chile's Torres del Paine without doubling back on yourself.

Parque Nacional Laguna San Rafael

ⓘ *US$6, at the glacier there is a small ranger station which gives information; a pier and 2 paths have been built, one path leads to the glacier.*

Some 150 nautical miles south of Puerto Aisén is the **Laguna San Rafael**, into which flows a glacier, 30 m above sea level and 45 km in length. The glacier has a deep blue colour, shimmering and reflecting the light. It calves small icebergs, which seem an unreal, translucent blue, and which are carried out to sea by wind and tide. The glacier is very noisy; there are frequent cracking and banging sounds, resembling a mixture of gunshots and thunder. When a hunk of ice breaks loose, a huge swell is created and the icebergs start rocking in the water. The glacier is disintegrating and is predicted not to last beyond 2011. Some suggest that the wake from tour boats is contributing to the erosion.

The thick vegetation on the shores, with snowy peaks above, is typical of Aisén. The only access is by plane or by boat. The glacier is equally spectacular from the air or the sea. The glacier is one of a group of four that flow in all directions from Monte San Valentín. This icefield is part of the Parque Nacional Laguna San Rafael (1,740,000 ha), regulated by Conaf. In the national park are puma, pudú (miniature deer), foxes, dolphins, occasional sealions and sea otters, and many species of bird. Walking trails are limited (about 10 km in all) but a lookout platform has been constructed, with fine views of the glacier.

● Sleeping

Lago General Carrera *p736*
Bahía Murta
E Residencial Patagonia, Pje España 64, Bahía Murta, T419600. Comfortable, serves food. Free camping by lake at Bahía Murta.

Puerto Río Tranquilo
B Hostal Los Pinos, 2 Oriente 41, Puerto Río Tranquilo, T411576. Better value lodging than Hostería Costanera.
C Hostería Costanera, next to bus stop, Puerto Río Tranquilo, T411121. Basic, overpriced, with breakfast.
E Cabañas Jacricalor, before the bridge, Puerto Río Tranquilo, T419500 (public phone). Hot shower, good meals, good information for climbers.

El Maitén
AL Cabañas Mallín Colorado, Carretera Austral Km 273, El Maitén, T(02) 234 1843, www.patagonia- pacific.cl. Comfortable cabañas in sweeping gardens, complete tranquillity, charming owners, 4-day packages available, including transfers from Balmaceda, horseriding, estancia trip, superb meals. Highly recommended.
A La Pasarela, just after the bright orange suspension bridge, El Maitén, T411425, utipatagonia@hotmail.com. Small comfortable rooms with bath, lakeside setting, welcoming staff, delicious food.
E pp Hospedaje (yellow house, unnamed), Mallín Grande, ask at the shop on the main road to Chile Chico. Basic, without breakfast, bathroom without shower, use of kitchen, very helpful owners.

Puerto Bertrand
AL Patagonia Baker Lodge and Restaurant, Puerto Bertrand, towards the south side of the lake, T411903, www.pbl.cl. Stylish cabañas in woodland, fishing lodge, fabulous views upriver towards rapids and the mountains beyond.
AL Río Baker Lodge, Puerto Bertrand, T411499, riobaker@hotmail.com. Full board, warmly recommended fishing lodge, also all-inclusive fishing packages.
C pp Hostería Campo Baker, Puerto Bertrand, T411447. Family cabañas in a woodland setting, boats, horse riding, and of course, fishing.
E Hospedaje Doña Ester, Casa No 8, Puerto Bertrand, T419900. Rooms in a pink house, good.
E pp Hostería Puerto Bertrand, Puerto Bertrand, T419900. With breakfast, other meals available, activities.

Puerto Guadal
AL Terra Luna Lodge, on lakeside, 2 km from Puerto Guadal, T431263, www.terra-luna.cl. Welcoming well-run place with restaurant.
A El Mirador Playa Guadal, 2 km from Puerto Guadal towards Chile Chico, T431222, www.patagoniaplayaguadal.cl. Cabañas near beach, fishing, walks to nearby waterfalls. Recommended.
D Hostería Huemules, Las Magnolias 382, Puerto Guadal, T431212. Breakfast, good views.
Camping Site at east end of village.

Chile Chico *p736*
D Hostería de la Patagonia, Camino Internacional s/n, Casilla 91, T411337, F411444. Good food, English, French and Italian spoken, trekking, horse-riding and whitewater rafting. Recommended.

66 99 The glacier is very noisy; there are frequent cracking and banging sounds, resembling a mixture of gunshots and thunder...

E pp Casa Quinta No me Olvides/Manor House Don't Forget Me, Sector Chacras, Camino Internacional s/n, T833 8006. Hospedaje and camping, cooking facilities, bathrooms, hot showers, honey, eggs, fruit and vegetables for sale, tours arranged to Lago Jeinimeni and Cueva de las Manos. Recommended.
E pp Hosp Don Luis, Balmaceda 175, T411384. Meals available, laundry service, helpful.
E pp Hospedaje at Tel Sur phone centre, in the middle of O'Higgins. Use of kitchen, helpful owners also sell bus tickets for La Unión buses to Los Antiguos and Comodoro Rivadavia.
Camping Free site at Bahía Jara, 5 km west of Chile Chico, then turn north for 12 km.

Cochrane *p737*
In summer it is best to book rooms in advance.
A Hostería Wellmann, Las Golondrinas 36, T/F522171. Comfortable, warm, good meals. Recommended.
D Residencia Cero a Cero, Lago Brown 464, T522158. With breakfast, welcoming.
D Res Rubio, Tte Merino 4, T522173. Very nice, breakfast included, lunch and dinner extra.
E pp Café Rogeri, Tte Merino 502, T522264. Cabañas, price includes breakfast, but principally an eating place.
E Res Cochrane, Dr Steffens 51, T522377. Also serves dinner, US$4.25, laundry, camping, hot shower, breakfast. Recommended. Also camping.
E Res El Fogón, San Valentín 651, T522240. Its pub is the only eating place open in low season, it's the best restaurant at any time of year.
E Res Sur Austral, Prat 334, T522150. Breakfast included, also very nice.

Caleta Tortel *p737*
There are several *hospedajes*. All prices are cheaper in the low season. For all T067-234815 (public phone).
E pp Hostal Costanera, Sra Luisa Escobar Sanhueza. Cosy, warm, attractive, lovely garden, full board US$21, breakfast US$2-2.50.
F pp Hosp Casa Rural Sra Elisa Urrutia Iníquez, full board US$18, breakfast US$2-2.50.
Camping Free site near the beach, 15-mins' walk south of main plaza, cold showers, drinking water, long drop, fire places and cooking area.

Villa O'Higgins *p737*
There are various cabañas and private lodgings.
E pp Hospedaje Patagonia, Río Pascua 191 y Lago Christie, T234813.
E pp Hospedaje y Residencial Apocalipsis 1:3, Pasaje Lago El Salto 345, T216927 or 234813. Good value.

🍴 Eating

Lago General Carrera *p736*
† † El Récor, Bahía Murta. Meals available here, US$4 for lunch.

Chile Chico *p736*
Cafés
Café Refer, O'Higgins 416. Good, despite the exterior.
Cafetería Loly y Elizabeth, PA González 25, on Plaza serves coffee and delicious ice cream and cakes.
   Also try the supermarket on B O'Higgins for lunch.

Caleta Tortel *p737*
Café Celes Salom, bar/restaurant serving basic meals, club night on Sat, occasional live bands.

🅰 Activities and tours

Cochrane *p737*
Don Pedro Muñoz, Los Ñadis 110, T522244, F522245. Hires horses for excursions in the surrounding countryside. Recommended. There are other places for horse hire.
Samuel Smiol, T522487. Offers tours to the icefields and mountains, English spoken.

⊖ Transport

Chile Chico *p736*
Bus Seguel, T431214, Mon, Fri to **Puerto Guadal**, US$10. See above for ferry to Puerto Ibáñez and connecting minibus to Coyhaique.

Border with Argentina: Chile Chico-Los Antiguos *p737*
Bus In summer, minibuses run from Chile Chico ferry to Los Antiguos on the Argentine side, US$3

(can pay in Argentine pesos), ½-1 hr including formalities: ask on quayside. **Trans Acuña**, T411553. Beware pirate vehicles which don't have the correct papers for crossing to Argentina.

Cochrane *p737*
Air Don Carlos to **Coyhaique**, Mon, Fri, US$70; also from **Balmaceda**.
Bus Company agencies: **Don Carlos**, Prat 344, T522150; **Los Ñadis**, Los Helechos 490, T522196. There are buses 6 days a week between Coyhaique and Cochrane, check with companies for current timetables, US$20. To **Villa O'Higgins**, Los Ñadis, Mon 0930, via Vagabundo, return Tue 0930, US$11. To **Tortel**, Acuario 13, Río Baker 349, T522143, daily US$10. Petrol is available, if it hasn't run out, at the **Empresa Comercial Agrícola** (ECA) and at the **Copec** station.

Caleta Tortel *p737*
Bus From **Cochrane**, see above.
Ferry Once a month there is a boat from Tortel to **Puerto Edén** (US$3, 24 hrs, rough, cold and uncomfortable, but very interesting). For the adventurous traveller who gets the timing right (ask the Municipalidad in Tortel in advance), you can catch the Navimag boat in Puerto Edén and continue to Puerto Natales. By going in stages from Puerto Montt to Tortel on the Carretera Austral, this works out cheaper than taking Navimag all the way.

Parque Nacional Laguna San Rafael *p738*
Air Taxi from Coyhaique (Aerohein), US$200 each if party of 5. Charters are also run by **Don Carlos**. The flights, which can be very rough, give a fine view before landing, after which there is a launch trip (5 hrs in all).
Ferry Cruises are run by : **Skorpios** (see under Puerto Montt); **Catamaranes del Sur**, **Compañía Naviera Puerto Montt** and **Navimag**'s Puerto Edén. Patagonia Express runs catamaran trips from Puerto Chacabuco to Laguna San Rafael via Termas de Puyuhuapi, in tours lasting 4-6 days, from Puerto Montt via Coyhaique including the catamaran service, the hotel stay at Termas de Puyuhuapi and the day excursion to Laguna San Rafael (see page 717). Also **Iceberg Express**, Av Providencia 2331, of 602, Santiago, T02-335 0580, 12-hr luxury cruises. Other charters are available. Private yachts can be chartered in Puerto Montt for 6-12 passengers.

❶ Directory

Chile Chico *p736*
Banks It's best to change money in Coyhaique. ATM in the middle of O'Higgins for Mastercard and Cirrus, not Visa. Dollars and Argentine pesos can be changed in small amounts in shops and cafés, including Loly y Elizabeth, at poor rates.
Post offices On the plaza.

Far south

This wild and wind-blown area, covering the glacial regions of southern Patagonia and Chilean Tierra del Fuego, is beautiful and bleak, with stark mountains and open steppe. Little vegetation survives here and few people; though it represents 17.5% of Chile's total area, it is inhabited by under 1% of the population. The southernmost city of Punta Arenas and the attractive, quiet port of Puerto Natales are the two main centres, the latter being the gateway to the Torres del Paine and Balmaceda national parks. In summer it is a wonderful region for climbing, hiking, boat trips and the southernmost crossings to Argentina.

Summers are sunny and very variable, with highs of 15° C. In winter snow covers the country, except those parts near the sea, making many roads more or less impassable, except on horseback. Cold, piercing winds blow, particularly in spring, when they may exceed 100 kph. Despite chilly temperatures, protection against the sun's ultraviolet rays is essential here and in summer, too, windproof clothing is a must.

Punta Arenas and around

→ *Phone code: 061. Colour map 9, grid C2. Population: Punta Arenas 150,000, Puerto Natales 20,500.*
About 2,140 km south of Santiago, Punta Arenas lies on the eastern shore of the Brunswick Peninsula facing the Straits of Magellan at almost equal distance from the Pacific and Atlantic oceans. Founded in 1843, it has grand neoclassical buildings and an opulent cemetery, testimony to its wealthy past as a major port and centre for exporting wool. In the late 19th

century, Salesian Missions were established to control the indigenous population so sheep farming could flourish. The city's fortunes slumped when the Panama Canal opened in 1924, but it remains a pleasant place, with attractive, painted wooden buildings away from the centre and superb fish restaurants. Good roads connect the city with Puerto Natales, 247 km north, and with Río Gallegos in Argentina.

Ins and outs

Tourist office Sernatur ① *Magallanes 960, T225385, infomagallanes@sernatur.cl. 0830-1745, closed Sat and Sun.* Much more helpful is the tourist information **kiosk** in the plaza, opposite Centro Español, T200610. Friendly staff, good town map with all hotels and

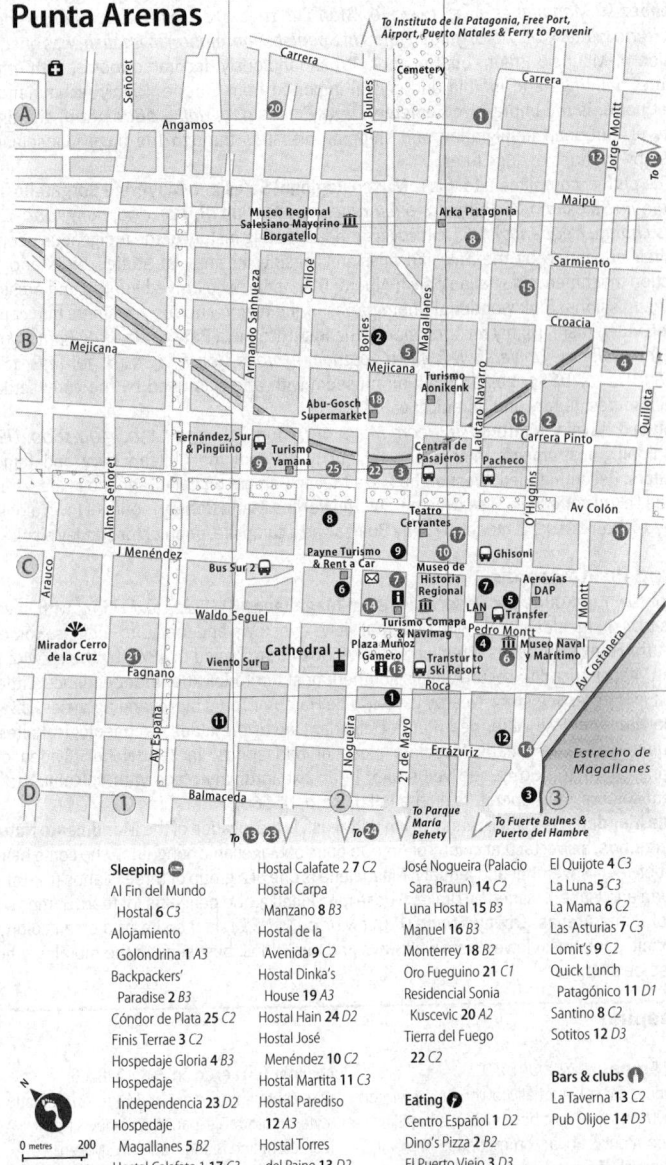

Punta Arenas

To Instituto de la Patagonia, Free Port, Airport, Puerto Natales & Ferry to Porvenir

Estrecho de Magallanes

To Parque María Behety

To Fuerte Bulnes & Puerto del Hambre

0 metres 200
0 yards 200

Sleeping
Al Fin del Mundo Hostal 6 *C3*
Alojamiento Golondrina 1 *A3*
Backpackers' Paradise 2 *B3*
Cóndor de Plata 25 *C2*
Finis Terrae 3 *C2*
Hospedaje Gloria 4 *B3*
Hospedaje Independencia 23 *D2*
Hospedaje Magallanes 5 *B2*
Hostal Calafate 1 17 *C3*

Hostal Calafate 2 7 *C2*
Hostal Carpa Manzano 8 *B3*
Hostal de la Avenida 9 *C2*
Hostal Dinka's House 19 *A3*
Hostal Hain 24 *D2*
Hostal José Menéndez 10 *C2*
Hostal Martita 11 *C3*
Hostal Paredizo 12 *A3*
Hostal Torres del Paine 13 *D2*

José Nogueira (Palacio Sara Braun) 14 *C2*
Luna Hostal 15 *B3*
Manuel 16 *B3*
Monterrey 18 *B2*
Oro Fueguino 21 *C1*
Residencial Sonia Kuscevic 20 *A2*
Tierra del Fuego 22 *C2*

Eating
Centro Español 1 *D2*
Dino's Pizza 2 *B2*
El Puerto Viejo 3 *D3*

El Quijote 4 *C3*
La Luna 5 *C3*
La Mama 6 *C2*
Las Asturias 7 *C3*
Lomit's 9 *C2*
Quick Lunch Patagónico 11 *D1*
Santino 8 *C2*
Sotitos 12 *D3*

Bars & clubs
La Taverna 13 *C2*
Pub Olijoe 14 *D3*

internet places marked, English spoken. Monday-Friday 0800-1900, Saturday 0900-1900, Sunday 0900-1300, informacionturistica@puntaarenas.cl. If coming from Argentina, note that Chile is twice as expensive. **Conaf**, Av Bulnes 0309, p 4, T238554, magallan@conaf.cl.

Sights

In the centre of the **Plaza Muñoz Gamero** is a striking statue of Magellan with a mermaid and two indigenous Fuegians at his feet. Around the plaza are a number of impressive neo-classical buildings, the former mansions of the great sheep ranching families of the late 19th century. **Palacio Sara Braun** (1895), now a hotel, has elegant rooms which are open to the public. Around the corner, on Magallanes is the **Teatro Cervantes** (now a cinema with beautifully decorated interior). The fascinating **Museo de Historia Regional Braun Menéndez** ① *Magallanes 949, T244216, Mon-Sat 1030-1700, Sun 1030-1400 summer (1100-1300 winter), US$1.50, guided tours in Spanish, information in English*, was once the mansion of Mauricio Braun, built in 1905. It has fabulously decorated rooms, with ornate furniture, paintings and marble and crystal imported from Europe. Highly recommended. Further north, is the impressive **Cemetery** ① *Av Bulnes 929, daily, 0800-1800*, charting a history of European immigration and shipping disasters through the huge mausoleums, divided by avenues of huge trees.

The perfect compliment to this is **Museo Regional Salesiano Mayorino Borgatello** ① *in the Colegio Salesiano, Av Bulnes 336 (entrance next to church), T241096, daily 1000-1800 (hours change frequently), US$2*. It covers the fascinating history of the indigenous peoples and their education by the Salesian missions, beside an array of stuffed birds and gas extraction machinery. The Italian priest, Alberto D'Agostini, who arrived in 1909 and presided over the missions, took wonderful photographs of the region and his 70-minute film can be seen on video (ask). Highly recommended. The **Instituto de la Patagonia** ① *Av Bulnes Km 4 north (opposite the University), T244216, outdoor exhibits Mon-Fri 0830-1130, 1430-1830, Sat 0830-1230, US$2*, has an open-air museum with artefacts used by the early settlers, pioneer homes, library and botanical gardens.

Museo Naval y Marítimo ① *Pedro Montt 981, Mon-Sat 0930-1230, 1500-1800, US$1*, has shipping instruments, maps, photos and relics from the Chilean navy and famous navigators. Recommended. West of the Plaza Muñoz Gamero on Calle Fagnano is the Mirador Cerro de La Cruz offering a view over the city. The **Parque María Behety**, south of town along 21 de Mayo, features a scale model of Fuerte Bulnes and a campsite, popular for Sunday picnics.

Around Punta Arenas

West of town (9 km) is the **Reserva Forestal Magallanes** ① *US$2, taxi US$4*, with several places to visit, including a hill with beautiful views over town and the surroundings. Some 56 km south, **Fuerte Bulnes** is a replica of the wooden fort erected in 1843 by the crew of the Chilean vessel Ancud to secure Chile's southernmost territories after Independence. Little to see but an interesting story. Nearby is Puerto de Hambre. Tours by several agencies, US$12. **Parque Nacional Pali Aike**, near Punta Delgada. One of the oldest archaeological sites in Patagonia (Pali Aike means 'desolate place of bad spirits' in Tehuelche). Evidence of aborigines from 10,000-12,000 years ago, in an extraordinary place with volcanic rock of different colours. Tour operators offer a full day trip, US$60.

Isla Magdalena, a small island 30 km northeast, is the location of the **Monumento Natural Los Pingüinos**, a spectacular colony of 60,000 pairs of Magellanic penguins, who come here to breed between November and January. Magdalena is one of a group of three islands (the others are Marta and Isabel), visited by Drake, whose men killed 3,000 penguins for food. Some 70 km north of Punta Arenas, **Otway Sound** ① *Oct-Mar only, US$4*, is the site of a small colony of Magellanic penguins, viewed from walkways and bird hides, best seen in the morning. Rheas can also be seen.

◉ Sleeping

Punta Arenas *p740, map p741*
Hotel prices are substantially lower during winter months (Apr-Sep). Most hotels include breakfast in the room price. For accommodation in private houses, usually **E** pp, ask at the tourist office.

LL Finis Terrae, Colón 766, T228200, www.hotelfinisterrae.com. Modern, international style, comfortable, panoramic views from restaurant and lounge, English spoken. Recommended.

LL José Nogueira, Plaza de Armas, Bories 959 y P Montt, in former Palacio Sara Braun, T248840, www.hotelnogueira.com. Best in town, stylish rooms, warm atmosphere, excellent service. Smart restaurant in the beautiful loggia. A few original rooms now a 'museum', with a portrait of Sara Braun (1000-1300, 1800-2030, US$2).

L Tierra del Fuego, Colón 716, T/F226200, www.patagoniahotels.com. Spacious, tasteful, TV, 2nd floor rooms have kitchenette. Popular Café 1900 downstairs, excellent restaurant open to non residents. Recommended.

A Cóndor de Plata, Av Colón 556, T247987, www.condordeplata.cl. Named after the aeroplane of German aviator and explorer Günther Plüschow, with relics, hot water, TV, café, laundry service, internet.

A Res Sonia Kuscevic, Pasaje Darwin 175, T248543, www.hostalsk.50megs.com. With breakfast, kitchen facilities, hot water, heating, parking. Good discount with Hostelling International card.

A-B Hostal de la Avenida, Colón 534, T247532. Attractive rooms, TV, pretty courtyard, welcoming.

B Hostal Carpa Manzano, Lautaro Navarro 336, T/F248864, carpamanzano@tie.cl. Comfortable rooms, quiet area. Recommended.

B Oro Fueguino, Fagnano 356, T061-249401, www.orofueguino.cl. Well-appointed and decorated, TV and phone, recommended. Often fills up with groups so book ahead.

B-C Hostal Calafate 2, Magallanes 926, T/F241281, www.calafate.cl. Rather shambolic, with simple rooms and dodgy bathrooms, on a noisy road but central, overpriced, internet, travel agency, English spoken. Also **Hostal Calafate 1**, Latuaro Navarro 850, T/F248415, same price, quieter.

C Hostal José Menéndez, José Menéndez 882, T/F221279. Convenient for Ushuaia bus, family-run, helpful, also dormitory.

C-D Hostal Dinka's House, Caupolicán 169, T244292, www.dinkashouse.cl. With bath, breakfast, use of kitchen, laundry, internet.

C-D Hostal Paradiso, Angamos 1073A, T224212. Lovely simple place, breakfast, parking, use of kitchen, great value, welcoming. Recommended.

D Hospedaje Magallanes, Magallanes 570, T228616. Nice rooms with shared bath, relaxed atmosphere. Recommended.

D Hostal Torres del Paine, Chiloé 1370 e Independencia, T245211. **E** with shared bath, lots of space in family home with 2 kitchens, luggage store, big sitting room.

D pp Luna Hostal, O'Higgins 424, hostalluna@hotmail.com. Quiet house with delightful rooms, comfy beds with duvets.

E pp Al Fin del Mundo Hostal, O'Higgins 1026, T710185, alfindelmundo@123.cl. Lovely house 2 blocks from plaza, run by young Chilean couple, shared bath, with breakfast, welcoming and helpful, English spoken, laundry, internet. Highly recommended.

E pp Alojamiento Golondrina, Lautaro Navarro 182, T229708. Hot water, kitchen facilities, meals served, English spoken. Recommended.

E pp Hosp Gloria, Mejicana 1174, T227678. Shared bath, good showers, quiet, use of kitchen.

E Hospedaje Independencia, Independencia 374, T227572, independencia@chileaustral.com. Use of kitchen, laundry. Highly recommended. Also good value cabañas away from the centre.

E Hostal Hain, José Nogueira 1600, remezona@hotmail.com. Convenient, secure, helpful, English spoken, kitchen facilities and internet, good.

E pp Hostal Martita, Colón 1195, T223131, alojamientobetty@hotmail.com. Without bath, good.

E pp Manuel, O'Higgins 646-8, T245441, turmanmi@entelchile.net. Big dormitories, kitchen, hot shower.

E pp Monterrey, Bories 621, T220636, monterrey@turismoaventura.net. Tiny rooms with TV, clothes washing, use of kitchen, comfortable, charming people, great breakfast.

F pp Backpackers' Paradise, Carrera Pinto 1022, T240104, backpackersparadise@hotmail.com. Popular, limited bathroom facilities, only curtains dividing the large dorms, not exactly comfortable, cooking and laundry facilities, internet, luggage store, can book *refugios* in Torres del Paine.

F pp Ely House, Caupolicán 75, T226660. Lovely, with breakfast, comfortable, heating and hot water, kitchen, collect from airport.

F pp Hosp Miramar, Almte Senoret 1190, T061-215446. Rooms and dorms, helpful staff, good breakfast, good views over the bay.

🍴 Eating

Punta Arenas *p740, map p741*

Many eating places close Sun. Some of the main hotels have good value set lunches and dinners. **Note**: *Centolla* (king crab) is caught illegally by some fishermen using dolphin, porpoise and penguin as live bait. There are seasonal bans on centolla fishing to protect dwindling stocks, do not purchase centolla out of season. At times centolla fishing is banned if the crabs are infected

---

For an explanation of the sleeping and eating price codes used in this guide, see inside the front cover. Other relevant information is found in Essentials pages 604-605.

with red tide, *marea roja*) a disease which is fatal to humans, and at these times bivalve shellfish must not be eaten. Mussels should not be picked along the shore because of pollution and the marea roja. Sernatur and the Centros de Salud have leaflets.

₸₸₸ El Puerto Viejo, O'Higgins 1205, T225103.Good seafood and pastas in bright, chic nautical surroundings.

₸₸₸-₸₸ Sotitos, O'Higgins 1138. An institution, famous for seafood in elegant surroundings. Book ahead in season.

₸₸ Las Asturias, Navaro 967. Recommended for seafood, imaginative Basque-inspired menu with meat dishes too, good value and service, popular with locals. Recommended.

₸₸ Centro Español, Plaza Muñoz Gamero 771, above Teatro Cervantes. Large helpings, limited selection.

₸₸ La Luna, O'Higgins 974. Fish, shellfish and local specialities, popular.

₸₸ La Mama, Sanhueza 720. Small *rotisería*, warm, friendly and convenient for buses.

₸₸ Santino, Colón 657. Good pizzas, large bar, good service.

₸₸ Quick Lunch Patagónico, Sanhueza 1198. Good, Mexican, vegetarian and Chinese.

₸ Dino's Pizza, Bories 557. Good value pizza in a cheerful fast food atmosphere. Lots of choice.

₸ El Quijote, Lautaro Navarro 1087. Good sandwiches and mid-range dinners, bright atmosphere. Recommended.

₸ Lomit's, Menéndez 722. Cheap snacks and drinks, open when the others are closed.

❶ Bars and clubs

Punta Arenas *p740, map p741*
Drive-In Los Brujos, Costanera, Km 7.5, T212600. Large disco.
Kamikaze, Bories 655. Popular club with visitors. Recommended.
Pub Olijoe, O'Higgins 1138. Like a traditional British pub, just off the Costanera, for beer in a lively atmosphere.
La Taverna, on the plaza at Magallanes y Roca. Good for evening drinks.

❂ Shopping

Punta Arenas *p740, map p741*
Punta Arenas has certain free-port facilities; but Zona Franca, 3½ km north of the centre, opposite Museo Instituto de la Patagonia, is not much cheaper than elsewhere. Closed 1230- 1500 and Sun (bus E or A from Plaza Muñoz Gamero; many colectivo taxis; taxi US$3).
Food and drink Cava de la Patagonia, Magallanes on the Plaza. For Chilean wines.

Chocolatta, Bories 852. Tasty handmade chocolate.
Handicrafts Artesanías Ñandú, O'Higgins 1401, **Artesanía Ramas**, Independencia 799, **Chile Típico**, Carrera Pinto 1015 and outdoor stalls at the bottom of Independencia, by the port entrance.
Outdoor clothing and camping Fagnano 675. Good quality clothes and wool goods. **Danilo** Jordán, O'Higgins 1120. For camping gas canisters.
Supermarkets Abu-Gosch, Bories 647, open daily 0900-2200. **Cofrima 2**, España 01375, 2 km from town. **Listo**, 21 de Mayo 1133. **Marisol**, Zenteno 0164.

▲ Activities and tours

Punta Arenas *p740, map p741*
Skiing Cerro Mirador, only 9 km west of Punta Arenas in the Reserva Nacional Magallanes, one of the few places where one can ski with a sea view. **Transtur** buses 0900 and 1400 from in front of Hotel Cabo de Hornos, US$3, return, taxi US$7. Daily lift pass, US$7; equipment rental, US$6. Mid-way lodge with food, drink and equipment. Season Jun-Sep, weather permitting. In summer there is a good 2-hr walk on the hill, with labelled flora. Contact **Club Andino**, T241479, about cross-country skiing facilities. Also skiing at Tres Morros.

Tour operators
Most tour operators organize trips to Torres del Paine, Fuerte Bulnes and the pingüinera on Otway sound.
Arka Patagonia, Magallanes 345, T248167, www.arkaoperadora.com. All types of tours, rafting, fishing, etc.
Payne Turismo y Rent a car, Menéndez 631, T240852, www.payne.cl. Treks to San Isidro lighthouse, birdwatching, Pali Aike all-day trips, Estancia Punta Delgada, including lunch, car hire.
Turismo Aonikenk, Magallanes 619, T228332, www.aonikenk.com. Excellent tailor-made, multi adventure and trekking tours for all levels of fitness, top of the market, French, German, English spoken. Highly recommended.
Turismo Aventour, J Nogueira 1255, T241197, aventour@entelchile.net. Specialize in fishing trips, organize tours to Tierra del Fuego, helpful, English spoken.
Turismo Comapa, Magallanes 990, T200200, www.comapa.com. Tours to Torres del Paine (responsible, well-informed guides), Tierra del Fuego and to see the penguins at Isla Magdalena. Also sell tickets for sailings Puerto Montt to Puerto Natales. Agents for Cruceros Australis (see below).
Turismo Yamana, Errázuriz 932, T710567, www.yamana.cl. Conventional tours, trekking in Torres del Paine, kayaking in the Magellan straits, multilingual guides, camping equipment provided. Recommended.

Viento Sur, Fagnano 585, T225167, www.viento sur.com. Horse riding, kayaking in the Magellan straits, and hiking at Pale Aike, mountain biking up Mt Fenton, plus Torres del Paine, good tours.

⊖ Transport

Punta Arenas *p740, map p741*
All transport is heavily booked from Christmas to Mar: advance booking strongly advised.
Air Carlos Ibáñez de Campo Airport, 20 km north of town. Bus service by **Buses Transfer**, Pedro Montt 966, T229613, scheduled to meet flights, US$2.50. Buses to **Puerto Natales** also stop. **DAP** have their own bus service to town, US$4. Taxi US$12. To **Santiago**, **LAN** and **Lan Express** daily, via **Puerto Montt** and **Temuco**. When no tickets are available, go to the airport and get on the standby list. To **Porvenir**, **Aerovías DAP** twice daily Mon-Sat, 12 mins, US$23. To **Puerto Williams**, twice weekly in summer, 1 hr, US$70. Also Puerto Natales-El Calafate (see below) and Antarctic trips including simple accommodation: Isla Rey Jorge 1 day, 2 days to 4 days, US$3,800. Services to Argentina: To **Ushuaia**, DAP twice a week, US$110 (schedules change frequently). **Note**: Take passport when booking tickets to Argentina.
Bus There's no central bus terminal; buses leave from company offices. Company offices: **Pingüino**, T221812, **Sur** and **Fernández**, Sanhueza 745, T242313, www.buses ernandez.com. **Pacheco**, Colón 900, T242174, www.busespacheco.com; Central de Pasajeros, Colón y Magallanes, T245811, office for booking all tickets, including Sur, T244464. **Bus Sur 2**, Menéndez 565, T242078. **Ghisoni**, Lautaro Navarro 971, T222078. Bus services: To **Puerto Natales**, 3½ hrs, **Fernández**, **Bus Sur**, and **Buses Transfer** several every day, last departure 2000, US$5.70, with pick-up at the airport, US$7.50. **Ghisoni** and **Austral** have services through Argentina to **Osorno** and **Puerto Montt**. Fares: to Puerto Montt or Osorno US$55 (cheaper off season), 36 hrs.
To **Río Gallegos**, Argentina, via Punta Delgada, **Pingüino** daily; **Ghisoni**, Mon, Wed, Thu, Sat; **Pacheco**, Sun, Tue, Fri. Fares US$9-12, officially 5 hrs, but can take up to 8, depending on customs, 15 mins on Chilean side, up to 2 hrs on Argentine side, including 30 mins lunch at Km 160. To **Río Grande** and **Ushuaia** via **Punta Delgada** (none via Porvenir) **Pacheco** and **Austral**, 7-9 hrs, US$20, heavily booked. US$29 to Ushuaia, 12-14 hrs. Book well in advance in Jan-Feb.
To **Otway Sound**: Bus with **Fernández** 1530, return 1930, US$12. Tours by several agencies, US$17, entry US$4. Useful tour goes on to

Puerto Natales, daily with **Patagonia Adventure Leaders** (see below).
Car hire Payne, José Menéndez 631, T245331, www.payne.cl **Internacional**, Waldo Seguel 443, T228323. **Note**: You need a hire company's authorization to take a car into Argentina. This takes 24 hrs (not Sat or Sun) and involves mandatory international insurance at US$240.
Ferry Services to **Porvenir** (Tierra del Fuego), daily except Mon, 0900, Sun 0930. Same boat goes on to penguin colony at **Isla Magdalena** (until Mar). US$35, includes guide: Agencia Broom, Bulnes 5075 (Tres Puentes), through Comapa, see Tour operators, above.
Shipping offices: Navimag, in the same office as **Comapa** Compañía Marítima de Punta Arenas), Magallanes 990, T200200, www.navimag.cl, www.comapa.com. **Shipping Services**: For Navimag services Puerto Montt-Puerto Natales, see under Puerto Montt (confirmation of reservations is advised). Highly recommended is the cruise from Punta Arenas through the Magellan Straits and the 'avenue of glaciers' to Ushuaia, Puerto Williams and Cape Horn on Mare Australis. Lots of opportunities to disembark and see wildlife, very comfortable, unforgettable experience. 7-12 days, can just go as far as Ushuaia. Details from Comapa, and www.australis.com US$1,600 in summer for 2 people. Advance booking (advisable) from **Cruceros Australis SA**, Santiago office, T02-442 3110, Buenos Aires office, T011-4325 8400.
To **Antarctica**: See under Santiago Tour Operators, page 620, otherwise, the only possibility is with the Chilean Navy. The Navy itself does not encourage passengers, so you must approach the captain direct. Spanish is essential. Two vessels, Galvarino and Lautaro, sail regularly (no schedule); usual rate US$80 pp per day, including 4 meals. isotop@mitierra.cl.
To **Monumento Natural Los Pingüinos**: The boat of Agencia Broom (see Ferries to Tierra del Fuego, below) booked through Comapa (see Activities and tours), sails on Tue, Thu and Sat at 1530 (Dec-Feb only), 2 hrs each way with 1 hr on the island. It returns at 2100, US$30; take your own refreshments, as they are expensive on board. Highly recommended, but the trip may be cancelled if it's windy.
Taxi Ordinary taxis have yellow roofs. Colectivos (all black) run on fixed routes, US$0.50 for anywhere on route. Reliable service from **Radio Taxi Austral**, T247710/244409.

ⓓ Directory

Punta Arenas *p740, map p741*
Airline offices LAN, Lautaro Navarro 999, T241232, www.lanchile.cl. Aerovías DAP,

O'Higgins 891, T223340, www.dap.cl. Open 0900-1230, 1430-1930. Helpful. **Sky**, T710645.
Banks Most banks and some supermarkets have ATMs; many on the Plaza. Banks open Mon-Fri 0830-1400. **Casas de cambio** open Mon-Fri 0900-1230, 1500-1900, Sat 0900-1230.
Consulates Argentina, 21 de Mayo 1878, T261912, open 1000-1530, visas take 24 hrs.
Belgium, Roca 817, Oficina 61, T241472. **Italy**, 21 de Mayo 1569, T221596. **Netherlands**, Magallanes 435, T248100. **Spain**, J Menéndez 910, T243566. **UK**, Cataratas de Nicaragua 01325, T211535. **Internet** All over the centre.

Medical services Hospitals: Hospital Regional Lautaro Navarro, Angamos 180, T244040. Public hospital, for emergency room ask for La Posta. Has good dentists. **Clínica Magallanes**, Bulnes 01448, T211527. Private clinic, minimum US$45. **Hospital Naval**, Av Bulnes 200 esq Capitán Guillermos. Open 24 hrs, good, friendly staff. Recommended.
Post offices Bories 911 y J Menéndez. Mon-Fri 0830-1930, Sat 0900-1400.
Telephones Several call centres in the centre; shop around as prices vary.

Puerto Natales and around

Beautifully situated on the calm waters of Canal Señoret fjord, an arm of the Ultima Esperanza Sound, edged with spectacular mountains, Puerto Natales, 247 km north of Punta Arenas, is a quiet town of brightly painted corrugated tin houses. It's the base for exploring the magnificent Balmaceda and Torres del Paine national parks, and although inundated with visitors in the summer, retains an unhurried feel, and is a place to relax for a few days.

Ins and outs

Tourist office Serantur office on the waterfront, Avenida Pedro Montt 19, T412125, infonatales@sernatur.cl. No English spoken, but good leaflets on Puerto Natales and Torres del Paine in English, and bus and boat information in the park. Monday-Saturday 0900-1900. Also at Municipalidad, Bulnes 285, T411263. **Conaf**, O'Higgins 584, T411843.

Sights

Museo Histórico ① *Bulnes 285, Mon-Fri 0900-1300, 1500-2000, weekends afternoon only, free*, has displays and photos of early colonizers There are lovely walks along the waterfront or up to Cerro Dorotea, which dominates the town, with superb views. Take any bus going east and alight at the road for summit (Km 9.5).

  Monumento Natural Cueva Milodón ① *25 km north, US$4 to enter park, camping allowed, getting there: regular bus from Prat 517, T412540, leaves 0945 and 1500, returns 1200 and 1700. US$5; taxi US$18 return or check if you can get a ride with a tour; both Adventur and Fernández tour buses to Torres del Paine stop at the cave*. In this cave (70 m wide, 45 m high and 270 m deep), formed by ice-age glacial lakes, remains were found of a prehistoric ground-sloth, together with evidence of occupation by early Patagonian humans some 11,000 years ago. There is a small, well-presented visitor centre, with toilets.

Parque Nacional Bernardo O'Higgins

Usually referred to as the **Parque Nacional Monte Balmaceda** ① *US$3.*, the park is at the north end of Ultima Esperanza Sound and can only be reached on boat trips from Puerto Natales (recommended). After a three-hour journey up the Sound, the boat passes the Balmaceda Glacier which drops steeply from the eastern slopes of Monte Balmaceda (2,035 m). The glacier is retreating; in 1986 its foot was at sea level. The boat docks one hour further north at Puerto Toro, from where it's a 1-km walk to the base of Serrano Glacier on the north slope of Monte Balmaceda. On the trip dolphins, sea-lions (in season), black-necked swans, flightless steamer ducks and cormorants can be seen. There's an optional three-hour boat trip by zodiac 35 km up the Río Serrano into PN Torres del Paine, which you can use to start trekking. Run by Onas (see Puerto Natales, Activities and tours) it takes about 7 hours, US$95, worth it for those with the budget and limited time (service starts on 1 November). Better going to the park than from the park (the view suddenly opens up and then just gets better and better).

Border with Argentina

There are three crossing points: **Villa Dorotea**, 16 km east of Puerto Natales. On the Argentine side the road continues to a junction, with alternatives south to Río Turbio and north to La

Esperanza and Río Gallegos. Chilean immigration is open all year 0800-2400. **Paso Casas Viejas**, 16 km northeast of Puerto Natales. On the Argentine side this joins the Río Turbio-La Esperanza road. Chilean immigration is open 0800-2400 in summer, 0800-2200 in winter. **Cerro Castillo**, 65 km north of Puerto Natales on the road to Torres del Paine, open 0800-2400 in summer, 0800-2200 in winter. On the Argentine side, Paso Cancha Carrera (14 km), the road leads to La Esperanza and Río Gallegos. All buses from El Calafate go via Cerro Castillo, making it possible to transfer to a bus passing from Puerto Natales to Torres del Paine. Chilean immigration is open all year 0800-2200, and the small settlement has several hospedajes and cafeterías. Sheep shearing in December, and rodeo and rural festival third weekend in January. See also Argentina, page 220.

⬤ Sleeping

Puerto Natales and around *p746, map p747*
In season cheaper accommodation fills up quickly after the arrival of the Magallanes ship from Puerto Montt. Hotels in the countryside open only in summer months: dates vary.
LL-L Costaustralis, Pedro Montt 262, T412000, www.costaustralis.com. Very comfortable, tranquil, lovely views, lift, English spoken, waterfront restaurant serves international and local seafood, much cheaper off season. Recommended.

L Cisne de Cuello Negro, T244506, T411498 (Av Colón 782, Punta Arenas). In a splendid lakeside setting, 5 km from town at Km 275 near Puerto Bories. Comfortable, excellent cooking.
L Hostería y Refugio Monte Balmaceda, T220174, aventour@entelchile.net or info@ aventouraventuras.com. Beautifully situated on Ultima Esperanza Sound, close to the Río Serrano. Comfortable rooms and refugio with well-lit, giant tents, beds and bathrooms, restaurant. Also organize tours and rent

Puerto Natales

To Punta Arenas & Parque Nacional Torres del Paine

Seno Ultima Esperanza

Estero Natales

To El Favorito

To Museo De Agostini

0 metres 100
0 yards 100

Sleeping
Aquaterra **17** C2
Blanquita **2** C2
Bulnes **3** B2
Casa Cecilia **4** B2
Casa Teresa **22** C2
Concepto Indigo **5** B1

Costaustralis **6** C1
Hospedaje Chila **20** C2
Hospedaje Dos
 Lagunas **7** B1
Hospedaje Nancy **8** C3
Hostal Lady
 Florence Dixie **9** B3
Hostal Sir Francis
 Drake **10** A2
Josmar 2 Camping **11** C2
Lago Sarmiento **12** C1
Los Inmigrantes **23** C2
Martín Gusinde **13** B2

Mwono Lodge **14** B1
Niko's **15** C3
Patagonia Adventure
 & Sendero Aventura **16** B2
Residencial Centro **25** B2
Residencial Dickson **18** C2
Residencial Gabriela **24** C2
Residencial Mundial **19** B2
Saltos del Paine **21** B1

Eating
Andrés **10** C1
Centro Español **1** B2

El Asador
 Patagónico **2** B2
El Living **3** B2
El Maritimo **4** B1
La Burbuja **5** B2
La Caleta Económica **6** B2
Los Pioneros **7** B1
Oveja Negra **11** B2

Bars & clubs
El Bar de Ruperto **8** B2
Kaweshkar **9** C1

equipment. Handy for boat trip up Río Serrano. Recommended.

L Hotel 3 Pasos, 40 km north on the way to Torres del Paine, T245494, www.hotel3pasos.cl. Good value in this simple, beautiful place.

L Martín Gusinde, Bories 278, T412770, www.austrohoteles.cl/martingusinde.html. American buffet breakfast included, ultra-modern, smart, parking, expensive restaurant.

AL Saltos del Paine, Bulnes 156, T 413607, www.saltosdelpaine.cl/. Modern, warm and cosy rooms, eclectic decor, breakfast included, a bit overpriced.

AL-A Aquaterra, Bulnes 299, T412239, www.aquaterrapatagonia.cl. New hotel, with good restaurant with vegetarian options, alternative therapy centre, nice decor, safe, warm, helpful and comfortable.

AL-A Hostal Lady Florence Dixie, Bulnes 659, T411158, www.chileanpatagonia.com/florence. Modern, hospitable. Recommended.

AL Weskar Patagonian Lodge, Ruta 9, Km 1, T410851, www.weskar.cl. New ecolodge (**A** in low season) with views of the fjord, onces and dinner served, internet, bicycles, boat trips, riding, birdwatching, fishing and other activities offered.

A Concepto Indigo, Ladrilleros 105, T413609, www.conceptoindigo.com. Relaxed atmosphere, on the water front, great views, small rooms simply furnished, cheaper without bath, breakfast included, café/restaurant serves good seafood and vegetarian dishes, internet access.

A Hostal Sir Francis Drake, Phillipi 383, T411553, www.chileaustral.com/francisdrake. Calm and welcoming, tastefully decorated, filling breakfast, good views. Recommended.

B Lago Sarmiento, Bulnes 90, T411542. Smart, simple, dodgy bathrooms, good value (**D** in low season), comfortable living room with good view.

B Bulnes, Bulnes 407, T411307, www.hostalbulnes.com. With breakfast, cheaper with shared bath, simple but charming, comfortable, laundry facilities, stores luggage.

C Blanquita, Carrera Pinto 409, T411674. Quiet, simple rooms, stores luggage. Recommended.

C-E Casa Cecilia, Tomás Rogers 60, T/F411797, redcecilia@entelchile.net. Welcoming, popular, with small simple rooms, some singles, other doubles **B** with bath, great breakfast. English, French and German spoken, rents camping equipment and bicycles, booking for tours and information for Torres del Paine, also shared rooms with bunk beds. Recommended. The annex is not so good.

D Hostal Patagonia, Patagonia 972, T412756. Helpful, tea and biscuits at any time, tours booked, laundry service, use of kitchen.

D Res Centro, Magallanes 258, T415033. With bath and breakfast, use of kitchen, helpful family.

D Res Dickson, Bulnes 307, T411871, lodgin@chileaustral.com. Good value, with breakfasts, helpful, internet, cooking and laundry facilities.

D-E pp Hosp Dos Lagunas, Barros Araña 104, T09-642 2407, doslagunas@hotmail.com. Lovely hospitable place with good breakfast, dinner available, shared bath, use of kitchen, TV and reading room, excursions and buses booked, lots of information.

D-E Mwono Lodge, Eberhard 214, T411018, mwonopatagonia@ze.cl. Nice, brightly decorated place with comfy shared rooms, breakfast included. Recommended.

D-E Niko's, E Ramírez 669, T412810, nikores idencial@hotmail.com. Breakfast extra, hospitable, basic, family-run, warm kitchen to use, luggage store, helpful, good meals.

D-E pp Niko's II, Phillipi 528, ½ block from Plaza de Armas, T411500, residencialnicosii@ hotmail.com. **C** with bath and TV, breakfast included, heating, English spoken, book exchange, information, tours to Paine and Perito Moreno glacier, tent rental.

D-E pp Patagonia Adventure, Tomás Rogers 179, T411028, www.apatagonia.com. Lovely old house, bohemian feel, shared bath, good value, homemade bread for breakfast, luggage store, equipment hire and tour arrangements for Torres del Paine.

D-E pp Res Mundial, Bories 315, T412476, elmundial@fortalezapatagonia.cl. Large breakfast, good value meals, use of kitchen when owners do not need it, luggage stored.

E pp Casa Teresa, Esmeralda 463, T410472, freepatagonia@hotmail.com. Good value, warm and quiet, breakfast included, also cheap meals, tours to Torres del Paine arranged.

E pp Hosp Chila, Carrera Pinto 442, T412328. Use of kitchen, welcoming, laundry facilities, luggage store, bakes bread. Recommended.

E pp Hosp Nancy, Ramirez 540, T410022, www.nataleslodge.cl. Good breakfast, shared bath, warm and hospitable, use of kitchen, information, internet, laundry service, runs tours and hires camping equipment. Recommended.

E pp Los Inmigrantes, Carrera Pinto 480, T413482, losinmigrantes@hotmail.com. Good breakfast, kitchen facilities, equipment rental, luggage store. Recommended.

E pp Res Gabriela, Bulnes 317, T411061. Good breakfast, owner Gabriela is very helpful, heating in rooms, luggage store. Recommended.

Camping Camping Daysee, Av España, Huerto no 70, T 411281. US$4 per site, all facilities, hot showers, laundry service, call from bus terminal for free pickup. Josmar 2, Esmeralda 517, in centre. Family run, convenient, hot showers, parking, barbecues, electricity, café, US$2.50 per site or **F** pp in double room.

Border with Argentina *p746*

B Hostería El Pionero, Cerro Castillo, T/F411646 or 691932 anexo 722, comfortable country house ambience, good service.

D pp **Hospedaje Loreto Belén**, Cerro Castillo, T413063, or 691932 (public phone, ask to speak to Loreto Belén). Rooms for 4, all with bath, breakfast included, also offers meals, good home cooking.

🍴 Eating

Puerto Natales *p746, map p747*

🍴 **El Asador Patagónico**, Prat 158 on the Plaza. Lamb on asado, salads, home-made puddings, attractive. Recommended.

🍴 **La Burbuja**, Bulnes 300. Great range of local seafood, eg king crab, filling portions, homely surroundings, try the fish soup.

🍴 **Centro Español**, Magallanes 247. Smart, local seafood, lamb. Recommended.

🍴 **El Marítimo**, on the waterfront. Excellent good value fish, friendly service, wonderful views. Recommended.

🍴 **El Rincón de Don Chicho**, Luis Martínez 206. The best parrilla in town, great fish too, authentic atmosphere with the charismatic Don Chicho.

🍴 **Los Pioneros**, Pedro Montt 166. Also good, seafood specialities in smart simple place, family welcome.

🍴 **Oveja Negra**, Tomás Rogers 169, Plaza de Armas. Excellent local food.

🍴 **Andrés**, Ladrilleros 381. Recommended for fish, nice owner, good service.

🍴 **La Caleta Económica**, Eberhard 261. Huge portions, fish, meat, good value.

🍴 **El Living**, Prat 156, Plaza de Armas, www.el-living.com. Just what you need: comfy sofas, good tea, magazines in all languages, book exchange, good music, delicious vegetarian food.

🍸 Bars and clubs

Puerto Natales *p746, map p747*

El Bar de Ruperto, Bulnes 371, T414302. Lively place with DJs, live music, lots of drinks (try the vodka with chillies) and some food. Open 2100-0500.

Disco Milodón, Blanco Encalada 854. Dancing in summer.

Kaweshkar, Bulnes 43, T415821, kaweshkar@yurhouse.com. Groovy laid-back bar, serving empanadas, hamburgers, vegetarian food. Try the parmesan molluscs tacos. Club at night with lounge music.

🛍 Shopping

Puerto Natales *p746, map p747*

Camping equipment Check all camping equipment and prices carefully. Average charges per day: whole set US$12, tent US$6, sleeping bag US$3-5, mat US$1.50, raincoat US$0.60, also cooking gear, US$1-2. (**Note**: Deposits required: tent US$200, sleeping bag US$100.) Camping gas is widely available in hardware stores, eg at Baquedano y O'Higgins and at Baquedano y Esmeralda. **Casa Cecilia**, Tomás Rogers 60, Recommended. **Fortaleza**, Tomás Rogers y Bulnes. Good equipment at a fair price. **Los Inmigrantes**, Carrera Pinto 480, T/F413482. Camping, climbing and mountain bikes. **Patagonia Adventures**, Tomás Rogers 179. **Las Rosas del Campo**, Baquedano 383, T410772. Some equipment, including wet weather gear for sale. **Turismo María José**, Bulnes 386. Rents good quality equipment, also arranges tours, internet access. **Handicrafts** **Hielo Azul** on Eberhard, for imaginative presents, lovely handmade jumpers. **Supermarkets** **El Favorito**, Bulnes 1085. **Super Dos** Bulnes y Balmaceda. Open 24 hrs, cheaper in Punta Arenas.

⚑ Activities and tours

Puerto Natales *p746, map p747*

Many agencies along Eberhard. Reports of the reliability of agencies, especially for their trips to Parque Nacional Torres del Paine, are very mixed. It is better to book tours direct with operators in Puerto Natales than through agents in Punta Arenas. Several agencies offer tours to the Perito Moreno glacier in Argentina, 1 day, US$40 without food or park entry fee. You can then leave the tour in Calafate to continue into Argentina. Recommended.

Bigfoot, Bories 206, T413247, www.bigfoot patagonia.com. Sea kayaking and ice hiking (½-day from Refugio Grey, includes 3 hr trek, learning about various glacial features, followed by a climb up a sheer ice wall, reasonable level of fitness required), not cheap but worth it, professional. Recommended.

Estancia Travel, Casa 13-b, Puerto Bories, Puerto Natales, T412221, www.estanciatravel.com. Based at the Estancia Puerto Consuelo, 25 km north of Puerto Natales, offer horseriding trips from 1 to 10 days around southern Patagonia and Torres del Paine, with accommodation at traditional estancias. Also kayaking trips, British run, bilingual, professional guides. Recommended.

Onas and **Andescape**, Eberhrd 595, T412707, www.onaspatagonia.com and T412592, www.andescape.cl. Tours of Torres del Paine, kayak trips. Onas offer boat trips to the Park by zodiak and Andescape run several refugios (see above).

Sendero Aventura, at Albergue Patagonia Adventure, Tomás Rogers 179, T415636, sendero_aventura@terra.cl. Adventure tours, including trekking to Torres del Paine, boats in Balmaceda PN, camping equipment and bike hire. Recommended.

Skorpios, address under Santiago, Ferry companies, www.skorpios.cl. Run Exploradores Kaweskar, and adventure tour from Puerto Natales to Puerto Edén, incorporating a seas journey on Skorpios 3 and expedition on the Campo Hielo del Sur.

⊖ Transport

Puerto Natales p746, map p747
Air Aerovías DAP flies from Puerto Natales to **El Calafate**, Mon-Fri, 40 mins, US$54.
Bus In summer book ahead. Buses leave from company offices: **Bus Fernández**, Eberhard 555, T411111. **Bus Sur**, Baquedano 534, T411325. **Transfer**, Baquedano 414, T421616. **Zaahj**, Prat 236, T412260.

To **Punta Arenas**, several daily, 3½ hrs, US$5.70, Fernández, Bus Sur and Transfer. To **Coyhaique**, Bus Sur Mon, US$45. To Argentina: to **Río Gallegos** direct, Bus Sur, El Pingüino and Ghisoni, 3 weekly each, US9-11, 4-5 hrs. Hourly to **Río Turbio**, Lagoper, Baquedano y Valdivia, and other companies, US$2.75, 2 hrs (depending on Customs – change bus at border). To **El Calafate**, US$20, **Cootra** via Río Turbio, daily, 6 hrs; or **Bus Sur** (2 a week) and **Zaahj** (3 a week) both operating a more direct service via Cerro Castillo. Otherwise travel agencies run several times a week depending on demand, US$50 one way, US$57 for return, not including Perito Moreno glacier entry fee (12 hr trip), shop around, reserve 1 day ahead.

Bus Sur also runs a bus to **Ushuaia** Oct-Apr, 15 hrs, US$40. **Note**: See Torres del Paine section for buses from Puerto Natales into the park, page 755.

Car hire Bien al Sur, Bulnes 433, T414025. **Motor Cars**, Blanco Encalada 330, T413593. **EMSA Avis**, Bulnes 6322, T410775. Hire agents can arrange permission to drive into Argentina, takes 24 hrs to arrange, extra insurance required.
Ferry See services from Puerto Montt. **Comapa**, Bulnes 533, T414300, www.comapa.com. **Navimag**, Manuel Bulnes 533, T414300, www.navimag.cl.

To **Parque Nacional Bernardo O'Higgins**: Sailings to **Balmaceda Glacier** daily at 0815 in summer, returning 1630, Sun only in winter (minimum 10 passengers), US$60. Including Río Serrano, US$85. Bookings direct from **Turismo 21 de Mayo**, Eberhard 560, T411476, www.turismo21demayo.cl. **Nueva Galicia**, Eberhard 169, T412352, or **Onas Turismo**, see Puerto Natales, Activities and tours. Expensive lunch extra, take picnic, drinks available on board. Heavily booked in high season. Take warm clothes, hat and gloves.

⊙ Directory

Puerto Natales p746, map p747
Banks Rates for TCs, which can't be changed into US$ cash, are poor. Banco Santiago, ATM; several others. Casas de cambio on Blanco Encalada, eg 266 (**Enio América**). Others on Bulnes and Prat. **Bicycle repairs** El Rey de la Bicicleta, Ramírez 540, Arauco 779. Good, helpful. **Internet** Several, including Blanco Encalada 23, also at Casa Cecilia, Concepto Indigo, see Sleeping; Bar de Ruperto, see Eating. Average US$1.50 per hr. **Post offices** Eberhard 417, open Mon-Fri 0830- 1230, 1430-1745, Sat 0900-1230. **Telephones** Telefónica, Blanco Encalada 23 y Bulnes. Phones, internet, fax. **Entel**, Baquedano y Bulnes.

Parque Nacional Torres del Paine → Colour map 9, grid B1.

Nothing prepares you for the spectacular beauty of Parque Nacional Torres del Paine. World renowned for its challenging trekking, the park's 181,414 ha contain 15 peaks above 2,000 m. At its centre is the glacier-topped granite massif Macizo Paine, from which rise the vertical pink granite Torres (Towers) del Paine and, below them, the Cuernos (Horns) del Paine, swooping buttresses of lighter granite under caps of darker sedimentary rock. From the vast Campo de Hielo Sur icecap on its western edge, four main glaciers (ventisqueros), Grey, Dickson, Zapata and Tyndall, drop into vividly coloured lakes formed by their meltwater: turquoise, ultramarine and pistachio expanses, some filled with wind-sculpted royal blue icebergs. Wherever you explore, there are constantly changing views of dramatic peaks and ice fields. The park enjoys a micro-climate especially favourable to wildlife and plants: there are 105 species of birds including condors, ibis, flamingoes and austral parakeets, and 25 species of mammals including guanaco, hares, foxes, pumas and skunks. Allow 5-7 days to see it all properly.

Ins and outs

Information The park is administered by **Conaf**: the Administration Centre (T691931) is in the south of the park at the northwest end of Lago del Toro (open 0830-2000 in summer, 0830-1230, 1400-1830 off season). There are entrances at Laguna Amarga, Lago Sarmiento and Laguna Azul, and you are required to **register** and show your passport when entering the park, since rangers (*guardeparques*) keep a check on the whereabouts of all visitors. You must also register before setting off on any hike. Phone the administration centre for information (in Spanish) on weather conditions. It also has videos and exhibitions with summaries in English of flora and fauna, but no maps to take away. There are six ranger stations (*guarderías*) staffed by rangers, who give help and advice. They will also store luggage (except at Laguna Amarga where they have no room). *Guarderías* at Camamentos Las Torrres, Italiano and Paso are open October-April only. Entry for foreigners: US$19 (10,000 pesos in 2006, payable only in pesos - will rise in 2006-07 season), less off-season – before 1 October (proceeds are shared between all Chilean national parks). The national park received about 100,000 visitors in 2005. The impact of huge numbers of visitors to the park is often visible in litter around the refugios and camping areas. Take all your rubbish out of the park including toilet paper.

Getting around and accommodation The park is well set up for tourism, with frequent bus services running from Puerto Natales through the park, to pick up and drop off walkers at various hotels, to start treks, and to connect with boat trips. For details, see Transport below. Accommodation is available on three levels: there are hotels (expensive, at least US$100 per night), seven well-equipped, staffed refugios, offering meals and free hot water for tea, soup etc (US$22-27 pp per night), and 14 campsites. All options fill up quickly in peak summer months, Jan-Feb, so plan your trip and book hotels and refugios in advance. Pay in dollars to avoid IVA (tax). See Sleeping for more details. **Note** Mice have become a problem around camping sites and the free refugios; do not leave food in packs on the ground. ⇥ *For further information, see Listings, page 753.*

Safety warning It is vital to be aware of the unpredictability of the weather (which can change in a few minutes, see Climate below) and the arduousness of some of the stretches on the long hikes. Rain and snowfall are heavier the further west you go and bad weather sweeps off the Campo de Hielo Sur without warning. The only means of rescue are on horseback or by boat; the nearest helicopter is in Punta Arenas and high winds usually prevent its operation in the park.

Forest fires are a serious hazard. Follow all instructions about lighting fires to the letter. An unauthorized campfire in 2005 led to the destruction of 10% of the northeast sector of the national park.

Equipment and maps A strong, streamlined, waterproof tent gives you more freedom than crowded refugios and is essential if doing the complete circuit. Also essential at all times of year are protective clothing against cold, wind and rain, strong waterproof footwear, a compass, a good sleeping bag, sleeping mat, camping stove and cooking equipment. Most refugios will hire camping equipment for a single night. Sun-screen and sunglasses are also necessary, and you'll want shorts in summer. At the entrance you are asked what equipment you have. Take your own food: the small shops at the Andescape refugios and at the Posada Río Serrano are expensive and have a limited selection. Maps (US$4) are obtainable at **Conaf** offices in Punta Arenas or Puerto Natales. Other Torres del Paine maps are published by Cartografía Digital, Mattassi and Patagonia Interactiva; all relatively accurate.

Climate Do not underestimate the severity of the weather here. The Park is open all year round, although snow may prevent access in the winter. The warmest time is December to March, but also the most unstable; strong winds often blow off the glaciers, and rainfall can be heavy. It is most crowded in the summer holiday season, January to mid-February, less so in December or March. In winter there can be good, stable conditions and well-equipped hikers can do some good walking, but some treks may be closed and boats may not be running.

Hikes

There are about 250 km of well-marked trails, and walkers must keep to the paths: cross-country trekking is not permitted. The times indicated should be treated with caution: allow for personal fitness and weather conditions.

El Circuito (Allow at least seven days) The main hike is a circuit round the Torres and Cuernos del Paine: it is usually done anticlockwise starting from the Laguna Amarga *guardería*. From Laguna Amarga the route is north along the west side of the Río Paine to Lago Paine, before turning west to follow the Río Paine to the south end of Lago Dickson. From here the path runs along the wooded valley of the Río de los Perros before climbing steeply to Paso John Gardner (1,241 m, the highest point on the route), then dropping to follow the Grey Glacier southeast to Lago Grey, continuing to Lago Pehoé and the administration centre. There are superb views, particularly from the top of Paso John Gardner.

Camping gear must be carried. The circuit is often closed in winter because of snow. The longest lap is 30 km, between Refugio Laguna Amarga and Refugio Dickson (10 hours in good weather; one campsite, Serón), but the most difficult section is the very steep slippery slope between Paso John Gardner and Campamento Paso, a section exposed to strong westerly winds. The major rivers are crossed by footbridges, but these are occasionally washed away.

Parque Nacional Torres del Paine

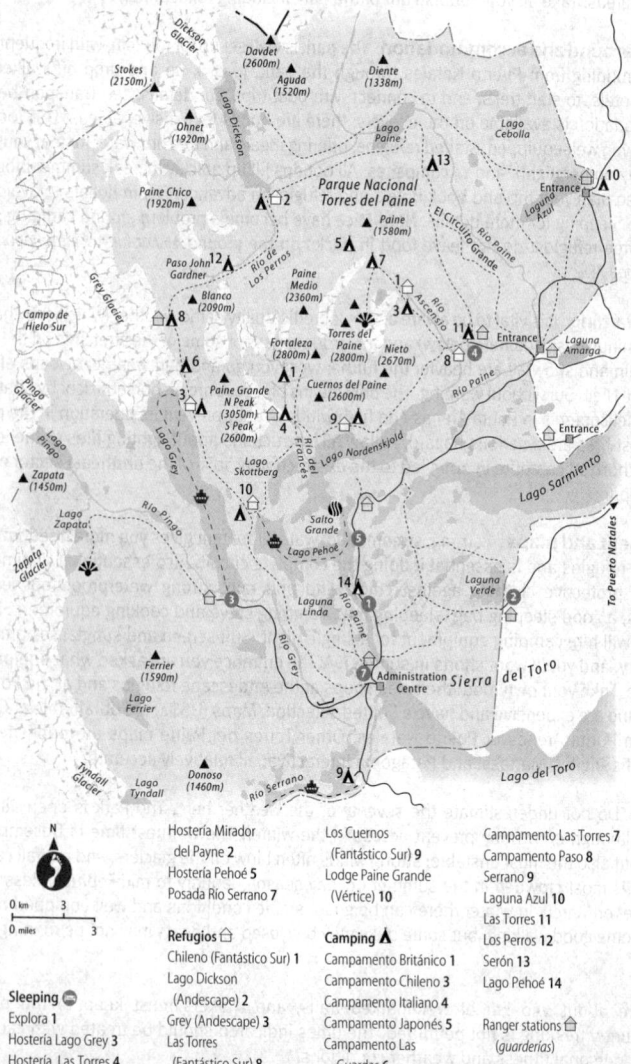

Hostería Mirador del Payne 2	Los Cuernos (Fantástico Sur) 9
Hostería Pehoé 5	Lodge Paine Grande (Vértice) 10
Posada Río Serrano 7	

Campamento Las Torres 7
Campamento Paso 8
Serrano 9
Laguna Azul 10
Las Torres 11
Los Perros 12
Serón 13
Lago Pehoé 14

Sleeping 🏠
Explora 1
Hostería Lago Grey 3
Hostería Las Torres 4

Refugios 🏠
Chileno (Fantástico Sur) 1
Lago Dickson (Andescape) 2
Grey (Andescape) 3
Las Torres (Fantástico Sur) 8

Camping ⛺
Campamento Británico 1
Campamento Chileno 3
Campamento Italiano 4
Campamento Japonés 5
Campamento Las Guardas 6

Ranger stations 🏠
(*guarderías*)

The W (Allow five days) The most popular route, it can be completed without camping equipment by staying in refugios, and can be done in either direction. It combines several of the hikes described separately below. From Laguna Amarga the first stage runs west via Hostería Las Torres and up the valley of the Río Ascensio via Refugio Chileno to the base of the Torres del Paine (see below). From here return to the Hostería Las Torres and then walk along the northern shore of Lago Nordenskjold via Refugio Los Cuernos to Campamento Italiano. From here climb the Valley of the Río del Francés (see below) before continuing to Lodge Paine Grande. From here you can complete the third part of the 'W' by walking west along the northern shore of Lago Grey to Refugio Grey and Glaciar Grey before returning to Lodge Paine Grande.

The Valley of the Río del Francés (Allow five hours each way) From Lodge Paine Grande this route leads north across undulating country along the west edge of Lago Skottberg to Campamento Italiano and then follows the valley of the Río del Francés, which climbs between (to the west) Cerro Paine Grande and the Ventisquero del Francés, and (to the east) the Cuernos del Paine to Campamento Británico. Allow 2½ hours from Lodge Paine Grande to Campamento Italiano, 2½ hours further to Campamento Británico. The views from the mirador, 20 minutes above Campamento Británico, are superb.

Up the Río Pingo valley (Allow four hours each way) From Guardería Grey (18 km west by road from the Administration Centre) follow the Río Pingo, via Refugio Pingo and Refugio Zapata (four hours), with views south over Ventisquero Zapata (plenty of wildlife, icebergs in the lake). It is not possible to reach Lago Pingo as a bridge has been washed away. Ventisquero Pingo can be seen 3 km away over the lake.

To the base of the Torres del Paine (Allow four to five hours each way) From Laguna Amarga the route follows the road west to Hostería Las Torres before climbing along the west side of the Río Ascensio via Campamento Chileno to Campamento Las Torres, close to the base of the Torres and near a small lake. Allow 1½ hours to Hostería Las Torres, then two hours to Campamento Chileno, two hours further to Campamento Torres where there is a lake: the path is well-marked, but the last 30 minutes is up the moraine; to see the towers lit by sunrise (spectacular, but you must have good weather), it's well worth humping camping gear up to Campamento Torres and spending the night. One hour beyond Campamento Torres is the good site at Campamento Japonés.

To Laguna Verde (Allow four hours each way) From the administration centre follow the road north 2 km, before taking the path east over the Sierra del Toro and then along the south side of Laguna Verde to the Guardería Laguna Verde. This is one of the easiest walks in the park and may be a good first hike.

To Laguna Azul and Lago Paine (Allow 8½ hours each way) This route runs north from Laguna Amarga to the west tip of Laguna Azul (following the road for 7km), from where it continues across the sheltered Río Paine valley past Laguna Cebolla to the Refugio Lago Paine (now closed) at the west end of the lake.

🌙 Sleeping

Parque Nacional Torres del Paine
p750, map p752

All the park's hotels are expensive, many feel overpriced. **Turismo Río Serrano**, Prat 258, Puerto Natales, T410684, and **Torresdelpaine.org**, T313 3389, hotelschile@terra.cl, offer accommodation, transfers and car hire, and **Experience Chile**, www.experiencechile.org offers hotels and tour itineraries.

LL Hostería Lago Grey, T410172, reservations T061-225986, www.austrohoteles.cl/lagogrey.html. Great views over Lago Grey, but small rooms and mediocre food, glacier walks

US$50 (reservations through Arka Patagonia in Punta Arenas). Accepts Visa.

LL Hostería Pehoé, T411390, www.pehoe.com, 5 km south of Pehoé ranger station, 11 km north of park administration. Beautifully situated on an island with spectacular view across Lago Pehoé, but rather run down. Closed Apr-Oct, restaurant (reservations: Turismo Pehoé in Punta Arenas or Antonio Bellet 77, of 605, Santiago, T235 0252, F236 0917).

LL Hotel Explora, T411247. The park's most expensive and exclusive is nestled into a nook at Salto Chico on edge of Lago Pehoé, spectacular views. Everything is included: pool, gym, horse riding, boat trips, tours, can arrange packages from Punta Arenas (reservations: Av Américo Vespucci 80, p 7, Santiago, T206-6060, www.explora.com).

LL-L Hostería Las Torres, head office Magallanes 960, Punta Arenas, T710050, www.lastorres.cl. Superb, comfortable rooms, beautiful lounge with wood fire and great views of the Cuernos, excellent restaurant with evening buffet (US$25), good service (but a bit of hard sell on the excursions etc), horse-riding (US$69 pp to the Torres and back), transport from Laguna Amarga ranger station, spa. Accepts Visa. Recommended. Visitor centre and confitería open to non-residents for sandwiches, but prices double after 1900.

AL Hostería Mirador del Payne, lovely location on Laguna Verde on east edge of the park, reservations from Fagnano 585, Punta Arenas, T061-228712, www.miradordelpayne.com. Comfortable, but inconvenient for park itself, riding, hiking, birdwatching.

AL-A Posada Río Serrano, an old estancia, reservations through Baqueano Zamora, Baquedano 534, Puerto Natales, T061-412911, www.baqueanozamora.com. Some rooms with bath, some without, near park administration, with expensive but good restaurant and a shop, may allow use of cooking facilities when quiet.

Refugios

Three companies between them run half of the refugios in the park, providing dormitory space only (bring your own sleeping bag, or hire one for US$6). Prices are US$20-27 pp, full board about US$25 extra. Refugios have kitchen facilities, hot showers, and space for camping. Andescape refugios hire tents for US$11 per night. Most refugios close in winter, although one or 2 may stay open, depending on the weather. Advance booking essential in high season; service can be poor.

Andescape refugios (Eberhard 599, Puerto Natales, T412877, www.andescape.cl).

Refugio Grey, on the eastern shore of Lago Grey (has facilities for ice climbing).

Refugio Lago Dickson, on the northern part of the circuit.

Fantástico Sur refugios (book through Las Torres, T061-710050, albergue@lastorres.com).

Refugio Chileno, in the Valley of the Río Ascencio, at the foot of the Torres (very expensive meals).

Refugio Las Torres, next to the Hostería Las Torres (see above), good facilities.

Refugio Los Cuernos, on the northern shore of Lago Nordenskjold.

Vértice refugios. Book through Vértice Patagonia, T061-414300, www.verticepatagonia.cl.

Lodge Paine Grande, on the northwest tip of Lago Pehoé (expensive food).

Camping

Fires may only be lit at organized camping sites, not at campamentos. The guarda- parques expect people to have a stove if camping. In addition to sites at the Andescape refugios there are the following sites: **Camping Lago Pehoé** and **Camping Serrano**, both run by Turismo Río Serrano (address above), US$20 per site at former (maximum 6 persons, hot showers) and US$15 per site at latter (maximum 6 persons, cold showers, more basic). **Camping Laguna Azul**, hot showers, US$19 per site. **Camping Los Perros**, run by Andescape, US$3 pp, shop and hot showers. **Camping Serón** and **Camping Las Torres** (at Hostería Las Torres) both run by Estancia Cerro Paine, US$4, hot showers. Free camping is permitted in 7 other locations in the park: these sites are known as campamentos. The wind tends to rise in the evening so pitch tent early. Beware mice, which eat through tents. Equipment hire in Puerto Natales (see above).

Punta Delgada

C Hostería Tehuelche, T061-694433 at Kamiri Aike, 17 km from the port, with restaurant.

E pp Hotel El Faro. In the town itself. There is also a cosy tea room Bahía Azul.

▲▲ Activities and tours

Parque Nacional Torres del Paine
p750, map p752

See under Puerto Natales, Activities and tours, page 749, for recommendations. There are increasingly mixed reports of tours. Before booking a tour, check carefully on details and get them in writing.

Boat trips From Refugio Lago Pehoé to Refugio Pudeto, US$15 one way with 1 backpack (US$8 for extra backpacks), from Pudeto 0930, 1200, 1800, from Pehoé 1000, 1300, 1900, 20 mins in high season, reserve in advance at the refugios at either end or at Catamarán Hielos Patagónicos, Los Arrieros 1517, Puerto Natales, T411380. Off-season, radio for the boat from Lodge Paine Grande. At all times check in advance that boats are running. See Parque Nacional Bernardo O'Higgins above for entry by 3-hr zodiac trip up the Río Serrano from Balmaceda glacier. Boat to face of glacier from **Hostería Grey** US$60 return. A one way trip can be made via the glacier face to/from the Hostería to the **Refugio Grey** for US$40.

✈ Transport

Parque Nacional Torres del Paine
p750, map p752

Bus The park is 145 km northwest of Puerto Natales. After mid-Mar there is little public transport and trucks are irregular. From early Nov-mid Apr, there are 3 companies running daily services into the park. To go to the Administration centre, all charge US$9 one way, US$15.25 open return (return tickets are not interchangeable between different companies). Buses will stop anywhere en route, but all stop at Laguna Amarga entrance, Salto Grande del Paine and administration centre near Posada Serrano. **JB**, Prat 258, T412824. **Fortaleza**, Prat 258, T410595. **Bus Sur**, Baquedano 534, T411325. Buses pass Guardería Laguna Amarga at 1030, Guardería Pehoé at 1130, arriving at Admin at 1230, leave Admin at 1320 (in high season the buses fill quickly so it is best to board at Admin), arrive in Puerto Natales 1650. All buses wait at Refugio Pudeto until 1345, when the boat from Refugio Lago Pehoé arrives. Travel between two points within the park (eg Pudeto- Laguna Amarga) US$3. At other times services by travel agencies are dependent on demand: arrange return date with driver to coincide with other groups to keep costs down. **Luis Díaz** is reliable, about US$12 pp, minimum 3 people. Hostería Las Torres sometimes runs an employee bus back to Puerto Natales at 1700, US$5, ask at reception.

In season there are frequent minibus connections within the park: from Laguna Amarga to Hostería Las Torres, US$6.50, and from the administration centre to Hostería Lago Grey. Other than these routes getting around the park without your own transport is difficult and expensive. From Torres del Paine to **Calafate** (Argentina): take the direct bus run by **Chaltén Travel**, US$40, or take services from Puerto Natales (see above); alternatively take a bus from the park to Cerro Castillo (106 km south of administration centre) then catch a direct service to Calafate, on Bus Sur or Zaahj (see Puerto Natales Buses).

Car hire Hiring a pick-up in Punta Arenas is an economical proposition for a group (up to 9 people): US$415 for 4 days. If driving there yourself, the road from Puerto Natales is being improved and, in the park, the roads are narrow and winding with blind corners: use your horn a lot. It takes about 3½ hrs from Puerto Natales to the administration, 3 hrs to Laguna Amarga. Petrol available at Río Serrano, but fill up in case.

Tierra del Fuego

The western side of this, the largest island off the extreme south of South America, belongs to Chile and the eastern to Argentina. Here the Andes cordillera runs from west to east, so that the north of the island is flat, covered with vast sheep farms, while the south has mountains, glaciers, lakes and forests. The major population centres, Ushuaia and Río Grande, are on the Argentine side, but Chile has the most southerly town in the world, Puerto Williams, on the island Isla Navarino below Tierra del Fuego. See Argentine Tierra del Fuego for Background.

Porvenir and around → *Phone code: 061. Colour map 9, grid C2. Population: 5,100.*
Porvenir is a quiet, pleasant place with many inhabitants of Croatian descent. Founded in 1894 in the gold boom, when many people came seeking fortunes from Croatia and Chiloé, it's a quiet, pleasant place with neat, painted tin houses and quaint, tall trees lining the main avenue. There is a small museum, the **Museo Fernando Cordero Rusque** *Samuel Valdivieso 402*, with archaeological and photographic displays on the Onas; good displays on natural history and the early gold diggers. There is a bank on the Plaza. **Tourist information** at the municipalidad, Zavattara 402, T580094, and at tiny kiosk on the waterfront, helpful, sells fine handicrafts, kuanip@entelchile.net. Porvenir is the base for exploring the wonderfully wild virgin territory of Tierra del Fuego. Fly fishing, until recently the secret of Hollywood stars, is becoming world-renowned. The area is rich in brown trout, sea-run brook trout and steelheads, weighing 2-14 kg. Excursions are likely to involve camping and travel on horseback.

Driving east along **Bahía Inútil**, a wonderful windswept bay, there are views of distant hills and the snow-capped Darwin range along the horizon. At Caleta Josefina, 98 km east, you can visit a handsome ex-estancia built in 1833, where some old buildings remain. Highly recommended is horseriding to the forests of the **Darwin range**, wild and challenging. Other options are sailing from Porvenir to **Río Cóndor** across Bahía Inútil, south of Cameron, with trekking or riding from Cameron to **Seno Almirantazgo**, a beautiful, wild and treeless place, where mountains sink into blue fjords with icebergs. Also sailing to

Marinelli glacier, where you can sail, kayak and dive. A recommended tour goes along the gold circuit, **Cordón Baquedano**, where you can see gold panning using the same techniques since mining began in 1881, a five-hour, 115-km round trip, good on horseback.

Border with Argentina → *Argentine time is 1 hr ahead of Chilean time, Mar-Oct.*

The only legal border crossing between the Chilean and Argentine parts of Tierra del Fuego is 142 km east of Porvenir at **San Sebastián**; open 0800-2200. On the Argentine side the road continues to Río Grande. **Note:** There are two settlements called San Sebastián, on each side of the border but they are 14 km apart; taxis are not allowed to cross. No fruit, vegetables, dairy produce or meat permitted on entry to Chile. For entry to Argentina, see page 225.

Puerto Williams → *Phone code: 061. Colour map 9, grid C2. Population: 2,500.*

Puerto Williams is a Chilean naval base on **Isla Navarino**, south of the Beagle Channel. About 50 km south east of Ushuaia (Argentina) at 54° 55' 41" south, 67° 37' 58" west, it is small, friendly and remote. The island is totally unspoilt and beautiful, offering great geographical diversity, thanks to **Dientes de Navarín** range, with peaks over 1,000 m, covered with southern beech forest up to 500 m, and, south of that, great plains covered in peat bogs, with many lagoons and abundant in flora. The island was the centre of the indigenous Yaganes culture and there are 500 archaeological sites, the oldest from 3,000 years ago. **Museo Martín Gusinde** ⓘ *Mon-Thu 1000-1300, 1500-1800, Sat-Sun1500-1800, Fri closed (subject to change), US$1*, is also known as the Museo del Fin del Mundo ('End of the World Museum'). It is full of information about vanished tribes, local wildlife, and voyages including Charles Darwin and Fitzroy of the Beagle, a must. The town has a bank, supermarkets and hospital. **Tourist information** ⓘ *Municipalidad de Cabos de Hornos, Pres Ibáñez 130, T621011, closed in winter*. Ask for maps and details on hiking.

Around Puerto Williams

For superb views, climb **Cerro Bandera** (3-4 hours' round trip, steep, take warm clothes). **Villa Ukika**, 2 km east of town, is where the last descendants of the Yaganes people live, relocated from their original homes at Caleta Mejillones. There is excellent trekking around the **Dientes de Navarín**, the southernmost trail in the world, through impressive mountain landscapes, with superb views of Beagle Channel (challenging, 53 km in five days, December-March only, good level of fitness needed). Charter flights are available over Cape Horn and to **King George Island** on northern tip of Antarctic peninsula, where you can see the curvature of the earth on the horizon, with excursions to penguin and sea lion colonies. No equipment rental on island.

Cape Horn

It is possible to catch a boat south from Isla Navarino to Cape Horn (the most southerly piece of land on earth apart from Antarctica). There is one pebbly beach on the north side of the island; boats anchor in the bay and passengers are taken ashore by motorized dinghy. A rotting stairway climbs the cliff above the beach, up to the building where three marines run the naval post. A path leads from here to the impressive monument of an albatross overlooking the wild, churning waters of the Drake Passage below.

● Sleeping

Porvenir *p755*

A Los Flamencos, Tte Merino, T580049, www.hosterialosflamencos.com. Best place to stay with good food, a pleasant place for a drink. Recommended.
D Rosas, Phillippi 296, T580088. Heating, restaurant and bar, internet. Recommended.
E pp España, Croacia 698, T580160. Good restaurant with fixed price lunch.

E pp Miramar, Santos Mardones 366. **D** with full board, heaters in rooms, good panoramic views.

E-F pp Hosp L y V Guaigino, Santos Mardones 333, T580491, wshere@hotmail.com. Helpful, safe, quiet, shared bath, with breakfast, use of kitchen.

● *For an explanation of the sleeping and eating price codes used in this guide, see inside the front* ● *cover. Other relevant information is found in Essentials pages 604-605.*

Border with Argentina: San Sebastián *p756*
B Hostería de la Frontera, T061-224731/09-4995331, frontera@entelchile.net. Where buses stop for meals and cakes, cosy, good food.
D ACA motel, T02964-425542,14 km east, across the border (open 24 hrs), in Argentine San Sebastián, basic; service station open 0700-2300.

Puerto Williams *p756*
A pp Pensión Temuco, Piloto Pardo 224, T621113. Full board (room only available), comfortable, hospitable, good food, hot showers. Recommended.
D pp Hostería Camblor, Vía 2 s/n, T621033, hosteriacamblor@terra.cl. Heavily booked up, rooms with bath, restaurant.
D pp Hostal Yagan, Piloto Pardo 260, T621334, hostalyagan@hotmail.com. Comfortable, includes breakfast, dinner available, family run by Daniel and Berta Yevenes, Daniel offers tours.
E pp Res Onashaga, Uspashun 15, T621564. Run by Señor Ortiz - everyone knows him. Cold, rundown, good meals, helpful, full board available. You can also stay at private houses.
Camping Near the Hostería.

Elsewhere in Chilean Tierra del Fuego
C Hostería Tunkelen Arturo Prat Chacón 101, Cerro Sombrero, T061-212757, hosteria_tunkelen@hotmail.com. Also dorm **D** pp.
Cerro Sombrero, 46 km south of Primera Angostura, is a village built to administrate oil drilling in the area, there's a bank, fuel and several other hotels (**E-F**).
D Posada Las Flores, Km 127 on the road to San Sebastián, reservations via Hostal de la Patagonia in Punta Arenas.
F Refugio Lago Blanco, on Lago Blanco, T061-241197. The only accommodation on the lake.

● Eating

Porvenir *p755*
♯ **Croacia Club** next to the bus stop on the waterfront. A lively place where you can get a good lunch for US$5.
♯ **Restaurante Puerto Montt**, Croacia 1169, for seafood. Recommended.
♯ **El Chispa**, on Señoret. For good cheap seafood and lamb. Many lobster fishing camps where fishermen will prepare lobster on the spot.

▲ Activities and tours

Porvenir *p755*
Turismo Cordillera de Darwin, Croacia 675, T09-640 7204, www.explorepatagonia.cl.

Puerto Williams *p756*
Boat trips Most recommended is the cruise around Cape Horn and on to Ushuaia, returning to Punta Arenas, run by **Cruceros Australis SA**, Santiago office T02-442 3110, www.australis.com. Book well in advance. **Victory Adventures**, Casilla 70, T061-621010, www.victory-cruises.com (Ben Garrett). You may get a lift on a yacht (unlikely); ask at the yacht club, 1 km west.

Tour operators
Karanka Expeditions, run by Maurice Van de Maele, T621127.
Sim Ltda, www.simltd.com. Sailing trips, trekking tours and many other adventure activities.

● Transport

Ferries to Tierra del Fuego
There are two crossings. The ferry company accepts no responsibility for damage to vehicles on the crossing.
Punta Arenas to Porvenir The **Melinka**, sails from Tres Puentes (5 km north of Punta Arenas, bus A or E from Av Magallanes, or colectivo 15, US$0.40; taxi US$3) at 0900, and an afternoon sailing Tue, Wed, Thu, 0930 Sun, no service Mon in season; less frequent sailings off season. 2½-hr crossing (can be rough and cold), US$6 pp, US$10 per bike, US$45 per vehicle. Return from Porvenir varying times in afternoon between 1300 and 1800, except Mon. Timetable dependent on tides and subject to change; check in advance. Reservations essential especially in summer (at least 24 hrs in advance for cars), obtainable from **Transboradora Austral Broom**, in Punta Arenas, Bulnes 5075, T218100, www.tabsa.cl.
Punta Delgada to Punta Espora (Bahía Azul) This crossing is via the Primera Angostura (First Narrows), 170 km northeast of Punta Arenas. Boats run every 90 mins, 0830-2215, for the 20-min crossing: foot passengers US$2, US$20 per car. The ferry takes about 4 trucks and 20 cars; before 1000 most space is taken by trucks. There is no bus service to or from this crossing. If hitching, this route is preferable as there is more traffic.

Porvenir *p755*

Air From Punta Arenas – weather and bookings permitting, **Aerovías DAP**, Señoret s/n, T580089, Porvenir, www.dap.cl, twice daily Mon-Sat, 12 mins, US$23. Heavily booked so make sure you have your return reservation confirmed.

Bus 2 a week between Porvenir and **Río Grande** (Argentina), Tue and Sat 1400, 5 hrs, **Transportes Gessell**, Duble Almeyda 257, T580488 (Río Grande 02964-425611), US$15, heavily booked, buy ticket in advance, or phone; Río Grande-Porvenir, Wed and Sun 0800.

Ferry Terminal at Bahía Chilota, 5 km west, see above for details. From bus terminal to ferry, taxi US$6, bus US$1.50.

Road All roads are gravel. Fuel is available in Porvenir, Cerro Sombrero and Cullen. Police may help with lifts on trucks to Río Grande; elsewhere is difficult as there is little traffic.

San Sebastián *p756*
Minibus From Porvenir to San Sebastián, US$14.

Puerto Williams *p756*
Air From Punta Arenas by air, **Aerovías DAP** (details under Punta Arenas) daily Mon-Sat, 1 hr, US$70 each way, in 7-seater Cessna, luggage allowance 10 kg. Book well in advance; long waiting lists (be persistent). The flight is beautiful (sit on right from Punta Arenas) with superb views of Tierra del Fuego, the Cordillera Darwin, the Beagle Channel, and the islands stretching south to Cape Horn. Also army flights available (they are cheaper), but the ticket has to be bought through DAP.

Ferry No regular sailings from Ushuaia (Argentina). Boats from Punta Arenas: **Ferry Patagonia** (Austral Broom), once a week, US$120 for seat, US$150 for bunk, including food, 36 hrs. www.tabsa.com. The Navarino leaves Punta Arenas in 3rd week of every month, 12 passengers, US$150 pp one way; contact the owner, **Carlos Aguilera**, 21 de Mayo 1460, Punta Arenas, T228066). The Beaulieu, a cargo boat carrying a few passengers, sails from Punta Arenas once a month, US$300 return, 6 days.

● Directory

Puerto Williams *p756*
Airline offices Aerovías DAP, Centro Comercial s/n, T621051, in the centre of town.
Post offices Close 1900.
Telephones Telefónica, Mon-Sat 0930-2230, Sun 1000-1300, 1600-2200.

Chilean Pacific Islands

Chile has two national parks in the Pacific: Juan Fernández Islands, a little easier to reach (and leave) now than in Robinson Crusoe's time, and the remarkable Easter Island.

Juan Fernández Islands → *Phone code: 032. Population: 500.*

This group of small volcanic islands is a national park administered by Conaf and is situated 667 km west of Valparaíso. They were declared a UN World Biosphere Reserve in 1977. They enjoy a mild climate and the vegetation is rich and varied. Fauna includes wild goats, hummingbirds and seals. The best time to visit is October-March; take insect repellent. The islands are named after Juan Fernández, the first European to visit in 1574. There are three islands, Robinson Crusoe, the largest, which was the home (1704-1709) of Alexander Selkirk (the original of Defoe's Robinson Crusoe), Alejandro Selkirk and Santa Clara, the smallest. Selkirk's cave on the beach of Robinson Crusoe is shown to visitors. The only settlement is San Juan Bautista on Robinson Crusoe Island, a fishing village of wooden frame houses, located on Bahía Cumberland on the north coast of the island: it has a church, schools, post office, and radio station. The islands are famous for langosta de Juan Fernández (a pincerless lobster) which is sent to the mainland.

Robinson Crusoe Island The remains of the **Fuerte Santa Bárbara**, the largest of the Spanish fortresses, overlook San Juan Bautista. The island has long been the target for treasure-seekers who claim that looted gold from Inca times is buried there. In September 2005 600 barrels of coins, jewels and statuary were said to have been found. Near Santa Bárbara are the **Cuevas de los Patriotas**, home to the Chilean independence leaders, deported by the Spanish after the Battle of Rancagua. South of the village is the **Mirador de Selkirk**, the hill where Selkirk lit his signal fires. A plaque was set in the rock at the look-out point by British naval officers from HMS Topaze in 1868; nearby is a more recent plaque placed by his descendants. (Selkirk, a Scot, was put ashore from HMS Cinque Ports and was taken off four years and four months later by a privateer, the Duke.) The Mirador is the only easy pass between the north and south sides of the island. Further south is the anvil-shaped **El Yunque**, 915 m, the highest peak on the island, where Hugo Weber, a survivor from the Dresden, lived as a hermit for 12 years. (The Dresden was a German cruiser, cornered by two British destroyers in Bahía Cumberland in 1915; the scuttled Dresden still lies on the bottom and a monument on the shore commemorates the event.) The only sandy beach on Robinson Crusoe is **Playa Arenal**, in the extreme southwest corner, two hours by boat from San Juan Bautista.

Each February, a **yachting regatta** visits the islands; setting out from Algarrobo, the yachts sail to Isla Robinson Crusoe, then to Talcahuano and Valparaíso. At this time Bahía Cumberland is full of colourful and impressive craft, and prices in restaurants and shops double for the duration. (Thomas G Lammers, Department of Botany, University of Miami.) There are no exchange facilities. Only pesos and US$ cash accepted. No credit cards, no traveller's cheques.

● Sleeping

Juan Fernández Islands *p758*
Lodging with villagers is difficult.
L-AL pp **Hostería El Pangal**, east of San Juan in Caleta Pangal, T02-273 1458. Half-board. Great views, bar and restaurant, best on the island.
A-B pp **Aldea Daniel Defoe Hotel**, Larraín Alcalde 449, T032-751075, ebeeche@terra.com. Half board, full board available, bar, laundry service, tours offered.
B-C pp **Hostal Charpentier**, Ignacio Carrera Pinto 256, T032-751020, hostalcharpentier@hotmail.com. Kitchen facilities, also has cabañas, half and full board available, tours offered.
C pp **Hostería Martínez Green**, El Castillo 116, T032-751039. Rooms with TV, full and half board available, views, tours.
C-D Hostería Villa Green, Larraín Alcalde 246, T032-751044. With breakfast and TV.

● Transport

Juan Fernández Islands *p758*
Air Air taxi daily in summer (subject to demand) from **Santiago** (US$400 round trip), by Transportes Aéreas Isla Robinson Crusoe, Av Pajaritos 3030, of 604, Maipú, Santiago, T/F531 4343, www.tairc.cl, from Los Cerrillos airport, and by **Lasa**, Av Larraín 7941, La Reina, Santiago, T273 4309, lassa@terra.cl, from Tobalaba Aerodrome in La Reina. The plane lands on an airstrip in the west of the island; passengers are taken by boat to San Juan Bautista (1½ hrs, US$2 one way).
Ferry A boat service from **Valparaíso**, is operated by **Naviera del Sur**, Blanco Encalada 1041, of 18, T594304. It is for cargo and passengers, modest accommodation, 36-hr passage. Also try **Agentur**, Esmeralda 940, Valparaíso, T032-250976. No fishing or cargo boats will take passengers.

Rapa Nui/Easter Island → *Phone code: 032. Always 2 hrs behind the Chilean mainland.*

Known as the navel of the world by the original inhabitants, this remote outpost is studded with giant carved statues that appear trance-like, their gaze fixed on a distant horizon on the Pacific. Isla de Pascua (Rapa Nui) is just south of the Tropic of Capricorn and 3,790 km west of Chile. Its nearest neighbour is Pitcairn Island.

Ins and outs
Information Tourist office Sernatur ① *Tu'u Maheke s/n esq Apina, T100255, ipascua@sernatur.cl.* **Websites** http://islandheritage.org (**Easter Island Foundation**). Average monthly temperatures vary between 15-17° C in August and 24° C in February, the hottest month. Average annual rainfall is 1,100 mm. There is some rain throughout the year, but the rainy season is March to October (wettest in May). The tourist season is from September to April. Anyone wishing to spend time exploring the island would be well-advised to speak to **Conaf** first (T100236); they also give good advice on special interests (biology, archaeology, handicrafts, etc).

The cultural development of Easter Island

Far from being the passive recipient of external influences, Easter Island shows the extent of unique development possible for a people left wholly in isolation. It is believed to have been colonized from Polynesia about AD 800: its older altars (*ahu*) are similar to those of (French) Polynesia, and its older statues (*moai*) similar to those of the Marquesas Island in the Pacific between 8°-10° S, 140° W.

The very precise stone fitting of some of the *ahu*, and the tall gaunt *moai* with elongated faces and ears for which Easter Island is best known were later developments whose local evolution can be traced through a comparison of the remains. Indigenous Polynesian society, for all its romantic idylls, was competitive, and it seems that the five clans which originally had their own lands demonstrated their strength by erecting these complex monuments.

The *moai* were sculpted at the Rano Raraku quarry and transported on wooden rollers over more or less flat paths to their final locations; their red topknots were sculpted at and brought from the inland quarry of Puna Pau; and the rounded pebbles laid out checkerboard fashion at the *ahu* all came from the same beach at Vinapu. The sculptors and engineers were paid out of the surplus food

produced by the sponsoring family: Rano Raraku's unfinished *moai* mark the end of the families' ability to pay. Over several centuries form about AD 1400 this stone work slowed down and stopped, owing to the deforestation of the island caused by roller production, and damage to the soils through deforestation and heavy cropping. The birdman cult represented at Orongo is a later development after the islanders had lost their clan territoriality and were concentrated at Hanga Roa, but still needed a non-territorial way to simulate inter-clan rivalry.

The central feature of the birdman cult was an annual ceremony in which the heads of the lineages, or their representatives, raced to the islets to obtain the first egg of the sooty tern (known as the Manatara), a migratory seabird which nests on Motu Nui, Motu Iti and Motu Kao. The winning chief was named Bird Man, Tangato Manu, for the following year. It appears that the egg of the tern represented fertility to the cult, although it is less clear what the status of the Tangata Manu actually was. The petroglyphs at Orongo depict the half-man, half-bird Tangata Manu, the creator god Make Make the symbol of fertility, Komari.

Background

The island is triangular in shape, 24 km across, with an extinct volcano at each corner. It is now generally accepted that the islanders are of Polynesian origin. The late Thor Heyerdahl's theories, as expressed in *Aku-Aku, The Art of Easter Island* (New York: Doubleday, 1975), are less widely accepted than they used to be, and South American influence is now largely discounted (see below). European contact with the island began with the visit of the Dutch admiral, Jacob Roggeven, on Easter Sunday 1722, who was followed by the British James Cook in 1774 and the French Le Perouse in 1786. The island was annexed by Chile in 1888.

The original islanders called the island *Te Pito o te Henua*, the navel of the world. The population was stable at 4,000 until the 1850s, when Peruvian slavers, smallpox and emigration to Tahiti (encouraged by plantation-owners) reduced the numbers. Now it is about 2,800, of whom about 500 are from the mainland, mostly living in the village of **Hanga Roa**. About half the island, of low round hills with groves of eucalyptus, is used for horses and cattle, and nearly one-half constitutes a national park (entry US$11, payable at Orongo). The islanders have preserved their indigenous songs and dances, and are extremely hospitable.

Tourism has grown rapidly since the air service began in 1967. Paid work is now more common, but much carving is still done. The islanders have profited greatly from the visits of North Americans: a Canadian medical expedition left a mobile hospital on the island in 1966, and when a US missile-tracking station was abandoned in 1971, vehicles, mobile housing and an electricity generator were left behind.

Sights

The unique features of the island are the 600 (or so) *moai*, huge stone figures up to 9 m in height and broad in proportion. One of them, on **Anakena** beach, was restored to its (probably) original state with a plaque commemorating Thor Heyerdahl's visit in 1955. Other moai have since been re-erected.

A tour of the main part of the island can be done on foot, but this would need at least two days, either camping at Anakena or returning to Hanga Roa and setting out again the next day. To see more, hire a horse or a vehicle. From Hanga Roa, take the road going southeast past the airport; at the oil tanks turn right to Vinapu, where there are two ahu and a wall whose stones are joined with Inca-like precision. Head back northeast along the south coast, past Vaihu (an *ahu* with eight broken moai; small harbour); Akahanga (ahu with toppled moai); Hanga Tetenga (one toppled moai, bones can be seen inside the ahu), Ahu Tongariki (once the largest platform, damaged by a tidal wave in 1960, being restored). Turn left to Rano Raraku (20 km), the volcano where the moai were carved. Many statues can be seen. In the crater is a small lake surrounded by reeds (swimming possible beyond reeds). Good views and a good place to watch the sunrise.

The road heads north past 'the trench of the long-ears' and an excursion can be made to **Poike** to see the open-mouthed statue that is particularly popular with local carvers (ask farmer for permission to cross his land). On Poike the earth is red; at the northeast end is the cave where the virgin was kept before marriage to the victor of ceremonies during the birdman cult . The road along the north coast passes Ahu Te Pito Kura, a round stone called the navel of the world and one of the largest moai ever brought to a platform. It continues to Ovahe, where there is a very attractive beach with pink sand, some rather recently carved faces and a cave.

From Ovahe, one can return direct to Hanga Roa or continue to Anakena, site of **King Hotu Matua's village** and Thor Heyerdahl's landing place. From Anakena, a coastal path of variable quality passes interesting remains and beautiful cliff scenery. At Hanga o Teo there appears to be a large village complex, with several round houses, and further on there is a burial place, built like a long ramp with several ditches containing bones. From Hanga o Teo the path goes west then south, inland from the coast, to meet the road north of Hanga Roa.

A six-hour walk from Hanga Roa on the west coast passes **Ahu Tahai** (a moai with eyes and topknot, cave house, just outside town). Two caves are reached, one inland appears to be a ceremonial centre, the other (nearer the sea) has two 'windows' (take a strong flashlight and be careful near the 'windows'). Further north is Ahu Tepeu (broken moai, ruined houses). Beyond here you can join the path mentioned above, or turn right to Te Pahu cave and the seven moai at Akhivi, which look straight into the setting sun. Either return to Hanga Roa, or go to Puna Pau crater (two hours), where the topknots were carved (good views from the three crosses at the top).

Rano Kau, south of Hanga Roa, is another important site to visit; one finds the curious Orongo ruins here. The route south out of Hanga Roa passes the two caves of Ana Kai Tangata, one of which has paintings. If on foot you can take a path from the Orongo road, just past the Conaf sign, which is a much shorter route to Rano Kau crater. 200 m below is a lake with many reed islands. On the seaward side is Orongo, where the birdman cult flourished, with many ruined buildings and petroglyphs. Out to sea are the 'bird islets', Motu Nui, Motu Iti and Motu Kao. It is very windy at the summit; good views at sunset, or under a full moon (it is easy to follow the road back to Hanga Roa in the dark).

In Hanga Roa is **Ahu Tautira**, next to a swimming area marked out with concrete walls and a breakwater (cold water). Music at the 0900 Sunday mass is 'enchanting'. **Museum** ① *near Tahai, US$6*, most objects are reproductions because the genuine articles were removed from the island, but it has good descriptions of island life. There is a cultural centre next to the football field, with an exhibition hall and souvenir stall.

⊕ Sleeping

Rapa Nui/Easter Island *p759*

Unless it is a particularly busy season, there is no need to book in advance; mainland agencies make exorbitant booking charges. The accommodation list at the airport information desk only covers the more expensive places. Flights are met by large numbers of hotel and residencial representatives with whom you can negotiate. Note that room rates, especially in residenciales can be much cheaper out of season and if you do not take full board.

LL Hanga Roa, Av Pont, T/F100299, www.hotelhangaroa.cl. Including all meals (120 beds), no credit cards.

LL Iorana, Ana Magara promontory, 5 mins from airport, T100312, ioranahotel@entelchile.net. Excellent food, convenient for visiting Ana Kai Tangata caves.

L-AL Poike, Petero Atamu, T100283, ngaeheehe @entelchile.net. Homely, hot water.

AL O'tai, Te Pilo Te Henua, T100250, otairapanui@entelchile.net. Pool, comfortable, family run. Recommended.

A Orongo Easter Island, Policarpo Toro, Hanga Roa, T100294, www.hotelorongo.com. Breakfast and dinner (excellent restaurant), good service, nice garden.

A Topo Ra'a, Heterki s/n, T100225, rapanui@ lava.net. 5 mins from Hanga Roa. Very good, helpful, excellent restaurant.

A Vai Moana, Atamu Tekena s/n, 3 blocks from museum, 2 from Tahai, owner Edgar Hereveri, T100626, www.vai-moana.cl. Cabañas with shared bath, good meals, French and English spoken. Recommended.

Private homes Many places offer accommodation and tours (rates ranging from US$18 to US$35 per person, includes meals):

AL Anita and Martín Pate's guesthouse, Hereveri, opposite hospital in Hanga Roa, T100593, hmanita@entelchile.net. With breakfast, hot water, TV, good food.

AL Res Apina Nui, Hetereki, T100292. **C** low season, but bargain, good food, helpful, English spoken.

A Chez Cecilia, Policarpo Toro y Atamu Tekema, T/F100499, PO Box 45, www.chezcecilia.co.cl. With breakfast, cabañas, quiet, internet, free airport transfer, camping, tours.

A Res Hanga Roa Reka, Simón Poao, T100433, miritoni@hotmail.com. Full board, good, camping.

B Res Tahai, Calle-Rei-Miro, T100395, rapanui@entelchile.net. With breakfast, **AL** full board, nice garden.

C pp **Ana Rapu**, C Apina, T100540,

jakota@hotmail.com. Includes breakfast, evening meal US$7, camping US$10, family-run, hot water (except when demand is heavy), English spoken, dirty.

C pp **Vai Kapua Guesthouse**, Te Pito Te Henua, Playa Anakena, T100377, vaikapua@entelchile.net. With bath, homely atmosphere, delicious home-cooked meals.

D pp **Chez Erika**, Tuki Haka Hevari s/n, T/F100474, chezerika@entelchile.net. With breakfast (**C** full board), big house, nice owners, can arrange tours, use of kitchen, horse and car rental, information, phone in advance for airport pick-up. Recommended.

D pp **Res Kona Tau**, Avareipua, T100321. Youth hostel, price includes bath and breakfast.

Camping Free in eucalyptus groves near the Ranger's house at Rano Raraku (with water tank), and at Anakena (also with water tank – purify it – has to be switched on at night), make sure tent is ant-proof. Officially, camping is not allowed anywhere else, but this isn't strictly enforced. Many people offer campsites in their gardens, US$5-10 pp, check availability of water first. Some families also provide food. Several habitable caves around the coast: eg between Anakena beach and Ovahe. If you must leave anything behind in a cave, leave only what may be of use to other campers, candles, oil, etc, certainly not rubbish. Camping equipment can be hired from a shop on Av Policarpo Toro, US$50 per day for everything. **Note**: Camping gas is expensive and poor quality.

⊕ Eating

Rapa Nui/Easter Island *p759*

Most residenciales offer full board. Vegetarians will have no problems on the island. Coffee is always instant. Beware of extras such as US$3 charge for hot water.

♈♈♈ Le Pecheur, Hanga Roa. French-run, expensive but worth it.

♈♈♈-♈ Ave Rei Pua, Hanga Roa. Limited menu.

♈♈ Atamu Tekena, at the harbour/caleta, T100382. Good view, good food.

♈♈ Kona Koa, Hanga Roa. Not cheap but good, live music.

♈♈ Mama Sabina, Av Policarpo Toro. Very tasty food, clean, welcoming.

♈♈ Pizzería, opposite post office. Moderately priced.

♈ Ariki o Te Pana, on Tuki Haka Hevari s/n. For delicious empanadas. Several others.

🌙 Bars and clubs

Rapa Nui/Easter Island *p759*
There are 2 in Hanga Roa. Action begins after 0100. Drinks are expensive: bottle of pisco US$9, canned beer US$2. **Piditi**, near airport. Open Thu-Sat. **Toroko**, Caleta Hanga Roa, near harbour (open Thu-Sat), US$1.25.

⚙ Festivals and events

Rapa Nui/Easter Island *p759*
Tapati, or Semana Rapa Nui, **end-Jan/ beginning-Feb**, lasts about 10 days. Dancing competitions, singing, sports (horse racing, swimming, modified decathlon), body-painting, typical foods (lots of small booths by the football field), necklace-making, etc. Only essential activities continue outside the festival.

⭕ Shopping

Rapa Nui/Easter Island *p759*
All shops and rental offices close 1400-1700. On Av Policarpo Toro, the main street, there are lots of small shops and market stalls (which may close during rain) and a couple of supermarkets, cheapest **Kai Kene** or **Tumukai** (good *panadería* next door).
Handicrafts Wood carvings, stone moais, best bought from the craftsmen themselves, such as Antonio Tepano Tucki, Juan Acka, Hipolito Tucki and his son (who are knowledgeable about the old culture). The expensive municipal market, left of church, will give you a good view of what is available – no compunction to buy. The airport shop is expensive. Good pieces cost between US$30 and 150. Souvenirs at **Hotu Matuu's Favorite Shoppe** are good, quite expensive, designs own T-shirts, fixed prices; also sells music. There is a mercado artesanal next to the church and people sell handicrafts at Tahai, Vaihu, Rano Raraku and Anakena. Bargaining is only possible if you pay cash. Food, wine and beer are expensive because of freight charges, but local fish, vegetables, fruit and bread are cheap.

▲ Activities and tours

Rapa Nui/Easter Island *p759*
Diving Mahigo Vai Kava, Puna Apa'u s/n, T551055. Run by Mike Rapu. **Orca**, Puan Apa'u s/n, T100375, F100448, run by Michael García. Both at the harbour, all equipment provided, packages US$50 and US$60 respectively. After a check dive you will go to more interesting sights; ask for dives that suit your experience.
Hiking Allow at least a day to walk the length of the island, one way, taking in all the sites. It is 5

easy hours from Hanga Roa to Rano Raraku (camp at ranger station); 5 hrs to Anakena (camp at ranger station, but ask first). You can hitch back to Hanga Roa, especially at weekends though there are few cars at other times.
Horse riding The best way to see the island, provided you are fit, is on horseback: horses, US$35 for 3½ hrs, US$210 for 2 days. A guide is useful. **Emilio Arakie Tepane**, also leads horseback tours of the island (Spanish only) T100504. Also **Cabalgatas Pantu**.

Tour operators
Many agencies, residenciales and locals arrange excursions around the island. The English of other tour guides is often poor. Maps are sold on Av Policarpo Toro for US$15-18, or at the ranger station at Orongo for US$10. A private tour of the island costs US$35 pp including guide.
Hanga Roa Travel, T551158, hfritsch@ entelchile.net. English, German, Italian and Spanish spoken, good value all-inclusive tours. Recommended.

⊖ Transport

Rapa Nui/Easter Island *p759*
Air The airport runway has been improved to provide emergency landing for US space shuttles! LAN fly 4 days a week in high season, twice a week low season, 3 hrs 20 mins. Most flights continue to **Papeete**, Tahiti. **LAN** office on Av Policarpo Toro, T100279, reconfirm flights here – imperative; do not fly to Easter Island unless you have a confirmed flight out (planes are more crowded to Tahiti than back to Santiago) and reconfirm your booking on arrival on the Island. For details of LAN's special sector fare to Easter Island and which must be purchased outside Chile, see Essentials. A round trip from Santiago is US$800, with occasional special deals through travel agents or the LAN website (eg fixed date return for under US$500). Students studying in Chile eligible for 30% discount. If flying to or from Tahiti, check if you can stay over till another flight or even if there is time for sightseeing before the flight continues. Airport tax: flying from Santiago to Easter Island incurs the domestic tax of US$13. Flying to Tahiti incurs the US$55 international flight departure tax.
Car hire A high-clearance vehicle is better-suited to the roads than a normal vehicle. If you are hiring a car, do the sites from south to north since travel agencies tend to start their tours in the north. Jeep hire: at **Sonoco** service station, Vaihu, T100325 or 100239, on airport road. **Hertz**, opposite airport. Many other vehicle hire agencies on the main street. US$40-60 per day. Chilean or international driving licence essential. There is no insurance available, drive at

your own risk (be careful at night, many vehicles drive without lights). Check oil and water before setting out. Motorbike hire: about US$40 a day including gasoline (Suzuki or Honda 250 recommended because of rough roads). Rentals from Av Policarpo Toro, T100326.

Taxi There are taxis and in summer a bus goes from Hanga Roa to Anakena on Sun at 0900, returning in the afternoon (unreliable). **Radiotaxi Vai Reva**, Sergio Cortés, Petero Atamu s/n, T100399, 24 hrs, reliable.

❶ Directory

Rapa Nui/Easter Island *p759*
Banks Changing money is best done in Santiago as local rates are poor. US dollars are widely accepted, again at poor rates. Prices are often quoted in dollars, but bills can be paid in pesos. The bank next to the tourist office, open 0900-1200 daily, charges high commission on changing TCs, but you can change as many TCs as you like (and they can be in different names). Also gives cash against Visa and has ATM. Cash can be exchanged in shops, hotels, etc, at about

5% less than Santiago. Poor rates on Amex TCs at **Sonoco service station**. Amex TCs also changed by **Kia-Koe Land Operator**, Hanga Roa Hotel. Amex credit cards cannot be used to obtain cash (but enquire at Sonoco service station), MasterCard can be used to get cash. Cards are rarely accepted for purchases. **Bicycle hire** Some in poor condition, are available for rent for US$20 on main street or from residenciales, or you can buy a robust one in Santiago (LanChile transports bikes free up to a limit of 20 kg) and sell it on the island after 4 days. **Internet** At Rapa Call US$3.80 per hr. **Medical facilities** There is a 20-bed hospital as well as 2 resident doctors, a trained nurse and 2 dentists on the island. **Post offices** 0900-1300, 1430-1800, Sat 0900-1230; only sends packages up to 1 kg. **Telephones** Phone calls from the Chilean mainland are subsidized, at US$0.35 per min. Calls to Europe cost US$10 for 3 mins, cheap rate after 1400. New phone and fax numbers are being introduced, with prefixes 550 and 551. If 100-numbers don't work, try one of those prefixes.

Colombia

Introduction

The adventurous will love this land of sun and emeralds, with its excellent opportunities for climbing, trekking and diving. The gold museum in Bogotá, the Lost City of the Tayrona and San Agustín have superb examples of cultures long gone. Among several fine colonial cities, the jewel is Cartagena, whose history of slavery and pirates can be seen in the massive fortifications. Today, pelicans share the beach with holiday-makers. Colombia's Caribbean, which stretches to the Panamanian isthmus, is the inspiration for Gabriel Garcia Márquez' world of magical realism and is the land of accordion-led vallenato music. Of the country's many snow-capped mountain ranges, the Sierra Nevada de Santa Marta with its secretive *indígenas*, is the most remarkable, rising straight out of the Caribbean. Also not to be missed is the cathedral inside a salt mine at Zipaquirá. There are mud volcanoes to bathe in, acres of flowers, coffee farms to visit and a CD library's worth of music festivals. In fact, dancing is practically a national pastime and having a good time is taken very seriously: as García Márquez once said, "five Colombians in a room invariably turns into a party." Despite the drug trade and the guerrilla violence which has scarred the minds and landscape of this beautiful country, Colombia is rebuilding its position on the tourist circuit.

★ Don't miss...

1 **Museo de Oro** One of the most significant museums in South America, with an awe-inspiring collection of pre-Columbian gold, page 782.

2 **Zipaquirá** Visit the cathedral carved out of a rock salt mine. This is truly one of the wonders of Colombia, page 792.

3 **Cartagena** A beautiful colonial city, with a fortified heart and fascinating history. Its other life is as a Caribbean beach resort, page 808.

4 **La Ciudad Perdida** Rising straight out of the Caribbean to over 5,000 m is the Sierra Nevada de Santa Marta. Hike through the forests of the Sierra's northern flank to the Lost City of the Tayrona civilization, page 827.

5 **La Zona Cafetera** Coffee has long been one of Colombia's top exports. Base yourself on a finca and enjoy the lovely countryside, page 848.

6 **San Agustín and Tierradentro** Mysterious statues carved out of stone look out over rolling green landscapes, while nearby the hills of Tierradentro are riddled with ancient burial chambers, page 861.

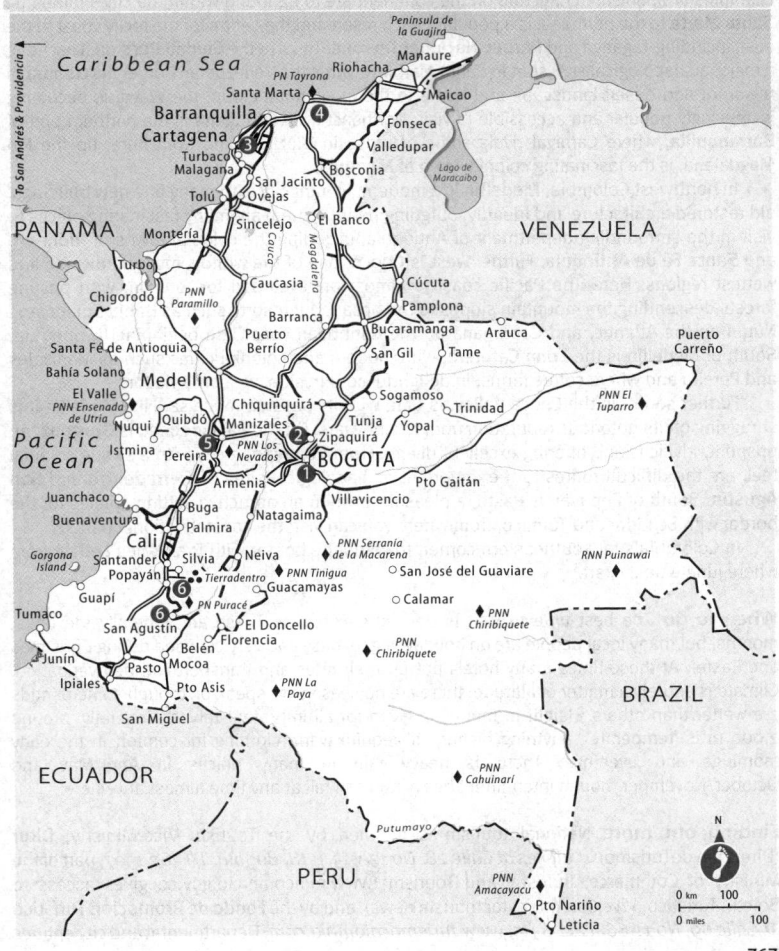

Essentials

Planning your trip

Where to go Bogotá, the capital, stands on a plateau in the eastern cordillera of the Andes. It epitomizes the juxtaposition of the historical and the modern, with many important colonial buildings and museums. Among its attractions are La Candelaria, the old centre of the city, and the magnificent Gold Museum, which houses a remarkable collection of prehispanic artefacts, one of the 'musts' of South America. Places to visit around Bogotá include the salt cathedral at Zipaquirá and the Chicaque Parque Natural, a fine preserved area of cloud forest.

Northeast from Bogotá, to Cúcuta on the Venezuelan border, the beautiful colonial town of **Villa de Leiva** is carefully preserved from the 18th century and well worth a visit. Further north, Santander department also has its attractions, including the most dramatic mountain scenery in Colombia in the **Parque Nacional Cocuy**. **Barichara** is one of the best kept colonial towns and nearby **San Gil** is an important adventure sports centre.

The obvious centre for exploring the north Caribbean coast and the tropical islands of San Andrés and Providencia is **Cartagena**. The city is a fashionable, modern beach resort and also the place where Colombia's colonial past can best be seen. Here are some of the greatest examples of Spanish architecture on the continent are to be found within the city's ramparts. **Santa Marta** to the northeast is a popular beach resort and the centre for the rocky coast to the east, including Taganga and **Parque Nacional Tayrona**. Treks to the **Ciudad Perdida** (Lost City), a major archaeological site, start in Santa Marta. Towards the Venezuelan border, **La Guajira**, a region of arid desert landscape and home to the indigenous group, the Wayú, is becoming increasingly popular and accessible to visit. Northeast from Cartagena is the northern port of **Barranquilla,** where Carnival rivals some of those in Brazil. Inland from here, up the Río Magdalena, is the fascinating colonial town of **Mompós**.

In northwest Colombia, **Medellín** is a modern, vibrant city with many fine new buildings, old restored architecture and friendly, outgoing people. There are many fascinating places to visit in the surrounding department of Antioquia, including the colonial towns of **Rionegro** and **Santa Fé de Antioquia**. Further west is **Chocó**, one of the world's most biodiverse and wettest regions. Here, the Pacific coast is almost undeveloped for tourism, with pristine forests descending the mountain slopes to the ocean, but resorts such as Bahía Solano and Nuquí on the Atlantic, and Capurganá on the Caribbean coast, are beginning to open up. South of Medellín is the **Zona Cafetera**, with modern and colonial cities such as Manizales and Pereira and where coffee farms, in delightful countryside, welcome visitors.

Further south, in the Cauca Valley, is **Cali**, with its passion for salsa. Like Medellín it is shrugging off its notorious reputation from recent years. Off the Pacific coast, is **Gorgona**, an unspoilt, idyllic island offering excellent diving. From **Popayán**, a city with a strong colonial feel, are the difficult routes to the important archaeological sites of **Tierradentro** and **San Agustín**. South of Popayán is Pasto, a pleasant town in an attractive setting, Ipiales for the border with Ecuador and Tumaco, from where you can visit the coastal national parks.

In Colombia's far southeastern corner, towards the border with Brazil, lies **Leticia** from where jungle treks start.

When to go The best time to visit is December-February. These are generally the driest months, but many local people are on holiday. It gets busy and very crowded during Christmas and Easter. At these times many hotels put up their rates and transport can be overloaded. Climate is entirely a matter of altitude: there are no seasons to speak of, though some periods are wetter than others. Height in metres is given for all important towns. Generally, around 2,000 m is 'temperate', anything higher will require warm clothing for comfort in the early mornings and evenings. There is heavy rain in many places in April/May and October/November though intermittent heavy rain can fall at any time almost anywhere.

Finding out more National tourism is handled by the Tourism Vice-Ministry, **Ditur** (Dirección de Turismo) ① *offices at Calle 28, No 13A-15, p 18, Bogotá, T/F382 1307*, part of the Ministry of Commerce, Industry and Tourism (www.mincomercio.gov.co gives access to Boletín Turístico, *Vive Colombia*, for tourism news), and by the **Fondo de Promoción Turístico** ① *Calle 69, No 11-66, T212 6315, www.turismocolombia.com*. Departmental and city entities have their own offices responsible for tourist information: see travelling text for local details. These offices should be visited as early as possible not only for information on accommodation and transport, but also for details on areas that are dangerous to visit. Regional tourist offices are better sources of information on safety than the Direccion de Turismo in Bogotá. Contact Colombia's representation overseas, see box for a list of addresses. See also Useful websites and Maps, below.

The National Parks service is the responsibility of the **Unidad Administrativa Especial del Sistema de Parques Nacionales Naturales** (UAESPNN) at the **Ministerio del Medio Ambiente, Vivienda y Desarrollo Territorial** (Ministry of the Environment) ① *Ecotourism office for information is in the Banco Agrario building, Carrera 10, No 20-30, p 1, Bogotá, T243 1634, www.minambiente.gov.co*, referred to in this guide as **MA**. A small selection of books, handicrafts, souvenirs, good videos and useful CDs about the national parks is available. At the Ecotourism office, it is possible to get up-to-date information about the security situation and which parks are closed. Permits to visit the parks are also obtainable here and at the many MA offices near the parks themselves (see text). If you intend to visit the parks, this is a good starting place. The national parks book, *Gran Libro de los Parques Nacionales de Colombia*, with superb photography and scientific information, costs US$50. Foreigners over 18 can participate on the voluntary park ranger programme. Details are available on the third floor of the UAESPNN offices in Bogotá (T341 3690). You will have to provide photocopies of ID documents and Colombian entry stamp in your passport. A good level of Spanish is required. See also their website www.parquesnacionales.gov.co (which does not give the security situation at individual parks – enquire at the Ecotourism office). Other useful address: **Red de Reservas Naturales** ① *Calle 21N, No 8-N18, Cali, T653 4538, F660 6133*. For private reserves around the country. **Instituto Colombiano de Antropología e Historia** (ICANH) ① *C 12, No 2-41, T561 9600, Bogotá, icanh@mincultura.gov.co, Mon-Fri 0800-1700*, very helpful.

Websites

www.cmi.com.co Up to date news and comment, in Spanish.
www.colombia.com Good Spanish portal, current affairs and entertainment news, information about national parks and festivals.
www.colombiajournal.org Interesting photo gallery and good selection of articles about Colombian current affairs, in Spanish and English.
www.conexcol.com Colombian search engine.
www.dfait-maeci.gc.ca/colombia/about-en.asp Canadian Embassy in Bogotá. Many useful pages and links.
www.etniasdecolombia.org Useful introduction to Colombia's indigenous groups and black communities, in Spanish.
www.humboldt.org.co Instituto Von Humboldt. Colombia's ecosystems and ethnic communities in Spanish.

www.ideam.gov.co Weather forecasts and climate information, in Spanish.
www.natura.org.co Fundación Natura, excellent conservation information.
www.poorbuthappy.com/colombia Reliable information on travel, jobs and safety, in English.
www.posadasturisticas.com.co Gives information about places to stay in Colombia, including Chocó.
www.presidencia.gov.co The government website. You can also access:
www.gobiernoenlinea.gov.co, in Spanish and English.
www.quehubo.com Colombian Yellow Pages site.
http://sinic.mincultura.gov.co/cultur activa/cons_culturactiva.asp?SECCION=8 Cultural events in Colombia, in Spanish

Maps Maps of Colombia are obtainable at the **Instituto Geográfico Agustín Codazzi** ① *Carrera 30, Bogotá, No 48-51, T369 4000, www.igac.gov.co*, or from their offices in other large cities. They have a wide range of official, country-wide and departmental maps and atlases. The topographical details of the walking maps are generally accurate, but trails and minor roads less so. In Bogotá, they are open Monday-Friday 0800-1630, maps are mainly from US$2.50 to US$6 and you pay at the bank next door. There is a library open until 1630 and refreshments available at lunchtime. The best current maps of Colombia, *Mapa Vial de Colombia* by Rodríguez, scale 1:2,000,000, 1994, costs about US$4. An excellent guide with good, detailed road maps across the country is the annual *Guía de Rutas por Colombia* available at major bookstores and toll booths. Drivers' route maps are included in the *AutoGuía*, by Publicación Legis, US$8 (1997). Esso and other maps from some service stations, US$2 and a *Guía Vial de Colombia*, US$3, available at bookshops.

Visas and immigration Tourists are normally given 90 days permission to stay on entry, though this is not automatic. If you intend to stay more than 30 days, make sure you ask for longer. If not granted at the border, extension (*salvoconducto*) can be applied for at the DAS (security police) office in any major city. The *salvoconducto* is only issued once for a period of 30 days and is usually processed within 24 hours. Best to apply two to three days before your visa expires. Bring two recent photos and copies of your passport. If you overstay on any type of visa, you will be charged a fine, minimum US$55 up to US$800. The **DAS** office in Bogotá is ① *C 100, No 11B-27, T601 7200, www.das.gov.co* (see under Bogotá, Useful addresses). Expect long queues and a painfully slow bureaucratic process. **Note** DAS does not accept cash payments; these are made at the appropriate bank with special payments slips. Alternatively, if you have good reason to stay longer (eg for medical treatment), apply at the embassy in your home country before leaving. If you wish to stay between seven to 10 days longer on a tourist visa, go to a DAS office with your onward ticket and they will usually grant you a free extension on the spot. An onward ticket may be asked for at land borders or Bogotá international airport. Visitors may be asked to prove that they have sufficient funds for their stay.

To visit Colombia as a tourist, nationals of Republic of Ireland, countries of former Eastern Europe (except Romania) and the Middle East (except Israel), Asian countries (except Japan, South Korea, Malaysia, Phillipines, Indonesia and Singapore), Haiti, Nicaragua, and all African countries need a visa. If in doubt, check regulations before leaving your home country. At the time of writing, nationals of Republic of Ireland were only being issued 15-day visas and getting extensions was very difficult. Visas are issued only by Colombian consulates. When a visa is required you must present a valid passport, three photographs, the application form (in duplicate), £30 or equivalent (price varies according to nationality), onward tickets, and a photocopy of all the documents (allow two weeks maximum).

If you are going to take a Spanish course, you must have a student visa. You may not study on a tourist visa. A student visa can be obtained while in Colombia on a tourist visa. Proof of sufficient funds is necessary (US$400-600 for a six-month stay is usually deemed sufficient). You must be first enrolled in a course from a bona fide university to apply for a student visa. Various business and other temporary visas are needed for foreigners who have to reside in Colombia for a length of time. The **Ministerio de Relaciones Exteriores** (not DAS) ① *Cra 13, No 93-68, of 203, T640 0974/640 8576, Mon-Fri 0730-1200*, processes student and some work visas. In general, Colombian work visas can only be obtained outside Colombia at the appropriate consulate and or embassy. You must register work and student visas at a **DAS** office within 15 days of obtaining them, otherwise you will be liable to pay a hefty fine. Visas must be used within three months. Supporting documentary requirements for visas change frequently. Check with the appropriate consulate in good time before your trip.

When entering the country, you will be given the copy of your DIAN (Customs) luggage declaration. Keep it; you may be asked for it when you leave. If you receive an entry card when flying in and lose it while in Colombia, apply to any DAS office who should issue one and restamp your passport for free. Normally passports are scanned by a computer and no landing card is issued, but passports still must be stamped on entry. Note that to leave Colombia you must get an exit stamp from the DAS. They often do not have offices at the small border towns, so try to get your stamp in a main city.

Note: It is highly recommended that you photocopy your passport details, including entry stamps which, for added insurance, you can have witnessed by a notary. Always carry a photocopy of your passport with you, as you may be asked for identification. This is a valid substitute for most purposes though not, for example, for cashing travellers' cheques or drawing cash across a bank counter. Generally acceptable for identification (eg to enter government buildings) is a driving licence, provided it is plastic, of credit card size and has a photograph. For more information, check with your consulate.

Colombian embassies and consulates Visit www.minrelext.gov.co for a full list of addresses.

Money The currency is the peso. There are coins of 50, 100, 200 and 500; there are notes of 1,000, 2,000, 5,000, 10,000, 20,000 and 50,000 pesos (the last can be difficult to change). Change is in short supply, especially in small towns, and in the morning. Watch out for forged notes. The 50,000-peso note should smudge colour if it is real, if not, refuse to accept it. Peso **exchange rate** with US$: 2,254 (March 2006); euro: 2,687. There is a limit of US$10,000 on the import of foreign exchange in cash, with export limited to the equivalent of the amount brought in.

Touching down

Airport and other taxes The airport departure tax for stays of over 60 days is US$51 (payable in US$, pesos; some airlines accept Visa). For stays of less than 60 days the tax is about US$26. You will need an exit tax exemption certificate from the *impuestos* desk (ground floor near check-in desks) to confirm you have been less than 60 days in the country. Travellers changing planes in Colombia and leaving the same day are exempt from this tax. When you arrive, ensure that all necessary documentation bears a stamp for your date of arrival; without it you will have to pay the full exit tax. There is also an airport tax on internal flights, US$2.30 (varies according to airport), usually included in the ticket price.

Business hours Offices Mon-Fri, 0800-1200 and 1400-1730 or 1800. Firms in the warmer towns such as Cali start at 0700 and finish earlier. **Government offices** generally follow the same hours as businesses, but prefer to do business with the public

in the afternoon only. **Embassy** hours for the public are 0900-1200 and 1400-1700 (Mon-Fri). **Banks** Mon-Fri 0900-1500, except the last working day in the month when they close at 1200 or all day. Some banks are now open on Sat. Outside Bogotá banks open 0800-1130, 1400-1630. **Shops** Mon-Sat 0900-1230 and 1430-1830.

In an emergency Police T112; civil defence T144 (640 0090 in Bogotá); DAS security T153;

International phone code +57. Ringing: equal tones with long pauses. Engaged: short tones with short pauses.

Official time Five hours behind GMT.

Tipping Upmarket restaurants 10%, often included in the bill. Porters, cloakroom attendants and hairdressers US$0.05-0.25. Taxis are not tipped.

VAT 16% on most items; 10% on some services.

Voltage 120 volts AC. Transformer must be 110-150 volt AC, with twin flat-prong plugs (all of same size).

Weights and measures Generally metric, but US gallons for petrol.

Plastic/TCs/banks Cash and travellers' cheques can in theory be exchanged in any bank, except the *Banco de la República*. Go early to banks in the smaller places to change cash or travellers' cheques. In most sizeable towns there are *casas de cambio* (exchange shops), which are quicker to use than banks but sometimes charge higher commission. It's best to use euros and, even better, dollars. It can sometimes be difficult to buy and sell sterling, even in Bogotá. Hotels may give very poor rates of exchange, especially if you are paying in dollars. It is dangerous to change money on the streets and you may well be given counterfeit pesos. Also in circulation are counterfeit US dollar bills. You must present your passport when changing money (a photocopy is not normally accepted). Take some US$ cash with you for emergencies.

Credit cards As it is unwise to carry large quantities of cash, credit cards are widely used, especially MasterCard and Visa; Diners Club is also accepted. American Express is only accepted in expensive establishments in Bogotá. Many banks accept Visa (Visaplus and ATH logos) and Cirrus/MasterCard (Maestro and Multicolor logos) to advance pesos against the card, or through ATMs. There are ATMs for Visa and MasterCard everywhere but you may have to try several machines. All Carulla supermarkets have ATMs. **Credit card loss or theft**: Visa call collect to (44) 20-7937 8091 or fax (44) 17-3350 3670, MasterCard T0800-912 1303. **Note** ATMs do not retain cards. If your card is not given back immediately, do not proceed with the transaction and do not type in your pin number. There are reports of money being stolen from accounts when cards have been retained. When getting cash advances on a Visa card at **Conavi** banks, you must show your passport and provide a photocopy. For cash advances on credit cards in banks, don't queue for the general cashiers, go directly to the customer services counter.

    Note Only use ATMs in supermarkets, shopping malls or those where a security guard is present. Be particularly vigilant in December as thieves tend to be on the prowl.

Travellers' cheques When changing TCs, a photocopy of your passport may be required as well as the original, so take a supply of photocopies with you. The procedure is always slow, maybe involving finger printing and photographs. Take dollar TCs in small denominations; better still, take a credit card (see above). Sterling TCs are practically impossible to change. To change Amex TCs, use major banks. You may have to provide proof of purchase. Obtaining reimbursement for lost American Express TCs can be straightforward if you have the numbers recorded (preferably proof of purchase), a police certificate (*diligencia de queja*) covering the circumstances of loss, and apply to their offices at C 85, No 20-32, T593 4949, Mon-Fri 0800-1800, Sat 0900-1200 (see Bogotá, Banks). Banks may be unwilling to change TCs in remote areas, take local currency. TCs are not normally accepted in hotels, restaurants, shops etc.

Cost of travelling Prices are generally lower than Europe and North America for services and locally produced items, but more expensive for imported and luxury goods. For the traveller prices are among the lowest in South America. Modest, basic accommodation will cost about US$10-12 pp per night in Bogotá, Cartagena, Santa Marta and colonial cities like Villa de Leiva, Popayán or Santa Fé de Antioquia, but a few dollars less elsewhere. A *comida corriente* (set lunch) costs about US$1.50-2 and breakfast US$1-1.75. *A la carte* meals are usually good value and fierce competition for transport keeps prices low. Typical cost of internet is US$1-4 per hour.

Safety Most travellers confirm that the vast majority of Colombians are honest and will go out of their way to help visitors and make them feel welcome. In general, anti-gringo sentiments are rare. However, in addition to the general advice given in the Essentials section at the beginning of the book, the following local conditions should be noted. Colombia is part of a major drug-smuggling route and still produces roughly 80% of the world's cocaine. Police and customs activities have greatly intensified and smugglers increasingly try to use innocent carriers. Do not carry packages for other people. Be very polite if approached by policemen in uniform, or if your hotel room is raided by police looking for drugs. Colombians who offer you drugs could be setting you up for the police, who are very active in Cali, on the north coast, San Andrés island and other tourist resorts.

There have been reports of travellers and Colombians being victims of *burundanga*, a drug obtained from a white flower, native to Colombia. At present, the use of this drug appears to be confined to major cities. It is very nasty, almost impossible to see or smell. It leaves the victim helpless and at the will of the culprit. Usually, the victim is taken to ATMs to draw out money. Be wary of accepting cigarettes, food and drink from strangers at sports events and in buses. In bars watch your drinks very carefully.

The internal armed conflict in Colombia is almost impossible to predict and the security situation changes from day to day. For this reason, it is essential to consult regularly with locals for up-to-date information. Taxi and bus drivers, local journalists, soldiers at checkpoints, hotel owners and Colombians who actually travel around their country are usually good sources of reliable information. Since 2002, incidents of kidnapping and homicide rates in major cities have been declining. Travelling overland between towns, especially during the holiday season and bank holiday weekends, has in general become much safer due to increased military and police presence along main roads. However, the government has launched a major offensive against the guerrilla (especially in the south) and in some areas fighting between the armed forces and guerrilla groups has intensified. The following areas are known as *zonas calientes* (hot zones) where there is active presence of guerrilla groups and/or paramilitaries: the rural areas down the eastern part of the country from Arauca and Casanare to Meta; Cáqueta and Putumayo; the Magdalena Medio and Norte de Santander; from Urabá near the border with Panamá into northwestern Antioquia and parts of Chocó; Sur de Bolívar and Carmen de Bolívar in the department of Bolívar; and in and around La Macarena national park. Travellers wishing to go into rural areas in Cauca and Nariño in the southwest should also seek advice. As a loose rule, the conflict is often most intense in coca growing areas, oil producing regions and along Colombia's borders. Guerrilla activity usually increases in the run up to local and national elections. Incidents in cities, including Bogotá, may also occur. Do not travel between towns by road at night. Parts of the motorway in the above areas maybe randomly closed at night between 1800 -0600 for security reasons. If venturing into rural areas and hot zones ask first at your embassy. It is essential to follow this up with detailed enquiries at your chosen destination. If arriving overland, go to the nearest hotel favoured by travellers (these are given in the text) and make enquiries. Note that rural hot zones are often littered with land mines.

Driving in Colombia

Road Signposting is poor and roads may be in poor condition. There are toll stations every 60-100 km on major roads: toll is about US$2.50. Motorcycles don't have to pay.

Safety Lorry and bus drivers tend to be reckless, and stray animals are often encountered. Always check safety information for your route before setting out. Police and military checks are frequent in troubled areas, keep your documents handy. In town, only leave your car in an attended car park (*parqueadero*). Only park in the street if there is someone on guard, tip US$0.20.

Documents International driving licences are advised, especially if you have your own car. To bring a car into Colombia, you must also have documents proving ownership of the vehicle, and a tourist card/transit visa. These are normally valid for 90 days and must be applied for at the Colombian consulate in the country which you will be leaving for Colombia. A *carnet de passages* is recommended when entering with a European registered vehicle. Only third-party insurance issued by a Colombian company is valid (around US$70); there are agencies in all ports. You will frequently be asked for this document while driving. Carry driving documents with you at all times.

Car hire In addition to passport and driver's licence, a credit card may be asked for as additional proof of identity and to secure a returnable deposit to cover any liability not covered by the insurance. If renting a Colombian car, note that major cities have the *pico y placa* system which means cars are not allowed entry in the city during morning and afternoon rush hour depending on the day and car number plate (does not apply during the weekends and public holidays).

Fuel 'Premium 95' octane (only in large cities), about US$2 per US gallon; 'corriente' 84 octane, US$1.50 per US gallon. Diesel US$1.30. The cost of petrol is up to 70% cheaper near and on the Venezuelan border, eg in La Guajira and Cúcuta.

Amazonas and to a lesser extent **Los Llanos** have always been difficult to visit because of their remoteness, the lack of facilities and the huge distances involved (these factors also apply to La Guajira in the north). Our text is limited to Villavicencio, Florencia and the Leticia region all of which are comparatively safe. They should only be visited by air, except Leticia where river routes are safe.

Getting around

Air Avianca, www.avianca.com, is the main internal airline. Other airlines are **Aires**, www.aires.com.co, and **AeroRepública**, www.aerorepublica.com.co. *Avianca* offers a domestic air pass ticket giving travel for 30 days, if arriving in Colombia by air from overseas. The pass must be bought outside Colombia in conjunction with an international air ticket and is also issued to passengers not travelling with Avianca from their original destination, at an additional US$35-50. There are reductions for children and infants. The air pass allows three stops (US$169), four (US$222) or five (US$272). An extra US$70 is charged for travel to Cartagena and San Andrés. The Air Pass is non-refundable unless the whole has been unused. You may not pass through each city more than once (except for transfers), and a proposed itinerary (not firm) must be submitted when buying the ticket. These prices and conditions change from time to time, enquire at any *Avianca* office. Sometimes there are good value reductions advertised in the press, eg weekend trips from Bogotá to the North coast and all-inclusive deals to San Andrés. Domestic airports vary in the services they offer and the tourist facilities tend to close early on weekdays, and all Sunday. It is almost impossible to change money at small regional airports. There is a 16% sales tax on one way tickets and an 8% tax on return trips. Local airport taxes are included in the ticket price. Security checks can be thorough, watch your luggage. **Satena** *www.satena.com*, fly to destinations in the south and remoter regions of Chocó, Los Llanos, Amazonas and Orinoquia and is generally slightly cheaper than Aires.

Bus Travel in Colombia is exciting. The scenery is generally worth seeing so travel by day: it is also safer and you can keep a better eye on your valuables. Almost all the main routes are paved, but the state of the roads varies considerably between departments. On main routes you usually have choice of company, and type, of bus. The cheapest (*corriente*) are basically local buses, stopping frequently, uncomfortable and slow but offering plenty of local colour. Try to keep your luggage with you. *Pullman* (each company will have a different name for the service) are long distance buses usually with a/c, toilets, hostess service, videos (almost always violent films, Spanish/Mexican or dubbed English) and limited stop. Sit near the back with your walkman to avoid the video and the need to keep the blinds down. Luggage is normally carried in a locked compartment against receipt. *Colectivos*, also known as *vans* or *busetas*, run by **Velotax**, **Taxis Verdes**, etc are usually 12-20 seat vehicles, maybe with a/c, rather cramped but fast, saving several hours on long journeys (so not for the faint-hearted!). You can keep your eye on luggage in the back of the van. Fares shown in the text are middle of the range where there is a choice but are no more than a guide. Note that meal stops can be few and far between, and short; bring your own food. Be prepared for climatic changes on longer routes and for the vagaries of a/c on buses, sometimes fierce, sometimes none. **If you entrust your luggage to the bus companies' luggage rooms, remember to load it on to the bus yourself; it will not be done automatically.** There are few interdepartmental bus services on holidays. If you are joining a bus at popular or holiday times, not at the starting point, you may be left behind even though you have a ticket and reservation. Always take your passport (or photocopy) with you: identity and luggage checks on buses are frequent and you may be body-searched at army roadblocks.

Cycling Cycling is a popular sport in Colombia. There are good shops for spares in all big cities, though the new standard 622/700 size touring wheel size is not very common. Take your own spare tyres. Around Calle13 with Cra 20 in front of La Sabana train station in Bogotá are several bicycle repair and accessory shops.

Hitchhiking Hitchhiking (*autostop*) is unadvisable. In safe areas, try enlisting the co-operation of the highway police checkpoints outside each town and toll booths. Truck drivers are often very friendly, but be careful of private cars with more than one person inside. Travelling on your own is not recommended.

Taxi Whenever possible, take a taxi with a meter and ensure that it is switched on. If there is no meter, bargain and fix a price. All taxis are obliged to display the additional legal tariffs that may be charged after 2000, on Sunday and fiestas. Don't take a taxi which is old; look for 'Servicio Público' on the side. It is safest to call a radio taxi, particularly at night, rather than hailing one down in the street. Bars, hotels and restaurants will gladly order taxis for customers. The dispatcher will give you the cab's number which should be noted in case of irregularities. The last two digits of the number from where the call was made is *el clave*, the security code. Remember it as taxi drivers will ask for the code before setting off. Never get into a taxi if there are already passengers in it. If the taxi 'breaks down', take your luggage out and find another taxi immediately.

Sleeping → *See inside front cover for our hotel grade price guide.*

Hotels The more expensive hotels are required to charge about 10% VAT (IVA). Some hotels add a small insurance charge (about US$0.75 per night). Between 15 December and 30 April, 15 June and 31 August and bank holidays (puentes) hotels in main holiday centres may increase prices by at least 20-30%. Prices are normally displayed at reception, but in quiet periods it is always worth negotiating.

Camping Sites are given in the text but also check locally very carefully before deciding to camp. Local tourist offices have lists of official sites, but they are seldom signposted on main roads. Permission to camp with tent, camper van or car is usually granted by landowners in less populated areas. Many haciendas have armed guards protecting their property: this can add to your safety. Vehicles may camp at truck drivers' restaurants, *balnearios campestres* with armed guards, or ask if you may overnight beside police or army posts.

Youth Hostels **Federación Colombiana de Albergues Juveniles**, Cra 7, No 6-10, Bogotá, T91-280 3041, www.fcaj.org.co. The (FCA) is affiliated to Hostelling International.

Eating → *See inside front cover for our Eating price guide.*

Eating out Colombia's food is regionally varied, but most major cities have restaurants with non-local Colombian food. Small towns do not cater for vegetarians. Restaurants in smaller towns often close on Sunday, and early on weekday evenings: if stuck, you will probably find something to eat near the bus station. If economising, ask for the excellent value *menú del día*, also known as *comida corriente* (daily set lunch). This consists of a filling three-course meal (juice, soup, meat or fish dish and dessert) for no more than US$2. If the menu states that 10% IVA is included in the price, this should not be added as an extra on the bill. Refuse to pay it.

Food A standard main course is *sancocho,* a filling combination of some root vegetable, including the tropical cassava and yam, with chopped fresh fish or any kind of meat. Colombia has its own variant of the inevitable *arroz con pollo* (chicken and rice) which is excellent. *Ajiaco de pollo* is a delicious chicken, maize, manioc, cabbage and potato stew served with cream and capers, and lumps of avocado; it is a Bogotá speciality; another Bogotá speciality is *sobrebarriga* (belly of beef). *Bandeja antioqueña* consists of meat grilled and served with rice, beans, potato, manioc and a green salad; *bandeja paisa* is a filling fry-up of minced beef with rice, beans, fried egg, chorizo, avocado; the simpler *carne asada* is cheaper. *Mazamorra*, boiled maize in milk, is a typical *antioqueño* sweet, and so is *salpicón*, a tropical fruit salad drink, also popular in Bogotá. (In Boyacá, however, *mazamorra* is a meat and vegetable soup.) *Lechona* (crispy sucking pig and herbs) is a speciality of Ibagué. Cartagena's rice is usually with coconut. In Nariño, guinea pig (*cuy, curí* or *conejillo de Indias*) is typical. *Tamales* are meat pies made by folding a maize dough round chopped pork mixed with potato, peas, onions, eggs and olives seasoned with garlic, cloves and paprika, and steaming the whole in banana leaves (which you don't eat); the best are from Tolima. From stalls in the capital and the countryside, try *mazorcas* (roast maize cobs), *arepas* (fried maize cakes), or *empanadas* (pies filled with meat and or cheese). On the Caribbean coast, eat an egg *arepa*, which consists of two layers of corn (maize) dough, fried with eggs in the middle. Also, try the popular *cazuela de mariscos*, a creamy, thick seafood casserole often served with grated cheese. Fried fish, including *mojarra* and *robalo* with rice and *patacones* (fried banana cakes) is the staple dish along the coast. *Huevos pericos*, eggs scrambled with onions/tomatoes, are popular for breakfast. *Pandebono*, best in Cali, is a delicious sour cheese-flavoured bread. Also from Cali, try the *pan de yuca*.

A good local sweet is the *canastas de coco*: pastry containing coconut custard flavoured with wine and surmounted by meringue. *Arequipe* is very similar to fudge, and popular (it is called *manjarblanco* in other parts of South America). *Brevas con arequipe*, figs filled with arequipe and covered in syrup, is a popular dessert from Cali. *Almojábanas*, a kind of sour-milk/cheese bread roll, are delicious if fresh. There is, indeed, quite an assortment of little fruit pasties and preserves. Then there are the usual fruits: bananas, oranges, mangoes, avocado pears, and (at least in the tropical zones) *chirimoyas, papayas*, and the delicious *pitahaya*, taken either as an appetizer or dessert. Colombia also has an abundance of other tropical fruits, all worth trying, eg the *guayaba* (guava), *guanábana* (soursop), *maracuyá* (passion fruit), *lulo* (*naranjilla*), *mora* (blackberry) and *curuba* (banana passion fruit). They make delicious juices, made with water, or with milk to make a *sorbete*, though *sorbetes* are best left alone unless you are satisfied the milk is fresh. There is also *feijoa*, a green fruit with white flesh, high in vitamin C. Fruit yoghurts are nourishing and cheap (try *Alpina* brand; *crema* style is best), or *kumis*, a kind of liquid yoghurt. Another drink you should try is *champús*, a corn base with lemon and other fruit.

Drink *Tinto*, the national small cup of black coffee, is taken at all hours and is usually sweetened. Colombian coffee is always mild. Coffee with milk is called *café perico*; *café con leche* is a mug of milk with coffee added. To make sure you get cold milk with your coffee, ask for it separately at an additional cost. *Agua de panela* is a common beverage (hot water with unrefined sugar), also made with limes, served with cheese. Many decent brands of beer are brewed,, including *Costeña, Aquila* and *Club Colombia*. Also popular is *Brava*. The local rum is good and cheap; ask for *ron* eg Santafe or Ron Viejo de Caldas. *Aguardiente* is a 'rougher' cane-based spirit served with or without aniseed (*aguardiente anisado*). Try *canelazo*, cold or hot *aguardiente* with water, sugar, lime and cinnamon, common in Bogotá. Local table wines include Isabella; none is very good. Wine is very expensive, US$15 in restaurants for an average Chilean or Argentine wine, more for European and other wines. If settling in at a bar or club for the night, order spirits by the bottle or half bottle, to cut down costs.

Colombia Essentials

Festivals and events

Public Holidays: there are some 18 public holidays throughout the year. The most important are: 1 January: Circumcision of our Lord; 6 January: Epiphany*; 19 March: St Joseph*; Maundy Thursday; Good Friday; 1 May: Labour Day; Ascension Day*; Corpus Christi*; Sacred Heart*; 29 June: SS Peter and Paul*; 20 July: Independence Day; 7 August: Battle of Boyacá; 15 August: Assumption*; 12 October: Columbus' arrival in America* (Día de la Raza); 1 November: All Saints' day*; 11 November: Independence of Cartagena*; 8 December: Immaculate Conception; 25 December: Christmas Day. When those marked with an asterisk do not fall on a Monday, or when they fall on a Sunday, they will be moved to the following Monday. Public holidays are known as *puentes* (bridges).

Bogotá

→ *Phone code: 91. Colour map 1, grid B3. Population: 7.19 million (2005). Altitude: 2,650 m. Mean temperature: 14° C.*

Bogotá, the eighth-largest city in Latin America, is a vast sprawling metropolis where, despite its modernity, it is not uncommon to see the horse and cart still in use on the streets. It is the cultural centre of the country with cosmopolitan restaurants and a vibrant night life. Predictably, there are staggering extremes of wealth and poverty, with the city segregated between the rich north and the poorer south. The capital has advanced in leaps and bounds since the mid-1990s, winning awards for its environmental efforts, libraries, transport systems as well as improving quality of life. Since 2001, the TransMilenio, a rapid, efficient north-south bus route has helped to unclog Bogotá's gridlocked streets. On Sundays, the city's main streets are closed to traffic for the benefit of cyclists, joggers and rollerbladers. Emerald sellers do deals on street corners, but for a safer view of all that glitters, visit the Gold Museum, one of the most stunning collections of pre-Columbian treasures in the Americas. The old centre of La Candelaria has countless well-preserved colonial buildings and important museums that lie along cobbled streets with fine views over the city. A windy mountain road above the city leads to La Calera, offering panoramic views, a popular place for lunch and horse riding at weekends. As Bogotá is Latin America's third highest city, it gets chilly at night. Warm clothes are needed.

Ins and outs

Getting there El Dorado **airport** has two terminals, El Dorado and Puente Aéreo, 15 km west of the centre. A taxi to the city costs about US$8, more at night and early morning. Make sure you get a registered taxi, normally yellow, outside the main terminal or **Avianca** terminal. Near the exit from the baggage area, there is a taxi office where you can state your destination and receive a computer slip detailing the fare (if not available, ask the driver to quote the fare beforehand). There are *colectivos* (US$1 plus luggage pp) from airport to centre; also buses in the daytime, US$0.25 (not easy with bulky luggage and they may refuse to take you). Be vigilant with your belongings when coming out of the arrivals hall into the street. The long-distance **bus terminal**, Terminal de Transportes, is in the same direction as the airport, but not as far out. To get into town from the terminal take buses marked 'La Candelaria', 'Centro' or 'Germania'; ask the driver where to get off (the 'Germania' bus goes up to the centre and La Candelaria). Note there are two areas called La Candelaria, one in the north of the city and one in the south. Be sure to ask for La Candelaria in 'el centro histórico'. To get to North Bogotá from the terminal, take a bus heading in that direction on Cra 68. If taking a taxi, obtain a slip (as at the airport), to fix the fare: to the centre, about US$6. At airport and bus terminal, unofficial taxis are dangerous and must be avoided. ▶ *For more information, see Transport, page 789.*

Getting around Bus: Several types of bus cover urban routes. All stop when flagged down. There are also the red **TransMilenio** buses on dedicated lanes. **Taxi**: have meters which calculate units starting at 25. Total units for journey are converted into pesos using a table which must be displayed in the taxi. Taxis are relatively cheap and easy to come by (apart from when it's raining). If you are carrying valuables and especially at night, call for a radio taxi rather than taking one on the street. For reliable and safe radio taxi companies

T311 1111 or 611 1111. **Street numbering**: The Calles (abbreviated 'C', or 'Cll') run at right angles across the Carreras ('Cra' or 'K'). It is easy enough to find a place once the address system, which is used throughout Colombia, is understood. The address Calle 13, No 12-45 would be the building on Calle 13 between Carreras 12 and 13 at 45 paces from Carrera 12; however transversals (Tra) and diagonals (Diag) can complicate the system. The Avenidas, are broad and important streets. One of the most important streets is Carrera 7, known as La Séptima, which runs from north to south of the city. Routes through the city are changing all the time, complicated by extensions of the TransMilenio. Potholes in both roads and pavements can be very deep: avoid them, especially when it is wet.

Orientation The mountains of the eastern cordillera always lie east, a useful landmark for getting your bearings. The city has three main interesting parts: La Candelaria, the well-preserved historic centre; Downtown Bogotá, known as 'El Centro', the old commercial centre with shops, high-rise offices and banks; and North Bogotá, where there has been great commercial expansion with the development of wealthy suburbs. **La Candelaria**, full of character, occupies the area bounded by Av Jiménez de Quesada, C 6, Cra 3 and Cra 10. There is some modern infill but many of the houses are well preserved in colonial style, of one or two storeys with tiled roofs, projecting eaves, wrought ironwork and carved balconies. The main colonial churches, palaces and museums are concentrated around and above the Plaza Bolívar. Some hotels are found in this part, more along the margins, eg Av Jiménez de Quesada. **Downtown Bogotá** runs in a band northeastwards along Cra 7 from Av Jiménez de Quesada to C26. It is a thorough mix of styles including modern towers and run-down colonial and later buildings, together with a few notable ones. The streets are full of life; they can be paralysed by traffic at busy times. The pavements can be congested too, particularly Cra 7 and Av 19. Many of the budget hotels and some of the better ones are found in this area. From C 50 to C 68 is **El Chapinero**, once the outskirts of the city and now a commercial district with a sprinkling of old, large, middle-class mansions. Next to the National Park, along La Séptima is **La Merced**, a cluster of English country-style houses. Beyond C 60, the main city continues north to a comparatively new district, **North Bogotá**. Most of the best hotels, restaurants and embassies are in this area which is regarded as the safest in Bogotá. **Maps** The best current maps of Bogotá are by *IGAC* (see Maps, in Essentials, Getting around), 1:30,000 published 2000, and *Cartur*, scale 1:25,000, 1994, about US$4 each. The **Instituto Distrital de Cultura y Turismo** (see below) gives out helpful street maps with attractions, of the city and La Candelaria.

Because of the **altitude**, go easy and be careful with food and alcoholic drinks for the first day or so. Using common sense and keeping vigilant, most travellers experience no problems walking Bogotá's streets; unless heading to Downtown or North Bogotá, do not go beyond the bounds of La Candelaria. It is unsafe to walk around La Candelaria at night, use a taxi instead. Care should be exercised anywhere after dark particularly in downtown Bogotá. Also take care on and around Av Caracas from C 26 to the centre at night as these streets become a favourite spot for prostitutes and drug dealers. Away from the centre, the whole of the south and west of the city should be avoided unless there are specific reasons for a visit. As in any city of this size, take care not to tempt thieves by careless display of money or valuables. Also, anyone approaching you with questions, offering to sell something or making demands, may well be a thief or a con-artist. The current favourite scam is a con-artist pretending to be a policeman demanding to see credit cards and money. Ignore them and walk on quickly.

Tourist offices Instituto Distrital de Cultura y Turismo, Cra 8, No 9-83, T327 4916, www.idct.gov.co, or www.bogotaturismo.gov.co. For information on Bogotá, including cultural events in La Candelaria. Also at the airport (both terminals) and bus terminal (helpful), operated by the city of Bogotá. Good local guide books and maps available. A useful website for information on Bogotá is www.terra.com.co/bogota (www.terra.com.co, also has pages on Cali and Medellín). The best monthly guide to what's on in the city, as well as lots of good info is *Plan B*, in bookshops, US$1.40, and *GO*, US$0.70, useful for trips outside Bogotá. **MA**, the National Parks Office, Cra 10, No 20-30, full details in Essentials, National Parks. Most museums are open and free on the last Sunday of the month. Many are free in August.

Sights

La Candelaria → *All museums are closed on Mon except where indicated.*

When the conquistadores first arrived in the 16th century, the area was inhabited by Chibcha Indians. The district, named after Nuestra Señora de la Candelaria, is where the conquistador Gonzalo Jiménez de Quesada founded Santafé (later renamed Bogotá) in 1538. Events in 1810 made La Candelaria synonymous with the Independence movement (see below), while the Franciscans and Jesuits founded schools and monasteries giving La Candelaria a reputation as a centre of learning. Among the oldest educational establishments is the **Colegio Nacional de San Bartolomé** ① *Calle 10, No 6-57*, across from the Chapel of **El Sagrario**, founded 1573, now a prestigious school. The **Colegio Mayor de Nuestra Señora del Rosario** ① *Calle 14, No 6-25* (1653), is a beautiful colonial building well worth a look (you can buy a good cheap lunch at the cafetería). The heart of the city and government is **Plaza Bolívar**, a good starting point from where to explore the colonial district. It is claimed that here stands the first ever statue of South America's liberator, Simón Bolívar. Around the Plaza are the narrow cobbled streets and mansions of the Barrio La Candelaria. On the northern side of the Plaza is the **Corte Suprema de Justicia** (the supreme court) destroyed by fire in 1985 after the now extinct M-19 guerrilla group stormed in. The court was wrecked and the present building was completed in

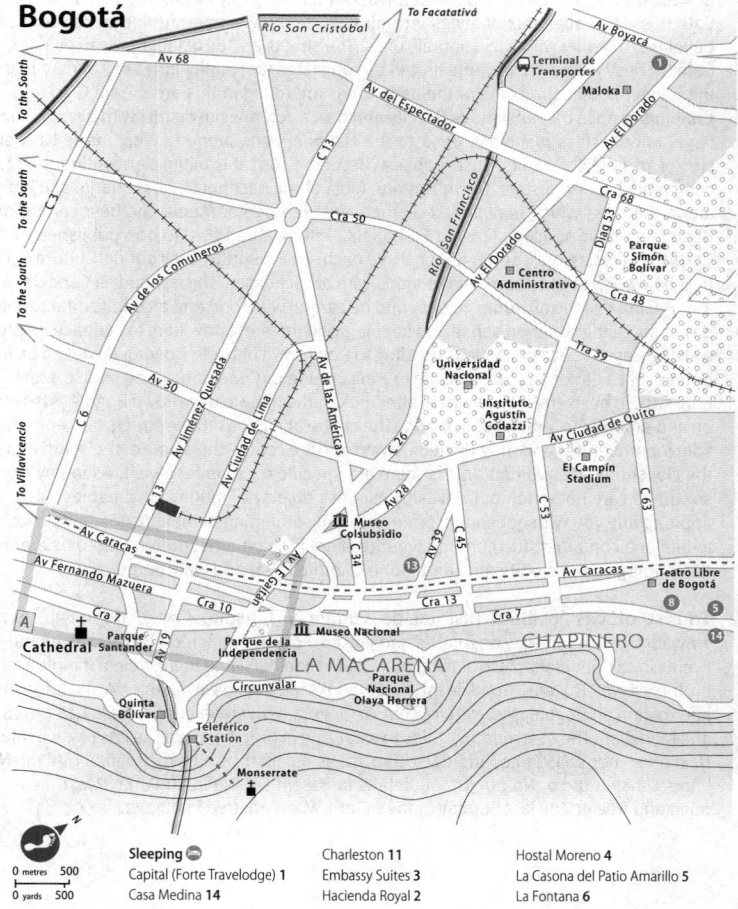

Bogotá

Sleeping 🛏

Capital (Forte Travelodge) **1**
Casa Medina **14**

Charleston **11**
Embassy Suites **3**
Hacienda Royal **2**

Hostal Moreno **4**
La Casona del Patio Amarillo **5**
La Fontana **6**

1999. On the west side of the plaza is the **Alcaldía Mayor de Bogotá** (the office of Bogotá's influential mayor and City Hall). On the south side is the **Capitolio Nacional** (congress), an imposing classical style structure with fine colonnades (1847-1925). A visit to the Capitolio Nacional can be arranged ⓘ *T382 3000/4000/5000.*

East of Plaza Bolívar On the eastern side of the plaza is the **Catedral**, rebuilt 1807-1823 in classical style. It has a notable choir loft of carved walnut and wrought silver on the altar of the Chapel of El Topo. Among its several treasures and relics is the banner brought by Jiménez de Quesada to Bogotá, now in the sacristy. There is a monument to Jiménez inside the Cathedral. In one of the chapels is buried Gregorio Vásquez de Arce y Ceballos (1638-1711), the most famous painter in colonial Colombia. Many of his paintings are in the Cathedral. Next door is the beautiful **Capilla del Sagrario** ⓘ *Mon-Fri 0700-1200, 1300-1730, US$2.20*, built at the end of the 17th century. It contains several paintings by Vásquez de Arce.

At the southeastern corner of the plaza is the **Palacio Arzobispal**, with splendid bronze doors. See the **Casa del Florero** or **Museo 20 de Julio** ⓘ *on the corner of Plaza Bolívar with Calle 11, Tue-Fri, 0900-1630, Sat-Sun 1000-1530, US$1.30 (reduction with ISIC).* It was here that the first rumblings of independence began and houses the famous flower vase that featured in the 1810 revolution. Its ten rooms display the history of Colombia's independence campaigns and boasts portraits and personal belongings of heroes such as Simón Bolívar and Antonio Nariño. It still has original early 17th century Spanish-Moorish balconies.

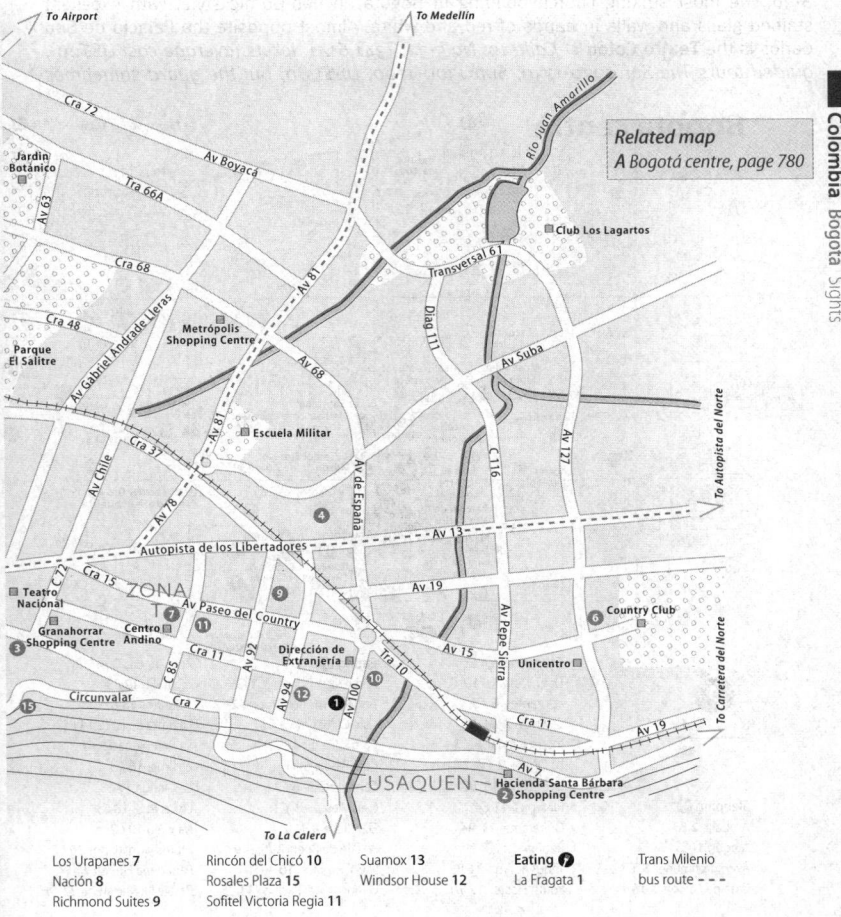

Related map
A Bogotá centre, page 780

Los Urapanes **7**
Nación **8**
Richmond Suites **9**

Rincón del Chicó **10**
Rosales Plaza **15**
Sofitel Victoria Regia **11**

Suamox **13**
Windsor House **12**

Eating ⓰
La Fragata **1**

Trans Milenio
bus route - - -

In the block behind it is the colonial **Plazuela de Rufino Cuervo**. Here is the house of Manuela Sáenz, the mistress of Bolívar. Inside is the **Museo de Trajes Regionales** ① *Calle 10, No 6-20, Mon-Fri 0930-1630, Sat 1000-1600, US$0.90, less with ISIC*, a small collection of traditional costumes from indigenous groups of Colombia. Beside it is the house in which Antonio Nariño printed in 1794 his translation of Thomas Paine's 'The Rights of Man' which had a profound influence on the movement for independence. You can read an extract of the text in Spanish on the wall of the building. Across from Plazuela de Rufino Cuervo is **San Ignacio**, a Jesuit church built in 1605 (being renovated in 2006). Emeralds from the Muzo mines in Boyacá were used in the monstrance and it has more paintings by Gregorio Vásquez de Arce. The **Museo de Arte Colonial** ① *Cra 6, No 9-77, Tue-Fri 0900-1700, Sat-Sun 1000-1600, US$0.90, less with ISIC*, is a fine colonial brick building. It belonged originally to the Society of Jesus, and was once the seat of the oldest University in Colombia and of the National Library. It has a splendid collection of colonial art and paintings by Gregorio Vásquez de Arce, all kinds of utensils, and two charming patios. Across Cra 6 is the **Palacio de San Carlos** ① *Calle 10, No 5-51, Mon-Fri 0900-1200, 1400-1700*, where Bolívar lived, which now houses the Foreign Ministry. Bolívar is said to have planted the huge walnut tree in the courtyard. On 25 September 1828, there was an attempt on his life. His mistress, Manuela, thrust him out of the window and he was able to hide for two hours under the stone arches of the bridge across the Río San Agustín (now Calle 7). Santander, suspected of complicity, was arrested and banished.

South of the Palacio de San Carlos is the **Iglesia de María del Carmen** ① *Cra 5, No 8-36*, the most striking church building in Bogotá, in neo-Gothic style, with excellent stained glass and walls in bands of red and white. Almost opposite the Palacio de San Carlos is the **Teatro Colón** ① *Calle 10, No 5-32, T341 6141 tickets (average cost US$20), guided tours Tue-Sat 0930-1730, Sun 1300-1700, US$1.80, but the guard sometimes*

Bogotá centre

Sleeping
Ambala 2 *C3*
Aragón 1 *C3*
Avenida Jiménez 3 *C3*
Casa de La Botica 18 *B2*

Centro Plaza 4 *C3*
Dann Colonial 19 *C3*
Dorantes 6 *C3*
El Virrey 7 *B4*
Internacional 8 *C3*
La Opera 9 *C2*
La Sabana 10 *B5*
Platypus 11 *C4*
Quiratama 13 *A4*
Regina 14 *C3*
Tequendama 16 *B5*
Youth Hostel 17 *B1*

Eating
Alina Pizza Gourmet 1 *C2*
Andante ma non Troppo 2 *C2*
Café Color Café 3 *C3*
Café L'Avenir 4 *C3*
Café Pasaje 5 *B3*
Candela Café 6 *C2*
Casa Vieja 7 *B5, C3*
El Boliche 8 *B6*
El Café de Buenos Aires 9 *C2*
El Champiñon 10 *A2*
El Rincón del Pacífico 11 *C3*

Empanadas Don Camillo 12 *C3*
Fulanitos 13 *C2*
La Barra de la 22 14 *B5*
La Berenjena 15 *A4*
La Bruja 16 *C3*
La Giralda 17 *B3*
Lotus Azul 18 *C3*
Mi Viejo 19 *C2*
Moros y Cristianos 20 *C2*
Panadería Florida 21 *B4*
Pasaje La Macarena 22 *B4*

allows a quick look around for free. It is considered the country's most prestigious theatre. Its opulent style is typical of late 19th-century Italian architecture. Opera, dance and ballet events are held here. One block northeast of here is the **Casa de la Moneda** (Mint) ① *Calle 11, No 4-93, Mon-Sat 0900-1900, Sun and holidays, 1000-1700, closed Tue, free.* The building dates back to 1620 when Felipe III of Spain ordered its construction, making this the first mint in the continent to produce gold coins. It houses Colombian and European art and sculptures and the machines used to produce gold and silver coins. The courtyard is worth seeing. Next door is the **Donación Botero Museum** ① *Calle 11, No 4-21/93, T343 1223, Mon-Sat 0900-1900, Sun 1000-1700, closed Tue, free.* This is a well-displayed, excellent collection of Botero's own donated sculptures and paintings, including his fine collection of modern and impressionist art including Picassos, Mirós, Dalís and Monets. Well worth a visit. In the same street is the Banco de la República's modern **Biblioteca Luis Angel Arango** ① *No 4-41, library 0800-2000, closed Sun, free,* one of the best endowed and arranged in South America, with three reading rooms, research rooms, art galleries and a splendid concert hall. There are exhibitions and regular concerts. There is good bookshop selling poster and CDs on the ground floor and a good cafetería on the sixth floor. Opposite the library is a Juan Valdez coffee shop in a pleasant terrace.

The **Palacio de Nariño** (1906), the presidential palace and offices, occupies a large space due south of Plaza Bolívar. It has a spectacular interior and a fine collection of modern Colombian paintings. It is occasionally open to the public; enquire. The guard ceremonially changes Wednesday, Friday and Sunday, normally at 1730. To the south is the Church of **San Agustín**, strongly ornamented (1637). It, too, has fine paintings by Vásquez Arce and the Image of Jesus, which was proclaimed Generalísimo of the army in 1812. South again is the **Santa Bárbara** church (mid-16th century), one of the most interesting colonial churches, with paintings by Gregorio Vásquez Arce.

Up Calle 7 from the Palacio Nariño is the **Museo Arqueológico** ① *Cra 6, No 7-43, T243 0465, www.musarq.org.co, Tue-Fri 0830-1700, Sat 0930-1700, Sun 1000-1600, US$1.30, ISIC discount,* a fine and extensive collection of Latin American, pre-Columbian pottery, in the restored mansion of the Marqués de San Jorge. The house itself is a beautiful example of 17th century Spanish colonial architecture. Below the Palacio Nariño is the **Museo del Siglo XIX** ① *Cra 8, No 7-93, Mon-Fri 0830-1730, Sat 0900-1300,* which has a fine collection of just about everything from the 19th century within a restored mansion. The nearby colonial church of **Santa Clara** ① *Cra 8, No 8-91, Mon-Fri 0900-1700, Sat-Sun 1000-1600,* has a fine interior. It is now a religious museum and concert hall.

Several blocks west of Plaza Bolívar is the **Parque Mártires** (Park of the Martyrs) ① *Cra 14 y C 10,* with a monument, on the site of the plaza in which the Spanish shot and killed many patriots during the struggle for independence.

Up the hill, east of Plaza Bolivar is **Plaza de Chorro de Quevedo**, the spot where Jiménez de Quesada and his weary troops stopped to quench their thirst at the humble fountain that still adorns the plaza. The square is a good place for people-watching and there are plenty of student bars. Storytellers and street musicians gather here on Sunday afternoons.

Pastelería Francesa **23** *C2*
Refugio Alpino **24** *B5*
Sociedad Económica **25** *B3*
Souk **26** *C2*

Churches ⛪
Catedral **1** *B2*
Capilla del Sagrario &
  Palacio Arzobispal **2** *B2*
La Tercera Orden **3** *B4*
La Veracruz **4** *B3*
Mária del Carmen **5** *C2*

San Augustín **6** *B2*
San Diego **7** *B5*
San Francisco **8** *B3*
San Ignacio **9** *B2*
Santa Bárbara **10** *B1*
Santa Clara **11** *B2*

Trans Milenio
bus route - - - - - -

Downtown Bogotá

Midway between Plaza Bolívar and Avenida Jiménez de Quesada, which marks the boundary between La Candelaria and Downtown, is the **Palacio de Comunicaciones** (Post and Telegraph building) ⓘ *Cra 7 y C 12A*, built on the site of the colonial church of Santo Domingo. Across the Avenida Jiménez de Quesada, in the commercial district, is **Parque Santander**, with a bronze statue of Santander, who helped Bolívar to free Colombia and was later its President. An artesan market is held here most day.

Next to Parque Santander is the **Banco de la República**, beside which is the wonderful **Museo del Oro** (the Gold Museum) ⓘ *C 16, No 5-41, T343 2222, www.banrep.gov.co/museo/, Tue-Sat 0900-1800, Sun and holidays (free) 1000-1600, closed 24 Dec-1 Jan, US$1.10, audioguides in English and French available*. This unique collection is a must and is a poignant reminder of why the *conquistadores* found Colombia and the rest of the continent so appealing. There are more than 35,000 pieces of pre-Columbian gold work in the total collection, most of which is held here. The rest are in other Museos de Oro sponsored by the Banco de la República throughout Colombia. The ancient gold objects discovered in Colombia were not made by the primitive technique of simple hammering alone, but show the use of virtually every technique known to modern goldsmiths. A tasteful light show in the Salón Dorado (The Gold Room) highlights some 8,000 pieces and should not be missed. The museum is undergoing expansion and the new version won't be completed until 2008. Opposite the Gold Museum is **Galería Artsenal de Colombia** ⓘ *Mon-Sun 0900-1900*, a permanent indoor art and crafts market.

Also around Parque Santander: **San Francisco** church (mid-16th century), with paintings of famous Franciscans, choir stalls, a famous ornate gold high altar (1622), and a fine Lady Chapel with blue and gold ornamentation. The remarkable ceiling is in Spanish-Moorish (mudéjar) style. Try to see this church when it is fully illuminated. **Palacio de San Francisco** ⓘ *Av Jiménez No 7-50*, built 1918-1933 in the Corinthian style on the site of the Franciscan friary, is now part of the Rosario University. Church of **La Veracruz**, first built five years after the founding of Bogotá, rebuilt in 1731, and again in 1904. In 1910 it became the Panteón Nacional e Iglesia de la República. José de Caldas, the famous scientist, was buried along with many other victims of the 'Reign of Terror' under the church. It has a bright white and red interior and a fine decorated ceiling. Fashionable weddings are held here. **La Tercera Orden** is a colonial church famous for its carved woodwork along the nave and a high balcony, massive wooden altar reredos, and confessionals, built by the Third Franciscan Order in the 17th century.

Continuing north along Carrera 7, at Calle 26 you reach **Parque de la Independencia**, adorned with wax palms. In the park is the **Planetarium**. ⓘ *Tue-Sun 1100, 1430 and 1630*. There is a good internet café (US$1 per hour) in the building, and good cappuccino served on a nice terrace overlooking the park. Behind is the impressive Moorish-style brick bullring, **La Santamaria**, see under Sports. Also at this junction (Carrera 7 and Calle 26) are the church and monastery of **San Diego**, a picturesque, restored old building. The Franciscan monastery with fine mudéjar ceiling was built in 1560 and the church in 1607 as its chapel. Local craft items are sold in part of the old monastery. Across the street is the **Tequendama Hotel**. Near the park is the **Biblioteca Nacional**, with its entrance on Calle 24. The **Museo de Arte Moderno** (Mambo) ⓘ *Calle 24, No 6-00, T286 0466, www.mambogota.com, Tue-Sat 1000-1800, Sun-holidays 1200-1700, US$1.80, students US$0.90*, is on the corner, a well displayed collection of Colombia's modern artists and foreign artists including Picasso, Dalí and Ernst. There is also a good bookshop. **Edificio Colpatria** ⓘ *Cra 7, No 24-89, US$1.20*, the tallest building overlooking this area and illuminated at night, is open Saturday, Sunday and holidays 1100-1700 for good views of the city from the top, 46 floors and 176 m up.

Museo Nacional ⓘ *Cra 7, No 28-66, T334 8366, www.museonacional.gov.co, Tue-Sat 1000-1800, Sun 1000-1600, US$1.30, students US$0.90 (pensioners free)*, is an old prison converted into a museum, founded by Santander in 1823. There is an excellent archaeological collection. Its top floor houses a fine art section, comprising national paintings and sculptures. The café, open 1100-1500, serves good salads and desserts.

Maloka ⓘ *Cra 68D, No 40A-51, near the bus terminal, www.maloka.org, Mon-Thu 0800-1800, Fri-Sun and holidays 0900-1900, US$4 without cinema entrance*, is a complex of science and technology exhibits for all ages, large screen cinema, internet café, all under a silver dome.

Monserrate

ⓘ T284 5700 (answer service in English too). The fare up to Monserrate is US$5 adult and child return. The funicular works Mon-Sat 0740- 1140; the cable car operates Mon-Sat 1200-2400 every 20 mins; both Sun and holidays 0530-1730. Times change frequently. There is a very good view of the city from the top of **Monserrate** (3,210 m), the lower of the two peaks rising sharply to the east. It is reached by a funicular railway and a cable car. The new convent at the top is a popular shrine and pilgrimage site. At the summit, near the church, a platform gives a bird's-eye view of the city's tiled roofs and of the plains beyond stretching to the rim of the Sabana. Sunrise and sunset can be spectacular. The Calle del Candelero, a reconstruction of a Bogotá street of 1887, has plenty of street stalls and snack bars. Behind the church are popular picnic grounds. There are two upmarket touristy restaurants at the top, both overpriced and closed Sunday. A good time to walk up is at the weekend about 0500, before the crowds arrive. There are enough people then to make it quite safe and you will catch the sunrise. The path is dressed stone and comfortably graded all the way up with refreshment stalls at weekends every few metres. It takes about 1¼ hours up (if you don't stop). On no account walk down in the dark. It is best not to go alone. On weekdays, it is not recommended to walk up and especially not down. You should also take a bus or taxi to the foot of the hill Monday-Friday and, at all times, from the bottom station into town. There are usually taxis waiting by the footbridge across the road. The walk up to Guadalupe, the higher peak opposite Monserrate, is not recommended.

At the foot of Monserrate is the **Quinta de Bolívar** ⓘ Calle 20, No 2-91 Este, T336 6419, Tue-Fri, 0900-1700, Sat-Sun 1000-1600, US$1.30, reductions for students and children, guided tours. This is a fine colonial mansion, with splendid gardens and lawns. There are several cannons captured at the battle of Boyacá. The elegant house, once Bolívar's home, is now a museum showing some of his personal possessions and paintings of events in his career. Opposite the Quinta is the attractive campus of the prestigious private university, Los Andes.

North Bogotá

In the link between Central and North Bogotá, is the country's leading state university, **Universidad Nacional** (about 13,000 students), which is housed in the Ciudad Universitaria shown on the orientation map. Be aware that the university's main entrance on Cra 30 is periodically the focal point of protests (sometimes violent) between students and riot police. Avoid the area during these times. There is an interesting, peaceful and well-organized **Jardín Botánico José Celestino Mutis** ⓘ Av 57, No 61-13, T437 7060, www.jbb.gov.co, daily 0900-1700, US$0.90, pensioners free, guided tours at weekends. It has a large collection of orchids, plus roses, gladioli and trees from all over the country (see map). North of Cra 68 is an expanding band of wealthy suburbs, shopping malls and classy restaurants. The area is regarded as relatively safe and the best hotels are here.

Colombia Bogotá Listings

● Sleeping

Book hotels in advance whenever possible. IVA tax of 10% is charged by middle and more expensive hotels. It is additional to the bill but included in our price classification. **Note**: Taxi drivers at the airport or bus station occasionally say that the hotel you have chosen is "closed", "not known" etc, especially the cheaper ones. Ask them to take you to the address we quote. There are any number of small, unregistered hotels and hostales in other parts of the city, not listed here, many of which are cheap, some of which are clean. Such areas may be unsafe for tourists and are remote from places of interest.

La Candelaria and Downtown p778, map p780

L Tequendama, Cra 10, No 26-21,T382 0300, www.ichotelsgroup.com/h/d/ic/1/en/hd/bogha. Large, elegant, modern business hotel in Intercontinental group, good location, used to be best in Bogotá, travel agencies, casa de cambio.

AL Casa de la Botica, C 9, No 6-45, T342 1108, hotelcasadelabotica@hotmail.com. Trendy boutique hotel in a restored colonial mansion, spacious comfortable suites, with breakfast, restaurant, excellent. The street is sealed off to traffic, so it's quiet and safe.

● For an explanation of the sleeping and eating price codes used in this guide, see inside the front
● cover. Other relevant information is found in Essentials pages 774-775.

AL La Opera, C 10, No 5-72, T336 2066, sales@hotelopera.com.co. Next to Teatro Colón, only good standard colonial hotel in centre, tastefully decorated small rooms, TV, with breakfast, 2 good restaurants, also conference facilities and business centre. Recommended.
A Dann Colonial, C 14, No 4-21, T314 1680, hoteldanncolonial@yahoo.es. Safe and well located, if somewhat uninspiring, restaurant, parking, other members of this group around the city.
B El Virrey, C 18, No 5-56, T334 1150. Modern, good value restaurant, parking. Recommended.
B La Sabana, C 23, No 5-23, T284 4830. Central, quiet, safe, carpeted rooms, a bit damp, English spoken, small restaurant, credit cards accepted.
C Ambala, Cra 5, No 13-46, T281 7124, www.hotelambala.net. Good value and a good choice, small rooms, central, safe, restaurant.
C Regina, Cra 5, No 15-16, T334 5137. Safe, good value.
D Avenida Jiménez, Av Jiménez, No 4-71, T243 6685. Helpful, sauna, safe.
D Dorantes, C 13, No 5-07, T334 6640. Cheaper without bath, hot water, high ceilings, 1950s decor, most rooms with good view of Monserrate, reasonable, safe.
D Quiratama, C 17, No 12-44, T282 4515, F341 3246. Very nice rooms, good service.
D-E Internacional, Cra 5, No 14-45, T341 8731. Cheaper without bath, hot water, kitchen facilities, free coffee, popular with Israelis (specify the address, there are other hotels with similar names).
D-E Platypus, C 16, No 2-43, T/F341 2874/ 3104, www.platypusbogota.com. In La Candeleria, run by helpful German who is an excellent source of information about travelling in Colombia, kitchen facilities, hot water, free coffee, dorms and private rooms, book exchange, good all-round travellers' guest house. Highly recommended.
E Aragón, Cra 3, No 14-13, T342 5239/284 8325. Shared bath, favoured by travellers, safe, honest, hot water, will store luggage, parking facilities.
E Centro Plaza, Cra 4, No 13-12, T243 3818, www.hotelcentroplaza.com. In La Candelaria, popular with Israelis, good, basic, hot water, colonial style, kosher restaurant, pool table, coin laundry service, adjacent internet café.
E pp Youth Hostel, Cra 7, No 6-10, 1 block beyond the Palacio de Nariño, T280 3041, F280 3460. The Federación Colombiana de Albergues Juveniles(FCA) is affiliated to the IYHA. Clean, well-run hostel with 90 beds, safe area, US$8 in dorm. Ask for full information about other hostels here.

North Bogotá p783, map p778
Most of the up-market hotels are located in North Bogotá.
LL Casa Medina, Cra 7, No 69A-22, T217 0288, reserv-casamedina@hoteles-charleston.com.

Bogotá's most stylish recent hotel, housed within a handsome old mansion, with great antique-feel. First-class service and French restaurant. Part of the Relais et Chateaux group.
LL Charleston, Cra 13, No 85-46, T257 1100, info@hoteles-charleston.com. Sister to the Casa Medina, slightly less expensive but no less extravagant, with 64 rooms and a fantastic restaurant, La Biblioteca.
LL La Fontana, Av 127, No 21-10, T615 4400. Distinctive, very good (**Los Arcos** restaurant in hotel, superb, elegant).
L Embassy Suites, C 70, No 6-22, T317 1313, F317 0464. Part of the Hilton group, good, safe location, all rooms comfortable, spacious mini-suites, restaurant and spa, business centre.
L Hacienda Royal, C 114, No 6a-02, T657 8950, F657 8913. Next to Santa Bárbara shopping centre, safe, modern, comfortable rooms, business centre, spa, restaurant and bar.
L Los Urapanes, Cra 13, No 83-19, T218 1188, www.hotellosurapanes.com.co. Very pleasant, smart, smaller hotel.
L Sofitel Victoria Regia, Cra 13, No 85-80, T621 2666, www.sofitel.com. Rooms and suites, elegant, good location, pool, restaurant, high quality.
L Windsor House, C 95, No 9-97, T616 6417, F617 0993. Large comfortable suites, elegant, restaurant, good service, safe, house taxis.
AL Capital (Forte Travelodge), Av El Dorado, No 69A-51, T423 3000, F423 3003. Close to airport, modern, comfortable.
AL Richmond Suites, C 93, No 18-81, T623 5623. Convenient, quiet, excellent rooms, spa.
AL Rosales Plaza, C 71A, No 5-47, T317 1100, www.hotelrosalesplaza.com. Spacious comfortable rooms, some with balcony, parking.
B Hostal Moreno, Transversal 33, No 95-28, T257 9127. Meals, house taxi driver, near TransMilenio stop, safe for left luggage, quiet, comfortable, hot water.
B La Casona del Patio Amarillo, Cra 8, No 69-24, T212 8805, www.lacasonadelpatio.net. Various room sizes, negotiate price, some with bath, quiet, family atmosphere, pleasant patio, safe residential area. Recommended.
B Nación, Cra 8, No 65-29/36, T249 5164, F347 5798. Just says hotel at the entrance, small rooms, safe, modern, good location.
B Rincón del Chicó, C101, No 13-32, T214 7430. Hot water, safe, family atmosphere, TV, helpful, good restaurant, free pick-up from airport and bus terminal.
B Suamox, C 38, No 16-07, T232 9800, suamox@empresario.com.co. Decent rooms, safe, fairly quiet area, restaurant.

❷ Eating

Many good value comedores on C 16 between Cras 4 y 5. Note that most restaurants that are open in the evenings in La Candelaria and Central Bogotá close around 2100. Many restaurants in La Candelaria are closed on Sundays.

La Candelaria *p778, map p780*
♥♥♥-♥♥ Casa Vieja, Avenida Jiménez, No 3-57. Friendly service in olde-worlde setting, with great typical dishes including *ajiaco*, *fritanga* and *mazamorra chiquita*. Also opposite the Hotel Tequendama, Cra 10, No 26-60.
♥♥♥-♥♥ El Café de Buenos Aires, C 9, No 2-17. 1940's BA in Bogotá, with great meat dishes. Tango shows and classes at the weekends.
♥♥♥-♥♥ La Barra de la 22, C 22, No 9-23, T342 9871. Close to bullring, favoured by media types and bullfight organizers during Dec, authentic Spanish, almost a museum, closed Sun and holidays.
♥♥♥-♥♥ Las Cazuelas de la 28, C 28, No 9-18. One of the best Spanish in town, try seafood *cazuela*.
♥♥♥-♥♥ Mi Viejo, C 11, No 5-41. Good upmarket Argentinian steak house, busy lunchtime atmosphere, closed Sun
♥♥ Alina Pizza Gourmet, C 9, No 2-81. Tasty pizzas in old colonial house setting.
♥♥ Fulanitos, Cra 3, No 8-61. Pretty antique decor with cooking from the Cauca Valley and a nice terrace. Now a chain with branches in the north, eg C 85, No 11-11. Good place for lunch, normally closed evenings.
♥♥ La Bruja, C 12, No 3-45. Mediterranean food in a converted monastery, closed Sun.
♥♥ Refugio Alpino, C 23, No 7-49, T284 6515. Good Swiss/French food.
♥♥ Sociedad Económica, C 11, No 6-42. Well-priced set lunches in a beautiful old mansión.
♥♥ Souk, Cra 6, No 10-82. Sushi, oriental food, good ribs, trendy decor, closed Sun.
♥♥-♥ El Boliche, C 27, No 5-66. Good value pastas, arty decor.
♥♥-♥ Along Cr 4 up to C 19 are rows of local fish and seafood restaurants with Caribbean and Pacific flavours, popular at the weekend, eg **El Rincón del Pacífico**, Cra 4 No 13-57.
♥ Andante ma non Troppo, Cra 3, No 10-92, La Candeleria. Excellent fresh Italian pasta, good value, Mon-Sat 1200-1500. Recommended.
♥ Boulevar Sesame, Av Jiménez No 4-64. A popular vegetarian.
♥ Candela Café, C 8, No 5-24. Located inside an old Carmelita chapel, with theatre to one side, good service.
♥ La Berenjena, C 19, No 34-37. Vegetarian, highly recommended, lunch US$2.50.
♥ El Champiñon, Cra 8, No 16-36, 2 other branches. Good vegetarian lunches, also fish.

♥ Empanadas Don Camillo, Cra 4, No 12-15. Excellent filled *arepas*. Warmly recommended.
♥ Lotus Azul, Cra 5 y C 14. Good quality vegetarian and good value.
♥ Moros y Cristianos, C7, No 5-66. Converted tall-ceilinged house, with bright, fun decor and good Cuban cooking, closed Sun.
♥ Pasaje La Macarena, C 19, No 8-62. Rows of indoor food stalls, cheap Colombian dishes and set lunches, popular with local workers.
Café Color Café, Cra 2, No 13-06, Plaza de Chorro. Cosy coffee shop and bar, rustic, try canelazo.
Café L'Avenir, C 11, No 2-98. French style, *crêpes* a speciality, salads, pleasant atmosphere, useful noticeboard, 1000-2200. Recommended.
Café Pasaje, Cra 6, No 14-25, Plazoleta del Rosario. An institution, has been on the block for 75 years, cheap beers, a good place for people watching.
La Giralda, Av Jiménez, No 7-91. Inside the handsome old Bancafé building, with cheap set lunches and piano tinkling at lunchtime. Another branch at the Museo del Siglo XIX, Cra 8, No 7-93.
Panadería Florida, Cra 7, No 21-46. Good pastries and is the place to try *chocolate santafereño*.
Pastelería Francesa, C 9, No 1-95. Charming bakery in colonial house with nice courtyard, good breakfasts, sandwiches and exquisite pastries.

Downtown Bogotá *p778, map p780*
Many good restaurants and cafes along Carrera 4 in Barrio La Macarena (behind the Bull Ring).
♥♥♥ Urbano Yo, Cra 4A, No 27-03, T334 1432. Trendy decor, Mediterranean menu, closed Sun.
♥♥♥-♥♥ El Patio Liberty, Cra 4A, No 27-48. Good French/Mediterranean food, cosy, intimate atmosphere.
♥♥♥-♥♥ Estrella de los Ríos Cocina, C 26B, No 4-50. Another intimate place, serves excellent dishes from the Caribbean coast, closed Sun.
♥♥ Clowns Deli, Cra 4, No 27-03. Restaurant chain, also in Cali. Good fresh food and crêpes, some vegetarian options.
♥♥ El Patio, Cra 4, No 27-86. Popular trendy pizzería with terrace.
♥♥ La Orilla, Cra 5A, No 26-04. Mon -Sat 1200-1530, popular seafood restaurant, excellent *cazuela de mariscos*. Recommended.
♥♥ Los Cauchos, C 26, No 3A-20. Excellent typical Colombian food served in colonial house, good lunch place. Try *bandeja paisa* and *sobrebarriga*.
♥♥-♥ La Hamburguesería, Cra 4A, No 27-27. Popular, good hamburgers, good value, terrace area. Try tortilla soup.
♥ Al Wadi, Cr 27, No 4A-14. Good Arab food, falafel.
♥ Andante coffee shop, Torres del Parque (behind Torre A) Cra 5, No 26-57. Excellent cheap breakfasts and fresh pastries under US$1.50. Recommended.

¶ Cositas Rápidas y Ricas. C 27, No 4-16. Good value and tasty *comida corriente*, popular with local office workers, nice decor, clean. Lunch only during the week.

¶ La Casa de la Abuela, C 27, No 4-75. Opposite and similar to Cositas Rápidas y Ricas. Both recommended.

North Bogotá *p783, map p778*

For great dining and lively bars, head to the Zona T, the pedestrianized area close to the CC Andino, around C 82 and Cra 13. There's also a good selection around the main in plaza in Barrio Usaquén, close to CC Santa Barbara; take bus marked Usaquén on Cra 7.

¶¶¶ Amarti, C 119, No 6-24 on Usaquén plaza. Very popular fashionable Italian, excellent pasta, buffet and deserts.

¶¶¶ Balzac, C 83, No 12-19 on La Zona T. Excellent French cuisine, good steaks, seafood and oysters, slick service.

¶¶¶ Claroscuro, C 69A, No 5-59. Fashionable and trendy, with a lounge bar upstairs.

¶¶¶ Club Colombia, Av 82, No 9-11. Impressive decor in English country style mansion with log fire, trendy, stylish lounge bar serving excellent but pricey cocktails and outside terrace area serving typical Colombian food. Open late, closed Mon. Try the *empanadas*, fruit juices, and *cazuelas*. Recommended.

¶¶¶ Di Lucca, Cra 13, No 85-32. Excellent fresh Italian food and cocktails, good service, pleasant courtyard, pricey but worth it. Open till late.

¶¶¶ La Fragata, C 100, No 8A-55. 12th floor of World Center, revolving. Also in Hotel Radisson, C 114, No 9-65, at Cra 13, No 27-98 and **Fragata Fish Market**, Cra 9, No 77-19. Excellent fish.

¶¶¶-¶¶ Gaira, Cra 13, No 96-11. Excellent Colombian food from the Caribbean coast, good atmosphere, fashionable, owned by the singer Carlos Vives. Mon-Thurs 1200-1800, Fri-Sat 1100- 2400.

¶¶¶-¶¶ Le Petit Bistrot, C 76, No 10-28, T249 4058. Excellent French cuisine.

¶¶¶-¶¶ Wok, C 93, No 12-28; Cra 13, No 82-74. Several branches of this highly-popular place serving oriental dishes.

¶¶ Fridays, C 93A, No 11-27. US$10-12. Good value, US-style bar and restaurant, good service.

¶¶ Houston's, Cra 17, No 93-17. Very popular, US-style, crowded Sun.

¶¶ Pizzería El Sol de Napolés, C 69, No 11-58, T345 3207. Small, cosy, excellent antipasto. Freshly made pasta, excellent cooking, open daily 1200-2400.

¶¶ Zhang, C 119, No 7-08. Trendy Chinese with terrace overlooking Usaquén plaza, good service.

¶¶-¶ Karen's Pizza, C 94 esq Cra 13, off Parque 93. Good fresh pizza and pasta, terrace area, good juices, popular with families, good value.

¶¶-¶ O'sole Mio, C 70A, No 10A-02 (Av Chile). Popular Italian restaurant for lunch.

¶ Crepes y Waffles, Cra 11, No 85-75. This is one of the nicest branches of this chain. Good fresh, cheap salad bar, excellent crêpes and ice-cream desserts, some vegetarian options. Branches across Bogotá and in other main cities. Recommended.

¶ El Integral Natural, Cra 11, No 96-31. Health food shop with a few tables at street level, vegetarian restaurant downstairs.

¶ Sopas de Mamá y Postres de la Abuela, Trv 19A, No 116-09. The name says it all, with regional dishes very well prepared, great value. Other branches in the city.

Café y Crepes, Diagonal 108, No 9A-11, T214 5312. Good food, good atmosphere, run by Mauricio Afanador, climbers meet here, also at Cra 16, No 82-17, T236 2688.

Café Juan Valdez, C 73, No 8-24 and C 11, No 4-15. Excellent 100% Colombian coffee but relatively expensive.

Café Oma, several locations, including Cra 15, No 82-58 and Av 19, No 118-78. Good food and coffee, nice atmosphere but relatively expensive, most are open late.

El Altillo del Sol, inside Santa Bárbara shopping centre, Plazoleta Zona B. Attractive, popular outside café serving snacks, good coffee and juices.

❶ Bars and clubs

Bogotá has good and varied nightlife, from classic salsa to heavy trance. Most clubs charge cover of US$6-9, check whether this includes a free drink. Partying starts on Wednesday night. There are many popular bars, discos etc in the Cra 11/13, C 80/86 region, known as the Zona Rosa, and on and around Parque 93. Others are on Cra 7, C 17/18, on Cra 5 with C 25, a relatively safe area, and around the plaza in Usaquén. For listings, check the *Plan B* events magazine.

In South Bogotá is an area known as Primero de Mayo, a working class neighbourhood with loads of lively bars and clubs popular at weekends. The atmosphere is less pretentious and prices are cheaper than in central Bogotá, but it is advised to go only with locals and use taxis there and back.

Downtown Bogotá *p778, map p780*

Cha Cha, Cra7, No 13-77, in former Hilton Hotel. The 'in' place at the time of writing, fashionable crowd, trendy velvet decor, excellent views of the city at night, House, techno. Thu-Sat, cover US$8.

Escobar y Rosas, Cra 4, No 15-01. One of the few good bars in La Candelaria. Converted old chemist, popular student hangout, packed Fri-Sat nights, trendy, DJs, acid jazz and funk. Wed-Sat 1730-0300.

Lounge, C 26A, No 4-42. Lively student bar in colonial house, well-priced drinks. Wed-Sat.

QuiebraCanto, Cra 5, No 17-76. In colonial house, world music, funk and salsa, best nights Wed, Thu, friendly crowd.

North Bogotá *p783, map p778*
Azul Café, C 93, No 12-73, Parque 93. Trendy lounge bar, live DJ Fri-Sat night, serves Arab food.
Bogotá Beer Company, Cra 11A, No 93-94 or C 82, No 12-10 in the Zona T. Decent British pints, very popular, European music, expensive bar food, happy hour 1600.
Café Village, Cra 8, No 64-29. Trendy and gay café.
Calles de San Francisco, Cra 13A, No 35-31. A popular gay bar.
Cameo, C 120A, No 4-90, Usaquén. Live house band, lively, friendly atmosphere.
Circa, C 69A, No 5-09. Lounge bar 2nd floor, fashionable and fancy drinks. Try the vodka and mango biche special.
Crab's Bar, Cra 13, No 73-23. One of the few bars offering live blues and jazz, best on Wed.
El Closet, Km 4.5 Vía La Calera (outside Bogota). Popular gay club.
El Salto del Angel, Cra 13, No 93A-45. Mexican restaurant and popular bar, attracts yuppie/embassy crowd, live music. Expect to queue to get in at the weekends. Cover US$7.
El Sitio, Cra 11A, No 93-52, just off Parque 93. Popular bar, good live house band at weekends, serves grills. Cover US$7
Galeria Café Libro, Cra 11ª, No 93-42 (off Parque 93) and Cr 15A No 46-38. Excellent salsa bar for salsa aficionados and couples, international salsa bands play here. Recommended.
Guararé, C 38, No 13A-91. Lively salsa club, open after 0300.
In Vitro, C 59, No 6-38, right on corner, 2nd floor. Packed Wed nights (get there before 2230), quiet rest of the week, attracts model/media crowd, friendly, good atmosphere. Cover US$8. Warmly recommended.
Kathmandu, Cr 6A, No 117-28, Usaquén. Attractive Asian decor, intimate, decent cocktails. Mon-Sat.
Salsa Cámara, Cra 14, No 82-66. Good salsa bar with live salsa at weekends. Good atmosphere.
Son Salomé, Cra 7a, No 40 -31, 2nd floor. Good local salsa bar, intimate, cosy atmosphere, Thu-Sat. Recommended.
Teatrón, C 58, No 10-32. In old large theatre, gay and mixed crowd, attracts international DJs, good atmosphere. Be careful coming out of the club at night, use a taxi. Cover US$8.
The Pub, Cra 12, No 83-48. English-style pub, popular, friendly place with good beers.
The Red Lion, Cra 12, No 93-64, off Parque 93. Another popular English-style pub.
Tienda de Café, C 119, No 6-16 on main square in Usaquén. Popular happy hour, arty decor, restaurant too.

⊙ Entertainment

Bogotá *p778, maps p778 and 780*
Cinema Consult *El Espectador* or *El Tiempo*, *PlanB* magazine; there are frequent programme changes. **Cine Bar Lumiere**, Cra 14, No 85-59, T636 0485, US$5 weekends and holidays, cheaper mid-week, comfortable airplane-style seats, food and drink. **Cine Bar Paraíso**, Cra 6, No 119B-56, Usaquén, T215 5361, foreign art films. **Cinemania**, Cra14, No 93A-85, mainstream and foreign art films. **Museo de Arte Moderno** shows Colombian and foreign films every day, all day.

There are cinema complexes in the principal shopping centres (see below). The best are **Centro Comercial Andino**, **Unicentro**, and **Atlantis**. Most have discounted rates on Tue. For programme times call *CineColombia* T404 2463. Foreign films, old and new, are shown on weekend mornings in some commercial cinemas and there are many small screening rooms running features. Admission, US$2-4. There is an international film festival in Oct (*Festival de Cine de Bogotá*) and a European film festival (*Eurocine*) in Apr/May.
Dance classes Galería Café Libro, Cra 11A, No 93-42, T218 3435. Weekly salsa classes at the club, about US$7 pp. **Punta y Taco**, Salón de Baile, Cra 14, No 75-15, T481 9534. Tango and salsa classes Mon-Sat 0800-1900, free first class, flexible class times. Individual class US$11, for a couple US$15.
Theatre Many of the theatres are in the Candelaria area. Tickets usually from about US$5 up. For **Teatro Colón**, see details on page 780.

⊛ Festivals and events

Bogotá *p778, maps p778 and 780*
There are many local religious festivals and parades at Easter and Christmas. One of the best is the **Jan Fiesta de Reyes Magos** (Three Kings) in the suburb of Egipto (up the hill to the east of Candelaria) with traditional processions.

In **Apr-May Feria Internacional del Libro** (book fair) is held in *Corferias*, Cra 40, No 22C-67, www.corferias.com. Bogotá hosts the biennial **Iberoamerican Theatre Festival** (next **2008**), www.festivaldeteatro.com.co. **Temporada de Opera y Zarzuela** held in the Teatro Colón in **May, Jun and Sep** with international artists. **Aug-Sep** is opera season. **Candelaria Festival** in **Sep** street theatre, music and dance events. In **Sep**, Festival Internacional de Jazz. In **Oct** there is **Rock al Parque**, the biggest annual rock festival in Latin America (www.rockal parque.gov.co). In **Dec** at Corferias is the **Expoartesanía** fair, an excellent selection of arts and crafts and regional food from across Colombia. Highly recommended.

O Shopping

Bogotá *p778, maps p778 and 780*

16% value-added tax on all purchases. Heavy duty plastic for covering rucksacks etc, is available at several shops around C 16 and Av Caracas; some have heat sealing machines to make bags to size. In Barrio Gaitán, Cr 30 y C 65, are rows of leather shops. This is an excellent area to buy made-to-measure leather jackets, good value; not safe at night, go during the day. Good buys can be had for designer labels such as Diesel and Levis which are cheaper in Colombia than in Europe.

Bookshops Ateneo, C 82, No 13-19, in the north of the city. Good selection of Colombian titles, knowledgeable staff. Exopotamia, C 70, No 4-47. Good selection of books and Latin music, also branch in *Biblioteca Luis Angel Arango* in Candelaria. Forum, C 93, No 13A-49, just off Parque 93. Foreign magazines, CDs, pleasant atmosphere. Librería Central, C 94, No 13-92. Some English and German books. Librería Francesa, Cra 8, No 63-45. Also imports English books. Librería Nacional bookstores across town eg Unicentro and Santa Bárbara shopping centres. Good Colombian history and current affairs section and some foreign press. Panamericana, Cra 7, No 14-09. Disorganized, but has some guidebooks and maps. Other branches in the city. Taschen, C 26, No 10-18, next to *Hotel Tequendama*. Art books, small selection of English books and foreign magazines. Also at Museum of Modern Art. Villegas Editores, Av 82, No 11-50, int 3. Great coffee-table books on Colombia.

Handicrafts Artesanías de Colombia, Claustro de Las Aguas, next to the Iglesia de las Aguas, Cra 3A, No 18-60; Cra 11 No 84-12 by CC Andino; and in Plaza de los Artesanos, Tr 48, No 63A-52. Beautiful but expensive designer crafts. Galerías Cano, Ed Bavaria, Cra 13, No 27-98 (Torre B, Int 1-19B), also at Unicentro, and Loc 218, Airport. Sell textiles, pottery, and gold and gold-plated replicas of some of the jewellery on display in the Gold Museum. Mercado de Pulgas (fleamarket) on Cra 7/C 24, in car park beside *Museo de Arte Moderno*, on Sun afternoons and holidays. A better fleamarket can be found at the Usaquén market around the plaza on Sun, also a good arts and crafts market at the top of the hill in Usaquén. Pasaje Rivas, C10 y Cra10. Persian-style bazaar. Hammocks, ceramics, cheap.

Jewellery The pavements and cafés along Av Jiménez, below Cra 7, and on Plazoleta del Rosario are used on weekdays (especially Fri) by emerald dealers. Rows of jewellers and emerald shops also along C 12 with Cra 6. Great expertise is needed in buying: bargains are to be had, but synthetics and forgeries abound. La Casa de la

Esmeralda, C 30, No 16-18. Wide range of stones. Emerald Trade Centre, Av Jiménez, No 5-43, p 1. German/English spoken. GMC Galería Minas de Colombia, C20, No 0-86, T281 6523, at foot of Monserrate diagonal from Quinta de Bolívar. Good selection of gold and emerald jewellery at reasonable prices.

Markets Paloquemao food market, Cra 27, entre C19 y 22. Bogotá's huge central market, good to visit just to see the sheer abundance of Colombia's tropical fruits and flowers. Cheap stalls serving *comida corriente*. Safe. San Andresito, Cra 38 y C12. Popular contraband market, cheap alcohol, designer sports labels, electrical goods, football shirts. Relatively safe.

Shopping centres Most have fast food malls, cinemas and *casas de cambio*. Atlantis Plaza, C 81, No 13-05. Upmarket centre with cafés, Hard Rock Café. Centro Comercial Andino, Cra 12, C 82/C 83. Upmarket shopping centre with cafes. Hacienda Santa Bárbara, Cra 7 y C 116. Charming converted colonial hacienda, Deprisa post office, Librería Nacional, internet café and Western Union agency. Metrópolis, Av 68, No 75A-50 (with Exito supermarket opposite). Palatino, Cr 7 No 139-07. New, best in North Bogotá. Unicentro, Cra 15, No 123-30 (take 'Unicentro' bus from centre, going north on Cra 10). Huge complex with Ley supermarket. Unilago, Cra 15, No 78-33. For all electrical goods, often give discounts if paying in cash.

Supermarkets Carulla supermarket chain is good for its salad and bakery counters, eg C 63, No 7-09, open 24 hrs with chemist. Exito supermarket chain, good selection of fruits and fast food counter, cheap clothes and underwear, eg Cra 59A, No 79-30. Ley, Cra 7, No 22-36 and Plaza de Bolívar Cra 7 No 11-30. Olímpico, Avenida Jiménez No 4-74. Pomona supermarket chain for expensive imported foods, eg Cra 11, No 9B-80.

▲▲ Activities and tours

Bogotá *p778, maps p778 and 780*

Bullfighting On Sun during the season (Jan), and occasionally for the rest of the year, at the municipally-owned Plaza de Toros de Santamaría, Cra 6, No 26-50, T334 1482, near Parque Independencia. In season, the bulls weigh over 335 kilograms; out of season they are "comparatively small and unprofessional". (Local bullfight museum at bullring, door No 6.)

Cycling The *Ciclovía* is a set of streets leading from Cra 7 to the west, closed to motor traffic every Sun morning and bank holidays, 0700-1400 for cyclists, joggers, rollerskaters etc. There is also the extensive *Cicloruta* paths. For days out by bike, see the *Ciclopaseo* website www.inssa.com.co.

Football Tickets for matches at El Campín stadium can be bought in advance at **Federación Colombiana de Futbol**, Av 32, No 16-22. It is not normally necessary to book in advance, except for the local Santa Fe- Millionarios derby, and of course, internationals. Take a cushion, matches Sun at 1545, Wed at 2000. Note that important matches can be rowdy and sometimes violent affairs.

Horse riding Cabalgatas Carpasos, Km 7 Vía La Calera, T368 7242, about US$15 per hr for groups of 4-5 (includes shots of aguardiente, but no food). Horse riding at night too.

Trekking Sal Si Puedes, hiking group arranges walks every weekend and sometimes midweek on trails in Cundinamarca, and further afield at national holiday periods eg Semana Santa; very friendly, welcomes visitors. Hikes are graded for every ability, from 6 km to 4-day excursions of 70 km or more, camping overnight. The groups are often big (30-60), but it is possible to stray from the main group. Reservations should be made and paid for a week or so in advance at Cra 7, No 17-01, offices 640, T283 3765, open 0800-1200 and 1400-1800. You are advised to check in advance if this service is operating as it is sometimes temporarily suspended. There are several other groups, good information on Fri in *El Tiempo* newspaper, *Eskape* section and in the monthly *Go Guía del Ocio* guide (has a small section in English and French). A recommended operator is **Caminar por Colombia**, Cra 7, No 22-31, of 226 B, T286 7487, caminarcolombia@hotmail.com, walks around the capital every Sun, US$10 for small groups, includes transport and guide.

Tour operators

Aviatur, Av 19, No 4-62, T234 7333, www.aviatur.com.co. Good, efficient, lots of branches across the country.

Bienvenidos, Cra 62, No 127-72, T/F271 4515, www.bienvenidosturismocolombia.com. Organizes cultural, trekking, beach and adventure tours and can advise on diving. Caters to tourists and business travellers, English spoken, helpful.

Eco-Guías, Cra 7, No 57-39, of 501, T347 5736/ 212 1423, 310-481 4090 (mob), www.ecoguias.com. Colombian/English team specializes in tailor made trips, ecotourism, adventure sports, trekking, riding and tourism on coffee fincas, efficient, knowledgeable and well-organized. Highly recommended.

Edutravel Victoria Reps, C 140, No 16-04, T648 3327, F274 4887. Efficient, helpful and knowledgeable, excellent English spoken by the owner, Victoria. Books hotels in Chocó and stays on coffee farms, open Sat morning. Recommended.

Oficina de Sueños, T677 7163, www.oficinadesuenos.org. Organizes good walking city tours, including La Candeleria and Zipaquirá, some with actors in period costume. Some guides speak English.

Somos Aventureros, T674 7016, T311 831 3591 (mob), www.somosaventureros.com. Arranges tours from Bogotá to Parque de los Nevados during bank holiday weekends, rafting, trekking, rock climbing

Trot@mundos, Cra 11, No 73-44, of 501, T345 7591, www.trotamundos.com.co. Student travel office, other branches around city.

Viajes Chapinero, Cra 10, No 26-33, T 566 9270. Helpful information, some English spoken.

⊖ Transport

Bogotá p778, maps p778 and 780

Air

There are 2 terminals on Av El Dorado, the Puente Aéreo terminal being 1 km before the main terminal (T425 1000 for flight information for both terminals). All **Avianca** domestic flights and some **Avianca** international flights use Puente Aéreo, which is comfortable but there is not as much duty-free shopping. **You must check which terminal your flight will use.** (See Ins and outs p for transport to the city.) The departure areas with the usual duty-free shops are of a high standard and comfortable. Many snack bars and restaurants on 1st floor. International calls can be made from **Telecom** on 1st floor open till 2100, credit cards accepted; post office in main arrivals lounge. Exchange rates are marginally lower in the city. Airport bank changes travellers' cheques, but is not open at holiday times. There is a *casa de cambio*, which changes cash only. When closed, ask airport police where to change money. Allow at least 2 hrs for checking in and security. Use only uniformed porters. Baggage deposit in the main terminal next to domestic arrivals exit (*llegadas nacionales*). There are 2 tourist offices, in international arrivals and in domestic arrivals, open late. Both are near respective exits for taxis.

For internal flights, which serve all parts of the country, see page 773. Sometimes, flights are overbooked, so check in well in advance. You must reconfirm all flights about 48 hrs before departure. For regional flights, it is sometimes possible to reserve flights over the phone and collect and pay for the ticket at the airport.

Bus

Local Fares start at US$0.40, depending on length of route and time of day. Most buses have day/night tariff advertised in the window. **Busetas** (green) charge US$0.45, US$0.65 after

2000. There are some *ejecutivo* routes (red and white) with plush seats, and *colectivos* (small vans), cramped but faster than others, charge a bit more. Fares are also higher on holidays. The **TransMilenio** (www.transmilenio.gov.co), an articulated bus system running on dedicated lanes connects North, Central and South Bogotá from C 170 (on the Autopista del Norte) to Portal de Usme (where the road to Villavicencio leaves the city). There is a spur to the west along Calle 80 and a link to Candelaria (Parque de Los Periodistas on Av Jiménez de Quesada with a stop at the Gold Museum). **Corriente** services stop at all principal road intersections, *expresos* limited stop only. The journey from the centre to the north takes less than 30 mins. More routes are planned. Journey cost US$0.50. Using the TransMilenio is a good, quick way of getting around the city but it tends to be crowded.

Long distance If going to towns in Boyacá or Cundinamarca for a long weekend, leave Bogotá before Fri 1200 as it can take 1½ hrs to get from Terminal to outskirts. Try to arrive back before 1300, or ask to be set down in North Bogota and take TransMilenio bus to centre.

The **Terminal de Transportes** is at C 33B, No 69-13, near Av Boyacá (Cra 72) between El Dorado (Av 26) and Av Centenario (C 13), T423 3600, www.terminaldetransporte.gov.co. There is also access from Cra 68. It is divided into modules serving the 4 points of the compass; each module has several bus companies serving similar destinations. If possible, buy tickets at the ticket office before travelling to avoid overcharging and to guarantee a seat, especially during bank holidays. Fares and journey times are given under destinations below. If you are travelling north, enquire if the bus company has a pick-up point on the Autopista del Norte around C 160. This saves considerable time, especially if already staying in North Bogotá. *Velotax busetas* are slightly quicker and more expensive than ordinary buses, as are colectivos, which go to several long-distance destinations. The terminal is well-organized and comfortable, but, as usual, watch out for thieves. Free self-service luggage trolleys are provided. There are shops and restaurants. There are showers at the terminal (between Nos 3 and 4), US$0.50, soap and towel provided. At the terminal's medical centre (modelo 4), it is possible to get yellow fever injections, Mon-Fri 0800-1700, Sat 0800-1400. To get there by bus, ask your hotel. Taxi around US$3.50.

International bus It is better not to buy a through ticket to Caracas with **Berlinas de Fonce** as this does not guarantee a seat and is only valid for 2 Venezuelan companies; moreover no refunds are given in Cúcuta. Ideally, if you have time, make the journey to Cúcuta in 2 stages to enjoy the scenery to the full. Bus connections from San Antonio de Táchira in Venezuela to Caracas are good. **Ormeño**, bus terminal modelo 2, T410 7522, www.grupo-ormeno.com/ colombia.htm, has a twice weekly Lima-Caracas service passes through Cúcuta (US$150 Lima-Cúcuta); there is also a Lima-Bogotá service weekly (US$130; Lima-Cali US$120). Bogotá-Caracas by this service US$60. International tickets with Ormeño can only be bought only at bus terminal.

Taxi
Minimum fare US$1. Average fare from North Bogotá to the centre US$3.50. Check for additional charges above what the meter states eg: night charge and rides to the airport. At busy times, empty taxis flagged down on the street may refuse to take you to less popular destinations. If you are going to an address out of the city centre, it is helpful to know the neighbourhood (barrio) you are going to as well as the street address, eg Chicó, Chapinero (ask at your hotel). Radio taxis are recommended for safety and reliability; when you call the dispatcher gives you a cab number, confirm this when it arrives, eg **Taxis Libres**, T311 1111; **Teletaxi** T611 1111. (The latest scam is for the driver and an accomplice to force passengers to go from ATM to ATM emptying their deposit or credit card account – *paseos milionarios*. At night it is not recommended to travel by taxi along the Av Circunvalar.) Tipping is not customary, but is appreciated.

---

❶ Directory

Bogotá *p778, maps p778 and 780*
Airline offices Domestic: AeroRepública, Cra 10, No 27-51, T320 9090, El Dorado airport T413 5421 . Aires, Cra 11, No 76-14, loc 210, T294 0300, El Dorado airport T413 9517. **Avianca**, Cra 7, No 16-36, T401 3434. **Satena**, Tequendama Hotel/Centro Internacional complex, T01-900-331 7100. International: Air France and KLM, Cra 9A, No 99-07, T413 9590. **American**, Cra 7, No 26-20, T343 2424. **Continental and Copa**, Tequendama Hotel/Centro Internacional complex, T01800-944 0219. **Delta**, Cra 7, Mp 99-11 loc 140, T01-800-9561 0352. Iberia, Cra 20, No 85-11, T616 6111. **Mexicana**, C 100, No 21a-41, inside Hotel Cosmos, T646 4000, Mon-Fri only. **Varig**, Cra 7, No 33-24, T350 5749.
Banks Some head offices are grouped around the Avianca building and the San Francisco church, others are in North Bogotá on or near C 72. **Banistmo**, Cra 8, No 15-46/60, T334 5088, and 20 local agencies, will cash Thomas Cook and Amex TCs (0900-1300, with passport), will give advances against Visa, and will accept sterling,

good rates. Most banks change TCs in the morning only. TCs can also be changed at the **Emerald Trade Centre**, Av Jiménez No 5-43. **Conavi** banks will give advances against Visa. There are countless ATMs accepting Visa and MasterCard. **BBVA** is good for Visa, **Carulla** supermarkets for MasterCard. There is a daily limit on how much money you can take out, usually US$170-260, depending on your bank account. Try **Davivienda** banks for a greater daily allowance. **Money changers: American Express:** for replacing lost Amex TCs, go to *American Express* (Expreso Viajes y Turismo), C 85, No 20-32, T593 4949 (has other branches), open 0800-1900, Sat 0900-1400 with full details, a police report of the loss and preferably proof of purchase. They first authorize cash advance on America Express cards and then direct you to the appropriate bank (**Banco Union Colombia**). Also exchange at **Cambios Country**, Cra 11, No 71-40, Of 201, and at El Dorado airport, T413 8979. Several other city offices, good rates, speedy service. **Orotur**, Cra 10, No 26-05 (very small, below *Hotel Tequendama* in pedestrian subway) is quick and efficient, cash only, including sterling. **Cambios New York Money**, in CC Unicentro, Av 15, No 123-30, loc 1-118, accepts sterling, efficient. **Titan**, C 19, No 6-19, p 2, open afternoons (when all banks have ceased foreign transactions), many other branches. Other *cambios* on Av Jiménez de Quesada, between Cras 6 and 11, and in the north of the city. On Sun exchange is virtually impossible except at the airport. **Car hire**: See Essentials, Car hire, for agencies with continent-wide distribution. Car hire is expensive in Colombia.

Cultural centres British Council, C 87, No 12-79, T618 7680, www.britishcouncil.org/es/colombia. Good TEFL library, British newspapers, the British Council runs a well-organized 2-week Spanish course for all levels in Cartagena, accommodation with a local family. Recommended. **Centro Colombo Americano**, C 19, No 2-49, T334 7640, www.colombobogota.edu.co. English and Spanish courses. Recommended. **Alianza Colombo-Francesa**, Cra 3, No 18-15, T341 3148 and Cra 7A, No 84-72, T256 3197, www.alianzafrancesa.org.co. Films in French, newspapers, library monthly bulletin etc. **Goethe Institut**, Cra 7, No 81-57, T254 7600, www.goethe.de/hn/bog/deindex.htm.

Embassies and consulates Opening times and rules for visas are changing continuously, phone before you go. Few embassies are open in the afternoon, best to go early morning. **Belgium**, Apt 3564, C 26, No 4A-45, p 7, T380 0380, bogota@diplobel.org. **Brazil**, C 93, No 14-20, T218 0800, secom2@brasil.org.co. **Canada**, Cra 7, No 115-33, p 14, T657 9800, open 0800-1630, www.dfait-maeci.gc.ca/bogota/. **Ecuador**, C 72,

No 6-30, p 7, T212 6512, mecucol@cable.net.co. **France**, Cra 11, No 93-12, T618 1400, www.ambafrance.gov.co. **Germany**, Cra 69, No 43B-44, T423 2600. **Israel**, Edif Caxdac, C 35, No 7-25, p 14, T327 7500. **Italy**, C 93B, No 9-92, T218 7206, ambitbog@cable.net.co. **Japan**, Cra 7, No 71-21, Torre B p 11, T317 5001. **Netherlands**, Cra 13, No 93-40, p 5, T638 4200 . **New Zealand Consulate**, Diagonal 109 No 1-39, Este, T629 8524, for emergencies only, Mon-Fri 0830-1730. **Panamanian Consulate**, C 92, No 7-70, T257 4452. Mon-Fri, 0900-1300. **Spain**, C 92, No 12-68, T622 0090. **Switzerland**, Cra 9, No 74-08, oficina 101, T255 3945, open Mon-Fri 0900-1200. **UK**, Cra 9, No 76-49, p 9, T326 8300, www.britain.gov.co. **USA**, C 22D bis, No 47-51, T315 0811, consulate/visas, T315 1566, http://bogota.usembassy.gov. **Venezuelan Consulate**, Av 13, No 103-16, T636 4011 (610 6622 visa information), 0830-1200. Visas can be collected the following day 1200-1630.

Internet There are internet centres all over the city, in commercial areas and in shopping centres. **Café del Cubo** in La Candelaria, Cr 4, No 13-57, Mon-Sat 0900-2200. **Foto and Internet Café**, Tequendama Hotel/Centro Internacional complex (2nd floor), loc 164, helpful, good service, Mon-Fri 0700-2000, Sat 0900-1600, US$0.90 per hour. Facilities also in hotels, eg *Hotel Platypus*. and *Centro Plaza*. Some fast and welcoming places in the North, include **Web Café**, Diag 27, No 6-81, Mon-Fri 0900-2000, Sat 1000-1800. **Coffeemail**, inside CC Santa Bárbara. Mon-Sat 1030-2000, Sun 1400-1800. Prices per hr range from US$1-2.

Language courses You may not study on a tourist visa. Make sure you have a student visa. Some of the best Spanish courses are in the **Universidad Nacional** (see map), T316 5000, www.unal.edu.co, about US$180 for 2 months, 8 hrs per week, or **Universidad de los Andes**, T339 4949, www.uniandes.edu.co, US$300, 6 weeks, and **Pontificia Universidad Javeriana**, T320 8320 ext 4620, www.javeriana.edu.co. Good value Spanish courses at the **Universidad Pedagógica**, C 72, No 11-86, T594 1894. Good reports, around US$90 for 40 hrs, 2 hrs per day. **Centro Latino Americano**, Departamento de Lenguas, Tr 4, No 42-00, p 4. Accommodation with local families can be arranged. Most other schools in Yellow Pages offer one-to-one private tuition at US$10-12 per hr.

Medical services 24-hr emergency health service, T125. **Cruz Roja Nacional**, Av 68, No 66-31, T428 0111. 0830-1800, consultations/inoculations US$12.50. **Santa Fe de Bogotá**, C 119, No 9-33, T629 3066, and **El Bosque**, C 134, No 12-55, T274 0577, are both modern, private hospitals, with good service. **Farmacity**, is a chain of new, well-stocked chemists open 24 hrs across the city. For 24-hr home deliveries in Bogotá, T530-0000, C 93A, No-13-41, off Parque de la 93, Cra 13, No 63A-67, among others.

Post offices Main Avianca ticket office and Deprisa airmail office in basement of Ed Avianca, Cra 7, No 16-36, open 0730-1900 Mon to Fri, 0800-1500 Sat, closed Sun and holidays (*poste restante* 0730-1800, Mon-Sat, letters kept for only a month, US$1 per letter). Parcels by air are sent from here too. Also Cra 7 y C 26-27, near Planetarium; C 140 between Cra 19 y Autopista. Parcels by air, contact *Avianca*. **Adpostal**, Cra 7, No 27-54, handles international parcels.

Telephones International calls from several *Telecom* offices in centre of Bogotá (eg in the *Tequendama Hotel*/Centro Internacional complex); all close within 30 mins of 2000. Purchase of phone cards recommended if you are using call boxes.

Useful addresses If you have problems with theft or other forms of crime, contact a **Centro de Atención Inmediata**, CAI, for assistance. Only at a CAI police office is it possible to report a theft and get the relevant paperwork, not at other police stations: downtown, C 60 y Cra 9, T217 7472, La Candelaria, Cra 7 y C6. There are many offices throughout the city, or T156. **Police**: T112 or 315 9188. **DAS**: Head office, Cra 28, No 17A-00, T208 6060, www.das.gov.co. Open 0730-1530, or T153. Cundinamarca office: C 58, No 10-55, T570 1077. **Dirección de Extranjería** (for extending entry permits): C 100, No 11B-27, T601 7200, open Mon-Thu 0730-1600, Fri 0730-1530. DAS will not authorize photocopies of passports; look in Yellow Pages for notaries, who will.

Useful numbers Ambulance: T125. Fire: T119. **Red Cross**: T132.

Around Bogotá

The basin on which Bogotá stands, with high ranges of the Cordillera to the east, is known as La Sabana de Bogotá and is the centre of Colombia's important cut-flower industry. Around La Sabana are many places of interest in nearby towns for weekend excursions out of the city.

Zipaquirá → *Phone code: 91. Colour map 1, grid B3. Population: 62,000. Altitude: 2,600 m.*

Twenty km beyond Chía, on La Sabana with its flower greenhouses and dairy farms, is the famous rock salt mine, still producing salt after centuries. Within the mines, the **Salt Cathedral** ① *Mon-Fri 0930-1600, Sat, Sun and holidays 0900-1700, Sun mass at 1200, admission by ticket, US$4.50, half price on Wed, including 1½ hr guided tour, car park US$1,* is one of the major attractions of Colombia. The entrance is in hills about 20 minutes' walk west of the town from Parque Villaveces. At the site, there is an information centre and the **Museo de la Salmuera** ① *US$0.50,* which explains how salt is produced. The original underground cathedral was dedicated in 1954 to Nuestra Señora del Rosario (patron saint of miners). Continuing deterioration made the whole cave unsafe and it was closed. A remarkable, new salt cathedral, minimalist in style, was opened on 16 December 1995. Inside, near the entrance, are the 14 Stations of the Cross, each sculpted by a different artist. Other sections of the cathedral follow to the Nave, 180 m below the surface, with huge pillars "growing" out of the salt. All is discretely illuminated and gives an austere impression.

Zipaquirá has a pleasant colonial plaza dominated by a brick cathedral. Tuesday is market day. In the town is the **Museo Quevedo Zornozo** ① *Calle 3, No 7-69, Tue-Fri 0930-1200, 1400-1600, Sat-Sun 0900-1700, US$1,* which displays musical instruments and paraphernalia including the piano of General Santander. The **Museo Arqueológico** ① *Calle 1, No 6-21, T852 3499, next to the Parque Villaveces entrance, Mon-Sun 0930-1800, US$1.30,* houses more than 1,500 pieces of pre- Columbian pottery. For eating and partying at weekends, a recommended place in **Chía** is **Andrés Carne de Res** (♔ Calle 2, No 11-94). This artsy, rustic restaurant and bar has become an institution with great typical food, highly-original decor and 'performers' to liven things up.

Around Zipaquirá

Nemocón, 15 km northeast of Zipaquirá, has salt mines (now closed) and a church with original 17th century frescos (currently under restoration). There is a small but interesting **Museo de Sal** ① *on the plaza, Tue-Sun 0800-1700, closed Tue after bank holiday, US$0.90,* which includes history of the salt industry in the time of the Chibcha Indians. ATM on main plaza. A side road connects with the Bogotá-Cúcuta highway. Some 8 km beyond Nemocón, with its own access to the main Tunja road, is **Suesca**, a centre of rock climbing on sandstone cliffs overlooking the Río Bogotá. ⏩ *See Transport listings page 795.*

Southwest of Bogotá

The Simón Bolívar Highway runs from Bogotá to Girardot; this 132 km stretch is extremely picturesque, running down the mountains. **Girardot**, the former main river port for Bogotá, is linked by road with the capital. Only small boats can go upriver from here. Girardot is a popular weekend and bank holiday haunt for Bogotanos looking for heat and sun. It's a relaxed place with a market on the main plaza. Cattle fairs are held on 5-10 June and 5-10 December. Across the bridge over the Río Magdalena towards Tolima is the small village of **Flandes**, known for its excellent local fish restaurants, eg **Club 60**, good river views, nice atmosphere, tasty fish platters, live music at weekends. Try the river fish *viuda de capaz*. From here launch rides on the river start from underneath the bridge; a one-hour trip to Isla del Sol is recommended (US$9). About 20 km along this road from the centre of Bogotá is Soacha, now the end of the built-up area of the city. A right fork here leads past the Indumil plant to the **Chicaque Parque Natural** ① *daily 0800-1600, US$9 for foreigners; take a bus to Soacha and ask for continuing transport to the park, T368 3114/3118, if driving, there is a better route via Mosquera on the Honda road, left towards La Mesa and in 11 km left again on the road to Soacha, the park sign is 6 km along this road*, a privately owned 300 ha park, principally cloud forest between 2,100 m and 2,700 m on the edge of the Sabana de Bogotá. It is a popular spot for walkers and riders at weekends with good facilities for day visitors and a Swiss-style *refugio*, about one hour down the trail from the entrance, which provides meals and accommodation for 70 or so costing US$20-25 per day including meals.

Northwest of Bogotá

The Sabana de Bogotá is dotted with white farms and groves of eucalyptus. The road passes through the small towns of Fontibón and Madrid, before reaching **Facatativá** (*Population*: 67,000. *Altitude*:1,800 m) 40 km from Bogotá. Some 3 km from Facatativá, on the road to the west, is the park of Piedras de Tunja, a natural rock amphitheatre with enormous stones, numerous indigenous pictographs and an artificial lake. **Villeta**, 71 km from Facatativá (*Population*: 13,000) is a popular weekend resort. The road continues to Honda, half way to which is the interesting historical town of **Guaduas** (*Population*: 23,000. *Altitude*: 1,000 m. *Phone code*: 91). In the main plaza is a statue of the liberator Policarpa Salavarrieta, the cathedral and one of several museums in the town. Sunday market. Best local dish is *quesillos*. Bus to Honda, US$2.50, one hour. The surrounding countryside is beautiful, including waterfalls at Versalles (10 km). Transport for Facatativá, Villeta and Guaduas: take Bogotá-Honda buses.

Honda On the west bank of the river, Honda is 32 km upstream from La Dorada. It is a pleasant old town with many colonial houses, an interesting indoor market and three museums. The streets are narrow and picturesque, and the town is surrounded by hills. El Salto de Honda (the rapids which separate the Lower from the Upper Magdalena) are just below the town. Several bridges span the Ríos Magdalena and the Guali, at whose junction the town lies. In February the Magdalena rises and fishing is unusually good. People come from all over the region for the fishing and the festival of the Subienda, the fishing season. There is a row of good cheap restaurants across the Río Magdalena bridge in Puerto Bogotá.

Gateway to the Llanos

Through Colombia's impressive longest tunnel, Buenavista, and along a 110-km road running southeast from Bogotá lies **Villavicencio**, capital of Meta Department. The region is known as Los Llanos (the plains) and is at the foot of the eastern slopes of the Eastern Cordillera stretching more than 800 km east as far as Puerto Carreño, on the Orinoco in Venezuela. Los Llanos is cowboy country and the never ending expanse of fertile flat plains makes it ideal for cattle raising, the area's main industry. The area is also rich in oil and the flames from oil refineries based in Puerto Rico can be seen flickering on the distant horizon. Villavicencio, a modern town, is a good base for visiting the Llanos. The region is also known for its good meats and local delicacies. Try *chigüiro*. See Safety, page 773.

● Sleeping

Zipaquirá *p792*
B Hostería del Libertador, Vía Catedral de Sal, T852 3060, F852 6851. Restored colonial

mansion, above the mine on top of the hill with nice views, good restaurant. Negotiate prices in low season.

C **Cacique Real**, Cra 6, No 2-12, T851 0209, www.hotelcaciquereal.com. Near Parque Villaveces entrance, 18th-century colonial style, rooms around pleasant patio, safe parking, helpful, with breakfast, good.
E **Colonial**, C 3, No 6-57, T852 2690. Showers, TV in some rooms, nice.

Around Zipaquirá: Suesca *p792*
B **La Esperanza,** Km 1 along railway from Suesca, T856 3339, www.hotella esperanza.com.co. Restaurant, conference centre, sauna, horse riding US$17 per hr, camping on grounds US$2.80.
D **Green Dream**, Vía Suesca Km 6, Vereda Teneria, T268 0596. Colonial style, nice patio area, spa, working farm.

Southwest of Bogotá: Girardot *p793*
B **Bachué**, Cra 8, No 18-04, T833 4790, F833 3830. Modern, large pool, a/c, restaurant, good.
AL **Tocarema**, Cr 5a, No 19-41, T835 0808, www.ghlhoteles.com. Stylish, elegant, art-deco style, airy and bright, lovely large pool area with views, tennis courts, restaurant, a/c. Recommended.
C-D **Rosmar**, C 16, No 9-37, T832 4437. Fan or a/c, central, TV, good.
D **Río**, Cra 10, No 16-31, T833 2805. Central near market, bit dirty, a/c, restaurant, laundry,
E **Bochica**, Cra 9, No 18-39, T833 3867. Basic, safe location, a bit shabby but cheap, fan, restaurant.

Northwest of Bogotá *p793*
Guadas
E **Hostería Colonial**, on plaza, T846 6041. Great value, delightful restored mansion, TV, bath.
E **Hotel La Posadita**, C 4, No 5-58. Basic, clean rooms, parking.

Honda
B **Campestre El Guali**, Vía Honda-Mariquita (entrada Colegio Pumarejo), Cra 32, No 12-293, T251 0000. Restaurant, pleasant pool area, parking, friendly staff.
D **Calle Real** , Cra 11, No 14-40, T251 7737. Central, safe, parking, restaurant, jacuzzi on rooftop. Recommended.
D **Campestre Vacari**, Km 5 Vía Honda-Mariquita T251 3615. Just outside town, rustic, comfortable rooms, safe, peaceful, helpful, English spoken, pool, good value, restaurant, parking. Recommended.
E **Dorantes**, C 14, No 12-57, T251 3423. With bath, TV, fan.

Gateway to the Llanos: Villavicencio *p793*
A **Villavicencio**, Cra 30, No 35A-22, T662 6434. A/c,

central, hot water, restaurant, helpful, roof pool.
D **Centauros**, C 38, No 31-05. Small rooms, reasonably clean and quiet.
E **Residencias Don Juan**, Cra 28, No 37-21 (Mercado de San Isidro). Attractive family house, with bath and fan, sauna, safe.
F **Residencias Medina**, C 39D, No 28-27. Shared shower, fair, washing facilities.
Youth Hostel Granja los Girasoles, Barrio Chapinerito. 160 beds, 3 km from the bus station. Several eating places sell typical local food, also Chinese restaurants in the centre; others, some with swimming pools, on the road to Puerto López.

🍴 Eating

Zipaquirá *p792*
🍴 **Parque Restaurante Funzipa**, C 1A, No 9-99. Colombian food served in a converted salt mill.
🍴 **Asadero Colonial**, C 5 y Cra 7. Good food, *arepas, bandejas*.
🍴 **El Mesón del Zipa**, main plaza. Good, cheap.

Southwest of Bogotá: Girardot *p793*
🍴 **Al Passo Pizzería**, Km 1 Vía Girardot-Bogotá, Ricaute. Good pizzas and grill in lovely patio.

Northwest of Bogotá: Guadas *p793*
🍴 **Zaguán del Virrey**, C 4, No 5-68. Good *comida corriente* in pleasant patio with art work.

🍸 Bars and clubs

Southwest of Bogotá: Girardot *p793*
Good nightlife on *puente* weekends (bank holidays).
Oasis Bar, inside Centro Comercial, Cra 10 y C 20. Popular rooftop bar, good atmosphere, small pool. Cover about US$5.

Gateway to the Llanos: Villavicencio *p793*
El Pentegrama Llanero, on Vía a Puerto López (in town). Good place to see *joropo* dancing and hear *llanero* music live on Fri and Sat nights.
Los Capachos, Vía Acacias (just out of town). The best, attracts young affluent crowd, popular, 2 floors, rustic setting. Cover charge US$7.

🎉 Festivals and events

Gateway to the Llanos: Villavicencio *p793*
International **Coleo** festival in mid **Oct**. Colourful event, rodeo style, cowboys attempt to make cattle fall down while on horseback. Bring hat and sunscreen. A string of festivals in **Dec**, with typical music (*joropo*) and beauty pageants.

● *For an explanation of the sleeping and eating price codes used in this guide, see inside the front*
● *cover. Other relevant information is found in Essentials pages 774-775.*
794

▲▲ Activities and tours

Around Zipaquirá: Suesca *p792*
Rock climbing For information call **Hernán Wilke**, T310-358 3606/T310-216 8119, or visit his climbing centre **Monodedo**, www.monodedo.com. In Suesca turn right at the entrance to Las Rocas, past *Rica Pizza* restaurant. He speaks English and German, experienced and knowledgeable. US$30 for half day climbing with guide, US$45 full day, open weekends and holidays 0830-2100. Also 5-day trips to Cocuy from US$70 pp per day. **Ricardo Cortés**, the owner of *Rica Pizza*, also arranges climbing trips and local accommodation.

◉ Transport

Zipaquirá *p792*
Bus Many buses from **Bogotá**: Cra 30 (Av Ciudad de Quito), marked 'Zipa', **Flota Alianza**, or others from the C 170 terminus of the TransMilenio in North Bogotá opposite *Exito* supermarket, US$2 each way, 1¼ hrs. The Zipaquirá bus station is 15 mins walk from the mines and cathedral. Zipaquirá can also be reached from Tunja (see page 796), by taking a Bogotá-bound bus and getting off at La Caro for connection to Zipaquirá, US$2.40. Note when arriving to C170 terminus from Zipaquirá you need to buy a TransMilenio bus ticket to leave the station. To avoid this, ask the driver to drop you off before the bus station.

Train La Sabana station at C 13, No 18-24. A slow tourist steam train runs on Sat, Sun and holidays at 0830 calling at Usaquén in the north of Bogotá (see map), going north to Cájica and Zipaquirá (1200), back in Bogotá, La Sabana at 1700. (All times variable.) Cost: adult US$11, child up to 10, US$6. Tickets should be bought in advance here, at La Sabana station, T375 0558, or from travel agents, or Usaquén station, C100 y Cr 10, or from travel agents.

Southwest of Bogotá: Girardot *p793*
Bus Most buses bypass the town, so ask for a bus that actually stops in Girardot. To **Bogotá**, 132 km, US$7, 3½-4 hrs. To **Neiva**, US$6, 3½ hrs.

Northwest of Bogotá: Honda *p793*
From **Bogotá** by **Velotax** and **Rápido Tolima**, US$9, 4 hrs. **Manizales**, US$6. **Rápido Tolima** run ½-hourly buses to **La Dorada** (1 hr), and beyond, to **Puerto Boyacá** (3 hrs), US$4.50.

Gateway to the Llanos: Villavicencio *p793*
Air **Aires** and **Satena** to **Bogotá** daily. Satena flies to Saravena, Arauca and Tame in the Llanos; for other flights ask locally. Taxi to town, US$4.50, bus US$0.50.
Bus Station outside town, taxi US$1.50. **La Macarena** and **Bolivariano** run from **Bogotá** about every 30 mins, US$4, 4 hrs, or colectivos **Velotax** or **Autollanos** who run every hr, US$4.20. Be prepared to queue for tickets back to Bogotá.

Bogotá to the Venezuelan border

The main road route from Bogotá to Venezuela has some beautiful stretches and passes through, or near, several colonial towns. In Cundinamarca and Boyacá it gives access to the Laguna de Guatavita, perhaps the nearest place the Spaniards came to finding their El Dorado, historical battle sites and the Sierra Nevada del Cocuy, excellent climbing and hiking country. Principal towns, both with a strong colonial heritage, are Tunja and charming Villa de Leiva.

The highway crosses Santander and Norte de Santander Departments on its way to Cúcuta. That this was an important route for the Spaniards can be seen in the colonial villages, like Barichara, and the more important centres like Bucaramanga and Pamplona. There is also some grand scenery in the Chicamocha canyon and the eastern cordillera, with possibilities for adventure sports.

Bogotá to Villa de Leiva

Guatavita ➜ *Phone code: 91. Colour map 1, grid B4. Population: 6,000. Altitude: 2,650 m.*
The modern town of Guatavita Nueva, 75 km from Bogotá,, is a popular haunt for Bogotanos. It was re-built in replica colonial style when the old town of Guatavita was submerged by the reservoir. There is a small bullring, cathedral and two small museums, one devoted to the Muisca Indians and the other to relics of the old Guatavita church. The many artisan shops are good places to buy ruanas. Market day is Sunday. The tourist information booth can find accommodation for visitors. **Laguna de Guatavita** ① *US$4, with guide,* a sacred lake of the Muisca Indians, is where the legend of El Dorado originated. The lake is a quiet, beautiful place;

The Gilded Man

The basis of the El Dorado (Gilded Man) story is established fact. It was the custom of the Chibcha king to be coated annually with resin, on which gold dust was stuck, and then to be taken out on the lake on a ceremonial raft. He then plunged into the lake and emerged with the resin and gold dust washed off. The lake was also the repository of precious objects thrown in as offerings; there have been several attempts to drain it (the first, by the Spaniards in colonial times, was the origin of the sharp cut in the crater rim) and many items have been recovered over the years. The factual basis of the El Dorado story was confirmed by the discovery of a miniature raft with ceremonial figures on it, made from gold wire, which is now one of the most prized treasures of the Museo del Oro in Bogotá. Part of the raft is missing; the story is that the gold from it ended up in one of the finder's teeth! (Read John Hemming's *The Search for El Dorado* on the subject.)

you can walk right round it, 1½ hours, or climb to the rim of the crater. Opinions differ on whether the crater is volcanic or a meteorite impact, but from the rim at 3,100 m there are extensive views over the varied countryside. Just before the road reaches Boyacá Department, it passes the Sisca reservoir where there is fishing and windsurfing. At the *Refugio de Sisca* restaurant, try the *empanadas de trucha* (cornmeal and trout snack), US$0.60, excellent.

Tunja → *Phone code: 98. Colour map 1, grid B4. Population: 120,000. Altitude: 2,820 m.*

Tunja, capital of Boyacá Department and 137 km from Bogotá, has some of the finest, well-preserved colonial churches of Colombia. When the Spaniards arrived in what is now Boyacá, Tunja was already an indigenous city, the seat of the Zipa, one of the two Chibcha kings. It was refounded as a Spanish city by Gonzalo Suárez Rendón in 1539. The **Cathedral** and five other churches are all worth visiting, particularly for their colonial woodwork and lavish decoration. These include **Santo Domingo**, begun in 1594, **Santa Bárbara** and the **Santa Clara La Real** chapel (1580).

The **Casa del Fundador Suárez Rendón** ① *Plaza de Bolívar, daily 0800-1200, 1400-1600, US$0.70,* is one of the few extant mansions of a Spanish *conquistador* in Colombia (1539-1543); peaceful courtyard with fine view of valley through gateway; see the unique series of plateresque paintings on the ceilings. The helpful **tourist office** is in the Casa del Fundador Suárez Rendón.

The market, near Plaza de Toros on the outskirts of town, is open every day (good for *ruanas* and blankets). Friday is main market day. During the week before Christmas, there is a lively festival with local music, traditional dancing and fireworks.

The battle of Boyacá was fought about 16 km south of Tunja, on the road to Bogotá. Overlooking the bridge at Boyacá is a large **monument to Bolívar** ① *daily 0800-1800, US$1.50 per car. There are several other monuments, an exhibition hall and restaurant at the site. Bus from Tunja, US$0.60, ask for "El Puente".* Bolívar took Tunja on 6 August 1819, and next day his troops, fortified by a British Legion, the only professional soldiers among them, fought the Spaniards on the banks of the swollen Río Boyacá. With the loss of only 13 killed and 53 wounded they captured 1,600 men and 39 officers. Only 50 men escaped, and when these told their tale in Bogotá the Viceroy Samao fled in such haste that he left behind him half a million pesos of the royal funds.

Villa de Leiva → *Phone code: 98. Colour map 1, grid B4. Population: 4,500. Altitude: 2,144 m.*

About 40 km west is the beautiful and unmissable colonial town of **Villa de Leiva** (also spelt Leyva) which has one of the largest plazas in the Americas. It is surrounded by cobbled streets, a charming, peaceful place. The town dates back to the early days of Spanish rule (1572), but unlike Tunja, it has been declared a national monument so will not be modernized. The first president of Nueva Granada, Andrés Días Venero de Leiva, lived in the town. Many of the **colonial houses** are now hotels, others are museums, eg the restored birthplace of the independence hero, **Casa de Antonio Ricaurte** ① *Cra 8 y C 15, Wed-Fri 0900-1200,*

1400-1700, Sat, Sun and holidays 0900-1300, 1400-1800. Ricaurte was born in Villa de Leiva and died in 1814 at San Mateo, Venezuela, fighting with Bolívar's army. The house has a nice courtyard and garden. **Casa de Nariño** ① *Cra 9, Mon-Sun 0900-1200, 1400-1700 (closed Wed)*, recently restored, displays documents from the Independence period. A **palaeontological museum** ① *15 mins' walk north of the town on Cra 9, Tue-Sat 0900-1200, 1400-1700, Sun 0900-1500, US$1.10*, is interesting and well displayed. The **Monasterio de las Carmelitas** ① *Calle 14 y Cra 10, Sat, Sun and holidays 1000-1300*, has one of the best museums of religious art in Colombia. Part of the monastery is the **Iglesia del Carmen** and the **Convento**, all worth a visit. The shops in the plaza and the adjoining streets have an excellent selection of Colombian handicrafts.

Some colonial houses close Monday-Friday out of season, but the trip is worthwhile for the views and for long, peaceful walks in the hills. Many places are closed Monday and Tuesday. Market day is Saturday, held in the Plaza de Mercado 0400-1300. During weekends and public holidays, the town is very crowded with Bogotanos. The **tourist office** ① *Cra 9, No 13-04 just off the plaza, T732 0232, Tues-Fri 0800-1230, 1400-1800, Sat, 1000-1700, Sun and holidays 1000-1400*, has local maps, gives advice on cheaper accommodation and bus schedules and is most helpful.

The wide valley to the west of Villa de Leiva abounds in fossils. Some 5 km along the road to Santa Sofía can be seen the fossil of a dinosaur (Kronosaurus) found in 1977, now with a museum built around it. A second fossil found in 2000 nearby has been put alongside. Look for road signs to **El Fósil** ① *daily 0700-1800, US$1.20*. About 2 km from El Fósil along this road is the turning for (1 km) the archaeological site of **El Infiernito** ① *0900-1200, 1400-1700, closed Mon, US$0.50*, where there are several carved stones believed to be giant phalli and a solar calendar. Some 6 km after the Infiernito turning is the **Monastery of Ecce-Homo** (founded 1620); note the fossils on the floor at the entrance. There are buses from Villa de Leiva (0800-1615) to Santa Sofía, US$1.20; it is 30 minutes to the crossing, then a

Villa de Leiva

To ⑨, Museo Paleontológico & Arcabuco

C 16
C 15
Iglesia del Carmen
Monasterio de Las Carmelitas
C 14
Av Circunvalar
Plazuela de San Agustín
Casa de Antonio Ricaurte
Museo Luis Alberto Acuña
Alcaldía
Casa del Primer Congreso
Plaza Mayor
Iglesia Parroquial
C 13
C 12
C 11
Parque Nariño
Plaza de Mercado
C 10
San Francisco

To Santa Sofía, Ecce-Homo & El Fósil
To ⑪ & Bogotá, via Tunja or Chiquinquirá
To ③

N
0 metres 100
0 yards 100

Sleeping 🛏
Colombian Highlands **9**
El Molino la Mesopotamia **1**
Hospedaje El Sol de la Villa **2**
Hospedaría El Marqués
  de San Jorge **4**
Hospedería Duruelo **3**

Hostal El Mirador **5**
Hostal La Candelaria **6**
Los Llanitos **7**
Plaza Mayor **8**
Posada La Villa de Alcalá **11**
Posada San Antonio **10**

Eating 🍴
Casa Blanca **2**
Dino's **1**
Los Arcos **3**
Sazón y Sabor **4**

2-km walk to the monastery. Beyond Santa Sofía is La Cueva de Hayal, a cave set in beautiful scenery. A tour of most of these attractions leaves the plaza at 0930, Saturday/Sunday, US$5.

About 20 km north of Villa de Leiva is a right turn for the **Iguaque Flora and Fauna Sanctuary** (3 km) run by MA ① *US$10 for foreigners, cars US$2.50; tourist centre with accommodation for 60; restaurant with good food US$1.80-2.20. Take a colectivo from Villa de Leiva-Arcabuco to the turn off to the park (1½ hrs' walk to ranger station); check for afternoon return times. (Camping is allowed, US$3 pp, safe.)* It contains oak woods, flora, fauna and lakes. There are guided paths and a marked trail to Lake Iguaque, a walk of 6½ hours. Best to arrive at the Sanctuary before 0900 to allow time to visit and return from the lake.

Ráquira → *Market day Sun.*

At **Ráquira**, 25 km from Villa de Leiva, locals make mainly earthenware pottery in several workshops in and around the village. The small town has charming rows of pastel coloured houses and a pleasant square. The ceramics, among the best-known in Colombia, are sold in about 10 shops on the main street. There is also a good selection of hammocks and handicrafts. At weekends it is possible to eat at the Museo de Artes y Tradiciones Populares. Accommodation along the main street (**D**).

About 7 km along a very rough road, which winds up above Ráquira affording spectacular views, is the beautiful 17th-century **Convento de La Candelaria** ① *daily 0900-1200, 1300-1700, US$1 with a guided tour which includes a simple but interesting museum.* On the altar of the fine church is the painting of the Virgen de La Candelaria, dating from 1597, by Francisco del Pozo of Tunja. The painting's anniversary is celebrated each 1 February, in addition to 28 August, the saint's day of San Agustín. Next to the church is the cloister with anonymous 17th-century paintings of the life of San Agustín

Chiquinquirá → *Phone code: 98. Colour map 1, grid B3. Population: 38,000. Altitude: 2,550 m.*

On the west side of the valley of the Río Suárez, 134 km from Bogotá and 80 km from Tunja, this is a busy market town for this large coffee and cattle region. In December thousands of pilgrims honour a painting of the Virgin whose fading colours were restored by the prayers of a woman, María Ramos, but the miracle took place in what is now the **Iglesia de la Renovación** *Parque Julio Flores*. In 1816, when the town had enjoyed six years of independence and was besieged by the Royalists, this painting was carried through the streets by Dominican priests from the famous monastery, to rally the people. The town fell, all the same. There are special celebrations at Easter and on 26 December, the anniversary of the miracle. The town is known for making guitars.

● Sleeping

Tunja *p796*
The area around bus station is not safe at night.
AL Hunza, C 21A, No 10-66, T742 4111. Best in town, modern, a bit bland, a/c, breakfast included, good restaurant,pool, sauna, parking.
C El Cid Plaza, Cra 10, No 20-78, T742 3458, F744 4417. Central, comfortable rooms, credit cards accepted.
D Americano, Cra 11, No 18-70, T742 2471. Hot water in bathrooms, cheaper with shared bath, attractive lobby. Restaurant serves light meals.
D Dux, C 19, No 10-78, next to *Saboy*, T742 5736. On pedestrianized road, one block from main plaza. Good rooms, hot water, good value.
D Hostería San Carlos, Cra 11, No 20-12, T742 3716. Colonial style, interestingly furnished, good restaurant at lunchtime. Highly recommended.
E Saboy, C 19, No 10-40, T742 3492. Nice covered patio, family-run.

Villa de Leiva *p796, map 797*
The town tends to be full of visitors at weekends and bank holidays when hotels increase their rates by around 10-30%. Booking is advisable (try bargaining Mon-Thu). It's essential to book in advance for the Festival of Light.
L Hospedería Duruelo, C 13, No 2-88, T732 0222. Large modern luxurious colonial style, beautiful views, nice gardens, also conference hotel, good food, 4 pools, gym, spa, tennis courts. Rents horses and bikes. Good family hotel.
AL El Molino la Mesopotamia, C del Silencio (top of Cra 8), T732 0235. A beautifully restored colonial mill filled with antiques, 10% rebate for booking 10 days ahead, excellent home cooking, beautiful gardens, fresh water pool, memorable. Recommended.
A Hostal La Candelaria, C 18, No 8-12, T732 0534. 7 rooms, delightful, excellent breakfast.
B Hospedaría El Marqués de San Jorge, C 14,

No 9-20, T732 048, F732 0240. Charming, well-kept colonial mansion, beautiful courtyard, parking, good.
B Los Llanitos, C 9, No 12-31, T732 0018. 5 mins' walk from main plaza, quiet, hot water, good food.
B Plaza Mayor, Cra 10, No 12-31, T732 0425 (T218 7741 Bogotá). Beautifully restored.
B Posada San Antonio, Cra 8, No 11-80, T732 0538. Tastefully restored, nice patio, meals served.
C Hospedaje El Sol de la Villa, Cra 8, No 12-28. Safe, hot shower, good breakfast. Recommended.
C Posada La Villa de Alcalá, Cra 9, No 5-104, T732 0989, F732 0671. Family atmosphere, charming colonial patio with fountain, arranges horse riding.
D Hostal El Mirador, Tra 8, No 6-94, T732 0941. New, good value, 4 blocks from main plaza.
D-E Colombian Highlands, 1 km from town, office in town at Cra 9, No 11-02, T732 1379. Run by knowledgeable Colombian biologist Oscar Giléde, speaks English. Rooms with bath and one dorm, camping on grounds, US$3 with tent, US$4.50 without tent, BBQ area, hammocks, kitchen facilities, Oscar runs a variety of trips (walking tours, horse rental and adventure sports). Recommended.
Camping Estadero San Luis, Av Circunvalar, T732 0617. Capacity 70. **Iguaque Campestre Camping Club**, Km 1 Vía Hipódromo, T732 0889, US$16 pp includes 2 meals (breakfast and dinner). Restaurant, parking.

Ráquira *p798*
B Nequeteba, on the Plaza, T732 0461. Converted and renovated colonial house, good, pool, restaurant, craft shop, helpful owner, parking.
D Norteño, also on the Plaza. Nice and clean, a good choice.

Chiquinquirá *p798*
B El Gran, C 16 No 6-97, T726 3700. Secure, comfortable, good restaurant, laundry service, parking.
C Sarabita, C 16, 8-12, T726 2068. Business hotel, pool, sauna (when working), restaurant, building is a national monument.
E Moyba, Cra 9, No 17-53, T726 2649, facing plaza. Cheaper without bath, dingy.

❼ Eating

Tunja *p796*
Fast food and pizza outlets in the pedestrianized streets near Plaza de Bolívar. Cafés on the plaza.
❸❸ La Buona Vita, Cra 9, No 23-45. Upmarket

Italian, open late, nice decor.
❸-❸ El Maizal, Cra 9 y C 20, near Cathedral. Good typical food.
❸ Pollo Listo, Cra 11, No 19-30. Good chicken.
❸ Sol y Luna, C 18, No 11-59. Vegetarian, good lunch US$2.50.

Villa de Leiva *p796, map 797*
Restaurants tend to close early in the evening, especially during the week.
❸❸ Nueva Granada, C 13, No 7-66. Good value, owner Jorge Rodríguez, plays classical guitar music if you ask.
❸❸ El Rincón Bachué, Cra 9, No 15-17. Interesting decoration with a china factory behind.
❸❸-❸ Casa Blanca, C 13, No 7-02. Decent typical food, *comida corriente*.
❸ Dino's, Cra 9, No 12-52, on Plaza Mayor T732 0803. Good *pizzeria* next to Iglesia Parroquial (also *hospedaría* **D** with shared bath, nice).
❸ La Misión, Centro Verarte, Cra 9, No 13-09. Salads, light meals.
❸ Los Arcos, Plaza Mayor. Excellent *pizzería*.
❸ Sazón & Sabor, on main Plaza. Mexican food, also bar at night, helpful owner Mónica Pineda arranges tours around Villa de Leiva. Closed Mon.
❸ Star de la Villa C 13, No 8-85. Cheap breakfast, decent *comida corriente*.
Café y que Café, C 12, No 8-88. Excellent *tinto*.
La Crepería, C 14, No 7-67. Antique decor, good.
La Galleta, C 13, No 7-17. Good desserts, pastries.
Panadería Francesa, Cra 10, No 11-82. Open 0800-1900, closed Wed, excellent.
Tienda de Teresa, Cra 10, 13-72. Good breakfasts.

Chiquinquirá *p798*
Plenty of reasonable places to eat around and near Parque Julio Flores including ❸❸ El Pórtico, Parque Julio Flores.

⊛ Festivals and events

Villa de Leiva *p796, map 797*
Virgen del Carmen, **13-17 Jul** annually. In **Aug** (check dates) an **international kite festival** is held in the Plaza Major and a popular **Festival of Light** is held every year in **mid-Dec**.

◯ Shopping

Chiquinquirá *p798*
Many delightful toys are made locally. Along the south side of the Basilica are shops specializing in musical instruments.

● *For an explanation of the sleeping and eating price codes used in this guide, see inside the front* ● *cover. Other relevant information is found in Essentials pages 774-775.*

⊙ Transport

Guatavita: Laguna de Guatavita *p795*
Bus Bogotá-Guatavita Nueva, **Flota Aguila**, at bus terminal, US$3, 2-3 hrs, several departures morning; last return bus at 1730. You can walk (2-3 hrs) or ride (US$7 per horse) from Guatavita Nueva to the lake. An easier approach is from a point on the Sesquilé-Guatavita Nueva road (the bus driver will let you off) where there is a sign 'via Lago Guatavita'. There is a good campsite and places to eat nearby. From the main road to the lakeside the road is paved as far as a school, about half way. Follow the signs. This road and subsequent track can be driven in a good car to within 300 m of the lake where there is a car park and good restaurant. Taxi tour from Bogotá US$60 full day.

Tunja *p796*
Bus Bus station is 400 m steeply down from city centre. From **Bogotá** Libertadores 2½ -3 hrs, 4½-5 hrs weekends and holidays, US$5.50. To **Bucaramanga**, frequent services, 7 hrs, US$19.

Villa de Leiva *p796, map 797*
Bus Station in 8th block of Cra 9. Advisable to book the return journey on arrival at weekends. Buses to/from **Tunja**, 1 hr, US$2 with **Cootax**, minibuses 45 mins, US$2, every 20 mins. To **Bogotá** with **Libertadores** 0500, 1400, more on Sun (recommended, most direct and comfortable),

good road takes 4-5 hrs (up to 6 on bank holiday weekends), US$6.50, several other companies, and via Zipaquirá and Chiquinquirá, US$6.70. To **Ráquira** *busetas* 4 daily US$2, taxi, US$4. Bus at 1000 from Leiva to **Moniquirá** connects with bus to Bucamaranga.

Ráquira *p798*
From Villa de Leiva, take the continuation south of Cra 9 past the bus station out of town to Sáchira, turn right to Sutamarchan and Tinjaca and left at Tres Esquinas for Ráquira, a further 5 km. The road from Tres Esquinas continues to Chiquinquirá.
Bus Ráquira is best reached from **Tunja**, 1 hr, US$2, although there are direct buses from Bogotá every 30 mins (**Rápido El Carmen**), US$7, 5-6 hrs. Last bus to Tunja 1330. If stuck after 1330, walk 5 km to Tres Esquinas, where buses pass between 1530-1630, mostly going east. There are busetas from **Villa de Leiva**.

Chiquinquirá *p798*
Bus To **Villa de Leiva** 1¾ hrs, US$5. To **Tunja**, 3 hrs, US$6. To **Zipaquirá**, US$6. To **Bogotá**, 2½ hrs, US$5.50.

⊙ Directory

Villa de Leiva *p796, map 797*
Banks 2 banks/ATMs in Plaza Mayor. **Post offices** Opposite *Telecom* building, C 13, No 8-26.

Tunja to Cocuy

Paipa and around
Along the road 41 km northeast of Tunja is **Paipa**, noted for the **Aguas Termales** complex ⓘ *3 km to the southeast, facilities daily 0600-2200, US$5, children US$3*. The baths and the neighbouring **Lago Sochagota** (boat trips possible) are very popular with Colombians and increasingly so with foreign tourists. From Paipa there is a minibus service, US$0.50, a taxi costs US$1.50, or you can walk in 45 minutes. There are innumerable hotels (**C-E**) and restaurants on the main street of Paipa and on the approach road to the Aguas Termales. Paipa is a good place to buy carpets, hammocks and handicrafts.

Sogamoso → *Phone code: 98. Colour map 1, grid B4. Population: 70,000. Altitude: 2,569 m.*
At Duitama, a town 15 km beyond Paipa known for basket weaving, turn right and follow the valley of the Río Chicamocha for **Sogamoso**, a large, mainly industrial town. This was an important Chibcha settlement, and a **Parque Arqueológico** ⓘ *Tue-Sun 0900-1300, 1400-1800, US$1.50, US$0.80 children*, has been set up on the original site. A comprehensive museum, describes their arts of mummification, statuary, and crafts, including gold working. Cafetería near the entrance. Camping possible in the grass car park opposite, with permission.

Lago de Tota and around
The main road south of Sogamoso climbs quite steeply to the continental divide at El Crucero at 3,100 m. At this point, the main road continues to Yopal. Turn right for **Lago de Tota** (3,015 m), ringed by mountains. Virtually all round the lake, onions are grown near water level, and the whole area has an intriguing 'atmosphere' of pine, eucalyptus and onion. **Aquitania** is the principal town on the lake. There are plenty of food shops, and restaurants including *Luchos*,

Tunjo de Oro and *Pueblito Viejo* together on corner of plaza, and a bright, restored church with modern stained glass windows. Above the town is a hill (El Cumbre) with beautiful views.

Monguí and around

Tópaga, 9 km northeast of Sogamoso, has a colonial church, unusual topiary in the plaza and the bust of Bolívar to commemorate the battle of Peñón of 11 July 1819. Turn south before Topagá to **Monguí**, which has earned the title of 'most beautiful village of Boyacá province'. The upper side of the plaza is dominated by the basilica and convent. There are interesting arts and crafts shops in all directions. Walk down Cra 3 to the Calycanto Bridge, or up C 4, to the Plaza de Toros. The **tourist office** is in the Municipalidad on the plaza, helpful. A recommended excursion is east to the **Páramo de Ocetá** with particularly fine *frailejones* and giant wild lupins. Local craftwork includes leather and wool items.

Sierra Nevada del Cocuy → *Entrance fee, US$10 for foreigners.*

For information contact **MA** ① *C 8 No, 4-74, Cocuy, T08-789 0359*, very helpful, provide maps.

By the bridge over the Río Chicamocha at **Capitanejo** is the turning to the attractive **Sierra Nevada del Cocuy** in the Eastern Cordillera, the best range in Colombia for mountaineering and rock climbing. The Sierra consists of two parallel north-south ranges about 30 km long, offering peaks of rare beauty, lakes and waterfalls. The flora is particularly interesting. Everyone wears ruanas, rides horses and is friendly. The most beautiful peaks are Ritacuba Negro (5,300 m), Ritacuba Blanco (5,330 m) and El Castillo (5,100 m). The main towns are to the west of the Sierra.

The centre for climbing the main peaks is **Guicán**, about 50 km east of Capitanejo. From *Cabinas Kanwara* (see Sleeping below), it is a steep three hours' walk on a clear trail to the snowline on Ritacuba Blanco. Rope and crampons recommended for the final section above 4,800 m. The *Cabinas* is the best starting place for the four- to five-day walk round the north end of the Sierra, which is surrounded by snowcapped mountains. Guicán is 1-1½ hours' drive by jeep from the mountains, so it is recommended to stay higher up (jeep hire about US$17 from José Riaño or 'Profe' in Guicán). Also, to get to the *Cabinas* you can take the milk truck ('el lechero') which leaves Guicán around 0500 via Cocuy for La Cruz, one hour's walk below the cabins, arriving 1100, getting back to Guicán around 1230, a rough but interesting ride. Alternatively you can take the path leading steeply east from Guicán which leads to the *Cabinas* in about 9 km.

The other main town is **Cocuy**. Above Cocuy you can sleep at *Hacienda La Esperanza* (four hours from Guicán) US$5 pp per night, meals US$3 or you can camp and take your own food. Also camping and horses available at a nearby finca. La Esperanza is the base for climbing to the Laguna Grande de la Sierra (seven hours round trip), a large sheet of glacier-fed water surrounded by five snowcapped peaks, and also for the two-day walk to the Laguna de la Plaza on the east side of the Sierra, reached through awesome, rugged scenery. Between Cocuy and La Esperanza is Alto de la Cueva where you can stay at El Himat meteorological station for US$6, basic, including three meals. There is a fine walk from here to Lagunillas, a string of lakes near the south end of the range (five hours return). Permission to camp can be obtained. Sketch maps from the Cucoy tourist office. It takes six to eight days to trek from one end to the other through the gorge between the two ranges; crampons, ice axe and rope are necessary for climbing. Be prepared for unstable slopes and rockfalls, few flat campsites and treacherous weather. The perpendicular rock mountains overlooking the Llanos are for professionals only. The views east towards the Llanos are stupendous. The best weather is from December to April.

● Sleeping

Paipa *p800*

L Casona del Salitre, Vía Toca, Km 3, T785 1508, www.casonadelsalitre.com. 5 mins' drive from town. A national monument and a memorable place to stay near the baths and lake in a well preserved hacienda where Simón Bolívar stayed before the Battle of Boyacá. Hot pools, spa, good restaurant, quiet, fireplace. Highly recommended.
B Cabañas El Portón, T785 0168. More expensive on bank holidays, hHot water, parking, restaurant.

Sogamoso *p800*

B Litavira, C 12, No 10-30, T770 2585, F770 5631. Discounts at weekends, including breakfast, cable TV, private parking, good value.
D Bochica, C 11, No 14-33, T770 7381. Good value, comfortable, hot water, TV, tourist info, restaurant.
E Valparaíso, C 11A, No 17-56, T771 6935, near bus station. With bath and TV.

Lago de Tota *p800*

A Camino Real, Km 20 Vía Sogamoso a Aquitania,

T770 0684, on the lake. Pleasant public rooms, colourful gardens, boat slipway, boats for hire.
A **Hotel Santa Inez**, Km 29 Sogamoso-Aquitania, 3 km before Aquitania, T779 4199, also cabins. Good position on lake, boats for hire/fishing, good food, helpful.
A **Pozo Azul**, 3 km beyond Camino Real, in a secluded bay on the lake, T619 3462 (Bogotá), also cabins up to 6. With breakfast. Suitable for children, comfortable, watersport facilities, good food.
F **Residencia Venecia**, C 8, No 144, Aquitania. Clean, basic, reasonable.
Camping Las Rocas Lindas campground, at Playa Blanca, southwest corner of lake. With bath and hot water, 2 cabins for 7, 1 for 8, boats for hire, dining room, bar, fireplaces. Recommended.

Monguí *p801*
C **Hostal Calycanto**, pink house next to the bridge. Lovely setting, restaurant, book in advance.
E **La Cabaña**, chalet on road beyond river (cross bridge, turn left). Basic, comfortable, food if advised.

Sierra Nevada del Cocuy *p801*
D **Cabinas Kanwara** at 3,920 m, 1,000 m above Güicán, 2 cabins for 15 people each, restaurant, open fires, electric showers, or camping F, horse rental and guide service. Highly recommended.
E **La Sierra**, Güicán. Good, meals available, information on the region, sketch map, jeep hire.
   Several hotels in Cocuy (D-E), eg E **Hospedaje Cocuy** (meals, laundry) and E **Villa Real**.

❼ Eating

Sogamoso *p800*
♈ **Susacá**, Cra 16, No 11-35, T770 2587. One of the best of several restaurants near the centre, open 1200-2030, Sun 1200-1700, specialities include trout, good *comida*, large portions.

⊜ Transport

Sogamoso *p800*
Bus To **Bogotá**, 4-4½ hrs, US$6; to **Yopal**, US$5, 4 hrs, several daily.

Lago de Tota *p800*
Bus From **Sogamoso**, US$2.80, 1½ hr; from **Bogotá** (Flota Alianzana), via Tunja and Sogamoso, goes round the lake to Aquitania, passing Cuitiva, Tota and the Rocas Lindas.

Monguí *p801*
Bus Office on plaza. To **Bogotá**, Libertadores daily, US$8, 4½-6 hrs. To **Sogamoso**, every 30 mins by buseta, US$1, 45 mins.

Sierra Nevada del Cocuy *p801*
Bus To **Bogotá**, from both Güicán and Cocuy, 6 buses a day start 0400, about US$17, 10-11 hrs; services by **Libertadores** (recommended) and others. From Cocuy to **Cúcuta**, one daily direct leaves in afternoon, 10-12hrs. Between Cocuy and Güicán, several buses a day, US$1.50, 1 hr. To go north, change at Capitanejo from where buses go to **Bucaramanga** and to **Cúcuta**. Or change at **Pamplona** for more connections to Bucaramanga. From Capitanejo a picturesque road goes north to Málaga (35 km north of Capitanejo, several hotels), Pamplona (see below) and Cúcuta. To Bucaramanga is another spectacular trip through the mountains, but the road is not good and is very tortuous.

To Bucaramanga and Cúcuta

Socorro → *Phone code: 97. Colour map 1, grid B4. Population: 23,020. Altitude: 1,230 m.*
The main road goes northeast for 84 km to Socorro, with steep streets and single storey houses set among graceful palms. It has a singularly large stone cathedral. The **Casa de Cultura** museum (opening hours vary) covers the local history and the interesting part played by Socorro in the fight for Independence. It is well worth a visit. There is a daily market.

San Gil → *Phone code: 97. Colour map 1, grid B4. Population: 28,000. Altitude: 1,140 m.*
About 21 km beyond Socorro, northeast on the main road to Bucaramanga, is San Gil, a colonial town with a good climate. The small town is an important centre for adventure sports (rafting, kayaking, parapenting, paragliding and caving) and is also a good place for biking, horse riding and walking. **El Gallineral** ① *daily 0800-1800, US$2*, a delightful riverside park with a fresh water swimming pool and beautiful trees covered with moss-like tillandsia (take insect repellent). Good view from La Gruta, the shrine overlooking the town (look for the cross). Visit the Juan Curi waterfalls, 20 minutes drive from town.

Barichara ➜ *Phone code: 97. Colour map 1, grid B4. Population: 10,000. Altitude: 1,300 m.*
From San Gil a paved road leads 22 km to Barichara, a beautiful colonial town founded in 1714 and designated as a national monument. Among Barichara's places of historical interest are the Cathedral and three churches, the cemetery and the house of the former president Aquiles Parra (the woman next door has the key). An interesting excursion is to **Guane**, 9 km away by road, or two hours' delightful walk by *camino real* (historic trail), where there are many colonial houses and an archaeological museum in the *casa parroquial*, collection of textiles, coins and a mummified woman (entry US$0.25). The valley abounds with fossils. There are morning and afternoon buses from Barichara. Another interesting trip is to the waterfall **Salto de Mica**, a 30-minute walk along a trail following the line of cliffs near Barichara. Between San Gil and Bucamaranga is the spectacular Río Chicamocha canyon, with the best views to the right of the road. At the time of writing, a cable car is being built across the canyon.

Bucaramanga ➜ *Phone code: 97. Colour map 1, grid B4. Population: 465,000. Altitude: 1,000 m.*
The capital of Santander, 420 km from Bogotá, was founded in 1622 but was little more than a village until the latter half of the 19th century. The city's great problem is space for expansion. Erosion in the lower, western side topples buildings over the edge after heavy rain. The fingers of erosion, deeply ravined between, are spectacular. The metropolitan area of this modern, commercial city, has grown rapidly because of the success of coffee, tobacco and staple crops. It is known as the 'city of parks'.

The **Parque Santander** is the heart of the modern city, while the **Parque García Rovira** is the centre of the colonial area. On it stands the city's oldest church, Capilla de Los Dolores, a national monument. Just off Parque García Rovira is the **Casa de Cultura**. The **Casa de Bolívar** ① *Calle 37, No 12-15, Mon-Fri 0800-1200, 1400-1730, Sat 0800-1200, US$0.50,* where Bolívar stayed in 1828. It is interesting for its connections with Bolívar's campaign in 1813. On the way out of the city northeast (towards Pamplona) is the **Parque Morrorico**, well-maintained with a fine view. There is a sculptured Saviour overlooking the park, a point of pilgrimage on Good Friday. The **tourist office** ① *(inside the mayor's office), C 30, No 26-117, T634 1132 (ext 123), Mon-Fri 0800-1200, 1400-1830,* is friendly and knowledgeable.

Around Bucaramanga
In **Floridablanca**, 8 km southwest, is the **Jardín Botánicao Eloy Valenzuela** ① *Mon-Sat 0500-1700, free, take a* Floridablanca *bus and walk 1 km; taxi from centre, US$3.50,* belonging to the national tobacco agency. **Girón** a tobacco centre 9 km southwest of Bucaramanga on the Río de Oro, is a quiet and attractive colonial town. Its white buildings, beautiful church, bridges and cobbled streets are well preserved and the town unspoilt by modernization. By the river are *tejo* courts and open-air restaurants with *cumbia* and *salsa* bands. Bus from Cra 15 or 22 in Bucaramanga, US$1.25. **Piedecuesta** is 18 km southeast of Bucaramanga. Here you can see cigars being handmade, furniture carving and jute weaving. Cheap, hand-decorated *fique* rugs can be bought. There are frequent buses to all the surrounding towns; taxi costs US$6. Corpus Christi processions in these towns in June are interesting. Bus from Cra 22, US$0.45, 45 mins.

Bucaramanga to Pamplona
The road (paved but narrow) runs east to Berlín, and then northeast (a very scenic run over the Eastern Cordillera) to Pamplona, about 130 km from Bucaramanga. **Berlín** is an ideal place to appreciate the grandeur of the Eastern Cordillera and the hardiness of the people who live on the *páramo*. The village lies in a valley at 3,100 m, the peaks surrounding it rise to 4,350 m and the temperature is constantly around 10°C, although on the infrequent sunny days it may seem much warmer. There is a tourist complex with cabins and there are several basic eating places. Camping (challenging but rewarding) is possible with permission. At the highest point on the road between Bucaramanga and Berlín, 3,400 m, is a café where you can camp on the porch.

Pamplona ➜ *Phone code: 975. Colour map 1, grid B4. Population: 43,700. Altitude: 2,200 m.*
Founded in the mountains in 1548, it became important as a mining town but is now better known for its university. It is renowned for its Easter celebrations. Pamplona is a good place to buy *ruanas* and has a good indoor market. The **Cathedral** in the spacious central plaza is worth a visit. The earthquake of 1875 played havoc with the monasteries and some of the churches: there is now a hotel on the site of the former San Agustín monastery, but it is possible to visit the ex-monasteries of San Francisco and Santo Domingo. The **Iglesia del Humilladero**, adjoining

the cemetery, is very picturesque and allows a fine view of the city. The **Casa Colonial** ① *Calle 6, No 2-56, Mon-Fri 0800-1200, 1400-1800; Sat 0800-1200, US$0.50*, archaeological museum, is a little gem. **Casa Anzoátegui** ① *Calle Real, No 7-48, Mon-Fri 0800-1200, 1400-1800*, houses a museum of the Independence period. One of Bolívar's generals, José Antonio Anzoátegui, died here in 1819, at the age of 30, after the battle of Boyacá. The state in northeast Venezuela is named after him. Tourist office ① *Calle 5 y Cra 6, on main plaza.*

Cúcuta → *Phone code: 97. Colour map 1, grid B4. Population: 526,000. Altitude: 215 m.*

Some 72 km from Pamplona is the city of **Cúcuta**, capital of the Department of Norte de Santander, 16 km from the Venezuelan border. Founded in 1733, destroyed by earthquake 1875, and then rebuilt, its tree-lined streets offer welcome respite from the searing heat, as does the **cathedral**, on Avenida 5 between Calles 10 and 11. The international bridge between Colombia and Venezuela is southeast of the city. The modern city is full of Venezuelan contraband and petrol and has some rough areas. See Warning, page 807. **Corporación Mixta de Promoción de Santander**, ① *Calle 10, No 0-30, Edif Rosetal, T571 8981*, helpful. Tourist police at the bus station and airport.

Just short of the border is the small town of **Villa Rosario**, where the Congress met which agreed the constitution of Gran Colombia in the autumn of 1821, one of the high points of the career of Simón Bolívar. The actual spot where the documents were signed is now a park beside which is the **Templo del Congreso**, in which the preliminary meetings took place. Also nearby is the **Casa de Santander**, where General Santander, to whom Bolívar entrusted the administration of the new Gran Colombia, was born and spent his childhood. The archaeological **museum** ① *Tue-Sat 0800-1200, 1400-1800, Sun 0900-1330*, is worth a visit. The **Casa de Cultura** (also known as Torre de Reloj) ① *Calle13 No 3-67*, has art exhibitions and incorporates the **Museo de la Ciudad** which covers the history of the city and its part in the Independence Movement.

Border with Venezuela → *Phone code: 97*
Venezuela is one hour ahead of Colombia. If you do not obtain an exit stamp, you will be turned back by Venezuelan officials and the next time you enter Colombia, you will be fined.

Colombian immigration ① *DAS, Av 1, No 28-57, daily 0800-1130, 1400-1730.* Take a bus from the city centre to Barrio San Rafael, south towards the road to Pamplona. Shared taxi from border is US$6, then US$1 to bus station. Exit and entry formalities are also handled at the DAS office in the white house before the international border bridge. DAS has a third office at the airport, which will deal with land travellers. For Venezuelan immigration, see page 1370. There is no authorized charge at the border.

Venezuelan consulate ① *Av Camilo Daza, Zona Industrial, near airport and Copetran terminal, T579 1967/1954/1956, Mon-Thu 0800-1100, 1300-1500, Fri 0800-1400, taxi US$1.50*. Nationals not requiring a visa are issued an automatic free tourist card by Venezuelan immigration officers at the border. Overland visitors requiring a visa to Venezuela can get one here, or at the Venezuelan Embassy in Bogotá, T610 6622 (visa information), although they may send you to Cúcuta. As requirements change frequently, it is recommended that all overland visitors (whether requiring a visa or not) check first with a Venezuelan consulate in advance. Apply for visa at 0800 to get it by 1300. If you know when you will be arriving at the border, get your visa in your home country.
Leaving and entering Colombia by private vehicle Passports must be stamped at DAS in town and car papers must be stamped at Aduana on the road to the airport, about 10 km from the border or at their office 40 m before the International Bridge.

● Sleeping

Socorro *p802*
B Tamacara, C 14, No 14-15, T727 3515. Swimming pool, restaurant, good services.
D Colonial, Cra 15, No 12-45, T727 2842. Fan, TV, restaurant, parking.
E Nueva Venezia, C 13, No 14-37, T727 2350. Shower, dining room, nice old rooms, good value.

San Gil *p802*
A Bella Isla, north of town, Vía Javel San Pedro, T724 2971. Large condominium, full services, great views, pool, beautiful gardens.
C Mansión Perla del Fonce, Cra 10, No 1-44, T724 3298. Outside of town, family hotel, includes breakfast, good views.

D Alcantuz, Cra 11, No 10-15, T724 3160.
Free coffee, fan, good location, a bit run-down.
E Macondo Guesthouse, C10, No 7-66,
T310-828 2095, macondohostal@hotmail.com.
Run by friendly Australian Shaun who also
owns an adventure sports company. Good
source of information on trips and activities.
Rooms and dorms in small house, kitchen
facilities, book exchange, patio, hammocks,
washing machine, best to call in advance to
reserve room, as hotel is not always fully staffed
due to adventure activities. Guests are given
a house key. Recommended.
E San Carlos, Cra 11, No 11-25, T724 2542.
Cheaper without bath, upstairs rooms are
preferable, basic.

Baricharas *p803*
Ask at the *Casa de Cultura* about staying
in private homes.
B Bahía Chalá, C 7, No 7-51, T726 7036.
Colonial, rooms around patio, restaurant,
price includes breakfast, helpful.
B Hostal Misión Santa Bárbara, C 5,
No 9-08, T726 7163. Old colonial house, quiet,
pool, suites, restaurant, parking, patio.
C Coratá, Cra 7, No 4-08, T726 7110.
Colonial, with a charming courtyard,
restaurant and lovely views of
the cathedral. Recommended.
D Diez Desitos, Cra 5, No 7-58, T726 7224.
Simple hostal, some rooms with bath, fan.
E Aposentos, C 6, No 6-40, T726 7294. Good
cheap option, on main plaza, with bath.

Bucaramanga *p803*
Since Bucaramanga is the site for numerous
national conventions, it is sometimes hard
to find a room. Wide variety of hotels on C 31,
between Cras 18-21.
AL Meliá Confort Chicamocha, C 34,
No 31-24, T634 3000, www.solarhoteles.com.
Luxury, a/c, swimming pool (non guests US$10).
C El Pilar, C 34, No 24-09, T634 7207.
Central, hot water, a/c, less with fan, quiet,
good service and food. Recommended.
D Residencias San Diego, Cra 18, No 54-71,
T643 4273. Quiet, basic.
E Residencias Amparo, C 31, No 20-29, T630
4089. With bath, comfy beds, will do laundry,
helpful, good.
F Residencia ABC, C 31, No 21-44. Basic,
cold water, private baths, cheap.

Around Bucaramanga: Girón *p803*
C Las Nieves, C 30, No 25-71, T646 8968.
Colonial house, central courtyard, balconies
overlooking central plaza, a/c, much cheaper
with fan, good restaurant.

Pamplona *p803*
Accommodation may be hard to find at
weekends, when Venezuelans visit the town.
C Cariongo, Cra 5, C 9, T568 1515.
Very good, excellent restaurant, US
satellite TV (locked parking available).
E Imperial, Cra 5, No 5-36, T568 2571,
on main plaza. Large rooms, hot water,
safe, restaurant.
E Orsúa, C5, No 5-67, T568 2470, on
main plaza. Cheaper without bath or TV,
good restaurant.
F Los Llanos, C 9, No 7-30, T568 3441.
Shared bath, cold water, simple rooms.
Recommended.

Cúcuta *p802, map p805*
AL Tonchalá, C 10, Av 0, T571 2005,
www.hoteltonchala.com. Good restaurant,
pool, a/c, sauna, casino, airline booking
office in hall.
A Casa Blanca, Av 6, No 14-55, T572 2888,
hotelcas@col1.telecom.com.co.
Good, a/c, pool, parking, reasonable restaurant.
B Acora, C 10, No 2-75, T572 4000, F573 1139.
A/c, comfortable, good restaurant, safe deposit,
cable TV, good value.

Cúcuta

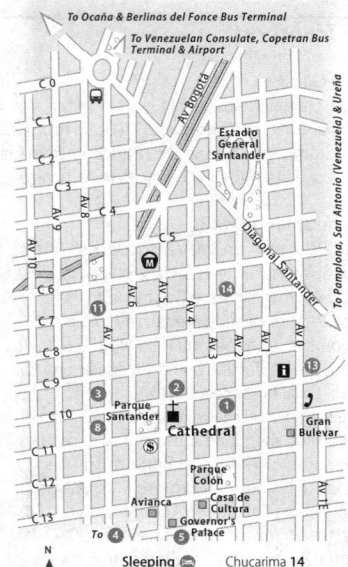

To Ocaña & Berlinas del Fonce Bus Terminal
To Venezuelan Consulate, Copetran Bus Terminal & Airport
Av Bogotá
Estadio General Santander
Diagonal Santander
To Pamplona, San Antonio (Venezuela) & Ureña
Parque Santander
Cathedral
Gran Bulevar
Parque Colón
Avianca
Casa de Cultura
Governor's Palace

N
0 metres 200
0 yards 200

Sleeping
Acora 1
Amaruc 2
Cacique 3
Casa Blanca 4
Chucarima 14
Internacional 5
Lord 8
Residencias Nohra 11
Tonchalá 13

B Chucarima, C 7, No 2-30, Barrio Latino, T583 2069. Central, very pleasant, new rooms, a/c, TV, safe, restaurant.

B Lord, Av 7, No 10-58, T571 3898. A/c, cheaper with fan, nice rooms, good restaurant, safe.

C Amaruc, Av 5, No 9-73, T571 7625, F572 1805. Less with fan, breakfast, parking.

C Cacique, Av 7, No 9-66, T571 2652, F571 9484. A/c, cheaper with fan, cold showers, reasonable.

D Internacional, C 14, No 4-13, T571 2718. Central, good value, pool, patio, restaurant, fan, helpful. Recommended.

F Residencias Nohra, C 7, No 7-52, T572 5889. Shared bath, quiet, basic.

🍴 Eating

San Gil *p802*
❚ **Casona China**, Cra 10, No 9-39. Decent Chinese.
❚ **El Maná**, C10, No 9-12. Good *comida corriente*.

Barichara *p803*
Light meals are available around the plaza.
❚ **La Casona**, C 6, No 5-68. Cheap, good food.

Bucaramanga *p803*
Try the *hormigas culonas* (large black ants), a local delicacy mainly eaten during Holy Week (sold in shops, not restaurants).
❚❚ **D'Marco**, C 48, No 28-76. Excellent meat.
❚ **Fonda**, C 33, No 34-42. Vegetarian, good.
❚ **Govinda**, Cra 20, No 34-65. Indian vegetarian, excellent lunch.
❚ **Los Notables**, Cra 18, C 34/35. Good breakfast.
❚ **Zirus**, C 56, No 30-88. Friendly, English spoken.
Berna, C 35, No 18-30. Café, good pastries.

Around Bucaramanga: Girón *p803*
❚❚ **Mansión del Fraile** on the plaza, in a beautiful colonial house. Good food, Bolívar slept here on one occasion, ask to see the bed.
❚ **La Casona**, C 28, No 27-47. Colonial setting, recommended. Try their *fritanga gironesa*.

Pamplona *p803*
❚ **Piero's Pizza**, Cra 5, No 8B-67. Good. See also Hotel Orsúa, above.
Angelitas, C 7 y Cra 7. Good coffee.
Cafetería La Malagueña, C 6, No 6. Good, cheap.
La Casa de las Tortas, C 6, No 5-92. Good bakery.
La Pamplonesa, C 7 y Cra 6. Bakery, breakfast.

Cúcuta *p802, map p805*
❚❚ **Madrigal**, C 11, No 1E-23, behind *Telecom*. Steaks, seafood.
❚ **La Brasa**, Av 5, C 7. Good *churrascos*, fair prices.
❚ **La Casa del Pollo**, Av 6, No 8-99. Chicken dishes, good lunch menus.
❚ **Don Pancho**, Av 3, No 9-21. Local menus.

🎉 Festivals and events

Bucaramanga *p803*
The annual international piano festival is held here in **mid-Sep** in the Auditorio Luis A Calvo at the Universidad Industrial de Santander, one of Colombia's finest concert halls. The university is worth a visit for beautiful grounds and a lake full of exotic plants. Part of the **Feria de Bucaramanga** includes an arts and crafts fair in **first 2 weeks of Sep**, in the Centro de Ferias y Exposiones.

🛍 Shopping

Bucaramanga *p803*
Handicrafts In Girón and typical clothing upstairs in the food market, C 34 y Cras 15-16. Similar articles (*ruanas*, hats) in San Andresito.

⛰ Activities and tours

San Gil *p802*
Colombia Rafting Expeditions, Cra 10, No 7-83, T283 8647, colombiakayak@hotmail.com, or contact Shaun at **Macondo** guest house, T311-828 2905 (mob). Offers rafting tours from 2 hrs to 4 days, all inclusive, US$13-200; kayaking courses US$150, rental US$25 per day; caving, 3 hrs, US$15; rappel, US$15; parapenting, courses US$350, 20-min flight US$30; mountain biking US$25; also trekking and horse riding. Good reports.

🚌 Transport

San Gil *p802*
Bus Station 5 mins out of town by taxi on road to Tunja. To **Bogotá**, US$17-19, 6-7hrs; **Bucaramanga**, US$6, 2½ hrs; **Barichara** from Cra 10 between C14/C15, US$1.40, 45 mins, hourly.

Bucaramanga *p803*
Air Palonegro, on 3 flattened hilltops south of city. Spectacular views on take-off and landing. Daily **Avianca** flights to **Bogotá** (also **AeroRepública** and **Satena**), and to principal Colombian cities. **Satena** (C36, No 15-56, T670 7087) flies to Cúcuta, Quibdó, Medellín and Cali.
Bus Local buses cost US$0.45.
The long distance terminal is on the Girón road, with cafés, shops and showers. Taxi to centre, US$2.30; bus US$0.45. To **Bogotá**, 8-11 hrs, US$25 (Pullman) with **Expreso Brasilia**. Same company to **Cartagena**, US$35, 12-13 hrs, 0830 and then frequent evening services 1900-2300. **Tunja**, 7-8 hrs, US$18. **Valledupar**, 8 hrs, US$23 at 1800. **Barranquilla**, 10-12 hrs, US$36. **Santa Marta**, 9-11 hrs, US$27, maybe more according to season, US$22 with **Expreso Brasilia**. To **Pamplona**, Expreso Brasilia, 4-5 hrs,

night buses (0100-0600), US$9. To **Cúcuta**, Expreso Brasilia, 6 hrs, US$12.50 and colectivo US$17. The trip to Cúcuta is spectacular in the region of Berlín. To **Barrancabermeja**, 3 hrs, US$7. To **El Banco** on the Río Magdalena, US$15, several companies, direct or change at Aguachica. Hourly buses to **San Gil**, with Expreso Brasilia, 2½ hrs, US$7. Other companies with local services to nearby villages on back roads, eg the folk-art buses of **Flota Cáchira** (C 32, Cra 33-34).

Taxi Most taxis have meters; beware of overcharging from bus terminals.

Pamplona *p803*
Bus To **Bogotá**, US$25, 13-16 hrs. To **Cúcuta**, US$4.20, 2½ hrs. To **Bucaramanga**, US$6.50, 4 hrs. To **Málaga** from main plaza, 5 a day from 0800, 6 hrs, US$6. To **Tunja**, US$22, 12 hrs (leaving at 0600). To **Berlín**, US$4. Buses leave from Cra 5 y C 4, minibuses to Cúcuta from Cra 5 y C 5.

Cúcuta *p802, map p805*
Air Do not buy airline 'tickets' from Cúcuta to Venezuelan destinations, all flights go from San Antonio: cross the border and fly from San Antonio airport (30 mins).

The airport is 5 km north of the town centre, 15 mins by taxi in normal traffic from the town and border, US$3. There are only domestic flights from Cúcuta airport. To **Bogotá** 3 daily and direct to other Colombian cities with **Avianca** and **Satena**. It is cheaper to buy tickets in Colombia for these flights than in advance in Venezuela.
Bus Bus station: Av 7 and C O (a really rough area). Taxi from bus station to town centre, US$1.50. **Berlinas de Fonce** and **Copetran** have their own terminals in the northwest of the city. Bus to **Bogotá**, hourly, 17-24 hrs, US$33, **Berlinas del Fonce** every 2 hrs from 0630 onwards, 2 stops, including 15 mins in **Bucaramanga** (US$2.50 extra for *cochecama*), or **Bolivariano**, 20 hrs. There are frequent buses, even during the night (if the bus arrives in the dark, sit in the station café until light). To **Cartagena**, **Brasilia** 1330 and 1730, 18 hrs, US$45. To **Bucaramanga**, US$12.50, 6 hrs, with Brasilia, 5 departures daily.
Warning Cúcuta and the surrounding area is a large centre for smuggling and guerrilla activity. Be careful. Travellers have been reporting for years that the bus station is overrun with thieves and conmen, who have tried every trick in the book. This is still true. You must take great care, there is little or no police protection. On the 1st floor there is a tourist office for help and information and a café/snack bar where you can wait in comparative safety. Alternatively, go straight to a bus going in your direction, get on it, pay the driver and don't let your belongings out

of your sight. For San Cristóbal, only pay the driver of the vehicle, not at the offices upstairs in the bus station. If you are told, even by officials, that it is dangerous to go to your chosen destination, double check. Report any theft to the DAS office, who may be able to help to recover what has been stolen. **Note**: Exceptions to the above are the **Berlinas del Fonce** and **Copetran** terminals, which are much safer.

Border with Venezuela *p804*
Bus **San Cristóbal**, US$1.40 (Bolivariano), colectivo US$3; **San Antonio**, taxi US$8, bus and colectivo from C 7, Av 4/5, US$0.50 to DAS office, then US$0.40 to ONIDEX in San Antonio. From Cúcuta to **Caracas**, go to San Antonio or (better) San Cristóbal and change. On any form of transport which is crossing the border, make sure that the driver knows that you need to stop to obtain exit/entry stamps etc. You will have to alight and flag down a later colectivo.

● Directory

Bucaramanga *p803*
Banks Bancolombia, by Parque Santander, will cash Thomas Cook and Amex TCs. Long queues (cheques and passports have to be photocopied). Other banks, many with cash machines. Cash (euros and US$) changed at **Cambiamos SA**, in *Vivero* supermarket, Viaducto La Flora, Mon-Sat 0900-1900, also MoneyGram agent for sending and receiving cash from abroad, no TCs.

Pamplona *p803*
Banks Banco de Bogotá, main plaza, gives Visa cash advances. Cash machines nearby. **Post offices** Cra 6 y C 6, in pedestrian passage. **Telephones** C 7 y Cra 5A.

Cúcuta *p802, map p805*
Banks Good rates of exchange at the airport, or on the border. Banco Ganadero/BBV and **Banco de Los Andes** near the plaza will give cash against Visa cards. Bancolombia changes TCs. Banco de Bogotá, Parque Santander, advances on Visa. There are money changers on the street all round the main plaza and many shops advertise the purchase and sale of bolívares. **Casa de Cambio** Cambiamos SA in *Vivero* supermarket, Av Demetrio Mendoza. Change pesos into bolívares in Cúcuta or San Antonio, difficult to change them further into Venezuela. **Internet** Centro Comercial, Gran Bulevar, across the street from Telecom, Opinonet, Internet Café oficina 606B. **Telephones** C 11 y Av 0.

Cartagena and the north coast

Caribbean Colombia is very different in spirit from the highlands: the coast stretches from the Darién Gap, through banana plantations, swamplands and palm plantations to the arid Guajira.

Cartagena → *Phone code: 95. Colour map 1, grid A2. Population: 746,000.*

Cartagena should not be missed. Besides being Colombia's top tourist destination and a World Heritage site, it is one of the most vibrant and beautiful cities in South America. It's an eclectic mix of Caribbean, African and Spanish tastes and sounds. The colonial heart of Cartagena lies within 12 km of ramparts. Within the walled city, El Centro, is a labyrinth of colourful squares, churches, mansions of former nobles and pastel houses along narrow cobbled streets. Most of the upmarket hotels and restaurants are found here. The San Diego quarter, once home to the middle classes, and Plaza Santo Domingo perhaps best capture the lure of Cartagena. Less touristy and developed is the poorer Getsemaní neighbourhood, where colonial buildings of former artisans are being rapidly restored. Here are most of the budget hotels. Immediately adjoining Getsemaní is the downtown sector known as La Matuna, where vendors and fruit juice sellers crowd the pavements and alleys between the modern commercial buildings and banks. Cartagena is also a popular beach resort and along Bocagrande and El Laguito are modern high-rise hotels on the sea front. It is also about glamour and during the high season the walled city becomes a playground for the rich and famous. Cruise ships dock at its port. Do not miss a drink by night in the cafés next to the city's oldest church, Santo Domingo, and in Plaza San Diego. Beyond Crespo on the road to Barranquilla is a fast-growing beach resort lined with luxury apartments. Trade winds during December-February provide relief from the heat.

Ins and outs

Getting there and around Rafael Núñez **airport** is 1½ km from the city in Crespo district, reached by local buses from Blas de Lezo, southwest corner of inner wall. Bus from one block from airport to Plaza San Francisco US$0.40. Taxi to Bocagrande US$4, to town US$3 (official prices). *Casa de cambio*, T656 4943, open, Mon-Fri 0830-2030, Sat 0830-1700, Sun 0830-2100, cashes Amex TCs but not *Bank of America*. Better rates in town. For information, ask at travel agents offices on upper level. Daily flights to all main cities and international destinations. **Bus terminal** is 30 mins from town on the road to Barranquilla, taxi US$5.50, or take city buses 'Terminal de Transportes', US$0.60. ▶▶ *For further information, see Transport, page 837.*

Information There is no official tourist office in Cartagena at present (2006). Ask at hotels, eg **Santa Clara** and **Casa Viena** are helpful. The **Instituto de Patrimonio y Cultura de Cartagena** ① *C del Curato de Santo Toribio No 38-161, Edif Aquilar, p 1, T664 5361, may provide information. See also www.cartagenacaribe.com (in Spanish)*. For maps, **Instituto Agustín Codazzi** ① *Calle 34, No 3-37, Edificio Inurbe.*

History

Cartagena de Indias was founded by Pedro de Heredia on 1 June 1533 and grew to be the most important port in the 'New World'. The core of the city was built on an island separated from the mainland by marshes and lagoons close to a prominent hill – the perfect place for a defensive port. There were then two approaches to it, Bocagrande, at the northern end of Tierrabomba island – the direct entry from the Caribbean – and Bocachica, a narrow channel at the south leading to the great bay of Cartagena, 15 km long and 5 km wide. (Bocagrande was blocked after Admiral Vernon's attack in 1741 – see box, The Sacking of Cartagena.) The old walled city lies at the north end of the Bahía de Cartagena, with the Caribbean Sea to the west.

Cartagena was one of the storage points for merchandise sent out from Spain and for treasure collected from the Americas to be sent back to Spain. A series of forts protected the approaches from the sea, and the formidable walls around the city made it almost impregnable.

Entering Bocachica by sea, the island of Tierrabomba is to the left. At the tip of a spit of land is the fortress of **San Fernando**. Opposite, right on the tip of Barú island, is the **Fuerte**

The sacking of Cartagena

Despite its daunting outer forts and encircling walls, Cartagena was challenged repeatedly by enemies. Sir Francis Drake, with 1,300 men, broke in successfully in 1586, leading to a major reconstruction of the ramparts we see today. Nevertheless the Frenchmen Baron de Pointis and Ducasse, with 10,000 men, beat down the defences and sacked the city in 1697. But the strongest attack of all, by Sir Edward Vernon with 27,000 men and 3,000 pieces of artillery, failed in 1741 after besieging the city for 56 days; it was defended by the one-eyed, one-armed and one-legged hero Blas de Lezo, whose statue is at the entrance to the San Felipe fortress.

San José. The two forts were once linked by heavy chains to prevent surprise attacks by pirates. Close to the head of the bay is Manga island, now a leafy residential suburb. At its northern end a bridge, **Puente Román**, connects it with the old city. This approach was defended by three forts: **San Sebastián del Pastelillo** built between 1558 and 1567 (the Club de Pesca has it now) at the northwestern tip of Manga Island; the fortress of **San Lorenzo** near the city itself; and the very powerful **Castillo San Felipe de Barajas** ① *daily 0800-1700, US$5, US$2.30 children and students; guides are available; few signs and little printed information*, the largest Spanish fort built in the Americas. Built on San Lázaro hill, 41 m above sea-level, to the east of the city, initial construction began in 1656 and was finished by 1741. Under the huge structure are tunnels lined with living rooms and offices. Some are open and lit; visitors pass through these and on to the top of the fortress. Good footwear is advisable for the damp sloping tunnels. Baron de Pointis, the French pirate, stormed and took it, but Admiral Vernon failed to reach it.

Yet another fort, **La Tenaza**, protected the walled city from a direct attack from the open sea. The huge encircling walls were started early in the 17th century and finished by 1798. They were on average 12 m high and 17 m thick, with six gates. They contained, besides barracks, a water reservoir.

In order to link Cartagena with the Río Magdalena, the most important route to the interior of the continent, the Spaniards built a 114 km canal from the Bahía de Cartagena to Calamar on the river. Called the Canal del Dique, it is still in use.

Independence Cartagena was the first Colombian city to declare independence from Spain, in 1811. A year later Bolívar used the city as a jumping-off point for his Magdalena campaign. After a heroic resistance, Cartagena was retaken by the royalists under Pablo Morillo in 1815. The patriots finally freed it in 1821.

Historic centre

The **Puente Román** leads from the island of Manga into Getsemaní. North of the bridge, in an interesting plaza, is the church of **Santísima Trinidad**, built 1643 but not consecrated until 1839. North of the church, at Calle Guerrero 10 lived Pedro Romero, who set the revolution of 1811 going with his cry of "Long Live Liberty". The chapel of **San Roque** (early 17th century), near the hospital of Espíritu Santo, is by the junction of Calles Media Luna and Espíritu Santo.

If you take Calle Larga from Puente Román, you come to the two churches and monastery of **San Francisco**. The oldest church (now a cinema) was built in 1590 after the pirate Martin Côte had destroyed an earlier church built in 1559. The first Inquisitors lodged at the monastery. From its courtyard a crowd surged into the streets claiming independence from Spain on 11 November 1811. The monastery is now used by the Corporación Universitaria Rafael Núñez. Originally part of the Franciscan complex, the **Iglesia de la Tercera Orden** *on the corner of C Larga*, is still an active church and worth a visit. Opposite is the **Centro Internacional de Convenciones**, an important modern conference centre.

Past the San Francisco complex is **Plaza de la Independencia**, with the landscaped **Parque del Centenario** beyond. At right angles to the Plaza runs the **Paseo de los Mártires**, flanked by the busts of nine patriots executed in the square on 24 February 1816 by the royalist Morillo when he retook the city. At its western end, the **Torre del Reloj** (clock tower) is one of Cartagena's most prominent landmarks. Through its arches (the main entrance to the inner

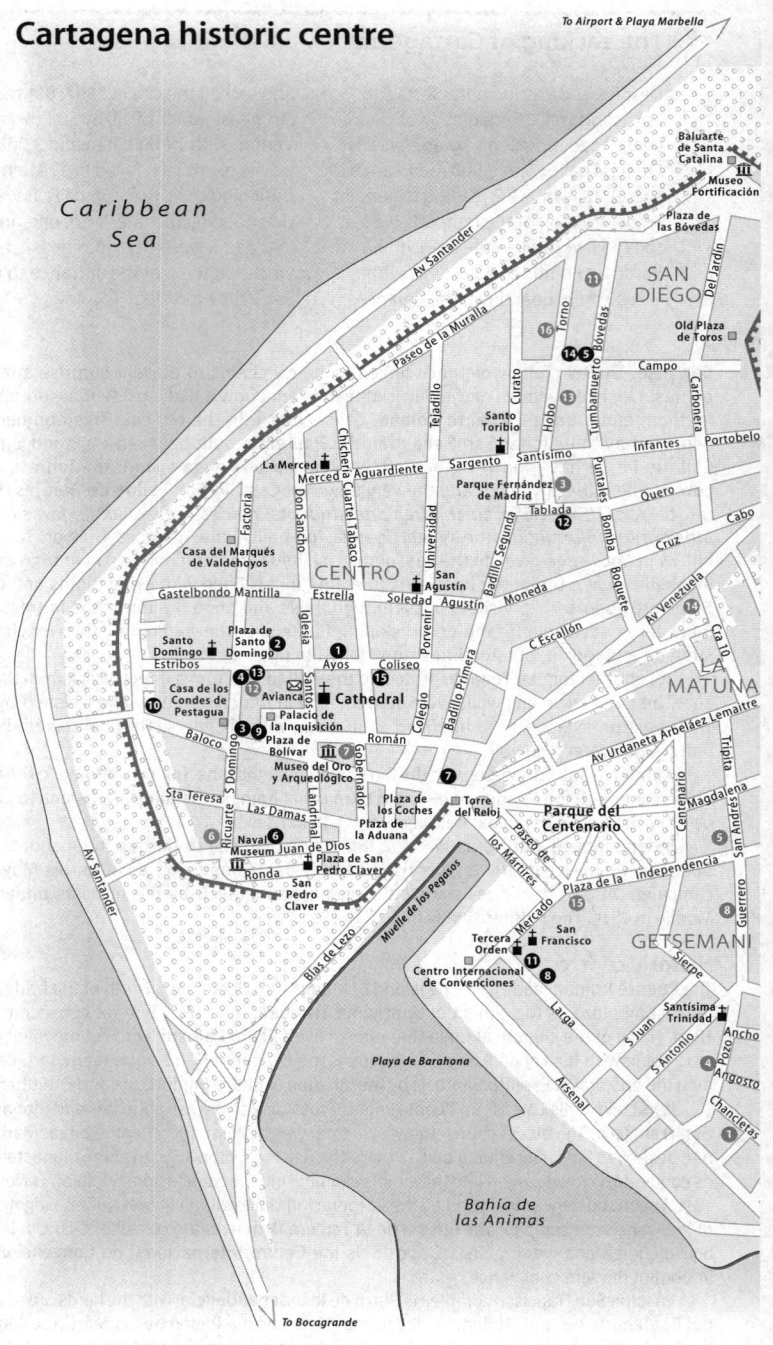

Cartagena historic centre

To Airport & Playa Marbella

Caribbean Sea

Baluarte de Santa Catalina

Museo Fortificación

Plaza de las Bóvedas

SAN DIEGO

Old Plaza de Toros

Av Santander

Paseo de la Muralla

Del Jardín

Campo

Carbonera

Portobelo

Santo Toribio

Parque Fernández de Madrid

Infantes

Quero

Cabo

La Merced

Chichería Aguardiente

Merced

Cuartel Tabaco

Don Sancho

Tejadillo

Universidad

Sargento

Santísimo

Tablada

Cruz

Av Venezuela

Factoría

Casa del Marqués de Valdehoyos

CENTRO

Estrella

Badillo Segunda

Bomba

Boquete

Cra 10

Gastelbondo Mantilla

San Agustín

Soledad

Agustín

Moneda

C Escallón

LA MATUNA

Santo Domingo Estribos

Plaza de Santo Domingo

Iglesia

Ayos

Coliseo

Porvenir

Badillo Primera

Casa de los Condes de Pestagua

Avianca

Cathedral

Colegio

Av Urdaneta Arbeláez Lemaitre

Baloco

Palacio de la Inquisición

Plaza de Bolívar

Román

Gobernador

Museo del Oro y Arqueológico

Sta Teresa

Las Damas

Plaza de los Coches

Plaza de la Aduana

Torre del Reloj

Parque del Centenario

Magdalena

Centenario

S Andrés

Ricaurte

S Domingo

Landrinal

Naval Museum

Juan de Dios

Plaza de San Pedro Claver

Paseo de los Mártires

Ronda

San Pedro Claver

Plaza de la Independencia

Guerrero

Av Santander

Blas de Lezo

Muelle de los Pegasos

Mercado

Tercera Orden

San Francisco

GETSEMANI

Sierpe

Centro Internacional de Convenciones

Larga

Santísima Trinidad

Ancho

S Juan

S Antonio

Lozano

Angosto

Playa de Barahona

Arsenal

Chancletas

Bahía de las Animas

To Bocagrande

Colombia Cartagena & the north coast

810

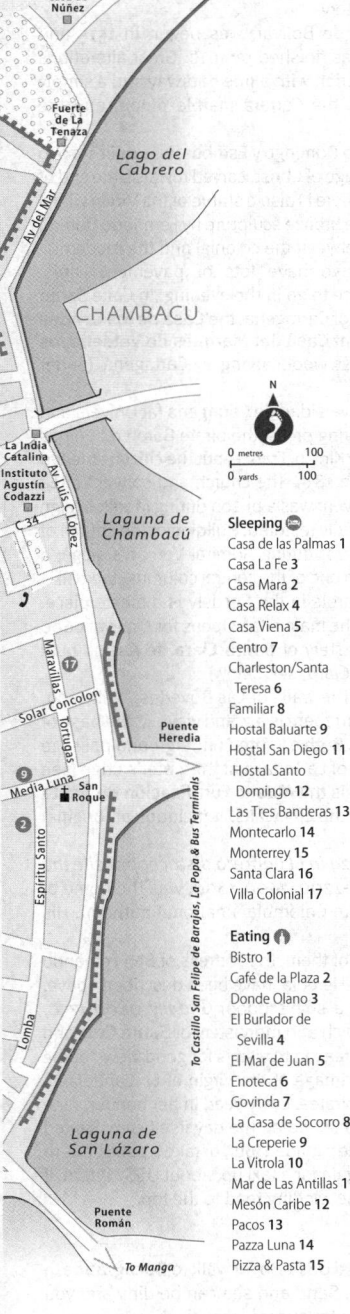

Casa de
Núñez

Fuerte
de La
Tenaza

Lago del
Cabrero

Av del Mar

CHAMBACU

La India
Catalina
Instituto
Agustín
Codazzi

N Luis C López

C 34

Laguna de
Chambacú

0 metres   100
0 yards   100

Maravillas

Solar Concolon

Tortugas

Puente
Heredia

9

Media Luna

2

San
Roque

Espíritu Santo

Lomba

To Castillo San Felipe de Barajas, La Popa & Bus Terminals

Laguna de
San Lázaro

Puente
Román

To Manga

Sleeping
Casa de las Palmas 1
Casa La Fe 3
Casa Mara 2
Casa Relax 4
Casa Viena 5
Centro 7
Charleston/Santa
  Teresa 6
Familiar 8
Hostal Baluarte 9
Hostal San Diego 11
Hostal Santo
  Domingo 12
Las Tres Banderas 13
Montecarlo 14
Monterrey 15
Santa Clara 16
Villa Colonial 17

Eating
Bistro 1
Café de la Plaza 2
Donde Olano 3
El Burlador de
  Sevilla 4
El Mar de Juan 5
Enoteca 6
Govinda 7
La Casa de Socorro 8
La Creperie 9
La Vitrola 10
Mar de Las Antillas 11
Mesón Caribe 12
Pacos 13
Pazza Luna 14
Pizza & Pasta 15

walled city), slaves from Africa were brought to the **Plaza de los Coches**, which served as a slave market. Around almost all the plazas of Cartagena arcades offer refuge from the tropical sun. On the west side of this plaza is the **Portal de los Dulces**, a favourite meeting place, where sweets are still sold. At night, the area becomes a popular place for an evening drink.

The **Plaza de la Aduana**, with a statue of Columbus, is flanked by the **Palacio Municipal** and the old Customs House. The **Museo de Arte Moderno** ① *Mon-Fri 0900-1200, 1500-1800, Sat 1000-1300, US$1.30*, exhibits modern Colombian artists and has a shop. The **Art Gallery and Museum** ① *Banco Ganadero, Plaza de la Aduana*, has contemporary Latin American paintings. Continue southwest to the **Church of San Pedro Claver and Monastery** ① *Mon-Sat 0800-1730, Sun 0830-1700, US$2.20 (reduction with ISIC), guides US$3 in Spanish, a little more in English*. Built by Jesuits in 1603, it was later dedicated to San Pedro Claver, a monk in the monastery, who was canonized 235 years after his death in 1654. Known as the Slave of the Slaves (El Apóstol de los Negros), he used to beg from door to door for money to give to the black slaves brought to the city. His body is in a glass coffin on the high altar and his cell and the balcony from which he sighted slave ships are shown to visitors. The monastery has a pleasant courtyard filled with flowers and trees in which Pedro Claver baptised slaves.

The church and convent of **Santa Teresa**, on the corner of C Ricaurte, was founded in 1609, but is now a hotel (opened 1997, renamed the **Charleston Santa Teresa**; see Sleeping). Opposite is the **Museo Naval del Caribe** *Tues-Sun 1000-1730, open Mon during high season, US$2.70, children half price*, displaying the naval history of Cartagena and the Caribbean.

The **Plaza de Bolívar** (the old Plaza Inquisición) has a statue of Bolívar. On its west side is the **Palacio de la Inquisición** ① *0900-1900, US$2.75, children half price*. First established in 1610, the present building dates from 1706. The stone entrance with its coats of arms and ornate wooden door is well preserved. The whole building, with its balconies, cloisters and patios, is a fine example of colonial baroque. It has been restored with air-conditioned rooms. The small museum contains photos of Cartagena from the 20th century, paintings of historical figures, fine scale models of colonial houses and a torture chamber (with reproductions of actual instruments). On the opposite side of the Plaza de Bolívar is the **Museo del Oro Zenú** ① *Tue-Fri 0800-1200, 1400-1800, Sat 0900-1700, free.* It has well displayed pre-Columbian gold and pottery.

The **Cathedral**, in the northeast corner of Plaza de Bolívar, was begun in 1575 and partially destroyed by Francis Drake. Reconstruction was finished by 1610. Great alterations were made between 1912 and 1923. It has a severe exterior, with a fine doorway and a simply decorated interior. See the gilded 18th century altar, the Carrara marble pulpit, and the elegant arcades which sustain the central nave.

The church and monastery of **Santo Domingo**, Santo Domingo y Estribos, was built 1570 to 1579 and is now a seminary. Inside, a miracle-making image of Christ, carved towards the end of the 16th century, is set on a baroque 19th century altar. There is also a statue of the Virgin with a crown of gold and emeralds. Opposite the church is a fine bronze sculpture by Fernando Botero, the *Gertrudis*, presenting an interesting juxtaposition between the colonial and the modern.

Plaza Santo Domingo and Calle Santo Domingo have lots of pavement cafés, restaurants and wandering musicians, an excellent place to go in the evening. In Calle Santo Domingo, No 33-29, is one of the great patrician houses of Cartagena, the **Casa de los Condes de Pestagua**. North of Santo Domingo is the magnificent **Casa del Marqués de Valdehoyos** *at C de la Factoría 36-57*, home of some of the best woodcarving in Cartagena (under refurbishment, not open to visitors).

The monastery of **San Agustín** (1580) is now the Universidad de Cartagena (at Universidad y La Soledad). From its chapel, today occupied by a printing press, the pirate Baron de Pointis stole a 500-pound silver sepulchre. It was returned by the King of France, but the citizens melted it down to pay their troops during the siege by Morillo in 1815. The church and convent of **La Merced**, Merced y Chichería, was founded 1618. The convent was a prison during Morillos reign of terror and its church is now the Teatro Heredia, beautifully restored. Building of the church of **Santo Toribio** (Badilla y Sargento) began in 1729. In 1741, during Admiral Vernon's siege, a cannon ball fell into the church during Mass and lodged in one of the central columns; the ball is now in a recess in the west wall. The font of Carrara marble in the Sacristy is a masterpiece. There is a beautiful carved ceiling (mudéjar style) above the main altar. Opens for Mass at 0600 and 1800, closed at other times. The church and monastery of **Santa Clara de Assisi**, built 1617-1621, have been converted into a fine hotel (*Santa Clara*, see below).

North of Santa Clara is the **Plaza de las Bóvedas**. The walls of Las Bóvedas, built 1799, are some 12 m high and 15 to 18 m thick. From the rampart there is a grand view. At the base of the wall are 23 dungeons, now containing tourist shops. Both a lighted underground passage and a drawbridge lead from Las Bóvedas to the fortress of La Tenaza at the water's edge (see above). In the neighbouring Baluarte de Santa Catalina is the **Museo Fortificación de Santa Catalina** ① *daily 0800-1800, US$1.50*, located inside the city walls. It includes an original well used for water storage during the siege of the city.

Casa de Núñez ① *just outside the walls of La Tenaza in El Cabrero district opposite the Ermita de El Cabrero, Calle del Coliseo, Mon-Fri 0800-1200, 1400-1800*, was the home of Rafael Núñez, president (four times) and poet (he wrote Colombia's national anthem). His grandiose marble tomb is in the adjoining church.

Four of the sights of Cartagena are off our map. Two of them, the Fortress of San Fernando and the Castillo San Felipe de Barajas, across the Puente Heredia, have been described above. At **La Popa** hill (named after an imagined likeness to a ship's poop) ① *daily 0800-1730, US$1.50, children US$0.75*, nearly 150 m high, is the church and monastery of **Santa Cruz** and restored ruins of the convent dating from 1608. The only reason to visit is for good views of the harbour and the city. In the church is the beautiful little image of the Virgin of La Candelaria, reputed a deliverer from plague and a protector against pirates. Every year, in her honour, nine days before 2 February thousands of pilgrims go up the hill and on the day itself carry lighted candles. It is dangerous to walk up on your own; either take a guided tour, or take a public bus to Teatro Miramar at the foot of the hill (US$0.50), then bargain for a taxi up, about US$7 return. If driving, take Cra 21 off Av Pedro de Heredia and follow the winding road to the top.

Beaches

Take a bus south from the Torre del Reloj (10 minutes), taxi US$1.80, or walk to **Bocagrande**, a spit of land crowded with hotels and apartment blocks. Sand and sea can be dirty and you may be hassled by vendors. But do not ignore the *palenqueras*, the black women who majestically carry bowls of fruits on their heads, serving excellent fruit salads on the beach. A better alternative is **Marbella**, a locals' beach, just north of Las Bóvedas. During the week, it is quieter and less crowded than Bocagrande. It is decent for swimming though subject at times to dangerous currents. Or try the beaches at the **Hilton** and **Las Américas** hotels, they are cleaner and have fewer vendors.

The **Bocachica** beach, on Tierrabomba island, is also none too clean. Boats leave from Muelle Turístico. The round trip can take up to two hours each way and costs about US$10. To ensure you are not stranded on the island do not pay the whole fare up front; pay the remainder on your return. *Ferry Dancing*, about half the price of the faster, luxury boats, carries dancing passengers. Boats taking in Bocachica and the San Fernando fortress include *Alcatraz*, which runs a daily trip from the Muelle Turístico. Recommended. The *Alcatraz* company goes to Islas del Rosario (see below), stops at the San Martín aquarium, then to Barú-Playa Blanca and leaves around 1530, returning to Cartagena around 1730.

Boats to the Islas del Rosario (see below) may stop at the San Fernando fortress and **Playa Blanca** on the Isla Barú for one hour. Many consider this to be the best beach in the region, with stretches of white sand and shady palm groves. Take food and water since these are expensive on the island. Playa Blanca is crowded in the morning, with armies of hawkers, but peaceful after the tour boats have left at 1500. There are several restaurants on the beach, go for the fish. If staying the night at Playa Blanca in *cabañas* or tents, take repellent against ferocious sandflies. Most restaurants allow you to camp on their premises for a nominal fee (but you must use their restaurant). If arriving by road (see Transport, below), turn right for cabañas. When taking boat trips be certain that you and the operator understand what you are paying for. You can arrange to be left and collected later, or you can try to catch an earlier boat on to Islas del Rosario or back to Cartagena with a boat that has dropped off people at the beach.

Islas del Rosario

The **Parque Nacional Corales del Rosario** embraces the Rosario archipelago (a group of 30 low-lying, densely vegetated coral islets 45 km southwest of the Bay of Cartagena, with narrow strips of fine sand beaches and mangroves) and the Islas de San Bernardo, a further 50 km south (see page 819). **Isla Grande** and some of the smaller islets are easily accessible by day trippers. Permits from *MA* in Cartagena or Bogotá are needed for the rest, US$2 entrance fee. **Rosario** (the best conserved) and **Tesoro** both have small lakes, some of which connect to the sea. There is an incredible profusion of aquatic and birdlife. The **San Martín de Pajarales Aquarium** ① *US$5.50, not included in boat fares (check that it's open before setting out)* is an open sea aquarium; there are guides, but also shark and dolphin shows (Footprint does not endorse dolphins in captivity, see www.wdcs.org/captivity). Many of the smaller islets are privately owned. Apart from fish and coconuts, everything is imported from the mainland, fresh water included. *Hotel Caribe* in Bocagrande has scuba lessons in its pool and diving at its resort on Isla Grande, US$230 and up. Enquire in Bocagrande for other places to stay on the islands. Diving permits are organized by diving companies and are included in the tour price.

North of Cartagena

The little fishing village of **La Boquilla**, northeast of Cartagena, is near the end of a sandy promontory between the Ciénaga de Tesca and the Caribbean, about 20 minutes past the airport. It is a popular weekend haunt and known for its many good fish restaurants on the beachfront (average US$8 for a meal). Sometimes people dance local dances, such as *la champeta*, on weekend evenings. Tours of the mangrove swamps are good for birdwatching, around US$12 for three-hour trip. Some restaurants allow camping for around US$3pp.

A good road continues beyond La Boquilla. On the coast, 50 km northeast, is **Galerazamba**, no accommodation but good local food. Nearby are the clay baths of **Volcán del Totumo** ① *US$1, a bathe will cost you US$2, masseurs available for a small extra fee*, in beautiful surroundings. The crater is about 20 m high and the mud lake, at a comfortable temperature, 10 m across, is reputed to be over 500 m deep.

⬤ Sleeping

Cartagena: Historic centre *p809, map p810*
Hotel prices rise substantially, up to 50%, during high season: Jun-Jul and 1 Nov-31 Mar, especially 15 Dec-31 Jan (dates are not fixed and vary

according to each hotel). Bargain in low season. Most budget hostels are on and around Calle Media Luna in Getsemaní. This area has been considered unsafe, but although it can be dirty and run down, safety is improving and it is still popular with travellers. Take care walking in and around Calle Media Luna and do not walk alone, especially at night

LL Santa Clara, Cra 8, No 39-29, T664 6070, www.hotelsantaclara.com. French Sofitel group, magnificently restored 16th- century convent, superb lunch buffet, lovely pool, garden with birds in cloisters, Aviatur office. A special place.

L Charleston/Santa Teresa, Cra 3A, No 31-23, T664 9494, F664 9448. Formerly a convent, elegantly converted, stylish pool on roof with great views of the colonial district and sea.

AL Casa La Fe, Parque Fernández de Madrid, Cra 7, No 36-125, T/F664 0306, www.casalafe.com. Discreet sign (pink building), run by English/Colombian team. Very pleasant converted colonial house, quiet, jacuzzi on roof, includes breakfast served in patio. Recommended.

AL Monterrey, Paseo de los Mártires Cra 8 B, No 25-103, T664 8560, www.hmonterrey.com. Colonial style, nice terrace with jacuzzi, business centre, comfortable rooms, a/c.

A Casa Mara C Espíritu Santo 29-139, Getsamaní, T664 8724. Private house owned by friendly Italian lady, small pool.

A Centro Hotel, C del Arzobispado, No 34-80, T664 0461, F664 2721. Central location, restored colonial building, a/c, spacious rooms, some with balcony overlooking street, safe.

A Hostal San Diego, C de las Bóvedas 39-120, T660 1433. Good location, safe, nice hotel decor and lobby but rooms don't match up.

B Casa Relax, Calle del Pozo No 25-105, Getsemaní. New, airy, bright hotel in colonial house, pool, internet, a/c, very pleasant, French and English spoken. Yacht available for rent.

B Las Tres Banderas, C Cochera de Hobo 38- 66, T660 0160. Off Plaza San Diego, helpful owner, very pleasant, safe, quiet, good beds, spacious rooms.

C Casa de las Palmas, C Larga (Callejón de las Palmas 25-51), Getsamaní, T664 3530. Charming colonial house filled with antiques, nice patio, small pool, good restaurant. Recommended.

C Hostal Santo Domingo, C Santo Domingo 33-46, T664 2268. Prime location, basic but clean rooms, popular with Colombians.

C Montecarlo, C 34, No 10-16, T673 5247. Modern, small rooms with a/c, safe, good location.

D Villa Colonial, C de las Maravillas 30-60, Getsamaní, T664 4996, F664 5919. Safe, well kept hostel run by friendly family, English spoken, a/c, cheaper with fan, TV.

E Hostal Baluarte, Calle Media Luna No 10-81, Getsemaní, T664 2208. Small basic rooms in colonial house, new rooms on 2nd floor, fan, TV, laundry service.

E-F Casa Viena, C San Andrés 30-53, T664 6242, www.casaviena.com. Popular traveller hostel, Austrian/Colombian run, owner, Hans, is an excellent source of information. Cooking facilities, washing machine, book exchange and internet, cheaper in dormitory. Enquire here for information about boats to Panama.

F Familiar, C El Guerrero No 29-66, Getsemaní, T664 2464. Very basic rooms and cooking facilities, some rooms with bath.

Houses to rent: Whole colonial mansions in El Centro for rent, luxurious, some with pool, 5-8 people, from US$900 a day. Contact Irma Seguerra de la Espriella (known as Wippy), T664 8790, T315-733 9725 (mob).

Beaches *p812*
Bocagrande
LL Hilton, Av Almte Brion, El Laguito, T665 0666, F665 2211. Excellent, family-oriented pool area, tennis courts, gym, spa, convention centre and restaurants. Overlooks the sea, own beach area.

L Caribe, Cra 1, No 2-87, T665 0155, www.hotel caribe.com. The first hotel to be built in Cartagena, retaining some splendour of bygone years. Tropical gardens with exotic animals, large pool, beach bar, rooms with sea view.

L Cartagena Millenium, Av San Martín No 7-135, T665 8499. Range of different suites and spacious rooms at various prices. New, chic and trendy, minimalist decor, small pool, restaurant, good service.

AL Charlotte, Av San Martín 7-126, T665 9201, www.hotelescharlotte.com. Colonial, Mediterranean style decor, small pool, comfortable rooms, a/c, good.

A San Martín, Av San Martín No 8-164, T665 4631, www.hotelsanmartincartagena.com. Bright and airy, small rooms some with balcony, pool.

B Internacional, Av San Martín 4-110, T665 8968. Price includes breakfast, helpful staff, TV, family atmosphere, comfortable rooms. Recommended.

B Leonela, Cra 3, No 7-142, T665 8595, F665 8868. One of the best *residencias* on Cra 3. Helpful staff, nice atmosphere, restaurant.

B Toledo, Cra 2, No 6-40, T665 3294, hoteltoledocartagena@yahoo.com. Prices include breakfast, a/c, cable TV, small pool, good restaurant, partially renovated (2006).

● *For an explanation of the sleeping and eating price codes used in this guide, see inside the front*
● *cover. Other relevant information is found in Essentials pages 774-775.*

Long stay El Conquistador, El Laguito, T665 0275/652 5015, opposite beach. Apartments for short and long term rent. Good services in building, internet, pool, cafeteria, laundry and phone centre but run down. Ask for Nidian Castro on the ground floor, local 4, who organizes rentals. Studio apartments from US$40 a night. Quality of apartments varies greatly. Best to see one first. Recommended for groups and long stays.

Marbella *p813*
There are several hotels and *pensiones* on the road to the airport, particularly at Marbella beach.
D Bellavista, Av Santander 46-50, T664 0691, F660 0379. Bohemian atmosphere, peaceful patio areas, good restaurant, English and French spoken by owner Enrique. Recommended for longer stays.

Playa Blanca *p813*
D Hostal Restaurante La Sirena, T310-889 1960 (mob), www.playa-blanca.net. Helpful co-owner Patrick speaks French, English and German, basic clean huts with electricity, some with private bath, fresh water showers,
G hammock space with mosquito nets and camping (US$2). Cheaper rates for children and free for children aged 0-6, food served.
E-F Wittenburg, ask for Gilberto, 'el francés', T 311-436 6215 (mob). Hammocks, dorms, rooms, limited fresh water showers, food served, including vegetarian.
E-F El Paraíso, beyond La Sirena. Basic.

Islas del Rosario *p813*
LL Kokomo, Isla Grande in Caño Ratón, T05-673 4450. Private beach resort, price is all-inclusive, including drinks and transport, cabins with bath and fan, also rooms with shared bath, bar, pool, restaurant, many European languages spoken.

● Eating

There is a wide range of excellent, up-market restaurants. All are busy during high season, reservations recommended.

Cartagena: historic centre *p, map p810*
♦♦♦ Donde Olano, C Santo Domingo y Inquisición, T664 7099, Tucked away, cosy, intimate atmosphere, great seafood with French influence.
♦♦♦ El Mar de Juan, Plaza San Diego. Seafood only, fine service and decor. Recommended.
♦♦♦ La Vitrola, C Baloco 2-01, El Centro, T660 0711. Attracts jet set crowd, great atmosphere, slick service, live Cuban band at weekends, good seafood and cocktails. Expensive but worth it, bok ahead. Recommended.
♦♦♦-♦♦ Enoteca, C San Juan de Dios, No 3-39, T664 3806. The best thin, crispy pizza in town, attractive patio, delicatessen and bustling atmosphere. Recommended.
♦♦♦-♦♦ La Casa de Socorro, C Larga, No 8B -112, Getsemaní, T664 4658. Busy at lunchtime, excellent Caribbean food. Try shark starter and *cazuela de mariscos*. Highly recommended.
♦♦♦-♦♦ Mar de Las Antillas, C Larga, No 8B- 26, Getsemaní, T664 5710. Popular, good seafood and service.
♦♦♦-♦♦ Pacos, Plaza Santo Domingo. Well-established, good Spanish and seafood, try aubergine starter.
♦♦ Bistro, C de Ayos, No 4-27/46, T664 1799. German run, nice atmosphere, open all day, good bakery, breakfasts, seafood and steak. Closed Sun.
♦♦ El Burlador de Sevilla, C Santo Domingo 33-88, T660 0866. Spanish, open late, excellent paella, attentive service, good.
♦♦ Pazza Luna, Plaza San Diego, next to and same owners as **El Mar de Juan**. Good pizza.
♦♦ San Pedro, Plaza de San Pedro Claver. Tables outside, a/c inside, Asian and fish specialities, good value. Recommended.

¶¶¶ **Dragón de Oro**, Av Venezuela 10-24. Chinese, good, inexpensive.

¶¶¶ **Fogón Costeño**, C de la Iglesia, No 35-48. Good value *comida corriente*, owner rents out spacious rooms upstairs (C). Parrots and surly monkey in patio.

¶¶¶ **Mesón Caribe**, C de La Tablada, No 7-62, San Diego, T660 2379. Popular with locals, good value lunches, nice atmosphere. Recommended.

¶¶¶ **Pizza & Pasta**, C del Arzobispado y C del Coliseo, T664 8960. Decent set lunch, open late and on Sun.

¶ **Govinda**, Plaza de los Coches 7-15. Vegetarian set lunch US$2. Recommended.

¶ **Marvel**, C del Colegio, No 34-25. Local, very simple, decent cheap set lunches for US$1.80.

¶ **Tienda Naturista**, C Quero 9-09. Good, cheap vegetarian.

Café de la Plaza, Plaza Santo Domingo. Great atmosphere, open all day.

La Creperie, Plaza de Bolívar. Generous salads, fruit juices.

Panadería La Mejor, Av Arbeláez. Good for breakfast, fine wholemeal bread, coffee, yoghurt, expensive.

Outside the centre

¶¶¶ **Club de Pesca**, San Sebastián de Pastelillo fort, Manga island, T660 5863. Wonderful setting, excellent fish and seafood. Recommended.

Beaches: Bocagrande *p812*

¶¶¶-¶¶ **Arabe**, Cra 3A, No 8-83, T665 4365. Excellent large steaks and Arab food, has belly dancer.

¶¶ **La Fonda Antioqueña**, Cra 2, No 6-161. Traditional Colombian.

¶¶¶ **Sandwich Qbano**, Av San Martín, No 9-124. Fast food chain, good sandwiches and salads.

¶ **Farah Express**, Cra 2 y C 9. Arab food, popular, also vegetarian dishes, open late, good value.

Coffee Bean Shop, Cra 2 y C 6. Coffee, drinks, snacks, internet.

La Dulcería, Cra 2, No 6-53. Good Arab desserts, snacks, popular.

✪ Bars and clubs

Cartagena *p808*
Good bars and clubs along C del Arsenal, Getsemaní, and along Portal de los Dulces, opposite the clock tower. Most clubs charge cover, US$7-9.

Bar Comarca, C Santo Domingo, No 3-38. Interesting naval decor, charismatic owner, speaks English, live music at weekends, attracts middle-aged crowd.

Café del Mar, on ramparts at end of C Estribos. Lounge bar, live DJ, young trendy crowd.

Excellent place for a drink at sunset, great views. Food served. Recommended.

La Carbonera, C del Arsenal, Getsemaní. Salsa and Colombian classics, no shorts allowed.

Mister Babilla, C del Arsenal, Getsemaní. The best known spot in this area, fierce a/c, salsa and Colombian classics.

Quiebra Canto, Parque Independencia, next to *Hotel Monterrey*, 2nd floor. Good salsa, nice atmosphere, balconies with good views. Recommended.

Tu Candela, 2nd floor bar, Portal de los Dulces. Range of music and salsa. Beware, pretty and friendly girls may be prostitutes.

Vía Apia, C Santo Domingo, No 33-46. Small bar, range of music. Popular with foreigners and Colombians. Tapas served.

☺ Festivals and events

Cartagena *p808*
La Candelaria, see La Popa. **Independence** celebrations, **2nd week of Nov**: men and women in masks and fancy dress roam the streets, dancing to the sound of *maracas* and drums. There are beauty contests, battles of flowers and general mayhem. This festival tends to be wild and can be dangerous. There is an **international film festival 2nd week of Mar**, www.festicinecartagena.com. The **Hay Literary Festival**, attracting international and Colombian writers, held its first event in Cartagena in 2006; the second will be **25-28 Jan 2007**.

⊙ Shopping

Cartagena *p808*
Bookshops Librería Nacional, Cra 7, No 36-27.

Handicrafts and jewellery In general shopping is better in Bogotá. Handicraft and emerald shops around Plaza de Bolivar and in the Plaza de las Bóvedas are good and have the best selection in Cartagena. In the Pierino Gallo building in Bocagrande are reputable jewellery shops. **El Centavo Menos**, C Román, No 5-08, Plaza de la Proclamación. Good selection of handicrafts from across Colombia.

Supermarket Supermarket Olympica, Cra 3, No 5-18, Bocagrande, open 24 hrs. **Vivero**, Av Venezuela y C del Boquete. A/c, with *cafetería*. Shopping malls with cinemas outside the city centre, eg **Los Caracoles** and **Santa Lucía**.

▲ Activities and tours

Cartagena *p808*
Bullfighting Bullfights take place mainly Jan-Feb in the new Plaza de Toros at the Villa Olímpica

on Av Pedro de Heredia, away from the centre. The old, wooden Plaza de Toros (in San Diego, see map) is a fine structure, but is no longer used. **Diving** Discounts are sometimes available if you book via the hotels, enquire. Recompression chamber at the naval hospital, Bocagrande. **Cultura del Mar**, C del Pozo, No 25-95, Getsemaní, T664 9312, www.culturadelmar.com. Run by team of young, well-organized Colombians, diving and tours to Islas del Rosario, English spoken. **Diving Planet**, Edif Alonso de Ojeda, 2-50, El Laguito, Bocagrande, T/F655 0154, also dive shop in Isla Grande (*Hotel Cocoliso*), www.divingplanet club.com. PADI open certificate course, 4 day, US$330, 2 dives including all equipment US$82, snorkelling trips, English spoken. **La Tortuga Dive Shop**, Edif Marina del Rey, Av del Retorno 2-23, El Laguito, Bocagrande, T/F665 6994, www.tortugadive.com. 2 dives US$70. Fast boat, which allows trips to Isla Barú as well as Los Rosarios, same price at *Hotel Caribe Dive shop*, T665 3517, www.caribedivenshop.com. **Windsurfing** Rental in Bocagrande, US$8 per hr.

⊖ Transport

Cartagena *p808*
Air
Flights to major Colombian cities and twice a week to Miami with **Avianca** T655 0736.To **San Andrés**, AeroRepública and Avianca. From Dec to Mar flights can be overbooked; even reconfirming and turning up 2 hrs early doesn't guarantee a seat; best not to book a seat on the last plane of the day. Flights to Panama.

Bus
Local Within the city large buses (with no glass in windows) cost US$0.30 (a/c buses US$0.50, green and white **Metrocar** to all points recommended). From bus terminal to centre, 30 mins with Metrocar, US$0.50.
Long distance To **Santa Marta**, US$8 (with **Brasilia**, C 32, No 20D-55, ticket office in Bocagrande, Edif Antillas, opposite *Hotel Caribe*), 4 hrs, also cheaper lines, US$7. To **Barranquilla** US$4.50 with **Transportes Cartagena**, 2½-3 hrs, or US$5 with **Expreso Brasilia** Pullman, 2 hrs. Pullman bus from Cartagena to **Medellín** 665 km, US$26 (Brasilia, or **Rápido Ochoa**, slightly cheaper, recommended). Several buses a day, but book early (2 days in advance at holiday times), takes 13-16 hrs. To/from **Bogotá** via Barranquilla and Bucaramanga with **Expreso Brasilia Pullman** (5 a day) or **Copetran**, US$40-45 (shop around), minimum 19 hrs (may take up to 28), depending on number of check-points.

To **Magangué** on the Magdalena US$12, 4 hrs with **Brasilia**; to **Mompós**, Unitransco, 0730 daily, 12 hrs including ferry crossing from Magangué, US$15. To **Valledupar** with **Expreso Brasilia**, Pullman US$13 (with a 30-min stop in Barranquilla), for Sierra Nevada and Pueblo Bello. To **Riohacha**, US$12. Bus to **Maicao** on Venezuelan border US$18 (with **Expreso Auto Pullman**, **Expreso Brasilia** at 2000, or **Unitrasco**), 10-12 hrs; the road is in good condition.

Ferry
There are boats leaving most days for points south along the coast, for example to **Turbo** cargo boats take 24 hrs, all in cost about US$25 pp. You can also go on up the Río Sinú to Montería, and up the Atrato as far as **Quibdó** (not recommended for safety reasons). For the trip to Quibdó see page 846. Enquire at **Club Náutico** for yachts to San Blas/Panama, about US$250 one way. There is good information at **Casa Viena** hotel. Get full independent advice before making direct arrangements with boat owners or captains. **Club Náutico**, Av Miramar, Isla Manga across the Puente Román, T660 4863, good for opportunities to crew or finding a lift to other parts of the Caribbean.

Taxi
Within the old city, US$1.80, a bit more at night; from Bocagrande to the centre US$2.20; for airport, see Ins and outs above. Set price before committing yourself, few use meters. A horse-drawn carriage can be hired for US$14, opposite *Hotel El Dorado*, Av San Martín, in Bocagrande, to ride into town at night (short ride). Also, a trip around the walled city, up to 4 people, US$16, from Torre del Reloj.

Beaches: Playa Blanca *p813*
If going only to Playa Blanca, there is a touristy, expensive **boat** from the tourist dock at 0830 which stop at Playa Blanca as part of its tour (but you will have to pay for the whole tour). Another goes at 0900 from near the Bazurto market, near La Popa, US$7 one way. Tell the taxi driver or bus driver that you want to go to Bazurto market via Av del Lago and not Av Pedro Heredia. An alternative is to group up with other tourists waiting at the market and hire a **vehicle**, US$65, with hard negotiating. The island is reached by a 5-min ferry crossing (US$ 3.50) over the Río Magdalena. From there, it is a 30-min ride over a rough dirt road to Playa Blanca. Do not give money or gifts to children dancing on the roadway.

Islas del Rosario p813

Travel agencies and the hotels offer launch excursions from the Muelle Turístico, leaving 0700-0900 and returning 1600-1700, costing from US$10 to US$25, lunch included; smaller boats take 50 mins less. Overnight trips can be arranged through agencies but they are overpriced. Do not buy tours from touts. Note that there is an additional 'port tax' of US$2 payable at the entrance to the *Muelle* or on the boat, and MA park entrance fee, US$2. Check around for prices and book in advance. Recommended are **Excursiones Roberto Lemaitre**, C 6, Edif Granada, loc 22, opposite El Almirante Hotel, Bocagrande, T665 5622 (owner of *Club Isla del Pirata*). **Yates Alcatraz** are more economical; enquire at the quay. The *Santa Clara Hotel* runs day trips to Isla Majagua, US$40 including lunch. For 5 or more, try hiring your own boat for the day and bargain for around US$16 pp. **Abraham David** boats stop at *Lizamar Hotel* on Isla Grande US$13 pp return (good fish lunch, tiny beach, monkeys and parrots in patio and comfortable rooms at Lizamar), the Aquarium (entry not included) and then Playa Blanca, well-organized tour. Recommended.

North of Cartagena: Volcán del Totumo p813

Bus from **Cartagena** (Mercado Bazurto) to Galerazamba in the morning, US$1.50, 2 hrs, ask to be dropped off at Lomo Arena and walk 2 km along the main road to a right turn signposted 'Volcán del Totumo', 1½ km along a poor road. Hitching possible. Many tour agencies, eg **Aviatur**, in the *Hotel Santa Clara*, organize trips to the volcano, including lunch and pickups from hotels; a good day trip.

● Directory

Cartagena p808

Banks Banco Unión Colombiana, Av Venezuela (C 35), No 10-26, La Matuna, changes American Express and Thomas Cook TCs. **Bancolombia**, good rates for TCs. **Bancafé**, gives money on Visa cards, both on Av Venezuela. **Banco Sudameris**, opposite conference centre, for Visa cash advances. **Citibank**, Centro Plazoleta, Av Venezuela, for MasterCard ATM. Many other ATMs in La Matuna along Av Venezuela and Bocagrande including supermarkets, eg *Carulla*. Also **A Toda Hora**, for Visa and MasterCard on Av Venezuela. **American Express** at branches of **Gema Tours**, eg Cabrera Cra 1, Av Santander, No 41-202, T660 2499. There are **cambios** in the arcade at Torre del Reloj and adjoining streets which change Amex TCs. **Caja de Cambio América**, Av Venezuela, No 8-48, La Matuna. Daily 1000-1800, changes sterling, also at Av San Martín, No 2-52, Bocagrande. **Cambios Santo Domingo**, C de la Iglesia, Edif Ayos, Cra 4, No 35-14, T664 4803, changes Bank of America TCs and sterling. **Never change money on the street, you will be ripped off.** TCs can be changed Sat morning (arrive early) at **Joyería Mora**, Román 5-39, and at El Portal nearby, in the old city. **Embassies and consulates** Panamanian Consulate, Cra 1, No 10-10, T665 1055. **Venezuela**, Cra 7, No 3-08, p7-B, T727 4076, F727 3967. Open Mon-Thu 0900-1300, Fri 0900-1500. Possible to get a visa the same day. **Internet** Café Punto com, El Laguito, Edif Belmar, loc 102, T665 5151. Good, also organizes apartment rentals. **Café Internet**, C Santo Domingo, No 35-40, broadband, US$0.90 per hr. Many others around town. **Post offices** in Avianca office near cathedral, open Mon-Fri 0800-1830, Sat 0800-1500. **Security** Carry your passport, or a photocopy, at all times. Failure to present it on police request can result in imprisonment and fines. Generally, central areas are safe and friendly (although Getsemaní is less secure, especially at night), but should you require the police, there is a station in Matuna (Central Comercial La Plazoleta), another in Barrio Manga. Beware of drug pushers on the beaches, pickpockets in crowded areas and bag/camera snatchers on quiet Sun mornings. At the bus station, do not be pressurized into a hotel recommendation different from your own choice. On the street, do not be tempted by offers of jobs or passages aboard ship: jobs should have full documentation from the Seamen's Union office. Passages should only be bought at a recognized shipping agency. **Telephones** Telecom, Av Urdaneta Arbeláez near corner of C 34; long distance phones behind this building; long distance also in Bocagrande. **Useful addresses** DAS: C 20B, No 29-18, T666 0438. MA (national parks office), C 4, No 3-204, Bocagrande, T665 5655, open 0800-1200, 1400-1800. **Volunteering**: If you are interested in working with local foundations/NGOs, contact cartagenitos@yahoogroups.com, www.cartagenitos.blogspot.com, who will find places for volunteers.

To Panama

Apart from the towns inland on the road to Medellín and the beaches around Tolú and Coveñas, this section is concerned with the troubled area of the Colombia/Panama border at Darién. Before going by road south of Cartagena, check the latest information on security.

South from Cartagena
The highway south towards Medellín goes through **Turbaco**, 24 km (**Botanical Garden** ① 1½ *km before village on the left, Tue-Sun 0900-1600*), **Malagana**, 60 km, and **San Jacinto**, 90 km, known for its cumbia music using gaitas and local craft work (hand woven hammocks).

Magangué and Mompós
A road runs east from the highway to **Magangué** (Phone code 952; Population: 65,000; Altitude: 30 m), on the western loop of the Río Magdalena. It is the port for the savannas of Bolívar. From here boats go to the small town of **Mompós**, also spelt Mompox (Phone code 952; Colour map 1, grid A3; Population: 33,000), a UNESCO World Heritage site on the eastern arm of the river. Due to its relative isolation, little has changed in this sweltering, humid town since Alfonso de Heredia (brother of the founder of Cartagena) founded it in 1540. Simón Bolívar stayed here frequently and wrote, "If I owe my life to Caracas, I owe my glory to Mompós." Today, Mompós is one of Colombia's most beautiful colonial towns. Opposite the river are the mansions of Spanish merchants for whom this was an important stopping-off point on the Cartagena trade route. Rows of well-preserved, white one-storey buildings have served as a backdrop in many Colombian films. Its six churches, cemetery and plazas are well signed. Mompós is packed during Easter week when visitors flock to see its ornate traditional processions. It is also known for its handworked gold and silver jewellery and goldsmiths are still to be seen working. The town is safe and peaceful and, with improved security in the surrounding area and roads, tourism has increased significantly. But it is still recommended to check safety before setting off. Guided tours of the city on foot or motortaxi cost US$6 per hour. Boat trips along the Río Magdalena have received good reports. Ferocious mosquitoes and the odd bat are a nuisance after dusk; take insect repellent and wear long sleeves.

Sincelejo to Turbo
The capital of Sucre Department, **Sincelejo**, is a hot, dusty town and cattle centre. The dangerous *Fiestas de Las Corralejas*, 15-20 January, involves bulls and men chasing each other around a ring. At Easter is the '*Fiesta del Burro*' where people dress up donkeys and prizes go to the best and the funniest (a three-day party). There are various hotels (**B-E**) and restaurants.

On the coast, 35 km northwest of Sincelejo is **Tolú**, a fast developing holiday town popular for its mud volcanoes, offshore islands and diving. From Cartagena, the best approach is south from Malagana through San Onofre. This is also an easier and safer way for cyclists. For safety reasons, it is recommended not to travel this route at night. From Tolú, a good trip is by boat three hours to Múcura island in the **Islas de San Bernardo**, about US$15 (details from *MA* sub-office in Tolú, or in Cartagena). If camping, take your own supplies. Trips to the mangrove lagoons also recommended. A good agency is **Club Náutico Los Delfines** *Av 1A, No 11-08, T288 5202*, daily tours to San Bernardo Islands 0800, back 1600, including aquarium on Isla Palma, US$30 lunch and transport, US$15 just transport. There are three diving agencies in Tolú along Avenida de La Playa. There are better beaches at **Coveñas**, 20 km further southwest (several *cabañas* on the beach and hotels). This is the terminal of the oil pipeline from the oilfields in the Venezuelan border area. Buses and *colectivos* from Tolú.

The main road south from Sincelejo passes **Caucasia** (194 km from Sincelejo, *Altitude*: 50 m), a convenient stopping place between Cartagena and Medellín.

Montería the capital of Córdoba Department, on the east bank of the Río Sinú, can be reached from Cartagena by air, by boat, or from the main highway to Medellín. It is the centre of a cattle and agricultural area. It has one fine church, picturesque street life and friendly people.

On the Gulf of Urabá is the port of **Turbo** (*Phone code 94; Colour map 1, grid A2; Population: 127,000*), an important centre of banana cultivation. It is a rough border community so it's best to move on quickly. **Before going to Turbo, or contemplating crossing Darién by land, please see below.**

North of Turbo, on the road to Necoli, is a turning off for **Los Arboletes**. Here is a huge mud volcano surrounded by mangrove swamps, well worth visiting.

Border with Panama

There are various routes involving sea and land crossings around or through the **Darién Gap**, which still lacks a road connection linking the Panamanian Isthmus and South America. Detailed descriptions of these routes are given in the *Mexico and Central America Handbook* and the *Colombia Handbook*. While maps of the region are available, there is no substitute for seeking informed local advice. In all cases, it is essential to be able to speak Spanish.

Latest information from Colombia is that armed groups, hostile to travellers including tourists, are active in the northwest corner of Colombia which includes the area on the Colombian and Panamanian sides of the border. If information has not improved before you set out to cross Darién by land either way, you are advised not to go. This warning includes visits to Los Katíos National Park (officially closed), the road south of Turbo to Dabeiba and the Río Atrato area up to Quibdó. The Río Atrato itself is widely used by both paramilitaries and guerrillas.

Colombian immigration DAS Office: see under Turbo directory below. If going from Colombia to Panama via Turbo you should get an exit stamp from the DAS office. You will also need a yellow fever certificate and an onward international ticket. There is also a DAS office in Capurganá (near *puesto de policia*, police booth), and a Panamanian consulate, but best not to leave it that late. If leaving Colombia, check the facts at any DAS office.

Entering Colombia Arriving from Panama, go to the DAS in Turbo for your entry stamp. Stamps from other DAS offices not accepted. A police stamp is no substitute, though can help.

Entering Panama Panamanian immigration at Puerto Obaldía will check all baggage for drugs and may ask for evidence of adequate funds for your stay: US$400, travellers' cheques or credit card. A ticket out of Panama is required, although a ticket from another Central American country may do. **Note**: Colombian pesos are impossible to change at fair rates in Panama.

Crossing Darién: Caribbean side

On the Caribbean side, the starting point is Turbo from where you must cross the Gulf of Urabá to Acandí, Capurganá and Zapzurro (all in Colombia) and Puerto Obaldía (Panama). **Acandí** (*Phone code: 9816; Population: about 7,000*) has several *residencias*. Most have their own electricity generators. A little further north is **Capurganá**, with spectacular, unspoilt white sand beaches and bays, including Cabo Tiburón (which featured in a recent Colombian reality show). The weather is generally drier and less humid than the Pacific coast of Chocó. The area's main attraction is the large marine turtles that come from Mexico to lay their eggs on the beaches from April to mid-June. Across the Panamanian border, **E Residencial Cande**, in Puerto Obaldía is good, with meals. Take advice on whether it is safe to hike along this coast: otherwise, take boats between coastal towns.

Overland from Turbo The aim is to cross the central Gap to Paya, from where there is a recognised route to Yaviza: Paya-Púcuro, six hours on foot; Púcuro-Boca de Cupe, by dugout; Boca de Cupe-Pinogana, also by dugout, plus a walk, two hours in all; Pinogana-Yaviza, walk and ferries/dugouts. From Yaviza (one hotel, **E Tres Américas**, basic) buses can be caught to Panama City, road subject to wash-outs. Alternatively you may be able to get a boat from Paya to Boca del Cupe and on to El Real, which has an airstrip for flights to Panama.

Although there are two main routes to Paya, we hesitate to suggest either. The first is to take a boat from Turbo across the Gulf of Urabá into the Río Tarena to **Unguía**, which has a couple of *residenciales* and basic restaurants. From here it is three or four hours to the border, then three hours to the Río Paya. You then hike down the Río Paya through dense jungle to Paya itself (about 12 hours). Do not attempt the Unguía-Paya route without a guide. The other main route to Paya, by motorboat from Turbo across the Bahía de Colombia, through the Great Atrato Swamp and up the Río Atrato should not be attempted in the current political climate. It is too dangerous. It can be very difficult to get an entry stamp anywhere before Panama City on this route; try at every opportunity as hikers have been detained in the capital for not having an entry stamp. It may help to prove you have adequate funds for your stay.

Los Katíos National Park

① *Go first to the MA office in Turbo (see Turbo directory below) for information: at present (early 2006) the park is closed.*
The park, extending in Colombia to the Panamanian border, contains several waterfalls: **Tilupo**, 125 m high; the water cascades down a series of rock staircases, surrounded by orchids and other fantastic plants, **Salto de La Tigra** and **Salto de La Tendal**. A full day's hike goes to Alto de Limón for a fine view of primary forest. Also in the park are the Alto de la Guillermina, a mountain behind which is a strange forest of palms called 'mil pesos', and the Ciénagas de Tumaradó, with red monkeys, waterfowl and alligators.

Crossing Darién: Pacific side

On the Pacific side, crossing into Panama involves travel by both boat and on foot, the quantity of each depending on the route chosen. Any routes through this part of Chocó are not advised because of violence, intense guerrilla and paramilitary activity and drug-running.

● Sleeping

Magangué *p819*
Several hotels and *residencias* (**B-E**). Few places to eat but very basic stalls along the riverfront serve decent cheap fish meals for breakfast and lunch.
B Avenida, Cra 3 y C 17, T687 7623. A/c, next to bus terminal.
D Julia, Cra 2A, No 12-37, T687 6160. Fan, more expensive with a/c.

Mompós *p819*
Malaria is endemic in the surrounding countryside. If staying overnight, mosquito nets and/or coils are a must. Essential to book in advance for Easter.
C Hostal Doña Manuela, C Real del Medío (Cra 2), No 17-41, T685 5142, F685 6175. A converted colonial merchant's house, a/c, quiet and peaceful, restaurant is the best in town, pool also open to the public for the day US$2. Good service and knowledge managers. Recommended.
E Casa Hotel La Casona, Cra 2, No 18-58, T685 5307. Colonial style, a/c, much cheaper with fan.
E Casa Hotel Villa de Mompós, Calle Real del Medio (Cra 2), No 14-108, T686 5208. Family-run, a/c, cheaper with fan.
E Residencias Aurora, Cra 2, No 15-65, T840102. One of the best budget options, pleasant, fan.
E San Andrés, Cra 2, No 18-23, T685 5886. Good option, friendly owner, a/c or fan, TV, restaurant.

Sincelejo to Turbo *p819*
Tolú
L Alcira, Av La Playa 21-40, T288 5016, F288 5036. Includes breakfast, cheaper off-season, a/c, TV, restaurant.
C Ibatama, Av La Playa 19-45, T288 5159, T/F288 5150. A/c, patio, restaurant.
C Mar Adentro, Av La Playa 11-36, T288 5481. With bath, a/c, helpful, much cheaper with fan, agency for trips to San Bernardo islands.
D-E Villa Babilonia, C 20, No 3-40, Barrio el Cangrejo, T288 6124. Run by Colombian/German team. Well-organized, dorms, new rooms with bath,

good restaurant, laundry service, good information on diving and island tours.
E El Turista, Av La Playa, No 11-68, T288 5145. With bath, TV, fan, basic, often full, best value.

Caucasia
B Caucasia, C 24, No 4-29, T839 3272. In centre, a/c, parking.
D Londres, C 19, No 2-27, T839 2879. A/c, laundry service, parking, restaurant, less with fan.

Montería
Many cheap dives around town.
L Sinú, Cra 3, No 31-38, T782 3355, F782 3980. The best, a/c, swimming pool, spa, TV, internet, restaurant. Discounts possible.
D Alcázar, Cra 2, No 32-17, T782 4900. Comfortable, a/c, cheaper with fan.

Turbo *p819*
B Castilla de Oro, T827 2185. Best, a/c, safe, good restaurant, modern, reliable water and electricity.
C Playa Mar, Av de la Playa, T827 2205. Good, but somewhat run down, a/c, cheaper with fan, TV.
C Hotel 2000, C 101, No 11-203, T827 2333. Near bus terminal, TV, bath, less with fan.

Crossing Darién: Caribbean side *p820*
C Hostal Marlin, Capurganá, T824 3611. One of the cheapest options, a small comfortable wooden lodge, with hammocks overlooking the beach. US$95 pp for a 3-night, all-inclusive package. Arranges guides, walks and snorkelling trips. There are also several luxury resort hotels.

● Eating

Sincelejo to Turbo: Tolú *p819*
Aroma de Café, Av 1, No 11-46. Good value *comida*. Other places to eat nearby, eg **Cafetería** on corner of Plaza, good cakes.

⊜ Transport

Magangué and Mompós *p819*
Air Flights to Montería from Mompós.
Bus and ferry Most *chalupas* (launches) and buses run in the morning. There is little public transport after 1400. From Magangué to Mompós: take a *chalupa* either direct to Mompós, 2 hrs, US$3.30, or to La Bodega, 30-45 mins, US$3, and then by taxi, frequent, 1½ hrs, US$3. The quickest and most comfortable route from Mompós to the coast is: taxi from Mompós to La Bodega, *chalupa* from La Bodega to Magangué, then taxi to **Barranquilla**, US$14, leave when full, 3-4 hrs direct to your destination in Barranquilla. **Brasilia** buses run from Magangué to Barranquilla. To **Cartagena** from Mompós with **Unitransco** at 0700, US$15, rough road in parts; also to Barranquilla.

To **Valledupar** and **Santa Marta**, either go from El Banco (further upriver), or cross the river at Talaigua (between Mompós and Magangué, *carritos* leave Mompós early morning) to **Santa Ana**. Buses leave Santa Ana 0700 for **Santa Marta** and **Valledupar**, first 2½ hrs unpaved, then paved; US$10 to Valledupar.

Sincelejo to Turbo *p819*
Tolú
Colectivo To **Cartagena**, 3hrs, US$9. Via Sincelejo, or direct from Cartagena. Several morning **buses**, 3-4 hrs, US$6. Also to **Medellín** with **Rápido Ochoa** and **Brasilia** 1100 and 1800, 10 hrs, US$32.

Caucasia *p819*
Bus From Caucasia to **Medellín** US$12, 6½-7 hrs, taxi US$18 (slightly quicker); to **Cartagena** US$20, 6-7 hrs.

Montería *p819*
Air Daily flights to **Bogotá**, **Barranquilla**, **Cartagena**, **Cúcuta** and **Medellín**.
Buses from **Cartagena**, US$13, 5 hrs, with **Brasilia**, has own terminal in Montería, or colectivo, US$11, 5 hrs.

Turbo *p819*
Air Small airport, few flights. More common to fly into Apartadó airport (30-min taxi ride, US$14, to Turbo, or microbus, US$1) where there are

more flight options, including 3 daily flights to/from **Medellín**. Local services to Caribbean and Pacific resorts with **Satena**.
Buses From **Medellín**, buses every 1½ hrs to Turbo, US$20, 10-12 hrs. Fewer from **Cartagena** (if stuck get a bus from Cartagena to Montería, 5 hrs, US$13 and then to Turbo). Checkpoints and bad road in parts. Check safety carefully before travelling by road from Turbo to Santa Fé de Antioquia.
Ferries Available to Cartagena and up the Río Atrato to Quibdó, but services are unreliable and dangerous.

To Panama *p819*
Air The simplest way is to fly from **Barranquilla**, **Bogotá**, **Cali**, **Cartagena**, **Medellín** or **San Andrés**.
Ferry Ask on the spot in Cartagena and in Colón if you wish to transport a vehicle between the two countries. Foot passengers may be able to travel on reputable cargo boats, but you must arrange with the captain the price and destination before departure. Small, irregular boats may well be contraband or arms runners and should not be used. See also under Cartagena, Ferry.

Crossing Darién: Caribbean side *p820*
Ferry From the small wharf, known as 'El Waffle', in Turbo take a daily launch direct to **Capurganá**. It leaves when its full, any time between 0800-1000, US$18, 2-3 hrs, an uncomfortable and bumpy ride. There is a DAS office at the wharf but it keeps very irregular hours, apparently open in the morning only. From Puerto Obaldía (see above on immigration), boats go to Porvenir (San Blas Islands) or Colón, planes to Panama City (Mon-Sat).

⊙ Directory

Turbo *p819*
Banks Banco Ganadero and others (ATMs available) but no banks are open for exchange of TCs on Mon or Tue; try exchanging money in stores. **Useful addresses/services** DAS: Postadero Naval, north of town just before the airport, take transport along Cra 13, open 0800-1630. **MA:** for information on Parque Nacional Los Katíos, office 1 km along the road to Medellín.

Barranquilla → *Phone code: 95. Colour map 1, grid A3. Population: 1,064,000.*

Barranquilla lies on the western bank of the Río Magdalena, about 18 km from its mouth, which, through deepening and the clearing of silted sandbars, makes it a seaport as well as a river port. During recent years, the city's commercial and industrial importance and its port have declined. Few colonial buildings remain. In the northwest of the city are pleasant leafy residential areas and parks. **Tourist office**: Fondo Mixto de Promoción del Atlántico ① *Vía 40, No 36-135, Edificio La Aduana, T351 0346*. Tourist information is also available at main hotels.

The main reason people visit Barranquilla is for its famous annual **Carnival**, held 40 days before Easter week, end-February/beginning of March. It's one of the oldest in Latin America and less commercial and touristy than the Rio Carnival. In 2003 UNESCO declared it a "masterpiece of the oral and intangible heritage of humanity". Pre-carnival parades and dances last through January until an edict that everyone **must** party is read out. Carnival itself lasts from Saturday, with the Batalla de las Flores, through the Gran Parada on Sunday, to the funeral of Joselito Carnaval on Tuesday. The same families going back generations participate, keeping the traditions of the costumes and dances intact. Prepare for three days of intense revelry and dancing with very friendly and enthusiastic crowds, spectacular float processions, parades and beauty queens. The main action takes place along, Calle 17, Carrera 44 and Vía 40. Tickets for the spectator stands are sold in major restaurants and bars, eg **Froggs Leggs** (see Bars and clubs). **La Casa de Carnaval** ① *Cra 54, No 49B-39, T379 6621, www.carnavaldebarranquilla.org*, is the official office and the best place to get information.

The church of **San Nicolás**, formerly the Cathedral, stands on Plaza San Nicolás, the central square, and before it is a small statue of Columbus. The new **Catedral Metropolitana** ① *Cra 45, No 53-120, opposite Plaza de la Paz*, has an impressive statue of Christ inside by the Colombian sculptor, Arenas Betancur. The commercial and shopping districts are round Paseo Bolívar, the main boulevard, a few blocks north of the old Cathedral, and in Avenida Murillo. The **Museo Romántico** ① *Cra 54, No 59-199*, covers the city's history with an interesting section on Carnival.

Barranquilla also attracts visitors because the most important national and international football matches are held here in Colombia's largest stadium, **Estadio Metropolitano** ① *Av Murillo, outside the city*. The atmosphere is considered the best in the country. Regular buses run from Paseo Bolívar and the church at Calle 33 y Carrera 41 to the attractive bathing resort of **Puerto Colombia**, 20 minutes. The **Pradomar Hotel** ① *Calle 2, No 22-61, T309 6011* (**B** good beach bar and restaurant), offers surfing lessons. South along the Magdalena, 5 km from the city, is **Soledad** (*Population: 16,000*); around the cathedral are narrow, colonial streets.

● Sleeping

Barranquilla *p823*
Hotel prices rise significantly during Carnival, essential to book well in advance.
LL El Prado, Cra 54, No 70-10, T369 7777. Original 1920s building, declared a national monument, far from the centre. Nice swimming pool, tennis courts, good restaurant.
AL Country Norte, Cra 52, No 75-30, T368 0495. New, stylish hotel, with pool and business centre, spacious comfortable rooms, good service. Substantial weekend discounts.
B Las Brisas, C 61, No 46-41, T340 2455. TV, breakfast included, noisy but recommended.
C San Francisco, C43, No 43-128, T379 2927,

F351 5532. Downtown, large rooms with fan, cable TV, fridge, laundry service, parking, good restaurant, pleasant.
D Colonial Inn, C 42, No 43-131, T379 0241. With bath, TV, good cheap restaurant, fan.
D Olímpico, Cra 42, No 33-20, T351 8310. With fan, more with a/c, TV, restaurant. Recommended.
E El Diamante, C 41, No 38-65, T379 0157. With fan, more with a/c, TV room, laundry, parking.
E Horizonte, Cra 44, No 44-35, T379 4893. With bath, quiet, fan, safe, but not welcoming.
F California, C 32 y Cra 44, T340 4795. Pleasant but about to fall down, power cuts, enjoy the chickens.

● *For an explanation of the sleeping and eating price codes used in this guide, see inside the front*
● *cover. Other relevant information is found in Essentials pages 774-775.*

❶ Eating

Barranquilla *p823*
Many places, for all tastes and budgets, on C 70 from Hotel El Prado towards Cra 42. At C 70 y 44B are several *estaderos*, bars with snacks and verandas. Many up-market restaurants along Carrera 53. There are numerous good Arab restaurants, especially Lebanese, in Barranquilla owing to waves of Arab immigration during the 20th century.
♥♥♥-♥♥ **Arabe Gourmet**, Cra 49C, No 76-181. More formal and expensive than others.
♥♥♥-♥♥ **La Cueva** C 59 y Cra 43. Formerly a high-class brothel and a favourite haunt of Gabriel García Márquez and his literati friends during the 1950s. Now its bohemian charm has gone, but it's still worth a visit for the interesting photos. Good typical food, live Cuban music at the weekends.
♥♥ **Arabe Internacional**, C 93, No 47-73, T378 2803. Good Arab cuisine in informal setting.
♥♥ **Crepes and Waffles**, Cra 51, No 76-47. Good fresh crêpes and salads as usual.

❶ Bars and clubs

Barranquilla *p823*
Froggs Leggs, C 93, No 43-122. Popular bar, good atmosphere.
Henry's Bar, C 80, No 53-18, CC Washington. Popular US-style bar, pizzería downstairs. Open daily from 1600.
   At weekends, opposite Buena Visita shopping mall is a park, a popular hang out with young people who pull up with their cars and turn on their huge stereos.

❍ Shopping

Barranquilla *p823*
Bookshop Librería Nacional, in CC Buenavista (see below). Small selection of English books.
Market San Andrecito, or Tourist Market, Vía 40, is where smuggled goods are sold at very competitive prices; a good place to buy film. Picturesque and reasonably safe. Any taxi driver will take you there.
Shopping centres Centro Comercial Buenavista, Cra 53, C 98, has a good selection of shops, cinemas and fast food outlets.

❍ Transport

Barranquilla *p823*
Air Ernesto Cortissoz airport is 10 km from the city. Daily flights to **Bogotá**, **Cartagena** and

Medellín, also to **Bucaramanga**, **Montería** and **Valledupar**. International flights to **Aruba**, **Curaçao**, **Miami** and **Panama City**. City bus from airport to town, US$0.35 (US$0.40 on Sun). Taxi to town, US$7 (taxis do not have meters, fix fare in advance). To town, take only buses marked 'centro' from 200 m to right when leaving airport; the bus to the airport (marked Malambo) leaves from Cra 44 up C 32 to Cra 38, then up C 30 to Airport. Taxi to Cartagena, US$15 pp, leave when full. Avianca, C 72, No 57-79, T353 4691, T334 8073 (at airport).
Bus The main bus terminal is south of the city near the Circunvalación. Some bus companies have offices around C 34 and Cra 45. Take a bus marked 'Terminal' along C 45. To **Santa Marta**, US$3.25, Pullman (less in non-a/c, **Coolibertador**), about 2 hrs, also direct to Santa Marta's Rodadero beach. To **Valledupar**, 5-6 hrs, US$10. To **Montería** direct, US$11, 7-8 hrs. To **Medellín** by Pullman, 16 hrs, US$40. To **Bucaramanga**, US$27 with **Copetran**, a/c, first class, departures at 1130 most days, 9 hrs. To **Bogotá**, 24 hrs, frequent, US$45 direct with Copetran. To **Caucasia**, US$17, 8-11 hrs. To **Maicao**, US$14.50, 6 hrs (with Brasilia, every 30 mins from 0100-1200). To **Cartagena**, 3 grades of bus, 2½-3 hrs (US$4.50 with Transportes Cartagena, US$5 with Expreso Brasilia, by *Brasilia Van Tours* mini-bus, from their downtown offices as well as the bus terminals), 2 hrs by colectivo US$7.
Taxi Taxis within the town cost US$1.60 (eg downtown to northern suburbs).

❶ Directory

Barranquilla *p823*
Banks Bancolombia, Banco de Bogotá, etc, and many ATMs. *Casa de cambio* El Cairo, C 76, No 48-30, T360 6433, and at C 34, No 43-177, Paseo Bolívar, T379 9441. TCs, euros, dollars but not sterling, Mon-Fri and Sat 0900-1200.
Consulates Germany, C73, Vía 40-270, T353 2078. **Netherlands**, Cra 77B, No 57-141, of 806, T368 8387. **USA**, C 77B, No 57-141, of 511, T353 2001 (visas obtainable only in Bogotá). **Venezuela**, Edif Bancafé, Cra 52, No 69-96, p 3, T358 0048, 0800-1500, visa issued same day, but you must be there by 0915 with photo and US$30 cash; onward ticket may be requested. **Post offices** Plaza Bolívar. **Useful addresses** DAS: C 54, No 41-133, T371 7500. **Tourist police:**, Cra 43, No 47-53, T351 0415/340 9903.

Santa Marta, Tayrona and Ciudad Perdida

Santa Marta is a port with strong historical associations and popular beaches. Nearby are the Tayrona national park with pre-Columbian remains and the unspoilt Sierra Nevada de Santa Marta coastal range.

Santa Marta → *Phone code: 95. Colour map 1, grid A3. Population: 309,000.*

Santa Marta is Colombia's third largest Caribbean port and capital of Magdalena Department. It lies on a deep bay with high shelving cliffs to the north and south, at the mouth of the Río Manzanares. The snow-clad peaks of the Sierra Nevada, less than 50 km east, are occasionally visible. The main promenade (Carrera 1) along the sea front is lined with hotels, restaurants and bars and a beach reaching the port. Much more attractive beaches are to be found around Taganga and Parque Nacional Tayrona. Santa Marta is the base for treks to La Ciudad Perdida.

For tourist information, go to **Turcol** ① *Cra 1C, No 20-15, T/F421 2256/433 3737*, arranges trips to Ciudad Perdida, Parque Tayrona and Pueblito and provides guide services (details in text); recommended. Beware of jungle tours, or boat trips to the islands sold by street touts.

Santa Marta, founded in 1525 by Rodrigo de Bastidas, was the first town founded by the *conquistadores* in Colombia. Most of the famous sea-dogs – the brothers Côte, Drake and Hawkins – sacked the city in spite of the forts built on the mainland and a small island at the entrance to the bay. It was here that Simón Bolívar, his dream of Gran Colombia shattered, came to die. Almost penniless, he was given hospitality at the *hacienda* of San Pedro Alejandrino, see below. He died, aged 47, on 17 December 1830, apparently from tuberculosis, and was buried in the Cathedral, but his body was taken to the Pantheon at Caracas 12 years later.

In the city centre, well-preserved clusters of colonial buildings and early churches still remain and more are currently being restored. On **Plaza de la Catedral** is the impressive white cathedral, claimed to be Colombia's oldest church and one of the oldest in Latin America. **Casa de la Aduana/Museo del Oro Tairona** ① *Calle 14, No 2-07 on main plaza, Mon-Fri 0800-1200, 1400-1800, Sat 0800-1300 (times change during the tourist season), free*, displays an excellent archaeological collection, exhibits on the Tayrona culture and some precolombian gold artefacts; visit recommended before going to Ciudad Perdida. **Museo Etnográfico de la Universidad de Magdalena** ① *Cra 1, C 22, 0800-1900, US$1*, is a new museum, tracing the history of Santa Marta, its port and the Tayrona culture, well-displayed.

Quinta de San Pedro Alejandrino ① *daily 0930-1630, US$3; take a bus or colectivo from the waterfront, Cra 1 C, in Santa Marta to Mamatoca and ask for the Quinta, US$0.25*, a 17th century villa surrounded by gardens 5 km southeast of the city. Here is the simple

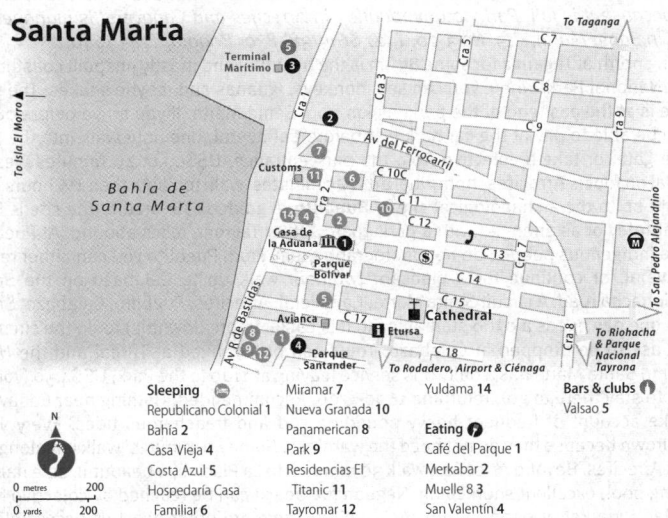

Santa Marta

Sleeping 🛏
Republicano Colonial 1
Bahía 2
Casa Vieja 4
Costa Azul 5
Hospedaría Casa
Familiar 6
Miramar 7
Nueva Granada 10
Panamerican 8
Park 9
Residencias El
Titanic 11
Tayromar 12
Yuldama 14

Eating 🍴
Café del Parque 1
Merkabar 2
Muelle 8 3
San Valentín 4

Bars & clubs 🍸
Valsao 5

0 metres   200
0 yards   200

room in which Simón Bolívar died, with a few of his belongings. Other paintings and memorabilia of the period are on display. This is a tasteful, elegant memorial to the man most revered by the Colombians.

Sandy beaches and headlands stretch all along this coast, surrounded by hills, green meadows and shady trees. The largest sandy bay is that of Santa Marta, with Punta Betín, a rocky promontory protecting the harbour to the north and a headland to the south. The rugged Isla El Morro lies 3 km off Santa Marta, topped by a lighthouse. **Playa El Rodadero** is a crowded, tacky beach resort, 4 km south of the city (local bus service, taxi, US$3). Many of the buses coming from Barranquilla and Cartagena stop at Rodadero on the way to Santa Marta.

Launches leave Rodadero beach every hour for the Aquarium, US$3 entry, last boat back 1600. From the Aquarium, it's a 10-minute walk to Playa Blanca where swimming is less crowded than elsewhere. Food is available at beach. At Punta Betín, behind the harbour, there is a marine eco-system research centre run by Colombian and German universities.

Around Santa Marta

The paved coast road to Santa Marta from Barranquilla passes salt pans and skirts the **Ciénaga de Santa Marta**, where all types of water birds, plants and animals may be seen. Cutting off the egress to the sea to build the coast road caused an ecological disaster, but a National Environment Programme is working to reopen the canals and restore the area. There are several villages built on stilts in the lake. On the east shore of the lagoon is **Ciénaga** (*Population: 75,000*), famous for *cumbia* music.

Aracataca, 60 km south of Ciénaga and 7 km before Fundación, is the birthplace of **Gabriel García Márquez**, fictionalized as Macondo in some of his stories (notably *100 Years of Solitude*). His home, now a modest museum, may be seen in the backyard of La Familia Iriarte Ahumada; it is 1½ blocks from the plaza, ask for directions. There are *residencias* (under US$3) and a restaurant, but it is better to stay in **Fundación**.

Taganga

Close to Santa Marta is the fishing village and beach of Taganga, set in a bay with good views. Swimming good, especially on Playa Grande, 25 minutes' walk round coast or US$2-3 by boat, but watch out for thieving. Taganga is quiet during week, but it is crowded on Sunday. Good fresh fish is served at places along the beach. Taganga is a popular place for diving. There is a good book exchange shop; no ATMs.

Parque Nacional Tayrona

① 0800-1700, US$9.50 foreigners, US$2.50 per car (more for larger vehicles), parking US$2.20 per day. During high season, the park is very crowded and sometimes temporarily closes because it is full. Park accommodation in Arrecifes and Cañaveral is managed by Aviatur, in Santa Marta, C15, No 3-20, T421 6615/3848, or Bogotá, T243 1640.

Stretching north of Taganga for some 85 km is the beautiful and mostly unspoilt coastline of Tayrona National Park, where you can see monkeys, iguanas and maybe snakes. The park entrance is at the east end of the park, 35 km from Santa Marta. If you arrive before 0800, you may be able to pay at the car park just before **Cañaveral**, one hour walk into the park from the gate, or take a colectivo from the park entrance, US$0.50. 40 minutes west of Cañaveral on foot is **Arrecifes**, from where it is 45 minutes' walk to Cabo, then 1½ hours on a clear path up to the archaeological site of **Pueblito**. A guided tour around the site is free, every Saturday or as arranged with a park guard. Other Tayrona relics abound. At Pueblito there are indigenous people; do not photograph them. From Pueblito you can either return to Cañaveral, or continue for a pleasant two-hour walk up to Calabazo on the Santa Marta-Riohacha road. A circuit Santa Marta, Cañaveral, Arrecifes, Pueblito, Calabazo, Santa Marta in one day needs a 0700 start at least. It is easier (more downhill) to do the circuit in reverse, ask to be dropped at Calabazo. Tours can be arranged at **Turcol** and the *Hotel Miramar* in Santa Marta has a daily bus service leaving at 1100 to the Park, US$4.50 (you do no have to stay there to go), returning 1600-1700. Recommended. Bathing near Cañaveral must take account of frequent heavy pounding surf and treacherous tides. Every year, people drown because they do not heed the warnings. Some 40 minutes' walk left along the beach is Arrecifes. Beyond Arrecifes, walk 30 minutes to La Piscina, a beautiful, safe natural swimming pool, excellent snorkelling. Neguangue beach can be reached by colectivo from Santa Marta Market at 0700, return 1600, US$7. There are other beaches accessible by coastal path, or by boat. **Beyond Cañaveral**, east along the coast, is **Palomino**. Tours can be arranged from there to *indígena* villages taking up to six days, cost around US$35 per day. Enquire at *Turcol* in Santa Marta (see page 825).

It is advisable to inform park guards when walking in the park. Wear hiking boots and beware of bloodsucking insects. Take food and water, but no valuables as robbery is common. You may be able to hire donkeys for the Arrecifes-Pueblito stretch, US$5 each way, but watch them as these animals eat everything. Generally, the main trails and campsites are badly littered. The best information on the Park is in Santa Marta. See Transport, below, for how to get there.

Sierra Nevada de Santa Marta

The Sierra Nevada, covering a triangular area of 16,000 sq km, rises abruptly from the Caribbean to 5,800 m snow peaks in about 45 km, a gradient comparable with the south face of the Himalaya, and unequalled along the world's coasts. Pico Colón is the highest point in the country. The area is a drugs-growing, processing and transporting region. For this reason, the reluctance of some local *indígenas* to welcome visitors, plus the presence of guerrilla and paramilitary groups makes much of the Sierra Nevada de Santa Marta a no-go area. This is a tragedy since here can be found the most spectacular scenery and most interesting indigenous communities in the country. For the latest information check with *MA* in Santa Marta and Bogotá, *ICANH* in Bogotá (see page 769), and the **Fundación Pro-Sierra Nevada** ① *C 17, No 3-83, Santa Marta, T431 0551*, for guidance on what may be possible. It is extremely unwise and very dangerous to enter the area on your own. If you must, always travel with an experienced guide. Trekking tours into the fringes of the Nevada de Santa Marta can from time to time be arranged in the Santa Marta and Valledupar areas, check with the respective tourist offices.

Ciudad Perdida → *Colour map 1, grid A3.*

Ciudad Perdida was called Teyuna by the Tayrona, meaning mother nature. The city covers 400 ha and was built around 700 AD. It was the political and trading centre of the Tayrona. The circular and oval stone terraces were once the living quarters for some 1,400-3,000 people. The city was also an important religious and burial site. The Tayrona built sophisticated irrigation systems and walls to prevent erosion. By around 1600, the Tayrona were almost wiped out by the conquistadores and the few who survived were forced to flee. For the next four centuries, the city disappeared under the forest growth. In 1973, tomb looters searching for gold known to exist in burial urns and graves, rediscovered the city by chance. By 1975, the city was officially re-found, attracting local and international anthropologists and archeologists who started to excavate, leading to the first tourist groups in 1984. Today the area is a protected indigenous reserve, where three main indigenous groups, the Koguis, Arhuacos and Arsarios, continue to live.

The 20-km trek to the Lost City is, at times, gruelling and challenging. It is not a leisurely walk, but is well worth the effort for a rewarding and memorable experience. The trek is perhaps more spectacular than the archeological site itself. Along with lush tropical humid and dry forests, abundant flora and fauna, there are crystal clear rivers, waterfalls and natural swimming pools. Watch out for snakes. Along the way, you will pass friendly Kogui villages. There are some 1,200 steep slippery steps to climb to the summit of the city. Wrap clothes in plastic bags to keep them dry and take a sleeping bag as it gets cold at night. At the time of writing, the area is controlled by the paramilitaries and it is likely that you will also pass them too. Do not take photos of them. Scores of tours leave Santa Marta every three to four days during the year, experiencing no problems.

● Sleeping

Santa Marta *p825, map p825*
If you arrive by bus, beware taxi drivers who take you to a hotel of their choice. Calle 10C (near the port, 2 blocks from the beach) has many budget hotels interspersed with brothels and has become a small gringo ghetto. Be careful here, especially at night. Around Rodedero beach is considered unsafe. For groups of 4 or more, ask about apartments for short rent. Essential to book ahead during high season.

In town
Av Rodrigo de Bastidas (Cra 1) has several high-rise hotels while Cra 2 and connecting streets have many budget *residencias*.
B Panamerican, Cra 1, No 18-23, T421 1238, F421 4751. A/c or cheaper with fan, safe, cafetería, modern holiday hotel.
B Tayromar, C 20, No 1C-71, T421 7324, one block from beach. New, helpful owners, well-organized, safety-deposit in rooms,

modern, a/c (cheaper with fan), parking, good service. Recommended.

B Yuldama, Cra 1, No 12-19, T421 0063, F421 4932. Bland modern hotel, a/c, conference centre, laundry.

C Bahía, C 12, No 2-70, T421 0193. A/c, cheaper without, modern, plain, safe deposit. Recommended.

C Casa Vieja, C 12, No 1-58, T421 4852. A/c, less with fan, good restaurant.

C Nueva Granada, C 12, No 3-17, T421 0685, www.hotelnuevagranada.com. Colonial building with rooms round a pleasant courtyard, quiet, cheaper with fan, pool, includes breakfast.

D Republicano Colonial (formerly Andrea Doria No 1), C 18, No 1C-90, T421 4329. Good service, some rooms with balcony, safe, luggage store, good value, cheaper with fan, parking.

D Park, Cra 1, No 18-67, T421 1215, F421 1574. On sea front, modern holiday hotel, popular with families, pool, stores luggage, helpful.

E Costa Azul, C 17, No 2-09, T421 2236. Fan, windows into courtyard, simple.

E Hospedaría Casa Familiar, C 10 C, No 2-14, T421 1697. Efficient, very helpful, family-run, safe, motorbike parking. Recommended.

F Miramar, C 10C, No 1C-59, T423 3276, 2 blocks from beach. Under new joint ownership, Jairo is very knowledgeable. Guides to the Ciudad Perdida hang around here, sells tours at the official price, also good for tours to Tayrona and Taganga (where they have *Hotel Ramarim*). Tends to be crowded, basic dorms and some nicer more expensive private rooms, luggage store, motorbike parking, internet, cheap restaurant. Often full. More refurbishment, activities and services in progress.

F Residencias El Titanic, C 10C, No 1C-68, T421 1947. Fan, basic, safe, good value, motorbike parking, tours to Ciudad Perdida can also be bought here.

Playa El Rodadero

L Irotama, Km 14, between airport and Rodadero Bay, T432 0600, www.irotama.com. Resort in tropical gardens with own beach, full service, several restaurants, convention facilities, rooms, suites and bungalows.

L Tamacá, Cra 2, No 11A-98, T422 7015. Direct access to beach, fair rooms with sea view, price includes 2 meals, good service, fine pool.

A Edmar, Cra 3, No 5-188, T422 7874, 2 blocks from beach. Price includes 2 meals, a/c, cafetería, welcoming, pool.

A La Guajira, Cra 4, No 23F-05, entrance to El Rodadero, T422 0918. Pleasant, modern, Wayúu manageress can advise about travel to La Guajira. Good breakfast, pool, safe parking, includes 2 meals.

B La Riviera, Cra 2, No 5-42, T422 7090. Small, safe, a/c, includes breakfast and TV.

C El Rodadero, C 11, No 1-29, T422 8295, Pool, helpful, restaurant, parking, some rooms with sea view, includes 2 meals.

D Tucuraca, Cra 2, No 12-53, T422 7493. Fan, will store luggage, helpful, TV.

D-F Hostería Tima Uraka, C 18, No 2-59, T422 8433. Shared rooms, nice garden, hammocks, laundry service.

Long-stay Cabañas de Gaira, C17, No 1-78, T422 8676, T300 897 9140 (mob). Patricia Valencia organizes cabins, flats and studios for rent, by the day or longer, fully furnished, 20 m from the beach. Good for groups for long stays. From US$45 per flat per night.

Around Santa Marta *p826*

F pp Carpe Diem, 15 km from Santa Marta at 400 m. Ecological farm run by Belgians Mathias and Elsa, guests collected from *Miramar* (see above) every 2 days. Private rooms, dormitory and hammocks, meals US$1.50-2 extra, horses riding, hiking, river bathing, tours to pre-Columbian sites, kitchen, book exchange, Dutch, French and English spoken. Recommended.

Fundación

E Caroli, Cra 8, No 5-30, T414 0273, is the best.

E Centro del Viajero, with a/c, good value. Also **Hotel Milán**, T414 0227.

Taganga *p826*

Travellers are increasingly staying here rather than in Santa Marta. Prices rise by around 30% during high season.

A La Ballena Azul, Cra 1, No 18-01, T421 9009. Attractive hotel with French riviera touch, comfortable, spacious rooms with sea views, also run boat tours to secluded beaches, horses for hire. Nice restaurant on the beach and good pancakes at the crêperie.

C Bahía Taganga, C 8, No 1-07, T421 9049/9151. Unmissable garish green sign on the cliff face. Overlooking bay, breakfast served on lovely terrace, hospitable, a/c, less with fan.

D Casa Blanca, near *La Ballena Azul*, T421 9232. On the beach, small rooms, some with good views, laundry.

D Techos Azules, look for the blue roofs at end of beach, T421 9141. Good sea views, hammock and terrace area, comfortable fully furnished studio apartments at US$10 pp.

D-E La Casa de Felipe, 3 blocks from beach, follow the signs, T421 9101/9120. Cosy traveller place run by knowledgeable French team of Jean Phillipe and Sandra Gibelin. Kitchen facilities, internet, laundry, hospitable, relaxing hammock area, studio apartments, dorms and rooms. Good information on trips to Tayrona (maps provided), English spoken. Recommended.

Parque Nacional Tayrona *p826*
Cañaveral
Cabins for 2-4 persons cost US$66 high season, US$45 low season, prices fixed by Aviatur, great views over sea and jungle, good restaurant. Campsite US$4.50 pp in 5-person tent; hammocks US$6.50; has facilities, but only one restaurant with a tiny store, take all supplies; attractive site but plenty of mosquitoes. Beware of falling coconuts and omnivorous donkeys.

Arrecifes
Cabins fit 6 people, camping and hammock hire available. Campsites charge about US$3 to hire a hammock. Rancho Bonito and El Paraíso are the best, with facilities and food. At *El Paraíso* there are cabins and a restaurant. The other 2 sites are basic. 200 m along the main road east of the park entrance is a truck stop where cyclists may be able to stay the night (US$5). On the path to Pueblito there is a campsite at Cabo where the path turns inland, small restaurant and hammocks for hire; there are other camping and hammock places en route. There is nowhere to stay at Pueblito. You can continue along the coast to beaches, but the going is difficult.

❶ Eating

Santa Marta *p825, map p825*
In town
¶¶-¶¶ Muelle 8, Cra 1, No 10A-12, at the port terminal, second floor. Upmarket, excellent seafood and local dishes.
¶¶ San Valentín, C 19, No 2-17 (Parque de los Novios). Decent Italian overlooking square, nice atmosphere.
¶¶-¶ Nuevo Toy San, C22, No 3-78, T421 4702. Decent Chinese, generous portions. Open Sun.
¶ El Jardín Paisa, C 20, No 1C-20. Good value *comida corriente* and service, popular. Also rents out rooms.
¶ Merkabar, C 10C, No 2-11. Family-run, pastas, great pancakes, good juices, café frappé, good value, tourist advice, popular with travellers. Near *Hotel Miramar.*

Playa El Rodadero
Many fast food restaurants, good juice kiosks and pizza stalls along the seafront promenades.
Café del Parque, Parque de Bolívar next to Casa de la Aduana. Great place for coffee and snacks, try *café frappé* (with ice), closed Sun.

❶ Bars and clubs

Santa Marta *p825, map p825*
La Escollera, C 5, No 4-107, outside of town at El Lago. Huge club under open straw roof, concerts.
La Puerta, C 17, between Cra 3 and 4. Excellent bar and atmosphere in colonial house. Highly recommended.
Valsao, Cra 1, No, 19A-12, at the port terminal, second floor. Upmarket open air restaurant and bar with good sea views.

Taganga *p826*
El Garaje, C 8, No, 2-127. Good popular bar.

▲ Activities and tours

Santa Marta *p825, map p825*
Tours Ask in hotels and tourist offices.

Taganga *p826*
Diving
There are several good, well-established dive shops in Taganga. Average prices: PADI course, 4 days, around US$200, 2 dives US$50. The standard of equipment varies, check everything carefully.
Calipso, C 12, No 1-40, T421 9146. Good reports.
Centro de Buceo Tayrona, C 18, No 1-45, T421 9195, T315-638 3307 (mob). 25 years experience, well-organized, daily dive trips 0900-1400, US$50 includes 2 dives, equipment and light lunch. PADI course, 3-4 days, US$210. English, Dutch, German spoken. Friendly owner José. Recommended.
Nautilos, C 16, Cra 1 on beach front, T421 9007.
Poseidon, C 18, No 1-69, T421 9224, www.poseidon divecenter.com. Another good option, experienced, good reports. Ask for German owner, Max.

Ciudad Perdida *p827*
Tours
We strongly recommend that you buy tours directly from Turcol in Santa Marta or Hotel Miramar. Turcol is the only tour operator allowed into Ciudad Perdida. The rest who offer tours are all middlemen. Tours take 5, 6 or 7 days, depending on how easy you want to take it and how much time spent at the site. Usually, 3 days hike there, 1 day at site, 2 days back. Turcol recommended guides: Edwin Rey very knowledgeable, warmly recommended, Wilson and Edilberto Montero, Walter Hinojoza and Eliezer Castro. All are well-organized, reliable and professional. No English speaking guides. Going on your own is almost impossible and

Colombia Santa Marta, Tayrona & Ciudad Perdida Listings

● *For an explanation of the sleeping and eating price codes used in this guide, see inside the front*
● *cover. Other relevant information is found in Essentials pages 774-775.*

very dangerous. For visiting Ciudad Perdida by helicopter, check with **Aviatur**, C 15, No 3-20, Santa Marta, T421 3848, www.aviatur.com.

⊖ Transport

Santa Marta *p825, map p825*
Air Simón Bolívar, 20 km south of city; bus, US$0.35, taxi from Santa Marta, US$6, from Rodadero, US$3. Daily flights to **Bogotá** and **Medellín**; connections to other cities. During the tourist season, get to the airport early and book well ahead.

Bus Terminal southeast of the city, towards Rodadero, minibus US$0.30; taxi US$2.50 to centre, US$3.50 to Rodadero. To **Bogotá**, about US$45, 6 a day with **Brasilia** (buses leaves from 1430-2000); if going direct, ask for **Vía La Dorada** buses which go by the new road, 15-18 hrs. **Coopetran** and Brasilia to **Bucaramanga** about 8-9 hrs, US$22. Journey time will be affected by the number of police checks. Buses to **Barranquilla**, every 15 mins, 2-3hrs, US$4.50. To **Cartagena**, 5 hrs US$7, or US$11, Brasilia. To **Riohacha** US$8.50, 4 hrs. Frequent buses to **Maicao**, US$12 a/c, also cheaper non a/c, 4-5 hrs. Brasilia runs a through bus to **Maracaibo**, daily at 1230, US$63. Brasilia buses direct to **Rodadero Beach** from Barranquilla, taking 2 hrs and costing US$2.50.

Car (port) Without a *carnet de passages*, it can take up to 4 working days to get a car out of the port, but it is usually well guarded and it is unlikely that anything will be stolen.

Around Santa Marta: Aracataca and Fundación *p826*
Bus Ciénaga-Fundación, US$1; Fundación-Aracataca, US$0.20; **Santa**

Marta-Aracataca, US$2.50, 90 mins; **Barranquilla** via Ciénaga, US$2.50.

Taganga *p826*
Minibus from **Santa Marta** US$0.35 (0600-2130), **taxi** US$2.70, 15-20 mins. Taxi from bus station, US$3.50.

Parque Nacional Tayrona *p826*
Bus To get to the park entrance in El Zaino, take a minibus from the market in Santa Marta, Cra 11 y C 11, about US$1.30, 45 mins, frequent service from 0700, last back about 2000 (check on the day with the bus driver). Tourist bus from *Hotel Miramar* in Santa Marta daily at 1100, US$4.50. This transport returns early afternoon; visitors normally stay overnight. Other hotels help in arranging tours, but there is no need to take guides (who charge US$20 or more pp for a day trip). A boat can be hired in Taganga to go to Arrecifes, about 2 hrs along the scenic coast, US$110 for 8.

❶ Directory

Santa Marta *p825, map p825*
Airline offices Avianca, Edif de los Bancos, Cra 2B y C 14,T214 4018, T432 0106 at airport. **Banks** Most banks and ATMs in Plaza Bolívar. eg Banco Occidente (good rates for MasterCard). Plenty of cash machines. *Casas de cambio* in 3rd block of C 14. **Internet** Mundo Digital, C 15, No 2B-19, Edif Los Bancos, just off Plaza Bolívar, Mon-Sat 0700-2000, Sun 0900-1700. International calls too. Dialnet Café, C 13, No 3-13. **Useful addresses** MA office, C 22, No 2A-33, T423 0704. DAS Office, Cra 8, No 26A-15, T421 4917. Mon-Fri, 0730-1200, 1400-1800. Sr Chávez, DAS director at Santa Marta, runs a tight ship and is not flexible.

To Venezuela

Roads head for the insalubrious border town of Maicao, but on the way is plenty of interest: lagoons where flamingos feed, the pleasant city of Valledupar, which is home to Colombia's famous vallenato music, and the arid, empty Guajira Peninsula with its wildlife and special Wayúu culture.

Riohacha and around → *Phone code: 95. Colour map 1, grid A4. Population: 142,000.*

The port of Riohacha, 160 km east of Santa Marta and capital of Guajira Department, comes alive at the weekend, when it fills with party-goers and music (almost always vallenato) springs up all over the place. It was founded in 1545 by Nicolás Federmann, and in early years its pearling industry was large enough to tempt Drake to sack it (1596). Pearling almost ceased during the 18th century and the town was all but abandoned. Today, there is a pleasant stretch of beach with shady palms and a long wooden pier. A promenade along the beachfront (Calle 1) is lined with banks, hotels, restaurants and tour agencies. Riohacha is a useful base for exploring the semi-desert landscape of La Guajira. Tourist office: **Dirección de Turismo de la Guajira** ① *Av La Marina, T727 1015*, little information, better to ask tour operators. Ask for the University of the Guajira, which has an excellent resource centre related to the region and the Wayuú culture (ID is necessary to get in).

Santuario Los Flamencos

① *Entry to the park is US$5.50. 95 km east of Santa Marta and 25 km short of Riohacha.*
There are several small and two large saline lagoons (Laguna Grande and Laguna de Navío Quebrado), separated from the Caribbean by sand bars. The latter is near Camarones (colectivo from Riohacha, new market) which is just off the main road. About 3 km beyond Camarones is 'La Playa', a popular beach to which some colectivos continue at weekends. Flamingoes normally visit the large lagoons between October and December, during the wet season, though some birds are there all year. They are believed to migrate to and from the Dutch Antilles, Venezuela and Florida. Across Laguna de Navío Quebrado is a warden's hut on the sand bar, ask to be ferried across by local fishermen or the park guards. **MA** has new, comfortable cabins (**D**) for up to eight, open all year. Showers available; meals at the tiendas by the entrance. There are several bars and two stores on the beach.

Valledupar → *Phone code: 955. Colour map 1, grid A4. Population: 260,000. Altitude: 110 m.*

South of Riohacha on an alternative road to Maicao and the Venezuelan border is **Cuestecita** (*Hotel Turismo*), where you can turn southwest to **Barrancas**, with one of the largest coal mines in the world, El Cerrejón. Continuing on this road, which takes you either round the Sierra Nevada to Barranquilla and Santa Marta via Fundación (see above) or south to Bucaramanga, you come to **Valledupar**, capital of César Department. Valledupar claims to be the home of the *vallenato* music. Each April (26-30), *La Festival de la Leyenda Vallenata* draws thousands of visitors. Casas de cambio on C 16.

Guajira Peninsula

Beyond Riohacha to the east is the arid and sparsely inhabited Guajira Peninsula. The *indígenas* here collect dividivi (the curved pods of trees used in tanning and dyeing), tend goats, and fish. They are Wayúu (or Guajiros), and of special interest are the coloured robes worn by the women. There language is Wayuunaiki; beyond Cabo de Vela little Spanish is spoken. Sunsets in the Guajira are magnificent.

Note: The Guajira peninsula is not a place to travel alone, parties of three or more are recommended. If going in your own transport, check on safety before setting out. Also remember it is hot, easy to get lost, and there is little cover and very little water. Locals, including police, are very helpful in giving lifts. Stock up with provisions and water in Riohacha or Maicao. Elsewhere, what little there is expensive.

To visit a small part of the Peninsula take a bus from Riohacha (twice a day from the indigenous market) to Manaure, US$3, three uncomfortable hours through fields of cactus but offering fine views of flamingoes and other brightly coloured birds. **Manaure** is known for its salt flats southwest of the town. If you walk along the beach past the salt works, there are several lagoons where flamingoes congregate the year round (take binoculars). Local children hire out bicycles for US$3 per day to travel to the lagoons and salt flats. Take plenty of sunblock and water and a torch/flashlight for returning in the evening. 14 km from Manaure in this direction is **Musichi**, an important haunt of the flamingoes, sometimes out of the wet season. From Manaure there are *busetas* to **Uribia** (US$1), which has a Wayúu festival in May (no other reason to stop here), and thence to Maicao. You can get *busetas* from Uribia to Puerto Bolívar (from where coal from El Cerrejón is exported) and from there transport to **Cabo de Vela**, where the lagoons seasonally shelter vast flocks of flamingoes, herons and sandpipers. It costs about US$3 from Uribia to Cabo de Vela. There are fine beaches, but very strong currents offshore. Good walks through desert scrubland, eg to Pan de Azúcar hill (one hour from beach) and El Faro, from where there are spectacular views of the coastline and desert. Tourism in Cabo de la Vela has boomed recently. To enjoy deserted beaches, avoid Christmas and Easter when the *cabañas* and beaches are crowded and full of cars. Jeep tours to Cabo de la Vela from Riohacha can be easily arranged.

Parque Nacional Macuira

① *Entry free.*
Towards the northeast tip of the Guajira peninsula is the Serranía de Macuira, a range of hills over 500 m which create an oasis of tropical forest in the semi-desert. Moisture comes mainly from clouds that form in the evening and disperse in the early morning. Its remoteness gives it interesting flora and fauna and indigenous settlements little affected by outsiders. To reach the area, you must travel northeast from Uribia either round the coast past Bahía Portete, or direct

about trips to Los Nevados and coffee farms. Recommended.

F Residencias Margarita, C 17 No 22-14. Safe but noisy, shabby rooms. More **F** range hotels around C 18, Cra 22-23.

Parque Nacional Los Nevados p848

A Hotel Termales del Ruiz, T897 2611, at 3,500 m. Comfortable, with restaurant and good thermal pools, only cash accepted. Camping US$11 pp. It is cold, you will need a good sleeping bag, but beautiful surroundings.
E Cabaña Potosí, Finca Campo Alegre, 35 km from Las Brisas. Accommodation at a farm, meals served, US$3 per meal. A *chiva* passes through Campo Alegre to Manizales, daily 0900.
Chalet Arenales, 4 km from the park entrance at 4,150 m. At the time of writing (Apr 2006), the chalet was closed, but hoped to reopen later in 2006.
E pp **El Cisne**, run by MA, 22 km from Las Brisas. One cabin, holds between 4-8, US$10-12pp.
Camping available in the park **F-G**. Breakfast, lunch and dinner available, US$2-3. Advance reservations recommended.

● Eating

Manizales p848

¶¶ **El Balcón del Arriero**, Cra 23, No 26-18. Good local dishes, reasonable prices.
¶¶ **Las Brasas**, Cra 23, No 75A-65. Good grill and *comida típica*.
¶¶ **Fonda Paisa**, Cra 23, No 72-130. Nice local dishes with local Andean music.
¶¶ **Las Redes**, Cra 23, No 75-97. Predominantly sea food, good but pricey.
¶ **Caballo Loco**, Cra 61, No 23-07. Good. Another with the same name at C 21, No 23-40 is mainly a bar but serves good pizzas.

● Entertainment

Manizales p848

Cinema and theatre Centro Cultural y Convenciones los Fundadores is a modern cinema-theatre auditorium. Interesting wood-carved mural by Guillermo Botero, who also has murals in the entrance hall of the *Club Manizales* and *Hotel Las Colinas*. Events held here and at other locations during Jazz and Theatre Festival in **Sep/Oct**. Free films at the *Universidad Nacional*, usually on Tue and Thu. Good way to meet students.

⊛ Festivals and events

Manizales p848

The Feria de Manizales held in early **Jan** includes a coffee festival, bullfights, beauty parades, folk dancing and general partying.

▲ Activities and tours

Parque Nacional Los Nevados p848

A warmly recommended guide is **Javier Echavarría Carvajal**, Manizales T874 0116/T880 8300, T311-310 9732 (mob), or at his office, **Ecosistemas**, Cra 21, No 23-21, Manizales, T880 8300. Charges US$35 for group of 4 to Los Nevados for a day. Longer trips to Los Nevados can be arranged.

⊖ Transport

Manizales p848

Air Avianca and Aires fly to **Bogotá**.
Bus Terminal with good restaurant, C 19 between Cras 15 and 17, T884 9183. Buses to **Medellín**: via Neira and Aguadas, 6 hrs, US$8; via Anserma, 10 hrs, 1st class US$8; colectivo to Medellín, US$10. Frequent buses to **Bogotá**, Pullman, Bolivariana, US$14, 7-9 hrs; *buseta*, US$11-12. To **Honda**, US$8. **Cali**, hourly, 6-7 hrs, US$11. **Pereira**, ¼-hourly, 1½ hrs, excellent road, beautiful scenery, US$3.50. **Armenia**, 3 hrs, US$7. To **Quibdó**, via Pereira, 14-17 hrs, US$18.

Parque Nacional Los Nevados p848

As the park entrance closes at 1430, it is advisable to start your journey to the park early in the morning. For those without transport, it is possible to catch a daily *chiva* which leaves opposite El Casino de Suboficiales del Batallón Ayacucho between 0430-0500, US$2.20. For further information contact **Mountain House** Hostel or Victor who runs the *chiva*, T880 9891, T311-380 0796 (mob). The **Rápido Tolima** bus daily, usually 1400, from the Terminal in Manizales to Murillo passes near the entrance to the Park, US$3, 2½ hrs. See under Pereira for access from there.

⊖ Directory

Manizales p848

Banks Banks are along Cra 23. **Useful addresses** DAS Office: C 53, No 25A-35, T885 1616, Mon-Fri, 0730-1200, 1400-1400. **MA**, Cra 23, No 54-04, T881 2210.

Pereira to Cartago

Still in the shadow of the Nevados, this is a region of modern cities (in several cases rebuilt after earthquakes), delightful scenery and a number of botanical parks and gardens. Coffee is still by far the most important agricultural product of the area, but there has been a good deal of diversification into other crops as varied as flowers, asparagus and even bamboo. Recently, coffee farms have been opening up to tourism, from day visits to overnight stays. No two fincas are the same; they range from beautiful historic country mansions to modest accommodation.

Pereira → *Phone code: 96. Colour map 1, grid B3. Population: 432,000. Altitude: 1,476 m.*

Capital of Risaralda Department and 56 km southwest of Manizales, Pereira stands within sight of the *Nevados* of the Cordillera Central. A severe earthquake on 5 February 1995 badly damaged several buildings and the city was also affected by the earthquake which devastated Armenia in 1999 (see below). Pereira is a pleasant modern city, founded in 1863. The central **Plaza de Bolívar**, is noted for the striking sculpture of a nude Bolívar on horseback, by Rodrigo Arenas Betancur. There are other fine works of his in the city. The **Cathedral** is unimpressive from the outside but has an elegant and interesting interior. The **Museo Quimbaya de Oro y La Cerámica** ① *in the Banco de la República building, Av 30 de Agosto/C 35*, is worth a short visit. The botanical garden, on the campus of Universidad Tecnológica de Pereria ① *T321 2523, US$4.50, Mon-Sat, 0700-1600, must book a visit in advance and use a guide*, is good for bird watching and has bamboo forests and 2-hour nature walks.

Tourist information: **Oficina de Fomento al Turismo** ① *Cra 7, No 18-55, 2nd floor, T324 8030.* **Corporación Autónomo Regional de Risaralda** (Carder) ① *Avenida de las Américas, C 46, T314 1456*, has information but does not deal with park permits. It will direct you to those who do. **Turiscafé** ① *C 19, No 5-48, office 901 (inside Novacentro shopping centre), T325 4157/58*, for good information on coffee farms in Risaralda.

Fifteen kilometres from Pereira is **Santa Rosa de Cabal**, from where several thermal pools can be reached, including Termales de Santa Rosa/Los Arbeláez ① *0800-2400, US$8.* An 9 km unpaved road from Santa Rosa leads to the hot baths (early morning *chiva* or taxi, US$9 to entrance). The Termales de Santa Rosa are surrounded by forests, with waterfalls and nature walks. It's packed at the weekend, quiet during the week. **Hotel Termales de Santa Rosa de Cabal** (attached to the hot baths, **A**), *T364 1322*, comfortable, chalet style, with restaurant. Further along this road, midway between Pereira and Manizales is **Chinchiná**, in the heart of the coffee zone. A coffee hacienda which takes day-visitors is **Finca Guayabal** ① *entry US$10, T06-840 1847, http://guayabal.tripod.com*, with a nature trail, full explanations of the coffee-growing process and lunch, US$12.

Northwest of Pereira, 30 km towards the Río Cauca, is **Marsella**, and the **Alexander von Humboldt Gardens**, a carefully maintained botanical display with cobbled paths and bamboo bridges. Just outside the town is **AL Ecohotel Los Lagos** *T368 6529, www.ecohotelloslagos.com*, previously a gold mine, then a coffee *hacienda*, now restored as a hotel and nature park with lakes.

Parque Ucumari

From Pereira it is possible to visit the beautiful **Parque Ucumari** ① *park office, T06-325 4781 for good information. If just visiting for the day and not staying overnight, entrance is free*, one of the few places where the Andean spectacled bear survives. From Pereria, a *chiva* leaves daily (0900, 1500, more frequently during high season) with Transporte Florida from C12, No 9-40 to the village of El Cedral. From El Cedral it is a 2-2½ hour walk to *La Pastora*, the park visitors' centre. There is excellent camping, US$2.20 per person or US$6 at a refuge, meals extra. From La Pastora it is a steep, rocky 1-2 day hike to Laguna de Otún through beautiful scenery of changing vegetation (see page 849). The **Otún Quimbaya** flora and fauna sanctuary forms a biological corridor between Ucumari and Los Nevados; it protects the last remaining area of Andean tropical forest in Risaralda. There are marked paths, *cabaña* accommodation, camping and meals available.

B Don Gregorio, Cra 5, No 9-59, T211 5111. A/c, pool, sauna, cheaper with fan, includes breakfast. **E Río Pul**, Diag 3, No 2-142, T211 0623. With fan and bath, TV. Recommended.

● Eating

Pereira *p851*

There are good restaurants on Av 30 de Agosto (the road west to the airport), and on Av Circunvalar going east.

▼▼ El Mesón Español, C 14, No 25-57. Spanish food.
▼▼ Mama Flor, Barrio Los Alpes. Typical food, good.
▼▼-▼ Pizza Piccolo, Av Circunvalar going east C 5, La Terraza. Good Italian food and pizzas. Recommended. Other restaurants in same block
▼ Mister Chuleta, C 5 y Cra 17, Pinares. Decent, good value *comida corriente*, good service. Others on same block.
Pastelería Lucerna, C 19, No 6-49. Large coffee shop, fountain/garden, good cakes, snacks, ice cream, clean.

Salento *p852*

▼▼▼-▼▼ El Portal de Cocora, 100m from Salento Vía Cocora, T759 3190. Memorable views, good food and atmosphere, try the trout. Recommended. Open Fri-Sun. Owners rent out 2 comfortable cabins opposite the restaurant, **A**.
▼▼-▼ El Rincón de Lucía, Calle Real. Popular, good.
▼ La Fonda de los Arrieros, on Plaza, next to police station. Typical dishes, good value, popular.

Armenia *p852*

▼▼▼ La Fogata, Av Bolívar No 14N-39, T749 5980. International, expensive but good.
▼▼▼-▼▼ Casa Verde, Cra 14 No 11A-25, T746 6093. Seafood and meat dishes, good.
▼▼ Parador Los Geranios, Cra 14, No 53N-34, T749 3474. Typical food, very popular, good value, speciality: *frijol garra picada*.
▼▼-▼ Cafetería Barú, Av Bolívar, No 22N-05. Light meals, salads, ice-cream.
Pastelería Lucerna, C 20, No 14-43. Light meals, good quality.

Ibagué *p852*

▼▼ La Vieja Enramada, Cra 8, No 15-03. Local and international dishes.
▼▼-▼ La Parilla de Marcos, Cra 5 with 43. Good meat grills.
▼▼-▼ La Mesa del Chef, C 69, No 4-73. Decent *comida corriente*.

⊕ Festivals and events

Ibagué *p852*

National Folklore Festival, in **Jun**. The Departments of Tolima and Huila commemorate

San Juan (**24 Jun**) and SS Pedro y Pablo (**29 Jun**) with bullfights, fireworks, and music. There are choral festivals biannually in **Dec**.

▲ Activities and tours

Pereira *p851*

D'p@seo, Cra 13, No 14-60, local 109, www.turis colombia.andes.com. Opposite **Hotel Pereira**. Arranges weekend trips to Los Nevados, trips on Río la Vieja. Mon-Sat 0800-1200, 1400-1900.

Armenia *p852*

Territorio Aventura, Av Bolívar, No 14N-80, of 207, T749 9568, www.territorioaventura.com. Organize kayaking, rafting, fishing trips.

● Transport

Pereira *p851*

Air Matecaña airport is 5 km to the south, bus, US$0.25. Daily flights to **Miami**, **Bogotá**, **Cali** and **Ibagué**; less frequent to other cities.
Bus Terminal is 1½ km south of city centre, stores luggage. Bus to **Armenia**, 1 hr, US$2, a beautiful trip. To **Cali**, US$8, 4½-5 hrs, buses by night, colectivo by day, same price. To **Medellín**, 6-8 hrs, US$10. To/from **Bogotá**, US$10-12, 7 hrs (route is via Girardot, Ibagué – both cities bypassed – and Armenia).

Pereira to Armenia: Salento *p852*

Bus To **Armenia** every 20 mins 0600-2000, US$1, 40 mins. To **Pereira**, 4 a day at weekends and public holidays, US$2.50, 1 hr. Jeep to **Cocora** valley US$8, or US$1.20 if you get a scheduled service.

Armenia *p852*

Air El Edén, 13 km from city. Daily flights to **Bogotá** and **Medellín** with Aires. Fog can delay flights.
Bus Terminal at C 35, No 20-68. To **Ibagué**, US$5.50 2½ hrs. To **Bogotá**, hourly, 7-9 hrs, US$15. To **Neiva**, US$12, 8 hrs. **Cali**, US$7, 3 hrs, frequent.

Ibagué *p852*

Air Daily Aires flights to **Bogotá**, **Cali** and **Medellín**, also to **Pereira.**
Bus Terminal is between Cras 1-2 and C 19-20. Tourist police at terminal helpful. Frequent services to **Bogotá**, US$8, 4 hrs. To **Neiva**, US$8-9, 3 hrs, and many other places.

Cartago *p853*

Bus To **Cali**, US$7, 3½ hrs. To **Armenia**, US$2, 2½-3 hrs. To **Pereira**, US$1.50, 45 mins. To **Medellín**, US$12, 7 hrs.

Pereira *p851*
Banks Banks around Plaza de Bolívar.
Most banks have ATMs which take
foreign cards. *Casas de cambio* change

Salento *p852*
Banks One bank which gives cash advance
against Visa card, no ATM, ash or TC exchange.

Cali and the Cauca Valley

*The narrow Cauca valley has as its focus Cali, the country's southern industrial centre but at
the same time one of Colombia's party hotspots. Cali calls itself the Salsa capital of the world,
and few would dispute that claim. The region is served by the Pacific port of Buenaventura. 56
km off the coast is the high-security prison turned national park of Gorgona Island.*

Cali → *Phone code: 92. Colour map 1, grid B2. Population: 1,780,000. Altitude: 1,030 m.*

Cali, Colombia's third city and capital of the Valle del Cauca Department, is the country's
self-declared salsa capital. So if you're looking for *la rumba* and wanting to join swinging salsa
couples on the dance floor, Cali should not to be missed. Sensuous, tropical rhythms are
ubiquitous, seeming to seep from every part of the city's being. Cali's other more contentious
claim is that it boasts the most beautiful girls in the country (though Medellín may beg to differ).
The region is set in a rich agricultural area producing sugar, cotton, rice, coffee and cattle. Cali
was founded in 1536, and until 1900 was a leisurely colonial town. Then the railway came, and
Cali is now a rapidly expanding industrial complex serving the whole of southern Colombia.

Ins and outs
Getting there Palmaseca **airport** is 20 km from city. It has *casa de cambio*. **Bus Terminal** is
at C 30N, No 2A-29, 25 minutes walk from the centre (leave terminal by the taxi stands, take first
right, go under railway and follow river to centre). Hotel information available, left luggage
US$0.60 per item, good food at terminal. Bus information, T668 3655. *Casa de cambio*, cash only.
Showers on second level (US$0.40). Buses between the bus station and the centre, US$0.30.
Taxi from centre to bus station, US$1.50. ▸▸ *For further information, see also Transport, page 858.*

Getting around Ensure that taxi meters are used. Prices, posted in the window, start at
US$0.30. Extra charge on holidays, Sun and at night.

Tourist offices Secretaría de Cultura y Turismo ① *Gobernación del Valle del Cauca
building, p 2, T620 0063/64, www.valledecauca.gov.co,* speak to Claudia Restrepo, helpful,
speaks English and French. See also www.caliescali.com (news, chat, entertainment, music
and tourist information on *La Guía* pages).

Sights
The city's centre is the **Plaza de Caicedo**, with a statue of one of the independence leaders,
Joaquín Caicedo y Cuero. Facing the plaza is the elegant **Palacio Nacional** and the **Cathedral**,
seat of the influential Archbishop of Cali. Nearby is the renovated church and 18th-century
monastery of **San Francisco** with a splendidly proportioned domed belltower. Cali's oldest
church, **La Merced** ① *Calle 7, between Cras 3 and 4*, has been restored by the Banco Popular.
The adjoining convent houses two museums: **Museo de Arte Colonial** (closed but the nuns
may let you in) and the **Museo Arqueológico** ① *Mon-Sat 0900-1300, 1400-1800, US$1,* with
pre- Columbian pottery. Another church worth seeing is the Gothic-style **La Ermita**, on the river
between Calles 12 and 13. **Museo del Oro** (also called Museo Calima) ① *Calle 7, No 4-69, Banco
de la República building, Mon-Sat 0800-1800, free,* has pre-Columbian gold work and pottery.

    Museo de Arte Moderno La Tertulia ① *Av Colombia, No 5-105 Oeste, Tue-Sun
1000-1800, US$1.80, children half price,* exhibits South American, including local, modern art.
To view the city, take a taxi to the **Monumento Las Tres Cruces**, northwest of the city or to the
Monumento Cristo Rey, 1,470 m, to the west of the city. The huge statue of Christ can be seen

50 km away across the Río Cauca. The neighbourhood of **San Antonio** (behind the **Intercontinental Hotel**) is the city's oldest area, where Cali's colonial past can still be felt. The area has a relaxed, bohemian atmosphere, especially at weekends when it's livelier. There are good views of the city from the 18th century church of San Antonio.

● Sleeping

Cali p855, map p856

Although the atmosphere in Cali is quite relaxed, carry your passport (or photocopy) at all times and be prepared for police checks. At night do not walk east or south of Cra 10 and C 15.

L Intercontinental, Av Colombia, No 2-72, T882 3225, www.intercontinental.com. Modern, central, pleasant, includes breakfast, tennis courts, pool, restaurants, good buffets.

AL-B Aparta Hotel Del Río, C 21N, No 2N-05, T660 2707, www.apartahoteldelrio.com. Comfortable, various suites and rooms with good facilities (gym, sauna, pool, laundry), safe, internet, good restaurant, parking.

A Aristi, Cra 9, No 10-04, T882 2521, www.hotel aristi.com.co. Weekend discounts and for stays over 5 days, cheaper with fan, art-deco style, turkish baths, rooftop pool, restaurant, central.

A Don Jaime, Av 6N, No 15N-25, T667 2828. Good location, modern, spacious rooms, with breakfast.

A Hostal Casa Republicana, C 7 No 6-74, T896 0949, F896 0840. Colonial house, nicely decorated, comfortable rooms, with breakfast, cable TV, restaurant, patio café. Recommended.

B Hostal San Fernando, C 3, No 27-87, T556 4820, near Parque del Perro (off map). Safe, pleasant, converted house, English spoken.

B Pensión Stein, Av 4N, No 3-33, T661 4927, www.hotelstein.com.co. Also houses the Swiss Embassy, run by very helpful Swiss consul, who speaks French, German and English. With breakfast, family-oriented, quiet, very safe, excellent food, small swimming pool, Alpine feel, parking. Recommended.

B Royal Plaza, Cra 4, No 11-69, T883 9243. On Plaza de Caicedo, good cheap rooftop restaurant with lovely views of the city, comfortable spacious rooms, nice atmosphere, credit cards accepted. Recommended.

Cali

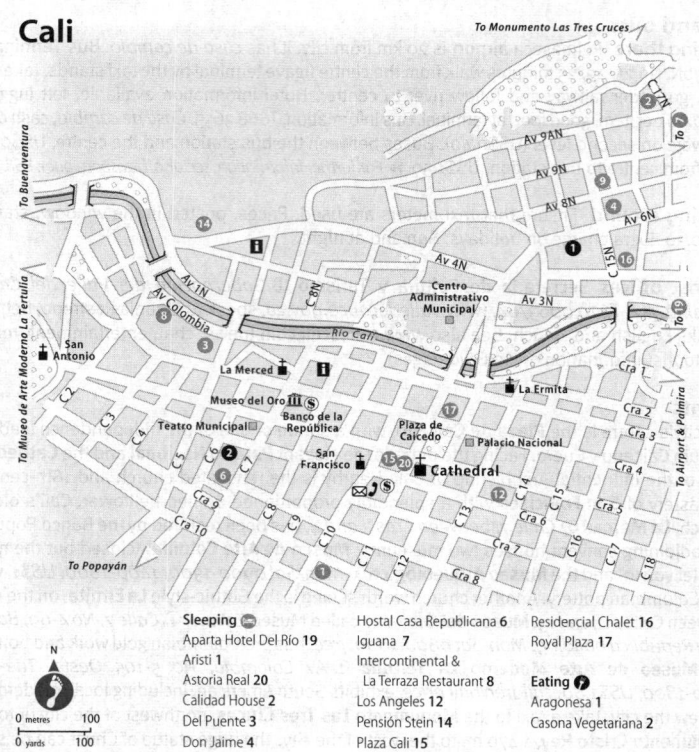

Sleeping ●
Aparta Hotel Del Río 19
Aristi 1
Astoria Real 20
Calidad House 2
Del Puente 3
Don Jaime 4

Hostal Casa Republicana 6
Iguana 7
Intercontinental &
La Terraza Restaurant 8
Los Angeles 12
Pensión Stein 14
Plaza Cali 15

Residencial Chalet 16
Royal Plaza 17

Eating ●
Aragonesa 1
Casona Vegetariana 2

Colombia Cali

C **Astoria Real**, C11, No 5-16, T883 0140, F880 5045. On corner of Plaza de Caicedo. Decent, bright, comfortable rooms, laundry.

C **Plaza Cali**, Cra 6, No 10-29, T882 2560. Modern, large rooms, can change money when manager is around, credit cards accepted, laundry, luggage stored, restaurant.

C **del Puente**, C 5, No 4-36, T893 8484, F893 8385. Airy, serves breakfast, stores luggage.

D **Los Angeles**, Cra 6, No 13-109, T391 5517, F391 5514. Modern, good value restaurant, spacious rooms, a bit noisy.

E **Iguana**, C 21N, No 9N-22, T661 3522. Some cheaper accommodation with shared shower, dorms and private rooms, nice patio area. Urs, the helpful Swiss manager, is a great source of local information. Laundry, internet, luggage store, kitchen facilities, motorcycle parking, excursions, language and salsa classes arranged, good travellers' guesthouse, safe area. Recommended.

E-F **Calidad House**, C 17N, No 9AN-39, T/F661 2338. Dorms and private rooms, recently renovated. Safe location, kitchen, laundry, will store luggage, pleasant, popular with travellers, 2 big dogs, good.

F **Residencial Chalet**, Av 4N, No 15N-43, T661 0029. Safe, basic, quiet, small dark rooms.

Out of town

L **Radisson**, Cra 100B, No 11A-99, T330 7777, F330 6477, in south of city, excellent service, pool, parking, restaurants, all Services.

B **Hotel Aeropuerto**, at the airport, T666 3229. Good, parking.

C **Turístico La Luna**, Autopista Sur, No 13-01, T558 2611, F558 6367. With breakfast, safe, large pool, restaurant, good parking.

● Eating

Cali *p855, map p856*
There are lots of sidewalk places to eat in the centre and along Av 6 in the north. Cafés and ice cream parlours abound near the university, across the river from the main part of town. Around Parque del Perro in San Fernando are upmarket restaurants and cafes. Good for an evening meal.

††† **Los Girasoles**, Av 6 N y C 35, T668 4646. Excellent Colombian menu, fish, ask for day's special. Recommended.

††† **Las Dos Parrillas**, Av 6N y C 35, T668 4646. Good steaks but expensive.

††† **La Terraza**, Av Colombia, No 2-72, T882 3225, in Intercontinental Hotel. Meat and international dishes, elegant, music and dance, nice atmosphere.

†† **Cali Viejo**, Cra 1, Parque El Bosque, T893 4927 (on south side of river near zoo). Colonial house, excellent local dishes.

†† **Pizza al Paso**, Cra 20 Este, No 2-55, El Peñón. Restaurant/bar with live music. Good reports.

†† **Rancho Alegre**, Av 15 Oeste, No 7-04, T893 4207. Colombian and international meat dishes.

†† **San Mango**, Cra 12, No 2-31, San Antonio. Modern decor in colonial house, good salads. Closed Mon.

††-† **Café Moro**, C 6, No 8-11. Arab food and grills, nice decor, decent daily buffet US$2.50.

††-† **Clowns Deli**, Av Colombia, No 5-105 (next to Museo de Arte La Tertulia). Fresh sandwiches and salads, nice terrace, good.

† **Aragonesa**, Av 6 N, No 13N-68. Good breakfasts, bakery.

† **Casona Vegetariana**, Cra 6, No 6-56. Good vegetarian food, juices and bread.

† **Comedor Vegetariano y Café**, Cra 5 No 7-38. Clean, vegetarian food and desserts, lunch only, closed Sun.

† **Govinda**, Cra 6, N 8-48. Vegetarian, lunch only.

† **Tales & Tales**, Cra 34, No 3A-03, Parque del Perro. Good value burgers.

Bread and pastry shops often have cafés or cafeterías eg **Punto Sabroso**, C 12, No 8-06; **Montecarlo**, Cra 5, No 14-22 in the centre.

● Bars and clubs

Cali *p855, map p856*
The nightlife along Av 6 N from C 16 upwards is safest and best known. There is a tour Fri-Sat on a *chiva* (open-sided bus) stopping off at various nightspots, US$14. Sometimes only couples are allowed into clubs.

Blues Brothers Bar, C 26N, No 5AN-51. Jazz and live rock bands. Good reports.

Costenita, Cra 15/C 15. Lots of local colour, Thu-Sun.

Kukaramakara, C 28N, No 2 Bis-97. The 'in' place at the time of writing. Live bands, mix of music.

Lotus, C 15N, No 9N-27. Lounge, electronic music.

Praga, Vía Cali-Yumbo. Popular, mix of music.

Tin Tin Deo, C 5 y Cra 22. Good atmosphere, small, intimate, salsa at weekends. Recommended.

Tropicali, Av 6 N, No 15-66, T667 1006. Serves food, has a range of entertainments. Many others nearby.

Zaperoco, Av 5N, No 16-46. Salsa, recommended.

Barrio Juanchito has a range of salsa bars and discos, from thatched roofs to huge, hi-tech salsatecas. It is worth visiting just to watch couples dancing salsa and to join in, if you dare! Go with locals and couples; groups of foreign male tourists might have a hard time getting in. Most advisable to take a registered radio taxi there and back; 15-min ride out of Cali, across the bridge over the Río Cauca.

● Entertainment

Cali *p855, map p856*
Cinema Alianza Colombo-Francesa, Av 6 N, No 21-34, T661 3431, and **Centro Colombo-**

clean public swimming pool, Las Moyas, T837 3804. US$3 pp with own tent, US$4.50 pp to hire tent, 1 large room with private bath, US$3.50pp, clean, pleasant, toilets, lights, laundry service, horse hire (see below).

Private houses Accommodation in private houses is available for less than US$3 pp. The farm of **Constantino Ortiz** is recommended, 3½ km from town, first turn on left after the Parque Arqueológico, 4 rooms, best to take a sleeping bag, meals and horses available, peaceful, good cooking, free morning coffee, also has camping, reservations at C 5, No 11-13 in town.

F **Casa de Nelly**, Vía la Estrella, 1½ km west along 2 Av, T837 3221. Attractive peaceful finca run by Nelly Haymann (French), hot water, good food nearby, free coffee. Recommended.

F **El Corcel**, C 5, No 11-09. Constantino Ortiz rents out simple rooms.

Just outside San Agustín

C **Hacienda Anacaona**, Vía al Estrecho del Magdalena, 2 km from town, T837 9390, www.anacaona-colombia.com. Elegant colonial style, attractive, beautiful views and garden, hammocks, hot water, restaurant, quiet. Camping allowed on grounds. Good.

D-E **El Maco**, 1 km from town, 400 m past Piscina Las Moyas, T837 3437. Swiss owned, working organic farm, rustic, peaceful and quiet, cosy cabins, also dorms, welcoming, basic kitchen facilities, laundry service, good restaurant.

E **Finca El Paraíso**, 1 km from Parque Arqueológico, T837 3575, T312-360 8564, ask for Riecuarte Urbano. Working farm with great views, good beds, shared bath, meals, hot water, laundry service, horses for rent, peaceful, free pick up from town. Camping on grounds, US$4.50 pp.

Around San Agustín: Alto de los Idolos and around *p868*

D **Parador de los Idolos**, 500 m from the Alto. 3 rooms, with bath and hot water.

D **Doña Tere**, C 5, No 4-36, Isnos. Opposite police station, off main plaza.

E **Casa Grande**, just off main plaza in Isnos. Central, cheaper without bath.

Bogotá to San Agustín: Neiva *p868*

A **Hostería Matamundo**, in old *hacienda* 3 km from centre, on road to Garzón and San Agustín, Cra 5, No 3S-51, T873 0217. A/c, swimming pool, restaurant, disco.

A **Tumburagua**, C 5A, No 5-40, T871 2406. With breakfast, a/c, TV, restaurant, discounts possible, helpful. Recommended.

C **Casa Pablo**, C 5, No 12-45, T872 3100. Good service, parking, laundry, much more with a/c.

870

F **Residencia Magdalena**, C 1A Sur, No 8A-57, T873 3586. Close to new bus station, cold water.

● Eating

Puracé *p865*
Two restaurants, one just above the church, meals around US$2.50.

Around Puracé: La Plata *p866*
Most eating places are closed by 2000. Good set meals opposite Banco Cafetero. Excellent bakery on main plaza.

♥ **Asadero Los Vikingos**, C 4, near *Hotel Cambis*, pizzas and all meals.

San Agustín *p867*
Tap water in San Agustín is not safe to drink.
♥♥ **Donde Richard**, 1 km from town towards Parque Arqueológico. Good steaks. Recommended.
♥♥-♥ **Surabhi**, C 5, No 14-09. Vegetarian dishes or meat, pizzas, *menú*, juices, desserts. Recommended.
♥♥-♥ **Pizza Mania**, Cra 3, No 3-43. Decent pizzas, also sold by the slice.
♥ **Brahama**, C 5, No 15-11. *Comida* including soup and drink, good fruit salads, vegetarian meals, cheap. Recommended.
♥ **El Fogón**, C 5 No 14-30. Family run, good *comida* and juices, fresh salads, Recommended.
♥ **The Tea Rooms**, 20 m from *Casa de Nelly*. Good food, roasts on Sun (sometimes).

Bogotá to San Agustin: Neiva *p868*
♥♥ **Avenida**, Av 26, opposite Red Cross. Decent *comida corriente*.
♥♥ **Barbacoa**, Cra 4 between C10-9. Good *comida corriente*.

● Bars and clubs

San Agustín *p867*
La Casa de Tarzan, C 2, No 8-04. Nice bamboo and wood interior, quiet.

● Festivals and events

San Agustín *p867*
Santa María del Carmenin **mid-Jul** (date varies) in San Agustín. 2 festivals in **Jun** are San Juan (24th) with horse races and dances, and San Pedro (29th) with horse races, dances, fancy dress, and more. In the **1st week of Oct**, the Casa de Cultura celebrates **La Semana Cultural Integrada**, with folklore events from all parts of the country.

Bogotá to San Agustin: Neiva *p868*
A local festival is **18-28 Jun**, when the Bambuco Queen is elected: folklore, dances and feasting.

▲ Activities and tours

San Agustín *p867*

Guides Authorized and recommended guides from World Heritage Travel Office: **Fabio Burbano**, T311-867 5665, professional, reliable and knowledgeable. **Jorge Hurtado**, T311-292 4241 (speaks English). They charge US$15 for a half day, US$30 for a full day, up to 10 people per guide. Make sure you are charged the correct price based on the number of people in your group. World Heritage Travel organises 90-min white-water rafting trips on the Río Magdalena, US$50 with group of 6. You can make your own arrangements, and it may cost less, but we have received many reports of unsatisfactory experiences of unregistered guides. If you have any problems, ask at World Heritage Travel.

Elvecio Silva Silva, T311-442 7403 (mob), has had positive recommendations.

Horse hire You are strongly advised to hire horses for trips around San Agustín through hotels or World Heritage Travel. Charges are about US$7 per half day, US$8 for a guide for the same time. If you require a guide, add the hire cost of his horse. There are fixed tariffs for 20 or so standard trips.

Vehicle tours Jeeps may be hired for between 4-6 people. Prices vary according to the number of sites to be visited, but the daily rate is about US$90. World Heritage Travel organises a good leisurely day trip to the Salto de Bordones and Mortiño waterfalls, Alto de Las Piedras and Alto de Los Idoles for US$15 (not including entrance fees, guide and lunch). Jeeps direct to Tierradentro can be hired for about US$115 between 5-6 people. For those who like a good walk, most sites can be reached on foot, see above.

◎ Transport

Puracé *p865*
Bus There are several daily to Puracé from **Popayán**, the last returning around 1730. The bus stops 3½ km from Pilimbalá.

Around Puracé *p866*
La Plata
Bus To **Bogotá**, via Neiva, **Coomotor**, 9 hrs, in the evening, **Cootranshuila**, 5 a day, US$18. To **Garzón**, bus or jeep 1½ hrs, US$3. To **Popayán** 0500 and others, US$6, 5½ hrs. To **San Agustín**, direct US$9 or take a colectivo to Garzón or Pitalito and change. For **Tierradentro** take a bus towards Popayán (leaves 0600-0630) and alight at the Cruce US$6. Private jeep hire La Plata- Tierradentro US$40, cheaper if you pick up other passengers. To **Pitalito**, 3½ hrs, US$7.

Florencia

Air Aires flies daily to **Neiva** and **Bogotá** (also *Satena*, 6 a week) and most days to **Cali**.
Bus There are regular services from **Neiva** (US$11, 4-6 hrs), **Garzón** and **Altamira** (bus Altamira to Florencia, US$5). To **Bogotá** US$25.

Pitalito

Bus At the bus stations, both off and on buses, in Pitalito, Garzón and Neiva (see below) , theft is common.

Plenty of buses and colectivos to **San Agustín**, US$2. Bus to **La Plata**, 3½ hrs, US$7. Buses in Pitalito go from the new bus station. **Taxis Verdes** from the main plaza (US$15 to Bogotá). Bus to **Mocoa** (in the Putumayo), US$10, 7-8 hrs, also jeeps from market square, 2 in morning. To **Parque Nacional Cueva de los Guácharos** take a bus/*chiva* to Palestina, US$2, 1 hr, and then a 40-min *chiva* to Mensura. From there it is an 8-km walk or horse ride to the Park visitors centre.

Parque Nacional Puracé *p866*

Bus All the places beyond Puracé village can be reached by bus from **Popayán** to La Plata or Garzón. The bus service can be erratic so check time of last daylight bus to Popayán and be prepared to spend a cold night at 3,000 m. The rangers will allow you to stay in the centre.

San Agustín *p867*

Bus To **Bogotá** by colectivo (**Taxis Verdes**, C 3, No 11-57) 4 daily, direct or change at Neiva, go early US$18, 9-11 hrs, or by bus (**Coomotor**, C 3, No 10-71), 1 a day, about US$18, 12-14 hrs. From **Bogotá**, Taxis Verdes will pick up at hotels (extra charge), T01-355 5555. Alternatively there are frequent services from Bogotá to **Neiva** as well as some to Pitalito (**Taxis Verdes** costs US$16). Most services going to Bogotá will stop at Garzón and Neiva. To **Tierradentro**, check first if any of the tourist offices is running a jeep (about US$120 for minimum 4 people), otherwise, **Taxis Verdes** or colectivos leave frequently to **Garzón** (US$3.50) or **Pitalito** (30 mins), then a colectivo jeep from Pitalito to **La Plata**, US$7, 3½ hrs. Usually you can get a **chiva**, bus or colectivo, 2-3 hrs to Tierradentro (San Andrés de Pisimbalá) the same day. Daily buses to **Garzón**, US$4.50, 2½-3 hrs, from where more buses go to La Plata for Tierradentro. Do not take a night bus to Tierradentro. There are 3 daily buses from San Agustín to Popayán via Paletará and Coconuco with **Cootranshuila** (office on C 3, No 10-81), slow, bad unpaved road, 6 hrs, US$12; some continuing to Cali (US$16) and **Coomotor** on this route to Cali, 9 hrs. Do not travel between San Agustín and Popayán at night. The road is isolated and dangerous. It's best to book seats and processing area. It is also the centre of the government-led coca eradication programme. Even if the authorities allow you to enter, you are strongly advised not to do so.

Ipiales → *Phone code: 927. Colour map 1, grid C2. Population: 72,000. Altitude: 2,898 m.*
Passing through deep valleys and a spectacular gorge, buses on the paved Pan-American Highway cover the 84 km from Pasto to Ipiales in 1½-2 hours. The road crosses the spectacular gorge of the Río Guáitara at 1,750 m, near El Pedregal, where *choclo* (corn) is cooked in many forms by the roadside. **Ipiales**, "the city of the three volcanoes", is famous for its colourful Friday morning indigenous market. The **Catedral Bodas de Plata** is worth visiting but the real attraction is the Sanctuary of the Virgin of **Las Lajas**, about 7 km east of Ipiales. Seen from the approach road, looking down into the canyon, the Sanctuary is a magnificent architectural conception, set on a bridge over the Río Guáitara: close up, it is very heavily ornamented in the gothic style. The altar is set into the rock face of the canyon, which forms one end of the sanctuary with the façade facing a wide plaza that completes the bridge over the canyon. There are walks to nearby shrines in dramatic scenery. It is a 10-15 minutes' walk down to the sanctuary from the village. There are great pilgrimages to it from Colombia and Ecuador (very crowded at Easter) and the Sanctuary must be second only to Lourdes in the number of miracles claimed for it. Colectivo taxis from Ipiales bus terminal go direct to Las Lajas (10 minutes), US$5.50 one way. Several basic hotels and a small number of restaurants at Las Lajas. You may also stay at the Casa Pastoral for about US$3 a night: amazing views of the Sanctuary.

Border with Ecuador

Ipiales is 2 km from the Rumichaca bridge across the Río Carchi into Ecuador. The border post stands on a concrete bridge, beside a natural bridge, where customs and passport examinations take place 0600-2100. All Colombian offices are in one complex: **DAS** (immigration, exit stamp given here), customs, **INTRA** (Dept of Transportation, car papers stamped here; if leaving Colombia you must show your vehicle entry permit) and **ICA** (Department of Agriculture for plant and animal quarantine). There is also a restaurant, Telecom, clean bathrooms (ask for key, US$0.10) and ample parking. See page 926 for the Ecuadorean side and see also Documents in Ecuador, Essentials, page 883. The **Ecuadorean consulate** ① *T773 2292, weekdays 0900-1230, 1430-1700*, is in the DAS complex. There are many money-changers near the bridge on both sides. Better rates on the Colombian side but check all calculations.

◉ Sleeping

Pasto *p872*
AL Don Saul, C 17, No 23-52, T723 0618, F723 0622. One block from main plaza. Comfortable, good restaurant, with breakfast. Recommended.
AL Cuellar's, Cra 23, No 15-50, T723 2879, F723 8274. Roomy, well-furnished, restaurant, breakfast included. Recommended.
A Galerías, Cra 26, No 18-71, p 3, T723 7390, F723 7069, above shopping mall. Comfortable, good restaurant, with breakfast, parking, central. Recommended.
B Casa Madrigal, C 26, No 15-37, T723 4592. Central, modern, with breakfast.
B El Dorado, C16A, No 23-42, T723 3260, With bath, quiet, TV.
C El Duque, Cra 20, No 17-17, T721 7390. Hot water, quiet, TV, good.
D Canchala, C 17, No 20A-38, T/F721 3965. Big, safe, hot water, TV, central.
D Koala Inn, C 18, No 22-37, T722 1101, koalainn@hotmail.com. Well-established, popular traveller hostal. Cheaper without bath, laundry facilities, speak to Luis Eduardo, very

helpful, hot water, book exchange, restaurant serves breakfast. Recommended.
E Aica, C 17, No 20-75, T721 5311. Near Macro Económico supermarket. Safe, cheaper with shared bath, hot water, TV, but dirty.
E Andino, Cra 19 y C 16, T721 1311. Good value, good beds, safe, restaurant.
E María Belén, C 13, No 19-15, Av de Las Américas, T723 0277. Central, safe, quiet, hot water.

Chachagüi
C Hotel Imperio de los Incas, 2 km form Pasto airport, T02-723 8054. With bath, hot water, pool, good value restaurant.

Tumaco *p873*
Children meet arriving buses to offer accommodation; most cheap places are in C del Comercio, many houses and restaurants without signs take guests – most have mosquito nets. Be very careful of food and water because there are many parasites.
B Villa del Mar, C Sucre, T727 2393. Modern, rooms and suites, a/c, cheaper with fan, with

shower and toilet, no hot water, good café below, also has well-equipped cabins with fan, a/c and all inclusive plans at El Morro Beach.
D El Dorado, C del Comercio, T727 2565, near water-front and *canoa* dock. Basic, TV, private and shared bath (half the price).

Ipiales *p874*
B Mayasquer, 3 km on road to the border, T773 2643. Modern, nice restaurant, very good.
C Los Andes, Cra 5, No 14-43, T734338. With hot water and breakfast, TV, restaurant, small pool, gym and spa, good, helpful.
D Bachué, Cra 6, No 11-68, T773 2164. Central, safe, hot water, with bath, TV.
D Castillo Real, C 14, No 4-36, T773 4610. Central, with bath, TV, hot water.
E Belmonte, Cra 4, No 12-111, T773 2771 (near *Transportes Ipiales*). Hot water, parking opposite, good value but crowded. Recommended.
E Dinar, Cr 4A, No 12A-18, T733 3659. Central, with hot water, bath, TV.
E Korpawasy, Cra 6, No 10-47, T732246. Plenty of blankets, hot water, with bath. Downstairs is a cafeteria.
E Rumichaca Internacional, C 14, No 7-14, T732692. Comfortable, central, good restaurant.

● Eating

Pasto *p872*
For local specialities, try *arepas de choclo*, made with fresh ground sweet corn, at the kiosks beside the main road going north. *Cuy*, grilled guinea pig, is another typical dish.

Centre
¶¶ Asadero de Cuyes Pinzón, Cra 40, No 19B-76, Barrio Palermo, T731 3228. Good place to try *cuy* (guinea pig). Open Sun.
¶¶ Las Dos Parrillas, Pasaje Dorado, No 23-22. Steaks, chicken, reasonable prices.
¶¶ Su Casa del Mar, C 21, No 4-65. Good seafood.
¶¶-¶ La Merced, Cra 22, No 17-37. Pizzas and local dishes, good.
¶ Gouranja, C14, No 25-09. Vegetarian.

Outside the centre
¶¶-¶ La Casa Vasca, C 12A, No 29-10. Spanish. Recommended.
¶¶-¶ Cokorín, bus terminal. Meat, chicken, local dishes.
¶¶-¶ Sausalito, Cra 35A, No 20-63. Seafood.

Tumaco *p873*
The main culinary attraction of the town is the fish, in the market and restaurants, fresh from the Pacific. A number of good restaurants on the main streets, C Mosquera and C del Comercio, though the best is probably **El Portón Marino** on C Sucre.

Ipiales *p874*
Plenty of cheap restaurants, better ones on Cra 7.
¶¶ Don Lucho (Los Tejados), Cra 5, No 14-13. For *antioqueño* food.
¶¶ La Herradura, outside town towards the border. Good food, reasonable prices, try their excellent *trucha con salsa de camarones* (rainbow trout with shrimp sauce).
Panadería Galaxia, C 15, No 7-89. Good cheap café, breakfast.

❀ Festivals and events

Pasto *p872*
During the new year's *fiesta* there is a **Día de los Negros** on **5 Jan** and a **Día de los Blancos** next day. On 'black day' people dump their hands in black grease and smear each others' faces. On 'white day' they throw talc or flour at each other. Local people wear their oldest clothes. On **28 Dec** and **5 Feb**, there is also a **Fiesta de las Aguas** when anything that moves gets drenched with water from balconies and even from fire engines' hoses. All towns in the region are involved in this legalized water war! In Pasto and Ipiales (see page 874), on **31 Dec**, is the **Concurso de Años Viejos**, when huge dolls are burnt; they represent the old year and sometimes lampoon local people.

○ Shopping

Pasto *p872*
Handicrafts Leather goods shops are on C 17 and C 18. Try the municipal market for handicrafts. Artesanía-Mercado Bomboná, C 14 y Cra 27. Artesanías Mopa-Mopa, Cra 25, No 13-14, for *barniz*. Artesanías Nariño, C 26, No 18-91. Casa del Barniz de Pasto, C 13, No 24-9.
Markets and supermarkets Ley on C 18. Supermercado Confamiliar de Nariño, C 16B, No 30-53. Recommended.
On main plaza (C 19 y Cra 25) is a shopping centre with many shops and restaurants.
Maps Maps of Colombia and cities from Instituto Geográfico Agustín Codazzi, C 18A, No 21A-18, limited selection.

● For an explanation of the sleeping and eating price codes used in this guide, see inside the front
● cover. Other relevant information is found in Essentials pages 774-775.

▲ Activities and tours

Pasto *p872*
Every Sun paddle ball is played on the edge of the town (bus marked 'San Lorenzo') similar to the game played in Ibarra, Ecuador.

⊙ Transport

Pasto *p872*
Air Daily with Satena to **Bogotá**, 3 a week to **Cali** and **Puerto Asís**. The airport is at Cano, 40 km from Pasto; by colectivo (beautiful drive), 45 mins, US$2.40 or US$13.50 by taxi. There are no currency exchange facilities, but the shop will change US$ bills at a poor rate.
Bus All interurban buses leave from the new terminal, Cra 6, C 16, 4 km from centre, taxi, US$1. To **Bogotá**, 18-23 hrs, US$35 (Bolivariano Pullman most direct, recommended). To **Ipiales**, 2 hrs, US$3, sit on the left for the views. To **Popayán**, ordinary buses take 10-12 hrs, US$7; expresses take 5-8 hrs, cost US$11. To **Cali**, US$11, expresses, 8½ to 10 hrs. To **Tumaco**, 9 hrs by bus, 7 hrs by minibus, US$10.

Around Volcán Galeras: Túquerres *p873*
Bus To **Pasto** US$4.50, 2 hrs, Trans Ipiales; jeep to **Ipiales** from Carrera 14, C 20, US$2, 1½ hrs.

Tumaco *p873*
Air There are daily flights to and from **Cali**, 40 mins, and **Medellín** with Satena.
Bus To **Pasto**, 6-9 hrs, US$11, with Supertaxis del Sur or Trans Ipiales, 4 a day, interesting ride; minibus 7 hrs. From Ipiales go to El Espino (US$0.75, colectivo, US$1.15) and there change buses for Tumaco (US$4.80).

Border with Ecuador: Tumaco *p873*
Boat Daily service at 1200 (times change) to **San Lorenzo**, 7 hrs (but can take 14) tickets from C del Comercio (protective plastic sheeting provided). Ask around the water-front at 0600, or try at the fishing centre, El Coral del Pacífico for a cheaper passage, but seek advice on safety before taking a boat (robberies reported). Fares: motorized canoe US$25; launch US$56.

The Putumayo: Laguna La Cocha *p873*
Taxi To La Cocha from **Pasto**, US$9, or colectivo from C 20 y Cra 20. Also you can take a **bus** to El Encano and walk the remaining 5 km to the chalets of Chalet Guamuez, or 20 mins from bus stop direct to lake shore and take a *lancha* to the chalets for US$3.

Ipiales *p874*
Air San Luis airport is 6½ km out of town. Aires and Satena to **Medellín**, **Bogotá** and **Puerto Asís**. Taxi to Ipiales centre, US$4.
Bus Bus companies have their individual departure points: *busetas/colectivos* mostly leave from the main plaza. To **Popayán**, Expreso Bolivariano, US$12, 7½-8 hrs, hourly departures, 0800-2000; also colectivo taxis, US$14-16. Expreso Bolivariano to **Cali**, US$15, 10-12 hrs. To **Pasto** US$3.50, 2-3 hrs. Frequent buses to **Bogotá** every 2 hrs, 20-24 hrs, US$35 (check if you have to change buses in Cali). To **Medellín**, 2 daily, 20-22 hrs, US$33. To **Túquerres**, 2 hrs, US$4.50.

Border with Ecuador: Ipiales *p874*
Bus From Ipiales to **Tulcán:** *colectivo* from C 14 y Cra 11, US$0.60 to the border (buses to Ipiales arrive at the main plaza – they may take you closer to the colectivo point if you ask). Colectivo from border to **Tulcán** US$0.70, to Tulcán bus station, US$1. Ask the fare at border tourist office. To go to bus terminal, take blue bus from central plaza, US$0.05. Easiest to take a taxi from Ipiales to the border, US$3.
Car If entering Colombia by car, the vehicle is supposed to be fumigated against diseases that affect coffee trees, at the ICA office. The certificate must be presented in El Pedregal, 40 km beyond Ipiales on the road to Pasto. (This fumigation process is not always carried out.) You can buy insurance for your car in Colombia at Banco Agrario, in the plaza.

⊙ Directory

Pasto *p872*
Banks For changing TCs, Bancolombia, C 19, No 24-52. Visa advances. Banco de Bogotá will change TCs 0930-1130. If going to Tumaco, this is the last place where TCs can be cashed. *Casas de cambio*, Titan, Cra 26, No 18-71, at Cra 25, No 18-97, and C 19, No 24-86, by the main plaza.
Post offices Cra 23, 18-42. **Telephones** Long distance calls, C 17 y Cra 23. **Useful addresses** DAS: C 17, No 29-70, T731 3981/1500, will give exit stamps if you are going on to Ecuador.

Ipiales *p874*
Banks It is not possible to cash TCs, but cash against Visa is no problem at Bancolombia, C 14, No 5-32. *Casa de Cambio* on the plaza. Money changers on street, in plaza and at border, but they may take advantage if the banks are closed. Coming from Ecuador, peso rates compare well in Ipiales with elsewhere in Colombia. **Telephones** International calls from Cra 6 y C 6/7.

Leticia and the Amazon

The extensive cattle lands from the Cordillera Central to the Orinoco are a good place to get away from it all in the dry season. Leticia, Colombia's port on the Amazon, is on the southern tip of a spur of territory which gives Colombia access to the great river, 3,200 km upstream from the Atlantic. There is a land border with Brazil a short distance to the east beyond which are Marco and Tabatinga. Directly south across the river is another important Brazilian port, Benjamin Constant, which is close to the border with Peru. On the north side of the Amazon, Colombia has a frontage on the river of 80 km to the land border with Peru.

Leticia → *Phone code: 9859. Colour map 3, grid A5. Population: 23,000. Altitude: 82 m.*

Capital of Amazonas Department, the city is clean, modern, though run down near the river. Parque Santander y Orellana is pleasant and is a popular meeting place. It is rapidly merging into one town with neighbouring Marco in Brazil. There is a modern, well-equipped hospital. The best time to visit the area is in July or August, the early months of the dry season. At weekends, accommodation may be difficult to find. Leticia is a good place to buy typical products of Amazon *indígenas* (for example *Artesanías Betel* in Centro Comercial Canoa), and tourist services are better than in Tabatinga or Benjamin Constant. The **Museo Etnográfico del Hombre Amazónico** *Cra 11 y Calle 9*, has local ethnography and archaeology, in a beautiful building with a library and a terrace overlooking the Amazon. For the border with Brazil, Colombia and Peru all information is given in the Brazil chapter, page 557, where Colombian, Brazilian and Peruvian procedures are detailed in one section. The **tourist office** is at ⓘ *C 10, No 9-86*. **Note:** There is an obligatory US$6 environment tax payable upon arrival in Leticia. You may also be asked for a yellow fever inoculation certificate on arrival; if you do not have this, an inoculation will be administered on the spot (not recommended).

Jungle trips from Leticia

Monkey Island Visits can be made to Yagua and Ticuna Indians. There are not many monkeys on the island now, those left are semi-tame. Agencies run overnight tours with full board.

Parque Nacional Amacayacu *0700-1700, US10 for foreigners*, 60 km upstream, at the mouth of the Matamata Creek. There is a jungle walk to a lookout (guides will point out plants, including those to avoid) and a rope bridge over the forest canopy, with wonderful views over the surrounding jungle (US$8). Boats go to a nearby island to see Victoria Regia water lilies. Accommodation in Parque Amacayacu is managed by Aviatur ⓘ *C 7, No 10-78, T592 6814 in Leticia (helpful) or T234 7333 (Bogotá)* The Leticia office will also give information and arrange transport to the park.

Puerto Nariño A small, attractive settlement on the Río Loretoyacu, a tributary of the Amazon, beyond the Parque Nacional Amacayacu. Where the two rivers meet is a popular place to watch dolphins. Tours include fishing, visits to *indígenas* and caiman watching.

● Sleeping

Leticia *p877*
AL Anaconda, Cra 11, No 7-34, T27119, www.hotel anaconda.com.co. Large a/c rooms, hot water, restaurant, good terrace and swimming pool.
AL Parador Ticuna, Av Libertador (Cra 11), No 6-11, T27243. Spacious apartments, hot water, a/c, sleep up to 6, swimming pool, bar and restaurant.
B Yurupary, C 8, No 7-26, T24743. A/c, TV.
C-D Residencias Fernando, Cra 9, No 8-80, T27362. Well-equipped, central, cheaper with fan. Recommended.
D Los Delfines, Cra 11, No 12-85, in front of fire station, T27388. Small, family atmosphere, spacious rooms, hammocks, patio.

D-E Mochillero/Casa de Viajeros, Cra 5, No 9-117, T25491, 310-604 0111 (mob). Good traveller hostel, hammocks, terrace with open air shower, quiet, laundry and kitchen facilities, private rooms and dorm. Speak to Javier about jungle trips.

Jungle trips from Leticia *p877*
Parque Nacional Amacayacu
Range of accommodation for 51 people. All prices given are in low season pp and include 2 meals (breakfast and dinner). Clean cabins with beds, US$23-45, private and or shared bath, and hammocks, US$18, suites (3 private rooms with bath), US$60, small handicraft shop run by the

local indigenous communities, restaurant and cafeteria. No camping allowed because of snakes.

Puerto Nariño
B Casa Selva, regularly used by tour groups, a/c.
E pp El Alto del Aguila, 20 mins' walk, 5 mins by boat. Comfortable cabins, trips arranged. Owner Hector (missionary and schoolteacher) is a good source of information.
E Brisas del Amazonas, charming location, simple rooms.

🍴 Eating

Leticia *p877*
Several small sidewalk restaurants downtown, serving good value *platos del día*. Cheap food (fried banana and meat, also fish and pineapples) is sold at the market near the harbour. Also cheap fruit for sale. Many café/bars overlook the market on the river bank. Take your own drinking water.
🍴 **Aquarias**, C 8 y Cra 7. Popular, restaurant/bar, good typical food.
🍴 **Tierras Amazónicas**, C 8, No 7-50. Also popular, restaurant/bar, good typical food.
🍴-🍴 **Sancho Panza**, Cra 10, No 8-72. Good value, good meat dishes, big portions, Brazilian beer.

🚶 Activities and tours

Leticia *p877*
If you choose to go on an organized tour, do not accept the first price and check that the equipment and supplies are sufficient for the length of the tour. The following tours are available: to Monkey Island; to Benjamin Constant to see a rubber plantation, 8 hrs; 3-6 day trips to visit indigenous communities with *Amazon Jungle Trips*, price depends on number of people in group. Companies include:
Amaturs, in lobby of *Hotel Anaconda*.
Amazon Jungle Trips, Av Internacional, No 6-25, T27377, amazonjungletrips@yahoo.com. Tailor-made packages (groups of up to 6 people), to visit Indian communities and trips along the Río Javary, stay at lodge owned by agency, US$70 per day all inclusive (food, transport, accommodation, pick ups from airport/hotel). Speak to owner Antonio (speaks English), well-organized.

Independent guides
Many guides can be found at the riverfront. They may be cheaper and better than organized groups, but you must seek advice about reputations and fix a firm price before setting out. The cheaper the guide, usually the less experienced he will be. Check that adequate first aid is taken and whether rubber boots are provided (or buy your own in Leticia, US$5-6). Recommended are:
Luis Daniel González (Cra 8, No 9-93, Apdo Aéreo 256, Leticia), or through *Residencias Fernando*. He is often to be found at the airport, knowledgeable, speaks Spanish, Portuguese, English, and runs various tours.
Luis Fernando Valera, T310-866 0124 (mob), contact through *Hotel Anaconda*. Experienced, he is often to be found at the airport, knowledgeable, speaks Spanish, Portuguese, English, and runs various tours.

⊖ Transport

Leticia *p877*
Air Airport is 1½ km from town, taxi US$2.40; small terminal, few facilities. Taxi direct to Brazilian immigration (Police Station) US$8. Expect to be searched before leaving Leticia airport, and on arrival in Bogotá from Leticia. **Aero República** flies to Leticia (Tabatinga airport if Leticia's is closed) from **Bogotá**, daily, about US$120 one way. Satena has several flights to local Amazonas destinations. **AeroSucre** allows passengers on its daily cargo flights Bogotá-Leticia, US$75. Go to their terminal about 3 km before the international airport in Bogotá (huge sign) and speak to the flight captain (no one else) 30 mins before take-off. Price is not negotiable and schedule changes each day, but usually at 0600. Regular minibus to Tabatinga, US$0.80.

Jungle trips from Leticia *p877*
Parque Nacional Amacayacu
Boat From Leticia US$1 one way, 2 hrs; 2 operators (check that your operator also runs the day you wish to return). *Rápido* launches leave the wharf (Puerto Civil) daily 1000 and 1400.

Puerto Nariño
Boat 2-hr trips from **Leticia** daily at 1000 and 1400 cost US$11.

⊙ Directory

Leticia *p877*
Banks There are street money changers, plenty of *cambios*, and banks for exchange. Shop around. TCs cannot be changed at weekends, and are hard to change at other times, but try Banco de Bogotá. **Internet** Very few places, slow connections. **Post offices** Adpostal, C 8, No 9-65, T592 7977.
Telephones Cra 11, near Parque Santander. **Useful addresses** DAS, C9, No 9-62, T24878, secamaadm@das.gov.co.

Ecuador

✷ Footprint features

Introduction

Tucked in between Peru and Colombia, this country is small enough for you to have breakfast with scarlet macaws in the jungle, lunch in the lee of a snow-capped peak and, at tea time, be eyeballed by an iguana whose patch of Pacific beach you have just borrowed.

A multitude of national parks and conservation areas emphasise the incredible variety of Ecuador. They include mangroves; an avenue of volcanoes – many of them active – striding across the Equator; forests growing on the dry Pacific coast, in the clouds and under the Amazonian rains; not forgetting all the animals and birds which flourish in these habitats. The capital, Quito, has become one of the gringo centres of South America, bursting at the seams with language schools, travel agencies and restaurants. The last remaining segment of the line from Quito to the Pacific port of Guayaquil, with spectacular zig-zags and switchbacks, is a highpoint of railway engineering. The exotic wildlife of the Galápagos Islands will also keep you enthralled, whether it's sympathizing with Lonesome George, the last giant tortoise of his race, watching an albatross take off on its flight path, or admiring the sexual paraphernalia of the magnificent frigate bird. If the Galápagos are beyond your budget, the Isla de la Plata is a more accessible alternative for seeing marine life.

★ Don't miss...

1 **Quito** The old centre is a World Heritage treasure trove of colonial art and architecture, while the new city is one of the places to which gringos gravitate to learn Spanish and get their bearings, page 889.
2 **Otavalo** This little town north of Quito is home to one of the largest and most colourful craft markets in South America, page 918.
3 **Nariz del Diablo** Although earthquakes and shortage of money have taken their toll on the famous railway from Quito to Guayaquil, one section is still run regularly. This, fortunately, is the part with the most amazing engineering and drama, page 949.
4 **Vilcabamba** In the far south of the Ecuadorean Andes is the fabled fountain of youth. Whether you'll live longer for going there or not, it's a great place to relax, or escape to the hills on foot or horseback, page 968.
5 **Northern jungles** Coca is the gateway to the northern Oriente, with some excellent lodges in the Yasuní National Park and the Cuyabeno Wildlife Reserve. Boating down a tributary of the Amazon to enter the rainforest is a great experience, page 1000.
6 **Galápagos Islands** Quite simply one of the world's most remarkable places, a sanctuary for wildlife that has evolved its own unique speciation and temperament. A visit here will surely be one of the highlights of a lifetime, page 1013.

Essentials

Planning your trip

Where to go The capital, **Quito**, boasts some of the best-preserved colonial architecture in South America in its 'Old Town', while the 'New City' is where you'll find most accommodation, restaurants, tour operators and language schools. From the capital many of the country's attractions are accessible by road in only a few hours. Day trips include nature reserves, hot springs, and, of course, the Equator. There is also good mountaineering and white-water rafting nearby. North of Quito is **Otavalo** with its outstanding handicrafts market, a regular one-day tour, but equally popular as a base for exploring nearby villages, more nature reserves and hiking or cycling routes. Carrying on towards the Colombian border is **Ibarra**, another good centre for visiting the north and the starting point for the journey to San Lorenzo on the Pacific.

In the Central Sierra, south of Quito is the national park surrounding **Cotopaxi**, one of Ecuador's most frequently climbed volcanoes. Further south is the **Quilotoa circuit**, a 200 km loop through small villages and beautiful landscapes, with lots of possibilities for trekking, cycling and riding. The starting point is Latacunga on the Pan-American Highway. On one of the main routes from the Sierra to the eastern jungle is **Baños**, a very popular spa town with climbing, hiking, riding and volcano watching opportunities close at hand. The heart of the central highlands is **Riobamba**, beneath Chimborazo volcano. This is another good base for climbing, biking and trekking, as well as the starting point for a very popular railway ride over La Nariz del Diablo (The Devil's Nose) – when the often-damaged line is open. The Inca ruin of **Ingapirca** is between Riobamba and **Cuenca**, a lovely colonial city in the Southern Sierra. Nearby is the Cajas National Park. En route from Cuenca towards Peru are the provincial capital of **Loja**, close to the Parque Nacional Podocarpus, and **Vilcabamba**, with a delightful climate and a favourite with backpackers. Several border crossings to Peru are accessible from Loja.

Ecuador's Pacific capital is **Guayaquil**, 45 minutes by air from Quito (eight hours by bus) and only four hours by bus south to the Peruvian border via Machala. It is the main jumping-off point for flights to the Galápagos. To the north stretch the **Pacific Lowlands** with beaches, pre-Columbian archaeological sites and peaceful little low-key resorts like Puerto López, Montañita, Canoa and Muisne, as well as a few highly developed ones like Bahía de Caráquez and Atacames. Near Puerto López the **Parque Nacional Machalilla** contains dry tropical forest, offshore islands and marine ecosystems. It is a good place for riding, diving, whale watching, birdwatching and relaxing on the beautiful Los Frailes beach.

The **Oriente** (eastern lowlands) offers good opportunities for nature tourism, with a number of specially designed jungle lodges, mainly in the north. A stay in one of these places is best booked in Quito or from home, but you can head for jungle towns like Coca, Lago Agrio, Tena, Puyo or Misahuallí to arrange a tour with a local agency or guide. The southern Oriente is less developed for tourism, but interest is growing, with Macas or Zamora as the places to aim for.

Ecuador is famous for its **hot springs** and, on either side of the Andes, there is great birdwatching in a wide variety of protected areas. Other special interest activities include diving, whitewater rafting and various volunteer programmes. The nature destination par excellence, though, is the **Galápagos Islands**, 970 km west of the mainland. Tours can be arranged in Quito, Guayaquil and from home, but if you have time and are on a more limited budget, last minute deals can sometimes be found in Puerto Ayora on Santa Cruz Island.

When to go Ecuador's climate is highly unpredictable. As a general rule, however, in the **Sierra**, there is little variation by day or by season in the temperature: this depends on altitude. The range of shade temperature is from 6°C to 10°C in the morning to 19°C to 23°C in the afternoon, though it can get considerably hotter in the lower basins. Rainfall patterns depend on whether a particular area is closer to the eastern or western slopes of the Andes. To the west, June to September are dry and October to May are wet (but there is sometimes a short dry spell in December or January). To the east, October to February are dry and March to September are wet. There is also variation in annual rainfall from north to south, with the southern highlands being drier. **Quito** is within 25 km of the Equator, but it stands high enough to make its climate much like that of spring in England, the days pleasantly warm and the nights cool. Rainy season is October to May with the heaviest rainfall in April. Rain usually falls in the afternoon. The day length (sunrise to sunset) is almost constant throughout the year.

Along the **Pacific coast**, rainfall also decreases from north to south, so that it can rain throughout the year in northern Esmeraldas and seldom at all near the Peruvian border. The coast, however, can be enjoyed year-round, although it may be a bit cool from June to November, when mornings are often grey with the *garúa* mists. January to May is the hottest and rainiest time of the year. Like the coast the **Galápagos** suffer from the *garúa* from May to December; from January to April the islands are hottest and brief but heavy showers can fall. In the **Oriente**, heavy rain can fall at any time, but it is usually wettest from March to September.

Ecuador's **high season** is from June to early September, which is also the best time for climbing and trekking. There is also a short tourist season in December and January. In resort areas at major fiestas, such as Carnival, Semana Santa and over New Year, accommodation can be hard to find. Hotels will be full in individual towns during their particular festivals, but Ecuador as a whole is not overcrowded at any time of the year.

Finding out more Ministerio de Turismo ① *Eloy Alfaro N32-300 Carlos Tobar, Quito, T250 7559, www.vivecuador.com.* Local offices are given in the text. Outside Ecuador, tourist information can be obtained from Ecuadorean Embassies. National parks, of which Ecuador has an outstanding array, are controlled by the **Ministerio del Ambiente** ① *Ministerio de Agricultura y Ganadería building, p 8, Amazonas y Eloy Alfaro, Quito, T250 6337.* The ministry has less information than the park offices in the cities nearest the parks themselves.

Websites

Www.ecuadorexplorer.com;www.ecuadortou rsonline.com; and www.ecuaworld.com are all travel guides.
www.saexplorers.org South American Explorers has information about how to become a member, the club's services and volunteering. See page 889 for address.

www.explored.com.ec General information about Ecuador in Spanish, including a guide to national parks.
www.quitogay.net Gay information.
www.thebestofecuador.com/volunt.htm Vo lunteering ideas page on a comprehensive guide to the country.

Maps and guide books Instituto Geográfico Militar (IGM) ① *Senierges y Tello Paz y Miño, Quito, T02-222 9075, www.igm.gov.ec, map sales room open Mon-Thu 0800-1600, Mon-Fri 0800-1300.* They sell country maps and topographic maps, covering most areas of Ecuador, in various scales, US$3 each. Maps of border areas and the seacoast are 'reservado' (classified) and not available for sale without a military permit (requires extra time). Buy your maps here, they are rarely available outside Quito. If one is sold out you may order a photocopy. Map and geographic reference libraries are located next to the sales room. The *IGM* is on top of the hill to the east of El Ejido park. From 12 de Octubre, opposite the *Casa de la Cultura*, take Jiménez (a small street) up the hill. After crossing Av Colombia continue uphill on Paz y Miño behind the Military Hospital and then turn right to the guarded main entrance; you have to deposit your passport or identification card. There is a beautiful view from the grounds. A good series of road maps, pocket maps and city guides by Nélson Gómez, published by **Ediguías** in Quito, are available in book shops throughout the country.

Visas and immigration All visitors to Ecuador must have a passport valid for at least six months and an onward or return ticket. The latter is seldom asked for, but can be grounds for refusal of entry. Citizens of the following countries do not require a visa to visit Ecuador as tourists: EU countries, North and South American countries (except Guyana, Suriname and Mexico), Australia, Israel, South Africa and Switzerland; contact your embassy for further details. New Zealanders apparently do need a visa, even though the Ministry of Foreign Relations website says they do not; check with an Ecuadorean consulate before arrival. Note that members of the Sikh religion, irrespective of nationality, may need a visa and should check with an Ecuadorean consulate before travelling. Upon entry all visitors must complete an international embarkation/disembarkation card, which is stamped along with your passport. Keep this card with your passport, losing it can cause all manner of grief when leaving the country.

Warning: you are required by Ecuadorean law to carry your passport at all times. Failure to do so can result in imprisonment and/or deportation. An ordinary photocopy of your passport is not an acceptable substitute and you will generally not be permitted to return

Touching down

Airport tax International flights at Quito airport US$31.60, US$25 at Guayaquil. 12% tax on air tickets for flights originating in Ecuador.
Business hours Banks Mon-Fri 0900-1600, cash advance and exchange limited hours, best in the morning. **Government offices** variable hours Mon-Fri, but most close for lunch. **Other offices** 0900-1230, 1430-1800. **Shops** 0900-1900; close at midday in smaller towns, open till 2100 on the coast.
International phone code: +593

In an emergency Police: 911 in Quito and Cuenca, 101 elsewhere.
Official time GMT -5 (Galápagos, -6).
Tipping In restaurants 10% included in the bill. In cheaper restaurants, tipping is uncommon but welcome. It is not expected in taxis. Airport porters, US$0.50-1, according to number of cases.
VAT/IVA 12%.
Voltage AC throughout, 110 volts, 60 cycles. Sockets are for twin flat blades, sometimes with a round earth pin.
Weights and measures Metric.

to your hotel to fetch the original document. A photocopy certified by your embassy or the immigration police may be acceptable, but you should also have your original passport close at hand. Tourists are not permitted to work under any circumstances.

Length of stay Tourists are entitled to visit Ecuador for up to 90 days during any 12 month period. This may be extended, at the discretion of the **Policía Nacional de Migración**. In practice, those travelling by land from Peru or Colombia are seldom granted more than 30 days on arrival, but this can usually be extended. When arriving at Quito or Guayaquil airport you will be asked how long you plan to stay. If you have no idea, ask for 90 days.

Extensions Extensions up to 90 days total stay may only be requested at the following locations: in Quito at the **Jefatura Provincial de Migración de Pichincha** ① *Isla Seymour 44-174 y Río Coca, T/F02-224 7510*. (**Note**: this is not the same as the *Dirección Nacional de Migración* listed below); in Guayaquil at the **Jefatura Provincial de Migración del Guayas** ① *Av Río Daule, near the* terminal terrestre, *T04-229 7010*; in Cuenca at the **Jefatura Provincial de Migración del Azuay** ① *Av Ordóñez Lazo y Los Cipreses, Edificio Astudillo*; in Baños, at Halflants y Rocafuerte, T03-274 0122; in Ibarra, Olmedo y LF Villamar, T06-295 1712; and in Puerto Baquerizo Moreno at the Jefatura Provincial de Migración de Galápagos, *at Charles Darwin y Española, T05-252 0129*. Extensions beyond 90 days and immigration problems may require a visit to immigration police headquarters in Quito: **Dirección Nacional de Migración** ① *Amazonas 171 y República, T245 4122*. The above offices are open Monday to Friday 0800- 1230 and 1500-1830. Immigration offices in provincial capitals other than the above can grant tourist visa extensions, but may not know the procedures. Obtaining an extension can take less than an hour, but do not leave it to the last minute. If you overstay your visa, you will be fined US$200. Regulations are subject to change. Polite conduct and a neat appearance are important.

Tourists attending a course at a language school do **not** need a student visa (unless staying more than 180 days). There are many options for foreigners who wish to stay in Ecuador longer than six months, but if you enter as a tourist you cannot change your status while in the country.

Note: In addition to your passport, all international travellers must carry an **international vaccination certificate**, although it is seldom asked for. An **International Student Identity Card (ISIC)** may help you obtain discounts when travelling. ISIC cards are sold in Quito by **Grupo Idiomas** ① *Roca 130 y 12 de Octubre, p 2, T250 0264*. They need a certificate from your university (minimum enrollment 20 hours/week), 2 photos and US$12.

Ecuadorean embassies and consulates For a complete list, visit www.mmrree.gov.ec.

Money The **US dollar** is the only official currency of Ecuador. Only US$ bills circulate. US coins are used alongside the equivalent size and value Ecuadorean coins. Ecuadorean coins have no value outside the country. Many establishments are reluctant to accept bills larger than US$20 because of counterfeit notes or lack of change. Counterfeit US$1 and Ecuadorean

50 cents coins also circulate, so check any bills and coins they receive as change. There is no substitute for cash-in-hand when travelling in Ecuador. Euros are slowly gaining acceptance, but **US$ cash** in small denominations is by far the simplest and the only universally accepted option. All other currencies are very difficult to exchange and fetch a very poor rate.

Plastic/traveller's cheques/banks (ATMs) The most commonly accepted credit cards are Visa, MasterCard, Diners and American Express. They can be used to obtain a cash advance at some branches of some banks. For large cash advances on any credit card, go to **Banco del Pacífico** on Naciones Unidas in Quito (see page 908). Most other banks and branches have a US$500 limit. Paying by credit card at most upscale establishments may incur a surcharge (at least 10%). MasterCard holders can obtain cash advances at the company's offices in Quito, Guayaquil, Cuenca and Ambato. Those with Visa cards can obtain cash advances at some branches of *Banco de Guayaquil* and *Banco del Pichincha*. Banks are increasingly discouraging the use of **traveller's cheques** and commissions are rising (it takes 8-15 days for the bank to be reimbursed by the issuing organization). TCs are still a good idea for emergency use, but the move is definitely towards credit cards and ATMs. Internationally linked **ATMs** are common, although they cannot always be relied on. The affiliations of banks to the Plus and Cirrus systems change often, so ask around. Debit cards are less easy to use. American Express has offices in Quito and Guayaquil; they sell TCs against an Amex card (or a cardholder's personal cheque) and replace lost or stolen TCs, but they do not give cash for TCs, nor TCs for cash. Their service is very efficient; a police report is required if TCs are stolen.

Funds may be rapidly wired to Ecuador by *Western Union*, but high fees and taxes apply. International bank transfers, however, are not recommended.

Cost of living/travelling Despite dollarization, prices remain modest by international standards and Ecuador is still affordable for even the budget traveller. A very basic daily travel

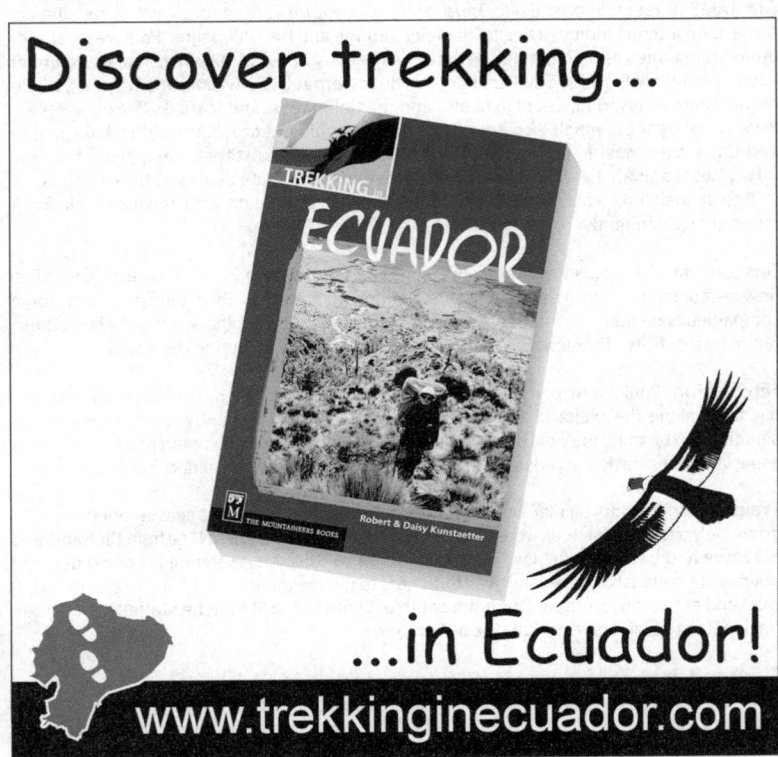

budget in 2006 was US$15-20 per person based on two travelling together. For US$50 a day you can enjoy a good deal of comfort. Internet use is about US$0.60-2 per hour.

Safety Urban street crime, bag snatching and slashing, and robbery along the country's highways are the most significant hazards. In an effort to fight crime, army and police patrols operate in some cities and along some highways. Don't be taken aback to see these troops on duty. Secure your belongings, be wary of con tricks, avoid crowds and travel during the daytime. The countryside and small towns are generally safest, but theft and robbery have been reported from several places where tourists gather. It is the big cities, Guayaquil, Quito, and to a lesser extent Cuenca, which call for the greatest care. The coast is more prone to violence than the highlands, and the northern border with Colombia, including the provinces of Esmeraldas, Carchi, and especially Sucumbíos, call for additional precautions. Armed conflict in Colombia has caused an influx of refugees, and parts of these provinces have come under the influence of insurgents. Enquire locally before travelling to and in any northern border areas.

Occasional social unrest is part of life in Ecuador and you should not overreact. Strikes and protests are usually announced days or weeks in advance, and their most significant impact on tourists is the restriction of travel. Activities in towns and especially the countryside often go on as usual. Stay put at such times and make the most of visiting nearby attractions, rather than trying stick to your original itinerary or returning to Quito – the situation will soon blow over. **Drugs use or purchase in Ecuador is punishable by up to 16 years' imprisonment**.

Ecuador's active volcanoes are spectacular, but have occasionally threatened nearby communities. The following have shown visible activity in recent years: Reventador northeast of Quito, Tungurahua near Baños, and Sangay southeast of Riobamba. Cotopaxi is also active. The **National Geophysics Institute** provides updates at **www.igepn.edu.ec**.

Getting around

Air TAME ① *reservations: Quito T290 9900, Guayaquil T269 2500, www.tame.com.ec*, is the main internal airline, flying to all major airports and the Galápagos. Enquire locally for up-to- date routes and timetables as they change constantly. TAME offices are listed under each relevant town or city. Smaller airlines include **Aerogal**, ① *www.aerogal.com.ec*, which serves Quito, Guayaquil, Cuenca, Manta and the Galápagos; and **Icaro** ① *T1-800-883567, www.ic aro.com.ec*, which flies from Quito to Guayaquil, Cuenca, Esmeraldas, Loja, Manta and Coca. Icaro has a cheap flight Monday-Friday to San Cristóbal, Galápagos, but only luxury boats operate here. For cheap boats or to find last-minute deals you have to add on a US$30 launch ride each way to get to Puerto Ayora. Confirm and reconfirm all flight reservations frequently.

Bus Bus travel is generally more convenient and regular than in other Andean countries. Several companies use comfortable air-conditioned buses on their longer routes; some companies have their own stations, away from the main bus terminals, exclusively for these better buses. **Note**: Throughout Ecuador, travel by bus is safest during the daytime.

Hitchhiking Public transport in Ecuador is so abundant that there is seldom any need to hitchhike along the major highways. On small out-of-the-way country roads however, the situation can be quite the opposite, and giving passers-by a ride is common practice and safe, especially in the back of a pickup or truck. A small fee is usually charged, check in advance.

Train Sadly, the spectacular Ecuadorean railway system has all but ceased operations. In 2006, only a few tourist rides were still being offered: over the Devil's Nose from **Riobamba to Sibambe** and back, and the lowland route **Huigra to Bucay** is operating on weekends and holidays (the Alausí to Huigra link was rumoured to be operating for the 2006 high season). A weekend excursion runs from **Tambillo, south of Quito to the El Boliche station** near Parque Nacional Cotopaxi, and a **45-km ride out of Ibarra**.

Sleeping → *See inside front cover for our hotel grade price guide.*
Hotels Outside the provincial capitals and a few resorts, there are few higher-class hotels. Service of 10% and tax of 12% are added to better hotel and restaurant bills. The cheaper hotels are beginning to apply the 12% tax, but check if it is included. Larger towns and tourist centres

🔹 Driving in Ecuador

Roads A good network of paved roads runs throughout the coast and highlands. Maintenance of major highways is franchised to private firms, who charge tolls of US$0.50-1. In the Oriente, most roads are dirt or gravel; some that appear paved are in fact crude oil sprayed onto compacted earth.

Safety Unexpected potholes and other obstructions, the lack of road signs, and local drivers' tendency to use the middle of the road make driving 'an experience'. Beware the bus drivers, who often drive very fast and rather recklessly. Driving at night is not recommended.

Documents Obtaining temporary admission to Ecuador for a car or motorcycle can be complex and time-consuming, as is shipping in a vehicle, especially through Guayaquil. A *carnet de passages* is an official requirement, but this rule is not consistently applied. Some drivers without it have been allowed to stay in the country, others have had to pass through to the Peruvian or Colombian border in three days. A valid driver's licence from your home country is generally sufficient to drive in Ecuador and rent a car, but an international driving licence is helpful.

Car hire To rent a car you must be 21 and have an international credit card. Surcharges may apply to clients aged 21-25. You may pay cash, which is cheaper and may allow you to bargain, but they want a credit card for security. You may be asked to sign two blank credit card vouchers, one for the rental fee itself and the other as a security deposit, and authorization for a charge of as much as US$3,500 may be requested against your credit card account. The uncashed vouchers will be returned to you when you return the vehicle, but the credit authorization may persist on your account (reducing your credit limit) for up to 30 days. Make sure the car is parked securely at night. A small car suitable for city driving costs around US$350 per week including tax and insurance. A 4WD (recommended for the Oriente and unpaved roads) can be more than twice as much.

Fuel There are two grades of petrol, 'Extra' (82 octane, US$1.48 per US gallon) and 'Super' (92 Octane, US$1.98). Both are unleaded. Extra is available everywhere, while Super may not be available in more remote areas. Diesel fuel (US$1.03) is notoriously dirty and available everywhere.

Ecuador Essentials

often have more hotels than we can list. This is especially true of Quito. The hotels that are included are among the best in each category, selected to provide a variety of locations and styles. Many hotel rooms have very low wattage bulbs, keen readers are advised to take a head torch.

Camping Camping in protected natural areas can be one of the most satisfying experiences during a visit to Ecuador. Organized campsites, car or trailer camping on the other hand are virtually unheard-of. Because of the abundance of cheap hotels you should never *have to* camp in Ecuador, except for cyclists who may be stuck between towns. In this case the best strategy is to ask permission to camp on someone's private land, preferably within sight of their home for safety. It is not safe to pitch your tent at random near villages and even less so on beaches. *Bluet Camping Gas* is easily obtainable, but white gas, like US Coleman fuel, is hard to find. Unleaded petrol (gasoline) is available everywhere and may be an alternative for some stoves.

Eating → *See inside front cover for our Eating price guide.*
Eating out Upmarket restaurants add 22% to the bill, 12% tax plus 10% service. All other places add the 12% tax, which is also charged on non-essential items in food shops. The cuisine varies with region. The following are some typical dishes.

In the highlands *Locro de papas* (potato and cheese soup), *mote* (corn burst with alkali, a staple in the region around Cuenca, but used in a variety of dishes in the Sierra), *caldo de patas* (cowheel soup with *mote*), *llapingachos* (fried potato and cheese patties), *empanadas de morocho* (fried snacks: a ground corn shell filled with meat), *sancocho de yuca* (vegetable soup with manioc root), roast *cuy* (guinea pig), *fritada* (fried pork), *hornado* (roast pork), *humitas* (tender ground corn steamed in corn leaves), and *quimbolitos* (similar to *humitas* but prepared with corn flour and steamed in *achira* lily leaves). *Humitas* and *quimbolitos* come in both sweet and savoury varieties.

On the coast *Empanadas de verde* (fried snacks: a ground plantain shell filled with cheese, meat or shrimp), *sopa de bola de verde* (plantain dumpling soup), *ceviche* (marinaded fish or seafood, popular everywhere, see below), *encocadas* (dishes prepared with coconut milk, may be shrimp, fish, etc, very popular in the province of Esmeraldas), *cocadas* (sweets made with coconut), *viche* (fish or seafood soup made with ground peanuts), and *patacones* (thick fried plantain chips served as a side dish).

In Oriente Dishes prepared with yuca (manioc or cassava root) and river fish.

Throughout the country If economizing ask for the set meal in restaurants, *almuerzo* at lunch time, *merienda* in the evening – very cheap and wholesome; it costs US$1.50-3. *Fanesca*, a fish soup with beans, many grains, ground peanuts and more, sold in Easter Week, is very filling (it is so popular that in Quito and main tourist spots it is sold throughout Lent). *Ceviche*, marinated fish or seafood which is usually served with popcorn and roasted maize (*tostado*), is very popular throughout Ecuador. Only *ceviche de pescado* (fish) and *ceviche de concha* (clams) which are marinated raw, potentially pose a health hazard. The other varieties of *ceviche* such as *camarón* (shrimp/prawn) and *langostino* (jumbo shrimp/king prawn) all of which are cooked before being marinated, are generally safe (check the cleanliness of the establishment). *Langosta* (lobster) is an increasingly endangered species but continues to be illegally fished; please be conscientious. Ecuadorean food is not particularly spicy. However, in most homes and restaurants, the meal is accompanied by a small bowl of *ají* (hot pepper sauce) which may vary in potency. *Colada* is a generic name which can refer to cream soups or sweet beverages. In addition to the prepared foods mentioned above, Ecuador offers a large variety of delicious fruits, some of which are unique to South America.

Drink The best fruit drinks are *naranjilla*, *maracuyá* (passion fruit), *tomate de árbol*, *piña* (pineapple), *taxo* (another variety of passion fruit) and *mora* (blackberry), but note that fruit juices are sometimes made with unboiled water. Main beers available are *Pilsener*, *Club*, *Biela*, *Brahma* and *Clausen*. Argentine and Chilean wines are available in the larger cities. Good *aguardiente* (unmatured rum, *Cristal* is recommended), also known as *puntas*, *trago de caña*, or just *trago*. The usual soft drinks, known as *colas*, are available. Instant coffee or liquid concentrate is common, so ask for *café pasado* if you want real coffee. In tourist centres and many upscale hotels and restaurants, good cappuccino and espresso can be found.

Festivals and events

1 January: New Year's Day; 6 January: Reyes Magos y Día de los Inocentes, a time for pranks, which closes the Christmas-New Year holiday season. 27 February: Día del Civismo, celebrating the victory over Peru at Tarqui in 1829. Carnival: Monday and Tuesday before Lent, celebrated everywhere in the Andes, except Ambato, by throwing water at passers-by: be prepared to participate. Easter: Holy Thursday, Good Friday, Holy Saturday. 1 May: Labour Day. 24 May: Battle of Pichincha, Independence. Early June: Corpus Christi. 24 July: Bolívar's birthday, some government offices close. 10 August: first attempt to gain the Independence of Quito. 9 October: Independence of Guayaquil. 12 October: Columbus' arrival in America. 2 November: All Souls' Day. 3 November: Independence of Cuenca. 6 December: Foundation of Quito. 25 December: Christmas Day.

Quito and around

→ Phone code: 02. Colour map 11, grid A4. Population: 1,399,378. Altitude: 2,850 m.

Few cities have a setting to match that of Quito, the second highest capital in Latin America after La Paz. The city is set in a hollow at the foot of the volcano Pichincha (4,794 m). The city's charm lies in its colonial centre – the Old City as it's known – a UNESCO World Heritage Site, where cobbled streets are steep and narrow, dipping to deep ravines. From the top of Cerro Panecillo, 183 m above the city level, there is a fine view of the city below and the encircling cones of volcanoes and other mountains.

North of the Old City is Modern Quito – or New City – with broad avenues lined with contemporary office buildings, fine private residences, parks, embassies and villas. Here you'll find Quito's main tourist and business area in the district known as Mariscal Sucre (or La Mariscal), bordered by Avenidas Amazonas, Patria, 12 de Octubre and Orellana.

Ins and outs

Getting there Mariscal Sucre airport is about 5 km north of the main hotel district. It is served by city buses, the trolley bus ('El Trole' – not designed for heavy luggage) and taxis (US$5 to the New City, US$6 to the Old City, recommended as the safest option). Most long-distance bus services arrive at the Terminal Terrestre at the junction of Maldonado and Cumandá, south of the Old City. It is safest to arrive and leave the terminal by taxi (US$4 to the New City), although the Cumandá stop of El Trole is nearby. Some luxury bus services run to their own offices in the New City. ▶▶ *For more detailed information, see Transport, page 906.*

Getting around Both the Old City and the New City can be explored on foot, but getting between the two requires some form of public transport, which is cheap and plentiful. The trolley bus (crowded at rush hour) runs north-south from Terminal Norte (north of the junction known as 'La Y') to Ciudadela Quitumbe. There are two parallel articulated-bus arteries, *La Ecovía*, mostly on Avenida 6 de Diciembre, running north-south from Río Coca to Plaza La Marín, and *Metrobus*, running north-south along Avenidas América and de la Prensa from La Ofelia to Santa Prisca. This is now the route to Mitad del Mundo, with a change of bus north of the airport. Robberies can occur on city buses and the Trole. Taxis are a cheap and efficient alternative; fares start at US$1, recommended at night. Authorized taxis display a unit number, driver's photograph and have a meter. **Note:** The Old City is closed to vehicles Sunday 0900-1600.

Orientation Most places of historical interest are in the Old City, while the majority of the hotels, restaurants, travel agencies and facilities for visitors are in the New City. In 1998, the city introduced a new street numbering system based on N (Norte), E (Este), S (Sur), Oe (Oeste), plus a number for each street and a number for each building. It has not been implemented for the whole city so both systems are in use.

Information Corporación Metropolitana de Turismo (*CMT*) ① *toll free T1-800-767767, www.quito.com.ec,* has information offices in the Old City at *Edificio El Cadisán, García Moreno N12-01 y Mejía, T257 2566,* at the airport *T330 0163,* in the New City in Parque Gabriela Mistral *Cordero y Reina Victoria, T255 1566,* and at the Museo Nacional del Banco Central in the *Casa de la Cultura, Av Patria y 6 de Diciembre, T222 1116.* Helpful and friendly, some staff speak English. The **Empresa de Desarrollo del Centro Histórico** ① *Pasaje Arzobispal at Plaza de la Independencia, ground floor, T258 6591, daily 0900-0000,* has an information office and a kiosk and runs walking tours of the colonial city, some English and French spoken. Tours last 2½-3 hours and cost US$5-10 (also horse-drawn carriage tours at night, US$12). The **Ministerio de Turismo** ① *Eloy Alfaro N32-300 Carlos Tobar (between República and Shyris), T250 7559, www.vivecuador.com, Mon-Fri 0830-1700,* has an information counter with brochures. Some staff speak English. **South American Explorers** ① *Jorge Washington 311 y Leonidas Plaza, Apdo 17-21-431, Eloy Alfaro, T/F222 5228, quitoclub@saexplorers.org, Mon-Fri 0930-1700, Sat 0900-1200.* Members may receive post and faxes, use internet and store gear. Local discounts with SAE card. They also have information on visiting non-Ecuadoreans in prisons. Prisoners rely on friends and families for support, so your help and gifts are much appreciated. Most have fallen foul of drugs laws. Take your passport, or a copy, and little of value.

Safety Efforts by the authorities have improved public safety in the city, but theft and armed robbery remain hazards. Both the Old City, apart from around Plaza Independencia, and the New City, including La Mariscal district, are dangerous after 2200 and pickpockets are active at all hours. Be careful on buses, the *Trole* and around the Terminal Terrestre. Always use taxis at night and whenever you are carrying anything of value. Do not walk through any city parks in the evening or in daylight at quiet times. **Tourist Police** ⓘ *HQ at Roca y Reina Victoria, T254 3983*, has information booths in La Mariscal and one at El Panecillo. Members of the **Policía Metropolitana**, who patrol the Old City on foot, speak some English and are very helpful.

Panecillo: neighbourhood brigades are patrolling the area, visitors are charged US$0.25 to finance this operation. Taking a taxi up is safer than walking up to the Virgin, which begins on García Moreno (where it meets Ambato). A taxi up and down with 30 minutes' wait costs US$5. Do not carry valuables and seek local advice before going on foot.

Despite efforts by the authorities, the city has a serious air and noise pollution problem. Because of the altitude, you may feel some discomfort, so slow your pace for the first 24 hours.

Sights

Old City

The heart of the Old City is **Plaza de la Independencia** or **Plaza Grande**, dominated by a somewhat grim **Cathedral** ⓘ *Mon-Sat, 1000-1600, Sun 1000-1400, US$1.50*, built 1550-1562, with grey stone porticos and green tile cupolas. On its outer walls are plaques listing the names of the founding fathers of Quito, and inside are the tomb of Sucre and a famous Descent from the Cross by the *indígena* painter Caspicara. There are many other 17th and 18th century paintings; the interior decoration shows Moorish influence. Facing the Cathedral is the **Palacio Arzobispal**, part of which now houses shops. Next to it, in the northwest corner, is the former **Hotel Majestic** (1930), with an eclectic façade, the first building in the old city with more than two storeys. It is being refurbished as a hotel (due to reopen late 2006 or 2007). On the northeast side is the concrete **Municipio**, which fits in quite well. The low colonial **Palacio de Gobierno** or **Palacio de Carondelet** ⓘ *visits with special permit only, Tue and Thu, 0930-1230, a written request must be presented several days in advance at the gate*, silhouetted against the flank of Pichincha, is on the northwest side of the Plaza. On the first floor is a gigantic mosaic mural of Orellana navigating the Amazon. The ironwork on the balconies looking over the main plaza is from the Tuilleries in Paris. You can only see the patio.

From Plaza de la Independencia two main streets, Venezuela and García Moreno, lead straight towards the Panecillo. Parallel with Venezuela is Calle Guayaquil, the main shopping street. These streets all run south from the main plaza to meet Calle Morales, or Calle La Ronda (after the district it's in), worth seeing for its cobbles and wrought-iron balconies. At night, though, it is a notorious red-light area. On García Moreno is the beautiful **El Sagrario** ⓘ *Mon-Sat, 0800-1800, Sun 0800-1330, free*, church with a gilded door. The **Centro Cultural Metropolitano** is at the corner of Espejo, housing temporary exhibits and the **Museo de Cera** ⓘ *T258 4363, Tue-Sun 0900-1700, US$1.50*, which depicts the execution of the revolutionaries of 1809 in the original cell. Well worth a visit, but it's not for the claustrophobic. The fine Jesuit church of **La Compañía** ⓘ *García Moreno by the corner of Sucre, Mon-Fri 1000-1700, Sat 1000-1600, Sun 1200-1600, US$2*, has the most ornate and richly sculptured façade and interior. Many of its most valuable treasures are in vaults at the Banco Central. Opposite is the **Casa Museo María Augusta Urrutia** ⓘ *García Moreno 760 y Sucre, T258 0107, Tue-Sun 0930-1800, US$2.50*, the home of a Quiteña who devoted her life to charity, showing the lifestyle of 20th century aristocracy (a restaurant serving Sra Urrutia's recipes is open in evening, T258 4173). Housed in the fine restored, 16th Century Hospital San Juan de Dios, is the **Museo de la Ciudad** ⓘ *T228 3882, Tue-Sun 0930-1730, US$3, students US$1.50, guide service US$6*. It takes you through Quito's history from prehispanic times to the 19th century, with imaginative displays.

Plaza de San Francisco (or Bolívar) is west of Plaza de la Independencia; here are the great church and monastery of the patron saint of Quito, **San Francisco** ⓘ *Mon-Fri 0800-1200, 1500-1800, Sat-Sun 0900-1200*. The church was constructed by the Spanish in 1553 and is rich in art treasures. A modest statue of the founder, Fray Jodoco Ricke, the Flemish Franciscan who sowed the first wheat in Ecuador, stands at the foot of the stairs to the church portal. See the fine wood-carvings in the choir, a high altar of gold and an exquisite carved ceiling. There are some paintings in the aisles by Miguel de Santiago, the colonial *mestizo* painter. The **Museo del Convento de San Francisco** ① *T228 1124, Tue-Sat 0900-1800, Sun 0900-1300, US$2*, has a collection of religious art. Adjoining San Francisco is the **Cantuña Chapel** ① *Mon-Fri 0800-1200, 1500-1800, Sat-Sun 0900-1700*, with sculptures. Not far away to the north along Calle Cuenca is the church of **La Merced** ① *Mon-Sat 0600-1200, 1230-1800*. In the monastery of La Merced is Quito's oldest clock, built in 1817 in London. Fine cloisters are entered through a door to the left of the altar. La Merced contains many splendidly elaborate

Quito Old City

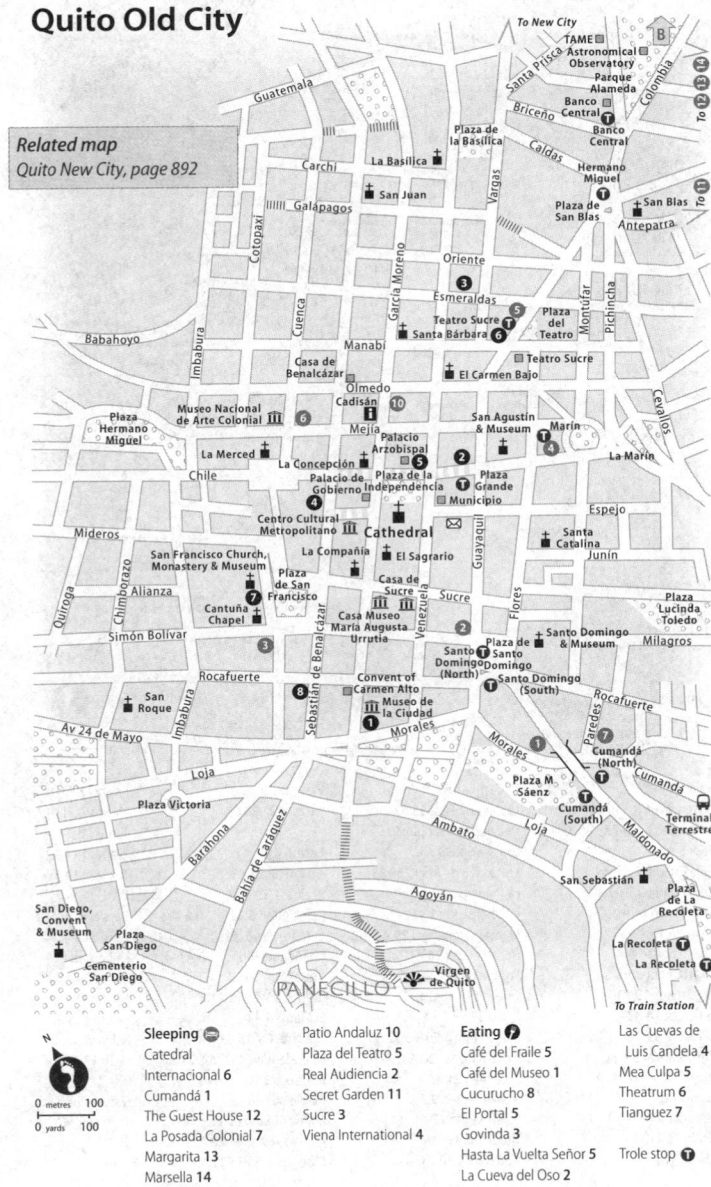

Related map
Quito New City, page 892

Sleeping 🛏
Catedral
Internacional **6**
Cumandá **1**
The Guest House **12**
La Posada Colonial **7**
Margarita **13**
Marsella **14**
Patio Andaluz **10**
Plaza del Teatro **5**
Real Audiencia **2**
Secret Garden **11**
Sucre **3**
Viena International **4**

Eating 🍴
Café del Fraile **5**
Café del Museo **1**
Cucurucho **8**
El Portal **5**
Govinda **3**
Hasta La Vuelta Señor **5**
La Cueva del Oso **2**
Las Cuevas de
 Luis Candela **4**
Mea Culpa **5**
Theatrum **6**
Tianguez **7**

Trole stop 🚎

Quito New City

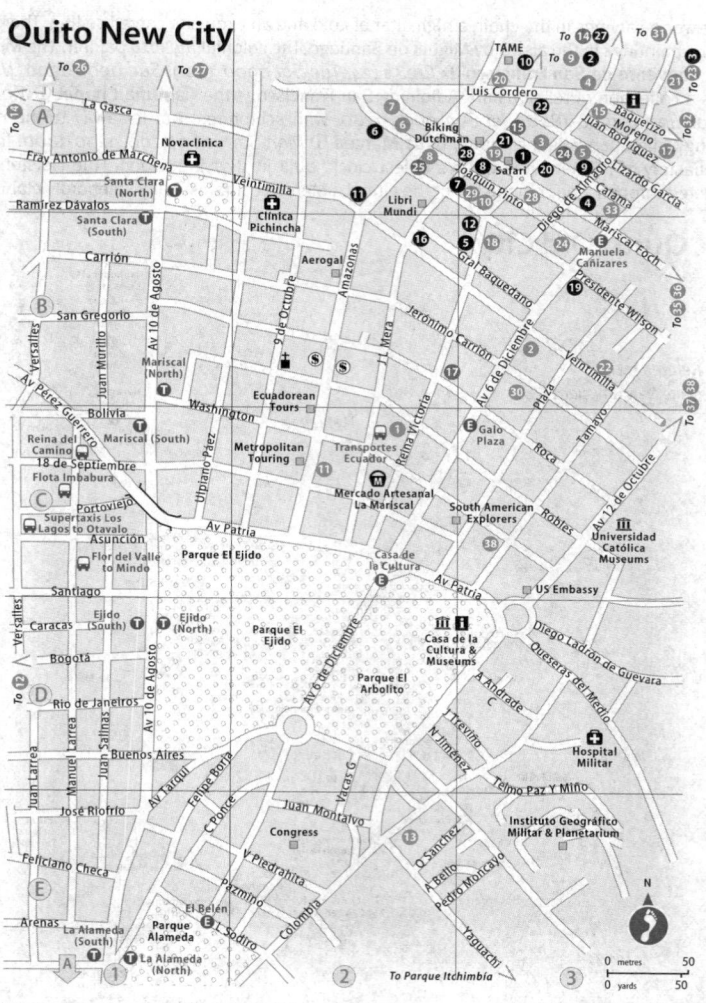

Sleeping

Adventure **6** *A2*
Amazonas Inn **8** *A2*
Bask **5** *A3*
Café Cultura **1** *C2*
Casa Helbling **2** *B3*
Casa Paxee **14** *A1*
Cayman **15** *A3*
Chalet Suisse &
  Restaurant **3** *A3*
Crossroads **19** *A3*
El Cafecito **4** *A3*
El Taxo **7** *A2*
Gan Eden **24** *B3*
Hostal de la Rábida **9** *A3*
Hostelling
  International **10** *A3*
Hothello **11** *C2*
Kinara **12** *D1*

La Cartuja **16** *C3*
La Casa de Eliza **35** *B3*
La Casa de Guápulo **38** *C3*
La Casa Sol **33** *A3*
La Casona de Mario **36** *B3*
La Pradera **31** *A3*
L'Auberge Inn **13** *E2*
Mansión del Angel **29** *A2*
Nuestra Casa **26** *A1*
Posada del Maple **17** *A3*
Queen's Hostel **18** *B3*
Quito **37** *C3*
Rincón Escandinavo **32** *A3*
Río Amazonas **20** *A3*
Sebastián **21** *A3*
Sierra Madre **22** *B3*
Sol de Quito **27** *A1*
Titisee **28** *A3*
Villa Nancy **30** *B3*

Villa Nancy **23** *C3*
Villantigua **38** *C3*

Eating

Adam's Rib **1** *A3*
Baalbeck **19** *B3*
Café Colibrí **6** *A2*
Café Trovero **7** *A3*
Chandani Tandoori **10** *A3*
Chez Alain **16** *B2*
Crêpes & Waffles **2** *A3*
El Maple **4** *A3*
Grain de Café **5** *B3*
La Bodeguita de Cuba **27** *A3*
La Choza **3** *A3*
Magic Bean **8** *A3*
Mama Clorinda **20** *A3*
Mango Tree Café **28** *A3*
Mongo's & Sushi **21** *A3*

Paléo **22** *A3*
Shorton Grill **9** *A3*
Terraza del
  Tártaro **11** *A2*
Tex Mex **12** *B3*

Bars & clubs

Ghoz **14** *A3*
La Boca del
  Lobo **24** *A3*
No Bar **15** *A3*
Patatu's **25** *A2*
Reina Victoria
  Pub **17** *B2*

Ecovía stop **E**
Trole stop **T**

styles; note the statue of Neptune on the main patio fountain. On the next block is the **Museo Nacional de Arte Colonial** ① *Cuenca y Mejía, T228 2297, undergoing restoration in 2006*, a collection of Ecuadorean sculpture and painting, housed in the 17th-century mansion of Marqués de Villacís.

At **Plaza de Santo Domingo** (or Sucre), southeast of Plaza de la Independencia, is the church and monastery of **Santo Domingo**, with its rich wood-carvings and a remarkable Chapel of the Rosary to the right of the main altar. In the monastery is the **Museo Dominicano Fray Pedro Bedón** ① *T228 2695, Mon-Fri 0830-1200, 1330-1700, US$2*, another fine collection of religious art. In the centre of the plaza is a statue of Sucre, pointing to the slopes of Pichincha where he won his battle against the Royalists. Nearby is the **Museo Histórico Casa de Sucre** ① *Venezuela y Sucre, T295 2860, Tue-Thu 0830-1600, Fri-Sat 0900-1300, US$1*, the beautiful house of Sucre.

On **Cerro Panecillo** ① *0900-1800, US$2 to enter the monument; also see Safety page 890*, there is a statue to the Virgen de Quito and a good view from the observation platform. In the museum of the monastery of **San Diego** (by the cemetery of the same name, just west of Panecillo) ① *Calicuchima 117 y Farfán, entrance to the right of the church, T295 2516, 0930-1300, 1430-1730 daily, US$2*, guided tours (Spanish only) take you around four colonial patios where sculpture and painting are shown. Of special interest are the gilded pulpit by Juan Bautista Menacho and the Last Supper painting in the refectory, in which a *cuy* and *humitas* have taken the place of the paschal lamb.

Many of the heroes of Ecuador's struggle for independence are buried in the monastery of **San Agustín** (Flores y Chile), which has beautiful cloisters on three sides where the first act of independence from Spain was signed on 10 August 1809. Here is the **Museo de San Agustín** ① *Chile y Guayaquil, T258 0263, Mon-Sat 0900-1200, 1500-1730 (not Sat), US$2*, with religious art. The **Basílica** ① *on Plaza de la Basílica, 7 blocks northeast of Plaza de la Independencia, 0930-1730, US$2*, is very large, has many gargoyles, stained glass windows and fine, bas relief bronze doors (under construction since 1926). A coffee shop in the clock tower gives good views over the city. To the west of the city, the **Museo del Agua**, called Yaku ① *Calle El Placer, T228 3883*, overlooks the Carcel García Moreno and has great views of the city. Its main themes are water and nature, society and heritage. The plan is for a small cable track to go there, but so far the best way is take a taxi or walk up Calle Chile, go under the tunnels road then left to El Placer. To the east of the colonial city is **Parque Itchimbía**, a natural lookout over the city with walking and cycle trails and a cultural centre housed in a 19th century "crystal palace" which came from Frankfurt, once one of the city's markets. In 2004, a *teleférico* (cable car) and tourist complex with lookout, restaurants and other amenities was built on Cruz Loma, US$4. Access is by special bus, US$1 from all the major 5-star hotels, round trip US$4 unless you are in a hurry and there is a queue, in which case pay for the express, US$7 to jump the queue. Further information from www.teleferiqo.com.

New City

Parque Alameda has the oldest **astronomical observatory** in South America ① *Mon-Fri 0900-1200, 1430-1730, US$0.50, ring bell; T257 0765 for details of observations on clear nights, 1900, US$1*. There is also a splendid monument to Simón Bolívar, lakes, and in the northwest corner a spiral lookout tower with a good view. A short distance north of Parque Alameda, opposite Parque El Ejido, at the junction 6 de Diciembre and Patria, there is a large cultural and museum complex housing the **Casa de la Cultura** ① *T222 3392, ext 320, Tue-Fri 0900-1700, Sat 1000-1400, US$3, good toilets*, and the Museo Nacional del Banco Central del Ecuador (see below). Museums belonging to the Casa de la Cultura are: **Museo de Arte Moderno**, paintings and sculpture since 1830; **Museo de Traje Indígena**, traditional dress and adornments of indigenous groups; **Museo de Instrumentos Musicales**, an impressive collection of musical instruments, said to be the second in importance in the world.

If you have time to visit only one museum in Quito, it should be the **Museo Nacional del Banco Central del Ecuador** ① *entrance on Patria, T222 3259, Tue-Fri 0900-1700, Sat-Sun 1000-1600, US$1.50, students with ISIC or national student card, US$0.50, guided tours in English, French or German by appointment*, also housed in the Casa de la Cultura. It has three floors, with five different sections. The **Sala de Arqueología** is particularly impressive with beautiful pre-Columbian ceramics. The **Sala de Oro** has a nice collection of prehispanic gold objects. The remaining three sections house art collections: the **Sala de Arte Colonial** (rich in paintings and sculptures especially of religious themes), the **Sala de Arte Republicano** and the

Ecuador Quito & around Sights

Sala de Arte Contemporáneo. There are also temporary exhibits, videos on Ecuadorean culture, a bookshop and cafeteria. Highly recommended. Near the Casa de la Cultura, in the Catholic University library building, is the **Museo Jijón y Caamaño** ① *12 de Octubre y Roca, T256 5627 ext 1242, Mon-Fri 0800-1600, US$0.60*, with a private collection of archaeological objects, historical documents, art, portraits, uniforms, etc, very well displayed.

The **Santuario de Guápulo** (1693), perched on the edge of a ravine east of the city, is well worth seeing for its many paintings, gilded altars, stone carvings and the marvellously carved pulpit. The **Museo Fray Antonio Rodríguez** ① *T256 5652, Mon-Sat 0900-1800*, has religious art and furniture, from the 16th to the 20th centuries. Guided tours (Spanish only) include a visit to the beautiful Santuario. Take bus 'Hospital del Sur-Guápulo' from Calle Venezuela by Plaza de la Independencia, 'Guápulo-Dos Puentes' eastbound along Av Patria, or walk down the steep stairway behind *Hotel Quito*. **Cima de la Libertad** ① *Tue-Fri 0830-1630, Sat-Sun 1000-1400, US$1, children and seniors US$0.25*, the museum at the site of the 1822 Battle of Pichincha, has great views. Take a taxi there as the suburbs are dangerous, or the trolley to El Recreo and a taxi from there.

Museo Guayasamín ① *Bosmediano 543, Bellavista, northeast of La Mariscal, T244 6455, Mon-Fri 1000-1700, US$3*, is highly recommended. As well as the eponymous artist's works there is a pre-Columbian and colonial collection. Works of art may be purchased (ask to see the whole collection) and also modern jewellery. It's easiest to take a taxi there. Also presenting Guayasamín's work and 5 blocks from the museum is **La Capilla del Hombre** ① *Mariano Calvache y Lorenzo Chávez, Bellavista, T244 8492, Tue-Sun 1000-1700, US$3, students and seniors US$2 (US$1 discount if visiting both sites)*, a collection of murals depicting the fate of Latin America from pre-Columbian to modern times.

In the eastern suburb of San Rafael is **La Casa de Kingman Museo** ① *Portoviejo y Dávila, 1 block from San Rafael park, Valle de los Chillos, T286 1065, www.fundacionkingman.com, Thu-Fri 1000-1600, Sat-Sun 1000-1700, US$3, students US$2, children under 7 free*. This is a collection of the renowned artist's work and other colonial, republican and 20th-century art. Take a taxi or a Sangolquí bus from La Marín as far as San Rafael park.

🅾 Sleeping

There are few good places to stay near the bus station and even fewer by the airport. Taxis are cheap so plan ahead about what type of lodgings and what part of town best suit you, and take a cab to your first choice.

Large international chain hotels are represented in the city and meet their international standards. For more information see: www.sheraton.com, www.radisson.com, www.swissotel.com, www.hilton.com, www.hotelesdann.com/html/dann_carlton_quito.html, www.hojo.com (Howard Johnson), http://marriott.com/default.mi, www.mercure.com, www.bestwestern.com, Compass (www.hotelquito.com.ec).

Old City *p890, map p891*
L Patio Andaluz, García Moreno N6-52 y Mejía, T228 0830, www.hotelpatioandaluz.com. 5-star 'boutique hotel', beautifully reconstructed colonial mansion, very nice place to stay, restaurant.
C Real Audiencia, Bolívar Oe3-18 y Guayaquil at Plaza de Santo Domingo Trole stop, T295 0590,

F258 0213. Includes breakfast, restaurant/bar on top floor, spacious, well furnished rooms, baggage stored, safety deposit box, great views. Highly recommended.
C Viena Internacional, Flores 600 y Chile, T295 9611, F295 4633. English spoken, good value, phone, good meals, secure.
D Catedral Internacional, Mejía 638 y Cuenca, T295 5438. In a colonial house, hot water, good rooms.
D Cumandá, Morales 449 y Av. Maldonado, T295 6984, www.hotel-cumanda.com. Restaurant, comfortable, garage, excellent service, safe, noisy from proximity to bus station but quieter at the back. Recommended.
D Plaza del Teatro, Guayaquil 1373 y Esmeraldas, T295 9462. Restaurant, parking, carpeted rooms, stylish, good service.
E La Posada Colonial, Paredes 188 y Rocafuerte, T228 2859. Cheaper without bath, simple hostel in a beautiful old building, parking. Recommended.
F Sucre, Bolívar 615 and Cuenca, Plaza San Francisco, T295 4025. Shared bath, laundry facilities, a bit noisy, has terrace with great

views over the Old City, restaurant, often full, also used for short-stay.

Apartments
A Apart-Hotel Amaranta, Leonidas Plaza N20-32 y Washington, T256 0585. Comfortable, well-equipped suites, from US$1,600 a month, good restaurant.

A Apart-Hotel Antinea, Rodríguez 175 y Diego de Almagro, T250 6839, www.hotelantinea.com. Suites and apartments, from US$800 per month, lovely rooms.

C Apartamentos Modernos, Amazonas N31-75 y Mariana de Jesús, T/F223 3766 ext 800, modernos@uio.satnet.net. From US$500 per month, good location near La Carolina park and Mall El Jardín, English spoken, spotlessly clean.

In between the new and old cities
C Kinara, Bogotá 534 y Av América, T/F222 8524, kinara@andinanet.net. Includes breakfast, cooking and laundry facilities, safe deposit boxes, library, English/ French spoken, free tea and coffee, spotless. Highly recommended.

D L'Auberge Inn, Av Colombia 1138 y Yaguachi, T255 2912, www.auberge-inn-hostal.com. Restaurant, cheaper without bath, parking, duvets on beds, fax service, garden, lovely terrace and communal area, helpful, good atmosphere.

D Secret Garden, Antepara E4-60 y Los Ríos, T295 6704, www.secretgardenquito.com. Australian-Ecuadorean run hostel, very popular, cheaper in dorm, terrace for dinner (also for non-residents, tasty meals, vegetarian choices), good reputation as a meeting place, double-check bookings, reception can be disorganized.

D The Guest House, Julio Castro 379 y Valparaíso, T252 2564, marcoatm@hoy.net. Hot water, kitchen and laundry facilities, sitting room, in a restored old house, comfortable rooms and great views, helpful.

E Margarita, Los Ríos 1995 y Espinoza, T295 0441. Parking, good beds, sheets changed daily, great value. Highly recommended.

E Marsella, Los Ríos 2035 y Espinoza, T295 5884. Cheaper without bath, parking, good rooftop terrace with views over Parque La Alameda, top floor rooms best but noisy, luggage stored, not a safe area, often full by 1700, safe deposit, notice board, good value, guard.

New City *p893, map p892*
L Mansión del Angel, Wilson E5-29 y JL Mera, T255 7721, F223 7819. Includes breakfast, refurbished old building, very elegant, lovely atmosphere.

L-AL Villa Nancy, 6 de Diciembre y Cordero, T255 0839, www.villanancy.com. In a quiet residential, homely, comfortable, helpful multilingual staff, includes breakfast, internet, airport transfers, lobby bar.

AL Café Cultura, Robles E6-62 y Reina Victoria, T/F250 4078, www.cafecultura.com. Beautiful garden, welcoming staff, restaurant with good food, safe deposit and luggage store (extra).

AL Río Amazonas, Cordero E4-375 y Amazonas, T255 6667, www.hotelrioamazonas.com. Buffet breakfast, restaurant, internet, pleasant, safe, all facilities.

AL Sebastián, Almagro N24-416 y Cordero, T222 2400, hotelsebastian@hotelsebastian.com. Restaurant, internet, comfortable, safe, garage, very good.

AL-A Sol de Quito, Alemania N30-170 y Vancouver, T254 1773, www.soldequito.com. Includes breakfast, lovely converted house, restaurant, helpful. Recommended.

A La Cartuja, Plaza 170 y 18 de Septiembre, T252 3577, www.hotelcartuja.com. Includes breakfast, restaurant, beautifully decorated, spacious comfortable rooms, safety deposit boxes, garden, very helpful and hospitable. Highly recommended.

Ecuador Quito & around Listings

A **Chalet Suisse**, Reina Victoria N24-191 y Calama, T256 2700, F256 3966. Includes breakfast, excellent restaurant, convenient location, rooms facing street noisy.

A **Hostal de la Rábida**, La Rábida 227 y Santa María, T222 1720, www.hotelrabida.com. Good restaurant, Italian-run, bright, comfortable. Highly recommended.

A **La Pradera**, San Salvador 222 y Pasaje Martín Carrión, La Carolina, T222 6833, www.hostallapradera.com. Includes breakfast, restaurant, comfortable, quiet, residential area.

A-D **La Casa Sol**, Calama 127 y 6 de Diciembre, T223 0798, www.lacasasol.com. Includes breakfast, small with courtyard, 24-hr cafetería, very helpful, hot water, suites available. Recommended.

B **Cayman**, Rodríguez E7-29 y Reina Victoria, T256 7616, www.hotelcaymanquito.com. Includes breakfast, good hotel with smallish rooms, bright breakfast room, sitting room with fireplace, garden, parking.

B **Hothello**, Amazonas N20-20 y 18 de Septiembre, T/F256 5835. Includes breakfast, restaurant, modern, heating, safety deposit, helpful, multilingual staff.

B **Savoy Inn**, Yasuni 304 y Av El Inca, close to airport, T246 0620, hsavoy@uio.satnet.net. American owned, internet, vehicle parking, safe.

B **Sierra Madre**, Veintimilla 464 y Luis Tamayo, T250 5687, www.hotelsierramadre.com. Hotel and restaurant, fully renovated old-style villa, comfortable, sun roof.

B **Villantigua**, Washington E9-48 y Tamayo, T252 8564, alariv@uio.satnet.net. Furnished with antiques, suites with fireplace more expensive, quiet, multilingual staff.

C **Posada del Maple**, Rodríguez E8-49 y Almagro, T254 4507, www.posadadel maple.com. Includes full breakfast, restaurant, laundry and cooking facilities, cheaper with shared bath or in dorm, warm atmosphere, free tea and coffee.

C **Rincón Escandinavo**, Leonidas Plaza N24-306 y Baquerizo Moreno, T/F222 5965, hotelres@ porta.net. Restaurant, small, modern, well-furnished, convenient location, English spoken.

C **Villa Nancy**, Carrión 335 y 6 de Diciembre, T256 3084, www.villa-nancy.com. Swiss-Ecuadorean owned, pleasant, includes breakfast, some rooms with shared bath, airport pickup, cooking facilities, travel info.

C-D **Casa Helbling**, Veintimilla E8-166 y 6 de Diciembre, T222 6013, www.casa helbling.de. Cooking and laundry facilities, cheaper with shared bath, helpful, German spoken, family atmosphere, good information, tours arranged.

C-D **Crossroads**, Foch E5-23 y JL Mera, T223 4735, www.crossroadshostal.com. Cheaper with shared bath, excellent hot showers, good restaurant for breakfast and snacks, videos.

C-D **Hostelling International**, Pinto 325 y Reina Victoria, T254 3995, www.hostelling-ecuador.org. Pricey modern hostel with capacity for 75. Double room with bath, cheaper in dormitory with lockers. Discounts for IYHF members and ISIC holders, restaurant, laundry service, coin-operated washing machines, hot water, safe deposit, luggage store, closed circuit TV security system.

D **Adventure**, Pinto E2-24 y Amazonas, T222 6340, rfcedeno@interactive.net.ec. Cheaper with shared bath, cooking facilities, simple, terrace, helpful.

D **Amazonas Inn**, Pinto E4-324 y Amazonas, T222 5723, amazonasinn@yahoo.com. Carpeted rooms, some sunny, 1st floor best, very nice.

D **El Cafecito**, Luis Cordero 1124 y Reina Victoria, T223 4862, www.cafecito.net. Cheaper in dorm, Canadian-owned, relaxed atmosphere, superb food in café including vegetarian, good information.

D **El Taxo**, Foch 909 y Cordero, T222 5593. Constant hot water, internet, cooking facilities, hostel-type, large family house, helpful, open fire, good meeting place.

D La Casa de Guápulo, C Leonidas Plaza (Guápulo), T/F222 0473. Includes breakfast, restaurant, parking, bar, peaceful area, multilingual staff, free transfer to airport.
D La Casona de Mario, Andalucía 213 y Galicia (La Floresta), T/F223 0129, lacasona@ punto.net.ec. Laundry and storage facilities, near Universidad Católica, sitting room, big garden, book exchange, several languages spoken, very helpful, popular.
D Nuestra Casa, Bartolomé de las Casas 435 y Versalles, T222 5470, mlmo@uio.satnet.net. Cooking facilities, converted family house, dinner available, camping in garden.
D Queen's Hostel, Reina Victoria 836 y Wilson, T255 1844, queen@uio.telconet.net. Cooking and laundry facilities, nice, smal, popular, fireplace.
D Titisee, Foch E7-60 y Reina Victoria, T252 9063. Nice place, helpful owner, cheaper with shared bath, large rooms, cooking facilities, lounge.
D-E Casa Paxee, Pasaje Navarro 364 (N 24-70) y La Gasca (entre Domingo Espinar y Lizarazu), T254 2663, www.hostal-casapaxi.com. Price includes breakfast, cooking and laundry facilities, discounts for longer stays.
E Bask, Lizardo García 537 y Reina Victoria, T250 3456. Cooking facilities, free coffee, cafeteria, nice atmosphere.
E La Casa de Eliza, Isabel La Católica N24-679 (La Floresta), T222 6602, manteca@ uio.satnet.net. Kitchen and laundry facilities, shared rooms, safety deposit, very popular and homely, no smoking.
E Gan Eden, Pinto 163 y 6 de Diciembre, T222 3480, ganeden163@hotmail.com. Restaurant serves cheap breakfast and good Israeli food, cheaper without bath, cooking facilities, double rooms or dorm, very helpful.

❼ Eating

Dining in Quito, especially in the New City, is excellent, varied, and increasingly cosmopolitan, though many restaurants close on Sun. In the Old City there are a number of elegant, upmarket places serving Ecuadorean and international food, plus many small, cheap places serving set meals. Most of these close by early evening. In all cases, assume good food, service and value. All have been recommended. Be very careful when choosing a seafood restaurant; some are less than hygienic.

Old City *p890, map p891*
♦♦♦ La Cueva del Oso, Chile Oe3-66 y Venezuela, across from the Plaza de la Independencia, T257 2786. Mon-Sat 1200- 0000, Sun 1200-1600. A good

place to sample Ecuadorean specialties in an elegant covered courtyard, art deco interior, great atmosphere.
♦♦♦ Mea Culpa, Plaza Independencia, upstairs in public part of Archbishop's Palace, T295 1190. Very elegant (formal dress code enforced), excellent international and Mediterranean food, reservations required.
♦♦♦ Theatrum, Plaza del Teatro, Teatro Sucre p 2, T228 9669. Mon-Fri 1230-1600, 1930-2330, Sat 1930-2330, Sun 1230-1600. Excellent creative gourmet cuisine in the city's most important theatre.
♦♦ Cucurucho, in the basement of the old Santa Clara market at Rocafuerte y Benalcázar, T228 5866. Ecuadorean specialities, reasonable prices, interesting building with brick arches and niches.
♦♦ Hasta la Vuelta Señor, Pasaje Arzobispal, p 3. Mon-Sat 1200-2300, Sun 1200-1600. A *Fonda Quiteña* perched on an indoor balcony with Ecuadorean *comida típica* and snacks.
♦♦-♦ Las Cuevas de Luis Candela, Benalcázar 713 y Chile. Spanish and Ecuadorean dishes, open daily 1100-1830, has cheap set lunch.
♦ Govinda, Esmeraldas y García Moreno. Vegetarian dishes and set meals, Mon-Sat 0800-1900.

Cafés
Café del Fraile, Pasaje Arzobispal, p 2, Mon-Sat 1000-0000, Sun 1100-1930. Snacks and drinks, on a balcony above one of the patios of the Palacio Arzobispal.
Café del Museo, García Moreno 572 at the Museo de la Ciudad, Tue-Sun 0930-1700. Snacks and soups, coffee, elegant decor.
El Portal, Pasaje Arzobispal, ground floor, enter from C Venezuela. Mon-Sat 1030-2030, Sun 1030-1800. Snacks, 20 varieties of coffee, drinks, modern decor with paintings.
Tianguez, Plaza de San Francisco. 0930-1830, Ecuadorean food, cafeteria, crafts, popular.

New City *p893, map p892*
♦♦♦ Avalón, Av Orellana 155 y 12 de Octubre, T250 9875, Tue-Sat 1200-1500, 1800-2300, Sun 1200-1700. Excellent seafood, upmarket, also serves meat.
♦♦♦ Chalet Suisse, Reina Victoria N24-191 y Calama, T256 2700, daily 1100-1500, 1900-2300. Steaks and some Swiss dishes, good service.
♦♦♦ El Cebiche, JL Mera 1236 y Calama, and Amazonas 2428 y Moreno Bellido, T252 6380, Tue-Sun 1000-1600. Delicious *ceviche*.
♦♦♦ El Galpón, Colón E10-53, behind Folklor Olga Fisch, T254 0209, Tue-Sun 1230-1500, 1830-2100. Very good Ecuadorean cooking, decorated with antiques, a pleasant place for relaxed dining.

Il Grillo, Baquerizo Moreno 533 y Almagro, T222 5531, Mon-Fri 1200-1500, 1900-2300, Sat 1900-2300. Great pizzas, upmarket.

Il Risotto, Eloy Alfaro N34-447 y Portugal, T224 6850. Very popular, very good, closed Sun evening.

La Bodeguita de Cuba, Reina Victoria 1721 y Pinta, T246 4517, Tue-Sat 1200-1600, 1830-2200, Sun 1130-1600. Good Cuban food and good music and snacks at *Varadero* bar next door.

La Choza, 12 de Octubre N24-551 y Cordero, T223 0839, Mon-Fri 1200-1600, 1900-2230, Sat-Sun 1200-1630. Traditional cuisine, good music and special decor.

La Cocina de Kristy, Whymper 1184 y Orellana, T250 1210, Tue-Sat 1230-1600, 1800-2300, Sun 1230-1600. Great food, upmarket, great view from the terrace. Recommended.

La Jaiba, Coruña y San Ignacio, T254 3887, Mon 1100-1530, Tue-Sat 1100-1600, 1900-2100, Sun 1100-1630. Varied seafood menu, an old favourite at new premises after 36 years, good service.

La Nueva Castilla, La Pinta 435 y Amazonas, T256 6979, Mon-Sat 1200-1500, 1900-2200. Typical Spanish fare, another old favourite in new premises.

La Paella Valenciana, República y Almagro, Tue-Sat 1200-1500, 1900-2300, Sun 1200-1600. Spanish, huge portions, superb fish and paella, an institution.

La Querencia, Eloy Alfaro N34-194 y Catalina Aldaz, T244 6654, Mon-Sat 1000-2300, Sun 1000-1800. Ecuadorean. Good views and atmosphere.

Los Troncos, Los Shyris 1280 y Portugal, T243 7377, Mon-Sat 1000-2200, Sun 1000-1600. Argentine, excellent for meats, fish, pasta, salads, busy on Sun.

Pavarotti, Av 12 de Octubre 1955 y Cordero, T256 6668, Tue-Sat 1200-1600,1900-2300, Sun 1200-1600. Creative Italian cuisine, good service.

Rincón de Francia, Roca 779 y 9 de Octubre, T255 4668, www.rincondefrancia.com, Mon-Fri 1200-1600, 2000-2300, Sat 1200-1530, 2000-2200. Excellent French cuisine but very expensive, reservation essential, slow service.

Rincón La Ronda, Belo Horizonte 406 y Almagro, T254 0459, daily 1200-2300. Nice atmosphere, huge Sun buffet, local and international, Sun evening folklore show.

Sake, Paul Rivet N30-166 y Whymper, T252 4818, Mon-Sat 1200-1530, 1900-2300, Sun 1230-1600. Sushi bar and other Japanese dishes, very trendy, great food.

Shorton Grill, Calama E7-73 y Almagro, and Urrutia N14-233 y Eloy Alfaro, T252 3645. Meat and seafood, salad bar, large portions, smart decor.

Swiss Corner, Los Shyris 2137 y El Telégrafo, T246 8007, Mon-Sat 0700-2030, Sun 0700-1600. Swiss dishes, also delicatessen and pastry shop, small quaint place.

Terraza del Tártaro, Veintimilla 1106 y Amazonas (no sign), top floor, T252 7987, Mon-Sat 1200-1600, 1800-2200, Sun 1200-1600. Steaks, pleasant atmosphere.

Raclette, Mall El Jardín, Amazonas y Mariana de Jesús, p 3, Mon-Sat 1130-2200, Sun 1200-1600. Swiss specialties including raclette and fondue with a great variety of ingredients to add, simple, modern decor.

Adam's Rib, Calama E6-16 y Reina Victoria. Closed Sat; happy hour 1730-2100. For steak, ribs and pecan pie.

Baalbeck, 6 de Diciembre y Wilson. Good Arabic food.

Capuletto, Eloy Alfaro N32-544 y Los Shyris, 0900-2400 (2200 on Sun). Excellent fresh pasta and desserts, Italian deli, lovely outdoor patio with fountain.

Crêpes & Waffles, La Rábida 461 y Orellana, opens 1200. Succulent savoury crêpes and salads and delicious desserts.

El Zócalo, JL Mera y Calama. Good choice on international menu, live music Fri, young crowd, popular.

Happy Panda, Cordero E9-348 e Isabel la Católica, Tue-Sat 1600-2200. Excellent Hunan specialties.

Hong Tai, La Niña 234 y Yanez Pinzón, Tue-Sat 1300-1500, 1900-2300, Sun 1300-1600. Good authentic Chinese cuisine.

La Casa de mi Abuela, JL Mera 1649 y la Niña, closed Sun afternoon/evening. Steak and other dishes, salads.

La Guarida del Coyote, Foch y JL Mera, Eloy Alfaro E25-94 y Catalina Aldaz, and Japón 542 y Naciones Unidas, Tue-Sun 1200-2300. Excellent Mexican food, live music.

Las Ensaladas/Mi Frutería, Quicentro Shopping. Gorgeous fresh fruit salads and coastal Ecuadorean food, daily 1000-2200.

Mama Clorinda, Reina Victoria 1144 y Calama, open 1200-2100 (1700 Sun-Mon). A la carte and set meals, filling, good value.

Mango Tree Café, Foch 721 y Amazonas. Salads, fruit juices, coffee, homemade bread and bagels, closed Sun and holidays.

Mongo's, Calama E5-10 y JL Mera, daily 1200-2200. Mongolian BBQ, select your ingredients and have them cooked on the grill.

Paléo, Cordero E5-48 y Reina Victoria, Mon-Sat 1230-1530 1830-2100. Authentic Swiss specialties such as rösti and raclette. Also serves a good economical set lunch. Recommended.

Pekín, Whimper 300 y Orellana, Mon-Sat 1200-1500, 1900-2230, Sun 1200-2030. Excellent Chinese food, very nice atmosphere.

Puerto Camarón, Av 6 de Diciembre y Granaderos, Centro Comercial Olímpico, Tue-Sat 1000-1500, 1800-2100, Sun 1000-1600. Varied seafood menu.

Sushi, Calama E5-104 y JL Mera, Mon-Sat 1200-2300, Sun 1200-1600. Sushi bar, pleasant atmosphere with nice balcony, good value happy hour 1700-1900.

Tex Mex, Reina Victoria 847 y Wilson, 1300-2200, closed Sun. The Tex Mex Mixta especially recommended, lively.

The Magic Bean, Foch 681 y JL Mera, Mon- Sat 1200-1530, 1900-2200, Sun 1200-1530. Specializes in fine coffees and natural foods, more than 20 varieties of pancakes, good salads, large portions, outdoor seating (also has popular lodging, **B-D**, T256 6181).

Café Colibrí, Pinto 619 y Cordero, daily 0800-1830. Large choice of breakfasts and German specialties, pleasant garden setting.

Chandani Tandoori, JL Mera N24-277 y Cordero, Mon-Sat 1100-2200. Simple little place, with good authentic Indian cuisine.

Chez Alain, Baquedano 409 y JL Mera, Mon-Fri 1200-1600, 1830-2200. Choice of good 4-course set meals at lunch, à la carte in the evening, pleasant relaxed atmosphere.

El Maple, Foch E8-15 y Almagro, daily 0730-2330. Varied vegetarian menu, good meals and fruit juices, set lunches, stylish decor. Recommended.

Grain de Café, Baquedano 332 y Reina Victoria, Mon-Sat 0700-2200. Meat or vegetarian set lunches, good cakes and coffee, cocktails, good service.

La Canoa Manabita, Calama y Reina Victoria, daily 1200-2100. Great seafood, very clean.

La Chacha, Foch y J L Mera. A small open air restaurant with heating, very good, cheap Italian fare, weekdays only.

Las Palmeras, Japón N36-87 y Naciones Unidas, opposite Parque la Carolina, daily 0800-1800. Good *comida esmeraldeña*, outdoor tables, good value.

Rincón Ecuatoriano Chileno, 6 de Diciembre N28-30 y Bello Horizonte, daily 1200-1600. Delicious, good value, busy at weekends.

Tomato, JL Mera E5-10 y Calama, daily 0800-0100. Good value buffet breakfast, choice of set lunches, pizza and pasta. Recommended.

Yu Su Café, Ed Torres de Almagro, Almagrro y Colón. Good sushi bar, Korean run, takeaway service.

Cafés

Bangalô, Foch y Almagro. Excellent cakes, quiches, coffees, Mon-Sat, open at lunchtime and 1600-2000, great atmosphere, good jazz at weekends.

Books & Coffee, JL Mera 12-27 y Calama. Cappuccino, espresso, sandwiches, local newspapers.

Café Trovero, JL Mera y Pinto, Mon-Fri 1230-2200, Sat 1330-2200. Espresso and sandwich bar, pastries, pleasant atmosphere, nicely decorated with plants.

Kallari, Wilson E4-266 y JL Mera, T223 6009, www.kallari.com. Fair trade and organic coffee, chocolate, breakfasts and lunches, handicrafts, all associated with a community project in Napo province, "great atmosphere and sound aims". Frequently recommended.

Mirador de Guápulo, Rafael León Larrea, behind Hotel Quito, daily 1000-0000. Snacks such as empanadas, crêpes, sandwiches, drinks, great views, portable heaters for outdoor seating at night.

⊙ Bars and clubs

New City *p893, map p892*

Cats, Lizardo García 537 y Reina Victoria. Informal disco-bar, varied music including rock, no latin music, popular.

El Pobre Diablo, Isabel La Católica y Galavis, 1 block north of Madrid, Mon-Sat 1600-0000. Relaxed atmosphere, jazz, sandwiches, Ecuadorean snacks and some meals, a good place to hang out and chill, popular.

Ghoz Bar, La Niña 425 y Reina Victoria. Swiss-owned, excellent Swiss food, pool, darts, videos, games, music, German book exchange.

La Boca del Lobo, Calama 284 y Reina Victoria. Café-bar, snacks and meals at mid-range prices, very laid-back, good meeting place, nice atmosphere, open Mon-Sat 1700-0000.

Matices Piano Bar, Av Isabel La Católica y Cordero. Excellent food, live piano music, owner is a well- known local pianist and composer, Dr Nelson Maldonado, open 1630-0200.

Matrioshka, Pinto 376 y JL Mera, Wed-Sat from 1900, but only gets started around 2200. Gay and lesbian bar.

Mayo 68, Lizardo García 662 y JL Mera. Salsoteca, small, an absolute must for all you authentic *salseros*. Highly recommended.

No Bar, Calama y JL Mera. Good mix of Latin and Euro dance music always packed on weekends, entry US$4 on weekends.

Oz, Maldonado y Pujilí, in the south near El Recreo Trole stop. Fine mix of music and people, huge, 5 dance halls, the 'in' place for dancing.

Patatu's, Wilson y JL Mera, 2030-0200, closed Sun. Good drinks, pool table, happy hour all night Mon, loud music, dancing (a place for those who want to show off their skills), owner speaks English and German.

Reina Victoria Pub, Reina Victoria 530 y Roca. Open Mon-Sat from 1700, darts, relaxed atmosphere, English style with microbrews and Irish and Scotch whisk(e)ys, happy hour 1800-2000, moderately priced bar meals, meeting point for British and US expats.
Seseribó, Veintimilla y 12 de Octubre. Caribbean music and salsa, open Thu-Sat 2100-0100. Recommended.
The Turtle´s Head Bar, La Niña 626 y JL Mera, Mon-Sat 1700-0200, Sun 1200-0200. Amazing microbrews, great fish and chips, chicken curry, also serves Sun lunch, pool table, darts.
Varadero, Reina Victoria 1721 y La Pinta, Mon-Fri 1200-0000, Sat 1800-0300. Bar-restaurant, live Cuban music Wed-Sat, meals and snacks, good cocktails, older crowd and couples.
Vauzá, Tamayo y F Salazar. Varied music, large bar in the middle of the dance floor, mature crowd, open Wed-Sat 2200-0100.

❻ Entertainment

Quito *p889, map p891 and 892*
For details of forthcoming events, see listings in *El Comercio* and other papers, also www.farras.com.

Cinema
Casa de la Cultura, Patria y 6 de Diciembre, T290 2272, http://cce.org.ec. Shows foreign films, often has documentaries, film festivals.
Ocho y Media, Valladolid y Guipuzcoa. Good for art films and specials, also has a café, programme available at *Libri Mundi* and elsewhere.
  There are several multiplexes, eg **Cinemark 7**, www.cinemark.com.ec, and **Multicines**, www.multicines.com.ec.

Dance schools
Ritmo Tropical, Amazonas N24-155 y Calama, T222 7094, ritmotropical5@hotmail.com. Salsa, merengue, cumbia, vallenato and folkloric dance.
Son Latino, Reina Victoria 1225 y García, T223 4340. Specializes in several varieties of salsa, 10-hr programmes US$40.
Tropical Dancing School, Foch E4-256 y Amazonas, T222 4713. Salsa, merengue and cumbia.

Music
Local folk music is popular in *peñas*. Most places do not come alive until 2230.
La Casa de la Peña, García Moreno 1713 y Galápagos, by the Basílica, T228 4179, lacasadelapenia@hotmail.com, Thu-Sun from 2130. Show of Quito legends, Sat at 2200. Popular with locals on Fri and Sat.

Ñucanchi, Av Universitaria Oe5-188 y Armero. Tue-Sat 2000-0200.
Concerts by the **Orquesta Sinfónica Nacional**, at Teatro Politécnico, Queseras del Medio, opposite Coliseo Rumiñahui, La Floresta, T256 5733, at **Teatro Sucre** (see below), or in one of the colonial churches. Occasional concerts at the **Auditorio de las Cámaras** (Chamber of Commerce), Amazonas y República, T226 0265/6 ext 231. Popular concerts at the **Plaza de Toros**, Amazonas y Juan de Azcaray, in the north, or **Coliseo Rumiñahui**, Toledo y Queseras del Medio, La Floresta, tickets are sold in advance. At **Plaza del Quinde**, Foch y Reina Victoria, there are concerts every Thu night starting 1800-1900.

Theatre
Agora, open-air theatre of Casa de la Cultura, 12 de Octubre y Patria. Stages many concerts.
Centro Cultural Afro-Ecuatoriano (CCA), Tamayo 985 y Lizardo García, T252 2318. Sometimes has cultural events and published material, useful contact for those interested in the black community.
Teatro Bolívar, Flores 421 y Junín, T258 2486, www.teatrobolivar.org. Despite restoration work there are still tours, presentations and festivals, the proceeds being used for the renovations.
Teatro Sucre, Plaza del Teatro, Manabí y Guayaquil, T228 1644, www.teatrosucre.com (has a listing of events for the year). Built in the 1880s, small and elegant, beautifully restored.

❻ Festivals and events

Quito *p889, map p891 and 892*
New Year, Años Viejos: life-size puppets satirize politicians and others. At midnight on 31 Dec a will is read, the legacy of the outgoing year, and the puppets are burnt; good along Amazonas between Patria and Colón, very entertaining and good humoured. On New Year's day everything is shut. The solemn **Good Friday** processions are most impressive. **24 May** is Independence, commemorating the Battle of Pichincha in 1822 with early morning cannonfire and parades, everything closes. **Aug**: Mes de Arte y Cultura, organized by the municipality, cultural events, dance and music in different places throughout the city. The city's main festival, Día de Quito, celebrated throughout the **week ending 6 Dec**, commemorates the foundation of the city with elaborate parades, bullfights, performances and music in the streets, very lively. Hotels charge extra, everything except a few restaurants shuts on 6 Dec. Foremost among **Christmas** celebrations is the **Misa del Gallo**, midnight mass. Over Christmas, Quito is crowded, hotels are full and the streets are packed with vendors and shoppers.

O Shopping

Quito p889, map p891 and 892
Shops open generally 0900-1900 on weekdays, some close at midday. Most shops shut Sat afternoon and Sun. Shopping centres are open at weekends.

The main shopping districts are along Av Amazonas in the north and C Guayaquil in the Old City. In the New City much of the shopping is done in huge US-style shopping malls (see list under Foodstuffs). For maps see Essentials, page 883.

Bookshops

Abya-Yala, 12 de Octubre 14-30 y Wilson. Good for books about indigenous cultures and anthropology, also has excellent library and museum.

Confederate Books, Calama 410 y JL Mera. Open 1000-1900, excellent selection of second-hand books, including travel guides, mainly English but also German and French.

Libri Mundi, JL Mera N23-83 y Veintimilla, and at Quicentro Shopping. Excellent selection of Spanish, English, French, German, and some Italian books, sells Footprint *Ecuador, South American Handbook* and other titles, knowledgeable and helpful staff, noticeboard of what's on in Quito, open Mon-Sat 0800-1800 (also Sun at Quicentro). Very highly recommended.

Libro Express, Amazonas 816 y Veintimilla, also at Quicentro Shopping and El Bosque. Has a good stock of maps, guides and international magazines.

Mr Books, El Jardín Mall, 3rd floor. Good stock, many in English including Footprint travel guides, open daily. Recommended.

Foreign newspapers are for sale at the news stands in luxury hotels and in some shops along Amazonas. *Lufthansa* will supply German newspapers if they have spare copies.

Camping

Camping gas is available many of the shops listed below, white gas (*combustible para lámpara Coleman*) at times from **Kywi**, Centro Comercial Olímpico, 6 de Diciembre, 2 blocks north of the stadium, and other locations.

Los Alpes, Reina Victoria N23-45 y Baquedano. Local and imported equipment, also rentals.

Altamontaña, Jorge Washington 425 y 6 de Diciembre. Imported climbing equipment for sale, rentals, good advice.

The Altar, J L Mera 615 y Carrión. Imported and local gear for sale, good prices for rentals.

Antisana, Centro Comercial El Bosque, ground floor. Sales only.

Aventura Sport, Quicentro Shopping, top floor. Tents, good selection of glacier sunglasses, upmarket.

Camping Sports, Colón 942 y Reina Victoria. Sales only.

Equipos Cotopaxi, 6 de Diciembre 927 y Patria. Ecuadorean and imported gear for sale, no rentals, lockable pack covers, made to measure.

The Explorer, Reina Victoria E6-32 y Pinto. Sales and rentals, very helpful, will buy US or European equipment.

Tatoo, JL Mera 820 y Wilson. Quality backpacks and outdoor clothing.

Film processing

Many labs along Amazonas and in shopping centres for rapid film processing and printing; quality varies greatly. For professional work and slide processing, **Ron Jones**, Lizardo García E9-104 y Andrés Xaura, 1 block east of 6 de Diciembre, T250 7622.

Foodstuffs

La Feria supermarket, Bolívar 334, entre Venezuela y García Moreno sells good wines and spirits, and Swiss, German and Dutch cheeses.

Mi Comisariato, another well-stocked super-market and department store, at Quicentro Shopping (Naciones Unidas y Shyris) and García Moreno y Mejía in the Old City.

Santa María, at Santa Clara, La Ofelia, Villa Flora and several in south Quito. A growing chain of supermarkets, good value and no membership, so you don't pay a surcharge if you don't have a card.

Supermaxi well-stocked supermarket and department store with a wide range of local and imported goods, at the Centro Comercial Iñaquito (Amazonas y Naciones Unidas), **Centro Comercial El Bosque** (Av Occidental), **Centro Comercial Plaza Aeropuerto** (Av de la Prensa y Homero Salas), **Megamaxi** (6 de Diciembre y Julio Moreno), **Multicentro** (6 de Diciembre y La Niña), **El Recreo** and at **Mall El Jardín** (Amazonas y Mariana de Jesús); all open Mon-Sat 1000-2000, Sun 1000-1300 (some until 1800).

Handicrafts

A wide selection can be found at the **Mercado Artesanal La Mariscal**, on Jorge Washington, between Reina Victoria and JL Mera. This interesting and worthwhile market, built by the municipality to house street vendors, is open daily 1000-1800. There are also souvenir shops on García Moreno in front of the Palacio Presidencial in the colonial city. **El Indio**, Roca E4-35 y Amazonas, T2555227, daily 0900-1900. A craft market with stalls selling a variety of products, also has a coffee shop. **Museo de Artesanía**, 12 de Octubre 1738 y Madrid, Mon-Fri 0900-1900, Sat 0900-1700. Another craft market with many vendors and products. There is an exhibition and sale of paintings in **Parque El Ejido**, opposite *Hotel Hilton Colón*, on Sat and Sun mornings.

Local garments (for natives rather than tourists) can be seen and bought on the north end of the Plaza de Santo Domingo and along the nearest stretch of C Flores.

Recommended shops with a wide selection are: **La Bodega**, JL Mera 614 y Carrión. Recommended for antiques and handicrafts **Camari**, Marchena 260 y Versalles. Direct sale shop run by an artisan organization. Member of the Fair Trade organization.
Folklore, Colón E10-53 y Caamaño, the store of the late Olga Fisch. Attractive selection of handicrafts and rugs, expensive as designer has international reputation; also at *Hotel Hilton Colón* and *Hotel Patio Andaluz*.
Galería Latina, JL Mera 823 y Veintimilla. Fine selection of alpaca and other handicrafts from Ecuador, Peru and Bolivia, visiting artists sometimes demonstrate their work.
Hilana, 6 de Diciembre 1921 y Baquerizo Moreno. Beautiful unique 100% wool blankets with Ecuadorean motifs, excellent quality, purchase by metre possible, inexpensive.
Marcel Creations, Roca 766, entre Amazonas y 9 de Octubre. Panama hats.
Homero Ortega, Isabel La Católica N24-100. Outlet for one of the Panama hat manufacturers in Cuenca.
Productos Andinos, Urbina 111 y Cordero. Artisan's co-op, good selection, including Panama hats.
Saucisa, Amazonas 2487 y Pinto, and a couple other locations in La Mariscal. Very good place to buy Andean music CDs and Andean musical instruments.
The Ethnic Collection, Amazonas N21-63 y Robles, T250 0155, www.ethniccollection.com. Wide variety of clothing, leather, bags, jewellery, balsa wood and ceramic items from across Ecuador.

Jewellery
Alquimia, Juan Rodríguez 139. High quality silversmith.
Argentum, JL Mera y Carrión. Also sells crafts and antiques, excellent selection, reasonably priced.
Hamilton, 12 de Octubre 1942 y Cordero. Fine silver and gold crafts and jewellery, native designs.
Jeritsa, Mall El Jardín, local 234. Good selection, prices and service.
Tinta, JL Mera 1020 y Foch. Good selection of silver jewellery, reasonable prices, good service.

Markets
Main produce markets, all accessible by Trole: **Mercado Central**, Av Pichincha y Olmedo (also on the Ecovía), **Mercado Santa Clara**, Versalles y Ramírez Dávalos and **Mercado Iñaquito**, Iñaquito y Villalengua. **Mercado Ipiales**, on Chile uphill from Imbabura, where clothing, appliances and stolen goods are sold (a particularly unsafe area). **Plaza Arenas** on Vargas, next to Colegio La Salle or along 24 de Mayo and Loja uphill from Benalcázar, is where you are most likely to find your stolen camera for sale (also try **Fotomania**, 6 de Diciembre N19-23 y Patria). Not surprisingly, these are unsafe parts of town.

▲ Activities and tours

Quito *p889, map p891 and 892*
Climbing and trekking
Climbs and trekking tours can be arranged in Quito and several other cities; the following Quito operators have been recommended (see Tour operators below for contact information):
Agama Expediciones, run by experienced climbing guide Eduardo Agama, also own Albergue Cara Sur on Cotopaxi.
Campo Base, run by Manuel and Diego Jácome, very experienced climbing guides, they also have a mountain lodge 15 km south of Sangolquí, near Sincholagua, good for acclimatization at 3050 m.
Compañía de Guías, English, German, French and Italian spoken.
Pamir Travel and Adventures, chief guide Hugo Torres is very experienced and speaks English.
Safari Tours, 2 climbers per guide, trekking tours, has own transport and equipment, large and small groups, several languages spoken, very knowledgeable, well organized and planned. Also runs a high altitude glacier school, with courses of 2-3 days with bilingual guides.
Sierra Nevada, chief guide Freddy Ramírez is fluent in French, English and German, has his own equipment, and takes mostly large groups.
Surtrek arranges guided climbs of most peaks, also rents and sells equipment, 2 climbers per guide, large and small group.
Independent guides do not normally provide transport or full service, ie food, equipment, insurance and, without a permit from the **Ministerio de Ambiente**, they might be refused entry to national parks.

The following are reputable guides: **Iván Rojas**, T255 8380; **Benno Schlauri**, T234 0709. **Local climbing clubs** welcome new members, but they do not provide free guiding service. It is not really worth joining if you are in Ecuador for only a few weeks.

The following all have climbing clubs: **Colegio San Gabriel**, **Universidad Católica**, **Nuevos**

Horizontes (Colón 2038 y 10 de Agosto, T255 2154) and **Club Sadday** (Alonso de Angulo y Galo Molina).

If planning to go to Cotopaxi with a Quito tour operator or guide, you must ensure that they have the requisite permits (*patentes*). A cheap tour may leave you stranded at the national park gates if your guide or transport does not have the correct papers.

Cycling and mountain biking

Quito has a couple of bike paths, **Ciclopaseos**, one around the perimeter of Parque La Carolina and a second one in the south, along Quebrada Ortega in the Quitumbe neighbourhood. The city organizes a ciclopaseo every fortnight. Key avenues are closed to vehicular traffic and thousands of cyclists cross the city in 24 km from north to south.

Aries, Wilson 578 y Reina Victoria, T/F290 6052, after hours T09-981 6003 (Mob), www.ariesbikecompany.com. 1-2 day mountain bike tours, all equipment provided.

Bicisport, in Quicentro Shopping, top floor and 6 de Diciembre 6327 y Tomás de Berlanga, T246 0894. Recommended stockist of imported bikes and parts.

Bike Tech, 6 de Diciembre N39-59 y El Telégrafo, T226 3421. A meeting place for long distance bikers. Owner Santiago Lara has informal 'meets' almost every weekend, anyone is welcome, no charge, they ride 20 or more routes around Quito, they also have a good repair shop and cheap parts.

Biking Dutchman, Foch 714 y JL Mera, T256 8323, T09-420 5349 (mob), www.biking dutchman.com. One and several-day tours, great fun, good food, very well organized, English, German and Dutch spoken, pioneers in mountain biking in Ecuador.

Ciclo Vivas 6 de Diciembre 2810 y Orellana, T256 6100. Stocks Jamis, Shimano and Wheeler.

Sobre Ruedas, Av 10 de Agosto N52-162, Ciudadela Kennedy, T241 6781. Repairs, tours, rentals and sales.
See also Safari, Tour operators below.

Jogging

Hash House Harriers, enquire at *Reina Victoria Pub*, T222 6369. Club for runners and walkers,

Paragliding

Escuela Pichincha de Vuelo Libre, Carlos Endara Oe3-60 y Amazonas, T02-225 6592 (office hours) T09-947 8349 (Mob), parapent@uio.satnet.net, is a good point of contact. Offers complete courses for US$350-500 and tandem flights for US$40-60.

Rugby

Friendly games are played when there are enough people, see noticeboard at the **Reina Victoria Pub.**

Swimming

There are a number of good, clean, heated public pools in the city. Swimming cap, towel and soap are compulsory for admission. One is in Miraflores, at the upper end of Av Universitaria, a 10-min walk from Amazonas. Open Tue-Sun 0900-1600. Another is at Batán Alto, on Cochapata, Ecovía to Los Sauces station and walk up Gaspar de Villaroel. The pool and sauna at Colegio Benalcázar are also open to the public, 6 de Diciembre y Portugal, Benalcázar stop on the Ecovía.

Tour operators

See also page 1018 for Galápagos boats and tour operators. Note that national park fees are rarely included in tour prices.

Advantage Travel, El Telégafo E10-63 y Juan de Alcántara, T246 2871, www.advantag ecuador.com. Run tours to Machalilla and Isla de la Plata. Also operate 4-5 day jungle tours on the

Manatee floating hotel, on the Río Napo.

Agama Expediciones, J Washington 425 y 6 de Diciembre, p 2, T290 3164. See Climbing and trekking above.

Alta Montaña, JL Mera 12-27 y Calama, T252 8769, donoso@andinanet.net. For climbing and trekking.

Anaconda Travel, Foch 635 y Reina Victoria, p 1, T/F222 4913, anacondaec@andinanet.net. Runs Anaconda lodge in the upper Napo, jungle trips, sell tours to Galápagos and other destinations.

Andando Tours – Angermeyer Cruises, Mariana de Jesús 326 y Pradera, T02-256 6010, www.andandotours.com.

Andes Explorer, Reina Victoria 927, T290 1493, www.andes_explorer.com.

Campo Base, Jacinto de Evia N60-121 (north of the airport), T259 9737, www.campobase turismo.com. Climbing, trekking and cycling tours, also have a mountain lodge, see Climbing and trekking above.

Canodros, Portugal 448 y Catalina Aldaz, T225 6759, www.canodros.com. Run luxury Galápagos cruises and jungle tours in the Kapawi Ecological Reserve, also have office in Guayaquil.

Compañía de Guías de Montaña, Jorge Washington 425 y 6 de Diciembre, T/F250 4773, www.companiadeguias.com. Climbing and trekking specialists, but sell other tours.

EcoAndes, Baquedano E5-27 y JL Mera, T222 0892, www.ecoandestravel.com. For classic tours, adventure travel, Galápagos and Amazon. Also have 2 hotels, **Fuente de Piedra I** and **II**, in La Mariscal district, and **Coraza** in Otavalo, www.ecuahotel.com.

Eco Tours, Magnolias 51 y Cristantemos, La Primavera, Cumbaya, Quito, T/F289 7316, www.EcotoursEcuador.com. Exclusive booking agent for the Napo Wildlife Center (www.NapoWildlifeCenter.com).

Ecuador Amazing, Pinto 521 y Amazonas, p6, T254 7257, www.ecuadoramazing.com. Full service tour operator and owner of a group of tour services. See advert for tours offered.

Ecuadorian Tours, Amazonas 329 y Washington, several other locations, T256 0488, www.ecuador iantours.com. (Also Amex representative.) Airline tickets and tours in all regions.

Enchanted Expeditions, de las Alondras N45-102 y de los Lirios, T334 0525, www.enchantedexpeditions.com. Operate Galápagos cruises in various categories, jungle and trekking tours.

Galacruises Expleditions, 748 Jorge Washington y Amazonas, T/F250 9007, www.galacruises.com.

Galasam, Amazonas 1354 y Cordero 1354, T290 3909, www.galasam.com. Full range of day and multi-day tours in highlands, jungle trips to their own lodge on the Río Aguarico, Galápagos trips.

Geo Reisen, Yugoeslavia 265 y Azuay, T243 6081, www.georeisentours.com. Specializing in cultural, adventure and nature tours adapted for individuals, groups or families.

Green Planet, JL Mera N23-84 y Wilson, T252 0570, greenpla@interactive.net.ec. Ecologically sensitive jungle trips, lodge on Río Aguarico, good food.

Kapok Expeditions, Pinto E4-225, T/F255 6348, www.kapokexpeditions.com. Jungle tours to Cuyabeno and Yasuní, trekking, Machalilla, hacienda tours (participate in daily farm activities).

Kempery Tours, Ramírez Dávilos 117 y Amazonas, Ed Turismundial, p 2, T250 5600, www.kempery.com. German, English and Dutch spoken, all kinds of tours, including Galápagos and jungle, good value.

Klein Tours, Eloy Alfaro N34-151 y Catalina Aldaz, also Shyris N34-280 y Holanda, T226 7000, www.kleintours.com. Galápagos cruises and mainland tours, tailor-made, English, French and German spoken.

Metropolitan Touring, República de El Salvador N36-84, also Amazonas 239 y 18 de Septiembre and other locations, T298 8200, www.metro politan-touring.com. Galápagos tours, arranges climbing, trekking expeditions led by world-known climbers, as well as tours of Quito, Parque Nacional Machalilla, rail journeys, jungle camps.

Palmar Voyages, Alemania 575 y Av Mariana de Jesús, T256 9809, www.palmarvoyages.com. Small specialist company, custom-made itineraries to all areas of Ecuador or Peru, good rates.

Pamir Travel and Adventures, JL Mera 721 y Veintimilla, T254 2605, F254 7576. Galápagos cruises, climbing and jungle tours.

Positiv Turismo, Voz Andes N41-81, T244 0604, www.positivturismo.com. Swiss-Austrian-run company offers trips to Galápagos, cultural trips, trekking and special interest tours.

Quasar Náutica, Brasil 293, Edif IACA p 2, T244 6996, www.quasarnautica.com. High-quality Galápagos cruises. In USA: 7855 NW 12th St, Suite 221, Miami, Florida 33126.

Rainforestur, Amazonas 420 entre Roca y Robles, T223 9822, rainfor@interactive.net.ec. Also have an office in Baños. Offers climbing and jungle trips to Cuyabeno and the Puyo area.

Safari, Foch E5-39 y JL Mera, T255 2505, www.safari.com.ec. Jean Brown and Pattie Serrano, excellent adventure travel, personalized itineraries, mountain climbing, cycling, rafting, trekking and cultural tours. They also book Galápagos tours, sell jungle trips and run a high-altitude glacier school. Great source of travel information. Daily 0930-1830. Recommended.

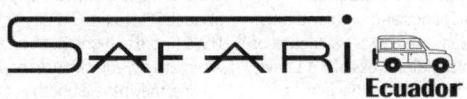

Sangay Touring, Amazonas N24-196 y Cordero, T T2508922, www.guide2galapagos.com. Run by Martin and Robin Slater, operate a variety of custom designed tours and sell Galápagos trips, efficient service.

Sierra Nevada, Pinto 637 y Cordero, T255 3658, snevada@accessinter.net. Climbing, rafting, jungle expeditions, experienced multi-lingual guides.

Surtrek, Amazonas 897 y Wilson, T256 1129, www.surtrek.com. Climbing, trekking expeditions, jungle and Galápagos tours, also flights.

Tierra de Fuego, Amazonas N2323 y Veintmilla, T250 1418, www.ecuadortierradefuego.com. Travel agency and tour operator with a small fleet of vehicles to provide land services and tours throughout the country.

Tours Unlimited, Julio Castro 379 y Valparaíso, T222 2564, www.tours-unlimited.com. Custom-made itineraries in all regions, specializing in trips for honeymooners.

Tropic Ecological Adventures, República E7-320 y Diego de Almagro, Edif Taurus, dpto 1-A, T222 5907, www.tropiceco.com. Run by Andy Drumm and Sofía Darquea, naturalist guides with many years experience in Galápagos, who work closely with conservation groups. Winners of awards for responsible tourism in 1997 and 2000. Their ecologically responsible and educational tours are recommended for anyone seriously interested in the environment. Part of each fee is given to indigenous communities and ecological projects. Also sell Galápagos and highland trips.

TrueColorsTravel, Guayaquil N9-59 y Oriente, of 304, T/F295 5345. Horse riding treks of 1-11 days, including Inca Trail, rides between haciendas, volcano, páramo rides, cloud forest trails.

Via Tierra, Pasaje Los Angeles 106 y Alemania, T223 7842, andresteran3@hotmail.com. Trekking, horse riding and other adventure tours to less frequented areas such as Tulipe and Sincholagua.

Zenith Travel, JL Mera 453 y Roca, T252 9993, www.zenithecuador.com. Runs a variety of tours in Ecuador and Peru, Galápagos tours, specializing in the GLBT market. Good value.

Whitewater rafting

Row Expediciones, Pablo Arturo Suarez 191 y Eloy Alfaro, T223 9224, www.row expediciones.com. 6-day trips on the Upano Nov-Feb, guides from Idaho, USA.

Sierra Nevada (see Tour operators below), excellent trips from 1 to 3 days, chief guide Edison Ramírez (fluent English/French) is certified by *French Association*.

Yacu Amu/Ríos Ecuador, Foch 746 y JL Mera, T290 4054, www.yacuamu.com. Australian-owned (Steve Nomchong), guide Gynner Coronel, very professional, rafting trips of 1-6 days, also kayak courses, good equipment. Highly recommended.

All these outfits charge US$50-70 per day.

⊖ Transport

Quito *p889, map p891 and 892*
Air
Mariscal Sucre Airport. The safest and easiest way to travel between town and the airport is to take a **taxi**. You can catch one from the rank right outside arrivals. The fare from the airport to the New City is about US$5; to the Old City or to a first-class hotel US$6 (more at night, but beware of overcharging). Alternatively, you can use the **Trans-Rabbit** van service, they have a booth at international arrivals, T227 6736, US$2-3 pp to the New City in a van with room for up to 15 passengers. This is good value if there are a few people sharing. **Public buses** are not recommended unless you have

Ecuador Quito & around Listings

virtually no luggage or are desperately low on funds. Buses and trolley alike are too crowded to enter with even a small backpack so the risk of theft is very high. The bus stop is 1 block west of terminal, in front of Centro Comercial Aeropuerto. For the New City take a southbound bus marked 'Carcelén- Congreso' or 'Pinar Alto-Hotel Quito', these run along Av Amazonas and later JL Mera, US$0.25. For the Old City and parts of the New City, take a bus from the Aeropuerto stop or a green *alimentador* (feeder bus line) to the northern terminus of the trolley; both from the same location as above. There is no bus or trolley service late at night when most flights from North America arrive. Beware of self-styled porters who grab your luggage in the hope of receiving a tip, legitimate porters wear a name tag. Left luggage facilities are just outside international arrivals. There are duty-free shops in the international departure lounge. Details of internal services are given in the respective destinations.

Bus

Local Quito has 3 parallel bus lines running from north to south on exclusive lanes, covering almost the length of the city. The fare is US$0.25. **Trole** (T266 5016, Mon-Fri 0500-2345, weekends and holidays 0600-2145) is system of trolley buses, with feeder bus lines (*alimentadores*, painted turquoise) from the suburbs. It runs along Av 10 de Agosto in the north of the city, C Guayaquil (southbound) and C Flores (northbound) in the Old City, and mainly along Av Pedro Vicente Maldonado in the south. The northern terminus is north of 'La Y', the junction of 10 de Agosto, Av América and Av de la Prensa; at El Recreo, on Av Maldonado is an important transfer station, known as Terminal Sur, and the southern terminus, Morán Valverde, is in Ciudadela Quitumbe in the far south. Trolleys have a special entrance for wheelchairs. **Ecovía** (T2430726, Mon-Sat 0500-2130, Sun and holidays 0600-2100) is a line

of articulated buses running along Av 6 de Diciembre, from La Marín near the Old City to the Estación Río Coca, at C Río Coca east of 6 de Diciembre, in the north. Ecovía feeder buses are dark red. **Metrobus Corredor Santa Prisca-La Ofelia** (Mon-Fri 0600-2200, weekends and holidays 0600-2100) also runs articulated buses along Av América and Av de la Prensa from Santa Prisca, at the southern end of the New City, to La Ofelia, a suburb in the north. There are also 3 types of **city buses**: *selectivos* are red, take mostly sitting passengers and a limited number standing, US$0.25. *Bus Tipo* are royal blue, take sitting and standing passengers, US$0.25. There are few *populares* left, these are light blue, US$0.18, can get very crowded. Many bus lines go through La Marín at the north end of the Old City. Extra caution is advised here: it is a rough area, pickpockets abound and it is best avoided at night.

Short distance Outer suburbs are served by *Interparroquial* buses painted green. Those running east to the valleys of Cumbayá, Tumbaco and beyond leave from the Estación Río Coca (see Ecovía above). Buses southeast to Valle de los Chillos leave from La Marín. Buses going northwest leave from San Blas, those north from C Larrea and Asunción and those going south from Villaflora.

Long distance The Terminal Terrestre, at Maldonado y Cumandá (south of Plaza Santo Domingo), handles most long-distance bus services and is really the only place to get information on schedules, 24-hr luggage store US$1.75 per day. US$0.20 to enter platforms. It is unsafe at all hours, worst at night. To or from the Terminal Terrestre, take a taxi (highly recommended), or the trolley bus (unsafe with luggage). There are company booking offices but staff shout destinations of buses leaving; you can get on board and pay later (but confirm fare in advance). For buses out of Quito it is sometimes advisable to reserve the day before (eg on holiday weekends). See under destinations for fares and schedules.

907

Several companies run better quality coaches on the longer routes, those with terminals in the New City are: **Flota Imbabura**, Manuel Larrea 1211 y Portoviejo, T223 6940, for Cuenca and Guayaquil; **Transportes Ecuador**, JL Mera 330 y Jorge Washington, T250 3642, to Guayaquil; **Transportes Esmeraldas**, Santa María y 9 de Octubre, T250 5099, for Esmeraldas; **Reina del Camino**, Larrea y 18 de Septiembre, T258 5697, for **Portoviejo**, **Bahía** and **Manta**; **Panamericana Internacional**, Colón 852 y Reina Victoria, T250 1585, for **Huaquillas**, **Machala**, **Cuenca**, **Loja**, **Guayaquil**, **Manta** and **Esmeraldas**, they also run 'international' bus to **Bogotá** (change buses in Tulcán and Ipiales, US$70, 28 hrs) and **Lima** (change buses in Aguas Verdes and Tumbes, US$70, 38 hrs). **Ormeño Internacional**, from Perú, Shyris N34-432 y Portugal, T246 0027, twice a week to **Lima** (US$70, 36 hrs), **La Paz**, US$150, **Santiago** (US$165, 4 days) and **Buenos Aires** (US$200, 1 week). It is quicker and cheaper to take a bus to the border and change. The route to **Peru** via Loja and Macará takes much longer than the Huaquillas route, but is more relaxed. Do not buy Peruvian (or any other country's) bus tickets here, they are much cheaper outside Ecuador.

Taxi

Taxis are a safe, cheap and efficient way to get around the city. Be reasonable and remember that the majority of taxi drivers are honest and helpful. For airport taxis, see above. From the Terminal Terrestre to the New City is US$4; and journeys around the New City cost from US$1. Expect to pay US$1-2 more at night. All taxis must have working meters by law, but make sure the meter is running (if it isn't, fix the fare before). Also insist that the taxi drops you precisely where you want to go. All legally registered taxis have the number of their co-operative and the individual operator's number prominently painted on the side of the vehicle and on a sticker on the windshield. They are safer and cheaper than unauthorized taxis. Note the registration and the licence plate numbers if you feel you have been seriously overcharged or mistreated. You may then complain to the transit police or tourist office. At night it is safer to use a radio taxi, there are several companies including: **Taxi Amigo**, T222 2222; **City Taxi**, T263 3333; and **Central de Radio Taxis**, T250 0600. Make sure they give you the taxi number so that you get the correct taxi and can trace anything you may leave behind. To hire a taxi by the hour costs from US$7. For trips outside Quito, agree the fare beforehand: US$90-100 a day. Outside the luxury hotels co-operative taxi drivers have a list of agreed excursion prices and most drivers are knowledgeable. For taxi tours with a guide, try **Hugo Herrera**, T226 7891. He speaks English and is recommended.

Train

Regular passenger service has been discontinued throughout the country. A tourist train runs from **Tambillo**, south of Quito, to the **Cotopaxi** station in Area Nacional de Recreación El Boliche, Sat and Sun 0800, return 1430, 3 hrs, US$4.60 return (children under 12 half price). Purchase tickets for passenger carriages in advance as it is a popular ride: from Bolívar 443 y García Moreno, T258 2927, Mon 1300-1630, Tue-Fri 0800-1600, passport number required for each passenger. Last minute sales at Tambillo are for box cars only, same price. If you wish to return by bus, it is a 2 km walk from the Cotopaxi station to the Pan-American highway. **Metropolitan Touring**, see above, offers various tours involving train travel.

● Directory

Quito *p889, map p891 and 892*
Airline offices National: Aerogal, Av Amazonas 7797 y Juan Holguin, opposite the airport, T292 0495, www.aerogal.com.ec. Atesa, Guipúzcoa E16-139 y Gerona, T230 3242, seconaca@pi.pro.ec. Icaro, Palora 124 y Amazonas, T245 0928. TAME, Amazonas 13-54 y Colón, Colón y Rábida y 6 de Diciembre N26-112, T290 9900. International: Air Europa, Reina Victora 1539 y Colón, Edif Banco de Guayaquil p 6, T256 7646. Air France and KLM, 12 de Octubre N26-27 y Lincoln, T298 6859. Air Madrid, Los Shyris y Bélgica, T227 4919. American Airlines, Amazonas 4545 y Pereira, T226 0900. Avianca, Coruña 1311 y San Ignacio, T1-800-003434. Continental, 12 de Octubre 1830 y Cordero, World Trade Center, No 1108, T225 0905. Copa, República de El Salvador 361 y Moscú, edif Aseguradora del Sur, T227 3082. Iberia, Eloy Alfaro 939 y Amazonas, edif Finandes, p 5, T256 6009. Lan, Pasaje Río Guayas E3-131 y Amazonas, Edif Rumiñahui, opposite Parque La Carolina, T299 2300. Lufthansa, Amazonas N27-205 y Palora, T226 7705. Santa Bárbara, Portugal 794 y República de El Salvador, T225 3972 TACA, República de El Salvador N36-139 y Suecia, T292 3170. **Banks** See page 885 for note on travellers's cheques. Banco del Austro, Amazonas y Santa María. Cash advances on Visa. Banco de Guayaquil, Colón y Reina Victoria, p 3. Cirrus, Maestro or Plus ATM, cash advances on Visa, fast and efficient. Mastercard headquarters, Naciones Unidas 825, next door to Banco del Pacífico. Cash advances, efficient service. Banco del Pacífico, main branch at Naciones Unidas entre Los Shyris y Amazonas (best branch for getting cash against a credit card), also

Amazonas y Roca, Mall El Jardín and Centro Comercial El Bosque. MasterCard and Visa through Cirrus and Maestro ATMs. **Banco del Pichincha**, Amazonas 13-54 y Colón, Venezuela y Espejo, half block from Plaza de la Independencia and many other branches. Cash through Cirrus ATM only. **Mutualista Pichincha**, 18 de Septiembre y JL Mera, García Moreno 1130 y Chile and other branches. Cash advances on Mastercard 0900-1630. **Produbanco**, Amazonas N35-211 y Japón (opposite CCI), Amazonas y Robles (also open Sat 0900-1300), Benalcazar 852 y Olmedo (cash advances only) and at the airport. Cash and TCs in various currencies, good service, cash advance on MasterCard. Mon-Fri 0830-1500. The **American Express** representative is **Ecuadorian Tours**, see above, sells and replaces Amex TCs, does not change TCs or give cash advances. **Casas de cambio: Vazcorp**, Amazonas N21-147 y Roca, T252 9212. Also changes other currencies and sells TCs. Mon-Fri 0845-1745, Sat 0900-1300. **Car hire** All the main car rental companies are at the airport. For multinational rental agencies, see Essentials, page 43. City offices of local companies: **Ecuacars**, Colón 1280 y Amazonas, T252 9781. **Expo**, Av América N21-66 y Bolívia, T222 8688. Good value. **Trans-Rabbit**, at the international arrivals section of the Airport, rent vans for up to 10 passengers, with driver, for trips in Quito and out of town, T223 2133; also **Achupallas Tours**, T330 1493, vanrent@andinanet.net. **Cultural** centres **Alliance Française**, at Eloy Alfaro N32-468, T245 2017, www.afquito.org.ec. French courses, films and cultural events. **Casa Humboldt**, Vancouver E5-54 y Polonia, T254 8480, www.asociacion-humboldt.org. German centre, Goethe Institute, films, talks, exhibitions. **Embassies and consulates** Austria, Gaspar de Villaroel E9-53 y Los Shyris, p 3, T244 3272, 1000-1200. **Belgium**, República de El Salvador 1082 y Naciones Unidas, p 10, T227 6145, ambelqui@ecnet.ec. Mon-Thu 0900-1200,

Mon-Wed 1430-1700. **Canada**, 6 de Diciembre 2816 y Paul Rivet, edif Josueth González p 4, T223 2114, 0900-1200. **Colombia**, Colón 1133 y Amazonas, T222 2486, 0900-1300, 1400-1600. **Denmark**, Rep de El Salvador 733 y Portugal, T243 7163. **Finland**, Whimper N30-91 y Coruña, T290 1501. **France**, L Plaza 107 y Patria, T256 0789, francie@andinet.net. **Germany**, Naciones Unidas E10-44 y República de El Salvador, edif City Plaza, T297 0820, alemania@interactive.net.ec. 0830-1130. **Israel**, 12 de Octubre y Salazar, Edif Plaza 2000, p 9, T223 7474, israemb@interactive.net.ec. 1000-1300. **Italy**, La Isla 111 y H Albornoz, T256 1077, www.ambitalquito.org. 0830-1230. **Japan**, JL Mera N19-36 y Patria, T256 1899, japembecq@uio.satnet.net. 0930-1200, 1400-1700. **Netherlands**, 12 de Octubre 1942 y Cordero, World Trade Center, p 1, T222 9229, 0830-1300, 1400-1730. **Norway**, Rep de El Salvador 1082 y Naciones Unidas, T246 1523. **Peru**, República de El Salvador 495 e Irlanda, edif Irlanda, T246 8410, embpeecu@uio.satnet.net. 0900-1300, 1500-1800. **Spain**, La Pinta 455 y Amazonas, T256 4373, embespec@uio.satnet.net. 0900-1200. **Sweden**, República de El Salvador N39-399 e Irlanda, T227 8189. **Switzerland**, Amazonas 3617 y Juan Pablo Sanz, edif Xerox, p 2, T243 4949, vertretung@qui.rep.admin.ch. **United Kingdom**, Naciones Unidas y República de El Salvador, edif Citiplaza, p 14, T297 0800, britembq@impsat.net.ec. Mon-Thu 0730-1230, 1300-1600, Fri 0830-1230. **USA**, 12 de Octubre y Patria, T256 2890, 0800-1230, 1330-1700. **Internet** Quito has very many cyber cafés, particularly in the Mariscal tourist district. Rates start at about US$0.60 per hr, but US$1 is more typical. **Language schools** The following schools have received favourable reports. **In the New City: Academia Latinoamericana de Espanol**, Noruega 126 y 6 de Diciembre, T225 0946, www.latinoschools.com. **Amazonas**, Washington 718 y Amazonas, edif Rocafuerte, p3, T252 7509,

Ecuador Quito & around Listings

www.eduamazonas.com. **Bipo & Toni's Academia de Español**, Carrión E8-183 y L Plaza, T/F255 6614, www.bipo.net. **Colón**, Colón 2088 y Versalles, T256 2485, www.colonspanish school.com. **Escuela De Espanol Simón Bolívar**, Leonidas Plaza 353 y Roca, T250 4977, www.simon-bolivar.com. **Equinoccial**, Reina Victoria 1325 y García, T/F256 4488, www.ecuadorspanish.com. Small school. **Galápagos**, Amazonas 1004 y Wilson, p 1, T256 5213, www.galapagos.edu.ec. **Pichincha**, Carrión N4-37 y 6 de Diciembre, T222 0478, www.pichinchaspanishschool.com. **Quito**, Marchena Oe1-30 y 10 de Agosto, T255 3647, www.academiaquito.com.ec. **La Lengua**, Colón 1001 y JL Mera, p 8, T/F250 1271, www.la-lengua.com. **Mitad del Mundo**, Patria 640 y 9 de Octubre, Edif Patria 1204, T254 6827, www.mitadmundo.com.ec. Repeatedly recommended. **Simón Bolívar**, Leonidas Plaza 353 y Roca, T/F223 6688, www.simon-bolivar.com. Have their own travel agency. **Sintaxis**, 10 de Agosto 15-55 y Bolivia, edif Andrade, p 5, T252 0006, www.sintaxis.net. Consistently recommended. **South American Language Center**, Amazonas N26-59 y Santa María, T/F254 2715, www.southamerican.edu.ec. **Superior**, Darquea Terán 1650 y 10 de Agosto, T222 3242, www.instituto-superior.net. They also have a school in Otavalo (Sucre 1110 y Morales, p 2, T06-292 2414), in Galápagos (advanced booking required) and can arrange voluntary work. **Universidad Católica**, 12 de Octubre y Roca, contact Carmen Sarzosa, T222 8781, csarzosa@puceuio.puce.edu.ec. **In the Old City**: **Beraca School**, García Moreno 858 between Sucre and Espejo, Pasaje Amador, p3, T228 8092, also at Amazonas 1114 y Pinto in the New City, T295 8687. **Los Andes**, García Moreno 1245 y Olmedo, p2, T295 5107, quitocolonial@

yupimail.com, has schools outside Quito and can arrange volunteer work. **San Francisco**, Sucre 518 y Benalcázar (Plaza San Francisco), p3, T228 2849, Iso at Amazonas 2262 y Ramírez Dávalos, New City, T255 3476, sanfranciscoss@ latinmail.com. **Medical services** Most embassies have the telephone numbers of doctors and dentists who speak non-Spanish languages. **Hospitals: Hospital Voz Andes** Villalengua Oe 2-37 y Av 10 de Agosto, T226 2142 (reached by Trole, la Y stop). Emergency room, quick and efficient, fee based on ability to pay, run by Christian HCJB organization, has out-patient dept, T243 9343. **Hospital Metropolitano**, Mariana de Jesús y Occidental, just east of the western city bypass, T226 1520, ambulance T226 5020, catch a Quito Sur-San Gabriel bus along América, or the Trole (Mariana de Jesús stop) and walk up, or take a taxi. Very professional and recommended, but expensive. **Clínica Pichincha**, Veintimilla E3-30 y Páez, T256 2296, ambulance T250 1565. Another very good, expensive hospital. **Clínica Pasteur**, Eloy Alfaro 552 y 9 de Octubre, T223 4004. Also good and cheaper than the above. **Novaclínica Santa Cecilia**, Veintimilla 1394 y 10 de Agosto, T254 5390, emergency T254 5000. Reasonable prices, good. **Med Center Travel Clinic** (Dr John Rosenberg), Foch 476 y Almagro, T252 1104, 09-973 9734. General and travel medicine with a full range of vaccines, speaks English and German, very helpful GP. **Fybeca** is a reliable chain of 33 pharmacies throughout the city. Their 24-hr branches are at Amazonas y Tomás de Berlanga near the Plaza de Toros, and at Centro Comercial El Recreo in the south. **Farmacia Colón**, 10 de Agosto 2292 y Cordero, T222 6534, also open 24 hrs. **Post offices** All branches open Mon-Fri 0800-1800, Sat 0800-1200. In principle all branches provide all services, but

⬛ Language schools in Quito

Quito is one of the most important centres for Spanish language study in Latin America with about 80 schools operating. There is a great variety to choose from. Identify your budget and goals for the course: rigorous grammatical and technical training, fluent conversation skills, getting to know Ecuadoreans or just enough basic Spanish to get you through your trip.

Visit a few places to get a feel for what they charge and offer. Prices vary greatly, from US$4 to US$10 per hour, but you do not always get what you pay for. There is also tremendous variation in teacher qualifications, infrastructure and resource materials. Schools usually offer courses of four or seven hours tuition per day. Many correspondents suggest that four is enough. Some schools offer packages which combine teaching in the morning and touring in the afternoon. A great deal of emphasis has traditionally been placed on one-to-one teaching, but remember that a well-structured small classroom setting can also be very good.

The quality of homestays likewise varies, the cost including meals runs from US$12 to US$25 per day. Try to book just one week at first to see how a place suits you, don't be pressed into signing a long term contract right at the start. For language courses as well as homestays, deal directly with the people who will provide services to you, and avoid intermediaries. Always get a detailed receipt whenever you make a payment.

If you are short on time then it can be a good idea to make your arrangements from home, either directly with one of the schools or through an agency, who can offer you a wide variety of options. If you have more time and less money, then it may be more economical to organize your own studies after you arrive. *South American Explorers* provides a free list of recommended schools and these may give club members discounts.

We list schools for which we have received positive recommendations each year. This does not imply that schools not mentioned are not recommended.

your best chances are at Colón y Almagro in the Mariscal district, and at the main sorting centre on Japón near Naciones Unidas, behind the CCI shopping centre. The branch on Eloy Alfaro 354 y 9 de Octubre frequently loses mail; best avoided. There is also a branch in the Old City, on Espejo entre Guayaquil y Venezuela, and between the old and New Cities at Ulloa and Ramírez Dávalos, behind the Mercado Santa Clara. This is the centre for parcel post, and you may still be directed there to send large packages. *Poste Restante* at the post offices at Espejo and at Eloy Alfaro (less efficient). All *poste restante* letters are sent to Espejo unless marked 'Correo Central, Eloy Alfaro', but you are advised to check both *postes restantes*, whichever address you use. Letters can be sent care of American

Express, Apdo 17-01-0265, Quito. *South American Explorers* hold mail for members. **Telephones** There are cabins (*cabinas*) all over the city operated by the **Alegro, Andinatel, Movistar** and **Porta** companies, for national and international calls. There are also debit card cell phones throughout the city. **Useful addresses** Emergencies: T911 for all types of emergency in Quito. **Immigration Offices**: see Essentials. Police: T101. **Policía de Turismo**, Reina Victoria y Roca, T254 3983.Report robberies at **Dirección de Seguridad Pública**, Cuenca y Mideros, T295 4604, in the Old City or **Policía Judicial**, Roca 582 y JL Mera, in La Mariscal, T255 0243.

Around Quito

Mitad del Mundo and around

The location of the equatorial line here (23 km N of Quito, nearest town San Antonio de Pichincha) was determined by Charles-Marie de la Condamine and his French expedition in 1736, and agrees to within 150 m with modern GPS measurements. The monument forms the focal point of a park and leisure area built as a typical colonial town, with restaurants, gift shops, Post Office with philatelic sales, travel agency, and has a very interesting **ethnographic museum** inside ① *Mon-Thu 0900-1800, Fri-Sun 0900-1900 (very crowded on Sun), US$1.50, children US$0.75, includes entrance to the pavilions; entry to the ethnographic museum US$3 (includes guided tour of museum in Spanish or English).* In the museum; a lift takes you to the top, then you walk down with the museum laid out all around with different indigenous cultures every few steps. There is a **Planetarium** *US$1.50 for planetarium, US$1 for model*, with hourly 30-minute shows and an attractive and interesting model of old Quito, about 10 m square, with artificial day and night, which took seven years to build. **Museo Intiñan** ① *200 m north of the monument, T239 5122, 0930-1730 daily, US$2,* shows the exact location of the equator, with certificates for visitors, eclectic and very interesting. Two minutes' walk before the Monument is the restaurant *Equinoccio*, about US$10 a meal, live music on Sunday, open 1000-1600 daily, T239 4091. Available at the restaurant or at stalls outside are 'certificates' recording your visit to the Equator (free with a meal).

Pululahua and Rumicucho

① *US$5.* A few kilometres beyond the Monument, off the paved road to Calacalí, is the Pululahua crater which can be seen from a lookout on the rim. It is a geobotanical reserve. Try to go in the morning, there is often cloud later. There is a rough track down from the rim to the crater. To get to the park and experience the rich vegetation and warm micro-climate inside, continuing past the village in the crater, turn left and follow an unimproved road up to the rim and back to the main road, a 15-20 km round trip.

Also in the vicinity of the Monument, 3 km from San Antonio, are the Inca ruins of **Rumicucho** *US$0.50*. Restoration is poor, but the location is magnificent. Start early if you want to visit all these in one day.

Protected areas northwest of Quito → Altitude: 1,200-2,800 m.

Despite their proximity to the capital (two hours from Quito), the western slopes of **Pichincha** and its surroundings are surprisingly wild, with fine opportunities for walking and especially birdwatching. Four roads drop into the western lowlands from Quito; each has a unique character, and each has interesting ecotourism reserves.

The cloud forest in the 18,500-ha **Maquipucuna Biological Reserve** contains a tremendous diversity of flora and fauna, including over 325 species of birds. The reserve has trails of varying length, from 15 minutes to full day (US$5 per person). Full board accommodation available (**L**), for transport see next paragraph. For reservations: **Fundación Maquipuicuna** ① *Baquerizo Moreno E9-153 y Tamayo, Quito, T02-250 7200, www.maqui.org*, supports the conservation of biodiversity and sustainable use of natural resources.

At Km 62 on the old road to Mindo via Tandayapa is **Bellavista**, with excellent birdwatching and botany at the *Hostería Bellavista*. For Maquipucuna and Bellavista take a bus to Nanegalito then hire a pick-up (US$15-20), or arrange everything with the lodges (see Sleeping, below) or in Quito.

Bosque Protector Mindo-Nambillo → Colour map 10, grid A3

Mindo, a small town surrounded by dairy farms and lush cloud forest climbing the western slopes of Pichincha, is the main access for the 19,200-ha Bosque Protector Mindo-Nambillo. The reserve, which ranges in altitude from 1,400 to 4,780 m, features beautiful flora (many orchids and bromeliads), fauna (butterflies, birds including the cock of the rock, golden-headed quetzal and toucan-barbet) and spectacular cloud forest and waterfalls. A controversial new oil pipeline built right through the heart of the reserve in 2002 has not diminished the area's many attractions. **Amigos de la Naturaleza de Mindo** ① *½ block from the Parque Central, T/F276 5463,* runs the **Centro de Educación Ambiental** (CEA), 4 km from town, within the 17 ha buffer zone, capacity for 25-30 people. Guide service, lodging and food are available (entry US$1).

Lodging **E-F** per person, full board including excursion **C** per person. Take sleeping gear (none provided) and food if you wish to prepare your own (nice kitchen facilities). Arrangements have to be made in advance. During the rainy season, access to the reserve can be rough. Vinicio Pérez (T390 0412, vinicioperez@andinanet.net) is an excellent birding guide, a little English spoken, recommended. Mindo also has orchid gardens and a butterfly farm 3 km from town. Activities include rappelling in the La Isla waterfalls, and 'tubing' regattas in the rivers.

West of Mindo
The road continues beyond the turn-off to Mindo, descending to the subtropical zone north of Santo Domingo de los Colorados. Known as the Eco-Ruta del Quinde, it goes via San Miguel de los Bancos and Pedro Vicente (PV) Maldonado to La Independencia on the Santo Domingo-Esmeraldas road. There are many new hostales and places to visit along the route, of particular interest to birdwatchers. There are tours from Quito. See Sleeping, below, for resorts.

On the shores of the lovely Río Caoni is **Puerto Quito**, a small town which was once intended to be the capital's port (hotels **D-F**, simple *comedores*). The main road bypasses the centre of town to the south. Along the Caoni and other rivers in the region are several reserves and resorts. This is a good area for birdwatching, swimming in rivers and natural pools, walking, kayaking, or simply relaxing in pleasant natural surroundings.

Papallacta
At the **Termas de Papallacta** ① *64 km east from Quito, 1 km from the road to Baeza, 0700-2100, T02-256 8989, www.papallacta.com.ec* there are ten thermal pools, three large enough for swimming, and four cold plunge pools, the best developed hot springs in the country. There are two public complexes of springs: the regular pools ① *US$6 pp*, and the spa centre ① *US$15 (massages and other special treatments extra)*. For accommodation, the hotel (**AL**) has heated rooms with private bath (one with private jacuzzi) surrounding small private pools (access only to guests). A set of cabins for families or groups of up to six people (**L**), surround more private pools. Guests are provided with identification and can enter any part of the pools; massages and other treatments at the spa centre have 50% discount. Meals are extra. For weekends book a room at least a week in advance; holiday weekends a month or more in advance. The complex is tastefully done and recommended. The view, on a clear day, of Antisana while enjoying the thermal waters is superb. There are several excellent self-guided routes in the reserve behind the pools ① *US$1 and US$2 pp*. Access to the road to Oyacachi, 45 km, is beside the information centre. It is advisable to obtain permission before trying to go through; call the Ministerio del Medio Ambiente in Cayambe, T211 0370. Likewise call the same office to use the guest cabin in the Cayambe-Coca reserve and fish in several of the lakes.

Sangolquí
About 20 minutes from Quito by bus is Sangolquí, in the Valle de los Chillos. It has a beautifully restored colonial plaza and a busy Sunday market (and a lesser one on Thursday) selling mainly food. There are few tourists.

Refugio de Vida Silvestre Pasochoa
① *Foreigners US$7, very busy at weekends, 45 mins southeast of Quito by car.*
This natural park set in humid Andean forest is run by the **Fundación Natura** ① *República 481 y Almagro, T250 3391.* The reserve has more than 120 species of birds (unfortunately some of the fauna has been frightened away by the noise of the visitors) and 50 species of trees, situated between 2,700 m and 4,200 m. There are walks of 30 minutes to eight hours. Camping is permitted in the park (US$3 per person). Take food and water as there are no shops and take your rubbish away with you. There is also a refuge (US$5 per person per night, with shower, has cooking facilities), but you will need a sleeping bag.

● Sleeping

Mitad del Mundo and around *p912*
C Hostería Alemana, Av Manuel Córdoba Galarza, 700 m south of the complex, in San Antonio de Pichincha, T239 4243. Very good restaurant, recommended.

Protected areas northwest of Quito *p912*
L-AL Hostería Bellavista (Cabins in the Clouds, Natural Sanctuary), Bellavista, T211 6947 (Bellavista), office at Jorge Washington E7-23 y 6 de Diciembre, Quito, T290 3165, www.bella

vistacloud forest.com. Full board, hot showers, excellent birdwatching and botany, **E** pp in research station (bunk beds, meals extra, kitchen facilities), camping US$5 pp, book in advance.
B Hostería San Jorge, Km 4 Vía Antigua Cotocollao-Nono, Bosque Protector Pichincha, T249 4002, www.hostsanjorge.com.ec. On the safe, northeast side of Rucu Pichincha, private protected land. On a traditional farm, restaurant, quiet, peaceful, pool, sauna and much else, horse riding, excellent birdwatching. Recommended.

Mindo *p912*

L El Monte. 2 km from Mindo on road to CEA, then cross river on cable car near the butterfly farm, contact office in town beforehand, T276 5427, www.ecuadorcloudforest.com. Includes 3 meals and some excursions, birdwatching, tubing, walking, swimming.
L Mindo Gardens, 3 km from Mindo on road to CEA, T225 2488. Includes 3 meals, very good food, expensive restaurant open to the public, also snack bar serving pizza, comfortable, tastefully decorated cabins, beautiful setting, good birdwatching.
AL El Carmelo de Mindo, in 32 ha 1 km west of town, T276 5449, www.mindo.com.ec. Includes 3 meals, restaurant, pool, rooms, cabins and tree houses, camping US$5, fishing, horse rental, excursions, mid-week discounts.
A Finca Mindo Lindo, On the main Calacalí-La Independencia road by Mindo turnoff, T245 5344, puntos_verdes@hotmail.com. Includes breakfast, restaurant, day visits and overnight stays, guided tours, meals available. Recommended.
A Hacienda San Vicente, 'Yellow House', 500 m south of the plaza, T276 5464. Including breakfast and dinner, family-run, nice rooms, good walking trails nearby, great value. Recommended.
B-D Jardín de las Orquídeas. 2 blocks from church, T276 5471. Includes breakfast, restaurant, vegetarian meals available, nice.
B-C El Descanso, 300 m from main street, take 1st right after bridge, T276 5383, www.eldes canso.net. Comfortable, cheaper in loft with shared bath, includes breakfast, parking. Recommended.
D-E El Bijao, Av Quito near entrance to town, T276 5470. Cheaper with shared bath, family run, laundry, restaurant, simple but nice, good value.
D-F Casa de Cecilia, 2 blocks from plaza, T276 5453, casadececilia@gmx.net. Cheap meals available, shared bath, hot water, internet, US$2 for use of kitchen, cheaper in dorm with mattresses on floor, popular with volunteer groups.
E Flor del Valle, on lane beside church. Shared bath, hot water, good value, basic.

West of Mindo *p913*

LL Arasha resort, in the biologically rich Chocó region, 4 km from Pedro Vicente Maldonado, Km

141, T276 5347. Quito office: Los Shyris N39-41 y Río Coca, 8th floor, T225 3937, www.arasha resort.com. Beautiful, top-of-the-range centre with excellent facilities, good birdwatching, trails in secondary and primary forest, spa, world-class food. Elegant and very upscale.
A Reserva Río Guaycuyacu, accessed from PV Maldonado, advance booking essential, write to: Galápagos 565, Quito, guaycuyacu@yahoo.com. An exotic fruit farm with 400 varieties of fruit and birdwatching. Includes 3 hearty vegetarian meals a day, maximum 8 guests. One-month agricultural apprenticeships can be arranged. From PV Maldonado take a *ranchera* to Cielo Verde (0600, 1300 and sometimes 1600, returning 2 hrs later, US$2, 2 hrs), from where it is a 30-min hike. From Quito 1 daily bus to Cielo Verde at 1300, **Trans Minas**, Los Ríos y Julio Castro.
E pp **Mirador del Río Blanco**, San Miguel de Los Bancos, T09-944 4665. Accommodation, good restaurant and hiking opportunities, great views.

Puerto Quito *p913*

A Cabañas Don Gaucho, 22 km from Puerto Quito and 6 km east of the junction with the Santo Domingo-Esmeraldas road, T/F233 0315 (Quito), www.ecuador- sommerfern.com. Comfortable, well furnished rooms with bath and hot water, fan, balcony, includes breakfast, restaurant specializing in Argentinian *parrilladas*, nice grounds on the shores of the Río Salazar. Tours to tropical forest, fruit plantations, Colorado Indians.
A La Isla, about 1½ km past *Aldea Salamandra*, along the same road, T276 5281. On an island between the Caoni and Achiote rivers, cabins, treehouses and comfortable cottages, with bath, cold water, price includes meals and excursions.
C pp **Aldea Salamandra**, about 2½ km east of Puerto Quito, take a dirt road going southeast for 650 m, T256 1146 (ext 294) (Quito), aldeasalamandra@yahoo.com. A 5-ha forest reserve with simple bamboo and thatch cabins, in a lovely setting by the river. Price includes all meals and excursions.

Papallacta *p913*

There are 8 other hotels in town and springs valley, **B-F** pp. The car park of the Termas complex allows vehicle camping for a small fee.
C Antisana, up the hill close to the Termas, T06-232 0626. Cheaper with shared bath and cold water, simple, some new rooms.
D La Choza de Don Wilson, junction of main road with road to Termas, T06-232 0627. Hot water, good restaurant, pool, spa, good service. Several simple places to eat, trout is a speciality.
D Coturpa, next to public baths in Papallacta town, T06-232 0640. New, includes breakfast, thermal pool, sauna, good value.

E Rincón El Viajero, in Papallacta town. Basic, shared bath, hot water, good value, restaurant with reasonable meals.

East of Papallacta
L Guango Lodge, reservations needed, Quito T254 7403, www.ecuadorexplorer.com/sanisidro. Including 3 good meals. Situated in temperate forest, grey-breasted mountain toucans are regularly seen here along with many other birds.

Sangolquí *p913*
AL La Carriona, Km 2½ via Sangolquí- Amaguaña, T233 1974, www.lacarriona.com. Beautiful hacienda, with breakfast, pool, spa, horses, restaurant.
AL Hostería Sommergarten, Chimborazo 248 y Riofrío, Urb Santa Rosa, T233 0315, www.ecuador-sommerfern.com. Bungalow resort, including breakfast, lots of activities, sauna, pool.

❼ Eating

Pululahua *p912*
El Cráter, on the rim of the crater, signed access before (east) the road to the mirador, T223 9399, daily 1230-1700. Popular upscale restaurant with excellent views; new hotel beside the restaurant.

▲▲ Activities and tours

Mitad del Mundo *p912*
Calimatours, Manzana de los Correos, Oficina 11, Mitad del Mundo, T239 4796, calima@andinanet.net. Tours to all the sites in the vicinity, US$8 per person for 2 hrs. Offers beautiful certificates to record your visit. Recommended.

Pululahua *p912*
Horse riding The Green Horse Ranch, Astrid Muller, T02-237 4847, www.horseranch.de.

❻ Transport

Mitad del Mundo and around *p912*
Bus A paved road runs from Quito to the Monument; take a 'Mitad del Mundo' *interparroquial* bus from the Av del Maestro stop on the Santa Prisca-La Ofelia line. An excursion by **taxi** to Mitad del Mundo (with 1 hr wait) and Pululahua is US$30 per taxi. Just a ride from the New City costs about US$12.

Pululahua *p912*
Bus For the rim, from Mitad del Mundo you can take a **Calacalí** bound bus and alight at the turnoff (infrequent). There is plenty of traffic at weekends for hitching a lift. There is no public transport to the reserve.

Mindo *p912*
Bus From **Quito**, Cooperativa Flor del Valle (Cayambe), M Larrea N10-44 y Asunción, T252 7495. Mon-Fri at 0800, 1545, Sat-Sun at 0700, 0800, 0900, 1545; US$2.50, 2½ hrs. To Quito, Mon-Fri 0600, 1200, Sat-Sun 1400, 1500, 1600, 1700. Weekend buses fill quickly, buy ahead. **Cooperativa Kennedy** from **Santo Domingo** at 0720, 1140 and 1400, returning at 0700, 1300 and 1700, US$3.50, 3½ hrs. If buses to Quito are booked, try taking a Santo Domingo-bound bus to the main highway or to **San Miguel de los Bancos** and transfer there. The most direct access from Quito is along the Calcalí-La Concordia road; at Km 79 to the south is the turn-off to Mindo. Taxis wait here till 1930 for the 7 km ride to town.

Papallacta *p913*
Bus From **Quito**, Terminal Terrestre, 2 hrs, US$2; ask to be let off at the road to the springs; it's a steep 30-min walk up to the baths.

Ecuador Around Quito Listings

915

Refugio de Vida Silvestre Pasochoa *p913*

Bus From Quito buses run from La Marín to Amaguaña US$0.40 (ask the driver to let you off at the 'Ejido de Amaguaña'); from there follow the signs. It's about 8-km walk, with not much traffic except at weekends.

Car Take the highway to Los Chillos, at San Rafael (2nd traffic light) continue straight towards Sangolquí and on to Amaguaña; 1.4 km past the entrance to Amaguaña turn left onto cobblestone road and follow the signs to Pasochoa, 5.4 km to the park. Take a taxi to Amaguaña from Quito, US$20, the a pick-up truck from Amaguaña, about US$6 for up to 3 people. There is a **Movistar** public phone at the information centre (take a debit card) to call **Cooperativa Pacheco Jr** in Amaguaña, T287 7047.

Northern Ecuador

The area north of Quito to the Colombian border is outstandingly beautiful. The landscape is mountainous, with views of the Cotacachi, Imbabura, and Chiles volcanoes, as well as the glacier-covered Cayambe, interspersed with lakes. The region is also renowned for its artesanía.

Quito to Otavalo

On the way from the capital to the main tourist centre in northern Ecuador, the landscape is dominated by the Cayambe volcano.

Quito to Cayambe

Calderón, 32 km north of the centre of Quito, is the place where figurines are made of bread. You can see them being made, though not on Sunday, and prices are lower than in Quito. Especially attractive is the Nativity collection. Prices range from about US$0.50 to US$8. On 1-2 November, the graves in the cemetery are decorated with flowers, drinks and food for the dead. The Corpus Christi processions are very colourful. Many buses leave from Santa Prisca and along Avenida América in Quito.

The Pan-American Highway goes to Guayllabamba where two branches split, one goes through Cayambe and the second through Tabacundo before rejoining at Cajas. At 8 km before Cayambe a concrete globe marks the spot where the Equator crosses the Pan-American Highway. At 10 km past Guayllabamba and 8 km before Tabacundo, just north of the toll booth, a cobbled road to the left (signed Pirámides de Cochasquí) leads to Tocachi and further on to the **Tolas de Cochasquí** ① *US$3, entry only with a 1½ hr guided tour; 0830-1630,* archaeological site. The protected area contains 15 truncated clay pyramids, nine with long ramps, built between AD 950 and 1550 by the Cara or Cayambi-Caranqui Indians. Festivals with dancing at the equinoxes and solstices. There is a site museum. Be sure to take a bus that goes on the Tabacundo road and ask to be let off at the turnoff. From there it's a pleasant 8-km walk. If you arrive at the sign around 0800, you could get a lift from the site workers. A taxi from Cayambe costs US$10 for the round trip.

Cayambe → *Phone code: 02. Colour map 11, grid A4. Population: 30,473.*

Cayambe, on the eastern (righthand) branch of the highway, 25 km northeast of Guayllabamba, is overshadowed by the snow-capped volcano of the same name. The surrounding countryside consists of rich dairy farms and flower plantations. The area is noted for its *bizcochos* (biscuits) served with *queso de hoja* (string cheese). On the edge of town are the pyramids of the Sun and Moon at Puntiachil, entrance at Olmedo 702, US$1 includes guided tour in Spanish. There is a *fiesta* in March for the equinox with plenty of local music; also Inti Raymi during the summer solstice blends into the San Pedro celebrations on June 29. Market day is Sunday, in the traditional plaza up the hill on Calle Rocafuerte.

Volcán Cayambe → *Altitude: 5,790 m.*

Cayambe, Ecuador's third highest peak, lies within the **Reserva Ecológica Cayambe-Coca** *US$10.* It's the highest point in the world to lie so close to the Equator (3¼ km north).

About 1 km south of Cayambe is an unmarked cobbled road heading east via Juan Montalvo, leading in 26 km to the Ruales-Oleas-Berge refuge at about 4,800 m. The *refugio* costs US$17 per person per night, can sleep 37 in bunks; bring a sleeping bag, it is very cold. There is a kitchen, fireplace, running water, electric light and a radio for rescue. The standard route, up from the west, uses the refuge as a base. The climb is heavily crevassed, especially near the summit, and is much more difficult and dangerous than Chimborazo or even Cotopaxi.

Northern Ecuador

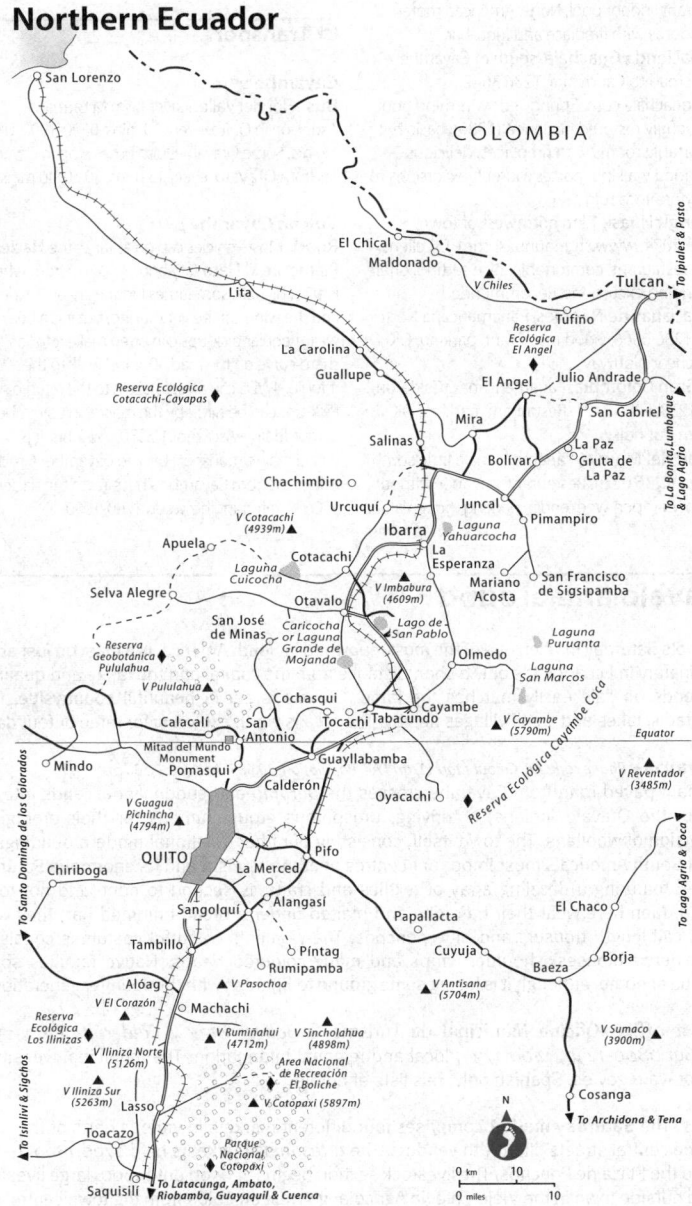

● Sleeping

Cayambe *p916*

Hotels may be full on Fri during Jun-Sep and during the week before Valentine's Day (high season at the flower plantations).

AL Jatun Huasi, Panamericana Norte Km 1½, T236 3775, F236 3832. Includes breakfast, restaurant, indoor pool, North American motel style, rooms with fireplace and frigo-bar.

A-B Hacienda Guachala, south of Cayambe on the road to Cangahua, T236 3042, www.guachala.com. Spring-fed swimming pool, a beautifully restored hacienda (1580), basic but comfortable rooms with fireplaces, delicious food, good walking, horses for rent, excursions to nearby pre-Inca ruins.

C Shungu Huasi, 1 km northwest of town, T/F279 2094, www.shunguhuasi.com. Excellent Italian restaurant, comfortable, nice setting, offers horse riding excursions. Recommended.

C-D Cabañas de Nápoles, Panamericana Norte Km 1, T236 0366. Good restaurant, parking, OK cabins near highway.

D La Gran Colombia, Panamericana y Calderón, T236 1238, F236 2421. Restaurant, parking, OK, modern but noisy.

E Mitad del Mundo, Panamericana a little south of town, T236 0226. Restaurant, cheaper without bath, pool (open weekends), parking, good value.

● Eating

Cayambe *p916*

♕♕♕ Casa de Fernando, Panamericana Norte Km 1.5. Varied menu, good food. Recommended.

♕ Aroma, Bolívar 404 y Ascázubi. Large choice of set lunches and à la carte, variety of desserts, very good, open until 2100, Sun until 1800, closed Wed.

● Transport

Cayambe *p916*

Bus Flor del Valle, leaves from M Larrea y Asunción in Quito, every 10 mins, 0500-1900, US$1, 1½ hrs. Some Otavalo-Quito buses stop in Cayambe. To/from **Otavalo**, every 15 mins, $0.60, 40 mins.

Volcán Cayambe *p916*

Road Most vehicles can go as far as the **Hacienda Piemonte El Hato** (at about 3,500 m) from where it is a 3-4 hr walk, sometimes longer if heavily laden, and the wind can be very strong, but it is a beautiful walk. Regular pick-ups can often make it to 'la Z', a sharp curve on the road 30-mins' walk to the refugio. 4WDs can often make it to the refugio. Pick-ups can be hired by the market in Cayambe, corner Junín y Ascázubi, US$30, 1½-2 hrs. It is difficult to get transport back to Cayambe. A milk truck runs from Cayambe's hospital to the hacienda at 0600, returning between 1700-1900.

Otavalo and around

Otavalo's Saturday market, one of the most renowned in South America, is a must on just about any itinerary in Ecuador. It's only a short distance from the capital and the range and quality of the goods on sale easily matches the fame. Otavalo is set in beautiful countryside, with mountains, lakes and small villages nearby. The area is worth exploring for three or four days.

Otavalo → *Phone code: 06. Colour map 11, grid A4. Population: 30,965. Altitude: 2,530 m.*

The main paved road from Cayambe crosses the *páramo* and suddenly descends into the land of the Otavalo Indians, a thriving, prosperous group, famous for their prodigious production of woollens. The town itself, consisting of rather functional modern buildings, is one of South America's most important centres of ethno-tourism and its enormous Saturday market, featuring a dazzling array of textiles and crafts, is second to none and not to be missed. Men here wear their hair long and plaited under a broad-brimmed hat; they wear white, calf-length trousers and blue ponchos. The women's colourful costumes consist of embroidered blouses, shoulder wraps and many coloured beads. Native families speak Quichua at home, although it is losing some ground to Spanish with the younger generation.

Tourist office Oficina Municipal de Turismo ⓘ *Bolívar 8-34 y Calderón, T292 1313, Mon-Sat 0800-1230, 1400-1730,* local and regional information. The municipal website is www.otavalo.gov.ec, Spanish only, has lists of hotels.

Sights The **Saturday market** comprises four different markets in various parts of the town with the central streets filled with vendors. The *artesanías* market is held 0700-1800, based around the Plaza de Ponchos. The livestock section begins at 0500 until 1000: large livestock is sold outside town in the Viejo Colegio Agrícola; go west on Colón from the town centre. The small animal market is held on Atahualpa by the bus terminal. 87The produce market lasts from 0700 till 1400, in Plaza 24 de Mayo. The *artesanías* industry is so big that the Plaza de Ponchos is filled with vendors every day of the week. The selection is better on Saturday but prices are a little higher than other days when the atmosphere is more relaxed. Polite bargaining is appropriate in the market and shops. Otavaleños not only sell goods they weave and sew themselves, but they bring crafts from throughout Ecuador and from Peru and Bolivia. Indigenous people in the market respond better to photography if you buy something first, then ask politely. Reciprocity and courtesy are important Andean norms. The **Instituto Otavaleño de Antropología** ① *Av de los Sarances y Pendoneros, 1 block west of the Panamericana Norte, T292 0321, Mon-Thu 0830-1200, 1430-1800, Fri 0830-1200, 1430-1700, free,* has a library, an archaeological museum with artifacts from the northern highlands, a collection of musical instruments, and a good ethnographic display of regional costumes and traditional activities. **Museo de Tejidos El Obraje** ① *Sucre 608 y Olmedo, T292 0261, US$2, Mon-Sat 0800-1200, 1400-1700,* shows the process of traditional Otavalo weaving from shearing to final products. Traditional weaving lessons are available. The **Museo Arqueológico César Vásquez Fuller**, with an excellent collection from different regions in Ecuador, was sold to the municipality and is awaiting a new location.

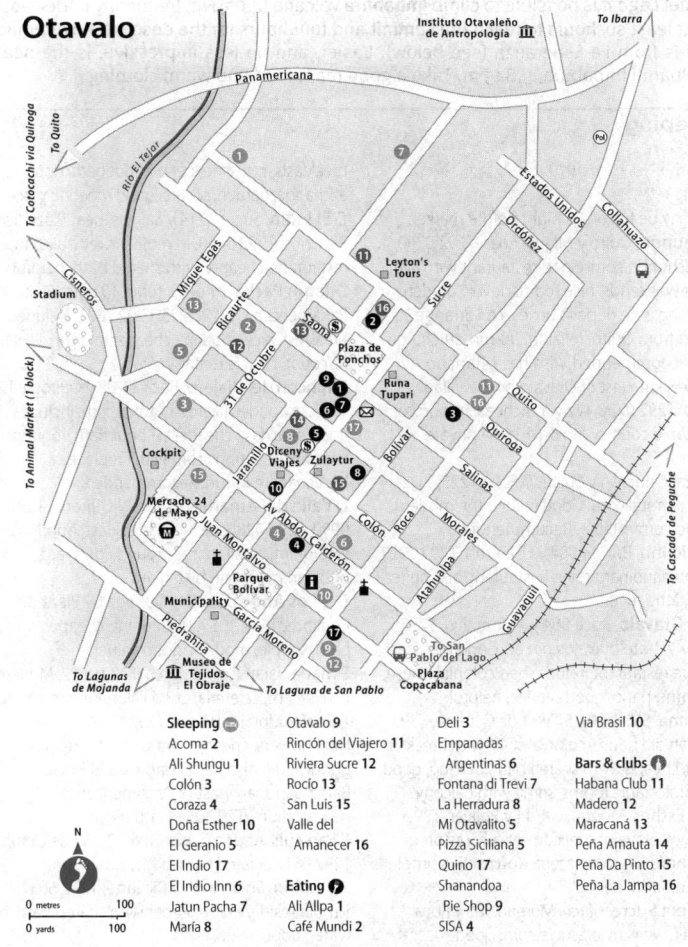

Otavalo

Sleeping	Otavalo 9	Deli 3	Via Brasil 10
Acoma 2	Rincón del Viajero 11	Empanadas	
Ali Shungu 1	Riviera Sucre 12	Argentinas 6	**Bars & clubs**
Colón 3	Rocío 13	Fontana di Trevi 7	Habana Club 11
Coraza 4	San Luis 15	La Herradura 8	Madero 12
Doña Esther 10	Valle del	Mi Otavalito 5	Maracaná 13
El Geranio 5	Amanecer 16	Pizza Siciliana 5	Peña Amauta 14
El Indio 17		Quino 17	Peña Da Pinto 15
El Indio Inn 6	**Eating**	Shanandoa	Peña La Jampa 16
Jatun Pacha 7	Ali Allpa 1	Pie Shop 9	
María 8	Café Mundi 2	SISA 4	

Around Otavalo

Otavalo weavers come from dozens of communities. The easiest to visit are Ilumán (visit the Conterón-de la Torre family of *Artesanías Inti Chumbi*, on the northeast corner of the plaza; there are also many felt hatmakers in town and *Yachag*, or shamen, mostly north of the plaza - look for signs); Agato (the Andrango-Chiza family of *Tahuantinsuyo Weaving Workshop*, gives weaving demonstrations and sells textiles); Carabuela (many homes sell crafts including wool sweaters); Peguche (the Cotacachi-Pichamba family, off the main plaza behind the church, sells beautiful tapestries). These villages are only 15-30 minutes away and all have a good bus service; buses leave from the Terminal and stop at Plaza Copacabana (Atahualpa y Montalvo). You can also take a taxi. Allow 1-1½ hours each way.

To reach the **Cascada de Peguche** *US$1*, from Peguche's plaza, facing the church, head right and continue straight until the road forks. Take the lower fork to the right, but not the road that heads downhill. From the top of the falls (left side, excellent views) you can continue the walk to Lago de San Pablo. The *Pawkar Raimi* festival is held in Peguche during carnival.

Lago de San Pablo

There is a network of old roads and trails between Otavalo and Lago de San Pablo, none of which takes more than two hours to explore. It is worth walking either to or back from the lake for the views (if you take the main road, beware traffic fumes and litter). From **San Pablo del Lago** it is possible to climb **Imbabura** volcano (4,630 m, frequently under cloud), allow at least six hours to reach the summit and four hours for the descent. An alternative access is from La Esperanza (see below). Easier, and no less impressive, is the nearby Cerro Huarmi Imbabura, 3,845 m. Take a good map, food and warm clothing.

⊜ Sleeping

Otavalo *p918, map p919*
In town
Hotels may be full on Fri night before market.
A Ali Shungu, Quito y Miguel Egas, T292 0750, www.alishungu.com. Good restaurant with live music at weekends, nice rooms, lovely garden, no smoking, safe deposit boxes, can arrange transport from Quito, reliable. US-run, surcharge for TCs. Recommended. Also has **L** Rancho Ali Shungo, 5 km west of Otavalo by the village of Yambiro, T292 0750, www.ranchoalishungu.com. Comfortable country inn on a 16 ha private reserve.
B Coraza, Calderón y Sucre, T/F292 1225, www.ecuahotel.com. Good restaurant, modern, quiet and comfortable. Recommended.
B El Indio Inn, Bolívar 904 y Calderón, T292 2922, hindioinn@andinanet.net. Restaurant, also suites, spotless, attractive.
B Hotel Otavalo, Roca 504 y J Montalvo, T292 3712, www.hotelotavalo.com.ec. Good breakfast, expensive restaurant, refurbished colonial house, large rooms, patio, good service, helpful.
B-D Acoma, Salinas 07-57 y 31 de Octubre, T292 6570. In an old house, colonial style, with breakfast, cafeteria, cheaper with shared bath, parking, good value, comfortable rooms, some with balcony.
C Doña Esther, Montalvo 4-44 y Bolívar, T292 0739, www.otavalohotel.com. Nicely restored colonial house, good pizzeria downstairs, simple rooms, colourful decor.
C-D Riviera Sucre, García Moreno 380 y Roca, T292 0241, www.rivierasucre.com. Good

breakfasts, café, cheaper without bath, book exchange, garden, secure, good meeting place.
D El Indio, Sucre 1214 y Salinas, near Plaza de Ponchos, T292 0060. In multi-storey building, restaurant, cheaper with shared bath, helpful.
D Jatun Pacha, 31 de Octubre 19 entre Quito y Panamericana, T292 2223, F292 2871. Includes breakfast, nice, modern, cheaper in dorm, IYHF discount, bicycle rentals.
D Rincón del Viajero, Roca 11-07 y Quiroga, T292 1741, rincondelviajero@hotmail.com. Includes good breakfast, cheaper without bath, rooftop hammocks, sitting room with fireplace, US/Ecuadorean-run. Recommended.
D Valle del Amanecer, Roca y Quiroga, T292 0990, F292 0286. Includes breakfast, good restaurant, small rooms around courtyard, popular, mountain bike hire.
D-E Los Andes, Sucre y Quiroga by Plaza de Ponchos, T292 1057. Restaurant, cheaper without bath, simple, modern, good value.
E María, Jaramillo y Colón, T/F292 0672. Modern, convenient, cafeteria, good value. Recommended.
E Rocío, Morales y Egas, T292 0584.
Hot showers, cheaper without bath, helpful, good value. Also has **D** Cabañas El Rocío, Barrio San Juan west of Panamericana, near stadium, T292 0584, attractive.
E San Luis, Abdón Calderón 6-02 y 31 de Octubre, T292 0614. Shared bath, basic, family-run.
E-F Colón, Colón 7-13 y Ricaurte, T292 6037. Simple residencial, cheaper with shared bath, hot water, good value.

E-F **El Geranio**, Ricaurte y Colón, T292 0185, hgeranio@hotmail.com. Breakfast available, cheaper without bath, cooking and laundry facilities, quiet, family-run, helpful, popular, value, runs trips. Recommended.

Out of town
LL **Casa Mojanda**, Vía Mojanda Km 3.5, T292 2986, www.casamojanda.com. Includes breakfast and one other meal, beautiful setting on 10 ha of forested gorge, organic garden, comfortable, quiet, horse riding, mountain bikes. Highly recommended.
L **Hacienda Pinsaquí**, Panamericana N Km 5, T294 6116, www.haciendapinsaqui.com. With breakfast, restaurant, 300 m north of the turn-off for Cotacachi. Beautiful antiques, lovely dining room, lounge with fireplace, colonial ambience, gardens, horse riding.
L **Vista del Mundo**, Panamericana at Pinsaquí toll, halfway between Otavalo and Ibarra, T294 6333, www.thegoldenspa.com. Luxury hotel, spa, built around the theme of world peace. Includes breakfast, dinner and use of heated pool, elegant expensive restaurant serves good food. Unusual.
A **Las Palmeras**, outside Quichinche, 15 mins by bus from Otavalo, T292 2607, www.laspalmeras inn.com. With breakfast, restaurant, cheaper without bath, tranquil rural setting, nice grounds.
B **La Casa de Hacienda**, Entrance at Panamericana Norte Km 3, then 300 m east, T292 3105, www.casadehacienda.com. Includes breakfast, restaurant, tasteful cabins with fireplace, advance reservations required for horse riding.
D **La Luna de Mojanda**, Vía Mojanda Km 2, T/F09-973 7415, la lunaecuador@yahoo.co.uk. Pleasant country hostel, restaurant, cheaper in dorm, parking, some rooms with fireplace and private bath, terrace with hammocks, pleasant dining room-lounge, camping possible, taxi from Otavalo US$3 or take Punyaro city bus, excursions arranged, popular. Recommended.
E **Posada Río Blanco**, on the road to Quiroga, near the Fuente de la Salud baths, T09-983 9692, ruthy_71@yahoo.es. Pleasant, rural setting, meals available, hot water, parking, small rooms with single bed or bunks, take a Cotacachi bound bus which goes via Quiroga, horse riding and excursions with advance arrangements.

Around Otavalo: Peguche p920
C **Aya Huma**, on the railway line, T292 2663, www.ayahuma.com. Restaurant, cooking facilities, quiet, pleasant atmosphere, Dutch-run, live folk music on Sat. Highly recommended.
C **Peguche Tío**, near centre of the village, T/F292 2619, peguchetio@mail.com. With breakfast, restaurant, internet, nice lounge with fireplace, decorated with works of art, interesting museum, sports fields, caters for groups.

Lago de San Pablo p920
L **Hacienda Cusín**, in a converted 17th-century *hacienda* on the east side of the lake, San Pablo del Lago, T291 8013, www.haciendacusin.com. With fireplace, including breakfast, fine expensive restaurant, sports facilities (horses, mountain bikes, squash court, pool, games room), library, lovely grounds, book in advance, British-run, German spoken. Recommended.
AL **Puerto Lago**, Panamericana Sur, Km 6, on the west side of the lake, T292 0920, www.puerto lago.net. Modern, lovely setting, good expensive restaurant, rooms and suites with fireplaces, very hospitable, includes the use of row-boats, pedalos and kayaks, other water sports extra.
A **Jatun Cocha**, 5½ km from the Panamericana on the east side of the lake, T/F291 8191, www.ranfturismo.com. Rooms with fireplaces, breakfast included, restaurant, kayaks, windsurfing, bicycles.

● Eating

Otavalo *p918, map p919*
♥ **Quino**, Roca 740 y Juan Montalvo, daily 1100-2300. Traditional coastal cooking and some meat dishes, pleasant seating around a patio.
♥ **Via Brasil**, Sucre y Abdón Calderón, p 2, Wed-Sun 1200-2200. Brazilian rodizio with a nice salad bar, feijoada, caipirinha, nicely decorated, authentic, Brazilian- Ecuadorean run.
♥-♥ **Fontana di Trevi**, Sucre 12-05 y Salinas, p 2, 1130-2200. Good pizza and pasta, nice juices, friendly service.
♥-♥ **Pizza Siciliana**, Morales y Sucre. A very popular eating place.
♥-♥ **SISA**, Calderón 409 y Sucre, open 0700-2200. Cultural centre, restaurant on second floor serves excellent set meals and à la carte, coffee shop with cappuccino, slow service, also bookstore, weekly international films, live music Fri-Sun.
♥ **Ali Allpa**, Salinas 509 at Plaza de Ponchos. Good value set meals and à la carte, trout, vegetarian, meat. Recommended.
♥ **Café Mundi**, Quiroga 608 y Jaramillo, Plaza de Ponchos. Good food and value, nice atmosphere, vegetarian available.
♥ **La Herradura**, Bolívar 10-05. Good set meals and à la carte, outdoor tables.
♥ **Mi Otavalito**, Sucre y Morales. Good for lunch also international food à la carte.
Deli, Quiroga y Bolívar, Open Fri and Sat only. Small place serving Mexican snacks such as tacos.
Empanadas Argentinas, Morales 502 y Sucre. Good savoury and sweet *empanadas*.
Shanandoa Pie Shop, Salinas y Jaramillo. Good pies, milk shakes and ice cream, expensive, good meeting place, recommended for breakfast, book exchange, daily movies at 1700 and 1900.

🕸 Bars and clubs

Otavalo *p918, map p919*
Otavalo is generally safe until 2200. Avoid
deserted areas. Peñas are open Fri-Sat from 2200,
entrance US$2. On Fri and Sat nights there are
nightlife tours on a *chiva* (open sided bus with a
musical group on board), it stops at the Plaza de
Ponchos and ends its route at the *Habana Club*.
Habana Club, Quito y 31 de Octubre. Lively disco,
live music some weekends, cover US$2.
Madero, Morales 10-60 y Ricaurte. Live folk
music, drinks, also dancing.
Maracaná, Salinas 6-12 y Jaramillo. Disco, varied
music, some live at weekends, young crowd.
Peña Amauta, Morales 5-11 y Jaramillo. Good
local bands, welcoming, mainly foreigners.
Peña Da Pinto, Colón 4-10 y Bolívar,
www.dapinto.com. Colourfully decorated, live
Latin music at weekends, drinks and snacks.
Peña la Jampa, Jaramillo y Quiroga. Very
popular for Andean and dancing music.

🕸 Festivals and events

Otavalo *p918, map p919*
The **end of Jun** combines the Inti Raymi
celebrations of the summer solstice (**21 Jun**), with
the Fiesta de San Juan (**24 Jun**) and the Fiesta de
San Pedro y San Pablo (**29 Jun**). These combined
festivities are known as Los San Juanes and
participants are mostly indigenous. The celebration
begins with a ritual bath in the Peguche waterfall (a
personal spiritual activity, best carried out without
visitors and certainly without cameras). Most of the
action takes place in the smaller communities
surrounding Otavalo. Groups of musicians and
dancers compete with each other as they make
their way from one village to another over the
course of the week; there is much drinking along
the way. In Otavalo, indigenous families have
costume parties, which at times spill over onto the
streets. In the San Juan neighbourhood, near the
Yanayacu baths, there is a week-long celebration
with food, drink and music. Fiesta del Yamor and
Colla Raimi **1st 2 weeks of Sep**, local dishes are
cooked, amusement parks are set up, bands in the
plaza and there are sporting events including
bullfights. Mojandas Arriba is an annual 2-day hike
from Quito over Mojanda to reach Otavalo for the
31 Oct foundation celebrations.

🔺 Activities and tours

Otavalo *p918, map p919*
Mountain bikes Several tour operators rent
bikes and offer cycling tours. **Hostal Valle del
Amanecer** (see Sleeping), US$8 per day. **Jatun
Pacha** (see Sleeping, above). Bikes for hire US$4

per hr, includes helmet. **Taller Ciclo Primaxi**,
García Moreno 2-49 y Atahualpa and at the
entrance to Peguche, has good bikes for rent,
US$1 per hr.
Rafting River People, T288 8383. Arrange trips
to the Río Apuela with mountain bike of hot
springs combinations.

Tour operators
Most common tours are to native communities,
Cuicocha and Mojanda, US$20-30 pp.
Independent travel to the Lagunas de Mojanda is
not recommended because of armed robbery and
public safety problems. Only go with a tour.
All about Eq, Colón 412 y Sucre, T292 3633,
www.all-about-ecuador.com (a merger of
Chachimbiro Tours and Suni Tours). Works with
native communities in the Chachimbiro and
Piñán region to foster sustainable development
through tourism. Offers trekking, horse riding,
cycling and climbing, as well as visits to the
Chachimbiro thermal baths.
Diceny Viajes, Sucre 10-11 y Colón, T292 1217,
zulayviajes@hotmail.com. Run by Zulay Sarabino,
an indigenous Otavaleña, knowledgeable native
guides. Recommended.
Leyton's Tours, Quito y Jaramillo, T292 2388,
leytontour@yahoo.com. Horseback and bike tours.
Runa Tupari, Sucre y Quiroga, Plaza de Ponchos
T/F292 5985, www.runatupari.com. Arranges
indigenous homestays in the Cotacachi area,
US$20 pp per day, half board, includes transport
(see Cotacachi), also the usual tours at higher-
than-average prices, English and French spoken.
Zulaytur, Sucre y Colón, p 2, T292 1176, F292
2969. Run by Rodrigo Mora, English spoken,
information, map of town, slide show, horse
riding. Recommended.

⊖ Transport

Otavalo *p918, map p919*
Note: Never leave anything in your car or taxi,
even if it is being watched for you.
Bus Terminal at Atahualpa y Ordóñez (see
map). To **Quito** 2 hrs, US$2, every 10 mins; all
depart from the Terminal Terrestre in Quito,
Coop Otavalo and **Coop Los Lagos** go into
Otavalo, buses bound for Ibarra drop you off at
the highway, this is not safe at night. From **Quito**
by taxi takes 1½ hrs, US$40; shared taxis with
Supertaxis Los Lagos (in Quito, Asunción y
Versalles T256 5992; in Otavalo, Roca 8-04, T292
3203) who run a hotel (in the New City only) to
hotel service and will divert to resorts just off the
highway; hourly Mon-Fri 0700 to 1900, Sat
0700-1600, Sun 0800-1800, 2 hrs, US$7.50 pp,
buy ticket the day before. They continue to
Ibarra, every 15 mins, US$0.50, 45 mins. To

Peguche, city bus on Av Atahualpa, every 15 mins, bus stops in front of the terminal and at Plaza Copacabana, US$0.18. To the **Intag region**, 5 daily.

Lago de San Pablo *p920*
Bus From **Otavalo**-San Pablo del Lago every 30 mins, more often on Sat, US$0.18; taxi US$4.

O Directory

Otavalo *p918, map p919*
Banks Banco del Pacífico, Bolívar 614 y García Moreno. **Banco del Pichincha**, Bolívar y Piedrahita. **Vaz Corp**, Jaramillo y Saona, Plaza de Ponchos,

Tue-Sat 0900-1700. TCs with commission, also change Euros and Colombian pesos.
Internet Prices about US$1 per hr.
Many in town, specially on C Sucre. **Language schools** Spanish classes run about US$4 per hr. Fundación Jacinto Jijón y Caamaño, Bolívar 8-04 y Montalvo, p 2, T292 0725.Spanish and Quichua lessons. **Instituto Superior de Español**, Sucre 11-10 y Morales, p 2, T299 2414, www.instituto- superior.net (see also Quito language schools). **Mundo Andino**, Salinas 509, p 3, Plaza de Ponchos, T292 5478, mundo andinoinn@hotmail.com. Also dancing and cooking lessons. Recommended. **Post offices** Corner of Plaza de Ponchos, entrance on Sucre, 1st floor.

Otavalo to the Colombian border

The route passes the Cotacachi-Cayapas reserve and then divides into two roads beyond the city of Ibarra. A detour heads down the mountains into the lush Chota valley and beyond, into the tropical lowlands and the coastal city of San Lorenzo. The Panamericana reaches the border at the busy town Tulcán, with its fantastic topiary.

Cotacachi

West of the road between Otavalo and Ibarra is Cotacachi, where leather goods are made and sold. There is access along a road from Otavalo through Quiroga. The **Casa de las Culturas** ① *Bolívar y 9 de Octubre*, a beautifully refurbished 19th century building is a monument to peace. It houses a library, internet café, the tourist information office, ① *T291 5140, www.cota cachi.gov.ec*, temporary exhibits and shows. The **Museo de las Culturas** ① *García Moreno 13-41 y Bolívar, Mon-Fri 0900-1200, 1400-1700, Sat 1400-1700, Sun 1000-1300, US$1*, has good displays about early Ecuadorean history, regional crafts and traditions (some English explanations). Local festivals include *Inti Raymi/San Juan* in June and *Jora* during the September equinox.

Laguna Cuicocha → *Altitude: 3,070 m.*
① *15 km from Cotacachi. US$1 to visit the lake and visitor centre, which has good natural history and cultural displays. US$5 park fee must be paid if going on longer hikes into the national park.*
The area is part of the **Reserva Ecológica Cotacachi-Cayapas**, which extends from Cotacachi volcano to the tropical lowlands on the Río Cayapas in Esmeraldas. This is a crater lake with two islands, although these are closed to the public for biological studies. There is a well-marked, 8-km path around the lake, which takes 4-5 hours and provides spectacular views of the Cotacachi, Imbabura and, occasionally, Cayambe peaks. The best views are in the morning, when condors can sometimes be seen. There is lookout at 3 km, two hours from the start. It's best to go anticlockwise; take water and a waterproof jacket. Motor boat rides around the islands, US$1.50 per person for minimum five persons.

Warnings There have been armed robberies of people walking around the lake. Do not take valuables. Always enquire locally before heading out. Do not eat the berries which grow near the lake, as some are poisonous. The path around the lake is not for vertigo sufferers.

To the northwest of Otavalo lies the lush subtropical region of **Intag**, reached along a road that follows the southern edge of Cuicocha and continues to the town of **Apuela**. Beyond, are pleasant thermal baths at **Nangulví**. The area is rich in cloudforest and has several nature reserves. On the southwest boundary of the Cotacachi-Cayapas reserve is **Los Cedros Research Station**, 6,400 ha of pristine cloudforest, with abundant orchids and bird life. Full board in **A** range. Contact ① José at loscedros@ecuanex.net.ec, for details (or try Safari Tours in Quito).

Ibarra and around → *Phone code: 06. Colour map 11, grid A4. Pop: 108,535. Altitude: 2,225 m.*

Once a pleasant colonial town (founded in 1606), Ibarra is the main commercial centre of the northern highlands, with an increasingly big city feel. The city has an interesting ethnic mix, with blacks from the Chota valley and Esmeraldas alongside Otavaleños and other highland *indígenas*, mestizos and Colombian immigrants. The city has two plazas with flowering trees. **Tourist offices: Ministerio de Turismo** ① *García Moreno 376 y Rocafuerte, T295 8547, www.imbabura.gov.ec*. Very helpful, free city map and tourist leaflets, English spoken, open Monday-Friday 0830-1300, 1400-1700. **Cámara Provincial de Turismo de Imbabura** ① *Oviedo y Bolívar, of 102, T/F264 2531, www.imbaburaturismo.com*. Regional information, very helpful, Spanish only, Monday-Friday 0800-1300, 1500-1800.

On **Parque Pedro Moncayo**, stand the Cathedral, the Municipio and Gobernación. One block away is the smaller Parque 9 de Octubre, at Flores y Olmedo, more commonly called **Parque de la Merced** after its church. Some interesting paintings are to be seen in the church of **Santo Domingo** and its museum of religious art, at the end of Simón Bolívar. On Sucre, at the end of Avenida A Pérez Guerrero is the **Basílica de La Dolorosa**. A walk down Pérez Guerrero leads to the large covered **Mercado Amazonas** ① *on Cifuentes, by the railway station. Daily, busiest Sat and Sun*. The **Museo Arqueológico de la Sierra Norte** ① *Sucre 7-21 y Oviedo, T295 2777, Mon-Sat, 0830-1330, 1430-1630, US$0.50*, run by the Banco Central, has interesting displays about cultures from northern Ecuador. Virgen del Carmen festival is on 16 July and Fiesta de los Lagos is in the last weekend of September, Thursday-Sunday.

Off the main road between Otavalo and Ibarra is **San Antonio de Ibarra**, well known for its wood carvings. Bargaining is difficult. It is worth seeing the range of styles and techniques and shopping around in the galleries and workshops. Buses leave from Ibarra, 13 km, 10 minutes. About 10 km from Ibarra is **La Esperanza**, a pretty village in beautiful surroundings. Ask in town for makers of fine clothes and embroidery. You can climb **Cubilche** volcano in three hours from La Esperanza for beautiful views. From the top you can walk down to Lago de San Pablo (see page 920), another three hours.

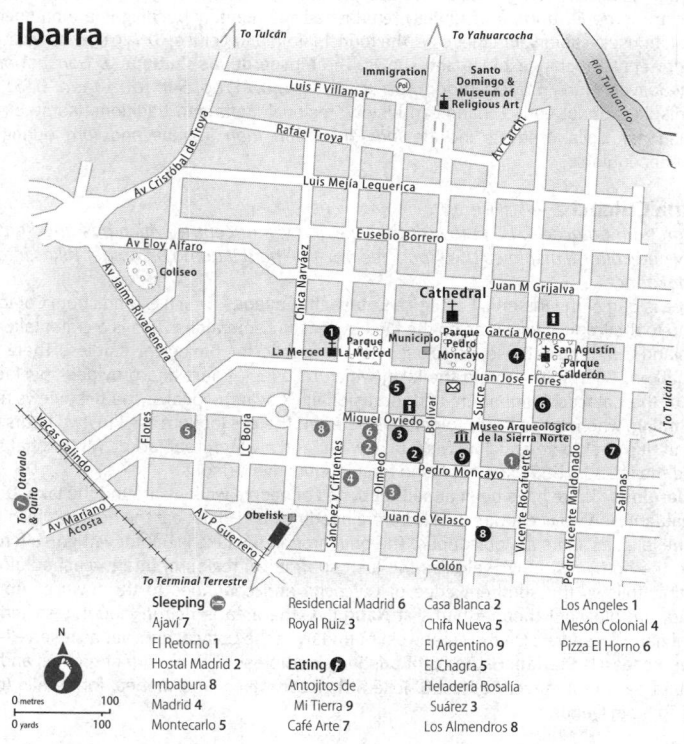

Ibarra

Sleeping
Ajaví 7
El Retorno 1
Hostal Madrid 2
Imbabura 8
Madrid 4
Montecarlo 5
Residencial Madrid 6
Royal Ruiz 3

Eating
Antojitos de
Mi Tierra 9
Café Arte 7
Casa Blanca 2
Chifa Nueva 5
El Argentino 9
El Chagra 5
Heladería Rosalía
Suárez 3
Los Almendros 8

Los Angeles 1
Mesón Colonial 4
Pizza El Horno 6

0 metres 100
0 yards 100

Ibarra to the coast

The spectacular train ride from Ibarra to San Lorenzo on the Pacific coast (see page 995) no longer operates, but an *autoferro* (motorized rail-car) runs for 45 km out of Ibarra to Primer Paso, just beyond **Tulquizán**, an interesting excursion through nice scenery (see Transport, below). From Tulquizán (the **Hostería Tulquizán**, across the river, T06-264 1989, was closed for repair in 2006; **C** pp **Cañon del Primer Paso**, T06-260 9325, alonso539@yahoo.com, price includes meals) you can continue by bus to San Lorenzo.

Some 24 km north of Ibarra is the turnoff west for Salinas and the very scenic paved road down to San Lorenzo on the Pacific coast (**safety**: enquire locally before undertaking this journey); 15 minutes beyond Salinas is Tulquizán (see above), further ahead is **Guallupe** and **El Limonal** (see Sleeping, below). There is an immense variety of wildlife in the surrounding tropical forest. In **Lita**, 20 km from Guallupe, there is an adequate *residencia* (**F**) and several restaurants about 1 km uphill from the train station. The remaining 93 km through a scenic area are prone to landslides during the rainy season.

North to Colombia

The Pan-American highway goes past Laguna Yahuarcocha (with a few hotels and restaurants) and then descends to the hot dry Chota valley. Beyond the turn-off for Salinas and San Lorenzo, 30 km from Ibarra, is a police checkpoint at **Mascarilla** (have your documents at hand), which has an interesting black community project 500 m towards El Angel (ceramic mask-making project, small friendly hostal **E** per person full-board). After Mascarilla the highway divides. One branch follows an older route through Mira and El Angel to Tulcán on the Colombian border. This road is paved and in good condition as far as El Angel, but deteriorates thereafter. It is passable with 4WD and is a great mountain bike route. IN the dry season cars with high clearance can get through to Tulcán.

Along the old Panamericana is **El Angel** (*Population: 4,400; altitude: 3,000 m*), with a Monday market. The main plaza retains a few trees sculpted by José Franco (see Tulcán Cemetery, below). The **Reserva Ecológica El Angel** ① *T/F297 7597, US$10 for foreigners, the reserve's office in El Angel is at the Municipio, information and pamphlets are available*, nearby protects 15,715 ha of *páramo* ranging in altitude from 3,400 to 4,768 m. The reserve contains large stands of the velvet-leaved *frailejón* plant, also found in the Andes of Colombia and Venezuela. Also of interest are the spiny *achupallas* with giant compound flowers. The fauna includes *curiquingues* (birds of prey), deer, foxes, and a few condors. There are several small lakes scattered throughout the reserve. It can be very muddy during the rainy season and the best time to visit is May to August.

From El Angel follow the poor road north towards Tulcán for 16 km to **El Voladero** ranger station, where a self-guided trail climbs over a low ridge (30 mins' walk) to two crystal-clear lakes. Camping is possible here, but you must be self-sufficient and take great care not to damage the fragile surroundings. Pickups or taxis can be hired in the main plaza of El Angel for a day trip to El Voladero, US$15 return with short wait. A longer route follows an equally poor road to Cerro Socabones, beginning in the town of **La Libertad**, 3½ km north of El Angel. This route climbs gradually to reach the high *páramo* at the centre of the reserve and, in one hour, the **El Salado** ranger station. Another hour ahead is **Socabones**, from where you can trek or take pack animals to the village of **Morán** (the local guide Hugo Quintanchala can take you further through the valley). There are many paths criss-crossing the *páramo* and it is easy to get lost. Transport from El Angel to Cerro Socabones, US$25 return, a helpful driver is **Sr Calderón**, T297 7274. A third access to the reserve, from the north along the Tufiño-Maldonado road, is not recommended because of its proximity to the Colombian border (see Tulcán Safety, below).

Eastern route to the border

The second branch (the modern Pan-American Highway), in good repair but with many heavy lorries, runs east through the warm Chota valley to Juncal, before turning north to reach Tulcán via Bolívar and San Gabriel. West of **Juncal** are several tourist complexes with accommodations (**AL-D** ranges), restaurants, swimming, horse riding; popular with Colombian and Ecuadorean tourists. A good paved road runs between Bolívar and El Angel, connecting the two branches.

Bolívar is a neat little town where the houses and the interior of its church are painted in lively pastel colours. There is a Friday market, a basic hotel (**F**) one block north of the plaza and two restaurants by the highway. Five kilometres north of Bolívar is the turn-off east for the town of **La Paz**, from which a steep but good cobbled road descends for 5 km to the **Gruta de La Paz**.

Views along the road are breathtaking, including two spectacular waterfalls. The place is also called *Rumichaca* (Quichua for rock bridge) after the massive natural bridge which forms the *gruta* (grotto); not to be confused with the Rumichaca on the Colombian border. The area is a religious shrine, receiving large numbers of pilgrims during Holy Week, Christmas, and especially around 8 July, feast day of the Virgin of La Paz. There are thermal baths nearby.

Some 10 km north of La Paz is **San Gabriel**, an important commercial centre. There are hotels (**D-F**) and restaurants. The spectacular 60-m high **Paluz** waterfall is 4 km north San Gabriel, beyond a smaller waterfall. Follow C Bolívar out of the main plaza and turn right after the bridge, or take a taxi (US$6,25).

East of San Gabriel by 20 km is the tiny community of **Mariscal Sucre**, also known as Colonia Huaquenia, the gateway to the **Guandera Reserve and Biological Station** ① *the reserve is part of the Fundación Jatun Sacha. Reservations should be made at Pasaje Eugenio de Santillán N34-248 y Maurian, Quito, T02-243 2246, www.jatunsacha.org.* You can see bromeliads, orchids, toucans and other wildlife in temperate forest and *frailejón páramo*. There is a lodge (**C**), take warm clothes as it gets very cold. From San Gabriel, take a taxi to Mariscal Sucre, one hour, then walk 30 minutes to the reserve, or make arrangements with Jatun Sacha.

Tulcán → *Phone code: 06. Colour map 11, grid A4. Population: 47,359. Altitude: 2,960 m.*

The chilly town of Tulcán is the busy capital of the province of Carchi. There is a great deal of informal trade here with Colombia, a textile and dry goods fair takes place on Thursday and Sunday. The old and new branches of the Panamericana join at Las Juntas, 2 km south of the city. In the cemetery, two blocks from Parque Ayora, the art of topiary is taken to beautiful extremes. Cypress bushes are trimmed into archways, fantastic figures and geometric shapes in *haut* and *bas* relief. To see the stages of this art form, go to the back of the cemetery where young bushes are being pruned. The artistry, started in 1936, is that of the late Sr José Franco, born in El Angel (see above), now buried among the splendour he created. The tradition is carried on by his sons.

Safety Don't wander about after 2200. The area around the bus terminal is unsafe. Tulcán and the traditionally tranquil border province of Carchi have seen an increase in tension due to the guerrilla conflict in Colombia. Do not travel outside town (except along the Panamericana highway) without advance local inquiry. The **tourist office**, Unidad de Turismo ① *entrance to the cemetery, T298 5760, Mon-Fri 0800-1300, 1500-1800*, is helpful, some English spoken, .

Border with Colombia

The border is open 0600-2200 for vehicles, 24-hours for pedestrians. It is well organized. There is an *Andinatel* office for phone calls, a tourist information office with maps and general information (Monday-Friday 0830-1700) and a snack bar. Try to ask for 90 days on entering Ecuador if you need them, although you will most likely only be given 30. See page 873 for Colombian immigration.

● Sleeping

Cotacachi *p923*
LL La Mirage, 500 m west of town, T291 5237, www.mirage.com.ec. Includes breakfast and dinner, lovely expensive restaurant, pool and gym, converted hacienda with luxurious facilities, beautiful gardens, antiques, conference facilities, and spa. Recommended.
C Sumac Huasi, Montalvo 11-09 y Moncayo, T291 5873, sumac_h@imbanet.net. Includes breakfast, large well-furnished rooms, nice roof top terrace.
D Munaylla, 10 de Agosto y Sucre, T291 6169. Modern, comfortable, good value.
D Plaza Bolívar, Bolívar 12-26 y 10 de Agosto, p 3, T291 5755, marcelmun@yahoo.es. Indoor parking, refurbished older building, stores luggage, helpful, knowledgeable owner.

E Bachita, Sucre 16-82 y Peñaherrera, T291 5063. Simple, quiet, cheaper with shared bath.

To promote rural/ethno-cultural tourism, the municipality has set up an interesting system of indigenous homestays in nearby villages. Visitors experience life with a native family by taking part in daily activities. The comfortable rooms have space for 3, fireplace, bathroom and hot shower. US$20 per person including breakfast, dinner and transport from Otavalo. Arrange with *Runa Tupari* (see below) or other Otavalo tour operators.

Laguna Cuicocha *p923*
A Los Pinos de Cuicocha, Hacienda Sta Rosa, Km 4 Via a Intag, T09-900 1516, 02-280 4867, www.lospinosdecuicocha.com. Comfortable

heated rooms in a working farm, includes breakfast and horse riding, restaurant (♦♦), parking, nice grounds but no views of the lake from rooms, English and German spoken.
B La Laguna, by the pier on the lakeshore, T264 8040, fgarces@andinanet.net. Modern comfortable rooms overlooking the lake, includes breakfast and dinner, restaurant with lake views (♦♦).
D El Mirador, on a lookout above the pier, follow the trail, T264 8039. Simple rooms in a great location, some with fireplace, good cheap restaurant, trout is their specialty, parking, transport provided to Quiroga (US$4) or Otavalo (US$10), owner Ernesto Cevillano is knowledgeable about the area and arranges trips to the Piñan Lakes or to climb Cotacachi.

Ibarra *p924, map p924*
The better class hotels tend to be fully booked during holidays and at weekends.
A Ajaví, Av Mariano Acosta 16-38 y Circunvalación, T295 5221, h-ajavi@imbanet.net. Comfortable, restaurant, pool, on main road to town from south.
B El Prado, Barrio El Olivo, off the Panamericana at Km 1.5, T/F295 9570. Includes breakfast, restaurant, pool, spa, set in fruit orchards.
C Montecarlo, Av Jaime Rivadeneira 5-61 y Oviedo, T295 8266, F295 8182. Restaurant, heated pool open weekends only, a better class hotel near the obelisk.
C Royal Ruiz, Olmedo 9-40 y P Moncayo, T264 1999, h.royalruiz@andinanet.net. Modern, includes breakfast, *Gourmet de Luc* restaurant, solar heated water, parking, comfortable.
D El Retorno, Pasaje Pedro Moncayo 4-32 entre Sucre y Rocafuerte, T295 7722. Restaurant, cheaper without bath, nice views from terrace. Recommended.
D Hostal Madrid, Olmedo 8-69 y Moncayo, T264 4918, rubenmoncayo@hotmail.com. Parking, modern and comfortable. Recommended.
D Hotel Madrid, Moncayo 7-41 y Olmedo, T295 9017, F295 0796. Comfortable rooms in multi-storey building.
E Res Madrid, Oviedo 85-7 y Olmedo, T295 1760. Simple, with bath and hot water.
F Imbabura, Oviedo 933 y Sánchez y Cifuentes, T295 0155. Long-time backpackers', in a colonial building, shared bath, basic, stores luggage.

Around Ibarra
Along the Pan-American Highway south towards Otavalo are several country inns, some in converted haciendas. From south to north are:

A Chorlaví, Panamericana S Km 4, T293 2222, chorlavi@andinanet.net. In an old hacienda, with breakfast, pool, expensive restaurant, excellent parrillada. Popular. Folk music and crafts on Sun.
B Natabuela, Panamericana Sur Km 293 2032, sproano@andinanet.net. Restaurant, covered pool, sauna, comfortable rooms.
D Casa Aída, La Esperanza, with bath, hot water, Aída speaks some English and cooks good vegetarian food, recommended.

Ibarra to the coast: El Limonal *p925*
D Finca Forestal Bospas, 800 m uphill from the main square of El Limonal, T06-264 8692, www.bospas.org. Includes breakfast, simple rooms with bath on an organic fruit farm, trekking and horse riding, volunteer opportunities, Belgian/Ecuadorean run. Recommended.

North to Colombia: El Angel *p925*
A pp Polylepis Lodge, on Morán road out of El Angel after the guard station, info@polylepislodge.com. New, price is full board, excellent forest and trails.
C Hostería El Angel, at entrance to village, T/F297 7584, www.ecuador-sommerfer.com. Includes breakfast, meals available on request, caters for groups, reservations required, contact Quito T/F222 1480. Offers trips into El Angel reserve and also has Cotinga Lodge in the Río Morán valley, a good place for birdwatching.
E Los Faroles, José Grijalva 5-96 on the plaza, T297 7144. Above OK restaurant, simple rooms, shared bath, hot water.

Tulcán *p926*
Many hotels are located on C Sucre.
B Sara Espíndola, Sucre y Ayacucho, on plaza, T298 5925, F298 6209. Comfortable rooms, best hotel with nicest restaurant in town.
C Machado, Bolívar y Ayacucho, T298 4221, F298 0099. Includes breakfast, comfy, parking.
D Lumar, Sucre y Rocafuerte, T298 0402. Modern, comfortable.
D Torres de Oro, Sucre y Rocafuerte, T298 0296. With breakfast, restaurant, parking, modern, nice.
E Los Alpes, JR Arellano next to bus station, T298 2235. Restaurant, hot water, OK, good value.
E Sáenz Internacional, Sucre y Rocafuerte, T298 1916. Very nice, modern, hot water, good value. Recommended.
E-F Florida, Sucre y 10 de Agosto, T298 3849. Cheaper without bath, hot water, modern section at back, good value.

● For an explanation of the sleeping and eating price codes used in this guide, see inside the front
● cover. Other relevant information is found in Essentials pages 886-888.

❶ Eating

Cotacachi *p923*

A local specialty is *carne colorada* (spiced pork).

⍡ Asadero La Tola, Rocafuerte 0-18 y 9 de Octubre. Grill, in an old courtyard.

⍡ El Leñador, Sucre 10-12 y Montalvo. Varied menu, mid-range prices.

⍡-⍡ La Marqueza, 10 de Agosto y Bolívar, daily 0730-2130. 4 course set lunches and à la carte.

⍡ El Viejo Molino, 10 de Agosto 10-65 y Moncayo. Set meals and à la carte, good value and quality.

Ibarra *p924, map p924*

⍡ Café Floralp, Av Teodoro Gómez 7-49 y Atahualpa. Crêpes, fondue, good breakfast, bread, yoghurt, cold cuts, excellent coffee, good selection of Chilean wines, the 'in place' to meet and eat, Swiss-owned. Warmly recommended.

⍡ El Argentino, Sucre y P Moncayo, at Plazoleta Francisco Calderón, Tue-Sun. Good mixed grill and salads, small, pleasant, outdoor seating when the weather permits.

⍡ Los Almendros, Velasco 5-59 y Sucre. Good set lunches and à la carte.

⍡ Mesón Colonial, Rocafuerte 5-53, at Parque Abdón Calderón. In a colonial house, extensive à la carte menu, good food and service, closed Sun. Recommended.

⍡ Pizza El Horno, Rocafuerte 6-38 y Flores. Good Italian dishes, live music Sat night, closed Mon.

⍡ Casa Blanca, Bolívar 7-83. Excellent, family run, located in colonial house with seating around a central patio with fountain, delicious food, closed Sun. Warmly recommended.

⍡ Chifa Nueva, Olmedo 7-20. Reasonable Chinese food, large portions.

⍡ El Chagra, Olmedo 7-44. *Platos típicos*, good trout. Recommended.

⍡ Los Angeles, Sánchez y Cifuentes 7-35 next to the Iglesia de la Merced. Good set lunches.

Cafés and heladerías

There are others at Olmedo y Flores.

Antojitos de Mi Tierra, Sucre y P Moncayo, at Plazoleta Francisco Calderón, afternoons. Outdoor seating, local drinks and snacks.

Café Arte, Salinas 5-43 y Oviedo, daily 1700 until late. Café-bar serving drinks, Mexican snacks, sandwiches and some à la carte dishes.

Café Pushkin, Olmedo 7-75. For breakfast, with good bread, opens 0730, a classic.

Heladería Rosalía Suárez, Oviedo y Olmedo. Excellent homemade *helados de paila* (fruit sherbets made in large copper basins), try *mora* or *guanábana* (soursop) flavours, an Ibarra tradition since 1896. Highly recommended.

La Bermejita, Olmedo 7-15.

Tulcán *p926*

⍡ Café Tulcán, Sucre 52-029 y Ayacucho. Café, snacks, desserts, juices.

⍡ El Patio, Bolívar 50-050 y 10 de Agosto. For Colombian specialities.

⍡ Los Leños, Olmedo y Ayacucho. Set meals and à la carte.

⍡ Mama Rosita, Sucre entre Boyacá y Atahualpa. Typical Ecuadorean dishes.

⍡ Tequila, Sucre entre Junín y Boyacá. Varied à la carte menu.

❶ Bars and clubs

Ibarra *p924, map p924*

Bar Buda, Sucre y Pedro Moncayo, at Plazoleta Francisco Calderón. Outdoor seating, a good place for an afternoon drink.

El Encuentro, Olmedo 9-59. Piano bar, interesting drinks, very popular, pleasant, unusual decor.

El Zarape, Circunvalacíon. *Peña* and restaurant.

Clubs include **Sambuca**, **Oviedo y Olmedo** and **Studio 54** at Laguna Yaguarcocha.

❶ Shopping

Ibarra *p924, map p924*

Supermarkets Akí, Bolívar y Colón. **Supermaxi**, south of the centre on road to Otavalo. **Supermercado El Rosado**, Olmedo 9-46.

⛰ Activities and tours

Ibarra *p924, map p924*

Paddle ball A unique form of paddle ball is played at weekends near the railway station and other places; ask around for details. Players have huge studded paddles for striking the 1 kg ball.

Swimming **Balneario Primavera**, Sánchez y Cifuentes 3-33, T295 7425, heated pool, Turkish bath, also aerobics classes and remedial massage.

Tour operators

Intipungo, Rocafuerte 6-08 y Flores, T295 7766, intiibr@interactive.net.ec. Regional tours.

Metropolitan Touring, Flores 5-76 y Sucre, see Quito.

Nevitur, Bolívar 7-35 y Oviedo, T295 8701, F264 0040. Excellent travel guides, van trips throughout the country.

❶ Transport

Cotacachi *p923*

Bus Terminal at 10 de Agosto y Salinas by the market. Frequent service from the Otavalo terminal, US$0.20, 20 mins; service alternates between the Panamericana and the Quiroga roads. To **Ibarra**, every 15 mins, US$0.45, 45 mins.

Laguna Cuicocha *p923*
Pick-ups From **Otavalo** US$10. From **Cotacachi**
market, US$4 one way, US$8 return with short
wait. From **Quiroga** US$4. Return service from
the lake available from **Cabañas El Mirador**,
same rates.

Los Cedros Research Station
Bus Access by morning Trans Minas San José
de Minas bus to Chontal from the new depot at
Los Ríos y Julio Castro, US$4, 4 hrs. Then a 4-5 hr
walk from Chontal, which is north of Pacto and
west of García Moreno.

Ibarra *p924, map p924*
Bus Terminal is at Av Teodoro Gómez y
Av Eugenio Espejo, to the south of the centre, T264
4676. At the terminal there are small shops, two
food courts and a telephone office. All inter-city
transport runs from here. City buses go from the
terminal to the centre or you can walk in 15 mins.
To/from **Quito**, frequent service, US$2.50, 2½ hrs.
Shared taxis with Supertaxis Los Lagos (Quito
address and schedules under Otavalo above, in
Ibarra at Flores 924 y Sánchez Cifuentes, Parque La
Merced, T295 5150), buy ticket at their office the
day before travelling, US$7.50 pp, 2½ hrs. To
Tulcán, hourly, US$2.50, 2½ hrs. To **Otavalo**,
frequent service, US$0.50, 45 mins. To **Cotacachi**,
US$0.45, 45 mins, some continue to **Quiroga**. To
the coast several companies leave from the
Terminal Terrestre, some go all the way to **San
Lorenzo** US$4, 3 hrs, others only as far as **Lita**,
US$3.50, 2 hrs. To **Ambato**, CITA goes via El
Quinche and bypasses Quito, 5 daily, US$5, 5 hrs.
To **La Esperanza** Bus from Parque Germán
Grijalva (east of the Terminal Terrestre, follow C
Sánchez y Cifuentes, south from the centre), every
30 mins, US$0.25, 30 mins.
Train Autoferro to **Primer Paso** (see above),
US$3.80 one way, leaves Mon-Fri 0700, returning
1400, Sat-Sun 0800, returning 1600, minimum 15
passengers, T295 5050.

North to Colombia: El Angel *p925*
Bus From **Ibarra** Terminal Terrestre to **Mira**,
every 30 minutes, US$0.90, 1 hr; to **El Angel**,
hourly, US$1.30, 1½ hrs. From **El Angel** to **Mira**,
every 30 min, US$.50, 20 minutes. From El Angel
to **Tulcán**, US$1.30, 1½ hrs. From El Angel to
Quito, US$4, 4 hrs.

Eastern route to the border *p925*
San Gabriel
Bus From **San Gabriel** to **Tulcán**, vans and jeeps
US$0.60, shared taxis US$0.80, 30 mins, all from
the main plaza. From San Gabriel to **Ibarra**, buses,
US$1.65, 2 hrs. From San Gabriel to **Quito**, buses,

US$3.50, 3½ hrs. For **La Paz**, public transport
from Tulcán and San Gabriel on weekends only;
you must hire a taxi at other times.

Tulcán *p926*
Air TAME (Sucre y Ayacucho, T298 0675) flies
Mon, Wed and Fri to **Quito** (US$36) and to **Cali** in
Colombia (US$78).
Bus The bus terminal is 1½ km uphill from
centre; best to take a taxi, US$1. To **Quito**, US$4, 5
hrs, every 15 mins. To **Ibarra**, 2½ hrs, US$2.
Otavalo, US$3, 3 hrs (make sure the bus is going
to Otavalo; if not get out on the Highway at the
turnoff), or transfer in Ibarra. To **Guayaquil**, 20 a
day, 11 hrs, US$13. To **Lago Agrio**, 1 a day with
Putumayo (tickets from **Gacela** office), US$7, 8
hrs, spectacular, but it does go close to the
Colombian border.

Border with Colombia: Tulcán-Ipiales
p926
Bus Minivans and shared taxis Tulcán-border
leave when full from Parque Ayora (near the
cemetery) US$0.80 pp, private taxi US$4. **Note**:
These vehicles cross the international bridge and
drop you off on the Colombian side, where
Colombian transport waits. Remember to cross
back over the bridge for Ecuadorean
immigration.

❶ Directory

Ibarra *p924, map p924*
Banks Banco del Pacífico, Moncayo y
Olmedo. Banco del Austro, Colón 7-51.
Banco del Pichincha, Bolívar y Mosquera.
Internet Prices US$1 per hr, several places in
town centre. **Language courses** Centro
Ecuatoriano Canadiense de Idomas (CECI),
Pérez Guerrero 6-12 y Bolívar, T295 1911,
US$3.50 per hr. CIMA, Obelisco Casa No 2, p 2.
Medical services Clínica Médica del Norte,
Oviedo 8-24, T295 5099, open 24 hrs. **Post
offices** Flores opposite Parque Pedro
Moncayo, 2nd floor.

Tulcán *p926*
Banks Banco del Pichincha, at Plaza de la
Independencia. Banco del Austro, Bolívar y
Ayacucho. Few places accept credit cards.
Nowhere in Tulcán to change TCs. Pesos
Colombianos can easily be changed on Plaza de
la Independencia. **Consulates** Colombia:
Bolívar 386 y Junín, T298 7302, visas require up to
20 days, Mon-Fri 0800-1300, 1430-1530.
Internet Prices US$1 per hr, many places in
town. **Post offices** Bolívar 53-27.

Cotopaxi, Latacunga and Quilotoa

An impressive roll call of towering peaks lines the route south of Quito, appropriately called the Avenue of the Volcanoes. This area obviously attracts its fair share of trekkers and climbers, while the less active tourist can browse through the many colourful indígena markets and colonial towns that nestle among the high volcanic cones. The Panamericana heads south from Quito towards the central highlands' hub of Ambato. The perfect cone of Cotopaxi volcano is ever-present and is one of the country's main tourist attractions. Machachi and Lasso are good places to acclimatize, while Latacunga is a good base for the region, and for the impossibly beautiful Quilotoa circuit of small villages and vast expanses of open countryside.

Cotopaxi and Latacunga

Machachi → *Phone code: 02. Colour map 11, grid A3. Population: 12,500. Altitude: 2,900 m.*
In a valley between the summits of Pasochoa, Rumiñahui and Corazón, lies the town of **Machachi**, famous for its mineral water springs and cold, crystal clear swimming pool (open 0800-1530 daily). The water, 'Agua Güitig', is bottled in a plant 4 km from the town and sold throughout the country (free tours 0800-1200, take identification). Machachi is in the middle of an important dairy area; annual highland 'rodeo', El Chagra, third week in July.

Reserva Ecológica Los Ilinizas
Machachi is a good starting point for a visit to the northern section of the **Reserva Ecológica Los Ilinizas** *US$5*. There is a *refugio*, a shelter below the saddle between the two peaks, at 4,750 m, with beds for 12 and cooking facilities, take a mat and sleeping bag, US$8 per night (check at the **Hostal Llovizna** on the way out of Chaupi, if Vladimir or his assistant is not at the hut, then they key is at the Hostal). Iliniza Norte (5,126 m) can be climbed without technical equipment in the dry season but a few exposed, rocky sections require utmost caution, allow 2-4 hours for the ascent from the refuge, take a compass, it's easy to mistake the descent. Iliniza Sur (5,245 m) has some ice climbing, but the glacier is disappearing fast: full climbing gear and experience are absolutely necessary. Access to the reserve is through a turnoff west of the Panamericana 6 km south of Machachi, from where it is 7 km to the village of El Chaupi. A dirt road continues from here to 'La Virgen' (statue) about 9 km beyond. Nearby are woods where you can camp.

Parque Nacional Cotopaxi → *Colour map 11, grid B4.*
ⓘ *Visitors to the park must register at the main entrance. Entrance fee: US$10. Park gates are open 0700-1500, although you can stay until 1800. The park administration, a small museum (0800-1200, 1300-1700), Hostal Paja Blanca, T02-231 4234 and a restaurant serving typical food, are 10 km from the park gates, just before Limpio Pungo. (See also Transport section below.) The museum has a 3D model of the park and stuffed animals.*
Cotopaxi volcano (5,897 m) is at the heart of a much-visited national park. This scenic snow-covered perfect cone is the second highest peak in Ecuador and a very popular climbing destination. Cotopaxi is an active volcano, one of the highest in the world, and its most recent eruption took place in 1904. Volcanic material from former eruptions can be seen strewn about the páramo surrounding Cotopaxi; there is a high plateau with a small lake (Laguna Limpio Pungo), a lovely area for walking and admiring the delicate flora, and fauna including wild horses and native bird species such as the Andean Lapwing and the Chimborazo Hillstar hummingbird. The lower slopes are clad in planted pine forests, where llamas may be seen.

The **main entrance** to the Parque Nacional Cotopaxi is approached from Chasqui, 25 km south of Machachi, 6 km north of Lasso, and is marked by a Parque Nacional Cotopaxi sign. At the gate this route is joined by the **El Boliche access**, starting 16 km south of Machachi. This begins near a sign for the Clirsen satellite tracking station, which has a museum for visitors. This route goes past Clirsen then via **Area Nacional de Recreación El Boliche** (shared entry with Cotopaxi, pay only once) for over 30 km along a signposted dirt road. This road skirts the western flanks of Rumiñahui volcano; it starts higher and stays higher making it a longer but easier approach, especially for cyclists. Once through the national park gates, go past Laguna Limpio Pungo to a fork, where the right branch climbs steeply to a parking lot (4,600 m). From here it is 30 minutes to one hour on foot to the José Ribas refuge, at 4,800 m; beware of altitude sickness. Walking from the highway to the refuge takes an entire day or more. **A third entrance**, from the northwest, goes from Machachi via Santa Ana del Pedregal (21 km from the Panamericana), 35 km in total to the car park. There are infrequent buses to Pedregal (2 a day) then the hike in is shorter but still a couple of hours. For more details, and equipment, ask Quito tour operators who run tours here, or *South American Explorers* in Quito. The **Ticatilín access** approaches Cotopaxi from the south. From the Panamericana, 1 km north of Lasso, at 'Aglomerados Cotopaxi' (the northern access to Saquisilí) a road goes to the village of San Ramón and on to Ticatilín where a contribution is expected to open the chain at the access point (US$1-2 per vehicle). If coming from the south, San Ramón is accessed from Mulaló. It leads to a less impacted páramo and the private Albergue Cotopaxi Cara Sur. Walking 4 hours from here you reach Campo Alto, a tent camp used by climbers. There are other access points from the north, east and south, which go through private land and combine with the Cotopaxi circuit trek.

Climbing Cotopaxi The ascent from the refuge takes 5-8 hours, start climbing at 0100 as the snow deteriorates in the sun. A full moon is both practical and a magical experience. Check out snow conditions with the guardian of the refuge before climbing. Equipment and experience are required. Take a guide if you're inexperienced on ice and snow. The best season is December-April. There are strong winds and clouds in August-December but the ascent is still possible for experienced mountaineers. Climbing guides can be hired through operators in Quito, Latacunga, Riobamba and Baños. Just north of Cotopaxi are the peaks of Sincholahua (4,893 m), Rumiñahui (4,712 m) and Pasochoa (4,225 m). To the southeast is Quilindaña (4,878 m). The southwest flank has not received as much impact as the north side. There is good walking, and you can climb Morurco (4,881 m) as an acclimatization hike. Condors may sometimes be seen. To climb to the summit in one day you have to stay at Campo Alto (see above, and Sleeping below). The route is reported easier and safer than the north face, but a little longer. The last hour goes around the rim of the crater with impressive views.

Lasso → *Phone code: 03. Colour map 11, grid B3. Altitude: 3,000 m.*
The railway and the Pan-American Highway cross one another at Lasso, a small town, 33 km south of Alóag, with a milk-bottling plant and some simple eateries. In the surrounding countryside are several *hosterías*, converted country estates offering accommodation and meals. Along the Panamericana are *paradores* or roadside restaurants.

Latacunga → *Phone code: 03. Colour map 11, grid B3. Population: 51,689. Altitude: 2,800 m.*
The capital of Cotopaxi Province is a place where the abundance of light grey pumice has been artfully employed. Volcán Cotopaxi is much in evidence, though it is 29 km away. Provided they are not hidden by clouds, which unfortunately is all too often, as many as nine volcanic cones can be seen from Latacunga; try early in the morning. The colonial character of the town has been well preserved. The central plaza, **Parque Vicente León**, is a beautifully maintained garden (locked at night). There are several other gardens in the town including **Parque San Francisco** and **Lago Flores**. **Casa de los Marqueses de Miraflores**, Sánchez de Orellana y Abel Echeverría, in a restored colonial mansion has a modest museum, with exhibits on Mama Negra (see Festivals and events, below), colonial art, archaeology, numismatics and a library (free).

Casa de la Cultura ① *Antonia Vela 3-49 y Padre Salcedo T281 3247, Tue-Fri 0800-1200, 1400-1800, Sat 0800-1500, US$1*, built around the remains of a Jesuit Monastery and the old Monserrat watermill, houses an excellent museum with pre-Columbian ceramics, weavings, costumes and models of festival masks; also art gallery, library and theatre. It has week-long festivals with exhibits and concerts for all the local festivities. There is a Saturday **market** on the Plaza de San Sebastián (at Juan Abel Echeverría). Goods for sale include *shigras* (fine stitched, colourful straw bags) and homespun wool and cotton yarn. The produce market, Plaza El Salto has daily trading and larger fairs on Tuesday and Saturday.

Tourist offices: Cámara de Turismo de Cotopaxi ① *Sánchez de Orellana y Guayaquil, at Plaza de Santo Domingo, T281 4968, Mon-Fri 0800-1200, 1400-1700*, local and regional information, Spanish only. **Oficina de Turismo**, at the Terminal Terrestre, second floor ① *Mon-Fri 0900-1200, 1330-1800, Sat 0900-1600, Sun 0900-1400*, staffed by high school students, local and some regional information.

⊜ Sleeping

Machachi *p930*

C La Estación de Machachi, 3 km west of the Panamericana, by Aloasí, T230 9246. Beautiful old house, family-run, fireplaces, access to Volcán Corazón, reserve in advance.

C-D Papa Gayo, in Hacienda Bolívia, 500 m W of the Panamericana, T231 0002, h_eran@ yahoo.com. Chilly old farmhouse, nice communal area with fireplace and library. Restaurant, cheaper with shared bath, parking, homely atmosphere, excursions arranged, popular.

D Chiguac, Los Caras y Colón, 4 blocks from the main park, T231 0396, germanimor@punto.net.ec. Small family run hostel, comfortable, includes breakfast, restaurant, shared bath.

E La Estancia Real, Luis Cordero y Panzaleo, 3 blocks east of park, T231 5760. Hot water, parking, OK.

Reserva Ecológica Los Ilinizas *p930*

C Hacienda San José del Chaupi, 3 km southwest of El Chaupi, T09-971 3986 (mob). Converted farm house and cabins, including breakfast, shared bath, hot water, meals available if requested in advance, horse riding.

E pp Hostal Llovizna, on the road to the *refugio*, on the left just after town. Owned by the operator of the *refugio* who gives a discount if you stay there and at the refuge. Hostal Llovizna arranges horses for transport to the *refugio*.

E-F Posada El Chaupi, in front of bus-stop, T02-286 0830. Meals with family on request, shared bath, electric shower, run by the Salazar family, basic and very friendly.

Parque Nacional Cotopaxi *p930*

All these inns are good for acclimatization at altitudes between 3,100 and 3,800 m.

There are 2 very basic *cabañas* and a couple of campsites below Limpio Pungo (US$2 per tent, no facilities). The **José Ribas refuge** (entry US$1) has a kitchen, water, and 30 bunks with mattresses; US$17 pp per night, bring sleeping bag and mat, also padlock for your excess luggage when you climb, or use the lockable luggage deposit, US$2.50. **Albergue Cotopaxi Cara Sur** on the southwest flank at 4,000m, capacity 40 in bunk beds, showers, US$12 pp, simple meals US$2-5, contact *Agama Expediciones* in Quito, see Tour operators. They also have a tent camp, *Campo Alto*, at 4,780 m, US$6 pp, 4 hrs walk up from the *Albergue*. Horses are available to carry gear to the tent camp, US$12 each.

Outside the park

LL Hacienda San Agustín de Callo, entrance from the Panamericana 1.6 km north of the southern park access, marked by a painted stone, 10 min ride from the highway, T03-271 9160, www.incahacienda.com. Some rooms in ancient Inca structure, with fireplaces, bathtub, breakfast and dinner included, horse and bicycle hire.

To the southeast of the park lies an area of rugged *páramos* and mountains dropping down to the jungle. The area has several large

Latacunga

haciendas which form the Fundación Páramo, a private reserve with restricted access.

L Hacienda Yanahurco, reservations: Quito, T02-224 1593, www.ecuador-yanahurco.com. Ranch-style rooms, fireplace or heater, meals, tours, yearly rodeo in Nov. Access is through the park so US$10 entry fee has to paid.

A-C Albergue Cuello de Luna, El Chasqui, Panamericana Sur Km 65, 2 km northwest of park entrance on a dirt road, at 3,125 m, T/F09-970 0330, www.cuellodeluna.com. Including breakfast, dorm cheaper, restored *hacienda*, restaurant, transport, tours.

B Tambopaxi, within the park at 3,750 m, 3 km south of the northern entrance (1 hr drive from Machachi) or 4 km north (left) of the turnoff for the climbing shelter, Quito T02-222 0242. Bunk beds, duvet blankets, shared bath with hot shower, good restaurant with set meals and Swiss specialities, llama trekking, camping US$5 pp. Access is through the park so US$10 entry fee has to paid.

Lasso *p931*
AL-A Hostería La Ciénega, 2 km south of Lasso, west of the Panamericana, T271 9052, www.geocities.com/haciendaec/. An historic *hacienda* with nice gardens, an avenue of massive eucalyptus trees, nice rooms with heater, good expensive restaurant.

A-B San Mateo, 4 km south of Lasso west of the Panamericana, T/F271 9471, www.hosteria sanmateo.com. Bright rooms, pricey restaurant, horse riding included, small but nice, adjoining working *hacienda* can be visited.

B Posada del Rey, opposite *Hostería La Ciénega*, T271 9319. Carpeted rooms, restaurant with choice of 3 set meals, covered pool, clean but a bit characterless and overpriced.

E Cabañas Los Volcanes, at the south end of Lasso, T271 9524. Nice rooms with shared bath, hot water, transport to mountains.

Latacunga *p931, map p932*
C Makroz, Valencia 8-56 y Quito, T280 0907, F280 7274. Restaurant (closed Sun), parking, modern, comfortable.

C Rodelú, Quito 16-31, T280 0956, rodelu@ uio.telconet.net. Includes breakfast, excellent restaurant (closed Sun), parking, comfortable.

D Cotopaxi, Padre Salcedo 5-61 on Parque Vicente León, T280 1310. Cafeteria, hot water after 0700, rooms with view over plaza are noisy at weekends.

D Estambul, Belisario Quevedo 6-46 y Padre Salcedo, T280 0354. Cheaper without bath, luggage store, tours. Recommended.

D Rosim, Quito 16-49 y Padre Salcedo, T280 2172, hotelrosim@hotmail.com. Carpeted

rooms, quiet, comfortable, discounts for IYHF members and in low season.

D Tilipulo, Guayaquil y Belisario Quevedo, T281 0611. Comfortable, helpful, parking, cafeteria, noisy at weekends. Recommended.

D-E Santiago, 2 de Mayo 7-16 y Guayaquil, T280 0899. Pleasant hotel, cheaper with bath outside the room (not shared), small but comfortable rooms, good value.

E-F Los Nevados, Av 5 de Junio 53-19 y Eloy Alfaro, near bus terminal, T280 0407. Restaurant, parking, modern, spacious rooms, good value but unpleasant area.

E-F Amazonas, Valencia 47-36 y Amazonas on Plaza El Salto, T281 2673. Simple, overlooking the market, cheaper with shared bath, electric shower, adequate rooms, gets noisy early in the morning.

❷ Eating

Machachi *p930*
♦♦♦-♦♦ Café de la Vaca, 4 km south of town on the Panamericana. Very good meals using produce from own farm, open daily for breakfast and lunch until 1600, very popular.

♦♦ El Chagra, take the road that passes in front of the church, on the right-hand side, about 5 km from church. Good typical food, reasonably priced.

♦ El Mesón del Valle, near the Parque Central. Good food, helpful owner.

Lasso *p931*
♦ Express, by the railway station. Serves simple, hearty Ecuadorean meals.

♦ Parador Chalupas, 5 km south of Lasso at La Avelina. Popular cafetería, busy at weekends.

♦ Parador La Avelina, 5 km south of Lasso, opposite Chalupas. Known for its cheese and ice cream, a traditional stopping place.

Latacunga *p931, map p932*
The local speciality is *chugchucaras*, pork skins served with corn, plantain, popcorn and small pieces of roast pork, all deep fried. Few places are open on Sun.

♦♦ Finca Parador Don Diego, south of the train station and the Rumipamba bridge on the Panamericana. Trout, steak, chicken, clean, classy, great service.

♦♦-♦ Los Copihues, Quito 14-25 y Tarqui. International menu, 4-course set lunch, good generous portions, Mon-Sat 1000-2200. Recommended.

♦♦ Pizzería Los Sabores de Italia, Quito 16-57 next to Hotel Rosim. Good pizza and Italian dishes, open daily 1200-2200.

♦ Chifa China, Antonia Vela 6-85 y 5 de Junio. Chinese, large portions, open daily to 2200.

Pizzería Buon Giorno, Sánchez de Orellana y
Gral Maldonado. Great pizzas and lasagne, huge
selection, 1300-2300, closed Sun.

Cafés
Café Precolombino, Belisario Quevedo 6-31 y
Padre Salcedo, Mon-Sat 0800-1400, 1500-
2200. Breakfast, snacks, desserts and sweets,
pleasant atmosphere.
Café-Libro Volcán, Belisario Quevedo 5-56 y
Padre Salcedo, Mon-Fri 1400-2200, Sat
1400-2000. Snacks, tacos, drinks, board games,
a place to hang around.
Cafetería El Pasaje, Padre Salcedo 43-16, p 2,
on pedestrian mall, Mon-Sat 0830-2030. Snacks,
burgers, coffee and other drinks.
Pingüino, Quito 73-106, 1 block from Parque
Vicente León. Good milk shakes and coffee.
    For *chugchucaras*: Rosita, Eloy Alfaro 31-226 on
the Panamericana. Don Pancho, Quijano y
Ordoñez y Rumiñahui. Also try *allullas con queso
de hoja*, biscuits with string cheese.

❶ Bars and clubs

Latacunga *p931, map p932*
Beer Center, Sánchez de Orellana 74-20.
Good atmosphere, bar and disco.
Kahlúa Bongo Bar, Padre Salcedo 4-56, on
pedestrian mall. Bar, open Wed-Sat 1900-0100.

❀ Festivals and events

Latacunga *p931, map p932*
The Fiesta de la Mama Negra is held on
24 Sep, in homage to *the Virgen de las Mercedes*.
It celebrates the black slaves brought by the
Spanish to work on the plantations with dancing
in the streets and colourful costumes. The
civic festival of Mama Negra is on the 1st Sun
in Nov.

❍ Shopping

Latacunga *p931, map p932*
Azul, Padre Salcedo 4-20, on pedestrian mall.
Ceramics, bronze and wooden items.
La Mama Negra, Padre Salcedo 4-43, on
pedestrian mall. A variety of crafts.

▲ Activities and tours

Latacunga *p931, map p932*
All operators and some hotels offer day trips to
Cotopaxi and Quilotoa (US$35 pp, includes
lunch and a visit to a market town if on Thu or
Sat); prices for 3 or more people. Climbing trips to
Cotopaxi are US$120-130 pp for 2 days (includes
equipment, park entrance fee, meals, refuge

fees), minimum 2 people. **Note**: Many agencies
require passport as deposit when renting
equipment. Trekking trips to Cotopaxi, Ilinizas,
etc US$30-40 pp, per day.
Metropolitan Touring, Guayaquil y Quito,
T280 2985. See Quito Tour operators. Makes
airline reservations.
Neiges, Guayaquil 5-19 y Quito, T/F281 1199.
Day trips and climbing.
Ruta de los Volcanes, Padre Salcedo 4-55 y
Quito, T281 2452. Tour to Cotopaxi follows a
secondary road through interesting country,
instead of the Panamericana.
Selvanieve, Padre Salcedo 4-38, T281 2895,
selvanieve1@hotmail.com. Various tours,
climbing, also has an agency in Baños, runs tours
throughout Ecuador.
Tovar Expediciones, Guayaquil 5-38 y Quito,
T281 1333. Climbing and trekking, Fernando Tovar
is an experienced mountain guide.

❺ Transport

Machachi *p930*
Bus To Quito, 1 hr, US$0.55 from Av Amazonas
1 block south of the park – *especiales* go to the
Terminal Terrestre, *populares* to El Recreo, 2-3
blocks before the Trole station of that name. To
Latacunga, from the obelisk at the
Panamericana, US$0.55, 1 hr.

Reserva Ecológica Los Ilinizas *p930*
Bus There is a frequent bus service from
Av Amazonas opposite the market in Machachi
to El Chaupi (30 min, US$0.30), from where you
can walk to the *refugio* in 7-8 hrs. Horses can be
hired at *Hacienda San José* or ask around the
village (see also Hostal Llovizna, above). A
pick-up from Machachi to 'La Virgen' takes about
45 mins (US$25), where it takes 3 hrs to walk
with a full pack to the *refugio*.

Parque Nacional Cotopaxi *p930*
To the Main park entrance and Refugio
Ribas, take a Latacunga bus from Quito
and get off at the main access point. Do
not take an express bus as you can't get off
before Latacunga. At the turnoff to the park
there are usually vehicles from Cooperativa
Zona Verde which go up to the park. US$20
to the parking lot before the refuge for up
to 5 passengers. From Machachi, pick-ups
go via the cobbled road to El Pedregal on
to the Limpio Pungo and the refugio
parking lot, US$35. From Lasso, pick-up
US$25 one-way to the refugio parking lot,
1½ hrs, US$40 return with 1 hr wait.
    To Cara Sur from Quito, Agama
Expediciones offer transport to the Albergue

Cara Sur, US$60 per vehicle up to 5 passengers. Alternatively take a Latacunga bound bus and get off at **Aceropaxi** (the entrance to Mulaló) and take a pick-up from there, US$15 per vehicle for up to 5 passengers.

Latacunga p931, map p932

Bus Buses leave from the terminal on the Panamericana just south of 5 de Junio, except Coop Santa, which has its own terminal at Eloy Alfaro 28-57 y Vargas Torres, 3 blocks north of the Terminal Terrestre along the Panamericana, T281 1659, serving **Cuenca**, **Loja**, and **Guayaquil** via Riobamba and Pallatanga. To **Quito**, every 15 mins, 2 hrs, US$1.75. To/from **Ambato**, 1 hr, US$1. To **Guayaquil**, US$6.50, 6 hrs. To **Saquisilí**, every 20 mins (see below). To **Quevedo**, 8 a day, US$4, 3½ hrs. Through buses do not stop at Latacunga

Terminal but use a bypass 3 blocks to the west or 3 to the south of the terminal. Taxi US$1. Buses on the Zumbahua, Quilotoa, Chugchilán, Sigchos circuit are given below. **Note**: On Thu most buses to nearby communities leave from Saquisilí market instead of Latacunga.

❶ Directory

Latacunga p931, map p932

Banks Banco de Guayaquil, Maldonado y Sánchez de Orellana. For Visa and MasterCard. Mutualista Pichincha, Quito 1497 y Maldonado. For MasterCard. **Internet** Prices around US$1 per hr. **Medical services** Hospital: at southern end of Amazonas y Hnos Páez, T281 2502, good service. **Post offices and telephones** Both at Belisario Quevedo y Maldonado.

Quilotoa Circuit

The popular and recommended round trip from Latacunga to Pujilí, Zumbahua, Quilotoa crater, Chugchilán, Sigchos, Isinliví, Toacazo, Saquisilí, and back to Latacunga can be done in two to three days by bus (times given below are approximate; buses are often late owing to the rough roads or requests for photo stops). It is 200 km in total. It is also a great route for biking and only a few sections of the loop are cobbled or rough. The best access is from Lasso or Latacunga.

Latacunga to Zumbahua

A fine paved road leads west to **Pujilí** ① *15 km, bus US$0.25*, which has a beautiful church. Good market on Sunday, and a smaller one on Wednesday. Colourful Corpus Christi celebrations. Beyond Pujilí, many interesting crafts are practised by the *indígenas* in the **Tigua** valley: paintings on leather, hand-carved wooden masks and baskets. **Chimbachuco**, also known as Tigua, is home to the Toaquiza family, most famous of the Tigua painters. Here is a gallery and comfortable, community-run hostal, **Samana Huasi**. The road goes on over the Western Cordillera to Zumbahua, La Maná and Quevedo. This is a great downhill bike route. It carries very little traffic and is extremely twisty in parts but is one of the most beautiful routes connecting the highlands with the coast. Beyond Zumbahua are the pretty towns of **Pilaló** (two restaurants and petrol pumps), **Esperanza de El Tingo** (two restaurants and lodging at *Carmita's*, T03-281 4657) and **La Maná**.

Zumbahua

Zumbahua lies ½ km from the main road, 37 km from Pujilí. It has an interesting Saturday market (starts at 0600) for local produce, and some tourist items. You can find a cheap meal in the market. Just below the plaza is a shop selling dairy products and cold drinks. Friday nights involve dancing and drinking. Take a fleece, as it can be windy, cold and dusty. There is a good hospital in town, Italian-funded and run. The Saturday trip to Zumbahua market and the Quilotoa crater is one of the best excursions in Ecuador.

Quilotoa

Zumbahua is the point to turn off for a visit to Quilotoa, a volcanic crater filled by a beautiful emerald lake, to which there is a steep path from the rim. From the rim of the crater several snowcapped volcanoes can be seen in the distance. The crater is reached by a paved road which runs north from Zumbahua (about 12 km, 3-5 hours' walk). There's a 300-m drop down from the crater rim to the water (US$1 to visit lake). The hike down takes about 30 minutes (an hour or more to climb back up). The trail starts to the left of the parking area down a steep, canyon-like cut; if unsure, take a guide. You can hire a mule to ride up from the bottom of the crater, but arrange it before heading down. Take a stick to fend off dogs. Everyone at the crater tries to sell the famous naïve Tigua pictures and carved wooden masks, so expect to be besieged (also by begging children). Be prepared, too, for sudden changes in the weather, it gets very cold at night.

Chugchilán, Sigchos and Isinliví → Phone code: 03.

Chugchilán, a poor village in one of the most scenic areas of Ecuador, is 22 km by road from the Quilotoa crater. It is a six-hour walk; or walk around part of the crater rim, then down to Guayama, and across the canyon (Río Sigüi) to Chugchilán, 11 km, about five hours. Take care of your belongings in this area and watch out for minor rip-offs.

Continuing from Chugchilán the road runs through Sigchos, the starting point for the Toachi Valley walk, via Asache to San Francisco de las Pampas (0900 bus daily to Latacunga). Southeast of Sigchos is Isinliví, on the old route to Toacazo and Latacunga. It has a fine woodcarving shop and a pre-Inca pucará. Trek to the village of Guantualó, which has a fascinating market on Monday. You can hike to or from Chugchilán (4 hours), or from Quilotoa to Isinliví in 7-9 hours.

The road east to Toacazo (E pp La Quinta Colorada, T716122, rooms or dorms, meals available, very nice) is cobbled and from there to Saquisilí it is paved (there are petrol stations at Toacazo and Yalo, below Sigchos).

Saquisilí → Phone code: 03.

Some 16 km south of Lasso, and 6 km west of the Panamericana is the small but very important market town of Saquisilí. Its Thursday market (0700-1400) is famous throughout Ecuador for the way in which its seven plazas and some of its streets become jam-packed with people, the great majority of them local *indígenas* with red ponchos and narrow-brimmed felt hats. The best time to visit the market is between 0900 and 1200 (0700 for the animal market). Be sure to bargain, as there is a lot of competition. Saquisilí has colourful Corpus Christi processions.

● Sleeping

Latacunga to Zumbahua p935

Pujilí

E Res Pujilí, Rocafuerte ½ block from highway, T272 3648. Simple, with bath, restaurant.

Tigua

B Posada de Tigua, 3 km east of Tigua-Chimbacucho, 400 m north of the road, T281 3682, laposadadetigua@latinmail.com. Refurbished hacienda, part of a working dairy ranch, 5 rooms, wood-burning stove, includes 3 tasty home-cooked meals, shared bath, pleasant family atmosphere, horses for riding, trails, nice views.

C-D Samana Huasi, in Tigua-Chimbacucho, Km 53 from Latacunga, T281 4868 or 02-2563175 (Quito), www.tigua.org. Community-run lodge, includes breakfast and dinner, shared composting toilets, some rooms with fireplace or wood burning stove, cheaper in dorm, nice views.

Zumbahua p935

There are only a few phone lines in town, which are shared among several people. Expect delays when calling to book a room.

E Cóndor Matzi, T281 4611 (hospital) to leave message, shared bath, hot water, best place

around, reserve ahead, serves Fri supper, other meals on request.

E Hostal Richard, opposite the market on the road in to town, T281 4605 (at Oro Verde). Modern but still missing some finishing touches, some rooms with toilet, hot water in shared shower, laundry and cooking facilities, parking, family run, owners can provide transport to Quilotoa.

E Quilotoa, at the north side (bottom) of the plaza, next to the abattoir. Fancy fixtures but already a bit run down, private bath, hot water, not too clean.

E-F Res Oro Verde, first place on the left as you enter town, T281 4605. Shared bath, hot water, has small store, Fri and Sat meals, others on request.

Quilotoa p935

A-B Quiltoa Crater Lake Lodge, T02-252 7835 (Quito), T09-497 9069, www.quiltoalodge.com. New in 2006, atop the Quilotoa volcanic peak at 3891 m, price includes breakfast. Fantastic views, clean comfortable rooms with private bath and hot water. Restaurant, bar, reading areas.

D Cabañas Quilotoa, T03-281 2044. Owned by Humberto Latacunga. Basic, very cold, wool blankets, electric shower, includes breakfast and dinner, Humberto will lead treks and provide mules, he is a good painter and has a small store.

D Hostal Pachamama, at the top of the hill by the rim of the crater, T09-873 0716 (Latacunga). A couple of rooms will have private bath, includes breakfast and dinner, electric shower.
D Princesa Toa, at the top of the hill by the rim of the crater. A community run hostel with accommodation in a large room with a fireplace and several beds. The area will be subdivided, price includes breakfast and dinner.

Chugchilán p936
A The Black Sheep Inn, a few mins below the village, T281 4587, www.blacksheepinn.com. Run by Andy Hammerman and Michelle Kirby, 6 private rooms with wood stove, tree house, **C-D** in new bunk room, new toilets, price includes 3-course vegetarian dinner plus breakfast or lunch and drinking water and hot drinks all day, hot showers, excellent vegetarian cooking, book exchange, internet, organic garden, sauna, 5% discount for ISIC, seniors or SAE members, llama treks, horse riding arranged, a good base for hiking. Highly recommended, advance reservations advised.
D Hostal Mama Hilda, 100 m from centre of Chugchilán towards Sigchos, T281 4814. Shared bath, hot water, homely, including dinner and breakfast, good food, warm atmosphere, arrange horse riding and walking trips. Highly recommended.
E Hostal Cloud Florest, next to Mama Hilda, T281 4808. Includes dinner and breakfast, shared bath, hot water, delicious local food, helpful owners.

Sigchos p936
F La Posada, Los Ilinizas y Galo Arteaga, T271 4224. A modern, simple hotel, restaurant downstairs, private bath, hot water.
F-G pp Res Sigchos, Carlos Hugo Páez y Rodrigo Iturralde, T271 4107. Basic but clean, large rooms, shared bath, hot water.
F Residencial Turismo, Tungurahua y Los Ilinizas, T271 4114. Basic hotel, some rooms with private bath, hot water, parking.

Isinliví p936
D-E Llullu Llama, T281 4790, www.isinlivi. safari.com.ec. Nicely refurbished house, cosy sitting room with woodburning stove, good hearty meals available (not included in price). Shared composting toilet with great views, abundant hot water, private, semi-private and dorm (cheaper) accommodations, nicely decorated rooms (some are a bit small), organic herb garden, warm and relaxing atmosphere, a lovely spot. Recommended.

Saquisilí p936
C Rancho Muller, 5 de Junio y González Suárez, south end of town, T272 2320, www.berosareisen.com. Cabins with bath and TV, expensive restaurant, German owner organizes tours and rents vehicles.
D pp Gilocarmelo Eco-hostal, 3 blocks east of the crafts market, T272 2223. New in 2006.
D San Carlos, Bolívar opposite the Parque Central, T272 1057. With electric shower, view of plaza, cheap breakfast, parking, good value, watch your valuables.
F Pensión Chavela, Bolívar by main park, T272 1114. Shared bath, water problems,very basic.
F Salón Pichincha, Bolívar y Pichincha. Shared bath, warm water, cheap, restaurant-bar below, basic.

⊖ Transport

Zumbahua p935
Bus Many daily on the Latacunga-Quevedo road (0500-1900, US$2, 2 hrs). Buses on Sat are packed full; ride on roof for best views, get your ticket the day before. A pick-up truck can be hired from Zumbahua to **Quilotoa** for US$15; also to **Chugchilán** for around US$30. On Sat mornings there are many trucks leaving the Zumbahua market for Chugchilán which pass Quilotoa.

Taxi Day-trip by taxi to Zumbahua, Quilotoa, return to **Latacunga** is US$40.

Quilotoa *p935*
Bus From the terminal terrestre in Latacunga Trans Vivero daily at 1000, 1100, 1200 and 1300, US$2.50, 2½ hrs. Note that this leaves from Latacunga, not Saquisilí market, even on Thu. Return bus to Latacunga around 1230 and 1330. Buses returning around 1430 and 1530 go only as far as Zumbahua, from where you can catch a Latacunga bound bus at the highway. Also, buses going through Zumbahua bound for Chugchilán will drop you at the turnoff, 5 mins from the crater, where you can also pick them up on their way to Zumbahua and Latacunga.

Chugchilán *p936*
Bus From **Latacunga**, daily at 1130 (except Thu) via Sigchos, at 1200 via Zumbahua; on Thu from **Saquisilí market** via Sigchos around 1130, US$2.50, 3½-4 hrs. Buses return to Latacunga daily at 0330 via Sigchos or Quilotoa. On Sun there are 2 extra buses to Latacunga leaving 0900-1000. There are extra buses going as far as Zumbahua Wed 0500, Fri 0600 and Sun between 0900-1000; these continue towards the coast. Milk truck to Sigchos around 0900-1000. On Sat also pick-ups going to/from market in Zumbahua and Latacunga. Taxi from Latacunga US$60. From **Sigchos**, through buses as indicated above, US$0.60, 1-1½ hrs. Pick-up hire to Sigchos US$25, up to 5 people, US$5

additional person. Pick-up to **Quilotoa** US$25, up to 5 people, US$5 additional person.

Sigchos *p936*
Bus From **Latacunga** frequent daily service US$1.50, 2-2½ hrs. From/to **Quito** direct service on Fri and Sun, US$3, 3 hrs. To **La Maná** on the road to Quevedo, via Chugchilán, Quilotoa and Zumbahua, Fri at 0500 and Sun at 0830, US$3.50, 6 hrs (returns Sat at 0730 and Sun at 1530). To **Las Pampas**, at 0330 and 1400, US$2.50, 3 hrs. From Las Pampas to **Santo Domingo**, at 0300 and 0600, US$2.50, 3 hrs.

Isinliví *p936*
From **Latacunga** daily (except Thu) at 1245 (**14 de Octubre**) via Sigchos and 1300 (**Trans Vivero**, 1030 on Sat) direct, on Thu both leave from Saquisilí market around 1030, US$1.80, 2 hrs. Both buses return to Latacunga at 0330, except Sun 0700 via Sigchos, 1200 direct, Mon one at 1430, Wed one at 0700. Connections to Chugchilán, Quilotoa and Zumbahua can be made in Sigchos. Bus schedules are posted on www.isinlivi.safari.com.ec.

Saquisilí *p936*
Bus Frequent service between **Latacunga** and Saquisilí, US$0.30, 20 mins; many buses daily to/from **Quito**, depart from the bus terminal, 0530 onwards, US$2, 2hrs. Buses and trucks to many outlying villages leave from 1000 onwards. Bus tours from Quito cost US$45 pp, taxis charge US$60, with 2 hrs wait at market.

Ambato → *Phone code: 03. Colour map 11, grid B3. Population: 154,095.*

Almost completely destroyed in the great 1949 earthquake, Ambato lacks the colonial charm of other Andean cities, though its location in the heart of fertile orchard-country has earned it the nickname of 'the city of fruits and flowers' (see annual festival below). It is also the principal supply town of the central highlands and a major centre for the leather industry. **Tourist office: Ministerio de Turismo** ① *Guayaquil y Rocafuerte, T282 1800. Open Mon-Fri 0830-1300, 1430-1730*, helpful.

The modern cathedral faces the pleasant **Parque Montalvo**, where there is a statue of the writer Juan Montalvo (1832-1889) who is buried in a neighbouring street. His **house** ① *Bolívar y Montalvo, T282 4248, US$1*, is open to the public and has a good restaurant. In the **Colegio Nacional Bolívar** is the **Museo de Ciencias Naturales Héctor Vásquez** ① *Sucre entre Lalama y Martínez, T282 7395, Mon-Fri 0800-1200, 1400-1730, closed for school holidays, US$1*, with stuffed birds and animals and items of local historical interest, recommended. The **Quinta de Mera** ① *Wed-Sun 0830-1600, US$1, take bus from Espejo y 12 de Noviembre*, an old mansion in beautiful gardens, is in Atocha suburb. The main **market**, one of the largest in Ecuador, is held on Monday, with smaller markets on Wednesday and Friday. They are interesting, but have few items for the tourist.

Ambato to Baños
To the east of Ambato, an important road leads to **Salasaca** (two hostales), where the *indígenas* sell their weavings; they wear distinctive black ponchos with white trousers and

broad white hats. Further east is **Pelileo**, the blue jean manufacturing capital of Ecuador with good views of Tungurahua. (**E Hostal Pelileo** ① *Eloy Alfaro 641, T03-287 1390*, shared bath, hot water.) From Pelileo, the road descends to Las Juntas, where the Patate and Chambo rivers meet to form the Río Pastaza. About 1 km east of Las Juntas bridge, the junction with the closed road to Riobamba is marked by a large sculpture of a macaw and a toucan (locally known as Los Pájaros). It is a favourite volcano watching site, with a *tarabita* ('shopping basket' cable car). The road to Baños then continues along the lower slopes of the volcano.

Eight kilometres northeast of Pelileo on a paved side-road is **Patate**, centre of the warm, fruit growing Patate valley. There are excellent views of Volcán Tungurahua from town and its surroundings. *Arepas*, sweets made of squash (unrelated to the Colombian or Venezuelan variety), are the local delicacy; sold around the park. The fiesta of Nuestro Señor del Terremoto is held on the weekend of **4 February**, featuring a parade with floats made with fruit and flowers.

Ambato to Guaranda

To the west of Ambato, a paved road climbs through tilled fields, past the páramos of Carihuairazo and Chimborazo to the great Arenal (a high desert at the base of the mountain), and down through the Chimbo valley to Guaranda (see page 948). This spectacular journey on the highest paved road in Ecuador takes about three hours. It reaches a height of 4,380 m and vicuñas can be seen.

Ambato to Riobamba

After Ambato, the Pan-American Highway runs south to Riobamba (see page 947). About half way is **Mocha**, where guinea pigs (*cuy*) are bred for the table. You can sample roast *cuy* and other typical dishes at stalls and restaurants by the roadside, *Mariadiocelina* is recommended. The highway climbs steeply south of Mocha and at the pass at **Urbina** (one hostal) there are fine views in the dry season of Chimborazo and Carihuairazo.

● Sleeping

Ambato *p938*
There are a lot of cheap residenciales, hotels and restaurants around Parque 12 de Noviembre, the area is not safe at night. The suburb of Miraflores is a pleasant walk from the centre, or bus to Av Miraflores.
AL Miraflores, Av Miraflores 1527, T284 3224, www.hmiraflores.com.ec. Includes breakfast, good restaurant, heating, suites with jacuzzi.
A Ambato, Guayaquil 0108 y Rocafuerte, T242 1791, www.hotelambato.com. Includes breakfast, good restaurant, casino, squash court, best in city centre. Recommended.
A-B Florida, Av Miraflores 1131, T242 2007. Includes breakfast, restaurant with good set meals, pleasant setting.
C Cevallos, Montalvo y Cevallos, T282 4877. Includes breakfast, restaurant, parking, good.
C Colony, 12 de Noviembre 124 y Av El Rey, near the bus terminal, T282 5789. Modern, large rooms, includes breakfast, parking.
D Pirámide Inn, Cevallos y Mariano Egüez, T284 1920, F242 1066. Includes breakfast, parking, comfortable, English and Italian spoken.

D Portugal, Juan Cajas 01-36 y 12 de Noviembre, T282 2476. Near bus station, hot water, good value.
D Royal, Cevallos 05-60 y Vargas Torres, T282 3528. A small modern hotel, rooms are small, comfortable and clean, good value.
D San Ignacio, Maldonado y 12 de Noviembre, T284 4370. Cafeteria, good value.
E-F Madrid, Juan Cajas y Calderón, T282 8679. Adequate hostel convenient to the bus terminal, restaurant, cheaper with shared bath, hot water, disco.

Ambato to Baños: Patate *p938*
AL Hacienda Leito, on de road to El Triunfo, T285 9329, llanganates@andinanet.net. Farm accommodation, includes breakfast and dinner, classy, facing Tungurahua, good.
A Hacienda Los Manteles, in the Leito valley on the road to El Triunfo, T09-871 5632, manteles@interactive.net.ec. Converted farm house, restaurant, great views, horse riding, hiking.
A Hostería Viña del Río, 3 km from town on the old road to Baños, T/F03-287 0314. Cabins, restaurant, pool, spa, good views, horse riding and mini golf.

● *For an explanation of the sleeping and eating price codes used in this guide, see inside the front*
● *cover. Other relevant information is found in Essentials pages 886-888.*

D Jardín del Valle, M Soria y A Calderón, 1 block from the main park, T03-287 0209. Nicely furnished, good breakfast available, good value. Recommended.

E-F Hospedaje Altamira, Av Ambato y J Montalvo, on the road from Pelileo. Shared bath, hot shower, basic.

Ambato to Riobamba: Urbina *p939*
D Posada de la Estación, in the solitary old railway station at 3,619 m, Urbina (signed), 2 km west of the highway, T/F03-294 2215, aventurag@ch.pro.ec. Meals available, shared bath, hot water, magnificent views, clean and comfortable but very cold at night. This is a good place for acclimatization, friendly and helpful, horses, trips and equipment arranged. Recommended.

❶ Eating

Ambato *p938*
¶¶ El Alamo Chalet, Cevallos 1719 y Montalvo, open 0800-2300 (2200 Sun). Ecuadorean and international food. Set meals and à la carte, Swiss-owned, good quality.
¶¶ El Coyote Disco Club, Bolívar y Guayaquil. Mexican-American food, disco at weekends.
¶¶ Farid, Bolívar 705 y JL Mera. Grilled meat served in middle eastern sauces.
¶¶ La Buena Mesa, Quito 924 y Bolívar. French, elegant. Recommended.
¶¶ Miramar, Quito y Rocafuerte. Good seafood.
¶ Gran Pacífico, Mariano Egüez y 12 de Noviembre. A good cheap *chifa*.
¶ La Fornace, Cevallos 1728 y Montalvo. Wood oven pizza.
¶ Mama Miche, 13 de Abril y JL Mera, Centro Comercial Ambato. 24-hr cheap cafeteria.
¶ Nueva Hong Kong, Bolívar 768 y Martínez. Good cheap *chifa*.

Cafés
Café Marcelo´s, Rocafuerte y Castillo, daily 0900-2100. Good cafeteria serves hamburgers and other snacks, also ice cream.
Pastelería Quito, JL Mera y Cevallos. Coffee and pastries, good for breakfast.

⊛ Festivals and events

Ambato *p938*
Ambato has a famous festival in **Feb** or **Mar**, the **Fiesta de frutas y flores**, during carnival when there are 4 days of bullfights, festivities and parades (best Sun morning and Mon night). It is impossible to get a hotel room unless you book ahead.

◯ Shopping

Ambato *p938*
Leather Many stores for leather shoes along Bolívar. Leather jackets, bags, belts on Vela between Lalama and Montalvo. Take a local bus up to the leather town of Quisapincha for the best deals, everyday, but big market on Sat.

▲ Activities and tours

Ambato *p938*
Metropolitan Touring, Centro Comercial Caracol, Local 59-62, T282 0211, www.metro politan-touring.com. A branch of the large Quito operator, also sells airline tickets.

⊖ Transport

Ambato *p938*
Bus The main bus station is on Av Colombia y Paraguay, 2 km north of the centre. Town buses go there from Plaza Cevallos in the city centre, US$0.20. To **Quito**, 2½ hrs, US$2.50. To **Cuenca**, US$7, 7 hrs. To **Guayaquil**, 6 hrs, US$6. To **Baños**, 1 hr, US$0.80. To **Riobamba**, US$1.25, 1 hr. To **Guaranda**, US$2, 2 hrs. To **Santo Domingo de los Colorados**, 4 hrs, US$3. To **Tena**, US$5, 6 hrs. To **Puyo**, US$3, 3 hrs. To **Macas**, US$7, 6½ hrs. To **Esmeraldas**, US$8, 8 hrs. To **Loja**, US$11, 11 hrs. To **Machala**, US$8, 9 hrs.

❶ Directory

Ambato *p938*
Banks Banco de Guayaquil, Sucre y JL Mera, for Visa. **Banco del Pacífico**, Cevallos y Lalama, and Cevallos y Unidad Nacional. Visa. **Produbanco**, Montalvo y Sucre. MasterCard. **Banco del Pichincha**, Lalama y Cevallos, on Parque Cevallos and Av El Rey y Av de las Américas, near the bus terminal. Visa. **Internet** Rates about US$0.90-1.20 hr. Several in the centre of town, along Castillo, also Montalvo. **Post offices** Castillo y Bolívar, at Parque Montalvo; 0730-1930.

Baños and Riobamba

Baños and Riobamba are both good bases for exploring the Sierra and their close proximity to high peaks gives great opportunities for climbing, cycling and trekking (but check for volcanic activity before you set out). The thermal springs at Baños are an added lure and the road east is one of the best ways to get to the jungle lowlands. On the other hand, anyone with the faintest interest in railways stops in Riobamba to ride the train on the last remaining section of the famous line from the Andes to Guayaquil, around the Devil's Nose.

Baños and around

→ *Phone code: 03. Colour map 11, grid B4. Population: 10,440. Altitude: 1,800 m.*

Baños is nestled between the Río Pastaza and the Tungurahua volcano, only 8 km from its crater. Baños bursts at the seams with hotels, *residenciales*, restaurants and tour agencies. Ecuadoreans flock here on weekends and holidays for the hot springs, to visit the Basílica and enjoy the local *melcochas* (toffees), while escaping the Andean chill in a sub-tropical climate (wettest in July and August). Visitors are also frequent, using Baños as a base for climbing Tungurahua (in quieter times), volcano watching, organizing a visit to the jungle, making local day-trips or just plain hanging out.

Ins and outs

Tourist offices iTur ① *Oficina Municipal de Turismo, at the Municipio, Halflants y Rocafuerte, opposite Parque Central, Mon-Fri 0830-1230, 1400-1700, Sat-Sun 0800-1600.* Helpful, have colourful maps of the area, some English spoken. There are several private 'tourist information offices' run by travel agencies near the bus station; high-pressure tour sales, maps and pamphlets available. Local artist, J Urquizo, produces an accurate pictorial map of Baños, 12 de Noviembre y Ambato, also sold in many shops. Take care near the San Francisco bridge and on the paths to Bellavista and Runtún – visitors have occasionally been robbed in these locations.

After over 80 years of inactivity, Tungurahua began venting steam and ash in 1999 and Baños was evacuated because of the threat of a major eruption between October and December of that year. Volcanic activity gradually diminished during 2000, former residents and tourists returned, and the town recovered its wonderful resort atmosphere. At the time of writing volcanic activity continues. **Tungurahua is closed to climbers** and the road to Riobamba is closed, but all else is normal. Since the level of volcanic activity can change, you should enquire locally before visiting Baños. The National Geophysics Institute posts reports on the web at www.igepn.edu.ec.

Baños

The **Manto de la Virgen** waterfall at the southeast end of town is a symbol of Baños. The **Basílica** attracts many pilgrims. The paintings of miracles performed by Nuestra Señora del Agua Santa are worth seeing; also a **museum** ① *Wed-Sun 0700-1600, US$0.50*, with stuffed birds and Nuestra Señora's clothing. Six sets of thermal baths are in the town. The **Baños de la Virgen** ① *0430-1700, US$1*, are by the waterfall opposite the *Hotel Sangay*. The water in the hot pools is changed three times a week, and the cold pool is chlorinated (best to visit very early morning); two small hot pools open evenings only (1800-2200, US$1.25), their water is changed daily. The **Piscinas Modernas** *US$1*, with a water slide are next door and are open weekends and holidays only, 0800-1700. **El Salado baths** ① *0430-1700, US$1* (several hot pools with water changed daily, plus icy cold river water) are 1½ km out of town off the Ambato road (this is a high-risk area during volcanic activity). The **Santa Clara baths** ① *at the south end of C Rafael Vieira, 0800-1800, US$1*, are tepid, popular with children and have a gym and sauna. **Eduardo's baths** ① *0800-1800, US$1, spa US$2.50*, are next to Santa Clara, with a 25-m cold pool (the best for serious swimming) and a small warm pool. The **Santa Ana baths** ① *weekends and holidays 0800-1700, US$1*, have hot and cold pools, just east of town on the road to Puyo. All the baths can be very crowded at weekends and holidays; the brown colour of the water is due to its high mineral content.

Around Baños

There are many interesting **walks** in the Baños area. The **San Martín shrine** is a 45-minute easy walk from town and overlooks a deep rocky canyon with the Río Pastaza thundering below. Beyond the shrine, crossing to the north side of the Pastaza, is the **Ecozoológico San Martín** T274 0552, www.sanmartinzoo.org, 0800-1700. US$1, 50 m beyond which is a path to the **Inés María waterfall**, cascading down, but polluted. You can also cross the Pastaza by the new **Puente San Francisco** road bridge, behind the kiosks across the main road from the bus station (a larger vehicular bridge has been built here). From here a series of trails fans out into the surrounding hills, offering excellent views of Tungurahua from the ridge-tops in clear weather. A total of six bridges span the Pastaza near Baños, so you can make a round trip.

On the hillside behind Baños, it is a 45-minute hike to the **statue of the Virgin** (good views). Go to the south end of Calle JL Mera, before the street ends, take the last street to the right, at the end of which are stairs leading to the trail. A steep path continues along the ridge, past the statue. Another trail begins at the south end of JL Mera and leads to the *Hotel Luna Runtún*, continuing on to the village of Runtún (five- to six-hour round-trip). Along the same hillside, to the **Bellavista cross**, it is a steep climb from the south end of Calle Maldonado, 50 minutes. There's a café at the cross. You can continue from the cross to *Hotel Luna Runtún*.

On the Puyo road the first town you reach beyond the Agoyán generating station is Río Blanco. Beyond is the hamlet of La Merced with a lookout and a trail with a swingbridge over the Pastaza going to the base of the lovely **Manto de La Novia** waterfall, on the Río Chinchín Chico. A new cable car goes right over the falls. About 1 km beyond is the *tarabita* (cable car)

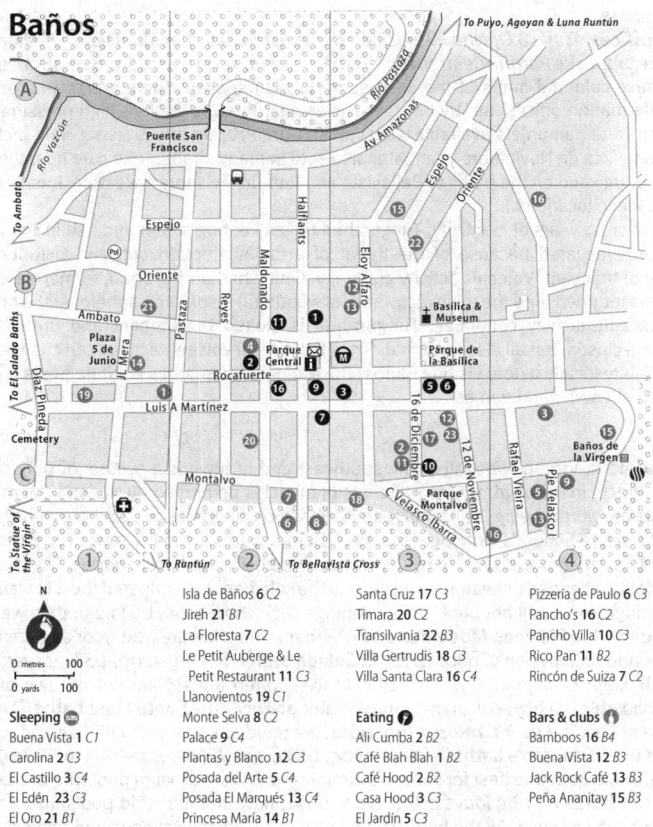

Baños

N

0 metres 100
0 yards 100

Sleeping
Buena Vista **1** *C1*
Carolina **2** *C3*
El Castillo **3** *C4*
El Edén **23** *C3*
El Oro **21** *B1*
Flor de Oriente **4** *B2*
Isla de Baños **6** *C2*
Jireh **21** *B1*
La Floresta **7** *C2*
Le Petit Auberge & Le
  Petit Restaurant **11** *C3*
Llanoviertos **19** *C1*
Monte Selva **8** *C2*
Palace **9** *C4*
Plantas y Blanco **12** *C3*
Posada del Arte **5** *C2*
Posada El Marqués **13** *C4*
Princesa María **14** *B1*
Sangay **15** *C4*

Santa Cruz **17** *C3*
Timara **20** *C2*
Transilvania **22** *B3*
Villa Gertrudis **18** *C3*
Villa Santa Clara **16** *C4*

Eating
Ali Cumba **2** *B2*
Café Blah Blah **1** *B2*
Café Hood **2** *B2*
Casa Hood **3** *C3*
El Jardín **5** *C3*
Mariane **9** *C2*

Pizzería de Paulo **6** *C3*
Pancho's **16** *C2*
Pancho Villa **10** *C3*
Rico Pan **11** *B2*
Rincón de Suiza **7** *C2*

Bars & clubs
Bamboos **16** *B4*
Buena Vista **12** *B3*
Jack Rock Café **13** *B3*
Peña Ananitay **15** *B3*

crossing the Pastaza to the village of San Pedro; it is powered by an old lorry engine, US$1. From the cable car you have nice views of the Pastaza and the **San Pedro falls** on the river of the same name. Several other *tarabitas* are being installed along this road.

About 3 km beyond and 17 km from Baños is the town of **Río Verde**, at the junction of the Verde and Pastaza rivers. The Río Verde has crystalline green water with several waterfalls on its course. The most spectacular are **El Pailón del Diablo** (the Devil's Cauldron). In Río Verde, cross the river and take the path to the right after the church, then follow the trail down towards the suspension bridge; before the bridge take a side trail to the right (small entry fee) which leads you to a viewing platform above the falls (kiosk, drinks sold). Five minutes' walk along a different trail are the smaller **San Miguel falls**; in town cross the bridge and take the first path to the right. It is also possible to hire bikes for the day from Baños and cycle downhill, passing El Pailón del Diablo and numerous other waterfalls on the way. Then take a bus back to Baños; several snack bars and restaurants in Río Verde let you leave the bike while you visit the falls.

● Sleeping

Baños *p941, map p942*
Baños has plenty of accommodation in but can fill during holiday weekends.
LL Luna Runtún, Caserío Runtún Km 6, T274 0882, www.lunaruntun.com. Includes dinner and breakfast, restaurant, internet, beautiful setting overlooking Baños, very comfortable rooms with balconies, gardens. Excellent service, English, French and German spoken. Hiking, horse riding and biking tours, travel agency, sports and nanny facilities. Highly recommended.
A-B Palace, Montalvo 20-03, T274 0470, hotelpalace@hotmail.com. Includes breakfast, restaurant, nice garden and pool, nicely old-fashioned, front rooms with balcony. Pools and spa open to public, US$5.
A-B Sangay Spa, Plazoleta Ayora 100, opposite the waterfall and thermal baths, T274 0490, www.sangayspahotel.com. Includes breakfast, good restaurant, pool and spa open to non-residents 1600-2000 (US$5), tennis and squash courts, attentive service, 3 categories of rooms. Recommended.
B Monte Selva, Halflants y Montalvo, T274 0566, www.hosteriamonteselva.com.

Includes breakfast, restaurant, warm pool, cabins, bar, spa, excellent service.
B-C Isla de Baños, Halflants 1-31 y Montalvo, T/F274 0609, islabanos@andinanet.net. European breakfast, internet, some suites more expensive, spa, nice atmosphere, garden with parrots and monkeys. Recommended.
B-C Le Petit Auberge, 16 de Diciembre y Montalvo, T274 0936, lepetitbanos@yahoo.com. Includes breakfast, good restaurant, parking, French-run, rooms with fireplace, patio, quiet.
B-C Posada del Arte, Pasaje Velasco Ibarra y Montalvo, T274 0083, www.posadadelarte.com. Cosy, includes breakfast, good restaurant (mid-range), nice sitting room, more expensive rooms with fireplace.
C La Floresta, Halflants y Montalvo, T274 1824, la_floresta_hospedaje@hotmail.com. Excellent breakfast, good restaurant, parking, comfortable rooms, nice garden. Recommended.
C Villa Gertrudis, Montalvo 2975, T274 0441, F274 0442. Includes breakfast, pool, classic old resort, lovely garden, reserve in advance. Recommended.

Ecuador Baños & around Listings

D El Castillo, Martínez y Rafael Vieira, T274 0285. Simple, quiet, restaurant serves filling 4-course meal, parking.

D El Edén, 12 de Noviembre y Montalvo, T2740616, hostaleleden@andinanet.net. Pleasant wheelchair-accessible hotel with a patio. Includes breakfast, restaurant, parking, rooms with balconies.

D El Oro, Ambato y JL Mera, T274 0736. Includes breakfast, cooking and laundry facilities, good value. Recommended.

D Flor de Oriente, Ambato y Maldonado on Parque Central, T274 0418, www.florideoriente. banios.com. Includes breakfast, very good but can be noisy at weekends, cafetería, parking.

D Posada El Marqués, Pasaje Velasco Ibarra y Montalvo, T274 0053, posada_marques@ yahoo.com. Spacious, good beds, garden, quiet area. Recommended.

D-E Buena Vista, Martínez y Pastaza, T274 0263. Hot water, quiet, simple, good value, discounts in low season.

D-E Llanovientos, Martínez 1126 y Sebastián Baño, T274 0682, gvieirah@hotmail.com. A modern breezy hostel with wonderful views, comfortable, cafetería, hot water, cooking facilities, parking, nice garden. Recommended.

D-E Plantas y Blanco, 12 de Noviembre y Martínez, T/F274 0044, option3@hotmail.com. Excellent breakfast on roof terrace, good restaurant, French-run, steam bath 0730-1100 (US$3), luggage store. Warmly recommended.

D-E Timara, Maldonado 381 y Martínez, T2740599, arte_con_natura@hotmail.com. Small, simple family-run hostel, shared bath, internet, laundry and cooking facilities, nice garden.

D-E Villa Santa Clara, 12 de Noviembre y Montalvo, T274 0349. Includes breakfast, basic cooking facilities, parking, simple rooms and cabins, nice garden.

E Carolina, 16 de Diciembre y Martínez, T274 0592. Hot water, cooking facilities, terrace, good value. Recommended.

E Jireh, Ambato y León, T274 0321. Pleasant, large rooms, hot water, laundry and cooking facilities, parking, good.

E Princesa María, Rocafuerte y Mera, T274 1035. Hot water, laundry and cooking facilities, popular meeting place, bicycle hire, good value. Frequently recommended.

E Santa Cruz, 16 de Diciembre y Martínez, T274 0648. Includes breakfast, café, modern and comfortable.

E Transilvania, 16 de Diciembre y Oriente, T2742281, hostal.transilvania@gmail.com. Simple rooms, includes breakfast, Middle Eastern restaurant, hot water, nice views from balconies, luggage storage, good value.

Around Baños *p942*

B Pequeño Paraíso, 1½ km east of Río Verde, west of Machay, T09-981 9756 (mob), www.geocities.com/pequeno_paraiso/. Comfortable cabins in lovely surroundings, abundant hot water, includes breakfast and dinner, tasty vegetarian meals, small pool, camping possible, climbing wall, Swiss-run. Recommended.

● Eating

Baños *p941, map p942*
Most establishments serve international food for foreign visitors, at mid-range prices. Those serving local fare and set meals are usually cheap. Those listed below open daily, unless stated otherwise.

₩₩₩ Le Petit Restaurant, 16 de Diciembre y Montalvo. Tue-Sun 0800-1500, 1800-2200. Parisian owner, excellent food, including vegetarian, great atmosphere.

₩₩ El Jardín, 16 de Diciembre y Rocafuerte. International and some vegetarian food, juices, also bar, good atmosphere and nice garden.

₩₩ Higuerón, Arrayanes y Oriente. Good European, local and vegetarian food, nice garden.

₩₩ Mariane, Halflants y Rocafuerte. French cuisine, large portions. Recommended.

₩₩-₩ Buon Giorno, Ambato y Pasaje Ermita de la Vírgen west of the market, and at Rocafuerte y 16 de Diciembre, Tue-Sun 1130-2230. Good, authentic Italian dishes.

₩₩-₩ Pancho Villa, Montalvo y 16 de Diciembre, Mon-Sat 1230-2130. Very good quality Mexican food, good service. Recommended.

₩₩-₩ Pizzería de Paolo, Rocafuerte at Parque de la Basílica. Good pizza, pasta and salads.

₩₩-₩ Pizzería El Napolitano, 12 de Noviembre y Martínez. Good pizza and pasta, pleasant atmosphere, pool table.

₩ Ambateñito, Ambato y Eloy Alfaro. Good set meals and barbecued chicken.

₩ Café Hood, Maldonado y Ambato, at Parque Central. Excellent vegetarian food, fruit juices, also meats, nice atmosphere, English spoken, always busy. Also rents rooms.

₩ Casa Hood, Martínez between Halflants and Alfaro, closed Wed. Varied vegetarian menu including Indonesian and Thai dishes, some meat dishes, juices, good desserts, travel books and maps sold, book rental and exchange, repertory cinema. Recommended.

₩ Chifa Shan He, Oriente y Alfaro. Chinese-run chifa, large portions.

₩ El Paisano, Rafael Vieira y Martínez. Variety of vegetarian meals and herbal teas.

La Puerta de Alcalá, Av Amazonas (main highway), ½ block downhill from bus terminal. Good value set meal.
C Ambato, has many restaurants serving economical set meals and local fare, the *picanterías* on the outside of the market serve local delicacies such as *cuy* and *fritada*.

Cafés
Ali Cumba, Maldonado opposite Parque Central, daily 0700-1800. Excellent breakfasts, fruit salads, filtered coffee, espresso, muffins, large sandwiches. Pricey but good, Danish-Ecuadorean run.
Café Blah Blah, Ambato y Halflants. Good coffee, snacks, small, cosy, sidewalk seating, popular meeting place.
Pancho's, Rocafuerte y Maldonado, at Parque Central. Snacks, hamburgers, coffee.
Rico Pan, Ambato y Maldonado. Good breakfasts, hot bread, good fruit salads, pizzas and meals.
Rincón de Suiza, Martínez y Halflants, Tue-Sun 0900-0000. Snacks, drinks, good coffee, cappuccino, best cakes and pastries in town. Pleasant atmosphere, books, games, pool table, ping-pong. Swiss-Ecuadorean run. Recommended.

● Bars and clubs

Baños *p941, map p942*
Eloy Alfaro, between Ambato and Oriente has many bars including:
Bamboos Bar, Barrio Los Pinos, off C Oriente, at east end of town. Popular for salsa, live at weekends.
Buena Vista, Alfaro y Oriente. A good place for salsa and other Latin music.
Jack Rock Café, Alfaro y Ambato. A favourite travellers' hangout, fantastic *piña colada* and juices.

● Entertainment

Baños *p941, map p942*
Córdova Tours has a *Chiva Mocambo*, an open-sided bus, cruises town playing music, it will take you to different night spots.
Peña Ananitay, 16 de Diciembre y Espejo. Good live music and dancing.

● Festivals

Baños *p941, map p942*
During Carnival and Holy Week hotels are full and prices rise.
Oct: Nuestra Señora de Agua Santa with daily processions, bands, fireworks, sporting events

and partying through the month. Week-long celebrations ending **16 Dec**: the town's anniversary, parades, fairs, sports, cultural events. The night of **15 Dec** is the **Verbenas**, when each *barrio* hires a band and there are many parties.

● Shopping

Baños *p941, map p942*
Look out for jaw-sticking toffee (taffy, known as *melcocha*) made in ropes in shop doorways, or the less sticky *alfeñique*.
Camping equipment **Varoxi**, Maldonado 651 y Oriente. Quality packs, repairs luggage.
Handicrafts Crafts stalls at Pasaje Ermita de la Vírgen, off C Ambato, by the market. Nice tagua (vegetable ivory made of palm nuts) crafts at several shops on Maldonado between Oriente and Espejo. Leather shops on Rocafuerte entre Halflants y 16 de Diciembre.
Galería de Arte Contemporáneo Huillac Cuna, 12 de Noviembre y Montalvo. Modern art exhibits, sells paintings and coffee-table books.
José Masaquiza, Halflants y Rocafuerte, next to Andinatel. For Salasacan weaving.
La Tienda de Mercedes, 12 de Noviembre y Ambato, good quality handicrafts and T-shirts, reasonable prices.
Las Orquídeas, Ambato Y Maldonado by the Parque Central and at *Hostal El Floresta*. Excellent selection of crafts, some guide and coffee-table books.
Pusanga Women's Cooperative, Halflants y Martínez. Crafts and musical instruments from the Oriente.
Recuerdos, at the south end of Maldonado. For painted balsa-wood birds. You can see crafts-people at work here.
Tucán Silver, Ambato esq Halflants. For jewellery.

● Activities and tours

Baños *p941, map p942*
Safety standards cannot be relied upon in adventure sports: it is your responsibility to check the quality of equipment and the qualifications of guides.
Canyoning **Pequeño Paraíso**, Río Verde (see above), T09-981 9756 (Mob), US$35. Contact Franco.
Climbing Due to the erratic nature of volcanic activity Tungurahua is officially closed to climbers. This does not prevent people entering the zone. Seek impartial advice from the municipal tourist office and do not be bullied into a climb. Anyone foolish enough to try climbing should be aware that rescue services are **not** available if something goes wrong.

Cycling Many places rent bikes, quality varies, rates from US$6 per day; check brakes and tyres, find out who has to pay for repairs, and insist on a helmet, puncture repair kit and pump. The following have good equipment:

Adrián Carrillo, 12 de Noviembre y Martínez. Rents mountain bike and motorcycles, reliable machines, helmets.

Hotel Isla de Baños runs cycling tours.

Horse riding There are several places, but check their horses as not all are well cared for. Rates average US$5 per hr. The following have been recommended:

Angel Aldaz, Montalvo y JL Mera (on the road to the statue of the Virgin).

José and Two Dogs, Maldonado y Martínez, T274 0746. Flexible hours.

Hotel Isla de Baños, see above. Horses for rent; 6 hrs with a guide and jeep transport costs US$25 per person, English and German spoken.

Ringo Horses, 12 de Noviembre y Martínez (*Pizzeria Napolitano*).

"Puenting" Many operators offer this bungee-jumping-like activity from the bridges around Baños, US$10-15 per jump, heights and styles vary.

River rafting Fatal accidents have occurred, but not with the agencies listed here. The Chambo, Patate and Pastaza rivers are all heavily polluted.

Geotours, see below, merged with Río Loco, a company which for many years ran rafting tours. Half day, US$35, US$60 for full day (rapids and calm water in jungle).

Tour operators

There are very many tour agencies in town, some with several offices, as well as 'independent' guides who seek out tourists on the street (the latter are generally not recommended). Quality varies considerably; to obtain a qualified guide and avoid unscrupulous operators, it is best to seek advice from other travellers who have recently returned from a tour. We have received some critical reports of tours out of Baños, but there are also highly respected and qualified operators here. In all cases, insist on a written contract. Check any mountaineering or other equipment carefully before heading out. Most agencies and guides offer trips to the jungle (US$30-50 per day pp) and 2 day climbing trips to Cotopaxi (approximately US$140 pp) or Chimborazo (approximately US$160 pp). There are also volcano-watching, trekking and horse tours, in addition to the day-trips and sports mentioned above. The following agencies and guides have received positive recommendations but the list is not exclusive and there are certainly others.

Córdova Tours, Maldonado y Espejo, T274 0923, www.cordovatours.banios.com. Tours on board their *chiva mocambo*, an open-sided bus (reserve ahead): waterfall tour, along the Puyo road to Río Verde, 0930-1430; Baños and environs, 1400-1600; night tour with music and volcano watching, 2100-2300 (they will drop you off at the night spot of your choice).

Deep Forest Adventure, no storefront, T09-837 4530 (mob), deepforestadventure@hotmail.com. Eloy Torres, speaks German, English and French, organizes jungle and trekking tours.

Expediciones Amazónicas, Oriente 11-68 y Halflants, T274 0506, www.amazonicas. banios.com. Run by Hernán and Dosto Varela, the latter is a recommended mountain guide.

Explorsierra, Halflants y Oriente, T274 0628, explorsierra1@hotmail.com. Guido Sánchez. Tours and equipment rental.

Geotours, Ambato y Halflants, next to Banco del Pichincha, T274 1344. Geovanny Romo offers various tours, and rafting.

Huilla Cuna, there are 2 agencies of the same name: at Ambato y Halflants, T274 1292, huilacuna@yahoo.es. Marcelo Mazo organizes jungle trips; and at Rafael Vieira y Montalvo, T274 0187, Luis Guevara runs jungle and mountain trips.

Willie Navarrete, at *Café Higuerón*, Los Arrayanes y Oriente, T274 1482, is a highly recommended guide for climbing.

Rainforestur, Ambato 800 y Maldonado, T/F274 0743, www.rainforestur.com.ec. Run by Santiago Herrera, guides are knowledgeable and environmentally conscious.

Vasco Tours, Alfaro y Martínez, T274 1017, vascotours@andinanet.net. Juan Medina, experienced naturalist guide, speaks English.

Transport

Baños *p941, map p942*

Bus City buses run between 0600 and 1830. To **El Salado** every 15 mins from Rocafuerte behind market. To **Agoyán** every 15 mins from Alfaro y Martínez. To **Río Verde** take any Puyo bus from Maldonado y Amazonas, opposite Baños bus station, 20 mins, US$0.50.

The long distance bus station is on the Ambato-Puyo road (Av Amazonas) a short way from the centre, and is the scene of vigorous volleyball games most afternoons. To/from **Quito**, via Ambato, US$3.40, 3½ hrs, frequent service; going to Quito sit on the right for views of Cotopaxi, buy tickets early for weekends and holidays. To **Ambato**, 1 hr, US$0.80. To **Riobamba**, landslides caused by Tungurahua's volcanic activity damaged the direct Baños-Riobamba road, buses go via Ambato,

2 hrs, US$2. To **Latacunga**, 2 hrs, US$2. To **Puyo**, 1½ hrs, US$2; pack your luggage in plastic as all goes on top of the bus which drives through waterfalls; delays possible because of construction work. Sit on the right. You can cycle to Puyo and take the bus back (passport check on the way). To **Tena**, 5 hrs, US$4.20. To **Misahuallí**, change at Tena, or at the Río Napo crossing, and **Macas**, 7 hrs, US$6 (sit on right).

⊙ Directory

Baños *p941, map p942*
Banks Banco del Pacífico, Halflants y Rocafuerte by the Parque Central. Visa and MasterCard ATM, Mon-Fri 0845-1600. **Banco del Pichincha**, Ambato y Halflants, Visa and MasterCard advances, Mon-Fri

0900-1300. **Cooperativa de Ahorros de Ambato**, Maldonado y Espejo. **Don Pedro**, Ambato y Halflants, hardware store opposite Banco del Pichincha. **Internet** Plenty of cyber cafés in town, prices US$2 per hr. **Language classes** Spanish lessons cost US$4.50-5 per hr. **Baños Spanish Center**, Julio Cañar y Oriente, T274 0632, elizbasc@ uio.satnet.net. Elizabeth Barrionuevo, English and German-speaking, flexible, salsa lessons, recommended. **Instituto de Español Alternativo IDEA**, Montalvo y Alfaro, T/F274 1315. **International Spanish School**, 16 de Diciembre y Espejo, T/F274 0612, Martha Vaca F. **Mayra's**, Martínez y Halflants, T274 2850, www.mayra school.com. **Raíces**, 16 de Diciembre y Pablo A Suárez, T274 0090, racefor@hotmail.com. **Post offices** Halflants y Ambato, across from Parque Central.

Riobamba and around

Guaranda and Riobamba are good bases for exploring the Sierra. Riobamba is the bigger of the two and is the starting point for what remains of the famous railway which used to go to Guayaquil. Because of their central location Riobamba and the surrounding province are known as 'Corazón de la Patria' – the heartland of Ecuador – and the city boasts the nickname 'La Sultana de Los Andes' in honour of lofty Mount Chimborazo.

Riobamba → *Phone code: 03. Colour map 11, grid B3. Population: approx 150,000. Altitude: 2,750 m.*
The capital of Chimborazo Province is built in the wide **Tapi Valley** and has broad streets and many ageing but impressive buildings. **Tourist office: Ministerio de Turismo** ⊙ *Av Daniel L Borja y Brasil, next to the Municipal Library, T/F294 1213, Mon-Fri 0830-1330, 1430-1700.* Very helpful and knowledgeable, English spoken. Also a small office in the terminal terrestre.

The main plaza is **Parque Maldonado** around which are the **Santa Bárbara Cathedral**, the **Municipality** and several colonial buildings with arcades. The Cathedral has a beautiful colonial stone façade and an incongruously modern interior. Four blocks northeast of the railway station is the **Parque 21 de Abril**, named after the Batalla de Tapi, 21 April 1822, the city's independence from Spain. The park, better known as **La Loma de Quito**, affords an unobstructed view of Riobamba and Chimborazo, Carihuairazo, Tugurahua, El Altar and occasionally Sangay. It also has a colourfully dressed tile tableau of the history of Ecuador. The **Convento de la Concepción** ⊙ *Orozco y España, entrance at Argentinos y J Larrea, T296 5212, Tue-Sat 0900-1200, 1500-1800, US$2, the guides are friendly and knowledgeable (tip expected)*, is now a religious art museum. The priceless gold monstrance, Custodia de Riobamba Antigua, is the museum's greatest treasure, one of the richest of its kind in South America. **Museo del Banco Central** ⊙ *Veloz y Montalvo, T296 5501, Mon-Sat 0830-1330, 1430-1630, US$0.50*, has well displayed exhibits of archaeology and colonial art. **Museo de la Ciudad** ⊙ *Primera Constituyente y Espejo, at Parque Maldonado, T295 1906, Mon-Fri 0800-1230, 1430-1800, Sat 0900-1600, free*, opened in 2004 in a beautifully restored colonial building, has displays on regional national parks, temporary exhibits, and Friday evening concerts. There is a **Museo Militar Casa Histórico** at the Galápagos military base on the ring road ⊙ *open weekdays, free*.

Riobamba is an important **market** centre where indigenous people from many communities congregate. Saturday is the main market day when the city fills with colourfully dressed *indígenas* from many different parts of the province of Chimborazo, each wearing their distinctive costume; trading overflows the markets and buying and selling go on all over town. Wednesday is a smaller market day. The 'tourist' market is in the small **Plaza de la Concepción or Plaza Roja** ⊙ *Orozco y Colón, Sat and Wed only, 0800-1500*, south of the Convento de la Concepción (see above). It is a good place to buy local handicrafts and authentic indigenous clothing. The main produce markets are **San Alfonso**, Argentinos y 5 de

Junio, which on Saturday spills over into the nearby streets and also sells clothing, ceramics, baskets and hats, and **La Condamine** ⓘ *Carabobo y Colombia, daily*, largest market on Fridays. Other markets in the colonial centre are **San Francisco** and **La Merced**, near the churches of the same name.

Guano is a carpet-weaving, sisal and leather working town 8 km north of Riobamba. Many shops sell rugs and you can arrange to have these woven to your own design. Buses leave from the Mercado Dávalos, García Moreno y New York, every 20 minutes, US$0.25, last bus returns to Riobamba at 1800. Taxi US$4.

Guaranda → *Phone code: 03. Colour map 11, grid B3. Population: 21,000. Altitude: 2,650 m.*

This quaint town, capital of Bolívar province, proudly calls itself 'the Rome of Ecuador' because it is built on seven hills. There are fine views of the mountains all around. Locals traditionally take an evening stroll in the palm-fringed main plaza, **Parque Libertador Simón Bolívar**, around which are the Municipal buildings and a large stone **Cathedral**. Although not on the tourist trail, there are many sights worth visiting in the province, for which Guaranda is the ideal base. Of particular interest is the highland town of **Salinas**, with its community development project (good cheeses), as well as the *subtrópico* region, the lowlands stretching west towards the coast. Towering over the city, on one of the hills, is an impressive statue of **El Indio Guaranga**, a local *indígena* leader after whom the city may have been named; museum (free), art gallery and auditorium. Take a taxi (US$1); or take a 'Guanujo' bus to the stadium, walk past the stadium to Av La Prensa and follow it till you reach the first turning on the right (10 minutes' walk).

Market days are Friday (till 1200) and Saturday (larger), when many indigenous people in typical dress trade at the market complex at the east end of Calle Azuay, by Plaza 15 de Mayo (9 de Abril y Maldonado), and at Plaza Roja (Avenida Gen Enríquez). Carnival in Guaranda is among the best known in the country. **Tourist office**: **Oficina Municipal de Información Turística** ⓘ *García Moreno entre 7 de Mayo y Convención de 1884, Mon-Fri 0800-1200, 1400-1800*. Information, maps, guided tours, horse riding and camping, Spanish only.

The Devil's Nose Train

Train service is very limited, but the most spectacular part of the trip – the **Devil's Nose** and **Alausí Loop** – can still be experienced. The train usually leaves **Riobamba** three days a week (see Transport, below) and goes via **Alausí** to **Sibambe** before returning to Alausí. Riding on the roof is fun, but hang on tight and remember that it's very chilly early in the morning. It's also a good idea to sit in the middle on the roof to avoid getting covered in oil from the exhaust. The train service is subject to frequent disruptions and timetables are always changing, best enquire locally about current schedules. The railway administration office is on Espejo, next to the Post Office, where information is available during office hours, T296 0115, or at the station itself T296 1909. On the days when the train is not running, you can still experience the Devil's Nose and the scenery, by walking along the tracks down from Alausí; a pleasant day trip. Horse rides in the area are also offered.

Alausí → *Phone code: 03. Colour map 11, grid B3. Population: 5,565. Altitude: 2,250 m.*

This is the station where many passengers join the train for the amazing descent over *La Nariz de Diablo* to Sibambe. There is a Sunday market, in the plaza by the church, just up the hill from the station; and a *Fiesta de San Pedro* on 29 June.

Climbing Chimborazo → *See also Riobamba Tour operators.*

ⓘ *US$10 entrance fee.* At 6,310 m, this is a difficult climb owing to the altitude. No-one without mountaineering experience should attempt the climb, and rope, ice-axe and crampons must be used. It is essential to have at least one week's acclimatization above 3,000 m. The best seasons are December and June-September. Ice pinnacles, *penitentes*, sometimes prevent climbers reaching the main, Whymper summit.

Sangay

Riobamba provides access to the central highland region of **Parque Nacional Sangay** *US$10*, a beautiful wilderness area with excellent opportunities for trekking and climbing. A controversial new road runs from Guamote to Macas in the Oriente, cutting through Parque Nacional Sangay. Now complete, it makes a spectacular ride, with five-hour bus services Riobamba-Macas. Deforestation and colonization of the area have begun. Sangay is an active volcano; **South**

The railway from the coast to the Sierra

The spectacular 464-km railway line (1.067 m gauge), which was opened in 1908, passes through 87 km of delta lands and then, in 80 km, climbs to 3,238 m. At Urbina on the summit, it reaches 3,609 m, then falls and rises before reaching the Quito plateau at 2,857 m.

Unfortunately, in 1997/98 El Niño damaged the lowland section between Durán and Sibambe, which is unlikely to be repaired owing to lack of funds. On a more positive note, the line's greatest achievements, the Alausí loop and the Devil's Nose double zigzag (including two V switchbacks), are on the part of the line open to trains, Sibambe to Riobamba. **Sibambe**, the current turning point of the train, has no hotels or bus service, so you must return by train to Alausí. Shortly after leaving Sibambe the train starts climbing the famous Nariz del Diablo (Devil's Nose),

a perpendicular ridge rising in the gorge of the Chanchán to a height of 305 m. This almost insurmountable engineering obstacle was finally conquered when a series of switchbacks was built on a 5½% grade.

Next comes **Alausí**. After crossing the 120 m long Shucos bridge, the train pulls into **Palmira**, on the crest of the first range of the Andes crossed by the railway. One by one the great snow-capped volcanoes begin to appear: Chimborazo, Carihuairazo, Altar and the burning heads of Tungurahua and Sangay, all seeming very close because of the clear air.

The best views are from the roof, but dress warmly and protect clothes from dirt. On the train, lock all luggage, even side pockets, as pilfering is common. The train is popular, especially at weekends and public holidays, so you'll have to queue early.

American Explorers has information on organizing a trip; equipment, helmet, etc, and guide essential. This seven-day trek is tough: expect long, hard days of walking and severe weather. Protection against falling stones is vital. With a little coaching a *mecánica* can make shields, arm loops welded to an oil drum top. December/January is a good time to climb Sangay. Porters can be hired in the access towns of Alao and Guarguallá. Guarguallá also has a community tourism project with accommodation and native guides. For information go to the **Ministry of the Environment**, Avenida 9 de Octubre y Quinta Macají, at the western edge of Riobamba, north of the roundabout at the end of Avenida Isabel de Godin, T296 3779; the office is only open in the early morning, be there before 0800. From town take city bus San Gerardo-El Batán.

Also in Sangay National Park is the beautiful **El Altar** volcano, whose crater is surrounded by snowcapped peaks. The most popular route begins beyond Candelaria at Hacienda Releche.

🌐 Sleeping

Riobamba *p947, map p950*
Many of the upmarket hotels are out of town.
A Abraspungu, Km 3 on the road to Guano, T294 0820, www.hosteria-abraspungu.com. Beautiful house in country setting, comfortable, good service, excellent restaurant.
A El Troje, 4½ km on the road to Chambo, T296 0826, www.eltroje.com. Good restaurant, pool and sauna, internet, nice rooms, good views.
A La Andaluza, 16 km north of Riobamba along the Panamericana, T294 9370, www.hosteria-andaluza.com. Includes breakfast, good restaurant, nice rooms in old hacienda, with heaters and roaring fireplaces, lovely views, good walking.

B El Cisne, Av Daniel L Borja y Duchicela, T296 4573, F294 1982. Restaurant, modern, helpful.
B Rincón Alemán, Remigio Romero y Alfredo Pareja, Ciudadela Arupos del Norte, T260 3540, arupo@gmx.de. Family-run hotel in a quiet residential area. Includes breakfast, laundry and cooking facilities, parking, garden, sauna, fitness room, fireplace, German spoken. Recommended.
B Zeus, Av Daniel L Borja 41-29, T296 8036, hotelzeus1@hotmail.com. Restaurant, jacuzzi, gym, bathtubs with views of Chimborazo, parking. Recommended.
B-C Montecarlo, Av 10 de Agosto 25-41 entre García Moreno y España, T296 0557. Includes

Ecuador Riobamba & around Listings

breakfast, nice house in colonial style, restaurant, parking, central.

D Canadá, Av de la Prensa 23-31 y Av Daniel L Borja, T/F296 4677, hotelcanada@lasernet.net. Near bus terminal, modern, restaurant, parking.

D La Estación, Unidad Nacional 29-15 y Carabobo, T295 5226. A nicely refurbished building, convenient for the train station, good beds, sitting rooms, terrace with hammocks and good views, restaurant, good value.

D Los Shyris, Rocafuerte 21-60 y 10 de Agosto, T/F296 0323, hshyris@yahoo.com. Cheaper without bath, hot water 0500-1100 and 1700-2300, internet, laundry facilities, good rooms, service, and value. Rooms at the back are quieter.

D Majestic, Av Daniel L Borja 43-60 y La 44, T296 8708. Rooms vary, cafeteria, electric shower, parking, near bus terminal.

D Oasis, Veloz 15-32 y Almagro, T296 1210, F294 1499. Small, pleasant, family-run, quiet location, laundry facilities, some rooms with kitchen and fridge, parking, nice garden, pick-up service from the Terminal. Recommended.

D Tren Dorado, Carabobo 22-35 y 10 de Agosto, T/F296 4890, htrendorado@hotmail.com. Convenient for the train station, early breakfast available, restaurant serves good vegetarian lunch, reliable hot water, modern, nice large rooms, very good value. Recommended.

D Whymper, Av Miguel Angel León 23-10 y Primera Constituyente, T296 4575, F296 8137. Hot water, parking, spacious rooms, a bit rundown.

D-E Imperial, Rocafuerte 22-15 y 10 de Agosto, T296 0429. Cheaper without bath, hot water,

stores luggage, good beds, basic, loud music from bar on Fri and Sat nights, good value.

Guaranda *p948*

B La Colina, Av Guayaquil 117, on road to Ambato, T/F298 0666. Bright, attractive rooms, lovely views, restful, includes breakfast, best in town but restaurant mediocre and expensive (good for Sun lunch though), covered pool.

C Hostal de Las Flores, Pichincha 402 y Rocafurete, T298 4396. Renovated colonial house with covered courtyard, well-decorated rooms.

D Bolívar, Sucre 704 y Rocafuerte, T298 0547. Good restaurant (closed Sun), parking, simple but pleasant, small courtyard.

D Cochabamba, García Moreno y 7 de Mayo, T298 1958, vviteriv@gu.pro.ec. A bit faded but good service, best restaurant in town, parking.

D Márquez, 10 de Agosto y Eloy Alfaro, T298 1306, F298 1101. Pleasant, family atmosphere, parking, a bit kitsch with grandmother-style furnishings, good value.

E Acapulco, 10 de Agosto y Amazonas, T298 1953. Basic, small rooms, restaurant, cheaper with shared bath.

Alausí *p948*

D Europa, 5 de Julio y Orozco, T293 0200. Nicely refurbished, rooms vary from functional to comfortable, best in town, restaurant, ample parking. Recommended.

D San Pedro, 5 de junio y 9 de Octubre, T293 0086. Parking, modern and comfortable but rooms are a bit bare.

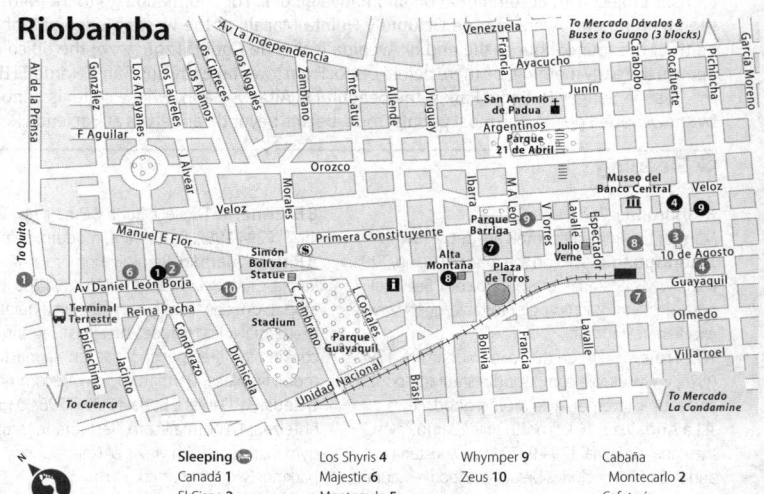

Riobamba

Sleeping	Los Shyris 4	Whymper 9	Cabaña
Canadá 1	Majestic 6	Zeus 10	Montecarlo 2
El Cisne 2	Montecarlo 5		Cafetería
Imperial 3	Oasis 11	Eating	Montecarlo 2
La Estación 7	Tren Dorado 8	Bonny 3	El Delirio 4

0 metres 100
0 yards 100

D-E Alausí, 5 de Junio 142 y Orozco, T293 0361. Cheaper without bath, electric shower, simple.

D-E Panamericano, 5 de Junio y 9 de Octubre, near the bus stop, T293 0278. Cheap restaurant, rooms cheaper without bath, hot showers, quiet at the back.

E Tequendama, 5 de Junio 152, T293 0123. Shared bath, electric shower, basic but clean and welcoming.

Sangay *p948*

D Hostal Capac Urcu, at Hacienda Releche, about 2 km outside Candelaria, at the entrance to the national park, T294 9761 (296 0848 Riobamba). Pleasant and relaxing small working hacienda. Use of kitchen (extra charge) or good meals on request, rents horses for the trek to Collanes, US$6 per horse each way, plus US$6 per muleteer. Also runs the E *refugio* at Collanes, by the crater of El Altar: rustic shelters, use of kitchen with gas stove and all utensils US$6. No hot water or blankets, take a warm sleeping bag. Recommended.

● Eating

Riobamba *p947, map p950*

Most places closed after 2100 and on Sun.

₩₩₩ El Delirio, Primera Constituyente 2816 y Rocafuerte (Bolívar stayed in this house). Ecuadorean and international dishes, popular with tour groups and overpriced, closed Mon and Sun.

₩₩ D'Baggio, Daniel León Borja 34-24 Diagonal, T296 1832. Excellent pizzería, very popular, good salads, too.

₩₩ Cafetería Montecarlo, 10 de Agosto 25-45 y García Moreno. 0700-1200, 1600-2200 (0500 breakfast can be arranged before train ride). Ecuadorean and international, good breakfasts, snacks and complete meals, nice atmosphere.

₩₩ La Gran Havana, Daniel León Borja 42-52 y Duchicela, daily 1100-2300. Economical set lunch, very good Cuban and international food à la carte.

₩₩ Parrillada de Fausto, Uruguay 2038 y Av Daniel L Borja. Good meat and fish, nice atmosphere.

₩₩-₩ Bonny, Villarroel 1558 y Almagro. 1000- 2000 daily. Cheap set meals and very good seafood (mid-range, à la carte), very popular.

₩₩-₩ Cabaña Montecarlo, García Moreno 21-40 y 10 de Agosto, Tue-Sat 1200-2100, Sun-Mon 1200-1500. Good value set lunch, pricier à la carte, good service, large portions, 'old Riobamba' atmosphere, popular with locals.

₩₩-₩ Mónaco Pizzería, Diego Ibarra y Av Daniel L Borja, Mon-Fri 1400-2200, Sat-Sun 1200-2300. Delicious pizza and pasta, nice salads, very good food, service and value.

₩ Natural Food, Tarqui entre Veloz y Primera Constituyente. Set meals only, vegetarian available.

₩ Restaurante Montecarlo, Colón y Primera Constituyente, daily 1200-1500, at night to 0100. Cheap set meals at midday and *comida típica* at night, popular.

₩ Sierra Nevada, Primera Constituyente y Rocafuerte, Mon-Sat 0800-2200, Sun 0800-1600. Excellent value set lunch, vegetarian on request. Nice atmosphere. Recommended.

Cafés and bakeries

Helados de Paila, Espejo y 10 de Agosto. Homemade ice cream, café, sweets, popular.

La Abuela Rosa, Brasil y Esmeraldas, Tue-Sat 1600-2100. Cafetería in grandmother's house serving typical Ecuadorian snacks. Nice atmosphere and good service.

Pynn's, Espejo 21-20 y Guayaquil, Mon-Sat 0900-1930. Tacos and lasagne, also set lunches.

Guaranda *p948*

See also Sleeping. Most places closed on Sun. Many simple *comedores* around Plaza Roja serve cheap set meals.

₩ Balcón Cuencano, Convención de 1884 entre García Moreno y Azuay. Breakfast, lunch and dinner, set meals and à la carte, good.

₩ La Estancia, García Moreno y Sucre. Good quality and value set meals and à la carte, nicely decorated, pleasant atmosphere.

₩ Mentuccia, Olmedo y Convención de 1884. Cosy Italian restaurant, white linen tablecloths.

₩ Pizza Buon Giorno, Av Circunvalación 2 blocks from Plaza Roja towards bus terminal. Pizza, salad.

₩ Rumipamba, Gen Enríquez 308, Plaza Roja. Grilled chicken, set meals and à la carte, juices.

● Bars and clubs

Riobamba *p947, map p950*
Gens-Chop Bar Av Daniel L Borja 42-17 y
Duchicela. Bar, good music and sport videos,
open daily, popular. Recommended.
Romeo Bar, Vargas Torres y Av Daniel León
Borja, US$2 cover. Popular, nice bar and club,
from Latin to Rythym and Blues, pleasant
sitting area on the second floor.
San Valentín, Av D L Borja y Vargas Torres. Good
Mexican dishes, pizza, hamburgers and other
snacks, bar and disco with a dance floor large
enough for 2-3 couples. Very popular.
Vieja Guardia Av Flor 40-43 y Av Zambrano.
Bar and open air disco, US$1 cover.

● Entertainment

Riobamba *p947, map p950*
Casa de la Cultura, 10 de Agosto y Rocafuerte,
T296 0219. Sometimes has a good *peña* on
Thu-Sat evenings.

● Festivals and events

Riobamba *p947, map p950*
Fiesta del Niño Rey de Reyes, with street parades,
music and dancing, starts in Dec and culminates
on **6 Jan**. Around **21 Apr** there are **independence**
celebrations lasting several days, hotel prices rise.
11 Nov is the Foundation of Riobamba.

● Shopping

Riobamba *p947, map p950*
Camping gear Some of the tour operators
hire camping and climbing gear. Julio Verne tour
operator also sells Camping Gaz. **Hobby Sport**,
10 de Agosto y Rocafuerte. Sleeping bags, tents,
fishing supplies. Directly opposite is a store which
also has some camping supplies, including
Camping Gaz. **Protección Industrial**, Rocafuerte
24-51 y Orozco, T296 3017. For waterproof
ponchos and suits, fishing supplies, ropes.
Handicrafts Crafts are sold at the Plaza Roja
on Wed and Sat (see above). Nice tagua carvings
and other crafts are on sale at *Alta Montaña* (see
Tour operators below); tagua also at shops on
Daniel León Borja near the train station. **Almacén
Cacha**, Orozco next to the Plaza Roja. A
co-operative of native people from the Cacha
area, sells woven bags, wool sweaters, other
crafts and honey, good value (closed Sun-Mon).
Artesanías Ecuador, Carabobo y 10 de Agosto.
Good selection of crafts, ceramics, wood, tagua.
Supermarkets Camari, Espejo y Olmedo,
opposite La Merced market. Small crafts section,
woollens. **La Ibérica**, Av Daniel L Borja 37-62.

▲ Activities and tours

Riobamba and around *p947*
Mountain biking Pro Bici, at Primera
Constituyente 23-40 or 23-51 y Larrea, T295 1759,
www.probici.com. Run by guide and mechanic,
Galo Brito. Bike trips and rental, guided tours with
support vehicle, equipment, US$35 pp per day,
excluding meals and overnight stays. **Julio Verne**
(see Tour operators), rental US$10 per day; tours
including transport, guide, meals, US$30 per day.

Tour operators
Most companies offer climbing trips (from
US$160 per person for 2 days) and trekking (from
US$50 per person per day). **Note**: Many hotels
offer tours, not all are run by qualified guides.
Alta Montaña, Av Daniel L Borja 35-17 y Diego
Ibarra, T294 2215, aventurag@ch.pro.ec. Trekking,
climbing, cycling, birdwatching and horse riding
tours in mountains and jungle, transport,
equipment rental, English spoken. Recommended.
Andes Trek, Rocafuerte 22-66 y 10 de Agosto,
T294 0964, www.andes-trek.com. Climbing,
trekking and mountain-biking tours, transport,
equipment rental, English and German spoken.
Marcelo Puruncajas is a known climber.
Expediciones Andinas, Vía a Guano, Km 3,
across from *Hotel Abraspungo*, T296 4915,
www.expediciones-andinas.com. Climbing
expeditions, operate Chimborazo Base Camp on
south flank of mountain. Cater for groups,
contact well in advance, German spoken, run by
Marco Cruz, a certified guide of the *German
Alpine Club*. Recommended.
Julio Verne, El Espectador 22-25 y Daniel L Borja,
2 blocks from the train station, T296 3436,
www.julioverne-travel.com. Climbing, trekking,
cycling, jungle and Galápagos trips, transport to
mountains, equipment rental, Ecuadorean-
Dutch-run, uses official guides. Recommended.
Metropolitan Touring, Av Daniel L Borja
y Miguel Angel León, T296 9600,
www.metropolitan-touring.com. Railway tours,
airline tickets, DHL and Western Union
representatives.
Veloz Coronado, Chile 33-21 y Francia, T296
0916, best reached after 1900. Enrique Veloz
Coronado, a recognized climber, is very helpful,
his sons are also guides and work with him.

● Transport

Riobamba *p947, map p950*
Bus Terminal Terrestre on Epiclachima y Av
Daniel L Borja for buses to Quito, Guayaquil,
Ambato, etc. Buses from Baños and the Oriente
arrive at the Terminal Oriental, Espejo y Córdovez.
Taxi from one terminal to another, US$1. **Quito**,

US$3.75, 4 hrs, about every 30 mins. To **Guaranda**, US$2, 2 hrs; the road is paved to San Juan, from where there are 2 scenic routes: via Gallo Rumi, unpaved, or via the Arenal, partly paved (some *Flota Bolívar* buses take this route), sit on the right for the beautiful views on either route. To **Ambato**, US$1.25, 1 hr, sit on the right. To **Alausí**, see below. To **Cuenca**, 6 a day via Alausí, 6 hrs, US$6. This road is paved but landslides are a constant hazard and the road is often under repair. To **Guayaquil**, frequent service, US$4.50, 5 hrs, the trip is really spectacular for the first 2 hrs. To **Baños**, see above. To **Puyo**, also via Ambato, US$3.75, 4 hrs direct. To **Macas** 5 hrs.

Guaranda *p948*
Bus Terminal at Eliza Mariño Carvajal, on road to Riobamba and Babahoyo; if you are staying in town get off closer to the centre. Many daily buses to: **Ambato**, US$2, 2 hrs. **Riobamba**, see below. **Babahoyo**, US$3, 3 hrs, beautiful ride. **Guayaquil**, US$4, 4 hrs. **Quito**, 3 companies run almost 30 daily services, US$4.50, 5 hrs.

The Devil's Nose Train *p948*
The train usually leaves **Riobamba** on Wed, Fri and Sun at 0700, arrives in **Alausí** around 1100, reaches **Sibambe** about 1130-1200, and returns to Alausí by 1330-1400. From Riobamba to Sibambe and back to Alausí costs US$11; Alausí-Sibambe-Alausí US$7; Alausí back to Riobamba US$3.40. Tickets go on sale the day before departure, or the same morning at 0600, seats are not numbered, best arrive early. You can rent cushions for US$1. In **Alausí** tickets go on sale around 0900. To check if it's running, T293 0126. (See box, page 949.) Metropolitan Touring operates a private *autoferro* (motorized rail-car) on the Riobamba-Sibambe route. They require a minimum number of passengers but will run any day and time convenient to the group. Approximately US$120 pp.

The continuation of the line from Alausí to **Huigra** was expected to be running in high season, 2006, and the line from Huigra to **Bucay** has a tourist service at weekends on holidays.

Alausí *p948*
Bus From **Riobamba**, 1¾ hrs, US$1.50, 84 km. To **Quito**, from 0600 onwards, about 20 a day, 5½ hrs, US$5-6; often have to change in

Riobamba. To **Cuenca**, 4 hrs, US$5. To **Ambato** hourly, 3 hrs, US$3. To **Guayaquil**, 3 a day, 5 hrs, US$5. **Coop Patria** and Trans Alausí have offices on 5 de Julio. Many through buses don't go into town, but have to be caught on the highway.

Chimborazo *p948*
There are no buses that will take you to the shelters. You can arrange transport with a tour operator or taxi from Riobamba (about US$25 one way). You can also take a bus travelling between Riobamba and **Guaranda** which goes on the Vía del Arenal (Flota Bolívar 8 daily, 0700-1800, check that it is taking this route; from Riobamba US$0.90, 1 hr), alight at the turn-off for the refuges and walk the remaining steep 5 km to the first shelter. To the eastern slopes, there are trekking tours, arrange transport from an agency or take a bus between Riobamba and **Ambato**, get off at the turnoff for Posada La Estación and Urbina.

Sangay *p948*
The most common access point for climbing Volcán Sangay is the town of **Alao**. Buses leave Riobamba for Alao from Benalcázar corner Primera Constituyente, Mon, Wed, Fri and Sat 1100 and 1630, Tue and Thu 1230, Sun 0600 and 1100, 2 hrs. All departure times approximate, be there at least 1 hr beforehand and wait. To **Candelaria** 1 bus most days around noon from Parque La Libertad, Benalcázar y Primera Constituyente, opposite Mercado San Francisco, 1½ hrs, US$1.25.

❶ Directory

Riobamba *p947, map p950*
Banks Banco del Pacífico, Av D L Borja y Zambrano. **Banco del Pichincha**, Primera Constituyente y García Moreno. **Banco de Guayaquil**, Primera Constituyente 2626 y García Moreno. **Produbacno**, Veloz y Gracía Moreno. **Internet** Many places, rates about US$1 per hr. **Post offices** 10 de Agosto y Espejo.

Guaranda *p948*
Internet Compumás, 10 de Agosto y 7 de Mayo. Another at Sucre y 10 de Agosto, near Parque Bolívar. Price US$1. **Post offices** Azuay y Pichincha.

The **Cathedral** and **Santo Domingo church** *Bolívar y Rocafuerte*, have painted interiors. **El Valle** church, on the south edge of the city is colonial, with a lovely interior. Housed in a beautifully restored house on the main park is the **Centro Cultural Loja** home of the **Museo del Banco Central** ① *10 de Agosto 13-30 y Bolívar, T257 3004, Mon-Fri 0900-1300, 1400-1700, US$0.40*, with well displayed archaeology, ethnography, art, and history halls. There are also temporary exhibits, a library and an auditorium. The **Monasterio de las Concepcionistas de Loja** ① *10 de Agosto y Bernardo Valdivieso, T258 4032, Mon-Sat 0900-1700. US$1*, has a religious art museum with paintings and sculptures. Loja is famed for its musicians and has one of the few musical academies in the country and two symphonic orchestras. Musical evenings and concerts are often held around the town. The **Museo de Música** ① *Valdivieso 09-42 y Rocafuerte, T2561342. Mon-Fri 0900-1300, 1500-1900, free*, housed in the restored Colegio Bernardo Valdivieso, honours ten Lojano composers. It also has rotating exhibits, not necessarily about music, and a café. **Mercado Centro Comercial Loja** (Mercado Modelo) ① *10 de Agosto y 18 de Noviembre, Mon-Sat (the main market day) 0600-1630, Sun 0600-1330*, is worth a visit. It is efficient and the cleanest in Ecuador. At Puente Bolívar, by the northern entrance to town, is a fortress-like monument and a lookout over the city, known as **La Entrada de la Ciudad** ① *Mon-Fri 0830-2130, Sat-Sun 0900-2130*. It has art exhibits at ground level and a small café upstairs, a good place to take pictures. Also in the north of the city, a couple of blocks east of the Terminal is the **Parque Recreacional Jipiro**, a well maintained, clean park, good to walk and relax in. It is popular at weekends. Take the city bus marked 'Jipiro', a five-minute ride from the centre.

Parque Educacional Ambiental y Recreacional de Argelia ① *0800-1200, 1400-1800, US$1, take a city bus marked 'Capulí-Dos Puentes' to the park or 'Argelia' to the Universidad Nacional and walk from there* is superb, with trails through the forest to the *páramo*. It is 500 m before the police checkpoint on road south to Vilcabamba. Across the road and 100 m south is the **Jardín Botánico Reynaldo Espinosa** ① *Mon-Fri 0900-1600, Sat-Sun 1300-1800, US$ 0.60*, which is nicely laid out.

Parque Nacional Podocarpus

① *Park entry is US$10, valid for 5 days at all entrances. Entrances to the upper section: at Cajanuma, about 8 km south of Loja on the Vilcabamba road. From the turnoff it is 8 km uphill to the guard station. At San Francisco, 24 km from Loja along the road to Zamora. The southwestern section of the park can be reached by trails from Vilcabamba, Yangana and Valladolid. Entrances to the lower section: Bombuscara can be reached from Zamora; the other entrance is at Romerillos, 2 hrs south of Zamora. Information from Ministerio del Ambiente in Loja, Sucre entre Quito e Imbabura, T/F258 5421, podocam@easynet.net.ec. In Zamora contact the Ministerio at T/F260 6606. Their general map of the park is not adequate for navigation. Conservation groups working in and around the park include: Arcoiris, Segundo Cueva Celi 03-15 y Clodoveo Carrión, T/F07-257 2926, www.arcoiris.org.ec; Fundación Ecológica Podocarpus, Catacocha entre Olmedo y Juan José Peña, T2585924, podofund@loja.telconet.net; Naturaleza y Cultura Internacional, Av Pío Jaramillo y Venezuela, T2573691, www.natureandculture.org.*

Podocarpus (950 to 3,700 m) is one of the most diverse protected areas in the world. It is particularly rich in birdlife, including many rarities and some newly discovered species, and includes one of the last major habitats for the spectacled bear. The park protects stands of *romerillo* or podocarpus, a native, slow-growing conifer. The park is divided into two areas, an upper premontane section with spectacular walking country, lush tropical cloud forest and excellent birdwatching, and a lower subtropical section, with remote areas of virgin rainforest and unmatched quantities of flora and fauna. Both zones are quite wet, making hiking or rubber boots essential. There are sometimes periods of dry weather October to January. The upper section is also very cold, so warm clothing and waterproofs are indispensable year-round. **Cajanuma** is the trailhead for the eight-hour hike to **Lagunas del Compadre**, 12 lakes set amid rock cliffs, camping is possible there. At **San Francisco**, the *guardianía* (ranger's station), operated by Fundación Arcoiris offers nice accommodation (see below). This section of the park is a transition cloud forest area at around 2,160 m, very rich in birdlife. This is the best place to see the podocarpus trees: a trail (four hours return) goes from the *guardianía* to the podocarpus.

Zamora → *Population: 10,500.*
The scenic road to the Oriente crosses a low pass and descends rapidly to Zamora, an old mission settlement about 65 km away at the confluence of the Ríos Zamora and Bombuscaro. The road is beautiful as it wanders from *páramo* down to high jungle, crossing mountain ranges of spectacular cloud forest, weaving high above narrow gorges as it runs alongside the Río Zamora. The town itself is a midway point for miners and gold prospectors heading further into the Oriente. There are two *orquidearios*, **Tzanka** ① *José Luis Tamayo y Jorge Mosquera, T260 5692, US$2* and **Paphinia** ① *Av del Ejército Km 2, T260 5911*. The best month is November, but except for April-June, when it rains almost constantly, other months are comfortable.

Loja to the Peruvian border
An alternative to the Huaquillas border crossing is the quieter and more scenic route via Macará. Leaving Loja on the main paved highway going west, the airport at **La Toma** (1,200 m) is reached after 35 km. If flying to or from La Toma, it's best to stay at **Catamayo** ① *taxi to airport US$1, or 20 mins walk*, nearby. At Catamayo, where you can catch the Loja-Macará-Piura bus, the Pan-American Highway divides: one branch runs west, the other south.

On the paved western road, at San Pedro de La Bendita, a secondary road climbs to the much-venerated pilgrimage site of **El Cisne**, dominated by its large incongruous French-style Gothic church. There is a small museum, several basic *pensiones* and places to eat. Vendors and beggars fill the town and await visitors (see Festivals and events, below). Continuing on the western route, **Catacocha** is spectacularly placed, a town built on a rock. There are pre-Inca ruins around the town. From Catacocha, the paved road runs south to the border at Macará.

The south route from Catamayo to Macará is via Cariamanga, fully paved. The road goes to **Cariamanga**, via **Gonzanamá**, a pleasant, sleepy little town (basic *hostales*), famed for the weaving of beautiful *alforjas* (multi-purpose saddlebags). It's 27 km to Cariamanga (six hotels, banks), then the road twists along a ridge westwards to **Colaisaca**, before descending steeply through forests to **Utuana** and Sozoranga (one hotel), then down to the rice paddies of **Macará**, on the border. There is a choice of accommodation here and good road connections to Sullana and Piura in Peru.

Border with Peru Ecuadorean immigration is open 24 hours. Formalities last about 30 minutes. It is a much easier crossing than at Huaquillas. During the day there are money changers dealing in soles at the international bridge and in Macará at the park where taxis leave for the border. The international bridge over the Río Macará is 2½ km from town. There is taxi and pick-up service (US$0.25 shared, US$1 private). On the Peruvian side, minivans and cars run La Tina-Sullana (try to avoid arriving in Sullana after dark).

● Sleeping

Saraguro *p963*
E Samana Wasi, 10 de Marzo near the Panamericana, T220 0315. Clean, modern, with good beds and hot showers.
E Sara Allpa, Antonio Castro y Loja, T220 0272. Several types of room, good beds, hot showers, family-run.
F Res Saraguro, Loja No 03-2 y A Castro, T220 0286. Cheaper with shared bath, nice courtyard, hot water, basic, good value.

Loja *p963*
There are a few basic *residenciales* in our **F** range on Rocafuerte, also some along Sucre with mostly short stay customers.
L-AL La Casa Lojana, París 00-08 y Zoilo Rodríguez, T258 5984, casalojanahotel @utpl.edu.ec. Refurbished in elaborate colonial style, but plain rooms, includes breakfast, elegant

dinning room, lovely grounds and views. Staffed by students of the Universidad Particular de Loja.
A Andes del Prado, Mariana de Jesús entre 10 de Agosto y Rocafuerte, T258 8271. Refurbished modern home overlooking the city, bright comfortable rooms, includes breakfast, internet, parking.
A Libertador, Colón 14-30 y Bolívar, T257 0344, hlibloja@impsat.net.ec. Comfortable, central, includes buffet breakfast, good restaurant, pool and spa, parking, suites available.
A-B Bombuscaro, 10 de Agosto y Av Universitaria, T257 7021, www.bombuscaro.com.ec. Comfortable rooms and suites, includes buffet breakfast, restaurant, internet, airport transfers, car rental, good service. Recommended.
B Hostal Del Bus, Av 8 de Diciembre y Flores, T257 5100, hdelbus@easynet.net.ec. Opposite the terminal, carpets, restaurant.

B Vilcabamba Internacional, Iberoamérica y Pasaje la FEUE, T257 3393, F256 1483. Includes breakfast, on the river, pleasant, restaurant, discount for *Handbook* users.

C Acapulco, Sucre 7-61 y 10 de Agosto, T257 0651. Pleasant, central, nicely furnished small rooms, includes breakfast, cafeteria, first floor rooms are quieter.

C Aguilera Internacional, Sucre 01-08 y Emiliano Ortega, T257 2894, F258 4660. North of centre, comfortable rooms, includes breakfast, restaurant, parking, sauna, gym.

D Chandelier, Imbabura 14-82 y Sucre, T256 3061, chandelierhotel@hotmail.com. Cheaper with shared bath, electric shower, parking, hospitable, OK.

D San Luis, Sucre 04-62 y Quito, T257 0370. Large adequate rooms, parking for small car, simple but clean.

E Internacional, 10 de Agosto 15-30 entre Sucre y 18 de Noviembre, T257 8486. Cheaper with shared bath, electric shower, older place but refurbished and OK.

E Londres, Sucre 7-51 y 10 de Agosto, T256 1936. Well-maintained old house, shared bath, hot water, basic, good value.

Parque Nacional Podocarpus *p964*
At **Cajanuma**, there are cabins with beds and mattresses, US$3 pp per night, bring warm sleeping bag, stove and food. At **San Francisco**, the *guardianía* (ranger's station), operated by **Fundación Arcoiris** offers nice accommodation with shared bath, hot water and kitchen facilities, US$8 pp if you bring a sleeping bag, US$10 if they provide sheets. At **Bombuscara** there is a cabin with kitchen facilities, US$3 pp.

Zamora *p965*
B-D Copalinga, Km 3 on the road to the Bombuscara entrance of Podocarpus national park, T260 5043 or T09-347 7013, jacamar@impsat.net.ec. Comfortable cabins (some with bath) in a lovely setting, meals available if arranged in advance, excellent birdwatching, English and French spoken, Belgian run, helpful. Recommended.

D Betania, Francisco de Orellana entre Diego de Vaca y Amazonas, T260 7030, hotelbetaniaz@hotmail.com. Includes breakfast, parking, modern.

D Orillas del Zamora, Diego de Vaca y Alonso de Mercadillo, T260 5754. Modern, comfortable, good value. Recommended.

E Seyma, 24 de Mayo y Amazonas, T260 5583. Shared bath, cold water, basic.

Loja to the Peruvian border *p965*
Catamayo
C Bellavista, in Trapichillo village, Catamayo valley, T267 7255. Quiet, with pool, sauna, restaurant.

C-D Los Almendros, on main road west of town, T267 7293, F257 0393. Pleasant resort with range of rooms, cheaper without breakfast or fridge, restaurant and bar, 2 pools, parking.

D-F Rossana, Isidro Ayora y 24 de Mayo, T267 7006. Cheaper with shared bath, cold water, also cheaper annexe next door.

Macará
D El Conquistador, Bolívar y Calderón, T269 4057. Includes breakfast, hot water, fan, parking, modern and comfortable.

D Espiga de Oro, C Ante opposite the market, T269 5089. Cold water, fan, OK.

D Santigyn, Bolívar y Rengel, T269 5035. Hot water, fan, some rooms with fridge, modern, comfortable.

D Terra Verde, Lázaro Vaca s/n, near the Hospital Civil, T269 4540, patricioluzuriaga@hotmail.com. Quiet location 2 blocks from the Coop Loja bus station. Includes breakfast, a/c, rooftop terrace, helpful.

E Bekalus, Valdivieso entre 10 de Agosto y Rengel, T269 4043. Cheaper with shared bath, cold water, simple, good value.

E Hostal del Sur, Veintimilla y Loja, T269 4189. With bath, cold water, modern, small.

● Eating

Saraguro *p963*
Several restaurants around the main plaza serve economical meals.

Loja *p963*
℣ 200 Millas, Juan José Peña y 10 de Agosto. Good fish and seafood, open 0900-1500.

℣ José Antonio's, Eguiguren 12-24 y Olmedo, 2nd floor. International and French cuisine, enthusiastic chef, open 1000-2200. Highly recommended.

℣ Parrilladas El Fogón, 8 de Diciembre y Flores, across from the bus station. Good grill and salad bar.

℣ Parrilladas Uruguayas, Juan de Salinas y Av Universitaria, Mon 1800-0000, Tue-Sat 1100-0000, Sun 1100-1800. Good grilled meat, helpful owner.

℣-℣ Café Azul, Eguiguren entre Bolívar y Sucre, Mon-Fri 0900-1230, 1500-2200, Sat 1500-2100. Breakfasts, crêpes, salads, sandwiches, lasagna and other pasta, drinks.

℣ Casa Sol, 24 de Mayo 07-04 y José Antonio Eguiguren, daily 0900-0000. Economical set meals and à la carte. Pleasant seating on a balcony overlooking the small Parque Cristóbal Ojeda.

¶ **Diego's**, Colón 14-88 y Sucre, 2nd floor. Very good cheap set lunch and mid-range à la carte, very popular, open daily 0730-2200. Recommended.

¶ **El Arbol de Oro**, Bolívar y Lourdes, opposite Mercado San Sebastián. Good cheap Chinese food.

¶ **El Paraíso**, Quito 14-50 y Bolívar, daily 0700-2100. Good vegetarian food, set meals and some à la carte dishes.

¶ **Mi Tierra**, Zoilo Rodríguez y 24 de Mayo, Tue-Sun 1000-2200. Typical *comida lojana* and international dishes in a very nice setting, great views.

¶ **Pizzería Forno di Fango**, Bolívar 10-98 y Azuay, Tue-Sun 1200-2230. Excellent wood-oven pizza.

¶ **Tamal Lojano**, 18 de Noviembre y Imbabura. Cheap set lunches, good tamales and other local snacks in the evening, Mon-Sat 0930-1330, 1630-2000. Recommended.

Cafés
El Jugo Natural, J Eguiguren 14-18 y Bolívar. Very good fresh juices and breakfast. Closed Sun.
Topoli, Bolívar 13-78 y Riofrío. Best coffee and yoghurt in town, good for breakfast, Mon-Fri 0800-2100, Sat 0800-2000.

Zamora *p965*
♦♦ **Don Pepe**, Sevilla de Oro y Pío Jaramillo, opposite the hospital, daily 0600-2100. Good set meals and à la carte.

¶ **Spiga Pan**, 24 de Mayo, ½ block downhill from the plaza. Great bakery with a variety of hot breads, cream cakes and fresh fruit yoghurt. Best choice in town.

❂ Festivals and events

Loja *p963*
16-20 Aug Fiesta de la Virgen del Cisne, the statue of the Virgin spends a month each year travelling around the province; the most important peregrination is the 3-day 70 km walk from El Cisne to Loja cathedral, beginning **17 Aug**. End-May, the last 2 weeks of Aug and the 1st week of Sep are crowded.

▲ Activities and tours

Loja *p963*
Aratinga Aventuras, Lourdes 14-80 y Sucre, T/F258 2434, aratinga@loja.telconet.net. Specializes in birdwatching tours, overnight trips to cloud forest. Pablo Andrade is a knowledgeable guide.

Biotours, Pasaje E, off Emiliano Ortega entre Colón y Azuay, T257 9387. City, regional and jungle tours, airline tickets.

Zamora *p965*
Discovery Zamora, T260 6207. Vinici Macanchi rents kayaks and organizes rafting trips on the Ríos Zamora and Bombuscara, US$40 pp per day. **Wellington Valdiviezo**, T260 5132 (office hours), manacus_manacus@yahoo.es. Naturalist guide who can organize tours to the Alto Nangaritza. Contact well in advance.

❂ Transport

Saraguro *p963*
Bus To and from **Cuenca** throughout the day, US$4.50, 3 hrs; to **Loja**, US$1.50, 2 hrs. Check if your bus is leaving from the plaza or the Panamericana.

Loja *p963*
Air The airport is at La Toma (Catamayo), 35 km west, shared taxi US$5-6 pp (see Loja to the Peruvian border above). There are **TAME** flights to Quito direct (US$63), 3 a week to Guayaquil (US$49). Flights are often cancelled due to strong winds or fog. The *TAME* office is at 24 de Mayo y E Ortega, TT257 0248, Mon-Fri 0830-1300, 1430-1800, Sat 0900-1300.
Bus All buses leave from the Terminal Terestre at Av Gran Colombia e Isidro Ayora, at the north of town, some companies also have ticket offices in the centre. From terminal buses every 2 mins to/from centre, 10 mins journey; left luggage, information desk, shops, US$0.15 terminal tax. Taxi from centre, US$1. To **Cuenca**, 4½ hrs, 7 a day, US$7.50. **Machala**, 10 a day, 6 hrs, US$6 (3 routes, via Piñas, for **Zaruma**, unpaved and rough but very scenic; via Balsas, fully paved and also scenic; and via Alamor, for **Puyango petrified forest**, military checkpoints on route). **Quito**, US$14, 14 hrs. **Guayaquil**, 8 hrs, US$10. To **Huaquillas**, US$5, 6 hrs direct. To **Macará**, 5 hrs, US$6.25. To **Piura (Peru)**, luxury coach service with **Transportes Loja**, via Macará, at 0700, 1300, 2230 and 2300 daily, US$8, 8 hrs including border formalities (make sure the bus stops for passport stamps); buy ticket 24 hrs in advance. Also **Unión Cariamanga** at 0300 and 0600.

Parque Nacional Podocarpus *p964*
For **Cajanuma**, take a Vilcabamba bound van or *taxiruta*, get off at the turnoff, US$1-1.20, it is a 8-km walk from the turnoff. Direct transport by taxi to the park gate, about US$10 (may not be feasible in the rainy season) or with a tour from Loja. You can arrange a pick up later from the guard station. To the **lower section**: there are 2 possible

entrances. Bombuscaro can be reached from **Zamora**: take a taxi US$6 to the entrance, then walk 1 km to the refuge. The other entrance is at **Romerillos**, 2 hrs south by bus. Bus departs Zamora 0630 and 1415, return to Zamora at 0815 and 1600. A 3-5 day hike is possible into this part of the park, contact the **Ministerio del Ambiente** in Zamora (see above) or **Fundación Maquipucuna** in Quito, Baquerizo Moreno E9-153 y Tamayo, T02-250 7200, www.maqui.org.

Zamora p965
Bus Leave from Terminal Terrestre. To **Loja**, frequent, 2 hrs, US$2.50; to **Gualaquiza**, US$3.50, 5 hrs, where you can change buses for Macas.

Loja to the Peruvian border p965
Macará
Bus Coop Loja and Cariamanga have frequent buses, daily from Macará to **Loja**; 6 hrs, US$5.80. **Transportes Loja** buses, which have 4 direct buses daily Loja-**Piura**, can also be boarded in Macará, US$4 to Piura, 3 hrs. Likewise **Unión Cariamanga** buses on the Loja-Piura route. *Coop Loja* also has service to **Quito**, US$15, 15 hrs, and **Guayaquil**, US$11-12, 8 hrs.

⊕ Directory

Loja p963
Banks Banco de Guayaquil, Eguiguren y Valdivieso, Euros, Visa and MasterCard. Banco del Austro, Eguiguren 14-12 y Bolívar, Visa and MasterCard, 4% commission. Mutualista Pichincha, Bolívar y Eguiguren, MasterCard. Comercial Karen's, 18 de Noviembre 06-80 y José Antonio Eguiguren, T257 2140, Mon-Sat 0900-1300, 1500-1900. Changes Peruvian Soles and Euros. **Embassies and consulates** Peru, Sucre y Azuay, T257 1668. **Internet** US$1 per hr. **Post offices** Colón y Sucre; no good for sending parcels.

Vilcabamba to Peru

Vilcabamba → *Phone code: 07. Colour map 11, grid C3. Altitude: 1,520 m.*
Once an isolated village, Vilcabamba has become increasingly popular with foreign travellers, an established stop along the gringo trail between Ecuador and Peru. The whole area is beautiful and tranquil, with an agreeable climate (17°C minimum, 26°C maximum, the rainy season is October to May, March and April are the rainiest; July and August can be very windy). There are many places to stay and several good restaurants. There are many great day-walks and longer treks throughout the area, as well as ample opportunities for horse riding. A number of lovely private nature reserves are situated east of Vilcabamba, between it and Parque Nacional Podocarpus. Trekkers can continue on foot through orchid-clad cloud forests to the high cold *páramos* of Podocarpus. **Tourist office: i Tur** ① *Unidad Municipal de Turismo, Diego Vaca de Vega y Bolívar, at the Casa Comunal on the main plaza, T264 0890, daily 0800-1300, 1500-1800.* Sketch map of Vilcabamba and surroundings, helpful.

Climbing **Mandango**, 'the sleeping woman' mountain ① *US$1.50, includes a small bottle of mineral water and a small bag of panela, local raw sugar,* is a popular and scenic half-day walk. The signed access is along the highway, 250 m south of the bus terminal. Regrettably, there have been several armed holdups of tourists in 2006: do not take valuables and enquire locally before heading out.

Note: Vilcabamba has become famous among travellers for its locally-produced hallucinogenic cactus juice called **San Pedrillo** (or San Pedrito). In addition to being illegal, it is more dangerous than it may seem because of flashbacks which can occur months or years after use.

Vilcabamba to Peru
Many daily buses run from Loja or Vilcabamba to **Zumba** (see Loja, Transport), 112 km south of Vilcabamba; **F San Luis,** T07-230 8121, is the only halfway decent place in town. It is a 1½ -hour rough ride by *ranchera* (open-sided bus, 0800, 1430, US$1.75) from Zumba to **La Balsa**, where there is an immigration post (supposedly open 24 hours). Passports are checked also just north of Zumba and 20 minutes north of La Balsa. A new vehicle bridge has been built over the river to the Peruvian border post (open 0800-1300, 1500-2000); entering Peru, visit immigration and the PNP office. On the Peruvian side a minibus service runs to **Namballe**, 15 minutes away, and cars run to Namballe and **San Ignacio** (Peru) when full, two hours, from where there is transport to **Jaén**. This opens a faster, more direct route between **Vilcabamba and Chachapoyas**, which can now be done, with luck, in two days, but it's a very rough ride.

Alternative border crossing

From Cariamanga (see above), a rough, unpaved road runs two hours south to **Amaluza**, a pleasant town, with a nice plaza and imposing modern church. There are two hotels (best is **D Guambo Real**, Av Chigua y Manuel Enrique Rojas, 1 block from the church, T2653061, comfortable rooms with small bath, cold water), and several well stocked shops. *Unión Cariamanga* has eight daily buses from Loja to Amaluza, US$4.75, 5 hours. There are six *rancheras* a day from the plaza at Amaluza to **Jimbura**, US$1, 1 hour. Jimbura is a nice quiet town, with **F Residencial Central**, on the main street, basic, and a few places to eat. It is a 6-km walk to the international bridge and a further 2 km to the Peruvian village of Espíndola (taxi US$7). Ecuadorean immigration is just outside Jimbura, open 24 hours. Peruvian immigration in Espíndola is also open 24 hours, but you may have ask for the officer. There are no services at all at the border bridge, but shopkeepers in Jimbura change soles at poor rates. To Ayabaca (Peru), a pickup leaves Espíndola about 0500 daily; if staying in Jimbura, go to Espíndola and let the driver know, he will pick you up in the morning. There is no fixed schedule during the day, patience is required on this route.

● Sleeping

Vilcabamba *p968, map p969*
Note: You may be approached by people touting for hotels. For its size, Vilcabamba has one of the best selections of accommodation in all Ecuador,

so you are better off choosing on your own.
AL-C Madre Tierra, 2 Km north on road to Loja, follow signs, T264 0269, www.madretierra1.com. From elaborate suites to simple cabins and dorms,

Vilcabamba

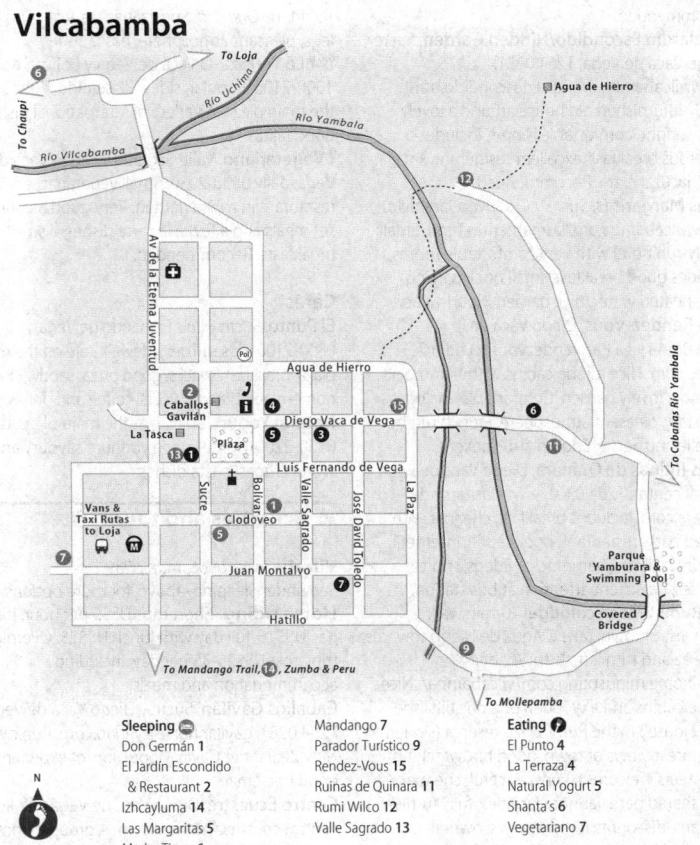

Sleeping ●
Don Germán **1**
El Jardín Escondido
  & Restaurant **2**
Izhcayluma **14**
Las Margaritas **5**
Madre Tierra **6**

Mandango **7**
Parador Turístico **9**
Rendez-Vous **15**
Ruinas de Quinara **11**
Rumi Wilco **12**
Valle Sagrado **13**

Eating ●
El Punto **4**
La Terraza **4**
Natural Yogurt **5**
Shanta's **6**
Vegetariano **7**

969

each distinctively decorated, includes breakfast and dinner, superb home cooking, vegetarian to order, non-residents must reserve meals a day in advance. Nice grounds, pool, spa (extra charge). Under new US management, English and French spoken, popular. Recommended.

C-D Izhcayluma, 2 km south on highway, T264 0095, www.izhcayluma.com. Comfortable cabins with terrace and hammocks, cheaper with shared bath, includes very good breakfast available all day, excellent restaurant with European specialties, nice grounds, pool, dining area with wonderful views, pleasant bar, games, includes use of bikes to get to town. English and German spoken, helpful. Highly recommended.

D Cabañas Río Yambala, Yamburara Alto, 4 km east of town, www.vilcabamba.cwc.net. Beautiful tranquil setting on the Río Yambala. Some cabins with kitchen facilities, meals also available, cheaper with shared bath (one simple cabin in **F** range). Access to *Las Palmas* private nature reserve with good birdwatching. English spoken, friendly owners Charlie and Sarah. Recommended.

D El Jardín Escondido/Hidden Garden, Sucre y Diego Vaca de Vega, T264 0281, www.vilcabamba.org/jardinescondido.html. Nicely refurbished old house around a lovely patio, bright, comfortable rooms, includes generous breakfast, excellent restaurant, small pool, jacuzzi extra. Recommended.

D Las Margaritas, Sucre y Clodoveo Jaramillo, www.vilcabamba.org/lasmargaritas.html. Small family-run hotel with very comfortable rooms, includes good breakfast, small pool, parking, solar-heated water, nice garden. Good value.

D Le Rendez-Vous, Diego Vaca de Vega 06-43 y La Paz, rendezvousecuador@ yahoo.com. Nice adobe cabins with hammocks around a lovely garden. Comfortable, includes breakfast, pleasant atmosphere, French run by Isabelle and Serge, English also spoken.

D Las Ruinas de Quinara, Diego Vaca de Vega east of centre, T264 0301, www.lasruinasde quinara.com. Includes breakfast, cheaper with shared bath, restaurant, pool, sauna, internet, laundry facilities, hammocks, videos, sports facilities, persistent attention at bus station.

D-E Rumi Wilco Ecolodge, 10-min walk northeast of town, take C Agua de Hierro towards C La Paz and turn left, http://kober press.home.mindspring.com/vilcabamba/. Nice adobe cabins and a wooden one on stilts (the 'Pole House') in the Rumi Wilco reserve (signed trails, great views of town, good birdwatching, volunteers welcome). Very peaceful, cheaper with shared bath, laundry facilities, fully furnished kitchens, discounts for long stays, owners Orlando and Alicia. Recommended.

E Don Germán, Bolívar y Clodoveo Jaramillo (no sign), T267 3130. Shared bath, hot water, laundry/cooking facilities, simple, family run, friendly owner: Sra Líbia Toledo.

E Mandango, Guilcopamba y Juan Montalvo behind the market. Cheaper with shared bath, electric shower, small pool, laundry/cooking facilities, internet.

E Parador Turístico, at the southeast end of town, T/F267 3122. One of Vilcabamba's first hotels, lovely grounds and views. Includes breakfast, restaurant, bar, pool, parking, a bit faded but good value outside holiday times.

F Valle Sagrado, Luis Fernando de Vega y Av de la Eterna Juventud, T264 0386, www.vilcabamba.org/ vallesagrado.html. Ample grounds, basic rooms, cheaper with shared bath, electric shower, laundry and cooking facilities, parking.

🍴 Eating

Vilcabamba *p968, map p969*

♦ **Shanta's**, on the road to Yamburara opposite *Ruinas de Quinara*. Specialities are trout and frog legs, pleasant atmosphere, has laundry.

♦♦-♦ **La Terraza**, D Vaca de Vega y Bolívar, daily 1000-2100. Popular, sidewalk seating, right on the main plaza. A variety of international dishes, good fajitas.

♦ **Vegetariano**, Valle Sagrado y Diego Vaca de Vega, daily 0830-2030. Small vegetarian restaurant in a nice garden. Very good 3 course set meals and a few à la carte dishes, also breakfasts. Recommended.

Cafés

El Punto, Sucre y Luis Fernando de Vega, 0800-2100, closed Tue. Sidewalk café on the main plaza, breakfast, snacks, good pizza, sandwiches on home-made bread, sweets, coffee and drinks.

Natural Yogurt, Bolívar, at the main plaza, daily 0800-2200. Home-made yoghurt, savoury and sweet crêpes, pasta dishes.

▲ Activities and tours

Vilcabamba *p968, map p969*
See under Sleeping, above, for more options.
Horse riding Short trips US$5 per hour, half day US$15, full day with lunch US$25. Overnight trips cost US$25-35 per day, including accommodation and meals.

Caballos Gavilán, Sucre y Diego Vaca de Vega, T264 0281, gavilanhorse@yahoo.com. Run by New Zealander Gavin Moore, lots of experience, good horseman.

Centro Ecuestre, Diego Vaca de Vega y Bolívar, centroecuestre@hotmail.com. A group of local guides, helpful.

La Tasca, Diego Vaca de Vega y Sucre, T258 0888, latascatours@yahoo.fr. Riding tours with experienced guide, René León.

Nambija runs Loja-**La Balsa** 0000, passes Zumba 0600, arrives at the border 0800; return 2030 from La Balsa, US$7.50.

⊖ Transport

Vilcabamba *p968, map p969*
Loja to Vilcabamba, a spectacular 1½-hour bus ride; from Loja's Terminal Terrestre, Vilcabambaturis vans and mini-buses, every 15 min, 0545-2045, US$1, 1 hr; or *taxirutas* (shared taxis) from La Tebaida, south of the centre, near Av Iberoamérica y Chile, US$1.20, 45 min. Taxi from/to Loja US$15.

To **Zumba** via Vilcabamba, with 4 companies, several daily (1st at 0500), 6-7 hrs, US$5-7, shop around. First from Vilcabamba 0700, same fare, 5-6 hrs. If the road is dry and passable, **Trans**

⊕ Directory

Vilcabamba *p968, map p969*
Banks There are no banks, ATMs or places to exchange TCs in Vilcabamba. **Internet** US$1.20 per hr, **Mandango**, at the hostel, 0900-2100. **Language schools** La Cumbre, Juan Montalvo 07-36 y José David Toledo, T264 0283, www.cumbrevilcabamba.com. Spanish lessons, 1 to 1 US$8 per hr, 2 students US$6 pp, per hr, 3-10, US$4.50 pp, per hr. Also German lessons. **Telephones** Pacifictel, Bolívar y Diego Vaca de Vega, near the park, but due to move to Sucre y Clodoveo Jaramillo.

Guayaquil and south to Peru

→ *Phone code: 04. Colour map 11, grid B2. Population: 2,000,000. Altitude: sea level.*

Guayaquil is hotter, faster and brasher than the capital. It is Ecuador's largest city and the country's chief seaport; an industrial and commercial centre, some 56 km from the Río Guayas' outflow into the Gulf of Guayaquil. Founded in 1535 by Sebastián de Benalcázar, then again in 1537 by Francisco Orellana, the city has always been an intense political rival to Quito. Guayaquileños are certainly more lively, colourful and open than their Quito counterparts. Since the late 1990s there have been organized movements for autonomy of Ecuador's coastal provinces, spearheaded by Guayaquil, and since 2000, Guayaquil has been working hard to attract more tourism. The Puerto Marítimo handles three-quarters of the country's imports and almost half of its exports. Industrial expansion continually fuels the city's growth.

Thriving and ever increasing banana plantations, with shrimp farms among the mangroves, are the economic mainstay of the coastal area bordering the east flank of the Gulf of Guayaquil. Rice, sugar, coffee and cacao are also produced. The Guayas lowlands are subject to flooding, humidity is high and biting insects are fierce. Mangroves characterize the coast leading south to Huaquillas, the main border crossing to Peru.

Ins and outs

Getting there Simón Bolívar International **airport** is 10 minutes north of the city centre by taxi (recommended for safety, US$3-4). US$0.25 by bus; No 2 to Malecón, No 69 to Plaza Victoria, but buses are neither safe nor practical with luggage. If going straight on to another city, get a cab directly to the **Terminal Terrestre** (bus station), which is close by; a taxi from the airport to the bus terminal is US$2. If you are arriving in Guayaquil and need a taxi from the airport, walk ½ block from the terminal out to Avenida Las Américas, where taxis and camionetas wait for passengers and charge about half the fare of the airport taxi cooperative, but not recommended at night. A great many local buses go from the bus terminal to the city centre. Taxi fare US$3-4. ▶▶ *For more detailed information see Transport, page 979.*

Getting around Because of traffic congestion, it is often quicker to walk short distances in the centre, rather than take a bus or taxi (but don't walk after dark). Public transport is essential for getting to the airport and bus station and to the northern residential and restaurant districts. Fare on city buses is US$0.25; also minibuses (*furgonetas*), US$0.25, which post up their routes in the windscreen. Buses are only permitted in a few streets in the centre; northbound buses go along the Malecón and on Rumichaca, southbound along Boyacá. Bus No 15 from the centre to Urdesa, 13 to Policentro, 14 to Albanborja, 74 to La Garzota and Sauces. Taxis have

❶ Bars and clubs

Esmeraldas *p994*
El Portón, Colón y Piedrahita. *Peña* and disco.
El Guadal de Ña Mencha, 6 de Diciembre y
Quito. *Peña* upstairs, marimba school at
weekends; good.

❷ Transport

Muisne *p994*
Bus All buses go from El Relleno, across
the Río Muisne. To/from **Esmeraldas** every 30
mins, US$2.50, 2 hrs. There are 2 direct buses to
Quito at night. For **Pedernales**, take a bus to **El
Salto**, US$0.50, 30 mins, on the Esmeraldas road,
from where there are buses going south to
Chamanga, US$1.50, 1½ hrs, where you change
again for Pedernales, US$1.60, 1½ hrs. At 0600
there is a direct bus Muisne-Chamanga.

North to Atacames *p994*
Bus To **Playa Escondida**: take a ranchera or bus
from Esmeraldas for Punta Galera, 5 a day, US$2, 2
hrs. A taxi from Atacames costs US$12 and a
pick-up from Tonchigüe US$5. To **Súa** and **Same**:
Buses every 30 mins to and from **Atacames; La
Costeñita**, 15 mins, 18 km, US$0.35. Make sure it
drops you at Same and not at Club Casablanca. To
Muisne, US$0.60, 30 mins.

Atacames *p994*
Bus To/from **Esmeraldas**, every 15 mins,
US$0.80, 40 mins; to **Guayaquil**, US$8, 8 hrs.
To **Quito**, 3 daily, US$8, 6½ hrs.

Esmeraldas *p994*
Air Gen Rivadeneira Airport is on the road to La
Tola. Taxi to centre, 30 km, about US$6, buses to
the Terminal Terrestre from the road outside the
airport pass about every 30 mins. Daily flights
except Wed, Sat to **Quito** with TAME (Bolívar
y 9 de Octubre, T272 6863), 30 mins, US$40.
Check in early, planes may leave 30 mins
before scheduled time.
Bus To **Quito** and **Guayaquil** there is *servicio
directo* or *ejecutivo*, a better choice as they are
faster buses and don't stop for passengers. To
Quito, US$7, 6 hrs, via Santo Domingo, frequent
service on a good paved road, with
Trans-Esmeraldas (10 de Agosto y Sucre, at main
park, recommended), **Occidental** (9 de Octubre y
Olmedo) and **Aerotaxi** (near the main park); also

with **Panamericana** (Colón y Piedrahita) twice
daily, slow but luxurious. To **Ibarra**, 8½ hrs,
US$9.50, via Borbón and San Lorenzo, **Flota
Imbabura**. To **Santo Domingo**, US$3.50, 3 hrs.
To **Ambato**, 5 a day with *Coop* Sudamericana,
US$8, 8 hrs. To **Guayaquil**, hourly, US$8.50,
directo, 8 hrs. To **Bahía de Caráquez**, via Santo
Domingo de los Colorados, US$8, 8 hrs. To
Manta, US$8, 10 hrs. La Costeñita (Malecón y 10
de Agosto) to/ from **La Tola** 7 daily, US$3, 3 hrs. To
Borbón, frequent service, US$3, 3 hrs. To **San
Lorenzo**, 8 daily, US$4, 4 hrs. To **Muisne**, see
above. To **Súa**, **Same** and **Atacames**, every 15
mins from 0630-2030, to Atacames US$0.80, 1 hr.

Limones *p995*
Ferry There are launches between **La Tola** and
Limones every 1½ hrs, US$3, 1 hr, and 3 daily
Limones-**San Lorenzo**, 1 hr US$3. A hired launch
provides a fascinating trip through mangrove
islands, passing hundreds of hunting pelicans;
US$10 per hr. From Limones you can also get a
canoe or boat to **Borbón**. Launches between La
Tola and Limones connect with buses to/from
Esmeraldas.

Inland from Limones: Borbón *p995*
Bus To/from **Esmeraldas**: frequent service,
US$3, 3 hrs.
Ferry 4 motor launches a day run to different
communities upriver, leaving 1030-1200. Check
how far each one is going as only the 1st one to
leave goes as far as **San Miguel**.

San Lorenzo *p995*
Bus To **Ibarra**, 10 daily, 4 hrs, US$4. They leave
from the train station or near *Hotel San Carlos*. To
Esmeraldas, via Borbón, 8 daily, US$4, 3 hrs.
Ferry Two companies that offer launch service
are Coopseturi, Calle Imbabura, T/F278 0161;
and Costeñita, on the same street. All services
are subject to change and cancellation. To
Limones, 3 daily, 2 hrs, US$3. To **La Tola**,
US$6, 4 hrs. To **Palma Real**, for beaches,
2 daily, US$3, 3 hrs.

❸ Directory

Esmeraldas *p994*
Banks Banco de Guayaquil, Bolívar y
Rocafuerte. Banco del Pichincha, Bolívar y
9 de Octubre. **Internet** Many in town.

The Oriente

East of the Andes the hills fall away to tropical lowlands, sparsely populated with indigenous settlements along the tributaries of the Amazon. Agricultural colonists have cleared parts of the forest for cattle rearing, while even more isolated areas are major oil producers, leading to the gradual encroachment of towns into the jungle.

The Oriente is currently at a crossroads. Ecuador's ever-increasing demand for land and resources must be weighed against the region's irreplaceable biodiversity and traditional ways of life. Yet the majority of this beautiful green wilderness, comprising the provinces of Sucumbíos, Orellana and Napo in the north, Pastaza in the centre, Morona Santiago and Zamora Chinchipe in the south, remains unspoiled and unexplored. Fortunately for the tourist, it is relatively accessible.

Ins and outs

Getting there Ecuador's eastern tropical lowlands can be reached by several road routes, from Quito, Ambato, Riobamba, Azogues, Cuenca or Loja. Apart from 3 km around the Papallacta bypass, Quito to Baeza is paved; from Baeza the route to Tena is half paved, likewise Tena to Puyo. Baños to Puyo and Loja to Zamora are fully paved. Otherwise roads are narrow and tortuous and subject to landslides in the rainy season, but all have regular, if poor bus services and all can be attempted in a jeep or in an ordinary car with good ground clearance. Several of the towns and villages on the roads can be reached by air services from Quito, and places further into the immense Amazonian forests are generally accessible by river canoe or small aircraft from Shell or Macas. The latest road, from Guamote, south of Riobamba, to Macas is complete, but remains controversial due to its impact on Parque Nacional Sangay. Finally, a road runs from Tulcán to Lago Agrio, a short trip but very close to the Colombian border and therefore unsafe.

Jungle tours These fall into three basic types: **lodges**; **guided tours** and **indigenous ecotourism**. When staying at a jungle lodge (normally a *cabaña* complex located in a natural setting), you will need to take a torch, insect repellent, protection against the sun and a rain poncho that will keep you dry when walking and when sitting in a canoe. Rubber boots can be hired. See also Jungle lodges on the Lower Napo, below. **Guided tours** of varying length are offered by tour operators, river cruise companies and independent guides. These should be licensed by the Ecuadorean **Ministerio de Turismo**. Tour operators and guides are mainly concentrated in Quito, Baños, Lago Agrío, Coca, Puyo, Tena and Misahuallí. A number of indigenous communities and families offer **ecotourism** programmes on their properties. These are either community-controlled and operated, or organized as joint ventures between the indigenous community or family and a non-indigenous partner. These programmes usually involve guides who are licensed by the Ministerio de Turismo as *guías nativos* with the right to guide within their communities. Though economically attractive, touring without a local, knowledgeable guide is not encouraged: from an ecotourist perspective, it does not contribute adequately to the local economy and to intercultural understanding and it may be environmentally damaging. Furthermore, it involves a greater risk of accident or injury. Moreover, a guide is obligatory in national parks and reserves.

Safety There are frequent military checks in the Oriente, so always have your passport handy. The Ecuadorean Amazon has traditionally been safe and peaceful and the few incidents which have taken place mostly involved foreign oil workers rather than tourists. A heavily armed holdup of tourists did take place in Cuyabeno national park in late 2005, but agencies operating in the area have changed their routes. Baeza, Tena, Misahuallí, Puyo and their surroundings, as well as jungle areas to the south, have experienced no difficulties. The northern Oriente, however, is at risk of being affected by conflict in neighbouring Colombia. Always enquire about public safety before visiting remote sites, particularly north of the Río Napo, and avoid areas immediately adjacent to the Colombian border. **Health:** Yellow fever vaccine and anti-malaria precautions (tablets, net and effective repellent) are recommended for all visitors.

Northern Oriente

Much of the Northern Oriente is taken up by the Parque Nacional Yasuní, the Cuyabeno Wildlife Reserve and most of the Cayambe-Coca Ecological Reserve. The main towns for access are Lago Agrio and Coca.

Quito to the Oriente

From Quito, through Pifo, to Baeza, the road is almost entirely paved via the Papallacta pass (4,064 m) and the turn to the Papallacta hot springs. It crosses the Eastern Cordillera at the pass, just north of **Volcán Antisana** (5,705 m), and then descends via the small villages of Papallacta (see page 913) and Cuyuja to the old mission settlements of Baeza and Borja. The trip between the pass and Baeza has beautiful views of Antisana (clouds permitting), high waterfalls, tropical mountain jungle, *páramo* and a lake contained by an old lava flow. **Antisana** gets vast quantities of snow and is very difficult to climb, experience is essential.

Baeza

The mountainous landscape and high rainfall have created spectacular waterfalls and dense vegetation. Because of the climate, orchids and bromeliads abound. Baeza, in the beautiful setting of the Quijos pass, is about 1 km from the main junction of the Lago Agrio and Tena roads. Get off the Lago Agrio bus at the petrol station and walk up the hill; the Tena bus goes through the town. Baeza Colonial (Old Baeza) is being replaced by Andalucía (New Baeza), where the post office and *Andinatel* are located. There are many hiking trails in this region which generally can be done without a guide.

Beyond Baeza

At Baeza the road divides. One branch heads south to Tena, with a branch road going directly via Loreto to Coca (seven hours). The other goes northeast to Lago Agrio, following the Río Quijos past the villages of **Borja**, a few kilometres from Baeza, and **El Chaco** (cabins on the edge of town and excellent food at the restaurant on the road) to the slopes of the still active volcano **Reventador**, 3,560 m (the area is not safe for climbing or trekking). At the village of Reventador there is a basic *Pensión de los Andes* and a restaurant.

The road winds along the north side of the river, past the impressive 145-m **San Rafael Falls**, believed to be the highest in Ecuador. To get to the falls take a Quito-Baeza-Lago Agrio bus. About two to three hours past Baeza, look for a covered bus stop and a disused construction camp. It's an easy 1½-hour round trip to the falls through cloudforest. A trail to the bottom of the falls is steep and slippery. Many birds can be spotted along the trail, including Cock-of-the-Rock, and there are swimming holes and waterfalls near a new *hostería*, **El Hotelito**.

Lago Agrio → *Phone code: 06 Colour map 11, grid A5 Population: 34,000.*

The capital of Sucumbíos is primarily an oil town with improving infrastructure and sanitation. The name comes from Sour Lake, the US headquarters of Texaco, the first oil company to exploit the Ecuadorean Amazon, but the town's official name is Nueva Loja.

Lago Agrio is among the places in Ecuador which has been most affected by the conflict in neighbouring Colombia. Although there is a border crossing to Colombia north of Lago Agrio, it is very dangerous. **You should not enter this area owing to the presence of guerrillas and paramilitaries.** As well as violence, the area is threatened by the spraying of broad-spectrum herbicides to destroy coca plantations across the border. Seek local advice from **Cámara de Turismo de Sucumbíos**, Av Quito y Pasaje Gonzanamá, T283 2502.

Cuyabeno Wildlife Reserve

US$20. Down the Aguarico from Lago Agrio is an extensive jungle river area on the Río Cuyabeno, which drains eventually into the Aguarico 150 km to the east. In the national park there are many lagoons and abundant wildlife. Transport is mainly by canoe and motorboat, except for one road to Río Cuyabeno, three hours by truck from Lago Agrio. Tourist pressure has been heavy in Cuyabeno and it is becoming increasingly rare to see many animals close to the big lake. Many agencies offer trips and most take up to 12 in a group (which is too many). If your aim is to see animals, then look for a smaller tour (maximum eight people) which keeps away from the most heavily visited areas and adheres to responsible practices. As in Coca, it is very difficult to find a cheap tour in Lago Agrio.

Coca → Phone code: 06. Colour map 11, grid A5. Population: 19,000.

Officially named **Puerto Francisco de Orellana**, Coca is a hot, dusty oil town at the junction of the Ríos Coca and Napo. It is the capital of the province of Orellana and is a launch pad from where to visit more exciting jungle parts. The view over the water is nice, and the riverfront can be a pleasant place to spend time around sunset. As a tourist centre, however, Coca offers few attractions other than being closer to undisturbed primary rainforest than the main jungle towns further west. Considering its relative isolation, food and supplies are not that expensive.

Jungle tours from Coca Most of the Coca region is taken up by the **Parque Nacional Yasuní** and **Reserva Huaorani**. This area is unsuited to tours of less than three days owing to the remoteness of its main attractions. Shorter visits of 3-4 days are worthwhile in the Coca-Yuturi segment of the Río Napo, where the lodges are concentrated. Tours to the park and reserve really need a minimum of five days. Wildlife in this area is under threat: insist that guides and the party take all litter back and ban all hunting and shooting; it really can make a difference.

A common misconception is that it is always easy to find a cheap tour in Coca . For people travelling alone in the low season (especially February to May) it is difficult to find a big enough group to get a bargain rate. Most jungle tours out of Coca cost US$40-60 per person per day. Furthermore, you should beware of cut-rate operators who may compromise on safety or quality. The cheaper the tour, the larger the group is likely to be. Maximum group size should not exceed 8. Check what precisely is being offered and that the price includes items such as rubber boots, tents, mosquito nets, cooking equipment and food, and transport. For a trip of any length take suitable footwear (rubber boots, or two pairs of light shoes – keep one pair dry), light sleeping bag, rain jacket, trousers (not shorts), binoculars, insect repellent, sunscreen, water-purifying tablets, sticking plasters. Wrap everything in plastic bags. **South American Explorers** provides updated information on how to arrange your trip. **Note:** If a guide offers a tour to visit the Huaorani, ask to see his/her permission to do so. The only guides permitted to take tourists into Huaorani territory are those who have made agreements with the Huaorani organization *ONHAE*.

Coca to Nuevo Rocafuerte and Iquitos

Pañacocha is halfway between Coca and Nuevo Rocafuerte, near the magnificent lagoon of Pañacocha on the Río Panayacu. This has been declared a protected forest region. Several agencies and guides run tours from Coca (see Tour operators). Basic local accommodation is available in Pañacocha.

Following the Río Napo to Peru is rough, adventurous and requires plenty of patience. Talk of introducing tourist boats on this route has, as yet (June 2006), come to nothing. A motorized canoe service from Coca goes to **Nuevo Rocafuerte** on the border. See Transport, page 1005. Nuevo Rocafuerte has one basic hotel with a dormitory, and equally basic options for eating. There is an Ecuadorean immigration office for exit stamps and boats can be hired for the 2-hour trip down river to the Peruvian border town of **Pantoja**, US$60 per boat, try to share the ride. Peruvian entry stamps are given in Pantoja and, although there is no hotel, you can arrange to stay with a family for a small charge. In addition to immigration, you may have to register with the navy on either side of the border so have your passport at hand.

● Sleeping

Baeza *p1000*
D Casa Bambú, in the New City. Cheaper with shared bath, hot water, OK.
D Mesón de Baeza, on the plaza in the Old City. Shared bath, electric shower, popular with kayakers.
E Hostal San Rafael, in the New City, T232 0144. With bath, hot water, spacious, helpful, parking. Recommended.

E-F Samay, in the New City. Shared bath, electric shower, basic.

Around Baeza
LL Cabañas San Isidro, in the Cosanga Valley, reservations necessary: T02-254 7403, www.ecuadorexplorer.com/sanisidro. Price includes 3 excellent meals. This is a 1,200 ha private reserve with rich bird life, comfortable

accommodation, private bath, hot water and warm hospitality, reservation required. Recommended.

C The Magic Roundabout, 12 km south of Baeza, T09-934 5264, www.themagicround about.org. Cabins or cheaper dorm, includes good breakfast and supper, shared bath, horse riding available, British-Ecuadorean run, "the only English pub for miles".

Lago Agrio *p1000*
Virtually everything can be found on the main street, Av Quito.

AL-A Arazá, Quito 610 y Narváez, T283 0223, arazahot@uio.satnet.net. Includes breakfast, restaurant, a/c, secure, best in town. Recommended.

B El Cofán, 12 de Febrero 2-12 y Av Quito, T283 0526, F283 2409. Includes breakfast, restaurant, a/c, fridge, parking, well cared-for and nice.

B Gran Hotel de Lago, Km 1½ Vía Quito, T283 2415. Includes breakfast, restaurant, pool, internet, cabins, nice gardens, quiet. Recommended.

C Gran Colombia, Quito y Pasaje Gonzanamá, T283 1032, F283 1031. Restaurant, a/c, cheaper with fan and cold water, parking, convenient location.

C D'Mario, Quito 171, T283 0172, F283 0456. Restaurant, a/c, cheaper with fan, central, a meeting place. Recommended.

D Lago Imperial, Colombia y Quito, T283 0453. A/c cheaper with fan, convenient, good value.

D Machala 2, Colombia entre Quito y Añazco, T283 0673. Good restaurant, cold water, fan, parking, safe.

E Americano, Quito 118 y Colombia, T283 0555. With bath, cold water, fan, small rooms but good value.

E Casa Blanca, Quito y Colombia, T283 0181. With bath, hot water, fan, nice bright rooms, good value.

Coca *p1001*
Many hotels and *residencias* are populated by oil workers and range from basic to barely habitable.

A-C El Auca, Napo entre Rocafurte y García Moreno, T288 0600, www.interactive.net.ec/ hotel-auca. A/c, cheaper with fan, hot water, comfortable, big garden with hammocks, manager speaks English, good meeting place to make up a tour party, restaurant and disco.

B La Misión, by riverfront, T288 0260, F288 0263. A/c, English spoken, internet, pool, restaurant and disco, arranges tours. Recommended.

B Puerto Orellana, Av Alejandro Labaka, at the entrance to town from Lago Agrio, T288 0129, jesseniabrito@andinanet.net. Electric shower, a/c, parking, out of the way but modern and very nice. Popular, best book in advance.

B-C Amazonas, 12 de Febrero y Espejo, T288 0444. Nice relaxed setting by the river, away from centre, restaurant, a/c, cheaper with fan, parking, quiet, good.

C-D San Fermín, Bolívar Y Quito, T288 0802. A/c, cheaper with fan and cold water, parking, modern and comfortable, good value.

D Coca, Inés Arango entre Cuenca y Rocafuerte, T288 1841. Cold water, fan, parking, modern and nice.

D-E Oasis, between the bridge and La Misión, T288 0206. Electric shower, fan, parking, quiet, simple but adequate.

Lodges on the lower Río Napo *p1001*
All Napo area lodges count travel days as part of their package, which means that often a "3-day tour" spends only one day actually in the forest. Also, the return trip must start before dawn if it is

to connect with that day's Coca-Quito flight; if it starts later it will be necessary to spend the night in Coca. Most lodges have fixed departure days from Coca (eg Mon and Fri) and it is very expensive to get a special departure on another day.

Bataburo, a lodge near Parque Nacional Yasuní is on the Río Tigüino, a 3-6 hr canoe ride from the end of the Vía Auca out of Coca. Quito office: **Kempery Tours**, see Quito Tour operators, page 903. Some cabins have private baths, others share showers. There are shared shower facilities. Guides are mostly local people. The birds here have been little studied but macaws and other large species are present. The mammal population also appears to be quite good. Prices are US$230 for 5 days/4 nights.

Napo Wildlife Center, for information contact Norby López, Quito T02-289 7316, www.napo wildlifecenter.com. Operated by and for the local Añangu community, across the Río Napo from La Selva, 2½ hrs downstream from Coca. This area of hilly forest is rather different from the low flat forest of some other sites, and the diversity is slightly higher. There are big caimans, good mammals, including giant otters, and the birding is excellent. The local guide, Giovanny Rivadeneyra, is one of the most knowledgeable birders in the Oriente.

La Selva, Quito office: San Salvador E7-85 y Martín Carrión, T02-255 0995, www.laselvajungle lodge.com. An upmarket lodge 2½ hrs downstream from Coca, professionally run, on a picturesque lake surrounded by excellent forest (especially on the far side of Mandicocha). Bird and animal life is exceptionally diverse. Many species of monkey are seen regularly. A total of 580 bird species can be found here, one of the highest totals in the world for a site at a single elevation, and some of the local guides (eg José) are very good at finding them. There is a biological station on the grounds (the Neotropical Field Biology Institute) as well as a butterfly farm. Cabins have private bathrooms and hot water. Meals are excellent. Usually the guides are biologists, and in general the guiding is of very high quality. A new canopy tower was built in 2004. Four-night packages from Quito including all transport, lodging, and food, cost US$756 pp.

Sacha, Quito office, Julio Zaldumbide 375 y Valladolid, T02-256 6090, www.sachalodge.com. Another upmarket lodge close to La Selva, 2½ hrs downstream from Coca, in a 5000-acre private reserve. Comfortable cabins with private bath and hot water, excellent meals. The bird list is outstanding, and they have a local bird expert,

Oscar Tapuy (T06-288 1486), who can be requested in advance by birders. Guides are generally knowledgeable. Boardwalks through swamp habitats allow access to some species that are difficult to see at other lodges, and nearby river islands provide another distinct habitat. They also have a butterfly farm and a canopy tower, and a self-standing rigid suspension canopy walk, believed the be the first of its kind anywhere. Several species of monkey are commonly seen. A 5-day package costs US$750 pp, excluding flight from Quito.
Sani, Quito office: Roca 736 y Amazonas, Pasaje Chantilly, T02-255 8881, www.sanilodge.com. Also near *La Selva*. All proceeds go to the Sani Isla community, who run the lodge with outside help. It is on a remote lagoon which contains 4-5 m long black caiman. This area is rich in wildlife and birds, including many species such as the Scarlet Macaw which have disappeared from most other Napo area lodges. There is good accommodation and a canopy tower. The lodge is accessible to people who have difficulty walking as it can be reached by canoe (total 4 hrs from Coca) without a walk. 5 days/4 nights costs US$493, good value.
Yuturi Forest Lodge, 4 hrs downstream from Coca. Quito office: Amazonas N24-240 y Colón, T/F250 4037, www.yuturilodge.com. Birdwatching is excellent, and there are some species (eg Black-necked Red Cotinga) that are difficult to find at other lodges. There is a wide variety of habitats and wildlife is good. The guides are usually local people accompanied by translators. 4 nights cost US$350, exclusive of airfare. Visits can be combined with **Yarina**, the closest lodge to Coca, about 1 hr down the Napo. Thatched roof cabins and a 40-ft canopy tower (4 days/3 nights US$200).

On the Río Pastaza (accessed from Coca)
Kapawi Ecological Reserve is a top-of- the-line jungle lodge located on the Río Pastaza in the heart of Achuar territory. Operated by **Canodros**, Guayaquil, T04-228 5711, www.kapawi.com. Or book through agencies in Quito or abroad. It is accessible only by small aircraft and motor canoe. The lodge was built in partnership with the indigenous organization OINAE and offers flexible programmes. It is also built according to the Achuar concept of architecture, using typical materials, and emphasizes environmentally friendly methods such as solar energy, bio-degradable soaps and rubbish recycling. It is in a zone rich in biodiversity, with many opportunities for seeing the forest and its inhabitants. 4 nights in a double cabin costs US$835, plus US$200 for transport to and from Quito. The location, quality of service, cabin accommodation and food have all been highly recommended.

⊘ Eating

Baeza *p1000*
🍴 **Gina**, the best restaurant, cheap, great trout.
🍴 **El Viejo**, next to *Hostal San Rafael*. A good place to eat.

Coca *p1001*
There are good restaurants at the larger hotels (see above). There are also many cheap *comedores*.
🍴🍴 **El Portón**, Bolívar y Quito. Expensive grill.
🍴🍴 **Parrilladas Argentinas**, Cuenca y Amazonas. Argentine-style grill.
🍴🍴-🍴 **Pizza Choza**, Rocafuerte y Napo. Good pizza, friendly service, English spoken. Daily 1700-2200.
🍴 **Media Noche**, Napo, in front of *Hotel El Auca*. Cheap chicken dishes.
🍴 **Ocaso**, Eloy Alfaro between Napo and Amazonas. Good set meals and à la carte

▲ Activities and tours

Cuyabeno Wildlife Reserve *p1000*
To visit Cuyabeno it is best to shop around in Quito, as few operators have offices in Lago Agrio (see Quito Tour operators, page 903). Some agencies can be found on C Quito in Lago Agrio. The following have been recommended for jungle trips to Cuyabeno:
Dracaena, Pinto 446 y Amazonas, Quito, T02-254 6590, dracaena@andinanet.net. Popular agency.
Ecuador Verde País, Calama E6-19 y Reina Victoria, T02-222 0614, www.cabanasjamu.com. Run *Jamu Lodge* in Cuyabeno, good service, 4 days/3 nights US$180 pp, plus transport and park fees, starting in the village of Cuyabeno.
Green Planet, see page 903.
Kapok Expeditions, see page 903.
Neotropic Turis, Av Amazonas N24-03 y Wilson, Quito, T02-252 1212, www.neotropicturis.com. Operate the *Cuyabeno Lodge*; US$295 pp for 4 days and 3 nights (including meals, guides – who speak English – but not transport to and from Lago Agrio and park fee).

Coca *p1001*
Jungle tours from Coca
Wymper Torres, T288 0336, ronoboa@ latinmail.com. He specializes in the Río Shiripuno and Pañacocha areas, Spanish only.

Tour operators in Quito *see also p903*
Almost all Quito agencies offer tours out of Coca. **Emerald Forest Expeditions**, Pinto E4-244 y Amazonas, T09-730 1413, www.emeraldexped itions.com. Guide Luis Alberto García has many years experience, speaks English, and runs tours to Pañacocha area (insist on him being your guide).

Kempery offers good 4 to 15-day tours to Huaorani villages.
Tropic Ecological Adventures runs ecologically-sound tours with local and bilingual naturalist guides, and works closely with Cofan, Secoya and Huaorani communities.

⊖ Transport

Baeza *p1000*
Bus Many to **Tena** (see below) and **Coca**, best to board the bus at the market, although you may be lucky waiting outside the *Hostal San Rafael* if the bus is not full. Buses to **Quito** go from the Old Baeza, near the former *Hotel Jumandí*, now the Registro de Propriedad.

Lago Agrio *p1000*
Air TAME and Icaro flights to **Quito** (not Sun), book 1-2 days in advance, US$51 one way.
Bus *Terminal terrestre* is north of town, but buses for Coca leave from the market area on Orellana, 3 blocks south of Av Quito. To **Quito**, US$7.50, 11 hrs. **Baeza**, US$8.70, 7 hrs. **Coca**, US$3, 2 hrs. To **Tena**, US$11, 9 hrs.

Coca *p1001*
Air Flights to **Quito** with Icaro (office in *Hotel La Misión*, T288 0546) and TAME (T288 1078), US$51, 2-3 daily, reserve as far in advance as possible, flights in and out of Coca are heavily booked, military and oil workers have priority on standby.
Bus Long distance buses depart from company offices in town; local destinations, including Lago Agrio, are served from the terminal, a 20-min walk north from *Hotel Auca* (ask to be let off in town). To **Quito**, 8 hrs, US$10, several daily 1030-2200, **Trans Baños, Trans Esmeraldas** and **Zaracay** depart from their offices near junction of Napo y Cuenca. To **Lago Agrio**, see above. To **Tena**, 6 hrs, US$7. To **Baeza**, US$7.50, 8 hrs. To **Baños**, US$11, 11 hrs.

Ferry To **Nuevo Rocafuerte** on the Peruvian border, motorized canoes go Mon, Tue, Thu before 0800, 10-12 hrs, US$15, stopping on route at **Pompeya** and **Pañacocha**. Contact Cooperativa Transporte Fluvial Orellana, T06-288 0087.

Departure dates of boats from **Pantoja** to **Iquitos** are irregular. Four *lanchas* operate the route, but they only come upriver as far as Pantoja when they have sufficient cargo, so several weeks can go by without any boat calling on the town. Try calling Iquitos in advance, to inquire when the next boat will sail from Pantoja: T+51-65-242082 for the **Victor** and the **Camila**, or T+51-65-266159, 51-65-9613049 (mob) for the **Jeisawell** and the **Siempre Adelante**. They have no berths, only deck space to hang your hammock and are very unsanitary by the end of the trip. The 5-7 day trip from Pantoja all the way to Iquitos costs US$30 including very basic food, but it may be possible to pick up faster transport at **Santa Clotilde**, about half way to Iquitos, or **Mazán**. Take a hammock, cup, bowl, cutlery, extra food and snacks, drinking water or purification, insect repellent, toilet paper, soap, towel, etc. Cash dollars and soles in small notes are indispensable, but soles cannot be purchased in Coca.

⊖ Directory

Lago Agrio *p1000*
Banks Impossible to change TCs or use credit cards take US$ cash.
Coca *p1001*
Banks Casa de Cambio, Napo y García Moreno, commission charged on TCs. Banco de Pichincha, Bolívar y 9 de Octubre, Visa cash advances only. Banks won't change TCs.
Immigration Rocafuerte y Napo, Edificio Amazonas, p 3, 0730-1230, 1500-1800.
Internet Prices around US$2 per hr.

Central and southern Oriente

Quito and Baños are the starting points for the cental Oriente. To the south, in addition to the roads from Cuenca and Zamora, there are new routes leading down from the Sierra, from Riobamba and Azogues . There are many different options for visiting the jungle here.

Archidona → *Phone code: 06. Colour map 11, grid B4. Population: 4,200.*
Roads from both Baeza and Coca go south to Archidona, 65 km from Baeza. It has a striking, small painted church and not much else but there are some excellent trips in the surrounding area. The road leaving Archidona's plaza to the east goes to the village of San Pablo, and beyond to the Río Hollín. Along this road, 7 km from Archidona, is the **Reserva Ecológica Monteverde** ① *entry for day visits US$2*, a 25 ha reserve with primary and secondary forest, and medicinal plants. There are walking trails, river bathing, fishing,

Puyo *p1007*

A-B Hostería Safari, outside town at Km 5 on the road to Tena, T288 5465. Includes break- fast and dinner, ample grounds, peaceful.

B Hostería Turingia, Ceslao Marín 294, T288 5180, www.hosteriaturingia.com. Restaurant, fan, small pool, parking, comfortable, nice garden.

D Gran Hotel Amazónico, Ceslao Marín y Atahualpa, T288 3094, F288 4753. Small rooms, fan, includes breakfast, restaurant downstairs.

D Hostal El Colibrí, C Manabí entre Bolívar y Galápagos, T288 3054, cascadayanarumi@ yahoo.es. Away from centre, cold water, parking, modern, good value. Recommended.

D Libertad, Francisco de Orellana opposite the Coliseo Municipal, T288 3282. Restaurant, electric shower, parking, basic but clean and good value.

D-E El Araucano, Ceslao Marín 576, T288 5686, F288 3834. Restaurant, fan, many different types of rooms at various prices, ranging from simple to basic.

E Chasi, 9 de Octubre y Orellana, T288 3059. Cold water, basic.

Shell *p1007*

D Los Copales, west of Shell on the road to Baños, T279 5290. Comfortable cabins with electric shower, restaurant.

D Germany Hostal, on a side street, T279 5134. Cabins are set in nice gardens, main entry is down side street or though restaurant on main street, hot water, family run.

D-E Esmeraldita, on main road, T279 5133. Restaurant, cheaper with shared bath, simple but clean.

E-F Azuay, on main road, T279 5574. Restaurant, cheaper with shared bath, simple but adequate.

Macas *p1007*

AL Cabañas Ecológicas Yuquipa, a 3-km walk from Km 12 on the road to Puyo, T270 0071. Includes breakfast, restaurant, minimum 3 days' stay. Package includes accommodation, guides, meals and transport. Contact *Pancesa* bakery at Soasti y 10 de Agosto.

B-C Manzana Real, at southern entrance to town, T270 0191. Includes breakfast in more expensive rooms, restaurant, pool, parking, suite available.

D California, 29 de Mayo at south end of town, T/F270 1237. Cheaper with shared bath, electric shower, some rooms have fan, parking, modern.

D Casa Blanca, Soasti 14-29 y Sucre, T270 0195, F270 1584. Includes breakfast, comfortable, very helpful. Recommended, book in advance.

D La Orquídea, 9 de Octubre 13-05 y Sucre, T270 0970. Cheaper with cold water, quiet.

D Milenium, Amazonas y Tarqui, T270 0805. Cheaper with shared bath, small modern rooms,

bottled water and coffee on tap on small terrace, good value.

D-E Esplendit, Soasti 1518 y D Comín, T270 0120. Cheaper with shared bath, parking, new section is nice and comfortable, older rooms cheap and basic. Parking, modern.

F Residencial Macas, 24 de Mayo 14-35 y Sucre, T270 0254. Above *Restaurante Chaplin* (good set meals), cheaper with shared bath, cold water, old wooden building, simple, good value.

Sucúa *p1007*

C Arutam, Vía a Macas Km 1, north of town, T274 0851. Restaurant, pool and spa, modern and comfortable, very nice.

D Don Guimo, Domingo Comín y Kiruba, T/F274 0483. Includes breakfast, cheaper with shared bath, hot water, parking, modern and comfortable. Recommended.

E Karina, on the southwest corner of the plaza, T274 0153. Cheaper with shared bath, hot water, bright.

Sucúa to Zamora *p1008*
Méndez

D Interoceanico, C Quito on the plaza, T276 0245, F276 0082. Modern, good value, best in town, parking.

D-E Hostal Los Ceibos, C Cuenca 1 block west of the plaza, T276 0133. Cheaper with shared bath, modern, small rooms.

E Los Sauces, C Cuenca 1 block west of the plaza, T276 0165. Cheaper with shared bath, hot water, rooms are small but OK.

Limón

D-E Residencial Dianita, C Quito, T277 0122. Cheaper with shared bath, cold water, basic.

E Limón, C Quito, T277 0114. Shared bath, cold water, basic, front rooms noisy.

F pp Dream House, Quito y Bolívar, T277 0166. New, with shared bathrooms.

Gualaquiza

D Internacional, C Cuenca y García Moreno, T278 0637, F278 0781. Restaurant, cheaper with cold water, most rooms have fan, best in town.

E Guadalupe, Gonzalo Pesántez 8-16 y García Moreno, T278 0113. Cheaper with shared bath, cold water, indoor parking, simple, popular, good value.

E Wakis, Orellana 08-52 y Domingo Comín, T278 0138. *Aroma Café* downstairs, cheaper with shared bath, cold water, small rooms, enthusiastic owner Antonio Quezada speaks English and organizes tours.

F Amazonas, Domingo Comín 08-65 y Gonzalo Pesantes, on main plaza, T278 0715. Shared bath, cold water, basic.

🍴 Eating

Archidona *p1005*
There are few decent places to eat, though **Restaurant Los Pinos**, near *Res Regina*, is good.

Tena *p1006*
There are several *chifas* in town.
🍴 **Chuquitos**, García Moreno by Plaza. Popular, good food, à la carte only, on a balcony overlooking the river.
🍴 **Pizzería La Massilia**, Malecón y 9 de Octubre, by the river, open from 1700 onwards. Really nice pizza.
🍴 **Cositas Ricas**, 15 de Noviembre, next to *Traveller's Lodging*. Tasty meals, vegetarian available, good fruit juices, also has new, upscale a/c restaurant on third floor.

Misahuallí *p1006*
🍴 **Doña Gloria**, Arteaga y Rivadeneyra by corner of plaza. Open 0730-2030 daily, very good set meals. Recommended.
🍴 **La Posada**, at the Plaza. Varied à la carte menu, good food, nice porch setting, slow service.

Puyo *p1007*
🍴 **El Alcázar**, 10 de Agosto 936 y Sucre, T288 5330, Mon-Sat 0900-2300, Sun 0900-1600. Very good, Spanish-European flavour in the Ecuadorean Amazon. Good value set meals and varied à la carte. Recommended.
🍴 **El Jardín**, on the Paseo Turístico in Barrio Obrero. Tue-Sun 1200-2200. Pleasant setting and atmosphere, international food.
🍴 **Pizzería Buon Giorno**, Orellana entre Villamil y 27 de Febrero, Mon-Sat 1200-2300. Good pizza and salads, very popular.
🍴 **La Posada de Gurmiek**, Ceslao Marín y 27 de Febrero, daily 0730-2200. Nice place, good value set lunch.
🍴 **Panadería Susanita**, Ceslao Marín y Villamil. Bakery, also serves breakfast and set lunch.
🍴 **Sal y Pimienta**, Atahualpa y 27 de Febrero. Grilled meats, popular.
🍴 **Heladería Haboud**, 27 de Febrero y Atahualpa. Good ice-cream.

Shell *p1007*
There are several cheap and simple *comedores* on the main street.

Macas *p1007*
🍴 **Chifa Pagoda China**, Amazonas y Domingo Comín. Very good Chinese food, open 1130-2230.

🍴 **La Italiana**, Bolívar 6-07 y Soasti, daily 1000-0000. Pizza and pasta.
🍴 **Chifa Welcome**, Soasti 14-34. Very cheap set lunch.

Sucúa *p1007*
There are several cheap and basic places in town.
🍴 **Gyna**, Domingo Comín ½ block south of the park. Set meals and à la carte.
🍴 **La Orquidea**, 8 de Diciembre y Domingo Comín. Very cheap set meals, good.

▲ Activities and tours

Tena *p1006*
Amarongachi Tours, address as for **Traveller's Lodging**, above.
Ríos Ecuador-Yacu Amu, Av Francisco de Orellana y Pano (Malecón), T288 6727, www.riosecuador.com. Highly recommended white-water rafting and kayak trips and a 5-day kayak school. Has the best safety records and standards.
Runa Ñambi, JL Mera 628 y Abdón Calderón, T288 6318, runanambi@yahoo.com.

Misahuallí *p1006*
Ecoselva, T289 0019, Santander on the plaza, ecoselva@yahoo.es. Recommended guide Pepe Tapia González speaks English and has a biology background. Trips from 1-6 days, well organized and reliable.
Quindi Tour, Napo opposite the plaza (in *La Posada*), T289 0031. Run by Carlos Santander and his brothers. Friendly, good food.

Puyo *p1007*
All of the following offer jungle tours of varying lengths. Prices range from US$25-50 pp per day.
Amazonía Touring, Atahualpa y 9 de Octubre, T288 3064.
Entsa Tours, T09-801 6642. Mentor Marino is helpful and knowledgeable.
Nave de Santos, at the Terminal Terrestre, T288 3262, F288 3267.
Papangu Tours, 27 de Febrero y Sucre, T288 7684, papangu@andinanet.net. Operated by the Organización de Pueblos Indígenas de Pastaza (OPIP), visits to local reserves and longer trips.

Macas *p1007*
Rodmor Tours, Domingo Comín 7-35 y Soasti, T270 1328. Run by Taylor Rodríguez.
Winia Sunka, Domingo Comín y Amazonas, the kiosk in front of *Chifa Pagoda China*, T/F270 0088, pablovguias@hotmail.com. Owner **Pablo Velín** is a recommended guide.

Every foreign visitor has to pay a **national park tax of US$100** on arrival, cash only. Be sure to have your passport to hand. Do not lose your park tax receipt; boat captains need to record it. A 50% reduction on the national park fee is available to children under 12, but only those foreigners who are enrolled in an Ecuadorean university are entitled to the reduced fee for students. The cost of living in the Galápagos is higher than the mainland, particularly in the peak season (December, July and August). **Note**: Do not touch any of the animals, birds or plants. Do not transfer sand, seeds or soil from one island to another. Do not leave litter anywhere; it is highly undesirable in a national park and is a safety and health hazard for wildlife. Do not take raw food on to the islands. Uninhabited islands are no-smoking zones.

What to take A remedy for seasickness is recommended; the waters south of Santa Cruz are particularly choppy. A good supply of sun block and skin cream to prevent windburn and chapped lips is essential, as are a hat and sunglasses. You should be prepared for dry and wet landings, the latter involving wading ashore. Take plenty of film or memory cards with you; the birds are so tame that you will use far more than you expected; a telephoto lens is not essential, but if you have one, bring it. Also take filters suitable for strong sunlight. Snorkelling equipment is particularly useful as much of the sea-life is only visible under water. Most of the cheaper boats do not provide equipment and those that do may not have good snorkelling gear. If in doubt, bring your own, rent in Puerto Ayora, or buy it in Quito. It is possible to sell it afterwards on the islands.

Tipping A ship's crew and guides are usually tipped separately. The standard suggestion is 10% of what you paid for the cruise, which is divided between guide and crew. The percentage is lower on economic and tourist class boats. It is, however, a very personal matter, but the key factor should always be the quality of service received.

If you have problems See below for complaints regarding itineraries. If a crew member comes on strongly to a woman passenger, the matter should first be raised with the guide or captain. If this does not yield results, a formal complaint, in Spanish, giving the crew member's full name, the boat's name and the date of the cruise, should be sent to **Sr Capitán del Puerto**, Base Militar de Armada Ecuatoriana, Puerto Ayora, Santa Cruz, Galápagos. Failure to report such behaviour will mean it will continue. To avoid pilfering, never leave belongings unattended in Puerto Ayora, or on a beach when another boat is in the bay.

Best time to visit The Galápagos climate can be divided into a hot season (December-May), when there is a possibility of heavy showers, and the cool or *garúa* (mist) season (June-November), when the days generally are more cloudy and there is often rain or drizzle. July and August can be windy, force 4 or 5. Daytime clothing should be lightweight. (Clothing generally, even on 'luxury cruises', should be casual and comfortable.) At night, however, particularly at sea and at higher altitudes, temperatures fall below 15°C and warm clothing is required. Boots and shoes soon wear out on the lava terrain. The sea is cold July-October; underwater visibility is best January-March. Ocean temperatures are usually higher to the east and lower at the western end of the archipelago. The islands climate and hence its wildlife are also influenced by the El Niño phenomenon. Despite all these variations, conditions are generally favourable for visiting Galápagos throughout the year.

Organizations and useful websites The **Galápagos Conservation Trust** ① *5 Derby St, London W1J 7AB, T020-7629 5049, www.gct.org*, publishes a quarterly Newsletter for its members. *Galapagos News* is a twice-yearly publication about science and conservation in the islands. It is the official publication of the Charles Darwin Foundation. 'Friends of the Galápagos' receive the journal as a part of their membership. For information, contact the site of the **Charles Darwin Research Station** and the **Galápagos Conservation Trust**, www.galapagos.org, which has links and news articles. Also visit **www.darwinfoundation.org**.

Choosing a tour
There are two ways to travel around the islands: a *tour navegable*, where you sleep on the boat, or shore-based tours on which you take day trips to the islands. On the former you travel at night, arriving at a new landing site each day, with more time ashore. On the latter you have to pay for hotel accommodation, even if the tour itself is cheaper, you spend less time at the

Ecuador Galápagos Islands Ins & outs

Near the reserve is the **Butterfly Ranch** (Hacienda Mariposa) ① *US$3, including a cup of hierba luisa tea, or juice,* where you can see giant tortoises in the pastures, but only in the dry season. In the wet season the tortoises are breeding down in the arid zone. Vermillion flycatchers can be seen here also. The ranch is beyond Bellavista on the road to Santa Rosa (the bus passes the turn-off).

San Cristóbal: Puerto Baquerizo Moreno → *Phone code: 05. Pop: 6,500.*

Puerto Baquerizo Moreno, on San Cristóbal island to the east, is the capital of the archipelago. The island is being developed as a second tourist centre. It is a pleasant place to spend a few days, with interesting excursions in the area.

In town, the **cathedral** ① *on Av Northía, 2 blocks up from the post office, 0900-1200, 1600-1800,* has interesting mixed-media relief pictures on the walls and altar. To the north of town, opposite Playa Mann, is the Galápagos National Park visitors' centre or **Centro de Interpretación** ① *T252 0138, ext 102, 0700-1800, free.* It has an excellent display of the natural and human history of the islands.

A good trail goes from the Centro de Interpretación to the northeast through scrub forest to **Cerro Tijeretas**, a hill overlooking town and the ocean, 30 minutes away (take water). Side trails branch off to some lookouts on cliffs over the sea. Frigate birds nest in this area and can be observed gliding about, there are sea lions on the beaches below. To go back, if you take the trail which follows the coast, you will end up at **Playa Punta Carola,** a popular surfing beach, too rough for swimming. Closer to town is the small **Playa Mann** (follow Avenida Northía to the north), more suited for swimming and in town is **Playa de Oro,** where some hotels are located. Right in the centre of town, along the sand by the tidal pool, sea lions can be seen, be careful with the male who 'owns' the beach. To the south of town, 20 minutes' walk past the airport, is **La Lobería,** a rocky bay with shore birds, sea lions and marine iguanas. You can continue along the cliff to see tortoises and rays, but do not leave the trail.

Around San Cristóbal There are five buses a day inland from Puerto Baquerizo Moreno to **El Progreso** ① *6 km, 15 mins, US$0.20,* then it's a 2½ hour walk to El Junco lake, the largest body of fresh water in Galápagos. There are also frequent pick-up trucks to El Progreso ① *US$2,* or you can hire a pick-up in Puerto Baquerizo Moreno for touring: US$20 to El Junco, US$40 continuing to the beaches at Puerto Chino on the other side of the island, past a man-made tortoise reserve (the road is poor). Prices are return and include waiting. At El Junco there is a path to walk around the lake in 20 minutes. The views are lovely in clear weather but it is cool and wet in the *garúa* season, so take adequate clothing. Various small roads fan out from El Progreso and make for pleasant walking. An interesting trail runs down from El Progreso via Cerro Mundo to **Puerto Ochoa,** near Isla Lobos on the west coast. It is some 4 hours down and 8 back up, so you must arrange for a boat to pick you up at the beach or take all provisions (including water) and camping gear. Note that it is easy to get lost, see below.

It's a three-hour hike from the landing site at **Caleta Tortuga,** on the northwest shore of the island, to **La Galapaguera Natural** where you can see tortoises in the wild. **Isla Lobos** is an islet with a large sea and nesting site for sea birds northeast of Puerto Baquerizo Moreno. It is also a dive site.

Boats go to **Puerto Ochoa,** 15 minutes, for the beach; to **Punta Pitt** in the far north where you can see all three species of booby (US$65 for tour). Off the northwest coast is **Kicker Rock** (León Dormido), the basalt remains of a crater; many seabirds, including Nazca and blue-footed boobies, can be seen around its cliffs (five hour trip, including snorkelling, recommended, US$35).

Note: Always take food, plenty of water and a compass or GPS when hiking on your own on San Cristóbal. There are many crisscrossing animal trails and it is easy to get lost. Also watch out for the large-spined opuntia cactus and the poisonwood tree (*manzanillo*), which is a relative of poison ivy and can cause severe skin reactions.

Isabela Island

This is the largest island in the archipelago, formed by the extensive lava flows from six volcanoes. Five of the volcanoes are active and each have (or had) their own separate sub-species of giant tortoise. Isabela is slowly developing for tourism. If you have a few days to spare and are looking for tranquillity, in a South-Pacific-island setting this may be just the place. Most residents live in **Puerto Villamil.** In the highlands, there is a cluster of farms at Santo

Tomás. There are several lovely beaches right by town, but mind the strong undertow and ask locally about the best spots for swimming. It is 2½ hours walk west to **Muro de las Lágrimas**, a gruesome place built by convict labour under hideous conditions. Along the same road 30 minutes from town is the **Centro de Crianza**, a breeding centre for giant tortoises surrounded by lagoons with flamingos and other birds. In the opposite direction, 30 minutes east toward the *embarcadero* (fishing pier) is **Concha Perla Lagoon**, with a nice access trail through mangroves and a little dock from which you can go swimming with sea lions and other creatures. Fishermen can take you to **Las Grietas**, a set of small islets in the harbour where white-tipped reef sharks may be seen in the still crystalline water (about US$10 per boat). **Sierra Negra Volcano** has the largest basaltic caldera in the world, 7½ x 12 km. It is 18 km (1 hour) by pickup truck to El Cura, where you switch to horses for the 1½ hr beautiful ride to the crater rim at 980m. It is a further 1½ hrs walk along bare brittle lava rock to **Volcán Chico**, with several fumaroles and more stunning views. The round trip takes a full day but there are only two buses a day along the road, no water, and it is easy to get lost, so going on your own is not advised. Tours can be arranged by most hotels, or contact Antonio Gil at *Hotel San Vicente*, T252 9140; about US$20 per person, minimum 4 people. **Note** Sierra Negra began erupting in late 2005; ask if visits are safe. A visit to **Punta Moreno**, on the southwest part, starts with a dinghy ride along the beautiful rocky shores where penguins and shore birds are usually seen. After a dry landing there is a hike through sharp lava rocks. **Elizabeth Bay**, on the west coast, is home to a small colony of penguins living on a series of small rocky islets and visited by dinghy.

Floreana Island

Floreana, the island with the richest human history has 90 inhabitants, most in Puerto Velasco Ibarra, the rest in the highlands. Unless you visit with one of the few boats which land at Black Beach for a few hours, it is difficult to get onto and off the inhabited part of the island. Services are limited; you should be very flexible about travel times and self-sufficient, unless staying with the Wittmers (delightful, see below). The pace of life is gentle and locally produced food is good, but you will not be entertained. Margret Wittmer died in 2000, however you can meet her daughter and granddaughter. The climate in the highlands is fresh and comfortable, good for birdwatching. Places to visit include the **Devil's Crown** snorkelling site, **Punta Cormorant**, a green beach near which is a lake normally inhabited by flamingoes and **Post Office Bay**, on the north side. There is a custom for visitors to Post Office Bay since 1793 to place unstamped letters and cards in a barrel, and deliver, free of charge, any addressed to their own destinations.

● Sleeping

Puerto Ayora *p1020*
Hotel space at the upper end of the market is limited. Reservations essential in high season.
LL Finch Bay, on a small bay south of Puerto Ayora, accessible only by boat, T252 6297, www.finch bayhotel.com. Remodelled, restaurant, pool, lovely beach, bar, good service, comfortable rooms. Book through **Metropolitan Touring** in Quito.
LL Royal Palm, Km 18, Vía Baltra, T252 7409, www.millenniumhotels.com. Exclusive, super-luxury resort in the highlands, all facilities including internet access in rooms, pool, private saunas, jacuzzis etc, massage, museum, sports, VIP landing services at airport.
LL-L Red Mangrove Inn, Darwin y las Fragatas, on the way to the research station, T252 7011, www.redmangrove.com. Full of character, restaurant, jacuzzi, deck bar. Owner Polo Navaro offers day tours and diving. Warmly recommended.
L Silberstein, Darwin y Piqueros, T252 6277, www.hotelsilberstein.com. Spacious rooms, lovely grounds, includes breakfast, pool, meals available, tours, diving.

AL Fernandina, 12 de Noviembre y Los Piqueros, T252 6499, F252 6122. Includes breakfast, pool (open weekends to non guests), jacuzzi, restaurant.
AL Las Ninfas, Los Colonos y Berlanga, T252 6127, galaven@pa.ga.pro.ec. Includes breakfast, good restaurant, full range of services, has its own boat at reasonable price for day trips, helpful with arrangements.
AL Red Booby, Av Plazas y Charles Binford, T252 6485, www.hotelredbooby.com.ec. A/c, hot water, tiled floors in spacious rooms, safe, pool, restaurant, internet, tours and sports options.
AL-C Lobo de Mar, 12 de Febrero y Darwin, T252 6188, www.lobodemar.com.ec. Includes breakfast, a/c, cheaper with fan, small pool, the new section is modern and comfortable, older rooms are simpler but good value, attentive service.
A-B Palmeras, Berlanga y Naveda, T252 6139, F252 6373. Restaurant, a/c, cheaper with fan, pool, good value.
A-C Sol y Mar, Darwin y Binford, T252 6281, F252 7015. Fan, variety of rooms in different categories, very pleasant.

B-C Castro, Los Colonos y Malecón, T252 6113, F252 6508. Restaurant, a/c cheaper with fan, owner Miguel Castro arranges tours, he is an authority on wildlife.

B-C Estrella de Mar, Darwin y 12 de Febrero, T252 6427, F252 6080. Includes breakfast, fan, spacious rooms (more expensive with sea view), communal sitting area.

B-C Fiesta, Brito y Las Ninfas, T/F252 6440, www.islasdefuego.com. Quiet, next to Laguna Las Ninfas, a 5-min walk from the seafront. A/c, cheaper with fan, pleasant garden, pool, patio, hammocks, nice grounds.

D España, Berlanga y Naveda, T252 6101. Cold water, fan, big rooms, small sitting area with hammocks, good value.

D Flamingo, Berlanga y Naveda, T/F252 6556. Cold water, courtyard, basic but adequate.

D Lirio del Mar, Naveda y Berlanga, T252 6212. Cafetería, pleasant, fan, good value.

D Los Amigos, Darwin y 12 de Febrero, T252 6265. Small place with 4-bed rooms, shared bath, cold water, laundry facilities, noisy bar below, basic but good value.

D New Elizabeth, Darwin y Berlanga, T/F252 6178. Reasonable, fan, owner very helpful.

D Peregrina, Darwin e Indefatigable, T252 6323. A small, simple family-run place. Some rooms have a/c, some have hot water, small garden.

D Salinas, Naveda y Berlanga, T252 6107, F252 6072. Cheaper with cold water, fan, pleasant and good value.

D Sir Francis Drake, Herrera y Binford, T252 6221. Fan, cold water, good value.

E Darwin, Herrera y Binford, T252 6193. OK, cold water, basic, don't leave valuables in your room.

Puerto Baquerizo Moreno *p1022*

A Orca, Playa de Oro, T/F252 0233. A/c, comfortable, fridge, good food, often filled with groups, has its own boat for cruises.

A-B Hostal Galápagos, at Playa de Oro, T252 0157, www.galahost.com. Rooms are a bit small and faded, a/c, fridge, also rents by the month.

B Alojamiento en Hogares, for information and bookings contact Berenice Norris, T252 0258, 09-414 8924 (mob), berenicenorris@gmail.com. An association of community bed & breakfasts offering accommodation in private homes. Includes breakfast, airport transfers, the use of kitchen and laundry facilities. Long stays also available.

B Northía, Northía y 12 de Febrero, T/F252 0041. Includes breakfast, a/c, pleasant, pricey.

B-C Chatham, Northía y Av de la Armada Nacional, on the road to the airport, T252 0137. Patio with hammocks, some rooms with a/c and fridge, cheaper with fan, adequate.

C Islas Galápagos, Esmeraldas y Colón, T252 0203, F252 0162. A/c, a bit run down but OK.

C Mar Azul, Northía y Esmeraldas, T252 0139, F252 0384. A/c, cheaper with fan, on the road to the airport, nice gardens, good value. Recommended.

D Cabañas Don Jorge, above Playa Mann, T252 0208. Fan, simple cabins in a quiet setting overlooking the ocean, shared kitchen, helpful.

D Los Cactus, Juan José Flores y Av Quito, T252 0078. Near Pacifictel, family run, simple.

D San Francisco, Malecón Charles Darwin y Villamil, T252 0304. Cold water, fan, rooms in front are nicer, simple, good.

Isabela Island *p1022*

AL La Casa de Marita, east end of village, T252 9238, www.galapagosisabela.com. Definitely upscale, even chic, for its location. Includes breakfast, other meals on request, a/c and fridge, right on the beach, very comfortable. Recommended.

B-C Ballena Azul and Isabela del Mar, Conocarpus y Opuntia, T252 9030, www.hosteriaisabela.com.ec. An older wooden building next to modern cabins, both are very nice. Solar hot water, fan, large balcony, pleasant, Swiss run, helpful. Recommended.

B-C Cormorant Beach House, Antonio Gil y Los Flamencos, T252 9192, albemarle20@ hotmail.com. Nice location on the beach. A/c, cheaper with fan, fridge and use of cooking facilities, modern and comfortable, small terrace with hammock, very pleasant.

D San Vicente, Cormoranes y Pinzón Artesano, T252 9140. Cold water, fan, fridge and use of cooking facilities, meals on request, good value and popular.

There are a couple of other basic places to stay in town.

Floreana *p1023*

L Pensión Wittmer, right on Black Beach, T252 9506. Includes 3 delicious meals, fan (when there is electricity), simple and comfortable, a very special place.

---

❶ Eating

Puerto Ayora *p1020*

🍴🍴🍴 **Angermeyer's Point**, at the end of Barranco, access by watertaxi, T252 6452, Tue-Sat 1900-2200, Sun brunch 1100-1600. In the old home of the Angermeyer family, popular and fashionable, innovative menu.

🍴🍴🍴 **La Garrapata**, Charles Darwin entre 12 de Febrero y Tomás de Berlanga, closed Sun. Good food, attractive setting and good music, juice bar and sandwiches during the day, choice of 2 set meals at lunch, and la carte at night.

♥ Café Habana, Charles Darwin y Naveda, daily 0900-0130. Restaurant and bar with music at night, cheap set lunch, varied à la carte menu.

♥ Hernán, Av Baltra y Opuntia, 0730-2230 daily. Restaurant and bar, international menu, includes pizza, burgers, capuccino.

♥ New Island, Charles Darwin y Charles Binford, Mon-Sat 0900-2100. Breakfast, fruit juices, seafood, ceviches.

♥ Trattoria de Pippo, Charles Darwin entre Indefatigable e Isla Floreana, also 'El Patio' at Charles Darwin entre Naveda y 12 de Febrero, daily 1700-2200. Italian and seafood, pleasant atmosphere, attentive owner.

♥-♥ Media Luna, Charles Darwin y Los Piqueros, 1500-2200, closed Tue. Good pizza and pasta, also sandwiches, excellent brownies.

♥ Capricho, Charles Darwin y Isla Floreana by the tortoise roundabout, daily 0630-2200, Mon till 1700. Good vegetarian, salads and juices, breakfast.

♥ Chocolate Galápagos, Charles Darwin entre Tomas de Berlanga y Charles Binford. Good breakfasts, soups, burgers and snacks.

♥ El Descanso del Guía, Charles Darwin y Los Colonos, near bus company offices, no sign. Good value set meals, popular with locals.

♥ El Manaba, Herrera y Tomás de Berlanga. Clean place, good set meals.

♥ Salvavidas, on the waterfront overlooking the pier. Good set lunch, breakfast and seafood. Recommended.

La Casa del Lago, Moisés Brito y Juan Montavo, in Barrio Las Ninfas, a quiet area away from the main drag, evenings only. Drinks and snacks, live music, cultured atmosphere.

Limón y Café, Charles Darwin y 12 de Febrero. Good snacks and drinks, lots of music, pool table, open evenings only, popular.

Santa Fe, Charles Darwin y Los Colonos. Bar and grill, drinks, sandwiches and snacks, pleasant.

Tikki Takka, Charles Binford y Charles Darwin, Mon-Sat 0800-2000. Breakfast and snacks, bread flown in from Cyrano bakery in Quito, plus pastries.

Along Charles Binford, near Padre J Herrera are a series of kiosks selling traditional food at economic prices; **Tía Juanita** cooks well, seafood.

Puerto Baquerizo Moreno *p1022*

♥ La Playa, Av de la Armada Nacional, by the navy base. Nice location, varied menu, popular.

♥ Miconia, Darwin e Isabela. Varied menu, meat, fish, pizza, Italian.

♥-♥ Rosita Ignacio de Hernández y General Villamil. Set meals and varied à la carte menu, very good.

♥ Albacora, Av Northía y Española. Good set meals, cheap.

♥ Barracuda, Charles Darwin y 12 de Febrero. Grilled meat and *menestras*.

♥ Pizzería Bambú, Ignacio de Hernández y General Villamil. Pizza as well as other dishes.

Cabaña El Grande, Villamil y Darwin. Fruit juices are the specialty, also burgers and snacks. Popular.

Heladería Sula Sula, Charles Darwin y Herman Melville. Ice cream and snacks, nice terrace.

Panadería Fragata, Northía y Rocafuerte. Excellent bread and pastries, good selection.

Patagonia, Charles Darwin y Teodoro Wolf. Drinks and snacks.

Isabela Island *p1022*

♥ El Encanto de la Pepa, Conocarpus y Pinzón Artesano. Lots of character, good food, attractive setting, pleasant.

♥-♥ La Choza, Antonio Gil y Las Fragatas. Order your pizza 1 hr in advance, dough is made fresh.

♥ Caballito de Mar, Los Cactos y Las Escalecias. Good set meals.

♥ La Ruta, on the beach between 16 de Marzo and Las Fragatas. Good quality and value set meals.

♥ Caracol, kiosk on Calle Conocarpus, next to police station. Simple set meals.

♠ Bars and clubs

Puerto Ayora *p1020*

La Panga, Av Charles Darwin y Berlanga and **Bar Bongo**, upstairs at the same location; both are popular. Also see **Café Habana** under eating and **La Casa del Lago** above.

Puerto Baquerizo Moreno *p1022*

El Barquero, Hernández y Manuel J Cobos. Bar and *peña*, open daily.

Neptuno, Charles Darwin y Herman Melville. Disco, young crowd, open Tue-Sat 2030-0300.

♦ Shopping

Do not buy items made of black coral as it is an endangered species.

Puerto Ayora *p1020*

Most basic foodstuffs generally can be purchased on the islands, but cost more than on the mainland. **The Proinsular** supermarket opposite the pier is the best place. The *mercado municipal* is on Padre J Herrera, beyond the telephone office, on the way out of town to Santa Rosa. There is a wide variety of T-shirt and souvenir shops along the length of Av Charles Darwin.

Puerto Baquerizo Moreno *p1022*

A good little supermarket is **Dos Hermanos**, Quito y Juan José Flores; a small produce market is located a block away at Juan José Flores y 12 de Febrero. There are a few souvenir shops along the Malecón selling T-shirts and crafts.

Ecuador Galápagos Islands Listings

▲ Activities and tours

Puerto Ayora *p1020*

Cycling Mountain bikes can be hired from travel agencies in town, US$8-16 per day; or at the **Red Mangrove Inn**, US$5 per hr.
Galápagos Tour Center, T252 6245, runs cycling tours in the highlands, US$16 per day.

Diving Please help to maintain standards by not disturbing or touching underwater wildlife. There are several diving agencies in Puerto Ayora offering courses, equipment rental, dives within Academy Bay (2 dives for US$90), and other central islands (2 dives, US$140), daily tours for 1 week in the central islands and several day live-aboard tours. There is a hyperbaric chamber in Puerto Ayora to treat divers in case of decompression sickness (US$850 per hr): 12 de Noviembre y Rodríguez Lara, T252 6911, sss@puertoayora.com, www.sssnetwork.com. Ask dive operators if they are affiliated with a plan that allows their clients to use the chamber in case of emergency. Agencies that offer all services and have been repeatedly recommended are:
Galápagos Sub-Aqua, Av Charles Darwin by Pelican Bay, T252 6633 (Quito: Pinto 439 y Amazonas, office 101, T02-256 5294), www.galapagos-sub-aqua.com. Instructor Fernando Zambrano offers full certificate courses up to divemaster level (PADI or NAUI).
Scuba Iguana, www.scubaiguana.com, is a long-time reliable and recommended dive operator who was changing premises and telephones at the close of this edition. Check the website for new contact information.
Horse riding For riding at ranches in the highlands, enquire at **Moonrise Travel**.
Kayaking and windsurfing Equipment rental and tours available from the Red Mangrove Inn, US$10 per hr.
Snorkelling: masks, snorkels and fins can be rented from travel agencies and dive shops, US$5 a day, US$30 per week, deposit required. Closest place to snorkel is by beaches near Darwin Station.
Surfing There is surfing at Tortuga Bay (see Excursions) and at other more distant beaches accessed by boat. **Note** There is better surfing near Puerto Baquerizo Moreno on San Cristóbal. **Galápagos Tour Center** rents surfboards US$15 per day.

Tour operators

Touts sometimes approach tourists at the airport or in the street, claiming to represent well-known agencies and offering cheap tours. Their services are generally not recommended. Tour operators in Puerto Ayora run excursions to the highland sites for US$20-30 pp, depending on the number of sites visited and the size of the group. These may include visits to ranches such as Rancho Mariposa (enquire at **Moonrise Travel**). Bay excursions in glass-bottom boats visit sites near Puerto Ayora such as Isla Caamaño, Punta Estrada, Las Grietas, Franklin Bay and Playa de los Perros. You are likely to see sea lions, birds, marine iguanas and marine life including sharks. Snorkelling can be part of the tour. Full-day tours (0900-1600) are US$25 pp and can be arranged through travel agencies.

Andando Tours, Mariana de Jesús E7-113 (326) y Pradera, Quito, T323 7186, www.andandotours.com.

Andes Explorer, Reina Victoria 927 (entre Pinto y Wilson), Quito, T290 1493, www.andes-explorer.com. Experienced tour operator

specializing in the Galápagos, with over 60 cruise ships from economy to luxury.

Enchanted Expeditions, De las Alondras N45-102 y de los Lirios (Monteserrin), Quito, T334 0525, www.enchantedexpeditions.com. 30 years' experience of Galápagos cruises. Adventure and special interest tours throughout Ecuador.

Galacruises Expeditions, N22-118 9 de Octubre y Veintimilla, ground floor, El Trebol building, Quito, T252 3324, www.galacruises.com. Yachts and catamarans, cruises and expeditions. Scuba diving, snorkelling and sea kayaks.

Galapagos Network-Ecoventura, 5805 Blue Lagoon Dr, Suite 160, Miami, Florida, 33126, USA, T262 6264, www.ecoventura.com. Full-week itineraries accompanied by 2 expert naturalist guides, 20-passenger yachts or 16-passenger dive-liveaboard packages.

Galápagos Tour Center, Padre J Herrera, opposite the hospital, T252 6245. Bicycle rentals and tours, surfboards, snorkelling gear, motorcycle rentals. Run by Victor Vaca who speaks several languages and arranges last-minute tours.

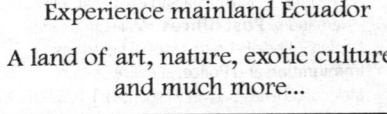

Galaptour, Rodríguez Lara y Genovesa, T252 6088, F252 7021. Last-minute cruise bookings.
Metropolitan Touring, Av República de El Salvador N36-84, Quito, www.metropolitan-touring.com. See Quito, page 905, for details.
Moonrise Travel, Av Charles Darwin, opposite Banco del Pacífico, T252 6348, sdivine@pa.ga. pro.ec. Last-minute cruise bookings, day tours to different islands, bay tours, highland tours, airline reservations. Knowledgeable, helpful and reliable.
Rolf Wittmer Turismo Galapagos, Foch e 7-81 y Diego de Almagro, La Mariscal, Quito, T252 6938, www.rwittmer.com. Tailor-made tours throughout Ecuador and the Galápagos.
Quasar Expeditions, T1-800 247 2925 (USA), T020 7871 4239 (UK), T225 7822 (Ecuador) www.quasarexpeditions.com. Galápagos cruises and mainland expeditions.

Puerto Baquerizo Moreno *p1022*
Cycling Bikes can be hired from travel agencies.
Diving There are several dive sites around San Cristóbal, most popular being Kicker Rock, Roca Ballena and Punta Pitt (at the northeastern side). Gonzalo Quiroga of **Chalo Tours** is a divemaster offering tours to these sites, however he is not always available. **Amparito y Angel**, who run a new diving agency at Teodoro Wolf y Darwin, are reported more dynamic. The nearest hyperbaric chamber is in Puerto Ayora.
Galakiwi, T252 1562, www.galakiwi.com. Multisport options, with dives, kayaks, hikes, horse rides etc. Also offer a selection of one-day dives from Cristóbal.
Surfing There is good surfing in San Cristóbal, the best season is Dec-Mar. **Punta Carola** near town is the closest surfing beach; popular among locals. There is a championship during the local *fiesta*, the 2nd week of Feb.

Tour operators
Chalo Tours, Malecón Charles Darwin y Villamil, T252 0953. Bay tours to Kicker Rock and Isla de los Lobos, boat tours to the north end of the island, highland tours to El Junco and Puerto Chino beach, occasional diving tours, bike rentals, snorkelling gear, surf boards, book exchange.

⊖ Transport

Puerto Ayora *p1020*
Bus From the new terminal on the edge of Puerto Ayora (taxi to town US$1), 3 daily buses leave for **Bellavista** (17 km, US$0.25, 10 mins) and **Santa Rosa** (23 km, US$0.50, 20 mins). There is a ticket office by the pier. Pick-up trucks may be hired for transport throughout town and up to the highlands, US$2-3, agree on the fare in advance.

❶ Directory

Puerto Ayora *p1020*
Airline offices Aerogal, Padre J Herrera y 10 Mayo, T252 1118, Mon-Fri 0800-1200, 1300-1700, Sat 0900-1300. Baltra airport counter, T252 0405, daily 0800-1300. TAME, Av Charles Darwin north of 12 de Febrero, T252 6165. Mon-Fri 0700-1200, 1300-1800, Sat 0900-1200. Emetebe, Av Charles Darwin opposite the port, 3rd floor of post office building, T252 6177. **Banks** Banco del Pacífico, Av Charles Darwin by Pelican Bay. Mon-Fri 0800-1530, Sat 0930-1230. US$5 commission for TCs, maximum US$500 per transaction. ATM for Mastercard only, cash advances on Visa Mon-Fri. A hefty surcharge may be applied to credit card purchases and many places do not accept credit cards. Most boats accept TCs. **Embassies and consulates** British Consul, David Balfour, c/o Etica, Barrio Estrada, Puerto Ayora, T252 6159.
Laundry Lavagal, by football stadium, machine wash and dry US$1.50 per kg, good, reliable, US$1 taxi ride from town. **Medical services** Hospitals: there is a hospital on Padre Herrera. For anything serious, locals usually fly to the mainland. See also under Diving, above. **Post offices** By the port. Post Office often runs out of stamps (never leave money and letters). DHL courier and Western Union, across the street from Hotel Silberstein. **Useful addresses** Immigration: at the police station on 12 de Febrero. They are usually able to extend tourist visas up to 90 days, but always check well before your time expires.

Puerto Baquerizo Moreno *p1022*
Airline offices Aerogal, at the airport, T252 1118. Icaro, at the airport, T252 1063. TAME, Charles Darwin y 12 de Febrero, T25 21351. Airport counter T252 1089.Emetebe, at the airport terminal, T252 0615. Mon-Fri 0700-1300, 1500-1730, Sat 0700-1300. **Banks** Banco del Pacífico, Charles Darwin entre Española y Melville. Same services as in Puerto Ayora. Open Mon-Fri 0800-1530, Sat 1000-1200. **Internet** US$1.50-3 per hr. **Laundry** Lavandería Limpio y Seco, Av Northía y 12 de Febrero. Wash and dry US$2. Open daily 0900-2100. **Medical services** There is a hospital providing only basic medical services. Dr David Basantes, opposite Hotel Mar Azul, T252 0126, is a helpful GP. Farmacia San Cristóbal, Villamil y Hernández. **Post offices** Malecón Charles Darwin y 12 de Febrero. **Useful services** Immigration and Police: at Police Station, Malecón Charles Darwin y Española, T/F252 0129.

Isabela Island *p1022*
Airline offices Emetebe, Antonio Gil y Las Fragatas, T252 9155, Mon-Fri 0730-1300, 1500-1730, Sat 0730-1300.

Paraguay

Introduction

An air of mystery hangs over this under-explored pocket of
South America, a country of farmland, forest and folklore. From
the hot, wild impenetrable Chaco in the north to the lush tropical
south, there is great birdlife, rivers to navigate and opportunities
for rural tourism. Land-locked Paraguay has had a strange history
of charismatic leaders, steadfastness and isolation. Its music, too,
marks it apart from its neighbours, sentimental songs and European
dances accompanied by virtuoso harp players and guitarists. Now,
though, the country is part of the Mercosur economic union, with
trade routes to Argentina and Brazil well-established. Moreover,
the road to Bolivia is gradually becoming easier – in the dry season,
at least: the Trans-Chaco is one of the great road adventures in
South America.

The remains of the Mission settlements built by Jesuits near the
banks of the Río Paraná are testimony to one of the major social
experiments on the continent. It is also renowned for a vigorous
line in contraband and a dedication to the consumption of *mate*
second to none. The indigenous language, Guaraní, is officially
recognised, but all those odd-looking names cannot hide the
warmth of Paraguayan hospitality.

★ Don't miss...

1 **Plaza de los Héroes, Asunción** Central Asunción has several squares, parks and historic buildings, but none more loaded with memory than that commemorating all those who died in the tragic wars that have punctuated Paraguay's independent history, page 1039.

2 **Itaipú** This huge hydroelectric scheme is shared with Brazil. You can visit the facilities on either side of the border and the Iguaçu Falls are within easy reach, page 1050.

3 **Jesuit missions** Near Encarnación on the Río Paraná are the remains of the Jesuit reductions which flourished in the 18th century. At Trinidad and Jesús are vestiges of the beautiful craftsmanship of the Guaraní Indians who were the Jesuits' flock, page 1055.

4 **The Chaco** Inhabited only by a few Mennonite communities, groups of indigenous peoples and scattered military outposts, Paraguay's western half is the best place to see wildlife. Its marshes give way to a thorny wilderness, where it is not advisable to venture alone (if at all), page 1060.

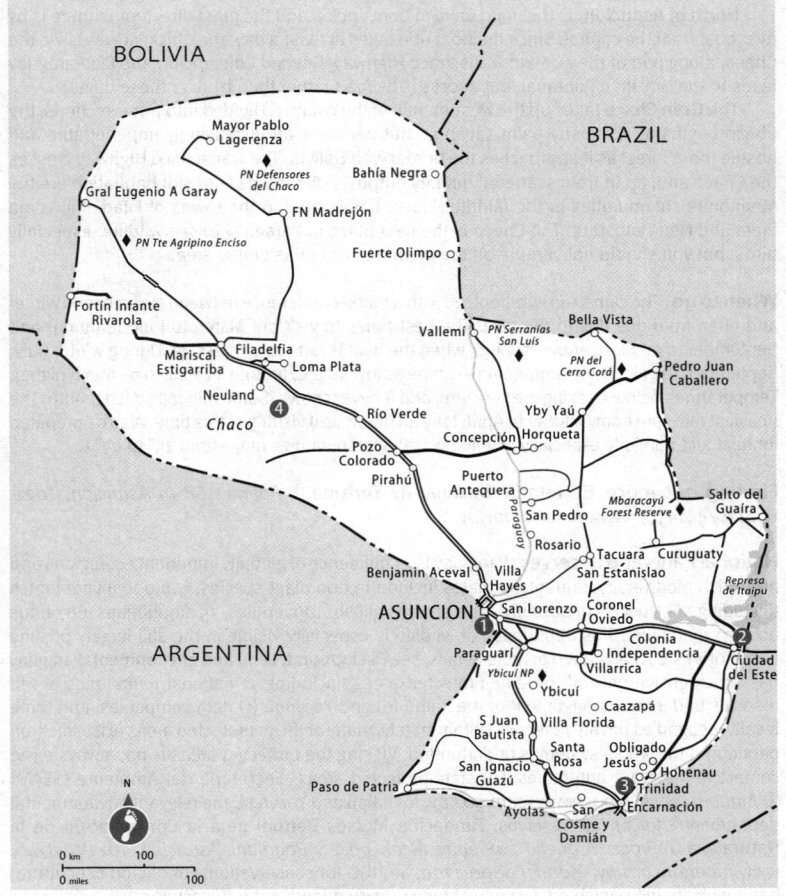

Paraguay

Essentials

Planning your trip

Where to go The capital, **Asunción**, stands on a bay on the eastern bank of the Río Paraguay and is the largest city in the country, followed by three smaller cities: Encarnación to the south, Ciudad del Este to the east and Concepción to the north. Asunción is the political and commercial heart and much of its architecture dates from the early 19th century. Paraguayan history is marked by bloody wars and charismatic dictators but what really sets this country apart is the warmth and tranquillity of its people. Paraguayans are proud of their Guaraní culture, which includes widespread use of the indigenous language which is still taught in schools today

East and south of Asunción is the fertile agricultural part of the country. The towns and villages are quiet and traditional in their way of life. Many have unique crafts associated with them. There are also many signs of the Jesuit heritage, which is best exemplified in the ruins of the reductions at Trinidad and Jesús, which are close to the city of Encarnación. From here you can cross the Río Paraná to the Argentine city of Posadas in the province of Misiones. Paraguay's eastern border with Brazil has several frontier posts, but the principal one is Ciudad del Este, a duty-free shopper's paradise (or hell, depending on your point of view). Across the Friendship Bridge from Ciudad del Este is Foz do Iguaçu in Brazil, where you can visit Itaipú, the largest hydroelectric dam in the world, and the magnificent Iguaçu Falls.

North of Asunción is the main town of Concepción and the most direct route there is by river boat from the capital. Since the boat ride takes at least a day, the quickest way is via the Chaco, along part of the 400-km Transchaco Highway. Beyond Concepción, the Río Paraguay leads to the Brazilian Pantanal, but access is by road rather than by river these days.

The Gran Chaco takes up the western half of the country. Divided into three sections, the Chaco begins as a marshy palm savanna, but becomes an increasingly impenetrable and hostile thorn forest as it approaches the border with Bolivia. The Transchaco Highway crosses the Chaco and, apart from scattered military outposts, the main centres of habitation are the Mennonite communities in the Middle Chaco, based around the towns of Filadelfia, Loma Plata and Neu-Halbstadt. The Chaco is the best place in Paraguay to see wildlife, especially birds, but you should not venture off the beaten track in this empty area.

When to go The climate is sub-tropical, with a marked difference between summer and winter and often from one day to the next. The best times to visit are March to June (autumn) and September to mid-December (spring), when the heat is not too oppressive. During winter (July-September) the nighttime temperature can be as low as 2°C, though it can also be much higher. Temperatures below freezing are very rare, and it never snows. Some rain falls each month. The heaviest rains are from October to April; take an umbrella if visiting at this time. Also be prepared for heat and humidity especially in January, when temperatures range from 25° to 43° C.

Finding out more Secretaría Nacional de Turismo ① *Palma 468 in Asunción, T021-494110/441530, www.senatur.gov.py.*

National Parks and Reserves Paraguay is a confluence of globally important ecoregions and has a rich biodiversity. Current estimates include 13,000 plant species, 100,000 invertebrates (including 765 species of butterfly), 300 species of fish, 100 reptiles, 75 amphibians, 687 birds and 171 mammals. This abundance of wildlife is especially visible in the still largely pristine Chaco of western Paraguay. For more details, see **Background, Land and environment**. Paraguay has an extensive network of state-protected areas, including 11 national parks, plus seven reserves under the management of the Itaipú (6) and Yacyretá (1) dam companies, and three legally recognized private reserves. Unfortunately, many of these protected areas exist solely on paper, and the whole system is underfunded. Visiting the protected areas is not always easy; contact the relevant authorities. For state-protected areas: **Secretaría del Ambiente** (SEAM) ① *Madam Lynch 3500, www.seam.gov.py*; for Itaipú and Yacyretá: the relevant environmental departments; for private reserves: **Fundación Moisés Bertoni para la Conservación de la Naturaleza** ① *Prócer Argüello 208 entre Mcal López y Boggiani, Asunción, T021-608740, www.mbertoni.org.py, Mon-Fri 0800-1700*, an NGO for conservation. **Fundación Ecocultura**, has a website in Spanish on a variety of topics, www.quanta.net.py/ecocultura.

Touching down

Airport tax US$25, payable on departure in US$ or guaraníes (cheaper). **Business hours** Shops, offices and businesses open around 0630-0700. Siesta is from 1200-1500. Commercial office hours are 0730-1100 or 1300, and 1430 or 1500-1730 or 1900. **Banks:** 0845-1500, closed Sat-Sun. **Government offices:** 0630-1130 in summer, 0730-1200 in winter, open Sat.
In an emergency Ambulance and Police emergency number T911.
International phone code +595. Ringing: equal tones with long pauses. Engaged: equal tones with equal pauses.

Official time 3-4 hours behind GMT (clocks go forward one hour in summer, Oct-Feb/Mar, dates change annually).
Tipping Restaurants, 10%. Porters US$0.15 a suitcase. Taxis, 10%. Porters at docks US$0.40 a suitcase. In supermarkets, tip the check-out boys who pack bags; they are not paid.
VAT/IVA 10%
Voltage Nominally 220 volts AC, 50 cycles, but power surges and voltage drops are frequent. European two round pin plugs are used.
Weights and measures Metric.

Websites

www.paraguay-hotel.com/py Links to tourist information as well as hotels.
www.pla.net.py Commercial links, information on going out, bus times, links to other sites.
www.paraguayglobal.com Business and cultural news in Spanish and English.

www.paraguay.com News in English and links to news services.
www.presidencia.gov.py The official site of the presidency (in Spanish).
www.terere.com Paraguayan portal with news and links.

Maps The best maps, including ones of the Chaco, are available from **Instituto Geográfico Militar**, Av Artigas casi Av Perú, take passport (an IGM map of the country can be bought at bookshops in Asunción). Small national maps, made by the Army, can be bought from the TACP (see Driving in Paraguay box below), at bookshops and bus terminals.

Visas and immigration A passport is required to enter Paraguay and tourist visas are issued at the point of entry for a stay of up to 90 days. Visitors are registered on arrival by the immigration authorities and get their documents back immediately. This procedure applies to those who do not require visas in advance, including citizens of: Austria, Belgium, Denmark, France, Germany, Italy, Israel, Japan, Netherlands, Norway, South Arica, Spain, Sweden, Switzerland and the UK. All others (including Australia, Canada, Ireland, New Zealand and USA) must apply for a visa before they travel, which costs £36 (US$60, or equivalent), multiple entry costs £52, presenting a valid passport and two photographs (for a business visa, a supporting letter from one's employer should suffice). Double check at a consulate or www.mre.gov.py before arrival which nationalities need a visa and which Paraguayan consulates issue them. Make sure you are stamped in and out of the country to avoid future problems. If you do not get an entrance stamp in your passport you can be turned back at the border, or have to pay a fine when leaving Paraguay.

Embassies and consulates See www.mre.gov.py, the Ministry of Foreign Affairs website.

Money The guaraní (plural guaraníes) is the unit of currency, symbolized by the letter G (crossed). There are bank notes for 1,000, 5,000, 10,000, 50,000 and 100,000 guaraníes and coins for 50, 100 and 500 guaraníes. The Guaraní **exchange rate:** US$1 = 6,098, 1 euro = 7,384 (Apr 2005). Get rid of all your guaraníes before leaving Paraguay; there is no market for them elsewhere (except in some cambios in Buenos Aires or Montevideo). If you receive dirty and/or torn US$ bills, a bank such as Lloyds TSB will replace all legitimate bills with acceptable ones.

Sights

Historic centre

At the bottom of Colón, just above where it joins El Paraguayo Independiente, are the colonial façades of **La Recova**, shops selling local arts and crafts. **La Aduana** (Customs) is at this same junction. Continue along El Paraguayo to a small plaza on your left with a statue of the former dictator, Alfredo Strossener. After his deposition, the statue was crushed and placed inside a block of concrete, only his hands and face protruding. Next to this is the **Palacio Gobierno**, built in the style of Versailles by Alan Taylor as a palace for Francisco Solano López (1860- 1869). During the later years Taylor was forced to use child labour as all adult men were enlisted to fight in the Triple Alliance War. It now houses government departments. Down the side of the palace towards the river is a platform for viewing the back of the building. Directly opposite the Palace is the **Manzana de la Rivera** ① *Ayolas 129 y El Paraguayo Independiente, Mon-Sat 0700-2000, library Mon-Fri 0700-1900, Sat 0800-1200*, nine restored buildings dating from 1700s including **Casa Viola** with Museo Memoria de la Ciudad with historical photos and city information, **Casa Clari**, with exhibition halls and a bar, and **Casa Vertua**, the municipal library.

Next to the Palace is the new **Congreso Nacional**, built in steel and glass representing a huge ship moored on the river bank and incorporating part of the old congress building. On **Plaza de la Independencia** there is a small memorial to those who died in the struggle for democracy (also look out for statues of the frog and the dog). On the Plaza are the **Antiguo Colegio Militar** (1588) originally a Jesuit College, now home to government ministries, the **Cabildo** ① *Mon-Fri 0900-1900, Sat 0800-1200, free*, now the **Centro Cultural de la República**, with temporary exhibitions, indigenous and religious art, museum of music, film and video on the top floor, and the **Catedral Metropolitana** (mid-17th century, rebuilt in the mid-19th century) ① *not always open, possible to view the interior before, after or during mass, usually*

Asunción

0 metres 200
0 yards 200

around 1100 daily. The altar, covered in Jesuit and Franciscan silver, is very beautiful. Between the river and the historical buildings is **La Chacarita**, a shanty town which is home to many poor families who have moved from the countryside in search of work. From the Plaza turn right onto Alberdi and to your right is the **post office**, a colonial building with a lovely planted courtyard; it also has public toilets and a small museum. At Alberdi and Eligio Ayala is the **Teatro Municipal**, currently being restored, due for completion late 2006. The **Estación San Roque** ① *Ayala y México, left of Plaza Uruguaya, T447848,* was built in 1856 with British and European help. Paraguay had the first passenger carrying railway in South America. No trains now run from the station but it has a small **museum** ① *0700-1200, free,* featuring the old ticket office, machinery from places like Wolverhampton and Battersea and the first steam engine in Paraguay, the **Sapucai** (1861). **Plaza Uruguaya** with its prostitutes, shady trees and fountain is another spot to stop and rest. From here take Mcal Estigarribia towards Plaza de Los Héroes. The **Museo Nacional de Bellas Artes** ① *Estigarribia e Iturbe, T447716, Tue-Fri 0700- 1900, Sat-0700-1200, closed Sun-Mon,* has some interesting 20th-century Paraguayan art and a good small collection of European paintings including works by Tintoretto and Murrillo.

Estigarribia becomes Palma at the intersection with Independencia Nacional (the names of all streets running east to west change at this point). On **Plaza de los Héroes** is the **Panteón Nacional de los Héroes** ① *Palma y Chile, open daily,* which is based on Les Invalides in Paris, begun during the Triple Alliance War and finished in 1937. It contains the tombs of Carlos Antonio López, Mariscal Francisco Solano López, Mariscal Estigarribia, the victor of the Chaco War, an unknown child-soldier, and other national heroes. The child-soldiers honoured in the Panteón were boys aged 12-16 who fought at the battle of Acosta Ñu in the War of the Triple Alliance, 15 August 1869. Most of the boys died and 9 out of 10 adult Paraguayan men were killed during the war. On the Plaza at Chile y Oliva (Plaza Libertad) there are **covered market stalls** selling traditional Paraguayan arts and crafts in wood, cotton and leather. Along Palma Maca Indian women sell colourful woven bags, beads and baskets. You may be approached by Maca men selling whistles, bows and arrows or feather headdresses. A few blocks further along Palma is the **tourist information office**; it has craft stalls for those not wishing to buy on the street. On Saturday morning, till 1200, Palma becomes a pedestrian area, with stalls selling arts, crafts, clothes and during the summer there is entertainment outside the tourist office. On Sunday there are stalls selling second-hand or antique items around Plaza de los Héroes. From Palma turn right at 14 de Mayo to the **Casa de la Independencia** ① *14 de Mayo y Pres Franco, Mon-Fri 0700-1830, Sat 0800-1200, free,* (1772), with a historical collection; this was where the 1811 anti-colonial revolution was plotted.

Heading out of the centre along Mariscal López

The **Museo Histórico Militar** ① *in the Ministry of National Defence, Mcal López y 22 de Septiembre (surrender passport on entry),* has articles from both the Triple Alliance and the Chaco Wars. These include gunshot-holed, blood-stained flags from the Triple Alliance as well as clothes and personal possessions of Franciso Solano López and his Irish mistress, Eliza Lynch. The national cemetery, **Cementerio Recoleta** ① *Av Mcal López y Chóferes del Chaco,* resembles a miniature city with tombs in various architectural styles. It contains the tomb of Madame Lynch (ask guide to show

Da Vinci **6** *B2*
Estrella **7** *B2*
La Flor de
  la Canela **8** *B5*
Le Saint Tropez **10** *B4*
Lido **11** *B3*
Metropol **12** *B6*
Oliver's (Hotel
  Presidente) **14** *C3*
San Roque **17** *B5*

Taberna Española **18** *C1*

Bars & clubs 🎵
Britannia Pub **19** *B5*

you the location), and, separately, the tomb of her baby daughter Corrine (Entrada 3 opposite Gran Unión supermarket). Eliza Lynch's home at the corner of Yegros and Mcal Estigarribia was, until 1999, the Facultad de Derecho.

The **National Universidad de Agronomía** ① *campus of the Universidad Nacional, Mon-Fri 0800-1530, closed Jan, free,* has natural history collections. Ask guard at gate for directions

On the outskirts of Asunción is **San Lorenzo** (Km 12). Reached via Ruta 2 (Mariscal Estigarribia Highway) or take buses 12, 56, 26 and get off at central plaza with blue, 18th-century neo-Gothic church. The **Museo Guido Boggiani** ① *Bogado 888, 1½ blocks from plaza, small sign, daily until 1900, ring the bell if door is shut,* is staffed by a very helpful lady who explains the exhibits and history. It has a well-displayed collection of tribal items from the northern Chaco from the turn of the 20th century. The shop across the road sells crafts at good prices. There's also a small Museo Arqueológico near the church and a daily market.

Heading out of the centre along Avenida España

Museo Etnográfico Dr Andrés Barbero ① *España y Mompox, T441696, Mon-Fri 0700-1100, Mon, Wed, Fri 1500-1700, free,* is anthropological with a good collection of tools and weapons of the various Guaraní cultures. The Centro de Artes Viuales includes the **Museo del Barro** and the **Museo de Arte Indígena** ① *Grabadores del Cabichuí entre Cañada y Emeterio Miranda, T607996, www.museodelbarro.org.py, daily, except Sun and holidays, 1600-2030, take bus 30 or 44A from the centre past Shopping del Sol, ask driver for Cañada.* Contains both contemporary and indigenous art, café. Highly recommended.

Luque (take bus 30), founded 1636, has an attractive central plaza with some well-preserved colonial buildings and a pedestrianized area with outdoor cafes. It is famous for the making of Paraguayan harps and guitars (**Guitarras Sanabria** ① *Km 13, T021-2291,* is one of the best-known firms), and for fine filigree jewellery in silver and gold at very good prices, many shops on the main street (ask for Alberto Núñez). Tourist information at Plaza Gral Aquino. There are some fine musical instrument shops on the road to Luque along Av Aviadores del Chaco.

Other Sights

The best of several parks is **Parque Carlos Antonio López**, set high to the west along Colón and, if you can find a gap in the trees, with a grand view. Good views are also offered from **Cerro de Lambaré**, 7 km south (buses 9 and 29 from Gral Díaz).

The **Jardín Botánico** (250 ha) 6 km east, on Av Artigas y Primer Presidente, lies along the Río Paraguay, on the former estate of the López family. The gardens are well-maintained, with signed walks, a rose garden and an 18-hole golf course. In the gardens are the former residences of Carlos Antonio López, a one-storey typical Paraguayan country house with verandas, which now houses a **Museo de Historia Natural** and library, and of Solano López, a two-storey European-inspired mansion which is now the **Museo Indigenista**. ① *Both museums are free, Mon-Sat 0730-1130, 1300-1730, Sun 0900-1300. Getting there: by bus (Nos 2, 6, 23, and 40, US$0.15, 35 mins from Luis A Herrera, or Nos 24, 35 or 44B from Oliva or Cerro Corá).* Neither is in good condition. The beautiful church of **Santísima Trinidad** (on Santísimo Sacramento, parallel to Avenida Artigas), where Carlos Antonio López was originally buried, dating from 1854 with frescoes on the inside walls, is well worth a visit. Nearby is the wreck of the **Ycuá Bolaños supermarket** ① *Santísima Trinidad y Estigarribia,* which was destroyed by fire in August 2004, killing over 700 people when the doors were locked to prevent looting. It is now a memorial with a donation box for the families of the dead. The **Maca Indian reservation** ① *US$0.30, guide US$0.50, getting there: take bus 42 or 44,* is north of the Botanical Gardens. The *indígenas*, who live in very poor conditions, expect you to photograph them (US$0.15).

Around Asunción

Many villages close to Asunción can be visited on a day trip, Aregua and San Bernadino on Lago Ypacari (see page 1048), Altos, great views over the lake, Itauguá. Alternatively take a tour from any travel agent (see Activities and tours below) of the **Circuito de Oro**: destinations vary but tend to include, Itá, Yaguarón, Paraguarí, Piribebuy, Caacupé, San Bernardino, Aregua, Itauguá, 200 km on paved roads, seven hours. The route goes through the hills, no more than 650 m high, which is beautiful, with hidden waterfalls and a number of spas. Chololó, Piraretá (near Piribebuy) and Pinamar (between Piribebuy and Paraguarí) are the most developed. The **Camino Franciscano** is similar, including the historical towns of Ypané, Altos, Itá, Atyra, Yaguarón, Piribebuy, Tobatí, Caacupé, Valenzuela, Villarrica, Caazapá and San Juan Neopomuceno.

● Sleeping

The hotel bill does not usually include a service charge. Look out for special offers.

Asunción *p1038, map p1038*

LL Hotel Casino Yacht y Golf Club Paraguayo, 12 km from town, at Lambaré, on its own beach on the Río Paraguay, PO Box 1795, T906117/121, www.hotelyacht.com.py. 3 restaurants, super luxury, with pool, gym, golf, tennis, airport transfers, etc; many extras free and special deals.

L Excelsior, Chile 980, T495632, www.excelsior.com.py. Luxurious, stylish, gym, pool, tennis, internet, cell phone rental, bar and restaurant.

L Granados Park, Estrella y 15 de Agosto, T497921, www.granadospark.com.py. Luxury, top quality hotel, with breakfast, all facilities, good restaurant *Il Mondo*.

L Sabe Center, 25 de Mayo y México, T450093, www.sabecenterhotel.com.py. Luxury hotel in modern tower, with all facilities, discounts available.

AL Cecilia, Estados Unidos 341 y Estigarribia, T210365, www.hotelcecilia.com.py. Comfortable, internet, good restaurant *La Preferida* (ᵽᵽᵽ), but pool may be dirty.

AL Chaco, Caballero 285 y Estigarribia, T492066, www.hotelchaco.com.py. With breakfast, parking nearby, rooftop swimming pool, bar, good restaurant (ᵽᵽᵽ)

AL Paramanta, Av Aviadores del Chaco 3198, T607053, www.paraguay-hotel.de. 4-star, mid-way between airport and centre, buses stop outside, with bath, TV, internet access, bar, restaurant, pool, gym, gardens, and many other services. English and German spoken.

A Aspen Apart Hotel, Ayolas y Gral Díaz, T493097. With breakfast, pool, sauna, gym, internet, lower price for longer stays.

A Bavaria, Chóferes del Chaco 1010, T600966, www.bavaria.f2s.com. Comfortable, beautiful garden, pool, a/c, good value, German spoken.

A El Lapacho, República Dominicana 543, casi Av España, T210662. Family-run, welcoming, comfortable, a bit run down, rooms available at lower prices. Convenient for local services, 10 mins from centre by bus, pool, 24-hr internet access.

A Portal del Sol, Av Denis Roa y Santa Teresa, T609395, www.hotelportaldelsol.com. Comfortable hotel with breakfast, free airport pick-up and internet, pool.

A Westfalenhaus, Sgto 1 M Benítez 1577 y Stma Trinidad, T292374, www.paraguay-hotels.com. Comfortable, German-run, service and facilities of international quality (certificate ISO 9001-2000), with pool, internet (wireless LAN), safe deposit box, a/c, international restaurant, *Piroschka*, gym, massage and spa, English, German and Spanish spoken. Also has travel information and a travel agency: www.paraguay-travel.de.

B Amalfi, Caballero 877, T494154, www.hotelamalfi.com.py. Modern, comfortable, spacious rooms, breakfast included, internet and restaurant. Recommended.

B Asunción Palace, Colón 415 y Estrella, T/F492151, www.geocities.com/aphotel. With breakfast, very helpful, elegant, colonial style, laundry, internet, older rooms may be available at backpacker rates.

B Gran Armele, Palma y Colón, T444686, www.hotelarmele.com.py. With breakfast, a/c, gym, sauna, restaurant, pool, used by tour groups.

B Trigo del Sur, Mayor Infante Rivarola 653Y, Bertoni, Villa Morra, T602389, www.trigodelsur.com. Small guesthouse with garden, a/c, comfortable, spacious rooms, pool, breakfast included, English spoken. Weekly rates available, in a residential area close to Shopping Villa Morra y Paseo Carmelitas, phone or email in advance for pick-up (US$12 from airport), restaurants and shops nearby.

C City Hotel, Humaitá 209, T491497, www.cityhotel.com.py. A/c, good, with breakfast in City Cafetería in lobby.

Paraguay Asunción Listings

Crafts Check the quality of all handicrafts carefully, lower prices usually mean lower quality. Many leading tourist shops offer up to 15% discount for cash. For leather goods there are several places on Colón and on Montevideo including: **Boutique Irene**, No 463; **Boutique del Cuero**, No 329; **La Casa Del Portafolio**, No 302, and **Galería Colón 185** (recommended).
Artes de Madera at Ayolas 222. Wooden articles and carvings. **Casa Overall 1**, Mcal Estigarribia y Caballero, good selection. Also **No 2** at 25 de Mayo y Caballero, T447891, http://overall. pyglobal.com. **Casa Vera**, Estigarribia 470, for Paraguayan leatherwork, cheap and very good. **Doña Miky**, O'Leary 215 y Pres Franco, recommended. **Folklore**, Mcal Estigarribia e Iturbe, T/F494360, good for music, woodcarvings and other items. **Victoria**, **Arte Artesanía**, Iturbe y Ayala, interesting selection of wood carvings, ceramics etc. Recommended.
Markets Mercado Cuatro on Pettirossi, a large daily market selling food, clothing, electrical items, DVDs, CDs, jewellery, toys, is a great place to visit. Good, cheap Chinese restaurants nearby. There is a daily market on Av Dr Francia, best visited during the week, and a Sat one on Plaza de la Independencia, where the nuns from Villeta sell handmade clothing for children. See also under Historic centre, Sights. Shopping Mariscal López (see below) has a fruit and vegetable market, Tue, in the car park, and a small plant/flower market, including orchids, Thu, at the entrance.
Shopping centres Asunción has a number of modern Shopping Malls with shops, ATMs, cafés, supermarkets, cinemas and *patio de comidas* all under one a/c roof. **Shopping Villa Morra** (Av Mcal López y San Roque González, www.shoppingvillamorra.com.py). **Shopping Mariscal López** (Quesada 5050 y Charles de Gaulle, behind Shopping Villa Morra, www.mls.com.py). **Shopping del Sol** (Av Aviadores de Chaco esq D F de González, www.delsol.com.py). **Mall Excelsior** (Chile y Manduvirá, www.mallexcelsior.com.py).
Supermarkets Hiperseis at Boggiani y Mcal López; **Stock** at Shopping del Sol and Mall Excelsior. **Superseis** at Shopping Villa Morra; **Casa Rica**, Av San Martín y Aviadores del Chaco, good for speciality foods and some European imports. **Real**, Boggiani y Av Argentina, has an imported food aisle, mainly USA.
Cheap electronic goods in the Korean-run shops.

▲ Activities and tours

Asunción *p1038, map p1038*
Football Asunción is the permanent home of the South American Football Confederation, on the Autopista heading towards the airport, opposite Ñu Guazú Park. At the moment this

imposing building with its striking 'football' fountain houses only offices and a small football library but a new museum at the site is due for completion in 2007. T645781 in advance for visits. **Estadio Defensores del Chaco**, Mayor Martínez y Alejo García, T480409, is the national stadium, hosting international, cup and major club matches
Horse riding Club Hípico Paraguayo, Av Gral Andrés Rodríguez y Cleto Romero, Barrio Mariano Roque Alonso, T756148. Members club open to the public. US$50 per month but daily rates available. Friendly and helpful.
Rural tourism *Turismo rural* has become one of the most enjoyable ways to visit the country and get a feel for a Paraguayan way of life that revolves around agriculture and ranching. The **Touring y Automóvil Club Paraguayo** (25 de Mayo y Brasíl, T210550, www.tacpy.com.py) is officially in charge of rural tourism, through the **Paraguayan Rural Tourism Association** (APATUR) T210550-3, int 126-7, or www.turismorural.org.py, and its own travel agency, **Touring Viajes**. They organize visits to ranches and farms all over Paraguay. One-day tour prices start at about US$50 pp including accommodation, food and drink (not alcohol); tours of three or more days for groups of 2-12, US$30-100. All the ranches listed under APATUR have good facilities. Transport to and from these ranches from Asunción is sometimes included in the package. Visitors experience living and working on a ranch, can participate in a variety of activities, and enjoy typical food, horse riding, photo safaris and nature watching.
Tennis Academia de Tenis at Parque Seminario, 25 de Mayo y Kubicheck, T206379 to reserve a court. Price US$4 per hr daytime and US$5 per hr evening. Coaching available.

Tours
Many agencies offer day tours of the Circuito de Oro or Camino Franciscano (from US$50). Trips to local estancias, Encarnación and the Jesuit Missions, Itaipú and Iguazú or the Chaco region are all offered as 1 or 2-day tours. Prices from US$100. Most agencies will also provide personalized itineraries on request. City tours also available. For more information contact **Dirección General de Turismo** or the **Paraguayan Association of Travel Agencies and Tourism** (ASATUR), Juan O'Leary 650, p 1, T491755/491728.
Alda Saguier, Yegros 941, p 2, T446492. English and German spoken.
Aries Travel, Rodríguez de Francia 140 e Yegros, T442334, ariestravel@emociones.org.py.
Canadá Viajes, Rep de Colombia 1061, T2211192, canada.viajes@quanta.com.py. Good Chaco tours.
Inter Tours, Perú 436 y España, T211747, www.intertours.com.py. Tours to Chaco, Iguazú

and Jesuit missions. Recommended.
Itra Travel, Venezuela 663 y España, T450722, itra@itra.com.py. Also offer ecotourism.
Menno Travel, Rep de Colombia 1042 y Brasil, T493504, mennotravel@gmx.net. German spoken.
Siboney, 25 de Mayo 2140 y 22 de Septiembre, T214018, www.siboney.com.py.
Time Tours, 15 Agosto y Gral Díaz, T449737, Villa Morra T601780, timetour@conexion.com.py. Fluent English, runs Camino Franciscano tours. Recommended.
Vips Tour, México 782, T/F441199, vipstours@telesurf.com.py.

⊕ Transport

Asunción p1038, map p1038
Air Silvio Pettirossi Airport, T645600. Several agencies have desks where you can book a taxi to your hotel, US$15-20. Bus 30 goes every 15 mins between the red bus stop outside the airport and Plaza de los Héroes, US$0.25, difficult with luggage. Minibus service from your hotel to airport run by Tropical, T424486, book in advance, US$8 (minimum 2 passengers, or pay for 2). The terminal has a tourist office (free city map and hotel information), bank (turn right as you leave customs – better rates in town), post office (0800-1800), handicraft shop, restaurant and several travel agencies who arrange hotel bookings and change money (very poor rates). Left luggage US$3 per day per item.
Bus City buses: Journeys within greater Asunción US$0.25. Buses are busy at rush hours. Turnstiles are awkward for large backpacks. Keep your ticket for inspection until you leave bus.
Long-distance: The Terminal de Omnibus is south of the centre at República Argentina y Fernando de la Mora (T552154/ 551737). Local bus No 8 is the only direct one from Oliva, which goes via Cerro Corá and Av Brasil from the centre, and stops outside the terminal, US$0.25. From the terminal to the centre it goes via Av Estados Unidos, Luis A Herrera, Antequera and E Ayala; get off at Chile y Díaz. Other buses Nos 10, 25, 31, 38 and 80, follow very circuitous routes. Taxi to/from centre, recommended if you have luggage, US$3.25, journey time depends on the amount of traffic, about 20 mins. The terminal has a bus information desk, free city/country map, restaurant (quite good), café, casa de cambio (poor rates), post office, phone booths and shops. There are many touts for bus companies at the terminal. Allow yourself time to choose the company you want and don't be bullied, or tricked, into buying the wrong ticket. Main companies: Nuestra Señora de la Asunción, T551667, www.nsa.com.py. RYSA, T444244, rysa1@supernet.com.py. Bus company offices on the top floor are in 3 sections:

short-distance, medium and long. Local departures, including for Yaguarón and Paraguarí from the basement. Hotels nearby: turn left from front of terminal, 2 mins' walk. Bus times and fares within Paraguay are given under destinations.
To Uruguay COIT (Eligio Ayala 693, T492473) runs to **Montevideo**, 1000, Sat and Wed, 20 hrs, US$40. **Brújula/Cynsa** (Pres Franco 995, T441720) Tue and Fri, with a 3rd service on Sun in summer, 1330, US$40 (the route is Encarnación, Posadas, Paso de los Libres, Uruguaiana, Bella Unión, Salto, Paysandú – the only customs formalities are at Bella Unión; passport checks here and at Encarnación).
To Argentina There is a road north from Asunción (passing the Jardín Botánico on Primer Presidente) to a concrete arch span bridge (Puente Remanso – US$1 toll, pedestrian walkway on upstream side, 20 mins to cross) which leads to the border at Puerto Falcón (about 40 km) and then to **Clorinda** in Argentina. The border is open 24 hrs; local services are run by Empresa Falcón to Puerto Falcón (US$0.50, every hr, last bus from Falcón to the centre of Asunción 1830; from Falcón to Clorinda costs US$0.25), but it is cheaper to book direct from Asunción to Argentina. Buses don't wait for you to go through formalities: wait for the same company's next bus, or buy a new ticket.
Buses to **Buenos Aires** (18 hrs) daily, many companies, via Rosario and Santa Fe (average fare US$53 luxury, US$33-40 diferencial, US$27-30 común). To **Formosa**, 4 a day, Brújula/La Internacional (T551662, US$5.40, plus US$0.50 luggage) many drug searches on this road; to **Posadas**, Singer, 3 a week at midnight. To **Salta**, take Brújula at 0600 to **Resistencia**, 8 hrs, then change to La Veloz del Norte, 1800.
To Brazil Many Paraguayan buses advertise that they go to destinations in Brazil, when, in fact you have to change buses and book again at the frontier. Note also that through services to **Campo Grande** (US$18) and **Corumbá** via Pedro Juan Caballero and Ponta Porã do not stop for immigration formalities. Check all details carefully. Crucero del Este, Nuestra Señora and Rysa, and the Brazilian companies Pluma (T445024) and Unesul, have services to Ciudad del Este, continuing to **Foz do Iguaçu** (Brazil), US$8, 5-7 hrs, 6 direct buses a day in all. Seat reservations recommended. To **Curitiba**, with Pluma, buses daily, 15½ hrs. To **São Paulo**, Rápido Yguazú, Pluma and Brújula, 20 hrs, Sun-Thu, US$27-29 (leito, US$61). Pluma to **Rio de Janeiro**, US$50; to **Porto Alegre**, Unesul, 4 a week, US$24; Nacional Expresso (Santa Rosa 1116, T669966, F557369) to **Brasília** 3 a week. Services also to **Blumenau** (Catarinense, T551738, Tue, Thu and Sat, 17 hrs, US$19) and **Florianópolis**, US$22, 20 hrs, daily (Pluma and Catarinense).

East of Asunción

Main roads head through rural Paraguay to the borders with Brazil and Argentina. But within the heartland side roads lead to ruined Jesuit missions, German colonies, pockets of native forest and small towns associated with the country's bloody past. In contrast to the quiet of the countryside, Ciudad del Este is a crossroads for all manner of merchandise, while the giant Itaipú dam has irreversibly changed the landscape. Just over the border are the Iguazú Falls.

Itauguá → *Population: 5,400.*

At Km 30, founded in 1728, Itauguá is where the famous ñandutí, or spiderweb lace, is made. There are over 100 different designs. Prices are lower than in Asunción and the quality is better; try the Taller Artesanal (Km 29), the Mutual Tejedoras (Km 28), or Casa Miryam (Km 30, T0294 20372). To watch the lace being made, ask around. The old town lies two blocks from the main highway. Worth seeing are the **market** ① *0800-1130, 1500-1800, closed Sun*, the church and the **Museo de Historia Indígena** ① *Km 25, daily 0800-1130, 1500-1800, US$0.60*, a beautiful collection of carvings of Guaraní myths, and the **Museo Parroquial San Rafael** ① *daily 0800-1130, 1500-1800*, with a display of indigenous art and Franciscan artefacts. There is a four-day festival in early-July, including processions and the crowning of Señorita Ñandutí.

Aregua

At Capiatá (Ruta 2, Km 20, fine colonial church), a left turn goes via a toll road (US$0.75) 7 km to Aregua. Founded in 1541 this is a pretty village on the slopes above Lago Ypacaraí with beautiful colonial houses and an attractive church at the highest point in town. It has an interesting ceramics co-operative, a museum, arts and crafts exhibition and a convent. There is a good German-run restaurant in the centre of the village. From here boat trips run across the lake at weekends to San Bernadino and the tourist steam train comes here each Sunday from Asunción.

San Bernardino and Lago Ypacaraí → *Phone code: 0512.*

At Km 40 on Ruta 2 a branch road, 8 km long, leads off to **San Bernardino**, originally a German colony, known locally as 'San Ber', on the east bank of Lago Ypacaraí. The lake, 24 km by 5 km, has facilities for swimming and watersports and a sandy beach. Ask locally about pollution levels in the water. There are frequent cruises from the pier during the tourist season. This has become *the* vacation spot for Asunción from December-February, which means that it is lively and crowded at weekends in the summer, with concerts, pubs and nightclubs, but it is also getting very built up and commercialized. During the week and off season it continues to be a tranquil resort town. Boats can be hired and there is good walking in the neighbourhood, for example from San Bernardino to **Altos**, which has one of the most spectacular views of the lake, wooded hills and valleys (round trip three hours). Shortly after the turn off from the main road towards San Bernardino is a sign to **La Gruta**; turn right here to a secluded park (Ypacaraí). There are grottos with still water and overhanging cliffs. No buses run after 2000 and taxis are expensive. Tourist information is in the centre of town between Gral Morinigo and Emilio Hassler.

Caacupé → *Phone code: 0511. Colour map 6, grid C6. Population: 9,105.*

At Km 54 on Ruta 2, this is a popular resort and religious centre on the Azcurra escarpment. The centre is dominated by the modern Basilica of Our Lady of the Miracles, with copper roof, stained glass and polychrome stone esplanade, which was consecrated by the Pope in 1988 (US$0.20 to climb the tower). There is an ATM on the plaza between the supermarket and Hotel El Mirador (no other ATM accepts international credit cards between here and Asunción).

Thousands of people from Paraguay, Brazil and Argentina flock to the shrine, especially for the **Feast of the Immaculate Conception** on 8 December. Besides fireworks and candlelit processions, pilgrims watch the agile gyrations of Paraguayan bottle-dancers; they weave in intricate measures whilst balancing bottles pyramided on their heads. The top bottle carries a spray of flowers and the more expert dancers never let drop a single petal.

Tobati, a town north of Caacupé, specializes in woodwork. A *villa artesenal* is a short walk from the bus stop outside the house of Zenon Páez, a world famous sculptor. There are some amazing rock formations on the way to Tobati. To get there, take a bus from the corner below the park on the main Asunción road in Caacupé; ask the driver to let you off at Páez' house.

Piribebuy

At Km 64 beyond Caacupé a paved road runs 13 km southeast to the small town of Piribebuy, founded in 1640 and noted for its strong local drink, *caña*. In the central plaza is the church (1640), with fine sculptures, high altar and pulpit. The town was the site of a major battle in the War of the Triple Alliance (1869), commemorated by the **Museo Histórico Pedro Juan Caballero**, *free*, which contains artefacts from the Chaco War. Buses from Asunción by Transportes Piribebuy. Near the town are the attractive falls of Pirareta. The road continues via Chololó, 13 km south, and reaches Ruta 1 at Paraguarí, 28 km from Piribebuy (see page 1053).

Vapor Cué National Park

A turn-off from Eusebio Ayala (Km 72) goes 23 km to Caraguatay, 5 km from which is the Vapor Cué National Park, where boats from the War of the Triple Alliance are preserved. Although officially a national park, it is more of an open-air museum. Next to the (indoor) museum is a pleasant hotel, called Vapor Cué (T0521-395). Frequent buses run from Asunción to Caraguatay.

Coronel Oviedo and around → *Phone code: 0521. Colour map 6, grid C6. Population: 21,80.0*

An important route centre, although not worth a stop, 3 km south of the junction of west-east highway and the major north-south Ruta 8; buses drop passengers at the junction (El Cruce). Ruta 8) runs north to **Mbutuy**, continuing as Ruta 3 to Yby Yaú, where it meets Ruta 5 (Concepción-Pedro Juan Caballero). At Mbutuy (Km 56, parador, restaurant, petrol station) Ruta 10 branches off northeast to the Brazilian frontier at Salto del Guaíra.

    Salto del Guaíra (Phone code 046) is named after the waterfalls now under the Itaipú lake. There is a 900-ha wildlife reserve, Refugio Biológico Mbaracayú. Salto del Guaíra, a free port, can also be reached by a paved road which runs north from Hernandarias, via Itaquyry to meet Ruta 10 at Cruce Carambey. **Note:** There is nowhere to change travellers' cheques here.

    Mbaracayú Forest Reserve ① *To visit you must book and pay in advance, and sign a disclaimer at the Moisés Bertoni Foundation in Asunción (see National Parks, page 1034); entry US$5, lodging US$15 pp, camping US$10 per tent, take your own food, cook available US$8 per day plus US$3 per day for gas, transport US$0.28 per km. You must hire a guide for US$20 per day. There is public transport to Villa Igatimi from where they pick you up, 20 km to the park. Pay ahead for transport you will require within the park. Buses from Asunción to Curuguaty: La Coruguateña and Santa Ana, 0900 and 1430, 6 hrs, US$5. From Curuguaty to Iguatimi local buses take 1 hr.* One of the finest national parks (not to be confused with Refugio Biológico further east), the reserve boasts 64,406 ha of protected rainforest and is the largest area of representative ecosystems in good conservation status in Paraguay. It contains 48% of all mammal species and 63% of all bird species (over 400) found in eastern Paraguay. There are trails, waterfalls and spectacular view points. There are also two groups of indigenous community, the Aché and Guaraní. There is a visitor centre and small museum at Igatimi.

    At Santa Rosa, 143 km north of Mbutuy, there is petrol, pensión and restaurants. A dirt road runs southwest for 27 km to **Nueva Germania** founded in 1866 by Bernhard Förster and Elisabeth Nietzsche (the philosopher's sister) to establish a pure Aryan colony. This road goes on to San Pedro and Puerto Antequera on the Río Paraguay (88 km). A further 23 km north of Santa Rosa, a dirt road runs northeast through jungle to the interesting **Capitán Badó** (120 km), which forms the frontier with Brazil. From here a road follows the frontier north to Pedro Juan Caballero (100 km). About 50 km north of the turn off to Capitán Badó is Yby Yaú, see page 1058.

Villarrica → *Phone code: 0541. Colour map 6, grid C6. Population: 21,210.*

Villarrica, 42 km south of Coronel Oviedo, is delightfully set on a hill rich with orange trees. A very pleasant, friendly place, it has a fine cathedral, built in traditional style with veranda, and various pleasant parks. The museum (closed weekends) behind the church has a foreign coin collection; please contribute. Products of the region are tobacco, cotton, sugar, yerba mate, hides, meat and wine produced by German settlers. There is a large student population.

German colonies near Villarrica

Some 7 km north is an unsigned turn off to the east, then 20 km to tiny **Colonia Independencia**, which has some beautiful beaches on the river (popular in summer). German-speaking travellers can also visit the German co-operative farms. A great mate and wine producing area and, at harvest time, there is a wine festival. They also have beer festival in October.

East from Coronel Oviedo

The paved Ruta 7 runs 195 km through cultivated areas and woods and across the Caaguazú hills. Ruta 7 continues from here to the spectacular 500-m single span 'Friendship Bridge' across the Paraná (to Brazil) at Ciudad del Este.

Ciudad del Este → *Phone code: 061. Colour map 7, grid C1. Population: 133,900.*

Originally founded as Ciudad Presidente Stroessner in 1957, this was the fastest growing city in the country until the completion of the Itaipú hydroelectric project, for which it is the centre of operations. Ciudad del Este has been described as the biggest shopping centre in Latin America, attracting Brazilian and Argentine visitors who find bargain prices for electrical goods, watches and perfumes. Don't buy perfume on the street and , it's only coloured water. And make sure that shops pack what you actually bought. The main shopping street is Avenida San Blas, lined with shopping malls and market stalls, selling a huge variety of goods, both original and imitations – usually the latter. Watch the exchange rates if you're a short-term visitor. Parts are of the city are dirty and frantic during business hours, but away from the shopping arcades people are friendly and more relaxed. The leather market is well worth a visit, be sure to bargain.

Around Ciudad del Este The **Monday falls** ① *US$0.30, taxi US$20 return*, where the Río Monday drops into the Paraná Gorge, are worth seeing. Nearby is the popular beach resort and biological refuge **Tatí Yupí**. There are two biological reserves bordering the Itaipú dam, **Itabó** and, further north, **Limoy**. Take the unpaved road north from Ciudad del Este towards Salto del Guaíra. Itabó is at the first turn off to Dorila, and Limoy the turnoff at Colonia San Lorenzo.

Border with Brazil

The border crossing over the Friendship Bridge to Foz do Iguaçu is very informal. No passport stamps are required to visit Ciudad del Este for the day. The Friendship Bridge is jammed with vehicles and pedestrians all day long. Motorcycle taxis (helmet provided, hang on tight) are a good option if you have no luggage. Otherwise, to enter Paraguay here, hire a taxi and go very early in the morning, or take your gear to the Paraguayan bus terminal (left luggage facilities) by city bus, then shuttle back and forth on foot to get passport stamped; long and tiring. (Do not fail to get a Paraguayan entry stamp; without it you will be fined. If you do get fined, get a receipt.) Paraguay and Brazilian immigration formalities are dealt with on opposite sides of the bridge. There is a friendly tourist office in the customs building on the Paraguayan side. Note that Adjust your watch to local time (Brazil is one hour ahead). The **Brazilian consulate** ① *Ciudad del Este, Pampliega 337, T500984/510636, F500985, Mon-Fri 0700*, opens to issue visas. The Argentine Consulate is at ① *Av Adrián Jara y Boquerón, Edificio Oriental, T500638/500945.*

Itaipú and around

① *www.itaipu.gov.py. Mon-Fri 0730-1200, 1330- 1700. Sat, Sun and holidays 0800-1100. Bus tours Mon-Fri 0800, 0900, 1400, 1500, 1600 (morning only at weekends and holidays). Free tours of the project with film show (several languages – ask). Take passport. Buses going to Hernandarias will drop you at the visitor centre.*
The Itaipú project (a huge hydroelectric project covering an area of 1,350 sq km) is close to Ciudad del Este, and well worth a visit.

On the way to Itaipú is **Flora y Fauna Itaipú Binacional** ① *0730-1130, 1400-1700*, zoo and museum containing animals and plants; it is about 2 km from the visitor's centre on the road back to Ciudad del Este. At the Centro Ambiental de Itaipú is the new **Museo de la Tierra Guaraní**, which offers a view of the science and culture of the Guaraníes via natural history displays and interactive screens.

Hernandarias, north of Ciudad del Este grew rapidly with the building of Itaipú. A paved road runs north to Cruce Carambey, where it meets Ruta 10 (see above, page 1049). From Hernandarias, boat trips on Lago Itaipú go to Puerto Guaraní where there is a museum.

● Sleeping

San Bernardino *p1048*
There are plenty of hotels other than those listed, many with good restaurants (eg **de Sol** and **Los Alpes**, US$3.30 for buffet lunch and use of pool).

Wander around and see what takes your fancy.
LL Sol de San Ber, E A Garay y Decond, Opposite Del Lago, T2024/2161, pueblo@telesurf.com.py. New, super luxury.

A-B San Bernardino Pueblo, Paseo del Pueblo y Mbocayá, T2195. Swimming pool, a/c, by the lake. Weekend packages, 2 nights for US$55 pp.
C Del Lago, near lake in town, T2201. With breakfast, attractive 19th-century building but run down, pool, lovely gardens.
C Los Alpes, Ruta Gral Morínigo Km 46.5, 3 km from town, T2083 or 0981-552066. A/c, cable TV, lovely gardens, 2 pools, excellent self-service restaurant, children's playground, beach 1 km away, frequent buses to centre.
Camping At Km 43 is **Casa Grande Camping Club** with all facilities. For info, Corfín Paraguaya, Ayolas 437 y Estrella, T492360/1, Asunción, or direct, T0511-649. **San Vicente**, 1km off Ruta 2, excursions, horse riding and birdwatching, T2274.

Caacupé *p1048*
Cheaper than Lago Ypacaraí. Prices increase during the Feast of the Immaculate Conception.
C Virgen Serrana, plaza, T2366. A/c, **D** with fan.
D El Mirador, T2652, on plaza. With bath.
D Katy María, Eligio Ayala y Dr Pino, T2860/2441, beside Basílica. Well-kept, welcoming.
Camping Club de Camping Melli, 1 km east of town, all facilities, T2313. West of Tobati

Ciudad del Este

To Itaipú
To Asunción
Cap Miranda
Emiliano Fernández
Camilo Recalde
Cnel Toledo
To Foz do Iguacu (Brazil)
Av San Blas
Ruta 7 Internacional
Av Mñor Rodríguez
Nanawa
Av Adrián Jara
Av Carlos López
Rgto Piribebuy
Boquerón
Abay
Rgto Itá Ybaté
Av Paí Pérez
García
Av Domingo Robledo
Curupayty
Pamplinga
Francisco Cedzich
Av Mñor
Nicanor Pamplinga
A Matiauda
Carlos López
Av Bernardino Caballero
Av Alejo García
Av Vicente Pamplinga
Pamplinga
Oscar Ribas Ortellado

To Monday Falls

N
0 metres 100
0 yards 100

Sleeping		
Austria 1	Munich 7	
California 2	New Cosmos	
Caribe 3	Apart-Hotel 8	
Convair 4	Panorama Inn 9	
Executive 5	Puerta del Sol 10	
	Tía Nancy 11	

is **Atyrá** (15km from Caacupé), 2 camp grounds: **Chorro Carumbey** and **Balneario Atyrá**.
Tourism farm Estancia Aventura, Km 61.5, Ruta 2, T0981-441804, www.estancia-aventura.com. 225 acres of countryside, worth spending a few days. Good, horse riding, tennis swimming, can arrange airport pickup from Asunción.

Piribebuy *p1049*
F Pensión Santa Rosa. Basic.
F Rincón Viejo, T0515-2251. Reasonable.

Coronel Oviedo and around *p1049*
Salto del Guaíra
C-D Peralta, Av Paraguay y Capitán Capii Pery, T2235. Pleasant, with breakfast and bath, **E** without.

Villarrica *p1049*
B Villarrica Palace Hotel, T43048, Ruta 8 Blas Garay, turn right on road entering Villarrica. New hotel, restaurant, parking, pool, sauna.
C Ybytyruzú, C A López y Dr Bottell, T2390, F2769. Best in town, breakfast, more with a/c, restaurant.
E La Guairana, Mcal López y Talavera, T42915. With bath and a/c, cheaper with fan, friendly.
E-F Central Comuneros y Pa'i Anasagasti, by Plaza Ybaroty at entrance to town. With bath, a/c, electric shower, family run.

German colonies near Villarica *p1049*
Colonia Independencia
C-D Hotel Tilinski, out of town, peaceful, German spoken, swimming pool (filled with river water), meals for residents.
Hotel Restaurant Panorama, set on top of a hill on the road 12 km from Colonia Independencia. German chalet style accommodation, also a good restaurant.
There is camping nearby at Melgarejo.

Between Coronel Oviedo and Ciudad del Este *p1050*
A pp **Estancia Golondrina**, José Domingo Ocampo, Km 235. Contact manager Gustavo Helman (no English, but helpful) at T0527-20122 or 0971-410200 (mob), haraslapaz@ges golondrina.com.py, or Asunción office T/F026-2238/2893/2894 (weekdays only), acsilvero@ gesgolondrina.com.py, or through APATUR (see Rural tourism, page). Take the unpaved road to the right, 17km to the ranch. A good place for combining rural and ecotourism. The ranch has extensive agricultural land as well as 12,000 ha of protected virgin forest and abundant wildlife. There are trails for walking or horse riding, boat trips on the river, and picturesque accommodation (a/c, private bathroom, very comfortable) overlooking the river. Price includes all meals and transportation from the main road.

Parque Nacional Ybycuí

At **Carapeguá**, Km 84 (*hospedaje* on main street, basic, friendly; blankets and hammocks to rent along the main road, or buy your own, made locally and cheaper than elsewhere), a road turns off to Acahay, Ybycuí and the **Parque Nacional Ybycuí** ① *0800-1700, for camping get a permit from the Environmental Department, Madame Lynch 3500, in Asunción (see National parks, page 1034)*, 67 km southeast, one of the most accessible National Parks, if you have a car and one of the few remaining areas of rainforest in eastern Paraguay. Founded in 1973, the 5,000 ha park includes one of the few remaining areas of rainforest in eastern Paraguay. Good walks, a beautiful campsite and lots of waterfalls. At the entrance is a well set out park and museum, plus the reconstructed remains of the country's first iron foundry (La Rosada). Crowded on Sunday but deserted the rest of the week. Guides available. The only shops (apart from a small one at the entrance selling drinks, eggs, etc, and a good T-shirt stall which helps support the park) are at **Ybycuí**, 30 km northwest.

San Ignacio Guazú and around

At Km 226, this is a delightful town on the site of a Jesuit *reducción* (*guazú* is big in Guaraní). Several typical Hispano-Guaraní buildings survive. Each Sunday night at 2000 a folklore festival is held in the central plaza, free, very local, "fabulous". The **Museo Jesuítico** ① *daily 0800-1130, 1400-1730, US$0.60*, housed in the former Jesuit art workshop, reputedly the oldest surviving civil building in Paraguay, contains an important collection of Guaraní art and sculpture from the missionary period. The attendant is very knowledgeable. Nearby is the **Museo Histórico Sembranza de Héroes** ① *Mon-Sat 0745-1145, 1400-1700, Sun 0800-1100*, with displays on the Chaco War. For tours of the area or to visit local ranches contact Emi Tours, T078-220286.

Santa María is 12 km northeast along a cobbled road. Here there is another fine **museum** ① *0900-1300, 1500-1800, US$0.30*, in restored mission buildings containing 60 Guaraní sculptures among the exhibits. The modern church has a lovely altar-piece of the Virgin and Child (the key is kept at a house on the opposite side of the plaza). Good local artesanía shop.

At **Santa Rosa** (Km 248), founded 1698, only a chapel of the original church survived a fire. The chapel houses a museum; on the walls are frescoes in poor condition; exhibits include a sculpture of the Annunciation considered to be one of the great works of the Hispanic American Baroque (ask at the parroquia next door for entry). Buses from San Ignacio Guazú.

A road at Km 262 leads 52 km southwest to **Ayolas** and the Yacyretá hydroelectric scheme. At Km 18 **Santiago** is another important Jesuit centre (1669) with a modern church containing a fine wooden carving of Santiago slaying the saracens. More wooden statuary in the small museum next door (ask around the village for the key-holder). There is an annual **Fiesta de la Tradición Misionera**.

At Km 306 a road turns off the highway to **San Cosme y Damián**, 25 km south. When the Jesuits were expelled from Spanish colonies in 1767, the **church and ancillary buildings** ① *0700-1130, 1300-1700 US$1*, here were unfinished. A huge completion project has followed the original plans. Some of the *casas de indios* are still in use.

Encarnación → *Phone code: 071. Colour map 6, grid C6. Population: 60,000.*

A bridge connects this busy port on the Alto Paraná (founded 1614) with the Argentine town of Posadas. The old town was badly neglected at one time as it was due to be flooded when the Yacyretá-Apipé dam was completed. Since the flooding, however, what is not under water has been restored and a modern town has been built higher up. This is less interesting than the lower part, which formed the main commercial area selling a wide range of cheap goods to visitors from Argentina and Brazil. The town exports the products of a rich area: timber, soya, mate, tobacco, cotton, and hides; it is fast losing its traditional, rural appearance. The town is a good centre for visiting the nearby Jesuit missions of San Cosme y Damián, Trinidad and Jesús. The cost of living is higher than in most other parts of Paraguay. The **tourist office** ① *by Universidad Católica, T203508, 0800-1200*, is very helpful and has a street map. In the afternoon maps available from the Municipalidad, Estigarribia y Kreusser, oficina de planificación.

Border with Argentina

The new San Roque road bridge connects Encarnación with **Posadas**. Formalities are conducted at respective ends of the bridge. Argentine side has different offices for locals and foreigners; Paraguay has one for both. **Note:** Paraguay is one hour behind Argentina, except during Paraguayan summer time.

Encarnación to Ciudad del Este

Jesuit Missions → *50 km from the Argentine border.*

From Encarnación a paved road (Ruta 6) goes northeast to Ciudad del Este. On this road is **Trinidad**, the hilltop site of a **Jesuit reducción** ① *US$0.20, Oct-May 0700-1900, Apr-Sep 0700-1730*, built 1706-1760, now a UNESCO World Cultural Heritage Site. The Jesuit church, once completely ruined, has been partially restored. Note the restored carved stone pulpit, the font and other masonry and relief sculpture. Also partially rebuilt is the bell-tower which is near the original church (excellent views from the top). You can also see another church, a college, workshops and indigenous living quarters. It was founded in 1706 by Padre Juan de Anaya; the architect was Juan Bautista Prímoli. For information or tours (in Spanish and German), ask at the visitor centre. The Jesuito Snack Bar at the turn off from the main road has decent food. 1 km from Trinidad is **Ita Cajón**, an enormous clearing where the stone was quarried for the Jesuit reducción.

About 10 km northwest of Trinidad, along a rough road (which turns off 300 m north from Trinidad entrance) is **Jesús**, now a small town where another group of Jesuits settled in 1763. In the five years before they were expelled they commenced a massive construction programme including church, sacristy, residencia and a baptistry, on one side of which is a square tower. ① *Oct-May 0700-1900, Apr-Sep 0700-1730, US$0.20.* (Camping permitted at entrance to ruins.) There is a fine front façade with three great arched portals in a Moorish style. The ruins have recently been completely cleaned and restored. Beautiful views from the main tower.

Encarnación

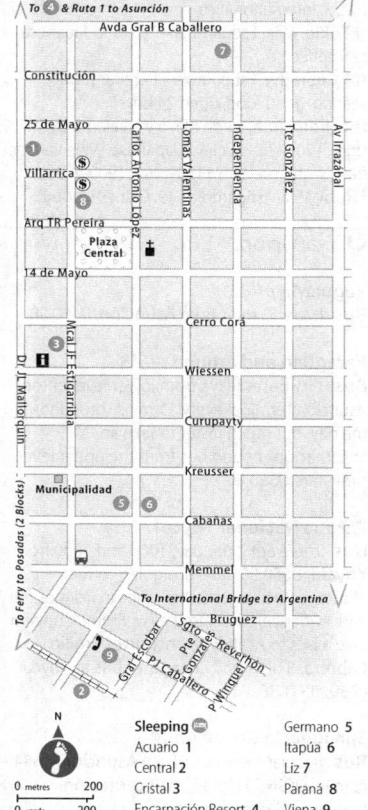

Sleeping 😴
Acuario **1**
Central **2**
Cristal **3**
Encarnación Resort **4**
Germano **5**
Itapúa **6**
Liz **7**
Paraná **8**
Viena **9**

0 metres 200
0 yards 200

From Trinidad the road goes through or near a number of German colonies including **Hohenau** (Km 36) and **Parque Manantial** ① *Km 35, 500 m from main road, T075-32732, F075-32250*. The park is in a beautiful location and has two swimming pools (0830-2200), a good restaurant, bar, camping ground and complete facilities (US$5 per day including use of pool and all facilities), horse riding, tour of the local countryside by jeep and cross country tours to the nearby Jesuit ruins. A good place to stop off on the way to Ciudad del Este. Owner Rubén Pretzle is always willing to help visitors, whatever the problem. Major credit cards accepted, phone calls can be made at no extra charge.

The next colony is **Obligado**; it has an ATM in the centre of town. About 5 km further north is **Bella Vista** (Km 42, ATM), where it is possible to visit various yerba mate plantations. The most geared for visitors is **Pajarito** ① *T0767-240240, www.pajarito.com.py. For those interested in mate see www.yerba-mate.info.*

● Sleeping

Paraguarí and around *p1053*
F Hospedaje Bonanza, Gral Caballero ½ block from highway, T531-32320. Shared bath, fan, nice patio, basic. Owner Juan Aliendre is a composer, he plays and teaches the harp.

Ybycuí *p1054*
D Hotel Pytu'u Renda, Av General Caballero 509. Good food, cooking facilities.
Pensión Santa Rosa and **San Juan**, both **E**, latter has no sign but is nice.

San Ignacio Guazú and around *p1054*
C **Parador Piringó**, T082-262. Modern, on outskirts, with a/c, E pp without, recommended, restaurant open 24 hrs.
E **La Casa de Loli**, T082-2362, on outskirts, Mcal López casi Calle Última. Nice atmosphere, pool, a/c, with breakfast, other meals on request.
E **Gran Katmandu**, Estigarribia e Iturbe (by plaza), T082-2001. A/c, hot water, pleasant, restaurant downstairs.
E **Hospedaje San Antonio**, T082-404. Fan, basic.
E pp **Unión**, T082-544. With bath, a/c and breakfast.
F pp **Pensión San José**, Santa María. Basic.
Camping is possible outside the town.

Encarnación *p1054, map p1055*
B **Encarnación Resort Hotel**, Villa Quiteria on outskirts Ruta 1, Km 2, T207264, erhotel@ ita.com.py. First class, comfortable, very well run. Highly recommended.
C **Paraná**, Estigarribia 1414, T204440. Good breakfast, helpful. Recommended.
D **Cristal**, Mcal Estigarribia 1157, T/F202371, cristalh@telesurf.com.py. Pool, restaurant, TV and a/c, helpful staff.
D **Viena**, PJ Caballero 568, T203486, beside Copaco. With breakfast, German-run, good food, garage.
E **Acuario**, J L Mallorquín 1550 casi 25 de Mayo, T/F202676. Pool, a/c, with breakfast.
E **Central**, Mcal López 542, Zona Baja, T203454. With breakfast, nice patio, German spoken.
E **Germano**, Cabañas y C A López, opposite bus terminal, T3346. F without bath or a/c, German and Japanese spoken, small, very accommodating. Highly recommended.
E **Itapúa**, C A López y Cabanas, T/F205045, opposite bus station. Dark rooms, modern.
E **Liz**, Av Independencia 1746, T202609. Comfortable, restaurant, recommended.

Encarnación to Ciudad del Este *p1055*
A **Hotel Tirol**, at Km 20, by Capitán Miranda, T071-202388, erik@hoteltirol.com.py. Has chalets, swimming pools filled freezing cold spring water, restaurant with plain cuisine, and beautiful views.
F pp **León**, a good hotel and restaurant next to the entrance to the hilltop site of a Jesuit reducción at Trinidad.
Centro Social, Trinidad. Food and shower available, take sleeping gear.
Camping is permitted behind the souvenir stall at Trinidad. No facilities and beware theft.

Obligado
A **Biorevital Hotel and Spa**, Av Mcal López 275, T0717-20073, www.spa-kur.com.py. German run, includes all meals, all organic food, swimming pools with mineral water, yoga, internet, homeopathic treatments.

Bella Vista
A-B **Papillón**, Km 44, T0767-235/280/559, www.paraguay-hotel.com/papillon. A/c, internet, pool, gardens, very pleasant, German, French, English, Flemish spoken, excellent and popular restaurant, full and half-board available. Highly recommended. Organizes excursions in the area including in a light aircraft.
D **Hotel Bella Vista Plaza**, Samaniego 1415, T0757-236.

❼ Eating

Paraguarí and around *p1053*
La Frutería, about 2½ km before the town. Wide selection of fruit, outdoor seating and a restaurant serving *empanadas*, hamburgers, beer, fruit salad.

Encarnación *p1054, map p1055*
♥♥ **American Grill**, Av Irrazábal just before International Bridge. Good *churrasquería*.
♥♥ **Parrillada las Delicias**, Estigarribia 1694. Good steaks, comfortable, Chilean wines.
♥♥ **Provenza**, Dr Mallorquín, just past the rail tracks. International cuisine.
♥♥ **Tokio**, Mcal Estigarribia 472. Good Japanese, real coffee.
♥♥-♥ **Cuarajhy**, Estigarribia y Pereira. Terrace seating, good food, open 24 hrs.
♥♥-♥ **Hiroshima**, 25 de Mayo y L Valentinas (no sign), T206288. Excellent Japanese, wide variety, fresh sushi, Tue-Sun 1130-1400, 1900-2330.
♥ **Rubi**, Mcal Estigarribia 519. Chinese, good.

❺ Transport

Yaguarón *p1053*
Bus Every 15 mins from **Asunción**, US$0.50.

Paraguarí and around *p1053*
Bus City buses leave from lower level of the Asunción terminal every 15 mins throughout the day, but much faster to take an Encarnación- bound bus from the upper level, same fare US$0.80.

Parque Nacional Ybycuí *p1054*
Bus There are 2 per day, 1000 and 1600 from **Ybycuí**, US$0.50, take bus going to the Mbocaya Pucú colony that stops in front of the park entrance. Hitching is easy. From Asunción take a bus to Acahay, **Transportes Emilio Cabrera**, 8 daily and change, or bus to Ybycuí, 0630, US$1.30.

San Ignacio Guazú *p1054*
Bus Regular services to/from **Asunción**, US$4 común, US$6.50 rápido; to **Encarnación**, frequent, US$5 común, US$7.50 rápido.

Santa María
Bus From **San Ignacio** from the Esso station, 6 a day from 0500, 45 mins.

San Cosme y Damián
Bus From **Encarnación**, La Cosmeña and Perla del Sur, US$2.50, 2½ hrs.

Encarnación *p1054, map p1055*
Bus The bus terminal is at Estigarribia y Memmel. Good cheap snacks. To/from **Asunción**, Alborada, Encarnaceña (recommended, T203448), Flecha de Oro, Rysa, Nuestra Señora de la Asunción, all except latter at least 4 a day, 6 hrs, US$12. Stopping (común) buses are cheaper, but much slower (6-7 hrs). To **Ciudad del Este**, US$5, several daily, 4 hrs.

Border with Argentina *p1054*
Bus Take any 'Posadas/Argentina' bus from opposite bus terminal over the bridge, US$0.60, 30 mins. Bus passengers should keep all luggage with them and should retain bus ticket; buses do not wait. After formalities (queues common), use ticket on next bus. **Taxi** costs US$5. **Cycles** are not allowed to use the bridge, but officials may give cyclists a lift. **Ferry** costs US$1: immigration formalities must be undertaken at the main offices.

Jesuit missions: Trinidad and Jesús *p1055*
Bus Many go from Encarnación to and through

Trinidad, take any bus from the terminal marked Hohenau or Ciudad del Este, US$1 (beware overcharging). A taxi tour from Encarnación costs about US$20. Bus direct Encarnación-**Jesús** 0800; buses run Jesús-Trinidad every hr (30 mins, US$0.40), from where it is easy to get back to Encarnación, so do Jesús first. Last bus Jesús-Trinidad 1700; also collective taxis, return Trinidad- Jesús US$3.50. No buses on Sun. Enquire locally as taxis try to overcharge.

❶ Directory

Encarnación *p1054, map p1055*
Banks Most banks now in the upper town, eg Banco Continental, Mcal Estigarribia 1418, Visa accepted. Lloyds TSB Bank, Mcal Estigarribia y Av G Caballero, Visa ATM, Mon-Fri 0845-1215. Citibank, Mcal Estigarribia y Villarrica, ATM. Casas de cambio for cash on Mcal Estagarribia (eg Cambios Financiero at No 307, Cambio Iguazú at No 211). Cambio Chaco Irrazábal casi Memmel, inside Superseis supermarket. Money changers at the Paraguayan side of the bridge but best to change money in town. **Consulates** Argentina, Mallorquín 788, T3446. Brazil, Memmel 450, T3950. Germany, Memmel 631, T204041, F202682. Japan, C A López 1290, T2287, F5130.
Telephones Copaco, Capitán PJ Caballero y Mcal López, 0700-2200, only Spanish spoken.

North of Asunción

The winding Río Paraguay is 400 m wide and is the main trade route for the products of northern Paraguay. Boats carry cattle, hides, yerba mate, tobacco, timber and quebracho, a tree that provides the purest form of tannin. On the river, a boat trip to Concepción is one of the most interesting ways to see the country. East of the river, towards Brazil, is the historically significant Cerro Corá national park.

Asunción to Concepción
North from Asunción by river, you pass Villa Hayes where the bridge marks the beginning of the Trans-Chaco Highway. Further upstream is Puerto Antequera and 100 km beyond is Concepción. **By road there are two alternative routes**. One is via the Trans-Chaco Highway and Pozo Colorado. The Pozo Colorado-Concepción road, 146 km, is now completely paved. This route offers spectacular views of birdlife. Via Ruta 2 to Coronel Oviedo, Ruta 3 to Yby Yaú (paved) and thence west along Ruta 5 (paved). North of Coronel Oviedo, at Tacuara (Km 225), a road heads west to Rosario, from where you can visit the Mennonite community of **Colonia Volendam**, nine hours by bus from Asunción (two a day, San Jorge, US$3). German and Spanish are spoken here.

Concepción → *Phone code: 031. Colour map 6, grid B6. Population: 35,000.*
A free port for Brazil, Concepción, 312 km north of Asunción, stands on the east bank of the Río Paraguay. To appreciate the colonial aspect of the city, walk away from the main commercial streets. At Plaza La Libertad are the Catedral and Municipalidad (undergoing restoration in 2006). Sunsets from the port are beautiful. The town is the trade centre of the north, doing a considerable business with Brazil. The Brazilian Vice Consulate is at Franco 972, T42655, issues visas Monday- Friday 0800-1400. The market, a good place to try local

food, is east of the main street, Agustín Pinedo (which is a kind of open-air museum). From here Avenida Pres Franco runs west to the port. Along Avenida Agustín Pineda is a large statue of María Auxiliadora with Christ child. There are stairs to balconies at the base of the monument which offer good views of the city. The **Museo Municipal** ① *Mcal López y Cerro Corá, Mon-Fri 0700-1200*, contains a collection of guns, religious art and other objects. Plaza Agustín Fernando de Pinedo has a permanent craft market. About 9 km south is a bridge across the Río Paraguay, which makes for an interesting walk across the shallows and islands to the west bank, about an hour return trip, taxi US$6. The island in the Río Paraguay facing Concepción is Isla Chaco'I, where you can stroll through the fields. Row boats take passengers to the island from the shore next to the port, US$0.20 per person.

East of Concepción
There is a 215-km road (Ruta 5 – fully paved) from Concepción, eastwards to the Brazilian border. This road goes through Horqueta, Km 50, a cattle and lumber town of 10,000 people. Further on the road is very scenic. From **Yby Yaú** (junction with Ruta 8 south to Coronel Oviedo) the road continues to Pedro Juan Caballero.

Six kilometres east of Yby Yaú a road branches off to the very pleasant, uncrowded **Parque Nacional Cerro Corá** (22,000 ha), which is the site of Mariscal Francisco Solano López' death and the final defeat of Paraguay in the War of the Triple Alliance. There is a monument to him and other national heroes; the site is constantly guarded. It has hills and cliffs (some with pre-Columbian caves and petroglyphs), camping facilities, swimming and hiking trails. The rocky outcrops are spectacular and the warden, Carmelo Rodríguez, is helpful and will provide free guides. When you have walked up the road and seen the line of leaders' heads, turn right and go up the track passing a dirty-looking shack (straight on leads to a military base). Administration office is at Km 180 on Ruta 5, 5 km east of the main entrance.

Pedro Juan Caballero → *Phone code: 036. Colour map 7, grid B1. Population: 65,000.*
Pedro Juan Caballero This border town is separated from the Brazilian town of Ponta Porã, by a road (Dr Francia on the Paraguayan side, on the Brazilian side either Rua Marechal Floreano or Av Internacional: anyone can cross as they please (see below for immigration formalities). Ponta Porã is the more modern and prosperous of the two. In addition to liquor and electronics, everything costs less on the Paraguayan side. **Shopping China** is a vast emporium on the eastern outskirts of town and **Maxi** is a large well stocked supermarket in the centre. You can pay in guaraníes, reais or US$, at good exchange rates. **Arte Paraguaya**, Mariscal López y Alberdi, has a good selection of crafts from all over the country.

Border with Brazil
This is a more relaxed crossing than Ciudad del Este. For day crossings you do not need a stamp, but passports must be stamped if travelling beyond the border towns. Paraguayan **migraciones** ① *T36-72195, Mon-Fri 0700-2100, Sat 0800-2100, Sun 1900-2100, take bus line 2 on the Parguayan side, or any Brazilian city bus that goes to the Rodoviaria, taxi US$4*, is in the customs building on the eastern outskirts of town near *Shopping China*. Then report to Brazilian federal police in Ponta Porã (closed Sat-Sun). The Brazilian consulate is it Mcal Estigarribia, casi Carlos Antonio López (T/F36-72218, consbras-pjc@uol.com.br, Mon-Fri 0800-1300), visa fees payable only in guaraníes, take passport and a photo, go early to get visa the same day. There is another crossing to Brazil at Bella Vista on the Río Apá, northwest of PJ Caballero; buses run from the Brazilian border town of Bela Vista to Jardim and on to Campo Grande. There is Paraguayan **migraciones** at Bella Vista there but no Brazilian Policia Federal in Bela Vista. To cross here, get Paraguayan exit stamp then report to the local Brazilian police who may give a temporary stamp, but you must later go to the Policia Federal in either Ponta Porã or Corumbá.

● Sleeping

Asunción to Concepción *p1057*
A pp **Estancia Jejui**, set on the Río Jejui, 65 km north of Tacuara on Ruta 3, address in Asunción, Telmo Aquino 4068, T021-600227, www.coinco. com.py/jejui. All rooms with a/c,

bathroom and hot water, fishing, horse riding, tennis, boat rides extra, US$60 pp including all meals.

E pp **Hotel Waldbrunner**, Colonia Volendam, T0451-20175. Bath, **F** without a/c, good restaurant.

Concepción *p1057*
C Francés, Franco y C A López, T42383. With a/c,
D with fan, breakfast, rooms are aging, nice grounds
with pool (US$1.50 non-guests), restaurant, parking.
C Victoria, Franco y Caballero, T42256. Nice rooms,
a/c, fridge, **D** with fan (basic), restaurant, parking.
D Concepción, Don Bosco y Cabral near market,
T42506. With simple breakfast, a/c, **E** with fan,
family run, good value.

Pedro Juan Caballero *p1058*
A Hotel Casino Amambay, Av Dr Francia 1 at
the west end of town, T71140, hcassino@
uol.com.br. A posh establishment centred
around its casino, simple rooms compared to its
surroundings, include buffet breakfast, a/c, fridge,
balcony, lovely grounds with large pool.
B-C La Siesta, Alberdi 30 y Dr Francia, T73021.
With breakfast, a/c, fridge, balcony, restaurant,
pool, aging but still OK, rooms in upper floor have
been refurbished and are nicer.
C Eiruzú, Mcal López y Mcal Estigarribia, T72435.
With breakfast, a/c, fridge and pool, starting to
show its age but still good.
E La Victoria, Teniente Herrero y Alberdi, near bus
station, T72733. With breakfast, electric shower
and a/c, cheaper with fan, family run, simple.

🍴 Eating

Concepción *p1057*
❦ **Hotel Francés**, good value buffet lunch, à la
carte in the evening.
❦ **Hotel Victoria**, set lunches and à la carte, grill
in *quincho* across the street.
❦ **Pollería El Bigote**, Pdnte Franco y E A Garay.
Simple, good chicken, sidewalk seating.
❦ **Ysapy**, Yegros y Mcal Estigarribia at Plaza
Pineda. Pizza and ice-cream, terrace or sidewalk
seating, very popular, 1630-0200 daily.

Pedro Juan Caballero *p1058*
❦ **Mr. Grill** at *Maxi* supermarket, Mcal López y J
Estigarribia. Good quality buffet by the kilo.
❦ **Pepes**, Dr Francia y Alberdi. Buffet, à la carte.
❦ **Pizza House**, Mcal López y José de J Martínez.

🚌 Transport

Concepción *p1057*
Bus The terminal is on the outskirts, 8 blocks north
along Gral Garay, but buses also stop in the centre,
Av Pinedo, look for signs Parada Omnibus. A shuttle
bus (Línea 1) runs between the terminal and the
port. Taxi from terminal or port to centre, US$1.75;
terminal to port US$2.50. To **Asunción**, 7 a day with
Nasa/Golondrina, 2 with Santaniana, plus other
companies, US$10, 5½ hrs via Pozo Colorado, 9 hrs
via Coronel Oviedo. To **Pedro Juan Caballero**,

frequent service, several companies, Amambay is
best, US$4.50, 4-5 hrs. To **Horqueta**, 1 hr, US$1. To
Filadelfia, Nasa/ Golondrina direct at 0730 daily,
US$10, 5 hrs, otherwise change at Pozo Colorado. To
Ciudad del Este, García direct at 1230 daily, US$12,
9 hrs, otherwise change at Coronel Oviedo.
Boat To **Asunción**, the Cacique sails Sun 0700
(in theory), 22 hrs, tickets sold on board in advance
of departure (fares and other services on p 1046).
To **Fuerte Olimpo**, **Bahía Negra**, and
intermediate points along the upper Río Paraguay,
the **Río Aquidabán** sails Tue 1100, arriving Bahía
Negra on Fri morning and returning immediately
to arrive back in Concepción on Sun, US$15 to
Bahía Negra plus US$8.50 for a berth if you want
one. Take food and water. Tickets sold in office just
outside the port, T42435, Mon-Sat 0700-1200.
There is no regular boat service beyond Bahía
Negra for Bolivia or Brazil. *Desplizadores* (motor
launches) may be hired but beware overcharging
and seek advice from the Prefectura Naval. **Note**
Since there is no immigration office in Concepción
nor further upriver, the last place to get an exit
stamp is Asunción, although they may refuse and
send you to a land border instead. In all, a time
consuming, adventurous and expensive journey.

Pedro Juan Caballero *p1058*
Air TAM, Curupayty y Mariscal López, T74501,
to **Asunción**, Mon-Fri, US$55. Airport is 30 km
from town on road to Yby Yaú, TAM has free
shuttle bus before flights, taxi US$17.
Bus To **Concepción**, frequent, 4-5 hrs, US$4.50.
To **Asunción**, 5-6 hrs via 25 de Diciembre, 7½
hours via Coronel Oviedo. Santaniana has nicest
buses, *bus cama* US$12; *semicama* US$10.
Amambay 0700 via Oviedo US$10, twice via 25 de
Diciembre, US$11. **Nasa** 2 a day US$10. To **Bella
Vista**, Perpetuo Socorro 3 a day, US$4.20, 4 hrs.
To **Campo Grande** Amambay 3 a day, US$13, 5
hrs, they stop at Policia Federal in Ponta Porã for
entry stamp. **Nacional Expresso** to **Brasília** via
Campo Grande and Goiânia, US$55, 22 hrs.

🗂 Directory

Concepción *p1057*
Banks Nowhere to change TCs. Norte Cambios,
Pres Franco y 14 de Mayo, Mon-Fri 0830-1700, Sat
0830-1100, fair rates for US$ and euros, cash only.
Financiera Familiar, Pres Franco y Gral Garay, US$
cash only. **Internet** Cybercom Internet Café,
Pres Franco casi 14 de Mayo, open until 2230.
Post office Presidente Franco. **Telephone**
Copaco and other cabinas on Pres Franco.

Pedro Juan Caballero *p1058*
Banks Many *cambios* on the Paraguayan side,
especially on Curupayty between Dr Francia and

Mcal López. Good rates for buying guaraníes or reais with US$ or euros cash, better than inside Brazil, but TCs are difficult to change and there is only one ATM. Banks on Brazilian side do not change cash or TCs but have a variety of ATMs. BBVA, Dr Francia y Mcal Estigarribia. Mon-Fri 0845-1300, changes US$ cash to guaraníes only,

and Cirrus ATM. **Norte Cambios**, Curupayty entre Dr Francia y Mcal López, Mon-Fri 0830- 1630, Sat 0830-1100, fair rates for cash, 3% commission for TCs. **Internet** Several places including **Maxi** supermarket, spacious, quiet, a/c, US$0.80 per hr. **Telephones** Copaco, behind the bus station, plus many *cabinas*.

The Chaco

West of the Río Paraguay is the Chaco, a remarkable area of marshes and farmland, with a substantial population of indigenous peoples. Birdlife is spectacular and common. Apart from the large cattle estancias, agriculture in the Chaco has been developed by German-speaking Mennonites. Through this partly-tamed land the Trans-Chaco Highway runs to Bolivia. Most of the region is pristine, perfect for those who want to escape into the wilderness with minimal human contact and experience nature at its finest.

Ins and outs
Getting there The Paraguayan Chaco covers 24 million ha, but once away from the vicinity of Asunción, the average density is less than one person to the sq km. A single major highway, the Ruta Trans-Chaco, runs in a straight line northwest towards the Bolivian border. It is paved and in excellent condition as far as La Patria, 125 km beyond Mariscal Estigarribia (Paraguayan immigration post). Paving continues between La Patria and Infante Rivarola on the Bolivian frontier. Until paving is completed, those travelling by bus are advised to take their own food and water for a few days as buses may get stuck for a week or more. They depart regardless of road conditions and simply go until they get bogged, then wait for a tractor to pull them out. When completed (no firm date) the Trans-Chaco will be part of a *corredor bi-oceánico*, connecting ports on the Pacific and Atlantic oceans. The elevation rises very gradually from 50 m opposite Asunción to 450 m on the Bolivian border. ›› *For further information, see Transport, page 1064.*

Getting around Most bus companies have some a/c buses on their Chaco routes (a great asset December-March), enquire in advance. There is very little local public transport between the three main Mennonite towns, you must use the buses headed to/from Asunción to travel between them as well as Mariscal Estigarribia. No private expedition should leave the Trans-Chaco without plentiful supplies of water, food and fuel. No one should venture onto the dirt roads alone. (And since this is a major smuggling route from Bolivia, it is unwise to stop for anyone at night.) In the Middle and Low Chaco, there are service stations at regular intervals along the highway; beyond Mariscal Estigarribia there is one stop for diesel. Winter temperatures are warm by day, cooler by night, but summer heat and mosquitoes can make it very unpleasant (pyrethrum coils – espirales – are available throughout the region).

Information Consejo Regional de Turismo Chaco Central (CONRETUR) coordinates tourism development of the three cooperatives and the private sector. Contact Hans Fast, T492-52422, Loma Plata, fast@telesurf.com.py. The **Fundación para el Desarrollo Sustentable del Chaco**, in Loma Plata, T492-52235, www.desdelchaco.org.py, operates conservation projects in the area and has useful information but does not offer tours. For tour operators, see page 1064. See also under individual towns for local tourist offices.

Background
The Low Chaco (the most highly populated part of the Chaco) is just west of Asunción across the Río Paraguay. It is a picturesque area of palm savanna, much of which is seasonally inundated because of the impenetrable clay beneath the surface, although there are 'islands' of high ground. Cattle ranching on gigantic estancias is the prevailing economic activity; some units lie several hundred kilometres down tracks off the highway. Remote estancias have their own airfields, and all are equipped with two-way radios.

In the **Middle Chaco**, the natural vegetation is scrub forest, with a mixture of hardwoods, and cactus in the north. The palo borracho (bottle-tree) with its pear-shaped, water-conserving, trunk, the palo santo, with its green wood and beautiful scent, and the tannin-rich quebracho (axe-breaker) are the most important native species. This is the best area in Paraguay to see large mammals, especially once away from the central Chaco Mennonite colonies.

The **High Chaco** is characterized by low dense thorn forest which has created an impenetrable barricade of spikes and spiny branches resistant to fire, heat and drought, very tough on tyres. Towards Bolivia cactus becomes more prevalent as rainfall decreases. There are a few estancias towards the south, where the brush is bulldozed into hedges and the trees left for shade. Summer temperatures often exceed 45°C.

Reserva de la Biósfera del Chaco

This 7.4 million-ha biosphere reserve in the Chaco and Pantanal eco-systems includes six national parks, monuments and indigenous reserves: Defensores del Chaco, Médanos del Chaco, Teniente Enciso, Cerro Cabrera-Timane, Cerro Chovoreca, and Río Negro. All are north of the Trans-Chaco and most are along the Bolivian border. Teniente Enciso is the smallest park and the only one accessible by public transport, although not easily, see below. The others can only be visited with a private 4WD vehicle or on expensive tours from Loma Plata and Asunción. Most of the country's remaining jaguars are found here. Puma, tapir and peccary also inhabit the area, as well as taguá (an endemic peccary) and a short-haired guanaco, possibly a new sub-species (discovered in Médanos del Chaco in 2003). The best time to see them is, with great patience, around water holes at nightfall. Cerro León (highest peak 600m), the only hilly area of the Chaco, is located in the park. This road from Filadelfia is very rough, 4WD vehicles only.

Parque Nacional Defensores del Chaco, some 220 km from Filadelfia, has three visitors sites with accommodation, a/c, kitchen, shared bath. Distances are long between sites, visitors may be able to travel with rangers, but cannot count on this. **Parque Nacional Teniente Enciso**, 20 km from La Patria, has a nice visitor's site with free accommodation, one room with bath, others shared, a/c, take sleeping bag and all food. **Nasa** mini-bus from Filadelfia to Teniente Enciso via Mariscal Estigarribia and La Patria, see Transport

The Trans-Chaco Route

To reach the Ruta Trans-Chaco, you leave As unción by the route across the Río Paraguay to Villa Hayes. Birdlife is abundant and visible in the palm savanna, but other wild animals are usually only seen at night, and otherwise occur mostly as road kills. The first service station after Asunción is at Km 130. **Pirahú**, Km 252, has a service station and is a good place to stop for a meal; it has a/c, good empanadas and fruit salad. The owner of the parador owns an old-fashioned carbon manufacturing site 2 km before Pirahú. Ask for him if you are interested in visiting the site. At Km 271 is **Pozo Colorado**, the turning for Concepción (see page 1057). There are two restaurants, a basic hotel (**F** pp with fan, cheaper without), supermarket, hospital, a service station and a military post; for hitching, try truck drivers at the truck stop. The Touring y Automóvil Club Paraguayo provides a breakdown and recovery service from Pozo Colorado (T093-516). At this point, the tidy Mennonite homesteads, surrounded by flower gardens and citrus orchards, begin to appear. At Km 282 is one of the most pleasant places to stay or eat, Rancho Buffalo Bill, 14 km northwest of Pozo Colorado, T021-298381.The restaurant, set beside a small lake, is in a picturesque thatched roof log cabin. Excellent homemade food, a/c. The estancia has 10,000 ha, limited but good accommodation (**D**), ask at restaurant. Horse riding, ecological walks and camping possible. At Km 320 is **Río Verde**, with fuel, police station and restaurant. The next acceptable place to stay or eat on the Trans-Chaco is **Cruce de los Pioneros**, at Km 415, a weekend excursion from Asunción where accommodation (**D Los Pioneros**, T491- 32170, hot shower, a/c), limited supermarket, vehicle repair shop, and fuel are available. A new paved road is being built from Cruce Boquerón, northwest of Cruce de los Pioneros, to Loma Plata.

The Mennonite communities

The Middle Chaco near Filadelfia has been settled by Mennonites, Anabaptists of German extraction who began arriving in the late 1920s. There are three administratively distinct but adjacent colonies: Menno (from Russia via Canada); Fernheim (directly from Russia) and Neuland (the last group to arrive, also from Russia, after the Second World War). Among themselves, the Mennonites speak 'plattdeutsch' ('Low German'), but they readily speak and understand 'hochdeutsch' ('High German'), which is the language of instruction in their

Mariscal Estigarribia *p1063*

C-D **Parador Arami**, northwest end of town and far from everything, also known as *la terminal*, T0494-247230. Functional rooms, a/c, meals on request, agents for Stel Turismo and Nasa bus lines.

E **La Laguna**, next to the Municipio. With bath, a/c, E with fan, very small rooms, mosquitoes, nice garden but otherwise neglected.

❶ Eating

Filadelfia *p1062*

ℸℸ **El Girasol**, Unruh 126-E y Hindenburg. Good buffet and *rodizio*, cheaper without the meat. Mon-Sat 1100-1400, 1800-2300, Sun 1100-1400.

Loma Plata *p1062*

ℸℸ **Chaco's Grill**, Av Dr Manuel Gondra, T52166. Open daily for buffet and *rodizio* plus à la carte, very good, patio, live music at weekends.

ℸ **Norteño**, almost opposite supermarket. Good, simple, lunch till 1400 then open for dinner.

ℸ **Pizzería San Marino**, Av Central y Dr Gondra. Pizza and German dishes, daily 1800-2300.

Mariscal Estigarribia *p1063*

ℸℸ **Italiano**, at the southwest end of town behind the Shell station, T0494-247231. Excellent cooking with a European touch, top quality meat, large portions, an unexpected treat in the outback. Italian owner Mauricio is friendly and helpful, open daily for lunch and dinner.

▲ Activities and tours

Many agencies in Asunción offer Chaco tours. Note that some are just a visit to Rancho Buffalo Bill and do not provide a good overview of the natural or cultural attractions. Hans Fast and Harry Epp also run tours to national parks. In Loma Plata ask around for bicycle hire to explore nearby villages.

❶ Transport

Filadelfia *p1062*

Bus From **Asunción**, Nasa/Golondrina, 5 daily; Stel Turismo, 1 overnight; Ovetense 2 daily; all 6-7 hrs, US$11. To **Loma Plata**, Nasa/Golondrina 0800 going to Asunción, 0600 and 1900 coming from Asunción, 1 hr, US$1.75. To **Neuland**, local service Mon-Fri 1130 and 1800, 1 hr, US$1.75. Also Stel Turismo at 1900 and Nasa/Golondrina at 2115, both coming from Asunción. To **Mariscal Estigarribia**, Ovetense at 1800 coming from Asunción, 1½ hrs, US$2. Also Nasa at 0500 Mon and Fri, continuing to La Patria and Parque Nacional Teniente Enciso (see page 1061), 5-6 hrs, US$8.50, returns around 1300 same day (new service in 2006, confirm all details in advance).

Loma Plata *p1062*

Bus Asunción, Nasa/Golondrina, 3 daily, 7-8 hrs, US$11. To **Filadelfia**, Mon-Fri 1300, Sat 1100, Sun 1200, daily 2130, all continuing to Asunción, 1 hr, US$1.75.

Neuland *p1062*

Bus To **Asunción**, Nasa/Golondrina 1t 1945, and Stel Turismo at 1800, via Filadelfia, 7-8 hrs, US$11. Local service to Filadelfia, Mon-Fri 0500, 1230, 1 hr, US$1.75.

Mariscal Estigarribia *p1063*

Bus From **Filadelfia** Nasa/Golondrina 1100 daily, **Ovetense** 1200 and 2000 daily; **Asunción** Nasa/Golondrina, Sun-Fri 2 daily, Sat one bus; Ovetense 2 daily, 7-8 hrs, US$11.0700. Buses from Asunción pass through town around 0300-0400 en route to Bolivia: **Yaciretá** on Tue, Thu, Sat, Sun (agent at Barcos y Rodados petrol station, T0494-247320); **Stel Turismo** daily (agent at Parador Arami, T0494-247230). You can book and purchase seats in advance but beware overcharging, the fare from Mariscal Estigarribia should be about US$10 less than from Asunción.

❶ Directory

Filadelfia *p1062*

Banks There are no ATMS in the Chaco, neither in the Mennonite colonies nor in Mariscal Estigarribia. **Fernheim Cooperative Bank**, Hindenburg opposite the Cooperative building, changes US$ and euro cash, no commission for US$ TCs. **Internet** At Shopping Portal del Chaco and opposite Radio ZP30. **Telephone** Copaco on Hindenburg, opposite supermarket, Mon-Sat 0700-2100, Sun 0700-1200, 1500-2000.

Loma Plata *p1062*

Banks Chortitzer Komitee Co-op, Av Central, Mon-Fri 0700-1730, Sat 0700-1100, good rates for US$ and euros, US$1 commission per TC. **Internet** Microtec, Fred Engen 1229, Mon-Sat 0800-1130, 1400-2200, US$0.80 per hr. **Telephone** Copaco, Av Central across from supermarket, Mon-Sat 0700-2000, Sun 0700-1200, 1500-2000.

Neuland *p1062*

Banks Neuland Cooperative changes US$ cash and TCs, Mon-Fri 0700-1130, 1400-1800, Sat 0700-1130.

Mariscal Estigarribia *p1063*

Banks No banks or cambios. Shell station has best rates for US$, cash only, small bills preferred. **Telephones** Copaco, one street back from highway, ask for directions.

☷ Footprint features

Introduction

Cuzco, capital of the Inca world, is now South America's gringo hangout, with its access to Machu Picchu, the Sacred Urubamba Valley and a buzzing nightlife. On the border with Bolivia is Lake Titicaca, blessed with a magical light and fascinating islands. But in Peru, the Egypt of the Americas, this is just the tip of the pyramid. The coastal desert may sound uninhabitable, yet pre-Inca cultures thrived there. They left their monuments in sculptures etched into the surface of the desert, most famously at Nasca. Civilization builders welcomed gods from the sea and irrigated the soil to feed great cities of adobe bricks. After the Incas came the Spanish *conquistadores*, who left some of their own finest monuments. You can trek for ever amid high peaks and blue lakes, cycle down remote mountainsides, look into canyons deeper than any others on earth, or surf the Pacific rollers. There are enough festivals to brighten almost every day of the year, while the spiritual explorer can be led down mystical paths by a shaman. East of the Andes the jungles stretch towards the heart of the continent with some of the richest biodiversity on earth. And, should you tire of nature, there is always Lima, loud, brash, covered in fog, but with some of the best museums and liveliest nightlife in the country.

★ Don't miss...

1 **Cordillera Blanca** Region of jewelled lakes and sparkling mountains, attracting mountaineers, cyclists and rafters in their thousands, page 1116.
2 **Kuélap** The greatest pre-Columbian fortress in the Americas, buried high in jungle-clad mountains, once home to the Cloud People, page 1155.
3 **Nazca Lines** Take a flight over the lines to see giant whales, spiders and hummingbirds mysteriously etched into the desert, page 1169.
4 **Colca Canyon** At the rim of one of the deepest canyons on earth, you can come face-to-face with the condor, page 1184.
5 **Machu Picchu** The Inca spirit and majesty of its setting rise above today's tourist demands, with the gringo capital of Cuzco nearby, page 1235.
6 **Manu Biosphere Reserve** One of the world's largest protected areas of rainforest, home to jaguars, giant otters and countless birds, page 1274.

Essentials

Planning your trip

Where to go Lima, the sprawling capital, is daunting at first sight, but worth investigating for its museums, colonial architecture and nightlife. Routes radiate in every direction and great steps have been taken to improve major roads linking the Pacific with the highlands. Travelling overland does, however, take time, so if on a short visit, flying is the best option.

North of Lima it is only seven hours to Huaraz, in the Cordillera Blanca, the country's climbing and trekking centre. Mountaineering and hiking can be easily linked with the archaeological site at Chavín, east of Huaraz, or with the pre-Inca cities Sechín, Chan Chán and the Huaca de la Luna, the last two close to the colonial city of Trujillo. Heading up the coast, there is plenty of evidence of pre-Columbian culture, particularly around Chiclayo, beaches for surfing (eg Chicama) or watching traditional fishing techniques, and wildlife parks in the far north near Tumbes. (Tumbes, and the nearby Piura-Sullana route are the gateways to Ecuador.) In the northern highlands, Cajamarca is a pleasant base for exploring more archaeological sites, thermal baths and beautiful countryside. From here, or by a route from Chiclayo, there is access to the remote Chachapoyas region where a bewildering number of prehispanic cities and cultures are beginning to be opened up to visitors. Going east from here is one of the less-travelled, but nonetheless beautiful roads into the jungle lowlands.

South of Lima are Peru's most deservedly famous tourist destinations. The chief focus is Cuzco, where Spanish colonial and Inca architecture are united, and the Sacred Valley of the Incas, with the mountain-top city of Machu Picchu as the highlight of a historical and cultural treasure trove. Regular trips from Cuzco extend to Puno on the shores of Lake Titicaca (on the overland route to Bolivia), in which islands are frequently visited to see a unique way of life. Arequipa, a fine city at the foot of El Misti volcano, gives access to the canyons of Colca and, for those with more time, the even deeper Cotahuasi. A much-travelled railway links Cuzco, Puno and Arequipa, but the Cuzco-Puno road has now been paved, offering new opportunities for exploring these high altitude regions. On the southern coastal route is the Paracas Peninsula (near Pisco), reputed to be home to the largest sea-lion colony on earth, and offshore Ballestas islands, one of the best places to see marine birdlife in the world. The mysterious Nazca Lines, whose meanings still stir debate, etched in the stony desert, should not be missed if you are on the Lima-Arequipa road, or taking the Pan-American Highway south to Tacna and Chile.

The **Central Highlands** can be reached by roads from Lima, Pisco and Nazca, the main centres being Huancayo, Huancavelica and Ayacucho. There is much of historical interest here and the Mantaro Valley, and Ayacucho are good areas for buying handicrafts. From Ayacucho you can continue to Cuzco by plane or, if willing to rough it, by bus. Roads in this part of the Sierra are being improved considerably, but check conditions if going far off the beaten track.

Another route into the **Peruvian jungle** runs from the Central Highlands to Pucallpa, but the most popular journeys are by air to the Amazon city of Iquitos, from where boats can be taken to Brazil, or from Cuzco to the spectacular Manu Biosphere Reserve and the Tambopata area (accessed from Puerto Maldonado). This has some of the highest levels of biodiversity in the world, providing wonderful opportunities for animal and plant lovers.

When to go Each of Peru's geographical zones has its own climate. The **coast**: December-April, summertime, temperatures from 25° to 35°C; hot and dry. These are the best months for swimming. Wintertime, May-November; the temperature drops a bit and it is cloudy. On the coast, climate is determined by cold sea-water adjoining deserts: prevailing inshore winds pick up so little moisture over the cold Peruvian current that only from May to November does it condense. The resultant blanket of cloud and sea-mist extends from the south to about 200 km north of Lima. This *garúa* dampens isolated coastal zones of vegetation (called *lomas*) and they are grazed by livestock driven down from the mountains. During the *garúa* season, only the northern beaches near Tumbes are warm enough for pleasant swimming.

The **sierra**: April-October is the dry season, hot and dry during the day, around 20°-25°C, cold and dry at night, often below freezing. November-April is the wet season, dry and clear most mornings, some rainfall in the afternoon, with average temperatures of 18°C (15°C at night).

Peru's high season is June-September, which is the best time for hiking the Inca trails or trekking and climbing elsewhere in the country. At this time the days are generally clear and sunny, though nights can be very cold at high altitude. The highlands can be visited at other times of the year, though during the wettest months November-April some roads become impassable and hiking trails can be very muddy.

The **jungle**: April-October, dry season, temperatures up to 35°C. This is the best time to visit the jungle. In the jungle areas of the south, a cold front can pass through at night. November-April, wet season, heavy rainfall at any time, humid and hot. During the wet season, it only rains for a few hours at a time, which is not enough to spoil your trip, but enough to make some roads virtually impassable.

Finding out more Tourism promotion and information is handled by **PromPerú** ① *Edif Mincetur, C Uno Oeste 50, p 13, urb Córpac, San Isidro, T01-224 3131, www.peru.org.pe, or www.peru.info. PromPerú runs an information and assistance service, **i perú** ① T01-574 8000 (24 hrs). The main office in Lima is at Jorge Basadre 610, San Isidro, T421 1627, iperulima@promperu.gob.pe, Mon-Fri 0830-1830. There is a 24-hr office at Jorge Chávez airport; there are offices around the country, addresses of which are given in the text.*

There are offices in most towns, either run by the municipality, or independently, which provide tourist information. Outside Peru, information can be obtained from Peruvian embassies and consulates. **Indecopi** ① *in Lima T224 7777, rest of Peru 0800-44040 (not available from payphones), www.indecopi.gob.pe,* is the government-run consumer protection and tourist complaint bureau. They are friendly, professional and helpful. An excellent source of information is **South American Explorers**, in Lima (see page 1079) and Cuzco. See also Essentials, page 32. They have information on travellers held in prison, some for up to one year without sentencing, and details on visiting regulations. A visit will be really appreciated!

Websites

www.conam.gob.pe National Environmental Commission (Spanish).
www.perucultural.org.pe Information on cultural activities, museums textiles (Spanish).
www.yachay.com.pe Red Científica Peruana, click 'Turismo' to get to travel page.
www.adonde.com and
www.perulinks.com are portals.
www.terra.com.pe Click 'Turismo' to get to travel page (in Spanish).
http://travel.peru.com/travel/english Peru.Com's travel page (English).
www.traficoperu.com Online travel agent with lots of information (Spanish and English).
www.livinginperu.com Informative guide in English for people living in Peru.
www.perurail.com Peru Rail.
www.geocities.com/perutraveller/ (English)
www.aboutcusco.com,

www.cuscoonline.com,
www.cuscoperu.com, and
www.cusco.net websites about Cuzco.
www.machu-picchu.info On Machu Picchu
www.isidore-of-seville.com/machu Lots of links to sites about Machu Picchu.
www.yachay.com.pe/especiales/nasca Nazca lines (in Spanish).
www.arequipa-tourism.com On Arequipa.
www.andeanexplorer.com and
http://huaylas.com For Huaraz and the Callejón de Huaylas, both in English.
www.perunorte.com Northern Peru (La Libertad, Cajamarca and Lambayeque), in Spanish, English and German.
www.xanga.com/TrujilloPeru Mainly for the north of the country, packed full of links.
www.caretas.com.pe The most widely-read weekly magazine, *Caretas*.

Maps The **Instituto Geográfico Nacional** in Lima sells a selection of maps, see page 1096. Lima 2000's *Mapa Vial del Perú* (1:2,200,000) is probably the most correct road map available. Maps can be obtained from the **South American Explorers**, who will give good advice on road conditions. The **Touring y Automóvil Club del Perú** ① *Av César Vallejo 699, Lince, Lima, T221 2432, www.touringperu.com.pe*, with offices in most provincial cities, gives news about the roads and hotels (for the most up-to-date information also try bus and colectivo offices). It sells a very good road map at US$5 (Mapa Vial del Perú, 1:3,000,000, Ed 1980) and route maps covering most of Peru. The *Guía Toyota* (Spanish), which is published annually, is one of the best guides for venturing off the beaten track. Other maps can be bought from street vendors in Colmena and Plaza San Martín, Lima. 'Westermanns Monatshefte; folio Ecuador, Peru, Bolivien' has excellent maps of Peru, especially the archaeological sites.

A good tourist map of the Callejón de Huaylas and Cordillera Huayhuash, by Felipe Díaz, is available in many shops in Huaraz, including Casa de Guías. **Alpenvereinskarte Cordillera Blanca Nord 0/3a** at 1:100,000 is the best map of that region, US$12, available in Huaraz and Lima, but best bought outside Peru. **Cordillera Huayhuash map**, 1:80,000 (The Alpine Mapping Guild, 2nd ed, 2004) is recommended, available in Huaraz at Café Andino, US$15.

Visas and immigration Tourist cards: no visa is necessary for citizens of countries in the EU, Asia, North and South America, and the Caribbean, or for citizens of Norway, Switzerland, Australia, New Zealand and South Africa. A Tourist Card is free on flights arriving in Peru, or at border crossings for visits up to 90 days. Insist on getting the full 90 days. The form is in duplicate, the original given up on arrival and the copy on departure, and may be renewed (see below). A new tourist card must be obtained for each re-entry or when an extension is given. If your tourist card is stolen or lost, get a new one at **Inmigraciones** ① *Av España 700 y Av Huaraz, Breña, Lima, Mon-Fri 0900-1330*.

Tourist visas For citizens of countries not listed above, cost £21.60 (approx US$38) or equivalent, for which you require a valid passport, a departure ticket from Peru (or a letter of guarantee from a travel agency), two colour passport photos, one application form and proof of economic solvency. Keep identification, preferably a passport, on you at all times. You must present your passport when reserving tickets for internal, as well as, international travel. An alternative is to photocopy the important pages of your passport – including the immigration stamp, and have it legalized by a 'Notario público' (US$1.50). This way you can avoid showing your passport. We have received no reports of travellers being asked for an onward ticket at the borders at Tacna, Aguas Verdes, La Tina, Yunguyo or Desaguadero. Travellers arriving by air are not asked for an onward flight ticket at Lima airport, but it is possible that you will not be allowed to board a plane in your home country without showing an onward ticket.

⁝ Touching down

Airport taxes US$30 on international flight departures, payable in dollars or soles; US$6 on internal flights (when making a domestic connection in Lima, you don't have to pay airport tax; contact airline personnel at baggage claim to be escorted you to your departure gate). 19% state tax is charged on air tickets; it is included in the price of the ticket.

Business hours Shops: 0900 or 1000-1230 and 1500 or 1600-2000. In the main cities, supermarkets do not close for lunch and Lima has some that are open 24 hours. Some are closed on Sat and most are closed on Sun. **Banks**: most banks around the country are open 0930-1200 and 1500-1800. Banks in Lima are open 0900-1800. Many banks in Lima and Cuzco have Sat morning hours from 0930-1230. **Offices**: Continuous hours 0900-1700 and most close on Sat. **Government offices**: Mon-Fri 0830-1130, Jan-Mar. The rest of year Mon-Fri 0900-1230, 1500-1700, but this changes frequently.

In an emergency Tourist Police Administrative office at Jr Moore 268, Magdalena at the 38th block of Av Brasil, Lima, T460 1060, daily 24 hrs; for public enquiries etc, Jr Pachitea at the corner of Belén, Lima, T424 2053. You should come here if you have had property stolen. They are friendly, helpful and speak English and some German

International phone code +51.

Time GMT -5.

Tipping Restaurants: service is included in the bill, but if someone goes out of his way to serve tips can be given. Give the tip to the person you want to receive it. Taxi drivers, none (bargain the price down, then pay extra for good service). Cloakroom attendants and hairdressers (very high class only), US$0.50-1. Airport or railway porters, US$0.50. Car wash boys, US$0.30, car 'watch' boys, US$0.20. If going on a trek or tour, it is customary to tip the guide as well as the cook and porters.

VAT/IVA 19%.

Voltage 220 volts AC, 60 cycles throughout the country, except Arequipa (50 cycles). Most four- and five-star hotels have 110 volts AC. Plugs are either American flat-pin or twin flat and round pin combined.

Weights and measures Metric.

Renewals and extensions To extend a tourist card at Immigration in Lima (address above), go to the third floor and enter the long narrow hall with many 'teller' windows. Go to window number 5 and present your passport and tourist card. The official will give you a receipt for US$20 (the cost of a one-month extension) which you will pay at the Banco de la Nación on the same floor. Then go down to the first floor and buy form Foo7 for S/.24 (US$6.75). Fill out the form and return to window 5 on the third floor. Give the official the paid receipt, the filled-out form, your passport and tourist card. Next, you will wait two minutes for your passport to be stamped and signed. **Note** three extensions like this are permitted, although it's unlikely that you will be allowed to buy more than one month at a time. Peruvian law states that a tourist can remain in the country for a maximum of six months, after which time you must leave. Crossing the border out of Peru and returning immediately is acceptable. You will then receive another 90 days and the process begins all over again.

If you let your tourist visa expire you can be subject to a fine of US$20 per day, but this is up to the discretion of the immigration official. You can extend your visa in Lima, Cuzco, Puno, Puerto Maldonado, and Iquitos, but in the provinces it can take more time.

Business visas If a visitor is going to receive money from Peruvian sources, he/she must have a business visa: requirements are a valid passport, two colour passport photos, return ticket and a letter from an employer or Chamber of Commerce stating the nature of business, length of stay and guarantee that any Peruvian taxes will be paid. The visa costs £21.60 (or equivalent) and allows the holder to stay 90 days in the country. On arrival business visitors must register with the *Dirección General de Contribuciones* for tax purposes.

Student visas To obtain a one year student visa you must have: proof of adequate funds, affiliation to a Peruvian body, a letter of recommendation from your own and a Peruvian Consul, a letter of moral and economic guarantee from a Peruvian citizen and four photographs (frontal and profile). You must also have a health check certificate which takes four weeks to get and costs US$10. Also, to obtain a student visa, if applying within Peru, you have to leave the country and collect it in La Paz, Arica or Guayaquil from Peruvian immigration (it costs US$20).

Peruvian embassies and consulates Visit www.rree.gob.pe, the Ministry of Foreign Affairs website for details of Peruvian embassies and consulates.

Money

Currency The new sol (s/) is divided into 100 céntimos. Notes in circulation are: S/200, S/100, S/50, S/20 and S/10. Coins: S/5, S/2, S/1, S/0.50, S/0.20, S/0.10 and S/0.05 (being phased out). Some prices are quoted in dollars in more expensive establishments, to avoid changes in the value of the sol. You can pay in soles, however. Try to break down large notes whenever you can. Sol **exchange rate** with US$: 3.27; with euro: 4.23 (June 2006).

Warning A large number of forged US dollar notes (especially US$20 and larger bills) are in circulation. Soles notes and coins are also forged. Always check your money when you change it, even in a bank (including ATMs). Hold notes up to the light to inspect the watermark and that the colours change according to the light. The line down the side of the bill spelling out the bill's amount should appear green, blue and pink. Fake bills are only pink and have no hologram properties. There should also be tiny pieces of thread in the paper (not glued on). In parts of the country, forged one-, two- and five-sol coins are in circulation. The fakes are slightly off-colour, the surface copper can be scratched off and they tend to bear a recent date. Posters in public places explain what to look for in forged soles. There is a shortage of change in museums, post offices, railway stations and even shops, while taxi drivers are notorious in this regard – one is simply told 'no change'. Do not accept this excuse.

Credit cards, traveller's cheques (TCs), Banks and ATMs Visa (by far the most widely-accepted card in Peru), MasterCard, American Express and Diners Club are all valid. There is often an 8-12% commission for all credit card charges. Most banks are affiliated with Visa/Plus system; those that you will find in almost every town and city are **BCP** and **BBVA Continental**. **Interbank** ATMs accept Visa, Plus, MasterCard, Maestro, Cirrus and American Express. **Banco Wiese Sudameris** ATMs accept Visa, Plus, MasterCard, Maestro and Cirrus. There are also **Red Unicard** ATMs which accept Visa, Plus, Mastercard, Maestro and Cirrus. ATMs usually give dollars if you don't request soles and their use is widespread. The compatibility of ATMs across Peru is increasing all the time. Your card has to be pretty obscure not to be able to obtain cash from an ATM, but availability decreases outside Cuzco and other large towns. In smaller towns, go prepared with cash. Businesses displaying credit card symbols, on the other hand, are less likely to take foreign cards. For credit card loss: **American Express** ① *Travex SA, Av Santa Cruz 621, Miraflores, Lima, T01-690 0900, info@travex.com.pe*; **Diners Club** ① *Canaval y Moreyra 535, San Isidro, T01-221 2050*; **Mastercard** ① *Porta 111, p 6, Miraflores, T01-311 6000, T0800-307 7309*; **Visa** ① *Travel Assistance, T108 and ask the operator for a collect call (por cobrar) to 410-902 8022 (English), T581 0120/9754 (Spanish), or T420-937 8091.*

US dollars and euros are the only currencies which should be brought into Peru from abroad (take some small bills). There are no restrictions on foreign exchange. Banks are the most discreet places to change travellers' cheques into soles. Some charge commission from 1% to 3%, some don't, and practice seems to vary from branch to branch, month to month. The services of the BCP have been repeatedly recommended. Changing money at a bank always gives a lower rate than with *cambistas* (street changers) or *casas de cambio* (exchange houses). Always count your money in the presence of the cashier. Street changers give the best rates for changing small amounts of dollars or euros cash, avoiding paperwork and queuing, but take care: check your soles before handing over your dollars, check their calculators, etc, and don't change money in crowded areas. If using their services think about taking a taxi after changing, to avoid being followed. Street changers usually congregate near an office where the exchange 'wholesaler' operates; he will probably be offering better rates than on the street. Soles can be exchanged into dollars at the exchange desks at Lima airport, and you can change soles for dollars at any border. Dollars can also be bought at the various borders. **Note**: No one, not even banks, will accept dollar bills that look 'old', or are in any way damaged or torn.

American Express will sell travellers' cheques to cardholders only, but will not exchange cheques into cash. Amex will hold mail for cardholders at the Lima branch only. They are also very efficient in replacing stolen cheques, though a police report is needed. Most of the main banks accept American Express travellers' cheques and BCP, Interbank and BSCH accept Visa travellers' cheques. Citibank in Lima and some BSCH branches handle Citicorp cheques. Travellers have reported great difficulty in cashing travellers' cheques in the jungle area, even Iquitos, and other remote areas. Always sign travellers' cheques in blue or black ink or ballpen.

Cost of travelling The approximate budget is US$25-35 per person a day for living comfortably, including transport, or US$12-US$15 a day for low budget travel. Your budget will be higher the longer you stay in Lima and depending on how many flights you take between destinations. Accommodation rates range from US$3-4 per person for the most basic *alojamiento* to over US$150 for luxurious hotels in Lima and Cuzco. For meal prices, see Eating, below. Living costs in the provinces are from 20% to 50% below those in Lima, although Cuzco is more expensive than other, less touristy provincial cities. For a lot of low income Peruvians, many items are simply beyond their reach. The price of using the internet is generally US$0.60-1 per hour, but where competition is not fierce, rates vary from US$1.50 to US$4.

Students can obtain very few reductions in Peru with an international students' card, except in and around Cuzco. To be any use in Peru, it must bear the owner's photograph. An ISIC card can be obtained in Lima from **Intej** ① *Av San Martín 240, Barranco, T477 2846, or Portal de Panes 123, of 107 (CC Los Ruiseñores), Cuzco, T084-256367, www.intej.org.*

Safety The following notes on personal safety should not hide the fact that most Peruvians are hospitable and helpful. For general hints on avoiding crime, please see the Security, Essentials, page 55. All the suggestions given there are valid for Peru. Always use licensed taxis: anyone can stick a taxi label on the windscreen and pick up a fare, but "pseudo taxis" are not safe. The police presence in Lima and Cuzco, and to a lesser extent Arequipa and Puno, has been greatly stepped up. Nevertheless, there has been an alarming increase in aggressive assaults in Lima and centres along the Gringo Trail. Places like Arequipa, Puno and in particular Cuzco have, at times, been plagued by waves of strangle muggings. Outside the Jul-Aug peak holiday period, there is less tension, less risk of crime, and more friendliness. A friendly attitude on your part, smiling even when you've thwarted a thief's attempt, can help you out of trouble.

Although certain illegal drugs are readily available, anyone carrying any is almost automatically assumed to be a drug trafficker. If arrested on any charge the wait for trial in prison can take a year and is particularly unpleasant. If you are asked by the narcotics police to go to the toilets to have your bags searched, insist on taking a witness. **Drug use or purchase is punishable by up to 15 years' imprisonment. The number of foreigners in Peruvian prisons on drug charges is still increasing.**

Tricks employed to get foreigners into trouble over drugs include slipping a packet of cocaine into the money you are exchanging, being invited to a party or somewhere involving a taxi ride, or simply being asked on the street if you want to buy cocaine. In all cases, a plain clothes 'policeman' will discover the planted cocaine, in your money, at your feet in the taxi, and will ask to see your passport and money. He will then return them, minus a large part of your cash. Do not get into a taxi, do not show your money, and try not to be intimidated. Being in pairs is no guarantee of security, and single women may be particularly vulnerable. Beware also thieves dressed as policemen asking for your passport and wanting to search for drugs; **searching is only permitted if prior paperwork is done**.

Insurgency The activities of Sendero Luminoso and MRTA seem to be a thing of the past, although it would be wrong to say that either organization was completely non-functional. It is still important to inform yourself of the latest situation before going, but in 2005-06 it was safe to travel to all parts of Peru except the Huallaga Valley and jungle areas east of Ayacucho because of drug trafficking and terrorism.

For up-to-date information contact the **Tourist Police**, see Touching down Box, your embassy or consulate, fellow travellers, or **South American Explorers**, who issue the pamphlet *How Not to Get Robbed in Peru* (T Lima 445 3306, Cuzco 245484, or in Quito). You can also contact the **Tourist Protection Bureau (Indecopi)** Details above in **Finding out more** and in **Tourist offices** sections in the text. As well as handling complaints, they will help if you have lost, or had stolen, documents.

Getting around

Air The main national carrier serving the most travelled routes (Arequipa, Cajamarca, Chiclayo, Cuzco, Iquitos, Piura, Puerto Maldonado, Pucallpa, Tacna, Tarapoto, Trujillo and Tumbes) are **WayraPerú**, *www.wayra.com.pe* (founded in 2006) and **Star Perú**, www.starperu.com. For destinations such as Andahuaylas, Arequipa, Ayacucho, Cajamarca, Iquitos, Pucallpa and Tacna flights are offered by **Aerocóndor** *www.aerocondor.com.pe*, and **LC Busre** *www.lc busre.com.pe*. **Lan** *www.lan.com* (part of the group formerly known as Lan Chile) flies to major cities and **Grupo Taca** *www.grupotaca.com*, offers a service on the Lima-Cuzco route. See page 1102 for airline phone numbers. Flights generally cost US$66-99 one-way anywhere in the country from Lima. Prices often increase during holiday times (Semana Santa, May Day, Inti Raymi, 28-29 July, Christmas and New Year), and for elections. During these times you should book early, especially on the Lima-Cuzco-Lima route. Flight schedules and departure times often change and delays are common. In the rainy season cancellations occur. Flights into the mountains may well be put forward one hour if there are reports of bad weather. Flights to jungle regions are also unreliable. Always allow an extra day between national and international flights, especially in the rainy season. Internal flight prices are fixed in US dollars (but can be paid in soles) and have 19% tax added. Time-keeping tends to be better early morning than later.

Note: If possible travel with hand luggage only (48 cm x 24 cm x 37 cm) to avoid the risk of losing baggage. Flights must be reconfirmed in the town you will be leaving from at least 24 hours in advance; be at the airport well ahead of your flight. About 30 minutes before departure, the clerk is allowed by law to let standby passengers take the seats of those who haven't turned up.

Bus Services along the coast to the north and south as well as inland to Huancayo, Ayacucho and Huaraz are good. There are direct (*ejecutivo*) service buses to major centres (different companies use different titles for their top class or executive services, eg *Imperial, Ideal, Royal*). As well as *ejecutivo*, many bus companies have regular (local) service and the difference is often great. Many buses have bathrooms, movies and reclining seats (*bus cama*). **Cruz del Sur** is thought to have the best service with the most routes. It accepts Visa cards and gives 10% discount to ISIC and Under26 cardholders. **Ormeño** and **Civa** also offer extensive coverage. For bus lines, see Lima Transport. For long journeys take a water bottle. Blankets and emergency food are a must in the mountains. Where buses stop it is possible to buy food on the roadside. With the better companies or *ejecutivo* service you will get a receipt for your luggage, which will be locked under the bus. On local buses there will be lots of people loading and unloading bags, so watch your luggage and always carry your valuables with you. If your bus breaks down and you are transferred to another line and have to pay extra, keep your original ticket for refund from the first company. If possible, on country buses avoid the back seats because of the bumpiness, and the left side because of exhaust fumes.

Combis operate between most small towns on one- to three-hour journeys. This makes it possible, in many cases, just to turn up and travel within an hour or two. On rougher roads, combis are minibuses, while on better roads there are also slightly more expensive and much faster car colectivos. Colectivos usually charge twice the bus fare. They leave only when full. They go almost anywhere in Peru; most firms have offices. Book one day in advance and they pick you up at your hotel or in the main plaza. Trucks are not always much cheaper than buses. Always try to arrive at your destination in daylight: much safer.

Note: Prices of bus tickets are raised by 60-100%, 2-3 days before Semana Santa, 28 Jul (Independence Day - Fiestas Patrias) and Christmas. Tickets are sold out 2-3 days in advance at this time and transport is hard to come by.

Hitchhiking Hitchhiking is difficult. Freight traffic has to stop at the police *garitas* outside each town and these are the best places to try (also toll points, but these are further from towns). Drivers usually ask for money but don't always expect to get it. In mountain and jungle areas you usually have to pay drivers of lorries, vans and even private cars; ask the driver first how much he is going to charge, and then recheck with the locals. Private cars are very few and far between. Readers report that mining trucks are especially dirty to travel in, avoid if possible.

Taxi Taxi prices are fixed in the mountain towns, about US$1-1.20 in the urban area. Fares are not fixed in Lima although some drivers work for companies that do have standard fares. Ask locals what the price should be and always set the price beforehand; expect to pay US$1.50-3 in the capital. The main cities have taxis which can be hired by phone, which charge a little more, but are

: Driving in Peru

Road About 10% of Peru's roads are paved, including the Pan-American Highway which runs north-south through the coastal desert. Mountain roads dirt, some good, some very bad. Each year they are affected by heavy rain and mud slides, especially on the east slopes of the mountains. Repairs can be delayed because of a shortage of funds. Some of these roads can be dangerous or impassable in the rainy season. Check beforehand with locals (not with bus companies, who only want to sell tickets) as accidents are common at these times.

Documents You must have an international driving licence and be over 21 to drive in Peru. If bringing in your own vehicle you must provide proof of ownership; a *libreta de pasos por aduana* or *carnet de passages* is officially required, but seldom asked for. You cannot officially enter Peru with a vehicle registered in someone else's name, but it is possible with a notarized letter of authorization and insurance documents stating that Peru is incorporated. On leaving Peru there is no check on the import of a vehicle.

Organizations The **Touring y Automóvil Club del Perú**, Av César Vallejo 699, Lince, T01-221 2432, www.touringperu.com.pe, offers help to tourists and particularly to members of the leading motoring associations. Good maps available of the whole country; regional routes and the South American sections of the Pan-American Highway available (US$5).

Car hire The minimum age for renting a car is 25. If renting a car, your home driving licence will be accepted for up to six months. Car hire companies are given in the text. Prices reflect high costs and accident rates. Hotels and tourist agencies will tell you where to find cheaper rates, but you will need to check that you have such basics as spare wheel, toolkit and functioning lights etc.

Fuel 84 octane petrol/gasoline costs US$3.45/gallon; 90 octane, US$3.85; 95 octane, US$4.48; 97 octane, US$4.72. Diesel costs US$3.27. Unleaded fuel is available in large cities and along the Panamericana, but rarely in the highlands.

reliable and safe. Many taxi drivers work for commission from hotels. Choose your own hotel and get a driver who is willing to take you. Taxis at airports are more expensive; seek advice about the price in advance. In some places it is cheaper to walk out of the airport to the main road and flag down a cab. Keep all hand luggage out of sight in taxis; smash-and-grab thieves are very quick. Another common form of public transport is the mototaxi, a three- wheel motorcycle with an awning covering the double-seat behind the driver. Fares are about US$1.

Train The main railways are Puno-Juliaca-Cuzco, and Cuzco-Machu Picchu, administered by **PerúRail SA** *www.perurail.com*, and Lima-Huancayo, with a continuation to Huancavelica in the Central Highlands. The Lima-Huancayo service is run by **Ferrovías Central Andina**, *www.ferroviasperu.com.pe*, at weekends. Trains run daily Huancayo-Huancavelica.

Sleeping → *See inside front cover for our hotel grade price guide.*

Hotels All deluxe and first class hotels charge 19% in state sales tax (IGV) and 10% service charges. Foreigners should not have to pay the sales tax on hotel rooms. Neither is given in the accommodation listings, unless specified. By law all places that offer accommodation now have a plaque outside bearing the letters H (Hotel), Hs (Hostal), HR (Hotel Residencial) or P (Pensión) according to type. A hotel has 51 rooms or more, a hostal 50 or fewer; the categories do not describe quality or facilities. Many hotels have safe parking for motor cycles. All hotels seem to be crowded during Christmas and Easter holidays, Carnival and at the end of July; Cuzco in June is also very busy. For upmarket hotels, www.hotelesenperu.com has information on accommodation with direct links to the hotels themselves. Take a torch and candles, especially in remoter regions. **iPeru** advises that all accommodations registered with them are now listed on their web site: www.peru.org.pe.

Camping Camping is easy in Peru, especially along the coast. There can be problems with robbery when camping near a small village. Avoid such a location, or ask permission to camp in a backyard or *chacra* (farmland). Most Peruvians are used to campers, but in some remote places, people have never seen a tent. Be casual about it, do not unpack all your gear, leave it inside your tent (especially at night) and never leave a tent unattended. Camping gas in little blue bottles is available in the main cities. Those with stoves designed for lead-free gasoline should use *ron de quemar*, available from hardware shops (*ferreterías*). White gas is called *bencina*, also available from hardware stores.

Youth hostels Contact **Asociación Peruana de Albergues Turísticos Juveniles** ① *Av Casimiro Ulloa 328, Miraflores, Lima, T446 5488, www.limahostell.com.pe.*

Eating → *See inside front cover for our Eating price guide.*
Eating out A normal lunch or dinner costs US$5-8, but can go up to about US$80 in a first-class restaurant, with drinks and wine. Middle and high-class restaurants may add 10% service, but not include the 19% sales tax in the bill (which foreigners do have to pay); this is not shown on the price list or menu, check in advance. Lower class restaurants charge only tax, while cheap, local restaurants charge no taxes. Lunch is the main meal and most restaurants serve one or two set lunch menus, called *menú ejecutivo* or *menú económico* (US$1.50-2.50). The set menu has the advantage of being served almost immediately and it is usually cheap. The *menú ejecutivo* costs US$2 or more for a three-course meal with a soft drink and it offers greater choice and more interesting dishes. Chinese restaurants (*chifas*) serve good food at reasonable prices. For really economically-minded people the *comedores populares* in most cities of Peru offer a standard three-course meal for US$1.

Coastal cuisine The best coastal dishes are seafood based, the most popular being *ceviche*. This is a dish of raw white fish marinated in lemon juice, onion and hot peppers. Traditionally, *ceviche* is served with corn-on-the-cob, *cancha* (toasted corn), yucca and sweet potatoes. *Tiradito* is *ceviche* without onions made with plaice. Another mouth-watering fish dish is *escabeche* – fish with onions, hot green pepper, red peppers, prawns (*langostinos*), cumin, hard-boiled eggs, olives, and sprinkled with cheese (it can also be made with chicken). For fish on its own, don't miss the excellent *corvina*, or white sea bass. You should also try *chupe de camarones*, which is a shrimp stew made with varying ingredients. Other fish dishes include *parihuela*, a popular bouillabaisse which includes *yuyo de mar*, a tangy seaweed, and *aguadito*, a thick rice and fish soup said to have rejuvenating powers.

    A favourite northern coastal dish is *seco de cabrito*, roasted kid (baby goat) served with the ubiquitous beans and rice, or *seco de cordero* which uses lamb instead. Also good is *aji de gallina*, a rich and spicy creamed chicken, and duck is excellent. *Humitas* are small, stuffed dumplings made with maize. The *criollo* cooking of the coast has a strong tradition and can be found throughout the country. Two popular examples are *cau cau*, made with tripe, potatoes, peppers, and parsley and served with rice, and *anticuchos*, which are shish kebabs of beef heart with garlic, peppers, cumin seeds and vinegar.

    Highland cuisine The staples of highland cooking, corn and potatoes, come in a remarkable variety of shapes, sizes and colours. Two good potato dishes are *causa* and *carapulca*. Causa is made with yellow potatoes, lemons, pepper, hard-boiled eggs, olives, lettuce, sweet cooked corn, sweet cooked potato, fresh cheese, and served with onion sauce (it can be made with tuna, avocado or prawns). You will also find *causa* on coastal menus: the mashed potato is wrapped around the filling, which often contains crabmeat. Another potato dish is *papa a la huancaína*, which is topped with a spicy sauce made with milk and cheese. *Ocopa* is a similar dish in which slices of potato are served with a sauce made from milk, herbs and pecan nuts. *Papa rellena* is a deep-fried mashed potato ball stuffed with vegetables, egg and meat. The most commonly eaten corn dishes are *choclo con queso,* corn on the cob with cheese, and *tamales*, boiled corn dumplings filled with meat and wrapped in a banana leaf.

    Meat dishes are many and varied. *Ollucos con charqui* is a kind of potato with dried meat; *sancochado* is a meat and all kinds of vegetables stewed together and seasoned with ground garlic. A dish almost guaranteed to appear on every restaurant menu is *lomo saltado*, a kind of stir-fried beef with onions, vinegar, ginger, chilli, tomatoes and fried potatoes, served with rice. *Rocoto relleno* is spicy bell pepper stuffed with beef and vegetables, *palta rellena* is avocado filled with chicken salad, Russian salad or prawns. *Estofado de carne* is a stew which often contains wine and *carne en adobo* is a cut and seasoned steak. Others include *fritos*, fried pork, usually eaten in the morning, *chicharrones*, deep fried chunks of pork ribs and chicken or fish, and *lechón*, suckling pig. A delicacy in the highlands is *cuy*, guinea pig.

Filling and good value are the many kinds of soup, such as *yacu-chupe*, a green soup made from potato, with cheese, garlic, coriander, parsley, peppers, eggs, onions, and mint, *and sopa a la criolla* containing thin noodles, beef heart, egg, vegetables and pleasantly spiced.

Tropical cuisine The main ingredient in jungle cuisine is fish, especially the succulent, dolphin-sized *paiche*, which comes with the delicious *palmito*, or palm-hearts, and yucca and fried bananas. *Juanes* are a jungle version of tamales, stuffed with chicken and rice.

Desserts *Cocada al horno* – coconut, with egg yolk, sesame seed, wine and butter; *picarones* – frittered cassava flour and eggs fried in fat and served with honey; *mazamorra morada* – purple maize, sweet potato starch, lemons, various dried fruits, sticks of ground cinnamon and cloves and perfumed pepper; *manjar blanco* – milk, sugar and eggs; *maná* – an almond paste with eggs, vanilla and milk; *alfajores* – shortbread biscuit with *manjar blanco*, pineapple, peanuts, etc; *pastelillos* – yuccas with sweet potato, sugar and anise fried in fat and powdered with sugar and served hot; and *zango de pasas*, made with maize, syrup, raisins and sugar. *Turrón*, the Lima nougat, is worth trying. *Tejas* are pieces of fruit or nut enveloped in *manjar blanco* and covered in chocolate or icing sugar – delicious. The various Peruvian fruits are of good quality: they include bananas, the citrus fruits, pineapples, dates, avocados (*paltas*), eggfruit (*lúcuma*), the custard apple (*chirimoya*) which can be as big as your head, quince, papaya, mango, guava, the passion-fruit (*maracuyá*) and the soursop (*guanábana*).

Drink The most famous local drink is *pisco*, a clear brandy which, with egg whites and lime juice, makes the famous pisco sour. The most renowned brands come from the Ica valley. Also popular are *chilcano*, a longer refreshing drink made with *guinda*, a local cherry brandy; and *algarrobina*, a sweet cocktail made with the syrup from the bark of the carob tree, egg whites, milk, pisco and cinnamon. The best wines are from Ica, Tacama and Ocucaje; both come in red, white and rosé, sweet and dry varieties. Tacama blancs de blancs and brut champagne have been recommended, also Gran Tinto Reserva Especial. Viña Santo Tomás, from Chincha, is reasonable and cheap. Casapalca is not recommended. Beer is best in lager and porter types, especially the *Cusqueña* and *Arequipeña* brands (lager) and *Trujillo Malta* (porter). In Lima only *Cristal* and *Pilsener* (not related to true Pilsen) are readily available, others have to be sought out. Look out for the sweetish 'maltina' brown ale, which makes a change from the ubiquitous pilsner-type beers. *Chicha de jora* is a maize beer, usually homemade and not easy to come by, refreshing but strong, and *chicha morada* is a soft drink made with purple maize. The local rival to Coca Cola, the fluorescent yellow *Inca Cola*, is made from lemon grass. Peruvian coffee is good, but the best is exported. Many cafés only serve coffee in liquid form or Nescafé. It is often brought to the table in a small jug accompanied by a mug of hot water to which you add the coffee essence. There are many different kinds of herb tea: the commonest are *manzanilla* (camomile) and *hierbaluisa* (lemon grass). *Mate de coca* is frequently served in the highlands to stave off the discomforts of altitude sickness.

Festivals and events

Two of the major festival dates are **Carnaval,** which is held over the weekend before Ash Wednesday, and **Semana Santa** (Holy Week), which ends on Easter Sunday. Carnival is celebrated in most of the Andes and Semana Santa throughout Peru. Another important festival is **Fiesta de la Cruz**, held on the first of May in much of the central and southern highlands and on the coast. In Cuzco, the entire month of June is one huge *fiesta*, culminating in **Inti Raymi**, on 24 June, one of Peru's prime tourist attractions. Another national festival is **Todos los Santos** (All Saints) on 1 November, and on 8 December is **Festividad de la Inmaculada Concepción**. A full list of local festivals is listed under each town.

Apart from the festivals listed above, the main holidays are: 1 January, New Year; 6 January, **Bajada de Reyes;** 1 May, Labour Day; 28-29 July, Independence (Fiestas Patrias); 7 October, Battle of Angamos; 24-25 December, Christmas.

Note: Most businesses such as banks, airline offices and tourist agencies close for the official holidays while supermarkets and street markets may be open. Sometimes holidays that fall during mid-week will be moved to the following Monday. The high season for foreign tourism in Peru is June to September while national tourism peaks at Christmas, Semana Santa and Fiestas Patrias. Prices rise and accommodation and bus tickets are harder to come by.

Lima → *Phone code: 01. Colour map 3, grid C2. Population: 8 million (metropolitan area).*

Lima's colonial centre and suburbs, shrouded in fog which lasts eight months of the year, are fringed by the pueblos jóvenes which sprawl over the dusty hills overlooking the flat city. It has a great many historic buildings, some of the finest museums in the country and its food, drink and nightlife are second to none. Although not the most relaxing of South America's capitals, it is a good place to start before exploring the rest of the country.

Ins and outs

Getting there All international flights land at Jorge Chávez **airport**, 16 km northwest of the Plaza de Armas. Transport into town by taxi or bus is easy. If arriving in the city by **bus**, most of the recommended companies have their terminals just south of the centre, many on Av Carlos Zavala. This is not a safe area and you should take a taxi to and from there. ▸▸ *For more detailed information including getting away from the airport, see Transport, page 1099.*

Getting around Downtown Lima can be explored on foot by day; at night a taxi is safest. Miraflores is 15 km south of the centre. Many of the better hotels and restaurants are here and in neighbouring San Isidro. Transport between the centre and the suburbs is not a problem. Three types of bus provide an extensive public transport system; all vehicles stop when flagged down. The route of the bus is posted on a coloured sticker on the windscreen; ignore destinations written on the side. **Taxis** do not use meters. Agree the price of the journey beforehand and insist on being taken to the destination of your choice. On both buses and taxis be ready to pay the exact fare. At night, on Sunday and holidays expect a surcharge of 35-50% is made in taxis.

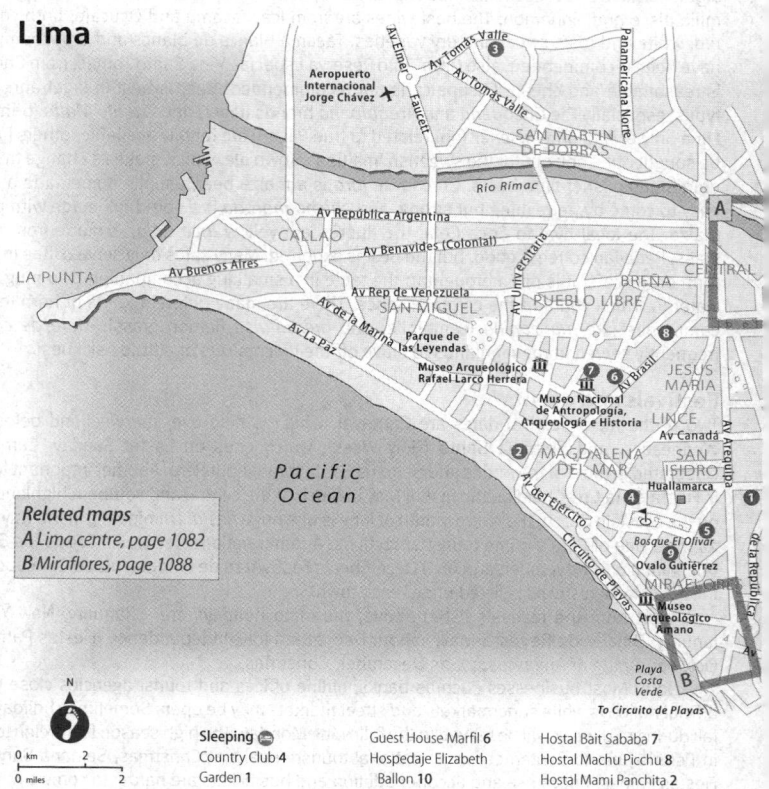

Lima

Related maps
A Lima centre, page 1082
B Miraflores, page 1088

0 km 2
0 miles 2

Sleeping 🛏
Country Club 4
Garden 1

Guest House Marfil 6
Hospedaje Elizabeth
Ballon 10

Hostal Bait Sababa 7
Hostal Machu Picchu 8
Hostal Mami Panchita 2

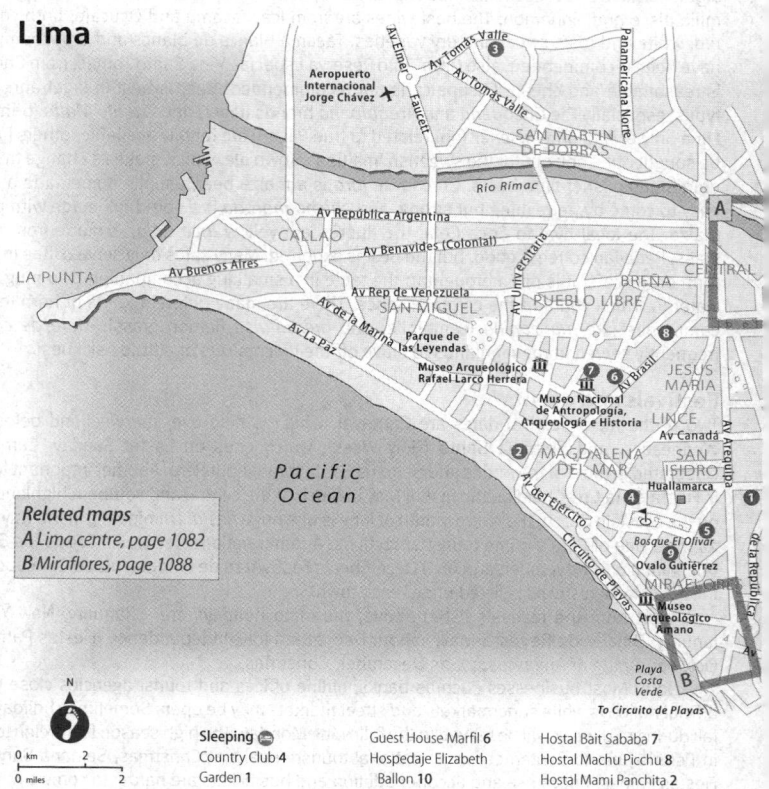

Addresses Several blocks, with their own names, make up a long street, a jirón (often abbreviated to Jr). Street corner signs bear both names, of the jirón and of the block. New and old names of streets are used interchangeably: Colmena is also Nicolás de Piérola, Wilson is Inca Garcilaso de la Vega, and Carabaya is also Augusto N Wiese. The city's urban motorway is often called 'El Zanjón' (the ditch) or Vía Expresa.

Climate Only 12° south of the equator, one would expect a tropical climate, but Lima has two distinct seasons. The winter is May-November, when a damp *garúa* (Scotch mist) hangs over the city, making everything look grey. It is damp and cold, 8-15°C. The sun breaks through around November and temperatures rise to as high as 30°C. Note that the temperature in the coastal suburbs is lower than the centre because of the sea's influence. Protect against the sun's rays when visiting the beaches around Lima, or elsewhere in Peru.

Tourist information i perú has offices at Jorge Chávez international airport ① *T574 8000, open 24 hrs*; Casa Basadre ① *Av Jorge Basadre 610, San Isidro, T421 1627, Mon-Fri 0830-1830*; and Larcomar shopping centre ① *Módulo 14, Plaza Gourmet, Miraflores, T445 9400, 1200-2000*. **Info Perú** ① *Jr de la Unión (Belén) 1066, of 102, T424 7963, infoperu@ qnet.com.pe, Mon-Fri 0930-1800, Sat 0930-1400*, is helpful with lots of advice, English, French spoken. Ask for the free, *Peru Guide* published in English by Lima Editora, T444 0815, available at travel agencies. **Fertur Peru**, has lots of information, see under Tour operators. **South American Explorers** ① *Piura 135, (Casilla 3714), Miraflores, T445 3306 (dial 011-51-1 from USA) www.saexplorers.org*. See also Essentials, page 32.

Background

Lima, capital of Peru, is built on both sides of the Río Rímac, at the foot of Cerro San Cristóbal. It was originally named *La Ciudad de Los Reyes*, in honour of the Magi, at its founding by Spanish conquistador Francisco Pizarro in 1535. From then until the independence of the South American republics in the early 19th century, it was the chief city of Spanish South America. The name Lima, a corruption of the Quechua name *Rimac* (speaker), was not adopted until the end of the 16th century.

The Universidad de San Marcos was founded in 1551, and a printing press in 1595, both among the earliest of their kind in South America. Lima's first theatre opened in 1563, and the Inquisition was introduced in 1569 (it was not abolished until 1820). For some time the Viceroyalty of Peru embraced Colombia, Ecuador, Bolivia, Chile and Argentina. There were few cities in the Old World that could rival Lima's power, wealth and luxury, which was at its height during the 17th and early 18th centuries. The city's wealth attracted many freebooters and in 1670 a protecting wall 11 km long was built round it, then destroyed in 1869. The earthquake of 1746 destroyed all but 20 houses, killed 4,000 inhabitants and ended its pre-eminence. It was only comparatively recently, with the coming of industry, that Lima began to change into what it is today.

Modern Lima is seriously affected by smog for much of the year, and is surrounded by 'Pueblos Jóvenes', or settlements of squatters who have migrated from the Sierra. Villa El Salvador, a few

Hostal Residencial Victor **3**   Sonesta Posada del
Libertador **4**   Inca El Olivar **5**
Sofitel Royal Park **9**

kilometres southeast of Lima, may be the world's biggest 'squatters' camp' with 350,000 people building up an award-winning self-governing community since 1971.

Over the years the city has changed out of recognition. Many of the hotels and larger business houses have relocated to the fashionable suburbs of Miraflores and San Isidro, thus moving the commercial heart of the city away from the Plaza de Armas.

Half of the town-dwellers of Peru now live in Lima. The metropolitan area contains eight million people, nearly one-third of the country's total population, and two-thirds of its industries. Callao, Peru's major port, runs into Lima; it is a city in its own right, with over one million inhabitants. Within its boundaries is the Jorge Chávez airport. The docks handle 75% of the nation's imports and some 25% of its exports. Callao has a serious theft problem, avoid being there in the evening.

Sights

The traditional heart of the city, at least in plan, is still what it was in colonial days. Although parts of it are run down, much of the old centre is undergoing restoration and many colonial buildings have been cleaned. It is worth visiting the colonial centre to see the architecture and works of art. Most of the tourist attractions are in this area. Churches open between 1830 and 2100 unless otherwise stated. Many are closed to visitors on Sunday. Some museums are only open 0900-1300 from January-March, and some are closed in January.

Plaza de Armas

One block south of the Río Rímac lies the Plaza de Armas (also called Plaza Mayor since 1998), which has been declared a World Heritage Site by UNESCO. Running along two sides are arcades with shops: Portal de Escribanos and Portal de Botoneros. In the centre of the plaza is a bronze fountain dating from 1650. The **Palacio de Gobierno** (Government Palace) ① *T311- 3908, Mon-Fri entry at 0845, 0945, Sat entry at 0900, 1000, 1100, 45 mins, free, to take a tour in English or Spanish, register a day in advance, or go to the PR office, Ed Palacio 269, of 201 (ask guard for directions)*, was totally rebuilt In 1937. The changing of the guard is at 1200, on the north side of the Plaza, stands on the site of the original palace built by Pizarro.

The **Cathedral** ① *T427 9647, Mon-Sat 0900-1630, US$1.50*, was reduced to rubble in the earthquake of 1746. The reconstruction, on the lines of the original, was completed 1755. Note the splendidly carved stalls (mid-17th century), the silver-covered altars surrounded by fine woodwork, mosaic-covered walls bearing the coats of arms of Lima and Pizarro and an allegory of Pizarro's commanders, the 'Thirteen Men of Isla del Gallo'. The supposed remains of Franscisco Pizarro lie in a small chapel, the first on the right of the entrance, in a glass coffin, though later research indicates that they reside in the crypt. Museo de Arte Religioso in the cathedral, free guided tours (English available, give tip), ask to see the picture restoration room. Next to the cathedral is the **Archbishop's Palace**, rebuilt in 1924, with a superb wooden balcony.

Around the Plaza de Armas

Just off the plaza is the **Philatelic Museum** ① *at the Central Post Office, Mon-Sun 0815-1300, 1400-1800, free*. Incomplete collection of Peruvian stamps and information on the Inca postal system. There is a stamp exchange in front of the museum every Saturday and Sunday, 0900-1300. Commemorative issues can be bought here. Nearby is the **Casa Aliaga** ① *Unión 224. Lima Tours has exclusive rights to include the house in its tours (T424 5110).* It is still occupied by the Aliaga family but has been opened to the public. The house contains what is said to be the oldest ceiling in Lima and is furnished entirely in the colonial style.

The baroque church of **San Francisco** ① *on the 1st block of Jr Lampa, corner of Ancash, a few blocks from the Plaza de Armas, T427 1381, daily 0930- 1730, church and monastery US$1.50, US$0.50 children, only with guide, Spanish and English (recommended)*, was finished in 1674 and withstood the 1746 earthquake. The nave and aisles are lavishly decorated in Mudéjar style. The monastery is famous for the Sevillian tilework and panelled ceiling in the cloisters (1620). The Catacombs under the church and part of the monastery are well worth seeing. (Fire severely damaged San Francisco in 2005; not all parts may be open to visitors.) The late 16th-century **Casa de Jarava** or **Pilatos** ① *Jr Ancash 390*, is opposite San Francisco church. Close by, **Casa de las Trece Monedas** ① *Jr Ancash 536*, still has the original doors and window grills.

1080

The **Palacio Torre Tagle** (1735) ① *Jr Ucayali 363, Mon-Fri during working hours,* is the city's best surviving example of secular colonial architecture. Today, it is used by the Foreign Ministry, but visitors are allowed to enter courtyards to inspect the fine, Moorish-influenced wood-carving in balconies and wrought iron work. **Casa de la Rada**, or **Goyoneche** ① *Jr Ucayali 358*, opposite, is a fine mid- 18th-century French-style town house which now belongs to a bank. The patio and first reception room are open occasionally to the public. **Museo Banco Central de Reserva** ① *Av Ucayali 291 and Lampa, 1 block from San Pedro Church, on same side as Torre Tagle Palace, T427 6250, ext 2660, Tue-Fri 1000-1630, Sat-Sun 1000-1300. Photography prohibited.* This is a large collection of pottery from the Vicus or Piura culture (AD 500-600) and gold objects from Lambayeque, as well as 19th and 20th-century paintings: both sections highly recommended. **San Pedro** ① *3rd block of Jirón Ucayali, Mon-Sat 0930-1145, 1700-1800,* finished by Jesuits in 1638, has marvellous altars with Moorish-style balconies, rich gilded wood carvings in choir and vestry, and tiled throughout. Several Viceroys are buried here; the bell called La Abuelita, first rung in 1590, sounded the Declaration of Independence in 1821.

Between Avenida Abancay and Jr Ayacucho is **Plaza Bolívar**, where General José de San Martín proclaimed Peru's independence. The plaza is dominated by the equestrian statue of the Liberator. Behind lies the Congress building which occupies the former site of the Universidad de San Marcos; visit recommended. Behind the Congress is Barrio Chino, with many *chifas* and small shops selling oriental items. **Museo del Tribunal de la Santa Inquisición** ① *Plaza Bolívar, C Junín 548, near the corner of Av Abancay, Mon-Sun 0900-1700, free, students offer to show you round for a tip; good explanations in English.* The main hall, with a splendidly carved mahogany ceiling, remains untouched. The Court of Inquisition was held here from 1584; 1829-1938 it was used by the Senate. In the basement there is a recreation *in situ* of the gruesome tortures. A description in English is available at the desk.

The 16th-century **Santo Domingo church and monastery** ① *T427 6793, monastery and tombs open Mon-Sat 0900-1230, 1500-1800; Sun and holidays morning only, US$0.75,* is on the first block of Jr Camaná. The Cloister, one of the most attractive, dates from 1603. The second Cloister is less elaborate. Beneath the sacristy are the tombs of San Martín de Porres, one of Peru's most revered saints, and Santa Rosa de Lima (see below). In 1669, Pope Clement presented the alabaster statue of Santa Rosa in front of the altar. Behind Santo Domingo is **Alameda Chabuca Granda**, named after one of Peru's greatest singers. In the evening there are free art and music shows and you can sample foods from all over Peru. A few blocks away, **Casa de Oquendo** or **Osambela** ① *Conde de Superunda 298, 0900-1300,* stages art exhibitions. A few blocks west is **Santuario de Santa Rosa** ① *Av Tacna, 1st block, T425 1279, daily 0930-1300, 1500-1800, free to the grounds,* a small but graceful church. A pilgrimage centre; here are preserved the hermitage built by Santa Rosa herself, the house in which she was born, a section of the house in which she attended to the sick, her well, and other relics. Nearby, **Casa La Riva** ① *Jr Ica 426,* has an 18th-century porch and balconies, a small gallery with 20th-century paintings.

San Agustín ① *Jr Ica 251, T427 7548, daily 0830-1130, 1630-1900, ring for entry,* is west of the Plaza de Armas: its façade (1720) is a splendid example of churrigueresque architecture. There are carved choir stalls and effigies, and a sculpture of Death, said to have frightened its maker into an early grave. The church has been restored after the last earthquake, but the sculpture of Death is in storage. **Las Nazarenas Church** ① *Av Tacna, 4th block, T423 5718, daily 0700-1200, 1600-2000,* is built around an image of Christ Crucified painted by a liberated slave in 1655. This, the most venerated image in Lima, and an oil copy of El Señor de los Milagros (Lord of Miracles), encased in a gold frame, are carried on a silver litter the whole weighing nearly a ton through the streets on 18, 19, and 28 October and again on 1 November (All Saints' Day). *El Comercio* newspaper and local pamphlets give details of times and routes.

North of Plaza de Armas

From the Plaza, passing the Palacio de Gobierno on the left, straight ahead is the **Desamparados** ① *free,* railway station, which now houses fascinating exhibitions on Peruvian themes. **The Puente de Piedra**, behind the Palacio de Gobierno, is a Roman-style stone bridge built in 1610, crossing the Río Rímac to the district of that name. On Jr Hualgayoc is the bullring in the **Plaza de Acho**, inaugurated on 20 January 1766, with the **Museo Taurino** ① *Hualgayoc 332, T482 3360, Mon-Sat 0800-1800, US$1, students US$0.50, photography US$2.* Apart from matador's relics, the museum contains good collections of paintings and engravings, some of the latter by Goya. There are two bullfight seasons: October to first week

in December and during July. They are held in the afternoons on Sunday and holidays. The
Convento de Los Descalzos ① *on the Alameda de Los Descalzos in Rímac, T481 0441, daily
1000-1300, 1500-1800, except Tue, US$1, guided tour only, 45 mins in Spanish (worth it),*

Lima centre

Sleeping	Hostal San Francisco 2	La Choza Náutica 7
Familia Rodríguez 3	Kamana 11	L'Eau Vive 8
Granada 5	Lima Sheraton 13	Machu Picchu 9
Hostal Belén 6	Maury 14	Manhatten 10
Hostal de las Artes 8	Pensión Ibarra 15	Natur 11
Hostal España 7		Neydi 6
Hostal Iquique 9	Eating	Salon Capon 12
Hostal La Posada	Antaño 8	San Martín 13
del Parque 12	Cordano 3	Wa Lok 14
Hostal Roma	El Maurito 4	
& Café Carrara 10	Govinda 5	

was founded in 1592. It contains over 300 paintings of the Cuzco, Quito and Lima schools which line the four main cloisters and two ornate chapels. The chapel of El Carmen was constructed in 1730 and is notable for its baroque gold leaf altar. The museum shows the life of the Franciscan friars during colonial and early republican periods. The cellar, infirmary, pharmacy and a typical cell have been restored.

Cerro San Cristóbal ① *Sat and Sun 1000-2100; departures every 15 mins, US$1.50*, dominates downtown Lima and can be visited in a one-hour tour, run by *Ofistur*, departing from in front of Santo Domingo, Jr Camaná. It includes a look at the run-down Rímac district, passes the Convento de los Descalzos (see above), ascends the hill through one of the city's oldest shanties with its brightly painted houses and spends about 20 minutes at the summit, where there is a small museum and café. Excellent views on a clear day.

South of Plaza de Armas

The Jr de La Unión, the main shopping street, runs to the Plaza de Armas. It has been converted into a pedestrian precinct which teems with life in the evening. In the two blocks south of Jr Unión, known as C Belén, several shops sell souvenirs and curios. **La Merced** ① *Unión y Miró Quesada, T427 8199, 0800-1245, 1600-2000 (Sun 0700-1300, 1600-2000); monastery daily 0800-1200 and 1500-1730*, is in Plazuela de la Merced. The first mass in Lima was said here on the site of the first church to be built. The restored façade is a fine example of colonial Baroque. Inside are some magnificent altars and the tilework on some of the walls is noteworthy. A door from the right of the nave leads into the Monastery. The cloister dates from 1546. Jr de la Unión leads to **Plaza San Martín**, which has a statue of San Martín in the centre. The plaza has been restored and is now a nice place to sit and relax.

Museo de Arte ① *9 de Diciembre 125, T423 6332, Thu-Tue 1000-1700, US$3.65, free guide, signs in English*, is in the Palacio de la Exposición, built in 1868 in Parque de la Exposición (designed by Gustave Eiffel). There are more than 7,000 exhibits, giving a chronological history of Peruvian cultures and art from the Paracas civilization up to today. It includes excellent examples of 17th- and 18th-century Cuzco paintings, a b4eautiful display of carved furniture, heavy silver and jewelled stirrups and also pre-Columbian pottery. The Filmoteca (movie club) is on the premises and shows films just about every night. See the local paper for details, or look in the museum itself. The **Gran Parque Cultural de Lima** ① *0800-2030*, is in the grounds. Inaugurated in January 2000, this large park has an amphitheatre, Japanese garden, food court and children's activities. Relaxing strolls through this green, peaceful and safe oasis in the centre of Lima are recommended.

Museo de Arte Italiano ① *Paseo de la República 250, T423 9932, Mon-Fri 1000-1700, US$1*, is in a wonderful neo-classical building, given by the Italian colony to Peru on the centenary of its independence. Note the remarkable mosaic murals on the outside. It consists of a large collection of Italian and other European works of art and houses the Instituto de Arte Contemporáneo, which has many exhibitions.

San Borja

Museo de la Nación ① *Javier Prado Este 2465, T476 9878, Tue-Sun 0900-1700, closed major public holidays, US$1.80. 50% discount with ISIC card*, in the huge *Banco de la Nación* building, is the museum for the exhibition and study of the art and history of the aboriginal races of Peru. It contains the **Museo Peruano de Ciencias de la Salud** ① *from Av Garcilaso de la Vega in downtown Lima take a combi with a "Javier Prado/Aviación" window sticker. Get off at the 21st block of Javier Prado at Av Aviación. From Miraflores take a bus down Av Arequipa to Av Javier Prado (27th block), then take a bus with a "Todo Javier Prado" or "Aviación" window sticker. Taxi from downtown Lima or Miraflores US$2*, which has a collection of ceramics and mummies, plus an explanation of pre-Columbian lifestyle. There are good explanations in Spanish and English on Peruvian history, with ceramics, textiles and displays of almost every ruin in Peru. Guided tours in English/Spanish. It is arranged so that you can follow the development of Peruvian precolonial history through to the time of the Incas. A visit is recommended before you go to see the archaeological sites themselves. There are displays of the tomb of the Señor de Sipán, artefacts from Batán Grande near Chiclayo (Sicán culture), reconstructions of the friezes found at Huaca La Luna and Huaca El Brujo, near Trujillo, and of Sechín and other sites. Temporary exhibitions are held in the basement, where there is also an Instituto Nacional de Cultura bookshop. The museum has a cafetería.

Pueblo Libre

The original museum of anthropology and archaeology is **Museo Nacional de Antropología, Arqueología e Historia** ① *Plaza Bolívar in Pueblo Libre, not to be confused with Plaza Bolívar in the centre, T463 5070, Tue-Sat 0900-1700, Sun and holidays 0900-1600, US$3, photo permit US$5, guides available, some displays in English.* On display are ceramics of the Chimú, Nazca, Mochica and Pachacámac cultures, various Inca curiosities and works of art, and interesting textiles. **Museo Nacional de Historia** ① *T463 2009, take any public transportation vehicle on Av Brasil with a window sticker saying "Todo Brasil." Get off at the 21st block called Av Vivanco. Walk about 5 blocks down Vivanco. The museum will be on your left. From Miraflores take bus SM 18 Carabayllo-Chorrillos, marked "Bolívar, Arequipa, Larcomar", get out at block 8 of Bolívar by the Hospital Santa Rosa, and walk down Av San Martín 5 blocks until you see the 'blue line'; turn left. The 'blue line' marked on the pavement, a bit faded in places, links the Museo Nacional de Antropología, Arqueología e Historia to the Museo Arqueológico Rafael Larco Herrera (see below), 10 mins' walk. Taxi from downtown US$2; from Miraflores US$3,* in a mansion occupied by San Martín (1821-1822) and Bolívar (1823-1826) is next door. It exhibits colonial and early republican paintings, manuscripts and uniforms.

   Museo Arqueológico Rafael Larco Herrera ① *Av Bolívar 1515, T461 1312, http://museo larco.perucultural.org.pe, 0900-1800; texts in Spanish, English and French, US$6.35 (half price for students), disabled access, photography not permitted, Take any bus to the 15th block of Av Brasil. Then take a bus down Av Bolívar. From Miraflores, take the SM 18 Carabayllo-Chorrillos, see above, to block 15 of Bolívar. Taxi from downtown, Miraflores or San Isidro, 15 mins, US$2.50. Follow the 'blue line' marked on the pavement to the Museo Nacional de Antropología, Arqueología e Historia (see above), 10 mins' walk.* Located in an 18th-century mansion, itself built on a seventh-century pre-Columbian pyramid, this museum has a collection which gives an excellent overview on the development of Peruvian cultures through their pottery. It has the world's largest collection of Moche, Sicán and Chimú pieces. There is a Gold and Silver of Ancient Peru exhibition, a magnificent textile collection and a fascinating erotica section. It is surrounded by beautiful gardens.

San Isidro

To the east of Avenida La República, down C Pancho Fierro, is **El Olivar**, an olive grove planted by the first Spaniards which has been turned into a park (best in daylight). Between San Isidro and Miraflores, is **the Pan de Azúcar**, or **Huallamarca** ① *C Nicolás de Rivera 201 and Av Rosario, 0900-1700, closed Mon, US$1.50. Take bus 1 from Av Tacna, or minibus 13 or 73 to Choquechaca, then walk.* An adobe pyramid of the Maranga culture, it dates from about AD 100-500. There is a small site museum. There are many good hotels and restaurants in San Isidro; see Sleeping, page 1087 and Eating, page 1076.

   South of San Isidro is the rundown seaside resort of **Magdalena del Mar**, inland from which is **Pueblo Libre**, where many museums are located. **Parque las Leyendas** ① *T464 4282, daily 0900-1730, US$2, getting there: take bus 23 or colectivo on Av Abancay, or bus 135. A or colectivo from Av La Vega, is reached from the 24th block of Av de La Marina in San Miguel: take Av Parque Las Leyendas to the entrance on Av La Mar,* is arranged to represent the three regions of Peru: the coast, the Sierra, and the tropical jungles of the Selva, with appropriate houses, animals and plants, children's playground. It gets very crowded at weekends.

Miraflores

Avenida Arequipa continues to the coast, to the most important suburb of Lima (see Sleeping, page 1087, Youth hostel, page 1091 and eating, page 1076). Together with San Isidro and Barranco this is now the social centre of Lima.

   Parque Kennedy, the Parque Central de Miraflores is located between Avenida Larco and Avenida Mcal Oscar Benavides (locally known as Avenida Diagonal). This extremely well kept park has a small open-air theatre with performances Thursday-Sunday and an arts and crafts market most evenings of the week. The house of the author **Ricardo Palma** ① *Gral Suárez 189, T445 5836, Mon-Fri 0915-1245, 1430-1700, small entrance fee,* is now a museum. At the end of Avenida Larco and running along the Malecón de la Reserva is the renovated **Parque Salazar** and the very modern shopping centre called **Centro Comercial Larcomar**. Here you will find expensive shops, hip cafés and discos and a wide range of restaurants, all with a beautiful ocean view. The 12-screen cinema is one of the best in Lima and even has a 'cine-bar' in the twelfth theatre. Don't forget to check out the Cosmic Bowling Alley with its black lights and fluorescent balls. A few hundred metres to the north is the famous **Parque del Amor** where on just about any night you'll see at least one wedding party taking photos of the newly weds.

Museo Arqueológico Amano ① *Retiro 160, 11th block of Av Angamos Oeste, Miraflores), T441 2909, visits by appointment Mon-Fri in afternoons only, free (photography prohibited).* The collection is of artefacts from the Chancay, Chimú and Nazca periods, owned by the late Mr Yoshitaro Amano. It has one of the most complete exhibits of Chancay weaving, and is particularly interesting for pottery and pre-Columbian textiles, all superbly displayed and lit. Take a bus or colectivo to the corner of Avenida Arequipa y Avenida Angamos and another one to the 11th block of Avenida Angamos Oeste. Taxi from downtown US$2; from Parque Kennedy US$1.

Poli Museum ① *Almte Cochrane 466, T422 2437, guided tours (in Spanish only and delivered very fast) by Sr Poli or his son cost US$10 pp irrespective of the size of the group; allow 2 hrs, phone in advance to arrange tours.* This is one of the best private collections of colonial and pre-Columbian artefacts in Peru, including material from Sipán.

At Borgoña, eighth block s/n, turn off Avenida Arequipa at 45th block, is **Huaca Pucllana** ① *free, 0900-1700, closed Tue,* a 5th-8th-century AD, pre-Inca site which is under excavation. Guided tours in Spanish only (give tip); small site museum but few objects from the site itself, handicrafts shop (see Eating, below).

Barranco

This suburb further south was already a seaside resort by the end of the 17th century. Nowadays, a number of artists have their workshops here and there are several chic galleries. The attractive public library, formerly the town hall, stands on the plaza. Nearby is the interesting *bajada*, a steep path leading down to the beach. The **Puente de los Suspiros** (Bridge of Sighs), leads towards the Malecón, with fine views of the bay. Barranco is quiet by day but comes alive at night (see Eating and Bars sections) in the bars focussed around the main plaza. Take a colectivo to Miraflores then another. Some run all the way to Barranco from Lima centre; check on the window or ask. The 45-minute walk from Miraflores to Barranco along the Malecón is nice in summer. **Museo de Arte Colonial Pedro de Osma** ① *Av Pedro de Osma 421, Barranco, T467 0141, Tue-Sun 1000-1330, 1430-1800, US$3. Only 10 visitors at any one time, Take bus 2, 54 or colectivo from Av Tacna.* A private collection of colonial art of the Cuzco, Ayacucho and Arequipa schools,

Lima beaches

In summer (December-April) the city's beaches get very crowded at weekends and lots of activities are organized. Even though the water of the whole bay has been declared unsuitable for swimming, Limeños see the beach more as part of their culture than as a health risk. Do not camp on the beaches as robbery is a serious threat and, for the same reason, take care on the walkways down. Don't take any belongings with you to the beach, only what is really necessary.

The *Circuito de Playas*, which begins with Playa Arica (30 km from Lima) and ends with San Bartolo (45 km from Lima), has many great beaches for all tastes. If you want a beach that's always packed with people, there's El Silencio or Punta Rocas. Quieter are Señoritas or Los Pulpos. Punta Hermosa has frequent surfing and volleyball tournaments.

Around Lima

Pachacámac

① *T430 0168, http://pachacamac.perucultural.org.pe, and www.ulb.ac.be/philo/ychsma, 0900-1700, closed 1 May, US$1.50, includes the museum, guide US$6.*
When the Spaniards arrived, Pachacámac in the Lurín valley was the largest city and ceremonial centre on the coast. A wooden statue of the creator-god, after whom the site is named, is in the site museum. Hernando Pizarro was sent here by his brother in 1533 in search of gold for Inca emperor Atahualpa's ransom. In their fruitless quest, the Spaniards destroyed images and killed the priests. The ruins encircle the top of a low hill, whose crest was crowned with a **Temple of the Sun**, now partially restored. Hidden from view is the reconstructed **House of the Mamaconas**, where the 'chosen women' spun fine cloth for the Inca and his court. An impression of the scale of the site can be gained from the top of the Temple of the Sun, or from walking or driving the 3-km circuit (the site is large and it is expected that tourists will be visiting by car - there are six parking spots).

Puruchuco

① *End of Av Javier Prado Este, www.museopuruchuco.perucultural.org.pe, 0900-1600, closed 1 May and 28 Jul, US$3.65.*

In the eastern outskirts of Lima, near La U football stadium, is Puruchuco, the reconstructed palace of a pre-Inca Huacho noble. There is a very good museum, Jiménez Borja, with ceramics and textiles from the lower Rímac or Lima valley. This is also the site of a major archaeological find (2002): under a shanty town called Túpac Amaru, over 2,000 intact mummy bundles have been uncovered in an Inca cemetery known as **Puruchuco-Huaquerones**. The quantity and completeness of the mummies, plus the tens of thousands of accompanying objects, should reveal a wealth of information about the last century of Inca society before the Spanish conquest. To see the tombs, ask the guards on Saturday morning if you can visit the archaeologists at work.

● Sleeping

Central Lima is not as safe at night as the more upmarket areas of Miraflores, San Isidro and Barranco. If you are only staying a short time and want to see the main sites, it is convenient, but do take care. San Isidro is the poshest district while Miraflores has a good mix of places to stay, great ocean views, bookstores, restaurants and cinemas. From here you can then commute to the centre by bus (30-45 mins) or by taxi (20-30 mins). Barranco is a little further out. All hotels in the upper price brackets charge 19% state tax and service on top of prices. In hotels foreigners pay no tax and the amount of service charge is up to the hotel. Neither is included in the prices below, unless otherwise stated. All those listed below have received good recommendations.

Near the airport *p1078, map p1078*

A-B Hostal Residencial Victor, Manuel Mattos 325, Urb San Amadeo de Garagay, Lima 31, T567 5083, hostalvictor@terra.com.pe. 5 mins from the airport by taxi, or phone or email in advance for free pick-up, large comfortable rooms, with bath, hot water, cable TV, free luggage store, free internet and 10% discount for Footprint book owners, American breakfast, evening meals can be ordered locally, mall with restaurants, fast food and gym nearby, very helpful, owner Víctor Melgar has a free reservation service for Peru and Bolivia.

Central Lima *p1080, map p1082*

LL Lima Sheraton, Paseo de la República 170, T315 5022, reservas@sheraton.com.pe. *Las Palmeras* coffee shop is good, daily buffet breakfast, good Italian restaurant, casino, all you'd expect of a 5-star hotel.

A Maury, Jr Ucayali 201, T428 8188, hotmaury@amauta.rcp.net.pe. Fancy, secure, breakfast included, most luxurious hotel in the historical centre.

A-B Kamana, Jr Camaná 547, T426 7204, www.hotelkamana.com. Rooms with TV, comfortable, safe, French and some English spoken, very helpful staff.

B Hostal La Posada del Parque, Parque Hernán Velarde 60, near 2nd block of Av Petit Thouars, Santa Beatriz, between centre and San Isidro, T433 2412, www.incacountry.com. Run by Sra Mónica Moreno and her husband Leo Rovayo who both speak good English, a charmingly refurbished old house in a safe area, elegant, cable TV, excellent bathrooms, breakfast US$3 extra, airport transfer 24 hrs for US$14 for up to 3 passengers, very good value.

C Granada, Huancavelica 323, T/F427 9033. Includes breakfast, hot water, English spoken, safe, laundry facilities.

D Hostal Roma, Jr Ica 326, T/F427 7576, www.hostalroma.8m.com. With bath, **E-F** off season, **F** without bath, hot water all day, safe to leave luggage, basic but clean, laundry service, free internet, airport transfer, book exchange, often full, motorcycle parking, *Café Carrara* open 0700-2200, Errol Branca speaks English (*Roma Tours*, helpful for trips, reservations, flight confirmations).

D-E Hostal de las Artes, Jr Chota 1460, Breña, T433 0031, artes@terra.com.pe. **F** without bath (no singles with bath), **G** pp in dormitory, Dutch owned, English spoken, safes in rooms and safe luggage store, nice colonial building, solar hot water system, book exchange, airport transfer US$12.

D-E Hostal Iquique, Jr Iquique 758, Breña (discount for SAE members), T433 4724, www.barrioperu.terra.com.pe/hiquique. **E** without bath, noisy and draughty, otherwise good, use of kitchen, warm water, storage facilities, rooms on the top floor are best.

E Hostal San Francisco, Jr Azángaro 127, T426 2735, hostalsf@lanpro.com.pe.

● *For an explanation of the sleeping and eating price codes used in this guide, see inside the front*
● *cover. Other relevant information is found in Essentials pages 1075-1077.*

Dormitories with and without bathrooms, new, safe, Italian/Peruvian owners, good service, internet and cafeteria.

F pp **Familia Rodríguez**, Av Nicolás de Piérola 730, p 2, T423 6465, jotajot@ terra.com.pe. With breakfast, popular, some rooms noisy, will store luggage, also has dormitory accommodation with only one bathroom (same price), transport to airport US$10 pp for 2 people, US$4 pp for 3 or more, good information, secure.

F Hostal Belén, Belén 1049, just off San Martín, T427 8995. Discount for groups of 3 or more but give prior notice, Italian spoken, basic breakfast extra, hot water, basic, noisy.

F Hostal España, Jr Azángaro 105, T427 9196, www.hotelespanaperu.com. **E** with bath (3 rooms), **G** pp in dormitory, fine old building, hot showers, English spoken, internet service, motorcycle parking, luggage store (free) and lockers, laundry service, don't leave valuables in rooms, roof garden, good café, can be very busy.

F Pensión Ibarra, Av Tacna 359, p 14-16, T/F427 8603 (no sign), pensionibarra@ekno.com. Breakfast US$2, discount for longer stay, use of kitchen, balcony with views of the city, very helpful owner, hot water, full board available (good small café next door).

G pp **Hostal Machu Picchu**, Av Juan Pablo Fernandini 1015 (block 10 of Av Brasil), Breña, T9794 4257. Family run, shared bath, hot water, kitchen facilities, cable TV, laundry service, excellent value.

Pueblo Libre p1084

F pp **Guest House Marfil**, Parque Ayacucho 126, at the 3rd block of Bolívar, T261 1206, cosycoyllor@ yahoo.com. English spoken, breakfast, kitchen facilities and laundry free of charge, internet, Spanish classes arranged, family atmosphere.

F Hostal Bait Sababa, Av San Martín 743, near the hospital, T01-261 4990, www.geocities.com/ sababalodgelimaperu/index.html. The home of a Jewish family who speak Spanish, English and Hebrew, very helpful, Fri evening meal provided, restaurants, laundry, internet and phone nearby.

San Isidro p1084

LL Country Club, Los Eucaliptos 590, T611 9000, www.hotelcountry.com. Excellent, fine service, luxurious rooms, safes in rooms, cable TV, free internet for guests, good bar and restaurant, classically stylish.

LL Sonesta Posadas del Inca El Olivar, Pancho Fierro 194, T712 6060, www.sonestaperu.com. Luxury, one of the top 5-star hotels in Lima, modern, many eating options, bar, garden, swimming pool, quiet, popular with business visitors.

L Libertador Hotels Peru, Los Eucaliptos 550, T421 6666, www.libertador.com.pe (reservations: Las Begonias 441, office 240, T442 1995/444 3720). Golden Tulip hotel, overlooking the golf course, full facilities for the business traveller, comfortable rooms, fine service, good restaurant. A rich collection of true hospitality and Peruvian culture with hotels in Arequipa, Cuzco, Huaraz, Lima, Mancora, Puno, Tambopata, Trujilla, Valle del Colca, Urubamba and Valle Sagrado.

L Sofitel Royal Park, Av Camino Real 1050, T215 1618, www.sofitel.com. Excellent rooms, charming, part of the French group, prices can be negotiated.

AL Garden, Rivera Navarrete 450, T442 1771, reservas@gardenhotel.com.pe. Includes breakfast, good beds, small restaurant, ideal for business visitors, convenient, free internet, good value.

D Hospedaje Elizabeth Ballon, Av del Parque Norte 265, San Isidro, T980 07557, hospedajeebr@ yahoo.fr. Family house in residential area 7 mins' walk from Cruz del Sur bus station. Shared or private bathrooms, TV room, laundry, luggage storage, breakfast included, airport transfers US$13.

San Miguel

C Hostal Mami Panchita, Av Federico Gallessi 198, T263 7203, raymi_travels@ perusat.net.pe. Dutch-Peruvian owned, English, French, Dutch, Spanish and German spoken, includes breakfast and welcome drink, comfortable rooms with bath, hot water, living room and bar, patio, email service, book exchange, Raymi Travel agency (good service), 15 mins from airport, 15 mins from Miraflores, 20 mins from historical centre. Frequently recommended.

Miraflores p1084, map p1088

LL Miraflores Park, Av Malecón de la Reserva 1035, T242 3000, www.mira-park.com. An Orient Express hotel, excellent service and facilities, beautiful views over the ocean, top class.

L La Hacienda, 28 de Julio 511 y Av Larco, T444 4346, reservas@bwlahacienda.com. English spoken, excellent service, breakfast included, has casino.

AL Antigua Miraflores, Av Grau 350 at C Francia, T241 6116, www.peru-hotels-inns.com. A small, elegant hotel in a quiet but central location, very attentive service, tastefully decorated, gym, cable TV, good restaurant.

AL Colonial Inn, Cmdte Espinar 310, T241 7471, coloinn@terra.com.pe. Colonial style, excellent service, noisy from traffic, parking, includes breakfast and tax.

AL José Antonio, 28 de Julio 398 y C Colón, T445 7743, www.hotelesjoseantonio.com. Good in all respects, including the restaurant, huge rooms, jacuzzis, internet, swimming pool, business facilities, helpful staff speak some English.

spoken, laundry service, internet, safe, near Plaza Vea hypermarket. Can help with bus and plane tickets, connected to other *hostales* in Peru.

C Hospedaje Atahualpa, Atahualpa 646c, T447 6601. Cheaper without bath, including breakfast, long-stay rates available, parking, hot water, cooking and laundry facilities, luggage stored, taxi service.

D pp **Inka Lodge**, Elias Aguirre 278, T242 6989, www.inkalodge.com. Also with dorms (**E** pp), convenient, excellent breakfast included, internet, laundry, very helpful.

D pp **Residencial El Castillo Inn**, Diez Canseco 580, T446 9501. All rooms with bath and hot water, family home, use of lounge, negotiate for longer stay.

E pp **Albergue Verde**, Grimaldo del Solar 459, T445 3816, www.albergueverde.com. Nice small hostal, comfortable beds, **C** pp in double, friendly owner, Arturo Palmer, breakfast included, airport transfers US$15.

E pp **Flying Dog Backpackers**, Diez Canseco 117, T445 6745, www.flyingdog.esmart web.com. Price includes breakfast in *El Parquetito* café, dormitories or private rooms, shared bath (**C**) in en suite room), very popular so reserve through the web, central, comfortable, hot water, secure, free internet and local calls, book exchange, kitchen facilities. Full transport information and tickets can be arranged.

E pp **Stop and Drop**, Berlín 168, p2, T243 3101, www.stopandrop.com. **C** double rooms with private bath. Backpacker hotel and guest house, also Spanish school. Bar, kitchen facilities, luggage store, laundry, TV, movies, internet, games, comfortable beds, safe, hot showers 24 hours, adventure sports and volunteer jobs. Airport pick up US$17.

E Wayruro's Backpackers, Enrique Palacios 900, T444 1564, www.wayruros.com. B&B, comfortable dorms, kitchen facilities, free tea and coffee, cheap bar, 24-hr hot water, laundry service, luggage storage, internet, TV, airport pick-up.

F pp **Eurobackpackers**, Manco Cápac 471 (no sign, look for the cat with the world on his stick), www.eurobackpackers.com. Dormitory, also doubles, breakfast included, family atmosphere, comfortable, safe, internet. Good reputation.

F pp **Explorer's House**, Av Alfredo León 158, by 10th block of Av José Pardo, T241 5002, explorers_ house@yahoo.es. No sign, but plenty of indications of the house number, with breakfast, dormitory with shared bath, or double rooms with bath, hot water, use of kitchen, laundry service, Spanish classes, English spoken, very welcoming.

F Friend's House, Jr Manco Cápac 368, T446 6248, friendshouse_peru@yahoo.com.mx. Dormitory accommodation with hot water, cable TV, use of kitchen, includes breakfast, very popular with backpackers, near Larcomar shopping centre,

plenty of good information and help. Highly recommended. They have another branch at José Gonzales 427, T446 3521. **E** pp with bath, same facilities, except private rooms only and more like a family home. Neither branch is signed.

F pp **Hogar del Mochilero** (Backpacker's Home), Jr Cesareo Chacaltana 162, T446 3268, maurosilva@hotmail.com. Rooms for 5-6 people, with bath and hot water, internet access a little extra, pleasant, quiet, a short walk from all main facilities, airport transfer, use of kitchen, Mauro speaks English, he and his wife, Mila, are very helpful.

F pp **Lex Luthor's House**, Porta 550 (look for the green lights), T242 7059, luthorshouse@ hotmail.com. Breakfast included, pleasant house, small and basic but clean, use of kitchen, good value.

Barranco *p1085*

B pp **Suites California**, or Villa Barranquina, Martínez Pinillos 129, corner with San Martín, T477 0772, hcalifor@viabcp.com. If you are looking for a flat, this would be a good choice, fully-equipped flatlets in a fascinating 1906 mansion, kitchen, lounge with sofa beds, bathroom, good bedrooms. Also has restaurant and laundry services.

C Domeyer, C Domeyer 296, T247 1413, domeyerhostel@peru.com. Hot water 24 hrs, laundry service, secure, welcomes gay and lesbian travellers.

C-D La Quinta de Alison, Av 28 de Julio 281, T247 1515, www.hotel-laquinta.com.pe. Breakfast extra, modern, lovely rooms with TV and bath, hot water, some rooms with jacuzzi (extra), excellent value, parking.

D Safe in Lima, Alfredo Silva 150, T252 7330, www.safeinlima.com. Quiet, Belgian-run hostal with family atmosphere in new premises, with breakfast, very helpful, airport pick-up US$14, good value, reserve in advance, lots of information for travellers.

E pp **Barranco's Backpackers Inn**, Malecón Castilla 260, T247 1326, www.barrancobackpackers.com. All rooms shared, with lockers,
hot water in bathrooms, breakfast included. **C** for double room, kitchen, laundry service, internet access, modern.

E pp **Mochileros Hostal**, Av Pedro de Osma 135, 1 block from main plaza, T247 8643, fenallo@hotmail.com. Beautiful house, completely redecorated, English-speaking owner, huge shared rooms with lockers, gay friendly, use of kitchen, good pub on the premises, a stone's throw from Barranco nightlife.

E-F pp **The Point**, Malecón Junín 300, T247 7997, www.thepointhostels.com. Rooms range from doubles to large dormitories, all with shared bath, very popular with backpackers (book in advance at weekends), breakfast included, internet, cable TV, laundry, kitchen facilities, gay-friendly, party atmosphere most of the time, *The Pointless Pub* open 2000 till whenever, weekly barbecues, therapeutic massage next door, can arrange bungee jumping, flight tickets and volunteering. Now has hostels in Arequipa and Cuzco (brand new 2006).

Youth hostels *map p1088*
F Albergue Juvenil Malka, Los Lirios 165 (near 4th block of Av Javier Prado Este), San Isidro, T442 0162, hostelmalka@terra.com.pe. Youth hostel, 20% discount with ISIC card, dormitory style, 4-8 beds per room, English spoken, cable TV, laundry, kitchen, climbing wall, nice café.
F pp Albergue Turístico Juvenil Internacional, Av Casimiro Ulloa 328, San Antonio, T446 5488, www.limahostell.com.pe. Dormitory accommodation, **C** in a double private room, basic cafeteria, travel information, cooking (minimal) and laundry facilities, swimming pool often empty, extra charge for kitchen facilities, safe, situated in a nice villa; 20 mins walk from the beach. Bus No 2 or colectivos pass Av Benavides to the centre; taxi to centre, US$2.50.

❶ Eating

19% state tax and 10% service will be added to your bill in middle and upper class restaurants. Chinese is often the cheapest at around US$5 including a drink.

Central Lima *p1080, map p1082*
♦♦ Antaño, Ucayali 332, opposite the Torre Tagle Palace. Good, typical Peruvian food, nice patio. Recommended.
♦♦ L'Eau Vive, Ucayali 370, also opposite the Torre Tagle Palace, T427 5612. Run by nuns, open Mon-Sat, 1230-1500 and 1930- 2130, fixed-price lunch menu, Peruvian-style in interior dining room, or à la carte in either of dining rooms that open onto patio, excellent, profits go to the poor, Ave Maria is sung nightly at 2100.
♦♦ Manhatten, Jr Miró Quesada 259. Open Mon-Fri 0700-1900, low end executive-type restaurant, local and international food from US$5-10, good.
♦♦-♦ El Maurito, Jr Ucayali 212, T426 2538. Peruvian/international, good pisco sours.
♦♦-♦ San Martín, Av Nicolás de Piérola 890, off Plaza San Martín. Typical Peruvian food from both coast and highlands, good value, reasonably cheap.
♦ Centro de Medicina Natural, Jr Chota 1462, next door to *Hostal de las Artes*. Very good vegetarian.

♦ Cordano, Jr Ancash 202. Typical old Lima restaurant/watering hole, slow service and a bit grimy but full of character. Definitely worth the time it takes to drink a few beers.
♦ Govinda, Av Garcilaso de la Vega 1670, opposite Gran Parque de Lima. Vegetarian, also sells natural products, good.
♦ Machu Picchu, near *Hostal Europa* at Jr Ancash 312. Huge portions, grimy bathrooms (to say the least), yet very popular, closed for breakfast.
♦ Natur, Moquegua 132, 1 block from Jr de la Unión, T427 8281. Vegetarian, the owner, Humberto Valdivia, is also president of the South American Explorers' board of directors, good for food and casual conversation.
♦ Neydi, Puno 367. Good, cheap seafood, open daily 1100-2000, popular.

Cafés
Café Carrara, Jr Ica 330, attached to *Hostal Roma*. Open daily until 2300, multiple breakfast combinations, pancakes, sandwiches, nice ambience, good.

Chinatown
There are many highly recommended *chifas* in the district of Barrios Altos. For example:
♦♦ Wa Lok, Jr Paruro 864, T427 2656. Owner Liliana Com speaks fluent English, very friendly. Has another branch at Av Angamos Oeste 703, T447 1280, good food in a tasteful, modern setting, ♦♦♦-♦♦.
♦ Kin Ten, Ucayali y Paruro. Excellent vegetarian options.
♦ Salon Capon, Jr Paruro 819. Very good. Has another branch in Larcomar shopping centre, Miraflores, which is ♦♦♦, elegant.

Breña *map p1082*
♦♦ La Choza Náutica, Jr Breña 204 behind Plaza Bolognesi. Good *ceviche* and friendly service.
♦ Azato, Av Arica 298, 3 blocks from Plaza Bolognesi, T423 4369. Excellent and cheap Peruvian dishes.

Pueblo Libre *p1084*
♦♦-♦ Antigua Taberna Quierolo, Av San Martín 1090, 1 block from Plaza Bolívar. Atmospheric old bar with glass-fronted shelves of bottles, marble bar and old photos, owns bodega next door. Serves simple lunches, sandwiches and snacks, good for wine, does not serve dinner.
♦♦-♦ Café del Museo, Av Bolívar 1515, T461 1312, in Museo Larco. Same chef as *Astrid & Gastón*, specially designed interior, open same hours as museum for Peruvian cuisine, has lunch and dinner specials.

San Isidro p1084

Ⓣ Alfresco, Santa Lucía 295 (no sign), T422 8915. Best known for its tempting seafood and *ceviche*, also pastas and rice dishes, expensive wines.

Ⓣ Antica Pizzería, Av Dos de Mayo 728, T222 8437. Very popular, great ambience, excellent food, Italian owner. Also **Antica Trattoria** in Barranco at Alfonso Ugarte 242, and an excellent bar, **Antica Taberna**, with a limited range of food at Conquistadores 605, San Isidro, very good value, fashionable, get there early for a seat.

Ⓣ Asia de Cuba, Conquistadores 780, T222 4940. Popular, serving a mix of Asian, Cuban and Peruvian dishes. It also has a reputation for its bar and nightclub; try the martinis.

Ⓣ Matsuei, C Manuel Bañon 260, T422 4323. Sushi bar and Japanese dishes, very popular, among the best Japanese in Lima.

Ⓣ Valentino, Manuel Bañon 215, T441 6174. One of Lima's best international restaurants, formal, look for the tiny brass sign.

Ⓣ Chez Philippe, Av 2 de Mayo 748, T222-4953. Pizza, pasta and crêpes, wood oven, rustic decor (same owners as Pizza B&B in Huaraz).

Ⓣ Chilis, Ovalo Gutiérrez. A branch of the American chain with a Peruvian twist, popular, like most of the places on the Ovalo.

Ⓣ Delicass, Miguel Dasso 131. Great deli with imported meats and cheeses, good coffee, open late, slow service.

Ⓣ Segundo Muelle, Av Conquistadores 490, T421 1206, and Av Canaval y Moreyra (aka Corpac) 605. Excellent *ceviche* and other very good seafood dishes, popular with the younger crowd.

Ⓣ MiniMarket Kasher, Av Pexet 1472. Kosher products, excellent, cheap *chala* bread every Fri.

Cafés

Café Olé, Pancho Fierro 115 (1 block from *Hotel Olívar*). Huge selection of entrées and desserts, very smart with prices to match.

Café Positano/Café Luna, Miguel Dasso 147. Popular with politicians, café and bistro.

News Café, Av Santa Luisa 110. Great salads and desserts, popular and expensive.

Miraflores p1084, map p1088

Calle San Ramón, known as 'Pizza Street' (across from Parque Kennedy), is a pedestrian walkway lined with outdoor restaurants/bars/discotheques open until the small hours of the morning. It's very popular, with good-natured touts trying to entice diners and drinkers with free offers.

Ⓣ Astrid y Gaston, Cantuarias 175, T444 1496. Excellent local and international cuisine, one of the best.

Ⓣ Las Brujas de Cachiche, Av Bolognesi 460, T447 1883. An old mansion converted into bars and dining rooms, traditional food (menu in Spanish and English), best Lomo Saltado in town, live *criollo* music.

Ⓣ Café Voltaire, Av Dos de Mayo 220. International cuisine with emphasis on French dishes, beautifully-cooked food, pleasant ambience, good service, closed Sun.

Ⓣ Cuarto y Mitad, Av Espinar 798. Popular Grill, also serves seafood.

Ⓣ La Gloria, Atahualpa 201. Very smart, excellent food and service.

Ⓣ Huaca Pucllana, Gral Borgoña cuadra 8 s/n, alt cuadra 45 Av Arequipa, T445 4042. Facing the archaeological site of the same name, contemporary Peruvian fusion cooking, very good food in an unusual setting.

Ⓣ El Kapallaq, Av Petit Thouars 4844, T444 4149. Prize-winning Peruvian restaurant specializing in seafood and fish, excellent *ceviches*. Open Mon-Fri 1200-1700 only.

Ⓣ El Rincón Gaucho, Av Armendáriz 580, T447 4778. Good grill, renowned for its steaks.

Ⓣ Rosa Náutica, T445 0149, www.larosa nautica.com, built on old British-style pier (Espigón No 4), in Lima Bay. Delightful opulence, finest fish cuisine, experience the atmosphere by buying an expensive beer in the bar at sunset, open 1230-0200 daily.

Ⓣ El Señorío de Sulco, Malecón Cisneros 1470, T441 0183, http://senoriodesulco.com. Overlooking a clifftop park, with ocean views from upstairs. Forget the Footprint grading, this is a 'five-fork' restaurant which some believe is the best in Lima, all Peruvian food, à la carte and buffet, piscos, wines, piano music at night.

Ⓣ Las Tejas, Diez Canseco 340. Open 1100-2300 daily, good, typical Peruvian food, recommended for ceviche.

Ⓣ La Tranquera, Av Pardo 285. Argentine-owned steak house, very good.

Ⓣ La Trattoria, Manuel Bonilla 106, 1 block from Parque Kennedy. Italian cuisine, popular, good cheesecake.

Ⓣ El Beduino, Av 28 de Julio 1301. Good, authentic Arabic food.

Ⓣ Bohemia, Av Santa Cruz 805, on the Ovalo Gutiérrez. Large menu of international food, great salads and sandwiches. Also at Av El Polo 706, p 2, and at Pasaje Nicolás de Rivera 142, opposite the main post office near the Plaza de Armas, Lima centre, T427 5537.

Ⓣ Café Tarata, Pasaje Tarata 260. Good atmosphere, family-run, good varied menu.

Ⓣ Dalmacia, San Fernando 401. Spanish-owned, casual gourmet restaurant, excellent.

Ⓣ Makoto Sushi Bar, Larcomar shopping centre, also at Las Casas 145, San Isidro. Very good.

La Palachinke, Av Schell 120 at the bottom of Parque Kennedy. Recommended for pancakes.
Il Postino, Colina 401, T446 8381. Great Italian food.
Ricota, Pasaje Tarata 248. Charming café on a pedestrian walkway, huge menu, big portions.
Sí Señor, Av Angamos Oeste 598. Mexican food, fun, loud. Also at Bolognesi 706, cheerful.
Dino's Pizza, Av Cdte Espinar 374 and many other branches. Great pizza at a good price, delivery service.
Madre Natura, Chiclayo 815. Natural foods shop and eating place, very good, closes 2100.
Pardo's Chicken, Av Benavides 730. Chicken and chips, very good and popular (branches throughout Lima).
El Parquetito, Diez Canseco 150. Good cheap menu, serves breakfast, eat inside or out.
Sandwich.com, Av Diagonal 234. Good, cheap sandwiches with interesting combinations of fillings.
Super Rueda, Porta 133, also Av Pardo 1224. Mexican food a-la Peru, fast-food style.

Cafés

Café Café, Martin Olaya 250, near the Parque Kennedy roundabout. Very popular, good atmosphere, over 100 different blends of coffee, good salads and sandwiches, very popular with 'well-to-do' Limeños. Also in Larcomar.
Café de la Paz, Lima 351, middle of Parque Kennedy. Good outdoor café right on the park, expensive, great cocktails.
Café Zeta, Mcal Oscar R Benavides 598 y José Gálvez. American owned, excellent Peruvian coffee, teas, hot chocolate, and the best homemade cakes away from home, cheap too.
C'est si bon, Av Cdte Espinar 663. Excellent cakes by the slice or whole, best in Lima.
Chef's Café, Av Larco 763. Nice place for a sandwich or coffee. Also has a little cart in Parque Kennedy until 2200 with good hot coffee to go.
Dove Vai, Diagonal 228. A bright *heladería* in this block of eating places; try the *encanto* with lumps of chocolate brownie.
Haiti, Av Diagonal 160, Parque Kennedy. Open almost round the clock daily, great for people watching, good ice cream.
Heladería 4D, Angamos Oeste 408. Open 1000-0100 daily, Italian ice cream, at other locations throughout Lima.
Mi Abuela, Angamos 393. Open 0900-2100 for probably the best yoghurt in Lima, and a large selection of natural foods.
San Antonio, Av Angamos Oeste 1494, also Vasco Núñez de Balboa 770, Rocca de Vergallo 201, Magdalena del Mar and Av Primavera 373, San Borja. Fashionable *pastelería* chain, good, not too expensive.

Tapas Bar, Manuel Bonilla 103, T242 7922. Expensive but very good tapas bar behind huge wooden doors, the tapas are a meal in themselves, extensive wine list, reserve a table at weekends.
La Tiendecita Blanca, Av Larco 111 on Parque Kennedy. One of Miraflores' oldest, expensive, good people-watching, very good cakes, European-style food and delicatessen.
Vivaldi, Av Ricardo Palma 260, 1 block from Parque Kennedy. Good, expensive, reminiscent of a gentlemen's club. Also **Vivaldi Gourmet**, Conquistadores 212, San Isidro, an international restaurant.
Zugatti, Av Larco 361, across from Parque Kennedy. Good Italian gelato.

Barranco *p1085*

Canta Rana, Génova 101, T477 8934. Open daily 1200-1700, good *ceviche* but expensive, small portions.
La Costa Verde, on Barranquito beach, T441 3086. Excellent fish and wine, expensive but recommended as the best by Limeños, open 1200-2400 daily, Sun buffet.
Manos Morenas, Av Pedro de Osma 409, T467 0421. Open 1230-1630, 1900-2300, creole cuisine with shows some evenings (cover charge for shows).
Ñaylamp, Av 2 de Mayo 239, T467 5011. Good seafood and ceviche, fashionable.
Festín, Av Grau 323, T247 7218. Huge menu, typical and international food.
El Hornito, Av Grau 209, on corner of the main plaza, T477 2465. Pizzería and creole food.
Las Mesitas, Av Grau 341, open 1200-0200. Traditional tea rooms-cum-restaurant, serving creole food and old sweet dishes which you won't find anywhere else.

✪ Bars and clubs

Central Lima *p1080, map p1082*
The centre of town, specifically Jr de la Unión, has many discos. It's best to avoid the nightspots around the intersection of Av Tacna, Av Piérola and Av de la Vega. These places are rough and foreigners will receive much unwanted attention.
720 Downtown, Av Uruguay 183. Exclusively gay, best in the centre, this is a rough neighbourhood so take a taxi to and from the club.
Estadio Futbol Sports Bar, Av Nicolás de Piérola 926 on the Plaza San Martín, T428 8866. Beautiful bar with a disco on the bottom floor, international football theme, good international and creole food.
Imperio, Jr Camaná 9th block. Exclusively gay, one of the older gay clubs in Lima, taxi recommended.

Piano Bar Munich, Jr de la Unión 1044 (basement). Small and fun.

Queirolo Bar, Jr Camaná 900 at Jr Quilca. Excellent for local colour. Opposite is the Centre's version of **La Noche** (see above).

El Rincón Cervecero, Jr de la Unión (Belén) 1045. German pub without the beer, fun.

San Isidro *p1084*

Palos de Moguer, Av Emilio Cavenecia 129, T221 8363. Brews 4 different kinds of beer, typical bar food.

Punto G, Av Conquistadores 512. Very popular, really small.

Miraflores *p1084, map p1088*

Barcelona, in Larcomar, T445 4823. One of the best pubs in the city.

Barra Brava, Av Grau 192. Lot's of fun, sports bar(ish).

The Clash, Psje Tello 269, Miraflores, T444 3376. Pub and gallery, excellent drinks, friendly staff, great decor, exclusively gay with shows and events.

Cocodrilo Verde, Francisco de Paula 226 near corner with Bellavista, Miraflores. Relaxed, stylish bar, slightly pricey but worth it for the Wed night jazz, and live music at weekends, occasionally charges cover for music at weekends.

Dionygreeks Pub, Av Dos de Mayo 385. Nice pub with Greek decor.

Media Naranja, Schell 130, at the bottom of Parque Kennedy. Brazilian bar with typical drinks and food.

Murphys, C Schell 627. Great Irish pub, "a must", also doing food such as fish'n'chips.

The Old Pub, San Ramón 295 (Pizza Street). Cosy, with live music most days.

Santa Sede, Av 28 de Julio 441. Very popular, great music, fun crowd, gay friendly.

Satchmo, Av La Paz 538, T442 8425. Live jazz, creole and blues shows.

Teatriz, Larcomar shopping center, T242 3084. Modern, expensive, very popular.

Voluntarios Pub, Independencia 131, T445 3939, www.voluntariospub.org. All staff are volunteers from non-profit organizations which benefit by receiving 90% of the profits made by the pub. Good atmosphere, music and drinks, nice to know that while you are partying other people are benefiting.

Barranco *p1085*

Barranco is the capital of Lima nightlife. The following is a short list of some of the better bars and clubs. Pasaje Sánchez Carrión, right off the main plaza, used to be the heart of it all. Watering holes and discos line both sides of this pedestrian walkway, but crowds and noise are driving

people elsewhere. Some places have been closed for safety reasons. Av Grau, just across the street from the plaza, is also lined with bars, eg El Ekeko, Av Grau 266, and Las Terrazas, Av Grau 290. Many of the bars in this area turn into discotheques as the evening goes on.

Bosa Nova, Bolognesi 660. Chilled student- style bar with good music.

El Dragón, N de Piérola near corner with Grau. Popular bar and venue for music, theatre and painting.

El Grill de Costa Verde, part of the *Costa Verde* restaurant on Barranco beach. Young crowd, packed at weekends.

Juanitos, Av Grau, opposite the park. Barranco's oldest bar, and perfect to start the evening.

La Noche, Bolognesi 307, at Pasaje Sánchez Carrión. A Lima institution and high standard, live music, Mon is jazz night, kicks off around 2200 (also in Central Lima).

La Posada del Angel, three branches on Pedro de Osma between 164 and 222. These are popular bars serving snacks and meals.

La Posada del Mirador, near the Puente de los Suspiros (Bridge of Sighs). Beautiful view of the ocean, but you pay for the privilege.

Sargento Pimienta, Bolognesi 755. Live music, always a favourite with Limeños. Opposite is the relaxed **Trinidad**.

◉ Entertainment

Lima *p1080, maps p1082 and p1088*
Cinemas

The newspaper *El Comercio* lists cinema information in the section called *Luces*. Most charge US$2 in the centre and around US$4-5 in Miraflores; two tickets for the price of one often offered on Tue. The cultural institutions (see below) usually show films once a week. Most films are in English with Spanish subtitles. The best cinema chains in the city are **Cinemark**, **Cineplanet** and **UVK Multicines**. Also good is **Multicine Starvision El Pacífico**, on the Ovalo by Parque Kennedy, Miraflores, T445 6990. Some *Cine Clubs* are **Cine Club Miraflores**, Av Larco 770, in the Miraflores Cultural Centre building, T446 2649. **Filmoteca de Lima**, Av 9 de Diciembre 125 (better known as Colón), T331 0126.

Peñas

Las Brisas de Titicaca, Pasaje Walkuski 168, at 1st block of Av Brasil near Plaza Bolognesi, T332 1881. A Lima institution.

De Cajón, C Merino 2nd block, near 6th block of Av Del Ejército, Miraflores. Good *música negra*.

La Candelaria, Av Bolognesi 292, Barranco, T247 1314. A good Barranco *peña*, open Fri-Sat 2130 onwards.

Del Carajo, San Ambrosio 328, Barranco, T241 7977. All types of traditional music.

La Estación de Barranco, at Pedro de Osma 112, T477 5030. Good, family atmosphere, varied shows.

Peña Poggi, Av Luna Pizarro 578, Barranco, T247 5790/885 7619. Over 30 years old, traditional.

Sachun, Av Del Ejército 657, Miraflores, T441 0123/4465. Great shows on weekdays as well.

Theatre

Most professional plays are staged at **Teatro Segura**, Jr Huancavelica 265, T427 9491. There are many other theatres in the city, some of which are related to Cultural centres (see below). The press gives details of performances. Theatre and concert tickets booked at Teleticket, T242 2823. Credit cards only.

⊛ Festivals and events

Lima *p1080, maps p1082 and p1088*
18 Jan: Founding of Lima. Semana Santa, or Holy Week, is a colourful spectacle with processions. **28-29 Jul**: is **Independence**, with music and fireworks in the Plaza de Armas on the evening before. **30 Aug**: Santa Rosa de Lima. **Oct**: is the month of **Our Lord of the Miracles**; see Las Nazarenas church, above page 1081.

O Shopping

Lima *p1080, maps p1082 and p1088*
Bookshops
Crisol, Ovalo Gutiérrez, Av Santa Cruz 816, San Isidro, T221 1010, Below *Cine Planet*. Large bookshop with café, titles in English, French and Spanish. Also in Jockey Plaza Shopping Center, Av Javier Prado Este 4200, Surco, T436 004.

La Familia, Av Diagonal 382, T01-447 8353, and Schell 279, T01-444 3993, Miraflores. Has a good selection of books on a wide variety of topics, helpful staff. Other branches at *La Tertulia*, CCPUCP, Av Camino Real 1075, San Isidro, and in the Jockey Plaza and El Polo commercial centres in Surco.

Ibero Librerías, Av Diagonal 500, T01-242 2798, Larco 199, T01-445 5520, and in Larcomar, Miraflores. Stocks Footprint Handbooks as well as a wide range of other titles.

Special Book Services, Av Angamos Oeste 301, Miraflores, T01-241 8490, www.sbs.com.pe. Also at Av Miguel Dasso 163, San Isidro, T2215464. The latter holds stock of international books in several languages.

Virrey chain has a great selection, but few in English: Larcomar Shopping Center (local 210), Miraflores, Pasaje Nicolás de Rivera, Lima centre behind the Municipalidad, T427 5080, and

Miguel Dasso 141, San Isidro (next door is **Librería Sur**, No 143).

Zeta, Av Cdte Espinar 219, T446 5139 and at airport. Stocks Footprint and other guide books.

For magazines, whether in downtown Lima or Miraflores, almost all street kiosks sell magazines in English. For the most recently published magazines and newspapers, try **Mallcco's** on Av Larco 175, on the Parque Kennedy roundabout, open daily 0800-2100. In front of Café Haiti by Parque Kennedy, men sell newspapers taken from arriving international flights; bargain hard.

Camping equipment

It's better to bring all camping and hiking gear from home. Camping gas (in small blue bottles) is available from any large hardware store or bigger supermarket, about US$3.

Alpamayo, Av Larco 345, Miraflores at Parque Kennedy, T445 1671. Sleeping mats, boots, rock shoes, climbing gear, water filters, tents, backpacks etc, very expensive but top quality equipment. The owner speaks fluent English and offers good information.

Camping Center, Av Benavides 1620, Miraflores, T242 1779. Selection of tents, back- packs, stoves, camping and climbing gear.

Huantzan, Jr Tarapacá 384, Magdalena, T460 6101. Equipment sales and rentals, MSR stoves, backpacks, boots.

Mountain Worker, Centro Comercial Camino Real, level A, store 17, San Isidro, T813 8367. Quality camping gear for all types of weather, made to order products as well.

El Mundo de las Maletas, Preciados 308, Higuereta-Surco, T449 7850. 0900-2200 daily for suitcase repairs.

Outdoor Peru, Centro Comercial Chacarilla, store 211, on Av Caminos del Inca 257, Surco, T372 0428. Decent selection.

Todo Camping, Av Angamos Oeste 350, Miraflores, near Av Arequipa, T447 6279. Sells 100% deet, bluet gas canisters, lots of accessories, tents, crampons and backpacks.

Handicrafts

Since so many artisans have come to Lima, it is possible to find any kind of handicraft in the capital - quality is high. Miraflores is a good place for high quality, expensive handicrafts; there are many shops on and around Av La Paz.

Agua y Tierra, Diez Canseco 298 y Alcanfores, Miraflores, T444 6980. Fine crafts and indigenous art.

Artesanía Santo Domingo, Plaza Santo Domingo, by the church of that name, in Lima centre, T428 9860. Good Peruvian crafts.

La Casa de la Mujer Artesana, Juan Pablo Ferandini 1550 (Av Brasil cuadra 15), Pueblo

Libre, T423 8840. Specialising in hand-made paper, some beautiful items, including from the rainforest and made from local materials, open Mon-Fri 0900-1300, 1400-1700.

Centro Comercial El Alamo, corner of La Paz y Diez Canseco, Miraflores. *Artesanía* shops with good choice.

Kuntur Wasi, Ocharan 182, Miraflores, T444 0557. English-speaking owner very knowledgeable about Peruvian textiles, often has exhibitions of fine folk art and crafts.

Las Pallas, Cajamarca 212, 5th block of Av Grau, Barranco, T4774629, Mon-Sat 0900- 1900. Very high quality handicrafts, English, French and German spoken.

Luz Hecho a Mano, Berlín 399, Miraflores, T446 7098, www.luzhechoamano.com. Lovely hand made handbags, wallets and other leather goods including clothing which last for years and can be custom made.

Alpaca There are bargains in clothing made from high quality Pima cotton. Shops selling alpaca items include:

Alpaca 111, Av Larco 671, Miraflores, T447 1623, www.alpaca111.com. High quality alpaca, baby alpaca and vicuña items.

Alpaca 859, Av Larco 859, Miraflores. Good quality alpaca and baby alpaca products.

Alpaka Studio, Av Larco 1144, Store 9, Miraflores. Fashionable alpaca garments.

Da Capo, Aramburú 920, dpto 402, San Isidro, T441 0714. Beautiful alpaca scarves and shawls in new designs.

La Casa de la Alpaca, Av La Paz 665, Miraflores, T447 6271. Open Mon-Fri 0930-2030.

Orígenes Andinos, Larcomar, Miraflores, T241 8472, www.origenesandinos.com. T-shirts and polo shirts made from Peruvian cotton with designs from the Nazca, Chimú, Moche, Mochica, Inca and other cultures.

Silvania Prints, Diéz Canseco 337A, Miraflores. Modern silk-screen prints on Pima cotton with pre-Columbian designs.

For modern designer crafts:

Dédalo, Paseo Sáenz Peña 295, Barranco, T477 0562. A labyrinthine shop selling furniture, jewellery and other items, as good as a gallery. It also has a nice coffee shop and has cinema shows.

Jewellery Ilaria, Av 2 de Mayo 308, San Isidro, T221 8575. Jewellery and silverware with interesting designs. There are other branches in Lima, Cuzco and Arequipa. Recommended. On Calle La Esperanza, Miraflores, dozens of shops offer gold and silverware at reasonable prices.

Maps

Instituto Geográfico Nacional, Av Aramburú 1190, Surquillo, T475 3030, ext 119, www.ign peru.gob.pe. Open Mon-Fri 0800-1730. It has topographical maps of the whole country, mostly at 1:100,000, political and physical maps of all departments and satellite and aerial photographs. They also have a new series of tourist maps for trekking, eg of the Cordillera Blanca, the Cuzco area, at 1:250,000.

Instituto Geológico Minero Y Metalúrgico (Ingemmet), Av Canadá 1470, San Borja, T225 3128, www.ingemmet.gob.pe. Open Mon-Fri 0800-1300, 1400-1600. Sells a huge selection of geographic maps ranging from US$12 to US$112. Also satellite, aeromagnetic, geochemical and departmental mining maps. Enquire about new digital products.

Lima 2000, Av Arequipa 2625, Lince (near the intersection with Av Javier Prado), T440 3486, www.lima2000.com.pe. Open Mon-Fri 0900-1300 and 1400-1800. Has an excellent street map of Lima (the only one worth buying), US$10, or US$14 in booklet form. Provincial maps and a country road map as well. Good for road conditions and distances, perfect for driving or cycling.

Ministerio de Transporte, Av 28 de Julio 800, Lima centre, T433 7800, www.mtc.gob.pe. Open Mon-Fri 0800-1230, 1400-1600.
Maps and plans of land communication routes, slow and bureaucratic.

Servicio Aerofotográfico Nacional, Av Las Palmas s/n, Barranco, T477 3682, informes@ sanperu.com. Open Mon-Fri 0800-1400. Aerial photographs available from mid- 1950's aerial survey, but they are expensive. Expect a waiting period as short as 1 day or as long as 2 weeks.

Markets

All are open 7 days a week until late.

Artesanía Carabaya, Jr Carabaya 319 at the Plaza de Armas.

Av Petit Thouars, in Miraflores. At blocks 51-54 (near Parque Kennedy, parallel to Av Arequipa). An unnamed crafts market area with a large courtyard and lots of small flags. This is the largest crafts arcade in Miraflores. From here to Calle Ricardo Palma the street is lined with crafts markets.

Feria Artesanal, Av La Marina y Av Sucre, in Pueblo Libre. Smaller than it used to be but is cheaper than Av Petit Thouars. It is no longer regarded as a safe area.

Parque Kennedy, the main park of Miraflores, hosts a daily crafts market from 1700-2300.

Polvos Azules, on García Naranjo, La Victoria, just off Av Grau in the centre of town. The 'official' black market, sells just about anything; it is generally cheap and very interesting; beware pickpockets.

La Portada del Sol, on cuadra 54 of Petit Thouars, has a small café with reasonable prices and good coffee.

Supermarkets

Lima's supermarkets are well stocked and carry a decent supply of imported goods. **Santa Isabel**, on Av Pardo in Miraflores is open 24 hrs.

▲▲ Activities and tours

Lima *p1080, maps p1082 and p1088*

Cycling

Best Internacional, Av Cdte Espinar 320, Miraflores, T446 4044 and Av Sucre 358, Magdalena, T470 1704. Open Mon-Sat 1000-1400, 1600-2000. Sells leisure and racing bikes, also repairs, parts and accessories.
Biclas, Av Conquistadores 641, San Isidro, T440 0890. Open Mon-Fri 1000-1300, 1600- 2000, Sat 1000-1300. Knowledgeable staff, tours possible, good selection of bikes, repairs and accessories, cheap airline boxes for sale.
BikeMavil, Av Aviación 4023, Surco, T449 8435, www.bikemavil.com. Open Mon-Sat 0930-2100. Rental service, repairs, excursions, selection of mountain and racing bicycles.
Casa Okuyama, Manco Cápac 590, La Victoria, T330 9131, www.biciperu.com. Open Mon-Fri 0900-1300, 1415-1800, Sat 0900-1300. Repairs, parts, try here for 28-in tyres, excellent service.
Neuquén, Jr Paruro 875, El Cercado, T427 2379. For Shimano parts.
Perú Bike, 28 de Julio 1381, Miraflores, T241 6367, www.perubike.com. Experienced agency leading tours, professional guiding, mountain bike school and workshop. **Willy Pro** (Williams Arce), Av Javier Prado Este 3339, San Borja, T346 4082. Open Mon-Sat 0800-2000. Selection of specialized bikes, helpful staff.

Diving

AquaSport, Av Conquistadores 645, San Isidro, T221 7270, www.aquasportperu.com. Owner is a CMAS instructor, gear for rent, tours and courses offered and quality equipment for sale.
Peru Divers, Av Huaylas 205, Chorrillos, T251 6231, www.perudivers.com. Open Mon-Fri 0900-1900, Sat 0900-1700. Owner Lucho Rodríguez is a certified PADI instructor who offers certification courses, tours and a wealth of good information.

Horse racing

Hipódromo Monterrico, on Tue and Thu evenings (1900) and Sat and Sun (1400) in summer, and in winter on Tue evening and Sat and Sun afternoons. For *Caballos de Paso*, which move in 4-step amble, extravagantly paddling their forelegs, **National Paso Association**, Miraflores, T447 6331.

Mountaineering

Asociación de Andinismo de la Universidad de Lima, Universidad de Lima, Javier Prado Este s/n, T437 6767. Meetings on Wed 1800-2000, offers climbing courses.
Club de Montañeros Américo Tordoya, Francisco Graña 378, Magdalena, T460 6101, http://es.geocities.com/clubamericotordoya/. Meetings Thu 2000, contact Gonzalo Menacho. Climbing excursions ranging from easy to difficult.
Club de Montañismo Camycam, see www.camycam.org for contact numbers. Expeditions, climbing, trekking, courses, guiding and help with community projects.
Trekking and Backpacking Club, Jr Huáscar 1152, Jesús María, Lima 11, T01-423 2515, 9987 4193 (mob), www.angelfire.com/mi2/ tebac. Sr Miguel Chiri Valle, treks arranged, including in the Cordillera Blanca.

Parapenting

Fly Adventure, Jorge Chávez 658, Miraflores, T9816 5461 (mob) (Luis Munarriz), 9900 9150 (Eduardo Gómez). US$25 for 15-min tandem flight over the cliffs, 4 to 6-day courses US$250-350. Recommended.

Surfing

Focus, Leonardo Da Vinci 208, San Borja, T475 8459. Shaping factory and surf boards,

knowledgeable about local spots and conditions, rents boards.

Klimax, José González 488, Miraflores, T447 1685. Sells new and secondhand boards, knowledgeable.

Wayo Whiler, Av 28 de Julio 287, Barranco, T247 6343, www.wayowhilar.com.pe. Makes all kinds of boards, sells clothing and materials, rentals and repairs, email in advance to have a board ready for when you arrive, can also organize excursions and runs a surf school with his brother (US$100 per month).

Tour operators

Do not conduct business anywhere other than in the agency's office and insist on a written contract. Bus offices or the airport are not the places to arrange and pay for tours. You may be dealing with representatives of companies that either do not exist or which fall far short of what is paid for.

Most of those in Lima specialize in selling air tickets, or in setting up a connection in the place where you want to start a tour. Shop around and compare prices; also check all information carefully. It is best to use a travel agent in the town closest to the place you wish visit; it is cheaper and they are more reliable.

Andean Tours, Schell 319 oficina 304-305, Miraflores, T444 8665, www.andean-tours.com. Recommended for bespoke arrangements.

AQP, Los Castaños 347, San Isidro, T222 3312, www.saaqp.com.pe. Comprehensive service, tours offered throughout the country.

Aracari Travel Consulting, Av Pardo 610, No 802, Miraflores, T242 6673, www.aracari.com. Regional tours throughout Peru, also 'themed' and activity tours, has a very good reputation.

Class Adventure Travel (CAT), San Martin 800, Miraflores; also Centro Comercial Sol Plaza, Av El Sol 948, Office 311, Cuzco, www.cat-travel.com. Dutch-owned and run, one of the best, with 10 years experience of tailor-made travel solutions throughout the continent. Highly recommended.

Coltur, Av José Pardo 138, Miraflores, T241 5551, www.coltur.com.pe. With offices in Cuzco and Arequipa, very helpful, well-organized.

Dasatariq, Jr Francisco Bolognesi 510, Miraflores, T447 7772, www.dasatariq.com. Also in Cuzco. A well-organized company with a good reputation and helpful staff.

Domiruth Travel Service S.A.C, Jr Rio de Janeiro 216-218, Miraflores, Lima 18, T0051-1 610 6022, www.domiruth.com.pe. Tours throughout Peru, from the mystical to adventure travel.

Explorandes, C San Fernando 320, T445 8683, www.explorandes.com.pe. Award-winning company. Offers a wide range of adventure and cultural tours throughout the country. Also offices in Cuzco and Huaraz (see page 1115).

Fertur Peru, Jr Junín 211, near Plaza de Armas, T427 1958, and Schell 485, Miraflores, T445 1974, http://ferturperu.tripod.com. Open 0900-1900. Highly recommended is Siduith Ferrer Herrera, CEO of this agency, not only offers up to date, correct tourist information on a national level, but also great prices on national and international flights, discounts for those with ISIC and Youth cards and **South American Explorers** members (of which she is one). Other services include flight reconfirmations, hotel reservations and transfers to and from the airport or bus stations. Also tours.

Hada Tours, 2 de Mayo 529, Miraflores, T446 8157, www.hadatours.com.pe. 20 years of experience.

Highland Peru Tours, Atahualpa 197, Miraflores, T/F242 6292, www.highlandperu.com.

Ideas, Ampay 036, San Miguel, T451 3603, ideas-mz@amauta.rcp.net.pe. Alternative tours of Lima, putting Inca and pre-Inca culture in its present context.

InkaNatura Travel, Manuel Bañon 461, San Isidro, T420 2022, www.inkanatura.com. Also in Cuzco, offers good tours with knowledgeable guides, special emphasis on sustainable tourism and conservation.

Lima Tours, Jr Belén 1040, Lima centre, T424 5110. Recommended for tours in the capital and around the country. Also has an office in San Isidro: Av Pardo y Alliaga 698, T222 2525, www.limatours.com.pe.

Masi Travel Sudamérica, Porta 350, Miraflores, T446 9094, www.masitravel.com. Tours throughout Peru, plenty of information on the website. Contact Verónika Reategui for an efficient service.

Peru Expeditions, Av Arequipa 5241 - 504, Lima 18, T447 2057, www.peru-expeditions. com. Specializing in expeditions in 4x4 vehicles and Andes crossings.

Peru For Less, ASTA Travel Agent #900144402, US office: T1-877-269 0309; UK office: T0203 002 0571; Peru (Lima) office: T272 0542, www.peru forless.com. Will meet or beat any published rates on the internet from outside Peru.

Peru Travel Bureau, Sebastián Tellería 45, San Isidro, T222 1909, www.ptb.com.pe. Recommended.

Roma Tours, Jr Ica 330, next to Hostal Roma, T/F427 7572, dantereyes@hotmail.com. Good and reliable. Administrator Dante Reyes is very friendly and speaks English.

Rutas del Peru SAC, Av Enrique Palacios 1110, Miraflores, www.rutasdelperu.com. Tailor-made trips and overland expeditions in trucks.

Viajes Pacifico (Gray Line), 163 La Mar St, Pacific Hse, Miraflores (Lima 18), T2413444, F2413319, www.graylineperu.com.

Victor's Travel Service, Jr de la Unión (Belén) 1068, T431 4195, 24 hr line 867 6341, victortravel@terra.com.pe. Hotel reservations (no commission, free pick-up), free maps of Lima and Peru, Mon-Sat 0900-1800, very helpful.

Viracocha, Av Vasco Núñez de Balboa 191, Miraflores, T445 3986, F447 2429. Very helpful, especially with flights, adventure, cultural and mystical tours.

Private guides The MITINCI (Ministry of Industry Tourism, Integration and International Business) certifies guides and can provide a list. Most are members of AGOTUR (Asociación de Guías Oficiales de Turismo), Baltazar La Torre 165, depto 101-D, San Isidro, T422 8937, agoturlima@ yahoo.com. Book in advance. Most guides speak a language other than Spanish.

Escorted Economic Overland Peru, T/F567 5107, victormelgar777@yahoo.com. Run by experienced tour guide Víctor Melgar (of **Hostal Victor** - see Sleeping), who escorts individuals, families and groups throughout Peru and Bolivia, safely and economically.

● Transport

Lima *p1080, maps p1082 and p1088*
Air
Arrivals or departures flight information T511 6055, www.lap.com.pe. Jorge Chávez Airport, 16 km from the centre of Lima. At the customs area, explain that you are a tourist and that your personal effects will not be sold in Peru; items such as laptops, cameras, bicycles, climbing equipment are exempt from taxes if they are not to be sold in Peru. The airport has been completely remodelled (2006).

Transport from the airport *Remise* taxi (**Mitsui** or **CMV**) from desks outside International Arrivals and National Arrivals, US$11.75 to centre, US$14.50 to San Isidro and Miraflores, US$17.50 to Barranco. There are many taxi drivers offering their services outside Arrivals with similar or higher prices (more at night). **Taxi Green** have been recommended as reliable and economical. See below for other taxi fares. There is a service called **Urbanito**, from the airport to the centre, Breña and San Miguel US$3, Pueblo Libre, San Isidro and Miraflores US$5 (slow, as it calls at all

hotels), T424 3650, 9957 3238 (mob), urbanito@terra.com.pe. Local buses (US$0.35) and colectivos run between the airport perimeter and the city centre and suburbs, their routes are given on the front window (eg 'Miraflores' for Miraflores). Outside the pedestrian exit are the bus, colectivo and taxi stops. At busy times (ie anytime other than late at night or early in the morning), luggage may not be allowed on buses. **Note** Do not take the cheapest, stopping buses to the centre along Av Faucett. They are frequently robbed. Pay more for a non-stop bus. If you are feeling confident and not too jet-lagged, go to the car park exit and find a taxi outside the perimeter, by the roundabout. They charge US$3-6 to the city centre. The security guards may help you find a taxi.

There are **ATMs** accepting American Express, Visa, MasterCard and the Plus, Maestro and Cirrus systems. There are **Casas de Cambio** (money changing desks) in the airport. They are open 24 hrs and change all types of travellers' cheque (they claim) and most major currencies. There are also exchange facilities for cash in the international arrivals hall.

Public telephones are everywhere in and around the airport. There is also a **Telefónica del Peru** office, open 0700-2300 daily. Fax service is available and internet facilities at US$3 per hr. **City Café** has fast computers for internet access at US$1.75 per hr (there is another one in departures, once through all the gates). There are two post offices.

Information desks can be found in the national and international foyers. There is also a helpful desk in the international arrivals hall. It can make hotel and transport reservations. The Zeta book kiosks have a selection of English language guidebooks.

Internal air services: to most destinations there are daily flights (most options are given in the text) but flights may be cancelled in the rainy season.

Bus

Local The bus routes are shared by buses, combis (mid-size) and colectivos (mini-vans); the latter run from 0600-0100, and less frequently through the night, they are quicker and stop wherever requested. All charge US$0.35. On public holidays, Sun and from 2400 to 0500 every night, a small charge is added to the fare. The principal routes are from the centre of Lima to Miraflores, San Isidro, Pueblo Libre, central market and airport.

Buses to **Miraflores**: Av Arequipa runs 52 blocks between the downtown Lima area and Parque Kennedy in Miraflores. Public transport has "Todo Arequipa" on the windscreen. When heading towards downtown from Miraflores the window

sticker should say "Wilson/Tacna". To get to Parque Kennedy from downtown look on the windshield for "Larco/Schell/Miraflores," "Chorrillos/ Huaylas" or "Barranco/ Ayacucho". On Vía Expresa, buses can be caught at Avs Tacna, Garcilaso de la Vega, Bolivia and Ugarte (faster than Av Arequipa, but watch for pickpockets). The main stop for Miraflores is Ricardo Palma, 4 blocks from Parque Kennedy. Taxi US$2.

Long distance There are many different bus companies, but the larger ones are better organized, leave on time and do not wait until the bus is full. For approximate prices, frequency and duration of trip, see destinations. **Note**: In the weeks either side of 28/29 Jul (Independence), and of the Christmas/ New Year holiday, it is practically impossible to get bus tickets out of Lima, unless you book in advance. Bus prices double at these times.

Cruz del Sur, Jr Quilca 531, Lima centre, T424 6158, www.cruzdelsur.com.pe. This terminal has routes to many destinations in Peru with *Ideal* service, quite comfortable buses and periodic stops for food and bathroom breaks, a cheap option with a quality company. They go to: **Ica, Arequipa, Cuzco, Puno, Chiclayo, Trujillo, Chincha, Camaná, Ilo, Moquegua, Pisco** and **Juliaca**. The other terminal is at Av Javier Prado Este 1109, San Isidro, T225 6163. This terminal offers the *Imperial* service (luxury buses), more expensive and direct, with no chance of passengers in the aisle, and *Cruzero* service (super luxury buses). They go to: **Tumbes, Sullana, Huancayo, Piura, Chiclayo, Trujillo, Huaraz, Jauja, Camaná, Arequipa, Moquegua, Ilo, Tacna, Cuzco** and **La Paz** (change buses in Arequipa). *Imperial* buses stop at the central terminal when going north and *Ideal* buses stop at the Javier Prado terminal when going south.

The following buses are all owned and operated by **Ormeño**: *Expreso Ancash* (routes to the **Huaraz area**), *Expreso Continental* (routes to **the north**), *Expreso San Cristóbal* (to **the southeast**), *Expreso Chinchano* (to the **south coast** and **Arequipa**) and *Expreso Internacional* (despite the name, to destinations throughout Peru). These depart from and arrive to: Av Carlos Zavala 177, Lima centre, T427 5679; also Av Javier Prado Este 1059, Santa Catalina, T472 1710, www.grupo-ormeno.com. **Ormeño** also offers *Royal Class* and *Business Class* service to certain destinations. These buses are very comfortable with bathrooms, hostess, etc. They arrive and depart from the Javier Prado terminal, but *Business* buses stop at both terminals. Javier Prado is the best place to buy any Ormeño ticket.

Other companies include: **Transportes Atahualpa**, Jr Sandia 266, Lima Centre, T428 7732. Direct to **Cajamarca** continuing on to

Celendín. Transportes Chanchamayo, Av Manco Cápac 1052, La Victoria, T265 6850. To **Tarma, San Ramón** and **La Merced**. CIVA, Paseo de La República 569-571, La Victoria, T332 5236, www.civa.com.pe. To all parts of the country. Has *Servicio Imperial* (executive service), but mixed reports about this company. **Ettsa**, Paseo de la República cuadra 7. Good service to the north, **Chiclayo, Piura, Tumbes**. **Flores**, Paseo de la República cuadra 6. Good buses to the south. **Transportes León de Huánuco**, Av 28 de Julio 1520, La Victoria, T424 3893. Daily to **Huánuco, Tingo María** and **Pucallpa**. **Línea**, José Gálvez 999, Lima Centre, T424 0836, www.transportes linea.com.pe. To destinations in the **north**. **Expreso Molina**, Av Nicolás de Arriola 2090-92 y Av San Luis 750, San Luis, T324 2137. Good service to **Ayacucho** via Pisco. **Móvil Tours**, Av Paseo de La República 749, Lima Centre near the national stadium, T332 0024 (has a second terminal at Los Olivos, very close to the airport, good for those who are short in time for a bus connection after landing in Lima). To **Huaraz** and **Chiclayo** by *bus cama*, and Chachapoyas (should you want to go straight through). **PerúBus/Soyuz**, Av México 333, T266 1515, www.soyuz.com.pe. To **Ica** every 8 mins, well-organized. **Rodríguez**, Av Roosevelt 393, Lima Centre, T428 0506. **Huaraz, Caraz, Yungay, Carhuaz**. Recommended to arrive in Huaraz and then use local transportation to points beyond. Good. Various levels of bus service. **Royal Tours**, Av Paseo de la República 3630, San Isidro, T440 6624. To **Huánuco, Tingo María** and **Pucallpa**.

Bus or colectivo to Pachacámac from Lima: From the Pan American Highway (south-bound) take a combi with a sticker in the window reading "Pachacámac/ Lurín" (US$0.85). Let the driver know you want to get off at the ruins. A taxi will cost approximately US$4.30, but if you don't ask the driver to wait for you (an extra cost), finding another to take you back to Lima may be a bit tricky. For organized tours contact one of the tour agencies listed above. **International buses**: Ormeño, Av Javier Prado 1059, Santa Catalina, T472 1710. To: **Guayaquil** (29 hrs with a change of bus at the border, US$50), **Quito** (38 hrs), **Cali** (56 hrs, US$115), **Bogotá** (70 hrs, US$130), **Caracas** (100 hrs), **Santiago** (54 hrs, US$130), **Mendoza** (78 hrs), **Buenos Aires** (90 hrs, US$140). A maximum of 20 kg is allowed pp. Depending on the destination, extra weight penalties range from US$1-3 per kg. **El Rápido**, Av Rivera Navarrete 2650, Lince, T447 6101. Service to Argentina and Uruguay only. Bear in mind that international buses are more expensive than travelling from one border to another on national buses.

Warning The area around the bus terminals is very unsafe; thefts and assaults are more common in this neighbourhood than elsewhere in the city. You are strongly advised either to take a bus from a company which has a terminal away from the Carlos Zavala area (eg Cruz del Sur, Ormeño, CIVA), or to take a taxi to and from your bus. Make sure your luggage is well guarded and put on the right bus. It is also important not to assume that buses leave from the place where you bought the tickets. Finally, check you change very carefully when paying in cash.

Taxi
The following are taxi fares for some of the more common routes, give or take a sol.
From downtown Lima to: Parque Kennedy (Miraflores), US$2. Museo de la Nación, US$2. South American Explorers, US$2. Archaeology Museum, US$2. Immigration, US$1.15. From Miraflores (Parque Kennedy) to: Museo de la Nación, US$2. Archaeology Museum, US$3. Immigration, US$2, Barranco, US$3. From outside airport terminal to centre US$3-6, San Isidro/Miraflores US$6-8. Whatever the size or make, yellow taxis are usually the safest since they have a number, the driver's name and radio contact. A large number of taxis are white, but as driving a taxi in Lima (or for that matter, anywhere in Peru) simply requires a windshield sticker saying "Taxi", they come in all colours and sizes. Licensed and phone taxis are safest and, by law, all taxis must have the vehicle's registration number painted on the side. There are several reliable phone taxi companies, which can be called for immediate service, or booked in advance; prices are 2-3 times more than ordinary taxis; eg to the airport US$15-20, to suburbs US$7-8. Some are **Taxi América**, T265 1960; **Moli Taxi**, T479 0030; **Taxi Real**, T470 6263; **Taxi Tata**, T274 5151; **TCAM**, run by Carlos Astacio, T9983 9305, safe, reliable. If hiring a taxi for over 1 hr agree on price per hr beforehand. Recommended, knowledgeable drivers: **César A Canales N**, T436 6184, T9687 3310 (mob) or through *Home Perú*, only speaks Spanish, reliable. **Hugo Casanova Morella**, T485 7708 (he lives in La Victoria), for city tours, travel to airport, etc. **Mónica Velásquez Carlich**, T9943 0796 (mob), vc_monica@hotmail.com. For airport pick-ups, tours, speaks English, most helpful. **Note**: Drivers don't expect tips; give them small change from the fare.

Train
Service on the Central Railway to Huancayo has been revived as a tourist route. Details are given under Huancayo, page 1249.

❶ Directory

Lima *p1080, maps p1082 and p1088*
Airline offices Domestic: Aero Cóndor, Av
Elmer Faucett 2112, San José, T452 5852, or 614
6014. **Lan**, Av José Pardo 513, Miraflores, T213
8200. **LC Busre**, Los Tulipanes 218, Lince, T619
1313. **Star Perú**, Av José Pardo 485, Miraflores,
T705 9000. **Taca Perú**, Av Cdte Espinar 331,
Miraflores, T511 8222. **WayraPerú**, Av Javier
Prado Oeste 2501, T261 4400, and Av José Pardo
140, Miraflores, T243 3123. **International**:
Aerolíneas Argentinas, Av José Pardo 805, p 3,
Miraflores, T444 0810. **Air France**, Av José Pardo
601, Miraflores, T444 9285. **Air Madrid**, Martín
Olaya 401, of 201, or Tika Tours, Pje Champagnat
139, Miraflores, T446 3644. **American Airlines**, Av
Canaval y Moreyra 390, San Isidro, and in Hotel
Las Américas, Av Benavides y Av Larco, Miraflores,
T211 7000. **Avianca**, Av Paz Soldán 225, of C5,
San Isidro, T445 0506. **Continental**, Víctor
Belaúnde 147, oficina 101, San Isidro, and in the
Hotel Marriott, 13th block of Av Larco, Miraflores,
T221 4340. **Copa**, Av 2 de Mayo 741, Miraflores,
T610 0810. **Delta**, Víctor Belaúnde 147, San Isidro,
T211 9211. **Iberia**, Av Camino Real 390, p 9, San
Isidro, T411 7800. **KLM**, Av José Pardo 805, p 6,
Miraflores, T421 9500. **Lacsa**, Av Cdte Espinar
331, Miraflores, T446 0758. **Lan Chile**, see Lan,
above. **Lloyd Aéreo Boliviano**, Av José Pardo
231, Miraflores, T241 5510. **Lufthansa**, Av Jorge
Basadre 1330, San Isidro, T442 4455. **Tame**,
Andalucía 174, Miraflores, T422 6600. **Varig**, Av
Camino Real 456, p 8, San Isidro, T221 0628.

Banks BCP, Jr Lampa 499, Lima Centre (main
branch), Av Larco at Pasaje Tarata, Miraflores, and
others. Amex TCs only, accepts Visa card and
branches have Visa/Plus ATM. **Banco de
Comercio**, Jr Lampa 560, Lima Centre (main
branch), Av Larco 265, Miraflores. Amex TCs only,
ATM accepts Visa/Plus. **BBVA Continental**, corner
of Av Larco and Av Benavides and corner of
Av Larco and Pasaje Tarata, Miraflores, Jr Cuzco
286, Lima Centre near Plaza San Martín. TCs
(Amex), Visa/Plus ATM. **Banco Financiero**, Av
Ricardo Palma 278, near Parque Kennedy (main
branch). TCs (Amex), ATM for Visa/Plus. **Banco
Santander Central Hispano (BSCH)**, Av Augusto
Tamayo 120, San Isidro (main branch), Av Pardo
482 and Av Larco 479, Miraflores. TCs (Visa and
Citicorp). ATM for Visa/Plus. **Banco Wiese
Sudameris**, Av Diagonal 176 on Parque Kennedy,
Av José Pardo 697, Miraflores, and others. TCs
(Amex only), ATM for Mastercard, Maestro and
Cirrus. **Citibank**, in all *Blockbuster* stores, and at Av
28 de Julio 886, Av Benavides 23rd block and Av
Emilio Cavenecia 175, Miraflores, Av Las Flores 205
and branch in Centro Comercial Camino Real, Av
Camino Real 348, San Isidro. *Blockbuster* branches

open Sat and Sun 1000-1900. **Interbank**, Jr de la
Union 600, Lima Centre (closed Sat morning),
also Av Pardo 413, Av Larco 690 and in Larcomar,
Miraflores, Av Grau 300, Barranco, and others
including *Metro* supermarkets *Wong* and *Metro*.
Amex TCs only, ATM for Visa/Plus,
Mastercard/Maestro/Cirrus and Amex.

Exchange houses There are many *casas de
cambio* on and around Jr Ocoña off the Plaza San
Martín. On the corner of Ocoña and Jr Camaná is a
large concentration of *cambistas* (street changers)
with huge wads of dollars, euros and soles in one
hand and a calculator in the other. They should be
avoided. Changing money on the street should
only be done with official street changers wearing
an identity card with a photo. This card doesn't
automatically mean that they are legitimate but
you're less likely to have a problem. Around Parque
Kennedy and down Av Larco in Miraflores are
dozens of official *cambistas* with ID cards and,
usually, blue, sometimes green vest. There are also
those who are independent, dressed in street
clothes, but it's safer to use an official changer.
There are a few places on Jr de la Unión at Plaza
San Martín that will accept worn, ripped and old
bills, but the exchange will be terrible. A
repeatedly recommended *casa de cambio* is **LAC
Dolar**, Jr Camaná 779, 1 block from Plaza San
Martín, p 2, T428 8127, also at Av La Paz 211,
Miraflores, T242 4069. Open Mon-Sat 0930-1800,
good rates, very helpful, safe, fast, reliable, 2%
commission on cash and TCs (Amex, Citicorp,
Thomas Cook, Visa), will come to your hotel if
you're in a group. Another recommended *casa de
cambio* is **Virgen P Socorro**, Jr Ocoña 184, T428
7748. Open daily 0830-2000, safe, reliable and
friendly. **American Express**, *Travex SA*, Av Sant
Cruz 621, Miraflores, T690 0900,
info@travex.com.pe. Mon-Fri 0830-1800, Sat
0900-1300. Replaces lost or stolen Amex cheques
of any currency in the world. Can purchase Amex
cheques with Amex card only. Or branches of
Viajes Falabella, eg Jr Belén 630, T428 9779, or Av
Larco 747-753, Miraflores, T444 4239,
lgutierrez@viajesfalabella.com.pe. **MasterCard**,
Porta 111, p 6, Miraflores, T242 2700. **Moneygram**,
Ocharan 260, Miraflores, T447 4044. Safe and
reliable agency for sending and receiving money.
Locations throughout Lima and the provinces.
Exchanges most world currencies and TCs.
Western Union Main branch: Av Petit Thouars
3595, San Isidro, T422 0036. Av Larco 826,
Miraflores, T241 1220 (also *TNT* office). Jr Carabaya
693, Lima centre, T428 7624. **Car rental** Most
rental companies have an office at the airport,
where you can arrange everything and pick up and
leave the car. It is recommended to test-drive
before signing the contract as quality varies. It can
be much cheaper to rent a car in a town in the

Sierra for a few days than to drive from Lima; also companies don't have a collection service. See page 43 for international rental agencies. Cars can be hired from: **Paz Rent A Car**, Av Diez Canseco 319, of 15, Miraflores, T446 4395, 9993 9853 (mob). Prices range from US$40 to US$60 depending on type of car. Make sure that your car is in a locked garage at night. **Cultural centres** Alianza Francesa, Av Arequipa 4595, Miraflores, T446 5524, www.alianzafrances alima.edu.pe. Various cultural activities, library. **British Council**, Torre Parque Mar, p 22, Av José Larco 1301, T617 3060, www.britishcouncil.org/peru.htm. **CCPUCP** (cultural centre of the Universidad Católica), Camino Real 1075, San Isidro, T616 1616, http://cultural.pucp.edu.pe. One of the best in Lima, with an excellent theatre (tickets US$7.15), European art films (US$1.45 Mon- Wed), galleries, good café and a bookshop selling art and literature titles. Recommended. **Centro Cultural de España**, Natalio Sánchez 181-85, Santa Beatriz, T330 0412. Has an art gallery and a cinema. **Centro Cultural Peruano Japonés**, Av Gregorio Escobedo 803, Jesús María, T463 0606, postmast@ apjp.org.pe. Has a concert hall, cinema, galleries, museum of Japanese immigration, cheap and excellent restaurant, lots of activities. Recommended. **Goethe Institute**, Jr Nazca 722, Jesús María, T433 3180, www.goethe.de/hn/lim/deindex.htm. Mon-Fri 0800- 2000, library, German papers. **Instituto Cultural Peruano-Norteamericano**, Jr Cuzco 446, Lima Centre, T428 3530, with library. Central office at Av Angamos Oeste 120, Miraflores, T242 6300, www.icpna. edu.pe. Theatre productions and modern dance performances are just a couple of the activities the ICPNA offers. Also Spanish lessons; see Language schools, below. **Embassies and consulates Note**: During the summer, most embassies only open in the morning. Australia, Av Víctor Andrés Belaúnde 147, Vía Principal 155, Ed Real 3, of 1301, San Isidro, Lima 27, T222 8281, info.peru@ austrade.gov.au. **Austria**, Av Central 643, p 5, San Isidro, T442 0503. **Belgian Consulate**, Angamos Oeste 392, Miraflores, T422 8231. **Bolivian Consulate**, Los Castaños 235, San Isidro, T442 3836, postmast@emboli.org.pe (0900-1330), 24 hrs for visas (except those requiring clearance from La Paz). **Brazilian Consulate**, José Pardo 850, Miraflores, T421 5650, Mon-Fri 0930-1300. **Canada**, Libertad 130, Casilla 18-1126, Lima, T444 4015, lima@ dfait-maeci.gc.ca. **Chilean Consulate**, Javier Prado Oeste 790, San Isidro, T611 2211, embchile@mail.cosapidata.com.pe. Open 0900-1300, need appointment. **Colombian Consulate**, Av Jorge Basadre 1580, San Isidro, T441 6922. Mon-Fri 0800-1400. **Ecuadorean Consulate**, Las Palmeras 356, San Isidro (6th block of Av Javier Prado Oeste), T212 4161, embjecua@

amauta.rcp.net.pe. **Finnish Embassy**, Av Víctor Andrés Belaúnde 147, Torre Real Tres of 502, Centro Empresarial Real, San Isidro, T222 4466. **French Embassy**, Arequipa 3415, San Isidro, T215 8400, france.embajada@computextos.com.pe. **Germany**, Av Arequipa 4202, Miraflores, T212 5016, emergency number 9927 8338. **Israel**, Natalio Sánchez 125, p 6, Santa Beatriz, T433 4431. **Italy**, Av G Escobedo 298, Jesús María, T463 2727. **Japan**, Av San Felipe 356, Jesús María, T218 1462. **Netherlands Consulate**, Av Principal 190, Santa Catalina, La Victoria, T476 1069, open Mon-Fri 0900-1200. **New Zealand Consulate**, Av Camino Real 390, Torre Central, p 17 (Casilla 3553), San Isidro, T221 2833, reya@nzlatam.com. Open Mon-Fri 0830-1300, 1400-1700. **Spain**, Jorge Basadre 498, San Isidro, T212 5155, open 0900-1300. **Sweden**, C La Santa María 130, San Isidro, T442 8905, konslima@terra.com.pe. **Switzerland**, Av Salaverry 3240, Magdalena, Lima 17, T264 0305, embsuiza@correo.tnet com.pe. **UK**, Torre Parque Mar, p 22, T617 3000, www.britishembassy.gov.uk/peru. Open 1300-2130 (Dec-Apr to 1830 Mon and Fri, and Apr-Nov to 1830 Fri), good for security information and newspapers. **USA**, Av Encalada block 17, Surco, T434 3000, for emergencies after hrs T434 3000, http://lima.usembassy.gov. The Consulate is in the same building. **Internet** Lima is completely inundated with internet cafés, so you will have absolutely no problem finding one regardless of where you are. An hour will cost you S/2-3 (US$0.60-0.90). **Language schools** Instituto Cultural Peruano-Norteamericano, see Cultural centres, above. Classes are on Mon-Fri from 0900 to 1100, US$80 per month, no private classes offered. **Instituto de Idiomas (Pontífica Universidad Católica del Perú)**, Av Camino Real 1037, San Isidro, T442 8761. Classes Mon-Fri 1100-1300, private lessons possible. Recommended. **Esit Idiomas**, Av Javier Prado Este 4457, Lima 33, T434 1060, www.esit-peru.com. **El Sol School of Languages**, Grimaldo del Solar 469, Miraflores, T242 7763, http://elsol.idiomas peru.com. US$15 per hr for private tuition, small groups US$195 per week. Family homestays and volunteer programmes available. **Independent teachers** (enquire about rates): Sra Lourdes Gálvez, T435 3910. Highly recommended, also Quechua. **Sra Georgelina Sadastizágal**, T275 6460. Recommended. Also Sr Mariano Herrera and Sr Dante Herrera: all these 4 can be contacted through peruidiomas@ LatinMail.com. **Srta Susy Arteaga**, T534 9289, T9989 7271 (mob), susyarteaga@ hotmail.com, or susyarteaga@ yahoo.com. Recommended. **Srta Patty Félix**, T521 2559, patty_fel24@yahoo.com. **Luis Villanueva**, T247 7054, www.acspanishclasses.com. Flexible, reliable, helpful. **Medical services** (It's also worth contacting your consulate for

recommendations.) **Hospitals: Clínica Anglo Americano**, Av Salazar 3rd block, San Isidro, a few blocks from Ovalo Gutiérrez, T221 3656. Stocks Yellow Fever for US$18 and Tetanus for US$3. Dr Luis Manuel Valdez recommended. **Clínica Internacional**, Jr Washington 1471 y Paseo Colón (9 de Diciembre), downtown Lima, T433 4306. Good, clean and professional, consultations up to US$35, no inoculations. **Instituto Médico Lince**, León Velarde 221, near 17th and 18th blocks of Av Arenales, Lince, T471 2238. Dr Alejandro Bussalleu Rivera speaks English, good for stomach problems, about US$28 for initial consultation. Repeatedly recommended. **Instituto de Ginecología y Reproducción**, part of Clínica Montesur, Av Monterrico 1045, Monterrico parallel to Av Polo, T434 2130. Recommended Gynaecologists are **Dra Alicia García** and **Dr Ladislao Prasak. Instituto de Medicina Tropical**, Av Honorio Delgado near the Pan American Highway in the Cayetano Heredia Hospital, San Martín de Porres, T482 3903. Cheap consultations, good for check-ups after jungle travel. Recommended. **Clínica del Niño**, Av Brasil 600 at 1st block of Av 28 de Julio, Breña, T330 0066. **Centro Anti-Rabia de Lima**, Jr Austria 1300, Breña, T425 6313. Open Mon-Sat 0830-1830. Consultation is about US$2.50.
Clínica Padre Luis Tezza, Av El Polo 570, Monterrico, T435 6990, emergency 24 hrs T437 1310. Top quality clinic specializing in a wide variety of illnesses/disorders etc, expensive; for stomach or intestinal problems, ask for Dr Raul Morales (speaks some English, US$28 for first consultation). **Clínica Santa Teresa**, Av Los Halcones 410, Surquillo, T221 2027. **Dr José Luis Calderón**, general practitioner recommended. **Backpackers Medical Care**, T9735 2668, backpackersmc@yahoo.com. The `backpackers' medic', Dr Jorge Bazán, has been recommended as professional and good value, about US$13 per consultation. **International Chiropractors Center**, Av Santa Cruz 555, Miraflores, T221 4764. **Pharmacy**: Pharmacy chains are modern, well-stocked, safe and very professional. They can be found throughout the city, often in or next to supermarkets. Some offer 24-hr delivery service. **Boticas Fasa**, T475 7070; **Boticas Torres de Limatambo**, T444 3022; **Farmacentro Tassara**, T251 0600; **Superfarma**, T440 9000. **Pharmax**, Av

Salaverry 3100, San Isidro, Centro Comercial El Polo, Monterrico (near the US embassy). Pharmacy/hypermarket, with imported goods (Jewish food products sometimes available at Av Salaverry branch, which is open 24 hrs). **Farmacia Deza**, Av Conquistadores 1140, San Isidro. Open 24 hrs. **Post offices** The central post office is on Jr Camaná 195 in the centre of Lima near the Plaza de Armas. Mon-Fri 0730-1900 and Sat 0730-1600. Poste Restante is in the same building but is considered unreliable. In Miraflores the main post office is on Av Petit Thouars 5201 in Miraflores (same hours). There are many small branches around Lima, but they are less reliable. For express service: **DHL**, Los Castaños 225, San Isidro, T215-7500. **UPS**, Av del Ejército 2107, San Isidro, T264 0105. **Federal Express**, Av Jorge Chávez 475, T242 2280, Miraflores, C José Olaya 260, Miraflores. **EMS**, next to central post office in downtown Lima, T533 2020/2424/2005. When receiving parcels from other countries that weigh in over 1 kg, they will be automatically sent to one of Lima's 2 customs post offices. Take your passport and a lot of patience as the process can (but not always) take a long time: Teodoro Cárdenas 267, Santa Beatriz (12th block of Av Arequipa); and Av Tomás Valle, Los Olivos (near the Panamerican Highway). **Note** Long trousers must be worn when going to these offices. **Telephones** Easiest to use are the many independent phone offices, *locutorios*, all over the city. They take phone cards, which can be bought in *locutorios*, or in the street nearby. There are payphones all over the city. Some accept coins, some only phone cards and some both. **Useful addresses** Tourist Police, Jr Moore 268, Magdalena at the 38th block of Av Brasil, T460 1060, open daily 24 hrs. For public enquiries, Jr Pachitea at the corner of Belén (Jr de la Unión), Lima, T424 2053. They are friendly and very helpful, English spoken. It is recommended to visit when you have had property stolen. **Immigration:** Av España 700 y Jr Huaraz, Breña, open 0900-1330. Procedure for extensions is described on page 1071. Provides new entry stamps if passport is lost or stolen. **Intej**, Av San Martín 240, Barranco, T477 2846. They can extend student cards, change flight itineraries bought with student cards. **National library**, Av Abancay 4th block, with Jr Miró Quesada, T428 7690. Open Mon-Sat 0800-2000, Sun 0830-1330.

Huaraz and the Cordilleras

The spectacular Cordillera Blanca is an area of jewelled lakes and snowy mountain peaks attracting mountaineers and hikers in their thousands. Huaraz is the natural place to head for. It has the best infrastructure and the mountains, lakes and trails are within easy reach. This region, though, also has some sites of great archaeological significance, the most notable of which must be Chavín de Huantar, one of Peru's most important pre-Inca sites.

Lima to Huaraz

From the coastal desert north of Lima a series of roads climb up to Huaraz, in the Callejón de Huaylas, gateway to Parque Nacional Huascarán. The Pan-American Highway parallels the coast all the way to the far north, and feeder roads branch from it up the various valleys. Just north of the beach resort of Ancón, the Pasamayo sand dune, stretching for 20 km, comes right down to the seashore. The old road which snakes above the sea is spectacular, but is now closed except to commercial traffic. The toll road, which goes right over the top, is safer, with incredible views over the coast and valleys.

Huaura Valley
The Pan-American Highway is four-lane (several tolls, US$0.75) to Km 101, at **Huacho**, 19 km east of **Puerto Huacho** (several hotels in Huacho, but none at the port). The beaches south of the town are clean and deserted. The journey inland from Huacho, up the Huaura valley, is splendid. Beyond Sayán the road follows the Huaura valley which narrows almost to a gorge before climbing steeply to **Churín**, with hot, sulphurous springs which are used to cure a number of ailments, and various hotels and restaurants. The climate is dry with temperatures ranging from 10° to 32°C. The area is famous for cheese, yoghurt and other natural products. Other hot springs nearby are **Huancahuasi**, **Picoy** (both new) and **Chiuchín** (neglected).

Barranca, Caral and Paramonga → *Phone code: 01.*
At Barranca (Km 195) the beach is long and not too dirty, though windy. There are various hotels **(D-F)** and **Banco de la Nación** accepts travellers' cheques (good rates). A few kilometres before Barranca (158 km from Lima) a turning to the right (east) leads to **Caral** ① *Proyecto Especial Caral, Unión 1040, Lima 1, T332 5380, www.caralperu. gob.pe, US$3, US$1 with student card; US$6 per group with guide, all visitors must report to the tourist post in the car park, see Listings for tours and transport.* This ancient city, 20 km from the coast, dates from about 2,600 BC. Many of the accepted theories of Peruvian archaeology have been overturned by Caral's age and monumental construction. It appears to be easily the oldest city in South America. The dry, desert site lies on the southern fringes of the Supe valley, along whose flanks there are many more unexcavated ruins. Caral covers 66 ha and contains eight significant pyramidal structures. To date seven have been excavated by archaeologists from the University of San Marcos, Lima. They are undertaking careful renovation on the existing foundations to re-establish the pyramidal tiers. It is possible to walk around and, in some cases, up on to the pyramids. A viewpoint provides a panorama across the whole site. Detailed, illustrated, bilingual (Spanish/English) information panels are located around the site. The site is well organized, criss-crossed by marked paths which must be adhered to. Allow at least two hours to visit the site.

Some 4 km beyond the turn-off to Huaraz, beside the Highway, are the well preserved ruins of the Chimú temple of **Paramonga** ① *US$1.20; caretaker may act as guide.* Set on high ground with a view of the ocean, the fortress-like mound is reinforced by eight quadrangular walls rising in tiers to the top of the hill.

Casma and Sechín → *Phone code: 043. Colour map 3, grid B2.*
Casma has a pleasant Plaza de Armas, several parks and two markets including a good food market. It is a base from where to explore **Sechín** ① *www.xanga.com/sechin, the site is open daily 0800-1800, photography best around midday, US$1.50 (children and students half price); ticket also valid for the Max Uhle Museum by the ruins and Pañamarca, an archaeological site in the Nepeña Valley, north of Casma, getting there: frequent colectivos*

leave from in front of the market in Casma, US$0.30 pp, or motorcycle taxi US$1, one of the most important ruins 5 km away on the Peruvian coast. It consists of a large square temple completely faced with about 500 carved stone monoliths narrating, it is thought, a gruesome battle in graphic detail. The style is unique in Peru for its naturalistic vigour. The complex as a whole is associated with the pre-Chavín Sechín culture, dating from about 1600 BC. Three sides of the large stone temple have been excavated and restored, but you cannot see the earlier adobe buildings inside the stone walls because they were covered up and used as a base for a second storey, which has been completely destroyed.

Chimbote → *Phone code: 043. Colour map 3, grid B2. Population: 35,900.*

The port of Chimbote serves the national fishing industry and the smell of the fishmeal plants is overpowering. As well as being unpleasant it is also unsafe. Take extensive precautions, always use taxis from the bus station to your hotel and don't venture far from the hotel. The modern Municipal building has a small **art gallery** *0900-2000*. **Note**: The main street, Avenida Víctor Raul Haya de la Torre, is also known by its old name, José Pardo. At weekends two-hour boat trips go around the bay to visit the cliffs and islands to see the marine birdlife and rock formations. www.laindustria.com (local newspaper) has a section on Chimbote.

● Sleeping

Casma and Sechín *p1105*
C Hostal El Farol, Túpac Amaru 450, T711064, hostalfaro@yahoo.com. Very nice, cheaper in low season, hot water, swimming pool, pleasant garden, good restaurant, parking, information.
E Gregori, Luis Ormeño 530, T711073. Cheaper without bath, café downstairs.
E Monte Carlo, Nepeña 370, T711421. TV, internet, laundry, good value.
E Rebeca, Huarmey 377, T711258. Modern, hot water only at night, good.
F Las Dunas, Luis Ormeño 505, T/F711057. A converted family home, friendly, upgraded and enlarged in 2002.
F Hostal Celene Ormeño 595, T711065. Large new rooms.

Chimbote *p1106*
Plenty of hotels, so try to negotiate a lower rate.
A Cantón, Bolognesi 498, T344388. The most modern, luxury hotel in the city, has a good but pricey chifa restaurant.
B Ivansino Inn, Haya de la Torre 738, T321811, ivansino@hotmail.com. Including breakfast, comfortable, modern.
C D'Carlo, Villavicencio 376, on the plaza, T/F321047. Friendly, TV, mini-bar, restaurant.
C San Felipe, Haya de la Torre 514, T323401. Hot water, comfortable, restaurant.
D Felic, Haya de la Torre 552, T325901. Recommended.
E without bath, quiet. Recommended.
D Hostal Karol Inn, Manuel Ruiz 277, T/F321216. Hot water, good, family run, laundry, cafetería.
D Residencial El Parque, E Palacios 309, on plaza, T323963. Converted old home, hot water, nice, secure.
E Hostal El Ensueño, Sáenz Peña 268, 2 blocks from Plaza Central, T328662. **F** without bath, very good, safe, welcoming.

E Tany, Palacios 553, T/F323411. Includes breakfast, TV, good value.
F Hostal Persia, L Prado 623, T/F342540. TV, good, but near market.

● Eating

Casma and Sechín *p1105*
Cheap restaurants on Huarmey. The local ice-cream, *Caribe*, is available at Ormeño 545.
♥ Tío Sam, Huarmey 138. Specializes in fresh fish.
♥ Venecia, Huarmey 204. Local dishes, popular.

Chimbote *p1106*
♥ Aquarius, Haya de la Torre 360. Vegetarian.
♥ Chifa Jin Lon, adjoining *Hostal Karol Inn*. Well-prepared Chinese food, popular.
♥ Delca, Haya de la Torre 568. Excellent bakery.
♥ Las Flores, Jr Enrique Palacios, 2 blocks west of the Plaza. Open 24 hrs, good breakfasts.
♥ Recutecu, L Prado 556. Good set lunch with a wide choice, popular with locals.

▲ Activities and tours

Barranca, Caral and Paramonga *p1105*
For tours to Caral from Lima: **Expedition de la Vega, Aventuras de oro**, Malecón Miramar 207, Punta Hermosa, Lima 24, T01-230 7246, 9728 7061 (mob), www.aventuras-de- oro.com. Fenny is the contact here; she is Dutch, married to a Peruvian.

Casma and Sechín *p1105*
Sechín Tours, in Hostal Monte Carlo, Casma, T711421. Organizes tours in the local area. The guide, Renato, only speaks Spanish but has knowledge of local ruins and can be contacted on T712528, renatotours@yahoo.com. US$3 per hr, including use of mototaxi.

⊝ Transport

Huara Valley p1105
Bus To **Huacho** from **Lima** 2½ hrs, US$2, or Comité 18, daily colectivos, US$2.50. To **Churín** Estrella Polar, Espadín and Beteta have several times a day from **Lima**, 4-5 hrs, US$5.

Barranca, Caral and Paramonga p1105
Bus To **Barranca** stops opposite the service station (*el grifo*) at the end of town. From **Lima** to Barranca, 3½ hrs, US$3. As bus companies have their offices in Barranca, buses will stop there rather than at Pativilca or Paramonga. Bus from Barranca to **Casma** 155 km, several daily, 2½ hrs, US$3. From Barranca to **Huaraz**, 4 hrs, US$6, daily buses or trucks. The good, paved road to Huaraz turns off the Panamericana just past Pativilca. **Caral** is best visited from Barranca or Supe. Colectivos leave from Av Lima, 2 blocks from the market, in Barranca for the village of Caral from 0700, 1½ hrs, US$1.50. The ruins are 25 km along a rough road which runs up the Supe valley. A path leads from the road across the valley to the ruins, though the river may be impassable Dec-Mar, 30 mins. Colectivos can also be picked up in Supe or at the signposted turn-off to the ruins on the Panamericana at Km 185, if they have room. A taxi in Barranca or Supe costs US$20, including a 2-hr wait. Another approach is from the south along a rough road, 28 km, through the Granja Toshi chicken farm: no regular transport but taxis wait at the Km 160 turn-off on the Panamericana, 2 hrs, US$20, including a 2-hr wait. This route is unsigned but may be the only way in the rainy season.

Buses run only to Paramonga port (3 km off the Highway, 4 km from the Paramonga ruins, about 15 mins from Barranca). **Taxi** From Paramonga to the ruins and return after waiting, US$4.50, otherwise take a Barranca-Paramonga port bus, then a 3 km walk.

Casma and Sechín p1105
Bus Half hourly from **Lima** to **Chimbote** which can drop you off in Casma, 370 km, 6 hrs, US$5. If going to **Lima** many of the buses from Trujillo and Chimbote stop briefly opposite the petrol station, block 1 of Ormeño or, if they have small offices, along blocks 1-5 of Av Ormeño. To **Chimbote**, 55 km, it is easiest to take a **Los Casmeños** colectivo, huge old Dodge cars, which depart when full from in front of the petrol station, block 1 of Ormeño, or from Plaza Poncianos, 45 mins, US$1.20. To **Trujillo** it is best to go first to Chimbote bus station and then take an **América Express** bus. To **Huaraz** (150km), via Pariacoto, buses come from Chimbote, 7 hrs, US$6. Transportes Huandoy, Ormeño 166, T712336, departs at 0700, 1100 and 1400, while Yungay

Express, Ormeño 158, departs at 0600, 0800 and 1400. This difficult but beautiful trip is worth taking in daylight. From Casma the first 30 km are paved, a good dirt road follows for 30 km to **Pariacoto** (basic lodging). From here to the **Callán pass** (4,224 m) the road is rough (landslides in rainy season), but once the Cordillera Negra has been crossed, the wide, gravel road is better with lovely views of the Cordillera Blanca (150 km to Huaraz). Most Huaraz buses go via Pativilca, which is further but the road is much better, 7 hrs, US$6, **Móvil Tours** and **Trans Chinchaysuyo**, all run at night.

Chimbote p1106
Warning Under no circumstances should you walk to the centre: minibus costs US$0.30, taxi US$1.30. There are no hotels near the terminal; some companies have ticket offices in the centre. **Bus** The station is 4 km south on Av Meiggs. From **Lima**, to Chimbote, 420 km, 6 hrs, US$7-9, several buses daily, **Trans Isla Blanca** has the most frequent service. To **Trujillo**, 130 km, 2 hrs, US$1.50, **América Express** buses every 20 mins. To **Huaraz** most companies, with the best buses, go the 'long way round', ie down the Panamericana to Pativilca, then up the paved highway, 7 hrs, US$6. The main companies start in Trujillo and continue to **Caraz**. To Huaraz via Pariacoto, 7 hrs, US$6, **Trans Huandoy** (Etseturh), T354024, at 0600, 1000 and 1300, 7 hrs, US$5.50, and **Yungay Express** at 0500, 0700 and 1300. To **Caraz** via Cañón del Pato, 7-8 hrs, US$7.60, **Yungay Express** at 0830 (for a description of this route see above). Sit on the left-hand-side for the best views. If arriving from Caraz via the Cañón del Pato there is usually time to make a connection to Casma or Trujillo/Huanchaco and avoid overnighting in Chimbote. If travelling to Caraz, however, overnighting in Chimbote is almost unavoidable. Casma is near enough to stay in but you will need to buy your Caraz ticket the day before; the bus station is on the Casma side of Chimbote.

⊕ Directory

Casma and Sechín p1105
Banks Good rates for cash and TCs, no commission, at BCP, Bolívar 181. **Internet** Café on west side of Plaza, 0900-2100. **Post offices** Fernando Loparte, ½ block from Plaza de Armas.

Chimbote p1106
Banks BCP and Interbank, both on Bolognesi and M Ruiz, for TCs and cash. **Casa Arroyo**, M Ruiz 292, cash only. There are other *casas* and street changers along M Ruiz between Bolognesi and VR Haya de la Torre. **Internet** At Palacios 518, Aguirre 278 and J.Pardo 660.

Huaraz → *Phone code: 043. Colour map 3, grid B2. Population: 80,000. Altitude: 3,091 m.*

The main town in the Cordillera Blanca, 420 km from Lima, Huaraz is expanding rapidly as a major tourist centre, but it is also a busy commercial hub, especially on market days. It is a prime destination for hikers and a Mecca for international climbers.

Ins and outs
Tourist office iPerú ① *Luzuriaga on Plaza de Armas, T428812, iperuhuaraz@promperu. gob.pe, Mon-Fri 0800-1300, 1700-2000, Sat-Sun 0800-1300. Policía de Turismo Av Laredo y Laredo 716, T421341, Mon-Fri 0900-1300, 1600-1900, Sat 0900-1300,* is the place to report all crimes and mistreatment by tour operators, hotels, etc. Huaraz has its share of crime, especially since the arrival of mining in the area and during the high tourist season. On no account should women go to surrounding districts and sites alone.

Callejón de Huaylas and the route to Huaraz → *See also p.*
Probably the easiest way to reach the Callejón de Huaylas is to take the paved road which branches east off the Pan-American Highway north of Pativilca (see page 1105), 203 km from Lima. The road climbs increasingly steeply to the chilly pass at 4,080 m (Km 120). Shortly after, Laguna **Conococha** comes into view, where the Río Santa rises. A dirt road branches off from Conococha to **Chiquián** (see page 1124) and the **Cordilleras Huayhuash** and **Raura** to the southeast. After crossing a high plateau the main road descends gradually for 47 km until **Catac**, where another road branches east to Chavín and on to the **Callejón de Conchucos** (the eastern side of the Cordillera Blanca). Huaraz is 36 km further on and the road then continues north between the towering Cordillera Negra, snowless and rising to 4,600 m, and the snow-covered Cordillera Blanca. This valley, the Callejón de Huaylas, has many picturesque villages and small towns, with narrow cobblestone streets and odd-angled house roofs. The alternative routes to the Callejón de Huaylas are via the Callán pass from Casma to Huaraz (see page 1107), and from Chimbote to Caraz via the Cañon del Pato (page 1118).

The valley's focus is **Huaraz**, capital of Ancash department. It was almost completely destroyed in the earthquake of May 1970. The Plaza de Armas has been rebuilt, with a towering, white statue of Christ. A new **Cathedral** is still being built. The setting, at the foot of the Cordillera Blanca, is spectacular. The main thoroughfare, Avenida Luzuriaga, is bursting at the seams with travel agencies, climbing equipment hire shops, restaurants, cafés and bars. A good district for those seeking peace and quiet is La Soledad, 6 blocks uphill from the Plaza de Armas on Avenida Sucre. Here, along Sucre as well as Jr Amadeo Figueroa, every second house seems to rent rooms, most without signs.

Museo Regional de Ancash ① *Instituto Nacional de Cultura, Plaza de Armas, 0800-2000, US$1.45,* contains stone monoliths and *huacos* from the Recuay culture, well labelled. The **Sala de Cultura SUNARP** ① *Av Centenario 530, Independencia, T421301, Mon-Fri 1700-2000, Sat 0900-1300, free* , often has interesting art and photography exhibitions by local artists.

About 8 km to the northeast is the **Willkawain** ① *US$1.50, take a combi from 13 de Diciembre and Comercio, US$0.55 direct to Willkawain. If walking, go past the Hotel Huascarán. After crossing a small bridge take a second right marked by a blue sign, it is about 2 hrs uphill walk; ask directions as there are many criss-crossing paths used regularly by local people,* archaeological site. The ruins (AD 700-1000, Huari Empire) consist of one large three-storey structure with intact stone roof slabs and several small structures. About 500 m past Willkawain is Ichiwillkawain with several similar but smaller structures. Take a torch if it's late. There is also an alternative road from the ruins to Monterrey.

North of Huaraz, 6 km along the road to Caraz, are the thermal baths at **Monterrey** (Altitude 2,780 m). ① *The lower pool is US$0.85; the upper pool, which is nicer (closed Mon for cleaning), US$1.35; also individual and family tubs US$1.35 per person for 20 mins; crowded at weekends and holidays. There are restaurants and hotels (B-C). City buses along Av Luzuriaga go as far as Monterrey (US$0.22), until 1900; taxi US$2-3.*

● Sleeping

Huaraz *p1108, maps p1110 and p1111*
Hotels fill up rapidly during high season (May-Sep), especially during public holidays and special events when prices rise (beware overcharging). Unless otherwise stated, all hotels listed are recommended.

AL Andino Club, Pedro Cochachín 357, some way southeast from the centre (take a taxi after dark), T421949, www.hotelandino.com. The best in town, affiliated to the Libertador group, expensive restaurant, safe parking, free internet for guests, Swiss run, 2nd floor rooms with balconies and views of Huascarán are more expensive, climbing and hiking gear for hire.

B El Tumi, San Martín 1121, T/F421784, www.hoteleltumi.com. Good restaurant (serves huge steaks), completely remodelled and upgraded in 2005, advance reservations advised.

B-C Hostal Montañero, Plaza Ginebra 30-B, T426386, www.trekkingperu.com. Hot water, modern, comfortable, good value, climbing equipment rental and sales.

C Albergue Churup, Jr Figueroa 1257, T422584, www.churup.com. Price includes breakfast, **E** in dormitory without breakfast, fully refurbished, hot water, fire in sitting room on 4th floor with mountain views, roof terrace, internet, cafeteria, use of kitchen, lots of information and travel agency, luggage store, laundry, book exchange, English spoken, Spanish classes, extremely helpful, motorcycle parking. Recommended.

C Edward's Inn, Bolognesi 121, T/F422692. Cheaper without bath, hot water, laundry, food available, popular, Edward speaks English and knows a lot about trekking and rents gear (not all guides share Edward's experience).

C Hostal Colomba, Francisco de Zela 278, just off Centenario across the river, T421501, colomba@terra.com.pe. Lovely old hacienda, bungalow, garden, safe car parking.

D Alojamiento Soledad, Jr Amadeo Figueroa 1267, T421196, ecuadros@viabcp.com. Breakfast extra, shared bath, hot water, kitchen, cafeteria, internet, secure, nice rooftop for sitting out, with washing facilities, trekking information. Recommended for value and service.

D La Casa de Zarela, J Arguedas 1263, T421694, www.lacasadezarela.com. Hot water, use of kitchen, laundry facilities, popular with climbers and trekkers, owner Zarela who speaks English organizes groups and is very knowledgeable.

D Olaza Guest house, J Arguedas 1242, T422529, www.andeanexplorer.com/olaza. Breakfast included, on rooftop terrace with great views, pick-up from bus station with room

reservation, mountain biking trips arranged (owned by Tito Olaza).

D Residencial Cataluña, Av Raymondi 622, T422761. Hot water, TV, **E** for more basic rooms, restaurant open only in the high season, safe, noisy.

D-E The Way Inn, Jr Buenaventura Mendoza 821, near Parque Fap, T428714, thewayinn@hotmail.com. No fixed fee for staying, people are asked to pay what they think it's worth. Run by Alex and Bruni, all mattresses are orthopaedic, fully-functioning kitchen (including oven and fridge), huge video library, laundry facilities, camping equipment for hire, free information on treks, places to eat, hanging out/etc, a health food bar, sauna and steam facilities as well as exercise equipment to help with the acclimatization.

E Alojamiento Marilla, Sucre 1123, T428160, alojamaril@latinmail.com. Good views, modern, rooms with and without bath, also dormitory, hot water, laundry and breakfast available, kitchen facilities, luggage store, knowledgeable owners.

E Alojamiento Nemy's, Jr Figueroa 1135, T422949. Secure, hot shower, breakfast US$2.40, good for climbers, luggage store. Recommended.

E Familia Meza, Lúcar y Torre 538, T426367, familiameza_lodging@hotmail.com. Shared bath, hot water, use of kitchen, laundry facilities, popular with trekkers, mountaineers and bikers.

E Hostal Copa, Jr Bolívar 615, T422071, F422619. Cheaper without bath, hot water, laundry facilities, owner's son Walter Melgarejo is a well-known guide, popular with trekkers, restaurant, travel agency with local tours.

E Hostal Estoico, San Martín 635, T422371. Cheaper without bath, safe, hot water, laundry facilities, good value.

E Hostal Gyula, Parque Ginebra 632, opposite the Casa de Guías, T421567, hotelperu@infoweb.com.pe. Hot water, helpful but noisy at weekends, has good information on local tours, stores luggage.

E Hostal Quintana, Mcal Cáceres 411, T426060. Cheaper without bath, hot shower, laundry facilities, basic, stores luggage, popular with trekkers.

E Hostal Tany, Lúcar y Torre 468A, T422534. Cheaper without bath, hot water at night, spotless, money exchange, tours, café/restaurant.

E Hostal Yanett, Av Centenario 164, at the north end of town across the river, T427150. Hot water, large rooms, breakfast restaurant.

E Jo's Place, Jr Daniel Villayzan 276, T425505. Safe, hot water at night, nice mountain views, garden, terrace, kitchen facilities, English owner, warm atmosphere.

E **Lodging Caroline**, Urb Avitentel Mz D-Lt 1, T422588, 20 min walk from centre. Price includes breakfast, free pick-up from bus station (phone in advance), hot water, kitchen facilities, tourist information and guides, laundry, very helpful. Frequently recommended.

E **Lodging Casa Sucre**, Sucre 1240, T422264, F421111. Private house, kitchen, laundry facilities,

Huaraz

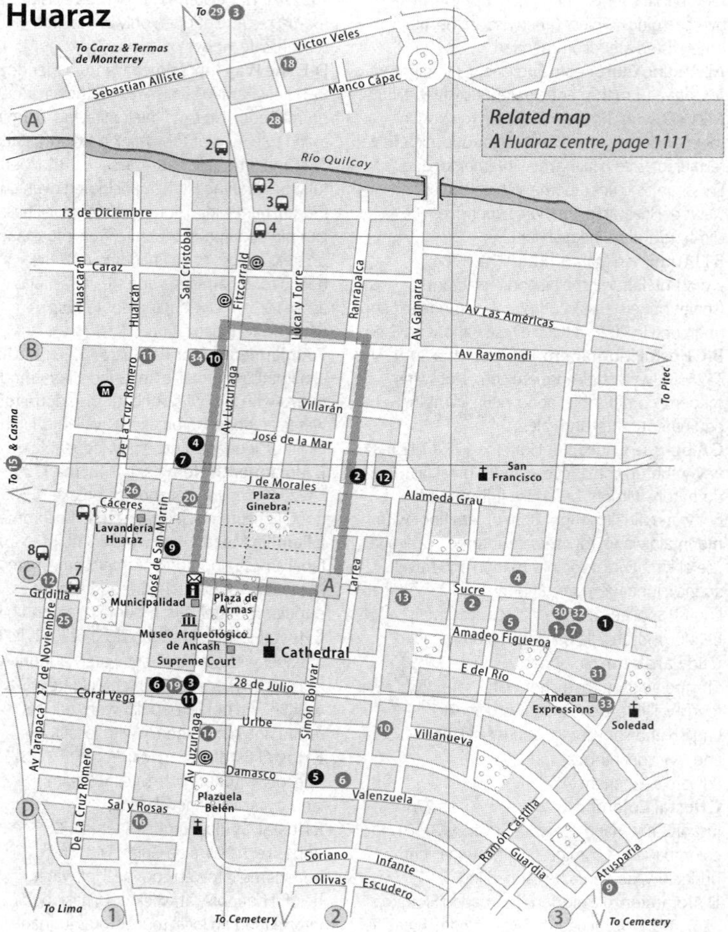

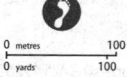

Related map
A Huaraz centre, page 1111

N

| 0 metres | 100 |
| 0 yards | 100 |

Sleeping 🛏
Albergue Churup **1** C3
Alojamiento El Jacal **2** C3
Alojamiento Marilla **4** C3
Alojamiento Nemy's **5** C3
Alojamiento Norma **6** D2
Alojamiento Soledad **7** C3
Andino Club **9** D3
Angeles Inn **10** D2

Backpackers **11** B1
Casa de Jaimes **12** C1
Casa Jansy's **13** C2
Edward's Inn **15** B1
El Tumi **16** D1
Hostal Colomba **18** A2
Hostal Continental **19** C1
Hostal Estoico **20** C1
Hostal Mi Casa **25** C1
Hostal Quintana **26** C1
Hostal Yanett **28** A2
Jo's Place **29** A1
La Cabaña **30** C3
La Casa de Zarela **31** C3
La Estancia **3** A2

Lodging Casa
Sucre **32** C3
Olaza Guesthouse **33** D3
Residencial Cataluña **34** B1

Eating 🍴
Bistro de los Andes **2** C2
Café California **6** C1
Café El Centro **3** C1
Fuente de Salud **4** B1
Huaraz Querido **5** D2
Las Puyas **7** B1
Pachamama **9** C1
Pepe's Place **10** B1
Pizza Bruno **11** D1

Siam de Los Andes **12** C2
Sucre **1** C3

Bars & clubs 🍸
Extreme **14** D1

Transport 🚌
Chavín Express **1** C1
Combis to Caraz **2** A1, A2
Combis to Wilcawain **3** A2
Terminal Terrestre
   Transportistas
   Zona Sur **7** C1
Trans Rodríguez **8** C1
Trans Huandoy **4** A2

hot water, English and French spoken,
mountaineering guide, Filiberto Rurush,
can be contacted here.
E Oscar's Hostal, La Mar 624, T/F422720,
marciocoronel@hotmail.com. Hot water, cheap
breakfast next door, good beds, cheaper in low
season, helpful.
E-F Alojamiento El Jacal, Jr Sucre 1044. With
or without shower, hot water, helpful family,
garden, use of kitchen, laundry facilities,
luggage store, internet café.
E-F La Cabaña, Jr Sucre 1224, T423428,
www.huaraz.org/lacabana. Shared and double
rooms, hot showers, laundry, kitchen, computer,
DVD, popular (especially with Israelis), safe for
parking, bikes and luggage.
E-F Casa Jansy's, Jr Sucre 948. Hot water, meals,
laundry, owner Jesús Rivera Lúcar is a mountain
guide. Recommended.
F Alojamiento Norma, Pasaje Valenzuela 837,
near Plaza Belén, T421831. Includes breakfast,
cheaper without bathroom, hot water.
Recommended.
F Casa de Jaimes, Alberto Gridilla 267,
T422281, 2 blocks from the main plaza.
Dormitory with hot showers, laundry facilities,
has maps and books of the region, use of
kitchen. Noisy but recommended.
F Casa María, Av Confraternidad Internacional
Oeste 674, T424061, www.shelektrek.com.
Small family guesthouse, very caring, use of
kitchen, includes breakfast, has travel agency
Shelek Tours in front.
F La Estancia, Jr Huaylas 162, Centenario,
T423183. With shared shower, luggage store,
safe motorcycle parking, good value.
F Hostal Continental, 28 de Julio 586
near Plaza de Armas, T424171. Hot water,
cafeteria serving good breakfasts.
Recommended but avoid rooms on
street as there are 2 noisy *peñas* nearby.
F pp Hostal Mi Casa, Tarapacá 773 (Av 27 de
Noviembre), T423375, bmark@ddm.com.pe.
Includes breakfast, cheaper in low season, hot
water, English spoken, very pleasant, owner Sr
Ames is an expert on glaciers, his son is a
climbing and rafting guide.
F-G Angeles Inn, Av Gamarra 815, T422205,
solandperu@yahoo.com. No sign, look for *Sol
Andino* travel agency in same building
(www.solandino.com), kitchen and laundry
facilities, garden, hot water, owners Max and Saul
Angeles are official guides, helpful with trekking
and climbing, rent equipment.
G pp Backpackers, Av Raimondi 510, T421773,
http://huaraz.com/backpackers. Includes
breakfast, spacious, hot showers, good views,
a real bargain.
G pp Lodging House Ezama, Mariano Melgar

623, Independencia, T423490, 15 mins' walk
from Plaza de Armas (US$0.50 by taxi). Light,
spacious rooms, hot water, safe, helpful.

Youth hostels
F pp Alojamiento Alpes Andes, at Casa de
Guías, Plaza Ginebra 28-g, T421811, casa_de_
guias@hotmail.com. Member of the Peruvian
Youth Hostel Association, 1 dormitory with 14
beds and another with 6 beds, hot water, with

Huaraz centre

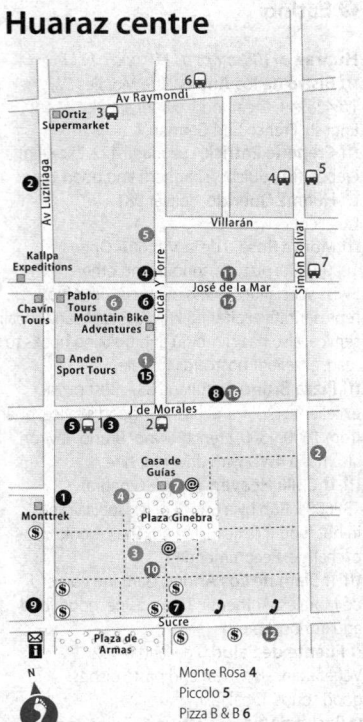

Monte Rosa **4**
Piccolo **5**
Pizza B & B **6**
Pizzería Landauro **7**
Rinconcito Minero **8**
Sabor Salud **9**

Sleeping
Alojamiento Alpes
  Andes **7**
Familia Meza **1**
Hostal Copa **2**
Hostal Gyula **3**
Hostal Montañero **4**
Hostal Tany **5**
Oscar's Hostal **6**

Eating
Café Andino **15**
Chifa Jim Hua **1**
Créperie Patrick **2**
El Querubin **8**
Las Tapas y Chimichurri **3**

Bars & clubs
Amadeus **10**
Makondo's **11**
Monttrek Disco **12**
Taberna Tambo **14**
Vagamundo **16**

Transport
Chinchaysuyo **1**
Civa **2**
Cruz del Sur **7**
Línea **5**
Móvil **4**
Renzo **6**
Yungay Express
  Los Andes **3**

very good restaurant (open 0700-1100, 1700-2300), laundry, free luggage store, the owner Sr López speaks English, French and German and is very helpful, he is the mountain guides administrator.

F El Tambo, Av Confraternidad Internacional Interior 122-B, T425144, marielafm@yahoo.com. Shared bath, free coffee and tea, laundry service, use of kitchen, book exchange, luggage store, safe, helpful.

● Eating

Huaraz p1108, maps p1110 and p1111

ͲͲͲ Bistro de los Andes, J de Morales 823, T/F426249. Great food, owner speaks English, French and German.

ͲͲͲ Créperie Patrick, Luzuriaga 422. Excellent crepes, fish, quiche, spaghetti and good wine.

ͲͲͲ Huaraz Querido, Bolívar 981. Excellent *cevichería*.

ͲͲͲ Monte Rosa, J de la Mar 661. Open 1000-2300, pizzería, fondue and other Swiss specialities. Swiss owner is Victorinox representative, offering knives for sale and repair service, also has climbing and trekking books to read, excellent postcards for sale.

ͲͲͲ Pizza Bruno, Luzuriaga 834. Best pizza, excellent crêpes and pastries, good service, open from 1600-2300, French owner Bruno Reviron also has a 4WD with driver for hire.

ͲͲͲ-ͲͲ Chilli Heaven, Parque Ginebra, T396085. Run by a British biker, specializing in hot food (Mexican, Indian, Thai), book exchange. Recommended.

ͲͲͲ-ͲͲ Siam de Los Andes, Gamarra corner J de Morales. Authentic Thai cuisine, good food and atmosphere.

ͲͲ Fuente de Salud, J de la Mar 562. Vegetarian, also meat and pasta dishes, good soups, breakfast.

ͲͲ Pachamama, San Martín 687. Bar, café and restaurant, concerts, art gallery, garden, nice place to relax, good toilets, pool table and table-tennis, information on treks, Swiss-owned. Recommended.

ͲͲ Pepe's Place, Raymondi 624. Good pizza, chicken, meat, warm atmosphere, run by Pepe from *Residencial Cataluña*.

ͲͲ Pizza B&B, La Mar beside laundry of same name. Recommended for its traditional sauces for pizza and pasta, and desserts.

ͲͲ Pizzería Landauro, Sucre, on corner of Plaza de Armas. Very good for pizzas, Italian dishes, sandwiches, breakfasts, nice atmosphere, closed 1200-1800 and Sun.

ͲͲ Rinconcito Minero, J de Morales 757. Swiss-run, breakfast, lunch, vegetarian options, coffee and snacks.

ͲͲ Sabor Salud, Luzuriaga 672, upstairs. Restaurant and pizzería specializing in vegetarian and Italian food.

ͲͲ-Ͳ Chifa Jim Hua, Luzuriaga 645, upstairs. Large, tasty portions, *menú* US$1.15, open Mon-Sat 0900-1500, 1800-2400, Sun 1800-2200.

ͲͲ-Ͳ Encuentro, Parque Ginebra, off Luzuriaga cuadra 6. Opens 0700, breakfast, lunch and dinners, very busy, good.

ͲͲ-Ͳ Piccolo, J de Morales 632. Pizzería, very popular with gringos.

Ͳ Las Puyas, Morales 535. Popular with gringos, good *sopa criolla* and trout, also serves breakfast.

Ͳ El Querubín, J de Morales 767. Good breakfast and set meals, also vegetarian, snacks and à la carte.

Ͳ Sucre, Sucre 1284, La Soledad. Good simple *menú* for quality, variety and value.

Cafés

Café Andino, Lúcar y Torre 538, cafeandino@hotmail.com. American- run café and bar, book exchange, extensive lending library in many languages, a nice place to relax, great atmosphere, good meeting place, owner guides treks in Cordillera Huayhuash.

Café California, 28 de Julio 562, http://huaylas.com/californiacafe/california.htm. Excellent book exchange. Californian owner is a good source of information on trekking in the Cordillera Huayhuash and security issues.

Café El Centro, 28 de Julio 592. Good breakfast for US$1.30-2, great chocolate cake and apple pie.

Comedor 14, San Martín 525. Good value breakfasts, sandwiches, teas, etc.

Las Tulpas y Chimichurri, J de Morales 660. Open 0730-2300, good breakfasts, free internet for customers.

● Bars and clubs

Huaraz p1108, maps p1110 and p1111

Amadeus, Parque Ginebra. Bar-disco.

La Cascada, Luzuriaga 1276. Disco tavern.

Extreme, Jr Gabino Uribe, near Luzuriaga, upstairs. Popular with *gringos*, soft music, open 1900-0200.

Makondo's, José de la Mar, opposite Cruz del Sur bus station. Bar, nightclub and restaurant, safe, popular. Above is **13 Buhos**, with good music, games, nice atmosphere.

Monttrek Disco, Sucre just off Plaza de Armas. In converted cinema, reasonable prices.

Taberna Tambo, José de la Mar 776. Folk music daily, disco, open 1000-1600, 2000-0200, knock on door to get in.

Vagamundo, J de Morales 753. Popular bar with snacks and football tables.

✹ Festivals and events

Huaraz *p1108, maps p1110 and p1111*
Patron saints' day, **El Señor de la Soledad**, week starting **3 May**. Semana del Andinismo, in **Jun**, international climbing and skiing week. **San Juan** and **San Pedro** throughout the region during the last week of **Jun**.

○ Shopping

Huaraz *p1108, maps p1110 and p1111*
Clothing For local sweaters, hats, gloves and wall hangings at good value, Pasaje Mcal Cáceres, off Luzuriaga, in the stalls off Luzuriaga between Morales and Sucre, Bolívar cuadra 6, and elsewhere. **Andean Expressions**, Jr J Arguedas 1246, near La Soledad church, T422951, olaza@ qnet.com.pe. Open 0800-2200, run by Lucho, Mauro and Beto Olaza, recommended for hand-printed clothing and gifts.
Markets The central market offers a wide variety of canned and dry goods, as well as fresh fruit and vegetables. Beware pickpockets in this area.
Supermarkets Ortiz, Luzuriaga 401 corner Raymondi (good selection).

▲ Activities and tours

Huaraz *p1108, maps p1110 and p1111*
Agencies
Anden Sport Tours, Luzuriaga 571, T421612. Have a basic practice wall behind the office. They also organize mountain bike tours, ski instruction and river rafting.
Andeno Viaggio, Av Luzuriaga 627, T428047, www.andenoviaggio.com. Day tours plus trekking and climbing, reputable.
Baloo Tours, Bolívar 471, T423928. Organizes tours and rents gear.

Cordillera Blanca Adventures, owned and run by the Mejía Romero family, T424352. Experienced for trekking and climbing, good guides and equipment.
Explorandes, Av Centenario 489, T421960, postmast@exploran.com.pe.
Galaxia Expeditions, Jr Mcal Cáceres 428, T425691, galaxia_expeditions@hotmail.com. Reputable agency with tours, equipment rental.
Hirishanka Sport, Sucre 802, T422562. Climbing, trekking, horse riding, 4WD hire, they also rent rooms, **E** pp, with bath, hot water, breakfast.
Huascarán, T424504, peruhuascaran@yahoo.com. Contact Pablo Tinoco Depaz, one of the brothers who run the company, 4-day Santa Cruz trip recommended. Good food and equipment, service professional and friendly, include free loan of waterproofs and pisco sour on last evening.
Kallpa, Luzuriaga 479, T427868, www.peruviantrek.com. Organizes treks, rents gear, arranges *arrieros* and mules, very helpful.
Montañero, Parque Ginebra 30-B, T426386, www.trekkingperu.com. Run by veteran mountain guide Selio Villón, German, French and English spoken.
Monttrek, Luzuriaga 646, upstairs, T421124, F426976. Trekking and climbing information, advice and maps, run ice and rock climbing courses (at Monterrey), tours to Lago Churup and the 'spectacular' *Luna Llena* tour, conscientious guides, good equipment; they also hire out mountain bikes, run ski instruction and trips, and river rafting. Next door in the Pizzería is a climbing wall, maps, videos and slide shows. For new routes and maps contact Porfirio Cacha Macedo, 'Pocho', at *Monttrek* or at Jr Corongo 307, T423930.
Peruvian Andes Adventures, Jr José Olaya 532, Huaraz, T421864, www.peruvianandes.com. Run by Hisao and Eli Morales, with an agency in New Zealand, professional, registered mountain and

Peru Huaraz Listings

trekking guides. All equipment and services for treks of 3-15 days, climbing technical and non-technical peaks, or just day walks. Vegetarians catered for.

Guides
Some guides speak English and are friendly but lack technical expertise; others have expertise but lack communicative ability. For maps and books see Books in Background chapter, page 1520.
Casa de Guías, Plaza Ginebra 28-g in Huaraz, T421811, casa_de_guias@hotmail.com. Mon-Sat 0900-1300, 1600-1800, Sun 0900-1300. This is the climbers' and hikers' meeting place. Has a full list of all members of the Asociación de Guías de Montaña del Perú (AGMP) throughout the country. It is useful with information, books, maps, arrangements for guides, arrieros, mules, etc. There is a notice board, postcards and posters for sale.
Ted Alexander, Skyline Adventures, Jr José de San Martín 637, T427097, www.sladventureschool.com. American, Outward Bound instructor, very knowledgeable, lots of information.
Koky Castañeda, T421694, or through La Casa de Zarela or Café Andino. Speaks English and French, AGMP certified.
Aritza Monasterio, through Casa de Guías. Speaks English, Spanish and Euskerra.
Augusto Ortega, Jr San Martín 1004, T424888, is the only Peruvian to have climbed Everest.
Filiberto Rurush Paucar, Sucre 1240, T422264 (Lodging Casa Sucre), speaks English, Spanish and Quechua.
Hugo Sifuentes Maguiña and his brother César (speaks English and a little French), at Siex (Sifuentes Expeditions), Av Centenario 687, T426529, www.siex.org.
Irma Angeles, T422205 (Sol Andino agency), speaks some English, knows Huayhuash well.
Christopher Benway, La Cima Logistics, T421203, cafeandino@hotmail.com. American, leads treks in the Huayhuash.
Vladimiro and Máximo Hinostrosa, Mountain Shop Chacraraju, T969 2395. Trekking guides with knowledge of the entire region.
Tjen Verheye, Jr Carlos Valenzuela 911, T422569, is Belgian and speaks Dutch, French, German, and reasonable English, runs trekking and conventional tours and is knowledgeable about the Chavín culture.
Genaro Yanac Olivera, T422825, speaks good English and some German, also a climbing guide.
Prices: The Dirección de Turismo issues qualified guides and arrieros (muleteers) with a photo ID. Always check for this when making arrangements; note down the name and card number in case you should have any complaints.

Prices for specific services are set so enquire before hiring someone. Prices: arriero, US$10 per day; donkey or mule, US$5 per day; trekking guides US$35-50 per day (more for foreign guides); climbing guides US$70-120 per day (more for foreign guides), depending on the difficulty of the peak; cooks US$20-30 per day. You are required to provide or pay for food and shelter for all arrieros, porters, cooks and guides.
Camping gear The following agencies are recommended for hiring gear: **Anden Sport Tours**, **Monttrek**, **Kallpa** and **Montañero**. Also **Skyline**, **Alpandes**, Luzuriaga 557, T424646, and **MountClimb**, Jr Mcal Cáceres 421, T426060, mountclimb@yahoo.com. Casa de Guías rents equipment and sells dried food. Check all camping and climbing equipment very carefully before taking it. Gear is of variable quality and mostly second hand, left behind by others. Also note that some items may not be available, so it's best to bring your own. All prices are standard, but not cheap, throughout town. All require payment in advance, passport or air ticket as deposit and will only give 50% of your money back if you return gear early. Many trekking agencies sell camping gaz cartridges. White gas is available from ferreterías on Raymondi below Luzuriaga and by Parque Ginebra. Campers have complained that campsites are dirty, toilet pits foul and that rubbish is not taken away by groups.

Horse riding
Posada de Yungar, at Yungar (about 20 km on the Carhuaz road), T421267, Swiss run. Ask for José Flores or Gustavo Soto. US$4.50 per hr on nice horses; good 4-hr trip in the Cordillera Negra with fabulous views.
Sr Robinson Ayala Gride, T423813. Contact well in advance for half-day trips (enquire at El Cortijo restaurant, Km 6.5 on road to Caraz). He is a master paso rider.

Mountain biking
Mountain Bike Adventures, Lúcar y Torre 530, T424259, www.chakinaniperu.com. Contact Julio Olaza. Hires good quality bikes, highly recommended, Julio speaks excellent English, US$20 for 5 hrs, various routes.

River rafting and canoeing
Ario Ferri, T9961 3058 (mob, between 1800-2000), www.yurakyaku.com, or through Café Andino. Multilingual rafting guide and certified kayak instructor.

Rock climbing
Several of the agencies, independent guides and Casa de Guías run courses at Monterrey

(behind *Hotel Baños Termales Monterrey*), Chancos, Recuay and Huanchac (30 mins' walk from Huaraz).

Tour operators
Chavín Tours, Luzuriaga 502, T421578, F724801. All local tours, long-standing agency.
Pablo Tours, Luzuriaga 501, T421142/ 421145. For all local tours (eg day trips to Llanganuco and to Pastarouri, both about US$10; good but long days).

☉ Transport

Huaraz *p1108, maps p1110 and p1111*
Bus To/from **Lima**: 7-8 hrs, US$6-14. There is a large selection of ordinary service and luxury coaches throughout the day. Many of the companies have their offices along Av Raymondi and on Jr Lúcar y Torre. Some recommended companies are: **Cruz del Sur**, Bolívar y José de la Mar, T423969; **Transportes Rodríguez**, Tarapacá 622, T421353; **Civa**, Morales opposite Lúcar y Torre; **Móvil**, Bolívar 452, T422555 (2 standard and 2 cama services a day); **Empresa 14**, Fitzcarrald 216, T421282, terminal at Bolívar 407.

Other long distance buses: To **Casma** via the Callán pass and Pariacoto (150 km) 7 hrs, US$6, the lower section of the road is very poor, landslides and closures are common (sit on the left for best views): Transportes Huandoy, Fitzcarrald 261, T427507 (terminal at Caraz 820), daily at 0800, 1000 and 1300. Yungay Express, Raymondi 744, T424377, 3 a day. They continue to Chimbote, 185 km. To Chimbote via Caraz and the Cañon del Pato (sit on the right for the most exciting views) *Yungay Express*, daily, US$7, 10 hrs. Other companies go to **Chimbote** via Pativilca; US$6, 7 hrs (to **Pativilca**, 160 km, 4 hrs, US$3.50). Most continue to **Trujillo**, all buses go at night, 8-9 hrs, US$8.60; Chinchaysuyo (J de Morales 650, T426417), Línea (Simón Bolívar 450, T426666), Móvil and Empresa 14, addresses above.

Within the Cordillera Blanca: Several buses and frequent minivans run daily, 0500- 2000, between Huaraz and **Caraz**, 1¼ hrs, US$1.35, from the parking area under the bridge on Fitzcarrald and from the open space beside the bridge on the other side of the river (beware of thieves here). To **Chavín**, 110 km, 2 hrs (sit on left side for best views), US$3: Chavín Express, Mcal Cáceres 338, T424652, 3 a day; Trans Río Mosna, Tarapacá 576,

T726632, 0700 and 1300. Both companies have buses that go on to Huari, 6 hrs, US$5. **Renzo**, Raymondi 821, T424915, runs to Chacas and San Luis (0615 Mon-Sat, 0645 Sun), Yanama, Piscobamba and Pomabamba (0630, best service). **Los Andes**, same office as Yungay Express, T427362, goes daily at 0630 to Yungay, US$0.75, Lagunas de Llanganuco, US$3.45, Yanama, US$3.45, Piscobamba, US$5.20 and Pomabamba, US$6 (8 hrs). Also to **Pomabamba** via Yungay, Lakes Llanganuco and Yanama, Transvir, Caraz y Comercio, and La Perla de Alta Mayo, 0630, 8 hrs, US$6. To Sihuas, Chavín Express, twice a week, and Perú Andino, once a week, 8 hrs, US$7. Colectivos to **Recuay**, US$0.45, and **Catac**, US$0.55, leave daily at 0500-2100, from Gridilla, just off Tarapacá (Terminal de Transportistas Zona Sur). To **Chiquián** for the Cordillera Huayhuash (see below). To **Huallanca** (Huánuco), the route now taken is the paved road through Conococha, Chiquián, Aquia to Huansala, then by good dirt road to Huallanca and La Unión. Departs Huaraz 0800, 1300, 1500, 6 hrs, with **Trans El Rápido**, Bolognesi 216, T043-422887. There are regular colectivos from Huallanca to La Unión from the corner of Comercio y 28 de Julio, 1 hr, US$0.75.
Taxi Standard fare in town is about US$0.60, US$0.70 at night; radio taxis T421482 or 422512.

☉ Directory

Huaraz *p1108, maps p1110 and p1111*
Banks BCP, on Plaza de Armas, closed 1300-1630, changes cash, 3.25% commission on TCs into soles, good rates, into cash dollars 5% commission, cash advance on Visa, Visa ATMs. Interbank, on Plaza de Armas, no commission on TCs into soles, Mastercard ATM. Banco Wiese, Sucre 766, changes cash and TCs. Casa de Cambio: Oh Na Nay, opposite *Interbank*, cash only, good rates. Street changers and *casas de cambio* on Luzuriaga (be careful).
Internet There are internet places everywhere, US$0.30 per hr on average. Sayuri, Bolívar 683. As well as internet, has digital photo services and international phone calls. **Post offices** Serpost, Luzuriaga opposite Plaza de Armas, open 0800-2000 daily. **Telephones** Telefónica, Sucre y Bolívar, Plaza de Armas, national and international phone and fax, open 0700-2300 daily. Many calling centres on Luzuriaga.

Cordillera Blanca

Apart from the range of Andes running along the Chile-Argentina border, the highest mountains in South America lie along the Cordillera Blanca and are perfectly visible from many spots. From Huaraz alone, you can see over 23 snow-crested peaks of over 5,000 m, of which the most notable is Huascarán (6,768 m), the highest mountain in Peru. Although the snowline is receding, the Cordillera Blanca still contains the largest concentration of glaciers found in the world's tropical zone and the turquoise-coloured lakes, which form in the terminal moraines, are the jewels of the Andes. Here also is one of Peru's most important pre-Inca sites, at Chavín de Huantar.

Parque Nacional Huascarán

Established in July 1975, the park includes the entire Cordillera Blanca above 4,000 m, with an area of 3,400 sq km. It is a UNESCO World Biosphere Reserve and part of the World Heritage Trust. The park's objectives are to protect the flora, fauna, geology, archaeological sites and scenic beauty of the Cordillera. Take all your rubbish away with you when camping. The park office charges visitors US$1.25 for a day visit. For visits of up to seven days (ie for trekking and climbing trips) a permit costing US$20 (65 soles) must be bought. If you stay longer than seven days, you will need another permit. Fees for visiting the national park are collected at rangers posts at Llanganuco and Huascarán (for the Llanganuco to Santa Cruz trek), and at Collón on the way up the Quebrada Ishinca. The park office is at Jr Federico Sal y Rosas 555, by Plazuela Belén, T422086; open Monday-Friday 0830-1300, 1430-1700. It is principally administrative.

Trekking and climbing in the Cordillera Blanca

The Cordillera Blanca offers popular backpacking and trekking, with a network of trails used by the local people and some less well-defined mountaineers' routes. Most circuits can be hiked in five days. Although the trails are easily followed, they are rugged with high passes, between 4,000 and nearly 5,000 m, so backpackers wishing to go it alone should be fit and acclimatized to the altitude, and carry all equipment. Essential items are a tent, warm sleeping bag, stove, and protection against wind and rain (the weather is unreliable and you cannot rule out rain and hail storms even in the dry season). Trekking demands less stamina since equipment can be carried by donkeys. The season is from May to September, although conditions vary from year to year. The rainy season in Huaraz is December-March.

Advice to climbers The height of the Cordillera Blanca and the Callejón de Huaylas ranges and their location in the tropics create conditions different from the Alps or even the Himalayas. Fierce sun makes the mountain snow porous and glaciers move more rapidly. The British Embassy advises climbers to take at least six days for acclimatization, to move in groups of four or more, reporting to the Casa de Guías (see above) or the office of the guide before departing, giving the date at which a search should begin, and leaving your embassy's telephone number, with money for the call. International recommendations are for a 300m per day maximum altitude gain. Be wary of agencies wanting to sell you trips with very fast ascents (few, if any, ask if you are acclimatized). The **Policía Nacional de Perú** ① T043-393327/333/291, usam@ pnp.gob.pe, has a 35-member rescue team in Yungay, with 24-hour phone service and vhf/uhf radio dispatch. They have two helicopters and trained search-and- rescue dogs. At present, they will rescue anyone – climbers, trekkers, tourists – without asking for cash up front. PNP rescues are currently free for uninsured climbers. They will bill insured climbers, but do not ask for any cash up front. Since this policy may change, and because they will only take the injured person as far as Huaraz hospital (from where additional costly medical evacuation may be required), it remains imperative that all climbers carry adequate insurance (it cannot be purchased locally).

Be well prepared before setting out on a climb. Wait or cancel your trip when the weather is bad. Every year climbers are killed through failing to take weather conditions seriously. Climb only when and where you have sufficient experience.

Note: Before heading out on any route, always enquire locally about public safety. The Cordillera Blanca is generally safe, but muggings have taken place on the way to Laguna Churup, to the Mirador Rataquena above Huaraz, the Mirador above Monterrey, and at Wilkawain. Local authorities and trekking operators have been investigating ways to improve public safety.

On all treks in this area, respect the locals' property, leave no rubbish behind, do not give sweets or money to children who beg and remember your cooking utensils and tent would be very expensive for a *campesino*, so be sensitive and responsible.

Huaraz to Chavín → *For Guides and prices, see Listings, page 1124.*

South of Huaraz is **Olleros** (Altitude 3,450 m). The spectacular and relatively easy three to four-day hike to Chavín, along a pre-Columbian trail, starts from Olleros. Some basic meals and food supplies available. At 38 km via the main road from Huaraz is **Catac** (two basic hotels and a restaurant), where a paved road branches east for Chavín. About 7 km south of Catac on the main road is **Pachacoto** from where a road goes to **Huallanca** (Huánuco) on the other side of the Cordillera Blanca (133 km, 4½ hours). Buses to Huallanca do not take this route, but the paved road via Chiquián.

A good place to see the impressive Puya Raimondi plants is the Pumapampa valley. 14 km gravel road from Pachacoto to park entrance (4,200 m), then 2 km to plants. Daily tours from Huaraz run to the **Pastoruri** valley, which is now a reserve with basic tourist facilities, to see the Puya Raimondi plants, lakes and the Pastoruri glacier (which is receding rapidly), a steep one-hour walk up from the car park, US$7 per person, 0900-1800. Take extra clothing. You can hike up the trail from Pachacoto to the park entrance – 2½ hours – where there is a park office. You can spend the night here. Walking up the road from this point, you will see the gigantic plants, whose flower spike, which can reach 12 m in height, takes 100 years to develop. The final flowering (usually in May) is a spectacular sight. Another good spot, and less visited, is the **Queshque Gorge**. Follow the Río Queshque from Catac (see above); it's easy to find.

From Catac to Chavín is a magnificent journey. The road passes Lago Querococha, has good views of the Yanamarey peaks and, at the top of the route, is cut through a huge rock face, entering the Cahuish tunnel at 4,550 m. (The tunnel has no light and is single lane; a small stream runs inside. Cyclists must have a strong light so that trucks and buses can see them.) On the other side it descends the Tambillo valley, then the Río Mosna gorge before Chavín.

Chavín de Huantar

① *Daily 0800-1700 (check if open Sun), US$3, US$5 for a group with Spanish-speaking guide (many at the entrance).*

Chavín de Huantar, a fortress temple, was built about 800 BC. It is the only large structure remaining of the Chavín culture which, in its heyday, is thought to have held influence in a region between Cajamarca and Chiclayo in the north to Ayacucho and Ica in the south. In December 1985, UNESCO designated Chavín a World Heritage Trust Site. The site is in good condition despite the effects of time and nature. The main attractions are the marvellous carved stone heads and designs in relief of symbolic figures and the many tunnels and culverts which form an extensive labyrinth throughout the interior of the structures. The carvings are in excellent condition, though many of the best sculptures are in Huaraz and Lima. The famous Lanzón dagger-shaped stone monolith of 800 BC is found inside one of the temple tunnels. In order to protect the site some areas are closed to visitors. All the galleries open to the public have electric lights. The guard is also a guide and gives excellent explanations of the ruins. There is a small museum at the entrance, with carvings and some Chavín pottery.

In high season, the site is busy with tourists all day through. You will receive an information leaflet in Spanish at the entrance.

The town of Chavín (Altitude 3,140 m), just north of the ruins has a pleasant plaza with palm and pine trees. There is nowhere to change money in town. Local *fiesta* July 13-20. There are four hot sulphur baths and a cooler pool (**Baños Termales de Chavín** ① *US$0.65*) about 2 km south of Chavín at Km 68 in the village of Quercos. Camping is possible here.

Chavín to Pomabamba → *225 km in total, gravel road, parts rough.*

From Chavín one circuit by road back to Huaraz is via Huari, San Luis, Yanama and Yungay (see page 1119) but the bus service is infrequent. The road north from Chavín descends into the Mosna river canyon. The scenery is quite different from the other side of the Cordillera Blanca, very dry and hot. After 8 km it reaches **San Marcos**, a small, friendly town with a nice plaza and a few basic restaurants and *hostales*. Further on 32 km is **Huari**, perched on a hillside at 3,150 m, with various basic hotels (**F**) and restaurants. *Fiesta of Nuestra Señora del Rosario* first two weeks of October.

There is a spectacular **two-three days' walk** from Huari to Chacas via Laguna Purhuay. Alberto Cafferata of Caraz writes: "The Purhuay area is beautiful. It has splendid campsites, trout, exotic birds and, at its north end, a 'quenoal' forest. This is a microclimate at 3,500 m, where the animals, insects and flowers are more like a tropical jungle, fantastic for ecologists and photographers." A day walk to Laguna Purhuay is possible for those who don't want the longer walk to Chacas, but this does not allow time to walk above the lake. A new road has been built to the lake.

In **Chacas**, 10 km south of San Luis, off the main road, is a fine church. The local *fiesta patronal* is in mid-August, with bullfights, a famous *carrera de cintas* and fireworks. Seek out the Taller Don Bosco, a woodcarving workshop run by an Italian priest. There are a few basic shops, restaurants, a small market and two or three basic hostels.

It is a three-day hike from Chacas to Marcará via the Quebradas Juytush and Honda (lots of condors to be seen). The Quebrada Honda is known as the Paraíso de las Cascadas because it contains at least seven waterfalls. From Huari the road climbs to the Huachacocha pass at 4,350 m and descends to **San Luis** at 3,130 m, 60 km from Huari (one basic hotel, **G**, a few basic restaurants, shops and a market).

Some 20 km north of San Luis, a road branches left to **Yanama**, 45 km from San Luis, at 3,400 m. It has one marked hotel outside and one unmarked hotel, **G**, on the plaza; ask at the pharmacy. Food is available, but no electricity in the village, which is beautifully surrounded by snow-capped peaks. A day's hike to the ruins above the town affords superb views.

A longer circuit to Huaraz can be made by continuing from San Luis 62 km to **Piscobamba**. There is a basic, but clean and friendly hotel, and one other, both **G**; also a few shops and small restaurants.

Beyond Piscobamba by 22 km, is **Pomabamba**, worth a visit for some very hot natural springs (the furthest are the hottest). There are various hotels (**F-G**) near the plaza and restaurants.

Several good walks into the Cordillera Blanca start from near Pomabamba, some day walks, others of several days, eg: via Palo Seco or Laurel to the Lagunas Safuna. From there you can go on to Nevado Alpamayo, dubbed 'the most beautiful mountain in the world'. The glacier of Alpamayo is an incredible sight. From there, continue down to Santa Cruz and Caraz.

From Pomabamba a dusty road runs up the wooded valley crossing the puna at Palo Seco, 23 km. The road then descends steeply into the desert-like Sihuas valley, passing through the village of Sicsibamba. The valley is crossed half an hour below the small town of **Sihuas**, a major connection point between the Callejón de Conchucos, Callejón de Huaylas, the upper Marañón and the coast. It has a few **F** hotels and places to eat. From Sihuas it is now possible to travel, via Huancaspata, Tayabamba, Retamas and Chahual to Huamachuco along a road which is very poor in places and involves crossing the Río Marañón twice. The building of a new bridge over the river means that it is now possible to travel from Cuzco to Quito through the Andes entirely by public transport. This journey is best undertaken in this direction though the road may be almost impassable in the wet season.

Cañón del Pato to Huaraz

Route from Chimbote via the Santa Valley Just north of Chimbote, a road branches northeast off the Pan-American Highway and goes up the Santa valley following the route of the old Santa Corporation Railway which used to run as far as **Huallanca** (Ancash – not to be confused with the town southeast of Huaraz), 140 km up the valley. At Chuquicara, three hours from Chimbote (paved - very rough thereafter), is Restaurante Rosales, a good place to stop for a meal (US$1-1.30 – you can sleep here, too, but it's very rough). At Huallanca there are also places to stay and eat. Fuel is available. At the top of the valley by the hydroelectric centre, the road goes through the very narrow and spectacular **Cañon del Pato**. You pass under tremendous walls of bare rock and through 35 tunnels, but the flow of the river has been greatly reduced by the hydroelectric scheme. After this point the road is paved to the Callejón de Huaylas and the road south to Caraz and Huaraz.

An alternative road for cyclists (and vehicles with a permit) is the 50-km private road known as the 'Brasileños', used by the Brazilian company Odebrecht which has built a water channel for the Chavimochic irrigation scheme from the Río Santa to the coast. The turn-off is 35 km north of the Santa turning, 15 km south of the bridge in Chao, on the Pan-American Highway at Km 482. It is a good all-weather road via Tanguche. Permits are obtainable from the Chavimochic HQ at San José de Virú, US$6.50, or from the guard at the gate.

Caraz → *Altitude: 2,290 m. Colour map 3, grid B2.*

This pleasant town is a good centre for walking, parasailing and the access point for many excellent treks and climbs. Tourist facilities are expanding as a more tranquil alternative to Huaraz, and there are great views of Huandoy and Huascarán as well as the northern Cordilleras in July and August. In other months, the mountains are often shrouded in cloud. Caraz has a milder climate than Huaraz and is more suited to day trips. The ruins of **Tunshukaiko** are 1 km from the Plaza de Armas in the suburb of Cruz Viva, to the north before the turn-off for Parón. There are seven platforms from the Huaraz culture, dating from around 2000-1800 BC. The tourist office, at Plaza de Armas, in the municipality, T791029, has limited information. On 20 January is the fiesta *Virgen de Chiquinquirá*. In the last week of July is *Semana Turística*.

Treks from Caraz

A good day hike with good views of the Cordillera Blanca is to **Pueblo Libre** (about four hours round trip, or you can take a colectivo back to Caraz). A longer day walk of six to seven hours in total with excellent views of Huandoy and Huascarán follows the foothills of the Cordillera Blanca, from Caraz south. It ends at Puente Ancash on the Caraz-Yungay road, from where transport goes back to Caraz.

A large stand of **Puya Raimondi** can be seen in the Cordillera Negra west of Caraz. Beyond Pueblo Libre the road which continues via Pamparomas and Moro joins the coastal highway between Casma and Chimbote. After 45 km (two hours) are the Puya Raymondi plants at a place called **Winchos**, with views of 120 km of the Cordillera Blanca and to the Pacific ① *getting there: most popular is to rent a bike (US$15/day), go up by public transport (see below), and ride back down in 3 hrs. Or form a group (eg via the bulletin board at Pony's Expeditions, Caraz) and hire a car which will wait for you. From Caraz, a combi for Pamparomas leaves from Grau y Ugarte between 0800 and 0900, or a bus from Ramón Castilla y Jorge Chávez, also 0800-0900, US$2, 2 hrs. From the pass (El Paso) or El Cruce - transport may take 1 of 2 routes - it is a short walk to the plants. Return transport also takes 1 of 2 routes between 1230 and 1300. If you miss the bus, you can walk back to Pueblo Libre in 4 hrs, to Caraz in 6-8 hrs, but it is easy to get lost and there are not many people to ask directions along the way.* The plants are usually in flower May or October. Take warm clothing, food and water. You can also camp near the puyas and return the following day.

Laguna Parón From Caraz a narrow, rough road goes east 32 km to Laguna Parón, in a cirque surrounded by several, massive snow-capped peaks, including Huandoy, Pirámide Garcilazo and Caraz. The water level has been lowered to protect Caraz, and the water from the lake is used for the Cañon del Pato hydroelectric scheme. The gorge leading to it is spectacular. It is a long day's trek for acclimatized hikers (25 km) up to the lake at 4,150 m, or a 4-5 hour walk from the village of Parón, which can be reached by combi. Camping is possible next to the Duke Energy refuge.

Santa Cruz Valley One of the finest treks in the area is the 4-5 days route over the path from the Santa Cruz valley, by Mount Huascarán to the Lagunas de Llanganuco (described below). The most popular way to do this famous hike starts at Cashapampa in the Santa Cruz valley (see Transport below). It takes four to five days over the pass of Punta Unión, 4,750 m, to Vaquería or the Llanganuco lakes. Many recommend this 'anticlockwise' route as the climb is gentler, giving more time to acclimatize, and the pass is easier to find. You can hire an *arriero* and mule in Cashapampa, prices given in Listings, Activities and tours, below. Campsites are at Llamacorral and Taullipampa before Punta Unión, and Quenoapampa (or Cachina Pampa) after the pass. You can end the hike at Vaquería on the Yanama-Yungay road, or, a day later with a night at the Paccha Pampa campsite, at the Llanganuco lakes, from where cars go back to Yungay.

Yungay → *Colour map 3, grid B2.*

The main road goes on 12 km south of Caraz to Yungay which was completely buried during the 1970 earthquake by a massive mudslide; a hideous tragedy in which 20,000 people lost their lives. The earthquake and its aftermath are remembered by many residents of the Callejón de Huaylas. The original site of Yungay, known as Yungay Viejo, desolate and haunting, has been consecrated as a *camposanto* (cemetery). The new settlement is on a hillside just north of the old town, and is growing gradually. It has a pleasant plaza and a concrete market, good on Wednesday and Sunday. October 17 is the *Virgen del Rosario* fiesta and October 28 is the anniversary of the founding of the town. The tourist office is on the corner of the Plaza de Armas.

Lagunas de Llanganuco

The Lagunas de Llanganuco are two lakes nestling 1,000 m below the snowline beneath Huascarán and Huandoy. The first you come to is Laguna Chinancocha (3,850 m), the second Laguna Orconcocha (3,863 m). The park office is situated below the lakes at 3,200 m, 19 km from Yungay. Accommodation is provided for trekkers who want to start the Llanganuco- Santa Cruz trek from here, US$2 per person. From the park office to the lakes takes about five hours (a steep climb). For the last 1½ hours, a nature trail, Sendero María Josefa (sign on the road), takes 1½ hours to walk to the western end of Chinancocha where there is a control post, descriptive trail and boat trips on the lake. Walk along the road beside the lake to its far end for peace and quiet among the quenoal trees, which provide shelter for 75% of the birdlife found in the park

Carhuaz → *Colour map 3, grid B2.*

After Yungay, the main road goes to **Mancos** (8 km south, 30 minutes) at the foot of Huascarán. There is a dormitory at *La Casita de mi Abuela*, some basic shops and restaurants. From Mancos it is 14 km to Carhuaz, a friendly, quiet mountain town with a pleasant plaza. There is very good walking in the neighbourhood (eg to thermal baths; up the Ulta valley). Market days are Wednesday and Sunday (the latter is much larger). The local fiesta of *Virgen de las Mercedes*, 14 -24 September, is rated as among the best in the region.

⏺ Sleeping

Olleros *p1117*

C Altas Montañas, at edge of village, T422569, altasmont@yahoo.es. Small 3-star lodge, Belgian-run, with hot showers, good breakfast included, dinner available, bar, birdwatching, guided treks, information, laundry, recommended for start or end of trek, phone 24 hrs in advance, preferably at 2000, to arrange free pick-up from Huaraz.

Chavín *p1117*

D La Casona, Wiracocha 130, Plaza de Armas, T754048, lacasonachavin@peru.com. In a renovated house with attractive courtyard, cheaper without bath, insufficient hot water, 1 double room, motorcycle parking.
D Ri'kay, on 17 de Enero 172N, T754068, www.sorem.com.pe/rickay. Set around 2 patios, modern, best in town, TV, hot water, restaurant serving Italian food in the evening. Recommended.
E Hostal Chavín, Jr San Martín 141-151, half a block from the plaza, T/F754055. Pleasant courtyard, hot water, will provide breakfast for groups, best of the more basic hotels but beds are poor.
E Hotel Chavín, Roca 151 y Tello, T754055. Modern, hot water, all rooms with bath and TV.
E Inca, Wiracocha 160. In a renovated house, **F** without bath, good beds, hot water on request, nice garden.
Camping Inside park gates at archaeological site for vehicles, ask for permission.

Caraz *p1119*

A-B O'Pal Inn, Pativilca/Caraz Km 265.5, T043-391015, www.opalsierraresort.com. Scenic, bungalows and rooms, swimming pool. Recommended.

C Chamanna, Av Nueva Victoria 185, 25 mins walk from centre, T978 1094 (mob), www.chamanna.com. Cabañas in beautiful garden, hot water, secure, excellent French and international cuisine in expensive restaurant, German run. Recommended.
C-E Los Pinos, Parque San Martín 103, 5 blocks west of plaza, T391130, lospinos@ apuaventura.com. Rooms with and without bath, hot water, comfortable and airy, garden open to all travellers, camping US$2.50, use of internet US$0.50 per hr, use of kitchen US$3, laundry service, safe, book exchange, information and travel agency Apu-Aventura. Breakfast and dinner are available, bar with movies every night. Recommended.
D La Alameda, Av Noé Bazán Peralta 262, T391177, jtorres@viabcp. com.pe. Comfortable rooms, hot water, breakfast, parking, gardens. Recommended.
D Caraz Dulzura, Sáenz Peña 212, about 10 blocks from the city centre, T391523, hostalcarazdulzura@hotmail.com. Modern building in an old street, hot water, cheaper without bath and TV, comfortable, great service, airy rooms, breakfast extra. Recommended.
D La Perla de los Andes, Plaza de Armas 179, T/F392007. Comfortable rooms, hot water, TV, helpful, average restaurant, has a large new annex 1 block up San Martín.
E Chavín, San Martín 1135 just off the plaza, T391171, hostalchavin66@hotmail.com. Warm water, good service but a bit grubby, breakfast extra, guiding service, tourist info.
E Regina, Los Olivos s/n y Gálvez, at the south end of town, 1 block west of road to Yungay, T391520. Modern, hot water, good value.

E **Restaurant Oasis**, Raymondi 425. Small, hot water, welcoming, good value, TV.

F **Alojamiento Caballero**, D Villar 485, T391637, or ask at *Pony's Expeditions* on the plaza. Shared bath, hot water, laundry facilities, stores luggage, basic, family run.

F **Familia Aguilar**, San Martín 1143, T391161. Basic, shared bath, owner is Prof Bernardino Aguilar Prieto, who has information on bee-keeping and trekking in the Cordillera Negra.

F **Hostal La Casona**, Raymondi 319, 1 block east from the plaza, T391334. F without bath, hot water, lovely little patio.

Yungay *p1119*

E pp **Complejo Turístico Yungay** (COMTURY), Prolongación 2 de Mayo 1019, 2.5 km south of the new town, 700 m east of main road in Aura, the only neighbourhood of old Yungay that survived, T969 1698 (mob). Nice bungalows, pleasant country setting, hot water, fireplace, restaurant with regional specialities, camping possible.

E **Hostal Gledel**, Av Arias Graziani, north past plaza, T393048, rugamboa@viabcp.com. Owned by Sra Gamboa, who is hospitable and a good cook, shared bath, hottish water, no towels or soap, cheap meals prepared on request, nice courtyard.

E **Hostal Las Rosas**, T393073. Pleasant, hot water.

E **Hostal Sol de Oro**, Santo Domingo 07, T393116. With bath, hot water, comfortable, good value, best in town.

E **Pan de Azúcar**, Jr La Merced 32, on a back street behind the hospital, T043-393057, pandeazucar@yahoo.com. Includes breakfast, shared bath, small and quiet, garden, good.

F **Complejo Turístico Huascarán**, Leoncio Prado s/n, T043-393023, www.huascaran peru.com. With bath, hot water and parking, modern but uninspiring.

F **Hostal Mery**, T313007. Hot water, simple but OK, rooms at front noisy.

Carhuaz *p1120*

B **El Abuelo**, Jr 9 de Diciembre y Tumbes, T394149, www.elabuelohostal.com. Modern, comfortable but overpriced, café, parking, ask at *Heladería El Abuelo* on main plaza.

C pp **Casa de Pocha**, 1 km out of town towards Hualcán, at foot of Nevado Hualcán, ask directions in town, T961 3058 (mob, 1800-2000), lacasadepocha@hotmail.com. Including breakfast and dinner, country setting, entirely solar and wind

energy powered, hot water, sauna and pool, home-produced food (vegetarian available), horses for hire, camping possible, many languages spoken. Recommended. Book in advance.

E **Hostal Señor de Luren**, Buin 549, 30 m from Plaza de Armas. Hot water, TV, safe motorcycle parking, very hospitable. E four family run *hospedajes* have been built as part of a community development project. All have private bath and hot water. The better 2 are: **Hospedaje Robri**, Jr Comercio 935, T394505. Modern. **Alojamiento Las Torresitas**, Jr Amazonas 603, T794213.

F **Hostal La Merced**, Ucayali 724, T394241 (Lima 442 3201). Hot water (usually), "like going back to the 1950s", luggage store.

❼ Eating

Chavín *p1117*

♦♦♦ **Chavín Turístico**, middle of 17 de Enero. The best in town, good *menú* and à la carte, delicious apple pie, nice courtyard, internet.

♦♦♦ **La Portada**, towards south end of 17 de Enero. In an old house with tables set around a pleasant garden. Recommended.

♦ **La Ramada**, towards north end of main street, 17 de Enero. Regional dishes, also trout and set lunch.

Caraz *p1119*

♦♦♦ **La Punta Grande**, D Villar 595, 10 mins' walk from centre. Best place for local dishes, closes 1700.

♦ **Esmeralda**, Av Alfonso Ugarte 404. Good set meal, breakfast. Recommended.

♦ **Heladería Caraz Dulzura**, D Villar on the plaza. Excellent home made ice cream, good value meals, pastries.

♦ **Jeny**, Daniel Villar on the plaza. Good food at reasonable prices.

♦ **El Mirador**, Sucre 1202 on the plaza. Nice view from terrace, good set lunch and BBQ chicken at night, popular. Recommended.

♦ **La Olla de Barro**, Sucre 1004. Good set meal.

Cafés

Café de Rat, Sucre 1266, above *Pony's Expeditions*. Serves breakfast, vegetarian dishes, pizzas, drinks and snacks, darts, travel books, nice atmosphere. Recommended.

El Turista, San Martín 1117. Open in morning and evening only. Small, popular for breakfast, ham omelettes and ham sandwiches are specialities.

● *For an explanation of the sleeping and eating price codes used in this guide, see inside the front*
● *cover. Other relevant information is found in Essentials pages 1075-1077.*

Yungay *p1119*

♦♦ Alpamayo, Av Arias Graziani s/n.
At north entrance to town, good for local
dishes, lunchtime only.
♦ Café Pilar, on the main plaza. Good for
juices, cakes and snacks.

Carhuaz *p1120*

♦♦ El Abuelo, Plaza de Armas. International and
local food , produce from own garden including
all natural ice cream.
♦♦ La Bicharra, just north of Carhuaz on main
road, T978 0893 (mob). Innovative North
African/Peruvian cooking, lunch only, busy at
weekends, call ahead to check if they are
open on weekdays.

♠ Bars and clubs

Caraz *p1119*

Taberna Disco Huandy, Mcal Cáceres 119.
Good atmosphere.

○ Shopping

Caraz *p1119*

Camping supplies Fresh food in the market.
Some dried camping food is available from
Pony's Expeditions, who also sell camping gaz
canisters and white gas.

▲ Activities and tours

Caraz *p1119*

Agencies in Caraz arrange treks in the Cordillera
Huayhuash, as well as more local destinations.
Apu-Aventura, D Villar 215, T392159,
www.apuaventura.com. Offer all sorts of
adventure sports and equipment rental.
Pony's Expeditions, Sucre 1266, near
the Plaza de Armas, T/F391642,
www.ponyexpeditions.com. Mon-Sat 0800-2200,
English, French and Quechua spoken, reliable
information about the area. Owners Alberto and
Aidé Cafferata are knowledgeable about treks
and climbs. Local tours and trekking with guides
are arranged, maps and books for sale, also
equipment for hire, mountain bike rental (US$15
for a full day). Highly recommended.
Mariano Araya is a trekking guide who is also
keen on photography and archaeology.

⊕ Transport

Chavín *p1117*

Bus It is much easier to get to Chavín (even
walking!) than to leave the place by bus. All buses
to **Huaraz** originate in Huari or beyond. They pass
through Chavín at irregular hours and may not

have seats available. Buying a ticket at an agency
in Chavín does not guarantee you will get a seat or
even a bus. For buses from **Huaraz**, see under
Huaraz. **Chavín Express** passes through around
1200, 1600 and 1700 daily; **Río Mosna** around
0430, 1600, 1800, 2000, and 2200 daily. Bus to
Huaraz takes 2 hrs, US$3. To **Lima**: 438 km, 12 hrs,
US$9, with **Trans El Solitario** and **Perú Andino**
daily. Most locals prefer to travel first to Huaraz and
then take one of the better companies from there.

To other destinations in the Callejón de
Conchucos, either use buses coming from Huaraz
or Lima, or hop on and off combis which run
between each town. To **San Marcos**, 8 km, and
Huari, 38 km, take one of the combis which leave
regularly from the main plaza in Chavín, 20 mins
and 30 mins respectively. There are buses during
the day from Lima and Huaraz which go on to
Huari, with some going on to **San Luis**, a further
61 km, 3 hrs; **Piscobamba**, a further 62 km,
3 hrs; and **Pomabamba**, a further 22 km,
1 hr; such as El Solitario which passes through
Chavín at 1800. Gasoline is available at north
end of Chavín.

Huari *p1117*

Bus Companies have their offices around
Parque Vigil. Getting there: To **Huaraz**, 5-6 hrs,
US$3.75, departures through the day. Services
also to **San Luis** and **Lima**.

Yanama *p1118*

Bus Daily between **Yungay** and Yanama over
the 4,767 m Portachuelo de Llanganuco (3 hrs,
US$4), continuing to Pomabamba.

Pomabamba *p1118*

To **Piscobamba**, combis depart hourly, 1 hr,
US$1.20. There are no combis from Piscobamba
to San Luis. To **Lima**, 18 hrs, US$11, via San Luis
(4 hrs, US$3), Huari (6 hrs, US$4) and Chavín (9
hrs, US$6) with El Solitario Sun, Mon and Thu at
0800; via **Yungay** and **Huaraz** with La Perla del
Alto Mayo, Wed, Thu, Sat, Sun, 16 hrs, US$11.

Sihuas *p1118*

Bus To **Pomabamba**, combis at 0700 and
1100, 4 hrs, US$3. To **Huaraz**, via Huallanca, with
Transvir, daily at 0830, 8 hrs, US$7; **Trans Chavín
Express**, Wed and Sat, and **Perú Andino** on Tue,
1100, 8 hrs, US$7. To **Tayabamba**, for the
Marañón route north to Huamachuco and
Cajamarca: **Andía** passes through from Lima on
Mon, Wed and Sat at 0100-0200, **La Perla del
Alto Mayo** passes through Wed and Sat
0000-0200; also twice a week with **Garrincha** and
once a week with **San Antonio de Padua**; all 7-8
hrs, US$6, the beginning of a long wild ride. To
Huacrachuco, **Trans Andina**, daily at 1000. To

Chimbote, La Perla de Alta Mayo on Tue, Thu and Sun, 10 hrs, US$9. To **Lima** (17 hrs, US$9) via Chimbote, **Andía** daily around 0200-0500; confirm all times locally.

Caraz *p1119*

Bus From Caraz to **Lima**, 470 km, 5 companies on D Villar and Jr Córdova, daily, US$7 (**El Huaralino, Expreso Ancash**, T791509, **Móvil, Rodríguez**, T391184), 10-11 hrs. All go via Huaraz and Pativilca. To **Chimbote**, Yungay Express (D Villar 318), via Huallanca and Cañon del Pato 0830 every day, US$6.60, 8 hrs. Sit on right for best views. To **Trujillo**, via Huaraz and Pativilca, **Chinchaysuyo** (Córdova 830, T391930), 1845 daily, US$9.10, 11-12 hrs, stops in Casma (US$7.60) and Chimbote (US$7.60). To **Huaraz**, combis leave 0400-2000, 1¼ hrs, US$1.35 . They are supposed to leave from a terminal on the way out of town, but if there is no police control they pick up passengers by the market and along Jr José Gálvez. To **Yungay**, 12 km, 15 mins, US$0.30. To **Huallanca** (for the Cañon del Pato), combis and cars leave from Córdova y La Mar, 0700-1730, US$1.50.

Laguna Parón *p1119*

To the village of **Parón** pickups from Santa Cruz y Grau by the market, Mon to Sat 0500 and 1300, Sun 0300 and 1300, 1 hr. They return from Parón at 0600 and 1400. From **Caraz**, colectivos go to the lake if there are enough passengers and only in the dry season, US$3-4 pp. Pony's Expeditions have a pool of well-trained drivers who make daily departures to Laguna Parón at 0800, US$25 for 4, including 1-hr visit to the lake and 1-hr walk downhill to the bridge, where diver will pick up the group (extra hours at US$3). Also, you can hire a bike (US$15 per day), take a car up (US$6 with 4 passengers) and ride back down.

Santa Cruz Valley *p1119*

To **Cashapampa** (Quebrada Santa Cruz) buses from R Castilla y J Chávez, Caraz, hourly from 0830 to 1530, 2 hrs, US$1.30. Yanama to Yungay buses can be caught at Vaquería between 0800-0900, US$4, 3 hrs. Also combis Vaquería-Yungay US$2.25.

Yungay *p1119*

Buses, colectivos and trucks run the whole day to **Caraz**, 12 km, US$0.30, and **Huaraz**, 54 km, 1½ hrs, US$1. To lakes **Llanganuco**, combis leave when full, especially 0700- 0900, from Av 28 de Julio 1 block from the plaza, 1 hr, US$1.50. To **Yanama**, via the Portachuelo de Llanganuco Pass, 4,767m, 58 km, 3 hrs, US$4; stopping at

María Huayta (for the Llanganuco-Santa Cruz trek), after 2 hrs, US$2. To **Pomabamba**, via Piscobamba, **Trans Los Andes**, daily at 0800, the only company with a ticket office in Yungay; **Transvir** and La Perla de Alta Mayo buses coming from Huaraz, 0730, stop if they have room, 6-7 hrs, US$6. After passing the Llanganuco lakes and crossing the Portachuelo the buses descend to Puente Llacma, where it is possible to pick up buses and combis heading south to San Luis, Chacas and Huari.

Carhuaz *p1120*

All transport leaves from the main Plaza. There are **trucks** (only 1 or 2 a day) and 1 minivan (0800) going up the Ulta valley to **Chacas** (see page 1118), 87 km, 4-5 hrs, US$4.50. The road works its way up the Ulta valley to the pass at Punta Olímpica from where there are excellent views. The dirt road is not in a very good condition owing to landslides every year (in the wet season it can be closed). The trucks continue to **San Luis** (see page 1118), a further 10 km, 1½ hrs. Each Thu, a **bus** (Transportes Huandoy) does the trip from Carhuaz to Chacas and returns, US$6 one way, 5 hrs. To **Huaraz**, colectivos and buses, 0500-2000, US$0.75, 40 mins; to **Caraz**, 0500-2000, US$0.75, 1 hr.

● Directory

Chavín *p1117*

Internet Librería Aquariu's, 17 de Enero y Túpac Yupanqui, US$1 per hr. **Post offices** 17 de Enero 365N; open 0630-2200.
Telephones Payphones all over town.

Huari *p1117*

Post offices Luzuriaga 324 by Parque Vigil.
Telephones Libertad 940, open 0700-2200 daily.

Caraz *p1119*

Banks No ATM in town. BCP, D Villar 217, cash and TCs at good rates, no commission, cash withdrawals on credit card. **Pony's Expeditions** (see above) cash only. **Importaciones América**, Sucre 721, T391479, good rates and service, open weekends and evenings. **Internet** Many places around the Plaza and throughout town, US$0.30. **Post offices** San Martín 909.
Telephones National and international phone and fax at Raymondi y Sucre. Also several others, eg at Sucre y Santa Cruz, and on Plaza de Armas next to *Jeny*. No collect calls can be made except from private lines. Very few of the coin boxes take phone cards.

Cordillera Huayhuash

The Cordillera Huayhuash, lying south of the Cordillera Blanca, has azure trout-filled lakes interwoven with deep quebradas and high pastures around the hem of the range and is perhaps the most spectacular cordillera for its massive ice faces that seem to rise sheer out of the Puna's contrasting green. You may see tropical parakeets in the bottom of the gorges and condors circling the peaks. The complete circuit is very tough; allow 10-12 days. Trekkers have to pay in total US$17.50 to the different communities in charge of security (*rondadores*) along the whole loop; this has greatly improved security. The trail head is at **Cuartel Huain**, between Matacancha and the **Punta Cacanan** pass (the continental divide at 4,700 m). There are up to eight passes over 4,600 m, depending on the route. A half-circuit is also possible, but there are many other options. Both ranges are approached from Chiquián in the north, **Oyón**, with links to Cerro de Pasco to the southeast, **Churín** in the south or Cajatambo to the southwest. The area offers fantastic scenery and insights into rural life.

Chiquián is a town of narrow streets and overhanging eaves. *Semana Turística*: first week of July. Buy all your food and supplies in Huaraz as there are only basic supplies in Chiquián and almost nothing in the hamlets along the route. **Mule hire** It may take a day to bring the mules to your starting point from Llamac or Pocpa where they are kept. (Very basic supplies only can be bought in either village.) Ask for mules (US$5 per day) or horses (US$7 per day) at the hotels or restaurants in Chiquián. A guide for the Huayhuash is **Sr Delao Callupe**, ask for him in Chiquián.

Cajatambo is the southern approach to the Cordillera Huayhuash, a small market town with a beautiful 18th-century church and a lovely plaza. There are various hotels (**F-G**) and some good restaurants around the plaza. Note that the road out of Cajatambo is not for the fainthearted. For the first 3-4 hours it is no more than a bus-width, clinging to the cliff edge.

● Sleeping

Cordillera Huayhuash *p1124*
E Gran Hotel Huayhuash, Figueredo y 28 de Julio, Chiquián, T747049. Private bathroom, hot water, TV, restaurant, laundry, parking, modern, great views.

E Hostal San Miguel, Jr Comercio 233, Chiquián, T747001. Nice courtyard and garden, clean, many rooms, popular.

G pp Los Nogales de Chiquián, Jr Comercio 1301, T747121 (in Lima T460 8037), hotel_nogales_chiquian@yahoo.com.pe. Cheaper without bath, hot water, cable TV, cafeteria, parking. Recommended.

Cordillera Huayhuash *p1124*
Ŷ **Panificadora Santa Rosa**, Comercio 900, on the plaza, Chiquián, for good bread and sweets, has coin-operated phones and fax.
Ŷ **El Refugio de Bolognesi** and **Yerupajá**, on Tarapacá, both offer basic set meals.

● Transport

Cordillera Huayhuash *p1124*
Coming from Huaraz, the road is now paved beyond Chiquián to Huansala, on the road to Huallanca (Huánuco). Four bus companies run from Huaraz to Chiquián, 120 km, 3½ hrs: **El Rápido**, at Bolognesi 216, T422887, at 1345; **Virgen del Carmen**, around the corner from Huascarán on Raymondi; **Chiquián Tours**, on Tarapacá behind the market; and **El Amigo del Milenio**, opposite the Frigorífico de Huaraz on Bolognesi. From Chiquián to Huaraz: all buses leave the plaza at 0500 daily, and **El Rápido**, Jr Figueredo 216, T747049, at 0500 and 1330. The companies have pretty good buses, US$1.75 (except El Rápido, US$3.65). Also colectivo Chiquián-Huaraz 1500, 3 hrs, US$2.45 pp. There is also a connection from Chiquián to Huallanca (Huánuco) with buses coming up from Lima in the early morning and combis during the day, which leave when full, 3 hrs, US$2.50. From Huallanca there are regular combis on to La Unión, 1 hr, US$0.75, and from there transport to Huánuco. From Cajatambo buses depart for **Lima** at 0600, US$8.80, daily with **Empresa Andina** (office on plaza next to Hostal Cajatambo), **Tour Bello**, 1 block off the Plaza, and **Turismo Cajatambo**, Jr Grau 120 (in Lima, Av Carlos Zavala 124 corner of Miguel Aljovin 449, T426 7238).

● For an explanation of the sleeping and eating price codes used in this guide, see inside the front ● cover. Other relevant information is found in Essentials pages 1075-1077.

1124

North coast

The north of Peru has been described as the Egypt of South America, as it is home to many
ruined pre-Inca treasures. Many tourists pass through without stopping on their way to or
from Ecuador, missing out on one of the most fascinating parts of the country. Along a
seemingly endless stretch of desert coast lie many of the country's most important pre-Inca
sites: Chan-Chán, the Moche pyramids, Túcume, Sipán, Batán Grande and El Brujo. The main
city is Trujillo, while Chiclayo is more down-to-earth, with one of the country's largest
witchdoctors' market. The coast is also famous for its deep-sea fishing, surfing, and the
unique reed fishing boats at Huanchaco and Pimentel. Inland lies colonial Cajamarca, scene
of Atahualpa's last stand. Further east, where the Andes meet the jungle, countless
unexplored ancient ruins await the more adventurous traveller.

Trujillo and around → Phone code: 044. Colour map 3, grid B2. Population: 850,000.

The capital of La Libertad Department, 548 km from Lima, disputes the title of second city of
Peru with Arequipa. The compact colonial centre, though, has a small-town feel. The greenness
surrounding the city is a delight against the backcloth of brown Andean foothills and peaks.
Founded by Diego de Almagro in 1534 as an express assignment ordered by Francisco Pizarro, it
was named after the latter's native town in Spain. Nearby are some of Peru's most important
Moche and Chimú archaeological sites and a stretch of the country's best surfing beaches.

Ins and outs
Getting there The **airport** is west of the city; the entry to town is along Avenida Mansiche.
There is no central bus terminal. **Bus stations** are spread out on three sides the city beyond
the inner ring road, Avenida España. Companies are moving to new premises north and
south along the Panamericana. There are few hotels around them, but plenty of taxis and
colectivos. Insist on being taken to your hotel of choice. ▶▶ *For more detailed information, see
Transport, page 1146.*

Getting around Trujillo is best explored on foot. Taxis in town charge US$0.55-70; always use
official taxis, which are mainly yellow. The major sites outside the city, Chan Chán, the Moche
pyramids and Huanchaco beach are easily reached by public transport, but take care when
walking around. A number of recommended guides run tours to these and other places. **Note**:
The city is generally safe but be careful at bus stations when arriving or leaving. Also take care
beyond the inner ring road, Avenida España, and in the Sánchez Carrión district at night.

Tourist offices i perú ⓘ *Municipalidad building, Pizarro 402, p 2, Plaza Mayor, T294561,
iperutrujillo@promperu.gob.pe, Mon-Sat 0800-1900, Sun 0800-1400.* Useful websites:
www.xanga.com/TrujilloPeru and www.laindustria.com/industria. **Tourist Police** have an office
at Independencia 630, Casa Ganoza Chopitea, T224025, policia_turismo_tru@ hotmail.com,
open year-round, they provide useful information. **Indecopi** ⓘ *Jr Bolivia 251, Urb El Recreo,
T295733, ldiaz@indecopi.gob.pe,* for tourist complaints. Maps available from **Touring and
Automobile Club** ⓘ *Argentina 258, Urb El Recreo, T290736, trujillo@touringperu.com.pe.*

Sights
The focal point is the pleasant and spacious **Plaza Mayor**. The prominent sculpture
represents agriculture, commerce, education, art, slavery, action and liberation, crowned by
a young man holding a torch depicting liberty. Fronting it is the **Cathedral**, dating from 1666,
with its museum of religious paintings and sculptures next door. Also on the Plaza are the
Hotel Libertador, the colonial style Sociedad de Beneficencia Pública de Trujillo and the
Municipalidad. The **Universidad de La Libertad**, second only to that of San Marcos at Lima,
was founded in 1824. Two beautiful colonial mansions on the plaza have been taken over.
The Banco Central de Reserva is in the Colonial-style **Casa Urquiaga (or Calonge)** ⓘ *Pizarro
446, Mon-Fri 0900- 1500, Sat-Sun 1000-1330, free 30-min guided tour, take passport,*

Trujillo

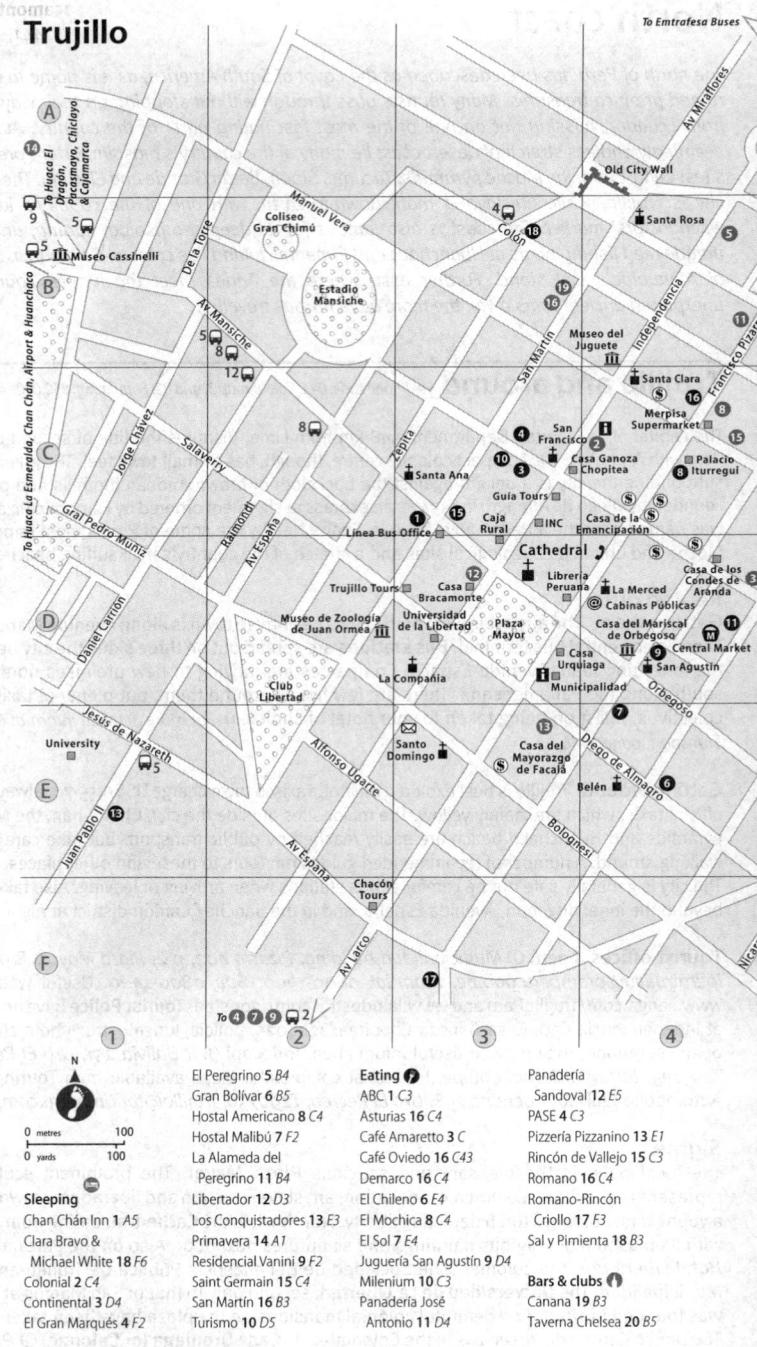

To Emtrafesa Buses

To Huaca El Dragón, Pacasmayo, Chiclayo & Cajamarca

To Huaca La Esmeralda, Chan Chán, Airport & Huanchaco

Manuel Vera

Coliseo Gran Chimú

Estadio Mansiche

De la Torre

Av Mansiche

Jorge Chávez

Salaverry

Gral Pedro Muñíz

Raimondi

Daniel Carrión

Av España

Jesús de Nazareth

Juan Pablo II

Av España

Av Larco

Colón

San Martín

Zepita

Independencia

Francisco Pizarro

Old City Wall

Santa Rosa

Museo del Juguete

Santa Clara

Merpisa Supermarket

Museo Cassinelli

San Francisco

Casa Ganoza Chopitea

Palacio Iturregui

Santa Ana

Guía Tours

Caja Rural

INC

Casa de la Emancipación

Casa de los Condes de Aranda

Línea Bus Office

Cathedral

Librería Peruana

La Merced

Trujillo Tours

Casa Bracamonte

Museo de Zoología de Juan Ormea

Universidad de la Libertad

Plaza Mayor

Cabinas Públicas

Casa del Mariscal de Orbegoso

Central Market

La Compañía

Casa Urquiaga

San Agustín

Club Libertad

Municipalidad

Diego de Almagro

Orbegoso

University

Santo Domingo

Casa del Mayorazgo de Facalá

Belén

Bolognesi

Alfonso Ugarte

Chacón Tours

Nicara

To

Sleeping

Chan Chán Inn **1** A5
Clara Bravo & Michael White **18** F6
Colonial **2** C4
Continental **3** D4
El Gran Marqués **4** F2
El Peregrino **5** B4
Gran Bolívar **6** B5
Hostal Americano **8** C4
Hostal Malibú **7** F2
La Alameda del Peregrino **11** B4
Libertador **12** D3
Los Conquistadores **13** E3
Primavera **14** A1
Residencial Vanini **9** F2
Saint Germain **15** C4
San Martín **16** B3
Turismo **10** D5

Eating 🍴

ABC 1 C3
Asturias **16** C4
Café Amaretto **3** C
Café Oviedo **16** C43
Demarco **16** C4
El Chileno **6** E4
El Mochica **8** C4
El Sol **7** E4
Juguería San Agustín **9** D4
Milenium **10** C3
Panadería José Antonio **11** D4
Panadería Sandoval **12** E5
PASE **4** C3
Pizzería Pizzanino **13** E1
Rincón de Vallejo **15** C3
Romano **16** C4
Romano-Rincón Criollo **17** F3
Sal y Pimienta **18** B3

Bars & clubs 🍸

Canana **19** B3
Taverna Chelsea **20** B5

0 metres 100
0 yards 100

N

Peru Trujillo & around

which contains valuable pre-Columbian ceramics. The other is **Casa Bracamonte (or Lizarzaburu)** ⓘ *Independencia 441*, with occasional exhibits. Opposite the Cathedral on Independencia, is the **Caja Rural** (officially known as Casa Garci Olguín), recently restored but boasting the oldest façade in the city and Moorish-style murals. The buildings that surround the Plaza, and many others in the vicinity, are painted in bright pastel colours. Near the Plaza de Armas is the spacious 18th- century **Palacio Iturregui**, now occupied by the **Club Central** ⓘ *Jr Pizarro 688, Mon-Sat 1100- 1800, free entry to patio, US$1.45 to see the ceramics.* An exclusive and social centre of Trujillo, it houses a private collection of ceramics.

Other mansions, still in private hands, include **Casa del Mayorazgo de Facalá** ⓘ *Pizarro 314*, now Banco Wiese. **Casa de la Emancipación** ⓘ *Jr Pizarro 610 (Banco Continental), daily 0900-1300, 1700-2000*, is where independence from Spain was planned and was the first seat of government and congress in Peru. The **Casa del Mariscal de Orbegoso** ⓘ *Orbegoso 553, banking hours, free*, is the Museo de la República owned by the BCP bank. **Casa Ganoza Chopitea** ⓘ *Independencia 630*, architecturally the most representative house in the city.

One of the best of the many churches is the 17th-century **La Merced** ⓘ *at Pizarro 550, US$2*, with picturesque moulded figures below the dome. **El Carmen** ⓘ *at Colón y Bolívar, Mon-Sat 0900-1300, US$0.85, church is open for mass Sun 0700-0730*, church and monastery, has been described as the 'most valuable jewel of colonial art in Trujillo'. Next door is the Pinacoteca Carmelita. **La Compañía** ⓘ *near Plaza de Armas*, is now an auditorium for cultural events.

Museo de Arqueología ⓘ *Junín 682 y Ayacucho, Casa Risco, T249322, www.uni tru.edu.pe/arq/indice.html, Tue-Fri 0900-1300, 1500-1900, Sat-Sun 0930-1600, US$1.45*, houses a large and interesting collection of thematic exhibits. The basement of the **Cassinelli** ⓘ *garage on the fork of the Pan-American and Huanchaco roads, 0830-1600, US$1.50*, contains a superb private collection of Mochica and Chimú pottery, recommended. Demonstrations of the whistling *huacos* are given. The **Museo del Juguete** ⓘ *Independencia 705 y Junín, Tue-Sat 1000-1800, Sun 1000-1300, 1500-1800, US$0.85, children US$0.30, café open 0900-2300*, is a toy museum containing examples from prehistoric times to 1950, collected by painter Gerardo Chávez. Downstairs is the Espacio Cultural Angelmira with a café bar; in a restored *casona*, worth a visit. **Museo de Zoología de Juan Ormea** ① *Jr San Martín 368, Mon-Fri 0700-1900, US$0.60, has interesting displays of Peruvian animals.*

Huacas del Sol and de la Luna

① *0830-1600 (last entry, but site open till sunset), US$3 with guide, some of whom speak European languages (students half price, children US$0.30), good visitor centre.*

A few kilometres south of Trujillo are the huge and fascinating Moche pyramids, the Huaca del Sol and the Huaca de la Luna. Until the Spaniards destroyed a third of it in a vain search for treasure, Huaca del Sol was the largest man-made structure in the western hemisphere, at 45 m high. It consisted of seven levels , with possibly six remodellings over the first six centuries AD. Today, about two-thirds of the pyramid have been lost and it is closed to the public. Huaca de la Luna, 500 m away, received scant attention until extensive polychrome moulded decorations were found throughout the 1990s. The colours on these remarkable geometric patterns and deities have faded little and it is now possible to view impressive friezes of the upper four levels on the northern exterior wall of the huaca. The highest mural is a 'serpent' which runs the length of the wall, beneath it there are repeated motifs of 'felines' holding decapitated heads of warriors, then repeated motifs of 'fishermen' holding fish against a bright blue background and, finally, huge 'spider/crab' motifs. Combined with intricate, brightly painted two- dimensional motifs in the sacrificial area atop the huaca, and with new discoveries in almost every excavation, Huaca de la Luna is now a truly significant site well worth visiting.

Chan Chán

① *5 km from Trujillo. 0830-1700, last entry 1600. Site may be covered up if rain is expected. Tickets cost US$2.85 (discount with ISIC card), include entrance fees for Chan Chán, site museum, Huaca El Dragón and Huaca La Esmeralda (for 2 days). A guide costs US$5.80 per hr – worth it; map and leaflet in English US$0.75. See note about safety, page 1133*

These vast, unusually decorated crumbling ruins of the imperial city of the Chimú domains are the largest adobe city in the world. The ruins consist of nine great compounds built by Chimú kings. The 9-m high perimeter walls surrounded sacred enclosures with usually only one narrow entrance. Inside, rows of storerooms contained the agricultural wealth of the kingdom, which stretched 1,000 km along the coast from near Guayaquil to the Carabayllo Valley, north of Lima.

Most of the compounds contain a huge walk-in well which tapped the ground water, raised to a high level by irrigation further up the valley. Each compound also included a platform mound which was the burial place of the king, with his women and his treasure, presumably maintained as a memorial. The Incas almost certainly copied this system and transported it to Cuzco where the last Incas continued building huge enclosures. The Chimú surrendered to the Incas around 1471 after 11 years of siege and threats to cut the irrigation canals.

The dilapidated city walls enclose an area of 28 sq km containing the remains of palaces, temples, workshops, streets, houses, gardens and a canal. What is left of the adobe walls bears well-preserved decorations of fish and other animals, and painted designs have been found on pottery unearthed from the debris of a city ravaged by floods, earthquakes, and *huaqueros* (grave looters). Owing to the damage, many of the interesting mouldings are closed to visitors. The **Ciudadela of Tschudi** has been restored (20 mins walk from the road).

The **site museum** ① *0830-1600*, on the main road, 100 m before the turn-off, has a son et lumière display of the growth of Chan Chán as well as objects found in the area.

The partly-restored temple, **Huaca El Dragón** ① *0900-1630 (in theory), it is on the west side of the Pan-American Highway in the district of La Esperanza; combis from Huayna Cápac y Los Incas, or Av España y Manuel Vera marked 'Arco Iris/La Esperanza', taxi costs US$2, dating from Huari to Chimú times (AD 1000-1470), is also known as* **Huaca Arco Iris** (rainbow), after the shape of friezes which decorate it.

The poorly preserved **Huaca La Esmeralda** is at Mansiche, between Trujillo and Chan Chán, behind the church (not a safe area). Buses to Chan Chán and Huanchaco pass the church at Mansiche.

El Brujo

① *US$3.50. www.unitru.edu.pe/arq/index.html or www.research.ibm.com/peru/brujo.htm.*
A complex collectively known as **El Brujo**, 60 km north of Trujillo, is considered one of the most

important archaeological sites on the north coast. Covering 2 sq km, it was a ceremonial centre for up to 10 cultures, including the Moche. Huaca Cortada (or El Brujo) has a wall decorated with high relief stylized figures. Huaca Prieta is, in effect, a giant rubbish tip dating back 5,000 years, which once housed the very first settlers. Huaca Cao Viejo has extensive friezes, polychrome reliefs up to 90 m long, 4 m high and on five different levels. In front of Cao Viejo are the remains of one of the oldest Spanish churches in the region. It was common practice for the Spaniards to build their churches near these ancient sites in order to counteract their religious importance. Excavations will continue for many years. Trujillo travel agencies run tours. There are exhibitions at the Chan Chán site museum, Banco Wiese and Museo de la Nación in Lima.

Huanchaco and around

An alternative to Trujillo is this fishing and surfing village, full of hotels, guest houses and restaurants (but little nightlife). It is famous for its narrow pointed fishing rafts, known as *caballitos* (little horses) *de totora*, made of totora reeds and depicted on Mochica, Chimú and other cultures' pottery. Unlike those used on Lake Titicaca, they are flat, not hollow, and ride the breakers rather like surfboards (fishermen offer trips on their *caballitos* for US$1.50, be prepared to get wet; groups should contact Luis Gordillo, El Mambo, T461092). You can see fishermen returning in their reed rafts at about 0800 and 1400 when they stack the boats upright to dry in the fierce sun. Overlooking Huanchaco is a huge church from the belfry of which are extensive views. Post Office at Manco Capac 306, open 1300-1800 in theory.

Puerto Malabrigo (Chicama), is known by surfers as the best surf beach in Peru, claiming that it has the longest left-hand point-break in the world. It is 70 km north of Trujillo. There are several basic places to stay and eat.

● Sleeping

Trujillo *p1125, map p1126*
Trujillo has confusing double street names: the smaller printed name is that generally shown on maps, in guide books and in general use.
L Libertador, Independencia 485, Plaza de Armas, T232741, trujillo@libertador.com.pe. Including tax, pool (can be used by non-guests if they buy a drink), cafetería and restaurant, breakfast US$5, excellent buffet lunch on Sun. Recommended.
AL Los Conquistadores, Diego de Almagro 586, T203350, losconquistadores@ viabcp.com. Includes American breakfast, internet, bar, restaurant, very comfortable.
AL El Gran Marqués, Díaz de Cienfuegos 145-147, Urb La Merced, T/F249366, www.elgran marques.com. Price includes breakfast, modern, free internet connection in rooms, pool, sauna, jacuzzi, restaurant. Recommended.
A-B Gran Bolívar, Bolívar 957, T222090, www.granbolivarhotel.com. Includes breakfast, airport transfer and welcome drink, in converted 18th-century house, internet, café, bar, parking.
B La Alameda del Peregrino, Jr Pizarro 879, T470512, www.perunorte.com/alameda peregrino. Includes breakfast, cable TV, internet service, restaurant, bar, café, safe, money exchange. Recommended. Also **El Peregrino**, Independencia 978, T203990, www.elperegrino hotel.com, which is convenient for Lima buses.
B Hostal Malibú, Av Larco 1471-1474, T284811, www.hostalmalibu.com. Variety of rooms, restaurant, room service, mini-bar, laundry,

massage, currency exchange. Also sister hotel of same name at Av Larco 1000, Huanchaco.
B Saint Germain, Junín 585, T208102, www.perunorte.com/saintgermain. Price includes breakfast, hot water, TV, internet, laundry, safe, parking.
C Continental, Gamarra 663, T241607, F249881. Opposite market, good breakfast, helpful, safe.
C-D Colonial, Independencia 618, T258261, hostalcolonialtruji@hotmail.com. Attractive but small rooms, hot showers, basic breakfast, good restaurant, especially for set lunch. Recommended.
D Residencia Vanini, Av Larco 237, outside Av España, T200878. Good but not central, 9 rooms.
D San Martín, San Martín 749, T/F252311, www.publinet.com.pe/hotelsanmartin. Good value, attractive, TV, small restaurant, good for breakfast, noisy, otherwise recommended.
D Turismo, Gamarra 747, T244181. Includes continental breakfast, central, good services TV, restaurant, parking, travel agency.
E Hostal Americano, Pizarro 764, T241361. Vast, rambling building, most rooms without window, can be noisy, cold water, rundown, mixed reports.
E Primavera, Av N de Piérola 872, Urb Primavera, T231915, F257399. Hot water, restaurant, bar, pool.
F pp Chan Chán Inn, Av Ejército 307, T/F294281, mocheperu@hotmail.com. Close to several bus terminals, includes breakfast (cheaper without), popular with backpackers, luggage store, café, laundry, internet, money exchange, information.

F pp **Clara Bravo and Michael White**, Cahuide 495, T243347, www.xanga.com/trujilloperu. Meals on request, very helpful, lots of information, many languages spoken (see Guides, below). Restaurants and fast internet nearby. Recommended.

Huanchaco *p1129*
B **Las Palmeras**, Av Larco 1150, sector Los Tumbos, T461199, www.lasplamerasdehuanchaco.com. One of the best, rooms with terrace, bath, TV, hot water, dining room, pool and gardens.

C **Caballito de Totora**, Av La Rivera 219, T/F651828, totora@terra.com.pe. Includes taxes, D in low season (when restaurant is closed), surfers' room F, pool, English spoken, nice garden, restaurant with good food and coffee, off site parking, good value, noisy. Recommended.

C **Hostal Bracamonte**, Los Olivos 503, T461162, www.hostalbracamonte.com. Comfortable chalets with bath B, pool, own water supply, emergency generator, rents bicycles, secure, good restaurant, English spoken. Camping. Highly recommended.

C **Hostal Huanchaco**, Larco 287 on Plaza, T461272, huanchaco_hostal@terra.com.pe. With breakfast, TV, hot water, pool, good but expensive cafetería, video, pool table. Recommended.

D **Las Brisas**, Raymondi 146, T461186, lasbrisas@hotmail.com. Hot water, café, cable TV, comfortable.

D **Hostal Los Esteros**, Av Larco 618, T461300, losesteros@trujillobusiness.com. Hot water, restaurant, safe motorcycle parking, can arrange surfing and *caballitos de totora* trips.

D **Hostal Sol y Mar**, Los Pinos 570, T461120. With pool, restaurant, friendly, garden. Recommended.

E **Naylamp**, Prolongación Víctor Larco 3, northern end of seafront in El Boquerón, T461022, naylamp@terra.com.pe. Rooms set around a courtyard, dorms F pp, hammocks, garden, good beds, hot water, camping US$1.45, US$2.30 to hire tent, laundry, safe, kitchen at campsite, many languages spoken, Italian food, good breakfasts. Recommended.

F pp **Casa Gaviotas**, Los Pinos 535, T461858. Small, comfortable, snacks, restaurant, cocktails.

F **Casa Hospedaje Los Ficus**, Los Ficus 516, T461719, www.huanchaco.net/losficus. Cheaper with shared bath, family run, hot water, use of kitchen, breakfast, laundry.

F pp **Golden Club**, Av La Rivera 217, T461306. Gym, pool, restaurant, use of kitchen, popular with surfers, laid back, excellent value.

F **Hostal Solange**, Los Ficus 484, 1 block from the beach, T461410, hsolange@yahoo.es. Hot showers, good food, laundry facilities, limited use of kitchen, popular meeting point.

F pp **Huanchaco's Garden**, Av Circunvalación Mz 'U', lote 3, T461194, huanchacogarden@yahoo.es. Bungalows around a small pool, also camping, 1 block from beach, TV, use of kitchen, hot water, many good reports.

F pp **La Casa Suiza**, Los Pinos 451, T461285, www.huanchaco.net/casasuiza. 3 blocks from the beach, German and English spoken, hot water, nice roof balcony, breakfast US$1.50, surf boards to rent, book exchange, internet, mixed reports.

G pp **Sra Mabel Díaz de Aguilar**, Túpac Amaru 248, T461232, mabel_minerva@ hotmail.com. Near football ground, shared bath, hot water, English spoken.

G pp **Hospedaje El Boquerón**, R Palma 330, T461968, maznaran@hotmail.com. 1 block from beach, modern, shared bathrooms, hot water, fully equipped kitchen, laundry, internet, French spoken.

● Eating

Trujillo *p1125, map p1126*
Many places close 1330-1630. There are cheap seafood restaurants at Plazuela El Recreo, at the end of Pizarro. For really cheap meals try the central market at Grau y Ayacucho.

₮₮ **Demarco**, Pizarro 725. Good food, excellent desserts, one of a cluster of eateries in the centre.

₮₮ **El Mochica**, Bolívar 462. Good typical food and occasional live music.

₮₮ **Pizzería Pizzanino**, Av Juan Pablo II 183, Urb San Andrés, opposite University. Recommended for pizzas, pastas, meats, desserts, evening only.

₮₮ **Romano**, Pizarro 747. International food, good *menú*, poor salads, breakfasts, coffee, excellent milkshakes, cakes, slow service.

₮₮ **Romano-Rincón Criollo**, Estados Unidos 162, Urb El Recreo, 10-min walk from centre, T244207. Northern Peruvian cuisine, *menú* for US$2, smart.

₮ **ABC**, Orbegoso 290 y San Martín. Good chicken.

₮ **Asturias**, Pizarro 741. Nice café with excellent meals, good juices and snacks.

₮ **Café Oviedo**, Pizarro 737. With vegetarian options, good salads and cakes, helpful.

₮ **Juguería San Agustín**, Bolívar 526. Good juices, good *menú*, popular, excellent value.

₮ **Milenium**, Gamarra 316. Vegetarian, good.

₮ **PASE**, Gamarra 353, T/F234715, Mon-Sat 1300- 1600, Thu-Sat 1900-2300. Restaurant school and hotel, good *menú* US$1.70-2.25, small portions.

₮ **Rincón de Vallejo**, Orbegoso 303. Good *menú*, typical dishes, very crowded at peak times.

₮ **Sal y Pimienta**, Colón 201. Very popular for lunch, US$1 and US$1.85, close to buses for Huanchaco and Chan Chán.

₮ **El Sol**, Pizarro 660. The original and best vegetarian, but not exclusively, cheap set meals, also serves other dishes.

Café Amaretto, Gamarra 368. Smart, good selection of real coffees, "brilliant" cakes, sweets, snacks and drinks.

Cafetería Buenos Aires, Pizarro 332. Substantial breakfasts, very busy at peak times.
El Chileno, Ayacucho 408. Café and ice cream parlour, popular.
Fitopán, Bolívar 406. Good selection of breads, also serves lunches.
Panadería José Antonio, Ayacucho 561-65, in the Mercado Central. Good selection of breads.
Panadería Sandoval, Orbegoso 822. Good selection of breads.

Huanchaco *p1129*

There are about 30 restaurants on the beachfront. Many close in the low season.
₶₶₶ **Big Ben**, Víctor Larco 836, near A Sánchez, T461869. Seafood and international, very good.
₶₶₶ **El Mochica**, Av Larco, next to *Mamma Mia*. Same owners and quality as this restaurant in Trujillo, very nice dining area and panorama.
₶₶₶ **El Mococho**, Bolognesi 535. One of the best seafood restaurants, expensive, caters for groups.
₶₶₶-₶₶ **Club Colonial**, La Ribera 171, T461015. On the seafront, fish, chicken or meat, excellent.
₶₶ **El Anzuelo**, next door to *Estrella Marina*. Good ceviche, offers 'taster' dishes at lower prices.
₶₶ **La Esquina**, C Unión 299. Recommended for local food (also has accommodation **G** pp).
₶₶ **Mamma Mia**, seafront. Good value Italian food and delicious homemade pasta and ice-cream, English spoken, closed Mon lunchtime, good lodging (**F**, shared showers) next door.
₶₶ **Estrella Marina**, Av Víctor Larco, seafront. Great value for fish.
₶₶ **El Tramboyo**, on the little plaza opposite the pier. Good food, helpful staff.
₶₶-₶ **Otra Cosa**, Av Larco 921, T461346, www.otracosa.info. New vegetarian restaurant, Dutch run, which also has a volunteering agency, massage, internet, tourist information and surfing services, Wed-Sun 0900-2000. Recommended.
₶ **Sabes?**, V Larco 920, ysabes@yahoo.com. Pub with food, internet café, popular, American run.
₶ **Casa Tere**, Víctor Larco 280, Plaza de Armas. Best pizzas in town, also pastas, burgers and breakfasts.
₶ **Chelita**, Los Abetos 198. Good value *menú*, fish dishes are best.
₶ **Piccolo**, Los Abetos 142. Friendly, live folk music weekend evenings, excellent, also has a surf and art shop.

❶ Bars and clubs

Trujillo *p1125, map p1126*
Canana, San Martín 788. Bars and restaurant, disco, live music at weekends (US$1.50-3), video screens (also has travel agency). Recommended, but take care on leaving.
Taverna Chelsea, Estete 675, T257032. Bar, restaurant, live Salsa at weekends (US$4 entry),

exclusive and lively. Highly recommended.
Las Tinajas, Pizarro 389, Plaza Mayor. A pub-disco with live rock music and *peña* on Sat.

❀ Festivals and events

Trujillo *p1125, map p1126*
The 2 most important festivals are the **National Marinera Contest** (end of **Jan**) and the **Festival Internacional de La Primavera** (last week of **Sep**), with cultural events, parades, beauty pageants and Trujillo's famous **Caballos de Paso**.

Huanchaco *p1129*
In the 1st week of **May** is the **Festival del Mar**, a celebration of the disembarkation of Taycanamo, the leader of the Chimú period. A procession is made in Totora boats. **30 Jun**, San Pedro, patron saint of fishermen: his statue is taken out to sea on a huge totora-reed boat. Also the annual **Olímpiadas Playeral** and **El Festival Internacional de la Primavera** (see Trujillo above). There are also surf competitions. Carnival and New Year are also popular celebrations.

❍ Shopping

Trujillo *p1125, map p1126*
Bookshops Librería Adriatica, Jr Junín 565, T044-291569, libreria@adriaticaperu.com. A very good bookshop, stocks Footprint. **Librería Peruana**, Pizarro 505, just off the Plaza. Best selection in town, ask for Sra Inés Guerra de Guijón.
Handicrafts APIAT, craft market, Av España near Zela. The largest craft market in the city, good for ceramics, totora boats, woodwork and leather, competitive prices. **Artesanía del Norte**, Independencia 616, 2 blocks from Plaza Mayor. Also in Huanchaco, Los Olivos 504, marycortijo@usa.net. Sells items mostly to her own design.
Markets Mercado Central, on Gamarra, Ayacucho and Pasaje San Agustín. **Mercado Mayorista**, between Sinchi Roca and Av Los Incas (not a safe zone). **Merpisa**, Pizarro y Junín. The best supermarket.

⛰ Activities and tours

Trujillo *p1125, map p1126*
Tour operators
Prices vary and competition is fierce so shop around for the best deal. Few agencies run tours on Sun and often only at fixed times on other days. To Chan Chán, **El Dragón** and **Huanchaco**, 3 hrs for US$8.50 pp. To **Huacas del Sol** and **de la Luna**, 2 hrs for US$7 pp. To **El Brujo**, US$17 pp. **City tours** cost US$5.65 pp (min of 2 people; discounts for 4 or more). Prices do not include entrance fees.
Chacón Tours, Av España 106-112, T255212. Sat

afternoon and Sun morning. Recommended. **Guía Tours**, Independencia 580, T234856, guitour@amauta.rcp.net.pe. Also Western Union agent. Recommended.

Tesores del Perú, Pizarro 575, of 03, T044-582381, oscarcampos10@hotmail.com. Oscar Campos Santa María organizes custom-made tours to archaeological sites, as far as Lambayeque. **Trujillo Tours**, San Martín y Almagro 301, T257518, ttours@pol.com.pe. Works with *Lima Tours*.

Guides
Many hotels work on a commission basis with taxi drivers and travel agencies. If you decide on a guide, make your own direct approach and always agree what is included in the price. The Tourist Police (see Directory) has a list of guides; average cost US$7 per hr. **Clara Bravo**, Cahuide 495, T243347, www.xanga.com/TrujilloPeru. An experienced tourist guide who speaks Spanish, English, German and understands Italian. She takes tourists on extended circuits of the region (archaeological tour US$16 for 6 hrs, city tour US$7 pp, US$53 per car to El Brujo, with extension to Sipán, Brüning Museum and Túcume possible). Clara works with English chartered accountant **Michael White** (same address, microbewhite@yahoo.com, also speaks German, French and Italian), who provides transport. He is very knowledgeable about tourist sites. They run tours any day of the week; 24-hr attention, accommodate small groups. **Laura Durán**, T281590, lauraduran@ yahoo.com. Speaks English, German and some Hebrew, lots of information, very accommodating. **Zaby Miranda Acosta**, Camelias 315, Huanchaco, T01-996 66421, zabymiranda@hotmail.com. Works at the tourist office, speaks German, Italian, US$10 per day. **Oscar and Gustavo Prada Marga**, Miguel Grau 169, Villa del Mar, or at Chan Chán. Both are experienced guides. **Pedro Puerta**, T960 9603 (mob). Works with Guía Tours and independently. **Jannet Rojas Sánchez**, Alto Mochica Mz Q 19, Trujillo, T934 4844, jannarojas@hotmail.com. Speaks English, enthusiastic, works independently and for *Guía Tours*. **Celio Eduardo Roldán**, celioroldan@hotmail.com. Helpful and informative taxi driver. **José Soto Ríos**, Atahualpa 514, dpto 3, T251489. He speaks English and French.

Huanchaco *p1129*
Surfing
Un Lugar, Bolognesi 457, T957 7170, unlugarsurfingschool@hotmail.com. Ask for English-speaking Juan Carlos.
Picolo, Los Abetos 142. For rental and instruction, wet suits and boards, owner is a local champion.
The Wave, Av Larco 525. With small Mexican restaurant, staff speak English.

Yenth Ccora, Av Larco 468, T940 38711, ycc_mar@hotmail.com. Surfing equipment manufacture, repair, rental and surfing school.

⊖ Transport

Trujillo *p1125, map p1126*
Air To **Lima**, 1 hr, daily flights with **Lan** and **WayraPerú** (also to **Talara** and **Tumbes**). Star Perú Mon-Sat to Lima and **Chiclayo**. Taxi to airport, US$4; or take bus or colectivo to Huanchaco and get out at airport turn-off (US$0.25) and walk 2 km.
Bus On all local city routes, US$0.25-0.35; colectivos are safer as there are fewer people and fewer pick-pockets. To and from **Lima**, 561 km, 8 hrs in the better class buses, average fare US$14.30- 18.50, 9-10 hrs in the cheaper buses, US$7.15-11.50. There are many bus companies doing this route, among those recommended are: **Ormeño**, Av Ejército 233, T259782, 3 levels of service, 5 daily (also runs north as far as Tumbes); **Cruz del Sur**, Amazonas 437 near Av Ejército, T261801; **Turismo Díaz**, Nicolás de Piérola 1079 on Panamericana Norte, T201237, leaves at 2230; **Línea** (recommended), Av América Sur 2855, T297000, ticket office at San Martín y Orbegoso, T245181, 3 levels of service, also to **Chimbote** hourly, **Huaraz** 2100, 9 hrs, US$8.65, **Cajamarca** 5 a day, US$4.25-10, **Chiclayo**, hourly, US$3.35 (from Carrión by Av Mansiche, T235847, on the hour), and **Piura**, 2300, US$7. Also Flores (Av Ejército 350, T208250), Ittsa (Av Mansiche 145, T251415; No 431 for northern destinations – good service, T222541), **Móvil**, Av América Sur 3959, T286538. Oltursa, Av Ejército 342, T263055, *bus cama* service to Lima, 2200.

Small **Pakatnamú** buses leave when full, 0400-2100, from Av N de Piérola 1092, T206564, to **Pacasmayo**, 102 km, 1¼ hrs, US$2. To **Chiclayo**, 3 hrs from Trujillo, US$3.35, several companies. Among the best are **Emtrafesa**, Av Túpac Amaru 285, T471521, on the half-hour every hour; to **Piura**, 6 hrs, US$7; and **Tumbes**, US$8.50, 8 hrs. Other companies include: **Transportes El Dorado**, Av América Norte opposite Díaz (old terminal next to Línea on Mansiche), T291778, leave at 1245, 2220 to **Piura** and **Sullana**, US$4.30/5.75.

Direct buses to **Huaraz**, 319 km, via Chimbote and Casma (169 km), with **Línea** and **Móvil**, 8 hrs, US$8.60 special. Also **Chinchaysuyo**, Av Mansiche 391, at 2030, 10 hrs. There are several buses and colectivos to **Chimbote**, with **América Express** from Lloque 162, 135 km, 2 hrs, US$1.20, departures every 30 mins from 0530 (ticket sales from 0500); then change at Chimbote (see above – leave Trujillo before 0600 to make a connection from 0800). Ask Clara Bravo and Michael White (see Guides, above) about transport to Caraz avoiding Chimbote (a very worthwhile trip via the Brasileños road and Cañon del Pato).

To **Cajamarca**, 300 km, 7-8 hrs, US$5.75- 8: with **Línea**, **Emtrafesa**, see above, at 1000, 2230, and **Tur Díaz** 6 a day. To **Huamachuco**, 170 km, 6 hrs, US$6, **Trans Agreda**, J B Farfán 647, 0800, 1300, **Negreiros**, Prol Vallejo block 13, 0900, 1300 (good service) and **Trans Gran Turismo**, Prol Vallejo 1368, T425391, 4 a day. To **Chachapoyas**, *Móvil* (see above) daily 1600 and 0130 en route from Lima, US$11.50, via Chiclayo, also to Tarapoto.

To **Tarapoto**, via Moyobamba, Tarapoto Tours, Av N de Piérola 1221, T221493, at 2230, US$14.30, and **Ejetur** Av N de Piérola 1238, T222228, at 1100, 1315, US$15, also to Yurimaguas at 0900, US$20, and to Jaén at 1600, US$7.50.

Taxi Town trip, US$0.55 within Av España and US$0.70 within Av América. To airport US$4. Beware of overcharging, check fares with locals. Taxi from in front of Hotel Libertador, US$7 per hr, about the same rate as a tour with an independent guide or travel agent for 1-2 people.

Huaca del Sol and Huaca de la Luna *p1128*
Combis (yellow and blue) every 30 mins from Suárez y Los Incas to the visitors centre, US$0.35. It's safer to catch the bus from Huayna Cápac, southeast of Av Los Incas. Taxis about US$3; plenty at site for return, or US$9.50 return with 1 hr wait.

Chan Chán *p1128*
Buses and combis leave from Huayna Cápac y Av Los Incas or (less safely) Zela on the corner of Los Incas, near the market (114A) or corner of España and Manuel Vera (114B) in **Trujillo**; US$0.35, 20 mins to the turn-off to the ruins. A **taxi** is US$3 from Trujillo, US$0.85 from museum to ruins, US$2.85 to Huanchaco from ruins. **Note**: It is not safe to walk on the dirt track from turn-off to site, unless in a group, 20 mins. There have been reports of robbery even within the site itself. On no account walk the 4 km to, or on, Buenos Aires beach near Chan Chán as there is serious danger of robbery and of being attacked by dogs.

El Brujo *p1128*
The complex can be reached by taking one of the regular buses from Trujillo to Chocope, US$0.55, and then a colectivo (every 30 minutes) to Magdalena de Cao, US$0.45, then a taxi to the site, including wait, US$4.50, or a 5 km walk to the site.

Huanchaco *p1129*
Combis between **Trujillo** and Huanchaco are routes A, B and C, 0500-2100 every 5-10 mins. A and B do an anti-clockwise circuit of Huanchaco and enter Trujillo by the roundabout on Av Mansiche, 3 blocks northwest of Av España in front of the Cassinelli museum, then A goes round the west side of Trujillo onto Av 28 de Julio, while B goes round the east side on Av Manuel Vera, España as far as Bolívar. At night they go only to España y Grau. US$0.35, 20-min journey. Slower 'micros', B and H, follow similar routes to América; leaving Trujillo B goes north of the centre on España, H goes south (convenient stops are shown on the Trujillo map), in daylight only. Colectivos and taxis minimum US$3, more likely US$4-5.

Puerto Malabrigo/Puerto Chicama *p1129*
Combis and colectivos from the Santa Cruz terminal at Av Santa Cruz y Av América Sur.

❶ Directory

Trujillo *p1125, map p1126*
Airline offices Aerocóndor, T255212. Lan, Pizarro 340-42, T221469. WayraPerú, Jr Alfonso Ugarte 310, T245935. **Banks** BCP, Gamarra 562. No commission on cash into soles, but US$12 fee on TCs or changing into dollars, cash advance on Visa card, ATM (Visa). Interbank, Pizarro y Gamarra. Good rates for cash, no commission on Amex TCs into soles, reasonable rate, Visa cash advance, quick service, also has Visa, Mastercard and Maestro ATMs (doesn't close for lunch). Banco Wiese Sudameris, Pizarro 314, *Casa de Mayorazgo de Facalá*. Good rates for Amex TCs, 2% commission into soles or dollars, ATM for Visa/Plus. BBV Continental, Pizarro 620. Amex TCs and Visa card accepted, US$10 commission up to US$500. Note that banks close 1300-1615. There is little difference between the rates for cash dollars given by banks and street changers, *casas de cambio* and travel agencies. There are many *casas de cambio* and street changers on the plazoleta opposite the Casa de Condes de Aranda and all along the 600 block of Bolívar. **Western Union**, Almagro 581, España y Huayna Cápac, see also *Guía Tours*, above. **Cultural centres** Alianza Francesa, San Martín 858-62, T231232, www.ucv.edu.pe/alianzafrancesa-trujillo. Instituto de Cultura Peruano Norteamericano, Av Venezuela 125, Urb El Recreo, T232512, www.elcultural.com.pe. **Consulates** UK, Honorary Consul, Mr Winston Barber, Jesús de Nazareth 312, T235548, winstonbarber@ terra.com.pe. Mon-Fri 0900-1700. **Internet** There are internet offices all over the centre, mostly on Pizarro blocks 1 and 6, and Av España blocks 1 and 8. **Medical services** Hospital: Hospital Belén, Bolívar 350, T245281. Clínica Peruano Americana, Av Mansiche 702, T231261, English spoken, good. **Pharmacies** Several pharmacy chains in the centre (on Pizarro and Gamarra) and others on

either side of Belén hospital on Bolognesi. **Post offices** Independencia 286 y Bolognesi. 0800-2000, stamps only on special request. DHL, Almagro 579. **Telephones** Telefónica, headquarters at Bolívar 658. Private call centres at Pizarro 561, Ayacucho 625, Gamarra 450, on 5th block of Orbegoso and Av España 1530. **Useful**

addresses Immigration: Av Larco 1220, Urb Los Pinos. Open Mon-Fri 0815-1230, 1500-1630. Gives 30-day visa extensions, US$20 (proof of funds and onward ticket required), plus US$1 for *formulario* in Banco de la Nación (fixers on the street will charge more).

Chiclayo and around

Lambayeque department, sandwiched between the Pacific and the Andes, is a major agricultural zone, especially for rice and sugar cane. The boasts a distinctive cuisine and musical tradition, and an unparalleled ethnographic and archaeological heritage. Chiclayo's witchcraft market is famous and excavations at nearby adobe pyramid cities are uncovering fabulous treasures.

Chiclayo → *Phone code: 074. Colour map 3, grid B1. Population: 411,536.*
Since it was founded in 1560 by Spanish priests, Chiclayo has grown to become a major commercial hub. The city has an atmosphere all of its won and a distinctive musical tradition featuring Afro-indian rhythms, but is best known for the spectacular cache of archaeological treasures that lie at its doorstep. **Tourist offices: Centro de Información Turística** (CIT) ① *Sáenz Peña 838, T238112.* For complaints and tourist protection, **Indecopi** ① *Av Balta 506, T209021, ctejada@indecopi.gob.pe, Mon- Fri 0800-1300, 1630-1930.* The **tourist police** ① *Av Sáenz Peña 830, T236700, 24 hours a day,* are very helpful and may store luggage and take you to the sites themselves. There are tourist kiosks on the Plaza and on Balta.

In the city itself, on the Plaza de Armas, is the 19th-century neoclassical **Cathedral**, designed by the English architect Andrew Townsend. The **Palacio Municipal** is at the junction of Avenida Balta, the main street and the Plaza. The private **Club de la Unión** is on the Plaza at the corner of Calle San José. Continue five blocks north on Balta to the **Mercado Modelo**, one of northern Peru's liveliest and largest daily markets. Don't miss the handicrafts stalls (see *Monsefú*) and the well-organized section (off C Arica on the south side) of ritual paraphernalia used by traditional curers and diviners (*curanderos*): herbal medicines, folk charms, curing potions, and exotic objects including dried llama foetuses to cure all manner of real and imagined illnesses. At *Paseo de Artesanías*, 18 de Abril near Balta, stalls sell handicrafts in a quiet, custom-built open-air arcade.

Monsefú and the coast

The traditional town of **Monsefú**, southwest, is known for handicrafts; good market, four blocks from the plaza. Handicraft stalls open when potential customers arrive (see also Festivals above). Beyond Monsefú are three ports serving the Chiclayo area. **Pimentel**, 8 km from Chiclayo, is a beach resort which gets very crowded on Sunday. You can walk along the decaying pier for US$0.25. There are several seafood restaurants. The surfing between Pimentel and the Bayovar Peninsula is excellent, reached from Chiclayo (14½ km) by road branching off from the Pan-American Highway. Sea-going reed boats (*caballitos de totora*) are used by fishermen and may be seen returning in the late afternoon. Nearby **Santa Rosa** has little to recommend it and it is not safe to walk there from Pimentel. The most southerly is **Puerto Etén**, a quaint port 24 km by road from Chiclayo. Its old railway station has been declared a national heritage. In the adjacent roadstead, Villa de Etén, panama hats are the local industry.

The ruined Spanish town of **Zaña**, 51 km south of Chiclayo, was destroyed by floods in 1726, and sacked by English pirates on more than one occasion. There are ruins of five colonial churches and the convents of San Agustín, La Merced and San Francisco.

Lambayeque

About 12 km northwest from Chiclayo is Lambayeque, its narrow streets lined by colonial and republican houses, many retaining their distinctive wooden balconies and wrought iron grill-work over the windows. For example, on 8 de Octubre are **Casona Iturregui Aguilarte**, No 410, and, at No 328, **Casona Cúneo** with the only decorated façade in the town; opposite is **Casona Descalzi**, perhaps the best preserved. On Calle 2 de Mayo see especially **Casa de la**

Logia o Montjoy, whose 64 m long balcony is said to be the longest in the colonial Americas. Also of interest is the 16th-century **Complejo Religioso Monumental de San Pedro** and the baroque church of the same name which stands on the **Plaza de Armas 27 de Diciembre**. There are hotels in town, should you prefer not to stay in Chiclayo, and good value restaurants, including opposite Museo Brüning.

The reason most people visit is to see the town's two museums. The older of the two is the **Brüning Archaeological Museum** ① *closed late 2005*, in a modern building, specializing in Mochica, Lambayeque/Sicán and Chimú cultures. Three blocks east is the more recent **Museo de las Tumbas Reales de Sipán** ① *Tue-Sat 0900-1700, US$9, http://sipan.peru cultural.org.pe*, shaped like a pyramid. The magnificent treasure from the tomb of 'The Old Lord of Sipán' (see below), and a replica of the Lord of Sipán's tomb are displayed here. A ramp from the main entrance takes visitors to the third floor, from where you descend, mirroring the sequence of the archaeologists' discoveries.

Mórrope, on the Pan-American Highway 20 km north of Lambayeqye still produces pottery using prehispanic techniques. The beautifully restored 16th-century **Capilla de la Ramada Las Animas** is on the plaza.

Chiclayo

To Combis to Túcume (2 blocks)
To Combis to Batán Grande (1 block)

Peru Chiclayo & around

Sleeping		
Adriático 1 *B3*	Hostal Santa Victoria 9 *C3*	El Huaralino 4 *C1*
América 2 *B2*	Hostal Sicán 10 *C2*	Fiesta 6 *B1*
Costa del Sol 3 *C3*	Inca 11 *B2*	Govinda 7 *B3*
El Sol 4 *B1*	Kalu 12 *A3*	Hebrón 8 *C3*
Europa 5 *B2*	Mochicas 13 *C2*	Kaprichos 9 *A3*
Garza 6 *C3*	Paracas 14 *A3*	La Panadería 10 *B2*
Gran Hotel Chiclayo 7 *B1*	Paraíso 15 *A3*	La Parra 11 *C3*
Hospedaje San	Pirámide Real 19 *C3*	La Plazuela 12 *B1*
Eduardo 16 *C3*	Santa Rosa 17 *B2*	Las Américas 13 *B3*
Hostal San José 8 *A2*	Sol Radiante 18 *C2*	Mi Tía 14 *B2*
		Roma 15 *C3*
	Eating ◐	Romana 16 *C3*
	Boulevar 1 *B2*	Tradiciones 17 *C3*
	Café Astoria 2 *C2*	
	D'Onofrio 3 *C3*	

Transport ◻
Brüning Express to
Lambayeque 1 *B1*
Civa 2 *C3*
Colectivos to Lambayeque 3 *A2*
Colectivos to Monsefú 4 *A3*
Colectivos to Puerto Etén 5 *A3*
Combis to Pimental 6 *A2, B1*
Cruz del Sur 7 *C3*
Emtrafesa 8 *C3*
Flores/Cial 9 *C3*
Línea 10 *C2*
Oltursa 11 *B1*
Tepsa 12 *C3*
Transportes Chiclayo 13 *B1*

Sipán

① *Daily 0800-1600 and the museum is open 0800-1700, entrance for tombs and museum is US$2; guide at site US$2.85 (may not speak English). To visit the site takes about 3-4 hrs.*

At this imposing complex a short distance east of Chiclayo, excavations since 1987 in one of three crumbling pyramids have brought to light a cache of funerary objects considered to rank among the finest examples of pre-Columbian art. Peruvian archaeologist Walter Alva, leader of the dig, continues to probe the immense mound that has revealed no less than 12 royal tombs filled with 1,800-year-old offerings worked in precious metals, stone, pottery and textiles of the Moche culture (circa AD 1-750). In the most extravagant Moche tomb discovered, El Señor de Sipán, a priest was found clad in gold (ear ornaments, breast plate, etc), with turquoise and other valuables. A site museum features photos and maps of excavations, technical displays and replicas of some finds.

In another tomb were found the remnants of what is thought to have been a priest, sacrificed llama and a dog, together with copper decorations. In 1989 another richly appointed, unlooted tomb contained even older metal and ceramic artefacts associated with what was probably a high-ranking shaman or spiritual leader, called 'The Old Lord of Sipán'. Three tombs are on display, containing replicas of the original finds. You can wander around the previously excavated areas to get an idea of the construction of the burial mound and adjacent pyramids. For a good view, climb the large pyramid across from the Sipán excavation.

Túcume

① *Daily 0800-1600 (the site stays open till 1700), US$2; guides charge US$2.85.*

About 35 km north of Chiclayo, beside the old Panamericana to Piura, lie the ruins of this vast city built over 1,000 years ago. A short climb to the two *miradores* on **Cerro La Raya** (or **El Purgatorio**) offers the visitor an unparalleled panoramic vista of 26 major pyramids, platform mounds, walled citadels and residential compounds flanking a ceremonial centre and ancient cemeteries. One of the pyramids, Huaca Larga, where excavations were undertaken from 1987-1992, is the longest adobe structure in the world, measuring 700 m long, 280 m wide and over 30 m high. There is no evidence of occupation of Túcume previous to the Sicán, or Lambayeque people who developed the site AD 1000-1375 until the Chimú conquered the region, establishing a short reign until the arrival of the Incas around 1470. The Incas built on top of the existing structure of **Huaca Larga** using stone from Cerro La Raya. Among the other pyramids which make up this huge complex are: **Huaca El Mirador** (90 m by 65 m, 30 m high), **Huaca Las Estacas, Huaca Pintada** and **Huaca de las Balsas** which is thought to have housed people of elevated status such as priests. (Do not climb the fragile adobe structures.)

Excavations at the site, which were once led by the late Norwegian explorer-archaeologist Thor Heyerdahl of *Kon-Tiki* fame, challenged many conventional views of ancient Peruvian culture. Some suspect that it will prove to be a civilization centre greater than Chan Chán. **A site museum** (same entrance as site), contains architectural reconstructions, photographs and drawings. No excavations are visible at the site, where there is little shade. There is a good, new hostel, **E**, built of traditional materials, next to the huacas.

The town of Túcume is a 10-15 minute walk from the site. On the plaza is the interesting **San Pedro Church**. The surrounding countryside is pleasant for walks and swimming in the river. *Fiesta de la Purísima Concepción*, the festival of the town's patron saint, is eight days prior to Carnival in February, and also in September.

Ferreñafe and Sicán

The colonial town of **Ferreñafe**, 18 km northeast of Chiclayo, is worth a visit, especially for the **Museo Nacional Sicán** ① *T286469, Tue-Sat 0900-1700, US$2, US$4 per guide (Spanish only).* This excellent new museum is designed to house objects of the Sicán (Lambayeque) culture from near Batán Grande. **Tourist office**: helpful **Mincetur** office on the Plaza de Armas ① *T282843, citesipan@mincetur.gob.pe.*

The entrance to **El Santuario Histórico Bosque de Pómac** ① *visitors' centre, T963 2390, bosquepomac@ecoportal.zzn.com, 0700-1600, a guide (Spanish only) can be hired with transport, US$3 with motorbike and US$7 with mototaxi, which includes the entrance fee,* which includes the ruins of **Sicán**, lies 16 km beyond Ferreñafe along the road to Batán Grande. Visiting the sanctuary is not easy because of the arid conditions and distances involved: it is 10 km to the nearest huaca (pyramid). At the visitors' centre food and drinks are available and camping is permitted. The guide covers a two-hour tour of the area which includes at least two huacas, some of the most ancient algarrob trees and a mirador (viewpoint), which affords a beautiful view across the emerald green tops of the forest with the enormous pyramids dramatically breaking through. Sicán has revealed several sumptuous tombs dating to AD 900-1100. The ruins comprise some 34 adobe pyramids, arranged around a huge plaza, measuring 500 by 250 m. The city, of the Sicán (or Lambayeque culture) was probably moved to Túcume (see above), 6 km west, following 30 years of severe drought and then a devastating El Niño related flood in AD 1050-1100. These events appear to have provoked a rebellion in which many of the remaining temples on top of the pyramids were burnt and destroyed.

North of Chiclayo
On the old Pan-American Highway 885 km from Lima, **Olmos** is a tranquil place (several hotels and *Festival de Limón* last week in June). A paved road runs east from Olmos over the Porculla Pass, branching north to Jaén and east to Bagua Grande (see page 1162). The old Pan-American Highway continues from Olmos to Cruz de Caña and Piura. At Lambayeque the new Pan-American Highway, which is in good condition, branches off the old road and drives 190 km straight across the Sechura Desert to Piura. There is also a coast road, narrow and scenic, between Lambayeque and Sechura via Bayovar.

The Sechura Desert is a large area of shifting sands separating the oases of Chiclayo and Piura. Water for irrigation comes from the Chira and Piura rivers, and from the Olmos and Tinajones irrigation projects which bring water from the Amazon watershed by means of tunnels (one over 16 km long) through the Andes to the Pacific coast. Note Solo cyclists should not cross the desert as muggings have occurred. Take the safer, inland route. In the desert, there is no water, no fuel and no accommodation. Do not attempt this alone.

⊜ Sleeping

Chiclayo *p1134, map p1135*
AL Gran Hotel Chiclayo, Villareal 115, T234911, www.granhotelchiclayo.com.pe. With breakfast, a/c, pool, safe car park, changes dollars, jacuzzi, entertainments, restaurant. Recommended.
AL-A Garza, Bolognesi 756, T228172, www.garza hotel.com. A/c, excellent bar/restaurant, pool, car park, tourist office in lobby provides maps, information in English, car hire, jacuzzi. Recommended.
A Costa del Sol, Balta 399, T227272, www.costadelsolperu.com. New, smart, TV, non-smoking rooms, small pool, sauna, jacuzzi. *Páprika* restaurant, good value Sunday buffets US$7.50, vegetarian options.
B Inca, Av L González 622, T235931, www.incahotel.com. A/c, restaurant, garage, comfortable, helpful.
C América, Av L González 946, T229305, americahotel@latinmail.com. Comfortable, restaurant, good value but laundry and breakfast expensive. Recommended.
C Hostal Santa Victoria, La Florida 586, Urb Santa Victoria, T/F225074. Hot water, good, restaurant, free parking, exchange cash dollars, 15-20 mins' walk from the centre.
C-D El Sol, Elías Aguirre 119, T232120, hotelvicus@ hotmail.com. Hot water, big rooms, restaurant, pool by car park, TV lounge, comfortable, good value.
D Europa, Elías Aguirre 466, T237919, hotele uropachiclayo@terra.com.pe. Hot water **F** without bath (single rooms small), restaurant, good value.

D Kalu, Pedro Ruíz 1038, near the Mercado Modelo, T/F228767, hotelkalu@terra. com.pe. Comfortable, TV, laundry, safe, good.
D Mochicas, Torres Paz 429, T237217, mochcas1@ hotmail.com. Fan, TV, helpful, good service.
D Paracas, Pedro Ruíz 1046, near Mercado Modelo, T221611. TV, good value. Recommended.
D Paraíso, Pedro Ruíz 1064, near the Mercado Modelo, T/F222070, hparaiso@terramail. com.pe. Also comfortable and well- appointed, but can be noisy. Recommended.
D Pirámide Real, MM Izaga 726, T224036. Compact but spotless, good value, very central.
D Santa Rosa, L González 927, T224411. Hot water, fan, laundry, international phone service, breakfast downstairs in snack bar, good value.
E Hospedaje San Eduardo, 7 de Enero 235, Urb San Eduardo, T209423. A 10-min walk from the centre; no sign other than a little notice in the window. Family run, large rooms, quiet, safe, cable TV, hot water.
E Hostal Sicán, MM Izaga 356, T237618. With breakfast, hot water, TV, comfortable, welcoming and trustworthy.
E Sol Radiante, Izaga 392, T237858, robertoiza@ mixmail.com. Cold water, comfortable, TV, pleasant.
F-G pp Adriático, Av Balta 1009. Fairly clean but basic, cold water, the best of a bad bunch on Balta.
F-G Hostal San José, Juan Cuglievan 1370, 1 block from the Mercado Modelo. Basic, acceptable, cold water. There are many other cheap hotels near the Mercado Modelo.

● Eating

Chiclayo *p1134, map p1135*
For delicious, cheap ceviche, go to the Nativo
stall in the Mercado Central, a local favourite.
₦₦₦ **Fiesta**, Av Salaverry 1820 in 3 de Octubre
suburb, T201970. Local specialities, first class.
₦₦₦ **El Huaralino**, La Libertad 155, Santa Victoria.
Wide variety, international and creole.
₦₦ **Las Américas**, Aguirre 824. Open 0700-0200,
good service. Recommended.
₦₦ **Hebrón**, Balta 605. For more upmarket than
average chicken, but also local food and *parrilla*,
good salads. Also does an excellent breakfast
and a good buffet at weekends.
₦₦ **Kaprichos**, Pedro Ruíz 1059, T232721.
Chinese, delicious, huge portions.
₦₦ **Roma**, Izaga 706. Wide choice, also has a bar.
₦₦ **Romana**, Balta 512,T223598. First-class food,
usually good breakfast, popular with locals.
₦₦ **Tradiciones**, 7 de Enero Sur 105, T221192.
Open 0900-1700 daily. Good variety of local
dishes, including ceviche, and drinks, nice
atmosphere and garden, good service.
₦ **Boulevar**, Colón entre Izaga y Aguirre.
Good, friendly, *menú* and à la carte.
₦ **Café Astoria**, Bolognesi 627. Open 0800-1200,
1530-2100. Breakfast, good value *menú*.
₦ **Govinda**, Balta 1029. Good vegetarian,
open daily 0800-2000.
₦ **Mi Tía**, Aguirre 650, just off the plaza. Large
portions, very popular at lunchtime, but
not good for breakfast.
₦ **La Parra**, Izaga 746. Chinese and creole,
parrillada, very good, large portions.
₦ **La Plazuela**, San José 299, Plaza Elías Aguirre.
Good food, seats outside.
Greycy, Elias Aguirre y Lapoint. Good ice cream.
D'Onofrio, Balta y Torres Paz. Great ice cream.
La Panadería, Lapoint 847. Good choice of
breads, including *integral*, snacks and soft drinks.

● Festivals and events

Chiclayo *p1134, map p1135*
6 Jan: Reyes Magos in Mórrope, Illimo and
other towns, a recreation of a medieval pageant in
which pre-Columbian deities become the Wise
Men. On **4 Feb**: Túcume devil dances (see below).
Holy Week, traditional Easter celebrations and
processions in many villages. **2-7 Jun**: Divine
Child of the Miracle, Villa de Etén. **27-31 Jul**:
Fexticum in Monsefú, traditional foods, drink,
handicrafts, music and dance. **5 Aug**: pilgrimage
from the mountain shrine of **Chalpón** to **Motupe**,
90 km north of Chiclayo; the cross is brought down
from a cave and carried in procession through the
village. At **Christmas** and **New Year**, processions
and children dancers (*pastorcitos* and *seranitas*)

can be seen in many villages,
eg **Ferreñafe, Mochumi, Mórrope**.

▲ Activities and tours

Chiclayo *p1134, map p1135*
The Lambayeque's museums, Sipán and Túcume
(see Around Chiclayo) can easily be visited by
public transport. Expect to pay US$18-25 pp for a
3-hr tour to Sipán; US$25-35 pp for Túcume and
Lambayeque (5 hrs); Sicán is US$45-55 pp for a
full-day tour including Ferreñafe and Pómac; to
Zaña and coastal towns, US$35-55 pp. These prices
are based on 2 people; discount for larger groups.
Indiana Tours, Colón 556, T222991,
www.indianatoursperu.com. Daily tours to
nearby archaeological sites and museums and a
variety of other daily and extended excursions
with 4WD vehicles; English and Italian spoken,
Handbook users welcome, reservations for
national flights and hotels.
Peruvian Treasures Explorer, Balta 398,
T233435. Archeological tours, helpful.

● Transport

Chiclayo *p1134, map p1135*
Air José Abelardo Quiñones González airport 1
km from town, T233192; taxi from centre US$1.
Daily flights to/from **Lima** and **Piura** with Lan.
Bus No terminal terrestre; most buses stop
outside their offices on Bolognesi. To **Lima**, 770
km, US$12 and US$22 for *bus cama*: Civa, Av
Bolognesi 714, T223434; **Cruz del Sur**, Bolognesi
888, T225508; **Ormeño**, Haya de la Torre 242, 2
blocks south of Bolognesi; **Las Dunas**, Bolognesi
block 1, luxury service with a/c, toilet, meals, leaves
at 2000; **Línea**, Bolognesi 638, T222221, *especial*
and *bus cama* service; **Móvil**, Av Bolognesi 195,
T271940 (goes as far as Tarapoto); **Oltursa**, ticket
office at Balta e Izaga, T237789, terminal at Vicente
de la Vega 101, T225611; **Transportes Chiclayo**,
Av L Ortiz 010, T237984, www.transportes
chiclayo.com. Most companies leave from 1900
onwards. To **Trujillo**, 209 km, with **Emtrafesa**, Av
Balta 110, T234291, almost hourly from 0530-2015,
US$3.35, and *Línea*, as above. To **Piura**, US$3.65,
Línea and Transportes Chiclayo leave hourly
throughout the day; also Emtrafesa and buses
from the Cial/Flores terminal, Bolognesi 751,
T239579. To **Sullana**, US$4.35. To **Tumbes**,
US$5.75, 9-10 hrs; with **Cial**, or **Transportes
Chiclayo**; **Oltursa** overnight service at 2015, arrives
0530 (good for crossing to Ecuador the next day),
seats can be reserved, unlike other companies
which tend to arrive full from Lima late at night.
Many buses go on to the **Ecuadorean border** at
Aguas Verdes. Go to the *Salida* on Elías Aguirre,
mototaxi drivers know where it is, be there by

1900. All buses stop here after leaving their terminals to try and fill empty seats, so discounts may be possible. To **Cajamarca**, 260 km; **Línea**, normal 2200, US$4.55, *bus cama* 2245 US$7.60; many others from Tepsa terminal, Bolognesi y Colón, eg **Días**, T224448. To **Chachapoyas**, 460 km, US$7.60-10.60: **Civa** 1730 daily, 10-11 hrs; **Turismo Kuélap**, in Tepsa station, 1830 daily, **Móvil**, address above, at 1900. To **Jaén**, US$4.55-7.50: eg **Móvil**, **Civa**, and **Transcade**. To **Tarapoto**, 18 hrs, US$18.20, with **Móvil**, also Tarapoto Tours, Bolognesi 751, T636231.

Taxi Mototaxis are a cheap way to get around; US$0.50 anywhere in city, but they are not allowed in the very centre.

Monsefú and the coast *p1134*
Combis to **Monsefú** cost US$0.45 from Amazonas y 7 de Enero, beyond the Mercado Modelo; colectivos from 7 de Enero y Arica. The **ports** may be visited on a half-day trip. Combis leave from Vicente de la Vega entre Angamos y Av L Ortiz, Chiclayo, to Pimentel; others leave from González y L Prado, 20 mins, US$0.25. Colectivos to Etén leave from 7 de Enero y Arica.

Lambayeque *p1134*
Colectivos from **Chiclayo** US$0.45, 25 mins, from Pedro Ruíz at the junction with Av Ugarte. Also **Brüning Express** combis from Vicente de la Vega entre Angamos y Av L Ortiz, every 15 mins, US$0.20.

Sipán *p1136*
Buses to Sipán leave from Terminal Este Sur-Nor Este on C Nicolás de Piérola, east of the city (take a taxi, US$1; area can dangerous), US$0.45, 1 hr.

Túcume *p1136*
Combis from **Chiclayo**, Angamos y Manuel Pardo, US$0.70, 45 mins; a combi from Túcume to the village of **Come** passes the ruins, hourly. Combi Túcume- **Lambayeque**, US$0.35, 25 mins.

Ferreñafe and Sicán *p1136*
Colectivos from Chiclayo to the centre of Ferreñafe leave every few mins from 8 de Octubre y Sáenz Peña, 15 mins, U$0.30, take a mototaxi to the museum, US$0.50. Alternatively, combis for Batán Grande depart from the Terminal Nor-Este, Av N de Piérola in Chiclayo, and pass the museum every 15-20 mins, 20 mins, US$0.50.

❶ Directory

Chiclayo *p1134, map p1135*
Banks Beware of counterfeit bills, especially among street changers on 6th block of Balta, on Plaza de Armas and 7th block of MM Izaga. **BCP**, Balta 630, no commission on TCs for US$100 or more (US$12 commission if less), cash on Visa, Visa ATM. **Banco Wiese Sudameris**, Balta 625, changes Amex TCs, cash advance on Visa card, ATM for Visa/Plus. **Interbank**, on Plaza de Armas, no commission on TCs, OK rate, good rates for cash, Mastercard ATM. All open Sat morning. **Cultural centres** Alianza Francesa, Cuglievan 644, T237571, www.universidadperu.com/ alianza-francesa- de-chiclayo.php. **Instituto de Cultura Peruano-Norteamericana**, Av Izaga 807, T231241, icpnachi@mail.udep.edu.pe. **Instituto Nacional de la Cultura**, Av L González 375, T237261, occasional poetry readings, information on local archaeological sites, lectures, etc. **Internet** Lots of places, particularly on San José and Elías Aguirre, average price US$0.60 per hr. **Medical services** Ambulance: Max Salud, 7 de Enero 185, T234032, maxsalud@ telematic.edu.com. **Post offices** On 1 block of Aguirre, 6 blocks from Plaza. **Telephones** Telefónica, headquarters at Aguirre 919; bank of phone booths on 7th block of 7 de Enero behind Cathedral for international and collect calls. Phone card sellers hang around here.

Piura and around → *Phone code: 073. Colour map 3, grid A1. Population: 324,500.*

A proud and historic city, Piura was founded in 1532, three years before Lima, by the conquistadores left behind by Pizarro. The city has two well-kept parks, Cortés and Pizarro (with a statue of the *conquistador*, also called Plaza de las Tres Culturas), and public gardens. Old buildings are kept in repair and new buildings blend with the Spanish style of the old city. Three bridges cross the Río Piura to Castilla, the oldest from Calle Huancavelica, for pedestrians (Puente San Miguel), another from Calle Sánchez Cerro, and the newest from Avenida Panamericana Norte, at west end of town. The winter climate, May-September, is very pleasant although nights can be cold and the wind piercing; December to March is very hot.

Tourist offices Information at the tourist office on the Plaza de Armas, next to Municipio ① *open Mon-Fri 0900-1300, 1600-2000, Sat 0900-1300. Municipal website, www.munipiura.gob.pe.* **Dirección Regional de Turismo** ① *Av Fortunato Chirichigno, Urb San Eduardo, T327351,* at the north end of town, helpful when there are problems, open 0900-1300, 1600-1800. *Indecopi* is also here, T304045.

Sights

Standing on the **Plaza de Armas** is the **cathedral**, with gold covered altar and paintings by Ignacio Merino. A few blocks away is **San Francisco** (under reconstruction), where the city's independence from Spain was declared on 4 January 1821, nearly eight months before Lima. **María Auxiliadora** stands on a small plaza on Libertad, near Avenida Sánchez Cerro. Across the plaza is the **Museo de Arte Religioso**. The birthplace of Admiral Miguel Grau, hero of the War of the Pacific with Chile, is **Casa Museo Grau** ① *Jr Tacna 662, opposite the Centro Cívico, 0800-1300, 1600-1900, free.* It is a museum and contains a model of the *Huáscar*, the largest Peruvian warship in the War of the Pacific, which was built in Britain. It also contains interesting old photographs. Interesting local craftwork is sold at the **Mercado Modelo**. The small but interesting **Museo Municipal Vicús**, with archaeological and art sections, is on Sullana, near Huánuco. **Catacaos**, 12 km to the southwest of Piura, is famous for its *chicha* (quality not always reliable), *picanterías* (local restaurants, some with music, *La Chayo*, San Francisco 493,

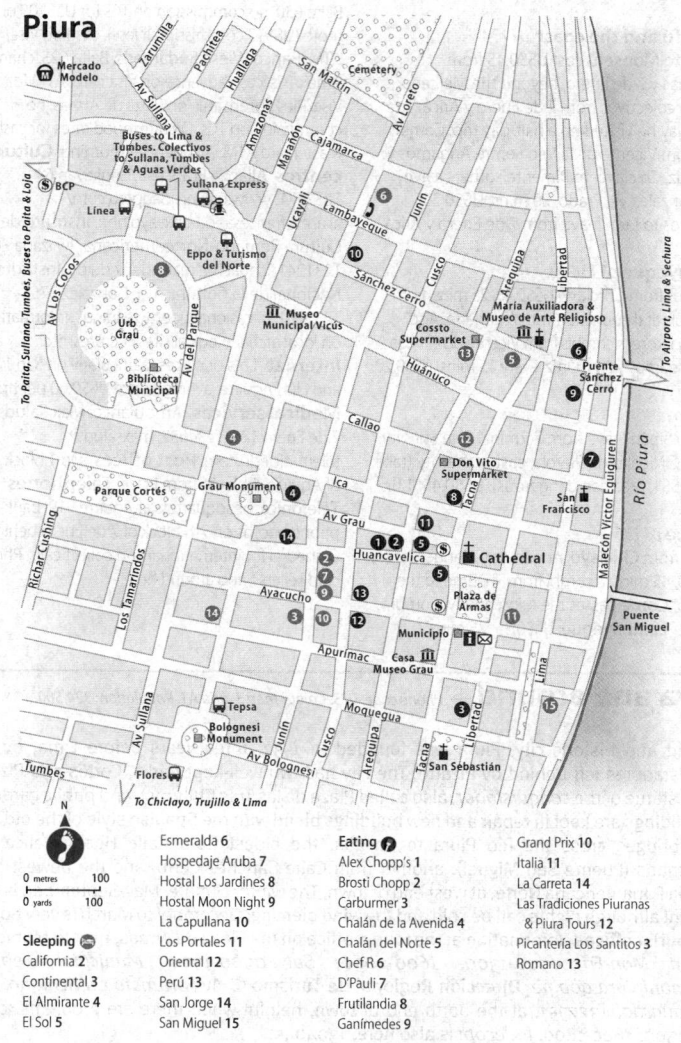

Piura

Sleeping
California **2**
Continental **3**
El Almirante **4**
El Sol **5**

Esmeralda **6**
Hospedaje Aruba **7**
Hostal Los Jardines **8**
Hostal Moon Night **9**
La Capullana **10**
Los Portales **11**
Oriental **12**
Perú **13**
San Jorge **14**
San Miguel **15**

Eating
Alex Chopp's **1**
Brosti Chopp **2**
Carburmer **3**
Chalán de la Avenida **4**
Chalán del Norte **5**
Chef R **6**
D'Pauli **7**
Frutilandia **8**
Ganímedes **9**

Grand Prix **10**
Italia **11**
La Carreta **14**
Las Tradiciones Piuranas
  & Piura Tours **12**
Picantería Los Santitos **3**
Romano **13**

Peru Piura & around

recommended), tooled leather, gold and silver filigree jewellery, wooden articles, straw hats (expensive) and splendid celebrations in Holy Week. About 2 km south of Catacaos is the **Narihualá** archaeological site.

The port for the area, 50 km from Piura, **Paita** exports cotton, cotton seed, wool and flax. Built on a small beach, flanked on three sides by a towering, sandy bluff, it is connected with Piura and Sullana by paved highways. It is a fishing port with a long history. Several colonial buildings survive, but in poor condition. Bolívar's mistress, Manuela Sáenz, lived the last 24 years of her life in Paita, after being exiled from Quito. She supported herself until her death in 1856 by weaving, embroidering and making candy, after refusing the fortune left her by her husband. Her house is on the road into town, adjoining a petrol station. On a bluff looming over Paita is a small colonial fortress built to repel pirates. Paita was a port of call for Spanish shipping en route from Lima to Panama and Mexico. It was a frequent target for attack, from Drake (1579) to Anson (1741).

● Sleeping

Piura *p1139, map p1140*
AL Los Portales, Libertad 875, Plaza de Armas, T321161. Includes breakfast and welcome cocktail, attractively refurbished, the city's social centre, elegant, a/c, hot water, pleasant terrace and patio, nice pool.
C Esmeralda, Loreto 235, T/F327109, www.hotelesmeralda.com.pe. Hot water, fan (**B** with a/c), comfortable, good, restaurant.
C San Miguel, Lima 1007, Plaza Pizarro, T305122. Modern, comfortable, TV, café.
D El Almirante, Ica 860, T/F335239. With fan, modern, owner is knowledgeable about the Ayabaca area.
D Perú, Arequipa 476, T333421. With fan, safe, laundry service, cold water, modern small rooms, all meals in restaurant are extra.
D San Jorge, Jr Loreto 960, T327514. With fan, cheaper without cable TV, hot water.
D El Sol, Sánchez Cerro 411, T324461. Hot water, small pool, snack bar, parking, accepts dollars cash or TCs but won't change them. Recommended.
E La Capullana, Junín 925, T321239. Some cheap single rooms, welcoming.
E Continental, Jr Junín 924, T334531. Some rooms with bath, comfortable, no breakfast.
E Hostal Los Jardines, Av Los Cocos 436, T326590. Hot water, TV, laundry, parking, good value.
E Hostal Moon Night, Junín 899, T336174. Comfortable, modern, spacious, **F** without bath or TV, cold water, good value.
F pp California, Jr Junín 835, upstairs, T328789. Shared bath, own water-tank, mosquito netting on windows, roof terrace, brightly decorated. Recommended (some short stay, though).
F Hospedaje Aruba, Junín 851, T303067. Small rooms but comfortable, shared bath, fan on request. Recommended.
F Oriental, Callao 446, T304011. Cheaper without bath and fan, good value but very noisy, TV in reception. Convenient for buses

● Eating

Piura *p1139, map p1140*
Local specialities *Majado de Yuca*, manioc root with pork; *Seco de Chavelo*, beef and plantain stew; and *Carne Seca*, sun-dried meat. Its best-known sweet is the delicious *natilla*, made mostly of goats' milk and molasses. Try *pipa fría*, chilled coconut juice drunk from the nut with a straw.
♥♥♥ Carburmer, Libertad 1014. Very good lunches and dinners, also pizza.
♥♥♥ Picantería Los Santitos, in the same precinct is Carburmer. Lunch only, wide range of traditional dishes in a renovated colonial house.
♥♥ La Carreta, Huancavelica 726. Popular for roast chicken.
♥♥ Chef R, Sánchez Cerro 210, near the bridge. Seafood.
♥♥ Alex Chopp's, Huancavelica 538. A la carte dishes, seafood, fish, chicken and meats, beer, popular at lunchtime.
♥♥ Brosti Chopp, Arequipa 780. Similar, but with lunch *menú* for US$1.45.
♥♥ Grand Prix, Loreto 395. Good food, reasonable prices.
♥♥ Romano, Ayacucho 580. Popular with locals, extensive menu, excellent set meal for US$1.55. Recommended.
♥♥ Las Tradiciones Piuranas, Ayacucho 579. Regional specialities, nice atmosphere, art gallery.
♥ Frutilandia, Jr Tacna 376. Good *menú*, good for breakfast, juices, ices and desserts.
♥ Ganímedes, Lima 440. A good vegetarian restaurant, very popular set lunch, à la carte is slow but well worth it, try the excellent yoghurt and fruit.
♥ Italia, Grau 172. For breakfasts, snacks, desserts and juices.

Cafés
Chalán del Norte several branches for sweets, cakes and ice cream, Tacna 520 on Plaza de Armas, Grau 173 and 450 (*Chalán de la Avenida*).
D'Pauli, Lima 541. Also for sweets, cakes and ice-cream, good.

▲ Activities and tours

Piura *p1139, map p1140*
Piura Tours, C Ayacucho 585, T328873,
piuratours@mail.udep.edu.pe. The manager
Mario speaks very good English.

⊖ Transport

Piura *p1139, map p1140*
Air Capitán Guillermo Concha airport is in
Castilla, 10 mins from the centre by taxi (US$1).
It has gift shops and two car rental agencies
(see below). Airport tax US$3.50. 2 daily
flights with Lan to **Lima** via **Chiclayo**.
Bus Most companies are on Av Sánchez Cerro,
blocks 11, 12 and 13. To **Lima**, 1,038 km, 14-16 hrs,
from US$7 (eg *Tepsa*), on the Panamericana Norte.
Most buses stop at the major cities on route;
Flores, Av Loreto 1210, T306664; **Ittsa**, Sánchez
Cerro 1142, T333982 (US$17.15 on top floor,
US$21.50 on lower floor); **Línea**, Sánchez Cerro
1215, T327821; **Tepsa**, Loreto 1198, T323721. To
Chiclayo, 190 km, 3 hrs, US$3.65, several buses
daily. Also several daily buses to **Trujillo**, 7 hrs, 487
km, US$7, to travel by day change in Chiclayo. To
Tumbes, 282 km, 4½ hrs, US$4.80, several buses
daily, eg **Cruz del Sur** (La Libertad 1176, T337094,
also to Lima), **Cial** (Bolognesi 817, T304250) and
Emtrafesa (Los Naranjos 235, T337093, also to
Chiclayo and Trujillo); also colectivos, US$5.75. To
Talara, US$2, 2 hrs, with **Eppo**, T331160. To **Paita**,
Trans Dora, Sánchez Cerro 1391, every 20 mins, 1
hr, US$0.75; also from Paita terminal on Av
Gullman, just off Sánchez Cerro. To **Máncora**,
US$3.15, 3 hrs, with **Eppo**.

To Ecuador: To **Machala** and **Guayaquil**,
the fastest route if you are heading directly to
Quito, **CIFA**, Los Naranjos y Sánchez Cerro
(cuadra 11-12) opposite Emtrafesa, T305925, 5 a
day, Machala US$6, 6 hrs, Guayaquil US$10, 9 hrs.
Otherwise, go to Tumbes and travel on from
there for the Aguas Verdes crossing. To **Loja**, the
best option if you want to visit the southern or
central highlands of Ecuador, **Transportes Loja**,
Sánchez Cerro 1480, T309407, at 0930, 1300,

2130, 2230, US$8, 8 hrs, to **Macará** US$4. Or
Unión Cariamanga, Sánchez Cerro (cuadra 18) y
Av Vice, Urbanización Santa Ana, T990 0135
(mob), at 1330 and 2000. Alternatively take a bus
to **Sullana**, 38 km, 30 mins (US$0.45), **Eppo,**
Sullana Express and **Turismo del Norte**, all on
1100 block of Sánchez Cerro; also colectivos
(US$1). To **La Tina** on the Ecuadorean frontier, is
a further 128 km, 1¾ hrs, US$2.85. It's best to take
an early bus to Sullana (start at 0430, leave when
full), then a colectivo (see under Sullana).

Catacaos *p1140*
Combis From **Piura** to Catacaos leave when
full from bus terminal at block 12 of Av Sánchez
Cerro, US$0.25, 20 mins.

❻ Directory

Piura *p1139, map p1140*
Banks BCP, Grau y Tacna. Cash and Visa and
Amex TCs (US$12 commission), cheques
changed in the mornings only, has ATM. BBV
Continental, Plaza de Armas. Changes Amex TCs
with US$10 commission. Interbank, Grau 170,
changes Visa TCs, ATM for Visa, Mastercard and
AmEx. *Casas de cambio* are at Arequipa 722, and
Ica 429 and 460. Street changers can be found on
Grau outside *BCP*. Look out for cheating when
changing money (forged dollar and sol notes,
rigged calculators, etc). **Car hire** Vicús,
T342051, www.vicusr entacar.com; Servitours,
T342008, www.servi tourspiura.com. Both at
airport, US$50 per day for a small vehicle; they
also provide transfers to Punta Sal US$80.
Consulates Honorary British Consul, c/o
American Airlines, Hancavelica 223, T305990,
F333300. Honorary German Consul, Jutta Moritz
de Irazola, Las Amapolas K6, Urb Miraflores,
Casilla 76, T332920, F320310. **Internet** At
Arequipa 728 and others in the centre. 10
machines in the Biblioteca Municipal, Urb Grau,
US$0.60 per hr. **Post offices** Libertad y
Ayacucho on Plaza de Armas. **Telephones**
Loreto 259, national and international phone and
fax. Also at Ovalo Grau 483.

North to Ecuador

Sullana, built on a bluff over the fertile Chira valley, is a busy, modern place 38 km north of
Piura. Here the Pan-American Highway forks. To the east it crosses the Peru-Ecuador border at La
Tina and continues via Macará to Loja and Cuenca. The excellent paved road is very scenic. The
more frequently used route to the border is the coastal road which goes from Sullana northwest
towards the Talara oilfields, and then follows the coastline to Máncora and Tumbes.

Border at La Tina-Macará The border crossing is problem-free; **Peruvian immigration** is
open 24 hours and officials are helpful. Go to Peruvian immigration at the end of the bridge,
get a stamp, walk across and then go to Ecuadorean immigration. There are no customs

searches (vehicles, including colectivos, are subject to full searches, though). There are banks at each side for changing cash only, Monday-Friday; rates are a little better in Macará. There is one *hospedaje* and several eating places on the road down to the bridge.

New border crossing beyond Ayabaca East from Piura or Sullana is Ayabaca (225 km northeast of Piura; several *hostales*), home of El Señor Cautivo de Ayabaca whose shrine is the most famous in northern Peru. From Ayabaca a rough road with great views goes via Samanguilla 64 km to **Espíndola**, a tiny frontier village with a satellite phone, a simple comedor and no other services. A very poor road continues 2 km to Peruvian immigration at the small international bridge over the Río Espíndola, open 24 hours. An equally poor road climbs 1 km to the hamlet of El Salado on the Jimbura-Zumba road. It's a further 4 km to Jimbura, with Ecuadorean immigration, open 24 hours (one basic residencial, a comedor, shops change soles at poor rates). There is regular transport from Jimbura to Loja via Amaluza.

To the border at Tumbes Talara, 112 km north of Piura, is the main centre of the coastal oil area. It has a State-owned, 60,000 barrel-a-day oil refinery and a fertilizer plant. Set in a desert oasis 5 km west of the Panamericana, the city is a triumph over formidable natural difficulties, with water piped 40 km from the Río Chira. La Peña beach, 2 km away, is unspoilt. There is a range of hotels and many cheap restaurants on the main plaza.

Máncora and Punta Sal
Máncora, a small, attractive resort stretching along 3 km of the Highway is a popular with young Limeños and as a stop-off for travellers, especially surfers, on the Peru-Ecuador route. Bathing is safe on a long, sandy beach and excellent beaches are being developed to the south (eg Las Pocitas). Surfing on this coast is best November-March and boards and suits can be hired from several places on Avenida Piura, US$1.50 each per hour. It is 32 km north of the port of Cabo Blanco. At 22 km further north of Máncora, at Km 1187, is the turn-off for **Punta Sal Grande**, 2 km, at the south end of beautiful Playa Punta Sal, a 3 km long sandy beach. The town is very upmarket, but quiet in the low season. Taxi from Máncora, 20 minutes, US$9, mototaxi 40 minutes, US$6, otherwise access is from a place called El Arco on the main road to Tumbes. **Zorritos**, 27 km south of Tumbes, is an important fishing centre with a good beach. At **Caleta La Cruz** is the only part of the Peruvian coast where the sea is warm all year, 16 km southwest of Tumbes. It was here that Pizarro landed in 1532. Regular colectivos, US$0.30 each way.

Tumbes → *Phone code: 072. Colour map 3, grid A1. Population: 34,000.*
ⓘ *Mosquito repellent is a must for Tumbes area. The water supply is poor.*
The most northerly of Peruvian towns (141 km north of Talara, 265 km north of Piura) has a long promenade, the Malecón Benavides, beside the banks of the Río Tumbes. It is decorated with arches and a monstrous statue called El Beso (the Kiss). There are some old houses in **Calle Grau**, and a colonial public library in the **Plaza de Armas** with a small museum. The **cathedral**, dating in its present incarnation from 1903, was restored in 1985. There are two pedestrian malls, Paseo de Los Libertadores on Bolívar and Paseo de la Concordia on San Martín, both leading north from the Plaza de Armas. Tumbes is a garrison town: do not photograph the military or their installations - they will destroy your film and probably detain you. **Tourist office**: Centro Cívico ⓘ *Bolognesi 194, 2nd level, on the plaza, T524940, tumbes@mincetur.gob.pe. Open 0800-1300, 1400-1800.* Helpful, provides map and leaflets. **Pronaturaleza**, Avenida Tarapacá 4-16, Urb Fonavi, T523412.

Excursions from Tumbes The Río Tumbes is navigable by small boat to the mouth of the river, an interesting two hour trip with fantastic birdlife and mangrove swamps. The **Santuario Nacional los Manglares de Tumbes** protects 3,000 ha of Peru's remaining 4,750 ha of mangrove forest. It contains examples of all five species of mangroves as well as being home to over 200 bird species, especially pelicans. It is best visited via the CECODEM centre near Zarumilla, but arrange day before with *Pronaturaleza* in Tumbes.

The **Parque Nacional Cerros de Amotape** protects 90,700 ha of varied habitat, but principally the best preserved area of dry forest on the west coast of South America. Species that may be sighted include the black parrot, white-backed squirrels, foxes, deer, tigrillos, pumas and white-winged turkeys. *Inrena* permission is needed to enter the area (which **Pronaturaleza** in Tumbes can arrange). All water must be carried which is why most visitors choose to visit by tour. Access is via the road which goes southeast from the Pan-American Highway at Bocapán (Km 1,233) to Casitas and Huásimo, it takes about two hours by car from Tumbes, and is best done in the dry season (July-November). Also access via Quebrada Fernández from Máncora and via Querecotilo and Los Encuentros from Sullana.

The **Zona Reservada de Tumbes** (75,000 ha) lies northeast of Tumbes between the Ecuadorean border and Cerros de Amotape National Park. It protects dry equatorial forest and tropical rainforest. Wildlife includes monkeys, otters, wild boars, small cats and crocodiles. The Río Tumbes crocodile, which is a UN Red-data species, is found at the river's mouth, where there is a small breeding programme (near Puerto Pizarro), and in its upper reaches. Access from Tumbes is via Cabuyal, Pampas de Hospital and El Caucho to the Quebrada Faical research station or via Zarumilla and Matapalo. The best accessible forest is around El Narango, which lies beyond the research station.

Border with Ecuador Immigration for those leaving Peru is at Zarumilla, at an office 4 km before the border; for those entering Peru, immigration is at the end of the international bridge, west side, at Aguas Verdes. PNP is on the east side. The border is open 24 hours a day and passports can be stamped on either side of the border at any time. There are virtually no customs formalities at the border for passengers crossing on foot, but spot-checks sometimes take place Lots of kids help with border crossing.

Peruvian immigration formalities are reported as relatively trouble-free, but if you are asked for a bribe by police officers on the Peruvian side of the international bridge, be courteous but firm. You should ask for 90 days. Porters on either side of the border charge too much; don't be bullied and check price beforehand. **Exchange** Changing money on either side of the border is a risky business. Rates are poor and cheating is common. Beware forged notes, especially soles. Change only enough money to get to a town with a reputable bank or cambio.

● Sleeping

North to Ecuador *p1142*
Sullana
Take care by the market. Do not arrive in town at night.
A Hostal La Siesta, Av Panamericana 400, T/F502264. At entrance to town, hot water, fan, **B** with cold water, pool, restaurant, laundry.
D El Churre, Tarapacá 501, T/F507006. TV, laundry, café. Recommended.
E Hospedaje San Miguel, C J Farfán 204, T502789. **F** without bath, basic, helpful, good showers, staff will spray rooms against mosquitoes, cafetería.
E Hostal Lion's Palace, Grau 1030, T502587. With fan, patio, pleasant, quiet, no breakfast.

Máncora and Punta Sal *p1143*
Máncora
The better hotels are at the southern end of town. Prices can increase by up to 100% in high season (Dec-Mar).
B Puerto Palos, along the old Pan-American Highway south of town (10 mins by mototaxi, US$1.45), T858199, www.puertopalos.com. Excellent, small, nice pool overlooking the ocean. Restaurant is good but expensive. Recommended.
B-C Las Olas on the beach in block 1 of Piura, T858109. Smart, cabin-style rooms, hammocks and gardens, half and full-board rates available.

(**El Mar** in the same area has the same prices and facilties.)
C Punta Ballenas, south of Cabo Blanco bridge at the south entrance to town, T858136. **B** in high season, lovely setting on beach, garden with small pool, includes breakfast, expensive restaurant. Recommended.
D Hostal Casa Azul del Turista, Av Piura 224, T858126. New, family-run, TV, roof terraces giving sea views. Recommended (but not at weekends or holiday times due to its proximity to the Sol y Mar disco).
D Sausalito, Piura block 4, T858058. Comfortable, quieter rooms at back, some rooms without windows, breakfast included.
E Sol y Mar, Piura block 2, on beach, T858106 (ask for Coqui Quiroga). With bath, fan and mosquito repellent extra, basic, restaurant, shop, internet café (very slow connection), occasionally host parties, noisy disco till 0600 at weekends and holidays.
E-F Hospedaje Crillon, Paita 168, 1 block back from Panamericana in centre, T858001. Basic rooms with 4 or more beds, shared bath, plenty of water. Recommended.

Punta Sal
C Los Delfines, T320251, near the beach at the entrance to Playa Punta Sal. Shared bathroom, clean, nice rooms, restaurant open in high season, meals on request in low season,

vegetarian available, Canadian-run, full board **AL** , more during high season for full board, **A** for a room only in high season. **C** pp **Hospedaje El Bucanero**, at the entrance to Playa Punta Sal, set back from the beach, T540118, htlelbucaneroptasal@hotmail.com. With a variety of rooms, pool, restaurant, bar, gardens and billiards, popular with travellers, great view.
D Huá, on the beach at the entrance to Playa Punta Sal, T540023, www.huapuntasal.com. **B** in the high season. A rustic old wooden building, pleasant terrace overlooking ocean, discount for IYHF card holders, camping permitted on the beach beside the hotel, meals available.
D pp **Las Terrazas**, opposite Sunset Punta Sal, T964 0353, lasterrazaspuntasal@yahoo.com. One of the more basic and cheaper hotels in Punta Sal, restaurant has sea view, some rooms better than others, not all with own bath.

E pp **Casa Grillo Centro Ecoturistico Naturista**, Los Pinos 563, between Bocapán and Los Pinos, 30 km from Tumbes, T/F072-544222, casagrillo@yahoo.es. Take colectivo from Tumbes market to Los Pinos, or get off bus on Pan-American Highway at Km 1236.5, Youth Hostel, excellent restaurant including vegetarian, great place to relax, 6 rooms for up to 4, made of local materials, shared bath, hot water, laundry, surfing, scuba diving, fishing, cycling, trekking, horse riding, camping available. Recommended.

Tumbes *p1143, map p1145*
Av Tumbes is still sometimes referred to by its old name of Teniente Vásquez. At holiday times it can be very difficult to find a room.
A Costa del Sol, San Martín 275, Plazuela Bolognesi, T523991, ventastumbes@costadel solperu.com. Best in town (but avoid noisy front rooms), hot water, minibar, fan, restaurant, good food and service, parking extra, nice garden with pool, helpful manager.
D Lourdes, Mayor Bodero 118, 3 blocks from main plaza, T522966. Fan, roof restaurant, slow service. Recommended.
D Roma, Bolognesi 425 Plaza de Armas, T524137. With fan, pleasant, convenient.
E Amazonas, Av Tumbes 317, T525266. With fan, noisy, water unreliable morning.
E Elica, Tacna 319, T523870. With fan, quiet.
E Estoril, Huáscar 317, 2 blocks from main plaza, T521360. With cold water, good, welcoming, discount for long stay.
E Hostal Tumbes, Grau 614, T522203. With cold water, fan, good value. Recommended.
E Toloa 1, Av Tumbes 430, T523771. With fan, safe, helpful.
E Toloa 2, Bolívar 458, T524135. With fan, OK.
F Sudamericano, San Martín 130, Paseo de la Concordia. Shared bath, basic but good value. Many other cheap hotels by the market.

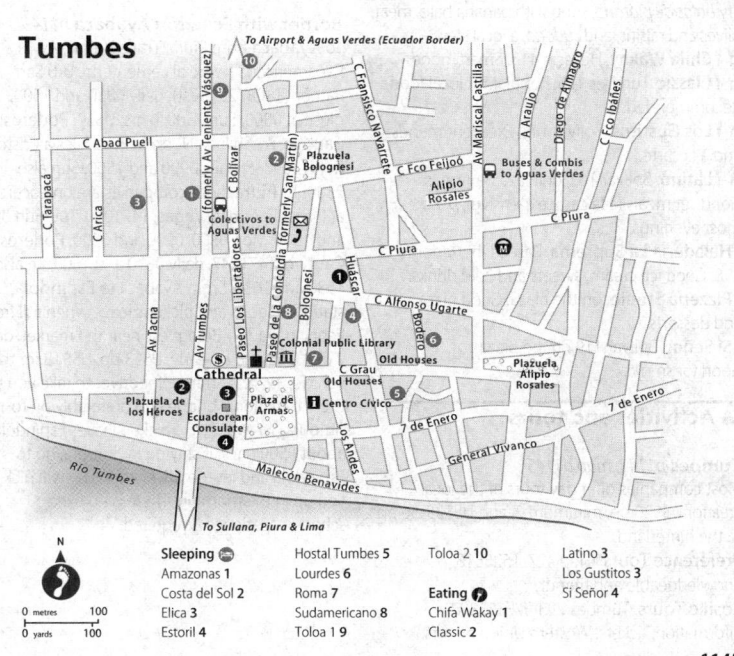

Tumbes

Border with Ecuador *p1144*
Zarumilla/Aguas Verdes

If stuck overnight in the border area there is a hotel in Aguas Verdes:

E **Hostal Francis**, Av República de Perú 220, T561177, OK. Aguas Verdes also has phone booths and airline ticket offices. There are 4 hotels in Zarumilla, at Km 1290 on the Pan-American Highway, 5 km south of Aguas Verdes.

❶ Eating

Máncora and Punta Sal *p1143*
Máncora

Café La Bajadita, is the best place in the evening to hang out, eat chocolate cake or *manjarblanco* and listen to rock and reggae.
Laguna Camp, T9401 5628, www.vivamancora.com/lagunacamp. 100m from the sea near the new breakwater, thatched roofs, hammocks, delicious food, breakfast, lunch and dinner, pizza and barbeque nights, has cabins sleeping up to 6 people, helpful. Recommended.
Stephanies, adjoining *Sol y Mar* hotel, overlooking beach. Serves *fuentes*, huge plates big enough for 2.

Also good are **La Espada** and **Don Pedro** on the highway. Several internet cafés on the highway.

Tumbes *p1143, map p1145*

There are inexpensive restaurants on the Plaza de Armas, Paseo de la Concordia and near the markets. Try *bolas de plátano*, soup with banana balls, meat, olives and raisins, and *sudado*, a local stew.
♛-♛ **Chifa Wakay**, Huáscar 413. Smart, good.
♛-♛ **Classic**, Tumbes 185. Popular for local food. Recommended.
♛-♛ **Los Gustitos**, Bolívar 148. Excellent menús and à la carte.
♛-♛ **Latino**, Bolívar 163, on Plaza de Armas. Good set meals (à la carte expensive), *peña* most evenings.
♛ **Heladería La Suprema**, Paseo Libertadores 298. Good ice cream, sweets and cold drinks.
♛ **Pizzería Studio**, on the plaza. Good pizza and desserts.
♛ **Sí Señor**, Bolívar 119 on the plaza. Good for snacks.

▲ Activities and tours

Tumbes *p1143, map p1145*

Most companies offer day tours of the local area for US$20 pp, minimum 2, and US$35-50 pp to the hinterland.
Preference Tours, Grau 427, T525518. Knowledgeable and friendly.
Rosillo Tours, Tumbes 293, T/F523892. Information, tickets, Western Union agents.

❸ Transport

Sullana *p1142*

Bus Several bus companies including **Ormeño** use a new Terminal Terrestre. To **Tumbes**, 244 km, 4-5 hrs US$5, several buses daily. To **Chiclayo** and **Trujillo** see under Piura. To **Lima**, 1,076 km, 14-16 hrs, US$9-18, several buses daily, most coming from Tumbes or Talara, luxury overnight via Trujillo with **Ittsa** (T501710) US$18, also with **Cruz del Sur** and **Ormeño**. To **Talara, Eppo** and **Emtrafesa**, Comercio, 1 block from Lama block 3, hourly, Eppo are faster but more expensive, US$1.25.
To **Máncora**, *Eppo*, 5 a day, 2½ hrs, US$3.

Border with Ecuador:
La Tina-Macará *p1142*

Buses leave frequently from Ecuadorean side for Loja, so if you are not taking the through bus (see under Piura), you can go from Sullana to Loja in a day. From the border to Sullana, cars may leave before they are full, but won't charge extra.
Combis Leave from Sullana to the international bridge from Terminal Terrestre La Capullana, off Av Buenos Aires, several blocks beyond the canal. They leave when full, US$2.85 per person, 1¾ hrs. It's best to take a taxi or mototaxi to and from the terminal. From the border to Macará is 4 km: walk over the bridge and take one of the pick-ups which run from the border (10 mins, US$0.30, or US$1.25 for whole car).

Border with Ecuador: Ayabaca *p1143*

To **Ayabaca** from Piura, **Trans Vegas**, Av Panamericana frente al cementerio, Urb San Ramón, T308729 (best), daily 0830 and 1500, plus Sat 0800, Sun 2300, 6 hrs, US$7. **Poderoso Cautivo**, Av Sullana Norte next to Iglesia Cristo Rey, T309888, daily 0900 and 1500, Sun also 2300. To **Piura**, both companies are on Cáceres at Plaza de Armas. **Vegas**, T471080, Tue-Sun 0830 and 1500, Mon 0800, 0900 and 1500. **Poderoso Cautivo**, T471247, daily 0830 and 1500, Fri also 1530 and 1630. From Ayabaca to **Espíndola**, station wagons and pickups leave when full from Leoncio Prado y Bolognesi, near the market, only 1 or 2 a day, so go early, US$3 pp, US$18 for the vehicle, 3½ hrs. Arrange for driver to take you to the international bridge and preferably on to Jimbura. To Ayabaca, a pickup leaves Espíndola about 0500 daily; if staying in Jimbura, go to Espíndola and let the driver know, he will pick you up in the morning. There is no fixed schedule, patience is required.

Talara *p1143*
Bus To **Tumbes**, 171 km, 3 hrs, US$3.50,
most coming from Piura and stopping at
major towns going north; several daily.
To **Piura**, 2 hrs, US$1.75.

Máncora and Punta Sal *p1143*
Bus Talara to **El Alto** (Cabo Blanco), 32 km, 30
mins, US$0.75, continuing to Máncora, 28 km, 30
mins, US$0.75. To **Talara/Sullana/ Piura** with
Eppo, 5 a day, US$3; to **Tumbes** (and points in
between), combis leave when full, US$1.50, 2 hrs.

Tumbes *p1143, map p1145*
Air Daily flights to and from **Lima** (Wayra
Perú, Av Tumbes Norte 270, T525020).
Bus Daily to and from **Lima**, 1,320 km, 18-20
hrs, depending on stopovers, US$12 (normal
service), US$25 (*Cruz del Sur*), US$34 (*Cruz del
Sur VIP* service). Several buses daily, all on Av
Tumbes: **Civa**, No 518, T525120; **Ormeño**, Av
Tumbes s/n, T522228; **Cruz del Sur**, No 519,
T522627; **Trans Chiclayo**, No 466, T525260.
Cheaper buses usually leave 1600-2100, more
expensive ones 1200-1400. Except for luxury
service, most buses to Lima stop at major cities
en route. Tickets to anywhere between Tumbes
and Lima sell quickly, so if arriving from Ecuador
you may have to stay overnight. Piura is a good
place for connections in the daytime. To **Sullana**,
244 km, 3-4 hrs, US$4.50, several buses daily. To
Piura, 4-5 hrs, 282 km, US$4.80 with **Trans
Chiclayo, Cruz del Sur, El Dorado** (Piura 459,
T523480) 6 a day; **Comité Tumbes/Piura**
(Tumbes N 308, T525977), US$7 pp, fast cars,
leave when full, 3½ hrs. To **Chiclayo**, 552 km, 6
hrs, US$5.75, several each day with *Cruz del Sur,
El Dorado*, and others. To **Trujillo**, 769 km, 10-11
hrs, US$7.15-14.35, *Ormeño, Cruz del Sur,
El Dorado, Emtrafesa*. Transport to the Border
with Ecuador, see below.

**Santuario Nacional los Manglares de
Tumbes** *p1143*
Combis From Tumbes market to **Zarumilla**,
20 mins, US$0.50. In Zarumilla hire a mototaxi
for the 7 km run (20 mins, US$1.50) to the
Centre. A 2½-hr guided visit costs US$12,
for up to 6 people.

Border with Ecuador *p1144*
Zarumilla/Aguas Verdes
Between Tumbes and the border Colectivos
leave from block 3 of Av Tumbes, US$1 pp or US$6
to hire car, and wait at the immigration office
before continuing to the border, 30-40 mins.
Colectivos can cross the bridge, taxis cannot (so
don't hire a Peruvian taxi to take you into Ecuador).

Note: Make sure the driver takes you all the way
to the border and not just as far as the complex 4
km south of the bridge. Returning from the
border, some colectivos leave from near the
bridge, but charge more than others which leave
2 blocks down along main street by a small plaza
opposite the church. Combis leave from the
market area along Mcal Castilla across from Calle
Alipio Rosales, US$0.50, luggage on roof. They
leave passengers at the immigration office. Old,
slow city buses ply the same route as combis,
US$0.40. Combis and buses return to Tumbes
from an esplanade 3 blocks east of the colectivo
stop, but don't wait at immigration. All vehicles
only leave when full. From the border to
Zarumilla by mototaxi costs US$0.50 pp. Taxi to
Tumbes, including wait at immigration, US$6.
Entering Peru It is easier to take a colectivo
to Tumbes and then a bus south, rather than
trying to get on a bus from the border to a
southern destination. When driving into Peru,
vehicle fumigation is not required, but there is
one outfit who will attempt to fumigate your
vehicle with water and charge US$10. Beware of
officials claiming that you need a *carnet* to
obtain your 90-day transit permit; this is not
so, cite Decreto Supremo 015-87-ICTI/TUR.
Frequent road tolls between Tumbes and Lima,
approximately US$1 each.

---

❶ Directory

Sullana *p1142*
Banks BCP, San Martín 685, will change cash
and TCs. *Casas de cambio* and street changers on
San Martín by Tarapacá. **Internet** At San Martín
798 and 847 (World Net, US$0.60 per hr), and at
Av José de Lama 125 and corner with Tarapacá.
Post offices At Farfán 326. **Telephones**
Telephone and fax at Miró Quesada 213. **Useful
addresses** Immigration: Grau 939.

Tumbes *p1143, map p1145*
Banks BBV Continental, Bolívar 121, cash and
Amex TCs only, US$5 commission. Cambios
Internacionales, Av Bolívar 161, cash only, good
rates. Money changers on the street (on Bolívar,
left of the Cathedral), some of whom are
unscrupulous, give a much better rate than banks
or *cambios*, but don't accept the first offer you
are given. None changes TCs. **Consulates**
Ecuadorean Consulate, Bolívar 155, Plaza de
Armas, T523022, 0900-1300 and 1400-1630,
Mon-Fri. **Internet** Widely available in many
cheap cafés and major hotels. **Post offices**
San Martín 208. **Telephones** San Martín 210.

Northern Highlands

Leaving the Pacific coast behind, you climb in a relatively short time up to the Sierra. It was here, at Cajamarca, that the defeat of the Incas by the Spaniards began, bringing about cataclysmic change to this part of the world. But, unlike this well-documented event, the history of the Incas' contemporaries and predecessors has to be teased out of the stones of their temples and fortresses, which are shrouded in cloud in the 'Eyebrow of the Jungle'.

Trujillo to Cajamarca

To the northeast of Trujillo is Cajamarca, an attractive colonial town surrounded by lovely countryside and the commercial centre of the northern mountain area. It can be reached by the old road via Huamachuco and Cajabamba, or by paved road via Pacasmayo. The former road is being improved, but, for cyclists especially, is lonely, taking a couple of days by bus (as opposed to 7-8 hours via Pacasmayo, see below), but it is more interesting, passing over the bare puna before dropping to the Huamachuco valley.

Huamachuco → *Colour map 3, grid B2. Altitude: 3,180 m. Internet access at S Carrión 740.*
This colonial town formerly on the royal Inca Road, 181 km from Trujillo, has the largest main plaza in Peru, with fine topiary, and a controversial modern **cathedral**. There is a colourful **Sunday market**, with dancing in the plaza, and the Founding of Huamachuco festival, second week in August, with spectacular fireworks and the amazing, aggressive male dancers, called *turcos*. **Museo Municipal Wamachuko** ① *Sucre 195, Mon-Fri 0900-1300, 1500-1900, plus holiday weekends, free,* displays artefacts found at nearby Cerro Amauta (a hill-top system of wells and water worship) and **Marca Huamachuco** ① *free, access is via a poor vehicle road or a mule track (preferable for walking), off the road to Sanagorán, there is an archway at the turnoff, 5 km from Huamachuco, mototaxi to turnoff US$2; combis to Sanagorán in the morning.* These hilltop pre-Inca fortifications rank in the top 10 archaeological sites in Peru. They are 3 km long, dating back to at least 300 BC though many structures were added later. Its most impressive features are: El Castillo, a remarkable circular structure with walls up to 8 m high located at the highest point of the site, and El Convento complex, five circular structures of varying sizes towards the northern end of the hill. The largest one has been partially reconstructed.

The extensive Huari ruins of **Wiracochapampa** are 3 km north of town, 45 minutes' walk. Although much of the site is overgrown the Waman Raymi festival is held here on the second Sunday in August (a northern version of Cuzco's Inti Raymi).

Cajabamba is a small market town and a useful stop-over point between Cajamarca and Huamachuco.

Pacasmayo → *Colour map 3, grid A2. Population: 12,300.*
Pacasmayo, 102 km north of Trujillo and port for the next oasis north, is the main road connection from the coast to Cajamarca. The paved 180 km road branches off the Pan-American Highway soon after it crosses the Río Jequetepeque (bus Pacasmayo-Cajamarca US$4.30, five hours; to Chiclayo US$1.70, two hours). The river valley has terraced rice fields and mimosas may often be seen in bloom, brightening the otherwise dusty landscape.

A few kilometres northwest on the other side of Río Jequetepeque are the ruins of **Pacatnamú** comparable in size to Chan Chán pyramids, cemetery and living quarters of nobles and fishermen, possibly built in the Chavín or Moche periods. Taxi bus to Guadalupe, 10 km from ruins, then another taxi, US$20 to the site. Micros run in summer. Where the Pan-American Highway crosses the Jequetepeque are the well-signed ruins of **Farfán** (separate from those of Pacatnamú, but probably of the same period; no explanations at the site).

Cajamarca → *Phone code: 076. Colour map 3, grid B2. Population: 117,500. Altitude: 2,750 m.*
At Cajamarca Pizarro ambushed and captured Atahualpa, the Inca emperor. This was the first showdown between the Spanish and the Incas and, despite their huge numerical inferiority, the Spanish emerged victorious, executing Atahualpa in the process.

The nearby **Yanacocha gold mine** ① *www.yanacocha.com.pe*, has brought new wealth to the town (and major ecological concerns and social problems) and Cajamarca is the hub of tourism development for the whole of the northwest via the *Circuito Turístico Nororiental* (Chiclayo-Cajamarca-Chachapoyas). **Tourist offices**: **Dirección Regional de Turismo** and **Instituto Nacional de Cultura** ① *in the Conjunto Monumental de Belén, Belén 631, T822997, cajamarca@mitinci.gob.pe, www.inccajamarca.org, Mon-Fri 0730-1300, 1415-1900*. **Cámara Regional de Turismo (Caretur)** ① *José Gálvez 771, T831579, caretur cajamarca@regionalcaj.zzn.com*. The University tourist school has an office at Del Batán 289, T821546, offering free advice and leaflets, open daily 0700-1345. The **Indecopi** office is at Amalia Puga 516, T823315, caraujo@indecopi.gob.pe. **Tourist police** ① *Av 13 de Julio s/n, T363042*. All museums are closed on Tuesday but open at weekends.

Complejo Belén ① *0900-1300, 1500-1730, Sat-Sun 0900-1230, US$1.20, valid for more than 1 day, a ticket is also valid for the Cuarto de Rescate, a guide for all the sites costs US$2.85 (US$5.75-8.50 for guides in other languages).* The complex comprises the tourist office and Institute of Culture, a beautifully ornate church, considered the city's finest. See the inside of the dome, where eight giant cherubs support an intricate flowering centrepiece. In the same courtyard is the **Museo Médico Belén**, which has a collection of medical instruments. Across the street is a maternity hospital from the colonial era, now the **Archaeological and Ethnological Museum** (Junín y Belén). It has a range of ceramics from all regions and civilizations of Peru. The **Cuarto de Rescate** ① *entrance at Amalia Puga 750* is not the actual ransom chamber but in fact the room where Atahualpa was held prisoner. A red line on the wall is said to indicate where Atahualpa reached up and drew a mark, agreeing to have his subjects fill the room to the line with treasure. The chamber is roped off but can be viewed from the outside. Pollution and weather have had a detrimental effect on the stone.

You can also visit the plaza where Atahualpa was ambushed and the stone altar set high on **Santa Apolonia hill** ① *US$0.30, take bus marked Santa Apolonia/Fonavi, or micro A,*

Cajamarca

where he is said to have reviewed his subjects. There is a road to the top, or you can walk up from Calle 2 de Mayo, using the steep stairway. The view is worth the effort, especially at sunrise (but go in a group).

The **Plaza de Armas**, where Atahualpa was executed, has a 350-year- old fountain, topiary and gardens. The **Cathedral**, opened in 1776, is still missing its belfry, but the façade has beautiful baroque carving in stone. On the opposite side of the plaza is the 17th century **San Francisco Church**, older than the Cathedral and with more interior stone carving and elaborate altars. The attached **Museo de Arte Colonial** ① *Mon-Sat 1430-1800, US$0.85, entrance is unmarked on far left corner of church*, is filled with colonial paintings and icons. The guided tour of the museum includes entry to the church's spooky catacombs.

The city has many old colonial houses with garden patios, and 104 elaborately carved doorways: see the **Bishop's Palace**, across the street from the Cathedral; the **palace of the Condes de Uceda**, at Jr Apurímac 719 (now occupied by BCP bank); and the **Casa Silva Santiesteban** (Junín y 2 de Mayo).

Museo Arqueológico Horacio H Urteaga ① *Del Batán 289, Mon-Fri 0700-1445, free, donations accepted*, of the Universidad Nacional de Cajamarca, has objects of the pre-Inca Cajamarca and other cultures. The university maintains an experimental arboretum and agricultural station, the **Museo Silvo-agropecuario** ① *Km 2.5 on the road to Baños del Inca*, with a lovely mural at the entrance.

Excursions About 6 km away are the sulphurous thermal springs of **Los Baños del Inca** ① *0500-1900, closed Mon and Fri, US$0.60, combis marked Baños del Inca cost US$0.30, 15 mins, taxis US$1.40.* The water temperature is 78° C. Atahualpa tried the effect of these waters on a festering war wound and his bath is still there. The complex is renewed regularly, with gardens and various levels of accommodation (see Sleeping, below). The main baths have units A, B, C (US$1); Turistas (US$1.20); and Imperial (US$1.50); all with private tubs and no pool. Sauna US$3, massage US$3 (take your own towel; soaps are sold outside). Only spend 20-30 minutes maximum in the water; obey instructions; many of the facilities allow bathers in shifts, divided by time and/or sex.

Other excursions include **Llacanora**, a typical Andean village in beautiful scenery (13 km southeast; nice walk downhill from Baños del Inca, two hours). **Ventanillas de Otusco** ① *0800-1800, US$1, combi US$0.15*, part of an old pre-Inca cemetery, has a gallery of secondary burial niches. There are good day walks in this area; local sketch maps available.

A road goes to **Ventanillas de Combayo** ① *occasional combis on weekdays; more transport on Sun when a market is held nearby, 1 hr*, some 20 km past the burial niches of Otusco. These are more numerous and spectacular, being located in an isolated, mountainous area, and distributed over the face of a steep 200 m high hillside.

Cumbe Mayo, a *pampa* on a mountain range, is 20 km southwest of Cajamarca. It is famous for its extraordinary, well-engineered pre-Inca channels, running for 9 km across the mountain tops. It is said to be the oldest man-made construction in South America. The sheer scale of the scene is impressive and the huge rock formations of Los Frailones ('big monks') and others with fanciful names are strange indeed. On the way to Cumbe Mayo is the Layzón ceremonial centre. There is no bus service; guided tours run from 0900-1300 (recommended in order to see all the pre-Inca sites); taxi US$15. To walk up takes 3-4 hours (take a guide, or a tour, best weather May-September). The trail starts from the hill of Santa Apolonia (Silla del Inca), and goes to Cumbe Mayo straight through the village and up the hill; at the top of the mountain, leave the trail and take the road to the right to the canal. The walk is not difficult and you do not need hiking boots. Take a good torch. The locals use the trail to bring their goods to market.

The **Porcón** rural cooperative, with its evangelical faith expressed on billboards, is a popular excursion, 30 km northwest of Cajamarca. It is tightly organized, with carpentry, bakery, cheese and yoghurt-making, zoo and vicuñas. A good guide helps to explain everything. If not taking a tour, contact **Cooperativa Agraria Atahualpa Jerusalén** ① *Chanchamayo 1355, Fonavi 1, T/F825631, granjaporcon@yahoo.com.*

Some 103 km east of Pacasmayo is the mining town of Chilete, 21 km north of which on the road to San Pablo is **Kuntur Wasi**. The site was devoted to a feline cult and consists of a pyramid and stone monoliths. Extensive excavations are under way and significant new discoveries are being made (excellent site museum). There are two basic *hostales* in Chilete; very limited facilities.

● Sleeping

Huamachuco *p1148*

B-D Hostal Real, Bolívar 250, T441402, hostalreal@hotmail.com. New, TV, sauna, internet, many of the fittings are of wood. Recommended.

C-D Hostal Santa Fe, San Martín 297, T441019, santa_fe@hotmail.com. New, TV, hot water. Recommended.

D Hostal Colonial, Castilla 537, T441334, colonialgrill@yahoo.com. An attractive old colonial house, with hot water, TV, restaurant is good value. Recommended.

E Huamachuco, Castilla 354, on the plaza, T441393. With hot showers (**F** without), good value, has parking.

F pp Hostal Kaseci, Jr San Martín 756, T441571, kasecihostal@peru.com. Hot water, cable TV nice garden, peaceful, good value.

Cajabamba *p1148*

E Hostal La Casona, Jr Alfonso Ugarte 586, Plaza de Armas, T848385. Small rooms, electric shower, with restaurant.

E Jhoel, Jr Grau 633, T851653. With electric shower, patio, pleasant, good value.

Pacasmayo *p1148*

F Panamericano, Leoncio Prado 18, T522521. With private cold shower, basic, small, safe, reasonable restaurant downstairs.

F San Francisco, Leoncio Prado 21, T522021. Opposite and cleaner than the *Panamericano*, still basic, OK.

Cajamarca *p1148, map p1149*

L Posada del Puruay, 5 km north of the city, T827928, postmast@p-puruay.com.pe. A 17th-century *hacienda* converted into a 'hotel museum', high standards and beautiful colonial furnishings. Recommended.

A El Ingenio, Av Vía de Evitamiento 1611-1709, T/F827121. With solar-powered hot water, spacious, very relaxed, helpful. Highly recommended.

B El Cumbe Inn, Pasaje Atahualpa 345, T826858, elcumbeinn@terra.com. Includes breakfast and tax, comfortable, bright rooms, hot water, small gym, will arrange taxis. Recommended.

B El Portal del Marqués, Del Comercio 644, T/F828464, portalmarques@terra.com.pe. Attractive converted colonial house, TV, laundry, safe, parking, restaurant *De Caña y Barro*. Recommended.

C Los Balcones de la Recoleta, Amalia Puga 1050, T/F823302, hslosbalcones@ speedy.com.pe. Beautifully restored 19th-century house, central courtyard full of flowers, some

rooms with period furniture, breakfast extra.

C El Cabildo, Junín 1062, T/F827025, cabildoh@ latinmail.com. Includes breakfast, in historic monument with patio and modern fountain, full of character, elegant local decorations, comfortable, breakfast served, gym. Recommended.

C Casa Blanca, Dos de Mayo 446 on Plaza de Armas, T/F822141. Safe, nice old building with garden, good restaurant.

C Hostal Cajamarca, colonial house at Dos de Mayo 311, T822532, F821432. Sizeable rooms, hot water, food excellent in *Los Faroles* restaurant (T825113) which also has good local music and disco/pub. Recommended.

C Hostal Los Pinos, Jr La Mar 521, T/F825992, pinoshostal@yahoo.com. Includes breakfast, lovely colonial house with a new extension, decorated in old style, comfortable, other meals on request, very nice.

C Portada del Sol, Pisagua 731, T823395, PortadadelSol@terra.com.pe. Good rooms, tastefully decorated, hot water, comfortable beds. Also has *Portada del Sol Hacienda* at Km 6 on road to Cumbe Mayo (**C**). Good choice.

D Colonial Inn, Av Los Héroes 350, T825300, F827249. Hot water, cheaper with shared bath, English spoken, meals extra, convenient for buses.

D Hostal Becerra, Del Batán 195, T827867. With hot water and TV, modern, pleasant, will store luggage until late buses depart.

D Hostal Los Jazmines, Amazonas 775, T821812, assado@hotmail.com. In converted colonial house with courtyard and café, 3 rooms with bath, 2 without, all funds go to handicapped children, some staff are handicapped, guests can visit the project's school and help. Recommended.

E Hostal Atahualpa, Pasaje Atahualpa 686, T827840. Hot water 0600-1100 (usually), a bit run-down but clean, meals extra, restaurant 0800-2200.

E Hostal Dos de Mayo, Dos de Mayo 585, T822527. Shared bath, hot water, simple, quite dark, good value *menú* in the restaurant.

E Hostal Pepe, Av Atahualpa 343, T821887. Most convenient for buses on Atahualpa. Cheaper without bath, hot water, no breakfast, noisy from all-night traffic.

E Hostal San Carlos, Av Atahualpa 324, T822600. Similarly convenient for buses on Atahualpa. Also cheaper without bath, hot water, no breakfast, noisy from all-night traffic.

F pp Casa pensión Karimbó, Dos de Mayo 700, T829888. Full board, shared rooms, some with bath.

Baños del Inca

L-AL Laguna Seca, Av Manco Cápac 1098, T894600, www.lagunaseca.com.pe. In pleasant surroundings with thermal streams (atmospheric misty mornings), private hot thermal baths in rooms, swimming pool with thermal water, good restaurant, bar, health spa with a variety of treatments (US$10-48), disco, horses for hire. Recommended.

B Hostal Fundo Campero San Antonio, 2 km off the Baños road (turn off at Km 5), T/F838237, hcsanantonio@terra.com.pe. An old *hacienda*, wonderfully restored, with open fireplaces and gardens, 15 mins walk along the river to Baños del Inca, includes breakfast, riding on *caballos de paso*, own dairy produce, fruit and vegetables, catch your own trout for supper; try the *licor de sauco*. Recommended.

B-C Los Baños del Inca, address above. **B** bungalows with thermal water, TV, fridge; **D** pp Albergue Juvenil, IH, rooms with 3 bunk rooms, with bath, basic, overpriced. Camping possible. **C La Hispana**, Jr Manco Cápac 1031, T838489. Includes breakfast, new, with restaurant, swimming pool, gym, sauna, pool table, free internet, very comfortable. Recommended. **F La Notte**, Manco Cápac 450. Parking, nice patio, 2 thermal baths, sauna, large bare rooms with electric shower or thermal bath, basic, good value.

● Eating

Huamachuco *p1148*
† La Casona, Sánchez Carrión 294. Open daily 0700-0900, 1200-1430, 1900-2030. Serves good value and quality set meals and local dishes, popular. Also places on the Plaza de Armas.
† Bar Michi Wasi, San Román 461 on the plaza. Attractive bar and good place to meet locals who know the area.

Cajabamba *p1148*
†† Don Lucho, Jr Leoncio Prado 227. Good local trout and other à la carte dishes.
† Unnamed restaurant at Bolognesi 790. Good *almuerzo*.

Cajamarca *p1148, map p1149*
††† El Batán Gran Bufet de Arte, Del Batán 369, T826025. International dishes and nouvelle cuisine, good wine list and wide choice of drinks, local dishes on non-tourist menu, some of the staff speak English, live music at the weekend, art gallery on the 2nd floor.
††† Querubino, Amalia Puga 589. Mediterranean-style decoration with American and French influence in the cooking, specializes in fish, breakfasts, cocktails, coffees, expensive wines.

†† El Cajamarqués, Amazonas 770. Has good value *menú* available after 1300, elegant colonial building with garden full of exotic birds.
†† Don Paco, Amalia Puga 390. Opposite San Francisco. Typical, including novo andino and international dishes, tasty food, desserts, drinks.
†† Om-Gri, San Martín 360, near the Plaza de Armas. Good Italian dishes, small, friendly, French spoken, opens 1300 (1830 Sun).
†† El Pez Loco, San Martín 333. Recommended for fish.
†† Pizzería El Marengo, Junín 1201. Good pizzas and warm atmosphere, T828045 for delivery.
†† Salas, Amalia Puga 637, on the main plaza. A Cajamarca tradition, open 0700-2200. Fast service, excellent local food (try their *cuy frito*), best *tamales* in town; also has a branch in Baños del Inca (1100-1600, Fri-Sun and holidays).
††-† El Zarco, Jr Del Batán 170, T823421. Open Sun-Fri 0700-2300. Very popular, also has short *chifa* menu, good vegetarian dishes, excellent fish, popular for breakfast; also *El Zarco Campestre*, off road to airport, use own produce, recommended for pork.
† Chifa Central, Del Batán 149. Great value, authentic Chinese.

Cafés

El Capulí, Jr Junín, in the Complejo Belén. Open 0900-1300, 1500-2000 (2400 Fri-Sat). Coffee, drinks, sandwiches and snacks. Lovely atmosphere for a quiet coffee.
Casa Luna, 2 de Mayo 334. Café with couches, also has a bar, live music Fri night, closed Sun.
Cascanuez, Amalia Puga 554. Great cakes, extensive menu including *humitas*, breakfasts, ice creams and coffees.
Heladería Holanda, Amalia Puga 657 on the Plaza de Armas, T830113. Dutch-owned, easily the best ice-creams in Cajamarca, 50 flavours (but not all on at the same time), try *poro poro*, *lúcuma* or *sauco*, also serves coffee. Also has a branch in Baños del Inca.
Sanguchón.com, Junín 1137. Best burgers in town, sandwiches, also popular bar.

The area is renowned for its cheese, *manjar blanco*, butter, honey, etc: try **El Tambo**, Dos de Mayo 576, **La Collpa**, Romero 124, **Los Alpes**, Junín 965, or **Porcón**'s shop (see Excursions) on Chancahmayo 1355, take a mototaxi.

⊛ Festivals and events

Cajamarca *p1148, map p1149*
The **pre-Lent Carnival** is very spectacular and regarded as one of the best in the country; it is also one of the most raucous. In Porcón, 16 km to the northwest, **Palm Sunday** processions are worth seeing. On **24 Jun**: is San Juan in

Cajamarca, Chota, Llacanora, San Juan and Cutervo. An agricultural fair is held in **Jul** at Baños del Inca; on the first Sun in **Oct** is the **Festival Folklórico** in Cajamarca.

O Shopping

Cajamarca *p1148, map p1149*
Handicrafts Cheap, but bargain hard. Specialities including gilded mirrors and cotton and wool saddlebags (*alforjas*). Items can be made to order. The market on Amazonas is good for *artesanía*; also daily handicraft market on block 7 of Belén. There are several shops on 300 block of Dos de Mayo.

▲▲ Activities and tours

Cajamarca *p1148, map p1149*
Agencies around the Plaza de Armas offer trips to local sites and further (eg Kuntur Wasi, Kuélap), trekking on Inca trails, riding *caballos de paso* and handicraft tours. Average prices: Cumbe Mayo, US$6, Ventanillas de Otusco US$4.50, Porcón US$6.
Cajamarca Tours, Dos de Mayo 323, T/F822813 (also DHL, Western Union and flight reconfirmations).
Cajamarca Travel, 2 de Mayo 570, T830074, cajamarcatravel@hotmail.com.
Clarín Tours, Del Batán 161, T/F826829, clarintours@yahoo.com.
Cumbemayo Tours, Amalia Puga 635 on plaza, T/F822938, cumbemayotours@ usa.net. Guides in English and French.
Inca Baths Tours, Amalia Puga 667, T/F824310, incablaz@hotmail.com.
Socio Adventures, contact via www.socioadventures.com. They offer a Stove Trek Tour, where you donate materials and help a local family build a cooking stove while taking a 5-day, 5-night guided tour of the area. You stay at their lodge called the *Blur Poncho* near Chota, excellent food and accommodation.
Variservice, Silva Santisteban 134, T822228, variservice@infonegocio.net.pe. An office where flights can be reconfirmed.

⊕ Transport

Huamachuco *p1148*
Bus From **Trujillo**, 170 km, 6 hrs, US$6: **Agreda** (Balta 865) at 0800, 1300, 1800, **Gran Turismo** (Balta 798), 4 a day, **Negreiros** (Balta y Suárez), 0900, 1300. To **Cajabamba**, **Trans Los Andes**, Psje Hospital 109, 4 combis a day, 3 hrs, US$2.

Cajabamba *p1148*
Bus To/from **Cajamarca**, US$3, 4 hrs, several companies.

Cajamarca *p1148, map p1149*
Air To/from **Lima**: Aerocóndor (Dos de Mayo 323, T825674) daily, **Atsa** (2 de Mayo 570, T828642) daily except Sun, and **LC Busre**, daily except Sat. Airport 3 km from town; taxi US$1.50, mototaxi US$0.75.
Bus Buses in town charge US$0.15. To **Lima**, 856 km, 12-14 hrs, *económico* US$10-11.45, to US$14.30-20 on **Civa's** double-deckers, to US$20-26 for **Cruz del Sur's** luxury service (includes taxi to your lodging in Lima), several buses daily. The road is paved. To **Pacasmayo**, 189 km, 5-6 hrs, US$7, several buses and hourly colectivos. To **Trujillo**, 296 km, 6½ hrs, US$4.30-10, regular buses daily 0945-2230 most continue to Lima. To **Chiclayo**, 260 km, 4½ hrs, US$4.55-7.60, several buses daily; you have to change buses to go on to Piura and Tumbes. To **Celendín**, 112 km, 4 hrs, US$3.50, at 0700 and 1300 (**Atahualpa**), 0900 and 1300 (**Royal Palace's**, poor minibuses). The route follows a fairly good dirt road through beautiful countryside. Among the bus companies are: **Atahualpa**, Atahualpa 299, T823060 (Lima, Celendín, Cajabamba); **Civa**, Ayacucho 753, T821460 (Lima); **Cruz del Sur**, Atahualpa 600, T821737 (Lima). **Emtrafesa**, Atahualpa 447, T829663 (to Trujillo); **Línea**, Atahualpa 318, T823956 (Lima, Trujillo, Chiclayo). **Royal Palace's**, Atahualpa 339, T825855 (Lima, Trujillo, Celendín); **Rojas**, Atahualpa 405, T820548 (to Cajabamba, buses not coming from Lima); **Turismo Días**, Sucre 422, T828289 (to Lima, Chimbote, Trujillo, Chiclayo).
Taxi US$0.60 within city limits. Mototaxis US$0.30

O Directory

Cajamarca *p1148, map p1149*
Banks BCP, Apurímac 719. Changes Amex TCs without commission, cash advance on Visa, Mascercard and Amex, 0.5% commission, Visa and Mastercard ATM. **Banco Wiese**, Amazonas 650. Accepts Amex TCs, US$3 commission, cash advance and ATM for Visa and Mastercard. **Interbank**, 2 de Mayo 546, on Plaza. Accepts Visa TCs without commission if paid in soles, US$5 if in dollars, Visa ATM. **Telebanco 24 Horas** ATM (Visa) at the gas station next to Cial buses on Av Atahualpa. Dollars can be changed in most banks and travel agencies on east side of Plaza, but euros hard to change. Casa de cambio in **Casa del Artefacto** musical and electrical store at Amazonas 537. Good rates, cash only. **Street changers** on Jr Del Batán by the Plaza de Armas and at Del Batán y Amazonas. **Internet** There are cabins everywhere, US$0.35 per hr. **Post offices** Serpost, Amalia Puga 778. Open 0800-2045. **Telephones** Public phone offices can be found all over the centre.

Chachapoyas Region

Cajamarca is a convenient starting point for the trip east to the province of Amazonas, which contains the archaeological riches of the Chachapoyans, also known as Sachupoyans. Here lie the great pre-Inca cities of Vilaya (not yet developed for tourism), Cerro Olán and the immense fortress of Kuélap, among many others. The road is in terrible condition to Chachapoyas, and barely passable in the rainy season because of landslides. It follows a winding course through the north Andes, crossing the wide and deep canyon of the Río Marañón at Balsas. The road climbs steeply with superb views of the mountains and the valleys below. The fauna and flora are spectacular as the journey alternates between high mountains and low rainforest.

Celendín → *Phone code: 076. Colour map 3, grid B2.*
East from Cajamarca, this is the first town of note, with a pleasant plaza and cathedral. Festival 16 July (Virgen del Carmen). There is also an interesting local market on Sunday where you can buy cheap sandals and saddlebags. The **Museo Cultural Huauco** in the nearby village of Sucre ① *Bolívar 211, T552096,* is interesting for local history (friendly curator).

Leymebamba and around
There are plenty of ruins around this pleasant town, many of them covered in vegetation. The *Comité Turístico* on the plaza is the place to go for all information on how to reach sites, including Laguna de los Cóndores (see below), for guides and horse hire.

La Congona, a Chachapoyan site, is well worth the effort, with stupendous views. It consists of three hills: on the easterly, conical hill, the ruins are clustered in a small area, impossible to see until you are right above them. The other hills have been levelled. La Congona is the best preserved of three sites, with 30 round stone houses (some with evidence of three storeys) and a watch tower. The two other sites, El Molinete and Pumahuanyuna, are nearby. It is a brisk three hours' walk from Leymebamba along a clearly marked trail which starts at the end of the street with the hotels. All three sites can be visited in a day but a guide is advisable; ask in the Comité Turístico.

At **Laguna de los Cóndores** ① *museum Mon-Sat 0900-1200, 1400-1700, US$4.35, http://centromallqui.org.pe for information,* in 1996, a spectacular site consisting of six burial *chullpas*, containing 219 mummies and vast quantities of ceramics, textiles, woodwork, *quipus* and everyday utensils from the late Inca period, was discovered near a beautiful lake in a jungle setting. The trip to Laguna de los Cóndores takes 10-12 hrs on foot and horseback from Leymebamba, nine hours return. All the material was moved to a new museum at San Miguel (3 km south of Leymebamba - 30-40 minutes' walk, take the footpath and ask directions constantly, the road is much longer). It is beautifully laid-out, very informative and has a café.

The road to Chachapoyas (being paved) crosses the Utcubamba River, passes through **Palmira** and heads north. Before Puente Santo Tomás there is a turn-off which heads east beyond **Duraznopampa** to the small town of **Montevideo** (basic *hospedaje*). Another Chachapoyan site is **Cerro Olán**, reached by colectivo to San Pedro de Utac, a small village beyond Montevideo, then a 30 minute walk. From the Plaza a clear trail rises directly into the hills east of town to the ruins, which can be seen from the village. Here are the remains of towers which some archaeologists claim had roofs like mediaeval European castles.

Further north are the towns of **Yerbabuena** and **Puente Santo Tomás**, which is at the turn-off for the burial *chullpas* of **Revash**, of the Revash culture (AD 1250).

The attractive town of **Jalca Grande** (or La Jalca as it is known locally), at 2,800 m, lies between Montevideo and Tingo, up on the east side of the main valley. In the town itself, one block west of the Plaza de Armas, is the interesting and well-preserved Chachapoyan habitation of **Choza Redonda**, which was inhabited until 1964. There is one very basic *hostal*, otherwise ask the mayor. Take a torch.

Tingo → *Phone code: 041. Colour map 3, grid B2. Altitude: 1,800 m.*
Situated in the Utcubamba valley, 25 km from Leymebamba, 37 km south of Chachapoyas by road, much of this village was washed away in the floods of 1993. About 3½ km above Tingo in the hills is **Tingo Nuevo**. There is a petrol station here, the only one between Celendín and Chachapoyas.

Kuélap → *Altitude: 3,000 m.*

ⓘ *0800-1700, US$3 (50% discount for students with identification). A small Centro de Interpretaciones is open 0800-1630; it has a good model of the site. There is a toilet block. The ruins are locked; the guardian, Gabriel Portocarrero, has the keys and accompanies visitors. He is very informative.*

Kuélap is a spectacular pre-Inca walled city which was re-discovered in 1843. It was built over a period of 200 years, from AD 900 to 1100 and contained three times more stone than the Great Pyramid at Giza in Egypt. The site lies along the summit of a mountain crest, more than 1 km in length. The massive stone walls, 585 m long by 110 m wide at their widest, are as formidable as those of any pre-Columbian city. Some reconstruction has taken place, mostly of small houses and walls, but the majority of the main walls on both levels are original, as is the inverted, cone-shaped dungeon. The structures have been left in their cloud forest setting, the trees covered in bromeliads and moss, the flowers visited by hummingbirds. Guides are available; pay them what you think appropriate.

Chachapoyas → *Phone code: 041. Colour map 3, grid B2. Population: 25,000. Altitude: 2,234 m.*

The capital of the Department of Amazonas, founded in 1538, was an important crossroads between coast and jungle until the 1940s. Archaeological and ecological tourism in the 1990s is slowly bringing in new economic benefits. The modern cathedral stands on the spacious Plaza de Armas. **INC Museum** ⓘ *Ayacucho 904, Mon-Fri 0800-1300, 1400-1645, free,* contains a small collection of artefacts and mummies in display cases, with explanations in Spanish.
Tourist offices: iperú ⓘ *Jr Ortiz 588, Plaza de Armas, Chachapoyas, T777292, iperuchachapoyas@promperu.gob.pe, Mon-Sat 0800-1300, 1500-1900.* **Dirección Regional de Turismo** ⓘ *Jr Triunfo 1051, T041-778355, www.regionamazonas.gob.pe.*

Chachapoyas

Sleeping
Belén 1 *A1*
Casa Vieja 2 *A1*
Casona Monsante 12 *B2*
El Dorado 3 *A1*
El Tejado 4 *B2*
Gran Vilaya &
  Café de Guías 5 *B2*

Hostal El Danubio 7 *B1*
Johumaji 8 *B2*
Kuélap 9 *B1*
Laguna de los
  Cóndores 10 *A2*
Puma Urcu & Café Café 13 *B2*
Revash 11 *B2*

Eating
Chacha 1 *B2*
Chifa Chuy Xien 3 *B2*
Dulcería Santa Helena 11 *B2*
El Edén 5 *A2*

Kuélap 4 *B2*
Las Rocas 6 *A2*
La Tushpa 2 *B1*
Mari Pizza 10 *A2*
Mass Burguer 7 *B1*
Matalache 8 *B3*
Panadería San José 9 *B2*

Transport
Buses to Celendín 11 *A3*
Cars to Pedro Ruiz &
  Bagua Grande 2 *A2*
Civa Buses 3 *A2*

Colectivos to Pedro Ruiz,
  Huancas & Mendoza 1 *A2*
Combis to
  Leymebamba 4 *B2*
Combis to Pedro
  Ruiz 7 *A2*
Rollers colectivos to Kuélap
  & Santo Tomás 6 *A2*
San Juan de Luya
  Combis 8 *A2*
Trans Zelada 9 *A2*
Turismo Kuélap 10 *A1*

Huancas ① *colectivos leave from Jr Ortiz Arrieta y Libertad; 20 min, US$0.60 (0700-1800),* which produces rustic pottery, can be reached by a two-hour walk on the airport road. Walk uphill from Huancas for a magnificent view into the deep canyon of the Río Sonche.

Levanto was built by the Spaniards and was their first capital of the area, directly on top of the previous Chachapoyan structures. Although the capital was moved to Chachapoyas a few years later, Levanto retained its importance for a while, but is now an unspoilt colonial village overlooking the massive canyon of the Utcubamba River. Kuélap can, on a clear day, be seen on the other side of the rift. There are two small bar-bodegas in the village. A 30-minute walk from Levanto are the partly cleared ruins of **Yalape**, which seems to have been a massive residential complex, extending over many hectares. The local people will guide you to the ruins.

East of Chachapoyas

On the road to Mendoza via Pipus and Cheto are the pre-Inca ruins of **Monte Peruvia** (known locally as Purunllacta), hundreds of white stone houses with staircases, temples and palaces. The ruins have been cleared by local farmers and some houses have been destroyed. A guide is useful as there are few locals of whom to ask directions. If you get stuck in Pipus, ask to sleep at restaurant *Huaracina* or the police station next door. There are no hotels in Cheto but a house high up on the hill above the town with a balcony has cheap bed and board. The same family also has a house on the Plaza. The ruins are two-hour walk from Cheto.

The road east from Chachapoyas continues on to **Mendoza**, the starting point of an ethnologically interesting area in the Guayabamba Valley, where there is a high incidence of fair-skinned people.

Northwest of Chachapoyas

On a turn-off on the road 37 km from Chachapoyas to Pedro Ruíz, is **Lamud**, which is a convenient base for several interesting sites, such as San Antonio and Pueblo de los Muertos. About 20 minutes' drive south of Lamud, on the same road, is the village of **Luya**. From here, more sites can be reached: **Chipuric** and **Karajía**, where remarkable, 2½-m high sarcophagi set into an impressive cliff face overlook the valley (entry at Karajía US$1; mototaxi to sarcophagi US$1.65 round trip). In a lush canyon, 1½ hours' walk from the road to Luya is **Wanglic**, a funeral site with large circular structures built under a ledge. Nearby is a beautiful waterfall, a worthwhile excursion. Ask for directions in Luya. Best to take a local guide (US$3.50-5 a day). Buses and combis to Lamud and Luya are listed under Chachapoyas, Transport. The road is unpaved but in reasonable condition.

● Sleeping

Celendín *p1154*

E **Hostal Celendín**, Plaza de Armas, T855041. Hot water, TV, pleasant, good restaurant.
E **Loyer's**, José Gálvez 410, T855210. Cheaper without bath, patio, nice.
F **Maxmar**, Dos de Mayo 349. Cheaper without bath, hot shower extra, basic, clean, parking, good value, owner Francisco is very helpful.
F **Raymi Wasi**, Jr José Gálvez, beside La Reserve, T855374. With bath, hot water, TV, large rooms, has patio, quiet, clean, parking, good value.

Leymebamba *p1154*

D **Hostal La Casona**, Jr Amazonas 221, T770261. With hot water, breakfast available on request.
E **Hostal La Petaca**, Jr Amazonas 461, opposite the church, T770288. With bath, hot water.
E **Laguna de los Cóndores**, Jr Amazonas, half a block from plaza, T770271, www.chachapoyasperu.com.pe/hostallagunadeloscondores.htm. Cheaper without bath, warm water, a good choice.

Tingo *p1154*

F pp **Albergue León**, Jr Saenz Peña s/n, no sign, walk 50 m from police checkpoint to corner and turn left, it's the third house on left (right-hand door), T999390. Basic, run by Lucho León, who is very knowledgeable.

Kuélap *p1155*

Walking up from Tingo, the last house to the right of the track (**El Bebedero**) offers very basic rooms with bed, breakfast and evening meal from US$6, friendly, helpful). The **Instituto Nacional de Cultura** (INC) hostel is 100 m below the ruins, with a dorm for 12, US$1.75 pp, no running water, lovely setting, simple meals. Free camping.

Choctámal

F pp **Choctámal Lodge**, kuelap@msn.com. With sheets and towels, E in room with hot tub, G pp with own sleeping bag. Cold at night. Meals from US$1. Ask for Norma Cruz or reserve ahead with **Chachapoyas Tours** in Chachapoyas.

Chachapoyas *p1155, map p1155*
C Gran Vilaya, Ayacucho 755, T777664, hotelvilaya@viabcp.com. The best in town, comfortable rooms with firm beds, parking, English spoken, all services.
C-D Casona Monsante, Jr Amazonas 746, T777702, www.casonamonsante.com. Converted colonial house with patio, cable TV, cafeteria, breakfast US$1.50.
D Belén, Jr Ortiz Arrieta 540, T777830, www.hostalbelen.com.pe. On the plaza, modern, hot water, nicely furnished.
D Casa Vieja, Chincha Alta 569, T777353, www.casaviejaperu.com. In a converted old house, very nicely decorated, family atmosphere, hot water, cable TV, *comedor*, continental breakfast, internet and library. Recommended.
D Kuélap, Amazonas 1057, T777136, kuelphotel@hotmail.com. Hot water, cheaper without TV, cheaper still with shared bath and cold water, basic breakfast, parking.
D Puma Urcu, Jr Amazonas 833, T777871, hotelpumaurcu@peru.com. Modern, carpeted rooms, hot water, cable TV, *Café Café* next door, both hotel and café receive good reports.
D Revash, Grau 517, Plaza de Armas, T777391, www.chachapoyasperu.com.pe. Hot showers, patio, helpful, laundry, sells local items, good local information, restaurant, local tours sold. Recommended.
E El Dorado, Ayacucho 1062, T777047. Hot water, helpful.
E El Tejado, Grau 534, Plaza de Armas, T777654. On 1st floor, same entrance as restaurant, electric shower, laundry, aging but OK.
F Hostal El Danubio, Tres Esquinas 193 y Junín 584, Plazuela Belén, some distance from centre, T777337. Hot water, cheaper with shared bath and cold water, meals can be ordered in advance.
F Hostal Johumaji, Ayacucho 711, T777279, olvacha@ddm.com.pe. Hot water, cell-like, basic, cheaper without TV, meals extra.
F Laguna de los Cóndores, Salamanca 941, T777492. Very basic, shared bath, cold water.

Levanto *p1156*
F pp Levanto Lodge, kuelap@msn.com. **G pp** with own sleeping bag; hot shower, lounge with fireplace and kitchen, meals US$1. Small groups of are welcome and beds and bedding are provided in the mayor's office and village meeting hall.

Northwest of Chachapoyas
D Hostal Kuélap, Garcilaso de la Vega 452, on the plaza, Lamud. Cheaper without bath or hot water, basic. A few doors down is **Restaurant María**, cheap, excellent value, popular, the owner's son is a good local guide and charges around US$10 per day.

G Hostal Jucusbamba, Luya. Basic accommodation

❼ Eating

Celendín *p1154*
♥-♥ La Reserve, José Gálvez 313. Good quality and value.
♥ Bella Aurora, Gran 485. Good food.
♥ Jalisco, Jr Unión, on plaza. Good value breakfasts and other meals, but beware of overcharging.
♥ Santa Isabel, Jr José Gálvez 512. Clean, OK.

Leymebamba *p1154*
♥ Cely Pizza's, Jr La Verdad 530, 2 blocks from Plaza de Armas, opposite the health centre. Good value, 2-course set meals for US$2.50, regional food, pizzas take 20 mins unless you book in advance, vegetarian meals at 24 hrs notice, great for breakfast.
♥ El Sabor Tropical, 16 de Julio. Good chicken and chips, friendly.

Tingo *p1154*
Restaurant Kuélap, at the junction of the main road with the road on the south bank of the Río Tingo. Two other eating places.

Chachapoyas *p1155, map p1155*
♥♥-♥ El Tejado, upstairs at Grau 534, Plaza de Armas. Good quality, nice view and atmosphere.
♥ Chacha, Grau 541, Plaza de Armas. Popular with locals, but nothing out of the ordinary.
♥ Chifa Chuy Xien, Amazonas 848. Authentic Chinese, daily specials and à la carte.
♥ El Edén, Grau y Ayacucho. Vegetarian, good, large helpings, open by 0830, closed Sat afternoon/evening.
♥ Kuélap, Ayacucho 832. Good food.
♥ Mari Pizza, Ayacucho 912. Serves good pizza.
♥ Matalache, Amazonas y Grau. Good and very popular, huge portions.
♥ Panadería San José, Ayacucho 816. Good breakfasts and other meals, good regional snacks.
♥ Las Rocas, Ayacucho 932 on Plaza. Popular, local dishes, open Sun evening.
♥ Tinkuy Wasi, Prolongación Jr Kuélap, Barrio Santa Rosa, above El Mirador del Colorado. Very good regional food, in a country setting above town, lovely views.
♥ La Tushpa, Jr Ortiz Arrieta 753. Open for lunch and dinner. The best in town, international food, good meats, *platos criollos*, wine list, spotless kitchen. Recommended.
Café de Guías, in *Hotel Gran Vilaya*, serves snacks, meals and organic coffee, also has lots of local information, good.
Dulcería Santa Helena, Amazonas 800. Very good for sweets.

Mass Burguer, Ortiz Arrieta, Plaza de Armas.
Excellent juices, cakes, fruit salads.

▲▲ Activities and tours

Chachapoyas *p1155, map p1155*
Tours in the surrounding area include: city tour,
Levanto, Yalape (0800-1530, US$8.65), Kuélap
(see page 1155), Karajía, La Jalca, Leymebamba
(all full day, US$12-20, depending on distance
and number of passengers, including guide and
food), Revash (by vehicle to Santo Tomás, then
2-hr hike), Gran Vilaya or Laguna de los Cóndores
(4-5 days each, depending on size of group),
Mendoza (groups of 6 to 8).
Andes Tours, address as **Hostal Revash**. Daily
trips to Kuélap, other conventional tours to ruins
and caves in the area and trekking to Gran Vilaya,
Laguna de los Cóndores, etc, combining travel by
car, on horseback and walking.
Chachapoyas Tours, Grau 534, Plaza Armas, p 2
(Hotel El Tejado), T778078, www.kuelapperu.com,
or in the USA T1-866-396- 9582, Int T001-407-583
6786. Reliable, English-speaking guide, good
service. Recommended.
Vilaya Tours, c/o Gran Hotel Vilaya, Jr Grau 624,
T777506, www.vilayatours.com. All-inclusive
area treks throughout northern Peru catering
to international clientele, mostly booked
from abroad.
Excellent guides: Robert Dover is British,
contact him through **Vilaya Tours**, or the
Café de Guías (see Eating, above). Vilaya
Tours has a regular newsletter and also
work in conjunction with community
projects. Recommended.

⊖ Transport

Celendín *p1154*
Bus To **Cajamarca**, 107 km, 4-5 hrs:
with **Atahualpa**, 2 de Mayo 707, Plaza de
Armas, T855256, at 0700 and 1300 daily,
US$3; **Royal Palace's**, Jr Unión 333, Plaza de
Armas, at 0645 and 1300 daily, poor minibuses,
US$3.50. To **Chachapoyas** via Balsas and
Leymebamba, 12-15 hrs (may be much longer
in the rainy season, take warm clothing, food
and water): **Virgen del Carmen**, Cáceres 117,
and **Paraíso del Oriente** alternate on Sun
and Thu at 1100, US$8.50. Other local
transport leaves from the market area.

Leymebamba *p1154*
Bus From **Chachapoyas** to **Celendín** pass
Leymebamba about 3½ hrs after departure; no
guarantee of a seat. There are also combis,
minibuses and trucks.

Jalca Grande *p1154*
Combis from **Chachapoyas** at about 1300 daily
(except Sat); 3½ hrs, US$3.65; return from La Jalca
at 0500 daily.

Tingo *p1154*
For transport from **Chachapoyas** to Tingo, see
Chachapoyas, Transport. Several combis (from
0500) daily to Chachapoyas. Tingo to
Leymebamba takes 2 hrs, US$1.75.

Kuélap *p1155*
There are 4 options: 1) Take a tour from
Chachapoyas. 2) Hire a vehicle with driver in
Chachapoyas, US$35 per vehicle. 3) Take a
combi from Chachapoyas to María or Quizanga,
or to Choctámal, the mid-point on the 36 km
tortuous road from Tingo to Kuélap, which has
been improved (see under Chachapoyas for
details). You can stay in Choctámal with a family
or at the Tambos Chachapoyanos lodge (see
above), then walk 19 km (4-5 hrs) along the
road to the site. In María there are several
hospedajes, **F** pp with hot water. Alternatively,
go early from Chachapoyas to Tingo, hike up to
Kuélap then walk down to María (2-3 hrs) and
spend the night there. 4) Take a combi from

Chachapoyas to Tingo, spend the night, then take the 3½-4 hrs' strenuous walk uphill from Tingo; take waterproof, food and drink, and start early as it gets very hot. Only the fit should try to ascend and descend in one day on foot. In the rainy season it is advisable to wear boots; at other times it is hot and dry (take all your water with you as there is nothing on the way up).

Chachapoyas *p1155, map p1155*

Bus To **Chiclayo** (10 hrs), **Trujillo** and **Lima** (22 hrs), the best option is **Móvil**, Libertad 464, T778545, to Lima 1230 daily, US$24; to Trujillo 2000 daily, US$12, to Chiclayo US$10.60, on either schedule. **Zelada**, Jr Ortiz Arrieta 310, to Lima, 1100 daily, US$20. **Civa**, Salamanca 956, T778048, to Lima at 1230 Mon, Wed, Fri, US$17; to Chiclayo, 1800 daily, US$7.60. **Turismo Kuélap**, Ortiz Arrieta 412, T778128, to Chiclayo, at 1700 daily, US$9. To **Celendín**, **Virgen del Carmen** and **Paraíso del Oriente** alternate on the route from Av Salamanca 650, on Tue and Fri at 0600, 12-15 hrs (or more), US$9.50. To **Pedro Ruíz**, for connections to Chiclayo or Tarapoto, combis (US$2.15, 2 hrs, 0800-1800) and cars (US$3, 1¾ hrs) leave from Grau y Salamanca and also from Ortiz Arrieta and Libertad. To **Bagua Grande**, 0430-1800, cars US$7, 2½ hrs, from Grau 355 y Libertad. To **Mendoza** (86 km), **Trans Zelada** from Ortiz Arrieta 310, 1100 daily, US$3.65, 3 hrs; cars 0400-2000, from Ortiz Arrieta, cuadra 3 (uphill from Zelada), US$4.55, 3 hrs. For **Kuélap**, **Roller's**, Grau 302, combis or cars, at 0500 and 1400, from Kuélap to Chacha at 1200 and 1700. **Kuélap** US$3.65, 3 hrs; **Yumal** US$3.65, 3 hrs; **María** US$3, 2½ hrs; **Lónguita** US$2.42, 2 hrs; **Tingo** US$1.50, 1½ hrs. Combis to **Tingo** from Grau y Salamanca, US$2.25, 1½ hrs. To **Santo Tomás**: Comité Interprovincial Santo Tomás, Grau, by the cul-de-sac between Salamanca and Libertad, 0800-1600, Santo Tomás, US$2.75, 3 hrs; Cruce de Revash US$2.75, 2½ hrs; Tingo US$2.25, 1½ hrs. To **Leymebamba**, combis and small buses from 2 de Mayo y Libertad, 1200, 1600

(also from cuadra 8 of Libertad), US$3, 2½ hrs. To **Jalca Grande**, Comité Interprovincial Santo Tomás, departures about 1300 onwards (few if any on Sat), US$3.65 (return in morning). To **Luya** and **Lamud**, from San Juan de Luya, Ortiz Arrieta 364, cars 0400-2000, US$2.25, 1 hr to Lamud, same price to Luya. Taxis may be hired from the Plaza for any local destination.

Levanto *p1156*

Levanto is 2 hrs by truck or 6 hrs walk from **Chachapoyas**. Trucks leave from the market in Chachapoyas most days at 0600, US$0.90; trucks and combis from outside Bodega El Amigo on Jr Hermosura at 1400. The nicest way to get there is by the Inca Road, 4-5 hrs. Take the road out of Chachapoyas for 40 mins, then take the stone path on the left. It is in pretty good shape, with one 15-m long stone stairway in excellent condition. A taxi from Chachapoyas to Levanto and back, including driver waiting while you look around, is US$14.50.

Monte Peruvia/Purunllacta *p1156*

There is no direct transport from Chachapoyas. Take a combi at 0930 and 1500 from Jr Salamanca, 4th block down from market, to Pipus, at the turn-off to Cheto; 1½ hrs, US$1.35. A camioneta leaves Pipus for Cheto early morning, US$0.90; or a 2 hr walk on a rough road.

⊙ Directory

Chachapoyas *p1155, map p1155*
Banks BCP, Ortiz Arrieta 576, on plaza, gives cash on Visa card, changes cash and TCs, Visa ATM. No Mastercard ATM or agent. There are two well-signed places on Ayacucho, Plaza de Armas, which change cash. **Internet** Many places around the plaza and elsewhere, US$0.45 per hr. **Post offices** Grau on Plaza de Armas. **Telephones** Ayacucho 926, Plaza de Armas, and Grau 608.

Chachapoyas to the Amazon

From Chachapoyas the road heads north through the beautiful river canyon for 2-3 hours to a small crossroads, **Pedro Ruíz** (three hotels; basic restaurants), where you return to the coast or continue to Yurimaguas, making the spectacular descent from high Andes to high jungle. The road, which goes through **Rioja** (198 km, with basic hotels) is paved as far as Tarapoto. In the rainy season, the road may be subject to landslides.

Moyobamba → *Phone code: 042. Colour map 3, grid B2. Population: 14,000. Altitude: 915 m.*

Moyobamba, capital of San Martín department, is a pleasant town, in the attractive Río Mayo valley. The area is renowned for its orchids and there is a Festival de la Orquídea over three days around 1 November. Among several places to see orchids is **Orquideario Wakanki**

① 0900- 1700, US$0.60, where the plants have been placed in trees. Just beyond are **Baños Termales** ① *San Mateo, 5 km southeast, 0500-2200, US$0.30*, which are worth a visit. There are **sulphur baths** ① *6.5 km west, 0500-1800, US$0.30*, at Oromina. **Puerto Tahuishco** is the town's harbour, a pleasant walk seven blocks north of the centre, where boat trips can be taken.

Tourist offices: Mincetur ① *Jr San Martín 301, on the plaza, T562043, www.turismo sanmartin.com*. Helpful, some leaflets and a map. **Oficina Municipal de Información** ① *Jr Pedro Canga 262, T562191, www.munimoyobamba.gob.pe*, Tue-Sun 0900-1300, 1600-2000, very helpful. Information on excursions and hikes is available from the **Instituto Nacional de Cultura** ① *Jr Benavides 352, Mon-Fri 0800-1300, 1400-1700*, which also has a small departmental museum.

Tarapoto → *Phone code: 042. Colour map 3, grid B2. Altitude: 500 m.*

Tarapoto is a very friendly place, eager to embrace tourism and agricultural development with a good local market 1½ blocks from Plaza de Armas on Av Raimondi. **Información turística** office at the Municipalidad ① *Jr Gregorio Delgado 260, open 0730-1330, 1500-1800*. The 109 km from Moyobamba to Tarapoto is heavily used by trucks, with fuel and meals available. At 35 km from Tarapoto towards Moyobamba a road leads off to **Lamas** where there is a small **museum** ① *US$0.60, custodian will show you round*, with exhibits on local indigenous community (Lamistas). In the town, **Rolly's** ① *San Martín 925, just off the plaza, getting there: take a colectivo from Tarapoto, 30 mins, US$0.85, from Paradero Lamas on road to Moyobamba (take mototaxi from centre, US$0.45)*, serves good food, Rolly is friendly.

About 14 km from Tarapoto on the spectacular road to Yurimaguas are the 50-m falls of **Ahuashiyacu** ① *US$0.30, toilets US$0.15, can be visited by tour from Tarapoto (US$4.50 by mototaxi)*. This is a popular place at lunchtimes and weekends. The entire falls can be seen from the *recreo turístico El Paraíso Verde*, with a restaurant serving typical food, drinks, toilets, swimming pool (US$0.60), also popular. There are many other waterfalls in the area.

On the road to Yurimaguas, after Ahuashiyacu, there is a tunnel, after which you descend through beautiful forest perched on rocky cliffs to Pongo de Caynarachi (several basic *comedores*), where the flats start and the road widens and improves. The government promised to pave the road to Yurimaguas in 2005. Even so, the route is prone to hold-ups and travellers should only during daylight hours.

● Sleeping

Moyobamba *p1159*

A Puerto Mirador, Jr Sucre, 1 km from centre, T/F562050, www.barrioperu.terra.com.pe/ pmirador. Includes breakfast, nice location, lovely grounds and river views, pool, good restaurant.
C La Casona, Alonso de Alvarado 682, T563858. Nicely refurbished old home, lovely courtyard with orchids, comfortable rooms, includes breakfast. Recommended.
C Marcoantonio, Jr Pedro Canga 488, T/F562045, www.altomayoperu.com. Smartest in the town, includes breakfast, hot water, TV, restaurant.
D Hostal Atlanta, Alonso De Alvarado 865, T562063. Hot water (**E** without), TV, fan, good but noisy, no breakfast.
E Hostal Cobos, Jr Pedro Canga 404, T562153. With bath, cold water, simple but good.
E Hostal Country Club, Manuel del Aguila 667, T562110. Hot water, comfortable, garden, has travel agency. Recommended.
E Hostal Royal, Alonso de Alvarado 784, T562662, F562564. Hot water, TV, laundry, café.

Tarapoto *p1160*

A Nilas, Jr Moyobamba 173, T527331, http://linka web.tripod.com/nilas.html. Modern, breakfast, hot water, a/c, TV, fridge, internet access, pool, jacuzzi, gym, airport transfer, very well appointed.
A Río Shilcayo, Pasaje Las Flores 224, 1 km east of town in La Banda de Shilcayo, T522225, F524236 (in Lima T447 9359). Excellent meals, non-residents can use the swimming pool for a fee.
B Lily, Jiménez Pimentel 405-407, T523154, F522394. Hot water, a/c, TV, includes breakfast and tax, laundry, sauna, restaurant.
C La Posada Inn, San Martín 146, T522234, laposada@terra.com.pe. Central, comfortable, hot water, fridge, TV, some rooms with a/c, nice atmosphere, breakfast and lunch.
D El Mirador, Jr San Pablo de la Cruz 517, T522177. 5 blocks uphill from the plaza, cold water, fan, TV, very welcoming, laundry facilities, breakfast (US$2) and hammocks on roof terrace with good views, also offers tours. Recommended.
E Edinson, Av Raimondi y Maynas, 10 m from Plaza Mayor, T523997, T/F524010. Cheaper

without bath and a/c, cold water, breakfast, comfortable, karaoke bars and disco.
E July, Jr Alegría Arias de Morey 205, T522087. Cold water, TV, fridge, no breakfast.
F Hostal San Antonio, Jr Jiménez Pimentel 126, T522226. With TV, fan, courtyard, no breakfast. Noisy but recommended.
G pp Alojamiento Santa Juanita, Av Salaverry 602, Morales (20 mins from centre). Good beds, fan, family run, English spoken, safe.

● Eating

Moyobamba *p1159*
♥♥-♥ La Olla de Barro, Pedro Canga y S Filomeno. Typical food, the most expensive but still good value. Open for breakfast. Also owns ♥♥ **La Tullpa de Mamá**, at Punta de Tahuishco.
♥ La Buena Salud, off Jr Callao, block 8. Opposite the market, vegetarian set meals and à la carte.
♥ Chifa Kikeku, Pedro Canga 451. Chinese.
♥ Edén, down the stairs at the end of Jr San Martín, 1 block from the Plaza de Armas. Vegetarian.
♥ Rocky's, Pedro Canga 402. Typical food, good, has cheap *menú*. Open for breakfast.

Tarapoto *p1160*
♥♥ Real, on Moyobamba on the Plaza. One of the best in town, but expensive.
♥ Helados Regionales La Muyuna, Jr Ramón Castilla 271. Good natural ice cream and drinks made with jungle fruits, 0900-2300 except closed Fri from 1800 and Sat until 1815.
♥ El Maguaré, Jr Moyobamba corner Manco Cápac. Choice of set meals and à la carte, good food and service.

● Transport

Chachapoyas to the Amazon *p1159*
Pedro Ruíz to Moyobamba Many buses to and from **Chiclayo**, **Tarapoto** (9-10 hrs) and **Chachapoyas** all pass through town. There is no way to reserve a seat and buses are usually full. Better to take combis (US$1.75) and cars (US$2.75) to **Bagua Grande**, 1½ hrs; to **Moyobamba** US$5.75, 4 hrs. Combis (US$2.15) and cars (US$3) also go to Chachapoyas, 2 hrs.
   Pedro Ruíz to **Nueva Cajamarca**, US$4.55 (combi), 2 hrs, then a further 20 mins, US$0.90 to **Rioja**. There are regular combis from Rioja to **Moyobamba** (21 km, US$0.90, 20 mins).

Moyobamba *p1159*
Bus Terminal Terrestre, about a dozen blocks from the centre on Av Grau, which leads out of town (mototaxi to the centre US$0.30). To **Tarapoto** (many companies including Tarapoto Tours, T563307, **Móvil**), US$3.60, 2 hrs. Buses en

route from Tarapoto to Pedro Ruíz and Chiclayo (US$7.60-15, 12 hrs) arrive at about 1030, but they will not sell you a ticket the day before if you are going to an intermediate destination such as Pedro Ruiz (US$6-7.60, 3½-4 hrs), they do take you if they have room when the bus arrives. **Combis** Transportes y Turismo Selva, Jr Callao entre Benavides y Varacadillo: to **Tarapoto** US$3, 2½ hrs. **Colectivos** Transportes y Turismo Cajamarca, Serafín Filomeno y Benavides, and Empresa San Martín, Benavides 276; to **Tarapoto**, US$6, 2 hrs, to **Rioja** US$0.90, 20 mins, to **Nueva Cajamarca**, US$1.50, 40 mins. There is no service direct to Pedro Ruiz or Yurimaguas unless you have enough people to fill a car.

Tarapoto *p1160*
Air US$3 per taxi airport to town, US$1.50 mototaxi (no bus service, but no problem to walk). To **Lima**, 1 hr, with **Lan**, Ramírez Hurtado, at the Plaza Mayor, daily, **Star Perú** and LC Busre.
Bus To the west leave from Av Salaverry, Morales, 10 mins by mototaxi from the Plaza. Many companies to **Moyobamba**, 116 km, US$3.65, 2 hrs, **Pedro Ruíz**, US$7.20 (US$8.65 Tarapoto Tours and **Paredes Estrella**) 6 hrs, **Chiclayo**, 690 km, 12 hrs, US$18.20, **Trujillo**, 15 hrs, US$21.20, and **Lima**, 24 hrs, US$27.30-32 (all fares **Móvil**, Salaverry 858, other companies less). Combis to Moyobamba leave from **Turismo La Selva**, Av Salaverry. Cars to Moyobamba, US$6. Buses to **Yurimaguas** leave from the eastern side of Tarapoto, US$3.65, 7-8 hrs, several companies (same price by combi, 5 hrs); pick-ups, daily, US$4.55 in front, US$2.50 in the back; cars US$7.50.

● Directory

Moyobamba *p1159*
Banks BCP, Alonso de Alvarado 903 y San Martín. ATM for Visa/Plus. **BBV Continental**, San Martín 494. **Novedades D'Valeria**, San Martín 481, good rates for cash.

Tarapoto *p1160*
Banks BCP, Maynas 134. Efficient, changes TCs, ATM for Plus/Visa. **BBV Continental**, Ramírez Hurtado, Plaza Mayor, with Visa/Plus ATM. **Interbank**, Grau 119, near the Plaza, for MasterCard. Charges no commission on changing TCs for soles. There are many street changers near the corner of Maynas and Jiménez Pimentel, on the Plaza Mayor.
Internet 4 places close to each other: at San Martín y Arias de Morey, Arias de Morey 109 and 136, and San Martín 129.

Chachapoyas to Ecuador and the coast

The road from Pedro Ruiz (see page 1159) goes west to Bagua Grande and then follows the Río Chamaya. It climbs to the Abra de Porculla (2,150 m) before descending to join the old Pan-American Highway at Olmos (see page 1137). From Olmos you can go southwest to Chiclayo, or northwest to Piura. **Bagua Grande** is the first town of note heading west and a busy, dusty place with many hotels and restaurants on the main street.

To Ecuador

Some 50 km west of Bagua Grande, a road branches northwest at Chamaya to **Jaén** (Phone code: 076. Colour map 3, grid B2. Population: 25,000), a convenient stopover en route to the jungle. It is a modern city and a centre for growing rice. Festival, *Nuestro Señor de Huamantanga*, 14 September.

A road runs north to **San Ignacio** (109 km, being paved), near the border with Ecuador (*fiesta* 30 July, Semana Turística, third week in September). San Ignacio is a pleasant town with steep streets and a modern plaza in the centre of a coffee growing area. The nearby hills offer excursions to waterfalls, lakes, petroglyphs and ancient ruins. From San Ignacio the narrow, unpaved road runs 45 km through green hills to **Namballe**. Just to the north a dirt road goes west to the **Santuario Tabaconas-Namballe** ① *reserve office at San Martín 332, Jaén, T846166, snntabaconasnamballe@yahoo.es*, a 29,500-ha reserve, at 1,200-3,800 m protecting several Andean eco systems. The border is 15 minutes from town at **La Balsa**, a handful of houses on either side of the international bridge. A few shops sell drinks and basic items and there are money changers. To leave Perú head directly to immigration, open 0800-1300, 1500-2000. (When entering Peru you have to stop at the PNP after immigration.) Ecuadorean immigration is supposedly open 24 hours, knock on the door or ask for the officer if not in sight. From the frontier transport goes to Zumba and then to Vilcabamba and Loja. See Transport, page 1163.

● Sleeping

To Ecuador p1162
Jaén
C **Hostal Valle Verde**, Mcal Castilla 203 on Plaza de Armas, T732201, hostalvalleverde@ hotmail.com. Modern, large comfortable rooms and beds, a/c, **D** with fan, hot water, frigobar, parking, includes breakfast. Recommended.
C **Prim's**, Diego Palomino 1341, T731039. Comfortable, a/c, hot water, pool. Recommended.
D **Cancún**, Diego Palomino 1413, T733511. Pleasant, hot water, fan, restaurant, pool. Recommended.
D **César**, Mesones Muro 168, T731277, F731491. Spacious rooms, comfortable, fan, TV (cheaper without), parking, nice.
E **Hostal Diego**, Diego Palomino 1267, T803125. With bath, fan, TV, views over the river, good value.
F **Hostal Santa Elena**, Sánchez Carrión 142, T803020. With bath, cold water, fan, simple, nice, good value.

North of Jaen
D **Sol de la Frontera**, 1½ km north of Namballe, 5 km from La Balsa , isabelayub@yahoo.es. Being built by a British woman, Isabel Wood. Some rooms open, bath tubs with plugs, gas water heaters, continental breakfast included, rural setting in 2.5 ha of countryside.

E **El Olivar**, Av San Ignacio 145, San Ignacio, T076-8446052. **F** with shared bath, cold water, basic, restaurant.
E **La Posada**, Jr Porvenir 218, San Ignacio, T/F 076-8846180. Best in town, some rooms with hot water, **F** with shared bath, simple, pleasant, helpful, decent restaurant.
F **Hostal Maldonado**, near the Plaza, Namballe, T076-330011 (community phone). Shared bath, cold water, basic. And a couple of other basic places.

● Eating

To Ecuador: Jaén p1162
♥ **Claudy Chicken**, Diego Palomino 1284. Selection of set meals (*comida criolla*) at midday, Chinese in the evening, *pollo a la brasa*.
♥ **Lactobac**, Bolívar 1382 at Plaza de Armas. Variety of à la carte dishes, snacks, desserts, very popular, also open for breakfast. Recommended.

● Transport

Chachapoyas to Ecuador & the coast p1162
Cars (US$2.75) and combis (US$1.75) depart from Jr B Alcedo at the east end of Bagua Grande when full to **Pedro Ruíz**, 1 hr.

To Ecuador p1162
Jaén
Bus Arrange bus transport at Mesones Muro, block 4; enquire where the bus leaves from as some companies also have ticket offices in the centre. To **Chiclayo**, 6 hrs: Móvil, bus cama at 1700, US$7.60, 5½ hrs; regular service at 2330, US$6.65. Civa at 1330 and 2230, US$4.55. Transcade at 1000 and 2100, US$4.55. In front of the bus terminal at Mesones Muro are cars, to Chiclayo US$9, 5 hrs. To **Lima**: Móvil bus cama at 1700, US$21.20, 15½ hrs; regular service at 2330, US$18.20. Civa at 1700, US$18.20, 16 hrs. Service to Lima also goes through Trujillo. To **Piura**, 8 hrs, US$7.60: Tarapoto Tours at 2200; Sol Peruano, at 2230. To **Pedro Ruiz**, US$4.55, 3hrs; **Moyobamba**, US$5.45, 7 hrs, and **Tarapoto**, US$ 7.60, 9 hrs: Jaén Express at 1730, Tarapoto Tours at 1930, Sol Peruano at 2030. To **Bagua Grande**: cars US$1.80, 1hr; combis US$1.50, 1¼ hrs. To **San Ignacio**, combis from Av Pinillos 638, 0400-1900, US$3.65, 3 hrs.

North of Jaén
Bus From San Ignacio to **Chiclayo**, daily with Turismo Adriazén, Av San Ignacio 406, and Ramírez Tours, Cajamarca 179. To **Jaén**, combis from Av Mariano Melgar, block 3, US$3.65, 3 hrs. To **Namballe** and **La Balsa** (border with Ecuador),

cars from Jr Santa Rosa corner Progreso: Namballe US$2.45 1¾ hrs; La Balsa US$3, 2 hrs. Ranchera from La Balsa to **Zumba** at 1230 and 1730, US$1.75. There are no pickups, no *carreras* to Zumba. If it has not been raining and the road is passable, there is one bus (Transportes Nambija) which goes from La Balsa directly to Loja at 2030, US$7.50, 8-9 hrs. There are military controls at Pucapamba, 20 min north of La Balsa and just north of Zumba, keep passport to hand.

❶ Directory

To Ecuador p1162
Jaén
Banks BCP, Bolívar y V Pinillos. Cash only; ATM (Visa/Plus - no MasterCard ATM). BBV Continental, Ramón Castilla y San Martín. Cash, US$5 commission for TCs. Cambios Coronel, V Pinillos 360 (*Coronel* across the street at 339). Cash only, good rates. Others on plaza, next to public phones. Cash only. **Internet** Fotocenter Erick, Pardo Miguel 425. US$1.15 per hr.

North of Jaén
Banks Centro Comercial Unión, Av San Ignacio 393, San Ignacio, for exchange. **Internet** Places in both San Ignacio and Namballe.

South coast

Peru South from Lima

The Pan-American Highway runs all the way south from Lima to the Chilean border. This part of Peru's desert coast has its own distinctive attractions. The most famous, and perhaps the strangest, are the mysterious Nazca Lines, whose origin and function continue to puzzle scientists the world over. But Nazca is not the sole archaeological resource here: remains of other pre-Columbian civilizations include outposts of the Inca empire itself. Pisco and Ica are the main centres before Nazca. The former, which is near the famous Paracas marine reserve, is named after the latter's main product, the pisco grape brandy and a number of places are well-known for their bodegas.

South from Lima

Beyond the beaches which are popular with Limeños the road passes near several towns worth a stop: eg Chincha with its Afro-Peruvian culture. The Paracas peninsula, near Pisco, is one of the world's great marine bird reserves and was home to one of Peru's most important ancient civilizations. Further south, the Ica valley, with its wonderful climate, is home to that equally wonderful grape brandy, pisco.par. Most beaches have very strong currents and can be dangerous for swimming; if unsure, ask locals.

Lima to Pisco
The first 60 km from Lima are dotted with a series of seaside resort towns and clubs: El Silenco (Km 30), **Punta Hermosa** (Km 35), Punta Negra (Km 40) and **San Bartolo** (43 km). At Km 60 is the charming fishing village of **Pucusana**.

Near the prosperous market centre of **San Vicente de Cañete**, 150 km south of Lima on the Río Cañete, another beach worth a stop is Cerro Azul (**B** *Hotel Los Palmeras* is best, directly on the beach).

Cañete valley

A paved road runs inland from Cañete, mostly beside the Río Cañete, to **Lunahuaná** (40 km). It is 8 km beyond the Inca ruins of **Incawasi**, which dominated the valley. You can taste the wines of the *bodegas* (wine cellars) in the valley. *Fiesta de la Vendimia*, grape harvest, first weekend in March. At the end of September/beginning October is the *Fiesta del Níspero* (medlar festival). Several places offer rafting and kayaking: from November-April rafting is at levels 4-5. May-October is low water, levels 1-2 only. Excellent kayaking is 2½ hours upriver. A festival of adventure sports is held every February. There are several hotels, ranging from **A** to **E**, and restaurants in Lunahuaná and surrounding districts.

Beyond Lunahuaná the road ascending the Cañete valley leaves the narrow flood-plain and runs through a series of gorges to the market town of **Yauyos** (basic accommodation, 5 km off the road). After the attractive village of **Huancaya**, the valley is transformed into one of the most beautiful upper valleys in all Peru, on a par with Colca. Above Huancaya the high Andean terrain lies within the **Nor-Yauyos National Reserve** and the river descends through a series of absolutely clear, turquoise pools and lakes, interrupted by cascades and white-water rapids. Culturally, the valley is fascinating for its dying indigenous languages and perhaps the best pre-Columbian terracing anywhere in Peru. Further upstream **Llapay** is a good base because it is in the middle of the valley (**G** *Hostal Llapay*, basic but very friendly, will open at any hour, restaurant). Places to visit include the village of Laraos and the pre-Inca ruins of Huamanmarca (2-hour walk from village of Carania, which is a 1-hour drive from Llapay). 17 July Fiesta Nor-Yauyina in Llapay, large and popular. Beyond Llapay, the Cañete valley narrows to an exceptionally tight canyon, with a hairy road squeezed between nothing but rock and rushing water for the steep climb to the 4,600-m pass. Beyond, the road drops to Huancayo (see page 1245).

Pisco → *Phone code: 056. Colour map 3, grid C3. Population: 82,250.*

The largest port between Callao and Matarani is a short distance to the west of the Pan-American Highway and 237 km south of Lima. The two parts of town, Pisco Pueblo with its colonial-style homes, and Pisco Puerto, which, apart from fisheries, has been replaced as a port by the deep-water Puerto General San Martín, have expanded into one.

In Pisco Pueblo, half a block west of the quiet Plaza de Armas, with its equestrian statue of San Martín, is the **Club Social Pisco** *Av San Martín 132*, the headquarters of San Martín after he had landed at Paracas Bay. There is an old Jesuit church on San Francisco, one block from the plaza, separated from the Municipalidad by a narrow park. The newer **Cathedral** is on the main plaza. Avenida San Martín runs from the Plaza de Armas to the sea.

Chincha Alta, 35 km north of Pisco, is a fast-growing town where the negro/criollo culture is still alive. The famous festival, *Verano Negro*, is at the end of February while, in November, the *Festival de las Danzas Negras* is held in the black community of El Carmen, 10 km south. Chincha is a good place to sample locally produced wine and pisco and local *bodegas* have guided tours.

Paracas National Reserve

ⓘ *US$1.50 pp.* Down the coast 15 km from Pisco Puerto is the bay of **Paracas**, sheltered by the Paracas peninsula. (The name means 'sandstorm' - they can last for three days, especially in August; the wind gets up every afternoon, peaking at around 1500.) Paracas can be reached by the coast road from San Andrés, passing the fishing port and a large proportion of Peru's fishmeal industry. Alternatively, go down the Pan-American Highway to 14.5 km past the Pisco turning and take the road to Paracas across the desert. After 11 km turn left along the coast road and one km further on fork right to Paracas village. The peninsula, a large area of coast to the south and the Ballestas Islands is a National Reserve, and one of the best marine reserves, with the highest concentration of marine birds in the world. It's advisable to see the peninsula as part of a tour it is not safe to walk alone and it is easy to get lost.

Return to the main road for the entrance to the Reserve (ask for a map here). There's the **Julio Tello site museum** ⓘ *daily 0900-1700, US$2, a shop (guide books, film, drinks), a visitors' centre and a natural history museum.* A *mirador* offers views of flamingoes feeding in Paracas bay, but you need binoculars (boat trips do not go to see flamingoes; in January-March the flamingoes go to the Sierra). The tiny fishing village of **Lagunilla** is 5 km from the museum across the neck of the peninsula; its beaches are free from sting rays but not very clean. The eating places tend to be overpriced. A network of firm dirt roads, reasonably well signed, crosses the peninsula (details from Park Office or ask for 'Hoja 28-K' map at Instituto Geográfico Militar in Lima). Other sights on the peninsula include **Mirador de los Lobos** at Punta El Arquillo, 6 km from Lagunilla, with view of sea lions; and a rock formation in the cliffs called **La Catedral**, 6 km from Lagunilla in the opposite direction. About 14 km from the museum is the pre-Columbian Candelabra (**Candelabro** in Spanish) traced in the hillside, at least 50 m long, best seen from the sea.

Ballestas Islands

Trips to the **Islas Ballestas** leave from the jetty at El Chaco, the beach and fishing port by Paracas village. The islands are spectacular, eroded into numerous arches and caves (*ballesta* means bow, as in archery), which provide shelter for thousands of seabirds, some of which are very rare, and hundreds of sea lions. The book *Las Aves del Departamento de Lima* by Maria Koepcke is useful.

Few tours include **Isla San Gallán**, where there are thousands of sea lions. You will see, close up, thousands of inquisitive sea lions, guano birds, pelicans, penguins and, if you're lucky, dolphins swimming in the bay. Most boats are speedboats with life jackets, some are very crowded; wear warm clothing and protect against the sun. The boats pass Puerto San Martín and the Candelabra en route to the islands.

Inland from Pisco

A 317 km paved road goes to Ayacucho in the sierra, with a branch to Huancavelica. At Castrovirreyna it reaches 4,600 m. The scenery on this journey is superb.

Tambo Colorado *US$1.50*, one of the best-preserved Inca ruins in coastal Peru, is 48 km from Pisco, up the Pisco valley. It includes buildings where the Inca and his retinue would have stayed. Many of the walls retain their original colours. On the other side of the road is the public plaza and the garrison and messengers' quarters. The caretaker will act as a guide, he has a small collection of items found on the site.

Ica → *Phone code: 056. Colour map 3, grid C3. Population: 161,400.*

Ica, 70 km southeast of Pisco, is Peru's chief wine centre and is famous for its *tejas*, a local sweet of *manjarblanco*. The **Museo Regional** ① *southwest of the centre, Mon-Sat 0800-1900, Sun 0900-1800, US$3/75, students US$0.65, US$1.25 to take photos, take bus 17 from the Plaza de Armas (US$0.50)*, has mummies, ceramics, textiles and trepanned skulls from the Paracas, Nazca and Inca cultures; a good, well-displayed collection of Inca counting strings (*quipus*) and clothes made of feathers. Behind the building is a scale model of the Nazca lines with an observation tower; a useful orientation before visiting the lines. The kiosk outside sells copies of motifs from the ceramics and textiles. Some tourist information is available at travel agencies. Also try **Touring y Automóvil Club del Perú** ① *C Fermín Tangüis 102, Urb San Miguel, T219393, ica@touringperu.com.pe.* **Tourist police** ① Av Elias cuadra 4, T227673.

Wine bodegas that you can visit are: **El Carmen**, on the right-hand side when arriving from Lima (has an ancient grape press made from a huge tree trunk). **El Catador** ① *José Carrasco González, T403295, 1000-1800, US$1.50, 10 km outside Ica, in the district of Subtanjalla, combi from the 2nd block of Moquegua, every 20 mins, US$0.40, taxi takes 10 mins, good tours in Spanish,* has a shop selling home-made wines and pisco, and traditional handicrafts associated with winemaking. In the evening it is a restaurant-bar with dancing and music, best visited during harvest, late February to early April, wine and pisco tasting usually possible. Near El Catador is **Bodega Alvarez**, whose owner, Umberto Alvarez, is very hospitable and won the gold medal for the best pisco in Peru in 1995. Ask about *pisco de mosto verde* and the rarer, more expensive *pisco de limón*.

About 5 km from Ica, round a palm-fringed lake and amid amazing sand dunes, is the oasis and summer resort of **Huacachina** ① *take a taxi from Ica for under US$1*, an increasingly popular gringo spot to warm up after the Andes. Its green sulphur waters are said to be curative and thousands of visitors come to swim here. There are lots of eating places and bars with music around the lake. Sometimes the water and shore get dirty and polluted. **Sandboarding** on the dunes is a major pastime here; board hire US$1.50 per hour. **Note:** For the inexperienced, sandboarding can be dangerous on the big dunes. **Dune buggies** also do white-knuckle, rollercoaster tours for US$12, or you can hire a buggy and scare yourself for US$6 per person for three to four hours.

● Sleeping

Lima to Pisco p1163

C **Posada del Mirador**, Malecón San Martín 105, San Bartolo, T430 7822. Price is for a bungalow, **A** for full board. Footprint users welcome.

C-D **Casa Resort Peñascal**, Av Las Palmeras 258, San Bartolo, T430 7436, www.surfpenascal.com. Relaxing, surf specials, with breakfast, hot water, laundry, right on the sea.

D **Casa** Barco, Av Punta Hermosa 340, Punta Hermosa, T230 7081, www.casabarco.com. Funky little hostel with a pool, great art work, rooms with views and cable TV. It's a short walk from where buses drop passengers off at the beginning of Punta Hermosa.

D-E **El Mirador - Centro Turístico Belvedere**, Pucusana, T430 9228, elmiradordepucusana@ hotmail.com. Owned by hospitable Adolfo del Campo, on hill overlooking the whole village and harbour, a cheap haven for travellers. Adolfo cooks with whatever is available, depending on when the boats come in.

Pisco p1164

B **Hostal Villa Manuelita**, San Fransisco 227, T/F535218, hostalvillamanuelita@ hotmail.com. Elegantly decorated colonial mansion converted into hotel with cafeteria and restaurant, cable TV, fan, helpful, tranquil.

C **Regidor**, Arequipa 201, T/F535220/219, regidor@mail.cosapidata.com.pe. With TV, fan, jacuzzi, café and restaurant, sauna, very good, price negotiable at quiet times.

D **Hostal San Isidro**, San Clemente 103, T/F536471, www.hostalsanisidro.com. **E** without bath, hot water, safe, laundry facilities, use of kitchen, English spoken, pool, parking, arranges dune buggies. Recommended.

D **Posada Hispana Hostal**, Bolognesi 236, T536363, www.posadahispana.com. Rooms with loft and bath, also rooms with shared bath (**G** pp), hot water, can accommodate groups, comfortable, breakfast extra, information service, English, French, Italian and Catalan spoken. Recommended.

D-E **Hostal Los Inkas Inn**, Prol Barrio Nuevo Mz M Lt 14, Urb San Isidro, T536634, los_inkas_inn@hotmail.com. 5 blocks from the Plaza de Armas, comfortable and straightforward, private rooms or dorms with shared bath, pool (not always full), internet, cafetería, sauna, laundry service, garage. Tours can be arranged.

E **El Condado**, Arequipa 136, Plazuela Belén, T533623, hostalcondado@hotmail.com. Hot water, cable TV, laundry, good if a bit noisy, expensive breakfast, tours to Ballestas arranged.

E **Hostal Belén**, Arequipa 128, Plazuela Belén, T533046. Basic, a bit outdated, but safe, hot water. Better rooms in new annex.

E **Hostal La Portada**, Alipio Ponce 250, T532098, hostallaportada@terra.com. Free coffee, hot water, TV, laundry service. Recommended.

E **Pisco**, on Plaza de Armas, T536669, hotelpisco@terra.com. **F** without bath, cold water and poor plumbing, breakfast US$1.75, safety box, internet, parking for motorcycles.

F pp **Hostal Pisco Playa** (Youth Hostel), Jr José Balta 639, Pisco Playa, T532492. Kitchen and laundry facilities, quite nice, breakfast US$1.50.

Chincha Alta p1164

AL **Hacienda San José**, 17th-century ranch-house, 9 km south of town in El Carmen district, T056-221458, hsanjose@ terra.com.pe. Full board (cheaper Mon-Thu), beautiful buildings, but overpriced, pool, garden, small church, colonial crafts, the tunnels believed to link up with other ranches and the catacombs, where many slaves were interred, can be visited, US$3 pp, very busy at weekends.

Paracas National Reserve p1164

A **Paracas**, bungalows on beach, T545100, hparacas@terra.com.pe. Good food, not cheap, good buffet lunch on Sun US$25, fine grounds facing the bay, it is a good centre for excursions to the Peninsula and flights over Nazca, tennis courts, open-air pool (US$2 for non-residents), also houses the Masson ceramics collection which is worth seeing. 2-hr dune-buggy trips can be arranged for US$25 pp.

C **El Mirador**, at the turn-off to El Chaco, T545086, www.elmiradorhotel.com. Hot water, good service, boat trips arranged, meals available, sometimes full board only.

E **Hostal Los Frayles**, Av Paracas Mz D, Lote 5, P2, T545141. Good value, nice terrace, no TV.

Ica p1165

Hotels are fully booked during the harvest festival and prices rise greatly.

AL **Las Dunas**, Av La Angostura 400, T256224, www.lasdunashotel.com. Lima offices: Malecón Armendáriz 193, Miraflores, Lima, T241 8000. Prices do not include service, about 20% cheaper on weekdays. Highly recommended, in a complete resort with restaurant, swimming pool, horse riding and other activities, it has its own airstrip for flights over Nazca, 50 mins.

C **Sol de Ica**, Lima 265, T236168, 1 block from Plaza de Armas, www.hotelsoldeica.com. Quite comfortable, breakfast extra, swimming pool, tour agency.

C-D **Hostal Siesta I**, Independencia 160, T233249. Hot water, hospitable owner, noisy. **Siesta II**, T234633, similar.

D Princess, Urb Santa María D-103, T212515, www.geocities.com/hotel_princess. Taxi ride from the main plaza, small rooms, hot water, TV, pool, tourist information, helpful, peaceful, very good.
D-E Arameli, Tacna 239, T239107. A good choice, cable TV, 1 block from Plaza, clean.
F Hostal Paraíso, Bolívar 418, T227582. Clean, quiet but thin walls, basic.

Huacachina *p1165*
Don't be bullied by taxi drivers: insist on going to the hotel of your choice.
A Mossone is at the east end of the lake, T213660, reserva@derrama.org.pe. Elegant, hacienda-style, full board available, lovely patio, pool, bicycles and sandboards for guests' use. Recommended.
B Hostería Suiza, Malecón 264, T238762, hostessuiza@terra.com.pe. Overlooking lake, lovely grounds, quiet, includes breakfast, safe parking. Recommended.
E Casita de Arena, T215274, casadearena@hotmail.com. Basic rooms, **G** without bath, bar, small pool, laundry facilities, board hire, popular with backpackers, check your bill and change carefully, don't leave valuables unattended.
E Hostal Rocha, T222256. Hot water, **F** without bath, family run, kitchen and laundry facilities, board hire, small pool, popular with backpackers, but a bit run-down.
F Hostal del Barco, Balneario de Huacachina 180. A very relaxed place with hammocks on the front terrace, basic rooms, bar, use of kitchen, can arrange tours.
F Hostal Salvatierra, T232352. A grand old place being renovated, not on waterfront, charming, pool, relaxing courtyard, rents sandboards, good value.
G Hostal Titanic, T229003. Small rooms, pool and café, clothes washing, board hire, good value for lodging and set meals.

🍴 Eating

Pisco *p1164*
There are seafood restaurants along the shore between Pisco and San Andrés and in San Andrés itself.
♥♥-♥ As de Oro, San Martín 472. Good food, decent prices, closed Mon, disco and karaoke on Sat.
♥♥-♥ El Bossa Nova, Av San Martín 176, p 2. Stylish café/bar for an espresso or your favourite trago, good night and day.
♥♥-♥ La Casona, San Martín. Good value, new, specializing in grilled meats, large portions.
♥ Don Manuel, Comercio 179, US$2-4 main dish.
♥ El Dorado, main plaza opposite Cathedral. Good value local dishes.

Cafés
Panadería/Café San Fransisco, next to Zarcillos Tours on the main Plaza. Good empanadas and baked goods, with a restaurant next door, cheap.

Ica *p1165*
♥♥-♥ Las Brujas de Cachiche, Cajamarca 118. Serves local dishes.
♥♥-♥ Chifa Karaoke Central, Urb Los Viñedos de Santa María E-25, T221294. Excellent Chinese.
♥♥-♥ El Otro Peñoncito, Bolívar 255. Set lunch (US$6) in a pleasant atmosphere, good toilets.
♥♥-♥ Pizzería Venecia, Lima 252. Best pizzas in town.

Cafés
Café Mogambo, Tacna 125. A good place for breakfast.
Pastelería Velazco, on Plaza de Armas. Good service, recommended for caffeinated drinks.
Tejas Helena, Cajamarca 137. The best *tejas* in town are sold here.
Tejas Ruthy, Cajamarca 122. Also good and a bit cheaper.

⊛ Festivals and events

Ica *p1165*
Wine harvest festival in early **Mar**. The image of El Señor de Luren, in a fine church in Parque Luren, draws pilgrims from all Peru to the twice-yearly festivals in **Mar** and **Oct (15-21)**, when there are all-night processions.

▲▲ Activities and tours

Ballestas Islands *p1165*
A full day tour of the islands and Paracas Peninsula costs US$20 pp; a half-day boat tour to the islands US$9-10 pp, usually starting at 0730, returning 1100 to avoid rougher seas in the afternoon; out of season tours are a lot cheaper. The main hotels in Pisco and Paracas will arrange tours (eg *Hotel Paracas*, US$18 in their own speedboat, 0900-1700). Often, agencies will put clients together in one boat. Don't book tours on the street. Recommended operators for trips to Islas Ballestas:
Amigos Adventure Travel Agency, Jr Progreso 167, p 2, T311984, amigos_adventures@ hotmail.com. Island tours, Reserve tours, sandboarding, many languages spoken.
Ballestas Travel Service, San Francisco 251, Pisco, T535564.
Blue Sea Tours, Chosica 320, San Andrés, Pisco, also at El Chaco. Guides Jorge Espejo and Hubert Van Lomoen (speaks Dutch) are frequently recommended, no time limit on tours.

The Zarcillo Connection, San Francisco 111, Pisco, T536543, www.zarcilloconnections.net. For Paracas National Reserve, Tambo Colorado, trekking and tours to Ica, Chincha and Nazca.

Ica *p1165*

Desert Adventures, T01-981 69352, Huacachina, desertadventures@ hotmail.com. Frequently recommended for sandboarding and trips into the desert, French, English and Spanish spoken.
Ica Desert Trip, icadeserttrip@yahoo.es. Roberto Penny Cabrera (speaks Spanish and English) offers 1, 2 and 3-day trips off-road into the desert, archaeology, geology, etc. US$50 pp per day, 4 people maximum, contact by email in advance. Take toilet paper, something warm for the evening, a long-sleeved loose cotton shirt for daytime and long trousers. Recommended, but "not for the faint-hearted".
La Ruta del Pisco, Lima travel agencies arrange 3-day, 2-night tours from Lima including transport, accommodation and visits to bodegas, from US$70-100.

⊖ Transport

Cañete valley *p1164*

The road from Cañete to Huancayo is being improved, so buses may become more frequent. ETAS run from **Cañete** (in front of AEDO petrol station, T01-287 8831 or 01-9771 1254) to **Huancayo** (Loreto 744, T215424). Information about ETAS buses on posters in the villages. Daily bus from **Lunahuaná** between 1900-2200 to **Yauyos** stops at a shop on the road on request. Bus from Yauyos to **Llapay** between 0100-0230, arrives 0200-0400, final destination **Huancayo** arriving 0900.

Pisco *p1164*

Bus If arriving by bus, make sure it is going into town and will not leave you at the Repartición which is a 5-km, 10 min mototaxi, US$0.50, or taxi ride, US$1, from the centre. To **Lima**, 242 km, 3-4 hrs, US$4, buses and colectivos every hour. Company offices in Pisco are: **Ormeño**, San Francisco, 1 block from plaza, **San Martín**, San Martín 199, and **Soyuz**, Callao on the Plaza. To **Ayacucho**, 317 km, 8-10 hrs, US$7.55-15.15, several buses daily (**Molina** recommended), leave from San Clemente 10 km north on Panamericana Sur, take a colectivo (20 mins), book in advance to ensure seat and take warm clothing as it gets cold at night. To **Huancavelica**, 269 km, 12-14 hrs, US$7, with **Oropesa**, coming from Ica. To **Ica**, US$0.90 by bus, 45 mins, 70 km, with **Ormeño**, also **Saky** (Pedemonte y Arequipa). To **Nazca**, 210 km, take a bus to Ica and then change to a colectivo. To **Arequipa**, US$12, 10-12 hrs, 2 daily. **Taxi** On Plaza de Armas. Transport from Repartición (see above) stops at Comercio by Plaza Belén.

Paracas National Reserve *p1164*

There's no public transport on the peninsula, although **Ormeño** passes by the Hotel Paracas at 1630, US$15 to Nasca (compared with US$6 on the same Royal Class bus from Ica).
Taxi From **Pisco** to Paracas about US$2.50-3; combis to/from **El Chaco** beach (marked 'Chaco-Paracas-Museo') when full, US$0.50, 25 mins. The last one returns at about 2200.

Tambo Colorado *p1165*

Bus From near the plaza in Pisco, 0800, US$1.60, 3 hrs; also colectivos, US$1.20 pp. Alight 20 mins after the stop at Humay; the road passes right through the site. Return by bus to Pisco in the afternoon. For transport back to Pisco wait at the caretaker's house. **Taxi** From Pisco US$25. Tours from Pisco agencies US$10-15 with guide, minimum 2 people.

Ica *p1165*

Bus All bus offices are on Lambayeque blocks 1 and 2 and Salaverry block 3. Beware of thieves when changing buses and around the Plaza de Armas. To **Pisco**, 70 km, several daily; **Saky** buses from opposite *Ormeño*, 45 mins to centre of Pisco, US$0.90. To **Lima**, 302 km, 4 hrs, US$5-10, several daily including **Soyuz** (Av Manzanilla 130 - every 8 mins 0600-2200), **Flores** and **Ormeño** (at Lambayeque 180). See also Lima, Transport. To **Nazca**, 140 km, 2 hrs, several buses (US$1.50) and colectivos (US$3.75) daily, including **Ormeño**, **Flores**, 4 daily, and **Cueva** (José Elias y Huánuco), hourly on the hour 0600-2200. To **Arequipa** the route goes via Nazca, see under Nazca.

⊙ Directory

Pisco *p1164*

Banks ATMs at banks on Plaza, mostly Visa. **BCP**, on Plaza de Armas gives good rates, for Amex and cash. Also on Plaza, **Interbank**, for Mastercard.
Telephones Telephone and fax office on Plaza de Armas between Av San Martín y Callao.

Ica *p1165*

Banks Avoid changing TCs if possible as commission is high. If necessary, use **BCP**.
Post offices At Callao y Moquegua.
Telephones at Av San Martín y Huánuco.

Nazca and around

Set in a green valley amid a perimeter of mountains, Nazca's altitude puts it just above any fog which may drift in from the sea. The sun blazes the year round by day and the nights are crisp. Nearby are the mysterious, world-famous Nazca Lines. Overlooking the town is Cerro Blanco (2,078 m), the highest sand dune in the world, popular for sandboarding and parapenting.

Nazca Town → *Phone code: 056. Colour map 3, grid C3. Population: 50,000. Altitude: 598 m.*

In the town of Nazca (140 km south of Ica via Pan-American Highway, 444 km from Lima) there are two important museums. **Museo Antonini** ① *Av de la Cultura 600, eastern end of Jr Lima, T523444, cahuachi@terra.com.pe, 0900-1900, ring the bell, US$3, including guide. 10-min walk from the plaza, or short taxi ride.* This museum houses the discoveries of Professor Orefici and his team from the huge pre-Inca city at Cahuachi (see below), which, Orefici believes, holds the key to the Nazca Lines. Many tombs survived the *huaqueros* and there are displays of mummies, ceramics, textiles, amazing *antaras* (panpipes) and photos of the excavations. In the garden is a prehispanic aqueduct. Recommended. The **Maria Reiche Planetarium** ① *Hotel Nazca Lines, T522293, shows usually at 1900 and 2100; US$6 (students half price), very good,* was opened in May 2000 in honour of Maria Reiche (see below). Stimulating lectures are given every night about the Nazca Lines, based on Reiche's theories, which cover archaeology and astronomy. The show lasts about 45 minutes, after which visitors are able to look at the moon, planets and stars through sophisticated telescopes. There is a small market at Lima y Grau and the Mercado Central at Arica y Tacna. The *Virgen de la Guadalupe* festival takes place 29 August-10 September . **Tourist police** ① *Av Los Incas cuadra 1, T522442.*

Nazca Lines

Cut into the stony desert about 22 km north of Nazca, above the Ingenio valley on the Pampa de San José, along the Pan-American Highway, are the famous Nazca Lines. Large numbers of lines, not only parallels and geometrical figures, but also designs such as a dog, an enormous monkey, birds (one with a wing span of over 100 m), a spider and a tree. The lines, best seen from the air, are thought to have been etched on the Pampa Colorada sands by three different groups – the Paracas people 900-200 BC, the Nazcas 200 BC-AD 600 and the Huari settlers from Ayacucho at about AD 630.

The Nazcas had a highly developed civilization which reached its peak about AD 600. Their polychrome ceramics, wood carvings and adornments of gold are on display in many of Lima's museums. The Paracas was an early phase of the Nazca culture, renowned for the superb technical quality and stylistic variety in its weaving and pottery. The Huari empire, in conjunction with the Tiahuanaco culture, dominated much of Peru from AD 600-1000.

Origins of the lines The German expert, Dr Maria Reiche, who studied the lines for over 40 years, mostly from a step ladder, died in June 1998, aged 95. She maintained that they represent some sort of vast astronomical pre-Inca calendar. In 1976 Maria Reiche paid for a platform, the mirador, from which three of the huge designs can be seen - the hands, the Lizard and the Tree. Her book, *Mystery on the Desert*, is on sale for US$10 (proceeds to conservation work) in Nazca. In January 1994 Maria Reiche opened a small **museum** ① *US$1. 5 km from town at the Km 416 marker, take micro from in front of Ormeño terminal, US$0.70, frequent.* Viktoria Nikitzhi, a colleague of Maria Reiche, gives one-hour lectures about the Nazca Lines at **Dr Maria Reiche Center** ① *Av de los Espinales 300, 1 block from Ormeño bus stop, T969 9419, viktorianikitzki@hotmail.com. She also organizes tours in Jun and Dec (phone in advance to confirm times). See the Planetarium, above.* Another good book is *Pathways to the Gods: the mystery of the Nazca Lines,* by Tony Morrison (Michael Russell, 1978), available in Lima.

Other theories abound: Georg A von Breunig (1980) claims that the lines are the tracks of running contests, and a similar theory was proposed by the English astronomer Alan Sawyer; yet another is that they represent weaving patterns and yarns (Henri Stirlin) and that the plain is a map demonstrating the Tiahuanaco Empire (Zsoltan Zelko). *The Nazca Lines - a new perspective on their origin and meaning* (Editorial Los Pinos, Lima 18), by Dr Johan Reinhard, brings together ethnographic, historical and archaeological data, including current use of straight lines in Chile and Bolivia, to suggest that the Lines conform to fertility practices throughout the Andes.

Another theory is that the ancient Nazcas flew in hot-air balloons, based on the idea that the lines are best seen from the air, and that there are pieces of ancient pottery and tapestry showing balloonists, and local legends of flying men (see *Nazca, The flight of Condor 1*, by Jim Woodman, Murray, 1980, Pocket Books, NY 1977). This in part accords with research carried out by the BBC series 'Ancient Voices'. Clues to the function of the lines were found in the pottery and textiles of the ancient Nazcans, some of which show a flying creature emitting discharge from its nose and mouth. This is believed to portray the flight of the shaman who consumes certain psycho-active drugs that convince him he can fly and so enter the real world of spirits in order to rid sick people of evil spirits. In this way, the lines were not designed to be seen physically from above, but from the mind's eye of the flying shaman. This also explains the presence of creatures such as a monkey or killer whale which possess qualities needed by the shaman in his spirit journeys.

After six years' work at La Muña and Los Molinos, Palpa (43 km north of Nazca), and using photogrammetry (mapping from aerial photographs), Peruvian archaeologist Johny Isla and Markus Reindel of the Swiss-Liechtenstein Foundation deduced that the lines on both the Palpa and Nazca plains are offerings dedicated to the worship of water and fertility. These two elements were paramount to the coastal people in this arid environment and they expressed their adoration not only in the desert, but also on their ceramics and on the engraved stones of the Paracas culture. Isla and Reindel believe that the Palpa lines predate those at Nazca and that the lines and drawings themselves are scaled up versions of the Paracas drawings. In addition, objects in the shape of drops of water, whales and chilis, found in the grave of El Señor de Palpa, are repeated in the desert. This new research proposes that the Nazca culture succumbed not to drought, but to heavy rainfall, probably during an El Niño event.

Other excursions
The Nazca area is dotted with over 100 cemeteries and the dry, humidity-free climate has perfectly preserved invaluable tapestries, cloth and mummies. At **Chauchilla** ① *30 km south of Nazca, last 12 km a sandy track*, grave robbing *huaqueros* ransacked the tombs and left bones, skulls, mummies and pottery shards littering the desert. A tour takes about two hours and should cost about US$7 per person with a minimum of three people. Gold mining is one of the main local industries and a tour usually includes a visit to a small family processing shop where the techniques used are still very old-fashioned. Some tours also include a visit to a local potter's studio. That of Sr Andrés Calle Benavides, who makes Nazca reproductions, is particularly recommended.

To the Paredones ruins and aqueduct: the ruins, also called Cacsamarca, are Inca on a pre-Inca base. They are not well preserved. The underground aqueducts, built 300 BC-AD 700, are still in working order and worth seeing. By taxi it is about US$10 round trip, or go with a tour.

Cantalloc is a 30 minutes to one hour walk through Buena Fe, to see markings in the valley floor. These consist of a triangle pointing to a hill and a *tela* (cloth) with a spiral depicting the threads. Climb the mountain to see better examples.

Cahuachi, to the west of the Nazca Lines, comprises several pyramids and a site called **El Estaquería** ① *to visit the ruins of Cahuachi costs US$10, minimum 2 people. See also the Museo Antonini, above.* The latter is thought to have been a series of astronomical sighting posts, but more recent research suggests the wooden pillars were used to dry dead bodies and therefore it may have been a place of mummification.

The road from Nazca towards Cuzco
Two hours out of Nazca on the newly paved road to Abancay and Cuzco is the **Reserva Nacional Pampas Galeras** at 4,100 m, which has a vicuña reserve. There is an interesting Museo del Sitio, also a military base and park guard here. No banks or ATMs, but several internet places. It's best to go early as entry is free. At Km 155 is **Puquio**, then it's another 185 km to **Chalhuanca**. Fuel is available in both towns. There are wonderful views on this stretch, with lots of small villages, valleys and alpacas.

South of Nazca
Chala (Phone code 054), 173 km from Nazca, is a fishing village with beaches. There are dozens of restaurants. There are several hotels (**C-F**), all in Chala Sur, 10 minutes' walk south from where the buses stop in Chala Norte. No banks or ATMs, but several internet places. Colectivos from Nazca cost US$3.50. Lima-Arequipa buses pass Chala about 0600.

About 10 km north of Chala are the large pre-Columbian ruins of **Puerto Inca** on the coast.

This was the port for Cuzco. The site is in excellent condition: the drying and store houses can be seen as holes in the ground (be careful where you walk). On the right side of the bay is a cemetery, on the hill a temple of reincarnation, and the Inca road from the coast to Cuzco is clearly visible. The road was 240 km long, with a staging post every 7 km so that, with a change of runner at every post, messages could be sent in 24 hours. The site is best appreciated when there is no *garúa* (ie when the sun is shining).

● Sleeping

Nazca *p1169, map p1171*
If arriving by bus beware of being told that the hotel of their choice is closed, or full, and no longer runs tours. This applies particularly to Alegría. If you phone or email the hotel they will pick you up at the bus station free of charge day or night.
L-A Maison Suisse, opposite airport, T/F522434, maisonsuisse@infonegocio.net.pe. Comfortable, safe car park, expensive restaurant, pool, suites with jacuzzi, accepts Amex, good giftshop, shows video of Nazca Lines. Also has camping facilities.
AL Casa Andina, Jr Bolognesi 367, T523563, www.casa-andina.com. One of this new chain of hotels, which all offer standardized services in distinctive style. Bright, modern decor, a/c, pool, TV, internet, restaurant open all day.
AL Nazca Lines, Jr Bolognesi, T522293, reservanasca@derramajae.org.pe. With a/c, comfortable, rooms with private patio, hot water, peaceful, American breakfast included, restaurant, good but expensive meals, safe car park, pool (US$4.50 for non-guests, or free if having lunch), they can arrange package tours which include 2-3 nights at the hotel plus a flight over the lines and a desert trip. Recommended.

B De La Borda, an old hacienda at Majoro about 5 km from town past the airstrip, T522750. Lovely gardens, pool, restaurant, serene surroundings but unpredictable service.
B Nido del Cóndor, opposite the airport, Panamericana Sur Km 447, T522424, contanas@terra.com.pe. Large rooms, hot water, good restaurant, bar, shop, swimming pool, camping US$3, parking, English, Italian German spoken, free pick-up from town, reservation advised.
C-E pp Hotel Alegría, Jr Lima 168, T/F522702, www.nazcaperu.com. Rooms with bath, a/c, continental breakfast, bungalows with hot shower, shared bath (**G** pp), hot water, café, garden, pool, English, Italian, German and Hebrew spoken, laundry facilities, safe luggage deposit, book exchange, email facilities for US$2 per hr, netphone also US$2, free video on the Lines at 2100, very popular. Recommended. Efraín Alegría also runs a tour agency and guests are encouraged to buy tours (see Activities and tours), flights and bus tickets arranged.
D Hostal Las Líneas, Jr Arica 299, T522488. Spacious, cheaper without bath, restaurant. Recommended.

Nazca

| 0 metres | 200 |
| 0 yards | 200 |

To ❷ ❽ ⓬ ⓮ Airport, Puquio & Cuzco

Sleeping 🛏
Alegría 1
Casa Andina 17
De La Borda 2
Estrella del Sur 3
Hostal Alegría 4
Hostal Las Líneas 5

Internacional 7
Maison Suisse 8
Mirador 9
Nasca 10
Nasca Lines 11
Nido de Cóndor 12
Posada Guadalupe 13
Rancho Park 14
Sol de Nasca 15

Via Morburg 16

Eating 🍴
Chifa Guang Zhou 2
Concordia 3
El Portón 1
El Puquio 4
Fuente de Soda
Jumbory 5

Kañada 6
La Carreta 13
La Púa 7
La Taberna 8
Los Angeles 9
Panadería 11
Picante's 14
Plaza Mayor 12
Rico Pollo 10

D Internacional, Av Maria Reiche, T522744, hostalinternacional@hotmail.com. Hot water, garage, café and nice bungalows.

D Mirador, Tacna 436, T523121, F523714. On main plaza, comfortable, cheaper with shared bath, TV, new, modern.

D Nasca, C Lima 438, T/F522085. Hot water, cheaper without bath, clothes washing facilities, luggage store, new annexe at the back, nice garden, safe motorcycle parking.

E Estrella del Sur, Callao 568, T522106. Small rooms, welcoming, TV, breakfast. Recommended.

E pp Hostal Alegría, Av Los Incas 117, opposite *Ormeño* bus terminal, T522497. Basic, hot water, hammocks, nice garden, camping, restaurant.

E Hostal Restaurant Via Morburg, JM Mejía 108, 3 blocks from Plaza de Armas, T522566, www.walkoninn.com. Under new ownership as The WalkOn Inn. With fan, hot water, small swimming pool, TV room, internet, provides tours and flights, information, excellent and cheap restaurant for breakfast and lunch. Recommended.

E Posada Guadalupe, San Martín 225, T522249. Family run, lovely courtyard and garden, **F** without bath, hot water, good breakfast, relaxing (touts who try to sell tours are nothing to do with hotel).

E Rancho Park, on Panamericana 1 km from town towards the airport, T521153. On farmland, 2 swimming pools (1 for children), entry to pools US$1, popular at weekends, good restaurant.

E Sol de Nasca, Callao 586, T522730. Rooms with and without hot showers, TV, restaurant, pleasant, don't leave valuables in luggage store.

The road from Nazca to Cuzco *p1170*

F Hostal Central, Av Castilla 625, Puquio. Shared bath, hot water, restaurant, motorbike parking.

Hostal Josef, also in Puquio, good value, friendly.

F Hostal Victoria, Jr Arequipa 305, Chalhuanca, T083- 321301. Shared bath, clean, comfortable.

South of Nazca *p1170*

A Puerto Inka, 2 km along a side road from Km 610 Panamericana Sur (for reservations T Chala 551055), www.puertoinka.com.pe. Bungalows on the beautiful beach, hammocks outside, great place to relax, boat hire, diving equipment rental, camping US$3, low season discounts, used by tour groups, busy in summer. Price reflects the location.

❶ Eating

Nazca *p1169, map p1171*

ᵠᵠ-ᵠ La Carreta, Bolognesi, next door to Los Angeles. Nuevo Andino dishes using traditional ingredients, rustic, lively atmosphere, live music.

ᵠᵠ-ᵠ La Choza, Bolognesi 290. Nice atmosphere with woven chairs and thatched roof, all types of food, live music at night.

ᵠᵠ-ᵠ Concordia, Lima 594. Good, also rents bikes at US$1 an hour.

ᵠᵠ-ᵠ Plaza Mayor, on the Plaza. Specializes in barbecue of all types, roasted chicken, steaks, anticuchos and great salads. Recommended.

ᵠᵠ-ᵠ El Portón, Moresky 120, in front of Hotel Nazca Lines. Popular with tours, specializes in Peruvian food of all types, indoor/outdoor setting. Recommended.

ᵠᵠ-ᵠ El Puquio, Bolognesi 50 m from plaza. Good food, especially pastas, pleasant atmosphere, good for drinks, popular.

ᵠᵠ-ᵠ La Taberna, Jr Lima 321, T521411. Excellent food, live music, popular with gringos, it's worth a look just for the graffiti on the walls.

ᵠ Los Angeles, Bolognesi 266. Good, cheap, try *sopa criolla*, and chocolate cake.

ᵠ Chifa Guang Zhou, Bolognesi 297, T522036. Very good.

ᵠ Kañada, Lima 160, nazcanada@ yahoo.com. Cheap, good *menú*, excellent pisco sours, nice wines, popular, display of local artists' work, email service, English spoken, helpful. Recommended.

ᵠ La Púa, Jr Lima, next to *La Taberna*. Good espresso, also pizzas, pastas and sandwiches.

ᵠ Rico Pollo opposite *Hostal Alegría*. Good local restaurant, cheap.

Fuente de Soda Jumbory, near the cinema. Good *almuerzo*.

Panadería, Bolognesi 387.

Picante's, Av Bolognesi 464. Delicious real coffee, good cakes. The owner, Percy Pizzaro is very knowledgeable about the Lines.

▲ Activities and tours

Nazca *p1169, map p1171*

All guides must be approved by the Ministry of Tourism and should have an official identity card. As more and more touts (*jaladores*) operate at popular hotels and the bus terminals, they are using false ID cards and fake hotel and tour brochures. They are all rip-off merchants who overcharge and mislead those who arrive by bus. Only conduct business with agencies at their office, or phone or email the company you want to deal with in advance. Some hotels are not above pressurising guests to purchase tours at inflated prices. Taxi drivers usually act as guides, but most speak only Spanish. Do not take just any taxi on the plaza for a tour, always ask your hotel for a reputable driver.

Air Nasca Travel, Jr Lima 185, T521027, guide Susi recommended. Very helpful and competitive prices. Can do all types of tours around Nazca, Ica, Paracas and Pisco. Recommended.

Algería Tours, Lima 186, T522444, www.naz caperu.com. Offers inclusive tours which have been repeatedly recommended. Guides with radio contact and maps can be provided for hikes to nearby sites. Guides speak English, German, French and Italian. Tours go as far as Ica, Paracas and the Ballestas Islands. *Alegría* run a bus from Nazca to Pisco every day at 1000 (returns at 1000 from Pisco's Plaza de Armas), via Ica, Huacachina and *bodegas*.

Andean Tempo, Ignacio Morsesky 126, Parque Bolognesi, T522379, 969 9255 (mob), andeantempo@hotmail.com. Run by Enrique Levano Alarcón, adventure tours, many off the beaten track. Recommended.

Jesús Erazo Buitrón, Juan Matta 1110, T523005. Very knowledgeable, he speaks a little English but his Spanish is easy to follow.

Fernández family, who run the *Hotel Nasca*, also run local tours. Ask for the hotel owners and speak to them direct.

Nanasca Tours, Jr Lima 160, T/F522917, T962 2054 (mob), nanascatours@yahoo.com. Very helpful.

Nasca Trails, Juan Tohalino Vera, Bolognesi 550, T522858, nascatrails@terra.com.pe. English, French, German and Italian spoken. Recommended.

Félix Quispe Sarmiento, `El Nativo de Nazca', Fedeyogin5@hotmail.com. He has his own museum, Hantun Nazca, at Panamericana Sur 447 and works with the Instituto Nacional de Cultura, tours off the beaten track, can arrange flights, knowledgeable, ask for him at Kañada restaurant. Recommended.

Tours of the Nazca Lines

On land Taxi-guides to the mirador, 0800-1200, cost US$4-6 pp, or you can hitch, but there is not always much traffic. Travellers suggest the view from the hill 500 m back to Nazca is better. Go early as the site gets very hot. Or take a taxi and arrive at 0745 before the buses.

By air Small planes take 3-5 passengers to see the Nazca Lines. Flights last 30-35 mins and are controlled by air traffic personnel at the airport to avoid congestion. The price for a flight is US$40-50 pp. You also have to pay US$3 airport tax. It is best to organize a flight with the airlines themselves at the airport. Flights are bumpy with many tight turns – many people get airsick so it's wise not to eat or drink just before a flight. Best times to fly are 0800-1000 and 1500-1630 when there is less turbulence and better light (assuming there is no fog). Make sure you clarify everything before getting on the plane and ask for a receipt. Also let them know in advance if you have any special requests. Taxi to airport, US$1.35, bus, US$0.10. These companies are recommended; there are others.

Aerocóndor, Panamericana Sur Km 447, T522404, or their office opposite Hotel Las Dunas in Ica, T256230 – see also Lima listings, www.aero condor.com.pe. From Lima, they offer flights over the lines in a 1-day tour (lunch in Nazca) for US$260 pp; or flights from Ica for US$130 pp.

Aero Ica in Jr Lima and at the airport. In Lima, T445 0839, aeroica@terra.com.pe. Offers flights over the lines from Lima in a 1-day tour (lunch in Nazca) for US$260 pp; or flights from Ica for US$130 pp. Aero Ica also offers a night in Maison Suisse plus flight for US$65, book 48 hrs in advance.

Alas Peruanas, T522444, www.alasperuanas.com. Flights can also be booked at Hotel Alegría. Experienced pilots. They also offer 1-hr flights over the Palpa and Llipata areas, where you can see more designs and other rare patterns (US$60 pp, minimum 3). They can also organize flights from Pisco (US$130) and Ica (US$120). All *Alas Peruanas* flights include the BBC film of Nazca.

⊖ Transport

Nazca *p1169, map p1171*

Bus It is worth paying the extra for a good bus - reports of robbery on the cheaper services. Over-booking is common.

To **Lima**, 446 km, 6 hrs, several buses and colectivos daily. Ormeño, T522058, *Royal Class* at 0530 and 1330 US$20 from Hotel Nazca Lines, normal service from Av Los Incas, 6 a day, US$5.50; **Civa**, Av Guardia Civil, T523019, normal service at 2300, US$6; **Cruz del Sur**, Av Guardia Civil 290, T523713, 4 daily, US$6. Ormeño's *Royal Class* arrives in Santa Catalina, a much safer area of Lima.

Ormeño to **Ica**, 2 hrs, US$1.50, 4 a day. For **Pisco** (210 km), 3 hrs, buses stop 5 km outside town (see under Pisco, Transport), so change in Ica for direct transport into Pisco. To **Arequipa**, 565 km, 9 hrs: Ormeño 1530, 2000, 2400, from Av Los Incas, US$10, with *Royal* Class at 2130, US$20, 8 hrs. **Cruz del Sur** has 4 buses daily between 1900 and 2400, US$10-27. Civa, US$20, 8 hrs. Flores has 9 buses daily, US$15, but trip takes 15-16 hrs. Delays are possible out of Nazca because of drifting sand across the road or because of mudslides in the rainy season. Travel in daylight if possible. Book your ticket on previous day.

Buses to **Cuzco**, 659 km, via **Chalhuanca** and **Abancay** (13 hrs). On the **Lima-Nazca-Abancay-Cuzco** route Expreso Wari have 6 services a day, normal US$17, and *Imperial* service US$20. Their offices are at the exit from Nazca on the road to Puquío. The highway from Nazca to Cuzco is paved and is safe for bus travellers, drivers of private vehicles and motorcyclists. Also buses to Cuzco with Ormeño, US$27, and Cruz del Sur, 2015, 2100, US$27, but via Arequipa.

Puerto Inca *p1170*

Taxi from **Chala** US$5, or take Yauca **colectivo**, US$0.50, to Km 603 and walk down, 3 km, or walk from Chala, 2 hrs. 1-day tour from Nazca, US$10 pp.

Banks BCP, Lima y Grau, changes cash and Visa TCs, cash advance on Visa, decent rates, Visa ATM. Some street changers will change TCs for 8% commission. **Internet** Many places on Jr Bolognesi. **Migsu Net**, Arica 295, p 2. Open daily 0800-2400, good, fast machines, US$1 per hr. Facilities at *Hotel Alegría* and *Casa Andina*. **Post offices** At Fermín de Castillo 379, T522016. **Telephones** Telefónica for international calls with coins on Plaza Bolognesi; also on Plaza de Armas and at Lima 359. **Useful addresses** Police: at Av Los Incas, T522105, or T105 for emergencies.

Arequipa and the far south

The colonial city of Arequipa, with its guardian volcano, El Misti, is the ideal place to start exploring southern Peru. It is the gateway to two of the world's deepest canyons, Colca and Cotahuasi, whose villages and terraces hold onto a traditional way of life and whose skies are home to the magnificent condor. From Arequipa there are routes to Lake Titicaca and to the border with Chile.

Arequipa → *Phone code: 054. Colour map 6, grid A1. Population: 1 million. Altitude: 2,380 m.*

The city of Arequipa, 1,011 km from Lima, stands in a beautiful valley at the foot of El Misti volcano, a snow-capped, perfect cone, 5,822 m high, guarded on either side by the mountains Chachani (6,057 m), and Pichu-Pichu (5,669 m). The city has fine Spanish buildings and many old and interesting churches built of sillar, a pearly white volcanic material almost exclusively used in the construction of Arequipa. The city was re-founded on 15 August 1540 by an emissary of Pizarro, but it had previously been occupied by Aymara Indians and the Incas. It is the main commercial centre for the south, and its people resent the general tendency to believe that everything is run from Lima. It has been declared a World Cultural Heritage site by UNESCO.

Ins and outs
Getting there Transport to and from the **airport** (7 km west) is described below under Transport. It takes about half an hour to town. The main **bus terminal** is south of the centre, 15 minutes from the centre by colectivo, 10 minutes by taxi. ▶▶ *For more detailed information, see Transport, page 1190.*

Getting around The main places of interest and the hotels are within walking distance of the Plaza de Armas. If you are going to the suburbs, take a bus or taxi. A cheap tour of the city can be made in a *Vallecito* bus, 1½ hours for US$0.30. It is a circular tour which goes down Calles Jerusalén and San Juan de Dios.

Climate The climate is delightful, with a mean temperature before sundown of 23°C, and after sundown of 14½°C. The sun shines on 360 days of the year. Annual rainfall is less than 150 mm.

Security There has been an increase in street crime in Arequipa in 2005-2006, with many reports of taxi drivers in collusion with criminals to rob both tourists and locals. The police are conspicuous, friendly, courteous and efficient, but their resources are limited.

Tourist office i-perú ① *Casona Santa Catalina, C Santa Catalina 210, T221228. i perú also has an office in the airport, 2nd floor, T444564, daily 0630-1800.* **Tourist office** ① *San Agustín 115, www.arequipa-tourism.com.Indecopi*, the tourist protection bureau, has two offices: ① *Moral 316, T212054, mcornejo@indecopi.gob.pe* and ① *Quezada 104, Yanahuara, T270181. Or To800-42579, 24 hours, toll-free.* **Tourist Police** ① *Jerusalén 315, T201258*, very helpful with complaints or giving directions.

Sights
The elegant **Plaza de Armas** is faced on three sides by arcaded buildings with many restaurants, and on the fourth by the massive **Cathedral**, founded in 1612 and largely rebuilt

in the 19th century. It is remarkable for having its façade along the whole length of the church (entrance on Santa Catalina and San Francisco). Inside is the fine Belgian organ and elaborately carved wooden pulpit. In the June 2001 earthquake which devastated much of southern Peru, one of the cathedral's twin towers famously collapsed. It has been rebuilt. Behind the Cathedral there is an alley with handicraft shops and places to eat.

Santa Catalina Convent ① *Santa Catalina 301, T229798, www.santacatalina. org.pe, 0900-1600, US$7.25. There are tours of 1½ hrs, no set price, many of the guides speak English or German (a tip of US$2.85 is expected). There is a good café, which sells cakes made by the nuns and a special blend of tea.* This is by far the most remarkable sight, opened in 1970 after four centuries of mystery. The convent has been beautifully refurbished, with

Arequipa

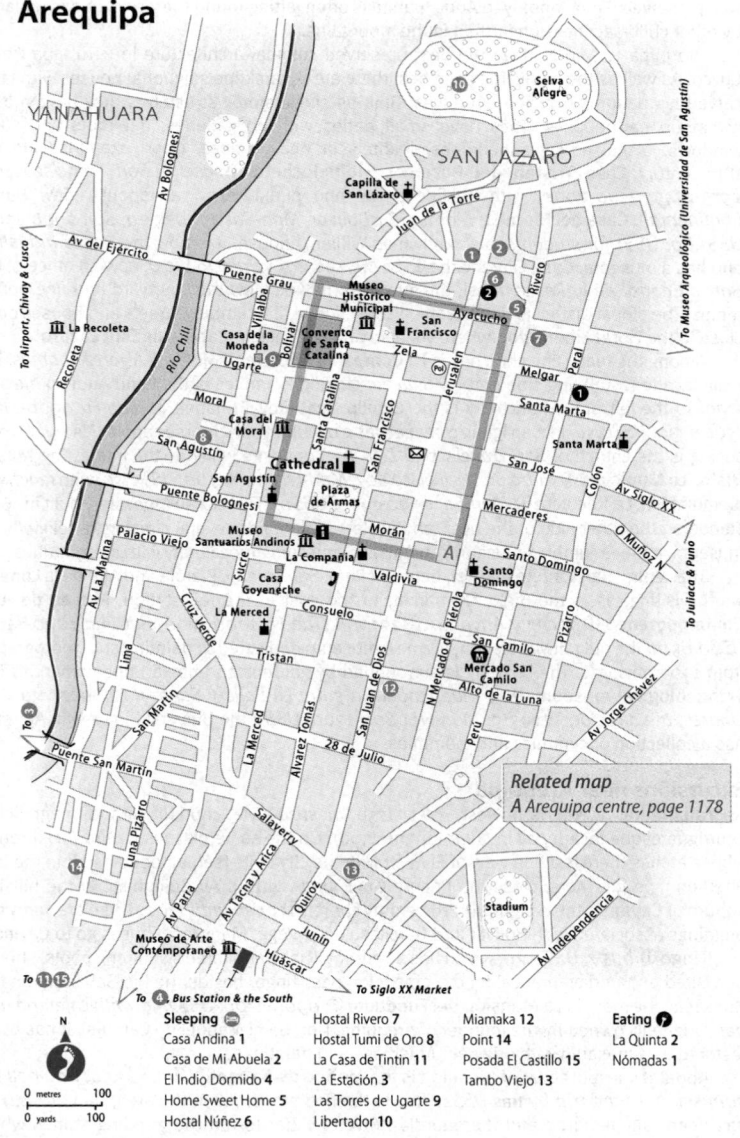

N

0 metres 100
0 yards 100

Sleeping	Hostal Rivero 7	Miamaka 12	Eating
Casa Andina 1	Hostal Tumi de Oro 8	Point 14	La Quinta 2
Casa de Mi Abuela 2	La Casa de Tintin 11	Posada El Castillo 15	Nómadas 1
El Indio Dormido 4	La Estación 3	Tambo Viejo 13	
Home Sweet Home 5	Las Torres de Ugarte 9		
Hostal Núñez 6	Libertador 10		

period furniture, pictures of the Arequipa and Cuzco schools and fully equipped kitchens. It is a complete miniature walled colonial town of over 2 ha in the middle of the city at Santa Catalina 301, where about 450 nuns lived in total seclusion, except for their women servants. The few remaining nuns have retreated to one section of the convent, allowing visitors to see a maze of cobbled streets and plazas bright with geraniums and other flowers, cloisters and buttressed houses. These have been painted in traditional white, orange, deep red and blue.

Museo Santuarios Andinos ① *La Merced 110, T200345, www.ucsm.edu.pe/santury, Mon-Sat 0900-1800, Sun 0900-1700, US$5 includes a 20-min video of the discovery in English followed by a guided tour in English, French, German, Italian or Spanish (tip the guide), discount with student card, in all the tour lasts 1 hr.* It contains the frozen Inca mummies found on Mount Ampato; the mummy known as 'Juanita' is fascinating as it is so well preserved. From January to April, Juanita is often jetting round the world, and is replaced by other child sacrifices unearthed in the mountains.

Arequipa is said to have the best preserved colonial architecture in Peru, apart from Cuzco. As well as the many fine churches, there are several fine seignorial houses with large carved tympanums over the entrances. Built as single-storey structures, they have mostly withstood earthquakes. They have small patios with no galleries, flat roofs and small windows, disguised by superimposed lintels or heavy grilles. Good examples are the 18th-century **Casa Tristán del Pozo**, or **Gibbs-Ricketts house** ① *San Francisco 108, 0915-1245, 1500-2000*, with its fine portal and puma-head waterspouts (now *Banco Continental*). **Casa del Moral** ① *Moral 318 y Bolívar, Mon-Sat 0900-1700, Sun 0900-1300, US$1.80, US$1 for students*, also known as Williams house. It is now the *Banco Industrial* and has a museum. **Casa Goyeneche** ① *La Merced 201 y Palacio Viejo*, now an office of the *Banco Central de la Reserva*, ask the guards to let you view the courtyard and fine period rooms. The oldest district is **San Lázaro**, a collection of tiny climbing streets and houses quite close to the **Hotel Libertador**, where you can find the ancient **Capilla de San Lázaro**.

Among the many fine churches is **La Compañía** ① *General Morán y Alvarez Thomas*, the main façade (1698) and side portal (1654) are striking examples of the florid Andean *mestizo* style. To the left of the sanctuary is the **Capilla Real** (Royal Chapel) ① *Mon-Fri 0900-1130, 1500-1730, US$0.50*. Its San Ignacio chapel has a beautiful polychrome cupola. Also well worth seeing is the church of **San Francisco** ① *Zela 103*, opposite which is the interesting **Museo Histórico Municipal** ① *Plaza San Francisco 407, Mon-Fri 0900-1700, US$0.50*, with much war memorabilia. **La Recoleta** ① *Mon-Sat 0900-1900, US$1*, a Franciscan monastery built in 1647, stands on the other side of the river, on Recoleta. It contains several cloisters, a religious art museum, a pre-Columbian museum, an Amazon museum and a library with many rarities

The central **San Camilo market**, between Perú, San Camilo, Piérola and Alto de la Luna, is worth visiting, as is the Siglo XX market, to the east of the rail station. **Museo de Arte Contemporaneo** ① *Tacna y Arica 201, T221068, Tue-Fri 1000-1700, Sat-Sun 1000-1400, US$0.85*, in the old railway station, is a new museum dedicated to painting and photography from 1900 onwards. The building is surrounded by gardens and has a Sunday market. The **archaeological museum** ① *Av Independencia entre La Salle y Santa Rosa, apply to Dr E Linares, the director, T229719, Mon-Fri 0800-1300, US$1*, the Universidad de San Agustín, has a collection of ceramics and mummies.

Excursions near Arequipa

At **Yanahuara**, 2 km northwest, is a 1750 *mestizo*-style church, with a magnificent churrigueresque façade, all in *sillar* (opens 1500). On the same plaza is a *mirador*, through whose arches there is a fine view of El Misti with the city at its feet, a popular spot in the late afternoon. To get there, cross the Puente Grau, turn right up Av Bolognesi. In the hillside suburb of **Cayma** is the delightful 18th-century church ① *open until 1700*. There are many old buildings associated with Bolívar and Garcilaso de la Vega. Many local buses go to Cayma.

Tingo ① *bus 7, US$0.20*, which has a very small lake and three swimming pools, should be visited on Sunday for local food. Some 3 km past Tingo, beside the Río Sabandía on the Huasacanche road, is **La Mansión del Fundador** ① *0900-1700, US$2.50, with cafetería and bar*. Originally owned by the founder of Arequipa, Don Garcí Manuel de Carbajal, it has been restored as a museum with original furnishings and paintings.

About 8 km southeast of Arequipa is the **Molino de Sabandía** ① *US$1.50, ring bell for admission; round trip by taxi US$4*. This is the first stone mill in the area, built in 1621. It has been fully restored and the guardian diverts water to run the grinding stones when visitors arrive. The well-kept grounds have old willow trees and the surrounding countryside is pleasant. Adjoining Sabandía is **Yumina** ① *tourist fee of US$6 payable, which may be asked for on the bus to Chivay*, with many Inca terraces which are still in use and between Sabandía and Arequipa is Paucarpata, with an old church and views of terraces, El Misti and Chachani.

Climbing El Misti At 5,822 m, El Misti volcano offers a relatively straight- forward opportunity to scale a high peak. Start from the hydroelectric plant, after first registering with the police there, then you need one day to the Monte Blanco shelter, at 4,800 m. Start early for the 4-6 hours to the top, to get there by 1100 before the mists obscure the view. If you start back at 1200 you will reach the hydroelectric plant by 1800. Alternatively, take a jeep at 3,300 m to the end of the rough road, then 4-5 hours' hike to the campground at 4,600 m. Only space for three tents. Be sure to take plenty of food, water and protection against the weather; it takes two days to reach the crater. Remember that the summit is at a very high altitude and that this, combined with climbing on scree, makes it hard going for the untrained. Recent reports of hold-ups of climbers make it inadvisable for you to go alone. Join a group or take a guide. Further information is available from travel agencies and Miguel and Carlos Zárate (address below, Climbing, page 1181).

● Sleeping

Arequipa *p1174, maps p1175 and p1178*
When arriving by bus, do not believe taxi drivers who say the hotel of your choice is closed or full. This applies to *El Indio Dormido*, *La Reyna* and *Tambo Viejo*. Ring the door bell and check for yourself.
LL-L Libertador, Plaza Simón Bolívar, Selva Alegre, T215110, www.libertador.com.pe. Safe, large comfortable rooms, good service, swimming pool (cold), gardens, good meals, pub-style bar, cocktail lounge, squash court.
AL Sonesta Posada del Inca, Portal de Flores 116, T215530, www.sonesta.com. On the Plaza de Armas, all the services associated with this chain, Inkafé café and bar with good views, restaurant, tiny outdoor pool, business centre with internet.
AL-A Casa Andina, C Jerusalén 603, T202070, www.casa-andina.com. Part of the attractive Casa Andina chain, with breakfast, comfortable and colourful, central, modern, good restaurant, safe, cable TV, phones, car parking.
B Casa de Mi Abuela, Jerusalén 606, T241206, www.lacasadmiabuela.com. Safe, hot water, laundry, cable TV, internet, swimming pool, rooms at the back are quieter and overlook the garden, **D** without bath, self-catering if desired, English spoken, parking, internet access US$3 per hr, tours and transport organized in own agency (*Giardino*, T221345, www.giardinotours.com), which has good information (expensive), small library of European books, breakfast or evening snacks on patio or in beautiful garden.
B De La Fuente, Urb La Campiña Paisajista D-14A, San Lázaro, T203996, delafuente_ hostal@hotmail.com. With breakfast, family-style, welcoming, cable TV, free internet, safe.

B Hostal Solar, Ayacucho 108, T/F241793, solar@star.com.pe. Nice colonial building, TV, bath, hot water, includes good breakfast served in nice patio, sun lunge on roof, very secure, quiet.
B-C Posada el Castillo, Pasaje Campos 105, Vallecito, T201828, www.posadaelcastillo.com. Newly built Dutch-owned hotel in colonial style 15 mins walk south of Plaza de Armas. Variety of rooms and suites, some with balcony and view of El Misti, free internet, TV, pool, wonderful breakfast, laundry. Recommended.
C Los Balcones de Moral y Santa Catalina, Moral 217, T201291, losbalcones@ hotmail.com. Convenient, 1 block from Plaza de Armas and close to Santa Catalina, large rooms, comfortable beds, hot water, laundry, café, tourist information.
C Casa de Melgar, Melgar 108, T/F222459, www.lared.net.pe/lacasademelgar. Excellent rooms, 18th-century building, with bath, hot water (solar panel), safe, nice courtyard, good breakfast in café open in the morning and 1730-2100. Good taxi driver (Angel). Recommended.
C La Casa de Margott, Jerusalén 304, T229517, lacasademargotthostal@hotmail.com. Bright with a massive palm tree in patio, spacious, convenient, small bar/café, cable TV, phone, security box. Recommended.
C La Casa de Tintin, Urbanización San Isidro F1, Vallecito, T284700, www.hoteltintin.com. 15 mins' walk, 5 mins by taxi from the Plaza de Armas, Belgian/Peruvian owned, hot water, cable TV, garden, terrace, sauna, laundry service, restaurant, café and bar and internet, mountain bike rental, very pleasant and comfortable, breakfast included. Recommended.

C Miamaka, San Juan de Dios 402, T241496, hotel_miamaka@terra.com.pe. Excellent service, helpful, cable TV, English spoken.

D La Estación, Loreto 419, Umacollo, T273852, www.backpackerperu.com. Unusual dormitory accommodation in 2 train carriages, includes breakfast, hot water, restaurant next door. 10 mins' walk from Plaza, ask directions for 'el Ovalo del Vallecito', English spoken.

D Home Sweet Home, Rivero 509A, T405982, www.homesweethome-peru.com. Run by María and daughter Cathy, who runs a travel agency and speaks Spanish, English, Italian, French, very helpful, warm and inviting atmosphere, substantial fresh breakfast included. Private or shared bath, hot water all day, simple rooms.

D Hospedaje El Caminante Class, Santa Catalina 207-A, 2nd floor, T203444. Cheaper without bath, hot water, comfortable, laundry service and facilities, sun terrace, very helpful owners. Recommended.

D Hostal Le Foyer, Ugarte 114 y San Francisco, T286473, hoastallefoyer@ yahoo.com. Comfortable, hot water, laundry, luggage store, helpful, but disco below.

D Hostal Núñez, Jerusalén 528, T233268, hostal_nunez@terra.com.pe. Hot water, TV, laundry, safe, small rooms, breakfast on roof terrace overlooking the city.

D Hostal Regis, Ugarte 202, T226111. Colonial house, French-style interior, hot water all day, cooking and laundry facilities, sun terrace with good views, safe deposit, luggage store, video rental, tours arranged, but poor breakfast.

D Hostal Tumi de Oro, San Agustín 311A, 2½ blocks from the Plaza de Armas, T/F281319. French and English spoken, hot water, roof terrace, book exchange, tea/coffee facilities, safe.

D Lluvia de Oro, Jerusalén 308, T214252, lluvia_de_oro@hotmail.com. Cheaper without bath, English-spoken, breakfast US$2, laundry service, good views.

D La Posada del Cacique, Puente Grau 219, T202170, posadadelcacique@yahoo.es. Old house with tall ceilings, teeny patio, sun terrace, hot water, English spoken, family atmosphere, **E** without bath, also dorm accommodation, safe storage facilities, breakfast available, laundry service, will pick up from terminal. Recommended.

D Las Torres de Ugarte, Ugarte 401, T/F283532, hostaltorresdeugarte@star.com.pe. Next to Santa Catalina convent, occasional hot water, cable TV, laundry service, roof terrace, parking, safe, luggage store, price includes breakfast.

D-F Tambo Viejo, Av Malecón Socabaya 107, IV Centenario, T288195, www.tamboviejo.com. 5 blocks south of the plaza near the rail station. Rooms vary and range from double with bath to dormitory, quiet, English and Dutch spoken,

walled garden, hot water, breakfast extra, expensive laundry service, cable TV, safe deposit, coffee shop, bar, book exchange (2 for 1), money changed, tourist information for guests, use of kitchen, internet, phone for international calls, bike rental, popular with young travellers, luggage store extra, tours and volcano climbs arranged. For a small fee, you can use the facilities if passing through. Telephone the hostel and they will pick you up free of charge from 0500-2100 as it's some distance from centre and not the safest area.

Arequipa centre

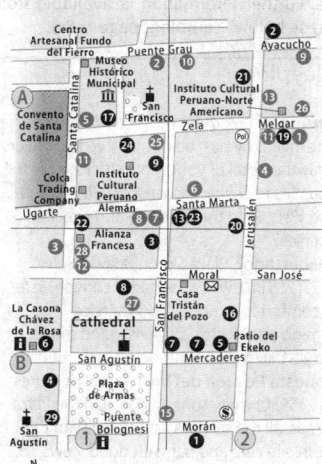

E Casa Itzhak, Av Parra 97, T204596, T994 6643 (mob). With and without bath, includes breakfast, cable TV, laundry service, restaurant, free transport to bus station, very helpful.
E Colonial House Inn, Puente Grau 114, T/F223533, colonial houseinn@hotmail.com. Hot water, quieter rooms at the back, laundry facilities and service, kitchen facilities, roof terrace, good choice of breakfasts, owners speak English.
E Hostal La Reyna, Zela 209, T286578. With or without bath, two more expensive rooms at the top of the house, hot water, the daughter speaks English, laundry, breakfast for US$1.15, pizza available at any hour, rooftop seating, will store luggage, ask about rips to the Colca Canyon and volcanoes.
E Hostal Rivero, Rivero 420, T229266, www.ciudadblanca.net/hostalrivero. Cheaper with shared bath, hot water, cable TV extra, sunny patio, medical assistance, laundry facilities, very helpful, good value.
E pp **The Point Arequipa**, Av Lima 515, Vallecito, T286920, arequipa@thepoint hostels.com. Sister hostel to The Point in Barranco (Lima), in same style, free internet, opened 2005.
F La Casita de Ugarte, Ugarte 212, T204363. English/Peruvian run, large basic rooms in a colonial building, new, good value.
F La Fiorentina, Puente Grau 110, T202571. **G** without bath, hot water, comfortable, family atmosphere, tours arranged, laundry facilities, use of kitchen extra.
F pp **El Indio Dormido**, Av Andrés Avelino Cáceres B-9, T427401, the_sleeping_indian@ yahoo.com. Close to bus terminal, free transport to centre, some rooms with bath, TV, very helpful.

Youth hostels
D Premier, Av Quiroz 100, T/F227821, www.hostalpremier.com. HI-affiliated, **E** pp for HI members or in dormitory, cultural and other trips offered.
F Youth Hostel Arequipa, Zela 313, T669253. Dormitory accommodation, kitchen, cosy lounge, cable TV, laundry facilities, very helpful, luggage stored.

⊘ Eating

Arequipa *p1174, maps p1175 and p1178*
Several restaurants overlook the Plaza de Armas on its west side; their staff may pounce on you good-naturedly as you walk by.

♥♥♥ La Quinta, Jerusalén 522. Excellent food, large portions of local food, tourist-oriented, quiet garden. Also for *peña* folklore music, weekends mainly, US$1.50 cover.
♥♥♥ Tradición Arequipeña, Av Dolores 111, Paucarpata, T246467. Restaurant serving excellent food, popular with tourists and locals alike, also dance hall. There are many other restaurants and discos on this avenue.
♥♥ Ary Quepay, Jerusalén 502. Excellent local meat and vegetarian dishes, open 1000-2400, very touristy but fun.
♥♥ Café-Restaurante Bóveda San Agustín, Portal San Agustín 127-129. Attractive, good value breakfasts and lunches, evening specials, opens at 0700.
♥♥ La Casita de José Antonio, Plaza San Francisco 401 y Zela. *Cevichería*, fish and seafood, lunchtime only.
♥♥ Nómadas, Melgar 306. Swiss and South American owned, breakfasts, wide menu including vegetarian, sandwiches.
♥♥ Pizzería Los Leños, Jerusalén 407. Excellent, good atmosphere, evenings only, popular, especially with tourists.
♥♥ Sonccollay, Portal de San Agustin 149. Serving 'Inca and Pre-Inca' dishes, stone-cooked alpaca steaks and meats are a speciality, entertaining owner, plenty of homemade *chicha*.
♥♥ Zig Zag, Zela 210. In a colonial house, European (including Swiss) and local dishes, meats include ostrich and alpaca, delicious. They also have **crêperies** in the Alianza Francesa and at Santa Catalina 208.
♥ Café El Buho, in Casona Chávez de la Rosa (UNSA), San Agustín. Evenings only. Recommended.
♥ Casa Vegetariana, Moral 205. Vegetarian and Asian, typical local food as well as western dishes.
♥ Colibri Café, San Francisco 225. Excellent value set lunches and dinners, open plan, attractive, good coffee.
♥ Lakshmivan, Melgar 104, T228768. Set vegetarian lunch for US$1.25, pleasant courtyard, good value, healthy, slow service.
♥ Mandala, Jerusalén 207. Good value, vegetarian, breakfast, 3 set menus for lunch, buffet, dinner, friendly staff. Recommended.
♥ El Turko, San Francisco 216. Kebabs, coffee, breakfasts recommended, good sandwiches, open 0700-2200. Also **♥♥ El Turko II** at San Francisco 315, also very good.

● *For an explanation of the sleeping and eating price codes used in this guide, see inside the front*
● *cover. Other relevant information is found in Essentials pages 1075-1077.*

Cafés

Café Capriccio, Mercaderes 121. Not that cheap, but excellent coffee, cakes, stuffed baked potatoes, pastas, sandwiches and juices, also has internet.

Café Manolo, Mercaderes 107 and 113. Great cakes and coffee, also cheap lunches.

Café Valenzuela, Morán 114. Fantastic coffee, locals' favourite.

La Canasta, Jerusalén 115. Bakes excellent baguettes twice daily, also serves breakfast and delicious apple and brazil nut pastries, courtyard seating.

Pushkin, Ugarte 121B. Good for set breakfasts, crêpes, burgers, very friendly and pleasant. Typical Arequipeño food is available at the San Camilo market. A good local speciality is Mejía cheese. You should also try the *queso helado*, which is frozen fresh milk mixed with sugar and a sprinkling of cinnamon. The local chocolate is excellent: La Ibérica, in Patio del Ekeko, Mercaderes 141 (see Shopping), is top quality, but expensive. The toffee and the fruit drinks called *papayada* and *tumbada* are also local specialities in the market and restaurants.

Bars and clubs

Arequipa *p1174, maps p1175 and p1178*
There are many good dancing spots on Av Ejército in Yanahuara, but most night-owls head to Av Dolores, a short taxi ride away (US$1).

Blue Margarita, Melgar 119. Large club with several areas, good mix of music.

Le Café Art Montreal, Ugarte 210. Canadian-run jazz/blues restaurant/ bar with live music Wed and Sat, good atmosphere.

Déjà Vu, San Francisco 319-B. Café/restaurant and bar, good food, DJ evenings, shows movies, popular, 2000-2400.

Farren's Irish Bar, Pasaje Catedral (as in Chivay). Good meeting place, pool table, great music.

Forum, San Francisco 317. Rock café, live music Thu-Sat 1800-0400, disco, pool tables, US$5 cover if band is playing, includes 1 drink, drinks US$1.50, popular.

Las Quenas, Santa Catalina 302. For *peña* music, Mon-Fri 2100.

Siwara, Santa Catalina 210. Trendy hangout, lively in the evening, good food and some live music.

Festivals and events

Arequipa *p1174, maps p1175 and p1178*
A full list of the department's many festivals is available locally.

10 Jan: Sor Ana de Los Angeles y Monteagudo, festival for the patron saint of

Santa Catalina monastery. **Mar-Apr**: Semana Santa celebrations involve huge processions every night, culminating in the burning of an effigy of Judas on Easter Sunday in the main plazas of Cayma and Yanahuara, and the reading of his will, containing criticisms of the city authorities. **27 Apr**: the celebration of the apostle Santiago. **May** is known as the **Mes de Las Cruces**, with ceremonies on hilltops throughout the city. **3 Aug**: a procession through the city bearing the images of Santo Domingo and San Francisco. **6-31 Aug**: Fiesta Artesanal del Fundo El Fierro is a sale and exhibition of *artesanía* from all parts of Peru, taking place near Plaza San Francisco. **6-17 Aug**: celebration of the city's anniversary (the 15th, many events including a mass ascent of El Misti). **2 Nov**: Day of the Dead celebrations in cemeteries.

Shopping

Arequipa *p1174, maps p1175 and p1178*
Bookshops
For international magazines, look along C San Francisco, between Mercaderes and San José.

Librería El Lector, San Francisco 211. Wide selection, including of Peruvian authors, book exchange in various languages (2 for 1), stocks Footprint.

Librerías San Francisco has branches at Portal de Flores 138, San Francisco 102-106 and 133-135. Books on Arequipa and Peru, some in English.

Handicrafts
Alpaca 21, Jerusalén 115, of 125, T213425. Recommended.

Colca Trading Company, Santa Catalina 300B, T242088, colcatradingperu@yahoo.com. Sells a wide variety of naturally coloured cotton and alpaca clothing for adults and children.

Michell y Cia, Juan de la Torre 101, T202525, www.michell.com.pe. Factory outlet, excellent place for alpaca yarn in huge variety of colours, also a clearance room for baby and adult alpaca yarn is sold. They also sell other types of wool. Alpaca garments also for sale. 1920s machinery on display.

Millma's, Pasaje Catedral 117 and 112 opposite, millmas@hotmail.com. 100% baby alpaca goods, run by Peruvian family high quality, beautiful designs, good prices.

Markets
The covered market opposite the Teatro Municipal in C Mercaderes is recommended for knitted goods, bags, etc.

Fundo del Fierro, the large handicraft market behind the old prison on Plaza San Francisco, is also worth a visit. Shop 14 sells alpaca-wool handicrafts from Callalli in the Colca canyon.

Shopping centres
Patio del Ekeko, Mercaderes 141, www.patiodelekeko.com. A commercial centre with upmarket handicrafts, *Alpaca 111* (recommended for high-quality alpaca and vicuña products), jewellery, *La Ibérica* chocolate shop, café, internet, cinema and *Museo de Arte Textil* upstairs.

▲▲ Activities and tours

Arequipa *p1174, maps p1175 and p1178*
Climbing, cycling and trekking
International recommendations are for a 300m per day maximum altitude gain. Be wary of agencies wanting to sell you trips with very fast ascents.
Colca Trek, Jerusalén 401 B, T206217, www.trekinperu.com. Run by the knowledgeable and English-speaking Vlado Soto, recommended for climbing, trekking and mountain biking in the Colca Canyon. Vlado is one of the best guides for the Cotahuasi Canyon. He also rents equipment and has topographical maps.
Julver Castro, who has an agency called *Mountrekk*, T601833, julver_mountrekk@ hotmail.com. A climbing guide recommended as experienced and "full of energy".
Naturaleza Activa, Santa Catalina 211, T204182, naturactiva@yahoo.com. Experienced guides, knowledgeable, climbing and trekking.
Peru Adventures Tours, Jerusalén 410, T221658, www.peruadventurestours.com. Downhill mountain biking with 4WD support, 3-hr trip into Misti and Chachani mountains,

stopping along the way for sightseeing. Cycle ride starts at Azufrero, 5,000 m, finishing in Arequipa at 1600, all equipment, oxygen and snack provided, English-speaking guide. Also other adventure sports, in southern Peru.
Selern Services, Urb Puerta Verde F13, José LB y Rivero, Arequipa, T348685, www.selernexpediciones.com. Trekking, adventure tourism, mountain climbing.
Volcanyon Travel, C Villalba 414, T205078, mario-ortiz@terra.com.pe. Trekking and some mountain bike tours in the Colca Canyon, also volcano climbing.
Zárate Expeditions, Santa Catalina 204, of 3, T202461/263107. Run by Carlos Zárate of the Mountaineering Club of Peru. Specialist mountaineering and exploring, with information and advice and some equipment rental. Carlos also runs trips to the source of the Amazon.

Tour operators
Many agencies on Jerusalén, Santa Catalina and around Plaza de Armas sell air, train and bus tickets and offer tours of Colca, Cotahuasi, Toro Muerto and city. Prices vary greatly so shop around. As a general rule, you get what you pay for, so check carefully what is included in the cheapest of tours. Always settle the details before starting the tour and check that there are enough people for the tour to run. Travel agents frequently work together to fill buses (even the more expensive agencies may not have their own transport) and there are lots of touts. Many tourists prefer to contract tours through their hotel. If a travel agency puts you in touch with a guide, make sure he/she is official. The following have been recommended as helpful and reliable.

A.I. Travel Tours, Santa Catalina 203, Office 1, T222052, www.aitraveltours.com. Peruvian-Dutch tour operator offering cultural and adventure tours for groups or individuals, volunteer work and Spanish courses, large book exchange.

Castle Travel, Santo Domingo 302, castle@castletravel.com.pe. Good for local tours.

Eco Tours, Jerusalén 409, T202562, ecotours@terra.com.pe. Regular and adventure tours, recommended for Colca tours, Spanish lessons, accommodation arranged.

Holley's Unusual Excursions, T/F258459 (home) any day 1700-0700, or all day Sat and Sun, or Mon-Fri 0800-1600 T222525 and leave a message, angocho@terra.com.pe. Expat Englishman Anthony Holley runs trips in his Land Rover to El Misti, Toro Muerto, the desert and coast.

Pablo Tour, Jerusalén 400-A, T203737, 961 1241 (mob), www.pablotour.com. Father-and-son agency that owns several hostals in Cabanaconde; they know the area well, 3-day mixed tours in the Colca Canyon with mountain biking, trekking and rafting, free tourist information, maps for sale, bus and hotel reservation service.

Santa Catalina Tours, Santa Catalina 219-223, T216994. Offer unique tours of Collagua communities in the Colca Canyon, open daily 0800-1900.

Servicios Aéreos AQP SA, head office in Lima, Los Castaños 347, San Isidro, T01-222 3312, tours@saaqp.com.pe. Offers tours to Arequipa, Colca and to all parts of the country.

Transcontinental Arequipa, Puente Bolognesi 132, of 5, T213843, transcontinental-aqp@terra.com.pe. Cultural and wildlife tours in the Colca Canyon.

⊙ Transport

Arequipa *p1174, maps p1175 and p1178*
Air
Rodríguez Ballón airport is 7 km from town, T443464. To and from **Lima**, 1 hr 10 mins, several daily with **Lan**, **Aero Cúndor**, **Star Perú**, **Taca** and **WayraPerú**. Lan also serve **Juliaca**, 30 mins, and **Cuzco**, 40 mins.

A reliable means of transport to and from the airport to the hotel of your choice is with **King Tours**, T243357/283037, US$1.30 pp; give 24 hrs notice for return pick-up from your hotel; journey takes 30-40 mins depending on traffic. Transport to the airport may be arranged when buying a ticket at a travel agency, US$1 pp, but not always reliable. Local buses go to about ½ km from the airport.

Bus
There are 2 terminals at Av Andrés A Cáceres s/n, Parque Industrial, south of the centre, 15 mins by colectivo US$0.20, or taxi US$1.75. The older Terminal Terrestre contains a tourist office, shops and places to eat. The newer Terrapuerto, across the carpark, has a tourist office (which makes hotel reservations) and its own hostal (**E** without breakfast), T421375. Terminal tax US$0.30. Buses may not depart from the terminal where you bought your ticket. All the bus companies have offices in Terminal Terrestre and several also have offices in Terrapuerto. Some companies also have offices around C San Juan de Dios (5-6 blocks from the Plaza de Armas), where tickets can be bought in advance. Addresses are given below.

Note: Theft is a serious problem in the bus station area. Take a taxi to and from the bus station and do not wander around with your belongings. No one is allowed to enter the terminal 2100-0500, so new arrivals cannot be met by hoteliers between those hours; best not to arrive at night.

To **Lima**, 1,011 km, 16-18 hrs, 'normal' service US$8.70, 'imperial' US$17.40, 'crucero' US$23-29 several daily; **Enlaces** (T430333, office only in Terrapuerto), **Flores** (T238741), **Ormeño** (T424187) and **Cruz del Sur** (T217728) are recommended (prices quoted are of Cruz del Sur). The road is paved but drifting sand and breakdowns may prolong the trip.

To **Nazca**, 566 km, 9 hrs, US$10 (US$20-27 on luxury services), several buses daily, mostly at night and most buses continue to Lima. Also US$7.25 to **Chala**, 8 hrs. Some bus companies charge the same fare to Nazca as to Lima. To **Moquegua**, 213 km, 3½ hrs, US$5.50, several buses and colectivos daily. To **Tacna**, 320 km, 6-7 hrs, US$6.50-9.50, several buses daily, most with *Flores*.

To **Cuzco**, all buses go via Juliaca or Puno, US$15-18, 10 hrs. Most companies use double-decker buses (toilet, TV, hostess, etc), eg **Enlaces**, **Cruz del Sur**, **Cial** and **Ormeño**, running one morning and, some companies, one afternoon bus. There is a new, quick paved road to **Juliaca**, US$3 via Yura and Santa Lucía, 5 hrs, and **Puno**, 6 hrs, US$4.50-6. Most buses and colectivos continue to Puno. **Flores**, **Sur Oriente** and **Julsa** recommended.

Taxi
US$4-5 airport to city (can be shared). US$0.70-0.85 around town. **Nova Taxi**, T252511; **Taxi 21**, T212121; **Telemóvil**, T221515; **Taxitur**, T422323.

Train
The railway system goes from **Arequipa** to **Juliaca**, where it divides, 1 line going north to

Cuzco, the other south to **Puno**. With the opening of the new Arequipa-Juliaca highway, passenger services no longer run to Juliaca.

● Directory

Arequipa *p1174, maps p1175 and p1178*
Airline offices Lan, Santa Catalina 118-C, T201100. **Star Perú**, Santa Catalina 105A, T221896. **Taca**, Av Cayma 636 y Av Ejército, p 1 Banco Wiese Sudameris, T0800 18222. WayraPerú, Portal de San Agustín 113, T222627. Most tour agencies sell air tickets.
Banks Interbank, Mercaderes 217. Mastercard representative and ATM. **BCP**, San Juan de Dios 125, accepts Visa Card and gives good rates, no commission, Visa ATM. **BBV Continental**, San Francisco 108. Visa ATM. **BSCH**, C Jerusalén, close to Post Office, will change TCs, low rates, Visa ATM. Also *cambios* on Jerusalén and San Juan de Dios, and several travel agencies. **Sergio A del Carpio D**, Jerusalén 126, T242987, good rates for dollars. **Via Tours**, Santo Domingo 114, good rates. **Casa de Cambio**, San Juan de Dios 109, T282528, good rates. It is almost impossible to change TCs on Sat afternoon or Sun; try to find a sympathetic street changer. Better rates for cash dollars in banks and *casas de cambio*.
Consulates Bolivia, Rivero 408, of 6, T213391. Mon-Fri 0900-1400, 24 hrs for visa (except those needing clearance from La Paz), go early. **Chile**, Mercaderes 212, p 4, Of 401-402, Galerías Gameza, T/F233556, entrance to lift 30m down passageway down Mercaderes on left. Mon-Fri 0900-1300, present passport 0900-1100 if you need a visa. **Italy**, La Salle D-5, T221444, 1130-1300; in the afternoon T254686 (home). **Netherlands**, Centro Comercial Cayma, of 36, T251840. Mon-Fri 0900-1300, 1630-1830. **Spain**, Ugarte 218, p 2, T205747 (home T224915). Mon-Fri 1100-1300, Sat 0900-1300. **Sweden**, Av Villa Hermosa 803, Cerro Colorado, T259847. Mon-Fri 0830-1300, 1500-1730. **Switzerland**, Av Miguel Forga 348, Parque Industrial, T232723. UK, Mr Roberts, Tacna y Arica 156, T241340, gerencia@gruporoberts.com. Mon-Fri 0830-1230, 1500-1830, reported as very friendly and helpful.
Cultural centres Alianza Francesa, Santa Catalina 208, T215579, www.afarequipa. org.pe. Instituto Cultural Peruano-Norte Americano, Casa de los Mendiburo, Melgar 109, T891020, www.ccpna.edu.pe, has an English Library. Instituto Cultural Peruano Alemán, Ugarte 207, T218567, icpa@terra. com.pe. **Instituto Nacional de Cultura**, Alameda San Lázaro 120, T213171.
Internet Many places throughout the centre,

about US$0.50 per hr. **Language courses** Centro de Intercambio Cultural Arequipa (CEICA), Urb Universitaria G-9, T/F231759, www.ceica-peru.com. Individual classes at US$6 per hr, US$4.50 for groups, accommodation with families arranged, with board (US$70 per week) or without (US$30), also excursions. Recommended. **Escuela de Español Ari Quipay (EDEAQ)**, T257358, 999 2995 (mob), www.edeaq.com. Peruvian- Swiss run, experienced, multilingual staff, recognized by Peruvian Ministry of Education, in a colonial house near the Plaza de Armas, one-to-one and group classes, home stay available. **Silvana Cornejo**, 7 de Junio 118, Cerrito Los Alvarez, Cerro Colorado, T254985, silvanacornejo@ yahoo.com. US$6 per hr, negotiable for group, she speaks German fluently and is recommended. Her sister Roxanna charges US$3 per hr. **Liz and Edwin Pérez**, T264068, edwinett@mixmail.com. US$5 per hr one-to-one tuition, will go to the hotel you are staying at. Classes are also available at the Instituto Peruano-Norte Americano and Instituto Cultural Peruano Alemán (see Cultural Centres), the latter is US$4 per hr, compared with US$10 at the former, good. **Carlos Rojas Núñez**, Filtro 405, T285061, carlrojas@mixmail.com. Private or group lessons to students of all levels, encourages conversation, knowledgeable on culture and politics. Recommended. **Medical services** Hospitals: **Regional Honorio Delgado**, Av A Carrión s/n, T238465/231818 (inoculations). **Central del Sur**, Filtro y Peral s/n, T214430 in emergency. Clinics: **Clínica Arequipa SA**, esq Puente Grau y Av Bolognesi, T253424, fast and efficient with English-speaking doctors and all hospital facilities, consultation costs US$18, plus US$4 for sample analysis and around US$7 for a course of antibiotics. **Paz Holandesa**, Av Jorge Chávez 527, T/F206720, www.pazholandesa.com. Dutch foundation dedicated to helping the impoverished, which also has a travel clinic for tourists. Dutch and English spoken, 24-hour service. Highly recommended (see their website if you are interested in volunteering). Emergencies: Ambulance T289800. Pharmacy: **Farmacia Libertad**, Piérola 108, owner speaks English.
Post offices The central office is at Moral 118, opposite *Hotel Crismar*. Letters can only be posted at the Post Office during opening hours: Mon-Sat, 0800-2000, Sun 0800-1400. DHL, Santa Catalina 115, T234288 for sending documents and money, also Western Union rep.
Telephones Alvarez Thomas y Palacio Viejo.

Colca Canyon → Tourist tax US$11, payable to park rangers at various points in the Canyon.

The Colca Canyon is twice as deep as the Grand Canyon. The Río Colca descends from 3,500 m above sea level at Chivay to 2,200 m at Cabanaconde. The roads on either side of the canyon are at around 4,000 m. In the background looms the grey, smoking mass of Sabancaya, one of the most active volcanoes in the Americas, and its more docile neighbour, Ampato (6,288 m). Unspoiled Andean villages lie on both sides of the canyon, inhabited by the Cabana and Collagua peoples, and some of the extensive pre-Columbian terraced fields are still in use. High on anyone's list for visiting the canyon is an early-morning trip to the Cruz del Cóndor, to see these majestic birds at close quarters. From January to April is the rainy season, but this makes the area green, with lots of flowers. This is not the best time to see condors. May to December is the dry, cold season when there is more chance of seeing the birds. Conditions vary annually, though.

From Arequipa there are two routes to **Chivay**, the first village on the edge of the Canyon: the old route, via Cayma, and the new route, through Yura, following the railway, longer but quicker. It can be cold in the morning, reaching 4,825 m in the Pata Pampa pass, but the views are worth it. Cyclists should use the Yura road; better condition and less of a climb at the start. The main road from Arequipa to Chivay has been paved. The old dirt route runs north from Arequipa, over the altiplano. About an hour out of Arequipa is the **Aguada Blanca National Vicuña Reserve**. If you're lucky, you can see herds of these rare animals near the road. This route affords fine views of the volcanoes Misti, Chachani, Ampato and Sabancaya.

Chivay is the chief linking point between the two sides of the canyon; there is a road bridge over the river here (others at Yanque and Lari). The road continues northeast to **Tuti**, where there is a small handicrafts shop, and **Sibayo**, with a *pensión* and grocery store. A long circuit back to Arequipa heads south from Sibayo, passing through **Puente Callalli, Chullo** and **Sumbay**. This is a little-travelled road, but the views of fine landscapes with vicuña, llamas, alpacas and Andean duck are superb.

Crossing the river at Chivay going west to follow the canyon on the far side, you pass the villages of **Coporaque, Ichupampa** (a footbridge crosses the river between the two villages and foot and road bridges connect the road between Coporaque and Ichupampa with Yanque), **Lari, Madrigal** (footbridge to Maca) and **Tapay** (connected to Cabanaconde by a footbridge).

Chivay to Cabanaconde

Chivay (3,600 m) is the gateway to the canyon. The hot springs of **La Calera** ① *US$3, regular colectivos (US$0.25) or a 1 hr walk from town,* are 4 km away and are highly recommended after a hard day's trekking.

From Chivay, the main road goes west along the Colca Canyon. The first village encountered is **Yanque** (8 km, excellent views), with an interesting church and a bridge to the villages on the other side of the canyon. A large thermal swimming pool is 20 minutes walk from the plaza, beside the renovated Inca bridge on the Yanque-Ichupampa road, US$0.75. The road continues to **Achoma** and **Maca**, which barely survived an earthquake in November 1991. New housing has been built. The Mirador, or **Cruz del Cóndor** ① *rangers collect the tourist tax here,* is at the deepest point of the canyon. The view is wonderful and condors can be seen rising on the morning thermals (0900, arrive by 0800 to get a good spot) and sometimes in the late afternoon (1600-1800). Camping here is officially forbidden, but if you ask the tourist police in Chivay they may help. The 0500 bus from Chivay to Cabanaconde will stop here briefly at 0630 (if not, ask), US$0.75. Take the return bus from Cabanaconde (0730) and ask to be dropped off at the Mirador.

From the Mirador it is a 20-minute ride (or three-hour walk) to **Cabanaconde** (3,287 m), a friendly, typical village, but very basic (it does have 24-hour electricity). It is the last village in the Colca Canyon. The views are superb and condors can be seen from the hill just west of the village, a 15-minute walk from the plaza. A path winds down into the canyon and up to the village of Tapay. There's a tourist information office, T280212, attended by friendly locals willing to give plenty of advice, if not maps. It's a good place to find trekking guides and muleteers (mule hire US$30 a day including guide).

● Sleeping

Colca Canyon p1184
Families in the Colca Canyon offer meals for about US$1 and lodging at US$2 Banco de la Nación on plaza will change dollars.
AL Colca Lodge, between Coporaque and Ichupampa, T054-202587, www.colca-lodge.com. Very pleasant and relaxing, with beautiful hot springs beside the river, spend at least a day to make the most of the activities on offer. Recommended.

Chivay to Cabanconde p1184
Chivay
AL Estancio Pozo del Cielo, over the Puente Inca from Chivay amid pre-Inca terraces, T531144, www.pozodelcielo.com.pe. Very comfortable, warm rooms, good views, good service and restaurant. Recommended.
A Casa Andina, Huayna Cápac s/n, T531020, www.casa-andina.com. Attractive cabins with hot showers and a cosy bar/dining area, another member of this recommended hotel chain, heating, internet, parking.
C Wasi Kolping, 10 blocks south of town opposite Plaza de Toros, T521076. Comfortable cabins with hot shower, quiet, good views.
C-D La Casa de Lucila, M Grau 131, T054-607086. Comfortable, coffee, guides available.
D La Posada del Inca, Salaverry 330, T521032. Modern, with hot showers, carpeted rooms, safe.
E Hostal Anita, north side of plaza, T531114. Rooms with bath look onto a small garden. Recommended.
F Hospedaje Jessy, Zarumilla 218, 1 block from market. Simple, clean, excellent showers, **G** without bath, helpful, parking.
F Hospedaje Restaurant Los Portales, Sucre, T521101. Good accommodation, breakfast US$0.75, same price for dinner in restaurant.
G pp **Rumi Wasi**, Sucre 714, 6 blocks from plaza (3 mins' walk), T531114. Good rooms, breakfast included, hot water, helpful, mountain bike rental (in poor condition).

Between Chivay and Yanque
AL El Parador del Colca, T288440, www.paradordelcolca.com. 3½ km from Yanque, 10 km from Chivay, owned by Orient Express. Built of local materials, with solar power, on an old estate, the hotel offers lots of activities; comfortable cabin-like suites, typical food and home-grown vegetables, meals extra. Recommended.

Yanque
C Tradición Colca, on main road. Contact Carelia and Emmanuel Derouet, Jerusalén 300C, T205336, www.tradicioncolca.com. Price is per unit, **D** in low season, includes breakfast, with gardens, restaurant, bar, games room, also has backpackers' rooms and a travel agency. Recommended.
E La Casa de la Bella Flor, Cuzco 303, T280454. Charming small lodge run by Sra Hilde Checca, flower-filled garden, tasteful rooms, good meals (also open to non-residents), Hilde's uncle, Gregorio, guides visitors to pre-Columbian sites.

Cabanaconde
B Kuntur Wassi, on the hill above the plaza, T252989, kunturwassi@terra.com.pe. New, attractive and original, restaurant/bar, great views, helpful. Recommended.
C Posada del Conde, C San Pedro, T440197, pdelconde@yahoo.com. Cheaper in low season, with hot shower, excellent value, very good restaurant.
F Hostal San Pedro, 2 blocks from plaza. Bright rooms, no shower.
F Hostal Valle del Fuego, 1 and 2 blocks from the plaza, T280367, www.pablotour.com. Good, hot showers, has two places, both with restaurants serving meals for around US$3. The owner and his son, both Pablo Junco, are a wealth of information and give passes for free entry to swimming pools at the Oasis.
G Virgen del Carmen, 5 blocks up from the plaza. Hot showers, may even offer you a welcoming glass of chicha. Recommended.

● Eating

Chivay p1184
♛-♛ Casa Blanca, on main plaza. Good, main dishes US$2.50-7.50, also has *peña*.
♛-♛ Fonda del Cazador, north side of plaza. Good food including alpaca.
♛-♛ Lobos Pizzería, on the plaza. Good pizzas and fast food, internet access, pool, and a happy hour bar.
♛-♛ Los Sismos, by the petrol station. Great alpaca steaks, often has live folklore shows.
♛-♛ Witete, Siglo XX 328. Good international food and some local dishes.
♛ Farren's, Peruvian/Irish owned bar, handmade Guinness sign outside. Good selection of drinks, sandwiches and music, also bikes for hire.

● For an explanation of the sleeping and eating price codes used in this guide, see inside the front
● cover. Other relevant information is found in Essentials pages 1075-1077.

R **La Pascana**, near the Plaza de Armas. Another place serving local food; also has lodging (**D**).

Cabanaconde *p1184*

There are several basic restaurants around the plaza, including **Rancho del Colca**, which is mainly vegetarian, and **Don Piero**, signposted just off main plaza, excellent choice and good information.

❀ Festivals and events

Colca Canyon *p1184*

Many in the Colca region: **2-3 Feb**: Virgen de la Candelaria, Chivay, Cabanaconde, Maca, Tapay. **Feb**: Carnaval, Chivay. Semana Santa. **3 May**: Cruz de la Piedra, Tuti. **13 Jun**: San Antonio, Yanque, Maca. **14 Jun**: San Juan, Sibayo, Ichupampa. **21 Jun**: anniversary of Chivay. **29 Jun**: San Pedro y San Pablo, Sibayo. **14-17 Jul**: La Virgen del Carmen, Cabanaconde. **25 Jul**: Santiago Apóstol, Coporaque. **26 Jul-2 Aug**: Virgen Santa Ana, Maca. **15 Aug**: Virgen de la Asunta, Chivay. **8 Dec**: Immaculada Concepción, Yanque, Chivay. **25 Dec**: Sagrada Familia, Yanque. Many of these festivals last several days and involve traditional dances and customs.

▲ Activities and tours

Colca Canyon *p1184*
Trekking

There are many hiking possibilities in the area, with *hostales* or camping for longer treks. Make sure to take enough water, or purification, as it gets very hot and there is not a lot of water available. Moreover, sun protection is a must. Some treks are impossible if it rains heavily in the wet season, but this is very rare. Check beforehand. Ask locals for directions as there are hundreds of confusing paths going into the canyon. Buy food for longer hikes in Arequipa. Topographical maps are available at the *Instituto Geográfico Militar* in Lima, and good information from *South American Explorers*. From Chivay you can hike to Coporaque and Ichupampa, cross the river by the footbridge and climb up to Yanque, a 1-day hike. It is a 2-hr walk from the Mirador to Cabanaconde (or the other way round - horses can be hired) by a short cut, following the canyon instead of the road, which takes 3 hrs. It takes 2-3 days to walk from Chivay to Cabanaconde (70 km), you can camp along the route, then take a bus back.

Four hours below Cabanaconde is Sangalle, an 'oasis' of palm trees, swimming pools and modern huts with beds, US$1.50-4 (3-4½ hrs back up, ask for the best route in both directions, horses can be hired to carry your bag up, US$5.85), recommended. A popular hike involves walking east on the Chivay road to the Mirador de Tapay (5 km before Cruz del Cóndor), then descending to the river on a steep track (4 hrs, take care). At the village of San Juan you can stay and eat at **E Hostal Roy**, solar-powered showers, simple meals, recommended. 3 other *hostales* in the village, with electricity. From there you go to the oasis, spend the night and return to Cabanconde on the third day.

Tours

Travel agencies in Arequipa arrange a 'one-day' tour to the Mirador at Cruz del Cóndor for about US$18-20: depart Arequipa at 0400, arrive at the Cruz del Cóndor at 0800-0900, expensive lunch stop at Chivay and back to Arequipa by 2100; for many, especially for those with altitude problems, this is too much to fit into one day (the only advantage is that you don't have to sleep at high altitude). Two-day tours are about US$30 pp with an overnight stop in Chivay; more expensive tours range from US$45 to US$90 with accommodation at the top of the range. Allow at least 2-3 days to appreciate the Colca Canyon fully, more if planning to do some trekking.

Chivay *p1184*

Colca Adventures, 22 de Agosto 101, T531137, rcordova@terra.com.pe. For bike hire and rafting tours. Good machines and equipment, very helpful.

❀ Transport

Colca Canyon *p1184*

Bus Cristo Rey, La Reyna (recommended) and Andalucia have 7 departures daily from Arequipa to **Chivay**, continuing to **Cabanaconde** after a few hours' wait in Chivay; a further 75 km, 2 hrs, US$1. La Reyna has the quickest service, about 6 hrs, US$3.85, others US$3. Buses return to Arequipa from the market. **Chivay-Cabanaconde** Bus at 0500. Combis run infrequently in each direction, none on Sun. Buses leave Cabanaconde for Arequipa from 0730 to 2300. It is difficult to go to Cuzco from Chivay: you have to go to the police checkpoint on the Arequipa-Juliaca road and change to a *Carhuamayo* bus there. Best to go back to Arequipa and get a Juliaca bus.

Cotahuasi Canyon

Toro Muerto

① US$2; entrance 10 mins' drive from the petroglyphs.

West of Arequipa, a dirt road branches off the Pan-American to Corire, Aplao and the Río Majes valley. The **world's largest field of petroglyphs** at Toro Muerto is near Corire, where there are several hotels and restaurants near the plaza. For Toro Muerto, turn-off on the right heading back out of Corire; one hour walk; ask directions. The higher you go, the more interesting the petroglyphs, though many have been ruined by graffiti. The designs range from simple llamas to elaborate human figures and animals. The sheer scale of the site is awe-inspiring and the view is wonderful (UNESCO World Heritage Site). Take plenty of water, sunglasses and sun cream.

Cotahuasi Canyon

Beyond Aplao the road heads north through **Chuquibamba** (festivals 20 January; 2-3 February; 15 May) traversing the western slopes of Nevado Coropuna (6,425 m), before winding down into **Cotahuasi** (*Phone code 054, Population 3,200, Altitude 2,600 m*). The peaceful colonial town nestles in a sheltered hanging valley beneath Cerro Huinao. Its streets are narrow, the houses whitewashed. Local festival is 4 May.

Several kilometres away a canyon has been cut by the Río Cotahuasi, which flows into the Pacific as the Río Ocuña. At its deepest, at Ninochaca (just below the village of Quechualla), the canyon is 3,354 m deep, 163 m deeper than the Colca Canyon and the deepest in the world. From this point the only way down the canyon is by kayak and it is through kayakers' reports since 1994 that the area has come to the notice of tourists (it was declared a Zona de Reserva Turística in 1988). There is little agriculture apart from some citrus groves, but in Inca times the road linking Puerto Inca and Cuzco ran along much of the canyon's course. Note that the area is not on the tourist route and information is hard to come by.

Following the Río Cotahuasi to the northeast up the valley, you come to **Tomepampa** (10 km), a neat hamlet at 2,700 m, with painted houses and a handsome chapel. The hotsprings of **Luicho** *① 18 km from Cotahuasi, 24 hrs, US1.50*, are a short walk from the road, across a bridge. Beyond is **Alca** (20 km, one hostal), above which are the small ruins of Kallak, Tiknay and a 'stone library' of rock formations. All these places are connected by buses and combis from Cotahuasi. Buses leave Alca for Arequipa around 1400, combis when full. **Puica** *① connected to Alca by combi (2 hrs, US$1.50*, is the last village of any significance in the valley, hanging on a hillside at nearly 3,700 m. Nearby attractions include: Churca and a vast prairie of Puya Raimondi cacti; the Ocoruro geysers; and the ruins of Maucallacta. Horses can be hired for US$3 a day, and locals can act as guides. Puica's fiesta is on 28 July.

One of the main treks in the region follows the Inca trade road from Cotahuasi to Quechualla. From the football pitch the path goes through Piro, the gateway to the canyon, and Sipia (three hours, two suspension bridges to cross), near which are the powerful, 150 m high Cataratas de Sipia (take care near the falls if it is windy). Combis from Cotahuasi go to within an hour's walk of the Cataratas; they leave 0600 and 1930, return 0900 and 1400. It's best to visit at midday. A road is being built from this point to the falls, and may be complete by the time you read this. The next three-hour stretch to Chaupo is not for vertigo sufferers as the path is barely etched into the canyon wall, 400 m above the river in places. At Chaupo ask permission to camp; water is available. Next is Velinga, then the dilapidated but extensive ruin of Huña, then **Quechualla**, a charming village and administrative capital of the district. Ask Sr Carmelo Velásquez Gálvez for permission to sleep in the schoolhouse.

⦿ Sleeping

Cotahuasi *p1187*

E Hostal Alcalá II, Arequipa 116, T581090. Very good, hot showers, excellent beds, doubles and triples. Recommended. Run by same family as **E-F Hostal Alcalá**, Alca, T280224. One of the best hostales in the valley, 2 rooms with shower, others shared, hot water, restaurant, good food. Prices vary according to season and demand.

F Alojamiento Chávez, Jr Cabildo 125, T581029. Basic rooms around a flower-filled courtyard, Sr José Chávez is helpful on places to visit.

F Hostal Fany Luz, Independencia 117, T581002. Basic but amenable, shared hot showers, double room available with cold water only.

F Hostal Villa, Independencia 118, off the plaza, T581018. Basic, bathroom away from the rooms.

🍴 Eating

Cotahuasi *p1187*
Three small restaurants/bars on Jr Arequipa offer basic fare, best is **BuenSabor**, opposite Hostal Alcalá II. There are many well-stocked tiendas, particularly with fruit, vegetables and local wine.
† **El Pionero**, Jr Centenario. Clean, good menú.
† **Las Quenas** and **Las Delicias**, both on main square, have decent menus.

🚍 Transport

Toro Muerto *p1187*
Empresa Del Carpio buses to **Corire** leave from **Arequipa** main terminal hourly from 0500, 3-4 hrs, US$3. Ask to be let out at the beginning of the track to Toro Muerto, or from the plaza in Corire take a taxi, US$6-10 including 2-hr wait.

If walking note that it takes 2 hrs to walk around the site, a lot in the heat.

Cotahuasi *p1187*
Buses daily from **Arequipa** bus terminal, 11-12 hrs, US$9: **Alex** at 1530; **Reyna** at 1600; all return from the plaza in Cotahuasi at the same times. They stop for refreshments in Chuquibamba, about halfway. Both companies continue to Alca.

🅾 Directory

Cotahuasi *p1187*
Useful services No money exchange. PNP, on plaza; advisable to register with them on arrival and before leaving. **Maps:** some survey maps in Municipalidad and PNP; they may let you make photocopies (shop on the corner of the plaza and Arequipa). Sr Chávez has photocopies of the sheets covering Cotahuasi and surroundings.

South to Chile

Moquegua → *Phone code: 053. Colour map 6, grid A1. Population: 110,000. Altitude: 1,412 m.*
This town 213 km from Arequipa in the narrow valley of the Moquegua River enjoys a sub-tropical climate. The old centre, a few blocks above the Pan-American Highway, has winding, cobbled streets and 19th-century buildings. The Plaza de Armas, with its mix of ruined and well-maintained churches, colonial and republican façades and fine trees, is one of the most interesting small-town plazas in the country. **Museo Contisuyo** ① *on the Plaza de Armas, within the ruins of the Iglesia Matriz, T461844, http://bruceowen.com/contisuyo/Museo E.html, Mon-Sun 0800-1300, 1430-1730, Tue 0800-1200, 1600-2000, US$0.45,* covers the cultures which thrived in the Moquegua and Ilo valleys, including the Huari, Tiahuanaco, Chiribaya and Estuquiña, who were conquered by the Incas. Artefacts are well-displayed explained in Spanish and English. Día de Santa Catalina, 25 November, is the anniversary of the founding of the colonial city. There are several email offices on or near the Plaza de Armas. Municipal **tourist office** on the plaza ① *Ayacucho y Ancash, Mon-Fri 0800-1600.*

A highly recommended excursion is to **Cerro Baúl** ① *30 mins by colectivo, US$1.70,* 2,590 m, a tabletop mountain with marvellous views and many legends, which can be combined with the pleasant town of Torata, 24 km northeast.

The Carretera Binacional, from the port of Ilo to La Paz, has a breathtaking stretch from Moquegua to Desaguadero at the southeastern end of Lake Titicaca. It skirts Cerro Baúl and climbs through zones of ancient terraces to its highest point at 4,755 m. On the altiplano there are herds of llamas and alpacas, lakes with waterfowl, strange mountain formations and snow-covered peaks. At Mazo Cruz there is a PNP checkpoint where all documents and bags are checked. Approaching Desaguadero the Cordillera Real of Bolivia comes into view. The road is fully paved and should be taken in daylight.

Tacna → *Phone code: 052. Colour map 6, grid A1. Population: 174,366. Altitude: 550 m.*
Only 36 km from the Chilean border and 56 km from the international port of Arica, Tacna has free-trade status. It is an important commercial centre and Chileans come for cheap medical and dental treatment. Around the city the desert is gradually being irrigated. The local economy includes olive groves, vineyards and fishing. Tacna was in Chilean hands from 1880 to 1929, when its people voted by plebiscite to return to Peru. Above the city (8 km away, just off the Panamericano Norte), on the heights, is the **Campo de la Alianza**, scene of a battle between Peru and Chile in 1880. The cathedral, designed by Eiffel, faces the Plaza de Armas, which contains huge bronze statues of Admiral Grau and Colonel Bolognesi. They stand at either end of the Arca de los Héroes, the triumphal arch which is the symbol of the city. The

bronze fountain in the Plaza is said to be a duplicate of the one in the Place de la Concorde (Paris) and was also designed by Eiffel. The **Parque de la Locomotora** ① *daily 0700-1700, US$0.30; knock at the gate under the clock tower on Jr 2 de Mayo for entry*, near the city centre, has a British-built locomotive, which was used in the War of the Pacific. There is a very good railway museum at the station. The house of **Francisco Zela** ① *Zela 542, Mon-Sat 0830-1230, 1530-1900*, who gave the Cry of Independence on 20 July 1811, is a museum.

Tourist office, **Dircetur** ① *Blondell 50, p3-4, T422784, tacna@mincetur.gob.pe, Mon-Fri 0730-1515*. Also by the Centro Cultural Miculla ① *Blondell y Francisco Lazo, Mon-Fri 0800-1300, Spanish only,* has city map and regional information, at the Terminal Terrestre Nacional ① *T427007, 0600-2200;* and at the Terminal Internacional ① *Mon-Fri 0800-1500, Sat 0800-1200,* city map, helpful, list of official taxi rates; www.mincetur.gob.pe/regiones/tacna. **Tourist police** ① *Jr Callao 121, T414141, ext 245.* **Touring y Automóvil Club del Perú** ① *Av 2 de Mayo 67, T744237, tacna@touringperu.com.pe.*

Border with Chile

There is a checkpoint before the border, which is open 0800-2300 (24 hours Friday and Saturday). You need to obtain a Peruvian exit stamp and a Chilean entrance stamp; formalities are straightforward (see below). If you need a Chilean visa, you have to get it in Tacna (address below). Peruvian time is 1 hour earlier than Chilean time March-October; 2 hours earlier September/October to February/March (varies annually). No fruit or vegetables are allowed into Chile or Tacna.

Crossing by private vehicle For those leaving Peru by car buy *relaciones de pasajeros* (official forms, US$0.45) from the kiosk at the border or from a bookshop; you will need four copies. Next, return your tourist card, visit the PNP office, return the vehicle permit and finally depart through the checkpoints.

Exchange See under Banks, below. Changers can also be found at counters in the international bus terminal; rates are much the same as in town.

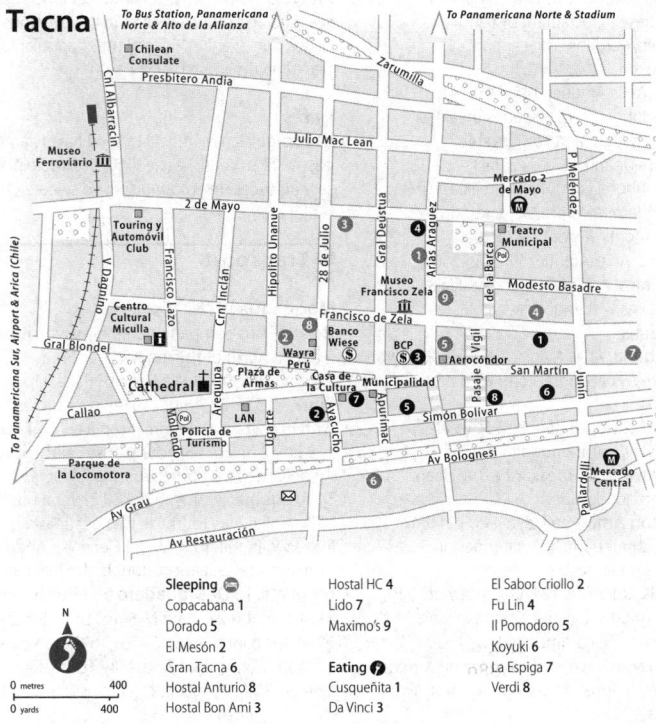

Tacna

Sleeping ⌂
Copacabana 1
Dorado 5
El Mesón 2
Gran Tacna 6
Hostal Anturio 8
Hostal Bon Ami 3

Hostal HC 4
Lido 7
Maximo's 9

Eating ⑦
Cusqueñita 1
Da Vinci 3

El Sabor Criollo 2
Fu Lin 4
Il Pomodoro 5
Koyuki 6
La Espiga 7
Verdi 8

0 metres 400
0 yards 400

N

1189

◎ Sleeping

Moquegua *p1188*

Hotels do not serve breakfast.

C Alameda, Junín 322, T463971.
Includes breakfast, large comfortable
rooms, welcoming.

D Arequipa, Jr Arequipa 360, T461338,
javierhotelarequiupa@hotmail.com. Clean
and pleasant, hot water sometimes.

D Hostal Adrianella, Miguel Grau 239,
T/F463469. Hot water, TV, safe, helpful,
tourist information, close to market and buses,
a bit faded.

D Hostal Plaza, Ayacucho 675, T461612.
Modern and comfortable, good value.

E Hostal Carrera, Jr Lima 320 (no sign), T462113.
Hot water (**F** shared bath, solar-powered hot
water, best in afternoon), laundry facilities on
roof, good value. Recommended.

F pp **Hospedaje Cornejo**, Tarapacá 281-A,
T507681. Shared bath, electric showers, basic
but clean.

Tacna *p1188, map p1189*

A Gran Hotel Tacna, Av Bolognesi 300,
T424193, www.derrama.org.pe. Includes
breakfast, internet access in rooms US$1/hr,
pool open to non-guests with minimum
US$8 purchase in restaurant or bar,
best in town, gardens, safe car park,
English spoken.

B Dorado, Arias Araguez 145, T415741,
www.doradohotel.com. Includes breakfast,
restaurant, modern and comfortable.

C El Mesón, Unánue 175, T425841,
www.mesonhotel.com, . With breakfast, TV,
central, modern, comfortable, safe, wireless
internet in rooms. Recommended.

C Maximo's, Arias Araguez 281, T242604,
www.maximoshotel.com. With breakfast,
modern rooms with frigo-bar, wireless
internet, sauna.

D Copacabana, Arias Araguez 281 y 2 de Mayo,
T421721, www.copahotel.com. With breakfast,
good rooms.

D Hostal Anturio, 28 de Julio 194 y Zela,
T244258, www.anturiohostaltacna.com.
Cafeteria downstairs, breakfast extra, clean,
modern and good value.

E Hostal Bon Ami, 2 de Mayo 445, T244847.
Cheaper without bath, hot water best in
afternoon, simple, secure.

E Hostal HC, Zela 734, T242042. Hot water, TV,
family run, good value, discounts available,
laundry service. Recommended.

E Lido, San Martín 876-A, near Plaza de Armas,
T577001. With hot showers, no breakfast, simple
but adequate.

◐ Eating

Moquegua *p1188*

Several eating places, including *chifas*,
in town.

♥♥ Pizzería Casa Vieja, Moquegua 326.
Mon-Sat 1830-2300, pizza and other
Italian dishes.

♥ Moraly, Lima y Libertad. The best place for
meals. Breakfast, good lunches, *menú* US$1.75,
open Mon-Sat 1000-2200, Sun 1000-1600.

Tacna *p1188, map p1189*

♥♥ DaVinci, San Martín 596 y Arias Araguez.
Mon-Sat 1100-2300, pizza and other varied
dishes, nice atmosphere, Leonardo bar upstairs
Tue-Sat 2000-0200.

♥♥ Il Pomodoro, Bolívar 524 y Apurimac. Closed
Sun evening and Mon midday, upscale Italian
serving set lunch on weekdays, pricey à la carte
in the evening, attentive service.

♥ Cusqueñita, Zela 747, 1100-1600, excellent
4-course lunch, large portions, good value,
variety of choices. Recommended.

♥ El Sabor Criollo, Ayacucho 86-C. A popular
lunch-time restaurant.

♥ Fu-Lin, Arias Araguez 396 y 2 de Mayo,
Mon-Sat 0930-1600, vegetarian Chinese.

♥ Koyuki, Bolívar 718. Generous set lunch daily,
sea food and other à la carte in the evening,
closed Sun evening. Several other popular lunch
places on the same block.

Cafés

La Espiga, San Martín 431. Good bakery and
pastry shop. Verdi, Pasaje Vigil 57. Simple place
serving excellent *empanadas* and sweets, also
set lunch.

◎ Transport

Moquegua *p1188*

Bus All bus companies are on Av Ejército,
2 blocks north of the market at Jr Grau,
except **Ormeño**, Av La Paz casi Balta. From
Lima, US$15-30, 15 hrs, many companies
with executive and regular services. To **Tacna**,
159 km, 2 hrs, US$3, hourly buses with **Flores**,
Av del Ejército y Andrés Aurelio Cáceres.
To **Arequipa**, 3½ hrs, US$5.50, several buses
daily. Colectivos for these two destinations
leave when full from Av del Ejercito y Andrés
Aurelio Cáceres, almost double the bus fare -
negotiate. To **Desaguadero** and **Puno**, San
Martín-Nobleza, 4 a day, 6 hrs, US$7.50; the
2130 bus continues to Cuzco; to **Cuzco** direct
at 1100, 13 hrs, US$13.50. **Mily Tours**, Ev
Ejército 32-B, T464000, colectivos to
Desaguadero, 4 hrs, US$15.

Tacna *p1188, map p1189*

Air The airport (T314503) is at Km 5 on the Panamericana Sur, on the way to the border. To go from the airport directly to Arica, call the bus terminal (T427007) and ask a colectivo to pick you up on its way to the border, US$4. Taxi from airport to Tacna centre US$2-3. To **Lima**, 1½ hrs; daily flights with **Lan** (Av San Martín 259, T428346) and **WayraPerú** (28 de Julio 102, T426642). **Aerocóndor** (Arias Araguez 135, T248187) to Lima via **Arequipa** on Tue, Thu, Sat, direct on other days.

Bus Two bus stations on Hipólito Unánue, T427007, 1 km from the plaza (colectivo US$0.25, taxi US$0.60 minimum). One terminal is for international services (ie Arica), the other for domestic, both are well-organized, local tax US$0.30, baggage store, easy to make connections to the border, Arequipa or Lima. To **Moquegua** (prices above) hourly buses with **Flores** (Av Saucini behind the Terminal Nacional, T426691). To **Arequipa**, 6 hrs, US$6.50-9.50, several buses daily, most with Flores. To **Nazca**, 793 km, 12 hrs, several buses daily, en route for Lima (fares about US$3 less than to Lima). Several companies daily to **Lima**, 1,239 km, 21-26 hrs, US$15-20 regular, US$30-40 *bus-cama*, eg **Flores**, **Cruz del Sur** and **Ormeño** (on Arias Araguez by the petrol station), recommended. Buses to **Desaguadero, Puno** and **Cuzco** leave from Terminal Collasuyo (T312538), Av Internacional in Barrio Altos de la Alianza neighbourhood; taxi to centre US$0.75. **San Martín-Nobleza** (T952 4252) is recommended, 4 a day to **Desaguadero** and **Puno**, US$8, 8-10 hrs; 1900 bus continues to **Juliaca** and **Cuzco**; to Cuzco direct at 0830, US$15, 15 hrs, or change in Moquegua.

At **Tomasiri**, 35 km north of Tacna, passengers' luggage is checked, whether you have been out of the country or not. Do not carry anything on the bus for anyone else, just your own belongings. Passports may be checked at Camiara, a police checkpoint some 60 km from Tacna.

To **La Paz**, Bolivia, the quickest and cheapest route is via Moquegua and Desaguadero; it also involves one less border crossing than via Arica and Tambo Colorado.

Border with Chile: Tacna *p1188*
Road 56 km, 1-2 hrs, depending on waiting time at the border. Buses to Arica charge US$1.80 and colectivo taxis US$3.60 pp. All leave from the international terminal in Tacna throughout the

day. Colectivos which carry 5 passengers only leave when full. As you approach the terminal you will be grabbed by a driver or his agent and told that the car is "just about to leave". This is hard to verify as you may not see the colectivo until you have filled in the paperwork. Once you have chosen a driver/agent, you will be rushed to his company's office where your passport will be taken from you and the details filled out on a Chilean entry form. You can change your remaining soles at the bus terminal. It is 30 mins to the Peruvian border post at Santa Rosa, where all exit formalities are carried out. The driver will hustle you through all the procedures. A short distance beyond is the Chilean post at Chacalluta, where again the driver will show you what to do. All formalities take about 30 mins. It's a further 15 mins to Arica's bus terminal. A Chilean driver is more likely to take you to any address in Arica.

Train Station is at Av Albaracín y 2 de Mayo. *Autoferro* to Arica, Mon-Sat 0545 and 1600 (from Arica at 0900 and 1800 Peruvian time), US$1.50, 1½ hrs, customs and immigration at railway stations. Ticket office 0800-0900 and 1430-1600, for the morning train best buy the morning before as it sells out.

⊙ Directory

Moquegua *p1188*
Banks **BCP**, Moquegua y Tarapacá. Changes TCs, advances money on Visa, Visa ATM. Street changers at Mercado Central. **Internet** Many places all over town, US$0.35 per hr.

Tacna *p1188, map p1189*
Banks BCP, San Martín 574, no commission for TCs (Amex, Citicorp) into soles. Similarly at **Banco Wiese**, San Martín 476. **Interbank**, San Martín 646, has ATM for Visa/Plus, Mastercard/Cirrus and Amex. Several *casas de cambio* at San Martín y Arias Araguez, all offering good rates for dollars cash, also change euros, pesos chilenos and bolivianos. Street changers stand outside the Municipalidad. **Consulates** Bolivia, Av Bolognesi 1751 y Piura, T245121, Mon-Fri 0900-1500. Chile, Presbítero Andía block 1, TT423063. Open Mon-Fri 0800-1300. **Internet** Many on San Martín, several open 24 hrs. Others around the centre. Average price US$0.35 per hr. **Post offices** Av Bolognesi 361. Open Mon-Sat 0800-2000. **Telephones** Public *locutorios* everywhere; shop around for best prices.

Lake Titicaca

Straddling Peru's southern border with Bolivia are the sapphire-blue waters of mystical Lake Titicaca, a huge inland sea which is the highest navigable lake in the world. Its shores and islands are home to the Aymara and Quechua, who are among Peru's oldest peoples. Here you can wander through traditional villages where Spanish is a second language and where ancient myths and beliefs still hold true. Newly paved roads climb from the coastal deserts and oases to the high plateau in which sits Lake Titicaca (Arequipa-Yura-Santa Lucía-Juliaca-Puno; Moquegua- Desaguadero-Puno). The steep ascents lead to wide open views of pampas with agricultural communities, desolate mountains, small lakes and salt flats. It is a rapid change of altitude, so be prepared for some discomfort and breathlessness.

Puno → *Phone code: 051. Colour map 6, grid A2. Population: 100,170. Altitude: 3,855 m.*

On the northwest shore of Lake Titicaca, Puno is capital of its department and Peru's folklore centre with a vast array of handicrafts, festivals and costumes and a rich tradition of music and dance. The **Cathedral**, completed in 1657, has an impressive baroque exterior, but an austere interior. Beside the Cathedral is the **Balcony of the Conde de Lemos** ① *Deústua esquina Conde de Lemos,* where Peru's Viceroy stayed when he first arrived in the city. The **Museo Municipal Dreyer** ① *Conde de Lemos 289, Mon-Fri 0730-1330, US$1,* has been combined with the private collection of Sr Carlos Dreyer. A short walk up Independencia leads to the **Arco**

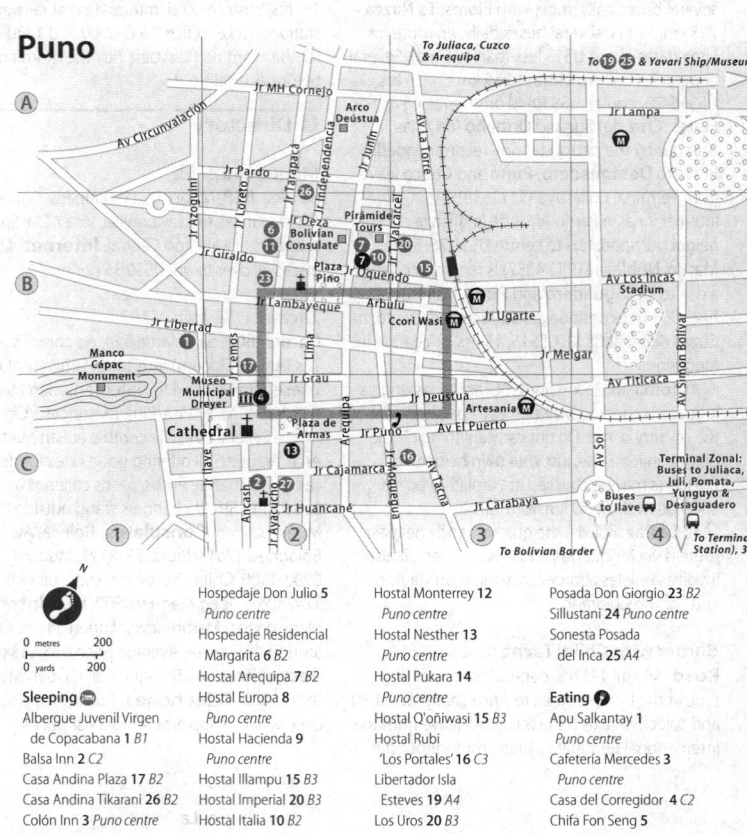

Puno

Deústua, a monument honouring those killed in the battles of Junín and Ayacucho. Nearby, is a mirador giving fine views over the town, the port and the lake beyond. The walk from Jr Cornejo following the Stations of the Cross up a nearby hill, with fine views of Lake Titicaca, has been recommended, but be careful and don't go alone (the same applies to any of the hills around Puno, eg Huajsapata).

The *Yavari*, the **oldest ship on Lake Titicaca** ① *free but donations welcome to help with maintenance costs. Project addresses: England: 61 Mexfield Rd, London SW15 2RG, T/F44-20-8874 0583, info@yavari.org. Peru/Lima: Giselle Guldentops, T01-9998 5071, Yavari. gulden@dwp.net; in Puno: Asociación Yavari, c/o Capitán Carlos Saavedra, T051-369329, carlosalberto@yavari.org. For general information, volunteering, donations, etc, visit www.yavari.org, museum 0800-1700,* is berthed near the entrance to the Sonesta Posada del Inca hotel and is now open as a museum. The ship was built in England in 1862 and was shipped in kit form to Arica, then by rail to Tacna and by mule to Lake Titicaca. The journey took six years. The *Yavari* was launched on Christmas Day 1870. Visitors are very welcome on board. In the harbour is Hull (UK)-built MS *Ollanta*, which sailed the lake from 1926 to the 1970s. **PerúRail** has restored the vessel. A new Malecón Bahía de los Incas, near the port, is a pleasant place for a stroll with views of the lake. The bay by Puno is, however, noticeably polluted. There is also a small museum ① *US$0.15,* at the jetty, displaying stuffed birds and fish from the lake.

Tourist offices: **i perú** ① *Jr Lima y Deústua, near Plaza de Armas, T365088.* They are friendly and helpful with general information and maps. **Indecopi**, the tourist protection bureau, has an office at ① *Lima y Fermín Arbulú, p 2, T/F366138, odipun@indecopi.gob.pe.* **Tourist police** ① *Jr Deústua 538, T364806. www.punored.com,* is a portal for the Puno area. Puno gets bitterly cold at night: from June to August the temperature at night can fall to -25°C, but generally not below -5°C.

Around Puno

Anybody interested in religious architecture should visit the villages along the western shore of Lake Titicaca. An Inca sundial can be seen near the village of **Chucuíto** (19 km), which has an interesting church, La Asunción, and houses with carved stone doorways. Visits to Chucuíto usually include the Templo de la Fertilidad, **Inca Uyo**, which boasts many phalli and other fertility symbols. The authenticity and original location of these objects is the subject of debate.

Juli, 80 km, has some fine examples of religious architecture. **San Pedro** on the plaza, designated as the Cathedral, has been extensively restored. It contains a series of paintings of saints, with the Via Crucis scenes in the same frame, and gilt side altars above which some of the arches have baroque designs. No opening hours are displayed. **San Juan Letrán** ① *mornings only, US$1.15,* has two sets of 17th-century paintings of the lives of St John the Baptist and of St Teresa, contained in sumptuous gilded frames. San Juan is a museum. It also has intricate *mestizo* carving in pink stone. **Santa Cruz** is partly roofless, with scaffolding and a shelter protecting what remains of the tower. It is completely closed to visitors, but there is a view of the lake from the plaza in front. The fourth church, **La Asunción** *US$0.85,* is also a museum. The nave is empty, but its walls are lined with colonial paintings with no labels.

Peru Lake Titicaca

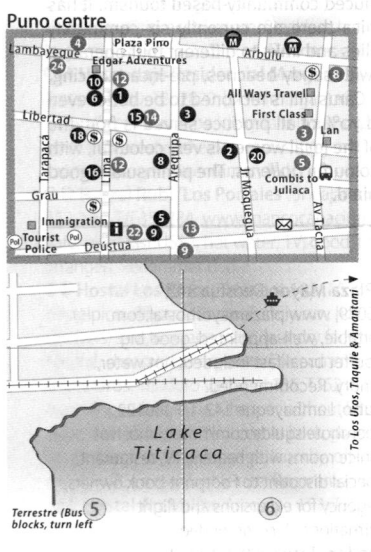

Puno centre

Lake Titicaca

Terrestre (Bus ⑤ blocks, turn left)

⑥

To Los Uros, Taquile & Amantani

Chifa Nan Hua **7** *B2*
Don Piero **6** *Puno centre*
Govinda **9** *Puno centre*
IncAbar **10** *Puno centre*
Internacional **20**
    Puno Centre
La Caywa Andean
    Cuisine Bar **8** *Puno centre*
Lago de Flores **1** *Puno centre*
La Plaza **13** *C2*
Pizzería El Buho **15**
    Puno centre

Remembranzas **2**
    Puno Centre
Ricos Pan **16**
    Puno centre
Vida Natural **18**
    Puno centre

Bars & clubs ⚐
Pub Ekeko's **12**
    Puno Centre

1193

††-† Lago de Flores, Lima 357. Local dishes and pizza, very good food, open fire in the shape of a pizza oven keeps diners warm.

††-† Don Piero, Lima 360. Huge meals, live music, try their 'pollo coca-cola' (chicken in a sweet and sour sauce), slow service, popular, tax extra.

††-† Pizzería El Buho, Lima 349 and at Jr Libertad 386. Excellent pizza, lively atmosphere, open 1800 onwards, pizzas US$2.35-3.

† Chifa Fon Seng, Arequipa 552. Good food, service and value, Chinese, popular.

† Chifa Nan Hua, Arequipa 167, 1 block from Plaza de Armas. Tasty Chinese, big portions.

† Govinda, Deústua 312. Cheap vegetarian lunch menus, closes at 2000.

† Remembranzas, Jr Moquegua 200. Pizzas as well as local food. Open 0630-2200.

† Vida Natural, Libertad 449. Open for breakfast, salads, fruits, yoghourt.

Cafés

Cafetería Mercedes, Jr Arequipa 351. Good menú US$1.50, bread, cakes, snacks, juices.

Casa del Corregidor, Deústua 576, aptdo 2, T051-355694. In restored 17th-century building, sandwiches, good snacks, coffee, good music, great atmosphere, nice surroundings with patio.

Panadería Una, Lima 317 and Arequipa 144. For croissants, fresh bread and cakes.

Ricos Pan, Jr Lima 424. Café and bakery, great cakes, excellent coffees, juices and pastries, breakfasts and other dishes, Mon-Sat 0600-2300, . Branches at Av Titicaca 155 and Moquegua 330.

❶ Bars and clubs

Puno *p1192, map p1192*

Dómino, Libertad 443. "Megadisco", happy hour 2000-2130 Mon-Thu, good.

Peña Hostería, Lima 501. Good music, also restaurant. Recommended.

Pub Ekeko's, Lima 355. Live music every night, happy hour 2000-2200.

❸ Festivals and events

Puno *p1192, map p1192*

Feb: at the **Fiesta de la Virgen de la Candelaria**, 1st 2 weeks in **Feb**, bands and dancers from all the local towns compete in a *Diablada*, or Devil Dance. The festivities are better at night on the streets than the official functions in the stadium. Check the dates in advance as Candelaria may be moved if pre-Lentern carnival coincides with it. A candlelight procession through darkened streets takes place on **Good Friday**. **3 May**: Invención de la Cruz, an exhibition of local art. **29 Jun**: colourful festival of **San Pedro**, with a procession at Zepita (see page 1194); also **20 Jul**.

4-5 Nov: pageant dedicated to the founding of Puno and the emergence of Manco Cápac and Mama Ocllo from the waters of Lake Titicaca.

❺ Shopping

Puno *p1192, map p1192*

Markets Beware pickpockets in the market. You will be hassled on the street and outside restaurants to buy woollen goods, so take care.

In the covered part of the market mostly foodstuffs are sold (good cheeses), but there are also model reed boats, attractive carved stone amulets and Ekekos (household gods). This central market covers a large area and on Saturday it expands down to the stadium (mostly fruit and vegetables) and along Av Bolívar (potatoes and grains). The markets between Av Los Incas and Arbulu (*Ccori Wasi*) and on the railway between Av Libertad and Av El Puerto are 2 of the best places in Peru for llama and alpaca wool articles, but bargain hard, especially in the afternoon. **Ichuña**, Libertad 113, www.ichunia.org. A cooperative selling weavings from a village 90 km from Puno.

▲ Activities and tours

Puno *p1192, map p1192*

Watch out for unofficial tour sellers, *jalagringos*, who offer hotels and tours at varying rates, depending on how wealthy you look. They are everywhere: train station, bus offices, airport and hotels. Ask to see their guide's ID card. Only use agencies with named premises, compare prices and only hand over money at the office, never on the street or in a hotel.

Agencies organize trips to the Uros floating islands (see page 1198) and the islands of Taquile and Amantaní, as well as to Sillustani, and other places. Make sure that you settle all details before embarking on the tour. We have received good reports on the following:

Allways Travel, Tacna 234, T/F355552, www.titicacaperu.com. Very helpful, kind and reliable, speak German, French, English and Italian. They offer a unique cultural tour to the islands of Anapia and Yuspique in Lake Wiñaymarka, beyond the straits of Tiquina, "The Treasure of Wiñaymarka", departures Thu and Sun.

Arcobaleno, Jr Lambayeque 175, T/F351052. Local tours, Western Union representative.

Ecoturismo Aventura, Jr Lima 458, T355785. Very helpful.

Edgar Adventures, Jr Lima 328, T/F353444 (office)/354811 (home), edgaradventures@ terra.com.pe. English, German and French spoken, very helpful.

Nayra Travel, Jr Lima 419, of 105. T364774, www.nayratravel.com. Small but very helpful staff, offering local tours.

Pirámide Tours, Jr Rosendo Huirse 130, T366107, www.titikakalake.com. Out of the ordinary and classic tours, flexible, personalized service, modern fast launches, very helpful, works only via internet, overseas clients.

Titikaka Explorers, Av La Torre 339-4, T355219, peru-titikaka@hotmail.com. Good service, helpful.

Turpuno, Lima 208, stand 8-II, upstairs in Gallery, T352001, www.turpuno.com. Very good service for local tours, transfers and ticketing, DHL and Western Union agent.

⊖ Transport

Puno *p1192, map p1192*

Bus All long-distance buses, except some Cuzco services and buses to La Paz (see below), leave from the Terminal Terrestre, which is between Av Simón Bolívar and the lake, southeast of the centre. It has a tourist office, snack bars and toilets. Platform tax US$0.30. Small buses and colectivos for Juliaca, Ilave and towns on the lake shore between Puno and Desaguadero, including Yunguyo, leave from Av Bolívar between Jrs Carabaya and Palma. Daily buses to **Arequipa**, 6 hrs via Juliaca, 297 km, most buses take this route, US$4.50-6 (**Cruz del Sur**, **Best Way**, **Destinos**, **Julsa**, **Señor de Milagros**, or **Sur Oriente**, most have a morning and evening bus – better quality buses go at night). To **Moquegua**, US$4.50-6, and **Tacna**, US$8. To **Lima**, 1,011 km, 22 hrs, US$21-25, *bus cama* US$30, all buses go through **Arequipa**, sometimes with a change of bus. See Arequipa, page 1190. To **Juliaca**, 44 km, 45 mins, US$0.60.

Note If you wish to travel by bus and cannot get on a direct bus, it is no problem to take separate buses to Juliaca, then to Sicuani, then to Cuzco.

To **Cuzco**, 388 km, 5-7 hrs, **Tour Perú**, at Terminal, T352991, tourperu@mixmail.com, 0830, 2000, both US$4.50-6 (less in low season); **Libertad**, at Terminal, T363694, 4 a day, **Cisnes**, at Terminal, T368674, 2 a day, and others. **First Class** (Jr Puno 675, T365192) and **Inka Express** (Jr Tacna 314-B, T365654), both at 0830 arriving 1800, US$20, 10 hrs, daily. This service leaves a little later than the train and is comfortable, with a good lunch stop and visits to Pukará, La Raya, Raqchi and Andahuaylillas en route. **Note** We have received many reports of robbery on night buses on the Juliaca- Puno-Cuzco route; travel by day, or by train.

Boats on Lake Titicaca Boats to the islands leave from the terminal in the harbour (see map); *trici-taxi* from centre, US$1.

Taxi 3-wheel 'Trici-Taxis', cost about US$0.20 per km and are the best way to get around.

Trains The railway runs from Puno to Juliaca (44 km), where it divides, to Cuzco (381 km) and Arequipa (279 km; no passenger service). To

Cuzco on Mon, Wed and Sat at 0800, arriving in Juliaca at 0910 and in Cuzco at about 1800 (try to sit on the right hand side for the views). The train stops at La Raya. In the high season (Jun especially), tickets sell well in advance. In the wet season services may be cancelled for short periods. Always check. **Fares**: Puno-Cuzco, *turismo*, US$16.66; *1st class*, US$119 including meal. The ticket office is open from 0630-1030, 1500-1700 Mon-Sat, and on Sun in the afternoons only. Tickets can be bought in advance, or 1 hr before departure if there are any left. The station is well guarded by police and sealed off to those without tickets.

Llachón *p1194*

Boats Only one weekly public boat from Llachón to Puno, Fri 0900, returning to Llachón Sat 1600. The daily 0800 boat to Amantantí may drop you off at Colata (at the tip of the peninsula), a 1 hr walk from Llachón, confirm details in advance. Returning to Puno, you can try to flag down the boat from Amantaní which passes Colata between 0830 and 0930. All fares US$3 one way. **Combis** run daily from Bellavista market in Puno to Capachica, from 0700 to1200, 1½ hrs, US$1, where you get another *combi* or bus to Llachón, leave when full, 30 mins, US$0.30. The unpaved road to the peninsula branches east from the main road half way between Puno and Juliaca.

⊕ Directory

Puno *p1192, map p1192*

Banks BCP, Lima 510. Changes TCs before 1300 without commission, cash advance on Visa and Visa ATM. **Banco Continental**, Lima 411. Visa ATM. **Interbank**, Lima 444, changes TCs morning and afternoon, 0.5% commission, Visa ATM. **Banco Wiese Sudameris**, Lima y Deústua, Mastercard ATM. For cash go to the *cambios*, the travel agencies or the better hotels. Best rates with money changers on Jr Lima, many on 400 block, and on Tacna near the market, eg Arbulu y Tacna. Check your Peruvian soles carefully. Exchange rates from soles to bolivianos and vice versa are sometimes better in Puno than in Yunguyo; check with other travellers. **Consulates** Bolivia, Jr Arequipa 136, T351251, consular visa on the spot, US$10, open 0830-1400 Mon to Fri. **Internet** There are offices everywhere in the centre, upstairs and down. Average price US$0.45 per hr; many have overnights. **Post offices** Jr Moquegua 267. **Telephones** Telefónica at Puno y Moquegua for local and international calls. Another phone office at Lima 489. **Useful addresses** Immigration: Ayacucho 280, T357103, for renewing entry stamps, etc. The process is very slow and you must fill in 2 application forms at a bank, but there's nothing else to pay.

The islands

The Uros

The people of Uros or the 'floating islands' in Puno Bay fish, hunt birds and live off the lake plants, most important of which are the reeds they use for their boats, houses and the very foundations of their islands. Visitors to the floating islands encounter more women than men. These women wait every day for the tour boats to sell their handicrafts. The few men one does see might be building or repairing boats or fixing their nets. The rest are out on the lake, hunting and fishing. The Uros cannot live from tourism alone, and the extra income they glean from tourists merely supplements their more traditional activities. They appreciate gifts of pens, paper, etc for their two schools. Many tourists find that, though the people are friendly, they are very poor and a few subject visitors to a hard-sell approach for handicrafts and the replacement of "invalid" entry tickets. The islands visited by tour boats are little more than 'floating souvenir stalls'. All the same, this form of tourism on the Uros Islands is now well-established and, whether it has done irreparable harm or will ultimately prove beneficial, it takes place in superb surroundings. Take drinking water as there is none on the islands.

Taquile

Isla Taquile, 45 km from Puno, on which there are numerous pre-Inca and Inca ruins, and Inca terracing, is only about 1 km wide, but 6-7 km long. Ask for the (unmarked) **museum of traditional costumes**, which is on the plaza, and also where you can see and photograph local weaving. There is a co-operative shop on the plaza that sells exceptional woollen goods, which are not cheap, but of very fine quality. Shops on the plaza sell film, postcards, water and dry goods. You are advised to take some food, particularly fruit, bread and vegetables, water, plenty of small-value notes, candles and a torch. Take precautions against sunburn. Easter, from 2-7 June, the *Fiesta de Santiago* over two weeks in mid-July, and 1 and 2 August are the principal festival days, with many dances in between.

Amantaní

Another island worth visiting, is Amantaní, very beautiful and peaceful. There are six villages and ruins on both of the island's peaks, **Pacha Tata** and **Pacha Mama**, from which there are excellent views. There are also temples and on the shore there is a throne carved out of stone, the **Inkatiana**. On both hills, a fiesta is celebrated on 15 January (or thereabouts). The festivities are very colourful, musical and hard-drinking. There is also a festival the first Sunday in March with brass bands and colourful dancers. The residents make beautiful textiles and sell them quite cheaply at the Artesanía Cooperativa. They also make basketwork and stoneware. The people are Quechua speakers, but understand Spanish. Islanders arrange dances for tour groups (independent travellers can join in), visitors dress up in local clothes and join the dances. Small shops sell water and snacks, but more expensive than Puno.

Anapia and Yuspique

In the Peruvian part of the Lago Menor are the islands of **Anapia**, a friendly, Aymara-speaking community, and **Yuspique**, on which are ruins and vicuñas. The community has organized committees for tourism, motor boats, sailing boats and accommodation with families (All Ways Travel, see page 1196, arranges tours). To visit Anapia independently, take a colectivo from Yunguyo to Tinicachi and alight at Punta Hermosa, just after Unacachi. Boats to Anapia leave Punta Hermosa on Sunday and Thursday at 1300 (they leave Anapia for Yunguyo market on the same days at 0630); bus from Puno Sunday, Tuesday, Thursday, US$3. It's two hours each way by boat. On the island ask for José Flores, who is very knowledgeable about Anapia's history, flora and fauna. He sometimes acts as a guide.

⊜ Sleeping

Taquile *p1198*
Average rate for a bed is US$3 pp, plus US$1.50 for breakfast. Other meals cost extra. Several families now have sizeable *alojamientos* (eg

Pedro Huille, on the track up from the north entry, with showers, proper loos). Instead of staying in the busy part around the main square, the Huayllano community is hosting visitors. This is on the south side of the island. Contact **Alipio Huata Cruz**, T952 4650 (mob, you can leave a voicemail that he will retrieve from Puno as there is no reception on the island) or you can arrange a visit with **Allways Travel**.

Amantaní *p1198*

There are no hotels, you stay with local families. Ask your boat owner where you can stay. Accommodation, including 3 meals, is US$6 pp. Some families have mainland addresses for booking, eg **Hospedaje Jorge Wasi**, basic, but nice family, great view of lake from room, or j.manani.cari@eudoramail.com; or **Familia Victoriano Calsin Quispe**, Casilla 312, Isla Amantaní, T051-360220 or 363320.

❶ Eating

Taquile *p1198*

There are many small restaurants around the plaza and on the track to the Puerto Principal (eg Gerardo Hualta's **La Flor de Cantuta**, on the steps; **El Inca** on the main plaza). Meals are generally fish (the island has a trout farm), rice and chips, tortilla and *fiambre*, a local stew. Meat is rarely available and drinks often run out. Breakfast consists of pancakes and bread.

Amantaní *p1198*

There is 1 restaurant, **Samariy**. Food at the family lodgings is frequently reported to be dreadful (a reflection of the artificially low price), so take your own supplies, especially bread and fruit.

❸ Transport

The Uros *p1198*

Boat Motorboats from the dock charge about US$3 pp for a 2-hr excursion. Boats go about every 30 mins from about 0630-1000, or whenever there are 10 or more people to fill the boat. The earlier you go the better, to beat the crowds of tourists. Almost any agency going to the other islands in the lake will stop first at Los Uros.

Taquile *p1198*

Boats Leave Puno daily at 0700 and 0800; 3 hrs, return 1430 and 1500, US$3 one way. This doesn't leave enough time to appreciate the island fully (if you buy a return ticket, don't get charged again for the return leg). Organized tours can be arranged for about US$10-16 pp, but only give you about 2 hrs on the island. Tour boats usually call at Uros on the outward or return journey.

Amantaní *p1198*

Boats Leave from the harbour in Puno at 0800 daily, return 0800, arriving in Puno around 1200, US$4.50 one way. The journey takes 4-5 hrs, take water and seasickness pills. A 1-day trip is not possible. Several tour operators in Puno offer 2-3 day excursions to Amantaní, Taquile and a visit to the floating islands, starting at US$12 pp (price depends on the season and size of group); including meals, 1 night on Amantaní and 3-4 hrs on Taquile. Despite what touts may tell you, it is possible to visit the islands independently and at your own pace. In this way the islands reap most of the reward from visitors, but that doesn't make it any cheaper. The majority of tour companies are owned in Puno. To visit both Taquile and Amantaní, it is better to go to Amantaní first; from there a boat goes to Taquile around 0800 when full, US$2.50 pp.

To Cuzco

Juliaca → *Phone code: 051. Colour map 6, grid A2. Population: 134,700. Altitude: 3,825 m.*

Freezing cold at night, Juliaca, 289 km northeast of Arequipa, is not particularly attractive. As the commercial focus of an area bounded by Puno, Arequipa and the jungle, it has grown very fast into a chaotic place with a large impermanent population, lots of contraband and more *tricitaxis* than cars. Monday, market day, is the most disorganized of all. On the huge Plaza Melgar, several blocks from the main part of the town, is an interesting colonial church. A Sunday woollens market, La Dominical, is held near the exit to Cuzco. The handicrafts gallery, *Las Calceteras*, is on Plaza Bolognesi. Túpac Amaru market, on Moquegua seven blocks east of railway line, is a cheap market. There are several internet places in the centre. **Tourist office, Dircetur** ① *Jr Noriega 191, p 3, T321839.*

The unspoiled little colonial town of **Lampa**, 31 km northwest of Juliaca is known as the 'Pink City'. It has a splendid church, La Inmaculada, containing a copy of Michelangelo's 'Pietà'. Also of interest is the Museo Kampac, Ugarte 462, a museum with sculptures and ceramics from the Lampa and Juli areas; the owner lives next door. It also has a good Sunday market. Buses and trucks daily, one hour, US$0.65, from Plaza de Armas in Juliaca.

Puno to Cuzco

On the way from Puno to Cuzco there is much to see from the train, which runs at an average altitude of 3,500 m. At the stations on the way, people sell food and local specialities, eg pottery bulls at Pucará (rooms available at the station); knitted alpaca ponchos and pullovers and miniature llamas at Santa Rosa (rooms available). There are three hotels in **Ayaviri**.

The railway crosses the altiplano, climbing to **La Raya**, the highest pass on the line; 210 km from Puno, at 4,321 m. Up on the heights breathing may be a little difficult, but the descent along the Río Vilcanota is rapid. To the right of **Aguas Calientes**, the next station, 10 km from La Raya, are steaming pools of hot water in the middle of the green grass; a startling sight US$0.15. The temperature of the springs is 40° C, and they show beautiful deposits of red ferro-oxide. Communal bathing pools and a block of changing rooms have been opened. At **Marangani**, the river is wider and the fields greener, with groves of eucalyptus trees.

You can travel to Cuzco from Puno by road which is paved all the way and consequently bus services are an acceptable alternative to the train.

At 38 km beyond La Raya pass is **Sicuani** (Phone code 084, Altitude 3,690 m), an important agricultural centre. Excellent items of llama and alpaca wool and skins are sold on the railway station and at the Sunday morning market. Around Plaza Libertad there are several hat shops. (For more information about places between Sicuani and Cuzco, see page 1227.)

● Sleeping

Juliaca *p1199*
There are water problems in town, especially in the dry season. Many cheap hotels near the corner of Nuñez and Cuzco.
AL Suites Don Carlos, Jr M Prado 335, on the outskirts of town, T321571, www.hotelesdon carlos.com. Good facilities, continental breakfast US$6.50, lunch or dinner US$13.
B Hostal Don Carlos, Jr 9 de Diciembre 114, Plaza Bolognesi, T323600, www.hotelesdon carlos.com. Comfortable, modern facilities, hot water, TV, heater, good service, breakfast included, restaurant and room service. Recommended.
B Royal Inn, San Román 158, T321561, www.royalinnhoteles.com. Decent place with hot water, heaters, TV, safe, laundry, good restaurant La Fonda del Royal (₸₸-₸). Recommended.
C Karlo's Hostal, Unión 317, T321817, lanzap@hotmail.com. Comfortable if overpriced, firm beds, hot water, TV, laundry, restaurant *Che Karlín* attached.
D Hostal Luquini, San Brasesco 409, Plaza Bolognesi, T321510. **E** without bath, patio, helpful, reliable hot water in morning only, good value, motorcycle parking. Recommended.
F Hostal La Casona, on the Plaza in the village of Lampa, T360228, mariaelenafd@hotmail.com. In newly refurbished old house, very nice.

Sicuani *p1200*
The bus terminal is in the newer part of town, which is separated from the older part and the Plaza by a pedestrian walkway and bridge. At the 'new' end of the bridge, but also close to the centre of town, are several *hostales* advertising hot water and private bathrooms.
E Obada, Tacna 104, T351214. Large, hot showers, has seen better days.

E Royal Inti, Av Centenario 116, T352730. West side of old pedestrian bridge, modern.
E Samariy, next to *Royal Inti*, Av Centenario 138, T352518. Good value.
G José's, Av Arequipa 143, T351254. With bath, good.

● Eating

Juliaca *p1199*
₸₸-₸ **Trujillo**, San Román 163. Extensive menu, daily specials, US$3-5.50 for main dishes, US$7.50 for fish.
₸ **Asador**, Unión 119. Chicken, grill and pizza, pleasant atmosphere.
Ricos Pan, San Román. Bakery with café, popular. Recommended.

Sicuani *p1200*
El Fogón, C Zevallos. Good chicken and chips, smart.
Pizzería Ban Vino, 2 de Mayo 129, p 2. Good Italian.
Mijuna Wasi, Jr Tacna 146. Closed Sun. Serves local dishes in a dilapidated, atmospheric courtyard.

● Transport

Juliaca *p1199*
Air Airport is small but well organized, airport tax US$3. To/from **Lima**, 2¼ hrs via **Arequipa** (30 mins) or **Cuzco**, twice daily with **Lan** (T322228 or airport T324448). **StarPerú** also daily via Arequipa (San Román 175, T327478). Minibuses 1-B, 6 and 14 to airport from 2 de Mayo at either Núñez or San Román, US$0.15; from airport to town they take you to your hotel. Beware overcharging for

transport from Juliaca airport. If you have little luggage, combis stop just outside the airport parking area. Taxi from Plaza Bolognesi, US$1.75. Tourist buses run direct from Puno to the airport and vice versa; US$3.50 pp, 1 hr. You can book ahead with **Rossy Tours**, T366709. Also taxis, US$11.75. If taking a public colectivo from Puno to Juliaca for a flight, allow plenty of time as they drive around Puno looking for passengers to fill the vehicle first.

Bus Terminal Terrestre is at Jr Mantaro y San Agustín: go down San Martín 10 blocks and cross Av Circunvalación. Lots of companies serve **Desaguadero**, **Moquegua**, **Arequipa** (US$3), **Lima** (US$17- 43) and **Cuzco** (US$3-4). To **Cuzco**, 344 km, 5-6 hrs, with **Tour Perú** (tourperu@ mixmail.com), day and night buses, prices as from Puno. **First Class** and **Inka Express** (inkaex@ yahoo.com) have pullman tourist buses which stop for sightseeing and lunch, with guide, see

under Puno. The road is paved and in good condition. To **Puno**, 44 km, 1 hr, US$0.60; small buses leave from Piérola y 18 de Noviembre, 2 companies. **Note**: We have received many reports of robbery on night buses on the Juliaca-Puno-Cuzco route; travel by day, or by train. Combis to Puno leave from Terminal Terrestre on Plaza Bolognesi, also US$0.60. See below for how to get to the Bolivian border and page 1202 for transport.

Train See information under Puno or Cuzco. The station at Juliaca is the junction for services between **Arequipa** (no passenger services), **Puno** and **Cuzco**. Prices to Cuzco are the same as from Puno. There is no ticket office. You can get on the train in Juliaca, but you must buy the ticket in Puno or Cuzco.

Sicuani *p1200*
Bus To **Cuzco**, 137 km, US$1.25.

Border with Bolivia → *Peruvian time is one hour behind Bolivian time.*

There are four different routes across the border:
Puno-La Paz via Yunguyo and Copacabana Peruvian immigration is five minutes' drive from **Yunguyo** and 100 m from the Bolivian post; open 24 hours a day (but Bolivian immigration is only open 0830-1930). Ninety days is normally given when entering Peru. Be aware of corruption at customs and look out for official or unofficial people trying to charge you a fee, on either side of the border (say that you know it is illegal and ask why only gringos are approached to pay the 'embarkation tax').

Bolivian consulate is at Jr Grau 339, T856032, near the main plaza in Yunguyo, open Monday-Friday 0830-1500, for those who need a visa; some nationalities have to pay. For **Bolivian immigration**, see page 266. Rates of exchange can be poor unless you negotiate for current rates; find out what they are before you arrive. For those entering Peru cash can be changed in the main plaza in Yunguyo. Travellers' cheques can be exchanged in the *cambio* here, poor rates. See also Puno, Banks.

Puno-Desaguadero Desaguadero is an unscrupulous place, with poor restaurants and dubious accommodation. Tuesday and Friday are *feria* days, busy with locals and their contraband. There is no need to stop in Desaguadero as all roads to it are paved and if you leave La Paz, Moquegua or Puno early enough you should be at your destination before nightfall. Combis and minibuses Puno-Desaguadero hourly 0600-1900, 2½ hrs, US$1.80. Taxi US$33. **Border offices** are open 0830-1230 and 1400-2000. It is easy to change money on the Peruvian side. This particular border crossing allows you to stop at Tiahuanaco en route.

Along the east side of Lake Titicaca This is the most remote route, via **Huancané** and **Moho** (several *hostales*, **F-G**). Some walking may be involved as there is little traffic between Moho and **Puerto Acosta**, Bolivia. Make sure you get an exit stamp in Puno, post-dated by a couple of days. From Juliaca there are buses to Huancané, Moho and Tilali, the last village in Peru with basic lodgings (see Transport, above). The road is paved to Huancané, then poor (improvement supposed to be due), but the views are wonderful. From Tilali it is 2-km walk to the **Peruvian customs** post and a further 2-km steep climb to the international frontier at Cerro Janko Janko, on a promontory high above the lake with magnificent views. Here are hundreds of small stone storerooms, deserted except during the busy Wednesday and Saturday smugglers' market. Puerto Acosta in Bolivia is a further 10 km. You must get a preliminary entry stamp at the police station on the plaza, then the definitive entry stamp at Migración in La Paz.

Sleeping

Yunguyo *p1201*
A few places to stay in **G** range.
G Hostal Isabel, San Francisco 110, near Plaza de Armas, T856019, shared bath, hot water, modern, good value, will change money and arrange transport.

North shore of Lake Titicaca
LL Hotel Isla Suasi, T051-
962 2709, a Casa Andina Private Collection hotel, www.casa-andina.com. The hotel is the only house on this tiny, tranquil island. There are beautiful terraced gardens, best Jan-Mar. The non-native eucalyptus trees are being replaced by native varieties. You can take a canoe around the island to see birds and the island has six vicuñas, a small herd of alpacas and one vizcacha. The sunsets from the highest point are beautiful. Facilities are spacious, comfortable and solar-powered, rooms with bath, hot water, hot water bottles. Price includes full board, good Andean nouvelle cuisine, lots of vegetables. Spa planned; internet US$20 per hr. Private boats from Puno are expensive and take 4-6 hrs (2½ hrs by fast boat, US$450 up to 15 passengers), but you can call at the islands or Llachón en route. A car for 4 people will cost US$75. Otherwise take public transport from Juliaca to Tilali (see below) or Conima bus (Mon 1300, Thu 1300, Sun 0800, 2½-3 hrs, US$1.80) and alight in Cambría, about 20 min past Moho. Walk down to the shore and take a rowing boat to Suasi, 10 mins, US$1.50 pp.

Transport

Border with Bolivia: Yunguyo *p1201*
Bus The road is paved from Puno to Yunguyo and the scenery is interesting. In Puno 3 companies sell bus tickets for the direct route from Puno to La Paz, taking 6-8 hrs (fare does not include the Tiquina ferry crossing, US$0.25): **Colectur**, Tacna 221, T352302, 0730, US$6.50, combines with *Galería* in Bolivia; **Panamericano**, Tacna 245, T354001, 0700, US$7.35, combines with *Diana Tours*; **Tour Perú** (address under Puno Transport), 0700 from your hotel, US$8.75, combines with *Combi Tour* (fares rise at holiday times) They stop at the borders and 1 hr for lunch in Copacabana, arriving in La Paz at about 1700. You only need to change money into Bolivianos for lunch on this route. Bus fare Puno-Copacabana US$4.40-5.80. To

Yunguyo, from the Terminal Zonal in Puno, combis and mini buses hourly 0600-1900, 2½ hrs, US$1.80. From Yunguyo to the border (Kasani), colectivos charge US$0.25 pp. From the border it is a 20-min drive to Copacabana; colectivos and minibuses leave from just outside Bolivian immigration, US$0.50 pp. Taxi from Yunguyo to Copacabana costs about US$1.50 pp. **Note** Don't take a taxi Yunguyo-Puno without checking its reliability first, driver may pick up an accomplice to rob passengers.

To La Paz by hydrofoil or catamaran There are luxury services from Puno/Juli to La Paz by **Crillon Tours** hydrofoil, with connections to tours, from La Paz, to Cuzco and Machu Picchu. In Puno their office is at **Arcobaleno Tours** (see Activities and tours), or contact head office in La Paz, see page 256 for details. The itinerary is: Puno- Copacabana by bus; Copacabana-Isla del Sol-Huatajata (Bolivia) by hydrofoil; Huatajata-La Paz by bus; 13 hrs. Similar services, by catamaran, are run by **Transturin**, whose dock is at Chúa, Bolivia; bookings through **Transturin** in La Paz.

Along the east side of Lake Titicaca *p1201*
Combis to from Juliaca to **Huancané**, 51 km, from Grifo San Juan del Oro, Sucre y Ballón, US$0.45, 1 hr. From Hunacané, combis leave for Julica when full throughout the day. Buses to **Moho** (40 km from Huancané), from Moquegua y Ballón, past Túpac Amaru market, 4 daily, 2-2½ hrs, US$1.50. From Moho to Juliaca, buses leave at 0130, 0800 and 1300 daily. Buses to **Tilali**, **Transportes Lucero**, 1 or 2 daily in early morning, **Aguila del Sur**, 1 daily in morning, both from Circunvalación y Lambayeque, 4 hrs, US$2.50 (schedules change daily; ask in advance). Daily buses from Tilali to Juliaca, around 0100, plus a morning bus, 0800-1000 on Sun, Tue and Fri. On market days trucks go to Puerto Acosta and La Paz. Try hitching to catch bus from Puerto Acosta to La Paz (daily) about 1400 (note Bolivian time is 1 hour ahead of Peru), more frequent service on Sun, 5 hrs, US$3.75. If you are in a hurry and miss the bus, ask the truck to drop you off 25 km further in Escoma, from where there are frequent minivans to La Paz. Buses leave La Paz for Puerto Acosta at 0600 daily. Transport from Puerto Acosta to border only operates on market days, mostly cargo trucks.

Cuzco → *Phone code: 084. Colour map 3, grid C4. Altitude: 3,310 m.*

The ancient Inca capital is said to have been founded around AD 1100, and since then has developed into a major commercial and tourism centre of 275,000 inhabitants, most of whom are Quechua. The city council has designated Qosqo (Cuzco in Quechua) as the official spelling. Today, colonial churches, monasteries and convents and extensive pre-Columbian ruins are interspersed with countless hotels, bars and restaurants that cater for the hundreds of thousands of visitors. Almost every central street has remains of Inca walls, arches and doorways; the perfect Inca stonework now serves as the foundations for more modern dwellings. This stonework is tapered upwards (battered); every wall has a perfect line of inclination towards the centre, from bottom to top. The curved stonework of the Temple of the Sun, for example, is probably unequalled in the world.

Ins and outs

Getting there The **airport** is to the southeast of the city and the road into the centre goes close to Wanchac station, at which **trains** from Juliaca and Puno arrive. The **bus terminal** is near the Pachacútec statue in Ttio district. Transport to your hotel is not a problem from any of these places by taxi or in transport arranged by hotel representatives. ▶▶ *For more detailed information, see Transport, page 1224.*

Getting around The centre of Cuzco is quite small and possible to explore on foot. Taxis in Cuzco are cheap and recommended when arriving by air, train or bus and especially when returning to your hotel at night. Cuzco is only slightly lower than Puno, so respect the altitude: two or three hours rest after arriving makes a great difference; avoid meat and smoking, eat lots of carbohydrates and drink plenty of clear, non-alcoholic liquid; remember to walk slowly. To see Cuzco and the surrounding area properly (including Pisac, Ollantaytambo, Chinchero and Machu Picchu) you need five days to a week, allowing for slowing down because of altitude.

Tourist information Official tourist information ① *Portal Mantas 117-A, next to La Merced church, T263176, open 0800-2000*. There is also an **i perú** tourist information desk at the airport ① *T237364, open daily 0600-1300*, and another at ① *Av Sol 103, of 102, Galerías Turísticas, T234498, daily 0830-1930*. **Dircetur** ① *Av de la Cultura 734, p 3, T223701, open Mon-Fri 0800-1300*. Other information sources include **South American Explorers** ① *Choquechaca 188, apto 4 (2 blocks behind the Cathedral), T245 484, www.saexplorers.org, Mon-Fri 0930-1700, Sat 0930-1300, closed Sun, but May-Sep open Mon-Sat 0930-1700, Sun 0930-1300*. As with SAE's other clubhouses, this is the place to go for specialized information, member-written trip reports and maps. For full details on South American Explorers, see page 32. Many churches close to visitors on Sunday; 'official' opening times are unreliable. No photographs are allowed in any museums. **Automóvil Club del Perú** ① *Av Sol 349, nivel 2, T/F224561, cusco@ touringperu.com.pe*, has some maps. Motorists beware; many streets end in flights of steps. There are very few good maps of Cuzco available. **Maps and**

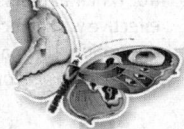

Cuszo was the capital of the Inca empire – one of the greatest planned societies the world has known – from its rise during the 11th century to its death in the early 16th century. (See John Hemming's *Conquest of the Incas* and B C Brundage's *Lords of Cuzco* and *Empire of the Inca*.) It was solidly based on other Peruvian civilizations which had attained great skill in textiles, building, ceramics and working in metal. Immemorially, the political structure of the Andean *indígena* had been the *ayllu*, the village community; it had its divine ancestor, worshipped household gods, was closely knit by ties of blood to the family and by economic necessity to the land, which was held in common. Submission to the *ayllu* was absolute, because it was only by such discipline that food could be obtained in an unsympathetic environment. All the domestic animals, the llama and alpaca and the dog, had long been tamed, and the great staple crops, maize and potatoes, established. What the Incas did – and it was a magnificent feat – was to conquer enormous territories and impose upon the variety of *ayllus*, through an unchallengeable central government, a willing spiritual and economic submission to the State. The common religion, already developed by the classical Tiwanaku culture, was worship of the Sun, whose vice-regent on earth was the absolute Sapa Inca. Around him, in the capital, was a religious and secular elite which never froze into a caste because it was open to talent. The elite was often recruited from chieftains defeated by the Incas; an effective way of reconciling local opposition. The mass of the people were subjected to rigorous planning. They were allotted land to work, for their group and for the State; set various tasks (the making of textiles, pottery, weapons, ropes, etc) from primary materials supplied by the functionaries, or used in enlarging the area of cultivation by building terraces on the hill-sides. Their political organization was simple but effective. The family, and not the individual, was the unit. Families were grouped in units of 10, 100, 500, 1,000, 10,000 and 40,000, each group with a leader responsible to the next largest group. The Sapa Inca crowned the political edifice; his four immediate counsellors were those to whom he allotted responsibility for the northern, southern, eastern and western regions (suyos) of the empire.

Equilibrium between production and consumption, in the absence of a free price mechanism and good transport facilities, must depend heavily upon statistical information. This the Incas raised to a high degree of efficiency by means of their *quipus*: a decimal system of recording numbers by knots in cords. Seasonal variations were guarded against by creating a system of state barns in which provender could be stored during years of plenty, to be used in years of scarcity. Statistical efficiency alone required that no one should be permitted to leave his home or his work. The loss of personal liberty was the price paid by the masses for economic security. In order to obtain information and to transmit orders quickly, the Incas built fine paved pathways along which couriers sped on foot. The whole system of rigorous control was completed by the greatest of all their monarchs, Pachacuti, who also imposed a common language, Quechua, as a further cementing force.

guidebooks: maps of the city, the Inca Trail and the Urubamba Valley are available at tour companies. There are information booklets on Machu Picchu and the other ruins at the bookshops. See Books, page 1520.

Visitors' tickets A combined entry ticket to most of the sites of main historical- cultural interest in and around the city, called *Boleto Turístico General* (BTG), costs 70 soles for 10 days,

US$21 approximately, and 40 soles for one day (either just museums, or just archaeological sites), US$12 approximately, payable in soles only. It permits entrance to: Santa Catalina Convent and Art Museum, Museo de Sitio Qoricancha (but not Santo Domingo/Qoricancha itself), Museo Histórico Regional (Casa Inca Garcilazo de la Vega), Museo Palacio Municipal de Arte Contemporáneo, Museo de Arte Popular, Centro Qosqo de Arte Nativo, Monumento Pachacútec; the archaeological sites of Sacsayhuaman, Qenqo, Puka Pukara, Tambo Machay, Pisac, Ollantaytambo, Chinchero, Tipón and Piquillacta. The tickets can be bought at the **OFEC office** ① *Casa Garcilaso, Plaza Regocijo, esquina Calle Garcilaso, T226919, Mon-Sat 0800-1600, Sun 0800-1200; Av Sol 103, T227037, Mon-Fri 0800-1800, Sat 0830-1230*, or at any of the sites included in the ticket. There is a 50% discount for students with a green ISIC card, which is only available at the OFEC office (Casa Garcilaso) upon presentation of the ISIC card. Take your ISIC card when visiting the sites, as some may ask to see it. Photography is not allowed in the churches, and museums.

Entrance tickets for the Cathedral, Santo Domingo/Qoricancha, the Inka Museum (El Palacio del Almirante), Museo de Arte Religioso del Arzobispado and La Merced are sold separately. Machu Picchu ruins and Inca trail entrance tickets are sold at the **Instituto Nacional de Cultura** (INC) ① *San Bernardo s/n entre Mantas y Almagro, T236061, Mon-Fri 0900-1300, 1600-1800, Sat 0900-1100*.

Security Police patrol the streets, trains and stations, but one should still be vigilant. On no account walk back to your hotel after dark from a bar or club, strangle muggings and rape are frequent. For safety's sake, pay the US$0.85 taxi fare, but not just any taxi. Ask the club's doorman to get a taxi for you and make sure the taxi is licensed. Other areas in which to take care include Santa Ana market (otherwise recommended), the San Cristóbal area, and at out-of-the-way ruins. Also take special care during Inti Raymi.

The **Tourist Police**, T249654, offices at Ovalo de Pachacútec, Tandapata at Plaza de San Blas and on C Saphi. If you need a *denuncia* (a report for insurance purposes), which is available from the Banco de la Nación, they will type it out. Always go to the police when robbed, even though it will cost you a bit of time. The Tourist Protection Bureau (**Indecopi**) is at the tourist office at Portal Carrizos, Plaza de Armas (see above). Toll free 0800-42579 (24-hour hotline, not available from payphones).

Sights

The heart of the city in Inca days was *Huacaypata* (the place of tears) and *Cusipata* (the place of happiness), divided by a channel of the Saphi River. Today, Cusipata is Plaza Regocijo and Huacaypata is the Plaza de Armas, around which are colonial arcades and four churches. To the northeast is the early 17th-century baroque **Cathedral** ① *until 1000 for genuine worshippers – Quechua mass is held 0500-0600. Tourists may visit Mon, Tue, Wed, Fri, Sat 1000-1130, 1400-1730, Thu and Sun 1400-1730. US$3*. It is built on the site of the Palace of Inca Wiracocha (*Kiswarcancha*). The high altar is solid silver and the original altar *retablo* behind it is a

masterpiece of Andean wood carving. The earliest surviving painting of the city can be seen, depicting Cuzco during the 1650 earthquake. In the far right hand end of the church is an interesting local painting of the Last Supper replete with *cuy*, *chicha*, etc. In the sacristy are paintings of all the bishops of Cuzco. The choir stalls, by a 17th-century Spanish priest, are a magnificent example of colonial baroque art. The elaborate pulpit and the sacristy are also notable. Much venerated is the crucifix of El Señor de los Temblores, the object of many pilgrimages and viewed all over Peru as a guardian against earthquakes. The tourist entrance

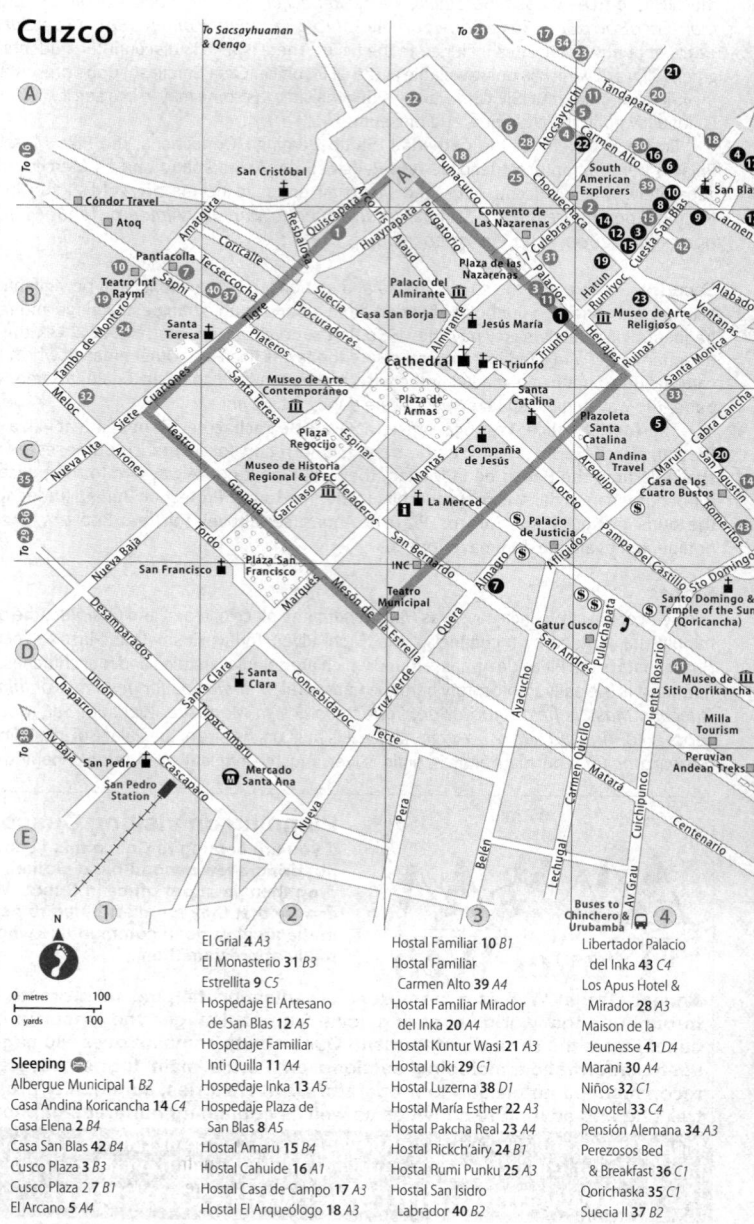

Cuzco

Sleeping

Albergue Municipal **1** *B2*
Casa Andina Koricancha **14** *C4*
Casa Elena **2** *B4*
Casa San Blas **42** *B4*
Cusco Plaza **3** *B3*
Cusco Plaza 2 **7** *B1*
El Arcano **5** *A4*

El Grial **4** *A3*
El Monasterio **31** *B3*
Estrellita **9** *C5*
Hospedaje El Artesano
  de San Blas **12** *A5*
Hospedaje Familiar
  Inti Quilla **11** *A4*
Hospedaje Inka **13** *A5*
Hospedaje Plaza de
  San Blas **8** *A5*
Hostal Amaru **15** *B4*
Hostal Cahuide **16** *A1*
Hostal Casa de Campo **17** *A3*
Hostal El Arqueólogo **18** *A3*

Hostal Familiar **10** *B1*
Hostal Familiar
  Carmen Alto **39** *A4*
Hostal Familiar Mirador
  del Inka **20** *A4*
Hostal Kuntur Wasi **21** *A3*
Hostal Loki **29** *C1*
Hostal Luzerna **38** *D1*
Hostal María Esther **22** *A3*
Hostal Pakcha Real **23** *A4*
Hostal Rickch'airy **24** *B1*
Hostal Rumi Punku **25** *A3*
Hostal San Isidro
  Labrador **40** *B2*

Libertador Palacio
  del Inka **43** *C4*
Los Apus Hotel &
  Mirador **28** *A3*
Maison de la
  Jeunesse **41** *D4*
Marani **30** *A4*
Niños **32** *C1*
Novotel **33** *C4*
Pensión Alemana **34** *A3*
Perezosos Bed
  & Breakfast **36** *C1*
Qorichaska **35** *C1*
Suecia II **37** *B2*

0 metres 100
0 yards 100

N

Peru Cuzco

to the Cathedral is through the church of **Jesús María** (1733), which stands to its left as you face it. Its gilt main altar has been renovated. **El Triunfo** (1536), on its right of the Cathedral, is the first Christian church in Cuzco, built on the site of the Inca Roundhouse (the *Suntur Huasi*). It has a statue of the Virgin of the Descent, reputed to have helped the Spaniards repel Manco Inca when he besieged the city in 1536.

On the southeast side of the plaza is the beautiful **La Compañía de Jesús**, built on the site of the Palace of the Serpents (*Amarucancha*, residence of Inca Huayna Capac) in the late 17th century. Its twin-towered exterior is extremely graceful, and the interior rich in fine murals, paintings and carved altars. Nearby is the **Santa Catalina** church ① *Arequipa at Santa Catalina Angosta, daily 0900-1200, 1300-1700, except Fri 0900-1200, 1300-1600,* convent and museum. There are guided tours by English-speaking students; tip expected.

La Merced ① *on Calle Márquez, church 0830-1200, 1530-1730; monastery and museum 1430-1700, except Sun, US$0.85.* The church was first built 1534 and rebuilt in the late 17th century. Attached is a very fine monastery with an exquisite cloister. Inside the church are buried Gonzalo Pizarro, half-brother of Francisco, and the two Almagros, father and son. The church is most famous for its jewelled monstrance, which is on view in the monastery's museum during visiting hours.

Much **Inca stonework** can be seen in the streets and most particularly in the Callejón Loreto, running southeast past La Compañía de Jesús from the main plaza. The walls of the *Acllahuasi* (House of the Chosen Women) are on one side, and of the *Amarucancha* on the other. There are also Inca remains in Calle San Agustín, to the east of the plaza. The stone of 12 angles is in Calle Hatun Rumiyoc halfway along its second block, on the right-hand side going away from the Plaza. The **Palacio Arzobispal** stands on Hatun Rumiyoc y Herrajes, two blocks northeast of Plaza de Armas. It was built on the site of the palace occupied in 1400. It contains the **Museo de Arte Religioso** ① *Mon-Sat, 0830-1130, 1500- 1730, US$3, US$1.50 for students,* a collection of colonial paintings and furniture. The collection includes the paintings by the indigenous master, Diego Quispe Tito, of a 17th-century Corpus Christi procession that used to hang in the church of Santa Ana.

The **Palacio del Almirante**, just north of the Plaza de Armas on Ataud, is impressive. It houses the **Museo Inka** ① *Mon-Sat 0800-1730, US$2.40,* which is run by the Universidad San Antonio de Abad, the museum exhibits the development of culture in the region from pre-Inca, through Inca times to the present day: textiles, ceramics, metalwork, jewellery, architecture,

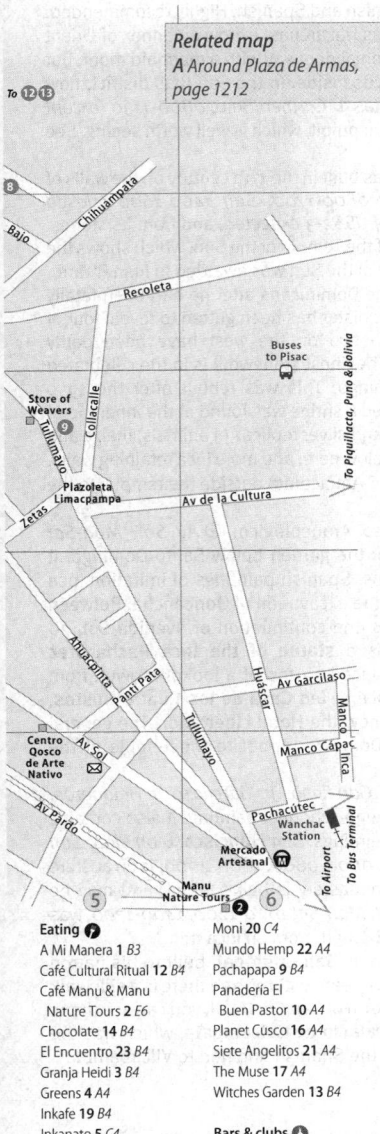

Related map
A Around Plaza de Armas, page 1212

To ⑫⑬

⑧

Chihuampata

Bajo

Recoleta

Buses to Pisac

To Piquillacta, Puno & Bolivia

Store of Weavers ⑨

Collacalle
Tullumayo

Plazoleta Limacpampa

Zetas

Av de la Cultura

Ahuacpinta

Panti Pata

Tullumayo

Huascar

Av Garcilaso

Manco

Centro Qosco de Arte Nativo ✉

Av Sol

Manco Cápac

Inca

Av Pardo

Pachacutec

Wanchac Station

Mercado Artesanal Ⓜ

To Airport

To Bus Terminal

⑤

Manu Nature Tours ②❷ ⑥

Eating 🍴
A Mi Manera **1** *B3*
Café Cultural Ritual **12** *B4*
Café Manu & Manu
 Nature Tours **2** *E6*
Chocolate **14** *B4*
El Encuentro **23** *B4*
Granja Heidi **3** *B4*
Greens **4** *A4*
Inkafe **19** *B4*
Inkanato **5** *C4*
Jack's Café **15** *B4*
La Bodega **6** *A4*
Los Toldos **7** *D3*

Moni **20** *C4*
Mundo Hemp **22** *A4*
Pachapapa **9** *B4*
Panadería El
 Buen Pastor **10** *A4*
Planet Cusco **16** *A4*
Siete Angelitos **21** *A4*
The Muse **17** *A4*
Witches Garden **13** *B4*

Bars & clubs 🍸
Km 0 (Arte y Tapas) **18** *A4*
Mandela's **11** *B3*

Peru Cuzco

technology. See the collection of miniature turquoise figures and other offerings to the gods. Weaving demonstrations are given in the courtyard. On the northwest side of the Plaza de las Nazarenas is **Museo de Arte Precolombino** ① *daily 0900-2200, US$6, US$3 with student card, shops, MAP Café (see Eating, below)*, housed in the **Casa Cabrera**. This beautiful museum is set around a spacious courtyard and contains many superb examples of pottery, metalwork (largely in gold and silver), wood carvings and shells from the Moche, Chimú, Paracas, Nazca and Inca cultures. There are some vividly-rendered animistic designs, giving an insight into the way Peru's ancient people's viewed their world and the creatures that inhabited it. Every exhibit carries explanations in English and Spanish. Highly recommended. The **Convento de las Nazarenas**, also on Plaza de las Nazarenas, is now an annex of Orient Express' *Monasterio* hotel. You can see the Inca-colonial doorway with a mermaid motif, but ask permission to view the lovely 18th-century frescos inside. In the San Blas district, now firmly on the tourist map, the small church of **San Blas** ① *Carmen Bajo, 0800-1130 (except Thu), 1400-1730*, has a beautiful carved *mestizo* cedar pulpit, which is well worth seeing. See Shopping Local crafts, below.

Santo Domingo, southeast of the main Plaza, was built in the 17th century on the walls of the **Qoricancha, Temple of the Sun** ① *Mon-Sat 0800-1700, Sun 1400-1600 (closed holidays), US$1.50, English-speaking guides, tip of US$2-3 expected*, and from its stones. Excavation has revealed more of the five chambers of the Temple of the Sun, which shows the best Inca stonework to be seen in Cuzco. The Temple of the Sun was awarded to Juan Pizarro, the younger brother of Francisco, who willed it to the Dominicans after he had been fatally wounded in the Sacsayhuaman siege. The baroque cloister has been gutted to reveal four of the original chambers of the great Inca temple - two on the west have been partly reconstructed in a good imitation of Inca masonry. The finest stonework is in the celebrated curved wall beneath the west end of Santo Domingo. This was rebuilt after the 1950 earthquake, at which time a niche that once contained a shrine was found at the inner top of the wall. Below the curved wall was a garden of gold and silver replicas of animals, maize and other plants. Excavations have revealed Inca baths below here, and more Inca retaining walls. The other superb stretch of late Inca stonework is in C Ahuacpinta outside the temple, to the east or left as you enter.

Museo de Sitio Qorikancha (formerly Museo Arqueológico) ① *Av Sol, Mon-Sat 0900-1200, 1300-1700, Sun 0800-1400*, is under the garden below Santo Domingo. It contains a limited collection of pre-Columbian items, Spanish paintings of imitation Inca royalty dating from the 18th century, and photos of the excavation of Qoricancha. Between the centre and the airport on Alameda Pachacútec, the continuation of Avenida Sol, 20 minutes walk from the Plaza de Armas, there is a **statue of the Inca Pachacútec** ① *1000-2000, small galleries and coffee shop*, placed on top of a lookout tower, from which there are excellent views of Cuzco. The palace called **Casa de los Cuatro Bustos**, whose colonial doorway is at San Agustín 400, is now the **Hotel Libertador**. The general public can enter the Hotel from Plazoleta Santo Domingo, opposite the Temple of the Sun/Qoricancha.

Museo de Historia Regional ① *in the Casa Garcilaso, Jr Garcilaso y Heladeros, 0730-1700*, tries to show the evolution of the Cuzqueño school of painting. It also contains Inca agricultural implements, colonial furniture and paintings. **San Francisco** ① *on Plaza San Francisco, 3 blocks southwest of the Plaza de Armas, 0600-0800, 1800-2000*, is an austere church reflecting many indigenous influences. Its monastery is being rebuilt and may be closed. **San Pedro** ① *in front of the Santa Ana market, Mon-Sat 1000-1200, 1400-1700*, was built in 1688. Its two towers were made from stones brought from an Inca ruin.

Above Cuzco, on the road up to Sacsayhuamán, is **San Cristóbal**, built to his patron saint by Cristóbal Paullu Inca. The church's atrium has been restored and there is a sidewalk access to the Sacsayhuamán Archaeological Park. North of San Cristóbal, you can see the 11 doorway-sized niches of the great Inca wall of the **Palacio de Colcampata**, which was the residence of Manco Inca before he rebelled against the Spanish and fled to Vilcabamba.

● *Archaeologists are investigating the possibility of a tunnel between Qoricancha and Sacsayhuman,*
● *supporting the belief that the lost treasures of the Inca empire are buried beneath Cuzco.*
1208

Sacsayhuaman

① *Daily 0700-1730; free student guides, give them a tip.*
There are some magnificent Inca walls in this ruined ceremonial centre, on a hill in the northern outskirts. The Incaic stones are hugely impressive. The massive rocks weighing up to 130 tons are fitted together with absolute perfection. Three walls run parallel for over 360 m and there are 21 bastions. Sacsayhuaman was thought for centuries to be a fortress, but the layout and architecture suggest a great sanctuary and temple to the Sun, which rises exactly opposite the place previously believed to be the Inca's throne - which was probably an altar, carved out of the solid rock. Broad steps lead to the altar from either side. The hieratic, rather than the military, hypothesis was supported by the discovery in 1982 of the graves of priests, who would have been unlikely to be buried in a fortress. The precise functions of the site, however, will probably continue to be a matter of dispute as very few clues remain, owing to its steady destruction. The site is about a 30-minute walk up Pumacurco from Plaza de las Nazarenas.

Along the road from Sacsayhuaman to Pisac, past a radio station, is the temple and amphitheatre of **Qenqo** with some of the finest examples of Inca stone carving *in situ*, especially inside the large hollowed-out stone that houses an altar. On the same road are **Puka Pukara** (Red Fort, but more likely to have been a *tambo*, or post-house), wonderful views; and the spring shrine of **Tambo Machay**, which is in excellent condition. Water still flows by a hidden channel out of the masonry wall, straight into a little rock pool traditionally known as the Inca's bath. Take a guide to the sites and visit in the morning for the best photographs. Carry your multi-site ticket, there are roving ticket inspectors. You can visit the sites on foot, a pleasant walk of at least half a day through the countryside; take water, sun protection, and watch out for dogs.

Alternatively, take the Pisac bus up to Tambo Machay (US$0.35) and walk back, or arrange a horseback tour with an agency.

● Sleeping

Cuzco *p1203, maps p1206 and p1212*
In Jun and other busy times, double-booking occurs so double-check reservations. Book more expensive hotels well in advance, particularly for the week or so around Inti Raymi, when prices are greatly increased. Prices given are for the high season in Jun-Aug. When there are fewer tourists hotels may drop their prices by as much as half. Always check for discounts. Train passengers are approached by unlicensed hotel agents for medium-priced hotels who are often misleading about details; their local nickname is *jalagringos* (gringo pullers), or *piratas*. Taxis and tourist minibuses meet the train and (should) take you to the hotel of your choice for US$0.60, but be insistent. Since it is cold here and many hotels have no heating, ask for an *estufa*, a heater which some places will provide for an extra charge.
LL El Monasterio, C Palacios 136, Plazoleta Nazarenas, T241777, www.monasterio.orient-express.com.com. 5-star, beautifully restored Seminary of San Antonio Abad (a Peruvian National Historical Landmark), including the Baroque chapel, spacious comfortable rooms with all facilities (some rooms offer an oxygen-enriched atmosphere to help clients acclimatize, US$25 extra), very helpful staff, price includes buffet breakfast (US$19 to non-residents, will fill you up for the rest of the day), good restaurants, lunch and dinner à la carte, business centre with email for guests (US$3 per hr).

LL Libertador, Plazoleta Santo Domingo 259, T231961, www.libertador.com.pe. 5-star, price includes buffet breakfast, good, especially the service, warm and bright, *Inti Raymi* restaurant, excellent, folk music in the evening.
LL Novotel, San Agustín 239, T881030, reservations@novotel.cusco.com.pe. 4-star, cheaper in modern section; price includes buffet breakfast, one of the best hotels converted from a colonial house, beautiful courtyard, roofed in glass, spacious rooms, cable TV, central heating, 2 restaurants and a French chef.
L Sonesta Posadas del Inca, Portal Espinar 108, T712 6060, www.sonestaperu.com. Includes buffet breakfast, warmly decorated rooms with heating and cable TV, safe, some rooms on 3rd floor with view of Plaza, very helpful, English spoken, restaurant with Andean food, excellent service.
AL Casa San Blas, Tocuyeros 566, just off Cuesta San Blas, T237900, www.casasanblas.com. A new 'boutique' hotel, bright, airy rooms decorated with traditional textiles, breakfast and internet included, attentive service.
AL Casa Andina Plaza, Portal Espinar 142, T231733, www.casa-andina.com. Near the plaza, this new hotel has 40 rooms with cable TV, private bathroom and safe deposit box. Equally recommendable are **Casa Andina Koricancha**, San Agustín 371, T252633, and **Casa Andina Catedral**, Santa Catalina Angosta 149, T233661, both of which are in the same price range.

Foundation (www.stichtinghope.org), which builds schools, helps teachers and hospitals, good value, great cause.

D El Arcano, Carmen Alto 288, San Blas, T232703. Cheaper in low season and with shared bath, hot water, safe to leave luggage, laundry, good beds, cheap breakfast.

D El Balcón Colonial, Choquechaca 350, T238129, balconcolonial@hotmail.com. Accommodation for 11 people in 6 rooms, hot

Around Plaza de Armas

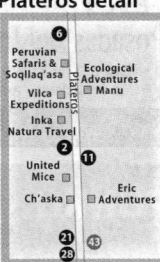

Plateros detail

Sleeping 🛏
Casa Andina
  Catedral **16** C3
Casa Andina Plaza**15** C2
El Procurador
  del Cusco **1** A2
Hostal Q'Awarina **6** A2
Hostal Resbalosa **7** A3
Hostal Royal Frankenstein
  & Tangible Myth **8** B1
Marqueses **2** B1
Pensión Loreto **9** C2
Royal Inka I **12** B1
Royal Inka II **13** A1
Sonesta Posada
  del Inca **3** B2

Eating 🍴
Al Grano **1** C3
Ama Lur **2** Plateros detail
Auliya **18** B1
Blueberry Lounge **3** B3
Café Ayllu **4** B3
Café Halliy **6**
  Plateros detail
Chez Maggy Clave
  de Do **7** A2

Chez Maggy El
  Corsario **8** B2
Chez Maggy La
  Antigua **9** A2
Cicciolina **44** C3
Due Mondi **10** C3
El Encuentro **12** C3
El Truco & Taberna
  del Truco **13** B1
Fallen Angel **14** B3
Inka Grill **15** B2
Kintaro **16** B1
Kusikuy **17** B3
La Retama **19** B2
Los Candiles & Café
  Amaru **21** Plateros detail
MAP Café **47** B3
Mia Pizza **24** A2
Paccha **23** B2
Pachacútec Grill
  & Bar **25** B2
Paititi **26** C3
Pomodoro **46** C2
Pucará **28** Plateros detail
Sunset Video Café **22** A2
The Real McCoy **11**
  Plateros detail

Trotamundos **31** B2
Tupananchis **5** C1
Tunupa & Cross
  Keys Pub **32** B2
Varayoc **33** B2
Victor Victoria **34** A2
Yaku Mama **35** A2

Bars & clubs 🍸
Big Blue Martini **30** A2
Corruption **20** A2
El Garabato Video Music
  Club **42** B2
Extreme **27** B3
Kamikaze **36** B2
Los Perros **37** A2
Magtas **27** B3
Mama Africa **45** B2
Mama América **38** C3
Norton Rat's
  Tavern **39** C2
Paddy Flaherty's **40** C3
Rosie O'Grady's **41** C3
Ukuku's **43** Plateros detail

showers, breakfast, kitchen and laundry facilities all extra, comfortable, safe, generous hosts.

D Hostal Familiar, Saphi 661, T239353.
E without bath, hot water, good beds, popular.

D (E pp) Hostel Loki, Cuesta Santa Ana 601, T243705, info@lokihostel.com. Huge, funky new hostel in a restored viceroy's residence on the steep Cuesta Santa Ana, dorms and rooms set around a beautiful courtyard, comfortable beds, hot water, free internet. A great meeting place.

D Hostal Pakcha Real, Tandapata 300, San Blas, T237484, pakcharealhostal@ hotmail.com. Family run, hot water, relaxed. Breakfast, cooking and laundry facilities extra. Airport/train/bus pick-up, but call ahead if arriving late.

D Hostal Rickch'airy, Tambo de Montero 219, T236606. **F** with shared bath, hot water in the morning, laundry service, free luggage store, breakfast available, nice garden with good views, will collect guests from train station, tourist information, mixed reports.

D Hostal Royal Frankenstein, San Juan de Dios 260, 2 blocks from the Plaza de Armas, T236999, ludwig_roth@hotmail.com. Eccentric, memorably-decorated, hot water, safe, cooking (US$0.30/day) and laundry facilities, German-owned, German and English spoken.

D Qorichaska, Nueva Alta 458, some distance from centre, T228974, qorichaska77@yahoo.com. Hot water, includes breakfast, use of kitchen, will store luggage, safe, great value.

D Hostal Resbalosa, Resbalosa 494, T224839. Cheaper without bath, hot water in the mornings and evenings, ask for a room with a view, luggage stored, laundry facilities, full breakfast for US$1.45.

D Suecia II, Tecseccocha 465, T239757. **F** without bath, good security, breakfast US$1.40 from 0500, beautiful building, good meeting place, water not always hot or bathrooms clean, best to book in advance (but if full they will find alternative accommodation, which may not be as good).

D-E Hostal Familiar Mirador del Inka, Tandapata 160, off Plaza San Blas, T261384, miradordelinka@latinmail.com. Cheaper without bath, hot water, laundry, son Edwin rents trekking equipment.

D-E Hospedaje Plaza de San Blas, Plazoleta San Blas 630, T235358, psanblas@cori huasi.com. Welcoming, good location, breakfast included, has a 4-bed family room.

E Estrellita, Av Tullumayo 445, parte Alta, T234134. Includes breakfast, basic kitchen for guests, most rooms with shared bath, 2 with private bath, basic but excellent value, safe parking available for bikes.

E Hostal Familiar Carmen Alto, Carmen Alto 197, T224367, 1st on the right down steps (there is no sign), 3 blocks from central plaza. If there's no answer at the bell, go to the shop next door. Tranquil and full of character, family run, use of kitchen and washing machine, breakfast US$2, shared bath.

E Hostal Luzerna, Av Baja 205, near San Pedro train station (take a taxi at night), T232762. Hot water, safe to leave luggage, good beds, nice family, with breakfast, use of kitchen.

E pp Perezosos Bed and Breakfast, Nueva Alta 424. Comfortable new hostel in the English B&B style. Excellent beds with duvets, good hot water, helpful owner, Indian restaurant downstairs.

F Hospedaje El Artesano de San Blas, Suytucato 790, San Blas, T263968, manosandinas@yahoo.com. Many bright and airy rooms, taxis leave you at Plaza San Blas, walk steeply uphill for 5-10 mins.

F pp Hospedaje Inka, Suytuccato 848, T231995. Like *El Artesano*, you need to walk up from Plaza San Blas, 5-10 mins, or phone the hostal. Includes breakfast, wonderful views, spacious rooms, owner Américo is very helpful.

F Hospedaje Familiar Inti Quilla, Atocsaycuchi 281, T252659. Shared rooms around a pleasant little courtyard, hot water 24 hrs, no breakfast or kitchen.

Peru Cuzco Listings

Youth hostels

D Maison de la Jeunesse (affiliated to HI), Av Sol, Cuadra 5, Pasaje Grace, Edif San Jorge (down a small side street opposite Qoricancha) T235617, www.hostellingcusco.com. French/Peruvian run, dormitories and private rooms, TV and video room, cooking facilities and very hot water, includes breakfast.

D-E El Procurador del Cusco, Coricalle 440, Prolongación Procuradores, T243559. Price includes use of the basic kitchen (no fridge) and laundry area, basic rooms, but upstairs is better, helpful, good value. Recommended.

E Albergue Municipal, Quiscapata 240, San Cristóbal, T252506, albergue@municusco.gob.pe. Dormitories and double rooms, helpful staff, luggage store, great views, bar, cafeteria, laundry, safe deposit, discount for members.

● Eating

Cuzco p1203, maps p1206 and p1212

♦♦♦ Cicciolina , Triunfo 393, 2nd floor, T239510, cicciolinacuzco@yahoo.com. Sophisticated, focusing largely on Italian/Mediterranean cuisine, excellent dishes, impressive wine list. Good atmosphere and great for treat.

♦♦♦ Fallen Angel, Plazoleta Nazarenas 221, T258184. International and Novo Andino gourmet cuisine, decor juxtaposes the modern and the kitsch with colonial surroundings, memorable special events throughout the year, Sun open 1500-2400.

♦♦♦ Inka Grill, Portal de Panes 115, Plaza de Armas, T262992. According to many the best food in town, specializing in Novo Andino cuisine (the use of native ingredients and 'rescued' recipes), also homemade pastas, wide vegetarian selection, live music, excellent coffee and homemade pastries 'to go'.

♦♦♦ MAP Café, in Museo de Arte Precolombino, Plaza de las Nazarenas 231, café 1000-1830. From 1830-2200 it's a 1st class international and Peruvian-Andean cuisine, innovative children's menu

♦♦♦ Pachacútec Grill and Bar, Portal de Panes 105, Plaza de Armas. International cuisine, including seafood and Italian specialities, excellent value *menú* for US$2.50, folk music nightly.

♦♦♦ Paititi, Portal Carrizos 270, Plaza de Armas. Live music, good atmosphere, Inca masonry, excellent pizzas.

♦♦♦ La Retama, Portal de Panes 123, 2nd floor. Good food (also Novo Andino) and service, live music and dance, art exhibitions.

♦♦♦ El Truco, Plaza Regocijo 261. Excellent local and international dishes, buffet lunch 1200-1500, nightly folk music at 2045, next door is **Taberna del Truco**, open 0900-0100.

♦♦♦ Pomodoro, Loreto 125, T221397. Almost certainly the best Italian food in Cuzco, a bastion of 'slow food', with all pasta and pizza hand made on the spot. Superb.

♦♦♦ Tunupa, Portal Confiturias 233, p 2, Plaza de Armas (same entrance as *Cross Keys*). Large restaurant, small balcony overlooking Plaza, international, Peruvian and Novo Andino cuisine, good buffet US$15, nicely decorated, cocktail lounge, live music and dance at 2030.

♦♦♦ Tupananchis, Portal Mantas 180, T976 4494. Tasty Novo Andino and Fusion cuisine in a sophisticated atmosphere. Recommended.

♦♦ A Mi Manera (Culturas Peru), Triunfo 393, T222 219, www.culturasperu.com. Remodelled in 2006, imaginative Novoandina cuisine with open kitchen. Great hospitality and atmosphere.

♦♦ Blueberry Lounge, Portal de Carnes 236, Plaza de Armas, T221397. In a beautifully restored colonial house, open fires in the evening, cosy place to read, listen to music, watch TV or videos, menu specializes in Asian dishes, with touches of the Novo Andino, good for breakfast, vegetarian options.

♦♦ Al Grano, Santa Catalina Ancha 398, T228032. Authentic Asian dishes, menu changes daily, excellent food, best coffee in town, vegetarian choices, open 1000-2100, closed on Sun.

♦♦ Greens, Tandapata 700, behind the church on Plaza San Blas, T243820. International food with some vegetarian, curries, Sunday roasts, relaxing atmosphere, games, book exchange, reservation required.

♦♦ Inkanato, San Agustín 280, T222926, www.perou.net. Good food, staff dressed in Inca outfits and dishes made only with ingredients known in Inca times, calls itself a "living museum".

♦♦ Jack's Café, Choquechaca y San Blas. Excellent varied menu, generous portions, relaxed atmosphere, can get very busy at lunchtime.

♦♦ Kintaro, Heladeros 149. Japanese and vegetarian, homemade and low fat food, good for high altitude, Japanese owner, closed Sun.

♦♦ Kusikuy, Suecia 339, T292870. Open 0800-2300 Mon-Sat, local, national and international dishes, good service, set lunch unbeatable value at only US$2.

♦♦ La Bodega, Carmen Alto 146, San Blas. Snug Dutch and Peruvian-owned café/restaurant, good food, salads, drinks.

♦♦ Los Toldos, Almagro 171 and San Andrés 219. Grilled chicken, fries and salad bar, also *trattoria* with homemade pasta and pizza, delivery T229829.

♦♦ Macondo, Cuesta San Blas 571, T229415. Interesting restaurant with an imaginative menu, good food, well-furnished, gay friendly.

♦♦ Pachapapa, Plazoleta San Blas 120, opposite church of San Blas, T241318, www.cuscorestaurants.com. A beautiful patio restaurant in a colonial house, good Cusqueña dishes, at night diners can sit in their own, private colonial dining room. Recommended.

Pucará, Plateros 309. Peruvian and international food, open 1230-2200, closed Sun, nice atmosphere.

The Real McCoy, Plateros 326, 2nd floor, T261111. A retreat for homesick Brits and Aussies, good value breakfast buffet (US$2), English classics for dinner, puddings too.

Varayoc, Espaderos 142, T232404. Swiss restaurant, including Peruvian ingredients (cheese fondue US$10-13); also has a variety of pastas, good desserts, literary atmosphere.

Witches Garden, Carmen Bajo 169, T962 3866. Good Novo Andino and international food and desserts, warmly decorated, videos for patrons to choose.

Mundo Hemp, Qanchipata 596, www.mundohemp.com. Foccacia bread, interesting savoury pancakes, quiche and good fresh juices. Nice atmosphere with a beautiful sunny courtyard, but the food's a bit overpriced. Also has a shop with a range of hemp products.

The cheapest food can be found around the Mercado Santa Ana and San Pedro station.

Ama Lur, Plateros 325. Very good menú for US$2, pleasant atmosphere.

Auliya, Garcilaso 265, p 2. Excellent vegetarian food in a renovated colonial house, also stocks dried food for trekking.

Café Cultural Ritual, Choquechaca 140. Good value and tasty vegetarian food, including some good Indian dishes, US$ 2.20.

Chez Maggy, 3 branches: **La Antigua** (the original) at Procuradores 365, **El Corsario** No 344 and **Clave de Do** No 374 (open at 0700 for buffet breakfast).

El Encuentro, Santa Catalina Ancha 384 and Choquechaca 136. One of the best value eateries in Cuzco, 3 courses of good healthy food and a drink for US$1.35, very busy at lunchtime.

Inkafe, Choquechaca 131. Great food and value in a nice setting, English spoken.

Mia Pizza, Procuradores 379. Good range of economical menus, including one with a reasonable curry.

Paccha, Portal de Panes 167. Good for breakfast, bookstore, posters for sale, English and French spoken.

Víctor Victoria, Tigre 130. Israeli and local dishes, first-class breakfasts, good value. Many good, cheap restaurants on Procuradores, Plateros (eg **Los Candiles**, No 323) and Tecseccocha.

Cafés

Amaru, Plateros 325, 2nd floor. Limitless coffee, tea, great bread and juices, even on 'non-buffet' breakfasts (US$1.15 for simple), colonial balcony. Also has bar.

Café Ayllu, Portal de Carnes 208. Classical/folk music, good atmosphere, superb range of milk products, wonderful apple pastries, good selection for breakfast, great juices, quick service.

Café Halliy, Plateros 363. Popular meeting place, especially for breakfast, good for comments on guides, has good snacks and 'copa Halliy' - fruit, muesli, yoghurt, honey and chocolate cake, also good vegetarian menú and set lunch.

Café Manu, Av Pardo 1046. Good coffee and good food too.

Chocolate, Choquechaca 162, T974 9343. Good for coffee and cakes, fresh gourmet chocolates.

Granja Heidi, Cuesta San Blas 525. German owner Carlos serves up delicious yoghurt, granola, ricotta cheese and honey and other great breakfast options, good vegetarian dishes.

Moni, San Agustín 311, T231029. Peruvian/English-owned, good fresh food and breakfast, British music, magazines, bright and comfortable.

The Muse, Tandapata 682, Plazoleta San Blas. Funky little café with fresh local coffee, good food, including vegetarian lasagne and carrot cake, smoothies, often has live music, helpful English owner. Will refill water bottles for a small charge in an attempt to minimise plastic waste.

Planet Cuzco, Carmen Alto 162, T223010. Great buffet breakfast in a stylish atmosphere, plus 10 mins free internet.

Sunset Video Café inside *Hostal Royal Qosqo*, turn left at the top of Procuradores. 3 films a day: 1600, 1900, 2130, good sound, popcorn and other snacks. US$0.70.

Trotamundos, Portal Comercio 177, 2nd floor. Balcony overlooking the plaza, nice atmosphere, especially at night with open fire, good coffees and cakes, safe salads, internet service, open Mon-Sat 0800-2400.

Yaku Mama, Procuradores 397. Good for breakfast, unlimited fruit and coffee.

Panaderías and heladerías

Due Mondi, Santa Catalina Ancha (near *Rosie O'Grady's*). Open 1000-2100. At just US$0.30 per delicious Italian scoop, this is an absolute must for ice cream lovers.

Panadería El Buen Pastor, Cuesta San Blas 579. Very good bread and pastries, proceeds go to a charity for orphans and street children.

❶ Bars and clubs

Cuzco *p1203, maps p1206 and p1212*
Bars
Big Blue Martini, Tecseccocha 148, T248839. Sophisticated, split-level sofa bar with funky lighting, very good cocktails, food and a lively music scene, jazz sessions on Thu, and on Sat a guest DJ.

Cross Keys Pub, Plaza de Armas, Portal Confiturías 233 (upstairs). Open 1100-0130, run by Barry Walker of **Manu Expeditions**, a Mancunian and ornithologist, darts, cable sports, pool, bar meals, plus daily half price specials Sun-Wed, great pisco sours, very popular, great atmosphere.

Km 0 (Arte y Tapas), Tandapata 100, San Blas. Mediterranean themed bar tucked in behind San Blas, good snacks and tapas, with live music every night (around 2200 - lots of acoustic guitar etc).

Los Perros Bar, Tecseccocha 436. Great place to chill out on comfy couches, excellent music, welcoming, good coffee, tasty meals available (including vegetarian), book exchange, English and other magazines, board games, open 1100-0100.

Mandela's Bar, Palacio 121, p 3, T222424. Bar/restaurant with an African theme, good atmosphere and lots of space to relax. Serves breakfast, lunch and drinks in the evening, also Sun barbecues and special events through the year. Great 360° panorama from the rooftop.

Norton Rat's Tavern, Loreto 115, p 2, same entrance as Hostal Loreto, T246204. Also serves meals, cable TV, popular, English spoken, fine

balcony, pool, darts, motorcycle theme with information for motorcyclists from owner, Jeffrey Powers.

Rosie O'Grady's, Santa Catalina Ancha 360, T247935. Good music, tasty food, English and Russian spoken, good value, open 1100 till late (food served till midnight).

Paddy Flaherty's, Triunfo 124 on the corner of the plaza. Irish theme pub, deservedly popular, open 1300-0100, good grub.

Clubs
Corruption, Calle Tecseccocha, just below **Los Perros** on the same side of the street. Wide range of music, very en vogue with Israeli backpackers.

Extreme, Suecia, next to Magtas's. Movies in the late afternoon and early evening, but after midnight this place really gets going with an eclectic range of music, from 60's and 70's rock and pop to techno and trance.

El Garabato Video Music Club, Espaderos 132, p 3. Open daily 1600-0300, dance area, lounge for chilling, bar, live shows 2300-0030 (all sorts of styles) and large screen showing music videos.

Kamikaze, Plaza Regocijo 274, T233865. *Peña* at 2200, good old traditional rock music, candle-lit cavern atmosphere, entry US$2.50.

Magtas Bar, Suecia 302 on the corner of the plaza. With chill-out section and dance floor, lots of salsa and Latin beats, but the odd pop-classic slips in.

Mama, Portal Belén 115, 2nd floor. The mother of all clubs in Cuzco, Mama Africa, has become 2 separate entities: **Mama América** is decorated in a jungle theme, with a dance floor and large video screen, although people dance anywhere they can. The music is middle of the road, from local music through '70s classics to the latest releases. **Mama Africa** now resides in the Portal de Harinas, 2nd floor. Cooler music and more of a serious clubber's spot, it claims.

Siete Angelitos, Siete Angelitos 638. Tiny club, just a couple of rooms, but spectacular cocktails, a friendly owner by the name of Walter and an awesome atmosphere when things get going.

Tangible Myth, San Juan de Dios 260, p 2 (next to Hostal Frankenstein), T260519. Live jazz, sometimes edging into funk and Latin rhythms, Mon-Sat, usually warming up at around 2100. This is a great place to enjoy a relaxed night out.

Ukuku's, Plateros 316. US$1.35 entry, very popular, good atmosphere, good mix of music including live shows nightly.

❷ Entertainment

Cuzco *p1203, maps p1206 and p1212*
Folklore Regular nightly folklore show at **Centro Qosqo de Arte nativo**, Av Sol 604, T227901. Show from 1900 to 2030, entrance on BTG ticket. **Teatro**

Inti Raymi, Saphi 605, nightly at 1845, US$4.50, well worth it. **Teatro Municipal**, C Mesón de la Estrella 149 (T227321 for information 0900- 1300 and 1500-1900). Plays, dancing and shows, mostly Thu-Sun. They also run classes in music and dancing from Jan to Mar which are great value.

⊛ Festivals and events

Cuzco *p1203, maps p1206 and p1212*
Carnival in Cuzco is a messy affair with flour, water, cacti, bad fruit and animal manure being thrown about in the streets (Carnival is lively along the length of the Sacred Valley). **Easter Monday**: procession of **El Señor de los Temblores** (Lord of the Earthquakes), starting at 1600 outside the Cathedral. A large crucifix is paraded through the streets, returning to the Plaza de Armas around 2000 to bless the tens of thousands of people who have assembled there. **2-3 May**: Vigil of the Cross takes place at all mountaintops with crosses on them, a boisterous affair. **Jun**: Q'Olloriti, the Snow Star Festival, is held at a 4,700 m glacier north of Ocongate (Ausangate) 150 km southeast of Cuzco. Several agencies offer tours. (The date is moveable.) On **Corpus Christi** day, the Thu after Trinity Sunday, all the statues of the Virgin and of saints from Cuzco's churches are paraded through the streets to the Cathedral. The Plaza de Armas is surrounded by tables with women selling *cuy* (guinea pig) and a mixed grill called *chiriuchu* (*cuy*, chicken, *tortillas*, fish eggs, water-weeds, maize, cheese and sausage) and lots of Cusqueña beer. **24 Jun**: the pageant of **Inti Raymi**, the Inca festival of the winter solstice, is enacted in Quechua at 1000 at the Qoricancha, moving on to Sacsayhuaman at 1300. Tickets for the stands can be bought a week in advance from the Emufec office, Santa Catalina Ancha 325, US$35. Standing places on the ruins are free but get there at about 1030 to defend your space. Travel agents can arrange the whole day for you, with meeting points, transport, reserved seats and packed lunch. Those who try to persuade you to buy a ticket for the right to film or take photos are being dishonest. On the night before Inti Raymi, the Plaza de Armas is crowded with processions and food stalls. Try to arrive in Cuzco 15 days before Inti Raymi for the Cusqueña beer festival (US$6 entry) and other festivals, parades etc. **28 Jul**: Peruvian Independence Day. Prices shoot up during these celebrations. **Aug**: on the last Sun is the **Huarachicoy** festival at Sacsayhuaman, a spectacular re-enactment of the Inca manhood rite, performed in dazzling costumes by boys of a local school. **8 Sep**: Day of the Virgin is a colourful procession of masked dancers from the church of Almudena, at the southwest edge of Cuzco, near Belén, to the Plaza de San Francisco. There is also a splendid fair at Almudena, and a free bull fight on the following day. **1 Nov**: All Saints Day, celebrated everywhere with bread dolls and traditional cooking. **8 Dec**: Cuzco day, when churches and museums close at 1200. **24 Dec**: Santuranticuy, 'the buying of saints', with a big crafts market in the plaza, very noisy until early hours of the 25th.

○ Shopping

Cuzco *p1203, maps p1206 and p1212*
Arts and crafts
In the Plaza San Blas and the surrounding area, authentic Cuzco crafts still survive. A market is held on Sat. Many leading artisans welcome visitors. Among fine objects made are Biblical figures from plaster, wheatflour and potatoes, reproductions of pre- Columbian ceramics and colonial sculptures, pious paintings, earthenware figurines, festive dolls and wood carvings.
 Cuzco is the weaving centre of Peru and excellent textiles can be found at good value. Be very careful of buying gold and silver objects and jewellery in and around Cuzco.
Agua y Tierra, Plazoleta Nazarenas 167, and also at Cuesta San Blas 595, T084-226951. Excellent quality crafts from lowland rainforest communities.
Coordinadora Sur Andina de Artesanía, C del Medio 130, off Plaza de Armas, has a good assortment of crafts and is a non-profit making organization.
La Mamita, Portal de Carnes 244, Plaza de Armas, sells the ceramics of Pablo Seminario (see under Urubamba, page 1230), plus cotton, basketry, jewellery, etc.
Mercado Artesanal, Av Sol, block 4, is good for cheap crafts.
Pedazo de Arte, Plateros 334B. A tasteful collection of Andean handicrafts, many designed by Japanese owner Miki Suzuki.
La Pérez, Urb Mateo Pumacahua 598, Huanchac, T232186. A big co-operative with a good selection; they will arrange a free pick-up from your hotel.

Bookshops
Centro de Estudios Regionales Andinos Bartolomé de las Casas, Limacpampa Grande 565, T234073, www.cbc.org.pe. Good books on Peruvian history, archaeology, etc, Mon-Sat 1100-1400, 1600-1900.
Jerusalem, Heladeros 143, T235408. English books, guidebooks, music, postcards, book exchange (3 for 1).
Book exchange, 1 for 1, at **The Sun**, Plazoleta Limacpampa Chico 471, a café/restaurant, maintained by an Australian.

Camping equipment

For renting equipment, there are several places around the Plaza area. Check the equipment carefully as it is common for parts to be missing. An example of prices per day: tent US$3-5, sleeping bag US$2 (down), US$1.50 (synthetic), stove US$1. A deposit of US$100 is asked, plus credit card, passport or plane ticket. White gas (*bencina*), US$1.50 per litre, can be bought at hardware stores, but check the purity. Stove spirit (*alcoól para quemar*) is available at pharmacies; blue gas canisters, costing US$5, can be found at hardware stores and camping shops. You can also rent equipment through travel agencies.
Soqllaq'asa Camping Service, owned by English-speaking Sra Luzmila Bellota Miranda, at Plateros 365 No 2F, T252560, is recommended for equipment hire, also buy and sell camping gear and make alpaca jackets, open Mon-Sat 0900-1300, 1600- 2030, Sun 1800-2030.

Fabrics and alpaca clothing

Alpaca 3, Ruinas 472 (English spoken). For quality items.
Alpaca 111, Plaza Regocijo 202, T243233. High quality alpaca clothing with outlets also in hotels *El Monasterio, Libertador* and *Machu Picchu Sanctuary Lodge*.
The Center for Traditional Textiles of Cuzco, Av Sol 603-A, T228117, www.incas.org. A non-profit organization that seeks to promote, refine and rediscover the weaving traditions of the Cuzco area. Tours of workshops, weaving classes, you can watch weavers at work. Over 50% of the price goes direct to the weaver. Recommended.
Josefina Olivera, Portal Comercio 173, Plaza de Armas. Sells old textiles and weavings, expensive but worth it to save pieces being cut up to make other items, open daily 1100-2100. Store of Weavers (Asociación Central de Artesanos y Artesanas del Sur Andino Inkakunaq Ruwaynin), Av Tullumayo 274, T233466, www.cbc.org.pe/tejidosandinos. A store administered by 6 local weaving communities, some of whose residents you can see working on site. All profits go to the weavers themselves.

Food

Casa Ecológica Cusco, Triunfo 393, www.casaecologicacusco.com. Organic foods, wild honey, coffee, granola. Casa Ecológica also offers natural medicines, indigenous art and weavings.
La Cholita, Portal Espinar 142-B and at airport. Extra-special chocolates made with local ingredients.

Jewellery

Carlos Chaquiras, Triunfo 375 y Portal Comercio, T227470, www.carlos chaquiras.com. Very upmarket, with lots of Inca figures, among other designs.
Ilaria, Portal Carrizos 258, T246253. Branches in hotels *Monasterio, Libertador* and at the airport. For recommended jewellery and silver.
H Ormachea, Plateros 372, T237061. Handmade gold and silver.
Spondylus, Cuesta San Blas 505 and Plazoleta San Blas 617, T226929. A good selection of interesting gold and silver jewellery and fashion tops with Inca and pre-Inca designs.

Music

Taki Museo de Música de los Andes, Hatunrumiyoq 487-5. Shop and workshop selling and displaying musical instruments, knowledgeable owner, who is an ethnomusicologist. Recommended for anyone interested in Andean music.

Markets

Wanchac, Av Garcilaso (southeast of centre) and **Santa Ana Market**, opposite Estación San Pedro, sell a variety of goods.

Supermarkets

La Canasta, Av La Cultura 2000 block. Very well-stocked, takes credit cards, ATM outside.
D'Dinos Market, Av La Cultura 2003, T252656 for home delivery. Open 24-hrs, well-supplied, takes credit cards.
Dimart, Matará 271, also at Av La Cultura 742. Open daily 0700-2200, credit cards accepted.
Gato's Market, Portal Belén 115.

▲ Activities and tours

Cuzco *p1203, maps p1206 and p1212*
For a list of recommended Tour operators for Manu, see page 1280.

There are many travel agencies in Cuzco. The sheer number and variety of tours on offer is bewildering and prices for the same tour can vary dramatically. Always remember that you get what you pay for and that, in a crowded market, organization can sometimes be a weak point. In general you should only deal directly with the agencies themselves. You can do this when in town, or you can raise whatever questions you may have in advance (or even in Cuzco), and get replies in writing, by email. Other sources of advice are visitors returning from trips, who can give the latest information, and the trip reports for members of the South America Explorers. Students will normally receive a discount on production of an ISIC card. Do not deal with guides who claim to be employed by agencies listed below without verifying their credentials. City tours cost about US$6 for 4 hrs; check what sites are included and that the guide is experienced.

Only a restricted number of agencies are licensed to operate **Inca Trail** trips. INRENA, Av José Gabriel Cosio 308, Urb Magisterial, 1 etapa, T229297, will verify operating permits, and all relevant information (agencies and guides with permits, regulations, reservations, etc) can be found on the INC website, www.inc-cusco.gob.pe: go to "Sistema de Reservas RCI" (see Visitors' tickets, above, for INC office). Unlicensed agencies will sell Inca Trail trips, but pass clients on to the operating agency. This can cause confusion and booking problems at busy times. There is a quota for agencies and groups to use the Trail, but modifications to the procedures encouraged some agencies to make block bookings way in advance of departure dates. This made it much harder for agencies to guarantee their clients places on the Trail. Current advice is to book your preferred dates as early as possible, between 2 months and a year in advance, depending on the season when you want to go, then confirm nearer the time. There have been many instances of disappointed trekkers whose bookings did not materialise. Don't wait to the last minute and check your operator's cancellation fees. **Note**: See page 1239, under The Inca Trail, for regulations governing the Trail.

Inca Trail and general tours
Amazing Peru, Av Tullumayo 213, T262720 (9 Alma Road, Manchester M19 2FG, T0808 2346805), www.amazingperu.com. Highly recommended, professional and well-organized, "perfect tour", knowledgeable guides.
Andina Travel, Plazoleta Santa Catalina 219, T251892, www.andinatravel.com. Specializes in trekking and biking, notably the Lares Valley, working with traditional weaving communities. Recommended.
Big Foot, Triunfo 392 (oficina 213), T238568, www.bigfootcusco.com. Tailor-made hiking trips, especially in the remote corners of the Vilcabamba and Vilcanota mountains; also the Inca Trail.
Ch'aska, Plateros 325, 2nd floor, T240424, www.chaskatours.com. Dutch-Peruvian company offering cultural, adventure, nature and esoteric tours. They specialize in the Inca Trail, but also llama treks to Lares, treks to Choquequirao.

Peru Cuzco Listings

Cóndor Travel, C Saphi 848-A, T225961, www.condortravel.com.pe (for flights diviajes@condortravel.com.pe). A high- quality, exclusive agency that will organize trips throughout Peru and the rest of the world. Also adventure travel and international flight tickets.

Destinos Turísticos, Portal de Panes 123, oficina 101-102, Plaza de Armas, T228168, www.destinosturisticosperu.com. The owner speaks Spanish, English, Dutch and Portuguese and specializes in package tours from economic to 5-star budgets. Advice on booking jungle trips and renting mountain bikes. Very helpful.

Ecotrek Peru, Totorapaccha 769, T247286, T972 7237 (mob), www.ecotrekperu.com. Run by Scot and long-term Cuzco resident Fiona Cameron, environmentally friendly, wide range of adventures bookable through website, specializing in little visited areas such as the Pongo de Mainique and Espíritu Pampa/Vilcabamba Vieja. Fiona's partner, David Ugarte, is a mountain biking specialist, and will tailor two-wheeled adventures, speaks English, T084-974 4810 (mob).

Enigma Adventure, Jirón Clorinda Matto de Turner 100, Magisterio 1a Etapa, Cuzco, T222155, www.enigmaperu.com. Run by Spaniard Silvia Rico Coll. Well-organized, innovative trekking expeditions, Inca Trail and a variety of challenging alternatives. Also cultural tours to weaving communities, Ayahuasca Therapy, climbing and biking itineraries on demand.

Explorandes, Av Garcilaso 316-A (not to be confused with C Garcilaso in the centre), T238380, www.explorandes.com. Experienced high-end adventure company. Arrange a wide variety of mountain treks; trips available in Peru and Ecuador, book through website. Also arranges tours across Peru for lovers of orchids, ceramics or textiles. Award-winning environmental practices.

Flamenco Travels, Portal de Confiturias 265, oficina 3, info@ponyexpeditions.com. Associated with **Pony 's Expeditions** of Caraz, Classic Inka Trail pooled trek with daily departures (average of 8-10 people). Also the 5-day Salkantay trek.

Gatur Cusco, Puluchapata 140 (a small street off Av Sol 3rd block), T223496, www.gaturcusco.com. Esoteric, ecotourism, and general tours. Owner Dr José (Pepe) Altamirano is knowledgeable in Andean folk traditions. Excellent conventional tours, bilingual guides and transportation. Guides speak English, French, Spanish and German. They can also book internal flights.

Hiking Peru, Portal de Panes 109, office 6, T247942/965 1414 (mob), www.hikingperu.com. 8-day treks to Espíritu Pampa; 7 days/6 nights around Ausangate; 4-day/3-night Lares Valley Trek.

Inca Explorers, Ruinas 427, T241070, www.inca explorers.com. Specialist trekking agency for small

group expeditions in socially and environmentally responsible manner. Also 2-week hike in the Cordillera Vilcanota (passing Nevado Ausangate), and Choquequirao to Espíritu Pampa.

Liz's Explorer, Medio 114B, T246619, www.lizexplorer.com. 4-day/ 3-night Inca Trail trek (minimum group size 10, maximum 16), other lengths of trips available. Liz gives a clearly laid out list of what is and what is not included. If you need a guide who speaks a language other than English let her know in advance. Reports of good trips but haphazard organization.

Machete Tours, Tecseccocha 161, T224829, T963 1662 (mob), info@machetetours.com. Many innovative trekking trips: eg 9-day traverse of the Cordillera Vilcabamba, expeditions to Espíritu Pampa, Ausangate and the Inca Trail. They have recently opened a rainforest lodge on the remote Río Blanco, south of the Manu Biosphere Reserve. Not all guides speak English so check this before trip details are confirmed.

Peruvian Andean Treks, Av Pardo 705, T225701, www.andeantreks.com. Manager Tom Hendrickson has 5-day/4-night Inca Trail for US$500 using high-quality equipment and satellite phones. His 7-day/6-night Vilcanota Llama Trek to Ausangate includes a collapsible pressure chamber for altitude sickness. Also organizes interesting extended trekking itineraries.

Peru Treks and Adventure, C Garcilaso 265, Office 11, 2 blocks from main square, T505863, www.perutreks.com. Trekking agency set up by Englishman Mike Weston and his wife Koqui González. They pride themselves on good treatment of porters and support staff and have been consistently recommended for professionalism and customer care, a portion of profits go to community projects. Treks offered include Salkantay, the Lares Valley and Vilcabamba Vieja. Mike also runs the **Andean Travel Web**, www.andeantravelweb.com.

Q'ente, Garcilaso 210, int 210b, T222535, www.qente.com. Their Inca Trail service is recommended. Also private treks to Salkantay, Ausangate, Choquequirao, Vilcabamba and Q'eros. Horse riding to local ruins costs US$35 for 4-5 hrs. Very good, especially with children.

Sky Travel, Santa Catalina Ancha 366, interior 3-C (down alleyway next to Rosie O'Grady's pub), T261818, www.skyperu.com. English spoken. General tours around city and Sacred Valley. Inca Trail with good-sized double tents and a dinner tent (the group is asked what it would like on the menu 2 days before departure). Other trips include Vilcabamba and Ausangate (trekking).

SAS Travel, Portal de Panes 143, T237292 (staff in a 2nd office at Medio 137, mainly deal with jungle information and only speak Spanish), www.sas travel.com. Discount for SAE members and students. Inca Trail includes the bus down from Machu Picchu to Aguas Calientes and lunch on the last day. SAS have their own hostel in Aguas Calientes. Offer alternatives to the classic Inca Trail, including Salkantay and Santa Teresa. Also mountain bike, horse riding and jungle tours. All guides speak English to some degree. They can book internal flights at cheaper rates than from overseas. SAS has had a solid reputation for good equipment and food on the trail, but reports increasingly mixed for office organization.

Tambo Tours, 20919 Coral Bridge Lane, Suite 225-A, Spring, TX 77388, USA, T1-888-2-GO-PERU (246-7378), www.2goperu.com. Long established adventure and tour specialist with offices in Peru and the US. Customized trips to the Amazon and archaelogical sites of Peru and Ecuador.

Trekperu, Ricaldo Palma N-9, Santa Mónica, T252899, www.trekperu.com. Experienced trek operator as well as other adventure sports and mountain biking. Offers 'culturally sensitive' tours.

Cusco Biking Adventure includes support vehicle and good camping gear (but providing your own sleeping bag).

Tucan Travel, T241123, cuzco@tucantravel.com. Offer adventure tours and overland expeditions.

United Mice, Plateros 351y Triunfo 392, T221139, www.unitedmice.com. Inca Trail and alternative trail via Salkantay and Santa Teresa, including entrance to Machu Picchu. Good English-speaking guides; Salustio speaks Italian and Portuguese. Discount with student card, good food and equipment. City and Sacred Valley tours and treks to Choquequirao. Cheaper than most.

Wayki Trek, Procuradores 3512nd floor, T224092, www.waykitrek.net. Budget travel agency, recommended for their Inca Trail service. Owner Leo grew up in the countryside near Ollantaytambo and knows the area very well. Treks to several almost unknown Inca sites and interesting variations on the 'classic' Inca Trail with visits to porters' communities. Also treks to Ausangate, Salkantay and Choquequirao.

Rafting, mountain biking and trekking

When looking for an operator please consider more than just the price of your tour. Competition between companies in Cuzco is intense and price wars can lead to compromises in safety as corners are cut or less experienced (and therefore cheaper) guides are hired. Consider the quality of safety equipment (lifejackets, etc) and the number and experience of rescue kayakers and support staff. On a large and potentially dangerous river like the Apurímac (where fatalities have occurred - the latest in 2006), this can make all the difference.

Amazonas Explorers, Av Collasuyo 910, Miravalle, PO Box 722, Cuzco, T252846 or 976 5448 (mob), www.amazonas-explorer.com. Experts in rafting, hiking and biking; used by BBC. English owner Paul Cripps has great experience, but takes most bookings from overseas (in England, T01437-891743). However, he may be able to arrange a trip for travellers in Cuzco. Rafting includes Río Apurímac and Río Tambopata including Lake Titicaca and Cuzco, with all transfers from Lima. Also 5-day/4-night Inca Trail, 14-day expedition to the Río Tuichi in Bolivia, and an excellent variation of the Ausangate Circuit. All options are at the higher end of the market and are highly recommended.

Apumayo, Av Garcilaso 316, Wanchaq, T084-246018, www.apumayo.com. Mon-Sat 0900-1300, 1600-2000. Urubamba rafting (from 0800-1530 every day); 3- to 4-day Apurímac trips. Also mountain biking to Maras and Moray in Sacred Valley, or from Cuzco to the jungle town of Quillabamba. This company also offers tours for disabled people, including rafting.

Atoq, C Saphi 704, T084-253902, www.atoq offroad.com. Specialists in innovative biking trips, from novice level to hardcore suicidal! Road and single-track tours range from day-trips to multi-week expeditions; prices depend on number of clients and the level of service/support required. Professional guides and excellent equipment.

Eric Adventures, Plateros 324, T234764, www.ericadventures.com. Specialize in adventure activities. They clearly explain what equipment is included in their prices and what you will need to bring. Rafting; mountain biking to Maras and Moray; Inca Trail to Machu Picchu, rent motorcross bikes for US$45 (guide is extra). Prices are more expensive if you book by email. A popular company.

Enigma Adventure, Jiron Clorinda Matto de Turner 100, Urb Magisterial 1a etapa, T222155, www.engmaperu.com. Specializes in small group treks and customer itineraries.

Instinct/Land of the Inkas, www.instinct-travel.com or www.landoftheinkas.com. Run by the very experienced Juan and Benjamín Muñiz,

this company now largely operates through web-based bookings, arranging multi-week expeditions and shorter adventures for those already in the Cuzco area. For many years a rafting specialist, **Instinct** now offers activities as diverse as surf safaris on Peru's north coast to multi-day horse riding tours in the Sacred Valley.

MAYUC Ecological Tourism Adventure Travel, Portal Confiturías 211, Plaza de Armas, T232666, www.mayuc.com. One of the longest-running river rafting companies. Departures are on the 1st and 3rd Sun of every month May-Nov. **Mayuc** now have a permanent lodge, **Casa Cusi**, on the upper Urubamba, which forms the basis of 2-day, Class III-IV trips in the area. Other tours include Inca Trail and alternative routes into Machu Picchu.

Medina Brothers, contact Christian or Alain Medina on T225163 or 965 3485/969 1670(mob). Family-run rafting company with good equipment and plenty of experience. They usually focus on day rafting trips in the Sacred Valley, but services are tailored to the needs of the client.

Swissraft-Peru, Plateros 369, T264124, www.swissraft-peru.com. This company has professionally-run tours on the Apurímac and Urubamba rivers, with the focus above all on safety. Equipment is new and of good quality.

Cultural tours

Milla Tourism, Av Pardo 689 and Portal Comercio 195 on the plaza, T234181/231710, www.millaturismo.com. Mon-Fri 0800-1300, 1500-1900, Sat 0800-1300. Mystical tours to Cuzco's Inca ceremonial sites such as Pumamarca and The Temple of the Moon. Guide speaks only basic English. They also arrange cultural and environmental lectures and courses.

Mystic Inca Trail, Unidad Vecinal de Santiago, bloque 9, dpto 301, T221358, ivanndp@ terra.com.pe. Specialize in tours of sacred Inca sites and study of Andean spirituality. This takes 10 days but it is possible to have shorter 'experiences'.

Spiritually Peru, based at Perezosos Restaurant/ Bed and Breakfast, Nueva Alta 424, T255341, www.spiritually-peru.com. Owner Jane Evans is highly qualified in Reiki, Karuna and Hypnotherapy. She combines these skills with journeys tailored to clients' needs, including hikes to Choquequirao and Vilcabamba, river journeys to the Pongo de Mainique and rafting on the Tambopata.

Shamans and drug experiences

San Pedro and Ayahuasca have been used since before Inca times, mostly as a sacred healing experience. If you choose to experience these incredible healing/teaching plants, only do so under the guidance of a reputable agency or shaman and always have a friend with you who is not partaking. If the medicine is not prepared

correctly, it can be highly toxic and, in rare cases, severely dangerous. Never buy from someone who is not recommended, never buy off the streets and never try to prepare the plants yourself. **Another Planet**, Triunfo 120, T084-229379, www.anotherplanetperu.net. Run by Lesley Myburgh (who also runs **Casa de La Gringa**, C Pensamiento E-3, Urb Miravalle, 5 mins by taxi from plaza, sleeping in D range), who operates all kinds of adventure tours and conventional tours in and around Cuzco, but specializes in jungle trips anywhere in Peru. Lesley is an expert in San Pedro cactus preparation and she arranges San Pedro journeys for healing at physical, emotional and spiritual levels in beautiful remote areas. The journeys are thoroughly organized and a safe, beautiful, unforgettable experience.
Eleana Molina, T975 1791 (mob), misticanativa@ yahoo.com. For Ayahuasca ceremonies.

Paragliding and ballooning
Richard Pethigal, T993 7333 (mob), www.cloudwalkerparagliding.com. For a condor's-eye view of the Sacred Valley, from May-Sep Richard runs half-day tandem paraglider flights, very experienced, high-quality equipment. Magnificent scenery, soaring close to snowcapped mountains makes this an awesome experience. He is licensed and charges US$70, but if weather conditions are good, for US$120 he can fly you all the way back to Cuzco, touching down in the ruins of Sacsayhuaman above the city.
Globos de los Andes, Av de la Cultura 220, suite 36, T232352, www.globosperu.com. Hot-air ballooning in the Sacred Valley and expeditions with balloons and 4WD lasting several days.

Private guides
As most of the sights do not have any information or signs in English, a good guide can really improve your visit. Either arrange this before you set out or contract one at the sight you are visiting. A tip is expected at the end of the tour. Set prices: City tour US$15-20 per day; Urubamba/Sacred Valley US$25-30, Machu Picchu and other ruins US$40-50 per day.

⊙ Transport

Cuzco *p1203, maps p1206 and p1212*
Air
The airport is at Quispiquilla, near the bus terminal, 1.6 km from centre, airport information T222611/601. **Note**: Sit on right side of the aircraft for the best view of the mountains when flying Cuzco-Lima; check in 2 hrs before flight. Reconfirm 48 hrs before your flight. Cuzco-Lima, flights may be delayed or cancelled during the wet season. Planes may leave early if the weather is bad. To **Lima**, 55 mins, daily flights with **Taca**, **Star Perú** and **Lan**. Flights are heavily booked in school holidays (May, Jul, Oct and Dec-Mar) and national holidays. To **Arequipa**, 30 mins daily with **Lan**. To **Puerto Maldonado**, 30 mins, with **Lan**. To/from **La Paz**, LAB but not daily. Taxi to and from the airport costs US$2 (US$3.50 by radio taxi). Colectivos cost US$0.20 from Plaza San Francisco or outside the airport car park. Many representatives of hotels and travel agencies operate at the airport, with transport to the hotel with which they are associated. Take your time to choose your hotel, at the price you can afford.

Bus
Long distance Terminal on Av Vallejo Santoni, block 2 (Prolongación Pachacútec), colectivo from centre US$0.20, taxi US$0.60. Platform tax US$0.30. All direct buses to **Lima** (20-24 hrs) go via **Abancay**, 195 km, 5 hrs (longer in the rainy season), and **Nazca**, on the Panamerican Highway. This route is paved but floods in the wet season often damage large sections of the highway. If prone to travel sickness, be prepared on the road to Abancay, there are many, many curves, but the scenery is magnificent. At Abancay, the road forks, the other branch going to **Andahuaylas**, a further 138 km, 10-11 hrs from Cuzco, and **Ayacucho**, another 261 km, 20 hrs from Cuzco. On both routes at night, take a blanket or sleeping bag to ward off the cold. All buses leave daily from the Terminal Terrestre. **Molina**, who also have an office on Av Pachacútec, just past the railway station, have buses on both routes. They run 3 services a day to Lima via Abancay and Nazca, and one, at 1900, to Abancay and Andahuaylas; **Expreso Wari** has 4 buses a day to Abancay, Nazca and Lima. **Cruz del Sur**'s *Ideal* service to Lima via Abancay leaves at 0730 and 1400, while their more comfortable *Imperial* service departs at 1500 and 1600. **San Jerónimo** and **Los Chankas** have buses to Abancay, Andahuaylas and Ayacucho at 1830. **Turismo Ampay** and **Turismo Abancay** go 3 times a day to Abancay, and **Expreso Huamanga** once. **Bredde** has 5 buses a day to Abancay. Fares: Abancay US$3.40, Andahuaylas US$6, Ayacucho US$12, Nazca US$17-20, Lima US$20 (*Cruz del Sur,*

Ideal Class) to US$32 (*Cruz del Sur, Imperial* Class). In Cuzco you may be told that there are no buses in the day from Abancay to Andahuaylas; this is not so as **Señor de Huanca** does so. If you leave Cuzco before 0800, with luck you'll make the connection at 1300 – worth it for the scenery.

To Lake Titicaca and Bolivia: To **Juliaca**, 344 km, 5-6 hrs, US$3-4. The road is fully paved, but after heavy rain buses may not run. To **Puno**, 44 km from Juliaca, US$4.50-6; there is a good service with **Ormeño** at 0900, US$10, 6 hrs. **First Class**, Av Sol 930, have a bus at 0800, calling at Andahuayllillas church, Raqchi and Pucará, US$20, lunch but not entrance tickets included. Other services are run by **Tour Perú** and **Libertad** (both at night), 6½-8 hrs. **Note**: We have received many reports of robbery on night buses on the Juliaca-Puno-Cuzco route; travel by day, or by train.

To **Arequipa**, 521 km, **Cruz del Sur** use the direct paved route via Juliaca and have 3 *Ideal* services leaving daily, 10½ hrs, US$7, and 1 *Imperial* service at 2000, 10 hrs, US$15. **Ormeño**'s fare is US$18. Other buses join the new Juliaca-Arequipa road at Imata, 10-12 hrs, US$7.75 (eg **Carhuamayo**, 3 a day).

To the **Sacred Valley**: To **Pisac**, 32 km, 1 hr, US$0.85, from Calle Puputi on the outskirts of the city, near the Clorindo Matto de Turner school and Av de la Cultura. Colectivos, minibuses and buses leave whenever they are full, between 0600 and 1600. Buses returning from Pisac are often full. The last one back leaves around 2000. An organized tour can be fixed up with a travel agent for US$5 pp. Taxis charge about US$20 for the round trip. To Pisac, **Calca** (18 km beyond Pisac) and **Urubamba** a further 22 km, buses leave from Av Tullumayo 800 block, Wanchac, US$1. Combis and colectivos leave from 300 block of Av Grau, 1 block before crossing the bridge, for **Chinchero**, 23 km, 45 mins, US$0.45; and for **Urubamba** a further 25 km, 45 mins, US$0.45 (or US$1 Cuzco- Urubamba direct, US$1.15 for a seat in a colectivo taxi). To **Ollantaytambo** from Av Grau, 0745, 1945, US$2.85, or catch a bus to Urubamba. Tours can be arranged to Chinchero, Urubamba and Ollantaytambo with a Cuzco travel agency. To Chinchero, US$6 pp; a taxi costs US$25 round-trip. Usually only day tours are organized for visits to the valley, US$20-25. Using public transport and staying overnight in Urubamba, Ollantaytambo or Pisac allows more time to see the ruins and markets.

Taxi
In Cuzco they are cheap and recommended when arriving by air, train or bus. They have fixed prices: in the centre US$0.60 (after 2200 US$0.90); to the suburbs US$0.85-1.55. In town it is safest to take taxis which are registered; these have a sign with the company's name on the roof, not just a sticker

in the window. Taxis on call are reliable but more expensive, in the centre US$1.25: **Ocarina** T247080, **Aló Cuzco** T222222. Trips to **Sacsayhuaman** US$10; ruins of **Tambo Machay** US$15-20 (3-4 people); day trip US$40-70.

Recommended taxi drivers: **Manuel Calanche**, T227368, T969 5402 (mob), enthusiastic, attentive (Spanish only). **Carlos Hinojosa**, T251160. **Angel Marcavillaca Palomino**, Av Regional 877, T251822, amarcavillaca@yahoo.com. Helpful, patient, reasonable prices. **Movilidad Inmediata**, Juan Carlos Herrera Johnson, T962 3821 (mob), local tours with English-speaking guide. **Ferdinand Pinares Cuadros**, Yuracpunco 155, **Tahuantinsuyo**, T225914, T968 1519 (mob), English and French spoken, reasonable prices. **Angel Salazar**, Marcavalle 1-4 Huanchac, T224679, English speaking, helpful, arranges good tours. **Milton Velásquez**, T222638, T968 0730 (mob), an anthropologist and tour guide who speaks English.

Train

There are 2 stations in Cuzco. To Juliaca and Puno, **Perú Rail** trains leave from the Av Sol station, Estación Wanchac, T238722. When arriving in Cuzco, a tourist bus meets the train to take visitors to hotels whose touts offer rooms. Machu Picchu trains leave from Estación San Pedro, opposite the Santa Ana market.

The train to **Juliaca/Puno** leaves at 0800, Mon, Wed and Sat, arriving at Puno at 1800, sit on the left for views. The train makes a stop to view the scenery at La Raya. Always check whether the train is running, especially in the rainy season, when services may be cancelled. Fares are given under Puno, Transport. Ticket office is open Mon-Fri 0800-1700, Sat 0900-1200. You can buy tickets on www.perurail.com, or through a travel agent. Meals are served on the train. To **Ollantaytambo** and **Machu Picchu**, see page 1237.

☉ Directory

Cuzco *p1203, maps p1206 and p1212*
Airline offices Aerocóndor, at airport, T252774. LAB, Santa Catalina Angosta 160, T222990, airport 229220. Lan, Av Sol 627-B, T225552. Star Perú, Av Sol 679, of 1, T234060. Taca, Av Sol 602, T249921. **Banks** Most of the banks are on Av Sol, and all have ATMs from which you can withdraw dollars or soles. BCP, Av Sol 189, cash advances on Visa, changes TCs to soles with commission, 3% to dollars; Visa ATM. Interbank, Av Sol y Puluchapata, no commission on TCs, Mastercard and Visa ATM. Next door Banco Continental, Visa ATM, US$4 commission on TCs. BSCH, Av Sol 459, Amex TCs, reasonable rates, ATM for Visa and MasterCard. Banco Wiese, Maruri entre Pampa del Castillo y Pomeritos, gives cash advances on Mastercard and Visa in dollars. There are ATMs around the Plaza de Armas and on Av La Cultura. Many travel agencies and *casas de cambio* (eg on Portal de Comercio, Plaza de Armas, and Av Sol) change dollars; some of them change TCs as well, but charge 4-5% commission. LAC Dollar, Av Sol 150, T257969, Mon-Sat 0900-2000, with delivery service to central hotels, cash and TCs. The street changers hang around Av Sol, blocks 2-3, every day; they will also change TCs. In banks and on the street check the notes. Dollars are accepted at many restaurants and at the airport. Western Union, Santa Catalina Ancha 165, T233727, money transfers in 10 mins; also at DHL, see below.
Consulates Belgium, Av Sol 954, T221098, F221100. France, Jorge Escobar, C Michaela Bastidas 101, p4, T233610. Germany, Sra Maria-Sophia Júrgens de Hermoza, San Agustín 307, T235459, Casilla Postal 1128, Correo Central, open Mon-Fri, 1000-1200, appointments may be made by phone, also book exchange. Ireland, Charlie Donovan, Santa Catalina Ancha 360 (Rosie

Peru Cuzco Listings

O'Grady's), T243514. **Italy**, Sr Fedos Rubatto, Av Garcilaso 700, T224398. Mon-Fri 0900-1200, 1500-1700. **Netherlands**, Sra Marcela Alarco Zegarra, Av Pardo 854, T264103, 965 0204 (mob). **Spain**, Sra Juana María Lambarri, T965 0106 (mob). **UK**, Barry Walker, Av Pardo 895, T239974, bwalker@amauta.rcp.net.pe. **US Agent**, Dra Olga Villagarcía, Apdo 949, Cuzco, T222183, F233541 or at the Binational Center (ICPNA), Av Tullumayo 125, Wanchac. **Internet** You can't walk for 5 mins in Cuzco without running into an internet café, and new places are opening all the time. Most have similar rates, around US$0.60 per hr, although if you look hard enough you can find cheaper places. The main difference between cafés is the speed of internet connection and the facilities on offer. The better places have scanners, webcams and CD burners, among other gadgets, and staff in these establishments can be very knowledgeable. **Language schools** Academia Latinoamericana de Español, Av Sol 580, T243364, www.latino schools.com. The same company also has schools in Ecuador (Quito) and in Bolivia (Sucre). They can arrange courses that include any combination of these locations using identical teaching methods

and materials. Professionally run with experienced staff. Many activities per week, including dance lessons and excursions to sites of historical and cultural interest. Good homestays. Private classes US$170 for 20 hrs, groups, with a maximum of 4 students US$125, again for 20 hrs. **Acupari**, the German-Peruvian Cultural Association, San Agustín 307, T242970, www.acupari.com. Spanish classes are run here. **Amauta Spanish School**, Suecia 480, T262345, PO Box 1164, www.amautaspanishschool.org. Spanish classes, one-to-one or in small groups, also Quechua classes and workshops in Peruvian cuisine, dance and music, US$10.50 per hr one-to- one, but cheaper and possibly better value for group tuition (2-6 people), US$98 for 20 hrs. They have pleasant accommodation on site, as well as a free internet café for students, and can arrange excursions and can help find voluntary work. They also have a school in Urubamba and can arrange courses in the Manu rainforest, in conjunction with Pantiacolla Tours SRL. **Amigos Spanish School**, Zaguán del Cielo B-23, T/F242292/225053, www.spanish cusco.com. Certified, experienced teachers, friendly atmosphere. All profits support a

foundation for disadvantaged children. Private lessons for US$8 per hr, US$108 for 20 hrs of classes in a small group. Comfortable homestays and free activities available, including a 'real city tour' through Cuzco's poor areas. **Cusco Spanish School**, Garcilaso 265, of 6 , p 2, T226928, www.cuscos panishschool.com. US$175 for 20 hrs private classes, cheaper in groups. School offers homestays, optional activities including dance and music classes, cookery courses, ceramics, Quechua, hiking and volunteer programmes. They also offer courses on an *hacienda* at Cusipata in the Vilcanota valley, east of Cuzco. **Excel Language Center**, Cruz Verde 336, T235298 , www.excel-spanishlanguage programs-peru.org. Very professional, US$7 per hr for private one-to-one lessons. US$229 for 20 hrs with 2 people, or US$277 with homestay, one-on-one for 20 hrs. **La Casona de la Esquina**, Purgatorio 395, corner with Huaynapata, T235830, www.spanish lessons.com.pe. US$5 per hr for one-to-one classes. **Mundo Verde Spanish School**, C Nueva Alta 432-A, T221287, www.mundoverdespanish.com. Spanish lessons with the option to study in the rainforest and the possibility of working on environmental and social projects while studying. Some of your money goes towards developing sustainable farming practices in the area. US$250 for 20 hours tuition with homestay. **San Blas**

Spanish School, Tandapata 688, T247898, www.spanish schoolperu.com. Private classes US$7 per hr, groups, with 4 clients maximum, US$80 for 20 hrs tuition. **Medical services** Clinics: **Hospital Regional**, Av de la Cultura, T227661, emergencies 223691. **Clínica Pardo**, Av de la Cultura 710, T240387, T993 0063 (mob). 24 hrs daily, trained bilingual personnel, complete medical assistance coverage with international insurance companies, highly regarded. **Clínica Paredes**, Lechugal 405, T225265. Director: Dr Milagros Paredes, whose speciality is gynaecology. **Motorcycle hire** Perú Mototours, Saphi 578, alc@ perumototours.com. Helpful, good prices and machines. **Post offices** Av Sol, block 5, Mon-Sat 0730-2000; Sun and holidays 0800-1400. Stamps and postcards available. *Poste restante* is free and helpful. DHL, Av Sol 627, T244167. **Telephones** Phone offices around town. Telefónica, Av Sol 386, for telephone and fax, open Mon-Sat 0700-2300, Sun and holidays 0700-1800. International calls by pay phone or go through the operator (long wait possible), deposit required. **Useful addresses** Migraciones, Av Sol s/n, block 6 close to post office, T222740, Mon-Fri 0800-1300 (for extending stay in Peru.) ISIC-Intej office, Portal de Panes 123, of 107 (CC Los Ruiseñores), T256367. Issues international student cards.

Southeast from Cuzco

There are many interesting villages and ruins on this road. **Tipón** ruins, between the villages of Saylla and Oropesa, are extensive and include baths, terraces, irrigation systems, possibly an agricultural laboratory and a temple complex, accessible from a path leading from just above the last terrace (5 km climb from village; take a combi from Cuzco to Oropesa, then a taxi, or taxi from Cuzco US$6). **Oropesa** church contains a fine ornately carved pulpit.

At **Huambutío**, north of the village of Huacarpay, the road divides; northwest to Pisac and north to **Paucartambo**, on the eastern slope of Andes. This remote town, 80 km east of Cuzco, has become a popular tourist destination. The *Fiesta de la Virgen del Carmen* is a major attraction, with masked dancers enacting rituals and folk tales: 15-17 July. (There is basic accommodation in town.) From Paucartambo, in the dry season, you can go 44 km to **Tres Cruces**, along the Pilcopata road, turning left after 25 km. Tres Cruces gives a wonderful view of the sunrise in June and July: peculiar climactic conditions make it appear that three suns are rising. Tour agencies in Cuzco can arrange transport and lodging.

Further on from Huacarpay are the Huari (pre-Inca) ruins of **Piquillacta** ① *daily 0700-1730*, a large site, with some reconstruction in progress. Buses to Urcos from Avenida Huáscar in Cuzco will drop you at the entrance on the north side of the complex, though this is not the official entry. The Piquillacta Archaeological Park also contains the Laguna de Huacarpay (known as Muyna in ancient times) and the ruins that surround it: Kañarakay, Urpicancha and the huge gateway of Rumicolca. It's good to hike or cycle and birdwatch around the lake.

Andahuaylillas is a village 32 km southeast from Cuzco, with a fine early 17th-century church (the 'Andean Sistine Chapel'), with beautiful frescoes, a splendid doorway and a gilded main altar. Taxis go there, as does the *Oropesa* bus (from Avenida Huáscar in Cuzco) via Tipón, Piquillacta and Rumicolca. The next village, **Huaro**, also has a church whose interior is entirely covered with colourful frescoes.

66 99 Tres Cruces gives a wonderful view of the sunrise in June and July: peculiar climactic conditions make it appear that three suns are rising...

Beyond Andahuaylillas is **Urcos**. There are three very basic hostales. A spectacular road from Urcos crosses the Eastern Cordillera to Puerto Maldonado in the jungle (see page 1275). Some 47 km after passing the snow line Hualla-Hualla pass, at 4,820 m, the super-hot thermal baths of **Marcapata** ① *173 km from Urcos, US$0.10,* provide a relaxing break.

Some 82 km from Urcos, at the base of **Nevado Ausangate** (6,384 m), is the town of **Ocongate**, which has two hotels on the Plaza de Armas. Beyond Ocongate is **Tinqui**, the starting point for hikes around Ausangate and in the Cordillera Vilcanota. On the flanks of the Nevado Ausangate is Q'Olloriti, where a church has been built close to the snout of a glacier. This place has become a place of pilgrimage (see Cuzco, Local festivals, page 1217).

Hiking around Ausangate The hike around the mountain of Ausangate takes six days: spectacular, but quite hard, with three passes over 5,000 m, so you need to be acclimatized. Temperatures in high season (April-October) can drop well below zero at night. It is recommended to take a guide or *arriero*. *Arrieros* and mules can be hired in Tinqui for US$7 per day for an *arriero*, US$6 for a mule, but more for a saddle horse. *Arrieros* also expect food. Make sure you sign a contract with full details. Buy all food supplies in Cuzco. Maps are available at the **IGM** in Lima or **South American Explorers**, who also have latest information.

From Urcos to Sicuani (see page 1200), the road passes **Cusipata** (with an Inca gate and wall), **Checacupe** (with a lovely church) and **Tinta**, 23 km from Sicuani (church with brilliant gilded interior and an interesting choir vault). There are frequent buses and trucks to Cuzco, or take the train from Cuzco.

Continuing to Sicuani, **Raqchi** is the scene of the region's great folklore festival starting on 24 June, *Wiracocha*, when dancers come from all over Peru. Raqchi is also the site of the **Viracocha Temple** ① *US$1.75, getting there: take a bus or truck from Cuzco towards Sicuani, US$1.50.* John Hemming wrote: "What remains is the central wall, which is adobe above and Inca masonry below. This was probably the largest roofed building ever built by the Incas. On either side of the high wall, great sloping roofs were supported by rows of unusual round pillars, also of masonry topped by adobe. Nearby is a complex of barracks-like buildings and round storehouses. This was the most holy shrine to the creator god Viracocha, being the site of a miracle in which he set fire to the land - hence the lava flow nearby. There are also small Inca baths in the corner of a field beyond the temple and a straight row of ruined houses by a square. The landscape is extraordinary, blighted by huge piles of black volcanic rocks."

◉ Sleeping

Ausangate *p1228*
G Ausangate, Tinqui. Very basic, but warm, friendly atmosphere. Sr Crispin (or Cayetano), the owner, is knowledgeable and can arrange guides, mules, etc. He and his brothers can be contacted in Cuzco on F227768. All have been recommended as reliable sources of trekking and climbing information, for arranging trips and for being very safety-conscious.
G Hostal Tinqui Guide, on the right-hand side as you enter Tinqui. Meals available, the owner can arrange guides and horses.

◉ Transport

Paucartambo *p1227*
Bus A minibus leaves for Paucartambo from Av Huáscar in **Cuzco**, every other day, US$4.50, 3-4 hrs; alternate days Paucartambo- Cuzco. Trucks and a private bus leave from the Coliseo, behind Hospital Segura in Cuzco, 5 hrs, US$2.50. Private car hire for a round trip Cuzco-Paucartambo on 15-17 July, US$30; travel agencies in Cuzco arrange this.

Ausangate *p1228*
Bus from Cuzco, to **Tinqui** leave Mon-Sat 1000 from C Tomasatito Condemayta, near the Coliseo Cerrado; 172 km, 6-7 hrs, US$3.50.

Sacred Valley of the Incas

The name conjures up images of ancient rulers and their god-like status, with the landscape itself as their temple. And so it was, but the Incas also built their own tribute to this dramatic land in monuments such as Machu Picchu, Ollantaytambo, Pisac and countless others. For the tourist, the famous sights are now within easy reach of Cuzco, but the demand for adventure, to see lost cities in a less 21st-century context, means that there is ample scope for exploring. But if archaeology is not your thing, there are markets to enjoy, birds to watch, trails for mountain-biking and a whole range of hotels to relax in. The best time to visit is April to May or October to November. The high season is June-September, but the rainy season, from December to March, is cheaper and pleasant enough.

Pisac → *Phone code 084. Colour map 3, grid C4.*

Pisac, 30 km north of Cuzco, has a traditional Sunday morning **market**, at which local people sell their produce in exchange for essential goods. It is also a major draw for tourists who arrive after 0800 until 1700. Pisac has other, somewhat less crowded but more commercial markets on Tuesday and Thursday morning. Each Sunday at 1100 there is a Quechua mass. On the plaza are the church and a small interesting **Museo Folklórico**. There are many souvenir shops on Bolognesi. Local fiesta: 15 July.

High above the town on the mountainside is a superb **Inca fortress** ⓘ *0700-1730, guides charge about US$5, if you do not show your multi-site ticket on the way up, you will be asked to do so by the warden.* The walk up to the ruins begins from the plaza (but see below), past the Centro de Salud and a new control post. The path goes through working terraces, giving the ruins a context. The first group of buildings is Pisaqa, with a fine curving wall. Climb then to the central part of the ruins, the Intihuatana group of temples and rock outcrops in the most magnificent Inca masonry. Here are the Reloj Solar ('Hitching Post of the Sun') – now closed because thieves stole a piece from it, palaces of the moon and stars, solstice markers, baths and water channels. From Intihuatana, a path leads around the hillside through a tunnel to Q'Allaqasa, the military area. Across the valley at this point, a large area of Inca tombs in holes in the hillside can be seen. The end of the site is Kanchiracay, where the agricultural workers were housed. Road transport approaches from this end. The descent takes 30 minutes. At dusk you will hear, if not see, the *pisaca* (partridges), after which the place is named. Even if going by car, do not rush as there is a lot to see and a lot of walking to do. Road transport approaches from the Kanchiracay end. The drive up from town takes about 20 minutes. Walking up, although tiring, is recommended for the views and location. It's at least one hour uphill all the way. The descent takes 30 minutes on foot. Horses are available for US$3 per person. Combis charge US$0.60 per person and taxis US$3 one way up to the ruins from near the bridge. Then you can walk back down (if you want the taxi to take you back down negotiate a fare). Overnight parking allowed in the parking lot.

Pisac to Urubamba

Calca, 2,900 m, is 18 km beyond Pisac. The plaza is divided in two: Urubamba buses stop on one side; and Cuzco and Pisac buses on the other side of the dividing strip. *Fiesta de la Vírgen Asunta* 15-16 August. There are basic hotels and eating places in town.

The **Valle de Lares** is beautiful for walking and cycling, with its magnificent mountains, lakes and small villages. You start near an old hacienda in Huarán (2,830 m), cross two passes over 4,000 m and end at the hot springs near Lares. From this village, transport runs back to Calca. Alternatively, you can add an extra day and continue to Ollantaytambo. Several agencies in Cuzco offer trekking and biking tours to the region and some offer this trek as an alternative Inca Trail.

About 3 km east of Urubamba, **Yucay** has two grassy plazas divided by the restored colonial church of Santiago Apóstol, with its oil paintings and fine altars. On the opposite side from Plaza Manco II is the adobe palace built for Sayri Túpac (Manco's son) when he emerged from Vilcabamba in 1558. In Yucay monks sell fresh milk, ham, eggs and other dairy produce from their farm on the hillside.

Urubamba → *Phone code 084. Altitude: 2,863 m.*

Like many places along the valley, Urubamba is in a fine setting with snow-capped peaks in view. Calle Berriózabal, on the west edge of town, is lined with pisonay trees. The large market square is one block west of the main plaza. The main road skirts the town and the bridge for the road to Chinchero is just to the east of town. *Banco de la Nación* is on M Castilla at the start of the 2nd block; *Serpost* is on the Plaza de Armas. Visit **Seminario-Bejar Ceramic Studio** ① *Berriózabal 111, T201002, kupa@ terra.com.pe*, in the beautiful grounds of the former Urpihuasi hostal. They investigate and use pre-Columbian techniques and designs, highly recommended. Internet at **Connections** *Av M Castilla y Av La Convención*. For local festivals, May and June are the harvest months, with many processions following ancient schedules. Urubamba's main festival, *El Señor de Torrechayoc*, occupies the first week of June.

About 6 km west of Urubamba is **Tarabamba**, where a bridge crosses the Río Urubamba. Turn right after the bridge to **Pichingoto**, a tumbled-down village built under an overhanging cliff. Also, just over the bridge and before the town to the left of a small, walled cemetery is a salt stream. Follow the footpath beside the stream to Salinas, a small village below which are a mass of terraced Inca salt pans which are still in operation; there are over 5,000. The walk to the salt pans takes about 30 minutes. Take water as this side of the valley can be very hot and dry.

Chinchero and Moray

Chinchero (3,762 m) ① *site 0700-1730, on the combined entrance ticket (see page 1204)*, is just off a direct road to Urubamba. It has an attractive church built on an Inca temple. The church has been restored to reveal in all their glory the interior paintings. The ceiling, beams and walls are covered in beautiful floral and religious designs. The church is open on Sunday for mass and at festivals; ask in the tourist office in Cuzco for other times. Recent excavations there have revealed many Inca walls and terraces. The food market and the handicraft market are separate. The former is held every day, on your left as you come into town. The latter, on Sunday only, is up by the church, small, but attractive. On any day but Sunday there are few tourists. Fiesta, day of the Virgin, on 8 September.

At Moray, there are three 'colosseums', used by the Incas, according to some theories, as a sort of open-air crop nursery, known locally as the laboratory of the Incas. The great depressions contain no ruined buildings, but are lined with fine terracing. Each level is said to have its own microclimate. It is a very atmospheric place which, many claim, has mystical power. The scenery is absolutely stunning. The most interesting way to get to Moray is from

The Sacred Valley

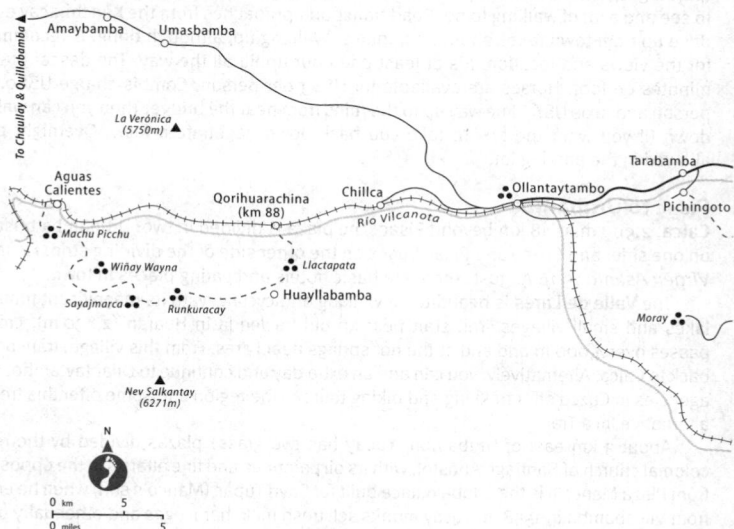

Urubamba via the Pichingoto bridge over the Río Urubamba. The climb up from the bridge is fairly steep but easy. The path passes by the spectacular **salt pans**, still in production after thousands of years, taking 1½-2 hours to the top. The village of Maras is about 45 minutes further on, then it's 9 km by road or 5 km through the fields to Moray. Tour companies in Cuzco offer cycle trips to Moray. There are no hotels at all in the area, so take care not to be stranded. (See Transport, below, for further details on how to get there.)

Ollantaytambo → *Phone code 084. Colour map 3, grid C4. Altitude: 2,800 m.*

ⓘ *0700-1730. If possible arrive very early, 0700, before the tourists. Admission is by combined entrance ticket, which can be bought at the site (otherwise US$6.50).*

The Inca town, or *Llacta*, on which the present-day town is based is clearly seen in the fine example of Inca *canchas* (blocks), which are almost entirely intact and still occupied behind the main plaza. Entering Ollantaytambo from Pisac, the road is built along the long wall of 100 niches. Note the inclination of the wall: it leans towards the road. Since it was the Inca's practice to build with the walls leaning towards the interiors of the buildings, it has been deduced that the road, much narrower then, was built inside a succession of buildings. The road out of the plaza leads across a bridge, down to the colonial church with its enclosed *recinto*. Beyond is a plaza (and car park) with entrances to the archaeological site.

The so-called **Baño de la Ñusta** (bath of the princess) is of grey granite, and is in a small area between the town and the temple fortress. Some 200 m behind the Baño de la Ñusta along the face of the mountain are some small ruins known as Inca Misanca, believed to have been a small temple or observatory. A series of steps, seats and niches have been carved out of the cliff. There is a complete irrigation system, including a canal at shoulder level, some 6 ins deep, cut out of the sheer rock face (under renovation). The flights of terraces leading up above the town are superb, and so are the curving terraces following the contours of the rocks overlooking the Urubamba. These terraces were successfully defended by Manco Incas warriors against Hernando Pizarro in 1536. Manco Inca built the wall above the site and another wall closing the Yucay valley against attack from Cuzco. These are visible on either side of the valley.

The temple itself was started by Pachacútec, using Colla Indians from Lake Titicaca - hence the similarities of the monoliths facing the central platform with the Tiahuanaco remains. The massive, highly finished granite blocks at the top are worth the climb to see. The Colla are said to have deserted half-way through the work, which explains the many unfinished blocks lying about the site.

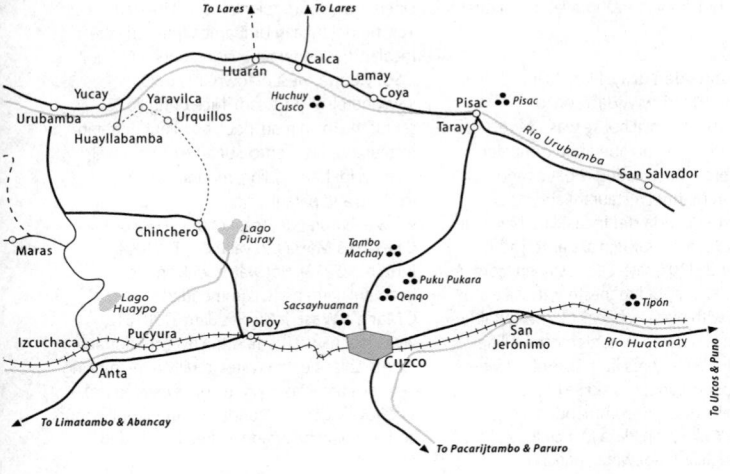

The real Pacaritambo?

Recently a 'pyramid' has been identified on the west side of the main ruins of Ollantaytambo. Its discoverers, Fernando and Edgar Elorietta, claim it is the real Pacaritambo, from where the four original Inca brothers emerged to found their empire (an alternative creation legend). Whether this is the case or not, it is still a first-class piece of engineering with great terraced fields and a fine 750 m wall aligned with the rays of the winter solstice, on 21 June. The mysterious 'pyramid', which covers 50-60 ha, can be seen properly from the other side of the river. This is a pleasant, easy one-hour walk, west from the Puente Inca, just outside the town. There are great views of the Sacred Valley, the river and the snowy peaks of the Verónica massif as a backdrop.

El Museo Catcco ① *1 block from plaza in the Casa Horno, T084-204024, www.ollantay tambo.org, 0900-1800, US$1.45*. The museum has good displays of textiles, findings from local ruins, ethnographic and archaeological information. Tourist information and details of heritage trails are available in the museum. Internet *Ollanta*, just before Plaza Ruinas on the left-hand side, opposite Santiago Apóstol church. There is an ATM in the cream building at the exit of the plaza towards the town.

On the west side of the main ruins, a two-dimensional 'pyramid' has been identified in the layout of the fields and walls of the valley. A fine 750 m wall aligns with the rays of the winter solstice on 21 June. It can be appreciated from a high point about 3.5 km from Ollantaytambo.

● Sleeping

Pisac *p1229*
AL Royal Inka Pisac, Carretera Ruinas Km 1.5, T203064, www.royalinkahotel.com/pisac.html. Including breakfast, converted hacienda with pool, sauna, very pleasant, provides guides.
F Res Beho, Intihuatana 642, T/F203001. Ask for room in main building, good breakfast for US$1, owner's son will act as guide to ruins at weekend.
G pp Parador, on the Plaza, T203061. Shared bathrooms, breakfast extra, hot water, restaurant.

Yucay *p1229*
L-AL La Casona de Yucay, Plaza Manco II 104, Yucay, T084-201116, www.lacasonade yucay.com. This colonial house was where Simón Bolívar stayed during his liberation campaign in 1824. With breakfast, heating, 2 patios and gardens, Don Manuel restaurant and bar.
L-AL Sonesta Posada del Inca, Plaza Manco II de Yucay 123, on the same plaza as the adobe palace, T084-201107, sales@sonestaperu.com. A converted 300-year-old monastery, it is like a little village with plazas, chapel, 69 comfortable, heated rooms, restaurant, conference facilities, price includes buffet breakfast. Lots of activities can be arranged, canoeing, horse riding, mountain biking, etc. Recommended.
B-C Hostal Y'Llary, on Plaza Manco II, T201112. Including breakfast, hot water, parking.

Urubamba *p1230*
L Casa Andina Private Collection Sacred Valley, Yanahuara, between Urubamba and Ollantaytambo, T976 5501, www.casa-andina.com. In its own 3-ha estate, with all the facilities associated with this chain, god restaurant, adventure options.
L Libertador Valle Sagrado Lodge, Yanahuara, 5ta paradero, T961 3316, http://en.valles agradolodge.com/about/. Affiliated to the Libertador group, colonial style. Libertador's **Tambo del Inka** in Urubamba (formerly the Incaland) is under renovation until mid-2007.
L Sol y Luna, west of town, T201620, www.hotelsolyluna.com. Nice bungalows set off the main road, pool, excellent buffet in restaurant. Has **Viento Sur** adventure travel agency, for horse riding, mountain biking, trekking and paragliding, www.aventurasvientosur.com.
C Las Tres Marías, Zavala 307, T201004 (Cuzco 225252). Hot water, welcoming, beautiful gardens. Recommended.
C Mach'a Wasi, Jr Nicolás Barre, T201612, www.machawasi.com. Attractive, comfortable rooms, solar-heated water, totally non-smoking, delicious breakfast extra (vegans catered for), safe, lovely garden, laundry, mountain-bike tours and treks can be arranged. Recommended.

D pp **Las Chullpas**, 3 km from town, T968 5713, www.geocities.com/laschullpas/. Very peaceful, includes excellent breakfast, vegetarian meals, English and German spoken, Spanish classes, natural medicine, treks, riding, mountain biking, camping US$3 with hot shower. Mototaxi from town US$0.85, taxi (ask for Querocancha) US$2.
F Capulí, Grau 222. With hot water and TV, or **G** per bed with shared bath.
F Hostal Urubamba, Bolognesi 605. Basic, pleasant, cold water, **G** without bath.

Chinchero *p1230*

F Hotel Restaurant Antabaraj, just beyond ticket control, T/F306002 (Patricia Cagigao), antabaraj@hotmail.com. Basic rooms, take sleeping bag, kitchen facilities, good views, food at reasonable prices.

Ollantaytambo *p1231*

AL Ñustayoc Mountain Lodge and Resort, about 5 km west of Ollantaytambo, just before Chillca and the start of the Inca Trail, T204098, www.nustayoclodge.com. Large lodge in a wonderful location with great views of Verónica and other peaks. Lovely flower- filled grounds, nicely decorated, spacious rooms, includes continental breakfast.
AL Pakaritampu, C Ferrocarril s/n, T204020, www.pakaritampu.com. Includes breakfast, modern, TV room, restaurant and bar, internet service for guests, laundry, safe and room service. Adventure sports can be arranged. Meals are extra: buffet US$13, dinner US$12-15. Excellent quality and service.
C El Albergue Ollantaytambo, within the railway station gates, T/F204014, www.rumbosperu.com/elalbergue/. Owned by North American Wendy Weeks, the Albergue has 8 rooms with shared bathrooms. Price includes breakfast; box lunch costs US$4, full dinner US$7 on request. Rooms are full of character and are set in buildings around a courtyard and lovely gardens. Great showers (24 hrs a day) and a eucalyptus steam sauna (US$5). The whole place is charming, very relaxing and homely. See the office-cum-shop-cum-exhibition where interesting handicrafts can be bought. Also for sale is Wendy's digestif, *Compuesto Matacuy*. It's very convenient for the Machu Picchu train and good place for information. Private transport can be arranged to the salt mines, Moray, Abra Málaga for birdwatching and taxi transfers to the airport. Recommended.

C Hostal Munay Tika, on the road to the station, T204111, munaytika@latinmail.com. Price includes breakfast, dinner served by arrangement, sauna US$5 with prior notice. Also has a nice garden, very good.
C-D Albergue Kapuly, at the end of the station road, T204017. Prices are lower off season, quiet, spacious rooms, some without bath, nice garden, price includes decent continental breakfast. Recommended.
D-E Hospedaje KB Tambo, between the main plaza and the ruins, T204091. French run, pleasant rooms, hot water, flower-filled garden, very good restaurant (♥♥).
E Hostal Chaskawasi, up Chaupicalle (also called Calle Taypi) north of the Plaza, T208085, anna_machupicchu@hotmail.com. Hostal snuggled away in the small alleys behind the Plaza. Owner Anna is very helpful.
E Hostal La Ñusta, C Ocobamba, on the right hand side in between the plaza and the bridge, T204035. Ask in the shop/restaurant of the same name on the plaza, decent if uninspiring budget option. Proprietor Rubén Ponce loves to share his knowledge of the ruins with guests. You get a good view of the ruins from the balcony. See below for the restaurant.
E Hostal Ollanta, on the south side of the Plaza, T204116. Basic, but great location. All rooms with shared bath.
E pp **Las Orquídeas**, near the start of the road to the station, T204032. Good accommodation, price includes breakfast and meals are available.
F Hostal Chuza, just below the main plaza in town, T204113. Very pleasant, safe motorcycle parking, TV in front room for guests, ask for the room with the view of the ruins and Nevado Verónica. Recommended.
G pp **Hostal Tambo**, just walk up the street called Lari that heads north from the Plaza. After 20 m or so you'll see an unmarked blue door on the left-hand side... bang on the door. If this doesn't work keep walking, turn left down the first small alley and bang on that blue door instead! Once past this unassuming exterior you enter a mini Garden of Eden, full of fruit trees, flowers, dogs, cats and domesticated parrots in the trees. No hot water and only 3 basic rooms, but the family is very friendly and the Señora is a real character.

● *For an explanation of the sleeping and eating price codes used in this guide, see inside the front*
● *cover. Other relevant information is found in Essentials pages 1075-1077.*

⊘ Eating

Pisac *p1229*

† **Doña Clorinda**, Bolognesi at the plaza, tasty food, including vegetarian.
Bakery, Mcal Castilla 372. Sells excellent cheese and onion *empanadas* for US$0.25, suitable for vegetarians, and good wholemeal bread.
Ulrike's Café, Plaza de Armas 828, ulrikescafe@terra.com.pe. Has possibly the best apple crumble with ice cream, excellent coffee, smoothies and a wide range of international dishes. A good place to chill out. See also Sleeping listings above.

Urubamba *p1230*

††† **Tunupa**, on road from Urubamba to Ollantaytambo, on riverbank, zappa@ terra.com.pe. Same owners as Tunupa in Cuzco, colonial-style hacienda, excellent food and surroundings, pre-Columbian and colonial art exhibitions, buffet lunch 1200-1500, US$15, dinner 1800-2030.
†† **La Casa de la Abuela**, Bolívar 272. Fine restaurant around a courtyard, helpful, trout a speciality. Recommended.
†† **El Fogón**, Parque Pintacha, T201534. Peruvian food. Recommended.
†† **El Maizal**, on the main road, before the bridge, T201454. Country-style restaurant, buffet service with a variety of Novo Andino and international choices, beautiful gardens, open daytime only. Recommended.
† **Pintacha**, Bolognesi 523. Pub/café serving sandwiches, burgers, coffees, teas and drinks, games, book exchange, cosy, open till late.
† **Pizzonay**, Av Mcal Castilla 2nd block. Pizzas, excellent lasagne.

Ollantaytambo *p1231*

†† **Bar/Restaurant Gran Tunupa**, corner of C Ocobamba and Bentinerio, right hand side between the Plaza and the bridge. Nice view and reasonable food, including pizzas.
†† **Il Cappuccino**, just before the bridge on the right hand side. The best cappuccino in town, good continental and American breakfasts, slightly more sophisticated than many other establishments in town.
†† **Fortaleza**, 2 branches, one on Plaza Ruinas, the other on the north side of the main Plaza. Basic but good food, breakfasts, pizza and pasta – gringo favourites and some local dishes.
†† **Kusicoyllor**, on the Plaza Ruinas.
The same owners as Il Cappuccino, serving pizza, pasta and good coffee.
†† **Mayupata**, Jr Convención s/n, across the bridge on the way to the ruins, on the left, T204083 (Cuzco). International choices and a selection of Peruvian dishes, desserts, sandwiches and coffee, opens 0600 for breakfast, and serves lunch and dinner. The bar has a fireplace; river view, relaxing atmosphere.
† **Alcázar Café**, C del Medio, 50m from Plaza, T204034. Vegetarian, but also offers meat and fish, and pasta. Arranges excursions to Andean communities.
† **Bahía**, on the east side of the Plaza. Vegetarian dishes served on request.
† **La Ñusta**, on the Plaza, with the same owner as the hostel – see above. Popular, good food; snacks available.

⊛ Festivals and events

Ollantaytambo *p1231*

On the Sun following Inti Raymi, there is a colourful festival, the **Ollanta-Raymi**.
6 Jan: the Bajada de Reyes Magos (the Magi), with dancing, a bull fight, local food and a fair.
End-May/early-Jun: 50 days after Easter, Fiesta del Señor de Choquekillca, patron saint of Ollantaytambo, with several days of dancing, weddings, processions, masses, feasting and drinking. **29 Oct**: the town's anniversary is celebrated with lots of dancing in traditional costume and many local delicacies for sale.

▲ Activities and tours

Urubamba *p1230*

Horse riding Perol Chico, 5 km from Urubamba at Km 77, T962 4475, office 054-213386, www.perolchico.com.
Dutch/Peruvian owned, 1- to 14-day trips out of Urubamba, good horses, riding is Peruvian Paso style. Recommended.
Trekking Haku Trek, contact Javier Saldívar, T961 3001, www.hakutrek.com. Cooperative tourism project in the Chicón valley (the mountain valley above Urubamba), run by residents of the community, 1 and 2-day hiking trips based at a simple eco-lodge; profits are used to fund reforestation of the area.

⊖ Transport

Urubamba *p1230*

Bus Terminal, west of town on the main road, about 3 km from centre. From Urubamba to **Calca**, **Pisac** (US$0.80, 1 hr) and **Cuzco**, about 2 hrs, US$1, with Caminos del Inca, from 0530; also buses to Cuzco via Chinchero. Combis run to **Ollantaytambo**, 45 mins, US$0.30.
Train See under Machu Picchu for the Sacred Valley Railway from Urubamba to Aguas Calientes, page 1237.

Chinchero and Moray *p1230*
Road There is a paved road from the main road
between Chinchero and Urubamba to the village
of Maras and from there an unmade road in good
condition leads to Moray, 9 km. Ask in Maras for
the best route to walk, other than on the main
road. There is public transport from Chinchero to
Maras; it stops running between 1700 and 1800;
US$0.60. Taxi to Moray, 1-hr wait then take you to
the salt pans, from where you can walk back to
the Urubamba-Ollantaytambo road, US$10.

Ollantaytambo *p1231*
Bus Direct bus Ollantaytambo to **Cuzco**
at 0715 and 1945, US$2.85. The station is
10-15 mins walk from the plaza. There are
colectivos at the plaza for the station when
trains are due. Check in advance the time
trains pass through here (see also under
trains to and from Machu Picchu, page 1234).
You won't be allowed on the station unless
you have previously bought a ticket (and it
is best to buy tickets in Cuzco).

Machu Picchu → *Colour map 3, grid C4.*

There is a tremendous feeling of awe on first witnessing Machu Picchu. The ancient citadel
(42 km from Ollantaytambo by rail) straddles the saddle of a high mountain (2,380 m) with
steep terraced slopes falling away to the fast-flowing Urubamba river snaking its hairpin
course far below in the valley floor. Towering overhead is Huayna Picchu, and green jungle
peaks provide the backdrop for the whole majestic scene. Machu Picchu is a complete Inca
city. For centuries it was buried in jungle, until Hiram Bingham stumbled upon it in 1911. It was
then explored by an archaeological expedition sent by Yale University. The ruins – staircases,
terraces, temples, palaces, towers, fountains and the famous Intihuatana (the so-called
'Hitching Post of the Sun') – require at least a day. Take time to appreciate not only the
masonry, but also the selection of large rocks for foundations, the use of water in the channels
below the Temple of the Sun and the surrounding mountains.

Ins and outs

Entrance to Machu Picchu The site is open from 0700 to 1730. Entrance fee is 79.50 soles
(35 with ISIC card), US$24 approximately, payable only in soles. Tickets must be bought in
advance from **Instituto Nacional de Cultura** (INC) in Aguas Calientes ① *Av Pachacútec cuadra
1, 0500-2200*, or Cuzco (see p 1205), www.inc-cusco.gob.pe. You can deposit your luggage at
the entrance for US$0.50. Guides are available at the site, they are often very knowledgeable
and worthwhile, US$15 for 2½ hours (but may take groups of up to 15). Site wardens are also
informative, in Spanish only. Permission to enter the ruins before 0600 to watch the sunrise
over the Andes, which is a spectacular experience, can be obtained from the
(www.inc-cusco.gob.pe), but it is often possible if you talk to the guards at the gate. After 1530
the ruins are quieter, but note that the last bus down from the ruins leaves at 1730. Monday and
Friday are bad days because there is usually a crowd of people on guided tours who are going or
have been to Pisac market on Sunday. The hotel is located next to the entrance, with a
self-service restaurant. Take your own food and drink if you don't want to pay hotel prices, and
take plenty of drinking water. Note that food and drink are not officially allowed into the site. In
the dry season sandflies can be a problem, so take insect repellent and wear long clothes.

Information Apart from the INC (see above), the agency officially responsible for the site is
Unidad Gestión de Machu Picchu ① *C Garcilaso 223, Cuzco, T242103*. It is an excellent
source of information on Machu Picchu and this is the place to which any complaints or
observations should be directed.

Around the site

Huayna Picchu, the mountain overlooking the site (on which there are also ruins), has steps to
the top for a superlative view of the whole site, but it is not for those who are afraid of heights
and you shouldn't leave the path. The climb takes up to 90 minutes but the steps are
dangerous after bad weather. The path is open 0700-1300, with the latest return time being
1500; and you must register at a hut at the beginning of the trail (400 visitors maximum per
day). The other trail to Huayna Picchu, down near the Urubamba, is via the Temple of the
Moon, in two caves, one above the other, with superb Inca niches inside. For the trail to the
Temple of the Moon: from the path to Huayna Picchu, take the marked trail to the left. It is in

good shape, although it descends further than you think it should. After the Temple you may proceed to Huayna Picchu, but this path is overgrown, slippery in the wet and has a crooked ladder on an exposed part about 10 minutes before reaching the top (not for the faint-hearted). It is safer to return to the main trail to Huayna Picchu, although this adds about 30 minutes to the climb. The round trip takes about four hours. Before doing any trekking around Machu Picchu, check with an official which paths may be used, or which are one-way.

The famous Inca bridge is about 45 minutes along a well-marked trail south of the Royal Sector. The bridge (on which you cannot walk) is spectacularly sited, carved into a vertiginous cliff-face. East of the Royal Sector is the path leading up to **Intipunku** on the Inca Trail (45 minutes, fine views).

Aguas Calientes

Those with more time should spend the night at Aguas Calientes and visit the ruins early in the morning, when no one's around. Most hotels and restaurants are near the railway station, on the plaza, or on Avenida Pachacútec, which leads from the plaza to the **thermal baths** ① *0500-2030, US$3.15, 10 mins walk from the town* (a communal pool, smelling of sulphur) good bar for cocktails in the pool. You can rent towels and bathing costumes (US$0.65) at several places on the road to the baths; basic toilets and changing facilities and showers for washing *before* entering the baths; take soap and shampoo, and keep an eye on valuables.

● Sleeping

Machu Picchu *p1235*
LL Machu Picchu Sanctuary Lodge, reservations as for the *Monasterio Hotel* in Cuzco, which is under the same management (Peru Orient Express Hotels), T211039, www.monasterio.orient-express.com. Comfortable, good service, helpful staff, food well-cooked and presented. Electricity and water 24 hrs a day, will accept American Express travellers' cheques at the official rate, restaurant for residents only in the evening, but the buffet lunch is open to all. The hotel is usually fully booked well in advance, try Sun night as other tourists find Pisac market a greater attraction.

Aguas Calientes *p1236*
LL Pueblo Hotel, T211122, Km 110, 5 mins walk along the railway from the town. For reservations: Jr Andalucia 174, San Isidro, Lima, T01-610 0404; in Cuzco at Plaza las Nazarenas 211, T245314, www.inkaterra.com. Beautiful colonial-style bungalows in village compound surrounded by cloud forest, lovely gardens, pool, expensive restaurant, also campsite with hot showers at good rates, offer tours to Machu Picchu, several guided walks on and off the property, great buffet breakfasts for US$12. Also has the Café Inkaterra by the railway line. Recommended, but there are a lot of steps between the public areas and rooms. The hotel is involved in a project to rehabilitate Spectacled Bears, and re-release them into the wild.
A Presidente, at the old station, T211034 (Cuzco T/F244598), presidente@terra.com.pe. Adjoining Hostal Machu Picchu, see below, more upmarket but little difference, rooms without river view cheaper, price includes breakfast.

B Hostal Pachakúteq, up the hill beyond *Hostal La Cabaña*, T/F211061. Hot water, good breakfast, quiet, family-run. Recommended.
B La Cabaña, Av Pachacútec M20-3, T/F211048. With breakfast, hot water, café, laundry service, helpful, popular with groups.
B Gringo Bill's (**Hostal Q'oñi Unu**), Colla Raymi 104, T/F211046, gringobills@yahoo.com. With breakfast, hot water, laundry, money exchange, luggage stored, good beds, lots of coming-and-going (so watch belongings) and uncommunicative staff, good but expensive meals in *Villa Margarita* restaurant, breakfast from 0530, US$4 packed lunch.
C Hostal Machu Picchu, at the old station, T211212. Functional, quiet, Wilber, the owner's son, has travel information, hot water, nice balcony over the Urubamba, grocery store, price includes breakfast and taxes. Recommended.
C Rupa Wasi, Huanacaure 180, T211101, http://perucuzco.com/rupawasi/lodge_english.htm. Charming 'eco-lodge' up a small alley off Collasuyo, laid back, comfortable, great views from the balconies, purified water available, organic garden under development, good breakfasts US$3.
C-D Jardín Real, Wiracocha 7, T/F211234, jardinrealhotel@hotmail.com. Modern, hot water, good value, price negotiable (same owner as the Pizzería Los Jardines on Pachacútec).
D Hospedaje Quilla, Av Pachacútec between Wiracocha and Tupac Inka Yupanki, T/F211009. Price includes breakfast, hot water, rents bathing gear for the hot springs.
D Hostal Wiracocha Inn, C Wiracocha, T211088. Hot water, breakfast included, small garden, helpful, popular with groups.

D Las Orquídeas, Urb Las Orquideas A-8, T211171. From Av Pachacútec, cross the bridge over the river to the football pitch, find a small dirt path on the right. With bath, hot water, quiet, pleasant.

D-E Hospedaje Inca Tambo, Huanacaure s/n, T211135, hostalinkatambo@latinmail.com. Basic but clean, just below *Rupa Wasi* (see above); negotiate for a good price.

D-E pp Las Bromelias, Colla Raymi, T211145, just off Plaza before Gringo Bill's. Cheaper without bath, small, hot water.

E Hostal Samana Wasi, C Tupac Inka Yupanki, T211170, quillavane@hotmail.com. Hot water 24 hrs, cheaper without bath, pleasant place.

Camping The only official campsite is in a field by the river, just below Puente Ruinas station. Do not leave your tent and belongings unattended.

❶ Eating

Aguas Calientes *p1236*
Pizza seems to be the most common dish in town, but many of the pizzerías serve other types of food as well. The old station and Av Pachútec are lined with eating places. At the station are, among others: **Aiko**, recommended; **La Chosa Pizzería**, good value, mixed reports; **Las Quenas**, café and baggage store (US$0.30 per locker); and 2 branches of **Pizza Samana Wasi**.

TTT Café Inkaterra, on the railway, just below the Machu Picchu Pueblo Hotel. US$15 for a great lunch buffet with scenic views of the river.

TT Indio Feliz, C Lloque Yupanqui, T/F211090. Great French cuisine, excellent value and service, set 3-course meal for US$10, good pisco sours. Highly recommended.

TT Inka's Pizza Pub, on the plaza. Good pizzas, changes money and accepts traveller's cheques. Next door is **Illary**, which is popular.

TT Inca Wasi, Av Pachacútec. A very good place to eat.

TT Pueblo Viejo, Av Pachacútec (near Plaza). Good food in a spacious but warm environment. Price includes use of the salad bar.

TT Toto's House, Av Imperio de los Incas, on the railway line. Same owners as Pueblo Viejo. Good value and quality *menú*.

T Clave de Sol, Av Pachacútec 156. Same owner as Chez Maggy in Cuzco, serving Italian food for about US$4, changes money, also has a vegetarian menu, open 1200-1500, 1800-whenever.

T Govinda, Av Pachacútec y Túpac Inka Yupanki. Vegetarian restaurant with a cheap set lunch. Recommended.

❶ Bars and clubs

Aguas Calientes *p1236*
Waisicha Pub, C Lloque Yupanqui. For good music and atmosphere.

❷ Transport

Machu Picchu *p1235*
Bus Buses leave **Aguas Calientes** for Machu Picchu every 30 mins from 0600 until 1300, 25 mins; they return 1200-1730. US$12 return, US$6 single, valid 48 hrs. The walk up from Aguas Calientes takes about 2½ hrs, following the Inca path.

Train PerúRail trains to Machu Picchu run from San Pedro station in Cuzco. They pass through Poroy and Ollantaytambo to Aguas Calientes (the official name of this station is 'Machu Picchu'). The station for the tourist trains at Aguas Calientes is on the outskirts of town, 200 m from the Pueblo Hotel and 50 m from where buses leave for Machu Picchu ruins. The ticket office is open Mon-Fri 0700-1700, Sat, Sun and holidays 0700-1200; there is a guard on the gate. There is a paved road in poor condition between Aguas Calientes and the start of the road up to the ruins.
Note Train schedules may be affected by mudslides in the rainy season. Delays occur.

There are 3 classes of tourist train: **Vistadome** (US$105 return, US$62 one-way); **Backpacker** (US$68 return, or US$44 one-way); and the new luxurious **Hiram Bingham** service (US$495 return). These trains depart from Cuzco; Hiram Bingham departs from Poroy and, on the other two services you can disembark at Poroy for a quicker bus ride into Cuzco on the return. The **Sacred Valley Railway Vistadome**, a different service, runs from Urubamba to Machu Picchu and costs US$71.50 return, while there are further Vistadomes and Backpackers from **Ollantaytambo** to Machu Picchu, at US$71.50 and US$53 return, respectively.

The **Vistadome** leaves **Cuzco** daily at 0600 and 0700, stopping at Ollantaytambo some 2hrs after Cuzco, and Machu Picchu at 0940 or 1105. It returns from Machu Picchu at 1530 and 1700, passing Ollantaytambo at 1700 and 1830, reaching Cuzco at 1920 and 2130. The Backpacker leaves Cuzco at 0615, passing Ollantaytambo at 0840 and Machu Picchu at 1010. It returns at 1555, passing Ollantaytambo at 1740, getting to Cuzco at 2020.

The **Sacred Valley Railway Vistadome** leaves Urubamba at 0610, reaching Machu Picchu at 0820, returning at 1645, reaching Urubamba at 1910. The Ollantaytambo Vistadomes leave at 1030 and 1455, arriving at 1145 and 1615, returning from Machu Picchu at 0845 and 1320, reaching Ollantaytambo at 1005 and 1440. The

Ollantaytambo Backpacker leaves at 0925, arriving at 1100, returning from Machu Picchu at 1700, reaching Ollantaytambo at 1840. Seats can be reserved even if you're not returning the same day. The Vistadome tickets include food in the price. These trains have toilets, video, snacks and drinks for sale. Tickets for all trains should be bought at Wanchac station in Cuzco, on Av Pachacútec. You must have your original passport to travel on the trains to Machu Picchu. Several Urubamba and Yucay hotels offer free transport to and from the Urubamba station, which is in the grounds of the **Libertador Tambo del Inka** hotel. Tickets can be bought through PerúRail's website, www.perurail.com and from travel agents. Services other than those listed above are entirely at the discretion of PerúRail. Note that the timetable and prices are subject to frequent change.

The new **Hiram Bingham** service departs Poroy at 0900 Mon-Sat, brunch is served on board, and arrives at Machu Picchu 1215 (the timing is good because you can enter the site at a time when most visitors are leaving for their journey back to Cuzco). The return journey is at 1800 (pre-dinner cocktails in bar accompanied by live entertainment, and then a 4-course dinner) reaching Poroy at 2125 with bus service to Cuzco hotels.

There is a cheap way to travel by train to Machu Picchu, but it is not advertised on Peru Rail's website. A Backpacker Noche train leaves Ollantaytambo at 2000, arriving Aguas Calientes 2120. It returns from Aguas at 0545, arriving Ollantaytambo at 0740. Tickets cost US$44 return, 30 one-way, they can be bought at the Wanchac

station in Cuzco or in Ollantaytambo. If you use this service you have to stay two nights in Aguas Calientes if you want to see Machu Picchu.

Tourists may not travel on the local train to Machu Picchu, but there is a way to avoid the train altogether: Take a bus from Cuzco towards Quillabamba at 1900, US$4. Get out at **Santa María** where minibuses wait to go to **Santa Teresa**, 2 hrs, US$1.50. Your reach Santa Teresa by sunrise in time to buy breakfast. Walk 6 km to the Central Hidroeléctrica, a nice, flat road, or hitch a ride on workers' truck, US$0.60. From the Hidroeléctrica train station it's 40 mins on the local train to Aguas Calientes at 1520, US$1.50 for tourists, or you can walk along the railway in 2-3 hrs. To return, at 0600 walk from Aguas Calientes to Santa Teresa to catch a bus at 1000 to Santa María, arrive at 1200. At 1300 take a bus back to Cuzco, arriving between 1900-2000. Or take the local train from Aguas Calientes to Santa Teresa at 1210, stay in a hostal, then take the 1000 bus to Santa María.

❶ Directory

Aguas Calientes *p1236*
Banks Several banks with ATMs in town.
Internet Many interent shops, average price US$1 per hr; slow connection. **Post offices** Serpost agencies: just off the plaza, between the Centro Cultural Machu Picchu and Galería de Arte Tunupa. **Telephones** Office is on Calle Collasuyo and there are plenty of phone booths around town. The town has electricity 24 hrs a day.

Inca trails

The most impressive way to reach Machu Picchu is via the centuries-old Inca Trail that winds its way from the Sacred Valley near Ollantaytambo, taking three to five days. The spectacular hike runs from Km 88, Qorihuayrachina (2,299 m), a point immediately after the first tunnel 22 km beyond Ollantaytambo station. A sturdy suspension bridge has now been built over the Río Urubamba. Guided tours often start at Km 82, Piscacucho, reached by road. New rules for hiking the trail are detailed below. What makes this hike so special is the stunning combination of Inca ruins, unforgettable views, magnificent mountains, exotic vegetation and extraordinary ecological variety.

Ins and outs
Equipment The Inca Trail is rugged and steep (beware of landslides), but the magnificent views compensate for any weariness which may be felt. It is cold at night, however, and weather conditions change rapidly, so it is important to take not only strong footwear, rain gear and warm clothing but also food, water, water purification for when you fill bottles from streams, insect repellent, a supply of plastic bags, coverings, a good sleeping bag, a torch/flashlight and a stove for preparing hot food and drink to ward off the cold at night. A stove using paraffin (kerosene) is preferable, as fuel can be bought in small quantities in markets. A tent is essential, but if you're hiring one in Cuzco, check carefully for leaks. Walkers who have not taken adequate equipment have died of exposure. Caves marked on some maps are little better than overhangs, and are not sufficient shelter to sleep in.

All the necessary equipment can be rented; see page 1218 under Camping equipment and Activities and tours. Good maps of the Trail and area can be bought from South American Explorers in Lima or Cuzco. If you have any doubts about carrying your own pack, reasonably priced porters/guides are available. Carry a day-pack for your water, snacks etc in case you walk faster than the porters and you have to wait for them to catch you up.

Tours Travel Agencies in Cuzco arrange transport to the start, equipment, food, etc, for an all-in price. Prices vary from about US$200 to US$300 per person for a four day/three night trek. If the price is under US$180, you should be concerned as the company will be cutting corners and may not be paying the environment the respect the new rules were designed to instil. All are subject to strict rules introduced in 2001 and must be licensed. Tour operators taking clients on any of the Inca Trails leading to the Machu Picchu Historical Sanctuary have to pay an annual fee. Groups of up to seven independent travellers who do not wish to use a tour operator will be allowed to hike the trails if they contact an independent, licensed guide to accompany them, as long as they do not cotact any other persons such as porters or cooks. There is a maximum of 500 visitors per day allowed on the trail. Operators pay US$10 for each porter and other trail staff; porters are not be permitted to carry more than 25 kg. Littering is banned, as is carrying plastic water bottles (canteens only may be carried). Pets and pack animals are prohibited, but llamas are allowed as far as the first pass. Groups have to use approved campsites only.

Trail tickets: on all hiking trails adults must pay US$58 (students and children under 15 US$29), except Salkantay to Huayllabamba and Km 88, where the fee is US$29 per adult (US$17.45 students and children). All tickets must be bought at the INC office on Calle San Bernardo in Cuzco; none is sold without evidence that you are going with a licensed tour operator. None is sold at the entrance to any of the routes. See page 1219 on the need to reserve your place on the Train in advance. You can save a bit of money by arranging your own transport back to Ollantaytambo in advance, either for the last day of your tour, or by staying an extra night in Aguas Calientes and taking the early morning train, then take a bus back to Cuzco. If you take your own tent and sleeping gear, some agencies give a discount. Make sure your return train ticket to Cuzco has your name on it for the tourist train, otherwise you have to pay for any changes.

The Annual Inca Trail Clean-up takes place usually in September. Many agencies and organizations are involved and volunteers should contact South American Explorers in Cuzco for full details of ways to help. **The Trail is closed each February for cleaning and repair.**

Timing and climate Four days would make a comfortable trip (though much depends on the weather) and you would not find yourself too tired to enjoy what you see. Allow a further day to see Machu Picchu when you have recovered from the hike. You are not allowed to walk back along the trail, though you can pay US$4.50 at Intipunku to be allowed to walk back as far as Wiñay-Wayna. You cannot take backpacks into Machu Picchu; leave them at ticket office, US$0.50.

The first two days of the Trail involve the stiffest climbing, so do not attempt it if you're feeling unwell. Leave all your valuables in Cuzco and keep everything inside your tent, even your shoes. Security has, however, improved in recent years. Avoid the July-August high season and check the conditions in the rainy season from November to April (note that this can vary). In the wet it is cloudy and the paths are very muddy and difficult. Also watch out for coral snakes in this area (black, red, yellow bands).

The trail

The trek to the sacred site begins either at Km 82, **Piscacucho**, or at Km 88, **Qorihuayrachina**, at 2,600 m. In order to reach Km 82 hikers are transported by their tour operator in a minibus on the road that goes to Quillabamba. From Piri onward the road follows the riverbank and ends at Km 82, where there is a bridge. You can depart as early as you like and arrive at Km 82 faster than going by train. The Inca Trail equipment, food, fuel and field personnel reach Km 82 (depending on the tour operator's logistics) for the Inrena staff to weigh each bundle before the group arrives. When several groups are leaving on the same day, it is more convenient to arrive early. Km 88 can only be reached by train, subject to schedule and baggage limitations. The train goes slower than a bus, but you start your walk nearer to Llaqtapata and Huayllabamba. Note that the route from Km 82 goes via **Cusichaca**, rather than Llaqtapata. (See below for details of variations in starting points for the Inca Trail.)

The walk to **Huayllabamba**, following the Cusichaca River, needs about three hours and isn't too arduous. Beyond Huayllabamba, a popular camping spot for tour groups, there is a camping place about an hour head, at **Llulluchayoc** (3,200 m). A punishing 1½ hour climb further is **Llulluchapampa**, a meadow for camping. If you have the energy to reach this point, it will make the second easier because the next stage, the ascent to the first pass, **Warmiwañuska** (Dead Woman's Pass) at 4,200 m, is utterly exhausting, 2½ hours.

Afterwards take the steep downhill to the Pacamayo valley. Beware of slipping on the Inca steps after rain. You camp by a stream at the bottom (1½ hours from the first pass). It is no longer permitted to camp at **unkuracay**, on the way up to the second pass (a much easier climb, 3,850 m). Magnificent near the summit in clear weather. A good overnight place is about 30 minutes past the ruins at **Sayacmarca** (3,500 m) about 1 hour on after the top of the second pass.

A gentle two-hour climb fine the highway leads this Inca tunnel to the third pass. Near the top there's a spectacular view of the entire Vilcabamba range. You descend to Inca ruins at **Phuyopata** (3,650 m), well worth a long visit camping overnight. There is a tourist bathroom where water can be collected (it before drinking). From the steps go up to the impressive ruins of **Wiña** (2,700 m), with views of the recently cleared of Inipata. Access is possible trail is not easily visible. There is a basic hostel with bunk beds, F per person, is a small restaurant. There is a small campsite of the hostel. After Wiñay-Wiña's no water and no camping till **Machu Picchu**.

The path from this goes more or less level through the steep staircase up to the **Intipunku** (two how there there's a magnificent view Picchu, especially at dawn, with the sun later in and out, clouds so during the ruins, sometimes leaving them clear views but in any case Get to **Machu Picchu** as early as possible, preferably befor Intipunku; guards may confiscate your tent. You may only can in the field by the river station.

Alternative Inca Trails

The **Camino Real de los Inkas** starts at K 104, where a footbridge access the ruins of Chachabamba and the trail which asends, passing above t of Chuesuysuy to connect with the main trail at Wiñay Wiña. This first part is a continus ascent of three hours (take water) and the trail is narrow and exposed in any peop recommend this short **Inca Trail**. Good hiking trails fro Aguas Calientes (see 6) have been opened along the left bank of the Urubamba, foray hikes crossing the bri the hydelectric plant to Choquesuysuy. A three-night trek goes from Km 82 to Km 88, then g the Ru Urubamba to Pacamayo Bajo and Km 104, from where you take the Camino Real los Inkas.

Two classic treks involve routes from **Salantay**: one, known as high Inca Trail joins the classic Trail at Huayllabamba then proceeds as before on hin Trail hrough Wiñay Wayna to Machu Picchu. To get to alkantay, you have the trek in Mollepata, northwest of Cuzco in the Aurimac valley. Ampoy buses run rom Arcopata on the Chinch ero road, or you can tae private transport to Mollata (thee hours from Cuzco). Salkantay to Machu Picchu th way takes three nights. The cond alkantay route, known as the Santa Teresa Trek, tes four days and crosses t 4,500m Huamantay Pass to reach the Santa Teresa valley which you follow to its confince with the Urubamba. The goal is the town of Santa Tersa from where you can go to Hidroelétrica station for the local train to Aguas Calientes.

There are other routes with approach the Inca Trails achu Picchu, such as Km 77, Chillca cocha route. A common in the Qente valley, which commonly called the Lago Anca cocha route. A common starting point for this trek is the mmunity of Huarocondo. You can walk this trek either at Huayllabamba, where you join the assic Inca Trail (for further g), or at the railway line at Km 82 (for transport to the Sacd Valley) or Km 88 (for the train Aguas Calientes). Then there is another access through the Millpo Valley in the Salkantay area. From the Vilcabamba mountain range, one can reach Machu Picchu by hiking down from Huancacalle to Chaulla by road, getting to Santa Teresa and walking to La Hidroeléctrica station. Touroperators which specialize in trekking can advise on these routes.

All the necessary equipment can be rented; see page 1218 under Camping equipment and Activities and tours. Good maps of the Trail and area can be bought from **South American Explorers** in Lima or Cuzco. If you have any doubts about carrying your own pack, reasonably priced porters/guides are available. Carry a day-pack for your water, snacks etc in case you walk faster than the porters and you have to wait for them to catch you up.

Tours Travel Agencies in Cuzco arrange transport to the start, equipment, food, etc, for an all-in price. Prices vary from about US$200 to US$300 per person for a four day/three night trek. If the price is under US$180, you should be concerned as the company will be cutting corners and may not be paying the environment the respect the new rules were designed to instil. All are subject to strict rules introduced in 2001 and must be licensed. Tour operators taking clients on any of the Inca Trails leading to the Machu Picchu Historical Sanctuary have to pay an annual fee. Groups of up to seven independent travellers who do not wish to use a tour operator will be allowed to hike the trails if they contact an independent, licensed guide to accompany them, as long as they do not contact any other persons such as porters or cooks. There is a maximum of 500 visitors per day allowed on the trail. Operators pay US$10 for each porter and other trail staff; porters are not be permitted to carry more than 25 kg. Littering is banned, as is carrying plastic water bottles (canteens only may be carried). Pets and pack animals are prohibited, but llamas are allowed as far as the first pass. Groups have to use approved campsites only.

Trail tickets: on all hiking trails adults must pay US$58 (students and children under 15 US$29), except Salkantay to Huayllabamba and Km 88, where the fee is US$29 per adult (US$17.45 students and children). All tickets must be bought at the INC office on Calle San Bernardo in Cuzco; none is sold without evidence that you are going with a licensed tour operator. None is sold at the entrance to any of the routes. See page 1219 on the need to reserve your place on the Trail in advance. You can save a bit of money by arranging your own transport back to Ollantaytambo in advance, either for the last day of your tour, or by staying an extra night in Aguas Calientes and taking the early morning train, then take a bus back to Cuzco. If you take your own tent and sleeping gear, some agencies give a discount. Make sure your return train ticket to Cuzco has your name on it for the tourist train, otherwise you have to pay for any changes.

The Annual Inca Trail Clean-up takes place usually in September. Many agencies and organizations are involved and volunteers should contact South American Explorers in Cuzco for full details of ways to help. **The Trail is closed each February for cleaning and repair.**

Timing and climate Four days would make a comfortable trip (though much depends on the weather) and you would not find yourself too tired to enjoy what you see. Allow a further day to see Machu Picchu when you have recovered from the hike. You are not allowed to walk back along the trail, though you can pay US$4.50 at Intipunku to be allowed to walk back as far as Wiñay-Wayna. You cannot take backpacks into Machu Picchu; leave them at ticket office, US$0.50.

The first two days of the Trail involve the stiffest climbing, so do not attempt it if you're feeling unwell. Leave all your valuables in Cuzco and keep everything inside your tent, even your shoes. Security has, however, improved in recent years. Avoid the July-August high season and check the conditions in the rainy season from November to April (note that this can vary). In the wet it is cloudy and the paths are very muddy and difficult. Also watch out for coral snakes in this area (black, red, yellow bands).

The trail

The trek to the sacred site begins either at Km 82, **Piscacucho**, or at Km 88, **Qorihuayrachina**, at 2,600 m. In order to reach Km 82 hikers are transported by their tour operator in a minibus on the road that goes to Quillabamba. From Piri onward the road follows the riverbank and ends at Km 82, where there is a bridge. You can depart as early as you like and arrive at Km 82 faster than going by train. The Inca Trail equipment, food, fuel and field personnel reach Km 82 (depending on the tour operator's logistics) for the Inrena staff to weigh each bundle before the group arrives. When several groups are leaving on the same day, it is more convenient to arrive early. Km 88 can only be reached by train, subject to schedule and baggage limitations. The train goes slower than a bus, but you start your walk nearer to Llaqtapata and Huayllabamba. Note that the route from Km 82 goes via **Cusichaca**, rather than Llaqtapata. (See below for details of variations in starting points for the Inca Trail.)

The walk to **Huayllabamba**, following the Cusichaca River, needs about three hours and isn't too arduous. Beyond Huayllabamba, a popular camping spot for tour groups, there is a camping place about an hour ahead, at **Llulluchayoc** (3,200 m). A punishing 1½ hour climb further is **Llulluchapampa**, an ideal meadow for camping. If you have the energy to reach this point, it will make the second day easier because the next stage, the ascent to the first pass, **Warmiwañuska** (Dead Woman's Pass) at 4,200 m, is utterly exhausting, 2½ hours.

Afterwards take the steep path downhill to the Pacamayo valley. Beware of slipping on the Inca steps after rain. You could camp by a stream at the bottom (1½ hours from the first pass). It is no longer permitted to camp at **Runkuracay**, on the way up to the second pass (a much easier climb, 3,850 m). Magnificent views near the summit in clear weather. A good overnight place is about 30 minutes past the Inca ruins at **Sayacmarca** (3,500 m), about an hour on after the top of the second pass.

A gentle two-hour climb on a fine stone highway leads through an Inca tunnel to the third pass. Near the top there's a spectacular view of the entire Vilcabamba range. You descend to Inca ruins at **Phuyopatamarca** (3,650 m), well worth a long visit, even camping overnight. There is a 'tourist bathroom' here where water can be collected (but purify it before drinking).

From there steps go downhill to the impressive ruins of **Wiñay-Wayna** (2,700 m), with views of the recently cleared terraces of Intipata. Access is possible, but the trail is not easily visible. There is a basic hostel with bunk beds, **F** per person, showers and a small restaurant. There is a small campsite in front of the hostel. After Wiñay-Wayna there is no water and no camping till Machu Picchu.

The path from this point goes more or less level through jungle until the steep staircase up to the **Intipunku** (two hours), where there's a magnificent view of Machu Picchu, especially at dawn, with the sun alternately in and out, clouds sometimes obscuring the ruins, sometimes leaving them clear.

Get to Machu Picchu as early as possible, preferably before 0830 for best views but in any case before the tourist train arrives at 1030. **Note:** Camping is not allowed at Intipunku; guards may confiscate your tent. You may only camp in the field by the river below Puente Ruinas station.

Alternative Inca Trails

The **Camino Real de los Inkas** starts at Km 104, where a footbridge gives access to the ruins of Chachabamba and the trail which ascends, passing above the ruins of Choquesuysuy to connect with the main trail at Wiñay-Wayna. This first part is a steady, continuous ascent of three hours (take water) and the trail is narrow and exposed in parts. Many people recommend this short Inca Trail. Good hiking trails from Aguas Calientes (see page 1236) have been opened along the left bank of the Urubamba, for day hikes crossing the bridge of the hydroelectric plant to Choquesuysuy. A three-night trek goes from Km 82 to Km 88, then along the Río Urubamba to Pacaymayo Bajo and Km 104, from where you take the Camino Real de los Inkas.

Two treks involve routes from **Salkantay**: one, known as the **High Inca Trail** joins the classic Trail at Huayllabamba, then proceeds as before on the main Trail through Wiñay Wayna to Machu Picchu. To get to Salkantay, you have to start the trek in **Mollepata**, northwest of Cuzco in the Apurímac valley. *Ampay* buses run from Arcopata on the Chinchero road, or you can take private transport to Mollepata (three hours from Cuzco). Salkantay to Machu Picchu this way takes **three nights**. The second Salkantay route, known as the **Santa Teresa Trek**, takes four days and crosses the 4,500-m Huamantay Pass to reach the Santa Teresa valley, which you follow to its confluence with the Urubamba. The goal is the town of Santa Teresa from where you can go to La Hidroeléctrica station for the local train to Aguas Calientes.

There are other routes which approach the Inca Trails to Machu Picchu, such as Km 77, Chillca, up the Sillque ravine in the Qente valley, which is commonly called the Lago Ancascocha route. A common starting point for this trek is the community of Huarocondo. You can end this trek either at Huayllabamba, where you join the Classic Inca Trail (for further walking), or at the railway line at Km 82 (for transport to the Sacred Valley) or Km 88 (for the train to Aguas Calientes). Then there is another access through the Millpo Valley in the Salkantay area. From the Vilcabamba mountain range, one can reach Machu Picchu by hiking down from Huancacalle to Chaulla by road, getting to Santa Teresa and walking to La Hidroeléctrica station. Tour operators which specialize in trekking can advise on these routes.

Vitcos and Vilcabamba

The Incas' last stronghold is reached from **Chaullay**, a village on the road and railway between Ollantaytambo and Quillabamba. No trains run beyond Machu Picchu, so you must take the road which passes through Peña, a place of great beauty with snowy peaks on either side of the valley. Once out of Peña, the climb to the pass begins in earnest - on the right is a huge glacier. Soon on the left, Verónica begins to appear in all its huge and snowy majesty. After endless zig-zags and breathtaking views, you reach the Abra Málaga pass. The descent to the valley shows hillsides covered in lichen and Spanish moss. At Chaullay, the road crosses the river on the historic Choquechaca bridge.

From Chaullay you can drive, or take a daily bus or truck (4-7 hours) to the village of **Huancacalle**, the best base for exploring the nearby Inca ruins of **Vitcos**, with the palace of the last four Inca rulers from 1536 to 1572, and **Yurac Rumi** (or **Chuquipalta**), the impressive sacred white rock of the Incas. There are a few restaurants, shops and basic places to stay at Huancacalle. There is a hostal, **F-G Sixpac Manco** (managed by the Cobos family). Alternatively villagers will let you stay on their floor, or you can camp near the river below the cemetery. Allow time for hiking to, and visiting Vitcos. It takes one hour to walk from Huancacalle to Vitcos, 45 minutes Vitcos-Chuquipalta, 45 minutes Chuquipalta-Huancacalle. Horses can be hired.

The road from Chaullay continues to **Vilcabamba La Nueva**. You can also hike from Huancacalle; a three-hour walk through beautiful countryside with Inca ruins dotted around. There is a missionary building run by Italians, with electricity and running water, where you may be able to spend the night.

Vilcabamba Vieja

Travellers with ample time can hike from Huancacalle to **Espíritu Pampa**, the site of the **Vilcabamba Vieja** ruins, a vast pre-Inca ruin with a neo-Inca overlay set in deep jungle at 1,000 m. The site is reached on foot or horseback from Pampaconas. From Chaullay, take a truck to Yupanca, Lucma or Pucyura: there rent horses or mules and travel through breathtaking countryside to Espíritu Pampa.

From Huancacalle a trip will take 3-4 days on foot, with a further day to get to Chaquiri and transport back to Quillabamba. It is advisable to take local guides and mules. Maps are available from the South American Explorers in Cuzco and Lima. Ask around in Huancacalle for guides. The Sixpac Manco hostal has various guides and other people in the village will offer their services. Distances are considerable and the going is difficult. Essential reading, *Sixpac Manco*, by Vincent R Lee (available in Cuzco), has accurate maps of all archaeological sites in this area, and describes two expeditions into the region by the author and his party, following in the footsteps of Gene Savoy, who first identified the site in the 1960s. His book, *Antisuyo*, which describes this and other expeditions, is also recommended reading.

The best time of year is May to November, possibly December. Outside this period it is very dangerous as the trails are very narrow and can be thick with mud and very slippery. Insect repellent is essential, also pain-killers and other basic medicines.

⊖ Transport

Huancacalle *p1241*
Bus Four companies leave Cuzco's bus terminal for **Quillabamba**, taking 8-14 hrs for the 233 km, depending on season, US$4. Then take a **combi** from Jr San Martín near Plaza Grau in Quillabmba, 0900 and 1200, US$2.50 to Huancacalle, 4-7 hrs. On Fri they go all the way to Vilcabamba.

West from Cuzco

Beyond Anta on the Abancay road, 2 km before Limatambo at the ruins of **Tarahuasi**, a few hundred metres from the road, is a very well-preserved **Inca temple platform**, with 28 tall niches, and a long stretch of fine polygonal masonry. The ruins are impressive, enhanced by the orange lichen which give the walls a honey colour.

Along the Abancay road 100 km from Cuzco, is the exciting descent into the Apurímac canyon, near the former Inca suspension bridge that inspired Thornton Wilders' *The Bridge of San Luis Rey*.

Choquequirao

Choquequirao is another 'lost city of the Incas', built on a ridge spur almost 1,600 m above the Apurímac. Although only 30% has been uncovered, it is reckoned to be a larger site than Machu Picchu, but with fewer buildings. The main features of Choquequirao are the **Lower Plaza**, considered by most experts to be the focal point of the city. The **Upper Plaza**, reached by a huge set of steps or terraces, has what are possibly ritual baths. A beautiful set of slightly curved agricultural terraces run for over 300 m east-northeast of the Lower Plaza.

Usnu is a levelled hilltop platform, ringed with stones and giving awesome 360-degree views. The **Ridge Group**, still shrouded in vegetation, is large collection of unrestored buildings some 50-100 m below the Usnu. The **Outlier Building**, isolated and surrounded on three sides by sheer drops of over 1½ km into the Apurímac Canyon, possesses some of the finest stonework within Choquequirao. **Capuliyoc**, nearly 500 m below the Lower Plaza, is a great set of agricultural terraces, visible on the approach from the far side of the valley.

There are three ways in to Choquequirao. None is a gentle stroll. The shortest way is from **Cachora**, a village on the south side of the Apurímac, reached by a side road from the Cuzco-Abancay highway, shortly after Saywite. It is four hours by bus from Cuzco to the turn-off, then a two-hour descent from the road to Cachora (from 3,695 m to 2,875 m). Guides (Celestino Peña is the official guide) and mules are available in Cachora. From the village you need a day to descend to the Río Apurímac then seven hours to climb up to Choquequirao. Allow 1-2 days at the site then return the way you came. The second and third routes take a minimum of eight days and require thorough preparation. You can start either at Huancacalle, or at Santa Teresa, between Machu Picchu and Chaullay. Both routes involve an incredible number of strenuous ascents and descents. You should be acclimatised for altitudes ranging from 2,400 m to between 4,600 and 5,000 m and be prepared for extremes of temperature. In each case you end the trail at Cachora. It is possible to start either of these long hikes at Cachora, continuing even from Choquequirao to Espíritu Pampa. Cuzco tour companies are now offering this adventure.

Saywite → *3 km from the main road at Km 49 from Abancay, 153 km from Cuzco, US$3. Altitude 3,500 m.*
Beyond the town of Curahuasi, 126 km from Cuzco, is the large carved rock of Saywite. It is a UNESCO World Heritage site. The principal monolith is said to represent the three regions of jungle, sierra and coast, with the associated animals and Inca sites of each. It is fenced in, but ask the guardian for a closer look. It was defaced, allegedly, when a cast was taken of it, breaking off many of the animals' heads. Six further archaeological areas fall away from the stone and its neighbouring group of buildings. The site is more easily reached from Abancay than Cuzco.

⏺ Sleeping

Choquequirao *p1242*
G pp **La Casona de Ocampo**, Jr San Martín 122, Cachora, T084-237514, lacasonade ocampo@yahoo.es. Hot shower, free camping, owner Carlos Robles organizes treks to Choquequirao. 2 other places in the village.

⏺ Transport

Choquequirao *p1242*
Buses run from Abancay (Jr Prado Alto entre Huancavelica y Núñez) to **Cachora** at 0500 and 1400, return 0630 and 1100, 3 hrs, US$1.50. Cars run from the Curahuasi terminal on Av Arenas, Abancay, US$15 for whole vehicle. Trek from Cachora to Choquequirao.

Central Highlands

The Central Andes are remote mountain areas with small, typical villages. The vegetation is low, but most valleys are cultivated. Roads, all dirt, are in poor condition, sometimes impassable in the rainy season; the countryside is beautiful with spectacular views and the people are friendly. The road into the central Andes has been improved and is paved throughout, offering fine views. Huancayo lies in a valley which produces many crafts; the festivals are very popular and not to be missed.

Lima to Huancayo

The Central Highway more or less parallels the course of the railway between Lima and Huancayo (335 km). With the paving of roads from Pisco to Ayacucho and Nazca to Abancay, there are now more options for getting to the Sierra and the views on whichever ascent you choose are beyond compare. You can also reach the Central Highlands from Cuzco (via Abancay and Andahuaylas) and from Huaraz (via La Unión and Huánuco), so Lima is not the sole point of access overland.

Chosica and Marcahuasi

Chosica (Population 31,200, Altitude 860 m) is the real starting place for the mountains, 40 km from Lima. It's warm and friendly and a great place to escape Lima's grey cloud. Beyond the town looms a precipitous range of hills almost overhanging the streets. There are four basic *hostales*, all with water problems.

Up the Santa Eulalia valley 40 km beyond Chosica, is **Marcahuasi**, a table mountain about 3 km by 3 km at 4,200 m, near the village of **San Pedro de Casta**. The *meseta* (US$3), was investigated by the late Daniel Ruzo. There are three lakes, a 40-m high 'monumento a la humanidad', and other mysterious lines, gigantic figures, sculptures, astrological signs and megaliths which display non-American symbolism. Ruzo describes this pre-Incaic culture in his book, *La Culture Masma*, Extrait de l'Ethnographie, Paris, 1956. Others say that the formations are the result of wind erosion.

The trail starts behind the village of San Pedro, and bends to the left. It's three hours to the *meseta*; guides cost about US$3 a day and are advisable in misty weather. Mules for carrying bags cost US$4 to hire, horses US$4.45. Tourist information at the municipality on the plaza sells a map of the plateau for US$1.50. At a shop on the plaza in San Pedro you can buy everything for the trip, including bottled water. Tours can be arranged with travel agencies in Lima.

Chosica to Huancayo

For a while, beyond Chosica, each successive valley looks greener and lusher, with a greater variety of trees and flowers. Between Río Blanco and **Chicla** (Km 127, 3,733 m), Inca contour-terraces can be seen quite clearly. After climbing up from **Casapalca** (Km 139, 4,154 m), there are glorious views of the highest peaks, and more mines, at the foot of a deep gorge. The road ascends to the Ticlio Pass, before the descent to **Morococha** and **La Oroya**. A large metal flag of Peru can be seen at the top of Mount Meiggs, not by any means the highest in the area, but through it runs Galera Tunnel, 1,175 m long, in which the Central Railway reaches its greatest altitude, 4,782 m. The railway itself is a magnificent feat of engineering, with 68 bridges and 71 tunnels, passing beautiful landscapes. It is definitely worth the ride on the new tourist service (see Transport, below).

La Oroya (Phone code 064, Altitude 3,755 m) The main smelting centre for the region's mining industry is full of vitality. It stands at the fork of the Yauli and Mantaro rivers. Any traveller, but asthmatics in particular, beware, the pollution from the heavy industry causes severe irritation. (For places to the east and north of La Oroya, see page 1257.)

The old town of **Jauja** (*Phone code 064, Population 105,000, Altitude 3,330 m*), 80 km southeast of La Oroya, was Pizarro's provisional capital until the founding of Lima. It has a very colourful Wednesday and Sunday market. There is an **archaeological museum**, which is recommended for the Huari culture. A modernized church retains three fine 17th-century altars. The **Cristo Pobre** church is claimed to have been modelled after Notre Dame and is something of a

curiosity. On a hill above Jauja there is a fine line of Inca storehouses, and on hills nearby the ruins of hundreds of circular stone buildings from the Huanca culture (John Hemming). There are also ruins near the **Paca lake**, 3½ km away. The western shore is lined with restaurants, many of which offer boat trips at weekends, US$0.75 (combi from Avenida Pizarro US$0.30).

On the road to Huancayo 18 km to the south, is **Concepción** (*Altitude 3,251 m*), with a market on Sunday. From Concepción a branch road (6 km) leads to the **Convent of Santa Rosa de Ocopa** ① *0900-1200 and 1500-1800, closed Tue, 45-min tours start on the hour, US$1.10, colectivos from the market in Concepción, 15 mins, US$0.25*, a Franciscan monastery set in beautiful surroundings. It was established in 1725 for training missionaries for the jungle. It contains a fine library with over 20,000 volumes, a biological museum and a large collection of paintings.

● Sleeping

Chosica *p1243*
F Hospedaje Chosica, Av 28 de Julio 134, T01-361 0841. Rooms with and without bath. Recommended.
F La Posada, Jr Trujillo y Salaverry, just off main road. Comfortable, hot water.

San Pedro de Casta *p1243*
Locals in town will put you up for US$0.60 pp; ask at tourist information at the municipality on the plaza, T01-571 2087. Take all necessary camping equipment for Marcahuasi trek.
E Marcahuasi, just off the plaza. **F** pp without bath, the best hotel in San Pedro; it also has a restaurant. There are 2 other restaurants.

La Oroya *p1243*
F Hostal Chavín, Tarma 281. Shared bath, cheap restaurant.
F Hostal Inti, Arequipa 117, T391098. Shared bath, warm water, basic.

Jauja *p1243*
E pp Hostal Manco Cápac, Jr Manco Cápac 575, T361620, niegemannilse@hotmail.com. Central, good rooms, good breakfast and coffee, German run. Recommended (reserve at weekends).
E Hostal María Nieves, Jr Gálvez 491, 1 block from the Plaza de Armas, T362543. Safe, helpful, price includes large breakfast, hot water all day. Recommended.
F Hostal Los Algarrobos, Huancayo 264, T362633. Shared bath, hot water in the morning, good value.

● Eating

La Oroya *p1243*
There are lots of *pollerías* in front of the train station in C Lima.
♈♈♈ **El Tambo**, 2 km outside town on the road to Lima. Good trout and frogs, recommended as the best restaurant.
♈ **La Caracocha**, Lima 168. Cheap good *menú*.

Jauja *p1243*
♈ **Centro Naturista**, Huarancayo 138. Fruit salad, yoghurt, granola, etc.
♈ **Ganso de Oro**, R Palma 249. Good restaurant in hotel of same name, US$2-4 per meal, the best in town.
♈ **Marychris**, Jr Bolívar 1166, T362386. Lunch only, excellent.
♈ **La Rotunda**, Tarapacá 415. Good lunch menú and pizzas in the evening.

● Transport

Chosica *p1243*
Colectivos for Chosica leave from Av Grau, **Lima**, when full, between 0600 and 2100, US$0.60. Most **buses** on the Lima-La Oroya route are full; colectivo taxi to La Oroya US$3.60, 3 hrs; very scenic, passing the highest railway in the world.

San Pedro de Casta/Marcahuasi *p1243*
Bus To San Pedro de Casta leave **Chosica** from Parque Echerique, opposite market, 0900 and 1500, 4 hrs, US$2; return 0700 and 1400.

La Oroya *p1243*
Bus To **Lima**, 4½ hrs, US$5.20. To **Jauja**, 80 km, 1½ hrs, US$1; and on to **Huancayo**, a further 44 km, 1 hr, US$1. To **Tarma**, 1½ hrs, US$1.35. To **Cerro de Pasco**, 131 km, 3 hrs, US$2.20. To **Huánuco**, 236 km, 6 hr, US$4.35. Buses leave from Zeballos, adjacent to the train station. Colectivos also run on all routes.

Jauja *p1243*
Bus To **Lima**: with Cruz del Sur, Pizarro 220, direct, 5 hrs, US$8. Most companies have their offices on the Plaza de Armas, but their buses leave from Av Pizarro. To **Huancayo**, 44 km, takes 1 hr and costs US$1.25. To **Cerro de Pasco**, Oriental leave from 28 de Julio 156, and Turismo Central from 28 de Julio 150, 5 hrs, US$3.55. Oriental and Turismo Central also go to **Huánuco**, 7 hrs, US$5.35. To **Tarma**, US$2, hourly with Trans Muruhuay and ET San Juan from Jr Tarma; the latter continues to **Chanchamayo**, US$4.50.

than BCP (no TCs). **Internet** All along
Junín blocks 9 to 12. **Post offices** Jr Bolívar.
Telephones Bolognesi 546; also at Ricardo
Palma, opposite *Hotel Ganso de Oro*, better
service and prices.

Huancayo and around

→ *Phone code: 064. Colour map 3, grid C3. Population: over 500,000. Altitude: 3,271 m.*

The city is in the beautiful Mantaro Valley. It is the capital of Junín Department and the main commercial centre for inland Peru. All the villages in the valley produce their own original crafts and celebrate festivals all year round. At the important festivals in Huancayo, people flock in from far and wide with an incredible range of food, crafts, dancing and music. The Sunday market gives a little taste of this every week (it gets going after 0900), but it is better to go to the villages for local handicrafts. Jr Huancavelica, 3 km long and four stalls wide, still sells clothes, fruit, vegetables, hardware, handicrafts and traditional medicines and goods for witchcraft. There is also an impressive daily market behind the railway station and a large handicrafts market between Ancash and Real, block 7, offering a wide selection.

Tourist offices Huancayo: Dirección Regional de Turismo, Dircetur, Av Libertad 204, T433007, junin@mincetur.gob.pe. Has information about the area and is helpful; 0900-1400, 1600-2000 Monday-Friday. There is a less informative office by the post office between Calles Real and Ancash (no English spoken here). **Touring y Automóvil Club del Perú**, Jr Lima 355, T231204, huancayo@touringperu.com.pe.

The **museum** ⓘ *at the Salesian school, Tue, Thu, Fri and Sun 0815-1100, 1415-1700, Wed 0815-1100, Sat 1415-1600, US$0.60,* has over 5,000 pieces, including a large collection of jungle birds, animals and butterflies, insects, reptiles and fossils. Recommended. The **Parque de Identidad Wanka** ⓘ *on Jr San Jorge in the Barrio San Carlos northeast of the city, entry free, but contributions are appreciated,* is a fascinating mixture of surrealistic construction interwoven with indigenous plants and trees and the cultural history of the Mantaro Valley.

Mantaro Valley

The whole Mantaro valley is rich in culture. On the outskirts of town is **Torre-Torre**, impressive, eroded sandstone towers on the hillside. Take a bus to Cerrito de la Libertad and walk up. The ruins of **Warivilca** (15 km) ⓘ *1000-1200, 1500-1700 (museum mornings only), US$0.15, take a micro for Chilca from C Real* are near **Huari**, with the remains of a pre-Inca temple of the Huanca tribe. Museum in the plaza, with deformed skulls, and modelled and painted pottery of successive Huanca and Inca occupations of the shrine. Between Pilcomayo and Huayo (15 km) is the **Geophysical Institute of Huayo**, on the 'Magnetic Equator' 12½° south of the geographical equator (best to visit in the morning, or when the sun is shining). Take bus from Jr Giráldez to Chupaca, but get out by bridge before Chupaca, where the road splits, then take a colectivo.

East of the Mantaro River The villages of **Cochas Chico** and **Cochas Grande**, 11 km away, are where the famous *mate burilado*, or gourd carving, is done. You can buy them cheaply direct from the manufacturers, but ask around. Beautiful views of the Valle de Mantaro and Huancayo. *Micros* leave from the corner of Amazonas and Giráldez, US$0.25.

Hualahoyo (11 km) has a little chapel with 21 colonial canvases. **San Agustín de Cajas** (8 km) makes fine hats, and **San Pedro** (10 km) makes wooden chairs; **Hualhuas** (12 km) fine alpaca weavings which you can watch being made. The weavers take special orders; small items can be finished in a day. Negotiate a price.

The town of **San Jerónimo** is renowned for the making of silver filigree jewellery; Wednesday market. Fiesta on the third Saturday in August. There are ruins 2-3 hours' walk above San Jerónimo, but seek advice before hiking to them.

Between Huancayo and Huancavelica, **Izcuchaca** is the site of a bridge over the Río Mantaro. On the edge of town is a fascinating pottery workshop whose machinery is driven by a water turbine (plus a small shop). A nice hike is to the chapel on a hill overlooking the valley; about one to 1½ hours each way.

🛏 Sleeping

Huancayo *p1245, map p1246*
Prices may be raised in Holy Week. **Note**: The
Plaza de Armas is called Plaza Constitución.
B Presidente, C Real 1138, T231736,
same email as *Turismo*. Helpful, safe, serves
breakfast. Recommended.
B Turismo, Ancash 729, T231072, hotelhyo@
correo.dnet.com.pe. Old building, some rooms

small, quiet, good meals for US$3.50.
C El Marqués, Puno 294, T219026, F219202. With
TV and free internet access, good value, efficient,
popular with local business travellers, safe parking.
C Retama Inn, Ancash 1079, T219193,
retamainn73@hotmail.com. All amenities,
comfortable beds, TV, café/bar, helpful, internet
US$1.50 per hr, breakfast US$2.

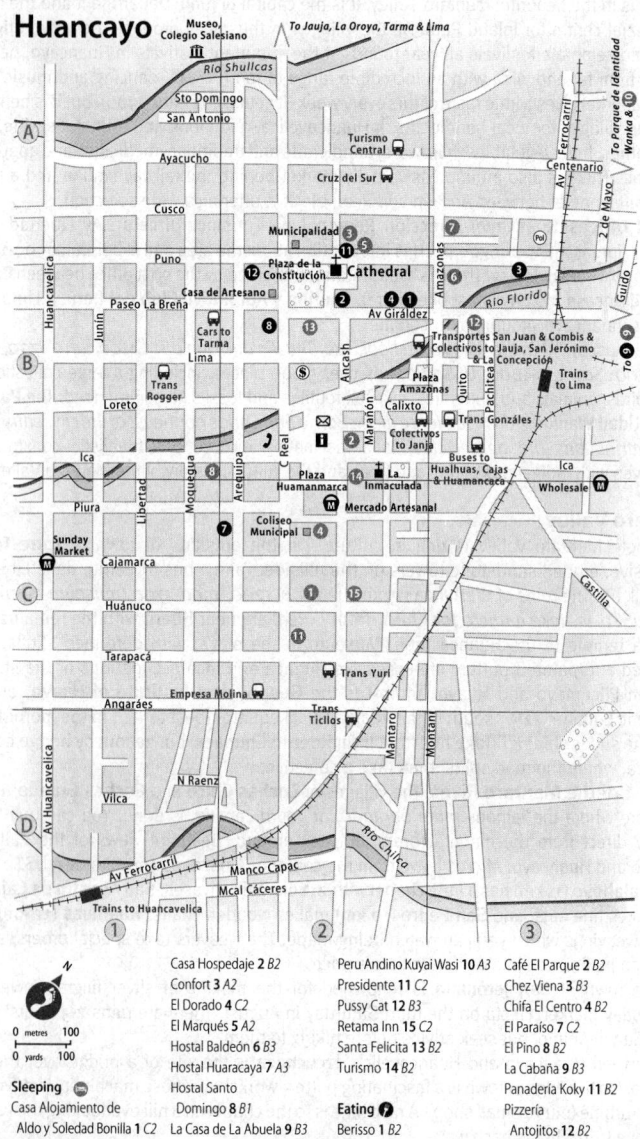

Huancayo

Museo,
Colegio Salesiano

To Jauja, La Oroya, Tarma & Lima

To Parque de Identidad Wanka &

Río Shullcas

Sto Domingo
San Antonio

Ayacucho

Turismo
Central

Cusco

Cruz del Sur

Municipalidad

Puno

Plaza de la
Constitución

Cathedral

Casa de Artesano

Paseo La Breña

Av Giráldez

Cars to
Tarma
Lima

Trans
Rogger

Loreto

Plaza
Amazonas

Calixto

Trans Gonzáles

Transportes San Juan & Combis &
Colectivos to Jauja, San Jerónimo &
La Concepción

Trains
to Lima

Ica

Colectivos
to Janja

Piura

Libertad

Plaza
Huamanmarca

La
Inmaculada

Buses to
Hualhuas, Cajas
& Huamancaca

Ica

Wholesale

Sunday
Market

Cajamarca

Coliseo
Municipal

Mercado Artesanal

Huánuco

Tarapacá

Trans Yuri

Angaráes

Empresa Molina

Trans
Ticllos

Vilca

N Raenz

Río Chilca

Av Ferrocarril

Manco Capac

Mcal Cáceres

Trains to Huancavelica

Huancavelica   Junín   Moquegua   Arequipa   C Real   Marañón   Ancash   Amazonas   Quito   Pachitca   Río Florido   Guido   Castilla   Centenario   Av Ferrocarril   2 de Mayo   Mantaro   Montano

N

0 metres 100
0 yards 100

Sleeping 🛏
Casa Alojamiento de
  Aldo y Soledad Bonilla **1** *C2*

Casa Hospedaje **2** *B2*
Confort **3** *A2*
El Dorado **4** *C2*
El Marqués **5** *A2*
Hostal Baldeón **6** *B3*
Hostal Huaracaya **7** *A3*
Hostal Santo
  Domingo **8** *B1*
La Casa de La Abuela **9** *B3*

Peru Andino Kuyai Wasi **10** *A3*
Presidente **11** *C2*
Pussy Cat **12** *B3*
Retama Inn **15** *C2*
Santa Felicita **13** *B2*
Turismo **14** *B2*

Eating 🍴
Berisso **1** *B2*

Café El Parque **2** *B2*
Chez Viena **3** *B3*
Chifa El Centro **4** *B2*
El Paraíso **7** *C2*
El Pino **8** *B2*
La Cabaña **9** *B3*
Panadería Koky **11** *B2*
Pizzería
  Antojitos **12** *B2*

Peru Huancayo & around Listings

C **Santa Felicita**, Giráldez 145, Plaza Constitución, T235285. Hot water, good.

D pp **Casa Alojamiento de Aldo y Soledad Bonilla**, Huánuco 332, half block from Mcal Cáceres bus station, T232103. Cheaper with- out full board, colonial house, owners speak English, laundry, secure, relaxing, nice court- yard, can arrange tours, best to book ahead. D **El Dorado**, Piura 452, T223947. Hot water, some rooms with TV in **C** category.

D **Hospedaje César Ada**, Pasaje Santa Teresa 294, El Tambo-3 Esquinas, 5 km from centre, T235615 for pick-up, wadaycesar@latin mail.com. Quiet, shared bath, garden, meals available, use of kitchen, breakfast included.

E **Confort**, Ancash 231, 1 block from the main Plaza, T233601. Rooms with hot water are nicer, but more expensive than those with cold water, all rooms good value, safe for bicycles, car parking US$1.

E **Hostal Huaracaya**, Amazonas 323. Hot water and TV, good value.

E **La Casa de la Abuela**, Av Giráldez 693, T223303. Hot shower, breakfast included, some rooms with antique beds, dormitory **F**, laundry facilities, meals available, sociable staff.

E **Pussy Cat**, Giráldez 359, T231565. **F** without bath, hot water, safe, luggage stored, comfortable beds.

F pp **Hostal Baldeón**, Amazonas 543, T231634. Kitchen and laundry facilities, nice patio, hot shower on request, basic rooms, safe, good value.

F **Hostal Santo Domingo**, Ica 655, T235461. Set around 2 pleasant patios, basic, good value.

F pp **Peru Andino Kuyai Wasi**, Pasaje San Antonio 113-115, on Av Centenario go 3 blocks from 2 de Mayo to San José, then 3 blocks left (north), 10-15 mins walk from the centre (if taking a taxi, stress that it's *Pasaje* San Antonio), T223956, www.geocities.com/ peruandino_1. Including breakfast, hot showers, several rooms with bath, safe area, cosy atmosphere, run by Sra Juana, daughter speaks some English, owner Luis runs trekking and mountain bike tours, cooking and laundry facilities, Spanish classes. Highly recommended.

G pp **Casa hospedaje**, Huamanmarca 125, T219980. Central, small, comfortable, hot water, shared showers, family run, nice atmosphere.

Mantaro Valley *p1245*
Izcuchaca has 1 hotel on the plaza, no bathroom, you have to use the public bath by the river; the other is just off

the plaza, a yellow 3-storey house, **G**, no shower, toilet suitable for men only, chamber pot supplied, only blankets on bed, cold.

❶ Eating

Huancayo *p1245, map p1246*
Breakfast is served in Mercado Modelo from 0700. Better class, more expensive restaurants, serving typical dishes for about US$4-5, plus 18% tax, drinks can be expensive. Lots of cheap restaurants along Av Giráldez serving set *menú*.

❦❦ **La Cabaña**, Av Giráldez 652. Pizzas, ice cream, *calentitos*, and other dishes, folk music at weekends.

❦❦ **Pizzería Antojitos**, Puno 599. Attractive, atmospheric pizzeria with live music some nights.

❦ **Chifa El Centro**, Giráldez 238. Chinese food, good service and atmosphere.

❦ **El Pino**, Real 539. Typical dishes for about US$2-3 and fixed price *menú*.

Cafés
Berisso, Giráldez 258. Good for cakes and quiche, friendly.

Café El Parque, Giráldez y Ancash, on the main plaza. Smart place to take coffee and cake.

Chanchamayo, Puno 209. Good little family café, cheap, good for breakfast.

Chez Viena, Puno 125. Another smart place serving good coffee and cakes.

Panadería Koky, Ancash y Puno. Good for breakfasts and pastries during the day.

El Paraíso, Arequipa 429. Good vegetarian food and service, great value.

Mantaro Valley *p1245*
❦ **Restaurant El Parque** on plaza, Izcuchaca. Opens 0700, delicious food.

❶ Bars and clubs

Huancayo *p1245, map p1246*
Café Billar, Paseo de Breña 133. Open 0900-2400, serves beer and snacks, pool tables.

El Cereco, Puno just below Plaza, near **Fuente de Soda El Inca**, good for late-night drinks, sandwiches, music videos, popular.

Clubs Most open around 2000 and close at 0200. Some charge an entrance fee of US$3-4.

Peñas All the *peñas* have folklore shows with dancing, open normally Fri, Sat and Sun from

● *For an explanation of the sleeping and eating price codes used in this guide, see inside the front*
● *cover. Other relevant information is found in Essentials pages 1075-1077.*

1300 to 2200. Entrance fee is about US$2 pp. Eg **Ollantaytambo**, Puno, block 2, and **Taki Wasi**, Huancavelica y 13 de Noviembre.

☺ Festivals and events

Huancayo *p1245, map p1246*
There are so many festivals in the Mantaro Valley that it is impossible to list them all. Nearly every day of the year there is some sort of celebration in one of the villages. This is a selection:

Jan: 1-6, New Year celebrations; 20, **San Sebastián y San Fabián** (recommended in Jauja). **Feb**: there are carnival celebrations for the whole month, with highlights on 2, **Virgen de la Candelaria**, and 17-19 **Concurso de Carnaval**. **Mar-Apr**: Semana Santa, with impressive Good Friday processions. **May**: Fiesta de las Cruces throughout the whole month. **Jun**: 15 **Virgen de las Mercedes**; 24, **San Juan Bautista**; 29, **Fiesta Patronal**. **Jul**: 16, **Virgen del Carmen**; 24-25, Santiago. **Aug**: 4, **San Juan de Dios**; 16, **San Roque**; 30, **Santa Rosa de Lima**. **Sep**: 8, **Virgen de Cocharcas**; 15, **Virgen de la Natividad**; 23-24, **Virgen de las Mercedes**; 29, **San Miguel Arcángel**. **Oct**: 4, **San Francisco de Asís**; 18, **San Lucas**; 28-30 culmination of month-long celebrations for **El Señor de los Milagros**. **Nov**: 1, **Día de Todos los Santos**. **Dec**: 3-13, **Virgen de Guadalupe**; 8, **Inmaculada Concepción**; 25, **Navidad** (Christmas).

☉ Shopping

Huancayo *p1245, map p1246*
Thieves in the market hand out rolled up paper and pick your pocket while you unravel them.
Crafts All crafts are made outside Huancayo in the many villages of the Mantaro Valley, or in Huancavelica. The villages are worth a visit to learn how the items are made.
Casa de Artesano, on the corner of Real and Paseo La Breña, at Plaza Constitución. Has a wide selection of good quality crafts.

▲ Activities and tours

Huancayo *p1245, map p1246*
Incas del Perú, next to La Cabaña restaurant (Av Giráldez 652), www.incasdelperu.com. Offers artesan and archaeological day tours, walking tours and mountain biking trips, US$35, which can include visits to Huamancaca prison on Fri. Incas del Perú also have maps and a book exchange, bicycle hire (US$15 per day).
Peruvian Tours, Puno 488, on the main plaza, T213069. Reputable organizer of tours to a variety of places in the Mantaro Valley.

Turismo Huancayo, C Real 517 oficina 6, T233351. Organizes local tours.
Wanka Tours, Real 550, T231743. Reputable organizer of tours to a variety of places in the Mantaro Valley.

⊙ Transport

Huancayo *p1245, map p1246*
Bus A new bus terminal for all buses to all destinations is planned 3 km north of the centre. There are regular buses to **Lima**, 6-7 hrs on a good paved road, US$10-13. Travelling by day is recommended for the fantastic views and, of course, for safety. If you must travel by night, take warm clothing. Recommended companies: **Ormeño**, Av Mcal Castilla 1379, El Tambo; **Cruz del Sur**, Ayacucho 281, T235650, and **Transportes Rogger**, Lima 561, T212687, *cama* and *semi-cama* at 1300 and 2330, comercial at 2230.

To **Ayacucho**, 319 km, 9-10 hrs, US$6.65-7.55. Molina, C Angaráes 334, T224501, 3 a day, recommended. The road is paved for the first 70 km, then in poor condition and is very difficult in the wet. Take warm clothing. (**Note**: If driving to Ayacucho and beyond, roads are "amazingly rough". Don't go alone. Count kilometres diligently to keep a record of where you are: road signs are poor.) After Izcuchaca, on the railway to Huancavelica, there is a good road to the Quichuas hydroelectric scheme, but thereafter it is narrow with hair-raising bends and spectacular bridges. The scenery is staggering.

To **Huancavelica**, 147 km, 5 hrs, US$2.85. Many buses daily, including **Transportes Yuri**, Ancash 1220, 3 a day. The road is in poor condition and takes much longer in the wet. The scenery is spectacular.

To **Cerro de Pasco**, 255 km, 5 hrs, US$4. Several departures. Alternatively, take a bus to La Oroya, about every 20 mins, from Av Real about 10 blocks north of the main plaza. From La Oroya there are regular buses and colectivos to Cerro. The road to La Oroya and on to Cerro is in good condition. To **Huánuco**, 7 hrs, **Turismo Central** at 2115, US$6, good service.

To **Chanchamayo**: Empresa San Juan, Ferrocarril 161 and Plaza Amazonas, and Tans Muruhuay each have an hourly service via Jauja to Tarma, 3 hrs, US$2.50, some of which continue on to La Merced, 5 hrs, US$4.

Some trucks and a few buses travel to **Cañete**, 289 km, 10 hrs, US$4. It is a poor road, with beautiful mountain landscapes before dropping into the valley of Cañete.

To **Jauja**, 44 km, 1 hr. Colectivos and combis leave every few mins from Huamanmarca y Amazonas, and Plaza Amazonas, US$1.50. Ones

via San Jerónimo and Concepción have 'Izquierda' on the front. Most buses to the Mantaro Valley leave from several places around the market area. Buses to **Hualhuas** and **Cajas** leave from block 3 of Pachitea. Buses to **Cochas** leave from Amazonas y Giráldez.
Train There are 2 unconnected railway stations. The Central station serves **Lima**, via La Oroya: Service on this railway with trains at weekends run by **Ferrocarril Centro Andino**, T01-361 2828, ext 222, www.ferroviasperu.com (at time of going to press, no details of service after Nov 2006). The fare is US$48 return. The train leaves Lima Fri 0700, arrives Huancayo 1800, returns Sun 1800, arrives Lima 0500. Coaches have reclining seats, heating, restaurant, tourist information, toilets, and nurse with first aid and oxygen.

From the small station in Chilca suburb (15 mins by taxi, US$1), trains run to **Huancavelica**, on a narrow gauge (3 ft). There are 2 trains: the *autovagón* (*expreso*) at 1300 daily, US$4, has 1st class and Buffet carriages. This "classic" Andean train journey takes 7 hrs and has fine views, passing through typical mountain villages where vendors sell food and crafts. There are 38 tunnels and the line reaches 3,676 m. The local train leaves at 0630 daily and takes 5 hrs. There are 1st, US$2.55, 2nd, US$2.20, and Buffet, US$4, classes. Services are often suspended, especially in the rainy season.

Mantaro Valley *p1245*
Train From **Huancavelica** arrive in Izcuchaca at 0800 and 1400-1430, then continue to **Huancayo**; US$1.70. Trains from Huancayo pass at around 0900 and 1600. They tend to be very crowded. Daily **colectivo** to Ayacucho at 1000-1100, 8 hrs.

❶ Directory

Huancayo *p1245, map p1246*
Banks BCP, Real 1039, changes TCs with no commission, cash advance on Visa. Banco Wiese, Real casi Ica. ATM does not accept international cards, poor rates for TCs. Interbank and Banco Continental are on block 6 of Real. There are several *casas de cambio* on Ancash; street changers hang out in front of Hotel Kiya. **Internet** Numerous places round Plaza Constitución on Giráldez, Paseo La Breña (eg Cyberwanka, No 173, very good) and Real; average price under US$0.75 per hr. **Language classes** Incas del Perú (see Activities and tours, above) organizes Spanish courses for beginners for US$100 per week, including accommodation at **Hostal La Casa de La Abuela**, Av Giráldez 691, and all meals, also homestays and weaving, playing traditional music, Peruvian cooking and lots of other things. **Katia Cerna** is a recommended teacher, T225332, katiacerna@hotmail.com. She can arrange home stays; her sister works in adventure tourism.

Huancavelica → *Phone code: 064. Colour map 3, grid C3. Population: 37,500. Altitude: 3,660 m.*

Huancavelica is a friendly and attractive town, surrounded by huge, rocky mountains. It was founded in the 16th century by the Spanish to exploit rich deposits of mercury and silver. It is predominantly an indigenous town, and people still wear traditional costume. There are beautiful mountain walks in the neighbourhood. The Cathedral, located on the Plaza de Armas, has an altar considered to be one of the finest examples of colonial art in Peru. Also very impressive are the five other churches in town. The church of San Francisco, for example, has no less than 11 altars. Sadly, though, most of the churches are closed to visitors. **Tourist office:** Dircetur ① *Jr Victoria Garma 444, T752938, huancavelica@mincetur.gob.pe.* Very helpful.

Bisecting the town is the Río Huancavelica. South of the river is the main commercial centre. North of the river, on the hillside, are the **thermal baths** ① *0600-1500, US$0.15 for private rooms, water not very hot, US$0.10 for the hot public pool, also hot showers, take a lock for the doors*. The handicraft sellers congregate in front of the Municipalidad on M Muñoz and the Biblioteco on the Plaza de Armas (V Toledo). Most handicrafts are transported directly to Lima, but you can still visit craftsmen in neighbouring villages. The Potaqchiz hill, just outside the town, gives a fine view, about one hour walk up from San Cristóbal. *Instituto Nacional de la Cultura*, Plaza San Juan de Dios, is a good source of information on festivals, archaeological sites, history, etc. Gives courses on music and dancing, and lectures some evenings. There is also an interesting but small **Museo Regional** ① *Mon-Sat 1000-1300, 1500-1900*.

Huancavelica to Ayacucho

The direct route from Huancavelica to Ayacucho (247 km) goes via **Santa Inés** (4,650 m), 78 km. Out of Huancavelica the road climbs steeply with switchbacks between herds of llamas and alpacas grazing on rocky perches. Around Pucapampa (Km 43) is one of the highest habitable *altiplanos* (4,500 m), where the rare and highly prized ash-grey alpaca can be seen. Snow-covered mountains are passed as the road climbs to 4,853 m at the Abra Chonta pass, 23 km before Santa Inés. By taking the turnoff to Huachocolpa at Abra Chonta and continuing for 3 km you'll reach the highest drivable pass in the world, at 5,059 m. Nearby are two lakes (Laguna Choclacocha) which can be visited in 2½ hours. 52 km beyond Santa Inés at the Abra de Apacheta (4,750 m), 98 km from Ayacucho, the rocks are all the colours of the rainbow, and running through this fabulous scenery is a violet river. See Transport, below, for road services and lodging options on this route.

There is another route to Ayacucho from Huancayo, little used by buses, but which involves not so much climbing for cyclists. Cross the pass into the Mantaro valley on the road to **Quichuas** . Then to **Anco** and **Mayocc** (lodging). From here the road crosses a bridge after 10 km and in another 20 km reaches **Huanta** (see page 1252). Then it's a paved road to Ayacucho.

● Sleeping

Huancavelica *p1249*
C **Presidente**, Plaza de Armas, T952760. Cheaper without bath, lovely colonial building, overpriced.
E **Camacho**, Jr Carabaya 481. Best of the cheap hotels, cheaper without bath, hot shower morning only, good value, safe.
E **San José**, Jr Huancayo, at top of Barranca (past Santo Domingo), T752958. Hot water 1700-1900, G without bath, nice beds, helpful.
F **Santo Domingo**, Av Barranca 366, T953086. Very basic, shared bath, cold water.
F **Savoy**, Av Muñoz 294 (no sign). Very basic, shared bath, cold water.

Huancavelica to Ayacucho *p1249*
G **Alojamiento Andino**, Santa Inés, a very friendly restaurant, El Favorito, where you can sleep, and several others.
G **Hostal Recreo Sol y Sombra**, Quichuas. Charming, small courtyard, helpful, basic.
G **Hostal Gabi**, Anco. Appalling, but better than anything else.

● Eating

Huancavelica *p1249*
There are lots of cheap, basic restaurants on C Muñoz and Jr Virrey Toledo. All serve typical food, mostly with set *menú*, US$1.50. There are also *chifas* on Virrey Toledo. ♦♦-♦ **Mochica Sachún**, Av Virrey Toledo 303. Great *menú* US$1.50, otherwise expensive.
♦ **Cami**, Barranca y Toledo. No sign, small, lively, good set menus and juices.
♦ **La Casona**, Jr Virrey Toledo 230. Cheap and good *menú*, also a *peña*.

● Festivals and events

Huancavelica *p1249*
The whole area is rich in culture. Fiesta de los Reyes Magos y los Pastores, 4-8 Jan. Fiesta del Niño Perdido is held on **2nd Sun in Jan**. Pukllaylay Carnavales, celebration of the first fruits from the ground (harvest), **20 Jan-mid Mar**. Semana Santa, Holy Week. Toro Pukllay festival **last week of May, 1st week of Jun**. Fiesta de Santiago is held in **May and Aug** in all communities. Los Laygas or Galas (scissors dance), **22-28 Dec**.

● Transport

Huancavelica *p1249*
Bus All bus companies have their offices on, and leave from the east end of town, around Parque M Castilla, on Muñoz, Iquitos, Tumbes and O'Donovan. To **Huancayo**, 147 km, 5 hrs, US$2.85, rough road, Transportes Yuri and Transportes Ticllas (O'Donovan 500). To **Lima** via Huancayo, 445 km, 13 hrs minimum, US$5.70. Most buses to Huancayo go on to Lima, there are several a day. The other route is to **Pisco**, 269 km, 12 hrs, US$7 and **Ica**, US$8, 1730 daily, with Oropesa, O'Donovon 599. Buy your ticket 1 day in advance. The road is poor until it joins the Ayacucho-Pisco road, where it improves. Most of the journey is done at night. Be prepared for sub-zero temperatures in the early morning as the bus passes snowfields, then for temperatures of 25-30°C as the bus descends to the coast.
Train See under Huancayo; the *autovagón* leaves for Huancayo daily at 0630, the local train at 1300, daily.

Huancavelica to Ayacucho *p1249*
There is no direct transport from Huancavelica to Ayacucho, other than 0430 on Sat with **San Juan Bautista** (Plazoleta Túpac Amaru 107, T803062), US$5.70. Otherwise you have to go to **Rumichaca** just beyond Santa Inés on the paved Pisco-Ayacucho road, also **San Juan Bautista** 0430, 4 hrs, then wait for a passing bus to Ayacucho at 1500, US$2, or try to catch a truck. Rumichaca has only a couple of foodstalls and some filthy toilets. This route is the highest continuous road in the world. The journey is a cold one but spectacular as the road rarely

drops below 4,000 m for 150 km. The best alternative is to take a colectivo Huancavelica-**Lircay**, a small village with **F** unnamed hostal at Sucre y La Unión, with bath and hot water, much better than Hostal El Paraíso, opposite, also with bath, **G** without (**Transportes 5 de Mayo**, Av Sebastián Barranca y Cercado, US$4.55, 2½ hrs, leave when full). The same company runs from Lircay Terminal Terrestre hourly from 0430 to Julcamarca (colonial church, **Hostal Villa Julcamarca**, near plaza, no tap water, really basic), 2½ hrs, US$3, then take a minibus from Julcamarca plaza to Ayacucho, US$2, 2 hrs; beautiful scenery all the way. Another option is to take the train to Izcuchaca, stay the night and take the colectivo (see above).

❶ Directory

Huancavelica p1249
Banks BCP, Virrey Toledo 300 block. There is a *Multired* ATM on M Muñoz in front of the Municipalidad. **Internet** Despite what they say, internet places open around 0900 till 2100-2200. There are places on V Toledo and M Muñoz. **Librería Municipal**, Plaza de Armas, US$0.60 per hr. **Post offices** Ferrua box, at block 8 of M Muñoz. **Telephones** Carabaya y Virrey Toledo.

Ayacucho → *Phone code: 066. Colour map 3, grid C3. Population: 105,918. Altitude: 2,748 m.*

A week can easily be spent enjoying Ayacucho and its hinterland. The climate is lovely, with warm, sunny days and pleasant balmy evenings, and the people are very hospitable. Semana Santa celebrations are famous throughout South America. Ayacucho was founded on 9 January 1539. On the Pampa de Quinua, on 9 December 1824, the decisive Battle of Ayacucho was fought, bringing Spanish rule in Peru to an end. In the middle of the festivities, the Liberator Simón Bolívar decreed that the city be named Ayacucho, 'City of Blood', instead of its original name, Huamanga.

The city is built round the Plaza Mayor, the main plaza, with the Cathedral, Municipalidad, Universidad Nacional de San Cristóbal de Huamanga (UNSCH) and various colonial mansions facing on to it. It is famous for its Semana Santa celebrations, its splendid market and its 33 churches. **Tourist offices**: i perú ① *Portal Municipal 48, on the Plaza, T818305, iperuayacucho@promperu.gob.pe, daily 0830-1930, Sun 0830-1430*. Very helpful. **Dirección Regional de Industria y Turismo** (Dircetur) ① *Asamblea 481, T812548. Mon-Fri 0800-1300*, friendly and helpful. **Tourist Police** ① *Arequipa cuadra 1, T312055.*

Sights

The **Cathedral** ① *daily 1700-1900, Sun 0900-1700*, built in 1612, has superb gold leaf altars. It is beautifully lit at night. On the north side of the Plaza Mayor, on the corner of Portal de la Unión and Asamblea, are the **Casonas de los Marqueses de Mozobamba y del Pozo**, also called Velarde-Alvarez. The **Museo de Arte Popular Joaquín López Antay** ① *Portal de la Unión 28, in the BCP building, museo@ unsch.edu.pe, Tue-Fri 1030-1700, Sat 1030-1230*, displays local craft work. North of the Plaza is **Santo Domingo** (1548) ① *9 de Diciembre, block 2, Mass daily 0700-0800*. Its fine façade has triple Roman arches and Byzantine towers.

Jr 28 de Julio is pedestrianized for two blocks. A stroll down here leads to the prominent **Arco del Triunfo** (1910), which commemorates victory over the Spaniards. Through the arch is the church of **San Francisco de Asís** (1552) ① *28 de Julio , block 3, daily for morning mass and 1730-1830*. It has an elaborate gilt main altar and several others. Across 28 de Julio from San Fancisco is the **Mercado de Abastos Carlos F Vivanco**, the packed central market. As well as all the household items and local produce, look for the cheese sellers,the breads and the section dedicated to fruit juices.

Santa Clara de Asís ① *Jr Grau, block 3, open for Mass*, is renowned for its beautifully delicate coffered ceiling. It is open for the sale of sweets and cakes made by the nuns (go to the door at Nazarenas 184, it's usually open). On the 5th block of 28 de Julio is the late 16th-century **Casona Vivanco**, which houses the **Museo Andrés A Cáceres** ① *Jr 28 de Julio 508, T066-812360, Mon-Sat 0900-1300, 1400-1800. US$1.25*. The museum has baroque painting, colonial furniture, republican and contemporary art, and exhibits on Mariscal Cáceres' battles in the War of the Pacific. Further south still, on a pretty plazuela, is **Santa Teresa** (1683) ① *28 de Julio, block 6, daily Mass, usually 1600*, with its monastery. The nuns here sell sweets and crystallized fruits and a *mermelada de ají*, made to recipe given

Peru Ayacucho

to them by God; apparently it is not picante. **San Cristóbal** ① *Jr 28 de Julio, block 6, rarely open*, was the first church to be founded in the city (1540), and is one of the oldest in South America. With its single tower, it is tiny compared with Santa Teresa, which is opposite.

The 16th-century church of **La Merced** ① *2 de Mayo, block, open for Mass*, is the second oldest in the city. The high choir is a good example of the simplicity of the churches of the early period of the Viceroyalty. **Casa Jáuregui**, opposite, is also called **Ruiz de Ochoa** after its original owner. Its outstanding feature is its doorway, which has a blue balcony supported by two fierce beasts with erect penises.

Museo de Anfasep (Asociación Nacional de Familiares de Secuestrados Detenidos y Desaparecidos del Perú) ① *Prol Libertad 1226, www.dhperu.org/anfasep, 15 mins' walk fro Mercado Artesanal Shosake Nagase, or mototaxi, entry free but give a donation*, provides an insight into the recent history of this region during the violence surrounding the Sendero Luminoso campaign and the government's attempts to counter it.

For a fascinating insight into Inca and pre-Inca art and culture, a visit to **Barrio Santa Ana** is a must. The district is full of *artesanía* shops, galleries and workshops (eg **Galería de Arte Latina** ① *Plazuela de Santa Ana 105, T528315, wari39@ hotmail.com*, and **Wari Art Gallery** ① *Jr Mcal Cáceres 302, T812529*). Galleries are closed on Sunday.

Excursions

The Inca ruins of **Vilcashuamán** are 120 km the south, beyond Cangallo. John Hemming writes: "There is a five-tiered, stepped *usnu* platform faced in fine Inca masonry and topped by a monolithic two-seat throne. The parish church is built in part of the Inca sun temple and rests on stretches of Inca terracing. Vilcashuamán was an important provincial capital, the crossroads where the road from Cuzco to the Pacific met the empire's north-south highway." Tours can be arranged with Travel Agencies in Ayacucho, US$13 per person, only with eight passengers, full day tour (0500-1800), including **Intihuatana** (Inca baths about one hour uphill from the village of Vischongo, one hour from Vilcashuamán, five from Ayacucho, also Puya Raimondi plants); alternatively stay overnight (three hotels, **G**, basic but clean). Market day is Wednesday. Buses and colectivos run from Avenida M Castilla, daily 0400-1500, four hours, US$3.

A good road going north from Ayacucho leads to **Huari** ① *22 km from Ayacucho, 0800-1700, US$0.90*, dating from the 'Middle Horizon'(AD 600-1000), when the Huari culture spread across most of Peru. This was the first urban walled centre in the Andes. The huge irregular stone walls are up to 3-4 m high and rectangular houses and streets can be made out. The most important activity here was artistic: ceramics, gold, silver, metal and alloys such as bronze, which was used for weapons and for decorative objects. The ruins now lie in an extensive *tuna* cactus forest (don't pick the fruit). There is a museum at the site.

Quinua village, 37 km northeast of Ayacucho, has a charming cobbled main plaza and many of the buildings have been restored. There is a small market on Sunday. Nearby, on the Pampa de Quinua, a 44 m-high obelisk commemorates the battle of Ayacucho. The village's handicrafts are recommended, especially ceramics. Most of the houses have miniature ceramic churches on the roof. San Pedro Ceramics, at the foot of the hill leading to the monument, and Mamerto Sánchez, Jr Sucre, should be visited, but there are many others. *Fiesta de la Virgen de Cocharcas*, around 8 September. Trips can be arranged to Huari, La Quinua village and the battlefield; US$7.55 per person, minimum four people. Combis leave from Paradero a Huari Quinua, corner of Jr Ciro Alegría and Jr Salvador Cavero, when full from 0700; 40 minutes to Huari, US$0.75, then on to Quinua, 25 minutes, US$0.50 (US$1 from Ayacucho - ask the driver to go all the way to the Obelisco for an extra US$0.50).

The Huanta valley is a picturesque region, 48 km northeast of Ayacucho. The town of Huanta is one hour from Ayacucho, on the road to Huancayo (US$0.90 by combi). From Huanta, several lakes can be visited (difficult in rainy season), also the valley of Luricocha, 5 km away, with its warm climate. Huanta celebrates the *Fiesta de las Cruces* during the first week of May. Its Sunday market is large and interesting. There are places to stay and eat around the Plaza.

On the road to Huanta 24 km from Ayacucho, is the site of perhaps the oldest known culture in South America, 20,000 years old, evidence of which was found in the cave of **Pikimachay**. The remains are now in Lima's museums.

Ayacucho

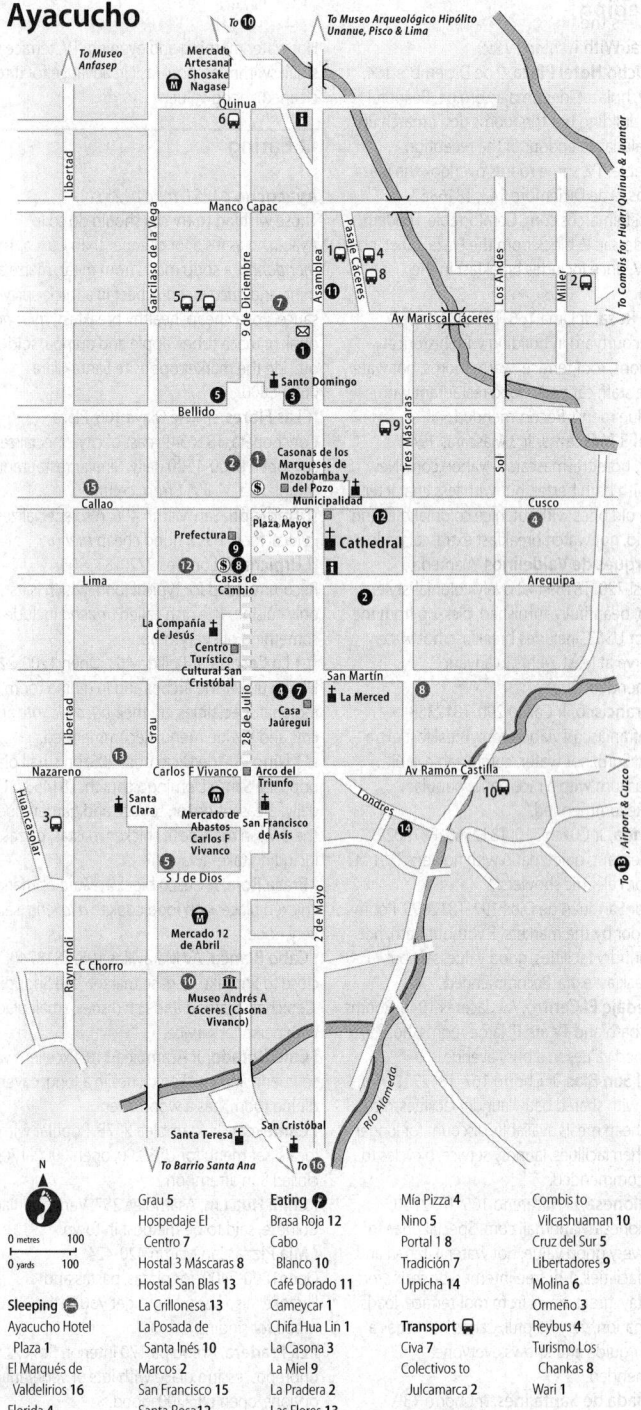

To 🔟

To Museo Arqueológico Hipólito Unanue, Pisco & Lima

To Museo Anfasep

Mercado Artesanal Shosake Nagase Ⓜ

Quinua

6 🚌

🅸

Manco Capac

Libertad

Garcilaso de la Vega

9 de Diciembre

Asamblea

Pasaje Cáceres

Los Andes

Miller

To Combis for Huari Quinua & Juantar

5 🚌 7 🚌

7 ⓘ

1 🚌 4
8
11

2 🚌

Av Mariscal Cáceres

✉ ①

Santo Domingo 🕆 ①
③

Bellido

⑤

Tres Máscaras

Sol

9 🚌

② ① Casonas de los Marqueses de Mozobamba y del Pozo
Ⓢ Municipalidad

Cusco

Callao

⑮

Prefectura

12 🅿

Lima

12 ⑨ Ⓢ ⑧ Casas de Cambio

Plaza Mayor 🏛

Cathedral 🕆

ⓘ

② Arequipa

④

La Compañía de Jesús 🕆

Centro Turístico Cultural San Cristóbal

28 de Julio

Grau

Libertad

Casa Jaúregui ④ ⑦

San Martín

La Merced 🕆

⑧ ②

Peru Ayacucho

Nazareno

⑬

Carlos F Vivanco ⓘ Arco del Triunfo

Av Ramón Castilla

Londres

Huancasolar

3 🚌

🕆 Santa Clara

Mercado de Abastos Carlos F Vivanco Ⓜ

San Francisco de Asís 🕆

10 🚌

14

To ⑬ **, Airport & Cuzco**

S J de Dios

⑤

2 de Mayo

Raymondi

C Chorro

Mercado 12 de Abril Ⓜ

Museo Andrés A Cáceres (Casona Vivanco) 🔟 🏛

Río Alameda

Santa Teresa 🕆

San Cristóbal 🕆

Santa Ana

To Barrio Santa Ana

To ⑯

N 👣

0 metres 100
0 yards 100

Grau **5**	**Eating** 🍴	Mía Pizza **4**
Hospedaje El Centro **7**	Brasa Roja **12**	Nino **5**
Hostal 3 Máscaras **8**	Cabo Blanco **10**	Portal 1 **8**
Hostal San Blas **13**	Café Dorado **11**	Tradición **7**
La Crillonesa **13**	Cameycar **1**	Urpicha **14**
Sleeping 🛏	La Casona **3**	**Transport** 🚌
Ayacucho Hotel Plaza **1**	La Miel **9**	Civa **7**
El Marqués de Valdelirios **16**	La Pradera **2**	Colectivos to Julcamarca **2**
Florida **4**	Las Flores **13**	

La Posada de Santa Inés **10**
Marcos **2**
San Francisco **15**
Santa Rosa **12**

Chifa Hua Lin **1**

Combis to Vilcashuaman **10**
Cruz del Sur **5**
Libertadores **9**
Molina **6**
Ormeño **3**
Reybus **4**
Turismo Los Chankas **8**
Wari **1**

1253

● Sleeping

Ayacucho *p1251, map p1253*

A **Ayacucho Hotel Plaza**, 9 de Diciembre 184, T812202, hplaza@derramajae.org.pe. Beautiful colonial building but the rooms don't match up to the palatial splendour of the reception, comfortable, TV, some rooms overlook the plaza.
C **Marcos**, 9 de Diciembre 143, T816867, www.hostalmarcos.com. Comfortable, modern, in a cul-de-sac ½ block from the Plaza, quiet, hot water, TV, price includes breakfast in the cafetería.
C **Santa Rosa**, Jr Lima 166, T812083. Lovely colonial courtyard in building with historical associations, roof terrace, warm rooms, hot water, attentive staff, car park, good restaurant with good value menú. Recommended.
D **Hostal 3 Máscaras**, Jr 3 Máscaras 194, T812921, hoteltresmascaras@yahoo.com. New rooms with bath better, but with less character, than the old ones without, nice colonial building with patio, hot water, breakfast extra, car park.
D **El Marqués de Valdelirios**, Alameda Bolognesi 720, T818944. Lovely colonial-style mansion, beautifully-furnished, pick-up from the airport for US$3, includes breakfast, hot water, bar, reserve at least 24 hrs in advance. Recommended.
D **San Francisco**, Jr Callao 290, T812353, hotelsanfrancisco@viabcp.com. Breakfast extra (none on Sun), hot water, comfortable, a bit like a museum with a nice patio, popular choice. Recommended.
D-E **Florida**, Jr Cuzco 310, T812565, F816029. Small, pleasant, quiet, patio with flowers, TV, hot water from electric showers.
E **Grau**, Jr San Juan de Dios 192, T812695. Rooms on 3rd floor by the markets, F without bath, hot water, laundry facilities, good value, safe but noisy, breakfast extra. Recommended.
E **Hospedaje El Centro**, Av Cáceres 1048. Rooms without bath and TV are F, large rooms, hot water, good value, on a busy avenue.
E **Hostal San Blas**, Jr Chorro 167, T812712. Hot water, F with shared bath, laundry facilities, nice rooms, cheap meals available, discount for longer stay, kitchen facilities, laundry service, bicycles to lend. Recommended.
E **La Crillonesa**, El Nazareno 165, T812350, hotelcrillonesa@latinmail.com. Special price for tourists, very good value, hot water, kitchen and laundry facilities, 1 hr free internet, discount for longer stay, great views from roof terrace, loads of information, very helpful, Carlos will act as a local tour guide and knows everyone. Recommended.
F **La Posada de Santa Inés**, Jr Chorro 139, T819544, posada_staines@hotmail.com.

Hot water morning and evening, TV, terrace with small swimming pool (ask in advance for it to be cleaned), good value.

● Eating

Ayacucho *p1251, map p1253*

Those wishing to try *cuy* should do so in Ayacucho as it's a lot cheaper than Cuzco. Try *mondongo*, a soup made from meat, maize and mint, and *puca picante*, beef in a thick, spicy sauce. For a cheap, healthy breakfast, try *maca*, a drink of maca tuber, apple and quinoa, sold outside the market opposite Santa Clara, 0600-0800.

♍ **Las Flores**, Jr José Olaya 106, Plaza Conchopata, T816349, east of city. Specializes in *cuy*, open 0900-1900 daily. Similar restaurants on this plaza, taxi US$1 from centre.
♍ **Tradición**, San Martín 406. Also specializes in local food; has a good cheap *menú*.
♍ **Urpicha**, Jr Londres 272, T813905. Recommended for typical food, which is its only cuisine. The dish called *urpicha* includes something of everything.
♍-♉ **La Casona**, Jr Bellido 463. Open 1200-2200. Dining under the arches and in dining room, regional specialities, try their *puca picante* and *cuy*, and a wide menu. Recommended.
♍-♉ **Nino**, Jr 9 de Diciembre 205, on small plaza opposite Santo Domingo church, T814537. Open daily, pleasant decor, terrace and garden (look for the owls in the trees); chicken, pastas, pizzas, including take-away.
♉ **Brasa Roja**, Jr Cuzco block 1. More upmarket chicken place with food cooked *a la leña*, salads, very good.
♉ **Cabo Blanco**, Av Maravillas 198, T818740, close to Shosaku Nagase market (see Shopping). Cebiches, seafood and fish dishes, small place with personal service.
♉ **Café Dorado**, Jr Asamblea 310. Excellent value set menu and chicken dishes in a long, cavernous dining room, has a wood oven.
♉ **Cameycar**, Jr Asamblea 257B. Popular with locals, set menu for US$0.90, open 0900-1700, closed Sun afternoon.
♉ **Chifa Hua Lin**, Asamblea 257. Very popular Chinese, said to be the best in town.
♉ **Mía Pizza**, San Martín 420-424. Open1800-2400, for pizzas, pastas and karaoke (also has a bar to get you in the mood for singing).
♉ **La Pradera**, Arequipa 170 interior. Basic, unprepossessing place with lots of vegetarian options, open till 2200, good.

Cafés

Centro Turístico Cultural San Cristóbal, 28 de Julio 178, some expensive cafés (eg **Lalo's**, No 115, open 0900-2100, **New York**, No 114) as well as other restaurants; all have tables in the pleasant courtyard.

La Miel, Portal Constitución 11-12, 2 locations. Good coffee, hot drinks, juices, shakes, cakes and snacks, also ice creams.

Portal 1, Portal Constitución 1. A good café on the corner of the plaza serving snacks, light meals and ice cream.

⊛ Festivals and events

Ayacucho *p1251, map p1253*
The area is well-known for its festivals throughout the year. Almost every day there is a celebration in one of the surrounding villages. Check with the tourist office. **Carnival in Feb** is reported as a wild affair. **Semana Santa** begins on the Fri before Holy Week. There follows one of the world's finest Holy Week celebrations, with candle-lit nightly processions, floral 'paintings' on the streets, daily fairs (the biggest on Easter Saturday), horse races and contests among peoples from all central Peru. All accommodation is fully booked for months in advance. Many people offer beds in their homes during the week. Look out for notices on the doors, especially on Jr Libertad. **25 Apr**: anniversary of the founding of Huamanga province.

⊙ Shopping

Ayacucho *p1251, map p1253*
Handicrafts Ayacucho is a good place to buy local crafts including filigree silver, which often uses *mudéjar* patterns. Also look out for little painted altars which show the manger scene, carvings in local alabaster, harps, or the pre-Inca tradition of carving dried gourds. The most famous goods are carpets and *retablos*. In both weaving and *retablos*, scenes of recent political strife have been added to more traditional motifs. For carpets, go to Barrio Santa Ana, see under Sights above. **Familia Pizarro**, Jr San Cristóbal 215, Barrio Belén. Works in textiles and *piedra huamanga* (local alabaster), good quality.
Mercado 12 de Abril, Chorro y San Juan de Dios. For fruit and vegetables **Shosaku Nagase**, on Jr Quinua. A large new handicraft market.

▲ Activities and tours

Ayacucho *p1251, map p1253*
Urpillay Tours, Portal Independencia 62, T815074, urpillaytours@terra.com. All local tours

and flight tickets. **Wari Tours**, Portal Independencia 70, T811415. Recommended for local tours. Also handles Ormeño bus tickets and Western Union. **Warpa Picchu**, Portal Independencia 66, T815191, www.warpa picchu.com. All the regular tours, but with an ecotourism angle. **Willy Tours**, Jr 9 de Diciembre 107, T814075. Personal guides, also handles flight and bus tickets.

⊙ Transport

Ayacucho *p1251, map p1253*
Air From/to **Lima** with Aerocóndor (9 de Diciembre 123, T813060), 3 times a week, and to **Andahuaylas** once a week. LC Busre (Jr Lima 178, T816012) flies from/to Lima daily.
Bus To **Lima**, 9-10 hrs on a good paved road, via Ica (7 hrs). For **Pisco**, 332 km, 6 hrs, take a Ica/Lima bus and get out at San Clemente, 10 mins from Pisco, and take a bus or combi (same fare to San Clemente as for Ica). Companies include: **Wari**, Pasaje Cáceres (opposite ReyBus), US$5.15 at 1800; and **Reybus**, Pasaje Cáceres 166, US$5.80. More expensive are **Libertadores**, Tres Máscaras 493, T813614, **Molina**, Jr 9 de Diciembre 458, T812984, 6 a day US$7.55-15.15; **Ormeño**, Jr Libertad 257, T812485, US$7.55 and US$12; **Civa**, Av Mcal Cáceres 1242, T819948, US$10, and **Cruz del Sur**, Av Mcal Cáceres 1264, T812813, US$15.15.

To **Huancayo**, 319 km, 9-10 hrs, US$6.65- 7.55. Daily with **Molina**, 3 a day. The road is paved but poor as far as Huanta, thereafter it is rough, especially in the wet season, except for the last 70 km (paved). The views are breathtaking.

For **Huancavelica**, take an Ormeño 0730 bus as far as **Rumichaca**, US$2, where combis wait at 1030 for Huancavelica, 4 hrs. Otherwise take a Huancayo bus as far as **Izcuchaca**, then take another bus, a longer route.

⊙ Directory

Ayacucho *p1251, map p1253*
Banks BCP, Portal Unión 28. No commission on TCs, cash advance on Visa, Visa ATM. Interbank, Jr 9 de Diciembre 183. ATM for Visa, Mastercard/Cirrus and AmEx. Opening hours 0915-1315, 1630-1830, Sat 0930-1230. Many street changers and *casas de cambio* at Portal Constitución on Plaza, good rate for cash.
Internet All over the centre. Connections and machines are good, average price is US$0.60 per hr, some charge US$0.90 at night. All 0800-2300 daily. **Post office** Asamblea 293. **Telephones** Many phone offices in the centre.

Ayacucho to Cuzco

A week can easily be spent enjoying Ayacucho and its hinterland. The climate is lovely, with warm, sunny days and pleasant balmy evenings, and the people are very hospitable. Semana Santa celebrations are famous throughout South America. Beyond Ayacucho are two highland towns, Andahuaylas and Abancay, which are possible stopping, or bus-changing places on the road to Cuzco. The road towards Cuzco climbs out of Ayacucho and crosses a wide stretch of high, treeless páramo before descending through Ocros to the Río Pampas (6 hours from Ayacucho). It then climbs up to **Chincheros**, 158 km from Ayacucho, and Uripa (good Sunday market).

Andahuaylas is about 80 km further on, in a fertile valley. It offers few exotic crafts, but beautiful scenery, great hospitality and a good market on Sunday. On the north side is the Municipalidad, with a small **Museo Arqueológico**, which has a good collection of pre-Columbian objects, including mummies. A good nearby excursion is to the **Laguna de Pacucha** ① *colectivo from Av Los Chankas y Av Andahuaylas, at the back of the market, US$0.75, 40 mins*. On the shore is the town of Pacucha and various places to eat. A road follows the north shore of the lake and a turn-off climbs to **Sóndor** ① *US$0.60 (beware overcharging by the guardian)*, an Inca archaeological site at 3,300 m. Various buildings and small plazas lead up to a conical hill with concentric stone terracing and, at the summit, a large rock or *intihuatana*. Each 18-19 June Sóndor Raymi is celebrated. Taxi from Andahuaylas, US$10; walk from Pachuca 8-10 km, or take a colectivo to Argama (also behind Andahuaylas market), which passes the entrance. With any form of public transport you will have to walk back to Pacucha, unless very lucky. **Tourist office: Dircetur** ① *Av Túpac Amaru 374, T721627*.

Nestled between mountains in the upper reaches of a glacial valley, the friendly town of **Abancay** *(Phone code: 084, Altitude 2,378 m)* is first glimpsed when you are many kilometres away. The town is growing in importance now that the paved Lima-Nazca-Cuzco road passes through. **Tourist office: Dircetur**, Av Arenas 121, p 1, T321664. **Santuario Nacional de Ampay**, north of town, has lagoons called Angasccocha (3,200 m) and Uspaccocha (3,820 m), a glacier on Ampay mountain at 5,235 m and flora and fauna typical of these altitudes. By public transport, take a colectivo to Tamburco and ask the driver where to get off. To get to the glacier you need two days trekking, with overnight camping. See page 1241 for sites of interest between Abancay and Cuzco, eg Saywite, page 1242.

⬤ Sleeping

Andahuaylas *p1256*

C El Encanto de Oro, Av Pedro Casafranca 424, T723066, www.encantodeoro.4t.com. Modern, comfy, good facilities, breakfast included, TV, hot water, laundry service, restaurant, organizes trips on request. Reserve in advance.

D Sol de Oro, Jr Juan A Trelles 164, T721152, soldeorohotel@hotmail.com. Includes breakfast, hot water, TV, laundry service, garage, tourist information, restaurant alongside, near buses.

E El Encanto de Apurímac, Jr Ramos 401 (near Los Chankas and other buses), T723527. With bath, hot water, TV, very helpful.

F Las Américas, Jr Ramos 410. Also near buses, a bit gloomy in public areas, but rooms are fine if basic, **G** without bath, hot water, helpful.

G Hostal Waliman, Av Andahuaylas 266. Basic, cold water in shared bathrooms, helpful, may have vegetarian restaurant by now.

Abancay *p1256*

B-D Turistas, Av Díaz Barcenas 500, T321017, hotursa@terra.com.pe. New block added to the

original building, totally refurbished, quiet, gardens, travel agency, internet, parking, good restaurant.

C-D Imperial, Díaz Barcenas 517, T321578. Great beds and hot water, spotless, very helpful, parking, good value, rooms also available without bath or breakfast.

D-E El Dorado, Jr Arenas 131, T322005. A good place to stay, with a small garden, comfortable rooms have an oriental feel, hot water, TV, breakfast extra.

F Apurímac Tours, Jr Cuzco 421, T321446. New building, rooms with bath have tiny bathrooms, hot water, breakfast and lunch extra in *comedor* in courtyard, good value, helpful.

❶ Eating

Andahuaylas *p1256*

❢ **El Dragón**, Jr Juan A Trellas 279. A recommended chifa serving huge portions, excellent value (same owner as Hotel El Encanto de Apurímac).

¶ Il Gatto, Jr G Cáceres 334. A warm pizzería, with wooden furniture, pizzas cooked in a wood-burning oven.

¶ Nuevo Horizonte, Jr Constitución 426. Vegetarian and health food restaurant, open for breakfast.

Abancay *p1256*

¶ Focarela Pizza's, Díaz Bárcenas 521. Simple but pleasant decor, pizza from a wood-burning oven, popular.

¶ Il Giardino, Díaz Bárcenas 500 block opposite Hotel Turistas. *Pollo a la leña*, typical dishes, *parrilladas* and other specials in smart atmosphere.

¶ Los Portales, Av Arenas at the plazuela opposite Hotel El Dorado. Good chifa with friendly service (one staff member speaks English), lunches are excellent value and other dishes are plentiful.

▲ Activities and tours

Abancay *p1256*

Hotel Turistas runs one and two-day tours to Santuario Nacional de Ampay: 1-day, 7 hours, US$40 pp for 1-2 people (cheaper for more people).

Karlop Andean Trek, T961 4297, karlop_36@ hotmail.com. Guides tours to local sites, camping equipment, horse riding.

Carlos Valer, guide in Abancay - ask for him at Hotel Turistas, very knowledgeable and kind.

⊖ Transport

Ayacucho to Cuzco *p1256*

Ayacucho to Andahuaylas, 261 km, takes 10-11 hrs (more in the rainy season), the road is unpaved but in good condition when dry, but landslides occur in the wet. The scenery is stunning. Daytime buses stop for lunch at Chumbes (4½ hrs), which has a few restaurants, a shop selling fruit, bread and refrescos, and some grim toilets. **Molina** passes through from Lima en route to Andahuaylas at 2200, check if there is a seat; **Wari** at 0400; **Los Chankas**, Pasaje Cáceres 144, T812391, at 0630 (good) and 1900, all US$7.55. Only Los Chankas' 1900 service is direct to **Cuzco**, US$12, but you still

have to change buses in Andahuaylas. There are no other direct buses to Abancay or Cuzco.

Andahuaylas to Ayacucho: Wari, Av José María Arguedas opposite El Piloto petrol station, at 0800; **Los Chankas**, Av José María Arguedas y Jr Trelles, T722441, 0600 and 1800 or 1840, one coming from Cuzco. To **Abancay**, Señor de Huanca, Av Martinelli 170, T721218, 3 a day, 5 hrs, US$3.40; **Los Chankas** at 0630, US$4. To **Cuzco**, San Jerónimo, Av José María Arguedas 425, T801767, via Abancay, 1800 or 1830, also 1900 Sun, US$6, and **Los Chankas**. To **Lima**, buses go via Abancay or Pampachiri and Puquio: **Wari** take the latter route, 3 a day, US$15.15. **Molina**, Av José María Arguedas y Av Lázaro Castilla, over the bridge, takes both routes to Lima, 1000 via Ayacucho, 1045 and 1600 via Pampachiri, US$15.15. Also to Abancay and Cuzco at 1900. On all night buses, take a blanket.

In **Abancay**, 138 km from Andahuaylas, 5 hrs, the new Terminal Terrestre is on Av Pachacútec, on the west side of town. Taxi to centre US$0.60, otherwise it's a steep walk up to the centre. Several companies have offices on or near the El Olivo roundabout at Av Díaz Bárcenas y Gamarra, others on Av Arenas. Buses go to **Cuzco, Andahuaylas,** and **Nazca** (464 km, via Chalhuanca and Puquio), continuing to **Lima**. To **Cuzco**, 195 km, takes 4½ hrs, US$4.55. The scenery en route is dramatic, especially as it descends into the Apurímac valley and climbs out again.

Bus companies, all leave from Terminal Terrestre; office addresses are given: Bredde, Gamarra 423,T321643, 5 a day to Cuzco. **Cruz del Sur**, Díaz Bárcenas 1151, T323028. **Los Chankas,** Díaz Bárcenas 1011, El Olivo, T321485. **Molina**, Gamarra 422, T322646. 3 a day to Lima US$13.65-16.65, 3 a day to Cuzco, to Andahuaylas at 2330. **San Jerónimo**, to Cuzco at 2130 and Andahuaylas at 2130. **Señor de Huanca** (Av Arenas 198, T322377), 3 a day to Andahuaylas. **Wari**, Díaz Bárcenas 1147, 6 a day to Lima, also to Andahuaylas. Several others to Lima and Cuzco.

⊙ Directory

Ayacucho to Cuzco *p1256*

Andahuaylas and **Abancay** have ATMs, casas de cambio and plenty of internet cabins.

East and north of La Oroya

A paved road heads north from La Oroya towards Cerro de Pasco and Huánuco. Just 25 km north of La Oroya a branch turns east towards Tarma, then descends into the relatively little-visited jungles of the Selva Central. This is a really beautiful run. North of La Oroya the road crosses the great heights of the Junín pampa and the mining zone of Cerro de Pasco, before losing altitude on its way to the Huallaga Valley. On this route you can connect by road to the Cordillera Blanca via La Unión.

Tarma → *Phone code: 064. Colour map 3, grid C3. Population: 105,200. Altitude: 3,050 m.*
Founded in 1538, Tarma, 60 km from La Oroya, is now growing, with garish modern buildings, but still has a lot of charm. The **Semana Santa celebrations** are spectacular, with a very colourful Easter Sunday morning procession in the main plaza. Accommodation is hard to find at this time, but you can apply to the Municipalidad for rooms with local families. The town is also notable for its locally made fine flower-carpets. Good, friendly market around C Amazonas and Ucayali. The surrounding countryside is beautiful. **Tourist office** ① *2 de Mayo 775 on the Plaza, T321010, turistarma@hotmail.com, very helpful. Mon-Fri 0800-1300, 1600-1800.*

Around Tarma

Around 8 km from Tarma, the small town of **Acobamba** has *tapices* made in San Pedro de Cajas which depict the Crucifixion. There are festivities during May. About 2 km up beyond the town is the **Santuario de Muruhuay,** with a venerated picture painted on the rock behind the altar.

Beyond Tarma the road is steep and crooked but there are few places where cars cannot pass one another. In the 80 km between Tarma and La Merced the road, passing by great overhanging cliffs, drops 2,450 m and the vegetation changes dramatically from temperate to tropical.

The towns of San Ramón and La Merced are collectively known as **Chanchamayo** (*Population 7,000*). **San Ramón** is 11 km before La Merced and has several hotels (**B-F**) and restaurants. There are regular combis and colectivos between the two towns.

La Merced (*Population 15,000*), lies in the fertile Chanchamayo valley. Campa Indians can usually be found around the central plaza selling bows, arrows, necklaces and trinkets. There is a festival in the last week of September. There are several hotels (**C-F**) and restaurants.

About 22 km north from La Merced is **San Luis de Shuaro**, from where the road has been extended over an intervening mountain range. A turn-off east leads to **Puerto Bermúdez**. This is a great base for exploring further into the San Matías/San Carlos national reserve in the Selva Central Peruana, with trips upriver to the Ashánincа communities. Tours arranged by **Albergue Humboldt** cost US$18-28 a day, depending on group size. Boat passages possible from passing traders. To go further downriver to Pucallpa, there is transport via Puerto Palcazu, US$10.

North of La Oroya

A paved road runs 130 km north from La Oroya to Cerro de Pasco. It runs up the Mantaro valley through canyons to the wet and mournful Junín pampa at over 4,250 m, one of the world's largest high-altitude plains. An obelisk marks the battlefield where the Peruvians under Bolívar defeated the Spaniards in 1824. Blue peaks line the pampa in a distant wall. This windswept sheet of yellow grass is bitterly cold and the only signs of life are the youthful herders with their sheep and llamas. The road follows the east shores of the Lago de Junín. The town of **Junín** lies some distance south of the lake and has the somewhat desolate feel of a high puna town, bisected by the railway.

The **Lago Junín National Reserve** ① *US$5, ticket from Inrena in Junín,* protects one of the best bird-watching sites in the central Andes where the giant coot and even flamingos may be spotted. It is easiest to visit from the village of Huayre, 5 km south of Carhuamayo, from which it is a 20-minute walk down to the lake. Fishermen are usually around to take visitors out on the lake. Carhuamayo is the best place to stay: *Gianmarco*, Maravillas 454, and *Patricia*, Tarapacá 862, are the best of several basic *hostales*. There are numerous restaurants along the main road.

Cerro de Pasco → *Phone code: 063. Population: 29,810. Altitude: 4,330 m.*

This long-established mining centre, 130 km from La Oroya, is not attractive, but is nevertheless very friendly. Copper, zinc, lead, gold and silver are mined here, and coal comes from the deep canyon of Goyllarisquisga, the 'place where a star fell', the highest coal mine in the world, 42 km north of Cerro de Pasco. The town is sited between Lago Patarcocha and the huge abyss of the mine above which its buildings and streets cling precariously. Nights are bitterly cold. *BCP* is on Jr Bolognesi. Money changers can be found on Jr Bolognesi between the market and the Cathedral.

Southwest of Cerro de Pasco by 40 km is **Huayllay**, near which is the **Santuario Bosque de Piedras** ① *US$1, payable only if the guides, Ernesto and Christian, are there, camping is permitted within the Sanctuary.* These unique weathered limestone formations are in the shape of a tortoise, elephant, alpaca, etc. At the Sanctuary (4,100-4,600 m), four tourist circuits through the spectacular rock formations have been laid out. The village of Huallay is 30 minutes beyond the sanctuary entrance.

The Central Highway from Cerro de Pasco continues northeast another 528 km to Pucallpa, the limit of navigation for large Amazon river boats. The western part of this road (Cerro de Pasco-Huánuco) has been rebuilt into an all-weather highway.

The sharp descent along the nascent **Río Huallaga** is a tonic to travellers suffering from *soroche*. The road drops 2,436 m in the 100 km from Cerro de Pasco to Huánuco, and most of it is in the first 32 km. From the bleak high ranges the road plunges below the tree line offering great views. The only town of any size before Huánuco is **Ambo**.

Huánuco → *Phone code: 062. Colour map 3, grid B3. Population: 118,814. Altitude: 1,894 m.*
This is an attractive Andean town on the Upper Huallaga with an interesting market. The two churches of **San Cristóbal** and **San Francisco** have both been much restored. The latter has some 16th-century paintings. **Museo de Ciencias** ① *Gen Prado 495, Mon-Fri 0900-1200, 1500-1900, Sat-Sun 1000-1200, US$0.50.* The natural history museum claims to have 10,000 exhibits. **Tourist office** ① *Gen Prado 716, on the Plaza de Armas, T512980.* A website giving local information is www.webhuanuco.com.

About 5 km away on the road west to La Unión is **Kótosh** (*Altitude 1,912 m*) ① *US$0.75, including a guide around a marked circuit which also passes through a small botanical garden of desert plants, taxi US$5 from the centre, with 30 mins' wait.* At this archaeological site, the Temple of Crossed Hands, the earliest evidence of a complex society and of pottery in Peru, dates from 2000 BC.

From Huánuco, a spectacular but very poor dirt road leads to **La Unión**, capital of Dos de Mayo district. It's a friendly, fast developing town with a couple of hotels (**E** to **G**) and restaurants, but electricity can be a problem and it gets very cold at night. On the pampa above La Unión are the Inca ruins of **Huánuco Viejo** ① *US$1.50, allow 2 hrs,* a 2½ hour walk from the town, a great temple-fortress with residential quarters. It has impressive Inca stonework and a fine section of Inca road running south.

The route to the Callejón de Huaylas goes through **Huallanca (Huánuco)**, an attractive town, with mining projects nearby. Check local political conditions before taking this route. See Transport, below.

● Sleeping

Tarma *p1258*
A Los Portales, Av Castilla 512, T321411, F321410. Out of town, hot water, heating, quiet, includes breakfast, good restaurant.
B Hacienda La Florida, 6 km from Tarma, T341041, www.haciendalaflorida.com. 18th-century, working hacienda, with hot water, includes breakfast, other meals extra, owned by German-Peruvian couple Inge and Pepe who arrange excursions. Recommended. Also camping for US$3.
B Hacienda Santa María, 2 km out of town at Sacsamarca 1249, T321232, www.haciendasantamaria.com. A beautiful (non-working) 17th-century hacienda, beautiful gardens and antique furniture. Includes breakfast and light evening meal. Excellent guides for local day trips. Recommended.
C Hostal Campestre Auberge Normandie, beside the Santuario de Muruhuay, Acobamba, T341028, www.normandie.com.pe. 16 cabins with hot water, TV, bar, restaurant.

C-D El Caporal, Lima 616, T323636, hostalel caporal@yahoo.es. Includes breakfast, good location, hot water, cable TV. Recommended.
E Albania, Amazonas 534, T321399. Small rooms, hot water.
E La Colmena, Jauja 618, T321157. Old building, convenient for Huancayo buses.
E Hostal Central, Huánuco 614, T310149. Shared bath, hot water, laundry facilities, a bit rundown but popular, has an observatory which opens Fri at 2000.
E Hostal El Márquez, Huaraz 389, T321060. Old building with character, shared showers, hot water.
F Hostal El Dorado, Huánuco 488, T321598. Hot water, **G** without bath, rooms set round a patio, first floor rooms better, reasonable.

Puerto Bermúdez *p1258*
E Albergue Cultural Humboldt, by the Río Pachitea at La Rampa, T063-720267, www.geocities.com/puerto_bermudez. US$4 extra for 3 meals a day. The owner, Basque writer Jesús, has created a real haven for backpackers,

● *For an explanation of the sleeping and eating price codes used in this guide, see inside the front*
● *cover. Other relevant information is found in Essentials pages 1075-1077.*

with maps, library and book exchange. Recommended. Jesús will arrange tours, from day trips to camping and trekking in the primary forest. Ask him about volunteering at a local Asháninka school.

Cerro de Pasco *p1258*
D Wong, Carrión 99, T721515. Hot water 24 hrs, TV, run-down and noisy but friendly, motorcycle parking.
E Hostal Arenales, Jr Arenales 162, near the bus station, T723088. Modern, TV, hot water in the morning.
E Welcome, Av La Plata 125, opposite the entrance to the bus station, T721883. Some rooms without window, hot water 24 hrs.

Huánuco *p1259*
B Gran Hotel Huánuco, Jr D Beraun 775, T514222, hotel.huanuco@terra.com.pe. Restaurant, pool, sauna, gym, parking. Recommended.
D Hostal Caribe, Huánuco 546, T513645, and adjoining it **D Hostal Mariño**. Two large modern hotels with big rooms, TV.
D Hostal Quintito, 2 de Mayo 987, T512691. Modern hotel with big rooms and TV.
E Hostal Beijing, Abtao 770, close to Plaza. Small, clean TV, hot water. Recommended.
E Las Vegas, 28 de Julio 936, on Plaza de Armas, T/F512315. Hot water, TV.
F Imperial, Huánuco 581, T513203. With cold shower (intermittent water), quiet.
F El Roble, Constitución 629, T512515. Slightly cheaper without bath, good value.

Huallanca (Huánuco) *p1259*
D Hotel Milán, 28 de Julio 107. Modern, TV and hot water in all rooms, best in town, good restaurant.
F Hostal Yesica, L Prado 507. Hot water, shared bathroom, the best of the basic ones.

❶ Eating

Tarma *p1258*
There are several places on Lima, including a vegetarian. The *manjarblanco* of Tarma is famous, as well as *pachamanca*, *mondongo* and *picante de cuyes*. Good places to buy local produce are **El Tarmenito**, Lima 149, and **La Pastora**, Arequipa 656.
❙ Chifa Roberto Siu, Lima 557. A good option for Chinese food, popular with locals.
❙ Comedor Vegetariano, Arequipa 695. Open 0700-2100, vegetarian, small and cheap, sells great bread.
❙ Lo Mejorcito de Tarma, Arequipa 501. Open 0700-2300. Good set menú US$1.50, local

specialities, also has tourist information.
❙ El Sabor Criollo, Huaraz 296. Local restaurant.
❙ Señorial/Pollería Braserita, Huánuco 138. Good *menú*, extensive choice, open late.

Cerro de Pasco *p1258*
❙ Los Angeles, Jr Libertad, near the market. Excellent *menú* for US$1.50. Recommended.
❙ San Fernando, bakery in the plaza. Opens at 0700 for first-rate hot chocolate, bread and pastries.

Huánuco *p1259*
❙❙-❙ Pizzería Don Sancho, Prado 645. Best pizzas in town.
❙ Chifa Men Ji, 28 de Julio, block 8. Good prices, nice Chinese food.
❙ Govinda, 2 de Mayo 1044. Reckoned to be the best vegetarian restaurant.
❙ La Olla de Barro, Gral Prado 852, close to main plaza. Serves typical food, good value.

⊛ Festivals and events

Huánuco *p1259*
20-25 Jan: is Carnaval Huanuqueño. **3 May**: La Cruz de Mayo. **16 Jul**: Fiesta de la Virgen del Carmen. **12-18 Aug**: Tourist Week in Huánuco. **28-29 Oct**: Fiesta del Rey y del Señor de Burgos, the patron of Huánuco. **25 Dec**: Fiesta de los Negritos.

⊖ Transport

Tarma *p1258*
Bus To **Lima**, 231 km (paved), 6 hrs, US$5.50. Transportes Chanchamayo, Callao 1002, T321882, recommended, 3 a day, en route from Chanchamayo; **Transportes Junín**, Amazonas 667, 3 a day, with *bus cama* night bus. **Trans La Merced**, Vienrich 420, 3 a day. , **Trans Muruhuay**, Huaraz y Amazonas, (several daily) start in Tarma. To **Jauja** and **Huancayo**, Transportes San Juan, from the stadium hourly on the half hour, buses coming from Chanchamayo; **Trans Muruhuay** leave when full, 0500-1800, to Jauja 2 hrs, US$2. All buses continue to Huancayo, 3 hrs, US$3. Colectivos depart when full from Callao y Jauja, 2 hrs, US$4, and 3 hrs, US$6, respectively. To **Cerro de Pasco**, Empresa Junín, Amazonas 450, 4 a day, 3 hrs, US$2.50. Also colectivos when full, 2 hrs, US$4. Buses to **La Oroya** leave from opposite the petrol station on Av Castilla block 5, 1 hr, US$1.25, while colectivos leave from the petrol station itself, 45 mins, US$2. To **Chanchamayo**, Transportes San Juan from the stadium every hour on the half hour, 1½ hrs, US$1.50 to San Ramón, and 2 hrs, US$1.75 to La Merced. Also, colectivos, 1-1¼ hrs, US$3 and US$3.50 respectively.

Colectivos and yellow Canary **buses**
to **Acobamba** and up to **Muruhuay** every
10 mins, US$0.25.

San Ramón p1258

Air Flights leave from San Ramón. There is a small
airstrip where **Aero Montaña**, T064-339191,
rfmamsa@hotmail.com, has air taxis that can be
chartered (*viaje especial*) to the jungle towns, with a
maximum of 3 people, but you have to pay for the
pilot's return to base. Flights cost US$250 per hr.
Puerto Bermúdez takes 33 mins. You can also
just go to the air base, across the river, on the east
side of town.

La Merced p1258

Bus Many buses go here from **Lima**: Expreso
Satipo, Trans Lobato, Junín, La Merced and
Chanchamayo (recommended) each have several
buses during the day, 8 hrs, US$6.50. To **Tarma**
Transportes San Juan, hourly,
2½ hrs, US$1.75, or **Selva Tours** colectivos, just
over 1 hr, US$3.50. To **Puerto Bermúdez**
Empresa Transdife, **Villarrica** and **Servicio**
Especial all have 4WD pick-ups or minibuses and
go at 0330 and 0430 (or when full). You can buy
your tickets in advance at the bus terminal,
US$8.80; standing in the back of pick-up US$7;
seat in pick-up cabin, US$10. This is not a paved
road and takes around 8 hrs in the dry season.

Huayllay p1258

Minibuses to Huallay from Cerro de Pasco's
terminal leave throughout the day, about
1 hr, US$1. They return until 1800-1900.

Cerro de Pasco p1258

Bus There is a large bus station. To **Lima** several
companies including **Carhuamayo** and
Transportes Apóstol San Pedro, hourly
0800-1200, plus 4 departures 2030-2130,
8 hrs, US$4-5. If there are no convenient daytime
buses, you could change buses in
La Oroya. To **Carhuamayo, Junín** and
La Oroya: buses leave when full, about every
20-30 mins, to Carhuamayo 1 hr, US$1; to Junín
1½ hrs, US$1; to La Oroya, 2½ hrs, US$2.
Colectivos also depart with a similar frequency,
1½ hrs, US$2.50, to La Oroya.
To **Tarma**, Empresa Junín, 0600, 1500, 3 hrs,
$2.50. Colectivos also depart hourly, 1½ hrs,
US$4. To **Huancayo**, various companies leave
throughout the day, 5 hrs, US$4. To **Huánuco**,
buses and cars leave when full, about half hourly,
2½ hrs and 1½ hrs, US$2 and US$4 respectively.

Huánuco p1259

Air From **Lima**, Aerocóndor (2 de Mayo 1253,
T517090), Tue, Thu, Sat, 50 mins, US$70. There

are connecting flights to Tingo María, Tocache,
Juanjui, Pucallpa, Saposoa and other jungle
towns. Check all flight details in advance. Flights
may be cancelled in the rains or if not full.
Bus To **Lima**, US$9, 8 hrs. León de Huánuco,
Malecón Alomía Robles 821, 3 a day. Also **Bahía**
Continental, Valdizan 718, recommended,
Transportes El Rey, 28 de Julio 1215 (28 de Julio
1192, La Victoria, Lima). The majority of buses of
all companies leave 2030-2200, most also offer a
bus at 0900-1000. A colectivo to Lima, costing
US$20, leaves at 0400, arriving at 1400; book the
night before at Gen Prado 607, 1 block from the
plaza. Recommended. To **Cerro de Pasco**, 3 hrs,
US$2, colectivos under 2 hrs, US$4. All leave
when full from the Ovalo Carhuayna on the north
side of the city, 3 km from the centre. To
Huancayo, 7 hrs, US$6: **Turismo Central**,
Tarapacá 530, at 2100. Colectivos run to **Tingo**
María, from block 1 of Prado close to Puente
Calicanto, 2½ hrs, US$5. Also **Etnasa**, 3-4 hrs, US2.
For **Pucallpa**, take a colectivo to Tingo María,
then a bus from there. This route has many
checkpoints and robberies can occur. Travel by
day and check on the current situation regarding
safety. To **La Unión**, Transportes El Niño,
Aguilar 530, colectivos, depart when full, 5 hrs,
US$7.15. This is a rough road operated by old
buses of which **Transportes Vitor**, Tarapacá 448,
and **Transportes Rosario**, Tarapacá 330, 0730, 6
hrs, US$4, are the more reliable.

La Unión p1259

Bus To **Huánuco**: El Niño colectivos,
Jr Comercio 12, T062-515952, 5 hrs, US$7.15; bus
companies leave at 0630 (no afternoon/evening
departures), 5-6 hrs, US$4.
To **Huallanca (Huánuco)**, combis leave from
the market, about half hourly, when full and follow
the attractive Vizcarra valley, 1 hr, US$0.75. Then
take an *El Rápido* bus to Huaraz. Combis leave
when full about half hourly, from the corner of
Comercio y 28 de Julio in Huallanca for La Unión.

Directory

Tarma p1258
Banks BCP, Lima 407, changes Amex TCs.
Internet Internet offices all along Av Lima and
Malecón José Gálvez. **Telephones** On the
Plaza de Armas.

Huánuco p1259
Banks BCP, at Dos de Mayo 1005, Visa ATM.
Internet Next to the Cathedral on the Plaza.
Many on Jr 2 de Mayo, 3 blocks southwest of Plaza.
Post offices 2 de Mayo on the Plaza. Open
0800-2000 Mon-Sat, 0800-1400 Sun.
Telephones 28 de Julio 1170.

Amazon Basin

Cooled by winds sweeping down from the Andes but warmed by its jungle blanket, this region contains important tropical flora and fauna. In the north of the region, Iquitos, on the Amazon itself, is the centre of jungle exploration. It is a very varied landscape, with grasslands and tablelands of scrub-like vegetation, inaccessible swamps, and forests up to 2,000 m above sea level. The principal means of communication in the jungle is by its many rivers, the most important being the Amazon, which rises high up in the Andes as the Marañón, then joins the Ucayali to become the longest river in the world.

The northern tourist area is based on the River Amazon itself with, at its centre, a sizeable city, Iquitos. Although it has lost its rubber-boom dynamism, Iquitos is still at the heart of life on the river. There are jungle lodges upstream and down, each with its own speciality and level of comfort, but none more than half a day away by fast boat. To get right into the wilds, head for Peru's largest national reserve, Pacaya-Samiria, accessed by boat from Iquitos or the little town of Lagunas.

North from Huánuco to Pucallpa

Huánuco to Tingo María

The journey to Tingo María from Huánuco, 135 km, is very dusty but gives a good view of the jungle. Some 25 km beyond Huánuco the road begins a sharp climb to the heights of Carpish (3,023 m). A descent of 58 km brings it to the Huallaga River again; it then continues along the river to Tingo María. The road is paved from Huánuco to Tingo María, including a tunnel through the Carpish hills. Landslides along this section are frequent and construction work causes delays. Although this route is reported to be relatively free from terrorism, robberies do occur and it is advisable to travel only by day.

Situated on the middle Huallaga, in the Ceja de Montaña, on the edge (literally 'eyebrow') of the mountains, **Tingo María** (*Phone code 062, Population 20,560, Altitude 655 m, Annual rainfall 2,642 mm*) is isolated for days in the rainy season. The altitude prevents the climate from being oppressive. The Cordillera Azul, the front range of the Andes, covered with jungle-like vegetation to its top, separates it from the jungle lowlands to the east. The mountain which can be seen from all over the town is called La Bella Durmiente, the Sleeping Beauty. The meeting here of highlands and jungle makes the landscape extremely striking. Bananas, sugar cane, cocoa, rubber, tea and coffee are grown. The main crop of the area, though, is coca, grown on the *chacras* (smallholdings) in the countryside, and sold legitimately and otherwise in Tingo María. A small university outside the town, beyond the *Hotel Madera Verde*, has a little **museum-cum-zoo** ① *free but a small tip would help to keep things in order*; it also maintains botanical gardens in the town. About 6½ km from Tingo, on a rough road, is a fascinating cave, the **Cueva de las Lechuzas** ① *US$0.90 for the cave, take a torch, and do not wear open shoes, getting there: take a motorcycle-taxi from town, US$1.75; cross the Río Monzón by new bridge.* There are many oilbirds in the cave and many small parakeets near the entrance. **Tourist office:** on the northwest side of the Plaza de Armas, in the municipal building, friendly, loads of free information, T-shirts with pictures of local views sell for US$3.45. Note that Tingo María is a main narco-trafficking centre and although the town is generally safe, it is not safe to leave it at night. Always keep to the main routes.

Tingo María to Pucallpa

From Tingo María to the end of the road at Pucallpa is 255 km, with a climb over the watershed - the Cordillera Azul - between the Huallaga and Ucayali rivers. The road is in poor shape for most of the journey, but some paving is in progress. Travel by day: it is safer the views are tremendous as you go from the high jungle to the Amazon Basin. Sit on the righthand side of the bus. When the road was being surveyed it was thought that the lowest pass over the Cordillera Azul was over 3,650 m high, but an old document stating that a Father Abad had found a pass through these mountains in 1757 was rediscovered, and the road now goes through the pass of Father Abad, a gigantic gap 4 km long and 2,000 m deep.

At the top of the pass is a Peruvian Customs house; the jungle land to the east is a free zone. Coming down from the pass the road bed is along the floor of a magnificent canyon, the Boquerón Abad. It is a beautiful trip through luxuriant jungle, ferns and sheer walls of bare rock, punctuated by occasional waterfalls plunging into the roaring torrent below. East of the foot of the pass the all-weather road goes over the flat pampa, with few bends, to the village of **Aguaytía** (narcotics police outpost, gasoline, accommodation in the **F Hostal San Antonio**, clean, and two restaurants). From Aguaytía the road continues for 160 km to Pucallpa - five hours by bus. There is a service station three hours before Pucallpa.

Pucallpa → *Phone code: 061. Colour map 3, grid B3. Population: 400,000.*

Pucallpa is a rapidly expanding jungle town on the Río Ucayali, navigable by vessels of 3,000 tons from Iquitos, 533 nautical miles away. The town's newer sections have paved streets, sewers and lights, but much of the frontier atmosphere still exists. The floating ports of La Hoyada and Puerto Italia are about 5 km away and worth a visit to see the canoe traffic and open-air markets. (When river levels are low, boats leave from a different port, Pucallpillo.) The economy of the area includes sawmills, plywood factories, a paper mill, oil refinery, fishing and boat building. Large discoveries of oil and gas are being explored, and gold mining is underway nearby. Local festivals are *Carnival* in February, *San Juan* on 24 June, and the Ucayali regional fair in October. The town is hot and dusty between June and November and muddy from December to May. **Note:** There is narcotics activity in the area. The city itself is safe enough to visit, but don't travel at night. **Museo Regional** ⓘ *Jr Inmaculada 999, 0800-1200, 1600-1800,US$0.90,* has some good examples of Shibipo ceramics, as well as some delightful pickled snakes and other reptiles. **Tourist office Dirección Regional de Turismo** ⓘ *Jr 2 de Mayo 111, T571303, ucayali@mincetur.gob.pe, Mon-Fri 0730-1300, 1330-1515.* Information also at **CTAR-Ucayali**, Raimondi block 220, T575018, oppto-ucayali@pres.gob.pe.

Around Pucallpa The Hospital Amazónico Albert Schweitzer, which serves the local *indigena*, is on picturesque Lake **Yarinacocha** ⓘ *20 mins by colectivo or bus from the market in Pucallpa, US$0.30, or 15 mins by taxi, US$2,* the main tourist attraction near Pucallpa. River dolphins can be seen in the lake. There are many restaurants on the waterfront and near the plaza. A good place to swim is at **San José**; take the road out behind the power station.

San Francisco and **Santa Clara** can be visited at the far end of the lake on its western arm. Both are Shibipo villages still practising traditional ceramic and textile crafts. In San Francisco a nice place to spend the night is in the house of Alberto Sánchez Ríos, *Casa Artesanal Shibipo*, which is very friendly and warmly recommended. To reach these villages take one of the motorized canoes, *peke-pekes*, which leave from Puerto Callao when full, US$0.90.

The beautifully located reserve, **Jardín Botánico Chullachaqui** *free*, can be reached by boat from Puerto Callao, the port on Lake Yarinacocha, to Pueblo Nueva Luz de Fátima, 45 minutes, then one hour's walk to the garden. For information about traditional medicine contact Mateo Arevalomayna, San Francisco de Yarinacocha (president of the group Ametra; T573152, or ask at Moroti-Shobo).

⦿ Sleeping

See also Activities and tours below for more information on lodges. Hotels are often ful,.

Tingo María *p1262*
B Madera Verde, Av Universitaria s/n, out of town on the road to Huánuco, near the University, T/F561800, maverde@ terra.com.pe. Chalets in beautiful surroundings, with and without bath, restaurant, swimming pool.
C Hospedaje Agroturístico Villa Jennifer, Km 3.4 Carretera a Castillo Grande, 10 mins from Tingo María, T960 3509, www.villa-jennifer.com. Danish-Peruvian owned, includes breakfast, weekend packages and tours

to local sites, birdwatching, restaurant, laundry service. Rooms are surrounded by local flora, with lots of birdlife.
E Hostal Marco Antonio, Jr Monzón 364, T562201. Quiet, restaurant of the same name next door.
E Nueva York, Av Alameda Perú 553, T562406. Cheaper without bath and TV, laundry, good value, restaurant.

Pucallpa *p1263*
AL Sol del Oriente, Av San Martín 552, T/F575510, www.dhperu.net/eng/ pucallpa.html. Price includes breakfast, pool, minizoo, good restaurant.

D Arequipa, Jr Progreso 573, T571348. Good but no a/c, comfortable, safe, TV, restaurant.
D Mercedes, Raimondi 601, T575120. Good, but noisy with good bar and restaurant attached, swimming pool.
E Barbtur, Raimondi 670, T572532. **F** without bath, central, good beds.
E Komby, Ucayali 360, T571184. Comfortable, swimming pool, excellent value.
E Sun, Ucayali 380. Cheaper without bath, good value, next to *Komby*.

Yarinacocha *p1263*

B La Cabaña Lodge, T616679, F579242. Full board, including transport to and from Yarinacocha harbour, run by Ruth and Leroy from USA, great food, jungle trips US$50 per day including boat, guide and food.
B-C pp La Perla, next door to La Cabaña Lodge. Price includes all meals, German- Peruvian owned, English and German spoken, no electricity after 2100, jungle tours organized.
C Jana Shobo Amazonian Lodge, Lake Yarinacocha, T596943, www.janashobo.tk. Small lodge is set in 10 ha of forest on the lakeshore. Price includes meals and airport transfer, packages and tours available. Camping possible, living room, reading room and kitchen.
D-E Los Delfines, T571129. With bath, fan, fridge, some with TV.
F El Pescador, in Puerto Callao, cheapest in town, restaurant.

🍴 Eating

Tingo María *p1262*

🍴 **El Antojito 2**, Jr Chiclayo 458. Local food.
🍴 **Girasol**, Av Raimondi 253, T562065. Chicken, burgers, cakes and fruit juices.

Pucallpa *p1263*

Typical dishes *Patarashca* is barbecued fish wrapped in *bijao* leaves; *zarapatera*, a spicy soup made with turtle meat served in its shell, but consider the ecological implications of this dish; *chonta salad*, made with palm shoots; *juanes*, rice with chicken or fish served during the San Juan festival; *tacutacu* is banana and sauces. The local beer 'San Juan' has been recommended.
🍴 **El Alamo**, Carretera Yarinacocha 2650, T571510. Good typical food.

🎵 Bars and clubs

Pucallpa *p1263*

Billy's Place, on Arica, on the street east of Jr Mcal Cáceres. A decent bar run by an American called Rick (Billy is his pet jaguar). He only sells beer, has TV and pinball. All the locals know it; the area is very dark late at night.

🛍 Shopping

Pucallpa *p1263*

Many Shibipo women carry and sell their products around Pucallpa and Yarinacocha.
Agustín Rivas, at Jr Tarapacá 861, above a small restaurant whose entrance is at No 863 (ask for it). For local wood carvings visit the workshop of this sculptor, whose work is made from huge tree roots. **Artesanías La Selva**, Jr Tarapacá 868, has a reasonable selection of indigenous craftwork.

🏔 Activities and tours

Tingo María *p1262*

Tingo María Travel Tours, Av Raimondi 460, T562501. For local excursions.

Pucallpa *p1263*

If organizing a group tour with the boatmen on the waterfront, expect to pay around US$30 per day pp. Only use accredited guides. **Laser Viajes y Turismo**, Raimondi 470, T571120, F573776. Helpful, recommended for planning a jungle trip.

⊖ Transport

Tingo María *p1262*

Bus To **Huánuco**, 119 km, 3-4 hrs, US$2 with Etnasa (not recommended - theft and drug-trafficking); take a micro, US$2, or colectivo, US$5, 2 hrs, several daily. Direct buses continue to Lima, 12 hrs, with **Trans Rey**, US$15 *bus cama*, **León de Huánuco** and **Bahía** (T01-424 1539), US$11. To **Pucallpa**, 255 km, 12 hrs, US$4.30-8.50. Ucayali Express colectivos leave from Raimondi y Callao. There are other colectivos and taxis, which all leave in the early morning in convoy.

Pucallpa *p1263*

Air To **Lima**, 1 hr, daily flights with **WayraPerú** (Jr Coronel Portillo 522, T592715) and **Star Perú** (7 de Junio 865, T590585). Airport to town, bus US$0.25; *motos* US$1; taxi US$2-3.
Bus There are regular bus services to **Lima**, 812 km, 18-20 hrs (longer in the rainy season, Nov-Mar), US$11. To **Tingo María**, 255 km, 7-9 hrs, US$4.30-8.50, combis leave at 0600, 0700 and 0800 with Ucayali Express, 7 de Junio y San Martín. All buses have police guard and go in convoy. Take blankets as the crossing of the Cordillera at night is bitterly cold.
Ferry To **Iquitos** the trip takes 3-5 days, and costs US$20 pp for hammock space, or US$30 for a bed in a cabin.

You must ask around for the large boats to Iquitos; they can be docked at Puerto La Hoyada, Puerto Italia or Pucallpillo. A mototaxi to any of the ports costs US$0.75 from the Plaza de Armas, taxis charge US$3. The Capitanía on the waterfront may give you information about sailings, but this is seldom reliable. Departure times are marked on chalk boards on the deck. Schedules seem to change almost hourly. Do not pay for your trip before you board the vessel, and only pay the captain. Some boat captains may allow you to live on board a couple of days before sailing. Bottled drinking water can be bought in Pucallpa, but not cheaply. See General hints for river travel, page 1272.

❶ Directory

Tingo María *p1262*
Internet Several places on Raimondi and near Plaza de Armas, fast and cheap but strange hours.

Pucallpa *p1263*
Banks It is easy to change dollars cash at the banks, travel agencies, the better hotels and bigger stores. There are also lots of street changers (watch them carefully). BCP, Raimondi y Tarapacá, is the only place to change Tcs, cash on Visa. Also at Interbank. **Cultural centres** Art school: Usko Ayar Amazonian School of Painting, in the house of artist Pablo Amaringo, a former *vegetalista* (healer), Jr LM Sánchez, Cerro 465-467, www.egallery.com/coll/amazon.php. The school provides art classes for local people, and is dependent upon selling their art. The internationally renowned school welcomes overseas visitors for short or long stays to study painting and learn Spanish and/or teach English with Peruvian students. **Police** Policia Nacional, Jr Independencia 3rd block, T575211.

Yurimaguas and Pacaya-Samiria

Yurimaguas

The Río Huallaga winds northwards for 930 km. The Upper Huallaga is a torrent, dropping 15.8 m per km between its source and Tingo María. The Lower Huallaga moves through an enervation of flatness, with its main port, Yurimaguas, below the last rapids and only 150 m above the Atlantic Ocean, yet distant from that ocean by over a month's voyage. Between the Upper and Lower lies the Middle Huallaga: the third of the river which is downstream from Tingo María and upstream from Yurimaguas.

Downriver of Tingo María, beyond Bellavista, the orientation is towards **Yurimaguas** (Phone code 065, Population 25,700), which is connected by road with the Pacific coast, via Tarapoto and Moyobamba (see page 1160). It's a very relaxed jungle town and, as the roadhead on the lower Río Huallaga, is an ideal starting point for river travel in the Peruvian Amazon. It has a fine church of the Passionist Fathers, based on the Cathedral of Burgos, in Spain. A colourful market is held from 0600-0800, full of fruit and animals. Excursions in the area include the gorge of Shanusi and the lakes of Mushuyacu and Sanango. Tourist information is available from the Consejo Regional building (which also has a small archaeological museum) on the main plaza, T352676.

Pacaya-Samiria

All river traffic to Iquitos stops at **Lagunas**, 12 hours from Yurimaguas. From here there are good jungle trips from Lagunas to the **Pacaya-Samiria Reserve** ① *Reserve office in Iquitos, Ricardo Palma 113, p 4, T232980, Mon-Fri 0800-1300, 1500-1800, has general information and an updated list of tour operators authorized to enter the reserve. You must go here to obtain proof of payment for the park entry fee (US$33), payment itself must be made at Banco de la Nación.* Pacaya-Samiria Reserve, at 2,080,000 ha, is the country's largest protected area. It is bounded by the rivers Marañón and Ucuyali, narrowing to their confluence near the town of Nauta. The reserve's waterways and wetlands provide habitat for manatee, tapir, river dolphins, giant otters, black cayman, boas, 193 species of fish and some 330 bird species. Many of the animals found here are in danger of extinction. Trips are mostly on the river, sleeping in hammocks, and include fishing. The main part of the reserve is off-limits to tourists, who may only be taken to forest surrounding the reserve. Iquitos operators enter through Nauta to Yarina where there is a shelter, also through Requena. Another entry point is the village of **Leoncio Prado** (with a couple of *hospedajes*), on the Marañón, opposite the outflow of the Río Samiria.

● Sleeping

Yurimaguas *p1265*
C Hostal Residencial El Naranjo, Arica 318, T351560, hotel_elnaranjo@hotmail.com. Best in town, a/c (**D** with fan), hot water, comfortable, small pool, with good restaurant.
D Luis Antonio, Av Jaúregui 407, T352061, antonio@vibcp.com. With fan **C** with a/c), cold water, balconies overlooking small pool, very helpful. Recommended.
E Hostal El Caballito, Av Jaúregui 403, T352427. Cold water, fan, pleasant, good value.
E Leo's Palace, Sgto Lores 106, Plaza de Armas, T351499. Good, reasonable value (**C**) with a/c), restaurant.

Lagunas *p1265*
F Hostal Isabel, Miraflores 1 block from plaza. Shared bath, cold water, basic, meals available. Several other basic places in town.
F Hostal La Sombra, Jr Vásquez 1121. Shared bath, basic, good food.

▲▲ Activities and tours

Yurimaguas *p1265*
Manguares Expeditions, Sargento Lores 126, near Plaza de Armas.
Nilo Hidalgo, Jr Elena Pardo 115, T352832, www.nilotour.cjb.net. US$70-100 per person per day.

Pacaya-Samiria *p1265*
There are 5 registered operators in Lagunas. These include **Manuel Rojas**, T401116, and **Gamaniel Valles**, T401007. Guides charge US$15 per day. Trips to Pacaya-Samiria can also be arranged in Iquitos. Expeditions must be booked in advance, all equipment and food is provided. **Asiendes** (Asociación Indígena en Defensa de la Ecología Samiria), asiendesperu@hotmail.com, or contact through **Yellow Rose of Texas** restaurant in Iquitos. A local association which runs trips into Pacaya-Samiria, promoting the jungle and benefiting the community, from 4 to 7 days, US$50 per day, all inclusive except boat passage from Iquitos and price of entry to the park. You stay at rangers' stations or can camp, very good experience, respectful of wildlife, knowledgeable and accommodating guides. Recommended.

● Transport

Yurimaguas *p1265*
Bus There are plans to pave the road to Tarapoto, which would considerably shorten the journey. **Paredes Estrella**, office on 5th block of Mariscal Cáceres, 0700 daily to **Tarapoto** (8 hrs, US$3.65), **Moyobamba** (10 hrs, US$7.50), **Pedro Ruiz** (for Chachapoyas, 16 hrs, US$10.50), **Chiclayo** (24 hrs, US$15), **Trujillo** (28 hrs, US$18), and **Lima** (34 hrs, US$24). Also Huamanga and Sol Peruano, offices on same street. If travelling only as far as Tarapoto, faster alternatives to the bus are colectivos (cars, 4 hrs, US$7.50), pickups (5 hrs, US$4.55 in cab, US$2.50 in the back), and combis (5 hrs, US$3.65).
Ferry To **Iquitos**, 2 days and 2 nights, **Eduardo** company is best, Elena Pardo 114, T351270 (see under Iquitos, Transport).

● Directory

Yurimaguas *p1265*
Banks Interbank or travel agents charge poor rates. **Negocios Zerimar**, Jaúregui ½ block from plaza, changes US$ cash, Mon-Sat 0700-2100, Sun 0700-1500. **Internet** Café on Plaza de Armas, US$1.70 per hr.

Iquitos and around → *Phone code: 065. Colour map 3, grid A4. Population: 600,000.*

Iquitos stands on the west bank of the Amazon and is a chief town of Peru's jungle region. Some 800 km downstream from Pucallpa and 3,646 km from the mouth of the Amazon, the city is completely isolated except by air and river. Its first wealth came from the rubber boom (late 19th century to second decade of 20th century). The main economic activities are logging, commerce and petroleum and it is the main starting point for tourists wishing to explore Peru's northern jungle. **Tourist offices**: i perú ① *Napo 232, on the Plaza de Armas, in the Municipal building, T236144, iperuiquitos@promperu.gov.pe, 0830-1930 daily,* also at the airport, 0800-1300, 1600-2000 daily. Both offices are helpful. If arriving by air, go first to this desk. They will give you a list of clean hotels, a map, tell you about the touts outside the airport etc. **Dircetur**① *Ricardo Palma 113, p 5, T234609, loreto@mincetur.gob.pe.* The local paper is **La Región**, www.diariolaregion.com. **Indecopi**, the tourism protection service, is at ① *Huallaga 325, T243490, ameza@indecopi.gob.pe.* **Tourist police**① *C Sargento Lores 834, T231851.*

The incongruous **Iron House/Casa de Fierro** stands on the Plaza de Armas, designed by Eiffel for the Paris exhibition of 1889. It is said that the house was transported from Paris by a local rubber baron and is constructed entirely of iron trusses and sheets, bolted together and painted silver. It now houses a restaurant and snack bar.

Belén, the picturesque, lively waterfront district, is worth visiting, but is not safe at night. Most of its huts are built on rafts to cope with the river's 10 m change of level during floods (January-July); now they're built on stilts. On Pasaje Paquito are bars serving local sugar cane rum. The main plaza has a bandstand made by Eiffel. In the high season canoes can be hired on the waterfront for a tour of Belén, US$3 per hour. The market at the end of the Malecón is well worth visiting, though you should get there before 0900 to see it in full swing.

Of special interest are the older buildings, faced with *azulejos* (glazed tiles). They date from the rubber boom of 1890 to 1912, when the rubber barons imported the tiles from Portugal and Italy and ironwork from England to embellish their homes. Werner Herzog's film *Fitzcarraldo* is a *cause célèbre* in the town and Fitzcarrald's house, the **Casa de Barro**, still stands on the Plaza de Armas. **Museo Amazónico**, in the renovated Prefectura, Malecón Tarapacá y Morona, has displays of native art. Next door to the tourist office on the Plaza is a **City Museum** *free*, with stuffed animals and wood carvings of local native peoples.

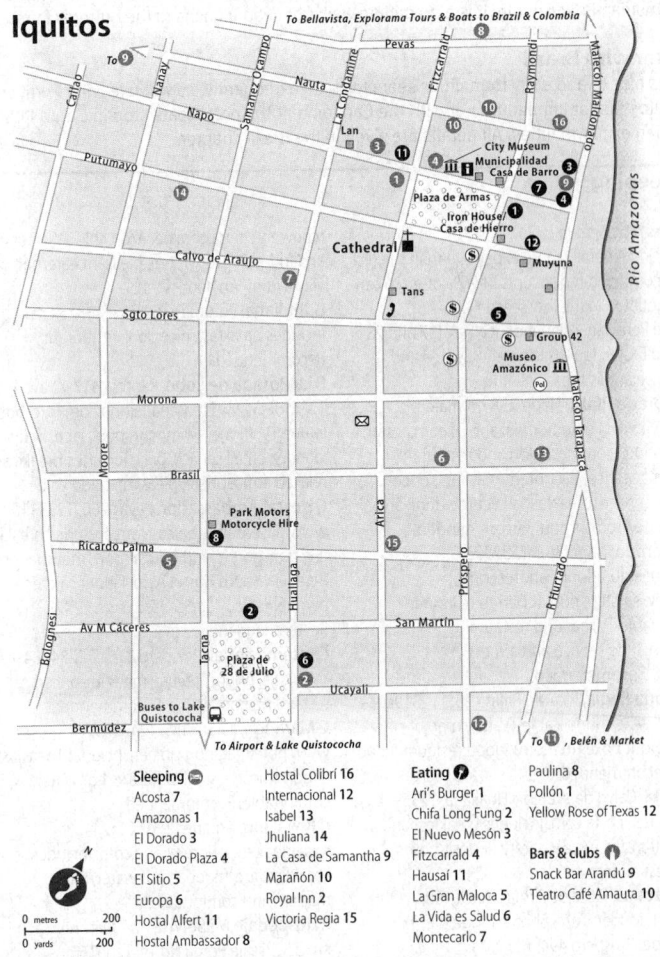

Iquitos

Excursions

There is a beach at **Bellavista**, which is safe for swimming and popular at weekends in summer. Boats can be hired from here to see the meeting of the Nanay and Amazon rivers, and to visit villages en route. There are lots of food stalls selling typical local dishes. Take a bus from Jr Próspero to 'Bellavista Nanay', 15 minutes, US$0.40.

Allpahuayo-Mishana Reserve ① *Iquitos office at Instituto de Investigaciones de la Amazonía Peruana (IIAP), Av Quiñones on the way to the airport, T265515.* Some 22 km south of Iquitos by road or 2-3 hours by boat from Bellavista, this reserve protects the largest concentration of white sand jungle (*varillales*) in Peru. Part of the Napo ecoregion, biodiversity here is among the highest in the Amazon basin. It has several endangered species including two primates, several endemic species; the area is rich in birds.

The beautiful **Lake Quistococha** in lush jungle is 4 km south of the city, with a fish hatchery at the lakeside. There's a good two-hour walk through the surrounding jungle on a clearly marked trail. See particularly the *paiche*, a huge Amazonian fish whose steaks (*paiche a la loretana*) you can eat in Iquitos' restaurants. There are also bars and restaurants on the lakeside and a small beach. Boats are for hire on the lake and swimming is safe but the sandflies are vicious, so take insect repellent. A map and information is available from zoo's ticket office. The **zoo** ① *US$1.30 0900-1700*, itself is squalid.

Pilpintuhuasi Butterfly Farm ① *near the village of Padre Cocha, T232665, www.amazon animalorphanage.org, Tue-Sun 0900-1600, US$5*, as well as butterflies, has a small well-kept zoo, Austrian-Peruvian run. It is a 20-minute walk from Padre Cocha to the butterfly farm.

Border with Brazil

Details on exit and entry formalities seem to change frequently, so when leaving Peru, check in Iquitos first at Immigration or with the Capitanía at the port. Boats stop in Santa Rosa for Peruvian exit formalities. All details are given in the Brazil chapter.

⬤ Sleeping

Iquitos *p1266, map p1267*

Hotels are generally more expensive than the rest of the country, but discounts of 20% or more can be negotiated in the low season (Jan-Apr). Around Peruvian Independence Day (27 and 28 Jul) and Easter, Iquitos can get crowded and prices rise at this time.

L El Dorado Plaza, Napo 258 on main plaza, T222555, www.eldoradoplazahotel.com. 5 star, very good accommodation and restaurant, excellent service, bar, internet access, prices include service, breakfast, welcome drink and transfer to/from airport. Recommended.

A El Dorado, Napo 362, T232574, dorado@eldoradoplazahotel.com. Same ownership, pool (open to restaurant users), cable TV, bar and restaurant, prices include service and airport transfer. Recommended.

A Victoria Regia, Ricardo Palma 252, T231983, F232499. A/c, fridge, cable TV, free map of city, safe deposit boxes in rooms, good restaurant and pool. Recommended.

B Acosta, Calvo de Araujo y Huallaga, T235974, www.hotelacosta.com. Includes breakfast and airport transfer, a/c, TV, safety deposit boxes, good restaurant.

B Amazonas, Plaza de Armas, Arica 108, T242431. Modern, a/c, phone, fridge bar, TV.

B Europa, Próspero 494, T231123,

rcpowerv@terra.com.pe. A/c, cable TV, phone and fridge in every room, pleasant café/bar, good views from 5th floor.

B Jhuliana, Putumayo 521, T/F233154. Includes breakfast, nice pool, restaurant. Recommended.

B La Posada de Lobo, Pantoja 417 y Yavari, T236140, www.laposadadelobo.com. A/c, hot water, TV, fridge, swimming pool, jacuzzi, gym, laundry, email service, price includes breakfast, relaxed atmosphere, pleasant, good value.

C Hostal Ambassador, Pevas 260, T233110, www.paseosamazonicos.com. Includes breakfast, a/c, transport to and from airport, member of Peruvian Youth Hostel Association, cafeteria, owns Sinchicuy Lodge (see page 1272). Recommended.

C Internacional, Próspero 835, T/F234684. A/c, TV, fridge, phone, secure, medium-priced restaurant, good value. Recommended.

C Marañón, Nauta 285, T242673, www.hotelmaranon.cjb.net. Includes breakfast, airport transfer, small pool, a/c, hot water, comfortable. Recommended.

C Royal Inn, Aguirre 793, T224244, royalinn_casinohotel@terra.com. Includes breakfast, a/c, frigobar, hot water, bidet, modern and comfortable.

E Hospedaje Mi Selvita, Av Quiñónez Km 3.5, Pasaje Roma No 14, T260165,

raxafe@operamail.com. A charming small *hostal* in lovely gardens, run by Aydee Ríos Cárdenas, who is a travel agent (she speaks some English). Near the airport, simple rooms with cool shower, fan, TV, meals.
E El Sitio, Ricardo Palma 541, T234932. Fan, cafeteria, spotless. Highly recommended.
E Hostal Alfert, García Sanz 01, T234105. Hard beds, good views of river, safe, but in market area, arranges jungle trips but not an authorized operator.
E Hostal Colibrí, Nauta 172, T241737. One block from Plaza and 50 m from the river, new building, TV, fan, hot water, secure, good value, helpful staff, a/c rooms more expensive.
F La Casa de Samantha, Nauta 787, T231005. Shared bath, cold water, small place, family-run, helpful.
F Isabel, Brasil 156, T234901. Good, but plug the holes in the walls, secure, often full.

🍴 Eating

Iquitos *p1266, map p1267*
Local specialities Try palm heart salad (*chonta*), or *a la Loretana* dish on menus; also try *inchicapi* (chicken, corn and peanut soup), *cecina* (fried dried pork), *tacacho* (fried green banana and pork, mashed into balls and eaten for breakfast or tea), *juanes* (chicken, rice, olive and egg, seasoned and wrapped in bijao leaves and sold in restaurants) and the *camu-camu*, an acquired taste, said to have one of the highest vitamin C concentrations in the world. Try the local drink *chuchuhuasi*, made from the bark of a tree, which is supposed to have aphrodisiac properties (for sale at Arica 1046), and *jugo de cocona*, and the alcoholic *cola de mono* and *siete raíces* (aguardiente mixed with the bark of 7 trees and wild honey), sold at **Exquisita Amazónica**, Abtao 590.

Many private homes offer set lunch, look for the board outside.
♦♦♦♦ Fitzcarrald, Malecón Maldonado 103 y Napo. Smart, best pizza in town, also good pastas and salads.
♦♦♦♦ La Gran Maloca, Sargento Lores 170, opposite Banco Continental. A/c, high class.
♦♦♦♦ Montecarlo, Napo 140. Next to the casino, said to be the best in town.
♦♦ Ari's Burger, Plaza de Armas, Próspero 127. Medium-priced fast food, good breakfasts, popular with tourists.
♦♦ Chifa Long Fung, San Martín at Plaza 28 de Julio. Good Chinese if a little expensive, a/c, 1200-1500, 1900-000 daily.

♦♦ El Nuevo Mesón, Malecón Maldonado 153. Local specialities include wild boar, alligator, turtle, tapir and other endangered species, has lots of regular dishes, too.
♦♦ Pollón, next door to *Ari's Burger*. Chicken and chips, open in the daytime.
♦♦ The Regal, in the *Casa de Hierro*, Plaza de Armas, Próspero y Putumayo, 2nd floor. Nice location, good set lunch US$2.30, other meals more expensive.
♦♦ Yellow Rose of Texas, Putumayo 180. Run by the ex-director of the tourist office, Gerald W Mayeaux, very helpful. Varied food including local dishes, Texan atmosphere. Open 24 hrs so you can wait here if arriving late at night, good breakfasts, lots of information, also has a bar, Sky TV and Texan saddle seats.
♦ Huasaí, Napo 326. Varied and innovative *menú*, popular and recommended, 0730-1600 daily.
♦ Paulina, Tacna 591. Good set lunch, popular but noisy.
♦ La Vida es Salud, Aguirre 759 on Plaza 28 de Julio. Vegetarian, simple little place, good value, open daily.

Cafés
Heladería, Próspero 415. Good ice-cream (try local flavour *aguaje*). **Juguería Paladar**, Próspero 245. Excellent juices.

🍸 Bars and clubs

Iquitos *p1266, map p1267*
Noa Noa, Pevas y Fitzcarrald. Popular disco, varied music, open Tue-Sat.
La Ribereña, Raymondi 453. With terraced seats on a newly-built plaza.
Snack Bar Arandú, Malecón Maldonado. Good views of the Amazon river.
Teatro Café Amauta, Nauta 248. Live music, open 2200-2400, good atmosphere, popular, small exhibition hall.
Tuspa, Raimondi block 2. Light rock, lively, good place to listen to music.

🎉 Festivals and events

Iquitos *p1266, map p1267*
5 Jan: founding of Iquitos. **Feb-Mar**: Carnival.
3rd week in Jun: tourist week.
24 Jun: San Juan. **28-30 Aug**: Santa Rosa de Lima. **8 Dec**: Immaculate Conception, celebrated in Punchana, near the docks.

⚙ Shopping

Iquitos *p1266, map p1267*
Hammocks in Iquitos cost about US$6. **Amazon Arts & Crafts**, Napo block 100. **Artesanías de la Selva**, R Palma 190. **Mad Mick's Trading Post**, next to the Iron House, hires out rubber boots for those going to the jungle. **Mercado Artesanal de Productores**, 4 km from the centre in the San Juan district, on the road to the airport, take a colectivo. Cheapest in town with more choice than elsewhere.

▲ Activities and tours

Iquitos *p1266, map p1267*
Jungle tours from Iquitos All agencies are under the control of the local office of the Ministry of Tourism. They arrange one day or longer trips to places of interest with guides speaking some English. Package tours booked in your home country, over the internet or in Lima are much more expensive than those booked locally. Take your time before making a decision and don't be bullied by the hustlers at the airport (they get paid a hefty commission). You must make sure your tour operator or guide has a proper licence (the Municipalidad's *Iquitos Guía Turística* gives a full list). Do not go with a company which does not have legal authorization; there are many unscrupulous people about. Find out all the details of the trip and food arrangements before paying (a minimum of US$45 per day). Speed boats for river trips can be hired by the hour or day at the Embarcadero Turístico, at the intersection of Av de la Marina and Samánez Ocampo in Punchana. Prices vary greatly, usually US$10-20 per hr, and are negotiable. In fact, all prices are negotiable, except **Muyuna**, who do not take commissions.

General information and advice Take a long-sleeved shirt, waterproof coat and shoes or light boots on jungle trips and a good torch, as well as espirales to ward off the mosquitoes at night – they can be bought from pharmacies in Iquitos. Premier is the most effective local insect repellent. The dry season is from Jul-Sep (Sep is the best month to see flowers and butterflies).
Amazon Lodge and Safaris, Av La Marina 592A, T251078, www.theamazonlodges.com. 48 km down-river from Iquitos. Comfortable; 3 days/2 nights, US$200 pp for 2-4 people, US$50 per person for additional nights.
Amazon Tours and Cruises, Requena 336, T231611, www.amazontours.net. An American-owned company. Luxury cruises on the *Andrea* Iquitos-Leticía-Manaus-Iquitos, US$5,150 per person, 9 days, and to Belém, US$6,950, 15 days; the *Río Amazonas* sails

Iquitos-Leticia-Iquitos, US$765; *Amazon Explorer* to Pacaya-Samiria, US$795. They also offer nature cruises and rugged expeditions.
Amazon Wilderness Expeditions, Jr Putumayo 163, altos 202, T34565, 967 4397 (mob). Good tours to Emerald Forest Camp, on Río Yanayacu, 185 km from Iquitos, US$65 per day. Comfortable, simple accommodation (no shower – wash in river), good food. Ask for guide Juan Carlos Palomino Berndt, T993 5472 (mob).
Blue Morpho Tours, Moore 144, T231 168, T961 9801 (mob), www.bluemorphotours.com. A rustic camp on the Río Aucayacu, a tributary of the Ucayali 300 km south of Iquitos. Centre for shamanic studies and workshops, tours US$80 pp per day, all inclusive except for bar and snacks.
Cumaceba Lodge and Expeditions, Putumayo 184 in the Iron House, T/F232229, www.cumaceba.com. Tours of 2-8 days to their lodges on the Amazon and Yarapa rivers, good birdwatching guides, 3 days/2 nights for US$120 pp. Very good all round.
Explorama Tours, by the riverside docks on Av La Marina 340, PO Box 446, T253301, www.explorama.com, are highly recommended as the most efficient and, with over 40 years in existence, certainly the biggest and most established. Their sites are: **Ceiba Tops**, 40 km (1½ hrs) from Iquitos, is a resort providing 'an adventure in luxury', 75 a/c rooms with electricity, hot showers, pool with hydromassage and beautiful gardens. The food is good and, as in all Explorama's properties, is served communally. There are attractive walks and other excursions, a recommended jungle experience for those who want their creature comforts, US$200 pp for 1 night/2 days, US$98 for each additional night (1-2 people).
Explorama Lodge at Yanamono, 80 km from Iquitos, 2½ hrs from Iquitos, has palm-thatched accommodation with separate bathroom and shower facilities connected by covered walkways, cold water, no electricity, good food and service. US$285 for 3 days/2 nights and US$85 for each additional day (1-2 people).
Explornapo Lodge at Llachapa on the Sucusai creek (a tributary of the Napo) is in the same style as Explorama Lodge, but is further away from Iquitos, 160 km (4 hrs), and is set in 105,000 ha of primary rainforest, so is better for seeing wildlife, US$395 for 3 days/2 nights. Nearby is the impressive canopy walkway 35 m above the forest floor and 500 m long, 'a magnificent experience and not to be missed'. It is associated with the **Amazon Center for Tropical Studies (ACTS)**, a scientific station, only 10 mins from the canopy walkway.
Explor Tambos, 2 hrs from Explornapo, offer more primitive accommodation, 8 shelters for 16

peru Iquitos & around Listings

campers, bathing in the river, offers the best chance to see rare fauna. Close to Explornapo is the ReNuPeRu medicinal plant garden, run by a curandero. Members of South American Explorers are offered 15% discount.

Heliconia Lodge, Ricardo Palma 242, T231959, www.amazonriverexpeditions.com. On the Río Amazonas, 1½ hrs from Iquitos, the lodge has hot water, electricity for 3 hrs a day, good guiding and staff; rustic yet comfortable, 3 days/2 nights US$180. Under same management as Zungarocoha, see below, and in same group as Hotels Victoria Regia and Acosta, see above. They organize trips to Allpahuayo-Mishana, to Pacaya-Samiria with Amazon Tours and Cruises, see above, and to the ACTS canopy walkway.

Jungle Bike, Libertad 549, T266631, www.junglebike.net. For cycle tours through the jungle.

Muyuna Amazon Lodge, Putumayo 163, T242858, 993 4424 (mob), www.muyuna.com. 120 km from Iquitos, also on the Yanayacu, before San Juan village. Packages from 1 to 5 nights available, 2 nights/3 days US$300, but users of this Handbook should make reservations in person for discounted price (similarly SAE members, 10%). Everything is included in the price. Good guides, accommodation, food and service, very well organized and professional, flexible, radio contact, will collect passengers from airport if requested in advance. They offer a 7-day birdwatching trip, combining several areas including Allpahuayo-Mishana Reserve; also have a new underwater microphone for listening to dolphins. Highly recommended.

Paseos Amazónicos Ambassador, Pevas 246, T/F231618, operates the **Amazonas Sinchicuy Lodge**, US$70 per person per night. The lodge is 1½ hrs from Iquitos on the Sinchicuy river, 25 mins by boat from the Amazon river. The lodge consists of several wooden buildings with thatched roofs on stilts, cabins with bathroom, no electricity but paraffin lamps are provided, good food, and plenty activities, including visits to local villages. Recommended. They also organize visits to Lake Quistococha.

Tahuayo Lodge, Amazonia Expeditions, 10305 Riverburn Drive, Tampa, FL 33647, toll free T800-262 9669, www.perujungle.com. Near the Reserva Comunal de Tamshiyacu- Tahuayo on the Río Tahuayo, 145 km upriver from Iquitos, comfortable cabins with cold shower, buffet meals, good food, laundry service, wide range of excursions, excellent staff. A 7-day programme costs US$1,295, all inclusive, extra days US$100. Recommended. The lodge is associated with the Rainforest Conservation Fund, see www.rain forestconservation.org.

Zungarocoha Amazon Lodge, Ricardo Palma

242, T/F231959 (see Heliconia, above). A recreation centre on the Río Nanay, 35 mins from Iquitos. Comfortable lakeside bungalows reached by road (12 km), swimming pool, watersports, mini-zoo, full day US$40, 1 night/2 days US$95.

⊖ Transport

Iquitos *p1266, map p1267*

Air Francisco Secada Vigneta airport, T260147. Taxi to the airport costs US$2.85; *motocarro* (motorcycle with 2 seats), US$2. A bus from the airport, US$0.20, goes from the main road; most go through the centre of town. To **Lima**, daily; **Lan** and **Star Perú**. Grupo 42 flies once a week to **Lagunas** for Pacaya Samiria (US$50), **Yurimaguas** (US$55), **Tarapoto** (US$80) and **Pucallpa** (US$60). Iquitos flights are frequently delayed; be sure to reconfirm your flight in Iquitos, as they are often overbooked, especially over Christmas; check times in advance as itineraries frequently change.

Airline offices Grupo 42, Sgto Lores 127, T233224. **Lan**, Napo 374, T232421. Star Perú, Próspero 428, T236208.

Ferry General hints for river travel: large passenger and cargo vessels are called *lanchas*, smaller faster craft are called *rápidos* or *deslizadores* (speedboats). You can find information on boats and tickets at **Bellavista**, Malecón Tarapacá 596; or in the Puerto Masusa district of Puchana, at Av La Marina with Masusa (take a bus from the centre, 10 mins).

All *lanchas* leave from Masusa, 2 km north of the centre, a dangerous area at night. All sailings around 1800-2000, the first night's meal is not included. Always deal directly with boat owners or managers, avoid touts and middle-men. All fares are negotiable. You can buy either a ticket to sling your hammock on deck, or for a berth in a cabin sleeping four people.

A hammock is essential. A double, of material (not string), provides one person with a blanket. Board the boat many hours in advance to guarantee hammock space. If going on the top deck, try to be first down the front; take rope for hanging your hammock, plus string and sarongs for privacy. On all boats, hang your hammock away from lightbulbs (they aren't switched off at night and attract all sorts of strange insects) and away from the engines, which usually emit noxious fumes. Guard your belongings from the moment you board. It's safer to club together and pay for a cabin in which to lock your belongings, even if you sleep outside in a hammock. There is very little privacy; women travellers can expect a lot of attention. There are adequate washing and toilet facilities, but the food is rice, meat and beans (and whatever can be picked up en route) cooked in river water. Stock up on drinking water, fruit and tinned food. Vegetarians must take their own supplies. There is a good cheap bar on board. Take plenty of prophylactic enteritis tablets; many contract dysentery on the trip. Also take insect repellent and a mosquito net. If arriving in Iquitos on a regular, slow boat, take extreme care when disembarking. Things get very chaotic at this time and theft and pickpocketing is rife.

Lanchas serve all of the following destinations: **Pucallpa**, 3-5 days up river along the Amazon and Ucayali, hammock US$22, berth US$35. To **Yurimaguas**, 3-4 days up river along the Amazon, Marañón and Huallaga, 2nd class hammock space US$18, 1st class hammock space US$25, berth US$35. **Eduardo** company is recommended, **Eduardo IV and V** are their newest vessels. **Islandia** for **Leticia** (Colombia) and **Tabatinga** (Brazil), 2-3 days down river on the Amazon, hammock space US$15, berth US$22. **Gran Diego** is a nice vessel. Passengers disembark in Peru for immigration formalities (no exchange facilities), then take another US$1 boat to **Marco**, the port for **Tabatinga**. Most boats for **Manaus** depart from Marco.

To **Pantoja** (for Ecuador), 5-7 days up river on the Napo, hammock space US$30, no berths. There are 4 basic boats: **Victor** and **Camila** (same owner, T242082) and **Jeisawell** and **Siempre Adelante** (same owner, T266159, T961 3049, mob). Each sails twice a month, but will not go all the way to Pantoja unless there is cargo. To reduce the voyage by a day, take a small boat to **Indiana** and cross to Mazán to catch the lancha on the Napo, but there may not be much space left onboard. Alternatively, you can take a rápido from Mazán to **Santa Clotilde** (5 hrs, US$24, less than half-way to Pantoja, one *hospedaje*, **F**) and wait for the *lancha*, or try to find a smaller boat going to Pantoja. The trip requires plenty of time and patience.

Rápidos for **Tabatinga** (Brazil) leave from El Embarcadero Turístico, at 0600 daily except Mon, 11 hrs, US$60. There are no boats direct to Manaus. Boats go to **Santa Rosa** on the border, opposite **Tabatinga**. They leave most days at 0600-0615; be at the port at 0445 for customs check. They go to Santa Rosa for immigration formalities then take passengers across to Tabatinga, US$2. Purchase tickets in advance from company offices: **Transtur**, Raymondi 384, T231278, transtur@terra.com.pe; **River Fox**, Raymondi 344, T243404 (not recommended). All include a small breakfast of a sandwich and coffee, a passable lunch and mineral water (ask for it). All carry life jackets and have clean bathrooms. Luggage limit is 15 kg. Most travel agencies sell tickets. Hotels have details of sailings; ask around which boats are reliable.

Lake Quistococha *p1268*
Combis leave every hour until 1500 from Plaza 28 de Julio, Iquitos; the last one back leaves at 1700. Alternatively take a **motocarro** there and back with a 1 hr wait, which costs US$6. Perhaps the best option is to hire a **motorbike** and spend the day there. The road can be difficult after rain.

● Directory

Iquitos *p1266, map p1267*
Banks BCP, Plaza de Armas. For Visa, also cash and TCs at good rates, Visa ATM around the corner on Próspero. **BBV Continental**, Sgto Lores 171. For Visa, 1% commission on TCs. **Banco de la Nación**, Condamine 478. Good rates. **Casa de cambio** at **Tienda Wing Kong**, Próspero 312, Mon-Sat 0800-1300, 1500-2000, Sun 0900-1200. Western Union, Napo 359, T235182. **Note**: Don't change money on the streets. **Consulates** Consulates: Colombia, Calvo de Araujo 431, T231461. UK, Casa de Hierro (Iron House), Putumayo 182A, T222732, F223607, Mon-Fri 1100-1200. **Note**: There is no Brazilian consulate. If you need a visa, you must get it in Lima. **Internet** There are places everywhere, US$0.80 per hr. **Medical services** Clínica Loreto, Morona 471, T233752, 24-hr attention, recommended, but only Spanish spoken. **Motorcycle hire** Park Motors, Tacna 579, T/F231688. Addresses of others from tourist office, see above. **Post offices** On the corner of C Arica with Morona, near Plaza de Armas, daily 0700-1700. **Telephones** Arica 276. Cheap private cabins at Próspero 523, national and international calls, helpful staff. **Useful addresses** Immigration: Mcal Cáceres 18th block, T235371. Tourist police: Sargento Lores 834, T242081, helpful with complaints. In emergency T241000 or 241001.

Southeastern jungle

The southern selva is in Madre de Dios department, which contains the Manu National Park (2.05 million ha), the Tambopata National Reserve (254,358 ha) and the Bahauja- Sonene National Park (1.1 million ha). The forest of this lowland region (Altitude 260 m) is technically called Sub-tropical Moist Forest, which means that it receives less rainfall than tropical forest and is dominated by the floodplains of its meandering rivers. The most striking features are the former river channels that have become isolated as ox-bow lakes. These are home to black caiman and giant otter. Other rare species living in the forest are jaguar, puma, ocelot and tapir. There are also howler monkeys, macaws, guans, currasows and the giant harpy eagle. As well as containing some of the most important flora and fauna on Earth, the region also harbours gold-diggers, loggers, hunters, drug smugglers and oil-men, whose activities have endangered the unique rainforest. Various conservation groups are working to protect it.

Ins and outs

Access to Manu The multiple use zone of Manu Biosphere Reserve is accessible to anyone and several lodges exist in the area (see Lodges in Manu below). The reserved zone is accessible by permit only. Entry is strictly controlled and visitors must visit the area under the auspices of an authorized operator with an authorized guide. Permits are limited and reservations should be made well in advance. In the reserved zone the only accommodation is in the comfortable Manu Lodge or in the comfortable but rustic Casa Machiguenga in the Cocha Salvador area. Several companies have tented safari camp infrastructures, some with shower and dining facilities, but all visitors sleep in tents. The entrance fee to the Reserved Zone is 150 soles pp (about US$40) and is included in package tour prices.

Useful addresses In Lima Asociación Peruana para la Conservación de la Naturaleza (APECO) ① *Parque José Acosta 187, p 2, Magdalena del Mar, To1-264 0094, www.ape co.org.pe.* **Pronaturaleza** ① *Av Alberto de Campo 417, Lima 17, To1-264 2736, and in Puerto Maldonado, Jr Cajamarca cuadra 1 s/n, To82-571585, www.pronaturaleza.org.* **In Cuzco** Perú **Verde** ① *Ricardo Palma J-1, Santa Mónica, To84-226392, www.peruverde.org.* This is a local NGO that can help with information and has free video shows about Manu National Park and Tambopata National Reserve. Friendly and helpful and with information on research in the jungle area of Madre de Dios. Further information can be obtained from the **Manu National Park Office** ① *Av Micaela Bastidas 310, Cuzco, To84-240898, pqnmanu@terra.com.pe, open 0800-1400.* They issue a permit for the Reserved Zone which costs about US$40.

Climate The climate is warm and humid, with a rainy season from Novemer to March and a dry season from April to October. Cold fronts from the South Atlantic, called *friajes*, are characteristic of the dry season, when temperatures drop to 15-16° C during the day, and 13° at night. Always bring a sweater at this time. The best time to visit is during the dry season when there are fewer mosquitoes and the rivers are low, exposing the beaches. This is also a good time to see nesting and to view animals at close range, as they stay close to the rivers and are easily seen. Note that this is also the hottest time. A pair of binoculars is essential and insect repellent is a must.

Manu Biosphere Reserve

No other reserve can compare with Manu for the diversity of life forms; it holds over 1,000 species of birds and covers an altitudinal range from 200 to 4,100 m above sea-level. Giant otters, jaguars, ocelots and 13 species of primates abound in this pristine tropical wilderness, and uncontacted indigenous tribes are present in the more remote areas, as are indigenous groups with limited access.

The reserve is one of the largest conservation units on Earth, encompassing the complete drainage of the Manu River. It is divided into the **Manu National Park** (1,692,137 ha), where only government sponsored biologists and anthropologists may visit with permits from the Ministry of Agriculture in Lima; the **Reserved Zone** (257,000 ha) within the Manu National Park, set aside for applied scientific research and ecotourism; and the **Cultural Zone** (92,000 ha), which contains acculturated native groups and colonists, where the locals still employ their traditional way of life. Among the ethnic groups in the Cultural Zone are the Harakmbut, Machiguenga and Yine in the Amarakaeri Reserved Zone, on the east bank of the Alto Madre de Dios. They have set up their own ecotourism activities. Associated with Manu are other areas protected by conservation groups, or local people (for example the Blanquillo reserved zone) and some cloud forest parcels along the road. The **Nahua-Kugapakori Reserved Zone**, set aside for these two nomadic native groups, is the area between the headwaters of the Río Manu and headwaters of the Río Urubamba, to the north of the alto Madre de Dios.

Cuzco to Puerto Maldonado via Mazuko

This route is Cuzco-Urcos-Quincemil-Mazuko-Puerto Maldonado. Bus and truck details are given under Transport, below. It's a painfully slow journey on an appalling road; trucks frequently get stuck or break down. **Quincemil**, 240 km from Urcos on the road to Mazuko, is a centre for alluvial gold-mining with many banks. Accommodation is available in **F Hotel Toni**, friendly, clean, cold shower, good meals. Quincemil marks the half-way point and the start of the all-weather road. Gasoline is scarce in Quincemil because most road vehicles continue on 70 km to Mazuko, which is another mining centre, where they fill up with the cheaper gasoline of the jungle region. The changing scenery is magnificent and worth the hardship and discomfort.

To Puerto Maldonado via Pilcopata and Itahuania

The arduous 255 km trip over the Andes from Cuzco to Pilcopata takes about 16-18 hours by bus or truck (20-40 hours in the wet season). On this route, too, the scenery is magnificent. From Cuzco you climb up to the pass before Paucartambo (very cold at night), before dropping down to this mountain village at the border between the departments of Cuzco and Madre de Dios. The road then ascends to the second pass (also cold at night), after which it goes down to the cloud forest and then the rainforest, reaching **Pilcopata** at 650 m.

Pilcopata to Itahuania After Pilcopata, the route is hair-raising and breathtaking, passing through **Atalaya**, the first village on the Alto Madre de Dios River and tourist port for hiring boats to Boca Manu (basic accommodation). The route continues to Salvación, where a Park Office and Park Entrance are situated. There are basic hostals and restaurants. Basic restaurants can be found in Pilcopata and Atalaya.

The end of the road, which bypasses the previous port of **Shintuya**, is **Itahuania**, the starting point for river transport. It won't be long before the port moves down river as the road is being built to Nuevo Eden, 11 km away, and there are plans to extend to Diamante by end-2006, beginning 2007, with the road one day planned to reach Boca Colorado. **Note:** It is not possible to arrange trips to the Reserved Zone of the National Park from Itahuania, owing to park regulations. All arrangements, including permits, must be made in Cuzco.

Itahuania to Puerto Maldonado Cargo boats leave for the gold mining centre of Boca Colorado on the Río Madre de Dios, via Boca Manu, but only when the boat is fully laden (see Transport below). Very basic accommodation can be found here, but it is not recommended for lone women travellers. From Colorado you then catch a boat to Laberinto, 6-7 hours, from where regular combis run to Puerto Maldonado.

Boca Manu is the connecting point between the rivers Alto Madre de Dios, Manu and Madre de Dios. It has a few houses, an air strip and some food supplies. It is also the entrance to the Manu Reserve and to go further you must be part of an organized group. The park ranger station is located in Limonal. You need to show your permit here. Camping is allowed if you have a permit. There are no regular flights from Cuzco to Boca Manu. These are arranged the day before, if there are enough passengers. Check at Cuzco airport; or with the tour operators in Cuzco.

To the Reserved Zone Upstream on the Río Manu you pass the *Manu Lodge* (see Sleeping, below), on the Cocha Juárez, 3-4 hours by boat. You can continue to Cocha Otorongo, 2½ hours and Cocha Salvador, 30 minutes, the biggest lake with plenty of wildlife. From here it is 2-3 hours to Pakitza, the entrance to the National Park Zone. This is only for biologists with a special permit.

Between Boca Manu and Colorado is **Blanquillo**, a private reserve (10,000 ha). Bring a good tent with you and all food if you want to camp and do it yourself, or alternatively accommodation is available at the *Tambo Blanquillo* (full board or accommodation only). Wildlife is abundant, especially macaws and parrots at the macaw lick near *Manu Wildlife Centre*. There are occasional boats to Blanquillo from Shintuya; US$10, 6-8 hours.

Puerto Maldonado → *Phone code: 082. Colour map 3, grid C5. Pop: 40,000. Altitude: 250 m.*
Puerto Maldonado is an important starting point for visiting the south eastern jungles of the Tambopata Reserve or departing for Bolivia or Brazil. It overlooks the confluence of the rivers Tambopata and Madre de Dios and its isolation makes it relatively expensive and because of the gold mining and timber industries, the immediate surrounding jungle is now cultivated.

The beautiful and tranquil **Lago Sandoval** is a one-hour boat ride along the Río Madre de Dios, and then a 5-km walk into the jungle (parts of the first 3 km are a raised wooden walkway; boots are advisable). Entry to the lake coasts US$5. You must go with a guide; this can be arranged by the boat driver. Boats can be hired at the Madre de Dios port for about US$25 a day, minimum two people (plus petrol) to go to Lago Sandoval (don't pay the full cost in advance).

Jungle tours from Puerto Maldonado
Trips can be made to **Lago Valencia**, 60 km away near the Bolivian border, four hours there, eight hours back. It is an ox-bow lake with lots of wildlife. Many excellent beaches and islands are located within an hour's boat ride. Mosquitoes are voracious. If camping, take food and water.

It is quite easy to arrange a boat and guide from Puerto Maldonado (see Tour operators below) to the **Tambopata National Reserve** (TNR) ① *Jr Cuzco 165, Puerto Maldonado, T573278, US$9 to enter the TNR, US$20 if going beyond the Malinowski/ Tambopata confluence, this is included in lodge packages*, between the rivers Madre de Dios, Tambopata and Heath. Some superb ox-bow lakes can be visited and the birdwatching is wonderful. All visitors must pay *Inrena* (the protected areas institute).

The **Bahuaja-Sonene National Park**, declared in 1996, stretches from the Heath River across the Tambopata, incorporating the Río Heath National Sanctuary. It is closed to visitors.

To the Bolivian border

Take the boat to Puerto Heath, but get a tourist visa at the Bolivian immigration office in Puerto Maldonado. It can take several days to find a boat going all the way to the Bolivian border. Motorized dugout canoes go to Puerto Pardo on the Peruvian side (five hours, US$4.50 per person, no hotels or shops). Wait here for a canoe to Puerto Heath. It is fairly hard to get a boat from the border to Riberalta; a wait of up to three days is not uncommon. The journey takes three days and costs US$15-20. Alternatively, go to the naval base at América, then fly.

To Iberia and Iñapari

Daily public transport runs on the improved dirt road which begins across the Río Madre de Dios and runs to **Iberia** and **Iñapari** on the border with Brazil. In the wet season the road may only be passable with difficulty, especially between Iberia and Iñapari. In the dry, though, it is a fast road and dangerous for motorcyclists because of passing traffic. Along the road there remains no primary forest, only secondary growth and small *chacras* (farms). There are also picturesque *caseríos* (settlements) that serve as processing centres for the brazil nut. Approximately 70% of the inhabitants in the Madre de Dios are involved in the collection of this prized nut.

Iberia, Km 168, has two hotels, the best is **F Hostal Aquino**, basic, cold shower. Just outside the town the local rubber tappers association has set up an interesting Reserve and Information Centre.

Iñapari, at the end of the road, Km 235, has two basic hotels and a restaurant, but **Assis Brasil** across the border is much more attractive and has a much nicer basic hotel (**F**) on the main plaza. In the dry season it is possible to walk across the Rio Acre to Assis, otherwise take the ferry. A suspension bridge is being built (due for completion 2006).

There is a road from Assis Brasil into Brazil and connections to Cobija in Bolivia from Brasiléia. It can be cold travelling this road, so take a blanket or sleeping bag. There are no exchange facilities en route and poor exchange rates for Brazilian currency at Iñapari. Crossing between Peru and Bolivia on this route is not easy.

Crossing to Brazil

Take one of the car colectivos that leave for Iñapari from Puerto Maldonado between 0700-0800, 5-5½ hours, US$10 (three companies). The cars stop near **immigration in Iñapari**. Exit stamps are obtained at immigration, open 0800-1830. In Assis Brasil, there is no Policía Federal office. You have to travel on to Brasiléia to obtain your Brazil entry stamp at Policía Federal in the Rodoviária (bus station). You must have a yellow fever certificate to enter Brazil.

● Sleeping

Manu Biosphere Reserve *p1274*
Lodges in Manu
Amazonia Lodge, on the Río Alto Madre de Dios just across the river from Atalaya. In Cuzco at Matará 334, T/F084-231370, amazonia1@ correo.dnet.com.pe. An old tea hacienda run by the Yabar family, famous for its bird diversity and fine hospitality, a great place to relax, contact Santiago in advance and he'll arrange a pick-up.
Casa Machiguenga, near Cocha Salvador, upriver from Manu Lodge. Contact **Manu Expeditions** or Apeco NGO, T084-225595. Machiguenga-style cabins run by local communities with NGO help.
Cock of the Rock Lodge, on the road from Paucartambo to Atalaya at 1,500 m, next to a Cock of the Rock *lek*, 8 double rooms and some private cabins, run by the **Perú Verde** group (see Ins and outs, above).
Erika Lodge, on the Alto Madre de Dios, 25 mins from Atalaya, offers basic accommodation and is cheaper than the other, more luxurious lodges.

Contact **Manu Ecological Adventures** (see below).
Manu Cloud Forest Lodge, at Unión, at 1,800 m on the road from Paucartambo to Atalaya, owned by **Manu Nature Tours**, 6 rooms with 4 beds.
Manu Lodge, on the Manu river, 3 hrs upriver from Boca Manu towards Cocha Salvador, run by **Manu Nature Tours** and only bookable as part of a full package deal with transport.
Manu Wildlife Centre, 2 hrs down the Río Madre de Dios from Boca Manu, near the Blanquillo macaw lick. Book through **Manu Expeditions** or InkaNatura. 22 double cabins, with private bathroom and hot water. Also canopy towers for birdwatching and a Tapir lick.
Pantiacolla Lodge, 30 mins down-river from Shintuya. Owned by the Moscoso family. Book through **Pantiacolla Tours** (see page 1281).

To Puerto Maldonado via Pilcopata and Itahuania *p1275*
C Boca Manu Lodge, book through **Emperadores Tours**, Procuradores 190, Cuzco,

T084-239987. Run by Juan de Dios Carpio, who owns a general store in Boca, reasonably priced.
F Unnamed place of Sra Rubella, Pilcopata. Very basic but friendly.

Tambo Amana, 30 mins from Shintuya on foot, tamboamana@yahoo.com. Run by the indigenous Chinipa family, a cultural as opposed to wildlife tour, learning about Harakmbut culture. If you make your own way there, this is a very economical jungle trip at US$190 for 5 days/ 4 nights for those prepared to rough it a bit. Jessica Bertram de Sasari helps the Chinipa family with marketing and is a good source of information. You can contact her at **Hospedaje Mario's**, C Choquechaca 469, Cuzco, T084-225500, jessicabertrampe@yahoo.com. Perudiscovery sell the trip with a stay in the cloudforest and a mountain biking descent, www.peru discovery.com. If contacting the family direct, you need to speak Spanish (or Harakmbut!).

Yine Lodge, next to Boca Manu airport. A cooperative project between **Pantiacolla Tours** and the Yine community of Diamante.
F pp Hostal in Boca Manu run by the community. Basic accommodation.

Puerto Maldonado p1276

A Wasai Lodge & Expeditions, Billinghurst opposite the Capitanía; reservations: Las Higueras 257, Residencial Monterrico, La Molina, Lima 12, T/F572290, www.wasai.com. In a beautiful location overlooking the Madre de Dios River, with forest surrounding cabin-style rooms, a/c, TV, shower, small pool with waterfall, good restaurant (local fish a speciality). Recommended. They can organize local tours and also have a lodge on the Río Tambopata.
C Cabañaquinta, Cuzco 535, T571045, cabanquinta@webcusco.zzn.com. Fan, good restaurant, lovely garden, very comfortable, airport transfer. Recommended.
C Don Carlos, Av León Velarde 1271, T571029. Nice view over the Río Tambopata, a/c,

restaurant, TV, phone, good.
D Amarumayo, Libertad 433, 10 mins from the centre, T573860. Comfortable, with pool and garden, good restaurant. Recommended.
E Hospedaje Español, González Prada 670, T572381. Comfortable, set back from the road, in a quiet part of town.
E Hospedaje La Bahía, 2 de Mayo 710, T572127. Cheaper without bath or TV, new, large rooms, a good choice.
E Rey Port, Av León Velarde 457, T571177. With bath, fan, front rooms noisy, good value.
E Royal Inn, 2 de Mayo 333, T571048. Modern and clean, very good.
F Hostal El Astro, Velarde 617, T572128. Clean, safe, family run.

Tambopata p1276

Some of the lodges along the Tambopata river offer guiding and research placements to biology and environmental science graduates. For more details send an SAE to **TReeS**: UK - J Forrest, PO Box 33153, London, NW3 4DR, www.geocities.com/treesperu

Lodges on the Río Madre de Dios

C Casa de Hospedaje Mejía, to book T571428, visit **Mejía Tours**, L Velarde 333, or just turn up. Attractive rustic lodge on Lago Sandoval, full board can be arranged, canoes are available.
El Corto Maltés, Billinghurst 229, Puerto Maldonado, T/F573831, cortomaltes@ terra.com.pe. On the Madre de Dios, halfway to Sandoval which is the focus of most visits. Hot water, huge dining-room, well run.
Eco Amazonia Lodge, on the Madre de Dios, 1 hr down-river from Puerto Maldonado. In Lima: Av Larco 1083, of 408, Miraflores, T242 2708, www.ecoamazonia. com.pe. Basic bungalows and dormitories, good for birdwatching, has its own Monkey Island with animals taken from the forest, US$150 for 3 days/2 nights.

Jungle Lodge, bungalows 15 km out on the Madre de Dios. Book through **Cuzco-Maldonado Tour**, Pasaje de Harinas 177, T/F244054, Cuzco. Jungle programmes from US$90 pp in low season, tours visit Lago Sandoval.

Reserva Amazónica Lodge, 45 mins by boat down the Madre de Dios. To book: **Inkaterra**, Andalucía 174, Lima 18, T01-610 0404; Cuzco T084-245314; Puerto Maldonado T082- 572283, www.inkaterra.com. Tastefully redecorated hotel in the jungle with suites and bungalows, solar power, good food in huge dining room supported by a big tree. Jungle tours in its own 10,000 ha but most tours are to Lago Sandoval, US$150 pp for 2 days/1 night package, up to US$450 for 5 days/4 nights, negotiable out of season. The lodge has Isla Rolín for the recovery of primates, which are readapted to their natural environment.

Sandoval Lake Lodge, 1 km beyond *Mejía* on Lago Sandoval, book through **InkaNatura**, address under Manu, Tour operators. Usual access is by canoe after a 3-km walk or rickshaw ride, huge bar and dining area, electricity, hot water. From US$140 pp for 2 days/1 night, to US$270 for 4 days/3 nights.

Lodges on the Tambopata

Lodges on the Tambopata are reached by vehicle to Bahuaja port, 15 km up river from Puerto Maldonado by the community of Infierno, then by boat.

Albergue Inatowa, T082-572511, www.inotawaexpeditions.com. Just downstream from Explorer's Inn, visits to nearby Lago Tres Chimbadas. Part of a scheme to show visitors the life of long-term colonists in the Tambopata area; facilities are quite basic, transport, food, mosquito net and Spanish-speaking guides.

Caiman Lodge, to book T082-571045, Puerto Maldonado, www.webcusco.com/sachavacasinn. 2 bungalows for up to 20 people, between Explorer's Inn and Libertador Tambopata Lodge. Visits are made to Lago Sachavacayoc.

Casa de hospedaje Picaflor, Casilla 105, Puerto Maldonado, picaflor_rc@yahoo.com. A small, family-run guest house with solar lighting, a good library, great cakes and fresh bread baked

daily. Just downriver from **Libertador Tambopata Lodge**, guiding in English/ Spanish, good trail system, visits also made to Lake Condenados. Suited to backpackers and birders, US$20pp per night plus TNR fee and transport. Special arrangements also for researchers and volunteers wanting to stay 4 or more weeks.
Explorers Inn, book through Peruvian Safaris, Alcanfores 459, Miraflores, Lima, T01-447 8888, or Plateros 365, T084-235342, Cuzco, or Fitzcarrald 136, Puerto Maldonado, T/F082-572078, www.peruviansafaris.com. Adjoining the TNR, in the part where most research work has been done, 58 km from Puerto Maldonado. 2½ hrs up the Río Tambopata (1½ hrs return), one of the best places in Peru for seeing jungle birds (580 plus species have been recorded), butterflies (1,230 plus species), also giant river otters, but you probably need more than a 2-day tour to benefit fully from the location. Offers tours through the adjoining community of La Torre. The guides are biologists and naturalists undertaking research in the reserve. They provide interesting wildlife-treks, including to the macaw lick (*collpa*). US$180 for 3 days/2 nights, US$165 in the low season.
Libertador Tambopata Lodge, on the Río Tambopata, to make reservations T01-442 1995, www.libertador.com.pe. Rooms with solar- heated water, good guides, excellent food. Trips go to Lake Condenado, some to Lake Sachavacayoc, and to the Collpa de Chuncho, guiding mainly in English and Spanish, package US$210 pp for 3 days/2 nights, naturalists programme provided.
Posada Amazonas Lodge, on the Tambopata river, 2 hrs upriver from Puerto Maldonado. Book through **Rainforest Expeditions**, Aramburú 166, of 4B, Miraflores, Lima 18, T01-421 8347, or Portal de Carnes 236, Cuzco, T084-246243, www.peru nature.com. A collaboration between the tour agency and the local native community of Infierno. Attractive rooms with cold showers, visits to Lake Tres Chimbadas, with good birdwatching including the Tambopata Collpa. Offers trips to a nearby indigenous primary health care project where a native healer gives guided tours of the medicinal plant garden. Service and guiding is very good. Recommended. Prices start at US$190 for a 3 day/2 night package, or US$690 for 5 days/4 nights including the **Tambopata Research Centre**, the company's more intimate, but comfortable lodge. Rooms are smaller than Posada Amazonas, shared showers, cold water (TRC has had to be renewed because of river encroachment, but is as good as ever). The lodge is next to the famous Tambopata macaw clay lick. Tapir are often seen on the bank opposite the collpa.
Tambo Tres Chimbadas, T082-571898, www.junglehouseperu.com. A small open-plan lodge, adjoining Lake Tres Chimbadas, no

electricity, communal bath. 10 km of trails and lake trips in dugout canoes. 3 days/2 nights costs US$144 pp, plus US$40 per extra day.
Wasai Lodge and Expeditions, Río Tambopata, 120 km (3½ hrs) upriver from Puerto Maldonado, T082-572290, T1436 8792 (Lima) 1½ hrs return, owned by Hotel Wasai, www.wasai.com. 20 km of trails around the lodge, guides in English and Spanish. The Collpa de Chuncho, one of the biggest macaw licks in the world, is only 1 hr up river; 3 day/2 night trips US$275, 4 day/3 nights US$375, both including a visit to Lake Sandoval plus 2 nights in Puerto Maldonado.

🍴 Eating

Puerto Maldonado *p1276*
🍴¶ **El Califa**, Piura 266. Some regional specialities. Recommended.
🍴¶ **El Hornito/Chez Maggy**, on the plaza. Cosy atmosphere, good pizzas, very popular at weekends.
¶ **El Buen Paladar**, González Prada 365. Good value lunch menu.
¶ **La Casa Nostra**, Velarde 515. Sells huge fruit juices for US$0.50, as well as *tamales, papas rellenas* and enormous fancy cakes.
¶ **La Estrella**, Velarde 474, the smartest and best of the *pollos a la brasa* places.

🍸 Bars and clubs

Puerto Maldonado *p1276*
Bar Amnesia, on the south side of the plaza.
Le Boulevard, behind **El Hornito**. Live music.
Discoteca Anaconda, on east side of plaza.
El Witite, Velarde 153. Open Fri and Sat, good popular disco, Latin music.

▲ Activities and tours

Manu Biosphere Reserve *p1274*
Warning Beware of pirate operators on the streets of Cuzco who offer trips to the Reserved Zone of Manu and end up halfway through the trip changing the route "due to emergencies", which, in reality means they have no permits to operate in the area. The following companies organize trips into the Multiple Use and Reserved Zones. Contact them for more details.
Amazon Trails Peru, C Tandapata 660, San Blas, Cuzco, T084-437499, or 974 1735 (mob), www.amazontrailsperu.com (owner Abraham Huamán and his German wife, Ulrike). Well-organized tours including visits to macaw and tapir licks, also trekking.
Expediciones Vilca, Plateros 363, Cuzco, T/F084-251872, www.cbc.org.pe/manuvilca/. Offers tours at economical prices.

InkaNatura, in Cuzco: C Plateros 361, T084-255255, in Lima: Manuel Bañón 461, San Isidro, T01-440 2022, www.inkanatura.com. Tours to Manu Wildlife Centre and Sandoval Lake Lodge (see above).

Manu Ecological Adventures, Plateros 356, Cuzco, T084-261640, www.manu adventures.com. This company operates one of the most physically active Manu programmes, with options for a mountain biking descent through the cloudforest and 3 hrs of white-water rafting on the way to **Erika Lodge** on the upper Río Madre de Dios.

Manu Expeditions, Humberto Vidal Unda G-5, p 2, Urb Magisterial, Cuzco, T084-226671, www.manuexpeditions.com. Owned by ornithologist, Barry Walker, 3 trips available to the reserve and Manu Wildlife Centre.

Manu Nature Tours, Av Pardo 1046, Cuzco, T084-252721, www.manuperu.com. Owned by Boris Gómez Luna, run lodge-based trips, owners of Manu Lodge and part owners of Manu Cloudforest Lodge; Manu is the only lodge in the Reserved Zone, open all year, situated on an ox-bow lake, providing access to the forest, US$130 per night including meals, guides available; activities include river-rafting and canopy-climbing, highly recommended for experiencing the jungle in comfort.

Oropéndola, Santa Teresa 379, interior 2do piso, T084-241428, www.oropendolaperu.org. Guide Walter Mancilla is an expert on flora and fauna. Uses lodges run by indigenous communities. Good reports of attention to detail and to the needs of clients.

Pantiacolla Tours SRL, Saphy 554, Cuzco, T084-238323, www.pantiacolla.com. Run by Marianne Von Vlaardingen and Gustavo Moscoso. They have tours to the Pantiacolla Lodge (see Sleeping, above) and also 8-day camping trips. Pantiacolla has started a community-based ecotourism project, called the Yine Project, with the people of Diamante in the Multiple Use Zone.

Puerto Maldonado p1276
Guides

All guides should have a carnet issued by the Ministry of Tourism (DIRCETUR), which also verifies them as suitable guides for trips to other places and confirms their identity. Check that the carnet has not expired. Reputable guides are **Hernán Llave Cortez**, **Romel Nacimiento** and the **Mejía** brothers, all of whom can be contacted on arrival at the airport, if available. Boat hire can be arranged through the Capitanía del Puerto (Río Madre de Dios), T573003.

⊖ Transport

To Puerto Maldonado: via Urcos and Mazuko p1275

Bus There is a daily bus from **Cuzco** with Transportes Huareño, which takes 24-30 hours to Puerto Maldonado. It costs US$15. Another option is to go from Cuzco to **Urcos**, 1 hr, US$2.25, then look for the **Transportes Juan Carlos** bus in Urcos' main plaza. This is a Volvo truck modified with seats and windows. In the dry season this takes 26 hrs to Puerto Maldonado, US$13; it leaves about 1500 daily. There are also daily buses from **Mazuko** to Puerto Maldonado with Transportes Bolpebra and **Transportes Señor de la Cumbre**, 8 hrs, US$5.

To Puerto Maldonado: via Pilcopata and Itahuania p1275

Road From the Coliseo Cerrado in Cuzco 3 bus companies run to **Pilcopata** Mon, Wed, Fri, returning same night, US$10. They are fully booked even in low season. Trucks to Pilcopata run on same days, returning Tue, Thu, Sat, 10 hrs in wet season, less in the dry. Only basic supplies are available after leaving Cuzco, so take all your camping and food essentials, including insect repellent. Transport can be disrupted in the wet season because the road is in poor condition (tour companies have latest details). *Camioneta* service runs between Pilcopata and **Salvación** to connect with the buses, Mon, Wed, Fri. The same *camionetas* run **Itahuania-Shintuya-Salvacion** regularly, when sufficient passengers, probably once a day, and 2 trucks a day. On Sun, there is no traffic whatsoever. To **Boca Manu** you can hire a boat in Atalaya, US$212 for a *peke peke*, or US$400 for a motor boat. It's cheaper to wait or hope for a boat going empty up to Boca Manu to pick up passengers, when the fare will be US$12.50 per passenger. Itahuania-Boca Manu in a shared boat with other passengers is US$6.25. A private, chartered boat would be US$105. From Itahuania, cargo boats leave for the gold mining centre of **Boca Colorado** on the Río Madre de Dios, via Boca Manu, but only when the boat is fully laden; about 6-8 a week, 9 hrs, US$15. From Colorado you can catch a boat to **Laberinto**, 6-7 hrs, US$12, from where regular combis run to **Puerto Maldonado**, 1½ hrs, US$2.50.

Tour companies usually use own vehicles for the overland trip from Cuzco to Manu.

Puerto Maldonado p1276

Air To Lima, daily with Aerocóndor and Lan via Cuzco. A moto-taxi from town to the airport is US$2, combi US$0.60, 8 km. **Airline** offices **Lan**, Av León Velarde y 2 de Mayo, T573677. **Aerocóndor**, Loreto 222, T571733.

Road and ferry A standard journey by **moto-taxi** in town costs US$0.75, a ride on a **motorbike** US$0.30. Routes from Cuzco are given above. Most **boats** leave from **Laberinto** (see above) for Colorado, 8 hrs; from there you continue to Boca Manu and Itahuania, 9-10 hrs.

⦿ Directory

Puerto Maldonado *p1276*
Banks Open 0900-1300, 1700-1900. BCP, cash advances with Visa, ATM, no commission on TCs. Banco de la Nación, cash on Mastercard, quite good rates for TCs. The best rates for cash are at the *casas de cambio* on Puno 6th block, eg *Cárdenas Hnos*, Puno 605. **Consulates** Bolivian Consulate, on the north side of the plaza. **Internet** All over town. **Language schools** Tambopata Language Centre, T573935, www.tambopata-language.com. It is now possible to learn Spanish while living close to the rainforest and this is a cheaper option than studying in Cuzco. **Motorcycle hire** Scooters and mopeds can de hired from San Francisco and others, on the corner of Puno and G Prado for US$1.15 per hr or US$10 per day. This is the standard rate in town. Passport and driver's licence must be shown. **Post offices** Serpost: at Velarde 6th block, 0800-2000, 0800-1500 Sun. **Telephones** Telefónica, on west side of Plaza, next to Municipalidad. Another on the Plaza next to *El Hornito*, sells phone cards for national and international calls. **Useful addresses** Peruvian immigration, Ica y 28 de Julio, get your exit stamp here.

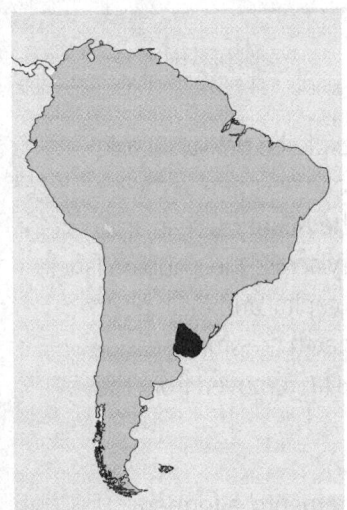

Uruguay

Introduction

Uruguay is a land of rolling hills, best explored on horseback, or by staying at the many estancias that have opened their doors to visitors. It also has its feet in the Atlantic Ocean and one of the best ways to arrive is by ferry across the shipping lanes of the Río de la Plata. Montevideo, the capital and main port, is refurbishing its historical centre to match the smart seaside neighbourhoods, but its atmosphere is far removed from the cattle ranches of the interior.

West of Montevideo is Colonia del Sacramento, a former smuggling town turned gambling centre, and a colonial gem where race horses take their exercise in the sea. Up the Río Uruguay there are pleasant towns, some with bridges to Argentina, some with thermal springs. Also by the river is Fray Bentos, a town that lent its name to corned beef for generations, which is now an industrial museum.

Each summer, millions of holidaymakers flock to Punta del Este, one of the most famous resorts on the continent, but if crowds are not your cup of *mate* (the universal beverage), go out of season. Alternatively, venture up the Atlantic coast towards Brazil for empty beaches and fishing villages, sea lions, penguins and the occasional old fortress. And anywhere you go, take your binoculars because the birdwatching is excellent.

★ Don't miss...

1 **Mercado del Puerto** Montevideo is a major port, as well as the capital. The 19th-century market building, near the docks, has been turned into a hive of restaurants serving one of Uruguay's staples – grilled meat. Lunchtimes are best, especially Saturday when you'll find live music, too, page 1295.

2 **Estancia tourism** Uruguay's agricultural heartland is ideal for estancia tourism (staying on a farm). Many welcome visitors, some for the day, others overnight. You can join in the work, or do absolutely nothing, but if you can do it on horseback, so much the better, page 1298

3 **Colonia del Sacramento** The only remnant of colonial architecture in this part of the continent, Colonia is a well-preserved historical gem on a small peninsula jutting into the Río de la Plata. The town also happens to be a short ferry ride from Buenos Aires, page 1302.

4 **Punta del Este** The premier South American beach resort, which bursts at the seams from December to February. There are quieter Atlantic beaches nearby and, out of season, you may have the coast pretty much to yourself, page 1313.

Uruguay

Essentials

Planning your trip

Where to go **Montevideo**, the capital, is the business heart of the country and has an interesting Ciudad Vieja (old city). The highlights are Mercado del Puerto, the former dockside market, which has become an emporium for traditional food and drink, and the magnificently restored Teatro Solís and the pedestrian Calle Sarandí. Within the city's limits are a number of beaches, which continue along the north shore of the Río de la Plata and on to the Atlantic seaboard. The most famous resort is **Punta del Este** which, in season (December-February), is packed with Argentines, Brazilians and locals taking their summer break. Beyond Punta del Este, there are quieter beaches with less infrastructure, but with sand dunes and other natural features. Along the coast, impressive villas and condominiums blend with their surroundings, a sort of museum of contemporary South American architecture under the open sky.

West of the capital is **Colonia del Sacramento**, a unique remnant of colonial building in this part of the continent. It is well preserved, standing on a small peninsula, and has one of the principal ferry ports for passenger traffic from Buenos Aires. Consequently it is a popular, but costly place, but well worth a visit. Continuing west you come to the confluence of the Río Uruguay with the Plata estuary. Up river are the last vestiges of the meat canning industry at **Fray Bentos**, which has a museum commemorating what used to be one of Uruguay's main businesses. Up river are towns such as **Paysandú** and the historic **Salto**, from which you can cross to Argentina, and the hot springs which have been developed into resorts.

The centre of the country is mainly agricultural land, used for livestock and crops. Many *estancias* (farms) throughout the country accept visitors, some just for the day, others for longer stays. Daytrips out of Montevideo, Punta del Este, or Colonia, for instance, to an *estancia*, usually involve a meal, handicraft shopping and educational element. Those ranches which offer lodging let you take part in the daily work (as these are working farms); you can do as much or as little as you like. Horse riding is the main activity and is usually suitable for all abilities.

When to go The climate is temperate, if somewhat damp and windy, and summer heat is tempered by Atlantic breezes. Winter (June-September) temperatures average 10-16°C, but can sometimes fall to below freezing. It is generally humid and hardly ever snows. Summer (December-March) temperatures average 21-27°C. There is always some wind and the nights are relatively cool. The rainfall, with prolonged wet periods in July and August, averages about 1,200 mm at Montevideo and some 250 more in the north, but the amount varies yearly.

Most tourists visit during the summer, which is also high season, when prices rise and hotels and transport need advance bookings. Seasonal variations for Montevideo and Punta del Este are given on pages 1294 and 1313. In the low season on the coast many places close.

Finding out more Ministry of Tourism ① *Edif Depósito Santos, Rambla 25 de Agosto y Yacaré, T02-188 5100, www.turismo.gub.uy and www.uruguaynatural.com.*

Websites

www.eltimon.com A good Uruguayan portal.
www.turismodeluruguay.com A tourism portal in English, Spanish and Portuguese.

www.brecha.com.uy *La Brecha*, a progressive weekly listing films, theatres and concerts in Montevideo and provinces, US$3. Recommended.

Maps **Automóvil Club del Uruguay** (see box page 1289), publishes road maps of the city and country, as do **Esso** and **Ancap**. A good road map of Uruguay and Montevideo (all in one) is published by **Silveira Mapas**, *Mapa de la República Oriental del Uruguay/Plano de la capital Montevideo*, US$6.40. **ITM** of Vancouver also publish a country map (1:800,000). Official maps are issued by **Instituto Geográfico Militar** ① *Abreu y 8 de Octubre, T801 6868, 0800-1230.*

Visas and immigration A passport is necessary for entry except for nationals of most Latin American countries and citizens of the USA, who can get in with national identity documents for stays of up to 90 days. Visas are not required for a stay of less than three months by nationals of all EU countries (except Estonia), Argentina, Australia, Bahamas, Barbados,

Belize, Bolivia, Brazil, Canada, Colombia, Costa Rica, Chile, Dominican Republic, Ecuador, El Salvador, Guatemala, Honduras, Israel, Iceland, Jamaica, Japan, Liechtenstein, Malaysia, Mexico, New Zealand, Nicaragua, Norway, Panama, Paraguay, Peru, South Africa, Switzerland, Trinidad and Tobago, Turkey, USA, Venezuela. Visas cost £27 (or equivalent), and you need a passport photo and a ticket out of Uruguay. Visa processing may take 2-4 weeks. For those living in a country with no Uruguayan embassy, a visa can be applied for online and collected at any Uruguayan consulate before entering the country. Visas are valid for 90 days and usually single entry. Tourist cards (obligatory for all tourists, obtainable on entry) are valid for three months, extendable for a similar period at the **Migraciones office** ① *C Misiones 1513, T916 0471, www.dnm.minterior.gub.uy.*

Uruguayan embassies and consulates Visit www.mrree.gub.uy/mrree/Embajadas_y_ Consulados/Misiones/misiones.htm for a complete list.

Money The currency is the *peso uruguayo*. Bank notes issued are for 5, 10, 20, 50, 100, 200 (don't confuse with old peso 2,000 notes – pre-1993, which are now worth 2 pesos), 500 (don't confuse with 50), and 1,000 pesos uruguayos. Coins: 1, 2 and 5 pesos. Any amount of currency can be taken in or out. Rates change often because of the floating **exchange rate** and inflation differentials against the $US. Peso exchange rate in April 2006: US$1=25.10, €1=30.40.

There is no restriction on foreign exchange transactions (so it is a good place to stock up with US$ bills, though American Express and some banks refuse to do this for credit cards; most places charge 3% commission for such transactions). Those banks which give US$ cash against a credit card are given in the text. Most ATMs in Montevideo can dispense both Uruguayan pesos and US$. Dollars cash can be purchased when leaving the country. Changing Argentine pesos into Uruguayan pesos is usually a marginally worse rate than for dollars. Brazilian *reais* get a much worse rate. US$ notes are accepted for some services.

Credit cards In some places there is a 10% charge to use a credit cards Visa and MasterCard ATMs can be found at branches of Redbanc and ABN Amro. Many other banks have Visa ATMs. Most ATMs have the Cirrus sign, but that system is not always available. MasterCard emergency line call collect to USA, T1-636-722 7111. Visa emergency line, call collect T00-044-20-7937 8091. Most of the cheaper hotels outside major cities do not accept credit cards.

Cost of travelling Uruguay is comparatively inexpensive. Prices vary considerably between summer and winter, Punta del Este being one of the most expensive summer resort in Latin America. Someone staying in a cheap hotel, eating the *menú del día* and travelling by bus, should allow US$20-30 per day. Internet costs US$0.75-US$1 per hour.

Safety Personal security offers few problems in most of Uruguay. Be aware that gang robbery may occur in Montevideo (don't show any signs of obvious wealth). Adult and child beggars are often seen in restaurants, cafes, public places and buses, trying to sell small items or simply asking for money. They are not dangerous, but watch your belongings. The Policía Turística patrol the streets of the capital.

Uruguay Essentials

Touching down

Airport tax US$6 on all air travellers leaving Uruguay for Buenos Aires, Aeroparque, but US$25 to Ezeiza; US$25 for all other countries (payable in US$ or local currency), US$0.50 on internal flights, and a tax of 3% on all tickets issued and paid for in Uruguay.

Business hours Department stores: Mon-Fri 0900-1200 (or 1230), 1400 (or 1430)-1900, Sat 0900-1230. **Businesses:** 0830-1200, 1430-1830 or 1900. **Banks:** 1300-1700 in Montevideo; there are special summer hours (1 Dec-15 Mar) in Montevideo (1330-1730), in the interior (0800-1200) and in Punta del Este and Maldonado (1600-2000); banks close Sat. **Government offices:** mid Mar-Nov Mon- Fri 1300-1830 ; otherwise 0700-1230.

In an emergency T109. Tourist police, Colonia T1021, Montevideo, T0800-8226, or 908 3303. Ambulance T105 or 400 1111. Fire service, T104. Road information T1954.

International phone code +598. Ringing: long equal tones, long pauses. Engaged: short tones, short pauses.

Official time GMT -3 (Sep-Mar -2).

Tipping Hotel and restaurant bills normally include a service charge, but an additional 5-10% is expected. Porters at the airport: US$1 per piece of luggage. Taxis: 5-10% of the fare. Cafés: 10%.

VAT/IVA 23%.

Voltage 220 volts 50 cycles AC. Various plugs used: round 2-pin, flat 2-pin (first two most common), oblique 2-pin with earth, 3 round pins in a line.

Getting around

Flight connections If flying from Uruguay to make an international connection in Buenos Aires, make sure your flight goes to Ezeiza International Airport (eg on United, American Airlines or TAM), not Aeroparque (almost all Aerolíneas Argentinas or Pluna flights). Luggage is not transferred automatically to Ezeiza and you will have to travel one hour between the airports by taxi or bus. If you need visa to enter Argentina, you must get a transit visa (takes up to four weeks to process in Montevideo), just to transfer between airports.

Bus and road All main cities and towns are served by good companies, but driving your own or a rented vehicle (see Box) is the best way to explore Uruguay, as it allows flexibility and access to many places not served by public transport. There are good services to neighbouring countries. Details are given in the text. **Hitching** is not easy.

Train The only passenger services are Tacuarembó-Rivera (sporadic) and slow commuter services Montevideo to Progreso, Canelones, Santa Lucía and 25 de Agosto (Florida department).

Sleeping → *See inside front cover for our hotel grade price guide.*

Camping There are lots of sites. Most towns have municipal sites (quality varies). Many sites along the Ruta Interbalnearia, but most of these close off season. The Tourist Office in Montevideo issues a good guide to campsites and youth hostels; see references in main text. The annual Guía de Verano is good for sites and prices, particularly at the beach resorts.

Youth hostels Red Uruguaya de Hostels ① *Canelones 935, Montevideo, T900 5749, www.hosteluruguay.org/hostelsuy.html,* operates eight hostels (HI members) around Uruguay.

Eating → *See inside front cover for our restaurant price guide.*

Eating out Dinner in 'top class restaurants' is served 2000-0100. In less formal restaurants service starts at 1930. Restaurants usually charge *cubierto* (bread), costing US$0.30-US$1 in Punta del Este. A *confitería* is an informal place which serves meals at any time, as opposed to a *restaurante*, which serves meals at set times. Many serve *preparación*, a collection of hors d'oeuvres. Uruguay does not have a great selection of international restaurants. Vegetarians may have to stick to salads, as even the dishes which are meatless elsewhere (*arroz a la cubana, tortilla española*) are served with bacon and sausages in Uruguay.

Driving in Uruguay

Road Driving is very expensive by South American standards: fuel costs are high and many roads have tolls (one-way tolls Montevideo-Colonia US$5.35). Roads are generally in good condition; 23% are paved and a further 60% all-weather. In rural areas, motorists should drive with their headlights on even in daylight, especially on major roads. Uruguayans are polite drivers: outside Montevideo, trucks will move to the shoulder to let you pass and motorists will alert you of speed traps.

Documents 90-day temporary admission is usually given without any problems. Entry is easier and faster with a *carnet de passages*, but it is not essential. Without it you will be given a temporary import paper which must be surrendered on leaving the country. Insurance is not required by law.

Organizations **Automóvil Club del Uruguay**, Yí y Colonia, Montevideo, T02-902 1691 (head office: Av Libertador General Lavalleja 1532, T02-902 4792, acu@netgate.com.uy). Reciprocity with foreign automobile clubs is available; members do not have to pay for affiliation.

Fuel All gasoline is unleaded: 97 octane, US$1.32 per litre, 95 octane, US$1.28, *especial* 87 octane, US$1.22 per litre; diesel, US$0.45 per litre. Many filling stations close at weekends.

Food Beef is eaten at almost all meals. Most restaurants are *parrilladas* (grills) where the staple is beef. *Asado* (barbecued beef) is popular; the main cuts are *asado de tira* (ribs); *pulpa* (no bones), *lomo* (fillet steak) and entrecote. To get a lean piece of *asado*, ask for *asado flaco*. *Costilla* (chop) and *milanesa* (veal cutlet) are also popular; usually eaten with mixed salad or chips. *Chivitos* are Uruguayan steak burgers; *chivitos canadienses* are sandwiches filled with slices of meat, lettuce, tomato, etc (normally over US$2, very filling). Two other good local dishes are *puchero* (beef with vegetables, bacon, beans and sausages) and local varieties of pizza. Other specialities are barbecued pork, grilled chicken in wine, *cazuela* (or stew) usually with *mondongo* (tripe) or seafood (such as squid, shark – *cazón*, mussels – *mejillones*). The sausages are very good and spicy (*chorizos, morcillas, salchichas*). *Morcilla dulce*, a sweet black sausage, made from blood, orange peel and walnuts, is tasty; so is the *morcilla salada*, which is savoury. For snacks, *media lunas mixtas* are a type of croissant filled with ham and cheese, either hot or cold; toasted sandwiches are readily available; *panchos* are hot dogs, *húngaros* are thin spicy sausage hot dogs. An excellent dessert is *chajá*, from Paysandú, a type of sponge-cake ball with cream and jam inside, also with peaches – very sweet; others are *massini* (a cream sponge), *Martín Fierro* (*dulce de membrillo* with cheese) and the common lemon pie. Pastries are very good indeed, and crystallized egg-yolks, known as *yemas*, are popular sweets. Ice cream is excellent everywhere.

Drink The beers are good. Local wines are very varied. 'Del museo' indicates the bodega's vintage reserve. *Uvita* is a sweet, potent liquor served in some old bars of Montevideo. The local spirits are *caña* and *grappa*. In the Mercado del Puerto, Montevideo, a *medio medio* is half still white wine, half sparkling white (elsewhere a *medio medio* is half *caña* and half whisky). *Espillinar* is a cross between whisky and rum. Try the *clérico*, a mixture of wine and fruit juices. Very good fresh orange and grapefruit juices (*exprimidos*). *Mate* is the favourite drink between meal hours. Coffee is good: a *cortado* is strong and white, *café con leche* is milk with a little coffee.

Festivals and events
Public holidays 1 Jan; 6 Jan; Carnival (see below); Easter week; 19 Apr; 1, 19 Jun; 18 Jul; 25 Aug; 12 Oct; 2 Nov; 25 Dec. (8 Dec is a religious holiday which also marks the official start of the summer holiday.) **Carnival** week is officially the Monday and Tuesday preceding Ash Wednesday, but many firms close for the whole week. Business also comes to a standstill during **Holy Week**, which coincides with La Semana Criolla (horse-breaking, stunt riding by cowboys, dances and song). Department stores close only from Good Friday. Banks and offices close Thursday-Sunday. Easter Monday is not a holiday.

Uruguay Essentials

Montevideo → Phone code: 02. Colour map 8, grid B6. Population: 1,311,976.

Montevideo is many cities rolled into one. It is an international port at its western end and, in the east, a seaside resort with sandy streets and pine forests. In between are the faded Old City, the country's financial heart and the posh residential areas along the coast. Everything blends together: myriad architectural styles; café society and tango music; theatres; pizza, parrillada and wines; outdoor markets and indoor malls; agricultural fairs; football, vintage cars and traffic. This is where all the elements of Uruguay meet on the shores of the Río de la Plata.

Montevideo, the capital, was founded in 1726. The original site is on a promontory between the Río de la Plata and an inner bay, though the fortifications have been destroyed. In addition to some colonial Spanish and Italian architecture, French and Art Deco styles can be seen. Many buildings in the centre exhibit fine stone and ironwork. The city not only dominates the country's commerce and culture: it accounts for 70% of industrial production and handles almost 90% of imports and exports. It is also a summer resort and the point of departure for a string of seaside resorts to the east. The city's population, indeed that of the entire country, is decreasing due to emigration and a very low birth-rate.

Ins and outs
Getting there Carrasco international **airport** is east of the centre, to which connections by bus or taxi are easy. It takes about 50 minutes by bus, 30 minutes by taxi, but there is a longer, more scenic route, by the coast, which may have fewer delays, but is more expensive (ask for the quick route if you want). Many arrive in Montevideo by boat from Buenos Aires. The **ferry terminal** is in the heart of the city, at the docks not far from the Mercado del Puerto. The **bus terminal**, Tres Cruces, is 10-15 minutes by city bus from the centre. It has good facilities and is used by bus companies. ▶▶ *For more detailed information, see Transport, page 1298.*

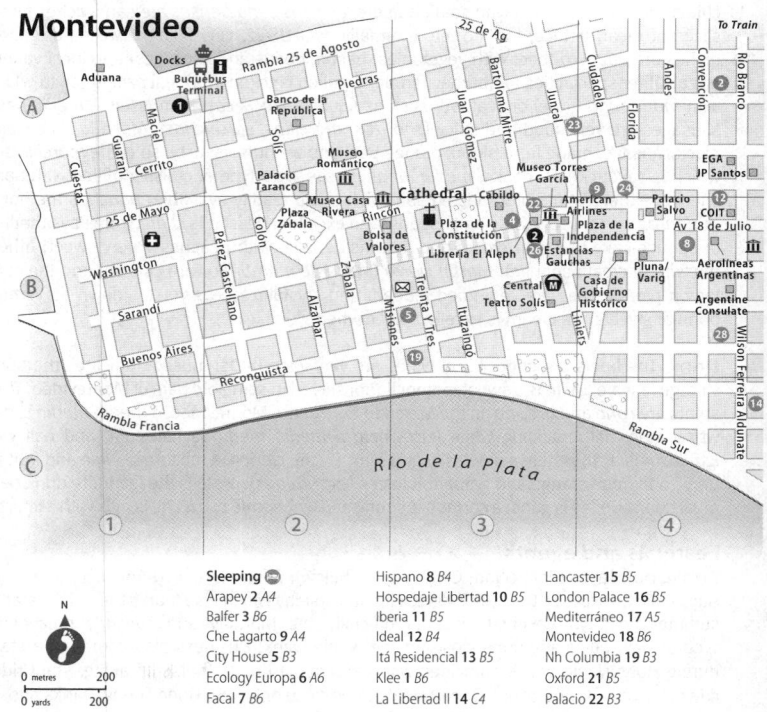

Montevideo

Río de la Plata

Sleeping 🛏
Arapey **2** *A4*
Balfer **3** *B6*
Che Lagarto **9** *A4*
City House **5** *B3*
Ecology Europa **6** *A6*
Facal **7** *B6*

Hispano **8** *B4*
Hospedaje Libertad **10** *B5*
Iberia **11** *B5*
Ideal **12** *B4*
Itá Residencial **13** *B5*
Klee **1** *B6*
La Libertad II **14** *C4*

Lancaster **15** *B5*
London Palace **16** *B5*
Mediterráneo **17** *A5*
Montevideo **18** *B6*
Nh Columbia **19** *B3*
Oxford **21** *B5*
Palacio **22** *B3*

Getting around The Ciudad Vieja can be explored on foot as it is not large. From there it is not far to Plazas de la Independencia, Fabini and Cagancha, but buses are plentiful along Avenida 18 de Julio, connecting all these places. To get to other parts of the city and the beach districts there are many buses, some running on express routes. There are two types of taxis, the ordinary ones, which are not expensive, but which charge more on Sunday and holidays, and *remises*, which operate out of offices and from the airport, and are more expensive. Full details are given in Local Transport, below. **Note** Some plazas and streets are known by two names: for instance, Plaza de la Constitución is also called Plaza Matriz. Streets whose names have been changed may not be marked as such on all maps: Michelini was Cuareim; Hector Gutiérrez Ruiz was Ibicuy; Convención was Latorre; Wilson Ferreira Aldunate was Río Branco.

Tourist offices Tourist information is at the Tres Cruces bus terminal (T409 7399); at Colonia 1021, north side of Plaza Fabini (Monday-Friday 0900-1830), at the Ministry of Tourism, Rambla 25 de Agosto y Yacaré, for whole country, separate desk for Punta del Este; and in the plaza outside Palacio Municipal, 18 de Julio y Ejido, mainly for Montevideo, all helpful. Also at Carrasco international airport, T604 0386. Ask for details of the downtown walking tour, signposted, from the Mercado del Puerto to Plaza Independencia. For the Tourist Police, T901 9102. The *Guía del Ocio*, a weekly guide with Friday edition of *La República*, has information on museums, cultural events and entertainment. Recommended. See also www.eltimon.com for entertainment details. The website of the municipality is www.montevideo.gub.uy.

Maps Best street maps of Montevideo are at the beginning of the *Guía Telefónica* (both white and yellow page volumes). Free maps of the centre can be obtained at almost all city museums, including a cultural map *Ciudad Vieja: pasado, presente y futuro*. The municipality's website, www.montevideo.gub.uy, has good maps. *Eureka Guía De Montevideo* is recommended for streets, with index and bus routes (US$4.75 from bookshops). Kiosks sell the *Atlas* bus guide.

Sights

Plaza Fuerte **4** *B3*
Príncipe **23** *A3*
Radisson Victoria
    Plaza **24** *A4*
Red Hostel **20** *C6*
Royal **25** *B5*
Solís **26** *B3*

The Place **27** *C5*
Youth Hostel **28** *B4*

Eating 🍴
Café Bacacay **2** *B3*
Mercado del Puerto **1** *A2*
Roma Amor **2** *B3*

City centre
In the **Ciudad Vieja** is the oldest square in Montevideo: the **Plaza de la Constitución**. Here on one side is the **Catedral** (1790-1804), with the historic **Cabildo** (1804) ① *JC Gómez 1362, T915 9685, Tue-Sun 1430-1900*, opposite. It contains the **Museo y Archivo Histórico Nacional**. The Cabildo has several exhibition halls, as well as the small **Museo del Carnaval**. On the south side is the **Club Uruguay** (built in 1888, now crumbling), which is worth a look inside. See also the unusual fountain, dating from 1881, made by Italians who misspelt the Spanish inscription at the base.

Still further west along Calle Rincón is the small **Plaza Zabala**, with a monument to Bruno Mauricio de Zabala, founder of the city. North of this Plaza are: the **Banco de la República** ① *Cerrito y Zabala* and the **Aduana** ① *Rambla 25 de Agosto*. Several historic houses belong to the Museo Histórico Nacional: **Casa de Montero-Roosen, Museo Romántico** ① *25 de Mayo 428, T915 5361, Tue-Fri 1100-1600, Sat 1100-1600*, first built in 1728, rebuilt by Antonio Montero in 1831, contains late 19th, early 20th century furniture, furnishings and portraits. **Museo Casa Rivera** ① *Rincón 437, T915 1051, Mon-Fri 0900-1700, Sat 1100-1600,* is an 1850 mansion of the first president of the republic. Its rooms are dedicated to various stages of Uruguayan history. Another house belonging to the Museo Histórico Nacional in the Ciudad Vieja, **Museo Casa de Lavalleja** ① *Zabala 1469, Mon-Fri 1200-1700, Sat 1100-1600* (1783) has historical mementoes and furniture. Also in the Ciudad Vieja is the **Palacio Taranco, Museo de Artes Decorativos** ① *25 de Mayo y 1 de Mayo, T915 1101, Mon-Sat 1215-1800, Sun 1400-1800, free,* whose garden overlooks Plaza Zabala, a palatial mansion in turn-of-the-century French style, sumptuously-decorated ground floor rooms, museum of Islamic and Classical pottery and glass in the basement. It was first built as a theatre in 1793; in 1908 it was bought by the Ortiz de Taranco family.

Three blocks north of Plaza Zabala are the docks, while three blocks south is the Río de la Plata. The seafront road, the Rambla, has been opened round the point to the port. In the port (which one can visit on Saturday from 1300 till sunset and on Sunday from 0800 till sunset), the ship's bell of HMS *Ajax* has been set up to commemorate the scuttling of the *Graf Spee*; it is in an open-air museum on the opposite side of the road from the Port Administration, 50 m to the right next to a large military building (you may have to persuade the sailors to let you see it). The anchor of the *Graf Spee* was erected inside the port area in 1964 to commemorate the 25th anniversary of the battle. In the Ciudad Vieja, many of the street names have descriptive plaques, but a number of the old buildings are in a poor state of repair. Significant effort (some funds are coming from European Union) is now being made to restore the old city to its former glory. The area west of C Pérez Castellano is still in disrepair and is not recommended after dark. During the day, long Paseo Escollera Sarandí leads to the Río de la Plata, offering good views of the old city, port and huge cargo ships passing by.

Between the Ciudad Vieja and the new city is the largest of Montevideo's squares, **Plaza de la Independencia**, a short distance east of Plaza de la Constitución along the pedestrianized Calle Sarandí. New cafés and boutiques open by the month on Peatonal Sarandí, which has been extended to Alaibar. Two small pedestrian zones full of cafés, live music (mostly after 2300) and restaurants, Peatonal Bacacay and Policia Vieja, lead off Sarandí. In the middle of Plaza de la Independencia is the subterranean marble mausoleum of Artigas, with his statue (1923) dominating the square above. Just west of the plaza is **Museo Torres García** ① *Sarandí 683, T916 2663, Mon-Fri 1000-1900, Sat 1000-1600, bookshop, donation requested (US$1).* It has an exhibition of the paintings of Joaquín Torres García (1874-1949), one of Uruguay's foremost contributors to the modern art movements of the 20th century, and five floors dedicated to temporary exhibitions of contemporary Uruguayan and international artists. At the eastern end is the **Palacio Salvo** ① *Plaza Independencia 846-848,* built 1922-28. Architectural masterpiece for some, monstrosity for others, it was the first skyscraper in Uruguay. It houses an entire universe, with condominiums, art exhibitions, offices and dilapidated bars where couples dance tango between pool tables. On the southern side is the **Casa de Gobierno Histórico** (Palacio Estévez). ① *Mon-Fri 1000-1700.* The modern block to the west of the Casa de Gobierno is the new Palacio de Justicia, still unfinished for lack of funds. The Casa de Gobierno, well-restored, is now used for ceremonial purposes only as the executive offices have been moved. Just off the plaza to the west is the splendid **Teatro Solís** (1842-69) ① *Reconquista y Bartolomé Mitre, T1950 3323, www.teatrosolis.org.uy.* It has been entirely restored to perfection, with added elevators, access for disabled people, marble flooring and impressive attention to detail. Built as an opera house, Teatro Solís is now used for many cultural events, including ballet, classical music, even the best tango performances. Check press for listings.

The Avenida 18 de Julio runs east from Plaza de la Independencia. The **Museo de Arte Contemporaneo** ① *18 de Julio 965, T900 6662, daily 1400-2000 except Thu 1400-1830,* holds temporary exhibitions. The **Museo del Gaucho y de la Moneda** ① *Av 18 de Julio 998, Edif Banco de la República, T900 8764, Mon-Fri 0900-1700, free,* was renovated in early 2003. Museo de la Moneda has a survey of Uruguayan currency and a collection of Roman coins; Museo del Gaucho is a fascinating history of the Uruguayan gaucho and is highly recommended. Between Julio Herrera and Río Negro is the **Plaza Fabini**, or **del Entrevero**, with a statue of a group of *gauchos* engaged in battle, the last big piece of work by sculptor José Belloni. Beneath the plaza is the **Salón Municipal de Exposiciones** ① *daily 1700-2100, free,* temporary exhibitions of contemporary art, photography, etc. In the **Plaza Cagancha** (or Plaza Libertad) is a statue of Liberty. An excellent new Paseo de los Artesanos and cultural centre is in the restored **Mercado de la Abundancia** ① *San Jose 1312,* with handicrafts downstairs (good quality and price), four traditional restaurants on the first floor and tango one night a week. The **Palacio Municipal** (La Intendencia) is on the south side of Avenida 18 de Julio, just before it bends north, at the statue of **El Gaucho**. It often has interesting art and photo exhibitions. The best view of the city is from the top of the Palacio Municipal; external glass elevators take you up to a *mirador* (glass-fronted terrace) on the 22nd floor. The road which forks south from the Gaucho is Constituyente, and leads to the beach at Pocitos. **Museo de Historia de Arte** ⓘ *18 de Julio 1360, T908 0456, Tue-Sun 1430-2000* is also in the Palacio Municipal. **Centro de Exposiciones** ⓘ *Palacio Municipal (Soriano entrance), Tue-Sun 1600-2000*, has temporary modern art exhibitions.

The immense but dilapidated **Palacio Legislativo** ⓘ *Mon-Fri 0830-1830, free, getting there: reached from Plaza Fabini along Av del Libertador Brig Gen Juan Lavalleja (normally known as Av Libertador), 5 blocks east of Plaza de la Independencia (buses 150, 173, 175 from C Mercedes)*, was built 1908-1925 from local marble: there are 55 colours of Uruguayan marble in the Salón de los Pasos Perdidos, 12 types of wood in the library. Other rooms are beautiful.

Outside the centre

Museo Nacional de Antropología ⓘ *Av de las Instrucciones 948, T359 3353, Mon-Fri 1300-1800, Sat, Sun and holidays 1000-1800, take bus 149 from Ejido*, has a modest but well-presented anthropological collection in the hall of a superb, late 19th century mansion, the ex-Quinta de Mendilaharsu (see, among other things, the Music Room with its huge Chinese silk tapestry). **Museo Municipal de Bellas Artes Juan Manuel Blanes** ⓘ *Millán 4014 esq Arroyo, T336 2248, Tue-Sun 1300-1900, free, take buses 146, 148, 149, 150 from Mercedes*, in the ex-Quinta Raffo (a late 19th century mansion) dedicated to the work of the artist Blanes (1830-1901), plus a room of the works of Pedro Figari (1861-1938), a lawyer who painted strange, naive pictures of peasant life and negro ceremonies, also work by other Uruguayan artists; has a room with paintings by Courbet, Vlaminck, Utrillo, Dufy, etchings by Orozco and engravings by Goya; temporary exhibitions. **Museo Zoológico** ⓘ *Rambla República de Chile 4215, Buceo, T622 0258, Tue-Sun 1300-1700, free, take bus 104 from 18 de Julio*, is well-displayed and arranged, recommended, great for children too.

Museo Naval ⓘ *Rambla Costanera y Luis A de Herrera, T622 1084, Mon-Fri 0800-1200, 1400-1800, free*, has a small display of naval history from War of Independence onwards, documentation on Battle of the River Plate and sinking of the *Graf Spee*, and on the sailing ship *Capitán Miranda*, which circumnavigated the globe in 1937-8. This ship is now in the port (can be visited Saturday and Sunday), bus 104 from 18 de Julio.

In **Parque Batlle y Ordóñez** (reached eastwards of Avenida 18 de Julio), are several statues: the most interesting group is the very well-known **La Carreta** monument, by José Belloni, showing three yoke of oxen drawing a wagon. In the grounds is the **Estadio Centenario**, the national football stadium with a seating capacity of 70,000 and a football museum, an athletics field and a bicycle race-track (bus 107). The **Planetarium** ⓘ *next to the Jardín Zoológico, free, gives good, 40-min shows on Thu at 1730, Sat and Sun at 1630 and 1730, getting there: buses 141, 142 or 144 from San José*, is southeast of this park at Avenida Gral Rivera 3254.

From the Palacio Legislativo, Avenida Agraciada runs northwest to **Parque Prado**, the oldest of the city's many parks, about 5 km from Avenida 18 de Julio (bus 125 and others). Among fine lawns, trees and lakes is a rose garden planted with 850 varieties, the monument of **La Diligencia** (the stage coach), the Círculo de Tenís and the Sociedad Rural premises. Part of the park is the adjacent **Jardín Botánico**. ⓘ *Mon-Fri 0800-1830, guided tours, T336 4005. It is reached via Av 19 de Abril (bus 522 from Ejido next to Palacio Municipal), or via Av Dr LA de Herrera (bus 147 from Paysandú)*. The largest and most popular park is **Parque Rodó**, on Rambla Presidente Wilson. Here are an open-air theatre, an amusement park, and a boating lake studded with islands. At the eastern end is the **Museo Nacional de Artes Visuales** ⓘ *Tomás Garibaldi 2283, T711 6124, Wed-Sun 1500-1900, free*, a collection of contemporary plastic arts, plus a room devoted to Blanes. Recommended.

Among the main seaside residential areas are **Pocitos** and **Carrasco**, the city's poshest suburb and a delightful place behind the beach of the same name at the end of the Rambla Sur. It is backed by the forest of the **Parque Nacional Roosevelt**, a green belt stretching north to the marshes of Carrasco (which are being drained). The city itself is expanding beyond Roosevelt. The international airport is nearby. The express bus DI runs every 30 minutes along Avenida 18 de Julio; this service, which costs slightly more (US$1) is about 30 minutes quicker to Carrasco.

At the western end of the bay is the **Cerro** ⓘ *getting there: bus from centre to Cerro: 125 'Cerro' from Mercedes, or boat Sat and Sun 1500-1900, US$5, T601 8601/2*, or hill, 139 m high (from which Montevideo gets its name), with the Fortaleza General Artigas, an old fort, on the top. It is now the **Museo Militar** ⓘ *T487 3121, Tue-Sun 1100-1730, free, getting there: bus 125 from Mercedes goes near*. It houses historical momentos, documentation of War of Independence. The Cerro is surmounted by the oldest lighthouse in the country (1804).

Nine sandy bathing **beaches** stretch along almost the whole of the metropolitan water front, from Playa Ramírez in the west to Playa Carrasco in the east. Along the whole waterfront runs the Rambla Naciones Unidas, named along its several stretches in honour of various nations. Bus 104 from Aduana, which goes along Avenida 18 de Julio, gives a pleasant ride (further inland in winter) past Pocitos, Punta Gorda and all the beaches to Playa Miramar, beyond Carrasco, total journey time from Pocitos to Carrasco, 35 minutes. The seawater, despite its muddy colour (sediment stirred up by the Río de la Plata), is safe to bathe in and the beaches are clean. Lifeguards are on duty during the summer months.

● Sleeping

Hotels sometimes add a 14% charge to bills, on top of which there is 23% VAT, although these charges are often included in the bill in cheaper and mid-range establishments. During the tourist season, 15 Dec-15 Mar, book in advance. At the beaches many hotels offer full board-only during high season. After 1 Apr prices are greatly reduced and some hotel dining rooms shut down. For Carnival week prices are raised by 20%. The city is visited by Argentines at weekends: many hotels increase prices. Midweek prices may be lower than those posted. Always ask in advance. When not included, breakfast (*café completo*) costs US$2 or more in a hotel. Almost all hotels **D** and above have cable TV and a mini bar or fridge.

The tourist office has information on the more expensive hotels. For more information and reservations contact Asociación de Hoteles y Restaurantes del Uruguay, Gutiérrez Ruiz 1213, T902 3990, ahru@montevideo.com.uy.

City centre *p1291, map p1290*
AL-A Plaza Fuerte, Bartolomé Mitre 1361, T915 9563, www.visit-uruguay.com/plazafuerte. Restored 1913 building, historical monument, each room different, a/c, safe, internet, restaurant, pub.
A Nh Columbia, Reconquista 470, T916 0001, F916 0192. 1st class, breakfast, IDD phone in every room, minibar, TV, restaurant, sauna, music show.
D Solís, Bartolomé Mitre 1314, T915 0279, hotelsolis@hotmail.com. Some rooms with bath and a/c, safe, bike rental, excursions, internet, bar, good value and location, but lots of street noise.
D Palacio, Bartolomé Mitre 1364, T916 3612, fpelaez@internet.com.uy. Well kept old hotel, with bath, safe, balconies, laundry service, stores luggage. Highly recommended.
D Ciudad Vieja Hostel, Ituzaingó 1436, T915 6192, www.ciudadviejahostel.com. New hostel

with lots of services (Spanish lessons, bike hire, city tours, laundry, theatre and show tickets, football, massage), internet, safes, kitchen, airport transport.
D-E pp, Che Legarto Hostel, Plaza independencia Av 713, www.chelegarto.com. Including breakfast, new HI hostel in excellent location over Plaza Independencia. 36 rooms, most with private toilet, in a colonial building with terrace and river views. Restaurant/pub and common areas. Internet, 24-hr check in. credit cards welcome.
E City House, Buenos Aires 462 (opposite Correos), T915 6427. With bath, bar, remodelled, good value (prices rise at weekend). **E Príncipe**, Juncal 1434, T908 5310, F902 6167. A/c, fridge, café, parking, prices rise on Fri and Sat.

East of Ciudad Vieja
L-AL Radisson Victoria Plaza, Plaza Independencia 759, T908 1048, www.visit-uruguay.com/radissonmontevideo.htm. A/c, excellent restaurant (rooftop, fine views), less formal restaurant in lobby, luxurious casino in basement, new 5-star wing fully open, art gallery, business centre (for guests only).
A Oxford, Paraguay 1286, T902 0046, www.visit-uruguay.com/oxford.htm. Modern, with good breakfast, safes, laundry service, parking, discount if booked on internet. Recommended.
B Balfer, Z Michelini 1328, T902 1418, F902 4228. Good, TV, safe deposit, excellent breakfast.
B Embajador, San José 1212, T902 0012, www.hotelembajador.com. Sauna, swimming pool in the summer, restaurant, TV with *BBC World*, excellent. Recommended.
B Facal, Paseo Yí y 18 de Julio 1363, T902 8833, F902 8828. A/c, safe, TV, convenient, pleasant, terrace restaurant.
B Lancaster, Plaza Cagancha 1334, T902 1054, F902 1117. A/c, breakfast, fridge/bar, good service.

● *For an explanation of the sleeping and eating price codes used in this guide, see inside the front*
● *cover. Other relevant information is found in Essentials pages 1288-1289.*

B London Palace, Río Negro 1278, T902 0024, F902 1633. Reliabl, excellent breakfast, parking.
B-C Hispano, Convención 1317, T/F900 3816. A/c, with breakfast, comfortable, laundry, parking.
B-C Klee Internacional, San José 1303, T902 0606, www.multi.com.uy/hotelklee. Very comfortable, good value, spacious rooms, includes internet use, breakfast, a/c, heater, minibar, good view, satellite TV. Highly recommended.
C Mediterráneo, Paraguay 1486, T900 5090. With breakfast, TV, comfortable.
C Montevideo, Aquiles Lanza 1309, T902 4634. Recommended. Small garage.
C Red Hostel, San José 1406, T908 8514, www.red hostel.com. By the Intendencia, new hostel with double rooms and dorms (**E**), cheerful, cable TV, internet connection in rooms, computers, safe, breakfast, bike rental, roof terrace and kitchen.
D Arapey, Av Uruguay 925, near Convención, T900 7032, www.visit-uruguay.com/arapey.htm. Good location, on route to airport, variety of rooms with bath, TV, fan, heating, no breakfast.
D Ecology Europa, Colonia 1341, T902 1222. A good choice in this price range.
D Iberia, Maldonado 1097, T901 3633. Modern, parking, US$1 for breakfast.
D Ideal, Colonia 914, T901 6389. Hot water, no breakfast, quiet, basic, higher rates on Sat.
D Itá Residencial, San José 1160, T901 3363. Quiet, 10% discount if you stay more than a week.
D The Place, Maldonado 1080, T900 6047, F908 2198. New hotel, a/c, large rooms, airy, old-style feel.
E Hospedaje Libertad, Gutiérrez Ruiz 1223, T901 4548. Simple, TV, and, same owner, **E La Libertad II**, Maldonado 980, T901 7665. **F** with shared bath, darker, but front rooms OK.
F Youth hostel (members only), Canelones 935, T908 1324, montevideo@hosteluruguay.org, www.hostel uruguay.org. Open all year. US$7 pp (seasonal variations, breakfast included, sheets US$1 extra), doors locked at 2400 (but security lax), clean, dormitory style, kitchen, lots of hot water, but shortage of bathrooms and noisy, bicycle hire.

Outside the centre *p1293*
Near Tres Cruces bus terminal
A Days Inn, Acevedo Díaz 1821-23, T400 4840, www.Daysinn.com.uy. A/c, with breakfast, safe, coffee shop and health club.
B Royal Palace, Acevedo Díaz 1697, T401 7227. 3-star, with TV, phone, 24-hr bar.
B Tres Cruces, Miguelete 2356 esq Acevedo Díaz, T402 3474, www.hoteltrescruces.com.uy. A/c, TV, safe, coffee shop.

East of the centre *p1293*
LL Sheraton, Victor Solino 349, T710 2121, www.sheraton.com. Beside Shopping Punta Carretas, all facilities, good views, access to Golf

Club. There is also a **Four Points Sheraton** at Ejido 1275, T901 7000, in the centre (**L-AL**).
AL Oceania, Mar Artico 1227, Playa Los Ingl eses, Punt Gorda, T600 0444, F600 2273. Pleasant view, good restaurant and night club. Highly recommended.

Carrasco *p1293*
LL Belmont House, Av Rivera 6512, Carrasco, T600 0430, www.belmonthouse.com.uy. 5-star, includes breakfast, small, beautifully furnished, top quality, excellent restaurant, pub/bar Memories, pool, 4 blocks from beach. Recommended.
L-A Pedro Figari, Rambla Rep de México 6535, Carrasco, T600 8824, www.hotelpedrofigari.com. Best Western hotel. A/c, buffet breakfast, cable TV, good for business visitors, convenient for airport, very pleasant.
A Regency Suites, Gabriel Otero 6428, T600 1383, www.regency.com.uy. Good boutique-style hotel with all services, free internet, safety deposit, fitness centre, pool, restaurant and pub, a couple of blocks from the beach.
Camping Parque Roosevelt, near Carrasco, US$3 pp, free, hot showers, safe, no electricity, 15 km from centre, open all year. For vans and caravans only at Punta Ramírez on Rambla República Argentina, free for stays under 48 hrs, central, basic facilities, 24 hr security.

🍴 Eating

There is a 23% added tax on restaurant bills, plus 14% service. In Montevideo, expensive (♥♥♥) = over US$12, mid-range (♥♥) = US$7-12, cheap (♥) = under US$7.

City centre *p1291, map p1290*
♥♥♥ **La Silenciosa**, Ituzaingó 1426, T915 9409. In a converted Jesuit convent (18th-century), later a prestigious fashion house (19th-century), now a historical monument, excellent food, international and French, open Mon-Fri for lunch and Thu-Sat for dinner. Highly recommended.
♥♥♥-♥♥ **Mercado del Puerto**, opposite the Aduana, Calle Piedras, between Maciel and Pérez Castellano (take 'Aduana' bus). Don't miss eating at this 19th-century market building, closed Sun, delicious grills cooked on huge charcoal grates (menus are limited to meat). It is best to go at lunchtime, especially Sat; the atmosphere is great, including buskers outside.
♥♥ **Café Bacacay**, Bacacay 1310 y Buenos Aires. Good music and atmosphere, food served, try the specials. Recommended.
♥♥ **Roma Amor**, Bacacay 1331. Closed Sun, great antipasti lunchtime buffet, US$3. Recommended.
Roldós, sandwiches, most people start with a *medio medio* (half still, half sparkling white wine).

La Estancia del Puerto (No 34, 36), Río Alegre (No 33), La Proa (touristy), Don Tiburón, Cabaña Verónica (No 38), La Pradera and Las Tablitas (No 46, also at Costa Rica 2105, Carrasco) have been recommended.

Plaza Cagancha

♦♦ **Anticuario**, Maldonado 1602. Atmospheric, fish and *parrilla*.

♦♦ **Facal Café Resto Bar**, 18 de Julio 1245, T908 7741. Good food, open until early in the morning, tango performances in front; daily (see Tango a Cielo Abierto, below). **El Mundo de las Tapas Españolas**, 18 de Julio, is next door.

♦♦ **Las Brasas**, San José 909. Good typical food.

♦♦ **El Fogón**, San José 1080. Good value, very friendly, always full.

♦♦ **Gran China**, San José 1077. Good Chinese.

♦♦ **Viejo Sancho**, San José 1229. Excellent, popular, complimentary sherry or vermouth to early arrivals, tearoom by day.

♦♦-♦ **Tío Chef**, Carlos Quijano 1334, T900-0130. Great authentic Chinese food.

Centro Cultural Mercado de la Abundancia, San Jose 1312 (see Sights, above) has good authentic local eateries upstairs, with lunch specials. Highly recommended.

♦ **Cantón Chino**, at Tres Cruces bus terminal, also at Roque Graseras 740, Pocitos, and Shopping Punta Carretas. Good Chinese.

♦ **Il Mondo della Pizza**, several locations, including 18 de Julio 1105, T900 0680, and 18 de Julio 922, T900 4416. Great pizza.

♦ **Subte Pizzerías**, Ejido 1327, T902 3050. An institution, cheap and good. Recommended.

♦ **Vegetariana**, Av Brasil 3086, Pocitos, and other locations (Yí 1334, 18 de Jhulio y Carlos Roxio and 25 de Mayo 462). Closed daily 1500-1900, 2000 on Sat, Sun 1200-1500. Excellent, self-service buffet.

♦ Restaurant on 6th floor of YMCA building, Colonia 1870. Reasonable for lunch, with good views, ask for Asociación Cristiana de Jóvenes.

Outside the centre *p1293*
Playa Ramírez (near Parque Rodó)

♦♦♦-♦♦ **Trattoria Di Piu**, Garibaldi 2570. Recommended for excellent seafood.

♦♦♦-♦♦ **'W' Lounge**, Rambla Wilson y Requena García. Fashionable place for young people with a range of foods and prices.

In and around Pocitos *p1293*

♦♦♦ **Doña Flor**, Artigas 1034. Classy French restaurant, limited menu but good, moves to Punta del Este in summer.

♦♦♦ **Spaghetería 23**, Scosería 2584. Tue-Sun, very good Italian.

♦♦ **El Entrevero**, 21 de Septiembre 2774. Excellent value, beef, take bus 522 from the centre.

♦♦ **El Puesto de Joaquín**, Williman 637. Popular, good atmosphere, varied menu.

♦♦ **Italiano Peck**, 21 de Septiembre 2721, T712 4628. One of the best Italian restaurants in the city, set lunch specials.

Carrasco *p1293*

♦♦♦ **Bungalow Suizo**, Costa Rica 1688, T601 1073. Very good.

♦♦ **La Casa Violeta**, P Murillo 6566 (other branches at Rambla Armenia 3676, Pocitos Nuevo). Help yourself, fixed price.

♦♦ **Dackel**, Dr Gabriel Otero 6438, T6006211. German/Swiss/Austrian food, good prices.

Confiterías **Café Brasileiro**, Ituzaingó 1447, T915 8120, half a block from Plaza Matriz towards the port. Small entrance; easy to miss. A must, one of the oldest cafés in Montevideo and a permanent hangout of one of the greatest Latin American writers, Eduardo Galeano. Others include: **Café Iberia**, Uruguay esq Florida. Locals' bar. **Cake's**, José Ellauri 1067, Pocitos. Expensive. Recommended. **Oro del Rhin**, Convención 1403. 0830-2100, good cakes. **La Pausa**, Sarandí 493. Books and magazines on Uruguayan art and literature. **Soko's**, Av 18 de Julio 1250. Popular, good food, expensive, good coffee, till 0100, Sat 0400. Sorocabana, Av 18 de Julio No 1008. 1400-2330. **Universal Bar**, Piedras y Gómez. Last of the real dock bars, worth a visit.

There are many good, cheap bakeries in Montevideo selling breads and a variety of sandwiches and local pastries. Most of them are takeaway only, but some have tables.

Heladerías **Batuk**, 26 de Marzo y Pérez, Pocitos, and at 18 de Julio y Yí. Both open daily 1000-0200. **La Cigale**, R Graseras 845 (Pocitos), Ejido 1368 and several other locations. **Las Delicias**, Schroeder 6454, Carrasco. **Papitos**, 18 de Julio 1060. Excellent but pricey.

🌓 Bars and clubs

Montevideo *p1290, map p1290*
Boliches
Café-Concerts/Peñas/Folk-Pubs, offering the most typical local nightlife:
Amarcor, Julio Herrera y Obes 1321. Thu-Sat 2100 onwards, traditional pop music.
Clyde's, Costa Rica y Rivera. Live music.
Flannagans Pub, Luis B Cavia 3082, Pocitos. Lively but small, pop, rock and salsa.
Fun-Fun, Ciudadela 1229, behind Teatro Solís, T915 8005. Hangout of local artists, founded in

1895, used to be frequented by Carlos Gardel, where *uvita*, the drink, was born. Great music on Fri and Sat. Recommended.
Lobizón, Michelini 1329. Good food and price.
Subterráneo Magallanes, Gonzalo Ramírez 1701, T419 1075. Daily 0800-2400, Fri and Sat 2230-0315, book in advance.

Boites
These are the more expensive discos which provide live music for dancing; prices, US$15-30. See www.eltimon.com for recommendations.
Palacio Sud América, Yatay 1429, near Palacio Legislativo. Thousands crowd into the 3 dance salons here every Sat, from 2400 till morning, Caribbean music on 1st floor, Tango on 2nd, tickets half price before 2400.

❸ Entertainment

Montevideo *p1290, map p1290*
Cinema Very popular. During the week no cinemas open before 1730. Films are released quite soon after the UK and USA, and often before they get to Buenos Aires. Details in *Guía del Ocio* and monthly *Cinemateca Uruguaya* (free). At least half of Montevideo's cinemas show blue films – marked *sexo explícito*. **Cine Universitario**, 2 halls: Lumière and Chaplin, Canelones 1280, also for classic and serious films. **Cinemateca** film club has 4 separate cinemas: Cinemateca 18, 18 de Julio 1286, T900 9056; Cinemateca Salas 1 y 2, Dr L. Carnelli 1311, T418 2460; Linterna Mágica, Soriano 1227, T902 8290; and Cinemateca Uruguaya Asociación Civil, A Chucarro 1036, T708 2957. The Cinemateca shows great films from all over the world and has an extended film archive. It organizes an international film festival, **Festival de invierno**. Entrance is US$2.50 for 6 months, which often admits 2.
Tanguerías La Vieja Cumparsita, C Gardel 1811. Nightly 2330-0500, no singles admitted, also has *candombe* shows, book ahead. **Tango a Cielo Abierto**, Tango Under the Open Sky, in front of Café Facal, Paseo Yi and 18 de Julio, T908 7741 for information. Free and very good Uruguayan tango shows every day on a wooden stage, Mon-Fri 1200-1300 and 1700-1800, Sat 1300-1400 and 2000-2100, Sun 1300-1400 and 1700-1800. Highly recommended. Besides tango and *candombe*, other popular music forms are Música Campestre-Folklórica (of gaucho origin), Música del Caribe by Uruguayan orchestras dedicated to dance music from Puerto Rico, and "the best New Orleans Dixieland Jazz Bands" in Latin America writes John Raspey. **La Escuela Universitaria de Música**, Sala Zitarrosa, 18 de Julio 1012. Good, free classical music concerts.

Theatres Montevideo has a vibrant theatre scene. Most performances are only on Fri, Sat and Sun, others also on Thu. Apart from **Teatro Solís** (see Sights, above), recommended are **Teatro del Centro Carlos E Sheck**, Plaza Cagancha 1162, T902 8915, and **Teatro Victoria**, Río Negro y Uruguay, T901 9971. See listings in the daily press and *La Brecha*. Prices are around US$4; performances are almost exclusively in Spanish starting at 2100 and at 1900 on Sun. **Teatro Millington-Drake** at the Anglo (see Cultural centres) puts on occasional productions, as do the theatres of the Alianza Uruguay-Estados Unidos and the Alianza Francesa (addresses below). Many theatres close Jan-Feb.

○ Shopping

Montevideo *p1290, map p1290*
The main shopping area is Av 18 de Julio. Many international newspapers can be bought on the east side of Plaza Independencia.
Bookshops The Sun market on Paysandú is good for second-hand books. The following have a few English and American books, but selection in Montevideo is poor: **Bookshop SRL**, JE Rodó 1671 (at Minas y Constituyente), T400 9954, Cristina Mosca. The only shop with exclusively English stock, very friendly staff, also at Montevideo Shopping Center; specializes in travel. **Roberto Cataldo**, Juan Carlos Gómez 1327, elgaleon@netgate.com.uy. **Ibana**, International Book and News Agency, Convención 1479. Specializes in foreign publications. **Librería Barreiro y Ramos**, 25 de Mayo y JC Gómez, 18 de Julio 937, 21 de Septiembre (Pocitos) and Av Arocena 1599 (Carrasco). **Librería Británica**, Sarandí 580. Specializes in language and children's books. **Plaza Libros**, Av 18 de Julio 892. Has a wide range of international books, travel guides, and gay literature. Also at 1185 on the same avenue. **Puro Verso**, 18 de Julio 1199, T901 6429, puroverso@adinet.co.uy. Very good selection is in Spanish, small secondhand section in English, excellent small café, chess tables. Others include: **Librería El Aleph**, Bartolomé Mitre 1358. Used and rare books in Spanish. **Librería Mosca Hermanos**, Av 18 de Julio 1578 and Av Arocena 1576 (Carrasco). Extensive stock. **Librería Oriente Occidente**, Cerrito 477. Used and rare books, also has English books, exchange of books in perfect condition. **Linardi y Risso**, Juan Carlos Gómez 1435, lyrbooks@linardiyrisso.com. **Mercado de Todo la Cultura Uruguaya**, Plaza Fabini. For books on Uruguay in Spanish and Uruguayan music.
Galleries There are many good art galleries. **Galería Latina**, Sarandí 671, T916 3737, is one of the best, with its own art publishing house.

Handicrafts Suede and leather are good buys. There are several shops and workshops around Plaza Independencia. Amethysts, topazes, agate and quartz are mined and polished in Uruguay and are also good buys. For authentic, fairly-priced crafts there is a marquee on Plaza Cagancha (No 1365), and at Mercado de la Abundancia, San José 1312, T901 0550, auda@minetuy.com. **Casa Mario**, Piedras 641. Suede and leather retailer, expensive. **Exculsividades Artesanales**, Av 18 de Julio 1197, Río Negro 1320 L 2, T908 3118. For leather and woollen goods, good prices. **Montevideo Leather Factory**, Plaza Independencia 832. Recommended. **Mundo Mineral**, Sarandí 672. Recommended for amethysts, topazes, agate and quartz. **Benito Sityá**, Sarandí 650 (Ciudad Vieja). Topazes amethysts, agate and quartz. Recommended.

Markets Calle Tristán Narvaja, opposite Facultad de Derecho on 18 de Julio. On Sun, 0800-1400, there is a large, crowded street market on this street, good for silver and copper, and all sorts of collectibles. **Plaza de la Constitución**, a small Sat morning market and a Sun antique fair are held here. **Villa Biarritz**, on Vásquez Ledesma near Parque Rodó, Pocitos. A big market selling fruit, vegetables, clothes and shoes (Tue and Sat 0900-1500, and on Sun in Parque Rodó, 0800-1400).

Shopping malls The Montevideo Shopping Center, on the east edge of Pocitos (Herrera 1290 y Galanza, 1 block south of Rivera). Open daily 1000-2100 and has a self-service restaurant, a cinema and *confiterías*. It also has wide range of shops selling leather goods, Foto Martín, bookshop, supermarkets and more (bus 141 or 142 from San José). **Punta Carretas Shopping**, Ellauri 306, close to Playa Pocitos in the former prison. Open 0900-2200, is large, modern, with all types of shop, also cinema complex and good food patio, popular. Take bus 117 or 121 from Calle San José. Other shopping centres at Portones in Carrasco, the Tres Cruces bus station and Plaza Arozena Shopping Mall.

▲ Activities and tours

Montevideo *p1290, map p1290*
The Palacio Municipal organizes city tours, Sat-Sun, US$5, T903 0648/9, Mon-Fri 1000-1800. A project run by the tourist office is *Caminando Montevideo*, a historical walking tour of the city lasting 1¾-2 hrs, departing from the fountain in Plaza Fabini, Tue-Fri 1330 in Spanish, 1545 in English, Sat 1300 in Spanish, 1505 in English. Tickets cost US$6 from Andes 1387 casi Colonia, T900 0586.
TransHotel, Acevedo Diaz 1671, T402 9935, www.e-transhotel.com. Accommodation, eco-tourism, sightseeing and tailor-made itineraries.
Estancia tourism Information on *estancias* can be found at **Lares**, Wilson Ferreira 1341, T901

9120, www.lares.com.uy, an organization that represents 30-odd *estancias* and *posadas*; at the tourist offices in Montevideo; or general travel agencies and those that specialize in this field:
Estancias Gauchas, Cecilia Regules Viajes (address below), agent for an organization of 80 estancias offering lunch and/or lodging, English, French and Portuguese spoken. Full list of estancias at www.turismo.gub.uy (click on Operadores, then Estancias Turísticas).
Jetmar, Plaza de la Independencia 725-7, T902 0793. A helpful tour operator.
Mundo Turismo Natural, Colonia 926, T/F902 0862. Adventure and nature tourism specialists, mainly to Maldonado and Rocha departments.
Cecilia Regules Viajes, Bacacay 1334, T/F916 3011, T09-968 3608 (mob), regulesv@adinet.com.uy or uy21333@antel.com.uy, very good, knowledgeable, specialist in *estancia*, tango and railway tourism in Uruguay, and skiing in Argentina.
Rumbos, Galería del Libertador, Rio Branco 1377, p 7, T900 2407, rumbouno@adinet.com.uy. Also at World Trade Center, Luis A de Herrera 1248, T628 5555, rumbodos@adinet.com.uy. Caters specifically for independent travellers, very helpful.
JP Santos, Colonia 951, T902 0300. Helpful agency.
Turisport Ltda, San José 930, T902 0829, turispor@netgate.com.uy. American Express for travel and mail services, good; sells Amex dollar TCs on Amex card and personal cheque at 1 commission. 1-day tours of Punta del Este are organized by many travel agents and run from several hotels, US$40-100 including meals.
Marian Whitaker, T700 6842, F701 5411. Bilingual guide for tours of Montevideo and Uruguay, riding, hiking, camping, fishing, also visits to Santa Sofia *estancia* in Río Negro.

● Transport

Montevideo *p1290, map p1290*
Air
The main airport, is at Carrasco, 21 km outside the city, T601 1757; with coffee shop and children's play area in departure lounge; left luggage about US$1 per day per item; exchange facilities, but if closed, buses will accept dollars for fares to town. If making an advance hotel reservation, ask them to send a taxi to meet you; it's cheaper than taking an airport taxi. To Montevideo 30 mins by taxi or *remise* (US$12-20, depending on destination in the city – may be able to pay taxi driver in Argentine pesos or in dollars, or charge it to hotel bill if without cost); about 50 mins by bus. Buses, Nos 700, 701, 704, 710 and 711, from Terminal Brun, Río Branco y Galicia, go to the airport US$1 (crowded before and after school hours); dark brown 'Copsa' bus terminates at the airport. **COT** buses connect

airport and Punta del Este, US$5. **Pluna** has a bus service from *Hotel Victoria Plaza*, Plaza Independencia to airport at 30 mins past the hour (only for **Pluna** and **Varig** passengers). **IBAT** bus service T601 0209/0943 2373. **Concorde Travel** (Robert Mountford), Germán Barbato 1358, apto 1302, T902 6346/8, has a service from hotel to plane (almost) US$10-25.

Air services to **Argentina**: for the Puente Aéreo to Buenos Aires, check in at Montevideo airport, pay departure tax and go to immigration to fill in an Argentine entry form before going through Uruguayan immigration. Get your stamp out of Uruguay, surrender the tourist card you received on entry and get your stamp into Argentina. There are no immigration checks on arrival at Aeroparque, Buenos Aires. For flights via Colonia see page 1310.

Bus

Local City buses are fairly comfortable and convenient. Pay your fare to the driver or to conductor in the centre of the bus, US$0.40; express buses D2 US$0.40, D3, 5, 8, 10, 11 US$0.50, D1 (see Sights Carrasco, above) US$1. There are many buses to all parts from 18 de Julio; from other parts to the centre or old city, look for those marked 'Aduana'. For Pocitos from city centre take bus No 121 from Calle San José. **Remises**: US$8 per hr; **Remises Montevideo**, Joaquín Requena 1303, F401 1149; **Libertad**, Plaza Cagancha 1126, T902 4393; **Juan Mastroianni**, T099-639865 (mob), good, safe, reasonably-priced; **Guillermo Muñoz**, Bartolito Mitre 2636, T707 3928.
Long distance During summer holidays buses are often full; it is advisable to book in advance (also for Fri and weekend travel all year round).
Buses within Uruguay: excellent terminal, Tres Cruces, Bulevar Artigas y Av Italia, T408 8710 (10-15 mins by bus from the centre, Nos 21, 64, 180, 187, 188 – in Ciudad Vieja from in front of Teatro Solís); it has a shopping mall, tourist office, internet café, restaurants, left luggage (free for 2 hrs at a time, if you have a ticket for that day, then US$0.70 up to 4 hrs, 24 hrs US$1.75), post and phone offices, toilets, good medical centre, **Banco de Montevideo** and **Indumex** cambio (accepts MasterCard). Visit www.tushopping.com.uy/tc/index.jsp for bus schedules. For nearby hotels, see Sleeping, above. Fares and journey times from the capital are given under destinations.
To Argentina (ferries and buses) You need a passport when buying international tickets. Direct to **Buenos Aires**: Buquebus, at the docks, in old customs hall, T130, Colonia y Florida, T902 0526, Terminal Las Cruces, Local 28/29, T408 8120, in the Sheraton and Punta Carretas Shopping. 1-2 daily, 3 hrs, US$53 tourist class, US$63 1st class. At Montevideo dock, go to Preembarque 30 mins before departure, present

ticket and pay exit tax; then go to Migración for Uruguayan exit and Argentine entry formalities. The terminal is like an airport and the seats on the ferries are airplane seats. On board there is duty-free shopping, video and poor value food and drinks. **Services via Colonia**: bus/ ferry services by **Buquebus**: 2 crossings daily 2 hrs from Colonia, US$18 tourist, US$24; **Ferrylíneas Sea Cat**, bookable through Buquebus, or T409 8198, fast service: 2-3 day, 1 hr, 1st class US$30 tourist, US$36 1st class, both with bus Montevideo-Colonia from Tres Cruces 2½ hrs, US$5 extra. Cars are carried on either route, US$74-84 **Montevideo**, US$31-36 and 51-56 (depending on size of vehicle and boat) **Colonia**; motorcycles US$55 Montevideo, US$20 Colonia. Schedules and fares can be checked on www.buquebus.com. Fares increase in high season, Dec-Jan, when there are more sailings. Break of journey in Colonia on all services is allowed; cheaper, if you do this, to buy bus ticket only in Montevideo, and then ferry ticket in Colonia. Services to **Carmelo** and **Tigre** (interesting trip): bus/ motor launch service by **Trans Uruguay/ Cacciola**, 2 a day (morning and afternoon), at Tres Cruces T401 9350, US$12.50 (22 return). Bus service via **Fray Bentos**, Bus de la Carrera (Terminal Tres Cruces 25/26, T402 1313), 1000, 2200, 2230 (dormibus) and 2300 daily, US$27, 7 hrs. Bus services also nightly with Cauvi (T401 9196) and **Belgrano** (T401 4764). Advanced booking is advisable on all services at busy periods. On through buses to Brazil and Argentina, you can expect full luggage checks both by day and night.
To Paraguay, Brazil, Chile If intending to travel through Uruguay to Brazil, do not forget to have Uruguayan entry stamped in your passport when crossing from Argentina. Without it you will not be able to cross the Brazilian border. To **Asunción**, Paraguay, US$67, 18 hrs: twice a week (Wed and Sat, plus Mon in summer) by **COIT**, Río Branco 1389, T908 6469, or Tres Cruces, T401 5628, and 2 a week by **Brújula**, T401 9196, both services recommended, meals served. Alternatively take bus to **Santa Fe**, Argentina (US$36), via Paysandú bridge, for easy access to Asunción. The through bus route is via Paysandú, Salto, Bella Unión, Uruguaiana, Paso de los Libros, Posadas, Encarnación, to Asunción (there are no passport or customs formalities except passport checks at Bella Unión and at Encarnación). There are very comfortable buses to **Porto Alegre** (US$44, 10 hrs, daily) and **São Paulo** (US$96, 32 hrs via Florianópolis, US$65, Camboriú, US$68, a good place to stop over, and Curitiba, US$79, Wed, Fri, Sun at 1600) with **EGA** (recommended), **Tres Cruces**, T402 5164, or **Río Branco** 1409, T902 5335, egakeg@andinet.com.uy. **TTL** (**Tres Cruces** or **Río**

Branco 1375, T901 7142/401 1410) also serves São Paulo, Florianópolis and Porto Alegre. A cheaper alternative route (which also avoids the risk of being stranded at the border by through-bus drivers) is to Chuy, eg COIT, T409 4949, or Plaza Cagancha 1124, T902 4004 (US$13, 4½ hrs), then catch an onward bus to Porto Alegre (7½ hrs, US$13 if paid in reais), either direct or via Pelotas.

Taxi
The meter starts at US$0.70. In the central area fares are about US$2-4. Fares are shown on the meter by a number which determines the cost according to a table displayed by the passenger's seat; make sure the meter starts at zero, even in radio taxis. There is a small charge for each piece of luggage. Tipping is not expected but welcomed. Prices go up on Sat, Sun, holidays and late at night.

Train
Uruguayan railways, AFE, use outdated trains, but interesting rides for enthusiasts. The old train station has been abandoned, replaced by a small, glass and steel terminus at the north end of Calle Río Negro (with Cerro Largo). Commuter trains run north to 25 de Agosto (Florida), passing some of the most desperate neighbourhoods in Uruguay. Mon-Fri depart to 25 de Agosto 1515, 1725 and 1920, returning to Montevideo 0350, 0450 and 0650. On Sat, to 25 de Agosto at 0830, 1425 and 1725, return from 25 de Agosto 0350, 0630 and 1810. Most commuter trains run only between Montevideo and Progreso. You can take the train to Santa Lucía, the stop before 25 de Agosto, and return by bus (2 hrs, US$2); the train goes via Canelones also: Montevideo-Progreso: US$0.80 one way. Progreso-Santa Lucia: US$0.70. Ferrotransporte (T924 1387) arrange return trips to Florida, with lunch and tours. On Sun, short excursions – one stop – by train (same carriages as used by commuter trains but pulled by a steam-engine; US$1.

● Directory

Montevideo *p1290, map p1290*
Airline offices Aerolíneas Argentinas, Av Cabildo 2900, T901 9466. American Airlines, Sarandí 699 bis y Plaza Independencia, T916 3979. ASATEJ Uruguay, Student Flight Centre, Río Negro 1354, p 2, of ½, T908 0509. Aviasur, at airport, T601 4618. Iberia, Colonia 673/75, T908 1032, F902 3284. KLM, Andes 1217, T902 5057. LAN T902 3881. Pluna (T604 4080, www.pluna.com.uy) and Varig, office on south side of Plaza Independencia, Fast Track check-in and bus at *Victoria Plaza* hotel, Plaza Independencia, near the driveway off Florida, T902 1414/600 0750. Uair, Plaza Independencia

759, p 7, T903 2223. United, Plaza Independencia 831, p 5, T902 4630. For information on all flight arrivals and departures, T601 1991. **Banks** Don't trust the few black market money changers offering temptingly good rates. Many are experienced confidence tricksters. Casas de cambio on Plaza Cagancha open daily until 2200, including Sun, but banks open only from 1230 to 1730. Many banks give cash advances against Visa and MasterCard. Airport bank open every day 0700- 2200. Lloyds TSB Bank, Calle Zabala 1500, and 11 city agencies. Citibank, Colonia 1329 and 26 de Marzo 3509, no commission on own cheques, Visa ATM. ABN Amro, 25 de Mayo 501 and 18 de Julio 1300 (MasterCard and Visa ATM); 22 other branches. 2 branches of *Redbanc* for Visa and MasterCard ATMs: Colonia 758, *Victoria Plaza*, and Galicia 963 y Río Branco. Branches of *Banco de Crédito* take Visa, with ATM, eg Río Branco 1450 y Mercedes. American Express Bank, Rincón 473, T916 0092/916 1162, does not change cash or TCs (see Turisport under Tour operators). Western Union, Río Negro y 18 de Julio, opposite *McDonalds*. The MasterCard office is in Edif Torre Libertad, Plaza Cagancha 1335, p 3. There are exchange houses, especially along 18 de Julio, eg Almar at 1077, Bacacay, near Plaza Independencia, La Favorita (Amex agents) at 1459, Suizo at 1190, Zito at 1841, but shop around for best rates (rates for cash are better than for TCs, but both are often better than in banks, and quicker service). Brimar, Misiones 1476; Durazno, 25 de Mayo 481, and Delta, Río Negro 1341, have been recommended. **Car hire** Without chauffeur, from US$36 to US$85 per 24 hrs (insurance included); guarantee of US$500 required. It is possible to negotiate small car for as little as US$39 per day, free mileage, including insurance and collision damage waiver, if you are hiring a car for at least 3 days (rates are much lower out of season and vary according to size of vehicle). Cheaper weekly rates available. Best to make reservations before arrival. It is wise to hire a small car (1.3 litre engine) as Uruguay is relatively flat and gas prices are high. Punta Car, Cerro Largo 1383, T900 2772, also at Aeropuerto Carrasco. Snappy, Andes 1363, T900 7728 or 099-660660. Sudancar, Piedras 533, T915 8150; many others. See Essentials, page 43 for international agencies. Most car companies don't allow their cars to be taken abroad. To travel to Argentina or Brazil, you can use Maxicar rentals in Salto, see pag 1311. **Cultural centres** Alianza Cultural Uruguay-Estados Unidos, Paraguay 1217, T902 5160, www.alianza.edu.uy, library open Mon-Fri, 1400-2000, US publications and books (excellent selection), theatre, art gallery. Instituto Cultural Anglo-Uruguayo (known as the 'Anglo'), San José 1426, T902 3773, www.anglo.edu.uy (theatre, recommended, library open Mon-Fri 0930-1200,

1430-1930); café at No 1227. **Alliance Française**, Av 18 de Julio 1772, T408 6012, www.alianzafrancesa. edu.uy (theatre, concerts, exhibitions in French and Spanish, library, excellent bookshop). **Goethe Institut**, Canelones 1524, T400 5813, F410 4432 (open Mon, Tue, Thu, Fri 1000-1300, 1600-1930). **Instituto Italiano de Cultura**, Paraguay 1177, T900 3354, iicmdeo@adinet.com.uy. **Embassies and consulates** Argentine Consulate, Wilson Ferreira Aldunate 1281, T902 8623, http://emb-uruguay.mrecic.gov.ar. Open 1400-1900, visa US$15, 1 day wait, English spoken. **Austrian Consulate-General**, Misiones 1372, T916 0152/916 0718, F915 1283. **Belgium**, Leyenda Patria 2880, Apt 202, T710 1265. **Brazilian Consulate**, Bulevar Artigas 1328, T707 2115, F707 2086, www.brasmont.org.uy. Consulate: Convención 1343, piso 6, T900 6282, F900 0348, Open 0930- 1230, 1430-1730 (service for visas takes 24 hrs and the procedure is more complicated than Buenos Aires – need photo, onward ticket, entry ticket, proof of finances). **Canada**, Plaza Independencia 749, of 102, T902 2030, F902 2029, www.dfait- maeci.gc.ca/uruguay. **Chile**, Andes 1365, T902 6316. Open 0900-1400, visa US$5, same day. **France**, Uruguay 853, T902 0077, www.amb-montevideo.fr. **Germany**, La Cumparsita 1417-35, T902 5222, F902 3422, www.deutschebotschaft-montevideo.info/ de/home/index.html. Open 0930-1230. **Israel**, Blvd Gral Artigas 1585, T400 4164. **Italy**, JB Lamas 2857, T708 4916, F708 4148, www.ambitalia.com.uy. **Netherlands**, Leyenda Patria 2880, Apt 202, T700 1631. **New Zealand Consulate**, Bulevar Artigas 1074, T785925, F780509. **Paraguayan Consulate**, Blvd Artigas 1191, T408 5810. Open 0900-1200

summer, 1400-1730 winter. **Portugal**, Av Dr F Soca 1128. **Spanish Consulate**, Libertad 2750, T708 0048. **Sweden**, Av Brasil 3079, piso 6, Pocitos, T708 0088. **Switzerland**, Ing Federico Abadie 2934-40, T710 4315. **UK**, Marco Bruto 1073, T622 3630, F622 7815, bemonte@ internet.com.uy. **US Embassy** and **Consulate**, Lauro Muller 1776, T408 777, F418 8611, http://uruguay. Usembassy.gov. **Internet** At Santiago de Chile 1286. **Cyber Enter**, San José 1334, near Municipalidad, Mon-Sun 1000-0400, US$0.75 per hr. **Millennium Café**, Paraguay 1325, local 53, in mall, US$1 per hr. **Cyber Café Nacho**, Av del Libertador 1607 y Cerro Largo, T903 9070. Open till 2200. **Cyber Café Uruguay**, Colonia 1955. Also pub and dancing. **Medical services** Hospital Británico, Av Italia 2420, T400 9011. Recommended. **Post offices** Misiones 1328 y Buenos Aires; 0800-1800 Mon-Fri, 0800-1300 Sat and holidays; philatelic bureau on 1st floor sells back issues. **Poste restante** at main post office will keep mail for 1 month, 2 if authorized in advance by administrator. Next to Pluna office on Av Libertador, next to Montevideo Shopping Center, 0800-1300, and under Intendencia at corner of Av 18 de Julio and Ejido, Mon-Fri 1000-2000, Sat 1700-2200. **Telephones** Antel, Fernández Crespo 1534 (headquarters) and at San José 1102 (Plaza), Arocena 1666 (Carrasco), Ariel 4914 (Sayago), Cádiz 3280 (Mercado Modelo), Garzón 1806 (Colón), José Belloni 4445 (Piedras Blancas); for international phone calls (including USA Direct Express), telex, fax, cables, daily 0800-2000. Long distance operator T120; for Latin America T0007, other countries T0008; special service T124. **Useful numbers** Information: T141.

Western Uruguay

West of Montevideo, Route 1, part of the Pan-American Highway, heads to the beautiful UNESCO World Heritage Site of Colonia del Sacramento and, beyond, the tranquil town of Carmelo. Off the road are historic sites like the old British mining town of Conchillas and the Jesuit mission at Calera de las Huérfanas. Other routes lead to the Río Uruguay, Route 2 from Rosario to Fray Bentos, and Route 3 via San José de Mayo and Trinidad to the historic towns of Paysandú and Salto. The latter passes through the real Uruguay, farms and wide-open spaces with cattle and sheep, man-made lakes and eventually the river itself. There are many hot-spring resorts in this part of the country, some humble, others luxurious.

Colonias Valdense and Suiza

Route 1 to Colonia de Sacramento is being made into a four-lane highway. At Km 121 from Montevideo the road passes Colonia Valdense, a colony of Waldensians who still cling to some of the old customs of the Piedmontese Alps. Tourist information T055-88412. A road branches off north here to Colonia Suiza, a town of Swiss settlement also known as **Nueva Helvecia** (*Population 9,000, Phone code 0552*), with lovely parks, gardens and countryside. In the town is the Santuario de Nuestra Señora De Schonstatt, all walls are covered by plants, and the first steam mill in Uruguay (1875).The Swiss national day is celebrated with great enthusiasm.

The highway skirts **Rosario** (Phone code 052, 140 km from Montevideo, 60 before Colonia del Sacramento), called "the first Uruguayan Museum of Mural Art". There are dozens of impressive murals around the city, some depicting bullfights, others with abstract designs.

Colonia del Sacramento → *Phone code: 052, from Bs As: 022. Colour map 8, grid B5. Population 22,000.*

① *All museums 1115-1645, closed Wed, combined tickets bought from Museo Municipal, US$0.20; not all may be open on the same day.*

Founded by Portuguese settlers from Brazil in 1680, Colonia del Sacramento was an important centre for smuggling British goods across the Río de la Plata into the Spanish colonies during the 17th century. The small historic section juts into the Río de la Plata, while the modern town extends around a bay. It is a lively place with streets lined with plane trees, a pleasant Plaza 25 de Agosto and a grand Intendencia Municipal (Méndez y Avenida Gen Flores – the main street). The town is kept very trim. The best beach is Playa Ferrando, 2 km to the east (buses from Gen Flores every two hours). There are regular sea and air connections with Buenos Aires and a free port. In the old city, visit the *Mercado Artesanal*, del Comercio y de la Playa and the *Rincón del Turista*, Santa Rita. In the third week of January, festivities mark the founding of Colonia.

Colonia del Sacramento

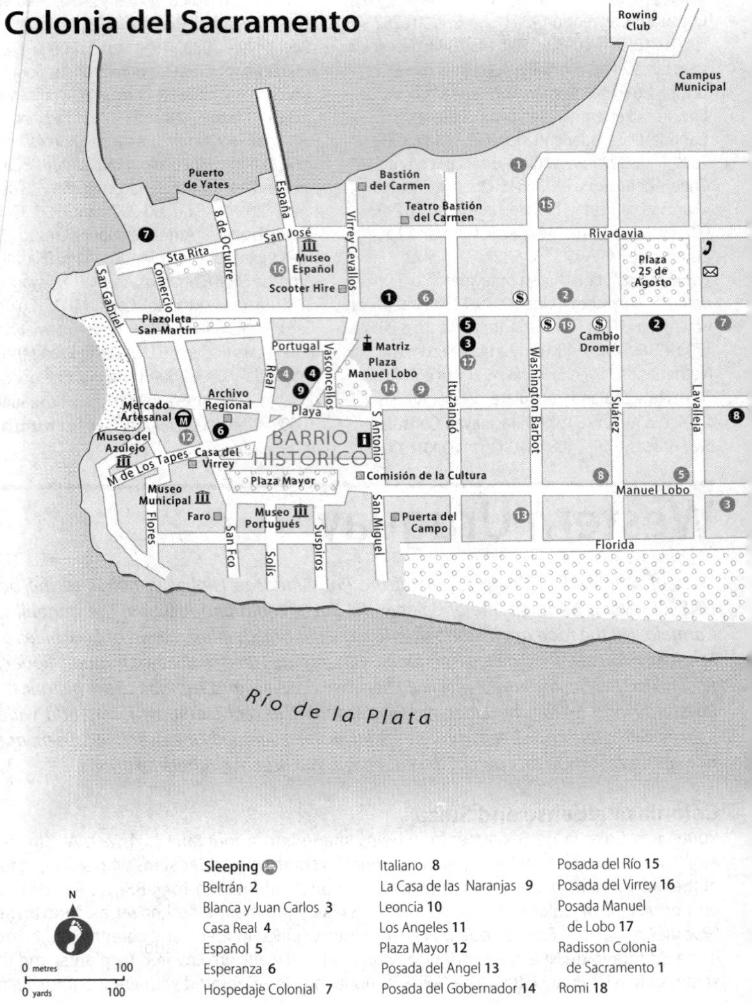

[map of Colonia del Sacramento showing Barrio Histórico, Plaza Mayor, Plaza 25 de Agosto, Río de la Plata and street grid]

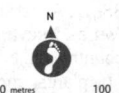

Sleeping		
Beltrán 2	Italiano 8	Posada del Río 15
Blanca y Juan Carlos 3	La Casa de las Naranjas 9	Posada del Virrey 16
Casa Real 4	Leoncia 10	Posada Manuel
Español 5	Los Angeles 11	de Lobo 17
Esperanza 6	Plaza Mayor 12	Radisson Colonia
Hospedaje Colonial 7	Posada del Angel 13	de Sacramento 1
	Posada del Gobernador 14	Romi 18

The **Barrio Histórico**, with its narrow streets (see Calle de los Suspiros), colonial buildings and reconstructed city walls, is charming because there are few such examples in this part of the continent. It has been declared Patrimonio Cultural de la Humanidad by UNESCO. The old town can be easily seen on foot in a day (wear comfortable shoes on the uneven cobbles), but spend one night there to experience the illuminations by nostalgic replica street lamps. The **Plaza Mayor** is especially picturesque and has parakeets in the palm trees. Grouped around it are the **Museo Municipal** in the former house of Almirante Brown (18th century; with indigenous archaeology, historical items, paleontology, natural history), the **Casa Nacarello** next door (18th century; depicting colonial life), the **Casa del Virrey**, the **Museo Portugués** (1720) and the ruins of the Convento de San Francisco, to which is attached the **Faro** (lighthouse, entry US$1, daily till 1730 – on a clear day you can see Buenos Aires). At the eastern end is the **Puerta del Campo**, the restored city gate and drawbridge. Just north of the Plaza Mayor is the **Archivo Regional** (1750), collection of maps, police records 1876-1898. The **Iglesia Matriz**, on Calle Vasconcellos (beside the Plaza de Armas/Manuel Lobo), is the oldest church in Uruguay. At the end of Calle Misiones de los Tapes, the Casa Portuguesa is now the tiny **Museo del Azulejo** (original floor, collection of French and Catalan tiles, plus the first Uruguayan tile from 1840). The house of Gen Mitre, Calles de San José y España, houses the **Museo Español**. At the north edge, the fortifications of the **Bastión del Carmen** can be seen; nearby is the Centro Cultural Bastión del Carmen, Rivadavia 223, with frequent theatre productions (US$1.65).

Around the bay is **Real de San Carlos** ① *5 km, take blue bus from Av Gen Flores y A Méndez, 30 mins, US$0.40*, an unusual, once grand but now sad tourist complex, built by Nicolás Mihanovic 1903-1912. The elegant bull- ring, in use for a mere two years, is falling apart (closed to visitors, bullfighting is banned in Uruguay). The casino, the nearest to Buenos Aires (where gambling was prohibited), failed when a tax was imposed on Mihanovic's excursions; also disused the huge Frontón court. Only the racecourse (Hipódromo) is still operational (men US$1, women free) and you can see the horses exercising and swimming in the sea.

Tourist offices ① *Flores y Rivera, T26141/ 23700, Mon-Fri 0800-1830, Sat-Sun 0900- 2200, www.colonia.gub.uy*, good maps of the Barrio Histórico. Also beside Plaza Mayor ① *Paseo de San Antonio, T/F21118, open 1000-1600, but Mon and Tue often closed in afternoon and Wed and Thu in morning, Sun 1100-1500*. Also at passenger terminal at the dock, T24897. Visit www.guiacolonia.com.uy.

Conchillas, 50 km from Colonia and 40 km from Carmelo, is a former British mining town from the late 19th century. It preserves dozens of buildings constructed by C H Walker and Co Ltd. The tourist office is open until 1700 and the police station is a good source of information. Direct buses from Colonia; road well marked on Route 21.

To Real de San Carlos

Alberto Méndez

Av Gen Artigas

Cnl Arroyo

Rivera

Dr D Fosalba

V García

To Playa Ferrando (2 km)

Budget
Intendencia Municipal **18**
10

To Real de San Carlos

Punta Rent a Car

Plaza de Deportes

Av General Flores

18 de Julio

AV F D Roosevelt

To **11** & Montevideo

PUERTO

To Buenos Aires

Royal **19**

Eating ❷
Almacén del Túnel **1**
Club Colonia **2**
El Asador **3**
El Drugstore & Viejo Barrio **4**

La Amistad **8**
Mercosur **5**
Mesón de la Plaza **9**
Pulpería Los Faroles **6**
Yacht Club **7**

Wreckers, revolutionaries and gauchos

Uruguay's passion for rural life began with Hernando Arias and the first shipment of cattle and horses to the Banda Oriental in 1603.

Today, a typical day on an *estancia* begins at the hearth, perhaps with a warming *mate*, before a horseride. The fireplace may be decorated with signs of present and past ownership, each brand burnt into the fireplace representing a personal history, but one element unites them all: the myth of the gaucho.

You might be forgiven for imagining yourself a latter-day gaucho as you put your foot in the *copa* (a cupped stirrup) and mount a sturdy Uruguayan horse, perhaps of the same breed as the one that Napoleon had shipped back to carry him around a wintry Europe. However, your thick poncho might well be the only piece of gaucho gear that you are wearing. Gauchos sometimes used ponchos as shields in knife fights, but on the ride you probably won't be needing a *facón* (a large dagger), nor a pair of *bombachas* (baggy trousers gathered at the ankle) or *culero* (an apron of soft leather tied around the waist, open on the left side) to avoid lacerations from a lasso during branding and gelding. Horses on tourism estancias are used to novice riders, and *rebenques* (short whips) are best kept unused by your side. You'll find the Uruguayan horse a compliant platform for launching your *boleadoras* (three stones, covered with hide, on ropes tied at the middle, are used for entangling the legs of cattle). At this point you may learn whether your horse is a *pingo*, a gaucho's favourite horse, or *flete*, an ordinary cargo beast.

Riding along extensive *cuchillas* (ridges) and crossing rivers will bring to mind the nomadic gaucho lifestyle, and the revolutionary guerrilla bands, manned largely by gauchos. A *montonera* was a band of gauchos organized to drive the Brazilians and Argentinians out of Uruguay. Patriot leader Artigas was a gaucho-caudillo (boss).

Uruguayan life is built from livestock, sometimes quite literally. Houses were occasionally made from cattle hide. And cattle were put to other uses: coastal ranchers in Maldonado Department in the 19th century placed lights on the horns of their cows to lure ships onto the rocks for plunder.

Carmelo → *Phone code 0542. Population 18,000.*

From Colonia, Route 21 heads northwest to Carmelo (74 km) on the banks of Arroyo Las Vacas. A fine avenue of trees leads to the river, crossed by the first swing bridge built 1912. Across the bridge is the Rambla de los Constituyentes and the Fuente de las Tentaciones. The church, museum and archive of El Carmen is on Plaza Artigas (named after the city's founder). In the Casa de Cultura Ignacio Barrios (IMC), 19 de Abril 246, is a tourist office and museum. Historically a mining centre, it is said that many luxurious buildings in Buenos Aires were made from they grey granite of Cerro Carmelo (mines are now filled with water and used for watersports). It is one of the most important yachting centres on Río de la Plata and its microclimate produces much wine.

Calera de Las Huérfanas (Estancia de las Vacas) is the remains of one of the area's main Jesuit missions. Vines were introduced and lime was exported for the construction of Buenos Aires. After the expulsion of the Jesuits, it became an orphanage for girls. It's in relatively good state and is best reached by car (exit from Route 21 clearly marked, some 10 km before Carmelo).

Mercedes → *Phone code: 0532. Colour map 8, grid B5. Population: 37,000.*

This livestock centre is best reached by Route 2 from the main Colonia-Montevideo highway. Founded in 1788, it is pleasant town on the Río Negro, a yachting and fishing centre during the season. Its charm (it is known as 'the city of flowers') derives from its Spanish-colonial appearance, though it is not as old as the older parts of Colonia. There is an attractive *costanera* (riverside drive). Some 4 km west of town is the Parque Maúá, dating from 1757. It has a mansion which contains the **Museum of Palaeontology** ⓘ *daily 1100-1800, free,* on the ground floor. The building is worth wandering around to see the exterior, upper apartments and stable block. Camping is possible in season. It takes 45 minutes to walk to the park, a pleasant route passing Calera Real on the riverbank, dating back to 1722, the oldest industrial ruins in the country (lime kilns hewn out of the sandstone). **Tourist office**: At Colón, on the plaza, maps and hotel lists available. **Fray Bentos**: The tourist office is at Puente General San Martín, T28369.

Fray Bentos → *Colour map 8, grid B5. Population: 22,000.*

Route 2 continues westwards (34 km) to Fray Bentos, the main port on the east bank of Río Uruguay 193 km from Buenos Aires. Here in 1865 the Liebig company built its first factory producing meat extract. The original plant, much extended and known as **El Anglo**, has been restored as the **Museo de La Revolución Industrial and a business park** ⓘ *T3607, daily except Mon, entry by guided tour only, US$1, 1000, 1430 (1000, 1130 and 1700 in summer), tour 1½ hrs in Spanish, may provide leaflet in English, restaurant (Wolves) and disco (Fuel Oil).* The office block in the factory has been preserved complete with its original fittings. Many machines can be seen. Within the complex is the Barrio Inglés, where workers were housed, and La Casa Grande, where the director lived. There are **beaches** to the northeast and southwest and also at *Las Cañas* (see Sleeping, below).

Crossing to Argentina

About 9 km upriver from Fray Bentos is the San Martín International Bridge, the most popular overland route with Argentina, toll US$4 per car (tourist office). Bicycles are not allowed to cross, but officials will give you a lift if there is no other traffic. Formalities are separate, at opposite ends of the bridge. The Argentine consulate is at Sarandí 3195, Fray Bentos.

Paysandú → *Phone code: 072. Colour map 8, grid A5. Population: 100,000.*

North of Fray Bentos, 130 km, is this undulating, historic city on the east bank of the Río Uruguay. Along Route 3, it's 380 km from Montevideo. Temperatures in summer can rise as high as 42°C. The **cathedral** ⓘ *Mon-Fri 1100-1300, closed Tue; Sat-Sun 0800-1300,* is 19th-century. **Museo Histórico Municipal** ⓘ *Zorilla y Leandro Gómez, Mon-Fri 0800-1645,*

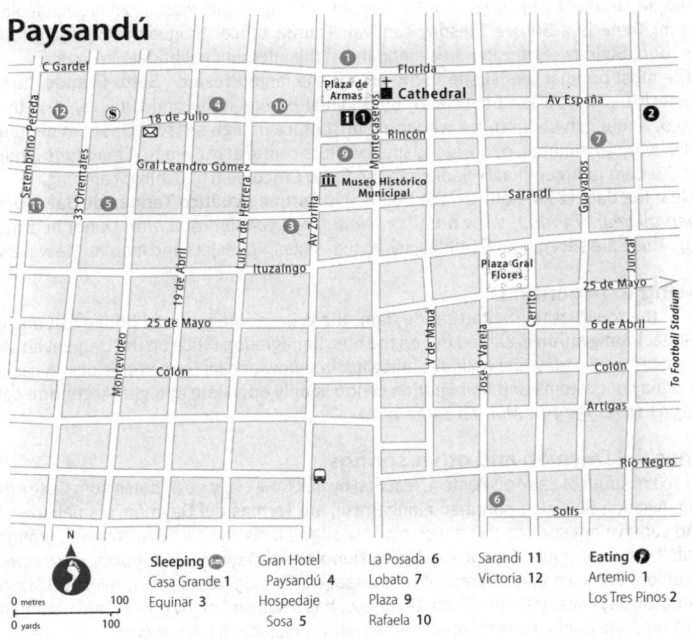

Paysandú

Sleeping	Gran Hotel	La Posada 6	Sarandí 11	Eating
Casa Grande 1	Paysandú 4	Lobato 7	Victoria 12	Artemio 1
Equinar 3	Hospedaje	Plaza 9		Los Tres Pinos 2
	Sosa 5	Rafaela 10		

Sat 0900-0230, has good collection of guns and furniture from the time of the Brazilian siege of 1864-65, well-documented. **Museo de la Tradición** ① *north of town at the Balneario Municipal, 0900-1800 daily, reached by bus to Zona Industrial*, gaucho articles, is also worth a visit. **Museo Salesiano** ① *Florida 1278, Mon-Fri 0830-1130* attached to Cathedral, interesting. **Tourist office** ① *Plaza de Constitución, 18 de Julio 1226, T26221, Mon-Fri 0800-1900, Sat-Sun 0800-1800, and at the Puente Gen Artigas, T27574.* Local website: www.paysandu.com.

Around Paysandú

The **Termas del Guaviyú** *US$0.50, getting there: 1½ hrs by bus, US$2, 4 a day,* thermal springs 50 km north, with four pools, restaurant, motel (**B-D**) and excellent cheap camping facilities. Along Route 90, 80 km east, are the **Termas de Almirón**, two pools, with camping and motels. The **Meseta de Artigas** ① *90 km north of Paysandú, 13 km off the highway to Salto, no public transport, free,* is 45 m above the Río Uruguay, which here narrows and forms whirlpools at the rapids of El Hervidero. It was used as a base by General Artigas during the struggle for independence. A terrace with a fine view, but the rapids are not visible from the Meseta. The statue, with Artigas' head topping a tall shaft, is very original.

Crossing to Argentina

The José Artigas international bridge connects with Colón, Argentina (toll US$4 per car), about 8 km away. Immigration for both countries is on the Uruguayan side in the same office. Migración officials board the bus, but non-Argentine/Uruguayans should get off bus for stamp.

Salto → *Phone code: 073. Colour map 8, grid A5. Population: 80,000.*

A centre for cultivating and processing oranges and other citrus fruit, Salto is a beautifully kept town 120 km by paved road north of Paysandú. The town's commercial area is on Calle Uruguay, between Plazas Artigas and Treinta y Tres. There are lovely historic streets and nice walks along the river. Next to Club Uruguay, Calle Uruguay, is the *Farmacia Fénix*, "la más antigua de Salto", over 100 years old. See the beautiful but run down **Parque Solari** (on Ruta Gral Artigas, northeast of the centre) and the **Parque Harriague** (south of the centre) with an open-air theatre. The **Museo de Bellas Artes y Artes Decorativas** ① *Uruguay 1067, 1400,* in the French style mansion of a rich *estanciero* (Palacio Gallino), well worth a visit. **Museo del Hombre y La Tecnología** ① *Brasil 514, free,* is also very interesting; it includes a small archaeological museum. There is a Shrove Tuesday carnival. **Tourist office:** Uruguay 1052, T34096, open 0800-2000, Sunday 0800-1200, free map; and at the international bridge, T28933.

The most popular tourist site in the area is the large **Presa de Salto Grande** dam and hydroelectric plant 20 km from Salto, built jointly by Argentina and Uruguay; taxi to dam US$5.50. A tour can be arranged with the tourist office in high season, US$2, minimum five people, every 30 minutes, 0700-1400; small visitors centre at the plant. A road runs along the top of the dam to Argentina. By launch to the **Salto Chico** beach, fishing, camping.

Near the dam (2 km north on the Route 3) is **Parque Acuático Termas de Salto Grande** ① *open all year, T30902, www.hotelhoracioquiroga.com/parque.htm,* (4 ha) in a natural setting. There are several pools, slides, hydro massages, water jets and man-made waterfalls.

Crossing to Argentina

North of the town, at the Salto Grande dam, there is an international bridge to Concordia, Argentina. **Immigration** is carried out on the bus. Immigration office on the Uruguayan side is often closed on Sunday and holidays, allowing free-flow of cars from both sides. A casino at the Uruguayan customs and immigration centre is only open late at night. **Argentine consul** ① *Artigas 1162, T32931, Mon-Fri 1300-1700.*

Termas del Daymán and other springs

About 10 km south of Salto on Route 3, reached by bus No 4 every 30 minutes from Calle Artigas, or from Avenida Sauzal at port then along Brasil, are **Termas del Daymán**, a small town built around curative hot springs. It is a nice place to spend a night; several restaurants around the beautifully laid out pools. **Complejo Médico Hidrotermal Daymán** ① *T69090, www.complejo* medicohidrotermal.com.uy, therapeutical massage US$11.65 pesos for 20 mins, US$17.50 for 40 mins, full day water treatment from US$17.50, has a spa and many specialized treatments in several separate pools (external and internal), showers, jacuzzis and rooms.

The road to **Termas del Arapey** branches off the partially paved Route 3 to Bella Unión, at 61 km north of Salto, and then runs 35 km east and then south. Pampa birds, rheas and metre-long lizards in evidence. Termas del Arapey is on the Arapey river south of Isla Cabellos (Baltazar Brum). The waters at these famous thermal baths (five pools) contain bicarbonated salts, calcium and magnesium.

To the Brazilian border: Artigas → *Phone code 0642. Colour map 8, grid A6.*

From near Bella Unión Route 30 runs east to Artigas, a frontier town in a cattle raising and agricultural area (excellent swimming upstream from the bridge). The town (Population 40,000) is known for its good quality amethysts. There is a bridge across the Río Cuaraim to the Brazilian town of Quaraí. The Brazilian consul is at Lecueder 432, T5414, F4504. Border crossing is straightforward, but you cannot get a Brazilian entry stamp in Quaraí. You have to get it at the airport in Porto Alegre (daily bus Quaraí-Porto Alegre at 2200).

● Sleeping

Nueva Helvecia *p1301*
L-AL Nirvana, Av Batlle y Ordóñez, T44081, www.hotelnirvana.com. Restaurant (Swiss and traditional cuisine), dinner included mid-week off-season, sports facilities, gardens. Recommended.
C Del Prado, Av G Imhoff, T45812, www.hoteles colonia.com/prado/index2.htm. Open all year, huge buffet breakfast, TV, pool.
Camping Campsite in a park at the turnoff for Col Suiza, on main road, free, toilets (locked after 2100), no showers.
Tourism farms AL pp **Estancia Los Macachines**, Km 93.5, Ruta 1, T0340-9074 (or Montevideo 600 1950, Nariño 1604, CP 11500), overnight or day visits (US$45), typical meals, horse riding, sports, *estancia* tours.
A pp **Estancia Don Miguel**, Ruta 1 Km 121 y Ruta 52, T0550-2041, esmiguel@adinet.com.uy. Book through **Cecilia Regules Viajes**. Rustic, working farm, full board, transport extra, good activities, little English spoken.
El Terruño, Ruta 1, Km 140, 35 km before Colonia, T/F0550-6004. Full day tours US$20, including rural safari, lunch.

Colonia del Sacramento *p1302, map p1302*
Choice is good including several recently renovated 19th-century posada hotels.

Barrio Histórico
L-AL Plaza Mayor, Del Comercio 111, T25316, www.colonianet.com/plazamayor/. In a 19th-century house with patio gardens, lovely rooms with a/c or heating, *confitería*, English spoken.
AL Casa Real, Real 170, T094-462472, www.casareal-hotel.com. Prices lower Sun-Thu, historical building with 3 rooms, a/c, jacuzzi, patio, includes breakfast, *Parrilla del Barrio* restaurant at no 166; also has 4-room section on Ruta 21, Km 180.9, a/c, restaurant, beauty suite. Cash only.
AL Posada del Gobernador, 18 de Julio 205, T22918, podelgob@adinet.com.uy. With breakfast, charming.

Centre
L Radisson Colonia de Sacramento, Washington Barbot 283, T30460, www.radisson.com/coloniauy. Great location overlooking the bay, includes buffet breakfast, internet, 2 pools, 1 indoors, very good.
AL Beltrán, Gral Flores 311, T22955, www.colonianet.com/hbeltran/principal.htm. In a 19th-century building, rooms with bath.
AL Esperanza, Gral Flores 237, T/F22922 (**B** weekdays). A charming place to stay with good restaurant.
AL-A Posada del Virrey, España 217, T/F22223, www.posadadelvirrey.com. Large rooms, some with view over bay (cheaper with small bathroom and no balcony), with breakfast. Recommended.
A Posada Manuel de Lobo, Ituzaingó 160, T22463, www.hotelescolonia.com/ manueldelobo/manueldelobo.htm. Built in 1850. Large rooms, huge baths parking, smaller rooms **B**, nice breakfast area inside and out.
B Italiano, Lobo 341, T22103. **C** without bath, good restaurant, hot water but no heating. Recommended.
B Leoncia, Rivera 214, T22369, F22049, www.hotelleoncia.com/.A/c, modern, good.
B Royal, General Flores 340, T22169, www.guiacolonia.com.uy/ royal/index.htm. With breakfast, comfortable, good restaurant, pool, noisy a/c but recommended.
C Los Angeles, Roosevelt 213, T22335. Small rooms, no restaurant, English spoken.
C La Casa de Las Naranjas, 18 de Julio y Ituzaingó, www.hotelescolonia.com/losnaranjos/index.htm. In an old house, a/c, small pool, family rooms US$5 more, comfortable, reasonable size rooms.
C Posada del Angel, Washington Barbot 59, T/F24602, www.hotelescolonia.com/posada delangel/index.htm. Early 20th-century house, breakfast, pleasant and helpful, gym, sauna, pool.
D Posada del Río, Washington Barbot 258, T/F23002, hdelrio@adinet.com.uy. A/c, small breakfast included, terrace overlooking bay.

D Romi, Rivera 236, T/F30456, www.hoteles colonia.com/ romi/index.htm. With breakfast, old posada-style downstairs (19th-century), airy modernist upstairs with large glass roof. Recommended.
E pp Hospedaje Colonial, Flores 436, T/F30347. HI affiliated, hot showers, kitchen, restaurant below (ice cream parlour next door), free internet access and bicycle use (all ancient machines). Recommended.
E Español, Lobo 377, www.guiacolonia. com.uy/espanol/espanol.htm. Good value, cheaper with shared bath, breakfast US$1.50, meals US$5. Recommended.
Camping D Municipal site at Real de San Carlos, T24444, US$3.50 pp, in mini-cabañas, electric hook-ups, 100 m from beach, hot showers, open all year, safe, excellent. Recommended.
Family hospedajes These are good value: **E pp** 18 de Julio 481, T25813. With breakfast, bath, cable TV. **E** Domingo Baque 571, T26354, ter@ adinet.com.uy. Includes breakfast, bath and cable TV, comfortable, nice family.

Carmelo *p1304*
LL Four Seasons, Ruta 21, Km 262, T9000, T Buenos Aires 4321 1690, carmelo@fours easons.com. A luxurious resort between Carmelo and Nueva Palmira. Has a superb dining room, but if not a guest you will have to negotiate entry at the gate.
B Timabe, 19 de Abril y Solís, T5401, www.ciudadcarmelo.com/timabe. Near the swing bridge, with a/c or fan, TV, dining room, parking, good.
Camping At Playa Seré, hot showers.

Mercedes *p1304*
D Club de Remeros, on riverside, T2534. Kitchen and laundry.
F Hospedaje y Cafetería Mercedes, F Sánchez 611, T23804, opposite hospital. Shared bath, without breakfast, very helpful.
Camping Site at Mercedes, on an island in mid-river, reached by a small road, toilets, showers, US$2.20.
Tourism Farm B Estancia La Sirena Marinas del Río Negro, Ruta 14, Km 4, T0530-2726, www.lasirena.com.uy. *Estancia* dating from 1830, picturesque, on the river, birdwatching, fishing, waterskiing, accommodation, meals, price is per person, full board (**D** pp bed and breakfast) friendly owners Rodney, Lucia and Patricia Bruce: all information from Calle Pittaluga 6396, Montevideo 11500, T02-606 2924. Warmly recommended.

Fray Bentos *p1305*
B Las Cañas, 8 km south, T2224. A tourist complex with a beach, entry US$1; pleasant, but crowded in summer. Accommodation in motel rooms with kitchenette and bath, cheaper without kitchen, all with a/c, TV, fridge. Camping US$8.50 per day minimum.
B Plaza, 18 de Julio y 25, T2363. Comfortable.
E Colonial, 25 de Mayo 3293, T2260. Attractive old building with patio.
Camping At the Club Remeros, near the river and at Colegio Laureles, 1 km from centre, T2236.

Paysandú *p1305, map p1305*
Book hotels in advance during Holy Week.
L Gran Hotel Paysandú, 18 de Julio y 19 de Abril, T23400. A/c, with breakfast, comfortable.
AL Casa Grande, Florida 1221 at Plaza Constitución, T24994, www.paysandu.com/ hotelcasagrande/. A/c, welcoming, parking, very good.
A Lobato, Gómez 1415, T22241. With breakfast, a/c, modern, good.
B-C Rafaela, 18 de Julio 1181, T24216. With breakfast, large rooms, modern.
C Plaza, Leandro Gómez 1211, T22022, F33545. A/c, balcony, with breakfast, parking.
C-D Hotel La Posada, José Pedro Varela 566, T/F27879. Some rooms a/c, heating, garden, family rooms available.
D Sarandí, Sarandí 931, T23465. Good, comfortable.
E Equinar, Sarandí 1190, T28188. Nice communal area with open fire, parking, breakfast US$2. **E pp Victoria**, 18 de Julio 979, T24320. Cheaper without bath, very helpful. Highly recommended.
F Hospedaje Sosa, Sarandí y Montevideo. Basic, family run.
Camping Balneario Municipal, 2 km north of centre, by the river, no facilities. Camping Club de Pescadores, Rambla Costanera Norte, T26220, US$2 per day, showers. Also at the Parque Municipal.
Tourism farms AL pp La Calera, near Guichón, 89 km east of Paysandú (T Montevideo 916 3011, or 0740-2292, Mara Morán, Colonia 881, piso 10, www.lacalera.com). 20 luxurious suites with fireplace, full board, dining room with home made food, swimming pool, riding, rodeo, conference facilities. Highly recommended.

Salto *p1306*
L Hotel Horacio Quiroga, near Salto Chico, T34411, www.hotelhoracioquiroga.com. Best I n town although some distance from centre, at the Termas complex, sports facilities, staffed by nearby catering school, special packages offered in season.

B Gran Hotel Salto, 25 de Agosto 5, T34333, www.www.todotermas.8k.com. With breakfast, a/c, good restaurant, reasonably priced. Recommended.

C Argentina, Uruguay 892, T29931. With breakfast, a/c, cafetería, comfortable.

D Concordia, Uruguay 749, T/F32735. Oldest hotel in Uruguay, founded 1860, Carlos Gardel stayed here, fine courtyard, pleasant breakfast room.

D pp Plaza, Plaza Treinta y Tres, T33744. Includes breakfast, fans, good location, simple, old-fashioned. Recommended.

E Hostal del Jardín, Colón 47, T33009. Comfortable, TV, fridge, very helpful, local breakfast available, simple but spacious garden.

F Club Remeros de Salto, Rambla Gutiérrez y Belén (by the river) T33418. Open all year, no cooking facilities, pool (US$4 per day), poor value.

Termas del Daymán *p1306*

B Hotel Termas Daymán, T69250, F69870, in front of the public spa; next door is **El Tritón**, T073-52250, open 0700 for breakfast. Highly recommended.

C Estancia La Casona del Daymán, 3 km east of the bridge at Daymán, T32735. Well-preserved, but non-operational farm, horse riding.

C La Posta del Daymán, Ruta 3, Km 487, T69618, www.lapostadeldayman.com. A/c, full board, **C** half-board or breakfast only (**C-D** low season, hostel accommodation about half price), thermal water in more expensive rooms, thermal swimming pool, good restaurant, discounts for long stay, camping. Recommended. This hotel also has a hydrothermal complex.

D Bungalows El Puente, near the bridge over the Río Dayman, T69271, includes entry to thermal baths.

D La Canela, Route 3, Km 488.3, T073-32121. Good value.

Camping Campsite at Estancia San Niconor, T/F0730-2209, 12 km from Termas de Daymán at the Termas de San Nicanor, Km 485, Route 3, good facilities; and *Cascadas*, US$3pp, T35245, Km 487, Route 3, closer to Daymán.

Termas de Arapey *p1307*

L Barceló Arapey Thermal Spa & Casino, T0768-2008, www.barcelo.com. Hotel with pool, good restaurant, also has cottages (can book rooms in combination with Buquebus tickets from Buenos Aires).

Camping US$1 per person, good facilities

Artigas *p1307*

Club Deportivo Artigas, Pte Berreta and LA de Herrera, 4 km from city, T0772-3860/2532. Open all

year, communal room, camping, restaurant, no cooking facilities, closes early.

Camping At Paseo 7 de Septiembre (by river), T2261, and at Club Zorrilla, T4341.

🍴 Eating

Nueva Helvecia *p1301*

♥♥-♥ **Don Juan**, main plaza. Snack bar/ restaurant excellent food, pastries and bread.

Colonia del Sacramento *p1302, map p1302*

♥♥-♥ **Almacén del Túnel**, Flores 227, T24666. Good meat dishes.

♥♥-♥ **Club Colonia**, Gen Flores 382, T22189. Good value.

♥♥-♥ **El Asador**, Ituzaingó 168. Good *parrillada* and pasta, nice atmosphere, value for money.

♥♥-♥ **El Drugstore**, Vasconellos 179. Very hip establishment, food is a fusion of Latin American, European and Asian (Japanese), good and creative. Music and show.

♥♥-♥ **La Amistad**, 18 de Julio 448. Good value local grill.

♥♥-♥ **Mesón de la Plaza**, Vasconcellos 153, T24807. 140-year old house, elegant dining, good traditional food.

♥♥-♥ **Mercosur**, Flores esq Ituzaingó, T24200. Popular with locals, varied dishes.

♥♥-♥ **Viejo Barrio** (VB), Vasconcellos 169, T25399. Very good for home-made pastas, also main dishes and fish, popular with famous people, Italian-Uruguayan run, famous live shows.

♥♥-♥ **Yacht Club** (at Puerto de Yates), T22197. Good.

Cafés

Arcoiris, Av Gral Flores at Plaza 25 de Agosto. Very good ice cream.

Restaurant El Torreón, Flores 19. Despite its name, more a café with very good homemade cakes and coffee.

Pulpería Los Faroles, Misiones de los Tapes 101, just off Plaza Mayor, old town, T25399.

Mercedes *p1304*

La Brasa, Artigas 426. Serves good food.

Círculo Policial, C 25 de Mayo. Another place with good food.

El Emporio de los Panchos, Roosevelt 711. Good range of dishes.

Fray Bentos *p1305*

♥ **Olla**, 18 de Julio near Plaza Constitución. Seafood and pasta, good value.

Several other cafés and pizzerías on 18 de Julio near Plaza Constitución.

Paysandú *p1305, map p1305*

♥ **Artemio**, 18 de Julio 1248. "best food in town"

♥♥ **Los Tres Pinos**, 19 Av España 1474.
Parrillada, very good.

Salto *p1306*
♥♥ **La Caldera**, Uruguay 221, T24648. Good
parillada, also seafood, closed Mon lunchtime.
♥♥ **Pizzería La Farola**, Brasil 895 esq Soca.
♥♥-♥ **Don Diego**, Chiazzaro 20. Pasta.
♥ **Club de Uruguay**, Uruguay 754. Breakfast
and good value meals.

Cafés
Café Arabache, Uruguay 702. Daytime hangout.

Artigas *p1307*
♥♥-♥ **Donatello**, Lecueder. Good bar, pizza.
♥ **Deportivo**, Herrera. Good value.

○ Shopping

Colonia del Sacramento *p1302, map p1302*
Colonia has a large artist community, Uruguayan
and international, with several good galleries,
including **Galería del Bastión**, Rivodavia 214.
The best paintings can be seen and bought at
Asociación Artistas Plásticos, Florida 203, near
old city gate. **Artesanías del Sacramento**, Calle
de la Playa 128, and **Oveja Negra**, Calle de la
Playa 113, 2 of several good galleries and artisan
shops on this street.

○ Transport

Nueva Helvecia *p1301*
Bus Montevideo-Colonia Suiza, frequent,
with COT, 2½ hrs, US$5; **Turil**, goes to Colonia
Suiza and Valdense; to **Colonia del
Sacramento**, frequent, 1 hr, US$1.85. Local
services between Colonia Valdense and Nueva
Helvecia connect with Montevideo/ Colonia del
Sacramento buses.

Colonia del Sacramento *p1302, map p1302*
Book in advance for all sailings and flights in
summer, especially at weekends.
Air Flights to Aeroparque, **Buenos Aires**,
most days, fare includes connecting bus services
to/from Montevideo, generally quicker than
hydrofoil. The airport is 17 km out of town along
Route 1; for taxi to Colonia, buy ticket in building
next to arrivals, US$2.
Road Roadworks on Route 1 west of Montevideo
make for slow driving. There are plenty of filling
stations. If driving north to Paysandú and Salto,
especially on Route 3, fill up with fuel and drinking
water at every opportunity, stations are few and far
between. From Colonia to Punta del Este by
passing Montevideo: take Ruta 11 at Ecilda
Paullier, passing through San José de Mayo,

Santa Lucía and Canelones, joining
the Interbalnearia at Km 46.
Bus All leave from bus terminal between the
ferry port and the petrol station (free luggage
lockers). to **Montevideo**, 2½ hrs, COT, T23121
(slower, several stops en route), 11 per day
0530-2200, and **Turil**, half- hourly service
between the two, US$4; **Chadre** US$6. **Turil**
to Col Valdense, US$2. To **Carmelo**, 1½ hrs,
Tauriño, 4 a day (not Sun), US$2. **Chadre/
Agencia Central** to Carmelo, **Salto**, 8 hrs, US$12
and on to **Bella Unión** en route from the capital,
0555 and 1430. **Turil** to **Tacuarembó**, US$10,
Rivera, US$13, and **Artigas**, US$15.
Ferry To **Buenos Aires**: 6 crossings daily,
with **Buquebus** (T052-22975/ 23364), cars
carried, and **Ferryturismo**, fares and schedules
given under Montevideo.
Taxi A Méndez y Gral Flores, T22920.
Tours City tours available with Colonia
Abierta, T30271, or **Guided Tours**, T23148.

Carmelo *p1304*
Bus To **Montevideo**, US$5.75, **Intertur**,
US$6.50, **Chadre**. To **Fray Bentos**, **Salto**, from
main plaza 0710, 1540. To **Colonia**, **Tauriño**, 4 a
day, 1½ hrs, US$2. To **Argentina**: via Tigre, across
the Paraná delta, an interesting bus/boat ride
past innumerable islands: **Cacciola** 3 a day; office
in Carmelo, Constituyente 263, T0542-8062, see
under Montevideo page 1299.

Mercedes *p1304*
Bus To **Paysandú**, with Sabelín, Sánchez 782,
T3937, 2½ hrs, US$3.85; also **Chadre** on the Monte-
video-Bella Unión route US$7.50. To **Argentina** and
Montevideo, CUT, Artigas (on plaza).

Fray Bentos *p1305*
Bus Terminal at 18 de Julio y Blanes, buses call
here, but do not alight as buses also call at company
offices around Plaza Constitución. To/from
Montevideo, CUT, 4½ hrs, 6 a day, US$7.50, also
Chadre, US$8.25. To **Mercedes**, ETA, US$0.65,
frequent, 30 mins. To **Paysandú**, US$3.15.

Crossing to Argentina
Bus To **Gualeguaychú** (Argentina), ETA, 2 a
day, 1 hr, US$3.15, passports inspected on bus.
To **Buenos Aires**, 3½ hrs, US$12.

Paysandú *p1305, map p1305*
Air Aviasur flights to **Montevideo** (US$80
return; **Pluna**, Florida 1249, T23071).
Bus It can be difficult to get a seat on long-
distance buses going north. Terminal at Zorilla y
Artigas, T23225. To/from **Montevideo**, US$9
(Núñez, Copay, T22094, 3 a day), 5-6 hrs, also
Chadre/Agencia Central, US$10, many buses. To

Salto US$3.15, 6 a day. To **Rivera**, US$9.35, Copay, 0400 daily and Sun-Fri,1700 (Sat only as far as Tacuarembó). To **Fray Bentos**, 4 a day, 1½ hrs direct, 4 hrs via Young, US$3.15. To **Paso de los Toros** 1430 (return 0430), US$4, or by **Alonso** bus to **Guichón** at 0600, 1100, 1430 and change. To **Colonia** by Chadre, 1700, 6 hrs, US$4.75.

Fray Bentos: Crossing to Argentina *p1306*
Bus To **Colón** and **Concepción del Uruguay**, 3 a day (**Copay** 0815, 1645, **Paccot** 1445), 2 on Sun (**Copay** 1645), US$1.50 to Colón, US$2.50 to Concepción.

Salto *p1306*
Air Aviasur flights to/from the capital. **Pluna**, Uruguay 657, T2724. Bus to airport, US$2.
Bus Terminal 15 blocks east of centre at Batlle y Blandengues, café/restaurant, shopping centre in same building with *casa de cambio*. Take taxi to centre. To/from **Montevideo**, 6 hrs, US$12 (**Bus del Norte**, **Núñez** and **Chadre**, 4 a day). To **Termas del Arapey**, 2 hrs, daily, US$3. **Paysandú** US$3.15, 2 hrs, 6 a day. To **Rivera**, US$10. To **Bella Unión**, 2 hrs, US$3.75, 6 a day. To **Colonia** by Chadre, 0555, 1555, 8 hrs, US$12; to **Fray Bentos**, same times, US$6.50.

Salto: Crossing to Argentina *p1306*
Bus To **Concordia**, Chadre (0800,1400, return 1200,1800) and **Flecha Bus**, 2 a day each, not Sun, US$3. To **Buenos Aires**, US$29, **Flecha Bus**. To **Posadas** night buses only, to **Puerto Iguazú**, 12 hrs, US$44.
Ferry To **Concordia**, Sanchristobal/Río Lago joint service, Mon-Sat several daily, fewer on Sun, US$2, depart port on C Brasil, 15 mins; immigration either side of river, quick and easy.

Artigas *p1307*
Air Airport at Bella Unión (**Tamu** to Montevideo US$30); **Pluna**, Garzón y Baldomir, T2545.
Bus To **Salto**, 225 km, Oribe 279, US$4.25. **Turil** and others from **Montevideo** via Durazno, Paso de los Toros and Tacuarembó, US$15.

⚙ Directory

Colonia del Sacramento *p1302, map p1302*
Banks Banks open in afternoon only. If on a day trip from Buenos Aires, there is no need to change money as most museums and restaurants accept Argentine pesos or US dollars, but rarely euros. Banco Acac, Flores y Barbot. Banco Comerical, on plaza, gives cash against Visa. Cambio Dromer, Flores 350, T22070. Cambio Viaggio, outside the ferry dock (with car hire), Mon-Sat 0900-1200, 1300-1800, Sun 1000-1300. Cambio Colonia and Banco de la República Oriental del Uruguay at

the ferry port (dollars and South American currencies). Exchange rates at the ferry port are far worse than in town. Many establishments accept Argentine pesos. **Car hire** Eleven, Puerto de Colonia, T30574. Punta, Puerto de Colonia, T22353; also car hire at airport. Thrifty, Flores 172, T22939, and at airport. Motorcycle and bicycle hire at Flores y Rivera and outside ferry dock, US$5 per hr, US$15 per day, recommended as a good way of seeing the town, traffic is slow. Scooter hire: Cevallos just off Flores. **Consulates** Argentine Consulate and Cultural Centre, Flores 209, T22093, open weekdays 1200- 1700. **Internet** Compuservice, Flores 547, T30728, US$1.20 per hr. **Post offices** On main plaza.
Telephones Antel, Rivadavia 420, open till 2300, does not accept foreign money.

Carmelo *p1304*
Banks Banco de la República, Zorilla 361, for exchange and ATM.

Mercedes *p1304*
Banks Cambio Fagalde, Giménez 709. Banco Comercial on Colón (just off plaza) and Banco de la República, on plaza.

Fray Bentos *p1305*
Banks For exchange, there is Cambio Fagalde, Plaza Constitución, open Mon-Fri 0800-1900, Sat 0800-1230.

Paysandú *p1305, map p1305*
Banks Several *casas de cambio* on 18 de Julio, including **Cambio Fagalde**, No 1004; **Cambio Bacacay**, No 1008; both change TCs, open Sat 0830-1230. Also Banco de la República, 18 de Julio y 19 de Abril, and others on 18 de Julio. **Consulates** Argentina, Gómez 1034, T22253, Mon-Fri 0800-1300. **Internet** 'paysandu.com', 18 de Julio 1250, on plaza, T/F28526. US$2 per hr, open Mon-Fri 0900-1300, 1430-2030, Sat 0900-1300, 1600-2100. **Post offices** 18 de Julio y Montevideo. **Telephones** Antel, Montevideo 875, T22100. **Tour operators** Viñar Turismo, Artigas 1163.

Salto *p1306*
Banks Banco Pan de Azúcar does cash advances on Visa and MasterCard. Banco de Crédito. Both on Uruguay, several exchange houses on Uruguay. **Car** hire Maxicar, Paraguay 764, T35554, 099-73436 (mob), maxirent@adinet.com.uy. 24 hours, their cars are allowed to travel to Argentina and some to Brazil. **Internet** Café Arabache, Uruguay 702 esq Sarandí, T32337. **Post offices** Treinta y Tres y Artigas. **Scooter hire** Agraciada 2019, T29967.

Eastern Uruguay

Resort after resort lines the coast from Montevideo to Punta del Este, the ultimate magnet for summer holidaymakers, especially from Argentina. Out of season, things quieten down and you can almost have the beaches to yourself, which is pretty much the case the closer you get to Brazil the year round. Inland are cattle ranches, some of which welcome visitors, and hills with expansive views.

East from Montevideo

This beautiful coast consists of an endless succession of small bays, beaches and promontories, set among hills and woods. The beach season is from December to the end of February. An excellent four-lane highway leads to Punta del Este and Rocha, and a good two-lane highway to Chuy. This route will give you a chance to see the most important Uruguayan beach resorts, as well as Parque Nacional Santa Teresa and other natural attractions. If driving there are three tolls each way (about US$2), but this route is the easiest and the most comfortable in Uruguay with sufficient service stations along the way.

Piriápolis → *Phone code: 043. Colour map 8, grid B6. Population: 6,000.*

This resort set among hills, 101 km from Montevideo, is laid out with an abundance of shady trees, and the district is rich in pine, eucalyptus and acacia woods. It has a good beach, a yacht harbour, a country club, a motor-racing track (street circuit) and is particularly popular with Argentines. It was, in fact, founded in the 1890s as a bathing resort for residents of Buenos Aires. Next to the marina is a small cable car (with seats for two) to the top of **Cerro San Antonio** ① *US$2.50, 10 mins ride, free car park and toilets at lower station*. Magnificent views of Piriápolis and beaches, several restaurants. Recommended, but be careful when disembarking. North of the centre, at **Punta de Playa Colorada**, is a **marine rescue centre** ① *T22960, sos-faunamarina@adinet.com.uy*, that looks after injured sea creatures before releasing them to the wild. **Tourist office**, Asociación de Turismo ① *Rambla de los Argentinos 1348, 0900-2100 in summer, 1000-1800 in winter, T22560*.

About 6 km north on the R37 is **Cerro Pan de Azúcar** (Sugar Loaf Hill) ① *getting there: take bus 'Cerro Pan de Azúcar' and get off after 6 km*, crowned by a tall cross with a circular stairway inside, fine coastal views. There is only a steep path, marked by red arrows, up to the cross. Just north of Piriápolis R 37 passes the La Cascada Municipal park (open all year) which contains the house of Francisco Piria, the founder of the resort, **Museo Castillo de Piria** ① *open daily in summer, weekends in winter, 1200-2000*. About 4 km beyond Cerro Pan de Azúcar is the village of Pan de Azúcar, which has a **Museo al Aire Libre de Pintura** where the walls of the buildings have been decorated by Uruguayan and Argentine painters, designers and writers with humorous and tango themes (direct bus every hour from Piriápolis).

Portezuelo and Punta Ballena

R93 runs between the coast and the Laguna del Sauce to Portezuelo, which has good beaches. The **Arboreto Lussich** ① *T78077, 1030-1630*, on the west slope of the Sierra de la Ballena (north of R93) contains a unique set of native and exotic trees. There are footpaths, or you can drive through; two *miradores*; worth a visit. From Portezuelo drive north towards the R9 by way of the R12 which then continues, unpaved, to Minas. Just off R12 is *El Sosiego* ① *1 km east from Solanas, then 4 km north, T042-236288, www.lapataiatambojazz.com.uy*, a dairy farm open to the public, selling goats' cheese, ice cream, *dulce de leche*, homemade pizzas and pastas, and has an international jazz festival in January.

At Punta Ballena there is a wide crescent beach, calm water and very clean sand. The place is a residential resort but is still quiet. At the top of Punta Ballena there is a panoramic road 2½ km long with remarkable views of the coast. **Casa Pueblo**, the house and gallery of Uruguayan artist Carlos Páez Vilaro, is built in a Spanish-Moroccan style on a cliff over the sea; the gallery can be visited (US$5), there are paintings, collages and ceramics on display, and for sale; season: 1 November to 1 April. Walk downhill towards the sea for a good view of the house.

Maldonado → *Phone code: 042. Colour map 8, grid B6. Population: 33,000.*
The capital of Maldonado Department, 140 km E of Montevideo, is a peaceful town, sacked by the British in 1806. It has many colonial remains and the historic centre is being restored (2005). It is also a dormitory suburb of Punta del Este. Worth seeing is the **El Vigia watch tower** ① *Gorriti y Pérez del Puerto*; the Cathedral (started 1801, completed 1895), on Plaza San Fernando; the windmill; the **Cuartel de Dragones exhibition centre** ① *Pérez del Puerto y 18 de Julio, by Plaza San Fernando*, and the **Cachimba del Rey** ① *on the continuation of 3 de Febrero, almost Artigas*, an old well – legend claims that those who drink from it will never leave Maldonado. **Museo Mazzoni** ① *Ituzaingó 787, T21107, daily 1300-1830, Sun 1600- 2200* has regional items, indigenous, Spanish, Portuguese and English. **Museo de Arte Americano** ① *José Dodera 648 y Treinta y Tres, T22276, summer only 1800-2200*, a private museum of national and international art, interesting. **Tourist office** at the bus station, T225701. For information on concerts and exhibitions in summer T222276.

Punta del Este → *Phone code: 042. Colour map 8, grid B6.*
About 7 km from Maldonado and 139 km from Montevideo (a little less by dual carriageway), facing the bay on one side and the open waters of the Atlantic on the other, lies the largest and best known of the resorts, **Punta del Este**, which is particularly popular among Argentines and, recently, Brazilians. The narrow peninsula of Punta del Este has been entirely built over.

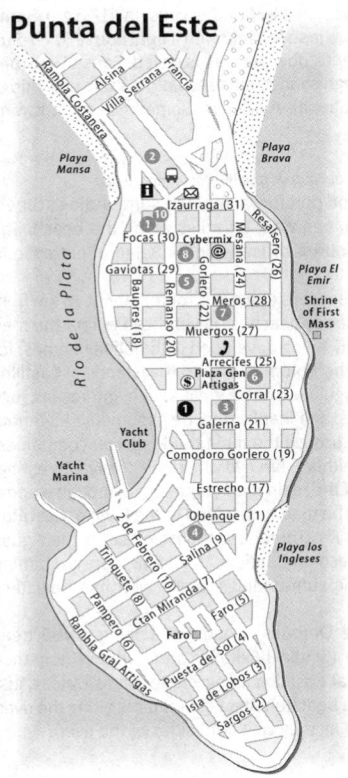

Punta del Este

Sleeping 🛌
1949 **1**
Alhambra **7**
El Hostal **6**
Embajador **2**
Iberia **3**
Palace **4**
Príncipe **8**
Remanso **5**
San Martín **6**
Tánger **10**

Eating 🍴
Lo de Tere **1**

N

0 metres   200
0 yards   200

On the land side, the city is flanked by large planted forests of eucalyptus, pine and mimosa. Two blocks from the sea, at the tip of the peninsula, is the historic monument of El Faro (lighthouse); in this part of the city no building may exceed its height. On the ocean side of the peninsula, at the end of Calle 25 (Arrecifes), is a shrine to the first mass said by the Conquistadores on this coast, 2 February 1515. Three blocks from the shrine is Plaza General Artigas, which has a *feria artesanal* (handicraft market); along its side runs Avenida Gorlero, the main street. There are two casinos, a golf course, and many beautiful holiday houses. **Museo Ralli of Contemporary Latin American Art** ① *Curupay y Los Arachanes, Barrio Beverly Hills, T483476, Tue-Sun 1700- 2100 in Jan-Feb, Sat-Sun 1400-1800 rest of year, free*. Worth a visit but a car is needed.

Punta del Este has excellent bathing **beaches**, the calm *playa mansa* on the bay side, the rough *playa brava* on the ocean side. There are some small beaches hemmed in by rocks on this side of the peninsula, but most people go to where the extensive *playa brava* starts, opposite the *Hotel Playa*. Papa Charlie beach on the Atlantic (Parada 13) is preferred by families with small children as it is safe. Quieter beaches are at La Barra and beyond.

There is an excellent yacht marina, yacht and fishing clubs. There is good fishing both at sea and in three nearby lakes and the Río Maldonado. The *Muriel*, a late-19th-century yacht, makes three sailings daily, lasting three hours, US$35. **Tourist information** ① *Liga de Fomento, Parada 1, T45979, open 0800-2000; in bus station T494042; at Parada 24, Playa Las*

Delicias (Mansa side), T230050; and at airports. See the websites www.puntaweb.com, www.puntadeleste.com and www.vivapunta.com.

Isla de Gorriti, visited by explorers including Solís, Magellan and Drake, was heavily fortified by the Spanish in the 1760's to keep the Portuguese out. The island, densely wooded and with superb beaches, is an ideal spot for campers (boats from 0800-1700, return 0915-1715, US$4.50, T441716; *Don Quico*, also does fishing trips, T443963). On **Isla de Lobos**, which is a government reserve within sight of the town, there is a huge sea-lion colony; excursions, US$30. Ticket should be booked in advance (T441716). See also Activities and tours, below.

Beaches east of Punta del Este

Between the Peninsula and the mouth of the Río Maldonado, a road runs along the coast, passing luxurious houses, dunes and pines. Some of the most renowned architects of Uruguay and Argentina design houses here. The river is crossed by a unique undulating bridge, like a shallow M, to **La Barra**, a fashionable place, especially for summer nightlife, with beaches, art galleries, bars and restaurants (bus from Punta del Este terminal; taxi US$15). The new **Museo del Mar Sirenamis** ① *1 km off the coast road, watch for signs, T771817, www.viva punta.com/museomar; summer daily 1000-2030; winter Sat, Sun and holidays 1100-1700, but will open other times for minimum 3 people if you call in advance, US$2.20*, has an excellent collection on the subject of the sea, its life and history and on the first beach resorts (it claims to have 5,000 exhibits). The coast road climbs a headland here before descending to the beaches further north, Montoya and **Manantiales** (reached by Condesa bus; taxi US$23). Some 30 km from Punta del Este is the fishing village of **Faro José Ignacio** with a **lighthouse** ① *Fri-Sun 1700-1900*, a beach club and other new developments, now the road is paved. Coastal R10 runs some way east of José Ignacio, but there is no through connection to La Paloma as a new bridge across the mouth of the Lago Garzón is not operational. A car ferry sometimes runs; rowing boats will take pedestrians and cyclists across.

La Paloma and around → *Phone code: 0473. Colour map 8, grid B6. Population: 5,000.*

Protected by an island and a sandspit, this is a good port for yachts. The surrounding scenery is attractive, with extensive wetlands nearby. You can walk for miles along the beach. The pace here is more relaxed than Punta del Este. **Tourist office** is on Av Solari at entrance to town, very helpful, T6088.

Coastal R10 runs to Aguas Dulces (regular bus services along this route). About 10 km from La Paloma is **La Pedrera**, a beautiful village with sandy beaches. Beyond La Pedrera the road runs near pleasant fishing villages which are rapidly being developed with holiday homes, for example **Barra de Valizas**, 50 minutes north. At **Cabo Polonio**, visits to the islands of Castillos and Wolf can be arranged to see sea lions and penguins. It has a great beach, interesting rock formations with crashing waves, souvenir stands and haphazard development. All-terrain vehicles run across the dunes from a number of stops on the main road (several companies, US$5). Ask locally in Valizas about walking there, either 8 km over the dunes (very interesting, but hot, unless you go early), or along a dirt road off the main road (at Km 257), through woods, then 2-3 km across the dunes. From **Aguas Dulces** the road runs inland to the town of **Castillos** (easy bus connections to Chuy), where it rejoins R9. There is a tourist office at the Aguas Dulces/Castillos crossroads on R9 with details on accommodation. At Km 298 there is a turning for **Punta del Diablo**, a fishing village in dramatic surroundings, again with fine beaches, popular with young people in high season.

From Castillos it is 16 km to the **Bosque de Ombúes**, woods containing *ombú* trees (Phytolacca dioica – the national tree), *coronilla* (Scutia buxifolia) and *canelón* (Rapanea laetevirens). The woods are reached by turning off at Castillos along R16 to Aguas Dulces, just before which you turn onto R10 to the bridge. Take a boat from here, 30 minutes along the river, US$5 including tour (*Monte Grande* recommended as they visit both sides of the river).

Parque Nacional Santa Teresa

① *100 km from Rocha, 308 km from Montevideo, www.parquesantateresa.com.uy, 1000-1700 except Mon, US$1.20 (check opening times, maybe 1300 on weekdays).*
This park has curving, palm-lined avenues and plantations of many exotic trees. It also contains botanical gardens, fresh-water pools for bathing and beaches which stretch for many kilometres (the surf is too rough for swimming). It is the site of the impressive colonial fortress of Santa Teresa, begun by the Portuguese in 1762 and seized by the Spanish in 1793.

The fortress houses a **museum** ⓘ *1000-1700 except Mon (winter hours shorter), US$0.30, tickets from restaurant* La Posada del Viajero, *opposite, recommended,* of artefacts from the wars of independence. On the inland side of Route 9, the strange and gloomy Laguna Negra and the marshes of the Bañado de Santa Teresa support large numbers of wild birds. A road encircles the fortress; it's possible to drive or walk around even after closing hours. From there is a good view of Laguna Negra.

There are countless campsites (open all year), and a few cottages to let in the summer (usually snapped up quickly). At the *capatacia*, or administrative headquarters, campers pay US$2 pp for 3 nights (tickets are collected for each night stayed). Here there are also a small supermarket, greengrocer, butcher, bakery, medical clinic, petrol station, auto mechanic, post and telephone offices, and the *Club Santa Teresa*, where drinks and meals are available, but expensive. Practically every amenity is closed off-season. Tour by taxi (US$12, daily) can be made to Santa Teresa fortress, Laguna Negra, and the collection of native and exotic plants from the bathing resort of **La Coronilla** (10 km north of Santa Teresa, 20 south of Chuy; several hotels and restaurants most closed in winter). Montevideo-Chuy buses stop at La Coronilla.

Chuy → *Phone code: 0474. Colour map 7, inset. Population: 9,000. For details of Chuí in Brazil see page 455.*
At Chuy, 340 km from Montevideo, the Brazilian frontier runs along the main street, Avenida Internacional, which is called Avenida Brasil in Uruguay and Avenida Uruguaí in Brasil. The Uruguayan side has more services, including supermarkets, duty-free shops and a casino.

On the Uruguayan side, on a promontory overlooking Laguna Merín and the gaúcho landscape of southern Brazil, stands the restored fortress of **San Miguel** ⓘ *US$0.40, closed Mon, bus from Chuy US$0.45, Rutas del Sol buses from Montevideo go here after passing through Chuy,* dating from 1734 and surrounded by a moat. It is set above a 1500-ha wetland park, which is good for birdwatching and is 7km north of Chuy along Route 19 which is the border. There is a small museum of *criollo* and *indígena* culture, displaying, among other artefacts, old carriages and presses. Not always open in low season. A fine walk from here is 2 km to the Cerro Picudo. The path starts behind the museum, very apparent. Tours (US$9 from Chuy) end for the season after 31 March.

Border with Brazil → *From October to February, Uruguay is 1 hour behind Brazil.*
Uruguayan passport control is 2½ km before the border on Ruta 9 into Chuy, US$2 by taxi, 20 minutes' walk, or take a town bus; officials friendly and cooperative. Ministry of Tourism kiosk here is helpful, especially for motorists, T42554. Tourists may freely cross the border in either direction as long as they do not go beyond either country's border post. Taking a car into Brazil is no problem if the car is not registered in Brazil or Uruguay. (Uruguayan rental cars are not allowed out of the country. Although you can freely drive between Chuy and Chuí, if you break down/have an accident on the Brazilian side, car rental insurance will not cover it: park in Chuy, even if only one metre from Brazil, and walk.) From the border post, Ruta 9 bypasses the town, becoming BR-471 on the Brazilian side, leading to Brazilian immigration, also outside town. The Brazilian consulate is at Tito Fernández esq Laguna Merín, T2049, Chuy. For buses to Brazilian destinations, go to the rodoviária in Chuí (details in the Brazil chapter, page 455). The bus companies that run from Chuy into Brazil ask for passports – make sure you get yours back before boarding the bus.

Entering Uruguay You must have a Brazilian exit stamp and a Uruguayan entry stamp (unless visiting only Chuí), otherwise you will be turned back at customs or other official posts. Those requiring a visa must have a medical examination before a visa can be issued in Chuí, cost about US$20 and US$10 respectively.

● Sleeping

Piriápolis *p1312*
Many hotels along the sea front, most close end-Feb until mid-Dec. Reservation is advisable in high season. Many others than those listed in our price ranges **D** and up.
A Argentino, Rambla de los Argentinos y Armenia, T22791. A fine hotel and landmark

designed by Piria with casino, 2 restaurants and medicinal springs, ice rink and pool open to public for US$2.50 (in low season), also sauna.
C Centro, Sanabria 935, T/F22516. With breakfast, cafetería, helpful about local sites.
C Danae, Rambla 1270 y Freire, T22594. **E** out of season, bath, breakfast, heating.

C **Rivadavia**, Rambla 1208, T22543. Open all
year (**E** in winter), hot water.
D **Luján**, Sanabria 939, T22216. Simple rooms,
family run, some rooms have balconies,
homeopathist on top floor.
D-F pp **Youth hostel Albergue de Piriápolis**,
behind Hotel Argentino, Simón del Pino
1106/1136, T20394. Rooms for 2, 3 and 4 people
(open all year), 270 beds, hot showers, cooking
facilities, student cards accepted.
Camping International YMCA camp on the slope
of Cerro del Toro, double rooms in bungalows, and
tents. Site at Misiones y Niza, just behind bus station.
Poor showers, smelly toilets, US$4.

Portezuelo and Punta Ballena *p1312*
LL **Casa Pueblo**, T579386, www.aluruguay.com/
Shotelcasapueblo.htm. Highly recommended
hotel, also time-share apartments, restaurant
and, lower down the hill, a *parrillada*.
LL **Hotel-Art Las Cumbres**, Ruta 12 Km 3.9, 4 km
inland on a wooded hill, T578689, www.cum
bres.com.uy. Some rooms **L** out of season, themed
as an artist's house-studio, pool with great views
over Laguna del Sauce and the coast, restaurant
and tea room (very expensive but popular).
Campsite Near Arboreto Lussich, turn off at
Km 128 on Interbalnearia, T427 8902/ 24181, or
Montevideo 480 1662. US$5.60 for 2 with tent,
many facilities, very clean.

Maldonado *p1313*
Hotel accommodation is scarce in summer;
cheaper than Punta del Este, but you will have to
commute to the beach. Basic 1-2 star places
(**C-E**), open all year, include: **Catedral**, Florida 830
casi 18 de Julio, T242513, central, **Colonial**, 18 de
Julio 841 y Florida, T223346, and **La Reja**, 18 de
Julio y JP Varela, T223717.
D **Celta**, Ituzaingó 839, T/F230139. Helpful,
Irish owner, No 7 bus stop outside.
E **Hospedaje Isla de Gorriti**, Michelini 884,
T225223. Nice courtyard. Recommended.
Camping Parque El Placer, T270034, free.

Punta del Este *p1313, map p1313*
Note Streets on the peninsula have
names and numbers; lowest numbers at the
tip. Hotels are plentiful but expensive: we
list only those with positive confirmations.
Rates in those few hotels that are open after
the end of Mar are as much as halved.
Visitors without a car are forced to take a
hotel on the peninsula, unless they want
to spend a fortune on taxis.

On the peninsula
L **Remanso**, C 20 y 28, T447412, www.visit-
uruguay.com/es/remanso.htm. **A** low season,
comfortable, businesslike, pool, safe, open all
year (alsohas suites in **LL** range). Recommended.
L-AL **Iberia**, C 24, No 685, T440405, www.visit-
uruguay.com/ es/iberia.htm. **A** out of season,
breakfast included, open all year, garage opposite.
AL-A **Palace**, Av Gorlero esq 11, T441919,
www.visit-uruguay.com /es/palace.htm (closed
in winter). 3-star. Breakfast only (expensive
restaurant, *La Stampa*, in the hotel), well kept.
AL-B **Tánger**, C 31 entre 18 y 20, T440601,
www.visit-uruguay.com /es/tanger.htm. Open
all year, a/c, safe, disabled access, 2 pools.
A **Alhambra**, C 28, No 573, T442084,
www.alhambra.com.uy. Open all year,
comfortable, TV, safe, parking, cafetería,
continental breakfast. In same group are
Príncipe, C 20 No 938, T440351, and **San Martín**,
C 24 on Plaza Artigas, T441617, both **A-B**.
B pp **Alicia Lorenzo**, Parada 5, T480781. Bed and
breakfast room with bath, barbecue.
B **Embajador**, C Risso, parada 1, by bus terminal,
T481008, F486750. 2-star. Good, closed in winter.
D **Youth hostel 1949**, C 30 y 18, info@1949
hostel.com. 100 m from bus station, near the
Information Centre. Small, **A** in double room,
kitchen, bar, TV and DVD, close to beaches.
E pp **Youth hostel El Hostal**, C 25 No 544 y 24,
T441632, elhostalpunta@yahoo.com. Includes
breakfast, lockers, central, basic.

Beaches east of Punta del Este *p1314*
San Rafael (Parada 12)
L-A **San Marcos**, Av Mar del Plata 191, T482251,
www.hotelsanmarcos.com. Pool (covered
in winter), half price in low season, also has
backpacker options (**D**) with weekly rates, bicycle
hire, internet US$4, very pleasant.
AL **La Capilla**, Viña del Mar y Valparaíso, behind
San Marcos, T484059, www.lacapilla.com.uy. Half
price in low season, includes breakfast, kitchenette
in some rooms, safes in rooms, gardens, pool,
good but has seen better days.
AL-B **San Rafael**, Lorenzo Batlle y Pacheco,
Parada 11 Brava, T482161, www.hotelsan
rafael.com.uy. Large hotel, open all year, one of
the cheaper options, a/c, heating, safe, TV, spa.
Camping Camping San Rafael, T486715.
Good facilities, US$7, bus 5 from Maldonado.

La Barra
LL **Mantra**, Ruta 10, Parada 48, T771000,
www.mantraresort.com. Probably the best

● *For an explanation of the sleeping and eating price codes used in this guide, see inside the front*
● *cover. Other relevant information is found in Essentials pages 1288-1289.*

in town (5 star) , but you will still need a car to move around, although the place has everything. Open all year, great pool, casino, restaurants, concerts, even it's own cinema and wine bar. Recommended.

L La Posta del Cangrejo hotel and restaurant, Ruta 10 Km 160, T770021, F770173. Nice location, smart, if a bit old. Recommended.

L-AL La Ballenera Bed and Breakfast, Km 162, just off coast road ½ km east of the hilly promontory, behind Playa Montoya, T771079, T09-444 7935 (mob), http://laballenera.net/english/index.html. Half price in low season, big old wooden mansion, lovely breakfast terrace, kitchen and internet.

B-D Backpacker de La Barra, C 9, No 2306, ½ km off main road, T/F772272, http://backpacker delabarra.com/espanol/index.html. Closed in low season, youth hostel style, price depends on package, café and restaurant, internet, laundry.

C Hostal de la Barra, Ruta 10, Km 161.300, T771521, www.hostaldelabarra.net. A cheaper option for hostel accommodation, but neat.

Camping There are 2 campsites after the bridge, the second is cheaper, US$9.75, good showers and toilets.

Manantiales

Resorts include: **LL-L Las Dunas**, Ruta 10 Km 163, T771211, F771210, 5-star, opulent, and **L Las Olas**, Ruta 10, Km 162.5, T770466, www.lasolasresort.com.uy, 4-star.

D Manantiales Hostel, Ruta 10, Km 164, T774427, www.manantialeshostel.com. **C** end Dec to end Jan. Free pick-up from bus station, kitchen, bikes and surfboards for rent, lockers, DVDs, laundry, free internet, bar, open 1 Nov to 15 Apr.

La Paloma p1314

D Bahía, Av del Navio, between Solari and Del Sol, T/F0479-6029. With breakfast, clean and simple.

D Embeleco, De La Virgen, just off Solari, T0479-6108. With breakfast, half price in winter, welcoming.

Youth hostels F at Parque Andresito, T6396, lapaloma@hosteluruguay.org. 50 beds, US$6-7 pp, clean, friendly, good meals available, kitchen facilities, Nov-Apr.

Palma de Mallorca, on Playa La Aguada, in nearby La Aguada, luxury hotel, T0479-6739, right on the ocean. Family discounts and 7-day packages offered. heated pool.

Camping In Parque Andresito, T6107, US$11.75. Overpriced, thatched *cabañas* for rent, US$22-38 per day with maid and kitchen facilities, sleep 4-6. *Grill del Camping* for *parrillas*. La Aguada, T6239, 2 km east of town, 300 m from beach, US$5. Good, each site with own barbecue, tap, sink, water and electricity.

Northeast of La Paloma

Ask around Barra de Valizas for cottage rental at US$25 per day, sleeps 4, fully equipped. At Cabo Polonio you can camp or stay in basic rooms cheaply.

A Cabañas Buenavista, Punta del Diablo, 4 blocks from shore, T099-370807, mcontini@adinet.com.uy. 2 nice bungalows for 5, **C** in low season, equipped except for linen, terrace with ocean view, book in advance.

A Hostería del Pescador, Punta del Diablo, T0472-1611 LD17. Private house for 4, US$50 per day.

A Hotel La Pedrera, La Pedrera, T0479-2001. Swimming pool, tennis, comfortable rooms.

A La Perla, Cabo Polonio, T0470-5125, T099-872360 (mob), www.mayoral.com.uy/laperla.htm. Meals US$8-11. Houses or rooms to rent; informal camping at your own risk. No electricity, cooking gas, or phone.

A Posada Eirete, Barra de Valizas. Small, tasteful, good breakfasts, owned by painter María Beloso. Recommended.

B Mariemar, Cabo Polonio. Nice owners, own electricity generator, only hotel open off-season. Recommended.

D-E Hotel Gainford, Aguas Dulces, with restaurant, and others, including breakfast. Lots of cheap cabins for rent.

Reserva Ecológica La Laguna, about 2 km from Aguas Dulces, T099-602410/0475-2118. Private reserve on a 25 ha lake, with cabins for 4-6 (**B**), meals extra, open all year, English, German, French, Italian, Spanish spoken, pick-up from bus stop in jeep or horse-drawn carriage, tours arranged, activities. (Rutas del Sol bus from Montevideo, US$10).

Youth hostels Barra de Valizas, Calle Principal, valizas@hosteluruguay.org. US$6 pp, open Nov-Apr (all year for groups). 50 beds, kitchen for members, also has restaurant.

Camping Camping Esmeralda, at Km 280.5, 17 km north of Castillos.

La Palomita, 8 blocks from the sea, La Pedrera. Wooded, electricity, US$5, summer only.

Chuy p1315

All hotels are open the year round.

AL Parador Fortín de San Miguel, Paraje 18 de Julio, near San Miguel fortress, T/F2207, www.elfortin.com. Excellent, **A** with dinner off season, colonial-style hotel. Beautiful rooms, gym, pool, difficult 9-hole golf course, fine food and service. Highly recommended. You don't have to go through Uruguayan formalities to get there from Brazil.

B Nuevo Hotel Plaza, Artigas y Arachanes, T/F2309. On plaza, bath, good buffet breakfast, TV, very helpful, good, restaurant *El Mesón del Plaza*.

C Alerces, Laguna de Castillos 578, T/F2260, 4 blocks from border. Bath, TV, breakfast, heater, nice.
F Vittoria, Numancia 143, T2280. Price includes breakfast, simple and clean, parking.
Camping From Chuy buses run every 2 hrs to the Barra del Chuy campsite, Ruta 9 Km 331, turn right 13 km, T2425. Good bathing, many birds. *Cabañas* for up to 4 persons cost US$20 daily or less, depending on amenities.

⑦ Eating

Piriápolis *p1312*
Many small restaurants near the harbour.

Portezuelo and Punta Ballena *p1312*
₸₸₸ Medio y Medio, Cont Camino Lussich s/n, Punta Ballena, T578791. Jazz club and restaurant, music nightly and good food.
₸₸₸-₸₸ Las Vertientes, Camino de Los Ceibos, 2 km on the Route 9, T042-669997. Country restaurant, fresh food which all comes from own farm, good salads and sweets.

Maldonado *p1313*
Best ice cream at Popy's.
₸₸₸-₸₸ Taberna Patxi, Dodera 944, T238393. Very good Basque food with authentic recipes.
₸₸₸-₸₸ Lo de Rubén, Santa Teresa 846, T223059. *Parrillada*, best restaurant in town.
₸₸ Al Paso, 18 de Julio 898, T222881. *Parrillada*, moderate prices.
₸₸ Piano-Bar JR Pizzetas, Rincón y Gutiérrez Ruiz. Pizzas and pasta, under US$12 pp.

Punta del Este *p1313, map p1313*
Many enticing ice cream parlours on Gorlero.
₸₸₸ Blue Cheese, Rambla y 23, T440354. For steaks and unlimited salads, good value.
₸₸₸ Bungalow Suizo, Av Roosevelt y Parada 8, T482358. Excellent Swiss, must book.
₸₸₸ Cantón Chino, C 28 y Gorlero, T441316. Creative Chinese food, good.
₸₸₸ Company Bar, C 29 entre 18 y 20, T440130. Live music in the evening, home made pasta, fish. Breakfast, lunch and dinner.
₸₸₸ Daiquiri Fondue, Rambla Williman y Parada 19, T226451, and C 9 entre 8 y 10, T488901. Good Swiss food including fondue.
₸₸₸ Los Caracoles, Calle 20 y 28, T440912. Excellent food (international, *parrilla*, seafood) at good prices.
₸₸₸ El Ciclista, Calle 20 y 27. Long-standing, with international cuisine, Italian, *parrilla* and seafood.
₸₸₸ Gure-etxe (also in La Coronilla), C 9 y 12. Seafood and Basque cuisine.
₸₸₸ Kika's Café, Rambla Artigas y C 28, T440951. Excellent fish, delicious Spanish dishes, sea view, but lunch specials are not a bargain.
₸₸₸ Lo de Charlie, 12 y La Salina, T444183. Fish.

₸₸₸ Lo de Tere, 20 y 21, T440492, www.lode tere.com. Good local food, open all year but closed Wed in winter, 20% discount if eating lunch before 1300 or dinner before 2100.
₸₸₸ La Tuttie, C 9, No 607, T447044. Restaurant and fishmonger, fresh fish, popular with locals.
₸₸₸ Solomio, Rambla. Artigas, Playa El Emir, T553268. Good fusion seafood.
₸₸₸ Viejo Marino, Calle 11 entre 14 y 15, Las Palmeras. Fish restaurant, very busy so go early.
₸₸₸ Virazón, Rambla Artigas y C 28, T443924. Good food and great view, but expensive.
₸₸₸ Yatch Club Uruguayo, Gral Artigas y 8, T441056. Very good, fish, seafood, continental, views over the port (not to be confused with the exclusive Yacht Club).
₸₸ Il Barreto, C 9 y 10, T447243. Italian vegetarian, good value, live Italian and Latin music some evenings, open weekends only in low season.
₸₸ Tutto Sapori, Parada 2 y Francia, T490599. Italian specialities, terrace, accordion music.

Beaches east of Punta del Este *p1314*
La Barra
₸₸₸ Deli Café Baby Gouda, Ruta 10, Km 161, T771874. Alternative food, yoga and Arab dances.
₸₸₸-₸₸ Bistro de Mar, Ruta 10, Km 162, ½ km over the promontory, T771356. Old-style, Italian and French as well as local dishes, good wine selection. Claims to be the only "real" bistro in Punta del Este

Faro José Ignacio
₸₸₸ 121, Los Teros and Zorzales, T0486-2009. Great location next to the lighthouse, good food and tranquil environment with private library which can be used by guests.
₸₸₸ Parador Santa Teresita, T0486-2004. Very popular, US$25 pp.

La Paloma *p1314*
₸₸₸ Arrecife, on main street. First class.
₸₸₸ Da Carlos, Av Solari. Moderate prices, pizzas plus Uruguayan food.
₸₸₸ La Marea, near tourist office. Very popular, has outstanding seafood.

Northeast of La Paloma
There are several restaurants in Castillos including **₸₸₸ La Strada**, 19 de Abril, and several restaurants in Punta del Diablo, eg **₸₸₸ La Posada**, highly recommended.
₸₸₸ Chivito Veloz, Aguas Dulces. Good, large portions for US$5.

Parque Nacional Santa Teresa *p1314*
₸₸ La Ruta, La Coronilla. This small round restaurant at the entrance to town may be your only option if you are driving in the evening and

off season from Chuy to Punta or Montevideo. Good meat dishes. Off season, other restaurants in Coronilla are closed.

Chuy *p1315*
¶¶-¶ **Parrillada/Pizzería Javier**, Arachanes on plaza. Quite good.
¶¶-¶ **Restaurant Jesús**, Av Brasil y L Olivera. Good value and quality.

⊕ Bars and clubs

Punta del Este *p1313, map p1313*
Sophia Caffe Concert, C 27 entre Gorlero y 24, T449505 to reserve. Can be packed in high season. Latin jazz, Bossa Nova, international music.

▲ Activities and tours

Punta del Este *p1313, map p1313*
Diving Punta Divers, C 32, No 626, T482481, www.ssila.com. US$290 for 8 dives to caves at Punta Ballena and Gorriti, and to wrecks (eg HMS *Agamemon*, Nelson's favourite ship), courses offered. Trips include refreshments. Also offer dive in a gold mine near Minas. To see right whales at end-Aug to Nov, US$18.
Riding Nueva Escuela de Equitación, at Cantegril Country Club, Av Saravia, T223211. Classes, guided rides for all levels and ages.

⊖ Transport

Piriápolis *p1312*
Road Piriápolis may be reached either by following the very beautiful R10 from the end of the Interbalnearia, or by taking the original access road (R37) from Pan de Azúcar, which crosses the R93. The shortest route from Piriápolis to Punta del Este is by the Camino de las Bases which runs parallel to the R37 and joins the R93 some 4 km east of the R37 junction.
Bus Terminal on Misiones, 2 blocks from Hotel Argentino. To/from **Montevideo**, US$2.50, 1½ hrs. To **Punta del Este**, US$1.50, 50 mins. To **Maldonado**, US$1.20. For **Rocha**, **La Paloma** and **Chuy**, take bus to Pan de Azúcar and change.

Maldonado *p1313*
Bus Av Roosevelt y Sarandí, T225026. To/from **Montevideo**, US$3.50; to **Minas**, 2 hrs, 5 a day, US$2.35. To **San Carlos** take a local bus 3 blocks from the main bus station, US$0.50.

Punta del Este *p1313, map p1313*
Air Direct daily Boeing 737 flights from Buenos Aires to brand new Punta del Este airport during the high season. Laguna del Sauce, Capitán Curbelo (T559777), which handles flights to

Buenos Aires (**Pluna** and **Lapa**, 40 mins). Airport tax US$20. Exchange facilities, tax-free shopping. Regular bus service to airport from Punta del Este (will deliver to and collect from private addresses and hotels), US$4, 90 mins before departure, also connects with arriving flights. Taxi US$25; *remise* US$18-US$38 depending on destination (T441269 or Punta del Este 443221). El Jagüel airport is used by private planes.
Bus Local: Traffic is directed by a one-way system; town bus services start from C 5 (El Faro), near the lighthouse. www.puntaweb.com has details of bus routes. **Long distance**: terminal at Av Gorlero, Blvd Artigas and C 32, T486810 (served by local bus No 7); has toilets, newsagent, café and *Casa de Cambio Nelson*. To/from **Montevideo** via Carrasco airport, COT (T486810) or Copsa (T489205), US$6.50, just over 2 hrs, many in the summer; 19 a day in winter. To **Piriápolis**, US$1.50. To **San Carlos** (US$1.45) for connections to Porto Alegre, Rocha, La Paloma, Chuy. Direct to **Chuy**, 4 hrs, US$4.75. Local bus fare about US$0.50. For transport Montevideo-Buenos Aires, **Buquebus** T484995/488380, at bus terminal, weekend buses to connect with ferries at Montevideo, US$6.30.

La Paloma *p1314*
Bus Frequent to and from **Rocha**, US$0.60, and to and from **the capital** (5 hrs, US$5). 4 buses daily to **Chuy**, US$3, 3½ hrs, 2 a day to San Carlos, Pan de Azúcar and Aguas Dulces, all with Rutas del Sol company. Northeast of La Paloma, some Montevideo-Chuy buses go into **Punta del Diablo**, 4 km from the main road.

Chuy *p1315*
Bus To **Montevideo** (COT, Cynsa, Rutas del Sol, Turismar) US$12, 5 hrs, may have to change buses in San Carlos; to **Maldonado** US$5. International buses which passing through en route from Montevideo to Brazil either stop in Chuy or at the border. Make sure the driver knows you need to stop at Uruguayan immigration. Sometimes everybody must get off for customs check. If looking for onward transport, if there is a free seat, most companies will let you pay on board.

⊕ Directory

Piriápolis *p1312*
Banks Banco de Uruguay on Rambla Argentinos changes TCs; Casa de Cambio Monex, Argentinos s/n, T25295. **Post offices** Av Piria y Tucumán.

Maldonado *p1313*
Banks Banco Pan de Azúcar, accepts Master-Card. Cambio Bacacay, Florida 803, good rates, TCs.

Punta del Este *p1313, map p1313*
Airline offices Aerolíneas Argentinas, Galería Santos Dumont locales 2 y 3, T444343, Laguna del Sauce, T559777; **Pluna-Varig**, Av Roosevelt y Parada 9, T490101. U**air**, international airport, Punta Ballena, T0800-8247. **Banks** Best rates of exchange from Banco de la República Oriental de Uruguay, which opens earlier and closes later than the other banks and accepts MasterCard, but no TCs. Many ATMs at banks on the peninsula and at Punta Shopping (Roosevelt). Also *casas de cambio*, eg Indumex, Av Gorlero y 28, **Brimar**, C 31 No 610. **Car hire** Punta Car, Continuación Gorlero s/n, *Hotel Playa*, T482112, puntacar@puntacar.com.uy. **Uno**, Gorlero y 21, T445018, unonobat@movinet.com.uy. And others. See Essentials, for international agencies. **Internet** Cybermix Café, Gorlero y 30, T447158, US$5 per hr. **Spot**, Gorlero y 30, T447290, open 0900-0200, US$6 per hr. **Post offices** Av Gorlero entre 31 y 32, 0900-1400, 1600-1900, daily (shorter hours out of season). **Scooter hire** US$10 per hr, US$25 per day, with drivers licence (US$50 fine if caught without it) and ID documents, one place opposite bus terminal, others on same street as *Taller Los Angeles*, Parada 2 casi Blvr Artigas, T486732. **Los Angeles** rents scooters and bicycles (US$1.50-US$2.20 per hr, US$5.15-US$6 per day depending on number of gears, padlock and chain included, leave ID as deposit). **Telephones** telephone and fax on Calle 24 at Calle 25, by the plaza.

La Paloma *p1314*
Internet Arrecife, Solari, US$1.50 per hr, open 0900-1200, 1600 until late. **Useful services** Bike rental opposite the casino, US$3.50 a day; horses can be hired. One bank which changes TCs; also a supermarket and post office.

Chuy *p1315*
Banks Several *cambios* on Av Brasil, eg Gales, Artigas y Brasil, Mon-Fri 0830-1200, 1330-1800, Sat 0830-1200, and in World Trade Center, open 1000-2200; on either side of *Gales* are *Aces* and *Val*. All give similar rates, charging US$1 plus 1% commission on TCs, dollars, pesos and reais exchanged. On Sun, try the casino, or look for someone on the street outside the *cambios*. Banco de la República Oriental Uruguay, Gen Artigas, changes TCs. No problem spending reais in Chuy or pesos in Chuí. **Internet** Nemar Informática, Numancia 139, T2980. US$3.50 per hr, open 0900-1200, 1500-2100, Fri closes at 2000, Sat at 1300. **Post offices** On Gen Artigas. **Telephones** Antel, S Priliac almost Artigas, open 0700-2300.

Montevideo north to Brazil

Two roads run towards Melo, heart of cattle-ranching country: Route 8 and Route 7, the latter running for most of its length through the Cuchilla Grande, a range of hills with fine views. Route 8 via Minas and Treinta y Tres, is the more important of these two roads to the border and it is completely paved.

Minas and around → *Phone code: 0442. Colour map 8, grid B6. Population: 34,000.*

This picturesque small town, 120 km north of Montevideo, is set in wooded hills. Juan Lavalleja, the leader of the Thirty-Three who brought independence to the country, was born here, and there is an equestrian statue to Artigas, said to be the largest such in the world, on the Cerro Artigas just out of town. The church's portico and towers, some caves in the neighbourhood, and the countryside around are worth seeing. Good confectionery is made in Minas; the largest firm, opposite *Hotel Verdun*, shows tourists round its premises. *Lloyds TSB Bank* and national banks are open 1300-1700 Monday-Friday. There is a tourist office at the bus station.

The Parque Salus, on the slopes of Sierras de las Animas, is 8 km to the south and very attractive; take the town bus marked 'Cervecería Salus' from plaza to the Salus brewery, then walk two km to the mineral spring and bottling plant (**C** pp *Parador Salus*, half board, good). It is a lovely three-hour walk back to Minas from the springs. The Cascada de Agua del Penitente waterfall, 11 km east off Route 8, is interesting and you may see wild rheas nearby. Hard to get to in the off-season.

To the Brazilian Border

Route 8 continues north via **Treinta y Tres** (population 28,000) to Melo (also reached by Route 7), near Aceguá close to the border. In **Melo** (population 42,000, Phone code 0462), there are places to stay and exchange rates are usually better than at the frontier.

At 12 km southeast of Melo is the Posta del Chuy (2 km off Route 26). This house, bridge and toll gate (built 1851 by two Frenchmen) was once the only safe crossing place on the main road between Uruguay and Brazil. Nowadays it houses a display of gaucho paintings and artefacts relating to its history.

Río Branco was founded in 1914, on the Río Yaguarón. The 1 km-long Mauá bridge across the river leads to Jaguarão in Brazil. The Brazilian consulate is at 10 de Junio 379, T2003, bravcrb@adinet.com.uy. For road traffic, the frontier at Chuy is better than Río Branco or Aceguá. There is a toll 68 km north of Montevideo.

An alternative route to Brazil is via Route 5, the 509-km road from Montevideo to the border town of Rivera, which runs almost due north, bypassing Canelones and Florida before passing through Durazno. After crossing the Río Negro, it goes to Tacuarembó. South of the Río Negro is gently rolling cattle country, vineyards, orchards, orange, lemon and olive groves. North is hilly countryside with steep river valleys and cattle ranching. The road is dual carriageway as far as Canelones.

East of Florida, Route 56 traverses the countryside eastwards to **Cerro Colorado**, also known as Alejandro Gallinal, which has an unusual clock tower.

Durazno → *Phone code: 0362. Colour map 8, grid B6. Population: 28,000.*
On the Río Yí 182 km from Montevideo, Durazno is a friendly provincial town with tree- lined avenues and an airport. There is a good view of the river from the western bridge.

Dams on the Río Negro have created an extensive network of lakes near **Paso de los Toros** (Population: 13,000; 66 km north of Durazno, bus from Montevideo US$6.50), with camping and sports facilities. Some 43 km north of Paso de los Toros a 55-km road turns east to **San Gregorio de Polanco**, at the eastern end of Lago Rincón del Bonete. The beach by the lake is excellent, with opportunities for boat trips, horse riding and other sports.

Tacuarembó → *Phone code: 0632. Colour map 8, grid B6. Population: 40,000.*
This is an agro-industrial town and major route centre 390 km north of Montevideo. The nearby Valle Edén has good walking possibilities. Some 23 km west of Tacuarembó, along Route 26, is the **Carlos Gardel Museum** *US$0.40*, a shrine to the great tango singer who was killed in an air crash in Medellín (Colombia). Uruguay, Argentina and France all claim him as a national son. The argument for his birth near here is convincing.

Brazilian border
Rivera (*Population 55,400, Phone code 0622*) is divided by a street from the Brazilian town of Santa Ana do Livramento. Points of interest are the park, the Plaza Internacional, and the dam of Cañapirú. Uruguayan immigration is in the Complejo Turístico at Sarandí y Viera, 14 blocks, 2 km, from the border (take bus along Agraciada). There is also a tourist office here, T5899. Luggage is inspected when boarding buses out of Rivera; there are also 3 checkpoints on the road out of town. The Brazilian consulate is at Ceballos 1159, T3278, and the Argentine one is at Ituzaingó 524, T3257. Remember that you must have a Uruguayan exit stamp to enter Brazil and a Brazilian exit stamp to enter Uruguay.

● Sleeping

Minas *p1320*
D Ramos, 18 de Julio near bus station. Basic (discount for HI members).
D-E Las Sierras, 18 de Julio 486, T3631. Including breakfast, very good value.
F Hostel de Villa Serrana, Calle Molle s/n off Route 8, Km 145, in small village of Villa Serrana, vserrana@hosteluruguay.org. US$6-7 pp a night (open all year), 28 km beyond Minas on road to Treinta y Tres. In a thatched house, kitchen for members, horses for hire, basic, take plenty of food and drink as there is no shop. Direct bus from Montevideo or Minas, ask driver to set you

down and walk 3 km to Villa Serrana; essential to book through Montevideo office.
Camping Arequita, T161170, beautiful surroundings, US$6.
Tourism farm B pp **Posada El Abra**, Puntas de Santa Lucía, 25 km from Minas, T0440-2869, mcontini@adinet.com.uy. Small *estancia* in hills at the headwaters of the Río Santa Lucía, price is full board, including transport, guides, horses for riding, good walking, remnant of native flora nearby, swimming in river, expansive views.

Treinta y Tres *p1320*
D pp Cañada del Brujo, Km 307.5, Ruta 8, Sierra del Yerbal, 34 km north of Treinta y Tres, T0452-2837, T099-297448 (mob), cdelbrujo@latinmail.com. An isolated hostel without electricity, basic but "fantastic", dormitory accommodation, local food, owner Pablo Rado drives you there, canoeing, trekking on foot or horseback, trips to Quebrada de los Cuervos.

Melo *p1320*
AL Gran Hotel Virrey, J Muñiz 727, T2411. Better rooms in new part, TV, minibar, café.

Cerro Colorado *p1321*
L San Pedro del Timoteo, 14 km west of Cerro Colorado, T/F0598-310 8086. A famous *estancia* hotel, colonial-style, like a village with its own church, landscaped park, 3 pools, cinema, gym, horseriding, good restaurant, still a working ranch.
AL Arteaga, 7 km off Route 7 north of Cerro Colorado. Typical European *estancia*, equally famous, beautiful interior, pool.

Durazno *p1321*
There are a few hotels (**C-E**).
Camping At 33 Orientales, in park of same name by river, T2806, nice beach, hot showers, toilets, laundry sinks.
Tourism Farm Estancia Albergue El Silencio, Ruta 14 Km 166, 10 km west of Durazno, T2014 (or T0360-2270, member of IH), silencio@adinet.com.uy. About 15 mins walk east of bridge over Río Yí where bus will stop: clean rooms, very friendly, riding, swimming, bird watching. Recommended.

Paso de los Toros *p1321*
A Los Médanos, T0369-4013, with breakfast, nicely furnished, swimming pool, jacuzzi, good value, its restaurant is across the road.
A-B Las Cañadas, north of Paso de Los Toros and then off a branch road to the west. A typical small ranch, comfortable and homely, offering an insight into the way the majority of *estancias* used to look. Recommended.

Tacuarembó *p1321*
B Tacuarembó, 18 de Julio 133, T2104. Breakfast, central.
D Plaza, 25 de Agosto 247, T27988. A/c, TV, small rooms.
E Hospedaje 25, 25 de Mayo 358. Basic, garden.
Camping Campsites 1 km out of town in the Parque Laguna de las Lavanderas, T4761, and 7 km north on R26 at Balneario Iporá.

Rivera *p1321*
A Casablanca, Sarandí 484, T3221. Shower, breakfast, a/c, comfortable, pleasant.
B-C Comercio, Artigas 115. Comfortable, **C** without bath. **B-C Sarandí**, Sarandí 777, T3521. Fan, good, **C** without bath.
Camping In Municipal site near AFE station, T3803, and in the Parque Gran Bretaña 7 km south along Route 27.

❶ Eating

Minas *p1320*
Recommended eating places are: **San Francisco**, 25 de Mayo 586, and **El Portal**, Aníbal del Campo 743, for *parrillada*.
Irisarri, C Treinta y Tres 618. The best pastry shop known for *yemas* (egg candy) and *damasquitos* (apricot sweets).

Tacuarembó *p1321*
Parrilla La Rueda, W Beltrán 251. Good.

❷ Transport

Minas *p1320*
Bus To **Montevideo**, US$3.75 (Núñez, Rutas del Plata), US$3 (Minuano, CUT), 2½ hrs. To **Maldonado**, US$2.45, 5 a day, 2 hrs.

Melo *p1320*
Bus From **Montevideo** US$10 (Núñez). Several buses daily to Río Branco.

Durazno *p1321*
Bus From **Montevideo** US$4.75, Núñez, US$4.10, Turismar, Nossar.

Tacuarembó *p1321*
Bus From **Montevideo**, US$10 (Turil, Núñez).
Train Service to **Rivera** at 0600 (see below).

Rivera *p1321*
Air Aviasur from Montevideo; Pluna, Paysandú 1079, T3404.
Bus Terminal at Uruguay y Viera (1½ km from the terminal in Santa Ana). To/from **Montevideo**, US$13 (Turil, Núñez). To **Paysandú**, Copay, T23733, at 0400, 1600, US$10. To **Tacuarembó**, US$2.85 (Núñez, Turil), no connections for Paysandú. To **Salto**, Mon and Fri 1630, 6 hrs, US$11. For **Artigas**, take bus from Livramento to Quaraí, then cross bridge.
Train Passenger service to **Tacuarembó** leaves Rivera 1700, Mon-Sat, 3½ hrs; depart Tacuarembó 0600, US$3. The train passes countryside abundant with wildlife.

Venezuela

Footprint features

Introduction

Venezuela is where the Andes meet the Caribbean. The Orinoco river separates great plains from the table-top mountains of the Gran Sabana, where waterfalls tumble in sheer drops into the forest and lost worlds are easy to imagine. More recent innovations – cablecars up to the high peaks, hang gliders for jumping off them – are now part of the scene at Mérida, capital of Venezuela's Andes. Lying at the heart of the country – geographically and spiritually – are the *llanos* (plains), a vast area of flat savannah the size of Italy and home to an immense variety of birds, exotic mammals and reptiles, such as caiman (alligators), giant anacondas, anteaters, pumas, jaguars and giant otters, to name but a few.

These plains flood seasonally, but when the waters retreat, the birds and animals share their territory with cattle and the *llanero* cowboys, renowned for their hospitality towards visitors who can stay at one of the many luxurious *hatos* – cattle ranches – or rough it on a budget tour from Mérida. If the sea is more to your taste, head for the country's seductive coastline – the longest in the Caribbean at over 2,500 km. Venezuela's waters play host to some of the best (and least known) diving in the region with three marine national parks. Pick of the bunch are Islas Los Roques, an archipelago of emerald and turquoise lagoons and dazzling white beaches. At the other end of the country, the Amazon is home to humid rainforests and rare plants and animals as well as over 20 different ethnic groups. This part of Venezuela is very much frontier territory and remains wild and untamed, as it was when the country received its first foreign visitor back in 1498. So overwhelmed was Columbus by what he saw that he described it as 'Paradise on Earth'.

★ Don't miss...

1 **Henri Pittier National Park** This stunning landscape of tumbling mountain streams and steep rugged hills is a birdwatcher's heaven, page 1347.

2 **Sierra Nevada National Park** From the city of Mérida, the highest cable car in the world wings its way up to the summit of the Andes. There is great trekking in the *páramo* and agricultural highlands, page 1368.

3 **Los Llanos** Another excellent area for wildlife watching. The great plains of the Orinoco are cowboy country and many of the cattle ranches offer themselves as bases, page 1373.

4 **Mochima National Park** A string of beautiful beaches, sandy coves and islets, backed by lush, forested hills. This is one of the most accessible of Venezuela's protected areas, so hire a boat and spend a day snorkelling and sunbathing, page 1381.

5 **Los Roques** Emerald lagoons and dazzling sands surrounded by 20 km of coral reef make this Caribbean archipelago one of Venezuela's top attractions, page 1398.

6 **Angel Falls** From a table-top mountain, a waterfall tumbles for almost 1 km. It's an adventure to get to the base and a major expedition to get to the top, unless of course you just hop on a little plane and fly over, page 1404.

Caribbean Sea

TRINIDAD

GUYANA

BRAZIL

COLOMBIA

Essentials

Planning your trip

Caribbean coast Venezuela has the longest coastline in the Caribbean with numerous palm-fringed beaches of white sand. **Caracas** is hidden from the Caribbean by Monte Avila, one of Venezuela's national parks, but you don't have to go too far beyond the mountain to find good beaches. Only a few hours west of the capital are some lovely little beaches, ideal if you have a few spare days before flying out, or on arrival. Further west is the Parque Nacional Morrocoy, with many islands close to the shore. North of Morrocoy is the historic town of Coro, surrounded by sand dunes, and the Paranaguá Peninsula. Parque Nacional Mochima, east of Caracas, has some excellent beaches and a multitude of islets to explore. Further east are unrivalled beaches on the Paria Peninsula, but they are harder to reach. Besides those islands already mentioned, there is Isla de Margarita, one of the country's principal destinations for local and foreign tourists. The Islas Los Roques, 166 km due north of the central coast, is a beautiful archipelago, still unspoilt despite the growth in tourist interest.

The Andes Venezuela's Andes have some gorgeous scenery, with snow-capped peaks and remote villages. The main centre for visitors is Mérida, in the middle of the Sierra Nevada of the same name. It is well provided with accommodation, other services and tour companies which can help with arranging treks, climbing and other excursions. Two of its claims to fame are the highest cable car in the world, ascending the 4,776-m Pico Espejo, and the shop selling the largest number of ice cream flavours in the world.

The Llanos Life in the *llanos* revolves around the cycle of wet and dry seasons; the movement of cattle, the mainstay of the region's economy, depends on it. In the flat grasslands are slow running rivers which flood in the rainy season, creating a huge inland sea. When the rains cease, the whole area dries out completely. South of the cattle lands are forests and the tributaries of the Río Orinoco. Just after the May-November wet season, this is a paradise for nature lovers, with a spectacular variety of birds, monkeys, big cats, anaconda, river dolphins, caiman and capybara. Tours to the *llanos* are run from Mérida and there are ecotourism ranches which offer you the chance to get to know the lifestyle of the plains.

Guayana and the Orinoco Above the grasslands of the Gran Sabana rise *tepuis*, flat-topped mountains from which spring magnificent waterfalls and rivers. The Angel Falls, the highest in the world, are one such wonder, usually seen from a plane, but also reachable by a 2-3 day trip upriver. There are many other falls in the Gran Sabana and a few places to stay, the most popular being Canaima camp on a lagoon on the Río Carrao. Where Venezuela meets Brazil and Guyana is Mount Roraima; to reach its summit is one of the most adventurous excursions to be made in the country. The Orinoco delta is remote, but trips can be made from the small town of Tucupita. Amazonas too, is well off the beaten track, but here again trips can be made, from Puerto Ayacucho. Much of the rainforest is protected and permission from the authorities is required to visit areas beyond the reach of a tour company.

When to go The climate is tropical, with changes between the seasons being a matter of wet and dry, rather than hot and cold. Temperature is determined by altitude. The dry season in Caracas is December to April, with January and February the coolest months (there is a great difference between day and night temperatures at this time). The hottest months are July and August. The Caribbean coast is generally dry and rain is particularly infrequent in the states of Sucre, in the east, and Falcón, in the northwest. The lowlands of Maracaibo are very hot all year round; the least hot months are July to September. South of the Orinoco, in the Gran Sabana and Parque Nacional Canaima, the dry season is November to May. The same months are dry in the *llanos*, but the best time to visit is just after the rains, when the rivers and channels are still full of water and the humidity is not too high. In the Andes, the dry season is October to May, and this is the best time for climbing or hiking. The days are clear, but the nights are freezing cold. The rains usually begin in June, but in the mountains the weather can change from day to day.

Finding out more In charge of tourism is the **Ministerio de Turismo**, Av Francisco de Miranda con Av Principal de La Floresta, Edif Mintur (Frente al Colegio Universitario de Caracas), Chacao, Caracas, T0212-208 4511, www.mintur.gob.ve. At the same address is **Instituto Nacional de Turismo - Inatur**, 0212-208 4872, which deals with tourism promotion.

For practical information, see the sites of the **Buró de Venezuela**, www.venezuela visitorsbureau.com, and www.burodevenezuela.com. Outside Venezuela, tourist information can be obtained from Venezuelan embassies and consulates (for addresses, see next page). Read and heed the travel advice, regularly updated, at www.britishembassy.gov.uk and www.travel.state.gov (go to Consular Information Sheets under Travel Warnings).

National parks Venezuela has 43 national parks, 21 national monuments and various other refuges and reserves, some of which are mentioned in the text. A full list is published by the **Instituto Nacional de Parques** (Inparques), al lado del Museo de Transporte, entre Avenida Francisco de Miranda y Autopista Francis Caracas, T285 4859 (Caracas), pnacionales@ inparques.gov.ve, www.inparques.gov.ve. Each park has a regional director and its own guards (*guardaparques*). Permits (free) are required to stay in the parks (up to five), although this is not usually necessary for those parks visited frequently. For further information on the national parks system, visit the **Ministerio del Ambiente y de los Recursos Naturales Renovables** (MARNR), Centro Simón Bolívar, Torre Sul, Caracas 1010, T481 2209, www.marnr.gob.ve. Ecotourism portal: **http://ecoportal.venezuela.com**, for ecotourism, sports, national parks and places to stay, lots of links and information in English, but confusing format. See also **www.parkswatch.org** for a good run down of the country's most important national parks.

Websites

www.gobiernoenlinea.ve Government site.
www.venezuelatuya.com Tourism, history, geography, cuisine, traditions and more.
www.auyantepuy.com, www.terra.com.ve, http://think- venezuela.net, www.venezuela voyage.com Ueful information and links.
http://venezuelatoday.net Access to any

medium, local, international, official and blogs.
www.vheadline.com, www.vcrisis.com and www.sumate.org A selection of the many sites with news and comment on current affairs.
www.bvonline.com.ve or www.venamcham.org VenAmCham's Business Venezuela.

Venezuela Essentials

Maps *Guía Vial de Venezuela*, edited by **Miro Popic** (Caracas 1999), US$25, is a motoring guide with road maps and tourist information. The best country map is the late Kevin Healey's, published by **International Travel Maps**, Vancouver, Canada; available at good travel agents.

Visas and immigration Entry is by passport and visa, or by passport and tourist card. Tourist cards (*tarjetas de ingreso*) are issued by airlines to visitors from Australia, Austria, Belgium, Canada, Denmark, France, Germany, Ireland, Italy, Japan, Norway, Netherlands, New Zealand, South Africa, Spain, Sweden, Switzerland, UK and USA. To check if you need a visa, contact www.mre.gov.ve/consular/visa_dex2.htm. Valid for 90 days, tourist cards cannot be extended. Overstaying your 90 days can lead to arrest and a fine when you try to depart. For a **tourist visa**, you need two passport photos, passport valid for six months, references from bank and employer, onward or return ticket, completed and signed application form. The fee is £22 (or equivalent, costs vary from country to country). For extensions go to **ONIDEX** ① *Av Baralt on Plaza Miranda in Caracas, T483 2070, www.onidex.gov.ve; office at Plaza Caracas, Torre Norte (Centro CB), mezzanine, Mon-Fri 0700-1230 (Fri 0800)*, take passport, tourist visa, photographs and return ticket; passport with extension returned at end of day. ONIDEX offices in many cities do not offer extensions. Transit visas, valid for 72 hours are also available, mostly the same requirements and cost (inward and onward tickets needed). ONIDEX in Caracas will not exchange a transit for a tourist visa. In Manaus you also need a yellow fever inoculation certificate. Consuls may give a one-year visa if a valid reason can be given. To change a tourist visa to a business visa, to obtain or to extend the latter, costs £44 or equivalent.

Work visas also cost £44 and require authorization from the **Dirección General Sectorial de Identificación y Control de Extranjeros** in Caracas. Student visas require a letter of acceptance from the Venezuelan institution, references from bank and university, completed and signed application form, two passport photos, onward or return ticket, passport valid for six months and US$60. It generally takes two days to issue any visa.

Note: If youa re not eligible for a tourist card, you must get a consular visa in advance. Carry your passport with you all the time you are in Venezuela as the police do frequent spot checks and anyone found without identification is immediately detained (carrying a certified copy is permissible, though not always accepted by officials). There are many military checkpoints, especially in border areas, at which all transport is stopped. Have your documents ready and make sure you know what entry permits you need; the soldiers may be unfamiliar with regulations for foreigners. Border searches are very thorough. Business visitors on short visits are strongly advised to enter the country as tourists, otherwise they will have to obtain a tax clearance certificate (*solvencia*) before they can leave. Do not lose the carbon copy of your visa as this has to be surrendered when leaving the country.

Venezuelan embassies and consulates Visit www.mre.gov.ve/misiones/dire.htm.

Money The unit of currency is the bolívar. There are coins for 10, 20, 50, 100 and 500 bolívares, and notes for 1,000, 2,000, 5,000, 10,000, 20,000 and 50,000 bolívares. Since the country changed its name in 1999, the Banco Central has been issuing the new 'República Bolivariana de Venezuela' notes. This does not help the foreign traveller. One now has to deal with two kinds of note for all denominations, all in different colours. Check notes carefully. Have small coins and notes to hand, since many shops and bars round up prices if you don't have the exact change. Similarly, on public transport, drivers may not be able to change big notes.

Venezuela has an exchange control regime for the bolívar. The government determines the 'official' rate, which has devalued slowly in relation to the dollar and other currencies since the measure was imposed in 2002. There is also a 'parallel' (ie black) market exchange of currencies. Any hard currency (eg dollar, euro – which is becoming popular) is difficult to buy officially. Even though changing bolívares for hard currency is punishable, it is common practice. If you do decide to change on the black market, a) find out what the unofficial rate is from as many sources as possible, and b) do the transaction with the most trusted person. Many travel agencies and hotels will not change on the black market openly. Rates of exchange in hotels are generally poor, but they may be your best bet for changing on the black market. When goods and services are priced in dollars, check the exchange rate if you intend to pay in bolívares, it is usually unfavourable. The *Daily Journal* newspaper publishes the unofficial rate on its mast-head. The official bolívar **exchange rate** in February 2006 was US$: 2,150; euro: 2,881. Prices in this guide are calculated with the official exchange rate.

Touching down

Airport tax International passengers pay a combined airport and exit tax of around US$61 at the official exchange rate (Bs58,800 for airport tax, payable in bolívares or dollars, and Bs73,500 exit tax; cash only). It goes up every March. Many airlines collect some of the tax in the ticket price, but you have to check what, if anything, has been paid. Children under two years do not pay tax. There is a 8% tax on the cost of all domestic flights, plus an airport tax of US$4.65. Exit stamps have to be paid by overland travellers. The fee differs at each border, eg US$11.60 Maracaibo- Maicao, US$15 San Antonia-Cúcuta, Colombia. Correct taxes are not advertised and travellers have experienced overcharging.

Business hours Banks: 0830-1530 Mon-Fri only. **Government offices:** 0800-1200 are usual morning hours, although they vary. Officials have fixed hours, usually 0900-1000 or 1500-1600, for receiving visitors. **Businesses:** 0800-1800 with a midday break. **Shops:** 0900-1300, 1500-1900, Mon-Sat. Generally speaking, Venezuelans start work early, and by 0700 in the morning everything is in full swing. Most firms and offices close on Saturday.

In an emergency T171 for the integrated emergency system.

International phone code +58. Ringing: long equal tones with equal long pauses. Engaged: short equal tones, with equal pauses.

Official time Four hours behind GMT, one hour ahead of EST.

Tipping Taxi drivers are not tipped if you have agreed the fare in advance. Usherettes are not tipped. Hotel porters, US$1; airport porters US$1 per piece of baggage. Restaurants 5-10% of bill.

VAT/IVA 14.5%.

Voltage 110 volts, 60 cycles. Plugs are either 2 flat pin, or 2 flat pin with a round earth pin.

Weights and measures Metric.

Plastic/TCs/banks (ATMs) Dollars cash and TCs can be changed in banks and *casas de cambio* at the official rate. To convert unused bolívares back into dollars upon leaving, you must present the original exchange receipt (up to 30% of original amount changed); only banks and authorized *casas de cambio* can legally sell bolívares. Some banks are reluctant to change either cash or TCs. *Casas de cambio* are a better bet, but their rates for TCs will be poor (because they use the official rate) and they insist on photocopying your passport, may ask for proof of purchase of TCs and may even photograph you. Beware of forged Amex TCs and US$ notes.

You can also use Visa or MasterCard for obtaining bolívares at the official rate. There are cash machines for Visa, MasterCard and Amex at Simón Bolívar airport although these may give a receipt but no cash. You should be wary of using cash machines throughout the country; Visa and MasterCard transactions inside banks, although slower, are much safer. Machines are often old or tampered with and queues at ATM machines attract thieves. In addition, few machines dispense cash to foreigners. *Corp Banca* is affiliated with American Express, no commission, some branches cash personal cheques from abroad on an Amex card; *American Express* travel services are handled by *Italcambio* and *Quo Vadis* agencies around the country. MasterCard assistance To800-1-002902. Visa assistance call collect +44-20-7937 8091 or F+44-17-3350 3670.

Cost of travelling On the cheapest possible budget you can get by on around US$25 pp per day, depending on which part of the country you visit. A less basic budget would be about US$50 per day, rising to US$100 and upwards for first class travel. The average cost for using the internet varies from US$0.50-0.80 outside Caracas to US$1-2 per hour in the capital.

Safety In Caracas and any popular tourist destination, especially on the coast, watch out for scams, cons and petty thieving. The beaches can be packed at weekends and, while empty on weekdays, the detritus left by the weekend crowds may not be cleared up. If you do find an isolated beach, it is wise to be on the look-out for unwanted attention from robbers. This may sound like a Catch-22, but there are quiet beaches where you will be undisturbed (simply make enquiries before setting out) and, in the main, Venezuelans are extremely hospitable.

Driving in Venezuela

Road Roads are generally poor, except for the four-lane *autopistas*.
Safety Use private car parks whenever possible. If you have an accident and someone is injured, you will be detained as a matter of routine, even if you are not at fault. Carry spare battery water, fan belts, the obligatory breakdown triangle, a jack and spanners.
Documents Minimum driving age is 18. A valid driving licence from your own country, or international driving licence (preferred) is required. Neither a *carnet de passages*, nor a *libreta de pasos por aduana* is officially required, but is recommended. Before shipping your vehicle to Venezuela, go to a Venezuelan consul to obtain all necessary documentation. You must also go to a Venezuelan consul in the country in which you land your car if other than Venezuela. An entry permit for a car costs US$10 and requires one photograph (takes 24 hours).
Organizations Touring y Automóvil Club de Venezuela, Torre Phelps, p 15, of A y C, Plaza Venezuela, Caracas, T0212-781 9743, tacvzla@cantv.net. Issues the *libreta de pasos por aduana*.
Car hire It is a good idea to hire a car; many of the best places are off the beaten track. You need a credit card to rent a vehicle. Basic rates for a car are US$75-100 per day, with insurance; discounts usually begin at seven days. Government tax of 17% is also added.
Fuel 91 and 95 octane, cost US$0.10-0.16 a litre; diesel, US$0.10 a litre. Oil costs US$0.60 a litre. **Warning** There is a US$20 fine for running out of fuel.

Getting around

Air Most big places are served by **Aeropostal** www.aeropostal.com, **Aserca** www.aserca airlines.com, **Avior** www.avior.com.ve, **Conviasa** www.conviasa.aero, **El Sol de América Láser** www.laser.com.ve, **Rutaca** www.rutaca.com.ve, and **Santa Bárbara** www.sbairlines.com. **Aereotuy** www.tuy.com, connects the coast, the Orinoco Delta and their camp in Canaima National Park, Arekuna. Apart from **Aserca**, which has been recommended, none is great. Lost luggage is a frequent problem. Internal airlines offer occasional family or student discounts, photocopies of ISIC card are useful. Beware of over-booking during holiday time, especially at Caracas airport; check in at least two hours before departure.

Bus and taxi Buses are relatively cheap. The quality of long-distance travel varies a lot, but some comfortable buses have been introduced on long journeys. There are numerous services between the major cities and many services bypass Caracas, so you don't have to change buses in the capital. Buses stop frequently, but there may not always be a toilet at the stop. For journeys in a/c buses take a sleeping bag or similar because the temperature is set to freezing. Also take earplugs against the loud stereo systems. The colectivo taxis and minibuses, known as *por puesto*, seem to monopolize transport to and from smaller towns and villages. For longer journeys they are normally twice as expensive as buses, but faster. They may be reluctant to take luggage and the ill-kempt. If first on board, wait for other passengers to arrive, do not take a *por puesto* on your own unless you want to pay for the whole vehicle. Outside Caracas, town taxis are relatively expensive. At peak periods *revendedores* (touts) will try to sell tickets at 2-3 times face value.

Hitchhiking Hitchhiking (*cola*) is generally safe, as Venezuelans are usually friendly and helpful if you know some Spanish. The best places to try are Guardia Nacional posts outside cities. It is illegal on toll roads and, theoretically, for non-family members in the back of pick up trucks. Some drivers may ask for money for the lift, especially if on a bus route.

Sleeping → *See inside front cover of the book for our hotel grade price guide.*

Value for money is generally not very high, with one or two exceptions, but many foreign-run, no-frills places catering for backpackers are opening up. The major cities, Isla Margarita, Los Roques, Guayana and Amazonas have higher room rates (eg US$15 in Caracas for a decent room). Add 10-15% for air-conditioning. In the Andean region prices are lower at around US$8 per person.

Camping Camping in Venezuela is a popular recreation, for spending a weekend at the beach, on the islands, in the Llanos and in the mountains. Camping, with or without a vehicle, is not possible at the roadside. If camping on the beach, for the sake of security, pitch your tent close to others, even though they play their radios loud.

Eating → *See inside front cover of the book for our restaurant price guide.*
Eating out Midday is the cheapest time to eat the main meal of the day and the best time to find fresh vegetables. Particularly good value is the three-course *menú ejecutivo* or *cubierto*. Minimum price for a meal is US$3-5, plus US$1 for drinks. Breakfast in your hotel is likely to be poor. It is better and cheaper in a *fuente de soda* and cheaper still in a *pastelería* or *arepería*.

Food There is excellent local fish (such as *pargo* or red snapper, *carite* or king fish), crayfish, small oysters and prawns. Although it is a protected species, turtle may appear on menus in the Península de Paraguaná as *ropa especial*. Of true Venezuelan food there is *sancocho* (a stew of vegetables, especially yuca, with meat, chicken or fish); *arepas*, white maize bread, very bland in flavour; toasted *arepas* served with various fillings or the local salty white cheese, are cheap, filling and nutritious; *cachapas*, a maize pancake wrapped around white cheese; *pabellón*, made of shredded meat, beans, rice and fried plantains; and *empanadas*, maize-flour pies containing cheese, meat or fish. At Christmas there are *hallacas*, maize pancakes stuffed with chicken, pork, olives, boiled in a plantain leaf. A *muchacho* (boy) on the menu is a cut of beef. *Ganso* is not goose but beef. *Solomo* and *lomito* are other cuts of beef. *Hervido* is chicken or beef with vegetables. *Contorno* with a meat or fish dish is a choice of fried chips, boiled potatoes, rice or yuca. *Caraotas* are beans; *cachitos* are filled *croissants*. *Pasticho* is what Venezuelans call Italian *lasagne*. The main fruits are bananas, oranges, grapefruit, mangoes, pineapple and pawpaws. Venezuelan names for fruit: *lechosa* is papaya, *patilla* water melon, *parchita* passion fruit, and *cambur* a small banana. Excellent strawberries are grown at Colonia Tovar, 90 minutes from Caracas, and in the Andes. Delicious sweets are *huevos chimbos* – egg yolk boiled and bottled in sugar syrup, and *quesillo* - made with milk, egg and caramel. The *Daily Journal* lists reliable restaurants in Caracas and Maracaibo. **Note:** Venezuelans dine late!

Drink Venezuelan rum is very good; recommended brands are *Cacique, Pampero* and *Santa Teresa*. There are five good beers: *Polar* (the most popular), *Regional* (with a strong flavour of hops), *Cardenal* and *Nacional* (a *lisa* is a glass of keg beer; for a bottle of beer ask for a *tercio*); Brazilian *Brahma* beer (lighter than *Polar*) is now brewed in Venezuela. There are also mineral waters and gin. There is a good, local wine in Venezuela. The *Polar* brewery joined with Martell (France) to build a winery in Carora. Wines produced are 'Viña Altagracia' and 'Bodegas Pomar'. 'Bodegas Pomar' also produces a sparkling wine in the traditional champagne style. Liqueurs are cheap, try the local *ponche crema*. Coffee is very cheap (*café con leche* has a lot of milk, *café marrón* much less, *café negro* for black coffee, which, though obvious, is not common in the rest of Latin America); coffee is often served with sugar already added, ask for "sin azúcar". Visitors should also try a *merengada*, a delicious drink made from fruit pulp, ice, milk and sugar; a *batido* is the same but with water and a little milk; *jugo* is the same but with water. A *plus-café* is an after-dinner liqueur. Water is free in restaurants even if no food is bought. Bottled water in *cervecerías* is often from the tap; no deception is intended, bottles are simply used as convenient jugs. Insist on seeing the bottle opened if you want mineral water. *Chicha de arroz* is a sweet drink made of milk, rice starch, sugar and vanilla. Fruit juices are very good, but you must ask for "jugo natural, preparado en el momento" for absolutely fresh juice.

Festivals and events
National holidays include: 1 January, Carnival on the Monday-Tuesday before Ash Wednesday (everything shuts down Saturday-Tuesday; book accommodation in advance), Thursday-Saturday of Holy Week, 19 April, 1 May, 24 June (the feast day of San Juan Bautista, celebrated on the central coast where there were once large concentrations of plantation slaves who considered San Juan their special Saint; the best-known events are in villages such as Chuao, Cata and Ocumare de la Costa), 5 and 24 July, 24 September, 12 October, 25 December. From 24 December-1 January, most restaurants close and there is no long-distance public transport. On New Year's Eve, everything closes and does not open for a least a day. Business travellers should not visit during Holy Week or Carnival. Extra holidays for banks: 19 March, nearest Monday to 6 January, Ascension Day, 29 June, 15 August, 1 November and 8 December.

Caracas

➜ *Phone code: 0212. Colour map 1, grid A6. Population: nearly 5 million (city 1,825,000). Altitude: 960 m.*

Caracas is not the gentlest of introductions to South America; it's more like a slap in the face from a garishly-dressed, loud mestizo with a taste for all things American. Founded in 1567, it lies in a rift in thickly forested mountains which rise abruptly from a lush green coast to heights of 2,000-3,000 m. The small basin in which the capital lies runs some 24 km east and west. By way of escape, there are several nearby excursions to mountain towns, the Parque Nacional Monte Avila, beaches and Los Roques, a beautiful Caribbean atoll.

Ins and outs

Getting there The **airport** is 28 km from Caracas, near the port of La Guaira: Maiquetía and Aeropuerto Auxiliar for national flights and Simón Bolívar for international flights. There are three main **bus terminals** in different parts of the city; where you arrive depends upon where you travelled from. ▸ *See also Transport, page 1340.*

Getting around The metro is a/c, clean, safe, comfortable and quicker than any other form of city transport. Buses are overcrowded in rush hour and charge an additional fare after 2100. On longer runs these buses are better for those with luggage than a *por puesto* minibus. Minibuses are known as *busetas, carmelitas* or *carritos. Por puestos* run on regular routes; fares depend on the distance travelled within the city and rise for journeys outside. Many *por puesto* services start in El Silencio. For full details see Transport, page . In the centre, each street corner has a name: addresses are generally given as 'Santa Capilla a Mijares', rather than the official 'Calle Norte 2, No 26'. In the east, addresses are more obvious, 'y' or 'con' used for street intersections.

Orientation Since the Second World War, colonial buildings have given way to modern multi-storeyed edifices; many visitors find the city lacking in character. A 10-km strip from west to east, fragmented by traffic-laden arteries, contains several centres: Plaza Bolívar, Plaza Venezuela, Sabana Grande, Chacaíto, Altamira, La Floresta, Boleíta. The Avila mountain is always north.

Caracas

Sleeping	
CCCT Best Western **1**	La Floresta **5**
Continental **2**	Radisson Eurobuilding **4**
El Cid **3**	Residencia Montserrat **5**
	Tamanaco **6**

Tourist offices Inatur, Av Francisco de Miranda con Av Principal de La Floresta, Edif Mintur (Frente al Colegio Universitario de Caracas), Chacao, T208 4872. There is a smaller office at the airport (see below).

Climate Maximum 32° C July-August, minimum 9° C January-February.

Security You should be on the lookout from the moment you arrive in the country: there are many pirate taxis and rip-off merchants operating at the international airport. It is advisable not to arrive in Caracas at night and not to walk down narrow streets or in parks after dark. Avoid certain areas such as all western suburbs from the El Silencio monument to Propatria, the areas around the Nuevo Circo and La Bandera bus stations, the area around the *teleférico*, Chapellín near the Country Club, and Petare. Street crime is on the increase, even armed robbery in daylight. Even in a crowded place like Sabana Grande, bag slashing and mugging are not uncommon. Take care at all times and never carry valuables. Carry handbags, cameras etc on the side away from the road as motorcycle purse-snatchers are notorious. Car theft is common. Police searches are frequent and thorough, especially around Avenida Las Acacias after dark and in airports; always carry ID. If you have entered overland from Colombia, you can expect thorough investigation. Outside the capital, the atmosphere is much more relaxed, but as in any country you should be cautious at night.

Sights

Centre

The shady **Plaza Bolívar**, with its fine equestrian statue of the Liberator and pleasant colonial cathedral, is still the official centre of the city, though no longer geographically so. In the **Capitolio Nacional** ⓘ *Tue-Sun, 0900-1200, 1400-1700,* the Elliptical Salon has some impressive paintings by the Venezuelan artist Martín Tovar y Tovar and a bronze urn containing the 1811 Declaration of Independence. The present **Cathedral** dating from 1674 has a beautiful façade, the Bolívar family chapel and paintings by Michelena, Murillo and an alleged Rubens 'Resurrection'.

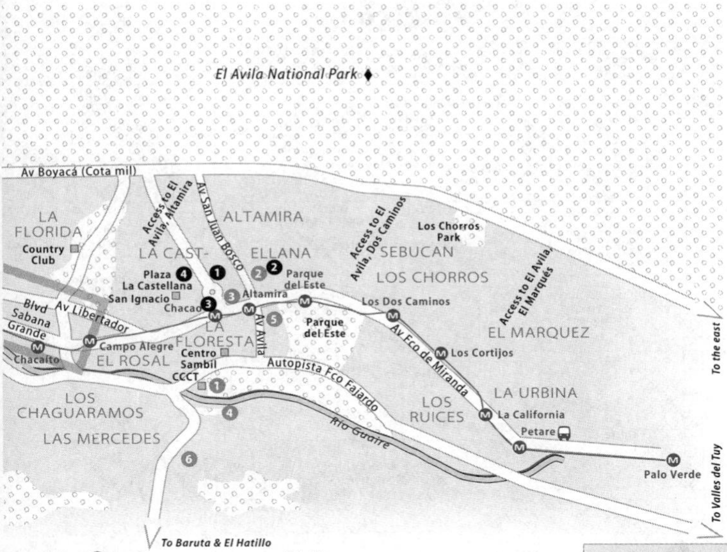

Eating
Chez Wong 1
Evio's Pizza 2
La Estancia 3
Primi 3
Spizzico 4

Related maps
A Caracas centre, page 1334
B Sabana Grande, page 1336

The **Consejo Municipal** (City Hall) on Plaza Bolívar contains three **museums** ① *all 3 open Tue-Fri 0930-1200, 1500-1800; Sat and Sun 0930-1800; informative guides are available*: a collection of the paintings of Emilio Boggio, a Venezuelan painter; the Raúl Santana Museum of the Creole Way of Life, a collection of miniature figures in costumes, all handmade by Raúl Santana; and the Sala de Arqueología Gaspar Marcano, exhibiting ceramics, mostly discovered on the coast.

Casa Natal del Libertador ① *Sur 1 y Este 2, Jacinto a Traposos, T541 2563, Tue-Fri 0900-1200, 1430-1700, Sun and holidays 1000-1700*: a reconstruction of the house where Bolívar was born (24 July 1783). It contains interesting pictures and furniture. The first house, of adobe, was destroyed by an earthquake. The second became a stable, and was later pulled down. **The Museo Bolivariano** is alongside the Casa Natal and contains the Liberator's war relics.

San Francisco ① *Av Universidad y San Francisco (1 block southwest of Plaza Bolívar)*, should be seen for its colonial altars; it's oldest church in Caracas, rebuilt 1641. **Santa Teresa** ① *between La Palma and Santa Teresa, just southeast of the Centro Simón Bolívar*, has good interior chapels and a supposedly miraculous portrait of Nazareno de San Pablo (popular and solemn devotions on Good Friday).

Panteón Nacional ① *Av Norte y Av Panteón, Tue-Sun 0900-1200,1400-1700*. The remains of Simón Bolívar, the Liberator, lie here in the Plaza Panteón. The tomb of Francisco Miranda (the Precursor of Independence), who died in a Spanish prison, has been left open to await the return of his body, likewise the tomb of Antonio José de Sucre, who was assassinated in Colombia. Every 25 years the President opens Bolívar's casket to verify that the remains are still there. Daniel O'Leary, Bolívar's Irish aide-de camp, is buried alongside.

Museo Histórico Fundación John Boulton ① *Torre El Chorro, 11th floor, Av Universidad y Sur 3, entre El Chorro y Dr Díaz, T564 4366, fjb@reacciun.ve Mon-Fri 0800-1200, 1300-1700, free, 2 tours a day by knowledgeable guides; underground parking on*

Caracas centre

Sleeping ⊜
Anauco Hilton **1**
Avila **2**
Caracas Hilton **3**

Inter **6**
Limón **7**
Plaza Catedral **8**
Renovación **9**

Eating ⨀
El Paso **1**
La Cocina Criolla
de Francy **2**

presentation of ID. Previously in La Guaira, this museum contains many historical items and a library of 19th-century research and commercial records of the Casa Boulton (easy access).

Museo de Arte Colonial ① *Quinta Anauco, Av Panteón, T551 4256, www.quinta deanauco.org.ve, Mon-Fri 0900-1130, 1400-1630, Sat-Sun 1000-1630, US$2. Guided tour in Spanish available, getting there: take por puesto from Bellas Artes metro (at the same stop as the metro bus), those bound for San Bernardino go past Quinta Anauco*. This delightful house in the beautiful suburb of San Bernardino, was built in 1720 and was formerly the residence of the Marqués del Toro. The museum holds chamber concerts most Saturdays at 1800.

Sabana Grande and east of the centre

In the **Parque Central**, between Avenida Lecuna (east end) and the elevated section of Avenida Bolívar there are four museums in a complex which includes two octagonal towers (56 floors each – ask the security guard to let you go up to the roof, leave passport and they will guide you, not Monday) and four large apartment buildings with shopping below: **Museo de Arte Contemporáneo** ① *Parque Central, Cuadra Bolívar, T573 4662, www.maccsi.org entrance beside Anauco Hilton, Tue-Sun 1000-1800, free.* It has a room devoted to five paintings by Picasso and his pen and ink drawings, and interesting modern sculptures. **Museo de los Niños** ① *Parque Central, next to east Tower, T575 0295, www.curiosikid.com/view/index.asp, daily 0900-1700, US$2, children US$1.50,* a highly sophisticated modern science museum, extremely popular. Also in the Parque Central complex, is the **Museo del Teclado** (keyboard instruments) ① *T572 0713, Mon-Fri 0900-1300, 1400-1600, Sat 1700-1900.*

Parque Los Caobos is peaceful and has a cafeteria in the middle. By the entrance in Avenida México is the cultural centre, **Ateneo de Caracas**, with a cinema, theatre, art gallery, concert room, bookshop and the imposing **Teresa Carreño theatre** complex. **Museo de**

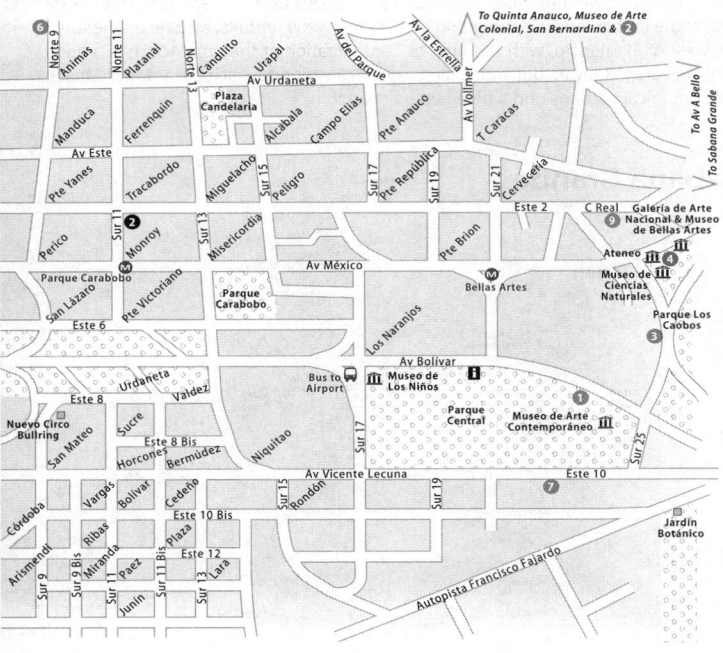

Plaza Mayor **3**

Bars & clubs 🎵
Café Rajatabla **4**

Bellas Artes ① *Plaza de los Museos in Parque Los Caobos, T578 1816 free, Mon-Fri 0900-1700, Sat-Sun 1000-1700*, the oldest museum in Caracas, designed by Carlos Raúl Villanueva. It contains works by mainly Venezuelan artists. Adjacent is the **Galería de Arte Nacional** ① *T578 1818, www.gan.org.ve, Mon-Fri 0900-1700, Sat-Sun 1000-1700*, which also houses the **Cinemateca Nacional** ① *Tue-Sun 1830 and 2130, Sun 1100 for children's films*. **Museo de Ciencias** ① *Plaza de los Museos, T577 5094, Tue-Fri 0900-1700, weekend 1000-1700*: archaeological, particularly pre-Columbian, zoological and botanical exhibits, interesting temporary shows.

Jardín Botánico ① *near Plaza Venezuela, entrance by Ciudad Universitaria, Tue-Sun 0800-1630, US$0.50, guide US$1 in English*, is worth a visit. There are extensive plant collections and a small area of 'natural forest'. Here you can see the world's largest palm tree (*Corypha Sp*) and the Elephant Apple with its huge edible fruit. In theory, you need permission to take photographs.

Parque Nacional del Este ① *closed Mon, opens 0530 for joggers, 0800 for others, till 1730, US$0.25, reached from Parque del Este metro station*, is a popular place to relax, especially at weekends. There is a boating lake, a replica of Columbus' Santa María (being renovated since 1991), the Humboldt Planetarium ① *T234 9188, weekend shows, US$0.50*, a number of different sunken lakes featuring caiman and turtles, monkeys, a caged jaguar and a Harpy Eagle in an upsettingly small cage, many types of water birds, a terrarium ① *Sat-Sun, US$0.25*. **Museo de Transporte** ① *Parque Nacional del Este (to which it is connected by a pedestrian overpass), T234 1621, Sun 0900-1630, US$0.25*, includes a large collection of locomotives and old cars.

Other parks

The heavily wooded **Parque Caricuao** ① *Tue-Sun 0900-1700, US$0.20: take metro to Caricuao Zoológico, then 5 min walk up Av Principal La Hacienda*, is at the southwest end of the Metro line, and forms part of the Parque Nacional Macuro. A pleasant day out. The **Parque Los Chorros** ① *US$0.25, getting there: take bus from Los Dos Caminos station to Lomas de Los Chorros*, at the foot of the Avila mountain has impressive waterfalls, also recommended. **El Calvario**, west of El Silencio, with the Arch of Confederation at the entrance, has a good view of Centro Simón Bolívar, but muggings have been reported. It has a small Museo Ornitológico, botanical gardens and a picturesque chapel.

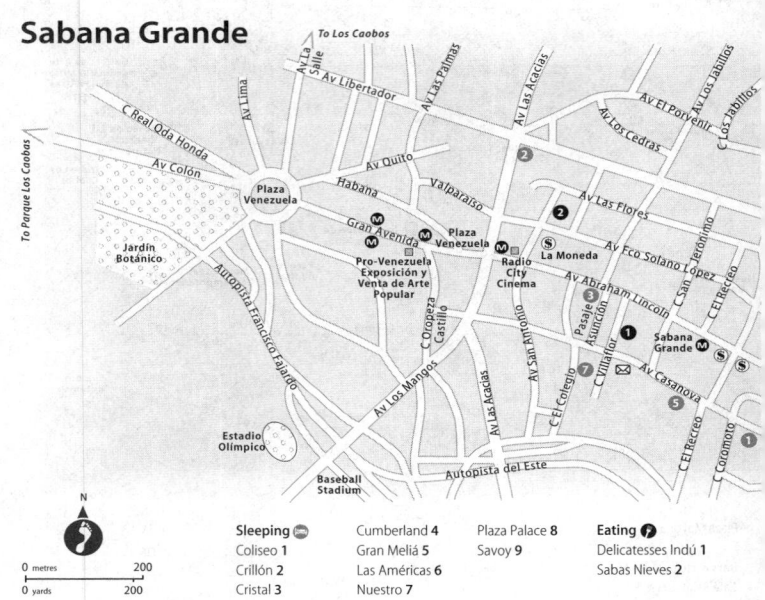

Sabana Grande

Sleeping	Cumberland **4**	Plaza Palace **8**	Eating
Coliseo **1**	Gran Meliá **5**	Savoy **9**	Delicatesses Indú **1**
Crillón **2**	Las Américas **6**		Sabas Nieves **2**
Cristal **3**	Nuestro **7**		

● Sleeping

Cheap *pensiones* are usually full of long-stay residents and have few rooms available for travellers. In the centre all cheap hotels take only short stay customers on Fri afternoon. The cheapest hotels are in the downtown area, but this is not a safe part of town at night, or even in the day with a backpack. Sabana Grande, which has a wide range of hotels, is not safe, either. If you don't want to stay in the suburbs, spend a little more and go to the Chacao, Altamira, La Castellana district. Hotels in the following list are recommended, apart from any minor points mentioned. Hotel prices below do not include 17% tax. The airport tourist office is very helpful and will book hotel rooms. If you book from abroad, make sure you receive written confirmation before beginning your journey. For apartment rental, consult *El Universal* daily paper, small ads columns. The business/ commercial district is southeast of the centre, not on metro.

Central area *p1333, map p1334*
The cheapest hotels are around the Nuevo Circo bus terminal (not a safe area).
LL Caracas Hilton, Av Sur 25 with Av Mexico, T503 5001, www.hiltoncaracas.com.ve. Ageing luxury hotel, excellent business centre, spectacular city views, especially at night, noisy (traffic and a/c), useful long-term luggage deposit and good

Bars & clubs ●
El Maní Es Así **3**

breakfast, nice pool, fax service open to non-residents, very helpful, good sushi bar.
A Plaza Catedral, Blvd Plaza Bolívar, next to Cathedral, T564 2111, hotelplazacatedral@cantv.net. Beautiful location in the colonial part of town, Amex accepted, a/c, some English spoken, good restaurant. Recommended.
D Renovación, Av Este 2 No 154, near Los Caobos and Bellas Artes Metro, T571 0133, www.usuarios.lycos.es/hotelrenovacion. With a/c, modern, lots of restaurants nearby.
E Inter, Animas a Calero, on corner of Av Urdaneta, near Nuevo Circo, T564 0251. Helpful, English spoken, very popular, poor restaurant, accepts credit cards.
E Limón, C Este 10, No 228, near metro Bellas Artes, T572 1968. Safe, parking, often recommended.

San Bernardino *map p1334*
A residential area 2 km north of Bellas Artes metro.
A Avila, Av Jorge Washington, T555 3000, www.hotel avila.com.ve. Set in tranquil gardens some distance from the centre, very pleasant, good service, most staff speak English and German, fans, mosquito screens, pool, Metrobus nearby, very good restaurant and poolside bar, travel agency, phones accept Visa/MasterCard.

Sabana Grande/Chacaíto *p1335, map p1336*
Many restaurants and shops here, but despite being well-placed for metro, safety has deteriorated greatly. Many hotels are in the Av Las Acacias/Av Casanova area, the majority are short-stay.
LL Gran Meliá, Av Casanova y El Recreo, T762 8111, gran.melia.caracas@solmelia.com. Top-ranking hotel with all facilities, business centre, restaurants (including Japanese and pizzería), gym, piano bar.
L Las Américas, C Los Cerritos, T951 7133, www.hotellasamericas.com.ve. Modern tower blocks, tiny roof pool and restaurant, taxi service to airport, good value.
AL Chacao Cumberland, Av Santa Lucía con Av Principal del Bosque, Chacaíto, T952 9833, www.hotelescumberland.com. Small, internet connections in rooms, bar and restaurant, good business facilities.
AL Coliseo, Av Casanova y Coromoto, T762 7916, www.hotelcoliseo.com.ve. A/c, good breakfast, more expensive rooms with internet connection, in the new tower, 100 m from Sabana Grande metro.
A Cumberland, 2da Av de las Delicias, T762 9961, www.hotelescumberland.com. Reasonable, nice restaurant, taxi service to airport.
B Crillón, Av Libertador, esq Av Las Acacias, T761 4411, www.hotelcrillon.com.ve. Highrise block, good service, comfortable, good bar.

El Libro Italiano, Pasaje La Concordia (between Sabana Grande pedestrian street and Av Fco Solano López). Italian bookshop.

Handicrafts Good quality Sun craft market between Museo de Bellas Artes and Museo de Historia Natural (metro Bellas Artes). Indian market on southwest corner of Plaza Chacaíto has selection of Venezuelan, Peruvian and Ecuadorean crafts.

Labady, Sabana Grande 98. Beautifully made gold jewellery, English spoken.

Pro-Venezuela Exposición y Venta de Arte Popular, on Gran Avenida, Plaza Venezuela (opposite Torre La Previsora). Sells Venezuelan crafts, very crowded, no prices, bargain hard.

Malls The CCCT shopping centre is worth a visit, as is the **Centro Comercial Plaza Las Américas**, mostly for fashion stores and beachwear.

Centro Sambil, Av Libertador, 1 block south of Chacao Metro. One of the largest in South America, with every type of shop.

San Ignacio, several blocks north of Chacao Metro. Very exclusive.

▲ Activities and tours

Caracas p1332, maps p1332, p1334 and p1336
Baseball Season is Oct-Jan. Sports clubs include the Social Centre of the **British Commonwealth Association**, Quinta Alborada, Av 7 with Transversal 9, Altamira, T261 3060, bar and swimming pool, British and Commonwealth visitors only, entry fee according to length of stay. The sports club run by the *Tamanaco Hotel* is open to non- guests and suitable for people staying a short time.

Tours
Alpitour, Torre Centro, Centro Parque Boyacá, of 11, Av Sucre, Los Dos Caminos, T283 1433, www.alpi-group.com.ve. Tours throughout Venezuela, English spoken, good for flights and advice. Also does 'flying safari' tours in private plane. Recommended.

Birding Venezuela, Edificio Meromary, p 3, of 3-C, C José Félix Rivas con Bolívar, T266 5766, www.birdingvenezuela.com. Run by experienced Englishman Chris Sharpe, also natural history tours.

Cacao Travel, C Andromeda, Qta Orquidea, El Peñón, T977 1234, www.cacaotravel.com. Tours and lodges throughout Venezuela, particularly Canaima, the Orinoco Delta, the Llanos and Los Roques. Recommended.

Candes Turismo, office in lobby of *Hilton* and Edif Celeste, Av Abraham Lincoln, T953 4710. Helpful, English, Italian, German spoken.

Cóndor Verde, Av Caura, Torre Humboldt, Prados del Este, T975 4306, www.condor verdetravel.com. Operate throughout the country, well-established, German run.

KuMeKa Tours, Torre Altocentro, C Negrín, p 1, T762 8356, F761 8538, kumekatours@cantv.net. Tours throughout Venezuela, helpful.

Lost World Adventures, Edif 3-H, p 6, Oficina 62, Av Abraham Lincoln, T761 1108, lwaccs@cantv.net. Tours to Roraima and Canaima.

Natura Raid, Av Libertador, Torre EXA Piso 1, Oficina 101, T740 6546, www.naturaraid.com. Travel and tourist agency.

Natoura Adventure Tours, C 24, 8-237, Merida 5101, T252 4216, www.natoura.com.

Orinoco Tours, Edif Galerías Bolívar, p 7, Blvd Sabana Grande, T761 8431, www.orinocotours.com. Flights and tours, very helpful, German run.

Selma Viajes, Av Blandín, Centro San Ignacio, Torre Este, p 3, La Castellana, T266 6489, www.selma.com.ve. Run recommended excursions to Canaima.

VenezuelaX, Av Sanz, Edif Carabobo p 4, El Marqués, T234 4106/ 0414-255 1591, www.VenezuelaX.com. Specializes in adventure of all types, on land, water and in the air, for all levels, good food, high standards. They have a base camp south of Barinas for trekking, mountain biking and rafting trips.

Tours to the Llanos Campamento La Llanada, Centro Integral Santa Rosa de Lima, p 1, of 103, Santa Rosa de Lima, T993 1315, www.lallanada.com.

◉ Transport

Caracas p1332, maps p1332, p1334 and p1336
Air
The airport, 28 km from Caracas at La Guaira port, has 2 terminals, Maiquetía (national) and Simón Bolívar (international), which are 5 mins' walk apart; taxis take a circular route, fare US$2.50; airport authorities run shuttle buses every 10 mins from 0700. Flight enquiries T031-355 2858; passenger assistance T031-355 1310; Maiquetía information T0212-303 1526; Police T031-355 1226. The helpful tourist office at the international airport has good maps and some is English spoken. Open 0700-2400. They will book hotels and reconfirm flights. The tourist office in the national terminal is open 0700-2100. Many facilities close 1 Jan, including duty free and money exchanges. Duty free shops close 2230. At Simón Bolívar: several *casas de cambio* open 24 hrs (count notes carefully); also *Banco Industrial* branch in international terminal and another, less crowded, in baggage reclaim area. If changing TCs you may be asked for your receipt of purchase;

commission 2.5%. There are cash machines for Visa, Amex and MasterCard. Best to change some cash at the official rate here, then find the parallel rate once at your destination. Pharmacy, bookshops, basement café (good value meals and snacks, open 0600-2400, hard to find); cafés and bars on 1st floor viewing terrace also good value. No official left luggage; so look after your belongings in both terminals. Direct dial phone calls to USA from AT&T booth in international departure lounge. CANTV at Gates 15 and 24, open 0700-2100, long-distance, international and fax services.

Always allow plenty of time when going to the airport, whatever means of transport you are using: the route can be very congested (2 hrs in daytime, but only 30 mins at 0430). Allow at least 2 hrs checking-in time before your flight. **Note** In early 2006 one of the bridges on the highway from the airport to Caracas collapsed. As a result traffic takes alternative routes, some of which go through unsafe areas. Moreover some flights are diverted to other airports, eg Valencia. At the time of writing the bridge was expected to reopen in Mar 2006. You are advised to check in advance, allow a minimum of 3 hrs to get to the airport and arrive, if possible, in daylight.

Freelance **taxi** drivers crowd the terminal and it is hard to verify their trustworthiness. Some are licensed, but some are pirates. **Warning** On no account go with an unlicensed driver. We have received reports of travellers being robbed at gunpoint in these cabs which may have a sign but no yellow number plates. To be safe, especially if a first-time visitor on your own, take an official taxi. These vehicles are all black, with an oval, yellow logo, which is also displayed at the counter in the arrivals hall. Buy a ticket for the journey into town and you will be accompanied to the taxi by a member of staff. Double check the driver's ID.Prices are listed by the sliding doors, outside

which the taxis wait. US$$15 to Caracas city centre, US$30 if late at night; US$23.50 to Altamira. Another option is to call a radio taxi. **Teletaxi**, T753 4155 have been recommended; they have an office inside the airport. Also **Aerotaxi**, T461 8586. If you think the licensed taxi driver is overcharging you, make a complaint to **Inatur**, or tell him you will report him to the Departamento de Protección al Consumidor. Drivers may only surcharge you for luggage (US$0.50 per large bag), but not if the fare is already agreed. From the city centre to the airport is around US$10-15.

The airport **shuttle bus** (blue and white with 'Aeropuerto Internacional' on the side) leaves from east end of terminal, left out of exit. To airport, catch it under the flyover at Bolívar and Av Sur 17, 250 m from Bellas Artes metro (poorly lit at night, not recommended to wait here in the dark); from 0700 to 2300, bus leaves when there are enough passengers, 1 hr or so, depending on traffic, US$3.50. If heading for a hotel in Chacao or Altamira on arrival, ask to be dropped off at Gato Negro metro station (same fare) and take metro from there (with luggage only at off-peak times). The shuttle bus or *por puesto* to airport can also be caught at Gato Negro metro station. Watch your belongings around Gato Negro.

Airport information Passengers leaving Caracas on international flights must reconfirm their reservations not less than 72 hrs in advance by telephone or in person; not less than 24 hours for national flights: if you fail to do this, you lose all rights to free accommodation, food, transport, etc if your flight is cancelled and may lose your seat if the plane is fully booked. Beware of counterfeit tickets; buy only from agencies. If told by an agent that a flight is fully booked, try at the airport anyway. International passengers must check in at least two hours before departure or they may lose their seat to someone on a waiting list.

Venezuela Caracas Listings

Bus

Local See Getting around, page 1332.

Long distance The *Terminal Oriente* at Guarenas for **eastern destinations** is clean, modern and relatively safe. City buses leave Nuevo Circo bullring every 30 mins, US$0.50, 45 mins, 1 hr in rush hour; or take *por puesto* from Petare metro station, an easier option but take a taxi at night. Taxi to terminal US$7.50. Bus from terminal to centre: turn left outside main entrance towards main parking area where buses wait; get off at Bellas Artes or El Silencio, US$0.50. Not recommended at night: take a taxi.

The La Bandera terminal for all **western** destinations is a 500 m, unsafe walk from La Bandera metro station on Line 3. City buses that pass are prominently marked 'La Bandera'. Give yourself plenty of time to find the bus you need although there are bus agents who will assist in finding a ticket for your destination. Tickets are sold in advance except for nearby destinations such as **Maracay** and **Valencia**, which leave as soon as full from a separate section (turn right on entering the terminal). For long distance buses use the stairs just inside the terminal entrance. Those first on get the best seats so it is advisable to arrive an hour before departure. Buses may also leave early. There is a left luggage office, telephone office, cash machines and a restaurant and many food and drink kiosks.

Buses to places near to Caracas leave from across the road from the old Nuevo Circo bus station, via the underpass (eg **Los Teques, Higuerote, Catia La Mar, La Guaira**). From La Hoyada metro, don't go under the bridge, walk straight down the road for 300 m.

On public holidays buses are usually fully booked leaving Caracas and drivers often make long journeys without stopping. Sat and Sun morning are also bad for travel into/out of Caracas. Always take identification when booking a long-distance journey. Times and fares of buses are given under destinations. Buses going west on the Panamericana route are not recommended because the old road suffers from many accidents.

Autoexpresos Ejecutivos, terminal at Av Principal de Bello Campo, Quinta Marluz (between Chacao and Altamira metro stops), T266 2321, www.aeroexpresos.com.ve, to **Maracay, Valencia, Barquisimeto, Maracaibo, Maturín** and **Puerto La Cruz**, reserve 2 days in advance, except for buses leaving on Fri (no left luggage). Fares are 3-4 times higher than other companies, but worth it. **Rodovias**, terminal at Av Libertador con Boulevard Amador Bendayan, between Plaza Venezuela and Colegio de Ingenieros metro, T577 7765/577 7011, www.rodovias.com.ve.

Excellent long distance buses to Ciudad Bolívar, Ciudad Guayana, Maturín, Carúpano, Cumaná, Puerto La Cruz and Valencia.

International buses Ormeño (T/F471 7205, www.grupo-ormeno.com) has 1 bus a week to **Bogotá** (US$75), **Cali** (US$90), **Quito** (US$110), **Guayaquil** (US$140), **Lima** (US$180); Mon 1300, safe, comfortable, a/c, video, toilet; terminal at Final Av San Martín detras del Bloque de Armas, 10 mins from Metro La Paz.

Car

Car hire Self-drive cars (Hertz, Avis, Budget, Dollar, ACO) are available at the airport (offices open 0700-2100, Avis till 2300, good service) and in town. They are cheaper than guided excursions for less than full loads. Rates are given on page .

Metro

Operates 0530-2300, no smoking, luggage allowed only at off-peak times. There are 3 lines: Line 1 (west-east) from Propatria to Palo Verde; Line 2 (north-south), from El Silencio to Las Adjuntas, with connection to Caricuao Zoológico; Line 3, south from Plaza Venezuela via La Bandera to El Valle, plus metrobus El Valle-Los Teques; www.metrodecaracas.com.ve. Tickets cost US$0.15-0.20 per journey; 10-journey tickets (Multi Abono) are available at US$1.65 (US$1.85 including Metrobus). Student discounts are available with ISIC card; apply at Parque del Este station. Metrobuses connect with the Metro system: get transfer tickets (*boleto integrado*, US$0.20) for services to southern districts, route maps displayed at stations - retain ticket after exit turnstile. Good selection of maps at shops in Altamira and La California stations. Line 4 is under construction, running from Capuchinos on Line 2 to Parque del Este, via Parque Central, Plaza Venezuela, Las Mercedes and Chuao.

Motorcycle

Motorcycles may not be ridden in Caracas between 2300 and 0500.

Taxi

Even though they are a legal requirement, taxi-meters are never used. Fares must be negotiated in advance; always offer 10% less than the driver's first quote. Most city trips are US$2 absolute minimum during the day (most fares US$5). Taxi drivers are authorized to charge an extra 20% on night trips after 1800, on Sun and all holidays, and US$1 for answering telephone calls. After 1800 drivers are selective about where they want to go. Beware of taxi drivers trying to renegotiate fixed rates because your destination is in 'a difficult area'. See warning above under Air about pirate taxis. See also under Air (or in Yellow Pages) for radio taxis. **Note**: Never tell a taxi driver it is your first visit to Caracas.

❶ Directory

Caracas *p1332, maps p1332, p1334 and p1336*
Airline offices Domestic: Aeropostal, Av Paseo Colón, Torre Polar Oeste, pb, Plaza Venezuela, T708 6222, or Torre Letonia, Av Principal La Castellana, T266 1059, or Hotel Tamanaco, or T800 284 6637. **Aereotuy**, Edif Gran Sabana, p 5, Av Lincoln y Blvd Sabana Grande, T761 6231. **Aserca**, Edif Taeca, C Guaicaipuro, El Rosal, T0800-648 8356, or 905 5333. **Avensa**, Edif Atlántida, Av Universidad (Metro La Hoyada), T976 5240, F975 444 (domestic airport T355 1479, international airport T355 1889). **Avior**, Torre Clemente, Av Venezuela, El Rosal, T955 3811. **Conviasa**, Simón Bolívar international airport, T355 12411, or T0500-2668 4272. **El Sol de América**, T959 1072. **Láser**, T0501-527 3700, airport T202 0100 ext 600. **Rutaca**, Centro Seguros La Paz, Av Fco de Miranda, Nivel Mezzanina, loc C-12, La California Sur, T235-6035, or T0800-788 2221. **Santa Bárbara**, Av Fco de Miranda, Centro Lido, Nivel Miranda, loc M25, T204 4000. See Getting around, page 1330 for websites. **International**: **Aerolíneas Argentinas**, Calle Guaicaipuro, Torre Hener p 1, of 1A, El Rosal, T951 3005. **Air France**, Parque Cristal, Torre Este, p 2, Los Palos Grandes, T285 2843, www.airfrance.com.ve, T0800-100 5655. **Alitalia**, Edif Atlantic, p 5, Av Andrés Bello, Los Palos Grandes, T312 5000, www.ali talia.com.ve. **American**, Torre ING Bank, p 7, Centro Letonia, T209 8111. **Avianca**, Av Tamanaco, Torre Norte del edif JW Marriott, loc 21 y 22, El Rosal, T200 5725. **British Airways**, Torre Copérnico (oeste), p 3, oficina 03-03, Centro San Ignacio, La Castellana, T266 0122. **Continental**, Centro Lido, Torre E, p 6, Av F de Miranda, T0800-100 3198. **Cubana**, Edif Atlantic, p 4, oficina 5, Av Andrés Bello y 1ra Transversal, T286 9890. **Delta**, Torre E, p 8, Centro Lido, Av Fco de Miranda, El Rosal, T0800-100 3453. **Iberia**, Av Fco de Miranda, edif Parque Cristal, Torre Este, p 9, Los Palos Grandes, T284 0020. **LAN**, Torre Kleper, of 3-1, Centro San Ignacio, Av Blandín, T267 9526. **Lufthansa**, Centro Torre Conaisa, p 1, Av San Felipe, La Castellana, T210 2100. **Varig**, Centro Emp Los Ruices, p 3, oficinas 316-317, Av Principal de Los Ruices, T202 2810. **Banks** See also Currency, page 1328. **Citibank** will exchange Citicorp cheques. **Unibanca** branches for **Visa** transactions. For Visa ATMs, branches of **Banco de Venezuela**. For cash advances on **MasterCard**, and ATM go to branches of **Banco Mercantil**. To change **American Express** TCs, try **Corp Banca**, Av Principal de La Castellana entre Blandín y Los

Chaguaramas, Torre Corp Banca, La Castellana, T206 2677, mornings and afternoons. They ask for ID and proof of purchase. For **exchange** and Amex travel services go to **Italcambio**. They also change Visa TCs, require proof of TC purchase, commission 0.50%, open Mon-Fri till 1630, Sat till 1200. Offices at: Veroes y Av Urdaneta (or **Visesta CA** opposite, highly recommended, accepts Eurocheques, also for travel arrangements, Walter Kleebinder speaks several languages and is very helpful, T562 4698/5333); Av Casanova entre 1 y 2 C Bello Monte (Sabana Grande), T761 8244; Edif Belmont, Av L Roche (Altamira Sur), T267 3389; Las Mercedes, Simón Bolívar Airport (may limit transaction to US$100, open public holidays), T288 7877, www.italviajes.com. Amex services also at **Quo Vadis**, Av Principal La Castellana, Banco Lara p 8, T261 7782, mmassimo@ quovadis.com.ve. **La Moneda**, Centro Financiero Latino, Urdaneta, p 8, and Av Fco Solano, 1 block from Plaza Venezuela metro, opposite El Molino Rosso restaurant and next to Banco Profesional, open Mon-Fri only. **Confinanzas**, Centro Comercial Paseo Las Mercedes, Local PA-CI, open 0800-1200, 1400-1700, 1% commission usually charged on TCs. **MVS Cambios**, Av Francisco Solano López, between C El Cristo and Los Manguitos, Edif Torre Oasis, Sabana Grande, less waiting, good rates. **Viajes Febres Parra**, Av Fco de Miranda, basement of Centro Lido (not well signed). Good rates for US$ and TCs, no queues.
Cultural centres British Council, Torre Credicard, p 3, Av Principal del Bosque, Chacaíto, T952 9965, F952 9651, www.britcoun.org/ venezuela. Great internet café, magazines, newspapers, film library, courses. El Centro Venezolano-Americano, Av Principal José Martí, Las Mercedes, T993 7911, www.cva.org.ve. Good free library of books in English, and free concerts. Also Spanish courses, 8 different levels, US$7.30 per hr, highly recommended. Asociación Cultural Humboldt (Goethe Institut), Av Jorge Washington con Juan Germán Roscio, San Bernardino, T552 7634, www.internet.ve/asohum. Library, lectures, films, concerts, Spanish courses.
Embassies and consulates Australia has no embassy in Caracas, see www.venezuela. embassy.gov.au. **Austria**, Edificio Plaza C, PH, Londres entre Caroní y New York, Las Mercedes, T993 9844, www.austria.org.ve. **Belgium**, 10a Transversal con 9a Transversal, Altamira, T263 3334, www.diplomatie.be/caracas. **Brazil**, Edif 'Centro Gerencial Mohedano', p 6, between C Los Chaguaramas y Av Mohedano, La Castellana, T261 5505, www.embajada brasil.org.ve/, Mon-Fri 0830-1230. Visa (valid for 3 months maximum) costs US$15, you need a photo, and it takes 24 hrs. **Canada**, Av Fco de Miranda con Altamira Sur, Altamira, T600 3000,

www.dfait-maeci.gc.ca/ latin-america/caracas.
Colombia, C Guaicaipuro entre Plaza Brion y Av
Casanova, Chacaíto, T951 3631,
colombia@net-uno.net, Mon-Fri 0800-1300 for
visas, you need a photo and US$12.50, the
process can take anything from 10 mins to 1 day.
Denmark, Av Fco de Miranda, Centro Seguros
Sudamérica, p 10, of 10 D, El Rosal, T952 8255,
www.dtccaracas.um.dk/da. Mon-Thu 0800-1600,
Fri 0800-1300. **Finland**, C Sorocaima entre Av
Venezuela y Av Tamanaco, Edif Atrium, p 1, El
Rosal, T952 4111. **France**, C Madrid and Av
Trinidad, Las Mercedes, T909 6500,
www.francia.org.ve. Mon-Thu 0800-1300,
1400-1700, Fri 0800-1415. **Germany**, Torre La
Castellana, p 10, Av Eugenio Mendoza con C José
Angel Lamas, La Castellana, T261 0181,
www.caracas.diplo.de/es/Startseite.html. Mon,
Tue, Thu 0715-1230, 1300-1545, Wed 0715-1230,
1300-1615, Fri 0715-1245. **Guyana**, Quinta
Roraima, Av El Paseo, Prados del Este, T977 1158,
www.guyana.org/spanish/venezuela_embassy.ht
ml. Open for visa Mon-Thu 0830-1530, Fri
0830-1500, issued on the same day if you're early,
need passport, airline ticket, yellow fever
certificate and 2 photos. **Israel**, Av Principal Los
Ruices at Av Fco de Miranda, Centro Empresarial
Miranda, of 4-D, T239 4511,
http://caracas.mfa.gov.il. Mon-Fri 0900-1200.
Italy, Edif Atrium, C Sorocaima entre Av
Tamanaco y Venezuela, El Rosal, T952 7311,
http://sedi.esteri.it/ambcaracas/. **Japan**, Av San
Felipe con 2da Transversal, Edif Bancaracas, p 12,
La Castellana, T261 8333,
www.ve.emb-japan.go.jp. **Netherlands**, Edif San
Juan, p 9, San Juan Bosco and Av Transversal 2,
Altamira, T276 9300, www.mfa.nl/car. **New
Zealand** ad honorem consul in Mexico, Wendy
Tipping, T+5 255 5283 1460, kiwimexico@
compuserve.com.mx. **Spain**, Av Mohedano, entre
1 y 2 Transversal, Quinta Marmolejo, La
Castellana, T263 2855, www.embespven.com.
Mon-Fri 0830-1330. **Sweden**, Torre Phelps, p 19,
Plaza Venezuela, T781 6976. **Switzerland**, Centro
Letonia, Torre ING-Bank, p 15, La Castellana,
T267 9585, vertretung@car.rep.admin.ch.
0900-1200. **Suriname**, 4a Av ES, Quinta 41,
Altamira, T263 8094, embsur1@cantv.net.
Trinidad, beside the Suriname Embassy, Quinta
Serrana, 4a Av, between 7a and 8a Transversal,

Altamira, T261 5796, www.embajadatt.com. Visa
costs US$20, you need 2 photos, it can take up to
1 week. **UK**, Torre La Castellana, p 11, Av Principal
La Castellana, T263 8411, emergency phone
T0416-626 2971, www.britain.org.ve. Mon-Thu
0800-1230, 1330-1630, Fri 0800-1315, consulate
Mon-Fri 0800-1230, plus Wed only 1330-1600.
USA, C F with C Suapure, Colinas de Valle Arriba,
take metro to Chacaíto then taxi, US$5, T975
6411, PO Box 62291, www.embajadausa.org.ve.
Internet   In CANTV Centros de
comunicaciones and independent outlets.
Average price US$1-2 per hr. **Cyber Café 2000**,
Galerías Bolívar, Blvd Sabana Grande, 0900-1900.
Cybercafé Madrid, Acuario floor, Centro Sambil,
Chacao. **Torre Capriles**, ground floor, Plaza
Venezuela, Mon-Fri 0900-1800. In food hall, **Torre
Centrum**, opposite McDonald's near Sabana
Grande metro. **Cyber Office 2020**, Av Casanova
near El Arabito, Sabana Grande. **MundoNet**, in
Altamira metro, Plaza Francia exit. See also **British
Council**, above.
Medical services   Hospital de Clínicas, Av
Panteón y Av Alameda, San Bernardino, T574 2011.
Post offices   Central at Urdaneta y Norte 4,
near Plaza Bolívar. Efficient overseas package
service; packages should be ready to send. **Lista
de correos** costs US$0.50, Mon-Fri 0700-1945,
Sat 0800-1700, Sun 0800-1200. *Ipostel* office in
Centro Comercial Cediáz, on Av Casanova
between C Villaflor and San Jerónimo, open
Mon-Fri office hrs, Sat till 1200; also at airport.
Telephones   CANTV, on 1st floor of Centro
Plaza on Francisco Miranda in the east (corner of
Andrés Bello between metros Parque del Este
and Altamira), open Mon-Sat 0800-1945, T284
7932, phone cards sold. Also public phones in the
Metro stations and along Blvd Sabana Grande
(Abraham Lincoln). Phone and fax at **Cables
Internacionales**, Santa Capilla a Mijares,
Edif San Mauricio, planta baja, Mon-Sat
0700-1900, near Capitolio Metro, 1 block east
of main Post Office then ½ block north.
Useful addresses   ONIDEX for visa renewal,
Av Baralt, Edif 1000, El Silencio, T483 2070.
Mon-Fri 0730-1630. (Don't believe anyone who
tells you visa extensions are not available.)
Touring y Automóvil Club de Venezuela, Torre
Phelps, p 15, of A y C, Plaza Venezuela, T781
9743, tacvzla@cantv.net.

Around Caracas

Between the capital and the Caribbean coast is the national park of El Avila, not only a popular recreational area for caraqueños, but also a refuge for wildlife within earshot of the city. The coast itself is also a favourite weekend escape, although don't expect get-away-from-it-all seclusion. Nor, at weekends, can you expect to have Colonia Tovar to yourself, a German immigrant town to which city folk flock for the local produce and pleasant climate.

Monte Avila → *Colour map 1, grid A6.*

The 85,192-ha **Parque Nacional El Avila** forms the northern boundary of Caracas. The green slopes rise steeply from both the city and from the central Caribbean coast. Despite being so close to the capital, the fauna includes red howler monkeys, jaguar and puma. There are also several species of poisonous snake. Access to the park is from Caracas where there are several marked entrances along the Cota Mil (Avenida Boyacá), which are designed for hikers. Access from the old Caracas-La Guaira road which crosses the park from north to south on the western side was damaged by the heavy rains of December 1999. The Caribbean side of the park was worst affected, but all parts of the park are open. For information see www.el-avila.com.

A **cable railway** (*teleférico*) ① *daily 1000-1930, US$9.35, US$5 for over 65s, free for children under 3*, runs up Monte Avila from Avenida Perimetral de Maripérez. The *Humboldt Hotel* on the summit has been refurbished, but not reopened (a casino and nightclub may be built). Camping is possible with permission. A dirt road runs from La Puerta section of San Bernardino to the summit, 45 minutes by 4WD. A recommended trip is to ride up in a vehicle and hike back down (note that it is cold at the summit, average temperature 13° C).

Listed below are three good places to start a hike in the park. Hikers should go in groups of at least three, for mountain and personal safety (Monte Avila is not a dangerous place, but the occasional thief lurks there). You should have a park permit from *Inparques* in Caracas to camp. Always take water and something for the cold at altitude. The unfit should not attempt any of the hikes. Full descriptions of the hiking routes are given in the *Footprint Venezuela*.

Pico Naiguatá (2,765 m) This is a very strenuous hike. Take the metro to La California, then a bus going up Avenida Sanz, ask for the Centro Comercial El Marqués. From there walk up Avenida Sanz towards Cota Mil (Avenida Boyacá), about four blocks. At the end of Avenida Sanz, underneath the bridge, is the entrance to the Naiguatá trail. In about 40 minutes you reach La Julia *guardaparques* station, where you have to pay US$0.50 entrance.

Pico Oriental (2,600 m) From the Altamira metro station take a bus to 'La entrada de Sabas Nieves', where the *Tarzilandia* restaurant is. From here a dirt road leads up to the Sabas Nieves *guardaparques* station (about 40 minutes). The path to Pico Oriental starts at the back of Sabas Nieves and is extremely easy to follow. **Note:** Paths beyond Sabas Nieves are shut in dry season (roughly February-June depending on the year) to prevent forest fires.

Hotel Humboldt (2,150 m) This is a relatively easy route of three hours. Take the metro bus from Bellas Artes station to El Avila stop, US$0.50; opposite is a grocery. Turn the corner and walk two blocks up towards the mountain. At the top of the street turn left; almost immediately on your right is the park entrance. **Note:** This area is not safe before 0800 or after dark. Plenty of people take this route, starting 0830-0900, giving enough time to get up and down safely and in comfort.

Litoral Central

The Litoral Central is the name given to the stretch of Caribbean Coast directly north of Caracas. A paved road runs east from Catia La Mar, past the airport and then through the towns of Maiquetía, La Guaira and Macuto. This became the state of Vargas in January 1999 and in December that year was the focus of Venezuela's worst natural disaster of the 20th century. Prolonged heavy rains on deforested hillsides caused flash floods and landslides, killing and causing to disappear an estimated 30,000 people and leaving 400,000 homeless. It is planned to turn the whole area into a national park. From La Guaira a panoramic road runs to the beaches at Chichiriviche de la Costa, Puerto Cruz (nice beach, no shade, bars) and Puerto Maya (very nice beach with shade and services).

La Guaira, Venezuela's main port dates back to 1567. It achieved its greatest importance in the 18th century when the Basque Guipuzcoana Company held the royal trading monopoly. Much of the city was severely damaged in the 1999 floods.

north of Maracay to the Caribbean, excluding the coastal towns of Ocumare, Cata and Choroní, and south to the valleys of Aragua and the villages of Vigírima, Mariara and Turmero. The dry season runs from December to March and the rainy season (although still agreeable) is from April to November. The variation in altitude gives a great range of vegetation, including lower and upper cloud forests. For information refer to *Parque Nacional de Henri Pittier - Lista de Aves*, by Miguel Lentino and Mary Lou Goodwin, 1993.

Two paved roads cut through the Park. The Ocumare (western) road climbs to the 1,128 m high Portachuelo pass, guarded by twin peaks (38 km from Maracay). At the pass is Rancho Grande, the uncompleted palace/hotel Gómez was building when he died (in a state of disrepair). It is close to the bird migratory routes, September and October are the best months. There are many trails in the vicinity. Permits to visit the park and walk the trails near the Rancho Grande biological research station are available here.

Aragua Coast

To Cata and Cuyagua The road to the coast from Rancho Grande goes through **Ocumare de la Costa** (*Population: 6,140, 48 km from Maracay*), to La Boca de Ocumare and **El Playón** (hotels and restaurants at both places). The road is very busy at weekends. 20 minutes west by boat is **La Ciénaga**, a pretty place, but little shade. A few kilometres east is **Bahía de Cata**, now overdeveloped, particularly at the west end, while the smaller beach at **Catita** is reached by fishing boat ferries (10 minutes, US$1). In Cata town (5 km inland, *population* of town and beach 3,120) is the small colonial church of San Francisco; devil dancers here fulfil an ancient vow by dancing non-stop through the morning of 27 July each year. Cuyagua beach, unspoilt, is 23 km further on at the end of the road. Good surfing, dangerous rips for swimmers. Devil dancers here too, on movable date in July or August.

To Choroní The second (eastern) road through the Parque Nacional Henri Pittier is spectacular and goes over a more easterly pass (1,830 m), to **Santa Clara de Choroní**, a beautiful colonial town. The Fiesta de San Juan on 31 May is worth seeing.

Choroní is a good base for walking. There are numerous opportunities for exploring the unmarked trails, many of them originate in picturesque spots such as the river pools, 'pozos', of El Lajao (beware of the dangerous whirlpool), and Los Colores, 6 km above Choroní. Other recommended 'pozos' are La Virgen, 10 km from Choroní, and La Nevera, 11 km away.

Puerto Colombia and around → *Phone code: 0243. Colour map 1, grid A6. Population: 7,000.*
Just beyond Choroní is the fishing village of **Puerto Colombia**, with the dazzling white beach of Playa Grande, five minutes' walk across the river. Bus journeys start and end here. At weekends drummers drum and dancers gyrate, and the beach gets crowded and littered. At other times it's peaceful and attractive, with brightly painted fishing boats in the river and frigate birds wheeling overhead. If swimming, beware the strong undertow. Many fishing boats are for hire in the harbour, US$55 for a day trip to one of several nearby beaches. Launches to **Cepe**, 30 minutes east, US$23, boats usually take 6-10 people, or *por puesto* fishing boat from the port US$2.35 per person. Many places serve fish, salad and *tostones* for about US$4.65. From the beautiful unspoiled beach there are fishing and scuba diving trips. The latter, with guide and equipment, explore the only bit of coral on this stretch of the coast. At Cepe's west end, you can climb the hill and descend to **Playa Escondida**, a deserted but more rocky beach. Other beaches include: to the east, before Cepe, Valle Seco (no services, no shade) and **Chuao**. To the west are: Diario (small, no shade), Aroa (lonely, with palms) and Uricao (also isolated); boat to Uricao US$20.

⊜ Sleeping

Maracay *p1347*
Budget hotels are located in the streets around Plaza Girardot.
AL Italo, Av Las Delicias, Urb La Soledad, T232 1576, www.hotelitalo.com.ve. A/c, 4-star, on bus route, very pleasant, small rooftop pool, good Italian restaurant, *El Fornaio*. Recommended.
B Posada El Limón, Calle de Pinal 64, El Limón suburb, near Parque Nacional Henri Pittier,

T283 4925, T0414-444 1915 (mob), caribean@ telcel.net.ve. Dutch owned, some way from centre, relaxed and very pleasant, family atmosphere, spacious rooms with a/c and hot water, laundry, pool, good restaurant, internet, excursions to Parque Nacional Henri Pittier in 4WD with guide US$100, airport pick-up/drop-off.
C Caroní, Ayacucho Norte 197, Bolívar, T554 4465. A/c, hot showers, comfortable. Recommended.

C **Princesa Plaza**, Av Miranda Este entre Fuerzas Aéreas y Av Bermúdez, T232 2052. Commercial hotel, 1 block east of Plaza Bolívar, convenient, inexpensive restaurant.
D **Central**, Av Santos Michelena 6, T245 2834. Safe and central.
D **San Luis**, Carabobo Sur 13, off the main shopping street. Well-kept, welcoming.

Parque Nacional Henri Pittier *p1347*
E pp **Rancho Grande biological research station**. Plenty of beds, US$7.50 pp per night, use of kitchen facilities, take warm sleeping bag, candles and food; nearest supplies at El Limón, 20 km before Rancho Grande.
F pp **El Cocuy Mountain Refuge** (price is for accommodation only, **A** full board), T0416-747 3833. Sleeping in hammocks, tours arranged with bi-lingual Spanish/ English guides.

Aragua Coast *p1348*
Ocumare de la Costa
AL **De La Costa Eco-Lodge**, California 23, , T993 1986, 0414-460 0655 (mob), www.eco venezuela.com. With bath, outdoor bar serving food, swimming pool, excursions, tours included in price, equipment hire, specialist bilingual guides.

Choroní
AL **Hacienda El Portete**, C El Cementerio, T991 1255, www.elportete.com. Colonial- style large grounds, a/c, hot water, restaurant, pool, many facilities for children, excursions.
A **Hacienda La Aljorra**, T0212-237 7462 (Caracas), panzades@cantv.net. Breakfast and dinner included, hot water, 200-year old cacao hacienda in 62 ha of wooded hillside, variable service.
C **La Gran Posada** , 5 km north of Choroní on a steep hillside above Maracay road, T217 0974. Neat, pleasant bar and restaurant.

Puerto Colombia and around *p1348*
A **Posada El Malecón**, El Malecón 1, T991 1107, www.geocities.com/posadaelmalecon. A/c, hot water, trips arranged, pricey but a cut above the average and 50% discount Mon-Thu.
A **Posada Pittier**, on road to Choroní, T/F991 1028, www.posadapittier.com. Small, immaculate rooms, a/c, good meals, helpful, garden. Recommended.
A-B **Posada de Choroní**, Calle Principal, 2 blocks from Malecón, T991 1191, www.laposadade choroni.3a2.com. Rooms with a/c and TV, cheaper without TV, cheaper still with fan, hot water, colonial with rooms off central garden, parking.
B **Brisas del Mar**, C Principal at the port. Noisy but comfortable, a/c, TV, a bit overpriced, but OK.
B **Hostal Vista Mar**, C Colón at western end, T991 1250, www.hostalvistamar.com. Pleasant, terraces with hammockas and sea view, fan, parking.

C **Costa Brava**, Murillo 9, near Malecón, T991 1059, suarezjf@cantv.net. Cheaper without bath, basic, ceiling fans, laundry facilities, parking, good food, English spoken, family-run. Recommended.
C **La Montañita**, Murillo 6, T991 1132, choroni_indio@hotmail.com. Popular, nice courtyard, charming owners, packages available (**B** including all meals).
C **Posada La Parchita**, Trino Rangel, T991 1233, 0416-832 2790 (mob). Including breakfast, rooms set around a lovely patio, very nice. Recommended, book in advance.
C **Posada Turpial**, José Maitin 3, T991 1123, www.turpialtravel.com. Cheaper without a/c, cosy, attractive, nice atmosphere, internet, German spoken. Recommended.
D **Hostal Colonial**, opposite the bus stop, T991 1087, hcolonial@choroni.net. With fan, laundry facilities, German owner, good value. Also good tours in the Pittier park. Recommended.
D **Posada Alfonso**, near checkpoint, T991 1037. German owner, quiet, hammocks, laundry facilities. Recommended.
E pp **La Abuela**, near bridge to Playa Grande. Basic, fan. Camping possible on the beach; beware of theft. Recommended.

Cepe and Chuao
There are several *posadas* in the village of Chuao, but it is some distance from the beach (those listed below are closer to the sea). **La Luzonera** (**C**), on the plaza, is the best, but there are others (**E**), unsigned, basic. Camping is permitted on the Chuao and Cepe beaches.
A **Posada Puerto Escondido**, Cepe, T241 4645. Includes 3 meals, drinks and boat from Puerto Colombia, spacious rooms, with bath, hot water and fan, peaceful and homely atmosphere, diving.
D **El Gran Cacao**, 200 m up the hill from the port at Chuao, T218 3604. New, comfortable, with a/c, some rooms with TV. Recommended.
D **Rincón del Marino**, near El Gran Chaco, basic, with fan.

🍴 Eating

Maracay *p1347*
Many excellent restaurants in the Av Las Delicias area; many are American style drive-up, fast-food outlets. Many reliable Chinese restaurants and *loncherías*, *tascas* and inexpensive restaurants in the streets around Plaza Girardot.
††† **Biergarten Park**, on east side of Plaza Bolívar. A pleasant, covered terrace with bar and restaurant, some German and Italian specialities, cheap and good.
† **El Indio Maecho**, Av 10 de Diciembre 114. Good cheap food, entertaining owner.

Puerto Colombia *p1348*

††† **Mango**, Trino Rangel. Delicious catch of the day, good *caipirinhas*. Recommended, but not that cheap for a full meal with wine.

††-† **El Abuelo**, just before bridge to Playa Grande. Very good food and value.

† **Café con Ron**, pizzas, coffee and cocktails.

† **El Tamaina Café**, on the road to Playa Grande. Family-run, nice, tranquil wooded setting, delicious vegetarian food. Recommended.

† **Terraza**, near bridge to Playa Grande. Tasty dishes, fresh fish, good cocktails.

● Transport

Maracay *p1347*
Bus The bus station is 2 km southeast of the centre, taxi US$3. *Por puesto* marked 'Terminal' for the bus station and 'Centro' for the town centre (Plaza Girardot). To **Maracaibo**, Expresos los Llanos, US$14. **Valencia**, US$0.75, 1 hr. **Caracas**, US$1.85 by *autobus*, US$2.30 by *microbus*, 1½ hrs, and US$4.65 by *por puesto*. **Barinas**, US$5.50, 7 hrs, Expresos Los Llanos. **Mérida** at 0800 and 2000, 12 hrs; **Ciudad Bolívar**, US$15, 10 hrs. To **Coro**, US$9, 7¾ hrs. Oriente destinations including **Margarita** served by Expresos Ayacucho, T234 9765, daily departure to Margarita, 1400, US$25 (including 1st class ferry crossing). Many buses to every part of the country, most leave 0600-0900 and 1800-2300.

Parque Nacional Henri Pittier *p1347*
Bus Depart from Maracay Terminal; pay full fare to **Ocumare** or hitch from the alcabala at El Limón. **Taxi** Can be hired at Maracay for a day's outing in the park for about US$40 (bargain hard).

Aragua Coast *p1348*
El Playón
Bus From **Maracay**, 2-2½ hours, US$2.50. To **Cata** from El Playón US$0.35 from plaza, from Ocumare de la Costa US$1.

Choroní
Bus Maracay-Choroní, beautiful journey, every 2 hrs from 0630-1700, more at the weekend, US$2.50, 2½ hrs. Taxis charge US$5.80.

Puerto Colombia *p1348*
Bus From **Maracay** bus terminal leave from platform 5. Buses to Maracay depart from the park near the police checkpoint every hour or so from 0500, last one at 1700, US$4, 2 hrs.
Taxi From **Maracay** US$50 for 4, 45 mins.

● Directory

Maracay *p1347*
Banks Italcambio (American Express), Av Aragua con C Bermúdez, C C Maracay Plaza, loc 10K, T235 6867. *Cambio* in **Air Mar** travel agency, ground floor of CADA Centro Comercial, Av 19 de Abril, Local 20, 2 blocks north of Plaza Girardot. 2.5 commission. **Internet** On Av 19 de Abril, opposite bullring and *Casa de Cultura* (art and cultural exhibitions, 2 blocks northwest of Plaza Bolívar).

Puerto Colombia *p1348*
Banks The nearest banks are in Maracay. Some *posadas* and restaurants change cash/TCs at poor rates, or give cash against credit cards (passport required). *Licorería San Sebastián*, by the bridge, changes cash and TCs and sells phone cards.

Valencia and around

Founded in 1555, Valencia is the capital of Carabobo State and Venezuela's third largest city. It's the centre of its most developed agricultural region and the most industrialized. Near the city are several groups of petroglyphs while the coast has some very popular beach areas. Best known of these is the Morrocoy national park, but you have to seek out the quiet spots.

Valencia → *Phone code: 0241. Colour map 1, grid A5. Population: 1,350,000. Altitude: 480 m.*
A road through low hills thickly planted with citrus, coffee and sugar runs 50 km west from Maracay to the valley in which Valencia lies. It is hot and humid with annual rainfall of 914 mm. Like its Spanish namesake, Valencia is famous for its oranges.

The **Cathedral** ① *daily 0630-1130, 1500-1830, Sun 0630-1200, 1500-1900*, built in 1580, is on the east side of **Plaza Bolívar**. The statue of the Virgen del Socorro (1550) in the left transept is the most valued treasure; on the second Sunday in November (during the Valencia Fair) it is paraded with a richly jewelled crown. See also **El Capitolio** ① *Páez, between Díaz Moreno y Montes de Oca*, the **Teatro Municipal** *Colombia y Av Carabobo*, the old **Carabobo University** building and the handsome **Plaza de Toros** *south end of Av Constitución beyond the ring road*, which is the second largest in Latin America after Mexico City. The magnificent former **residence of General Páez** (hero of the Carabobo battle) ① *Páez y Boyacá, Mon-Fri, free*, is now a museum. Equally attractive is the **Casa de los Celis** (1766) ① *Av Soublette y C Comercio, http://mipagina.cantv.net/casacelis, Tue-Sun 0800-1200, 1500-1700* which houses the Museo de Arte e Historia, with pre-Columbian exhibits. Most of the interesting sights are closed on Monday.

Around Valencia

Most important of the region's petroglyphs can be found at the **Parque Nacional Piedras Pintadas**, where lines of prehispanic stone slabs, many bearing swirling glyphs, march up the ridges of Cerro Pintado. The new **Museo Parque Arqueológico Piedra Pintada** ① *at the foot of Cerro Las Rosas, T041 571 596, Tue-Sat 0900-1700, Sun 1000-1600, Herodoto78@ hotmail.com, for guide Williams Hernández*, contains 165 examples of rock art and menhirs (guided tours, parking, café).

Other extensive ancient petroglyphs have been discovered at **La Taimata** near Güigüe, 34 km east of Valencia on the lake's southern shore. There are more sites along the west shore, and on the rocks by the Río Chirgua, reached by a 10-km paved road from Highway 11 (turn north at La Mona Maraven gas station), 50 km west of Valencia. About 5 km past Chirgua, at the Hacienda Cariaprima, is the country's only geoglyph, a remarkable 35 m-tall humanoid figure carved into a steep mountain slope at the head of the valley.

At 30 km southwest of Valencia on the highway to San Carlos is the site of the **Carabobo** battlefield, an impressive historical monument surrounded by splendid gardens. The view over the field from the *mirador* where the Liberator directed the battle in 1814 is impressive. Historical explanations are given on Wednesday, weekends and holidays.

Some 18 km from Valencia, the road passes the decaying spa of **Las Trincheras** (*Population 1,350*) ① *facilities 0800-1800 daily, US$2, getting there: frequent buses from Valencia,* which has three baths (hot, hotter, very hot – at 98° C these are the second hottest sulphur springs in the world), a mud bath and a Turkish bath; delightful setting.

Coast north of Valencia

Puerto Cabello (Colour map 1, grid A5, Phone code 0242, Population 185,000), 55 km from Valencia, is Venezuela's second most important port. Plaza Bolívar and the colonial part of town are by the waterfront promenade at Calle 24 de Julio. The **Museo de Historia** ① *C Los Lanceros 43, Tue-Fri 0900-1600, Sat 0900-1230,* is in one of the few remaining colonial houses (1790), in the tangle of small streets between Plaza Bolívar and the sea.

To the east is **Bahía de Patanemo**, a beautiful, tranquil horseshoe-shaped beach shaded by palms. It has three main sectors, Santa Rita, Los Caneyes and Patanemo itself, with the village proper, further from the beach than the other two. All three have lodging, but it may be difficult to find meals midweek (try at posadas). Offshore is the lovely Isla Larga (no shade or facilities), best reached by boat from Quizandal, US$3.75. From Puerto Cabello, take a *por puesto* from the terminal, 20 minutes, US$0.70, a taxi US$4.65.

Parque Nacional Morrocoy → *Colour map 1, grid A5.*

Palm-studded islets and secluded beaches make up Parque Nacional Morrocoy. The largest and most popular of the islands within the park is **Cayo Sombrero**. It is very busy at weekends but has some deserted beaches, with trees on which to sling a hammock. **Playuela** is beautiful, it has a restaurant at weekends and there's a nice walk to Playuelita. **Boca Seca** is also pleasant, with shade and calm water suitable for children, but it can be windy. **Cayo Borracho**, one of the nicest islands, has become a turtle-nesting reserve, closed to visitors. With appropriate footwear it is possible to walk between some of the islands. Calm waters here are ideal for water-skiing while scuba diving is best suited to beginners. Two things to note, though: a chemical spill in the 1990s destroyed about 50% of the coral in the park, so snorkellers will see very little. Only by diving to deeper waters will you see coral, although in all locations there are still fish to watch. Secondly, take insect repellent against *puri puri* (tiny, vicious mosquitoes) and flies. A number of muggings have been reported around Playa Sur.

Adjoining the park to the north is a vast nesting area for scarlet ibis, flamingoes and herons, the **Cuare Wildlife Sanctuary**. Most of the flamingoes are in and around the estuary next to Chichiriviche, which is too shallow for boats but you can walk there or take a taxi. Birds are best watched early morning or late afternoon.

Coro and around

The relaxed colonial city of Coro, with its sand-dune surroundings, sits at the foot of the arid, windswept Paranaguá Peninsula. Inland from Coro, the Sierra de San Luis is good walking country in fresher surroundings.

Coro → *Phone code: 0268. Colour map 1, grid A5. Population: 158,760. Mean temperature: 28°C.*

Founded in 1527, Coro, 177 km from Tucacas, is clean and well kept and the colonial part is lovely with many beautiful buildings and shaded plazas. The **tourist office** is on Paseo Alameda, T251 8033, secturfal@hotmail.com. English spoken, helpful. See also **www.coroweb.com** (in English, French and Spanish).

The **Cathedral**, a national monument, was begun in 1583. **San Clemente** church has a wooden cross in the plaza in front, said to mark the site of the first mass said in Venezuela; it is believed to be the country's oldest such monument. It is undergoing reconstruction. There are several interesting colonial houses: **Los Arcaya** ① *Zamora y Federación, Tue-Sat 0900-1200,1500-1800, Sun 0900-1300, free*, one of the best examples of 18th-century architecture, houses the **Museo de Cerámica**, small but interesting, with a beautiful garden. **Los Senior** ① *Talavera y Hernández*, where Bolívar stayed in 1827, houses an extension of the **Museo de Arte** of the Universidad Francisco de Miranda, whose main branch is on Paseo Talavera entre Bolívar y Comercio. **Las Ventanas de Hierro** ① *Zamora y Colón, Tue-Sat 0900-1200, 1500-1800, Sun 0900-1300, US$0.20*, built 1764-1765, now the **Museo de Tradición Familiar**. Just beyond is the **Casa del Tesoro** *C Zamora, T252 8701, free*, an art gallery showing local artists' work. The **Jewish cemetery** ① *C 23 de Enero esq C Zamora*, is the oldest on the continent.

The **Museo de Coro 'Lucas Guillermo Castillo'** ① *C Zamora opposite Plaza San Clemente, T251 1298, Tue-Sat 0900-1200, 1500- 1800, Sun 0900-1330, US$0.25*, is in an old monastery, and has a good collection of church relics, recommended.

Coro is surrounded by sand dunes, **Los Médanos de Coro**, which form a **national park** ① *www.losmedanos.com/; getting there: take bus marked 'Carabobo' from C35 Falcón y Av Miranda, or up Av Los Médanos and get off at the end, just after Plaza Concordia, from there walk 500 m to entrance, or take a taxi.* The place is guarded by police and is generally safe, but stay close to the entrance and on no account wander off across the dunes. Kiosk at entrance sells drinks and snacks; open till 2400.

On the road to the town's port, **La Vela de Coro**, near the turning, is the **Jardín Botánico Xerofito Dr León Croizat** ① *T277 8451, Mon-Fri 0800-1200, 1300-1600, Sat-Sun 0900-1700, free, getting there: take Vela bus from corner of C Falcón, opposite Banco Coro, and ask to be let off at Pasarela del Jardín Botánico – the bridge over the road.* It is backed by UNESCO and has plants from Africa, Australia, etc. A very interesting place to visit, with tours in Spanish.

Coro

Posada La Casa de los Pájaros 4
Taima Taima 5
Vila Antigua 7
Zamora 6

Eating ❼
Barra del Jacal 1
Dulzura y algo más 2
El Portón de Arturo 3
Mersi 5
Posada Don Luis 6

Sleeping 🛏
Colonial 1
El Gallo 2
Intercaribe 3
Miranda Cumberland 6
Posada Don Antonio 7

Venezuela Coro & around

Paraguaná Peninsula → *Phone code: 0269. Colour map 1, grid A5. Population: 125,000.*

Punto Fijo and around This area is a must for windsurfers and is a great place for walking and flamingo-spotting. The western side of the peninsula is industrialized, with oil refineries at Cardón and Amuay connected by pipeline to the Lago de Maracaibo oilfields. The main town is **Punto Fijo**, a busy, unappealing place. 5 km away is the residential area of **Judibana**, a much nicer place to stay, with shopping centre, cinema and restaurants. Beaches around Los Taques are at least 30 minutes north of Punto Fijo, many are accessible by car, few visitors, good camping but no shade or facilities.

Adícora A quiet little resort on the east side of the peninsula. The beaches are very windswept and not great but they are popular with windsurfers. There are three windsurfing schools in town. Adícora is also a good base for exploring the peninsula.

Cerro Santa Ana (830 m) is the only hill on the peninsula and commands spectacular views. The entrance is at El Moruy; take bus to Pueblo Nuevo (0730-0800), then take one to Punto Fijo and ask to be dropped off at the entrance to Santa Ana. From the plaza walk back to the signpost for Pueblo Nuevo and take the dirt road going past a white building; 20 m to the left is Restaurant La Hija. Walk 1 km through scrubby vegetation (watch out for dogs) to the *Inparques* office (closed Monday-Friday but busy at weekends). Register here before attempting the steep three-hour climb. It's safer to go at weekends.

Laguna Boca de Caño (also known as Laguna Tiraya) is a nature reserve north of Adícora, inland from Supi, along a dirt track normally fit for all vehicles. Bird life here is abundant, particularly flamingoes. It is the only mangrove zone on the east side of the peninsula.

Sierra de San Luis

South of Coro, on the road to Barquisimeto, the Sierra includes the **Parque Nacional Juan C Falcón**. The area is a paradise for nature lovers and hikers, with tropical forest, caves and waterfalls. The picturesque village of **Curimagua** is best for visiting the park; jeeps leave from Coro terminal, US$2. The lovely colonial town of **Cabure** is the capital of the Sierra. Jeeps leave from Coro terminal, 58 km, 1¼ hours, US$3. As well as hotels, Cabure has restaurants, bars, a bakery, supermarket and pharmacy. A few kilometres up the road is a series of beautiful waterfalls, Cataratas de Hueque. **The Spanish Road** is a fantastic three-hour walk through orange groves and tropical forest from Curimagua to Cabure. Take water; very muddy in rains, take insect repellent and good shoes, be prepared to get wet. Ask at any of the hotels listed below. To walk the Spanish Road from Coro in one day, take transport to Cabure, ask to be dropped at the turn off for the **Posada El Duende** (see below) and walk uphill about 1 km to the Posada, where you begin the trek along the Spanish Road. The path eventually comes out at the Curimagua-Coro paved road, where you can take transport or hitch back to Coro.

Sleeping

Coro *p1354, map p1354*

AL-A Miranda Cumberland, Av Josefa Camejo, opposite old airport, T252 2111, www.hoteles cumberland.com. Beautiful hotel, good value, restaurant, swimming pool.

C Intercaribe, Av Manaure entre Zamora y Urdaneta, T251 1844. Expensive food, good, pool, a/c, small rooms.

D Casa Tun Tun, Zamora 92, entre Toledo y Hernández, T404 0347, casatuntun@hotmail.com. To open in 2006, small, rooms with or without bath, fan, 2 patios, laundry.

D Posada Don Antonio, Paseo Talavera 11, T253 9578. Central, small rooms, a/c, internet, parking.

D Posada La Casa de los Pájaros, Monzón 74 entre Ampies y Comercio, T252 8215,

rstiuv@cantv.net. Colonial house about 6 blocks from the city centre, being restored by the owners with local art and antiques, rooms with and without bath, camping US$4, tents for rent, hammock space US$2.50, breakfast US$2-4, 30 mins free internet, use of kitchen for small fee, laundry service, offers trips to local sights of interest. Recommended.

D Taima Taima, C 35 Falcón (some distance from centre, off our map), T252 1215, hospedajetaimataima@hotmail.com. Small rooms, a/c, TV, some hot water, parking.

D Villa Antigua, C 58 Comercio 46, T251 6479/0414-683 7433. A/c, TV, fountain in courtyard, restaurant, public phones.

● *For an explanation of the sleeping and eating price codes used in this guide, see inside the front* ● *cover. Other relevant information is found in Essentials pages 1330-1331.*

D **Zamora**, C 33 Zamora, entre C 48a y 50 Colina, T251 6005. Cold water but no shortages, a/c, TV, huge rooms with table, also dorms, modern.

E pp **Colonial**, Paseo Talavera, T252 4179. Beside the cathedral, basic, with a/c.

E **El Gallo**, Federación 26, T252 9481. French/ Venezuelan owned, relaxed atmosphere, courtyard with hammocks, use of kitchen, English spoken, see Eric for tours.

Camping About 30 km east of Coro at La Cumara, nice, good beach and dunes, US$2 pp.

Paraguaná Peninsula *p1355*
Punto Fijo

D **Caribe**, Comercio 21-112 near Expresos Occidente terminal, T245 0421. With a/c, TV, restaurant, accepts Mastercard.

E **Miami**, C Falcón entre Av México y Bolivia, T245 8532. Recommended.

Judibana

C **Jardín**, on Av Mariscal y C Falcón, near airport, T246 1727. A/c, pool, restaurant, accepts credit cards, changes US$ cash.

C **Luigi**, C 10 next to Banco de Venezuela, T246 0970. A/c, pleasant, good restaurant, changes US$ cash, accepts credit cards.

Adícora

B **Hacienda La Pancha**, about 5 km from Adícora in the hills, T0414-969 2649, www.venaventours.com/haciendalapancha/defa ult.asp. Beautiful old house with original decor, nice owners, swimming pool, no children.

C **Posada Kitzburger**, on Malecón, T988 8004. Fan, German owners, no single rooms, good restaurant. Recommended.

C-D **Posada Montecano**, on western outskirts, T988 8174, glpr267@cantv.net. Great value and delicious food, all new.

Sierra de San Luís *p1355*
Curimagua

C **Apolo**, with restaurant, runs tours in park.

D **El Trapichito**, 2 km outside Curimagua, T416 1989. A good place to stay.

E-F **Finca El Monte**, 5 km from the village, T416 0622, fincaelmonte@yahoo.com. Run by a Swiss couple on an ecological basis, hot water, meals, Ernesto takes tours round the park. Highly recommended.

Cabure

C-D **Hotel El Duende**, 20 mins uphill from village, T808 9066, 0414-661 1079 (mob). A beautiful 19th-century posada and garden, price depends on size of room, fan, cold water, good restaurant, horse riding, walking, peaceful. Recommended.

In town are D **Camino Viejo**, and E **La Montaña**.

❶ Eating

Coro *p1354, map p1354*

₮₮ **Barra del Jacal**, Av Manaure y C 29 Unión. Outdoors, pizza and other dishes.

₮₮ **Mersi**, C 56 Toledo y Zamora. Good pizzas, *empanadas*.

₮₮ **El Portón de Arturo**, C 56 Toledo, towards Plaza Falcón. All kinds of regional meat.

₮₮ **Posada Don Luis**, opposite airport. Serves local speciality, *chivo*, goat.

₮ **Chupulún**, Av Manaure esq C Monzón. Recommended for lunch, homemade *chicha*.

Cafés

Dulzura y algo más, on corner of Paseo Alameda. Good ice cream and typical sweets. **Panadería Costa Nova**, Av Manaure, opposite *Hotel Intercaribe*. Good bread and pastries, poor coffee.

Paraguaná Peninsula: Punto Fijo *p1355*

₮ **Colonial**, C Libertad entre Colombia y Ecuador. Cheap, recommended, lunch only.

₮ Good *panadería* opposite bus terminal.

⊛ Festivals and events

Coro *p1354, map p1354*

26 Jul, Coro Week. **9-12 Oct**, state fair. **24-25 Dec**, Tambor Coriano and Parranda de San Benito (Coro, La Vela and Puerto Cumarebo). Aug Regatta, Curaçao to La Vela, competitors from USA, Holland, Caribbean take part, ask at Capitanía (Port Captain's office).

⛰ Activities and tours

Coro *p1354, map p1354*

Aeromar, C Ciencias, CC Miranda, local 4, T251 3187, tremont1@cantv.net.

Kuriana Travel, C Zamora opposite Museo Diocesano, T/F251 3055. Local tours with English-speaking guide; ask for Mercedes Medina, who has an excellent campsite nearby (*Llano Largo*, Vía Siburna, T0416-868 1374), highly recommended, specializing in ecotourism.

❷ Transport

Coro *p1354, map p1354*

Air Airport open for domestic flights; see also Las Piedras, below, for flights.

Bus Terminal is on Av Los Médanos, entre Maparari y Libertad, buses go up C 35 Falcón, US$0.25, taxi US$2. To/from **Caracas** US$12-15, 10 hrs; **Maracaibo**, US$8, 4 hrs, *por puesto* US$12; **Tucacas**, every 20 mins, US$6, 3 hrs; **Punto Fijo**, *por puesto* US$2.

Paraguaná Peninsula *p1355*
Punto Fijo
Air Airport is at **Las Piedras**: *por puestos* from C Garcés y Av Bolívar (don't believe taxi drivers who say there are no *por puestos* from airport to town); taxi from Punto Fijo US$5, from bus terminal US$3. 4 flights a day to **Aruba**, **Avensa** and **Santa Bárbara**, 2 a day to **Curaçao**, Dutch Caribbean Express. Domestic flights to **Caracas**, **Mérida** and **Maracaibo** with Santa Bárbara.
Bus Terminal on C Peninsular entre Colombia y Ecuador; *por puestos* to **Pueblo Nuevo, Adícora, Coro, Valencia** and **Maracaibo**. To **Maracay, Barquisimeto, Maracaibo** and **Caracas**: Expresos Occidente, on C Comercio entre Ecuador y Bolivia; to **Mérida, Barinas** and **Caracas**, Expresos San Cristóbal, C Carnevali just behind Hotel América; **Expresos Alianza**, on Av Colombia between Carnevali and Democracia, to many destinations.

Adícora *p1355*
Bus Several daily to and from **Coro**, from 0630-1830, US$1.25, 50 mins; to and from **Pueblo Nuevo** and **Punto Fijo**, several daily from 0600-1730.

❶ Directory

Coro *p1354, map p1354*
Banks Banco Mercantil, C 35 Falcón y C 50 Colina, ATM and cash on Visa or Mastercard. Banco Venezuela, Paseo Talavera. ATM and cash on Visa. Try hotels and travel agents for cash and TCs. **Internet** Internet Coro CC Punta del Sol, C 35 Falcon y Av Manaure. Also at CANTV Centro de Comunicaciones on Av Los Médanos, opposite bus terminal, also international calls.

Paraguaná Peninsula: Punto Fijo *p1355*
Banks Many banks on Av Bolívar y Comercio accept Visa, MasterCard and other cards, eg Banco de Venezuela, Banesco. Banco Mercantil, Av Bolívar y C Girardot. Changes Citicorp TCs. **Casa Fukayama**, Av Bolívar entre C Altagracia y Girardot. Changes US$ cash. **Consulates** Dutch Consul in Judibana at Urb La Laguna, C Mucubaji 38, Roque Hernández, T246 0430, open weekdays 1600-1700. **Post offices** Ipostel at C Páez y Av Panamá, collection every 10 days. **Telephones** CANTV at C Falcón y Av México.

From Maracaibo to Colombia

To the heart of Venezuela's oil business on the shores of Lake Maracaibo: not many tourists find their way here. Those that do are usually on their way to Colombia via the border crossing on the Guajira Peninsula to the north. If you've got the time to stop, though, and can handle the heat, Maracaibo is the only town or city in Venezuela where you'll see indigenous people in traditional dress going about their business and nearby are reminders of prehispanic and oil-free customs.

Maracaibo → *Phone code: 0261. Colour map 1, grid A4. Population: 1,800,000.*
Venezuela's second largest city, and capital of the State of Zulia, is the country's oil capital, with 70% of the nation's output coming from the Lago de Maracaibo area. Maracaibo is a modern commercial city with wide, clean streets and, apart from the intense heat, is pleasant to walk around, especially around Plaza Bolívar. The hottest months are July to September, but there is usually a sea breeze from 1500 until morning. Just north of the regional capital is a lagoon where you can still see the stilt houses that inspired the Spanish invaders to christen it 'Little Venice'. In the southwest is the Catatumbo delta, a huge swamp brimming with wildlife and one of the most fascinating trips in the whole country (best reached by tour from Mérida). Its nightly displays of lightning have yet to be explained. The **tourist office** is Corzutur ① *T783 4928, zuliaturistica@cantv.net.* See **www.zuliaturistica.com** for more sights, events and advice.

Sights The traditional city centre is **Plaza Bolívar**, on which stand the **Cathedral** (at east end), the **Casa de Gobierno**, the **Asamblea Legislativa** and the **Casa de la Capitulación** (or Casa Morales) ① *Mon-Fri, 0800-1600, tour free,* a colonial building and national monument. The Casa has a large library dedicated to the Liberator. Next door is the 19th-century **Teatro Baralt**.
　　Running west of Plaza Bolívar is the **Paseo de las Ciencias**, a 1970s development which levelled all the old buildings in the area. Only the **Iglesia de Santa Bárbara** stands in the Paseo. **Calle Carabobo** (one block north of the Paseo de las Ciencias) is a very good example of a colonial Maracaibo street. One block south of the Paseo is **Plaza Baralt** *Av 6, stretching to C 100 and the old waterfront market* (**Mercado de Pulgas**). The **Centro de Arte de Maracaibo Lía Bermúdez** ① *in the 19th-century Mercado de Pulgas building, Mon-Fri 0800-1200, 1400-1600, Sat-Sun 0930-1700*, displays the work of national artists. It is a/c, a good place to

escape the midday heat and makes a good starting place for a walking tour of the city centre. The new part of the city round **Bella Vista** and towards the University is in vivid contrast with the **old town** near the docks. The latter, with narrow streets and brightly-painted, colonial style adobe houses, has hardly changed from the 19th century, although many buildings are in an advanced state of decay. The buildings facing **Parque Urdaneta** (three blocks north of Paseo de las Ciencias) have been well-restored. Also well-preserved are the church of **Santa Lucía** and the streets around. This old residential area is a short ride (or long walk) north from the old centre. **Parque La Marina**, on the shores of the lake, contains sculptures by the Venezuelan artist, Jesús Soto (1923-2005). More of his work can be seen in the **Galería de Arte Brindhaven** (free), near Santa Lucía.

Paseo de Maracaibo, or del Lago, is a lakeside park built in the late 1970s, near the *Hotel del Lago*. It offers walks along the shores of the Lake at its narrowest point, spectacular views of the Rafael Urdaneta bridge and of oil tankers sailing to the Caribbean. The park attracts a wide variety of birds. To get there take a 'Milagro' *por puesto* or a 'Norte' bus northbound and ask the driver to let you off at the entrance, which is well-marked. Opposite is the Mercado de los Indios Guajiros (see Shopping).

Maracaibo to Colombia

About one hour north is the Río Limón. Take a bus (US$0.70, from terminal or Avenida 15 entre C 76 y 77) to **El Moján**, riding with the Guajira Indians as they return to their homes on the peninsula. From El Moján, *por puestos* go to **Sinamaica** (US$1.40; taxi US$5). Beyond Sinamaica, a paved road passes the Sinamaica Lagoon and leads to the border with Colombia. Along the way you see Guajira Indians, the men with bare legs, on horseback; the women with long, black, tent-shaped dresses and painted faces, wearing the sandals with big wool pom-poms which they make and sell, more cheaply than in the tourist shops. The men do nothing: women do all the work, tending sheep and goats, selling slippers and raising very little on the dry, hot, scrubby Guajira Peninsula. Because of the proximity of the border, across which drug trafficking occurs, it is best not to stay in this area after 1600.

Border with Colombia → *Colombia is 1 hr behind Venezuela.*

The border opens at 0800. You need an exit card, US$11.60, to leave Venezuela, payable in bolívares only. Ask for 90 days on entering Colombia. For information on entering Colombia, see page 832. To enter Venezuela by land a visa may be asked for, even for those who don't officially require one. Only 72-hour transit visas are issued at this border; *tarjetas de turismo* must be obtained from *ONIDEX* in Maracaibo (Edif Banco Maracaibo, Plaza Baralt, C Comercio, T721 1984 – not an easy task. Get a visa in advance. Expect searches at the border and en route to Maracaibo.

● Sleeping

Maracaibo *p1357*

It is best to reserve well in advance.
AL Kristoff, Av 8 Santa Rita entre C 68 y 69, T796 1000, www.hotelkristoff.com. A/c, nice pool open to non-residents US$6, disco, laundry service, restaurant, changes US$ cash at terrible rates.
A Gran Hotel Delicias, Av 15 esq C 70, T797 6111, F797 3037. A/c, recommended restaurant, good value, pool, disco, accepts credit cards.
C Doral, C 75 y Av 14A, T797 8385. A/c, helpful. Recommended.
C Paraíso, Av 93, No 82-70, sector Veritas, T797 6149. With small sitting room, a/c, cable.
D Acuario, C 78 (also known as Dr Portillo) No 9-43, Bella Vista, T797 1123. A/c, shower, safe, small rooms, safe parking, basic.
D San Martín, Av 3Y (San Martín) con C 80, T791 5095. A/c, restaurant next door, accepts credit cards.
E Victoria, Av 6-14, Plaza Baralt, T722 9466. With bath, no hot water, a/c.

● Eating

Maracaibo *p1357*

Most restaurants are closed on Sun. Many restaurants on *palafitos* (stilts) in Santa Rosa de Agua district, good for fish (*por puesto* US$0.35 to get there).
₸₸₸ El Zaguán, on C Carabobo (see above). Serves traditional regional cooking, expensive and difficult to find at night.
₸₸ El Carite, C 78, No 8-35, T71878. Excellent selection of fish and seafood, delicious and moderately-priced.
₸₸ Mi Vaquita, Av 3H con C 76. Texan steak house, popular with locals, good atmosphere. Recommended.
₸₸ Pizzería Napoletana, C 77 near Av 4. Excellent food but poor service, closed Tue.
₸ Bambi, Av 4, 78-70. Italian run with good cappuccino, pastries, recommended.
₸ Chips, Av 31 opposite Centro Comercial Salto Angel. Regional fast food, *tequeños* and *patacones*.

Recommended. There are many other good restaurants around the Plaza de la República, C77/5 de Julio and Av 31, in Bella Vista.
⟡ **La Friulana**, C 95 con Av 3. Good cheap meal, closes 1900. Repeatedly recommended.

Cafés and panaderías
Kabuki, C 77 entre Av 12 y 13. Nice café with good food.
La Habana, Av Bella Vista (Av 4) near C 76. Good salads and milkshakes, open 24 hrs.
Larga Vida, Av 13A entre C 75 y C 76. Health food store.
Panadería Bella Vista, 1 block from *Bambi* on Av 4, near C 76. Recommended for *quesillo* and *tiramisu*.

☸ Festivals and events

Maracaibo *p1357*
Virgen del Rosario, **5 Oct**; **24 Oct**; **18 Nov**, NS de Chiquimquira (La Chinita), processions, bullfights – the main regional religious festival.

⚙ Shopping

Maracaibo *p1357*
Bookshops Librería Cultural, Av 5 de Julio. Best Spanish language bookstore in town. Librería Italiana, Av 5 de Julio, Ed Centro América. Postcards and foreign publications. Librería Universal, Av 5 de Julio y Av 4. Maps, stationery, Caracas newspapers, poor selection of books. Staff at the public library, Av 2, are helpful to tourists.
Handicrafts and markets El Mercado de los Indios Guajiros, open market at C 96 y Av 2 (El Milagro). A few crafts, some pottery, hammocks, etc. **Las Pulgas**, south side of C 100 entre Av 10 y 14. The outdoor market, enormous, mostly clothes, shoes, and general household goods. Most of the shops on **C Carabobo** sell regional crafts, eg *La Salita*.

⚙ Transport

Maracaibo *p1357*
Air La Chinita airport is 25 km southwest of city centre. Taxis charge US$8-10, there are no *por puestos*. Good bookshop in arrivals sells city map; *Italcambio* for exchange, open 0600-1800 daily, no commission; car hire offices outside. There are frequent flights with **Aserca, Aeropostal, Avior, Láser** and Santa Bárbara to **Caracas, Valencia, Barquisimeto, Mérida, San Antonio** (be early to guarantee seat), **Barcelona, Las Piedras** and **Porlamar**. International flights to **Aruba** (*Santa Bárbara*) and **Miami** (*American, Aeropostal*).
Bus The bus station is 15 mins walk from centre, 1 km south of the old town. Ask for buses into

town, local services are confusing. There are several fast and comfortable buses daily to **Valencia**, US$13.50 by **Expresos del Lago**. **San Cristóbal**, US$11.50, 6-8 hrs, *por puesto*, US$23. **Barquisimeto**, 5½ hrs, US$8.75. **Coro** US$8, 4 hrs. **Caracas**, US$18, 10-13 hrs, *por puesto* US$40. **Mérida**, 2300, US$8, 5-7 hrs, or *por puesto*, US$12, 6½ hrs; **Aeroexpresos Ejecutivos** 6 a day from Av 15 con C 90 (Distribuidor las Delicias), T783 0620.
Local *Por puestos* go up and down Av 4 from the old centre to Bella Vista. Ruta 6 goes up and down C 67 (Cecilia Acosta). The San Jacinto bus goes along Av 15 (Las Delicias). Buses from Las Delicias also go to the centre and terminal. From C 76 to the centre *por puestos* marked 'Las Veritas' and buses marked 'Ziruma'. Look for the name of the route on the roof, or on the front window, passenger's side. A ride from downtown to Av 5 de Julio in a 'Bella Vista' *por puesto* costs US$0.35. Taxis US$2.50-3.50.

Border with Colombia *p1358*
Maracaibo-Maicao
Bus Busven direct at 0430. Otherwise by colectivo taxi from Maracaibo bus terminal (5 passengers), US$6 pp - shop around, plus US$1.50 road toll. Lots of police checks en route, but no luggage checks; a straight- forward crossing. Some drivers are unwilling to stop for formalities; make sure the driver takes you all the way to Maicoa and arrive before the last bus to Santa Marta or Cartagena (1630).

☎ Directory

Maracaibo *p1357*
Banks Banco Mercantil, on corner of Plaza de la República. Cash advance on Visa and MasterCard. Branches of **Banco de Venezuela**, including at airport, for Visa ATMs. Best for dollars and TCs is **Casa de Cambio de Maracaibo**, C 78 con Av 9B. Italcambio, C C Montielco, loc PA 1-1, entre Av 20 y C 72, T7832682, Amex rep. Citibank, Av 15 (Las Delicias) con C 77 (5 de Julio) for Citicorp TCs. All banks shut at 1630, exchange morning only. *Cambio* at bus terminal will change Colombian pesos into bolívares at a poor rate. **Consulates** France, Av 3F y C70, T791 2921. Germany, C77 No 3C-24, Edif Los Cerros p 9, T791 2406. Italy, Av 3H No 69-79, T791 9903. Netherlands, Av 3C y C67, La Lago, Unicentro Virginia, office 6, p 2, T/F792 2885. Norway, Km 1 Carretera a Perijá, Sector Plaza Las Banderas-Los Haticos. Spain, Av Sabaneta y C El Prado No 9B-55. Sweden, Av 15 Las Delicias No 88-78. Switzerland, Av 9B No 75-95. UK, Av 2G No 67-49, Sector El Lago, Urbanización Virginia, T791 5589, georgep@inspecciones.com. 0800-1230. USA, Centro Venezolano Americano del Zulia, C

63, No 3E-60, T291 1860. **Internet** Cyber Estudio, Av 10 No 66-110, 1100-2300, US$3 per hr. **Medical services** Doctors: Dr García, *Hospital Coromoto*, Av 3C and C 72, T790 0366, speaks English, as does **Dr Carlos Febres**, a dentist, Av 8, No 84-129, Mon-Fri 0900-1200, 1500-1800, T221504. **Post offices** Av

Libertador y Av 3. **Telephones** CANTV, C 76 near Av 3E, Bella Vista, open 0700-2330, Mon-Fri. Servicio de Telecomunicaciones de Venezuela, C 99, esq Av 3. Payphones for local calls only. If offices are closed, phone cards are available at the desk of the nearby *Hotel Astor*, south side of Plaza de la República.

Barquisimeto and around

→ *Phone code: 0251. Colour map 1, grid A5. Population: 900,000. Altitude: 565 m. Mean temperature: 25°C*

The arid, fruit-growing area around the city of Barquisimeto leads to the lush Andean foothills of Trujillo state. Venezuela's fourth largest city was largely destroyed by an earthquake in 1812, but is a nice enough place to spend a few days when visiting the area. For information: **División de Turismo y Recreación** ① *Av Libertador, Edif Fundalara p 2, T255 9321/6580, dirtur@cantv.net (take a No 12 bus)*. See also www.barquisimeto.com.

Many fascinating corners have been preserved and a law prohibiting demolition of older buildings means that more are being restored. The **Museo de Barquisimeto** ① *Av 15 between C 25 and 26, Tue-Fri 0900-1700, Sat-Sun 1000-1700, free*, displays the town's history, also contemporary art. More old buildings are a block away around **Plaza Jacinto Lara**. The **San Francisco church** faces the plaza. On the opposite side is the small **Ateneo cultural centre** ① *Cra 17 y C 23, Mon-Fri 0830-1200, 1500-1830, Sat 0900-1200, free*, which has temporary exhibitions in an 18th-century house. It also has a restaurant and occasional evening concerts. The **Cathedral** *C 30 y Cra 26 (Venezuela)*, is a modern structure of reinforced concrete and glass. At the heart of the old city is **Plaza Bolívar**, with a statue of the Liberator and the white-painted **Iglesia Concepción** on the south side. Also on the plaza, the **Palacio Municipal** ① *Cra 17 y C 25*, is an attractive modern building. **Parque Ayacucho** ① *Cra 15 (Av Francisco de Miranda) between C 41-43*, has lush vegetation, paths, fountains and a bronze statue of Mariscal Sucre.

About 24 km southwest of Barquisimeto is the busy agricultural centre of **Quíbor** (*Phone code 0253, Population 53,525*). Festivals on 18 January (NS de Altagracia) and 12 June (San Antonio de Padua). The **Centro Antropológico de Quíbor** exhibits work of the *indígenas* who used to live in the region. South of Quíbor and 40 minutes from Barquisimeto is **Sanaré** (1,360 m), on the edge of the **Parque Nacional Yacambú**, where you can hike through tropical forest up the Fumerola, a sleeping volcano. About 60 km east of Barquisimeto is **Chivacoa** (Population 40,400). South of the town is the sacred mountain of the María-Lionza cult, practised throughout Venezuela. Celebrations are held there at weekends with 12 October (Día de la Raza) being the most important day. There is a Catholic festival, La Inmaculada Concepción, from 8-14 December.

● Sleeping

Barquisimeto *p1360*
B Príncipe, Av 18 entre C 22 y C 23, T231 2344. Pool, restaurant.
C Hevelin, Av Vargas entre 20 y 21. Hot water, a/c.
D La Casona, Av 17 con C 27 near Plaza Bolívar, T231 5311. A/c, hot water, restaurant. **D Lido**, Av 15 entre C26 y 27. Hot water, a/c or fan.

Sanaré *p1360*
E-D Posada Turística El Cerrito, T0253-449 0011, manager speaks English, small restaurant and bar, tours to local sights and Yacambú, highly recommended.

● Eating

Barquisimeto *p1360*
♥ **Barquipán**, C 26 entre Cras 17 y 18. Good breakfasts, snacks.
♥ **Majestic**, Av 19 con C 31. Breakfast and vegetarian meals.
♥ **Sabor Vegetariano**, on C 24 entre Av 20 y 21, next to *El Rincón Griego* restaurant. Snacks.

● Festivals and events

Barquisimeto *p1360*
On **28 Dec** (morning) is the fiesta of La Zaragoza, when colourfully clad participants and children pass through the streets accompanied by music and dancing. Huge crowds are attracted to the procession of La

Divina Pastora in early **Jan**, when an image of the Virgin Mary is carried from the shrine at Santa Rosa village into the city.

⊖ Transport

Barquisimeto *p1360*
Air Jacinto Lara international airport is 8 km southwest of the centre, 10 mins, US$5 by taxi. Local buses outside, US$0.25. Flights to **Caracas, Maracaibo, Mérida, San Antonio** and **Valencia**.
Bus Terminal is on the edge of the city at Carrera 25 y C 44: to **Mérida**, 3-4 a day, at 1020 and several between 2000 and 0200, 8 hrs via Agua Viva and El Vigía, US$8.50; to **Acarigua** (see page 1373), 1 hr, US$3. To **Barinas**, 5 hrs, US$4. To **Valera** *por puesto*, 3½ hrs, US$8.75. To

Tucacas every 2 hrs; to **Coro** at 1200 and by night, 7 hrs, US$8.75. To **Caracas**, US$8.75, 6 hrs.

❶ Directory

Barquisimeto *p1360*
Banks Banco Provincial, Av 20 entre C 31 y 32 and C 23 entre Avs 18 y 19, for Visa and MasterCard. **Banco de Venezuela**, Av 20 y C 31, No 31-08 (and other branches), Visa ATMs. Capital Express, Av Los Leones, Centro Comercial Paseo, next to C 90. Changes US$ cash at low rates. Italcambio, Av Los Leones, C C París, loc 1-40, T254 9790, and at airport for Amex. **Car hire** Volkswagen best at Av Pedro León Torres y C 56, also at airport. **Post offices** Av 17 con C 25. **Telephones** C 30 entre Avs 24 y 25.

Valera to Mérida

From the lowland heat of Valera, roads climb towards the mountains, passing colonial towns and entering an increasingly rugged landscape.

Valera → *Phone code: 0271. Colour map 1, grid A5. Population: 130,000.*
This is the most important town in the State of Trujillo. Here, you can choose between two roads over the Sierra, either via Timotes and Mucuchíes to Mérida, or via Boconó and down to the Llanos at Guanare. An agricultural and industrial fair is held in August. There are several upmarket business hotels, few decent budget ones, and lots of good Italian restaurants on the main street.

Trujillo → *Phone code: 0272. Colour map 1, grid A5. Population: 44,460. Altitude: 805 m.*
From Valera a road runs via the restored colonial village of **La Plazuela** to the state capital, Trujillo. This beautiful historic town consists basically of two streets running uphill from the Plaza Bolívar. It's a friendly place with a warm, sub-tropical climate. The **Centro de Historia de Trujillo**, on Avenida Independencia, is a restored colonial house, now a museum. Bolívar lived there and signed the 'proclamation of war to the death' in the house. A monument to the **Virgen de la Paz** ① *0900-1700, US$1* (47 m high, with elevator) was built in 1983; it stands at 1,608 m, 2½ hours walk from town and gives good views to Lake Maracaibo but go early. Jeeps leave when full from opposite *Hotel Trujillo*, 20 minutes, US$1.40 per person. For **tourist information**, T236 1455, ctt@cttutismo.org.

Boconó and Niquitao
From Trujillo there is a high, winding, spectacular paved road to the town built on steep mountain sides and famed for its crafts. The **Centro de Acopio Artesanal Tiscachic** is highly recommended for *artesanía* (turn left just before bridge at entrance to town and walk 350 m).

    Niquitao, a small town one hour southwest of Boconó, is still relatively unspoilt. Excursions can be made to the Teta de Niquitao (4,007 m), two hours by jeep, the waterfalls and pools known as Las Pailas, and a nearby lake. Southwest of Niquitao, by partly-paved road is **Las Mesitas**; continue up towards **Tuñame**, turn left on a good gravel road (no signs), cross pass and descend to **Pueblo Llano** (one basic hotel and restaurant), from where you can climb to the Parque Nacional Sierra Nevada at 3,600 m, passing Santo Domingo. Good hiking in the area; Johnny Olivo at the video shop on Plaza Bolívar is a knowledgeable guide.

Road to the high Andes

After **Timotes** the road climbs through increasingly wild, barren and rugged country and through the windy pass of **Pico El Aguila** (4,007 m), best seen early morning, otherwise frequently in the clouds. This is the way Bolívar went when crossing the Andes to liberate Colombia, and on the peak is the statue of a condor. At the pass is the tourist restaurant *Páramo Aguila*, reasonably priced with open fire; also food stalls, souvenir sellers and horses for hire. Across from the monument is a small chapel with fine views. A paved road leads from here 2 km to a *CANTV* microwave tower (4,118 m), continuing north as a lonely track to the **Piñango lakes** (45 km) and the traditional village of **Piñango** (2,480 m). Great views for miles around. The Aranjo family provides food and lodging and hires horses.

Santo Domingo (*Phone code 0274, Population 6,000, Altitude 2,178 m*), with good handicraft shops and fishing, is on the spectacular road up from Barinas to Mérida, before the Parque Nacional Sierra Nevada. Festival: 30 September, San Gerónimo. The tourist office is on the right leaving town, 10 minutes from the centre.

● Sleeping

Trujillo *p1361*
D**Los Gallegos**, Av Independencia 5-65, T/F236 3193. With hot water, a/c or fan, with or without TV. As well as several other places.

Boconó *p1361*
C**Estancia de Mosquey**, Mosquey, 10 km from Boconó towards Biscucuy, T/F0272-652 1555, 0414-725 0073 (mob). Family run, great views, good beds, good restaurant, pool, recommended. There are 3 other basic hotels in town.

Niquitao *p1361*
D**Na Delia**, T0271-885 2113, on a hill 500 m out of town, both have restaurants.
D**Posada Turística de Niquitao**, T0271-885 2042/0414-723 3925/0416-771 7860.

Road to the high Andes *p1362*
Timotes
C**Las Truchas**, north entrance to town, T/F0271-828 9158, www.andes.net/lastruchas.
D**Carambay**, Av Bolívar 41, T0271-828 9261..

Santo Domingo
AL**La Trucha Azul**, east end of town, T898 8140, 0416-674 8431 (mob). Rooms with open fireplace, expensive for what it offers.
A**Los Frailes**, between Santo Domingo and Laguna Mucubají at 3,700 m. Book through Hoturvensa, T/F0212-976 0530/976 4984, hoturvensa@cantv.net, but pay at hotel. Beautiful former monastery, international menu and wines.
B**Paso Real**, on the other side of the river from Los Frailes. Almost as good.
B**Hotel Moruco**, T898 8155, F898 8225, out of town. Beautiful, good value, food good, bar.
C**Hotel Tasca Halcón de Oro**, T898 8044. Cheap rooms for rent next door, opposite Panadería Santo Domingo.

● Eating

Niquitao *p1361*
††-†**La Estancia**, Plaza Bolívar. Owner Golfredo Pérez, helpful, kind, knows area well, pizzas.

● Transport

Valera *p1361*
Bus The bus terminal on the edge of town. To **Boconó**, US$4 3 hrs; to **Trujillo**, *por puestos*, 30 mins, US$0.75; to **Caracas**, 9 hrs, US$12 (direct at 2230 with **Expresos Mérida**); to **Mérida**, 4 daily with **Empresa Barinas** (0800, 1000, 1300, 1500), US$2.60, 4½ hrs; *por puestos* to **Mérida**, 3 hrs, US$6, leave when full; to **Maracaibo**, *micros* every 30 mins until 1730, 4 hrs, US$6.50.

Road to the high Andes *p1362*
Santo Domingo
Bus Buses or *busetas* pass through in either direction at approximately 2 hr intervals through the day. **Mérida** 2 hrs, US$4 *por puesto*; **Barinas** 1½ hrs, US$4.25.

● Directory

Valera *p1361*
Banks Corp Banca, Av Bolívar con C 5, changes Amex TCs, no commission. Banco de Venezuela, C 7 con Av 10, cash on Visa and MasterCard, very efficient and helpful.

Trujillo *p1361*
Banks Banco Provincial, on main plaza, cash on Visa and MasterCard. Banco de Venezuela, 1 block down from cathedral, has ATM.

Mérida and around

Venezuela's high Andes offer hiking and mountaineering, and fishing in lakes and rivers. The main tourist centre is Mérida (674 km from Caracas), but there are many interesting rural villages. The Transandean Highway runs through the Sierra to the border with Colombia, while the Pan-American Highway runs along the foot of the Andes through El Vigía and La Fría to join the Transandean at San Cristóbal.

The Sierra Nevada de Mérida, running from south of Maracaibo to the Colombian frontier, is the only range in Venezuela where snow lies permanently on the higher peaks. Several basins lying between the mountains are actively cultivated; the inhabitants are concentrated mainly in valleys and basins at between 800 m and 1,300 m above sea level. The towns of Mérida and San Cristóbal are in this zone.

Mérida → *Phone code: 0274. Colour map 1, grid A4. Population: 300,000. Altitude: 1,640 m.*

Mérida stands on an alluvial terrace – a kind of giant shelf – 15 km long, 2½ km wide, surrounded by cliffs and plantations and within sight of Pico Bolívar, the highest in Venezuela, crowned with a bust of Bolívar. The mountain is part of the snow-capped Five White Eagles group, which is visible from the city. Founded in 1558, the capital of Mérida State retains some colonial buildings but is mainly known for its 33 parks and many statues. From the tourist point of view, though, its claims to fame are the great opportunities for adventure sports and the buzz from a huge student population.

Ins and outs

Getting around Mérida may seem a safe place, but theft and robbery does occur. Avoid the Pueblo Nuevo area by the river at the stairs leading down from Avenida 2, as well as Avenida 2 itself and Viaducto Miranda. The **airport** is on the main highway, 5 km from the centre. *Por puesto* into town US$0.25, taxi US$2.50. The **bus terminal** is 3 km from the centre of town on the west side of the valley, connected by a frequent minibus service to Calle 25 entre Avenidas 2 y 3. Taxi from bus station to town centre US$2. ▶▶ *For further details, see Transport, page 1372.*

Information Tourist offices Corporación Merideña de Turismo, Avenida Urdaneta y C 45, next to the airport, T263 4701/2782. Low season 0800-1200, 1400-1800, high season 0800-1800, closed Sunday. They supply a useful map of the state and town (US$0.30). Also at the airport in the waiting lounge, very informative, same low season hours, 0730-1330 in high season; in the bus terminal, same hours, have a map of the city (US$0.30). At Jardín Acuario, Avenida Andrés Bello, low season 0800-1200, 1400-1800, high season 0830- 1830. A good website for information on Mérida is www.andes.net (Spanish), www.andesholidays.com (English). **Inparques** (National Parks) office on street parallel to Avenida Las Américas, opposite IVSS, T262 1356, drmerida@inparques.gov.ve, http://sierranevada.andigena.org. Map of Parque Nacional Sierra Nevada (mediocre) US$1; also at Teleférico for permits.

Sights

Among the city's parks, the **Parque de las Cinco Repúblicas** ① *C 13, between Avs 4 and 5, beside the barracks,* is renowned for having the first monument in the world to Bolívar (1842, replaced in 1988) and contains soil from each of the five countries he liberated (photography strictly prohibited). Three of the peaks known as the Five White Eagles (Bolívar, 5,007 m, Toro, 4,755 m, and León 4,740 m) can be clearly seen from here. The **Parque La Isla** contains orchids, basketball and tennis courts, an amphitheatre and fountains. In the **Plaza Beethoven**, a different melody from Beethoven's works is chimed every hour; *por puestos/busetas,* run along Avenida 5, marked 'Santa María' or 'Chorro de Milla', US$0.25. **Jardín Acuario**, beside the aquarium ① *high season daily 0800-1800, low season closed Mon, US$0.25; (busetas leave from Av 4 y C 25, US$0.25, passing airport),* is an exhibition centre, mainly devoted to the way of life and the crafts of the Andean *campesinos.*

Mérida has several museums: **Museo de Arte Colonial** ① *Av 4, Casa 20-8, T252 7860, daily in high season 0900-1600, low season Tue-Fri 0800-1200, 1400-1800, US$0.50.*

More interesting is the small **Museo Arqueológico** ① *Av 3, Edif del Rectorado de la Universidad de los Andes, just off Plaza Bolívar, T240 1111, Mon-Fri 0800-1100, Sat-Sun 1000-1900,* with pre-Columbian exhibits from the Andean region. **Museo de Arte Moderno** ① *between Avs 2 and 3, diagonally opposite Plaza Bolívar, Tue-Sun 0900-1700, free,* is in the Centro Cultural Don Tulio Febres Cordero, check here for cultural events. Roger Manrique has an impressive butterfly collection (over 10,000), also knowledgeable about Andean wildlife, contact through **Arassari Trek**, see Tour operators, page 1367.

Trekking The heart of Venezuelan mountaineering and trekking is the Andes, with Mérida as the base. A number of important peaks can be scaled and there are some superb hikes in the highlands. Bear in mind that high altitudes will be reached and acclimatization is essential. Similarly, suitable equipment is necessary and you may wish to consider bringing your own. Also in the Sierra Nevada you can find the following sports: mountain biking, white water rafting, hang-gliding, paragliding and horse riding. The companies listed in Activities and tours, below, will give an idea of what is available.

Mérida

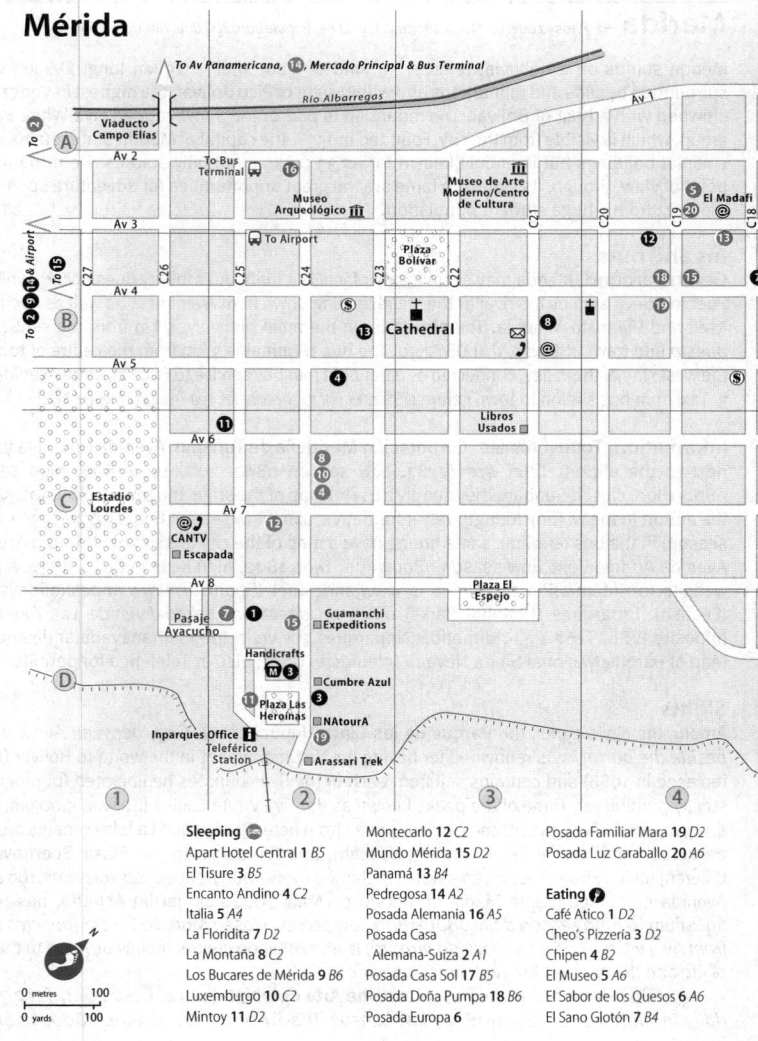

⊙ Sleeping

Mérida p1363, map p1364
Book ahead during school holidays and the Feria del Sol. Most hotels have a link on www.andes.net.
AL El Tisure, Av 4 entre C 17 y 18, T252 6072. Modern, colonial-style, very pleasant, disco.
A Pedregosa, off Av Los Próceres, T266 3181. On the edge of town, laid out like an Andean village with guests' cottages, pool, restaurant, good for families with children, safe, armed guards, National car hire office, horse riding, rowing boats and bicycle rental nearby.
B Mintoy, C 25 (Ayacucho), No 8-130, T252 0340. 10% discount for cash, comfortably

furnished, breakfast, good value, parking, suites with separate sitting area (sleeps 5).
C Apart Hotel Central, Av 3 entre C 16 y 17, T252 7629. Good apartments for 4 or 8 with TV and kitchen.
C Posada Casa Alemana-Suiza, El Encanto, Av 2 No 38-120, T263 6503, info@casa-alemana.com. Very nice, airport pick-up, parking, discount for long stays, laundry, English and German spoken.
C Montecarlo, Av 7 entre C 24 y C 25, T252 5981, F252 5910. Safe, parking, hot water, restaurant, ask for a back room with mountain view.
C Posada Casa Sol, Av 4 entre C15 y C16, T252 4164, info@posadacasasol.com. Renovated colonial-era house with lovely rooms, hot water, garden, free internet, food available, very helpful, English, German and Italian spoken. Recommended.
C Posada Luz Caraballo, Av 2 No 13-80, opposite La Plaza de Milla, T252 5441 (reserve by phone). Excellent cheap restaurant, good bar, hot water, colonial style old building.
C Posada Doña Pumpa, Av 5 y C 14, T/F252 7286. Good showers, spacious rooms, cable TV, quiet, very comfortable, English-speaking owner.
D Encanto Andino, C 24 No 6-53, entre Avs 6 y 7, T252 6929, F252 3580. Cheaper without bath, easy-going, fully-equipped kitchen, bicycle hire.
D La Montaña, C 24 No 6-4 entre Av 6 y 7, T252 5977, www.andes.net/lamontana/index.html. Laundry, English spoken, excellent restaurant.
D Los Bucares de Mérida, Av 4 No 15-5, T/F252 2841. Quiet, hot showers, TV, family rooms B nice patio with occasional live music, garage, safe.
D Luxemburgo, C 24, between Avs 6-7, T252 6865, www.luxemburgo.andes.net. Cold water, annex guesthouse used when hotel is full, safe.
D Posada Alemania, Av 2 entre C 17 y 18, No 17-76, T/F252 4067, info@posada-alemania.com. E without bath, quiet, family atmosphere, nice patio, busy, breakfast, laundry, kitchen, book exchange, tourist information, English and German spoken, German owner. Also runs good tours and activities as Carnaval Tours, T263 6503.
D Posada Europa, C 15 entre Avs 3 y 4, T252 4875, www.posada-europa.com. Rooms with shared bathrooms (with hot showers), terrace, kitchen facilities, Spanish lessons, English spoken.
D Posada Familiar Mara, C 24 No 8-215, T252 5507. Pleasant, hot water, luggage store.
E Italia, C 19 entre Av 2 y 3, T252 5737. Hot water, F in smaller rooms without bath, kitchen and laundry facilities, post box, travel agency, speak English, German and French, changes dollars.
E Mundo Mérida, C 24 y Av 8, on Plaza las Heroínas, T252 6844, jorgemda@hotmail.com. Hot water, shared bath, opposite *Guamanchi Tours*, luggage store, laundry, good.

Federico's **14** *B1*
Fonda Vegetariana **15** *B1*
Fortune **8** *B3*
Heladería Coromoto **9** *B1*
La Abadía **10** *A5*
La Esquina de
Pajarito **11** *C2*
La Mamma **12** *B4*
Lonchería Joseph **13** *B2*
T-Café **2** *B1*

Bars & clubs 🍸
Alfredo's **15** *B4*
Birosco Carioca **16** *A2*
Clubber **17** *B6*
El Hoyo del
Queque **18** *B4*
Gradas **19** *B4*
Kontiki **20** *A4*

E **Panamá**, Av 3 entre 18 y 19, T252 9156. Hot
water, popular with students and backpackers, TV.
F **La Floridita**, C 25, No 8-44, on Plaza las
Heroínas, T251 0452. Cheaper in shared room,
hot water, helpful, kitchen, well-kept, Cuban run.

Houses for rent

Finca La Trinitaria, a beautiful farm with
a 3-bedroom colonial house, 10 mins from the
town centre towards the Hechicera. Sleeps 6 in
comfort, self-catering, well-furnished and
equipped, US$50 per night, contact Ian and Mary
Woodward, T244 0760, IanWdwrd@netscape.net.

① Eating

Mérida *p1363*
Many places offer student set lunches for US$1-1.50.
†† **La Abadía**, Av 3 entre C 17 y 18, T251 0933.
Excellent, varied menu, 30 mins free internet
time with each meal.
†† **Chipen**, Av 5, C 24/C 23. Good meat.
†† **El Museo**, Av 3, C12-13. Nice patio, nostalgic
decorations, lots of graffiti, good food, pleasant
place for a drink.
††-† **La Mamma**, Av 3 and C 19. Good pizza,
pasta, set lunches and salad bar, popular in the
evening, live music at weekends, local wine.
† **Café Atico**, C 25 near Plaza Las Heroínas.
Excellent lunch for US$4. Recommended.
† **Cheo's Pizzería**, 3 separate restaurants on
Plaza Las Heroínas serving good pizzas.
† **Chino**, Av Los Chorros de Milla, a few hundred
metres before Parque Chorros de Milla, 15 mins
by bus. Excellent Chinese.
† **La Esquina de Pajarito**, C 25 esquina Av 6.
Simple but good local food, cheap set lunch.
† **Federico's**, Av 3, C27-28. Vegetarian and pizza.
† **Fonda Vegetariana**, C 29/Av 4. Recommended.
† **Fortune**, C 21 entre Av 4 y 5. Good Chinese
food, English and German spoken.
† **Lonchería Joseph**, C 23 entre Av 4 y 5.
Good *batidos*, cheap set meal, friendly Lebanese
owner speaks French.
† **La Montaña**, C 24 between Av 6 and 7 (next to
posada). Good, cheap food, pleasant setting.
† **El Sabor de los Quesos**, on Plaza de Milla. Very
good and cheap pizzería.
† **El Sano Glotón**, Av 4 y C 18. Vegetarian.
Recommended. Next door but one is a great
snack bar with excellent *empanadas*.
† **Zanzibar**, Av 4 entre C 19 y 20. Very good value
lunches under US$2, German chef.

Cafés

Heladería La Coromoto, Av 3 y C 29, T523525,
open 1400-2200, closed Mon, offers 750 flavours
of ice cream, at least 60 choices each day, eg,
trout, avocado, garlic, spaghetti!

Reina de los Andes, Av 5 entre C 21 y 22.
For arepas, juices and coffee.
T-Café, diagonally opposite Heladería
La Coromoto. Homemade food, juices,
coffee and cakes.

① Bars and clubs

Mérida *p1363*
There is no cover charge for nightclubs
but always take your passport or a copy.
Alfredo's, C 19 y Av 4. Bar, very popular, also
has vegetarian café (lunch US$1) and internet
access 0900-2300.
Birosca Carioca, Av 2 y C 24. Popular, with
live music, take care outside.
The Clubber, Av 4 entre C 14 y 15. Irish bar
with live music at weekends.
Gradas, opposite El Hoyo del Queque.
A US-style sports bar.
El Hoyo del Queque, across the road
from *Alfredo's*. Usually packed, good
meeting place.
Kontiki, Av 3 y C 19. Mérida's oldest club.

❀ Festivals and events

Mérida *p1363*
For 2 weeks leading up to Christmas there
are daily song contests between local students
on Plaza Bolívar, 1700-2200. **Feria del Sol**, held
on the week preceding Ash Wednesday. This
is also the peak bullfighting season. **1-2 Jan**,
Paradura del Niño; **15 May**, San Isidro.

① Shopping

Mérida *p1363*
Bookshops Librería Universidad, Av 3,
C 29/30. Superb. Libros Usados, J Santos,
Av 6, 21-45. Very good prices, including some
second-hand English, German and French books.
Camping shops 5007, Av 5 entre C 19
y 20, T252 6806. Cumbre Azul, C 22 opposite
Plaza Las Heroínas, T416 3231. Rents
mountaineering equipment (also sells fishing
tackle). Escapada, CC El Ramiral, C 26 entre
Av 7 y 8, T251 0523. Many tour operators
rent equipment.
Handicrafts Handicraft market on
La Plaza de Las Heroínas, opposite *teleférico*,
good café. Market on C 26 near Av T Febres
Cordero has expensive but beautiful and
unusual jewellery. Mercado Principal on
Av las Américas (buses for bus station pass by),
has many small shops, top floor restaurant has
regional *comida típica*, bargaining possible.
Music Discoteca Internacional, Av 3, Edif
Trujillo. Good record shop.

▲ Activities and tours

Mérida *p1363*
Paragliding Several agencies offer courses. Beginners must recognize that this is a dangerous sport and conditions in Mérida (lots of wind and thermals) are much better suited to those with experience. Accidents are not uncommon. Recommended is Raúl Penso of **Andes Fly Center**, T0414-746 5833, or through **Arassari Trek** (see below). Very experienced. Another experienced pilot is Oswaldo, T0414-717 5953.
Xtreme Adventours, Av 8, C24, T252 7241, www.xatours.com. For paragliding (latest equipment, safety) and many other adventure options, plus tours in the region.

Tour operators
Arassari Trek, C 24 No 8-301 (beside the teleférico), T/F252 5879, www.arassari.com Run by Tom and Raquel Evenou, English, French and German spoken, good tours with great guides at fair prices, very helpful and hospitable, highly recommended for trekking and climbing in the Sierra Nevada, horse riding, mountain biking, canyoning, caving, parapenting, rafting and canoeing. They also have a book exchange and cybercafé with excellent food. Angel Barreto can arrange domestic flights. Their Llanos tour (US$130-140 for 4 days) is excellent with many different activities, have their own, superb purpose-built camp. English-speaking guide Alan Highton is highly recommended for the tours of the Llanos and the Río Catatumbo.
Gravity Tours, C 24 entre Av 7 y 8, 1 block from cable car, T251 1279, 0414-737 7541 (mob), www.gravity-tours.com. Bilingual guides, natural history and adventure tours, some extreme, including rock climbing, rafting, biking, para-gliding, Llanos trips and Gran Sabana, good value.
Guamanchi Tours (owned by John and Joëlle Peña), C 24, No 8-39, T/F252 2080, www.guamanchi.com. German, French, Italian and English spoken, recommended for hiking, paragliding, horse riding, biking, birdwatching, equipment hire, exchange, information, mountain climbing, also tours to Llanos, Amazonia and Angel Falls, email service, free to customers.
NAtourA, C 24 No 8-237 beside the teleférico, T252 4216, www.natoura.com. Open daily 0830-1900, friendly company organizing tours throughout Venezuela, run by José Luis Troconis and Renate Reiners, English, French, German and Italian spoken, climbing, trekking, rafting, horse riding, mountain biking, birdwatching and equipment hire. Repeatedly recommended.
Ponciano Dugarte Sánchez, T266 5096/ 252 8416, recommended for jeep hire, English, German and Italian spoken. Also Lucio (T252

8416) and Nicolás Savedra (T271 2618) and Juan Medina, *Yagrumo*, C 24, mostalla@hotmail.com.

⊖ Transport

Mérida *p1363*
Air You can save a lot of time by checking in the day before flight. Daily flights to **Caracas** (1 hr direct), with **Santa Bárbara** (T263 2723); also to **Maracaibo, Barquisimeto, San Antonio** and **Valencia**. In the rainy season, especially on afternoon flights, planes may be diverted to San Antonio (3-5 hrs by road), or El Vigía (2½ hrs away). Airport tax US$1. *Casa de cambio* (see Banks below).
Bus To call a taxi ring bell on left just outside entrance as you leave. A small exit tax of US$0.25 is charged at the information desk, make sure you pay, officials check buses before departure. On interstate buses, it is essential to book in advance; for buses within the state you pay on board. **Bus companies**: Expresos Occidente, daily direct to **Caracas** at 0830, US$16, 12 hrs; via Valencia and Maracay at 0800; to **Coro/ Punto Fijo** at 0700, US$12, 12-14 hrs. Expresos San Cristóbal (T263 1881), daily direct to Caracas at 1930, 14 hrs, via Valencia and Maracay at 1700, 2030; to **Maracaibo**, at 1930, 8 hrs, US$8. **Expresos Mérida** (T263 3430/263 9918), to Caracas hourly from 1800, some direct others via Valencia and Maracay (10-11 hrs); also to **Barquisimeto** (US$8.50, 8 hrs), Maracaibo and Punto Fijo. **Transportes Barinas** (T263 4651), 4 daily to **Barinas** via Santo Domingo, US$3.50, 5 hrs; 3 to **Valera**, US$2.60, 5 hrs. **Táchira Mérida**, to **San Cristóbal** and **San Antonio** (US$8, 6 hrs). Expresos Los Llanos (T265 5927), to Caracas at 1900; to **San Fernando de Apure**, via Valencia and San Juan, at 2045, 18 hrs, US$30. Also *por puestos* leave from upper level of terminal to: Jají, Chiguará, Apartaderos (US$3), Barinas (US$4, 4 hrs), Maracaibo (US$12), Barquisimeto, Caracas, El Vigía, San Cristóbal (US$9), Valera (US$6).
Taxi In town about US$2. Línea Tibisay, outside *Park Hotel*, T263 7930. Recommended.

⊕ Directory

Mérida *p1363*
Banks Banco Mercantil, Av 5 y C 18. ATM takes Cirrus (commission lower than Visa). Banco Provincial, Av 4 y C 25, and Banco de Venezuela, Av 4 entre C 23 y 24, both ATM and cash advance on Visa and Mastercard at official rate. *Italcambio* at airport; this is often the easiest place to change cash and TCs. **Car hire** Several companies at the airport, including **Alquil Auto**, T263 1440, or **Dávila Tours**, Av Los Próceres opposite Urb la Trinidad, T266 0711, or airport T263 4510.
Consulates Colombia, Av Andrés Bello, CC San

Antonio, open 0800-1400. Visas take 10 min. **UK**, Professor Robert Kirby, honorary vice-Consul, Edif Don Chabelo, Apto PH-4, in front of Urb Humboldt, T266 2022, F266 3369.
Internet Places all over town, most with broadband, US$0.40-0.80 per hr. See *La Abadía* and *Arassari Trek* above. **El Madafi**, Av 3 entre C 18 y 19, open till midnight. **CANTV Centro de Comunicaciones**, Av 7 entre C 25 y 26. Also opposite *Ipostel*. **Language schools** Iowa Institute, Av 4 y C 18, T252 6404, www.iowa institute.com/locale.html. Run by Cathy Jensen de Sánchez, competitive prices, fully qualified teachers, homestays arranged. Recommended. **Latinoamericano de Idiomas**, CC Mamayeya, p 4, of C-5-38, T/F244 7808. Contact Marinés Asprino, Conjunto Residencial Andrés Bello, Torre C, p 5, Apt 6-1, T271 1209 for private lessons and cheap accommodation. Recommended. **Carolina Tenías**, 17 years' experience in private lessons for travellers, grammar and conversation; details at Posada Europa, C 15 entre Av 3 y 4; T252 4875/ T0416-876 5087. **Medical services** Doctor:

Dra María Yuraima C de Kirby at Clínica Médica, C 22 (opposite Cultural Centre), T521859. Speaks English. Recommended. **Post offices** Ipostel, C 21 entre Avs 4 y 5, 0800-1900 daily. Post office also in bus terminal, 0800-1200, 1400-1700, weekdays only. **Telephones** CANTV, C 21 y Av 5, Mon-Sat 0800-1930. **Useful addresses** Immigration office: ONIDEX, Av 4 y C 16. Tourist police: The Cuerpo Técnico de Policia Judicial (PTJ), will provide a *constancia* reporting the crime and listing the losses. Their office is on Av Las Américas, just below the Mercado Principal. Open daily but won't issue a *constancia* on Sun. To get there, take any bus marked 'Terminal Sur' or 'Mercado' leaving from C 25. You can also get a *constancia* from the *Prefectura Civil del Municipio Libertador*, but it can take all day and is only valid for a limited period of time; at Av 4 No 21-69, just off Plaza Bolívar; opening hours variable. The tourist offices are probably a better bet than the police if you need to register a theft for insurance purposes.

Sierra Nevada de Mérida

The Sierra is a mixture of the wild and isolated and the very touristy. In the latter group fall the cable car up Pico Espejo and villages designed to lure the shopper, but it is not difficult to escape the tour groups. There are routes from the mountains to the Llanos and to Colombia.

Parque Nacional Sierra Nevada (South)

Close to Mérida is the popular hiking area around Los Nevados, with the added attraction of the highest cable car in the world (if it's running). The further you go from Mérida, the greater the off-the-beaten-track possibilities for hiking and exploration that arise.

Since this is a national park, you need a permit to hike and camp overnight. It must be obtained from the *Inparques* (National Parks) office in Mérida (see Ins and outs). Permits are not given to single hikers (except to Los Nevados): a minimum of two people is required. It costs US$0.20 per person. Have your passport available. Return permit after your hike. If camping, remember that the area is between 3,500 and 4,200 m so acclimatization is necessary, as is warm clothing for night-time. (See Altitude, Health, Essentials, at the beginning of the book.) Some treks are very difficult so be sure to check with the tourist office before leaving. Water purification is also recommended. See also Mérida Tour operators and Parque Nacional Sierra Nevada (North) page 1369.

Pico Espejo ① *T252 5080/1997, F252 9174, 0700-1200 in high season, 0730-1200 low season, when there is no service Mon and Tue, tickets, US$20 return, must be bought in advance to avoid queues. Do not leave unattended baggage at the stations.* The world's highest and longest aerial cableway (built by the French in 1958) runs to Pico Espejo (4,776 m) in four stages. When operating, its final station is at Pico Espejo, with a change of car at Loma Redonda, the penultimate station, at 4,045 m. It operates haphazardly, but according to its website (www.telefericodemerida.com) it was running into Pico Espejo in June 2005.

Los Nevados From Los Nevados (*Altitude 2,711 m*), it is a very testing two-day trek to **Pico Espejo**; with a strong possibility of altitude sickness as the ascent is more than 1,600 m. It is best done November-June early in the morning (before 0830 ideally), before the clouds spoil the view. In summer the summit, with its statue to Nuestra Señora de las Nieves, is clouded and covered with snow and there is no view. It is a one-day return to Mérida. **Do not attempt Pico Espejo alone; go with a guide, it is easy to get lost**. Reputable trekking companies provide suitable clothing, temperatures can be as low as 0° C. August is the coldest month on the peaks. The glacier on Pico Bolívar can be seen clearly; so can Picos Humboldt and Bompland (4,883 m), forming the Corona, and to the east, on a clear day, the blue haze of the llanos.

From Los Nevados to **Loma Redonda** takes five to seven hours (14 km). The hike is not too difficult; breathtaking views; be prepared for cold rain in the afternoon, start very early. Mules do the journey daily, four hours; US$6 per mule.

You can walk down from Loma Redonda to **La Aguada** station (3,452 m) on a rough path, two hours; wear boots, walk slowly, not for children or the elderly, take water. From La Aguada you can walk to the main road to Mérida (three to five hours) and catch a *por puesto* to town. It is a 30-minute walk from La Aguada to Los Calderones' farm (accommodation and horses for hire). From La Aguada to the next station down, **La Montaña** (2,442 m), it's a tough 2½ hours walk (wet and overgrown). From La Montaña it's a 2½-3½ hour walk to Mérida. An alternative to the cableway is to take a jeep as far as the little hamlet of Los Nevados. All *posadas* will arrange food and mules for climbing to El Alto de la Cruz or to Loma Redonda.

The walk from Los Nevados to the village of **El Morro** (24 km) takes seven to nine hours (very steep in parts). (It's 47 km to Mérida; jeeps do the trip daily.) Sr Oviller Ruiz provides information on the history of the church and indigenous cemetery.

A recommended hike from Pico Espejo, is to the cloud forest at La Mucuy (see page 1369), two to three days walking at over 4,000 m altitude, passing spectacular snow peaks and several lakes. A tent and a warm sleeping bag are essential, as is a good map (local guides may lend theirs to photocopy).

Parque Nacional Sierra Nevada (North)
The Transandean highway snakes its way through the rugged mountain landscape, past neat, little towns of red-tiled roofs, steep fields and terraces of maize and potatoes. The snow-tipped peaks of the high sierras watch over this bucolic scene, with Pico Bolívar, at 5,000 m, lording it over them all. Throughout the park you will see a plant with felt-like leaves of pale grey-green, the *frailejón* (or great friar), which blooms from September to December. Be prepared for near-freezing temperatures if camping out.

Tabay From Plaza Bolívar in Tabay (10 km from Mérida) a jeep can be taken to the cloud forest at **La Mucuy** and to Aguas Calientes (or Termales), two warm pools in a stream (US$1.15).

Mucuchíes At Mucuchíes (*Phone code: 0274, Population: 9,175, Altitude: 2,980 m*) there is a trout farm. Beside the statue of the Liberator on Plaza Bolívar is a representation of the Indian boy, Tinajaca, and the Mucuchíes dog, Snowy, given to Bolívar in 1813 and, according to legend, devoted to him until their death on the same day at the Battle of Boyacá. The patron saint of Mucuchíes is San Benito; his festival on 29 December is celebrated by participants wearing flower-decorated hats and firing blunderbusses continuously. Tourist office on C 9 as you enter from Mérida; internet at C 9 Independencia.

Between Mucuchíes and Mérida is **Los Aleros**, a reconstruction of a 1930s town; entry US$5. Staff wear appropriate rustic costume (the drunks are not acting; they're paid by the government). Restaurant *El Caney*, colonial style, in front of bus stop, cheap, highly recommended, busy at weekends.

The road leads up from Mucuchíes to **San Rafael de Mucuchíes** (*Altitude: 3,140 m*), said to be the highest village in Venezuela. You should visit the remarkable church, pieced together from thousands of stones, by the late Juan Félix Sánchez and Epifania Gil. The picturesque road continues to Apartaderos, two hours from Mérida. It follows the Río Chama valley in the heart of the cultivated highlands and the fields extend up to the edge of the *páramo*, clinging to the steepest slopes.

Apartaderos (*Phone code 0274, Altitude 3,342 m*) is an unappealing tourist trap at the junction of Route 7 and the road over the Sierra Nevada to Barinas. About 3 km above Apartaderos, a narrow paved road (signposted) turns west off the highway at 'Escuela Estatal 121' and winds its way to **Llano del Hato** (at 3,510 m, the highest place in Venezuela served by road) and on to the three-domed **Centro de Investigaciones de Astronomía** (3,600 m) ① *the 4 telescopes and modern facilities are open to visitors daily 1000-2230 during school holidays, Easter Week, and in Aug and Dec; otherwise Sat 1000-2230, Sun 1000-1630 (check website for changes), US$2, www.cida.ve.* At least two viewing points on the way in give great views of the Lake Mucubají plateau. A good paved road descends 7 km from Llano del Hato to the Mérida highway at La Toma, just above Mucuchíes. Many prehispanic terraces and irrigation systems, adobe houses and ox-ploughed fields (*poyos*) are visible from the road.

A few kilometres beyond the junction of the roads from Barinas and Valera is the entrance to the **Parque Nacional Sierra Nevada** (*Trans Barinas* bus, two hours, or *por puesto* from Mérida US$3.50, two hours, 60 km). At the turn-off to the park is a motel, restaurant (good coffee and *arepas*) and shop. Near the entrance is **Laguna Mucubají**, at 3,600 m, with free but insecure campsite (visitors' centre, bookshop, good maps, interesting museum). A 1½-hour walk takes you to Laguna Negra. A permit is required from *Inparques* office at the entrance. A further 1½-hour walk from Laguna Negra is the very beautiful Laguna Los Patos. Horses can be hired (US$7.50 per person including guide). Guides (not absolutely necessary) can be found at Laguna Mucubají or at the hotels in Santo Domingo. (See Barquisimeto to the Andes section).

Southwest of Mérida

The continuation of the Trans-Andean Highway from Mérida to the Colombian border passes various small towns and the city of San Cristóbal. You can also drop down from this road eastwards to the Llanos.

Jají and around → *Phone code: 0274.*

Jají is famous for its colonial architecture, including an attractive main plaza. The plaza and adjoining streets are mainly given over to *artesanías* from all over the continent. There are a few basic hotels and good walking in the hills. *Buseta* from Terminal Sur, Mérida, hourly, 50 minutes, US$1. Off the road to Jají, 20 minutes from Mérida, is *Venezuela de Anteayer*, where regional culture is recreated in a series of displays, includes typical music and food, US$8. *Por puesto* from C 26, Mérida.

Continuing for 62 km – narrow, but mostly paved - beyond Jají, the Panamericana is reached 37 km east of El Vigía (several gas stations on the way). Transandean Route 7 leaves Mérida and passes through the Chama valley, heading for Lagunillas and Bailadores.

Tovar (*Phone code 0275, 96 km from Mérida*) is a nice little town with pleasant excursions, from where you can rejoin the Panamericana via Zea, itself a pleasant village, or tackle the wild and beautiful old mountain road over the Páramo de La Negra to San Cristóbal. From Tovar the road continues to **Bailadores** (fiesta from Christmas to Candlemas, bus US$1.25), and **La Grita**, a pleasant town (Sunday market, fiesta 6 August).

San Cristóbal → *Phone code: 0276. Colour map 1, grid B4. Population: 290,900. Altitude: 830 m.*

The capital of Táchira State was founded in 1561 and has been restored in the colonial style. A good road runs over the mountains to San Antonio towards the Colombian border, which is 55 km from San Cristóbal. Fiesta de San Sebastián, 7-30 January. **San Cristóbal**: Cotatur, Pabellones de Exposición, Avenida España, Pueblo Nuevo, T357 9655, cotatur@funtha.gov.ve. Helpful, José Gregorio speaks English. **Inparques**, Parque Metropolitano, Avenida 19 de Abril, T547 8347. **Touring y Automóvil Club**, Avenida Libertador C y Avenida Principal Las Lomas, Edif Olga.

San Antonio → *Phone code: 0276. Colour map 1, grid B4. Population: 42,630.*

The border town of San Antonio is connected by international bridge with Cúcuta on the Colombian side (about 16 km); continue by road or air to Bogotá. San Antonio has a colonial cathedral and some parks, but is not tourist-orientated. There is a festival on 13-20 May.

Border with Colombia Get a Venezuelan exit stamp at **ONIDEX** ① *Carrera 9 y Av 1 de Mayo, San Antonio*. The Colombian consulate is at 10 Centro Cívico San Antonio, p 2, open 0800-1400; better to go to Mérida for visas. **Note:** Venezuelan time is one hour ahead of Colombian.

Entering Venezuela, go to ONIDEX before buying a bus ticket to San Cristóbal. Taxi from ONIDEX to bus station US$1.50. If Venezuelan customs is closed at weekends, it is not possible to cross from Cúcuta. There is a customs post 5 km after San Antonio; be prepared for strip searches and for searches between San Cristóbal and Mérida.

If crossing by private vehicle, car documents are checked at ONIDEX. You must have a visa and a *carnet de passages* (but see page 43). See Cúcuta, Colombia, page 804, for details on exit formalities. Once in Venezuela, you may find that police are ignorant of requirements for foreign cars.

⊜ Sleeping

Parque Nacional Sierra Nevada (South) *p1368*
Los Nevados
Recommended *posadas* are:

E pp **Posada Bella Vista**, behind church. Hot water, hammocks, great views, restaurant.

E pp **Posada Guamanchi**, T252 2080, www.guamanchi.com. Owned by travel agency based in Mérida. Solar power, great views, cheaper with shared bath.

F pp **El Buen Jesús**, T252 5696. Hot water, meals available.

El Morro
E **Posada** run by Doña Chepa, as you enter from Los Nevados, warm. Recommended.

F pp **Posada El Orégano**, including meals, basic, good food. Recommended.

Parque Nacional Sierra Nevada (North) *p1369*
Tabay
D **La Casona de Tabay**, on the Mérida road 1½ km from the plaza, T0274-283 0089, posadalacasona@cantv.net. A beautiful colonial-style hotel, surrounded by mountains, comfortable, home cooking, family-run. Highly recommended. Take *por puesto*, 2 signposts.

D **Casa Vieja**, Transandina via Páramo, San Rafael de Tabay, inside the Parador Turístico El Paramito, T0274-417 1489, www.casa-vieja-merida.com. Colonial house with plenty of plants, owners are German and Peruvian, good double rooms, hot water, breakfast, use of kitchen, relaxing, very helpful, lots of information on independent trips from Tabay and transport, English, French and German spoken. Has travel agency, **Caiman Tours**, for Llanos, wildlife and adventure tours; see also www.birds-venezuela.de. From the bus terminal in Mérida take a bus via Mucuchíes or Apartaderos, 30 mins to Tabay, get off exactly 1.5 km after the gas station in Tabay village (just after you pass Plaza Bolivar); the bus stop is called "El Paramito". There is a sign on the road pointing left. Free pick up from the airport or terminal if you have a reservation. Recommended.

F pp **Posada de la Mano Poderosa**, T0414- 742 2862, dormitory rooms, lovely, quiet, hot showers, good food, great value, get off at La Plazuela then walk 15 mins towards Vivero Tutti Flor.

Mucuchíes
C **Los Conquistadores**, Av Carabobo 14, T/F872 0350. Good hotel with lots of facilities including pool and bicycle hire, ATM.

D **Posada Los Andes**, T872 0458, F872 0151. Old house above plaza, cosy rooms, hot water, shared bathrooms, excellent restaurant (closes 2030). Highly recommended.

San Rafael de Mucuchíes
D **El Rosal**, T872 0331. Hot water, good.

Apartaderos
B **Hotel y Restaurante Mifafi**, T888 0131. Good food, beautiful, no heating.

B **Parque Turístico**, T888 0094. Attractive modern chalet-style building, heating, very hot showers, helpful owner, expensive restaurant. Recommended.

E **Posada San Rafael del Páramo**, just outside Apartaderos on road to San Rafael, T872 0938. Cosy converted farmhouse, hot water, breakfast, restaurant in high season. Recommended.

E **Posada Viejo Apartaderos**, T888 0003, posadaviejoapartaderos@cantv.net. Good value, good restaurant with reasonable prices. Open only in high season.

Jají and around: Tovar *p1370*
D **Hostería Sabaneta**, Cra 3, T873 0611. With bath.

F **Pensión Ideal**, basic, laundry facilities.

San Cristóbal *p1370*
Several cheap hotels on Av 6A, just off the central plaza, and around Avs 5-7, C 4-8; **E-F** category.

A **Círculo Militar De Ferias El Tamá**, Av 19 de Abril, overlooking the town, T/F346 5175. Safe, spacious, good pool and gym. Recommended.

B **Del Rey**, Av Ferrero Tamayo, T343 0561, hotelrey@yahoo.com. Good showers, fridge, quiet. Recommended.

C **Korinu**, Cra 6, C 5, T344 9866. Laundry, restaurant, parking. Recommended.

D **Posada Turística Don Manuel**, Cra 10 No 1-104, Urb La Concordia, T347 8082. Hot water, family run, TV, fridge, kitchen facilities.

E **Ejecutivo**, C 6, No 3-45, T344 6298. Old and basic but clean and central.

E **Río**, outside bus station. Big rooms, hot shower.

San Antonio *p1370*
C **Neveri**, C 3, No 3-11, esq Carrera 3, T771 5702. A/c, TV, safe, parking nearby, by border.

D **Terepaima**, Carrera 8, No 1-37, T771 1763. Safe, good meals. Recommended.

E **Frontera**, C 2 y Carrera 9, No 8-70. Pleasant, good value. Many hotels near town centre.

Venezuela Sierra Nevada de Mérida Listings

● *For an explanation of the sleeping and eating price codes used in this guide, see inside the front*
● *cover. Other relevant information is found in Essentials pages 1330-1331.*

❶ Eating

Parque Nacional Sierra Nevada (North) *p1369*
El Morichal, 50 m from plaza, Tabay. Good, cheap.

Jají and around: Tovar *p1370*
Restaurant Kek Duna, Tovar. Hungarian owner speaks 6 languages and serves interesting food.

San Cristóbal *p1370*
Fuente de Soda La Bohème, Av García de Hevia y 7 Av, Centro Cívico. Expensive, breakfasts all day. **El Rancho de Esteban**, 500 m from *Hotel Del Rey*. Open-air with fine view over city, special barbecue dishes. Highly recommended.

San Antonio *p1370*
La Giralda de Sevilla, next door to Hotel Neveri. Only place open on Sun evenings. **Refugio de Julio**, Carrera 10. Value pizzas.

❷ Transport

Parque Nacional Sierra Nevada (South) *p1368*
Los Nevados
Jeep Los Nevados-**Mérida**, late afternoon (depart 0700 from Plaza Las Heroínas in Mérida), 5-6 hrs, US$10 pp, US$50 per jeep, very rough and narrow but spectacular.

Parque Nacional Sierra Nevada (North) *p1369*
Tabay
Regular *por puesto* service, buses from **Mérida** C 19 entre Avs 3 y 4. Gasoline in Tabay.

Apartaderos
Bus To **Mérida** from turn-off to Barinas; bus to **Barinas** on the road over the Sierra Nevada is unreliable, best to catch it in Mérida.

Jají and around: Tovar *p1370*
Bus From **Mérida** to Tovar, US$2.50.

San Cristóbal *p1370*
Air Airport at Santo Domingo, 40 km away. Taxi to San Cristóbal US$15, or walk 30 mins to highway and catch bus, 1 hr, US$0.50. Daily flights to/from **Caracas** with Aserca.
Bus The bus station is well-equipped; the information booth has little useful information. To **Maracaibo**, 6-8 hrs, US$11.50, *por puesto*, US$23. To **Mérida**, US$8, 6 hrs, US$9 by *por puesto*. To/from **Bailadores** US$2.50. To **Caracas**, US$20, 15 hrs (**Expresos Occidente**), executive service US$23.50; **Valencia**, US$17.50.

To **San Antonio**, 2½ hrs by bus, US$2, or *por puesto*, US$4, which continues to **Cúcuta**, stopping at Immigration in both countries, runs every 20 mins. By taxi to Cúcuta: US$19 to San Antonio, US$8 to wait at border, then US$12 to Cúcuta. To **Guasdualito**, US$10, 0650 bus connects with 1200 from Guasdualito to San Fernando de Apure.

San Antonio *p1370*
Air The airport has exchange facilities (mainly for Colombian pesos). Taxis run to ONIDEX (immigration) in town, and on to Cúcuta airport, US$15. *Por puesto* to airport, US$0.35. Internal flights: to **Caracas**, Aeropostal, **Aserca** and **Rutaca**. There are also flights to **Barcelona**, **Barquisimeto**, **Maracaibo**, **Mérida**, **Porlamar**, **Ciudad Bolívar**, **Puerto Ayacucho**, **Puerto Ordaz** and **Valencia**.
Bus **Caracas**-San Antonio US$23.50, a/c, to Caracas at 1600 and 1800, 12 hrs; to **Mérida** at 1200, 1700, US$8. Terminal tax US$0.10.

Border with Colombia
Air It is cheaper, but slower, to fly **Caracas**-San Antonio, take a taxi to Cúcuta, then take an internal Colombian flight, than to fly direct Caracas-Colombia. The airport transfer at San Antonio is well-organized and taxi drivers make the 25-min trip with all stops. Air tickets out of Cúcuta can be reserved in a Venezuelan travel agency.
Bus San Antonio to border bridge US$1.75, in bolívares or pesos. Taxi to Cúcuta, US$12. On any transport that crosses the border, make sure the driver knows you need to stop to obtain stamps. *Por puesto* drivers may refuse to wait. Taxi drivers will stop at all the offices. Just to visit Cúcuta, no documents are needed.

❸ Directory

San Cristóbal *p1370*
Banks Corp Banca (American Express), 5a Av, Edif Torre east. **Consulates** German, Edif Torovega, Carrera 8, La Concordia. **Post offices** Palacio Municipal, next to Cathedral. **Telephones** CANTV, on Carrera 23, C 10 y Pasaje Acueducto.

San Antonio *p1370*
Banks There is Amex at *Corp Banca*, on main plaza. TCs are difficult to change. *Casas de cambio* near the international bridge will not all change cheques and some will only change Colombian pesos, not even US$ cash. The exchange rate for bolívares to pesos is the same in San Antonio as in Cúcuta.

Los Llanos and Amazonas

A spectacular route descends from the Sierra Nevada to the flat llanos, one of the best places in the world to see birds and animals. This vast, sparsely populated wilderness of 300,000 sq km – one third of the country's area – lies between the Andes to the west and the Orinoco to the south and east. Southwest of the Guayana region, on the banks of the Orinoco, Puerto Ayacucho is the gateway to the jungles of Venezuela. Although it takes up about a fifth of the country, Amazonas and its tropical forests is largely unexplored and unspoilt.

Los Llanos

The *llanos* are veined by numerous slow running rivers, forested along their banks. The flat plain is only varied here and there by *mesas*, or slight upthrusts of the land. About five million of the country's 6.4 million cattle are in the *llanos*, but only around 10% of the human population. When the whole plain is periodically under water, the *llaneros* drive their cattle into the hills or through the flood from one *mesa* to another. When the plain is parched by the sun and the savanna grasses become inedible they herd the cattle down to the damper region of the Apure and Orinoco. Finally they drive them into the valley of Valencia to be fattened.

In October/November, when the vast plains are still partially flooded, wildlife abounds. Animals include capybara, caiman, monkeys, anacondas, river dolphins, pumas and many varieties of birds. Though it's possible to explore this region independently, towns are few and far between and distances are great. It's better to visit the *llanos* as part of a tour from Mérida (see Tour operators, page 1372), or stay at one of the ecotourism *hatos*, or ranches (see below).

Guanare → *Phone code: 0257. Colour map 1, grid B5. Population: 32,500.*
An excellent road goes to the western *llanos* of Barinas from Valencia. It goes through San Carlos, Acarigua (an agricultural centre and the largest city in Portuguesa state) and Guanare, which is a national place of pilgrimage with an old parish church containing the much venerated relic of the Virgin of Coromoto. Pilgrimages to Coromoto are on 2 January and 8 September and Candlemas is 1 February.

Barinas → *Phone code: 0273. Colour map 1, grid A5. Population: 240,000.*
The road continues to Barinas, the hot, sticky capital of the cattle-raising and oil-rich state of Barinas. A couple of colonial buildings remain: the Palacio del Marqués on the west side of the plaza and the Casa de la Cultura on the north side. On the south side of the plaza is the beautifully restored, 19th-century Escuela de Música; the cathedral is to the east. The shady Parque Universitario, just outside the city on Avenida 23 de Enero, has a botanical garden open Monday to Friday. **Tourist office** ① *Av Marqués del Pumar 5-42, southwest of Plaza Bolívar, T552 7091, corbatur@telcel.net.ve.* Helpful, maps, no English spoken; kiosks at airport and bus station.

San Fernando de Apure → *Phone code: 0247. Colour map 1, grid A6. Population: 135,000.*
At Lagua, 16 km east of Maracay, a good road leads south to San Fernando de Apure. It passes through San Juan de los Morros, which has natural hot springs; Ortiz, near the crossroads with the San Carlos-El Tigre road; the Guárico lake and Calabozo. Some 132 km south of Calabozo, San Fernando is the hot and sticky capital of the state of Apure and a fast-growing trade and transport hub for the region. There is *Corp Banca* for American Express, Avenida Miranda, and *Bancos Mercantil* (Paseo Libertador) and *Provincial* (Plaza Páez) with Visa and MasterCard ATM and cash advance. From San Fernando you can travel east to Ciudad Bolívar (see page 1400), or south to Puerto Ayacucho (see below).

San Fernando to Barinas
From San Fernando a road heads west to Barinas (468 km). It's a beautiful journey, but the road is in terrible condition between Mantecal, La Ye junction and Bruzual, a town just south of the Puente Nutrias on the Río Apure. In the early morning, many animals and birds can be seen, and in the wet season caiman (alligators) cross the road. **Mantecal** is a friendly cattle-ranching town with hotels and restaurants. *Fiesta*, 23-26 February.

Sleeping

Guanare *p1373*
C **Italia**, Carrera 5, No 19-60. A/c, bar and restaurant, off-street parking.
D **Colina**, near the river at bottom of town. Motel-style, comfortable, restaurant.

Barinas *p1373*
B **Varyná**, Av 23 de Enero, near the airport, T553 3984. A/c, restaurant, parking. Recommended.
D **Internacional**, C Arzobispo Méndez on Plaza Zamora, T552 2343. A/c, safe, good restaurant.
D **La Media Avenida**, Av 23 de Enero, near the airport, T552 2278. Cold showers, bar, restaurant, parking. Recommended.

Opposite bus terminal
D **Palacio**. A/c, good value.
E pp **Lisboa**. Basic, fan.

Staying at a tourist ranch
An alternative to travelling independently or arranging a tour from Mérida is to stay at one of the tourist ranches. Most of these are in Apure state and can be reached from Barinas or San Fernando de Apure.
LL pp **Doña Bárbara** ranch, book through *Doña Bárbara* travel agency, Paseo Libertador, Edif Hotel La Torraca, PB y Mezzanina, Apdo 55, San Fernando de Apure, T0247-341 3463, F341 2235, barbara@sfapure.c-com.net. Price includes 3 meals, 2 tours per day, bath, a/c or fan, clean, comfortable, or US$45 for a daytime visit.
LL-L pp **Hato Piñero**, contact number in Caracas: T0212-991 8935, F991 6668, www.hatopinero.com. This is a safari-type lodge at a working ranch near El Baúl (turn off Tinaco-El Sombrero road at El Cantón). Fully inclusive price, per day, packages can include return overland or air transport from Caracas. Free drinks, good room, bi-lingual nature guide for excellent bird- and animal- watching trips. Highly recommended. No public transport to ranch but ask police in El Baúl for ride with Hato Piñero workers. From Caracas the direct route is 6 hrs; from Ciudad Bolívar 9 hrs.
L **Hato El Cedral**, about 30 mins by bus from Mantecal (see above). Address: Av La Salle, edif Pancho p 5, of 33, Los Caobos, Caracas, T0212-781 8995, F793 6082, www.hatocedral.com. A 53,000-ha ranch where hunting is banned. Fully inclusive price, tax extra (high season 15 Nov to 30 Apr), a/c, hot water, land and river safaris, pool. Special offers at certain times of year.
L pp **Hato El Frío**, office in Achaguas, T0414-743 5329/0414-741 0022, F0247-882 1223. Also charges pp per night, including 3 meals, 2 tours per day (price rises 15 Nov-30 Apr), with bath, a/c or fan, clean, comfortable, US$45 for a daytime visit.

A pp **Reserva Privada de Flora y Fauna Mataclara**, on the road to El Baúl at Km 93 (next to Hato Piñero turn off). Address: Prof Antonio González-Fernández, Universidad de Los Llanos 'Unellez', Mesa de Caracas, Guanare 3323, Estado de Portuguesa, T0241-867 7254/ 0414-408 3514. Lodging with full board, horse riding, fishing and animal watching trips costs US$50 pp per day.
B pp **Río Caiman Camp**, contact Alexis Léon Rojas, Sector La Plazuela, San Rafael de Tabay, Mérida, T0414-974 5099 (mob), leontours@hotmail.com. Reached from Bruzual (see above), by road or by boat in the wet season (US$5). Fully inclusive, except horse riding and river rafting, accommodation in hammocks or tents, excursions, multilingual guides (mostly English and German).
B pp **Rancho Grande**, close to Mantecal, T0416-873-1192 (mob), aventura@aventuras ranchogrande.com. Run by very friendly and knowledgeable Ramón González. All inclusive, good wildlife spotting and horse riding trips.

San Fernando de Apure *p1373*
Most hotels are within 1 block of the intersection of Paseo Libertador and Av Miranda.
B **Gran Hotel Plaza**, C Bolívar, T342 1746, 2 blocks from the bus terminal. A/c, good.
C pp **El Río**, Av María Nieves, near the bus terminal, T341 1928. With a/c, good value.
C-D **La Fuente**, Miranda y Libertador, T342 3233. A/c, TV, phone, safe.
D **La Torraca**, Av Boulevard y Paseo Libertador by Plaza Bolívar, T342 2777. Excellent rooms, a/c, balcony overlooking centre of town. Recommended. D **Trinacria**, Av Miranda, near bus terminal, T342 3578. Huge rooms, a/c.

Eating

Guanare *p1373*
El Paisano, popular restaurant. **Restaurante Turístico La Casa Vieja**, good food and value.

Barinas *p1373*
♥♥♥ **El Estribo**, C Apure entre Av Garguera y Andrés Varela. Roast and barbecued local meat, good, open 1100-2400.
♥ **Don Enrique**, facing *Hotel Palacio*. Good, cheap.
♥ **Yoanna**, Av 7, 16-47, corner of Márques del Pumar. Arab owner, excellent.

San Fernando de Apure *p1373*
♥ **Comedor** in building beside CANTV. Has good *menú*, Mon-Fri, 1100-1200.
♥ **Gran Imperio Romano**, on Av Boulevard. Small, popular, good and cheap.
♥ **Punto Criollo**, Av Miranda. Good value.

⊖ Transport

Barinas *p1373*

Air Aeropuerto Nacional, Av 23 de Enero. Flights to **Caracas**.

Bus To **Mérida**, 6 a day with **Transportes Barinas**, US$3.25, spectacular ride through the mountains, 5-7 hrs (sit on right for best views); *por puesto*, US$4; also to **Valera** at 0730, US$5, 7 hrs. To **Caracas**, US$12.50, 8 hrs, several companies go direct or via **Maracay** and **Valencia**, regularly 0730-2300. To **San Cristóbal**, several daily, US$8.50, 5 hrs; to **San Fernando de Apure**, US$10, 9 hrs with **Expresos Los Llanos** at 0900, 2300; the same company also goes to **Maracaibo** (at 2000 and 2200, US$10, 8 hrs), **San Antonio** (at 2330) and **Puerto La Cruz** (3 a day, US$25, 16 hrs).

From Barinas there is a beautifully scenic road to Apartaderos, in the Sierra Nevada de Mérida (see page 1369). Motorists travelling east to Ciudad Bolívar can either go across the *llanos* or via San Carlos, Tinaco, El Sombrero, Chaguaramas, Valle de la Pascua (see below) and El Tigre. The latter route requires no ferry crossings and has more places with accommodation.

San Fernando de Apure *p1373*

Air Aeropuerto Las Flecheras, Av 1 de Mayo, T342 3356. Flights to **Caracas**.

Bus Terminal is modern and clean, not far from centre; US$2 taxi ride. To **Caracas**, US$11, 7 hrs; to **Barinas**, Expresos Zamora, 5 daily, 7 hrs (take food and drink), rough ride, day and night bus, US$10; to **Maracay**, US$7; to **Puerto Ayacucho**, US$15, 8 hrs; to **Calabozo**, 1½ hrs, US$3.

San Fernando to Barinas *p1373*

Bus San Fernando de Apure-Mantecal 3½ hrs, US$4.50; Mantecal-Barinas, 4 hrs, US$6.

⊕ Directory

Barinas *p1373*

Banks Banco Mercantil, Av Marqués del Pumar y Bolívar, and Banco Provincial, Av Marqués del Pumar y Carvajal, for MasterCard or Visa cash withdrawals.

Amazonas

Much of Amazonas is stunningly beautiful and untouched, but access is only by river. The more easily-accessible places lie on the course of the Orinoco and its tributaries. The best time to visit is October to December, after the rains, but at any season, this is a remote part of the country. On arrival in the Amazonas territory, it is necessary to register at a Guardia Nacional checkpoint about 20 km before Puerto Ayacucho. Around this area the national guard can be very strict and travellers are likely to be searched.

San Fernando to Puerto Ayacucho

Due south of San Fernando de Apure is **Puerto Páez** (*Population 2,600, Phone code 0247*) at the confluence of the Meta and Orinoco rivers; here there are crossings to Puerto Carreño in Colombia (see below), and to El Burro west of the Caicara-Puerto Ayacucho road. A road is being built from San Fernando to Puerto Páez; for 134 km it is paved, then from the Río Capanaparo it is dirt (two buses a day San Fernando-Puerto Páez, dry season, four ferry crossings). Between the Capanaparo and Cinaruco rivers is the **Parque Nacional Cinaruco- Capanaparo** (also called **Santos Luzardo**), reached only from this road. If this road is closed, to get to Puerto Ayacucho from San Fernando involves a 15-hour (minimum) detour via the Caicara ferry.

From Caicara a new paved road runs 370 km southwest to Puerto Ayacucho. The turn off to **El Burro**, where the boat crosses the Orinoco to Puerto Páez (ferry US$1, also to Puerto Carreño, Colombia), is 88 km north of Puerto Ayacucho (*taxi* El Burro-Puerto Ayacucho, two hours US$8).

Puerto Ayacucho →*Phone code: 0248. Colour map 1, grid B6. Population: 73,660.*

The capital of the State of Amazonas, 800 km via Orinoco from Ciudad Bolívar, has an area of 175,000 sq km and a population of 80,000. At the end of the dry season (April), it is very hot and sticky. It is deep in the wild, but no direct boats do the five day journey up river. **Museo Etnológico Monseñor Enzo Ceccarelli** ①*opposite church, Tue-Sat, Sun morning, US$1,* has a library and collection of regional exhibits, recommended. In front of the museum is a market, open every day, where *indígenas* sell handicrafts. One block away is the cathedral. The Salesian Mission House and boys' school on Plaza Bolívar may also be visited. Prices in Puerto Ayacucho are generally higher than north of the Orinoco. **Note:** Malaria is prevalent in this area; take precautions.

Venezuela Amazonas

Excursions Locals recommend October to December as the best time for trips, when the rivers are high but the worst of the rains has passed. In the low season, May-June, it may be difficult to organize tours for only a few days.

You can walk up **Cerro Perico** for good views of the town, or go to the Mirador, 1 km from centre, for good views of the Ature rapids. A recommended trip is to the village of Pintado (12 km south), where petroglyphs described by Humboldt can be seen on the huge rock **Cerro Pintado**. This is the most accessible petroglyph site of the hundreds scattered throughout Amazonas.

Some 35 km south on the road to Samariapo is the **Parque Tobogán de la Selva**, a pleasant picnic area with tables and refreshments based around a steeply inclined, smooth rock over which the Río Maripures cascades. This water-slide is great fun in the wet season; crowded on Sunday, take swimsuit, bathing shoes and food and drink (stick to the right to avoid crashing into the barrier, there are some painful rocks to the left near the bottom; few locals slide right from the top; also beware of broken glass). A small trail leads up from the slide to a natural jacuzzi after about 20 minutes. Taxi to Cerro Pintado and Parque Tobogán, US$15-20 return (be sure to organize your return with the driver, otherwise you may face a lengthy hike). Agencies in town arrange tours; easier but more expensive.

The well-paved road from Puerto Ayacucho to Samariapo (63 km) was built to bypass the rapids which here interrupt the Orinoco, dividing it into 'Upper' and 'Lower'; the powerful Maripures Rapids are very impressive.

Border with Colombia

Some 88 km north of Puerto Ayacucho a paved branch road leads west to El Burro, from where a ferry-barge crosses to Puerto Páez. On the south bank of the Meta opposite is Puerto Carreño in Colombia. Do not cross this border without first finding out what the security situation is on either side of the border. It is not recommended to enter the Llanos of Colombia at this time.

Tours in Amazonas

For starting out, the best base is Puerto Ayacucho. Do not travel alone. By ascending the Autana or Sipapo rivers, for example, you can see **Autana-tepuy**, a 1,200 m-high soaring mass of rock which no-one has yet climbed from the base. There are other *tepuis* in the region, including the great mass of the Sierra de la Neblina on the Brazilian border.

San Juan de Manapiare (Population: 3,700) is the regional centre for the middle Ventuari. A beautiful track winds around the Cerro Guanay to get there. The road starts at Caicara and goes through Guaniamo and Sabana de Cardona.

● Sleeping

Puerto Ayacucho p1375
A **Oriniquia Lodge**, on the Río Orinoco, 20 mins from airport, book through Cacao Travel, cacaotravel@cantv.net. Nice setting, comfortable.
C **City Center**, Av 23 de Enero, on roundabout at entrance to town, T521 0639. Pleasant, safe parking, takes credit cards.
D **Apure**, Av Orinoco 28, T521 0516, less than 1 km from centre. A/c, good restaurant. Recommended.
D **Guacharo's Amazonas Resort Hotel**, at end of Av Evelio Roa, 2 blocks from Av Río Negro, T521 0155. A/c, restaurant, attractive sitting room.
E **Res Internacional**, Av Aguerrevere 18, T521 0242. A/c (cheaper without), comfortable, shower, locked parking, safe but basic, not very clean, good place to find tour info and meet other travellers, if no room available you can sling up your hammock, bus drivers stay here and will drive you to the terminal for early morning journeys.
E **Tobogán**, Av Orinoco con Av Evelio Roa. With a/c, TV lounge, laundry facilities, helpful staff, English spoken, popular.

Private camps in Amazonas: There are a number of private river camps on the upper Orinoco but they do not welcome casual guests.

Near Puerto Ayacucho
LL pp **Jungle Camp Calypso**, run by *Calypso Tours*, T Caracas 0212-545 6009, F541 3036. In mixed jungle and dry forest setting, price is for 2 days including food, basic cabin accommodation, highly recommended, excursions in canoes.
B **Canturama Amazonas Resort**, T521 0266, or Caracas 0212-941 8813, F943 5160, 20 mins by vehicle south of town. On the banks of the Orinoco, 40 km from nearest jungle, highly recommended accommodation and food but beware biting insects by the river, full day tours US$10.
B **Dantos Adventure**. Very basic jungle refuge, accommodation and canoe tours, probably cheapest option available, also space for camping, run by English-speaking guide Reni Barrio, recommended, ask at *Aguas Bravas* (see below).

Río Manapiare area

LL Campamento Camani, in a forest clearing on the banks of the Río Alto Ventuari, 2 hrs by launch from San Juan de Manapiare, T521 4553. From Puerto Ayacucho daily aerotaxi takes 50 mins. Maximum 26 guests at any one time, mosquito nets, all amenities, excursions available. Price is for 3 day/2 night package.

LL Yutajé Camp, located on a tributary of the Río Manapiare due east of Puerto Ayacucho. The camp accommodates 30, with restaurant and bar, full board (in theory), fishing, canoes, horses, airboats, excursions to indigenous villages, expensive but professional, most welcoming. Reached by plane from Puerto Ayacucho or boat up the Ríos Manapiare and Corocoro (take something soft to sit on). Price is for 3 day/2 night package.

🍴 Eating

Puerto Ayacucho *p1375*

🍴 **Cherazad**, Aguerrevere y Av Orinoco. Arabic food, relatively expensive.

🍴 **El Padrino**, in Urb Andrés Eloy Blanco on Av Belisio Pérez off Av 23 de Enero. Good Italian.

🍴-🍴 **El Espagetazo**, Av Aguerrevere. Mainly pasta, most dishes US$3, popular with locals.

🍴-🍴 **Las Palmeras**, Av 23 de Enero, 2 blocks from the Redoma. Pizzas and fast food.

🍴 **Capi Fuente de Soda**, on Av Evelio Roa behind *gobernación*. Some vegetarian dishes.

🛍 Shopping

Puerto Ayacucho *p1375*

Handicrafts Good *artesanía* in the Plaza del Indio; also in **Artes Amazonas** on Av Evelio Roa, next to **Wayumi**, and in **Topocho** just up from Plaza del Indio. Many tourist souvenirs are on offer and Vicente Barletta, of **Típico El Casique**, Av Principal 583, Urb Andrés Eloy Blanco, has a good collection of masks (free); he also works as a guide, recommended, take own food and equipment.

🥾 Activities and tours

Tours in Amazonas *p1376*

It is strongly recommended to go on tours organized by tour agents or guides registered in the **Asocación de Guías**, in the Cámara de Turismo de Puerto Ayacucho, Casa de la Piedra, on the Arteria Vial de la Av Orinoco with Av Principal (the house on top of the large rock). Some independent guides may not have permission to visit Amazonas. Tours generally cost US$50-120 pp per day. Those listed below

will arrange permits and insurance but shop around.

Autana Aventura, Av Aguerrevere, 1 block from Av Orinoco. Owned by Julián Jaramillo.

Coyote Expediciones, Av Aguirrevere 75. Helpful, professional, English spoken, organizes trips staying in indigenous villages.

Expediciones Aguas Bravas Venezuela, Av Río Negro, No 32-2, in front of Plaza Rómulo Betancourt, T521 4458. Whitewater rafting, 2 daily from 0900-1200 and 1500-1800, 3-13 people per boat, reservations required at peak times, take insect repellent, sun protector, light shoes and swimsuit, US$5 pp.

Guaharibo CA, C Evelio Roa 39, in same building as *Wayumi*, T Caracas 952 6996, F953 0092. Manager Levis Olivo.

Tobogán Tours, Av 23 de Enero 24, near *Instituto del Menor*, T521 4865.

Yutajé Tours, in Urb Monte Bello, 1 block from Av Orinoco, past the Mercadito going out of town, T521 0664, turismoamazonas@cantv.net. Good value for money but organization erratic.

🚌 Transport

Puerto Ayacucho *p1375*

Air Airport 7 km southeast along Av Orinoco.

Bus Expresos del Valle to **Ciudad Bolívar** (US$12, 10 hrs; take something to eat, bus stops once for early lunch), **Caicara, Puerto Ordaz** and **San Félix**; Cooperativa Cacique to **San Fernando de Apure**, US$15, 8 hrs; both companies in bus terminal. Expresos La Prosperidad to **Caracas** and **Maracay** from Urb Alto Parima. Bus from **Caracas**, 2030, 2230 daily, US$21, 12 hrs (but much longer in wet season). *Por puesto* to Ciudad Bolívar, 3 daily, US$20, 10-12 hrs (Caicara Amazonas).

Ferry Ferry across the Orinoco, US$0.30. Boat to **Caicara**, 1½ days, US$18.75 including food, but bargain; repellent and hammock required.

🔧 Directory

Puerto Ayacucho *p1375*

Banks Unibanca, Av Orinoco No 37, has Visa ATM. Changing dollars is difficult; try *Hotel Tobogán*. **Car hire** Servicio Amazonas de Alquiler, Av Aguerrevere. **Internet** El Navegante, CC Maniglia, Av Orinoco, or on top floor of Biblioteca Pública Central, Av Río Negro. **Post offices** Ipostel on Av Aguerrevere 3 blocks up from Av Orinoco. **Telephones** International calls from CANTV, on Av Orinoco next to *Hotel Apure*; also from *Las Churuatas* on Av Aguerrevere y C Amazonas, 1 block from Plaza del Indio.

Barcelona p1378

C **Barcelona**, Av 5 de Julio, near Cathedral, T277 1065, F277 1076. TV, parking, 6th floor restaurant.
C **Neveri**, Av Fuerzas Armadas, T277 2376. Similar, good restaurant *Castillo del Oriente*.
D **Madrid**, just behind cathedral, T277 4043. With restaurant.
D **Plaza**, C Juncal opposite Cathedral, T277 2843. In a colonial building. Recommended.
D **Toledo**, Juncal y Av 5 de Julio. Basic, good value.

Puerto La Cruz p1379, map p1379

Newer, up-market hotels are at Lechería and El Morro; cheaper hotels are concentrated in the centre, though it's not easy to find a cheap hotel.
L **Gran Hotel Puerto La Cruz**, Paseo Colón, eastern edge of the centre, T500-3611, reservaciones. puertolacruz@hotelespremier.com. Best in this part of town, luxury hotel with all facilities.
A **Cristal Park**, Buenos Aires entre Libertad y Honduras, T267 0744, F265 3105. A/c, laundry, changes money at a god rate.
A **Rasil**, Paseo Colón y Rodriguez, T267 2535, rasilplc@hotmail.com. Rooms, suites and bungalows, 3 restaurants, bar, pool, gym, money exchange, car rental and other facilities, convenient for ferries and buses.
A **Senador**, Miranda y Bolívar, T267 3522, hotelsenadorplc@cantv.net. A/c, back rooms quieter, phone, restaurant with view, parking.
B **Caribbean Inn**, Freites, T267 4292, h-caribbean@convergence.com.ve. Big rooms, very well kept with quiet a/c, small pool, very good service.
B **Gaeta**, Paseo Colón y Maneiro, T281 4717, gaeta@telcel.net. Very modern, a/c, good location but very small rooms, restaurant, scooter rentals, *casa de cambio* (good rates).
B **La Marina**, Andrés Eloy Blanco, new ferry terminal. A/c, good views, waterside restaurant, parking for those using the Margarita ferry.
B **Riviera**, Paseo Colón 33, T267 2111, hotelriviera@cantv.net. Seafront hotel, noisy a/c, some rooms have balcony, phone, bar, watersports, very good location, poor breakfast.
C **Comercio**, Maneiro, 1 block from Paseo Colón, T265 7330. Phones, cold water only, a/c, safe.
C **Neptuno**, Paseo Colón y Juncal, T265 3261, F265 5790. A/c, hot water, TV, excellent restaurant, parking. Recommended.
D **Margelina**, Paseo Colón 109, next to *Neptuno*, T268 7545. Large rooms, a bit tatty, a/c, TV.
E **Pippo**, Freites y Municipal, T268 8810. Cold water, some rooms with TV, very noisy.

● Eating

Barcelona p1378

♥ **Bueno Pollo**, Av Miranda y C 5 Maturín. Good grilled chicken, pleasant atmosphere.

♥ **Lucky**, Av Miranda No 4-26, north of Plaza Bolívar. Chinese.

Puerto La Cruz p1379, map p1379

Many on Paseo Colón, eg **El Parador**, 2nd floor, excellent food and service. **Tío Pepe** and **Big Garden**, delicious sea food. **O Sole Mio**, cheap, excellent, wide variety.
♥♥ **El Guatacarauzo**, Paseo Colón near Pizza Hut. Live music, salsa, good atmosphere and value.
♥♥ **Maroco**, Av 5 de Julio 103. Good seafood.
♥ **Celeri**, on Av Municipal, 1 block from Guamaché. Vegetarian, open weekdays 1130-1530. Recommended.
♥ **El Farao**, east corner of main bus station. Excellent, authentic, spicy Arabic food.
♥ **El Teide**, Av 5 de Julio No 153, near Plaza Bolívar. Good local food, closes at 2000.
♥ **La Colmena**, next to *Hotel Riviera*. Vegetarian, worth trying.
♥ **La Granela**, Miranda y Honduras. Another vegetarian option.
♥ **La Taberna del Guácharo**, C Carabobo, east end of Paseo Colón. Excellent cheap Venezuelan cuisine, good service. Highly recommended.

Cafés

Heladería Tropic, Galería Colón on Paseo Colón. Good ice cream.
Sourdough Bakery and Grill, Paseo Colón. Indoor and outdoor seating, vegetarian options, excellent.

● Bars and clubs

Puerto La Cruz p1379, map p1379

Most nightspots have moved to El Morro and Lechería.
Casa Latina Av 5 de Julio. Good 1970s-style salsa.

▲ Activities and tours

Puerto La Cruz p1379, map p1379

Diving Several companies, mostly on Paseo Colón, run diving courses. They're a bit more expensive than Santa Fe and Mochima. Hotels and travel agents also organize trips. The nearest recompression chamber is on Isla Margarita. We have received favourable reports on the following:
Explosub, *Gran Hotel Puerto La Cruz*, T267 3256, www.puntonet.com.ve/explosub. Efficient, helpful, will dive with 1 person, US$75 for 2 dives, good 4-island tour.
Aquatic Adventures (formerly Lolo's Diving Center), at end of Paseo Colón in the Marina, T267 3963, T0414-820 8758 (mob), www.aquatic adven.com. Very experienced, English spoken, collect you from hotel and provide lunch, US$50 for 2 dives, 2-3 person minimum, 4-day PADI course US$300, rents snorkelling equipment.

Kayaking Jakera, www.jakera.com. Sea kayaks for rent from their lodge at Playa Colorada, trips to whole country arranged (lodge in Mérida too), Chris and Joanna helpful, English spoken.

Tour operators
Note: Do not buy tours from wandering salesmen not affiliated with a registered tour company. **Ma-Ci-Te**, CC Pasaje Colón, Paseo Colón, T268 8529, www.maciteturismo.com. Well-organized, helpful, local and national tours, also diving, English and Italian spoken.

◉ Transport

Barcelona *p1378*
Air The airport is 3 km south; also serves Puerto La Cruz. Many flights daily to Caracas, 40 mins, and daily flights to Porlamar, 30 mins, Maracaibo and Valencia (with **Aeropostal**, T286 4063, and **Aserca**). **Oficambio** exchange facilities (no TCs), *artesanía* shops, small museum, car rental agencies, **Inatur** booth (stays open late for some incoming flights, few handouts, friendly, cannot book hotels, a city map can be scrounged from **National Car Rental**). Taxi to airport from bus station US$3.50; taxi to Puerto La Cruz US$11.65.
Bus The Terminal de Pasajeros next to the Mercado Libre is used mostly by *por puestos*, with regular departures to Anaco, El Tigre, Maturín, Cumaná and other nearby destinations. Buses go to **Caracas** (5 hrs, 3 daily, US$8.75); **San Félix** (Ciudad Guayana); **Ciudad Bolívar** (6 daily); **Maturín** (2 daily). Buses for **Puerto La Cruz** (40 mins) run every few mins from another Terminal de Pasajeros, along Av 5 de Julio, past Plaza Bolívar.
Note: Take care around bus terminals.

Puerto La Cruz *p1379, map p1379*
Bus Bus terminal to the east of town; *por puesto* terminal at Av Juncal y Democracia. To **Caracas**, 5 hrs, US$8-14, at least 15 through the night, **Expresos Los Llanos** (T267 1373, recommended,

a/c, movies), **Sol de Margarita** (recommended), *por puesto*, depart 1550, 4 hrs, US$30; **Autoexpresos Ejecutivos** to/from **Caracas** 4 a day, US$22 (T267 8855, next to ferry terminal), highly recommended (also to Maracay, Valencia, Barquisimeto and Maturín). To **Mérida**, US$30, 16 hrs. To **Ciudad Bolívar** US$8; to **Ciudad Guayana** US$13.50. To **Cumaná**, bus US$3.50, *por puesto* US$7, 1½ hrs. To **Barcelona**, US$1.75, 40 mins. To **Carúpano**, US$7, 5 hrs. *Por puesto* to Playa Colorado US$2 and to Santa Fe about US$3. There are also services to San Félix, Maracay, Valencia, Barinas, San Cristóbal, Güiria. Along Av 5 de Julio runs a bus marked 'Intercomunal'. It links Puerto La Cruz with Barcelona and intervening points. Another Barcelona bus is marked 'Ruta Alternativa' and uses the inland highway via the Puerto La Cruz Golf and Country Club and Universidad de Oriente, US$0.20.
Ferry For details of ferries to **Isla Margarita**, see page 1397.

● Directory

Puerto La Cruz *p1379, map p1379*
Banks Corpbanca (American Express TCs), Av 5 de Julio, Local No 43. Italcambio, C C Paseo Mar, loc 6, C Sucre y Paseo Colón, T267 3623. Amex representative. Oficambio, Maneiro y Libertad, no commission on TCs, open 0800-1200, 1400-1730 Mon-Fri, or on the sea front between Buenos Aires and Sucre, Mon-Fri 0800-2100.
Consulates UK, *Hotel Maremares*, Av Américo Vespucio y Av R17, T811011, F814494.
Internet In Galería Colón, Paseo Colón, American Net and CANTV Centro de Comunicaciones. North American Connection, CC Paseo Plaza, C Carabobo, ½ block south of Hotel Puerto La Cruz. Fax and scanning facility as well as internet. Puerto Internet, C Maneiro.
Post offices and telephones CANTV and Ipostel, Freites y Bolívar, 1 block from Paseo Colón. Telephone office accepts Visa for calls.

Parque Nacional Mochima

Beyond the cities of Barcelona and Puerto La Cruz, the main focus is the Mochima national park, one of the country's most beautiful regions. Hundreds of tiny Caribbean islands, a seemingly endless series of beaches backed by some of Venezuela's most beautiful scenery and tiny coves tucked into bays, all offer excellent snorkelling, fishing and swimming.

Ins and outs Tour companies offer trips to the islands from Puerto La Cruz: for example **Passion**, Paseo Colón 47-B, T267 0242; passiontours@cantv.net, manager Gabriel Laclé, day tour around several islands with stops US$40, includes snorkelling equipment and soft drinks. Also **Aquatic Adventures**, see Puerto la Cruz Activities and tours, above. **Transtupaco**, next to *Gran Hotel Puerto La Cruz*, no tours, they act as a taxi to the islands. Alternatively, you can reach the islands with the *Embarcadero de Peñeros*, on Paseo Colón, behind the *Tejas Restaurant*. Departures from 0900-1000, return at 1600-1630; US$6 per person. Tourist office in Puerto La Cruz provides tour operators for day trips to various islands for swimming or snorkelling; six-hour trip to four islands costs US$25 per person, including drinks. The islands to the east (Isla de Plata, Monos, Picuda Grande and Chica and the beaches of Conoma and Conomita) are best reached from the port at **Guanta** (taxi from town, or *por puesto* from C Freites between Avenida 5 de Julio and C Democracia, and ask to be dropped off at the Urb Pamatacualito). **Note:** Boat trips to the islands are cheaper from **Santa Fe** or **Mochima** (see below). Bring your own food as the island restaurants are expensive.

Best time to visit At Christmas, Carnival and Easter this part of the coast becomes extremely congested so patience is needed as long queues of traffic can develop. Accommodation is very hard to find. It can also become littered and polluted, especially on the islands. Robbery may be a problem, but if you take care and use common sense the risk is minimal. Camping on the islands in Parque Nacional Mochima is not advisable.

Around the park Starting east from Puerto La Cruz is the Costa Azul, with the islands of the Parque Nacional Mochima offshore. Highway 9 follows the shore for much of the 85 km to Cumaná. The road is spectacular but if driving take great care between Playa Colorada and Cumaná. It passes the 'paradise-like' beaches of **Conoma** and **Conomita**. Further along is **Playa Arapito** (*posada*, **D**, restaurant, parking extra). Here boats can be hired to **La Piscina**, a beautiful coral reef near some small islands, for good snorkelling (lots of dolphins); US$15 per boat.

    Playa Colorada is a popular beach (Km 32) with beautiful red sands and palm trees (*por puesto* from corner of terminal in Puerto La Cruz, US$2, or hitch). Nearby are **Playa Vallecito** (camping free, security guard, car US$1, bar with good food and bottled water on sale, plenty of palm trees for hammock-slinging) and **Playa Santa Cruz**. At **Playa Los Hicacos** is a lovely coral reef. **Note**, robberies have been reported on the empty beach at the west end of Playa Colorada.

    In Sucre State 40 km from Puerto La Cruz is **Santa Fe** (*Phone code 0293*), larger and noisier than Mochima, but a good place to relax. The attractive beach is cleaned daily. It has a market on Saturday. Jeep, boat or diving tours available. Fishermen offer trips but their prices are usually high. Boat trips to Playas Colorada or Blanca cost US$15 per person; better to hire your own boat for half the price, or hitch down the road to Colorada.

    The little village of **Mochima** beyond Santa Fe, is 4 km off the main road (hitching difficult). It's busy at weekends but almost deserted through the week. The sea is dirty near the town. Boats take tourists to nearby beaches, such as Playa Marita and Playa Blanca (excellent snorkelling, take own equipment). Both have restaurants, but bring food and water to be safe. Boats to the islands cost US$11.50-15 (up to six people), depending on distance, eg **Semilla Tours** on the main street. Arrange with the boatman what time he will collect you. The tourist office arranges six hour, four-island trips with snorkelling and swimming, US$15. Canoeing trips are available and walks on local trails and to caves (ask for information, eg from Carlos Hernández, or Rodolfo Plaza - see Diving, below).

● Sleeping

Parque Nacional Mochima *p1381*
Playa Colorada
B **Villas Turísticas Playa Colorada**, Av Principal, T0416-681 6365 (mob). Clean pool, comfortable rooms, a/c, TV, also trailers for 4 (**B**), good restaurant, no credit cards, in Caracas T0212-992 7850.
D **Carmita**, Apdo 46/7, on road from beach to village. Excellent breakfast included, very helpful German-speaking owner. Highly recommended.
D **Posada Lemus**, Carretera Nacional, 200 m from entrance to town. Very clean, laundry, excellent food. Highly recommended.
E **Quinta Jaly**, C Marchán, T0416-681 8113 (mob). Run by Jack Allard, some a/c, shared bathroom, hot water, very quiet, also small bungalows, family

atmosphere, English and French spoken, use of kitchen, laundry facilities, good breakfast (US$2), multilingual library. Recommended.
E **Villa Nirvana**, 6-min walk uphill from beach, opposite *Jali*, run by Sra Rita who is Swiss, T0414-803 0101. Rooms with fan or a/c, also mini-apartments with kitchen for 2-4 people, hot water, kitchen facilities, English, French and German spoken, book exchange, breakfast US$2.50.

Santa Fe
B **Playa Santa Fe Resort and Dive Center**, T0414-773 3777, Santafe@telcel.net.ve. Renovated *posada* with various rooms and suites, laundry service, restaurant, owner Jerry Canaday speaks

English, diving trips US$65, transport to beaches, mountain bike rental.

D Bahía del Mar, T231 0073/0416-887 4307. Pleasant rooms with fan, upstairs rooms have a cool breeze, French and English spoken.

D Café del Mar. 1st hotel on beach, T231 0009. Fan, good restaurant, tours to islands US$5-10 pp, also to Gran Sabana, Orinoco Delta, owner Matthias Sauter, German spoken.

D La Sierra Inn, near *Café del Mar*, T231 0042/0414-993 3116. Rooms with fans, self-contained garden suite with fridge and cooker, run by Sr José Vivas, English spoken, helpful, tours to islands, recommended.

D Las Palmeras, T231 0008/0414-773 6152. Behind *Cochaima*, fan, room for 5 with fridge and cooker, French spoken.

D Posada Los Angeles, T0414-775 5445. With fan, room for 4 with fridge and cooker, Italian restaurant.

D Siete Delfines, on beach, T431 4166, dolphins@cantv.net. Cheaper without breakfast, safe, fan, laundry service, bar, good meals in restaurant, excursions, owner speaks German, English and Italian spoken.

E Cochaima, on beach, T0414-840 1615. Run by Margot, noisy, popular, fan, next to restaurant of same name (slow service), safe. Recommended.

E El Portugués, Sr Julio César, last *posada* on beach. Cooking facilities, very helpful. Recommended.

Mochima

B Posada Gaby, at end of road with its own pier next to sea, T431 0842/0414-773 1104. A/c or fan, breakfast available, lovely place, take guests to islands (included in the room price).

D Posada Mochimero, on main street in front of *Restaurant Mochimero*, T0414-773 8782. A/c or fan, rooms with bath, recently expanded.

D Villa Vicenta, Av Principal, T416 0916/0414-993 5877. Basic rooms with cold water and larger rooms with balcony, also cold water, dining room, owner Otilio is helpful.

Room to rent on the plaza from José Cruz, T416 6114 (his family also runs Posada Doña Cruz). A/c, TV, living room and bedroom. Recommended.

🍴 Eating

Parque Nacional Mochima *p1381*
Playa Colorada
🍴**Daniel's Barraca**, at east end of the beach, is good for cheap food.

Santa Fe
🍴**Club Naútico**, fish and Venezuelan dishes, open for lunch and dinner.
🍴**Los Molinos (Julios)**, open all day from 0800, beach bar serves sandwiches, hamburgers, beer and cocktails.

Mochima
🍴**El Mochimero**, on waterfront 5 mins from jetty. Highly recommended for lunch and dinner.
🍴**Il Forno de Mochima**, on the main street. Run by Roberto Iorio, for those who would like a change from seafood, homemade pastas and pizza.
🍴**Puerto Viejo**, on the plaza. Good food, if a bit pricey, good views.

⛰ Activities and tours

Parque Nacional Mochima *p1381*
Mochima
Diving Francisco García, runs a diving school and shop (*Aquatics Diving Center*, T416 0009/0414-777 4894), C La Marina at Plaza Apolinar. Equipment hire, courses, trips.
Rodolfo Plaza runs a diving school (*La Posada de los Buzos*, T432 3416/0414-777 1949, mochimarafting@hotmail.com) and hires equipment, also walking and canoeing trips around Mochima; contact him in Caracas (Los Palos Grandes, Av Andrés Bello entre 3a y 4a transversal, T0212-961 2531).

⊖ Transport

Parque Nacional Mochima *p1381*
Santa Fe
Getting there from **Cumaná**, take *por puesto* 1 block down from the Redonda del Indio, along Av Perimetral, US$1.75. It may be difficult to get a bus from **Puerto La Cruz** to stop at Santa Fe, take a *por puesto* (depart from terminal, US$3, 1 hr), or taxi, US$23 including wait.

Mochima
Bus From **Cumaná** to Mochima take a bus from outside the terminal and ask to be let off at the street where the transport goes to Mochima, US$1.50; change here to crowded bus or jeep (US$0.70). No buses between Santa Fe and Mochima, take a *por puesto*, bargain hard on the price, US$15-21 is reasonable. Bus to Cumaná, 1400, US$1.40.

Cumaná → *Phone code: 0293. Colour map 2, grid A1. Population: 280,000.*

Cumaná was founded in 1521 to exploit the nearby pearl fisheries. It straddles both banks of the Río Manzanares. Because of a succession of devastating earthquakes (the last in 1997), only a few historic sites remain. Cumaná is a charming place with its mixture of old and new, but the port area (1½ km from the centre) is not safe at night. Main festivals are 22 January, Santa Inés, a pre-Lenten carnival throughout the state of Sucre and 2 November, the Santos y Fideles Difuntos festival at El Tacal.

A long public beach, **San Luis**, is a short bus ride from the centre of town; take the 'San Luis/Los Chaimas' bus. The least spoilt part is the end by the *Hotel Los Bordones*.

The **Castillo de San Antonio de la Eminencia** (1686) has 16 mounted cannons, a drawbridge and dungeons from which there are said to be underground tunnels leading to the Santa Inés church. Restored in 1975, it is flood-lit at night (but don't go there after dark, it's not safe). The **Castillo de Santa María de la Cabeza** (1669) is a rectangular fortress with a panoramic view of San Antonio and the elegant homes below. **Convento de San Francisco**, the original Capuchin mission of 1514, was the first school on the continent; its remains are on the Plaza Badaracco Bermúdez facing the beach. The **Church of Santa Inés** (1637) was the base of the Franciscan missionaries; earthquakes have caused it to be rebuilt five times. A tiny 400-year-old statue of the Virgen de Candelaria is in the garden. The **home of Andrés Eloy Blanco** (1896-1955) ① *Mon-Fri 0800-1200, 1600-2000, Sat-Sun 0900-1200, 1600-2000, free,* one of Venezuela's greatest poets and politicians, on Plaza Bolívar, has been nicely restored to its turn-of-the-century elegance. On the opposite side of the plaza is **La Gobernación** around a courtyard lined by cannon from Santa María de la Cabeza; note the gargoyles and other colonial features. There are markets selling handicrafts and food on both sides of the river.

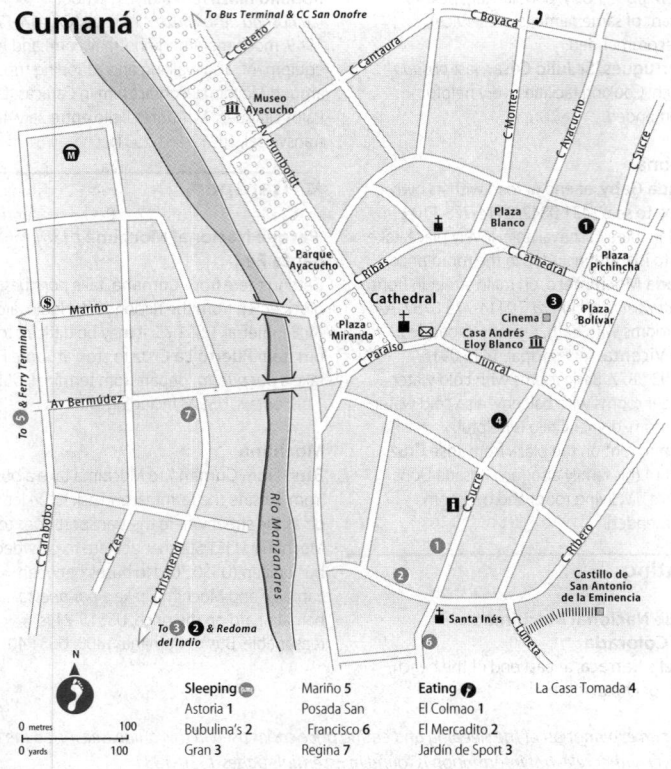

Cumaná

Sleeping ⊙
Astoria **1**
Bubulina's **2**
Gran **3**
Mariño **5**
Posada San Francisco **6**
Regina **7**

Eating ❷
El Colmao **1**
El Mercadito **2**
Jardín de Sport **3**
La Casa Tomada **4**

The **Museo Gran Mariscal de Ayacucho** ① *Consejo Municipal in Parque Ayacucho, Tue-Fri 0845-1130, 1545-1830; free tours,* commemorates the battle of Ayacucho: with portraits, relics and letters of Bolívar and José Antonio Sucre (Bolívar's first lieutenant). **Museo del Mar** ① *Av Universidad with Av Industrial, Tue-Sun 0830-1130, 1500-1800, US$0.75, getting there: take San Luis minibus from the cathedral,* has exhibits of tropical marine life, at the old airport.

For information contact **Dirección de Turismo** ① *C Sucre 49, T431 6051, fonmitur@venezuela.com.ve.* Very helpful, English spoken, only open in morning. Also **Fondoturismo de Sucre** ① *Edif Cámara de Comercio, Av Universidad, T451 2856, procatur_sucre@cantv.net.*

◎ Sleeping

Cumaná *p1384*
A **Nueva Toledo Suites**, end of Av Universidad, close to San Luis beach, T451 8118, www.nuevatoledo.com. A/c, hot water, TV, pool, beach bar, good value all-inclusive deals.
A **Los Bordones**, at end of Av Universidad on the beach, T451 3111. A/c, pool, restaurant, another hotel with all-inclusive options.
B **Bubulina's**, Callejón Santa Inés, half a block west of Santa Inés church, T431 4025/ 0414-393 8000, bubulinas@cantv.net. In the historic centre, beautifully restored colonial building, a/c, TV, hot water, good service, good restaurant with Venezuelan food. Recommended.
B **Gran Hotel**, Av Universidad near San Luis beach, T451 0671, F451 2677. A/c, pool, restaurant.
C **Mariño**, Mariño y Junín, T416 2462. Central, a/c, hot water, reasonable restaurant.
D **Posada San Francisco**, C Sucre, near Santa Inés, T431 3926. Renovated colonial house, court-yard, spacious rooms, hot water, a/c (cheaper with fan), very helpful, bar, restaurant. Recommended.
D **Regina**, Arismendi y Av Bermúdez, T431 1073. Hot water, a/c, restaurant, helpful, safe for valuables.
E-F **Astoria**, Sucre, T433 2708. A/c, shower, basic, bar, restaurant with good food cooked to order.

◎ Eating

Cumaná *p1384*
All central restaurants close Sun lunchtime
♯♯ **El Colmao** on Plaza Pichincha, C Sucre. Very good fish, charming service.
♯ **Ali Baba**, Av Bermúdez near corner of C Castellón. Excellent middle eastern food. Recommended.
♯ **El Mercadito** at Redoma del Indio. For excellent cheap lunches, fish and seafood.
La Casa Tomada, just off Plaza Bolívar on Sucre. A good *tasca* with reasonable prices.
Jardín de Sport, Plaza Bolívar. Outdoor café, good food, noisy atmosphere. Recommended.

▲ Activities and tours

Cumaná *p1384*
Piel Rojo, Sr Nelson Castro, T432 5416/0414- 840 7694, or in *Posada San Francisco*. Local tours, sailing, diving, many languages spoken.

Ya-Wei, in *Hotel Barceló* (see above), T451 9595, yawei@telcel.net.ve. Organizes launches to Araya Peninsula and beaches, diving, tours to Amazonas and Gran Sabana.

◎ Transport

Cumaná *p1384*
Bus Terminal 3 km northwest of the centre on Av Las Palomas, just before the junction with the peripheral road. Local bus into centre US$0.25, taxi US$2.50. *Por puesto* to **Puerto La Cruz**, US$7, bus US$3.50, 1½ hrs. To **Güiria**, US$8, **Expresos Los Llanos** once a day, *por puesto* US$15 (6-7 hrs), beware of overcharging, often stop in Irapa. To **Carúpano**, US$3, 2-3 hrs. To **Caripe**, you have to go to **Santa María**, south of Cariaco, and change to *por puesto* there. To **Caracas**, US$10-12 upwards depending on company (7-8 hrs), frequent service; many daily to **Ciudad Guayana** and **Ciudad Bolívar**, US$12.50 and 10 respectively. **Caribe** runs all the way to **Boa Vista** in Brazil. Other destinations include Maturín and Barcelona.
Ferry For Ferries to **Araya Peninsula** and **Isla Margarita**, see below and page 1397.

◎ Directory

Cumaná *p1384*
Banks For cash advance on Visa and MasterCard **Banco Mercantil**, Av Bermúdez, 2 blocks up from *Hotel Guaiqueri*. ATM and cash advance on Visa and Mastercard. Also Banco Venezuela, at Mariño y Rojas. **Corp Banca**, Av Bermúdez. Amex TCs changed at good rates, no commission. **Oficambio**, Mariño y Carabobo, Edif Funcal, 1 block from Plaza Estudiante. Cash and TCs at official rate (take passport and proof of purchase, may limit exchange to US$200), open weekdays 0800-1130 and 1415-1730, Sat 0830-1130.
Internet Centro de Comunicaciones CANTV, CC San Onofre at the end of Av Humboldt. Comiti, Edif Arismendi p2, Av Arismendi. **Post offices** Ipostel, next to Cathedral on C Paraíso. **Telephones** CANTV, on C Montés con Boyacá, 2 blocks from Plaza Blanco.

Playa Copey

C Posada Nena, 1 block from the beach, T331 7624, F331 7297. Fan, hot water, games room, good restaurant, public phone, good service, German spoken, owner Volker Alsen offers day trips to Cueva del Guácharo, Mochima, Medina and Pui Puy, US$25 pp. Recommended.

C-D Posada Casa Blanca, 5 mins from *Posada Nena*, T331 6896. Fan, hot water, safe, good family atmosphere, private stretch of beach illuminated at night, Spanish restaurant, German spoken, discounts for long stays.

Caripe *p1386*

C Finca Agroturística Campo Claro, at Teresén, T555 1013/0416-491 7654. Cabins with cooking facilities and bath, also rooms (**D**), restaurant for residents, horse riding.

C Samán, Enrique Chaumer 29, T/F545 1183, www.hotelsaman.com. Also has more expensive suites, comfortable, pool, parking, not so welcoming to backpackers.

E Plaza Centro, opposite church on Plaza Bolívar, T545 1018. Hot water, not very clean.

E Venezia, Av Enrique Chaumer 118, 5 mins from centre, T545 10325, F545 1875. No sheets, poor water and electricity supply, restaurant, owner speaks English.

Paria Peninsula *p1387*
Río Caribe

As well as those listed, there are other *posadas* and private, unmarked pensions; ask around.

B Posada Caribana, Av Bermúdez 25, T646 1242, www.caribana.com.ve. Beautifully restored colonial house, tastefully decorated, some a/c, otherwise fans, with breakfast, restaurant, bar, excursions.

C Mar Caribe, corner of boulevard next to pier, T646 1494. A/c, hot water, pool, restaurant.

C La Posada de Arlet, 24 de Julio 22, T/F646 1290. Price (US$30) includes breakfast, a/c, laundry service, English and German spoken, bar, offers day trips to local beaches and rents mountain bikes (only place in town that does, check bike carefully). Recommended.

D Posada de Angel, 2 km away from the beach at Playa Medina. Nice place to stay, with private bathrooms, fan, mosquito netting on windows.

E Posada Vanexa, on right as you enter village, T646 1670. Basic but clean, use of cooker.

F Pensión Papagayo, 14 de Febrero, 1 block from police station, opposite *liceo*, T646 18868. Charming house and garden, fan, shared bath with hot water (single sex), use of kitchen, German spoken, nice atmosphere, owner Cristina Castillo leads tours in the area.

San Juan de las Galdonas

B Las Pioneras, T0416 694 0113/964 0843. 4 star overlooking the main beach, fan or a/c, hot water, bar/restaurant, swimming pool, jacuzzi, parking.

C pp Habitat Paria, T0414-779 7955, www.habitatparia.vzla.org. With breakfast and supper, huge, splendid, zodiac theme, fan, hot water in some rooms, bar/restaurant, terraces, garden. The *posada* is right behind Barlovento beach on the right hand side of San Juan. Also run day trips by boat US$30 pp, min 5 passengers, packed lunch included.

C Posada Las Tres Carabelas, T0416-894 0914 (mob), carabelas3@hotmail.com. Fans and mosquito nets, restaurant, bar, wonderful view, owner Javier knowledgeable about local area. Ask about new *posada* at Guariquen, as yet untouched by tourism.

Güiria

C Playa Paraíso, 10 mins from town on road to Las Salinas, T982 0350, F982 0451. A/c, hot water, pool, restaurant, OK (but has caged toucan), boat trips to Macuro and Trinidad.

D Miramar, Turiparin, close to Banco República, T982 0732. A/c, cheaper with fan.

E Plaza, esq Plaza Bolívar, T982 0022. Basic, restaurant, luggage store.

La Posada de Chuchu, C Bideau, 2 blocks from plaza, T982 1266. A/c, hot water, TV, fridge, good *creole* restaurant. Recommended.

Macuro

E Posada Beatriz, C Mariño y Carabobo. Basic, clean, with bath, fan.

F Posada Marlo, C Mariño. Shared bath, fan.

● Eating

Araya *p1386*

Eat early as most places close before 2000. Hamburger stalls around the dock and 2 *panaderías*.

¶ **El Delfín**, at the dock. Good food and service.

¶ **La Monaguense**, 2 blocks from dock. Good value Venezuelan food.

¶ **Parador Turístico Eugenía**, in front of *Posada Helen*. For good value meals.

Carúpano *p1386*

¶¶-¶ **El Fogón de La Petaca**, Av Perimetral on the seafront. Traditional Venezuelan dishes, fish.

¶¶-¶ **La Madriguera**, Av Independencia close to Plaza Santa Rosa. Good Italian food, some vegetarian dishes, Italian and English spoken.

¶ **Bam Bam**, kiosk at the end of Plaza Miranda, close to seafront. Tasty hotdogs and hamburgers.

¶ **La Flor de Oriente**, Av Libertad, 4 blocks from Plaza Colón. Open from 0800, arepas, fruit juice

and main meals, good, large portions, good, food, reasonable prices, very busy at lunchtime.
El Oasis, Juncal in front of Plaza Bolívar. Open from 1800, best Arabic food in Carúpano.

Other options include the **food stalls** in the market, especially the one next to the car park, and the *empanadas* in the Plaza Santa Rosa.

Caripe *p1386*
Tasca Restaurante Río Colorado, G Blanco 77, T545 1243. Good, local food.
Trattoria de Stefano, C Cabello. Wide variety of good food, popular with locals and tourists.

Paria Peninsula*P1387*
Río Caribe
Doña Eva, Zea 46. Good food and is also a *posada*. **Mi Cocina**, on the road parallel to Av Bermúdez, 3 mins' walk from Plaza Bolívar. Very good food, large portions.

Güiria
Everywhere is closed Sun, except for kiosks on Plaza Bolívar. Restaurants include:
El Limón, C Piar, good value.
El Milagro, corner of Plaza Bolívar. OK.
Rincón Güireño, corner of Plaza Sucre. Good for breakfast (also rents rooms, **D-E**).

▲ Activities and tours

Carúpano *p1386*
Corpomedina, T331 5241, F331 3021, at the airport, associated with Fundación Thomas Merle (see Casa del Cable, above), reservations for cabins at Medina or Pui Puy beach: at Medina US$143 for 2, US$250 for 4, including meals, but not alcoholic beverages or transport; at Pui Puy US$51 for 2, US$80 for 4, including breakfast. Transport from the airport to Medina and return for 2 people US$95, to Pui Puy US$110.
Mar y Luna, T/F332 2668, louisa@cantv.net. Offer day trips to Medina, Pui Puy, Caripe, El Pilar, Los Pozos, specialist surfing and diving packages, walking and hiking in the Paria Peninsula, reconfirmation of international flights, reservations for national flights, reservations for *posadas*, reception of fax and email, general information and advice, English, French, Portuguese and a little Italian spoken, very helpful.

Paria Peninsula: Macuro *p1387*
A highly recommended **guide** is Eduardo Rothe, who put together, and lives at, the Museo de Macuro on Calle Bolívar, 1 block from *Posada Beatriz*. He'll take you on walking tours to the north coast, US$10-15 per person per day, or boat trips (US$60 per boat), or fishing trips (US$30 per person per day, including mangroves).

☉ Transport

Araya *p1386*
Ferry Cumaná-Araya ferry *la palita* shuttles back and forth from 0600 till 1700, US$1.85 pp, US$7.45 per car. At weekends it usually makes only 1 trip each way. Also **Naviarca** car ferry, 3 a day, T0800-227 2600/431 5577 or ferry terminal 433 3605. To get to ferry terminal take Conferry bus from **parador del centro**, just up from CANTV, in Cumaná (avoid walking; it can be dangerous). Alternatively, take a *tapadito* (passeger ferry in a converted fishing boat, leave when full, crowded, stuffy) to Manicuare and *camioneta* from there to Araya (15 mins). Return ferries from Araya depart from main wharf at end of Av Bermúdez. Ferries to **Isla de Margarita**, *tapaditos* depart from **Chacopata** (1 hr, US$10 one way). To get to Chacopata from Carúpano, take a *por puesto* at the stop diagonal to the market entrance (where the fish is unloaded), US$5, 1½ hrs.

Carúpano *p1386*
Air The airport is 15 mins' walk from the centre, US$5 by taxi. **Avior** (T331 2867) flies daily to **Caracas** and **Porlamar**, and less frequently to **Barcelona**, **Güiria** and **Tucupita**.
Bus To **Caracas**, US$15, 8 hrs, *Rodovías* directly into central Caracas close to Metro Colegio de Ingenieros. Most other buses only go as far as Terminal de Oriente. To **Maracay, Valencia**, US$20, 10 hrs. For other destinations such as **Cumaná**, US$3, 2 hrs, **Puerto La Cruz**, US$7, 4 hrs (Mochima/Santa Fé), **Güiria**, US$5, 3 hrs *por puestos* are a better option. They run more frequently and make fewer stops. Buses do not go from Carúpano to Caripe, you have to take a *por puesto* to **Cariaco**, US$2.80, then another to **Santa María**, US$2.10, then another to Caripe, US$1.70.

Caripe *p1386*
Bus Terminal 1 block south of main plaza. For **Carúpano**, take *por puestos* to Santa María and Cariaco (see above), similarly for **Río Caribe**. To get to **Cumaná**, go to Santa María and catch transport from there. Bus to **Maturín** direct, 0600, 2½ hrs, US$2; Maturín-**Caracas** costs US$12.55. *Por puesto* to Ciudad Bolívar 1500, 1½ hrs, US$3.50.

Cueva del Guácharo *p1386*
Bus Frequent from **Caripe** to the caves. If staying in Caripe, take a *por puesto* (a jeep marked Santa María - Muelle), at 0800, see the caves and waterfall and catch the Cumaná bus which goes past the caves between 1200 and 1230. Taxis from Caripe (US$2.35 - negotiate price), hitching possible. Bus from Cumaná direct to the Cueva del Guácharo leaves at 0715,

US$3.50 and stops right in front of the caves. *Por puesto* from Cumaná US$12.50, 2 hrs. Private tours can be organized from Cumaná for about US$15 per person, with guide.

Paria Peninsula *p1387*
Río Caribe and San Juan de las Galdonas
Bus Direct from **Caracas** (Terminal del Oriente) to Río Caribe with **Cruceros Oriente Sur**, 10 hrs, and from **Maturín** with Expresos Maturín. *Por puesto* Carúpano-Río Caribe, US$1.15. Buses depart Río Caribe from the other Plaza Bolívar, 7 blocks up from pier. Jeep Carúpano-San Juan de las Galdonas 1100, 1½ hrs; *camioneta* from Río Caribe from stop near petrol station, 0600 till 1300.

Güiria
Bus Depart Plaza Sucre, at top end of C Bolívar: **Expresos Maturín** to **Maturín** (US$6, 6 hrs), **Caripito, San Félix, Cumaná, Puerto La Cruz** and **Caracas**; also Expresos Los Llanos (recommended).
Ferry To **Macuro**: depart daily 1100-1200 from the Playita, US$3-5, return 0500, 2 hrs.
Travel to Trinidad A ferry leaves every Wed at 1500 for Chaguaramas, Trinidad (leaves Trinidad at 0900, Wed), 3½ hrs, US$80 return (plus tax). There is a US$23 exit tax from Venezuela (US$12.10 from Trinidad). Talk to Siciliano Bottini at the *Agencia Naviera* for other ships to Trinidad. Don't take any old boat that's going; however safe it may appear you may come under suspicion for drug running.

❶ Directory

Carúpano *p1386*
Banks It is not easy to change foreign currency in Carúpano. American Express TCs can be changed until 1400 at **CorpBanca**, next to Plaza Colón. Cash advance on Visa or MasterCard at **Banco Caribe**, Av Independencia, 4 blocks from Plaza Santa Rosa. ATMs are unreliable for European cards. Good exchange rate at the casino on the waterfront near the bus station. It may be possible to change dollars in *Hotels Lilma, San Francisco* or *Victoria*, but rates are not good. **Internet** Centro de Comunicaciones CANTV, C Juncal, opposite *Hotel San Francisco*, open 0800-2000. Cybercafé, C Las Margaritas entre Juncal y Carabobo, same hours. **Ebenezer**, CC Sahara, C San Félix. **Post offices and telephones** Both **Ipostel** and **CANTV** are at the end of Carabobo, 1 block up from Plaza Santa Rosa.

Paria Peninsula: Güiria *p1387*
Banks Corp Banca for American Express TCs, good rates, no commission. **Useful services** Immigration: visas can't be arranged in Güiria, should you need one; maximum length of stay 14 days (but check). For more than 14 days, get visa in Caracas. Remember to get exit stamp before leaving Venezuela. Officially, to enter Trinidad and Tobago you need a ticket to your home country, but a return to Venezuela is usually enough.

Isla de Margarita → *Colour map 2, grid A1*

Margarita is the country's main Caribbean holiday destination. Some parts are crowded but there are undeveloped beaches and colonial villages. Despite the property boom and frenetic building on much of the coast and in Porlamar, much of the island has been given over to natural parks. Of these the most striking is the Laguna La Restinga.

The western part, the Peninsula de Macanao, is hotter and more barren, with scrub, sand dunes and marshes. Wild deer, goats and hares roam the interior, but 4WDs are needed to penetrate it. The entrance to the Peninsula de Macanao is a pair of hills known as **Las Tetas de María Guevara**, a national monument covering 1,670 ha. There are mangroves in the **Laguna de las Marites** natural monument, west of Porlamar. Other parks are **Cerro El Copey**, 7,130 ha, and **Cerro Matasiete y Guayamurí**, 1,672 ha (both reached from La Asunción). The climate is exceptionally good; very little rain. The roads are good, and a bridge connects the two parts. Nueva Esparta's population is over 250,000, of whom 85,000 live in the main city, Porlamar. The capital is La Asunción.

Ins and outs
Getting there and around There are many flights from Caracas and other Venezuelan cities to **Isla de Margarita**, as well as international scheduled services and charter flights. There also ferries from La Guaira (Caracas), Puerto La Cruz and Cumaná in Venezuela. Car hire is a cheap way of getting around. The roads are generally good and most are paved. A bridge connects the two parts. Sign posts are often non-existent or poorly-positioned. It is best not to drive outside Porlamar after dark and women should avoid walking alone at night on the

island. Beware of robbery of hired vehicles. Public transport is available if you don't want to drive. ▸▸ *For more details, see Transport, page 1397.*

Information Isla de Margarita: The private **Cámara de Turismo** is at the seaward end of Avenida Santiago Mariño in Porlamar, T263 9024. They have free maps and are very helpful. A tourist information booth on Avenida 4 de Mayo, opposite the *Dugout* sports bar, has a good map, coupon booklet and *La Vista* tourist magazine. The **state tourism department** can be contacted on T262 2322/3638, corpoturmargarita@cantv.net. Travel agencies can also provide a tourist guide to Margarita. *MultiGuía de Margarita* (US$4) is published yearly and is a useful directory of tourist information and can be found in kiosks, *panaderías*, cafés, and bookshops. The best map is available from *Corpoven*. **Websites**: www.islamargarita.com and www.margaritaonline.com.

Porlamar →*Phone code: 0295.*
Most of the island's hotels are at Porlamar which is 20 km from airport and 28 km from Punta de Piedra, where ferries dock. If you're seeking sun and sand, then head for the north coast towns. Porlamar's beaches are nothing special, but it makes up for what it lacks in this department with its shops. The trendy Avenida Santiago Mariño and surroundings are the place for designer labels, but decent copies can be found on Blvds Guevara and Gómez and around Plaza Bolívar in the centre. For bargains on denims, t-shirts, shorts, swimming gear, bikinis and towels, take a bus to the *Conejeros* **market**. At Igualdad y Díaz is the **Museo de Arte Francisco Narváez**, displaying the work of this local sculptor. At night everything closes by 2300.

Ferries go from Punta de Piedra and *peñeros* from El Yaque and La Isleta to the **Isla de Coche** (11 km by 6), which has 4,500 inhabitants and one of the richest salt mines in the country (see Transport below). They also go, on hire only, to **Isla de Cubagua**, which is totally deserted, but you can visit the **ruins of Nueva Cádiz** (which have been excavated). Large private yachts and catamarans take tourists on day trips to Coche.

La Asunción →*Population: 30,000.*
The capital is a few kilometres inland from Porlamar. It has several **colonial buildings**, a **cathedral**, and the **fort of Santa Rosa** ① *Mon 0800-1500, other days 0800-1800*, with a famous bottle dungeon. There is a **museum** in the Casa Capitular, and a local **market**, good for handicrafts. Nearby is the **Cerro Matasiete** historical site, where the defeat of the Spanish on 31 July 1817 led to their evacuation of the island.

Beaches on Margarita
There are wild, isolated beaches, long white stretches of sand bordered by palms, developed beaches with restaurants and sunshades for hire, and beaches where you can surf or snorkel. Sunscreen is essential. The beaches of Porlamar suffer from their popularity at weekends. The **Bella Vista** beach, although crowded, is kept clean; lots of restaurants. **Playa Concorde** is small, sheltered and tucked away to the side of the marina. **Playa Morena** is a long, barren strip of sand serving the Costa Azul hotel zone to the east of the city. **La Caracola** is a very popular beach for the younger crowd.

The beaches on the **east coast** (see also Playa Guacuco below) are divided into ocean and calm beaches, according to their location in relation to the open sea. The former tend to be rougher (good surfing and windsurfing) and colder. Water is clear and unpolluted. Restaurants, *churuatas* (bars built like native huts), sunshades and deckchairs are widespread. Hire charges are not more than US$10.

Pampatar →*Population: 25,000.*
For a more Venezuelan atmosphere go northeast to Pampatar, which is set around a bay favoured by yachtsmen as a summer anchorage. Pampatar has the island's largest fort, **San Carlos de Borromeo,** built in 1662 after the Dutch destroyed the original. Visit also the church of **Cristo del Buen Viaje**, the **Library/Museum** and the **customs house**. There is an amusement park to the southwest of Pampatar, called **Diverland** ① *T267 0571, www.parquediverland.com, Fri-Sat 1800-2400, Sun 1700-2400, more frequently in peak holiday season, US$5 adults, US$3.35 children, all rides included (low season US$0.50 and each ride US$0.30-0.60).* Jet skis can be hired on the clean and pretty beach. A fishing boat

turn left after 300 m. Run by Matthias, ask for special dishes cooked by Yvonne, internet access (good rates).

El Paradiso, south end. Rents out cabins, small but comfortable.

Posada Shangri-Lá. Recommended.

Juan Griego *p1393*

El Buho, a French-owned pub open till 0600. Recommended.

Juan Griego Steak House, same building as *Hotel El Yare*. Good value. Recommended.

Restaurant Mi Isla. Recommended.

Viejo Muelle, good restaurant, live music, outside beach bar.

Viña del Mar, opposite *Hotel Fortín*. A/c, attractive, excellent food.

Playa El Yaque *p1393*

🍴**Fuerza 6** and **Gabi's Grill**, main meals US$6.

🍷 Bars and clubs

Porlamar *p1391*

Bahía, Av Raúl Leoni and Vía El Morro. Bar-restaurant, excellent value, live music.

Cheers, Av Santiago Mariño y Tubores. A popular sports bar.

Doce 34, Av 4 de Mayo. 2 dance floors. Highly recommended.

Dugout, Av 4 de Mayo. Popular sports bar.

Mosquito Coast Club, behind *Bella Vista Hotel*. Good merengue and rock music, bar outside, also does excellent Mexican meals (beware of overcharging on simple items like water).

Señor Frogs, one of 3 bar/clubs in the Centro Comercial Costal Azul on Av Bolívar. Popular.

Village Club, Av Santiago Mariño. Recommended disco, expensive drinks, cover charge.

Woody's Bar, Av 4 de Mayo. Spit and sawdust venue good for a drink and a dance.
Many of the hotels in Urb Costa Azul have relatively inexpensive **casinos**; the best are the Casino del Sol at the *Hotel Marina Bay*, and Gran Casino Hilton. Porlamar has many illegal casinos.

Playa El Yaque *p1393*

Several beach bars; best bar is **Los Surf Piratas**, drinks and dancing from 2130.

⊛ Festivals and events

Isla de Margarita *p, map p1392*

Many religious festivals on the island, including **19 Mar** at Paraguachí (*Feria de San José*, 10 days); **26 Jul** at Punta de Piedras; **31 Jul** (Batalla de Matasiete) and **15 Aug** (Asunción de la Virgen) at La Asunción; **1-8 Sep** at El Valle; **4-11 Nov** at Boca del Río, **4-30 Nov** at Boca del Pozo;

5-6 Dec at Porlamar; **27 Dec-3 Jan** at Juan Griego See map for locations.

◎ Shopping

Porlamar *p1391*

Margarita's status as a duty-free zone attracts Venezuelan shoppers, who go in droves for clothing, electronic goods and other items. Gold and gems are good value, but many things are not. Street sellers lay out their handicrafts on Av Santiago Mariño in the afternoon. When purchasing jewellery, bargain, don't pay by credit card (surcharges are imposed) and get a detailed guarantee of the item.

Del Bellorín, Cedeño, near Av Santiago Mariño. If you are not after duty-free shopping, this is a good place for handicrafts.

Sonia Gems, on Cedeño. Good jewellery.

▲ Activities and tours

Porlamar *p1391*

Diving Porlamar is a good place to book scuba diving and snorkelling trips: most go to Los Frailes, a small group of islands to the north of Playa Agua, and reputedly the best diving and snorkelling in Margarita, but it's also possible to dive at Parque Nacional La Restinga and Isla Cubagua. Prices from US$75 pp for an all-inclusive full day (2 dives), but bargaining is possible if you have a group of 4 or more. Snorkelling is always about half the price of scuba diving.

Aquanauts Diving, T267-1645, www.aqua nauts.com.ve. PADI school, scuba and snorkelling.

Enomis' Divers, at *Hotel Margarita Dynasty*, Los Uveros, and Caribbean Center Mall, Av Bolívar, T/F262 2977, enomisdivers@hotmail.com. Recommended.

Margarita Divers, at the Marina Concorde, T264 2350. ½ and 1-day dives and PADI courses.

Octopus, at *Hotel Hilton*, Los Uveros, and Av Bolívar 13, T264 6272, octopus@cantv.net.

Jeep tours   CC Tours, El Colegio, T264 2003. Tours taking in Cerro El Copey and La Restinga national parks, off-roading in Macanao Peninsula, and a couple of beaches, including food and drink.

Highberg Tours, *Hotel Margarita Princess*, Av 4 de Mayo, T/F263 1170, jeepsafari@ telcel.net. US$50 pp, guides in English, German, and Polish, tours around Margarita.

Sailing The private yachts **Viola Festival** and **Moon Dancer**, and the catamarans **Yemaya** and **Catatumbo** can be hired for mini cruises to the island of Coche or Isla Cubagua. Contact **Viola Turismo**, Caribbean Center Mall, Av Bolívar, T267 0552, **Enomis' Divers** or **Octopus** (see above). Expect to pay US$35-40 pp. They can also arrange fishing trips.

Trekking Moony Shuttle Service,
T263 5418, runs treks in Cerro El Copey.
Tours Most tours can be arranged through
travel agents.
Esparta Tours, Final de Av Santiago Mariño, near
Hotel Bella Vista, T261 5524.

La Restinga and around *p1393*
Peninsula de Macanao
Horse riding You can ride on the peninsula at
Hato San Francisco Cabatucan Ranch
(T0416-681 9348 (mob), cabatucan@telcel.net.ve)
and at El Saco with **Rancho Negro**, T242 3197,
T0414-995 1103 (mob). Prices US$35-US$45 pp.

⊖ Transport

Porlamar *p1391*
Air There are too many flight options to list
here: check with local offices for details. **Gen
Santiago Mariño Airport**, between Porlamar and
Punta de Piedras, has the international and
national terminals at either end. Taxi from
Porlamar US$10. There are scheduled flights to
Frankfurt and internal flights to almost all
Venezuela's airports. All national airlines have
routes to **Margarita**. Many daily flights to/from
Caracas, with Aeropostal, Láser, Santa Bárbara,
and **Aserca**, 45 mins flight; tickets are much
cheaper if purchased in Venezuela. Reservations
made from outside Venezuela are not always
honoured. To **Canaima** and to **Los Roques** with
Aereotuy and Rutaca.
Bus Local: *Por Puestos* serve most of the
island: to Punta de Piedras, from Maneiro,
Mariño a Arismendi, US$0.75; Airport, from
Centro Comercial AB, Av Bolívar (0530 and 2000
every day), US$1; La Asunción, from Fajardo,
Igualdad a Marcano, US$0.35; Pampatar, from
Fajardo y La Marina, US$0.25; La Restinga, from
Mariño, La Marina a Maneiro, US$1; Playa El
Agua, from Guevara, Marcano a Cedeño; Juan
Griego, from Av Miranda, Igualdad a Marcano,
US$0.65; El Valle, from Av Miranda, Igualdad a
Marcano; Playa Guacuco, from Fraternidad, La
Marina a Mérito (mornings), from Fajardo,
Igualdad a Velásquez (afternoons); El Conejeros,
Fraternidad, Igualdad a Velásquez.
Long distance: Several bus companies
in Caracas sell through tickets from Caracas to
Porlamar, arriving about midday. Buses return to
Caracas from La Paralela bus station in Porlamar.
Ferry From **Puerto La Cruz** to Margarita
(Punta de Piedras): **Conferry**, Los Cocos
terminal, Puerto La Cruz, T0281-267 7847,
www.conferry.com. Ferries to Margarita, depart
3 times a day (check times, extras when busy), 5
hrs, passengers US$7-9.30 one-way, children
2-7 half price (proof of age required), cars

US$15. Fast ferries, **Margarita Express** and
Cacique Express, take 2 hrs, US$18-27 one way.
Also from Terminal Marítimo, La Guaira, near
Caracas, T/F331 2053, US$37-51 one way.
Ferries not always punctual. Don't believe taxi
drivers at bus terminal who may tell you there's
a ferry about to leave. To get to terminal in
Puerto La Cruz, take 'Bello Monte' *por puesto*
from Libertad y Anzoátegui, 2 blocks from Plaza
Bolívar. From **Cumaná**, Conferry Terminal,
Puerto Sucre, T0293-433 1903, twice a day (may
wait until full of cars), US$10 one way for
passengers. **Conferry** freefone number for
reservations 0501-2663 3779. In Porlamar T261
6780; in Punta de Piedras T239 8340. **Gran
Cacique II** is a passenger-only hydrofoil service
that also runs from Puerto La Cruz, T0800-227
2600 (2 daily, US$19, 2 hrs), and Cumaná,
T0293-432 0011 (2 daily, US$16, 2 hrs). A ferry
operated by **Conferry** from Punta de Piedras to
Coche sails once a day, US$1.50, 1 hr. **Note**:
Ferries are very busy at weekends and Mon.
Taxi To hire a taxi for a day costs US$10-15
per hr. Always fix fare in advance; 30%
surcharge after 2100.

ⓘ Directory

Porlamar *p1391*
Airline offices Aeropostal, *Hotel Hilton*, Los
Uveros, T264 5877, T0800-284 6637. **Aereotuy**,
Edif Vista Bella, Av Santiago Mariño, T263 2211.
Aserca, CC Margarita Plaza, Av Santiago Mariño,
near *Hotel Bella Vista*, T261 6186, T0800-648
8356. **Avior**, Av 4 de Mayo, Edif Ofega, T416 8810.
Láser, Edif Bahía de Guaraguao, Av Santiago
Mariño, T269 1216, T0800-527 3700. **Rutaca**,
Galería La Rosa, Cedeño, T269 9236.
Banks National banks on Avs Santiago Mariño
and 4 de Mayo. (Banks are open 0830-1130,
1400-1630.) **Casas de cambio**: Cambio Cussco
at Velásquez y Av Santiago Mariño. Italcambio,
CC Jumbo, Av 4 de Mayo, Nivel Ciudad. **Bicycle
hire** US$6 per day from **Bicimanía**, Caribbean
Center Mall, Av Bolívar T/F262 9116,
bicimania@cantv.net. **Car hire** A cheap way of
getting around the island; several offices at the
airport and larger hotels, average US$35 per day.
Ramcar II, at airport and *Hotel Bella Vista*,
recommended as cheap and reliable, non-
deductible insurance (others on Av Santiago
Mariño). In all cases, check the brakes and
bodywork and check conditions and terms of hire
thoroughly. Scooters can also be hired. **Maruba
Motor Rentals**, La Mariña. English spoken, good
maps, US$16 bikes for 2, US$13 bikes for one.
Highly recommended. Motor cycles may not be
ridden between 2000 and 0500. **Note**: Make
sure to fill up before leaving Porlamar as service

old colonial house, a/c, fan, hot water, restaurant, and travel agency.

D Colonial, Paseo Orinoco, T632 4402, F632 3649. Has seen better days but good value, a/c, *Neckar* travel agency, nice restaurant on balcony overlooking river.

D Unión, Calle Urica, T632 3374. Clean, basic with fan, cable TV, helpful, filtered water, good value.

F Amor Patria, Amor Patria 30, T632 8819, plazabolivar@hotmail.com. Renovated colonial house, fan, shared bathrooms, kitchen, hammocks for hire (**G**. **Soana Travel** (see below) based here. German and English spoken. Recommended.

Near the bus terminal
D Universo, Av República, 2 blocks left out of terminal, T654 3732. A/c, hot water, TV, restaurant, accepts credit cards.

Outside town
D Posada La Casita, Av Ligia Pulido, Urb 24 de Julio, PO Box 118, T632 3223, T0414-854 5146 (mob), reservation@gekkotours-venezuela.de. Very nice rooms, with cold water, fan, hammock with mosquito net can be rented, **F**, space for tents, **G** Beautiful gardens (with small zoo), pool, laundry service, good food and drinks available, German and English spoken, helpful. Free pick up from airport or bus terminal (ring in advance). Free shuttle service into town. The owner runs **Gekko Tours** (see below).

● Eating

Ciudad Bolívar *p1400*
† Arabe-Venezolano, on Cumaná near Bolívar. Clean, a/c, good Arabic food, not cheap.
† Mirador Paseo Orinoco. *Comida criolla* with views over the river.
† † La Playa, C Urica entre Venezuela y Zea. Good for fish, reasonable prices.
† Flamingo, C Urica opposite Hotel Unión. Peruvian dishes, good value if they don't overcharge.
† La Carioca market, at the end of Paseo Orinoco, has series of small, cheap restaurants.
† Charly's, Venezuela. Good *fuente de soda*, cheap, fast service.
† Lonchería Ché, by *Hotel Colonial*. Good breakfast.
† Lonchería Urica, Urica, next to *Hotel Unión*. Good lunch for US$1.25, get there early.
† Mi Casa, C Venezuela. Open-air, good value.
† Pizzería La Casita Venezuela, opposite *La Casa de las Doce Ventanas*. Good value pizza and ice cream, views over Puente Angostura.

† Restaurant Vegetariano La Gran Fraternidad Amor Patria y Dalla Costa. Lunch only.
† Savoy, Venezuela y Dalla Costa. Good value breakfast.

○ Shopping

Ciudad Bolívar *p1400*
Camping equipment White gas (stove fuel) is available at **Lubriven**, Av República 16, near the bus terminal.
Handicrafts Arts and crafts from Bolívar state, including basketry from the Orinoco Delta can be found in **La Carioca** market, at the end of Paseo Orinoco and **Tienda Artesanía Guayanesa** at the airport.
Jewellery There are many jewellers on Pasaje Guayana, which runs off Paseo Orinoco and near *Hotel Colonial*.
Supermarket Close to the Museo Soto on Av Germania, large and well-stocked.

▲ Activities and tours

Ciudad Bolívar *p1400*
Competition is stiff in Ciudad Bolívar, and among the genuine companies roam phoney salesmen. You are more than likely to have someone attempt to sell you a tour at the bus station. Do not pay any money to anyone in the bus station or on the street. Always ask to be taken to the office. Always ask for a receipt (and make sure that it comes on paper bearing the company logo). Be suspicious of people offering tours that start in another town or city. If you are unfortunate enough to fall prey to a con artist, be sure to make a *denuncio* at the police station and inform genuine travel agents.

Ciudad Bolívar is the best place to book a tour to Canaima, but you may pick up cheaper deals for trips to Roraima and the Gran Sabana from Santa Elena. There are 2 main tours operators in Canaima who offer tours at backpacker prices – *Bernal Tours* and *Tiuna Tours*. Most agents in Ciudad Bolívar sell one of these two options, but sometimes add commission. Always ask who will be running the actual tour - it may be cheaper to book from the tour operator directly. Service seems to change with the seasons. For 3 days/2 nights tours to Canaima expect to pay around US$190-230 pp; 4 days/3 nights to Gran Sabana US$250. 5 days/ 4 nights; Río Caura US$250-300.

Asociación Cooperativa Yajimadu, Servicios y Excursiones Ecoturísticas, T615 2354, dichenedu@hotmail.com, or Miguel Estaba, T0414-099 0568. US$275 for 5-day trip to Río Caura, 10 and 15-day trips also available, small

---

● *For an explanation of the sleeping and eating price codes used in this guide, see inside the front*
● *cover. Other relevant information is found in Essentials pages 1330-1331.*

groups catered for, guides are Ye'kwana from villages on the river, knowledgeable, Spanish spoken (some guides learning English), sleeping in hammocks, very good.

Expediciones Dearuna, C Libertad 16 (above Inversiones Ruiz), T632 4635, www.total aventura.com. All usual tours at competitive prices, restructured in 2006.

Gekko Tours, run by Pieter Rothfuss at airport (also *Posada La Casita*), T632 3223, T0414-854 5146 (mob), www.gekkotours-venezuela.de. Gran Sabana, Canaima, Roraima, Orinoco Delta, rafting and river trips.

Miguel Gasca, T0414-923 5210/0166-629 4600 (mob), or look for him at *Hotel Italia*. Recommended for tours to Roraima, Gran Sabana and Canaima.

Sapito Tours (Bernal Tours), at airport, T0414-854 8234 (mob), bernaltours@ terra.com.ve. Canaima tours slightly more expensive (and not always up-to-scratch, eg unplanned changes of itinerary, poor camping), *indígena* guides. Also offer tours to Roraima, Gran Sabana, Orinoco Delta, Kavác and Río Caura.

Soana Travel, run by Martin Haars at *Hospedaje Amor Patria*, T632 8819, T0414 852 0373 (mob), soanatravel@gmx.de. Tours to Río Caura, Canaima and Gran Sabana, English and German spoken.

Tiuna Tours, at airport, T632 8697. Cheapest option for Canaima, have a camp that takes 180 people. Guides speak English, German and Italian.

Turi Express, at airport, T652 9764, T0414-893 9078 (mob), turiexpress@cantv.net. Range of tours plus Guri dam and fishing tours, good English.

◎ Transport

Air Minibuses and buses marked Terminal to town centre. Taxi to Paseo Orinoco US$2.25. To Caracas twice a week, 1½ hrs, **Aserca. Comeravia** and **Rutaca** (recommended for views) fly daily to **Canaima** and **Santa Elena**, US$55. Airport tax US$0.50. There are international phones at the airport, a good restaurant and car hire (Budget). Check where tours start from as some fly from Ciudad Guayana (**Turi Tours**), and charge passengers for taxi transfers.

Bus Terminal at junction of Av República and Av Sucre. To get there take bus marked Terminal going west along Paseo Orinoco (US$0.25). 10 daily to **Caracas** US$15 (student discount

available, night bus $17.50), 8-9 hrs, with Expresos Los Llanos, Rodovias, and Rápidos de Guayanesa, *por puesto* US$40. 10 daily to **Puerto La Cruz**, US$8 (student discount available), 5 hrs, with Caribe and Expresos San Cristobal, *por puesto*, US$17.50. 1 daily to **Cumaná**, US$10, 7 hrs with Caribe. Several daily to **Maracay**, US$15, and **Valencia**, via Maracay, US$15, 8-9 hrs, with Expresos Los Llanos and Rodovias. **Tumeremo** US$9; Tumeremo bus through to El Dorado US$9.50, 3 daily. To **Santa Elena de Uairén** direct with Caribe US$21 (3 daily), Expresos San Cristobal, US$15 (2 daily), stopping en route with Línea Orinoco, Transportes Mundial (5 daily), spectacular views of Gran Sabana, 12-13 hrs. 1 daily to **Boa Vista** with Caribe, US$33, 20 hrs. To **Ciudad Guayana** hourly from 0700, US$2, 1½ hrs, *por puesto*, US$5.50, 1½ hrs. To **Ciudad Piar**, US$4, 3 hrs, and **La Paragua**, US$8, 4 hrs, with Coop Gran Mcal Sucre. 2 daily to **Caicara**, US$6.50 (including 2 ferry crossings), 7-8 hrs, with Coop Gran Mcal Sucre. To **Maturín** with Unión Maturín. 2 daily to **Puerto Ayacucho**, US$12, 10-12 hrs with Coop Gran Mcal Sucre (*por puesto* US$20), take food.

Taxi US$1.50 to virtually anywhere in town. US$2 from bus station to town centre.

◎ Directory

Ciudad Bolívar *p1400*
Banks Note: TCs difficult to change. ATMs open only in banking hours. **Corp Banca**, Paseo Meneses, Edif Johanna, C Bolívar. Amex TCs. **Banco de Venezuela**, near *Hotel Colonial*. Cash on Visa, ATM. **Banco Mercantil**, east end of Paseo Orinoco. Changes TCs, has ATM. **Banco Provincial**, west end of Av Jesús Soto, opposite Mobil petrol station. Cash on Visa, ATM.

Consulates Denmark, Av Táchira, Quinta Maninata 50, of 319, T632 3490, 0800-1200, 1500-1700. Italy, Av 17 de Diciembre, Edif Terepaima, Local 1, T/F654 4335.

Internet Galaxia.com, C C Abboud Centre, Paseo Orinoco. Galaxy Computer, Av República y Jesús Soto, behind Mobil petrol station. **Post offices** Av Táchira, 15 mins walk from centre. **Telephones** *CANTV*, Av 5 de Julio, 100 m from Av Táchira (closed Sun).

Canaima and Angel Falls

→ Colour map 2, grid B1. Park entry US$6 pp paid to Inparques on arrival in Canaima.

At Canaima camp, the Río Carrao tumbles spectacularly over six waterfalls into the lagoon, which has beautiful tannin-stained water with soft beige beaches. It's a lovely spot, but it also has the airstrip and is the centre of operations for river trips to Angel Falls. The Falls are named after Jimmie Angel, the US airman who first reported their existence in 1935. Two years later he returned and crash-landed his plane, the *Río Caroní*, on top of Auyán Tepuy. The site is marked with a plaque. The sheer rock face was climbed in 1971 by three Americans and an Englishman, David Nott, who recounted the 10-day adventure in his book *Angels Four* (Prentice-Hall).

Canaima

There are several tourist lodges at Canaima and many package tours now visit on day trips. For orientation, **www.venezuelatuya.com/gransabana/mapacanaimaframes.htm** has a good map. For good information on the region, see **www.thelostworld.org**. Do not forget swimming costumes, insect repellent and sun cream; waterproof clothing may be advisable. There are dangerous undercurrents in the lagoon; people have drowned while swimming near the falls. Do not walk barefoot as there are chiggers, or *niguas*, in the lagoon's sand beaches.

Trips to the Angel Falls

The Angel Falls, the highest in the world (979 m – its longest single drop is 807 m), 70 km downriver from Canaima, are best reached by plane to Canaima from Caracas, Ciudad Bolívar or Ciudad Guayana. Trips by boat upriver to the Angel Falls operate May-January, depending on the level of the water in the rivers. Even during the rainy season, you may have to get out and push. Most trips make an overnight stop on one of the islands, continuing to the Falls the next day. There are also bottom-numbing, 12-hour day trips which cost around US$150. More relaxing, with more stops are beauty spots, are 44-hour, 'three day' trips, US$260. If you have a *permiso de excursionistas* from *Inparques*, you may be able to go on one tour and come back with another, giving yourself more time at the Falls, but you may have to pay extra to do this, up to US$50 (take all food and gear). Trips can be arranged with agencies in Ciudad Bolívar (see

Parque Nacional Canaima

above) or at Canaima airport. All *curiaras* (dugouts) must carry first aid, life jackets, etc. Take wet weather gear, swimwear, mosquito net for hammock and insect repellent, lots of film and a plastic bag to protect your camera/day bag. The light is best on the falls in the morning.

The cheapest way to fly over the falls is on scheduled flights from Ciudad Bolívar with Rutaca or Ciaca. From Canaima a 45-minute flight costs US$45 per person and does some circuits over and alongside the falls.

Kamarata

The largest of the tepuis, **Auyán Tepuy** (700 sq km) is also one of the more accessible. **Kamarata** is a friendly indigenous settlement with a Capuchin mission on the plain at the east foot of the tepuy. It has a well-stocked shop but no real hotels; basic rooms can be found for about US$6 per person, camping also possible at the mission (mosquito nets necessary and anti-malarial pills advised). Take food, although there is one place to eat, and locals may sell you dinner. The whole area is within the Parque Nacional Canaima.

Pemón families in Kamarata have formed co-operatives and can arrange *curiaras*, tents and porters for various excursions: see Activities and tours, below.

Kaváç

About a two-hour walk northwest of Kamarata, this is a new indigenous-run resort consisting of a dozen thatched huts (*churuatas*) for guests, a small shop, and an excitingly short airstrip serviced by Cessnas from Ciudad Bolívar, Santa Elena, and Isla Margarita; flights from the north provide excellent views of Angel Falls and Auyán Tepuy. There is a vehicle connection with Kamarata but it is expensive because all fuel has to be flown in. The prime local excursion is to **Kaváç Canyon** and its waterfall known as La Cueva, which can be reached by joining a group or by setting out early west up the Río Kaváç. A natural jacuzzi is encountered after a 30-minute wade along the sparkling stream, after which the gorge narrows dramatically until the falls are reached. Go in the morning to avoid groups of day-trippers from Porlamar. The sun's rays illuminate the vertical walls of the canyon only for a short time around 1100. Be prepared to get wet; bathing suits and shoes with good grip, plus a dry change of clothing are recommended; also insect repellent, as there is a mosquito and midge invasion around dusk. Late afternoon winds off the savannah can make conditions chilly. It costs US$16 per person to stay at the camp (cheaper in hammocks). The price includes the tour to the canyon. Take food with you.

Uruyén

South of Auyán Tepuy and west of Kamarata, **Uruyén** is similar to Kaváç, only smaller and more intimate. It also has a beautiful canyon and is the starting point for treks up Auyán Tepuy. The camp is run by the Carvallo family. Charter flights can be arranged through **AmazonAir** ① *To212-283 6960, www.amazonair.com.*

● Sleeping

Canaima *p1404*
LL Campamiento Canaima, T0212-976 0530, www.hoturvensa.com.ve. Comfortable cabins, with shower and toilet. Meals are poor value, but drinks are at regular prices. Tours are well organized. 1 night, US$355 (high season price, 1 Dec-30 Apr), pp in double room, including transfers, meals, boat trip and flight over the Angel Falls, weather permitting. The airfare is not included. Although the quickest and most convenient way to visit Canaima is on a package tour, it is much cheaper to travel independently.
LL Campamiento Ucaima Jungle Rudy, T0286-962 2359, www.junglerudy.com. Run by the daughters of the late 'Jungle' Rudy Truffino, full board available, 1 hr walk from Canaima above Hacha Falls.

LL Wakü Lodge (Canaima Tours), T0286-962 0559, www.canaimatours.com. The best new option in Canaima, romantic, comfortable, right on lagoon, various packages. Recommended.
L Camp Wey Tüpü, in the village, T0414-884 0993 (mob). Ring direct to the camp if you wish to reserve lodgings only, *Roymar* in Caracas handle reservations of all-inclusive packages run from the camp, T/F0212-576 5655, roymar@ cantv.net. Fan, shower, bar, price includes meals and flight over Falls.
L Parakaupa Lodge, 5 mins from airport, on southwestern side of lagoon, T0286-961 4963, parakaupa@etheron.net. Attractive rooms with bath, hammocks outside rooms, views over the lagoon and falls, restaurant, full board.

B **Kusary**, close to *Parakaupa Lodge*, near airport, T0286-962 0443. Basic but clean, with bath, fan, food available, ask for Claudio at *Tienda Canaima*. E pp **Kaikusé**, next to *Kusary*, T0414-884 9031. Basic, clean with bath, hammocks.

Some families in the village rent hammocks for US$5-10 per person. Travel agencies also rent hammocks for US$3-5 per person a night; ask at the airport. Best place to rent a hammock or camp is at **Campamento Tomas Bernal** (*Bernal Tours*) on Anatoly Island, T0414-854-8234 (mob), bernaltours@terra.com.ve, or try at **Campamento Tiuna** (*Tiuna Tours*).

Camping Camp for free, but only around the *fuente de soda*; fires are not permitted. Ask *Inparques* at the airport. No tents available for hire.

❼ Eating

Canaima *p1404*
Food is expensive at the *Campamiento Canaima* restaurant. A cheaper option is **Simon's** restaurant in the village which is used by many of the agencies, US$4-5 pp, breakfast US$3. It is advisable to take food, though there are various stores, both on the west side, **Tienda Canaima**, or in the indian village, selling mainly canned foods. A *fuente de soda* overlooks the lagoon. There is an expensive snack bar at the airport; also souvenir shop.

▲▲ Activities and tours

Canaima *p1404*
You can do walking expeditions into the jungle to indigenous villages with a guide, but bargain hard on the price. Other excursions are to the Mayupa Falls, including a canoe ride on the Río Carrao (US$50, half day), to Yuri Falls by jeep and boat (US$35, half day); to Isla Orquídea (US$75, full day, good boat ride, beach barbecue); to Saltos de Sapo and Sapito (3 hrs, US$25).
Guides in Canaima There is fierce competition at the airport but agencies pretty much offer the same thing at the same price. Some package tours to Canaima are listed under Caracas and Ciudad Bolívar Tour operators. Agents may tell you that guides speak English: some do, but many don't.
Bernal Tours (see above), with its own camp on Isla Anatoly in the lagoon, beds and hammocks, popular with travellers.
Kamaracoto Tours and **Tiuna Tours** for trips to Salto Sapo, Kavác, Salto Angel; they will also help with finding accommodation.

Kamarata *p1405*
Macunaima Tours (Tito Abati), **Excursiones Pemón** (Marino Sandoval), and **Jorge and Antonio Calcaño II** run local tours.

For details on climbing Auyán Tepuy, contact **Kamadac** in Santa Elena, run by Andreas Hauer (T0289-995 1408, T0414-886 6526 (mob), kamadac@cantv.net, www.abenteuer-venezuela.de) or **Alechiven**, run by Edith Rogge, which has a base and radio at Kamarata, T0414-211828.
Alechiven and Pemón, co-operatives run 6-day river trips from Kamarata to Angel Falls (May-Dec), descending the **Río Akanán** to the Carrao by motorized dugout then turning south up the 'Devil's Canyon' to the Falls; the tours continue downriver to Canaima. It costs about US$450 for the *curiara* (minimum 4 persons), not including flights to Kamarata or food – supply your own food. River trips in this region are easier in the rainy season. Guides for Auyán Tepuy can be hired here for about US$25 per day, if you have your own equipment. Contact Andreas Hauer at *Kamadac*.

❸ Transport

Canaima *p1404*
Air The return airfare from Caracas is US$300 with **Avior**, who fly daily from **Caracas**, 1 hr 40 mins direct. Do not rely on being able to change the return date on your flight and be even more wary of getting an open return. The airlines are quite happy to change your ticket, but the next available seat could be in 5 days time and Canaima is a very expensive place to kill time. Arrangements are best made through travel agencies. **Aereotuy** runs 1 day excursions by 19-seat Dornier aircraft out of **Ciudad Bolívar**, landing at Canaima. There is a connecting **Aereotuy** flight from **Isla Margarita** (0900, returning 1500) and direct excursions from Margarita (0730 departure returning 1800). They have a new camp near the foot of Nonon Tepuy, bookable only through **Aereotuy**, recommended (T0212-761 6231, www.tuy.com). Other flights from Margarita with **Rutaca**. From **Ciudad Bolívar** and **Puerto Ordaz**, Canaima Tours (see above under Wakü Lodge) has daily flights, US$130 and US$180 respectively. Various companies offer day excursions in 5-seater Cessnas to Canaima from **Ciudad Bolívar**, book early, 0630-0700 at airport, US$180 pp, including flight over Angel Falls, boat across lagoon, lunch and trip to Salto Sapo; flight only, US$55 one way with **Rutaca**, **Comeravia** and **Ciaca**, 2 hrs. Reductions are available for parties. Note that you may not even see the falls from the air in the rainy season – the additional cost of a trip to the Angel Falls may well bring the cost of your journey up to that of a package. Flight to **Santa Elena** from Canaima costs US$55, one way. Tours can also be made to **Kavác** (see Kavác section).

Kamarata *p1405*
Air Aereotuy, Rutaca and Comeravia fly from
Ciudad Bolívar (US$80 one way, 2 hrs), and
Rutaca and Comeravia fly from **Santa Elena de
Uairén** (US$140 one way).

Kavác *p1405*
Air A day excursion by light plane to Kavác
from **Canaima** (45 mins' flight) can be made

with any of the tour operators at the airport, and
costs around US$130-140 per person depending
on number of passengers. Flight only from
Ciudad Bolívar to Kavác or Kamarata costs
US$80 per person one way. Trips from Ciudad
Bolívar can be arranged with tour agencies in
town or at airport; around US$250 per person
including flight via Angel Falls, meals, and 1
night's accommodation.

Ciudad Guayana and the Orinoco Delta

Ciudad Guayana → *Phone code: 0286. Colour map 2, grid A2. Population: 700,000.*
In an area rich in natural resources 105 km downriver from Ciudad Bolívar, an entirely new
metropolis, known as Ciudad Guayana, is still being built. It is on the south bank of the
Orinoco and both sides of the Caroní River before it spills into the Orinoco. Four separate
centres, San Félix, Palúa, Puerto Ordaz and Matanzas, are being forged into one. East of the
Caroní are the commercial port of **San Félix** (work in progress to make a riverside walk and
park) and the Palúa iron-ore terminal of the railway from El Pao. Across the Caroní by the 470
m concrete bridge is **Puerto Ordaz** (airport), the iron-ore loading port connected by rail with
the famous Cerro Bolívar open-cast iron mine. The iron-tinted waterfall in the pretty Parque
Cachamay (20 minutes' walk from centre; closes 1700) is worth a visit.

Excursions Just up the Caroní is the Macagua hydroelectric plant; there are some truly
beautiful cataracts called **Salto Llovizna** as you enter the grounds (known as **Parque La
Llovizna**, taxi, US$5). There is a grand facility on the dam itself *0900-2100 daily, except Mon,*
housing an archaeological museum and exhibits on the construction of the dam (free), as well
as a coffee shop. Higher up the river is the massive **Guri dam**, powered by the world's second-
largest artificial reservoir, which is filled by the Paragua and Caroní rivers. The trip to Guri takes
90 minutes by taxi; the plant is open daily 0900-1030, 1415-1515, take your passport; the area
gets very full during holidays, Easter or carnival. You can also visit the rest of the complex
including the hotel (**C**, a/c, comfortable). *Por puesto* from Ciudad Bolívar, Route 70, US$20 one
way; for return, ask at Alcabala Río Claro (gatehouse) if they can get you a free lift.

Los Castillos, said to be where Sir Walter Raleigh's son was killed in the search for El
Dorado, are two old forts down the Orinoco from San Félix (one hour by *por puesto*, US$2.50,
or take a tour).

Tucupita → *Phone code: 0287, Colour map 2, grid A2, Population: 81,820.*
A worthwhile side trip along asphalted roads can be made to Tucupita (*Climate: very humid*),
on the Orinoco delta. Though capital of Delta Amacuro state and the main commercial centre
of the delta, there's a one-horse feel about it. There is a **tourist office** at Calle Dalla Costa
beside Sonido Color 2000. Tourists should go there first for information on tours. **Note:** Banks
won't change travellers' cheques.

For a 3-4 day **trip to see the delta**, its fauna and the indigenous *Warao*, either arrange
boats through the tourist office (see Ins and outs, above). Boats are not easy to come by and
are expensive except for large groups. Bargain hard and never pay up front.

Excursions often only travel on the main river, not in the *caños* where wildlife is most often
be seen. To avoid disappointment, be sure to determine where your guide intends to take you
before you leave. If the river level rises after a downpour, arrangements may be cancelled. On all
trips agree in advance exactly what is included, especially that there is enough food and water
for you and your guide. Hammocks and mosquito repellents are essential.

Barrancas → *Colour map 2, grid A2. Population: 13,000.*
An interesting and friendly village, founded in 1530, Barrancas is one of the oldest villages in
the Americas, but its precolonial past dates back to 1000 BC. Situated on the Orinoco, it can
be reached by road from Tucupita (63 km), or from Maturín. It has two basic hotels (**D**). The
village has a large community of Guyanese people who speak English. It is possible to take a
boat to the *Warao* villages of **Curiapo** and **Amacuro** (near Guyana border), check at harbour.

New Frontiers Adventure, also on
C Urdaneta next to *Tommy Town*, T995 1584,
T0414-886 6030 (mob), www.newfrontiers
adventures.com. Affiliated to the International
Ecotourism Society, ecotours and tours for small
groups. They offer all the usual tours at standard
prices, and 4-day, all-inclusive walking tours at
US$40 pp per day, taking in the different
ecosystems of the Gran Sabana, and staying in
Pemón villages. English, French, and German
spoken. Recommended.
Recommended guides Rawllins and his
brother, **Terry** (Guyanese) speak English,
excellent cooks, T0414-886 2669 (mob),
rawllins@yahoo.com, akawaio@hotmail.com.
Franklin Sierra, T995 1686, 0414-886 2448,
speaks English, Italian and other languages,
tailor-made tours, good service and value.

⊙ Transport

Tumeremo *p1410*
Bus To **Santa Elena**, US$15, 8-10 hrs, with
Líneas Orinoco, 2 blocks from plaza near *Leocar*);
El Dorado, US$2, 1½ hrs. Bus to **Ciudad Bolívar**,
US$9.25, 6 a day, 6½ hrs or *por puesto* (via San
Félix and Puerto Ordaz). Bus to **San Félix** (Ciudad
Guayana), US$3.60, *por puesto* US$8.75. To
Caracas, US$20, direct service at 1600, 14 hrs.
The road between Tumeremo and El Dorado is in
poor repair, but is passable with care.

El Dorado *p1410*
Bus All buses stop on main plaza. From
Caracas, Expresos del Oriente, at 1830 daily,
US$20, 14½ hrs, return at 1400 (925 km). The
Orinoco bus line connects with **Ciudad Bolívar**
(6 hrs) and **Santa Elena**, as does Transmundial
(better buses, leaving 1100, US$9.50 to **Santa
Elena**, US$5.50 to San Félix, 4 hrs).

El Dorado to Santa Elena de Uairén *p1410*
Km 88 (San Isidro)
Bus Km 88-Caracas, US$20; to **Ciudad Bolívar**
wait at gas station for buses from Las Claritas
(depart 0900, 1100, 1500, 1800). Frequent *por
puestos* from **El Dorado** to Km 88, 1 hr, US$3.50.
Most non-luxury buses stop at the petrol station
to refuel. Alternatively get a ride with jeeps and
trucks (little passes after 1030).

Santa Elena de Uairén *p1412, map p1411*
Air Airport, 8 km from the centre. **Rutaca** is the
only company currently serving the airstrip in
Santa Elena. Their 5-seater Cessnas leave once or
twice a day for destinations that include **Ciudad
Bolívar, Canaima, Kavác, Kamarata,** and
Kavanayen (US$70 one way), **Wonken** (US$40
one way), and **El Paují** and **Icabarú** (US$25 one

way). To calculate the price of chartering an
airplane from Santa Elena to any destination, take
the cost per passenger and multiply by 5.
Bus The new bus terminal on the road to Ciudad
Bolívar is about 4 km from town, taxi US$4-5. Get
to the terminal 15 mins in advance for the SENIAT
baggage check for contraband. From **Caracas** it is
best to go to Ciudad Bolívar and take a bus direct
to Boa Vista, or Santa Elena. 10 buses daily from
Santa Elena to **Ciudad Bolívar**, US$15, with
Expresos Los Llanos (recommended), San
Cristobal, and Línea Orinoco, 10-12 hrs. 10 daily
to **Ciudad Guayana** and **San Félix**, US$18, 10-11
hrs, with **Caribe** (recommended) and **Turgar**. 10
daily to **Puerto La Cruz**, US$21, 14 hrs, with **Caribe**
(recommended), **Turgar**, and **Línea Orinoco**.
Expresos Maturín goes to **Maturín** daily.
Expresos Los Llanos go to **Maracay** and
Valencia 3 times a day, US$22, 18-20 hrs. 3 buses
daily to **Boa Vista**, US$8, 4 hrs, with **Eucatur**; at
0700 to **Manaus** about 15 hrs, US$31.50 (make
sure ticket includes the exit tax). Take warm
clothing for buses with a/c (the driver may even
insist that the shades be closed throughout the
journey, so as not to affect the a/c).
Hitchhiking North from Santa Elena is
said to be easy. Stand at the roadside at
the garage just opposite the terminal. Expect
a charge of US$5.
Jeep To **El Paují** (US$10), **Canta Rana** (US$15),
and **Icabarú** (US$20) leave about 0700 from Plaza
Bolívar. Can also be caught at *Panadería Gran Café*,
C Icabarú. PDV gas station on road out of town,
open 0800-1900.

El Paují *p1413*
Air El Paují to **Santa Elena** (see above).
Road To get further than El Paují – to Canta
Rana and Icabarú – a 4WD vehicle is necessary.
From Santa Elena, US$8-10 by jeep if full, more if
not, daily at around 0600-0700 and 1500-1600
from Plaza Bolívar. Taxi US$10. **Hitching** from
the airport is possible, but normally ends in
tears of frustration. You may get lucky.
Jeep hire in El Paují, US$50 per day.

⊙ Directory

El Dorado *p1410*
Banks There is a Banco de Venezuela, which
accepts Visa and MasterCard; exchange is
possible with the gold buyer on the main street,
cash only, poor rates.

Santa Elena de Uairén *p1412, map p1411*
Banks Banco Industrial C Bolívar. Cash
advances on Visa. Try the shops in the centre for
dollars cash, reais or TCs, eg *Casa de Los
Cóchamos*, the gold shop south of main plaza,

which changes TCs at lower rate than bank. **Inversiones Fortaleza**, C Urdaneta on plaza, cash dollars, TCs or Brazilian currency. **La Boutique Zapatería** also changes TCs and cash at reasonable rates. Also grocery store **El Gordito**, C Urdaneta, for Brazilian currency (English and French spoken). Try at border with Brazilians entering Venezuela. Generally the rates are poor; check with travellers going in opposite direction what rates should be. For better rates you must wait until Ciudad Guayana, or Boa Vista if going to Brazil (change some money into Brazilian currency before the bus leaves).

Internet Global de Comunicaciones, C Icabarú y Urdaneta. Another place opposite **Panadería Rico Pan** on C Bolívar.

Telephones Global de Comunicaciones, CANTV at old bus terminal for international calls and faxes. To buy a card and call from a street phone is cheapest for international calls.

Mount Roraima → *Altitude: 2,810 m.*

An exciting trek is to the summit of Mt Roraima, at one time believed to be the '**Lost World**' made famous by Arthur Conan Doyle's novel. `Roroima' is a word in the Pemón Indian language meaning 'The great blue-green'. Owing to the tough terrain and extreme weather conditions, this hike is only suitable for the fit. Supplies for a week or more should be bought in Santa Elena. If your food is being supplied by a tour company, check what food you will be eating; often vegetarians go hungry.

San Francisco de Yuruaní
The starting point is this Pemón village, 9 km north of the San Ignacio military checkpoint (at which you must register). There are three small shops selling basic goods but not enough for Roraima hike. Meals are available and tents can be hired, US$3 each per day, quality of tents and stoves is poor; better equipment is available in Santa Elena.

Paraitepui
The road to Paraitepui (signposted), the nearest village to the mountain, leaves the highway 1 km south of San Francisco. It is in good condition, with three bridges; the full 25 km can be walked in seven hours. You can sleep free in the village if hiring a guide; camping is permitted. Few supplies available; a small shop sells basics. The villagers speak Tauripán, the local dialect of the Pemón linguistic group, but now most of them also speak Spanish.

Climbing Roraima
The foot trail winds back and forth on a more direct line than the little-used jeep track; it is comparatively straightforward and adequately marked descending from the heights just past Paraitepui across rolling hills and numerous clear streams. The goal, Roraima, is the mountain on the right, the other massive outcrop on the left is Mata Hui (known as Kukenán after the river which rises within it). If leaving the village early in the day, you may reach the Río Cuquenán crossing by early afternoon (good camping here). Three hours' walk brings you to a lovely bird-filled meadow below the foothills of the massif, another perfect camping spot known as *campamento base* (10 hours to base camp from Paraitepui). The footpath now climbs steadily upwards through the cloud forest at the mountain's base and becomes an arduous scramble over tree trunks and damp rocks until the cliff is reached. From here it is possible to ascend to the plateau along the 'easy' rock ledge which is the only route to the top. Walkers in good health should take about four hours from the meadow to the top. The summit is an eerie world of stone and water, difficult to move around easily. There are not many good spots to camp; but there are various overhanging ledges which are colourfully-known as 'hoteles' by the guides. Red painted arrows lead the way to the right after reaching the summit for the main group of these. A marked track leads to the survey pillar near the east cliff where Guyana, Brazil and Venezuela meet; allow a day as the track is very rough. Other sights include the Valley of the Crystals, La Laguna de Gladys and various sinkholes.

The whole trip can take anywhere between five days and two weeks. The dry season for trekking is November-May (with annual variations); June-August Roraima is usually enveloped in cloud. Do not remove crystals from the mountain; on the spot fines up to US$100 may be charged. Thorough searches are now made on your return. Take all your belongings and rubbish back down with you.

binoculars). Many of the animals are nocturnal and seldom seen. The region is scattered with Amerindian villages and a few large cattle ranches which date from the late 19th century: the descendants of some of the Scots settlers still live here. Links with Brazil are much closer than with the Guyanese coast; many people speak Portuguese and most trade is with Brazil.

Avoid the Rupununi in the wet season (mid-May to August); much of the Savannah floods and malaria mosquitoes and *kabura*/sandflies are widespread. The best time is October to April. River bathing is good, but beware of dangerous stingrays and black caiman. Note that a permit from the Home Affairs Ministry is usually required to visit Rupununi, unless you go with a tour operator. Check in advance if your passport is sufficient. A separate permit to visit Amerindian villages is needed from the Minister of Amerindian Affairs, the President's office in Georgetown.

Lethem A small but scattered town on the Brazilian border (see below), this is the service centre for the Rupununi and for trade with Brazil. There are many small stores, a small hospital (T772 2006), a police station (T772 2011) and government offices. A big event at Easter is the rodeo, visited by cowboys from all over the Rupununi. Prices are about twice as high as in Georgetown. About 2½ km south of town at St Ignatius there is a Jesuit mission dating from 1911. In the nearby mountains there is good birdwatching and there are waterfalls to visit.

Border with Brazil The Tacutu River separates Lethem from Bonfim in Brazil. The crossing is about 1.6 km north of Lethem and 2½ km from Bonfim. Small boats ferry foot passengers,

Sleeping

Georgetown *p1425, map p1426*

It's best to book in advance. There isn't much choice in the lower price categories and many small hotels and guesthouses are full of long-stay residents, while some are rented by the hour. If in doubt, go to a larger hotel for first night and look around next

AL-A Ariantze, 176 Middle St, T227 0152, www.ariantzesidewalk.com. Fans, or a/c in deluxe rooms. Includes small breakfast, see Eating, below. Very good but can be noisy from music and nightclub next door.
AL-B Grand Coastal Inn, 2 Area M Le

① US$20 pp pd for a day visit including entry to the walkway and qualified guide with good birding knowledge. www.iwokramacanopywalkway.com. The walkway allows visitors to walk among the tree-tops and see the birds and monkeys of the upper canopy, at the same time giving a different perspective on the middle and ground levels. Night excursions are available on the walkway. There is a library with birding books and a small arts and crafts shop.

run, modern, popular with backpackers, no a/c,
Arrowpoint Nature Resort, no Eping Av,
Bel Air Park, Georgetown, T225 9648,
www.roraimairways.com. In the heart of the Santa Mission Amerindian reservation, offers a "back to nature experience", with numerous activities such as mountain biking, canoeing.

Linden *p1428*
B Barrow's Dageraad Inn, 82 Manni St, Mackenzie, T444-6799, dunbarr@networksgy.com. Breakfast, US$3.50, all rooms are double/twin, hot water, a/c, TV, fridge.
B-C Hotel Star Bonnett, 671 Industrial Area, 1.5 km out of town on Georgetown Rd, T444 6505, F444 6829. Various standards of room, all with a/c and TV, clean, breakfast US$4, good lunches (US$4-5).

C-E Summit Hotel, 6 Industrial Area, McKenzie,

Corriverton *p1428*
A Par Park, in Skeldon. With bath and a/c, hot water, TV, no meals available.
B Mahogony, in Skeldon. With bath, TV, fridge, hot water, clean, lunch/dinner US$2.60-3.25. Recommended.
E pp Swiss Guest House, Springlands, T339 2329. Pakistani run, with bath and fan, no meals, helpful, simple accommodation.

Lake Mainstay *p1428*
AL Lake Mainstay Resort, T226 2975, www.lake mainstayresort.com. 40 cabins with a/c, cheaper without lake view, also single rooms, beachfront on the lake, restaurant, bars, swimming, boating, other sports, birdwatching and nature trails;

● For an explanation of the sleeping and eating price codes used in this guide, see inside the front cover. Other relevant information is found in Essentials page 1425.

special events and entertainment. Breakfast US$3.85, lunch and dinner US$7.20. Day trips can be arranged for US$51 per person (1-7 passengers), US$31 (8 and over) including entrance fees, road and boat transport, breakfast and lunch, but no drinks. Transport only is US$27.75 Georgetown-Parika return, US$83 return Parika-Supenaam in a regular speed boat, up to 10 people, US$33 return Supenaam-Lake Mainstay for up to 4 passengers.

Mabaruma p1428

There is a **Government Guest House**, 2 rooms with bath or shared bath, clean, book in advance.
D Kumaka Tourist Resort, Maburama, contact **Somwaru Travel Agency**, Georgetown, T225 9276. Meals, bath, run down; offers trips to Hosororo Falls, Babarima Amerindian settlement, rainforest, early examples of Amerindian art.

Bartica p1429

B Marin Hotel, 19 Second Ave, T455 2243. **A** with a/c, with bath, TV, phone, fridge, meals available (breakfast US$2.75, lunch and dinner US$6).
E Hi-Lo, on First Ave. Self-contained suites, also very basic rooms under US$3, crowded, no bath, claustrophobic.
E Modern, 9 First Ave, T455 2301, near ferry. 2 luxury rooms **C**, others basic, with bath and fan. Recommended. Good food, best to book ahead.
Mrs Payne's daughter, Third Ave next to Hospital. Basic rooms, clean.

Resorts near Bartica

LL-AL Baganara Island Resort, beautiful house on Baganara Island in Essequibo River a few miles south of Bartica, www.baganara.com. Price depends on season and standard of room, full board, private beach, watersports, airstrip; day trips US$60 pp (minimum 10), with meals, bar and activities. Transport to resort US$25 pp return.
AL Shanklands, booking office Middle and Camp Sts, Georgetown, T225 2678, www.shank lands.com. Dormitory accommodation available. On a cliff overlooking the Essequibo, 5 colonial style cottages. Activities include swimming, birdwatching, croquet, fishing, watersports, 1st class, US$60 pp for day trip (minimum 8 people), good food. *Shanklands* can be reached by boat from Parika or Bartica; the Baganara Island airstrip nearby; private transport by road can be arranged from *Timberhead* (see above).

South of Bartica p1429

A Rainbow River Safari, a 16,800 acre, independent conservation site on the Mazaruni River at Marshall Falls, very different from other jungle lodges (simple softwood cabins, basic bedding, pit latrines, washing in river), cooking over woodfire. Trails in unspoilt forest, waterfalls,

wildlife watching, gold and diamond panning, swimming and other activities. Day trippers have to pay G$1,000. For prices and tours contact **Mr E** Sabat, tedsabat@aol.com or tedsabat@yahoo.com.

Kaieteur Falls p1429

E The rest house at the top of the Falls is open for guests, but is basic; enquire and pay first at the National Parks Commission, Georgetown, T225 9142 (if planning to stay overnight, you must be self-sufficient, whether the guest-house is open or not; take your own food and a hammock, it can be cold and damp at night; the warden is not allowed to collect money).

Resorts in the Rupununi p1429

For both ranches below, contact *Wilderness Explorers*. All transport is arranged.
L pp Dadanawa Ranch, Duane and Sandy de Freitas, 96 km south of Lethem, one of the world's largest ranches, each bedroom has a verandah (being upgraded). They can organize trekking and horse riding trips, also camping with *vaqueros*. Tours also to the **Upper Rewa River**, minimum 14 day in conjunction with Wilderness Explorers: one of the most spectacular wildlife destinations in South America. Very remote and expensive but a high chance of seeing big cats, other large mammals and Harpy Eagle.
L pp Karanambu Ranch, Dianne McTurk, 96 km northeast of Lethem, on the Rupununi River, unique old home, cottages with bath, mosquito net, toiletries, good meals, fishing, excellent birdwatching and boat rides with guides. 24 km from Yupukari Amerindian village, trips possible. Dianne McTurk rears and rehabilitates orphaned giant river otters.

Lethem p1430

A number of places take guests, full board, organize tours and transport.
A pp Manari Ranch Hotel, 11 km north of Lethem on a creek (good swimming). US$60 per day, can accommodate about 20 people, reserve through the Airport Shop.
B-C Takutu, T772 2034. Simple a/c and fan-cooled rooms, also hammock space (**E**), fridge, clean, breakfast US$3.25-3.80. Lunch/dinner US$3.95-4.20.
C Savannah Inn, T772 2035 (Georgetown T227 4938), savannahinn@futurenetgy.com, or book through *Wilderness Explorers*. Including breakfast, a/c cabins with bath (cheaper with fan), phone, TV, fridge, clean, bar, breakfast US$3.05-4.30, lunch or dinner US$4.30, changes reais into Guyanese dollars, tours arranged, will take you to airport.
D Trail's End, book through the cybercafe at the airport shop, run by a '60-yr-old teenager', Patricia Rash. Ranch house atmosphere, comfortable rooms

with fan, mosquito nets, or hammock space (**B**.
Includes full cooked breakfast; lunch and dinner on
request and a range of tours in the Rupununi.
D-ECacique Guest House, T772 2083. With
bath, fan, clean, breakfast US$3.25-3.80,
lunch/dinner US$3.95-4.20.
The **Penthouse** at the **Airport Shop**,
T772 2085, is for backpackers, bathroom outside,
safe, can tie up hammock, basic; Don and Shirley
provide the most comprehensive information in
the Rupununi. They offer horse riding, tours in the
Rupununi and have a cybercafe.

Annai *p1430*
LThe Rock View Lodge, Annai, T226 5412,
www.rockviewlodge.com, to book, or through
Wilderness Explorers. Colin Edwards and family,
guesthouse with 8 self-contained rooms, bars,
zoo, natural rock swimming pool; in the
Pakaraima foothills, where the savannah meets
the Iwokrama Rainforest Programme (see below).
Pony treks to nearby foothills, nature tours for
painting, photography and fishing, regional
Amerindian and other local cooking, full board.
Recommended.
CThe Oasis, Rock View's second facility on the
Lethem-Georgetown road. With a bar,
churrascaria restaurant, shop, accommodation in
comfortable a/c rooms or hammock space (**G**.
Onward air tickets and buses can be booked from
here, as well as tours from Rock View or for
Surama/ Iwokrama. There is an interesting nature
trail in front of the Oasis up a forest covered hill -
sweeping views of the savannah - channel billed
toucans very common here.

Iwokrama *p1430*
ALpp Atta Rainforest Lodge. For visits to the
Iwokrama Canopy Walkway, guests stay overnight
facilities in hammock with a bar, dining area and
full bathroom facilities. Private rooms are
scheduled to be constructed in 2006. Mosquito
nets provided. New restaurant serves breakfast,
lunch and dinner. The overnight trip rate includes
entry to the Iwokrama Canopy Walkway, trained
guide, hammock accommodation, 3 meals. Visitors
can experience the dawn chorus and be on the
walkway at dusk and into the night.
   At **Iwokrama Field Station**, the rainforest
lodge is one of the most comfortable in South
America in a beautiful setting on the banks of
the Essequibo, next to pristine forest, full of
giant Moura trees and Kapoks. It has two types
of accommodation, in free standing cabins or in
a terrace of rooms. Tourists pay a fee for the bed
and a user fee. The cabins are comfortable, with
bath and veranda. Meals served in huge
thatched dining research area with fine views of
the river. All meals cost US$5 (take your own

alcoholic drinks). Reservations for all Iwokrama
lodges and information from **Wilderness
Explorers**, see Georgetown, Tour operators,
or from Rock View (see above).

Camps
Maparri Wilderness Camp. Contact **Wilderness
Explorers** for rates and bookings. It is on the
Maparri River, in the Kanuku Mountains,
recognized by Conservation International as one
of the few remaining pristine Amazonian areas,
rich in flora and fauna. It is easy to watch
macaws, herons, toucans, kingfisherm, maybe
harpy eagles. With luck, you can see tayra, labba,
ocelot, agouti, monkeys, tapir, even jaguar.
Various treks are arranged. It can only be reached
by a combination of air and river. **Maparri Camp**
is built of wood, with open sides, and has
hammocks with mosquito nets. The site
overlooks a waterfall; the river water is crystal
clear (unlike most rivers in Guyana) and the fall
and surrounding pools are safe for swimming.
The camp is merely a framework. Simple,
nutritional meals, supplemented by fish from the
river, are prepared over an open fire.

🍴 Eating

Georgetown *p1425, map p1426*
A 10% service may be added to the bill. Many
restaurants are closed on public holidays.
Restaurants are categorized according to their
most expensive dishes. All have much cheaper
options on menus.
¶¶¶Bottle Bar and Restaurant at *Cara Lodge*.
Very good, pleasant surroundings, must book,
also open for breakfast.
¶¶¶Golden Coast, Main and Middle Sts. Chinese,
good food, huge portions, classy.
¶¶¶-¶Arawak Steak House, in roof garden, near
Stabroek Market. Casual atmosphere, busy in
evening, good value, closes 2200.
¶¶¶-¶Coalpot in New Town. Good lunches
starting at US$1.80, up to US$13.15 (no shorts
allowed, cheaper cafetería).
¶¶¶-¶El Dorado, at *Le Meridien* hotel. Good
atmosphere, Caribbean, Continental, Guyanese.
¶¶¶-¶Excellence, 82 Robb St, Bourda, T226 8782.
Creole restaurant and night club (free entrance),
which also has apartments (**A-B**per day) and a
catering service.
¶¶¶-¶Hack's Halal, 5 Commerce St, T225 6798.
Specializing in West Indian food, with some
vegetarian and sweet dishes.
¶¶¶-¶New Court Yard, 35 Main St. Pleasant
outdoor bar and restaurant.
¶¶¶-¶New Thriving, Camp and Brickdam Sts. A/c,
buffet restaurant with large, oily portions.

ᵀᵀᵀ-ᵀ **Poolside**, at *Le Meridien*. BBQ, pizza, live bands.

ᵀᵀᵀ-ᵀ **Sidewalk Café and Jazz Club** in *Ariantze Hotel*, Middle St. Buffet lunches Mon-Sat.

ᵀᵀᵀ-ᵀ **Yue Yuan**, Robb St. Good Chinese.

ᵀᵀ **Brazil Churrascaria**, 208 Alexander St, Lacytown. All you can eat for US$7.20. Great.

ᵀᵀ **JR Burgers**, 3 Sandy Babb Str, Kitty. Popular.

ᵀᵀ **Kamboat**, 51 Sheriff St, Campbellville. Recommended for Chinese.

ᵀᵀ **Popeye's**, 1e Vissengen Rd and Duncan St, T223 6226. Serves chicken.

ᵀᵀ-ᵀ **Main Street Café**, at *Tower Hotel*. Good breakfast and other meals.

ᵀ **Jerries**, 228 Camp St near Middle St. Big portions, slow service, cheap beer. Also fresh daily baking.

ᵀ **Salt and Pepper Food Court**, 14-15 Croal and Longden Sts, T223 6172. Central, serves over 50 different Creole dishes (eg roti and curry, cook-up rice, pepper pot, etc).

ᵀ **Oasis Café**, 42 Croal and United Nations Place, Stabroek. Fast food, popular and safe.

ᵀ **Upscale**, 32 Regent and Hing St, T225 4721. Popular, poetry night Tue, comedy night Fri.

ᵀ **Waterchris**, see Sleeping. Very good breakfast, also lunch and dinner.

Cafés

Juice Power, Middle St, past the hospital. Excellent fruit juices, also sells drinking water.

Windies Sports Bar, 91 Middle St.

Corriverton *p1428*

Mansoor, in Skeldon. Good Indian food. Several good Chinese restaurants within a few blocks of Springlands town centre.

Bartica *p1429*

Riverview Beach Bar, at Goshan near Bartica (Camp Silo bible study centre). Popular hotel and bar, disco, nice beach, safe swimming.

Lethem *p1430*

The Airport Shop, good snacks, bar.

Foo Foods, T772 2010. Highly recommended for snacks.

● Bars and clubs

Georgetown *p1425, map p1426*

Surprisingly lively at night, mainly with gold miners, traders and overseas Guyanese throwing US$ around. Most nightclubs sell imported, as well as local Banks beer; many sell drinks by the bottle rather than shot, this works out cheaper. Don't walk home at night; take a taxi.

Jazzy Jacks, Alexander St, near the Kitty Market (this area is unsafe unless you go with locals). Open till 0400 at weekends, US$3 entry.

Latino Bar, at *Le Meridien Pegasus*. Fri-Sat, Cuban theme, very popular, lively, no cover charge.

Sidewalk Café and Jazz Club in *Ariantze Hotel*, Middle St. US$3 on Thu, major international artists US$6-12.

Trump Card, Church St, near St George's. Sometimes has a live band.

Sheriff St is some way from the centre but is 'the street that never sleeps' full of late night Chinese restaurants and has some good bars including **Tennessee Lounge** (no cover charge), **Burns Beat** (US$5.50 for night club section), **Avalanche**, large dance club, busiest Thu-Sat, very popular, **Royal Castle** (Sheriff and Garnett Sts) for chicken burgers, and **Buddy's Mei Tung** (No 137), restaurant, bar, nightclub, gym and pool hall.

● Entertainment

Georgetown *p1425, map p1426*
Cinema

Astor, Waterloo and Church Sts. US$1.05-2.65.

Strand, Charlotte St. US$1.60-2.65; 1 on Main St (protect against mosquitoes). There are 2 theatres.

○ Shopping

Georgetown *p1425, map p1426*

The main shopping area is Regent St.

Bookshops The Bookseller, Church St. Wide selection. Argosy and Kharg both on Regent St. Dimension, Cummings St. GNTC, Water St. Universal Bookstore on Water St, near Fogarty's. Good selection and cards.

Clothes Good T-shirts are sold at **Guyana Stores** (see below) and in the markets.

Crafts Items are a good buy: Amerindian basketwork, hammocks, wood carvings, pottery, and small figures made out of Balata, a rubbery substance tapped from trees in the interior. Look for such items in the markets, or craft shops. **Creations Craft**, Water St; **Amerindian Hostel**, Princess St, **Hibiscus Craft Plaza**, outside General Post Office. Others are advertised in the papers.

Department stores Guyana Stores, Church St, and Fogarty's, both of which stock a wide range of goods.

Film Films over ASA400 are normally not available; bring your own stock.

Gold Gold is sold widely, often at good prices but make sure you know what you are buying. Do not buy it on the street.

Markets Most Guyanese do their regular shopping at the 4 big markets: Stabroek (don't take valuables), Bourda, La Penitence and Kitty.

Touching down

Airport tax Exit tax US$35.
Business hours Shops and businesses: Mon-Fri 0900-1630, Sat 0900-1300. **Government offices**: Mon-Thu 0700-1500, Fri 0700-1430. **Banks**: Mon-Fri 0900-1400 (airport bank is open when flights operate).
In an emergency Police: Emergency T115; Other police numbers T471111/ 7777/3101. **First Aid centre**: Academic

Hospital, T442222. **Fire Brigade**: T473333/ 491111/451111.
International phone code +597. Ringing: equal tones and long pauses. Engaged: equal tones with equal pauses.
Official time GMT -3.
Voltage 110/127 volts AC, 60 cycles. Plug fittings: usually 2-pin round (European continental type).
Weights and measures Metric.

Finding out more Suriname Tourism Foundation ① *Dr J F Nassylaan 2, T410357*, www.suriname-tourism.org (in English). Also try **Stinasu** or **NV Mets**, see Paramaribo Tour operators. The **Suriname Planatlas**, maps with natural environment and economic development topics, each with commentary in Dutch and English, is out of print, but can be consulted at the **National Planning Office** on Dr Sophie Redmondstraat, www.planbureau.net.

Note Heavy rains in early 2006 caused severe flooding in parts of Suriname. Before heading to the interior, you should check if any facilities are closed.

Useful websites

Http://lanic.utexas.edu/la/sa/suriname The University of Texas site, lots of links.
www.kabinet.sr.org Office of the President.
www.nickerie.com Marlon Romeo's web page on district of Nickerie in English.
www.ci-suriname.org Conservation

International site. Information on Suriname, including the Central Suriname Nature Reserve.
www.stahm.com. The leading consultancy in ecotourism in the country with useful associations with a number of operators and NGOs. Helpful and informative.

Visas and immigration Visitors must have a valid passport and a visa. Nationalities which do not need a visa include: Israel, Japan and Switzerland. To obtain a visa in advance, apply to a Surinamese Embassy or Consulate at least two weeks before departure. You need to fill an application with a copy of your passport page, purpose of trip and flight number. You will then be issued a letter and another form to be completed with a passport photo. Procedures at consulates vary. Visas issued at the consulate in Cayenne normally take one day; two passport photos are required. In Georgetown, visa applications can be given in at any time, but only collected when the consular section is open on Monday, Wednesday and Friday morning. If applying when the consulate is open, visas are usually processed on the same day. A visa costs US$30 for two months (or €30 for one month; costs vary per nationality and where visa is bought). Make sure your name on the visa agrees in detail with that on your passport. On entry to Suriname (by land or air) your passport will be stamped by the military police indicating a brief period (usually 7-10 days) for which you can remain in the country, regardless of the length of stay authorized by your visa. If you are considering a longer visit, or want a multiple entry visa (US$60-175 costs vary for length of stay), you should go as soon as possible to the Alien Registration Office (Vreemdelingendienst) in Paramaribo to get a second stamp in your passport: address, van 't Hogerhuysstraat, Nieuwe Haven, Paramaribo, T597-403101/609, Monday-Friday, 0700-1430. Allow 1½ hours for this. You must also return here for any further extensions and for an exit authorization stamp (called 'stamp out') two days before you leave the country. The final exit stamp is again given by the military police at the airport or land border. Multiple entry visas may also be obtained at the Ministry of Foreign Affairs, consular section, Gravenstraat 23-25 (opposite Surinaamsche Bank), Paramaribo; passport and onward ticket required. These procedures are not usually explained to visitors on arrival. **Note:** Brazilians need a certificate of vaccination against yellow fever to be allowed entry.

Driving in Suriname

Roads 26% of roads are paved. East-west roads: From Albina to Paramaribo to Nieuw-Nickerie is paved. North-south roads: the road Paramaribo-Paranam-Afobaka-Pokigron is open. The road to the western interior, Zanderij-Apura, crosses the Coppename River; thereafter small bridges are in poor shape (take planks to bridge gaps). On the unpaved Moengo-Blakawatra road (eastern Suriname), the bridge across the Commewijne River is closed to traffic. **Road safety** Driving is on the left, but many vehicles have left-hand drive. There is a 24 hour emergency service for motorists: **Wegenwacht**, Sr Winston Churchillweg 123, T484691/487540.

Documents All driving licences accepted, but you need a stamp from the local police and a deposit. To drive a foreign registered vehicle requires no *carnet* or other papers. People wishing to travel from Suriname to either Guyana or Guiane by car need special vehicle insurance, available from **Assuria Insurance Company**, Gravenstraat 5-7, Paramaribo. T473400, www.assuria.sr. **Note**: Although an international driver's license is accepted in both Suriname and Guyana, a special permit is required to drive a vehicle in the two countries for longer than one month. **Fuel** Gasoline is sold as diesel, 'regular', unleaded, or super unleaded (more expensive): basic price SRD3 (US$1.10) per litre.

Suriname embassies and consulates See www.surinameembassy.org/embassy_consulate.shtml for a list of Suriname's representation abroad.

Money As of 1 January 2004, the unit of currency is the Suriname dollar (SRD, replacing the Suriname guilder (Sf) at the rate of 1,000 to 1, divided into 100 cents. There are notes for 1, 2.50, 5, 10, 20, 50 and 100 dollars. Coins are for 1 and 2.50 dollars and 1, 5, 10 and 25 cents (the 25-cent coin is usually known as a *kwartje*, 10-cent *dubbeltje* and 5-cent *stuiver*). In June 2006 the **exchange rate** was SRD2.78 = US$1, SRD3.52 = €1. Euros are readily exchanged in banks and with licensed money changers. On arrival, change a little money at the bank in the Johan Adolf Pengel Airport (where rates are poorer than in the city), then go to the main banks, or one of the many *cambios* in Paramaribo for further exchange. Officially visitors must declare their foreign currency on arrival. When arriving by land, visitors' funds are rarely checked, but you should be prepared for it. If entering Suriname from Guyana, you can change money at one of several banks in Nieuw-Nickerie. If arriving via Albina, the nearest bank, *Surinaamsche Bank* (www.dsbbank.sr), is in Moengo, otherwise *Hakrinbank* (www.hakrinbank.com) at Tamanredjo (Commewijne), or *Multitrack Money Exchange* not far from the Jules Albert Wijdenbosch bridge in Meerzorg Commewijne. On departure, you can change Suriname dollars into Guyanese or US dollars at Corriverton or in Georgetown. To check daily exchange rates for US dollars, euros, pounds sterling and Netherlands Antilles guilders, visit the **Central Bank site**, www.cbvs.sr/english/publicaties-dagkoers.htm.

Safety Street crime in Paramaribo has been much reduced. Although beggars are a nuisance at night, they are rarely dangerous. Generally, Paramaribo is much safer than Georgetown or Cayenne, but it's still wise to be cautious after dark nd take care around the markets and docks. Do not photograph military installations. If in doubt, ask first. Those travelling to the interior should ask in the capital about the safety situation in the areas they plan to visit.

Getting around
Air Internal services are run by **SLM**, **Gum Air** (T498760, www.gumair.com) and **Blue Wing** (T434393, www.bluewingairlines.com), small air charter firms. **Heli Jets** is a helicopter charter company at Zorg en Hoop airport (T432577).There are no scheduled flights, only charters. The air companies fly to several Amerindian and Maroon villages. Most settlements have an airstrip, but internal air services are limited. These flights are on demand.

Road Details of buses and taxis are given in the text below. **Hitchhiking** is not common, but it is possible.

Cycling Bicycles can be bought from **A Seymonson**, Rijwielhersteller, Rust en Vredestraat. Recommended rides from Paramaribo include: to Nieuw-Amsterdam, Marienburg, Alkmaar and back via Tamanredjo in the Javanese Commewijne district or from Rust en Werk to Spieringshoek to Reijnsdorp (3½ hours) and return to Leonsberg via ferry, whence it is a 30 minutes to Paramaribo.

Ferry The **Suriname Navigation Co** (SMS) has a daily service, leaving 0700, on the Commewijne River (a nice four hour trip; you can get off at **De Nieuwe Grond,** a plantation owned by an English couple, and stay overnight). The **SMS** ferry to Alliance/Reynsdorp leaves on Wednesday, Friday, Saturday or Sunday at 0700.

   Note: It is advisable to check the weather conditions and probabilities of returning on schedule before you set out on a trip to the interior. Heavy rains can make it impossible for planes to land in some jungle areas; little or no provision is made for such delays and it can be a long and hungry wait for better conditions.

Sleeping → *See inside front cover for our hotel grade price guide.*
Hotels (and restaurants) are rare outside the capital, but accommodation in the interior is excellent if organized through a tour operator. Many have their own resorts, such as the Mets' Awarradam complex near the Saramaka villages on Gran Rio. These resorts are usually very comfortable. Going alone, you usually have to supply your own hammock and mosquito net, and food. A tent is less useful in this climate. Travelling is cheap if you change cash dollars on the black market; taking hammock and food will reduce costs.

Eating → *See inside front cover for our eating price guide.*
Surinamese cuisine is as rich and varied as the country's ethnic makeup. Rice is the main staple and of very high quality. Cassava, sweet potatoes, plantain, and hot red peppers are widely used. *Pom* is a puree of the tayer root (a relative of cassava) tastily spiced and served with *kip* (chicken). *Moksie Alesie* is rice mixed with meat, chicken, white beans, tomatoes, peppers and spices. *Pindasoep* (peanut soup with plantain dumplings, also with plantain noodles) and *okersoep met tayerblad* (gumbo and cassava soup) are both worth a try. *Petjil* are vegetables cooked in peanut sauce. Well known Indonesian dishes include *bami* (fried noodles) and *nassie goreng* (fried rice), both spicy with a slightly sweet taste. Among the Hindustani dishes are *roti* (a crêpe wrapped around curried potatoes, vegetables and chicken), *somosa* (fried pastry filled with spicy potatoes and vegetables), and *phulawri* (fried chick-pea balls). Among the many tropical fruits of Suriname, palm nuts such as the orange coloured awarra and the cone shaped brown maripa are most popular.

Festivals and events
Public holidays 1 January, New Year; Holi Phagwa (Hindu spring festival, date varies each year, generally in March, very interesting but watch out for throwing of water, paint, talc and coloured powder); Good Friday; Easter (two days); 1 May (Labour Day); 1 July (Emancipation Day); Diwali (Hindu Festival of Light in October); 25 November (Independence Day); Christmas (two days). For Moslem holidays see note under Guyana.

Festivals Avond Vierdaagse starting on the first Wednesday after Easter is a carnival parade of the young and old dressed in traditional costume or simple clothes; it is organized by Bedrijven Vereniging Sport en Spel (BVVS), Johannes Mungrastraat 48, Paramaribo, T461020. **Surifesta** (www.surifesta.com) is a year-end festival, from mid- December to the first week of January, with shows, street parties, flower markets, culminating in **Het Vat** on 31 December. The **Suriname Jazz Festival**, www.surinamejazzfestival.com, is held annually in Paramaribo in October. Project manager: Ms Anne-Marie Hermelijn, an.hermelijn@surinamejazzfestival.com. **Nationale Kunstbeurs/National Art Fair/ National Art Exhibition**, held in Vormingscentrum Ons Erf, Prins Hendrikstraat, Paramaribo, www.suriname-fvas.org/activities.html.

Paramaribo → *Colour map 2, grid B5. Population: 257,000.*

The capital and chief port, lies on the Suriname River, 12 km from the sea. There are many attractive colonial buildings. The **Governor's Mansion** (now the Presidential Palace) is on Onafhankelijkheidsplein (also called Eenheidsplein and, originally, Oranjeplein). Many beautiful 18th- and 19th-century buildings in Dutch (neo-Normanic) style are in the same area. A few have been restored, notably along the waterfront.

Ins and outs
Getting there The airport is 47 km south. There is no central bus station. ▶▶ *For more detailed information see Transport, page 1450.*

Getting around There are very few regular **buses**; the few services that are left leave from Heiligenweg. There are privately run 'wild buses', also known as 'numbered buses' which run on fixed routes around the city; they are minivans and are severely overcrowded. **Taxis** generally have no meters. The price should be agreed on beforehand to avoid trouble. If hiring a taxi for touring, beware of overcharging. If you're a hotel guest, let the hotel make arrangements.

Tourist information **Suriname Tourist Foundation**, main office JF Nassylaan 2, T410357, www.suriname-tourism.org. Monday-Friday 0730-1500. Branch office at the Zeelandia Complex, T479200, Monday-Friday 0900-1530. You can also get information from operators like **Mets** or **Sun and Forest**.

Sights
Fort Zeelandia houses the Suriname Museum ① *T425871, Tue-Fri 0900-1400, Sun 1000-1400, US$0.75,* restored to this purpose after being repossessed by the military. The whole complex has been opened to the public again and its historic buildings can be visited. The fort itself now belongs to the Stichting (foundation) Surinaams Museum, and is generally in good condition. The old wooden officers' houses in the same complex have been restored with Dutch finance. Very few exhibits remain in the old museum in the residential suburb of Zorg en Hoop, Commewijnestraat. Look for Mr F H R Lim A Postraat if you wish to see what Paramaribo looked like only a comparatively short time ago. The 19th century **Roman Catholic St Peter and Paul Cathedral** (1885), built entirely of wood, is one of the largest wooden buildings in the Americas. This twin towered, neo-Gothic building with a rose window is both impressive and beautiful. Times of tours are given on the sign at the entrance. Continuing restoration is due with funds from the European Union. Much of the old town, dating from the 19th century, and the churches have been restored. Other things to see are the colourful **market** and the waterfront, **Hindu temples** in Koningstraat and Wanicastraat (finally completed after years of construction), one of the Caribbean's largest **mosques** at Keizerstraat (magnificent photos of it can be taken at sunset). There are two **synagogues**: one next to the mosque at Keizerstraat 88, the other (1854) on the corner of Klipstenstraat and Heerenstraat (closed, now houses an internet café and IT business unit). The new **Numismatich Museum** ① *Mr FHR Lim A Postraat 7, T520016, www.cbvs.sr daily 0800 – 1400,* displaying the history of Suriname's money, is operated by the Central Bank. A new harbour has been constructed about 1½ km upstream. Two pleasant parks are the **Palmentuin**, with a stage for concerts, and the **Cultuurtuin** (with poorly-kept zoo owing to lack of funds, US$1.20, busy on Sunday), the latter is a 20 minute walk from the centre. National dress is normally only worn by the Asians on national holidays and at wedding parties, but some Javanese women still go about in sarong and klambi. A university (Anton de Kom Universiteit van Suriname) was opened in 1968. There is one public swimming pool at Weidestraat, US$0.60 per person. There is an exotic Asian flavour in the market area. There is a Sunday morning flea market on Tourtonnelaan.

An interesting custom practised throughout Suriname is the birdsong competitions, held in parks and plazas on Sunday and holidays. People carrying their songbird (usually a small black tua-tua) in a cage are frequently seen; on their way to and from work, to a 'training session', or simply taking their pet for a stroll!

Outside Paramaribo

Excursions and day trips close to the city and the routes to the borders with Guyana and Guyane. There are some worthwhile nature reserves to visit.

Inland from Paramaribo

Accaribo resort, about one hour by car from the capital on the Suriname River, near the villages of La Vigilantia and Accaribo: seven rooms with bath, visit Amerindian settlement, pottery making, swimming in the river, Creole and Javanese cultures.

Powaka, about 90 minutes outside the capital, is a primitive village of thatched huts but with electric light and a small church. In the surrounding forest one can pick mangoes and other exotic fruit. An interesting half, or full day excursion is to take minibus four, or taxi, to **Leonsberg** on the Suriname River (**Stardust Hotel**, with mid-priced restaurant, coffee shop, swimming pool, games; restaurant **Rust Pelikan** on waterfront; at **Leonsberg** restaurant try *saoto* soup and other Javanese specialities, overlooking the river), then ferry to **Nieuw-Amsterdam**, the capital of the predominantly Javanese district of Commewijne. There is an open-air **museum** ① *open only in mornings except Fri, 1700-1900*, inside the old fortress which guarded the confluence of the Suriname and Commewijne rivers (badly rundown). There are some interesting old plantation mansions left in the Commewijne district. **Braamspunt**, a peninsula with nice beaches at the mouth of the Suriname River, is 10 km from Paramaribo. Boats from the Leonsberg scaffold go down river.

You can go by private car to **Jodensavanne** (Jews' Savannah, established 1639), south of Paramaribo on the opposite bank of the Suriname River, where a cemetery and the foundations of one of the oldest synagogues in the Western Hemisphere have been restored. There is no public transport and taxis won't go because of the bad road. It is still only 1½ hours with a

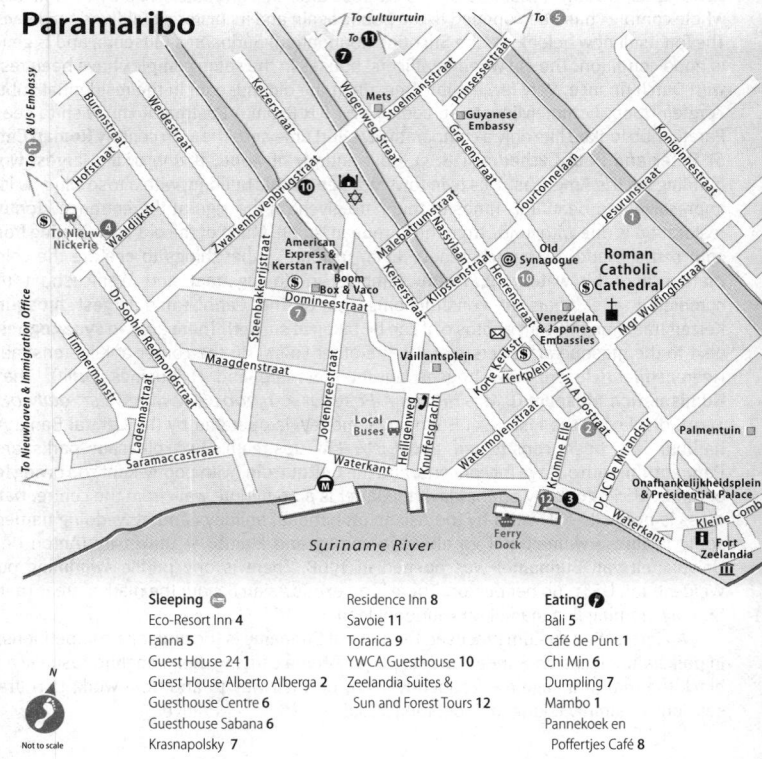

Paramaribo

Sleeping	Residence Inn 8	Eating
Eco-Resort Inn 4	Savoie 11	Bali 5
Fanna 5	Toravica 9	Café de Punt 1
Guest House 24 1	YWCA Guesthouse 10	Chi Min 6
Guest House Alberto Alberga 2	Zeelandia Suites &	Dumpling 7
Guesthouse Centre 6	Sun and Forest Tours 12	Mambo 1
Guesthouse Sabana 6		Pannekoek en
Krasnapolsky 7		Poffertjes Café 8

N

Not to scale

suitable vehicle (see above for tours). There is a bridge across the Suriname River to Jodensavanne. **Blakawatra** is said to be one of the most beautiful spots in all Suriname (shame about the amount of rubbish strewn around). This was the scene of much fighting in the civil war. A full day trip to Jodensavanne and Blakawatra, returning to Paramaribo via Moengo, has been recommended if you can arrange the transport. Bus to Blakawatra at 0800, three hours, US$0.20. Some 5 km from the International Airport there is a resort called **Colakreek** *US$0.20*, so named for the colour of the water, but good for swimming (busy at weekends), lifeguards, water bicycles, children's village, restaurant, bar, tents or huts for overnight stay. The village of **Bersaba**, 40 km from Paramaribo close to the road to the airport, is popular area for the Coropinakreek. Many people go there and the neighbouring village of Republiek at weekends and on holidays.

Approximately 30 km southwest of Paramaribo, via **Lelydorp** (*Hotel De Lely*, Sastrodisomoweg 41; *The Lely Hills* casino), is the Bush Negro village of **Santigron**, on the east bank of the Saramacca River. Minibuses leave Paramaribo at 0530 and 1500, two hours, US$0.10. They return as soon as they drop off passengers in the village, so make sure you will have a bus to return on; there is no accommodation in Santigron. Nearby is the Amerindian village of **Pikin Poika**. The two make a good independent day trip. Tour agencies also visit the area about twice a month, including canoe rides on the Saramacca River and a Bush Negro dance performance.

By bus or car to **Afobakka**, where there is a large hydroelectric dam on the Suriname River. There is a government guest house (price includes three meals a day) in nearby **Brokopondo**. Victoria is an oil-palm plantation in the same area.

The hills of **Brownsberg National Park** ① *US$1.20*, an hour by car from Brokopondo, overlook the Professor Dr Ir van Blommensteinmeer reservoir. It features good walking, ample opportunities to see wildlife and three impressive waterfalls. Stinasu run all-inclusive tours from Paramaribo (one and three-day tours, price includes transport, accommodation, food, and guide). Independent visits are possible. Minibuses for Brownsweg leave Saramaccastraat in Paramaribo daily when full, be there 0800-0900, two hours, US$5.55. Trucks converted into buses do the trip for US$3.70. Go to Stinasu at least 24 hours in advance and pay for accommodation in their guest houses (US$35, or US$5 to camp) or to arrange for a vehicle to pick you up in Brownsweg (US$30). Take your own food.

Tukunari Island, in van Blommesteinmeer lake, is about three hours drive from Paramaribo to Brokopondo then a two hours canoe ride. The island is near the village of Lebi Doti, where Aucaner Maroons live. Tours with NV Mets include fishing, visits to villages, jungle treks and visits to rapids.

Saramaka villages and **Awarradam**. There are many Saramaka villages along the Gran and Pikin Rios; both tributaries of the Suriname River. These are fascinating places, set up by escaped slaves in the 17th and 18th centuries who were originally from a part of Ghana and who preserve a ceremonial language, spirituality and traditions from Kromanti in that country. NV Mets have a very comfortable lodge on the Gran Rio at Awarradam, in front of a beautiful set of rapids in thick forest, and many other agencies, such as Sun and Forest, organize culturally sensitive tours to the villages. Freelance visitors are not welcome.

Power Smoothie 9
Roopram Rotishop 10
Spice Quest 11
'T Lekkerbekje 1
'T VAT' 2
Uncle Ray & Warungs 3
Zanzibar 1

Bars & clubs 🎵
Broki 12
Touché 4

Raleighvallen/Voltzberg Nature Reserve (78,170 ha) is a rainforest park, southwest of Paramaribo, on the Coppename River. It includes Foengoe Island in the river and Voltzberg peak; climbing the mountain at sunrise is unforgettable. The reserve can be reached by air, or by road (180 km) followed by a 3-4 hour boat ride. This reserve has been joined with Tafelberg and Eilerts de Haan reserves to create the **Central Suriname Nature Reserve** (1.592 million ha – 9.7% of Suriname's total land area). The Reserve is now part of the Unesco's World Heritage List (www.unesco.org). New tourist facilities have been opened. Stinasu does a US$10 tour, or can arrange all-inclusive tours with accommodation, transport, food and guides. **Stoelmanseiland**, on the Lawa River in the interior, and the Maroon villages and rapids in the area can be visited on an organized tour. Price US$170 per person for three days (five persons, minimum). They are, however, more easily reached by river from St-Laurent du Maroni and Maripasoula in Guyane.

Kasikasima and **Palumeu**, in the far south of Suriname, are a series of dramatic granite mountains rising out of pristine forest. The highest is Mount Kasikasima, near the Trio and Wajana Amerindian village of Palumeu. Mets have a comfortable river lodge here and organize trips up the mountain, as do other operators.

West of Paramaribo

A narrow but paved road leads through the citrus and vegetable growing areas of **Wanica** and **Saramaca**, linked by a bridge over the Saramaca River. At **Boskamp** (90 km from Paramaribo) is the Coppename River. The Coppename bridge crosses to **Jenny** on the west bank. The **Coppename Estuary** is a national park, protecting many bird colonies.

A further 50 km is **Totness**, where there was once a Scottish settlement. It is the largest village in the Coronie district, along the coast between Paramaribo and Nieuw-Nickerie on the Guyanese border. There is a good government guesthouse. The road (bad, liable to flooding) leads through an extensive forest of coconut palms. Bus to Paramaribo at 0600. 40 km further west, 5 km south of the main road is **Wageningen**, a modern little town, the centre of the Suriname rice-growing area. The road from Nickerie has been renewed. One of the largest fully mechanized rice farms in the world is found here (*Hotel de Wereld*, T0251544). The **Bigi-Pan** area of mangroves is a birdwatchers' paradise; boats may be hired from local fishermen.

Nieuw-Nickerie (Population over 8,000 (district 45,000, mostly East Indian) on the south bank of the Nickerie River 5 km from its mouth, opposite Guyana, is the main town and port of the Nickerie district and is distinguished for its rice fields. It is a clean and ordered town, but there are a lot of mosquitoes.

Border with Guyana

Ferry to Moleson Creek (for Springlands) From South Drain (Suriname, 40 km from Nieuw-Nickerie) to Moleson/Crabwood Creek (Guyana), it's a 30-minute crossing on the regular ferry. Immigration forms are handed out on the boat. See Transport below. The illegal 'Back Track' speedboat runs from a point 10 minutes from town, by a café on the beach. Seek local advice before using this route. **Note**: Suriname is 1 hr ahead of Guyana.

Apura on the Corantijn can be reached by sea-going vessels (**C**) with three meals, advance booking from Paramaribo advisable, good). **Blanche Marie Falls**, 320 km from Paramaribo on the Apura road, is a popular destination. There is a guesthouse, Dubois, see Sleeping below. **Washabo** near Apura, which has an airstrip, is an Amerindian village. No public transport runs from Paramaribo to the Apura-Bakhuis area, but frequent charter flights go to the Washabo airstrip. Irregular small boats sail from Apura to Nieuw-Nickerie and to Springlands (Guyana).

East of Paramaribo to Guyane

Eastern Suriname was the area most severely damaged during the civil war. A paved road connects Meerzorg (bridge across the river) with Albina, passing through the districts of Commewijne and Marowijne. There is little population or agriculture left here. **Moengo**, 160 km up the Cottica River from Paramaribo, was a bauxite mining and loading centre for Suralco. It can be reached by medium draught ships and by cars. The new bauxite mining centre is at Coermotibo, not far from Moengo.

There are two **nature reserves** on the northeast coast of Suriname. Known primarily as a major nesting site for sea turtles (five species including the huge leatherback turtle come ashore to lay their eggs), **Wia-Wia Nature Reserve** (36,000 ha) also has nesting grounds for some magnificent birds. The nesting activity of sea turtles is best observed April-July (July is a good month to visit as you can see adults coming ashore to lay eggs and hatchlings rushing to the sea at high tide). Since the beaches and consequently the turtles have shifted westwards out of the reserve, accommodation is now at **Matapica** beach, not in the reserve itself. (After a visit to the reserves send any comments to Stinasu. Your support is needed to keep the reserves functioning.) The SMS riverboat from Paramaribo stops at Alliance on its journey up the Commewijne River. You then transfer to a Stinasu motorboat for a one hour ride to Matapica. The motorboat costs US$50 for four people, round trip; a guide is the same price. Suitable waterproof clothing should be worn. Fishermen make the crossing for US$3-4. Book accommodation and boat through Stinasu or other agencies; keep your receipts or you will be refused entry. Early booking is essential. Stinasu has a lodge at Matapica. It can accommodate 8 people, facilities are basic and it costs US$53.

The **Galibi Nature Reserve** ① *www.biotopic.demon.nl/suriname/suriname.htm*, where there are more turtle-nesting places, is near the mouth of the Marowijne River. There are Carib Indian villages. From Albina it is a three hour (including 30 minutes on the open sea) boat trip to Galibi. There is new tourist lodge here: it has cooking facilities, a refrigerator, rooms with shower and toilet, powered mostly by solar energy. Make arrangements through Stinasu who run all-inclusive, four-day, three-night tours (you can save money by taking your own food and public transport to the river to meet the motorboat). Sun and Forest Tours also have tours here.

East of Moengo, the scars of war are most obvious. **Albina** is on the Marowijne River, the frontier with Guyane. Once a thriving, pleasant town and then a bombed-out wreck, it is now showing signs of recovery with new buildings, shops, a market and several restaurants. *The Creek Hotel* (eight rooms) is on the northern outskirts of town; the owner speaks English.

Border with Guyane
Customs and immigration on both sides close at 1900, but in Albina staff usually leave by 1700. Be wary of local information on exchange rates and transport to Paramaribo. Changing money on the Suriname side of the border is illegal; see Currency, page 1441. Suriname dollars are not recognized in Guyane; when crossing to Suriname, pay for the boat in euros, or get the minivan driver to pay and he will stop at a cambio before reaching Paramaribo so you can change money and pay him. Immigration is at either end, next to the ferry terminal. See Transport, below.

● Sleeping

Paramaribo *p1443, map p1444*
Service charge at hotels is 5-10%. Beware: many cheap hotels not listed are 'hot pillow' establishments. The Suriname Museum in Zorg-en-Hoop (see above) now has a good guest house; book in advance.
L Zeelandia Suites, Kleine Waterstraat 1a, T424631, www.zeelandiasuites.com. Smart, business-style suites with all mod cons next to a lively bar and restaurant area.
L-AL Krasnapolsky, Domineestraat 39, T475050, www.krasnapolsky.sr. A/c, central, travel agency, shopping centre, exhibition hall in the lobby, good breakfast and buffet, *Atrium* restaurant for local and international cuisine (mid-range), *Rumours Grand Café* (with jazz jam sessions on Tue and Fri), poolside bar, business centre with internet and conference facilities, takes Amex, swimming pool.
L-AL Torarica, Mr Rietbergplein, T471500, www.torarica.com. Best in town, very pleasant, book ahead, swimming pool and other sports facilities, sauna, casino, nightclub, tropical gardens, a/c, central, 3 expensive restaurants (*Plantation Room*, European; *Saramacca Bar*, with live entertainment; good poolside buffet on

Fri evening), superb breakfast, business centre with internet and conference facilities. Has subsidiary *Tangelo Bar and Terrace*, at Mr Rietbergplein 1.
AL Eco-Resort Inn, Cornelis Jongbawstraat 16, PO Box 2998, T425522, www.ecoresortinn.com/ website/html/index.php. Use of *Torarica* facilities, good atmosphere and value, restaurant (mid-range), bar, Ms Maureen Libanon is very helpful, business centre, with internet and fax.
A De Luifel, Gondastraat 13 (about 15 mins from centre), T439933, F439930. A/c, warm water, cable TV, mid-priced European restaurant, special 'business-to-business' deal: 1 night with breakfast, laundry, airport transfer, car hire and taxes included, US$99, Amex accepted.
A Savoie, Johannes Mungrastraat 25, T432495, www.cq-link.sr/bedrijven/ hotel-savoie. Breakfast extra.
A Residence Inn, Anton Dragtenweg 7, T472387, www.surinamevacations.com. TV, minibar, laundry, including breakfast, credit cards accepted, in a residential area, pool, tennis court, a/c bar and *Atlantis* restaurant, European and Surinamese food (mid-range).

A Shereday, Cornelis Prinsstraat 87, T434564, F463844, 5 km from centre. Exercise floor, swimming pool, restaurant/bar (mid-range).

B Guesthouse Amice, Gravenberchstraat 5 (10 mins from centre), T434289, www.guesthouse-amice.sr (in Netherlands, Robijndrift 47, 3436 BR Nieuwegein, T030-294 5229, amice@ worldonline.nl). Quiet neighbourhood, room with balcony more expensive, a/c, comfortable, internet, breakfast, airport transfer and tours available.

B Guesthouse Centre, Sommelsdijckstraat 4 (near *Hotel Torarica*), T426310. A/c, TV, new.

B-C ABC, Mahonielaan 55, T420851, www.hotel aabece.com. Small, simple, cosy and good, well-decorated, a/c, fridge, TV, kitchenette, safe.

C Guest House Alberto Alberga, Lim A Po Straat 13b, T/F520050, 888 6659 (mob), Sabina_floridia@yahoo.com. Central, above a doctor's clinic, very pleasant, decorated with Amerindian costumes, terrace and TV area, spick and span rooms with a/c or fan.

C Guesthouse Sabana, Kleine Waterstraat 7, T424158, F310022, opposite *Torarica*. A/c, safe, helpful.

D YWCA Guesthouse (pronounced Why-Ka) at Heerenstraat 14-16, T476981. Best for budget travellers. Cheaper weekly rates, full of permanent residents, essential to book in advance (office open 0800-1400), very accommodating, shared bath, cold water, safe, luggage store, cheap local snackbar, internet next door.

D-E Fanna, Prinsessestraat 31, T476789. From a/c with bath to basic, breakfast extra, safe, family run, English spoken.

E Guesthouse 24, Jesurunstraat 24. Simple but well-maintained apartments.

Inland from Paramaribo *p1444*
AL Overbridge River Resort, 1 hr south of the capital, via Paranam (30 km), then 9.5 km to Powerline mast 20-21, then 7.5 km to resort, or 60 km by boat down Suriname River, www.overbridge.net. Reservations, Anton Dragtenweg 352, Paramaribo-Noord, T/F456440. Cabins by the river, price includes breakfast, weekend and other packages available.

AL-B Hendrison Bungalows, Bersaba, contact address Andresietsstraat 4, Paramaribo T/F457391 (Rodenryselaan 403, 3037 XG Rotterdam, T104-66414), www.hendrison.com. Fully-furnished.

A-B Residence Inn, R P Bharosstraat 84, Nieuw Nickerie, PO Box 4330, T0210950/1, www.surinamevacations.com. Best in town, prices higher at weekend, central, a/c, bath, hot water, TV, business centre with email (US$5 per hr), internet access (US$7 per hr), fax (US$0.35 national only), laundry, good restaurants (*De Palm* and *Café de Tropen*, both **ℍ**), bar.

C Ameerali, Maynardstraat 32-36, Nieuw Nickerie, T0231212, F31066. A/c, good, restaurant (**ℍ**) and bar.

D Luxor, Gouverneurstraat, Nieuw Nickerie. Recently renovated, with mirror-glass frontage.

F Tropical, Gouverneurstraat 114, Nieuw Nickerie, T231796. Mostly short stay, noisy bar downstairs.

Hotel Frederiksdorp, T305003, frederiksdorp@ sr.net. Manager Mr Marcel Hagemeyer. In an old coffee plantation, apartments, bar, restaurant, museum, conference facilities and email.

Border with Guyana *p1446*
B Dubois, contact Eldoradolaan 22, Paramaribo T476904/2. Guesthouse near the Blanche Marie Falls, 320 km from Paramaribo on the Apura road.

● Eating

Paramaribo *p1443, map p1444*
Meat and noodles from stalls in the market are very cheap. There are some good restaurants, mainly Indonesian and Chinese dishes. Blauwgrond is the area for typical, cheap, Indonesian food, served in *warungs* (the Indonesian name for restaurants).

Indonesian
Try a *rijsttafel* in a restaurant such as **Sarinah** (open-air dining), Verlengde Gemenelandsweg 187. Javanese foodstalls on Waterkant are excellent and varied, lit at night by candles. Try *bami* (spicy noodles) and *petjil* (vegetables), recommended on Sun when the area is busiest. In restaurants a dish to try is *gadogado*, an Indonesian vegetable and peanut concoction.
ℍ Bali, Ma Retraiteweg 3, T422325. Very good food, service and atmosphere, check bill.
ℍ Jawa, Kasabaholoweg 7. Famous Indonesian restaurant.

Chinese
ℍ Chi Min, Cornelis Jongbawstraat 83. For well-prepared Chinese food. Recommended.
ℍ Dumpling, Dr JF Nassylaan 12. Simple, well-prepared Chinese dumplings and other such dishes. Generous portions, popular with children.

Others
ℍ Café De Punt, Kleine Waterstraat 17, opposite *Torarica*. Local and international cuisine, live entertainment at weekends.

● *For an explanation of the sleeping and eating price codes used in this guide, see inside the front*
● *cover. Other relevant information is found in Essentials page 1442.*

¶¶ **DOK 204**, Anton Dragenweg 204, T311461. Surinamese dishes in an intimate restaurant decorated with a nautical theme.

¶¶ **Mambo**, opposite *Torarica*, next to Sabana Guesthouse. Local and international cuisine.

¶¶ **Pannekoek en Poffertjes Café**, Sommelsdijckstraat 11. Speciality pancakes.

¶¶ **Spice Quest**, Dr Nassylaan. Romantic, candlelit dinners and Asian food, hippie feel.

¶¶ **'T Lekkerbekje**, Sommelsdijckstraat (near Guesthouse Centre). Specializes in fish.

¶¶ **'T VAT'**, opposite *Torarica*. A smart little square with lots of little bars and restaurants, popular after work for early evening meeting and drinking.

¶¶ **Zanzibar**, Sommelsdijckstraat 1, near Hotel Torarica, T471848. Surinamese and international cuisine, with entertainment, Tue-Sun 2000 till early morning.

¶¶-¶ **Roopram Rotishop**, Zwartenhovenbrugstraat 23, T478816. Rotis and accompanied fillings in an a/c fast-food style dining room, generous portions, *roti aard* particularly good.

¶ **Power Smoothie**, Zwartenhovenbrugstraat and Wilhelminastraat. Healthy fast food.

¶ **Uncle Ray** at Waterkant by the Javanese *warungs*, opposite Central Bank of Suriname. Local Creole food.

◑ Bars and clubs

Paramaribo *p1443, map p1444*
All are liveliest Thu-Sat.

Don Julio Muziek Eetcafe, Wilhelminastraat 8 (near Torarica). Popular spot, live entertainment, Sun-Thu 1600-0100, Fri-Sat 1600- 0300.

Ballrom Energy, L'Hermitageweg 25, T497534. Younger crowd.

Broki, Waterkant next to the Ferry Docks. Hammock bar, good food and atmosphere.

The Jungle, Wilhelminastraat 60-62. For all ages.

Millennium, Petrus Dondersstraat 2, Rainville suburb. Popular with all ages but mostly the over-30s; **Grill** restaurant inside.

Touché, Waaldijk/Dr Sophie Redmondstraat 60. Fri-Sat only 2300, small restaurant, the best disco.

◉ Entertainment

Paramaribo *p1443, map p1444*
There are many **casinos** in the city, including at major hotels. **Cinema Tower**, Heerenstraat. Showing recent productions.

◯ Shopping

Paramaribo *p1443, map p1444*
Arts and crafts Carvings (of Amerindian and Maroon origin) are better value at the workshops on Nieuwe Domineestraat and the Neumanpad.

Many jewellers' shops in the centre sell at reasonable prices. Local ceramics are sold on the road between the airport and Paranam, but they are rather brittle. Old Dutch bottles are sold. **Arts & Crafts**, Kersten Shopping Mall. Amerindian goods, batik prints, carvings, basket work, and drums. **Cultuurwinkel**, Anton de Komstraat. Bosneger carvings, also available at *Hotel Torarica*.

Bookshops Second-hand books, English and Dutch, are bought and sold in the market. Maps are hard to find, but try Vaco. The kiosk in Krasnapolsky Hotel sells books. **Boekhandel Univers NV**, Gravenstraat 61. Recommended for nature, linguistic and scholarly books on Suriname. **Hoeksteen**, Gravenstraat 17. **Kersten**, Domineestraat. One of the 2 main bookshops in the city, selling English- language books. **Vaco**, opposite Krasnapolsky. The other main bookshop, also selling English books.

Film Photo Max, 37 Domineestraat, next to Krasnapolsky Hotel. Cheap film.

Music The following sell international and local music on CD (the latter is heavily influenced by Caribbean styles): **Beat Street** in Steenbakkerijstraat, near Krasnapolsky Hotel. **Boom Box**, Domineestraat, opposite Krasnapolsky Hotel. **Disco Amigo**, Wagenwegstraat, opposite Theater Star.

Shopping centre Hermitage Shopping Mall, 5 mins in taxi from centre. The only place open until 2100, with chemists, money exchange, boutiques, coffee shops and music stores.

▲▲ Activities and tours

Paramaribo *p1443, map p1444*
If intending to take a tour to the jungle and either Amerindian or Maroon villages, check how much time is spent in the jungle itself and on the conditions in the villages. One such trip is to Palumeu, an Amerindian village (Trio, Wajana and Akurio peoples) due south of Paramaribo, not far from the Brazilian border. Four-day, 3-night packages include flights, food, accommodation, jungle hikes and boat trips.

Access Suriname Travel, Prinsessestraat 37, T/F424522, www.surinametravel.com. Sells all major tours in Suriname and can supply general travel information on the country, manager Syrano Zalman is helpful.

Arinze Tours, Prinsessestraat 2c, T425960, www.arinzetours.com. Tours to Maroon villages of Santigron, manager George Lazo.

Cardy Adventures and Bike Rental, Cornelis Jongbawstraat 31 (near Eco Resort), T422518, www.cardyadventures.com. Bicycle rental (bikerental@cardyadventures.com) and tours to Commewijne district, and tours to Brownsberg, Raleigh Falls, Matapica and jungle survival trips,

English spoken, very helpful and efficient, excellent food. Open Mon-Fri 0800-1600, Sat 0800-1300.

Danpaati Eco Lodges, Winchesterstraat 6, T/F401687, http://danpaati.net. Lodges in the Upper Suriname (Boven Suriname) on the island of Danpaati.

Eagle Tours, Albatrosstraat 10, T311355 or 09-978850, www.eagletours.info. Tours of Paramaribo, Nickerie, Para, Commewijne and Jodensavanne; also fishing trips.

Ma-Ye-Du, Matoeliestraat 22, T/F410348, mayedu@sr.net. For tours to Maroon villages in the Marowijne River.

Moonlight Jungle Tour, Julianastraat 36, T520709, www.surjungle.com. Jungle expeditions and cruises on Suriname River.

NV Mets (Movement for Eco-Tourism in Suriname), PO Box 9080, Dr JF Nassylaan 2, Paramaribo, T477088, F422322, mets@sr.net, www.surinamevacations.com. Also in Cayenne, 15 rue Louis Blanc, T317298, F305786; in Georgetown contact *Wilderness Explorers* (see page 1436). Trips to the interior, reasonable rates. Tours offered are City Tour, Rivercruise, Santigron (all day trips); 4/5 day trips to Tukunari Island; 4/5-day trips to Palumeu (see below) staying in lodges; 8-day trip to Mount Kasikasima in remote southern Suriname (all transport, food and guides – good – included, US$625). Excellent lodge at Awarradam for the Saramaka maroon villages. Can be booked through any **Surinam Airways** outside Suriname.

Stinasu is the Foundation for Nature Preservation in Suriname, Cornelis Jongbawstraat 14, T476597, PO Box 12252, Paramaribo, www.stinasu.sr. It offers reasonably priced accommodation and provides tour guides on the extensive nature reserves throughout the country. One can see 'true wilderness and wildlife' with them.

Sun and Forest Tours, Kleine Waterstraat 1B, T478383, www.surinamesunforest.net. Excellent tours to the interior, including the Central Suriname Nature Reserve, to the turtle nesting beaches near Galibi and Amerindian villages. Onward transport to and trips within Guyane or Guyana with associated operators. Good, reliable service.

Suriname Safari Tours, Dr S S Kaffiludistraat 27, T400925, safaritours@sr.net. Excursions to the interior.

Tojo Adventures, Gravenstraat 73, T422654, www.surinamevakanties.com. Ecotours, helpful tour guides, art, stock for Mr Boyke Tojo. Or through **Mena-Eng**, www.mena-suriname.com.

Waldo's Travel Service, Heerenstraat 8, T422530, www.waldostravel.sr. For all tours within Suriname.

Nieuw Nickerie *p1446*
Manoetje Tours, Crownstraat 11, Nieuw-Nickerie, T231991 (Hans Overeem). Boat tours to, among other places, Apura, Orealla, Corantijn.

⊖ Transport

Paramaribo *p1443, map p1444*
Air The Johan Pengel International Airport is 47 km south of Paramaribo. Minibus to town costs US$7.40 (eg De Paarl, T403610); bus costs US$8.25 with **Ashruf** taxi company, T454451 (it makes many stops), taxi proper costs US$14, but negotiate. *Hotel Torarica, Eco Resort Inn* and *Residence Inn* offer free transfers to and from the international airport for guests with room reservation. There is a guest house near the airport. Internal flights leave from Zorg en Hoop airfield in a suburb of Paramaribo (take minibus 8 or 9 from Steenbakkerijstraat). See Getting there and Getting around in Essentials, above, for airline offices.

Bus To **Nickerie** from Dr Sophie Redmondstraat, near *Hotel Ambassador*, minibuses leave when full between 0500 and 1000, US$3, 3 hrs. There are also buses after 1200, but the price then depends on the driver, 4-5 hrs, extra for large bag. (Taxis from the same area are slightly faster.) Verify fares in advance and beware overcharging.

Minibus taxis to **Albina** US$7.40, 2-3 hrs from Paramaribo cross the new bridge; there is also a bus from the station near the ferry services in Paramaribo at 0830, return 1300, US$1.65 (take an APB or PBA bus, which has a plainclothes policeman on board). **Taxis** are available, but dishonest (usually). There are irregular bus services to other towns. For full details ask drivers or enquire at the tourist office. There is much jostling in the queues and pure mayhem when boarding vehicles. They are all minivans and have no luggage space. Try to put bags under your seat or you will have to hold it in your lap.

Direct **buses** to **Georgetown** via South Drain (fare does not include ferry crossing), US$15-22: **Bobby's**, T498583 (very cramped), pick up and drop off at hotels; **Le Grand Baldew**, Tourtonnelaan 59, T474713, www.baldew.com (can organize trips through to Cayenne also), Master Card accepted. Also **Lambada Bus Service**, Keizerstraat 162. T411073, and **Bin Laden**, T0-210944/ 0-8809271 (mob).

Nieuw Nickerie *p1446*
Bus For bus services, see under Paramaribo. The bus station is next to the market on G G Maynardstraat.

Boat Ferry to Moleson Creek (for Springlands): from South Drain to Moleson/ Crabwood Creek (Guyana), ferry at 1100 only, US$10, cars US$15, pick ups US$20. T472447 to check if ferry is running on holidays. Taxi bus from Nickerie market to South Drain at 0730, but can pick you up from your hotel. Bus Paramaribo-South Drain: US$5.55, eg with **Le Grand Baldew**. See under Transport, Paramaribo, for other companies.

Border with Guyane *p1447*
Boat Pirogues take people across the river to **St-Laurent du Maroni** for around US$3.50-4.75, in euros. The car ferry charges US$3.50 for foot passengers, US$25-30 per car, payable only in euros. If you don't want to take a crowded minivan, or an expensive taxi (US$50) from Paramaribo, ask to join a Stinasu tour to Galibi to get to Albina. Albina-Paramaribo: a scrum meets the boats from Guyane, minibus taxis charge US$7.40, 2-3 hrs. A bus leaves at 1300, US$1.65.

ⓘ Directory

Paramaribo *p1443, map p1444*
Airline offices Surinam Airways, Dr Sophie Redmondstraat 219, T432700, www.slm.firm.sr (to/from Amsterdam, joint operation with KLM, HK. Hof-en Burenstraat 1, T411811, Miami - with Dutch Caribbean Airlines, www.flydca.net, and Caribbean). BWIA, Wagenstraat 36, T520034 (Port of Spain, www.bwee.com). Meta, Henck Arronstraat 61, T597 520120, www.voemeta.com.br (Brazil via Georgetown, schedules vary all the time). For Air France (flights between Cayenne and Europe), T473838.
Banks Finabank, Dr Sophie Redmondstraat 61, opposite Ambassador Casino. Hakrinbank, Dr Sophie Redmondstraat 11-13, 0700-1400. RBTT Bank, Kerkplein 1, www.rbtt.com. Cash on Visa and Mastercard. ATMs issue Suriname dollars, foreign exchange desk inside bank. De Surinaamsche Bank, Gravenstraat 26-30, www.dsbbank.sr. Cash on Visa and Mastercard. Surinaamse Postspaar Bank, Heiligenweg near bus station. Volks Credit Bank, Waterkant 104. Landbouwbank, Lim A Postraat 28-30, T475945, F410821. All banks except Finabank are closed on Sat. Amex agent is C Kersten and Co, NV, in Kersten Travel building opposite Hotel Krasnapolsky, T477148. Cambios for exchange, open evenings and on Sat: De Vries, Waterkant 92-94; Dallex, Keizerstraat 8; Multitrack Money Exchange, Mr Rietbergplein, opposite Torarica Hotel; Surichange, Dr Sophie Redmondstraat 71, Yokohama Drive Through, Saramaccastraat (open Sun), Surora Drive Through, Gravenstraat opposite 's Lands Hospitaal. **Bicycle hire** Fietsen in Suriname, FIS, Mijnhooplaan 21, T852 0021, info@fietsen-in-suriname.nl. Koen's Verhuur Bedrijf, Van Sommels- dijckstraat 6, T08-876106, open Mon-Sat 1000-1700, also rents scooters. See also Cardy's under Tour operators.
Car hire Avis, Fred O'Kirkstraat, T450447/807090, F456392; Hertz at Real Car,

Van 't Hogerhuysstraat 19, T402833, ckcmotor@sr.net; SPAC, Verl Gemenelandsweg 139A, T490877, www.spac.cq-link.sr. From US$30 per day, hotel delivery, drivers available. U-Drive, T490803, Wheelz, HD Benjaminstraat 20, T442929, 887 9366 (mob) or 8802361 after 1600 and at weekends, killit@sr.net. Mastercard accepted, US$35-110 daily (tax not included). And other agencies include: City Taxi, Purperhart, Kariem, Intercar. **Embassies and consulates** Brazil, Maratakkastraat 2, T400200, brasaemb1@sr.net. British Honorary Consul, c/o VSH United Buildings, PO Box 1300, Van't Hogerhuysstraat 9-11, T402870, united@sr.net. Canadian Honarary Consul, Wagen-wegstraat 50B, 1st floor, T424527, cantim@sr.net. France, 5-7 Henck Arronstraat, PO Box 2648, T475222. German Honorary Consul, Maagdenstraat 46, T474380. Guyana, Gravenstraat 82, T477985, guyembassy@sr.net. Israeli Honorary Consul, Klipstene- straat 2-10, T411998, F471154. Netherlands, Roseveltkade 5, T477211, nlgovprm@sr.net. USA, Dr Sophie Redmondstraat 129, PO Box 1821, T472900, consul T425788, consular parama@state.gov. Venezuela, Gravenstraat 23-25, T475401, resvensu@sr.net.
Internet All Telesur Dienstencentrum offices offer email (about US$2 per hour), fax (send and receive), local and international phones and computer services. Eg: Paramaribo-West, Zonnebloemstraat 50, T494555; Paramaribo-Noord, Hoek Jozel Israelstraat/ Kristalstraat, T550086; Paramaribo-Zuid (LATOUR), Latoruweg 57, T480093. The Browser Internet Café, Hoek Wilhelmina/HJ De Vriesstraat (opposite Pizza Hut), Paramaribo, T422977. Another important supplier of internet services is Carib, with branches in the synagogue as the Heerenstraat, the Hermitage Mall, Kwattaweg, also in Lelydorp and in Commewijne. Phone cards for cheap international calls are also available in newsagents, many shops and hotels throughout Paramaribo. These offer a far better deal than Telesur cards. These can be bought at Telesur, Heiligenweg 1, Paramaribo (near the fountain, downtown) and its branches, or in supermarkets nationwide, T474242, www.sr.net.

Nieuw Nickerie *p1446*
Banks There are 5 banks on the park, R P Bharosstraat with Landingstraat, and at the corner of Gouverneurstraat and Oost-Kanaalstraat. Finabank is in the Residence Inn Nickerie building. **Internet** At Surtel. Also Telesur Dienstencentrum, Oostkanaalstraat 3, T0-231391. **Post offices and telephones** Offices are on Oost- Kanaalstraat, between Gouverneurstraat and R P Bharosstraat. **Note**: If phoning within town, omit 0 from prefix.

Guyane

Essentials

Planning your trip

Where to go Guyane is an Overseas Department of France, upon which it is heavily dependent. The capital, Cayenne, is on an island at the mouth of the river of the same name. Like its neighbours, Guyane has a populated coastal strip and much of the country remains sparsely populated and underdeveloped despite French aid. The department is known internationally for its space station at Kourou, home to the European Ariane space programme, where economic activity and investment is concentrated. The site has been used to launch over half the world's commercial satellites and over 20,000 foreigners are employed there. Tourism is slowly being developed and is increasing, as in all the Guianas, with adventure trips into the forests making up for the lack of good beaches. Almost all visitors are from France and Belgium. Over 10,000 tourists arrive annually, but their numbers are dwarfed by the 60,000 other visitors, businessmen and those who work in the space programme. An unusual attraction is the remains of the former penal colony, notably the Iles du Salut.

When to go The best months to visit are between August-November. The climate is tropical with heavy rainfall. Average temperature at sea-level is 27° C, and fairly constant. There is often a cool breeze blowing in from the ocean. Night and day temperatures vary more in the highlands. The rainy season is from November to July, with (sometimes) a dry interruption in February and March. The great rains begin in May.

Finding out more The French Government tourist offices generally have leaflets on Guyane; also **Comité du Tourisme de la Guyane** ① *1 rue Clapeyron, 75008 Paris, T33-1-4294 1516, guyanaparis@wanadoo.fr*. In Guyane: **Comité du Tourisme de la Guyane** ① *12 rue Lallouette, BP 801, 97300 Cayenne, T05-94-296500, www.tourisme-guyane.com*. See also www.cr-guyane.fr. **Note**: The Amerindian villages in the Haut-Maroni and Haut-Oyapock areas may only be visited with permission from the Préfecture in Cayenne *before* arrival in Guyane.

Visas and passports Passports are not required by nationals of France and most French-speaking African countries carrying identity cards. For EU visitors, documents are the same as for Metropolitan France (that is no visa, no exit ticket required – check with a consulate in advance). EU passports must be stamped; be sure to visit immigration if arriving from Suriname or Brazil, it is easy to miss. No visa required for most nationalities (except for those of Brazil, Guyana, Suriname, some Eastern European countries, and Asian – not Japan – and other African countries) for a stay of up to three months, but an exit ticket out of the country is essential (a ticket out of one of the other Guianas is not sufficient); a deposit is required otherwise. If you stay more than three months, income tax clearance is required before leaving the country. A visa costs €35, or equivalent (US$44).

Embassies and consulates A full list of France's overseas representation will be found at www.expatries.diplomatie.gouv.fr/annuaires/repdipet.asp

Money The currency is the euro. Take euros with you; many banks do not offer exchange facilities, but ATMs are common. Good rates can be obtained by using Visa or MasterCard (less common) to withdraw cash from any bank in Cayenne, Kourou and St-Laurent du Maroni. It is possible to pay for most hotels and restaurants with a Visa or MasterCard. American Express, Eurocard and Carte Bleue cards are also accepted.

Getting around

Air Internal air services are by **Air Guyane** (see Airline offices, Cayenne). These flights are always heavily booked, so be prepared to wait, or phone. There are daily connections to Maripasoula, at 0930 and 1430, Saül at 1200 and St-Georges at 0745 and 1430. Baggage allowance 10 kg. There are also helicopter companies with domestic services.

⁝ Driving in Guyane

Roads The main road, narrow, but now paved, runs for 130 km from Pointe Macouris, on the roadstead of Cayenne, to Iracoubo. Another 117 km takes it to Mana and St-Laurent. It also runs to Régina and St-Georges de l'Oyapock on the Brazilian border.

Documents There are no formalities for bringing a private car across the Guyane-Suriname border.

Car hire A convenient way to get around. There are 14 agencies in Cayenne; those at the airport open only for flight arrivals. **Avis, Budget** and **Hertz** have offices (see page 43 for websites). A local agency is **Jasmin,** T308490, www.jasminrent-a-car.gf. All types of car available, from economy to luxury to pick-ups and jeeps. Cheapest rates are about US$25 a day, km extra, US$290 per week including km, insurance extra. Check insurance details carefully; the excess is very high.

Motorcycle hire, also a good way to get around, at Ave Pasteur and Dr Gippet, from US$30-US$35 per day.

Fuel Gasoline/petrol costs about US$0.85 a litre; diesel US$0.55 a litre.

Road There are no railways, and about 1,000 km of road. It is now possible to travel overland to Cayenne from Suriname and onwards to Macapá in Brazil. The latter takes about 24 hours from Cayenne with half a day's waiting in St-Georges de l'Oyapock for the Brazilian bus to leave. The roads are much improved. Combis (minivans) ply the coastal roads between St-Laurent, Cayenne and St-Georges de l'Oyapock. Transport is expensive, around US$2 per 10 km. **Hitchhiking** is reported to be easy and widespread.

Boat 1-3 ton boats which can be hauled over the rapids are used by the gold-seekers, the forest workers, and the rosewood establishments. Ferries are free. Trips by motor-canoe (*pirogue*) up-river from Cayenne into the jungle can be arranged.

Sleeping → *See inside front cover for our hotel grade price guide.*
There are no hotels under our **A** bracket and almost no restaurants under the ¶¶¶ bracket. Accommodation in Guyane is more expensive than Paris, but food is better value. The Comité du Tourisme de la Guyane (see Finding out more above) has addresses of furnished apartments for rent (*Locations Clévacances*) and *Gîtes*, which are categorized as *Gîtes d'Amazonie*, with accommodation in hammocks or *carbets* (imitation Amerindian huts), *Carbets d'Hôtes*, which include breakfast, and *Gîtes Panda Tropiques Label*, which are approved by the WWF. **Ecotourisme Guyane Expedition** (EGE - see page 1460) can reserve hotels and private flats throughout the country for a small fee. Full details on their website, www.ecotourisme.fr, or contact the owner, Marc (through the site). He speaks English.

Festivals and events
Public holidays These are the same as in Metropolitan France, with the addition of **Slavery Day,** 10 June. **Carnaval** (February or March). Guyane's Carnaval is joyous and interesting. It is principally a Créole event, but there is some participation by all the different cultural groups in the department (best known are the contributions of the Brazilian and Haitian communities). Celebrations begin in January, with festivities every weekend, and culminate in colourful parades, music, and dance during the four days preceding Ash Wednesday. Each day has its own motif and the costumes are very elaborate. On Saturday night, a dance called 'Chez Nana – Au Soleil Levant' is held, for which the women disguise themselves beyond recognition as 'Touloulous', and ask the men to dance. They are not allowed to refuse. On Sunday there are parades in downtown Cayenne. Lundi Gras (Fat Monday) is the day to ridicule the institution of marriage, with mock wedding parties featuring men dressed as brides and women as grooms. 'Vaval', the devil and soul of Carnaval, appears on Mardi Gras (Fat Tuesday) with dancers sporting red costumes, horns, tails, pitch-forks, et cetera. He is burnt that night (in the form of a straw doll) on a large bonfire in the Place des Palmistes. Ash Wednesday is a time of sorrow, with participants in the final parades dressed in black and white.

Monday-Saturday 0800, 0930, 1100, 1500, 1630, Sunday and holidays 0930-1100, chilling, buy tickets from tourist office here, US$4.65. Tourist office: **Office du Tourisme** ① *1 esplanade Laurent Baudin, 97393 St-Laurent du Maroni, T342398, www.97320.com. Mon-Fri 0730-1800, Sat 0800-1300, 1500-1800, Sun 0900-1300.*

Border with Suriname Make sure you obtain proper entry stamps from immigration, not the police, to avoid problems when leaving. Customs and immigration, 2 km south of the centre, close at 1900. There are aggressive touts on the St-Laurent and Albina piers. It is best to change money in the Village Chinois in St-Laurent (dangerous area); although rates are lower than in Paramaribo, it is illegal to change money in Albina. Beware theft at St-Laurent's black market.

Around St-Laurent About 3 km from St-Laurent, along the Paul Isnard road, is Saint-Maurice, where the rum distillery of the same name can be visited, Monday to Friday 0730-1130. At Km 70 on the same dirt road is access to **Voltaire Falls**, 1½ hours walk from the road 7 km south of St-Laurent on the road to St-Jean du Maroni is the Amerindian village of **Terre Rouge**; canoes can be hired for day trips up the Maroni River (see Maripasoula below).

Some 40 km north of St-Laurent du Maroni is **Mana**, a delightful town with rustic architecture near the coast. 20 km west of Mana following the river along a single track access road is **Les Hattes**, or Yalimapo, an Amerindian village. About 4 km further on is Les Hattes beach where leatherback turtles lay their eggs at night; season April to August with May/June peak. No public transport to Les Hattes and its beach, but hitching possible at weekends; take food and water and mosquito repellent. Despite the dryish climate Mana is a malaria region. The freshwater of the Maroni and Mana rivers makes sea bathing pleasant. It is very quiet during the week.

Aouara, or Awala, an Amerindian village with hammock places, is 16 km west of Les Hattes. It also has a beach where leatherback turtles lay their eggs; they take about three hours over it. Take mosquito nets, hammock and insect repellent.

There are daily flights from Cayenne to **Maripasoula**; details in Air transport, page 1452, local office T372141. It is up the Maroni from St-Laurent (2-4 day journey up river in *pirogue*). There may be freight canoes which take passengers (US$40) or private boats (US$150) which leave from St-Laurent; 5-6 day tours and other options with *Takari Tour* or other operators in Cayenne. Maripasoula has 5,000 inhabitants in town and its surroundings. Many bush negros live here.

South to Brazil

About 28 km southeast of Cayenne is the small town of **Roura**, which has an interesting church. An excursion may be made to the Fourgassier Falls several kilometres away (*L'Auberge des Cascades*, excellent restaurant). From Cayenne the road crosses a new bridge over the Comte River. Excursions can be arranged along the Comte River. Nearby is Dacca, a Laotian village, which has *La Crique Gabrielle*, T/F280104, a restaurant which also has rooms. For information about the area contact the **Syndicat D'Initiative de Roura**, T311104.

From Roura a paved road, RD06, runs southeast towards the village of **Kaw**, on an island amid swamps which are home to much rare wildlife including caimans. The village is reached from where the Roura road ends at the river at Approuague. Basic accommodation available; **Jacana Tour**, T380795, excursions by day or night on the river; take insect repellent.

At Km 53 on another road southeast to Régina is the turn-off to **Cacao** (a further 13 km), a small, quiet village, where Hmong refugees from Laos are settled; they are farmers and produce fine traditional handicrafts. The main attraction is the Sunday morning market with local produce, Laotian food, and embroidery. Canoe and kayak rental behind the *Degrad Cacao* restaurant, US$2.50 per hour, US$8.50 per day, good wildlife trips upriver. Halfway along the side road is the *Belle Vue* restaurant, which lives up to its name, because of the superb view over the tropical forest; the restaurant is open at weekends. Consult the Comité du Tourisme de la Guyane for *gîtes* in the area.

Southwest of Kaw on the river Approuague is **Régina**, linked with Cayenne by a paved road. A good trip is on the river to Athanase with G Frétique, T304551. An unpaved road, runs from Régina to St-Georges de l'Oyapock (difficult during the rainy season).

Saül This remote gold-mining settlement in the 'massif central' is the geographical centre of Guyane. The main attractions are for the nature-loving tourist. Beautiful undisturbed tropical forests are accessible by a very well-maintained system of 90 km of marked trails, including several circular routes. The place has running water, a radiotelephone, and electricity. Ten-day expeditions are run by Christian Ball, '*Vie Sauvage*', 97314 Saül, US$86 (30% in advance) per day with meals, maps of local trails provided, own hammock and bedding useful but not essential. It can be cold at night. Another fascinating overland route goes from Roura (see below) up the Comte River to Belizon, followed by a 14-16-day trek through the jungle to Saül, visiting many villages en route, guide recommended. Meals are arranged by the *mairée* at *Restaurant Pinot*. Two markets sell food.

Border with Brazil St-Georges de l'Oyapock, with its small detachment of the French Foreign Legion who parade on Bastille Day, is 15 minutes down river from Oiapoque in Brazil, US$4 per person by motorized canoe, bargain for a return fare. The tourist office is in the library to the left of the town hall. There are bars, restaurants, supermarkets with French specialities, a post office and public telephones which take phonecards. Thierry Beltran, Rue Henri Sulny, T370259, offers guided river and forest tours. A pleasant day trip is to the **Saut Maripa** rapids (not very impressive with high water), located about 30 minutes upstream along the Oiapock River, past the Brazilian towns of Oiapoque and Clevelândia do Norte. Hire a motorized *pirogue* (canoe) to take you to a landing downstream from the rapids. Then walk along the trolley track (used to move heavy goods around the rapids) for 20 minutes to the rundown huts by the rapids (popular and noisy at weekends). There are more rapids further upstream on the way to Camopi.

Immigration (*gendarmerie*) for entry/exit stamps at eastern end of town, follow signs, open daily 0700-1200, 1500-1800 (often not open after early morning on Sunday, in which case try the police at the airport); French, Portuguese and English spoken. One of the Livre Service supermarkets and *Hotel Chez Modestine* will sometimes change dollars cash into euros at poor rates; if entering the country here, change money before arriving in St-Georges. Brazilian currency is accepted in shops at poor rates.

⊕ Sleeping

Cayenne *p1454, map p1458*
Most hotels are in the centre. A few of the better ones are in the suburb of Monjoly, next to a coarse sand beach and muddy sea, but the best neighbourhood in Cayenne nonetheless. Hotels rarely add tax and service to their bill, but stick to prices posted outside or at the desk. Bed and breakfast accommodation (gîte) is available for about US$60 a night (breakfast included) – contact the tourist office for details.
LL-L Novotel, Route de Montabo, Chemin St. Hilaire, T303838, www.accor-hotels.com. Beach- side hotel 3 km from the centre set in a tropical garden, pool, 2 tennis courts and a respectable French and Creole restaurant. Car hire available.
L-AL Best Western Amazonia, 28 Av Gen de Gaulle, T288300, www.bestwestern.com. A/c, luggage stored, pool, central location, good buffet breakfast extra.
AL-A Hotel des Amandiers, Place Auguste-Horth, T289728. Pleasant, tranquil and breezy location next to a park on a little peninsula at the north end of town, a/c rooms.
A Central Hotel, corner rue Molé and rue Becker, T256565, www.centralhotel-cayenne.fr. Good location, 100m from the Place de Palmistes, a/c rooms and a terrace overlooking the street. Special prices for groups and business travellers. Book in advance through the net.

B Ket-Tai, Av de la Liberté corner Blvd Jubelin, T388777. The best cheapie in town at the very bottom end of this price range, simple a/c rooms with en suites, look at a few before deciding. Chinese restaurant.

Around Rémire-Montjoly
AL Motel du Lac, Chemin Poupon, Route de Montjoly, T380800, moteldulac@opensurf.net. In a protected area, very peaceful, garden, convenient for the airport, pool, bar, restaurant.

Near Matoury and the airport
A La Chaumiere, Chemin de la Chaumière (off the road to Kourou), 97351 Matoury, T255701, lachaumiere@wanadoo.fr. Set in gardens with thatched huts, restaurant, pool, at bottom end of this price range, good value, though cabs to town push up the cost.

Apartment rentals
A good option, but what is on offer changes frequently. It's best to reserve through the tourist office who publish a brochure, *Locations de Vacances*, with full details including pictures. Contact them in advance through the website. Write in French if possible.

Kourou p1455

Hotels are overbooked and raise prices when there's an Ariane rocket launch (1 a month).

LL Ariatel Kourou, Av de St-Exupéry, Lac Bois Diable, T328900, www.accor-hotels.com. Overlooking a lake, 9 hole golf course nearby, good restaurant and pool with snack bar.

L Mercure Inn, near Lac Bois Diable, T321300, www.accor-hotels.com. A/c, modern, pool, good restaurant, best value for business visitors.

AL Hôtel des Roches, Pointe des Roches, T320066, F320328. Fair, a/c, includes breakfast, pool with bar, beach, Le Paradisier restaurant, cybercafé.

AL-A Les Jardins D'Hermes, 56 rue Duchesne, T320183. In heart of old Kourou, a/c, modern, good, restaurant.

A Ballahou, 2-3 rue Amet Martial, T220022, ballahou@ariasnet.fr. Small hotel with 14 rooms, some with cooking facilities, a/c, TV, nice, modern, good restaurant. Book ahead.

Camping

At Km 17.5 south of Kourou on the Saramaca road is **Les Maripas**, tourist camp, T325548, F323660. River and overland excursions, **D** for tent, book at Guyane Excursion, 7 quartier Simarouba, near *Restaurant Saramaca*.

Iles du Salut p1455

A Auberge Iles du Salut, on Ile Royale (postal address BP 324, 97378 Kourou, T321100, F324223). A 60-bed hotel (**AL** full board), also hammock space US$20 per person; former guard's bungalow, main meals (excellent), minimum US$36, breakfast US$6; gift shop with high prices (especially when a cruise ship is in), good English guide book for sale.

Sinnamary p1455

AL Hôtel du Fleuve, 11 rue Léon Mine, T345400, www.hoteldufleuve.com. Gardens, restaurant, internet access, pool, one of the grandest hotels west of Cayenne.

A Chez Floria, 14 rue Ronda Silva, Iracoubo, T346385, F326378. Very simple guest house with plain a/c rooms with en suites about 40 km from Sinnamary.

St-Laurent du Maroni p1455

AL Le Relais des 3 Lacs, 19-23 Domaine du Lac Bleu, T340505, 23lacs@nplus.gf. A/c, cheaper with fan, shuttle to town centre, restaurant, gardens, pool.

A La Tentiaire, 12 Av Franklin Roosevelt, T342600, rioual.robert@wanadoo.fr. A/c, the best, breakfast extra, phone, pool, secure parking.

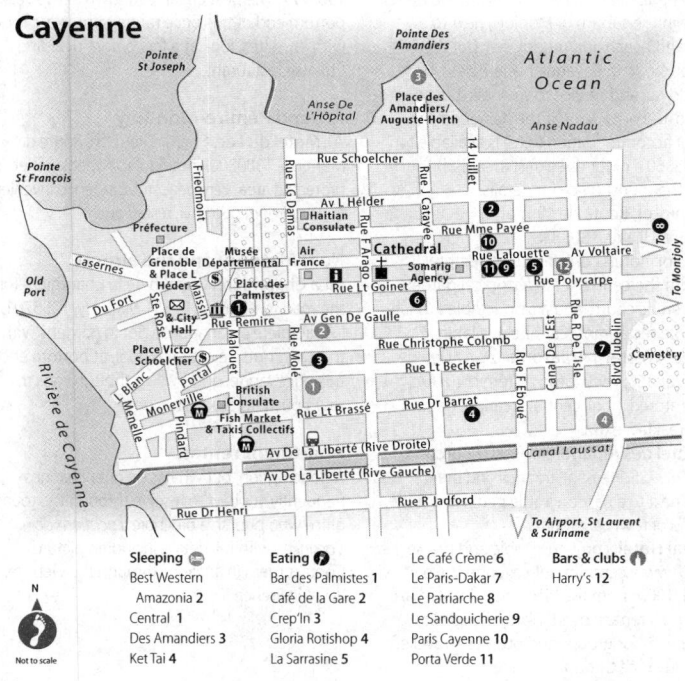

Cayenne

Sleeping	Eating		Bars & clubs
Best Western	Bar des Palmistes 1	Le Café Crème 6	Harry's 12
Amazonia 2	Café de la Gare 2	Le Paris-Dakar 7	
Central 1	Crep'In 3	Le Patriarche 8	
Des Amandiers 3	Gloria Rotishop 4	Le Sandouicherie 9	
Ket Tai 4	La Sarrasine 5	Paris Cayenne 10	
		Porta Verde 11	

B Chez Julienne, rue Gaston Monnerville, 200 m past Texaco station, T341153. A/c, TV, a/c, shower, good value.

B As, 109 rue Thiers, T341084. A/c, pool, cheaper rooms poor value, run down, cheap restaurant.

Voltaire Falls *p1456*

A pp Auberge des Chutes Voltaires, T00-874-762-945-774 satellite 1300-1600, 1900-2200. Also hammock space US$11, meals extra.

Mana *p1456*

Nuns next to the church rent beds and hammocks, US$8, clean and simple, T348270, F348415, Communauté des Soeurs de St-Joseph de Cluny, 1 rue Bourguignon.

C Le Bougainvillier, 3 rue des Frères, T348062, F348295, a/c, **D** with shared bath.

Gîte Angoulême, Mme Maryse Buira, PK 206/207 RN1 Saut Sabbat, T346496, F348688. Beside the river Mana, hammock space US$7.15, gîte **L** for weekend, breakfast US$5.

Les Hattes *p1456*

Three *gîtes*, all **C**: **Chez Jeanne**, T342982, F342071; **Chez Judith et Denis**, T342438; **Pointe les Hattes, chez Joseph**, T343806.

Maripasoula *p1456*

AL Campement Touristique de Saut Sonnelle, 48 rue Madame Payé, T314945. Full board.

C Chez Dedè, Av Leonard, T/F372074, US$4.50 for breakfast.

Roura *p1456*

C Auberge du Camp Caïman, RD06 29 km from Roura, T376034. Tourist camp (**F** to hang hammock), tours arranged to watch caiman in the swamps.

C Hotel Relais de Patawa, RD06 Km 36 from Cayenne, T280395. Rooms, or sling your hammock for US$4, cheaper rates for longer stays, highly recommended. The owners, M and Mme Baloup, who are entomologists, will show you their collection, take you on guided tours of local sights and introduce you to their pet anaconda.

Cacao *p1456*

C Restaurant La Lan, 1 room, good value, good food.

E M Levessier, T305122, has hammocks.

Régina *p*

E Albergue de l'Approuague, Lieu-dit Corossony, 97390 Régina. Price is for hammock space, meals expensive, great views of the forest.

Saül *p1456*

E pp Larozaly, a tourist camp in Saül, has running water, solar electricity, cooking facilities, and is a good place to stay.
Accommodation in Saul can be arranged through **Ecotourisme Guyane Expedition**, see Activities and tours, below.

St-Georges de l'Oyapock *p1457*

Accommodation is far cheaper on the Brazilian side.

B Caz Cale, rue E Elfort, 1 street back from the riverfront, just east of the main square, T/F370054. A/c, cheaper with fan.

B Chez Modestine, on the main square, T370013, F370214. A/c or fan, restaurant.

C Le Tamarin, rue Joseph Léandre, on the riverfront near the main square, T370884. With bath, fan, bar and restaurant.

● Eating

Cayenne *p1454, map p1458*

There are, sadly, very few decent French *patisseries* and *boulangeries*. Many restaurants close on Sun. There are many small Chinese restaurants dotted throughout the city all serving much the same fare: noodles, rice, soups etc.

ᵀᵀᵀ Bar des Palmistes, Place des Palmistes. Good spot for people watching, opposite the Place des Palmistes. Simple French and Creole fare and cold, draft Abbaye beer.

ᵀᵀᵀ Cric-Crac at *Motel Beauregard*, Créole cooking, lovely atmosphere.

ᵀᵀᵀ La Baie des Iles, Km 10 Route des Plages, Rémire-Montjoly, T386020. On the beach, good value seafood, 1000-midnight, closed Mon evening and Tue. Recommended.

ᵀᵀᵀ La Sarrasine, rue Lt Goinet 55, T317238. Good fish, salads, crêpes and quiches in an intimate little dining room. Respectable wine list and attentive service. At the bottom end of the price range.

ᵀᵀᵀ Le Kaz Kreol, 35 Av D'Estrées, T390697. Creole cooking served by waitresses in costume, delights include stuffed cassava, agouti stew and sauerkraut of papaya.

ᵀᵀᵀ Le Paris-Dakar, 103 rue Lt. Becker, T305517. Closed Sun, Mon lunch. African cooking from Senegal, Zaire, Benin and the Ivory Coast, like tropical fish slices on pureed aubergine, excellent vegetarian platter.

ᵀᵀᵀ Le Patriarche, rues Voltaire at Samuel Lubin, T317644. Excellent classical French and Creole cooking, one of the best in Guyane and very good value for this country. Reserve in advance.

● *For an explanation of the sleeping and eating price codes used in this guide, see inside the front*
● *cover. Other relevant information is found in Essentials page 1453.*

ⅲⅲ-ⅲ Marveen Snack Bar, rue Christophe Colomb, near Canal de L'Est. Food and staff pleasant, the patrons are very helpful (the elder of the 2 is a pilot for the Guyane Flying Club).

ⅲⅲ Paris-Cayenne, 59 rue de Lallouette, T317617. French cooking with tropical ingredients, nice decor.

ⅲⅲ Porta Verde, 58 rue Lt Goinet, T291903. Brazilian buffet, US$12 per kg, lunchtime only. Recommended.

ⅲⅲ-ⅲ Crep'In, 5 rue Lt Becker, T 302806. Street stall and little café with sweet and savoury crêpes, breakfast specials, and a range of fresh fruit juices and sandwiches.

ⅲⅲ-ⅲ Le Café Crème, 42 rue Justin Catayée, T281256. Pastries, superior sandwiches, juices, breakfasts and excellent coffee.

ⅲⅲ-ⅲ Café de la Gare, 42 rue Léopold Hélder, T350799. Great little restaurant with club playing classy live music every Thu and weekend. Good atmosphere, 20-40 something crowd.

ⅲⅲ Gloria Rotishop, 14 rue Dr Barrat, T251643. Surinamese style rotis with excellent fillings and West Indian and Indian breads. English speaking.

ⅲⅲ Le Sandouicherie, rue Félix Eboué at Lt Goinet, T289170. French bread sandwiches, snacks, juices and breakfasts, a/c.

Snacks

Vans around Place des Palmistes in evenings sell cheap, filling sandwiches.
Along the Canal Laussant there are Javanese snack bars: try *bami* (spicy noodles) or *saté* (barbecued meat in a spicy peanut sauce). Also along the canal are small, cheap Créole restaurants, not very clean.

Kourou *p1455*
ⅲⅲ Ballahou (see Sleeping). Best for fish and seafood (try *Guyabaisse*).

ⅲⅲ Le Bistrot du Lac, Hotel Mercure Ariatel, T328900. Named chef, Dominique Pirou, has one of the best tables in Guyane, serving French Creole dishes like Grouper in wild mushroom sauce and Tiger prawns in citrus. The hotel's **Le Ti-Gourmet** (ⅲⅲ-ⅲ) serves up-market snacks.

ⅲⅲ-ⅲ Le P'tit Café, 11 Place Monnerville, T228168. A good value set lunch and a respectable à la carte menu.

ⅲⅲ Le Karting, Zone Portuaire de Pariacabo (at the entrance to Kourou), T320539 (closed weekends). Excellent lunch set meal with a large choice of starters and mains and an evening BBQ on Tue and Fri.

ⅲ Many cheap Chinese (also takeaway), eg: **Le Chinatown**, rue Duchesne. Recommended. Many vans sell sandwiches filled with Créole food, good.

L'Hydromel, rue Raymond Cresson. Good pancakes. **Le Glacier des 2 Lacs**, 68 Ave des 2 Lacs. Ice cream, cakes, teas, very good.

St-Laurent du Maroni *p1455*
ⅲⅲ La Goelette, Balaté Plage, 2.5 km from St-Laurent, T342897. Housed in a converted fishing boat on the river and serving fish and game. Nice atmosphere in the evenings. Closed Sun evening and Mon.

ⅲ Le Mambari, 7 rue Rousseau, T343590. Pizzas and light French food served in a large, upmarket *palapa*. Open until late.

ⅲ Many cheap Chinese restaurants.

ⓘ Bars and clubs

Cayenne *p1454, map p1458*
Acropolys, Route de Cabassou, 3 km from town, T319781. Club music, Wed-Sat, 300-sq-m dance floor. **Harry's Bar**, 20 rue Rouget de l'Isle, T292958. Jazz, blues, Latin music and large selection of whiskies, also has English and Irish beer.

Kourou *p1455*
Clibertown, rue Guynemer, T323665; at the entrance to Kourou overlooking the lake. The most popular in town by far.

ⓞ Shopping

Cayenne *p1454, map p1458*
Bookshops Librairie AJC, 31 Blvd Jubelin, has an excellent stock of books and maps on Guyane (in French). There is a branch in *Drugstore des Palmistes*, Place des Palmistes.

▲ Activities and tours

Cayenne *p1454, map p1458*
Look under Tours Opérateurs on www.tourisme-guyane.com for listings of French and local tour operators. Tours to the interior cost about US$80-100 pp per day. Pick-ups from the airport and accommodation in Cayenne for a night or two are usually part of the package. Full details on the company web sites, some of it in English.

Ecotourisme Guyane Expedition (EGE), at **Takari Tour**, see below, www.ecotourisme.fr. Organize tours out of Cayenne, Kourou or St-Laurent du Maroni and book hotels throughout the country.

JAL Voyages, 26 Av Gen de Gaulle, T316820, www.jal-voyages.com. For a wide range of tours on the Mahury, Mana, Approouague rivers, on a houseboat on the Kaw marshes (US$85, very good accommodation, food and birdwatching) and to Devil's Island, a little English spoken. Recommended.

Takari Tour, 8 rue du Capitaine Bernard, BP 051397332, T311960, www.espace-amazonie. com. Recommended for inland tours, twinned with **Espace-Amazonie** in Kourou.
Thomas Cook, 2 Place du Marché, T255636. Flights, changes Thomas Cook traveller's cheques, English spoken.

Kourou *p1455*
Espace Amazonie, 7 Centre Commercial Simarouba, T323430, www.espace-amazonie.com.
Guyanespace Voyages, A Hector Berlioz, T223101, www.guyanespace.com.

St-Laurent du Maroni *p1455*
Ouest Guyane, 10 rue Féliz Eboué, T344444, ouestguyane@wanadoo.fr.
Youkaliba (Maroni) Expeditions, 3 rue Simon, T341645/312398. For canoe trips up the Maroni River. For example 1-night trip to Apatou, US$140; to Saut Anana on Mana River, 10 days, US$655.

⊖ Transport

Cayenne *p1454, map p1458*
Air Cayenne-Rochambeau Airport (T353882/89) is 16 km from Cayenne, 20 minutes by taxi, and 67 km from Kourou (US$60-80). There is a cambio changing US dollars and Brazilian reais as well as Cirrus and Visa Plus cashpoints for withdrawing Euros. No public transport; only taxis (US$25 daytime, US$30 night, but you can probably bargain or share). The cheapest route to town is taxi to Matoury US$10, then bus to centre US$2. The cheapest method of return to airport is by collective taxi from corner of Avenue de la Liberté and rue Malouet to Matoury (10 km) for US$2.40, then hitch or walk. On departure at the airport, once through the gate, there are no facilities (no duty free, exchange or restaurant).
Bus Terminal at corner of rue Molé and Av de la Liberté. Regular urban services run by SMTC, Place du Marché, T302100, Mon-Fri 0800-1200, 1500-1700. The only westbound bus is run by **Ruffinel & Cie**, 8 Av Galmot, T312666, as far as Kourou (US$12) leaves 0530 (not Sun). Minibuses to St-Laurent du Maroni leave when full from the terminal (can take up to 4 hrs waiting), 0400-1200, 2½ hrs, US$42-48. Service to **Mana** Mon and Thu only. To **Kaw**, Wed. To **Régina** US$25, and to **St-Georges del'Oyapock** US$45, 3 hrs, 4 daily. Arrive at the bus stop at 0700 to be sure of a seat. Be careful walking in this area - many drug addicts; take a cab to the bus stop.
Shared taxis (collectifs) Leave from the *gare routière* by the Canal Laussat early in the morning (Kourou US$12, St Laurent US$30-38). Other taxis can be found at the stand on Place des Palmistes, at the corner of Av Gen de Gaulle and Molé.

Kourou *p1455*
Taxi US$10, Lopez T320560, Gilles TT320307, Kourou T321444.
Bus To **Cayenne**, leaves Shell service station, corner Av de France, Av Vermont Polycarpe.
Share taxis To Cayenne 0600, 0630, 0700, 1330, US$12. Taxi to Cayenne or airport, US$60 (US$85 at night). To St-Laurent du Maroni US$27 by *taxi collectif* (irregular) or by minibus from Shell station.

Iles du Salut *p1455*
Boat Ferry from Kourou's port at the end of Av Gen de Gaulle, 4 km from the old centre US$53 return (children under 12 half price), leaves 0800 daily, returns from island at 1700 (book in advance, T320995/321100), additional sailing Sat and in high season, 1½-2 hr each way. Advance bookings are imperative in Jul and Aug. Tickets may be obtained from **EGE, JAL, Takari**, see Activities and tours; **Air Guyane Voyages**, 2 rue Lalouette, T317200; in Kourou from au Carbet des Roches, island only. Getting back to Cayenne late in the afternoon after the boat docks may be a problem if you don't have your own transport: ask other tourists for a lift. There are no regular boats from Ile Royale to Ile Saint-Joseph, which is wilder and more beautiful, with a small beach (this island had solitary-confinement cells and the warders' graveyard). It may be possible to hire a private boat at the ferry dock, or ask for James on the Kourou-Ile Royale ferry. There are no sailings between Ile Royale and Ile du Diable by law.

St-Laurent du Maroni *p1455*
Minibuses To Cayenne meet the ferry from Suriname, leaving when full from rue du Port, 3 hrs (maybe not until 1830 or 1900), US$42-48. Ask the minibus at rue du Port to pick up your luggage from your hotel.
Shared taxis To and from Cayenne, 8 people, US$42-48 a head, 3½ hr trip. Bus to Cayenne at 0600,same price.
Freight pirogues Sometimes take passengers inland along the Maroni River, but they can be dangerous as they tend to be overladen, often with dubious captains. Better to fly to Maripasoula and return on a pirogue as they are empty going down river. Alternatively a group can hire a *pirogue* for about US$200 a day.

Border with Suriname *p1456*
Boat Ferry for vehicles and passengers to Albina Mon, Thu, 0700, 0900, 1400, 1600, Tue, Wed, Sat 0700, 0900, Sun, 1530, 1600, 30 mins. Passengers US$4.40/€3.50 one-way, car US$25-30 one-way, payable only in euros. Speedboats US$3.50-US$4.75.

Minibuses and **taxis** Transport to/from Paramaribo meets the Albina ferry.

Cacao *p1456*
Minibus From **Cayenne**, Mon 1200; Fri 1800, return Mon 0730, Fri 1400.

Saül *p1456*
Air Service with **Air Guyane** from Cayenne or via Maripasoula (see above; local office T309111). Try at airport even if flight said to be full. By *pirogue* from Mana up Mana River, 9-12 days, then 1 day's walk to Saül, or from St-Laurent via Maripasoula along Moroni and Inini rivers, 15 days and 1 day's walk to Saül, both routes expensive.

St-Georges de l'Oyapock *p1457*
Air Aside from minibus, flying is the only option. For **Air Guyane** flights to Cayenne see Air transport in Essentials. **Air Guyane** office at airport open 0700-0730, 1400-1430 for check in, open 0800-1100 for reservations, T/F370360. Flights are fully booked several days in advance; you must check in at stated times. Extra flights are sometimes added. The police check that those boarding flights who have arrived from Brazil have obtained their entry stamp; also thorough baggage search.
Minibuses To **Cayenne**, US$45, 3 hrs; US$20 on the unpaved road to Régina, then US$25 to Cayenne.

Onward buses to **Macapá** leave in the late afternoon, 10 hrs: book as soon as you arrive in Oiapoque (Brazilian side). The road is generally good though rough in places.

---

❶ Directory

Cayenne *p1454, map p1458*
Airline offices Air Caraïbes, T293636 (flies to Pointe-à-Pitre, Fort-de-France, Port-au-Prince, plus Macapá and Belém in Brazil and Santo Domingo - Dominican Republic). Air France, 17-19 rue Lalouette, BP 33, Cayenne, T298787, F298790. Air Guyane, 2 rue Lalouette, 97300 Cayenne, T293630, F293631. Surinam Airways, 15 rue Louis Blanc, T293001, F305786. TAF, T303910 (French and Portuguese spoken, flights Cayenne-Macapá-Belém-Fortaleza twice a week). Book at least a week in advance (can be booked through travel agents like EGE - see

page 1460). **Banks** Banque Nationale de Paris-Guyane (BNPG), 2 Place Schoelcher; no exchange facilities on Sat. Banque Française Commerciale (BFC), 2 Place des Palmistes (best bank exchange rates). Crédit Populaire Guyanais, 93 rue Lalouette. Most banks have ATMs for cash withdrawals on Visa, sometimes MasterCard, never Amex. Banque Populaire, 5 Av Gen de Gaulle, Cirrus/ MasterCard ATM. Crédit Mutuel, 13 rue Léon Damas, Visa/Plus and Cirrus/ MasterCard ATM. Cambio Caraïbe, Av Gen de Gaulle near Catayée (best rates for US$). Guyane Change, Av Gen de Gaulle near rue F Eboué. The Post Office exchanges cash and TCs at good rates, but complicated and time- consuming. There is an exchange facility at the airport (see Airport information, above). Central drugstore may help when banks are closed. Almost impossible to change dollars outside Cayenne or Kourou.
Embassies and consulates British (Honorary), Mr Nouh-Chaia, 16 Ave Monnerville (BP 664, Cayenne 97300), T311034, F304094. Brazilian, 444 chemin St Antoine, T296010. Dutch (Honorary), Batiment Sogudem, Port of Dégrad des Cannes, BP139, Cayenne 97323, T354931, F354671. Haitian, 12 rue L Héder, at corner of Place des Palmistes, T311858, F312065, closed Sat. Suriname, 3 Ave L Héder, T282160, F317645, Mon-Fri 0900-1200. English spoken, visa takes 2 hrs, proof of travelout of Venezuela or Guyana acceptable. For USA and Canada, apply to embassies/ consulates in Paramaribo, Suriname. **Internet** Cybercafé des Palmistes, 1 Av Gen de Gaulle, US$15 per hr. **Post offices** Route de Baduel, 2 km out from town (US$2.25 by taxi or 20 mins on foot), crowded. Poste Restante letters are only kept for 2 weeks maximum. Also Poste Cayenne Cépéron, Place L Héder.

Kourou *p1455*
Banks Several in town, including Banque National de Paris Guyane, near the Mairie. **Post offices** Ave des Frères Kennedy.

St-Laurent du Maroni *p1455*
Banks BFC, 11 Av Félix Eboué, open Tue-Fri, Sat morning. Cambio COP, 19 rue Montravel, near BNP, T343823, changes Euros and Suriname and US dollars.

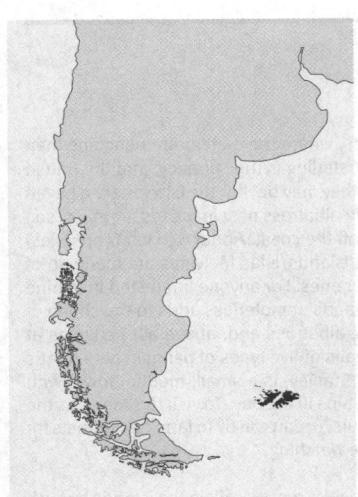

Falkland Islands / Islas Malvinas

Essentials → *Colour map 9, inset.*

Planning your trip

Where to go These remote South Atlantic outposts, where there are more penguins than people, are the only part of South America where UK sterling is the currency, and the British monarch's head appears on the stamps. Windswept they may be, but the islands are a haven for wildlife and a paradise for those who wish to see it: albatross nest in the tussac grass, sea lions breed on the beaches and Orca whales cruise off the coast. About 640 km (400 miles) east of the South American mainland, the Falklands Islands/Islas Malvinas are made up of two large islands, surrounded by hundreds of smaller ones. For anyone interested in marine mammals and birdlife, this is the place to go. The islands' remoteness adds to the charm of being able to see elephant seals, dolphins, whales, albatross and, above all, penguins at close range. There are said to be 494,500 breeding pairs of five types of penguin here (that's about 415 birds per human inhabitant). The capital, Stanley, is a small, modern town, with reminders of its seafaring past in the hulks of sailing ships in the bay. To visit the camp, as the land outside Stanley is known, 4WD vehicles make tours, or you can fly to farming outposts for warm hospitality, huge skies and unparalleled nature watching.

Note In accordance with the practice suggested by the UN, we are calling the islands by both their English and Spanish names.

When to go Best months to visit are Oct-Mar. Although the *Sunday Express* once referred to a mutton freezer in the Falklands as a Colonial Development project near the South Pole (8 March 1953), the Islands are in the same latitude south as London is north. The climate is cool and oceanic, dominated by persistent westerly winds which average 16 knots. Long periods of calm are rare except in winter. Though not always inclement, weather is very changeable but temperatures vary relatively little. At Stanley, the capital, the mean temperature in summer (January/February) is 15.4° C, but temperatures frequently exceed this on the islands. In winter (June/July) 3° C. Stanley's annual rainfall of about 600 mm is slightly higher than London's. In the drier camp, outside Stanley, summer drought sometimes threatens local water supplies. Snowfall is rare although a dusting may occur at any time of the year. Spring, autumn and winter clothing, as used in the UK, is suitable. Wind-protective clothing is recommended and sunblock is essential.

Finding out more The **Falkland Islands Tourist Board** ① *Old Philomel Store, Philomel St, Stanley, Falkland Islands, FIQQ 1ZZ, T22215, www.visitorfalklands.com.* They will provide all information on holidays on the islands, including organized tours. The **Falkland Islands Government London Office** ① *Falkland House, 14 Broadway, Westminster, London SW1H 0BH, T020-7222 2542*, will answer enquiries. See also **Tourist offices**, under Stanley, Ins and outs, below. Also try: **www.falklandislands.com, www.falklands.info** (Falkland Islands information portal), **www.falklands.gov.fk** (the Falkland Islands Government page), **www.falklandnews.com** (Falkland Islands News Network), **www.falklands.com** (Merco Press, South Atlantic's News Agency) and **www.penguin-news.com** (*Penguin News* newspaper).

Before you travel

Getting in All travellers must have full passports to visit the Falkland Islands/Islas Malvinas. Citizens of Britain, North America, Mercosur, Chile, and most Commonwealth countries and the European Union are permitted to visit the islands without a visa, as are holders of UN and International Committee of the Red Cross passports. Other nationals should apply for a visa from the Travel Coordinator at *Falkland House* in London (see above), the Immigration Department in Stanley (see Stanley, Useful addresses), or a British Embassy or Consulate. Visas cost £20. All visitors require a one-month visitor permit, normally provided on arrival upon presentation of a return ticket. Visitors are also asked to have pre-booked accommodation and sufficient funds to cover their stay. Work permits are not available. Do not stay beyond the valid period of your visa without applying to the Immigration Office for an extension.

Falkland Islands / Islas Malvinas Essentials

describing the Stanley wrecks is sold by the museum). At **Darwin** are the *Vicar of Bray* (last survivor of the California Gold Rush fleet), and another old iron ship, the *Garland*. There are interesting old French buildings and ruins at Port Louis (the road between Stanley and Port Louis is a boulder-strewn clay track, very tricky when wet).

From the Beaver hanger, Ross Rd West, walk past the various ships and monuments, along the harbour, up to the Falkland Islands Company offices. Here it is possible to walk onto the jetty and visit the after section of a 19th-century sailing vessel. Also below the jetty you will see a couple of 19th-century Welsh colliers. From here go east until you reach B slip, used by the British Forces during the 1982 conflict. Carry on east, past the floating harbour and around the head of the bay to the iron barque *Lady Elizabeth*. At low tide it is possible to walk out to her. Follow the bay round and eventually you will come to various penguin rookeries and Gypsy Cove (see below).

Outside Stanley
Sparrow Cove, **Kidney Cove**, and adjacent areas, only a short distance from Stanley by road, are good areas to see four species of penguin and other wildlife. **Gypsy Cove**, walking distance from Stanley, features a colony of burrowing Magellanic penguins and other shorebirds. Leopard seals, elephant seals and the occasional killer whale visit the area. **Note**: Observe minefield fences which prevent close inspection of the penguins (they are not unduly inhibiting, though). At **Cape Pembroke**, around the town airport and the renovated lighthouse you can see Gentoo penguins and ground-nesting birds such as dotterels, snipe, and Upland geese.

Volunteer Point, north of Stanley, is a wildlife sanctuary. It contains the only substantial nesting colony of King penguins outside of South Georgia (the most accessible site in the world). Gentoo penguins, Magellanic penguins, geese, ducks, and elephant seals are very tame and easily photographed. Access is by a track which is open November-March, weather permitting.

Sea Lion Island in the southeast is a delightful place to explore and relax. Throughout the austral summer the lodge accommodates a maximum of 23 visitors. Many Southern Sea Lions breed on the beaches; Southern Elephant Seals also breed here. A pod of Orca whales is seen almost daily cruising the kelp beds in search of an unsuspecting meal. The island also has

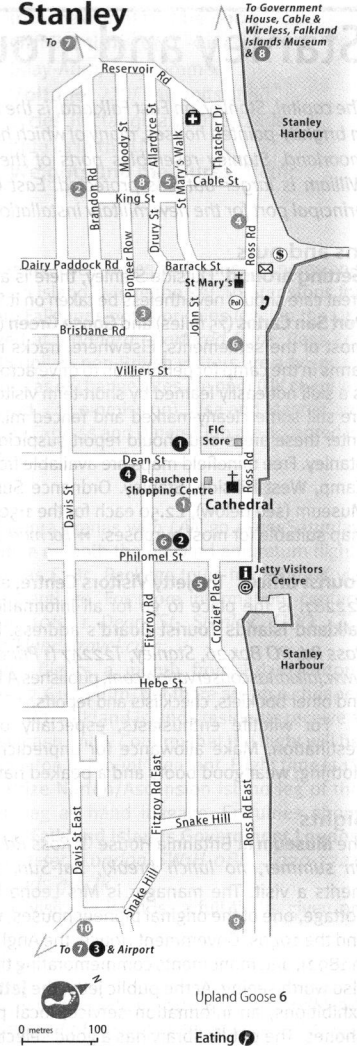

Stanley

Sleeping
- Bennett House **8**
- Dolphin's Guest House **1**
- Kay's B&B **3**
- Lafone Guest House **9**
- Malvina House **4**
- Scotia House **5**
- Shorty's Motel & Diner **10**
- Sue Binnie's **2**
- Tenacres **7**
- Upland Goose **6**

Eating
- Deano's Bistro **1**
- Falklands Brasserie **2**
- Lighthouse Seaman's Centre **3**
- Woodbine Takeaway **4**

Bars & clubs
- Globe **5**
- Narrows **7**
- Stanley Arms **8**
- Victory **6**

Falkland Islands / Islas Malvinas   Stanley & around

magnificent bird life: Gentoo, Magellanic and Rockhopper Penguins, Giant Petrels (known locally as stinkers), King Cormorants, the incredible flightless Steamer Duck, Black-crowned Night Herons, the friendly Tussock Bird, Oystercatcher (Magellanic and Black) and the rare Striated Caracara. Also on the island is the HMS *Sheffield* memorial.

The **smaller islands off West Falkland**, such as Carcass and New Island, are the most spectacular and attractive for wildlife and scenery. New Island is divided into two distinct properties, both of which are run as nature reserves. The New Island South, on the extreme west edge of the archipelago, is run as New Island South Conservation Trust, www.falklandswildlife.com. The northern half, owned by Tony Chater, has a small sheep farm. The island has a grass airstrip and is served by FIGAS on flights limited to three passengers (owing to the length of the strip). Carcass can be visited more easily and has accommodation (see below). Cruise ships stop here *en route* to Antarctica, but only for a few hours. **Saunders Island**, besides a representative sample of wildlife, contains the ruins of the 18th century British outpost at Port Egmont. It is run by **Suzan and David Pole-Evans** ① *T41298, davidpe@horizon.co.fk*. There is a small group of King Penguins at the Neck, about three-hour walk, 45 minutes by jeep from the settlement. Gentoo, Magellanic, Rock Hoppers and albatross can also be seen here. A further 1½-2 hours walk goes to the point where elephant seals can be seen. Another good place is the bay just north of the settlement with many Gentoo and Magellanic penguins and other wildlife.

Sleeping

Stanley *p1467, map p1468*
Note: Advance reservation of room is essential.
L pp **Malvina House**, 3 Ross Rd, T21355, malvina@horizon.co.fk. Very good, full board, power showers, hot drinks, central heating, TV, nice restaurant, bar, spa, laundry.
L **Upland Goose Hotel**, 20-22 Ross Rd, T21455, fic@horizon.co.fk. Some cheaper rooms, full board, lounge bar and restaurant.
B **The Dolphin's Guest House**, 46 John St, T/F22950, commersons@ horizon.co.fk. Refurbished in 2005 with a variety of rooms, shared facilities, cable TV in rooms, satellite TV in ounge, bar, dining room, conservatory for light meals.
C pp **Kay's B&B**, 14 Drury St, T/F21071, kay@horizon.co.fk. Dinner £5, lunch £2-3, excellent value, good food. Highly recommended (camping in her grounds).
All Stanley B&Bs are priced at around £25 pp or under. For a full list, see www.tourism.org.fk/stanley-acc.htm.
Bennett House, 14 Allardyce St, T22645, and **Scotia House**, 12 St Mary's Walk, T21191, www.scotiaandbennetthouse.co.fk. Both owned by Bob and Celia Stewart. Central, excellent home baking and breakfasts at both houses. Bennett House has recently refurbished rooms, good views, welcoming. Camping permitted at Scotia House.
Sue Binnie's, Brandon Rd, T21051. Central, 1 double room with shared bath, bed and breakfast, Spanish spoken.
Lafone Guest House, T22891, arlette@ horizon.co.fk. Owned and run by Arlette Betts, luxury bed and breakfast, panoramic views of the harbour, evening meals on request.
Lookout Lodge, Keil Canal Rd, contact John Birmingham, T22834, lookout@horizon.co.fk. Over 50 single rooms available. Originally built for contract workers, now offering simple accommodation and full catering facilities for breakfast, lunch and evening meals.
Shorty's Motel, Snake Hill, T22855, marleneshort@horizon.co.fk. All rooms en-suite, laundry facilities, internet. Shorty's Diner is next door.
Tenacres, see Activities and tours, below. Run by Sharon Halford. Excellent meals and home baking, thoughtful touches such as hair-dryers and bathrobes in rooms.
The Waterfront, 36 Ross Rd, T22331, thewaterfront@horizon.co.fk. Very helpful, with restaurant, evening meals and snack lunches on request. Recommended.

Outside Stanley *p1468*
The comfortable tourist lodges at Sea Lion Island, the most southerly inhabited island of the group (35 mins flight from Stanley), and Pebble Island (40 mins flight) are good bases to view wildlife. Each lodge has transport to the airstrip and points of interest nearby.
L-AL pp **Sea Lion Lodge**, Sea Lion Island, T32004 (manager Rob Mackay), sealion_lodge @horizon.co.fk or www.sealionisland.com. Price depends on season, full board, some rooms shared bath, modern, central heating, phone in rooms.
AL **Pebble Island Lodge**, Pebble Island, T41093, pebblelodge@horizon.co.fk. Jacqui Jennings and Allan White. En suite rooms, central heating, full board, lounge, TV and DVD, phone and internet, island tours.

AL pp Port Howard Lodge, Port Howard, West Falkland, T42187, porthowardlodge@ horizon.co.fk. Price depends on season, all rooms en suite, central heating, excursions extra, rod hire, Land Rover hire. Offers excellent trout fishing, a small but interesting war museum, and an opportunity to see the operations of a traditional large sheep station.

B Carcass Island Cottages, contact Rob McGill, Ross Rd East, Carcass Island, T41106, F41107, on West Falkland. Rooms in main farmhouse, full board with good food, and 1 self-catering cottage, on one of the wildlife jewels of the Falklands, open summer only.

B pp Saunders Island, address above, self-catering Portakabin at the Neck, including transport, basic. At the settlement are two self-catering cottages, **D** pp per night. Catering can be provided for groups.

Cobbs Cottage, Bleaker Island, contact Mike and Phyl Rendell, T21355, malvina@horizon.co.fk. 30-min flight south from Stanley, finished to a high standard throughout. Good wildlife.

Darwin House, Close to Goose Green, T32255, darwin.h@horizon.co.fk. Owners Bonnie and Ken Greenland. Close to the British and Argentine cemeteries and only 35 mins' drive from Mount Pleasant Airport, an excellent base for the start of a holiday. Fully-catered accommodation in the lodge, and 2 cottages for self-catering. Excellent home baking and evening meals. Battlefield tours available, also fishing, golf at nearby Goose Green, boat excursions.

Little Chartres, West Falkland, T42215, jandlwoodward@horizon.co.fk. New, operated by Lesley and Jim Woodward, who ensure you get the most from your visit. Tours available throughout West Falkland.

Port San Carlos Lodge, 2 hrs' drive from Stanley. Owned by Simon and Sandra Goss, T21315/41024, psclodge@horizon.co.fk. Tours and fishing can be organized.

Roy Cove, Crooked Inlet Farm, Danny and Joy Donnelly, T41102. A comfortable self-catering property, splendid sea views from the house overlooking the cove, where dolphins regularly play. Sea-trout and rock cod fishing nearby.

West Lagoons, West Falkland, full-board accommodation on a sheep farm, Shelley and Peter Nightingale. Contact through *International Tours and Travel*, see Tour operators.

● Eating

Stanley *p1467, map p1468*
The Bread Shop. Open Mon-Sat. Wide range of breads, sandwiches, snacks etc, all freshly baked daily on the premises.
Deano's bistro, John St. Bar snacks, including vegetarian menu.
Falklands Brasserie, Philomel St, centrally located near Public Jetty, T21159, brasserie@ horizon.co.fk. Innovative cooking with local produce, opens 1100.
Lighthouse Seamans' Centre, over the bridge next to FIPASS ('The Seaman's Mission'). Serves tea, coffee, snacks, home cooking and baking, lunches, open all day.
Michelle's Café, close to the Public Jetty. Open Mon-Sat, daytime and evening, home baking a speciality, all food cooked to order.
Woodbine Takeaway, 29 Fitzroy Rd, T21102. Fish and chips and pizza.
Closed Sun and Mon.

● Bars and clubs

Stanley *p1467, map p1468*
The pubs (open all day, except Sun only from 1200 to 1400, and 1900-2200) include: **Beagle Bar**, at Malvina House Hotel, **Narrows Bar**, Ross Rd East (welcomes families, serves freshly-prepared bar snacks and food), **Stanley Arms**, near Beaver Hangar, John Biscoe Rd, **The Globe**, near the public jetty, and **The Victory**, Philomel Hill.

▲ Activities and tours

Stanley *p1467, map p1468*
Sea-trout fishing is excellent on the islands. The season runs from 1 Sep to 30 Apr. A licence costs £10 per year.

Tour operators
Antarctic Cruises, Reservations: Vitacura 2771 of 904, Santiago, Chile, T236 5179, www.antarctic.cl.
Falkland Island Holidays (division of Stanley Services), Airport Rd, Stanley, T22622, www.falklandislandsholidays.com. Offer inbound tourist services, FIGAS flights, overland 4WD excursions from Stanley to various sights, bookings for lodgings and for fishing, riding and vehicle hire.

● *For an explanation of the sleeping and eating price codes used in this guide, see inside the* ● *front cover.*

International Tours and Travel, 1 Dean St, PO Box 408, Stanley, T22041, www.falklands travel.com. Handle inbound tourist bookings, book FIGAS flights, arrange tours etc and are the Falkland Island agents for **LAN**. Recommended.
South Atlantic Marine Services, Carol and Dave Eynon, PO Box 140, Stanley, T21145, sams@horizon.co.fk. Overland tours, boat trips, safaris and have a dive centre with deck recompression chamber (PADI courses).

Guided tours
Adventure Falklands, PO Box 223, T21383, pwatts@horizon.co.fk. Patrick Watts offers tours of battlefield and other historical sights, ornithological trips and more.
Cross Country Expeditions, T21494, scm@ horizon.co.fk. Wildlife and fishing tours, airport transfers and lodging with Sam Miller.
Discovery Falklands, T21027, www.discovery falklands.com. Tony Smith offers overland 4WD excursions from Stanley to various sights, specializes in battlefield tours.
Falkland Frontiers, T21561, falklandfrontiers @horizon.co.fk. Neil Rowlands offers overland and boat tours, also fishing guide.
France's Falkland Forays, 7 Snake Hill, T21624, france@horizon.co.fk. Graham France's city, golf, penguin watching and historical tours.
Kidney Cove Safari Tours, T31001, allowe@ horizon.co.fk. Adrian and Lisa Lowe, offer overland 4WD tours to see 4 species of penguins at Kidney Cove, close to Stanley.
Tenacres Tours, T21155, www.tenacrestours. horizon.co.fk. Sharon Halford offers overland 4WD excursions from Stanley. Also B&B, farmstay accommodation about 15 mins' walk from the centre, other meals available.

⊖ Transport

Falklands/Malvinas
Air
The **Falkland Islands Government Air Service** (FIGAS, T27219, fwallace@figas.gov.fk) operates 3 Islander aircraft to farm settlements and settled outer islands according to bookings, seat availability, and weather. En route you will see some spectacular sights from low-level flying. To book a seat, telephone FIGAS no later than the morning of the day before travelling; flight schedules are announced that evening on local radio (airfares range from £40-73; luggage limit 14 kg/30 pounds). FIGAS tickets are also available from **Stanley Services Travel** and **International Tours and Travel Ltd**, see Activities and tours, above. Regular service operates 7 days a week. Flights leave from Stanley Airport, 3 miles east of town on the Cape Pembroke peninsula. Passengers arriving on **LAN** can fly with FIGAS directly to Port Howard or Pebble Island with prior arrangement.

Car rentals
Falklands Islands Company, Travel Services, West Store, Stanley, T27600, www.the-falkland-islands-co.com (also Charrington House, The Causeway, Bishop Stortford, CM23 2ER, Herts, UK, T01279-461630). Rents Land Rovers.
Stanley Services Ltd, Travel Division, Airport Road, Stanley, T22622, info@falklandislandsholidays.com. Rents Mitsubishi Pajeros.

Ferry
MV Tamar FI, Island Shipping Ltd, Globe Offices, Philomel Hill, Stanley, T22345, www.shipping.horizon.co.fk, sails according to need, carrying inter-island cargo. It has 2 cabins,

Falkland Islands / Islas Malvinas Stanley & around Listings

Pre-independence history

Earliest settlement

It is generally accepted that the earliest settlers in South America were related to people who had crossed the Bering Straits from Asia and drifted through the Americas from about 50,000 BC. Alternative theories of early migrations from across the Pacific and Atlantic have been rife since Thor Heyerdahl's raft expeditions in 1947 and 1969-1970. The earliest evidence of human presence has been found at various sites: in the Central Andes (with a radiocarbon date between 12000 and 9000 BC), northern Venezuela (11000 BC), southeast Brazil, south-central Chile and Argentine Patagonia (from at least 10000 BC). After the Pleistocene Ice Age, 8000-7000 BC, rising sea levels and climatic changes introduced new conditions as many mammal species became extinct and coastlands were drowned. A wide range of crops was brought into cultivation and camelids and guinea pigs were domesticated. It seems that people lived nomadically in small groups, mainly hunting and gathering but also cultivating some plants seasonally, until villages with effective agriculture began to appear between 2500-1500 BC. The earliest ceramic-making in the western hemisphere was thought to have come from what is now Colombia and Ecuador, around 4000 BC, but fragments of painted pottery were found near Santarém, Brazil, in 1991 with dates of 6000-5000 BC.

The coast of central Peru was where settled life began to develop most rapidly. The abundant wealth of marine life produced by the Humboldt Current, especially north of today's Lima, boosted population growth and settlement in this area. Around 2000 BC climatic change dried up the *lomas* ('fog meadows'), and drove sea shoals into deeper water. People turned more to farming and began to spread inland along river valleys. As sophisticated irrigation and canal systems were developed, farming productivity increased and communities had more time to devote to building and producing ceramics and textiles. The development of pottery also led to trade and cultural links with other communities.

The earliest buildings constructed by organized group labour were *huacas*, adobe platform mounds, centres of some cult or sacred power dating from the second millennium BC onwards. During this period, however, much more advanced architecture was being built at Kotosh, in the central Andes near Huánuco, now in Peru. Japanese archaeological excavations there in the 1960s revealed a temple with ornamental niches and friezes. Some of the earliest pottery was also found here, showing signs of influence from southern Ecuador and the tropical lowlands, adding weight to theories of Andean culture originating in the Amazon. Radiocarbon dates of some Kotosh remains are as early as 1850 BC.

Andean and Pacific coastal civilizations

Chavín and Sechín For the next 1,000 years or so up to c900 BC, communities grew and spread inland from the north coast and south along the north highlands. Farmers still lived in simple adobe or rough stone houses but built increasingly large and complex ceremonial centres. As farming became more productive and pottery more advanced, commerce grew and states began to develop throughout central and north-central Peru, with the associated signs of social structure and hierarchies.

Around 900 BC a new era was marked by the rise of two important centres; Chavín de Huántar in the central Andes and Sechín Alto, inland from Casma on the north coast, both now in Peru. The chief importance of Chavín de Huántar was not so much in its highly advanced architecture as in the influence of its cult, coupled with the artistic style of its ceramics and other artefacts. The founders of Chavín may have originated in the tropical lowlands, as some of its carved monoliths show representations of monkeys and felines.

The Chavín cult This was paralleled by the great advances made in this period in textile production and in some of the earliest examples of metallurgy. The origins of metallurgy have been attributed to some gold, silver and copper ornaments found in graves in Chongoyape, near Chiclayo, which show Chavín-style features. But earlier evidence has been discovered at Kuntur Wasi (some 120 km east of the coast at Pacasmayo) where 4,000-year old gold has been found, and in the Andahuaylas region, dating from 1800-900 BC. The religious symbolism of gold and other precious metals and stones is thought to have been an inspiration behind some of the beautiful artefacts found in the central Andean area.

The cultural brilliance of Chavín de Huántar was complemented by its contemporary, Sechín, with which may have combined forces, Sechín being the military power that spread the cultural word of Chavín. Their influence did not reach far to the south where the Paracas and Tiwanaku cultures held sway. The Chavín hegemony broke up around 500 BC, soon after which the Nasca culture began to bloom in southern Peru. This period, up to about AD 500, was a time of great social and cultural development. Sizable towns of 5-10,000 inhabitants grew on the south coast, populated by artisans, merchants, government administrators and religious officials.

Paracas-Nasca Nasca origins are traced back to about the second century BC, to the Paracas Cavernas and Necropolis, on the coast in the national park near Pisco in Peru. The extreme dryness of the desert here has preserved remarkably the textiles and ceramics in the mummies' tombs excavated. The technical quality and stylistic variety in weaving and pottery rank them among the world's best, and many of the finest examples can be seen in the museums of Lima. The famous Nasca Lines are a feature of the region. Straight lines, abstract designs and outlines of animals are scratched in the dark desert surface forming a lighter contrast that can be seen clearly from the air. There are many theories of how and why the lines were made but no definitive explanation has yet been able to establish their place in South American history. There are similarities between the style of some of the line patterns and that of the pottery and textiles of the same period. In contrast to the quantity and quality of the Nasca artefacts found, relatively few major buildings belonging to this period have been uncovered in the southern desert. Alpaca hair found in Nasca textiles, however, indicates that there must have been strong trade links with highland people.

Moche culture Nasca's contemporaries on the north coast were the militaristic Moche who, from about AD 100-800, built up an empire whose traces stretch from Piura in the north to Huarmey, in the south. The Moche built their capital outside present day Trujillo. The huge pyramid temples of the Huaca del Sol and Huaca de la Luna mark the remains of this city. Moche roads and system of way stations are thought to have been an early inspiration for the Inca network. The Moche increased the coastal population with intensive irrigation projects. Skilful engineering works were carried out, such as the La Cumbre canal, still in use today, and the Ascope aqueduct, both on the Chicama River. The Moche's greatest achievement, however, was its artistic genius. Exquisite ornaments in gold, silver and precious stones were made by its craftsmen. Moche pottery progressed through five stylistic periods, most notable for the stunningly lifelike portrait vases. A wide variety of everyday scenes were created in naturalistic ceramics, telling us more about Moche life than is known about other earlier cultures, and perhaps used by them as 'visual aids' to compensate for the lack of a written language. A spectacular discovery of a Moche royal tomb at Sipán, made in February 1987 by Walter Alva, director of the Brüning Archaeological Museum, Lambayeque, included semi-precious stones brought from Chile and Argentina, and seashells from Ecuador. The Moche were great navigators.

The cause of the collapse of the Moche Empire around AD 600-700 is unknown, but it may have been started by a 30-year drought at the end of the sixth century, followed by one of the periodic El Niño flash floods (identified by meteorologists from ice thickness in the Andes) and finished by the encroaching forces of the Huari Empire. The decline of the Moche signalled a general tipping of the balance of power in Peru from the north coast to the south sierra.

Huari-Tiwanaku The ascendant Huari-Tiwanaku movement, from AD 600-1000, combined the religious cult of the Tiwanaku site in the Titicaca basin, with the military dynamism of the Huari, based in the central highlands. The two cultures developed independently but they are generally thought to have merged compatibly. Up until their own demise around AD 1440, the Huari-Tiwanaku had spread their empire and influence across much of south Peru, north Bolivia and Argentina. They made considerable gains in art and technology, building roads, terraces and irrigation canals across the country. The Huari-Tiwanaku ran their empire with efficient labour and administrative systems that were later adopted and refined by the Incas. Labour tribute for state projects practised by the Moche were further developed. But the empire could not contain regional kingdoms who began to fight for land and power. As control broke down, rivalry and coalitions emerged, and the system collapsed. With the country once again fragmented, the scene was set for the rise of the Incas.

Chachapoyas and Chimú cultures After the decline of the Huari Empire, the unity that had been imposed on the Andes was broken. A new stage of autonomous regional or local political organizations began. Among the cultures corresponding to this period were the Chachapoyas in northern highlands (see page 1154) and the Chimú. The Chachapoyas people were not so much an empire as a loose-knit 'confederation of ethnic groups with no recognized capital' (Morgan Davis 'Chachapoyas: The Cloud People', Ontario, 1988). But the culture did develop into an advanced society with great skill in road and monument building. Their fortress at Kuelap was known as the most impregnable in the Peruvian Andes. The Chimú culture had two centres. To the north was Lambayeque, near Chiclayo, while to the south, in the Moche valley near present-day Trujillo, was the great adobe walled city of Chan Chán. Covering 20 sq km, this was the largest pre-Hispanic Peruvian city. Chimú has been classified as a despotic state that based its power on wars of conquest. Rigid social stratification existed and power rested in the hands of the great lord *Siquic* and the lord *Alaec*. These lords were followed in social scale by a group of urban couriers who enjoyed a certain degree of economic power. At the bottom were the peasants and slaves. In 1450, the Chimú kingdom was conquered by the Inca Túpac Yupanqui, the son and heir of the Inca ruler Pachacuti Inca Yupanqui.

Cultures of the northern Andes What is today Ecuador was a densely populated region with a variety of peoples. One of the most important of these was the **Valdivia culture** (3500-1500 BC) on the coast, from which remains of buildings and earthenware figures have been found. A rich mosaic of cultures developed in the period 500 BC to AD 500, after which integration of groups occurred. In the mid-15th century, the relentless expansion of the Inca empire reached Ecuador. The **Cañaris** resisted until 1470 and the Quitu/Caras were defeated in 1492. Further north, most of the peoples who occupied Colombia were primitive hunters or nomad agriculturists, but one part of the country, the high basins of the Eastern Cordillera, was densely occupied by **Chibcha Indians** who had become sedentary farmers. Their staple foods were maize and the potato, and they had no domestic animal save the dog; the use they could make of the land was therefore limited. Other cultures present in Colombia in the precolumbian era were the **Tayrona, Quimbaya, Sinú** and **Calima**. Exhibits of theirs and the Chibcha (Muisca) Indians' gold-work can be seen at the Gold Museum in Bogotá and other cities.

Southern Andes Although there was some influence in southern Bolivia, northern Chile and northern Argentina from cultures such as Tiwanaku, most of the southern Andes was an area of autonomous peoples, probably living in fortified settlements by the time the Incas arrived in the mid-15th century. The conquerors from Peru moved south to the Río Maule in Chile where they encountered the fierce **Mapuches** (Araucanians) who halted their advance. Archaeological evidence from the Amazon basin and Brazil is more scanty than from the Andes or Pacific because the materials used for house building, clothing and decoration were perishable and did not survive the warm, humid conditions of the jungle. Ceramics have been found on Marajó island at the mouth of the Amazon while on the coast much evidence comes from huge shell mounds, called *sambaquis*. Although structured societies developed and population was large, no political groupings of the scale of those of the Andes formed. The Incas made few inroads into the Amazon so it was the arrival of the Portuguese in 1500 which initiated the greatest change on the Atlantic side of the continent.

The Inca Dynasty

The origins of the Inca Dynasty are shrouded in mythology and shaky evidence. The best known story reported by the Spanish chroniclers talks about Manco Cápac and his sister rising out of Lake Titicaca, created by the sun as divine founders of a chosen race. This was in approximately AD 1200. Over the next 300 years the small tribe grew to supremacy as leaders of the largest empire ever known in the Americas, the four territories of Tawantinsuyo, united by Cusco as the umbilicus of the Universe (the four quarters of Tawantinsuyo, all radiating out from Cusco, were Chinchaysuyo, north and northwest; Cuntisuyo, south and west; Collasuyo, south and east; Antisuyo, east).

At its peak, just before the Spanish Conquest, the Inca Empire stretched from the Río Maule in central Chile, north to the present Ecuador-Colombia border, contained most of Ecuador, Peru, west Bolivia, north Chile and northwest Argentina. The area was roughly equivalent to France, Belgium, Holland, Luxembourg, Italy and Switzerland combined, 980,000 sq km. For a brief description of **Inca Society**, see under Cusco. The first Inca ruler, Manco Cápac, moved to the fertile Cusco region, and established Cusco as his capital. Successive generations of rulers were fully occupied with local conquests of rivals, such as the Colla and Lupaca to the south, and the Chanca to the northwest. At the end of Inca Viracocha's reign the hated Chanca were finally defeated, largely thanks to the heroism of one of his sons, Pachacuti Inca Yupanqui, who was subsequently crowned as the new ruler.

From the start of Pachacuti's own reign in 1438, imperial expansion grew in earnest. With the help of his son and heir, Topa Inca, territory was conquered from the Titicaca basin south into Chile, and all the north and central coast down to the Lurín Valley. In 1460-71, the Incas also laid siege to the Chimú. Typical of the Inca method of government, some of the Chimú skills were assimilated into their own political and administrative system, and some Chimú nobles were even given positions in Cusco.

Perhaps the pivotal event in Inca history came in 1527 with the death of the ruler, Huayna Cápac. Civil war broke out in the confusion over his rightful successor. One of his legitimate sons, Huáscar, ruled the southern part of the empire from Cusco. Atahualpa, Huáscar's half-brother, governed Quito, the capital of Chinchaysuyo. In 1532, soon after Atahualpa had won the civil war, Francisco Pizarro arrived in Tumbes with 179 *conquistadores*, many on horseback. Atahualpa's army was marching south, probably for the first time, when he clashed with Pizarro at Cajamarca. **Francisco Pizarro**'s only chance against the formidable imperial army he encountered at Cajamarca was a bold stroke. He drew Atahualpa into an ambush, slaughtered his guards, promised him liberty if a certain room were filled with treasure, and finally killed him on the pretext that an Inca army was on its way to free him. Pushing on to Cusco, he was at first hailed as the executioner of a traitor: Atahualpa had ordered the death of Huáscar in 1533, while himself captive of Pizarro, and his victorious generals were bringing the defeated Huáscar to see his half-brother. Panic followed when the *conquistadores* set about sacking the city, and they fought off with difficulty an attempt by Manco Inca to recapture Cusco in 1536.

The Spanish conquest

Pizarro's arrival in Peru had been preceded by Columbus' landfall on the Paria Peninsula (Venezuela) on 5 August 1498 and Spanish reconaissance of the Pacific coast in 1522. Permanent Spanish settlement was established at Santa Marta (Colombia) in 1525 and Cartagena was founded in 1533. Gonzalo Jiménez de Quesada conquered the Chibcha kingdom and founded Bogotá in 1538. Pizarro's lieutenant, Sebastián de Belalcázar, was sent north through Ecuador; he captured Quito with Diego de Almagro in 1534. Gonzalo Pizarro, Francisco's brother, took over control of Quito in 1538 and, during his exploration of the Amazon lowlands, he sent Francisco de Orellana to prospect downriver. Orellana did not return, but drifted down the Amazon, finally reaching the river's mouth in 1542, the first European to cross the continent in this way. Belalcázar pushed north, founding Pasto, Cali and Popayán (Colombia) in 1536, arriving in Bogotá in 1538. Meanwhile, wishing to secure his communications with Spain, Pizarro founded Lima, near the ocean, as his capital in 1535. The same year Diego de Almagro set out to conquer Chile. Unsuccessful, he returned to Peru, quarrelled with Pizarro, and in 1538 fought a pitched battle with Pizarro's men at the Salt Pits, near Cusco. He was defeated and put to death. Pizarro, who had not been at the battle, was assassinated in his palace in Lima by Almagro's son three years later. In 1541, Pedro de Valdivia founded Santiago de Chile after a renewed attempt to conquer Chile. Like the Incas before them, the Spaniards were unable to master the Mapuches; Valdivia was killed in 1553 and a defensive barrier along the Río Biobío had to be built to protect the colony.

Since 1516 European seafarers had visited the Río de la Plata, first Juan de Solís, then Sebastian Cabot and his rival Diego García in 1527. An expedition led by Pedro de Mendoza founded Buenos Aires in 1536, but it was abandoned in 1541. Mendoza sent Juan de Ayolas up the Río Paraná to reach Peru from the east. It is not known for certain what happened to Ayolas, but his lieutenant Domingo Martínez de Irala founded Asunción on the Paraguay in 1537. This was the base from which the Spaniards relaunched their conquest of the Río de la Plata and Buenos Aires was refounded in 1580.

66 99 Given impetus by Napoleon's invasion of Spain in 1808, Simón Bolívar, El Libertador, led a revolution in the north and José de San Martín, with his Army of the Andes, led an uprising through Argentina and Chile. Both converged on Peru.

Treasure hunt As Spanish colonization built itself around new cities, the *conquistadores* set about finding the wealth which had lured them to South America in the first place. The great prize came in 1545 when the hill of silver at Potosí (Bolivia) was discovered. Other mining centres grew up and the trade routes to supply them and carry out the riches were established. The Spanish crown soon imposed political and administrative jurisdiction over its new empire, replacing the power of the *conquistadores* with that of governors and bureaucrats. The Viceroyalty of Peru became the major outlet for the wealth of the Americas, but each succeeding representative of the Kingdom of Spain was faced with the twofold threat of subduing the Inca successor state of Vilcabamba, north of Cusco, and unifying the fierce Spanish factions. Francisco de Toledo (appointed 1568) solved both problems during his 14 years in office: Vilcabamba was crushed in 1572 and the last reigning Inca, Túpac Amaru, put to death. For the next 200 years the Viceroys closely followed Toledo's system, if not his methods. The Major Government – the Viceroy, the *Audiencia* (High Court), and *corregidores* (administrators) – ruled through the Minor Government – Indian chiefs put in charge of large groups of natives: a rough approximation to the original Inca system.

Towards independence

The Indians of Peru rose in 1780, under the leadership of an Inca noble who called himself Túpac Amaru II. He and many of his lieutenants were captured and put to death under torture at Cusco. Another Indian leader in revolt suffered the same fate in 1814, but this last flare-up had the sympathy of many of the locally born Spanish, who resented their status: inferior to the Spaniards born in Spain, the refusal to give them any but the lowest offices, the high taxation imposed by the home government, and the severe restrictions upon trade with any country but Spain. This was a complaint common to all parts of the Spanish empire and it fostered a twin-pronged independence movement. Given impetus by Napoleon's invasion of Spain in 1808, Simón Bolívar, El Libertador, led a revolution in the north and José de San Martín, with his Army of the Andes, led an uprising through Argentina and Chile. Both converged on Peru.

Bolívar, born in Venezuela in 1783, was involved in the early struggle to free the region from Spanish rule. In 1811 Venezuela declared itself an independent republic, only to be defeated by Spain in 1812. Bolívar led a new revolt in 1813, which was crushed in 1815. He went into exile in Jamaica and Haiti, to return in 1816 with a new army which, in a bold move, he led over the Andes from Venezuela to liberate Nueva Granada (as Colombia was called) at the Battle of Boyacá in 1819. He proclaimed a new republic, Gran Colombia, taking in Colombia, Venezuela and Ecuador. Venezuela was freed at the Battle of Carabobo in 1821.

San Martín's Argentine troops, convoyed from Chile under the protection of the English admiral, Lord Cochrane, landed in southern Peru on 7 September 1820. San Martín proclaimed Peruvian independence at Lima on 28 July 1821, though most of the country was still in the hands of the Viceroy, José de La Serna. Bolívar sent Antonio José de Sucre to Ecuador where, on 24 May 1822, he gained a victory over La Serna at Pichincha. San Martín, after a meeting with Bolívar at Guayaquil, left for Argentina and a self-imposed exile in France, while Bolívar and Sucre completed the conquest of Peru by defeating La Serna at the battle of Junín (6 August 1824) and the decisive battle of Ayacucho (9 December 1824). For over a year there was a last stand in the Real Felipe fortress at Callao by the Spanish troops under General Rodil before they capitulated on 22 January 1826. Bolívar was invited to stay

The Jesuits

Between 1609, when they built their first reducción or mission in the region of Guaíra in present day Brazil, and 1767, when they were expelled from Spanish America, the Jesuits founded about 50 missions around the upper reaches of the Ríos Paraná, Paraguay and Uruguay. In 1627, the northern missions around Guaíra were attacked by slave- hunting Bandeirantes from São Paulo, forcing them to flee southwards. Some 10,000 converts, led by their priests, floated 700 rafts down the Río Parapanema into the Paraná, only to find their route blocked by the Guaíra Falls. Pushing on for eight days through dense forest, they built new boats below the Falls and continued their journey to reestablish their missions 725 km from their original homes.

Efficiently organized and strictly laid out, the missions prospered, growing indigenous and European crops and herding cattle. Their success and economic power attracted many enemies, from the Spanish crown to local landowners. When, in 1750, Spain and Portugal settled their South American border dispute, seven missions were placed under Portuguese control. This the Jesuits resisted with arms, fuelling further the suspicion of the order's excessive power. Under highest secrecy, King Carlos III sent instructions to South America in 1767 to expel the Jesuits. 2,000 were shipped to Italy, their property was auctioned and their schools and colleges were taken over by the Franciscans and Dominicans. By the early 19th century, many of the missions had fallen into disrepair.

Only four missions show signs of their former splendour: San Ignacio Miní in Argentina; Jesús and Trinidad in Paraguay; and São Miguel in Brazil.

in Peru, but in 1826 he left for Colombia where he tried to hold Gran Colombia together as a single state. He failed as internal divisions and political ambitions pulled the three new republics apart. While heading for exile, Bolívar died in 1830.

Brazil: from colony to independence

The Portuguese, Pedro Álvares Cabral, landed in Brazil on 22 April, 1500. He left after a week, shortly followed by Américo Vespucci who had been sent to explore further. The first system of government adopted by the Portuguese was a Capitania, a kind of feudal principality – there were 13 of them, but these were replaced in 1572 by a Viceroyalty. In the same year it was decided to divide the colony into two, north and south, with capitals at Salvador and Rio; it was not until 1763 that Rio became the sole capital.

Three centuries under the paternal eye of Portugal had ill-prepared the colonists for independent existence, except for the experience of Dutch invasion (1624 in Salvador, and 1630-1654 in Recife). The colonists ejected the Dutch from Brazil with little help from Portugal, and Brazilians date the birth of their national sentiment from these events. Resentment against Portuguese government and trade intervention led to the **Inconfidência**, the first revolution, masterminded by **Tiradentes** with 11 other citizens of Minas Gerais. They were unsuccessful (Tiradentes was executed), but when France invaded Portugal in 1807, King João VI was shipped to safety in Brazil, escorted by the British navy. Rio was temporarily declared the capital of the Portuguese Empire. The British, as a price for their assistance in the Portuguese war, forced the opening of Brazil's ports to non-Portuguese trade. King João VI returned to the mother country in 1821, leaving his son, the young Pedro, as Regent. Pedro refused to return control of Brazil to the Portuguese Côrtes (parliament), and on 13 May 1822, by popular request, he agreed to stay and assumed the title of 'Perpetual Defender and Protector of Brazil'. On 7 September he declared Brazil's independence with the cry 'Independence or Death' by the Rio Ipiranga; on 12 October he was proclaimed constitutional emperor of Brazil, and on 1 December he was crowned in Rio.

Post-independence history

Argentina

Independence from Spain

In 1778, Spain finally permitted Buenos Aires to conduct overseas trade. Before that it was controlled by the Viceroy in Lima and was merely a military outpost for Spain to confront the Portuguese settlement at Colonia, across the estuary. Its population then was only 24,203 and its main activity was smuggling. Following Spain's alliance with Napoleon, Britain attacked Buenos Aires in 1806 and again in 1807. The defeat of these attacks, known as the Reconquista, greatly increased the confidence of the *porteños* (the name given to those born in Buenos Aires) to deal with all comers, including the mother-country. On 25 May 1810, the *cabildo* of Buenos Aires deposed the viceroy and announced that it was now governing on behalf of King Ferdinand VII, then a captive of Napoleon. Six years later, in July 1816, when Buenos Aires was threatened by invasion from Peru and blockaded by a Spanish fleet in the Río de la Plata, a national congress held at Tucumán declared independence. The declaration was given reality by José de San Martín, who marched an Argentine army across the Andes to free Chile and embarked his forces for Peru, where he captured Lima, the first step in the liberation of Peru.

The formation of the republic

When San Martín returned home, it was to find the country rent by conflict between the central government and the provinces. On the one hand stood the Unitarist party, bent on central control; on the other the Federalist party, insisting on local autonomy. The latter had for members the great *caudillos* (the large landowners backed by the *gauchos*) suspicious of the cities. One of their leaders, Juan Manuel de Rosas, took control in 1829. During his second term as Governor of Buenos Aires he asked for and was given extraordinary powers. The result was a 17-year reign of terror which became an international scandal. When he began a blockade of Asunción in 1845, Britain and France promptly countered with a three-year blockade of Buenos Aires. In 1851 Justo José de Urquiza, Governor of Entre Ríos, one of his old henchmen, organized a triple alliance of Brazil, Uruguay, and the Argentine opposition to overthrow him. He was defeated in 1852 at Caseros, a few kilometres from Buenos Aires, and fled to England. Rosas had started his career as a Federalist; once in power he was a Unitarist. His downfall meant the triumph of federalism. In 1853 a federal system was finally incorporated in the constitution, but Buenos Aires refused to join the new federation until the city, led by Bartolomé Mitre, was finally defeated by the federal forces in 1880. Buenos Aires was consequently made into a special federal territory. The conquest at about the same time of all the Indian tribes of the pampas and the south by a young colonel, Julio A Roca, was to make possible the final supremacy of Buenos Aires over all rivals.

20th century

From 1916 to 1930 the Unión Cívica Radical (founded in 1890) held power, under the leadership of Hipólito Yrigoyen and Marcelo T de Alvear, but lost it to the military uprising of 1930. Though seriously affected by the world depression of the 1930s, Argentina's rich soil and educated population had made it one of the 10 wealthiest countries in the world, but this wealth was unevenly distributed, and the political methods followed by the conservatives and their military associates in the 1930s denied the middle and working classes any effective share in their own country's wealth and government.

Peronism and its legacy

A series of military coups in 1943-44 led to the rise of Col Juan Domingo Perón, basing his power on an alliance between the army and labour; his contacts with labour were greatly assisted by his charismatic wife Eva (since commemorated in the rock-opera and film *Evita*). In 1946 Perón was elected President. His government is chiefly remembered by many Argentines for improving the living conditions of the workers. Especially in its early years the government was strongly nationalistic, but also intolerant of opposition parties and independent newspapers. Although Perón was re-elected in 1951, his government soon ran into trouble: economic problems led to the introduction of a wage freeze, upsetting the labour unions, which were the heart of Peronist support; the death of Evita in 1952 was another blow. In September 1955 a military coup unseated Perón, who went into exile. Perón's legacy dominated the period 1955-1973: society was bitterly divided between Peronists and anti-Peronists; the economy struggled; the armed forces, constantly involved in politics, were also divided. In a climate of tension and guerrilla-inspired violence, the military bowed out in 1973. Elections were won by the Peronist candidate, Hector Campora. Perón returned from exile in Madrid to resume as President in October 1973, but died on 1 July 1974, leaving the Presidency to his widow, Vice-President María Estela Martínez de Perón (his third wife). The subsequent chaotic political situation, including guerrilla warfare, led to her deposition by a military junta, led by Gen Jorge Videla in March 1976.

The Dirty War and after

Under the military, guerrilla warfare and the other features of dissidence were repressed with great brutality: about 9,000 people (although human rights organizations believe the total is at least double this) disappeared without trace during the so-called 'dirty war'. Confidence in the military ebbed when their economic policies began to go sour in 1980. In 1982-83 pressure for a democratic restoration grew particularly after the Falklands (Islas Malvinas) War with Great Britain in 1982, when Argentina invaded the South Atlantic islands run by the British, in an attempt to reclaim them. General elections on 30 October 1983 were won by the Unión Cívica Radical (UCR), with Dr Raúl Alfonsín as president. During 1985 Generals Videla, Viola and Galtieri were sentenced to long terms of imprisonment for their parts in the 'dirty war'.

Menem and his legacy

When Alfonsín was defeated by Dr Carlos Saúl Menem of the Partido Justicialista (Peronists) in May 1989, Alfonsín stepped down early because of economic instability. Strained relations between the Peronist Government and the military led to several rebellions, which President Menem attempted to appease by pardoning the imprisoned Generals. His popularity among civilians declined, but in 1991-92 the Economy Minister Domingo Cavallo succeeded in restoring confidence in the economy and the Government as a whole. The key was a Convertibility Law, passed in 1991, fixing the peso against the US dollar, and permitting the Central Bank to print local currency only when fully backed by gold or hard currency. This achieved price stability; the annual average growth of consumer prices fell from 3,080% in 1989 to 3.9% in 1994 and remained in single figures until 2001. Having succeeded in changing the constitution to permit the re-election of the president for a second term of four years, Menem was returned to office in 1995 by an electorate favouring stability. But his renewed popularity was short-lived: unemployment remained high and corruption unrestrained. Menem failed to force another change to the constitution to allow him to stand for a third term, but his rivalry with the Peronists' eventual candidate, Eduardo Duhalde, was one of the factors behind the victory of Fernando de la Rúa of the Alliance for Work, Justice and Education (Alianza).

De la Rúa pledged to reduce joblessness, provide better healthcare and end corruption, but within a year was facing scandals and a series of economic crises. The peso became increasingly overvalued, but the government refused to modify the Convertibility Law. By the end of 2001, the country was in deep recession, unemployment was 20% and the government had practically run out of money to service its US\$132 billion debt. As faith in the banking system and the government plummeted, Argentines started to take back their savings from banks; on 30 November 2001 alone, US\$2 billion were withdrawn. The government imposed a US\$250 weekly limit on cash withdrawals, leading to rioting, looting and 27 deaths, which eventually forced de la Rúa out of office. Three subsequent presidents resigned. On 2 January 2002, Eduardo Duhalde was sworn in as Argentina's fifth president in two weeks. The mammoth task of dragging the economy out of recession and restoring confidence could not be achieved before elections in April 2003, although positive steps were taken. The devaluation of the peso in 2002, which saw the value of Argentines' savings plummet, did return the trade balance to surplus. Agriculture and tourism saw dramatic improvements and there was a slight fall in joblessness. Nevertheless, over half the population was living in poverty, desperate for work and food, many surviving thanks to barter clubs. Instead of a display of unity in the crisis, however, the Peronist party pulled itself apart prior to the elections, with the governor of Santa Cruz, Néstor Kirchner, running against ex-president Menem. In the first round, both polled more votes than liberal economist Ricardo López Murphy, but Menem, facing heavy defeat in the run-off, pulled out of the race at the last moment. This gave Kirchner the presidency but with the electoral support of just 22% of the vote from the first round (compared with 24% for Menem). By October 2005, Kirchner had gained sufficient popular support to win a substantial majority in mid-term congressional elections. At the same time, the economy recovered from a decline of 11% in 2002 to growth of 9% in 2003 and over 8% in 2004 and 2005, with similar results expected in 2006. Symbolic of that upturn was the cancellation of its US$9.8 billion debt facility, thus severing all ties with the Fund. Nevertheless, stresses remained as *piqueteros* (mostly jobless workers) continued to campaign for larger government handouts, antagonizing many with their strategies of disrupting transport and other forms of protest against poverty and unemployment. In addition, inflation increased to 12% in 2005, but the administration showed no signs of adopting policies which might represent a return to "orthodoxy" imposed by outside agencies.

Bolivia

Coups, mines and wars

Bolivian politics have been the most turbulent in Latin America. Although in the 19th century the army was very small, officers were key figures in power-struggles, often backing different factions of the landowning elite. Between 1840 and 1849 there were 65 attempted *coups d'état*. The longest lasting government of the 19th century was that of Andrés Santa Cruz (1829-1839), but when he tried to unite Bolivia with Peru in 1836, Chile and Argentina intervened to overthrow him. After the War of the Pacific (1879-1883) there was greater stability, but opposition to the political dominance of the city of Sucre culminated in a revolt in 1899 led by business groups from La Paz and the tin-mining areas, as a result of which La Paz became the centre of government.

Although silver had been of paramount importance in the colonial period, the Bolivian economy depended for much of the 20th century on exports of tin. The construction of railways and the demand for tin in Europe and the USA (particularly in wartime) led to a mining boom after 1900. By the 1920s the industry was dominated by three entrepreneurs, Simón Patiño, Mauricio Hochschild and the Aramayo family, who exercised great influence over national politics. The importance of mining and the harsh conditions in the isolated mining camps of the Altiplano led to the rise of a militant miners movement.

Since independence Bolivia has suffered continual losses of territory, partly because of communications difficulties and the central government's inability to control distant provinces. The dispute between Chile and Peru over the nitrate-rich Atacama desert in 1879 soon dragged in Bolivia, which had signed a secret alliance with Peru in 1873. Following its rapid defeat in the War of the Pacific Bolivia lost her coastal provinces. As compensation Chile later agreed to build the railway between Arica and La Paz. When Brazil annexed the rich Acre Territory in 1903, Bolivia was compensated by another railway, but this Madeira-Mamoré line never reached its destination, Riberalta, and proved of little use; it was closed in 1972. There was not even an unbuilt railway to compensate Bolivia for its next loss. A long-running dispute with Paraguay over the Chaco erupted into war in 1932. Defeat in the so-called Chaco War (1932-1935) resulted in the loss of three quarters of the Chaco (see page 1493).

Modern Bolivia

The Chaco War was a turning point in Bolivian history, increasing the political influence of the army which in 1936 seized power for the first time since the War of the Pacific. Defeat bred nationalist resentment among junior army officers who had served in the Chaco and also led to the creation of a nationalist party, the Movimiento Nacionalista Revolucionario (MNR) led by Víctor Paz Estenssoro. Their anger was directed against the mine owners and the leaders who had controlled Bolivian politics. Between 1936 and 1946 a series of unstable military governments followed. This decade witnessed the apparent suicide in 1939 of one president (Germán Busch) and the public hanging in 1946 of another (Gualberto Villarroel). After a period of civilian government, the 1951 elections were won by the MNR but a coup prevented the party from taking office.

The 1952 revolution In April 1952 the military government was overthrown by a popular revolution in which armed miners and peasants played a major role. Paz Estenssoro became president and his MNR government nationalized the mines, introduced universal suffrage and began the break-up and redistribution of large estates. The economy, however, deteriorated, partly because of the hostility of the US government. Paz's successor, Hernán Siles Zuazo (president from 1956 to 1964), a hero of the 1952 revolution, was forced to take unpopular measures to stabilize the economy. Paz was re-elected president in 1960 and

1964, but shortly afterwards in November 1964 he was overthrown by his vice president, Gral René Barrientos, who relied on the support of the army and the peasants to defeat the miners.

Military rule in the 1970s The death of Barrientos in an air crash in 1969 was followed by three brief military governments. The third, led by Gral Torres, pursued left-wing policies which alarmed many army officers and business leaders. In August 1971 Torres was overthrown by Hugo Banzer, a right-wing colonel who outlawed political parties and trade unions. After Banzer was forced to call elections in 1978, a series of short-lived military governments overruled elections in 1978 and 1979 giving victories to Siles Zuazo. One of these, led by Gral García Meza (1980-1981) was notable for its brutal treatment of opponents and its links to the cocaine trade, which led to its isolation by the international community.

Return to democracy In August 1982 the military returned to barracks and Dr Siles Zuazo assumed the Presidency in a leftist coalition government with support from the communists and trade unions. Under this regime inflation spiralled out of control. The elections of 1985 were won again by Víctor Paz Estenssoro, who imposed a rigorous programme to stabilize the economy. In the elections of 1989, Gonzalo Sánchez de Lozada of the MNR (chief architect of the stabilization programme) failed to win enough votes to prevent Congress choosing Jaime Paz Zamora of the Movimiento de la Izquierda Revolucionaria (MIR), who came third in the elections, as president in August 1989. Paz had made an unlikely alliance with the former military dictator, Hugo Banzer (Acción Democrática Nacionalista).

Although Gonzalo Sánchez de Lozada just failed to gain the required 51% majority to win the presidency in the 1993 elections, the other candidates recognized his victory. The main element in his policies was the capitalization of state assets, in which investors agreed to inject fresh capital into a chosen state-owned company in return for a 50% controlling stake. The other 50% of the shares were distributed to all Bolivians over 18 via a private pension fund scheme. As the programme gained pace, so did opposition to it. In the elections of 1 June 1997, Banzer and the ADN secured 22% of the vote and ADN became the dominant party in a new coalition with three other parties. In his first two years in office, Banzer pursued economic austerity and the US-backed policy of eradicating coca production. In 2000, however, economic hardship in rural areas, together with unemployment and anger at both the coca eradication and a plan to raise water rates led to violent protests and road blocks in many parts of the country. With the country's economic and social problems still severe, President Banzer was forced to resign in August 2001 because of cancer. His replacement, Vice-President Jorge Quiroga, had just a year left of Banzer's term to serve before new elections were held, in which a coalition led by former president Sánchez de Lozada won an extremely narrow victory. The runner-up was Evo Morales, leader of the coca growers, who campaigned for a restoration of traditional coca production and an end to free market reforms.

From the outset, Sánchez de Lozada faced economic crisis. In February 2003, mass demonstrations turned into riots over tax increases and the president was forced to flee the presidential palace in an ambulance. A week later, the cabinet resigned, the tax hikes were cancelled, police were awarded a pay rise and Sánchez de Lozada vowed to forego his salary. This failed to ease tension and in September a protest over the sale of Bolivian gas to the US became a national uprising against Sánchez de Lozada's free-market policies. Weeks of violent street protests led to Sánchez de Lozada's resignation on 17 October 2003. Vice president Carlos Mesa took over the presidency, but he managed to survive only until June 2005, when Supreme Court President Eduardo Rodríguez was appointed interim president until new elections were held on 18 December 2005. Evo Morales of Movimiento al Socialismo (MAS), self-styled "United States' worst nightmare", beat ex-president Quiroga by a clear majority.

Three main issues precipitated Mesa's demise: the continued opposition to gas sales abroad, linked with demands to renationalize the gas and oil industries; mass protests by the inhabitants of El Alto, calling for a more equal society and a new constituent assembly; and pressure from the business lobby in Santa Cruz for more autonomy for their region and a greater share of gas revenues. The first two, plus his support for coca growers, precipitated Morales' rise to power. Morales soon announced elections to a new constituent assembly and, in May 2006, sent troops into the gas fields prior to a renegotiation of all contracts with foreign hydrocarbon companies. This provoked consternation in many quarters, notably Brazil and Spain, but the move had the support of Hugo Chávez and Fidel Castro. The aim of any renationalization would be to eradicate poverty and high expectations rested on Morales acting swiftly. At the same time, he had to adopt caution in order not to alienate the Bolivian business lobby, foreign investors and aid donors. To this end he did not sever ties with the US, despite the latter's concern over some of his policies.

Brazil

Imperial Brazil

Dom Pedro the First had the misfortune to be faced by a secession movement in the north, to lose the Banda Oriental (today Uruguay) and to get too involved in his complicated love life. Finally, he abdicated as the result of a military revolt in 1831, leaving his five-year-old son, Dom Pedro the Second, in the hands of a regent, as ruler. On 23 July 1840, the lad, though only 15, was proclaimed of age. Dom Pedro the Second, a strong liberal at heart, promoted education, increased communications, developed agriculture, stamped on corruption and encouraged immigration from Europe. Under his rule the war with the dictator López of Paraguay ended in Brazilian victory. Finally, he declared that he would rather lose his crown than allow slavery to continue, and on 13 May 1888, it was finally abolished by his daughter, Princess Isabel, who was acting as Regent during his temporary absence.

There is little doubt that it was this measure that cost him his throne. Many plantation owners, who had been given no compensation, turned against the Emperor; they were supported by elements in the army and navy, who felt that the Emperor had not given due heed to their interests since the Paraguayan War. On 15 November 1889, the Republic was proclaimed and the Emperor sailed for Europe. Two years later he died in a second-rate hotel in Paris, after steadfastly refusing a pension from the conscience-stricken revolutionaries. At the time of the first centenary of independence in 1922 the imperial family was allowed to return to Brazil, and the body of Dom Pedro was brought back and buried in the cathedral at Petrópolis.

From Republic to dictatorship

The history of the 'Old Republic' (1889-1930), apart from the first 10 years which saw several monarchist rebellions, was comparatively uneventful, a time of expansion and increasing prosperity. Brazil declared war on Germany during both wars and Brazilian troops fought in the Italian campaign in 1944-1945. In 1930 a revolution headed by Getúlio Vargas, Governor of Rio Grande do Sul, who was to become known as 'the Father of the Poor', deposed President Wáshington Luís. Vargas assumed executive power first as provisional president and then as dictator. He was forced to resign in October 1945. In 1946 a liberal republic was restored and the following 18 years saw considerable economic development and social advance.

An increase in government instability and corruption prompted the military to intervene in civil affairs. From March 1964 until March 1985, the military governed Brazil using political repression and torture, yet achieving great economic success (up to 1980). Between 1964-1974 average growth was 10% a year, but the divide between rich and poor widened. Labour leaders were oppressed, dissenters were jailed and *favelas* mushroomed. Political reform did not occur until 1980 and free elections were not held until 1989.

Return to democracy

In January 1985 a civilian, Tancredo Neves, representing a broad opposition to the military régime, was elected President by the electoral college introduced under the military's 1967 constitution. He was unable, because of illness, to take office: the vice-president elect, Sr José Sarney, was sworn in as acting President in March 1985, and in April became President on Sr Neves' death. After complete revision by a Constituent Assembly in 1987-1988, Brazil's new constitution of 1988 permitted direct presidential elections in November 1989. These were won by Fernando Collor de Melo, of the small Partido da Reconstrução Nacional, who narrowly defeated Luis Inácio da Silva (Lula), of the Workers Party (PT). Just over half-way through his five-year term, Collor was suspended from office after a landslide congressional vote to impeach him over his involvement in corruption. He avoided impeachment by resigning on 29 December 1992. Vice-president Itamar Franco took over, but had scant success in tackling poverty and inflation until the introduction of an anti-inflation package which introduced the real as the new currency.

Recent developments

The success of the **real** plan was the principal reason for its architect, finance minister Fernando Henrique Cardoso, defeating Lula in the presidential elections of October 1994. Throughout 1997 and 1998, the financial crisis in Asia threatened Brazil's currency and economic stability. Cardoso was therefore obliged to introduce policies which, at the cost of slowing down economic growth, would prevent an upsurge in inflation and a devaluation of the currency. At

The Bandeirantes

Reviled in some quarters for their appalling treatment of Indians, revered in others for their determination and willingness to withstand extreme hardship in the pursuit of their goals, the bandeirantes are an indispensible element in the formation of Brazil.

The Portuguese knew that South America held great riches; their Spanish rivals were shipping vast quantities back to Europe from Peru. Legends proliferated of mountains of precious stones, golden lakes and other marvels, also of terrifying places, all in the mysterious interior. Regardless of the number of expeditions sent into the sertão which returned empty-handed, or failed to return at all, there was always the promise of silver, emeralds or other jewels to lure the adventurous beyond the coast.

The one thing that Brazil had in abundance was Indians. Throughout the colony there was a demand for slaves to work the plantations and farms, especially in the early 17th century when Portugal temporarily lost its African possession of Angola.

The men who settled in São Paulo proved themselves expert at enslaving Indians. Without official sanction, and certainly not blessed by the Jesuits, these adventurers formed themselves into expeditions which would set out often for years at a time, to capture slaves for the internal market. The Guaraní Indians who had been organized into reducciones by the Jesuits around the Río Paraguay were the top prize and there developed an intense rivalry between the bandeirantes and the Jesuits. The priests regarded the Paulistas as murderous and inhumane; the slavers felt they had some justification in attacking the missions because they were in Spanish territory and, in the 17th century, the entire western boundary of Brazil was in dispute.

This was one side of the coin. The other was that the bandeirantes were incredibly resourceful, trekking for thousands of kilometres, withstanding great hardships, travelling light, inspired not just by the desire to get rich, but also by a fierce patriotism. To uncover the sertão's riches, they demystified it, trekking into Minas Gerais, Goiás and Mato Grosso looking for precious metals. Through their efforts, the Minas Gerais gold rush began. In the bandeirantes' footsteps came settlers and cattle herders who took over the lands that had been emptied of their Indian population. Although Indians were exploited as labour and became a source of income for the Paulistas, they also intermarried with the Europeans, hastening the miscegenation process which became so evident throughout Brazil.

the same time, the President was still faced with the social imbalances which his government had failed to redress: rising unemployment, unequal income distribution, crime, the low level of police pay, lamentable prison conditions, poor services in the state-run health and education services, land reform and the violence associated with landlessness. These issues notwithstanding, Cardoso again defeated Lula in presidential elections in October 1998. As the new administration battled to enforce greater budgetary discipline, the economy finally succumbed to internal and external pressures in early 1999. Brazil's decision in mid-January to devalue the real by 9% sent shockwaves through world financial markets as it implied that an IMF rescue package of November 1998 had failed. As capital continued to leave the country, the Government was soon forced to let the real float freely. In March 1999 the IMF resumed lending to Brazil, with support from the USA, and as early as May 1999 the economy showed signs of having confounded all the worst expectations. Despite further external shocks in 2001, such as 11 September and the economic crisis in Argentina, the economy remained stable thanks largely to the external sector.

The recession had lowered Cardoso's popularity and thus his influence over his coalition partners. At last the door was open for Lula, who in 2002, at the fourth attempt, won the presidency in the run-off vote against José Serra. Contrary to forecasts that he would lead Brazil

Background Post-independence history

down a left-wing path unacceptable to many outside agencies and governments, his first months in power met with approval at home and abroad. Although passionately committed to social reform, Lula did not abandon orthodox economic policies. This pragmatism has been slow to bring the benefits for which poor and dispossessed Brazilians were hoping. One effect of the social inequalities in Brazilian society was the Primeiro Comando da Capital (First Capital Command or PCC) riots in São Paulo in May 2006. The PCC, a ruthless, nationwide criminal gang which has tried to improve the lot of prisoners, coordinated a wave of urban protests, attacks on police and prison uprisings largely to demonstrate power, but also to highlight humanitarian concerns. Their actions were met with a violent police backlash.

The Workers Party's self-proclaimed uncorruptibility was dealt a severe blow when a number of voting and bribery scandals emerged in 2005. Many heads rolled in revelations of the scope of the *mensalão* (vote-buying) scandal, including Lula's two main deputies, José Dirceu and Antonio Palocci (finance minister until March 2006). Lula himself did not escape untainted, but not enough to limit his chances of winning a second term in the October 2006 presidential elections.

Chile

Independence

In 1810 a group of Chilean patriots, including Bernardo O'Higgins – the illegitimate son of a Sligo-born Viceroy of Peru, Ambrosio O'Higgins, and a Chilean mother – revolted against Spain. This revolt led to seven years of war against the occupying troops of Spain – Lord Cochrane was in charge of the insurrectionist navy – and in 1817 Gen José de San Martín crossed the Andes with an army from Argentina and helped to gain a decisive victory. O'Higgins became the first head of state, but his liberal policies offended the dominant landed aristocracy, leading to his downfall in 1823. A period of anarchy followed, but in 1830 conservative forces led by Diego Portales restored order and introduced the authoritarian constitution of 1833. Under this charter, for almost a century, the country was ruled by a small oligarchy of landowners.

The War of the Pacific

During the 1870s disputes arose with Boliva and Peru over the northern deserts, which were rich in nitrates. Although most of the nitrates lay in Bolivia and Peru, much of the mining was carried out by Anglo-Chilean companies. In the ensuing War of the Pacific (1879-1883), Chile defeated its neighbours, gaining the Bolivian coastal region as well as the Peruvian provinces of Tarapacá and Arica. For the next 40 years it drew great wealth from the nitrate fields. In the south settlers began pushing across the Río Biobío in the 1860s, encouraged by government settlement schemes and helped by technological developments including repeating rifles, telegraph, railways and barbed wire. At the end of the War of the Pacific the large Chilean army was sent to subdue the Mapuches who were confined to ever-diminishing tribal lands. The territory was then settled by immigrants – particularly Germans – and by former peasants who had fought in the north.

The 20th century

The rule of the Right was challenged by the liberal regime of President Arturo Alessandri in 1920. Acute economic distress in 1924, linked to the replacement of Chilean nitrates with artificial fertilizers produced more cheaply in Europe, led to army intervention and some reforms were achieved. The inequalities in Chilean society grew ever sharper, despite the maintenance of political democracy, and gave rise to powerful socialist and communist parties. President Eduardo Frei's policy of 'revolution in freedom' (1964-1970) was the first concerted attempt at overall radical reform, but it raised hopes it could not satisfy. In 1970 a marxist coalition assumed office under Dr Salvador Allende; the frantic pace of change under his regime polarized the country into Left- and Right-wing camps. Increasing social and economic chaos formed the background for Allende's deposition by the army; he died on 11 September 1973. Chile was then ruled by a military president, Gen Augusto Pinochet Ugarte, and a four-man junta with absolute powers. In its early years particularly, the regime suppressed internal opposition by methods which were widely condemned. Despite economic prosperity and efforts to make the regime more popular, Pinochet's bid for a further eight years as president after 1989 was rejected by the electorate in a plebiscite in 1988.

Post-Pinochet

As a result, presidential and congressional elections were held in 1989. A Christian Democrat, Patricio Aylwin Azócar was elected President and took office in March 1990 in a peaceful transfer of power. While Aylwin's coalition held the Chamber of Deputies, the Senate majority was controlled by eight Pinochet appointees, who could block constitutional reform. Gen Pinochet remained as Army Commander although other armed forces chiefs were replaced. The new Congress set about revising many of the military's laws on civil liberties and the economy. In 1991 the National Commission for Truth and Reconciliation published a report with details of those who were killed under the military regime, but opposition by the armed forces prevented mass human rights trials. In December 1993 presidential elections were won by the Christian Democrat Eduardo Frei, son of the earlier president, but in Congress his party failed to achieve the required two-thirds majority to replace heads of the armed forces and end the system of designated senators. Oblivious to public sentiment, the military's position in the senate was strengthened when General Pinochet, who retired as army commander-in-chief in March 1998, took up a senate seat, as a former president who had held office for more than six years. Although ex-officio, Pinochet's presence, and therefore parliamentary immunity from prosecution for alleged crimes during his dictatorship, was offensive to parliamentarians who had suffered during his regime.

In October 1998, Pinochet's position came under threat from an unforeseen quarter when a Spanish magistrate filed for his extradition from London, where he was on a private visit, to face charges of torture against Spanish and Chilean citizens between 1973 and 1990. He was detained while the British judiciary deliberated and in March 1999 the Law Lords concluded that Pinochet should stand trial for criminal acts committed after 1988, the year Britain signed the international torture convention. In April, Home Secretary Jack Straw authorized the extradition, but throughout 1999 the process was subject to continuous legal disputes culminating in a health report which claimed that Pinochet was too ill to stand trial. On this evidence the Home Secretary was "minded" to allow Pinochet to return to Chile, which he did in January 2000. After arriving in Santiago apparently fully fit, Pinochet's health did decline, as did his seemingly untouchable status. Implications of his involvement in the torture and killings of the 1970s and 1980s began to surface and in June 2000 an appeals court stripped Pinochet of his immunity from trial.

Partly as a result of the Pinochet affair, but also because of economic recession, President Frei's standing suffered a sharp decline in 1999. The Concertación elected socialist Ricardo Lagos to be its December 1999 presidential candidate and he beat Joaquín Lavín only by the slimmest of majorities, thus becoming Chile's first socialist president since Salvador Allende. Despite positive economic results during his term, the main focus remained the legacy of Pinochet. While the former dictator enjoyed support from the military, the erosion of his position and image continued. Most damaging were admissions by former military personnel that, under orders from above, they had committed human rights abuses in the 1970s and 1980s. A protracted process of indictments against Pinochet was met with appeals that, among other things, he was too ill to stand trial. In December 2004 he did suffer a stroke, but he has been placed under house arrest on various charges, had his assets frozen and was charged in relation to the deaths of political opponents in 1975. The number of accusations lodged against him ensured that his past would remain in the spotlight for a long time to come, regardless of his seesawing fortunes in the courts. Furthermore, one of the leading contenders for the 2005 presidential election was Michelle Bachelet, who had survived torture while a political prisoner during the Pinochet regime. She was duly elected president in December 2005 and the Concertación coalition won majorities in both houses of congress.

Colombia

Colombia's divided society

After the collapse of Simón Bolívar's Republic of Gran Colombia in 1829/30, what is now known as Colombia was called Nueva Granada until 1863. Almost from its inception the new country became the scene of strife between the centralizing pro-clerical Conservatives and the federalizing anti-clerical Liberals. From 1849 the Liberals were dominant during the next 30 years of insurrections and civil wars. In 1885 the Conservatives imposed a highly centralized constitution which was not modified for over 100 years. A Liberal revolt in 1899 turned into a civil war, 'the War of the Thousand Days'. The Liberals were finally defeated in 1902 after 100,000 people had died. It was in 1903 that Panama declared its independence from Colombia, following US pressure.

After 40 years of comparative peace, the strife between Conservatives and Liberals was reignited in a little-publicized but dreadfully bloody civil war known as *La Violencia* from 1948 to 1957 (some 300,000 people were killed). This was ended by a unique political truce, decided by plebiscite in 1957 under which the two political parties supported a single presidential candidate, divided all political offices equally between them, and thus maintained political stability for 16 years. The agreement was ended in 1978. Belisario Betancur, the Conservative president from 1982-1986, offered a general amnesty to guerrilla movements in an attempt to end violence in the country. Following an initial general acceptance of the offer, only one of the four main guerrilla groups, the FARC, upheld the truce in 1985-1987. In May 1986, when the Liberal candidate, Sr Virgilio Barco, won the presidential elections, FARC's newly-formed political party, the Unión Patriótica (UP), won 10 seats in congress; the Liberal party took the majority. Right-wing groups refused to accept the UP and by the beginning of 1990, 1,040 party members had been killed in five years. During the campaign for the 1990 presidential both the Liberal Party and the UP presidential candidates, Luis Carlos Galán and Bernardo Jaramillo, were assassinated.

The narcotics trade
In Medellín and Cali, two cartels transformed Colombia's drugs industry into a major force in worldwide business and crime. Their methods were very different: Medellín being ostentatious and violent, Cali much more low-key. In 1986, President Barco instigated an international effort to bring them to justice, but opposition to extradition of suspects to the USA stymied progress. Pablo Escobar, the alleged leader of the Medellín drugs cartel, who had surrendered under secret terms in 1991, escaped from custody in July 1992. Despite a multi-million dollar reward offered for his recapture and renewed conditional offers of surrender, he remained at large until he was killed in December 1993.

Modern Colombia
Having won the presidential elections held on 27 May, 1990, César Gaviria Trujillo (Liberal), who took up the candidacy of the murdered Luis Carlos Galán, appointed a coalition government made up of Liberals from rival factions, Conservatives and the M-19 (Movimiento 19 de Abril).

The Gaviria government was unable to stem violence, whether perpetrated by drug traffickers, guerrillas or common criminals. Not surprisingly, this was one of the issues in the 1994 election campaign, in which Ernesto Samper (Liberal) defeated Andrés Pastrana (Conservative). The main thrust of Samper's programme was that Colombia's current economic strength should provide resources to tackle the social deprivation which causes drug use and insurgency. Most impetus was lost during 1995-1997, however, in the wake of revelations that Samper's election campaign had received about US$6 million from the Cali cartel. The debate over Samper's awareness of the funding lasted until June 1996, almost overshadowing the capture or surrender of most of the leading Cali drug lords. The USA, having decided in March 1996 to decertify (remove) Colombia from its list of countries making progress against drugs trafficking, denied Samper the right to a US visa and again decertified the country in March 1997, not least because the Cali cartel bosses were continuing their business from prison. Whatever progress was being made to eradicate drugs plantations and stocks, the denial of US aid through decertification permitted little scope for the establishment of alternative crops. Many rural communities were therefore left without means of support.

In 1998, congressional and presidential elections were relatively peaceful and a welcome boost to confidence was given when the US withdrew the 'decertification' restrictions. The new president, Andrés Pastrana, immediately devoted his efforts to bringing the guerrillas to the negotiating table. A stop-go process began with FARC in late 1998 and the insurgents were conceded a large demilitarized zone, based on San Vicente de Caguán in Caquetá. Not everyone was in favour of Pastrana's approach, especially since FARC violence and extortion did not cease. ELN, meanwhile, angry at being excluded from talks, stepped up its campaign, demanding similar treatment. Paramilitary groups, too, showed no signs of ending their activities. Pastrana also sought international aid for his Plan Colombia, aimed at combatting the drugs trade. The US$1.6 billion package, approved by the US Congress in May 2000, was to cover mainly military and anti-narcotics equipment, with the remainder destined for crop substitution and other sustainable agriculture projects. It has become clear that the policy of spraying drug crops has not achieved the desired result. Not only has the net area under cultivation increased, but the concentration on eradicating coca has permitted a dramatic expansion in the production of opium poppies. Furthermore, with both left-wing guerrillas and right-wing paramilitaries involved in the narcotics trade, the two fronts of fighting terrorism and drugs have become increasingly entangled.

Negotiations with the guerrilla groups continued unsuccessfully into 2002, but the terror campaigns of FARC and ELN increased the government's frustration and, with an eye on the approaching May 2002 elections, Pastrana abandoned his peace initative and sent in the Army. Strategic points in the demilitarized zone were quickly taken but the guerrillas melted away into the forests and countryside and the disruption and kidnapping continued.

The frontrunners for the 2002 presidential elections were both Liberals: Horacio Serpa was the official party candidate, while Alvaro Uribe Vélez left the Liberals to run under his own movement, Colombia First. The main thrust of Uribe's campaigning was that the time had come to stop pandering to the left-wing guerrillas and to use a firm hand to restore order and security. This struck a chord with many Colombians, not just those who supported Pastrana's later hard line, but also the illegal, right-wing paramilitary groups who are waging their own war against FARC and ELN. Consequently, Uribe won with over 50% of the vote in the first round. Despite (or maybe because of) Uribe's anti-guerrilla policies, and despite a decline in support for insurgents following numerous atrocities, violence continued, prompting a tough new anti-terrorism law. At the same time, and in the face of criticism, Uribe began peace talks with the AUC (United Self Defence Forces of Colombia), the paramilitary group implacably opposed to FARC and ELN and accused of some of the worst human rights abuses. Initially little progress was made, but in mid-2004, the AUC agreed to disarm and restrict itself to a small area of Córdoba province. Uribe then launched Plan Patriota, a huge military offensive against FARC in southern Colombia. The strength of FARC's response to the Plan continued right up to national elections in 2006, but, having altered the constitution to permit a second presidential term, Uribe won the May 2006 elections with a 62% majority. In March 2006 his supporters won most seats in the senate and chamber of deputies. Both results showed that public support for the hard-line apporach had not dwindled, if only because there seemed to be no alternative to breaking the impasse in Colombia's internal conflict.

Ecuador

After independence
Ecuador decided on complete independence from the Gran Colombia confederation in August 1830, under the presidency of Juan Flores.The country's 19th century history was a continuous struggle between pro-Church conservatives and anti-Church (but nonetheless devoutly Catholic) liberals. There were also long periods of military rule from 1895, when the liberal Gen Eloy Alfaro took power. During the late 1940s and the 1950s there was a prolonged period of prosperity (through bananas, largely) and constitutional rule, but the more typical pattern of alternating civilian and military governments was resumed in the 1960s and 1970s. Apart from the liberal- conservative struggles, there has been long-lasting rivalry between Quito and the Sierra on one hand and Guayaquil and the Costa on the other.

Return to democracy
Following seven years of military rule, the first presidential elections under a new constitution were held in 1979. The ensuing decades of democracy saw an oscillation of power between parties of the centre-right and centre-left. Governments of both political tendencies towed the international economic line and attempted to introduce neoliberal reforms. These measures were opposed by the country's labour organizations and, more recently, by the indigenous movement, which gained considerable political power. Against a backdrop of this tug-of-war, disenchantment with the political process grew apace with bureaucratic corruption and the nation's economic woes. In 1996 the frustrated electorate swept a flamboyant populist named Abdalá Bucaram to power. His erratic administration lasted less than six months.

Following an interim government and the drafting of the country's 18th constitution, Ecuador elected Jamil Mahuad, a former mayor of Quito, to the presidency in 1998. Mahuad began his term by signing a peace treaty to end the decades-old and very emotional border dispute with Peru. This early success was his last, as a series of fraudulent bank failures sent the country into an economic and political tailspin. A freeze on bank accounts failed to stop landslide devaluation of the Sucre (Ecuador's currency since 1883) and Mahuad decreed the adoption of the US Dollar in a desperate bid for stability.

Less than a month later, on 21 January 2000, he was forced out of office by Ecuador's indigenous people and disgruntled members of the armed forces. The first overt military coup in South America in over two decades, it lasted barely three hours before power was handed to vice-president Gustavo Noboa. Significantly, all of the foregoing years of social unrest were never accompanied by serious bloodshed.

Noboa, a political outsider and academic, stepped into Mahuad's shoes with remarkable aplomb. With assistance from the USA and the International Monetary Fund, his government managed to flesh out and implement the dollarization scheme, thus achieving a measure of economic stability at the cost of deepening poverty. Social unrest diminished, and Ecuadoreans instead attempted to bring about change through the ballot box. In November 2002, Colonel Lucio Gutiérrez, leader of the January 2000 *coup*, was elected president by a comfortable majority. He had run on a populist platform in alliance with the indigenous movement and labour unions, but began to change his stripes soon after taking office. His administration was lacklustre and only constantly shifting allegiances and high petroleum revenues managed to keep him in power. In late 2004, the dismissal of all the supreme court judges by unconstitional means - and tear-gas - drew local and international criticism. It was a thinly-veiled ploy to facilitate the return of exile ex-president Bucaram, the latest ally to prop up the foundering Gutiérrez régime. Popular opposition in Quito grew, with peaceful, well-attended protests. The president's response, using heavy-handed police repression, led to mass demonstrations which swept Gutiérrez from office in April 2005. Congress and the army ratified his overthrow and vice-president Alfredo Palacio replaced him. Lacking a political party base, Palacio found government no easy ride, having to face persistent strikes, especially in the Amazon region where protestors blocked oil pipelines to demand roads and other infrastructure projects promised by Gutiérrez. General elections were brought forward to October 2006.

Paraguay

Independence and dictatorship

The disturbances in Buenos Aires in 1810-16, which led to independence from Spain, enabled creole leaders in Asunción to throw off the rule of Buenos Aires as well as Madrid. The new republic was, however, subject to pressure from both Argentina, which blocked Paraguayan trade on the Río de la Plata, and Brazil. Following independence Paraguay was ruled by a series of dictators, the first of whom, Dr Gaspar Rodríguez de Francia (1814-1840) known as 'El Supremo', imposed a policy of isolation and self-sufficiency. The opening of the Río de la Plata after the fall of the Argentine dictator Rosas enabled de Francia's successor, Carlos Antonio López (1840-1862) to import modern technology: in 1856 a railway line between Asunción and Villarrica was begun; an iron foundry and telegraph system were also developed. Carlos López was succeeded by his son, Francisco Solano López (López II), who saw himself as the Napoleon of South America. Believing Paraguay to be threatened by Brazil and Argentina, Solano López declared war on Brazil in 1865. When Argentina refused permission to send troops through Misiones to attack Brazil, López declared war on Argentina. With Uruguay supporting Brazil and Argentina, the ensuing War of the Triple Alliance was disastrous for the Paraguayan forces who held on against overwhelming odds until the death of López at the Battle of Cerro Corá on 1 March 1870. Of a pre-war population of 400,000, only 220,000 survived the war, 28,000 of them males, mostly either very young or very old. In the peace settlement Paraguay lost territory to Brazil and Argentina, although rivalry between these neighbours prevented a worse fate.

After the war, Paraguay experienced political instability as civilian factions competed for power, often appealing to army officers for support. Although there were few policy differences between the two political parties (the National Republican Association, known as Colorados from its red banner, and the Liberal party who adopted the colour blue), rivalry was intense. Elections were held regularly, but whichever party was in government invariably intervened to fix the result and the opposition rarely participated.

The Chaco War

While Paraguayan leaders were absorbed with domestic disputes, Bolivia began occupying disputed parts of the Chaco in an attempt to gain access to the sea via the Río Paraguay. Although Bolivian moves started in the late 19th century, the dispute was given new intensity by the discovery of oil in the 1920s. In the five-year Chaco War (1932-1937) 56,000 Bolivians and 36,000 Paraguayans were killed. Despite general expectations Paraguayan troops under Mariscal Estigarribia pushed the Bolivian army out of most of the Chaco.

Victory in war only increased dissatisfaction in the army with the policies of pre-war governments. In February 1936 nationalist officers seized power and appointed the war hero, Colonel Rafael Franco as President. Although Franco was overthrown in a counter-coup in 1937, the so-called 'February Revolution' began major changes in Paraguay including the first serious attempt at land reform and legal recognition of the small labour movement. Between 1939 and 1954 Paraguayan politics were even more turbulent, as rival civilian factions and army officers vied for power. In 1946 civil war shook the country as army units based in Concepción fought to overthrow President Morínigo.

The Stroessner Years

A military coup in May 1954 led to General Alfredo Stroessner becoming President. Stroessner retained power for 34 years, the most durable dictator in Paraguayan history. His rule was based on control over the army and the Colorado party, both of which were purged of opponents. While a network of spies informed on dissidents, party membership was made compulsory for most official posts including teachers and doctors. In fraudulent elections Stroessner was re-elected eight times. Paraguay became a centre for smuggling, gambling and drug-running, much of it controlled by Stroessner's supporters. Meanwhile the government spent large amounts of money on transportation and infrastructure projects, including the giant hydroelectric dam at Itaipú. Although these projects brought employment, the completion of Itaipú in 1982 coincided with recession in Brazil and Argentina on whose economies Paraguay was heavily dependent. Meanwhile rivalry intensified within the regime over the succession, with Stroessner favouring his son, Gustavo. Opposition focussed around Gen Andrés Rodríguez, who was married to Stroessner's daughter. When Stroessner tried to force Rodríguez to retire, troops loyal to Rodríguez overthrew the 75-year old Stroessner, who left to live in Brazil.

Liberalization

Rodríguez, who became provisional president, easily won multi-party elections in May 1989. The commitment to greater democracy permitted opponents, who had previously boycotted, or been banned from elections, to gain an unprecedented number of seats in the legislative elections of the same date. Despite considerable scepticism over General Rodríguez's intentions, political liberalization became a reality. The presidential and congressional elections that he promised were held on 9 May 1993. The presidency was won by Juan Carlos Wasmosy of the Colorado Party and Domingo Laíno of the Authentic Radical Liberal Party came second.

The government's commitment to market reforms, privatization and to economic integration with Argentina and Brazil within Mercosur inspired protests from all quarters. 1994 saw the first general strike for 35 years. There were also demands for land reform. A worsening of relations between the military and the legislature in 1995 led to a critical few days in April 1996. Army commander General Lino Oviedo was dismissed for threatening a coup; Wasmosy offered him the defence ministry but then withdrew the offer after massive public protest. Oviedo was later arrested on charges of insurrection, but from jail he made many accusations about corruption at the highest level. To the dismay of the Colorado leadership, Oviedo was chosen as the party's candidate for the May 1998 presidential elections. This intensified the feud between Oviedo and Wasmosy who eventually succeeded in having Oviedo jailed by a military tribunal for 10 years for attempting a coup in 1996. A compromise ticket of Raúl Cubas Grau (Oviedo's running mate) and Luis María Argaña (Colorado party president and opponent of Wasmosy) won the election. Within a week of taking office in August 1998, Cubas released Oviedo from prison, provoking a constitutional crisis as the supreme court ruled that Oviedo should serve out his sentence. Matters came to a head when Vice President Argaña was shot in March 1999, just before the Senate was to vote on impeachment of Cubas. Intense diplomatic efforts, led by Paraguay's Mercosur partners, resulted in Cubas' resignation on 29 March. He was replaced by Luis González Macchi, the president of Congress. Cubas went into exile in Brazil, Oviedo in Argentina. In December 1999, Oviedo escaped from the Patagonian *estancia* where he was held and began verbal attacks on the government. Soldiers loyal to Oviedo staged an unsuccessful coup in May 2000. In the following month Oviedo was arrested in Brazil. The González Macchi administration, meanwhile, was facing economic recession, strikes and social discontent. The economic downturn and its repercussions worsened through 2002 as a result of Argentina's financial crisis. Unemployment stood at about 16% of the workforce and, according to the UN, one third of the population was living in poverty. In February 2003, González Macchi himself was discredited by, but avoided impeachment over, allegations of the misuse of state funds, fraud and the torture of leftwing militants. Nevertheless, in subsequent elections in April 2003, in which González Macchi did not stand, Paraguayans continued to back the Colorado Party and its candidate, Nicanor Duarte Frutos. Duarte's first act as president was to join other South American leaders in signing the Declaration of Asunción against drug trafficking. By 2005, however, strain between Paraguay and its larger Mercosur partners was appearing, partly because of the tade imbalances between the smaller members and Argentina and Brazil, partly because of Paraguay's permission for US troops to conduct excercises in Paraguay.

Peru

After independence

Important events following the ejection of the Spaniards were a temporary confederation between Peru and Bolivia in the 1830s; the Peruvian-Spanish War (1866); and the War of the Pacific (1879-1883), in which Peru and Bolivia were defeated by Chile and Peru lost its southern territory. The 19th and early 20th centuries were dominated by the traditional elites, with landowners holding great power over their workers. Political parties were slow to develop until the 1920s, when the socialist thinkers Juan Carlos Mariátegui and Víctor Raúl Haya de la Torre began to call for funadmental change. Haya de la Torre formed the Alianza Popular Revolucionaria Americana (APRA), but in the 1930s and 40s he and his party were constantly under threat from the military and the elilte.

To the Shining Path

A reformist military Junta took over control of the country in October 1968. Under its first leader, Gen Juan Velasco Alvarado, the Junta instituted a series of measures to raise the personal status and standard of living of the workers and the rural Indians, by land reform, worker participation in industrial management and ownership, and nationalization of basic industries, exhibiting an ideology perhaps best described as 'military socialism'. In view of his failing health Gen Velasco was replaced in 1975 by Gen Francisco Morales Bermúdez and policy (because of a mounting economic crisis and the consequent need to seek financial aid from abroad) swung to the Right. Presidential and congressional elections were held on 18 May 1980, and Fernando Belaúnde Terry was elected President for the second time. His term was marked by growing economic problems and the appearance of the Maoist terrorist movement Sendero Luminoso (Shining Path).

Initially conceived in the University of Ayacucho, the movement gained most support for its goal of overthrowing the whole system of Lima-based government from highland Indians and migrants to urban shanty towns. The activities of Sendero Luminoso and another terrorist group, Túpac Amaru (MRTA), frequently disrupted transport and electricity supplies, although their strategies had to be reconsidered after the arrest of both their leaders in 1992. Víctor Polay of MRTA was arrested in June and Abimael Guzmán of Sendero Luminoso was captured in September; he was sentenced to life imprisonment (although the sentence had to be reviewed in 2003 under legal reforms). Although Sendero did not capitulate, many of its members in 1994-1995 took advantage of the Law of Repentance, which guaranteed lighter sentences in return for surrender, and freedom in exchange for valuable information. Meanwhile, Túpac Amaru was thought to have ceased operations (see below).

The Fujimori years

The April 1985 elections were won by the APRA party leader Alán García Pérez. During his populist, left-wing presidency disastrous economic policies caused increasing poverty and civil instability. In presidential elections held over two rounds in 1990, Alberto Fujimori of the Cambio 90 movement defeated the novelist Mario Vargas Llosa, who belonged to the

Fredemo (Democratic Front) coalition. Fujimori, without an established political network behind him, failed to win a majority in either the senate or the lower house. Lack of congressional support was one of the reasons behind the dissolution of congress and the suspension of the constitution on 5 April 1992. With massive popular support, President Fujimori declared that he needed a freer hand to introduce free-market reforms, combat terrorism and drug trafficking, and root out corruption.

Elections to a new, 80-member Democratic Constituent Congress (CCD) in November 1992 and municipal elections in February 1993 showed that voters still had scant regard for mainstream political groups. A new constitution drawn up by the CCD was approved by a narrow majority of the electorate in October 1993. Among the new articles were the immediate re-election of the president (previously prohibited for one presidential term), the establishment of a single-chamber congress, the reduction of the role of the state and the favouring of foreign investment. As expected, Fujimori stood for re-election on 9 April 1995 and beat his independent opponent, former UN General Secretary, Javier Pérez de Cuéllar, by a resounding margin. The coalition that supported him also won a majority in Congress.

The government's success in most economic areas did not accelerate the distribution of foreign funds for social projects. Furthermore, rising unemployment and the austerity imposed by economic policy continued to cause hardship for many. Economic progress also began to falter, casting further doubt on the government's ability to alleviate poverty. Dramatic events on 17 December 1996 thrust several of these issues into sharper focus. 14 Túpac Amaru terrorist infiltrated a reception at the Japanese Embassy in Lima, taking 490 hostages and demanding the release of their imprisoned colleagues and new measures to raise living standards. Most of the hostages were released and negotiations were pursued during a stalemate that lasted until 22 April 1997. The president took sole responsibility for the successful, but risky assault which freed all the hostages (one died of heart failure) and killed all the terrorists. By not yielding to Túpac Amaru, Fujimori regained much popularity. But this masked the fact that no concrete steps had been taken to ease social problems. It also deflected attention from Fujimori's plans to stand for a third term following his unpopular manipulation of the law to persuade Congress that the new constitution did not apply to his first period in office. Until the last month of campaigning for the 2000 presidential elections, Fujimori had a clear lead over his main rivals. His opponents insisted that Fujimori that should not stand and local and international observers voiced increasing concern over the state domination of the media. Meanwhile, the popularity of Alejandro Toledo, a centrist and former World Bank official of humble origins, surged to such an extent that he and Fujimori were neck-and neck in the first poll. Toledo and his supporters claimed that Fujimori's slim majority was the result of fraud, a view echoed in the pressure put on the president, by the US government among others, to allow a second ballot. The run-off election, on 28 May 2000, was also contentious since foreign observers, including the Organization of American States, said the electoral system was unprepared and flawed, proposing a postponement. The authorities refused to delay. Toledo boycotted the election and Fujimori was returned unopposed, but with minimal approval. Having won, he proposed to "strengthen democracy".

This pledge proved to be worthless following the airing of a secretly-shot video on 14 September 2000 of Fujimori's close aide and head of the National Intelligence Service (SIN), Vladimiro Montesinos, handing US$15,000 to a congressman, Alberto Kouri, to persuade him to switch allegiances to Fujimori's coalition. Fujimori's demise was swift. His initial reaction was to close down SIN and announce new elections, eventually set for 8 April 2001, at which he would not stand. Montesinos, declared a wanted man, fled to Panama, where he was denied asylum. He returned to Peru in October and Fujimori personally led the search parties to find his former ally. Peruvians watched in amazement as this game of cat-and-mouse was played out on their TV screens. While Montesinos himself successfully evaded capture, investigators began to uncover the extent of his empire, which held hundreds of senior figures in its web. His activities encompassed extortion, money-laundering, bribery, intimidation, probably arms and drugs dealing and possibly links with the CIA and death squads. Swiss bank accounts in his name were found to contain about US$70 million, while other millions were discovered in accounts in the Cayman Islands and elsewhere. By early 2001 sightings of him were reported in Costa Rica, then Venezuela and Aruba. Meanwhile, Fujimori, apparently in pursuit of his presidential duties, made various overseas trips, including to Japan. Here, on 20 November, he sent Congress an email announcing his resignation. Congress rejected this, firing him instead on charges of being "morally unfit" to govern. An interim president, Valentín Paniagua, was sworn in, with ex-UN Secretary General Javier Pérez de Cuéllar as Prime

Minister, and the government set about uncovering the depth of corruption associated with Montesinos and Fujimori. It also had to prepare for free and fair elections. Further doubt was cast over the entire Fujimori period by suggestions that he may not have been born in Peru, as claimed, but in Japan. His hosts certainly declared that, through his parents, he was a Japanese national and therefore exempt from extradition. If he was indeed Japanese by birth as well as ancestry, he should never have been entitled to stand for the highest office in Peru.

After Fujimori

In the run-up to the 2001 elections, the front-runner was Alejandro Toledo, but with far from a clear majority. Ex-President Alan García emerged as Toledo's main opponent, forcing a second ballot on 3 June. This was won by Toledo with 52% of the vote. He pledged to heal the wounds that had opened in Peru since his first electoral battle with the disgraced Fujimori, but his presidency was marked by slow progress on both the political and economic fronts. With the poverty levels still high, few jobs created and a variety of scandals, Toledo's popularity plummeted. A series of major confrontations and damaging strikes forced the president to declare a state of emergency in May 2003 to restore order. Nor could Toledo escape charges of corruption being laid at his own door; accusations that he and his sister orchestrated voter fraud in 2000 were upheld by a congressional commission in May 2005, but no action was agreed.

The April 2006 elections were contested by Alán García, the conservative Lourdes Flores and Ollanta Humala, a former military officer and unsuccessful coup leader who claimed support from Venezuela's Hugo Chávez and Evo Morales of Bolivia. García and Humala won through to the second round, which García won, in part because many were suspicious, even critical of the "Chávez factor" and the latter's interference in Peruvian affairs. Many were equally suspicious fo García's ability to overcome his past record as president, but prior to taking office he pledged to rein in public spending and not squander the benefits of an economy that had shown strong growth in 2005.

All the while, the past continued to dog the present. From 2002 on, Montesinos was convicted of a number of crimes in a series trials and yet more prosecutions were in process. In 2004, prosecutors also sought to charge exiled Fujimori with ordering the deaths of 25 people in 1991 and 1992. This followed the Truth and Reconciliation Committee's report (2003) into the civil war of the 1980s-1990s, which stated that over 69,000 Peruvians had been killed. With attempts to extradite Fujimori from Japan coming to nothing, prosecution could not proceed. Meanwhile Fujimori himself declared that he would be exonerated and stand again for the presidency in 2006. To this end he flew to Chile in November 2005 with a view to entering Peru, but the Chilean authorities jailed him for seven months and then did not allow him to leave for Peru.

Uruguay

Struggle for independence

In 1808 Montevideo declared its independence from Buenos Aires. In 1811, the Brazilians attacked from the north, but the local patriot, José Gervasio Artigas, rose in arms against them. In the early stages he had some of the Argentine provinces for allies, but soon declared the independence of Uruguay from both Brazil and Argentina. Buenos Aires invaded again in 1812 and was able to enter Montevideo in June 1814. In January the following year the Orientales (Uruguayans) defeated the Argentines at Guayabos and regained Montevideo. The Portuguese then occupied all territory south of the Río Negro except Montevideo and Colonia. The struggle continued from 1814 to 1820, but Artigas had to flee to Paraguay when Brazil took Montevideo in 1820. In 1825 General Juan Lavalleja, at the head of 33 patriots (the Treinta y Tres Orientales), crossed the river and returned to Uruguay, with Argentine aid, to harass the invaders. After the defeat of the Brazilians at Ituzaingó on 20 February 1827, Britain intervened, both Argentina and Brazil relinquished their claims on the country, and independence was finally achieved in 1828.

19th-century upheavals

The early history of the republic was marked by a civil war (known as the Guerra Grande) which began as a conflict between two rival leaders, José Fructuoso Rivera with his Colorados and Manuel Oribe with his Blancos; these are still two of the three main parties today. Oribe was helped by the Argentine dictator, Juan Manuel de Rosas, but was overthrown in 1838. Blanco forces, backed by Rosas, besieged Montevideo between 1843 and 1851. Although Rosas fell from power in 1852, the contest between Colorados and Blancos continued. A Colorado, General Venancio Flores, helped by Argentina, became president and, in 1865, Uruguay was dragged into the war of the Triple Alliance against the Paraguayan dictator, López. Flores was assassinated in 1868 three days after his term as president ended.

Batlle y Ordoñez
The country, wracked by civil war, dictatorship and intrigue, only emerged from its long political turmoil in 1903, when another Colorado, a great but controversial man, José Batlle y Ordóñez was elected president. During Batlle y Ordóñez' two terms as president, 1903-1907 and 1911-1915, Uruguay became within a short space of time the only 'welfare state' in Latin America. Its workers' charter provides free medical service, old age and service pensions and unemployment pay. Education is free and compulsory, capital punishment abolished, and the church disestablished.

Guerrillas and military rule
As the country's former prosperity has ebbed away since the 1960s, the welfare state has become increasingly fictitious. The military promised to reduce bureaucracy and spend more on the poor and development after the turmoil of 1968-1973, the period in which the Tupamaros urban guerrilla movement was most active. In practice the military, which effectively wiped out the Tupamaros by 1972, expanded state spending by raising military and security programmes. Real wages fell to less than half their 1968 level and only the very wealthy benefited from the military regime's attempted neo-liberal economic policies. Less than 10% of the unemployed received social security payments. Montevideo began to sprout shanty towns, once unheard of in this corner of the hemisphere. Nevertheless, the country's middle class remains very large, if impoverished, and the return to democracy in 1985 raised hopes that the deterioration in the social structure would be halted. Almost 10% of the population emigrated for economic or political reasons during the 1960s and 1970s: the unemployed continue to leave, but the political and artistic exiles have returned.

Allying himself with the Armed Forces in 1973, the elected president, Juan M Bordaberry, dissolved Congress and stayed on to rule as the military's figurehead until 1976. Scheduled elections were cancelled in that year, and a further wave of political and trade union repression instituted. Unable to convince the population to vote for a new authoritarian constitution in 1980, the military became increasingly anxious to hand back power to conservative politicians.

Return to democracy
In August 1984 agreement was reached finally on the legalization of most of the banned leftist parties and elections were held in November. Under the moderate government of Julio María Sanguinetti (of the Colorado party) the process of national reconstruction and political reconciliation began with a widespread political amnesty (endorsed by referendum in April 1989). The moderate conservative Partido Nacional (Blancos) won November 1989 presidential and congressional elections and Luis Alberto Lacalle became president. There was considerable opposition to plans for wage restraint, spending cuts, social reforms and privatization. As a result, his Blanco Party lost the November 1994 elections: Colorado ex-president Sanguinetti was again victorious over the Blancos and the Frente Amplio, a broad left front. Each party won about a third of the seats in Congress. Soon after taking office in March 1995, President Sanguinetti managed to forge an alliance with the Blancos to introduce economic restructuring and steps towards implementing much needed social security reforms. While the coalition worked together to reduce the influence of the public sector, the Frente Amplio gained support for its aim of maintaining the welfare state.

In December 1996 a referendum was held on constitutional reforms, including changes to the presidential selection process which would restrict political parties to a single candidate for each election and the introduction of a second ballot for the presidency. The Blancos and Colorados were in favour of the changes, but the Frente, fearing that the two main parties would maintain their cooperation to keep it from power, was opposed. The electorate voted in favour of the changes. The first elections under the new system were held at the end of 1999 and the Frente Amplio candidate, Tabaré Vásquez, was narrowly defeated in the second ballot by Jorge Batlle of the Colorados. In congress, however, the Frente Amplio, in coalition with Encuentro Progresista, was the single party with the largest number of seats.

from the air. Coffee and cotton were the main crops until the late 18th century, but sugar had become the dominant crop by 1820. In 1834 slavery was abolished. Many slaves scattered as small landholders, and settlers had to find another source of labour: indentured workers from India, a few Chinese, and some Portuguese labourers. At the end of their indentures many settled in Guyana.

The end of the colonial period was politically turbulent, with rioting between the mainly Indo-Guyanese People's Progressive Party (PPP), led by Dr Cheddi Jagan, and the mainly Afro-Guyanese People's National Congress (PNC), under Mr Forbes Burnham. The PNC, favoured over the PPP by the colonial authorities, formed a government in 1964 and retained office until 1992. Guyana is one of the few countries in the Caribbean where political parties have used race as an election issue. As a result, tension between the ethnic groups has manifested itself mainly at election time.

On 26 May 1966 Guyana gained independence, and on 23 February 1970 it became a co-operative republic within the Commonwealth, adopting a new constitution. Another new constitution was adopted in 1980; this declared Guyana to be in transition from capitalism to socialism. Many industries, including bauxite and sugar, were nationalized in the 1970s and close relations with the USSR and Eastern Europe were developed. Following the death of President Forbes Burnham in August 1985, Desmond Hoyte became president. Since then, relations with the United States have improved.

Regular elections to the National Assembly and to the presidency since independence were widely criticized as fraudulent. In October 1992 national assembly and presidential elections, declared free and fair by international observers, the PPP/Civic party, led by Dr Jagan, won power after 28 years in opposition. The installation of a government by democratic means was greeted with optimism and prompted foreign investors to study potential opportunities in Guyana. An economic recovery programme, part of an IMF Enhanced Structural Adjustment Facility, stimulated several years of positive gdp growth, but also seriously eroded workers' real income and hit the middle classes very hard.

In March 1997, President Jagan died after a heart attack. In new elections on 15 December 1997, the PPP/Civic alliance was re-elected. Jagan's widow, Janet, was elected as president. The PNC, led by Desmond Hoyte, disputed the results and a brief period of violent demonstrations was ended when a Caricom (Caribbean Common Market) mission agreed to mediate between the two sides. Even though the PPP/Civic was sworn in to office on 24 December 1997, agreeing to review the constitution and hold new elections within three years, Hoyte refused to recognize Jagan as president. In August 1999 President Jagan resigned because of ill health and Minister of Finance, Bharrat Jagdeo was appointed in her place. New elections were eventually held in March 2001 and the PPP/Civic alliance and Jagdeo were returned to office. After the death of Desmond Hoyte in December 2002, Robert Corbin was elected leader of the opposition PNC/Reform. In May 2003, Jagdeo and Corbin agreed new terms for "constructive engagement", which included an end to the PNC/R's boycott of the National Assembly. Elections scheduled for August 2006 had to be postponed because of technical problems at the elections commission. Before a new date had been set (18 September), there was instability in the country and a stand-off between Jagdeo and Corbin. During the period of unrest, Agriculture Minister Satyadeow Sawh was murdered and violence generally was on the increase but whether these crimes were directly related to the elections was unclear.

Suriname

Although Amsterdam merchants had been trading with the 'wild coast' of Guiana as early as 1613 (the name Parmurbo-Paramaribo was already known) it was not until 1630 that 60 English settlers came to Suriname under Captain Marshall and planted tobacco. The real founder of the colony was Lord Willoughby of Parham, governor of Barbados, who sent an expedition to Suriname in 1651 under Anthony Rowse to find a suitable place for settlement. Willoughbyland became an agricultural colony with 500 little sugar plantations, 1,000 white inhabitants and 2,000 African slaves. Jews from Holland and Italy joined them, as well as Dutch Jews ejected from Brazil after 1654. On 27 February 1667, Admiral Crynssen conquered the colony for the states of Zeeland and Willoughbyfort became the present Fort Zeelandia. By the Peace of Breda, 31 July 1667, it was agreed that Suriname should remain with the Netherlands, while Nieuw-Amsterdam (New York) should be given to England. The colony was conquered by the British in 1799, only to be restored to the Netherlands with the Treaty of

Paris in 1814. Slavery was forbidden in 1818 and formally abolished in 1863. Indentured labour from China and Indonesia (Java) took its place.

On 25 November 1975, the country became an independent republic, which signed a treaty with the Netherlands for an economic aid programme worth US$1.5 billion until 1985. A military coup on 25 February 1980 overthrew the elected government. The military leader, Sergeant Desi Bouterse, and his associates came under pressure from the Dutch and the USA as a result of dictatorial tendencies. After the execution of 15 opposition leaders at Fort Zeelandia on 8 December 1982, the Netherlands broke off relations and suspended its aid programme, although bridging finance was restored in 1988.

The ban on political parties was lifted in late 1985 and a new constitution was drafted. In 1986 guerrilla rebels (the Jungle Commando), led by a former bodyguard of the promoted Lieutenant-Colonel Bouterse, Ronny Brunswijk, mounted a campaign to overthrow the government, disrupting both plans for political change and the economy. Nevertheless, elections for the National Assembly were held in November 1987. A three-party coalition (the Front for Democracy and Development) gained a landslide victory over the military, but conflicts between Assembly President Ramsewak Shankar and Bouterse led to the deposition of the government in a bloodless coup on 24 December 1990 (the 'telephone coup'). A military-backed government under the presidency of Johan Kraag was installed and elections for a new national assembly were held on 25 May 1991. The New Front of three traditional parties and the Surinamese Labour Party (SPA) won most Assembly seats and Ronald Venetiaan was elected president on 6 September 1991. Meetings between Suriname and the Netherlands ministers after the 1991 elections led to the renewal of aid in 1992. In August 1992, a peace treaty was signed between the government and the Jungle Commando.

It was only after the 1990 coup and a 25% fall in the price of alumina in 1991 that pressing economic issues such as unifying the complex system of exchange rates and cutting the huge budget deficit began to be addressed. In 1992 a Structural Adjustment Programme (SAP) was drawn up as a forerunner to a 1994-1998 Multi-Year Development Programme. A unified floating rate was introduced in 1994, but apart from that the New Front Government failed to reap any benefit from the SAP. New Front's popularity slumped as its handling of the economy foundered and corruption scandals undermined its claim to introduce 'clean politics'. Because of wide ideological differences, the opposition parties presented no concerted campaign against the New Front until the 23 May 1996 general election. Until then, much greater impetus was given to popular discontent by the economic decline, which reached catastrophic proportions by 1995. Although the New Front won a small majority in the National Assembly, Venetiaan did not hold enough seats to become president. Several parties defected to the NDP with the result that, in September 1996, the United Peoples Assembly elected by secret ballot Jules Wijdenbosch as president. Wijdenbosch, who had been a vice-president during Bouterse's regime, formed a coalition government of his own NDP and five other parties. Bouterse, for whom the special post of Councillor of State had been created in 1997, was dismissed by Wijdenbosch in April 1999 for failing to 'contribute to a healthy political climate'. At the same time Bouterse was tried *in absentia* in the Netherlands on suspicion of drug trafficking; he was convicted in July and is still sought there (Ronnie Brunswijk was convicted *in absentia* on similar charges).

Protests and strikes at the government's handling of the economy erupted in 1998-1999 and Wijdenbosch's position became precarious following the collapse of his coalition. He was forced to bring forward elections from 2001 to 25 May 2000 and was humiliated by the electorate, gaining a mere 9% of the vote. The New Front coalition led by ex-president Ronald Venetiaan won 47%. Venetiaan's most urgent priority was to stabilize the economy, which, by 2000 and with Dutch aid terminated, had fallen back into recession. From 2001, there were renewed signs of improvement, but the outlook remained grim for over 60% of the population estimated by the United Nations to be living in poverty. In January 2004, Suriname abandoned its currency, the guilder, in favour of the Suriname dollar, introduced at a rate of 2.8 to the US dollar. Exchange rates were also simplified with the aim of strengthening the currency and bringing confidence back to the economy. In general elections in May 2005, the outgoing New Front coalition won 23 seats, 10 fewer than previously. Bouterse's NDP won 15 seats, becoming the largest political party in the country. A new party, A-Combination (AC), won 5 seats, the People's Alliance for Progress (VVV) of former president Jules Wijdenbosch secured 5 seats and Alternative-1 (A-1) won 3. In August a special session of the People's Assembly reelected Venetiaan as president. In the first half of 2006 torrential rains caused flood damage estimated at US$25 million, destroying crops, houses and schools and displacing thousands of people in many areas.

Guyane

Several French and Dutch expeditions attempted to settle along the coast in the early 17th century, but were driven off by the native population. The French finally established a settlement at Sinnamary in the early 1660s but this was destroyed by the Dutch in 1665 and seized by the British two years later. Under the Treaty of Breda, 1667, Guyane was returned to France. Apart from a brief occupation by the Dutch in 1676, it remained in French hands until 1809 when a combined Anglo-Portuguese naval force captured the colony and handed it over to the Portuguese (Brazilians). Though the land was restored to France by the Treaty of Paris in 1814, the Portuguese remained until 1817. Gold was discovered in 1853, and disputes arose about the frontiers of the colony with Suriname and Brazil. These were settled by arbitration in 1891, 1899, and 1915. By the law of 19 March 1946, the Colony of Cayenne, or Guyane Française, became the Department of Guyane, with the same laws, regulations, and administration as a department in metropolitan France. The seat of the Prefect and of the principal courts is at Cayenne. Despite heavy dependence economically on France, unemployment is a serious problem. The colony was used as a prison for French convicts with camps scattered throughout the country; Saint-Laurent was the port of entry. After serving prison terms convicts spent an equal number of years in exile and were usually unable to earn their return passage to France. Majority opinion seems to be in favour of greater autonomy and there has been some civil unrest caused by a minority calling for change in the relationship with Metropolitan France. The French government has shown no inclination to alter the department's status. There is an independence movement, but it does not have a significant following.

Government

Argentina

The country's official name is La República Argentina, the Argentine Republic. The form of government has traditionally been a representative, republican federal system. Of the two legislative houses, the Senate has 72 seats, and the Chamber of Deputies 257. By the 1853 Constitution (amended most recently in 1994) the country is divided into a Federal Capital (the city of Buenos Aires) and 23 Provinces. Each Province has its own Governor, Senate and Chamber of Deputies. The municipal government of the Federal Capital is exercised by a Mayor who is directly elected. The Constitution grants the city autonomous rule.

Bolivia

The Constitution of 1967 vests executive power in the President, elected by popular vote for a term of five years, who cannot be immediately re-elected. Following the election of Evo Morales to the presidency in 2006, the process for drawing up a new constitution began. Congress consists of two chambers: the Senate, with 27 seats, and the Chamber of Deputies, with 130 seats. There are nine departments; each is controlled by a Prefecto appointed by the President. **Note:** Sucre is the legal capital, La Paz is the seat of government.

Brazil

The 1988 constitution provides for an executive president elected by direct popular vote, balanced by a bicameral legislature (81 seats in the Federal Senate, 513 seats in the Chamber of Deputies) and an independent judiciary. The vote has been extended to 16-year-olds and illiterates. Presidential elections are held every five years, with a second round one month after the first if no candidate wins an outright majority. Congressional elections are held every four years, the deputies being chosen by proportional representation.

Chile

The pre-1973 constitution was replaced, after a plebiscite, on 11 March 1981. This new constitution provided for an eight year non-renewable term for the President of the Republic, a bicameral Congress and an independent judiciary and central bank. In February 1994, the Congress cut the presidential term of office from eight years to six. Congress is composed of a 120-seat Chamber of Deputies and a 47-seat Senate. In 1974 the country was divided into 13 regions, replacing the old system of 25 provinces.

Colombia

Senators and Representatives are elected by popular vote. The Senate has 102 members, and the Chamber of Representatives has 165. The President, who appoints his 13 ministers, is elected by direct vote for a term of four years, but cannot succeed himself in the next term. Every citizen over 18 can vote. The 1886 Constitution was reformed by a Constituent Assembly in 1991. Administratively the country is divided into 32 Departments and the Capital District of Bogotá.

Ecuador

There are 22 provinces, including the Galápagos Islands. Provinces are divided into *cantones* which are subdivided into *parroquias* for administration.

Under the 1998 constitution, all citizens over 18 are both entitled and required to vote. The president and vice-president are elected for a four-year term and may be re-elected. The president appoints cabinet ministers and provincial governors. The parliament (Congreso Nacional) has 100 members who are elected for a four-year term at the same time as the president.

Paraguay

A new Constitution was adopted in 1992. The country has 19 departments. Executive power rests with the president, elected for five years. There is a two-chamber Congress (Senate 45 seats, Chamber of Deputies 80). Voting is secret and obligatory for all over 18.

Peru

Under a new constitution (approved by plebiscite in October 1993), a single chamber, 80-seat congress replaced the previous, two-house legislature. Men and women over 18 are eligible to vote; registration and voting is compulsory until the age of 60. Those who do not vote are fined. The President, to whom is entrusted the Executive Power, is elected for five years and may, under the constitution which came into force on 1 January 1994, be re-elected for a second term.

Uruguay

Uruguay is a republic with a bicameral legislature: a Senate with 31 seats and a Chamber of Representatives with 99 seats. The president, who is head of state and of the government, holds office for five years. The country is divided into 19 provinces.

Venezuela

Venezuela is a federal republic of 23 states, a Federal District and federal dependencies of over 70 islands. There is one legislative house, a chamber of deputies with 165 members who are elected every five years. A referendum was held on 15 December 1999 which voted to change the constitution and allow immediate reelection of the president. The constitution came into force on 30 December 1999. The country's name was changed to the Bolivarian Republic of Venezuela.

Guyana

A Prime Minister and cabinet are responsible to the National Assembly, which has 65 members, 53 of whom are elected for a maximum term of five years. The other 12 are appointed by local councils. The president is Head of State. The country is divided into 10 administrative regions.

Suriname

There is one legislative house, the National Assembly, which has 51 members, elected every four years. The President is both head of state and government. Suriname is divided into 10 districts, of which the capital is one.

Guyane

The head of state is the president of France; the local heads of government are Le Préfet (the Prefect), for France, and the presidents of the local General and Regional Councils. The General Council (19 members) and the Regional Council (31 members) are the two legislative houses. The main parties in the regional council are the Parti Socialiste Guyanais and the Front Democratique Guyanais. Guyane sends a representative to the French Senate and one to the National Assembly in Paris.

Culture

People

Argentina → *Population in 2004 was 38.2 million. Population growth 2000-2005 was 0.98%; urban population 90%; infant mortality rate 15 per 1,000 live births; GDP per capita US$3,375 (2003).*

In the Federal Capital and Province of Buenos Aires, where about 45% of the population lives, the people are almost exclusively of European origin. In the far northern provinces, colonized from neighbouring countries, at least half the people are *mestizos* though they form about 15% of the population of the whole country. It is estimated that 12.8% are foreign born and generally of European origin, though there are also important communities of Syrians, Lebanese, Armenians, Japanese and Koreans. Not surprisingly, the traditional image of the Argentine is that of the *gaucho*; *gauchismo* has been a powerful influence in literature, sociology and folklore, and is celebrated each year in the week before the 'Day of Tradition', 10 November.

In the highlands of the northwest, in the Chaco, Misiones and in the southwest, there are still some **indigenous groups**. The total of the Indian population is unknown; estimates vary from 300,000 to 500,000. The pampas Indians were virtually exterminated in the 19th century; the Indians of Tierra del Fuego are extinct. Surviving peoples include the Wichi and others in Salta and Jujuy provinces (see page 143), various Chaco Indians (see page 168) and tribes related to the Mapuche and Tehuelche nations in the southwest.

Bolivia → *Population in 2004 was 9.2 million. Population growth 2000-2005 was 1.98%; urban population 64%; infant mortality rate 56 per 1,000 live births; GDP per capita US$878 (2003).*

Of the total population, some two thirds are Indians, the remainder being *mestizos* (people of mixed Spanish and indigenous origin), Europeans and others. The racial composition varies from place to place: Indian around Lake Titicaca; more than half Indian in La Paz; three-quarters *mestizo* or European in the Yungas, Cochabamba, Santa Cruz and Tarija, the most European of all. There are also about 17,000 blacks, descendents of slaves brought from Peru and Buenos Aires in 16th century, who now live in the Yungas. Since the 1980s, regional tensions between the 'collas' (*altiplano* dwellers) and the 'cambas' (lowlanders) have become more marked. About two-thirds of the population lives in adobe huts. Under 40% of children of school age attend school even though it is theoretically compulsory between 7 and 14.

The most obdurate of Bolivian problems has always been that the main mass of population is, from a strictly economic viewpoint, in the wrong place, the poor Altiplano and not the potentially rich Oriente; and that the Indians live largely outside the monetary system on a self-sufficient basis. Since the land reform of 1952 isolated communities continue the old life but in the agricultural area around Lake Titicaca, the valleys of Cochabamba, the Yungas and the irrigated areas of the south, most peasants now own their land, however small the plot may be. Migration to the warmer and more fertile lands of the east region has been officially encouraged. At the same time roads are now integrating the food-producing eastern zones, with the bulk of the population living in the towns of the Altiplano or the west-facing slopes of the Eastern Cordillera.

The **highland Indians** are composed of two groups: those in La Paz and in the north of the Altiplano who speak the guttural Aymara (an estimated one million), and those elsewhere, who speak Quechua, the Inca tongue (three million – this includes the Indians in the northern Apolobamba region). Outside the big cities many of them speak no Spanish. In the lowlands are some 150,000 people in 30 groups, including the Ayoreo, Chiquitano, Chiriguano, Garavo, Chimane and Mojo. The **lowland Indians** are, in the main, Guaraní. About 70% of Bolivians are Aymara, Quechua or Tupi-Guaraní speakers. The first two are regarded as national languages, but were not, until very recently, taught in schools, a source of some resentment.

The Indian women retain their traditional costume, with bright petticoats (*polleras*), and in the highlands around La Paz wear, apparently from birth, a brown or grey bowler (locally called a *bombín*). Indians traditionally chew the coca leaf, which deadens hunger pains and gives a measure of oblivion. Efforts to control the cultivation of coca is one of many sources of friction between the indigenous population and the authorities; others include landlessness, and exploitation of labour. On feast days they drink with considerable application, wear the most sensational masks and dance till they drop.

Brazil

At first the Portuguese colony grew slowly. From 1580 to 1640 the population was only about 50,000 apart from the million or so indigenous Indians. In 1700 there were some 750,000 non-indigenous people in Brazil. Early in the 19th century Humboldt computed there were about 920,000 whites, 1,960,000 Africans, and 1,120,000 Indians and *mestiços*: after three centuries of occupation a total of only four million, and over twice as many Africans as there were whites.

Modern immigration did not begin effectively until after 1850. Of the 4.6 million immigrants from Europe between 1884-1954, 32% were Italians, 30% Portuguese, 14% Spanish, 4% German. Since 1954 immigrants have averaged 50,000 a year. There are some one million Japanese-descended Brazilians; they grow a fifth of the coffee, 30% of the cotton, all the tea, and are very active in market gardening. The total population according to the 2000 census was 169,799,170 (all population figures in the text are taken from the 2000 census); the UN gave the total population in 2004 as 181.6 million. Population growth 2000-2005 was 1.39%; urban population 84%; infant mortality rate 27 per 1,000 live births; GDP per capita US$2,700 (2003).

Today the whites and near-whites are about 54% of the population, people of mixed race about 40%, and Afro Brazilians 5%; the rest are Asians. There are large regional variations in the distribution of the races: the whites predominate in the south, which received the largest flood of European immigrants, and decrease more or less progressively towards the north.

Most of the German immigrants settled in the three southern states: Santa Catarina, Rio Grande do Sul, and Paraná. The Germans (and the Italians and Poles and other Slavs who followed them) did not in the main go as wage earners on the big estates, but as cultivators of their own small farms.

The arid wastes of the Sertão remain largely uncultivated. Its inhabitants are people of mixed Portuguese and Indian origin (*mestiço*); most live off the 'slash and burn' method of cultivation, which involves cutting down and burning the brushwood for a small patch of ground which is cultivated for a few years and then allowed to grow back.

Brazilian culture is rich in African influences. Those interested in the development of Afro-Brazilian music, dance, religion, arts and cuisine will find the whole country north of São Paulo fascinating, and especially the cities of Bahia and São Luís which retain the greatest African influences. Though there is no legal discrimination against black people, the economic and educational disparity – by default rather than intent of the Government – is such that successful Afro Brazilians are active almost exclusively in the worlds of sport, entertainment and arts. Black Pride movements are particularly strong in Bahia.

Rural and urban population The population has historically been heavily concentrated along the coastal strip where the original Portuguese settlers exploited the agricultural wealth, and further inland in the states of Minas Gerais and São Paulo where more recent development has followed the original search for gold, precious stones and slaves. Much of the interior of Pará, Amazonas, Goiás and the Mato Grosso has densities of one person per sq km or less. Internal migration has brought to the cities problems of unemployment, housing shortage, and extreme pressure on services; shanty towns – or *favelas*, *mocambos*, *alagados*, according to the region – are an integral part of the urban landscape. But while the northeast, because of its poverty, has lost many workers to the industries of the southeast, many rural workers from southern Brazil have moved north, drawn by the rapid development of Amazônia, creating unprecedented pressures on the environment.

Indigenous peoples It is estimated that, when the Portuguese arrived in Brazil, there were between three and five million Indians living in the area. Today there are only about 350,000. Tribal groups number 210; each has a unique dialect, but most languages belong to four main linguistic families, Tupi-Guarani, Ge, Carib and Arawak. A few tribes remain uncontacted, others are exclusively nomadic, others are semi-nomadic hunter-gatherers and farmers, while some are settled groups in close contact with non-Indian society. The struggle of groups such as the Yanomami to have their land demarcated in order to secure title is well-documented. The goal of the Statute of the Indian (Law 6.001/73), for demarcation of all Indian land by 1978, is largely unmet. It was feared that a new law introduced in January 1996 would slow the process even more. Funai, the National Foundation for the Support of the Indian, a part of the Interior Ministry, is charged with representing the Indians' interests, but lacks resources and support. There is no nationwide, representative body for indigenous people. Most of Brazil's indigenous people live in the Amazon region; they are affected by deforestation, encroachment from colonizers, small- and large-scale mining, and the construction of hydroelectric dams. Besides the Yanomami, other groups include the Xavante, Tukano, Kreen-Akrore, Kaiapó, Arawete and Arara.

Chile → *Population of Chile in 2004 was 16.1 million. Population growth 2000-2005 was 1.12%; urban population 87%; infant mortality rate 8 per 1,000 live births; GDP per capita US$4,523 (2003).*

There is less racial diversity in Chile than in most Latin American countries. Over 90% of the population is *mestizo*. There has been much less immigration than in Argentina and Brazil. The German, French, Spanish, Italian and Swiss immigrants came mostly after 1846 as small farmers in the forest zone south of the Biobío. Between 1880 and 1900 gold-seeking Serbs and Croats settled in the far south, and the British took up sheep farming and commerce in the same region. The influence throughout Chile of the immigrants is out of proportion to their numbers: their signature on the land is seen, for instance, in the German appearance of Valdivia, Puerto Montt, Puerto Varas, Frutillar and Osorno.

The population is far from evenly distributed: Middle Chile (from Copiapó to Concepción), 18% of the country's area, contains 77% of the total population. The Metropolitan Region of Santiago contains, about 39% of the whole population. The rate of population growth per annum, at 1.5% (1993-98), is slightly under the average for Latin America. Many Chileans live in slum areas called *callampas* (mushrooms), or *tomas* on the outskirts of Santiago and around the factories. It is estimated that 22% of the population lives in acute poverty. Unemployment in 2002 was 8.8%.

There is disagreement over the number of **indigenous people** in Chile. The Mapuche nation, 95% of whom live in forest land around Temuco, between the Biobío and Toltén rivers, is put at one million by Survival International, but much less by others, including official, statistics. There are also 15,000-20,000 Aymara in the northern Chilean Andes and 2,000 Rapa Nui on Easter Island. A political party, the Party for Land and Identity, unites many Indian groupings, and legislation is proposed to restore indigenous people's rights.

Colombia → *Population in 2004 was 45.3 million. Population growth 2000-2005 was 1.59%; urban population 77%; infant mortality rate 26 per 1,000 live births; GDP per capita US$1,744 (2003).*

The regions vary in their racial make-up: Antioquia and Caldas are largely of European descent, Pasto is Indian, the Cauca Valley and the rural area near the Caribbean are African or *mulato*. However, continual population migrations are evening out the differences. The birth and death rates vary greatly from one area to the other, but in general infant mortality is high. Hospitals and clinics are few in relation to the population. About 66% of the doctors are in the departmental capitals, which contain about half of the population, though all doctors have to spend a year in the country before they can get their final diploma. Education is free, and since 1927 theoretically compulsory, but many children, especially in rural areas, do not attend. There are high standards of secondary and university education, when it is available.

An estimated 400,000 **tribal peoples**, from 60 ethnic groups, live in Colombia. Groups include the Wayuú (in the Guajira), the Kogi and Arhauco (Sierra Nevada de Santa Marta), Amazonian indians such as the Witoto, the nomadic Nukak and the Ticuna, Andean indians and groups of the Llanos and in the Pacific Coast rain forest. The diversity and importance of indigenous peoples was recognized in the 1991 constitutional reforms when indians were granted the right to two senate seats; the National Colombian Indian Organization (ONIC) won a third seat in the October 1991 ballot. State recognition and the right to bilingual education has not, however, solved major problems of land rights, training and education, and justice.

Ecuador → *Population in 2004 was 13.0 million. Population growth 2000-2005 was 1.45%; urban population 62%; infant mortality rate 25 per 1,000 live births; GDP per capita US$2,108 (2003).*

Roughly 50% of Ecuador's people live in the coastal region west of the Andes, 45% in the Andean Sierra and 5% in Oriente. Migration is occurring from the rural zones of both the coast and the highlands to the towns and cities, particularly Guayaquil and Quito, and agricultural colonization from other parts of the country is taking place in the Oriente. There has also been an important flux of mostly illegal migrants out of Ecuador, seeking opportunities in the USA and Spain; 380,000 people (3% of the population) left between 1995 and 2001. Ecuador's national average population density is the highest in South America. Average *per capita* income rose rapidly in the 1970s and 80s, like other oil-exporting countries, but the distribution has become increasingly skewed. A few Ecuadoreans are spectacularly wealthy, while more than 70% of the population lives in poverty. Dollarization, at turn of the millennium, accentuated this imbalance.

There are 2-3 million Quichua-speaking **highland Indians** and about 70,000 **lowland Indians**. The following indigenous groups maintain their distinct cultural identity: in the Oriente, Siona, Secoya, Cofán, Huaorani, Zápara, Quichua, Shiwiar, Achuar and Shuar; in the Sierra,

Otavalo, Salasaca, Puruhá, Cañari and Saraguro; on the coast, Chachi (Cayapa), Tsáchila (Colorado), Awa (Cuaiquer) and Epera. Many Amazonian Indian communities are fighting for land rights in the face of oil exploration and colonization.

Paraguay → *Population in 2004 was 5.2 million. Population growth 2000-2005 was 2.37%; urban population 58%; infant mortality rate 37 per 1,000 live births; GDP per capita US$1,001 (2003).*
Since Spanish influence was less than in many other parts of South America, most people are bilingual, speaking both Spanish and Guaraní. Outside Asunción, most people speak Guaraní by preference. There is a Guaraní theatre, it is taught in private schools, and books and periodicals are published in that tongue, which has official status as the second national language. According to official figures, the **indigenous population** is about 39,000; non-government sources put it as high as 99,000 (see *Return of the Indian* by Phillip Wearne, London 1996, page 212). Two-thirds of them are in the Chaco, and one-third in the rest of the country. There are 17 distinct ethnic groups with five different languages, among which Guaraní predominates. The 1981 Law of Native Communities in theory guarantees Indian rights to ownership of their traditional lands and the maintenance of their culture. Contact Tierra Viva, Casilla de Correo 789, Asunción, T/F595-2185209.

Peru → *Population in 2004 was 27.6 million. Population growth 2000-2005 was 1.50%; urban population 74%; infant mortality rate 33 per 1,000 live births; GDP per capita US$2,238 (2003).*
Peruvian society is a mixture of native Andean peoples, Afro-Peruvians, Spanish, immigrant Chinese, Japanese, Italians, Germans and, to a lesser extent, indigenous Amazon tribes. The first immigrants were the Spaniards who followed Pizarro's expeditional force. Their effect, demographically, politically and culturally, has been enormous. Peru's black community is based on the coast, mainly in Chincha, south of Lima, and also in some working-class districts of the capital. Their forefathers were originally imported into Peru in the 16th century as slaves to work on the sugar and cotton plantations on the coast. Large numbers of poor Chinese labourers were brought to Peru in the mid-19th century to work in virtual slavery on the guano reserves on the Pacific coast and to build the railroads in the central Andes. The Japanese community, now numbering some 100,000, established itself in the first half of the 20th century. Like most of Latin America, Peru received many emigrés from Europe seeking land and opportunities in the late 19th century. The country's wealth and political power remains concentrated in the hands of this small and exclusive class of whites, which also consists of the descendants of the first Spanish families.

The **indigenous population** is put at about three million Quechua and Aymara Indians in the Andean region and 200,000-250,000 Amazonian Indians from 40-50 ethnic groups. In the Andes, there are 5,000 Indian communities but few densely populated settlements. Their literacy rate is the lowest of any comparable group in South America and their diet is 50% below acceptable levels. About two million Indians speak no Spanish, their main tongue being Quechua, the language of the Incas; they are largely outside the money economy. The conflict between Sendero Luminoso guerrillas and the security forces caused the death of thousands of highland Indians. Many Indian groups are under threat from colonization, development and road- building projects. Some have been dispossessed and exploited for their labour.

Uruguay → *Population in 2004 was 3.3 million. Population growth 2000-2005 was 0.72%; urban population 93%; infant mortality rate 13 per 1,000 live births; GDP per capita US$3,274 (2003).*
Uruguayans are virtually all European, mostly of Spanish and Italian stock. A small percentage in parts of Montevideo and near the Brazilian border are of mixed African and European descent. Less than 10% are mestizos. There was little Spanish settlement in the early years and, for a long time, the area was inhabited mainly by groups of nomadic *gauchos* who trailed after the herds of cattle killing them for food and selling their hides only. Organized commerce began with the arrival of cattle buyers from Buenos Aires who found it profitable to hire herdsmen to look after cattle in defined areas around their headquarters. By about 1800 most of the land had been parcelled out into large *estancias*. The only commercial farming was around Montevideo, where small *chacras* grew vegetables, wheat and maize for the near-by town. Only after 1828 did immigration begin on any scale. Montevideo was then a small town of 20,000 inhabitants. Between 1836 and 1926 about 648,000 immigrants arrived in Uruguay, mostly from Italy and Spain, some into the towns, some to grow crops and vegetables round Montevideo. The native Uruguayans remained pastoralists, leaving

commercial farming to the immigrants. More recent immigrants, however, Jewish, Armenian, Lebanese and others have chosen to enter the retail trades, textiles and leather production rather than farming.

Venezuela → *Population was 25.7 million in 2004. Population growth 2000-2005 was 1.82%; urban population 88%; infant mortality rate 18 per 1,000 live births; GDP per capita US$2,994 (2003).*
A large number are of mixed Spanish and Indian origin. There are some pure Africans and a strong element of African descent along the coast, particularly at the ports. The arrival of 800,000 European immigrants, mostly in the 1950s, has greatly modified the racial make-up in Venezuela. One in six of all Venezuelans is foreign born. Venezuela, despite its wealth, still faces serious social problems. Many rural dwellers have drifted to the cities; one result of this exodus is that Venezuelan farmers do not provide all the food the nation needs and imports of foodstuffs are necessary, even for items such as beans and rice. A very small proportion of the population (150,000) is **Indian**. Among the best-known are the Yanomami, who live in Amazonas, and the Bari in the Sierra de Perijá (on the northwest border with Colombia). An Indian Reserve gives the Bari effective control of their own land, but this has not prevented infringement from mining, plantation or settlers. Other groups do not have title to their territory. These groups include the Wayuu (in the Guajira), the Panare and the Piaroa.

Guyana → *According to the UN, total population in 2004 was 746,000. Population growth 2000-2005 was 0.20%; urban population 38%; infant mortality rate 49 per 1,000 live births; GDP per capita US$1,010 (2003).*
Until the 1920s there was little natural increase in population, but the eradication of malaria and other diseases has since led to rapid expansion, particularly among the East Indians (Asian), who, according to most estimates comprise about 50% of the population. The 1992 census showed the following ethnic distribution: East Indian 48.3%; black 32.7%; mixed 12.2%; Amerindian 6.3%; white 0.3%; Chinese 0.2%; other 0.02%. Descendants of the original **Amerindian inhabitants** are divided into nine ethnic groups, including the Akawaio, Makuxi and Pemon. Some have lost their isolation and moved to the urban areas, others keenly maintain aspects of their traditional culture and identity.

Suriname → *According to the UN, total population in 2004 was 487,000. Population growth 2000-2005 was 0.69%; urban population 77%; infant mortality rate 26 per 1,000 live births; GDP per capita US$2,240 (2003).*
The estimated composition of the population is: **Indo-Pakistanis** (known locally as Hindustanis), 37%; **Creoles** (European-African and other descent), 31%; **Javanese**, 15%; **Bush Negroes**, called 'Maroons' locally (retribalized descendants of slaves who escaped in the 17th century, living on the upper Saramacca, Suriname and Marowijne rivers), 10%; **Europeans, Chinese** and others, 3%; **Amerindians**, 3% (some sources say only 1%). About 90% of the existing population live in or around Paramaribo or in the coastal towns; the remainder, mostly Carib and Arawak Indians and Maroons, are widely scattered.The Asian people originally entered the country as contracted estate labourers, and settled in agriculture or commerce after completion of their term. They dominate the countryside, whereas Paramaribo is racially very mixed. Although some degree of racial tension exists between all the different groups, Creole-Hindustani rivalry is not as fundamental an issue as in Guyana, for example. Many Surinamese, of all backgrounds, pride themselves on their ability to get along with one another in such a heterogeneous country.

Guyane → *According to the UN, totoal population in 2004 was 187,226. Population growth 2000-2005 was 2.59%; urban population 75%; infant mortality rate 14 per 1,000 live births; GDP per capita US$9,705 (2003).*
There are widely divergent estimates for the ethnic composition of the population. Calculations vary according to the number included of illegal immigrants, attracted by social benefits and the high living standards. By some measures, over 40% of the population are Créoles, with correspondingly low figures for Europeans, Asians and Brazilians (around 17% in total). Other estimates put the Créole proportion at 36%, with Haitians 26%, Europeans 10% (of whom about 95% are from France), Brazilians 8%, Asians 4.7% (3.2% from Hong Kong, 1.5% from Laos), about 4% from Suriname and 2.5% from Guyana. The **Amerindian population** is put at 3.6% (over 4% by some estimates). The main groups are Galibis (1,700), Arawak (400), Wayanas (600), Palikours (500), Wayampis-Oyampis (600) and Emerillons (300). There are also bush negroes (Bonis, Saramacas, Djukas), who live mostly in the Maroni area, and others (Dominicans, St Lucians, etc) at 0.7%.

Music and dance

Argentina

Buenos Aires contains almost half of the country's population and its music is the **Tango**. Although also sung and played, the Tango was born as a dance just before the turn of the 20th century. The exact moment of the birth was not recorded by any contemporary observer and continues to be a matter of debate, though the roots can be traced. The name 'Tango' predates the dance and was given to the carnivals (and dances) of the black inhabitants of the Río de la Plata in the early 19th century. Elements of the black tradition were taken over by whites, as the black population declined into insignificance. However, the name 'Tango Americano' was also given to the Habanera (a Cuban descendant of the English Country Dance) which became the rage in Spain and bounced back into the Río de la Plata in the middle of the 19th century, not only as a fashionable dance, together with the polka, mazurka, waltz and cuadrille, but also as a song form in the very popular 'Zarzuelas', or Spanish operettas. However, the Habanera led not a double, but a triple life, by also infiltrating the lowest levels of society directly from Cuba via sailors who arrived in the ports of Montevideo and Buenos Aires. Here it encountered the Milonga, originally a Gaucho song style, but by 1880 a dance, especially popular with the so-called 'Compadritos' and 'Orilleros', who frequented the port area and its brothels, whence the Argentine Tango emerged around the turn of the century to dazzle the populace with its brilliant, personalized footwork, which could not be accomplished without the partners staying glued together. As a dance it became the rage and, as the infant recording industry grew by leaps and bounds, it also became popular as a song and an instrumental genre, with the original violins and flutes being eclipsed by the bandoneón button accordion, then being imported from Germany. In 1911 the new dance took Paris by storm and returned triumphant to Buenos Aires. It achieved both respectability and notoriety, becoming a global phenomenon after the First World War. The golden voice of the renowned Carlos Gardel soon gave a wholly new dimension to the music of the Tango until his death in 1935. After losing some popularity in Argentina, it came to the forefront again in the 1940s (1920-1950 is considered the real golden age). Its resurgence was assisted by Perón's decree that 50% of all music played on the radio must be Argentine, only to suffer a second, much more serious decline in the face of rock music over the past two decades. Fortunately, it has experienced another revival in recent years and the Tango and Milonga can once again be seen being danced in Buenos Aires. Apart from Carlos Gardel, other great names connected with the Tango are Francisco Canaro (Uruguayan), Osvaldo Pugliese and Astor Piazzolla, who has modernized it by fusion with jazz styles (nuevo tango).

If the Tango represents the soul of Buenos Aires, this is not the case in the rest of the country. The provinces have a very rich and attractive heritage of folk dances, mainly for couples, with arms held out and fingers clicked or handkerchiefs waved, with the 'Paso Valseado' as the basic step. Descended from the Zamacueca, and therefore a cousin of the Chilean Cueca and Peruvian Marinera, is the slow and stately Zamba, where the handkerchief is used to greatest effect. Equally popular throughout most of the country are the faster Gato, Chacarera and Escondido. These were the dances of the Gaucho and their rhythm evokes that of a cantering horse. Guitar and the bombo drum provide the accompaniment. Particularly spectacular is the Malambo, where the Gaucho shows off his dextrous footwork, the spurs of his boots adding a steely note to the rhythm.

Different regions of the country have their own specialities. The music of Cuyo in the west is sentimental and similar to that of neighbouring Chile, with its Cuecas for dance and Tonadas for song. The northwest on the other hand is Andean, with its musical culture closer to that of Bolivia, particularly on the Puna, where the Indians play the quena and charango and sound mournful notes on the great long erke. Here the dances are Bailecitos and Carnavalitos, while the songs are Vidalitas and the extraordinary high pitched Bagualas, the very essence of primeval pain. In the northeast provinces of Corrientes and Misiones, the music shares similarities with Paraguay. The Polca and Galopa are danced and the local Chamamé is sung, to the accordion or the harp, the style being sentimental. Santiago del Estero is the heartland of the Chacarera and the lyrics are often part Spanish and part Quichua, a local dialect of the Andean Quechua language. In the Province of Buenos Aires you are more likely to hear the Gauchos singing their Milongas, Estilos and Cifras and challenging each other to a Payada or rhymed duel. Argentina experienced a folk revival in the 50's and 60's and some of the most celebrated groups are still drawing enthusiastic audiences today. These groups include Los Chalchaleros and Los Fronterizos, the perennial virtuoso singer and guitarist, Eduardo Falú and, more recently, León Gieco from Santa Fe.

Bolivia

The heart of Bolivia is the Altiplano and it is the music of the Quechua and Aymara-speaking Indians of this area that provides the most distinctive Bolivian musical sound. Although there is much that is of Spanish colonial origin in the Indians' dances, the music itself has more Amerindian style and content than that of any other country in South America. It is rare to find an Indian who cannot play an instrument and it is these instruments, both wind and percussion, that are quintessentially Bolivian. The clear sounds of the quena and pinkullo, the deeper, breathier notes of the tarka, pututo and sicuri accompanied by huankaré, pululu and caja drums can be heard all over the Altiplano, the charango (a small, G-stringed guitar) being virtually the only instrument of European origin. The Indian dances are mainly collective and take place at religious fiestas. The dancers wear colourful costumes with elaborate, plumed headdresses and some of them still parody their ex-Spanish colonial masters.

The principal popular dances that can be regarded as 'national' in their countrywide appeal are the Cueca and Huayño. The Bolivian Cueca is a close relative of the Chilean national dance of the same name and they share a mutual origin in the Zamacueca, itself derived from the Spanish Fandango. The Huayño is of Indian origin and involves numerous couples, who whirl around or advance down the street, arm-in-arm, in a 'Pandilla'. Justly celebrated is the great carnival Diablada of Oruro, with its hordes of grotesquely masked devils, a spectacle comparable to those of Rio in Brazil and Barranquilla in Colombia. The region of Tarija near the Argentine border has a distinctive musical tradition of its own, based on religious processions that culminate with that of San Roque on the first Sunday in September. There are many professional folk groups on record, the best known being *Grupo Aymara, Los Runas, Los Laris, Los Masis, Kolla Marka* and *Bolivia Manta*, some of which have now established themselves in Europe and North America.

Brazil

Perhaps because of its sheer size, Brazil has a greater musical inventory than any other Latin American country, not only reflected in the immense regional spread of folk music but also in its successive waves of urban popular music. The Brazilian expresses themselves through music and dance to an extraordinary degree and the music covers the whole spectrum from the utmost rural simplicity to the ultimate state-of-the-art commercial sophistication.

The South In Paraná, Santa Catarina and Rio Grande do Sul, the music is strictly European in origin, rhythm and instrumentation. Rio Grande do Sul shares Gaucho dances such as the Pericom and song styles such as the Milonga, Trova and Pajada with neighbouring Uruguay and Argentina. The Chula is a competitive dance for men to show off (comparable to the Argentine Malambo), while the Pexinho is for men and women. The guitar and the accordion are favourite instruments, also true for Santa Catarina and Paraná, where the names of the dances denote their European origins: Mazurkas, Valsas, Chotes, Polquinhas and Rancheiras. The Chimarrita is a song style that came straight from the Azores. If you are feeling sentimental, you sing a Toada, if energetic, you stamp your feet to a Fandango. Except for the Batuque de Rio Grande do Sul in Porto Alegre, closely related to the Candombe of nearby Montevideo, there is no African influence in the music of this region and none of that classic Brazilian syncopation.

São Paulo, Rio de Janeiro, Minas Gerais Moving north into São Paulo, we enter an area rich in traditional folk dances and music, with the African admixture beginning to show up. At many religious festivals will be found the Congadas (European 'Moors and Christians', but danced by blacks) and Moçambique (a stick dance for men), while the Samba de Lenço, Fandango and Batuque are recreational dances for one or more couples. The instrumental accompaniment branches out into shakers (the ganzá), drums (caixas and tambores) and above all the guitar (viola). Try the great pilgrimage church at Aparecida do Norte on a Sunday. You might well see a group of religious dances. In the hinterland of Rio de Janeiro the Folias de Reis are out on the street from Christmas to Epiphany, singing from house to house, accompanying themselves on the caixa and adufe drums and the guitar, while in the old colonial towns of Paraty and Angra dos Reis are to be found the **Dança de Velhos** (the old men), performed to the accordion. The Jongo is a dance of African origin for men and women, naturally with a drum accompaniment. And there is hardly need to mention Rio at carnival and its Samba Schools. Further north again, we come to the states of Espíritu Santo, Minas Gerais and Goiás. In colonial Ouro Preto, in Minas, you can hear the old Modinha sung to the Portuguese guitar as a serenade and be transported into the past. Espíritu Santo is home to the Ticumbi, a kind of Congada, danced to the guitar and shakers (*chocalhos*). Goiás shares with Minas Gerais a very rich heritage of Portuguese derived religious folk song and dance, centred on Folias, Modas and Calangos.

Bahia Bahia is the heart of African Brazil and a very musical heart it is, born of the Yoruba religion that came with the slaves from what is now Nigeria. The resulting syncretic religion is known as Candomblé in Bahia and the gods or 'Orixás' are worshipped through song, dance and possession in the 'Terreiros', directed by the priests (Pais-de-Santo) and priestesses (Mães-de-Santo). The mainly female adepts, dressed entirely in white, circle gracefully to the background chant of 'Pontos' and the thunderous pounding of the atabaques, the tall drums. The two most revered priestesses are Mãe Olga de Alakêto and Mãe Menininha de Gantois. Similar syncretic African religions are found elsewhere in Brazil. Another vital African element in Bahian folk music is the spectacular dance-cum-martial arts form of Capoeira. Bodies whirl and cartwheel around to the sound of the berimbau (a one-stringed bow with resonator) and the accompanying chant. Related to the Capoeira is the stick dance Maculelê. Two of the best berimbau groups on record are *Camaféu de Oxóssi* and the *Cordão de Ouro*. Bahia has a carnival almost as celebrated as that of Rio and here you can see the Afoxé, a serious religious dance, performed to drums alone.

The North East North of Bahia is the Nordeste, with music that runs the whole gamut from black African to mediaeval Portuguese. In colonial times the church directed the peoples' musical energies into religious plays, songs and dances and a large number of these are still performed. The Bumba-Meu-Boi is a folk drama in the course of which a bull is killed and then brought back to life. Particularly popular in Piauí and Maranhão, its variants are found as far afield as Amazônia, where it is called the Boi-Bumbá, and Paraná in the far south, where it is known as Boi-Mamão. Also popular along the coast from Ceará to Paraíba is a nautical drama of Portuguese origin called Marujada or Nau Catarineta, a version of Moors and Christians, accompanied by Portuguese guitar (violão), drums and the ganzá scraper. In Alagoas, Sergipe and Pernambuco we find the sword dance called Reisado, danced after Christmas, the Caboclinhos, who are dressed like Indians and dance with bows and arrows, and the Guerreiros Alagoanos, a mixture of both. The last named are accompanied by the classical northeastern musical group called Terno de Pífanos, with the pífano vertical flute, accompanied by maracas and ganzá. The Banda de Pífanos of Caruaru in Pernambuco can be found on record. Recreational dance music in the Nordeste goes under the generic name of 'Forró', said to be derived from the expression 'For All', because the English companies operating at the turn of the century organized weekend dances for their workmen to which all comers were invited. Four very popular recreational folk dances of this region are the Ciranda (a round dance), the Coco, the Bate-Coxa (where the dancers bump bellies) and the Bambelô. Carnival in Recife, the largest city, is when and where to see the energetic and gymnastic Frevo, danced by young men with an umbrella in their hands, and the very stately and superbly costumed Maracatu dancers, with their queen and king. The Nordeste is equally rich in song styles, notably the Desafios, Emboladas, Cocos and Aboios. The Desafios are performed by so-called Repentistas or Violeiros, who accompany themselves on the Portuguese guitar and whose repertoire includes a large inventory of verse styles. They will sing about individual spectators, who then pay willingly for the compliment. The Emboladas and Cocos are similar, but faster and accompanied solely by tambourines, while the Aboios are songs related to cattle and cattlemen. Repentistas and Emboladores can be found at work in markets throughout the region. The premier Repentista is Otacílio Batista do Pajeú, who sang to the Pope during the latter's visit to Brazil. The music of the Nordeste has also been well propagated by more sophisticated groups that have based themselves on folk roots, such as the Quinteto Violado, Ariano Suassuna's Orchestra Armorial and Cussy de Almeida's Quinteto Armorial, not forgetting the veteran accordionist Luiz Gonzaga and Alceu Valença. As a result of the huge migration of nordestinos to the urban south, moreover, it is just as easy to hear this regional music in São Paulo as it is in Recife.

Pará and the Amazon Finally to Pará and the Amazon in the far north, where the music has been heavily influenced from the Caribbean. The most popular musical genre here is the Carimbó, danced to a Merengue-type rhythm and played on drums, wind or brass (usually the clarinet) and strings, particularly the banjo. Notable performers are Pinduca ('O Rei do Carimbó'), Veriquete and Vieira. It is the latter who thought up the term 'Lambada' for his particular version of the Carimbó, and the spectacular, thigh-entwining dance form introduced to the world in Paris by Karakos and Lorsac in 1988 had already been popular among young people at 'Forrós' throughout the region for some years. The very traditional island of Marajó in the mouth of the Amazon has preserved versions of 18th century dances, such as the Lundú and Chula.

Urban popular music The vast range of Brazilian regional folk music is only equalled by the chronological depth of its urban popular music, which surges like endless waves on a beach. For the origins we have to go back to Jesuit missions and Portuguese folk music, influenced and blended by African slaves, from which emerged the 19th century Lundús, Polcas and Maxixes that in turn gave way to the romantic and sentimental Choro song genre (from chorar, to weep), accompanied by guitar, flute and cavaquinho (small guitar), which became all the rage and indeed still has its adepts in Brazil today. A key figure in urban music was Ernesto Nazaré, composer and pianist, who occupied a special niche somewhere between popular and light classical, composing between 1880 and 1930 a vast number of Tangos Brasileiros (not to be confused with the Argentine variety), Mazurkas, Polcas, Waltzes and other popular songs.

Around the turn of the century the instrumentation turned to brass and Rio's urban Samba was born, a birth that was announced by the recording in 1917 of Donga's 'Pelo Telefone'. Names from this early period are Pixinguinha, Sinhô, Heitor dos Prazeres, Ary Barroso, Noel Rosa and of course Carmen Miranda, who took the Samba to Hollywood and the rest of the world. It also became intimately connected with the carnival in the form of Marcha Ranchos and Sambas de Enredo as the first samba schools were formed, of which Salgueiro, Mangueira, Partido Alto, Portela, Mocidade Independente and Beija-Flor are some of the most famous. With the Escolas de Samba came the Batucada or percussion groups playing the pandeiro (tambourine), atabaque and tamborim (drum), agogô (cowbell), reco-reco, chocalho, afoxê and cuíca. This is the real engine room of Samba. Listen to Lúcio Perrone or Mocidade Independente de Padre Miguel. A new phase was ushered in with an invasion from Bahia and the Nordeste in the early 1950s. From Bahia came Dorival Caymmi, who dropped his fishermen's songs in favour of the Samba, and Luiz Gonzaga, who brought his accordion, zabumba drum and triangulo, with which to play his Baiãos (his 'Asa Branca' is a classic) and almost put the Samba itself into eclipse for several years. Almost, but not quite, for out of the ashes there soon arose Bossa Nova – white, middle class and silky smooth. Vinícius de Moraes and Tom Jobim were its heroes; 1958 to 1964 the years; Copacabana, Ipanema and Leblon the scene; 'Samba de uma Nota Só', 'A Garota de Ipanema' and 'Desafinado' the songs and Nara Leão, Baden Powell, Toquinho, João Gilberto, Luis Bonfá and Astrud Gilberto the main performers. Stan Getz, the American jazz saxophonist, helped export it to the world. What was now being called MPB (Música Popular Brasileira) then took off in several directions. Chico Buarque, Edu Lobo and Milton Nascimento were protest singers. Out of Bahia emerged 'Tropicalismo' in the persons of Gilberto Gil, Caetano Veloso and his sister Maria Bethânia, Gal Costa, João Gilberto and 'Som Livre'. The words were important, but the rhythm was still there. Brazilian rock also now appeared, with such stars as Roberto Carlos, Elis Regina, Rita Lee, and Ney Mattogrosso. Heavy metal is a popular genre that continues to evolve as exemplified by the band *Sepultura*. Recently, in turning towards international black consciousness, the Bahianos have mixed Reggae and Samba to produce 'axê'. Still, Samba has survived, although now called 'Pagode' and amazingly, 40% of all Brazilian records sold are of Música Sertaneja, a highly commercialized pseudo-folk genre which is closer to American Country and Western than to most other Brazilian music. Listen to the 'Duplas' of Tonico and Tinoco, Jacó e Jacozinho, Vieira and Vieirinha, or Leonardo and Leandro (who died in 1998) and you'll see. In the meantime a series of brilliant Brazilian instrumentalists have become international names and often live abroad – Sérgio Mendes, the guitarist Sebastião Tapajós, flautist Hermêto Paschoal, saxophonist Paulo Moura, accordionist Sivuca, percussionists Airto Moreira and Nana Vasconcelos, singer Flora Purim and all-rounder Egberto Gismonti are but a few. On the top of a huge recording industry, we're now a long way from the grassroots and the haunting flute music of the forest Indians.

Chile

At the very heart of Chilean music is the **Cueca**, a courting dance for couples, both of whom make great play with a handkerchief waved aloft in the right hand. The man's knees are slightly bent and his body arches back. It is lively and vigorous, seen to best advantage when performed by a Huaso wearing spurs. Guitar and harp are the accompanying instruments, while handclapping and shouts of encouragement add to the atmosphere. The dance has a common origin with the Argentine Zamba and Peruvian Marinera via the early 19th century Zamacueca, in turn descended from the Spanish Fandango. For singing only is the Tonada, with its variants the Glosa, Parabienes, Romance, Villancico (Christmas carol) and Esquinazo (serenade) and the Canto a lo Poeta, which can be in the form of a Contrapunto or Controversia, a musical duel. Among the most celebrated groups are Los Huasos Quincheros, Silvia Infante with Los Condores and the Conjunto Millaray. Famous folk singers in this genre are the Parra Family from Chillán, Hector Pávez and Margot Loyola. In the north of the country the music is Amerindian and closely related to that of

Bolivia. Groups called 'Bailes' dance the Huayño, Taquirari, Cachimbo or Rueda at carnival and other festivities and precolumbian rites like the Cauzulor and Talatur. Instruments are largely wind and percussion, including zampoñas (pan pipes), lichiguayos, pututos (conch shells) and clarines. There are some notable religious festivals that attract large crowds of pilgrims and include numerous groups of costumed dancers. The most outstanding of these festivals are those of the Virgen de La Tirana near Iquique, San Pedro de Atacama, the Virgen de la Candelaria of Copiapó and the Virgen de Andacollo. In the south the Mapuche nation, the once greatly feared and admired 'Araucanos', who kept the Spaniards and Republicans at bay for 400 years, have their own songs, dance-songs and magic and collective dances, accompanied by wind instruments like the great long trutruca horn, the shorter pifilka and the kultrun drum. Further south still, the island of Chiloé, which remained in the hands of pro-Spanish loyalists after the rest of the country had become independent, has its own unique musical expression. Wakes and other religious social occasions include collective singing, while the recreational dances, all of Spanish origin, such as the Vals, Pavo, Pericona and Nave have a heavier and less syncopated beat than in central Chile. Accompanying instruments here are the rabel (fiddle), guitar and accordion.

Colombia

No South American country has a greater variety of music than Colombia, strategically placed where the Andes meet the Caribbean. The four major musical areas are (a) the mountain heartland (b) the Pacific coast (c) the Caribbean coast and (d) the Llanos or eastern plains. The mountain heartland covers the Andean highlands and intervening valleys of the Cauca and Magdalena and includes the country's three largest cities, Bogotá, Cali and Medellín. It is relatively gentle and sentimental music, accompanied largely by string instruments, with an occasional flute and a chucho or carángano shaker to lay down the rhythm. The preferred instrument of the highlands and by extension Colombia's national instrument, is the tiple, a small 12-stringed guitar, most of which are manufactured at Chiquinquirá in Boyacá. The national dance is the Bambuco, whose lilting sounds are said to have inspired Colombian troops at the Battle of Ayacucho in 1824. It is to be found throughout the countrys heartland for dancing, singing and instrumentalizing and has long transcended its folk origins. The choreography is complex, including many figures, such as la Invitación, Los Ochos, Los Codos, Los Coqueteos, La Perseguida and La Arrodilla. Other related dances are the Torbellino, where the woman whirls like a top, the more stately Guabina, the Pasillo, Bunde, Sanjuanero and the picaresque Rajaleña. Particularly celebrated melodies are the 'Guabina Chiquinquireña' and the 'Bunde Tolimense'. The following fiestas, among others, provide a good opportunity of seeing the music and dance: La Fiesta del Campesino, ubiquitous on the first Sunday in June, the Fiesta del Bambuco in Neiva and Festival Folklórico Colombiano in Ibagué later in the month, the Fiesta Nacional de la Guabina y el Tiple, held in Vélez in early August, the Desfile de Silleteros in Medellín in the same month and Las Fiestas de Pubenza in Popayán just after the New Year, where the Conjuntos de Chirimía process through the streets.

On Colombia's tropical Pacific coast (and extending down into Esmeraldas, Ecuador) is to be found some of the most African sounding black music in all South America. The Currulao and its variants, the Berejú and Patacoré, are extremely energetic recreational dances and the vocals are typically African-style call- and-response. This is the home of the marimba and the music is very percussion driven, including the upright cununo drum plus bombos and redoblantes. Wakes are important in this region and at these the Bundes, Arrullos and Alabaos are sung. Best known is the 'Bunde de San Antonio'. The Jota Chocoana is a fine example of a Spanish dance taken by black people and turned into a satirical weapon against their masters. The regional fiestas are the Festival Folklórico del Litoral at Buenaventura in July and San Francisco de Asís at Quibdó on 4 August. Quibdó also features a Fiesta de los Indios at Easter.

The music of Colombia's Caribbean coast became popular for dancing throughout Latin America more than 30 years ago under the name of 'Música Tropical' and has much more recently become an integral part of the Salsa repertory. It can be very roughly divided into 'Cumbia' and 'Vallenato'. The Cumbia is a heavily black influenced dance form for several couples, the men forming an outer circle and the women an inner one. The men hold aloft a bottle of rum and the women a bundle of slim candles called 'espermas'. The dance probably originated in what is now Panama, moved east into Cartagena, where it is now centred and quite recently further east to Barranquilla and Santa Marta. The most celebrated Cumbias are those of Ciénaga, Mompós, Sampués, San Jacinto and Sincelejo. The instrumental accompaniment consists of gaitas or flautas de caña de millo, backed by drums. The gaitas ('male' and 'female') are vertical cactus flutes with beeswax heads, while the cañas de millo are smaller transverse flutes. The most famous conjuntos are the Gaiteros de San Jacinto, the Cumbia Soledeña and the Indios Selectos. Variants of the Cumbia are the Porro, Gaita, Puya, Bullerengue and Mapalé, these last two being much faster and more energetic. Lately Cumbia has also become very much part of the Vallenato repertoire and is therefore often played on the accordion. Vallenato music comes from Valledupar in the Department of César and is of relatively recent origin. It is built around one instrument, the accordion, albeit backed by guacharaca rasps and caja drums. The most popular rhythms are the Paseo and the Merengue, the latter having arrived from the Dominican Republic, where it is the national dance. Perhaps the first virtuoso accordionist was the legendary 'Francisco El Hombre', playing around the turn of the century. Today's best known names are those of Rafael Escalona, Alejandro Durán and Calixto Ochoa. In April the Festival de la Leyenda Vallenata is held in Valledupar and attended by thousands. Barranquilla is the scene of South America's second most celebrated Carnival, after that of Rio de Janeiro, with innumerable traditional masked groups, such as the Congos, Toros, Diablos and Caimanes. The Garabato is a dance in which death is defeated. Barranquilla's carnival is less commercialized and more traditional than that of Rio and should be a must for anyone with the opportunity to attend. Other important festivals in the region are the Corralejas de Sincelejo with its bullfights in January, La Candelaria in Cartagena on 2 February, the Festival de la Cumbia in El Banco in June, Fiesta del Caiman in Ciénaga in January and Festival del Porro in San Pelayo (Córdoba). To complete the music of the Caribbean region, the Colombian islands of San Andrés and Providencia, off the coast of Nicaragua, have a fascinating mix of mainland Colombian and Jamaican island music, with the Calypso naturally a prominent feature.

The fourth musical region is that of the great eastern plains, the so-called Llanos Orientales between the Ríos Arauca and Guaviare, a region where there is really no musical frontier between the two republics of Colombia and Venezuela. Here the Joropo reigns supreme as a dance, with its close relatives the Galerón, the slower and more romantic Pasaje and the breathlessly fast Corrido and Zumba que Zumba. These are dances for couples, with a lot of heel tapping, the arms hanging down loosely to the sides. Arnulfo Briceño and Pentagrama Llanera are the big names and the harp is the only instrument that matters, although normally backed by cuatro, guitar, tiple and maracas. The place to see and hear it all is at the Festival Nacional del Joropo at Villavicencio in December.

Ecuador

Culturally, ethnically and geographically, Ecuador is very much two countries – the Andean highlands with their centre at Quito and the Pacific lowlands behind Guayaquil. In spite of this, the music is relatively homogeneous and it is the Andean music that would be regarded as 'typically Ecuadorean'. The principal highland rhythms are the Sanjuanito, Cachullapi, Albaza, Yumbo and Danzante, danced by Indian and mestizo alike. These may be played by brass bands, guitar trios or groups of wind instruments, but it is the rondador, a small panpipe, that provides the classic Ecuadorean sound, although of late the Peruvian quena has been making heavy inroads via pan-Andean groups and has become a threat to the local instrument. The coastal region has its own song form, the Amorfino, but the most genuinely 'national' song and dance genres, both of European origin, are the Pasillo (shared with Colombia) in waltz time and the Pasacalle, similar to the Spanish Pasodoble. Of Ecuador's three best loved songs, 'El Chulla Quiteño', 'Romántico Quito' and 'Vasija de Barro', the first two are both Pasacalles. Even the Ecuadorean mestizo music has a melancholy quality not found in Peruvian 'Música Criolla', perhaps due to Quito being in the mountains, while Lima is on the coast. Music of the highland Indian communities is, as elsewhere in the region, related to religious feasts and ceremonies and geared to wind instruments such as the rondador, the pinquillo and pifano flutes and the great long guarumo horn with its mournful note. The guitar is also usually present and brass bands with well worn instruments can be found in even the smallest villages. Among the most outstanding traditional fiestas are Inti Raymi in Cayambe and Ingapirca, the Pase del Niño in Cuenca and other cities, the Mama Negra of Latacunga, carnival in Guaranda, the Yamor in Otavalo, the Fiesta de las Frutas y las Flores in Ambato, plus Corpus Cristi and the Feast of Saint John all over the highlands. Among the best known musical groups who have recorded are Los Embajadores (whose 'Tormentos' is superb) and the Duo Benítez-Valencia for guitar. There is one totally different cultural area, that of the black inhabitants of the Province of Esmeraldas and the highland valley of the Río Chota in Imbabura. The former is a southern extension of the

Colombian Pacific coast negro culture, centred round the marimba xylophone. The musical genres are also shared with black Colombians, including the Bunde, Bambuco, Caderona, Torbellino and Currulao dances and this music is some of the most African sounding in the whole of South America. The Chota Valley is an inverted oasis of desert in the Andes and here the black people dance the Bomba. It is also home to the unique Bandas Mochas, whose primitive instruments include leaves that are doubled over and blown through.

Paraguay

The music of Paraguay is a curiosity. Although this is the only South American country, the majority of whose population still speak the original native tongue, the music is totally European in origin. The 17th- and 18th-century Jesuits found the Guaraní people to be highly musical and when their missions were established, the natives were immediately and totally indoctrinated into European music, of which they became fine performers, albeit not composers or innovators. A good example is Cristóbal Pirioby (1764-94), who changed his name to José Antonio Ortiz and moved to Buenos Aires to perform. At his death he left a large collection of musical instruments and sheet music of works by Haydn, Boccherini, etc. After the disastrous War of the Triple Alliance there was an abandonment of things national and even the national anthem was composed by a Uruguayan. Although black slaves were introduced to the country, they became quickly absorbed and there is no trace of black influence in the music. Neither is there any Guaraní element, nor infusion from Brazil or Argentina. Virtually the only popular instruments are the guitar and harp and it is the latter in particular that has come to be the hallmark of all that is musically Paraguayan, with the assistance of such brilliant performers as Félix Pérez Cardoso and Digno García. Paraguayan songs are notably languid and extremely sentimental and the present repertoire is not 'traditional', but of 20th century origin and by known composers. Of the three principal musical genres, two are slow and for singing, while one is lively and purely for dancing. The two singing genres are the Canción Paraguaya (or Purajhéi) and the Guarania, the former being a slow polka, of which the earliest and most famous example is 'Campamento Cerro León' about the War of the Triple Alliance. The Guarania was developed by José Asunción Flores as recently as the 1920s and includes most of the country's best loved and oft-repeated songs, such as 'India', 'Mi Dicha Lejana' and 'Recuerdos de Ypacaraí'. Equally celebrated and far more vigorous is that favourite of harp virtuosos, the wordless but onomatopeic 'Pájaro Campana'.

For dancing there are the lively Polca Paraguaya and Polca Galopada, first mentioned in print in 1858. They have similarities with the Argentine 'Gato' for instance and are not a true polka nor a gallop, the names of these popular European dances having been attached to an existing Paraguayan dance of unknown name. The Polca is a dance for couples, whilst the even livelier Galopa is usually danced by groups of women, the so-called 'Galoperas', who swing round barefoot, balancing a bottle or jar on their heads. This in turn has developed into the 'Danza de la Botella' or bottle dance, a more recent variant for virtuoso individual performance. Other less well known dances are the Valseadas (a local variant of the waltz), the Chopi or Santa Fé (for three couples), the Taguato, Golondrina, Palomita and Solito, the last named a kind of 'musical chairs'. Paraguayan music first came to global attention soon after the second world war and a number of artists such as Luis Alberto del Paraná and Los Paraguayos have achieved world fame. At the other end of the spectrum the four barefoot old men of the Banda Peteke Peteke from Guajayvity near Yaguarón play their own traditional music on two mimby flutes and two little drums, a small idiosyncratic island in an ocean of harp music.

Peru

Peru is the Andean heartland. Its musicians, together with those of Bolivia, have appeared on the streets of cities all over Europe and North America. However, the costumes they wear, the instruments they play, notably the quena and charango, are not typical of Peru as a whole, only of the Cusco region. Peruvian music divides at a very basic level into that of the highlands ('Andina') and that of the coast ('Criolla'). The highlands are immensely rich in terms of music and dance, with over 200 dances recorded. Every village has its fiestas and each fiesta has its communal and religious dances. Those of Paucartambo and Coylloriti (Q'olloriti) in the Cusco region moreover attract innumerable groups of dancers from far and wide. The highlands themselves can be very roughly subdivided into some half dozen major musical regions, of which perhaps the most characteristic are Ancash and the north, the Mantaro Valley, Cusco, Puno and the Altiplano, Ayacucho and Parinacochas.

66 99 Peru is the Andean heartland. Its musicians have appeared on the streets of cities all over Europe and North America.

There is one recreational dance and musical genre, the Huayno, that is found throughout the whole of the Sierra, and has become ever more popular and commercialized to the point where it is in danger of swamping and indeed replacing the other more regional dances. Nevertheless, still very popular among Indians and/or Mestizos are the Marinera, Carnaval, Pasacalle, Chuscada (from Ancash), Huaylas, Santiago and Chonguinada (all from the Mantaro) and Huayllacha (from Parinacochas). For singing only are the mestizo Muliza, popular in the Central Region, and the soulful lament of the Yaravi, originally Indian, but taken up and developed early in the 19th century by the poet and hero of independence Mariano Melgar, from Arequipa.

The Peruvian Altiplano shares a common musical culture with that of Bolivia and dances such as the Auqui-Auqui and Sicuris, or Diabladas, can be found on either side of the border. The highland instrumentation varies from region to region, although the harp and violin are ubiquitous. In the Mantaro area the harp is backed by brass and wind instruments, notably the clarinet, in Cusco it is the charango and quena and on the Altiplano the sicu panpipes. Two of the most spectacular dances to be seen are the Baile de las Tijeras ('scissor dance') from the Ayacucho/Huancavelica area, for men only and the pounding, stamping Huaylas for both sexes. Huaylas competitions are held annually in Lima and should not be missed. Indeed, owing to the overwhelming migration of peasants into the barrios of Lima, most types of Andean music and dance can be seen in the capital, notably on Sunday at the so-called 'Coliseos', which exist for that purpose. Were a Hall of Fame to be established, it would have to include the Ancashino singers La Pastorcita Huaracina and El Jilguero del Huascarán, the charango player Jaime Guardia, the guitar virtuoso Raul García from Ayacucho and the Lira Paucina trio from Parinacochas.

The flood of migration to the cities has meant that the distinct styles of regional and ethnic groups have become blurred. One example is Chicha, a hybrid of Huayno music and the Colombian Cumbia rhythm which comes from the pueblos jóvenes. More recent is Tecno-cumbia, which originated in the jungle region with groups such as Rossy War, from Puerto Maldonado, and Euforia, from Iquitos. It is a vibrant dance music which has gained much greater popularity across Peruvian society than chicha music ever managed.

The 'Música Criolla' from the coast could not be more different from that of the Sierra. Here the roots are Spanish and African. The popular Valsesito is a syncopated waltz that would certainly be looked at askance in Vienna; the Polca has also suffered an attractive sea change, but reigning over all is the Marinera, Peru's national dance, a rhythmic, graceful courting encounter, a close cousin of Chile's and Bolivia's Cueca and the Argentine Zamba, all of them descended from the Zamacueca. The Marinera has its 'Limeña' and 'Norteña' versions and a more syncopated relative, the Tondero, found in the north coastal regions, is said to have been influenced by slaves brought from Madagascar. All these dances are accompanied by guitars and frequently the *cajón*, a resonant wooden box on which the player sits, pounding it with his hands. Some of the great names of 'Música Criolla' are the singer/composers Chabuca Granda and Alicia Maguiña, the female singer Jesús Vásquez and the groups Los Morochucos and Hermanos Zañartu.

Also on the coast is to be found the music of the small black community, the 'Música Negroide' or 'Afro-Peruano', which had virtually died out when it was resuscitated in the 50s, but has since gone from strength to strength. It has all the qualities to be found in black music from the Caribbean – a powerful, charismatic beat, rhythmic and lively dancing, and strong percussion provided by the *cajón* and the *quijada de burro*, a donkey's jaw with the teeth loosened. Some of the classic dances in the black repertoire are the Festejo, Son del Diablo, Toro Mata, Landó and Alcatraz. In the Alcatraz one of the partners dances behind the other with a candle, trying to set light to a piece of paper tucked into the rear of the other partner's waist. Nicomedes and Victoria Santa Cruz have been largely responsible for popularizing this black music, and Peru Negro is another excellent professional group. The undoubted, internationally famous star, though, is Susana Baca. Finally, in the Peruvian Amazon region around Iquitos, local variants of the Huayno and Marinera are danced, as well as the Changanacui, accompanied by flute and drum.

1516

Uruguay

Most musical influences came with the European immigrants who arrived after the disappearance of the Amerindian population. The folk songs and dances are very closely related to those of the Argentine pampas, except in the north, where they are shared with the neighbouring Brazilian state of Rio Grande do Sul. The major song genres are the Estilo, Cifra, Milonga and Vidalita, whilst the 'national' dance is the stately Pericón for six or more couples. The Milonga is also danced, as are the Tango, Cielito, Media Caña and Ranchera. The guitar is the instrument that accompanies most country music and as in Argentina, the gauchos like to engage in Payadas de Contrapunto, where two singers vie with each other, alternating improvised verses. 19th century Europe introduced other popular dances into Uruguay, such as the polca, waltz, chotis and mazurca, all of which were given a local touch. In the northern departments a number of dances are shared with Brazil, such as the Chimarrita, Carangueijo and Tirana, which are also sung, either in Spanish or Portuguese or a mixture of both. There were many black slaves in the Río de la Plata during colonial times and the African ritual of the Candombe was practised in Montevideo until late in the 19th century. Less than 3% of the population is black and the only musical remains of African origin are to be found in the presence during carnival of the Morenada groups of up to 50 Candomberos, who take part in the procession, playing their tamboril drums, while smaller groups take part in these so-called 'Llamadas' from December through to Holy Week. There are four sizes of drums – chico, repique, piano and bajo – and the complex polyrhythms produced by the mass of drummers advancing down the street is both unexpected and impressive.

Venezuela

Venezuelan music is more homogenous than that of some of the other republics. Its highly distinctive sound is based on an instrumental combination of harp, cuatro (a small, four stringed guitar) and maracas. Many of the rhythms have a very fast, almost headlong pace to them, stimulating both to the senses and to the feet, music here being almost inseparable from dance. The recipe for Venezuelan music is a classic European/African/Amerindian mix. The country's national dance is the Joropo, a name deriving from the Arab 'Xarop', meaning syrup and which originally meant a country dance. This is a dance for couples with several sequences, such as the Valseao, Zapatiao, Escobillao and Toriao. Closely related to the Joropo are the Corrido, with a ballad content, Galerón (slow for singing or fast for dancing), Pasaje (lyrical, very popular in the Llanos) and Golpe, from the State of Lara, to all of which styles the Joropo may be danced in different parts of the country. Note that the little cuatro is normally referred to as 'guitarra' while the Spanish guitar is called the 'guitarra grande'. Some of the dance rhythms have been imported from abroad or are shared with neighbouring countries, such as the urban Merengue (introduced into Caracas in the 1920s), the Jota and Malagueña of Anzoátegui State, the Pasillo (shared with Colombia and Ecuador), the Polo of the Oriente and Isla Margarita and the Bambuco, found in Lara and Táchira states near the border with Colombia.

There is a wealth of dances and musical forms found in particular towns or states at religious festivities. Outstanding among these is the Tamunangue of Lara State, danced in the second fortnight of June to the accompaniment of drums and small guitars and made up of seven individual dances, varying from the 'Batalla', where men battle with sticks, to the 'Bella', a flirtatious dance for couples. Corpus Cristi is the time to visit San Francisco de Yare in Miranda State, 90 km from Caracas, and see the 80 or so male 'Diablos' of all ages, dressed entirely in red and wearing large horned masks, who dance in the streets to the sound of their own drums and rattles. The Bailes de Tambor take place among the largely black people of the Barlovento coast during the feasts of San Juan and San Pedro and at Christmas. This is brilliant polyrhythm on huge drums (cumacos, minas and curvetas) held between the legs. Also in Barlovento, but in May, can be heard the Fulias, chant-and-response songs addressed to a venerated saint or cross, to the accompaniment of cuatro, tambora drum and maracas. Christmas is a great period for music from the Gaitas of Zulia to the ubiquitous Aguinaldos, both in Merengue rhythm, with solo verses responded to by a chorus and varied instrumental accompaniment. Notable in the eastern states are the folk theatre dances of the Pájaro Guarandol (a hunter shoots a large bird that is brought back to life), Carite (from Margarita, using a large model fish), Chiriguare (a monster that is duly despatched) and Burriquita (a hobby horse). More surprising is to find the Calipso, played on steel bands by the black inhabitants of El Callao in the Orinoco region, whose ancestors came from Trinidad and who also perform the Limbo.

Venezuelans enjoy Salsa as much as other Hispanic peoples around the Caribbean, but they are also very keen on their own music, whether rustic 'folk' or urban 'popular'. The virtuoso harpist

Juan Vicente Torrealba has performed with his group Los Torrealberos for more than three decades, usually with Mario Suárez as vocal soloist. Another famous singer is Simón Díaz. Outstanding among the folk groups who strive for authenticity are Un Solo Pueblo, Grupo Vera and Grupo Convenezuela. Choral and contrapuntal singing of native music in a more sophisticated style has also been perfected by Quinteto Contrapunto and Serenata Guayanesa.

Books

Argentina
Reference/travel
Bigongiari, Diego (ed.) *Pirelli Guide*, including map for cultural, historical and nature information, highly recommended.

Hudson, W H *Far Away and Long Ago* and *Idle Days in Patagonia*, deal with this English writer's early life in the countryside.

Kirbus, Federico B *Guía de Aventuras y Turismo de la Argentina* (with comprehensive English index – 1989); and *La Argentina, país de maravillas*, Manrique Zago ediciones (1993), a beautiful book of photographs with text in Spanish and English; *Patagonia* (with **Jorge Schulte**) and *Ruta Cuarenta*, both fine photographic records with text (both Capuz Varela). Also by Kirbus, *Mágica Ruta 40* and *Quebrada de Humahuaca*; see www.magicaruta40.com.ar and www.kirbus.com.ar.

Lucas Bridges, E *Uttermost Part of the Earth*, about the early colonization of Tierra del Fuego.

Literature
Borges, Jorge Luis (1899-1986) Argentina's most famous writer, and at the forefront of avant-garde experimental and urban themes. He is best known for his teasing, revolutionary and poetic short stories, best seen in *Ficciones* (1944) and *El Aleph* (1949).

Cortázar, Julio (1914-1984) The leading Argentine representative of the 1960s 'boom'. His novel *Rayuela* (Hopscotch, 1963) typifies the experimentation, philosophy and freedom of the period.

Güiraldes, Ricardo (1886-1927) *Don Segundo Sombra*, a second great gaucho work (see Hernández below), further cementing the figure of the gaucho as national hero. **Hernández, José** *El gaucho Martín Fierro* (1872), an epic poem about the disruption of local communities by the march of progress; the eponymous hero and dispossessed outlaw came to symbolize Argentine nationhood.

Martínez, Tomás Eloy (1934-) Has written novels on two of Argentina's enduring 20th-century figures, *Santa Evita* (1995) and *La novela de Perón* (The Perón Novel, 1985), both highly acclaimed.

Portnoy, Alicia *The Little School*.

Puig, Manuel (1932-1990) A writer fascinated by mass culture, gender roles and the banal as art who expressed these ideas in novels such as *El beso de la Mujer Araña* (The Kiss of the Spider Woman, 1976 – made into a renowned film).

Sábato, Ernesto (1911-) Important Sixties writer whose most famous novel is *Sobre héroes y tumbas* (On Heroes and Tombs, 1961) and who also wrote the preface to *Nunca más* (Never again, 1984), the report of the commission into the disappearances in the 1970s 'dirty war'.

Soriano, Osvaldo (1943-1998) Another writer dealing with dictatorship and the 'dirty war' in *No habrá más penas ni olvido* (A Funny, Dirty Little War, 1982).

Valenzuela, Luisa (1938-) *Cola de lagartija* (The Lizard's Tail, 1983).

Bolivia
Reference
McFarren, Peter *An Insider's Guide to Bolivia* (Fundación Cultural Quipus, Casilla 1696, La Paz, 3rd edition, 1992).

Meadows, Anne *Digging up Butch and Sundance* (Bison Books, 1996), an account of the last days of Butch Cassidy and the Sundance Kid and the attempts to find their graves.

Trekking
Brain, Yossi *Bolivia – a climbing guide* (The Mountaineers, Seattle, 1999).

Brain, Yossi, North, Andrew and **Stoddart, Isobel** *Trekking in Bolivia* (The Mountaineers, Seattle, 1997).

Mesili, Alain *The Andes of Bolivia* (CIMA, La Paz, 2004, www.andes-mesili.com).

Murphy, Alan *Footprint Bolivia* (Footprint).

20th-century fiction and poetry
Arguedas, Alcides *Raza de Bronce* (1919); and **Mendoza, Jamie** *El las tierras de Potosí* (1911); both examine the life of the *campesino* in a society dominated by whites.

Céspedes, Augusto *Sangre de mestizos* (1936), a collection of short stories about the Chaco War.

Prado de Oropeza, Renato *Los fundadores del alba* (1969), inspired by Che Guevara's campaigns in the 1960s and *Antología del terror político* (1979), which deals with Bolivia under dictatorship.

Zamudio, Adela (1854-1928) Modernist poet.

Brazil

Reference/travel

Fawcett, Lt-Col P H *Exploration Fawcett*, arranged from his records by Brian Fawcett (Hutchinson, 1953).

Gott, Richard *Land without Evil. Utopian Journeys across the South American Watershed* (Verso, 1993).

Guillermoprieto, Alma *Samba* (Bloomsbury, 1991).

Plotkin, Mark J *Tales of a Shaman's Apprentice* (1993).

Robb, Peter *A Death in Brazil: A Book of Omissions* (Bloomsbury, 2004).

Waterton, Charles *Wanderings in South America*. Introduction by David Bellamy (Century, 1983).

The Amazon

Gheerbrant, Alain *The Amazon, Past and Present* (Thames & Hudson, 1992).

Goulding, Michael, **Smith, Nigel J H**, and **Mahar, Dennis J** *Floods of Fortune: Ecology & Economy of the Amazon* (Columbia University Press, 1996).

Hemming, John *Amazon Frontier. The Defeat of the Brazilian Indians* and *Red Gold. The Conquest of the Brazilian Indians* (Papermac 1987/1995 and 1995).

Brazilian literature

Abreu, Caio Fernando (1948-1996) One of the writers most effective in dealing with life in the Latin American megalopolis.

Amado, Jorge (1912-2002) Over a long career he published many bestsellers: he is sometimes criticized for producing an overly optimistic, sexily tropical view of the country.

Ângelo, Ivan (1936-) Has written much the best novel about the political, social and economic crisis at the end of the 1960s, the worst period of the military regime: *A festa* (1976) (The Celebration, Avon Books, 1992).

Bandeira, Manuel (1886-1968) A member of the Modernist movement and one of Brazil's greatest poets, master of the short, intense lyric. For a collection in English, see *This Earth, that Sky: Poems by Manuel Bandeira* (University of California Press, 1988).

de Andrade, Carlos Drummond (1902-1987) Perhaps Brazil's greatest poet, with a varied, lyrical, somewhat downbeat style. See, in English, *Travelling in the Family: Selected Poems* (Random House, 1986).

de Assis, Joaquim Maria Machado (1839- 1908) The classical satirical novelist of the Brazilian 19th century, one of the most original writers to have emerged from Latin America.

da Cunha, Euclides (1866-1909) *Os sertões* (1902) (Rebellion in the Backlands, University of Chicago Press, 1944, often reprinted, including Picador, 1995). The 'epic' story of the military campaign to crush the rebellion centred in Canudos in the interior of the State of Bahia. One of the great books about the Brazilian national make-up.

Lispector, Clarice (1920-1977) Brazil's greatest woman writer, now has a considerable following outside Brazil. Many of her stories and novels have been translated into English.

Ramos, Graciliano (1892-1953) The greatest of the novelists of the 1930s and 1940s.

Chile

Reference/travel

Green, Toby *Saddled with Darwin* (Phoenix, 2000).

Keenan, Brian and **McCarthy, John** *Between Extremes* (Transworld, 1999).

Swale, Rosie *Back to Cape Horn* (Fontana, 1988) desribes her epic horse ride through Chile.

Wheeler, Sara *Travels in a Thin Country* (Little, Brown and Co, 1994).

Poetry

Chile has produced some exceptional poets in the 20th century.

Huidobro, Vicente (1893-1948) Among many books, see *Altazor* (1931).

Mistral, Gabriela (1889-1957; Nobel Prize 1945) *Desolación* (1923). *Tala* (1938), *Lagar* (1954).

Neruda, Pablo (1904-1973; Nobel Prize 1971) Of Neruda's many collections, see *Veinte poemas de amor y una canción deseperada* (1924), *Tercer residencia* (1947), *Canto general* (1950) and his memoirs *Confieso que he vivido* (1974). See also **Feinstein, Adam**, *Pablo Neruda, a passion for life* (Bloomsbury, 2004).

Nicanor Parra (1914-) Brother of the famous singer and artist Violeta Parra *Poemas y antipoemas*, (1954).

20th-century prose

Allende, Isabel (born 1942) Novels such as *The House of the Spirits*, *Of Love and Shadows* and *Eva Luna* are world-famous.

Bolaño, Roberto *By Night in Chile* (Harvill, 2002).

Bombal, María Luisa (1910-80) *La última niebla* (1935).

Brunet, Marta (1901-1967) *Montaña adentro* 1923, *María Nadie* (1957).

Donoso, José (1924-1996) *El obsceno pájaro de la noche*.

Dorfman, Ariel (born 1942) *La muerte y la doncella* (Death and the Maiden), *La última canción de Manuel Sendero* (The Last Song of Manuel Sendero).

Eltit, Damiela (born 1949) *Vaca sagrada* (1991), *El cuarto mundo* (1988).

Skármeta, Antonio (born 1940) Best known for *Ardiente paciencia*, retitled *El cartero de Neruda* and filmed as *Il Postino* (The Postman).

Colombia
Reference
Hemming, John *The Search for Eldorado*.
Nicholl, Charles *The Fruit Palace*, an account of travelling in modern Colombia (specifically his adventures in the cocaine trade).
Smith, Stephen *Cocaine Train* (1999).
von Humboldt, Alexander *Travels* written after five years in South America (1799-1804).

Literature
García Márquez, Gabriel His novels and short stories have a reputation way beyond that of any other Colombian writer. *Cien años de* soledad (A Hundred Years of Solitude, 1967) was the novel that brought him to prominence in Latin America and worldwide. Previously he had published many short stories and novels, for instance *La hojarasca* (Leafstorm, 1955) and *El coronel no tiene quien le escriba* (No-one Writes to the Colonel, 1958), but it was *Cien años de soledad* which led to his recognition as one of the major exponents of the magic realism which characterized Latin American fiction from the 1960s onwards. Later novels have included *El otoño del patriaca* (The Autumn of the Patriarch, 1975), *Crónica de una muerte anunciada* (Chronicle of a Death Foretold, 1981), *El amor en los tiempos de cólera* (Love in the Time of Cholera, 1985), *Del amor y otros demonios* (Of Love and Other Demons, 1994) and *Memoria de mis putas tristes* (2004). He has also continued to publish short stories and journalism and was awarded the Nobel Prize for Literature in 1982.

Ecuador
Reference/travel
The Ecotourist's Guide to the Ecuadorean Amazon (1995).
Kunstaetter, Robert and Daisy *Trekking in Ecuador* (The Mountaineers, 2002).
Miller, Tom *The Panama Hat Trail* (Abacus, 1986).
Thomsen, Moritz *Living Poor* (Eland) and several other books on Peace Corps life.

Fiction
Adoum, Jorge Enrique *Entre Marx y una mujer desnuda* (1976). Ambitious.
Barrera Valverde, Alfonso *El País de Manuelito* (Editorial El Conejo, Quito, 1991), the country seen through the eyes of an orphaned child.
Burroughs, William *Queer* (1985).
Icaza, Jorge *Huasipungo* (1934; London, 1962), a harrowing tale of the hardships of Sierra Indians.

Vonnegut, Kurt *Galapagos* (1986).
Grupo de Guayaquil *Los que se van*, The compilation by 3 of the writers of this group (1st half of the 20th century), who focused on the people of the coast.

Paraguay
Reference
Cawthorne, Nigel *The Empress of South America* by (Heinemann, 2002), recent book on Elisa Lynch.
Gimlette, John *At the Tomb of the Inflatable Pig* (Hutchinson, 2003). An amusing account of Paraguayan history and culture.
Gott, Richard *Land Without Evil* (Verso 1993), on Jesuit history.
Greene, Graham *Travels With My Aunt*, includes a voyage to Paraguay by a retired bank manager and his eccentric aunt.
MacIntyre, Ben *Forgotten Fatherland*, about New Germany (Nueva Germania, page 1049) in Paraguay.
Rees, Siân *The Shadows of Elisa Lynch* (Headline, 2004) and **Tuck, Lily** *The News from Paraguay* (HarperPerennial, 2005). Two books on Elisa Lynch, the first a history, the second a novel.
Roa Bastos, Augusto Paraguay's most renowned contemporary novelist (1918-2005). Try *Yo, el Supremo* and *Hijo de hombre*.

Peru
Reference/trekking
Bartle, Jim *Parque Nacional Huascarán*, a beautiful soft-cover photo collection.
Davis, Morgan *The Cloud People*, an Anthropological Survey.
Muscutt, Keith *Warriors of the Clouds: A Lost Civilization in the Upper Amazon of Peru* (New Mexico Press, 1998; www.chachapoyas.com).
Person, David L and Beletsky, Les *Ecotraveller's Wildlife Guide: Peru* (London: Academic Press, 2001).
Savoy, Gene *Antisuyo (1970)*.
Sharman, David *Climbs of the Cordillera Blanca of Peru*, (1995). A climbing guide.
South American Explorers publishes a good map with additional notes on the popular Llanganuco to Santa Cruz loop.

Cuzco and Machu Picchu
Bingham, Hiram *Lost City of the Incas*, (available in Lima and Cusco, new illustrated edition, with introduction by Hugh Thomson, Weidenfeld & Nicolson, London, 2002).
Box, Ben *Footprint Cuzco and the Inca Heartland* (Footprint).
Frost, Peter *Exploring Cusco*, available in Cuzco bookshops.

Milligan, Max *In the Realm of the Incas* (Harper Collins, 2001). A recommended book with photographs and text.

Thomson, Hugh *The White Rock* (Phoenix, 2002), describes Thomson's own travels in the Inca heartland, as well as the journeys of earlier explorers and the history of the region. Thomson's latest book is *Cochineal Red: Travels through Ancient Peru* (Weidenfeld & Nicolson, 2006), an exploration of pre-Inca civilizations.

The southeastern jungle

MacQuarrie, Kim and **Bartschi, André and Cornelia** *Manu National Park*, an expensive, excellent book, with beautiful photographs.

TReeS *Birds of Tambopata – a checklist, Mammals, Amphibians and Reptiles of Tambopata*, *Ecology of Tropical Rainforesets: a layman's guide* and *Tambopata map guide*, all by TReeS, who also produce tapes of *Jungle Sounds* and *Bird Sounds of southeast Peru* (address on page 1278).

History and culture

Hemming, John *The Conquest of the Incas*, invaluable for the whole period of the Conquest.

Heyerdahl, Thor, **Sandweiss, Daniel H** and **Narváez, Alfredo** *Pyramids of Túcume*, (Thames & Hudson, 1995).

Kendall, Ann *Everyday Life of the Incas*, (Batsford, London, 1978).

Mosely, Michael E *The Incas and their Ancestors: The Archaeology of Peru*.

Travel

Murphy, Dervla *Eight Feet in the Andes* (1983).

Parris, Matthew *Inca-Kola* (1990).

Shah, Tahir *Trail of Feathers* (2001).

Wright, Ronald *Cut Stones and Crossroads: a Journey in Peru* (1984).

Fiction

Alegría, Ciro (1909-67) *El mundo es ancho y ajeno/Broad and Alien is the World* (1941).

Arguedas, José María (1911-1969) *Los ríos profundos/Deep Rivers* (1958).

Mathiessen, Peter *At Play in the Fields of the Lord* (1965).

Matto de Turner, Clorinda (1854-1909) The first writer of 'indigenist' fiction in Peru (see *Aves sin nido*). Others writers listed here followed in attempting to use fiction to address the issues of the ethnic majority.

Vargas Llosa, Mario (1936-) Peru's best known novelist has written many internationally acclaimed books, eg *La ciudad y los perros/The Time of the Hero* (1962), *La casa verde/The Green House* (1965), *La guerra del fin del mundo/The War of the End of World* (1981), *La fiesta del chivo/The Feast of the Goat* (2000) and *El paraíso en la otra esquina/The Way to Paradise* (2002).

Vallejo, César (1892-1938) Peru's outstanding 20th-century poet: his avant- garde collection *Trilce* (1922) is unlike any- thing before it in the Spanish language, but his work also has strong political commitment, as in *Poemas humanos* and *España, aparte de mí este cáliz*, both published posthumously.

Wilder, Thornton *The Bridge of San Luis Rey* (1927).

Uruguay

Reference

Bigongiari, Diego *Pirelli* of Argentina publishes a good guide to Uruguay (1996). Uruguay has a strong tradition of critical writing, for example: **Rodó, José Enrique** *Ariel* (1900); **Rama, Angel**, and **Galeano, Eduardo** *Venas abiertas de América Latina, Memoria del fuego, Días y noches de amor y de guerra*, etc.

de San Martín, Juan Zorilla Has been called Uruguay's greatest poet and his book *Tabare* the country's 'national book'.

Regules, Elías Gaucho stories.

Two other novelists who have gained international fame are **Juan Carlos Onetti** and **Mario Benedetti** (also a poet and critic).

Venezuela

Allende, Isabel *Eva Luna* (1987).

Brizuela, Ramón Antonio In the 1970s a new literary form known as *Testimonios* developed, incorporating genuine recorded material (usually dramatic social and political issues) into a semi-fictional account of a real event, eg *Soy un delincuente* and *Aquí no pasa nada* by **Zayo, Angela**.

Conan Doyle, Sir Arthur *The Lost World* (1912), is reputed to be set on Mount Roraima.

Conrad, Joseph *Nostromo* (1904), the Costaguana is said to be modelled on Venezuela.

de la Parra, Teresa (1890-1936) An early 20th-century writer.

Gallegos, Rómulo (1884-1969) The best known of all Venezuelan writers, and president briefly in 1947. Among his novels are *Doña Bárbara* (1929) and *Canaima* (1935).

Murphy, Alan and **Green, Dan** *Footprint Venezuela* (Footprint).

O'Hanlon, Redmond *In Trouble Again. A Journey between the Orinoco and the Amazon* (1988). An entertaining and sometimes alarming account of travelling in Venezuela.

St Aubin de Teran, Lisa *The Keepers of the House* (1982), *The Tiger* (1985) and *Otto: A Novel* (Virago, 2005).

Uslar Pietri, Arturo *Las lanzas coloradas* (1931).

von Humboldt, Alexander *Travels* (see Colombia, above).

Other Venezulan writers: **Miguel Otero Silva**, **Julián Padrón**, and **Adriano González León**.

Guyana
Brock, Stanley E *Jungle Cowboy* (1972).
Colchester, Marcus *Guyana Fragile Frontier* (Latin American Bureau, World Rainforest Movement and Ian Randle, 1997).
Durrell, Gerald *Three singles to Adventure*.
Melville, Pauline *The Ventriloquist's Tale* (1997). And works by: **Wilson Harris**, **Roy Heath** and **Fred D'Aguiar**.

Guyane
Cendrars, Blaise *Rhum*, by a French Guyanese writer, worth reading for its descriptions of the country's distinctive customs and traditions.

General
Birds and other wildlife
Bright, Michael *Andes to Amazon, A Guide to Wild South America*, (London: BBC, 2002). Good coverage of the subcontinent's wildlife, with a useful gazeteer.
Clements, J F and **Shany, Noam** *A Field Guide to the Birds of Peru* (Ibis, 2001).
Dunning, J *South American Birds*.
Hilty, S and **Brown, W** *A Guide to the Birds of Colombia* (Princeton University), an excellent field guide.
Krabbe, N and **J Fjeldsa** *Birds of the High Andes* (University of Copenhagen, 1990), on birds that live above 3,000 m.
Meyer de Schauensee, R *A Guide to the Birds of South America*.
Narosky, T and **Yzurieta, D** *Guía para la identificación de las aves de Argentina y Uruguay*, with drawings and colour illustrations.
Ridgely, R and **Greenfield, P** *Birds of Ecuador*, a definitive guide.

Climbing
Biggar, John *The Andes*, (Castle Douglas: Andes, 1999), a climbing guide for the entire Andean chain.

Cinema/film

The cinema in South America has been largely dominated by Hollywood, in the films that are on offer to the public and what cinema-goers choose to see. The cinema also has to compete with television and the huge popularity of *telenovelas* (soap operas). Despite enthusiasm for film-making since the beginnings of moving pictures, the industry in South America has been underfunded and has frequently had to confront repression and censorship. Individual countries can all claim a film industry at certain times and with certain motivations (eg in opposition to repression in Bolivia, Chilean cinema in exile after 1973), but Argentina and Brazil, together with Mexico, have been the leaders of film-making. Hugo Chávez, president of Venezuela, was intent in 2006 of overturning Hollywood's dominance of the Latin American cinema market. He launched a US$11 million Cinema Town studio with a view to producing films more representative of Latin America's own view of the continent, in parallel with the Telesur TV channel backed by Argentina, Cuba, Uruguay and Brazil, with Venezuela as major participant.

The earliest Argentine films were mostly silent documentaries, graduating into tango-led talkies in the 1930s. In the 1930s and 40s in Brazil, musicals were also the main box office draw. By the 1950s directors began to reject the old formulae and embraced 'new cinema' with its political and artistic messages. The chief exponents of this style in Argentina were Leopoldo Torre Nilsson (eg *La casa de ángel* – The House of the Angel – 1957) and Fernando Birri. One of the prominent directors in Brazil at this time was the neorrealist Nelson Perreira dos Santos (*Rio 40 Graus* – Rio 40º, 1955; *Vidas Secas* – Barren Lives, based on Graciliano Ramos' novel). *Cinema Novo* in Brazil reached its most fruitful period in the 1960s, especially in the work of Glauber Rocha (*O Cangaçeiro* – The Bandit, 1953, and *Deus e o Diabo no Terra do Sol* – God and the Devil in the Land of the Sun, 1963, both set in the Northeast; *O Barravento*). Before the descent into military dictatorship and censorship, 1966-68 saw production of the revolutionary four-hour documentary about Argentina, *La hora de los hornos* (The Hour of the Furnaces), directed by a group led by Fernando Solanas. This highly influential, politically-charged film confronted both Hollywood and the ideas of new cinema, but in the 1970s Solanas was forced into exile in France. The Radical government which took power after the demise of the Argentine generals in 1983 rejuvenated the National Film Institute, with the result that cinema flourished. Major films of this period were María Luisa Bemberg's *Camila* (1984), Luis Puenzo's *La historia oficial* (The Official Version , 1986 – the first Argentine film to win an Oscar) and Solanas' *Tangos, el exilio de Gardel* (Tangos the Exile

⁞ Ten of the best reads

Isabel Allende, *The House of the Spirits* (1982). A brilliant dynastic tale of 20th-century Chile, leading up to the events of 1973.

Jorge Amado, *Gabriela, Clove and Cinnamon* (1958). One of the Brazilian master storyteller's most popular books, set in Bahia.

Bruce Chatwin, *In Patagonia* (1977). A delightful, and not uncontroversial, mix of fact and fantasy.

Anne Enright, *The Pleasure of Eliza Lynch* (2002). A novel of the affair between Eliza Lynch and Francisco López, dictator of Paraguay, its excesses of passion and war.

Gabriel García Márquez, *One Hundred Years of Solitude* (1967). The Colombian novel which opened the world's eyes to South American magic realism.

John Hemming, *The Conquest of the Incas* (1970). A masterly account of the events that changed South America for ever.

Matthew Parris, *Inca Kola: A Traveller's Tale of Peru* (1993). A chronicle of Parris and three friends' bizarre adventures in Peru.

Ann Patchett, *Bel Canto*, (2001). The award-winning story of a kidnapping in an unnamed Latin American country.**Colin Thubron**, *To the Last City* (2002). A novel about the trek to Vilcabamba, how the trekkers react to each other, the landscape and its history, and their own demons.

Mario Vargas Llosa, *The War of the End of World* (1981). The Peruvian master's novel depicting the Canudos rebellion in Brazil.

of Gardel, 1985) and *Sur* (South, 1988). These and other films dealt, directly or by analogy, with the themes of the Dirty War, exile and the return to democracy. Recent successes from Argentina are Fabián Bielinsky's *Nueve Reinas* (Nine Queens, 2002), an award-winning tale of two small-time swindlers and their involvement in a once-in-a-lifetime scam, Carlos Sorín's *Bonbón el Perro* (2004), about a mechanic's attempts to overcome Argentina's economic collapse with a thoroughbred dog, and Solanas' 2005 film *La dignidad de los nadies* (The Dignity of the Nobodies), ten stories of people suffering in the economic collapse at the beginning of the 21st century.

In 1981, Hector Babenco's *Pixote, a Lei do Mais Fraco* was released (Pixote), a harrowing tale of Brazil's homeless children, marking a resurgence in Brazilian cinema. International recognition came in the 1990s with works such as Fábio Barreto's *O Quatrilho* (The Quadrille) and Bruno Barreto's *O Que é Isso, Companheiro* (from Fernando Gabiera's book about the kidnapping of the US ambassador in 1969). This success was followed by Walter Salles' *Central do Brasil* (Central Station – 1988) and *Behind the Sun* (2001) and, in 2003, Fernando Meirelles' compelling, violent drama of the Rio favelas, *Cidade de Deus* (City of God) and Hector Babenco's drama about prison life in São Paulo, *Carandiru*. Salles' admirable film of Che Guevara's *The Motorcycle Diaries* was a huge international success. Two further successes of 2005 were Breno Silveira's *Os Dois Filhos de Francisco* (The Two Sons of Francisco), a dramatised biography of the *sertanejo* singers Zezé di Camargo and Luciano, and Sérgio Bianchi's *Quanto Vale ou É por Quilo?* (What is it Worth?), a lacerating critique of neoliberalism and consumerism which makes parallels with slavery.

Some films with a South American theme

1959 *Orfeu Negro* (Black Orpheus) (**Marcel Camus**). The Orpheus and Eurydice legend retold during Rio Carnaval; music by Antônio Carlos Jobim and Luiz Bonfa.

1972 *Aguirre Wrath of God* (**Werner Herzog**). About Lope de Aguirre, the murderous conquistador and his journey down the Amazon; Klaus Kinski stars.

1982 *Missing* (**Constantin Costa Gavras**). An American activist goes missing in an unspecified South American country. His wife, Sissy Spacek, and father, Jack Lemmon, set out to find him, despite the country's dictator and the US consul's opposition.

1982 *Fitzcarraldo* (**Werner Herzog**). The epic story of one man's obsession (Klaus Kinski again) to build an opera house in the Peruvian jungle; includes the remarkable attempt to haul a 300-ton ship over a mountain. See also *Burden of Dreams* (1982, Les Blank), which documents Herzog's obsession in making of *Fitzcarraldo*.

1985 *Kiss of the Spider Woman* (O Beijo da Mulher Aranha) (**Hector Babenco**). Based on the novel by Manuel Puig, a two-hander between a homosexual and a terrorist in a prison cell.

1986 *The Mission* (**Roland Joffé**). Robert de Niro and Jeremy Irons as Jesuit priests in the Missions in Argentina and Paraguay at the time of the expulsion of the order from South America accompanied by a beautiful Ennio Morricone score.

1994 *Death and the Maiden* (**Roman Polanski**). Taken from Ariel Dorfman's play of the same name, this is a grim story of a woman (Sigourney Weaver) taking revenge on the man (Ben Kingsley) who, she believes, was her torturer several years earlier (country unnamed).

1994 *The Postman* (Il Postino) (**Michael Radford**) Taken from Antonio Skármeta's novel, *El cartero de Neruda* (originally called *Ardiente paciencia*); it weaves the story of a Chilean postman's love for a barmaid with the death of Pablo Neruda and the fall of Salvador Allende.

2002 *The Dancer Upstairs* (Pasos de baile) (**John Malkovich**) Javier Bardem plays a detective seeking a guerrilla leader in an unnamed South American country in this adaptation of Nicholas Shakespeare's novel about the nature of corruption.

Land and environment

The dominant feature of South America's geography is the Andes mountain range which defines the western, Pacific, side of the continent from 12°N to 56°S, with tablelands and older mountains stretching east to the Atlantic Ocean. The highest peaks of the Andes have no rivals outside the Himalaya. Dominant to the east are the vast river basins of the Orinoco, the Paraná and above all the Amazon. At least part of every country (except Uruguay) is in the tropics, though the southernmost tips of Chile and Argentina are close to Antarctica. No wonder the variety of scenery, climate and vegetation is immense.

The Andean countries

Colombia → *Land area: 1,242,568 sq km.*

Four ranges of the Andes (*cordilleras*) run from north to south. Between the ranges run deep longitudinal valleys. Roughly half of Colombia consists of these deep north-south valleys of the Andes and the coastal fringes along the Pacific and Caribbean shorelines. The remaining 620,000 sq km east of the Andes consists of the hot plains (*llanos*) to the north, running down to the Orinoco River, and the Amazon forests to the south. Near the foot of the Andes, the *llanos* are used for cattle ranching, but beyond is jungle. Except for the northwest corner where oil has been found, islands of settlement are connected with the rest of the country only by air and river; the few roads are impassable most of the year. Almost all Colombians live in the western 50% of the country.

The **cordilleras**, the main Andes ranges, run northwards for 800 km from the borders of Ecuador to the Caribbean lowlands. A few peaks in the Western Cordillera are over 4,000 m but none reaches the snowline. The Central Cordillera, 50-65 km wide, is much higher; several of its peaks, snow clad, rise above 5,000 m and its highest, the volcano cone of Huila, is 5,750 m. The Eastern Cordillera extends north across the border into Venezuela (see below), and includes the spectacular Cucuy ranges. Apart from the peaks (a few are active volcanoes), there are large areas of high undulating plateaux, cold, treeless and inhospitable, dissected by deep river gorges. They have interesting flora and fauna and many of these regions are protected as national parks. In a high basin of the Eastern Cordillera, 160 km east of the Río Magdalena, the Spaniards in 1538 founded the city of Bogotá at 2,560 m, now the national capital. The great rural activity here is the growing of food: cattle, wheat, barley, maize and potatoes. The **valleys** between the Cordilleras are deep and dominated by the Magdalena and Cauca Rivers. The upper sections are filled with volcanic ash and are very fertile. With the tropical range of temperature and rainfall, this is very productive land. Coffee dominates but almost every known tropical fruit and vegetable grows here. In the upper parts of the valleys, the climate is more temperate, with another wide range of crops. There is cattle production everywhere; sugar, cotton, rice and tobacco are common.

The **Caribbean lowlands** include three centres of population, Cartagena, Barranquilla and Santa Marta, behind which lies a great lowland, the floodplain of the Magdalena, Cauca and their tributaries. During the dry season from October to March great herds of cattle are grazed there, but for the rest of the year much of it is a network of swamps and lagoons with very little land that can be cultivated except for a few ranges of low hills near the coast. The **northeast** includes one more mountain group in Colombia, the Sierra Nevada de Santa Marta, standing isolated from the other ranges on the shores of the Caribbean. This is the highest range of all: its snow-capped peaks rise to 5,800 m within 50 km of the coast. Further northeast, is La Guajira, a strange region of semi-desert, salt-pans, flamingos and unusual micro- climates. The **Pacific coast** stretches for 1,300 km. Along the coast north of Buenaventura runs the Serranía de Baudó, the shortest of the Cordilleras, thickly forested. East of it is a low trough before the land rises to the slopes of the Western Cordillera. The trough is drained southwards into the Pacific by the Río San Juan, and northwards into the Caribbean by the Río Atrato, both are partly navigable. The climate is hot and torrential rain falls daily. The inhabitants are mostly black. The 320 km south of the port of Buenaventura to the border with Ecuador is a wide, marshy, and sparsely inhabited coastal lowland.

Ecuador → *Land area: 272, 045 sq km.*

The Andes, running from north to south, form a mountainous backbone to the country. There are two main ranges, the Central Cordillera and the Western Cordillera, separated by a 400-km long Central Valley, whose rims are about 50 km apart. The rims are joined together, like the two sides of a ladder, by hilly rungs, and between each pair of rungs lies an intermont basin with a dense cluster of population. These basins are drained by rivers which cut through the rims to run either west to the Pacific or east to join the Amazon. Both rims of the Central Valley are lined with the cones of more than 50 volcanoes. Several of them have long been extinct, for example, Chimborazo, the highest (6,310 m). At least eight, however, are still active including Cotopaxi (5,897 m), which had several violent eruptions in the 19th century; Pichincha (4,794 m), which re-entered activity in 1998 and expelled a spectacular mushroom cloud in October 1999; and Sangay (5,230 m), one of the world's most active volcanoes, continuously emitting fumes and ash. Earthquakes too are common.

The **sierra**, as the central trough of the Andes in known, is home to about 47% of the people of Ecuador, the majority of whom are indigenous. Some of the land is still held in large private estates worked by the Indians, but a growing proportion is now made up of small family farms or is held by native communities, run as cooperatives. Some communities live at subsistence level, others have developed good markets for products using traditional skills in embroidery, pottery, jewellery, knitting, weaving, and carving. The **costa** is mostly lowland at an altitude of less than 300 m, apart from a belt of hilly land which runs northwest from Guayaquil to the coast, where it turns north and runs parallel to the shore to Esmeraldas. In the extreme north there is a typical tropical rain forest, severely endangered by uncontrolled logging. The forests thin out in the more southern lowlands and give way to tropical dry forest. The main agricultural exports come from the lowlands to the southeast and north of Guayaquil. The heavy rains, high temperature and humidity suit the growth of tropical crops. Bananas and mango are grown here while rice is farmed on the natural levees of this flood plain. The main crop comes from the alluvial fans at the foot of the mountains rising out of the plain. Coffee is grown on the higher ground. Shrimp farming was typical of the coast until this was damaged by disease in 1999. The Guayas lowland is also a great cattle-fattening area in the dry season. South of Guayaquil the rainfall is progressively less, mangroves disappear and by the border with Peru, it is semi-arid.

The **Oriente** is east of the Central Cordillera where the forest-clad mountains fall sharply to a chain of foothills (the Eastern Cordillera) and then the jungle through which meander the tributaries of the Amazon. This east lowland region makes up 36% of Ecuador's total territory, but is only sparsely populated by indigenous and agricultural colonists from the highlands. In total, the region has only 5% of the national population, but colonization is now proceeding rapidly owing to population pressure and in the wake of an oil boom in the northern Oriente. There is gold and other minerals in the south. The **Galápagos** are about 1,000 km west of Ecuador, on the Equator, and are not structurally connected to the mainland. They mark the junction between two tectonic plates on the Pacific floor where basalt has escaped to form massive volcanoes, only the tips of which are above sea level. Several of the islands have volcanic activity today. Their isolation from any other land has led to their unique flora and fauna.

Peru → *Land area: 1,285,216 sq km.*

The whole of Peru's west seaboard with the Pacific is desert on which rain seldom falls. From this coastal shelf the Andes rise to a high Sierra which is studded with groups of soaring mountains and gouged with deep canyons. The highland slopes more gradually east and is deeply forested and ravined. Eastward from these mountains lie the vast jungle lands of the Amazon basin.

The **Highlands** (or Sierra), at an average altitude of 3,000 m, cover 26% of the country and contain about 50% of the people, mostly Indian, an excessive density on such poor land. Here, high-level land of gentle slopes is surrounded by towering ranges of high peaks including the most spectacular range of the continent, the Cordillera Blanca. This has several ice peaks over 6,000 m; the highest, Huascarán, is 6,768 m and is a mecca for mountaineers. There are many volcanoes in the south. The north and east highlands are heavily forested up to a limit of 3,350 m: the grasslands are between the forest line and the snowline, which rises from 5,000 m in the latitude of Lima to 5,800 m in the south. Most of the Sierra is covered with grasses and shrubs, with Puna vegetation (bunch grass mixed with low, hairy-leaved plants) from north of Huaraz to the south. Here the indigenous graze llamas, alpacas and sheep providing meat, clothing, transport and even fuel from the animals' dung. Some potatoes and cereals (*quinua*, *kiwicha* and *kañiwa*) are grown at altitude, but the valley basins contain the best land for arable farming. Most of the rivers which rise in these mountains flow east to the Amazon and cut through the plateau in canyons, sometimes 1,500 m deep, in which the climate is tropical. A few go west to the Pacific including the Colca and Cotahuasi in the south, which have created canyons over 3,000 m deep.

The **coast**, a narrow ribbon of desert 2,250 km long, takes up 11% of the country and holds about 45% of the population. It is the economic heart of Peru, consuming most of the imports and supplying half of the exports. When irrigated, the river valleys are extremely fertile, creating oases which grow cotton throughout the country, sugar-cane, rice and export crops such as asparagus in the north, grapes, fruit and olives in the south. At the same time, the coastal current teems with fish and Peru has in the past had the largest catch in the world. The **jungle** covers the forested eastern half of the Andes and the tropical forest beyond, altogether 62% of the country's area, but with only about 5% of the population who are crowded on the river banks in the cultivable land – a tiny part of the area. The few roads have to cope with dense forest, deep valleys, and sharp eastern slopes ranging from 2,150 m in the north to 5,800 m east of Lake Titicaca. Rivers are the main highways, though navigation is hazardous. The economic potential of the area includes reserves of timber, excellent land for rubber, jute, rice, tropical fruits and coffee and the breeding of cattle. The vast majority of Peru's oil and gas reserves are also east of the Andes.

Bolivia → *Land area: 1,098,581 sq km.*

A harsh, strange land, with a dreary grey solitude except for the bursts of green after rain, Bolivia is the only South American country with no coastline or even navigable river to the sea. It is dominated by the Andes and has five distinct geographical areas. The **Andes** are at their widest in Bolivia, a maximum of 650 km. The Western Cordillera, which separates Bolivia from Chile, has high peaks of between 5,800 m and 6,500 m and a number of active volcanoes along its crest. The Eastern Cordillera also rises to giant massifs, with several peaks over 6,000 m in the Cordillera Real section to the north. The far sides of the Cordillera Real fall away very sharply to the northeast, towards the Amazon basin. The air is unbelievably clear – the whole landscape is a bowl of luminous light.

The **Altiplano** lies between the Cordilleras, a bleak, treeless, windswept plateau, much of it 4,000 m above sea-level. Its surface is by no means flat, and the Western Cordillera sends spurs dividing it into basins. The more fertile northern part has more inhabitants; the southern part is parched desert and almost unoccupied, save for a mining town here and there. Nearly 70% of the population lives on it; over half of the people in towns. **Lake Titicaca**, at the northern end of the Altiplano, is an inland sea of 8,965 sq km at 3,810 m, the highest navigable water in the world. Its depth, up to 280 m in some places, keeps the lake at an even all-year-round temperature of 10° C. This modifies the extremes of winter and night temperatures on the surrounding land, which supports a large Aymara indigenous population, tilling the fields and the hill terraces, growing potatoes and cereals, tending their sheep, alpaca and llamas, and using the resources of the lake. The **Yungas** and the **Puna** are to the east of the Altiplano. The heavily forested northeastern slopes of the Cordillera Real are deeply indented by the fertile valleys of the Yungas, drained into the Amazon lowlands by the Río Beni and its tributaries, where cacao, coffee, sugar, coca and tropical fruits are grown.

Further south, from a point just north of Cochabamba, the Eastern Cordillera rises abruptly in sharp escarpments from the Altiplano and then flattens out to an easy slope east to the plains: an area known as the Puna. The streams which flow across the Puna cut increasingly deep incisions as they gather volume until the Puna is eroded to little more than a high remnant between the river valleys. In these valleys a variety of grain crops and fruits is grown.

The **tropical lowlands** stretch from the foothills of the Eastern Cordillera to the borders with Brazil, Paraguay and Argentina. They take up 70% of the total area of Bolivia, but contain only about 20% of its population. In the north and east the Oriente has dense tropical forest. Open plains covered with rough pasture, swamp and scrub occupy the centre. Before the expulsion of the Jesuits in 1767 this was a populous land of plenty; for 150 years Jesuit missionaries had controlled the area and guided it into a prosperous security. Decline followed but in recent years better times have returned. Meat is now shipped from Trinidad, capital of Beni Department, and from airstrips in the area, to the urban centres of La Paz, Oruro, and Cochabamba. Further south, the forests and plains beyond the Eastern Cordillera sweep down towards the Río Pilcomayo, which drains into the Río de la Plata, getting progressively less rain and merging into a comparatively dry land of scrub forest and arid savanna. The main city of this area is Santa Cruz de la Sierra, founded in the 16th century, now the second city of Bolivia and a large agricultural centre.

The Southern Cone

Chile → *Land area: 756, 626 sq km.*

Chile is a ribbon of land lying between the Andes and the Pacific. The Andes and a coastal range of highland take up from a third to a half of its width. There are wide variations of soil and vast differences of climate; these profoundly affect the density of population. Down virtually the whole length, between the Andes and the coastal ranges, is a longitudinal depression. For 1,050 km south of the capital Santiago this is a great valley stretching as far as Puerto Montt. South of Puerto Montt the sea has broken through the coastal range and drowned the valley, and there is a bewildering assortment of archipelagos and channels. The Andes, with many snow-capped peaks over 6,000 m, culminate near Santiago with several of almost 7,000 m. They diminish in height from Santiago southwards, but throughout the range are spectacular volcanoes right down to the southern seas, where the Strait of Magellan gives access to the Atlantic. Associated with the mountains are geological faults and earthquakes are common.

From north to south the country falls into five contrasted zones: The first 1,250 km from the Peruvian frontier to Copiapó is a rainless desert of hills and plains devoid of vegetation. Here lie nitrate deposits and several copper mines. There is almost no rain, just occasional mists. From Copiapó to Illapel (600 km) is semi-desert; there is a slight winter rainfall, but great tracts of land are without vegetation most of the year. Valley bottoms are cultivated under irrigation. From Illapel to Concepción is Chile's heartland, where the vast majority of its people live. Here there is abundant rainfall in the winter, but the summers are perfectly dry. Great farms and vineyards cover the country, which is exceptionally beautiful. The fourth zone, between Concepción and Puerto Montt, is a country of lakes and rivers, with heavy rainfall through much of the year. Cleared and cultivated land alternates with mountains and primeval forests. The fifth zone, from Puerto Montt to Cape Horn, stretches for 1,600 km. This is archipelagic Chile, a sparsely populated region of wild forests and mountains, glaciers, islands and channels. Rainfall is torrential, and the climate cold. South of Puerto Montt, the Camino Austral provides almost unbroken road access for more than 1,000 km. Chilean Patagonia is in the extreme south of this zone. A subdivision of the fifth zone is Atlantic Chile – that part which lies along the Magellan Strait to the east of the Andes, including the Chilean part of Tierra del Fuego island. There is a cluster of population here raising sheep and mining coal. Large offshore oilfields have been discovered in the far south.

Argentina → *Land area: 2, 780, 092 sq km.*

Argentina occupies most of the southern cone of the continent. There are four main physical areas: the Andes, the north and Mesopotamia, the Pampas, and Patagonia. Much of the country is comparatively flat which made modern communications easy. The **Andes** run the full length of Argentina, low and deeply glaciated in the Patagonian south, high and dry in the prolongation in northwest Argentina adjoining the Bolivian Altiplano. Though of modest height, Cerro Fitzroy and other peaks on the fringes of the Patagonia icecap are amongst the most dramatic on the continent, while many peaks in the north are over 6,000 m, including Aconcagua, the highest outside the Himalayas. To the east, in the shadow of the Andes, it is dry. Oases strung along the eastern foot of the Andes from Jujuy to San Rafael, including Tucumán and Mendoza, were the first places to be colonized by the Spaniards. Further south is the beautiful Lake District, with Bariloche at its heart. The mountain ridges and the many lakes created by the glaciers are now withdrawing under the impact of global warming. The **north** and **Mesopotamia** contains the vast plains of the Chaco and the floodplain lying between the rivers Paraná and Uruguay. Rice growing and ranching are widespread. The Province of Misiones in the northeast lies on the great Paraná plateau while the northwest Chaco has some of the highest temperatures in the continent.

The **Pampas** make up the heart of the country. These vast, rich plains lie south of the Chaco, and east of the Andes down to the Río Colorado. Buenos Aires lies on the northeast corner of the Pampas and is the only part of the country which has a dense population – about 40% of Argentines live in and around the capital. The Pampas stretch for hundreds of kilometres in almost unrelieved flatness, but get progressively wetter going east. Cattle and cereal growing dominate. **Patagonia** lies south of the Río Colorado – a land of arid, wind-swept plateaux cut across by ravines. In the deep south the wind is wilder and more continuous. There is no real summer, but the winters are rarely severe.

Uruguay → *Land area: 406,752 sq km.*

Unlike all other South American countries, Uruguay is compact (it's the smallest Hispanic country in South America), accessible and homogeneous. The **coast** along the Atlantic consists of bays, beaches and off-shore islands, lagoons and bars, the sand brought by currents north from the River Plate. Behind is a narrow plain which fringes most of the coast (but not near Montevideo). Behind is a line of mainly wooded hills (called *cuchillas*), the whole area extensively farmed with grain and cattle *estancias*. **Central Uruguay** up to the Brazilian border is pleasant, rolling country dissected by the Río Negro which rises in Brazil and on which a number of dams have been built. North of the river is agricultural and pasture country dominated by sheep. Near Minas there are stone quarries and other mining activity. **western Uruguay** is dominated by the River Plate from Montevideo round to Colonia, then north up the Río Uruguay which provides the frontier with Argentina. It consists of an alluvial flood plain stretching north to Fray Bentos where the first road crossing can be made. Thereafter, the general character of the land is undulating, with little forest except on the banks of its rivers and streams. The long grass slopes rise gently to far-off hills, but none of these is higher than 600 m. Five rivers flow westwards across the country to drain into the Río Uruguay, including the Río Negro. Cattle and wheat are the main traditional products.

Paraguay → *Land area: 406, 752 sq km.*

Paraguay is landlocked, divided into two distinct regions by the Río Paraguay. Eastern Paraguay combines habitats characteristic of three ecoregions: *cerrado* (a mosaic of dry forest and savanna habitats) in the north, humid Atlantic forest in the east, and natural grasslands and marshes in the south. West of the river lies the vast expanse of the Chaco, comprised of seasonally flooded palm-savannas in the south-east, semi-arid thorn scrub-forest to the west, and in the north, the Pantanal, part of the world's largest wetland. The Río Paraná forms part of the eastern and southern boundaries of the country but the rivers are so difficult to navigate that communication with Buenos Aires, 1,450 km from Asunción, has been mainly on land.

Eastern Paraguay is the 40% of the country east of the Río Paraguay, a rich land of rolling hills in which most of the population live. An escarpment runs north from the Río Alto Paraná, west of Encarnación, to the Brazilian border. East of this escarpment the Paraná Plateau extends across neighbouring parts of Argentina and Brazil. The Plateau, which is crossed by the Río Paraná, ranges from 300-600 m in height, was originally forest and enjoys relatively high levels of rainfall. West and south of the escarpment and stretching to the Río Paraguay lies a fertile plain with wooded hills, drained by several tributaries of the Río Paraná. Most of the population of Paraguay lives in these hilly lands, stretching southeast from the capital, to Encarnación. The area produces timber, cotton, hides and semi-tropical products. Closer to the rivers, much of the plain is flooded once a year; it is wet savanna, treeless, but covered with coarse grasses. The **Chaco**, about 60% of the country's area, is a flat, infertile plain stretching north along the west bank of the Río Paraguay. The marshy, unnavigable Río

Pilcomayo, which flows southeast across the Chaco to join the Río Paraguay near Asunción, forms the frontier with Argentina. The landscape is dominated by the alluvial material brought down in the past by the rivers from the Andes. As the rainfall diminishes westwards, the land can naturally support little more than scrub and cacti. The arrival of the Mennonites has led to some intense production of fruit and other crops.

Brazil and the north

Brazil → *Land area: 8,547,404 sq km.*

Brazil is one of the largest countries of the world. It stretches over 4,300 km across the continent but is one of the few in South America that does not reach the Andes. The two great river basins, the Amazon and the River Plate, account for about three-fifths of Brazil's area.

The **Amazon Basin**, in northern and western Brazil, takes up more than a third of the whole country. The basin borders the Andes and funnels narrowly to the Atlantic, recalling the geological period, before the uplift of the Andes, when the Amazon flowed into the Pacific Ocean. Most of the drained area has an elevation of less than 250 m. The rainfall is heavy: some few places receive from 3,750 to 5,000 mm a year, though over most of the area it is no more than from 1,500 to 2,500 mm. This heavy rain comes from the daily cycle of intense evaporation plus the saturated air brought by winds from the northeast and southeast, losing their moisture as they approach the Andes. Much of the basin suffers from annual floods. The region was covered by tropical forest, with little undergrowth except along the watercourses; it is now being rapidly cut down. The climate is hot and the humidity high throughout the year. The **Brazilian Highlands** lying southeast of the Amazon and northeast of the River Plate Basin form a tableland of from 300 to 900 m high, but here and there, mostly in southeast Brazil, mountain ranges rise from it. The highest temperature recorded was 42°C, in the dry northeastern states. The highest peak in southern Brazil, the Pico da Bandeira, northeast of Rio, is 2,898 m. The **Great Escarpment** is where the Brazilian Highlands cascade sharply down to the Atlantic, leaving a narrow coastal strip which is the economic heartland of the country. It runs from south of Salvador as far as Porto Alegre and in only a few places is this Escarpment breached by deeply cut river beds, for example those of the Rio Doce and the Rio Paraíba. Along most of its course, the Great Escarpment falls to the sea in parallel steps, each step separated by the trough of a valley. The few rivers rising on the Escarpment, which flow direct into the Atlantic are not navigable. Most of the rivers flow west, deep into the interior. Those in southern Brazil rise almost within sight of the sea, but run westward through the vast interior to join the Paraná, often with falls as they leave the Escarpment, including the spectacular Iguaçú. In the central area the Escarpment rivers run away from the sea to join the São Francisco River, which flows northwards parallel to the coast for 2,900 km, to tumble over the Paulo Afonso Falls on its eastward course to the Atlantic.

The **River Plate Basin**, in the southern part of Brazil, has a more varied surface and is less heavily forested than the Amazon Basin. The land is higher and the climate a little cooler. The **Guiana Highlands**, north of the Amazon, are ancient rock structures, some of the oldest in the world. The area is partly forested, partly hot stony desert. Slopes that face the northeast trade winds get heavy rainfall, but the southern areas are drier. The highest peak in all Brazil, the Pico da Neblina, 3,014 m, is on the Venezuelan border.

Guyane → *Land area: 83,900-86, 504 sq km (estimate).*

Guyane has its eastern frontier with Brazil formed partly by the river Oiapoque (Oyapock in French) and its southern, also with Brazil, formed by the Tumuc-Humac mountains (the only range of importance). The western frontier with Suriname is along the river Maroni-Litani. To the north is the Atlantic coastline of 320 km. The land rises gradually from a coastal strip some 15-40 km wide to the higher slopes and plains or savannahs, about 80 km inland. Forests cover the hills and valleys of the interior, and the territory is well watered, for over 20 rivers run to the Atlantic.

Suriname → *Land area: 163,820 sq km. (A large area in the southwest is in dispute with Guyana. There is a less serious border dispute with Guyane in the southeast.)*

Like its neighbours, Suriname has a coastline on the Atlantic to the north. The principal rivers are the Marowijne in the east, the Corantijn in the west, and the Suriname, Commewijne (with its tributary, the Cottica), Coppename, Saramacca and Nickerie. The country is divided into topographically quite diverse natural regions: the northern lowlands, 25 km wide in the east and 80 km wide in the west, have clay soil covered with swamps. There follows a region, 5-6 km wide, of a loamy and very white sandy soil, then an undulating region, about 30 km wide. It is mainly savanna, mostly covered with quartz sand, and overgrown with grass and shrubs. South of this lies the interior highland, almost entirely overgrown with dense tropical forest, intersected by streams. At the southern boundary with Brazil there are savannas.

Guyana → *Land area: 215,083 sq km.*

Guyana has an area of 215,083 sq km, nearly the size of Britain, but only about 2.5% is cultivated. About 90% of the population lives on the narrow coastal plain, either in Georgetown, the capital, or in villages along the main road running from Charity in the west to the Suriname border. The rivers give some access to the interior beyond which are the jungles and highlands towards the border with Brazil.

The **coastal plain** is mostly below sea level. Large wooden houses stand on stilts above ground level. A sea wall keeps out the Atlantic and the fertile clay soil is drained by a system of dykes; sluice gates, *kokers* are opened to let out water at low tide. Separate channels irrigate fields in dry weather. Most of the western third of the coastal plain is undrained and uninhabited. Four **major rivers** cross the coastal plain, from west to east they are the Essequibo, the Demerara, the Berbice, and the Corentyne. Only the Demerara is crossed by bridges. Elsewhere ferries must be used. At the mouth of the Essequibo River, 34 km wide, are islands the size of Barbados. The lower reaches of these rivers are navigable; but waterfalls and rapids prevent them being used by large boats to reach the interior. (The area west of the Essequibo River, about 70% of the national territory, is claimed by Venezuela.) The **jungles** and the **highlands** inland from the coastal plain, are thick rain forest, although in the east there is a large area of grassland. Towards Venezuela the rain forest rises in a series of steep escarpments, with spectacular waterfalls, the highest and best known of which are the Kaieteur Falls on the Potaro River. In the southwest is the Rupununi Savanna, an area of grassland more easily reached from Brazil than from Georgetown.

Venezuela → *Land area: 912, 050 sq km.*

Venezuela has 2,800 km of coastline on the Caribbean Sea and many islands. The Andes run up north-eastwards from Colombia, along the coast eastwards past Caracas, ending up as the north coast of the Caribbean island of Trinidad. In the northwest corner is the Maracaibo basin. South of the Andean spine is the vast plain of the Orinoco which reaches the sea near the Guyana border and to the southeast of that are the ancient rocks known as the Guayana Highlands.

The **Andes** are highest near the Colombian border where they are known as the Sierra Nevada de Mérida. Beyond they broaden out into the Segovia Highlands north of Barquisimeto, and then turn east in parallel ridges along the coast to form the Central Highlands, dipping into the Caribbean Sea only to rise again into the North Eastern Highlands of the peninsulas of Araya and Paria. This region has an agreeable climate and is well populated with most of the main towns. The **Maracaibo Lowlands** are around the fresh water lake of Maracaibo, the largest lake in South America, is 12,800 sq km. Considerable rainfall feeds the lake and many rivers flow through thick forest to create swamps on its southern shore. The area is dominated by the oil producing fields on both sides of the lake and beneath its surface. To the west, the Sierra de Perijá forms the boundary with Colombia and outside the lake to the east is the most northerly point of the country the peninsular of Paraguaná, virtually desert.

The **Llanos**, as the Orinoco plains are called, cover about one third of the country. They are almost flat and are a vast cattle range. The Orinoco river itself is part of Latin America's third largest river system. Many significant rivers flow from the Andes and Guayana Highlands to join the Orinoco, whose delta is made up of innumerable channels and thousands of forest-covered islands. The **Guayana Highlands**, which take up almost half the country, are south of the Orinoco. This is an area of ancient crystalline rocks that extend along the top of the continent towards the mouth of the Amazon and form the northern part of Brazil. In Venezuela they are noted for huge, precipitous granite blocks known as *tepuys*, many of which have their own unique flora, and create many high waterfalls including the Angel Falls, the world's highest.

Footnotes

Useful words and phrases

Greetings & courtesies	Spanish	Portuguese
hello/good morning	*hola/buenos días*	*oi/bom dia*
good afternoon/evening/night	*buenas tardes/noches*	*boa tarde/boa noite*
goodbye	*adiós/chao*	*adeus/tchau*
see you later	*hasta luego*	*até logo*
how are you?	*¿cómo está/cómo estás?*	*como vai você?/tudo bem?*
		tudo bom?
I'm fine	*estoy bien*	*tudo bem /tudo bom*
pleased to meet you	*mucho gusto/encantado*	*um prazer*
please	*por favor*	*por favor/faz favor*
thank you (very much)	*(muchas) gracias*	*(muito) obrigado (man speaking)*
		/obrigada (woman speaking)
yes/no	*sí/no*	*sim/não*
excuse me/I beg your pardon	*permiso*	*com licença*
I don't understand	*no entiendo*	*não entendo*
please speak slowly	*hable despacio por favor*	*fale devagar por favor*
what's your name?/	*¿cómo se llama?/me llamo_*	*Qual é seu nome?/ O meu*
I'm called_		*nome é_*
Go away!	*¡Váyase!*	*Vai embora!*

Basic questions

where is_?	*¿dónde está_?*	*onde está/onde fica?*
how much does it cost?	*¿cuánto cuesta?*	*quanto custa?*
when?	*¿cuándo?*	*quando?*
when does the bus leave/	*¿a qué hora sale/llega el*	*qa que hora sai/chega o*
arrive?	*autobus?*	*ônibus?*
why?	*¿por qué?*	*por que?*
how do I get to_?	*¿cómo llegar a_?*	*para chegar a_?*

Basics

police (policeman)	*la policía (el policía)*	*a polícia (o polícia)*
hotel	*el hotel (la pensión, el*	*o hotel (a pensão,*
	residencial, el alojamiento)	*a hospedaria)*
room	*el cuarto/la habitación*	*o quarto*
single/double	*sencillo/doble*	*(quarto de) solteiro*
with two beds	*con dos camas*	*com duas camas*
bathroom/toilet	*el baño*	*o banheiro*
hot/cold water	*agua caliente/fría*	*água quente/fria*
toilet paper	*el papel higiénico*	*o papel higiênico*
restaurant	*el restaurante*	*o restaurante (o lanchonete)*
post office/telephone office	*el correo/el centro de llamadas*	*o correio/o centro telefônico*
supermarket/market	*el supermercado/el mercado*	*o supermercado/o mercado*
bank/exchange house	*el banco/la casa de cambio*	*o banco/a casa de câmbio*
exchange rate	*la tasa de cambio*	*a taxa de câmbio*
travellers' cheques	*los travelers/los cheques de*	*os travelers/os cheques de*
	viajero	*viagem*
cash	*el efectivo*	*o dinheiro*
breakfast/lunch	*el desayuno/el almuerzo*	*o café de manhã/o almoço*
dinner/supper	*la cena*	*o jantar*
meal/drink	*la comida/la bebida*	*a refeição/a bebida*
mineral water	*el agua mineral*	*a água mineral*
beer	*la cerveza*	*a cerveja*
without sugar/without meat	*sin azúcar/sin carne*	*sem açúcar/sem carne*

Getting around

on the left/right	*a la izquierda/derecha*	*á esquerda/á direita*
straight on	*derecho*	*direito*
bus station	*la terminal (terrestre)*	*a rodoviária*
bus stop	*la parada*	*a parada*
bus	*el bus/el autobus/la flota/*	*o ônibus*
	el colectivo/el micro	
train/train station	*el tren/la estación (de*	*o trem*
	tren/ferrocarril)	
airport/aeroplane	*el aeropuerto/el avión*	*o aeroporto/o avião*
ticket/ticket office	*el boleto/la taquilla*	*o bilhete/a bilheteria*

Time

What time is it?	*¿Qué hora es?*	*Que horas são?*
at half past two/two thirty	*a las dos y media*	*as duas e meia*
it's one o'clock/ it's seven o'clock	*es la una/son las siete*	*é uma/são as sete*
ten minutes/five hours	*diez minutos/cinco horas*	*dez minutos/cinco horas*

Numbers

1	*uno/una*	*um/uma*
2	*dos*	*dois/duas*
3	*tres*	*três*
4	*cuatro*	*quatro*
5	*cinco*	*cinco*
6	*seis*	*seis*
7	*siete*	*sete*
8	*ocho*	*oito*
9	*nueve*	*nove*
10	*diez*	*dez*
11	*once*	*onze*
12	*doce*	*doze*
13	*trece*	*treze*
14	*catorce*	*catorze*
15	*quince*	*quinze*
16	*dieciseis*	*dezesseis*
17	*diecisiete*	*dezessete*
18	*dieciocho*	*dezoito*
19	*diecinueve*	*dezenove*
20	*veinte*	*vinte*
21	*veintiuno*	*vinte e um*
30	*treinte*	*trinta*
40	*cuarenta*	*quarenta*
50	*cincuenta*	*cinqüenta*
60	*sesenta*	*sessenta*
70	*setenta*	*setenta*
80	*ochenta*	*oitenta*
90	*noventa*	*noventa*
100	*cien, ciento*	*cem, cento*
1000	*mil*	*mil*

Footnotes Useful words & phrases

Spanish and Portuguese pronunciation

Spanish

The stress in a Spanish word conforms to one of three rules: 1) if the word ends in a vowel, or in n or **s**, the accent falls on the penultimate syllable (*ventana*, *ventanas*); 2) if the word ends in a consonant other than **n** or **s**, the accent falls on the last syllable (*hablar*); 3) if the word is to be stressed on a syllable contrary to either of the above rules, the acute accent on the relevant vowel indicates where the stress is to be placed (*pantalón*, *metáfora*). Note that adverbs such as *cuando*, 'when', take an accent when used interrogatively: *¿cuándo?*, 'when?'

Vowels: a not quite as short as in English 'cat'; **e** as in English 'pay', but shorter in a syllable ending in a consonant; **i** as in English 'seek'; **o** as in English 'cot' (North American 'caught'), but more like 'pope' when the vowel ends a syllable; **u** as in English 'food'; after 'q' and in 'gue', 'gui', u is unpronounced; in 'güe' and 'güi' it is pronounced; **y** when a vowel, pronounced like 'i'; when a semiconsonant or consonant, it is pronounced like English 'yes'; **ai**, **ay** as in English 'write'; **ei**, **ey** as in English 'eight'; **oi**, **oy** as in English 'voice'

Unless listed below **consonants** can be pronounced in Spanish as they are in English. **b**, **v** have an interchangeable sound and both are a cross between the English 'b' and 'v', except at the beginning of a word or after 'm' or 'n' when it is like English 'b'; **c** like English 'k', except before 'e' or 'i' when it is as the 's' in English 'sip'; **g** before 'e' and 'i' it is the same as j; **h** when on its own, never pronounced; **j** as the 'ch' in the Scottish 'loch'; **ll** as the 'g' in English 'beige'; sometimes as the 'lli' in 'million'; **ñ** as the 'ni' in English 'onion'; **rr** trilled much more strongly than in English; **x** depending on its location, pronounced as in English 'fox', or 'sip', or like 'gs'; **z** as the 's' in English 'sip'.

Portuguese

There is no standard Portuguese and there are many differences between the Portuguese of Portugal and the Portuguese of Brazil. If learning Portuguese before you go, get lessons with a Brazilian, or from a language course which teaches Brazilian Portuguese. Within Brazil itself, there are variations in pronunciation, intonation, phraseology and slang. This makes for great richness and for the possibility of great enjoyment in the language. Describing the complex Portuguese vocalic system is best left to the experts; it would take up too much space here. A couple of points which the newcomer to the language will spot immediately, however, are: the use of the til (~) over **a** and **o**. This makes the vowel a nasal vowel. Vowels also become nasal when a word ends in **m** or **ns**, when a vowel is followed by **m** + consonant, or by **n** + consonant. Another important point of spelling is that words ending in **i** or **u** are accented on the last syllable, though unlike Spanish no accent is used there. This is especially important in place names: Buriti, Guarapari, Caxambu, Iguaçu. Note also the use of **ç**, which changes the pronunciation of **c** from hard [k] to soft [s].

Note: In conversation, most people refer to **you** as "*você*", although in the south and in Pará "*tu*" is more common. To be more polite, use "*O Senhor/A Senhora*". For **us**, "*a gente*" (people, folks) is very common when it includes **you** too.

Map symbols

Administration

- ⬜ Capital city
- ○ Other city, town
- International border
- Regional border
- Disputed border

Roads and travel

- Motorway
- Main road (National highway)
- Minor road
- Track
- Footpath
- ⊷▬ Railway with station
- ✈ Airport
- 🚌 Bus station
- Ⓜ Metro station
- Cable car
- ⊦⊦⊦⊦ Funicular
- Ferry

Water features

- River, canal
- Lake, ocean
- Seasonal marshland
- Beach, sandbank
- Waterfall
- Reef

Topographical features

- Contours (approx)
- ▲ Mountain, volcano
- Mountain pass
- Escarpment
- Gorge
- Glacier
- Salt flat
- Rocks

Cities and towns

- Main through route
- Main street

- Minor street
- Pedestrianized street
- ⊃⊂ Tunnel
- → One way-street
- Steps
- ⋈ Bridge
- Fortified wall
- Park, garden, stadium
- ● Sleeping
- ❶ Eating
- ❶ Bars & clubs
- Building
- Sight
- ✝ Cathedral, church
- Chinese temple
- Hindu temple
- Meru
- Mosque
- Stupa
- ✡ Synagogue
- Tourist office
- 🏛 Museum
- ✉ Post office
- Police
- Ⓢ Bank
- @ Internet
- ♪ Telephone
- Market
- Medical services
- 🅿 Parking
- Petrol
- Golf
- A Detail map
- A Related map

Other symbols

- Archaeological site
- ♦ National park, wildlife reserve
- Viewing point
- ▲ Campsite
- Refuge, lodge
- Castle
- Diving
- Deciduous, coniferous, palm trees
- Hide
- Vineyard
- Distillery
- Shipwreck
- ✕ Historic battlefield

Map index

Advertisers' index

Footnotes Advertisers' index

1537

Index

Footnotes Index

1541

Footnotes Index

Footnotes Index

Credits

Footprint credits

Editor: Nicola Jones
Assistant editor: Angus Dawson
Map editor: Sarah Sorensen
Picture editor: Robert Lunn

Publisher: Patrick Dawson
Editorial: Sophie Blacksell, Felicity Laughton,
Alan Murphy
Cartography: Robert Lunn, Kevin Feeney,
Sarah Sorensen
Series development: Rachel Fielding
Design: Mytton Williams and Rosemary
Dawson (brand)
Sales and marketing: Andy Riddle,
Daniella Cambouroglou
Advertising: Debbie Wylde
Finance and administration:
Elizabeth Taylor

Photography credits

Front cover: Alamy
Back cover: SuperStock
Inside: Alamy, South American Pictures,
SuperStock

Print

Manufactured in Italy by LegoPrint
Pulp from sustainable forests

Footprint feedback

We try as hard as we can to make each
Footprint guide as up to date as possible but, of
course, things always change. If you want to let
us know about your experiences – good, bad or
ugly – then don't delay, go
to www.footprintbooks.com and send in your
comments.

Publishing information

Footprint South American Handbook
83rd Edition
© Footprint Handbooks Ltd
September 2006

ISBN 1 904777 68 6
CIP DATA: A catalogue record for this book is
available from the British Library

® Footprint Handbooks and the Footprint mark
are a registered trademark of Footprint
Handbooks Ltd

Published by Footprint

6 Riverside Court
Lower Bristol Road
Bath BA2 3DZ, UK
T +44 (0)1225 469141
F +44 (0)1225 469461
discover@footprintbooks.com
www.footprintbooks.com

Distributed in the USA by

Publishers Group West

Every effort has been made to ensure that the
facts in this guidebook are accurate. However,
travellers should still obtain advice from
consulates, airlines etc about travel and visa
requirements before travelling. The authors and
publishers cannot accept responsibility for any
loss, injury or inconvenience however caused.

Acknowledgements

For their assistance with the 2007 edition, the author wishes to thank all at Footprint, especially Nicola Jones, Alan Murphy and Sarah Sorensen.

In late 2005, the author travelled to Argentina, Bolivia and Chile. For their help and hospitality in Buenos Aires, Ben would like to thank Federico and Marlú Kirbus, Herbert Levi, Harry Ingham, and Brad Krupsaw; and in Chile, Patricia Vincent (Arica), Don Tomás Poblete (San Pedro de Atacama), and Janak Jani and Lorena Lara (Valparaíso). Warmest thanks go also to David Williamson for sharing a marvellous journey, and to Robert and Daisy Kunstaetter for joining us on an unforgettable adventure in southwest Bolivia. For the latter we should all like to thank Fabiola Mitru and family, Beatriz Michel Torres, Idel Huayta and Eusebia Huanca (all of Tupiza). Robert and Daisy also provided significant updates for the text of this edition, for Argentina; many parts of Bolivia (where they would like to thank Luis and Liliana Szwerdszarf, La Paz, Jacobo Cukierman, La Paz, Daniel Mairana, SERNAP, La Paz, Alistair Matthew, Gravity Assisted Mountain Biking, La Paz, Johny Resnikowski, Alatai Oasis, Sorata, Germán Gutiérrez, Hotel Samay Huasi, Oruro, Jesús Valencia Andrade, Oficina de Turismo, Oruro, and Roberto de Urioste, Ranking Bolivia, Uyuni); Brazil; Chile; Ecuador; Paraguay, where they updated the Trans Chaco route (with thanks to Alberto and María Fernanda Poletti in Asunción); Peru, where they updated the Titicaca region, the south coast and parts of the north (thanks to Jaime and Anita Lerner, Lima); and Uruguay.

Argentina: Nicolás Kugler (Buenos Aires), who would like to add his thanks to Natalia Westberg and Lautaro Lafleur for their help. Federico Kirbus (Buenos Aires).
Brazil: Alex Robinson (author of Footprint Brazil).
Chile: Janak Jani (author of Footprint Chile).
Colombia: Anastasia Moloney (Bogotá) updated the whole chapter.
Ecuador: Jean Brown (Quito).
Paraguay: Hilary Wheat and Joe South (Asunción).
Peru: Thanks are due to all those who contributed to Footprint's Cuzco and Inca Heartland, especially Steve Frankham (full acknowledgements are given in the 3rd edition). Many thanks also to Alberto Cafferata (Caraz) and to Sarah Cameron for preparing the update file.
Uruguay: Andre Vltchek.
Venezuela: Brad Krupsaw and Miriam Posz (Buenos Aires).
Guyana: Tony Thorne and Teri O'Brien (Wilderness Explorers, Georgetown).

The Health section was written by Prof Larry Goodyer, head of the Leicester School of Pharmacy and director of Nomad Medical.

Travellers whose emails and letters have been used this year (in part of in full): Chris Alger, UK (Bra, Ecu, Per); Alvaro Alliende, Chile (Per); Michael Anderson, UK (Arg, Bol, Ecu, Per); Nick Antram and Naomi Douglas, UK (Arg, Chi); Gale and Eve Bach, US (Per); Ignacio Ballen, Peru (Per); Julien Barber, UK (Per); Adrian Beck (Per); Hope Becker and Adrian, UK (Bol, Chi, Per); Paul Beckitt, UK (Col, Per); Nigel Bellamy, UK (Bol); Eva Berger, Germany (Per); Sandro and Sonya Bieder, Switzerland (Arg, Par, Uru); Roni Biller, Israel (Arg); Claudine Blum, Switzerland (Chi, Per); Peter Boers, The Netherlands (Per); Dieter Bongardt, Germany (Bra); Mari Borghesi, UK (Arg); Jamie Borley, UK (Chi); John Boyd, Eire (Per); Jim Bray, US (Bra); Andrew Bresler and Sara Andrews, UK (Bol); Timothy Brignall, UK (Bol, Per); Kim Bruce, Australia, (Col); Astrid Brucker, Germany (Per); Florian Brunner and Eva, Germany (Bol, Bra); Jayne Burrage Churchill, UK (Per); Leen Buysrogge (Per); Edward Cahill (Per); Jocelyn Cai, Singapore (Per); Juani Calderón (Chi); Tony and Patricia Cantor, UK (Par); Anne and Jerome Cardwell (Chi); Michael Carlton (Arg, Bol, Bra, Par, Per); Sara Carter, UK (Arg, Chi, Par); Marie Chabbert, UK (Chi); Francis Chambers (Arg, Bol, Bra, Chi, Per, Uru); Ursula Chan, US (Per); Steve Cheetham, UK (Chi); Caroline Chow and Mike Blanchard, USA (Bol, Chi); Jayne and Peter Churchill, UK (Bol, Per); John Clarke, UK (Ecu); Kate Comiskey, US; Alex Cooney (Chi); Kitty Couper (Ecu); Mairead Cussen, UK (Ecu); Helena Dahlenius, Sweden (Bol); Ann Daly, Australia (Chi); Christian Darchis, Chile (Chi); Ben Davies, UK (Chi); Mathieu de Patoul, Belgium (Chi); Elmer de Ronde,

Netherlands (Chi); Heleen de Smet, the Netherlands (Chi); Jeroen Decuyper, Belgium (Peru); Petra Deen, The Netherlands (Per); Leslie Derrick, US (Ecu); Richard Desomme and Catherine Koch (Arg, Bol, Chi, Ecu, Per); Christine Deutsch, Austria (Bra); Martin Dixon, UK (Ven); Hessel Dokkum (Per); Shannon Donovan, New Zealand (Per); Tadeusz Dubowicz (Arg, Par); Nicolas Dumoulin, France (Per); Liz Dunningham, UK (Arg); Ben Eastwood, Australia (Per); Walter Eberhart, Peru (Per); Yotam Ebert, Israel (Arg, Bra); Guy Edwards (Ecu); Pam Elliott, Canada (Per); Wolfram Engelhardt, Germany (Col, Ecu, Per); Louisa Ersanilli, Belgium (Bol); Aoife Farrelly with Eileen and Trish, Eire (Bol, Chi, Ecu, Per); Cristi Fedryna, Canada (Chi); Sunita, Shane and Sheldon Ferrao, Canada (Per); Simone and Peter Fink, Switzerland (Chi); Michael Fitzpatrick, Eire (Chi); Claudia Fliegner, Venezuela (Ven); Paul Focke, UK (Chi); Jo Fowler and Robert Dickson, UK (Arg, Bol, Per); Christian Furrer, Switzerland (Bra, Par, Uru); Sergio Galves, Spain (Arg); Alvaro Garcí, Uruguay (Ven); Claudia Geier, Austria (Chi); Eva Gengenbach, Germany (Per); Axel and Paty Gerke, France (Chi); Jean-François Girard, Switzerland (Chi); Chris Girdham, UK (Chi); Joachim Götz, Germany (Per); Oliver Greenall, UK (Per); Clare Gross (Ven);Jochen Hager, US (Per); Stuart Hambling and Nicole Booth, UK (Chi); Robin and Dierdre Hamill, UK (Par); Yves Hanotiau, Belgium (Chi); Anne Hay, UK (Per); Siobhan Healy, Eire (Ven); Hanneke Hendrickx, The Netherlands (Chi); Beata Hemer, Sweden (Per); Nienke Hensbroek, The Netherlands (Chi); Werner Hinz, Germany (Chi); Arno Hitzkopf, Austria (Chi); Jeremy Hoare, UK (Arg, Chi); Cooper Holoweski, US (Chi); Robert Hoogstad, The Netherlands (Chi); Valerie Hooper, US (Per); Clarisa Hopkins, Australia (Per); Bea Huber, Switzerland (Per); Jon Huber, USA (Bra); Gerhard Hucke, Germany (Chi); Maribel Tamara Huertas (Bra); Richard Hughes, UK (Bol); Kristin Hulaas Sunde and Andreas Sunde Corvalan, UK (Chi); Vicky Jacobs, UK (Bra, Ecu, Per); Sandro Jaeger, Switzerland (Chi); Beda Janeba, Australia (Chi); Roland Jesse (Chi); Marcelo Jiménez, Spain (Chi); Jens Jugelt, Germany (Arg, Chi); Peter Kalil, US (Chi); Judith Kane, UK (Bol); Tomas Kaving, Sweden (Bol); Alex and Janette Kernitsky and Kfar Ilan, Israel (Per); Angelene Kiel, US (Per); Robert Kittilsen, Norway (Bol); Maria Kochis and R Ryan Hammond, US (Chi); Antonella König and Serafin, Germany (Bol); Lauri Korhonen, Finland (Arg, Bra, Chi, Par, Per, Ven); Bernadette Kurte, Peru (Per); Catriona Lane, UK (Chi); Jodie Larson, US (Chi, Per); David Latham and Jo (Bol, Col, Per); Dan Lauritsen (Per); Edna Lazar, US (Per); Denis and Mary Anne Le Jeune (Bra, Uru); Sam and Thea Leavitt, US (Arg, Chi); Philippe Lefroid, France (Chi); Herbert Levi, Argentina (Arg, Uru); Johanna Lindman (Chi); Cornelis Lodewijk, Luxembourg (Chi); Rainer Loewen, Germany (Chi); Jonnie Lyle, UK (Per); Steve McElhinney, UK; Norma McGoldrick, UK (Chi); Sasha McInnes, Canada (Per); Sandra and Fraser McIver, UK (Arg, Chi, Ecu, Per); Andrea McNeal, US (Per); Kimberly Madson, US (Ecu); Ciara Maguire, Eire (Per); Joe Mailhot, US (Ecu); Robert E Manley, US (Bra, Per); Rebecca Martin, Eire (Per); Silvia Mattaveli, Italy (Chi); Michelangelo Mazzeo, Italy (Col); Jean-Pierre Mélon, Belgium (Per); Anna Molenaar, The Netherlands (Bol, Bra, Chi, Ecu, Per); Sean Morris (Per); Cathy Morton (Bra); Vicki Mountford, UK (Bol); Beat Mueller, Switzerland (Chi); Dennis Mulder, The Netherlands (Chi); John Murrihy, Eire (Chi); Eabhnat Ni Laighin, Eire (Chi); Henrike Niebaum, Germany (Chi); Anita and Patrick Obendrauf, Switzerland (Chi); Anthea Owen, UK (Chi); Naomi Paget, UK (Per); Mary Panagopoulos, UK (Uru); Eliott Parish, UK (Ecu); Jean-Paul Penrose, UK (Per); Jan Peters, US (Bol, Per); Mark Pfaff, UK (Bra, Chi); Jason Plevey, UK (Ven); Daniel Plewman, Eire (Per); Ricardo Poppeliers, The Netherlands (Arg); Babette Prick, The Netherlands (Per); Katia Prud'homme, Canada (Ven); Kathrin Raabe, Chile (Chi); Giorgio Raschio, Italy (Per); Ranjan Raychowdhury, UK (Per); Helen Reader, Czech Republic (Bol); Kathrin Reinke, Germany (Per); Joanna Richardson, UK (Arg); Andy Richmond, UK (Par); Isabelle Risom, Denmark (Bol); Felicity Roos, Australia (Chi); Anna Rosenkvist, Sweden (Chi); Norman Rudd, UK (Bra); David Rutkowski, US (Per); Jaime Salinas, Bolivia (Per); Philipp Schaab, Germany (Chi, Ecu, Per); Angela and Axel Schmitz, Germany (Ecu, Per); Inbar Schmulik, Israel (Chi); Martin Schoernig (Chi); Avi Shua (Per); Oliver Schuetz (Per); Dr Wolfgang Schürger, Germany (Bra); Susanne Schuster, UK (Arg, Bol, Bra, Per); David Schwartz, US (Per); Harvey Schwartz, US (Bra); Steve Scott, UK (Arg, Bol, Per); Peter Selley, UK (Per); Emma Sheppard, UK (Chi); Karen Siegel, Ecuador (Ecu, Per); Andre Siraa, US (Guy); Ole Skjerven, Norway (Arg, Bra, Ecu, Per); Birgit Sonnerer, Austria (Ven); Cath Smith, UK (Per); Josh Snyder, US (Per); David Sparkes, UK (Chi); Michael Spindler, US (Per); Wolf Staub, Chile (Chi); R Steffen, Switzerland (Arg, Bol); Peter Stollery, Canada (Uru); Nina Strandkjaer, Denmark (Per); Ariana Svenson, Australia (Per); Lior Tal, Peru (Per); Andrew Tester, New Zealand (Per); Thomas and Eva (Chi); Paul Thoreson, Colombia (Col); David Thovson, US (Per); Pearl Tom, US (Chi); Fabian Toonen, Netherlands (Per); Edward Tothill, UIK (Chi); Totte (Col,

Ecu); Silvia Tremolada, Italy (Chi); Terhi Tuominen and Teija Vaha, Finland (Arg, Chi, Per); Volker T Umpfenbach, Germany (Per); Jon Underdahl-Peirce, US (Chi); Bernie Upjohn and Eric Potter, Australia (Arg, Bol, Bra, Chi, Ecu, Per, Uru, Ven); Patterson Molina Vale, Brazil (Bol, Par, Per);Wibo van der Heide, The Netherlands (Chi); Marleen van der Veen, The Netherlands (Chi); Guy Vanackeren, Peru (Per); Dineke Veerman, Netherlands (Per); Jan Verhoek, The Netherlands (Chi); Jonna von Wendt, Finland (Chi); Clive Walker, Costa Rica (Chi); Beate Weber, Chile (Arg, Chi); Andrea and Russ Weedon, Switzerland (Arg, Chi); Alan Wehmann, USA (Col); Family Westra, The Netherlands (Bol, Ecu); Brian and Ruth Whiting, US (Per); Graham Williams, UK (Col, Ecu, Per); Stuart Williams, UK (Chi); Rudolf Winkler, Germany (Per); Amelia Wix (Per); Patrick Wohlfender, Switzerland (Arg, Chi); Sarah Woodruff and Fred Long, Chile (Chi); Stella Wong, Canada (Chi); Steve Wright, UK (Ecu); Susan Wright (Per); Mrs C Young, UK (Ecu); Elad Z (Per); Gabby Zegers and Joost Beltman, The Netherlands (Arg, Chi); Austin Zeiderman, US (Per); Marthe Zeldenrust, The Netherlands (Per); Monica Zihlmann, Switzerland (Chi); Paola Zimmermann, Germany (Per); Roland Zimmermann, Germany (Per).
Specialist contributors: Specialist contributors: Peter Pollard for Land and environment; Nigel Gallop for Music and dance; Katie Moore and Steve Frankham for Off the beaten track/Thirty ways to escape; Ashley Rawlings for Motorcycling; Hallam Murray for Cycling; Hilary Bradt for Hiking and trekking; Richard Robinson for World wide radio information; Mark Eckstein for Responsible travel.

About the author

One of the first assignments **Ben Box** took as a freelance writer in 1980 was sub-editing work on the *South American Handbook*. The plan then was to write about contemporary Iberian and Latin American affairs, but in no time at all the lands south of the Rio Grande took over, inspiring journeys to all corners of the sub-continent. Ben has contributed to newspapers, magazines and learned tomes, usually on the subject of travel, and became editor of the *South American Handbook* in 1989. He has also been involved in *Footprint Central America & Mexico, Footprint Caribbean Islands, Footprint Brazil* and *Footprint Peru* since their inception. In 2001 he wrote *Footprint Cuzco & the Inca Heartland*, on which he now collaborates with Steve Frankham. Having a doctorate in Spanish and Portuguese studies from London University, Ben maintains a strong interest in Latin American literature and as a cricketer he looks forward to the day his village side is invited to play anywhere in South America where there is a wicket (the new ground at Providence in Georgetown, perhaps?...One can but dream). .

Notes

About the author

The South American Handbook: 1924-2007

It was 1921

Ireland had just been partitioned, the British miners were striking for more pay and the federation of British industry had an idea. Exports were booming in South America – how about a Handbook for businessmen trading in that far away continent? The *Anglo-South American Handbook* was born that year, written by W Koebel, the most prolific writer on Latin America of his day.

1924

Two editions later the book was 'privatized' and in 1924, in the hands of Royal Mail, the steamship company for South America, became *The South American Handbook*, subtitled 'South America in a nutshell'. This annual publication became the 'bible' for generations of travellers to South America and remains so to this day. In the early days travel was by sea and the Handbook gave all the details needed for the long voyage from Europe. What to wear for dinner; how to arrange a cricket match with the Cable & Wireless staff on the Cape Verde Islands and a full account of the journey from Liverpool up the Amazon to Manaus: 5898 miles without changing cabin!

1939

As the continent opened up, *The South American Handbook* reported the new Pan Am flying boat services, and the fortnightly airship service from Rio to Europe on the Graf Zeppelin. For reasons still unclear but with extraordinary determination, the annual editions continued through the Second World War.

1970s

From the 1970s, jet aircraft transformed travel. Many more people discovered South America and the backpacking trail started to develop. All the while the Handbook was gathering fans, including literary vagabonds such as Paul Theroux and Graham Greene (who once sent some updates addressed to **"The publishers of the best travel guide in the world, Bath, England"**.)

1990s

During the 1990s Patrick and James Dawson, the publishers of *The South American Handbook* set about developing a new travel guide series using this legendary title as the flagship. By 1997 there were over a dozen guides in the series and the Footprint imprint was launched.

2000s

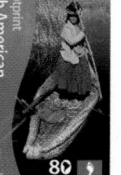

In 2003, Footprint launched a new series of pocket guides focusing on short-break European cities. The series grew quickly and there were soon over 100 Footprint travel guides covering more than 150 destinations. In January 2004, *The South American Handbook* reached another milestone as it celebrated its 80th birthday. Later that year, Footprint launched its first Activity guide: *Surfing Europe,* packed with colour photographs, maps and charts. This was followed by a new full-colour Discover series in 2005, and further Activity guides such as *Surfing Britain, Surfing the World, Diving the World* and *Snowboarding the World.*

The future

There are many more guides in the pipeline. To keep up-to-date with new releases check out the Footprint website for all the latest news and information, **www.footprintbooks.com.**

Complete title listing

Footprint publishes travel guides to over 150 destinations worldwide. Each guide is packed with practical, concise and colourful information for everybody from first-time travellers to travel aficionados. The list is growing fast and current titles are noted below. Available from all good bookshops and online www.footprintbooks.com

(P) denotes pocket guide

Latin America & Caribbean
Antigua & Leeward Islands (P)
Argentina
Barbados (P)
Discover Belize, Guatemala & Southern Mexico
Bolivia
Brazil
Caribbean Islands
Mexico & Central America
Chile
Colombia
Costa Rica
Cuba
Cusco & the Inca heartland
Dominican Republic (P)
Ecuador & Galápagos
Havana (P)
Jamaica (P)
Nicaragua
Discover Patagonia
Peru
Discover Peru, Bolivia & Ecuador
Rio de Janeiro (P)
St Lucia (P)
South American Handbook
Venezuela

North America
New York (P)
Vancouver (P)
Discover Western Canada

Africa
Cape Town (P)
East Africa
Egypt
Kenya
Libya
Marrakech (P)
Morocco
Namibia
South Africa
Tanzania
Tunisia
Uganda

Middle East
Dubai (P)
Israel
Jordan
Syria & Lebanon

What the papers say...

"I carried the South American Handbook from Cape Horn to Cartagena and consulted it every night for two and a half months. I wouldn't do that for anything else except my hip flask."
Michael Palin, BBC Full Circle

"My favourite series is the Handbook series published by Footprint and I especially recommend the Mexico, Central and South America Handbooks."
Boston Globe

"If 'the essence of real travel' is what you have been secretly yearning for all these years, then Footprint are the guides for you."
Under 26 magazine

"Who should pack Footprint—readers who want to escape the crowd."
The Observer

"Footprint can be depended on for accurate travel information and for imparting a deep sense of respect for the lands and people they cover."
World News

"The guides for intelligent, independently-minded souls of any age or budget."
Indie Traveller

Mail order
Available worldwide in bookshops and on-line. Footprint travel guides can also be ordered directly from us in Bath, via our website www.footprintbooks.com or from the address on the imprint page of this book.

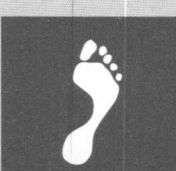

1557

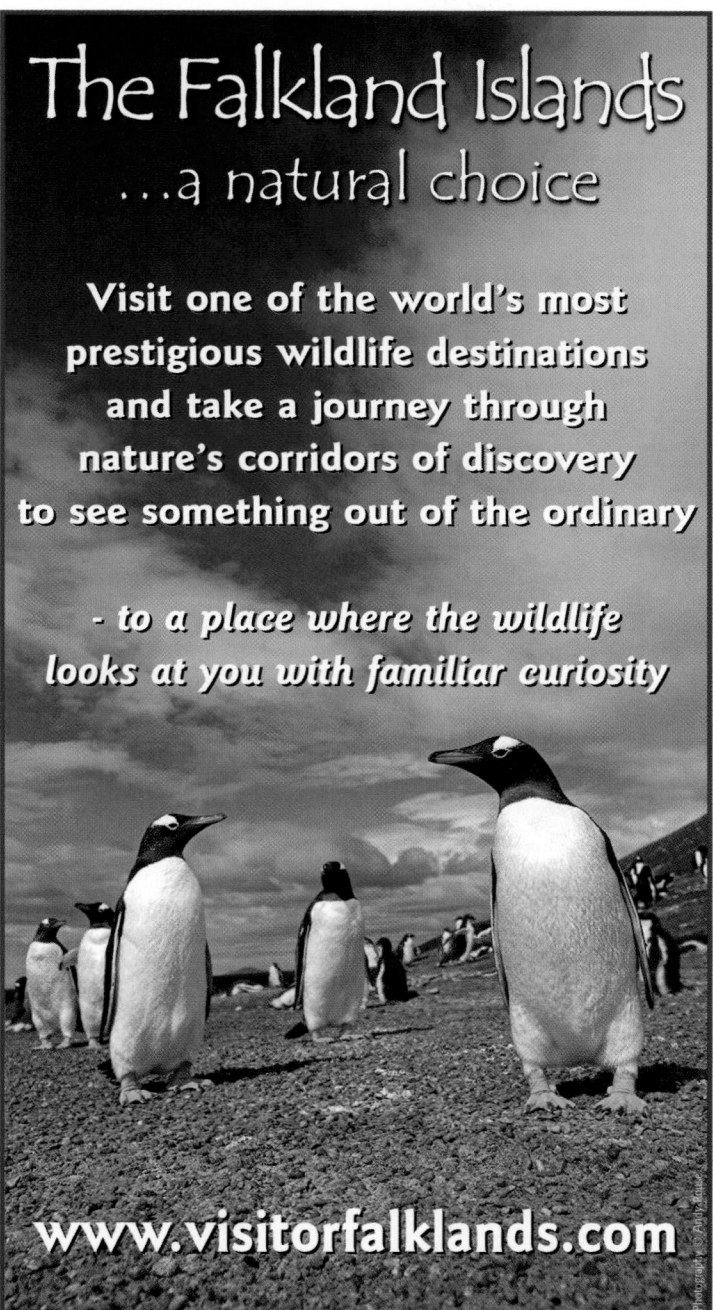
1559

PERURAIL

Exploring the Land of the Incas

Cusco - Lake Titicaca

A stunning rail journey beginning in Cusco and running south to the historic city of Puno and the famed Lake Titicaca. The gentle climb is breathtaking, with the first half of the journey dominated by magnificent Andean mountains, which slowly give way to the gentler, rolling Andean plains with their herds of vicuña and alpaca. There is a scenic stop at La Raya, the highest point of the journey.

An extraordinary destination deserves an extraordinary passage of way
Welcome aboard the Perurail's train services

Cusco - Machu Picchu

"In the variety of its charms and the power of its spell, I know of no place in the world which can compare with it. Not only has it great snow peaks looming above the clouds... it has also in striking contrast, orchids and ferns, the delectable beauty of luxurious vegetation, and the mysterious witchery of the jungle..."
Hiram Bingham ("Machu Picchu, The Lost City of the Incas")

reservas@perurail.com
Phone: 084-238722
Fax: 084-222114
www.perurail.com

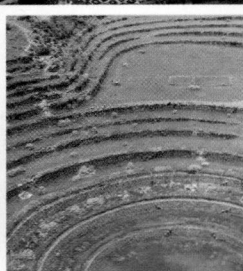

South America

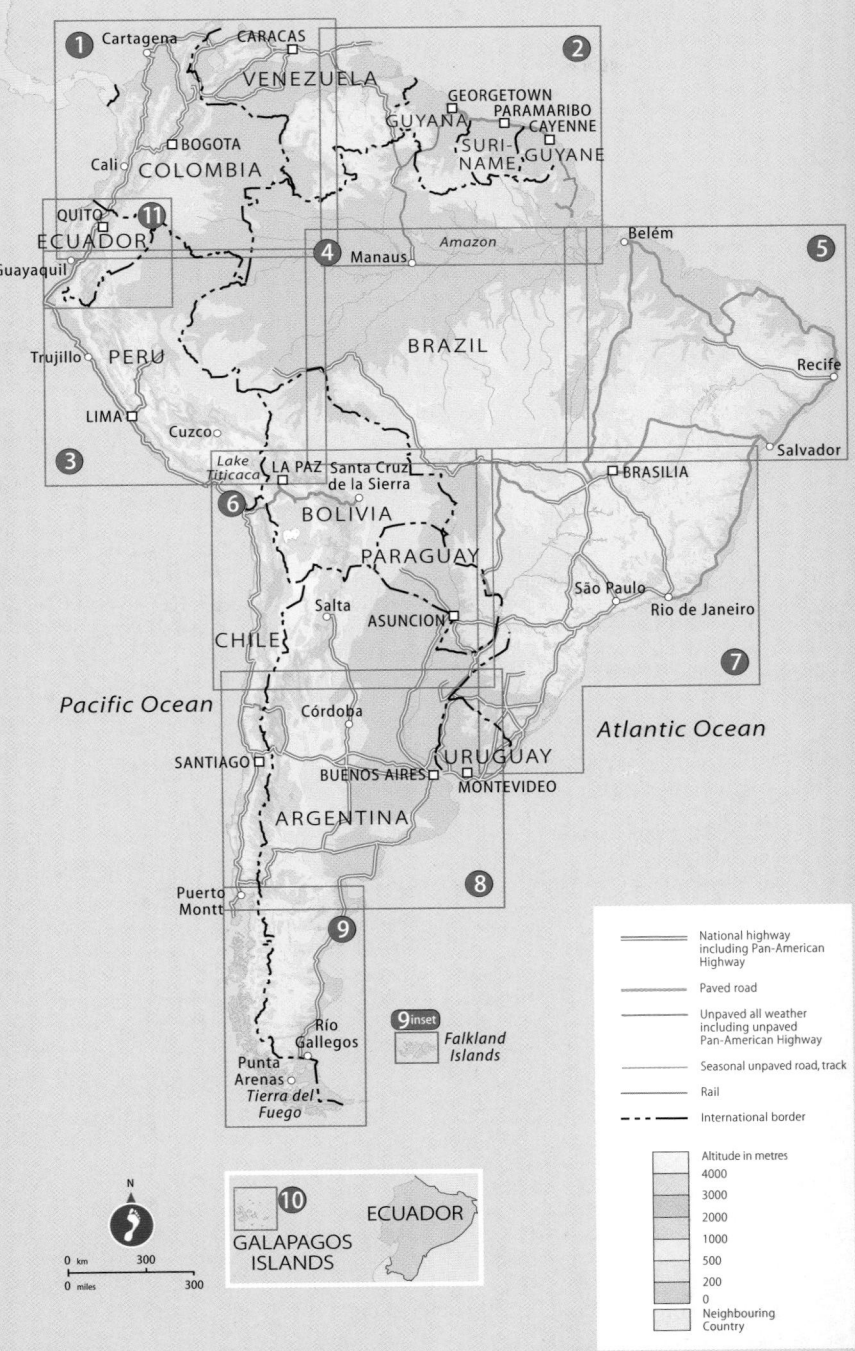

	National highway including Pan-American Highway
	Paved road
	Unpaved all weather including unpaved Pan-American Highway
	Seasonal unpaved road, track
	Rail
	International border

Altitude in metres
4000
3000
2000
1000
500
200
0
Neighbouring Country

Pacific Ocean

Atlantic Ocean

N

0 km 300
0 miles 300

Map 1

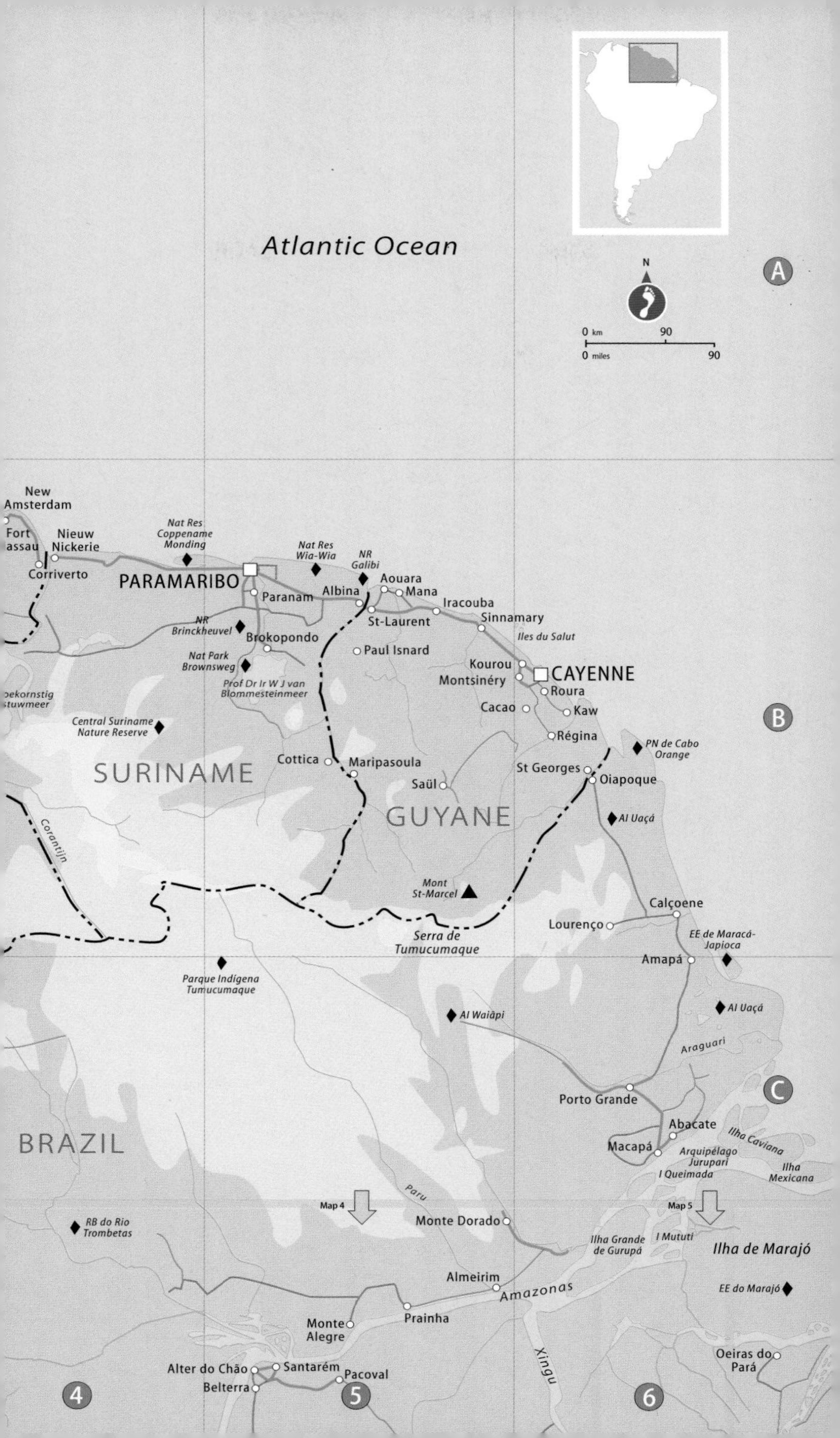

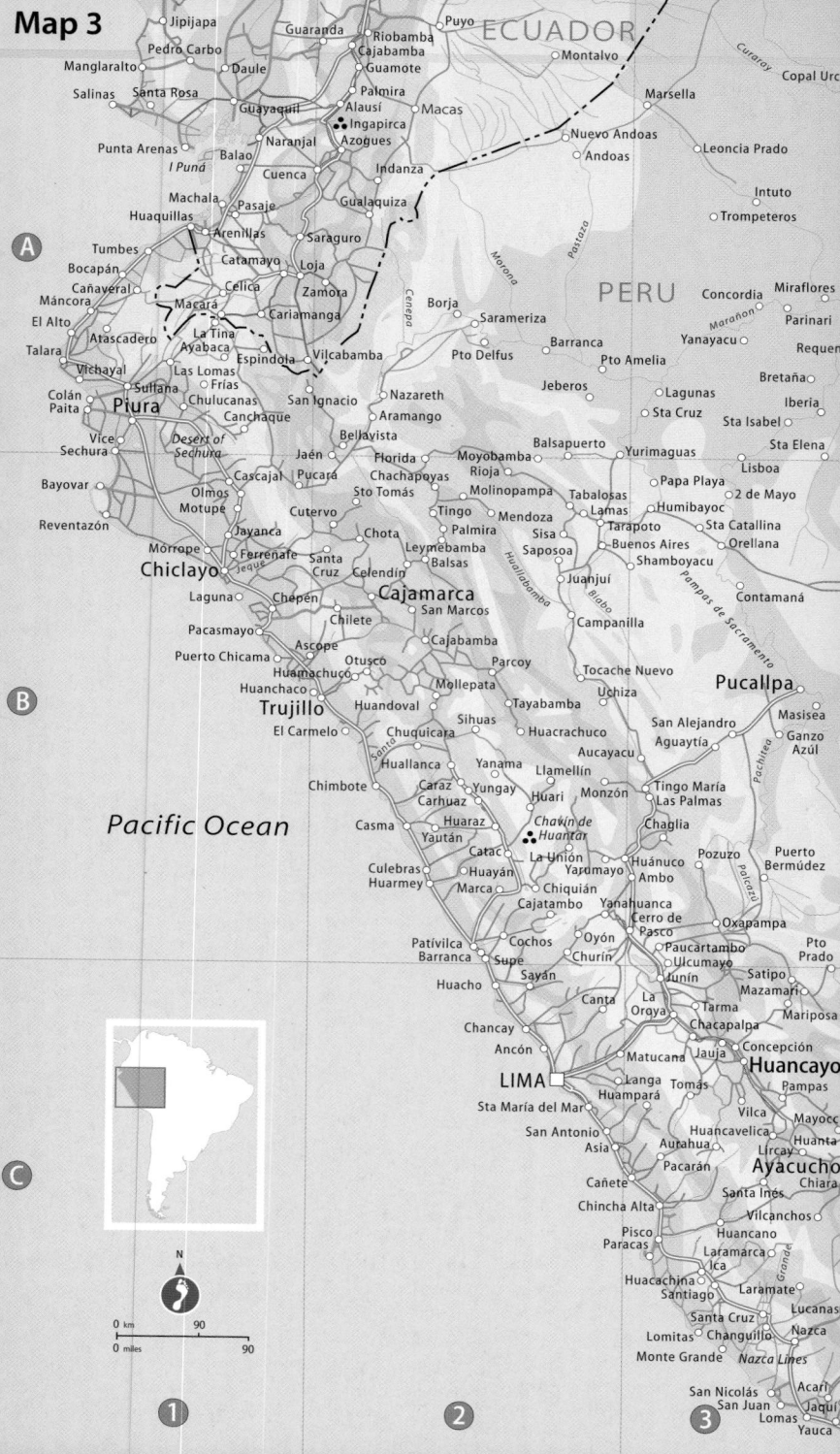

Map 3

ECUADOR

Jipijapa · Guaranda · Puyo
Pedro Carbo · Guamote · Riobamba · Cajabamba · Montalvo · Curaray · Copal Urc
Manglaralto · Daule · Palmira · Marsella
Salinas · Santa Rosa · Guayaquil · Guamote · Macas · Nuevo Andoas
Punta Arenas · Balao · Ingapirca · Azogues · Andoas · Leoncia Prado
I Puná · Naranjal · Cuenca · Indanza · Intuto
Machala · Pasaje · Gualaquiza · Trompeteros
Huaquillas · Arenillas · Saraguro · Marona
A · Tumbes · Catamayo · Loja · Zamora · Pastaza · Concordia · Miraflores
Bocapán · Cañaveral · Celica · Cariamanga · **PERU** · Parinari
El Alto · Máncara · Macará · Borja · Marañón · Yanayacu · Requen
Talara · Atascadero · La Tina · Espíndola · Vilcabamba · Saramériza · Barranca · Bretaña
Vichayal · Ayabaca · Las Lomas · Nazareth · Pto Delfus · Pto Amelia · Iberia
Colán · Sullana · Frías · Aramango · Jeberos · Lagunas · Sta Isabel
Paita · Piura · Chulucanas · Canchaque · Bellavista · Sta Cruz · Sta Elena
Vice · Desert of · Jaén · Florida · Moyobamba · Balsapuerto · Yurimaguas · Lisboa
Sechura · Sechura · Pucará · Chachapoyas · Rioja · Papa Playa · 2 de Mayo
Bayovar · Cascajal · Sto Tomás · Molinopampa · Tabalosas · Humibayoc · Sta Catalina
Reventazón · Olmos · Cutervo · Tingo · Mendoza · Lamas · Tarapoto · Orellana
Motupe · Chota · Palmira · Sisa · Buenos Aires
Mórrope · Jayanca · Leymebamba · Saposoa · Shamboyacu · Contamaná
Ferreñafe · Santa · Balsas · Juanjui · Pampas de Sacramento
Chiclayo · Cruz · Celendín · San Marcos · Campanilla
Laguna · Chepén · Chilete · **Cajamarca** · Pucallpa
Pacasmayo · Ascope · Cajabamba · Parcoy · Tocache Nuevo · Masisea
Puerto Chicama · Huamachuco · Otuzco · Mollepata · San Alejandro · Ganzo
B · Huanchaco · Huandoval · Sihuas · Tayabamba · Uchiza · Azúl
Trujillo · Chuquicara · Huacrachuco · Aguaytía
El Carmelo · Huallanca · Yanama · Llamellín · Tingo María · Pachitea
Chimbote · Caraz · Yungay · Huari · Monzón · Las Palmas
Casma · Carhuaz · Chavín de · Chaglla · Pozuzo · Puerto
Yaután · Huaraz · Huántar · Huánuco · Bermúdez
Culebras · Catac · La Unión · Ambo · Oxapampa
Huarmey · Huayán · Yarumayo · Pto
Marca · Chiquián · Cajatambo · Yanahuanca · Paucartambo · Prado
Patívilca · Cochos · Oyón · Cerro de · Ulcumayo · Satipo
Barranca · Supe · Churín · Pasco · Mazamari
Huacho · Sayán · Canta · Junín · Tarma · Mariposa
Pacific Ocean · Chancay · La · Chacapalpa · Concepción
Ancón · Oroya · Jauja · Huancayo
LIMA · Matucana · Pampas
Langa · Tomás · Vilca · Mayocc
Sta María del Mar · Huampará · Huancavelica · Huanta
San Antonio · Autahua · Lircay · **Ayacucho**
Asia · Pacarán · Santa Inés · Chiara
Cañete · Huancano · Vilcanchos
Chincha Alta · Laramarca · Lucanas
Pisco · Ica · Laramate
Paracas · Huacachina · Santa Cruz · Changuillo · Nazca
Lomitas · Monte Grande · Nazca Lines · Acarí
San Nicolás · San Juan · Jaquí
San Antonio · Lomas · Yauca

C

N

0 km 90
0 miles 90

① ② ③

Map 4

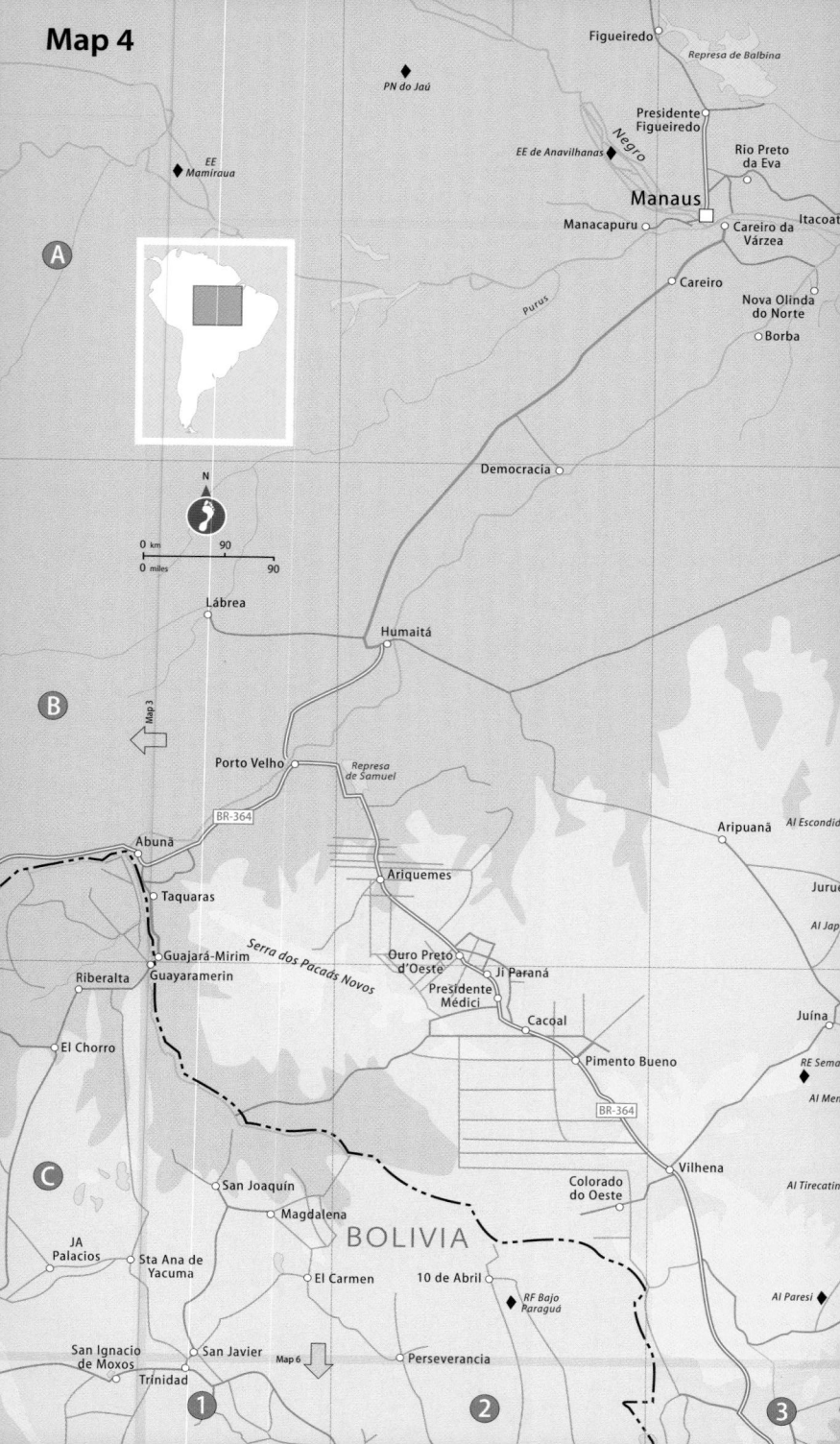

Figueiredo

Represa de Balbina

PN do Jaú

EE Mamiraua

Presidente Figueiredo

EE de Anavilhanas

Negro

Rio Preto da Eva

Manaus

Manacapuru

Careiro da Várzea

Itacoat

A

Purus

Careiro

Nova Olinda do Norte

Borba

N

0 km 90

0 miles 90

Democracia

Lábrea

Humaitá

Map 3

B

Porto Velho

Represa de Samuel

Aripuanã

AI Escondid

BR-364

Jurué

Abunã

AI Jap

Taquaras

Ariquemes

Serra dos Pacaás Novos

Ouro Preto d'Oeste

Ji Paraná

Juína

Guajará-Mirim

Guayaramerín

Presidente Médici

RE Sema

Riberalta

Cacoal

AI Meri

El Chorro

Pimento Bueno

BR-364

C

Vilhena

AI Tirecatin

San Joaquín

Colorado do Oeste

Magdalena

BOLIVIA

JA Palacios

Sta Ana de Yacuma

El Carmen

10 de Abril

RF Bajo Paraguá

AI Paresi

San Ignacio de Moxos

San Javier

Map 6

Perseverancia

Trinidad

1

2

3

Map 5

Ilha do Marajó

EE do Marajó ◆

Ponta de Pedras ○

Soure ○

Baia de Marajó

Curuça

Salinópolis

Castanhal

Belém

Capanema

Bragança

Viseu

Carutapera

I Sirituba

Oeiras do Para ○

Abaetetuba ○
Acará ○

Abaetetuba-Miri ○

Irituia ○

Concórdia do Pará ○

Tomé-Açu ○

Turiaçu ○

Cururupu ○

Sta Helena

Alcântara

São Luís
B de São Marcos
B de São José
Icatu ○

Humbe do Cam

PN do Le Maranh

Paragominas ○

Gurupi

Goianésia ○

Al Rio Pindaré ◆

Pindaré

Urban Santo

Represa de Tucuruí

Santa Luzía ○

Miranda do Norte ○

Chapadinh

RI Paracaná ◆

Açailândia ○

Arame ○

Bacabal ○

Pedreiras ○

Peritoró ○

Timbira

Marabá ○

Imperatriz ○

Presidente Dutra ○

Caxias

Map 4

Araguaia

Estreito ○

Barro do Corda ○

Sa das Alpercatas

Colinas ○

Tucuma ○

Xinguara ○

Araguaína ○

Carolina ○

Riachão ○

Balsas ○

Pastos Bons ○

Floria

Represal de Boa Esperança

Uruçuí ○

Conceição do ○

Bertolinia ○

Itaueí

Al Kraós ◆

BRAZIL

Flores Piau

Guaraí ○

RI Xerentes ◆

Miranorte ○

Miracema do Tocantins ○

Elisau Martins ○

Canto c Buriti

Cristino Castro ○

PN Se Cap

S Raimu Nona

PN do Araguaia ◆

Santa Teresinha ○

Gilbués ○

Palmas ○

Ilha do Bananal ◆

Fatimá ○

Porto Nacional ○

São Félix do Araguaia ○

Sta Rita de Cássia

Barrage Sobrad

Gurupi ○

Dianópolis ○

Ibiraba

Barra

PI do Araguaia ◆

Peixe ○

Conceição do Tocantins ○

Mimosa d'Oeste ○

Boqueirão ○

Xi
X

Alvorada ○

Taipas ○

Paranã ○

Taguatinga ○

Barreiras ○

Pirajaba ○

Ibotirama
Bro

Capix

Araguaçu ○

Arraias ○

Roda Velha ○

Brejolândia ○

São Miguel do Araguaia ○

Campos Belos ○

São Domingos ○

Santana ○

Mundo Novo ○

Crixás ○

Teresina de Goiás ○

PN Chapada dos Veadeiros ◆

Nova Roma ○

Correntina ○

Sta Maria da Vitória ○

Bom Jesus da Lapa ○

Mozorlândia ○

Niquelândia ○

Posse ○

Coribe ○

Espigão Mestre

São Francisco

1

2

Map 7

3

A

B

C

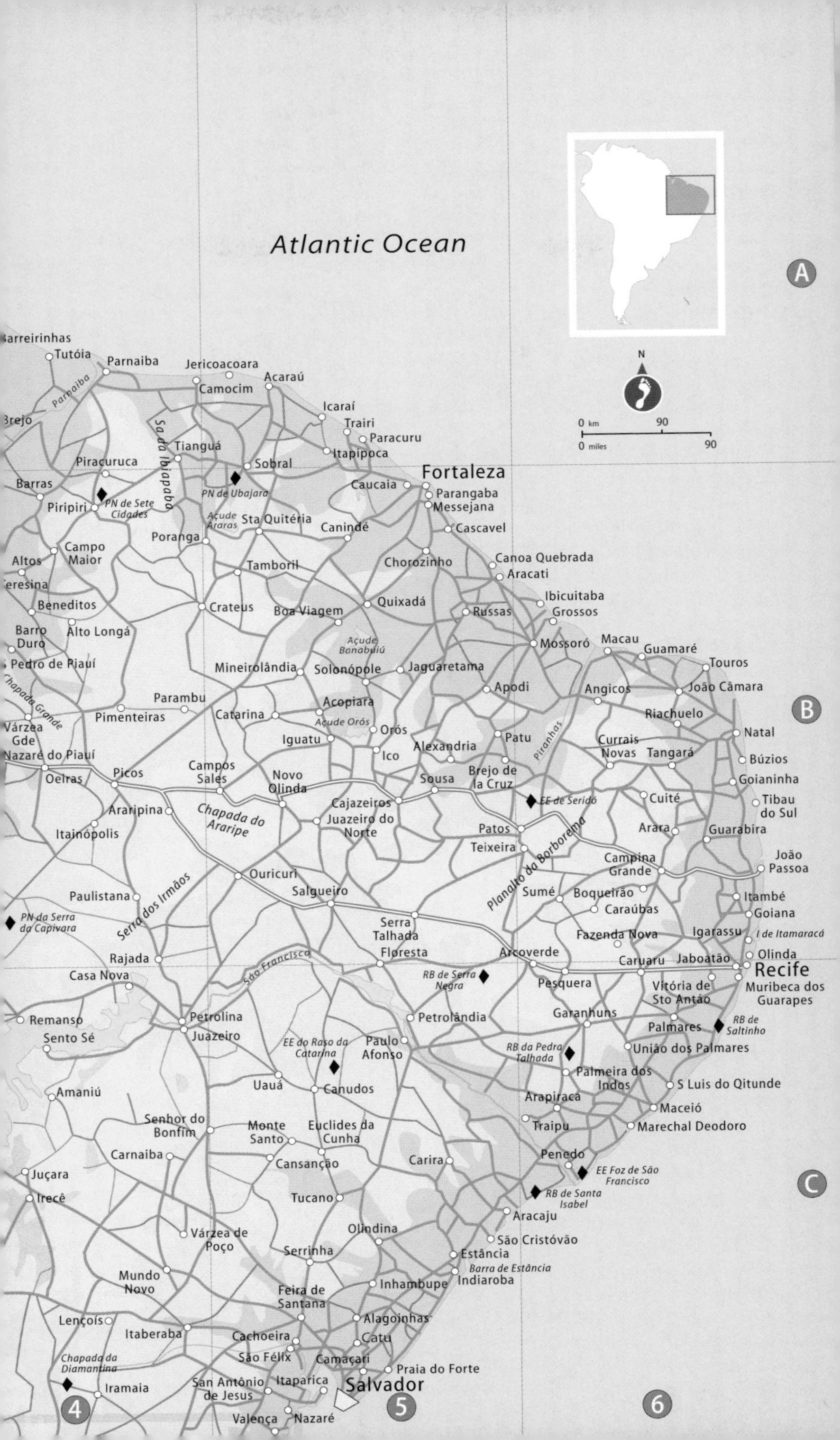

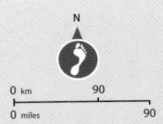

Map 6

PERU

Raqchi
Sta Rosa
Challa
Crucero
Ananea
Queara
Reyes
San Javi
Trinida
Yauri
Ayaviri
Azángaro
Apolo
Atén
Rurrenabaque
San Borja
San Ignac
de Moxos
Puica
Cailloma
Condoroma
Putina
Santa Rosa
Yucumo
Cotahuasi
Orcopampa
Moho
Consata
Mapiri
Chuquibamba
Colca Canyon
Chivay
Juliaca
Escoma
Guanay
Calhua
Lluta
Imata
Lago Titicaca
Carabuco
Alcoche
Caranavi
Iquipi
Yura
Pati
Puno
Ilave
Sorata
Zongo
Corire
Arequipa
Sorapa
Achacachi
Coroico
San José
Camaná
Mollebaya
Juli
Zepita
Huarina
Chulumani
Ocoña
Sta Rita
Omate
Desaguadero
Laja
LA PAZ
Mollendo
Cocachacra
Humajalso
Pisacoma
Guaqui
Viacha
Pto Villarr
Moquegua
San Andrés de Machaca
Calamarca
Patacamaya
Independencia
Villa Tunari
Toquepala
Tarata
Achiri
Umala
Sica Sica
Morochata
Tiraque
Sama Grande
Visviri
Curahuara de Carangas
Caracolla
Cochabamba
Epizana
Ilo
Ite
Tacna
PN Lauca
Putre
Lago Chungará
PN Sajama
Turco
Toledo
Oruro
Tarata
Sacaca
Totora
Aiquile
Arica
Guallatiri
Tambo Quemado
Sabaya
Corque
L Uru Uru
Machacamarca
Quiroga
Poconchile
Sacabaya
Huachacalla
Andamarca
Huanuni
Colquechaca
Codpa
Sabaya
Lago Poopó
Challapata
Ocurí
Cuya
Caraiña
Isluga
Colchane
Stgo de Huari
Sucre
Tarabuc
Pisagua
Chusmisa
Sevaruyo
Otuyo
Tarapacá
Mamiña
Llica
Potosí
Betanzos
Humberstone
Huara
Salar de Uyuni
Río Mulatos
Iquique
La Tirana
Colchane
Camargo
Pozo Almonte
Pica
Matilla
S Pedro de Quemes
Uyuni
Cerdas
Atocha
El Puente
Quillagua
Ollagüe
Río Grande
Julaca
Chiguana
San Vicente
Tupiza
Suipacha
San Pablo de Lípez
Mojo
Villazór
Soniquera
Villazór
San Pedro
Tocopilla
Chuquicamata
Toconce
San Antonio de Lípez
La Quiaca
Iruya
María Elena
Calama
El Tatio
Quetena
Abra Pampa
Cobija
Iturbe
San Pedro de Atacama
Toconao
Paso de Jama
Humahuaca
Mejillones
Carmen Alto
Salar de Atacama
Salar de Quisquiro
Susques
Tilcara
Bolsico
Baquedano
Socaire
Catúa
R Nt Olaruz Caucyhari
Antofagasta
Olacapato
Purmamarca
Jujuy
CHILE
R Nt de los Andes
San Antonio de los Cobres
Tastil
Salta
Socompa
Puna de Atacama
Cachi
Güeme
Desert of Atacama
Lumbre Meta
Paposa
Molinos
La Viña
Taltal
Agua Blanca (5,780m)
Angastaco
Rosario la Fronte
Parque Nacional Pan de Azúcar
Cerros de Piedra Parada (5,920m)
Antofagasta de la Sierra
Cafayate
El Tala
El Salvador
Chañaral
Río Salado
Potrerillos
Aimachá del Valle
Tráncas
Diego de Almagro
Paso San Francisco
Santa María
Tafí del Valle
Tucumá
Caldera
Bahía Inglesa
Copiapó
Laguna del Negro Francisco
Pissis (6,882m)
Fiambalá
Hualfín
Monteros
Chañarcillo
Veladero (6,436m)
Bonete (6,759m)
Belén
Andalgalá
La Madrid
Simoca
Las Juntas
Reserva Natural Laguna Brava
Tinogasta
Taco Pozo
Laval
S José

Pacific Ocean

Map 3

N

0 km   90
0 miles   90

Ⓐ Ⓑ Ⓒ

① ② ③

Map 7

Cuiabá
Cnl Ponce
Várzea Grande
São Vicente
Primavera
Alto Coité
Planalto do Mato Grosso
RI São Marcos
Map 4
Mozorlândia
Dois Irmãos
PN Brasi

Barao de Melgaço
Al Gomes Carneiro
Guiratinga
Rondonópolis
Barra do Garças
Goiás Velho
Jaraguá
Brazlândia
BRASÍLIA
Taguatinga
Gam

Map 6
Sonoro
Itiquira
Diamantino
Iporã
Pirenópolis
Anápolis

A

Pantanal Matogrossense
Alto Garças
Mineiros
Jataí
Rio Verde
Goiânia
Paraúna
Indiara
Edéia
Pontalina
S Domingos
Caldas Novas

Coxim
Placa dos Mineiros
PN das Emas
Serranópolis
Aparecida do Rio Doce
Itumbiara
Corumbaíba
Catalão
Batr Itumbiara
Rep de Emborcaç

Rio Verde de Mato Grosso
Paraiso
Aporé
Caçu
Barragem de S Simão
Ituiutaba

Capim Verde
Camapuã
Raimundo
Paranaiba
Uberlândia

Aquidauana
Campo Grande
Água Clara
Aparecida do Taboado
Jales
Fernandópolis
Votuporanga
BRAZIL
Grande
Barragem Água Vermelha
Uberuba

Nioaque
Três Lagoas
Castilho
Major Prado
Nhandeara
S José do Rio Preto
Barretos
Fran

B
Jardim
Serra de Maracaju
Maracaju
Nôvo Alvarada
Sta Rita do Pardo
Panorama
Araçatuba
Penápolis
Tietê
Ribeirão Preto

Cabeceira do Apá
Itaum
Dourados
Casa Verde
Bataguassu
Presidente Prudente
Tupã
Lins
Jacanga
Matão
Araraquara
San Carlos
Jaú

PN del Cerro Corá
Ponta Porã
Ivinhema
Sto Ignácio
Marília
Gália
Bauru
Rio Claro
Limeira
Piracicaba
American
Campir

Pedro Juan Caballero
Caarapá
Paranaponema
Bela Vista do Paraíso
Ubirajara
Ourinhos
Botucatu
Avaré

Amambaí
Paraná
Rep Capivari
Londrina
Sto Antônio da Platina
Piraju
Rep Armando
Itapetininga

Ygatimi
Mbaracayú Forest Reserve
Eldorado
Umuarema
Maringá
Represa de Xavantes
Capão Bonito
Sorocaba

Salto del Guairá
Guaíra
Palotina
Campo Mourão
Itapeva
Pedro Barras

Curuguaty
Campina
Têrmas de Jurema
Iretama
Alecrim
Jaguariaíva
Itapeva
Peruí
Iguape
Cananéia

Represa de Itaipu
Toledo
Pitanga
Piraí do Sul
Tunas
Registo

Cascavel
Catanduvas
Guarabuava
Ponta Grosso
Vila Velha
PN Marumbi
Guaraqueçaba

Medianeira
Laranjeiras do Sol
Irati
Curitiba
Morretes
PN de Superagüi
Paranaguá

C
Ciudad del Este
Foz do Iguaçu
Iguaçu
Represa de Salto Santiago
Areia Branca
S Botodo do Sol
Guaratuba

Caazapá
Puerto Iguazú
Warida
Pato Branco
Represa de Foz Areia
União de Vitória
Papanduva
Jaragua do Sol
Joinville
São Francisco do Sul

Eldorado
Campo Erê
Horizonte
Sta Cecilia
Blumenau
Camboriú

Obligado
Hohenau
San Pedro
Bom Jesus
Chapecó
Curitibanos
Rio do Sul

Jesús
Trinidad
Bella Vista
San Ignacio
Mocona
Exerim
Tupitanga
Florianópolis
Ilha de Santa Catarina

Encarnación
Posadas
Oberá
El Soberbio
Barragem Passo Fundo
Passo Fundo
La Vermelha
Lages
Sta Rosa de Lima

Azara
Garruchos
Map 8
Santo Angelo
Vacaria
PN São Joaquim
São Joaquim
Tubarão
Laguna

São Luís Gonzaga
São Lourenço das Missões
São Miguel das Missões
Cruz Alta
Soledade

Encruzilhada

1
2
3

Caxias do Sul

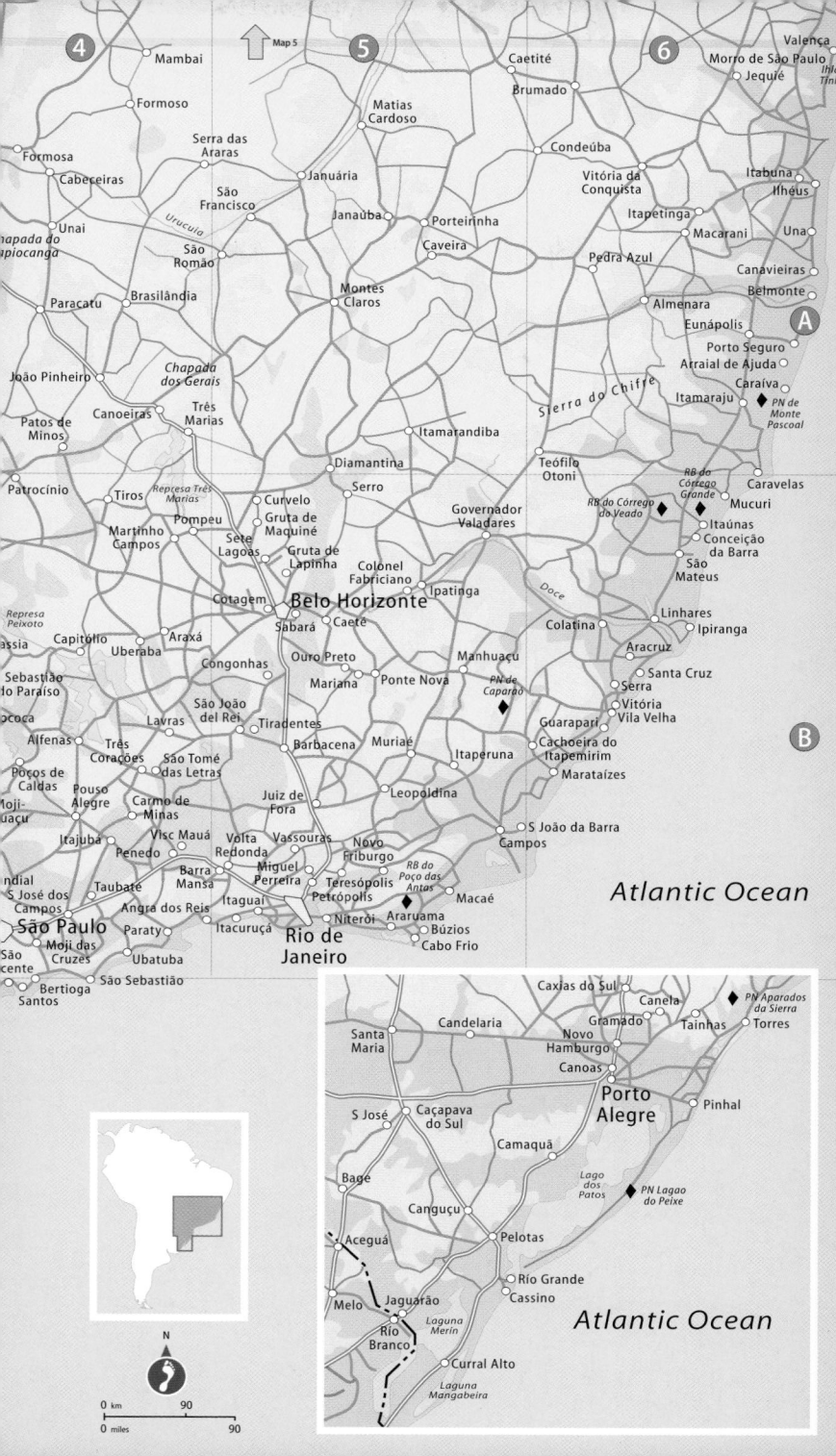

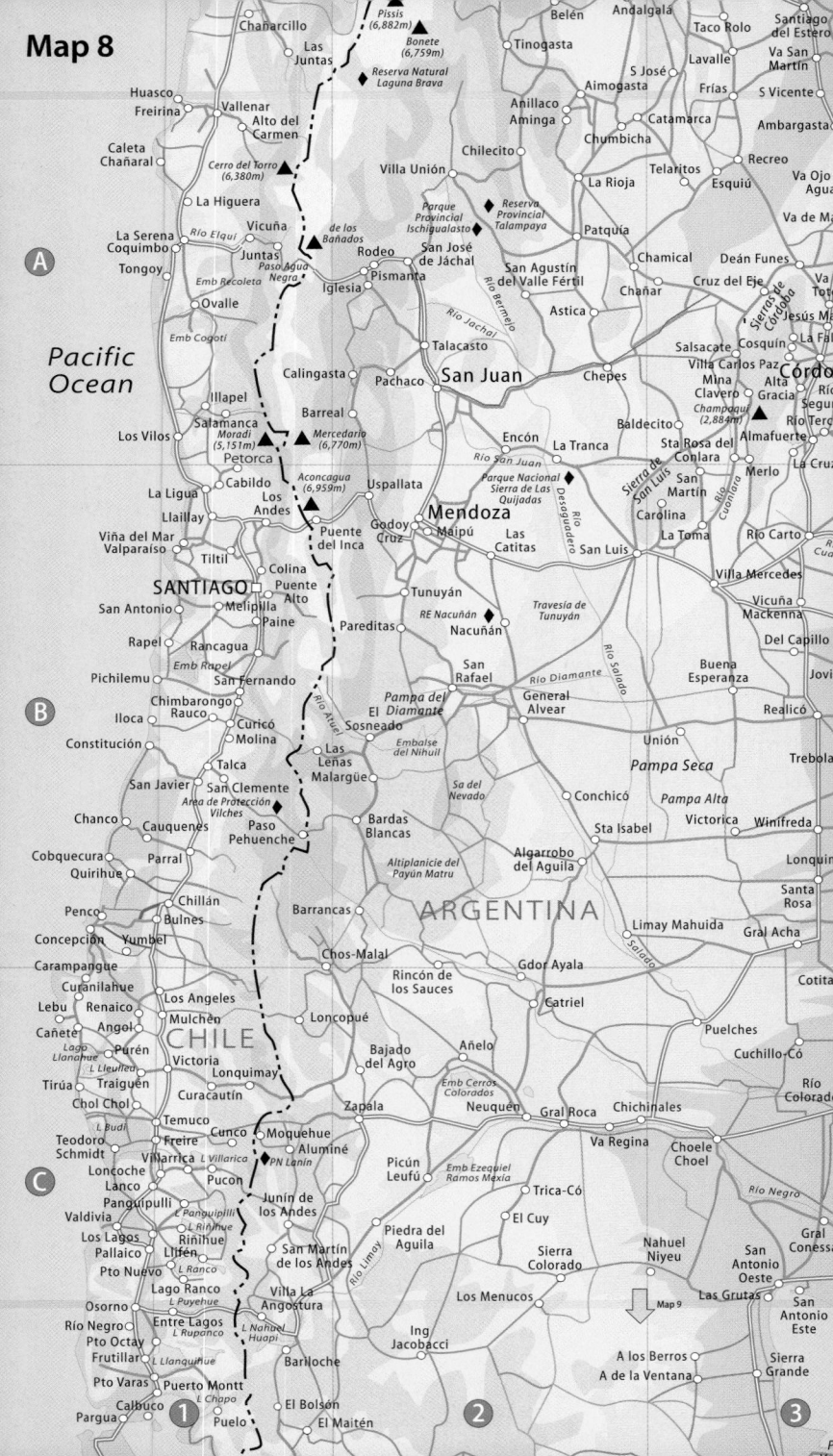

Map 8

Pacific Ocean

ARGENTINA

CHILE

Chañarcillo
Las Juntas
Pissis (6,882m)
Bonete (6,759m)
Belén
Andalgalá
Taco Rolo
Santiago del Estero
Va San Martín

Reserva Natural Laguna Brava
Tinogasta
S José
Aimogasta
Lavalle
Frías
S Vicente

Huasco
Freirina
Vallenar
Alto del Carmen
Anillaco
Aminga
Catamarca
Ambargasta

Caleta
Chañaral
Cerro del Torro (6,380m)
Chilecito
La Rioja
Recreo
Va Ojo Agua

La Higuera
Villa Unión
Parque Provincial Ischigualasto
Reserva Provincial Talampaya
Patquía
Telaritos
Esquiú
Va de Ma

Vicuña
de los Bañados
Rodeo
San José de Jáchal
Chamical
Deán Funes
Va Toto

La Serena
Coquimbo
Tongoy
Río Elqui
Juntas
Paso Agua Negra
Pismanta
Iglesia
San Agustín del Valle Fértil
Astica
Chañar
Cruz del Eje
Sierras de Córdoba
Jesús Ma
La Fal

Ovalle
Emb Recoleta
Río Bermejo
Río Jáchal
Salsacate
Cosquín
Córdo

Emb Cogotí
Calingasta
Pachaco
Talacasto
San Juan
Chepes
Villa Carlos Paz
Mina Clavero
Champaquí (2,884m)
Alta Gracia
Río Segur
Río Terce

Illapel
Barreal
Encón
Baldecito
Sta Rosa del Conlara
Almafuerte
La Cruz

Salamanca
Moradi (5,151m)
Petorca
Mercedario (6,770m)
Río San Juan
La Tranca
Parque Nacional Sierra de Las Quijadas
San Martín
Merlo

Los Vilos
Aconcagua (6,959m)
Uspallata
Mendoza
Carolina
Río Cuarto

La Ligua
Cabildo
Los Andes
Godoy Cruz
Maipú
Las Catitas
San Luis
La Toma
Río Carto

Lllaillay
Puente del Inca
Río Desaguadero
Villa Mercedes

Viña del Mar
Valparaíso
Tiltil
Colina
Puente Alto
Paine
Pareditas
RE Nacuñán
Nacuñán
Travesía de Tunuyán
Vicuña
Mackenna

SANTIAGO
Meliplla
Tunuyán
Río Diamante
Buena Esperanza
Del Capillo

San Antonio
Rapel
Rancagua
San Fernando
San Rafael
General Alvear
Río Salado
Realicó
Jovi

Pichilemu
Emb Rapel
Chimbarongo
Rauco
Pampa del Diamante
El Sosneado
Pampa Seca
Trebola

Iloca
Curicó
Molina
Río Atuel
Embalse del Nihuil
Sa del Nevado
Unión
Pampa Alta

Constitución
Talca
Las Leñas
Malargüe
Conchicó
Victorica
Winifreda
Lonquim

San Javier
San Clemente
Área de Protección Vilches
Bardas Blancas
Sta Isabel
Santa Rosa

Chanco
Cauquenes
Paso Pehuenche
Altiplanicie del Payún Matru
Algarrobo del Aguila
Gral Acha
Cotita

Cobquecura
Quirihue
Parral
Barrancas
Limay Mahuida
Salado

Penco
Chillán
Bulnes
Chos-Malal
Rincón de los Sauces
Gdor Ayala
Puelches
Cuchillo-Có

Concepción
Yumbel
Carampangue
Curanilahue
Los Angeles
Mulchén
Loncopué
Bajado del Agro
Añelo
Catriel
Río Colorado

Lebu
Cañete
Renaico
Angol
Purén
Victoria
Lonquimay
Zapala
Emb Cerros Colorados
Neuquén
Gral Roca
Chichinales
Va Regina
Choele Choel

Tirúa
Chol Chol
Lago Llanahue
L Lleulleu
Traiguén
Curacautín
Picún Leufú
Emb Ezequiel Ramos Mexía
Río Negro
Gral Conessa

Teodoro Schmidt
Temuco
Freire
Cunco
Moquehue
Aluminé
PN Lanín
Trica-Có
San Antonio Oeste
San Antonio Este

Loncoche
Lanco
Villarrica
L Villarica
Pucón
Junín de los Andes
Picún Leufú
El Cuy
Las Grutas

Valdivia
Panguipulli
L Panguipulli
L Rinihue
San Martín de los Andes
Piedra del Aguila
Sierra Colorado
Sierra Grande

Los Lagos
Pallaico
Pto Nuevo
Riñihue
Llifén
L Ranco
Lago Ranco
Villa La Angostura
Los Menucos
Nahuel Niyeu

Osorno
Río Negro
Pto Octay
Frutillar
Entre Lagos
L Puyehue
L Rupanco
L Nahuel Huapi
Map 9
A los Berros

Pto Varas
Calbuco
Pargua
L Llanquihue
Puerto Montt
L Chapo
Bariloche
El Bolsón
El Maitén
Ing Jacobacci
A de la Ventana

Puelo

1   2   3

A   B   C

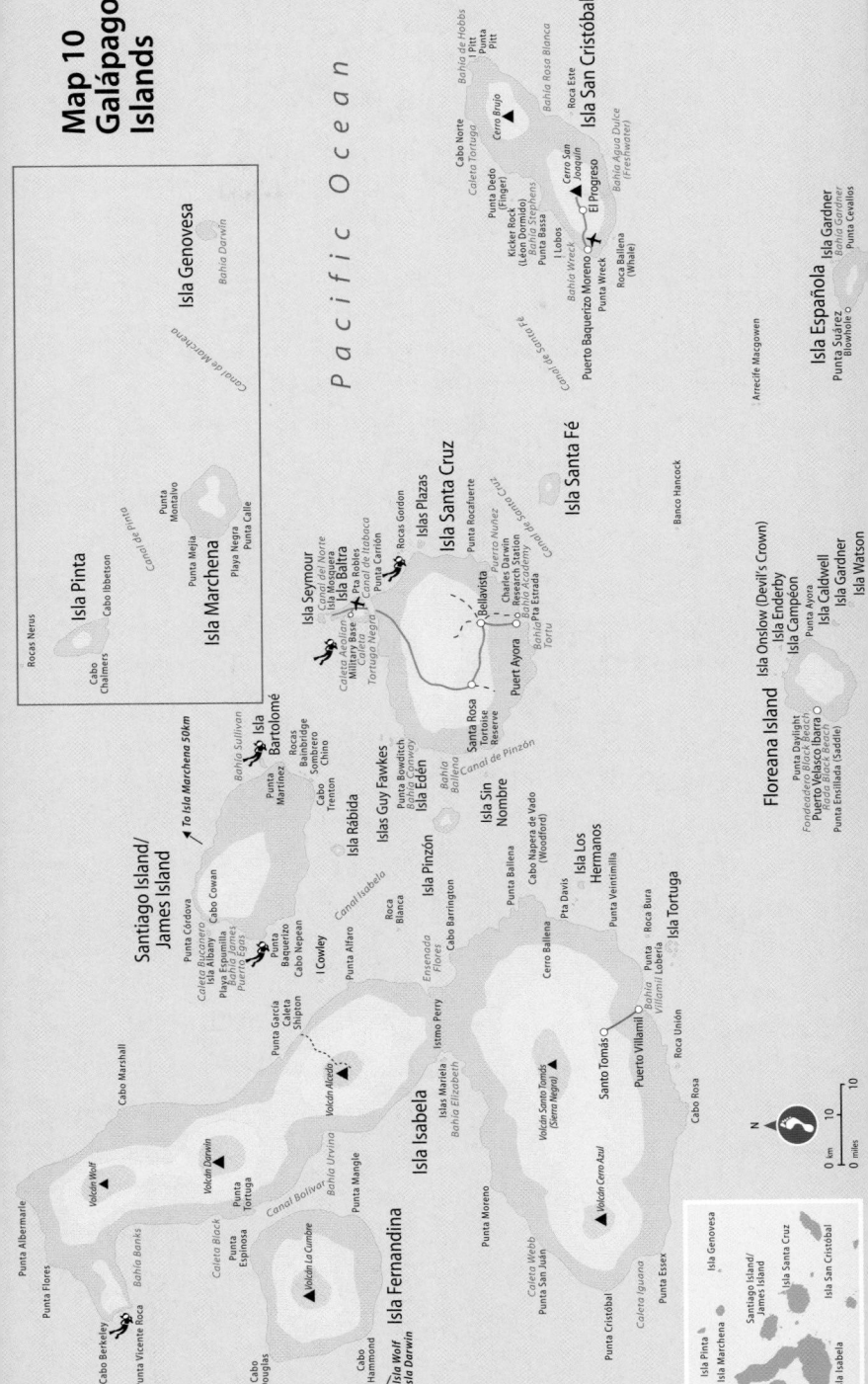

Map 10
Galápagos Islands

Pacific Ocean

Rocas Nerus

Isla Pinta
Cabo Ibbetson

Isla Genovesa
Bahía Darwin

Canal de Marchena

Cabo Chalmers

Punta Montalvo

Isla Marchena
Punta Mejía
Playa Negra
Punta Calle

Bahía de Hobbs
I Pitt
Punta Pitt

Bahía Rosa Blanca

Cabo Norte
Cerro Brujo
Caleta Tortuga

Roca Este
Isla San Cristóbal

Punta Dedo (Finger)
Kicker Rock (León Dormido)
Bahía Stephens
Punta Bassa
I Lobos
Bahía Wreck

Cerro San Joaquín
El Progreso
Bahía Agua Dulce (Freshwater)

Puerto Baquerizo Moreno
Punta Wreck
Roca Ballena (Whale)

Canal de Santa Fé

Arrecife Macgowen

Isla Gardner
Bahía Gardner
Punta Cevallos

Isla Española
Punta Suárez
Blowhole o

Rocas Bainbridge
Sombrero Chino

Santiago Island/ James Island

Punta Córdova
Caleta Bucanero
Isla Albany
Playa Espumilla
Bahía James
Puerto Egas
Punta Baquerizo
Cabo Nepean
I Cowley
Punta Alfaro

Cabo Cowan

Bahía Sullivan
Isla Bartolomé
Punta Martínez
Rocas
Cabo Trenton

To Isla Marchena 50km

Isla Seymour
Canal del Norte
Isla Mosquera
Military Base
Canal de Itabaca
Caleta Tortuga Negra
Canal de Pájaro

Rocas Gordon
Punta Rocafuerte

Islas Plazas
Isla Santa Cruz

Bellavista
Charles Darwin Research Station
Puerto Núñez
Bahía Academy
Bahía Estrada
Tortu
Puerto Ayora

Santa Rosa
Tortoise Reserve

Canal de Santa Cruz

Banco Hancock

Isla Santa Fé

Isla Guy Fawkes
Isla Edén
Bahía Borrero

Isla Rábida

Isla Pinzón
Bahía Canal de Pinzón

Isla Sin Nombre

Cabo Napea de Vado (Woodford)

Isla Onslow (Devil's Crown)
Isla Enderby
Isla Campeón

Punta Ayora
Isla Caldwell
Isla Gardner
Isla Watson

Floreana Island
Punta Daylight
Fondeadero Black Beach
Puerto Velasco Ibarra
Black Beach
Punta Ensillada (Saddle)

Roca Blanca
Cabo Barrington

Isla Los Hermanos
Punta Ballena
Pta Davis
Punta Veintimilla

Ensenada Flores

Canal Isabela

Punta García
Caleta Shipton
Volcán Alcedo

Istmo Perry
Bahía Elizabeth
Islas Mariela

Santo Tomás

Roca Bura
Isla Tortuga
Punta Lobería
Bahía Villamil
Punta
Puerto Villamil

Volcán Santo Tomás (Sierra Negra)

Volcán Cerro Azul

Roca Rosa

Cabo Rosa

Cabo Marshall

Isla Isabela

Volcán Wolf

Volcán Darwin
Punta Tortuga

Volcán La Cumbre

Isla Fernandina

Cabo Douglas
Cabo Hammond
To Isla Wolf & Isla Darwin

Punta Albemarle
Punta Flores

Cabo Berkeley
Punta Vicente Roca

Bahía Banks

Caleta Black
Punta Espinosa

Canal Bolívar

Punta Mangle

Bahía Urvina

Punta Moreno

Caleta Webb
Punta San Juan

Punta Cristóbal
Caleta Iguana
Punta Essex

N

0 km   10
0 miles 10

Isla Pinta   Isla Genovesa
Isla Marchena
Santiago Island/ James Island   Isla Santa Cruz   Isla San Cristóbal
Isla Isabela   Isla Española

Map 11 Ecuador

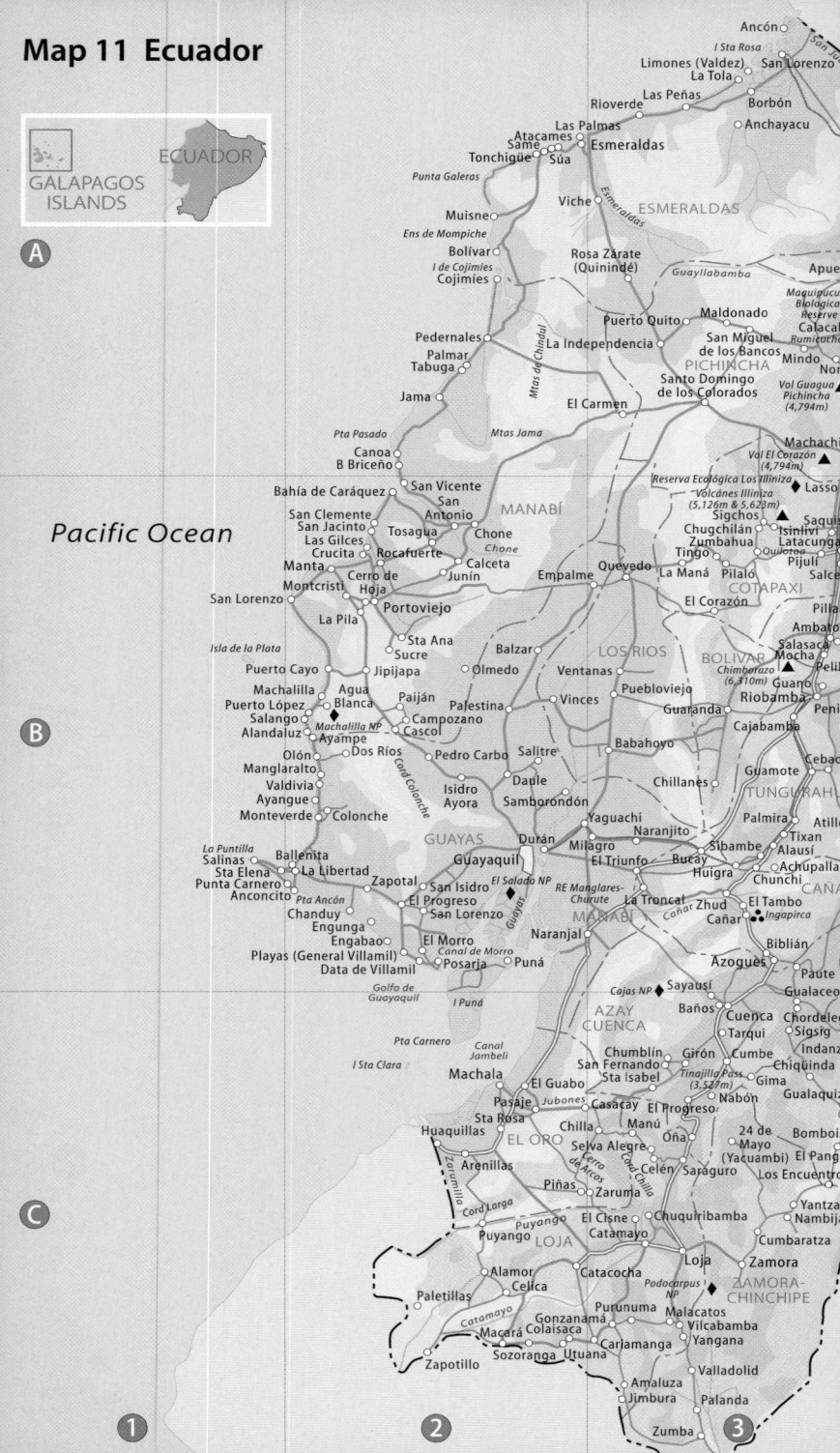

GALAPAGOS ISLANDS

ECUADOR

A

B

C

Pacific Ocean

1 **2** **3**

Ancón
I Sta Rosa
Limones (Valdez)
La Tola
San Lorenzo
Las Peñas
Borbón
Rioverde
Anchayacu
Las Palmas
Atacames
Same
Tonchigüe
Súa
Esmeraldas
Punta Galeras
Viche
ESMERALDAS
Esmeraldas
Muisne
Ens de Mompiche
Bolívar
I de Cojimíes
Cojimíes
Rosa Zárate
(Quinindé)
Guayllabamba
Apue
Maquipucu
Biological
Reserve
Calacal
Rumitachoc
Puerto Quito
Maldonado
San Miguel
de los Bancos
Mindo
Nor
Pedernales
La Independencia
PICHINCHA
Santo Domingo
de los Colorados
Vol Guagua
Pichincha
(4,794m)
Palmar
Tabuga
Machachi
(4,794m)
Jama
El Carmen
Val El Corazón
(4,794m)
Mtas de Chindul
Mtas Jama
Pta Pasado
Reserva Ecológica Los Illiniza
Lasso
Canoa
B Briceño
Volcánes Illiniza
(5,126m & 5,623m)
Saquis
San Vicente
Sigchos
Isinliví
Latacunga
Bahía de Caráquez
San
Antonio
MANABÍ
Chugchilán
Zumbahua
Quilorca
Pijuli
San Clemente
Chone
Tingo
Pilaló
Salce
San Jacinto
Las Gilces
Tosagua
Chone
La Maná
COTAXAXI
Crucita
Rocafuerte
Calceta
Pillar
Manta
Cerro de
Junín
Quevedo
El Corazón
Montcristi
Hoja
Empalme
Ambato
San Lorenzo
Portoviejo
Salasaca
La Pila
Mocha
Pelil
Isla de la Plata
Sta Ana
Balzar
LOS RIOS
BOLIVAR
Chimborazo
Guano
Sucre
(6,310m)
Riobamba
Puerto Cayo
Jipijapa
Olmedo
Ventanas
Peni
Machalilla
Agua
Paiján
Puebloviejo
Guaranda
Cajabamba
Puerto López
Blanca
Palestina
Vinces
Salango
Campozano
Babahoyo
Guamote
Alandaluz
Ayampe
Cascol
Pedro Carbo
Chillanes
Cebac
Olón
Dos Ríos
Salitre
TUNGURAHU
Manglaralto
Isidro
Daule
Valdivia
Ayora
Samborondón
Palmira
Atill
Ayangue
Colonche
Yaguachi
Naranjito
Sibambe
Tixan
Monteverde
GUAYAS
Durán
Milagro
Bucay
Alausí
La Puntilla
Guayaquil
El Triunfo
Huigra
Achupalla
Salinas
Ballenita
Zapotal
RE Manglares-
La Troncal
Chunchi
CAÑA
Sta Elena
La Libertad
San Isidro
El Salado NP
Churute
Zhud
El Tambo
Punta Carnero
Anconcito
El Progreso
MANABÍ
Cañar
Ingapirca
Chanduy
San Lorenzo
Naranjal
Engunga
El Morro
Canal de Morro
Biblián
Engabao
Posarja
Puná
Playas (General Villamil)
Data de Villamil
Azogués
Paute
Golfo de
Gualaceo
Guayaquil
I Puná
Cajas NP
Sayausí
AZAY
Baños
Cuenca
Chordelec
CUENCA
Tarqui
Sigsig
Pta Carnero
Canal
Chumblín
Girón
Cumbe
Indanz
Jambeli
San Fernando
Chiquinda
I Sta Clara
Machala
Sta Isabel
Tinajillo Pass
Gima
(3,527m)
Nábón
Gualaquiz
El Guabo
Casacay
El Progreso
Pasaje
Jubones
Chilla
Manú
24 de
Bomboia
Sta Rosa
Selva Alegre
Oña
Mayo
Huaquillas
Cerro
(Yacuambi)
El Pang
EL ORO
de Arcos
Saraguro
Los Encuentro
Arenillas
Cord Chilla
Piñas
Zaruma
Cord Larga
Puyango
Chuquiribamba
Yantza
Puyango
El Cisne
Catamayo
Nambija
LOJA
Cumbaratza
Alamor
Catacocha
Loja
Zamora
Paletillas
Celica
Podocarpus
ZAMORA-
NP
CHINCHIPE
Purunuma
Malacatos
Gonzanamá
Vilcabamba
Macará Colaisaca
Carlamanga
Yangana
Zapotillo
Sozoranga Utuana
Amaluza
Valladolid
Catamayo
Jimbura
Palanda
Zumba